EARLY
WEST TENNESSEE
MARRIAGES

Volume I

Grooms

By

Byron Sistler and Barbara Sistler

Janaway Publishing, Inc.
Santa Maria, California
2011

Early West Tennessee Marriages, Two Volumes

Copyright © 1989 by Byron Sistler and Barbara Sistler
All rights reserved.

Originally published, Nashville, 1989
by Byron Sistler and Associates, Inc.

by

Janaway Publishing, Inc.
732 Kelsey Ct.
Santa Maria, California 93454
(805) 925-1038
www.JanawayPublishing.com

2007, 2011

Two Volume Set, ISBN: 978-1-59641-039-8
Volume I, ISBN: 978-1-59641-226-2
Volume II, ISBN: 978-1-59641-227-9

Made in the United States of America

INTRODUCTION

We have attempted in these two books to set forth the essential data on all early West Tennessee marriages for which records have survived. The area included is outlined on the map on the next page; records published here are for 15 shaded counties. Official ante-bellum marriage records do not exist for the rest of them.

All pre-1861 marriages are set forth here. When feasible and convenient (primarily because of cutoff dates of the original books) we have also included later records as well.

The information in the brides book is a duplication of that in the grooms, the difference being in the order in which they appear. Each book is a single area-wide alphabetical listing of the records.

Where two dates appear on an entry, the first one is the date license was issued, the second (in parentheses) the date marriage was solemnized. If only one date, it usually means that the date of execution was the same as the date of license issuance.

It should be remembered that the entries are, in most cases, far from complete. They show names of the celebrants, county and dates, and no more. The original books and the books from which this information was extracted usually contained additional data, much of which can be of inestimable importance to the genealogist. Such data as names of bondsmen, ministers, justices of the peace, churches, etc. is omitted. In some cases age, names of parents, occupations and similar information are to be found with the source material cited in the Bibliography (at the end of each volume), or in the original marriage books.

At the end of each entry is a county symbol in brackets. Key to the county symbols is on the following page. Immediately before the county symbol may be a B or an *, or both. The B is for black or colored; the * means that the source material included additional information of sufficient importance that we urge the researcher to obtain a copy of the source books or microfilm if possible.

Almost all of the original marriage books are available on microfilm at the Tennessee State Library and Archives in Nashville. This, of course, is the nearest we can come to "truth" in the records. Keep in mind that the clerks who entered the data were fallible; glaring errors appear frequently. As in all genealogical searching, certainty or something near it requires corroborating records.

Byron Sistler
Barbara Sistler

Nashville, Tennessee
May, 1989

COUNTY SYMBOLS, COUNTIES, YEARS REPRESENTED

Be	Benton	1832-1869	Hn	Henry	1838-1867
Cr	Carroll	1838-1873	L	Lauderdale	1838-1867
Dy	Dyer	1860-1879	Ma	Madison	1823-1871
F	Fayette	1838-1871	Mn	McNairy	1861-1865
G	Gibson	1824-1870	O	Obion	1824-1877
Hr	Hardeman	1823-1861	Sh	Shelby	1819-1865
Hy	Haywood	1859-1878	T	Tipton	1840-1874
		We	Weakley	1843-1863	

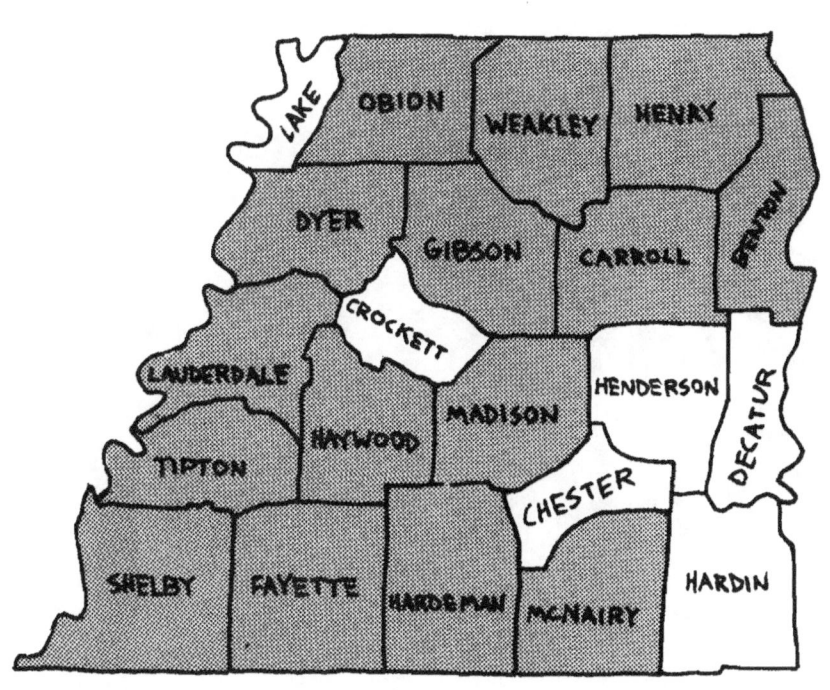

Aaron, W. B. to Sarah E. Reynolds 4-23-1863 Hn
Aaron, Wiley J. to Elvira J. Ablett 5-3-1866 Hn
Abbernathy, M. C. M. to Mary Donaldson 9-9-1846 (9-10-1846) F
Abbet, Henry to Caroline Poleston 8-28-1865 Be
Abbett, J. D. to Luellen Barksdale 1-6-1864 (no return) Cr
Abbey, Wm. D. to Martha C. Anlada 10-20-1859 (no return) Cr
Abbington, Henry to Nancy M. Cathey 11-28-1853 O
Abbington, W. B. to Miss Parrish 9-30-1850 We
Abbington, W. T. to Mary J. Plant 12-3-1866 (12-4-1866) F
Abbott, George to Matilda F. Giles 4-6-1842 Cr
Abbott, H. F. to Martha E. Norwood 10-8-1869 (10-10-1869) Cr
Abbott, Henry to Emma Rumley 2-2-1860 Cr
Abbott, Henry to Rebecca Dunston 1-10-1871 (1-13-1871) Dy
Abbott, J. D. to Elizabeth Green 9-5-1870 (9-6-1870) Cr
Abbott, James C. to Martha Jane Cole 3-2-1854 Be
Abbott, James T. to Rebecca E. Barton 4-8-1846 (4-10-1846) G
Abbott, John W. to Martha Jones 12-7-1863 (12-18-1863) Cr
Abbott, John to Frances Thompson 2-3-1852 Be
Abbott, L. B. to M. A. Jones 12-14-1866 (no return) Cr
Abbott, Richard H. to Elizabeth Cotheran 10-16-1855 Sh
Abbott, William H. to Mary J. Baker 8-16-1847 G
Abbott, William P. to Martha E. Taylor 6-3-1855 Hn
Abel, George F. to Clara Schindler 10-28-1845 Sh
Abel, J. M. to Mary F. Cowan 12-24-1867 (12-26-1867) F
Abel, William to Mary S. Coulter 8-9-1853 (no return) F
Abels, Joseph to Delilah Lindsey 10-1-1846 (10-4-1846) F
Abercrombie, Ephraim to Mary A. Maigue (Maguire?) 3-9-1853 Sh
Abercromby, C. S. to Ann Murphy 6-28-1858 (6-30-1858) Sh
Abernathy, A. K. to Sarah F. Parish 1-25-1865 Mn
Abernathy, Abraham to Ann Crawford 9-3-1869 (11-25-1869) F B
Abernathy, Buchanan to Mary A. Kesterson 5-28-1849 Sh
Abernathy, Daniel F. B. to Paralee Austin 4-7-1861 We
Abernathy, J. C. to Mary E. Carver 8-21-1853 Cr
Abernathy, James A. to Sarah E. Berry 3-4-1845 Cr
Abernathy, John S. to Matildy F. Robins 1-9-1843 Sh
Abernathy, Josiah C. to Sarah L. Swindle 5-26-1866 (5-7?-1866) Cr
Abernathy, R. J. to   12-15-1877 (12-16-1877) L
Abernathy, R. T. to Alice Overton 3-20-1873 Hy
Abernathy, Robert M. to Parthena A. Rhay 3-11-1874 (3-12-1874) L
Abernathy, Thos. E. to Nancy E. Ivey 11-6-1867 Hy
Abernathy, W. H. to Callie Barham 2-5-1886 (2-7-1886) L
Abernathy, Wm. to Nancy Kirkland 12-17-1850 Cr
Abinathey, S. D. to S. A. Brewer 12-11-1866 (12-16-1866) Cr
Abington, Hardamon to Margaretta Blair 9-19-1839 (9-26-1839) F
Abington, Jas. to Billy Waller 12-12-1851 (no return) F
Abington, John to Manda Olive 2-12-1874 O
Abington, Joseph H. to Lenora Dee Reid 5-14-1861 Sh
Abington, Nelson to Lucy Dunn 2-26-1868 (2-29-1868) O B
Able, H. C. to M. H. Bull 9-2-1867 (9-5-1867) F
Able, John F. to R. J. Tiller 10-19-1867 (10-23-1867) F
Able, John to Caroline Doebler 10-30-1855 Sh
Able, John to Mary Denny (Dennis) 12-10-1845 We
Able, Thomas P. to Nancy Oliver 11-2-1853 (11-3-1853) G
Ables, B. S. to Mary E. Gilbreth 7-8-1844 (no return) F
Ables, Chas. N. to N. S. Brown 2-3-1863 Sh
Ables, Chrs. to Martha Ann Nixon 7-5-1860 (7-8-1860) L
Ables, John W. to Lucinda Beavers 2-26-1839 F
Ables, Luther to Amanda P. German 4-10-1858 (4-13-1858) Hr
Ables, William to Mary Ann Templey 2-10-1869 L
Abnathy, Richard A. to Nancy Sample 3-8-1873 (3-9-1873) T
Abney, G. W. to Margaret L. McGee 10-29-1877 G
Abney, James M. to Mary Janes 3-1-1859 We
Abraham, J. W. B. to Arriemita Allison 11-16-1885 (11-17-1885) L
Abraham, Saml. N. to Ann E. Darnall 2-27-1860 (3-15-1860) Hr
Absteen, D. C. to M. J. Mabins 12-24-1878 Hy
Achtman(n), Joseph to Mary (Mrs.) Doerle 5-28-1863 Sh
Ackin?, Samuel J. to Sallie J. Chapman 4-18-1865 T
Acklin, Thomas to Marenah Robertson 11-9-1870 (11-10-1870) Dy
Aclin, Robert W. to Mary E. Cook 3-26-1861 We
Aclin, Thos. to Sarah Flowers 3-31-1869 Hy
Acock, A. A. to Sarah Carter 2-10-1848 Sh
Acre, Lewis to Anna Lambert 1-3-1839 (1-6-1839) Ma
Acre, Michie to Susan Copher 7-1-1843 (7-2-1843) Ma
Acre, Timothy J. to Martha C. Scarborough 4-25-1844 We
Acree, A. J. to Sarah A. Logan 4-19-1841 Sh
Acree, Wesley S. to Harriet A. Peters 1-4-1870 (1-6-1870) Ma
Acree, William J. to Ann Scott 8-14-1859 We
Acres, B. F. to P. McDaniel 2-10-1842 Be
Acres, James N. to Mary (Mrs.) Melley 6-6-1857 Ma
Acres, Thos. J. to Luzia D. Forest 7-25-1854 Cr
Acres, Uriah to Mary W. McCord 2-29-1847 Hn
Acuff, Isaac M. to Mary E. Golding 3-21-1856 (6-22-1856) L
Acuff, Isaac M. to Mary Jane Black 1-4-1870 (7-17-1870) L
Acuff, Isaac to Mary E. Golding 11-17-1854 L
Acuff, J. H. to J. F. Wilson 2-17-1877 (2-19-1877) L
Acuff, J. W. to F. E. Ledbetter 5-31-1884 (6-1-1884) L
Acuff, J. W. to Willie L. Watson 1-19-1884 (1-20-1884) L
Acuff, James C. to Frances H. Meadows 11-1-1849 L
Acuff, James C. to Sarah C. Norriss 6-24-1853 (no return) L
Acuff, Leander to Sarah Ray 7-10-1875 (7-12-1875) L
Acuff, R. W. to Lucy M. Crutchfield 10-11-1866 Hy
Acuff, W. R. to M. E. Shuck 4-2-1877 (4-3-1877) L
Acuff, W. R. to Melissa J. Scott .7-25-1882 (8-1-1882) L
Acuff, Wm. Robertson to Lucinda Sanders 12-3-1859 L
Adair, Benjamin M. to Elizabeth Shane 2-14-1833 G
Adair, James B. to Mary R. Cocke 1-20-1849 F
Adair, W. B. to Alethia Clipper 7-17-1850 Sh
Adair, William N. to Eliza C. Senter 1-1-1855 (1-4-1855) G
Adam, John to Minnie Barnes 2-27-1864 (2-29-1864) Sh
Adam, Tapley to Margaret A. Butler 8-24-1853 (8-25-1853) Ma
Adams, A. H. to Ann E. Upshaw 12-3-1847 F
Adams, A. H. to Rhoda (Rebecca) Jones 5-7-1829 Sh
Adams, A. H. to Sarah Price 9-13-1866 Hn
Adams, A. R. to Mary E. Blair 7-17-1853 Cr
Adams, Abraham to Martha Todd 10-22-1840 Hn
Adams, Alexander to Victoria Reeves 1-17-1867 Be
Adams, Allen D. to Elizabeth J. Adams 9-9-1858 We
Adams, Anderson to Martha Wilson 9-21-1870 (9-22-1870) T
Adams, Andrew to Leah Sherrell 3-17-1866 (3-25-1866) T
Adams, Ben to Sallie Brooks 3-28-1872 Hy
Adams, Benjamin to Mary Moon 9-10-1827 O
Adams, Bill to Chaney Nowell 3-2-1867 Hy
Adams, Bowlin to Cenus? Tipton 12-15-1870 Dy B
Adams, C. C. to A. R. Hammonds 5-1-1867 G
Adams, C. C. to M. E. Garner 12-20-1882 L
Adams, C. H. to Harriet Barber 1-17-1856 We
Adams, C. W. to Sarah E. Boaze 12-18-1851 We
Adams, Charles to Dephy Smith 1-1-1838 (1-6?-1838) Hr
Adams, Charles to Jane McKinney 9-2-1830 O
Adams, Chester T. to Nancy Oliver 10-30-1860 (11-1-1860) Ma
Adams, Claiborne to Mary White 1-24-1853 Sh
Adams, Collin H. to Evaline Harris (Haynes) 7-4-1849 O
Adams, D. R. to Catharin King 5-14-1866 (5-17-1866) Cr
Adams, David to Margaret Ralph 9-30-1873 (10-1-1873) T
Adams, David to Mildred L.(F?) Mayes (Meyer) 10-7-1863 Sh
Adams, David to Pricilla S. Walker 9-19-1855 (no return) F
Adams, David to Tabitha B. (Mrs.) Johnson 9-12-1859 (9-13-1859) Sh
Adams, Dennis L. to Susan F. C. Kirk 1-20-1845 Hn
Adams, Elijah S. to Susan Dortch 11-28-1852 Hn
Adams, Elijah to Priscilla Davis 7-10-1838 Cr
Adams, Ephraim B. to Mary Ann Bray 10-30-1841 (10-31?-1841) Hr
Adams, F. M. to E. A. Simmons 12-29-1855 (no return) Hn
Adams, F. M. to Emma Smith 11-26-1865 Hn
Adams, F. to Celia C. Smith 11-15-1844 Sh
Adams, G. W. to A. F. Merrick 6-24-1866 G
Adams, Garland to Elizabeth Cook 8-11-1838 (8-16-1838) G
Adams, George to Catherine Woodson 3-14-1876 (no return) Hy
Adams, George to Mary Ann Leggett 2-3-1847 Sh
Adams, Giles to Armon A. Fuqua 10-22-1850 Cr
Adams, Green to Jane Franklin 3-3-1874 T
Adams, Green to Mary Townsell 8-20-1845 Be
Adams, H. G. to Sarah C. Rainy 3-1-1858 Hr
Adams, H. to L. A. Nolen 11-14-1841 Be
Adams, Henry to Amanda Bell 12-31-1869 Cr
Adams, Howell to Darcus E. Allen 2-19-1848 G
Adams, Ira to Sarah Winston 11-4-1865 (11-14-1865) T
Adams, Isaac to Fanny Adams 4-10-1867 (no return) Hy
Adams, Israel to Mary Baldwin 3-12-1874 Hy
Adams, J. A. to Mattie J. Houston 10-17-1871 (10-19-1871) Cr
Adams, J. C. to M. J. Sanders 4-15-1859 (4-20-1859) F
Adams, J. G. to Isa L. Sherrill 12-4-1873 T
Adams, J. H. to Mollie J. Wainright 12-14-1871 (no return) Hy
Adams, J. J. to Louiza Ray 12-16-1866 Hn
Adams, J. K. to S. E. Carson 7-1-1880 L
Adams, J. M. to Cornelia A. Stafford 2-7-1866 F
Adams, J. N. to Alabama Swor 2-14-1867 Hn
Adams, J. W. to Lucy Akers 12-9-1882 (12-10-1882) L
Adams, J. W. to S. J. Eskew 12-12-1872 (no return) Cr
Adams, Jack to Jane Patterson 12-51867 G B
Adams, Jake to Alice Green 11-15-1877 Hy
Adams, James B. to M. E. Bradly 1-23-1860 (1-24-1860) F
Adams, James Goodram to Martha Susan Hopper 2-9-1849 (2-15-1849) T
Adams, James M. to Ellen Moseley 1-6-1876 Dy
Adams, James M. to Ellen Moseley 6?-6-1876? (with Apr 1876) Dy
Adams, James M. to Sarah F. Mosely 11-7-1872 Dy
Adams, James to Mary E. Bowden 11-22-1866 (no return) Hn
Adams, James to Mary E. Rollins 9-20-1854 (12-21-1854) Ma
Adams, James to Mary S. White 11-29-1848 Sh
Adams, Jesse F. S. to Sarah Willoughby 12-22-1859 (12-25-1859) Sh
Adams, Jno. to Elizabeth Wells 1-4-1838 (1-5-1838) Hr
Adams, Joe to George Ann Watkins 10-29-1874 Hy
Adams, Joe to Sarah Bishop 4-24-1872 Hy
Adams, John C. to Grisom E. Garrett 6-6-1866 (6-7-1866) Dy
Adams, John D. to Martha Hodges 3-4-1847 Hr

Grooms

Adams, John G. to Ann Wilson 1-9-1830 Sh
Adams, John G. to Mary Ann Walker 6-17-1849 Sh
Adams, John W. to Deborah L. Barfield 9-26-1865 L
Adams, John W. to Mary Montgomery 12-20-1846 Cr
Adams, John W. to Nancy Kennon 12-19-1868 (12-20-1868) Cr
Adams, John to Amanda Densford 4-6-1866 (4-7-1866) T
Adams, John to Mary Nunnally 12-24-1833 Hr
Adams, Leon to Alta Counsal 5-21-1846 (6-1-1846) G
Adams, Logan B. to Martha Bright 10-14-1851 Hr
Adams, Lonis? to Elizabeth V. Carroll 4-13-1833 (4-16-1833) Hr
Adams, Lysander to Lydia M. Bedford 7-23-1826 O
Adams, M. H. to Juantha B. King 5-8-1863 Hn
Adams, Marion to Martha Jane Harper 9-29-1852 (9-30-1852) O
Adams, Martin G. to Lucy Ann Gambriel 8-1-1840 Hr
Adams, Martin H. to Susan McConnell 1-16-1854 Sh
Adams, Martin H. to Susan McConnell 1-24-1854 (no return) F
Adams, Migugol? to Ella? Faucett 10-30-1869 T
Adams, Minus O. to Frances C. Butler 1-10-1859 (1-11-1859) Ma
Adams, N. H. to Amanda E. Chapman 11-26-1860 Hn
Adams, Nathan to Mary Stoveall 10-5-1843 (no return) We
Adams, Noah to Harriet Mathis 5-1-1873 Hy
Adams, Parham to Catharine Rose 5-29-1855 (5-31-1855) Sh
Adams, Parham to Sarah Hardaway 3-4-1853 Sh
Adams, Peter to Milly Shepherd 1-5-1867 G
Adams, R. A. to Julina Jane Abbett 7-3-1853 Be
Adams, R. H. to Elizabeth Layman (Sayman) 10-17-1866 G
Adams, R. L. to Levenia D. Neil 2-13-1861 Sh
Adams, Richard L. to Lucinda Vernatta 7-15-1848 O
Adams, Richard to Melinda Starks 4-26-1867 (no return) Hy
Adams, Richard to Milley Strong 9-30-1865 (10-28-1865) T
Adams, Richard to Ruth H. Alphan 2-14-1854 O
Adams, Robert G. to Susan Davis 3-17-1862 Ma
Adams, Robert H. to Sarah Ann Harris 11-9-1843 Sh
Adams, Robert S. to E. H. Fielder 9-22-1857 G
Adams, Robert to Fanny (Mrs.) Wales 1-26-1864 Sh
Adams, Robt. H. to Susie (Mrs.) McFarland 8-22-1871 (8-22-1871) Ma
Adams, S. J. to Sarah F. Foster 9-20-1865 G
Adams, S. to Elizabeth Price 11-15-1867 (no return) Hn
Adams, Sanco to Leanna Adams 12-24-1866 (no return) Hy
Adams, Simon to Martha Payne 12-26-1871 Hy
Adams, Sterling to Cath Kee 7-11-1839 Be
Adams, T. to Caroline Doorens 1-16-1845 Hn
Adams, Taylor to Mary Ann Cup 10-21-1869 (10-22-1869) T
Adams, Thomas E. to Mary Alston 10-8-1839 Sh
Adams, Thomas M. to Martha Sommers 9-18-1862 We
Adams, Thomas to Emma Read 12-28-1866 Hy
Adams, Thos. N. to M. E. Parker 4-20-1856 Be
Adams, Thos. S. to Charlotte Blow 11-18-1852 Cr
Adams, W. H. to Fannie Calhoon 1-4-1857 (1-6-1857) T
Adams, W. H. to Maggie A. Ware 2-5-1874 Hy
Adams, W. H. to Martha Brown 2-12-1873 (2-13-1873) T
Adams, W. H. to Ocie Caldwell 2-27-1867 (2-28-1867) O
Adams, W. S. to Elizabeth F. Mebene 4-23-1864 (4-24-1864) Cr
Adams, W. S. to Mary Ann Caff 1-14-1859 (1-17-1859) Sh
Adams, Warren to Martha Moore 1-11-1849 (no return) F
Adams, Was. to Lucy Mitchel 1-8-1840 Be
Adams, Washington to Mary Walden 2-18-1832 Hr
Adams, Whitmill P. to Rachel Pierce 11-16-1853 Ma
Adams, William A. to Unaty Adams 2-15-1861 We
Adams, William C. to Elizabeth E. Palmer 10-18-1853 Hn
Adams, William G. to Elvira Craig 11-7-1842 Hr
Adams, William Henry to Miranda Jane Massey 2-10-1859 (2-17-1859) Ma
Adams, William to Doretha E. Carnell 8-3-1857 (8-5-1857) L
Adams, William to Ellen McDearon 12-28-1871 L B
Adams, William to Jane Reynolds 7-31-1849 (no return) L
Adams, William to Martha S. Hale 8-6-1850 (no return) Hn
Adams, William to Mary Hooper 12-15-1858 (12-16-1858) L
Adams, William to Mollie Shade 1-11-1871 Hy
Adams, William to Zelpha Hale 8-6-1841 O
Adams, Williams to America Richardson 11-28-1868 (11-29-1868) L
Adams, Win to Matilda Cornelius 7-2-1827 (7-4-1827) Hr
Adams, Wm. C. to Eliza W. Newland 5-4-1846 (5-5-1846) Hr
Adams, Wm. G. to Allison E. Scott 1-18-1839 Sh
Adams, Wm. to Mary Ann Rose 5-28-1859 Sh
Adcock, A. M. to Caroline S. Mills 5-13-1863 (5-14-1863) Cr
Adcock, Allen to Mary E. Akin 12-10-1862 We
Adcock, Bowling to Elizabeth Shoemake 9-26-1860 Dy
Adcock, William to Elizabeth Litton 4-25-1846 (4-28-1846) O
Addison, J. E. P. to Frances E. Jones 4-17-1878 (4-18-1878) L
Adelbert, Thos. to M. Pursley 5-1-1869 O B
Aden, A. B. to Elizabeth C. Marchbanks 9-10-1854 Be
Aden, Bennett S. to Mary M. Yowell 7-12-1865 Hn
Aden, James S. to Anna E. Moore 1-10-1866 Hn
Aden, S. V. to Lydia Perkins 6-4-1844 Be
Aden, W. K. to J. Farrar 6-5-1842 Be
Adin, Clinton to M. M. Fuqua 5-28-1865 (6-8-1865) Cr
Adkins, Albert to Elizabeth Trobough 4-14-1866 T

Adkins, Benj. Tho. to Margaret Miller 10-2-1850 T
Adkins, Charles Howell to Harriet L. Wooton 9-11-1853 (9-13-1853) T
Adkins, Charles to Martha Weaver 7-26-1852 (7-27-1852) T
Adkins, F. B. to Elizabeth McLennan 3-7-1860 (3-8-1860) T
Adkins, Franklin to Susan J. McLester 10-22-1860 Hn
Adkins, George A. to Angeline Rutlidge 10-19-1843 G
Adkins, H. C. to Tilda Traylor 7-30-1870 (7-31-1870) Cr
Adkins, Isaac to Matilda Okelly 8-17-1867 F B
Adkins, James A. to Ruth R. Spitler 2-13-1839 Sh
Adkins, James L. to Jane Hill 2-3-1847 (2-10-1847) T
Adkins, John Henry to Sallie Davis 11-8-1870 G
Adkins, John to Annie Bledsoe 8-18-1874 (8-8?-1874) T
Adkins, Larkin to Mary Harvey 5-29-1851 (no return) F
Adkins, Moses to Ann Payne 1-7-1874 (1-8-1874) T
Adkins, Nathan to Louisa Coward 10-22-1874 (10-23-1874) T
Adkins, Phillip to Harriet Holmes 4-2-1866 (4-7-1866) T
Adkins, Robert to Mary Jane Alvis 4-4-1844 Sh
Adkins, Sam to Amy Robinson 2-14-1867 T
Adkins, Sam to Bettie Taylor 4-6-1867 (4-7-1867) F B
Adkins, Saml. Will to Lennie Thompson 12-29-1870 T
Adkins, Saml. to Matilda Gillum 1-11-1873 G
Adkins, Thomas to Ellen Rose 5-13-1846 (5-14-1846) Hr
Adkins, W. C. to Cinthia A. Birdsong 6-27-1851 (6-30-1851) F
Adkins, William H. to Frances A. Stuart 2-12-1842 (2-17-1842) Hr
Adkins, William to Gemema G. Grubb 12-31-1857 We
Adkins, William to Rosanna Holliday 7-9-1865 Hn
Adkins, William to Sally Oliver 11-26-1860 (11-27-1860) Ma
Adkins, William to Sarah E. F. Gannaway 11-24-1866 (11-25-1866) Ma
Adkinson, Calvin to Martha Wright 6-13-1868 (6-14-1868) O
Adkinson, John to Margaret E. String no date (with 1862) T
Adkinson, Levi to Minerva Sanders 1-2-1856 (1-6-1856) O
Adkinson, Matha to Sarah M. Vaughan 12-10-1850 We
Adkinson, William D. to Catherine Robins 6-28-1830 O
Adkison, Bynum to Eliza Easley 5-31-1858 (6-1-1858) T
Adkison, James to Mary Easley 11-20-1869 (11-23-1869) T
Adkison, William to Martha Littleton 6-25-1859 (6-26-1859) L
Adkisson, Isaac to Charlotte Cooper 3-6-1843 (3-9-1843) T
Admas?, Saml. to Judia Walker 3-17-1866 T
Aebly, Jacob to Christina Buckmuller 10-20-1860 Sh
Agassiz, Frederick to Ellen (Miss) Hagan 8-3-1863 Sh
Agee, C. C. to S. L. Connell 3-29-1865 G
Agee, Daniel T. to Luemma S. Conlee 3-13-1855 G
Agee, John D. to Tennessee A. Burrow 7-4-1865 G
Agee, Jonathan B. to Sarah E. Burrow 12-18-1850 G
Agee, Thomas H. to Jane Flowers 7-28-1861 G
Agee, Wm. T. to Martha A. Kelly 2-12-1857 G
Agnew, Robert to Martha Middleton 3-24-1846 (no return) Hn
Agnew, Samuel E. to Elizabeth Sinkler 2-23-1853 (2-24-1853) O
Agnew, Tennessee to Nancy Shelby 8-26-1865 O
Agnew, Thomas J. to Nancy Denham 1-2-1854 (1-4-1854) O
Agnew, William to Martha M. Caruthers 12-1-1840 O
Agnugh, Hugh to Mary J. Bookout 1-26-1859 We
Ahearn, Wm. to Ellen Burns 2-22-1854 Sh
Ahern, Patrick to Mary Owens 8-10-1847 Sh
Aiken, J. H. to S. J. Carroll 2-28-1871 (3-2-1871) Dy
Aiken, James to Ellen Johnson 4-4-1872 Hy
Aiken, Richd. to Sarah E. Sevier 12-13-1851 (no return) F
Aiken, T. H. to Lucinda Thompson 10-29-1868 (no return) Dy
Aikens, R. E. to Mattie C. Hurt 1-1-1866 (1-4-1866) T
Aikin, W. A. to Robina Brewer 8-27-1870 (8-28-1870) Cr
Aitkin, William N. to Nancy J. Nevill 11-21-1849 Sh
Akens, George T. to Ann E. Freeman 1-15-1861 (no return) Hy
Aker, Burges to Martha Forrest 2-6-1867 (no return) Hy
Aker, F. M. to S. G. Edwards 4-10-1866 O
Akers, Abner to Adeline Howard 2-28-1865 Hn
Akers, B. T. to Francis Childress 1-8-1862 Be
Akers, George to Mary J. E. Hening 12-2-1846 (12-3-1846) G
Akers, Harris to Parthena Rice 1-20-1872 (1-23-1872) Cr
Akers, Isaac to Sarah C. Gregson 3-6-1845 Hn
Akers, James to Nancy Snider 10-29-1865 Be
Akers, Jess to Susan C. Warren 1-2-1844 Cr
Akers, John to Martha Ann Bird 12-23-1852 Cr
Akin, A. C. to Amanda M. Hatch 8-23-1856 (8-24-1856) O
Akin, C. C. to Martha S. Phillips 9-1-1842 Sh
Akin, C. V. to Ellen M. Pickard 1-26-1885 (1-29-1885) L
Akin, Christopher to Anna Bumpass 11-29-1870 (12-3-1870) Dy B
Akin, F. M. to Tabitha E. Smith 7-4-1868 G
Akin, George W. to Sinah M. Mullins 8-21-1851 (8-22-1851) G
Akin, George to Martha Durham 2-8-1844 F
Akin, H. B. to R. O. Steward 1-18-1875 (1-20-1875) L
Akin, J. G. W. to S. C. Holland 9-4-1876 (no return) Dy
Akin, James E. to Mary F. Portice 12-25-1847 (12-30-1847) Hr
Akin, James to Mollie Setten 11-11-1876 (11-12-1876) L
Akin, Jas. M. to Louisa R. D. Mount 8-4-1870 G
Akin, Jeremiah to D. T. Martin 4-11-1843 Be
Akin, Joel to Oran Wyant 12-5-1842 Sh
Akin, John J. to Sallie J. Chapman 4-18-1865 (4-20-1865) T

Akin, John W. to Martha H. Stroud 11-21-1870 (11-23-1870) T
Akin, John to Easter Boyd 11-2-1868 T
Akin, John to Easter Boyd 11-7-1868 T
Akin, L. H. to N. M. Reed 3-6-1861 G
Akin, M. V. to S. A. McCutchen 9-4-1871 (9-5-1871) Dy
Akin, N. T.? to Tennessee E. Grimes 11-10-1874 (11-11-1874) T
Akin, Richard J. to Mary L. Nedry 6-3-1868 (6-4-1868) O
Akin, Saml. H. to Sarah Lashlee 12-11-1849 Be
Akin, T. R. to M. J. Ward 12-9-1874 (12-10-1874) Dy
Akin, Thomas A. to Nancy M. Reed 10-25-1855 G
Akin, Thomas J. to Louiza Bryant 3-17-1859 (3-18-1859) G
Akin, Wm. H. to Martha M. Jackson 9-23-1841 Sh
Akin, Z. T. to Sarah A. Smith 10-7-1863 (no return) Dy
Akins, Abner to Margaret M. Carver 12-12-1849 Cr
Akins, George to Margaret Holmes 7-17-1848 Cr
Akins, John T. to P. P. Perkins 3-24-1858 Cr
Akins, Taylor to Jane Boyd 12-22-1875 (no return) Hy
Akins, Thomas to Nancy Edwards 11-25-1843 (11-26-1843) G
Akins, Thos. to Syntha J. Stone 3-1-1847 Cr
Akins, William to Letty Smith 11-6-1839 Cr
Akins, Wm. to Mary Tomblinson 5-16-1871 (5-17-1871) Cr
Akins, Wm. to Sarah Smith 12-7-1852 Cr
Al---ty?, Elijah to Malvina Rumley 7?-7-1864 Be
Albea, Lewis to Mariah Atkins 12-30-1866 G
Albert, John P. to Augusta Yanike 7-28-1855 Sh
Alborn, James D. to Margarett (Miss) Wallacle 4-15-1864 Sh
Albrecht, John H. to Mary C. Weaver 10-13-1858 Sh
Albright, Austin J. to Mary Burns 2-4-1864 (no return) Cr
Albright, Austin J. to Mary Burrus 2-4-1864 (2-7-1864) Cr
Albright, C. I. W. to Sue P. Hardison 12-23-1868 G
Albrittain, David to Sarah F. Olds 12-15-1869 Dy
Albritten, Isaac to Sarah P. Simmons 7-25-1852 Hn
Albritton, Beverly E. to Sarah G. Moore 11-24-1861 Hn
Albritton, John H. to Elizabeth Spring 3-31-1852 Ma
Albritton, Sam P. to Martha J. Brown 6-1-1861 (no return) Dy
Albritton, Wm. A. to Virginia J. Hooper 5-9-1851 Hn
Alcebrook, Thomas C. to Frances P. Stone 12-22-1857 (no return) L
Alden, Jacob to Rosina Newbold 6-27-1848 Sh
Alderson, Joseph M. W. to Elizabeth C. Erwin 1-1-1841 Hn
Alderson, Lucius H. to Elizabeth Smith 11-11-1853 Hn
Alderson, William to Aloda Ann Scales 12-18-1833 O
Aldridge, David to Nancy Kimbrough 7-25-1841 Sh
Aldridge, George to Martha Furgerson 6-8-1870 (6-28-1870) L B
Aldridge, Henry to Bay C. Wallis 4-16-1869 G
Aldridge, Jessee to Rosa Jane Smith 6-30-1850 Sh
Aldridge, Josiah to Rebecca Williams 1-12-1843 Hn
Aldridge, Thos. to kSina Sanford 1-11-1866 (1-13-1866) T
Ales, Charly to Cylvia Anderson 10-13-1871 T
Alestock, James S. to Elizabeth Thurman 7-26-1837 Hr *
Alexander, Aaron to Sina Tapscott 12-30-1869 Hn
Alexander, Abner to Mary E. Davis 5-26-1853 (no return) F
Alexander, Athelbert to Henrietta Manly 8-23-1853 Sh
Alexander, B. E. to Lively A. Bratton 12-11-1852 (no return) Hn
Alexander, Barney to Emina Wilson 12-7-1874? T
Alexander, Benj. to Malinda Motion 12-18-1872 (12-19-1872) Cr B
Alexander, Berry P. to Mary Jane Alexander 1-27-1850 Hn
Alexander, C. B. to Mary D. Allison 3-13-1849 Sh
Alexander, C. G. to Nellie A. Wright 12-5-1865 Hn
Alexander, C. M. to L. E. Stegall 9-3-1862 Mn
Alexander, C. W. to Margaret M. Stratton 7-3-1858 (7-5-1858) Sh
Alexander, Charles to Lucy Berry 5-8-1873 Hy
Alexander, Charles to Penny Simpson 2-12-1876 (no return) Hy
Alexander, Charley to Lou Miller 11-12-1870 (11-17-1870) F B
Alexander, D. W. to Susan A. Tyner 12-25-1874 (12-27-1874) O
Alexander, Daniel to Mary Anne Powell 4-1-1847 Hn
Alexander, Daniel to Fanny Heaslet 12-24-1869 (no return) F B
Alexander, Dudley to Mary Pierce 5-5-1858 Ma
Alexander, Duncan L. to Hannah Chandler 1-31-1854 Ma
Alexander, E. R. to Maryann Provine 12-15-1841 (no return) F
Alexander, Edward F. to Julia A. Dodds 6-22-1870 Ma
Alexander, Elias to Clarentine M. Boyle 2-9-1847 (2-11-1847) Hr
Alexander, Elijah to Sarah E. Guinn 12-22-1868 (12-23-1868) Ma
Alexander, Emanuel to Noah Shephard 7-21-1869 (7-29-1869) F B
Alexander, Even S. to Urcilla Alsup 9-17-1844 Sh
Alexander, Ezekiel Z. to Mary E. Robinson 7-20-1846 (7-24-1846) Hr
Alexander, F. E. to Sarah E. Wall 4-4-1864 (no return) Hn
Alexander, Ferdinand to Ellen Smith 12-17-1879 L
Alexander, Franklin to Nancy B. Edwards 3-21-1844 Cr
Alexander, G. B. to M. A. Hart 10-3-1855 We
Alexander, G. L. to M. J. Wilkerson 1-19-1869 (no return) Hy
Alexander, G. W. to Elizabeth F. Grimes 4-13-1848 Hn
Alexander, G. W. to Margaret Mitchell 10-14-1861 Sh
Alexander, G. W. to Mary D. Baughs 8-24-1870 (no return) Hy
Alexander, Geo. to Leanna Olive 10-13-1847 Hn B
Alexander, George to Cornelia Faulkner 1-26-1874 (1-28-1874) Dy
Alexander, George to Rachel Bowden 12-23-1865 (no return) Hn
Alexander, George to Rachel Bowden 12-30-1865 (no return) Hn

Alexander, H. P. to Rebecca Mathis 1-3-1865 Hn
Alexander, Hamilton to Martha J. Mathis 9-16-1846 Hn
Alexander, Harvey M. to Malinda Maynard 12-16-1869 (12-17-1869) Ma
Alexander, Henry N. to Samantha B. Veazey 8-7-1867 Ma
Alexander, Henry to Betsy Tate 7-19-1867 (no return) F B
Alexander, Henry to Julia Smith 1-24-1878 Hy
Alexander, Henry to Mildred H. Carr 1-21-1846 Sh
Alexander, Henry to Tisha Roach 5-3-1869 (no return) Cr
Alexander, Hiram K. to Mary J. Davis 1-28-1858 O
Alexander, Hugh W. to Sarah L. Basford 8-5-1851 Be
Alexander, Ira to Sarah Hunt 12-8-1840 Hn
Alexander, Isaac W. to Nancy Berry 4-15-1831 (4-22-1831) Ma
Alexander, Isaack to Sarah Word 9-11-1838 G
Alexander, J. B. to M. J. Morris 2-3-1872 (2-4-1872) L
Alexander, J. E. to Mollie Cisco 1-27-1869 (1-28-1869) F
Alexander, J. F. to Louisa Jane Woods 12-28-1864 (no return) Hn
Alexander, J. H. to Mary E. Dickson 10-29-1839 Cr
Alexander, J. M. to Margaret A. Rudisill 2-22-1848 Sh
Alexander, J. M. to Mary (Miss) Ammen 7-25-1863 Sh
Alexander, J. M. to Mary L. Lewis 12-17-1839 (2-13-1840) L
Alexander, J. O. to Mary J. Jones 2-29-1848 Hn
Alexander, J. P. B. to Sarah G. Gillispie 12-15-1842 Sh
Alexander, Jack to Elizabeth Alexander 10-8-1873 (10-20-18730) T
Alexander, James F. to Elizabeth Jobe 6-17-1852 F
Alexander, James F. to Mary Jane F. Hall 11-17-1858 We
Alexander, James H. to Martha E. Pryor 9-14-1837 Hr
Alexander, James M. to Mary Elizabeth Rollings 3-15-1855 Ma
Alexander, James M. to Mary Jane Cobb 11-17-1871 Ma
Alexander, James M. to Narcissa D. Harris 8-29-1844 Ma
Alexander, James P. to Jane Patterson 2-20-1829 G
Alexander, James R. to Fannie S. Sanford 12-8-1858 T
Alexander, James S. to Elizabeth Elliott 12-20-1843 (12-21-1843) G
Alexander, James W. to Mary Jane (Mrs.) Rose 10-7-1841 Sh
Alexander, James to Amanda Allen 9-4-1860 Cr
Alexander, James to Amelia Ann Conn 1-24-1829 Ma
Alexander, James to Lucinda Creed 10-8-1825 O
Alexander, James to Martha Alexander 1-18-1841 (1-21-1841) F
Alexander, James to Mary Ann Young 6-5-1867 Be
Alexander, James to Peninah Teague 12-25-1856 Ma
Alexander, James to Percy Pope 6-8-1854 G
Alexander, Jasper to Eley Fisher 1-8-1872 (1-19-1872) L
Alexander, Jefferson to Eliza Alexander 3-9-1846 Hn
Alexander, Jess L. to Emily Martin 2-25-1863 Hn
Alexander, Jimms P. to Nancy P. Kell 10-24-1871 (10-25-1871) Ma
Alexander, John A. to Elizabeth A. Boswell 5-1-1865 F
Alexander, John B. to Margaret Allison 7-14-1866 (7-15-1866) Ma
Alexander, John B. to Nancy J. Lomax 1-20-1859 We
Alexander, John D. to Lutitia Mahala Hedin 9-1-1863 (no return) Dy
Alexander, John E. to Mary Ann Nobles 9-23-1847 G
Alexander, John E. to Rebecca A. Allen 1-11-1859 Hn
Alexander, John H. to Elizabeth Auff 3-5-1846 Hn
Alexander, John M. to Elizabeth J. Hutson 3-29-1860 (3-?-1860) O
Alexander, John M. to Lenory Dyal 11-23-1843 G
Alexander, John M. to Lydia M. Lewis 9-28-1848 Hn
Alexander, John M. to Mary E. Hutson 12-11-1860 O
Alexander, John P. to Emily Stephen 2-19-1848 (no return) Hn
Alexander, John W. to Sarah Jane Potts 12-18-1860 Hn
Alexander, John to Caroline Reeves 9-15-1859 O
Alexander, John to Julia Densmore 4-15-1857 Sh
Alexander, John to Sophia Ann Jones 6-16-1866 (no return) F B
Alexander, Joseph F. to Frances (Mrs.) Frieles 12-10-1868 (12-13-1868) Ma
Alexander, Joseph H. to Eliza E. Boyd 5-25-1843 L
Alexander, Josiah M. to Amanda McCaleb 11-23-1846 G
Alexander, M. D. to M. J. Hampton 6-25-1864 (6-26-1864) O
Alexander, M. V. B. to S. F. Barber 5-14-1863 We
Alexander, Madison to Betsey Ray 12-16-1865 Hn
Alexander, Martin D. to Mary Jane Alexander 5-14-1853 Ma
Alexander, Melville B. to Angeline J. Janes 12-21-1862 Hn
Alexander, Meredith to Nancy Gholston 11-15-1855 (no return) Hn
Alexander, Milus to Pleasan Small 2-28-1867 T
Alexander, Moses B. to Margaret Allen 10-26-1837 Sh
Alexander, N. C. to Sophia Hartsfield 11-28-1866 Hn
Alexander, N. W. to M. M. Miles 6-19-1869 (no return) Hy
Alexander, N.? to Margaret S. White 11-20-1867 (no return) Hn
Alexander, O. C. to Henrietta Alexander 5-31-1866 (no return) Hn
Alexander, P. C. to Lavina Delashment 11-11-1862 (11-13-1862) T
Alexander, P. H. to Eveline E. LeCog (Secog) 3-23-1849 Sh
Alexander, Philip D. to Jane Guinn 12-22-1869 (12-23-1869) Ma
Alexander, Poke to Parthenia Easley 3-2-1867 Hy
Alexander, Preston to Mattie Collier 3-13-1872 Hy
Alexander, R. B. to Sarah M. Taylor 3-29-1838 F
Alexander, R. H. to Ann E. Wicks 3-29-1852 (3-30-1852) G
Alexander, R. M. to Sarah M. Threldkel 11-11-1867 O
Alexander, Ralph G. to Nancy Gwinn 7-30-1839 (no return) Hn
Alexander, Remkin M. to Nelly Hart 11-5-1839 Hn
Alexander, Robert P. to Emily E. Anderson 7-31-1837 Hr
Alexander, Robert to Sallie Sloan 1-23-1860 Sh

Alexander, Russel to Charlotte Mask 12-30-1868 (12-31-1868) F B
Alexander, S. W. to Elizabeth Stiles 2-18-1852 Hn
Alexander, Sam to Jennie Ware 8-17-1872 Hy
Alexander, Sam to Sarah Jane Hays 1-15-1876 (no return) Hy
Alexander, Samuel D. to Colista E. Boon 1-27-1859 G
Alexander, Samuel P. to Emily E. Wray 12-23-1862 We
Alexander, Samuel W. to Edy C. Smotherman 4-2-1849 Hn
Alexander, Sandy to Tennessee Hess 7-19-1867 (no return) Hy
Alexander, Shelby to Pemelia Black 12-16-1840 Sh
Alexander, Simpson to Martha J. Haynes 2-27-1847 (no return) Hn
Alexander, T. J. to Jennie Lanier 9-2-1865 (9-3-1865) Cr
Alexander, T. J. to Lucinda H. Drinkard R. A. Maynard 2-20-1855 We
Alexander, T. P. to Elizabeth Chandler 2-12-1863 Mn
Alexander, Thadeus A. to Mary C. Howerton 1-19-1858 (1-20-1858) T
Alexander, Thomas B. to Jerusha L. Evans 4-8-1869 (no return) L
Alexander, Thomas to Dilsey Ware 11-25-1874 Hy
Alexander, Thomas to Jane Blan 2-27-1838 Hn
Alexander, Thos. to Catharine (Miss) Peak 1-28-1858 Sh
Alexander, U. (Dr.) to Elizabeth J. Lavis 1-27-1841 G
Alexander, Uriah M. to Ann Abernathy 1-30-1871 (2-1-1871) F
Alexander, W. H. R. to Luentia Butler 2-28-1850 (no return) Hn
Alexander, W. L. to Jane Wall 3-8-1866 O
Alexander, Wiley to Gracy Henderson 12-23-1871 (12-29-1871) L B
Alexander, William A. to Suzy Ann Irvin 3-21-1843 (3-23-1843) Ma
Alexander, William H. to Eliza J. Gaskins 10-24-1859 (no return) '
Alexander, William J. to Lucinda C. Faust 8-16-1860 Hn
Alexander, William M. to Francis M. Hubert 10-31-1860 O
Alexander, William R. to Elizabeth German 11-3-1829 (11-4-1829) Hr
Alexander, William R. to Susan Needham 4-30-1830 Hr
Alexander, William to Abitha Stephens 9-19-1846 Hn
Alexander, William to Nancy N. Guinn 3-18-1868 Ma
Alexander, Winslew to Julia Odem 9-30-1858 We
Alexander, Wm M. to J. M. Hart 3-28-1854 (no return) F
Alexander, Wm. J. to Mattie Kyle 11-27-1865 (no return) F
Alexander, Wm. to Mary J. Adams 10-18-1853 Sh
Alexander, Wright to Catherine Fitzpatrick 9-20-1869 (9-25-1869) L B
Alexander, Zinas to Nancy Given 5-14-1844 (5-16-1844) L
Alexander?, Rob. S. to Mary C. Alexander 11-15-1846 F
Alexandner, D. P. W. to M. C. Tyler 12-19-1866 G
Alexandner, D. V. to M. C. Melton 2-28-1870 G
Alexandner, Dick to Caroline McGregory 10-23-1869 G B
Alexandner, Ike to Harriet Mosely 1-20-1868 G B
Alexandner, Joseph N. to Mary E. Lett 7-11-1864 G
Alexandner, Saml. to Martha Hassell 12-22-1867 G
Alexandra, Sam to Artheria Harris 6-11-1870 (6-10?-1870) Dy
Aley, James A. to Louisa White 10-1-1876 Hy
Alfin, Ivy S. to Eliza Kenady 4-1-1841 (4-8-1841) G
Alford, B. to Mary E. Holland 1-17-1884 (1-21-1884) L
Alford, Burtis to Mary E. Nobles 10-11-1870 L
Alford, G. W. to Mary C. Ridout 5-19-1861 Sh
Alford, Green? to Patsey G. Callihan 6-18-1855 L
Alford, H. C. to Martha F. Dickson 9-11-1866 L
Alford, J. H. to Anna Sloan 12-14-1870 (12-15-1870) F
Alford, J. T. to Margaret Craig 3-12-1885 L
Alford, J. W. to Martha L. E. Dement 1-12-1863 G
Alford, James M. to Susan Lockard 9-1-1876 L
Alford, James to Jane Arnol 1-30-1850 (2-5-1850) G
Alford, James to Jane Vantrence 3-9-1841 Ma
Alford, James to Mariah Sellers? 3-31-1847 (4-1-1847) Hr
Alford, John to Lucinda Nobles 6-27-1857 (6-28-1857) L
Alford, Leander to Nancy Davis 1-30-1844 Ma
Alford, Lewis G. to Sarah Manley 11-29-1860 L
Alford, Lewis to Louisa Nobles 8-5-1852 L
Alford, Thomas J. to Frances Richardson 12-29-1845 (12-30-1845) G
Alford, Thomas J. to Martha R. Brightwell 7-5-1858 G
Alford, Willis to Annie Cook 9-22-1877 (no return) L
Alford, Wilson W. to Cora C. Stuckey 6-23-1854 L
Alford, Wm. Jasper to Mary E. Lewis 7-26-1859 Sh
Alford, Wm. to Martha Boney 1-16-1851 L
Alford, jr., Burtis to Margaret E. Nobles 8-4-1852 L
Algea, Jacob to Molly Shepherd 2-14-1870 (2-15-1870) Cr
Algea, R. H. to Frances B. Inman 4-29-1846 Cr
Algee, James A. to V. A. Lowrence 9-3-1857 Cr
Algee, James G. to Sarah E. Wilson 12-31-1840 Cr
Algee, John C. to Jane Brooks 10-5-1852 Cr
Algee, Lander D. to Martha A. Robinson 9-14-1846 Cr
Algee, R. W. to Josephine Anderson 4-6-1863 (no return) Cr
Algee, Robert C. to Margaret C. Mooring 12-27-1855 Ma
Algee, W. H. to M. E. Vaughter 6-28-1867 Cr
Alison, B. G. to Ellen Shaw 6-4-1862 (no return) Hy
Alison, B. W. to Julia A. Whitelaw 1-6-1875 Hy
Alison, B. W. to Mary Coltart 11-9-1865 Hy
Alison, Charley to Frances Smith 12-15-1872 Hy
Alison, Henry to Rachael Raylor 10-14-1865 (no return) Hy
Alison, Joseph to Caroline Loyd 1-3-1877 Hy
Alkins, J. G. to Nancy J. Smyth 6-8-1854 We
Allain (Allen), J. D. to Sarah Foster Mitchell 1-6-1844 Sh *

Allan, John to Mary (Mrs.) Stewart 1-21-1863 (1-22-1863) Sh
Allbright, George N. to Barbara E. Thompson 12-14-1865 (no return) Hy
Allbright, Jacob to Sarah L. Nelson 10-1-1827 Hr
Allbritten, Beverly G. to Rutha A. Etherage 4-13-1845 Hn
Allbritten, Beverly to Rebecca Gullage 4-20-1842 Hn
Allbritton, Jas. C. to Virginia C. Burton 12-27-1865 Hn
Allbritton, Van B. to Sallie H. Caldwell 12-1-1866 (no return) Hn
Allcock, Durin O. to Hannah R. Caldwell 12-16-1854 (11?-17-1854) O
Allcock, James C. to Ann Ashley 12-25-1851 O
Allder, Abraham N. to Martha J. Bruce 3-3-1860 Sh
Allen, A. J. to Lucinda H. Drinkard 3-7-1867 G
Allen, Abner to Nancy Yates 1-4-1864 (1-5-1864) O
Allen, Alex to Matilda McMurry 3-8-1868 G B
Allen, Alfred to Mary E. Rodgers 11-7-1850 Hr
Allen, Andrew A. to Ann B. Allen 12-22-1845 (12-23-1845) F
Allen, Andrew J. to Elizabeth Jane Cassell 6-27-1853 (6-30-1853) O
Allen, Andrew J. to Mary A. Russell 1-25-1870 Ma
Allen, Archer to Lucinda Adams 2?-17-1867 (3-26-1867) T
Allen, Arnold to Emma Pierson 11-12-1868 (no return) L B
Allen, Athan to Charllotty Oneal 12-9-1827 Ma
Allen, B. F. to C. E. Crawford 8-10-1865 G
Allen, B. F. to Cernelia Brown? 2-21-1863 (2-22-1863) Sh
Allen, B. F. to Martha A. Fletcher 7-26-1848 Sh
Allen, B. W. to Levonia F. Owen 12-15-1868 (12-16-1868) L
Allen, Benj. F. to Margaret A. Houston 12-1-1857 Sh
Allen, Benj. J. to Fannie R. Sims 11-6-1855 (no return) F
Allen, Benjamin to Susan (Mrs.) Blackburn 12-2-1872 Dy
Allen, Beverly A. to Elizabeth Gilliam 8-14-1856 (8-16-1856) O
Allen, Beverly S. to Mary E. Doherty 11-12-1856 Cr
Allen, C. A. to Sarah Jane Kluigh 10-29-1856 (10-30-1856) T
Allen, C. R. to S. M. Norrid 8-4-1866 O
Allen, C. T. to L. A. Fletcher 6-7-1865 (6-8-1865) Cr
Allen, Caleb D. (L.) to Susan A. Wilson 12-17-1863 G
Allen, Carlton to Rebecca Vaughan 4-3-1843 (4-4-1843) T
Allen, Carter L. to Elizabeth P. Gilbert 12-28-1858 We
Allen, Charles B. to Mollie A. Lane 7-28-1864 G
Allen, Charles H. to Penny E. Dozier 10-8-1862 G
Allen, Charles J. to Mary E. Townsend 6-23-1835 Hr
Allen, Charles to Alice Moore 9-11-1866 Hy
Allen, Charles to B. M. McCoy 12-27-1866 G
Allen, Charles to Rebecca Reinhardt 1-26-1848 Sh
Allen, Charley to Easter Mirks 3-2-1867 (no return) Hy
Allen, Charley to Hattie Brown 10-21-1880 L B
Allen, Charley to Permella Stephens 2-7-1871 (2-9-1871) F B
Allen, Chas. L. to Isabella H. (Miss) Bell? 6-25-1864 (6-26-1864) Sh
Allen, Christopher D. to Amanda E. Shaw 7-22-1868 G
Allen, Cyrus A. to Jane Richardson 2-27-1849 T
Allen, D. C. to Lizzie T. J. Hall 5-28-1879 (6-15-1879) L
Allen, D. S. to A. S. Vaughn 9-1-1842 Hn
Allen, David A. to Elmira C. Jones 10-7-1849 Sh
Allen, Edmond to Rebecca M. Smith 12-30-1838 F
Allen, Edward G. to Ann Vaughan 12-14-1844 (12-19-1844) T
Allen, Enos A. to Mariah J. E. Leete 5-9-1855 (5-11-1855) L
Allen, F. L. to E. S. Edmondson 12-15-1855 (12-25-1855) Sh
Allen, F. M. to Josphine Ward 8-2-1873 (8-3-1873) O
Allen, Fayett to Nannie Rogers 8-12-1874 Hy
Allen, Flemming S. to Allie Allen 8-19-1847 Hn
Allen, Francis M. to Mary A. Horton 8-28-1856 G
Allen, G. A. to Celia Smith 4-20-1847 Be
Allen, G. S. to Susan S. Clement 1-16-1850 (1-17-1850) G
Allen, G. W. to Jennie Dowdy 11-29-1870 (11-31?-1870) F
Allen, Geo. A. to Mary Sweeney 8-18-1850 Sh
Allen, George E. to Mary J. Moore 12-14-1877 (12-15-1877) L
Allen, George N. to Mary Sisco 11-24-1845 (no return) F
Allen, George W. to Martha Golden 7-27-1855 (no return) Hn
Allen, George to Ellen Betten 9-16-1871 (9-21-1871) T
Allen, George to Josafine Cannon 9-13-1870 (no return) Dy
Allen, Green to Hannah Bledsoe 8-31-1872 (9-1-1872) Cr
Allen, H. to Martha M. Gately 12-16-1849 G
Allen, Henderson to Jinny Brooks 12-26-1866 G
Allen, Henry to Eliza Cameron 1-7-1871 Hy
Allen, Henry to Love Carter 1-13-1867 (1-19-1867) F B
Allen, Henry to Milly Watkins 9-25-1869 (no return) F B
Allen, Hosea D. to Delpha Brewer 11-20-1851 Be
Allen, Isaac to Louisa Williamson 1-16-1871 (1-19-1871) F B
Allen, Isaac to Martha Bayless 1-10-1849 Cr
Allen, J. D. to Mollie T. Hicks 12-16-1874 (12-17-1874) L
Allen, J. F. to Martha W. Williamson 10-29-1862 G
Allen, J. W. J. to Martha E. Crabb 10-24-1871 (no return) Cr
Allen, J. N. to Mary Jane Williams 12-28-1859 (12-29-1859) Sh
Allen, J. S. to Sarah F. Darden 6-4-1879 (no return) Dy
Allen, J. W. to Mary J. Pickler 7-30-1863 Cr
Allen, J. W. to Mary J. Pickles 12-5-1863 Cr
Allen, Jack to Lindy Taylor 2-3-1867 Hy
Allen, James B. to Sarah J. Brown 8-3-1848 Sh
Allen, James D. to Permilee S. Forest 9-12-1852 Cr
Allen, James H. to Eliza A. Martin 2-3-1868 (no return) Hy

Allen, James M. to Laura E. Hawley 9-14-1852 (no return) F
Allen, James R. to A. Jane Diggs 8-31-1847 Hn
Allen, James W. to Jane Snow 4-20-1844 (4-23-1844) O
Allen, James to Amanda J. Brackins 8-26-1861 Be
Allen, James to Mahala Brown 1-23-1849 Cr
Allen, James to Naomi Spivey 2-14-1878 (no return) Hy
Allen, James to Setta Allen 10-29-1870 (11-2-1870) T
Allen, James to 9-29-1871 Cr
Allen, Jas. W. to Eliza J. James 12-28-1857 Hr
Allen, Jesse M. to Delphi Williams 3-5-1845 (3-12-1845) G
Allen, Jesse M. to Nancy Jane Nail 8-15-1868 G
Allen, Jesse to Martha J. Halstead 9-2-1855 Hn
Allen, John A. to Mary E. Kendall 11-17-1858 Hn
Allen, John B. to Nancy Wilson 1-27-1832 O
Allen, John C. to Jane Price 3-21-1844 (3-23-1844) F
Allen, John G. to Angelina Hughes 8-9-1837 (8-24-1837) Hr
Allen, John H. to Martha Nelson 12-10-1839 (12-12-1839) Ma
Allen, John H. to Mary Avenshire 2-3-1848 Cr
Allen, John H. to Susanna Peebles 3-1-1876 (no return) Hy
Allen, John N. to Martha A. Haun 1-8-1863 G
Allen, John W. to Frances L. Newhouse 9-10-1863 G
Allen, John to Haddy Bloyd 6-26-1848 Hn
Allen, John to Puss Wright 3-19-1870 (4-16-1870) F B
Allen, John to S. J. Strickland 3-17-1869 Be
Allen, John to Susanah R. Johnson 8-23-1852 (8-24-1852) Hr
Allen, John to Tennessee Allen 10-22-1859 Hn
Allen, Joseph D. to Eliza Stricklin 2-26-1844 Sh
Allen, Joseph to Elizabeth D. F. Grissom 12-27-1852 (no return) F
Allen, Josiah to Lucy J. Roberson 11-3-1842 G
Allen, L. D. to J. C. Stroud 1-2-1859 Hn
Allen, L. P. to S. L. O. Wilson 1-12-1861 Cr
Allen, Lacy to Mary Richardson 3-1-1857 Be
Allen, Lewis to Mary Jane Forester 1-13-1840 Sh
Allen, M. A. to C. S. Bayless 4-17-1860 (4-18-1864) Sh
Allen, M. C. to Mary (Mrs.) Dumay 11-4-1864 Sh
Allen, Marion to Roberta Gloster 4-25-1866 (6-17-1866) F B
Allen, Mathew D. to Rebecca J. Litton 12-23-1868 (no return) L
Allen, Miles S. to Elizabeth Berry 10-7-1848 (10-11-1848) G
Allen, Milton S. to Margaret J. Knott 11-9-1868 (no return) F
Allen, Montgomery to Ann Keaton 6-19-1869 G B
Allen, Moses R. to Mary J. Cooper 12-23-1862 Cr
Allen, Moses S. to Elizabeth C. Teague 4-17-1856 Ma
Allen, Moses to Rosina Calahan 1-9-1838 Hn
Allen, Nelson to Edy Johnson 12-7-1872 (no return) Cr B
Allen, Nicholas Lewis to Sallie C. Totten 3-6-1830 O
Allen, O. H. to Martha Jane Parker 3-21-1867 Hn
Allen, Peter J. to Nettie Phillips 9-8-1866 (9-9-1866) Ma
Allen, R. C. to Mary McBride 6-18-1856 G
Allen, R. E. to Tennie Hughs 11-21-1868 (no return) Hy
Allen, R. W. to Alice Cook 1-22-1868 G
Allen, R. to I. Allen 6-5-1865 O
Allen, Richard H. to Etha Jane Scott 12-4-1846 (12-6-1846) O
Allen, Richard to Nancy Hudson 2-4-1869 G B
Allen, Robert N. (W.) to Martha G. Williamson 9-14-1837 Sh
Allen, Robert S. to Mariah S. Griffin 1-13-1844 (1-25-1844) F
Allen, Robert to Rachel A. Morrow 8-26-1870 (8-28-1870) F B
Allen, Robt. to Emily Webb 12-20-1848 F
Allen, Robt. to Joanna McMahon 3-3-1859 Sh
Allen, Robt. to Mima Raines 5-6-1866 G
Allen, S. B. to Sarah Busby 1-19-1858 (no return) We
Allen, S. Lafayette to Margaret Estes 7-9-1862 Ma
Allen, S. R. to Margarett Orvenshire 4-10-1842 Cr
Allen, Sam to Allice Bentley 6-14-1867 (no return) F B
Allen, Sam to Lou Murrell 2-22-1868 (2-26-1868) F B
Allen, Sam to Millie Jennings 12-14-1883 (maybe 1882?) L
Allen, Sam'l (Sammy) to Martha Lewis 1-6-1868 G B
Allen, Saml. to Jane Williams 12-28-1870 T
Allen, Samuel A. to Elizabeth Rodgers 12-23-1840 Hn
Allen, Samuel B. to Kate D. Crocket 2-20-1861 (2-21-1861) Sh
Allen, Samuel B. to Sarah P. Russell 7-30-1839 (no return) Hn
Allen, Samuel to Martha Phillips 1-17-1868 T
Allen, Samuel to Mary Bailey 6-4-1831 Sh
Allen, Samuel to Sarah Wilson 12-13-1832 O
Allen, Scott to Caroline Jeffreys 3-11-1867 (no return) Hy
Allen, Sherwood to Mary E. (Miss) Clark 2-15-1864 Sh
Allen, Sidney to Harriett Top 8-3-1870 (no return) Hy
Allen, Sterling W. to Milija C. Carter 12-10-1850 Cr
Allen, T. J. to R. Hutchison 7-25-1866 G
Allen, T. Walker to Martha Appleby 5-20-1869 (5-23-1869) Ma
Allen, Theophalus W. to Martha Anderson 11-2-1859 Sh
Allen, Thomas H. to Ellen H. Shanks 6-30-1847 Sh
Allen, Thomas Jefferson to Mary Robinson 1-17-1843 (not executed) T
Allen, Thomas N. to H. M. Drenon 1-11-1870 (no return) Hy
Allen, Thomas to Adaline Sanders 11-21-1870 (11-23-1870) Ma
Allen, Thomas to Laura Reed 9-12-1867 (9-13-1867) O
Allen, Thomas to Mary Thompson 1-7-1869 F B
Allen, Thos. to R. V. Rogerse 12-30-1856 (1-1-1857) Sh
Allen, Tomlin P. to Rhoda Ann Nelson 12-22-1840 (12-24-1840) Ma
Allen, Vinson R. to Nancy R. Robertson 1-29-1839 (1-31-1839) G
Allen, W. A. to J. M. Dennis 1-5-1868 G
Allen, W. A. to Martha Winter 5-31-1862 (no return) We
Allen, W. H. to Mollie E. Veazey 12-28-1865 Hn
Allen, W. J. to Sallie L. Earle 9-28-1864 (10-1-1864) O
Allen, W. M. to Elizabeth J. Nelson 12-22-1858 T
Allen, W. M. to Elizabeth Nelson 12-22-1858 T
Allen, W. T. to Frances Nelson 4-16-1853 Ma
Allen, W. T. to Sarah E. Bodkin 2-11-1868 G
Allen, Walter to Mary Pain 5-24-1848 Sh
Allen, William A. to Jane Montgomery 9-1-1826) (9-7-1826) Hr
Allen, William B. to Rachel Clement 11-25-1841 Hn
Allen, William C. to Margaret M. Wall 12-23-1847 F
Allen, William C. to Sarah C. Dunbar 6-20-1846 (6-21-1846) F
Allen, William F. to Martha Boggs 6-11-1859 Hn
Allen, William H. to Nancy O. Kendall 12-14-1859 Hn
Allen, William I. to Martha L. Aldridge 12-31-1865 Mn
Allen, William J. to Mary J. Acuff 10-12-1885 (10-24-1885) L
Allen, William L. to D. E. Parker 11-6-1856 Hn
Allen, William M. to Amanda Hodgson 6-15-1839 (6-18-1839) Ma
Allen, William M. to Hulda Hicks 3-15-1870 (3-16-1870) Ma
Allen, William M. to Mary W. Watts 12-2-1847 (12-14-1848?) F
Allen, William M. to Sarah E. Menees 10-21-1847 (10-23-1847) F
Allen, William T. to Eliza J. Nelson 12-30-1844 Ma
Allen, William W. to Mary A. Clark 3-17-1841 Hn
Allen, William to Ann Bledsoe 1-25-1871 (1-26-1871) T
Allen, William to Drucilla Gay 3-12-1875 Hy
Allen, William to Jane Belton 3-12-1850 (3-14-1850) Ma
Allen, Willie to Catherine Grace 12-28-1828 Sh
Allen, Willy to Elizabeth Jones 2-13-1841 Cr
Allen, Wilson to Lottie Sneed 2-1-1871 (no return) F B
Allen, Wilson to Mary Rives 2-3-1841 (2-4-1841) F
Allen, Wm. F. to Mary C. Stewart 11-24-1842 Sh
Allen, Wm. G. to Mary Folks 9-29-1849 Cr
Allen, Wm. H. to F. E. (Miss) Rogers 1-21-1862 Sh
Allen, Wm. H. to Lizzie J. Yancey 5-14-1866 (5-15-1866) F
Allen, Wm. H. to Mary E. Stacy 4-3-1845 F
Allen, Wm. V. to E. Kate Bledsoe 12-30-1857 (1-6-1858) Sh
Allen, Wm.L. to Elizabeth (Miss) Wickham 7-24-1856 Sh
Allen, Y. W. J. to Susan Frances Cline 12-31-1868 G
Allen, Young W. to Mary Hammond 2-1-1850 G
Allen, Z. W. to N. A. Glass 1-8-1863 We
Allen, Zach to Pat Gause 1-18-1871 (1-19-1871) L
Allen, jr., John to Louisa Harwood 10-13-1857 G
Allender, Wm. F. to Molly L. (Miss) Jones 3-7-1864 (3-8-1864) Sh
Alley, F. M. to Nancy Broggton 1-5-1867 O
Alley, Stephen to Dicey M. Fowler 3-9-1845 Sh
Alley, Stephen to Hester V. Robertson 3-1-1842 Sh
Allgee, J. F. to M. L. J. Jones 1-1-1870 (1-2-1870) Cr
Allison, Charles to Laura A. McGinn 12-3-1866 (12-4-1866) Dy
Allison, Daniel M. to Amanda Mills 2-19-1870 (2-20-1870) Ma
Allison, Daniel R. to Nancy Watson 6-29-1843 Ma
Allison, David to Margaret Cox 5-16-1828 (5-22-1828) Hr
Allison, Elihu C. to Margaret Neely 9-11-1829 (9-17-1829) Hr
Allison, Henry T. to Sallie J. Duncan 10-12-1871 Ma
Allison, Henry to Caroline Fitzgerrald 10-27-1866 G
Allison, Henry to Kate Vaughn 9-21-1867 (9-21-1867) T
Allison, J. W. to Susan Taylor 5-8-1866 G
Allison, James W. to Martha P. Hamilton 7-2-1853 G
Allison, James to Delilah Howard 8?-31-1829 (8-6-1829) Hr
Allison, John W. to Elizabeth W. Hrrington 12-21-1849 (12-27-1849) G
Allison, John W. to Martha A. Betty 10-24-1859 Ma
Allison, John W. to Mary J. Armor 9-20-1858 O
Allison, Joseph to Agnus Estus 6-24-1870 (no return) L
Allison, Joseph to Lizzie Richardson 7-4-1872 L
Allison, Joseph to Mary Frances Johnson 7-16-1839 Ma
Allison, L. G. to Rosa E. Smith 1-30-1883 L
Allison, Milton J. to Rebecca Cole 3-10-1862 (3-22-1862) O
Allison, Milton J. to Synthey D. Davis 9-22-1840 (9-24-1840) O
Allison, R. J. to B. (Miss) Allen 9-12-1863 (9-16-1863) Sh
Allison, Robert F. to Mary M. Taylor 1-3-1871 (1-5-1871) F
Allison, Robert to Anna Morgan 12-30-1878 (no return) L
Allison, Robert to Sarah Henning 3-21-1873 L B
Allison, Robt. to Sarah Turner 11-5-1861 Sh
Allison, Samuel S. to Elizabeth S. Hurendon 4-20-1852 Be
Allison, Thomas J. to Mary Sloan 1-5-1857 (1-6-1857) O
Allison, Thomas to Beedy Brooks 1-31-1869 Hy
Allison, Thomas to Flora Johnson 8-3-1871 L
Allison, Thos. H. to Nancy T. Box 5-6-1864 (5-8-1864) O
Allison, W. L. to Elizabeth E. Poole 9-4-1865 (9-7-1865) O
Allison, William A. to Sarah C. Dunlap 3-6-1845 G
Allison, William Malichi to Agasy Caroline Adams 11-18-1857 Ma
Allison, William W. to Martha M. Edmonds 4-18-1837 (5-18-1837) O
Allison, William to Fannie Henning 8-25-1877 (no return) L
Allison, William to Sarah A. E. Robinson 8-20-1848 Ma
Allison, Wm. H. to Mary J. Smith 1-13-1876 (no return) Hy

Allison, Wm. to Mary Saunders 7-16-1843 Be
Alliston, William A. to L. C. Massengill 8-26-1865 Mn
Allman, William M. to Louisa J. Murphy 9-28-1858 We
Allmon, Aaron G. to Mary A. Willson 2-10-1862 We
Allmon, William E. to Miranda E. Gooden 5-7-1857 We
Allmond, A. G. to Elizabeth Boaz 1-7-1859 We
Allmond, James W. to Jane Cheek 10-16-1856 Hn
Allmore, Wesley H. to Zetton A. Roan 1-17-1854 Cr
Alloway, A. to C. Garrett? 9-7-1846 Hr
Allred, Jas. M. to Mary Goodman 3-2-1852 (3-4-1852) Sh
Allson, F. J. to Nannie S. Crawford 1-15-1868 Hy
Alman, Charles W. to Eleanor F. Anderson 11-10-1862 (no return) Hy
Almin, J. E. to Mary A. Newbery 1-21-1855 We
Almon, Charles W. to Rebecca Ford 5-23-1859 (5-26-1859) L
Almond, John A. to Angeline W. Kimble 8-30-1843 L
Almond, Nehemiah M. to Delphia Ann Russell 10-20-1858 Hn
Alphin, Hillard to Mary E. Fleming 2-15-1867 G
Alphin, Reuben to Mary Jane Douglas 8-13-1856 O
Alphin, Wm. B. to Hegal Spiven 1-12-1871 Hy
Alphine, A. B. to Nancy Pate 9-27-1863 G
Alsabrook, Robert to Minnie Sumerow 1-20-1886 (1-24-1886) L
Alsbrook, John to Adeline Helfer 7-14-1850 Sh
Alsbrook, Nathan F. (J) to Sarah C. Wood 11-1-1846 Sh
Alsobrook, James C. to Mary E. Somerow 9-12-1849 L
Alsobrook, Jesse H. to Amanda M. F. Robertson 6-23-1835 Sh
Alsobrook, Nathan to Savanah Soward 12-20-1883 L
Alsobrook, Simmonds D. to Susan C. Soward 1-28-1859 (2-2-1859) L
Alsop, David to Aby Nash 12-14-1845 Be
Alsop, David to Caroline L. Graham 2-9-1848 Be
Alsop, Sterling to Jane Reddick 11-7-1848 Be
Alsop, Thomas to Margaret C. McAuly 1-29-1852 Be
Alsten, Philip to Susan Blakemore 12-8-1846 We
Alsten, Sandy to Emerlin Watter 1-10-1867 T
Alston, Aaron to Jannie Avery 7-10-1869 (7-13-1869) T
Alston, Alexander to Judia McDermain 2-5-1869 (2-6-1869) L
Alston, Augustus B. to Judith F. Holt 3-14-1854 (3-15-1854) Ma
Alston, Ben to Mary Johnson 1-24-1870 T
Alston, Charles H. to M. A. Leach 11-6-1867 Dy
Alston, Furgus to Harriet Sherrill 1-7-1874 T
Alston, George to Ellen Evans 1-4-1871 T
Alston, George to Julia Smith 11-29-1866 (11-30-1866) T
Alston, J. H. to Nancy Rutherford 12-25-1869 Hy
Alston, John B. to Eliza B. Struthers 12-12-1866 Hy
Alston, John J. to Mary F. Lloyd 5-3-1859 (no return) L
Alston, John L. to Emily V. Conner 1-11-1870 L
Alston, John R. to Lydia Ann Tyson 3-8-1831 Ma
Alston, John R. to Martha Ann Beasley 11-8-1853 Be
Alston, Lawrence to Ellen Phelps 3-28-1874 T
Alston, Mat to Sarah Wilson 1-16-1871 T
Alston, Nelson to Millie Fowlkes 8-31-1871 Dy
Alston, Phil to Maria Angus 3-8-1867 (3-10-1867) T
Alston, Philip M. to Martha Booth 3-14-1844 Sh
Alston, Pink to Alabama Hamilton 7-8-1868 G B
Alston, Ray to Lucy Williams 2-3-1867 Hy
Alston, Richard to Mary Alston 12-27-1867 (12-2-1868?) T
Alston, Sam to Tennessee Norris 4-8-1885 L
Alston, Sam, jr. to Tennessee Norris 12-9-1884 L
Alston, Samuel J. to Martha Crider 10-17-1867 Hn
Alston, Samuel to Jesbella Lloyd 3-7-1874 (3-8-1874) L B
Alston, Sandy to Jennie Gray 12-16-1873 T
Alston, Sandy to Martha Lawrence 8-14-1868 G B
Alston, Soloman G. to Joanah C. Currie 12-11-1865 (12-12-1865) L
Alston, Thomas E. to Nancy C. Baines (Barnes?) 9-15-1852 (9-16-1852) L
Alston, Thomas P. to C. M. (Mrs.) Luckett 12-13-1872 (12-15-1872) L
Alston, Thomas P. to Elizabeth J. Bryant 11-5-1858 (11-6-1858) L
Alston, Thomas P. to Sarah J. Crook 10-2-1860 (10-3-1860) L
Alston, Thos. to Agnes Alston 12-30-1867 (12-2-1868?) T
Alston, Thos. to Martha J. English 3-3-1874 (3-26-1874) T
Alston, Volney S. to Mary Jane Russell 9-1-1860 (no return) L
Alston, W. M. to Mahala Childress 12-19-1859 L
Alston, Washington to Malissa Brown 7-8-1873 T
Alston, Whit F. to Isabella Smith 2-10-1873 (2-12-1873) T
Alston, William to Duley Taylor 5-6-1867 T
Alston, Willie E. to Sallie A. Thum 2-19-1861 (no return) L
Alston, Wylie to Katie Alston 9-28-1872 (9-29-1872) T
Alsup, Andrew to Susan Ann Alsup 7-26-1856 Be
Alsup, Benjamin to Dorothy Crain 1-20-1830 Hr
Alsup, Benjamin to Nancy Thomas 12-25-1833 Hr
Alsup, Burwell to Rebecca J. Wilson 8-10-1857 Be
Alsup, James J. to Elizabeth Cherry 9-3-1857 Be
Alsup, James to Martha Cole 9-14-1854 Be
Alsup, James to Polly Slaughter 10-24-1829 Hr
Alsup, O. M. to Lucy J. Jones 10-17-1844 Sh
Alsup, O. to Malinda Bullock 9-1-1863 Be
Alsup, Wm. to Catharine Buchanan 7-3-1861 Be
Alte, Chas. to Henriette Sophia Umhold 8-2-1861 Sh
Altman, Joel W. to Rachel A. Maddox 2-19-1849 (12-20-1849) Ma

Altom, Elisha to Hannah Williamson 4-16-1849 (4-6?-1849) Ma
Altom, J. B. to Z. Z. Bradley 5-25-1843 Sh
Altum, Andrew J. to Dolly J. Parr 12-5-1838 (12-13-1838) O
Alverson, Wade A. to Nancy Gilstrop 8-20-1847 (8-26-1847) L
Alvis, John to Sarah Crouch 5-10-1838 Sh
Alvis, Merradett to Mary Bradford 10-1-1838 (10-3-1838) G
Alvis, T. S. to Amanda Allen 12-3-1867 G
Alvis, Z. C. to Sarah Ann Burks 1-24-1853 (1-25-1853) Sh
Alvis, Zacariah C. to Lucretia W. Sulivant 8-26-1841 Sh
Ames, James to M. M. Keys 8-9-1858 G
Amick, A. J. M. to A. A. Searcy 3-16-1875 (3-17-1875) Dy
Amick, Eli to Mary Nance 8-30-1838 Hn
Amis, E. H. to A. H. Peviard? 6-26-1869 (6-27-1869) F
Amis, J. S. to S. J. Reames 11-14-1865 (11-16-1865) F
Amis, J. W. to A. L. Anderson 8-12-1867 (8-13-1867) F
Amis, Lewis to Catharine Lee 11-11-1839 F
Amis, Samuel S. to Clara Amis 12-10-1866 F
Amis, Thomas J. to Elizabeth A. Martin 1-26-1860 O
Amix, E. to Angeline Searcey 11-7-1874 (11-8-1874) L
Ammen, Peter to Mary Cooker 10-17-1843 (no return) F
Ammon, Hiram to Susan? Terry 11-1-1832 Hr
Ammon, Peter to Narcissa Kimbrough 1-10-1833 Sh
Ammons(Powell?), Wm. H. to Alice Powell 7-28-1847 (7-29-1847) Hr
Ammons, Doctor to Sarah Crawford 12-13-1854 (12-14-1854) Hr
Ammons, Dorriss to Jane Belote 7-10-1843 (no return) F
Ammons, E. to L. F. Sullivan 12-9-1854 (no return) F
Ammons, G. W. to Ann P. Rodgers 8-22-1851 (no return) F
Ammons, Jesse T. to Mary E. Rogers 10-28-1848 (10-29-1848) Hr
Ammons, Josiah to Clarissa A. Toller 3-8-1842 (3-16-1842) Hr
Ammons, William H. to Mary H. Boyte 1-6-1844 (1-11-1844) Hr
Ammons, Wm. H. to Elizabeth Ann Ammons 2-21-1837 (2-26-1837) Hr
Amones, James to Sarah J. Harris 9-12-1865 (9-13-1865) L
Amos, Jas. T. to Sudie Newel 11-14-1871 (11-15-1871) Ma
Amos, T. F. to Mary A. T. Johnson 12-2-1867 (12-5-1867) Ma
Amos, Thomas to Eliza Miller 1-14-1857 G
Amos, William L. to M. J. Wallis 12-2-1867 (12-5-1867) Ma
Amos, William to Lucritia Pierce 5-23-1875 L B
Ancromb, Charles to Agnes Hobson 12-11-1869 (no return) F B
Anders, A. T. to Cornelia M. Hurley 9-29-1856 (9-30-1856) L
Anderson (Andrews?), David B. to Martha Whittamore-Whittaman 1-23-1853 (11-24-1853) L
Anderson, A. B. to Mollie M. Kindred 7-24-1866 Hn
Anderson, A. C. to M. J. Harper 10-15-1867 (10-17-1867) O
Anderson, A. J. to Nancy P. Williamson 7-4-1853 (no return) F
Anderson, A. S. to Rachel Estes 10-14-1879 Dy
Anderson, A. W. to M. M. Thomson 12-20-1859 (12-21-1859) Sh
Anderson, Adolphus to Matilda Jones 11-2-1866 (11-3-1866) F B
Anderson, Alfred H. to Mary J. Denning 9-7-1860 We
Anderson, Amos to Susan Morris 5-9-1867 (no return) Hn B
Anderson, Anderson J. to Sarah E. Townsend 7-12-1869 (7-13-1869) T
Anderson, Andrew J. to Sarah E. Townsend 7-12-1867 T
Anderson, Andrew to Perlina Rivers 11-18-1869 (11-21-1869) F B
Anderson, Andrew to Virginia G. Crews 1-27-1869 (2-4-1869) F
Anderson, Andy to Victoria Mitchell 9-4-1865 (9-6-1865) F
Anderson, Ashley to Mary Jane Chism 2-26-1849 (2-28-1849) L
Anderson, Beverly to Nancy Smith 1-6-1844 Ma
Anderson, Bill to Caroline Jelks 2-21-1873 Hy
Anderson, Bill to Lucy Taylor 4-5-1871 (4-6-1871) F B
Anderson, Burrel to Jane Webb 12-24-1869 (12-25-1869) T
Anderson, C. C. to Callie V. White 12-20-1882 (12-21-1882) L
Anderson, Calvin to Emiline Hampton 2-25-1870 (no return) Dy
Anderson, Carrol to Delila King 7-20-1843 Sh
Anderson, Carter to Frances Lindsey 1-2-1869 (1-5-1869) F B
Anderson, Chamberlin H. to E. W. Perry 2-7-1845 (2-9-1845) Hr
Anderson, Charles to Frances Peebles 12-29-1866 Hy
Anderson, Charley to Sallie McCuller 2-1-1872 Hy
Anderson, Chas. to Eliza Anderson 11-18-1873 Hy
Anderson, D. W. to M. E. M. Eastham 3-7-1853 (no return) F
Anderson, Daniel B. to Laura M. Ragland 12-5-1842 Sh
Anderson, Dennie to Harriett Fullen 12-6-1881 L
Anderson, E. to Martha M. Smith 1-17-1861 Sh
Anderson, Ed. G. to Hassie A. Wright 12-30-1879 (1-1-1880) L
Anderson, Edward A. to Mary Jane Whitten 11-9-1846 (11-12-1846) F
Anderson, Edward H. to Mattie O. Evans 1-2-1871 (1-8-1871) F
Anderson, Edwin to Malinda Malone 1-13-1869 T
Anderson, Eli to Sarah Ann Oldham 12-19-1868 (12-20-1868) L
Anderson, Enoch to Emeline Smith 5-6-1847 Be
Anderson, Ezekiel to Marjiana A. Holte (Hault) 2-13-1851 (2-20-1851) Sh
Anderson, Fredrick to Bertha H. Britton 2-23-1846 (2-26-1846) Ma
Anderson, G. M. to Mary E. Pyland 12-13-1872 (12-15-1872) L
Anderson, G. W. to Hannah Richardson 10-22-1877 Hy
Anderson, Gabriel M. to Eliza G. Kerr 5-9-1849 Sh
Anderson, Gabriel M. to Rachel Talbot Barker 1-2-1855 (1-3-1855) T
Anderson, Garland to Julia Vernon 10-17-1854 Hr
Anderson, George to Amanda Ferguson 10-15-1873 (10-16-1873) Dy
Anderson, George to Eliza Coe 1-21-1874 T
Anderson, George to Josey Taylor 6-19-1869 G B

Anderson, George to Julia Peryear 1-6-1873 (1-9-1873) L
Anderson, George to Nancy Moody 12-22-1866 (no return) F B
Anderson, Green to Fannie Smith 12-22-1869 T
Anderson, H. C. to Cora Jones 1-1-1879 (1-8-1879) L B
Anderson, H. M. to Elizabeth V. Hundley 12-16-1858 (12-18-1858) Hr
Anderson, Hal to Margaret Poke 12-28-1869 (1-1-1870) F B
Anderson, Henry Clay to Elisabeth Hunter 11-17-1870 L B
Anderson, Henry to Dicie Jones 2-2-1871 Cr B
Anderson, Henry to Margaret Embry 4-27-1867 (5-2-1867) L B
Anderson, Herrod C. to Almira A. Cherry 4-11-1849 (4-24-1849) G
Anderson, Hiram to Susan Harp 5-8-1828 He
Anderson, Hugh N. to Mary C. Waters 1-30-1845 Ma
Anderson, Isaac to Annie Thompson 1-14-1869 Hy
Anderson, Isaac to Dicy Ann Mercer 4-26-1840 Cr
Anderson, Isaac to Jane Miller 1-28-1869 G B
Anderson, Isaac to Menervia Baine 7-22-1868 (no return) Hy
Anderson, Isah to Mary M. Neely 9-6-1848 Cr
Anderson, J. C. to Bettie C. Roberts 5-17-1861 (5-22-1861) Sh
Anderson, J. C. to Mary Duncan 10-19-1854 Be
Anderson, J. M. to C. C. Griffith 11-30-1866 (12-5-1866) L
Anderson, J. Patton to H. B. (Miss) Adair 4-28-1853 (4-30-1853) Sh
Anderson, J. R. to Elizabeth Camp? 11-11-1864 (no return) Hn
Anderson, Jabize S. to Mary J. Elder 12-4-1847 (12-7-1847) F
Anderson, Jack to Margaret Spence 6-2-1866 Dy
Anderson, Jacob to Felicia Mills 11-14-1872 L B
Anderson, Jacob to Jane Barbee 3-17-1866 Hy
Anderson, Jacob to Levina Ann May 4-28-1838 F
Anderson, James A. to Louisa C. Trent 5-24-1852 (no return) F
Anderson, James C. to Margaret L. Mathis 8-3-1872 (8-4-1872) L
Anderson, James M. to Nancy J. Black 7-13-1840 Ma
Anderson, James M. to Pernella Harp 12-20-1867 (no return) Hn
Anderson, James R. to Virginia Estes 10-8-1870 (10-13-1870) Ma
Anderson, James W. to Ellen B. Dunaway 5-8-1861 Ma
Anderson, James W. to Margarett C. Alexander 1-17-1842 (1-23-1842) F
Anderson, James W. to Amy Miller 8-13-1870 (8-14-1870) F B
Anderson, James to Nancy Miller 5-6-1836 Sh
Anderson, James to Nancy Redmon 5-18-1825 O
Anderson, Jas. W. to Annie E. (Miss) White 8-22-1864 Sh
Anderson, Jeff to Littie Loving 1-18-1869 Hy
Anderson, Jefferson to Narcissa Dew 5-11-1855 Ma
Anderson, Jno. C. to Lucy J. Richardson 10-3-1859 Hr
Anderson, Jno. to Anna Nelson 8-23-1870 Dy
Anderson, John A. to Julia A. Thompson 12-13-1870 (12-17-1870) F B
Anderson, John E. to Randa Weever 6-21-1870 Dy
Anderson, John J. to Matilda W. Fussell 9-8-1847 Ma
Anderson, John P. to Jane Gregory 1-13-1842 (1-15-1842) G
Anderson, John T. to Eliza Ann McLeod 12-21-1857 (no return) L
Anderson, John T. to Martha P. Johnson 7-15-1850 Ma
Anderson, John Tyler to Julia Ann Brown 10-9-1860 Ma
Anderson, John V. to Elizabeth Freeling 8-8-1831 Ma
Anderson, John W. to Tamsey Jane Overcast 8-1-1866 (no return) Hn
Anderson, John to Jennie Cobb 4-7-1868 (no return) Hy
Anderson, John to Jennie Wilson 10-10-1872 Hy
Anderson, John to Mary Ann Snowden 6-18-1846 Ma
Anderson, John to Mary Wood 1-27-1867 (no return) Dy
Anderson, John to Matilda Haynes 7-17-1838 Hn
Anderson, John to Mollie Graves 5-31-1877 (4?-1-1877) L
Anderson, John to Polly Henson 12-7-1843 Ma
Anderson, John to S. B. Barham 12-27-1865 Hn
Anderson, Jos. to Emily M. Bridgewater 2-24-1853 Sh
Anderson, Joseph B. to Permelia Harper 1-20-1845 (no return) F
Anderson, Josiah to Mary M. Pritchard 2-?-1862 (no return) Cr
Anderson, Julius to Adlinea Garrison 3-2-1878 (3-3-1878) L
Anderson, Kenneth B. to Elizabeth Whitson 11-7-1844 L
Anderson, Lee to Jane Rice 3-12-1874 H
Anderson, Leonidas to Margaret (Miss) Jerry 2-8-1858 Sh
Anderson, Lewis to Jane Cothrel? 9-20-1883 (9-24-1883) L
Anderson, Logan J. to Susan E. Franklin 12-8-1862 (12-9-1862) Ma
Anderson, M. D. L. to Louisa Cross 7-25-1856 (8-5-1856) Hr
Anderson, M. D. to C. C. Singletary 5-18-1863 (no return) Dy
Anderson, M. J. to M. A. Massey 10-27-1860 (10-28-1860) O
Anderson, M. L. to N. S. Pittman 1-17-1878 L
Anderson, M. Logan to Cordelia Smith 3-25-1870 (3-30-1870) F
Anderson, Marcus L. to Elizabeth C. Smith 3-7-1867 Be
Anderson, Marma D. to Sarah E. Oliver 12-23-1850 Ma
Anderson, Mitt to L. J. Leach 3-6-1855 Cr
Anderson, Montgomery to Alpha Webb 1-10-1844 Ma
Anderson, Montgomery to Cynthia E. Steward 8-8-1849 (8-16-1849) Ma
Anderson, Newman to Kattie Hill 3-12-1871 Hy
Anderson, Norman to Barthena Crockett 12-14-1869 (12-16-1869) L
Anderson, P. B. to Jennie Lewis Read 9-23-1874 Hy
Anderson, Peter to Maria Hardin 2-26-1883 (3-11-1883) L
Anderson, R. D. to Eliza A. Kerr 12-13-1865 Mn
Anderson, Redman to Elizabeth Vincent 7-30-1832 (8-3-1832) Hr
Anderson, Reuben to Fannie Crockett 2-14-1867 O
Anderson, Richard to Juliana Hartsfield 5-6-1840 Hn
Anderson, Richard to Nancy Fleet 3-20-1856 Hr
Anderson, Richd. to Dina Powell 8-30-1871 (no return) Hy
Anderson, Robert M. to Lucy A. Wyatt 8-18-1849 Sh
Anderson, Robert to E. E. Turner 1-31-1865 Be
Anderson, Robert to Hester Mann 12-24-1874 Hy
Anderson, Robert to Maria Johnson 10-10-1879 (10-12-1879) L B
Anderson, Robert to Nancy P. Luckey 2-1-1863 Hn
Anderson, Robly H. to Maggie M. Gray 4-19-1876 Hy
Anderson, Robt. D. to Sarah A. Womack 3-10-1868 (3-20-1868) Ma
Anderson, Ruben to Fannie Crockett 2-14-1867 O
Anderson, S. D. to Mary S. Smith 12-5-1861 Mn
Anderson, Samuel G. to Elizabeth C. Glenn 2-9-1860 Hn
Anderson, Samuel R. to Susan (Mrs.) Allen 2-13-1856 Sh
Anderson, Scott to Lucy Fowlkes 1-28-1880 Dy
Anderson, Sid to Victoria Twilla 7-16-1870 (7-17-1870) Dy
Anderson, T. B. to Martha Walker 12-18-1867 (no return) Hy
Anderson, T. S. to Bettie Garrett 12-28-1866 Hy
Anderson, T. S. to Mary E. Garrett 12-20-1871 (12-22-1871) L
Anderson, Theodore to M. J. Burdick 12-31-1859 (1-3-1860) Sh
Anderson, Thomas G. to Susan Cage 4-8-1838 F
Anderson, Thomas J. to Margaret Winiford 12-21-1842 Sh
Anderson, Thomas to Eliza Jane Harrison 8-7-1854 Ma
Anderson, Thornton F. to Margaret (Miss) Brooks 6-15-1853 Sh
Anderson, Thos. C. to Frances E. Otey 7-19-1858 Sh
Anderson, Thos. F. to Jane H. Gates 12-5-1834 (12-9-1834) Hr
Anderson, Tobias to Mary E. Morgan 11-6-1869 (11-9-1869) F B
Anderson, Turner M. to Eliza Jane McNaion 8-3-1869 Ma
Anderson, W. C. to Mar. Tittle 5-31-1839 Be
Anderson, W. C. to Matilda F. James 8-4-1859 Sh
Anderson, W. G. to Florence I. Johnson 7-27-1869 (7-29-1869) F
Anderson, W. H. to M. E. Harper 7-4-1866 (7-4-1866) O
Anderson, W. M. to Judy Ann Horton 4-3-1880 (4-4-1880) L B
Anderson, W. P. to Frances M. Moon(Moore) 12-26-1849 Hr
Anderson, W. T. to Mollid A. Green 7-6-1869 (7-8-1869) F
Anderson, W. V. to Fredonia Simpson 12-28-1852 (12-30-1852) Sh
Anderson, WM. J. to Sarah Rogers 3-9-1854 Cr
Anderson, Wash to Harriett Walker 5-26-1872 Hy
Anderson, Wash to Sarah Lawthon 3-13-1869 (3-14-1869) T
Anderson, Wash to Viney Holt 11-5-1881 (11-6-1881) L B
Anderson, Wesley to Sarah Manley 1-27-1858 Ma
Anderson, William A. to Caroline N. Smith 9-30-1856 Hn
Anderson, William C. to Ann G. Willis 8-7-1847 Hn
Anderson, William C. to Caroline Neal 10-19-1850 (10-20-1850) O
Anderson, William J. to Lucy Thornton? 5-26-1857 Be
Anderson, William J. to Martha A. Holmes 7-5-1859 G
Anderson, William L. to Amanda D. Vick 4-29-1848 Ma
Anderson, William to Adeline Edmunston 12-27-1843 (no return) F
Anderson, William to Celinda Fuller 1-22-1828 We
Anderson, William to Elizabeth Golden 6-3-1830 Ma
Anderson, William to Maria Jane Murray 1-6-1879 (1-7-1879) L
Anderson, William to Mary McMillan 1-6-1837 (1-12-1837) Hr
Anderson, William to Nancy Cates 11-26-1854 We
Anderson, William to Rebecca McGroom 6-22-1852 Ma
Anderson, William to Sarah Ann Gwin 1-13-1845 (no return) Hn
Anderson, William to Vic Cross 1-23-1867 Dy
Anderson, Wm. C. to Emeline Smith 8-8-1837 Sh
Anderson, Wm. J. to M. Caroline Dickinson 1-29-1867 (1-31-1867) Ma
Anderson, Wm. P. to Frances Cox 1-15-1870 (1-16-1870) F
Anderson, Wm. R. to Fanny Pace 9-12-1866 (9-13-1866) Ma
Anderson, Wm. R. to Permelia Reed 9-21-1839 Hr
Anderson, Wm. V. to Margery J. Simpson 8-5-1854 (8-30-1854) Sh
Anderson, Wm. W. to Mary Settle 3-16-1866 (no return) F
Anderson, Zedikiah to Joice Wesson 10-22-1857 Sh
Anderson, Ziba to Linda Pitts 12-24-1877 (12-25-1877) L B
Andlerson, Hiram to Harnett N. Isaacs 3-14-1842 Hr
Andrews, A. C. to Nancy A. Butler 1-24-1871 (no return) Dy
Andrews, Antonio to Bettie Givins 5-29-1867 G B
Andrews, Bryant to Dorcas Jackson 2-4-1834 G
Andrews, Bryant to Penina Wollard 10-15-1850 G
Andrews, Cullen to Mahaly C. Pollard 9-25-1856 G
Andrews, Elbert to Annie M. Gabbrough 1-1-1862 G
Andrews, Eli M. to Chrisriana Clark 6-28-1843 Hr
Andrews, George B. to Sarah Ann Lee 6-3-1848 Sh
Andrews, Henry to Mary Ann Simmons 8-27-1850 Be
Andrews, J. F. to Margaret Stalcup 6-22-1872 (6-21?-1872) Dy
Andrews, J. K. to Harriet J. Dixon 12-17-1861 Mn
Andrews, J. T. B. to Sarah Brooks 11-1-1848 Sh
Andrews, John D. to D. P. (Mrs.) Sullivan 8-30-1864 Sh
Andrews, John McHenry to Mary J. Bruce 8-8-1854 Be
Andrews, John to Effy W. Clement 10-31-1867 Be
Andrews, Ott to Elizabeth H. Cain 11-25-1850 Hr
Andrews, R. M. to Johnnie Mitchell 1-12-1886 (1-13-1886) L
Andrews, Robt. E. to Sarah Campbell 6-13-1846 (6-14-1846) Hr
Andrews, S. P. to Nancy S. T. Parsley 12-13-1870 Dy
Andrews, Saml. J. to Nany Kelzoe 10-18-1845 G
Andrews, Seth L. to Louretta E. Dillingham 11-26-1861 Be
Andrews, W. T. to E. B. Webb 12-13-1876 (no return) L
Andrews, Warren A. to Sarah U. Massey 12-30-1841 Sh

Andrews, Wm. H. to Julia A. (Miss) Grace 4-29-1858 Sh
Anerson?, Stark to Sarah Mosby 8-16-1870 (9-4-1870) T
Angel, Calvin to Laura A. Robinson 2-12-1866 (2-1?-1866) T
Angel, Henry to Nancy Fisher 12-17-1878 (12-18-1878) L
Angle, James to Louiza Grooms 7-11-1871 Cr
Anglemyer, Isaac to A. E. (Miss) Lourance 4-28-1859 Sh
Angus, Edward E. to Sarah Curlins 5-1-1860 Sh
Angus, Jacob to Ellen Hemphill 1-17-1871 (1-18-1871) T
Angus, Thomas L. to Eliz. Ann Corisar? 10-12-1846 (10-13-1846) T
Angus, Thomas Lowry to Eliza Jane Bowers 3-22-1851 (3-25-1851) T
Angus, Thos. to Sue Goodman 1-23-1869 (1-26-1869) T
Angus, William Werter to Jane Ralph 7-16-1849 (7-17-1849) T
Anington, W. T. to Emma C. Levy 1-18-1860 G
Aninston, George to Ann Rice 12-26-1878 L
Anker, Solomon to Ginnett Greenwall 6-21-1856 (no return) F
Annis, John to Sarah V. Campbell 3-28-1867 Hy
Anthoney, P. W. to R. J. Niece 2-18-1868 (no return) Dy
Anthony, A. S. to L. N. Anthony 11-26-1884 (11-27-1884) L
Anthony, Allen to Elizabeth V. Carnall 6-11-1866 (6-14-1866) L
Anthony, C. M. to Belle Walker 12-23-1879 (12-24-1880) L
Anthony, E. R. to Eddie Jones 10-15-1885 L
Anthony, Edwin to Susan F. Webber 12-11-1850 Sh
Anthony, Elias to Jennie Wilingham 1-20-1877 Hy
Anthony, Fred L. to Celia A. Kent 1-1-1877 (1-2-1877) Dy
Anthony, G. W. to Bamley Hollowell 11-8-1862 (not endorsed) F
Anthony, G. W. to Margaret A. Nolan 1-11-1883 (1-12-1883) L
Anthony, J. A. to M. A. Anthony 7-11-1877 Dy
Anthony, J. W. to Cynthia Johnson 5-27-1830 Ma
Anthony, J. W. to Willie E. Percival 1-3-1883 (1-4-1883) L
Anthony, James A. to L. Ida Young 12-18-1877 L
Anthony, John to Charlotte Green 4-18-1872 L
Anthony, John to Mollie Dickerson 10-18-1881 (10-19-1881) L B
Anthony, Marshall to Charity Cobb 1-27-1876 (no return) Hy
Anthony, Michael to Annie (Miss) Graham 9-1-1863 Sh
Anthony, Peter to Mary Bond 1-20-1877 Hy
Anthony, Peter to Sally Gammons 1-9-1869 (1-10-1869) F B
Anthony, Philip to Cora Hays 3-21-1878 (no return) Hy
Anthony, R. G. to Lillie Walker 10-26-1882 L
Anthony, R. N. to Martha F. Hamil 9-3-1861 (no return) Hy
Anthony, R. R. to Margaret E. Hamil 7-29-1866 Hy
Anthony, S. A. to C. J. Fenley 10-9-1883 (10-10-1883) L
Anthony, Sam to E. J. White 8-30-1877 (no return) L
Anthony, Samuel A. to Ema T. Sumerow 11-2-1874 L
Anthony, Samuel A. to Lura A. Huggins 5-15-1879 L
Anthony, Stephen to Jennie Dison 3-23-1872 Hy
Anthony, T. L. to M. A. Pleasant 10-29-1849 (11-4-1849) F
Anthony, T. S. to R. L. Shaw 11-3-1874 Hy
Anthony, Thomas A. to Susan M. Rice 6-21-1853 (6-22-1853) L
Anthony, Thos. C. to Mary A. Adams 4-11-1866 T
Anthony, Tony to Martha Comb 7-20-1866 O
Anthony, William A. to Julia S. (Mrs.) Boner 3-1-1858 (3-8-1858) Ma
Anthony, William J. to Margaret Ann Brimm 8-8-1859 (no return) L
Anthony, William to H. M. Robinson 7-1-1865 (no return) Hy
Anthony, William to Vina McClish 6-4-1866 (no return) Hy
Anthony, Wm. D. to Mary E. K. Crist 8-7-1867 (8-8-1867) Ma
Anthony, Wm. Linn to Josephine L. Anthony 9-11-1872 Hy
Anthony, Zack to Lizzie Shaw 3-24-1876 (no return) Hy
Anthony, jr., Thos. A. to Sallie E. Pickett 12-19-1877 Hy
Antonio, John Francisco to Esserline Simmons 5-16-1867 Hn
Antry, John C. to Mary C. Hammett 2-26-1861 (no return) Cr
Antwine, James to Susan Brown 3-17-1849 Hr
App, Joseph to Ottelaan Shleihan 6-14-1854 (6-15-1854) Sh
App, Mathias to Catherine Hezekiah 2-18-1850 Sh
Appel, Charles to Rosa Hill 1-2-1854 (1-3-1854) Sh
Appelton, Elija to Frances Morgan 12-2-1847 Cr
Apperson, Edward F. to Asenath Bell Robertson 6-24-1880 (no return) L
Applebee, John W. to Margaret M. Decker 10-3-1859 (10-12-1859) Sh
Appleberry, David A. to Mary A. McDaniel 4-5-1838 Sh
Appleberry, F. W. to Sarah F. Shaw 1-19-1859 (1-26-1859) Sh
Appleberry, J. D. to E. A. Privett 12-23-1863 (12-29-1863) F
Appleberry, J. N. to Paulina E. Johnson 1-7-1857 (1-8-1857) Sh
Appleberry, Joles S. to Ella Murphy 11-9-1884 L
Appleberry, R. G. to Matilda J. Privette 1-13-1865 (1-18-1865) F
Appleberry, Richd. to Mary L. Newton 9-21-1846 (no return) F
Appleberry, W. A. to Permelia Appleberry 12-18-1845 Sh
Appleberry, W. F. to Alsa Isom 7-27-1839 Sh
Applegate, E. W. to Nancy Frazier 1-24-1849 Sh
Applegate, Henry A. to Mary E. McMurry 10-31-1854 (11-1-1854) O
Applegate, James M. to Ellen Minton 8-20-1838 (8-22-1838) O
Applegate, R. F. to M. R. McGaugh 2-18-1861 (2-19-1861) O
Appleton, Jas. to Anan Daley 7-20-1852 Sh
Appleton, John S. to Elizabeth t. Gregory 3-11-1870 Ma
Applewhite, Jesse to Piety Killingsworth 4-10-1843 (4-12-1843) T
Applewhite, John to Nancy Jane McFerin 2-16-1841 (2-20-1841) T
Applewhite, W. H. to Alice White 12-25-1874 (no return) Dy
Applewhite, W. H. to R. A. Shumaker 6-22-1870 (6-23-1870) Dy
Aragon, Manuel to Octavia (Miss) Hourbeight 3-18-1857 (3-21-1857) Sh

Arant, Hugh to Nancy B. Hoggis 10-14-1840 Hn
Arbuckle, D. C. to Marion Lake 12-18-1852 (1-4-1853) Hr
Arbuckle, E. to Frances Alexander 2-8-1861 (no return) Hn
Arbuckle, Edward to E. C. Simmons 2-24-1848 Hr
Arbuckle, John W. to Mary Ann Smith 10-7-1852 (10-10-1852) G
Arbuckle, S. B. to Matilda A. Koen (Cohen) 11-24-1858 (11-30-1858) Sh
Archa, Thomas to Susan Delda 11-15-1838 Ma
Archard, Michael to Katharine Eagan 1-15-1856 Sh
Archard, Michael to Sobrina Daniels 12-25-1850 Sh
Archbell, Dave to Mary Shelton 12-26-1868 (12-28-1868) F B
Archer (Archsed?), Michael to Briget McGarth 8-24-1842 Sh
Archer, C. T. to Sarah B. Penny 2-20-1869 (2-24-1869) T
Archer, Charles W. to Susan Ann Walk 6-20-1855 T
Archer, D. B. to Aletha J. Shell 1-28-1867 (no return) Hn
Archer, David to Cressy Taylor 12-26-1866 (12-28-1866) F B
Archer, Henry A. to Sarah A. Blackburn 3-31-1865 G
Archer, James T. to Sarah J. Cunningham 9-21-1854 Hn
Archer, R. P. to M. M. Dobyns 12-27-1849 Sh
Archer, Richd. to Susan Howard 2-25-1869 T
Archer, W. A. to Selina C. Sanders 12-7-1859 G
Archer, W. H. to Margaret J. Corder 11-27-1861 (11-28-1861) T
Archer, W. H. to Matilda C. Manasco 2-8-1871 T
Archer, W. to Fannie Hitower 4-8-1874 (4-5?-1874) T
Archer, W. b. to Mary E. (Miss) Gillen 1-3-1863 (1-4-1863) Sh
Archer, Wm. Franklin to Margaret Ann Smith 12-5-1849 T
Archey, Matt to Famy Trigg 7-2-1872 (7-13-1872) T
Archibald, T. K. to Sue T. Neblett 7-6-1870 (no return) F
Archie, Rufus to Mary A. Motley 1-29-1861 (1-30-1861) F
Arendale, K.? H. to Sarah Jane Broche 3-26-1864 Sh
Arey, Gilbert to Sarah A. Darnell 8-20-1851 Hn
Argo, J. A. to Louvina Holmes 12-31-1847 Cr
Argo, J. W. to Margaret Jones 10-17-1859 Cr
Argo, Jasper N. to Malvina A. Johns 1-20-1870 G
Argo, John A. to Nancy Phipps 4-1-1841 Cr
Argo, John A. to Soniza Bullington 12-26-1848 (12-27-1848) G
Argo, John A. to Sonya Billingsly 12-2-1848 G
Argo, Solomon to E. J. Hays 11-7-1847 Cr
Argo, W. D. to Sarah E. Cribbs 9-8-1866 (no return) Cr
Arington, A. P. to Martha H. McCord 8-5-1873 (8-6-1873) Cr
Arington, B. F. to J.? A. Fussell 5-23-1861 (5-18-1861) Cr
Arington, Eli W. to S. F. Chandler 8-23-1866 Cr
Arl, Martin to Maggie Hipp 12-22-1885 (12-31-1885) L
Armfield, Bartlett Y. to Elizabeth Hamilton 2-20-1839 Sh
Armfield, I. A. to Mary J. Hendrix ?-?-1862? Mn
Armor, G. W. to Catharine Ballard 2-2-1865 Be
Armor, William to Sarah Ann Rushing 3-9-1845 Be
Armour, Alsey B. to Harriett Bloodworth 5-7-1845 Sh
Armour, David to Ann Cromwell 5-26-1828 Ma
Armour, David to Eliza G. Deaderick 11-20-1839 Sh
Armour, David to Sallie Jordan 3-29-1869 (4-1-1869) F B
Armour, J. C. to Elizabeth Bell 6-23-1853 Be
Armour, James L. to Mahala C. Cherry 5-28-1856 (6-2-1856) O
Armour, John D. to Achsa G. Wilkins 11-1-1849 Sh
Armour, John T. to Jacksy Baley 10-16-1844 (10-17-1844) G
Armour, Saml. James to M. C. Person 1-17-1855 Sh
Armour, Wm. C. to Susan E. Gardner 9-2-1850 (9-4-1850) F
Arms, William to Martha Huddleston 11-14-1839 Hr
Armstead, Geo. E. to Mary C. Caldwell 10-12-1860 (10-17-1860) Hr
Armstead, Geo. E. to Mary Jane Glass 2-8-1870 (2-9-1870) Ma
Armstrong, Abe to Fanny Alston 11-20-1871 911-23-1871) T
Armstrong, Alfred to Jollie? Mitchell 8-29-1870 (no return) F B
Armstrong, B. L. to Mary B. Rogers 10-4-1847 Sh
Armstrong, David to Amanda Jones 4-16-1873 (4-17-1873) Dy B
Armstrong, Elias to Annie Shaw 12-25-1848 Cr
Armstrong, Ezechal to Margarett Armfield 4-19-1839 (4-21-1839) G
Armstrong, George to Eliza Cole 7-18-1849 Sh
Armstrong, Isaac to Martha Jeter 12-31-1869 Hy
Armstrong, J. B. to M. E. Holland 1-13-1870 (1-18-1870) F
Armstrong, J. C. to Eliza Jane Anderson 12-20-1847 Hr
Armstrong, J. F. to Mollie A. Brock 3-14-1867 (3-19-1867) Dy
Armstrong, J. M. to L. J. Hill 4-28-1863 Mn
Armstrong, J. M. to M. A. White 11-10-1862 G
Armstrong, J. P. to E. C. Sharkman 12-23-1866 G
Armstrong, J. P. to Mary A. E. Flowers 6-6-1865 G
Armstrong, J. P. to Sarah Jacobs 6-7-1869 Cr
Armstrong, James H. to Lucy Ballard 4-12-1877 Hy
Armstrong, James Harvey to Juliann Minerva Clark 1-29-1842 (2-?-1842) T
Armstrong, James M. to Mary A. Bishop 3-26-1845 Hn
Armstrong, James M. to Rebecca A. Yarbrough 3-15-1849 G
Armstrong, James to Susan Vaughan 3-20-1871 G
Armstrong, Jehu H. to Jane Pankey 1-13-1844 (1-17-1844) Hr
Armstrong, John C. to Jane Nunnelly 10-18-1837 (?-19-?) Hr
Armstrong, John S. to Mollie A. Sloan 2-18-1864 G
Armstrong, John W. to Sarah (Miss) Willin 1-7-1858 Sh
Armstrong, Jonathan to Nancy Munn 2-11-1844 Cr
Armstrong, Marion to Elizabeth Parrish 9-19-1853 G
Armstrong, Martin T. to Fredonia O. Patrick 12-15-1857 Sh

Armstrong, R. M. to Mary A. Parker 3-14-1867 O
Armstrong, Robert E. to Ann E. Hathaway 8-4-1858 Ma
Armstrong, Robt. E. to Mary F. A. Cain 9-22-1853 Sh
Armstrong, Samuel W. to A. E. McBroom 2-13-1856 (2-14-1856) G
Armstrong, Thomas T. to Julia Ann Morgan 4-18-1845 Sh
Armstrong, Thomas to M. J. Foster 5-9-1868 (5-10-1868) O
Armstrong, W. C. to Sallie A. Phillips 10-21-1868 (10-22-1868) F
Armstrong, William to Elizabeth Forsythe 2-21-1850 Hn
Armstrong, Wm. R. to Annie Sophia (Miss) Young 3-14-1858 Sh
Arnett, Andrw J. to T Mayer 12-19-1844 Hn
Arnett, J. M. to Lucinda P. Jackson 1-1-1869 (1-14-1869) Cr
Arnett, J. M. to Sarah Smart 12-18-1858 (12-22-1858) Hr
Arnett, J. W. to Callie Whitley 5-13-1873 (5-14-1873) Dy
Arnett, James T. to Mary E. Dickens 9-11-1872 (9-12-1872) Dy
Arnett, R. M. to M. E. Hunt 5-13-1873 Dy
Arnett, W. H. to Nannie Cunningham 1-22-1874 Dy
Arnett, William P. to Cornelia F. Nancy 9-19-1860 Hn
Arnn, Crispin D. to Mary E. Griffin 1-2-1859 Hn
Arnn, E.? H. to Letitia L. McFadden 1-9-1863 Hn
Arnold, Aaron to Josephine Hawley 8-23-1853 Be
Arnold, Adsalom to P. J. Morris 5-9-1850 (no return) Hn
Arnold, Allen to Dixie Soward 1-15-1885 L
Arnold, Asa A. to Malvina Kimball 10-13-1859 Hn
Arnold, Asa to Racheal Hill 9-22-1828 Hr
Arnold, B. to Rebecca Finch 11-4-1856 G
Arnold, Benj. F. to Louisa Waldrop 3-30-1848 G
Arnold, Benjamin F. to Martha Ford 3-28-1853 (3-29-1853) G
Arnold, Charles to Catharine Schneider 8-23-1851 Sh
Arnold, Clark to Sally Ann Rogers 2-3-1853 Hn
Arnold, David to Siney Walker 8-10-1841 G
Arnold, Davis to Elizabeth Nichols 6-19-1837 (6-22-1837) O
Arnold, E. T. to M. J. Rankin 2-6-1858 We
Arnold, E. to L. A. Turley 1-25-1859 (2-21-1859) Sh
Arnold, E. to Suckey A. McDowd 8-5-1854 We
Arnold, Eli to Mary A. Lacy 2-26-1862 Sh
Arnold, Eli to Nancy A. Gill 2-19-1855 (8-9-1855) Sh
Arnold, Elijah M. to Sarah Jones 9-9-1857 (9-10-1857) O
Arnold, Elijah to Lucinda Snidere 8-12-1862 We
Arnold, Elisha to Martha J. Snider 2-26-1857 We
Arnold, Enoch P. to Nancy A. Gorden 1-12-1858 We
Arnold, Ezra I. to Margaret C. Patterson 3-10-1833 G
Arnold, F. M. to Clementine F. Golden 8-11-1861 Hn
Arnold, F. M. to Frances P. Golden 10-25-1863 Hn
Arnold, F. M. to Julia A. Wayman (Wagnore) 10-24-1849 Sh
Arnold, F. to Sarah Read 7-20-1854 We
Arnold, Francis N. to Mahala Thomas 9-29-1858 Ma
Arnold, Frank M. to Emma A. (Miss) Freeman 12-2-1863 Sh
Arnold, Geo. to Emma Strout? 9-22-1851 Sh
Arnold, George W. to Elvina A. Jackson 10-20-1853 Be
Arnold, George W. to Martha A. E. Arnold 9-27-1873 (9-29-1873) L
Arnold, H. W. to Mary D. Hart 12-25-1876 (12-26-1876) L
Arnold, H. W. to Mary Edwards 11-28-1884 (12-3-1884) L
Arnold, Hamilton to Winney Taylor 1-28-1865 O
Arnold, Henry to Clementine S. Petty 12-20-1858 (12-22-1858) G
Arnold, Henry to Sarah England 12-19-1853 Be
Arnold, J. A. to M. J. Calvin 10-5-1872 (10-6-1872) Dy
Arnold, J. G. to A. C. Price 10-15-1870 (10-16-1870) Cr
Arnold, J. G. to A. J. Radford 11-4-1874 (no return) Dy
Arnold, J. M. to N. C. Arnold 11-25-1880 L
Arnold, Jacob W. to Angaline K. Hamilton 12-27-1847 (1-25-1848) G
Arnold, James B. to Martha L. Steele 11-5-1867 (11-7-1867) Cr
Arnold, James D. to Eliza Thomas 12-17-1849 (12-17-1850?) Ma
Arnold, James P. to Mary E. Shane 1-5-1852 (1-6-1852) G
Arnold, James W. to Margaret Benson 9-21-1850 (9-25-1850) Hr
Arnold, James to Elizabeth Pafford 8-3-1855 Be
Arnold, James to Elizabeth West 8-3-1855 (8-5-1855) G
Arnold, James to Mary Thedford 4-6-1836 G
Arnold, James to Virginia Stewart 10-6-1845 T
Arnold, Jno. A. to Cornelia Shettleworth 1-8-1885 L
Arnold, Joel to Sarah Paris 12-28-1848 G
Arnold, John B. to E. C. Sharp 12-2-1869 G
Arnold, John B. to Mary A. Johnson 10-31-1849 (11-1-1849) G
Arnold, John H. to Sarah E. White 2-23-1853 (2?-1-1853) G
Arnold, John N. to Sarah Thomas Henning 1-5-1844 (1-2?-1844) Ma
Arnold, John to Matilda Rogers 12-19-1854 Hn
Arnold, John to Nancy Green 12-16-1868 O
Arnold, John to Nancy Honeycut 7-24-1846 We
Arnold, John to Nancy Simmonds 11-27-1848 Be
Arnold, L. A. to Elizabeth Finch 4-16-1863 O
Arnold, Littleberry B. to Sarah A. Lewis 3-9-1852 G
Arnold, Littleberry to Elizabeth F. Barnett 12-15-1862 (12-17-1862) Ma
Arnold, Martin B. to Elizabeth Knott 6-12-1845 G
Arnold, Miles to Mary Eliza Nevils 7-11-1846 (7-12-1846) L
Arnold, P. M. to Sarah J. Patrick 12-31-1846 Sh
Arnold, R. A. to A. J. Hall 9-5-1866 G
Arnold, Reddick to Lucy J. Floyd 10-14-1839 (10-24-1839) F
Arnold, Richard to Cordelia (Mrs.) Duvirage 9-17-1864 Sh

Arnold, Richardson to Polly Dickey 7-3-1843 (7-27-1843) G
Arnold, Robert to R. Brackins 2-10-1844 Cr
Arnold, S. C. to Eliza Ann Duggin 4-29-1870 G
Arnold, Theo. to Rebecca Walker 8-27-1839 (9-4-1839) Ma
Arnold, Thomas A. to Catherine Lankford 5-26-1859 Hn
Arnold, Thomas G. to Margaret J. Humphreys 9-14-1853 (9-15-1853) Ma
Arnold, Thomas to Malinda J. Walker 3-3-1838 (3-4-1838) L
Arnold, Thos. G. to Margaret J. Humphreys 9-4-1853 Ma
Arnold, Thos. S. to Martha Jane West 7-4-1861 Sh
Arnold, W. A. to Mary Wade 5-26-1868 Be
Arnold, W. B. to M. C. Bowie 8-23-1875 (8-24-1875) L
Arnold, W. F. to Nancy Patterson 10-30-1867 G
Arnold, William S. to Perlina C. Rogers 3-2-1854 Hn
Arnold, William to Drucilla Wright 11-11-1870 (no return) L
Arnold, William to Mary Butler 11-16-1843 We
Arnold, Wyatt to Virginia Biggs 12-29-1853 Be
Arnold], Wyatt to Martha Warick 2-21-1847 Be
Arragon, R. T. D. to Dennie Felts 6-26-1866 (7-4-1866) F
Arrington, A. to Rebeca Price 7-3-1865 (7-6-1865) Cr
Arrington, Benjamin to Emily Wrens 11-19-1857 Hn
Arrington, Jim to Malvina Alexander 9-1-1870 G B
Arrington, Wiley J. to Elizabeth Fuzzell 10-16-1856 Cr
Arrington, William to Caroline Nevils 3-14-1847 Sh
Arrington, Wm. H. to Eliza Jane Jones 8-1-1848 Cr
Arter, Wm. to Elizabeth Oliver 11-18-1838 F
Arthur, James P. to Lucy Ann Mullin 2-16-1867 (2-17-1867) L
Arthur, Philip to Mary Barnett 12-12-1857 (12-13-1857) L
Artrup, Joseph F. to Martha Ann McKiney 3-9-1869 (3-10-1869) L
Arun, David to Ann Babb 6-14-1853 Hn
Arun, George to Charlotte Lewry 1-11-1848 Hn
Arun, George to Louiza V. Lankford 9-8-1857 Hn
Arun, James M. to Amanda Bond 12-29-1848 Hn
Arun, John M. to Rebecca F. Morefield 9-20-1858 Hn
Arun?, John W. to Sarah J. Cole 10-20-1866 Hn
Arvinshire, William to Frances Lightle 7-15-1864 (7-17-1864) Cr
Arwood, Cornelias M. to Frances E. Johnson 1-16-1866 (1-17-1866) L
Arwood, J. A. to Mary E. Smith 8-19-1882 L
Arwood, Jessee A. to Cassanna Williams 2-14-1878 L
Ary, Gabriel to Rebecca Brown 10-20-1842 (10-21-1842) Hr
Ary, Thomas H. to Rebecca J. Thompson 11-12-1856 Hn
Asbel, Aaron to Letty Key 5-29-1850 O
Asbell, James to Amanda Polsgrove 4-29-1857 O
Asberry, Samuel to Nancy C. Shore 4-17-1858 (4-18-1858) O
Asbridges, Joseph H. to Elizabeth Sanders 12-17-1852 Cr
Asburry, L. L. to Bettie T. Gray 11-4-1858 Hr
Asbury, Henry F. to Caren Elizabeth Rowland 3-28-1857 (3-29-1857) O
Asbury, Willis to Charity Moorman 1-28-1870 (2-5-1870) F B
Ascue, James to Mary L. Crook 11-14-1855 (11-16-1855) L
Aselmeyer, Johannes (John) to Rachel Rimspah 11-6-1861 (11-7-1861) Sh
Ash, John L. to Ebby Jackson 8-4-1835 Hr
Ash, Thomas H. to Margaret Howe 7-17-1861 Sh
Ashbrook, Clarence P. to Hannah Coolidge 12-10-1861 Sh
Ashbrooks, Wade to Leah Goyle 1-21-1853 (1-22-1853) Sh
Ashby, Thos. T. to E. S. (Mrs.) Test 2-15-1860 (2-16-1860) Sh
Ashcraft, Wm. T. to Clementine C. Waddell 12-27-1852 (12-28-1852) Sh
Ashe, Gilford to Maria Wood 12-30-1874 Hy
Asher, David to Bertha Powell 5-23-1864 Sh
Asher, William to Jane Rodny 3-15-1857 Hn
Ashford, George W. to Eliza Jane Shuford 11-29-1856 (12-2-1856) Ma
Ashford, Jackson to Rebecca J. Okelly 12-6-1870 (12-7-1870) F
Ashford, W. J. L. to Mary E. (Miss) Smither 6-2-1858 Sh
Ashkettle, Wm. C. to Annie Chaffee 4-6-1864 (4-10-1864) Sh
Ashley, Calvin to Jemmina A. Gardner 11-4-1851 (11-6-1851) G
Ashley, Ed to Mary E. Rayger 6-26-1882 (6-27-1882) L
Ashley, G. M. to Mary Peebles 11-15-1860 Be
Ashley, Henry to Sally Tucker 2-18-1869 (2-21-1869) F B
Ashley, J. B. to C. L. Carlton 1-13-1859 G
Ashley, J. M. to Virginia Allen 1-15-1867 G
Ashley, L. H. to Harriet Jetton 2-27-1869 G
Ashley, R. M. to S. L. Draper 7-9-1865 G
Ashley, Wm. to Martha Garret 2-13-1856 (2-14-1856) Sh
Ashley, Young to Lydia C. Warren 4-18-1844 (no return) We
Ashlin, John to Margaret L. B. McDowell 7-25-1837 Hn
Ashlock, Benjamin F. to Sarah M. Willson 3-11-1851 Hn
Ashlock, Martha? to Elizabeth J. Thompson 4-19-1859 Hn
Ashmore, E. P. to Rutha Jane Goins 9-10-1873 L
Ashmore, John to Jenny Jones 12-3-1873 Hy
Ashmore, T. L. to Rejoiner Sistrunk 1-7-1869 (1-12-1869) L
Ashmore, Thomas to Caroline Riker 8-30-1878 (9-1-1878) L
Ashmore, W. D. to Mollie Cliatt 6-2-1879 (6-8-1879) L
Ashter, Manuel to Ann Mays 3-23-1867 Hy
Ashton, Emannuel to Mary Ella Anderson 3-15-1873 (3-18-1873) L B
Ashton, O. P. to Isabella Kendall 12-25-1867 Hn
Ashurst, Wm. to Mildred A. Jarson? 3-6-1873 (3-7-1873) T
Askew, Ashley to Martha Ann Nairon 1-21-1846 Hn
Askew, Ashley to Nancy A. Compton 4-3-1850 Hn
Askew, D. C. to Elizabeth Turner 1-7-1860 Be

Askew, James to Eliza Walton 10-20-1842 Cr
Askew, James to Sarah Pierce 3-15-1846 Hn
Askew, Joseph D. to Rutha J. Doherty 12-19-1857 Ma
Askew, Sandy to Edy Reddick 1-15-1869 (no return) F B
Askew, Thomas to Sarah Cash 6-22-1857 Ma
Askridge, J. D. to L. R. J. Thetford 8-10-1875 (8-11-1875) Dy
Asler, D. I. to Ann Barham 1-3-1850 (1-?-1850) G
Aslin, C. F. to J. M. Ford 11-30-1865 G
Aslin, J. B. to Nancy E. Patrick 9-9-1852 G
Aslin, James to Mary Ann Smith 12-24-1853 G
Aslin, John F. to Eliza Jones 1-4-1858 (1-7-1858) G
Aslin, Samuel to Angeline Hailey 3-17-1862 H
Aslin, Samuel to Mary A. Barham 12-19-1839 G
Aslin, T. N. to Margaret Williams 1-28-1866 G
Aslin, Thomas to Mary A. Morris 2-6-1861 G
Aslin, William A. to Delilah Morris 6-21-1866 G
Asmear (Azamire?), Conrad to Laney Wolfe 3-2-1855 (3-4-1855) Sh
Aspray, H. C. to S. C. Ray 1-15-1872 (no return) Dy
Aspy, James to Lucy C. Petty 11-4-1846 Cr
Astin, Augustus to Ann J. C. Vails 4-26-1854 (4-27-1854) Sh
Aston, C. S. to Martha M. Bell 12-6-1847 F
Aston, James to Sarah R. Hardin 2-14-1837 Hr
Aston, William to Frances R. Flippin 11-18-1845 F
Atcherson, J. to A. J. Hollowell 6-16-1842 Be
Atcherson, James L. to Levina Stanley 10-26-1827 Sh
Atcheson, Adam to Margaret A. Monroe 10-20-1839 Hn
Atcheson, Ezekial to Tabitha Jones 1-2-1844 Hn
Atcheson, G. P. to Alice Cora Gorman 9-11-1854 Be
Atcheson, J. to A. J. Hollowell 6-16-1842 Be
Atcheson, Jacob to Mary Yarbrough 1-5-1840 (no return) Hn
Atchison, C. W. to Mary J. Bingham 6-20-1866 Hn
Atchison, E. R. to E. E. Curd 9-16-1853 Hn
Atchison, George W. to Mary P. Lowry 6-23-1852 Hn
Atchison, Robert to Moley J. Higgins 8-18-1841 G
Atchison, William to Madlena McCracken 6-8-1839 (no return) Hn
Atchison, William to Threasy L. Davy 8-20-1831 Ma
Atchison, Willis to Susan C. Nance 7-10-1863 (no return) Hn
Atchison, jr., William to Sarah B. Knox 10-11-1848 G
Atertwim, J. A. to A. M. Avery 12-5-1866 G
Atherton, A. C. to C. M. Beavers 1-8-1866 (1-10-1866) F
Atkerson, P. to Emily Woods 5-16-1843 Cr
Atkerson, Thomas A. to Mary J. Tutor (Lutor) 10-16-1844 We
Atkin, E. F. to Sarah Jane Gowen 1-28-1848 (1-30-1848) F
Atkins, Abea to Mary Lanier 4-10-1848 (4-11-1848) F
Atkins, Asa A. to Mary M. Walker 12-14-1874 (12-15-1874) Dy
Atkins, Caleb to Amanda Jernigan 10-15-1866 Hn B
Atkins, Daniel L. to Amanda J. McAdoo 10-10-1850 (no return) Hn
Atkins, G. P. to Margaret S.? Waters 12-13-1871 T
Atkins, George M. to May M. Freeman 1-1-1868 Hn B
Atkins, Henry F. to Matilda Moore 2-23-1841 N
Atkins, Henry to Paramelia Frances McNabb 7-19-1856 (7-24-1856) Sh
Atkins, J. A. to Mollie Price 3-23-1869 (no return) Dy
Atkins, J. D. C. to E. P. Porter 11-23-1847 Hn
Atkins, J. J. to Clarissa M. Breedlove 12-19-1867 Hn
Atkins, James to Lavenia Tipton 2-14-1872 (2-4?-1872) Dy
Atkins, John B. to Elvira Smotherman 9-9-1845 Hn
Atkins, John B. to Perlina Bridges 12-16-1852 Hn
Atkins, John W. to Lucind Helms 11-30-1865 Dy
Atkins, Joseph to Melissa Ann Jackson 1-17-1861 Hn
Atkins, Lewis to Mary Ann Clark 3-26-1867 Hn B
Atkins, R. S. to O. C. Goldsby 10-19-1852 We
Atkins, Thomas J. to Elizabeth J. Phelts 9-28-1861 (no return) We
Atkins, W. G. to L. E. Aldridge 10-17-1864 Mn
Atkins, W. J. to Nancy Stewart 7-15-1860 Hn
Atkins, W. P. to Paulina Savage 2-1-1886 (2-9-1886) L
Atkins, William E. T. to Susan E. Cooper 4-20-1863 Hn
Atkins, William H. to Martha D. McCullough 5-13-1866 Hn
Atkins, William J. to Clementine Hall 12-3-1845 Hn
Atkinson, Ben H. to Jennie A. Robinson 3-29-1859 (3-30-1859) Sh
Atkinson, Calvin to M. E. Parnell (Pannell) 4-25-1876 (4-28-1876) O
Atkinson, Henry D. to Sarah S. Cook 11-20-1856 We
Atkinson, Ira to Catharine(Elisabeth) White 7-11-1859 Hr
Atkinson, Jno. R. (Dr.) to Bettie Lanier 12-6-1869 (12-8-1869) Ma
Atkinson, John W. to Sarah J. Parker 4-8-1852 Hn
Atkinson, Nathaniel to Ann E. Hunt 10-27-1837 (10-29-1837) Hr
Atkinson, R. A. to Arcena L. Biggs 1-14-1856 (1-21-1856) Sh
Atkinson, R. D. to Agnes Griggs 1-30-1869 (2-4-1869) F
Atkinson, R. W. to M. (Mrs.) McDearmon 11-11-1867 G
Atkinson, Robt. to Malinda Foster 3-1-1852 (3-2-1852) Sh
Atkinson, S. W. to Amanda J. Rosson 10-31-1871 (11-2-1871) O
Atkinson, Thomas to Mina Miller 6-22-1860 Hn
Atkinson, Thos. R. to Elizabeth Bond 1-4-1849 Sh
Atkinson, Wm. to Mary Jane Carneal 3-20-1863 Sh
Atkison, George to Caroline Hillsman 12-30-1869 (1-9-1870) Cr
Atkison, John to Margaret E. Strong 3-18-1862 (3-20-1862) T
Atkison, Robert A. to Levina Donald 10-30-1840 Ma
Atkison, S.? P. to Avarilla E. Call 1-31-1867 Hn

Attkisson, John to Fanney Bryant 10-20-1871 (10-25-1871) Cr
Attwood, Frederick J. to Rebecca Windiote 4-17-1854 (4-18-1854) Sh
Attwood, Josiah E. to Mary (Mrs.) Hile 12-12-1864 Sh
Atutwim, J. A. to A. M. Avery 12-5-1866 G
Atwood, Thomas to Mary A. Bedford 11-6-1851 (11-7-1851) Sh
Atwood, William W. to Mary C. Neely 6-9-1829 (6-10-1829) Hr
Aubrey, James H. to Mary Boon 8-23-1845 (8-25-1845) Ma
Auger, Herman to Helena Adler 10-3-1854 Hn
Augustus, S. W. to Mollie Bradley 3-3-1860 (3-5-1860) Hr
Austen, S. W. to Sarah E. Keltner 1-1-1863 L
Austin, Ananias to Sabry Shaw 2-16-1869 Hy
Austin, C. H. to Lavinia Dillard 12-5-1878 Hy
Austin, Charles to Paralee Butler 7-25-1870 (7-27-1870) Cr
Austin, Edwin K. to Marion W. Hanley 7-15-1845 (7-18-1845) F
Austin, Henry J. to Mary Ann Howell 9-30-1857 (10-1-1857) Ma
Austin, Hezekiah to Nancy Hamill 6-8-1854 L
Austin, John A. to Harrit A. Bumpass 1-5-1860 We
Austin, John A. to Mary P. Stout 5-25-1866 (5-27-1866) Ma
Austin, John R. to Luisa S. Castilaw 8-1-1863 (8-9-1863) L
Austin, John to Ann Barns 7-16-1857 Hr
Austin, John to Mattie Powell 12-4-1878 Hy
Austin, Joseph A. to Millie Davie 12-14-1871 Hy
Austin, Phillip G. to Mary A. Maxwell 7-4-1860 We
Austin, Prestin to Willie Nelson 12-25-1869 Hy
Austin, W. A. to Susan C. (Mrs.) Barker 9-12-1862 (9-13-1862) Dy
Austin, Wilson to Lizer J. Austin 7-16-1865 G
Austin, Wm. to Dirzean Watkins 3-22-1877 Hy
Auston, Sam to Jennie Howard 9-1-1870 (9-5-1870) L
Auterbridge, Dick to Ella Coggshall 12-26-1876 Hy
Autery, S. W. to Rilley Rogers 12-21-1863 (12-23-1863) Cr
Autney, Lauson to Martha Smith 1-15-1870 Hy
Autrey, B. P. to Sallie Templeton 12-6-1885 (no return) L
Autrey, G. E. to L. S. Roney 2-8-1848 (2-10-1848) O
Autrey, James to Susan Elizabeth Tanner 5-13-1856 O
Autrey, John L. to Sarah Jane Ray 4-11-1857 (4-12-1857) O
Autrey, William G. to Rosannah M. Roney 1-27-1858 (1-28-1858) O
Autry, C. to Ann E. Styers 1-16-1873 L
Autry, Dungan to Susan Hedges 10-24-1849 Cr
Autry, E. W. to M. E. McAuley 11-21-1868 (11-22-1868) Cr
Autry, James to Rebecca Cherry 8-7-1865 (8-10-1865) O
Autry, John A. to Winifred Parish 2-22-1844 Cr
Autry, John A. to Winnie W. Watson 9-19-1847 Cr
Autry, Samuel to Narcissa Roberds 1-14-1851 Cr
Autry, Tyson to Louiza Horn 11-26-1861 (no return) Cr
Autry, Wm. to Belinda Haywood 10-9-1848 Cr
Avant, Nelson to Martha Ann Person 1-23-1872 (1-28-1872) T
Avant, Peter A. to Margaret A. Traylor 2-19-1855 (2-21-1855) Hr
Avant, Saml. T. to Ella M. Alexander 1-13-1860 Hr
Avants, J. T. to A. M. Jackson 1-23-1872 (1-28-1872) Dy
Avenshire, Elias to Gatsey Stokes 12-12-1848 Cr
Avenshire, Moses to Nancy Stocker 2-1-1844 Cr
Avent, Drewry to Susan Gates 3-29-1845 (4-3-1845) Hr
Avent, Wash D. to Nanney McKinnie 11-17-1855 (11-19-1855) Hr
Averett, J. W. to E. W. Turner 8-14-1873 O
Avery, A. B. to J. C. Crawford 3-12-1865 G
Avery, A. H. to Henrieta E. Polk 4-10-1848 (4-12-1848) F
Avery, Albert to Rachal Moore 12-17-1869 (12-18-1869) T
Avery, Allen B. to Frances M. Nelson 3-25-1845 Sh
Avery, D. V. to S.(L.) C. Boswell 12-16-1866 G
Avery, Elisha to Jane C. Blan 9-29-1848 Hn
Avery, Frank to Ann Brasfield 2-27-1868 G B
Avery, Hammon to Isabella Tatum 3-3-1869 G B
Avery, Henry to Ann Burwell 3-25-1863 (3-25-1863) Dy
Avery, J. T. J. to Harriett A. T. Avery 10-2-1848 G
Avery, James to Martha C. Neckron 1-29-1846 Hn
Avery, Jas. F. A. M. to Nancy C. Gunner 12-5-1854 (12-7-1854) G
Avery, John W. to Margaret Hicks 1-8-1839 G
Avery, R. T. S. to Polly Babb 10-13-1836 G
Avery, Silas to Lucinda Pentegrass 6-18-1845 (6-23-1845) G
Avery, Walker to Bettie Nichols 7-27-1870 G
Avery, William M. to America E. Hardgraves 8-26-1867 Ma
Avery, Wm. A. G. to Sarah N. Rosamon 9-3-1866 (9-9-1866) Ma
Avetts, William to Caroline Webb 6-28-1846 Sh
Avey, John B. to M. J. G. Gillis 12-27-1871 Dy
Avrett, M. A. to M. E. Ward 11-6-1868 (11-8-1868) Dy
Axtell, W. H. to Sarah A. Mendenall 12-10-1857 Sh
Aycock, A. A. to Martha V. Farris 10-22-1864 (9-26-1864) T
Aycock, James W. to Tabitha N. Conyers 2-1-1843 (no return) Hn
Aycock, Jourden to Mary J. Upchurch 10-13-1846 Cr
Aycock, N. H. to Sarah C. Bell 12-11-1861 Dy
Aycock, R. G. to Mary M. Woods 6-22-1854 G
Aycock, R. R. to Amanda P. Guthrie 9-1-1853 Hn
Aycock, R. R. to Haseltine Barbee 7-15-1850 Hn
Aydelotte, Jackson L. to Mary E. Wortham 12-24-1851 Sh
Aydlett, Thomas P. to Susan M. Hutchings 6-12-1850 Sh
Aydlott, Stephen D. to Elizabeth Whitley 10-1-1851 (10-8-1851) Sh
Ayers, B. W. to Martha A. Heggie 3-24-1858 Be

Ayers, F. N. to Allice Reed 9-28-1864 O
Ayers, George C. to Temperance A. Patterson 11-25-1868 Ma
Ayers, George N. to Claresy A. Snowden 1-23-1845 Cr
Ayers, J. C. to Martha M. Nowlen 2-21-1858 We
Ayers, J. L. to D. F. Redus 4-16-1850 F
Ayers, J. W. to Campbell 3-2-1878 (no return) Dy
Ayers, James L. to Mary E. Yarbro 5-12-1858 T
Ayers, John A. to Sarah Campbell 10-15-1850 Cr
Ayers, John H. to Mary J. Williams ?-?-1861? Mn
Ayers, Josiah F. to Mary G. Wiatt 8-8-1846 Sh
Ayers, S. B. to M. S. Mott 12-13-1870 (12-21-1870) O
Ayers, Samuel W. to Elizabeth L. Cook 1-2-1850 Sh
Ayers, T. J. to Lucy Jane Lowery 9-28-1859 (10-2-1859) Hr
Ayers, W. F. to Ann Huddleston 7-27-1848 Hr
Ayers, W. L. to Martha H. Chambers 9-23-1872 (9-26-1872) O
Ayers, Wm. F. to Gray Howell 4-15-1858 T
Ayrens?, Wilie to Jane Cate 8-7-1871 Dy
Ayres, Allen to Mary Rosson 8-21-1830 (8-22-1830) Hr
Ayres, Amos to Elizabeth C. Fisher 8-10-1841 O
Ayres, Eli to Caroline Wilson 10-13-1829 (10-15-1829) Hr
Ayres, Wm. F. to Mary E. Howell 3-1-1854 (3-2-1854) Sh

B____, Bryant? to Elizabeth Whitten 6-17-1852 Hn
Babb, Benjamin to Mary (Mrs.) Kennedy 6-8-1859 (6-9-1859) Sh
Babb, David W. to Rachael Murphy 1-27-1852 (1-29-1852) Hr
Babb, Henry to Sarah A. E. Avery 11-28-1842 G
Babb, J. B. G. to Elizabeth T. Ragan 1-3-1866 G
Babb, James to Elizabeth Craig 3-6-1831 G
Babb, Mathew G. to Jane Catharine Lambert 2-5-1852 (2-8-1852) Hr
Babb, Peyton to Polly Gooden 7-13-1870 (7-14-1870) F B
Babb, Stephen to Alcy Hooper 6-6-1842 Hn
Babb, Stevin Oliver to Malinda E. Mayfield 5-3-1858 (5-4-1858) Hr
Babb, Thomas S. to Emily Davis 5-13-1845 (5-14-1845) O
Babb, Wm. F. to Mary M. Cooper 3-26-1860 (4-3-1860) Hr
Babbett, Thos. F. to Barbary A. Ward 5-16-1860 F
Babbs, Silas to Hester Montague 9-25-1869 (6-15-1870) F B
Babcock, Robert G. to Cynthia Anderson 10-29-1863 O
Baber, Alexander to Mary K. Harris 11-13-1838 (no return) Hn
Baber, B. G. to Willie Ann Pyron 6-4-1862 Sh
Baber, Francis J. to Janetta J. Day 10-6-1859 Ma
Bacchus, Charles L. to Elizabeth Bushart 11-2-1843 Hn
Bacchus, John A. to Rebecca Markrum 2-11-1855 Hn
Bachele, F. to F. Senn 6-2-1855 (6-7-1855) Sh
Bachelor, jr., John to Elizabeth Pearson 9-2-1865 (9-5-1865) L
Bachman, P. M. to Mary Ann Coyne 12-8-1862 Sh
Bacigalupo, Vincent to Mary Brizalaro 4-22-1852 (4-25-1852) Sh
Backer, Herm (Harmon) to Louisa Duttlinger 9-11-1863 (9-13-1863) Sh
Backloop, Joseph to Mary Abernatha 9-19-1865 (no return) Hy
Bacon, Harvey to Mary Allen 7-28-1831 Sh
Bacon, Joseph to Bettie Jones 3-22-1875 (3-24-1875) Dy
Bacon, T. J. to Minnie Landrum 10-16-1883 (10-22-1883) L
Baden, Robert to Sally Butler 4-25-1877 Hy
Badger, Wm. to Harriet N. Miller 12-3-1851 (12-24-1851) Sh
Badget, George to Fanny Hall 12-9-1844 G
Badgett, Zach to Millie Henderson 10-15-1880 (10-24-1880) Dy
Badinelli, Luzaro to Mary Rizzi 6-30-1857 Sh
Bady, Joyner W. to Lucenda J. Cassell 9-8-1851 (9-10-1851) G
Baenbridge, William B. to Jane Dean Campbell 11-15-1847 (11-16-1847) T
Bagbey, C. M. to Tina Balderson 1-3-1872 L
Bagby, Henry C. to Margaret E. Myares 2-15-1862 We
Bagby, James P. to J. F. Owen 12-8-1855 (12-12-1855) Hr
Bagby, James P. to Mary E. Lankford 12-11-1865 (12-14-1865) L
Bagby, Jim to Tilda Harrison 2-22-1871 Hy
Bagby, Timany to Ellen Black 6-3-1859 Hn
Bagby, T. E. to Mary Ann Oury 7-13-1852 Hn
Bagly (Bagby), Rufus W. to Mary Ann Eliza Jones 8-12-1850 Sh
Bagg, Mathew G. to Juliann Paterson 10-7-1854 (10-9-1854) Hr
Baggett, Benjamin B. to Susan A. Phillips 7-27-1843 Sh
Baggett, Bradford to Martha Yarbrough 1-11-1882 L
Baggett, H. W. to E. H. Ballowe 9-20-1854 Be
Baggett, Layfayette to Nancy Lann 2-23-1883 L
Baggett, Thos. D. to Martha M. Pyron 2-21-1853 (no return) F
Bagley, George A. (of Miss.) to Jemima Johnson 7-16-1861 Ma
Bagley, James to Mary A. High 4-12-1836 (4-14-1836) Hr
Bagley, T. E. to Mary Ann Oury 7-13-1852 Hr
Bagly (Bagby), Rufus W. to Mary Ann Eliza Jones 8-12-1850 Sh
Bagnell, Isaac to Mary A. Butts 1-24-1849 Ma
Bagwell, William to Susan Whitehead 2-14-1863 (2-16-1863) O
Bagwell, Wm. to Nancy Miller 8-16-1840 Hr
Bahanan, Lewis to Telitha T. Capps 6-4-1860 (no return) We
Bailey, A. J. to Phoeba Logue 1-11-1861 Sh
Bailey, Alpha to Elizabeth A. Sain 1-9-1855 (1-11-1855) Hr
Bailey, Alston to Martha Motly 12-2-1844 (12-26-1844) G
Bailey, Anderson to Angeline Frances Stewart 1-7-1867 (1-8-1867) Ma
Bailey, Andrew I. to Elizabeth Goodrich 2-8-1842 Ma
Bailey, Arter to Catharine Peebles 11-4-1869 (11-9-1869) F B
Bailey, Ben to Anna Johnson 10-20-1871 Hy
Bailey, Benj. A. to E. A. Clark 11-27-1855 (no return) F
Bailey, Benjamin A. to Mary Sain 10-26-1844 (10-29-1844) G

Bailey, Benjamin C. to Nancy Wade Sullivan 12-8-1845 (12-10-1845) T
Bailey, Boyd to Valenta Underwood 4-1-1892 Sh
Bailey, Burton to Mahina E. Carter 6-1-1843 Hr
Bailey, Carison to Elizabeth Denny 6-15-1850 Hr
Bailey, Charles to Alvira Wright 5-13-1845 (5-14-1845) O
Bailey, Charles to Mattie Shelton 12-23-1869 (no return) F B
Bailey, Cyrus J. to Mary F. Bailgar (Bilgar?) 8-6-1864 Sh
Bailey, Elijah to Hannah Norris 1-12-1837 Hr
Bailey, Elijah to Martha C. Bailey 12-28-1866 (12-31-1866) Ma
Bailey, G. T. to L. T. Long 11-15-1858 We
Bailey, George to Ailsey Green 1-3-1877 Hy
Bailey, George to Hester Anne Dawson 5-24-1869 (SB 1868?) G B
Bailey, George to Matilda Cage 1-8-1874 T
Bailey, Giles to Mandy Taylor 2-3-1867 Hy
Bailey, H. H. to Ann J. Fuller 2-4-1867 (2-5-1867) F
Bailey, Harris to Mary (Mrs.) Cotner 5-5-1852 (no return) F
Bailey, Harris to R. E. Baily 12-28-1859 F
Bailey, Henderson to Eliza Jackson 8-14-1845 (8-22-1845) G
Bailey, Isham to Sarah A. Betts 12-17-1854 G
Bailey, Ishmal to Mary Stephenson 5-24-1847 Cr
Bailey, J. F. to Eliza Books 12-17-1868 G
Bailey, J. G. to R. T. Brinkley 2-23-1878 (2-26-1878) Dy
Bailey, Jackson to Mary Ross 11-9-1867 G B
Bailey, James L. to Sarah Hartsfield 12-20-1851 (12-21-1851) T
Bailey, James M. to Martha J. Baker 1-21-1867 G
Bailey, James T. to Elizabeth Forbess 8-5-1856 (8-6-1856) Hr
Bailey, James to Ema Moorer 4-18-1873 Hy
Bailey, James to Sarah Bond 11-17-1877 Hy
Bailey, Jeremiah to Dizia Ann Bailey 6-22-1857 (6-23-1857) Ma
Bailey, Jerry to L. A. Holder 3-2-1857 G
Bailey, Jesse to Mary E. Slayton 9-26-1868 (9-27-1868) Dy
Bailey, John A. to Nancy Porter 7-4-1853 G
Bailey, John B.? to Sarah Ward 9-24-1864 (no return) Dy
Bailey, John C. to Sarah Ann E. Peal 2-3-1862 (no return) Dy
Bailey, John J. to Emma R. Parr 1-6-1851 F
Bailey, John W. to Mary Ann Phillips 4-21-1842 Sh
Bailey, John to Nancy Wyatt 12-29-1868 G B
Bailey, John to Sidny Holmes 10-14-1875 (10-15-1875) Dy
Bailey, Joseph E. to Martha Huckaby 1-6-1844 (1-8-1844) Hr
Bailey, Joseph to Harriet M. Jackson 12-18-1847 (12-20-1847) Ma
Bailey, Joshua to Elizabeth Cannon 1-3-1867 T
Bailey, Lewis to Jane Bishop 7-5-1869 G
Bailey, Mortica to Elizabeth McDurmit 4-7-1846 (4-8-1846) G
Bailey, Nathe. C. to Martha M. Thomas 12-26-1870 (12-27-1870) Ma
Bailey, Peleg to Eliza N. Bailey 9-13-1832 G
Bailey, Peleg to Margarett J. Donaldson 2-23-1846 (2-26-1846) G
Bailey, R. W. to T. J. McCullough 12-1-1873 T
Bailey, R. a. to S. E. Tucker 6-20-1868 G
Bailey, Robert B. to S. E. Philips 3-15-1843 (3-18-1843) F
Bailey, S. R. to M. F. Kibble 11-2-1875 (no return) Hy
Bailey, Silas to Sarah Ann Logan 11-13-1869 (11-14-1869) F
Bailey, Silvester to Julia C. Tyler 3-28-1833 Hr
Bailey, Soloman to Callie Young 12-27-1877 Hy
Bailey, Stephen Lewis to Harriet Jones 12-9-1885 (no return) L
Bailey, Tho. J. to Eliza Anderson 3-18-1835 (3-24-1835) Hr
Bailey, Tinsley T. to Sarah Baker 9-4-1872 (no return) L
Bailey, Tom to Mary Black 8-26-1868 (no return) F B
Bailey, W. C. to Tebitha Bucy 11-2-1848 Hn
Bailey, W. H. to J. J. McAuley 7-24-1869 (7-25-1869) Cr
Bailey, W. L. to Mary Wilkinson 1-4-1832 (1-5-1831?) Hr
Bailey, Wash to Nancy Richardson 1-25-1871 (1-26-1871) F B
Bailey, William A. to Mary Ann Stallcup 7-21-1863 (no return) Dy
Bailey, William C. to Mary Ann Bucy 11-20-1846 Hn
Bailey, William H. to Martha A. Biggs 12-20-1843 G
Bailey, William to Hollan Patrick 6-3-1839 (6-13-1839) G
Bailey, William to Mary A. Coleman 2-4-1846 (no return) Hn
Bailey, Wm. C. to Fanny P. Farrill 10-8-1849 (10-11-1849) F
Bailey, Wm. T. (Dr.) to Catharine Gwynne 4-9-1860 (4-10-1860) Sh
Bailey, Wyatt to Sallie Boyd 1-11-1871 F
Bailey, Wyatt to Sarah Dargan 2-15-1838 (no return) Hn
Baily, David to Martha Dove 11-29-1869 Dy
Baily, Henry to Jane Wiley 12-24-1872 T
Baily, John C. to Rosa Ann Binkly 4-11-1853 (4-12-1853) Hr
Baily, John to Caroline Glasper 8-28-1867 Hy
Baily, Solomon A. to Ellen Baily 4-5-1854 (4-13-1854) G
Baily, T. to Martha A. Elkins 10-31-1865 O
Baily, William W. to Paralee Wadley 8-18-1855 (8-19-1855) Ma
Bain, A. T. to Mary E. Ledbetter 10-20-1870 G
Bain, David L. to Ella Benton 7-27-1866 (10-15-1866) F
Bain, Henry T. to Mary Tompkins 1-25-1852 Be
Bain, James to Martha E. Joslin 4-18-1878 (4-21-1878) Dy
Bain, John to Matilda Bass 8-4-1837 Hr
Bain, S. C. D. to Emma Griffin 2-20-1878 Hy
Bain, William to Polly Knott 12-25-1843 (12-28-1843) G
Bain, Wm. W. to Julia B. Haynes 12-18-1866 (12-20-1866) Ma
Baines, B. F. to Susan Keller 2-25-1874 (3-1-1874) T

Baines, Frank to Tennessee Bowen 4-15-1872 (4-17-1872) Dy
Bains, William to Willie Brooks 3-6-1873 Hy
Bair, Joseph to Sidonia Wilbosern 5-22-1860 Dy
Baird, Andrew J. to Christian Gillis 1-19-1844 (1-21-1844) O
Baird, Babe to Margarett Coley 8-26-1869 G
Baird, C. W. to Linnie E. Anthony 2-18-1878 (no return) Hy
Baird, Charles G. to Nancy Hayns 11-20-1843 G
Baird, D. G. to Texana L. Cain 2-17-1870 G
Baird, David to Julia A. McAlister 5-14-1861 G
Baird, J. F. to J. A. Tombs 3-8-1860 O
Baird, J. H. to Jane Woodard 5-31-1864 (6-1-1864) O
Baird, J. Linsey to M. Bettie McQuiston 12-6-1870 (12-8-1870) T
Baird, J. S. to Penelope Newsom 9-24-1866 (9-25-1866) F
Baird, J. W. to Sarah J. Roe 9-19-1866 G
Baird, James M. to Sarah J. Baird 6-21-1852 G
Baird, Jas. M. to Julia F. Martin 6-7-1858 (6-8-1858) G
Baird, Jo to Mary E. Franklin 6-5-1866 (1?-6-1866) Dy
Baird, John to Eliza Miller 1-29-1868 T
Baird, Joihn to Lee Jones 10-17-1868 G B
Baird, Joseph to Susan Smith 2-25-1871 (2-26-1871) Dy
Baird, Josiah to Eliza Ann Misskelly 11-18-1856 (11-20-1856) L
Baird, Lewis to Martha J. Parks 4-12-1871 (no return) Dy
Baird, M. V. to Olly B. Hopper 3-30-1860 G
Baird, Marcus to Mary E. Bishop 7-2-1862 G
Baird, R. H. to A. L. Roe 2-7-1866 G
Baird, Richard W. to Catharine Taylor 9-13-1845 O
Baird, Stephen to Aneliza Hafford 12-6-1871 N
Baird, Thomas S. to Julia A. M. Thorn 10-17-1867 G
Baird, Thomas to Irena Stewart 5-11-1859 (5-12-1859) G
Baird, Thos. D. to Nancy A. M. Bryant 12-9-1850 (12-8?-1850) G
Baird, Vines to Balmy Johnson 6-21-1866 (6-22-1866) O
Baird, W. T. to M. C. Jones 2-4-1867 (2-12-1867) Cr
Baird, Wiley M. to Bettie Jordan 9-2-1866 G
Baird, William to Nancy Jane McQuiston 3-5-1844 T
Baird, Wm. C. to M. M. E. McDaniel 8-25-1873 (9-4-1873) T
Baird, Wm. to Earnest Drake 5-7-1876 Hy
Bairfield, Needham B. to Victoria Faine 5-2-1870 Dy
Baker, A. J. to Jamima Dewalt 5-14-1861 L
Baker, A. to Martha E. Farley 2-9-1846 (2-11-1846) F
Baker, Abijah to Arlamesa Holiday 5-18-1830 Hr
Baker, Abraham to Cholley Crawford 11-16-1858 (11-18-1858) Hr
Baker, Abram to Babette Lery 10-17-1853 (10-18-1853) Sh
Baker, Alexander to Mary Layne 7-9-1870 (7-10-1870) L
Baker, Alvis to J. H. Cresap 10-16-1858 (10-21-1858) G
Baker, Andrew to Mollie Inns 12-17-1870 Hy
Baker, Asa to Mary T. Garrett 10-29-1856 Sh
Baker, B. J. to Malinda C. Sanders 10-11-1849 Be
Baker, Calib to Katherine Moore 12-31-1868 (1-1-1869) F B
Baker, Christian to Mary Hoopert 1-11-1855 (1-15-1855) Sh
Baker, Daniel to Agnes Watson 12-17-1868 (12-25-1868) F B
Baker, David J. to Eliza Jane Sanders 2-3-1848 Be
Baker, Dick to Candis Strickland 4-4-1868 F B
Baker, Duke to Elizabeth Platt 2-11-1863 Dy
Baker, E. F. to Elizabeth Gooch 8-5-1859 Cr
Baker, E. H. to Lena H. Dawson 12-24-1874 Dy
Baker, Edward V. to Cynthia A. Wiley 10-9-1849 Sh
Baker, Emanuel to Mary E. Jennings 8-24-1838 Sh
Baker, Enoch to Nancy E. Ligen 5-15-1864 Hn
Baker, F. C. to M. E. Marchant 9-18-1866 (9-19-1866) Dy
Baker, Felix to Gussie Hamilton 2-2-1870 G B
Baker, Fetus to Judith Phelps 11-8-1842 (11-9-1842) Ma
Baker, George T. to Martha E. Hurt 9-27-1865 (9-28-1865) Dy
Baker, George W. to Arabella Barrett 8-15-1846 (8-17-1846) Ma
Baker, George W. to Mattie Potts 9-28-1873 Hy
Baker, German to Henrietta Crutcher 11-20-1854 (11-21-1854) Sh
Baker, Green L. to L. Snider 3-15-1849 Hn
Baker, Greenville A. J. to Sarah Catherine Weatherly 5-21-1866 (no return) Hn
Baker, H. B. to Eliza Powers 10-5-1856 We
Baker, H. B. to Louisa B. Thompson 3-5-1852 Hn
Baker, H. D. C. to D. E. Young 9-9-1867 (9-11-1867) T
Baker, Harris L. to Emma Bet. Dawson 12-25-1872 Dy
Baker, Harrison to Elizabeth A. Smith 4-19-1838 Hn
Baker, Henderson to Willey Jones 2-15-1841 (2-18-1841) G
Baker, Henry C. to Sarah A. Graves 6-23-1866 (6-24-1866) Ma
Baker, Henry T. to Sarah Edward 12-11-1867 G
Baker, Henry W. to Mary L. Kirk 1-20-1863 (1-22-1863) Dy
Baker, Henry to Elizabeth Read 8-3-1858 (8-12-1858) Ma
Baker, Henry to Pricilla Gray 2-5-1863 Mn
Baker, Henry to Susan T. Allen 1-10-1865 G
Baker, Henry to Tabitha Boyd 10-13-1856 T
Baker, Howard to Lucinda Powers 1-13-1860 Be
Baker, Isaac to Mary F. King 8-1-1853 (8-2-1853) Hr
Baker, Isaac to Pemela E. Garrett 1-7-1852 Sh
Baker, J. A. to M. C. Saunders 12-24-1846 Be
Baker, J. C. to Louisa A. Webber 4-2-1855 Sh
Baker, J. C. to M. J. E. Turner 2-1-1881 L
Baker, J. F. to S. A. Snead 1-6-1873 (1-7-1873) Cr

Baker, J. J. to E. B. Moore 8-24-1867 (8-25-1867) Dy
Baker, J. N. to Susan Adair 3-3-1859 Sh
Baker, J. S. to Martha Erwin 5-31-1866 O
Baker, J. W. to Elizabeth Adcocks 2-18-1882 (2-20-1882) L
Baker, Jacob to Rebecca Jackson 11-4-1850 Ma
Baker, James A. to Eliza Jane Waldrop 8-27-1843 Hn
Baker, James A. to Louisa V. Ligan 10-4-1849 Hn
Baker, James B. to Sarah J. Bram 6-19-1854 (no return) F
Baker, James F. to Amanda C. Deaton 7-26-1869 (7-28-1869) Ma
Baker, James H. to Elizabeth Glenn 12-27-1849 (12-29-1849) Ma
Baker, James J. to Eliza J. Pennington 7-21-1856 (8-4-1856) G
Baker, James J. to Martha A. D. Wilson 12-14-1847 (3-26-1848) Ma
Baker, James S. to Hursay Wortham 3-26-1845 (4-1-1845) G
Baker, James W. to Nancy Holt 8-23-1866 G
Baker, James to Ann Steely 2-24-1846 (no return) Hn
Baker, James to Nancy J. Powers 3-12-1856 Ma
Baker, James to Polly Mitts 1-8-1830 (1-14-1830) G
Baker, Jesse to Levena Golen 10-18-1840 F
Baker, Jesse to Martha E. Reynolds 12-4-1869 (12-5-1869) Dy
Baker, Jessee B. to Martha Herril 3-16-1876 Dy
Baker, John A. to Martha A. Hudson 8-20-1857 (8-26-1857) Hr
Baker, John A. to Martha Jane Shinn 5-31-1848 (6-8-1848) Hr
Baker, John C. T. to Sidney G. Lamb 11-11-1839 We
Baker, John C. to Sarah Davis 2-18-1874 (2-19-1874) L
Baker, John G. to Catherine Elliott 3-28-1850 Sh
Baker, John L. to S. J. (Mrs.) Goza 5-2-1866 G
Baker, John P. to Elizabeth J. Lockhart 11-11-1866 Be
Baker, John W. to Elizabeth F. Toones 9-16-1867 (9-18-1867) Ma
Baker, John W. to Mary C. Blain 2-13-1850 (2-14-1850) G
Baker, John W. to Mary E. Little 7-3-1852 (7-8-1852) Ma
Baker, John W. to Mary F. L.(S) Jones 5-21-1835 Sh
Baker, John W. to Mary Tatum 1-31-1842 (2-2-1842) F
Baker, John W. to Narcissa Lumpkins 10-31-1872 L
Baker, John to Anna Turner 12-22-1869 (no return) L
Baker, John to Clarisa Ann Wallice 6-5-1869 (no return) L
Baker, John to Elizabeth Dickerson 1-13-1858 Sh
Baker, John to Harriet Thompson 6-1-1867 (no return) L B
Baker, John to Hester Walker 10-19-1868 (10-30-1868) F B
Baker, John to Mary S. Womble 2-1-1860 We
Baker, John to Nancy Parker 12-7-1846 We
Baker, John to Peggy Keller 4-21-1857 (4-22-1857) Sh
Baker, John to Rebecca Burleson 12-15-1831 Hr
Baker, John to Sarah C. Henson 3-1-1850 (3-7-1850) Hr
Baker, Johonn (John) to Catherine Gayheart 8-27-1863 (8-28-1863) Sh
Baker, Jonas to Sary Hodge 10-30-1828 Hr
Baker, Jones to Lizzie Parish 4-24-1867 (4-28-1867) F B
Baker, Joseph to Amanda Shilling 12-31-1840 Be
Baker, Joseph to Catharine Powers 6-13-1860 Sh
Baker, Joseph to Nancy Green 7-25-1837 Hr
Baker, Joshua to Amanda J. Blankenship 12-4-1861 G
Baker, Joshua to Jennett West 11-3-1855 (11-6-1855) G
Baker, Joshua to Lucretia Perry 5-11-1839 Ma
Baker, Josiah to Mary Forester 12-2-1834 G
Baker, L. A. to Martha J. Good 6-12-1866 G
Baker, L. C. to Jane E. Goodman 11-10-1869 G
Baker, L. G. to Martha J. Wilkes 10-6-1847 Sh
Baker, Leonard to Martha A. C. Walker 1-10-1872 (1-11-1872) Dy
Baker, Lewis to Betsey Dudley 4-7-1845 (no return) We
Baker, Lorenso D. to Sarah Burleson 7-10-1834 (7-15-1834) Hr
Baker, Nathan N. to Eliza Fipps (Flippo) 12-7-1843 Sh
Baker, Newton to M. C. Oliver 8-11-1880 (8-12-1880) L
Baker, Noah to Malvina (Matilda?) Inman 3-16-1848 L
Baker, Noah to Matilda Dyal 10-21-1840 (no return) L
Baker, Patrick to Ellen Foley 10-31-1864 Sh
Baker, Peter to Elizabeth Browning 9-1-1841 Hn
Baker, Peter to Mary Elizabeth Rogers 7-21-1852 Sh
Baker, Peter to Rebecca A. Wiley 12-24-1845 Sh
Baker, Phinias G. to Sallie E. Bergman 6-13-1874 (6-14-1874) T
Baker, Pinkney to Mary A. Cunningham 8-25-1877 (8-29-1877) L
Baker, Pinkny to Nancy McDurmit 7-12-1842 (7-13-1842) G
Baker, R. B. to L. D. Carroll 11-30-1865 (12-5-1865) Cr
Baker, R. D. to Sarah Kemp 5-5-1863 (no return) We
Baker, Robert P. to E. A. Harrison 12-8-1866 G
Baker, Robert to Charlotte O. Lynn 1-29-1829 (1-30-1829) Ma
Baker, Robert to Martha Skipper 7-13-1858 (7-27-1858) L
Baker, Robt. M. to Annie J. Miller 3-22-1854 (3-23-1854) Sh
Baker, S. A. to M. A. (Mrs.) Harrold 10-2-1867 O
Baker, Sam to Lucinda Dowdy 12-27-1865 (no return) F B
Baker, Samuel A. to Eliza McDonald 1-16-1845 O
Baker, Samuel to Anne Forrester 5-25-1828 (5-29-1828) G
Baker, Samuel to Elmina Metheny 6-22-1853 Hn
Baker, Samuel to Malvina Evans 12-19-1881 (12-21-1881) L
Baker, Samuel to Mary J. Baker 12-6-1855 G
Baker, Shadrich to Mary Piercifull 1-14-1850 (1-17-1849?) Ma
Baker, Stephen to Laura Ann Wilson 7-5-1866 (7-6-1866) F B
Baker, Symon to Nancy E. Cooper 4-3-1860 Be
Baker, T. S. to Mary Logan 10-24-1874 (10-25-1874) T

Baker, Thomas A. to Belle Guaranes 1-27-1859 We
Baker, Thomas H. to Marinda James 4-22-1861 (no return) Cr
Baker, Thomas to Amanda Baker 10-9-1865 Hn
Baker, Thomas to Elizabeth Cook 3-4-1839 (3-5-1839) Ma
Baker, Thomas to Levina Smith 12-22-1829 (1-26-1830) G
Baker, W. D. to Emma E. Prince 12-10-1864 (12-14-1864) Cr
Baker, W. H. to J. Davidson 2-1-1865 G
Baker, W. H. to Mary A. Price 5-21-1864 (no return) L
Baker, W. R. to Lucy J. Maury 3-26-1855 (no return) F
Baker, W. T. to A. M. Abston 10-2-1866 Hy
Baker, W. T. to S. T. C. Drake 8-6-1866 (no return) Hy
Baker, Wam. A. to Mary E. Baker 3-28-1862 We
Baker, William G. to Mary A. D. Witherford 8-30-1854 G
Baker, William G. to Nancy J. Weatherford 12-27-1847 (12-28-1847) G
Baker, William M. to J. A. M. Anderson 3-17-1877 (3-18-1877) L
Baker, William M. to Susan J. Hartman 1-5-1850 Sh
Baker, William R. to Martha Ann Percy 12-13-1843 (12-15-1843) Ma
Baker, William W. to Elizabeth Phelps 1-8-1851 Hn
Baker, William to Cynthia Reagan 5-8-1828 (5-11-1828) Hr
Baker, William to Margarett Beard 1-25-1844 F
Baker, William to Margarett Wilkins 7-28-1846 Ma
Baker, William to Mary Kelly 7-14-1853 (7-31-1853) G
Baker, William to Nancy A. Hillis 2-4-1857 We
Baker, William to Nancy J. Hall 6-1-1870 (6-2-1870) Cr
Baker, Wily to Lena Lemmons 12-17-1873 Dy
Baker, Wm. C. to Frances A. E. Reeves 8-9-1869 (8-12-1869) Ma
Baker, Wm. H. to Mary Ann Price 5-21-1864 (5-22-1864) L
Baker, Wm. M. to Sarah F. Mount 3-19-1862 G
Baknet, Jos. to C. V. Ganbetti 12-8-1864 (12-14-1864) Sh
Balam, Tom to Caroline Lewis 12-25-1869 (12-20?-1869) F B
Balch, John K. to Amanda Wheatley 9-15-1830 G
Balderson, Joseph to Marth_ Payen (Payne?) 9-12-1838 (9-13-1838) L
Baldin, William B. to Johanna F. Gromes? 10-4-1855 (no return) Hn
Baldock, Derastus to Mary Jane Hill 12-26-1853 (1-2-1854) T
Baldock, James P. to Marinda J. Faulk 10-8-1855 Sh
Baldridge, Almus F. to Mary A. Stephens 9-21-1856 We
Baldridge, Andrew W. to Nancy Harper Minton 1-20-1831 O
Baldridge, Charles W. to Martha J. Baldridge 5-31-1854 (no return) We
Baldridge, Charles W. to Martha J. Baldridge 6-1-1854 We
Baldridge, Edmond T. to Amanda T. Fisher 2-27-1868 G
Baldridge, Francis to Mary A. Maxwell 5-8-1854 (no return) We
Baldridge, Franklin to Mary A. Maxwell 5-4-1854 We
Baldridge, H. P. to Mary J. Young 11-13-1856 We
Baldridge, J. L. to C. P. Lewis 8-12-1860 We
Baldridge, J. L. to M. E. Bolling 1-29-1866 Hy
Baldridge, James to Mary Brogdon 9-15-1857 Cr
Baldridge, John P. to M. E. Neal 12-23-1866 Hy
Baldridge, John S. to Martha Moore 10-5-1846 (10-6-1846) G
Baldridge, W. D. to Elizabeth Routen 5-14-1855 (5-15-1855) G
Baldridge, William H. to Elizabeth Nuckles 12-28-1846 (12-29-1846) G
Baldridge, William H. to Lucy E. H. Nichold 8-26-1850 G
Baldridge, William J. to Adaline Pearce 10-7-1870 G
Baldridge, William Thomas to Mary C. Hickman 12-24-1853 (12-27-1853) Ma
Baldridge, William to Elizabeth H. Clemer 3-13-1855 We
Baldrige, George to Eolino Hall 12-20-1866 (12-29-1866) Dy
Baldwin, Edwin to Margaret St. Leger 8-6-1845 Sh
Baldwin, G. W. to Emily P. Washington 4-30-1849 (5-2-1849) Hr
Baldwin, H. D. to Martha Champain 6-11-1865 Hn
Baldwin, John to Susan Powell 11-8-1871 (no return) Hy
Baldwin, Joseph T. to Clarecy A. Shaw 11-14-1851 (no return) F
Baldwin, Lewis to Sarah Lewis 3-22-1845 (no return) Hn
Baldwin, W. C. to M. C. Pickens 1-31-1842 (2-6-1842) F
Balentine, J. W. to Mary Gross 4-2-1877 (4-7-1877) L
Balentine, James to Margaret Ann Burrow 2-19-1857 Ma
Bales, Fed to Sarah Feild? 2-9-1867 T
Balew, John to Amanda E. Bryant 12-29-1858 (1-6-1859) G
Baley (Bagby), Bennett to Frances C. Lewis 10-4-1842 Sh
Baley, David to Nancy Reeves 12-27-1871 Hy
Baley, Elijah to Martha Lorance 9-5-1854 Cr
Baley, J. W. to E. J. Mitchell 11-2-1856 We
Baley, J. W. to Elizabeth Coffman 6-15-1864 Mn
Baley, James R. to Louisa J. Chrisman 1-13-1862 G
Baley, John C. to Matilda Sledman 12-4-1827 Ma
Baley, John W. to Nancy P. Shipman 12-20-1842 G
Baley, Johnathan to Mary Thompson 2-5-1845 G
Baley, Martin L. to Dizey Bledsoe 3-13-1846 (3-15-1846) G
Baley, Robert? C. to Elizabeth Childers 4-23-1861 (4-25-1861) Dy
Balinger, Henry C. to Lucinda J. Webb 11-21-1865 (no return) Cr
Ball, B. F. to Emily F. (Mrs.) Dunn 10-8-1860 Sh
Ball, Benj. F. to Martha J. Odell 2-3-1848 Sh
Ball, C. S. to S. E. Anthony 1-17-1868 Hy
Ball, Charles S. to Mary Goodwin 7-30-1860 Ma
Ball, D. J. to Sarah Thompson 7-14-1864 G
Ball, James P. to R. A. Roper 9-30-1863? 10-1-1859 O
Ball, James to Burline Wallice 12-2-1863 G
Ball, Jonaathan to Mary A. Robinson 9-20-1843 (no return) L
Ball, R. A. to Trophenia Hall 11-29-1864 Be
Ball, R. L. to Cordelia Davidson 11-10-1852 Sh
Ball, S. H. to M. M. Taylor 1-5-1876 Dy
Ball, Samuel to Martha J. Harris 12-8-1869 Hy
Ball, Stephen C. to Nancy C. Raper 11-28-1859 (11-29-1859) F
Ball, Tedrick to Rebecca Cooly 8-8-1844 Hn
Ball, W. H. to Mary A. Hassell 4-1-1867 (4-3-1867) Dy
Ball, William A. to Mary Bethune 9-3-1873 (9-24-1873) L
Ball, Willis to Marthy A. Crowder 12-29-1877 Hy
Ball, Wm. T. to Margarette Koonce 1-26-1865 G
Ballard, A. B. to Josephine W. Jones 2-8-1860 Sh
Ballard, Ben to Margarett Wilson 1-21-1867 G
Ballard, D. M. to Elizabeth Brinkley 1-6-1868 (1-8-1868) T
Ballard, Ed to Evey Hunter 12-12-1868 (12-21-1868) F B
Ballard, Edward M. to Sylvester C. Jenkins 4-22-1860 Hn
Ballard, G. K. to A. E. Rose 6-1-1883 (6-3-1883) L
Ballard, G. K. to Nannie Sexton 4-27-1885 (4-29-1885) L
Ballard, Geo. W. to Mary A. Williams 3-12-1850 Be
Ballard, George to Dilcy Harding 7-18-1869 G B
Ballard, H. G. to Hardenia A. Taylor 5-3-1847 (5-4-1847) F
Ballard, H. W. to E. J. Boyd 1-16-1845 (no return) Hn
Ballard, Henry M. to Eliza Williams 7-16-1861 (8-17-1861) T
Ballard, Henry to Mary Beaver 2-1-1867 (8-15-1867) F B
Ballard, Isaac N. to Talitha C. O'Neal 11-7-1866 Ma
Ballard, J. A. to Dicy Culbreath 2-23-1860 Sh
Ballard, J. A. to Dicy Galbreath 2-23-1860 T
Ballard, J. F. to Elizabeth Tate 3-24-1855 Sh
Ballard, J. W. to S. M. Johnson 6-29-1868 (7-1-1868) T
Ballard, James F. to Mary A. Foren 3-14-1859 (3-24-1859) Sh
Ballard, James M. to Elizabeth A. Ballard 11-17-1844 Hn
Ballard, James to Elizabeth Forbess 8-23-1838 Hn
Ballard, Jeff to Beckey Coker 6-11-1883 (6-17-1883) L
Ballard, John D. to Martha E. A. Ballard 7-26-1858 (7-18-1858) T
Ballard, John to Carolin Ballard 9-18-1865 (9-19-1865) T
Ballard, John to Margaret Lewellen 7-9-1866 (7-12-1866) T
Ballard, Milton Jackson to Arrianna Pernett Talley 4-5-1848 T
Ballard, Peter R. B. to Elizabeth Petty 2-10-1850 Sh
Ballard, Samuel O. to Mary F. Williams 3-25-1841 F
Ballard, T. A. to Laura J. Hicks 5-24-1874 Hy
Ballard, W. E. to Mary A Shinault 2-22-1866 F
Ballard, William to Lucinda Wilkinson 3-31-1863 O
Ballard, William to Nancy E. Shepherd 10-26-1846 (10-27-1846) F
Ballard, Willis to Frances Nichols 11-7-1842 (11-8-1842) G
Ballenger, Moses to Tabisha Williams 2-10-1845 F
Ballentine, J. W. to Sarah Ann Taylor 9-26-1865 G
Ballentine, Jessee to Elizabeth B. Bledsoe 8-26-1845 (8-27-1845) G
Ballentine, John W. to Martha S. Acklin 9-17-1858 (9-18-1858) G
Ballentine, John W. to Rebecca Barker 7-3-1845 G
Ballentine, Peter to Elizabeth C. Bunnell 12-17-1847 (12-22-1847) G
Ballentine, S.D. to S. J. Arnold 2-20-1865 G
Ballentine, W. M. to Harriet A. Stalcup 12-6-1867 (no return) Dy
Ballentine, William to Frances J. Holderfield 10-23-1858 (10-28-1858) G
Ballerson, Thomas to Caroline Johnson 6-13-1861 (no return) L
Balleu, James M. to Mary McClure 6-5-1837 G
Ballew, John G. to Mainard Mitchell 10-23-1860 (10-24-1860) Cr
Ballew, John to Mary Scott 3-2-1863 Cr
Ballew, John to Mary Scott 3-2-1863 (no return) Cr
Ballew, Richard to Urany (Mercury) Carter 2-10-1834 Sh
Ballew, Robert J. to Mary Puckett 11-1-1836 Sh
Balley, J. H. to Sallie B. Hunn? 12-12-1868 (12-10?-1868) T
Ballinger, Edward to Isabella McKinley 3-13-1858 (3-16-1858) L
Ballinger, Edward to Sarah McKinley 2-1-1843 (no return) L
Ballinger, Wm. D. to Mary Coleman 9-12-1860 Sh
Ballowe, John to Frances Pahol 12-30-1866 Be
Ballowe, William to Mary Cherry 9-30-1864 Be
Ballowe, Wm. N. to Martha H. Baggett 9-9-1850 Be
Balser, W. M. to Nannie Day 3-15-1879 (3-20-1879) Dy
Balser, Wm. S. to Amanda C. Blackburn 2-18-1878 Dy
Balthrop, John L. to Eliza T. Hinson 12-20-1869 (12-22-1869) F
Baltimore, Ruebin to Katie Jones 5-26-1866 (no return) Hy
Balton, James to Mary A. E. Sherrill 8-25-1859 Cr
Baltzunot, F. W. to Dora Benjes 4-6-1859 Sh
Balus, Wm. R. to Lucy Allen 2-14-1847 Be
Baly, Elisha to Martha C. Jackson 1-14-1852 (1-15-1852) Ma
Balylock, John M. to Martha M. Rowe 2-5-1867 Be
Bambridge, A. A. to J. V. Beaver 8-6-1870 (8-9-1870) T
Bancroft, Daniel to Elizabeth Senter 8-22-1840 (8-23-1840) Ma
Bancum, Newton C. to Matilda J. Kellow 7-11-1861 G
Band (Bard?), T. I. to Eugenia P. Roberts 8-15-1858 We
Banden, J. C. to Florence E. S. Motley? 8-21-1869 T
Bandy, G. W. to M. E. Gunter 9-?-1866 G
Bandy, J. F. to Nannie Wickersham 12-23-1875 (no return) L
Bandy, James H. to Margarett C. Bragg 1-28-1858 We
Bandy, James M. to Eliza Rebecca Harrison 3-22-1879 (3-23-1879) Dy
Bandy, Joseph W. to Louisa J. Dunlap 2-29-1860 We
Bandy, Josiah Washington to Mary Vanburen Driver? 8-28-1852 T
Bandy, Smith M. to Caroline Feezor 12-20-1851 (12-28-1851) T
Bandy, Woodford to Catharine Brogg 3-7-1859 (no return) We

Grooms

Bane, J. J. to Matilda Huzza 1-23-1848 Be
Bane, John to Fannie Palmer 3-5-1859 Cr
Banfield, James to Teresa Griffing 1-11-1849 Sh
Bangs, James to Josephine T. McCabe (McCake?) 7-29-1853 Sh
Bangues, B. A. to Lydia Ann Minter 3-8-1844 (3-12-1844) Hr
Banie, Henry to Mary E. Whitelaw 6-29-1872 Hy
Banister, Abram to Sally Herron 5-21-1869 (5-22-1869) Cr
Banister, J. W. to M. C. Wise 8-18-1869 G
Banister, James M. to Roda A. Hague 10-25-1859 (10-26-1859) G
Banister, William to Elizabeth Conell 12-18-1834 (12-23-1834) G
Banker, Joseph to Sallie A. Smith 11-15-1872 (11-17-1872) Dy
Bankhead, James to Martha Webster 2-5-1845 (2-6-1845) F
Bankhead, Robert to Nancy Oliphant 3-4-1846 (3-5-1846) F
Bankhead, Thos. R. to Dora McAnulty 10-10-1868 (10-11-1868) F
Banks, A. L. to Jemima Fodge 8-16-1864 (no return) Hn
Banks, Alfred to Pernecia L. Crews 10-2-1859 We
Banks, Frank to Nancy Manning 12-23-1869 Hy
Banks, Geo. F. to Zilpha Robertson 4-5-1868 Hy
Banks, George to Loucrecia Hart 11-14-1874 (no return) Hy
Banks, Gorton H. to Candis Baucom 4-26-1838 Cr
Banks, H. O. to Frances Strong 4-25-1871 (4-26-1871) T
Banks, H. to M. J. Gallaher 10-31-1874 (11-3-1874) Dy
Banks, H. to Patsy A. Turner 8-18-1869 G
Banks, Hiram H. to Martha Ann Bean 2-15-1837 (2-23-1837) G
Banks, J. H. to Harriett A. Lawrence 11-28-1867 Hn
Banks, J. L. to E. R. Tucker 9-18-1872 Dy
Banks, James H. to Mary Ann Farr 11-3-1838 Cr
Banks, James H. to Melissa L. Hopkins 1-30-1859 G
Banks, Jno. D. to Jane E. String 12-13-1864 (12-14-1864) T
Banks, John Will to Emily Vaughn 12-27-1864 (no return) Hn
Banks, John to Ella Harris 11-3-1870 G
Banks, Ro. M. to Louisa Elmira Strong 1-10-1853 (1-12-1853) T
Banks, Robt. to Lizzie Erck 10-12-1864 (10-13-1864) Sh
Banks, Saml. to Jane Clack 4-28-1866 Hy
Banks, W. A. to L. A. Wade 4-15-1868 G
Banks, W. T. to Valleria Ann Cage 10-14-1857 Sh
Banks, William H. to Josephine Hurt 12-18-1850 (no return) Hn
Banks, Wyatt to Mary Berry 12-25-1867 (no return) Hn B
Banner (Bonner), Alfred R. to Elizabeth H. Dye 10-9-1845 Sh
Banner, George W. to Jane E. McCalley 12-30-1868 (1-2-1869) T
Bannon, Edward to Susan Lyon 12-23-1873 T
Bannon, P. to Margaret Daley 5-5-1853 Sh
Bannon, Patrick to Maria Rice 12-1-1850 Sh
Bansfield(Bunsfield), N. T. to Rhoda M. Rhodes 12-7-1858 (12-9-1858) Hr
Bantau, H. D. to Elizabeth Walker 3-22-1851 (3-23-1851) O
Baptist, N. Wilson to Belle H. Boyd 1-11-1871 (1-18-1871) T
Baptiste, Benis (Berni?) J. to Caroline Bonear 3-13-1852 Sh
Baque, Peter to Margaret Palmer 4-21-1855 (4-22-1855) Sh
Bar, John to Mary Waisler 2-5-1857 Sh
Barbee, Ambrose to Mattie Campbell 9-11-1884 (10-4-1884) L
Barbee, Geo. A. to Virginia L. Harrison 9-30-1851 Sh
Barbee, James A. to Lucy Anthony 1-7-1866 Hy
Barbee, John to Catharine Carmack 10-1-1840 Hn
Barbee, John to Polly Armstrong 12-9-1846 (no return) Hn
Barbee, Joseph W. to Sarah G. Jenkins 1-7-1866 Hn
Barbee, Manuel to Mollie Edwards 12-5-1869 Hy
Barbee, Martin A. to Perlina Jane Dunn 9-27-1857 Hn
Barbee, Richmond to Harriet Shaw 10-9-1849 G
Barbee, Thomas to Caroline Winsett 12-4-1838 Hn
Barbee, W. R. to Sarah F. Step 1-14-1857 (1-15-1857) Sh
Barber, Billups to Mary J. Mizelle 12-18-1856 (12-19-1856) We
Barber, Carner to Sarah Elkins 6-24-1839 (6-27-1839) O
Barber, Carney to Flora Gillis 2-14-1838 O
Barber, Clark to Martha E. Jerry 2-18-1859 (3-17-1859) Sh
Barber, Clarke to Ann E. Jerry 1-18-1854 Sh
Barber, Henry to Caroline E. Jones 2-29-1868 Hy
Barber, James A. to Sarah C. Cress 3-4-1855 We
Barber, James to Nancy Miller 8-21-1861 L
Barber, Jas. M. to Sarah A. Lanier 3-5-1844 (3-6-1844) L
Barber, John C. to Nancy J. Bolding 3-13-1852 (3-17-1852) Sh
Barber, John R. to Jane E. Carlan 12-27-1859 We
Barber, Joseph to Justina Elder 7-17-1847 O
Barber, Joseph to Mary Ann Luttrell 7-28-1847 (7-29-1847) Hr
Barber, L. L. to Elizabeth J. Baker 6-4-1869 G
Barber, N. W. to Emma P. Laird 10-4-1884 (10-5-1884) L
Barber, Raleigh W. to Elizabeth Bettis 6-11-1842 (6-12-1842) L
Barber, Thomas to Mary Jane Horn 1-11-1849 Ma
Barber, Turner F. to Luraney Nichols 2-18-1837 O
Barberry, Mathew to Rebecca Ann Beaver 9-15-1842 F
Barbiere, jr., Joseph to Mary G. Levett 10-30-1855 Sh
Barbouor, Carney to Catherine Culbertson 6-18-1836 (6-20-1836) O
Barbour, Tap to Harriet Williamson 9-27-1870 G
Barcco, Jno. to Sarah A. Elliott 9-5-1850 Sh
Barchy, James to Nanny Evalinie 7-30-1830 (8-15-1830) Ma
Barcklay, Sam to Margaret Moody 1-11-1866 Ma
Barclay, James W. to Nancy Minerva Henderson 3-10-1857 (3-11-1857) Ma
Barcroft, D. to Covington M. L. 10-1-1873 Hy

Barcroft, James to Sarah Clark 2-2-1864 (no return) Hy
Barcroft, R. A. to E. A. Haralson 11-23-1871 Hy
Barcroft, R. A. to V. E. Dawson 3-24-1870 Hy
Barcroft, W. C. to Lavenia Smith 10-19-1875 (no return) Hy
Barcus, E. R. to Mary F. Smith 6-28-1852 Sh
Bard, Charles to Nancy C. Twiss 11-19-1857 We
Bard, Henry to Elizabeth Moss 10-26-1865 (10-29-1865) O
Barding, Alfred A. to Rebecca Waddell 12-30-1851 Sh
Barding, James to Pamely Jones 10-4-1840 Sh
Barding, Joseph G. to Elizabeth C. King 7-15-1856 Sh
Bardon, Wm. D. to Mary W. Cole 3-29-1863 Be
Bardwell, Brainard to Martha E. Rogers 1-11-1845 Sh
Barefield, Henry P. to Lucinda Pitts 3-28-1849 (3-29-1849) L
Barfield, B. W. to Virginia C. Baxter 1-9-1885 (1-12-1885) L
Barfield, Frederick to Mary Ann Benton Edny 2-6-1841 (2-9-1841) L
Barfield, George C. to Harriet Smith 1-30-1829 Ma
Barfield, H. J. to Ella Thum 10-30-1877 (10-31-1877) L
Barfield, H. P. to Harriet Bentley 2-26-1884 L
Barfield, I. J. to Hattie C. Burks 12-17-1884 L
Barfield, Ira G. to Eliza J. Thum 1-20-1851 (1-22-1851) L
Barfield, J. P. to Ella Mann 2-13-1878 (2-14-1878) L
Barfield, J. R. W. to Mary Jane Burks 12-17-1872 (12-18-1872) L
Barfield, John W. to Louisa Strain 12-24-1857 (no return) L
Barfield, Moses to Jimicy Tharpe 5-18-1866 (no return) Hn B
Barfield, R. D. to Ella Cobb 2-13-1878 (2-14-1878) L
Barfield, William D. to Virginia E. Lankford 10-30-1852 (11-4-1852) L
Barfoot, Turner to L. L. Mires 8-9-1842 Be
Barfoot, Turner to Susan Cole 11-10-1850 Be
Barger, Christian J. to Julian Skipper 6-30-1860 (7-1-1860) Dy
Barger, James S. to Margaret B. Wall 8-28-1855 Cr
Barger, James W. to Sarah C. Tarwater 1-3-1856 We
Barger, John N. to Rebecca E. Stewart 12-1-1860 (12-4-1861) We
Barger, Wm. S. to Martha Jane Atchison 6-19-1860 Be
Barham, Andrew J. to Clerda Page 11-29-1846 Cr
Barham, Andrew to Lena Fuller 8-23-1871 (8-24-1871) Cr B
Barham, Benjamin to Elizabeth Williams 5-24-1848 (5-25-1848) O
Barham, Edwin J. to Susan E. Cooper 11-8-1849 Hr
Barham, Ezekiel to Mollie McDonald 12-8-1869 (12-9-1869) Cr
Barham, I. H. to June Christian 2-14-1840 (2-16-1840) Ma
Barham, J. A. to A. C. Perkins 2-9-1843 Be
Barham, James A. to Mary Murdaugh 11-2-1853 (11-3-1853) Hr
Barham, James M. to Lucy Greer 8-21-1844 Hn
Barham, James to Sarah Ann Hale 1-15-1848 (1-18-1848) O
Barham, John A. to Mary a. Garley 7-11-1848 Cr
Barham, John C. to Gemima Conley 3-13-1839 (3-20-1839) O
Barham, John W. to Mary E. Turner 12-20-1865 Hy
Barham, John to Mary E. Dowiggin 12-16-1858 O
Barham, Joseph A. to Nancy E. Cody 9-10-1843 Cr
Barham, Joseph to Sarah A. Nichols 5-4-1863 (5-7-1863) Cr
Barham, L. B. to B. E. Jones 9-16-1871 (9-17-1871) Cr
Barham, L. F. to Elizabeth Mathis 1-28-1849 (no return) Hn
Barham, N. R. C. to M. M. J. McMichael 6-21-1863 We
Barham, Newton J. to Mary E. Foust 1-27-1859 Hn
Barham, Richard A. to Terissa S.? Cooper 3-28-1848 (3-30-1848) Hr
Barham, Sim to Harriett Wright 8-5-1873 (8-6-1873) Cr B
Barham, T. H. to B. E. Crockett 11-9-1867 O
Barham, Thomas C. to Louisa S. Orgain 2-28-1848 (3-1-1848) Ma
Barham, Thos. to Eliza J. Holloway 1-5-1848 F
Barham, W. H. to Sophia B. Carter 10-8-1848 Hn
Barham, Wm. to Rebecca McGinnis 11-30-1872 (12-1-1872) O
Barkdale, D. M. to F. E. Terry 10-27-1856 (no return) We
Barker (Baker), Joseph T. to Rachel Goyer 3-17-1858 Sh
Barker, A. L. to Prudie Thornton 9-24-1867 (no return) Hn
Barker, A. to Mary J. Butler 12-5-1857 Cr
Barker, Allen to Vilet Tanner 6-20-1842 (6-21-1842) O
Barker, Ben to M. A. Sparkman 12-23-1868 G
Barker, Benj. J. to Martha Jane Watson 8-10-1843 Be
Barker, Briggs to Nancy Adaline Harper 8-20-1862 Be
Barker, Briggs to Rachel A. Strickland 1-7-1852 Be
Barker, Brinkley B. to Rachel C. Shelby 9-5-1840 (9-6-1840) O
Barker, Brinkley to Julia Bledsoe 9-30-1865 G
Barker, D. W. to M. B. Barker 4-10-1842 Be
Barker, Edwin G. to Mary Barker 2-21-1869 G
Barker, Francis M. to Mary Ann Hawthorn 6-29-1856 Be
Barker, G. B. to Fannie V.? Roberts 12-1-1870 Hy
Barker, G. L. to Amanda J. Tate 4-29-1871 (4-30-1871) T
Barker, Gray B. to Nancy Taylor 1-7-1851 (1-8-1851) G
Barker, Gray to Celey Barker 9-1-1841 (9-2-1841) G
Barker, Hosea to Mary Smith 3-21-1841 Sh
Barker, Isaac to Martha J. Michell 11-19-1850 Cr
Barker, Israel M. L. to Diana W. Porter 11-27-1860 Hn
Barker, Israel M. L. to Mary H. Hassell 3-8-1852 (3-9-1852) G
Barker, J. W. to Martha Turner 3-11-1860 Be
Barker, James A. to Marilane Vinson 1-23-1863 Be
Barker, James A. to Sharlatta V. Crews 12-13-1860 We
Barker, James S. to Mary J. Stribling 3-22-1857 Cr
Barker, James Y. to Ann Maria Sparkman 7-5-1854 O

Barker, John A. to Margarette A. Bledsoe 1-26-1865 G
Barker, John W. to Margaret E. Stewart 7-17-1858 Cr
Barker, Joseph to Frances A. Purdy 6-23-1866 (6-28-1866) Dy
Barker, L. A. to Catherine A. Tims 6-3-1871 T
Barker, N. B. to Sally Holland 8-16-1865 Be
Barker, N. to Susan A. Williams 6-5-1853 Be
Barker, R. W. to Louisa Chitwood 1-16-1866 (1-17-1866) Dy
Barker, Robt. to Lizzie Darden 1-31-1876 (2-1-1876) Dy
Barker, Stephen C. to Susan A. Goodman 6-20-1857 (6-21-1857) G
Barker, Thomas E. to Joannah Ryan 8-31-1855 (9-1-1855) Sh
Barker, W. E. to Sallie E. Tinkle 1-23-1869 G
Barker, W. G. to Elizabeth Brame 1-8-1848 F
Barker, W. R. to N. B. Carroll 8-14-1867 (no return) Cr
Barker, Wesley G. to Nancy W. Wortham 12-13-1851 (12-14-1851) G
Barker, William E. to Mary E. Lea 4-10-1848 (4-17-1848) G
Barker, Wm. to Jane Scoby 1-7-1858 F
Barker, Zachariah D. to Caroline Gilaspie 7-4-1844 O
Barker, Zachariah D. to Caroline Gilaspie 7-9-1842 O
Barker, Zachary to Margaret M. A. Joyner 2-21-1861 (2-16?-1861) Cr
Barker, Zechariah to Sarah Mayfield 2-7-1865 Be
Barkley, Frank L. to Mary M. McConnell 11-19-1852 (11-22-1852) G
Barkley, Joseph to Sarah Ann Carrell 11-19-1870 L
Barksdale, David M. to Frances E. Terry 10-27-1856 We
Barksdale, G. T. to C. O. Barham 1-30-1871 (2-1-1871) Cr
Barksdale, Horace R. to Cenith C. Glason 10-27-1849 (10-28-1849) G
Barksdale, J. F. to O. V. Drake 2-20-1865 (no return) Cr
Barksdale, J. L. B. to Evelyn A. Lackey 12-31-1867 L
Barksdale, James G. to Sarah J. Gleason 12-8-1860 G
Barksdale, N. P. to Ella Hurt 1-15-1872 (1-18-1872) Cr
Barksdale, Nathan to Sarah S. Davis 7-25-1827 G
Barksdale, Nathaniel F. to Sarah C. Jones 5-20-1852 G
Barlow, J. H. to E. J. Campbell 12-18-1872 (12-19-1872) Cr
Barlow, John H. to Mary Scoby 2-1-1864 (2-11-1864) Cr
Barlow, John H. to Mary Scoby 2-1-1864 (no return) Cr
Barlow, Madison to Mary Lake 11-6-1880 (11-7-1880) L
Barlow, Robert to Manda Thogmortin 12-24-1867 (1-16-1868) Cr
Barman?, Charles to Sallie Smith 7-8-1867 (7-9-1867) T
Barmer?, Coleman to Harriet Grigsby 3-12-1874 T
Barmon, Henry to Eliza Bazzel 10-3-1849 (no return) F
Barnard, Albert A. to Sarah L. Whipple 1-6-1864 Sh
Barnard, Albert to Emma Phearce 10-3-1870 G B
Barnard, C. L. to A. J. Scarbrough 9-28-1852 (no return) F
Barne, Wm. C. to Delila Shilling 9-22-1848 Be
Barnell, James to Matilda Alston 1-28-1870 T
Barner (Barnes), Haman G. to Maria W. Brabst 1-25-1849 Sh
Barner, Pall to Elizabeth Smith 10-30-1870 G
Barner, Paul T. to Elizabeth J. Glisson 11-21-1853 (11-22-1853) G
Barnes (Baines?), Edward to J. Pope 4-4-1853 (4-16-1853) L
Barnes (Burnes?), Stephen G. to _____ Caras Given 9-27-1849 L
Barnes, Allen A. to Mary F. Lee 12-11-1862 Hn
Barnes, Allen to Jennie Elder 6-30-1883 L
Barnes, Andrew J. to Ruhamy Harris 9-18-1851 Be
Barnes, Asbury to Janey Stokely 2-4-1881 (2-26-1881) L B
Barnes, B. F. to V. P. Bell 1-12-1870 Hy
Barnes, B. S. to Emeline L. Earnest 3-28-1867 G
Barnes, C. L. to Margaret English 1-8-1873 (1-9-1873) T
Barnes, Charles to Amanda Byrn 11-26-1855 Be
Barnes, D. T. to M. C. Biggs 3-9-1869 G
Barnes, Dennis to Obedience Middleton 8-10-1865 Mn
Barnes, Edward to Matilda Anderson 5-1-1849 (5-3-1849) Ma
Barnes, Elijah to Fannie Henning 5-1-1885 (no return) L
Barnes, Gabriel to Phebi Jane Goodrich 12-28-1845 G
Barnes, George W. to Mildred A. Gaines 12-18-1883 (12-19-1883) L
Barnes, George to Mary F. Hernes 12-5-1867 F
Barnes, Granville to Caroline Rumley 2-23-1860 Cr
Barnes, H. B. to Sarah Cooper 2-28-1863 Be
Barnes, H. H. to I. F. Presnell? 12-16-1854 (12-24-1854) O
Barnes, Henry to Susan Hollomon 10-10-1850 Be
Barnes, Hilliard to Alice Stokely 3-7-1881 (3-18-1881) L B
Barnes, Houston to Martha Washama 11-17-1858 O
Barnes, Isaiah to Nancy McMurtry 10-16-1851 Be
Barnes, J. M. to Mary Rosson 7-8-1860 G
Barnes, J. W. to N. C. B. Berry 12-16-1850 Cr
Barnes, James H. to Anjaline Lewis 10-14-1866 Be
Barnes, James to Eliza Fowlkes 3-1-1877 Dy
Barnes, James to Elizabeth Hargrove 9-22-1845 (9-25-1845) F
Barnes, James to Harriett Morris? 3-16-1866 (no return) Cr
Barnes, James to Margaret Logan 1-6-1864 (1-7-1864) Sh
Barnes, John A. to Mary E. Burns 12-4-1851 Be
Barnes, John B. to Eliza V. Jones 1-22-1848 (1-23-1848) Hr
Barnes, John P. to Caroline Smothers 11-15-1868 Be
Barnes, John to Georgia McCutchen 3-7-1873 (3-25-1873) Dy
Barnes, Josephus to Rosanna Harmon 12-5-1867 Hy
Barnes, L. W. to M. C. Smith 10-8-1865 Mn
Barnes, M. B. to Julia F. C. Moore 11-5-1866 (11-12-1866) L
Barnes, Moses to Margaret E. Oxford 12-8-1850 Be
Barnes, Moses to Mary Shirley 8-29-1853 Be

Barnes, Peter to Gracy Smith 6-12-1867 Hy
Barnes, R. M. to Martha Kirk 8-13-1864 (8-16-1864) O
Barnes, Richard W. to E. J. Green 8-4-1853 Hn
Barnes, Rush to Cherry Turner 6-12-1878 Hy
Barnes, Samuel to Martha Ann Droke 3-12-1863 Mn
Barnes, T. A. to Mary Ann McKerly 3-23-1833 Hr
Barnes, Tho. J. to Mary Catharine Akin 3-12-1856 (3-13-1856) T
Barnes, Thomas V. to Lucenda C. Pitts 9-28-1861 (9-30-1861) L
Barnes, Thomas to Catherine Redden 4-4-1857 (4-5-1857) O
Barnes, Thomas to Elizabeth Nevill 8-20-1852 Ma
Barnes, Thomas to Nancy Jones 3-9-1843 (4-1-1843) G
Barnes, Thomas to Prudence Prince 6-29-1852 Hn
Barnes, Timothy J. to Laura L. Kirby 10-5-1869 (10-6-1869) Ma
Barnes, W. H. to Matilda A. Edwards 11-12-1866 G
Barnes, W. M. to Lucy Johnson 2-28-1881 L
Barnes, W. M. to Mollie L. Mangrum 3-8-1881 (no return) L
Barnes, Wesley to Mariah Haywood 7-21-1867 G
Barnes, William J. to Martha Brown 7-18-1862 (9-4-1866?) Cr
Barnes, Wm. Edwin to Ann Parsons 11-27-1855 Sh
Barnet, J. W. to Nancy Larimore 2-11-1868 (3-3-1868) T
Barnet, Jesse to Margaret Kerk (Kirk) 9-10-1829 Sh
Barnet, John M. to Jackey J. Harp 2-21-1855 (2-27-1855) Ma
Barnett(Bennett), John C. to Mary E. Morrow 2-21-1832 (2-23-1832) Hr
Barnett, A. E. to Margaret Holmes 1-5-1869 (no return) Cr
Barnett, A. J. to Mary J. Hubbs 8-1-1847 Be
Barnett, Achilles to James L. Harvey 7-20-1837 Sh
Barnett, C. G. to Elizabeth Ellis 1-15-1861 (1-24-1861) O
Barnett, Columbus to Nancy Pahell 11-30-1868 Be
Barnett, David P. to Mary Jane Allison 8-15-1853 (8-16-1853) G
Barnett, E. M. to M. J. Rouse 3-15-1863 G
Barnett, Edward to Mollie Hampton 10-2-1869 Cr
Barnett, Elias D. to Almira N. Key 3-22-1848 (3-28-1848) Ma
Barnett, Elizabeth J.? to Martha Houghton 10-20-1845 (10-21-1845) Ma
Barnett, Enos H. to Lucinda J. Henderson 8-17-1846 (8-20-1846) Ma
Barnett, Flint to Elizabeth McCoy 1-18-1859 O
Barnett, G. W. to Mollie Green 8-11-1874 (8-13-1874) T
Barnett, Henry to Lucinda Martin 1-2-1877 (1-3-1877) Dy
Barnett, Hyram to Sarah Webb 2-10-1832 (2-14-1832) Hr
Barnett, J. L. to Licetta A. Williams 2-14-1851 O
Barnett, J. Y. to Olivia L. Griffin 11-9-1864 (11-10-1864) Sh
Barnett, Jacob to Julia Biggs 12-22-1870 (1-1-1871) Dy
Barnett, James J. to Elizabeth Willie 3-22-1834 (3-27-1834) Hr
Barnett, James S. to Narcissa Box 10-22-1855 (10-24-1855) Hr
Barnett, John J. to Margaret E. Thompson 4-6-1867 (4-9-1867) Ma
Barnett, John M. to Lavanda Ferguson 3-20-1860 Hr
Barnett, John M. to Lidia J. Diggs 1-13-1860 Hn
Barnett, John W. to Mary Jacobs 6-7-1834 (6-12-1834) Hr
Barnett, John to Betty A. Johnson 4-17-1862 (4-19-1862) O
Barnett, John to Eliza Harris 6-10-1863 O
Barnett, Lawson T. to Dionitia A. Preston 1-5-1847 (no return) F
Barnett, Leroy to Naomi Gordon 9-25-1850 (10-1-1850) Ma
Barnett, Louis to Fannie Tipton 1-3-1877 (1-4-1877) Dy
Barnett, Matthew B. to Louisa Malinda Allen 3-19-1870 (3-22-1870) Ma
Barnett, Nathaniel T. to Catherine L. Barnett 5-26-1843 Hn
Barnett, Nelson to Rose Strain 12-9-1868 (no return) L
Barnett, Peter B. to Mahala V. E. Garrett 12-3-1860 (12-5-1860) Ma
Barnett, Peter B. to Susan J. Barnett 9-2-1859 (9-8-1859) Ma
Barnett, Peyton to Renzie Young 12-26-1843 O
Barnett, Robert M. to Ann E. Drake 10-15-1855 (10-18-1855) G
Barnett, Robert W. to Mary M. Alexander 12-4-1827 (12-6-1827) Hr
Barnett, S. C. to Margaret (Mrs.) Wilson 6-25-1859 (6-26-1859) Sh
Barnett, Samuel D. to Mary L. Fogg 5-25-1857 Ma
Barnett, Samuel to Tennessee Spence 8-11-1866 Dy
Barnett, Sanmartin to Camilee Wyly 5-31-1850 Be
Barnett, Stephen to Alice Graham 1-21-1867 Hy
Barnett, T. S. to Martha Duffer 11-1-1866 G
Barnett, Talton to Mary Burgent 10-11-1871 O
Barnett, Theron B. to Mary E. Nelson 4-15-1861 (4-18-1861) Ma
Barnett, Thomas to Eliza McLeary 2-8-1843 Ma
Barnett, Thomas to Manta Diggs 7-16-1874 T
Barnett, Thos. to Abagil Landers 8-6-1864 (8-7-1864) Sh
Barnett, William to Eveleni Lynn 7-2-1828 (7-3-1828) Ma
Barnette, Joseph P. (Joel B.) to Sally Ann Isler 8-30-1849 Sh
Barney, Jerry to Bule Halfacre 3-22-1876 (no return) L B
Barnhart, F. to Isabella Phillips 3-20-1852 Cr
Barnhart, J. C. to Margaret C. Rowland 4-?-1867 (4-21-1867) Cr
Barnhart, James to Roda Nanney 1-28-1858 Cr
Barnhart, Robert to Saphrona Palmer 7-2-1866 (7-4-1866) Cr
Barnhart, Robt. C. to Caroline Williams 1-22-1872 (no return) Cr
Barnhart, Robt. C. to Nannie C. Rodgers 12-20-1855 Cr
Barnhart, William to Mary E. Powel 8-19-1871 (8-21-1871) Cr
Barnhart, Wm. to Julia A. Rogers 1-17-1850 Cr
Barnhill, J. P. to Martha E. Steel (Stell) 8-20-1848 Sh
Barnhill, Lewis to Martha Capps 8-19-1851 (8-20-1851) O
Barnhill, Wm. A. to Caroline (Mrs.) Goodrich 2-16-1871 Ma
Barns, Anderson J. to Nancy Rooks 1-26-1842 (1-?-1842) T
Barns, Arther to Frances Shern 12-18-1838 (12-20-1838) G

Barns, B. to Harriet Wheeler 1-21-1866 G
Barns, Charles to Frances M. Herren 1-3-1863 Be
Barns, Daniel H. to Louisa J. Akins 11-29-1838 (12-6-1838) G
Barns, Daniel to Catharine Parker 1-22-1844 (1-25-1844) G
Barns, Henry to Susan Wyatt 4-19-1838 Cr
Barns, James W. to Judy Greenwood 5-28-1845 Cr
Barns, W.C. to Elila Pierce 11-29-1865 Be
Barns, William W. to Susan E. Cox 11-28-1868 (11-29-1868) Cr
Barns, Wilson to Sarah Rochell 10-31-1862 (no return) Cr
Barnwell, George to Mariah P. Hendley 8-19-1847 Hn
Barnwell, J. H. to Mary E. West 10-9-1865 G
Barnwell, J. W. to Mary J. Throgmorton 1-12-1848 Hn
Barquty, Jacob to Susan Watson 7-29-1847 Sh
Barr, Benjamin to Sarah R. Elrod 1-4-1843 Ma
Barr, F. M. to Arilla Nix 9-23-1846 (no return) Hn
Barr, Francis M. to Julina Magill 12-28-1847 Be
Barr, George W. to Indiana Woods 3-12-1865 Be
Barr, James A. to Eliza Cox 7-21-1841 Cr
Barr, James N. to Lucretia Ward 3-14-1838 (no return) Hn
Barr, John to Tabitha Sudberry 1-3-1871 (1-4-1871) Dy
Barr, T. N. to Martha A. Bruce 12-18-1853 Be
Barr, William M. to Sarah J. Russell 9-12-1859 (9-13-1859) Ma
Barr, William to Mary Gage 2-26-1863 Hn
Barr, Wilson to Carrie Grant 11-8-1840 Cr
Barret, Anthony R. to Rebecca Hill 8-7-1850 Sh
Barret, George Washington to Catherine Boyd 12-27-1870 (12-28-1871?) T
Barret, John H. to Isabella F. Smith 12-14-1870 T
Barret, Ned? to Maria Lippman 10-9-1868 (10-12-1868) T
Barret, Richard S. to Mary Matilda Harris 12-22-1847 T
Barret, T. J. to Rachael Jackson 1-2-1860 (1-5-1860) Hr
Barrett, A. G. to Sarah G. Seaton 4-13-1832 (4-16-1832) Hr
Barrett, A. J. to Finey Gold 1-24-1874 (1-25-1874) Dy
Barrett, Cornelius to Matilda Baker 10-13-1830 (10-14-1830) Hr
Barrett, George W. to Sarah A. Chance 11-7-1858 Hn
Barrett, J. D. to L. S. Bradford 12-4-1866 G
Barrett, J. M. C. to M. A. Jackson 12-16-1857 (12-17-1857) Hr
Barrett, J. T. to Ulissus Hopper 6-26-1873 Dy
Barrett, James M. to Ann Jane Sharp 4-3-1861 T
Barrett, James W. to Martha Hopper 2-16-1870 (2-17-1870) Dy
Barrett, John W. to Alvira Wood 5-17-1863 G
Barrett, Luther to E. L. Skiles 2-24-1869 G
Barrett, Michael to Margaret Eagan 5-25-1860 (5-27-1860) Sh
Barrett, T. O. to D. A. McCann 5-28-1863 Mn
Barrett, William S. to Prudence West 10-7-1854 (10-12-1854) O
Barrett, William to Mexico Barton 2-15-1850 G
Barrett, Wilson to Susan Robertson 6-4-1840 Hr
Barrette, J. W. to M. E. Dickey 11-8-1875 (11-10-1875) Dy
Barrier, Lafayette to Amanda Bingham 12-4-1860 Ma
Barriet, P. H. to Susie Lowry 12-4-1878 Hy
Barringer, Calvin L. to Tommie Patton 12-24-1862 (no return) F
Barringer, Richmond(Richard) L. to Mary Wilson 12-26-1853 (12-27-1853) O
Barrington, Dennis to Missouri Roberson 12-28-1867 (1-1-1868) F B
Barritt, W. F. to R. E. Burn 2-16-1867 G
Barrom, Thomas to Mary A. E. Mathews 2-28-1867 (3-5-1867) F
Barron, Alexander to Missouri Williams 5-2-1831 Ma
Barron, Amos W. to Sarah Jane Munn 10-25-1859 (11-1-1859) Ma
Barron, Andrew to ____ Chaney 10-10-1867 G
Barron, Arch B. to Casey L. Fletcher 1-17-1859 (1-20-1859) G
Barron, Francis M. to Canvass B. Russell 9-28-1858 G
Barron, John W. to Sarah Jane Noel 9-8-1853 (9-11-1853) G
Barron, Nathan to Elizabeth Sherron 12-17-1835 G
Barron, Patrick to Jeheno Lynch 5-26-1858 (5-26-1858) Sh
Barron, Philip to Johanna Cook 11-25-1858 Sh
Barron, Sanders to Mary Barron 9-18-1869 (no return) F B
Barron, W. J. to Mollie E. Culp 12-11-1866 (12-13-1866) F
Barron, William J. to Margarett F. Mathis 11-17-1856 G
Barrott, Franklin to Sarah Massee 10-3-1839 G
Barrott, John to Lucy Howell 6-9-1842 Cr
Barrott, Joseph to Sarah J. McBride 11-8-1843 G
Barrott, Marcus to Martha A. Thomas 3-19-1844 G *
Barrow, S. L. to E. A. Culp 12-20-1864 (12-24-1864) F
Barrow, W. H. to Mary J. West 1-21-1869 F
Barry (Burney?), David to Melinda Stuckey 5-4-1853 L
Barry, Danl. to Elisa J. Moore 5-29-1852 (5-30-1852) Sh
Barry, Danl. to Eliza J. Moore 12-3-1851 Sh
Barry, Edmond to Mary Real 8-11-1857 (8-18-1857) Sh
Barry, Henry A. to Nancy S. Taylor 5-17-1841 Sh
Barry, William A. F. to Francis Ann Taylor 5-27-1841 Sh
Bartcliff, John W. to Pelma Hamilton 3-2-1866 (3-4-1866) O
Barter?, Neel to Crotia Ann Robson 6-4-1829 Hr
Bartlet, Gabriel M. to Elizabeth G. Glasgow 12-3-1846 F
Bartlett, Edward G. to Sarah E. Wade 10-27-1856 (10-29-1856) Sh
Bartlett, Edward H. to Jane Armstrong 12-15-1856 Sh
Bartlett, Emanuel to Celia Hare 12-13-1869 (12-14-1869) F B
Bartlett, G. M. to Rebecca Cross 1-4-1854 (no return) O
Bartlett, J. M. to Josephine Baldridge 8-30-1864 O
Bartlett, John to Ann M. Morrison 8-19-1833 (8-20-1833) Hr

Bartlett, Wm. M. to Sarah Smith 5-18-1859 (5-19-1859) Sh
Barton, B. F. to Martha E. Morgan 5-11-1864 Sh
Barton, Christopher to Rosanna Quinn 4-29-1858 Sh
Barton, Edward to Sarah Ket 6-19-1843 Hn
Barton, F. M. to Susan Madden 11-17-1855 (11-18-1855) Sh
Barton, George W. to Melissa Mathis 8-22-1852 Hn
Barton, Greenberry to Joan Stephens 12-20-1855 Hn
Barton, H. C. to Mattie A. Becton 2-16-1869 G
Barton, H. L. M. to Susan Bobbett 9-15-1838 (9-16-1838) G
Barton, J. Wade to Louiza S. Bowden 3-22-1864 Hn
Barton, James D. to Martha A. McAdams 2-16-1861 (no return) We
Barton, James to Frances Paschall 1-10-1849 Hn
Barton, James to Permelia Mullins 3-8-1859 Cr
Barton, John A. to Sarah J. Lewis 12-23-1863 Hn
Barton, John L. to Mary J. Nichols 10-30-1867 (10-31-1867) Cr
Barton, John M. to Sarah J. Barrott 1-13-1847 (1-15-1847) G
Barton, John to Eliza J. Bateman 11-30-1848 Sh
Barton, Joseph H. to Catherine A. Harper 2-3-1849 Sh
Barton, Joseph to Mary E. Black 1-10-1863 Mn
Barton, Joseph to Sarah Davis 2-21-1839 Hn
Barton, Ned to Rebecca Robinson 1-23-1870 G B
Barton, Robert W. to Harratt E. Davidson 12-5-1839 G
Barton, Robert to Catherine Wells 7-3-1851 Hn
Barton, Roger to Eudora Barry 5-2-1832 Hr
Barton, Spencer G. to Mildred Ward 12-23-1841 G
Barton, T.J. to Martha Rice 11-23-1872 (11-26-1872) Cr
Barton, Thomas F. to Nancy Black 12-28-1847 (12-30-1847) Ma
Barton, W. H. to T. E. Mason 1-1-1856 (no return) Hn
Barton, W. M. to Sallie Duke 2-12-1870 (no return) Hy
Barton, William C. to Roeana P. Abbott 7-18-1844 G
Barton, William H. to Rebecca C. Orr 11-15-1865 Hn
Barton, William R. to Harrie A. Provine 11-4-1850 (11-6-1850) Ma
Barton, William to Mary L. Mitchell 4-30-1847 F
Barton, Willis S. to Elphady C. Wilson 9-19-1856 (9-23-1856) G
Barton, Wm. B. to Mary Simmons 3-15-1851 Cr
Barton?, John D. W. to Mary Buckley 10-11-1853 Hn
Barwell, D. M. to Ann E. Thompson 10-8-1860 (10-24-1860) F
Base?, John W. to Mary A. Cossett 8-21?-1843 (9-5-1843) F
Basford, Aaron C. to Clementina Stallings 7-1-1843 (7-2-1843) L
Basford, Isaac F. to Ellen (Mrs.) Dennis 7-25-1854 (7-26-1854) Sh
Basford, John to Margaret McQurry 5-5-1847 Be
Bashears, J. S. to S. J. Muligin 12-23-1874 T
Bashears, W. H. to Nancy M. Wilkerson 2-26-1862 Mn
Bashen?, Jackson to Elizabeth Nichols 4-10-1862 (no return) Cr
Basheres, Rufus T. to Martha Helen Davis 7-24-1843 T
Basinger, G. F. to Mary Hunt 11-28-1861 G
Ba(y)singer, George M. to Mary Jane Denney 12-27-1853 (1-3-1854) O
Basinger, George R. to Susan E. Ray 10-14-1868 G
Basinger, George to Eleanor Hawkins 6-24-1861 Mn
Basinger, William A. to Nancy J. Fields 1-3-1842 (1-7-1842) G
Baskerville, G. B. to Sallie L. Read 11-16-1869 Hy
Baskerville, Jno. T. (Rev.) to A. T. (Mrs.) Hare 1-7-1857 (1-8-1857) Sh
Baskerville, Richard to Frances Booker 12-22-1870 (12-28-1870) F B
Baskin, Turby to Eliza J. Baskin 2-26-1867 (2-28-1867) T
Baskins, David J. to Sallie Freeman 7-12-1864 (7-13-1864) T
Baskins, J. H. to M. J. Wallis 7-13-1864 (7-14-1864) T
Baskins, John B. to Malinda J. Kelly 12-16-1868 T
Baskins, W. L. to Elizabeth Jane Dawson 8-1-1866 (8-10-1866) T
Bason, Isaac to Mary Elizabeth Standley 12-26-1840 (12-29-1840) F
Bason, Richard to Ellen Warbane 7-15-1851 Sh
Bason, Richard to Elmyra Hale 11-12-1852 Sh
Bass, Allen to Mary Philips 6-9-1867 Hy
Bass, Anderson to Rosaella Edwards 12-28-1876 Hy
Bass, David S. to Agnes C. Ruffin 8-9-1866 (8-12-1866) F
Bass, Drury L. to Harriett P. Bass 12-5-1838 Sh
Bass, Edward to Elmina Jacobs 7-15-1828 (not executed) Hr
Bass, Edward to Nancy Hall 8-10-1847 (8-12-1847) G
Bass, G. W. to E. A. E. Hatler 12-29-1858 (no return) We
Bass, Gilbert to Ann Joy 2-15-1869 (3-8-1869) F B
Bass, Gilfin W. to Mary E. Hughes 8-8-1861 We
Bass, Hartwell W. to Jane E. Bethell 10-30-1844 Sh
Bass, Henry S. to Matilda Napey 11-19-1827 Ma
Bass, Isaac to Sarah Hunt 5-20-1850 (5-28-1850) G
Bass, James H. to Sarah A. Benthel 1-28-1845 G
Bass, Jas. H. to Marilu? E. Parker 4-3-1866 G
Bass, John E. to Mary E. Gray 10-16-1844 Sh
Bass, John to Sarah Sullenger 4-15-1826 (4-20-1826) Hr
Bass, Joseph J. to Elizabeth S. Hunt 5-9-1843 G
Bass, L. H. to Mary B. Dunevant 2-9-1874 (2-11-1874) Dy
Bass, Lewis to Marthy Jones 5-8-1877 Hy
Bass, R. C. to M. E. Dyson 10-17-1854 O
Bass, Redick to Manerva Ellis 4-27-1845 Sh
Bass, Reuben to Mary Matthews 12-18-1837 Hr
Bass, Richardson to Amanda Hale 8-16-1842 Sh
Bass, Rufus to Laura N. Clark 2-5-1868 (2-6-1868) F
Bass, Shade to Mollie Avery 3-14-1874 T
Bass, Solomon to Sarah Varnal 1-1-1839 Sh

Bass, Thomas A. to S. J. Dunn 4-12-1861 Hr
Bass, Thomas C. to Masa Williams 9-10-1832 Sh
Bass, W. B. to Jane H. Simmons 11-20-1869 G
Bass, Wm. H. to Lucy Henson 9-20-1859 Hr
Basset, Edward to Mary Burnes 7-8-1862 Mn
Bassett, Edward to Sarah Isabella Hill 6-18-1856 (no return?) Sh
Bassford, Aaron C. to Eliza Jane Ward 9-25-1856 Hn
Bassham, Drue F. to Louisa A. Russom 9-10-1865 Mn
Bassham, Eli to Polly Mosier 10-27-1830 O
Bassham, William to Agness Eastridge 1-20-1855 (1-22-1855) O
Bassmore, Anthony to Anna Woods 8-11-1877 (no return) Hy
Baswell, John to Susanah Davis 8-2-1848 (no return) F
Baswell, W. W. to M. A. D. Newton 3-17-1860 (3-22-1860) F
Batailly, Victor to Elise Orgelat 7-30-1864 Sh
Batchelor, Ansell to Susan Stanly 8-19-1874 Hy
Batchelor, Colonel to Amanda Oldham 1-8-1873 (no return) Hy
Batchelor, Green to Fannie Campbell 3-4-1873 Hy
Batchelor, J. A. B. to Mattie A. Harper 11-2-1869 (no return) Hy
Batchelor, James W. to Catherine A. Baty 4-17-1860 (no return) Hy
Bate, H. H. to N. D. Simpson 11-24-1873 (11-25-1873) T
Bate, John to Marina Bond 9-13-1872 (no return) Hy
Bate_, J. C. to Nancy E. Baggett 6-1-1856 Be
Bateman, Benihar to Louisa Massey 4-30-1856 Sh
Bateman, Edward M. to Mildred A. Dowell 2-16-1860 (2-20-1860) Sh
Bateman, Green to Lucindy C. Haywood 4-11-1847 Cr
Bateman, Harden W. to Mary E. Barton 7-27-1848 Sh
Bateman, Hugh to Penina Cantrell 9-?-1860 (9-7-1860) Cr
Bateman, Hugh to Peronia Cantrell 9-6-1860 (9-7-1860) Cr
Bateman, J. B. to Martha J. Polston 6-22-1869 (6-23-1869) Cr
Bateman, J. J. to T. J. Roberson 4-4-1867 Cr
Bateman, John T. to Bridget Fellson 8-1-1859 (8-2-1859) Sh
Bateman, John to Emily J. Roberts 11-15-1848 F
Bateman, Josiah to Caroline Singleton 9-23-1867 (no return) Cr
Bateman, Morgan M. to Ann E. Edwards 5-11-1854 Sh
Bateman, W. R. to Elizabeth R. Prewitt 6-25-1870 (6-26-1870) Cr
Bateman, W. R. to Louisa J. Stone 1-12-1885 (1-14-1885) L
Bateman, William to Rianna Parish 3-2-1871 (3-5-1871) Cr
Bateman, W. to Mary Haywood 1-30-1840 Cr
Bates, Ben, sr. to Chaney McFarland 12-24-1878 (1-2-1879) L B
Bates, Benjamin to Charlotte Eggleston 5-21-1870 (no return) L
Bates, Bevily to Sallie Vancleive 3-8-1872 (3-10-1872) Cr
Bates, Chalres T. to Pattie Barr 8-16-1871 (8-19-1871) Ma
Bates, Charles to Martha Owen 9-6-1874 Hy
Bates, Chas. to Ann Moore 12-26-1870 Hy
Bates, David C. to Martha B. Carruthers 10-9-1854 (10-10-1854) Hr
Bates, E. P. to Emaline Bowden 8-24-1849 Hn
Bates, Esau to Lucinda Honey 12-11-1843 (12-14-1843) F
Bates, Ewing P. to Flotilla Hartsfield 10-25-1852 Hn
Bates, J. to L. Campbell 4-21-1839 Be
Bates, James S. to E. J. Laycock 12-5-1872 Cr
Bates, James to Harriet New 3-7-1836 Hr
Bates, James to Mary W. North 5-8-1848 (5-9-1848) Hr
Bates, John C. to Mary Bowers 8-25-1835 G
Bates, John C. to Seley Chaplin 11-15-1849 O
Bates, John to Elizar Blalock 10-1-1858 (no return) We
Bates, John to Julia Baird 2-1-1867 (2-2-1867) F B
Bates, Major to Linda Jordan 9-1-1879 (no return) L
Bates, Nathaniel to Maria Jane Davis 11-29-1871 (no return) L
Bates, Robert to Francis Simms 1-24-1877 (1-29-1877) L B
Bates, S. D. to Barbara A. Hutson 1-24-1877 (no return) Dy
Bates, Stephen to Mary Condry 12-22-1865 (12-24-1865) L
Bates, Thomas M. to Mary Hutchins 5-6-1845 Sh
Bates, Thomas to Fannie Mitchell 12-27-1876 (12-29-1876) Dy
Bates, Thomas to Norah Scott 12-23-1873 (12-24-1873) L B
Bates, William to F. A. Sistrunk 1-13-1882 (1-17-1882) L
Batey, J. C. to C. C. Stewart 1-2-1871 (1-5-1871) T
Bathshears, William to Mary M. Langham 7-5-1856 (7-1-1856) G
Bats, George W. to Jane Linder 3-26-1863 We
Batsel, William E. to Emeline Wedington 3-20-1854 O
Batt, Jas. F. to Mary A. Wilkinson 10-14-1846 Sh
Batt, John M. to Elizabeth F. Woodfin 9-19-1840 (9-24-1840) F
Batte, Robert B. to Mary E. Dickerson 10-17-1866 (10-25-1866) T
Batten, G. C. to Louise Green 12-10-1849 Cr
Batten, J. R. to Sophia Butler 11-27-1869 (11-30-1869) Cr
Batter, Benj. to Rebecca F. Brown 3-18-1846 (no return) L
Battle, Alfred to Irene Taylor 12-11-1867 Hy
Battle, B. W. to T. S. Tooms 4-20-1865 G
Battle, George to Sallie Ann Adams 1-27-1867 Hy
Battle, H. to Eley Moore 8-2-1865 G
Battle, Henry to Martha Dunlap 7-14-1842 G
Battle, Jo to Lucinda Easley 7-18-1878 Dy
Battle, Lewis to Frances Sorrell 8-11-1860 (8-16-1860) Ma
Battle, Lewis to Rebecca Dotson 10-7-1872 (10-14-1872) Dy
Battle, W. B. to Elizabeth A. Bonner 8-1-1846 F
Batton, Wm. to Elizabeth Williams 7-28-1842 Cr
Batts, Garldas? to Nancy Duke 7-17-1844 Cr
Batts, J. F. to S. M. Foushee 11-28-1877 O

Batts, Pleasant to Emily Wilkes 1-26-1871 (1-28-1871) F B
Battson, J. J. to Mary E. Lamb 8-27-1855 (no return) Hn
Batty, James to Nancy C. Hicks 4-28-1859 Cr
Baty, H. B. to Elizabeth G. Wash 12-18-1838 (12-20-1838) F
Baty, William to Rebecca Aulton 4-8-1843 (4-9-1843) Hr
Baucom, Alfred to Susanna Evans 11-3-1866 (no return) Hy
Baucom, Cane to Harriet Crutchfield 4-19-1871 (4-20-1871) Cr B
Baucom, Chas. A. to Sarah F. Williams 8-21-1870 Hy
Baucom, Geo. to Joann Mitchell 8-31-1872 (9-1-1872) Cr
Baucom, John G. to Louisa Pace 12-8-1878 Hy
Baucum, Danl. to Isabella Graves 1-7-1841 (1-10-1841) F
Baucum, David C. to Elizabeth Meredith 12-24-1865 Hn
Baucum, Henderson to Mary M. Lee 5-22-1842 Hn
Baucum, Newton C. to Matilda J. Kellow 7-11-1861 G
Baucum, Samuel to Nelly Sparks 3-8-1877 Cr
Baucum, Sidney to Harriet Jackson 2-18-1852 (no return) Hn
Baucum, Wiley to M. E. Beard 12-21-1865 Mn
Bauden, John to Mary Smith 4-14-1842 Sh
Bauen (Baren?), H. M. to Pochahontas Davis 2-2-1860 (2-4-1860) Sh
Baugh (Baughman), James F. to Hannah Wap (Wass?) 5-21-1859 (5-22-1859) Sh
Baugh, Francis to Nancy (Mrs.) String 3-18-1863 Sh
Baugh, Jacob to Margaret M. Good 4-23-1857 Hn
Baugh, Jeremiah to Pamelia R. Cole 11-30-1848 Sh
Baugh, John R. to Fannie Baugh 4-6-1858 T
Baugh, Josiah R. to Sarahjennett Holloway 11-2-1847 F
Baugh, Theophass to Mary W. Howard 12-11-1856 We
Baugh, Thos. J. to Frances Stokes 7-26-1854 (1-?-1854) T
Baughman, Jacob to Emeline Sargeant 10-8-1857 Sh
Baulch, J. M. to M. L. Perry 11-11-1871 (11-16-1871) Dy
Baum, Felix to Angell Watkins 4-7-1849 Sh
Baum, Henry, sr. to Josephina Loeb 11-8-1884 (11-9-1884) L
Baum, John D. to Martha F. Margrove 6-26-1865 (6-27-1865) F
Baum, John to Lenora Som 3-25-1859 (3-26-1859) Sh
Baum, Thos. D. to Mary J. Hargrove 11-26-1849 F
Bauman, Adolph to Louisa Albert 1-16-1855 Sh
Baw, Edward B. to Martha Jane Shaw 1-15-1844 (1-18-1844) F
Baw, William A. to Julina Stone 1-13-1852 (no return) F
Baxter, A. to Sarah (Mrs.) Trice 11-17-1846 We
Baxter, Albert to Adaline Jones 1-9-1874 (no return) L
Baxter, Caleb E. to Emely Tansil 12-25-1843 We
Baxter, Calvin to Rebacca A. Foust 12-25-1866 (12-26-1866) Dy
Baxter, Dave to Zenobia? Tucker 2-1-1877 Dy
Baxter, Frederick to Mary E. Rose 7-31-1845 Sh
Baxter, G. W. to Lou Freeman 6-10-1872 Hy
Baxter, George W. to A. E. Moody 6-11-1859 (no return) Hy
Baxter, J. F. to Eliza E. Morton 1-7-1870 (1-13-1870) F
Baxter, J. P. to Lucy Puryear 3-20-1880 (3-21-1880) L
Baxter, James M. to Nancy A. Dougan 10-2-1850 (10-3-1850) Ma
Baxter, James to Sarah M. Simmons 12-27-1855 We
Baxter, James to Margarett Humphreys 7-20-1849 Ma
Baxter, James to Mary Heriod 11-28-1854 G
Baxter, Jno. Edwin to E. J. Tacket 11-13-1872 T
Baxter, John to Marassela C. Rollins 8-5-1865 (8-6-1865) Cr
Baxter, John to Mary W. Powell 5-1-1845 G
Baxter, John to Nancy J. McNail 1-20-1853 G
Baxter, Lafayette to Nancy J. Williams 9-1-1870 Hy
Baxter, Mit to Arteny Jones 2-17-1871 Dy
Baxter, Mit to Eliza Campbell 8-1-1870 Dy
Baxter, Nathan to Mary Yarbrough 8-31-1850 Cr
Baxter, Robert J. to Lucy J. Hughs 8-1-1866 (no return) Cr
Baxter, S. W. to A. V. Branch 12-19-1850 F
Baxter, Samuel M. to Halley A. Murphy 5-1-1855 We
Baxter, W. K.? to J. C. Algee 1-1-1861 (1-2-1861) Cr
Baxter, W. N. to S. E. King 7-7-1864 Sh
Baxter, W. s. to C. C. Clark 1-28-1874 Hy
Baxter, Wesley to Emily Trent 7-6-1867 (7-7-1867) F B
Baxter, William to Jane Wardlaw 12-18-1855 (12-19-1855) L
Baxter, William to Sarah Berry 1-7-1832 G
Baxter, Wm. to Malinda Houston 1-14-1847 Sh
Baylam?, J. to Hellen Taylor 2-26-1869 T
Bayles, Abraham to Eliza Warren 11-25-1826 (or 11-26?) Sh
Bayless, Samuel H. to Martha A. Hatley 7-22-1844 F
Bayley, Armstead to Martha Green 12-.7-1867 (12-25?-1867) L B
Bayley, Henry to Arcady F. Jones 6-12-.848 Ma
Bayley, Robt. to Lucinda F. Sneed 1-10-1872 (1-11-1872) T
Bayley, Wm. E. to Madeleine L. Roberts 2-16-1863 Sh
Bayliss, Bronson to Maria L. Lewis 10-15-1849 Sh
Bayliss, Elijah E. to Mary Garrett 5-23-1850 Hn
Bayliss, Thomas C. to Mary E. Cowardin 9-15-1853 We
Bayliss, Thomas H. to Mary Mask 4-8-1848 (4-13-1848) Hr
Bayn, D. B. to Ruth A. Hall 3-9-1858 (3-10-1858) G
Bayn, Mastin F. to Lucy Ann Owen 5-9-1846 (5-14-1846) G
Bayne, A. O. to Susan A. Biers 12-23-1861 G
Bayne, G. W. to Elizabeth R. Dubose 1-14-1856 (1-15-1856) Sh
Bayne, Matthew to Mary Ann Colt 2-24-1840 Sh
Bayne, Walter D. to Emily Buck 9-13-1842 Sh

Baynes, Henry to Sallie Maclin 8-8-1869 Hy
Baynes, J. L. to F. B. Tucker 6-23-1859 (6-30-1859) Sh
Baynes, Thomas F. to Swannanoa Lea 10-22-1873 Hy
Bays, W. S. to Aceneth E. Aikin 4-10-1861 (4-17-1861) T
Baysinger, James M. to Martha Dickerson 8-24-1844 (8-25-1844) G
Baysinger, Jno. to Mary Ann Morgan 11-10-1836 G
Baysinger, Thos. J. to Merris Horn 9-8-1838 (9-9-1838) G
Bazel, Bird to Mary Spurling 6-22-1827 (6-24-1827) Hr
Bazemore, Jesse to S. C. (Mrs.) Patrick 4-6-1864 Sh
Bazen, John R. to Mary Ellen Brogden 5-30-1859 (6-2-1859) L
Beacham, Abner C. to Lean G. Dibrill 9-4-1834 G
Beacham, Calvin to Mary An Armour 8-?-1842 (no return) F
Beacham, Henry to Rosetta Harris 1-24-1869 G B
Beachum, C. H. to Martha Ann Burnett 7-6-1854 Hr
Beachum, William to Jane Burleson 1-14-1833 (1-15-1833) Hr
Beadgit, Zach. to Eliza Bradway 10-21-1841 Cr
Beadles, Alex M. to Mary Fite 3-17-1847 G
Beadles, Brice H. to Emely A. Cavitt 3-4-1861 We
Beadles, Calhoun W. to Elizabeth H. Lawrence 12-26-1859 (no return) We
Beadles, Duke J. to Ann C. Harris 11-18-1857 Ma
Beadles, L. Y. to Charlotte A. Alexander 10-1-1866 (no return) Hn
Beadles, Marshal L. to E. H. Hapsens 1-12-1860 We
Beadls?, Dick to Martha Bledsoe 1-12-1868 T
Beak, Presley S. to Margaret A. Gammons 3-6-1861 Dy
Beakley, James H. to Sarah Jackson 2-19-1876 (2-20-1876) Dy
Beal, John to Mary Powers 9-4-1830 Sh
Beal, Lewis to Lucy Shepherd 7-4-1866 O
Beal, Simon to Jane Wilkinson 12-25-1843 Ma
Beal, W. H. to E. E. Baxter 12-12-1865 F
Beale, Enoch to Eliza Brown 2-22-1868 F B
Beamer, Jacob to Mary Edwards 12-20-1880 (12-30-1881?) L
Beamish, Jno. to Elizabeth Murray 3-27-1858 (4-4-1858) Sh
Bean (Beard), Joab (Jacob) to Peggy Grace? 6-27-1820 Sh
Bean, B. F. to P. M. Gay 8-1-1859 G
Bean, Benjamin to Eliza Bass 11-21-1836 (11-22-1836) G
Bean, George to Hamar Taylor 1-1-1872 (1-7-1872) T
Bean, McKelva to Martha A. T. Thompson 3-14-1842 G
Bean, Russell to Mary C. (Charlotte) Harkleroad 5-6-1820 Sh
Beany(Beny), Berry to Susannah Garner 10-23-1841 (10-24-1841) Hr
Bear, H. to Rebecca Davis 1-3-1845 Hn
Beard (Baird), S. M. to Julia Ann Jackson 1-26-1859 (1-27-1859) L
Beard, B. B. to Elizabeth D. McCommun? 12-16-1847 (12-23-1847) Hr
Beard, Eli to Elizabeth Wilson 3-5-1867 O
Beard, J. B. to Cordelia M. E. Newhall 6-27-1857 (6-28-1857) Sh
Beard, J. F. to M. E. Latham 5-26-1885 (5-27-1885) L
Beard, J. H. to Alice Hornbeak 2-8-1859 We
Beard, J. M. to Martha J. Beard 7-5-1867 Hn
Beard, J. W. to M. A. Smith 12-23-1863 Hn
Beard, James B. to Matilda J. Medlin 1-29-1861 (no return) Hy
Beard, James to Julia Ann Williams 10-3-1867 G B
Beard, James? H. to Mary A. Tyson 12-14-1848 Hn
Beard, Jno. C. to Crecy Longley 7-26-1873 Hy
Beard, John H. to Susan Jane Laughter 4-29-1846 (4-6?-1846) F
Beard, Lewis to Alice Halliburton 11-28-1883 L
Beard, Lewis to Alsie Wardlaw 2-14-1878 L
Beard, Peter to Laura Sumner 2-22-1871 Hy
Beard, Presley T. to Narcissa Pope 3-2-1857 G
Beard, R. C. to P. G. Bledsoe 7-30-1856 Sh
Beard, Sam to Bettie Miller 3-10-1870 (no return) Hy
Beard, T. C. to Nancy Boon 6-7-1852 (no return) F
Beard, T. L. to Elizabeth (Mrs.) Wilcox 11-12-1855 (11-13-1855) Sh
Beard, Thomas Y. to Martha J. Batt 12-7-1862 We
Beard, Thomas to Mary Easterwood 10-27-1846 G
Beard, Thomas to Matilda J. Booth 7-14-1854 Cr
Beard, Thomas to Sally Warren 7-10-1830 Hr
Beard, W. F. to Lucy Thurman 3-12-1863 Mn
Beard, William H. to Mary C. Amyett 1-17-1856 We
Beard, William W. to Maria Jane Lowrance 11-3-1855 (11-4-1855) Hr
Beard, William to Frances Reece 1-23-1861 (no return) Hy
Beard, Wm. E. to Ann C. McAlexander 4-20-1846 (4-26-1846) Hr
Beard, Wm. H. to Sarah J. Harpeth 1-3-1862 We
Bearden, G. W> to Sarah E. Dixon 11-13-1867 Hy
Bearden, J. D. to Mary E. Bradley 12-25-1869 Hy
Beardsley, S. E. to Mattie C. Chamberlain 1-13-1863 Sh
Beasely, Joseph L. to Martha J. Ballinger 12-30-1859 (1-1-1860) L
Beasley, Adam to Ellen Blanton 7-7-1866 Hn B
Beasley, Alez to Martha Ann Price 4-20-1852 We
Beasley, Andrew A. to Rhoda C. Thompson 10-25-1855 Be
Beasley, Charles to Mariah Walker 12-12-1868 (12-13-1868) F B
Beasley, Geo. W. to Jane Pulliam 9-29-1859 Hr
Beasley, Ira T. to Fannie C. Brown 10-14-1868 (10-15-1868) L
Beasley, Isam to Sarah Black 3-3-1845 (no return) F
Beasley, James W. to Martha Broom 10-1-1847 (10-2-1847) F
Beasley, James to Amelia Tripp 2-23-1867 (3-4-1867) F B
Beasley, James to Martha A. Florence 2-7-1858 Be
Beasley, John to M. C. Loyd 11-3-1856 Be
Beasley, John to Sarah Terrill 9-4-1862 (no return) Hy
Beasley, Marion to C. A. Winters 10-4-1852 We
Beasley, Reuben to Leathy White 12-3-1870 (12-29-1870) F B
Beasley, Robert E. to Mary Jane Barton 2-12-1839 Sh
Beasley, Rubin H. to Malesey D. Tailor 12-5-1855 We
Beasley, Rubin to Fannie Harden 3-30-1867 (4-2-1867) T
Beasley, Thos. J. to Agness Griffin 1-21-1867 (1-24-1867) F
Beasley, Thos. to Mary Hansel 3-18-1852 Be
Beasley, W. J to Emily Nelson 1-26-1860 (no return) Hy
Beasley, William to Mary Young 7-19-1870
Beasly, Bryant to Martha Balderson 12-16-1884 (12-19-1884) L
Beasly, Henry to L. A. O. Kelly 4-29-1865 (5-2-1865) F
Beaton, A. H. to Elvina Powell 2-7-1860 Be
Beaton, Christopher C. to Elizabeth Van Maning 12-26-1865 Be
Beaton, Cullen to Susanah A. French 3-25-1855 Be
Beaton, J. R. to Elizabeth Barnes 12-10-1865 Be
Beaton, M. A. to Caroline E. Debruce 9-24-1857 Be
Beaton, W. D. to Caroline H. Clement 11-23-1865 Be
Beaton, William S. to Mahala Cheshier 1-1-1850 Hr
Beats, Elijah to Fannie Garland 12-23-1873 T
Beattie, John D. to Elizabeth S. Parker 4-10-1856 Sh
Beatty, John W. to Mary Wilcox 12-10-1863 O
Beatus, Joseph to B. Klein 9-7-1864 Sh
Beaty, A. to Mary L. Bond 5-5-1856 (5-13-1856) Sh
Beaty, Cicero to Lucretia Turner 2-25-1861 Hr
Beaty, J. N. to Margaret Brown 7-26-1863 Mn
Beauchamp, Louis to Mary Ann Holliday 12-18-1827 Hr
Beauchamp, Wm. Thos. to Virginia C. Halstead 5-1-1861 Sh
Beaumont, Alex to Laura Tucker 8-11-1870 Dy
Beaumont, Frank to Amanda Clark 1-1-1866 Dy
Beauty, William to Harriet Weatherington 1-19-1860 T
Beaver, George M. to Eliza McCauley 1-22-1851 Cr
Beaver, H. W. to Julia C. Smith 10-29-1873 (11-3-1873) T
Beaver, H. W. to Margaret Long 5-1-1862 T
Beaver, Hiram to E. J. Phillips ?-?-1860 Cr
Beaver, Michael to Mildred J. Ralph 4-21-1853 T
Beaver, T. T. to M. E. Lewis 12-5-1871 Hy
Beaver, Thomas to Emaly Howard 11-8-1873 T
Beaver, Wilson T. to Martha W. Jackson 7-19-1841 (7-22-1842?) F
Beavers, Henry to Mary Ann Ralph 12-19-1846 (12-25-1846) T
Beavers, J. H. to Mary Ann Rece 6-27-1863 (7-5-1863) Cr
Beavers, J. P. to Dolly Ann Hickam 5-17-1857 Hn
Beavers, James G. to Nancy James 4-27-1843 Sh
Beavers, Jesse W. to Elizabeth Stuart 12-26-1852 Hn
Beavers, L. J. to Martha E. Fuller 9-21-1872 (9-22-1872) T
Beavers, Macal to Harriet Long 1-14-1868 (1-16-1868) T
Beavers, Michael to Mary Jackson 11-30-1839 (12-5-1839) F
Beavers, Samuel to Caroline E. Smith 7-11-1852 Hn
Beavers, Thos. B. to Angeline Jones 2-4-1858 G
Beavers, W. B. to Mary J. Harris 2-19-1866 (2-20-1866) F
Beavers, W. J. to Sophia F. Beabers(Biebers) 11-9-1858 Hr
Beaves, R. L. to Tersa McIlwaine 2-20-1873 T
Beazley, John to Mary Waldron 4-14-1840 Sh
Beazll, Harrison to Fanny Deaton 8-11-1863 Be
Beazly, John to Sarah Ann Little 4-19-1863 Be
Bechtol, William to Sarah M. Cooper 12-27-1867 (no return) L
Bechtold (Barthold), Jacob to Caroline Newbold 2-28-1845 Sh
Beck, F. M. to Elizabeth Odom 6-3-1862 Be
Beck, George to Easter Kelley 7-27-1833 Hr
Beck, George to Elizabeth Barker 8-19-1834 Hr
Beck, J. W. to Nancy J. Wrinkle 12-8-1865 Mn
Beck, James to Lucy Lennard 9-27-1836 H
Beck, Thomas to Caroline Hall 4-16-1849 (4-18-1849) F
Beck, William to Barbara Smith 1-25-1860 Sh
Beck, William to Winny Wimberley 3-4-1858 Hn
Becket, Charlie to Loula Fowlkes 9-22-1880 (9-23-1880) Dy
Becket, Lewis to Arabella McNeil 1-1-1855 Hr
Beckett, Letas to Frances Porter 5-30-1871 (6-1-1871) Dy
Beckett, Silas to Bettie Hale 1-3-1877 (1-4-1877) Dy
Beckley, James B. to Mary A. R. Barber 12-23-1858 We
Beckman, H. C. to M. J. (Mrs.) Wilson 12-20-1864 Sh
Beckman, Willis to Frances Abbott 2-23-1847 Cr
Becksterling, John to Jane Adams 8-18-1863 (8-20-1863) T
Becktel, William to Sallie Howell 11-3-1868 Hy
Beckwith, Jim to Martha Hunter 4-17-1844 We
Beckwith, Reuben to Mary Green 3-15-1880 (3-16-1880) L B
Becton, F. A. to Rose Green 5-29-1873 (6-1-1873) L B
Becton, F. E. to Pressilla Harper 2-17-1838 (2-18-1838) G
Becton, F. E. to Susan Thomas 7-16-1859 (7-17-1859) G
Becton, Fed to Eliza Bowers 1-1-1885 (no return) L
Becton, Frederick to Pherraby Hillard 2-18-1847 G
Becton, L. F. to H. A. Davidson 12-2-1866 G
Becton, S. M. to S. M. Marshall 12-26-1865 G
Becton, W. J. to Elizabeth McGill 1-10-1855 (1-11-1855) G
Becton, William J. R. to Margaret S. Greer 9-13-1853 (9-15-1853) G
Bedford, Alfred M. to Mary Wilson 10-23-1847 O
Bedford, James to E. M. Harris 3-14-1861 O
Bedford, James to Elizabeth Latimer 11-18-1854 (11-23-1854) O

Bedford, James to Jane Cunningham 5-19-1854 (5-21-1854) Sh
Bedford, James to Mary E. Harper 9-15-1850 (10-4-1850) O
Bedford, John to Eliza Parker 9-12-1862 (9-18-1862) F
Bedford, Julian to Virginia R. Kenney 8-4-1851 (8-5-1851) Sh
Bedford, Lawson P. to Susan S. Lovelace 12-27-1860 L
Bedingfield, S. W. to Sallie McClenahan 11-9-1874 (11-11-1874) T
Bedwell, Reuben to Mary J. T. Stigall 6-29-1858 Hn
Beechum, John H. to Susan Read 7-12-1859 Hr
Beehn, C. A. to Molly P. Torry 8-12-1861 (8-13-1861) Sh
Been?, Dempsey to Mary J. B. Beach 11-29-1849 Hn
Beer, A. to Matilda Albert 12-30-1862 Sh
Beesley, David to Lacy Rasbury 11-4-1839 Be
Behan, John to Bridget A. Lowrie 5-30-1862 Sh
Behmer, Jacob to Adaline Fannell 5-30-1877 (no return) Hy
Behns, John to Mary Ann Gibson 2-5-1870 Ma
Behrens, Conrad to Heding Finn 12-17-1855 Sh
Beim? (Benim?), Wm. to Mary Hines 1-31-1853 Sh
Beith (Birth), Robt. H. to Martha Powers 1-10-1856 Sh
Belan, Stephen to Lucy Brooks 10-5-1870 F B
Belch, Elisha to Mulinda Walls 1-6-1844 (2-3-1844) G
Beleau (Belew), Joseph to Mary A. Sexton 2-18-1850 Sh
Belerford, Rewbin to Millie Miller 4-27-1873 Cr B
Belew, Aaron W. to Jane Belew 3-6-1841 (3-9-1841) G
Belew, G. T. to Martha McCollum 5-25-1870 (5-26-1870) Cr
Belew, Giles to Martha Braswell 2-13-1864 Cr
Belew, Giles to Martha Braswell 2-13-1864 (no return) Cr
Belew, Giles to Tennessee Flippin 7-31-1856 (8-3-1856) Cr
Belew, Governor to Elizabeth Scott 11-13-1850 (11-14-1850) G
Belew, Governor to Sarah Ann Bryant 1-2-1854 (1-4-1854) G
Belew, Harvy to Rachal Holcomb 8-14-1839 Cr
Belew, Hosea to Wilmouth Murphy 1-23-1839 Cr
Belew, James M. to S. L. D. Capps 9-12-1867 G
Belew, James R. to Verona A. Hardy 12-22-1869 (12-23-1869) Cr
Belew, James W. to N. C. Pinckley 11-9-1870 (11-10-1870) Cr
Belew, James to Mariah Staten 11-19-1867 G
Belew, Jim to Mary Pratt 3-13-1869 G
Belew, John G. to Mamaret? Mitchell 10-?-1860 (10-24-1860) Cr
Belew, John, jr. to Mary Flippin 11-1-1866 G
Belew, Martin to Patsey Bryant 11-15-1853 (11-17-1853) G
Belew, N. H. to Currillea J. Hardy 11-23-1870 (no return) Cr
Belew, Oliver to Ellen Vaden 1-16-1869 G
Belew, R. to Polly Kittle 8-26-1838 Cr
Belew, Thos. to Elizabeth Phillips 2-13-1844 Cr
Belew, W. M. to M. A. Strong 1-31-1867 G
Belew, William M. to Vandelia Belew 1-15-1870 G
Belieu, Wm. C. to Sarale A. J. Neely? 4-15-1846 (4-16-1846) Hr
Beliles, Ira to Lucinda Smith 6-6-1835 Hr
Belinger, W. to Caroline Sorrells 11-29-1842 Sh
Bell, A. E. to M. E. Childress 5-20-1867 (5-21-1867) L
Bell, A. J. to Ruth E. Carter 1-6-1848 Cr
Bell, Aaron S. to Susanna W. Townsend 2-11-1851 (2-13-1851) T
Bell, Alexander to Louisa C. Corbitt 9-26-1858 Be
Bell, Alexander to Sarah Roberts 9-16-1871 T
Bell, Allen to Margaret J. Leach 12-26-1849 Cr
Bell, Anderson to Emaline Carson 12-27-1870 (1-2-1871) Cr B
Bell, Andrew D. to Alcy Mathis 2-21-1849 O
Bell, Andrew to Alcey Mathis 2-21-1849 O
Bell, Andrew to Alcy Mathis 2-21-1849 O
Bell, Andrew to Parolle Yeates 10-21-1852 G
Bell, B. to Elizabeth Smally 1-2-1856 Be
Bell, Ben to Cohaly? Bumpas 7-28-1866 (7-29-1866) T
Bell, Benjamin to Elizabeth Sneed 12-29-1860 (12-31-1860) Hr
Bell, Benjamin to Olivia Ervin 4-24-1857 Hr
Bell, Benjamin to Polly Fox 12-5-1834 Hr
Bell, Burrell to Mary Thomas 7-10-1852 Be
Bell, Burwell to D. Dary Nichols 8-21-1855 Be
Bell, C. C. to Tenny Lee 5-1-1870 G
Bell, Charly to Mary Adaline Yates 11-17-1852 Be
Bell, Cit L. to Sallie Webb 3-8-1871 Ma
Bell, David D. to Martha G. Gibbs 4-9-1846 Ma
Bell, David to Elisza Ornsby 8-21-1826 (8-23-1826) Hr
Bell, David to Mary A. S. Dinwiddie 12-23-1850 (no return) Hn
Bell, Davis N. to Melvina Fariss 11-21-1832 Hr
Bell, Dennis to Nancy Beasley 2-5-1855 Be
Bell, Durant H. to Mary S. Hill 3-12-1838 Sh
Bell, Eli M. to Martha King 4-16-1845 T
Bell, G. G. to Henrietta Pinkard 12-30-1854 (12-31-1854) Sh
Bell, George N. to Delizar Woods 12-20-1855 G
Bell, George W. to Martha Bragg 10-2-1845 T
Bell, George W. to Mary Gryson (Guyson) 6-16-1842 Sh
Bell, George to Emma Tinsley 9-7-1872 T
Bell, Harvey to Martha Bell 1-3-1871 (1-10-1871) Dy
Bell, Henry to Catharine Jones 5-25-1867 Dy
Bell, Henry to Martha Neel 11-1-1869 T
Bell, I. M. to L. E. Wallis 1-23-1867 O
Bell, Ira to Sritha Ann Wilson 9-15-1860 (9-16-1860) L
Bell, Ira to Winna Angeline Bassham 2-25-1844 O

Bell, Isaac to Jennie Johnson 12-24-1868 (12-28-1868) Cr
Bell, J. H. to Eizabeth Allen 12-14-1870 Hy
Bell, J. J. to Margaret Newbill 12-29-1857 Cr
Bell, J. P. to M. J. Radford 5-16-1867 Dy
Bell, Jackson to Lucinda Ritchie 1-29-1853 Sh
Bell, Jacob to Ellen Brown 12-28-1867 (12-13?-1868) F B
Bell, James C. to E. A. White 12-21-1853 Cr
Bell, James G. to Adelia Neely 4-26-1831 Hr
Bell, James G. to Ann M. Carney 2-17-1852 (2-19-1852) G
Bell, James L. to Francis J. Harris 9-27-1859 (no return) We
Bell, James to Michel Bell 5-8-1832 G
Bell, James to Susan J. Willis 9-26-1850 G
Bell, Jarret to Vicy Bassham 2-14-1839 O
Bell, Jarrett to Easter Wright 10-15-1845 (10-16-1845) O
Bell, John F. to Lenora King 12-24-1864 G
Bell, John G. to Mary C. Taylor 11-10-1856 Ma
Bell, John G. to Mary P. Holland 1-6-1862 (no return) Dy
Bell, John H. to Lucy A. Smith 10-9-1866 Ma
Bell, John N. to Elizabeth M. Serratt 5-14-1840 G
Bell, John N. to Ruth A. Raines 8-25-1859 G
Bell, John W. to Delia Hewett 2-13-1879 (2-16-1879) L
Bell, John W. to Flora Jones 5-6-1869 F B
Bell, John W. to Georgia E. Bond 7-29-1871 (no return) Hy
Bell, John W. to Sarah Bell 6-2-1849 (6-5-1849) G
Bell, John Wesley to Indiana A. Harwell 4-2-1877 (4-4-1877) Dy
Bell, John to Callie Holliday 2-10-1875 (no return) Hy
Bell, John to Caroline White 9-9-1849 Cr
Bell, John to Lucy Ann Blackwell 1-17-1847 Be
Bell, John to Mary Delany (Delary?) 11-13-1852 Sh
Bell, John to Racheal Box 5-17-1832 (5-24?-1832) Hr
Bell, John to Susan A. White 7-21-1862 (no return) Hy
Bell, Jonathan to Sarah Culp 10-27-1871 (no return) Cr
Bell, Joseph to Lucinda Hall 10-11-1845 Cr
Bell, Joseph to Mary Jane Montgomery 12-28-1840 Ma
Bell, Joshua to Louisa Bledsoe 10-19-1833 (10-22-1833) G
Bell, L. B. to Mary L. Shearin 9-28-1865 Hy
Bell, Lafayett to Elizabeth I. Hall 1-11-1859 We
Bell, Leroy to Martha Glascock 11-12-1838 G
Bell, M. (Dr.) to L. H. Strickland 4-23-1859 (not endorsed) Sh
Bell, M. M. to M. M. Bell 9-2-1858 Cr
Bell, M. to Sue H. Ligon 5-16-1865 (5-17-1865) T
Bell, Manroe to Sallie A. Jordan 9-12-1867 G
Bell, Martin to Mattie Wilson 8-19-1867 (8-24-1867) F B
Bell, Matthew to Rachael J. Penick 12-23-1840 Hn
Bell, Mayfield to Jane Morris 11-28-1855 (12-3-1855) Hr
Bell, Moses to Sarah Coleman 4-25-1867 (no return) F B
Bell, N. D. to Harriet G. Warfield 11-10-1857 Sh
Bell, Ned to Mollie Branch 12-17-1871 Hy
Bell, Peyton S. to Matilda (Mrs.) Oliver 8-4-1862 (8-10-1862) Ma
Bell, Pinckney to Malinda Russell 7-18-1866 O
Bell, R. D. to Elizabeth M. Shofner 1-10-1866 Cr
Bell, R. J. to U. J. Phillips 11-27-1868 (11-29-1868) Cr
Bell, Ransom H. to Zelphia J. Brigance 1-24-1870 (1-25-1870) Ma
Bell, Richard to Elvira Lang 4-4-1859 (4-7-1859) L
Bell, Robert B. to Katie Green 10-14-1876 (10-17-1876) L
Bell, Robert to Mary Owen 8-10-1870 (8-11-1870) T
Bell, Robert to Ruth A. New 2-15-1851 G
Bell, Robt. to Lue Clay 10-5-1870 (10-6-1870) Cr
Bell, S. M. to A. L. Cotheran 2-17-1874 (2-18-1874) T
Bell, Samuel H. to Sarah C. Bigham 9-28-1865 (10-22-1865) T
Bell, Samuel J. to Frances B. Montgomery 1-16-1849 Ma
Bell, Samuel J. to Rebecca Ann Cauley 7-20-1846 (7-22-1846) L
Bell, Samuel to Elizabeth R. E. A. Robinson 11-26-1846 Sh
Bell, Samuel to Mary Beard 12-2-1869 (12-4-1869) Cr
Bell, Spencer to Jane Mitchell 8-5-1869 (8-7-1869) F B
Bell, Surgeon S. J. to Harriet Craine 8-25-1864 Sh
Bell, T. N. to Sarah E. Spenser 10-3-1865 Hn
Bell, Tho. J. to Lucy A. Hudspeth 12-16-1845 (12-17-1845) F
Bell, Thomas C. to Martha Jane Bagby 1-9-1849 (no return) Hn
Bell, Thomas F. to Mary J. Reed 10-3-1869 G
Bell, Thomas H. to Jemima Duff 2-14-1833 Sh
Bell, Thomas H. to Sarena Beard 5-18-1861 Mn
Bell, Thomas W. to Mary A. Willis 12-5-1848 (not executed?) Sh
Bell, Thos. to Elizabeth Goodman 12-1'-1836 (12-22-1836) G
Bell, V. H. to Fanny Carter 1-23-1839 (-24-1839) G
Bell, V. H. to Narcissa Bradford 7-25-1859 G
Bell, Valentine to Precilla Holder 10-12-1850 (10-13-1850) G
Bell, Van S. to Elinder Rook 7-2-1833 (7-10-1833) Hr
Bell, Vollentine to Matilda T. McCall 3-10-1841 (3-21-1841) G
Bell, W. M. to June Asha Woodard 4-23-1849 Cr
Bell, W. S. to Martha J. Smith 2-22-1859 Hr
Bell, W. to J. Yarber 1-12-1842 Be
Bell, Walter D. to Susan Bondurance 9-27-1858 (9-28-1858) Sh
Bell, William J. to Nancy Roseman 9-19-1855 (9-20-1855) Ma
Bell, William to Ema Brooks 11-19-1865 G
Bell, William to Lucy Tucker 11-7-1878 (no return) Dy
Bell, William to Mary E. Whitlow 4-8-1843 (5-11-1843) G

Bell, William to Pernelia C. Morgan 4-1-1861 (4-3-1861) O
Bell, William to Sarah Alston 4-25-1872 (4-27-1872) T
Bell, Willis to Lavinia Patterson 1-27-1876 Dy
Bell, Wm. A. to Joe Winsett 10-19-1865 (10-22-1865) F
Bell, Wm. J. A. to Josephine S. Moore 9-29-1842 Sh
Bell, Wm. M. to Mary Jane James 2-25-1868 G
Bell, Wm. to Mary Greer 9-15-1861 Be
Bell, Wm. to Mary M. Bobby 10-12-1857 Cr
Bellamy, Chas. E. to Elizabeth W. Croom 5-11-1858 (5-12-1858) Sh
Bellar, Mosel? to Missouri Elder 3-1-1869 (3-3-1869) T
Bellew, Aaron to Nancy E. Quinn 5-22-1858 Cr
Bellew, J. F. to Martha C. Herron? 12-11-1865 (no return) Cr
Bellew, John L. to Susan H. Phillips 2-9-1862 (no return) Cr
Bellew, John W. to M. E. Black 12-26-1871 (12-27-1871) Cr
Bellew, R. A. to Elizabeth Fuqua 9-14-1866 Cr
Bellew, R. H. to E. J. Fite 9-17-1872 (9-18-1872) Cr
Bellfield, Wm. B. to Elizabeth Costillo 12-26-1861 Sh
Belliew, W. H. to Vandalia Belliew 9-10-1870 Cr
Bellows?, Z. T. to Penelope E. Burrow 10-3-1860 (10-7-1860) Cr
Bells, William B. to Sarah J. Sexton 1-3-1849 (1-4-1849) G
Bellue, Joseph to Mary McCleur 5-29-1837 G
Beloate, John M. to Mary F. Godbey 1-10-1871 (1-11-1871) F
Belote, Benj. R. to Mary J. Wooden 12-28-1856 Hr
Belote, Brown to Tennessee Ann Williams 8-28-1846 (no return) F
Belote, Charles R. to Nancy E. White 8-31-1854 Ma
Belote, George W. to Rachel S. Glass 6-2-1838 Hr
Belote, John to Mary J. Scott 12-10-1858 (12-14-1858) Sh
Belote, Smith C. to Lydia M. Rogers 7-15-1844 F
Belote, Smith C. to Maryann Williams 7-10-1848 (no return) F
Belotte, Clement to Rebecca Standback 7-23-1855 (8-16-1855) Hr
Belotte, John S. to Amanda Moore 2-11-1853 Hr
Belotte, William N. to Rebecca J. Williams 10-31-1854 (11-2-1854) Hr
Belton, J. P. to Nancy M. Ledbetter 12-6-1882 (12-7-1882) L
Belton, James to Julia Olds 1-8-1862 (1-9-1862) Dy
Belue, George to Sarah E. Dollar 6-7-1854 (6-8-1854) Ma
Beluw, J. M. to Martha Hall 1-9-1860 (1-10-1860) G
Bemis?, L. C. to Helen Spain 12-6-1873 (12-7-1873) Dy
Benchbark, T. G. to Catharine E. Tomlinson 7-8-1852 (no return) F
Bendall, Francis M. to Louisa J. Kirk ?-?-1861? Mn
Bender, Louis to Nancy Jane Lane 6-15-1861 Sh
Benderbis(Bardelis?), Fidelis (Felix) to Elizabeth Darrett (Dennett?) 8-22-1853 (9-4-1853) Sh
Benett, William to Julia Jefferson 4-5-1870 Hy
Benge, M. L. to Jane Strong 1-1-1840 Sh
Benge, S. D. to Demetria L. Marshal 12-16-1868 G
Benham, John W. to Mary E. Goodwin 12-30-1848 G
Benham, V. M. to Isabella S. Snow 7-27-1867 Dy
Beninger, William H. to Caroline C. Gate 12-25-1843 (12-28-1843) F
Benjamin, S. C. to Harriet D. May 12-9-1857 (12-10-1857) Ma
Benjes (Burgis), William to Catharine Wagner 4-22-1850 Sh
Benken, Jacob to Mary Frick 8-24-1854 Sh
Benner, John F. to Charlotte Heinz (Heiney) 9-10-1842 Sh
Bennet, Benjamin F. to Frances G. Kelley 2-19-1846 Sh
Bennet, Elijah to Mlda? B. Grant 7-3-1855 (7-4-1855) Ma
Bennett, A. A. to Asplie Morgan 8-6-1840 Cr
Bennett, A. D. to Irene E. Mitchell 1-17-1841 Cr
Bennett, A. M. to Martha A. Spellings 12-31-1872 (no return) Cr
Bennett, Alex to Martha Helms 8-24-1876 Hy
Bennett, Alexander to Jane Riley 11-12-1857 Cr
Bennett, Archibald to Nancy Taylor 7-25-1839 Cr
Bennett, Benjamine to Elizabeth McCain 12-6-1872 (12-7-1872) Cr
Bennett, Duwery to Nancy Bennett 8-28-1853 Be
Bennett, E. G. H. to Mary B. Dewitt 1-7-1866 Cr
Bennett, E. H. to Martha J. Allen 11-29-1870 (11-30-1870) F
Bennett, Elijah to Nelly Hanline 4-8-1841 Hn
Bennett, Elisha to Margaret Horton 1-23-1840 Cr
Bennett, Ezekiel to Nancy Durham 9-7-1849 Sh
Bennett, Ezekil to Rebecca Guardner 6-4-1855 (6-7-1855) T
Bennett, F. T. to Sarah S. Austin 1-7-1852 We
Bennett, Francis E. to Isabella P. Tranthan 3-3-1858 (3-4-1858) Sh
Bennett, Francis to Louisa Leslie 6-15-1852 Cr
Bennett, Franklin to Malinda Lee 10-31-1843 F
Bennett, G. W. to Nancy Edwards 9-17-1846 Cr
Bennett, Geo. W. to L. F. Regenn 12-1-1857 G
Bennett, George M. to Mary Kirby 4-15-1857 (4-16-1857) Ma
Bennett, George W. to Catharine Potter 12-18-1861 (no return) Hy
Bennett, George W. to Lutitia P. Palmer 12-19-1860 (12-20-1860) Cr
Bennett, Green to Mary Ammons 8-20-1845 (8-21-1845) F
Bennett, Hiram L. to Mary A. Brown 11-18-1866 Hn
Bennett, James F. to Sarah F. Taylor 8-4-1856 G
Bennett, James to Bridget Brady 4-9-1864 (4-11-1864) Sh
Bennett, John H. to Sarah Norwood 11-29-1858 Cr
Bennett, John N. to Nancy Webb 1-19-1856 Cr
Bennett, John T. to Elizabeth Bennett 8-21-1845 Hn
Bennett, John to Elizabeth Wilson 9-13-1848 Hr
Bennett, John to Jane Osborne 12-13-1853 (12-15-1853) Sh
Bennett, John to Margaret Shaw 5-8-1840 (5-12-1840) T

Bennett, John to Martha Webb 6-28-1871 Dy
Bennett, John to Nancy Cisco 10-26-1851 Be
Bennett, John to Susan Turner 3-25-1873 (3-27-1873) O
Bennett, Joseph to Eliza Taylor 3-24-1856 (3-25-1856) Sh
Bennett, Joshua E. to Adelia N. Garvin 3-18-1864 (3-22-1864) F
Bennett, Josiah to Marinda M. Brown 9-2-1850 (9-17-1850) Hr
Bennett, L. T. to Elizabeth N. Leremore 4-25-1854 Sh
Bennett, Larkin to Emaly Wilson 11-9-1857 Hn
Bennett, McKinney to Jane Edwards 2-22-1847 O
Bennett, Milam R. to Elizabeth Myers 12-3-1846 Cr
Bennett, Powhatton P. to Sue Matthews 12-16-1868 (12-19-1868) Ma
Bennett, Richard to Matilda Bass 7-31-1839 Ma
Bennett, S. P. to S. A. M. Caldwell 12-21-1843 Hn
Bennett, Samuel H. to Martha A. Williams 10-29-1868 Cr
Bennett, T. T. to Nancy Jane Lumpkin 8-24-1858 (8-25-1858) Sh
Bennett, T. W. to Ragile G. Hood 10-5-1848 (no return) F
Bennett, Vincent A. to Mary Edwards 9-7-1833 (9-8-1833) O
Bennett, W. C. to Eliza J. Snodgrass 10-18-1855 We
Bennett, W. G. to E. J. Mitchell 9-8-1860 Ma
Bennett, W. R. to Martha A. Hammett 4-19-1857 Cr
Bennett, W. T. to L. K. Price 6-25-1865 G
Bennett, W. T. to Matilda Scott 6-15-1856 Cr
Bennett, Whiten to Jottee Palmon 7-17-1869 Hy
Bennett, William A. to Lusinda Stations 7-22-1848 (no return) F
Bennett, William A. to Matilda Manaskco 12-28-1848 Sh
Bennett, William A. to Susan O. Land 11-12-1861 Hr
Bennett, William F. to Martha S. Cobb 12-8-1869 Cr
Bennett, William J. to Emma L. Cannon 11-2-1853 Hn
Bennett, William K. to Eliza A. Read 3-1-1849 (3-5-1849) Ma
Bennett, William to Elizabeth Simpson 5-8-1875 (no return) Hy
Bennett, William to J. C. Laxton 7-19-1873 (7-20-1873) T
Bennett, William to Winny Cunningham 11-11-1846 Be
Bennett, Wm. K. to Margaret Moore 2-24-1869 Hy
Bennett, Wm. to Elizabeth Pace 3-30-1871 Cr
Benns, L. C. to Emily Spain 12-6-1871 (12-7-1871) Dy
Benson, Benjamin B. to Rosa P. Farrar 8-14-1848 (8-?-1848) T
Benson, Cullen to Margaret Parmer 2-7-1839 Hr
Benson, Cullin to Edny Pate 7-1-1835 Hr
Benson, E. A. to Carrie C. Williamson 2-17-1862 (2-19-1862) Sh
Benson, Earby to Susan Stacy 9-25-1852 (no return) F
Benson, Geo. W. to Allice Bevel 11-25-1859 (11-27-1859) G
Benson, H. W. to M. E. Jamison 12-16-1873 (12-17-1873) T
Benson, Henry to Ellin Carter 9-2-1839 (no return) F
Benson, J. W. to Elizabeth Harden 1-20-1862 Mn
Benson, James R. to Elizabeth Pate 11-30-1836 Hr
Benson, James to Nancy E. Newman 10-2-1858 (10-7-1858) Hr
Benson, Jesse to Mary J. Eason 10-17-1846 (no return) F
Benson, Jessee C. to A. A. Byrd 2-14-1868 (2-20-1868) T
Benson, John W. to Mary A. Lee 3-7-1844 We
Benson, Martin to Martha J. Furgenson 12-3-1849 (12-4-1849) G
Benson, P. D. to A. J. Humphreys 8-18-1843 (9-8-1843) F
Benson, Pleasant Davis to Catharine Sharp 1-11-1850 (1-16-1850) T
Benson, R. C. to Emily F. Madden 2-26-1859 (3-1-1859) Sh
Benson, Ricahrd I. to Narcisas Smith 10-23-1849 G
Benson, Robt. W. to Frances D. Moore 5-4-1859 (5-5-1859) Hr
Benson, Tom to Rachel Rainor 1-18-1868 Hy
Benson, Uzzell to Cely Johnson 6-16?-1833 Hr
Benson, William A. to E. I. Blackmon 9-22-1842 Ma
Benson, William to Sarah E. Lawhorn 10-19-1858 (10-26-1858) Hr
Benthel, James L. to Louisa C. Adkins 4-22-1857 G
Benthel, James L. to Martha E. Bass 4-6-1848 G
Benthel, Laban to Teracey (Mrs.) Adcock 3-31-1846 G
Benthill, William to Frances A. Durley 1-12-1854 G
Bentley, David H. to Mary Williams 12-16-1834 Sh
Bentley, George B. to Minerva George 10-18-1848 Sh
Bentley, James A. to Elizabeth Coffee 12-15-1845 (12-18-1845) F
Bentley, John W. to Ellender George 3-14-1855 Sh
Bentley, K. H. to P. I. Ferguson 2-25-1861 (no return) Dy
Bentley, Nazareth J. to Mary T. Smith 9-19-1867 (9-20-1867) L
Bentley, W. R. to Martha M. Ferguson 12-14-1860 (12-19-1860) Dy
Bentley, Walter E. to Amanda E. Carnell 1-1-1884 (1-2-1884) L
Bentley, William J. to Edna C. Barnes 1-11-1881 (1-12-1881) L
Bently, D. H. to Elizabeth C. Phillips 12-27-1852 (no return) F
Benton, A. to Mary Ann Wardlaw 2-27-1839 (3-7-1839) L
Benton, B. L. to Sarah S. Brown 9-18-1869 (9-19-1869) Cr
Benton, Ben F. to Mattie Harper 12-2-1874 L
Benton, D. W. to E. Cotton 4-24-1842 Be
Benton, H. H. to Rebecca Jones 8-15-1866 (8-16-1866) Cr
Benton, J. F. to Mattie P. Sullivan 12-22-1874 (12-23-1874) T
Benton, J. W. to Eliza C. Taylor 2-18-1859 (2-20-1859) Sh
Benton, James to Martha Adams 7-31-1845 Hr
Benton, James to Nancy Fields 7-11-1837 Hr
Benton, Jas. M. to Martha J. Davis 9-25-1866 (9-27-1866) Cr
Benton, John B. to L. J. Rowland 12-30-1852 L
Benton, John T. to Sophronia A. Brown 11-22-1867 (11-23-1867) Cr
Benton, Nathaniel to Nancy A. Stribling 9-12-1848 (9-13-1848) Ma
Benton, R. M. Johnson to Fanny Sawyer 12-22-1869 (no return) Dy

Benton, Robert F. to Frances E. Barnes 8-31-1852 (no return) F
Benton, Robt. R. to Nancy Hill 12-23-1849 Be
Benton, Thomas H. to Mary E. Eason 7-1-1847 O
Benton, W. E. to S. J. Cole 2-20-1866 (2-21-1866) O
Benton, Wm. B. to Sarah J. McAuly 1-31-1856 Cr
Benton, Wm. C. to Mary Cupps 7-10-1838 Cr
Beram, M. to Wm. S. Wright 3-9-1847 (3-14-1847) O
Beranes?, James to Mary Monroe 12-6-1860 (11-6-1860?) O
Berdon, August to Mary Broeg 9-1-1859 (9-6-1859) Sh
Berdon, Gustavus to Martha T. Baugh 6-11-1867 (6-18-1867) F
Berdsell, Geo. to Mary Shannors 6-7-1864 Sh
Beretto, Alexander to Josephine Staggs 2-25-1854 (2-26-1854) Sh
Berg (Berry), August (Orguse) to Kate Makeman 4-11-1861 Sh
Berg, Henry to Catharine Alt 11-13-1860 Sh
Berge, Richard H. to Jane G. Hall 11-27-1834 G
Berges, E. G. to M. J. Hightower 12-15-1873 (12-16-1873) T
Bergmann, Geo. to Lisetta Baling 12-29-1858 (12-30-1858) Sh
Beriam, Robert to May Eller Hill 11-28-1871 (11-29-1871) T
Berkle (Ruckle?), Jacob to Rebecca Vorwerk 3-29-1860 Sh
Berkley, William B. to Lucy Ann Arun 9-5-1855 (no return) Hn
Berlen, Ben to Jenny Stokely 2-10-1876 (no return) Hy
Berman, Joseph to Alvina Beuhl 4-16-1857 Sh
Bernard, Adolph to Maria C. Rodner 10-6-1860 (10-7-1860) Sh
Bernard, Anthony to Alice Hall 3-27-1869 (3-28-1869) T
Bernard, Benj. to ___ane Hall 9-9-1865 T
Bernard, Chas. L. to Eliza (Mrs.) Stanback 11-26-1857 Sh
Bernard, Frank to Hager Murphy 2-6-1871 (3-5-1871) T
Bernard, Henry to Selina Middleton 9-18-1861 (9-19-1861) Sh
Bernard, Johnson to Felia Lowe 8-7-1872 (1-16-1872?) T
Bernard, Mingo to Lucy Harris 12-27-1871 (12-28-1871) T
Bernard, Saml. P. to Nancy Cotton 2-13-1854 T
Bernard, Samuel P. to Lucy B. McLemore 3-24-1846 Sh
Bernard, Vincent to Therace Baty (Batty, Bety?) 10-10-1863 Sh
Bernard, Wm. to Rachel Booker 12-24-1867 T
Berners, F. to Eliza A. Trenton 4-24-1861 Sh
Berry, A. S. to M. F. Hobday 8-4-1877 (no return) Dy
Berry, A. to Mariah Jenkins 5-3-1854 We
Berry, Abraham W. to Martha E. Thornton? 5-20-1849 F
Berry, Albert to Rosey Ann Vester 12-27-1855 Be
Berry, Alfred to Pernicy Nix 10-3-1839 Hn
Berry, Daniel D. to D. M. Guin? 4-12-1831 Hr
Berry, Edwin to Josie Hill 9-30-1863 (10-1-1863) Sh
Berry, Fenwick H. to Elizabeth Koen 10-8-1841 Sh
Berry, Isaac G. to Martha Melton 3-11-1851 Be
Berry, J. H. C. to Jennie Pursley 11-29-1863 O
Berry, J. L. to Martha J. E. Grier 2-20-1861 G
Berry, J. W. F. to Pheby Jane Melton 7-29-1850 Be
Berry, J. W. T. to M. M. Saxton 3-1-1868 G
Berry, James T. to Louisa J. Crocket 7-1-1858 We
Berry, James T. to Mary E. Bucy 1-22-1857 Hn
Berry, James to Martha Wheatley 3-1-1860 Be
Berry, James to Mary Holland 11-9-1852 Be
Berry, James to Tennessee C. Berry 12-5-1864 Be
Berry, John to Betheny Hill 1-25-1851 (1-26-1851) G
Berry, John to Mary Johnson 2-15-1872 Hy
Berry, M. S. to Nancy Rochell 11-21-1868 (11-22-1868) Cr
Berry, Martin R. to Jane Hallum 3-7-1863 (3-8-1863) Sh
Berry, Newton P. to Mary A. Lett 2-10-1862 (2-11-1862) Cr
Berry, Reddiee to Catherine Allen 12-12-1843 (12-13-1843) G
Berry, Reuben to Phebe Ann Flowers 8-14-1868 (8-29-1868) L *
Berry, Richard to Martha Berry 9-6-1858 G
Berry, Samuel J. S. to Julia A. E. Dickson 10-20-1855 (10-24-1855) G
Berry, Samuel S. to Elizabeth Anderson 3-7-1854 Be
Berry, Simon to Eliza J. Delany 1-13-1848 T
Berry, T. B. to Fannie Pugh 5-6-1871 (5-7-1871) Dy
Berry, Thomas D. to Kate L. Bacon 12-16-1867 O
Berry, Thomas F. to Mary Pearson 3-10-1870 Ma
Berry, Timothy to Margaret White 11-8-1859 Sh
Berry, W. J. to Angeline Williams 12-21-1868 (12-23-1868) T
Berry, Will H. to Sarah A. Crews 1-25-1845 Hn
Berry, William L. to Jennie Lampkins 10-10-1861 Hn
Berry, William M. to Sarah M. Bargo 10-24-1844 We
Berry, William P. to Jane Lyon 2-16-1841 (no return) Hn
Berry, William to Lucinda Kuykendall 9-14-1854 Hn
Berry, William to Mary Jane Vester 2-8-1854 Be
Berry, Wm. C. to Milly C. Runnels 4-3-1844 Cr
Berry, Z. H. to Andromedia Vickers 12-24-1872 Cr
Berry, Zachriah Richard to Martha Rodgers 9-6-1858 (9-16-1858) G
Berry, Zack to Mary Lankford 8-10-1867 G
Berryhill, A. A. to Jane Scott 12-16-1849 Cr
Berryhill, J. J. to C. C. Gwinn 10-11-1871 (10-12-1871) Cr
Berryhill, J. T. to N. P. Pettyjohn 2-20-1869 (2-21-1869) Cr
Berryhill, Jas. M. to Salina Vincent 12-8-1841 Sh
Berryhill, John to Everline Brawner 3-13-1863 (no return) We
Berryhill, W. J. to Jerlien Stanfield 8-9-1863 Cr
Berryhill, Wm. J. to Jerleen Stanfield 8-?-1863 (no return) Cr
Berson, Henry V. to Narcissa Harbert 11-28-1877 Hy

Berson?, Guilliame to Bassie Elder 4-8-1869 G
Bert?, Henry C. to Mary Wade 10-26-1844 (10-31-1844) F
Berten, Leon to Mary Maretto 12-8-1862 Sh
Berthold, W. F. to Mary Ann Pfisterer 10-30-1858 Sh
Berton, August to Louisa Hessing 6-27-1864 Sh
Bertow, Richard C. to Martha J. Powers 3-23-1848 Hn
Bertow, William L. to Martha W. Bertow 3-16-1848 Hn
Bertram, Benjamin F. to Martha Dodd 1-14-1849 Hn
Bertram, J. W. to Mary Belote 1-10-1872 (1-11-1872) Dy
Bertschi, Henry to Ida Kranche 2-11-1860 Sh
Bertschi, Rudolph to Jennie Brunschwiler 2-7-1862 (2-10-1862) Sh
Beson, James M. to Carolin Thomas 12-22-1869 (12-25-1869) T
Besor, Louis to Sarah Dunn 7-10-1855 (7-13-1855) Sh
Bess, Richard to Eleanor (Mrs.) McCrory 4-30-1857 Ma
Bessent, B. A. to Mollie Williamson 12-7-1877 (12-8-1877) Dy
Bessent, J. C. to S. E. Veazey 6-16-1869 G
Bessent, James to M. E. Cooper 3-17-1879 (3-18-1879) Dy
Bessent, Milton to Mary Richardson 10-2-1867 G
Bessent, Plesant R. to E. T. Morris 12-18-1867 (12-19-1867) Dy
Best, E. B. to Mary Smith 8-31-1882 (9-3-1882) L
Best, E. to Mary Smith 4-5-1882 (9-3-1882) L
Best, Ebenezer to Harriet Braden 8-7-1856 L
Best, Ebenezer to Mary Jane Sanders 7-7-1858 L
Best, Ebenzer to Sarah Mackey 12-24-1835 Sh
Best, Eligia to Ida Ashmore 7-16-1877 (7-17-1877) L
Best, J. W. to C. T. McMahan 10-6-1872 Hy
Best, J. W. to Elizabeth J. Hutchison 8-5-1861 (no return) L
Best, J. W. to Sarah Wiseman 2-5-1868 T
Best, Jno. C. to Winnie Miller 12-21-1871 Hy
Best, John W. to Martha A. Sanders 8-8-1849 Sh
Best, Jordan to Phoebe Mann 9-16-1879 (9-24-1879) L B
Best, R. H. to M. J. Dearren 11-6-1865 (11-14-1865) F
Best, Richard to Mary Moss 12-7-1853 (12-11-1853) G
Best, Richard to Minerva Bird 4-12-1863 G
Best, Robert A. to Flora M. McIntyre 10-14-1884 (10-16-1884) L
Best, William P. to Elizabeth J. Young 1-21-1847 Sh
Best, Wm. to Elizabeth Mackey 9-24-1847 Sh
Bethany, Charles H. to Martha A. Pierce 7-8-1861 Be
Bethel, William G. to Nancy M. Miles 8-26-1850 O
Bethell, Wm. D. to Julia Donaldson 10-30-1837 G
Bethewen, J. H. to D. A. Taylor 1-9-1873 (1-12-1873) Cr
Bethill, John M. to Mary M. Gee 2-12-1844 Cr
Bethshares, George to Louisa Thomas 3-19-1870 Ma
Bethshares, H. H. to Jane P. McFarland 9-24-1861 G
Bethshares, P. F. to Martha E. Carrick 7-28-1861 G
Bethsheres, Wm. to Exeline Hargett 3-9-1863 (no return) Hy
Bethune, Allen to Heneritta Busby 7-31-1830 (8-2-1830) Ma
Bethune, J. W. to L. F. Childs 7-12-1876 (7-13-1876) L
Bettis, Anderson C. to Fannie Pryor 11-26-1856 L
Bettis, B. C. to Theodosia Owen 9-11-1871 (9-12-1871) Dy
Bettis, Jno. to Martha Ann Julian 6-4-1864 (6-5-1864) T
Bettis, John B. to Sarah A. Webb 12-17-1848 Sh
Bettis, John G. to Nancy J. Stephens(on) 1-25-1859 (1-27-1859) O
Bettis, M. V. (Mo?) to L. V. Johnson 11-21-1866 (no return) Dy
Bettis, Shelby A. to Fady J. Womack 2-12-1850 Sh
Bettis, William to Sarah Pierce 8-1-1833 Sh
Bettis, Wyatt to Margaret Coble 11-14-1839 Sh
Betts, A. F. to Elizabeth J. Woods 10-14-1854 (10-19-1854) G
Betts, A. F. to Frances Grady 4-5-1860 G
Betts, Alen to Sally Parker 12-15-1829 G
Betts, Allen to Letty Richardson 7-2-1867 G
Betts, C. C. to H. A. Jones 10-3-1862 G
Betts, F. L. to Martha Ann Clutts 1-6-1867 Hn
Betts, J. C. to Adaline Gravitt 7-5-1867 G
Betts, J. L. to Nancy C. McKinnon 11-30-1869 Hy
Betts, James to Louisa McKinnon 1-9-1866 Hy
Betts, James to Louisa Mckinnon 1-1-1866 (no return) Hy
Betts, John H. to Martha E. Ford 6-9-1859 G
Betts, John to Mary Ann Edwards 8-7-1853 Hn
Betts, Theodore to Ann C. Shabel 5-15-1849 Sh
Betts, Thomas P. to Paralee Holt 12-25-1869 G
Betty, John to Martha Tarbutton 11-25-1830 (11-30-1830) Ma
Betty, Joseph A. to Sarah E. Alexander 2-2-1852 (2-10-1852) Ma
Betty, W. T. to Nancy E. Willeford 4-25-1868 G
Betty, Wyatt to Lucy Holcomb 1-4-1867 G
Beuford, Gideon J. to Mary S. May 3-29-1852 (no return) F
Beurer, F. to Clarrissa Seitz 4-10-1858 Sh
Beurer, F. to Theresa Dutlinger 7-11-1859 (7-12-1859) Sh
Beurer, Frederick to C. Denttinger-Dutlinger 11-28-1855 Sh
Beurer, Jacob to Rosina Binkle (Burkle?) 5-31-1852 Sh
Bevans, Wiley to Mary E. Moore 11-5-1857 Sh
Bevard, James to Elizabeth Thomerson 10-26-1844 Cr
Bevel, Henry to Elizabeth Mainard 5-2-1858 Cr
Bevell, Jerome to M. R. Leshlie 12-18-1872 (12-25-1872) Cr
Bevens, Fed to Puss Currie 5-16-1872 Hy
Beveridge, John T. to Amanda M. Bledsoe 12-20-1854 (12-21-1854) Ma
Bevett, Oren D. to Ann Ray 3-30-1863 Mn

Bevil, Henry L. to Nancy Malear 7-26-1845 Hn
Bevil, William M. to Julia Thomas 10-23-1851 Hn
Bevill, Andrew H. to Mollie Kirby 12-13-1866 Ma
Bevill, Elisha to Nancy Scott 10-9-1853 Hn
Bevill, George M. to Lucinda J. Rains 8-9-1855 (no return) Hn
Bevill, Harrison to Parthenia Cross 12-19-1843 Hn
Bevill, Hogekiah to Sarah A. Dunn 3-27-1856 Hn
Bevill, James to Emaline Hinchey 9-14-1851 Hn
Bevill, John to Harriet C. Whitlock 10-21-1850 Hn
Bevill, Marcus L. to Emily Brown 10-4-1860 Ma
Bevill, Newton J. to Martha J. Blackwood 6-21-1860 Hn
Bevill, Newton J. to Mary Ann Potter 3-16-1858 Hn
Bevill, Richard J. to Mary J. Lee 12-12-1867 (no return) Hn
Bevill, Thomas to Elizabeth Radford 9-15-1853 Hn
Bevill, Vivont to Melissa Capell 5-6-1859 (no return) Hy
Bevill, Wesley B. to Susan A. Roberts 10-9-1856 Ma
Bevill, William G. to Rebecca Malear 8-16-1844 Hn
Bevill, William M. to Elizabeth Hogan 6-12-1865 (no return) Hn
Bevils, Henry R. to Elizabeth G. Taylor 12-22-1832 Hr
Bevins, A. to Elizabeth Iley 12-18-1847 (12-17?-1847) F
Bevlin, Isaac to Lelia Alkire 2-13-1868 F
Bias, Cesario to Mary Jane (Mrs.) Kennedy 6-22-1846 Sh
Bibb, Alford T. to Mary E. Woodard 9-17-1857 (no return) L
Bibb, B. T. to Ann Hawkins 11-11-1867 Dy
Bibb, Benjamin F. to Mary Wilson 2-21-1851 Hr
Bibb, George I. to Lucy Wade Brooks 1-28-1847 Sh
Bibb, J. R. to H. A. Jinkens 3-1-1871 (3-2-1871) L
Bibb, John F. to Ann Eliza Hinton 3-9-1853 L
Bibb, John T. to Nannie (Mamie?) Austin 11-28-1883 L
Bibb, S. H. to Nancy Edney 2-9-1867 (2-10-1867) L
Bibb, S. R. to M. C. Childress 4-19-1882 (4-20-1882) L
Bibb, Samuel L. to M. C. Strain 7-14-1870 (7-17-1870) L
Bibb, Samuel L. to Martha L. Barnett 5-6-1847 Hn
Bibb, Stephen H. to Martha E. Forbiss 1-25-1856 (1-26-1856) L
Bibee (Jenkins?), Larkin to Mary Butler 5-22-1839 Sh
Bickers, Benjamin to Martha Woodard 8-15-1840 (8-17-1840) F
Bickers, H. E. to Jane R. Mason 7-25-1853 Hr
Bickers, Jefferson R. to Elizabeth Pace 12-22-1853 Hr
Bickers, John M. to Elizabeth Pace 8-29-1850 Hr
Bickers, John W. to D. Jane Mallay 8-7-1851 Hr
Bickers, Lewis A. to Susan Thompson 11-1-1848 Ma
Bickers, Robert to Isabella Thompson 11-1-1847 (11-18-1847) Ma
Bickers, W. H. to Cora Thompson 7-25-1882 (7-26-1882) L
Bickerstaff, H. B. to Lou A. Belote 10-19-1864 Sh
Bickerstaff, Sandford M. to California Lovell 4-13-1869 (4-14-1869) Ma
Bickerstaff, Seburn to Feliceann Gill 10-12-1826 (SB 10-26?) Sh
Bicknell, Frank to Darinda Meadows 3-23-1874 (3-25-1874) L
Bidden, Squire to Sarah Larrison 11-10-1868 G B
Biddix, J. H. to Harrett A. Latimer 8-18-1864 O
Biddle, William A. to Sarah E. Gillum 10-22-1866 (10-30-1866) Ma
Bierbrower, Charles to Joana Burk 6-26-1860 Sh
Bigby, John E. to Minerva Bigby 11-1-1874 O
Bigelow, A. W. to Bettie Nichols 11-4-1875 Dy
Bigelow, Horace to Amelia Platt 4-6-1869 Hy
Bigelow, James to Georgia Baker 2-15-1868 G
Biggart, Joseph S. to Martha E. T. Carter 3-5-1868 (no return) Cr
Biggers, A. J. to Martha E. Morrison 2-11-1850 (2-12-1850) F
Biggott, Joseph J. D. to Sarah E. Robinson 11-29-1865 G
Biggs, A. R. to Susie Jones 11-30-1870 (12-1-1870) Dy
Biggs, Benjamin to Rachel Horn 12-29-1833 Sh
Biggs, D. L. to Fannie Swinney 2-9-1843 Cr
Biggs, Henry R. to Tennessee Sanderlin 1-1-1855 (1-4-1855) Sh
Biggs, Henry to Cassanda H. Neville 4-3-1854 (no return) F
Biggs, Isaac J. to Julia Ann Greer 4-1-1852 G
Biggs, J. R. to Mollie Roberts 12-16-1864 (maybe 1863) G
Biggs, James B. to A. M. Northem 12-7-1863 G
Biggs, James H. to Mary A. McCombs 1-13-1859 G
Biggs, James to Elizabeth C. Thomasson 12-16-1847 G
Biggs, Jesse to Sophia J. Rutherford 7-18-1867 Ma
Biggs, Nehemiah to Gemima Ringold 7-8-1842 G
Biggs, Reuben W. to Miss Martha M. Hullum 12-24-1845 Hr
Biggs, Richard S. to Ellen T. Tisdale 10-17-1874 (10-18-1874) Dy
Biggs, Ruben W. to Elizabeth Sellars 3-2-1830 (3-22-1830) G
Biggs, S. T. to Martha J. Bridges 10-26-1864 Be
Biggs, Stephen J. to Elizabeth C. Lockheart 7-4-1836 (7-5-1836) O
Biggs, T. R. to Pathena Berry 11-29-1865 G
Biggs, W. H. to Katie A. Jones 7-25-1877 Dy
Biggs, William E. to Elvina Hix 10-22-1856 G
Biggs, Zachariah to Elizabeth Perteat 10-31-1840 (11-1-1840) G
Biggs, Zachariah to Martha A. Penney 11-23-1837 G
Biggs, Zacheriah to Sally Dunagan 7-10-1829 (7-16-1829) G
Biggs, Zack to Tabitha G. Ellis 7-9-1861 G
Biggs, Zack, jr. to Julia E. Raines 11-21-1865 G
Bigham, Ben to Adline Bigham 2-10-1872 Cr B
Bigham, Hugh M. to Rebeckha Taylor 2-19-1831 G
Bigham, John M. to Cynthia Lee 9-29-1865 (10-1-1865) Cr
Bigham, R. L. (Dr.) to Mollie D. Fly 5-22-1867 (5-23-1867) Cr
Bigham, Robert to Fanny New 12-10-1868 (12-11-1868) Cr

Bigham, S. Y. to Margarett Morris 5-14-1860 (5-16-1860) Cr
Bigham, Silas to Rachel Hurt 9-27-1871 (9-28-1871) Cr B
Bigham, W. A. to Violet Haynes 11-5-1840 Cr
Bigham, W. L. to Cathrine Brandon 10-24-1844 Cr
Bigham, Wm. M. to Mary F. Matthews 2-12-1857 Sh
Bigley, Peter G. to Kate Flaherty 9-22-1864 (9-27-1864) Sh
Bigloe, Alfred to Mary Ann Burnam 11-13-1854 (11-16-1854) Ma
Biglow, B. S. to Alice M. Keefe 7-27-1851 Sh
Biglowe, Alonza C. to Catherine D. Covington 12-17-1862 (no return) We
Bigord, Frederick to Catherina Baker 1-8-1857? (1-8-1856?) Sh
Bilberry, F. H. to Mary Roe 3-7-1848 Cr
Bilbrey, F. M. to Nancy E. Rogers 1-17-1865 Cr
Bilbrey, W. H. to Nancy R. Wadkins 12-29-1870 Cr
Bilbro, Thaddius T. T. to C. J. Shoulders 11-26-1853 Sh
Bilbry, James C. to Nancy A. Rowe 4-17-1871 (4-20-1871) Cr
Bilch, Elisha to Mary A. E. Word 2-9-1841 G
Biles, John S. to Frances M. Shaw 6-23-1845 (6-24-1845) F
Biles, R. S. to Mary A. Kimbro 7-1-1866 G
Biles, Thomas L. to Margarett Looney 6-10-1846 Hn
Bill, Geo. W. to Sarah Wallace 7-10-1850 (no return) F
Bill, L. C. to Nancy A. Buster 10-18-1854 (no return) We
Billberry, Josiah to Martha Swain 1-1-1866 (1-10-1866) Cr
Billeps, Hamp to Rachel Tatum 12-14-1869 (no return) F B
Billing, F. T. to M. R. Roan 11-25-1868 (11-26-1868) T
Billingly, John D. to Melinda Matlock 3-8-1841 Cr
Billings, Andrew J. to Elizabeth J. Little 4-16-1856 Hn
Billings, David M. to Martha E. Williams 1-13-1866 T
Billings, F. R. to Elizabeth Orr 6-17-1847 Sh
Billings, G. W. to Ada V. Kellar 11-29-1882 (11-30-1882) L
Billings, G. W. to Catharine Pearce 1-18-1855 Hn
Billings, G. W. to Sarah F. Walker 12-11-1865 (12-19-1865) T
Billings, George W. to Jane L. Walker 11-6-1847 (11-18-1847) T
Billings, George to Keziah Barnes 5-26-1873 (5-27-1873) T
Billings, Henry Y. to Nancy Smith 8-1-1855 T
Billings, Jas. Abner to Elizabeth Roe 11-21-1855 11-21-1855 T
Billings, John to Lydia Pinkston 1-10-1849 Cr
Billings, John to Martha Witherington 12-5-1846 (12-6-1846) T
Billings, John to Mary Ann Whitson 8-29-1850 L
Billings, Spinia? to Sharlott Roe 9-3-1856 T
Billings, William H. to Amanda Shankle 7-17-1868 (7-19-1868) T
Billings, Wilson to Eliza Violet Grace 5-3-1851 (5-4-1851) T
Billingsby, Baswell to Lucinda Cooper 1-29-1850 We
Billingsby, Warren to Elizar Walker 10-7-1860 We
Billingsley, Elijah to Emeline Northcott 2-21-1828 G
Billingsley, Elijah to Rebecca Pipkins 2-25-1828 (2-26-1828) G
Billingsly, David to Elizabeth Leeton 12-31-1856 Hr
Billingsly, Elisha to Martha Fite 12-14-1829 G
Billingsly, Robert to Frances R. Thomas 12-8-1846 Ma
Billingsly, Thomas J. to Amanda A. McKaugn 2-6-1849 (2-7-1849) Hr
Billingsly, Wm. B. to Eliza P. Wilson 5-19-1851 G
Billington, James E. to Margaret A. Stevenson 2-24-1864 Hn
Billington, John H. to Nancy Gaston 10-29-1866 (10-31-1866) Ma
Billips, William J. to Elizabeth Strain 11-10-1849 (11-15-1849) G
Billoate, R. H. to A. P. Shafner 9-1-1858 G
Bills, A. S. to Nancy Dodson 12-22-1853 (12-25-1853) Hr
Bills, J. H. to Frankie Davis 12-23-1878 (no return) Dy
Bills, Leonidas to Mary Miller 5-18-1857 Hr
Bills, Wallace to Louiza J. Hardin 1-23-1852 (1-27-1852) G
Bills, Wilson T. to Lucy C. Wood 12-2-1857 Hr
Billsbury, B. J. to Adaline Jones 6-19-1873 O
Bimmer? (Beimer?), Carl to Martha Carter 12-14-1864 Sh
Bingham, Jabez to Martha S. Patterson 10-1-1855 Ma
Bingham, Robert S. to Nancy M. Nance 5-4-1843 Hn
Binkley, R. W. to Mary Campbell 11-5-1874 (no return) Dy
Binkley, Rufus N. to Mary E. (Mrs.) Willett 2-18-1869 Ma
Binkly, John G. to Levanda Carley 3-2-1850 (3-3-1850) Hr
Binson, Patrick to Phoebe Ann Wilson 12-27-1861 Sh
Binyon, William B. to Lydia J. Turner 2-21-1843 G
Birch, George W. to Catherine Swan 12-13-1858 (12-16-1858) Ma
Birch, W. A. to Emma Ferguson 12-22-1880 (12-23-1880) L
Bird, Amos R. to Martha A. Boothe 10-4-1854 Hn
Bird, Bartlett F. to Sophronia Bostrick 12-18-1850 Ma
Bird, Blackman H. to Anna Longly 7-28-1832 (8-2-1832) O
Bird, Blackman H. to Nancy M. Thompson 6-17-1843 O
Bird, Coleman to Elizabeth K. Waddy 3-4-1827 (5-6-1827) O
Bird, David to Elizabeth Legate 1-5-1854 (1-12-1854) G
Bird, Dempsey to Sarah Jane Emerson 7-15-1848 (7-20-1848) Ma
Bird, Edward A. to Ellen M. A. Moore 3-20-1861 Sh
Bird, G. W. to M. L. Allen 10-15-1870 (10-17-1870) O
Bird, Governor to Pink Kirkpatrick 4-9-1866 (no return) F B
Bird, J. C. to Mary M. Short 12-11-1856 We
Bird, J. H. to P. F. McNat 11-8-1872 (11-12-1872) T
Bird, Jack to Emma Carnes 2-23-1873 Hy
Bird, James B. to Jonnah Payne 7-24-1851 G
Bird, James C. to Eliza D. Thomas 1-31-1847 Hn
Bird, John to Caroline Mills 12-4-1842 Hn
Bird, John to Nancy Williams 8-16-1859 Hr

Bird, Joseph D. to Margaret Rebecca Howell (Harvell) 11-21-1853 (11-23-1853) O
Bird, Joseph D. to Nancy Bird 1-3-1841 Cr
Bird, King to Lizzie Skipper 12-24-1869 (12-29-1869) F B
Bird, Lewis to Lizie Howell 7-23-1874 Hy
Bird, M. T. to A. J. Hamilton 11-20-1871 T
Bird, Pinkney to Mary A. Dilling 10-24-1855 We
Bird, Robert S. to Sarah O. McMin 12-16-1867 (12-18-1867) T
Bird, S. J. to Mary F. Olds 12-15-1873 (12-16-1873) Dy
Bird, Thomas to Martha J. Barham 3-30-1843 Cr
Bird, Thomas to Rebecca Bradley 6-7-1863 Mn
Bird, W. C. to L. J. Harper 6-2-1862 (no return) Hy
Bird, Wm. C. to Sarah Ross 8-31-1858 Cr
Bird, Wyatt to Alpha Measler 4-22-1842 Hn
Birdin, Spencer to Polly Conner 8-23-1830 Hr
Birdsong, H. B. to M. J. Newland 12-27-1845 (12-31-1845) Hr
Birdsong, Henry F. to Mary E. Sanders 3-19-1866 Ma
Birdsong, John C. to Gemina Thedford 11-23-1841 Ma
Birdsong, Patrick H. to Harrett Ann Moss 12-20-1852 (12-21-1852) Hr
Birdsong, Perry to Elizur Medland 10-12-1848 O
Birdsong, Thomas to J. D. Groves 10-22-1859 (8-12-1860) F
Birdsong, Thomas to Penny Balcum 9-29-1866 (9-30-1866) F
Birdsong, William J. G. to Virginia M. Sims 7-26-1862 (7-30-1862) Ma
Birdsong, William L. to Ann Mariah Jones 12-17-1849 (12-20-1849) Hr
Birdwell, Albert to Daney Ann Butler 4-5-1864 (4-6-1864) Cr
Birdwell, Calvin to Frances Ann Barham 12-20-1847 (12-21-1847) O
Birdwell, Felix J. to Emily S. Donald 1-9-1848 Cr
Birdwell, George to Artilla Martin 6-10-1850 O
Birdwell, Isaac S. to Polly Ann King 1-1-1851 Be
Birdwell, James M. to Margarett M. Brown 4-6-1853 (no return) F
Birdwell, John to Mary Powell 6-25-1858 Be
Birdwell, S. R. to Nancy Horn 12-3-1851 Cr
Birdwell, V. S. to Victoria Montgomery 1-8-1872 (1-10-1872) Cr
Birdwell, Wm. P. to Pricella Haywood 2-7-1852 Cr
Birkhead, D. S. to E. A. Sparks 8-17-1861 (8-19-1861) Hr
Birks, Jim to Dilcy Currie 12-26-1871 Hy
Birmingham, Daniel F. to Ann D. W. Cate 5-19-1846 Ma
Birmingham, Danl. J. (Gibson Co) to Sarah J. (Mrs.) Sykes 8-19-1869 Ma
Birmingham, E. B. to Mary T. Carver 6-17-1871 (6-18-1871) Cr
Birmingham, Edward L. to Caroline Frederick 7-6-1859 (7-7-1859) Ma
Birmingham, W. R. to E. M. Williamson 6-6-1866 (6-7-1866) O
Birnbaum, J. L. to Mary (May?) Powers 2-15-1859 (2-16-1859) Sh
Birthwright, C. E. to Louisa D. Harris 4-2-1846 (no return) We
Bishop, Alvin to Mary Jane Cox 10-15-1841 (10-21-1841) Hr
Bishop, Andrew to Amanda Smith 1-27-1869 Dy
Bishop, Asa to Elizabeth Stephens 5-23-1850 Hr
Bishop, David L. to Mary Ann Gilstrop 11-14-1842 (11-17-1842) L
Bishop, David to Louisa Grantham 10-1-1856 (10-2-1856) Hr
Bishop, Elias J. to Margaret B. Mitchel 10-12-1848 Hr
Bishop, G. F. to Elizabeth W. Burrow 3-27-1866 (3-29-1866) Cr
Bishop, George to Isabella Cooper 3-3-1857 (3-4-1857) Ma
Bishop, George to Margaret Revely 1-17-1853 (1-18-1853) Ma
Bishop, Hardeman to Elizabeth Prewitt 11-20-1855 (11-22-1855) Hr
Bishop, Harmon to Mary Williams 10-9-1834 Hr
Bishop, J. A. to M. J. Harrison 4-14-1880 L
Bishop, J. H. to Amanda Johnson 8-12-1869 F
Bishop, J. J. to A. H. Bowles 5-18-1853 Cr
Bishop, Jessey to Charlott Miller 4-10-1871 (no return) Hy
Bishop, John D. to Charity A. Daugherty 12-30-1868 (1-6-1869) F
Bishop, John W. to Elizabeth A. Moore 3-14-1844 L
Bishop, John W. to Emily Renfroe 2-4-1862 L
Bishop, Lewis to Rachel Barnes 4-27-1867 G
Bishop, Moses to Mary Sherod 5-18-1841 Cr
Bishop, Samuel A. to Ida Peebles 10-15-1873 Hy
Bishop, Squire to Martha Henry 12-15-1861 Me
Bishop, W. B. to Ann C. Lensdin 11-14-1856 Cr
Bishop, William to Mary A. Bryant 2-12-1845 (2-13-1845) G
Bishop, Willis to Mary Eliza McMullen 10-29-1840 Cr
Bishop, Wm. J. to Sarah P. Black 3-8-1849 (3-13-1849) F
Bishup, Henry to Jane Ann McHenry 1-17-1856 Be
Bissel, J. M. to B. C. Forsyth 3-5-1862 Mn
Bistwick, Henry to Martha A. Faldwell 9-20-1847 (9-26-1847) F
Bitter, James to E. Burns 12-13-1861 (12-15-1861) Y
Bittermann, Rudolph to Juliana (Mrs.) Baker 9-27-1858 Sh
Bittick, N. M. to Caroline Wilson 11-4-1865 (11-5-1865) O
Bittick, S. F. to Elizabeth Peppers 5-17-1866 O
Bittix, Green to M. A. Noah 7-31-1863 O
Bius?, John J. to Martha Lummicons 6-24-1868 (6-25-1868) T
Bivens, Jack to Elizabeth Epps 3-15-1871 (4-10-1871) T
Bivens, S. C. to Sarah A. Griffy 9-19-1849 G
Bivens, Wiley to Jane McFarlen 2-24-1858 (2-25-1858) G
Bivins, Albert to Mary Green 9-7-1867 (9-8-1867) L B
Bivins, David w. to Jane Parker 2-2-1846 (2-6-1846) Ma
Bivins, John L. to Virginia A. Roberson 2-6-1855 G
Bivins, John S. to Frances Elder 9-24-1867 (9-25-1867) L
Bivins, John to Margarett Farrow 12-19-1848 Be
Bivins, Lewis C. to Sarah E. (Mrs.) Booth 12-15-1864 (12-16-1864) Sh
Bivins, W. E. to Isabelle J. Johnson 10-20-1868 Be
Bivren, John to Sarah W. Bryan 1-22-1839 F
Bizzel, Raiford to Mary Bennett 1-23-1835 (1-29-1835) Hr
Bizzel, Stephen V.? to Martha A. Chitwood 11-27-1860 Dy
Bizzell, Henry to Nancy C. Tilmon 4-20-1857 Hr
Bizzell, W. H. to Frances Hutcherson 12-29-1868 Hy
Bizzle, Martin to Mary Margaret McKee 1-26-1850 (1-27-1850) Hr
Bizzle, Wm. to Nancy A. Daniel 12-22-1856 (12-23-1856) Hr
Black, A. A. to Rebecca J. Hunter 7-30-1853 (no return) F
Black, A. R. to Isabel P. Greer 12-23-1855 Be
Black, Alexander to Narcissa Bell 9-25-1833 (9-26-1833) G
Black, Alfred to Amanda Johnson 10-7-1865 Mn
Black, Amos to Jane M. Stephens 10-26-1857 Ma
Black, C. A. to Emma J. M. E. Lewis 7-2-1858 Hr
Black, C. R. to R. J. Irby 12-12-1866 (12-20-1866) T
Black, Charles E. to Ellen O'Brien 3-17-1855 Sh
Black, Charles R. to Elenor B. Benson 9-8-1864 (9-11-1864) F
Black, Cyrus to Emily H. S. Bailey 11-20-1843 Hr
Black, Duncan H. to Harrett Hopkins 7-23-1849 (7-25-1849) G
Black, Edward E. to Ellen Yoakum 11-17-1840 Sh
Black, Geo. B. to Sarah E. Harrison 12-22-1868 (12-24-1868) Ma
Black, Hamilton to Ann Eliza Russell 3-29-1854 (3-30-1854) Hr
Black, Henry to Charlotte Sullivan 12-30-1870 (no return) Hy
Black, J. F. to S. T. Smith 8-4-1876 (8-5-1876) Dy
Black, J. M. to O. J. Slaughter 1-29-1866 (2-1-1866) F
Black, J. P. to Mary Griggs 12-18-1883 (12-19-1883) L
Black, Jacob R. to Sirena Jolly 3-17-1841 Cr
Black, James A. to Angeline Hicks 4-11-1850 Cr
Black, James B. to Mary F. Martin 11-27-1865 (no return) Hy
Black, James M. to Sarah E. Adams 12-29-1858 (12-30-1858) T
Black, James R. to Mary Gibson 10-1-1857 Hr
Black, James R. to T. A. Smith 12-3-1872 L
Black, James W. to Isabella Adams 9-3-1847 Hr
Black, James W. to Nancy C. Alston 5-8-1848 F
Black, James to Leona Kee 12-16-1868 Be
Black, James to Mary H. Fonshee 9-26-1867 (no return) Dy
Black, James to Sarah Baker 2-18-1832 Ma
Black, Jasper to Emeline Kidd 7-12-1864 Sh
Black, John C. to Amanda Stewart 2-6-1854 Ma
Black, John S. to Emily Duncan 3-30-1863 Sh
Black, Joseph A. to Sarah Catharine Gibson 3-17-1859 Hr
Black, Joseph C. to Sarah J. R--- 12-17-1867 G
Black, L. to Louisa Walker 8-14-1854 (no return) F
Black, Leander to Mary A. S. (Mrs.) Harwell 5-20-1844 (5-29-1844) F
Black, Matthew to Margaret Reed 1-30-1828 (2-3-1828) Hr
Black, Mebane to Sarah McGinnis 2-2-1871 (2-11-1871) F B
Black, Middleton to Mary Scruggs 1-2-1849 Hr
Black, Peyton to Fanny Hodges 3-9-1839 Sh
Black, Porter to Mary Jane Smith 9-28-1865 Mn
Black, R. J. to Fannie M. Somerville 4-12-1869 (4-14-1869) T
Black, R. W. to Aminta J. Cross 10-22-1867 (10-23-1867) F
Black, Robert C. to Lydia A. Clendenen 8-15-1840 (8-21-1840) F
Black, Robert H. to Martha A. Cross 2-19-1867 (2-20-1867) F
Black, Robert R. to Eliza A. Toons 5-10-1855 F
Black, Robert to Charity Stephenson 7-10-1843 (9-26-1843) O
Black, Robt. to Mary E. Clark 11-18-1858 Sh
Black, Samuel to Sarah Sullivan 4-16-1850 Hr
Black, Shadrack to Elizabeth Brown 9-30-1854 (10-1-1854) L
Black, Sterling M. to Eugenia E. Burroughs 10-23-1869 (10-27-1869) F
Black, Thomas G. to Delia Graves 1-20-1869 G
Black, Thomas S. to Analiza Yancy 3-6-1852 (no return) F
Black, Thomas to Amanda Allison 12-2-1846 (12-3-1846) Ma
Black, Thomas to Cornelia P. Wood 10-18-1842 Sh
Black, Thomas to Elizabeth Guyn 10-21-1840 (12-6-1840) F
Black, Thomas to Loset M. York 2-21-1843 Ma
Black, Thomas to Pernissa R. A. Roberson 11-6-1865 (11-7-1865) Dy
Black, W. F. to Sallie J. Coppedge 4-16-1872 (no return) Hy
Black, W. G. to Tobitha A. Thomas 2-20-1860 G
Black, W. H. to Sarah A. Ferguson 12-11-1852 (12-22-1852) Hr
Black, W. J. to Martha Ann Berryhill 12-11-1858 (12-1_-1858) Sh
Black, William D. to Sarah E. Hamilton 1-1-1857 G
Black, William G. to Martha Hotchkiss 1-10-1850 Ma
Black, William to Bena Mollier 5-7-1862 Sh
Black, William to Catharine Barker 11-3-1835 (11-5-1835) Hr
Black, William to Mary Ann Pirtle 2-6-1854 (2-12-1854) Hr
Black, William to Sarah P. Chunn 10-29-1848 Hn
Black, Wm. F. to P. C. Murray 1-26-1858 Hr
Black, Wm. J. to Cairy Ann Bolton 1-14-1847 Sh
Black, Wm. to Arabella Ross 4-19-1851 F
Blackard, Radford F. to Sarah Ann Clift 7-30-1836 Hr
Blackard, Wiley F. to Terrissa M. Wyley 12-22-1855 (12-24-1855) Ma
Blackard, William T. to Martha J. Holt 2-11-1850 Ma
Blackbern, J. R. to Mary Ann Privett 10-29-1862 (10-30-1862) Dy
Blackburn, A. to M. E. Smith 8-1-1870 (8-5-1870) O
Blackburn, Daniel to Amanda Phelan 5-29-1858 Y
Blackburn, Geo. F. to Catharine White 6-23-1858 Sh
Blackburn, J. A. to E. F. (Mrs.) Parrott 2-9-1869 (no return) Dy

Blackburn, J. M. to Ople--- Whiten 9-20-1860 G
Blackburn, J. R. A. to Martha B. Gibbs 11-30-1854 G
Blackburn, James to Martha J. Ward 5-15-1845 G
Blackburn, Jessee to Flora Gunter 2-29-1848 (3-2-1848) G
Blackburn, Jessee to Sarah Bivens 8-21-1856 G
Blackburn, John C. to Ardinia? Reese 4-28-1841 (5-4-1841) T
Blackburn, M. F. to Dora (Dona) Mitchell 5-18-1874 O
Blackburn, Marcellus to Martha J. Baker 12-14-1848 Sh
Blackburn, Rufus to Jane C. Skiles 12-15-1853 G
Blackburn, T. M. to A. L. Clark 5-20-1867 G
Blackburn, Thomas to T. Cornelia 6-18-1858 Sh
Blackburn, Wesly to Sarah Brooks 12-29-1846 (12-31-1846) Ma
Blackburn, William to Mathena C. Hampton 2-14-1831 Hr
Blackburn, William to Nancy M. Ward 1-2-1845 G
Blackford-Blackwell, James T. to Margaret M. Rust (Rash) 6-8-1848 Sh
Blackley, M. S. to Mary F. Fusell 11-7-1857 (no return) We
Blackley, Samuel to Mulinda Treumen 1-28-1837 (2-2-1837) G
Blackley, Samuel to Winney Jack 1-16-1850 (1-17-1850) G
Blackly, James to Lydia Riddle 12-8-1866 O
Blackman, Bennett to Rachel A. Gurly 1-15-1865 O
Blackman, Burwell to Mary E. Watson 9-8-1846 (9-10-1846) Ma
Blackman, Henry to Martha Bell 7-27-1863 G
Blackman, J. P. to Elizabeth Walker 6-27-1866 (6-28-1866) O
Blackman, James to Miriam L. Anderson 1-4-1843 (1-5-1843) Ma
Blackman, M. F. to S. J. Coleman 8-11-1872 O
Blackman, Thos. to Mary Dinwiddie 9-24-1856 Cr
Blackmon, Fordham to Margarett C. Climer 2-26-1856 G
Blackmon, John to Eliza Reid 9-21-1842 (9-22-1842) Ma
Blackmore, A. J. to F. E. Hufstettler 8-21-1875 (8-23-1875) Dy
Blackmore, John? (Thos.?) to Hannah Shehan 6-27-1864 Sh
Blacknall, Charles H. to Eliza K. Edmondson 11-23-1852 (11-25-1852) Ma
Blacknall, Thos. Y. to Nancy H. Campbell 11-28-1855 (11-29-1855) G
Blackshar, J. C. to Nancy Maloney 3-1-1859 O
Blackshear, James C. to Elizabeth J. Blair 3-10-1853 G
Blackshear, Joel H. to Tabitha C. Blair 4-13-1854 G
Blackshear, Thomas N. to Angeline L. McElroy 12-11-1852 (1-5-1853) O
Blackshear, W. S. to Milly Miller 7-25-1854 Hn
Blackshere, Jesse B. to Mary A. Corbett 12-3-1860 (12-6-1860) O
Blackstock, Thos. to Martha J. Culp 1-4-1851 Cr
Blackstone, Wm. P. to Louisiana C. White 1-25-1849 Sh *
Blackwell, Andrew to Virginia Thompson 8-6-1875 (8-12-1875) L
Blackwell, Auren to Elizabeth Wells 1-24-1871 (1-25-1871) L
Blackwell, George W. to Margarette C. Harden 12-22-1858 (12-28-1858) G B
Blackwell, George W. to Mary Moore 7-30-1868 G B
Blackwell, George to Lucinda Glass 1-16-1867 (1-17-1867) L B
Blackwell, Georgge to Fanny Elder 1-3-1829 (1-8-1829) G
Blackwell, H. H. to Polly A. Scates 12-30-1866 (maybe 1870) G
Blackwell, J. B. to Ellen Bradford 12-6-1860 (no return) Hy
Blackwell, J. to Mary Medlin 12-29-1863 (no return) L
Blackwell, Jack to Caroline White 6-22-1868 (6-25-1868) T
Blackwell, James to Mary Ann Tyus 7-21-1862 (7-22-1862) L
Blackwell, John C. to Arimencia Hale 8-23-1830 (9-3-1830) Hr
Blackwell, John H. to Maggie Wright 10-19-1873 Hy
Blackwell, John P. to Mary C. Samford 3-24-1856 (no return) Hn
Blackwell, John T. to M. E. J. Kee 6-8-1872 (6-9-1872) Cr
Blackwell, John to Katy Granderson 11-17-1873 G
Blackwell, John to Loda? Cherry 8-28-1872 (no return) L B
Blackwell, John to Mary A. (Mrs.) Philpott 1-18-1843 (no return) F
Blackwell, John to Mary Philpott 11-2-1829 Hr
Blackwell, John to Winnie A. Henning 10-20-1867 (no return) L
Blackwell, Joseph to Mary Delph 12-2-1856 (12-7-1856) Ma
Blackwell, Reuben to Bell Moorer 12-30-1885 (12-31-1885) L
Blackwell, Robert J. to Charity E. Lockard 12-10-1858 (12-16-1858) L
Blackwell, Robert J. to F. A. Martin 3-6-1877 (3-7-1877) L
Blackwell, Stephen to Sallie Evans 1-21-1870 G B
Blackwell, T. J. to Annie Bramlett 12-25-1872 Hy
Blackwell, Thomas M. to A. S. C. Rice 3-1-1842 (no return) L
Blackwell, Thos. J. to Lilly Rice 12-16-1879 (12-18-1879) L
Blackwell, Warren to Margaret Dow 4-15-1871 (4-17-1871) F B
Blackwell, William A. to Nannie E. Rogers 1-11-1859 (1-12-1859) L
Blackwood, Anderson to Nancy Dunn 12-13-1857 Hn
Blackwood, Burress to Catherine Peterson 3-23-1841 Sh
Blackwood, George to Martha Peel 2-13-1860 Sh
Blackwood, Newton J. to Sarah A. Southerlin 2-15-1859 Hn
Blackwood, R. K. to Margaret Gibbs 6-15-1854 Sh
Blackwood, Reid to Martha Skelly 7-7-1856 Sh
Blackwood, Sidney W. to Green H. Lassiter 9-27-1857 Hn
Blackwood, William to Rebecca Kesterson? 1-11-1826 Hr
Blain, Nathanl. to Sarah J. Pleasants 4-9-1842 (4-14-1842) F
Blair, A. B. to Harriet A. Dunlap 9-28-1850 (10-10-1850) G
Blair, A. W. to Kate A. Reider 5-22-1870 G
Blair, Abnur to Eliza J. Craft 10-21-1853 (no return) F
Blair, Andrew to Ann Chapman 11-13-1868 (no return) Hy
Blair, Andrew to Martha I. Reaves 11-7-1855 Cr
Blair, Andrew to Nancy Sellars 10-8-1831 (10-9-1831) G
Blair, Andrew to Nancy Sellars 10-8-1835 G
Blair, David D. to Lucy R. Smith 6-18-1838 (6-21-1838) G

Blair, Ephraim to Polly C. Miller 4-12-1827 G
Blair, Ephraim to Polly C. Miller 4-12-1828 G
Blair, G. G. to Sarah M. Johnson 12-10-1868 Hy
Blair, Geo. D. to Nannie J. Potts 10-14-1868 Hy
Blair, George D. to Martha McGuire 2-9-1846 Ma
Blair, George W. to Ann H. Lewis 7-3-1848 (7-6-1848) Hr
Blair, J. R. to Lucy T. Claiborne 6-24-1874 Dy
Blair, James A. to Mary A. Blair 7-24-1849 Cr
Blair, James T. to Lizzie H. McDowell 2-26-1867 (2-28-1867) F
Blair, James to Nancy E. Coker 4-13-1876 Hy
Blair, John R. to Deborah Haltom 11-21-1855 Ma
Blair, John W. to Sophina A. Bigham 11-2-1854 Cr
Blair, John to Eliza Stone 9-19-1845 Ma
Blair, John to Fanny Jennings 10-15-1875 (no return) Hy
Blair, John to Sarah Brown 1-22-1839 Ma
Blair, Nelson to Laura Williams 2-22-1883 (no return) L
Blair, R. F. to Mollie S. Elam 12-12-1866 G
Blair, T. E. to N. C. McCutchen 7-28-1873 (7-31-1873) Dy
Blair, Thomas B. to Sally Holmes 12-8-1829 G
Blair, Thomas J. to Panthaer W. Williams 2-12-1855 (2-13-1855) G
Blair, Thomas to Nancy Barton 1-1-1868 (1-2-1868) Ma
Blair, W. C. to Mary L. Kee 10-11-1866 Cr
Blair, W. H. to J. J. Parker 3-29-1870 G
Blair, William A. to Jane E. Barker 10-20-1856 G
Blair, William J. to Nancy Suggs 2-6-1856 (2-7-1856) Hr
Blair, William to K. A. Burk 3-5-1856 We
Blake, B. R. to Elizabeth Walker 12-31-1850 Cr
Blake, Benjamin L. to Martha J. Carter 10-24-1838 O
Blake, Frederick to Nancy Jane Mays 4-21-1870 (4-24-1870) Ma
Blake, H. M. to Sarah E. Sanderlin 1-21-1856 Sh
Blake, Henry to Julia Blake 7-4-1866 G
Blake, Henry to Mary Jane (Mrs.) Childress 12-8-1862 (12-10-1862) Sh
Blake, J. J. to Harriett L. Diggs 12-27-1864 Hn
Blake, J. J. to Paralee Wakeland 5-22-1867 Hn
Blake, Leonard H. to Lucy Crittenden 12-18-1842 Hn
Blake, Leroy M. to Mary Forrest 11-19-1844 We
Blake, Samuel M. to Mary E. Dobbins 1-7-1855 Hn
Blake, W. A. to Susan Simmons 12-7-1865 G
Blake, W. S. to Isabell M. Williams 9-15-1840 Hn
Blake, William to Eliza J. Shaw 1-8-1852 (no return) F
Blake, Wm. R. to Aley A. Biddy 11-20-1867 (no return) F
Blakeley, P. A. to Gilly Keith 8-2-1858 (8-3-1858) O
Blakeley?, D. L. to Mary E. Morgan 5-14-1851 (5-15-1851) F
Blakely (Blakey), Henry to Merica McBroom 7-23-1878 (7-24-1878) L
Blakely, George to Tennie Dunnavant 7-22-1877 Hy
Blakely, John to Nancy Sexton 9-20-1863 G
Blakely, P. A. to Gilly Keith 8-2-1856 (8-3-1856) O
Blakely, Rufus to Ana Bond 8-29-1873 Hy
Blakeman, B. F. to A. J. Chester 1-14-1858 We
Blakeman, J. H. to Mary D. Adams 11-15-1854 We
Blakemon, Sam to Jona Shivers 2-20-1869 Hy
Blakemore, A. G. to Salena Bettis 8-10-1847 Sh
Blakemore, A. J. to Mollie Klyce 12-24-1861 (no return) Hy
Blakemore, Coley to Paralee Smith 8-1-1868 G B
Blakemore, J. H. to Fanny Chester 11-27-1867 G
Blakemore, J. H. to R. A. Corley 7-27-1878 (7-28-1878) Dy
Blakemore, James B. to Catharine Rucker 5-30-1839 G
Blakemore, James S. to Sarah King 3-22-1849 G
Blakemore, Jas. G. to R. C. Wade 3-8-1860 G
Blakemore, L. W. to C. F. H. McDowell 5-3-1854 G
Blakemore, Peter to Jenny Ivey? 7-18-1868 G B
Blakemore, Samuel to Missouri Martin 2-17-1872 (no return) Hy
Blakemore, Thomas J. to Malvina Rooers? 11-15-1858 We
Blakemore, W. F. to Martha D. Parker 6-7-1859 G
Blakemore, W. S. to Isabella M. Williams 9-15-1840 Hn
Blakemore, William D. to Ellen Ingram 6-30-1867 G
Blakemore, William T. to Mary J. H. Rolls 12-13-1834 G
Blakemore, William to Jane Evans 1-16-1860 (no return) Hy
Blakeny, Bery to Martha Smothers 3-9-1861 (3-10-1861) Cr
Blakley, L. Y. to Frances C. Smith 12-21-1865 Mn
Blaloch, Sampson to Sarah E. White 11-10-1851 G
Blalock, F. S. to Mary A. Linebarger 12-7-1868 (12-9-1868) F
Blalock, Horace to Caroline Kirkland 3-22-1870 (3-26-1870) F B
Blalock, Jesse to Rosana Lea 4-13-1833 (4-14-1833) Hr
Blalock, Richard A. to R. C. Winford 12-10-1870 (12-14-1870) T
Blalock, Sampson to Deca J. Moore 8-4-1857 We
Blalock, William H. to Ann E. Hawes 3-21-1866 Hn
Blancett, H. L. to Sallie G. Branch 5-5-1867 Hy
Blancett, Jessee to Elizabeth F. Baker 11-21-1843 G
Blanchard, Henry M. to Susan P. Fletcher 12-29-1865 (12-31-1865) O
Blanchard, J. H. to Mrs. M. A. McCreight 6-21-1866 T
Blanchet, John to Anney Baker 2-28-1844 G
Blanchet, Thomas D. to Martha Jane Fagg 11-4-1850 Ma
Blanchett, William to Charlotte Greer 10-22-1851 Hy
Bland, Addison W. to Elizabeth Massey 12-13-1848 Sh
Bland, Andrew to Sucky Macklin 2-4-1869 (no return) F B
Bland, Arthur to Elizabeth Mangrum 5-8-1841 (5-9-1841) Ma

Bland, B. F. to Lucy L. Luny 1-4-1844 Sh
Bland, Calin? Wm.? to Jane Barker 12-21-1860 (not executed) Sh
Bland, Calvin W. to Amanda E. Harrell 2-7-1863 (2-8-1863) Sh
Bland, Calvin W. to Mary T. Sanderford 11-12-1851 (11-13-1851) Sh
Bland, Charles A. to Louis S. Morrell 4-11-1846 (4-12-1846) Ma
Bland, Charles to Catharine Jackson 12-6-1854 (12-7-1854) Sh
Bland, Charles to Elizabeth Baird 1-30-1860 (no return) Hy
Bland, Daniel M. to Lucinda E. Peel 12-1-1853 (12-8-1853) Sh
Bland, George L. to Margaret Johnson 6-24-1848 Sh
Bland, Giles to Nancy Stokes 7-27-1871 (no return) Hy
Bland, Isaac to Tibitha Ellis 11-12-1834 Sh
Bland, Jack to Cornelia O'Kelly 8-10-1866 (8-11-1866) F B
Bland, James R. to Mary C. Ragan 10-26-1860 (10-27-1860) Hr
Bland, John to Nancy Wheeler 7-7-1836 Sh
Bland, L. D. to L. M. L. Whitson 8-24-1865 G
Bland, Nelson to Fannie Goin 1-4-1876 Dy
Bland, Newman to Nancy Trobough 12-9-1865 T
Bland, Theopholus to Adaline Adams 4-27-1834 Sh
Bland, Thos. Nash to Marietta Mason 5-10-1867 (5-11-1867) F B
Bland, William to Margaret Byram 5-22-1861 (5-24-1861) Sh
Bland, Wm. H. to Satira Gibson 6-30-1842 Sh
Blandit, James G. to Eulah A. Carnes 1-8-1860 Cr
Blane, A. J. to Mary Ann Butler 2-15-1864 F
Blane, G. D. to Martha C. Cockran 8-26-1863 Hn
Blane, George P. to June Ashlock 3-1-1848 Hn
Blaney (Blarney), R. L. to Mary Hicks 11-15-1849 Sh
Blankenship, Andrew to Elizabeth Culp 12-3-1850 Cr
Blankenship, Benj. to Martha R. Bobbett 8-29-1856 (9-1-1856) G
Blankenship, Calvin M. to Emelia Hays 9-22-1838 (9-23-1838) F
Blankenship, Colbert to Mary Allen 12-26-1863 (1-21-1864) Dy
Blankenship, D. H. to Syntha A. Parker 7-4-1865 G
Blankenship, E. H. to Emily A. Baxter 12-12-1865 F
Blankenship, F. W. to Susan F. Ragsdale 1-3-1869 G
Blankenship, Geo. W. to Martha A. Jackson 3-15-1847 (3-16-1847) G
Blankenship, J. D. to Ida Nixon 1-14-1878 (1-15-1878) L
Blankenship, J. E. to Mary J. Wright 11-28-1871 (12-20-1871) Dy
Blankenship, J. E. to S. J. Miller 8-29-1879 (8-31-1879) L
Blankenship, J. Y. to F. A. Reavis 1-22-1882 (1-24-1882) L
Blankenship, James to Rebecca Applewhite 1-14-1839 O
Blankenship, Jas. M. to Mary Irvin 2-17-1851 (2-15?-1851) G
Blankenship, Joel to Lou Bessent 2-27-1871 (2-28-1871) Dy
Blankenship, John to Lucinda Rooks 1-5-1859 (1-6-1859) G
Blankenship, Joseph R. to Susan J. (Mrs.) Grammer 10-17-1871 (no return) L
Blankenship, P. L. to Sarah J. Murray 6-15-1872 (6-16-1872) Dy
Blankenship, R. C. to Kate Millington 10-25-1858 Sh
Blankenship, R. G. to M. W. Stokes 10-5-1850 (no return) L
Blankenship, Raymond A. to Martha Thompson 7-17-1855 Ma
Blankenship, Thomas B. to Martha J. Bobbitt 7-2-1864 G
Blankenship, Thomas to Mary Jobe 11-2-1857 Sh
Blankenship, Thomas to Susan U. A. Blake 9-15-1867 O
Blankenship, Thos. R. to Martha A. Farris 1-5-1852 (1-6-1852) G
Blankenship, W. C. to Missouri Murray 10-16-1879 Dy
Blankenship, W. D. to Adaline Cunningham 11-8-1880 (no return) L
Blankenship, Wm. F. to Rebecca S. Holloway 11-7-1854 (no return) F
Blankenship, Wm. to Susan Jones 12-4-1853 Cr
Blankinship, David C. to Mary E. Carter 12-27-1859 (12-28-1859) G
Blankinship, James M. to Martha A. C. Blankinship 6-25-1868 G
Blankinship, James P. to Frances A. Hollingsworth 11-12-1866 (11-13-1866) Ma
Blankinship, Jesse S. to Elizabeth A. Blankinship 9-30-1853 (10-2-1853) G
Blankinship, John C. to Margaret Cannon 8-21-1845 (8-26-1845) G
Blankinship, John W. to Sarah G. Reeves 12-30-1850 (1-1-1851) G
Blankinship, T.(S?) K. to Alice L. Stamper 11-1-1883 L
Blankinship, W. D. to N. H. McCoy 3-12-1884 (3-13-1884) L
Blanks, James to Rebecca Burrow 10-7-1850 Cr
Blanks, Wm. to Mary P. Burrow 1-17-1859 Cr
Blann, William to Zaby McKnight 1-10-1832 (1-17-1832) G
Blanton, C. to K. L. Anderson 6-1-1858 We
Blanton, H. T. to Henrietta Stephens 6-7-1864 Hn
Blanton, H. T. to Susan E. Kane 8-18-1856 Hn
Blanton, Horace T. to Martha A. Lamb 7-4-1843 Hn
Blanton, John D. to Nancy Ann Harris 6-13-1868 (6-14-1868) O
Blanton, N. H. to Mary Sharp 8-31-1866 G
Blanton, W. W. to Martha Fielder 10-3-1869 G
Blanton, William to Martha Childress 1-20-1847 (2-16-1847) O
Blanton, William to Martha Childress 1-20-1848 (2-16-1848) O
Blanz, G. F. to G. M. Carr 10-6-1864 Sh
Blare, James to Mary C. McLeod 2-22-1851 (no return) F
Blasengame, James F. to Jane Carver 1-25-1863 Mn
Blasingame, Columbus to Mary J. Smith 4-14-1874 T
Blasingame, William S. to Amanda Duncan 12-21-1857 (2-12-1858) Hr
Blasingame, William to Pheby E. Watson 1-10-1876 (1-11-1876) L
Blasingham, Washington to Lidia Ann Boren 10-26-1842 Sh
Blassengame, H. P. to Elizabeth Calhoun 6-3-1861 O
Blay, M. D. to Amalia Yergon 7-1-1840 F
Blaydes, Anderson to Margaret Clark 2-24-1872 (no return) Hy
Blaydes, J. D. to Rebeccca Garrison 2-26-1866 (3-1-1866) F
Blaydes, J. J. to Emma Gregory 9-20-1870 Hy
Blaydes, J. J. to Malissa A. Montague 10-25-1865 Hy
Blaydes, James to Eveline Chaffin 7-3-1867 F B
Blaydes, James to Georgeanna Payne 12-25-1873 T
Blaydes, Samuel H. to Mary N. McLemore 11-23-1852 (11-25-1852) Ma
Blaydes, William to Celia Ross 1-19-1871 F B
Blaylock, D. H. to Sarah A. Ginor (Genoe) 7-9-1838 Sh
Blaylock, Sittlelen to Nancy Jane Andrew 1-11-1857 (1-13-1857) We
Bleckley, George to Ann Cain 8-13-1864 (8-14-1864) Sh
Bledsoe, A. B. to Mary Smith 7-4-1858 Cr
Bledsoe, A. T. to Mary T. Bolton 8-23-1849 Sh
Bledsoe, Aaron to Mary Witherington 9-11-1854 T
Bledsoe, Albert W. to Martha S. Vaden 10-31-1843 G
Bledsoe, Anthony T. to Lucasia Bolton 10-6-1841 Sh
Bledsoe, Anthony to Ann Weathington 2-26-1857 T
Bledsoe, Anthony to Drusilla Griffin 7-4-1842 (7-7-1842) Ma
Bledsoe, B. C. to B. J. Dumas 12-27-1855 (no return) Hn
Bledsoe, B. G. to Helen Crawford 5-17-1857 Cr
Bledsoe, Bart to Elizabeth Green 2-12-1873 (2-13-1873) T
Bledsoe, C. C. to M. Powers 1-10-1867 G
Bledsoe, Edward to Diner Anderson 10-21-1870 (10-23-1870) Cr
Bledsoe, Francis A. to Martha Ann Bledsoe 7-31-1837 G
Bledsoe, George W. to Sarah Lynch 8-4-1835 G
Bledsoe, Granderson to Freesaver? Yarbro 3-10-1873 (3-11-1873) T
Bledsoe, Hearvy to Mary L. Bledsoe 3-18-1833 (3-20-1833) G
Bledsoe, Isaac M. to Elizabeth Ray 4-7-1859 G
Bledsoe, Jacob D. to Mary W. Allen 11-19-1863 (no return) Cr
Bledsoe, Jamerson to Mary Nance 1-31-1843 Ma
Bledsoe, James M. to Annie Nolin 3-6-1866 Hy
Bledsoe, James W. to Sarah Ann Vaught 10-9-1838 Sh
Bledsoe, Job to Rebecca Moorland 4-30-1840 Sh
Bledsoe, John H. to Nancy E. McCutcheon 12-11-1844 G
Bledsoe, John R. to Sarah McDougald 4-27-1843 G
Bledsoe, John to W. E. Gamble 9-8-1877 (9-9-1877) Dy
Bledsoe, Joseph M. to Tabitha J. Thomas 12-29-1868 (12-31-1868) Ma
Bledsoe, Joshua to Eliza Craige 2-24-1841 G
Bledsoe, M. L. to Sarah Ferrill 5-16-1874 (5-17-1874) Dy
Bledsoe, Major to Centha Shaw 12-22-1837 G
Bledsoe, Major to Mary Welch 8-26-1847 G
Bledsoe, Marcus S. to Frances Ventreese 3-15-1856 Ma
Bledsoe, Marcus to Lucy Young 3-20-1850 (3-21-1850) Ma
Bledsoe, Ned to Earline Sweargim 7-23-1868 (7-29-1868) Cr
Bledsoe, Peter to Amanda Brevard 12-30-1872 Cr
Bledsoe, R. B. to Mattie A. King 2-11-1869 G
Bledsoe, R. M. to Jennie Finley 2-1-1877 Dy
Bledsoe, Sandy to Amanda Rose 12-20-1867 (12-27-1867) T
Bledsoe, Thomas A. to Mary Echols 8-31-1876 (9-1-1877?) Dy
Bledsoe, Wellington H. to Centhy Bledsoe 4-1-1838 (4-4-1838) G
Bledsoe, Wellington H. to Ellender Rust 1-19-1843 G
Bledsoe, William E. to Mary A. Clark 1-10-1860 G
Bledsoe, William to Fannie Berk 8-16-1864 G
Bledsoe, William to Julia Flowers 12-29-1870 (12-31-1870) F B
Bledsoe, William to S. J. Gamble 11-28-1877 (11-29-1877) Dy
Bledsoe, Wm. G. to Emeline Merritt 9-18-1839 G
Bledsoe, Wm. H. to Myra T. Allen 12-8-1864 (no return) Cr
Bledsoe, Zachariah to Phebe Turner Allen 10-22-1849 (10-21?-1849) G
Bledsow, Malekiah to E. J. Hendrix 5-19-1849 (5-24-1849) O
Blescot(Hescot?), B. J. to M. J. Adams 12-2-1874 T
Blessing, Jacob to Susan G. Walls 9-8-1856 (9-11-1856) G
Blevins, Hugh to Sarah Coopender 1-18-1840 (1-19-1840) Ma
Blincon (Blucon), George T. to Elizabeth Turner 9-1-1836 Sh
Bliss, Francis, jr. to Mary D. McDougle 7-5-1869 Hy
Bliss, Isaac W. to Mary M. Smith 8-5-1850 Sh
Block, Maurice to Anna Wilman 5-17-1848 Sh
Block, Nicholas to Caroline Hasler 8-16-1847 Sh
Blome, Edward H. to Mary A. Shirley 7-17-1870 Hy
Blood, James M. G. to Lucinda Flippo 6-24-1839 Sh
Bloodworth, Elisha to Elizabeth Bloodworth 1-4-1843 Sh
Bloodworth, F. M. to Lucy Ann Berry 1-29-1853 (2-2-1853) Sh
Bloodworth, H. W. to Martha J. L. Shaw 2-1-1848 Sh
Bloodworth, Hardy to Mary White 12-7-1848 Cr
Bloodworth, M. R. to Harriet Bane 11-10-1847 Be
Bloodworth, W. F. T. to Martha Ann Greer 8-6-1843 Be
Bloom, Marx to Rosa Strauss 5-12-1854 Sh
Bloomingdale, Charles B. to Fannie Harton 7-31-1871 Dy
Bloomingdale, Isaac D. to Maria Rothgerber 2-10-1859 Sh
Blount, Jesse F. to Martha Jane Ewill 1-11-1851 (1-12-1851) T
Blount, Jesse to Christiana Hight 9-7-1840 Hr
Blount, John G. to Kissiah A. Brewer 8-25-1853 Cr
Blount, John G. to Winnie R. King 2-24-1869 Cr
Blount, John to E. Brewer 1-7-1847 Cr
Blount, W. to Mary A. Gooch 1-14-1846 Cr
Blow, T. R.? to Sallie Mathis 2-?-1868 (2-6-1868) Cr
Blow, Wm. P. to Elizabeth Chambers 10-12-1843 Cr
Blowers, James to Tennessee Cooke 8-29-1842 Sh
Bloyce, Wm. to S. A. Price 10-3-1862 (10-5-1862) O
Bloyde, James E. to Malinda E. Payne 4-33-1866 T
Bloys, W. D. to Emily McKnight 12-18-1849 (12-23-1849) O

Bloys, William D. to Aurora Mitchell 7-18-1844 O
Bloys, William D. to Emily McKnight 12-18-1849 (12-23-1849) O
Bluck, Robert to Sally A. Etheridge 11-1-1854 Sh
Bludworth, J. P. to P. J. Taylor 7-6-1869 Be
Bludworth-Bloodworth, W. K. to Lucinda Black 9-3-1865 Be
Blum, F. L. to Mattie French 2-13-1871 Hy
Blume, Benj. H. to Hannah O. (Mrs.) Simmons 3-20-1867 Ma
Blunt, B. D. to Mary A. Christopher 11-17-1863 Be
Blunt, Edward J. to Elizabeth Stockdale 1-15-1868 Be
Blunt, Jno. W. to Serbnny? Hooper 12-25-1844 (12-26-1844) Hr
Blunt, Samuel to Agnis Perry 7-29-1877 Hy
Blurton, John W. to Catherine Faulkner 12-16-1870 (12-18-1870) Ma
Bly, L. A. to Elisabeth J. (Mrs.) Pickens 9-14-1864 Sh
Blydes, Jim to Harriet Read 1-6-1870 Hy
Blyne, Edward to Rosanna Alexander 10-11-1859 (no return) Hn
Blythe, H. T. to Mary J. Fisher 9-27-1842 (9-29-1842) L
Blythe, Joseph A. to Linda C. Bell 4-26-1844 Hn
Blythe, W. H. to Martha J. Lemons 9-23-1865 O
Blythe, William J. to Sarah P. Howard 8-26-1841 Hn
Boals, George W. to Nancy J. Hathaway 7-19-1859 (7-21-1859) Ma
Boals, J. W. to Janusy Curtis 3-4-1869 (no return) Dy
Boals, James to Desimony Moss 11-4-1829 (11-5-1829) G
Boals, John R. to Ann Eliza Jones 12-17-1860 (12-19-1860) Ma
Boals, John W. to Martha R. Nesbit 5-22-1869 (5-23-1869) F
Boals, Nelson to Harriet Hilliard 9-13-1867 (9-14-1867) F B
Boals, Nelson to Margaret Norman 5-12-1866 (no return) F B
Board, George to Adaline Lawson 6-19-1875 (6-20-1875) O
Boardman, Henry to Cornelia M. Griffin 11-20-1857 Sh
Boatman, Charles to Aussale? N.? Murray? 2-16-1834 Hr
Boatright, Wm. C. to Martha J. Ballowe 10-5-1856 Be
Boatwright, C. M. to M. E. Chamberlain 9-1-1870 Dy
Boatwright, David J. to Emerilla A. Fain 8-24-1847 Hn
Boatwright, Elias to Mary Ann King 12-8-1868 (12-8-1869?) L
Boatwright, J. T. to S. J. Davis 10-28-1873 (10-29-1873) Dy
Boatwright, William A. to Etta Chamberlain 4-13-1876 Dy
Boaz, C. D. to Susan Oury 5-11-1858 Hn
Boaz, George W. to Sophia Lorance 10-13-1866 (10-14-1866) Cr
Boaz, James to Martha J. Nix 11-15-1865 Hn
Boaz, S. T. to Margaret M. (Mrs.) Tomlinson 11-13-1867 (11-14-1867) Cr
Boaz, Thomas E. to Ella G. Stone 11-19-1872 Dy
Boaz, W. M. J. to T. A. White 3-2-1859 Cr
Boaz, William J. to Martha E. Glover 2-7-1862 (no return) Cr
Bobbett, Albert L. to M. I. S. S. Dickens 9-1-1854 (9-5-1854) G
Bobbett, B. F. to Mary E. Berry 12-27-1854 (12-28-1854) G
Bobbett, Benjamin F. to Martha A. Dinwiddie 2-13-1850 Hn
Bobbett, Davidson B. to Eliza C. Lett 2-2-1854 G
Bobbett, Isaac to Hasty Dickens 12-14-1846 (12-17-1846) G
Bobbett, J. (Dr.) to Elizabeth J. Wallace 12-31-1845 (1-1-1846) G
Bobbett, James to Lecia Wyatt 2-7-1854 G
Bobbett, Silas M. to Emma H. Mayfield 8-23-1852 (8-24-1852) G
Bobbett, Stephen J. to Lucy Holt 1-13-1845 (1-16-1845) G
Bobbit, Lewis to Sally Hooper 11-11-1831 Ma
Bobbit, Samuel to Jane Croom 12-8-1841 (12-9-1841) Ma
Bobbitt, Allen to Elizer Johnson 1-31-1867 G
Bobbitt, Charles to Margaret Atkins 11-23-1846 (12-1-1846) F
Bobbitt, Green W. to Sarah Plant 12-15-1845 (12-16-1845) F
Bobbitt, Hawood H. H. to Elizabeth C. Jinkins 2-20-1863 We
Bobbitt, Henry to Jane C. Dinwiddie 9-13-1838 Hn
Bobbitt, James R. to Susan A. Orr 1-19-1870 G
Bobbitt, James to Eliza A. Province 2-19-1845 Cr
Bobbitt, James to Sarah Boyd 5-31-1856 Cr
Bobbitt, John to Mary P. Province 12-10-1845 Cr
Bobbitt, Matthew G. to Martha Williams 12-14-1846 (12-15-1846) Ma
Bobbitt, Stephen J. to Jamima J. Tate 2-16-1863 G
Bobbitt, T. F. to S. D. Ward 1-6-1871 (1-10-1871) F
Bobbitt, W. D. to N. M. McMinn 10-23-1867 G
Bobins, John W. to Susan O'Kelly 5-3-1847 (5-13-1847) F
Bobo, Allen H. to Sarah Ann Hargus 6-3-1844 (no return) F
Bobo, B. H. to Sarah Z. Longley 7-14-1838 (7-15-1838) O
Bobo, D. F. to Mary Ann Alexander 11-16-1854 Hn
Bobo, Willis to M. J. Gregory 10-14-1851 Cr
Bocks?, David to Narcissa Houston 12-25-1867 (no return) Hn
Boddie, Van B. to Annie E. Jewell 4-3-1861 Sh
Boden, Andrew V. to Amanda White 12-1-1866 (no return) Hn
Boden, Bloomfield to Sarah Kimbrough 1-19-1838 (no return) Hn
Boden, Green to Virginia Tombs 5-6-1865 (no return) Hn
Boden, James W. to Mary Burnett 12-30-1863 (no return) Hn
Boden, James to Amanda Courts 8-24-1843 Hn
Bodkin, Daniel to Cordelia Eskew 11-21-1876 (11-22-1876) Dy
Bodkin, Levi to Elizabeth C. Hillard 8-30-1855 (8-31-1855) G
Bodkin, Steel to Nancy Meurhead 9-16-1835 G
Bodkin, W. F. to Nancy S. Shelby 3-19-1867 G
Bodkin, William L. to Fany C. Alexander 1-21-1847 G
Bodkins, Hugh to Susan E. G. Woodson 11-21-1867 G
Bodkins, J. F. to M. A. Woodson 3-28-1868 G
Bodkins, James S. to Sarah E. Johnson 7-29-1869 G
Bodkins, James to Elizabeth Speres 4-23-1833 (4-24-1833) G

Bodwell, B. H. to Elizabeth Poiner 10-25-1847 Hn
Bogard, Abe to Martha Robertson 7-18-1869 G B
Bogard, James to Annis Harris 7-14-1837 (7-27-1837) Hr
Bogards, Alexander to Frances A. A. Hudspeth 2-13-1861 (2-14-1861) Hr
Bogel, G. W. to Fannie Watts 12-25-1877 (12-27-1877) O
Boges, Smith A. to Virginia Guthery 9-25-1860 We
Bogg, William D. to Elizabeth H. Price 1-23-1853 (2-8-1853) O
Boggan, Wm. to Elizabeth M. Scruggs 4-16-1841 Hn
Boggess, Lemuel to Frances Atkins 10-24-1848 Hn
Boggs, J. W. P. to Susana Moody 11-11-1855 Hn
Boggs, Kitchen to Maggie Ray 12-7-1869 (12-8-1869) F
Boggs, Saml. to Mary Brown 1-5-1867 (1-6-1867) F
Boggs, William O. to Emeretta C. Nash 2-19-1856 (no return) Hn
Bogguss, Robt. R. to Mary Ann Tucker 9-6-1875 (9-9-1875) Dy
Bogin, Joseph to Caroline Arnold 4-19-1862 Sh
Bogino (Bojianno), Jas. to Mary Parnashia 3-28-1864 Sh
Bogle, John A. to Emeline Goodwin 1-10-1870 G
Bogle, L. F. to S. A. R. Wyatt 1-31-1862 G
Bogle, R. E. to B. B. (Mrs.) Williams 5-13-1871 (5-14-1871) Dy
Bogle, R. E. to Susan C. Giles 12-27-1868 (12-28-1868) Cr
Bogle, Robert to Mary F. Tucker 2-21-1844 (2-22-1844) G
Bogle, Thomas C. to Manarca F. S. J. W. Blankenship 11-13-1855 (11-14-1855) G
Bogle, Thomas H. to Nancy T. Johnson 7-31-1860 Hn
Bogle, Wm. to Susanna H. Gardner 7-19-1842 Cr
Bogles, William to Mollie Steel 3-1-1868 G B
Bogsen?, William to Elizabeth Jane Foust 2-20-1846 (2-22-1846) F
Boguss, Joseph J. to Frances Hamlet 9-24-1845 (9-27-1845) Hr
Bohanan, D. A. to Mary J. Lasiter 1-19-1858 Cr
Bohanan, Jackson to Mary Ann Vails 7-23-1848 G
Bohannan, James to Tobithia Hundey 7-10-1854 G
Bohannon, Hiram to Clarissa Barrett 8-31-1838 Hn
Bohannon, Hiram to Jane Campbell 3-19-1841 (no return) Hn
Bohannon, Joseph to Mary Nance 12-18-1836 Hn
Bohanon, D. L. to Mary E. Bibbs 3-6-1866 (3-8-1866) Cr
Bohanon, Jackson to Permelia Jane Sweeton 8-4-1841 Hr
Bohanon, John to Amanda Savage 11-18-1852 Hr
Bohlen, Phillip R. to Agnes Handiworker 10-7-1854 Sh
Boie, F. to Bertie Eyrich 7-20-1859 Sh
Boile, Washington to Hannah Buford 12-27-1869 (12-31-1869) F B
Boland, Green to Jane McMillin 4-2-1830 (4-?-1830) G
Boland, Solen to Eliza Hart 7-23-1839 Sh
Bolder, Gust to Dora Basin 12-17-1870 (12-24-1870) F B
Bolding, John J. to Lyde O. McChristie 1-3-1877 Hy
Bolem, J. C. to Matilda M. Smith 4-16-1868 Be
Bolen, John A. to Martha Jordan 12-30-1859 (1-3-1860) G
Bolen, John to Rebecca Hudspeth 5-27-1837 (5-30-1837) Hr
Bolen, Lewis Z. T. to Emma Moore 11-16-1870 (11-17-1870) Ma
Boles, G. M. to F. L. Auten 1-8-1863 Mn
Boles, Nathan to Louisa Norman 3-31-1845 (4-1-1845) F
Boles, Robert to Nancy Lamons 3-3-1830 G
Boles, Robert to Nancy Leamons 3-5-1831 G
Bolin, George A. to Nancy Parker 6-23-1856 (6-24-1856) Ma
Bolin, John to Mary Ann Sanders 8-31-1840 Hr
Bolin, Moses L. to Elizabeth Tuttle 12-5-1866 Hn
Bolin, William to Adaline Barham 10-26-1871 (10-31-1871) Cr
Boling, A. J. to Emily Whitteman 12-6-1865 (12-10-1865) Dy
Boling, A. J. to Emily Whittemore 12-6-1865 (12-10-1865) Dy
Boling, G. W. to Ann E. Stafford 1-14-1854 (no return) F
Boling, G. W. to Mary E. Permenter 3-15-1866 Hy
Boling, James to Jane Hanson 7-13-1830 (7-15-1830) Hr
Boling, Thomas to Sarah Hopkins 11-21-1827 G
Boling, William to Elizabeth Moss 9-23-1826 G
Bolles, George C. to Margaret Suplee 9-23-1858 (8?-26-1858) Sh
Bolling, Burgess to Mary A. Stamper 5-5-1851 (no return) G
Bolling, Clayton L. to Genevia Monom 7-1-1829 (7-2?-1829) Hr
Bolling, John to Penny Lewis 12-30-1866 Hy
Bolling, Thomas to Sarah Gee 10-23-1834 Sh
Bolling, Thornton to Dinah Houston 3-29-1866 (4-1-1866) F B
Bolling, W. T. (Rev.) to Mollie E. (Mrs.) Pearce 4-14-1870 G
Bollinger, Conrad to Magdelina Stoll 3-23-1859 Sh
Bolls, William to Perney E. Tyler 7-28-1857 (7-30-1857) G
Boltin, L. J. to Elizabeth Brawner 8-25-1856 (no return) We
Bolton, Isaac L. to Sanderilla Boulton 12-9-1835 Sh
Bolton, J. L. to Henrietta B. Polk 1-28-1861 (1-30-1861) Sh
Bolton, J. P. to Ann Keller 12-26-1867 L
Bolton, Jefferson to Julia Harris 1-20-1836 Sh *
Bolton, Jeremiah T. to Sarah E. Byers 9-20-1865 (9-21-1865) Cr
Bolton, John C. to Mary A. Bolton 8-31-1857 (9-25-1857) Sh
Bolton, John J. to Anna Reid Waller 11-10-1874 (11-11-1874) T
Bolton, John P. E. to Mary T. G. Person 6-9-1841 Sh
Bolton, John to Mary Sigler 1-6-1842 Sh
Bolton, Luck to Maria Bowles 7-15-1876 Hy
Bolton, Lucus L. to Martha Ann Mercer 8-28-1849 Sh
Bolton, Manuel to Ellen Smith 1-4-1868 G B
Bolton, Moses to Cindirilla Bolton 3-16-1861 Sh

Bolton, Moses to F. L. Bolton 6-28-1860 Sh
Bolton, Moses to Nancey Alsup 9-21-1848 Sh
Bolton, Richard T. to Malissa Boals 1-9-1849 (1-10-1849) Ma
Bolton, Wade H. to Lavinia A. Person 12-19-1836 Sh
Bolton, Wm. to Sallie Hobbs 8-16-1873 (no return) Hy
Boman, James to Frances Sumner 4-24-1860 (4-25-1860) Ma
Bomar, Beverly to Sarah E. Walker 10-20-1840 Cr
Bomar, Booker to Mary O. Daniel 12-17-1854 (no return) F
Bomar, Calvin to Sarah E. Bomar 10-17-1853 Cr
Bomar, Charles to Caroline Tipton 9-17-1850 Hn
Bomar, David T. to Rebecca Bomar 5-13-1843 Hn
Bomar, James to Julene M. Haynes 12-15-1842 Hn
Bomar, John F. to Martha A. Green 3-1-1854 Cr
Bomar, John R. to Drucilla Cooper 9-19-1849 Hn
Bomar, Reuben to Mary Ann Thomas 3-28-1844 Hn
Bomar, Reuben to Mary E. Irion 11-11-1866 Hn
Bomar, Robert J. to Martha A. H___ 1-9-1853 Be
Bomar, Spencer to Meria Hillsman 12-2-1844 Cr
Bomar, W. C. to S. E. Compton 9-7-1869 Cr
Bomar, W. N. to M. C. Etherage 1-21-1856 (no return) Hn
Bomar, W. S. to Dora A. Irion 11-11-1866 Hn
Bomar, Westley to Caroline Williams 1-2-1867 Hn B
Bomar, William to Anna E. J. Carter 12-23-1866 Hn
Bomar, William to Martha Ellis 6-25-1849 Hn
Bomberger, Isaac to Jeanette Hesse 12-6-1858 Sh
Boment, Sterling to Julia Scott 9-2-1870 G B
Bomer, Charles to Caroline Wood 12-9-1858 Hn
Bomer, David to Susan A. Caldwell 12-23-1857 Hn
Bomer, Elijah H. to Hulda Ann Garrett 8-28-1856 Hr
Bomer, Spencer to Salina Rushing 1-17-1839 Be
Bomer, Spencer to Sarah A. Barker 3-25-1851 Cr
Bomer, Wesley K. to Sarah Roland 10-24-1854 Hn
Bona, Ben Franklin to Elizabeth Nelson 9-11-1838 Ma
Bond(Vaughan), Benjamin to Elizabeth Mathis 6-26-1834 Hr
Bond, A. C. to C. C. Hunt 10-11-1866 G
Bond, A. L. to Susan C. Thomas 2-9-1869 Be
Bond, Albert to Adeline Garrett 12-28-1870 (no return) L
Bond, Alexander to Emiline Johnson 7-16-1874 Hy
Bond, Allen W. to Martha Wilson 2-2-1826 Sh
Bond, Allen to Lizzie Whartin 12-31-1869 (no return) Hy
Bond, Alstin to Mary Allen 7-28-1869 (no return) Hy
Bond, Alston to Sally Bradford 7-31-1875 Hy
Bond, Amus to Rachal Bond 3-30-1872 Hy
Bond, Ananias to Mattie Smith 3-5-1873 (no return) Hy
Bond, Andrew Jackson to Nancy Ross 6-29-1850 Cr
Bond, Andw. James to Aurelia Anderson 3-14-1878 Hy
Bond, Annias to Mattie Smith 3-15-1873 T
Bond, Antelpes? to Minerva Smith 5-5-1871 (5-7-1871) T
Bond, Arther to Judy Morris 3-4-1875 Hy
Bond, Ben to Caroline Johnson 2-12-1870 Hy
Bond, Benj. F. to Martha Bone 2-19-1861 Ma
Bond, Benj. F. to Mary A. Clark 11-11-1862 G
Bond, Benj. to Sarah Grigg 4-10-1878 Hy
Bond, Benjamin F. to Biddy (Mrs.) Scott 10-20-1858 (10-21-1858) Ma
Bond, Benjamin W. to Mary Gillum 4-24-1850 Sh
Bond, Benjamin to Mary Jane Estes 11-25-1865 (no return) Hy
Bond, Blunt to Liza Holaway 12-26-1867 (no return) Hy
Bond, Bob to Jane Barbee 8-21-1869 (no return) Hy
Bond, Brister to Jane Lea 11-9-1867 Hy
Bond, Buford to Martha A. Harris 2-16-1850 Cr
Bond, Burton to Laura Minor 4-18-1878 Hy
Bond, Bush to Winny Huggins 2-16-1874 Hy
Bond, Calvin to Eliza Sherrod 12-24-1866 (no return) F B
Bond, Calvin to Mary Ann Bethory 8-13-1849 Be
Bond, Cornelius to Eliza McQuister 1-23-1866 T
Bond, Daniel to Margaret W. Bond 1-9-1874 Hy
Bond, Eaton to Sarah S. Hare 7-27-1840 (no return) F
Bond, Edward to Julia Lacey 3-19-1867 (3-21-1867) F B
Bond, Elijah to Laura Curry 7-4-1874 (no return) Hy
Bond, Emanuel to Jane Garner 12-20-1880 (12-25-1880) L B
Bond, F. P. to Minnie Bond 8-2-1877 Hy
Bond, Francis A. to Martha L. Young 12-3-1850 Ma
Bond, G. T. to Matilda Headrick 10-15-1853 (10-16-1853) Sh
Bond, George W. to Mary J. Chester 10-6-1845 (10-7-1845) Ma
Bond, George to Emeline Ernest 1-25-1863 G
Bond, George to Francis Foster 5-3-1877 Hy
Bond, Gilbert to Minnie Hurt 3-9-1876 (no return) Hy
Bond, Gilbert to Paralle Bond 1-14-1876 (no return) Hy
Bond, Green to Ellen Sargent 12-27-1872 Hy
Bond, Harvey to Betsey Kelly 3-6-1873 Hy
Bond, Henry R. to Mrs. M. H. Mathews 7-12-1847 (7-15-1847) F
Bond, Henry to Ala Jane Clay 6-19-1870 Hy
Bond, Henry to Mattie Anthony 11-17-1874 Hy
Bond, J. M. to Pricilla P. Wynne 11-28-1853 (11-29-1853) Sh
Bond, J. P. to Sarah A. Clary 1-21-1867 (1-24-1867) F
Bond, Jacob to Phebee Jane Presson 4-29-1855 Be
Bond, Jake to Agnes Wise 12-27-1877 Hy
Bond, James (Junus?) to Nellie Wheeler 4-4-1885 (4-9-1885) L
Bond, James K. P. to Mary Cooper 11-17-1867 Be
Bond, James M. to Mary Gregory 7-7-1839 Hn
Bond, James O. to Lydia A. McCord 5-24-1867 Hy
Bond, James W. to Martha N. C. Wilkes 1-16-1856 (1-22-1856) Ma
Bond, James to Ada M. Batchelor 9-12-1877 Hy
Bond, Jeff to Callie Craighead 2-21-1871 Hy
Bond, Jim to Fannie Autney? 12-22-1871 Hy
Bond, Joe to Mollie Yancy 12-2-1871 Hy
Bond, John R. to Jennie V. Taylor 2-7-1872 Hy
Bond, John W. to Mary Ann J. Winn 1-26-1838 Sh
Bond, John to Elizabeth Ward 1-11-1843 Be
Bond, John to Feeby Reed no date (not issued) Hy
Bond, John to Martha Outlaw 5-31-1873 Hy
Bond, Joseph to Antoinette H. Snead 2-22-1848 Sh
Bond, Joseph to Nancy H. Williams 2-21-1843 Hn
Bond, L. to M. E. Freels 5-26-1870 (no return) Hy
Bond, Lewis B. to L. R. Hawkins 7-3-1860 (7-4-1860) Ma
Bond, Lewis to Fannie Boyd 12-3-1873 (12-5-1873) T
Bond, Louis to Jennie Davis 4-16-1872 Hy
Bond, Luke to Caroline Harrison 1-12-1870 (1-13-1870) L
Bond, Morris to Nancy Collman 1-28-1872 Hy
Bond, Moses to Lucinda Cherry 8-17-1876 (no return) Hy
Bond, Moses to Mary Livingston 3-26-1874 Hy
Bond, Neal to Carra Smith 1-1-1866 (no return) Hy
Bond, Nelson to Harriet Johnson 12-11-1867 Hy
Bond, Newton Henry to Martha Mary McCoy 2-9-1863 (2-10-1863) Sh
Bond, Nicholas P. to Ellen M. Priddy 9-11-1861 Sh
Bond, Noah to Emma Livingston 3-9-1871 Hy
Bond, Noah to Tempa Sherrod 2-10-1866 (2-15-1866) T
Bond, Norman to Sarah A. McDaniel 9-26-1847 Sh
Bond, Peter N. to Olivid? P. Branch 5-8-1865 (5-10-1865) T
Bond, Peter to Louisa Sherrod 12-6-1873 Hy
Bond, Rhoden to Ella Holmes 11-29-1873 Hy
Bond, Robert J. to Mariah P. Radford 7-24-1861 Be
Bond, Robert N. to Martha A. Harrill 2-16-1849 Sh
Bond, Robert N. to Sarah T. Sanderford 1-14-1829 Sh
Bond, Robert W. to Sallie F. Henning 2-17-1869 Ma
Bond, Robt. T. to Bettie P. Harrison 10-11-1864 (10-25-1865?) Sh
Bond, Rush to Lucy Moses (Masyl?) 3-23-1875 Hy
Bond, Silas to Lizzie Shaw 12-14-1876 Hy
Bond, Sylvester to Susan P. Sandiford 3-5-1839 Sh
Bond, T. E. to Carrie Bishop 7-17-1878 (no return) Hy
Bond, Tallassee G. to Margaret M. Giles 3-28-1844 Sh
Bond, Tallassee to Mary Greenhaw 3-14-1833 Sh
Bond, Theophilus to Laura Warlick 4-1-1852 Ma
Bond, Thomas to Ellen Jones 1-17-1878 (no return) Hy
Bond, Thomas to Rosa Taylor 2-19-1868 Hy
Bond, Thomas to Venis Bond 12-20-1871 Hy
Bond, W. T. to Caroline VanBuren 2-18-1861 (no return) Hy
Bond, Walter to Laura Rice 2-8-1884 (2-10-1884) L
Bond, Washington to Nancy J. Warren 5-23-1836 Sh
Bond, Washington to Rose Lee 12-13-1873 Hy
Bond, Washington to Sarah Clark 12-2-1866 Hy
Bond, Whitmell T. to Hannah O. Bond 5-3-1852 (5-4-1852) Ma
Bond, William L. to Eliza Chapman 12-2-1844 (12-4-1844) Ma
Bond, William to Ann Marie Vaughn 9-16-1831 Sh
Bond, William to Anna Midgett 3-24-1874 Hy
Bond, William to Catharine Stewart 10-11-1852 Sh
Bond, William to Rebecca Wiseman 4-6-1856 Be
Bond, William to Sinter Ann Presson 11-7-1855 Be
Bond, Willis to Siller Allen 3-17-1875 (no return) Hy
Bond, Wm. W. to L. S. Harbert 4-27-1854 (5-3-1854) Ma
Bond, jr., Eaton to Bell Penn 12-9-1867 Ma
Bond, jr., John to Jennie Davis 8-13-1872 (no return) Hy
Bond, jr., Watson to Bettie Sanders 2-4-1874 Hy
Bond, jr., Will P. to Sarah E. Read 12-18-1866 Hy
Bond?, S. D. to Caroline E. Bourne 4-24-1854 (no return) F
Bonds, A. J. to E. Glawson 12-1-1851 Cr
Bonds, G. W. to Nancy E. White 4-1-1868 O
Bonds, Granville to Martha Ross 2-3-1857 Be
Bonds, James R. to Mary Pinson 10-17-1841 Cr
Bonds, Jas. W. to Martha A. Rogers 9-5-1857 Hr
Bonds, John W. to Jane Gunter 7-27-1841 (no return) Hn
Bonds, John W. to Mary E. Turner 1-2-1860 (1-3-1860) Sh
Bonds, John to Marzella Ballentine 9-3-1862 (9-4-1862) Dy
Bonds, John to Nancy J. Wright 1-13-1852 Cr
Bonds, R. G. to Nancy J. Halmark 8-17-1852 Cr
Bonds, Wright to Nancy A. Craig 5-15-1861 Be
Bondurant, C. P. to Mary E. Etheridge 12-18-1845 We
Bondurant, D. R. to M. L. Knox 7-9-1874 (7-10-1874) O
Bondurant, P. M. to L. B. Hilliard 4-3-1854 (no return) F
Bondurant, Robert M. to Margarett Watkins 7-2-1847 (no return) F
Bondurant, Thomas C. to Sarah Chambers 1-7-1858 O
Bondurant, W. W. to Sallie P. Woodson 11-8-1869 (11-9-1869) F
Bondurant, Wiley B. to Martha C. Mays 7-21-1856 (7-23-1856) O
Bone, A. B. B. to Mary Ann Crosby 11-13-1855 Sh

Bone, Henry to Frances Ivie 11-12-1866 (12-1-1866) F B
Bone, Hugh Y. to Martha Jane Robb 4-25-1839 G
Bone, Josiah to Charlotte Dennis 8-14-1852 (8-15-1852) O
Bone, Josiah to Elizabeth Wynn 8-18-1849 (8-21-1849) O
Bone, Levi S. to Catharine Burrow 2-4-1839 (2-7-1839) O
Bone, Samuel J. to Emily Pettus 5-11-1855 (5-13-1855) G
Bone, Sherwood to Aga Davis 8-27-1839 (8-30-1839) O
Bone, W. S. to Louisa Neal 4-10-1867 G
Bone, William to Camilla T. Moore 11-2-1854 (11-24-1854) G
Boner, Booker to Susanah Notgrass 8-7-1851 (no return) F
Boner, Wm. to Julia Moore 12-23-1858 (12-30-1858) T
Boney, David to A. E. Halfacre 12-12-1882 (12-13-1882) L
Boney, James S. to Susannah E. Hunt 6-7-1838 (6-10-1838) Hr
Boney, John W. to Nancy Thrailkill 2-12-1842 (2-13-1842) Hr
Bonfels, L. F. to Mariah D. Whitlocke 7-26-1842 (7-27-1842) G
Bongerent, Nathan to Chester Berry 12-25-1867 (no return) Hn B
Bonne, P. A. to Virginia M. Boswell 8-6-1857 T
Bonner, Georg W. to Olivia Mason 2-6-1854 (2-7-1854) T
Bonner, George W. to Mary E. Newsom 7-21-1865 T
Bonner, Hosea to Mary W. Edwards 12-7-1853 Cr
Bonner, Thos. to Fannie Allison 2-28-1868 Hy
Bonner, William R. to Mary E. Griffin 2-6-1840 Hn
Bonner, William T. to Judy Mosley 7-25-1843 F
Bonner, Williamson to Frances B. Bentley 1-10-1837 Sh
Bonner, Willis R. to Feriba A. Harmon 4-23-1857 Hn
Booe, George A. to Sarah Ann Hainline 7-4-1839 Hr
Booe, Isaac to Julia Ann Anderson 1-13-1842 Hr
Booe, Radford to Sarah Elizabeth Jenkins 1-24-1857 Ma
Booker, A. G. to Parthenah S. Ross 4-8-1853 Be
Booker, A. T. to Lucinda Webb 1-21-1845 (no return) F
Booker, C. T. to E. R. Clements 11-16-1874 (11-18-1874) T
Booker, Edmund to Eliz. Anderson Perkinson 6-29-1846 (7-2-1846) T
Booker, J. B. to Isabella Jones 6-3-1851 (6-4-1851) F
Booker, James P. to Eliza C. Mallory 2-29-1860 Sh
Booker, Samuel to Stacy Cole 5-14-1854 Be
Booker, William Branch to Alethia Munford Jones 9-18-1852 (9-23-1852) T
Booker, William to Mary Bernard 12-27-1870 T
Booker, Wm. B. to Eliza F. Bailey 2-12-1862 (no return) Hy
Booker?, Edmond J. to Mary Ann White 8-3-1842 (8-4-1842) T
Bookout, J. F. to H. Ann Lemmon 12-31-1860 (1-1-1861) Dy
Bookout, John to Lucy A. Southern 6-28-1878 (no return) Hy
Boon, Alexr. to Martha Cross 10-13-1877 (10-14-1877) Dy
Boon, Benjamin F. to Martha Slaughter 2-27-1844 Sh
Boon, Benjamin to Mary E. Little 1-15-1850 G
Boon, Benjamin to Unicy T. Hunt 5-16-1838 (5-17-1838) G
Boon, Charles F. to M. E. Henderson 8-24-1869 Ma
Boon, F. M. to M. E. Kersey 11-27-1862 (11-28-1862) O
Boon, Frank to Jane Batts 11-18-1866 G
Boon, Gilbert to Nancy L. Hatchett 3-29-1839 (4-4-1839) G
Boon, Harrison to Malinda Curtner 9-9-1850 O
Boon, Henry to Frances E. Pierce 3-19-1862 Dy
Boon, Henry to Susan Golden 1-16-1830 Ma
Boon, J. S. to Lula S. Hartsfield 12-16-1869 G
Boon, J. T. to P. E. Hall 10-5-1869 Dy
Boon, Jackson to Sarah Miller 7-3-1838 (7-4-1838) O
Boon, James E. to Sarah B. Atkins 3-11-1845 G
Boon, James H. to Caroline C. Thomas 12-11-1850 (12-12-1850) G
Boon, James to G. F. Billingsley 4-27-1863 G
Boon, James to Harriet Warlick 11-19-1869 G B
Boon, James to Sousin Bradly 3-14-1848 Hr
Boon, Jas. to Mary Sanders 3-18-1872 Hy
Boon, Jesse to M. E. C. Pool 12-12-1865 (12-15-1865) F
Boon, John J. to Lucretia L. Lacy 3-28-1866 (3-29-1866) Ma
Boon, John J. to Martha E Johnson 7-10-1850 Ma
Boon, John P. to Jane Noblin 11-13-1843 (no return) We
Boon, John to Ann E. Lanier 7-28-1872 Hy
Boon, Milton to Mollie Richardson 3-25-1868 (3-31-1868) Ma
Boon, Owen to Sarah Shores 3-12-1845 Be
Boon, Ratliff to Lucrety C. Hopkins 5-6-1844 G
Boon, Robert D. to Martha A. Senter 10-20-1856 Ma
Boon, Robert H. to Ann A. Mitchell 11-1-1858 (11-4-1858) Ma
Boon, Samuel to Julia A. McAdoo 5-6-1870 G
Boon, Sebastian to Nancy Evans 8-6-1834 O
Boon, Sion W. to Mary Louisa Pyles 4-17-1856 (4-8?-1856) Ma
Boon, Sion to Mary A. Hatchett 6-6-1846 G
Boon, Thomas J. to Mary E. Patterson 10-21-1862 G
Boon, William M. to Sarah Todd 11-19-1866 (11-22-1866) Ma
Boon, Wm. A. to Almedia Prichard 1-17-1877 (1-18-1877) Dy
Boone, James L. to Catharine Gosey 7-22-1879 L
Boone, John to Caroline Cross 1-5-1876 Dy
Boone, Jordon B. to Elizabeth L. Short 1-8-1844 (1-11-1844) Ma
Boone, Marion to Clarissa Ann Magary 12-25-1871 (12-27-1871) Dy
Boone, Samuel to Celia Ann Fogg 8-22-1869 G B
Boone, Thomas to Susan Matlock 11-24-1867 Be
Boose, Andrew to Tennie Ferrill 5-18-1876 Dy
Booser, Ivason to Mary Smith 9-28-1871 T
Booth, B. F. to Sarah Hall 12-21-1859 (12-24-1859) Sh

Booth, D. C. to Josephine Ray 8-25-1882 (8-27-1882) L
Booth, D. C. to Sarah L. Fincher 3-17-1880 (3-21-1880) L
Booth, David C. to Amelia J. Jernigan 3-9-1839 (no return) F
Booth, David C. to Mary L. Menascoe 5-7-1866 (5-11-1866) T
Booth, David to Lucinda Tidwell 11-30-1865 Mn
Booth, Elam to Sarah Meadows 1-11-1874 Hy
Booth, Greenwood to Julia Ann Jane Shane 8-29-1849 (8-30-1849) G
Booth, H. C. to F. D. Avery 1-4-1860 (1-4-1860) G
Booth, J. B. to E. E. Clark 12-17-1878 Hy
Booth, James B. to Sarah C. Pearcy 7-5-1870 Hy
Booth, Joel to Martha Gregory 10-2-1851 Hr
Booth, John L. to Sarah E. Allison 8-6-1861 O
Booth, Peter to George A. Averet 4-6-1869 Hy
Booth, Purley M. to Nancy Owens 12-11-1839 Hn
Booth, Ratliff to Elizabeth Adkins 10-13-1846 G
Booth, Richard to Kate DeLaroque 11-1-1864 (11-3-1864) Sh
Booth, S. G. to Cynthia Tatum 10-18-1866 G
Booth, William to E. Davis 6-12-1857 Sh
Booth, William to Rebecca Dickson 10-23-1839 (10-31-1839) F
Booth, William to Sarah L. Bloodworth 2-21-1847 G
Booth, Wm. A. to Martha A. Moore 4-2-1845 F
Booth, Wm. to Mary F. Slaughter 2-12-1868 F
Boothe, Abijah H. to Melinda McCarley 2-2-1842 (2-3-1842) Hr
Boothe, Alvis to Lucy N. Brooks 4-18-1854 (no return) Hn
Boothe, James to Elizabeth Dunn 1-4-1842 Hn
Boothe, John L. to Sarah E. Birmingham 11-13-1856 O
Boothe, John S. to Martha E. Dortch 6-24-1852 Hn
Boothe, Warren J. to Sarah Ann Bromly 12-9-1852 Sh
Boothe, William B. to Mary A. Klutts 8-2-1858 (no return) Hn
Boothe, William D. to Melinda Roney 9-5-1855 (9-6-1855) O
Boothe, William H. to Caroline Hansel 6-2-1853 Hn
Boothe, William H. to Rebecca Hastings 10-25-1849 Hn
Boothe, William to Jane Barbee 3-9-1839 Hn
Bopford, John M. to Harriett C. Randle 12-22-1859 Hn
Bora, Antonio to Catharine DeLagorio 4-18-1855 (4-22-1855) Sh
Bordeaux, Anthony to Fannie Price 8-4-1869 (no return) F B
Borden, Luther to Amanda Wood 10-24-1861 Sh
Borden, S. R. to S. J. Williams 8-21-1861 Hn
Boren, Alfred to Nancy Clark 7-24-1827 Sh
Boren, Frank to Jane Batts 11-18-1866 G
Boren, H. J. to Martha J. Edwards 12-26-1865 (12-28-1865) Cr
Boren, Hosea to E. F. Thurmond 3-20-1878 Dy
Boren, James W. to Elizabeth Fussell 12-12-1867 Ma
Boren, Jas. F. to Anne Bethell 9-9-1845 Sh
Boren, Wm. A. to Permelia J. Jeffries 12-12-1870 (12-13-1870) Ma
Borihus, Nelson to Lucilla Gray 2-12-1863 Mn
Borin, Ozy to Elizabeth McFarlin 5-19-1870 (no return) Dy
Boring, Armistead to Nancy Greenlaw 9-17-1831 Sh
Bornemann, Gustavus to Beth Grone (Grove?) 7-3-1856 Sh
Boro, James to Sarah Weibel 7-26-1851 Sh
Boro, Vincent to Theresa Brignadello 1-7-1858 (1-10-1858) Sh
Borough, William B. to Mary J. Griffin 7-1-1862 (no return) Hy
Boroughs, Henry C. to Martha O. Bivins 12-23-1846 (12-24-1846) F
Boroum, Daniel P. to Mary A. K. Boyd 2-19-1842 (2-22-1843?) L
Borroughs, Aaron to Eliza S. Bradshaw 6-22-1835 (6-23-1835) Hr
Borsh, George to Fanny Parker 12-14-1865 G
Borsh, George to Susan Isabelle Rich 4-8-1869 G
Borthwick, M. S. to Almira A. Bocock 4-27-1861 Sh
Borum, Henry to Polly Thornton 8-2-1879 (8-3-1879) L B
Borum, J. Hubbard to Sallie E. W. Owen 6-15-1859 Hy
Borum, J. W. W. to Martha J. Butler 1-2-1869 (1-4-1869) Dy
Borum, James H. to Martha J. Durham 6-29-1868 (6-30-1868) L
Borum, James W. to Nancy E. Gains 6-17-1868 (6-18-1868) L
Borum, James to Mary Bolt 12-17-1838 Sh
Borum, Joseph H. to Ann C. Brooks 2-9-1841 T
Borum, Richd. to Julia A. Harris 1-4-1870 (no return) Hy
Borum, Sam to Jane Turpin 4-16-1885 (4-16-1886?) L
Borum, Toney to Ezilda Owen 10-31-1869 Hy
Borun, Thomas T. to Ann Notgrass 11-11-1847 (no return) F
Bosberne, John to Polly Hay(May) 9-9-1829 Hr
Bosch, Fred to Louisa Geneve Kowskie 7-2-1864 Sh
Boscheers, Ben Franklin to Louisa Patterson 8-14-1869 (3?-15-1869) Ma
Boshiers, Taylor to Nancy Edwards 7-1-1865 (7-2-1865) O
Bosler, Charles A. to Pulina Buck 11-10-1854 (11-12-1854) Sh
Bosler, John E. to Frances E. Buck 12-27-1852 (12-29-1852) Sh
Bossett (Bopett?), W. H. to Caroline H. Toon 2-14-1854 Sh
Bossie, Wm. to Lucy Cooper 8-10-1840 Cr
Bostian, J. C. to Louisa Price 10-5-1859 (10-6-1859) Hr
Bostic (Bolster), Hamon (Harmon?) to Olivia Eliz. Jane Powell 6-8-1843 Sh
Bostic, Allen to Annie Lee 11-2-1867 (11-9-1867) L B
Bostic, Anderson to Millie Curren 12-8-1877 (12-16-1877) L
Bostic, C. R. to Nancy Clark 11-20-1865 Hn
Bostic, William to Mary Ann Taylor 12-20-1843 Hn
Bostick, C. D. to A. F. Carr 2-5-1851 Hn
Bostick, Chas. D. to Rutha A. J. Owen 3-30-1848 (no return) Hn
Bostick, James H. to Lovenna S. Swearingain 3-31-1831 Sh

Bostick, Jas. R. to Ann Manning 8-5-1856 Sh
Bostick, John to Mary Carrington 12-30-1845 (12-31-1845) Ma
Bostick, John to Susanna B. Hudson 2-22-1841 (2-24-1841) Ma
Bostick, Levi to Caroline Carring 10-15-1846 Ma
Bostick, R. F. to Sarah J. Riggs 4-24-1861 We
Bostick, R. to Arrena Gray 12-20-1882 (12-21-1882) L
Bostick, Shade to Ellen Wright 12-27-1882 (12-28-1882) L
Bostick, Thos. A. to Rebecca J. Luckado 1-1-1850 (1-2-1850) F
Bostick, W. A. to Mary A. Bowden 9-11-1866 Hn
Boston, Jacob to Mary Ann Jenkins 6-30-1870 (7-2-1870) Cr
Boston, James S. to Ellen Fellows 6-18-1859 (6-19-1859) Sh
Boston, Jesse to Catharine E. Bunch 4-30-1870 (5-1-1870) Cr
Boston, John T. to Sarah M. Jones 9-17-1867 G
Boston?, M. L. to Martha A. Gee 12-13-1858 Cr
Boswell, Benjamin to Sarah P. Rowland 12-12-1860 Cr
Boswell, C. A. to R. A. Avery 3-28-1865 G
Boswell, Daniel Buford to Frances Dacus 9-27-1848 (9-28-1848) T
Boswell, G. W. to Ellen Fuqua 1-23-1871 (no return) Cr
Boswell, George W. to Mary Coleman 10-30-1848 Cr
Boswell, Henry C. to Candis Warmock 7-14-1844 Be
Boswell, J. M. to Mary H. Route 2-7-1857 (2-8-1857) Hr
Boswell, J. R. to Adelaide F. Brown 3-28-1861 (3-29-1861) Sh
Boswell, J. T. to Anne E. Rowland 3-20-1861 (no return) Cr
Boswell, J. Thomas to E. Jane Avery 1-7-1860 (1-8-1860) G
Boswell, James D. to Martha A. Kavanaugh 12-27-1877 Hy
Boswell, John D. to Amanda Dacus 9-3-1859 T
Boswell, John Davis to Martha L. Dacus 12-28-1854 T
Boswell, John J. to Sarah J. Allen 10-29-1856 Be
Boswell, John to Elizabeth Jane Dacus 2-11-1847 T
Boswell, Jonathan to Elizabeth Horne 10-30-1849 Ma
Boswell, M. T. to Mamie Beloate 1-12-1880 (1-13-1880) L
Boswell, N. H. to Catharine Merrit 10-12-1865 (11-6-1865) T
Boswell, Nicholas H. to Eliza Jane Baskins 6-9-1842 T
Boswell, Stephen to Celia Durden 4-16-1851 Be
Boswell, Stephen to Elizabeth Martin 9-17-1853 Be
Boswell, Thomas H. to Unie Chester 2-2-1859 We
Boswell, Thos. H. to Mary E. Tipping 11-11-1864 (11-12-1864) Sh
Boswell, Thos. L. to Charlete Jones 10-6-1837 G
Boswell, W. C. to Eliza McCarroll 10-1-1864 (10-2-1864) T
Boswell, W. H. to Harriett Burnett 12-5-1853 (no return) F
Boswell, Wm. to Mahaly C. Arnold 1-9-1850 Be
Bottem, James M. to Julia A. Hutcheson 12-18-1866 (12-5?-1866) L
Bottenberg, Andrew J. to Elizabeth McDonald 11-22-1864 Sh
Botto, Joseph to Margaret Botto 5-4-1860 (5-6-1860) Sh
Botto, Joseph to May Sangueneth 6-10-1847 Sh
Botto, Louis to Hattie Morse 5-24-1864 Sh
Bottom, Granville M. to Easter O'Daniel 12-21-1854 G
Bottoms, D. H. to Margarette N. Bowles 3-28-1865 G
Bottoms, J. K. to Mahulda J. Boyett 1-13-1868 G
Bottoms, James M. to Ann F. Davis 1-10-1855 G
Bottoms, P. A. to Mary Alphin 2-24-1865 G
Bottoms, Presley L. to Arvazena Keathley 7-25-1857 (7-26-1857) G
Bottoms, Starling S. to Adaline O'Daniel 12-23-1860 G
Bottoms, Thomas N. to Susanna Coplend 11?-6-1871 (9?-6-1871) L
Bottoms, W. S. B. to S. A. Gammon 11-3-1873 O
Bottoms, William A. to Mary F. Peel 1-29-1870 (no return) L
Bottoms, William to Elizabeth McBride 6-26-1848 (7-6-1848) Hr
Botts, James H. to Eliza Ann Klutts 9-?-1844 (no return) Hn
Botts, Jno. T. to Lyde Tomlin 12-1-1868 Ma
Boty, George to Roxan Chambers 2-26-1872 O
Bouchell, J. B. to Lucy J. Delony 9-30-1857 Sh
Boucher, Gilbert B. to Philadelphia Ann Hankley 12-1-1858 Hr
Bouchette, R. M. to Emma O. Polk 12-31-1842 (1-3?-1843) F
Bough, Johnathan to Sarah Maye 8-25-1866 T
Boughman, J. R. to Mary J. Orr 11-25-1844 We
Boughner (Beughner?), John to L. M. Smith 7-28-1864 Sh
Boughton, Wallace W. to Tabetha White 4-11-1863 Mn
Bouldin, G. W. to M. A. Mullins 4-13-1870 (4-14-1870) Cr
Boulger, Chas. to Mary Finnigan 12-31-1847 Sh
Boulin, Solomon to Lucinda Rogers 6-11-1825 O
Boult, John H. to Caroline Trotter 12-9-1839 (12-19-1839) F
Boulton, Charles to Sarah Campbell 6-6-1830 Sh
Boulton, James to Martha Dean 3-16-1825 Sh
Boulton, Washington to Sarah Dandridge 1-15-1833 Sh
Bounds, George to Ida A. Nobles 2-28-1870 (3-2-1870) F
Bounds, J. J. to Nisha A. Winfield 7-18-1865 F
Bounds, Joseph B. to Margarett A. Boales 9-21-1847 (10-10-1847) F
Bounds, Sterling to Marry A. East 8-29-1843 (9-5-1843) F
Bounds, Thomas to Margarett Floyed 12-7-1841 (12-9-1841) F
Bourk (Burke), John J. to Ann Donovan 8-15-1863 Sh
Bourk (Burke), Wm. to Margaret Burke 7-26-1856 (7-29-185_) Sh
Bourk, Patrick to Sarah McCullaf 2-21-1862 (2-24-1862) Sh
Bourland, James R. to Olivia J. (Mrs.) Lewis 2-20-1871 (2-21-1871) Ma
Bourland, W. P. to E. A. Dickson 12-22-1870 G
Bourn, P. A. to Lucy E. Moss 10-11-1870 (10-12-1870) T
Bovett, Charles to Ellen Reid 11-28-1843 Sh
Bowan, S. T. to Drusilla Price 12-25-1856 Hn

Bowden, A. J. to Eliza Leach 11-20-1853 T
Bowden, B. D. to Sarah A. Hamsbury 10-?-1842 Hn
Bowden, Balder D. to J. Anderson 9-5-1850 Hn
Bowden, Benjamin K. to Ann Raspberry 10-21-1857 Hn
Bowden, Dempsey to Rhoda Owen 1-10-1850 Hn
Bowden, Edward G. to Leuize Phillips 11-11-1846 Hn
Bowden, Elijah to Sarah Martial 12-23-1853 Hn
Bowden, G. W. to N. E. Buckley 3-31-1856 Hn
Bowden, J. H. to Elzada Carter 2-23-1851 Hn
Bowden, James C. to Artemesia Patterson 2-26-1855 (no return) Hn
Bowden, James J. to Elizabeth Poe 10-12-1848 Hn
Bowden, James M. to Sarah H. Cope 12-18-1856 (no return) Hn
Bowden, James M. to Sarah J. Petty 8-10-1854 Hn
Bowden, Jeremiah to Maria Myers 11-15-1853 T
Bowden, Jesse to Elizabeth Smith 2-19-1847 (no return) F
Bowden, John H. to Perlina Poiner 10-29-1845 (no return) Hn
Bowden, John to Mahala Porter 9-16-1865 Hn
Bowden, Lea to Mattie Clay 7-2-1874 (7-3-1874) L B
Bowden, Matthew T. to Amanda E. Atkins 11-13-1850 Hn
Bowden, R. D. to M. A. Roulet 5-20-1856 We
Bowden, Robert D. to Eliza J. Goode 12-29-1840 Hn
Bowden, Roderick to Ellen Hagler 2-15-1868 (no return) Hn
Bowden, Sumners D. to Martha C. Allen 1-12-1860 Hn
Bowden, Tandy to Nancy Hamilton 12-28-1868 G B
Bowden, Thomas P. to Mary Ellin Bonigle? 12-26-1866 (12-27-1866) T
Bowden, Thomas to Elizabeth Z. McKinnie 3-6-1843 (3-8-1843) Hr
Bowden, Thos. L. to Virginia Cardwell 5-4-1858 (5-6-1858) O
Bowden, Thos. P. to Mary J. Erwin 7-1-1874 T
Bowden, W. J. to L. H. Caton 10-1-1865 Hn
Bowden, William F. to Sophronia A. Cox 6-9-1859 Hn
Bowelen, J. W. to Mary F. Phillips 1-2-1867 Cr
Bowen, A. C. to M. J. Earle 2-21-1871 (no return) Dy
Bowen, Arthur to Phinity Parker 11-21-1848 Sh
Bowen, George to Mary Jane Jordan 3-11-1840 (no return) F
Bowen, J. P. to Laura Henderson 10-4-1870 (10-6-1870) Dy
Bowen, J. W. to Sophia Grimbley 3-21-1860 (3-22-1860) Sh
Bowen, James W. to Lucinda Adkins 9-13-1843 (9-14-1843) F
Bowen, James to Lutitia Parker 12-7-1872 O
Bowen, James to Narcissa Arnold 11-2-1870 (no return) Dy B
Bowen, John H. to Henrietta S. (Mrs.) Avery 7-19-1864 (7-20-1864) Sh
Bowen, John H. to Mary C. Armour 4-30-1845 Sh
Bowen, John H. to Sarah Cherry 9-18-1865 Hn
Bowen, John to E. J. E. Coopwood 4-22-1851 Sh
Bowen, Jonah to Martha Childers 11-9-1864 (11-10-1864) Dy
Bowen, Marcus to Fannie Porter 12-28-1872 (12-30-1872) Dy
Bowen, Mark to Fanny Rice 10-13-1866 (10-14-1866) Dy
Bowen, Mark to Lizzie Howell 4-15-1885 (no return) L
Bowen, P. H. to V. G. Polk 3-9-1864 (3-15-1864) F
Bowen, Thomas C. to Nancy C. Branden 3-13-1872 Hy
Bowen, W. E. to Nancy E. Thomas 1-17-1872 O
Bowen, William to Easter D. Craig 2-4-1833 (2-7-1833) G
Bowen, Wm. to S. M. Lemons 10-1-1867 (10-2-1867) Dy
Bowen, Zachariah to Hanah Holaway 9-21-1837 (9-28-1837) G
Bower, E. R. to Mary Ann Heath 12-6-1849 F
Bower, Elijah R. to Jane N. Keating 5-28-1845 (6-12-1845) G
Bower, James A. to Mary C. Jones 1-12-1867 (1-15-1867) T
Bowers (Bonner?), Timothy to Mary Needham 11-2-1853 (10?-3-1853) Sh
Bowers, A. C. to M. B. Perry 2-8-1866 Hn
Bowers, A. H. to Sidney Cox 2-2-1856 (2-4-1856) Sh
Bowers, A. J. to C. M. Abington 12-18-1843 O
Bowers, Albert to Emeline Byars 12-28-1870 (no return) Hy
Bowers, Algernon S. to Sarah Ann Rebecca Bowers 9-22-1840 Hr
Bowers, Allen to Jane O. K. Allen 7-20-1858 (7-21-1858) G
Bowers, Andy to Mary Baird 7-6-1867 (no return) F B
Bowers, B. to Susan H. Cunliffe 10-31-1859 (11-1-1859) F
Bowers, Billy to Liza Whitehead 6-24-1869 Hy
Bowers, Charles A. to Jane C. Winn 12-23-1847 Sh
Bowers, Charles to Lucy M. Clark 10-3-1867 G
Bowers, David to Polly Mayfield 2-10-1844 (2-13-1844) G
Bowers, Ed to Arena Hudson 3-28-1870 (3-29-1870) F B
Bowers, Finis to Ida Watson 12-26-1870 (no return) F B
Bowers, G. M. D. to F. E. A. Graves 11-1-1875 (no return) L
Bowers, G. M. D. to Mary E. Bowers 1-20-1868 (no return) L
Bowers, H. to Susan Robertson 11-9-1882 (no return) L
Bowers, Henry C. to Fanny E. Newton 8-22-1865 (8-23-1865) T
Bowers, Henry to Anna Flippin 12-17-1868 (no return) F B
Bowers, Isaac to Veniann Taylor 5-19-1868 F B
Bowers, Jacob to Margaret J. Allen 6-26-1850 Sh
Bowers, Jacob to Rebecca H. Doudy 4-2-1845 (4-9-1845) F
Bowers, James Henry to Cordelia Ann Joice 1-12-1846 (not executed) T
Bowers, James Henry to Marina Jane Acock 3-12-1846 Sh
Bowers, Joe to Julia Miller 9-7-1867 F B
Bowers, John A. to Amanda Whitaker 1-24-1831 Hr
Bowers, John H. to Mary A. Allen 2-16-1848 (2-17-1848) Hr
Bowers, John R. A. to Sudie A. Bradberry 12-29-1858 We
Bowers, John to Adaline Russell 10-28-1853 (no return) Hn
Bowers, John to Eliza Wiley 8-14-1867 (no return) Hn

Bowers, Joseph to Amanda Davidson 11-18-1871 (12-20-1871) L
Bowers, Lewis to Becky Pettus 12-27-1869 (12-23?-1869) F B
Bowers, Lewis to Emma Brown 12-27-1869 (12-23?-1869) F B
Bowers, Luke to Christianer Athens 4-22-1871 (4-23-1871) F B
Bowers, Mack to Susan Boyd 3-27-1869 (3-28-1869) F B
Bowers, Philemon Y. to Margaret McDougle 7-2-1829 G
Bowers, Robbin to Florrence Bowers 1-5-1867 F B
Bowers, S. T. to J. F. Chapman 3-19-1866 (3-31-1866) T
Bowers, Southerland to Louisa Bryan 12-14-1854 Sh
Bowers, Thomas to Lucinda Luttrell 12-28-1865 Mn
Bowers, Thos. R. to E. A. Jones 11-18-1851 Cr
Bowers, W. C. to Mary S. Wilcox 12-8-1846 We
Bowers, W. F. to Frances V. Tucker 11-24-1856 (11-25-1856) T
Bowers, W. H. to Amerca J. Brown 10-2-1865 (10-3-1865) T
Bowers, William M. to Harriet Murray 10-14-1844 (no return) Hn
Bowers, Wm. P. to C. G. Speckernagle 2-8-1858 (2-9-1858) Sh
Bowers, thomas to Obediance Baley 3-13-1833 (3-14-1833) G
Bowie, J. K. P. to Sarah E. Rush 1-9-1867 L
Bowie, John T. to Caroline Matilda Arnold 10-28-1874 L
Bowie, Thos. W. to Margaret Lawler 8-30-1856 Sh
Bowland, Alexander to Elizabeth Blessing 7-29-1841 F
Bowlen, John to Ann Smith 5-2-1859 Sh
Bowles, A. A. to Letty Bishop 11-2-1853 Cr
Bowles, Calvin to Nancy A. Sheets 5-30-1854 (6-1-1854) Hr
Bowles, Elijah B. to Maylissa G. C. Powers 12-30-1850 Hn
Bowles, Geo. W. to Martha A. Blankenship 11-7-1861 G
Bowles, J. S. to E. M. Turnage 3-21-1871 (3-23-1872?) T
Bowles, J. W. to Sarah P. Ellis 9-18-1844 Hn
Bowles, James B. to Melinda H. Null 9-30-1850 Cr
Bowles, James to Rebecca A. Gaylord 7-18-1860 G
Bowles, John R. to Betsy Ann McIver 1-30-1856 (2-5-1856) Ma
Bowles, John to Joanna Bond 3-5-1866 (no return) Hn
Bowles, Philip D. to Sarah Virginia Heart 10-27-1846 (10-28-1846) T
Bowles, Wm. B. to M. T. P. Ferrell 12-3-1864 (12-4-1867) T
Bowles, Zebulon P. to Elvira W. Montague 2-26-1845 Sh
Bowlin, Alec. to Amanda Warren 8-30-1862 (9-1-1862) Dy
Bowlin, Alex to Jerusha Watson 10-13-1847 Hn
Bowlin, Hiram to Abigill? Bell 5-16-1869 Hy
Bowlin, J. C. to Elizabeth Harris 1-4-1853 (1-5-1853) Sh
Bowlin, S. C. to E. J. Winstead 7-10-1856 We
Bowlin, Thomas to Mariah Weakley 10-29-1866 (maybe 1870) G
Bowlin?, Peter to Lethy House 5-15-1848 Hn
Bowling, Alexander to Sarah J. Davie 11-29-1850 Ma
Bowling, Andrw J. to Eliza Smith 9-17-1851 (9-18-1851) G
Bowling, Bernard to Olivia Bowers 2-13-1861 (2-14-1861) Hr
Bowling, E. H. to Almira Winstead 4-19-1844 (no return) We
Bowling, James A. to M. F. Farrow 1-2-1860 (no return) Hy
Bowling, Joe to Drucilla Strictlin 12-12-1870 (no return) Hy
Bowling, Phillip to Puss Sawyer 12-25-1871 (12-27-1871) Dy
Bowling, Powell to Susan Thomas 1-16-1861 G
Bowls (Rowls), Jackson to Atha Worf 2-16-1853 Sh
Bowls, Charles A. to Sarah A. Jackson 2-1-1855 (2-3-1855) G
Bowls, J. C. to N. A. Anders 4-25-1869 Hy
Bowls, John T. to Rachel B. Stubbs 8-9-1831 Ma
Bowls, Joseph to Mary E. Throgmartin 10-23-1861 (no return) We
Bowls, Joshua to Matilda Miller 2-3-1870 Hy
Bowls, Sampson to Ella Bromley 8-28-1877 (no return) Hy
Bowls, Willes to Sina Hill 7-26-1869 Hy
Bowls, William G. to Elizabeth A. Barrott 8-24-1860 G
Bowman, Alex to Lucy Bowman 5-23-1866 (no return) Hn
Bowman, Charley to Emma Evans 2-25-1873 Hy
Bowman, G. F. to Amanda B. Duke 5-13-1867 (5-14-1867) Dy
Bowman, Henry to China Bowman 5-23-1866 (no return) Hn
Bowman, J. G. to Nancy Powell 1-5-1870 Dy
Bowman, Joshua M. to Mary (Mrs.) Bowman 12-14-1867 (12-15-1867) Ma
Bowman, N. L. to Ella McCrackin 4-24-1875 (4-28-1875) Dy
Bowman, Samuel C. to Isabella P. Sanford 5-18-1856 Hn
Bowman, Simon to Annie Mann 1-30-1869 Hy
Bowman, Thos. C. to Fanny B. Bass 4-24-1867 F
Bowman, Wm. to Eliza G. Crisp 12-21-1837 G
Box, Charles to Eliza Watson 12-22-1861 Be
Box, Edward to Mary Ann Morrison 4-3-1847 O
Box, Edward to Nancy Medley 8-15-1845 (8-16-1845) O
Box, George to Sarah A. F. Butrum 11-3-1858 (11-4-1858) O
Box, James H. to Harriet A. Hood 9-25-1865 (10-18-1865) Cr
Box, James M. to Frances S. Hudson 10-7-1846 Hr
Box, James S. to Elizabeth Newton 8-4-1845 (8-6-1845) O
Box, James to Roxannah Johnson 10-7-1862 (10-8-1862) O
Box, Jeptha to S. E. (Mrs.) Shelton 12-10-1865 (12-18-1865) G
Box, Jess to Martha E. (Mrs.) Stewart 3-11-1870 (3-13-1870) Ma
Box, Joseph to Ruthey Morrison 2-22-1847 O
Box, Robert to Edny Ron? 7-31-1830 (8-10-1830) Hr
Box, Robert to Temperance Gray 1-4-1841 (1-7-1841) Hr
Box, Stephen to Elizabeth Harper 1-28-1835 Hr
Box, Steven to Adaline Moore 11-25-1854 (11-30-1854) Hr
Box, Thomas to Nancy Wynne 2-21-1866 Hr
Box, William to Elizabeth Stroud 4-18-1836 O

Boxley, D. S. to Agness W. Smith 11-23-1835 Hr
Boyaknir, Lynn to H. J. McLennahan 1-20-1871 (1-22-1871) T
Boyce, Alexander K. to Harriet E. Boyce 9-3-1848 Sh
Boyce, Jas. L. to Mary L. Boyce 9-3-1848 Sh
Boyce, Leonidas H. to Margaret A. Bass 12-31-1861 (1-5-1861) Hr
Boyce, Robt. to Amanda Harris 10-28-1871 (11-2-1871) T
Boyce, Wm. H. (Dr.) to Sarah W. Jones 12-20-1836 Sh *
Boyd, Aleck to Jane Morrow 3-28-1866 (3-31-1866) F B
Boyd, Alfred to Frances Leea? 6-5-1833 (6-6-1833) Hr
Boyd, Allen to Sallie Ann Barbee 1-20-1870 (no return) Hy
Boyd, Amos to Mary Williams 2-6-1861 (2-8-1861) Hr
Boyd, Archibald to Mary Ann Emerson 9-22-1858 (9-23-1858) Ma
Boyd, Armistead to Violet Ann Fults 2-2-1869 T
Boyd, B. K. to S. A. McFadden 4-11-1864 (4-12-1864) F
Boyd, B. P. to Elizabeth Taylor 9-10-1867 Hy
Boyd, Burril to Fannie Thomas 12-22-1866 T
Boyd, C. M. to Mary E. Hill 12-23-1856 Cr
Boyd, Dan to Ella Wilson 1-1-1871 Hy
Boyd, Dave to S. Thompson 7-16-1859 Cr
Boyd, David H. to Penelope C. Edwards 4-14-1840 Cr
Boyd, David to Tennessee Hunter 12-22-1875 (no return) Hy
Boyd, E. B. to Margaret C. Calahan 1-1-1864 (no return) Hn
Boyd, Elias B. to Sarah A. Rushing 9-18-1855 (no return) Hn
Boyd, Elisha T. to Matilda Jane Elkins 12-17-1868 Be
Boyd, Felix to Mary Crosby 1-6-1871 (no return) F
Boyd, George D. to Lizzie Nixon 1-3-1882 (1-4-1882) L
Boyd, George P. to Paralee R. Scott 2-1-1857 We
Boyd, George to Elizabeth Flemings 4-27-1867 Be
Boyd, George to Emily Pickett 12-1-1874 (no return) Hy
Boyd, George to Vina Hill 8-8-1873 T
Boyd, Hal to Catharine Williams 1-13-1859 (1-17-1859) Hr
Boyd, Henry Clay to Nannie Edwards 6-28-1867 (6-29-1867) Dy
Boyd, Henry to Amy Cobbs 2-6-1869 F B
Boyd, Henry to Lila Hampton 12-27-1877 Hy
Boyd, Hugh to Eliza Jane Ramsey 6-1-1859 Hn
Boyd, Hugh to Mary Lemons 2-5-1855 (2-7-1855) Ma
Boyd, J. P. to M. J. Colvin 10-14-1882 (10-18-1882) L
Boyd, J. T. to Elizabeth F. Orr 3-27-1867 G
Boyd, J. W. to Winney M. Rogers 7-12-1864 Hn
Boyd, J. Y. to Mollie R. Loving 1-29-1870 (no return) Hy
Boyd, J. Y. to Virginia A. Wray 1-1-1851 F
Boyd, Jabez T. to Emily M. Pinkston 8-25-1868 (8-26-1868) Cr
Boyd, James A. to Mary Jones 8-20-1850 Cr
Boyd, James G. to Manda C. Pinkston 2-24-1853 Cr
Boyd, James G. to Nancy M. Keykendall 7-16-1846 Cr
Boyd, James G. to P. Q. Alexander 3-17-1851 Cr
Boyd, James M. to Atila Paschall 11-7-1846 Hn
Boyd, James S. to Iva McMullen 5-7-1860 (5-10-1860) F
Boyd, James S. to Narcissa C. Pope 2-26-1851 L
Boyd, James W. to Caroline A. Malone 2-6-1845 (2-8-1845) Ma
Boyd, James to Ann Graiger 11-10-1852 Ma
Boyd, James to M. J. Farmer 12-20-1858 (12-22-1858) T
Boyd, Jessee to Emily Morrow 1-19-1867 F B
Boyd, Jno. T. to Sarah A. S. Posey 6-1-1843 L
Boyd, Jo L. to Harriett Bond 9-15-1880 (9-18-1880) L B
Boyd, Jo to Ellis Jones 11-13-1879 (not executed) L B
Boyd, Joe L. to Bedience Glenn 10-1-1876 Hy
Boyd, Joe L. to Bell Colman 2-12-1880 (no return) L
Boyd, Joe to Maggie Stewart 10-22-1871 Hy
Boyd, John C. to Sarah J. Myrick 11-30-1859 Hr
Boyd, John E. to Dora E. McLemore 5-12-1870 Ma *
Boyd, John G. to Martha J. Gardner 8-16-1858 Cr
Boyd, John George to Harriet Sitner 3-19-1872 T
Boyd, John to Elvira Poindexter 12-26-1867 (12-27-1867) F B
Boyd, John to M. E. Hendrix 1-30-1866 (1-31-1866) Dy
Boyd, John to Margaret Turnage 8-13-1873 (8-14-1873) T
Boyd, John to Martha Rust 2-18-1841 Cr
Boyd, Joseph B. to Mary A. Bridges 12-16-1862 Hn
Boyd, Joshua to Martha J. Butler 3-15-1847 Cr
Boyd, L. L. to Musadora Reeves 1-27-1866 (1-30-1866) F
Boyd, Lewis to Harriet Ware 1-4-1871 (no return) Hy
Boyd, Lorenza B. to Julian Dowell 12-11-1852 (12-15-1852) G
Boyd, Lovelace to Esther Taylor 8-24-1878 L
Boyd, Lovelace to Flora Walker 4-8-1876 (no return) Hy
Boyd, M. M. to Eliza Green 7-19-1865 F
Boyd, Marcellus to Myra Hay 5-19-1861 Hy
Boyd, Milton B. to Mary L. W. Becton 10-26-1850 (10-27-1850) Ma
Boyd, P. C. to Mary W. McSwain 4-8-1852 Hn
Boyd, Paschall to Nancy B. Salmon 5-8-1865 (no return) Hn
Boyd, Patrick to Sary Avery 4-8-1863 Mn
Boyd, Richd. to Gracy Walker 1-18-1876 (no return) Hy
Boyd, Robert R. to Harriet Black 12-3-1861 Sh
Boyd, Robert S. to Martha G. Jones 7-17-1861 (7-18-1861) Cr
Boyd, Robert to Elizabeth Cassles 2-11-1852 G
Boyd, Robert to Sarah Lipscomb 12-10-1873 Hy
Boyd, Robt. A. to Emily G. Bagley 11-8-1858 (11-11-1858) Hr
Boyd, S. W. to Annie W. Nixon 5-19-1869 (no return) Hy

Boyd, Sam to Vick Stewart 10-15-1871 Hy
Boyd, Samuel R. to Sarah C. Hoofman 10-25-1838 Hn
Boyd, Shepard to Mary Royester 12-14-1873 Hy
Boyd, Silas to Delia Adams 11-18-1871 Hy
Boyd, Taylor to Susan Taylor 9-18-1878 L B
Boyd, Thomas B. to Jane Haywood 12-22-1842 Cr
Boyd, Thomas W. to Margaret J. Sullivan 3-21-1861 Sh
Boyd, Thomas to Ann McNamee 12-30-1849 Sh
Boyd, Thomas to Lucy Mahon 9-1-1877 Hy
Boyd, Thomas to Selina Bennett 9-6-1838 Cr
Boyd, Tom to Sidney Curley? 12-17-1870 Hy
Boyd, Will to Elizabeth Wynn 12-22-1841 Hn
Boyd, William A. to Mary Hudgins 1-11-1844 Hn
Boyd, William E. to Martha J. McMahan 4-9-1850 Sh
Boyd, William H. to Mollie E. Halliburton 6-17-1873 (6-18-1873) L
Boyd, William R. to Frances Caroline Posey 6-1-1843 L
Boyd, William T. to America P. Robison 4-29-1870 (5-1-1870) Cr
Boyd, William to Margaret Parnell 12-13-1862 (12-16-1862) Dy
Boyd?, Adam to Nancy Peter 12-1-1865 (12-3-1865) T
Boydston, Armstead W. to Tennessee V. Henley 11-30-1868 (12-1-1868) L
Boydston, Armsted W. to Emma E. Durham 2-25-1874 L
Boydston, B. F. to Martha F. Ledbetter 12-28-1881 L
Boydston, B. F. to Mary E. Crenshaw 7-26-1838 Hn
Boydston, Benj. F. to Mary Wood 8-28-1843 (8-30-1843) L
Boydston, Benjamin J. to Elizabeth Jacobs 11-12-1825 (11-15-1825) Hr
Boydston, James K. P. to Sarah J. McClelland 10-3-1866 L
Boydston, W. to Mary Lusk 8-30-1838 L
Boydston, William to Eliza Priscilla Pierce 9-18-1862 (9-22-1862) L
Boyed, D. T. to Eliza A. Cloyed 12-6-1854 (no return) F
Boyed, John J. to Mary E. Dalton 5-25-1848 F
Boyed, Presley D. to Manervy Ann Trotter 10-28-1852 (no return) F
Boyed, Thomas G. to Julia A. Macon 9-17-1840 (9-24-1840) F
Boyed, Whitfield to Locky Mariah Henderson 2-25-1841 F
Boyer, L. to Margaret Baldwin 12-6-1854 (12-7-1854) F
Boyer, Sireneus W. to Susan F. Allen 10-27-1851 (10-28-1851) Sh
Boyers, Rodwier? J. to Missouri S. Turner 5-19-1843 (5-21-1843) F
Boyers, S. J. to Lucy A. Curlin 8-26-1871 O
Boyet, William W. to Elizabeth T. Grant 10-6-1851 (10-9-1851) Ma
Boyett, B. S. to Elizabeth Andrews 9-10-1853 (9-15-1853) G
Boyett, Baptist to Mary Ann Fentris 1-16-1848 O
Boyett, Cullen J. to Delilah Watts 2-12-1846 G
Boyett, D. G. to Charrinda Crews 8-17-1838 (8-20-1838) G
Boyett, E. W. to S. A. Mitchell 12-22-1859 (12-25-1859) G
Boyett, Ezekiel to Eliza Jane Massey 5-6-1848 (5-18-1848) Ma
Boyett, G. T. to Harrit S. Bottoms 1-13-1868 G
Boyett, J. W. to Mary Whitley 2-12-1861 G
Boyett, James E. to Mary E. West 2-13-1860 (2-16-1860) O
Boyett, James T. to Margarett J. Baker 7-7-1857 (7-8-1857) G
Boyett, Joseph P. to Manerva M. West 6-30-1849 (7-12-1849) G
Boyett, Lewis M. to Elmira Morrow 6-5-1852 O
Boyett, Lycurgus to Louiza E. Clark 12-27-1858 (12-29-1858) G
Boyett, S. A. to Martha A. Sloane 5-13-1869 G
Boyett, Stephen A. to Jane Holloman 2-23-1858 (2-25-1858) O
Boyett, Thomas F. to Louisa Elmira West 12-8-1852 (12-9-1852) O
Boyett, Thomas H. to Letty Nedry 9-21-1850 (9-22-1850) O
Boyett, Thomas to Elizabeth Harris 12-15-1839 (12-19-1839) Ma
Boyett, Thomas to Nancy Reeves 1-17-1838 (1-21-1838) O
Boyett, W. G. to Sarah Abington 9-20-1848 L
Boyett, William B. to Elizabeth A. Woddy 10-8-1858 (10-14-1858) G
Boyett, Wm. B. to N. L. Bynum 4-20-1865 O
Boykin, Carren E. to Mary E. Matthews 4-17-1854 (4-18-1854) Ma
Boykin, Edmund to Claricy Nevills 10-30-1869 F B
Boykin, James M. to Eliza E. Cox 12-6-1861 (12-8-1861) Ma
Boykin, John E. to Rosalie A. Wilson 11-6-1855 (11-7-1855) Ma
Boykin, Samuel B. to Mattie U. Ferrel 12-12-1870 (12-14-1870) Ma
Boykin, Thadius H. to S. J. Hilliard 10-10-1860 T
Boykin, William O. to Martha J. Lane 11-17-1852 Ma
Boykin, William to Lida Catten 11-26-1868 T
Boylan, Balam to Katie Stewart 2-18-1871 (no return) F B
Boylan, Isiah to Lina Tucker 4-8-1871 (no return) F B
Boylan, Joseph to Sarah E. McCoy 1-18-1870 (no return) L
Boylan, Michail to Mary Shea 2-12-1861 Sh
Boyle (Boyd), Thos. to Bridgett Bresinhan 10-31-1860 Sh
Boyle, Anderson to Mat Rivers 1-12-1869 (1-17-1869) F B
Boyle, John to Jennie P. Looney 9-17-1863 Sh
Boyle, Thomas to Margaret Owen 11-23-1847 (11-25-1847) Hr
Boyle, Thomas to Mary Browning 11-3-1846 Hr
Boyle, Thomas to Mary Jane Love 10-19-1841 (10-21-1841) Hr
Boyle, W. F. to Jenny E. Hills 12-17-1861 (12-18-1861) Sh
Boynton, Henry to Henrietta Mathews 12-12-1876 Hy
Boys, Henry to Anna Warrack 7-17-1839 Be
Boyt, Elijah to Susan Crane 4-25-1830 G
Boyt, Elijah to Susan Crane 4-25-1831 G
Boyte, Baptist to Mahulda Evan 5-3-1828 (5-9-1828) O
Boyte, John A. to Ann A. Butler 1-11-1854 (1-12-1854) Hr
Boyte, John B. to Nancy M. McKaughan 7-6-1842 (7-7-1842) Hr
Boyte, Ollen to Mary A. Turner 12-12-1848 (12-21-1848) Hr

Boyte, Patrick to Nancy McVay 8-3-1853 (8-4-1853) Hr
Bozzle, John to Clara Jackson 4-29-1851 (5-4-1851) Hr
Bracchus, E. F. to Mary A. Allen 11-22-1858 Sh
Brach, Green to Mary L. Delany 3-12-1863 (no return) Cr
Brack, Franklyn to Nancy E. Plunk 1-17-1863 Mn
Brack, Washington to Martha Purvis 3-28-1839 Hn
Brack, William to Eliza Bonner 8-5-1885 (8-7-1885) L
Bracken, Jerry to Lizzie A. Whitmore 1-1-1868 (2-3-1868) F B
Bracken, Tom to Eliza Boyd 5-19-1868 (5-22-1868) F B
Brackens, Felix H. to Lydie A. Wyatt 7-16-1869 (7-17-1869) Cr
Bracker, Anderson to Emma Leech 11-16-1871 Hy
Brackett, Charles H. to Helen Mead 9-31?-1862 Sh
Brackin, A. F. to Eliza Looney 4-15-1838 F
Brackin, H. to Lucinda Pinkston 7-7-1841 Cr
Brackin, J. M. to Georgia A. Stevens 4-10-1878 Dy
Brackin, John to Sarah Perkins 8-9-1853 Cr
Brackin, Preston to Susan Arnold 2-6-1840 Cr
Brackin, Wm. A. to J. P. Butler 8-28-1872 (8-29-1872) Cr
Bracklin, Daniel to Mary Jane Maupin 10-17-1870 (10-22-1870) L
Bradberry, Charles to Elizabeth Sanders 2-9-1843 F
Bradberry, J. P. to M. J. Jones 10-28-1866 G
Bradberry, J. R. to Francis Cook 5-16-1859 We
Bradberry, James J. to Matilda Bruff 1-6-1830 (1-7-1830) G
Bradberry, James M. to Nancy Cox 12-20-1843 Cr
Bradberry, John H. to Francis A. Bullock 1-15-1859 We
Bradberry, John to Martha Gardner 3-21-1846 (3-25-1846) G
Bradberry, Joseph to Mary Ford 9-10-1852 We
Bradberry, W. B. to Susan J. Pickler 1-27-1864 (1-31-1864) Cr
Bradburn, Michael to Mariah Mosier 5-6-1854 (5-12-1854) L
Bradbury, John M. to Martha F. Moore 3-16-1857 (3-18-1857) Ma
Bradbury, John to Martha Combs 2-19-1846 G
Braden, A. C. to M. F. Simpson 2-26-1878 (2-27-1878) L
Braden, Absolum C. to Joana A. Glimp 12-1-1868 (12-2-1868) L
Braden, Anderson to Martha M. Pugh 5-18-1867 (no return) L B
Braden, B. P. to Sarah Harris 2-3-1849 F
Braden, Edward to Martha H. Taylor 11-7-1871 T
Braden, Francis M. to Margaret E. Clark 11-15-1855 (no return) L
Braden, Frank to Jemima Johnson 2-28-1866 (no return) F B
Braden, George to Annie Williams 8-9-1867 (8-10-1867) F B
Braden, Gus to Mary Martin 8-27-1869 F B
Braden, H. B. to M. J. Glimp 2-7-1882 (2-8-1882) L
Braden, Henry to Parthenia Goldsby 7-13-1854 We
Braden, Isaac to Gilly Hunter 10-22-1842 (10-23-1842) L
Braden, J. B. to J. L. (Mrs.) Alexander 1-23-1878 L
Braden, Jack to Mallie Fisher 4-5-1879 (4-7-1879) L B
Braden, James P. to Laura Paine 11-10-1869 (11-11-1869) F
Braden, James W. to Jane E. Castellaw 9-17-1857 L
Braden, James W. to Mary Lavina Curtis 7-7-1871 (7-8-1871) L
Braden, James to M. V. Webb 5-13-1847 L
Braden, James to Martha Ann Brown 12-17-1855 (12-18-1855) L
Braden, Jas. Henry to Elizabeth Mullins 1-4-1870 (no return) Hy
Braden, John D. to Elisabeth Stewart 11-23-1848 (11-30?-1848) F
Braden, John J. (I?) to Elmira A. Crook 12-14-1869 (no return) L
Braden, John Y. to L. H. J. Hipp 7-5-1851 (7-6-1851) L
Braden, John to A. L. M. Webb 8-27-1846 L
Braden, Joseph P. to Elizabeth Melton 11-1-1843 (11-3-1843) F
Braden, Knob to Neely Holt 4-30-1878 (5-1-1878) L
Braden, Nick to Mary Parr 4-1-1880 L B
Braden, R. A. to N. J. Pollard 2-3-1879 (2-4-1879) L
Braden, Reuben to Alcinia Catherine Brown 1-20-1853 L
Braden, Robert W. to Meranda Brown 12-17-1860 (12-19-1860) L
Braden, Robert to Ellen Henning 5-25-1874 L B
Braden, Soloman to Civil H. Burns 11-15-1868 Hy
Braden, Wiley A. to Alethy Belt? 9-9-1859 (9-15-1859) L
Braden, William to Susan M. Shirman 8-3-1846 (8-4-1846) L
Bradford, Alfred to Julia Clark 12-27-1866 Hy
Bradford, Andrew to Lindy Lucas 3-16-1874 Hy
Bradford, B. M. to H. A. Taylor 10-3-1872 Hy
Bradford, Carrol J. to Elizabeth R. Gingery 8-9-1847 (8-17-1847) L
Bradford, Crawford to Lucinda Allen 11-16-1852 Hn
Bradford, David A. to Jane Jorden 12-11-1861 (no return) L
Bradford, David A. to Margaret Buck (Burk?) 2-11-1839 (2-12-1839) L
Bradford, David to Bethi Davis 5-20-1877 Hy
Bradford, Dick to Agnes Jackson 12-7-1870 T
Bradford, Dickson to Nancy Davis 7-21-1867 Hy
Bradford, Eli to Lucy A. Lucus 2-21-1874 (2-22-1874) L
Bradford, Elisha M. to Elizabeth Rice 4-3-1882 (4-15-1882) L
Bradford, Ephraim to Polly (Patsy) Farr 2-14-1850 (2-17-1850) O
Bradford, Ephram to Rebecca Williams 3-27-1834 (7-4-1834) O
Bradford, G. H. to Mary J. Coleman 1-18-1866 Hy
Bradford, G. H. to Rutha A. E. Batchellor 9-5-1883 (9-6-1883) L
Bradford, G. M. to Mahailey Leonard 4-4-1851 Cr
Bradford, G. M. to Martha M. Barkley 12-26-1864 G
Bradford, G. M. to Mary E. Stults 9-17-1855 G
Bradford, George to Dilsey Shepperd 1-11-1876 (no return) Hy
Bradford, H. B. to Jane Tiner 8-12-1864 G
Bradford, H. S. to S. C. McSwain 1-16-1856 (no return) Hn

Bradford, H. T. to Elizabeth Williams 7-15-1845 Hn
Bradford, H. W. to Amanda Gillespie 5-10-1854 G
Bradford, Harris to Annitha Wallice 8-20-1859 G
Bradford, Harris to Elen J. Briant 12-11-1856 (12-12-1856) G
Bradford, Harris to Elizabeth James 5-12-1845 (5-15-1845) G
Bradford, Henry D. to Permelia Rice 12-30-1874 (no return) L B
Bradford, Henry to Ailsey Richardson 5-20-1834 Sh
Bradford, Henry to Eveline F. Hansel 4-4-1853 Be
Bradford, Henry to Rachel Meritt 12-30-1867 G B
Bradford, Henry to Rebecca Guyman 6-6-1844 Hn
Bradford, Isaac to Emma Larson 3-22-1884 (3-26-1884) L
Bradford, Isaac to Mary J. Taylor 12-30-1875 Hy
Bradford, J. A. to Bettie P. Sutton 12-17-1878 (12-18-1878) L
Bradford, J. B. to Mildred Taylor 4-3-1873 Hy
Bradford, J. M. to Martha R. Dougherty 7-7-1860 O
Bradford, J. P. to A. E. Stephens 8-19-1866 G
Bradford, Jacob to Dony Brown 12-24-1868 Hy
Bradford, James C. to Ann Reeves 7-24-1855 Ma
Bradford, James C. to Arrilla Kelly 1-21-1860 (9-31-1868) T
Bradford, James C. to Lucy Usery 10-5-1844 Ma
Bradford, James C. to Mary Williams 12-9-1844 G
Bradford, James M. to Narcissa C. Nuckolls 2-25-1860 (2-26-1860) Hr
Bradford, James to Mary E. Powers 6-30-1842 Hn
Bradford, James to Susan Upchurch 11-6-1849 Hn
Bradford, Jno. S. to Caroline N. Browning 12-17-1855 Hr
Bradford, John to Emily Nuckolls 7-19-1849 Hr
Bradford, John to Miranda Mann 12-29-1866 (no return) Hy
Bradford, Johram to Mahala Thraneer? 5-23-1863 (5-24-1863) O
Bradford, L. H. to Susan Foot 2-11-1856 (2-12-1856) Hr
Bradford, Lea to Anny Taylor 7-21-1867 Hy
Bradford, Lee to Mollie Yancy 12-5-1878 Hy
Bradford, Lee to Viva Wilson 12-17-1870 (no return) Hy
Bradford, M. to Linda Sanders 2-3-1875 (no return) Hy
Bradford, Mack to May Jones 6-22-1867 Hy
Bradford, Madison to Sarah Jane Taylor 1-12-1867 Hy
Bradford, Mame to Tiller Bond 9-28-1868 (no return) Hy
Bradford, Middleton to Lydia Bell McCollum 11-26-1846 Sh
Bradford, Moses to Tracey Bond 10-15-1874 Hy
Bradford, Peter to Elizabeth Curren 1-12-1878 L
Bradford, Peter to Sarah Ann Williams 1-22-1867 Hn
Bradford, R. C. to Addie Tilman 2-12-1884 (2-14-1884) L
Bradford, Ray to Minerva J. Greer 1-21-1844 (1-1?-1844) O
Bradford, Robert N. to Delila Moore 11-27-1866 Hn
Bradford, Robert P. to Mary Bradford 3-25-1858 Sh
Bradford, Robert to Martha Ford 9-9-1857 Sh
Bradford, Robert to Mary Baker 10-22-1853 (10-23-1853) G
Bradford, Robert to Mary F. Hall 7-30-1851 Cr
Bradford, S. G. to V. S. Anderson 2-17-1869 (no return) Hy
Bradford, Saml. to Lizzie Moore 7-27-1878 (7-28-1878) L
Bradford, Saml. to Martha Ann Anderson 1-8-1873 (1-11-1873) L B
Bradford, Sanford to Bertie Taylor 12-29-1871 Hy
Bradford, Silas to Pheby A. Burton 2-22-1871 (no return) Hy
Bradford, Spincer to Eliza Summons 2-14-1842 G
Bradford, Stephen to Betsy M. Taylor 2-25-1871 (no return) Hy
Bradford, Stephen to Rosa Hammons 8-19-1880 L B
Bradford, Thomas to Mariah W. Gillespie 7-30-1850 G
Bradford, Thomas to Sarah J. McGree 10-2-1862 G
Bradford, Tom to Linda Dean 12-31-1875 (no return) Hy
Bradford, W. G. to Elisa Oates 8-6-1848 Hr
Bradford, W. R. to Lavinia A. Powell 12-12-1866 (12-19-1866) L
Bradford, Warren to Elizabeth Harmon 2-28-1839 Hn
Bradford, William G. to Matildy Wilie 1-24-1829 Hr
Bradford, William to Harriet E. Moore 10-2-1849 G
Bradford, William to Martila Sturdevant 2-18-1868 (2-20-1868) Ma
Bradford, Wm. H. to Martha C. Kent 12-23-1845 (12-24-1845) L
Bradford, Young to Catherine E. Wilkins 4-3-1860 (4-5-1860) Ma
Bradford, Young to Elizabeth Cox 11-24-1846 (11-25-1846) Ma
Bradhsaw, Ephraim to Elizabeth Brandon 1-19-1854 Hn
Bradhsaw, Richard to Martha Jane Chilcutt 1-13-1853 Hn
Bradley, A. W. to America London 2-1-1869 G
Bradley, Alexander to Amanda (Mrs.) Slate 1-12-1864 Sh
Bradley, B. to Jane Clay 4-11-1863 G
Bradley, Charles to Martha Atkins 4-22-1851 Hn
Bradley, Chas. E. to Addia Browning 12-1-1853 Hn
Bradley, Collins L. to Judith M. Totten 6-4-1834 O
Bradley, D. C. to T. S. Simmons 12-30-1863 Hn
Bradley, D. R. to Amanda Jane Lee 4-22-1866 Hn
Bradley, David C. to Mary F. Morris 5-11-1856 Hn
Bradley, David to T. P. Paton 6-10-1859 Cr
Bradley, Henry C. to Mary C. Coldwell 8-26-1876 L
Bradley, Ira V. to Priscilla Joyner 4-8-1851 (4-10-1851) O
Bradley, J. D. to K. J. Brashier 3-22-1873 (3-23-1873) Dy
Bradley, J. M. to Sarah A. Lowe 5-25-1873 (5-21?-1873) Dy
Bradley, James to Mary A. Shay 10-22-1860 Sh
Bradley, John J. A. to Christina Clay 10-9-1864 G
Bradley, John Q. to Martha A. Page 11-17-1869 T
Bradley, John W. to Mary J. Martin 4-2-1863 Hn

Bradley, John to Zosco Z. Stevens 1-1-1829 Sh
Bradley, W. M. to A. F. Singleton 10-23-1866 (10-24-1866) Dy
Bradley, William to Aminda James 3-13-1858 (3-14-1858) G
Bradley, William to Arvey Egenia? Williams 12-15-1873 (12-17-1873) L
Bradley, William to Kate Marks 3-8-1870 (3-9-1870) Ma
Bradley, Williams H. to Mary E. Henderson 1-15-1850 (1-17-1850) Ma
Bradley, Wm. P. to Sarah R. Miller 4-18-1855 (5-1-1855) Sh
Bradley, Wm. P. to Susan S. Featherston 6-26-1845 Sh
Bradlley, Jefferson K. to Mary J. Walton 6-30-1847 O
Bradshaw, A. to Tishie Harris 12-28-1870 (12-29-1870) Dy
Bradshaw, Asa to Almeda Jane Carnell 5-10-1879 (5-11-1879) L
Bradshaw, Asa to Frances Smith 2-28-1871 (3-3-1871) Dy
Bradshaw, Charles to Mary Gardner 4-16-1843 L
Bradshaw, G. W. to Sarah Martin 12-25-1863 (12-27-1863) Sh
Bradshaw, Geo. to Laura Tucker 11-25-1875 Dy
Bradshaw, J. B. to Sarah E. Roper 3-16-1878 (3-17-1878) Dy
Bradshaw, J. K.(E?) to P. P. Murray 3-15-1862 Sh
Bradshaw, J. M. to Isamiah Spuriers 8-13-1870 G
Bradshaw, J. M. to Sarah David 1-21-1860 (1-22-1860) G
Bradshaw, Jacob to Parthina Bowers 9-28-1867 (9-29-1867) T
Bradshaw, Jesse to Mary Ann Chilcutt 3-4-1849 Hn
Bradshaw, John to Mary Facen 4-27-1846 We
Bradshaw, Joseph R. to Elizabeth A. Randolph 7-2-1861 Mn
Bradshaw, Matt to Milly Foust 8-14-1872 Dy
Bradshaw, Matt to Ruth Foust 12-27-1869 (no return) Dy
Bradshaw, Moses J. to Frances Montague 3-12-1844 (3-28-1844) F
Bradshaw, Robert K. to Martha M. Wisdom 11-5-1850 Hr
Bradshaw, Saml. B. to Lenora Powell 9-15-1863 (no return) Dy
Bradshaw, Thomas E. to Sarah E. Ethridge 5-22-1859 Hn
Bradsher, Stephen G. to M. E. Boyd 12-7-1869 (12-16-1869) F
Brady, Alex to L. L. Dunn 1-4-1845 Cr
Brady, Alexander to Elizabeth A. Fowler 4-18-1852 Hn
Brady, Andrew to Catharine Plunkett 6-13-1853 Sh
Brady, Edward to May Heflin 9-12-1838 Hn
Brady, Hugh to Sarah L. Anthony 9-7-1857 (9-30-1857) Hr
Brady, James to Evaline Smith 1-8-1876 (no return) L
Brady, John C. to Sarah Milliner 10-15-1864 O
Brady, John C. to Settie Milliner 2-15-1865 (2-16-1865) O
Brady, Michael to Bridgett Harvey 11-24-1850 Sh
Brady, Ripley to Mary J. Robb 4-11-1855 (4-12-1855) G
Brady, Robert W. to Jane Muse 12-10-1855 (no return) Hn
Brady, Stephen M. to Catharine Brady 12-27-1844 We
Brady, T. A. to Mary E. Howard 11-14-1867 O
Brady, W. H. to Elizabeth A. Brewer 6-11-1865 O
Brady, William to Nancy Ward 2-22-1858 (2-24-1858) O
Brady, Wm. to Minervy P. Orr 10-27-1848 Cr
Bragg, Albert to Louise Jackson 1-11-1871? (2-11-1872) T
Bragg, Elmore to M. J. Hilliard 3-30-1858 Cr
Bragg, G. W. to Martha Ellen Seward 4-11-1869 G
Bragg, Henry to Betsey Gooding 2-21-1872 (2-22-1871? L B
Bragg, J. M. to M. D. Moore 1-7-1873 (1-9-1873) T
Bragg, Jas. B. to C. Carr 3-5-1838 (no return) Hn
Bragg, Jas. Dick to Violet Holloway 8-3-1871 (8-4-1871) T
Bragg, John to M. S. Thomasin? 1-1-1856 Hn
Bragg, M. to A. C. Howard 5-21-1870 (5-22-1870) T
Bragg, Robert to Eliza Harwell 8-6-1868 T
Bragg, Robt. J. to Luticia Bell 11-19-1845 T
Bragg, William to Junie Dunlap 8-13-1840 Hn
Bragg, William to Martha M. Howard 12-29-1869 (12-30-1869) T
Bragg, Wm. to Frances Wollerford 9-30-1850 (no return) F
Brake, A. J. to Lavince R. Tyrer 11-2-1859 (11-3-1859) O
Brake, Jesse to Emeline N. Boothe 10-21-1858 O
Brakefield, Wm. H. to Elizabeth A. Craigg 1-22-1846 F
Brambalow, William S. to Milly A. Self 10-18-1849 G
Bramblett, James to Isabella Norrid 8-31-1842 (9-1-1842) O
Bramblett, John to Sarah Gamble 4-13-1846 (8-18-1846) O
Bramblett, Larkan to S. A. S. J. Robbins 6-15-1850 (6-19-1850) O
Bramblett, Newton to Esther Hubert 7-4-1834 O
Bramblett, Redman to Candas Harris 2-6-1840 O
Bramblett, Sandford to Margaret Buchanan 9-15-1847 O
Bramblett, Sandford to Nancy Boon 10-17-1843 (10-18-1843) O
Bramblett, Wiley G. to Mary C. Snow 12-9-1844 (12-10-1844) O
Bramblett, _____ to Inda Downey 1-26-1830 O
Brame, C. B. to R. H. (Mrs.) Mitchel 8-20-1855 (no return) F
Bramlet, Elijah to D. M. Dickson 2-15-1873 (2-14?-1873) O
Bramlett, Ambrose to Francis J. Allison 6-7-1838 O
Bramlin, Abram to Ellen Kincaid 8-24-1871 O B
Branan, August to Martha J. Gallery 8-6-1855 (no return) F
Branch, Aaron to Catherine Harrison 12-5-1838 (12-6-1838) G
Branch, Abraham to Malinda Patten 12-17-1867 G B
Branch, Archelus B. to Martha E. Pate 4-17-1850 (4-21-1850) G
Branch, Benj. F. to Nancy Ann McKnight 10-13-1858 (10-14-1858) Ma
Branch, Benjamin C. to Sarah Pettyjohn 1-18-1845 G
Branch, Bogan to Elizabeth Branch 9-10-1842 (9-20-1842) Ma
Branch, Boling to Sarah E. T. Ingram 7-22-1840 (7-23-1840) Hr
Branch, Burrell to R. S. Appleton 12-18-1847 (no return) F
Branch, Danil to Mary Trusdile 11-4-1871 (11-5-1872?) T

Branch, Davy to Louisa Dowdy 12-28-1865 (no return) F B
Branch, Duke to Mollie Davis 12-8-1871 Hy
Branch, George to Amy L. McLin 8-19-1867 Hy
Branch, H. F. V. to S. F. Davis 12-5-1883 L
Branch, Hawood to Margaret Fleming 11-9-1838 Sh
Branch, Haywood to Mary Starks 8-28-1845 Sh
Branch, Hugh to Jena (Tena?) Davis 1-6-1874 (1-8-1874) L
Branch, J. M. to Sarah J. Johnson 12-23-1872 (12-24-1872) Cr
Branch, J. N. to Allis Davis 10-26-1875 (no return) Hy
Branch, J. Neehan to Mary Collin 6-24-1877 Hy
Branch, Jesse B. to Elizabeth Vinson 10-6-1842 Ma
Branch, Jessee L. to Sarah J. Gillespie 1-16-1844 (1-18-1844) G
Branch, Jonathan McF. to Elizabeth Sparkman 12-22-1856 Sh
Branch, Joseph to Nancy Willis 1-7-1864 (no return) Cr
Branch, Kinan to Lutita Smith 9-7-1869 Hy
Branch, L. H. C. to M. B. Allen 12-18-1865 (12-20-1865) F
Branch, Nathan to Mary Puryear 3-4-1886 L
Branch, Needham to Susan Bandin? 8-9-1837 (8-13-1837) O
Branch, R. to Eugene P. Dyer 5-11-1853 (no return) F
Branch, Terrell to Rebecca Hundley 9-3-1856 G
Branch, Thomas to Margaret J. Davis 12-19-1846 (no return) F
Branch, W. M. to L. R. Hoskins 6-18-1875 (6-21-1875) Dy
Branch, William D. to Mary Caruthers 12-23-1830 Ma
Branch, William to Polly Gordon 7-13-1866 (no return) F B
Branch, Wm. M. to Prisslor Vinsor 8-9-1857 Cr
Brand, John to Ann Jones 1-4-1873 (1-5-1873) G
Brand, Thomas to Catharine Sneed 7-15-1845 We
Brand, William A. to Eliza Wallace 11-20-1850 We
Branden, T. B. to Susan Ward 8-29-1860 We
Brandford, William C. to Mary Jane Turpin 3-24-1853 Hn
Brandon, Allen K. to Louisa A. E. Kennon 12-2-1869 Cr
Brandon, B. W. to Martha Joiner 11-11-1846 Cr
Brandon, B. W. to Sarah Roark 12-14-1850 Cr
Brandon, C. S. to Rosanna A. Benton 7-3-1861 (7-4-1861) Cr
Brandon, Christopher to Omy Swinford 3-13-1831 Sh
Brandon, D. W. to Judie R. Henning 1-25-1870 (1-26-1870) L
Brandon, G. L. to C. S. Williams 11-6-1872 Dy
Brandon, H. S. to Mary Webb 10-17-1866 Cr
Brandon, Henry to Lusinda Walker 3-23-1867 (3-24-1867) T
Brandon, J. B. to Elizabeth Grogan 11-7-1872 Cr
Brandon, J. P. to Elizabeth Lawrence 12-12-1852 Hn
Brandon, J. W. to Nancy Bradley 2-10-1863 (no return) Hn
Brandon, James L. to Mary Parker 12-17-1860 (no return) L
Brandon, James M.? to Sarah C. Johnson 12-28-1861 (1-6-1862) Cr
Brandon, Jerome B. to Mary Ann Syles 9-1-1847 (9-2-1847) L
Brandon, John D. to Martha J. Wall 4-27-1853 Cr
Brandon, Joseph A. to Sarah C. Carlton 2-12-1863 We
Brandon, Lackey to Joanna Shay 12-23-1868 (12-24-1868) Cr
Brandon, Lemuel to Sarah J. Lawrence 1-22-1855 Hn
Brandon, Matthew to Jane Miskelly 8-20-1838 (8-21-1838) L
Brandon, Michael to Issabella McCluskey 11-2-1864 (no return) Cr
Brandon, Murray A. to Margaret C. Wilson 2-2-1869 Cr
Brandon, S. C. to Mattie Hall 9-23-1868 G
Brandon, Samuel to Jane Crutcher 6-3-1839 Hn
Brandon, Thomas to Rebecca Daniel 4-18-1849 Hn
Brandon, Volantine C. to June White 8-7-1844 Hn
Brandon, W. M. to Nancy Taylor 4-17-1867 (4-18-1867) L
Brandon, William T. to Josephine Cloud 10-10-1871 (10-12-1871) O
Brandon, William to Martha Beck 1-7-1839 (no return) Hn
Brann, Colman to Mary J. Shanklin 10-22-1857 We
Brann, H. A. to Isabella F. Webb 11-5-1858 G
Brann, J. N. to Martha Price 12-17-1850 We
Brann, James M. to Ellen Price 11-16-1854 We
Brann, Melten to Nancy Stoker 11-3-1857 We
Brann, T. C. to Emily McGehee 11-5-1857 We
Brann, Thomas J. to Emaline E. Old 1-22-1863 We
Brann, William V. to Elizar J. Webb 8-18-1859 (8-21-1860) We
Brann, Wm. M. to Septima J. Stow 9-25-1855 We
Brannoch, J. M. to Sarah C. Gwinn 4-6-1852 Cr
Brannon, G. W. to Mollie A. Cowan 12-11-1862 (12-16-1862) F
Brannon, James R. to Elizabeth Ford 10-5-1859 Hn
Brannon, John W. to Martha A. Ashlock 1-26-1860 Hn
Brannon, Joseph to Sarah Weaks 8-4-1859 Hn
Brannon, Samuel S. to Margaret Tuggall 5-26-1846 (no return) Hn
Brannon, Thomas to Nancy Malone 1-16-1862 Hn
Brannon, William to Nancy Stewart 2-10-1864 (no return) Hn
Brannon?, Samuel S. to Margaret A. Tuggall 9-4-1846 Hn
Branoch, Austin to Tenness Boyd 11-23-1871 (11-25-1871) Cr B
Branon, John R. to Nancy Rutledge 7-29-1841 (8-11-1841) O
Bransford, Gideon M. to Jessie M. D. Patterson 11-8-1875 (11-11-1875) O
Bransford, James W. to Elizabeth Ridgeway 2-29-1852 O
Bransford, James W. to Katharine Scearce 3-12-1858 O
Bransford, T. L. to H. E. Catron 2-1-1872 (2-21-1872) O
Branson, J. S. to Lucy Powell 4-3-1866 G
Branson, Joab to A. H. Tinkle 1-21-1862 G
Branson, Nathan to Frances G. Weber 4-29-1839 Sh
Branson, T. W. to M. A. D. Lewis 8-10-1865 G

Branson, Tandy M. to Amedia A. Sigman 2-3-1852 G
Branson, Thomas W. to Martha H. Powell 1-3-1863 G
Branson, William to Susan E. Dodd 10-13-1860 G
Branson, Z. W. to Catharine Lanom 8-?-1862 G
Branstudd, John to Louisa Price 2-18-1863 Mn
Brantlen, J. G. to S. E. Lucas 2-28-1871 (2-29?-1871) Dy
Brantley, A. L. to M. C. Walter 8-13-1885 (not endorsed) L
Brantley, Charles to Missrie Fullen 8-18-1885 (8-20-1885) L
Brantley, Joseph J. to Susannah Clayton 7-19-1835 Hr
Brantley, Joseph to Louisa E. Balderidge 5-23-1857 (no return) We
Brantley, Joseph to Sarah Bell 1-24-1878 He
Brantly, Henry D. to Margaret R. Steel 3-27-1866 Hy
Brantly, Joe to Ann Read 4-8-1876 (no return) Hy
Brantly, Joe to Susan Chilton 7-29-1867 Hy
Brantly, Johns to Frances Poyner 6-20-1840 (6-27-1840) Hr
Brantly, Murph to Jane Elerson 11-3-1868 (no return) Hy
Brantly, Philip to Jemima Cox 7-9-1833 (7-11-1833) Hr
Brantly, S. N. to Nancy A. Leabnathy 8-12-1865 (no return) Hy
Brantly, William J. to Nancy A. Glass 12-31-1844 (1-2-1845) Hr
Brasfield, A. C. to Adalaida Bondurant 3-18-1857 We
Brasfield, C. J. A. to M. F. Jones 10-1-1855 (no return) We
Brasfield, Cullin to Sallie Fowler 5-2-1873 (5-6-1873) O
Brasfield, Geo. S. to Martha D. Kennedy 9-29-1847 Sh
Brasfield, George R. to Mary J. Roger 10-6-1848 (10-17-1848) Ma
Brasfield, John J. to Margaret Young 8-17-1850 (8-22-1850) Ma
Brasfield, L. E. to Lizzie Doer 1-12-1886 (1-13-1886) L
Brasfield, Lenard R. to Betty A. Jeter 9-2-1863 We
Brasfield, W. N. to Sarah N. Jones 2-2-1850 We
Brasfield, William N. to Mary E. Spearse 10-7-1846 We
Brasfield, William N. to Mary E. Spearse 10-8-1846 We
Brashears, John C. to Rebecca J. Hawkins 9-3-1867 Dy
Brasher, J. W. to V. R. Curren 10-22-1870 (10-23-1870) Cr
Brasher, Lomax to Tabitha Casey 6-6-1853 (6-7-1853) T
Brasier, Westly to Matilda E. Gee 1-1-1866 (1-4-1866) Cr
Brassel, Adolph to Margaretha Mueller 7-6-1861 Sh
Brassell, John to Mary C. Smith 10-24-1871 T
Brassell, John to Mary Gardner 12-6-1861 (12-7-1861) Sh
Brassfield, Albert to Francis Lucinda Oliver 3-2-1857 (3-5-1857) Ma
Brassfield, E. L. to Fannie Hollins 1-28-1868 (1-29-1868) Dy
Brassfield, George S. to Sarah Nunn 2-11-1846 (2-12-1846) G
Brassfield, Joshua E. to Amanda M. Oliver 1-2-1854 Ma
Brassfield, T. R. to Martha J. Canon 10-27-1864 G
Brassfield, Thomas to Charlotte Howell 2-18-1868 Dy
Braswell, C. P. to Mary Jane Harvey 10-25-1848 Hn
Braswell, M. D. to Araminta Delany 7-18-1860 (no return) Cr
Braswell, Marcus P. to Martha A. Reditt 7-20-1842 Sh
Braswell, Marcus P. to Sarah Nelson 7-14-1846 Sh
Braswell, Wm. to Ella Seymour 7-19-1866 (7-21-1866) F B
Bratton, Alexander to Eliza Williams 8-18-1860 (8-19-1860) Cr
Bratton, David G. to Martha J. Manley 6-3-1871 (6-4-1871) L
Bratton, J. F. to Isabella Caplinger 6-17-1861 (no return) L
Bratton, J. F. to Virginia Tucker? 1-4-1870 (1-5-1870) L
Bratton, James H. to Mary P. Fifer 4-29-1846 G
Bratton, John W. to Mary Ward 7-3-1834 G
Bratton, Robert W. to Martha J. Bratton 3-19-1879 (3-20-1879) L
Bratton, William H. to Martha J. Ross 2-8-1853 (2-10-1853) Ma
Bratton, William J. to Martha J. Phifer 6-27-1852 Ma
Bratton, William M. to Winaford Umstard 5-6-1848 (5-9-1848) G
Bratton, William to Mariah A. Kendrick 6-28-1838 (no return) Hn
Braun (Brann?), Jacob to Martha Huffman 6-5-1862 Sh
Braun, F. J. to Mary A. Crawford 6-15-1859 (6-16-1859) Sh
Brauner, Doger to Sarah Acree 1-14-1855 We
Brauner, John to Elizabeth Cravins 9-25-1858 We
Brawder, John to Malilda Baker 9-8-1859 We
Brawner, Henry P. to Zilla L. Crow 7-19-1844 We
Brawner?, H. D. to Louisa Morris 1-23-1869 (1-24-1869) Cr
Bray, Fielding G. to Melinda P. Williams 9-11-1855 We
Bray, H. L. to Sarah Phillips 10-13-1859 Hr
Bray, Henry C. to Mary A. Harmon 10-15-1854 Hn
Bray, Henry L. to Mary Elizabeth Day 3-15-1859 (not executed) Ma
Bray, James H. to Fanny A. Spence 8-14-1869 Ma
Bray, James to Margaret L. Powe 2-17-1853 Hn
Bray, John J. to Eliza Tillman 12-2-1854 (no return) We
Bray, Matthew to Louisa Allen 3-23-1858 Sh
Bray, Peter to Emily Algea 12-24-1868 G B
Bray, Samuel to Sarah Henry 12-10-1861 (12-11-1861) L
Bray, T. to Sarah Sheets 1-15-1857 Hr
Bray, Wm. H. to Margaret A. Hunter 5-15-1866 Ma
Brazeal, Jackson to Susannah Price 4-10-1836 (4-12-1836) Hr
Brazell, Martha to Merseny House 9-8-1838 Hr
Brazier, B. F. to K. J. Caliway 1-26-1870 Dy
Breaden, Andrew J. to Arvenia Hill 11-6-1854 Sh
Breaden, Gabriel to Sarah Ann Bennett 4-19-1853 Sh
Breaderick, David to Joanna Davis 9-2-1838 Hn
Bready, J. M. to Martha M. Reed 9-27-1866 G
Breakenridge, F. A. to Isabella C. Ready 6-1-1841 Sh
Brearton, James to Mary Finacy 11-21-1856 (11-23-1856) Sh

Brechieno, Thomas G. to Sarah Smith 6-14-1851 Cr
Breck?, James B. to Nancy Jane Willhellmis 3-20-1873 T
Bredon, T. O. to Elizabeth Williams 4-17-1855 Cr
Breeden, P. M. to S. A. E. Hickman 7-19-1865 Hn
Breeden, Russel to Mary (Mrs.) Bowles 3-18-1852 Sh
Breeding, Archibald to Lucinda Moore 11-15-1832 Hr
Breeding, Lott to Jemima Ragan 11-21-1833 Hr
Breedlove, J. M. to M. L. Vancleave? 3-1-1866 Hn
Breedlove, Larkin to Caroline Dinwiddie 2-25-1868 Hn
Breedlove, Martin to Ann Eliza Howard 8-16-1867 Hn B
Breedlove, S. C. to Mary J. Baker 1-9-1866 Hn
Breeze, J. R. to Susan C. Daugherty 5-6-1863 Mn
Brenn (Brown), Danl. W. to Anna Gorhan 5-9-1864 Sh
Brennen (Brannen), Edward to Elizabeth Lawler 1-23-1864 Sh
Brenner, Sebastian to Helena Koehler 9-15-1859 Sh
Brent, N. R. to Martha Morton 12-21-1865 Hn
Brent, William H. to Lethe Jane Mays 4-30-1860 (5-1-1860) Dy
Brent, William L. to Nancy E. Steward 12-9-1849 Ma
Brett, James to Laura T. Nelson 6-5-1862 Sh
Brevard, B. J. to Susan A. Henderson 12-8-1868 Cr
Brevard, Benj. J. to Martha C. Harrison 1-24-1851 Cr
Brevard, Wm. A. to Mary S. Warner 12-23-1858 Sh
Brewder, Henry to Louiza Carter 6-21-1871 (6-22-1871) Cr B
Brewer (Bisner), Wesley to Lucy Ann Williams 3-22-1848 Sh
Brewer, A. P. to M. E. Hull 3-27-1877 (3-29-1877) Dy
Brewer, Alfred to Martha A. Reycroft 2-27-1878 Dy
Brewer, B. H. to Barbra A. Jordan 2-24-1853 Be
Brewer, B. to Lucretia Tipton 10-30-1849 (11-2-1849) F
Brewer, Benj. to Frances Allen 2-22-1844 Cr
Brewer, Bradford to Sarah Holloway 4-30-1853 (5-1-1853) Sh
Brewer, Colemon to Mary Cox 6-30-1843 Be
Brewer, David to Frances Lanier 2-27-1861 (no return) Dy
Brewer, David to Sarah McGlown 9-4-1844 Be
Brewer, Enoch to Polly Ann (Mrs.) Kerly 12-28-1867 (1-2-1868) Cr
Brewer, G. W. to Margarett A. Gordon 11-11-1866 G
Brewer, George W. to Rebecca Hall 11-16-1850 (11-17-1850) G
Brewer, Henry C. to Sarah Ann J. Cartwright 7-24-1845 Sh
Brewer, Henry to Elizabeth Price 10-31-1839 (11-1-1839) Hr
Brewer, Henry to Sarah Hedge 12-27-1855 Cr
Brewer, Isaac N. to Dorthy Kirk 10-25-1865 (10-31-1865) Cr
Brewer, Isaac to Charlotte Harriss 3-13-1843 (3-14-1843) Hr
Brewer, J. M. to Luisa McGill 2-24-1864 Be
Brewer, J. M. to Mary Alsup 12-19-1867 Be
Brewer, J. M. to Rebecca C. McGill 7-8-1866 Be
Brewer, J. N. to M. F. Mitchell 1-20-1872 (1-22-1872) Cr
Brewer, J. W. to Rosina B. Skeggs 11-21-1866 (11-22-1866) F
Brewer, James M. to Drusey E. Bowers 10-24-1858 We
Brewer, James M. to Rebecca G. Richardson 10-3-1835 (10-7-1835) G
Brewer, James to Sarah Pope 2-12-1876 (2-10?-1876) Dy
Brewer, Jesse J. to Mary E. McDonald 7-19-1838 (7-20-1838) Hr
Brewer, John B. to Ida C. Key 9-16-1875 O
Brewer, John G. to Elizabeth Crossno 2-11-1863 Be
Brewer, John J. to Becca A. Box 12-1-1857 Be
Brewer, John M. to Emily Cunningham 10-22-1860 (no return) Dy
Brewer, John N. to Mahulda Brewer 8-21-1855 Be
Brewer, John to Drew Emery 5-18-1883 (5-21-1883) L
Brewer, John to Elizabeth Brewer 1-25-1865 Be
Brewer, Kit to Cathrine Littlejohn 3-1-1869 (3-5-1869) F B
Brewer, Malcom to Sarah A. Crossno 8-22-1861 Be
Brewer, Matthew to Mariah Tappan 3-1-1871 (3-2-1871) F B
Brewer, Moreau to Sophie Louise Trumpy 12-24-1857 Sh
Brewer, N. O. J. to Alsy Shipman 7-1-1847 Cr
Brewer, Nathaniel to Nancy Bird 5-30-1867 (no return) Cr
Brewer, P. B. to Alcy C. Horn 12-18-1865 (12-19-1865) Cr
Brewer, P. N. to Mary E. Wright 10-25-1855 Be
Brewer, Thomas to Milly Linzy 11-24-1870 (no return) Cr
Brewer, W. B. to M. E. Pate 11-24-1875 Dy
Brewer, W. S. to Nancy A. Collins 3-20-1867 Be
Brewer, Wm. C. to Absgullah H. Ragder 11-24-1851 G
Brewer, Wm. M. to Harriett A. Abernathy 2-21-1866 (2-22-1866) Cr
Brewerr, Benjamin J. to Eliza E. Ward 12-26-1867 Be
Brewr, T. to J. H. Brewer 9-30-1840 Be
Brewster, J. L. to Martha L. Witt 4-8-1855 Sh
Brewster, Richard Henry to Mary Rebecca Nevill 4-5-1854 (4-9-1854) Sh
Brewster, Richardson to Eliza J. Underwood 7-16-1856 (7-17-1856) Sh
Brewton, Chas. P. to Josephine Davis 4-2-1857 Hr
Briant, Adolphus to Lucy A. Prince 11-19-1868 Cr
Briant, Charles P. to Sarah J. Purvis 12-31-1868 Cr
Briant, Daniel M. to Mary L. McLemore 11-10-1866 (11-11-1866) Cr
Briant, Isah to Harriett Lorate 1-1-1872 (no return) Cr B
Briant, John jr. to Ardina Leach 10-18-1870 (10-23-1870) Cr
Briant, John to Matilda Jackson 1-12-1830 G
Briant, John to Recca Blanks 9-2-1867 (no return) Cr
Briant, Martin to Dicy Smith 1-28-1836 (2-5-1836) G
Briant, Noah to Bell Clark 12-9-1871 (no return) Cr
Briant, Richard H. to M. L. Mitchell 2-20-1861 (2-21-1861) Cr
Briant, Richd. H. to M. L. Mitchell 2-20-1861 (2-21-1861) Cr

Briant, T. J. to M. E. Noell 6-14-1866 Cr
Briant, W. B. to M. E. Edwards 2-14-1870 (2-15-1870) Cr
Briant, W. W. to M. E. Alley 11-15-1865 Hn
Briant, Z. B. to M. A. Browney 7-22-1864 (no return) Cr
Brice, J. D. to Margret Climer 8-18-1870 Hy
Brice, J. Y. to Nancy Climer 8-11-1870 Hy
Brice, T. A. to S. M. Crihfield 7-4-1885 (7-5-1885) L
Brice, Walter to Jane B. Moffatt 11-26-1858 O
Brickhouse, J. W. to Martha M. Edmundson 6-6-1861 G
Brickhouse, L. to M. C. Odom 10-3-1861 G
Brickhouse, Latima to Susan M. Tinkle 5-10-1854 (5-11-1854) G
Brickum, Harrison to Frances Whitley 3-14-1861 Mn
Brickum, R. S. to Marcy C. Lee 10-6-1864 Mn
Bridgeman, Daniel A. to M. H. W. Long 9-14-1850 Cr
Bridgeman, Marshall to Mary Cunagham 7-13-1871 Cr
Bridgeman, T. L. to Caroline Long 1-11-1850 Cr
Bridgemon, William A. to Elvira L. Roundtree 11-18-1834 G
Bridger, J. H. to Alfreda Bridger 10-18-1880 (10-19-1880) L
Bridger, J. H. to G. I. Margraves 7-10-1860 (no return) Hy
Bridger, Richd. C. to Elisabeth Dismukes 5-11-1870 (no return) Hy
Bridges, Alfred to C. Cartwell 3-31-1852 We
Bridges, Andrew J. to Martha Jane Phillips 8-11-1840 Cr
Bridges, Bradford to Eliza Jenkins 12-2-1849 Be
Bridges, C. A. to D. A. Rogers 4-1-1865 (no return) Cr
Bridges, Edmund to Melinda Spence 8-11-1831 Ma
Bridges, Geo. R. to Mariah V. Howard 11-6-1844 (11-8-1844) Hr
Bridges, H. B. to Martha E. Fowler 9-7-1854 Be
Bridges, H. T. to Elizabeth Adams 11-21-1856 We
Bridges, Henry to B. F. Cravens 6-2-1849 Cr
Bridges, J. A. to Halley White Huey 11-11-1855 Cr
Bridges, J. B. to L. Th? 1-2-1842 Be
Bridges, J. T. to M. J. Stewart 12-11-1872 Cr
Bridges, James H. to Nancy Jane Presson 8-26-1851 Be
Bridges, James H. to Rachael Poe 9-22-1846 Be
Bridges, James R. to E. A. Reding 12-23-1844 Cr
Bridges, James T. to Tennessee Elder 7-19-1865 (7-22-1865) O
Bridges, Jason A. to Elizabeth S.? Cross 6-23-1860 (6-25-1860) Cr
Bridges, John H. to Martha Taylor 2-16-1864 (no return) Cr
Bridges, Lewis to Nancy Barnes 11-10-1866 (no return) Hy
Bridges, Oliver to Mary J. Cannon 10-1-1842 (no return) Hn
Bridges, Porter to Martha Barnett 12-15-1864 Hn
Bridges, Reuben D. to Martha Jane Rumbley 10-26-1851 Be
Bridges, Rowan to Mary E. Ford 11-20-1866 Ma
Bridges, S. A. to L. Gordon 1-31-1859 Cr
Bridges, Thos. to Catharine Helms 3-31-1866 O
Bridges, W. A. C. to L. E. Cunningham 11-16-1867 (12-18-1867) Cr
Bridges, W. F. to Cordelia C. Smith 5-25-1865 (5-30-1865) Cr
Bridges, William A. to Margaret E. Gore? 1-13-1857 (1-14-1857) O
Bridges, William H. to Sarah B. Rust 10-18-1831 (10-20-1831) G
Bridges, William to Mary Lackey 10-20-1859 (no return) Hy
Bridges, William to Nancy J. Swor 11-13-1839 We
Bridges, Wm. H. to Eliza C. Richards 10-20-1857 Sh
Bridges, York to Abbie Crawford 11-11-1870 (11-20-1870) F B
Bridgett, George to Mary Shauners 6-7-1864 Sh
Bridgewater, W. H. to Lucinda J. Jerry (Jenny?) 1-23-1853 Sh
Bridgewater, William to Rocky (Rody) Hardin 2-2-1871 (2-8-1871) F B
Bridgwater, Wm. to Mary M. (Mrs.) Kennedy 8-2-1864 Sh
Bridjman, Wiley to Mary Babcox 8-19-1845 We
Brigance, Clinton to Sarah H. Bledsoe 10-12-1852 (10-13-1852) G
Brigance, Fayette (Fate) to Sarah J. Dority 1-24-1880 (1-25-1880) L
Brigance, J. A. to Mariah Westbrooks 8-4-1863 (no return) We
Brigance, J. C. to Cyntha J. Feley 11-2-1871 L
Brigance, James to Nancy Thompson 4-10-1859 Hy
Brigance, S. L. to M. A. (Mrs.) Haggard 7-25-1876 (no return) L
Brigance, William D. to Mary T. Spratt 3-14-1842 Ma
Briges, John H. to Martha Tayler 2-16-1864 (no return) Cr
Brigg, John J. to Rhonda A. Lucian? 2-7-1860 Cr
Briggance, J. F. to Minerva Cox 12-24-1867 G
Briggs, Francis to Diademy _____ 1-4-1827 O
Briggs, J. H. to Nancy C. Duncan 5-24-1875 Dy
Briggs, M. B. to Sallie Throgmorten 7-21-1867 Be
Briggs, Sterling H. to Sarah Crutcher 10-13-1842 Hn
Briggs, T. J. to Elisa Ladd 2-19-1870 (2-24-1870) T
Brigham, D. A. to Ella Bracken 5-1-1878 Dy
Brigham, David to Mary McGlohon 2-3-1846 Be
Bright, A. D. to A. R. Rives 10-18-1867 (10-24-1867) F
Bright, Arter to Cathrin Duckworth 2-6-1871 (no return) Hy
Bright, B. A. to Mary Jane Massey 3-15-1850 Cr
Bright, David to Ellinor E. Motheral 12-13-1842 O
Bright, Greenberry to Elizabeth Crisp 1-28-1830 Hr
Bright, James B. to Emma P. Adams 10-29-1873 (10-30-1873) T
Bright, John to Mary Jane Johnson 1-6-1859 Sh
Bright, Lemuel D. to America I. Turner 1-19-1860 We
Bright, Malica C. to Dilly Dinwoody 1-24-1848 T
Bright, Malichi C. to Sarah A. E. Dement 8-30-1851 (9-2-1851) Sh
Bright, R. S. (Dr.) to Mary L. Robertson 1-24-1867 G
Bright, Simeon W. to Levinia Mothershed 2-18-1853 Be

Bright, Simeon to Keziah Box 4-24-1828 (4-29-1828) Hr
Bright, Solomon P. to Prudence Harris 12-8-1833 O
Brightwell, Samuel to Manda Standley 11-10-1855 (11-11-1855) G
Brightwell, Thomas H. to Annie L. Shaw 1-14-1869 F
Brightwell, William J. to Mary M. Key 8-23-1858 G
Brignadello, James to Margaritta Maranda Kelly 9-8-1860 (9-16-1860) Sh
Briles, A. Layfett to Jenette Yeates 1-3-1859 (1-4-1859) Sh
Briley, Abraham to Eliza Jane Deats 3-17-1842 Hn
Briley, B. T. to Elizabeth Moore 10-4-1868 Hy
Briley, Henry to Moriah Young 4-20-1872 Hy
Briley, James to Mary L. Coble 12-5-1875 Dy
Briley, Jesse to Susan E. Jennings 1-18-1870 (no return) Hy
Briley, Jessie to _____ _____ 5-9-1838 Sh
Briley, William to Malvina Vines 4-1-1872 Hy
Briley, Wm. B. to Lucretia A. Braswell 10-3-1848 Sh
Briley, Wright to Mary Jane McCoy 8-20-1877 Hy
Brim, F. M. to Barsheeba Lowery 3-2-1856 We
Brim, James to Mary Ann Elizabeth Cup 7-27-183 (7-28-1833) Hr
Brim, John A. R. to Elizabeth I. Brame 6-14-1838 (no return) F
Brim, William to Mary Ann Hobbs 4-8-1834 Hr
Brimen, Geo. to Martha E. Smith 12-28-1878 (no return) Dy
Brimingham, John to Jane Massey 9-8-1852 Ma
Brimingham, Liberty W. to Mary S. Boaz 10-18-1859 (10-20-1859) Ma
Brimley, Wm. J. to Elizabeth Parsons 2-23-1857 (3-8-1857) T
Brimm, George to Amanda A. Harris 12-25-1871 Dy
Brimm, William to Elizabeth Millsap 6-8-1836 Hr
Brimmage, John H. to Sarah Wilson 4-10-1850 Cr
Brimmage, John to Nancy Fitzgerald 8-11-1855 Cr
Brimmage, John to Permia Matthews 12-15-1858 Cr
Bringadello, Dominie to Louisa Brissalara 2-7-1858 Sh
Bringanello, James to Nancy Corella 1-27-1855 (1-28-1855) Sh
Bringle, C. A. to Rosa J. Rich 1-2-1871 (1-5-1871) T
Bringle, James H. to Nancy J. White 11-11-1868 (11-12-1868) T
Bringle, James to Mollie Maxwell 2-14-1872 T
Bringle, John Nicholas to Margaret Billings 7-14-1846 T
Bringle, S. J. to Elizabeth J. Owen 4-28-1860 (4-29-1860) T
Brinkley, Anthony to M. Self 10-10-1847 Cr
Brinkley, Anthony to Piety Harris 7-24-1848 Cr
Brinkley, E. W. to Martha Garrison 12-13-1860 Dy
Brinkley, George A. to Nikolas Ann Perkins 3-26-1844 Hr
Brinkley, J. A. to Margaret Brinkly 9-22-1866 (9-23-1866) Dy
Brinkley, J. S. to Ann Eliza Millican 11-7-1867 Dy
Brinkley, J. S. to Mary J. Allen 5-1-1861 (5-2-1861) Dy
Brinkley, J. W. to L. C. Markus 3-24-1874 (8-27-1874) O
Brinkley, James H. to Elizabeth Edwards 4-28-1859 Cr
Brinkley, James to Sarah McCulley 3-1-1847 (3-3-1847) F
Brinkley, Jefferson to Texanna Manning 4-28-1868 (5-3-1868) Cr
Brinkley, Jeremiah to Sarah Brinkley 1-27-1849 (2-1-1849) F
Brinkley, M. A. to Lucy J. Johnson 2-23-1846 We
Brinkley, R. C. to Elizabeth Hempstead 12-24-1860 (12-31-1860) Cr
Brinkley, Richard to A. E. Sawyers 2-16-1842 (2-17-1842) F
Brinkley, Richd. to Mary Ann Weller 12-26-1848 (no return) F
Brinkley, Seth to America Allmon 8-27-1860 (8-28-1860) Cr
Brinkley, Thos. W. to Jennie Covington 10-18-1870 (10-20-1870) F
Brinkley, William to Malisa B. Hunt 12-2-1855 We
Brinkley, Wm. R. to Nancy Emily Floyed 2-1-1841 (no return) F
Brinkly, Levi S. to Adaline Mollen 1-2-1859 Cr
Brinkly, T. H. to Amanda Wright 1-7-1868 (1-8-1868) Dy
Brinnin, R. to Mary Williams 2-1-1865 O
Brinson, John to Julia Ann Nevils 2-10-1850 Ma
Brinson, Robert W. to Caroline C. Neville 3-22-1845 Ma
Brinson, Robert to Sarah Neville 10-20-1853 Ma
Brint, James B. to Alsy Boyte 9-13-1828 Hr
Brint, James H. to Leusi Powell 3-16-1850 (3-19-1850) Hr
Briscoe, Robert to Anny Parker 9-28-1873 L
Briscoe, Robert to Rachael Fitzpatrick 2-18-1884 L
Brisdendine, J. B. to Sarah L. Blackwell 1-20-1869 (1-29-1869) L
Briseman, Wm. E. to C. C. Woods 6-21-1859 (6-22-1859) T
Brisendine, William L. to Catherine Jobe 4-23-1844 Hn
Brisentine, Wm. to Bettie Browne 5-16-1868 (5-17-1868) T
Britingham, John to Sally Ormes 12-29-1829 G
Britt, A. to Lidda J. Avery 8-17-1865 (no return) Hy
Britt, Benj. (Joseph) to Martha Marshall 7-31-1869 (no return) Hy
Britt, Benj. W. to Mary S. Ewell 8-3-1846 (no return) F
Britt, E. B. to Sarah E. Stewart 12-2-1859 (12-15-1859) Sh
Britt, Edmund to Betsey Sammons 5-20-1829 (5-24-1829) G
Britt, G. W. to Elizabeth Davis 7-28-1873 (no return) Hy
Britt, J. Y. to N. A. Crawford 9-8-1869 (9-9-1869) Cr
Britt, James H. to Sarah E. Oliver 10-?-1861 (10-20-1861) Cr
Britt, Lamuel to Mary Rose 7-22-1839 (7-25-1839) Hr
Britt, Nathaniel to Amanda Jane Williams 8-26-1857 (8-27-1857) Ma
Britt, Peter to Fredonia Pearson 5-29-1871 (5-30-1871) Cr
Britt, Singleton to Charlotte Jones 6-20-1876 (6-22-1876) Dy
Britt, Wiley to Martha Oliver 9-9-1864 (9-11-1864) Cr
Britt, Wily to Martha Oliver 9-9-1864 Cr
Britt, Wm. A. to Judith O. Butler 5-14-1854 Cr
Britten, Adolpha to Sarah Sweeny 8-26-1841 Ma

Britten, John to City Scott 11-8-1871? Hy
Britton, Adolphus to Anne Sweeny 11-30-1852 (12-2-1852) Ma
Britton, Adolphus to Mary Barrier 9-27-1848 (11-27-1848) Ma
Britton, Bartholomew C. to Eliza Jane (Mrs.) Fawcett 7-27-1870 (7-28-1870) Ma
Britton, Bartholomew C. to Margaret E. Gilliland 4-11-1861 Ma
Britton, Bill to Sarah Pugh 3-11-1876 (no return) Hy
Britton, Harrison to _____ _____ no date (with Aug 1867) Dy
Britton, James W. to Susan Jane Scott 9-21-1854 (9-23-1854) O
Britton, Thomas to Frances Briton 4-1-1850 Ma
Britton, William to Patsy Cogbill 12-22-1870 (12-27-1870) F B
Brizendine, D. D. to J. D. Wade 1-7-1866 Hn
Brizendine, James H. to Barbery Lathis 10-18-1860 Hn
Brizendine, Robert to Isabella Hudgens 4-1-1847 Hn
Brizendine, Robert to Mary E. Lemonds 12-3-1856 Hn
Brizendine, W. C. to Sarah D. Hudgens 1-29-1867 Hn
Brizendine, W. M. to Cornelia A. Tucker 12-30-1865 (no return) Hn
Brizendine, William W. to Jemima G. Barton 12-3-1857 Hn
Broach, Addison to Nancy J. Hagler 11-20-1867 (no return) Hn
Broach, Barby to Caroline Lightfoot 12-18-1844 Hn
Broach, George to Isabella Bell 10-1-1839 Hn
Broach, Green to Jane W. Prince 5-10-1844 Cr
Broach, Green to Mary L. Delaney 3-12-1863 (no return) Cr
Broach, James to Jane Cunning 3-26-1844 Cr
Broach, Sidney to Lucie Swarigen? 9-12-1867 Cr
Broach, Sidney to Margaret B. Hamilton 1-27-1841 Cr
Broachy, John to Sarah Lovell 5-11-1858 (5-13-1858) Sh
Broaden, Thomas to Martha Ann Lattimore 1-12-1864 Be
Broadnax, Martin to Martha Broadnax 10-16-1869 F B
Broady, John to Harriett Jackson 1-14-1870 (1-16-1870) O
Brobbeck, J. R. to Jyncy Ballaw 9-20-1851 (no return) F
Brock, Benj. F. to Nancy A. Yeargain 12-31-1852 (1-2-1853) G
Brock, Benjamin F. to Sarah Pearce 10-27-1846 We
Brock, D. to Mattie Singleton 3-29-1875 Dy
Brock, Franklin to Sophronia Anderson 7-12-1853 (7-14-1853) Ma
Brock, Henry M. to Sarah Ann D. Kirk 6-22-1861 (6-30-1861) O
Brock, I. N. to Fannie Bennett 1-8-1875 (no return) Hy
Brock, Isaac to Sophronia Bly 11-17-1875 (no return) Hy
Brock, James Henry to Sarah U. Oliver 4-18-1870 L
Brock, Josephine to Logan Hopkins 11-16-1857 Ma
Brock, Moses to Elizabeth Warren 10-14-1854 (10-15-1854) Sh
Brock, S. Frank to Evelyn Green 2-24-1866 Dy
Brock, Wm. to Mary Crews 9-20-1846 Cr
Brock, jr., D. to F. A. Dickason 8-13-1872 (8-14-1872) Dy
Brockett, Benjamin F. to Lenora Mixon 11-22-1849 Sh
Brockman, Ben to Susan Bivens 4-9-1845 (4-10-1845) F
Brockman, John L. to Martha King 12-27-1865 (12-28-1865) Dy
Brockwell, James H. to Mary V. West 9-4-185? with 1858 O
Brockwell, John to Nancy Hogan 1-16-1839 (1-17-1839) O
Brockwell, Wm. to Martha A. Brockwell 6-2-1865 O
Broddie, Wesley to Martha Nixon 12-23-1867 (12-26-1867) L B
Brodenaux, Chas. to Mattie Smith 1-22-1875 Hy
Brodie, David to Mary Jane Oldham 12-25-1871 (12-26-1871) L
Brodie, H. S. to M. L. Sinclair 2-7-1872 L
Brodie, L. L. to Adalade E. Eggleston 7-8-1863 (7-9-1863) L
Brodnax, Jacob M. to Nancy Stevens 12-7-1874 T
Brodnax, Richard T. jr. to Sallie H. Taylor 1-18-1867 (1-23-1867) T
Brodnax, William F. to Mollie Bet. Taylor 12-24-1862 (12-25-1862) T
Brodnax, Wm. F. to Eliza S. Maclin 5-15-1865 T
Brody, Patrick to Ellen Raven 5-21-1864 (5-22-1864) Sh
Brody, Patrick to Margaret Morrissey 1-16-1859 Sh
Brody, Pattie to Ellen Raden 5-21-1864 (5-24-1864) Sh
Broeder, Joseph to Mary Flaherty 7-21-1860 (7-22-1860) Sh
Broens, Gerard to Mary E. Brand 4-30-1861 Sh
Brogden, Bennett B. to Margarette Ann Brewer 10-23-1865 G
Brogden, D. H. to Peninie Brown 4-17-1867 L
Brogden, David to Amanda Stevens 1-14-1868 Hy
Brogden, E. S. to Sarah Jane Haynes 1-7-1878 (1-9-1878) L
Brogden, George M. to Elizabeth Neill 10-18-1850 (10-20-1850) Hr
Brogden, George to Margaret Belton 12-26-1854 (12-27-1854) Ma
Brogden, Gideon to Cornelia J. Gidcum 9-9-1861 (9-11-1861) L
Brogden, Gideon to Martha E. Williams 7-5-1859 (no return) L
Brogden, H. H. L. to Elmena Thurman 12-14-1857 We
Brogdon, A. J. to Ann M. Brogdon 6-1-1853 Hn
Brogdon, Allen to Sidney Phillips 9-29-1847 G
Brogdon, George N. to Louisa F. Manus 6-17-1868 (12-3-1868) Ma
Brogdon, Gideon to Rebeca Saunders 7-6-1883 (7-8-1883) L
Brogdon, Henry H. to Elizabeth Hall 3-7-1842 Hn
Brogdon, Jacob J. T. to Sarah Clark 9-14-1854 Hn
Brogdon, James H. to Amanda Hennings? 5-3-1861 (no return) L
Brogdon, James H. to Annie R. Kelly 5-23-1866 (5-24-1866) L
Brogdon, James L. to Minerva Spencer 3-20-1839 Ma
Brogdon, John to Thursey Gerley 5-1-1846 (no return) Hn
Brogdon, Joseph J. to Araminta J. Baldridge 6-24-1858 We
Brogdon, L. H. to Alice Davidson 1-20-1885 (1-21-1885) L
Brogdon, Moses to Cherry Barnner 8-14-1845 Hn
Brogdon, N. G. to Mary Ann Palmer 11-1-1854 Hn
Brogdon, Robert to Mary Ann Hall 4-4-1848 Hn

Bromagen?, Joel E. to Elizabeth Moody 1-31-1859 Hn
Broman, P. C. to Mary E. Lea 2-16-1868 Hy
Bromly, James to D. Smith 11-26-1850 Cr
Bron (Broun?-Brow?), D. W. to Susan P. Barfield 3-3-1885 (3-5-1885) L
Bronaugh, T. B. to Drusilla T. Foster 1-11-1883 L
Bronaugh, Thomas B. to Martha A. B. Smith 5-17-1879 (5-23-1879) L
Bronaugh, W. J. to Margaret Mulherrin 12-19-1860 (no return) Hy
Bronte, Matthew to Jane Whitney 8-2-1842 F
Broocke, P. E. to A. L. Jeffryes 1-10-1871 Hy
Broocke, Philip E. to M. E. Herring 1-19-1876 (no return) Hy
Brook, J. D. to J. P. Hargess 1-16-1852 (no return) F
Brook, Josiah to Jane Stabough 5-20-1830 (5-25-1830) Hr
Brook, Silas to Rebecca H. Hays 1-6-1832 (1-5?-1832) Hr
Brook, Stephen L. to Jane Davis 8-6-1829 Hr
Brookes, James to Maria L. Davis 6-21-1842 (6-22-1842) F
Brooks, A. M. to Marthan Hansel 8-27-1847 Be
Brooks, A. P. to E. J. Reeves 6-15-1846 Sh
Brooks, A. T. to Louisa J. Leach 11-21-1850 Cr
Brooks, Aganza? Benton to Cynthia Jane Wright 11-27-1848 (11-30-1848) T
Brooks, Allen to Harriet Mann 7-17-1874 (no return) Hy
Brooks, Archie to Caroline Marr 12-28-1867 (no return) F B
Brooks, Ase to Sally Mawns 1-19-1868 Hy
Brooks, B. F. C. to E. E. Alexander 2-13-1855 (2-14-1855) Sh
Brooks, B. F. C. to Mary V. Steel 3-8-1858 Hr
Brooks, B. H. to Elizabeth Jones 6-8-1856 Hn
Brooks, Benjamin S. to Adaline Perry 5-23-1850 Ma
Brooks, Benjamin to Rhoda Merick 2-3-1835 Hr
Brooks, Braddock to Susan Mcguire 1-1-1867 (1-3-1867) F B
Brooks, Bud to Sarah Nunn 1-1-1876 (no return) Hy
Brooks, Cannon L. to Lucinda M. Edwards 9-11-1849 Sh
Brooks, Charles to Margaret Jones 11-26-1883 L
Brooks, D. D. to Margaret L. Gillaspie 11-27-1861 (no return) We
Brooks, D. L. to M. E. Cavitt 1-4-1860 (no return) We
Brooks, Danl. to Lizzie Davis 1-4-1874 Hy
Brooks, Delfras to Harritt Curtis 1-18-1877 (no return) L
Brooks, E. W. to Eliza Ralston 11-8-1858 Sh
Brooks, Edwin to Charlotte Baker 9-2-1840 T
Brooks, Elijah to Louisa M. G. Williamson 1-13-1836 Sh
Brooks, Elijah to Sarah H. Allen 1-26-1848 Sh
Brooks, Francis W. to Nancy Ann Curley 1-15-1842 Sh
Brooks, Frank to Malissa Lake 4-30-1883 (5-6-1883) L
Brooks, G. H. to Mary F. Leach 12-1-1856 Cr
Brooks, G. L. to Mary E. Atkins 12-16-1857 We
Brooks, George D. to Leona F. Rogers 9-5-1867 Hn
Brooks, George D. to Mary F. Price 12-1-1866 (no return) Hn
Brooks, George G. to Martha J. Smith 11-27-1862 (no return) Hy
Brooks, George K. to Lizzie H. Brooks 11-13-1866 Ma
Brooks, H. L. to Milly Jane Warmack 12-13-1866 Be
Brooks, Hampton to Geo. A. Nelson 12-30-1871 Hy
Brooks, Hartwell H. to Martha Ward 12-22-1846 (no return) Hn
Brooks, Henry H. to Freedonia Duncan 1-17-1855 Hr
Brooks, Henry R. to Laura E. Gill 12-21-1866 (12-30-1866) F
Brooks, Hugh W. to Martha J. Scott 1-16-1856 Sh
Brooks, J. A. to B. J. Parrish 1-26-1859 We
Brooks, J. P. to Emmer Estis 1-3-1878 Hy
Brooks, Jack to M. A. Batchelor 12-27-1869 (no return) Hy
Brooks, James E. to Bettie Johnson 7-9-1878 (no return) Dy
Brooks, James H. to Martha J. Lipe 2-20-1850 Cr
Brooks, James H. to Mary A. Leach 1-13-1853 Cr
Brooks, James J. to Margaret Wardlaw 12-21-1859 Sh
Brooks, James J. to Pollyann Mills 10-14-1853 (10-15-1853) O
Brooks, James M. to W. Mosella Rucker 7-31-1860 (no return) Hy
Brooks, James R. to Amanda E. Mitchell 11-25-1839 O
Brooks, James to Celia Morrison 8-8-1825 Sh
Brooks, James to Matilda Wooten 3-16-1861 T
Brooks, James to Sallie A. Mulherin 12-27-1860 (no return) Hy
Brooks, Jas. M. to Mary A. Moore 11-17-1847 Hn
Brooks, Jas. W. to Nannie B. Beal 2-9-1865 (6-23-1865) F
Brooks, Jno. to Eliza Joyes 1-10-1845 (1-12-1845) F
Brooks, Joel S. to Nancy L. Davis 7-4-1857 (7-7-1857) Sh
Brooks, John C. to Emaly Y. Montague 8-8-1848 F
Brooks, John H. to Margret J. Wright 1-28-1858 Sh
Brooks, John M. to Victoria J. L. Barnett 11-4-1856 (11-6-1856) Sh
Brooks, John P. to Lucretia W. Watson 9-20-1845 (9-25-1845) Ma
Brooks, John to Elizabeth Dollar 3-16-1853 (3-17-1853) Hr
Brooks, John to Sarah L. Action 12-7-1848 Ma
Brooks, Joseph A. to Sarah A. (Mrs.) Stanley 8-1-1860 (8-2-1860) Ma
Brooks, Joseph C. to Louisa Cobb 11-14-1861 T
Brooks, Joseph to Agnes Neilson Dandridge 2-22-1847 (2-25-1847) Hr
Brooks, Joseph to Rachel Kerr 8-16-1865 Mn
Brooks, Joseph to Mary Lacy 7-21-1842 F
Brooks, Joseph to Mattie Johnson 10-28-1862 (no return) Dy
Brooks, Len to Manerva Malone 1-18-1868 Hy
Brooks, Martin V. to Elizabeth Brown 7-29-1856 Hr
Brooks, P. H. to Isabella Jones 1-22-1857 We
Brooks, Phillip P. to G. A. Thompson 4-11-1883 (4-12-1883) L
Brooks, Preston to Mary Taylor 12-19-1873 Hy

Brooks, R. R. to Tabitha Geraldine Stroud? 1-1-1867 Hn
Brooks, Reuben to Mot Price 4-30-1872 (5-1-1872) O
Brooks, Robert M. to Margaret E. Langston 9-6-1866 Ma
Brooks, S. T. to Nancy M. Young 1-9-1862 Mn
Brooks, Saml. to Annie Young 1-23-1860 Sh
Brooks, Samuel C. to Elizabeth J. Tatum 3-23-1843 (3-24-1843) F
Brooks, Samuel R. to Frances Turner 10-13-1852 Hr
Brooks, Silas L. to S. A. Bowen 3-11-1869 (no return) Hy
Brooks, Stephen to Matilda Lackey 2-8-1840 (2-16-1840) Ma
Brooks, Thomas B. to Melinda A. Anderson 3-8-1855 Cr
Brooks, Thomas to C. F. Carter 11-1-1859 We
Brooks, Thomas to Dema Gardner 5-23-1885 (5-24-1885) L
Brooks, Thomas to Lucy Rutledge 12-1-1845 Sh
Brooks, Thomas to Sarah Jones 4-7-1867 Hy
Brooks, Thompson to Rachel Blackwood 8-10-1832 (8-14-1832) Hr
Brooks, Tob? to Lucy Alston 7-10-1868 (7-11-1868) T
Brooks, Travis C. to Elizabeth A. Morris 7-5-1828 (7-8-1828) Ma
Brooks, W. B. to Vina E. Robertson 2-9-1874 (2-11-1874) Dy
Brooks, W. G. to E. S. Smithson 12-31-1866 (no return) F
Brooks, W. H. M. to N. F. Gilbert 4-14-1857 We
Brooks, W. J. to Lizzie Hill 4-3-1850 Sh
Brooks, William C. to Caroline T. Dunn 2-6-1845 Hn
Brooks, William F. to Sarah E. Potts 11-14-1850 Sh
Brooks, William H. to Elizabeth Yates 10-13-1846 Hn
Brooks, William S. to Mary Ann E. Glaason 10-15-1849 (10-18-1849) G
Brooks, William to Berthena Bass 7-2-1832 (7-15-1832) Hr
Brooks, William to Dora Cummins 3-30-1870 (4-2-1870) F B
Brooks, William to Fannie Brooks 11-13-1866 Ma
Brooks, Wm. A. to Eliza Barding 10-2-1840 Sh
Brookshire, William to Nancy Mary 12-29-1841 (12-30-1841) Ma
Broom, Absolem to Rebecah Crawley 6-15-1847 (no return) F
Broom, John H. to Eliza Farris 4-1-1844 (no return) F
Broom, Julius to Lizy Flippin 11-26-1869 F B
Broom, Peterson P. to Mary C. Bowers 11-5-1838 (11-17-1838) F
Broom, Taylor to Mozella Blaw 12-21-1868 (12-25-1868) F B
Broom, Tho. M. to Susan T. King 1-19-1865 (1-24-1865) F
Broom, Thomas M. to Louisa E. V. Yancy 3-20-1860 (3-22-1860) F
Broomly, Alfred to Mildrid C. Stevens 12-23-1868 (12-24-1868) T
Brosnahier, Jerry to Mary Sweeny 8-29-1859 Sh
Brothers, Jackson F. to Susan F. Miller 1-6-1879 (no return) Dy
Brotherton, George L. to Jane Alexander 1-2-1830 Hr
Brotherton, John S. to Eliza Morris 6-13-1843 (6-15-1843) Hr
Brotherton, Logan D. to Henrietta Jobe 7-8-1835 Hr
Brotherton, William to Mary J. Jetton 7-4-1868 (7-5-1868) O
Brotly?, Daniel to Mary Foley 2-28-1843 Sh
Brotsepe, Jacob to Rosina Defeli 8-1-1854 Sh
Brough, Giles to Ellen O. Byram 8-12-1863 (8-16-1863) T
Brough, John H. to Eliza Woodard 1-16-1836 Hr
Broun, Samuel H. to Fannie H. Cooper 1-10-1860 (1-11-1860) Sh
Browder, H. H. to M. J. Pate 4-25-1863 (4-26-1863) Dy
Browder, J. W. to Elizabeth W. Fields 2-5-1857 Sh
Browder, John W. to Martha J. Simmons 9-3-1853 (9-5-1853) Ma
Browder, L. T. to M. A. Kelley 11-27-1872 (11-29-1872) O
Browder, Pitt C. to Nancy Susan Davis 12-9-1867 (12-10-1868?) Ma
Browder, R. A. to Phila Patterson 11-27-1871 (11-29-1871) O
Browder, Washington R. to Sarah T. Davis 10-17-1857 (10-18-1857) Ma
Browder, William T. to Martha A. Franklin 10-29-1840 (10-30-1840) Ma
Brower, Isham H. to Elvira Catherine Johnson 12-28-1855 (12-29-1855) Ma
Browery, Johnson to Bettie Washington 4-24-1873 Hy
Brown (Bronn?), Charles to Fanny Turner 6-9-1869 (6-10-1869) L B
Brown (Broom?), Illa G. B. to Nancy Abbett (Albert) 12-26-1837 Sh
Brown, A. M. to Frances (Mrs.) Jackson 1-10-1866 G
Brown, Abraham to Jennie Harper 5-26-1869 (5-29-1869) F B
Brown, Adam to Nerva Tucker 7-13-1867 (8-3-1867) F B
Brown, Adam to Ritter Seymore 2-22-1869 (2-28-1869) Cr
Brown, Addison to Ila Jones 4-26-1870 G
Brown, Albert to Nancy Kersey 12-22-1847 Sh
Brown, Amos to America Ridley 2-9-1878 (no return) L B
Brown, Anderson to Mahaly Hoover 11-25-1870 G B
Brown, Andrew L. to Melisa E. Hogge 8-31-1861 (no return) L
Brown, Andrew T. to Adeline E. Lock 12-2-1850 (12-5-1850) Ma
Brown, Andrew T. to Caroline M. Nobles 11-2-1846 Ma
Brown, Andrew to Eliza Scott 3-7-1872 T
Brown, Andrew to Josephine Sanders 6-24-1867 G
Brown, Anson to Polly Sellers 12-30-1835 (12-31-1835) Hr
Brown, Anson to Rachel Grantham 2-12-1831 (2-14-1831) Hr
Brown, Asa A. to Rebecca Anthony 2-15-1868 Hy
Brown, Asa A. to S. P. Rudd 2-10-1862 (no return) Hy
Brown, B. C. to Mary Booker 11-21-1855 Sh
Brown, B. C. to Rachel Caraway 1-12-1860 (1-26-1860) O
Brown, B. S. to Mary Jane Polk 1-29-1857 Sh
Brown, Bartholomew to Mary Brennon 2-14-1852 (2-15-1852) Sh
Brown, Belford to Mary A. Brown 12-30-1858 Cr
Brown, Benham H. (Dr.) to A. T. Mallory 12-22-1856 Sh
Brown, Benjamin F. to Emily C. Ray 11-14-1846 (11-15-1846) Ma
Brown, Benjamin to Elizabeth Philips 1-4-1838 Sh
Brown, Benjamin to Elizabeth Youngblood 1-20-1831 (1-22-1831) Ma

Brown, Benjamin to Peggy Lowdermilk 10-6-1829 Hr
Brown, C. F. to M. J. Brown 6-14-1875 (6-17-1875) Dy
Brown, C. H. to Eliza C. Childress 11-2-1869 (no return) L
Brown, C. M. to Sarah P. Adams 2-12-1872 (2-13-1872) T
Brown, C. to Jane Lefever 1-31-1849 Hn
Brown, Cairo to Mary Brown 12-24-1873 (12-25-1873) O
Brown, Calven S. to Nancy J. Rasco 9-16-1860 We
Brown, Calvin S. to Margaret A. Martin 9-9-1856 O
Brown, Charles A. to Martha Needham 12-21-1853 (12-22-1853) G
Brown, Charles G. to Sarah D. Thompson 10-19-1869 (10-21-1869) Cr
Brown, Charles H. to Johana Frank 6-28-1875 O
Brown, Charles H. to Priscella P. Holcomb 3-4-1859 (3-6-1859) G
Brown, Charles H. to Sarah C. Kyle 8-9-1854 Ma
Brown, Charles R. to Martha Curtis 6-22-1860 (6-25-1860) L
Brown, Charles to Laura Rice 8-14-1871 (8-27-1871) L B
Brown, Chas. P. to Martha F. Parks 2-4-1864 Sh
Brown, Clark to Jennie Jones 2-14-1884 L
Brown, Clark to Martha E. Calhoun 11-29-18?? (with 1866) O
Brown, Clark to Martha Richardson 1-3-1871 (1-5-1871) T
Brown, Cornelius to Rosanna Campbell 9-5-1872 (9-14-1872) T
Brown, D. A. to Martha A. Bestwick 12-26-1837 Sh
Brown, Daniel to Lucinda Jones 12-29-1843 (12-31-1843) Hr
Brown, Danl. W. to Nancy Pirtle 7-30-1859 Hr
Brown, David B. to Harriett Guess (Gross) 8-25-1841 Sh
Brown, David F. to Jane F. McNeal 10-14-1829 (10-15-1829) Hr
Brown, David to Julia Berry 12-24-1874 O
Brown, Dickson to Merica Fonville 7-30-1841 (8-2-1841) O
Brown, Dolphus to Polly L. Smith 9-23-1867 T
Brown, Dred to Sarah Tucker 12-22-1876 Hy
Brown, E. C. to Mary McGrath 8-2-1862 Sh
Brown, E. E. B. to Sarah Perkins 12-24-1866 (1-1-1867) Cr
Brown, Edmond to Rinda Holman 9-16-1873 O
Brown, Eli D. to Beanthur Crider 11-8-1862 (11-9-1862) Cr
Brown, Eli to Lucim Askew 3-13-1866 Ma
Brown, Elijah M. to Mariah? M. Brown 1-4-1866 (1-7-1866) L
Brown, Elijah V. to Elvira Hudson 6-12-1843 (6-13-1843) Hr
Brown, Elijah to Eliza Kitchen 2-26-1855 (2-27-1855) T
Brown, Elijah to Peggy Chism 5-16-1833 (5-17-1833) Hr
Brown, Eliphalet to Nancy Sain 1-6-1834 (1-9-1834) Hr
Brown, Ephraim N. to Nancy J. Thetford 2-24-1861 G
Brown, Ephraim to Mary Walker 5-31-1835 Sh
Brown, F. M. to Nancy J. Burks 8-17-1864 Mn
Brown, Frank to Ann Henry 12-27-1866 (no return) Dy
Brown, Frederick C. to Levisa Horton 5-13-1845 (5-18-1845) O
Brown, George W. to Elender K. Huffman 4-29-1841 Sh
Brown, George W. to Laura A. Crockett 5-23-1843 O
Brown, George W. to Mary A. Anderson 4-23-1860 (4-25-1860) Ma
Brown, George W. to Mattie Palmer 10-5-1864 (10-7-1864) Cr
Brown, Gilford to Nancy Davis 6-3-1877 Hy
Brown, Granison to Isadore Coe 2-26-1869 (no return) F B
Brown, H. C. to Lu (Lee?) Morris 10-28-1866 G
Brown, H. H. to E. Crockett 5-29-1867 (5-30-1867) L
Brown, H. W. to J. B. McFaddin 12-31-1849 (1-1-1850) F
Brown, Harper to Dousilla Bridgeman 2-5-1869 G B
Brown, Harrel to Julia A. Norton 9-14-1853 Hn
Brown, Harrison to Millie Jane Nat 3-2-1878 (no return) Hy
Brown, Harrison to Nancy Palmer 5-15-1879 L
Brown, Harrison to Rose Stewart 6-9-1868 (6-10-1868) F B
Brown, Harrison to Serilda Doughty 12-8-1838 (12-10-1838) Hr
Brown, Harvey W. to Mary Posey 1-28-1854 (no return) F
Brown, Harvey to Sarah Elmore 7-29-1847 F
Brown, Henry C. to Maie Glenn 5-19-1871 (5-22-1871) Ma
Brown, Henry H. to Mary Ann Dotson 2-11-1835 Hr
Brown, Henry H. to Sarah E. Wrenn 5-23-1842 (5-26-1842) Ma
Brown, Henry K. to Harriet E. E. Lawson 10-29-1857 O
Brown, Henry W. to Mary A. Fowler 7-4-1831 (7-7-1831) Hr
Brown, Henry to Elizabeth Alston 2-24-1872 (no return) L B
Brown, Henry to Mary Smith 12-30-1871 T
Brown, Henry to Sarah A. Mitchel 5-14-1828 G
Brown, Henry to Susan A. Robbins 8-20-1879 (8-21-1879) Dy
Brown, Hiram N. to Martha Johnson 1-27-1845 Hr
Brown, Hosea Carroll to Harriet Ford Leach 9-22-1852 T
Brown, Isaac to Della Randolph 1-2-1871 Hy
Brown, Isiah to Myra Johnson 12-28-1870 F B
Brown, J. A. to Lizzie Brown 12-29-1881 L
Brown, J. A. to Martha McClosky 4-6-1861 (5-2-1861) Sh
Brown, J. A. to S. A. J. Hampton 5-30-1864 (5-31-1864) Cr
Brown, J. B. to Mary E. Clary 7-19-1853 Hn
Brown, J. D. to Julie A. Brown 1-17-1866 Hn
Brown, J. E. to Ann J. Walker 12-28-1857 Cr
Brown, J. F. to B. F. Pope 4-9-1866 (no return) Cr
Brown, J. F. to Elizabeth Pearson 7-24-1854 (no return) F
Brown, J. J. to Belsia Abernathy 1-2-1871 (no return) F
Brown, J. L. to S. E. Sessem 10-15-1871 Sh
Brown, J. N. to Mary B. Penn 10-11-1848 Sh
Brown, J. R. to L. E. Moore 1-3-1866 Hn
Brown, J. W. to Clementine Bowden 5-4-1859 Hn

Brown, J. W. to E. J. Price 3-12-1874 L
Brown, J. W. to H. M. Jones 6-19-1855 (6-23-1856) Sh
Brown, J. W. to Martha Allen 1-11-1862 (no return) Cr
Brown, J. W. to Nancy Pentecost 7-14-1846 We
Brown, Jabez to Sarah McRee 8-22-1855 (8-23-1855) O
Brown, Jackson to Lyda Ann Bunnell 5-20-1839 G
Brown, James A. to Frannie T. Beasley 1-5-1869 L
Brown, James A. to Virginia A. Fletcher 7-14-1851 Sh
Brown, James C. to Elizabeth L. Flowers 1-28-1847 Be
Brown, James C. to Ruth P. Davidson 8-11-1843 (8-15-1843) O
Brown, James L. to Sarah J. Holly 9-11-1854 (9-12-1854) Hr
Brown, James M. to Louisa Clark 8-27-1857 (8-30-1857) L
Brown, James M. to Mary Ann D. Butram 8-11-1856 O
Brown, James M. to Mary W. Boon 5-3-1856 (5-4-1856) Ma
Brown, James M. to Susan M. Childress 3-17-1860 (no return) Hy
Brown, James Milton to Martha Louisa Clark 8-23-1873 (8-24-1873) L
Brown, James R. to Elizabeth Ruth 11-15-1862 Mn
Brown, James S. to E. T. Harrell 2-14-1854 Cr
Brown, James W. to Martha A. Killow 11-6-1845 Cr
Brown, James W. to Rebecca Anne Payne 2-3-1848 Sh
Brown, James W. to Sarah A. Russell 7-23-1850 (7-26-1850) O
Brown, James to Addie Manning 7-16-1868 Dy
Brown, James to Emily Allen 12-28-1866 (12-30-1866) F B
Brown, James to Julia G. Patterson 8-31-1860 Sh
Brown, James to Litha Robinson 1-13-1869 G B
Brown, James to Milla Reed 9-25-1868 F B
Brown, Jas. H. to Mahala Gunter 6-28-1832 Hr
Brown, Jas. L. W. to Susan S. Pearson 8-9-1854 (8-16-1854) G
Brown, Jas. R. to Caroline Mobley 12-22-1855 G
Brown, Jefferson to Catharine Lanningham 5-27-1873 Dy
Brown, Jeremiah to Margaret Welch 8-12-1857 Sh
Brown, Jesse A. to Amanda R. Woods 5-12-1857 Hn
Brown, Jesse A. to Bettie J. Essary 9-23-1868 Dy
Brown, Jesse A. to Elizabeth Warren 6-30-1839 Hn
Brown, Jesse B. to A. M. Buford 6-19-1840 (6-24-1840) F
Brown, Jesse G. to Louisa C. Daniels 2-27-1871 (2-22?-1871) T
Brown, Jesse G. to Mary E. Corbet 9-23-1868 (9-24-1868) T
Brown, Jesse to C. A. Clement 2-7-1861 (2-12-1861) T
Brown, Jno. L. to Serpeta P. Weaver 6-28-1841 Sh
Brown, Jno. S. to Rachell E. Baker 6-25-1850 We
Brown, Jo to Ann Chester 1-1-1873 (1-2-1873) L
Brown, Jo to Nancy McCuller 12-30-1873 L
Brown, John A. to Frances Grooms 1-20-1855 Cr
Brown, John A. to Pocahontas Durden 3-12-1879 (3-16-1879) Dy
Brown, John C. to Mary C. Neiley 1-8-1849 (1-10-1849) F
Brown, John C. to Mary Irwin 3-18-1841 We
Brown, John Calvin to Elizabeth Tillman 1-3-1852 (1-11-1852) Hr
Brown, John G. to Lucy Ann Norey 1-5-1860 Sh
Brown, John H. to Elizabeth Bedwell 4-13-1845 Hn
Brown, John H. to Kissiah H. Pipkins 12-28-1853 (12-29-1853) Hr
Brown, John I. to Mary F. Whitenton 11-16-1869 Ma
Brown, John L. to Mary J. Wade 12-5-1853 Hn
Brown, John M. to Turzey J. Reeves 12-2-1844 (12-3-1844) O
Brown, John Mathis to Paralee E. Love 4-13-1858 Hn
Brown, John R. to Elizabeth Simpson 1-10-1842 (1-11-1842) O
Brown, John S. to Elizabeth Anderson 10-29-1828 Ma
Brown, John T. to Angeline Wood 12-18-1841 (12-19-1841) Hr
Brown, John T. to Ann E. Butler 11-23-1859 (11-24-1859) Ma
Brown, John T. to C. F. Martin 11-5-1858 O
Brown, John T. to Susan Whitlock 4-16-1857 T
Brown, John W. to Henrietta L. Hauger 4-30-1855 (5-3-1855) G
Brown, John W. to Mary G. Andrews 2-22-1871 (2-23-1871) Dy
Brown, John W. to Narcissa Jane Brint 12-13-1853 (12-15-1853) Hr
Brown, John W. to Sarah A. Johnson 7-9-1846 Ma
Brown, John to A. A. King 1-13-1854 (1-20-1854) Sh
Brown, John to A. E. Mathis 2-23-1867 G
Brown, John to Amy C. Vaughn 7-3-1862 Mn
Brown, John to Charlotte Cogburn 6-5-1870 G
Brown, John to Clara M. Coleman 1-14-1832 Hr
Brown, John to Elizabeth Messer 7-16-1873 (7-17-1873) Cr
Brown, John to Elizabeth P. Alston 5-25-1840 (5-26-1840) F
Brown, John to Elizabeth Trump 6-23-1826 Sh
Brown, John to Evaline Blackman 7-20-1850 Sh
Brown, John to Margaret Jones 2-20-1873 (no return) Hy
Brown, John to Mariah Loving 4-2-1855 (4-5-1855) Sh
Brown, John to Martha Hall 9-6-1862 (9-8-1862) Cr
Brown, John to Mary Wilkeson 3-15-1836 Hr
Brown, John to Rachel Perry 12-28-1874 Hy
Brown, John to Rhoda Chandler 3-13-1828 Ma
Brown, John to Teula Rutherford 12-18-1873 Hy
Brown, Jonas to Mary Carroll 7-17-1837 G
Brown, Jos. J. to Sutilia C. Roberts 11-16-1858 (11-17-1858) G
Brown, Joseph F. to Martha J. Leonard 10-25-1856 Sh
Brown, Joseph S. to Mary E. Crider 12-20-1866 Cr
Brown, Joseph to Amanda Warren 12-24-1870 (12-25-1870) F B
Brown, Josiah W. to Sallie Knott 8-20-1867 (8-22-1867) Ma
Brown, L. W. to Mary E. Hensly 12-23-1858 Hr

Brown, Lacy L. to Elizabeth J. Davie 12-4-1857 (12-6-1857) Ma
Brown, Lacy L. to Nannie E. Wells 11-28-1866 Ma
Brown, Lawson W. to Elizabeth M. Hood 9-19-1843 Hr
Brown, Lenard to Nancy J. Johnson 11-8-1849 F
Brown, Levi to Martha H. Ferril 7-26-1848 (7-27-1848) G
Brown, Lewis to Marsha (Martha) Huffman 12-20-1842 Sh
Brown, Lewis to Mary E. Jones 2-9-1865 Mn
Brown, Lindsy B. to Elizabeth C. Burns 11-18-1852 Sh
Brown, Lot to Amelia Fowlkes 1-24-1879 (1-26-1879) Dy
Brown, Lucius to Nannie Mangrum 11-18-1869 (11-21-1869) Dy
Brown, Manuel to Ann Wrightout 9-25-1875 (no return) Hy
Brown, Mathew to Aira Gee 5-9-1833 Sh
Brown, Matthew to Mary C. Brooks 9-7-1849 Sh
Brown, Matthew to Nancy Hill 11-28-1853 (12-1-1853) Sh
Brown, Micajah Hillman to Arvazena Betts 8-22-1867 G
Brown, Milton A. to Mary Hathaway 10-4-1866 (10-9-1866) Ma
Brown, Milton to Moslie J. Smith 8-1-1866 G
Brown, Morris to Manda Carlton 11-7-1871 Hy
Brown, Mosses to Margarett A. Gren 5-7-1868 G B
Brown, Nathaniel to Adaline Nannie 3-30-1869 Cr
Brown, Neill S. to Elizabeth J. Gwynn 2-14-1871 F
Brown, Nelson D. to Nancy J. Gidcombe 11-7-1866 (no return) L
Brown, Neverson to Julian Stanton 5-19-1877 Hy
Brown, Noah to Matilda Wiseman 12-26-1865 (12-28-1865) T
Brown, O. D. to F. B. Matthews 1-3-1868 (1-7-1868) O
Brown, O. T. to M. P. Dickey 4-29-1847 O
Brown, Orlando to Josephine C. Cooper 3-17-1859 Sh
Brown, Osborn to Sarah Ann Goodman 3-29-1853 Sh
Brown, Osker to Frances Panky 12-27-1873 (12-30-1874?) O
Brown, Osmund R. to Racheal A. Morris (Harris) 8-25-1857 O
Brown, P. R. B. to Willietta Ferell 11-30-1859 Sh
Brown, Parson to Margaret E. Foster 3-10-1869 G B
Brown, Patrick to Alice Sweeny 7-23-1861 Sh
Brown, Perry H. to Ruthy Ledbetter no date (6-27-1852) L
Brown, Perry to Nancy Allen 12-31-1869 Hy
Brown, Perry to Nancy Thrailkill 4-18-1848 (4-20-1848) Hr
Brown, Peter to Mary A. Francis 12-31-1846 We
Brown, Pinkney to Sarah J. Wilson 12-1-1852 (12-4-1852) Sh
Brown, R. A. to Julia Patterson 3-22-1877 (3-23-1877) L
Brown, R. M. to Amanda Arnold 1-7-1875 (1-10-1875) Dy
Brown, R. P. to E. E. J. Rasbury 5-24-1863 Mn
Brown, R. T. to L. J. Carter 9-11-1868 Hy
Brown, Randolph H. to Arabella E. Clary 10-13-1854 Hn
Brown, Randolph H. to Delinda Irby? 2-14-1842 Hn
Brown, Ransom to Anna Lucas 9-28-1870 (no return) F B
Brown, Reddick to Eliza Jenkins 2-18-1867 F B
Brown, Reubin B. to Mary Ann Harrison 12-17-1855 (12-19-1855) Sh
Brown, Richard A. to Martha Williams 8-2-1854 G
Brown, Robert B. to Sarah Odum 9-12-1865 Mn
Brown, Robert C. to Nancy E. Watson 9-1-1869 L
Brown, Robert F. to Sarah A. Locke 7-12-1855 Ma
Brown, Robert F. to Susan E. Parker 10-18-1865 (10-25-1865) Dy
Brown, Robert H. to Elizabeth Stephens 10-29-1855 (11-1-1855) G
Brown, Robert M. to Isabella A. Mills 10-19-1854 O
Brown, Robert to Ann Eliza Pipkin 11-23-1857 Hr
Brown, Robert to Elizabeth Watts 7-4-1848 Sh
Brown, Robert to Mahala Houston 10-13-1855 Hn
Brown, Robert to Rebecca Roberts 4-5-1847 F
Brown, Robert to Susan Brown 3-25-1828 Ma
Brown, Royal F. to Mary J. Palmore 1-15-1847 (1-17-1847) F
Brown, Ruffin to Martha Pankey 7-22-1851 (7-24-1851) Hr
Brown, S. H. to Elizabeth Yarbro 6-5-1856 T
Brown, S. M. to Georgianna Malone 2-24-1858 (2-25-1858) Sh
Brown, S. R. D. to A. E. Alexander 12-15-1853 G
Brown, Samuel B. to Nancy Micheal 7-31-1847 (8-4-1847) Ma
Brown, Samuel R. to Eliza C. Blake 12-6-1838 Sh
Brown, Samuel R. to Sarah Ann Drake 6-19-1842 Sh
Brown, Samuel S. to Minerva L. Montague 11-15-1848 Sh
Brown, Tho. J. to Frances Branch 1-14-1846 (1-15-1846) F
Brown, Thomas C. to Sarah E. Rushin 12-3-1860 (12-9-1860) Cr
Brown, Thomas J. to Jane L. Reeves 9-29-1852 (9-30-1852) O
Brown, Thomas W. to Mary Hamlett 12-15-1838 (12-20-1838) F
Brown, Thomas to Anna Bond 9-7-1877 (no return) Hy
Brown, Thomas to Letty Saunders 2-28-1834 Sh
Brown, Thomas to Lucinda Blankenship 4-13-1868 G
Brown, Thomas to Mary C. Williams 10-3-1865 Mn
Brown, Thomas to Mary E. Brown 8-27-1872 Hy
Brown, Thomas to Mary Fedleton 9-27-1860 G
Brown, Thos. J. to Leavicy Hathcock 2-5-1845 (no return) L
Brown, Thos. K. to Elizabeth Ann Sellers 2-3-1847 (2-4-1847) Hr
Brown, Thos. to Lillie Hawkins 10-4-1868 Hy
Brown, Thos. to Rhoda Humphreys 1-4-1851 (1-5-1851) F
Brown, Tom to Sarah Young 8-31-1867 (9-7-1867) F B
Brown, W. E. to Tennessee O. Hamilton 3-10-1840 Cr
Brown, W. G. to Caroline Pankey 12-11-1850 Hr
Brown, W. H. to Sallie A. Leath 11-24-1870 G
Brown, W. M. to Ida F. McIntire 12-14-1878 (12-15-1879?) L
Brown, W. N. to Helen L. Allen 12-7-1859 Sh
Brown, W. P. to M. T. Siler 8-2-1873 (8-3-1873) T
Brown, W. P. to Mary Traylor 12-21-1871 Hy
Brown, Wesley C. to Lucy Kennedy 10-28-1836 Hr
Brown, Wesley H. to Martha J. Weatherall 5-22-1854 Sh
Brown, William A. to Lidia Rudd 11-18-1861 (no return) Hy
Brown, William A. to Martha T. Harper 9-1-1832 O
Brown, William A. to Mary Marberry 7-13-1849 Hn
Brown, William A. to Nancy H. Mills 9-8-1845 (9-9-1845) O
Brown, William J. to Susan Jane Palmer 2-3-1847 (2-4-1847) F
Brown, William M. to Martha A. Braden 12-20-1870 (12-21-1870) L
Brown, William P. to Agnes Reeves 11-2-1847 (11-3-1847) O
Brown, William S. to Mary A. Wilson 8-27-1846 (no return) F
Brown, William T. to Mary W. Mauldin 2-24-1851 (2-27-1851) Hr
Brown, William W. to Elizabeth A. Edmondson 11-24-1840 O
Brown, William to Christina Wade 12-28-1867 G
Brown, William to Elizabeth Moanings 1-5-1870 (no return) F
Brown, William to Judie B. Cook 7-18-1855 (7-19-1855) Ma
Brown, William to Louisa Brooks 7-23-1867 T
Brown, William to Mary Hullum 6-19-1829 (6-25-1829) Hr
Brown, William to Mary Mangrum 1-19-1867 (1-20-1867) Dy
Brown, William to Mary P. Durley 4-3-1865 G
Brown, William to Matilda A. Landrum 8-5-1873 (8-15-1873) Dy
Brown, William to Minney Jane Howell 5-14-1857 Hr
Brown, William to Racheal Lewdermilk 1-21-1834 (1-23-1834) Hr
Brown, William to Renie Perry 5-27-1871 (6-1-1871) Dy
Brown, William to Sallie Wiseman 1-7-1874 (1-10-1874) T
Brown, William to Sarah Cox 7-22-1834 (7-24-1834) Hr
Brown, William to Violet Lee 1-20-1870 (1-22-1870) F B
Brown, Wilson to Polly Glasscock 11-18-1828 G
Brown, Wm. A. to Julia A. Robinson 1-11-1855 Cr
Brown, Wm. C. to M. E. Burris 2-19-1865? O
Brown, Wm. C. to Mary Jane Williams 1-31-1863 (2-4-1863) L
Brown, Wm. F. to Priscilla P. (Mrs.) Boylan 3-14-1839 F
Brown, Wm. J. to Lydia M. Grantham 8-1-1857 (8-4-1857) Hr
Brown, Wm. James to Frances Parker 11-13-1860 (11-15-1860) Hr
Brown, Wm. R. to Martha A. Barrett 2-12-1875 (2-14-1875) Dy
Brown, Wm. W. to Mary Ann Craig 1-6-1859 L
Brown, Wm. W. to Mary E. Collier 12-15-1878 Hy
Brown, Wm. W. to Serilda W. Frain 12-28-1843 Sh
Brown, Wm. to Amanda Edwards 12-19-1867 Dy
Brown, Wm. to Catherine Kinnen 4-26-1862 Sh
Brown, Wm. to Maria Williams 4-20-1854 Sh
Brown, Wm. to Penni? Moore 1-11-1871 (1-15-1871) T
Brown, Wm. to Sarah Flaniken 7-3-1841 (10-17-1841) T
Brown, belton to Jennie Williams 9-17-1868 (9?-19-1868) F
Brown?, Silas to Julian Craig 7-22-1869 (7-25-1869) Dy
Brown?, Thomas to Ella Bumpass 12-11-1869 T
Browne, James M. to Elizabeth Jones 10-20-1859 We
Browne, Wm. A. to Mallissa C. Sherfield 11-29-1844 (11-30-1844) F
Browning, August to Lydia Ann Nix 1-6-1853 (no return) Hn
Browning, B. S. to Emeline Sykes 12-4-1845 Be
Browning, Cas to Hester Ann Sumerow 1-29-1878 (no return) L B
Browning, Edward D. to Margarette J. Swindell 9-28-1862 G
Browning, Francis O. to Mollie Beal 12-9-1867 Ma
Browning, George W. to Harrett Adams 10-16-1840 (11-17-1840) Hr
Browning, Guilford to Mary (Mrs.) Vaught 1-16-1868 G
Browning, Hosea D. to Malissa Davidson 5-16-1867 Be
Browning, Isiah to Mary M. McMahan 5-15-1842 Sh
Browning, J. A. to Penina Boswell 9-20-1849 Be
Browning, J. M. to Temperance Lashlee 1-13-1846 Be
Browning, James M. to Bettie Bradley 10-29-1874 Hy
Browning, James to Kate Eddie 4-27-1872 (4-29-1872) T
Browning, John M. to Caroline Durden 4-1-1858 Be
Browning, John R. to Julina Johnson 11-20-1856 Be
Browning, John T. to Eliza Balew 12-29-1852 F
Browning, M. R. to Susan E. Springer 1-21-1868 (no return) Cr
Browning, R. G. to L. D. Nixon 1-5-1886 (1-6-1886) L
Browning, Richard H. to Margaret J. Wright 3-18-1861 (3-20-1861) L
Browning, Robert C. to Caroline Holland 11-18-1861 Cr
Browning, Wm. to Rachell Leach 11-19-1857 Cr
Browning, Z. T. to M. T. Leach 8-5-1872 (8-8-1872) Cr
Brownings, Sampson to Pharuba Carns 4-19-1842 Cr
Brownlee, C. to Sarah A. Ferguson 7-4-1860 G
Brownlow, F. M. to L. P. Smith 6-2-1860 (6-7-1860) O
Brownlow, Franklin to M. A. Yant 8-17-1876 (8-20-1876) O
Brownlow, G. T. to R. M. Aker 4-3-1866 O
Brownlow, James J. to Edney J. Williams 7-13-1840 (no return) F
Broyhill, T. E. to Eliza Paine 9-24-1874 Hy
Broyles?, M. B. to Adeline W. Blain 11-30-1855 (no return) F
Broyls, L. G. to Sabra M. Farmer 9-4-1871 (9-10-1871) L
Bruce, A. to Atilla Sarrett 11-12-1840 Be
Bruce, Allen A. to Martha Hays 11-4-1850 Ma
Bruce, D. A. to Mary A. Turpin 2-6-1861 Be
Bruce, George W. to Emeline Adams 10-3-1840 (10-4-1840) F
Bruce, Henry to Tennessee Almon 2-11-1866 Hn
Bruce, J. C. to Sallie P. Buck 12-10-1872 Hy

Grooms

Bruce, J. H. to Mary J. Woods 9-24-1868 Be
Bruce, J. H. to Susan Harrison 4-7-1864 Be
Bruce, J. R. to H. E. Jackson 7-24-1848 (no return) F
Bruce, Lucian N. to D. P. Rutherford 3-2-1857 (3-3-1857) Sh
Bruce, N. S. to Ann Wyant 12-31-1851 (1-1-1852) Sh
Bruce, Philip to Nancy Winsett 6-15-1843 Hn
Bruce, S. B. to Mary A. Vickery 1-7-1853 Hn
Bruce, Thomas F. to Sarah Peacock 1-28-1846 (2-12-1846) O
Bruce, W. S. to Elizabeth Worland 1-27-1848 Sh
Bruce, W. W. to Minerva Harris 5-25-1861 (5-30-1861) Dy
Bruce, William A. to Mary Vandouser 11-25-1862 Ma
Bruce, William a. to Mary L. Jones 12-20-1859 (12-22-1860?) We
Bruce, Wilson to Malinda Winsett 10-17-1839 Hn
Bruff, Franklin J. to Martha J. Johns 6-8-1869 G
Bruff, Greenville M. to Sarah T. Murphy 6-8-1865 G
Bruff, S. H. to V. A. Cowsert 5-24-1866 (5-27-1866) O
Bruff, Thopson to Sarah Smith 3-12-1836 G
Bruhl, Edward to Ann Mulby 10-29-1859 (11-1-1859) Hr
Bruit?, H. G. to M. K. Hamilton 12-23-1866 G
Brumage, A. to Melinda Kemp 12-12-1848 F
Brumager, J. W. to Amanda J. Melton 1-3-1866 Be
Brumbelow, John to Theay Stamps? 8-28-1834 Hr
Brumett, W. H. to S. A. Measles 8-17-1881 (8-18-1881) L
Brumitt, D. A. to Bettie Brummett 2-6-1872 Hy
Brumley, A. J. to Sarah A. Campbell 8-20-1846 F
Brumley, C. H. to Analiza High 5-6-1841 F
Brumley, Hiram to Maria Mallory 9-1-1857 (9-3-1857) Sh
Brumley, J. H. to Margaret Moxley 6-5-1858 Sh
Brumley, W. J. to Eliza Jane Morphus 8-27-1861 (8-29-1861) Hr
Brummet, William to Mary Rushing 12-15-1867 Be
Brunche, Augustin to Martha Tubbs 12-2-1849 Sh
Brunderidge, Thos. to Elizabeth E. Eskridge 9-20-1857 We
Brundidge, Eli A. to America A. Seawright 8-3-1865 Hn
Brundige, James L. to Drusilla Jane Collins 8-6-1857 Hn
Brundridge, Calven S. to N. A. E. Brann 12-26-1858 We
Brundridge, J. W. to Elizabeth Price 7-3-1855 (no return) We
Brundridge, J. W. to Mary A. Brann 12-4-1856 We
Brundridge, John W. to Elizabeth Prince 7-4-1855 We
Bruner, Elias Edward to Susan W. Gladding 6-10-1850 Sh
Brunson, David Alexr. to Mary Coffy McClellan 1-12-1846 (1-13-1846) T
Brunson?, Joshua N. to Susan A. M. S. Easley 9-14-1840 (9-15-1840) T
Brunston, G. W. to Nancy A. Neules 2-19-1872 (2-20-1872) Dy
Brush, James to Mary Ann Freeman 9-11-1861 (9-12-1861) O
Brush, John W. to Mary A. Lambdin 1-9-1861 Sh
Brust, Jacob to Dora Manx (Maux) 11-16-1850 Sh
Bruton, Lenoir to Harriett E. Jones 11-16-1843 Ma
Bruton, William H. to Mollie F. Gill 12-18-1866 (12-20-1866) Ma
Brutus, Jeff to Molly McMurray 2-8-1867 G
Bryan, Andrew R. to Susan A. McCampbell 7-20-1859 Hn
Bryan, C. J. to M. E. Mise 10-30-1858 Sh
Bryan, Dennis to Sally Reid 11-6-1851 Sh
Bryan, Ellen F. to Mary Jourdan 12-31-1829 Hr
Bryan, Enoch to Margaret J. Boone 7-29-1840 Ma
Bryan, Finis E. to Elizabeth A. Jett 12-7-1868 Ma
Bryan, Hinton to Sarah Freeling 4-4-1842 (4-7-1842) Ma
Bryan, J. W. to Emmer Stickney 12-7-1868 Hy
Bryan, John A. to Margarett E. Teller 9-12-1854 (no return) F
Bryan, Jonathan T. to Elnory E. Watkins 3-23-1844 (3-28-1844) F
Bryan, Joseph to Julia Leonard 10-31-1856 (11-2-1856) Sh
Bryan, N. to Elizabeth M. Petty 11-26-1853 (11-27-1853) T
Bryan, Ransom H. to May Ann Cook 12-17-1838 (12-18-1838) Ma
Bryan, Robert H. to Ann E. Winston 12-17-1867 (12-19-1867) Ma
Bryan, Stephen R. to Barbara A. Harston 12-8-1856 (12-10-1856) Ma
Bryan, T. A. to M. A. Considine 11-29-1866 G
Bryan, T. M. to Mary A. Mosley 8-18-1858 (8-20-1858) G
Bryan, Thos. D. to G. A. Hester 11-21-1876 (11-23-1876) O
Bryan, W. A. to E. J. Simmons 4-26-1853 (no return) F
Bryan, William H. to Penelope Byrn 1-21-1843 (1-24-1843) Ma
Bryan, William O. to Mary S. Harris 12-16-1833 (12-18-1833) Hr
Bryan?, J. F. to Lodicia C. Starnes 9-19-1863 Be
Bryant, A. B. to J. A. Abbott 1-18-1858 Cr
Bryant, A. D. to Alethia M. Quinn 10-15-1866 (no return) Cr
Bryant, A. S. to Martha P. Nolton 8-31-1856 Cr
Bryant, A. W. to Louisa G. Davis 10-13-1847 (10-14-1847) Hr
Bryant, Alfred to Amey Bishop 12-31-1870 (1-5-1871) Cr
Bryant, Allen to Peninah Williams 4-15-1850 (4-18-1850) Ma
Bryant, B. O. to Nancy L. Muse 8-27-1870 (9-4-1870) Ma
Bryant, Barnett O. to Mary J. Norrid 3-8-1867 O
Bryant, Boyd F. to Sally Little 3-9-1829 G
Bryant, Boyd to Jane Jordan 1-18-1867 G
Bryant, Boyd to Mollie Algee 7-31-1873 (7-27?-1873) Cr
Bryant, C. H. to C. R. Baird 12-21-1878 (12-22-1878) L
Bryant, Caleb D. to Margaret C. Stone 4-10-1854 (4-18-1854) Ma
Bryant, Charles to Henrietta Lake 6-2-1883 (6-3-1883) L
Bryant, Clark to Mary Webb 6-15-1867 (6-20-1867) F B
Bryant, Columbus to Virginia Bell Frasier 10-21-1865 (10-22-1865) F
Bryant, David to Sarah Bishop 12-1-1842 Cr

Bryant, Edward to Fannie Winrow 5-25-1867 L B
Bryant, Elijah to E. E. Swindle 9-28-1865 G
Bryant, F. A. to Jane C. Babb 9-16-1861 Mn
Bryant, Franklin D. to Emily A. Pounds 1-12-1870 G
Bryant, Frederick to Martha Jones 7-27-1831 G
Bryant, G. H. to Martha A. Cocks 1-8-1866 G
Bryant, G. W. to Mary J. Bishop 11-6-1856 Cr
Bryant, Geo. W. to Martha A. Pollock 7-24-1865 (7-25-1865) F
Bryant, Harper to Martha Jordan 8-16-1867 G B
Bryant, Isaac T. to Martha Elizabeth Hale 12-31-1857 Sh
Bryant, James A. to Susan A. Wesson 10-1-1863 Sh
Bryant, James D. to Lavinia F. Tiller 1-27-1852 (no return) F
Bryant, James E. to Amanda S. Fortune 9-1-1858 (9-2-1858) Hr
Bryant, James H. to Cordelia Ball 3-29-1855 Sh
Bryant, James H. to Mary Ann Wilkins 4-9-1852 (4-16-1852) Ma
Bryant, James R. to Winniford A. Woodard 10-13-1849 Cr
Bryant, James S. to Mary Jane Freeman 8-7-1843 T
Bryant, Jesse to Mary L. Hicks 9-30-1856 (10-2-1856) Hr
Bryant, Jesse to Sarah Biddy 11-21-1866 (11-22-1866) F
Bryant, Jiles to Harriet Putman 2-28-1847 Cr
Bryant, Jim to Martha Lacy 8-31-1867 (9-7-1867) F B
Bryant, John D. to Nancy M. Hall 8-19-1867 T
Bryant, John J. E. to Susan Ann Stevens 8-1-1853 (8-3-1853) T
Bryant, John R. to Sarah A. Southerland 8-18-1853 Cr
Bryant, John S. to M. E. C. Burrow 1-19-1860 Cr
Bryant, John to Eliza Farris 11-19-1853 (11-20-1853) Sh
Bryant, John to Jane McDaniel 9-16-1850 (9-17-1850) Hr
Bryant, John to Rebecca Ann McFarland 3-13-1869 G
Bryant, John to Rody Flippin 1-10-1856 G
Bryant, John to Sarah Sumner 3-5-1849 (3-11-1849) F
Bryant, Josiah to Mary C. Clayton 12-20-1864 Mn
Bryant, L. G. to Frances V. Robinson 9-25-1860 Sh
Bryant, LaFayette to Louisa Richland 4-22-1858 Sh
Bryant, Laurel to Elizabeth McGarrity 3-18-1837 (3-20-1837) G
Bryant, Matthew S. to Armanda Jane Woods 10-4-1847 (9-6-1848) Ma
Bryant, N. A. D. to Virginia C. Ingram 5-27-1856 Hr
Bryant, P. D. to Sarah A. Wilkerson 4-22-1863 (no return) Hn
Bryant, Perryman to Nancy L. Whitby 7-29-1841 Sh
Bryant, Peter to Sarah Pentecost 11-24-1863 (11-25-1863) O
Bryant, S. L. to Mary Waynesberg 10-13-1859 Sh
Bryant, Thomas J. to Mary(Nancy) Walpole 12-29-1856 (1-1-1857) Hr
Bryant, Thomas J. to Nancy Revil 12-3-1857 Cr
Bryant, Thomas to Alvira Hersey 8-10-1854 G
Bryant, Thomas to Nancy Louisa Curtis 11-4-1866 Be
Bryant, W. J. to Anna Gibson 3-11-1868 (no return) Dy
Bryant, W. J. to Maggie Gibson 10-28-1871 (10-29-1871) Dy
Bryant, Washington to Mary Elizabeth Usery 4-30-1854 Hr
Bryant, William G. to Lucy A. D. Andrews 10-4-1859 (10-6-1859) G
Bryant, William H. to Alsa J. Parrish 12-30-1846 Ma
Bryant, William J. to Lilly A. Barton 9-24-1854 G
Bryant, William K. to Emily A. Blankenship 7-1-1854 G
Bryant, William R. to Frances C. Snodgrass 8-3-1861 (8-5-1861) Ma
Bryant, William R. to M. A. E. Roe 1-13-1859 G
Bryant, William to Catherine Parker 5-2-1867 Hn
Bryant, William to Eveline Hedleburg 11-4-1840 Ma
Bryant, Wm. A. to Nancy J. Elmore 10-22-1851 (10-23-1851) Hr
Bryant, Wm. A. to Rebecca A. Love 1-1-1866 (1-4-1866) F
Bryant, Wm. E. to Epps Neal 12-8-1873 (no return) Hy
Bryant, Wm. J. to Mary Stewart 12-20-1846 G
Bryant, Wm. J. to Susan Thomas 12-20-1870 (12-22-1870) Cr
Bryant, Wm. to Jan M. Glass 9-1-1845 (9-16-1845) Hr
Bryant, Zachariah to Elizabeth A. Floyd 1-8-1840 (1-9-1840) G
Bryant, Zachriah to Elizabeth Bishop 11-19-1858 Cr
Bryant, jr., Jno. to Martha Bullington 8-15-1861 G
Bryns, Richard to Martha L. Petty 11-24-1844 Cr
Bryson, David K. to Z. A. Dooley 3-22-1859 (no return) L
Buch, C. B. to N. A. Warren 11-1-1866 G
Bucham, John W. to Mary E. Plumley 5-30-1872 T
Buchanan, B. B. to Eliza Jane Smith 1-25-1847 Sh
Buchanan, Charles R. to Mary E. Murrah 12-23-1849 Sh
Buchanan, E. J. to Cofie Currey 11-7-1867 G
Buchanan, George to Amanda C. Freeland 10-31-1859 Hn
Buchanan, Harry to Harriet Sinclair 12-30-1869 G B
Buchanan, Harry to Lizzie Bowen 1-8-1872 (no return) Dy
Buchanan, Henry to Lucy Green 10-24-1885 (10-27-1885) L
Buchanan, Henry to Mary Ann Hutchson 4-22-1862 O
Buchanan, J. B. to Verginia Bright 9-4-1867 O
Buchanan, J. C. to N. A. Roney 8-6-1872 (no return) Cr
Buchanan, J. to M. J. Inman 3-1-1866 O
Buchanan, J. M. to S. J. Campbell 3-9-1864 (3-10-1864) O
Buchanan, J. T. to L. P. Myers 2-5-1867 (2-6-1867) O
Buchanan, J. W. to E. H. Walker 4-9-1857 Hn
Buchanan, J. W. to Lucretia Ann West 2-20-1862 O
Buchanan, James E. to Mary M. Freeland 1-6-1857 (no return) Hn
Buchanan, James L. to Martha Hood 2-14-1861 O
Buchanan, James W. to Tirzah Hood 1-17-1854 O
Buchanan, Jas. A. to E. M. Reeves 2-7-1865 (2-9-1865) O

Buchanan, John A. to Nancy Belle Edmonds 3-11-1856 O
Buchanan, John T. to Eliza Jane York 8-22-1866 (8-26-1866) Ma
Buchanan, John W. to Mary Ann Edmunds 4-11-1861 Hn
Buchanan, John to Margaret Legget 12-11-1867 O
Buchanan, Mecajah to Mary E. Allen 10-29-1865 (10-31-1865) O
Buchanan, Peter W. to Aratanna Clendenin 11-23-1859 Hn
Buchanan, T. C. (Capt.) to Sarah A. Bell 6-28-1875 (6-29-1875) Dy
Buchanan, T. C. to Emma Bell 4-26-1877 Dy
Buchanan, T. G. to Susan G. Maleer 1-28-1858 Hn
Buchanan, T. J. to Mary E. Ramsey 3-5-1867 O
Buchanan, Thomas A. to Grace S. Garrison 2-3-1857 O
Buchanan, Thomas to Molly Browning 8-26-1866 Hn B
Buchanan, William to Ruthy M. McKelvy 5-17-1859 G
Buchanan, Wm. H. to Jennie Rice 12-19-1878 Hy
Buchanan, Wm. H. to L. J. Buchanan 8-11-1861 G
Buchannan, Eli to Lucy Parker 6-30-1877 (7-1-1877) L
Buchannan, John C. to Luiza J. Goodwin 10-31-1854 G
Buchannan, Joseph E. to Nancy K. English 5-13-1859 (5-14-1859) Sh
Buchannan, Thos. E. to Susan V. Goodin 4-8-1856 G
Buchannon, D. A. to Caroline Wilson 12-7-1864 (12-8-1864) Cr
Buchannon, John to Nancy Clopton 9-27-1848 L
Buchanon, L. A. to Rutha An Sulivant 2-3-1848 (2-7-1848) F
Buck, A. T. to Caroline Foster 1-13-1848 Hn
Buck, Albert to Ann E. Johnson 1-2-1878 Hy
Buck, Anderson to Sallie Claybrook 8-27-1869 Hy
Buck, Calvin to Mandy Mann 1-18-1876 (no return) Hy
Buck, Edward to Sarah Davis 7-28-1848 (7-30-1848) F
Buck, Edwin C. to Sophona M. Phillips 11-7-1850 Sh
Buck, Hamsen to Hannah Williams 12-20-1871 (no return) Hy
Buck, Harrison to Mary Kinan? 3-17-1867 G
Buck, Hosea to Mary Helen Strother 7-17-1850 Sh
Buck, Jerry to Elva Johnson 1-23-1872 (no return) Hy
Buck, Ples to Fannie Claybrook 8-3-1870 (no return) Hy
Buck, R. to Rosalie Newmaier 1-31-1859 Sh
Buck, Robert to Malinda Anthony 1-23-1877 Hy
Buck, Silas to Jane Haralson 5-20-1841 Sh
Buckannan, D. A. to Caroline Wilson 12-7-1864 Cr
Buckannon, J. J. S. to Samantha M. Bucy 7-9-1863 Hn
Bucke, James G. to Mary Ann E. Reynolds 12-26-1854 (12-31-1854) Hr
Buckelew, R. F. to Elizabeth Johnson 8-30-1851 (no return) F
Buckett, David M. to Mary E. Pritchard 2-6-1853 Cr
Buckhannan, A. M. to B. O. Posey 12-4-1849 (12-5-1849) L
Buckhanon, H. C. to Bethena Young 9-10-1846 We
Buckingham, George J. to Elizabeth S. Arnis 12-18-1866 (12-19-1866) Ma
Buckingham, Henry G. to Eliza McIntosh 10-18-1843 Sh
Buckingham, J. M. to Lizzie Lewis 3-23-1874 (3-24-1874) Dy
Buckley (Burkley), William to Eliza Evans 6-7-1847 F
Buckley, B. B. to Fannie A. Wade 12-17-1874 (12-20-1874) O
Buckley, Benjamin B. to Martha A. Cobb 4-17-1857 (4-19-1857) O
Buckley, Henry L. to Laura Jane Tate 8-16-1831 Sh
Buckley, James to Caroline Parrish 2-13-1857 We
Buckley, John M. to Elizabeth Cole 11-13-1861 We
Buckley, Organ to S. M. Wagster 12-3-1867 O
Buckley, W. D. to Mary E. Phillips 3-20-1869 (3-23-1869) F
Buckley, William to Nancy A. Kelley 4-30-1850 (no return) F
Buckley?, James to Elizabeth Culbreath 12-4-1843 (12-?-1843) T
Buckleys, Warner (Warren?) L. to Evelina G. Redditt 11-14-1839 Sh
Buckly, Americus F. to Mary F. Cooper 1-13-1860 We
Buckly, Paschal to Synthia Redditt 5-3-1836 Sh
Buckly, Warner L. to Eliza M. Redditt 10-13-1834 Sh
Buckner, Charles to Charity Ruffian 1-24-1883 (no return) L
Buckner, Edward to Mary L. Coggins 8-14-1860 (8-15-1860) Ma
Buckner, Jonathan to Jane L. Wood 1-21-1846 (1-28-1846) F
Buckner, Wm. P. to Susan Barker 1-2-1851 Cr
Bucknor, John J. to Ann A. Russell 8-31-1850 (no return) Hn
Bucy, James A. to Nancy J. Champion 10-4-1855 (no return) Hn
Bucy, John M. to Emily McChristian 8-14-1843 (no return) Hn
Bucy, Monroe to Mary Burton 11-29-1865 Hn
Bucy, T. W. to Louisa J. Bullock 12-24-1867 Hn
Bucy, W. H. to Elizabeth Bucy 1-14-1866 Hn
Bucy, William R. to Elvcy D. Purnell 5-11-1840 Hn
Bucy, William to Nancy A. Moody 8-15-1852 Hn
Budgett?, Jonathan to Margaret? Alfred 12-29-1862 T
Buding?, Thomas to Mary Carter 1-9-1838 Hr
Bueckner, Charles to Frederica Fisher 4-25-1861 (4-26-1861) Sh
Buehl, Henry to Josephine G. Wild 2-8-1861 (2-9-1861) Sh
Buell, Henry to Susan J. Willis 3-16-1860 Hn
Buffalo, Mathew T. to Kezziah Brown 5-13-1839 (5-15-1839) Hr
Buffaloe, E. T. to Susan M. Taylor 1-9-1862 (no return) Hy
Buffaloe, Jno. W. to Martha J. Brown 11-30-1869 Hy
Buffaloe, W. A. to Mary J. Howell 12-17-1850 Sh
Buffalow, George D. to Udora J. Clements 2-20-1871 (2-21-1871) Ma
Buffum, Rufus E. to Eliza M. Laughorn 7-15-1846 F
Buford, Abram J. to Elvira J. Bryan 12-20-1852 (12-22-1852) Sh
Buford, Austin to Clara Jackson 1-8-1867 F B
Buford, Henry to Fanny Beasley 2-6-1867 (2-7-1867) F B
Buford, John O. H. to Caroline A. Black 11-2-1846 (11-5-1846) F

Buford, Mingo to Priscilla Maclin 4-1-1870 (12-28-1870) F B
Buford, Robt. C. to Martha D. Suttle 11-27-1848 (no return) F
Buford, Semion E. to Mary Ann Fields 4-20-1840 (4-22-1840) G
Buford, Smith to Mattie A. Hall 2-6-1866 (2-7-1866) T
Buford, W. L. to H. A. Hall 8-2-1859 (8-3-1859) T
Bugg, Albert to Mary Vaughan 9-30-1866 (SB 1870?) G
Bugg, Alex to Sarah A. Dock 5-3-1869 (no return) Dy
Bugg, Andrew M. to Louiza M. Jacobs 10-13-1866 Cr
Bugg, J. R. to Flomida Shefard? 12-27-1858 O
Bugg, J. R. to Florence Sheppard 12-27-1858 O
Bugg, James L. to H. F. McFall 11-20-1860 Sh
Bugg, Jas. H. to Martha Ann Somers 11-18-1872 O
Bugg, Jesse to Eliza Atcherson 12-13-1843 Hn
Buggs, Phillip to Kate Fields 8-30-1873 (8-31-1873) T
Buhse?, Leopold to Mary E. Pugh 8-22-1874 (8-26-1874) T
Buie, Archibald to Huldah Mason 11-7-1839 Hn
Buie, John F. to Sarina J. Charles 12-23-1860 Hn
Buirckman, Frances to Mary E. Stone 8-18-1865 (8-19-1865) O
Bukley, John L. to Appe Payne 2-4-1851 (2-5-1851) L
Bulger, Chas. to Sarah Morgan 12-19-1846 Sh
Bulger, Cornelius to Emily Waxter 6-20-1861 (6-21-1861) Hr
Bulger, James to M. E. Hays 1-30-1862 T
Bull, D. R. to M. F. Able 9-2-1867 (9-5-1867) F
Bull, Jeremiah to Edna F. Robertson 7-12-1851 (no return) F
Bull, R. C. to F. C. Jones 10-19-1852 Cr
Bull, William to Mary H. Bandy 11-16-1869 T
Bullard, Christopher to Mary Moon(Moore) 11-6-1844 (11-?-1844) Hr
Bullard, David C. to Jane C. Ferrell 2-4-1867 (2-5-1867) Dy
Bullard, James to Maranda Ferrell 7-27-1843 (7-28-1843) G
Bullard, John P. to Sarah Gantlett 5-25-1863 (5-26-1863) O
Bullen, George M. D. to Mary Hanks 2-28-1865 G
Bullin, J. W. to Nannie F. Walker 1-27-1873 O
Bulling, John to Minerva Wallis 12-13-1865 G
Bullington, B. F. to Mary M. Rose 3-31-1855 (4-?-1855) Hr
Bullington, D. A. to Ellen Browning 11-27-1869 (12-2-1869) Cr
Bullington, J. C. to Mary Bullington 12-29-1865 (12-31-1865) Cr
Bullington, J. S. to Lidy J. Meritt 12-15-1870 Cr
Bullington, Jasper to James Jones 12-24-1855 G
Bullington, John C. to Elizabeth Lee 2-11-1854 (2-16-1854) G
Bullington, Josiah C. to Mary A. C. McKinly 11-8-1850 (11-14-1850) Hr
Bullington, Lewis Jackson to Parilee Box 7-4-1850 (7-11-1850) Hr
Bullington, M. L. to Nancy J. Stribling 12-19-1871 (no return) Cr
Bullington, Mark to Nancy Browning 9-26-1837 G
Bullington, Paschal to Mary E. Hix 9-27-1860 G
Bullington, Richard E. to Sallie Peete 12-27-1869 T
Bullington, William C. to Sarah J. Browning 12-2-1862 (12-5-1862) Cr
Bullington, Wm. H. to Mary F. Tucker 8-8-1858 Cr
Bullock, Alex to Martha Davis 1-13-1878 Hy
Bullock, Amos to Kesiah Hopkins 10-16-1843 (no return) We
Bullock, Billey to Mary Ann Taylor 2-27-1868 T
Bullock, C. L. to Mary Carter 9-25-1854 (no return) F
Bullock, G. T. to N. A. Cope 2-27-1866 Hn
Bullock, Isaac J. to Cathrine M. Priest 11-27-1841 Cr
Bullock, John to Rhodie Mitchell 1-11-1868 (1-21-1868) F B
Bullock, Joshua to Mary Ann Cassles 4-3-1866 Hn
Bullock, Meciagah to Susan A. M. Brown 9-29-1841 Ma
Bullock, Obadiah to Penelope Nobles 4-16-1840 Be
Bullock, Richard M. to Fannie A. Twigg 1-10-1860 (no return) We
Bullock, Robert to Ann S. Mathews 9-24-1839 F
Bullock, Stephen to Lindy Love 12-27-1866 Hn B
Bullock, William L. to Ellen J. Boyd 7-12-1863 Hn
Bumpas, Anderson to Fannie Binam 11-11-1871 (11-24-1871) T
Bumpass, Alex. A. to Elizabeth T. Frazier 9-4-1848 Ma
Bumpass, Amos to Mollie Ward 6-18-1870 (6-19-1870) Dy
Bumpass, Benjamin to Lucinda Short 4-5-1829 (4-5-1829) Hr
Bumpass, E. Y. to Tennessee Cravens 2-25-1862 Hn
Bumpass, E.B. to Kate B. Willis 5-8-1859 Hn
Bumpass, Edward F. to Ethelenda Wade 10-10-1849 Hn
Bumpass, Ezekiel Green L. to Julia Carson 7-15-1838 Hn
Bumpass, Gabril to Susan Hateley 9-22-1844 Hr
Bumpass, George W. to S. A. Mayo 12-22-1868 (12-23-1868) F
Bumpass, James M. to Lucinda Hopper 8-9-1853 (8-10-1853) Ma
Bumpass, John J. to Margret Nelms 9-29-1842 (10-11-1842) O
Bumpass, Moses to Nancy Brantley 7-14-1826 (7-16-1826) Hr
Bumpass, R. E. to Elizah Mitchum 11-18-1870 (11-22-1870) Cr
Bumpbass, Julian to Lovy Coe 4-23-1870 T
Bumphass, Monroe to Matilda Wright 2-16-1874 (2-24-1874) T
Bumpious, William L. to Mary Ann Barber 2-19-1841 (2-23-1841) O
Bumpus, Alpha R. to Margarett M. Henry 1-3-1843 Ma
Bumpus, James M. to Marcha A. Frazier 3-15-1842 (3-17-1842) Ma
Bumpus, William L. to Catharine Hall 2-15-1858 O
Bunch, B. B. to Anna E. Williams 10-14-1866 Hn
Bunch, B. F. to Mary A. Boston 3-8-1870 Cr
Bunch, Fed to Chaney Outerbridge 6-15-1878 (no return) Hy
Bunch, Hiram D. to Nancy Butler 11-14-1829 Sh
Bunch, Jim to Chaney Fisher 2-6-1874 (no return) Hy
Bunch, John to Sally Butler 6-13-1827 Sh

Grooms

Bunch, Reuben to Julia Harris 1-29-1883 (not endorsed) L
Bunch, Samuel J. to Sallie Coe 12-1-1855 Sh
Bunch, Valentine to Elizabeth Taylor 9-28-1857 O
Bunch, Wiley to Mary Ann Butler 2-16-1837 Sh
Bunch, Zelliver to Fannie Nixune 2-15-1867 L B
Bundy, R. C. T. to Mannie Moody 9-18-1870 Hy
Bunicum, Wm. to Margarett Fitzgerald 4-4-1864 Sh
Bunn, Cader to Nancy Edwards 12-9-1845 Cr
Bunn, Calvin to Nancy J. Orrell 8-17-1841 (no return) Hn
Bunn, William to Fredonia Raines 2-3-1883 (2-4-1883) L
Bunn, William to Martha Bishop 9-12-1866 (no return) L
Bunn, William to Martha Bishop 9-26-1867 (9-12?-1867) L
Bunn, William to Mary Davidson 2-25-1868 (2-26?-1868) L
Bunnell, Wilson A. to J. T. Tarkington 7-31-1863 Dy
Bunpsups?, Edward J. to Elvinie Carroll 10-1-1857 We
Buns, William H. to Margaret E. Sorrell 7-2_-1866 (7-24-1866) L
Bunten, Daniel W. to Nancy P. Britton 5-12-1860 (5-?-1860) Ma
Buntin, Asa to Emma Montgomery 4-28-1866 Ma
Buntin, Council to Susan T. Davis 1-28-1867 Ma
Buntin, James H. to Susan A. B. Wilie 2-8-1870 Ma
Buntin, Joel to Nannie M. Hart 1-18-1871 (1-19-1871) Ma
Buntin, Reubin to Mary E. Davis 12-16-1850 (1-1-1851) Ma
Bunton, J. W. to Mary E. Cunningham 1-15-1860 Hn
Bunton, John to Axie Fulas 10-10-1840 Hn
Bunton, Johnson to Susan Brown 10-23-1845 F
Bunton, William to Lucy Mangrum 8-10-1855 Hn
Bunyon, Richard to Hannora O'Brien 5-20-1861 Sh
Bur?, John to Catherine Hudgins 1-8-1845 Hn
Burch, Abe to Harriet Tyus 12-23-1878 Hy
Burch, B. D. to Sallie B. Turner 5-12-1860 T
Burch, Chesley to Bettie Tucker 12-14-1873 Hy
Burch, David R. to Martha J. Love 8-21-1854 G
Burch, J. W. to Martha Jane Leiper 2-7-1856 Hn
Burch, S. to Nancy A. Mills 8-30-1870 Dy
Burch, W. N. to Narcissa Brom 2-7-1861 Be
Burch, Zach. to Mary Woodard 11-22-1844 Cr
Burchard, William to Margaret S. Conrad 8-2-1848 Sh
Burchet, P. to A. Burchet 7-27-1870 (9-1-1872?) T
Burchett, Henry to Cora Hays 5-7-1870 T
Burchett, Junior to Nancy J. Kindred 1-27-1855 O
Burchett, Junor to Jane Elder 9-9-1837 (9-21-1837) O
Burd, J. H. to Martha A. Hillyard 11-2-1867 Hn
Burd, James N.? to Mary Chandler 9-2-1866 Hn
Burd, William to S. Stoffle 3-30-1845 Hn
Burdell, William to Roxey Siver 12-14-1864 Sh
Burdet, John to Criddie Cody 8-31-1872 (no return) Cr B
Burdick, James L. to Dicy A. Sullivan 5-10-1861 (5-14-1861) T
Burdine, J.R. to Sarah A. Bonner 1-6-1855 (no return) Hn
Burdit, Robt. to Ann Carson 12-19-1870 (12-20-1870) Cr B
Burdon, Govner to Hannah Autney 12-27-1870 Hy
Burford, Andrew J. to Ann Lyle 11-17-1874 Hy
Burford, B. Franklin to S. R. Apperson 10-31-1863 Sh
Burford, F. M. to Cordelia A. Shaw 10-22-1849 (10-25-1849) Hr
Burford, Jesse S. to Martha M. White 5-9-1842 Hr
Burford, Pat to Penny Turner 12-29-1875 (no return) Hy
Burford, Philemon T. to Caroline J. Ingram 5-22-1839 (5-24-1839) F
Burford, Philemon T. to Frances A. Smith 3-4-1842 (no return) F
Burford, Phillip T. to Nancy C. W. Tally 5-19-1838 O
Burford, S. C. to E. F. Dickerson 1-10-1871 (no return) Hy
Burford, William to Loomy McLeod? 7-6-1844 (7-7-1844) F
Burge, Andrew to Sarah Gordon 4-27-1838 Ma
Burge, Saml. B. to Marthaan Wootten 10-20-1839 (10-24-1839) F
Burgess, James to Susan Markham 9-8-1855 (9-10-1855) T
Burgess, Robert E. to Mary Arnold 12-25-1850 (12-31-1850) G
Burgess, Thos. R. to _____ ?-?-1859 Hy
Burgess, W. H. to M. C. Taylor 12-14-1876 Dy
Burgett, J. W. to Emma J. Fadley 1-11-1861 Sh
Burgie, D. S. to J. E. Barnett 10-13-1869 Dy
Burgitt, Wm. Porter to Sarah Ann Withington 12-17-1855 (12-20-1855) T
Buris, James to Mary Watson 10-16-1875 (no return) Hy
Burk, Edward to Alice Stafford 4-5-1850 Sh
Burk, J. H. C. to Jane (Mrs.) Cocks 9-21-1870 G
Burk, Madison to Nancy Pane 2-1-1852 Hn
Burk, Michael to Catherine Loughman 4-26-1851 (4-28-1851) Sh
Burk, Michael to Margaret Stone 8-11-1859 Cr
Burk, Michael to Mary Easley 10-30-1859 Hn
Burk, Robert W. to Fredonia W. Williams 1-16-1872 (1-17-1872) L
Burk, Stephen A. to Martha A. Dixon 10-19-1850 Cr
Burk, Thos. to Joanna Murphy 5-20-1853 Sh
Burk, Timothy to Alice Stafford 11-31-1848 Sh
Burk, Virgil R. to Mary E. Greenwood 6-12-1863 Cr
Burk, Virgil R. to Mary E. Greenwood 6-12-1863 (no return) Cr
Burk, W. M. to S. A. Maxwell 2-29-1872 Cr
Burk, William to Bunavista Stephens 8-24-1870 G
Burk, William to Louisa Pate 3-26-1859 (no return) We
Burke, Edward to Ann Mack 4-28-1855 Sh
Burke, James to Margaret L. Atwell 9-7-1861 (9-8-1861) Sh

Burke, James to Marie Kane 1-4-1848 (SB 1849?) Sh
Burke, John M. to Eliza Jorden 12-20-1868 G B
Burke, John to Ellen Burke 7-18-1849 Sh
Burke, John to Mary Larkin 8-24-1842 Sh
Burke, Patrick to Bridget Foley 3-6-1843 Sh
Burke, Patrick to Kate (Mrs.) Whalen 9-27-1863 Sh
Burke, Robert A. to Elizabeth A. Jordan 1-10-1859 (1-12-1859) L
Burke, Saml. to Mary Jarrett 11-8-1845 Cr
Burke, William R. to Sarah E. Fewell 10-28-1868 G
Burke, Wm. Hartwell to Polly Butler 6-13-1827 Sh
Burkeen, A. J. to Vandelia Meadows 12-21-1870 Dy
Burkes, Alexander to Ellen O'Neal 11-1-1856 Sh
Burkes, Barney to George Ann Norton 2-18-1844 (12-24-1844) Ma
Burkes, Charles L. to Mary E. Eddins 3-4-1856 Sh
Burket, J. A. to M. E. Rogers 1-23-1878 (1-24-1878) Dy
Burket, J. to E. McFarlin 12-3-1841 Be
Burkett(Burkhead), Thomas O. to Nancy Willoughby 2-7-1839 (2-8-1839) Hr
Burkett, J. H. to Verginia Robertson 10-6-1870 (no return) Dy
Burkett, John M. to Eugenia Roberson 10-13-1869 (10-14-1869) Ma
Burkett, John W. to M. J. Harrison 2-2-1861 Be
Burkett, John to Mary Ann Dunevant 9-13-1877 Dy
Burkett, Wm. M. to Lucy A. Saners 1-25-1870 (1-26-1870) Ma
Burkhart, A. to Nancy J. Chambers 1-24-1855 (no return) F
Burkhart, Alexder. to Mary A. Harris 12-4-1856 (no return) F
Burkhart, J. F. to J. M. Reeves 8-29-1860 (9-4-1860) T
Burkhart, James Miles to Mary Ann Henderson 8-15-1843 (8-18-1843) T
Burkhead, A. Hamilton to Mary F. Walsh 1-28-1869 Ma
Burkhead, Andrew H. to Mamena? Willoughby 11-28-1844 Hr
Burkhead, Eliazer to Rhoda Jane Nailor 1-1-1856 (1-3-1856) Hr
Burkhead, Geo. G. to Sarah Roark 12-30-1847 Hr
Burkhead, L. M. to J. L. Wakefield 1-17-1877 L
Burkin, Andrew to M. E. Payne 4-3-1867 G
Burkitt, Ephraim to Temperance Council 3-7-1840 Be
Burkle, David to Caroline Brooker 11-24-1860 (11-28-1860) Sh
Burklen?, Church to Lizzie Connell 5-1-1876 Dy
Burkley, Peyton to Dora Ledsinger 5-11-1878 (5-15-1878) Dy
Burkley, W. M. to Sarah Ann Dunlap 9-3-1863 Hn
Burkley, William to Emeline Bulliner 9-20-1863 Mn
Burks, Allen to Allen? Fitzpatrick 7-7-1868 (7-8-1868) L
Burks, Anderson to Fannie Estis 4-19-1885 (4-22-1885) L
Burks, B. F. to Samtha O. Spence 8-4-1885 (8-5-1885) L
Burks, E. H. to Elizabeth Gary 10-24-1865 Hn
Burks, E. L. to Maggie Clemmons 12-24-1875 (12-26-1875) Dy
Burks, George to Cora Glass 1-26-1877 L
Burks, George to Sallie Currie 2-28-1877 Hy
Burks, H. T. to L. A. Chambers 2-23-1881 (2-24-1881) L
Burks, J. E. to Jessee Parsley 12-5-1883 L
Burks, J. E. to Nora Parsley 2-16-1886 L
Burks, J. R. to Eddie Wood 11-21-1885 (11-24-1885) L
Burks, James R. to Josephine E. Shorter 12-7-1857 Sh
Burks, James to Winney Edward Johnson 2-2-1867 (2-3-1867) L B
Burks, John T. to Sarah E. Reddick 7-17-1869 (7-19-1869) Cr
Burks, S. B. to Fannie E. Burks 1-15-1884 (1-16-1884) L
Burks, S. N. to M. A. Chambers 12-10-1878 (12-11-1879?) L
Burks, Sabert L. to Harriet A. McGaughy 10-20-1869 (10-21-1869) L
Burks, Seaton B. to Ann E. Wood 12-21-1843 (no return) L
Burks, Seaton B. to Laura Powell 4-29-1854 (5-2-1854) L
Burks, T. C. to Mary E. Erwin 2-11-1863 Mn
Burks, W. C. to C. B. Williams 11-28-1882 L
Burks, W. E. to Mollie E. McDearman 2-26-1872 (2-28-1872) L
Burks, William to Bell Badwell 12-24-1866 (12-25-1866) T
Burks, Wm. L. to Margaret Wessen 3-20-1862 L
Burlerson, Wm. L. to Eurind Holsouser? 12-20-1853 T
Burleson, Aaron to Minerva Jane Seaton 8-21-1838 (8-23-1838) Hr
Burleson, David A. to Frances E. Webb 1-4-1868 (1-5-1868) L
Burleson, Jacob to Elizabeth Burleson 12-24-1828 (1-8-1829) Hr
Burleson, James to Jackoleno Biggs 3-20-1830 Sh
Burleson, Jonathan to Elizabeth Nichols 2-4-1833 (2-7-1833) Hr
Burleson, Joseph to Ally M. Seaton 10-8-1827 (11-1-1827) Hn
Burleyson, Archey to Sarah Ann Hunsucker 12-21-1866 (12-22-1866) F
Burlison, Henry to Catharine Hemphill 2-15-1868 (2-6?-1868) T
Burlison, J. H. to Jennie Ballard 12-21-1873 T
Burn, Bennett to Charlotte Taylor 11-15-1844 (11-19-1844) Ma
Burn, Daniel R. to Martha J. Lambert 12-31-1849 (12-16?-1849) Ma
Burnam, H. T. to Rebecca A. Page 7-22-1839 (7-25-1839) G
Burnam, Henry T. to Ann H. Turner 6-3-1841 (6-9-1841) G
Burnam, Joshua to Lou Duncan 11-15-1865 (11-16-1865) Dy
Burne, George to Elizabeth Moore 8-30-1856 (8-31-1856) Sh
Burnes, Eli M. to Sarah A. Mathews 11-10-1874 (no return) L
Burnes, Nathan M. to Mary Jane Tipler 7-31-1846 (8-4-1846) Hr
Burnes, William A. to Cyntha May 10-28-1837 (10-31-1837) T
Burnes, William H. to Mary E. Magett 4-19-1847 (4-29-1847) F
Burnes, William to Frances A. Manley 1-3-1877 L
Burnet, Geo. L. to Amanda J. Gatewood 2-6-1858 (2-7-1858) Hr
Burnett (Burrett), Patterson to Elizabeth Morgan 10-19-1855 We
Burnett, B. F. to M. E. Donnell 4-17-1863 (4-19-1863) O
Burnett, Calvin to America Haywood 11-23-1869 Hy

Burnett, Charles J. to Nancy Vinson 2-24-1841 (2-26-1841) Hr
Burnett, Daniel H. to Pelina Davidson 2-4-1860 (no return) Hy
Burnett, Edmond to C. A. Boykin 7-20-1866 (8-11-1866) F B
Burnett, G. W. to N. A. Alexander 5-29-1860 (not endorsed) F
Burnett, Glenn O. to Sarah M. Rogers 1-4-1830 (2-1-1830) Hr
Burnett, Henry C. to Mattie A. Robinson 1-8-1866 G
Burnett, J. K. to Louisa Foster 6-11-1867 O
Burnett, J. T. to Macy Jones 8-29-1865 Hy
Burnett, J. T. to Mary E. Goodman 1-17-1871 (1-18-1871) Dy
Burnett, Jacob to Nancy C. Poston 1-8-1867 (1-9-1867) Dy
Burnett, James H. to America J. Wilson 6-19-1865 (6-27-1865) O
Burnett, James M. to Jane Parris 11-26-1853 (11-27-1853) G
Burnett, Jas. H. to M. L. Robinson 8-15-1864 O
Burnett, Jasper N. to Nancy Seawright 4-3-1851 Hn
Burnett, Joel B. to Sally Ann Isler 8-20-1849 Sh
Burnett, John A. to Susan B. Mankins 6-5-1859 Hn
Burnett, John W. to S. E. Thompson 2-9-1871 Hy
Burnett, Joseph to Emma Wilson 12-29-1877 Hy
Burnett, Leonard to Caroline Black 1-26-1869 (no return) F B
Burnett, Louis to M. L. Osburne 6-2-1862 (6-5-1862) O
Burnett, Peter H. to Harriett W. Rogers 8-13-1828 (8-20-1828) Hr
Burnett, R. T. to Minerva McRee 12-14-1866 (12-16-1866) O
Burnett, Stewart to Lizzie Watkins 4-25-1878 (no return) Hy
Burnett, T. B. to Louisa Lance 12-10-1867 O
Burnett, W. L. to Ellen J. Tomblinson 12-20-1852 (no return) F
Burnett, Wesley A. to Susan F. McFadin 10-12-1858 T
Burnett, William P. to Caroline Gatewood 12-26-1860 Hr
Burnett, William to Margarette White 12-12-1861 G
Burney, John F. to Nancy Ann M. Parks 7-9-1851 (7-13-1851) G
Burney, W. R. to Mary F. Webb 11-5-1877 (11-6-1877) L
Burney, William B. to Margaret A. Caruth 8-21-1844 (8-22-1844) L
Burnham, G. W. to Nancy P. Brunt 10-19-1872 (10-20-1872) Dy
Burnham, J. H. to M. F. Whitt 12-21-1870 (12-22-1870) Dy
Burnham, John to Harriet Bradshaw 11-16-1854 We
Burnham, W. C. to Tennessee Bailey 9-21-1875 (9-22-1875) Dy
Burnly, Edward to Elizabeth O. Trueheart 2-5-1851 Sh
Burns (Bunn?), J. H. to Mary Palmer Bishop 3-15-1867 (no return) L
Burns, A. M. to L. C. Cook 6-29-1856 We
Burns, A. T. to E. F. Porter 12-16-1872 (12-19-1872) Cr
Burns, Barney to Margaret Glenn 3-15-1862 (3-17-1862) Sh
Burns, Charles to Louisa Williams 1-10-1861 Hr
Burns, Citizen to Agnes W. Clark 7-20-1838 We
Burns, Columbus to Julia Estes 1-17-1880 (1-18-1880) L B
Burns, E. A. to Mary Ann E. Dayley 12-25-1848 (12-26-1848) F
Burns, E. T. to M. J. Gwin 11-10-1851 Cr
Burns, Edward to Ellen O'Shee 1-3-1860 Sh
Burns, Elias to Elizabeth E. Pritchard 3-15-1841 Cr
Burns, George G. to Mary Pettyjohn 9-12-1852 Hn
Burns, H. C. to Alice H. Newbill 12-19-1864 (no return) Cr
Burns, Isaac to Nancy Morrow 1-3-1861 O
Burns, J. P. to Lucinda Holms 11-12-1869 Hy
Burns, J. W. to Laurena L. Haynes 1-6-1886 L
Burns, James B. to Margaret E. Black 7-10-1865 Hn
Burns, James H. to Amanda E. McKiney 11-28-1866 (12-2-1866) Cr
Burns, James H. to Civil Falkner 11-2-1865 Hy
Burns, James M. to G. A. G. Griggs 5-26-1874 (5-27-1874) L
Burns, James to Elizabeth Williams 11-1-1879 (11-2-1879) Dy
Burns, Jno. P. to Edna M. Johnson 7-23-1868 (7-24-1868) F
Burns, John to Elizabeth Ray 3-29-1869 (no return) Dy
Burns, John to Susan Wails 7-15-1864 Sh
Burns, Nathan M. to Hannah T. Harrison 1-13-1840 Hr
Burns, Richard to Starry Bowden 4-3-1880 (no return) L B
Burns, Robert H. to Mary Jane Dungan 12-11-1862 Ma
Burns, Robert W. to Ruth Gibson 7-17-1839 (7-19-1839) Ma
Burns, Thomas V. to Matilda A. Darby 4-28-1868 Ma
Burns, W. B. to Eliza Wisenor 9-8-1854 G
Burns, W. M. to Eliza M. Koonce 12-18-1859 (12-21-1859) T
Burns, William H. to Caroline Griffin 9-17-1840 Hn
Burnside, H. S. to C. J. Hamilton 1-8-1875 (1-12-1875) Dy
Burnwant, Chesley L. to Elizabeth A. Bird 11-16-1850 (11-21-1850) G
Burr, A. B. to Minnie F. Backus 1-15-1861 Sh
Burr, Anderson to Sarah A. Worthy 2-7-1854 Sh
Burr, Luther S. to Cynthis Jane Fanan (France?) 1-3-1848 Sh
Burrel?, David to Sina Maclin 12-23-1872 (12-26-1872) T
Burrell, Isaac to Eliza F. (Mrs.) Edwards 12-23-1872 (no return) Dy
Burrell, John to Henretta Corss 2-15-1873 (2-16-1873) T
Burrell, Michael to Emma Taylor 12-30-1868 (12-31-1868) F B
Burrell, Peter to Rachell Moss 11-12-1873 T
Burrell, Richmond to Fannie Cage 5-9-1874 T
Burress, B. M. to Elizabeth Bryant 10-24-1861 G
Burress, George W. to Nancy O. Greer 9-29-1851 G
Burris, Henry to Ellen Picket 8-2-1851 (no return) F
Burris, James to Eliza A. Easterwood 7-27-1850 (7-29-1850) G
Burris, Joseph J. to Mary E. Haste 10-16-1866 G
Burris, Solomon to Rose Abington 12-22-1868 (12-23-1868) F B
Burris, Stephen A. to Malissa J. Honeycutt 4-22-1862 O
Burris, Thomas to Precilla Wright 3-5-1825 (3-6-1825) Hr

Burris, William A. to Elizabeth M. Long 6-10-1861 (6-16-1861) O
Burris, William J. to Martha Ann Campbell 11-7-1844 (11-9-1844) T
Burris, Wm. to Anna Campbell 11-3-1874 Hy
Burrough, John to Mary E. Buckley 10-4-1848 Sh
Burrough, K. L. A. to Eliza Dickson 8-17-1848 Cr
Burrow, Albert L. to Jane V. Bugg 11-28-1842 (11-22?-1842) Ma
Burrow, Banks M. to Elizabeth Richardson 10-11-1832 (10-12-1832) G
Burrow, Banks M. to Martha J. Mills 10-1-1867 (no return) Cr
Burrow, Daniel to Caroline Webb 2-13-1871 (2-16-1871) Cr
Burrow, Ephraim to Elizabeth Bobbett 4-2-1834 (4-5-1834) G
Burrow, Ephraim to Lu? Briant 2-1-1869 Cr
Burrow, F. S. to Sarah O. Cobell 10-27-1858 Cr
Burrow, Felix to Mollie Maclin 4-17-1882 L
Burrow, G. H. to Hattie E. McNight 3-28-1870 G
Burrow, George J. to Mary Oliver 7-13-1857 Cr
Burrow, Green to Martha Henley 5-19-1840 F
Burrow, Handsel W. to Fannie E. Gill 10-12-1857 (10-13-1857) Ma
Burrow, Hastings to Sarah Hargas 12-9-1842 Cr
Burrow, Henderson to Mary Cook 11-15-1871 (no return) Cr
Burrow, Henry to Sarah Burrow 11-23-1847 Cr
Burrow, Henry to Sarah Johnson 3-1-1832 Sh
Burrow, Isaac R. to Mary A. King 12-23-1847 G
Burrow, Isham to Elvira Chandler 2-14-1838 Ma
Burrow, J. B. to E. F. Agee 12-20-1865 G
Burrow, J. C. to E. J. Putman 11-30-1854 Cr
Burrow, J. L. to Amanda J. Hall 11-14-1874 O
Burrow, J. L. to Elizabeth R. Burrow 3-12-1859 (3-13-1859) Cr
Burrow, J. P. to Sarah C. Jones 9-16-1846 Cr
Burrow, J. T. to M. A. Woodard 8-13-1856 Cr
Burrow, James R. to Amanda T. Wilson 2-?-1845 Ma
Burrow, Jno. A. to R. F. Wright 10-3-1840 G
Burrow, John S. to Betsy Ann Ledbetter 12-21-1842 Ma
Burrow, John to Elizabeth Lanom 11-6-1864 G
Burrow, Jordan to Marry (Amey?) Smith 5-19-1871 (5-20-1871) Cr
Burrow, Martin to C. Jones 2-1-1866 G
Burrow, N. S. to Nancy J. London 1-2-1860 (1-4-1860) G
Burrow, N. S.(L.?) to Margaret J. Boon 8-28-1866 G
Burrow, Nimrod to Elizabeth Harper 11-15-1861 (no return) Cr
Burrow, Nimrod to Martha Laflor 2-16-1850 Cr
Burrow, Phillip to Rosa Ann Nisser 3-3-1842 Cr
Burrow, R. G. to Emily Lewis 12-23-1844 Hr
Burrow, Reuben to Permelia Murrell 3-7-1842 (4-5-1842) F
Burrow, Robert A. to Melora S. Pledge 7-25-1852 (9-8-1852) Hr
Burrow, Robt. H. to Mary Richardson 5-1-1873 (no return) Cr B
Burrow, Simon J. to Margaret McWilliams 1-6-1847 Cr
Burrow, Sol to Millie A. Cabe 12-23-1841 Cr
Burrow, Solomon to Scarlet J. Benton no date (not executed) Cr
Burrow, Starling to Dicy Barker 11-4-1837 (11-5-1837) Hr
Burrow, Sterling to Ruth Zamples 2-6-1834 Hr
Burrow, W. E. to E. J. Porterfield 3-2-1871 Cr
Burrow, Washington M. to Mary C. Tigert 8-18-1844 Ma
Burrow, William J. to Mary New 9-20-1854 (9-28-   ) G
Burrow, William to Emeline Smith 12-12-1848 (12-13-1848) Ma
Burrow, Wilson A. to Mary E. Montgomery 9-20-1855 Cr
Burrows, B. F. to Matilda Young 3-2-1866 (no return) F
Burrows, Thomas to Ellender McKey 7-9-1840 Sh
Burrows, William to Helen Taliaferro 8-22-1867 Hy
Burrus, Charles to Elizabeth Thompson 3-16-1835 (3-19-1835) Hr
Burrus, J. B. to S. C. Cherry 6-26-1868 (6-30-1868) O
Burrus, John to Eliza Smith 8-5-1856 (8-6-1856) G
Burrus, John to Elizabeth M. Goodrich 1-9-1849 Ma
Burruss, Benj. F. to Mary Elder 6-3-1851 (no return) F
Bursh, James to Theresa Thom 4-13-1840 (4-1-1840) Ma
Burson?, J. M. to Mary Scott Rateree 6-2-1851 (no return) Hn
Burt, Aaron to Mary Ann Land 1-27-1836 Sh
Burt, Ben to Missouri Boylan 8-31-1867 (no return) F B
Burt, Williamson N. to Cintha Boydston 7-19-1838 Hr
Burten, A. J. to Susan E. Pain 2-14-1855 We
Burten, Shedrick to Lucy Whitelaw 9-9-1871 (no return) Hy
Burten, Soloman E. to C. W. Guthrie 9-25-1860 We
Burtin, J. W. to Paralee Crow 10-14-1872 (10-17-1872) Dy
Burtis, Theodore to Nancy E. Chapman 6-15-1866 (6-19-1866) T
Burton, Albert C. G. to Eliza J. Hutchinson 2-15-1871 (no return) F B
Burton, Charles W. to Martha J. Altom? 10-9-1859 Hn
Burton, Charles to Sallie Furgerson 4-28-1867 Hn
Burton, Charlie to Louisa Morgan 1-31-1876 L B
Burton, Daniel W. to Sarah A. Ferris 12-9-1854 (12-10-1854) Ma
Burton, Drewry to Evalyn Dollahite 2-6-1838 (no return) Hn
Burton, Ed to Jane Haynes 1-8-1872 Hy
Burton, Fley O. to Caroline Bumpasss 2-25-1870 (no return) Dy
Burton, Frank A. W. to Elizabeth C. Willis 10-31-1844 Ma
Burton, Frank to Fannie Wilkins 12-2-1875 G
Burton, Franklin H. to Susan Mitchell 12-7-1864 Be
Burton, Frederick to Melvina Reed 12-28-1868 (12-29-1868) F B
Burton, George W. to Emily J. Ballew 12-30-1865 (12-31-1865) Cr
Burton, George to Elizabeth Johnson 1-21-1854 Cr
Burton, H. L. to A. A. Manier 2-4-1862 (2-10-1862) F

Burton, Henry to Laura Rudd 1-4-1870 (no return) Hy
Burton, Hezekiah to Mary Jane Bakers 11-15-1843 (11-16-1843) T
Burton, Isaiah to Lucinda Webb 10-16-1843 Hn
Burton, Iverson to Martha C. Dick 10-16-1850 (10-17-1850) Ma
Burton, J. B. to Franca? J. Drummond 4-3-1868 (4-5-1868) T
Burton, J. W. H. to Rachel Crow 10-15-1863 Be
Burton, James A. to Cordelia E. Pritchard 6-19-1871 (no return) Cr
Burton, James A. to Louiza F. Findley 1-30-1851 Hn
Burton, James L. to M. E. A. Taylor 8-1-1871 (8-2-1871) Ma
Burton, James Thos. to Ellen Akin 11-5-1867 (11-6-1867) T
Burton, James W. to Lucy W. Cocke 7-12-1865 F
Burton, James to Caroline Love 10-1-1855 Ma
Burton, Jefferson to Elizabeth C. Crop 11-17-1840 Ma
Burton, Jefferson to Martha J. Wales 5-27-1854 (5-28-1854) G
Burton, Jerimiah to Nancy Issabella Stevenson 12-10-1850 (12-13-1850) Hr
Burton, John A. to Caroline Travis 12-30-1843 (no return) Hn
Burton, John A. to Nancy Bucy 2-8-1844 Hn
Burton, John F. to Nancy Griffith 10-14-1850 (10-17-1850) Hr
Burton, John M. to Mary Halloway 11-4-1847 (11-5-1847) F
Burton, John W. to Nannie E. Whittenberger 2-24-1862 G
Burton, John to Martha P. Wells 6-28-1839 (6-29-1839) F
Burton, John to Sarah Kilby 12-4-1873 Hy
Burton, John to Victoria Jamerson 1-23-1861 (1-27-1861) Cr
Burton, L. A. to Martha Bennett 2-14-1865 Hn
Burton, Lewis H. to Tennessee Maloney 8-24-1867 O
Burton, M. H. to Hannah L. Colter 2-7-1870 (no return) Hy
Burton, Morris G. to Martha A. Overbray 7-29-1843 Hn
Burton, Richard C. to Lucy Ann E. Steel 8-11-1857 Hn
Burton, Samuel to Emeline Volentine 6-5-1855 Ma
Burton, Sherrod J. to Letta J. Valentine 11-30-1858 Hn
Burton, V. M. to M. E. Simpson 12-15-1864 Hn
Burton, W. B. to Alice L. Greaves 10-17-1877 (no return) Hy
Burton, William T. J. to Elizabeth Culbreath 6-6-1855 Hn
Burton, William to Charity Valentine 3-23-1854 Ma
Burton, William to Cynthia Baker 9-12-1829 Hr
Burton, William to Martha Carroll 10-24-1838 (no return) Hn
Burton, William to Nancy Morgan 2-13-1851 (no return) F
Burton, William to Sarah C. Watson 8-23-1848 F
Burton, Wm. C. to Mallissa Higgason 10-23-1860 (10-24-1860) F
Burtus, John S. to Sarah Word 7-27-1853 (no return) F
Busbee, G. to Sally Evans 2-14-1870 (2-17-1870) Cr
Busbee, Sidney to Ruth J. Smith 2-11-1862 Hn
Busby, Albert to Adeline Hager 7-22-1852 Sh
Busby, David to Martha Dunning 5-25-1859 (5-28?-1859) We
Busby, John to Patiance C. Mainor 10-31-1843 G
Busby, Josiah to Elizabeth Ward 9-20-1846 We
Busby, L. M. to Emily Murphy 2-27-1856 Sh
Busby, Merideth to Minerva Hunt 6-19-1826 Sh
Busby, Micajah to Dysy Barns 2-15-1830 Ma
Busby, Milet to Tabitha Herrod 3-20-1858 O
Busby, W. V. to Fanny Boone 12-13-1861 (12-15-1861) Sh
Busby, Wade to Martha Cole 3-7-1849 Be
Busby, William H. to Matilda Allen 10-27-1858 Hn
Buscamp, W. to Dinah Croger 6-1-1852 Sh
Busey, Edward T. to Martha A. Burton 1-3-1842 (no return) Hn
Busey?, W. P. to Frances Sauls 11-5-1865 Hn
Bush, B. J. to Nancy Harnsberry 1-4-1865 Hn
Bush, Bennett to Darcus Jones 8-8-1856 Be
Bush, C. B. to Malvina Melton 10-27-1855 (no return) Hn
Bush, Carter to Mollie Gause 7-6-1877 (no return) L
Bush, Elijah M. to Dorcus Frence 8-8-1838 (no return) Hn
Bush, Elijah M. to Jane Little 1-30-1839 (no return) Hn
Bush, Elisha J. to Nancy Daniel 2-20-1848 Be
Bush, Ephraim to Rena Cerry 12-24-1870 (no return) Dy
Bush, James B. to Fredericka Anderson 3-10-1874 Dy
Bush, James H. to Sarah Hollinsworth 9-10-1849 Hn
Bush, John J. to Nancy Jane Bush 12-3-1845 Be
Bush, John N. to Rachal Glisson 10-12-1847 G
Bush, John to Lucy Leigh 11-24-1861 O
Bush, John to Martha B. Rushing 5-2-1858 Be
Bush, John to Martha Gaines 10-12-1859 Cr
Bush, Joseph to Mary Daniel 12-5-1850 Be
Bush, Malachiah B. to Lacy Cole 1-11-1852 Be
Bush, Peter to Eda (Edna) C. Hill 9-18-1850 Sh
Bush, W. to Mary Emison 10-18-1855 Hn
Bush, William to Lucy Bragg 12-2-1852 Be
Bush, Wm. C. to Persnetia A. Gibson 3-10-1847 Cr
Bush, Wm. to Claney Bell 10-5-1843 Cr
Bush, Wm. to Priscilla A. Pethel 9-8-1856 Be
Bushart, Daniel R. to Louisa BRagg 8-17-1848 Hn
Bushart, Henry to Adaline Hull 12-26-1857 Hn
Bushart, Jacob to Elmyra Boldin 10-27-1846 Hn
Bushart, John P. to Eliza Hicks 9-24-1851 Hn
Bushart, John to Martha Thomas 4-30-1851 Hn
Bushart, John to Mary E. Griffin 5-26-1857 Hn
Bushart, William H. to A. Stokes 5-23-1852 Hn
Bushins?, David J. to Louisa Adkisson 8-5-1846 (8-6-1846) T

Busic, Thomas to Catherine Warthwait? 7-20-1872 (7-21-1872) T
Busick, Joseph M. to Eliza Smith 9-15-1858 (9-16-1858) O
Busick, Owen J. to Martha Kirby 9-25-1847 Ma
Busick, Thos. C. to Mary A. Boce 10-30-1844 Ma
Busick, William M. to Sarah E. Pace 1-6-1858 G
Buskamp, William to Elizabeth Wingerman 5-31-1856 (6-3-1856) Sh
Buson?, Guilliame to Bassie Elder 4-8-1869 G
Bussey, G. W. to Mary V. Garrett 5-6-1858 Sh
Buster, Samuel L. to Emily K. Lewis 11-15-1832 Sh
Butcher, J. F. to S. J. Jones 6-30-1874 O
Butcher, Joseph to Jane Burnes 5-6-1829 Hr
Butcher, Manuel to Netty Harvy 1-14-1870 (1-16-1870) F B
Butes, Newton to Julian Irvin 7-5-1841 Ma
Butler, A. G. to A. E. Wilson 12-5-1857 Cr
Butler, A. J. to Susan Bradbery 9-30-1867 (10-1-1867) Cr
Butler, A. L. to Matilda J. Landrum 12-11-1883 L
Butler, A. S. to Nancy Moon 10-24-1860 We
Butler, A. T. to Elizabeth Smith 3-11-1846 Cr
Butler, A. T. to Nancy J. Dickenson 1-26-1866 (1-28-1866) Cr
Butler, A. T. to Ruth Sherfield 3-28-1870 (3-30-1870) Cr
Butler, Anderson to Susan Garrett 8-18-1831 Ma
Butler, Atlas J. to Milly Huffman 1-3-1847 Cr
Butler, B. to Victoria Huffman 9-20-1848 Cr
Butler, Ben R. to Hollie J. Childress 11-17-1869 G
Butler, Brently to Minerva Sharp 3-6-1855 Cr
Butler, Burton (Birton) to Ellen Gibson 6-24-1866 G
Butler, C. K. to Nancy J. Boswell 9-13-1865 (9-15-1865) Cr
Butler, C. to Una Sedberry 10-14-1855 Cr
Butler, Carrol to Mary E. Johnson 2-2-1856 (2-5-1856) Hr
Butler, Charles E. to Louisa Lee 8-23-1852 (8-26-1852) G
Butler, Charles to Jane Graham 1-15-1853 Hr
Butler, Christopher C. to Eliza Jane Sexton 3-8-1851 G
Butler, Clark S. to Sarah Parks 1-19-1848 Cr
Butler, Daniel to Hannah Bains 10-29-1860 Ma
Butler, David M. to M. P. Green 10-8-1870 (10-9-1870) Cr
Butler, David T. to Ann A. Young 6-18-1852 (6-23-1852) Hr
Butler, Davis to Cheny Nelson 1-16-1873 Hy
Butler, E. A. to Martha E. Sexton 10-12-1850 (10-15-1850) G
Butler, E. C. to Aulenor Bower no date (with Jun 1864) G
Butler, E. C. to Rebecca E. Hix 7-11-1860 G
Butler, E. C. to Sarah Ann Sexton 9-14-1848 G
Butler, E. C. to Texan Patterson 5-15-1866 G
Butler, E. G. to D. E. Sturdivant 2-9-1865 G
Butler, Eli H. to Susan M. Messer 1-10-1839 Cr
Butler, Elias T. to Mary Jane McVey 7-10-1848 (7-13-1848) Ma
Butler, Ezekal to Catherin Eaton 4-3-1872 (4-4-1872) T
Butler, Francis to A. J. English 1-9-1866 Cr
Butler, G. W. to Matilda Lawrence 1-1-1856 We
Butler, G. W. to Milisa Hicks 12-25-1867 G
Butler, G. W. to Pinkey Kyle 10-29-1867 Cr
Butler, George to Irene Reed 10-12-1866 T
Butler, George to Parthena Ann Taylor 3-13-1856 T
Butler, Granvill H. to Mary A. Scott 2-6-1872 Cr
Butler, H. H. to Susan H. Medearis 9-12-1860 (no return) Cr
Butler, H. to Mary E. Whiteside 7-23-1845 Cr
Butler, Haratio to C. Smiley A. Lindy 8-29-1856 Cr
Butler, Henry C. to Nancy A. Jones 3-26-1856 Cr
Butler, Henry to Martha E. Revely 2-12-1845 Ma
Butler, Henry to Rose Dickinson 12-22-1867 G B
Butler, Hezekiah to I. E. Pearce 6-12-1859 Cr
Butler, J. C. to Nancy Parson 9-24-1868 G
Butler, J. F. to Martha E. Shane 9-18-1860 G
Butler, J. H. to Acinnath Crow 10-9-1860 Be
Butler, J. J. to Louisa C. Swindle 4-25-1861 Be
Butler, J.? P. to Narcissa Anderson 11-16-1867 (11-17-1867) Cr
Butler, Jackson G. to Elizabeth M. Butler 12-4-1852 (12-8-1852) Ma
Butler, Jacob H. to Sarah W. Nelson 12-23-1858 Hr
Butler, Jacob to Jane Parish 2-8-1873 (2-9-1873) Cr B
Butler, James C. to Elizabeth McCord 8-8-1843 Cr
Butler, James M. to A. L. Jones 1-6-1858 Cr
Butler, James M. to Susan J. McKelvey 9-20-1858 (9-22-1858) G
Butler, James P. to Louisa B. Butram 2-1860 O
Butler, James to Mary Biddy 12-9-1829 (12-10-1829) Hr
Butler, James to Susan Finler 12-22-1860 (no return) We
Butler, Jas. D. to Lizzie D. Bill 11-1-1855 Sh
Butler, Jas. L. to Hessie Yarbrough 2-27-1868 G
Butler, Jasper N. to Sarah Alexander 2-17-1857 (2-26-1857) Ma
Butler, Jno. to Charlotta Isham 11-6-1828 Sh
Butler, Joel A. to Frances Rogers 1-1-1868 (1-5-1868) Cr
Butler, John B. to Martha M. Cassell 8-1-1855 G
Butler, John F. to Mary M. Cates 2-25-1869 G
Butler, John F. to Nancy Holt 10-7-1868 G
Butler, John Madison to Mona Agnes Rice 7-17-1843 (7-19-1843) T
Butler, John to Mary (Mrs.) Jones 11-29-1862 (11-30-1862) Sh
Butler, John to May Parmer 11-5-1838 Ma
Butler, Jordon to Artimisa F. Whitley 3-2-1869 (3-10-1869) Cr
Butler, L. F. to C. J. Eason 6-8-1867 Cr

Butler, Lawrence to Susan Seats 11-15-1860 (11-18-1860) Ma
Butler, Lenord to Elizabeth Black 4-8-1851 Sh
Butler, Levi to Ella Rowland 8-24-1870 Cr
Butler, M. C. to Jennie A. Robinson 2-3-1885 L
Butler, M. J. to M. O. Jackson 4-3-1877 (4-4-1877) Dy
Butler, Manuel to Emily Spoon 8-19-1841 Cr
Butler, Marvell to Susan Liles 8-6-1860 Cr
Butler, Oliver to Mary Ann Hulsey 8-5-1848 Ma
Butler, P. T. to Mary A. McArthur 7-21-1862 (no return) Cr
Butler, Patrick to Ellen Honan 4-4-1864 (4-6-1864) Sh
Butler, Philip T. to Sarah C. Boyd 3-2-1864 (no return) Cr
Butler, Phillip F. to Frankie Taylor 12-23-1852 Cr
Butler, Phillip H. to Ednie McFarland 7-27-1866 G
Butler, Phillip T. to Sarah C. Butler 3-2-1864 (3-3-1864) Cr
Butler, Richard F. to Elizabeth Arnal 8-26-1854 (no return) We
Butler, Richard F. to Mary A. E. English 12-14-1859 G
Butler, S. H. to J. E. Pendygrass 9-28-1871 Cr
Butler, Simon to Abgret Cooper 4-6-1844 Cr
Butler, T. M. to S. A. Stewart 11-25-1868 Sh
Butler, T. S. to Martha J. Maderis 2-1-1850 Cr
Butler, Thomas J. to Mary C. Swink 1-19-1869 (1-21-1869) Ma
Butler, Thomas to Nancy E. B. Hall 10-29-1860 (10-30-1860) Cr
Butler, Thomas to Wilmurth Grooms 10-28-1824 Hr
Butler, Thos. M. to Elizabeth A. Lowrance 1-22-1859 Cr
Butler, Thos. T. to Eugenia Gates 6-1-1870 (6-11-1870) Ma
Butler, Tobias to Bridget Ryan 1-21-1856 Sh
Butler, W. H. to L. A. Walker 9-28-1869 G
Butler, W. M. to Mollie E. Ballard 2-28-1857 Sh
Butler, W. P. H. to Ada P. Glass 7-5-1876 L
Butler, W. P. H. to Joella Boram 11-9-1870 L
Butler, W. S. to Frances Mosier 11-26-1867 O
Butler, W. S. to Mary J. Jordan 10-23-1856 Be
Butler, William D. to Sarah P. Tilman 10-13-1868 (no return) L
Butler, William G. to Ann S. Skyles 9-27-1848 (9-28-1848) G
Butler, William H. to Amandia A. Travis 8-21-1862 Be
Butler, William M. to Lizzie Henning 12-21-1870 L
Butler, William to Frances Thomas 11-14-1868 Hy
Butler, William to Judith FitzGibbon 11-27-1854 Sh
Butler, William to Ruthy B. Skiles 3-10-1857 (3-11-1857) G
Butler, Wm. G. to E. M. Fergerson 2-25-1851 Cr
Butler, Wm. G. to Tempy Butler 12-21-1842 Cr
Butler, Wm. J. to Susan Crow 3-16-1850 V
Butler, Wm. S. to Jane Uptergrove 8-30-1854 Cr
Butler, Wm. W. to Sallie B. Wharton 11-8-1877 Hy
Butler, Wm. to Martha Hicks 7-15-1856 Cr
Butler, jr., Charlie E. to Narcissa C. Sinclair 11-7-1876 (11-8-1876) L
Butram, Andrew P. B. R. to Sarah M. Smith 10-27-1849 G
Butram, Franklin A. to Juda A. Reaves 5-25-1863 O
Butram, John H. to Sarah Dunlap 8-20-1846 G
Butram, John S. to Mary E. Cotton 11-18-1873 O
Butram, Simeon to Elizabeth Fletcher 2-5-1838 (2-14-1838) G
Butt, William N. to Elizabeth H. Harris 6-20-1856 Ma
Butt, Wm. A. to Julia F. Bowden 11-9-1859 Cr
Butterworth, David F. to Matilda Bunch 12-27-1845 Hn
Butterworth, Jesse T. to Maryann Branch 9-13-1847 (9-16-1847) F
Butterworth, R. T. to L. J. Butterworth 2-9-1872 (2-10-1872) Dy
Butterworth, William P. to Martha A. Branch 2-17-1843 (2-23-1843) F
Buttery?, James to Margaret Miller 12-16-1871 (12-17-1871) T
Butler, R. F. to Elizabeth Arnold 4-27-1854 (no return) We
Buttram, John to Frances Adeline Duncan 2-21-1855 (2-23-1855) Sh
Butts, Alexander to Nancy H. Meade 3-13-1855 (3-15-1855) O
Butts, Bob to Martha Green 3-2-1872 (11-20-1872) T
Butts, H. A. to Bettie Ridout 12-4-1875 (no return) Hy
Butts, Halsted to Elizabeth Worrell 11-18-1850 (11-20-1850) Ma
Butts, James R. to Martha Mahalda Yarbrough 8-23-1870 (8-25-1870) Ma
Butts, L. C. to Martha A. Martin 2-15-1844 (2-25-1844) F
Butts, Leroy D. to Mary Faw? 8-25-1851 (8-28-1851) Hr
Butts, R. F. to Mary F. Bond 12-3-1867 L
Butts, Richard F. to Cornelia A. Snowden 1-1-1855 Ma
Butts, Tillman to May Jane Manning 3-1-1867 L
Butts, William N. to Helen Harris 7-15-1852 Ma
Butts, Wm. C. to Martha Castle 12-31-1845 We
Buzbee?, W. T. to Eliza Gunnings 6-29-1861 Sh
Byars, Alexander to Susan Parkes 9-29-1858 We
Byars, Anderson to Icey Todd 7-20-1860 (no return) Hn
Byars, Andrew to Mary A. Winstead 12-23-1857 We
Byars, Cyrus D. to Elizabeth C. Griffin 7-17-1855 Hn
Byars, Gabriel to Letta Howard 3-8-1866 Hn B
Byars, H. D. to Sarah A. Lowry 5-25-1863 Hn
Byars, Jefferson to Anna Coltart 1-27-1872 Hy
Byars, Nicholas B. to Rebecca J. Beard 2-26-1852 Hn
Byars, Nicholas to Martha A. Hatten 6-18-1839 Hn
Byars, Sam to Manerva Cole 4-13-1867 Hn B
Byars, W. to Jno. Cordelia L. Dyke 9-6-1847 Sh
Byars, Wesley to Mary Ann Smith 11-14-1877 Hy
Byars, William H. to Nancy J. Bowden 12-9-1855 (no return) Hn
Byars, William to Joanna Smith 12-26-1871 Hy

Byars, William to Margarett Lowry 1-13-1847 Hn
Byars, Wm. to Martha Caps 7-15-1846 We
Byars, Z. P. to Sophia A. Groom 6-24-1863 Hn
Byassee, Peter to Paris Stallings 4-8-1871 (4-9-1871) Dy
Byers, Charles P. to Ann G. A. McAdoo 6-10-1851 Cr
Byers, James to Mary Jane Vincent 5-15-1851 T
Byers, William T. to Emily L. Carthel 10-12-1858 (10-13-1858) G
Byford, Billy to America Howard 8-25-1877 (8-26-1877) L
Byford, Irvin to L. J. Brady 1-9-1866 (1-10-1866) T
Byler, Benj. L. D. to Mary E. Perkins 1-14-1861 (1-15-1861) L
Byler, Jacob to Margaret Ellis 11-25-1851 L
Byler, James C. to Nancy L. Wilcox 6-6-1859 (6-9-1859) L
Byler, Thomas H. to Lucy A. Tillman 3-16-1869 (no return) L
Byler, William L. to Fannie E. L. Crocker 1-20-1875 L
Byles, Marcus to Mary Montgomery 8-26-1841 F
Bylor, J. A. to Cyntha T. Condry 12-19-1876 (12-20-1877?) L
Bynan, Guy to Frankie Tipton 11-4-1872 (11-5-1872) T
Byner, Andrew J. to Sarah Brook 9-1-1841 Ma
Bynum, D. W. to Bettie Ford 1-15-1857 Sh
Bynum, E. H. to M. A. Kinnard 3-7-1876 (3-9-1877) O
Bynum, Eli to Mary F. Brooks 9-13-1863 Hn
Bynum, G. L. to Sarah Newton 1-6-1844 We
Bynum, Guy to Laura Burchett 11-9-1871 T
Bynum, Joseph to Catharine Workman 6-26-1854 We
Bynum, Patrick to Mollie Owen 3-26-1868 T
Bynum, W. G. to S. J. Lancaster 3-6-1872 (3-7-1872) O
Bynum, W. I. to T. A. Gilbert 1-1-1867 O
Byram, John C. to Mary Tinsley 10-28-1855 (10-31-1855) Sh
Byram, John to Luella Gidcombe 4-26-1881 (4-27-1881) L
Byram, Ralph to Nancy A. Durner 2-6-1860 (2-9-1860) Hr
Byran, William A. to Mary Ann Eliza Massey 7-26-1844 Sh
Byran?, Joseph John to Emily Williams 4-24-1850 (4-25-1850) L
Byrd, C. C. to S. F. Timms 8-11-1874 (8-13-1874) T
Byrd, Jesse S. to Minirva Reynolds 11-21-1860 T
Byrd, Jesse to Mary Margaret Williams 6-14-1855 T
Byrd, Jethro L. to Elizabeth J. Haywood 2-26-1833 O
Byrd, Neapolheo? D. to Frances Jane Tam? 12-24-1846 (12-30-1846) T
Byrd, Thomas to Amanda Taylor 6-23-1857 O
Byrd, Wm. Thomas to Eliza Catharine Wallace 8-28-1867 (8-29-1867) Ma
Byrn, A. G. W. to Martha E. Braden ?-30-1839? (1-3-1840) L
Byrn, Benjamin to Charlotte Cleek? 12-25-1868 (12-26-1868) L B
Byrn, George W. to Hannah M. Lankford 10-8-1859 (10-9-1859) L
Byrn, Handy W. to Sally Haynest 8-31-1831 Ma
Byrn, J. P. to E. J. McRae 11-14-1855 Be
Byrn, James to Harriet Johnson 5-23-1872 L B
Byrn, James to Louverta Palmer 2-6-1869 (2-7-1869) L
Byrn, John A. J. to Hester E. Hinton 5-23-1866 L
Byrn, John to Ibernia Mathis 5-20-1876 L
Byrn, Joseph to Nancy Smith 10-24-1874 (4-4-1875) L
Byrn, R. J. E. to Amanda McCarver 4-25-1874 (4-26-1874) L
Byrn, R. J. E. to M. E. Beggs 11-16-1881 L
Byrn, R. J. M. to M. E. F. Thacker 3-27-1862 (no return) Dy
Byrn, R. M. to M. D. Chipman 12-17-1878 Cr
Byrn, Thomas J. to Deanna Price (Brice?) 2-1-1860 L
Byrn, Thomas J. to Theresa Carson 10-6-1866 (10-7-1866) L
Byrn, W. Green to Sarah E. Meacham 10-6-1877 (no return) L
Byrne, Michael T. to Ruth Bond 9-7-1847 Hn
Byrne, Ransom H. to Dolly Cocke 11-18-1828 G
Byrnes, Wilson to Cornelia Wetherington 8-17-1867 (8-18-1867) T
Byrns, Alexander T. to Rebecca A. Meridith 3-10-1831 Ma
Byrns, Calvin to Rebeca Crockett 9-9-1882 (9-10-1882) L
Byrns?, Richard H. to Darthula Pope 1-19-1869 (1-24-1869) Cr
Byrs, C. J. to Mahaley K. Collins 1-11-1858 We
Byrum, Bennett to Francis D. Hester 1-8-1878 Hy
Byrum, James to Sarah J. Williams 2-9-1858 (2-10-1858) L
Byrum, Jestice to Mary T. Fitzhugh 12-15-1852 Ma
Byrum, John T. to Lydia Glenn 11-1-1866 Ma
Byrum, John to Jane Brown 5-9-1867 L
Byrum, Thomas to Jane Vandygraff 3-13-1869 (no return) L
Byrum, Tom to Nancy Horton 12-8-1871 Hy
Byrum, Wade to Martha M. Dick 5-9-1861 Ma

Cabainess, William to Minty K. Shaw 8-5-1850 Hn
Cabe, David C. to Lucy Hoofman 11-23-1851 Hn
Cabe, George W. to Sarah Boyd 11-22-1841 Hn
Cabe, George to Sarah Nance 4-7-1859 Hn
Cabe, W. M. to Malica Aery 9-25-1850 (not endorsed) We
Cabell, Samuel J. to Elizabeth Harvill 6-1-1827 (6-3-1827) Hr
Cabler, John D. to Julia L. Davidson 3-15-1835 (3-17-1835) G
Cabler, Nicholas W. to Tibetha C. Harper 8-22-1838 G
Cabness, John to Rose Tucker 3-17-1869 (no return) F B
Caborne, James to Sarah Shipman 4-25-1826 Hr
Cadwallader, Edward to Isabella Robinson 9-2-1852 Sh
Cadwell, C. C. to Emily E. Ross 7-10-1849 Hn
Caffey, J. N. to Pernalia S. Cloyeds 7-6-1841 F
Caffrey, Thomas to Belinda Chaney 12-10-1850 Ma
Cage, David to Susanah Dowland 12-31-1855 G

Grooms

Cage, E. R. to Sarah F. Minter 1-20-1847 (1-21-1847) Hr
Cage, Hibrey? to Miss Peggy Hill 12-2-1865 T
Cage, Hilary to Pecella Lauderdale 3-5-1869 T
Cage, James O. to Sarah J. Henning 12-15-1852 (no return) L
Cage, Willis to Rebecca Turner 1-2-1881? (1-4-1882) L B
Cage, Wilson to Martha Ann Shuck 1-11-1855 (1-11-1856?) O
Cagle, G. W. to Mary Caroline Stockdale 4-5-1866 Be
Cagle, James A. to Mary Catharine Blanks 11-25-1865 Be
Cagle, Jefferson to Eden Keloe 6-25-1866 (6-27-1866) O
Cagle, M. G. to Susan C. Barkley? 5-24-1836 Hr
Cagle, Wm. T. to Elizabeth J. Liles 4-14-1860 (4-29-1860) Cr
Cahill, Patrick to Mary Maguire 6-9-1860 (6-10-1860) Sh
Cail, Isaac to Martha H. Beavers no date (with Jun 1853) G
Cail, John W. to Celia F. Fairless 4-29-1858 G
Cail, William H. to Letty M. Slayton 6-21-1855 G
Cain, Albert to Mary Carroll 10-4-1856 Sh
Cain, Alfred to Fannie Bond 5-8-1873 (no return) Hy
Cain, Dyes to Mary Harris 12-15-1832 (12-27-1832) Hr
Cain, E. W. to Nancy Jane Harper 8-10-1848 Be
Cain, Elijah C. to Eliza Newhouse 4-30-1862 (5-1-1862) O
Cain, George W. to Amanda J. Bell 9-9-1871 (9-10-1871) Ma
Cain, George to Luvenia Mount no date (1860-1870) G
Cain, Gideon Lewis to Su H. (Mrs.) Pearce 4-1-1868 G
Cain, Isaac to Catherine Bird 7-17-1856 Cr
Cain, John H. to Percilla Washburn 10-18-1829 Hr
Cain, John T. to Elizabeth J. Kent 6-13-1843 (no return) L
Cain, John T. to Sarah B. Ward 10-15-1852 We
Cain, Marcellius to Cindy R. Presson 1-27-1843 Be
Cain, Michael to Margaret O'Connell 4-29-1861 Sh
Cain, Obediah to Catharine Muse 1-25-1847 Hr
Cain, Robert F. to Margaret R. Haltom 5-18-1858 (5-19-1858) Ma
Cain, William to Ann Martin 1-30-1843 (2-1-1843) F
Cain, William to Elizabeth Moss 12-2-1865 (no return) Cr
Cain, William to Mary Farrell 10-25-1852 Sh
Cain, William to Sarah Ann Boatman? 6-4-1852 (no return) F
Caine, Calloway to Martha A. Nabors 4-13-1841 Hr
Cal, Bently to Chany Peebles 4-22-1867 F B
Calaway, Adam to Charlotte Adkins 6-15-1873 T
Caldwell, A. J. to Sarah J. Orsbourn 9-22-1866 (9-23-1866) O
Caldwell, A. W. to Mary Ann Walker 11-2-1868 (no return) F
Caldwell, Alex C. to Lizzie L. Taylor 8-20-1868 Ma
Caldwell, Alexr. C. to Mary W. Alexander 11-7-1860 Ma
Caldwell, Alfred to Susan Gentry 1-13-1879 (1-15-1879) L
Caldwell, Alonzo to Lucinda Green 11-24-1880 (no return) L
Caldwell, Charles to Permelia Jones 6-21-1866 Hn B
Caldwell, D. C. to M. M. Cunningham 3-2-1857 G
Caldwell, D. P. to Ann Lyghtner 2-2-1859 O
Caldwell, Daniel to Jane Mitchum 2-21-1870 G B
Caldwell, Davidson R. to Eleanor F. Hudson 1-6-1848 Sh
Caldwell, Douglass to Fannie Pierce 12-15-1857 Hn
Caldwell, E. S. to Margaret Jane Galoway 12-23-1857 (12-24-1857) Hr
Caldwell, E. W. to Lucy H. (Mrs.) Crenshaw 1-19-1859 (1-20-1859) Sh
Caldwell, Edmond W. to Nancy W. Davidson 3-20-1845 O
Caldwell, Freeland to Silva J. Pursley 7-20-1875 O
Caldwell, George H. to Mary E. Oglesby 11-20-1857 (11-24-1857) O
Caldwell, Haywood to Mariah Davis 1-3-1872 Hy
Caldwell, Henry to Letta Cowan 12-27-1867 Hn
Caldwell, Henry to Mary McClelland? 8-23-1843 (8-24-1843) L
Caldwell, I. M. to Sarah Walton 12-21-1866 (12-25-1866) O
Caldwell, Isaac W. to Sarah E. Whipple 12-27-1838 O
Caldwell, Isaac to Aggy Jordan 1-24-1867 (no return) L B
Caldwell, J. F. to Daisy E. Hill 10-19-1885 (10-20-1885) L
Caldwell, J. F. to Tabitha A. McCommon 2-20-1849 (2-22-1849) Hr
Caldwell, J. R. to E. A. Frazier 1-17-1855 Hn
Caldwell, J. R. to Lou Ann Nelson 12-30-1866 Hn
Caldwell, J. W. to Rachel A. Postin 10-17-1871 (no return) Hy
Caldwell, James B. to Sarah V. Knox 1-18-1858 We
Caldwell, James E. to Mollie Clark 2-24-1868 (2-27-1868) O
Caldwell, James S. to A. J. Riner 11-17-1861 Sh
Caldwell, James to Mary I. Twigg 9-21-1859 We
Caldwell, John C. to Lucretia B. White 4-15-1844 (4-16-1844) O
Caldwell, John Thomas to Caroline Sullivan 12-29-1868 G B
Caldwell, John W. to Elizabeth J. Crockett 1-23-1854 (1-29-1854) O
Caldwell, John to Elizabeth Markham 10-4-1851 T
Caldwell, John to Frances A. Blythe 8-1-1854 (no return) Hn
Caldwell, John to Mary Ann Harris 10-12-1827 Hn
Caldwell, Joseph E. to Elizabeth Cole 3-31-1858 (4-1-1858) O
Caldwell, Joseph to Mary Ann T. Adams 3-4-1830 Sh
Caldwell, L. M. to A. C. Cowan 1-10-1849 Hn
Caldwell, L. M. to Isabella Sharp 5-20-1868 G
Caldwell, N. J. to R. E. Davis 10-12-1856 Hn
Caldwell, Nathan G. to Martha D. Brown 8-14-1849 (8-16-1849) L
Caldwell, Nelson to Rachel Shad 5-10-1870 (5-14-1870) Cr
Caldwell, O. B. to Mary E. Houston 11-6-1850 G
Caldwell, R. D. to Emily Mitchum 11-23-1857 Cr
Caldwell, Robert D. to Adaline N. Hubberd (Hubert) 3-12-1858 (3-4?-1858) O
Caldwell, Robert J. to Rosannah S. Walker 9-26-1860 Hn
Caldwell, Robert P. to Harrett J. Wilkins 5-15-1851 (5-19-1851) G
Caldwell, Robert T. to Jane Bedford 3-15-1840 O
Caldwell, Robert to Susan Bolin 10-8-1856 G
Caldwell, Robt. to Mary E. Bumpass 11-3-1846 F
Caldwell, Saml. S. to Elizabeth Ray 1-1-1856 (1-3-1856) Hr
Caldwell, Samuel H. to Mary R. Thompson 12-24-1860 Hn
Caldwell, Samuel L. to Martha S. Stedvent 11-4-1851 Cr
Caldwell, Samuel P. to Sarah Jane Taylor 5-29-1855 (5-30-1855) Ma
Caldwell, Simon W. to Josaphine J. Dickason 1-23-1867 (1-30-1867) F
Caldwell, Theophilus to Elizabeth C. Hodges 1-19-1846 (no return) F
Caldwell, Thomas J. to Julia Ann Eliza Robertson 5-12-1835 Sh
Caldwell, Thomas to Elnora Rucker 12-28-1872 (1-2-1873) L
Caldwell, W. A. to Sallie E. Vaulx 1-13-1873 (no return) Hy
Caldwell, W. H. to Jane C. Park 4-24-1861 (4-25-1861) O
Caldwell, W. P. to Ada B. Gardner 9-21-1854 We
Caldwell, Walter H. to Elizabeth B. Morgan 5-30-1843 O
Caldwell, Wilie to Kesiah Hanks 7-11-1827 Hr
Caldwell, William H. to Grace Jane Robinson 1-21-1858 O
Caldwell, William P. to M. O. Williams 12-11-1851 Hn
Caldwell, William to Mary Ann Powell 5-13-1869 (5-16-1869) L
Caleb, Columbus W. to Elizabeth A. Patterson 1-12-1852 G
Caleb, Hansel to Louisa Haltum 1-7-1829 Ma
Calewell, Robert to Nancy S. Hargis 1-29-1844 (2-5-1844) F
Calhoon, Boyd to Becky Harris? 12-29-1865 (1-14-1866) T
Calhoon, J. A. C. to Elizabeth Anderson 12-22-1846 Sh
Calhoon, James A. to Elsey Larimore 9-17-1840 (10-15-1840) T
Calhoon, Stephen to Mary Alexander 12-12-1872 Hy
Calhoon, Steven to Mary Dent 2-4-1867 (no return) Hy
Calhoon, William S. to Eliza Bacyas? 4-2-1867 T
Calhoun, A. E. to Margaret E. Gray 8-21-1863 (8-23-1863) O
Calhoun, A. F. to Ann R. Morphis 4-10-1865 (4-13-1865) F
Calhoun, Alexander E. to Mary A. Chandler 11-11-1857 O
Calhoun, Austin to Susan Willis 11-30-1867 Hn B
Calhoun, Ben to Nancy C. Harris 1-5-1871 T
Calhoun, C. B. to Martha E. Paton 11-4-1863 (no return) Hn
Calhoun, Claborn to Alice Speers 8-11-1876 (8-12-1876) O
Calhoun, Dan to Rena Belford 5-16-1870 (5-18-1870) T
Calhoun, Grandison to Minerva Clement 12-29-1865 (12-30-1865) T
Calhoun, James C. to Blondina M. Kirtland 12-20-1858 (12-22-1858) Sh
Calhoun, James T. to Frances R. Vaughan 1-14-1854 (1-17-1854) Sh
Calhoun, John W. to Sallie A. Barret 1-19-1870 T
Calhoun, Pomp to Ellen Hawood 8-15?-1871 T
Calhoun, Pompey to Mary Yarbroh 9-29-1866 (10-29-1866) T
Calhoun, Robert C. to Elizabeth Cassa 6-12-1861 (6-18-1861) Sh
Calhoun, Robert to Ann Dunlap 4-29-1867 (no return) Hn
Calhoun, S. A. to Pheby E. Marshall 11-22-1864 (11-23-1864) O
Calhoun, S. S. to E. J. Dickey 3-14-1848 O
Calhoun, Sam'l. A. to Martha Hogue 11-30-1859 (12-1-1859) O
Calhoun, Samuel A. to Margaret Anderson 11-27-1855 (11-28-1855) O
Calhoun, Thomas C. to T. C. Hubbard 12-11-1860 (12-13-1860) Cr
Calhoun, Thos. to Sarah Bernard 6-5-1869 (6-6-1869) T
Calhoun, William F. to Margaret Jane Hogue 12-17-1853 (12-17-1853) O
Calhoun, William M. to Sarah M. Owen 4-19-1857 (4-21-1857) O
Call, Jas. A. to Mary E. Huffstutter 9-13-1865 O
Call, Salmon to Capy Cox 5-5-1857 Hn
Call, W. C. to Mary J. Rogers 2-13-1860 O
Call, William to Mary Lamb 12-16-1858 Hn
Callaghan, Denis to Elizabeth Campbell 11-19-1864 (11-23-1864) Sh
Callahan, A. M. to Eighty Eveline Neelly 3-1-1826 (3-7-1826) Hr
Callahan, James to H. Barry 6-26-1856 (6-28-1856) Sh
Callahan, John P. to Patsy Elizabeth Williams 5-28-1849 (6-7-1849) L
Callahan, Martin to Ellen Ryan 10-16-1852 (10-17-1852) Sh
Callahan, Peter to Delia Martin 2-16-1860 (2-17-1860) Sh
Callahan, R. M. to Susan A. Cox 1-28-1860 (1-29-1860) Hr
Callaway, R. S. to Viola Trousdale 9-13-1841 (no return) Ma
Callehan, Hawkins H. to Edy Throgmorton 10-2-1839 Hn
Callehen, Richard to Malinda Chitwood 1-3-1859 (1-6-1859) Sh
Callens, Thos. to Anne Maria Whalen 5-5-1862 Sh
Callhoon, Ghos. C. to Isonah Mitchell 12-20-1848 Cr
Callicoat, Thos. P. to Mary Ann Harper 5-29-1861 O
Callicott, Calvin H. to Agnes M. Harper 11-1-1849 O
Callicott, James H. to Emaly H. Tart 10-14-1846 Hn
Callicott, John W. to Harriet E. Walker 10-9-1851 Hn
Callicott, William F. to Mary Crittenden 10-8-1841 Hn
Callihan, Doke to Elizabeth Cariker 11-29-1852 (11-30-1852) Hr
Callis, Henry to Sabra Russell 4-4-1860 (4-5-1860) O
Callis, J. C. to Annie Wilson 10-2-1863 Sh
Callis, Thomas J. to Hariett Mason 2-20-1861 G
Callis, W. H. to Eliza R. Grist 12-25-1869 G
Callison, Carroll to Emaline Gunter 3-2-1863 We
Callison, John to Margaret Arnold 12-10-1860 (no return) We
Calloway, Benj. R. to E. J. (Mrs.) McDaniel 1-25-1869 (1-27-1869) Ma
Calloway, Chas. J. to Sarah J. Bond 12-13-1869 (12-14-1869) Ma
Calloway, James E. to Sarah E. Littleton 9-26-1857 Hn
Calloway, W. R. to M. E. Jackson 2-18-1866 Hn
Calloway, William J. to Emma C. Kirk 10-8-1867 Ma
Calloway, William S. to Elizabeth N. Brown 1-22-1840 Ma

Grooms

Calls, Jos. to Eliza Jane Cockram 12-2-1851 (12-16-1851) Sh
Calton, J. L. to M. E. Wherry 9-26-1874 (9-27-1874) Dy
Calvey, Luke to Bridget McAnally 1-18-1864 Sh
Calvin, Henry to Lucinda Ford 12-29-1850 Be
Calway, John to Rose Green 4-30-1868 (no return) F B
Cambell, Osa to Hanah Louis 9-22-1870 G B
Camel?, John to Virginia F. Craig 4-10-1871 (4-11-1871) T
Camerhorn, J. S. to Susan C. Wilkins 6-3-1868 G
Cameroans, William T. to Hararet M. Wiles 11-19-1859 Sh
Cameron, David to Judy Ann Waddle 1-6-1877 Hy
Cameron, Ewing to Mary Johnson 7-29-1874 O
Cameron, Hector to Zilpha Forrest 12-5-1878 Hy
Cameron, John J. to Sarah McMurry 12-4-1866 (no return) Hy
Cameron, John to Susan Shaw 4-3-1869 Hy
Camp, Aaron to Livinia Shields 12-1-1867 Hy
Camp, Benj. to Margaret Jackson 3-11-1852 Sh
Camp, G. A. to Mary Davidson 7-11-1856 Be
Camp, James W. to Lucy Johnson 12-28-1854 Be
Camp, W. H. to M. A. Ballaner 9-9-1840 Be
Camp, W. to Sarah Jane Tyner 2-21-1861 Be
Camp, Wm. S. to Mary Humphreys 11-19-1856 Sh
Campbell, A. B. to A. R. Scott 11-8-1864 Sh
Campbell, A. B. to E. V. Leech 6-13-1842 F
Campbell, A. to Josephine Daniel 2-7-1866 Hn
Campbell, Adam Dean to Eleanor B. Davis 12-3-1855 (12-4-1855) T
Campbell, Alex G. to Angelin R. Ashby 9-14-1852 (9-15-1852) Hr
Campbell, Alexander to Elizabeth Parker 12-26-1844 We
Campbell, Alexander to Martha A. Walker 9-6-1856 (9-7-1856) Hr
Campbell, Alfred W. to Sarah F. Giles 10-13-1851 (no return) F
Campbell, Allen to Eadie Harris 1-21-1873 (1-3?-1873) Dy
Campbell, Anderson to Harriet Browning 2-5-1869 (no return) L
Campbell, Anderson to Sallie Wright 8-17-1881 (8-18-1881) L
Campbell, Andy J. to Elmira Hall 3-3-1877 (3-4-1877) Dy
Campbell, Archabald to Louisa Skinner 12-24-1847 (12-30-1847) Hr
Campbell, Benj. M. R. to Mary I. Hart 12-22-1842 Cr
Campbell, Cains to Nancy Turner 12-16-1828 Ma
Campbell, Calvin to Pheby Stockton 11-3-1848 (11-9-1848) Hr
Campbell, Claiborne to Lucinda Hester 1-25-1836 (1?-7-1836) Hr
Campbell, D. G. to A. M. Cooly 3-4-1846 (no return) We
Campbell, Daniel to Ann Eliza Furgerson 8-19-1875 L B
Campbell, Daniel to Elvira E. Guise 12-21-1857 (12-23-1857) Hr
Campbell, David G. to Lavinia (Lousiana) Burns 8-13-1846 Sh
Campbell, David L. to Elizabeth J. Smyth 11-21-1844 We
Campbell, David to Judy Ann McDaman 3-8-1873 Hy
Campbell, E. S. to Levenia L. Penn 12-7-1864 G
Campbell, E. to M. M. Cooper 11-15-1844 Hn
Campbell, Edward to Sarah S. Wood 2-3-1848 Hn
Campbell, Edwin to Mary L. White 8-6-1860 (8-7-1860) Sh
Campbell, Erasmus kSydenham to Eliza Jane Mariner 6-1-1844 (6-4-1844) T
Campbell, Eugene to Emily Ann Lambert 10-27-1846 (10-30-1866) Ma
Campbell, F. A. to M. W. Brown 8-9-1869 (no return) Hy
Campbell, F. to Phebe Lindsey 11-18-1840 Be
Campbell, Francis W. to Mariah A. Womack 12-19-1859 (12-20-1859) Ma
Campbell, Frank to Parthenia Moses 5-22-1869 (no return) Hy
Campbell, G. D. to Tabitha Brigman 6-23-1857 Hr
Campbell, Garner D. to Elizabeth Rankin 11-11-1850 (11-14-1850) Hr
Campbell, Geo. E. to Callie Williamson 10-18-1871 Ma
Campbell, Geo. J. to Ellen M. Graham 6-21-1864 (6-22-1864) Sh
Campbell, George L. to Jane Molloy? 7-24-1828 (7-29-1828) Hr
Campbell, George W. to Flora Green? 11-3-1871 (11-6-1871) L
Campbell, George to Vina McDaman 7-11-1874 Hy
Campbell, Gilbert P. to Eliza E. Tillman 5-16-1861 We
Campbell, Grandison A. to N. J. Cloucher 4-2-1884 L
Campbell, Green to Francis Wright 12-20-1875 L B
Campbell, Henderson to Lucinda Jordan 7-20-1867 (no return) L B
Campbell, Henry W. to Martha C. Cheatham 2-14-1844 We
Campbell, Henry to Charlotte Burnett 12-18-1870 G B
Campbell, Henry to Cyntha Westbrook 3-17-1875 L B
Campbell, Henry to Tennessee Hunter 12-14-1867 (no return) Hy
Campbell, J. B. to Nancy Y. Boyne 1-25-1866 G
Campbell, J. B. to Tabitha A. R. Cillett 8-6-1878 Dy
Campbell, J. R. to Mary J. Patton 1-9-1858 Cr
Campbell, J. W. to Mary A. Eubanks 6-21?-1855 (no return) F
Campbell, J. W. to Mollie J. Miller 10-20-1871 (10-26-1871) T
Campbell, J.(I?) P. to Minerva Shelton 1-8-1845 Sh
Campbell, James H. to Judith K. Nichols 7-22-1828 Ma
Campbell, James M. to Lucinda E. Lovelace 7-8-1862 (no return) L
Campbell, James McHenry to Rosanah H. Tolbert 11-30-1864 (12-2-1864) L
Campbell, James to Betsy Butcher 12-18-1828 Sh
Campbell, James to Emma Brandon 8-28-1867 (no return) Hy
Campbell, James to Lou Ellen Mitchell 1-26-1877 (1-28-1877) Dy
Campbell, James to Martha A. Barfoot 2-3-1850 Hn
Campbell, James to Martha Henderson 1-18-1875 Hy
Campbell, James to Sarah Ann Sadler 12-21-1859 Hy
Campbell, Jas. B. to Caroline V. Black 1-30-1866 F
Campbell, Jno. Boyd to Eleanor Valentin Bambridge 2-1-1843 (2-7-1843) T
Campbell, John A. to Margaret S. Comer 9-7-1867 Hn

Campbell, John A. to Permelia J. Lilley 11-9-1852 (11-11-1852) O
Campbell, John W. to E. A. Crutchfield 2-24-1850 Hn
Campbell, John W. to Louisa A. Allen 4-27-1852 O
Campbell, John to Aley A. H. Welch 8-24-1837 L
Campbell, John to Anny Yeary 7-10-1828 (4-6-1829) Hr
Campbell, John to Elizabeth F. Brown 2-19-1856 (2-22-1856) O
Campbell, John to Frances Jane Hite 3-6-1869 (3-7-1869) T
Campbell, John to Molley Barber 4-24-1870 (no return) Cr
Campbell, John to Parisade Rogers 12-24-1869 (no return) F B
Campbell, Jonathan A. to Judith C. Sutton 2-9-1853 L
Campbell, Joseph to Aura? Love 1-30-1835 Hr
Campbell, Josiah B. to Ann Rebecca Frances Sawyer 9-18-1857 (9-23-1857) L
Campbell, Josiah B. to Drurie A. Mays 1-16-1867 L
Campbell, Josiah E. to Catherine E. McCord 6-22-1848 Sh
Campbell, Julian B. to Mattie White 12-22-1880 (12-23-1880) L
Campbell, L. M. to Elizabeth B. Stephens 9-8-1842 We
Campbell, Lawrence A. to Mary Thompson 4-26-1869 (4-27-1869) F
Campbell, Lemuel M. to Eliza Jane Bowles 12-1-1841 (12-2-1841) T
Campbell, Lewis to Maridna J. Tate 10-19-1860 (9?-19-1860) O
Campbell, Lewis to Mary Fitzpatrick 2-11-1871 (2-13-1871) L
Campbell, Lysander M. to Angelina R. Lee 6-15-1848 L
Campbell, M. F. to M. Tevilla 1-11-1871 Dy
Campbell, M. G. to Mary Parker 12-25-1867 O
Campbell, M. H. to Rosa Lee Chandler 9-24-1872 (no return) L
Campbell, Matt. to Leve Childs 12-31-1866 O
Campbell, Moses to Ann Eliza Camp 2-14-1854 Hr
Campbell, Narcus R. to Caroline Massey 7-28-1852 Ma
Campbell, Ned to Ella Drake 3-4-1874 Hy
Campbell, Peter to Sophronia Taylor 1-30-1882 (2-2-1882) L
Campbell, R. M. to Mary A. Clancy 7-1-1869 Hy
Campbell, R. S. to Polly Ann Brush 3-14-1876 (3-17-1876) Dy
Campbell, Richard A. to Virginia E. Dance 12-19-1872 Hy
Campbell, Richard to Amanda Lewis 1-26-1869 G B
Campbell, Robert A. to Mary Ann Davis 8-11-1847 (8-12-1847) Ma
Campbell, Robert C. to Mary L. Glass 12-12-1843 We
Campbell, Robert W. to Margaret J. Fleming 9-13-1859 (9-14-1859) O
Campbell, Robert to Elizabeth Vails 2-27-1847 Hr
Campbell, Robert to Sarah Ann McCarroll 4-13-1847 Be
Campbell, Robert to Sarah Lyon 3-17-1828 Ma
Campbell, Roland K. to Ruth J. Sample 1-18-1853 (2-7-1853) O
Campbell, Sandy to Delia Allen 3-4-1871 (no return) Hy
Campbell, Sidney F. to Sarah M. Allen 2-16-1859 (2-17-1859) G
Campbell, Simon to Eva Sutton 3-7-1873 (3-8-1873) L B
Campbell, Stephen to Eliza Jane Dodd 2-23-1846 (2-244-1846) O
Campbell, Thomas C. to Eliz. Mary Isabella Archer 12-5-1849 (12-6-1849) T
Campbell, Thomas to Lucinda Hardy 12-13-1852 Ma
Campbell, W. J. to A. C. Adams 5-21-1866 (no return) Hy
Campbell, W. O. to Amanda C. Alexander 2-12-1878 (2-13-1878) L
Campbell, Willes N. to Lewellen E. Cates 2-21-1853 (2-22-1853) G
Campbell, William B. to Jane Tilghman 11-26-1846 Sh
Campbell, William F. to Mary Bartlett 12-31-1849 (1-2-1850) T
Campbell, William H. to L. C. Fuller 2-4-1863 (2-5-1863) Dy
Campbell, William M. to Elizabeth V. Bass 5-2-1853 G
Campbell, William to Kezir? Smith 1-30-1866 (1-31-1866) T
Campbell, William to Mary A. Baker 7-3-1860 Dy
Campbell, William to Nartecea F. Dent 12-17-1856 We
Campbell, Wm. B. to Jane Gugman 11-23-1846 Sh
Campbell, Wm. E. to Rebecca Jane Anderson 6-2-1863 (6-4-1863) L
Campbell, Wm. to E. C. H. Holland 10-7-1845 Hr
Campbell?, W. C. to Syntha Utley 11-22-1848 Be
Campbill, D. T. to Malinda Oliver 9-16-1857 We
Campton, Richard to Sarah E. Hill 5-20-1854 (no return) F
Canada, A. B. to Lucy Spoon 12-20-1875 (12-21-1875) Dy
Canada, A. to S. M. Thurmon 8-20-1868 (8-23-1868) Dy
Canada, Daniel W. to Mary Seward 1-13-1852 (1-27-1852) Sh
Canada, George to Sarah Mitchell 11-9-1844 (11-20-1844) G
Canada, Isaac to Amanda Harris 9-6-1879 (9-7-1879) Dy
Canada, Isaac to Cordelia Davis 1-20-1877 (1-21-1877) Dy
Canada, J. P. to O. A. Greer 9-27-1867 G
Canada, J. U. to Elizer J. Larkin 12-23-1869 G
Canada, James to Partilla Yates 1-10-1849 (1-11-1849) G
Canada, John B. to Carolina I. Dennis 10-17-1850 Sh
Canada, John F. to Granville M. L. Cox 9-13-1859 (no return) Hy
Canada, Thos. S. to Mary Lay 4-8-1868 (no return) F
Canada, William J. to Susan E. Neal 1-15-1873 (1-16-1873) Dy
Canada, William to Hicksey G. Elsten 7-23-1866 G
Canaday, Hiram to Sarah Allen 11-10-1855 O
Canaday, Isaac to Mahala Yates 12-22-1847 (12-23-1847) G
Canaday, L. D. to Margaret E. McCorkle 6-30-1858 Hn
Canady, Alfred to Mariah Taylor 8-25-1845 (8-28-1845) O
Canady, Allen to Lucindy (Mrs.) Galespie 12-18-1853 (12-28-1853) Sh
Canady, Archabald to Eliza Pope 1-14-1842 (1-20-1842) L
Canady, Dennis to Margaret Murphey 6-1-1864 Sh
Canady, Elias J. to Malinda Moser 11-19-1857 O
Canady, Hiram to Bramley Griffin 10-22-1849 (10-23-1849) O
Canady, J. M. to Margaret J. Thomas 11-5-1863 Sh
Canady, James C. to Julia C. Brown 3-2-1863 G

Canady, Jas. C. to Mary J. Spencer 2-24-1859 G
Canady, L. H. to Mahaly C. Cassells 9-3-1857 G
Canady, Thomas to Elizabeth Herald 11-26-1877 Dy
Canady, Thos. to Elizabeth Canadey 4-6-1837 Hr
Canaghen, Michael to Bridget Burns 6-23-1864 Sh
Canahan, Peter to Mary Kelly 1-12-1863 Sh
Canaven, James to Telitha Piercy 12-17-1856 (12-18-1856) Ma
Canbrul, G. to Martha Gowan 2-19-1852 We
Candee, B. C. to Mary Mosier 5-4-1859 Sh
Candell, Buckner to Polly Craton 2-18-1828 Hr
Candenove, Jasper N. to Catherine Holmes 9-4-1856 Cr
Candis, Henry to Charlott Anderson 10-17-1868 (no return) Hy
Candler, W. J. C. to Mary E. McSwayne 8-30-1855 (no return) Hn
Cane, Henderson to Lucy Boothe 2-3-1843 (2-2?-1843) Hr
Canepa, Jno. to Benedetta Boro 6-1-1860 (6-3-1860) Sh
Caney, Ham to Elizabeth Wymmer 4-24-1860 We
Canmer, Wm. T. to Sarah Kern 1-12-1854 Cr
Cannaday, B. B. to Mary M. Ramsey 10-31-1857 Sh
Cannady, Allen to Mary Jane Cook 11-16-1870 (11-17-1870) Ma
Cannady, Calvin to Sarah Jones 6-13-1851 (6-18-1851) Sh
Cannady, Hugh to Malissa Duckworth 7-15-1828 Ma
Cannady, John to Martha Jane Norman 1-27-1870 (no return) Dy
Cannady, W. R. to Caroline Thomas 10-7-1864 (10-18-1864) Sh
Cannell, James to Harriet Hughes 1-30-1860 Hy
Cannie, John to Mary A. McAdoo 3-18-1868 Cr
Cannon (Camron), James F. to Martha M. Barnet 11-3-1827 Sh
Cannon, Alfred F. to Mary E. Cupp 3-7-1844 Cr
Cannon, Alfred to Laura J. Currie 2-20-1874 (no return) Hy
Cannon, Arthnald to Mary Rush 2-12-1852 Sh
Cannon, Benj. A. to Mary A. Temple 2-6-1860 (no return) Hn
Cannon, Bevely to Mary Gunter 2-10-1844 (2-15-1844) G
Cannon, Beverly to Nancy Pendergrass 6-22-1840 (6-23-1840) G
Cannon, Bryant to Margaret Murphy 10-10-1843 (10-12-1843) Hr
Cannon, C. C. to M. L. Wages? 3-13-1873 T
Cannon, Cornelius to Ellen Dooner 5-2-1861 (5-6-1861) Sh
Cannon, Daniel S. to Joana B. Gayler 1-13-1857 Hr
Cannon, E. A. to M. Campbell 10-7-1863 Sh
Cannon, E. M. to E. A. Hamilton 1-25-1849 Cr
Cannon, Elija to Louvenia Higgs 5-25-1850 (5-26-1850) Hr
Cannon, Erasmus to Emily Graham 9-27-1866 (no return) Hy
Cannon, Erasmus to Robertia Rix 1-25-1872 Hy
Cannon, Gabrial to Lavinia Gately 6-11-1841 (6-12-1841) Hr
Cannon, Gabriel to Clara J. Davis 2-24-1853 (no return) F
Cannon, H. L. to Mary Jane Taylor 10-8-1850 G
Cannon, Haywood to Elling Adams 1-1-1854 (no return) F
Cannon, Haywood to Louiza Stevens 10-29-1854 T
Cannon, Henry to Sarah Ann Glass 8-12-1858 T
Cannon, J. D. to S. E. Fulkerson 1-14-1882 (1-15-1882) L
Cannon, J. Q. to Mary E. (Mrs.) Samuels 6-30-1860 (7-1-1860) Sh
Cannon, J. T. to Mary E. Jackson 9-11-1857 G
Cannon, J. W. to Sarah G. Simmons 1-11-1855 (1-16-1855) G
Cannon, James A. to Mary A. M. Wimberley 9-8-1865 (no return) Hn
Cannon, James L. to Nancy King 9-21-1852 O
Cannon, James S. to Angevona C. Jones 10-5-1858 (10-6-1858) G
Cannon, James to Mary Pate 12-12-1846 (12-13-1846) G
Cannon, James to Mary Taylor 12-22-1840 G
Cannon, James to Sarah Cook 9-17-1850 (9-18-1850) G
Cannon, Jas. H. to Margarett Everett 12-18-1872 (no return) Cr
Cannon, Jas. T. to Elizabeth A. Doherty 10-12-1858 (10-13-1858) G
Cannon, Jasper G. to Arimetta B. Caviness 6-3-1861 Hn
Cannon, Jasper M. to Mary G. Bradford 8-29-1852 Cr
Cannon, Joe T. to Mary A. Jarman 10-27-1843 Cr
Cannon, John M. to Eliza A. McCrackin 12-26-1864 (12-27-1864) Cr
Cannon, John N. to Sarah A. Clark 11-15-1848 G
Cannon, John N. to Sarah F. Brown 12-4-1856 Hn
Cannon, John Q. A. to Tibetha B. Rison 1-15-1846 Cr
Cannon, John W. to Elizabeth Maclin 5-17-1867 (no return) Hy
Cannon, John Wesley to M. F. Fulkerson 2-9-1882 L
Cannon, John to Elizabeth McSwain 3-18-1846 (no return) Hn
Cannon, John to Martha Davis 3-24-1865 (3-28-1865) F
Cannon, Lee A. to M. V. Allison 11-11-1869 G
Cannon, Levi to Smith Ann Maclin 2-27-1867 T
Cannon, N. B. to Marietta Jackson 1-26-1874 (1-27-1874) O
Cannon, R. A. to Mary M. Wilson 11-6-1856 Hn
Cannon, Robt. to Nancy Orr 1-6-1848 Cr
Cannon, Socrates to Nancy Hooker 12-7-1853 Cr
Cannon, Spencer to Indiana Wortham 1-10-1870 T
Cannon, Stephen to Nancy Stafford 3-16-1866 (3-21-1866) F
Cannon, Steven to Annis Harris 3-11-1863 (3-17-1863) F
Cannon, Thomas to Susan McMahan 1-8-1867 (no return) Hy
Cannon, W. M. to Mary M. H. Everett 12-19-1866 T
Cannon, William F. to Mary C. Miller 9-5-1873 L
Cannon, William S. to Margaret C. D. Roberts 5-26-1860 We
Cannon, William to Eliza Ann Durley 10-18-1848 G
Cannon, William to Elizabeth Jonigan 2-7-1845 (5-14-1845) G *
Cannon, William to Mary Brown 12-31-1866 T
Cannon, William to Pemilia A. Blankenship 5-14-1845 (5-15-1845) G

Cannon, Wm. J. to Catharine Wirt 11-9-1854 (no return) F
Cannon, Wm. to Caroline Tillman 6-11-1861 (6-13-1861) Hr
Cannovan, John to Mary A. Coyle 2-1-1858 Sh
Canon, James A. to J. M. Dickson 1-3-1861 (1-6-1861) Cr
Canon, Travis B. to Lavinia A. Pettus 1-19-1860 (no return) Hy
Cantey, Henry to Mary C. Webb 12-6-1861 Sh
Cantlin, Jacob to Julia Ann Hoskins 2-12-1875 (2-25-1875) Dy
Cantrel, Berry to Mahaly Runalds 3-20-1841 (3-28-1841) G
Cantrel, John L. to Amanda Vetetoe 8-31-1862 Mn
Cantrel, John W. to Nancy Thetford 10-15-1862 G
Cantrell, A. J. to Nancy Todd 9-18-1866 Hn
Cantrell, A. P. to M. D. Roberts 9-21-1854 We
Cantrell, George to Mary Jones 9-18-1856 Be
Cantrell, J. K. P. to Martha Ann Holt 10-17-1860 (no return) We
Cantrell, John H. to Ablone Prist 1-24-1859 Cr
Cantrell, P. H. to Mary A. Thomas 12-10-1846 We
Cantrell, STephen to Amanda Ownbie 2-6-1851 Cr
Cantrell, W. C. to Lucinda Ivans 9-6-1845 (no return) We
Cantrell, W. M. to Rutha Crocker 4-15-1866 G
Cantrell, William W. to Jane Marcus 8-8-1859 (no return) We
Cantrell, Wm. C. to M. A. Clayborn 7-6-1850 Cr
Cantrell, Wm. to Margaret Creasy 12-17-1864 Be
Cantwell, E. to J. A. Tull 2-26-1881 (no return) L
Cantwell, Newton J. to Mary M. Latham 12-6-1855 We
Cantwell, Smith to Sarah Pratt 12-19-1850 Cr
Caolman, Alfred A. to Louisa R. Ivins 8-23-1846 We
Cap (Cass?), Hunter to Harriet Warton 1-3-1874 (1-4-1874) L B
Capaman, William to Caroline Venable 8-29-1868 G B
Capehart, William to Elizabeth Joiner 11-28-1853 T
Capel, Roberson to Elzira O. Moore 3-19-1851 Sh
Capell, Alx. to Hattie Pewett 4-16-1870 Hy
Capell, Hans to Susan Taylor 1-18-1843 Ma
Capell, J. T. to Kitty Bessent 10-15-1868 Dy
Capell, Louis to Mary A. Thomas 10-14-1868 Hy
Capell, Nelson to Moria Taylor 11-22-1877 Hy
Capell, Wm. F. to Lezinka Rogers 5-25-1876 Hy
Capella, James to Ann David 3-12-1860 Sh
Capers, F. G. to Victoria Woodward 3-16-1858 Sh
Capers, Gilmore to Sallie Moody 1-9-1873 Hy
Caperton, James B. to Nancy C. Brooks 10-15-1844 (no return) F
Capher, James to Emeline Boals 8-11-1847 (8-12-1847) Ma
Caple, Benjamin D. to Nancy H. Johnston 4-20-1852 G
Caple, Littleton to Polly Sanders 1-8-1840 (1-9-1840) F
Caple, Phillip to Julia Ann Ingram 9-6-1839 (no return) F
Caplinger, Andrew to Louisa Williams 12-1-1858 (no return) L
Caplinger, John to Susan Culpepper 4-6-1867 (no return) Hn
Caplinger, K. O. to T. C. Jenkins 1-19-1882 L
Capps, D. M. (SB F. M.) to A. M. Thompson 1-10-1864 Be
Capps, Finis to Angeline Rutledge 12-25-1868 G
Capps, J. G. to A. J. Jackson 1-12-1867 G
Capps, J. M. to M. C. Whitehurst 12-18-1868 G
Capps, James M. to Martha Peebles 4-14-1864 Be
Capps, James N. to Cathey Clifford 7-2-1839 Cr
Capps, James S. to Sarah P. Winn (Norrod) 8-28-1868 Cr
Capps, James to Sarah Justice 12-21-1839 Cr
Capps, Jesse J. to Ancy Roberson 7-29-1862 We
Capps, John to Susan P. Hayatte? 1-9-1865 (no return) L
Capps, Newten J. to Senly Busby 1-13-1858 (no return) We
Capps, Person to Sally Owens 10-10-1855 We
Capps, Pleasant to Nancy J. Cantrell 12-17-1856 Cr
Capps, Reuben to Eliza Farrar 8-18-1860 Be
Capps, Robert R. to Sarah A. Cochrin 9-9-1841 Cr
Capps, Simon M. E. to Martha J. Lorance 10-2-1866 G
Capps, W. N. to Sarah E. Denning (Dunning) 1-13-1858 (no return) We
Capps, William to A. Cochran 12-1-1856 (no return) We
Capps, William to E. C. Becten 3-24-1867 G
Capps, William to Mary C. Jones 2-18-1869 Cr
Capps?, P. B. to P. A. C. Bruce? 4-20-1867 (4-21-1867) Cr
Caps, Andrew to Sarah Ann Coleman 12-1-1855 (12-6-1855) Hr
Caps, P. B. to Sarah L. Rumage 9-13-1870 L
Caps, Wm. N. to Louisa A. Ghrum 8-15-1843 (no return) We
Car, Silas to Jane McDowel 4-14-1870 G B
Caradine, Andrew to America ___ 12-16-1846 Ma
Caradine, James to Frances Dent 12-27-1843 (12-28-1843) Ma
Caraline, Nickolas to Sabrina E. Doeble 5-11-1853 Sh
Caraway, Alexander to Mary E. Applewhite 8-9-1853 (8-12-1853) O
Caraway, B. to M. B. Tucker 1-8-1866 G
Caraway, Bryant to Rachael Peel 8-23-1852 (8-26-1852) G
Caraway, James Henry to Mary Love Edwards 12-28-1844 (1-2-1845) T
Caraway, James to Catharine Keathley 3-26-1843 (3-?-1843) O
Caraway, Jesse to Annie Ross 8-15-1866 G
Caraway, John to Pamelia P. Harris 8-28-1854 (9-4-1854) Sh
Caraway, John to Sarah Brown 5-30-1835 Hr
Caraway, Lovit to Orphia C. Bass 3-23-1856 We
Caraway, Matthew to Sarah Jane Wolf 5-4-1864 Sh
Caraway, T. F. to Martha E. Scates 5-3-1857 Cr
Caraway, Thomas B. to Lucy A. M. Pryor 1-5-1856 (no return) We

Caraway, Thomas B. to Lucy A. M. Pryor 1-6-1856 We
Caraway, V. to Susan Tucker 2-8-1866 G
Caraway, William to Louisa Catharine Lindsey 10-5-1866 Be
Caraway, Wm. to Almeda Alsup 8-13-1861 Be
Carberry, Thomas to Lou Harrissinger 10-18-1873 (10-19-1873) L
Carden, Jas. E. to Nancy A. Neighbours 12-18-1865 (12-19-1865) Cr
Cardinal, Lewis to Mary A. Shipan 7-26-1853 Sh
Cardinal, Louis to Jane Franklin 8-5-1849 Sh
Cardwell, Harry to Mollie Campbell 1-10-1878 Hy
Cardwell, Isaac L. to Nancy E. Rogers 3-12-1844 Hn
Cardwell, John W. to Amanda E. Diggs 2-3-1859 Hn
Cardwell, M. D. to Holly Ann Hicks (Kicks) 6-18-1846 (no return) We
Cardwell, Plivin to Elizabeth Ann Stone 1-20-1839 Cr
Cardwell, W. Y. to Margaret Moore 5-15-1863 Mn
Cardwell, William G. to Joannah Dew 5-4-1860 Ma
Cardwell, Wm. A. to Sarah J. Ussery 1-12-1857 Hr
Cardy, H. to Eliza Greathouse 9-19-1863 (9-20-1863) Sh
Careley, Martin F. to Elizabeth F. Davis 2-11-1868 Dy
Carelli, A. to Mary Brunus? 5-25-1853 Sh
Carelton, Calvin to Nancy M. Pierce 1-9-1861 (1-10-1861) F
Carey, Everett to Nancy Williams 11-11-1841 (11-12-1841) Ma
Carey, Felix to Nancy Brewer 5-14-1870 (5-18-1870) Cr
Carey, John to Eliza Nobles 3-6-1843 (3-7-1843) G
Carey, John to M. B. Finch 6-20-1865 O
Carey, Miles to Susan C. Wheatley 10-11-1839 Sh
Carey, Myer to Lina Carey 8-11-1866 O
Carey, P. S. to Mary J. Carr 8-4-1863 G
Carey, Patrick to Mary McMahan 2-15-1854 Sh
Cargal, Thomas H. to Sarah Jane Read 11-8-1851 (no return) F
Cargel, Wm. W. to Necia Simmons 12-28-1843 Cr
Cargil, Wiley T. to Josephine Hooks 12-13-1866 (12-24-1866) F
Cargil, Wily to Mary Folwell 7-7-1851 (no return) F
Cargil, Wm. W. to Penelope A. Brown 4-6-1849 (5-2-1849) F
Cargill, Tom to Lucinda Cargill 8-8-1867 (12-28-1867) F B
Caricker, Charles to Nancy Brown 7-28-1854 (7-30-1854) Hr
Carigton, Richard to D. P. Kerby 3-27-1867 (3-28-1867) Cr
Carington, J. T. to Georgie Ginn 3-22-1871 Hy
Carington, William L. to Nancy Carington 2-23-1848 Hn
Carithers, John A. to Mary Rudolph 8-22-1831 Hr
Carithers, Samuel to Eliza Hill 6-24-1865 (6-28-1865) O
Cariven, Thos. W. to Elizabeth Vaughn 1-18-1842 Cr
Carl, Jacob E. to Mary E. Norman 12-26-1853 (no return) F
Carlesly, Thomas to Melissa Lanny 1-13-1855 (1-14-1855) L
Carley, Jesse to Letty Roberts 8-17-1849 (8-19-1849) Hr
Carley, John W. to Milly Boothe 10-1-1840 (10-4-1840) Hr
Carley, John to Elizabeth Davis 1-27-1849 (2-4-1849) Hr
Carley, John to Polly Ann Savage 9-26-1840 (9-27-1840) Hr
Carley, Luke to Louisa Barham 4-21-1852 (4-22-1852) Hr
Carley, Peter K. to Susannah Liggett 1-26-1843 Hr
Carley, William to Malinda Binkley 8-10-1839 Hy
Carley, William to Sarah Carley 10-1-1840 (10-2-1840) Hr
Carlile, David to Jane Edward 8-8-1848 Sh
Carlington, Jas. to Mary Jane Ross 12-23-1846 Ma
Carlisle, James to Lucy Ann Wesson 7-4-1848 Sh
Carlisle, Wiley to Elizabeth R. H. Hardaway 12-30-1847 Sh
Carlisle, Wilie to Pauline (Mrs.) Thompson 1-12-1864 Sh
Carlo, Grismani to Margaret Botto 10-22-1863 Sh
Carlock, W. V. to M. C. Park 9-25-1866 O
Carlton, Albert M. to Mary C. Wills 1-4-1871 Hy
Carlton, Allen to Moriah Owen 12-25-1871 Hy
Carlton, Ambros to Alice Hawkins 1-9-1873 Hy
Carlton, B. O. to Iza J. Carlton 2-1-1863 G
Carlton, David C. to Sarah E. Cantrell 3-14-1861 We
Carlton, Jasper N. to Adeline Livingston 12-13-1859 (no return) Hy
Carlton, John B. to Sarah M. Wagster 10-28-1858 We
Carlton, John C. to Sarah J. Ashley 9-8-1859 G
Carlton, John F. to Mary Ann Hall 10-28-1861 (no return) Cr
Carlton, John H. to G. E. Demall 11-22-1856 Cr
Carlton, Newton J. to Emma Elmore 8-12-1868 G
Carlton, Obediah to Elizabeth Parks 12-8-1857 We
Carlton, P. J. to O. A. Webb 12-26-1869 G
Carlton, R. A. to I. J. Joyce 3-5-1861 G
Carlton, R. J. to Tobitha L. Slaton 10-20-1856 (10-21-1856) G
Carlton, Sterling to Julia Ann Scott 1-3-1867 (1-6-1867) F B
Carlton, Thomas to Martha A. Pool 10-28-1852 We
Carlton, Thomas to Naomi Patterson 2-23-1853 (2-24-1853) G
Carlton, W. F. to Susan A. E. Evans 2-2-1860 (no return) Hy
Carlton, Wm. H. to Phebe Brumfalow 8-22-1847 We
Carlton?, James D. to Ellen H. Rollins 2-8-1871 (2-9-1871) Cr
Carly, Philip D. to Nancy Dickson 10-27-1840 (10-29-1840) Ma
Carmack, Baccus to Mitta A. McCree 11-8-1867 (11-10-1867) F B
Carmack, G. L. to Mary A. Allen 10-22-1856 Cr
Carmack, J. W. to Benny Curtis 1-1-1868 (no return) Dy
Carmack, J. W. to J. A. Dodson 12-17-1875 (12-19-1875) Dy
Carmack, John to M. C. Moore 10-27-1860 (10-24?-1860) O
Carmack, P. P. to A. R. Fleming 1-23-1867 G
Carmack, W. J. to Eliza J. Cannon 4-24-1867 G

Carmack, W. T. to Sarah Ann Kelly 2-11-1856 (2-13-1856) Sh
Carmack, William to Caroline Cunningham 11-8-1825 O
Carmady, Patrick to Mary Shea 11-15-1851 Sh
Carman, Edward J. to Davie D. P. Malone 1-19-1866 Hy
Carman, Samuel to Susan King 6-28-1847 O
Carmichael, James to Catherine Cain 1-16-1861 Sh
Carn?, James Irwin to Ann Savanna? Gustins? 1-5-1843 (1-5-1843) T
Carnahan, George to Ruby R. Eastman 6-23-1854 Sh
Carnahan, James B. to Martha Bell 4-1-1831 (4-2-1831) G
Carnal, H. L. to Mattie A. Johnson 10-20-1875 (10-21-1875) L
Carnal, J. M. to L. E. Parker 3-13-1867 (3-15-1867) Cr
Carnal, James J. to Rachael L. Milam 1-26-1870 (1-27-1870) Cr
Carnal, James M. to Ellen Nichols 6-28-1869 (6-29-1869) Cr
Carnal, Joshua to Sarah Gordon 1-4-1853 Cr
Carnall, E. W. to Clementia Carnall 1-9-1849 (1-11-1849) L
Carnall, E. W. to Lizzie V. Hicks 8-22-1863 (8-23-1863) L
Carnall, J. L. to Sarah Jane Davis 11-11-1873 (11-13-1873) L
Carnall, Joseph to Caroline Long 12-19-1849 (12-20-1849) L
Carnall, W. L. to S. E. Parker 1-23-1873 Cr
Carnatzan, Charles E. to Mary E. D. Perry 9-9-1857 (9-10-1857) Ma
Carnatzer, James to Ellen Ferguson 12-26-1860 Ma
Carne, John D. to Jane E. Alexander 1-5-1864 G
Carnell, Brinkley to Sarah Williams 3-7-1859 Cr
Carnell, E. P. to Matilda Carnell 2-1-1865 (no return) L
Carnell, G. W. to M. A. Hooper 3-19-1879 (3-20-1879) L
Carnell, Isiah to Harrett J. Bennett 2-?-1848 Cr
Carnell, J. M. to M. A. Taliaferro 7-24-1880 (7-25-1880) L
Carnell, John N. to Mary Jane Fossett 12-18-1871 (12-20-1871) L
Carnell, R. A. to M. J. Cousins 11-11-1876 (11-12-1876) L
Carnell, R. A. to Minnie Burks 11-23-1883 L
Carnell, Wm. C. to Adeline Carnell 1-6-1872 (1-9-1872) L
Carnell, Wm. Samuel to Mary E. Garner? 5-5-1855 (5-7-1855) L
Carnelton, Jerimiah to Mary C. Brechum 12-10-1850 Cr
Carnes, A. R. to Mintie S. Rogers 3-5-1862 (3-6-1862) Cr
Carnes, David B. to Mary Steel 10-7-1828 (10-9-1828) Hr
Carnes, George to Lucy Walker 4-28-1866 (5-13-1866) F
Carnes, James A. to Elizabeth M. Jones 10-28-1840 (10-29-1840) F
Carnes, James to Mandy Mulherren 8-13-1868 (no return) Hy
Carnes, Robert W. to Prudence E. Steele 11-10-1842 Hr
Carnes, Stephen G. to Bettie B. Cooper 3-30-1869 F
Carnes, Thomas to Elizabeth McBride 6-26-1835 (6-28-1835) Hr
Carnetzer, William D. to Malvina Brimingham 12-29-1859 Ma
Carney, D. P. to Virginia Scott 11-4-1867 (11-5-1867) F
Carney, Edmond to Vick Sanders 9-1-1874 Hy
Carney, Henry to Jane Dancy 1-4-1873 Hy
Carney, J. L. to America Gardner 3-10-1874 Hy
Carney, Lawrence to Mary Morality 8-25-1855 (8-26-1855) Sh
Carney, Michael to Elizabeth Forrester 12-21-1854 (12-22-1854) O
Carney, Michael to Mary Price 1-2-1868 O
Carney, Pat to Susan Alltop 4-4-1871 (no return) Hy
Carney, Patrick to Ann McCormick 2-1-1859 (2-3-1859) Sh
Carney, Patrick to Margaret Cleary 4-24-1855 Sh
Carney, R. S. to A. E. Morris 3-5-1860 (no return) Hy
Carney, Thomas S. to Christiana Payne 6-6-1858 We
Carney, Wm. to Lizzie Payne 6-18-1878 (no return) Hy
Carnigay, Bryant to Hester Grady 1-16-1843 G
Carns, Absolum to Elizabeth Gunter 10-27-1842 (12-5-1842) G
Carny, Francis to Margarett Long 3-29-1864 (3-31-1864) Sh
Carolan, Bernard to Lizzie Fellowes 6-18-1861 Sh
Carooth, William to Elizabeth Jaine Lea 2-11-1852 L
Carotti, David to Mary Grace 1-1-1858 Sh
Carouth, Aquilla H. to Emily E. Robertson 5-23-1850 Hr
Caroway, James M. to Mary M. Carmichael 1-22-1863 We
Caroway, Jno. B. to Martha J. Smith 1-14-1868 (1-16-1868) F
Caroway, Lewis to Eliza Strong 1-27-1872 (2-6-1872) T
Carpender, Robert to Anna Read 8-1-1877 Hy
Carpenter, A. H. to M. E. Churchman 10-27-1874 (10-28-1874) Dy
Carpenter, A. M. F. to Henrietta Thompson 2-27-1861 (3-13-1861) O
Carpenter, Dangerfreld? to Ellin Kyle 3-7-1835 (3-8-1835) Hr
Carpenter, Fondell to Mary Jane (Mrs.) Bowes 5-28-1853 (no return) F
Carpenter, Frederick to Nancy N. Lynch 2-11-1850 O
Carpenter, Frederick to Sarah A. Duff 9-30-1862 (10-2-1862) O
Carpenter, George to Jane Dodson 3-24-1866 F
Carpenter, H. R. to M. S. Ray 5-11-1878 (5-13-1878) Dy
Carpenter, James F. to Mary Josephine Fletcher 1-29-1853 (1-30-1853) O
Carpenter, John C. to Maria L. Taylor 12-23-1857 (12-24-1857) Ma
Carpenter, John H. to Martha J. Tanner 11-11-1846 O
Carpenter, John H. to Martha Jane Tanner 11-11-1840 O
Carpenter, Mat to Alice Higgason 4-12-1871 F B
Carpenter, Nathaniel C. to Mary D. Smith 10-29-1849 (11-1-1849) Ma
Carpenter, O. K. to Sarah A. Hopper 12-10-1855 (12-11-1855) Ma
Carpenter, Samuel to Lilly Merrill 2-7-1860 (2-9-1860) Sh
Carpenter, W. C. to Nancy M. Baker 10-2-1868 (10-4-1868) Dy
Carpenter, Willis to Mary White 3-13-1883 (no return) L
Carpenter, Wm. to Eliza Fort 6-19-1869 (6-20-1869) F B
Carper, Alexander to Mary Huffman 5-19-1857 (5-22-1857) Hr
Carper, Jno. K. to R. A. Richardson 11-18-1869 Hy

Carper, William to Margaret Goforth 2-2-1861 (2-5-1861) Hr
Carr, Allen to Lucety Bools 1-4-1859 (1-5-1859) Ma
Carr, Anderson B. to Ann Kimbrough 7-24-1825 Sh
Carr, Andrew A. to Everlina Rony 9-12-1838 (9-14-1838) G
Carr, Arch to W. M. Suralle 7-16-1862 (7-17-1862) Sh
Carr, B. B. to Mary E. Tharpe 3-22-1876 (no return) Dy
Carr, Benjamin F. to Mary J. House 12-2-1848 Hn
Carr, C. C. to Susan W. Smith 5-26-1866 (5-29-1866) T
Carr, G. L. to Ann E. Black 12-28-1837 Sh
Carr, Gideon to Judith A. Collins 4-12-1856 (4-13-1856) Sh
Carr, H. M. to Sallie H. (Mrs.) Vickers 9-3-1863 Sh
Carr, Hardy to Mahulda Duberry 2-29-1840 (3-1-1840) Hr
Carr, Henry to Mary White 2-25-1838 Sh
Carr, James to Eliza Ann M. Carr 10-3-1849 (10-4-1849) G
Carr, Jerry to Mary Jane Green 9-23-1878 (7?-13-1879) L B
Carr, Jesse D. to Elizabeth Woods 5-23-1843 Sh
Carr, John A. to E. A. Jefferson 12-12-1877 Hy
Carr, John A. to Nancy A. Sigmor 12-17-1851 (12-18-1851) G
Carr, John H. to Sarah C. Anderson 1-18-1849 Sh
Carr, John to Mary L. Hodges 2-14-1849 Sh
Carr, Overton W. to Mary Hill 5-1-1820 Sh
Carr, R. D. to M. A. Smoot 10-14-1866 (no return) Cr
Carr, Robert H. to Elenor J. McDaniel 3-3-1853 G
Carr, Robert H. to Margaret A. Ellison 10-27-1845 (10-28-1845) G
Carr, Samuel to Mary Ann Elizabeth Reinhardt 6-18-1844 Sh
Carr, Silas to Ellen Stubbs 3-10-1885 (3-15-1885) L
Carr, Thomas to Mary M. Tatum 12-3-1853 (12-4?-1853) Ma
Carr, W. F. to Nancy Briant 1-24-1855 (1-25-1855) G
Carr, W. M. to L. A. Rowe 2-28-1860 (3-3-1860) Sh
Carr, William F. to Rebecca Olaver 8-9-1842 G
Carr, William to Emarilla J. Ruleman 12-23-1848 Sh
Carr, William to Harriet M. Berry 6-29-1852 Sh
Carr, Z. A. to Miranna Whitly 10-4-1847 Sh
Carradine, William to Emely Hall 1-21-1832 (2-23-1832) G
Carraway, Bryant C. to Sidney Hall 10-28-1843 (10-29-1843) G
Carraway, Bryant to Isabella King 1-9-1851 G
Carraway, Henry to Abacilla McKinnie 3-14-1843 Hr
Carraway, Jas. M. to Susan C. Casey 11-23-1858 (11-25-1858) Hr
Carray, Jesse to Elizabeth Keathly 4-16-1838 (4-17-1838) G
Carray, Thomas to Della Roberts 6-1-1867 (no return) Cr
Carrele, James to Sarah E. Mullins 4-8-1868 (4-12-1868) L
Carricker, Geo. M. to Mary E. Phillips 9-16-1857 Hr
Carricker, George M. to Elizabeth Gray 8-7-1852 Hr
Carrigan, James D. to Ellen Reosier 1-16-1877 (1-17-1877) L
Carrigan, James R. to Eliza A. Fitzpatrick 5-15-1860 (no return) L
Carrigan, James R. to Sarah A. E. Watkins 4-7-1857 (4-8-1857) L
Carrigan, John to Fa_ba Hicks 5-3-1863 L
Carrigan, L. C. to Mattie T. Glenn 3-26-1868 Hy
Carrigan, William to Sallie M. Henley 4-1-1879 (4-2-1879) L
Carrigan, William to Susan F. Durham 11-14-1866 L
Carrington, Charles W. to Eliza Hardin 3-12-1868 Ma
Carrington, J. B. to Elizabeth Springfield 6-21-1861 (6-22-1861) Hr
Carrington, James H.? to Sarah A. Simpson 3-28-1860 (no return) We
Carrington, Luke to Nannie Toone 12-10-1858 (1-11-1859) Hr
Carrington, Neal to Elizabeth E. Johnson 4-24-1852 Ma
Carrington, S. M. to Manassa Dickins 9-19-1856 (9-20-1856) G
Carrington, Scott to Louisa Freeman no date (Aug/Sep 1873) L
Carrington, Thos. A. to Synthan C. Hicks 8-14-1856 Cr
Carrington, Wiley A. to Martha Pirtle 4-30-1859 (5-2-1859) Hr
Carrington, William to Julia P. Harton 6-4-1842 Ma
Carriston?, William to Mariah A. Chaney 3-4-1871 T
Carrne, J. D. to Mary F. Sammons 2-5-1863 G
Carrol, C. to Emily O. Daniel 7-25-1856 (9-10-1856) G
Carrol, J. D. to Nancy J. Butler 3-26-1861 G
Carrol, J. R. to S. J. Needham 11-18-1857 G
Carrol, John to Sallie Plot 1-13-1862 Sh
Carroll, Alfred M. to Tennessee Cardwell 10-10-1862 We
Carroll, Allen to Jane Jones 2-2-1826 (2-4-1826) Hr
Carroll, Arthur to Jane Shearon 2-13-1850 (2-14-1850) O
Carroll, B. A. to F. Flack 3-11-1874 Dy
Carroll, C. H. to Susan M. Lippard 6-20-1866 O
Carroll, Chas. D. to Maudy Perry 6-2-1869 Ma
Carroll, Clemuel to Julia A. Patterson 8-21-1864 Mn
Carroll, D. C. to Jane Hurley 8-14-1858 Sh
Carroll, E. C. to S. E. Dougherty 10-12-1867 O
Carroll, Elias to Amelia L. Durham 1-29-1840 (1-30-1840) F
Carroll, Francis M. to Frances M. Lowe 7-25-1838 (7-26-1838) Hr
Carroll, Frank to Sarah Webb 7-17-1866 (7-26-1866) F
Carroll, Freeman A. to Frances A. Wesson 9-8-1848 Sh
Carroll, George W. to Lucy M. Carrol 12-13-1854 G
Carroll, George W. to Margarett Wallace 12-21-1870 (12-22-1870) F
Carroll, I. N. to Julia Hill 2-13-1867 G
Carroll, J. D. to E. M. Harris 1-14-1861 (1-15-1861) Dy
Carroll, J. E. to Louise Bailey 12-23-1861 (12-24-1861) O
Carroll, J. J. to N. H. Harper 2-13-1873 Cr
Carroll, James A. to Nancy Kensey 3-21-1841 G
Carroll, James C. to E. J. Ewing 10-20-1883 (10-21-1883) L

Carroll, James to Ann Munn 3-13-1844 Sh
Carroll, James to Mary Singleton 1-25-1834 G
Carroll, Jno. M. to Nancy Smith 1-1-1838 (1-2-1838) G
Carroll, John A. to Mary Ann McBride 9-3-1849 Sh
Carroll, John C. to Sarah Howard 1-2-1843 (1-5-1843) G
Carroll, John D. to Ferlea? U. Doggett 8-16-1853 (8-18-1853) Sh
Carroll, John D. to Racheal Rennick 1-28-1828 Hr
Carroll, John H. to Susan M. Bruce 11-27-1842 G
Carroll, John M. to Elizabeth Wilson 9-6-1852 (9-7-1852) G
Carroll, John to Louisa N. W. Manley 12-30-1847 Ma
Carroll, John to Mary Brissolary 5-2-1852 Sh
Carroll, Johnun? to Adaline Price 12-30-1839 (no return) F
Carroll, Joseph to Sarah McFadden 8-30-1842 (no return) F
Carroll, Josiah R. to Lavinia A. Thornton 6-11-1853 (6-26-1853) G
Carroll, Moladeous B. to Cornelia F. Henry 3-20-1848 (3-22-1848) G
Carroll, Nash to Margaret Sullivan 10-28-1854 Sh
Carroll, Owen to Cathorin Rian? 2-11-1851 Sh
Carroll, R. H. to B. J. (Mrs.) Roberson 10-21-1863 Sh
Carroll, R. H. to Caroline M. Thurmond 3-21-1836 (3-24-1836) Hr
Carroll, S. D. to Julia Ann Akin 11-28-1870 (11-30-1870) Dy
Carroll, Sydney S. to Lucy F. Hamilton 12-2-1858 Cr
Carroll, Thomas B. to Martha D. Linton 11-1-1866 (11-8-1866) Ma
Carroll, Thomas to Malinda Fuller 11-17-1841 Hn
Carroll, Thomas to Martha J. Simmons 6-16-1867 Hn
Carroll, W. A. to Mattie Blanton 8-9-1879 (no return) Dy
Carroll, W. B. to J. A. Gardner 9-4-1871 Cr
Carroll, W. B. to M. Peel 12-29-1869 G
Carroll, W. O. to Susana Stringer 8-22-1862 (9-3-1862) Sh
Carroll, W. R. J. to Permelia J. Nelson 7-6-1867 (no return) Cr
Carroll, Washington B. to Martha L. Mathis 1-1-1828 Hr
Carroll, William A. to E. A. Voncleave? 1-20-1851 G
Carroll, William A. to Frances Faircloth 2-9-1858 Hn
Carroll, William A. to Martha Crowder 12-1-1865 (no return) Hn
Carroll, William R. to Rebecca C. Moudy 8-25-1846 (8-27-1846) G
Carroll, William T. to Martha R. Thedford 10-23-1852 (10-28-1852) G
Carroll, William to Harriet Vaughn 9-3-1860 (9-5-1860) O
Carroll, William to Martha Lucas 8-25-1855 (no return) F
Carroll, Wm. J. to Terza Jane Ellington 1-10-1852 G
Carroll, (John H. to Martha Bruce 2-12-1845 (2-18-1845) G
Carron, Michael to Napkin Malony 2-9-1864 Sh
Carruth, J. J. to Mary Jane Clark 5-27-1858 (8-10-1858) Hr
Carruth, W. H. to Victoria E. Smith 11-23-1869 Hy
Carruthers, James N. to Elizabeth J. A. Benton 1-1-1845 Ma
Carruthers, James W. to Mary Ann Morrow 5-28-1846 Ma
Carry, Nathan to Ann Carry 11-26-1835 G
Carson, A. J. to Eliza A. Rosson 3-4-1856 (3-6-1856) Hr
Carson, Andrew J. to Matilda Tedford 2-28-1854 Hr
Carson, Andrew to Nicy Murray 2-6-1840 Hn
Carson, G. S. to Margaret T. Carpenter 7-3-1855 L
Carson, Irvin E. to Jane Redding 8-29-1846 (no return) Hn
Carson, James F. to Mary E. Pennington 12-16-1879 (no return) L
Carson, John B. to Louisa A. Stewart 7-9-1857 (no return) L
Carson, John P. to Sarah Ann Hagsett 5-5-1856 (5-6-1856) L
Carson, John to Sallie Branoch 3-28-1872 (no return) Cr B
Carson, R. A. to Mary F. Harris 10-5-1863 (no return) Hn
Carson, Richard to Louisa Barham 8-17-1868 (8-18-1868) Cr
Carson, Robert A. to Nannie B. Heathcock 3-3-1878 Hy
Carson, Robt. to Louisa Williams 8-3-1871 (no return) Hy
Carson, Samuel B. to Sarah B. Sampson 3-12-1868 Dy
Carson, Smith to Margaret Clay 9-2-1874 L B
Carson, Steward to Margarett Sparks 11-21-1872 Cr B
Carson, T. S. to Martha Thomas 8-15-1839 Be
Carson, Thomas C. to Suretta Cress 7-12-1867 (no return) Hn
Carson, Thomas to M. C. Davis 10-11-1865 T
Carson, Thos. J. to Elizabeth C. Sparks 11-22-1854 Cr
Carson, Thos. S. to Mary A. Glover 4-20-1853 (no return) F
Carson, W. M. to Sallie Ridley 1-14-1862 (no return) Cr
Carson, W. to Rebecca Ann Crow 7-8-1857 (7-9-1857) Sh
Carson, Washington to Alice C. Maguire 4-18-1861 Sh
Carson, William D. to Mary A. Meadows 3-4-1885 L
Carson, William H. to Elizabeth M. Reed 1-2-1845 Hn
Carson, William H. to Fanny Strickland 4-4-1855 Sh
Carson, William to Janie Green 6-26-1878 L
Carson, William to Mary Ann Gholson 12-10-1839 (12-12-1839) Ma
Carson, Wm. S. to Martha A. Jenkins 4-17-1860 (4-22-1860) Hr
Carson, Wm. to Martha A. Freeman 2-2-1859 (2-3-1859) T
Carswell, Thomas to Ellen (Mrs.) Black 7-26-1863 (7-27-1863) Sh
Cart, Andrew to Sarah Jane Ferrell 10-11-1870 Dy
Carten, James W. to Jane Harts 7-6-1837 G
Carter, A. E. to Eliza Moore 11-24-1855 Cr
Carter, Albert A. to Nancy C. Williams 10-12-1856 Cr
Carter, Alfred to Mary Newsom 8-26-1868 F B
Carter, Alfred to Nancy Campbell 10-17-1859 (10-18-1859) L
Carter, Allison E. to Jane L. Veazey 12-15-1841 Hn
Carter, Anderson to Cinthia Anderson 9-30-1885 L
Carter, Archibald W. to Sarah A. Bomar 7-26-1860 Hn
Carter, Augustine to Mary Halliburton 9-28-1848 (10-10-1848) Ma

Carter, Augustus C. to Menerva Shaw 2-12-1846 Cr
Carter, B. to Lititia Clancey 2-7-1865 F
Carter, Barons to Emma Clancy 1-1-1866 (no return) Hy
Carter, Berry to Fannie Prince 12-14-1872 (12-19-1872) Cr B
Carter, Beverly A. to Margaret McKenna 12-22-1853 Sh
Carter, Braxter to Martha Yates 12-29-1856 (12-30-1856) Sh
Carter, Braxton to Ivy Ann Pritchet 8-6-1845 Sh
Carter, Brooks to Mary Brown 11-30-1878 (12-1-1878) Dy
Carter, Calvin to Francis Capell 12-28-1874 L B
Carter, Charles to Cate Right 4-16-1870 G B
Carter, Charles to Elizabeth Lowery 1-18-1845 Hn
Carter, Charles to Francis E. Cooper 8-25-1859 We
Carter, Charles to Mattie Smith 4-11-1871 (4-15-1871) F B
Carter, Chas. W. to Martha J. Young 1-27-1862 (1-28-1862) Ma
Carter, Columbus to Harriet Fuller 1-21-1870 Cr
Carter, D. M. to Emma G. McMurray 2-14-1862 (2-19-1862) Sh
Carter, D. R. to Sarah E. Pled;ge 11-26-1855 (11-27-1855) Hr
Carter, Daniel N. to Martha J. Lindsey 12-15-1852 Cr
Carter, David to Mary A. Byron 8-27-1864 Sh
Carter, De L. to Martha Norton 2-24-1859 (2-25-1859) Ma
Carter, Drury (Fayette Co.) to Bella Shepard 8-19-1848 (8-21-1848) Ma
Carter, E. P. to M. J. Potter 11-18-1864 G
Carter, Edmond to Emaline Dowell 12-4-1873 T
Carter, Edward to Hannora Flaherty 7-19-1856 (7-20-1856) Sh
Carter, Elias to Eliza E. Crawford 10-17-1860 (no return) We
Carter, Elijah H. to Martha Ann Bailey 6-15-1867 (6-16-1867) Ma
Carter, Ephraim to Elizabeth Ross 7-16-1842 Cr
Carter, Frank C. to Kate A. Blair 1-25-1877 (no return) L
Carter, G. B. to Mary A. Young 1-18-1864 (1-19-1864) Sh
Carter, G. N. to Martha Leech 3-14-1861 (no return) Cr
Carter, George O. to Fannie Proctor 11-30-1876 Hn
Carter, George R. to Harriet Brown 2-2-1863 (no return) Hy
Carter, George to Catherine Joyner 3-24-1862 (3-26-1862) O
Carter, George to Sarah Fisher 12-9-1846 Cr
Carter, Gilbert to Nancy Sauls 2-?-1851 Cr
Carter, Green B. to Nancy Ann Crews 1-3-1839 Hr
Carter, Henry to Aramenta Finch 10-3-1861 (no return) Hn
Carter, Henry to Sarah A. Burrow 10-20-1847 Cr
Carter, Henry to Sarah C. French 10-30-1869 (10-31-1869) Cr
Carter, Isaac J. to Mary C. Morris 5-25-1844 F
Carter, Isaiah to Adaline Turner 12-23-1846 (no return) We
Carter, J. A. to Georgianna Burnett 1-8-1862 Sh
Carter, J. D. D. R. to Margarett Carlton 6-24-1848 Cr
Carter, J. D. to S. J. Eudaly 1-1-1873 Dy
Carter, J. F. to Sarah E. Reynolds 8-24-1868 (8-27-1868) L
Carter, J. M. to Mary F. Harman? 11-13-1867 Hn
Carter, J. W. to Arbella Wells 3-11-1846 Hn
Carter, J. W. to M. D. Williamson 1-14-1867 (no return) Cr
Carter, J.R. to M. W. Mullin 1-23-1878 Hy
Carter, Jacob to Julia Manley 2-6-1867 Hn
Carter, James D. to Sarah A. O. Shore 5-28-1846 (6-10-1846) F
Carter, James E. to Catherine Bowden 3-9-1842 Hn
Carter, James F. to Eliza Jane Bass 10-8-1858 Sh
Carter, James G. to Hulda E. Mayfield 1-12-1839 (1-15-1839) G
Carter, James L. to Josephine S. Meadows 10-1-1857 O
Carter, James M. to Sarah A. Lewis 8-31-1860 O
Carter, James R. to S. E. Diggs 12-4-1851 Hn
Carter, James T. to Ada Cisco 12-30-1867 (1-14-1868) F
Carter, James W. to Emily Kemp 11-13-1860 Hn
Carter, James W. to Mary E. Moorefield 2-15-1852 Hn
Carter, James to Elizabeth Davis 4-9-1833 O
Carter, James to Jane Hart 7-6-1836 G
Carter, James to Malvina Armstrong 12-22-1846 (12-24-1846) Ma
Carter, James to Mary Jane Babb 9-21-1847 Hn
Carter, James to Salina Dean 4-27-1836 Hr
Carter, Jefferson to Harriet Holmes 10-30-1866 (no return) F B
Carter, Jerome to Elizabeth Nix May 5-9-1839 Hn
Carter, Jesse A. to Anna Johnson 9-19-1857 Hr
Carter, John B. to Lydia B. Meadows 1-23-1863 O
Carter, John C. to Mary Ann Strong 12-21-1836 Sh
Carter, John E. R. to E. Lumsley 12-13-1844 (12-14-1844) F
Carter, John L. to Harriett F. Earls 1-28-1868 (1-30-1868) Cr
Carter, John M. to Sarah L. Carr 11-27-1866 Cr
Carter, John V. to S. V. Marshal 4-29-1868 O
Carter, John W. to Mary Angeline Crawford 8-16-1855 Hn
Carter, John to Charity Baucom 1-2-1840 Cr
Carter, John to Elizabeth McKnight 1-4-1848 (1-6-1848) Ma
Carter, John to Henrietta Conley 2-22-1878 L
Carter, John to Ibby Wilson 4-10-1840 (4-12-1840) F
Carter, John to Liser Taylor 1-8-1868 (no return) Hy
Carter, John to Martha Bush 3-15-1839 Cr
Carter, John to Martha R. White 11-14-1865 (11-15-1865) Cr
Carter, John to Mary Haskins 11-5-1857 Hn
Carter, John to Mincy Oldham 9-15-1885 L
Carter, Jos. John to Sarah Ann Sheckels? 12-27-1842 (12-28-1842) Hr
Carter, Joseph to Jinnie McDonald 9-15-1869 (9-20-1869) Cr
Carter, Joseph to Sarah B. Crowder 5-11-1848 Hn

Carter, L. G. to Sarah E. Harris 2-1-1863 G
Carter, L. H. to Cathorin Nichols 7-14-1873 Cr
Carter, L. to B. F. Jackson 10-2-1844 Hn
Carter, Laban to Nancy M. Snodgrass 9-3-1861 Hn
Carter, Lawson H. to Martha Nichols 2-6-1851 Cr
Carter, Moses to Mary Bell 7-8-1863 Sh
Carter, Orlando to Josephine Lambert 7-25-1859 (7-27-1859) Sh
Carter, Orvill to Jane Hall 5-13-1840 Hn
Carter, P. C. to Mary J. Cameron 12-1-1851 Sh
Carter, Perry G. to Emma W. Shaw 11-9-1843 (11-14-1843) Ma
Carter, Perry G. to George A. (Miss) Berry 3-8-1859 (3-17-1859) Sh
Carter, Perry to Nancy Enochs 5-23-1871 (5-25-1871) Dy
Carter, Philip B. to Susana E. Mathis 7-26-1837 (7-27-1837) G
Carter, Pinckney to Mary Maria Christenbury 3-21-1866 (no return) Hn
Carter, R. B. F. to M. J. Wilson 12-10-1868 Cr
Carter, R. B. to N. A. Fergerson 1-15-1851 Cr
Carter, R. S. to Sarah A. Wood 10-14-1862 (10-16-1862) Cr
Carter, R. W. to Josephina Norman 1-25-1860 Cr
Carter, R. to Rachel Pierce 1-14-1865 Be
Carter, Richard to Elizabeth Timberson 7-9-1840 Cr
Carter, Robert to Cynthia Totty 10-21-1844 Hn
Carter, Robert to Mary Nayce 1-2-1867 (no return) Hy
Carter, Robert to Rozy Ann Jones 9-5-1844 Hr
Carter, Ruben F. to Nancy E. Carter 2-24-1848 Cr
Carter, Sam to Lucy Carter 1-7-1867 (1-12-1867) F B
Carter, Samuel M. to Rachel Looney 10-29-1850 Hn
Carter, Samuel to Mary T. Burton 10-31-1843 Hn
Carter, Samuel to Mat Rucker 11-25-1870 Hy
Carter, Simon to Ann Palmer 10-22-1870 (10-23-1870) F B
Carter, Stephen L. to Nancy Howell 2-5-1851 F
Carter, T. B. to S. A. Waller 2-28-1866 (3-1-1866) Cr
Carter, T. J. to Tennessee Armstrong 12-29-1869 (12-30-1869) Dy
Carter, Thomas H. H. to Mary F. Hardy 12-18-1869 (12-19-1869) Cr
Carter, Thomas J. to Sarah C. McCulloch 11-12-1861 G
Carter, Thomas L. to Bettie Lackie 12-24-1867 (12-25-1867) Ma
Carter, Thomas L. to Mary Ann Carter 6-2-1869 Ma
Carter, Thomas L. to Mary Ann Pirtle 9-10-1859 Hr
Carter, Thomas to Mary Bently 12-17-1846 Sh
Carter, Thos. A. to Martha E. Williams 12-24-1855 Cr
Carter, Thos. M. to Martha Davis 10-31-1844 Cr
Carter, Thos. to Nancy Bragdon 12-17-1851 Cr
Carter, W. C. to Mary E. Thompson 5-7-1849 Cr
Carter, W. F. to Martha J. Hood 3-11-1849 (no return) F
Carter, W. H. to L. J. Broach 12-4-1872 Cr
Carter, W. H. to Tabitha L. Kemp 12-26-1863 (no return) Cr
Carter, W. L. to S. A. Gallion 3-6-1871 (3-7-1871) Dy
Carter, W. M. to Sarah A. Bloodworth 11-6-1854 (11-9-1854) Sh
Carter, Washington to Lucy Jackson 12-28-1867 (12-29-1867) F B
Carter, Wesley C. to Martha E. Williams 10-28-1857 O
Carter, Wiley S. to Levina Statum 8-4-1845 (8-5-1845) G
Carter, Wilkerson to M. Fowler 3-12-1860 Cr
Carter, William A. to Mary Ann Baker 7-14-1852 Sh
Carter, William B. to Christiana Smith 7-28-1839 Sh
Carter, William M. to Martha Ann Allguiar 8-9-1853 (8-10-1853) O
Carter, William Y. to Mary Ann Lackey 3-12-1859 Ma
Carter, William to Bridget Leonard 7-1-1854 Sh
Carter, William to Elizabeth Lovell 7-27-1831 Sh
Carter, William to Elizabeth Ward 5-7-1829 Sh
Carter, William to Eunita Browning 9-1-1841 Hn
Carter, William to Lucindy Lindsay 3-25-1824 O
Carter, William to Mary C. Duke 9-28-1869 (9-29-1869) Dy
Carter, Wm. A. M. to Julia A. Carter 3-1-1859 Cr
Carter, Wm. to Hannah A. Powers 11-10-1849 Cr
Carthel, J. to Jinsey Carthel 5-6-1866 G
Carthel, John T. to Minnie Neely 5-13-1857 Ma
Cartmell(Cartwell?), R. H. to Mary Jane Baldwin 3-26-1850 (3-27-1850) Hr
Cartmell, Martin to Jamima A. Sharp 10-25-1827 Ma
Cartwell, J. M. to Sophia William 11-6-1860 G
Cartwell, John to Johanna O'Harrell 8-28-1863 (8-30-1863) Sh
Cartwright, A. to Angeline Walker 1-19-1869 (2-5-1869) F B
Cartwright, G. C. to F. O. Penn 9-19-1865 G
Cartwright, Morgan to Bettie P. Halliburton 12-12-1871 L
Cartwright, Robert to Sarah Hamblin 4-7-1828 M
Cartwright, Timothy M. to Sallie W. McFerrin 11-7-1870 (11-10-1870) F
Cartwright, W. C. to Sarah Jane Brandon 4-1-1850 Ma
Cartwright, W. H. to L. A. Beckam 1-23-1864 G
Caruth, James to Rachael Swindle 9-1-1868 G
Caruth, Walter to Hanah E. Henry 12-23-1852 L
Caruthers, Dee to Daffne Walker 1-17-1868 F B
Caruthers, J. R. to Celia Ann Devault 9-11-1861 Mn
Caruthers, James H. to Fannie Hill 11-13-1858 (11-23-1858) Sh
Caruthers, James W. to Margaret A. Sharp 12-15-1856 (12-16-1856) Ma
Caruthers, John P. to Flora R. McNeil 7-29-1861 Sh
Caruthers, William J. to A. M. Bassham 7-27-1852 (7-26?-1852) O
Caruthers, William to Mary Jane Stoddert 6-6-1859 (6-7-1859) Ma
Caruthers, Willis to Katie Wade 7-14-1875 L
Carvan, Will to Lucinda Vails 1-1-1853 (1-2-1853) Hr

Carver, Franklin to Martha Abernathy 8-30-1855 Cr
Carver, James to Emaline Carver 2-18-1842 O
Carver, Robert T. to Matilda Valliant 12-10-1855 (12-12-1855) O
Carver, Sam B. to Julia E. Trapp 5-15-1862 (5-16-1862) Sh
Carver, W. G. to Linda Ann Eliza Steel 3-5-1870 (3-9-1870) Cr
Carver, W. H. to S. E. Smith 10-2-1871 O
Carvin, D. L. to Patsey Dove 11-3-1874 (11-4-1874) Dy
Carvin, J. H. to Caldonia White 2-24-1874 Hy
Cary, Geo. H. to M. J. Turner 10-29-1863 O
Cary, H. to Ella Rhea 5-1-1866 F
Cary, James to Elmira Wright 12-8-1849 (12-12-1849) O
Cary, James to Mary Vanatta 1-4-1849 O
Cary, James to Nancy Rushin 2-5-1851 (2-6-1851) O
Cary, John A. to Anna E. Sherrill 12-22-1874 (12-23-1874) T
Cary, Michael to Tabitha A. Watson 8-6-1843 Cr
Cary, Thomas to Elizabeth McLane 3-22-1847 Cr
Cary, William to Mary Vanatta 1-4-1849 (1-13-1849) O
Cary, Wm. to Caroline Hammett 12-10-1840 Cr
Case (Cash), F. M. to Elizabeth H. Drake 8-1-1850 Sh
Case, Alman to Mary A. Powell 8-6-1860 O
Case, Ezekiel to Margaret Nanny 7-14-1856 (7-15-1856) Ma
Case, Martin to Barbry Jackson 1-2-1845 Hr
Case, Mosses to Elizabeth Stafford 5-7-1863 We
Case, Thomas to Mary Jackson 6-24-1840 Hr
Case, William to Eliza Hubbard 12-5-1833 Sh
Case, Wm. H. to Lavina Chappell 5-16-1863 We
Casee, Mizo to Mary Brantly 2-16-1839 (2-23-1839) Hr
Caseldine, Leomiao to Amanda A. Yearwood 2-12-1863 Mn
Casey, G. W. to L. A. Forsyth 1-29-1871 Hy
Casey, Henry to Sarah Lovelace 12-25-1872 (12-26-1873?) L
Casey, Hiram D. to Ann Lax 5-21-1847 (5-23-1847) Hr
Casey, Jacob to Nancy Su. Mah. Eliz. Wynn 9-8-1867 Be
Casey, James A. to Margaret Honel 5-5-1829 Hr
Casey, James C. to Tennessee Casey 8-15-1870 (8-17-1870) Ma
Casey, James G. to Jane Harris 9-30-1861 (10-6-1861) Hr
Casey, James to Jane Savage 8-4-1829 Hr
Casey, John L. to Harriett Nunnelly 11-23-1836 (11-24-1836) Hr
Casey, John L. to Marilda Stewart 8-8-1844 Hr
Casey, John to Bridget Stephens 5-16-1864 Sh
Casey, John to Francis Houston 12-7-1843 Cr
Casey, John to Julia Spilman 2-1-1864 (2-2-1864) Sh
Casey, Joseph to Nancy Westbrook 7-16-1850 (7-21-1850) Hr
Casey, Lewis to Mary Burr 3-28-1863 Sh
Casey, Louis to Mary (Mrs.) Herney 5-3-1863? Sh
Casey, Michael to Catharine Ryan 7-11-1857 (7-12-1857) Sh
Casey, Michael to Elizabeth Carr 5-19-1860 (5-21-1860) Sh
Casey, R. D. to Cynthia G. Joyner 12-31-1857 (1-5-1858) Hr
Casey, Randolph to Gilly Dean 5-25-1828 (5-26-1828) Hr
Casey, S. W. to S. J. Holloway 10-18-1861 Hr
Casey, Solomon C. to Eliza Ann Hicks 9-8-1856 (9-11-1856) Hr
Casey, Thomas B. to Elizabeth R. Benson 10-11-1858 (10-13-1858) Ma
Casey, Timothy to Margaret Burke 1-28-1856 Sh
Casey, William L. to Mary E. Neal 1-11-1867 (1-15-1867) Ma
Casey, Zadoc to Amanda Foster 8-6-1841 Hr
Casey, lHiram to Sydney M. Hale 6-4-1861 (6-6-1861) Hr
Cash, Anderson to Martha Baker 2-29-1852 Hn
Cash, Benjamin to Mildred S. Dandrige 7-23-1838 (8-1-1838) Hr
Cash, Elkins to Ellen Evans 5-3-1845 (5-8-1845) F
Cash, G. B. to S. E. Pennel 12-7-1868 (12-9-1868) T
Cash, James L. to Mary J. Crain 6-24-1873 (6-26-1873) T
Cash, James to J. Emly Watt 8-24-1850 G
Cash, John J. to Julia A. Lyon 12-28-1859 Ma
Cash, Joseph H. to Italia A. Walsh 5-12-1859 Sh
Cash, Lorenza D. to Mary Wyatt 4-4-1843 (4-6-1843) Ma
Cash, Paul to Malinda Brown 4-26-1870 (4-30-1870) F B
Cash, T. to Maria Flannegan 8-8-1860 Sh
Cash, Thomas W. to Emily E. Outlaw 6-26-1840 (8-27-1840) O
Cash, W. D. to M. E. Pennel 1-21-1874 (1-24-1874) T
Cash, W. D. to S. E. Hunt 3-23-1869 (3-24-1869) T
Cash, Watt to Sarah Ann Stone 6-29-1850 (7-1-1850) Ma
Cash, William Lewis to Jarucia Ann Phallis 11-3-1853 G
Cashar, Martin F. to Mary E. Duberry 10-21-1849 G
Cashen, David to Susan Bergert 8-21-1859 (no return) We
Cashes, John to Jane Adams 5-21-1856 Cr
Cashien, Richard W. to Nancy Hampton 2-10-1842 O
Cashion, James L. to Minerva P. Hewlett 4-24-1855 (4-30-1855) O
Cashion, James P. to Nancy J. Nooner 11-9-1862 We
Cashion, Martin to Elizabeth A. Odle 3-24-1846 We
Cashon, James L. to Raussa Summers 2-13-1839 (2-21-1839) O
Cashon, Joseph Lell? to Delila Brann 9-11-1855 (no return) We
Caskins, Henry to Elizabeth E. Jones 7-29-1844 Ma
Caskins, James to Hellen Hindman 12-8-1861 T
Cason, Harrison E. to Elizabeth Moore 3-15-1858 (3-17-1858) O
Cason, William C. to Mary Jane Hamilton 6-26-1860 (6-27-1860) Ma
Cason, Willis to Lucy Williams 3-12-1883 (3-16-1883) L
Casoretti, John to Maria Solari 5-18-1860 (5-29-1860) Sh
Cass, Elijah to Caroline C. Alexander 12-29-1846 Ma

Cass, William to C. G. Patterson 12-31-1860 (1-1-1861) Sh
Cassan, Alexander to Margaret Williams 10-12-1867 T
Cassell, William to Elizabeth Montcreath 10-18-1852 (no return) F
Cassells, Jessee to Jane Craige 7-13-1846 (7-15-1846) G
Cassels, Henry C. to Martha Jane Boyd 1-7-1867 Ma
Cassels, J. B. to Arta M. Ford 2-18-1858 G
Cassels, James L. to Lucinda E. Fuqua 9-13-1848 (9-19-1848) G
Cassels, Thos. A. J. to Amanda Sanders 6-7-1851 G
Cassels, William H. to Polly A. N. E. Draper 8-24-1853 (8-25-1853) Ma
Cassian, Liston T. to Mary Newton 10-26-1836 (10-27-1836) O
Cassitt, F. D. to L. F. J. Malone 12-10-1844 Hr
Casson, John to Julia Armstrong 12-2-1833 Hr
Castagnere, Honore to Victorine Taylor 10-9-1854 Sh
Casteel, Pinckney A. to Elizabeth J. Allen 12-23-1866 Be
Castelaw, Benj. H. to May J. Singleton 10-22-1855 L
Castelbery, A. to Clara Iohe 5-5-1863 Sh
Castele (Castile), James M. to Mary J. Cole 9-23-1867 Be
Castell, Abram to Rachel Hays 8-2-1826 Hr
Castellaw, Alfred to Priscilla Fort 7-8-1833 Hr
Castello, W. D. to R. E. Taylor 11-27-1884 L
Castellow, I. F. to M. A. Blaydes 10-5-1865 Hy
Castellow, J. D. to Emily Thomas 6-15-1869 Hy
Castellow, J. E. to Mattie Coleman 10-25-1870 Hy
Castellow, T. J. to N. M. Johnson 8-16-1865 (no return) Hy
Castellowk, G. W. to Mollie E. Wateridge 11-25-1866 Hy
Castle, J. T. to M. L. Dodd 11-15-1862 (11-20-1862) O
Castle, Lyman C. to Sarah C. Bryan 12-5-1864 (12-6-1864) Sh
Castleberry, Stephen to Cathrine Moore 1-8-1867 (1-16-1867) F B
Castles, Green to Frances J. Holyfield 9-3-1846 (8?-3-1846) Ma
Castles, J. C. to E. W. McQuiston 12-12-1870 (12-15-1870) T
Castles, James to Harriet H. Welch 9-2-1828 (9-4-1828) G
Castles, John D. to L. A. Neel 10-19-1866 (10-23-1866) F
Castolow, James to Mary McDonnell 7-30-1860 G
Castor, W. W. to Sarah K. Rose 1-21-1861 (1-24-1861) Hr
Caswell, M. D. L. F. to Sarah Jane Cotton 5-13-1842 Sh
Caswell, T. to R. Williams 1-20-1842 Be
Cate, Atlas J. to Eliza F. Davidson 8-7-1866 (8-9-1866) Ma
Cate, Beverley F. to Elizabeth J. McCord? 9-30-1860 Hn
Cate, Charles L. to Amanda E. Peden 4-30-1844 Hn
Cate, Charles W. to Sarah Tyson 12-16-1845 (12-10?-1845) Ma
Cate, Daniel to Ann Peeples 1-13-1867 Hn B
Cate, J. H. to Mary E. Emerson 10-15-1865 Hn
Cate, James F. to Martha F. Hicks 12-26-1852 Hn
Cate, James H. to Mary Bragg 5-31-1841 (no return) Hn
Cate, Jesse C. to Lamira J. Hicks 12-2-1857 Hn
Cate, S. C. to Sarah Evans 8-22-1851 Cr
Cate, Simeon W. to Naomy E. Wilson 1-19-1858 Hn
Cate, Thomas F. to Clarissy Peel 11-16-1841 (no return) Hn
Cate, W. D. to Rebecca J. Hastings 10-10-1867 Hn
Cate, William to Martha Singleton 12-15-1852 Hn
Cate, William to Mary Barham 12-4-1866 Hn
Cate, William to Mary E. Wayson 11-30-1872 (12-4-1872) Dy
Cates, Anderson to Emily Peacock 8-5-1848 (8-13-1848) O
Cates, Anderson to Susan Box 12-8-1850 (12-15-1850) O
Cates, C. W. to Callie D. Ward 2-9-1885 (2-10-1885) L
Cates, Charles Franklin to Rebecca Alle Olds 7-27-1870 (7-28-1870) L
Cates, Columbus W. to Susan M. Olds 10-23-1877 L
Cates, Dolphin W. to Susan A. Campbell 9-12-1853 G
Cates, George S. to Margaret E. Myers 12-23-1873 T
Cates, J. W. to Z. M. Norvell 1-18-1872 Hy
Cates, John S. to Mary Lester 11-6-1845 Hn
Cates, John T. to M. J. Walker 1-4-1870 G
Cates, N. F. to E. F. Belton 4-1-1882 (4-5-1882) L
Cates, R. G. to M. A. Wainwright 7-12-1866 Hy
Cates, Riley to Patsey Avery 10-15-1867 G B
Cates, S. W. to Mary A. Fryar 11-5-1854 Hn
Cates, W. A. to Bettie E. Burk 7-20-1870 (no return) Hy
Cates, W. M. to Elizer A. Short 2-25-1869 G
Cates, William to E. S. Wilson 8-29-1871 (8-30-1871) T
Cates, William to Parthena Parrish 11-18-1839 Hr
Cates, Wm. M. to Genetha Ann Young 8-19-1846 We
Cathcart, F. N. to Sue M. Cokely 7-26-1870 G
Cathcart, W. T. to W. M. Cope 3-5-1879 (3-9-1879) Dy
Cather, Josiah to Cynthia Jones 12-25- 866 (12-26-1866) F B
Cathey, Alexander H. to Sarah J. Wats. n 2-9-1853 Ma
Cathey, G. L. to Sarah F. Neal 1-18-1855 We
Cathey, George T. to Sarah Dickinson 10-30-1856 O
Cathey, J. C. to M. A. Halford 2-16-1865 G
Cathey, J. H. L. to L. J. Smith 7-27-1871 (7-30-1871) O
Cathey, James W. to Alevy C. Gillaspie 2-23-1859 We
Cathey, Jas. A. to A. C. Purser 1-1-1874 O
Cathey, John A. to Narcissa Turnage 11-19-1835 Sh
Cathey, Joshua to Margarett Gilpin 8-5-1862 G
Cathey, Levett to Violett Reed 8-30-1866 G B
Cathey, Peter to Sarah Ann Crawford 9-17-1864 Sh
Cathey, Robert A. to Rebecca A. Exum 11-12-1856 Ma
Cathron, Wm. A. to Tabitha G. Wynne 2-20-1840 Sh

Cathy, John to Frances Zarman 12-27-1848 Sh
Cating, Barney to Hannah O. Gorman 1-14-1860 (1-15-1860) Sh
Catnar, Phillip to Mary M. Whitaker 11-14-1848 (11-16-1848) F
Cato, Robert H. to Phredonia Cross 12-23-1854 (12-24-1854) Sh
Caton, George a. to Mary Bohannon 8-15-1839 Hn
Caton, Henry to Fanny Fuller 2-15-1853 (2-17-1853) O
Caton, Henry to Mary Robbins 1-11-1868 G
Caton, James B. to July A. Matthews 10-2-1859 Cr
Caton, James to Marinda Shipman 11-10-1846 G
Caton, John M. to Nancy Biles 6-5-1849 Hn
Caton, Matthew D. to America Pybass 9-1-1868 G
Caton, Thos. A. to Sallie Dickson 2-17-1873 O
Caton, W. R. to S. J. Carter 2-16-1843 (no return) Hn
Caton, William to Rachael McNeeley 10-20-1857 (10-25-1857) O
Catron, John to Feddie Fraser 12-9-1868 F
Catron, William to Rebecca Catron 7-23-1870 (no return) F B
Catson, J. H. to Medora Ewing 3-28-1861 Sh
Cattrell, A. I. to Analiza Bene 8-18-1859 We
Caudele, S. C. to Mary E. Covington 11-27-1855 We
Caudell, J. B. to Jane (Mrs.) Riley 10-2-1867 O
Caudle, A. H. to L. B. Caldwell 10-14-1863 O
Caudle, A. H. to Sarah A. Orsburn 3-7-1865 O
Caudle, A. J. to Mary A. Cooper 8-1-1860 O
Caudle, James to Mary A. Portis 9-18-1840 Hn
Caudle, M. R. to Franky Wallis 11-8-1859 (11-10-1859) O
Caudle, W. H. to Nancy Shaver 1-11-1867 (1-17-1867) Cr
Caudle, William A. to Huldah Walace 11-18-1853 O
Caufman, M. D. to Alra Garrett 11-4-1884 (11-6-1884) L
Caughein, John C. to Mrs. Byrd 10-2-1869 T
Caughorn, W. to Susan Oar 8-6-1841 Be
Caulbreath, J. C. to Sarah J. Cockrill 4-11-1868 (4-12-1868) T
Causbey, Joseph to Elizabeth M. Drowup 12-7-1847 Hn
Causeby, John to Jane Norton 3-3-1825 Hr
Causey, John S. to Elizabeth Paul 11-22-1853 Hn
Causey, Wm. C. to Susan A. Fleshart 4-1-1843 Sh
Causler, Jas. C. W. to Sarah Ashworth 1-4-1869 (1-7-1869) Ma
Cave, Henry C. to Elizabeth Gilleland 11-10-1852 Hn
Cave, John to Martha Trousdale 2-24-1855 Hn
Cavenah, Wm. to Martha Miller 3-10-1852 Sh
Cavenar, J. W. to Amanda E. Clifton 12-26-1870 (12-27-1870) T
Cavender, J. M. to H. B. Nooner 1-31-1863 (12-24-1863?) We
Cavenness, James to Maryann Gaines 2-8-1840 (2-11-1840) F
Cavenor, William B. to Margaret E. Meeks 5-25-1853 (5-26-1853) Hr
Cavens, A. B. to Elizabeth Burton 12-22-1860 (12-24-1860) Hr
Caviness, Daniel H. to Eliza Jane Bailey 12-23-1851 (1-1-1852) Hr
Cavinor, J. B. to Elizabeth Ly_te 8-5-1874 (8-9-1874) L
Cavnes, Eli to A. Bridgewater 12-9-1869 (12-25-1869) F B
Cawbourn?, Hansell to Mariam Barrett 7-9-1839 (no return) F
Cawthon, E. W. to Mollie F. Croom 1-9-1866 (1-11-1866) Dy
Cawthon, J. L. to E. J. McCorkle 2-19-1877 (2-21-1877) Dy
Cawthon, John to Frances Jamerson 11-22-1866 Cr
Cawthon, William to Isabella F. Baldridge 12-30-1854 (1-1-1855) G
Cayce, Almon to Lavicey Wright 9-24-1855 (10-4-1855) O
Cayce, E. B. to J. E. McCulloch 4-23-1860 G
Cazort, Anthony Haywood to Rebecca Kerby 3-8-1848 (3-9-1848) Ma
Ceal, Sidney J. to Hannah M. Palmer 1-5-1854 Cr
Cearnall, E. M. to Malic K. Wilson 6-27-1869 Be
Cearnell, E. M. to Frances Gordon 7-20-1862 Be
Cenagan, Michael to Bridget Burn 6-23-1864 (6-24-1864) Sh
Center, John to Julia Springfield 3-19-1874 Hy
Center, Norah to Eliza Young 7-27-1873 Hy
Cerley, J. R. to Mariah (Mrs.) Warren 12-28-1872 (12-31-1872) Dy
Cerly, Jesse to Martha Davis 1-18-1849 Hr
Cerron, Sandy to Sindy Alison 10-16-1869 Hy
Cessel, James to Mary Ann Gidcum 8-25-1863 (no return) L
Cessna, William to Sarah McMahon 2-28-1837 Sh
Cester, E. A. Y. to D. T. Valentine 8-9-1865 Hn
Cesterson, Camel to Arina Bass 12-12-1832 (12-23-1832) Hr
Chaddick, James W. to Cyntha Mills 3-20-1837 (3-30-1837) Hr
Chadwick, Albertis to Elizabeth McGuire 7-16-1858 (no return) Hn
Chadwick, Iram to Martha Winberry 9-17-1870 (9-18-1870) Dy
Chaffin, D. L. to Sarah E. Stephens 1-30-1851 (1-31-1851) F
Chaffin, E. H. to L. A. White 2-9-1854 (no return) F
Chaffin, Harris to Charlotte Yancey 12-28-1868 F B
Chaffin, Harris to Keziah Battle 2-1-1871 (no return) F B
Chaffin, Haywood to Tillah Pettis 1-2-1873 F B
Chaffin, J. B. to Mary Jane Vaughn 11-30-1838 (no return) F
Chaffin, James to Bettie Bracken 2-13-1869 (2-16-1869) F B
Chaffin, Leonidas C. to Sallie J. Rives 12-20-1869 (12-21-1869) F
Chaffin, Talafaro B. to Jennet Riddle 12-27-1831 (12-29-1831) Hr
Chaill, James to Catharine Dunfey 1-25-1860 (1-29-1860) Sh
Chains, William B. to Nancy M. Roberts 2-12-1852 We
Chalk, G. D. to Febia Garrett 11-11-1872 (no return) L
Chalk, George D. to Ann M. Thomas no date (not executed) Hy
Chalk, George D. to Mary E. McLeod 12-23-1867 (12-25-1867) L
Chalk, John W. to Nellie Vowel 5-28-1872 (6-9-1872) L
Chalk, Napoleon B. to Siss Tipit 7-6-1862 We

Chamagne, G. R. to Sallie E. Jones 1-31-1860 (2-1-1860) Sh
Chamber, Daniel Webster to Maney Gracey 1-27-1866 T
Chamber, George to Susan Harper 10-16-1874 (10-17-1874) T
Chamberlain, C. A. to Melissa V. Davis 2-7-1859 Sh
Chamberlain, Charles D. to Sarah C. Cupp 10-9-1855 Ma
Chamberlain, D. M. to N. E. Farrer 3-10-1868 (no return) Dy
Chamberlain, Green T. to Frances J. Chamberlain 10-11-1858 Cr
Chamberlain, J. R. to Rosa P. McCombs 2-1-1877 Dy
Chamberlain, J. S. to Mary Walker 11-22-1877 Dy
Chamberlain, Jo to Lizzie Baxter 6-28-1871 (no return) Dy
Chamberlain, Lanson N. to Mary E. R. Camp 12-31-1855 Sh
Chamberlane, Charles to K. C. Murphy 3-5-1868 G
Chamberlin, A. G. to M. E. Haywood 7-11-1872 (7-13-1872) Cr
Chamberlin, A. M. to Jane Anderson 4-13-1837 O
Chamberlin, Alexander to Margaret Bailey 12-2-1863 (12-3-1863) Cr
Chamberlin, Alonzo M. to Margarett A. Henderson 4-14-1842 Ma
Chamberlin, C. F. to Margaret A. Alexander 12-24-1861 (12-25-1861) Sh
Chamberlin, Charles W. to Susan Chamberlin 1-13-1841 (1-14-1841) Ma
Chamberlin, Charles to Huldy Brinkley 12-27-1841 Ma
Chamberlin, Charles to Thera Harris 1-7-1847 (1-10-1847) Ma
Chamberlin, Ed to Parlee McCutchen 5-16-1872 Dy
Chamberlin, Has. to Mary Woodard 1-3-1842 Ma
Chamberlin, John to Elizabeth Stroud 4-7-1833 Ma
Chamberlin, John to Polly Hayes 8-18-1831 Sh
Chamberlin, W. A. J. to Lizzie White 2-4-1862 Sh
Chamberling, William D. to Polly Lane 9-5-1836 (9-8-1836) G
Chambers (Chalmers), E. G. to Annie M. Wever 7-3-1860 Sh
Chambers, A. B. to Louisiana Pitts 12-20-1842 (12-23-1842) L
Chambers, Albert to Isabella Cobb 8-10-1871 O
Chambers, B. F. to V. V. Martin 11-1-1871 (no return) Cr
Chambers, Benji. to Juatt? Edwards 9-22-1847 (9-16?-1847) F
Chambers, C. L. to Susan Amanda Atkins 7-4-1861 Mn
Chambers, C. S. to M. V. Rucker 12-20-1876 (12-21-1876) Dy
Chambers, Carroll to Nancy Moss 9-11-1845 We
Chambers, Edwin to Sylva Samuels 10-10-1868 T
Chambers, Elias to Sarah Atkinson 12-22-1866 (12-23-1866) F
Chambers, Francis to Milly F. Dean 12-26-1860 (no return) Hy
Chambers, G. W. to Fanny E. Ellis 7-23-1864 Sh
Chambers, Geo. to Jane Young 11-30-1872 (12-1-1872) T
Chambers, George W. to Amanda J. Thurmond 11-4-1874 L
Chambers, George W. to Amanda J. Walpole 1-22-1869 (2-1-1869) L
Chambers, Gloster to Palina Chambers 11-6-1869 (12-4-1869) F B
Chambers, Green B. to Margaret Edwards 5-26-1837 G
Chambers, Guss to Bettie Alexander 12-13-1873 (12-15-1873) T
Chambers, H. C. to M. J. Chambers 1-18-1843 Cr
Chambers, H. D. to A. E. Brewer 3-23-1868 (3-24-1868) O
Chambers, Henry to Mary Chambers 6-19-1869 G B
Chambers, Isham to Mattie Jinkens 12-30-1872 (1-2-1873) O
Chambers, J. G. to Mary F. Taylor 8-3-1859 F
Chambers, J. H. to Margaret Dickie 1-4-1868 (1-9-1868) L
Chambers, J. H. to Mattie Bethune 5-31-1876 (6-4-1876) L
Chambers, J. M. to A. R. Rucker 12-18-1872 (12-19-1872) Dy
Chambers, J. N. to D. F. Conklin 9-20-1879 (9-22-1879) Dy
Chambers, James H. to Martha J. _____ 8-26-1868 (no return) L
Chambers, James W. to Mollie E. Moore 8-24-1871 (8-26-1871) L
Chambers, James W. to Narcissa C. Espy 12-31-1839 (1-2-1840) L
Chambers, James W. to Sarah J. Gibson 1-22-1867 (1-23-1867) Dy
Chambers, James to Marthy Cobins 10-20-1867 Hy
Chambers, James to S. M. Warre 10-12-1868 (12-13-1868) Dy
Chambers, Jerry to Jane Coon 12-18-1874 Hy
Chambers, Joel M. to Mary J. Breechum 9-15-1857 Cr
Chambers, Joseph to Margaret Buckley 2-6-1855 Sh
Chambers, Josiah to Sarah P. Joyner 3-2-1863 (no return) Hy
Chambers, Josias M. to Sarah Caroline Walpole 12-29-1845 (1-1-1846) L
Chambers, M. L. to E. F. Wade 10-24-1859 (10-26-1859) L
Chambers, M. P. to M. A. Bowden 11-26-1878 (11-27-1879) L
Chambers, Madison H. to Martha Ann Laughn 12-8-1843 (no return) F
Chambers, Madison H. to Susan Crawley 9-1-1831 We
Chambers, R. F. to Elizabeth J. Adams 1-14-1867 (1-15-1867) L
Chambers, R. F. to Frances A. Thurmond 5-4-1868 (5-13-1868) L
Chambers, R. T. to Frances E. Davis 9-26-1866 (9-30-1866) Dy
Chambers, R. T. to Sallie R. Johnson 6-8-1878 (6-11-1878) Dy
Chambers, S. C. to Ann C. Allen 7-8-1858 O
Chambers, Samuel to Levina Anderson 11-20-1862 Mn
Chambers, Stephen to L. Vinson 9-21-1841 Cr
Chambers, T. J. to Louisa Polk 9-27-1858 (9-28-1858) Sh
Chambers, Thomas R. to Samella E. Raney 8-8-1876 (8-10-1876) T
Chambers, Thomas to Martha Mask 10-23-1846 (10-28-1846) Hr
Chambers, William to Ann Carter 1-22-1855 Sh
Chambers, Willis to Mollie Davis 11-12-1871 O
Chambers, Wm. B. to Lucy Ann Davis 2-20-1841 (2-25-1841) L
Chambers, Wm. B. to M. E. Espey 12-23-1843 (no return) L
Chambers, Wm. C. to M.J. Pinckley 2-2-1871 Cr
Chambers, Wm. G. to S. E. J. Glover 3-10-1863 (3-11-1863) O
Chambers, Wm. H. to Mary H. Royster 11-28-1849 Sh
Chambers, Wm. M. to Catharine Burrows 1-29-1855 (no return) F
Chambers, Wm. P. to Martha Spellings 10-13-1847 Cr

Chambers, Z. to Lucinda McAlpin 12-30-1862 Mn
Chambless, H. A. to P. C. Stewart 1-18-1870 Cr
Chambless, Hinton to Mary Jane Hurt 10-11-1869 (10-13-1869) Cr
Chambless, Seth H. to Winnie Brinkley 12-31-1840 Cr
Chamblin, T. S. to Ella Sweet 5-3-1870 Hy
Chambliss, Daniel R. to Sarah Ellen Overton 10-8-1849 (10-9-1849) Hr
Chambliss, John N. to Nancy M. Walker 6-4-1852 (6-6-1852) Hr
Chambliss, Orange to Ellen Lorance 1-10-1873 (no return) Cr
Chambliss, T. W. to C. J. Drinnon 6-3-1848 (6-4-1848) Hr
Chambliss, Thomas to Adelia C. Bell 9-7-1853 (9-8-1853) Hr
Chambliss, W. F. to P. T. Yancey 11-27-1866 F
Chambliss, W. L. to Henrietta M. King 5-23-1859 Sh
Chamlind-Chamberland, Wm. A. to Jane Castell 3-12-1860 (3-15-1860) Sh
Champ, Pleasant to Narissa Black 10-20-1853 (10-23-1853) L
Champee, P. R. to M. F. Mosely 1-27-1877 (1-29-1877) L
Champion, E. W. to Emeline Marshall 7-9-1868 F
Champion, Jack Thomas to Harriet A. Walls 3-10-1849 (3-13-1849) Hr
Champion, James to Minerva Oliver 11-11-1851 Hn
Champion, James to Parthena H. Champion(Anderson) 10-2-1833 Hr
Champion, Jourdan to Margaret Bucy 3-17-1843 Hn
Champion, Saml. E. to Allice E. Simms 3-4-1868 (3-5-1868) F
Champion, Saml. E. to Drucilla B. Witt 1-12-1871 F
Champion, W. C. to O. J. Alexander 10-22-1868 F
Champion, William to Catherine Robertson 11-25-1826 Hr
Chance, W. H. to Nannie Alexander 8-24-1870 (8-25-1870) Cr
Chandler, Archa B. to Elizabeth Niceler 6-22-1860 (no return) Cr
Chandler, Carroll A. to Mary E. Griggs 9-6-1859 (9-7-1859) L
Chandler, David to Mary M. Vaugh 10-23-1850 Cr
Chandler, E. M. to E. H. Ward (Word?) 9-30-1868 G
Chandler, Elhanon S. to Sophronia J. Steele 1-12-1853 L
Chandler, Eli C. to Hannah Irvine 6-5-1850 Ma
Chandler, G. E. to M. E. Walker 11-13-1874 (11-15-1874) O
Chandler, G. W. to Martha B. Scruggs 11-29-1869 G
Chandler, Gabriel to Elizabeth B. Gizzard 1-22-1855 (1-25-1855) Ma
Chandler, Ivy S. to Margaret Allgiar 12-6-1854 (12-7-1854) O
Chandler, Ivy to Sarah Ann Griggs 4-10-1844 (no return) L
Chandler, J. D. to Mary Stephens 8-11-1856 Cr
Chandler, Jabreal to Mary Putman 8-7-1854 Cr
Chandler, James A. to Mary A. N. Pace 7-27-1860 Cr
Chandler, James A. to Mary A. N. Pace 7-?-1861 (7-7-1860?) Cr
Chandler, James C. to Mary Maginis 11-22-1842 (11-23-1842) Ma
Chandler, James H. to Permelia Harpool 7-18-1846 (7-19-1846) O
Chandler, Jno. W. to Emily E. Guinn 3-14-1871 Ma
Chandler, John to Elizabeth W. Roach 5-4-1843 Cr
Chandler, John to Mary E. Turner 4-9-1866 (4-12-1866) Cr
Chandler, John to Minerva McNeil 9-8-1877 (no return) Dy
Chandler, John to Sarah Cockerham 5-21-1829 Sh
Chandler, L. C. to Jane Massey 4-17-1852 Cr
Chandler, Martin L. to Martha A. Holland 2-9-1869 (2-11-1869) Ma
Chandler, Miles P. to Helen Freeman 4-6-1847 Hn
Chandler, Miles P. to Mary J. Denny 10-18-1842 Ma
Chandler, O. L. to Mary McAlister 1-28-1857 G
Chandler, R. T. to Susan L. Foreman 1-21-1861 (1-23-1861) Hr
Chandler, Real J. to Mary A. E. Bibb 9-10-1850 (9-12-1850) L
Chandler, Richard to Lucy McMullen 1-31-1848 (2-1-1848) G
Chandler, Roy to Elizabeth Nelson 3-17-1842 Cr
Chandler, Ryland to Mary I. Wiggs 5-17-1838 Ma
Chandler, Saml. L. to Nancy Caroline Cloar 9-23-1857 O
Chandler, Stephen D. to Eliza A. Chilton 3-17-1869 (3-18-1869) Cr
Chandler, W. R. to L. E. Bibb 2-8-1876 (2-7?-1876) L
Chandler, William B. to Corilla Cooper 5-21-1849 Cr
Chandler, William Hutson to Mary Blount 8-15-1839 (8-15-1839) Hr
Chandler, William R. to Mary Thomas 7-21-1857 (7-2?-1857) Ma
Chandler, William to Eliza A. Birchett 9-24-1865 Mn
Chandler, Wm. F. to Martha Burney 7-21-1859 Hr
Chandler, Wm. to J. J. Perdice 8-7-1851 Cr
Chaney, C. C. to Mary E. Kelly 8-20-1862 G
Chaney, Charles to Lucy Kelly 1-3-1852 L
Chaney, D. S. to Mary L. Jones 11-27-1872 (11-28-1872) L
Chaney, Daniel to Ada Wright 12-20-1871 (12-21-1871) L B
Chaney, E. J. to Emma Jones 1-9-1878 (1-10-1878) L
Chaney, Ephraim to Caroline Cleaves 2-20-1869 (2-27-1869) F B
Chaney, Hesikaik to Bevy Bragdon 8-16-1853 Cr
Chaney, John N. to Fannie J. Hawkins 1-20-1870 Hy
Chaney, Joseph J. to Martha E. Arnold 10-16-1866 (10-17-1866) F
Chaney, N. H. to Susan Cheany 8-26-1865 (no return) Hy
Chaney, S. J. to M. A. Young 12-12-1850 Hn
Chaney, W. A. to Ann Verser 12-5-1857 (12-6-1857) T
Chany, F. W. to Sallie D. Hawkins 8-19-1863 (8-23-1863) L
Chapel, Asberry to Malvina E. Chipman 12-17-1838 (12-19-1838) O
Chapel, Benjamin to Eliza Ann Hall 7-17-1840 (7-19-1840) O
Chapel, James H. to Elizabeth Carter 10-16-1837 O
Chapell, S. W. to Living A. Chappell 1-25-1859 We
Chapman, Albartis to Matilda Gray 11-20-1828 Hr
Chapman, Alexander to Nancy Godlin 6-5-1846 (6-6-1846) Hr
Chapman, Bob to Sallie Haynes 11-25-1871 Hy
Chapman, C. A. (Dr.) to Bettie D. Wood 12-17-1866 (12-18-1866) Ma

Chapman, C. J. to N. J. Pryer 6-18-1868 O
Chapman, D. H. to Sarah G. Magivney 11-17-1864 Sh
Chapman, D. W. to Adaline Carpenter 8-28-1875 (8-29-1875) O
Chapman, David W. to Martha Ann Brown 8-16-1849 O
Chapman, Douglass to Cynthia Whitby (Whitley) 12-3-1846 Sh
Chapman, E. W. to Sarah C. Hawkins 9-13-1867 (no return) Dy
Chapman, Ed to Cate Jones 2-29-1868 G B
Chapman, Eli to Equilla Portis 3-1-1850 (3-3-1850) Hr
Chapman, Ervin to Ruth A. Halliburton 10-4-1867 Hy
Chapman, F. S. to V. L. Sinclair 3-8-1876 L
Chapman, Francis M. to Mary Ann Biggs 11-12-1842 (11-13-1842) T
Chapman, George J. to B. J. Norwood 4-7-1854 (no return) L
Chapman, George to Laura A. Currin 11-29-1856 Sh
Chapman, Harmon to Molinda Smith 11-7-1843 We
Chapman, J. B. to C. P. Bowers 11-10-1874 (11-11-1874) T
Chapman, J. G. to Nancy G. Coles 11-12-1845 Hn
Chapman, Jacob to Margarett E. McLaine 1-16-1855 (1-18-1855) G
Chapman, James C. to Mary Biebers 9-5-1845 (9-?-1845) Hr
Chapman, James P. to Ellen M. Johnson 11-3-1858 (11-4-1858) Sh
Chapman, Jessee R. to Nancy S. Sanders 5-8-1873 (5-14-1873) T
Chapman, John A. to Narcissa Carter 2-24-1869 T
Chapman, John David to Julia Ann Gardner 5-26-1879 (6-5-1879) L
Chapman, John H. to Mary Ann Ledbetter 9-14-1863 (9-15-1863) L
Chapman, Marion E. to Mary J. Bruce 11-3-1859 Hn
Chapman, Robert D. to Rebecca Hodges 10-6-1836 Hr
Chapman, T. O. to A. D. Deloach 1-31-1882 (2-?-1882) L
Chapman, Thomas M. to Nancy J. Brown 1-22-1856 Sh
Chapman, W. O. to Elizabeth A. Hutcherson 5-29-1861 G
Chapman, W. S. to Sarah E. Jordan 5-29-1861 G
Chapman, W. W. to Melinda Johnson 12-16-1878 (12-17-1879?) L
Chapman, William E. to Susie McMillen 12-20-1870 Dy
Chapman, William J. to Dicy Swades? 8-22-1842 Hn
Chapman, William to Maria Chapman 1-4-1847 Sh
Chapman, William to Martha Barrett 1-30-1862 G
Chapman, Williams to Caroline Todd 3-26-1850 Ma
Chapman, Willis to Texanna Mulherrin 12-22-1877 (no return) Hy
Chapman, Wm. N. to Nancy C. Shelton 4-24-1845 We
Chappel, Christopher to Ann Green 12-31-1838 (1-1-1839) Hr
Chappel, George W. to Mary A. (Mrs.) Wiseman 2-22-1870 Ma
Chappel, W. R. to Jacky N. Fowler 4-1-1855 (no return) We
Chappel, William M. to Angeline N. Swayne 7-20-1848 Hn
Chappell, Ancel to E. C. Carr 4-22-1865 (4-26-1865) O
Chappell, Asberry to Sarah J. Heatherington 5-25-1853 O
Chappell, Claudius E. to Mollie Hamerly 5-22-1867 Ma
Chappell, J. L. to N. J. Blair 1-6-1874 Dy
Chappell, Joel R. to A. W. Conger 9-23-1839 (9-24-1839) Ma
Chappell, John L. to Elmina Parrott 12-18-1838 Ma
Chappell, John P. to Patsy Davis 12-14-1839 (12-15-1839) Hr
Chappell, William H. to Elizabeth Smith 12-15-1855 (no return) Hn
Chappell, Wm. Thomas to Paralee Cole 4-11-1870 (4-5?-1870) Ma
Chapples, David M. to Mona J. Russell 9-7-1850 Cr
Charles, F. J. to Lucy Moorberry 11-19-1863 G
Charles, Joshua to Mary Jane Buie 2-26-1857 Hn
Charles, Needham to Amanda Scott 10-30-1861 (no return) Hn
Charles, T. J. to Mary A. J. Mooberry 12-24-1855 (no return) F
Charlton, A. B. to Nannie E. Hill 11-8-1859 We
Charlton, Edmond to Amanda F. Carr 10-18-1837 Sh
Charlton, John to Susan Adones 3-12-1828 G
Chase, James to Betsy Williams 2-7-1825 Sh
Chase, William to Mary Ann Joiner 10-3-1839 Sh
Chatham, George to Sarah Allmond 9-15-1849 Hn
Chatham, Jeptha to Mary Mackey 12-4-1842 Sh
Chatman, Columbus to Rissy Brown 3-29-1877 Hy
Chatten, Thomas to Fanny T. M y 7-7-1867 G
Chatten, Thomas to Mary Grant 8-7-1853 (9-8-1853) Ma
Cheairs, David B. to Eliz. Ann Wooley 11-30-1841 (12-1-1841) Hr
Cheairs, Joseph to Nancy Wilkerson? 11-7-1842 (no return) F
Cheairs, Nathaniel to Eliza Mask 3-7-1853 (3-10-1853) Hr
Cheairs, Wm. T. to P. Hitchcock 9-6-1847 Hr
Cheak, William to Elizabeth M. Rogers 1-30-1846 Hr
Cheaney, Ezra to Lucinda Jane Acuff 10-29-1859 L
Cheaney, Henry to Martha Witt 8-19-1865 (no return) Hy
Cheatham, D. F. to Mary Ann Stockdale 2-21-1856 Be
Cheatham, George W. to Mary E. Urbey 11-15-1860 (no return) We
Cheatham, Isaiah to Mary Davis 7-5-1858 Hn
Cheatham, J. J. to Mary Brewer 11-6-1862 Be
Cheatham, J. O. to Nancy J. Davis 3-24-1867 Hn
Cheatham, J. P. to Elizabeth Davis 4-30-1866 O
Cheatham, J. R. to Charlie Goss 10-13-1875 (10-14-1875) O
Cheatham, John A. to Jemima J. Smith 4-12-1860 Hn
Cheatham, Joseph to Elizabeth Simmons 1-11-1856 (1-12-1856) O
Cheatham, Robert B. to Nancy Smith 7-2-1857 Hn
Cheatham, Thomas to Elvira Hardy 8-8-1846 O
Cheek, Moses D. to Sarah Eliza McPherson 2-12-1844 Sh
Cheek, Boardmon R. to Tobitha E. Lloyed 2-10-1871 L
Cheek, Chris to Emily Housman 6-16-1884 (7-9-1884) L
Cheek, Chris to Manda Hardy 3-30-1876 (4-9-1876) L

Cheek, Christopher to Malinda A. Acuff 5-30-1874 (5-31-1874) L
Cheek, F. M. to M. T. Jones 10-13-1856 Hn
Cheek, Jacob to Sallie Calhoon 1-20-1866 (1-21-1866) T
Cheek, Jacob to Sallie Calhoun 1-20-1866 T
Cheek, John A. to Harriet Carr 1-8-1852 Sh
Cheek, M. C. to Susan B. Wilson 12-25-1849 Hn
Cheek, Thomas H. to Mary M. Reed 4-6-1859 Sh
Cheny, Robert A. to Sarah A. Farmer 9-18-1861 (9-20-1861) Dy
Cherry, A. J. to Rachael A. McCauly 12-17-1861 (no return) Hy
Cherry, Alfred to Harriet Taylor 12-2-1873 (no return) Hy
Cherry, C. W. to Anna M. Williamson 7-17-1849 (7-18-1849) F
Cherry, Calib to Emarilla Arnold 6-17-1876 (6-18-1876) O
Cherry, David A. to Eliza C. Knox 5-31-1854 (6?-1-1854) T
Cherry, Edward? James to Sarah Angeline Edwards 6-15-1857 (6-17-1857) O
Cherry, G. W. to Florence Albritton 1-5-1872 (1-7-1872) Dy
Cherry, G. W. to Miss A. S. Butler 7-18-1861 (7-19-1861) T
Cherry, George W. to Phillis Henly 12-20-1878 Hy
Cherry, Harrison to Ellen Morrow 12-26-1868 (12-?-1868) L
Cherry, Harry to Amanda Vaughn 1-17-1870 Hy
Cherry, Henry H. to Mary Ellen Parr 4-28-1877 (not executed) L
Cherry, Jeremiah to Sarah G. Buntin 11-6-1835 G
Cherry, John R. to Martha D. Stone 4-10-1849 F
Cherry, John Stanley to Analiza Floyd 5-13-1858 Be
Cherry, John T. to Martha Sarah Johnson 1-28-1858 Ma
Cherry, John to Hannah Adamson 9-10-1853 (9-11-1853) O
Cherry, John to Jane Roberts 12-17-1849 (1-8-1849?) G
Cherry, John to Mary Myers 4-1-1832 (4-5-1832) Hr
Cherry, L. C. to S. I. Coppedge 1-11-1875 (no return) Hy
Cherry, Lemuel L. to Susan R. Thompson 1-8-1859 (1-13-1859) Ma
Cherry, Lewis J. to Sarah J. Morris 5-28-1856 G
Cherry, Mauris Julien to Mary E. McBride 6-12-1863 Sh
Cherry, Miles to Edmonia Hays 7-23-1868 Hy
Cherry, R. W. to Cordela Barnett 12-14-1874 O
Cherry, Robert to Mariah Keller 2-21-1871 (2-22-1871) L
Cherry, W. B. to Sallie Darnell 1-20-1875 (1-21-1875) Hy
Cherry, W. H. to Caldonia Alsobrooks 7-25-1877 (8-2-1877) L
Cherry, W. P. to M. Burford 6-22-1875 (no return) Hy
Cherry, William J. to Elizabeth C. Dement 12-4-1852 G
Cherry, William S. to Elizabeth B. Reasons 8-30-1851 (8-31-1851) G
Cherry, William to Susan Mariah Oakes 9-10-1853 (9-11-1853) O
Chersey, John to Martha McNeill 11-9-1867 (no return) F B
Chesap, A. H. to Louisa J. Rust 3-1-1855 G
Cheshier, John to Nancy C. Fortune 11-28-1849 (11-29-1849) Hr
Cheshier, Johnathan to Ann E. Clements 2-15-1860 (2-16-1860) Hr
Cheshier, Washington D. to Rebecca Ann Pankey 8-31-1846 (9-1-1846) Hr
Cheshire, Hezekiah to Sarah J. McKinne 10-2-1854 (10-3-1854) Hr
Chester, Fil to Minerva Williamson 5-11-1868 (no return) F B
Chester, John to Apphia A. Taylor 10-24-1848 Ma
Chester, Robert H. to Mary J. Long 11-1-1853 Ma
Chester, Robert J. to Jane P. Donelson 1-22-1855 Sh
Chester, S. J. to Sallie Moore 11-21-1866 Hy
Chester, Samuel H. to Ella E. Ragland 6-18-1878 (no return) Hy
Chews, D. H. to Eliza Shaw 9-15-1853 Cr
Chilcott, J. R. to Caroline Koonce 12-31-1844 L
Chilcut, George to R. H. Gambol 2-1-1844 Be
Chilcut, James to Jane Ross 2-22-1851 (no return) Hn
Chilcut, Joseph W. to Sarah H. Robins 8-31-1859 (no return) Hn
Chilcut, W. F. to Frances Roberts 1-1-1856 (no return) Hn
Chilcut, W. F. to Sarah Jane Robbins 3-11-1865 (no return) Hn
Chilcutt, G. P. to M. W. Oliver 1-18-1848 Hn
Chilcutt, George W. to M. Wynn 7-8-1847 Hn
Chilcutt, Thomas J. to Mary Ann Shipley 9-3-1854 Hn
Childers, Alfred to Sarah Slayton 12-23-1867 Dy
Childers, Ezra to Ellinor Radford 4-1-1841 Hn
Childers, Jessee to Harrett Bledsoe 12-1-1848 (12-3-1848) G
Childers, Jno. M. to Mary Childers 12-28-1867 (no return) Dy
Childers, L. A. to Margaret E. Hawks 12-8-1845 Hn
Childers, S. C. to Mary P. Williams 8-11-1863 We
Childers, S. L. to Martha Ann Brown 3-24-1866 Hy
Childers, Sterling to Ausena Jenkins 10-24-1858 Hn
Childers, Thomas to Mary Melton 8-17-1848 Be
Childers, Thomas to Urilsa Young 3-6-1866 Hn
Childers, Zachariah D. to Sally Woods 4-24-1842 Hn
Childras, John to Eland McMillin 5-20-1830 (5-26-1830) G
Childres, ____ to Mary Davis 4-7-1863 Hn
Childress, A. B. to Mary W. Haley 11-20-1867 G
Childress, C. H. to S. M. Carson 12-9-1882 Hy
Childress, David to Sarah Buchanan 8-12-1841 O
Childress, Edward to Pattie Williamson 9-4-1879 (9-7-1879) Dy
Childress, Ellison to Sarah Simms 7-13-1829 Hr
Childress, Enoch B. to Mary R. Henndon 12-15-1873 L
Childress, George W. L. to Emily E. Hawks 10-28-1846 Hn
Childress, George W. to Sarah Johnson 8-30-1853 (no return) L
Childress, J. A. to Mary Wilson 8-20-1856 Be
Childress, J. M. to H. B. Reynolds 11-7-1881 (no return) L
Childress, J. S. to Josephine Gaiters 7-12-1882 L
Childress, J. W. to Cornelia Robertson 12-5-1882 (12-6-1882) L

Childress, J. W. to Mahala Jane Arwood 2-10-1873 L
Childress, James C. to Mary J. Hopkins 11-18-1849 Hn
Childress, James L. to Martha L.? Turner 12-16-1867 (12-18-1867) Cr
Childress, James T. to Mary C. Greer 6-30-1867 Be
Childress, James W. to Nancy J. Sorrels 7-25-1868 (7-26-1868) L
Childress, Jas. A. to Asa A. Coleman 1-3-1856 (SB 1857?) G
Childress, Jessie to Nancy Dillard 1-15-1829 Ma
Childress, John M. to Elizabeth Simpson 1-12-1871 Dy
Childress, John W. to Martha A. McCarter 5-15-1859 (6-16-1859) Hr
Childress, John to Ailsey Fitzgerald 1-1-1833 Sh
Childress, John to Willie Jane Privett 8-29-1869 G
Childress, L. A. to Martha B. Sanders 4-15-1865 (5-28-1865) T
Childress, N. G. to Mary D. Hawks 1-9-1845 Hn
Childress, Preston L. to Jane R. Panst 3-6-1841 (3-7-1841) Ma
Childress, Robert to Norra Cunningham 5-14-1863 Sh
Childress, S. H. to E. R. McKinley 2-27-1878 (2-28-1878) L
Childress, Stephen A. to Louisa J. McKinley 12-26-1855 (12-27-1855) L
Childress, Stephen P. to Mary J. Howard 1-8-1840 (1-9-1840) G
Childress, Stephen to Elizabeth Allen 2-29-1840 (3-3-1840) Hr
Childress, Thomas A. to Parmelia Moon 1-4-1849 Hn
Childress, Thomas A. to July Florence Cath. Baines (Barnes?) 3-19-1874 L
Childress, Thomas P. to Malissa J. Beazley 8-15-1867 Be
Childress, W. C. to Frances Herington 2-20-1860 G
Childress, W. O. to Mindie? Thompson 6-13-1879 (6-15-1879) Dy
Childress, W. R. to Mary F. Dennie 4-7-1883 (4-11-1883) L
Childress, Wesley to Barbery Riddick 10-2-1856 Be
Childress, Wesley to Mary Reddick 1-25-1867 Be
Childress, Will H. to Abigil Johnson 7-17-1856 (7-20-1856) Hr
Childress, William C. to Nancy Gateley 4-7-1856 (4-10-1856) Ma
Childress, William D. to Sarah L. Taylor 11-22-1850 (12-2-1850) G
Childress, William M. to Martha Ann Massey 3-30-1843 Sh
Childress, William to Lucinda Johnson 8-6-1847 (8-8-1847) Hr
Childress, William to Martha Baxter 3-31-1842 O
Childress, Wm. C. to Martha Kerby 12-18-1846 (12-19-1846) L
Childress, Wm. D. to N. E. Peeler 8-1-1861 Be
Childress, Wm. K. to Mary J. Thompson 1-18-1849 Sh
Childress, Z. F. to Amazon Brown 6-14-1856 (6-15-1856) L
Childs, C. V. to S. J. Garrett 12-28-1881 L
Childs, James H. to Mary Jane Bloodworth 11-28-1846 Be
Childs, Robert H. to Mary Bailey 1-29-1854 (1-19?-1854) Hr
Childs, Roland to Margarette M. Blair 8-16-1854 (8-17-1854) G
Childs, W. E. to Sarah H. Hinton 12-16-1884 (12-17-1884) L
Chiles, Henry B. to Arabella E. Mitchell 1-4-1851 (1-6-1851) F
Chiles, Henry C. to Mary E. Sanford 6-20-1861 O
Chiles, J. S. to Annie Van Wagnen? 5-13-1858 Sh
Chiles, J. T. to S. Miller 1-16-1868 O
Chiles, Silas M. to Permelia Hutchins 2-28-1838 F
Chiles, Williama to Octevy Simpson 1-30-1860 (1-31-1860) O
Chilsen, Henry to Virginia Grimes 12-26-1867 Hy
Chilton, Ceasar to Caroline Pearson 2-28-1883 L
Chilton, Cezar to Emily White 7-23-1870 Hy
Chilton, Granderson to Sarah E. Taylor 7-3-1878 (no return) Hy
Chilton, Henry to Violet David 10-8-1873 Hy
Chilton, James to Sallie Mabry 3-2-1870 Hy
Chilton, John C. to Minnie W. Henderson 7-22-1877 Hy
Chilton, John to Amanda Smith 1-10-1878 Hy
Chilton, Nat to Texanna Joyner 11-25-1875 (no return) Hy
Chilton, Samuel L. to Martha J. Smith 2-16-1870 Cr
Chilton, Solomon to Sarah Bell 12-31-1883 (1-1-1884) L
Chinesman, J. M. to Fanny Ellis 10-17-1866 Hn
Chipman, B. F. to Anna Shoemake 7-17-1879 L
Chipman, Frederick to Mary Ann Prendergrast 4-19-1852 (4-20-1853) Ma
Chipman, G. W. to Sarah E. Boothe 5-21-1864 (5-24-1864) O
Chipman, George to Bettie Witt 8-23-1862 L
Chipman, George to Francis Barnes 3-16-1861 (3-17-1861) O
Chipman, George to Mary Ann Jones 12-18-1852 Ma
Chipman, George, jr. to Mary Manning 9-7-1862 L
Chipman, Henry to Felicia Ann Wood 2-10-1872 (2-12-1872) L
Chipman, Henry to Sarah Hubbard 12-25-1882 (12-26-1882) L
Chipman, J. W. to Sarah E. Booth 5-21-1864 O
Chipman, Jo H. to Addie O'Steen 6-29-1881 L
Chipman, Joseph H. to Sarah A. Miller 8-30-1873 (8-31-1873) L
Chipman, T. J. to Amelia Pennington 11-24-1880 L
Chipman, Thomas J. to Nancy Tennessee Manning 9-27-1867 (9-19?-1867) L
Chipman, William R. to Angeline Maning 2-4-1867 (7-4-1867) L
Chisam, George to Nancy Roberts 12-4-1869 T
Chisem, William to Sarah Ditto 9-21-1870 L
Chisholm, J. M. to Sophronia Wilson 12-15-1884 (12-17-1884) L
Chisholm, Wm. R. to Eveline A. Meadows 3-2-1843 L
Chism, A. J. to Mary A. Grogan 3-10-1886 (3-11-1886) L
Chism, Clemmon C. to Sarah B. Job 7-9-1856 Sh
Chism, Elijah G. to Sarah Ledbetter 5-18-1842 L
Chism, George W. to Mary M. Meadows 6-4-1840 L
Chism, J. C. (or C. C.) to Eugene E. Chronister 1-22-1876 (1-24-1876) L
Chism, Jacob B. to Catharine M. Brookshire 11-23-1837 Sh
Chism, James W. to Mary Lockard 4-16-1853 (4-17-1853) L
Chism, John S. to Martha E. Ledbetter 9-29-1855 (9-30-1855) L

Chism, Moses B. to Nancy C. Lockard 9-16-1868 L
Chism, S. L. to Elinora T. Fields 9-23-1873 (9-24-1873) L
Chism, Thos. to Martha E. Coble 5-15-1861 L
Chism, Vann R. to Elizabeth Ann Dillingham 6-18-1836 Hr
Chism, W. R. to Mary C. Wells 8-14-1869 (8-15-1869) L
Chisty, Landon to Elizabeth Nelms 10-4-1856 Sh
Chisum, Henry T. to Jane Park 10-26-1829 Hr
Chisum, James L. to Caroline Henry 12-2-1867 Ma
Chisum, John D. to Mary R. Davis 12-24-1860 (12-27-1860) Hr
Chisum, John G. to Louisa Jane Purtle(Pirtle?) 6-3-1839 (6-6-1839) Hr
Chisum, John to Sarah Robinson 12-29-1834 Hr
Chisum, Thomas G. to Belinda Chisum 11-19-1829 Hr
Chisum, William W. to Mariah Olivia Caruthers 3-11-1867 Ma
Chisum, William to Caroline Vinson 1-3-1848 Ma
Chisum, William to Mary Ann Chisum 2-24-1828 Hr
Chitwood, Edmond to Rebecca A. Curtis 6-3-1868 (no return) Dy
Chitwood, Greenville to Elizabeth Anderson 9-19-1843 Sh
Chitwood, J. H. to S. A. Hendricks 11-27-1878 (11-28-1878) Dy
Chitwood, S. A. to M. A. Tatum 8-29-1866 (no return) Dy
Chitwood, S. H. to Emily Pursell 4-16-1867 (no return) Dy
Chitwood, William to Harriet Emeline Newberry 1-11-1862 (1-12-1862) Sh
Choat, Jno. W. to Permelia Moncreiff 9-19-1844 (9-20-1844) F
Choat, Layton to Frances Smith 12-22-1800 Sh
Choate, James to Nancy Cockran 1-2-1838 Sh
Chobell, Calvin to Sarah Frances Taylor 12-6-1867 G
Chowning, Tinsley to Julia Ann M. Taylor 5-11-1839 (6-12-1839) Hr
Chradick, Richard to Margarett S. Nobles 11-8-1849 (11-11-1849) G
Chrenshaw, Jacob to C. Donaldson 10-12-1870 G
Chrifield, D. F. to H. F. Garrett 5-6-1884 L
Chrisehall, John to Lucinda (Mrs.) Dove 1-30-1867 O
Chrisenberry, William A. to Catherine Wimberly 11-16-1865 Hn
Chrisenberry, William M. to Sarah S. Kirkland 10-7-1858 Hn
Chrisenberry, Wm. to Nancy Jenkins 6-18-1849 Hn
Chrisman, Anthony to Isadora Summers 5-1-1868 G B
Chrisman, F. H. to Mary H. Phillips 7-10-1848 L
Chrisman, J. L. to Mary E. Laster 10-31-1871 (11-3-1873?) Dy
Chrisman, T. W. to M. E. Bell 2-27-1877 Dy
Chrisp, Henry C. to Ida A. Wade 12-15-1869 G
Chrisp, J. J. (Dr.) to Addie J. Wilkins 5-8-1867 G
Chrisp, John W. to Elizabeth P. Mitchell 12-23-1847 (12-25-1847) Ma
Chrisp, S. G. to C. D. Simmons 4-30-1868 G
Christain, W. R. to Fannie E. Moore 11-20-1866 (11-23-1866) Cr
Christenberry, J. M. to Susan McLean 8-4-1862 G
Christenberry, W. _. to Betty Owensby 9-2-1870 G
Christenberry, Wm. to Susan Felts 10-31-1867 Hy
Christerbery, J. V. to Sallie Dill 2-7-1867 G
Christian, A. B. to H. R. Smith 6-24-1868 (6-25-1868) Cr
Christian, Frederick to Frances N. Robertson 10-13-1827 Sh
Christian, Gilbert T. to Sallie Snodgrass 4-9-1866 Ma
Christian, Harry B. to Mary America Moore 7-22-1839 (7-23-1839) Ma
Christian, J. B. to Mattie A. Wright 11-6-1866 G
Christian, James to Nancy Porter 7-16-1870 (5?-11?-1870) F B
Christian, John J. to Mary A. Vines 12-23-1848 Sh
Christian, John to E. P. Thomas 3-5-1838 Ma
Christian, Robt. N. to Valeria Shaw 7-28-1866 (8-?-1866) F
Christian, Thomas to Sarah B. Logan 8-25-1841 (8-26-1841) Ma
Christian, W. C. to L. A. Cawthan 12-1-1866 (no return) Cr
Christian, W. J. to Suphinia Grace 5-30-1869 G
Christian, William A. to Mary R. Sherman 1-15-1859 (1-20-1859) Ma
Christie, C. to Mary Ann Carlile 2-19-1867 O
Christie, W. O. to R. E. Reynolds 10-16-1877 Dy
Christie, Wm. H. to LeElla McNill 9-13-1866 Hy
Christmas, Ephraim to Elizabeth Hudson 8-5-1853 Sh
Christopher, Eli to Hariett R. Mosmon 4-2-1844 Be
Christopher, Eli to Lauretta J. Snider 5-31-1849 Be
Christopher, Henry to Bridget Carrol 10-5-1858 Sh
Christopher, Jessee to Mary Ann Ross 8-29-1860 Be
Christopher, John H. to Mary Ann M. Box 1-9-1866 Be
Christopher, John to Betsy Harlowe 3-2-1845 Hn
Christopher, Solomon to Isabella Snider 7-18-1850 Hn
Christopher, Westley to Nancy Avery 3-26-1851 Hn
Chromate, Thos. to Tersey E. Cox 10-27-1864 G
Chronister, Adam to Tinsey Garrison 1-5-1826 Hr
Chronister, T. P. to Nancy J. Stevenson 1-7-1868 Dy
Chronister, W. C. to Amelia Jones 10-17-1860 (10-8?-1860) Dy
Chronister, Wesley to Sarah Dodson 1-30-1866 (1-31-1866) Dy
Chub, John to Caroline Porter 7-3-1858 Sh B
Chumley, Bird to Rebecca Lax 9-26-1848 Hn
Chumley, W. H. to M. J. Teter 11-27-1865 (11-28-1865) O
Church, Geo. W. to Nannie Vick 9-5-1870 (9-11-1870) Dy
Church, James to Clara Rogers 4-2-1864 Sh
Church, R. J. to J. L. Vick 12-18-1867 G
Church, T. T. (F. F.)? (Dr.) to Mary Ann Sanders 9-10-1853 (9-11-1853) O
Churchill, Charles C. to Mary A Rivers 7-8-1857 (7-15-1857) T
Churchland, D. W. C. to I. Rosgarell Robinson 1-5-1857 Cr
Churchman, H. C. to Eugenie C. Robertson 12-16-1872 (12-17-1872) Dy
Churchman, H. L. to L. H. Oakley 7-31-1869 (8-1-1869) Dy

Churchman, J. R. to M. M. Baker 11-7-1865 (no return) Dy
Churchman, W. J. to E. J. Bell 2-2-1871 Dy
Churchwell, A. B. to P. A. Vickers 1-11-1849 Cr
Churchwell, James P. to Eliza Ann Davidson 5-17-1859 (5-19-1859) L
Churchwell, Jas. P. to Piecia Allen 5-10-1873 (5-11-1873) Cr
Churchwell, John E. to Frances K. Olive 3-12-1859 Hn
Churchwell, Robert to Louisa King 4-3-1856 Sh
Churchwell, Thomas G. to Ruth Pickard 3-12-1842 (3-13-1842) O
Churchwell, Wm. to Tissy Williams 8-29-1844 Cr
Cicallo, Paul B. to Helen Canapa (Cassapa?) 5-15-1854 (5-17-1854) Sh
Cically, James to Mary Collins 1-6-1857 (1-7-1857) Sh
Ciger, John to Julia A. Triggs 4-5-1856 We
Cirtis, William to Gillie Ann Humble 8-6-1866 (8-7-1866) L
Cissell, James to Jane Hines 4-30-1883 (5-1-1883) L
Citchins, Benjamin to Sarah A. M. Webb 10-18-1864 O
Claborn, Leonard A. to Sarah Jane Forest 3-7-1854 Be
Clabron, Mason to Damsel Harris 1-4-1868 Hy
Clabrun, Elias A. to Ellen P. Capps 1-14-1857 We
Clack, Henry C. to Susan E. Williams 1-1-1867 O
Clack, John B. to Jane Ayeres 12-9-1856 (12-10-1856) O
Clack, John B. to Mary Logan 6-22-1838 (6-23-1838) O
Clack, John to Tennessee Parkes 6-27-1863 (6-28-1863) O
Clack, Martin to Sarah Caffrey 2-21-1837 O
Clack, Peter S. to Sarah Green 8-23-1862 (8-24-1862) O
Clack, Peter S. to Susannah H. Logan 7-2-1839 O
Clack, Reynard to Louisa Carter 6-9-1847 O
Clack, Reynard to Lucinda B. Logan 7-1-1840 O
Claerben, W. C. to Mary J. Blackley 9-12-1854 We
Claiborn, C. L. to S. A. Light 12-30-1872 (12-31-1872) Dy
Claiborn, J. H. to C. A. Looney 4-21-1865 (no return) Cr
Claiborn, Jas. Henry to Amelia Vanclaire? Ryan 10-26-1852 T
Claiborn, Jesse M. to Elenor H. Markham 5-4-1859 T
Claiborn, Pat to Sarah Taylor 10-20-1865 Hy
Claiborne, Andy to Mary Bond 12-10-1870 Hy
Claiborne, Elias A. to Sarah Guthrie 1-11-1863 (no return) We
Claiborne, John A. to E. A. Taylor 12-18-1866 Hy
Claiborne, John C. to Mary Ann Green 2-21-1843 L
Claiborne, Philip R. K. to Mary Billingsley 1-18-1837 G
Claiborne, Robt. to Bettie Estis 12-15-1869 Hy
Claiborne, Thomas to Laura Ann Clark 9-24-1849 (10-4-1849) T
Claiborne, Wallace C. to Ellen N. Haskell 11-12-1853 Ma
Claiburne, Charles to Charlett Harrison 3-22-1869 T '
Claiburne, Harry to Emaline Bragg 9-11-1865 (9-14-1865) T
Clair, A. L. to Mary Jane Thomas 11-11-1852 Sh
Clampet, Victor to Martha J. Smith 10-17-1854 (no return) F
Clampet, William to Nancy Levesque 1-30-1839 (1-31-1839) F
Clampit, H. I. to Mary E. Riley 2-13-1849 Sh
Clampit, Samuel to Sarah E. Riley 1-16-1854 (1-18-1854) Sh
Clancy, Samuel C. to Rosalia Niederegger 1-18-1868 (1-19-1868) Cr
Clancy, T. J. to Fredonia Q. Belote 11-23-1857 Sh
Clanton, John J. to Susan T. Hicks 5-11-1870 (5-12-1870) Ma
Clanton, Josiah F. to Martha Deloach 9-6-1847 (9-9-1847) Ma
Clapp, Frederick B. to Amy M. Frost 3-2-1863 Sh
Clapp, Gilbert to Olia Campbell 1-4-1871 (2-14-1871) F B
Claridge, Alexander H. to Mary Jane Stephens 8-21-1854 Ma
Claridge, Henry B. to Rebecca J. Dyer 9-8-1853 Ma
Claridge, W. V. to Francis LeRoy 12-26-1863 (12-27-1863) Sh
Clark, A. F. to Angeline Ring 2-22-1861 (2-24-1861) O
Clark, A. S. to M. A. Boyett 1-30-1861 (1-31-1861) O
Clark, A. S. to Mary A. McRight 12-29-1862 O
Clark, A. V. to Mary E. Wilson 12-4-1866 Y
Clark, Adam to Margarett A. Vincent 11-25-1863 G
Clark, Alexander to Jane T. Mayfield 9-24-1850 (9-25-1850) G
Clark, Alexander to Martha B. Night 11-15-1866 Hy
Clark, Ambrose to Cinda Wyly 2-26-1867 Be
Clark, Andrew H. to Mary Ann Thompson 11-4-1871 (11-6-1871) Ma
Clark, Andrew J. to Sarah P. Lyle 4-15-1843 Hr
Clark, Asa S. to Elzada Nedry 12-30-1857 (12-31-1857) O
Clark, B. C. to Adline Griffin 4-2-1867 Cr
Clark, B. L. to Delia Elizabeth Calhon? 5-25-1872 T
Clark, Benjamin to Mary A. R. Willson 8-21-1851 Hn
Clark, Bob to Amanda Mulherin 6-13-1867 Dy
Clark, Bob to Matilda Shaw 1-1-1869 (no return) Hy
Clark, Bob to Susan Wynne 1-2-1879 Dy
Clark, Bowlen to Harriett Newbill 7-4-1870 (7-7-1870) Cr
Clark, C. C. to Bell Cameron 3-17-1868 Hy
Clark, C. N. to R. D. Wilson 4-12-18847 O
Clark, Cato to Sarah J. Bone 1-5-1870 G B
Clark, Charles to Missouri Jamison 1-8-1870 (1-9-1870) Cr
Clark, Christopher R. to Caroline Hynds 10-15-1846 We
Clark, Christopher T. to Hannah W. Wilson 9-2-1851 Hn
Clark, Christopher to Amanda Betts 6-4-1854 Hn
Clark, D. A. to Mollie R. Wolf 10-26-1858 Sh
Clark, D. C. to E. Hendrix 4-5-1865 (4-9-1865) O
Clark, D. C. to E. R. King 5-16-1865 (no return) Hy
Clark, David C. to Nora A. Young 11-22-1877 (11-25-1877) Dy
Clark, Edwin to Martha Childress 8-17-1852 Ma

Clark, Felix H. to Sarah Bradford 11-10-1869 (11-14-1869) Cr
Clark, Francis R. to Susan A. Lewis 12-2-1869 Hy
Clark, Geo. to Rose Benders 4-20-1872 Hy
Clark, George N. to Rody J. Hall 2-3-1873 (2-9-1873) L
Clark, George to Lucy Grigg 10-7-1865 Hy
Clark, Green to Tildy Roberson 7-5-1877 Hy
Clark, H. C. to Nannie D. Pyland 11-20-1883 (11-21-1883) L
Clark, Harrison to Elizabeth Williams 1-30-1841 (2-14-1841) Hr
Clark, Harvy S. to Cleopatra Robinson 9-16-1854 (10-19-1854) Hr
Clark, Henry E. to V. C. Gwyn 6-10-1857 Sh
Clark, Henry F. to Rhoda M. Rodgers 4-30-1870 (5-1-1870) Ma
Clark, Henry R. to Elizabeth R. L.____ 11-2-1865 G
Clark, Henry to Harriet Rhodes 12-20-1869 (12-22-1869) Cr
Clark, Henry to Jennie Rodner 9-26-1864 (9-27-1864) Sh
Clark, Henry to Molly Clark 12-18-1869 (12-23-1869) Cr
Clark, Isaac E. to Mary A. McCleary 9-30-1830 Ma
Clark, Isaac to Elizabeth Hart 12-27-1866 (12-13?-1866) T
Clark, Isaac to Lizzie Hart 12-29-1866 T
Clark, Isaac? to Rosa Clements 9-7-1872 (9-8-1872) T
Clark, J. J. to Amanda W. Yancey 11-19-1855 (11-22-1855) G
Clark, J. N. to Sarah E. Permenter 12-7-1871 Hy
Clark, J. P. to G. A. Hames 10-22-1874 Hy
Clark, J. P. to Martha S. Darby 11-3-1866 (11-5-1866) Cr
Clark, J. S. to Mary J. Stephens 11-14-1859 (no return) Hy
Clark, James H. to Seph W. Mathews 3-14-1866 G
Clark, James M. to Margaret B. Jones 12-4-1848 Cr
Clark, James R. to Elizabeth Lovin 6-24-1856 Sh
Clark, James S. to Nancy A.? Smith 2-6-1869 (2-10-1869) T
Clark, James W. to Mary E. Thomas 1-2-1866 (1-3-1867?) Ma
Clark, James to A. G. R. Bailey 11-19-1847 We
Clark, James to Ann B. Royster 1-31-1856 Sh
Clark, Jef to Eliza Joyner 4-27-1871 Hy
Clark, Jefferson to Elizabeth G. Samuel 11-24-1841 Ma
Clark, John A. to Hattie C. Moore 4-10-1867 G
Clark, John E. to Mary Jane Doake 1-25-1849 (1-30-1849) Ma
Clark, John H. to Malinda C. Prewitt 4-12-1860 Ma
Clark, John J. to Mary A. Morris 4-29-1851 Cr
Clark, John M. to Anna M. Porter 10-11-1853 Hn
Clark, John R. to Elizabeth May 2-13-1844 (2-15-1844) Ma
Clark, John R. to Malinda Sweeton 4-13-1832 (4-15-1832) Hr
Clark, John S. to Lucinday Ann Covington 11-2-1838 (11-4-1838) Hr
Claton, John W. to M. E. Wardlaw 11-24-1869 L
Clark, John Wesley to ____ Vanhook Darby 11-24-1842 (12-?-1842) T
Clark, John to Mahalia Curtis 1-23-1850 Sh
Clark, John to Smithy Burden 8-23-1853 (9-8-1853) Hr
Clark, John to Susan Lewis 4-6-1866 (no return) Hy
Clark, Joseph W. to Ann McFarland 7-24-1860 We
Clark, Joseph to Delila (Delile F.) Conrad 1-12-1847 Sh
Clark, Joseph to Louisa Witt 2-17-1848 Hn
Clark, Joshua D. to Sarah J. Brimage 7-3-1871 (7-6-1871) Cr
Clark, Joshua P. to Zerrah Lyons 4-17-1845 Cr
Clark, L. M. to Francis Jackson 11-25-1858 We
Clark, L. P. to Metilda Rosson 11-15-1860 G
Clark, L. W. to Miss Minerva Childress 11-4-1874 (11-8-1874) T
Clark, Lewis to Elizabeth Theraby (Pheraby) 6-14-1864 Sh
Clark, Lewis to Harriett Bomar 1-22-1873 (1-23-1873) Cr B
Clark, Logan to Amanda Richardson 3-2-1869 (3-3-1869) T
Clark, Louis R. to Sarah Johnson 11-18-1851 Cr
Clark, Malcum to L. Simmons 11-27-1867 G
Clark, Mary I. to Willis Overton 11-28-1842 Ma
Clark, Mitchell to Mollie Cunningham 12-5-1868 (12-6-1868) Cr
Clark, Moses C. to Mary A. Johnson 8-13-1846 (8-14-1846) F
Clark, Nelson to Frances Hammett 10-26-1861 (10-30-1861) Cr
Clark, Obediah to Helen W. Tylor 10-26-1848 O
Clark, P. T. to S. E. McClure 11-26-1853 Sh
Clark, R. H. to Fanny E. Scott 7-14-1868 G
Clark, R. R. to T. E. Richardson 5-3-1868 Hy
Clark, Richard G. to Mary H. Isler 7-1-1845 Cr
Clark, Richard P. to Martha L. Black 6-18-1862 (6-19-1862) L
Clark, Richd. to Patsey Whitelaw 11-30-1872 Hy
Clark, Robert T. to Martha J. Love 2-22-1848 Hn
Clark, Robert to Delia Bradberry 10-8-1870 Ma
Clark, Robert to Harriett Owen 12-19-1850 (no return) Hn
Clark, Robert to Jane Crockett 12-26-1840 (12-29-1840) G
Clark, Robert to Mary E. Smith 12-19-1863 (12-21-1863) Sh
Clark, Sam to Peggie Wardlaw 8-20-1885 (8-23-1885) L
Clark, Samuel C. to Cherrie C. Ellis 8-15-1870 G
Clark, Samuel P. to Sarah M. Shaw 9-3-1874 Hy
Clark, Silas S. to Frances G. McCullum 3-17-1841 Cr
Clark, Stuart to Lydia Taylor 12-22-1827 (12-23-1827) O
Clark, T. B. to N. A. Winbourn 1-17-1872 Hy
Clark, Thomas H. to Rachel Duncan 2-26-1846 Hn
Clark, Thomas L. to Artemissia Williams 9-8-1863 (no return) L
Clark, Thomas to Ellen Blythe 1-29-1866 Hn
Clark, Thomas to Frances Patterson 8-19-1845 Ma
Clark, Thomas to Lamira Ann Littlepage 12-8-1866 (12-16-1866) Ma
Clark, Thos. E. to Susan Patterson 4-26-1851 (4-30-1851) Sh

Clark, Thos. G. to Margier B. Rolyere? (Rogers?) 10-8-1838 (10-9-1838) F
Clark, W. A. to Madora L. Abernathy 12-13-1882 (12-14-1882) L
Clark, W. F. to N. H. Hutchinson 12-7-1859 (12-8-1859) O
Clark, W. G. to Elizabeth Powers 2-3-1851 Sh
Clark, W. H. to E. R. Neely 1-16-1871 (no return) Cr
Clark, W. to Rhody Forrest 11-23-1872 Hy
Clark, Wallace to Matilda Barret 2-4-1870 T
Clark, Wesley to Evaline Smith 12-30-1846 Sh
Clark, William D. to Kate L. Scurlock 5-24-1869 Ma
Clark, William F. to Malissa Jane Spencer 8-16-1866 Hn
Clark, William to Betsey Oliver 2-26-1856 (no return) Hn
Clark, William to Elizabeth Jane Whitehead 1-29-1839 F
Clark, William to Frances E. Warren 9-25-1867 (no return) Cr
Clark, William to Frances Harper 3-9-1850 Sh
Clark, William to Indiana Miller 1-20-1866 T
Clark, William to Jane Thompson 6-30-1866 (no return) F B
Clark, William to Lucy E. Stewart 9-26-1861 Mn
Clark, Winchester to Clora McNeal 9-20-1877 Hy
Clark, Wm. A. to Martha Wylie 9-28-1868 F
Clark, Wm. to Jennie Bowen 1-12-1870 (1-13-1870) Dy
Clark, jr., H. M. to Anna F. Anderson 9-11-1872 Hy
Clark, jr., T. L. to Margaret Davidson 11-1-1873 (11-2-1873) L
Clarke, Benj. F. L. to Harriet Thompson 2-13-1847 Hr
Clarke, E. to Mary Bledsoe 12-13-1866 G
Clarke, Geo. W. to Ester Dison 4-1-1871 (no return) Hy
Clarke, H. M. to Mary Irene Read 12-23-1839 (12-25-1839) Ma
Clarke, Henry C. to Mary Smith 5-25-1854 Sh
Clarke, Henry C. to Sarah Walker 3-21-1870 Hy
Clarke, J. W. to Sallie J. Hardison 1-26-1874 (1-27-1874) Dy
Clarke, James A. to Mary J. Tilghman 6-18-1856 Hn
Clarke, James to Louisa Alsobrook 3-12-1840 Ma
Clarke, John to Margaret Woodson 12-31-1869 Hy
Clarke, John to Martha Pritchett 3-30-1852 Sh
Clarke, Joshua to Mary E. Oliver 2-11-1858 Hn
Clarke, Julus to Jane Calhoun 12-30-1837 (12-31-1838) G
Clarke, Stuart to Lydia Taylor 12-22-1827 O
Clarke, Thompson C. to Nancy (Mary) Forester 8-20-1841 Sh
Clarke, V. D. to Helen W. Tyler 10-26-1848 O
Clarke, William to Louisa Smith 1-24-1863 (1-26-1863) Sh
Clarke, Wyatt to Theodosia (Theodora) White 1-23-1843 Sh
Clary (Cleary), W. to Johanna Meria 6-23-1845 Sh
Claton, J. D. to Polly Ann Edington 8-17-1865 Be
Claunch, William M. to Jane C. Gilmore 7-22-1844 (7-25-1844) F
Claunch?, Jerimiah S. to Harriet A. Hullum 4-24-1835 (4-27-1835) Hr
Claxton, Francis M. to Cary Ann Freeman 2-24-1857 Hr
Claxton, James A. to Elsworth Nelson 10-4-1865 (10-5-1865) F
Claxton, Jo. to Emily Gardner 4-9-1880 (no return) L
Claxton, John M. to Elmira Biddix 1-21-1867 O
Claxton, Lee to Mary Roberson 7-21-1880 L
Claxton, T.J. to A. M. Lemons 1-8-1866 T
Claxton, Wm. H. to Martha C. Stone 2-21-1859 (2-23-1859) G
Clay, A. I. to Any Bond 12-30-1876 Hy
Clay, Albert to Mary Harris 12-28-1870 (12-29-1870) T
Clay, Anthony to Laura Jones 1-20-1876 L
Clay, Austin to Eliza Campbell 11-9-1872 (11-10-1872) L
Clay, Charles to Minerva Lanningham 7-2-1873 (7-3-1873) Dy
Clay, Chas. to Hellen Sorrell 10-6-1864 (no return) Dy
Clay, E. H. to Sarah J. Sevier 4-10-1860 (no return) Hy
Clay, Elias to Mary Jayroe 3-7-1868 (3-8-1868) L B
Clay, George to Tilda McLemore 7-28-1870 Hy
Clay, Green B. to Mary Mizells 5-28-1851 (no return) L
Clay, Harry to Frances Halliburton 9-24-1870 (no return) L B
Clay, Harry to Mary Jane Sims 1-16-1877 (1-22-1877) L B
Clay, Harry to Piggy Turner 1-31-1872 (no return) L B
Clay, Henry to Amanda Currie 12-25-1865 Hy
Clay, Henry to Eliza Cartwright 12-20-1867 (no return) F B
Clay, Henry to Matilda Foster 10-8-1870 F B
Clay, Henry to Varna Jones 7-22-1871 (7-23-1871) Cr B
Clay, Hugh to Elen Gilliland 12-10-1873 (12-11-1873) L B
Clay, Hugh to Malinda Halliburton 10-8-1870 (10-9-1870) L
Clay, J. A. to Anna J. Cartwright 11-18-1867 (11-20-1867) F
Clay, J. A. to Roxey Sinthycorn 9-22-1869 Hy
Clay, J. H. to E. D. Craddoc 5-21-1873 (5-22-1873) Cr
Clay, J. H. to Mollie A. Sinthicum 12-24-1870 (no return) Hy
Clay, J. M. to Nancy T.(G?) (Mrs.) Tilman 2-27-1884 (2-28-1884) L
Clay, Jackson M. to Catherine P. Olds 6-10-1868 (no return) L
Clay, Jackson M. to Cynthia G. Guynn 12-14-1839 (12-15-1839) Hr
Clay, James R. to Frances M. Wheatley 5-16-1866 L
Clay, John H. to Mary E. Garrett 1-30-1868 Ma
Clay, John W. to Elizabeth Stanley 1-21-1861 (1-22-1861) L
Clay, John to Emaline Huggins 7-1-1865 (no return) L
Clay, Joseph Green to Jamima Olds 3-29-1873 (3-30-1873) L
Clay, Joseph to Narcissa H. Nelson 1-18-1854 L
Clay, Marcus to Margarett E. Turner 1-18-1859 (1-20-1859) G
Clay, Patrick to Coatney Byars 12-25-1870 Hy
Clay, Richard to Eliza Greer 4-19-1870 (4-20-1870) Cr
Clay, Richard to Ellen Campbell 5-15-1869 (5-22-1869) L

Clay, Sancho to Martha Patterson 9-21-1868 Cr
Clay, Simon to Becky Jones 12-26-1867 Hy
Clay, Squire to Arenar Dun 1-5-1870 (2-1-1870) F B
Clay, Willis to Jinny Clay 12-30-1865 (no return) Hy
Clay, Wm. to Jenny Clay 7-28-1866 Hy
Clayborn, Earnest to Ellen Capps 10-1-1854 Cr
Clayborn, Leonard A. to Sarah A. Capps 8-6-1858 Cr
Clayborn, Peter to Sarah Moody 5-4-1868 (no return) Hy
Claybrook, Allen to Amanda Briford 10-2-1868 (no return) Hy
Claybrook, Allen to Lucenda Greem 2-5-1869 Hy
Claybrook, Harry to Margaret Crichloe 12-11-1868 (no return) Hy
Claybrook, James to Lucinda A. Elam 12-12-1854 (12-15-1854) G
Claybrook, James to Susana R. Williams 6-7-1865 G
Claybrook, Jno. C. to Callie Walker 12-11-1869 (no return) Hy
Claybrook, Josiah L. to Elizabeth Jane McCollister 6-26-1849 (6-27-1849) G
Claybrook, Lewis to Ann Buck 4-5-1871 (no return) Hy
Claybrook, Peter to Lucy A. Blankinship 5-9-1866 G
Claybrook, Wm. to Eliza Buck 1-3-1878 Hy
Claybrooks, Peter to Rebecca (Mrs.) Estes 6-7-1841 (6-10-1841) G
Clayburn, Thomas to Harrit Clayburn 12-28-1868 Hy
Clayton, Alfred N. to Ann Maria Peters 9-10-1846 (10-16-1846) Hr
Clayton, Calvin to Winniford Jones 1-6-1842 Hr
Clayton, Dennis to Louisa J. Marcom 11-30-1860 Be
Clayton, F. M. to S. C. Naylor 12-1-1865 Mn
Clayton, G. W. to Mary M. Oneal 1-30-1863 Mn
Clayton, Henry to Louisa Williams 1-14-1869 (1-16-1869) F B
Clayton, Isham to Ellender J. Collins 7-18-1848 Hn
Clayton, J. C. to Marth E. Davis 10-21-1865 (10-25-1865) T
Clayton, J. F. to Amanda J. Cobb 5-2-1861 Mn
Clayton, James H. to H. T. Reeves 10-24-1855 (no return) F
Clayton, James H. to M. Alice Harris 3-6-1866 (3-7-1866) Ma
Clayton, James M. to Mary E. Barnes 10-19-1865 Mn
Clayton, James M. to Susan Bolan 1-3-1844 Sh
Clayton, Jesse to Martha Jane Isom 7-18-1860 Mn
Clayton, John A. to Cleopatria A. R. Han 10-18-1836 Sh
Clayton, John O. to Poilee Boyett 4-2-1866 (4-14-1866) O
Clayton, John T. to Zillie Isham 1-19-1857 Sh
Clayton, John to Jane Foster 1-10-1874 (1-11-1874) Dy
Clayton, John to Sarah Hutchens 11-11-1841 (no return) Hn
Clayton, Joseph A. to Amanda M. Pool 6-22-1847 Sh
Clayton, William to Eliza Whitfield 1-19-1854 Hn
Clayton, William to Elizabeth Floyd 12-28-1836 Hr
Clayton, William to Ellen Yarbrough 2-3-1871 F B
Clayton, Wm. L. to Mary E. Martin 3-1-1853 (no return) F
Clear, Robert to Clarissa Jones 1-13-1871 (no return) F B
Cleare, John to Julia Crockett 12-28-1870 (no return) F B
Cleaver, Albert to Charlotte Barnhart 7-29-1856 Cr
Cleaver, Daniel S. to Amanda A. M. Ward 3-20-1864 Hn
Cleaver, Frances M. to Malisha Shaw 12-25-1848 Cr
Cleaver, Frances M. to Sarah R. Sims 10-5-1854 Hn
Cleaver, W. W. to K. A. Trevathan 4-5-1854 (no return) Hn
Cleaver, Wesley W. to Mary C. Greer 12-31-1851 (no return) Hn
Cleaves, Clavin C. to Mary A. Strange 11-7-1844 Sh
Cleaves, George to Elizabeth Dolan 4-28-1852 G
Cleaves, Henry to Juda McDowell 1-6-1871 (1-16-1871) F B
Cleaves, James D. to Julia Sanderman? Bucy 5-11-1852 (no return) F
Cleaves, John D. to Sidney T.D.H.E. Mason 6-11-1852 (no return) F
Cleaves, William A. to Sarah R. Nevils 11-29-1843 L
Cleaves, William H. to Margarett Verser 3-8-1843 Ma
Cleavis, William to Martha Ann Mason 6-1-1842 (6-9-1842) Ma
Cleek, Jackson to Tempa N. Pyland 3-23-1868 Dy
Cleere, J. L. to Minerva Word 10-3-1854 (no return) F
Cleere, John to Liddie Dupree 12-26-1867 F B
Cleere, Mack to Malissa Jackson 2-12-1867 (2-14-1867) F B
Cleghorn, Robert G. to Mary Hanner 2-11-1833 Sh
Cleghorn, T. H. to Mary Hall 9-7-1840 Be
Clem, William to Sallie Morgan 12-28-1882 L
Clemens, Charles S. to Mary S. Moss 2-21-1860 We
Clemens, Clayborn to Millie Wills 10-29-1871 Hy
Clemens, Robt. S. to Martha A. Saddler 7-16-1860 Dy
Clement (Weakley Co), Thos. P. to Jane T. (Mrs.) Smith 3-16-1870 Ma
Clement, Abram to Mary Jane Dortch 9-14-1848 Hn
Clement, Anthony M. to Mary C. Patrick 11-1-1852 G
Clement, Anthony to Hanna Foster 12-30-1869 G B
Clement, Benjamin W. to Catherine E. Matthews 12-21-1858 (12-22-1858) Ma
Clement, Benjamin W. to Elizabeth W. Lock 6-21-1843 (6-22-1843) G
Clement, Calvin C. to Mary E. Lewis 7-10-1866 Ma
Clement, Edward R. to Mary A. T. McCullough 8-10-1859 Ma
Clement, Henry to Ann Eliza Artis 12-24-1868 G B
Clement, James to Anne Belle Strange 10-29-1874 G
Clement, James to Mary J. Stovall 12-9-1865 (12-13-1865) O
Clement, John M. to Anna J. M. Bingham 10-1-1863 Hn
Clement, Lenard to Rhody Ann Peete 6-1-1866 (6-2-1866) T
Clement, N. W. to A. M. Davidson 8-25-1853 (no return) Hn
Clement, Nathaniel C. to Nancy E. Bucy 1-1-1860 F
Clement, P. G. to Nancy Darlin 1-30-1855 We
Clement, Paul G. to Martha Goodman 1-11-1865 (no return) Dy

Clement, S. M. to Esther A. McDaniel 1-30-1868 Be
Clement, Stephen C. to Margaret Grayham 10-8-1862 Be
Clement, Stephen to Emily Shavers 1-22-1867 G
Clement, Stephen to Nancy Buchanon 9-10-1844 Be
Clement, Thos. to Adaline Davie 2-11-1873 O
Clement, W. G. to Elizabeth A. Arnold 10-28-1868 G
Clement, W. R. to Sarah J. Vancleave 12-23-1866 Hn
Clements (Gibson Co), Calvin C. to Mary A. Fly 11-10-1849 (11-13-1849) Ma
Clements, A. F. to Candis B. Herington 2-25-1845 (no return) We
Clements, A. J. to Susan L. Galbreath 4-4-1870 (4-5-1870) T
Clements, Abner to Caroline Galbreath 8-2-1858 (8-3-1858) T
Clements, Adam Dabney to Martha Ann Sherrod 5-3-1847 (5-6-1847) T
Clements, Asa to Nancy Elder 10-4-1841 (10-6-1841) F
Clements, Caleb R. to Barbia R. Patrick 7-15-1856 G
Clements, Charles A. to Ann Henry Williams 12-21-1847 (not executed) T
Clements, Claiborn to Winnie Bolton 10-4-1870 (10-8-1870) T
Clements, F. S. to America Catherine Bevill 8-26-1868 (8-27-1868) Ma
Clements, H. C. to I. F. Stovall 10-11-1865 O
Clements, Haywood to Minerva Henderson 12-28-1866 Hy
Clements, J. C. to Martha J. Mays 2-4-1862 Sh
Clements, J. C. to Mary A. Brown 2-8-1842 (no return) F
Clements, Jame J. to Nancy W. Smith 3-6-1871 (3-16-1871) T
Clements, James K. P. to M. T. Hart 8-31-1868 (9-3-1868) Cr
Clements, Jimion S. to Martha J. Locke 6-22-1847 T
Clements, L. J. to Jennie Applewhite 5-29-1878 Dy
Clements, Newton to Jennie Smith 6-21-1872 Hy
Clements, Paul to Alice Winford 8-31-1866 (9-13-1866) T
Clements, Saml. to Sarah Benton Dodson 8-9-1851 (8-10-1851) T
Clements, W. J. to Maria Cox 4-8-1858 (4-15-1858) Sh
Clements, William E. to Drucilla D. Drummons 12-19-1843 (12-21-1843) T
Clements, Wm. R. to Mary Jackson Hunt 9-9-1854 (9-14-1854) T
Clements, Worelson to Penelopee L. Driggers 12-1-1860 (12-25-1860) Cr
Clemmens, J. W. to S. A. Lawrence 9-16-1856 We
Clemment, Calvin C. to Mary E. Hamilton 12-9-1839 (12-10-1839) G
Clemmons, A. E. to Ella H. Thompson 10-24-1877 (no return) L
Clemmons, J. R. to M. A. Todd 12-29-1875 Dy
Clemmons, W. H. to Eliza J. Dudley 3-17-1874 Dy
Clemmont, Wm. H. to Mary A. Hail 12-26-1837 (1-17-1838) G
Clemomson, W. D. to Elizabeth Jackson 1-21-1858 T
Clemontine, Fredrick (Franch) to Jennie Ashmire 1-21-1873 (1-22-1873) L
Clenahan, Reubin to Susan Crowell 3-16-1873 Hy
Clendenin, J. F. to T. J. Wright 12-20-1865 Hn
Clendenin, James B. to Sallie A. Vancleave 10-30-1862 Hn
Clendenin, John to Nancy Ellinor 2-17-1839 Hn
Clendening, W. J. to Martha L. Love 2-4-1867 (2-5-1867) Dy
Cleveland, Handy to Laura Moore 6-21-1867 (6-22-1867) F B
Cleveland, John to Patsy Scott 10-27-1873 (no return) Hy
Cleveland, Wm. T. to Louiza J. (Mrs.) Clark 2-27-1864 (3-3-1864) Sh
Clever, Calvin to Margarette Swindle 5-15-1855 (5-16-1855) G
Clever, James to Lucy Manning 9-6-1849 Cr
Cliburn, Patrick H. to Elizabeth S. Epps 1-11-1833 (1-13-1833) Hr
Click, J. A. to Ellen Blakeley 3-18-1880 (no return) L
Click, Joseph to Lucretia Taylor 8-15-1855 Be
Click, Michael to Susan Cottingham 2-22-1853 Be
Click, Thomas to C. A. Linderman 1-10-1880 (1-11-1880) L
Click, William to Eliza Reddick 4-13-1847 Be
Click, William to Georgia Ann Bullen 7-29-1854 O
Clifford, Daniel to Bridget McGraw 4-8-1861 Sh
Clifford, George to Amanda Simons 7-21-1862 Mn
Clifford, Harvey F. to Sarah E. Romine 7-30-1874 (7-31-1874) L
Clifford, James to Mary McNerney 5-22-1856 (5-23-1856) Sh
Clifford, James to Sarah (Mrs.) Morrison 10-21-1858 Sh
Clifford, William to Emily Nobles 12-9-1847 Sh
Cliffordth?, Louis E. to Victoria Booth 7-4-1872 Hy
Clifft, B. A. to Sabella Prewett 2-19-1859 (2-22-1859) Hr
Clifft, Barnet to Alsey Allsup 1-23-1828 (1-24-1828) Hr
Clifft, Thomas J. to Lydia Ann Gay 2-11-1860 (2-13-1860) Hr
Clift, John W. to Clarissa M. Stanly 4-5-1832 Sh
Clift, Thos. J. to Mary Ann Barkley 4-4-1842 (4-7-1842) Hr
Clift, Willie to Temperance A. Sherron 11-30-1854 Hr
Clifto, Edward V. to V. L. Corbett 6-30-1868 (7-2-1868) O
Clifton, Daniel to Mary A. E. Mosley 2-12-1834 Sh
Clifton, J. D. to Nancy House 9-1-1851 (9-4-1851) Hr
Clifton, J. E. to V. E. Moore 11-17-1875 L
Clifton, J. H. to Mary C. Harris 5-15-1875 (5-16-1875) L
Clifton, John to Hannah Strothers 12-23-1841 (12-30-1841) Hr
Clifton, John to May Webb 9-28-1858 (10-7-1858) Hr
Clifton, Lemuel K. to Sarah J. Lyon 11-6-1845 Ma
Clifton, Ridley to Elizabeth Harris 4-11-1846 (no return) F
Clifton, Ridley to Mary O. Robertson 4-30-1860 T
Clifton, Thomas B. to Adaline Cupp 1-1-1855 (1-5-1855) Hr
Clifton, William Thos. to Araminta Catha 1-24-1847 Sh
Clifton, William to Mary Draper 9-22-1828 Ma
Climer, Carrol to Mary E. Vandygriff 1-22-1853 (1-30-1853) Hr
Climer, John W. to Gracy Simpson 11-27-1843 Hw
Climer, Milton to Barbara A. Oliver 12-22-1854 (12-25-1854) Ma
Clinard, Alexander to Arcenia Reddick 4-5-1860 (4-6-1860) Ma

Cline, Dennis to Allice Goode 1-5-1869 (1-6-1869) F B
Cline, Henry to Martha Wilson 8-13-1862 Mn
Cline, Jacob Daniel to Sarah Cline 3-30-1841 Ma
Cline, John to Nancy Bryant 7-11-1872 O
Cline, Marcus H. to Emoline Mitchell 9-14-1839 (9-15-1839) Ma
Clinton, Alex. M. to Mildred Rigsbey 2-6-1877 Hy
Clinton, David to Rebecca McKearly 6-11-1833 (6-13-1833) Hr
Clinton, John to Emily Barclay 8-7-1861 (no return) Hy
Clinton, Robert to Sarah Coonrod 3-8-1826 (3-9-1826) Hr
Clinton, William S. to Sarah Ann Coates 1-22-1850 Hr
Clinton, Wilson to Josie White 2-17-1876 (no return) Hy
Cload, J. H. to Elizabeth Stribling 1-5-1853 Cr
Cloar, Absolem to Susan Hubert 5-31-1834 O
Cloar, Green to Sarah J. Looney 1-31-1851 Hn
Cloar, John E. to Martha F. Glover 9-11-1865 (9-13-1865) O
Cloar, John to M. N. Butry? 7-22-1866 G
Cloar, John to Mary C. Cunningham 9-11-1865 (9-13-1865) O
Cloar, John to Matilda Hubert 8-13-1836 O
Cloar, T. C. to O. L. Glover 6-22-1865 O
Cloar, Thomas A. (J.) to Amanda Acock 1-31-1846 Sh
Cloar, William to Caroline J. E. Hubbard 12-24-1839 Sh
Cloar, Wm. to Nancy Lone 10-6-1845 We
Cloe, John to Penina Daniel 2-6-1844 Sh
Cloid, Newton F. to Mary L. Argo 1-17-1870 Cr
Clois, F. J. to C. V. Overby 10-31-1866 (no return) Hn
Clopton, J. P. to B. C. Brown? 2-12-1868 (2-13-1868) Cr
Clopton, R. A. to Margarett Guffee 3-4-1868 (3-15-1868) Cr
Clore?, Franklin to Elizabeth Byars 5-30-1864 (no return) Hn
Clouch, D. W. to Mary J. Kemp 2-24-1862 Mn
Cloud, Jason to Elizabeth Adams 1-2-1830 Hr
Cloud, Joseph F. to Jane M. Vaughn 1-22-1832 Hr
Cloud, Joseph to Elizabeth Short 2-24-1836 Hr
Cloud, Robert Evans to Angeline J. Mounts 1-17-1843 (not executed) T
Cloud, Samuel to Lucy Jane Underwood 5-13-1858 Ma
Clough, James C. to Mariah Burton 8-4-1846 Hn
Clowney, Samuel C. to Prudence Means 12-18-1835 Sh
Cloyd, Carey H. to Margaret Dunnegin 3-30-1857 (4-2-1857) O
Cloyd, John to Eliza A. (Mrs.) Murry 11-26-1855 (no return) F
Cloyd, S. P. to Elyna Kirby 1-21-1856 Cr
Cloyed, David P. to Eliza Hope 4-21-1841 F
Cloys, B. F. to Roxanna Miller 2-13-1851 O
Cloys, Charles P. to Mary W. Byrn 5-6-1850 (5-8-1850) O
Cloys, Hiram O. to Parmelia Ann Jones 9-15-1858 Hn
Cloys, M. C. to Mariah M. Roper 6-27-1858 O
Cloyse, Henry C. to Elizabeth Key 1-2-1846 Hn
Clutts, Lawson A. to F. J. Jenning 9-18-1846 We
Clyatt, Peter to Nancy A. Bell 7-10-1879 (7-16-1879) L
Clyne, Hiram to Elizabeth Miller 3-13-1843 Hr
Clyne, Matthew to Margaret Carrick 4-4-1853 Sh
Coachman, Robert to Ada Partee 7-8-1880 (no return) L B
Coachman, Robt. to Harriet Rice 6-28-1867 T
Coaker, Reding T. to Martha Crihfield 7-15-1865 (7-16-1865) L
Coakley, Allen to Frances Proctor 8-3-1867 G B
Coal, Wm. to Sarah Ann Spead 6-6-1846 (no return) We
Coalman, L. T. to Anne E. Smith 11-24-1871 Hy
Coalman?, Robert to June Mathis 5-7-1864 (no return) Hn
Coapland, N. W. to Isabella D. Kerr no dates (with Jun 1838) F
Coates, Caswell to Mary Allen 12-27-1841 (12-30-1841) Hr
Coates, Edward to Eliza H. Hart 9-13-1852 (no return) F
Coates, J. B. to Mary M. Roe 11-18-1871 (11-21-1871) T
Coates, J. H. to A. E. Roe 7-21-1871 (7-26-1871) T
Coates, James S. to Elizabeth Mooring 11-9-1852 (11-11-1852) Ma
Coates, James to Sarah P. Crook 2-22-1845 (2-26-1845) L
Coates, John to Adaline Coffey 10-31-1846 (11-11-1846) Hr
Coates, John to Eliza Jane Neely 2-26-1857 Ma
Coates, John to Mary Ann Jernigin 9-8-1847 (9-19-1847) Hr
Coates, John to Nancy C. Johnson 2-20-1839 Hr
Coates, John to Salina Boswell 4-21-1845 F
Coates, Thompson C. to Amanda S. M. Luggett 12-17-1845 Hr
Coates, William to N. E. Lile 7-13-1846 Hr
Coates, William M. to Elizabeth Sharp 7-24-1848 G
Coats, Alan to Elizabeth Boswell 12-24-1843 (12-26-1843) T
Coats, Berry to Gilly Eglentine Coats 11-1-1850 (11-3-1850) T
Coats, Boston to Kysiah Somervill 7-2-1866 T
Coats, Felty to Frances Jane Boswell 9-18-1845 T
Coats, Geo. Gideon to Frances America Harrison 9-2-1846 (9-3-1846) T
Coats, George to Martha Peeler 1-23-1866 T
Coats, Henry to Charlotte Frances Bibb 2-23-1847 T
Coats, Henry to Martha Coats 10-4-1845 (10-15-1845) T
Coats, Hillary to Sarah Ables 2-26-1858 (no return) L
Coats, James to Charlotte Hytower 1-24-1860 (1-26-1860) T
Coats, James to Sarah Askew? 2-26-1858 (no return) L
Coats, John to Mary E. Jayne 6-21-1849 Ma
Coats, John to Susan E. (Mrs.) Nipper 1-12-1867 (1-13-1867) Ma
Coats, Milton A. to Jerusha Ann Jane McGuice 11-7-1857 (11-10-1857) T
Coats, Newt to Scyntha Woods 1-15-1866 T
Coats, R. H. to Caroline Rigsby 12-9-1858 We

Coats, Solomon to Sarah Ann Oliver 12-8-1853 T
Coats, Thomas W. to Susan Jane Campbell 8-24-1841 (8-26-1841) T
Coats, William C. to Ella V. Moore 1-7-1867 (1-8-1866?) Ma
Coats, Wilson Wm. to Mary Cathrine Oliver 3-18-1854 (3-19-1854) T
Cobb(s), William to Mary Wilborn 2-13-1849 (2-21-1849) O
Cobb, Alfred to Sallie Ross 3-2-1867 (not endorsed) F B
Cobb, Barnett to Eliza Williams 12-29-1871 O
Cobb, Benjamin to Eliza Eggleston 3-10-1882 (3-12-1882) L
Cobb, Benjamin to Jenny Stokes 5-25-1841 (5-27-1841) T
Cobb, Charles to Flora Batchelor 1-15-1874 Hy
Cobb, Elis to Sisley King 12-16-1856 Cr
Cobb, Henry to Margaret E. Bragg 11-11-1844 T
Cobb, Hesekiah to Eliza J. P. Angus 11-2-1857 (11-3-1857) T
Cobb, Hezekiah to Lucy A. Halley 11-20-1849 Sh
Cobb, Hezekiah to Mary Ann Hatcher 11-22-1845 Sh
Cobb, Humphrey to H. T. Payne 11-26-1828 (no return) Sh
Cobb, J. D. to R. C. H. Hon 7-4-1869 Hy
Cobb, J. P. A. to C. A. White 6-21-1862 Mn
Cobb, J. T. to Sarah Cardwell 2-3-1863 Mn
Cobb, J. W. to M. C. Phelan? 12-13-1858 Sh
Cobb, Jackson D. C. to Ann Eliza Kirk 1-30-1861 Dy
Cobb, Jacob to Martha Fumbanks? 8-8-1860 (8-9-1860) Dy
Cobb, James M. to Mary Thom 10-23-1842 (10-25-1842) Ma
Cobb, Jas. E. to Emily E. Wallace 12-25-1873 Hy
Cobb, Jesse B. to Lucy Ann Jones 12-22-1847 (12-28-1847) Hr
Cobb, John H. to Agethy White 12-25-1873 Hy
Cobb, John to Rebecca Bell 9-4-1866 (9-15-1866) T
Cobb, John B. to Mary Ann Guthrie 5-27-1862 Ma
Cobb, Marion to Elizar O. Slaton no date (8-22-1869) Cr
Cobb, R. H. to Sarah Carman 1-27-1863 Mn
Cobb, R. T. to M. B. Worrell 11-9-1870 (11-10-1870) F
Cobb, S. A. to Elizabeth White 12-24-1864 (no return) Hy
Cobb, Therm B. to Delia Cobb 9-22-1825 Sh
Cobb, Thomas D. to Addie Johnston 12-10-1867 L
Cobb, W. C. to Emma J. Steele 8-12-1877 Hy
Cobb, W. T. to E. T. Outlaw 1-25-1866 Hy
Cobb, William C. to Ruth R. Cunningham 5-21-1866 (5-23-1866) L
Cobb, William H. to Nancy J. Edwards 3-27-1851 (4-13-1851) O
Cobb, William H. to Nancy A. Edwards 3-27-1851 (4-14-1851) O
Cobb, William to Jane E. Payne 12-17-1829 Sh
Cobb, William to Martha Jane Hammet 9-20-1852 O
Cobb, William to Mary Blake 5-13-1834 Sh
Cobb, William to Mary Wilborn 2-13-1849 O
Cobb, Wm. to Susan A. Grooms 9-27-1870 (10-16-1870) Cr
Cobb, Wylie to Nancy Whitley 6-25-1856 O
Cobbs, Edwin H. to Lucy H. Young 12-15-1845 (no return) F
Cobbs, Jas. H. to Mary T. Tanner 4-11-1850 F
Cobbs, Wm. to Callie Nelson 2-16-1867 F B
Cobel, Thomas J. to Susan (Mrs.) Williams 9-7-1867 (9-10-1867) Ma
Cobern, Abraham to Maria Cross 12-21-1868 (no return) F B
Cobern, Stanley D. to Eliza J. Baily 3-18-1866 Hy
Cobert, Daniel to Raines Atkins 3-13-1875 O
Coble, Hezekiah to Martha L. Owenby? 9-20-1866 (10-3-1866) Cr
Coble, James to Caroline (Mrs.) Crumpton 11-26-1862 (11-27-1862) Sh
Cobourn, James to Irene Turley 2-24-1857 (2-25-1857) Ma
Coburn, Henry G. to Mary Ann Lovell 8-30-1853 Sh
Coburn, James L. to Margaret Bradford 7-5-1855 Hr
Coburn, Wm. H. to Margaret A. Doyle 3-20-1861 Hr
Cochran, David to Martha Bradley 2-28-1846 Hn
Cochran, Dennis to Alpha T. Johnson 10-19-1844 We
Cochran, J. P. to Julia Shawn 1-14-1857 We
Cochran, John B. to Sarah L. Thomas 7-19-1844 (no return) We
Cochran, M. P. G. to F. E. White 10-26-1870 Hy
Cochran, Marcus E. to Sophia E. Leake 9-25-1849 Sh
Cochran, Michael to L. C. Ellis 4-19-1862 O
Cochran, Michael to L. C. Ellis 8-19-1862 (8-20-1862) O
Cochran, Peter to Laura Wilson 6-11-1868 (6-12-1868) O B
Cochran, R. L. to Anna E. Gates 10-27-1875 (no return) Hy
Cochran, S. W. to Ruth D. (Mrs.) Clark 9-12-1861 O
Cochran, Samuel S. to Calta E. J. Pope 1-15-1862 We
Cochran, Samuel W. to Caroline Cate 7-16-1860 Hn
Cochran, W. W. to Augustine Neal 12-27-1871 (12-28-1871) Dy
Cochran, William L. to Wincey (Nancy) Ann Boyett 1-28-1854 (1-29-1854) O
Cochrill, J. L. to Adaline Tate 1-30-1877 (1-31-1877) Dy
Cochron, Wm. E. to Eugenia A. White 12-19-1871 (no return) Hy
Cochrum, John A. to Mary E. Humphreys 1-12-1858 Hn
Cochrum, W. A. to Harriet J. Cochram 4-12-1866 Hn
Cochrum, William to Eliza A. Hunter 3-2-1845 Hn
Cock, Caswell C. to Mary M. Goodrick 11-4-1857 (11-5-1857) Ma
Cock, Edward to Harriett May 12-9-1858 Ma
Cock, James T. to Mary A. Kelton 1-29-1855 (1-30-1855) G
Cock, John L. to Mary Jane Shumate 2-26-1857 Ma
Cock, John R. to Amanda C. Trout 4-12-1867 G
Cock, John to Sirena Moore 12-18-1844 (12-19-1844) G
Cock, M. T. to Mary Ann Kelton 9-21-1852 (9-22-1852) Ma
Cock, Singleton to Pegy Dickson 7-11-1827 (7-17-1827) G
Cock, Thomas A. to Julia A. E. King 5-14-1849 (5-15-1849) Ma

Cocke, B. J. W. to L. V. Carpenter 9-17-1860 F
Cocke, Bowler to Mary E. Haralson 9-1-1842 Sh
Cocke, George W. to Laura A. Boon 1-15-1856 Ma
Cocke, H. C. to Bettie A. Marlar 5-11-1867 (no return) F
Cocke, Hal to Patience Jones 11-16-1869 (11-18-1869) F B
Cocke, Harmon to Celia Tudor 12-28-1829 (12-31-1829) Hr
Cocke, Henry M. to Fannie A. Herron 1-16-1861 F
Cocke, Henry to Cornelia Williamson 1-23-1869 F B
Cocke, J. D. to A. E. Ricketts 12-27-1864 (12-29-1864) F
Cocke, James H. to Mary P. Cocke 5-4-1870 (5-5-1870) F
Cocke, John to Ann King 3-22-1839 Sh
Cocke, Lindsey to Anikee McNeill 2-7-1868 (no return) F B
Cocke, N. J. to Lucy W. Pleasants 10-14-1845 (10-15-1845) F
Cocke, N. J. to Mary S. Higgarson 9-1-1847 F
Cocke, Ned to Martha McClain 1-5-1871 F B
Cocke, Robert to Watsie? Ann Link 9-15-1869 F B
Cocke, Smith K. to Mary E. Hutchans 2-27-1856 G
Cocke, Solomon to Lucy Martin 2-18-1869 (2-20-1869) F B
Cocke, Stephen W. to Ann Mariah Mann 4-2-1838 F
Cocke, Thomas R. to Mary Jane Jones 3-5-1840 F
Cocke, W. H. to Mattie E. Hudson 12-18-1871 (12-19-1871) T
Cockeram, Henry to Ruth Johnson 7-30-1828 (4-6-1829) Hr
Cockrahane, Daniel K. to Catharine A. Smith 5-17-1843 (5-18-1843) F
Cockram, J. T. to Nancy A. Coble 1-7-1864 Mn
Cockran, P. G. to Jane Shoop 1-9-1851 (1-11-1851) Sh
Cockran, Tecumseh to Josephine Allen 1-19-1870 F B
Cockrell, J. L. to M. E. McBride 2-10-1873 (2-11-1873) Cr
Cockrell, James Henry to Martha Ann Haynie 10-13-1847 T
Cockrell, Jesse to Sarah Cook 8-14-1861 O
Cockrell, R. H. M. to Maggie M. Starks 12-24-1858 Sh
Cockrell, Wm. to Loucinda Lashlee 10-17-1867 Be
Cockrill, Blunt to Mary Clements 1-10-1869 T
Cockrill, William G. to Amanda P. McMillen 7-1-1857 Ma
Cockrill, William G. to Laura J. Mayo 3-18-1867 (3-14?-1867) T
Cockrill, Wm. S. to Martha E. Bosley 7-31-1850 Sh
Cockron, A. D. to Martha A. Roberts 5-21-1857 Cr
Cockron, James to Fielder Smith 2-12-1839 Cr
Cocoran, Thomas to Susan Kirk 7-25-1840 Hr
Cocrum, John C. to Sarah Woods 2-23-1867 (3-11-1867) T
Coddy, Michael to Julia Powers 1-24-1863 Sh
Cody, F. M. to Mary A. Wilson 1-14-1860 (1-17-1860) F
Cody, James R. to Louisa F. Love 10-24-1848 Hn
Cody, James to Janie Colbert 4-19-1826 (4-20-1826) Hr
Cody, James to Lucy E. Exum 2-1-1870 (no return) F
Cody, John to Sarah Wilson 11-17-1853 Cr
Cody, Jos. L. to Harriet A. Cody 1-2-1868 (no return) F
Cody, Michael to Rosa Grant 2-7-1848 Sh
Cody, Steward to Lanah Crofford 10-27-1870 (10-28-1870) Cr B
Cody, Thomas D. to Lucinda Nichols 8-3-1831 Hr
Cody, Thomas J. to Martha L. Alexander 2-25-1856 (2-28-1856) Sh
Cody, William S. to Sarah Swan 12-8-1853 (12-13-1853) G
Coe, Harcus to Mary Frances Coe 5-31-1869 (6-13-1869) F B
Coe, Jesse to Alice E. Coe 2-16-1859 F
Coe, Levin H. to Lucy E. Stainback 12-20-1866 F
Cofer, John to Mary Ann Acre 6-29-1839 (7-2-1839) Ma
Coffee, A. B. to Annie Willis 2-11-1859 (2-12-1859) Sh
Coffey(Coffer?), James to Adalin Murry 3-2-1840 Hr
Coffey, D. M. to Anne E. Henly 12-12-1859 (no return) Hy
Coffey, Elijah to Eliza M. Fowler 7-15-1834 Sh
Coffey, Elijah to Polly King 2-17-1825 Sh
Coffey, Elijah to Polly McConell? 3-22-1847 Hr
Coffey, John G. to Octave B. Powell 11-2-1865 (11-8-1865) L
Coffey, Thomas D. to Alberter H. Newsom 12-7-1870 Hy
Coffman, Giles to S. A. Morris 12-24-1865 Hy
Coffman, Isaac R. to Isay Byars 3-4-1866 Hn
Coffman, J. M. C. to E. C. Cox 9-18-1866 (no return) Hn
Coffman, James M. to Nancy J. Coleman 2-4-1846 Hn
Coffman, James to America Stake 11-17-1874 (11-18-1874) T
Coffman, James to Mary A. Lee 11-24-1840 Hn
Coffman, L. J. to S. Y. Lundy 6-26-1862 (no return) Hy
Coffman, R. C. to Emma (Mrs.) Nash 12-3-1872 (12-5-1872) Dy
Coffman, W. F. to Susan P. Myers 7-18-1852 Hn
Coffman, William L. to A. J. Rainey 12-20-1870 (12-21-1870) L
Cofield, Thomas to Margaret Tharp 3-9-1870 (no return) F B
Cogan, John to Catherine (Mrs.) Greer 3-18-1863 Sh
Cogbell, Burrell to Verda Newby 2-11-1871 (no return) F B
Cogbill, C. H. to Frances L. McCauley 10-30-1854 (no return) F
Cogbill, C. H. to H. A. Ballard 7-21-1859 F
Cogbill, Henry to Adaline Heaslett 2-2-1867 (no return) F B
Cogbill, Jas. C. to Mollie C. Holman 1-2-1866 (1-11-1866) F
Cogbill, Thomas J. to Lucinda B. Dawson 8-21-1842 F
Cogbill, Thos. C. to Lucy A. Owen 10-18-1867 (10-30-1867) F
Cogburn, John C. to Malissa Bailey 10-15-1862 G
Cogchall, Charlie to Nancy Lewis 5-10-1883 L
Coggeshall, Boyd to Spencer A. Mitchell 12-15-1878 Hy
Coggschall, March to Martha Posey 9-4-1885 (9-5-1885) L
Coghill, George W. to Sarah E. Massey 6-25-1847 (6-29-1847) F

Coghill, Peter to Kate Morris 12-28-1871 O
Coghlan, William to Ellen Dencan (Duncan?) 12-27-1854 Sh
Cogshell, Boyd to Lucy Henning 3-31-1873 (4-1-1873) L
Cogswell, F. M. to Celia V. Bond 9-26-1854 (9-27-1854) Sh
Cohen, James to Kate Morton 1-25-1864 (1-26-1864) Sh
Cohn, David to P. D. A. L. Eskridge 1-17-1853 (no return) F
Cohorn, James to A. A. Coleman 3-18-1863 G
Cokeley, John to Delila S. Field 5-5-1849 (5-10-1849) G
Coker, Elija to Emer J. Criswell 9-10-1856 (9-11-1856) G
Coker, H. G. to Liley Short 8-19-1869 G
Coker, Hiram G. to Coly Ann Jones (Janes?) 11-20-1861 G
Coker, James Henry to Mary E. Robertson 1-16-1871 (1-17-1871) Dy
Coker, James to Mary Shaine 3-22-1844 (3-23-1844) F
Coker, James to Sarah Bradberry 6-20-1851 G
Coker, Jas. J. to Susie T. Scales 5-2-1870 (5-3-1870) Dy
Coker, Jimmy to Amanda Blakeley 3-5-1886 (3-6-1886) L
Coker, John E. to Nancy C. Anderson 1-2-1866 G
Coker, John E. to Sarah E. Boen 9-16-1859 (9-20-1859) G
Coker, Leonard to Sarah Nutt 7-11-1846 (7-12-1846) F
Coker, N. to Embra Fowlkes 2-7-1867 Dy
Coker, Nuton to Mary Jane Blair 4-14-1870 Hy
Coker, R. M. to Louisa Summers 9-6-1880 L
Coker, Robert to Susan Dunavant 4-20-1880 (not executed) L
Coker, W. T. to Lucas Avry 8-4-1874 Hy
Coker, William T. to Elizabeth Patterson 5-9-1860 (no return) Hy
Coker, Wm. H. to Eller Wells 12-11-1867 Hy
Colbert(Colvard), Wade H. to Lathey Gage 1-30-1830 Hr
Colbert, Frank to Mary Eudaly 12-12-1874 Dy
Colbert, James to Caroline Moore 1-22-1833 Sh
Colbert, James to Lou Mifflin 6-4-1866 Dy
Coldwell, Austin to Mariah Davis 4-10-1870 Hy
Coldwell, Dave to Margaret Walker 10-5-1872 (10-6-1872) T
Coldwell, Haywood to Mahala Graves 1-2-1873 Hy
Coldwell, John to Caroline Miller 1-9-1873 Hy
Coldwell, Vanburen to Elizabeth Turner 9-10-1870 Hy
Coldwell, W. P. to Ella Griffin 11-26-1872 (11-27-1873?) L
Cole, Alexander T. to Evelina Cook 10-26-1850 (10-28-1850) Ma
Cole, Allen A. to Minerva Finch 1-8-1850 Hy
Cole, Andrew W. to Cena D. Deaton 5-1-1872 Hy
Cole, B. G. M. to Margaret Jane Huffine 12-14-1876 Dy
Cole, B. R. to Martha E. Turner 12-30-1866 Be
Cole, C. A. to Susan E. Cowell 2-3-1856 Be
Cole, C. B. to M. B. Jones 6-9-1863 (6-10-1863) O
Cole, C. M. to M. J. Cardwell 11-21-1858 Hn
Cole, Calvin to Mary Ann Garett 9-27-1854 Be
Cole, Charles to Rhodie Williams 1-7-1877 Hy
Cole, Clem S. to Lydia A. Ross 12-17-1867 (12-19-1867) F B
Cole, David to Hannah Acklin 12-22-1871 (no return) Hy
Cole, David to Susan Elizabeth Bush 10-24-1845 Be
Cole, Davy to Sally Clark 7-27-1875 (no return) Hy
Cole, Dennis to Martha A. Hicks 10-17-1852 Be
Cole, E. M. to A. A. E. Small 2-21-1860 (2-29-1860) Sh
Cole, E. M. to F. A. Ross 12-2-1856 (12-3-1856) Sh
Cole, Francis M. to Elizabeth J. Baldwin 8-24-1860 Hn
Cole, Geo. B. to Celester A. Bryant 10-10-1872 (10-11-1872) Cr
Cole, George F. to Mary Bennett 6-2-1857 Cr
Cole, George W. to Lucy Ann Reynolds 5-14-1846 Sh
Cole, George W. to Susan Thompson 12-3-1849 Ma
Cole, Gillis to Milly Perkins 7-28-1867 Hy
Cole, H. J. to Mary Ann Stephens 5-16-1864 (no return) Hn
Cole, Harville to Lucinda Gammell 11-7-1836 O
Cole, Henderson to Laura Joyner 2-12-1876 Hy
Cole, Henry Clay to Lucinda Shackelford 5-14-1866 (no return) F B
Cole, Henry G. to Dorthula P. Lewis 8-17-1837 O
Cole, Ivy to Emiline Smith 11-3-1866 (11-4-1866) O
Cole, Ivy to Nancy Henry 5-25-1854 O
Cole, Ivy to Nancy Henry 5-25-1856 O
Cole, J. B. to Georgia A. Rhodes 9-25-1867 Hn
Cole, J. C. to Anna E. Perry 5-26-1857 (5-27-1857) Sh
Cole, J. E. to P. Benson 12-6-1859 (12-13-1859) F
Cole, J. J. to Eliza E. Marchbanks 7-17-1856 Be
Cole, J. M. to T. A. Maony? 3-2-1865 Hn
Cole, J. N. to Mary S. Carter 12-19-1867 Hn
Cole, J. P. to Nancy E. Strickland 6-26-1870 G
Cole, Jackson to Lucy Henderson 12-27-1870 (12-28-1870) Cr
Cole, Jake to Katie Bead 1-30-1872 (no return) Hy
Cole, James E. to Rebecca Dean 12-17-1846 (12-18-1846) G
Cole, James M. to Henryetta Aiden 8-24-1865 O
Cole, James M. to Mariah Mathews 6-1-1833 O
Cole, James M. to Sarah Carrington 12-31-1849 Cr
Cole, James R. to Phinela Whitlow 2-17-1842 Ma
Cole, James R. to Sarah A. Baker 11-11-1866 Be
Cole, James W. to Eliza A. Hudson 11-28-1866 (11-29-1866) F
Cole, James to Bet Short 8-13-1868 (no return) Hy
Cole, James to Jane Windsor 7-3-1853 Hn
Cole, James to Martha A. Ward 12-2-1860 We
Cole, James to N. J. Mitchell 1-4-1848 Be

Cole, Jas. A. to Mary A. Lindsey 1-20-1861 Be
Cole, Jas. M. to Rebecca Birdwell 10-3-1854 O
Cole, Jasper N. to Catharine A. Pruett 11-15-1865 (11-19-1865) Cr
Cole, Jasper S. to Sarah K. Gresham 8-27-1854 Hn
Cole, Jeptha to M. P. Bomer 3-19-1851 (no return) Hn
Cole, John A. to Levenia C. Edings 4-6-1865 G
Cole, John A. to Martha A. Swift 3-13-1843 (3-22-1843) F
Cole, John A. to Nancy Ann King 1-3-1865 O
Cole, John F. to Jane Shackelton 4-3-1866 (no return) Dy
Cole, John G. to Martha T. Borum 12-15-1849 (12-19-1849) L
Cole, John H. to Mary Ann Mathis 1-17-1848 Be
Cole, John J. to Lucinda Fry 9-19-1844 Hn
Cole, John J. to Mary Ann Marberry 1-17-1855 (no return) Hn
Cole, John S. to Mary Godwin 3-1-1859 Hn
Cole, John W. to Sarah Freeman 6-29-1857 O
Cole, John to Francis Mobley 12-1-1826 G
Cole, John to Lucy Waddell 1-24-1829 Ma
Cole, John to Mary A. Bivins 10-11-1852 Cr
Cole, John to Sarah Ann James 1-3-1849 (1-4-1849) G
Cole, John to Sarah England 9-18-1849 Be
Cole, John to Sarah Short 1-7-1841 Be
Cole, Joseph J. to Mary Ann Marchbanks 8-25-1848 Be
Cole, Josephus to Henrietta Newbern 12-9-1877 Hy
Cole, Kinchen G. to Cary Ann Marchbanks 11-15-1846 Be
Cole, Lewis to Nancy J. Berry 8-10-1854 Be
Cole, Logan T. to Matilda Beasley 6-14-1873 (6-17-1873) T
Cole, M. L. to Matildy Hollomon 9-28-1845 Be
Cole, Mark to Pheriby Cox 9-4-1853 Be
Cole, Minor C. to Winiford Fly 9-15-1837 G
Cole, Mumphred H. to Elizabeth Young 4-24-1840 (5-5-1840) F
Cole, Obadiaih to Martha A. Owen 8-24-1866 O
Cole, Phillip to Mollie V. Turner 2-1-1868 Ma
Cole, R. H. to E. J. Norman 11-28-1867 G
Cole, Rascar R. to Martha C. Jones 12-29-1852 Sh
Cole, Richard A. to Zilphana Jane Phillips 10-23-1844 Be
Cole, Richard J. to Rachael Odom 10-11-1846 Be
Cole, Richard R. to Martha Smith 5-1-1838 Cr
Cole, Robert W. to Martha M. Ray 10-11-1842 Hn
Cole, Robert to Eliza A. Boldin 11-5-1846 Hn
Cole, Ruffin to Lucy Mothershed 11-18-1852 Be
Cole, Samel E. to Martha O. Manees 4-3-1850 (no return) F
Cole, Samuel L. to Elizabeth Fry 8-13-1845 Hn
Cole, Samuel to Nancy M. J. Cook 2-17-1843 (2-21-1843) O
Cole, Shed to Manerva Dickinson 12-9-1870 F B
Cole, T. S. to E. O. Dixon 3-29-1859 (3-31-1859) Sh
Cole, Thomas B. to Nannie D. McLemore 5-13-1856 (5-14-1856) Ma
Cole, Thomas W. to Eliza Choate 9-30-1846 Sh
Cole, Thos. C. to Laura Ann (Mrs.) Jones 1-8-1864 Sh
Cole, W. D. to Elizabeth Smith 4-30-1863 Be
Cole, W. G. M. to Martha C. Sawyer 2-16-1871 Dy
Cole, W. H. to J. M. Henrietta Henning 3-29-1881 (3-30-1881) L
Cole, W. H. to M. Jorden 10-3-1837 Be
Cole, W. H. to Mary I. Smith 9-8-1866 O
Cole, W. H. to Susan F. Jones 1-7-1850 Hn
Cole, Will H. to Caroline Fortner 9-16-1846 (9-20-1846) Hr
Cole, William B. to Mary Settle 3-5-1840 Hn
Cole, William H. to Sarah Adams 11-4-1861 Hr
Cole, William L. to Sarah Burtus 12-22-1847 (12-23-1847) F
Cole, William to Eliza Stockton 6-17-1835 Hr
Cole, William to Ellin Crockett 2-26-1861 O
Cole, William to Harriet Simpson 8-31-1858 Hr
Cole, William to Sarah Fowler 11-15-1854 (11-16-1854) G
Cole, Wily to Ruth Ann Bryant 1-1-1877 Hy
Cole, Wm. A. to M. L. Arnold 1-14-1874 O
Cole, Wm. M. to Sarah E. Smith 12-11-1868 Be
Cole, Wm. N. to Martha J. House 1-12-1853 Cr
Cole, Wm. R. (Dr.) to Sallie E. Dunnaway 11-12-1870 (11-17-1870) Ma
Cole, Wm. T. to Laurie Ann England 4-19-1857 Hn
Cole____, I. to Nancy C. Vancleave 12-22-1859 Hn
Coleburn, William N. to Francis A. Perry 8-14-1854 (8-15-1854) Ma
Coleman (Callenan?), John to Bridget Ragan 4-28-1860 (4-29-1860) Sh
Coleman, A. A. to Louisa Neely 7-6-1859 Hr
Coleman, A. F. to Sarah E. Reeves 10-29-1861 G
Coleman, A. R. to Elizabeth A. Hoover 7-25-1860 G
Coleman, A. R. to Mary F. Trice 8-1-1853 Cr
Coleman, A. to Ella Daniel 2-5-1874 Hy
Coleman, Ammon to Nancy Belew 7-19-1831 Sh
Coleman, Ammon to Sarah Spain 12-20-1828 Sh
Coleman, Amos to Emma Morgan 11-3-1876 Hy
Coleman, Andrew J. to Nancy A. Wall 3-8-1842 Hn
Coleman, Archie R. to Nancy M. Price 10-29-1866 (no return) Hy
Coleman, Austin to Rainor Smith 12-24-1867 G B
Coleman, Benjamin L. to Elizabeth Yeates 11-14-1853 (11-17-1853) O
Coleman, Benjamin to Martha E. Rice 2-8-1858 (2-10-1858) L
Coleman, Campbell C. to Emily W. Harrell 1-13-1836 Sh
Coleman, Charles to M. E. Hancock 3-31-1879 (4-1-1879) Dy
Coleman, Cornelius to Mollie Hunter 12-25-1872 Hy

Coleman, E. G. to Margaret C. Patton 10-12-1847 F
Coleman, E. J. to Kate Younger 11-14-1865 (11-15-1865) Cr
Coleman, F. M. to Martha McCartay 6-9-1850 Hn
Coleman, G. C. to Nancy E. Lenier 1-21-1869 Hy
Coleman, G. W. to Levenia Neal 11-26-1865 G
Coleman, George to Ann Fields 9-14-1869 (no return) Dy B
Coleman, George to Louisa Brannock 9-4-1869 (9-19-1869) Cr
Coleman, George to Sarah E. Blythe 2-16-1848 L
Coleman, Green to Rena Hoggard 12-9-1868 (12-10-1868) Cr
Coleman, H.B. to A. F. Sammons? 2-20-1867 G
Coleman, Henry to Frances Cody 3-15-1871 (1-?-1872) F B
Coleman, Isham to Amelia Nixon 5-1-1879 L
Coleman, J. C. to A. D. Ore 3-22-1873 (3-25-1873) T
Coleman, J. C. to Sarah T. Crafton 12-8-1868 (12-10-1868) O
Coleman, J. D. to F. C. Smith 2-22-1864 O
Coleman, J. D. to Sue E. Gaines 3-11-1886 L
Coleman, J. F. to A. Neal 12-13-1866 G
Coleman, J. H. to Mattie H. Fowler 6-24-1870 (6-28-1870) Cr
Coleman, J. W. to Salina Keeth 11-23-1854 (12-1-1854) G
Coleman, James S. to Virginia C. Gains 12-20-1860 (no return) L
Coleman, James to Alabama Thomas 12-24-1867 (1-5-1868) Cr
Coleman, James to Ellen David 1-4-1853 (1-5-1853) Hr
Coleman, James to Susan E. Bayliss 5-31-1851 Sh
Coleman, Jeff to Eliza Williams 12-10-1870 (no return) Hy
Coleman, John A. to Mary A. Hilton 4-22-1859 (no return) L
Coleman, John E. to Verona May Cross 2-26-1879 (3-9-1879) L
Coleman, John T. to Celicia Perry 7-30-1855 (7-31-1855) Ma
Coleman, John T. to Elizabeth Merritt 2-2-1846 (2-3-1846) G
Coleman, John to Catharine Dooley 4-3-1860 (4-15-1860) Sh
Coleman, John to Elizabeth Harris 8-3-1857 Cr
Coleman, John to Julia Ann Aikins 2-17-1830 Sh
Coleman, Jonathan to Sarah E. Read 11-14-1853 (11-16-1853) O
Coleman, Jonathan to Susan E. Hardy 10-12-1851 (10-15-1851) O
Coleman, Jordan to Laura Westbrook 1-14-1873 Hy
Coleman, Joseph to Maggie Clark 3-20-1872 (no return) Cr B?
Coleman, Joshua to Elizabeth McBride 11-24-1855 (11-26-1855) Hr
Coleman, L. R. to Mary F. Pettus 1-18-1866 Hy
Coleman, Lovelace to Jane Thompson 10-10-1877 Hy
Coleman, Marion to Winney Higgins 4-1-1870 (4-2-1870) Cr
Coleman, Melton to Sarah Resiner 11-8-1832 Sh
Coleman, Mooreman T. to Mary Carter 1-22-1831 Sh
Coleman, N. A. to Anna L. Alvis 4-14-1867 G
Coleman, P. J. G. V. to Louisa H. Taylor 9-10-1838 (no return) Hn
Coleman, R. S. to F. A. Williams 11-7-1855 Hn
Coleman, R. T. to Cora E. Shaw 10-25-1876 Hy
Coleman, R. T. to H. E. Norman 12-1-1851 Cr
Coleman, Robert to Maria Harris 12-28-1869 Cr
Coleman, S. C. to Sarah E. Hughs 1-25-1860 Cr
Coleman, Solomon to Alice Whitelaw 12-26-1874 Hy
Coleman, T. S. to Alice Oury 1-2-1861 Hn
Coleman, Thomas to Emily Owen 9-23-1871 T
Coleman, Thos. W. to Lousinia Thomas 1-19-1846 Cr
Coleman, Travis C. to Frances J. Wilson 10-4-1854 Hn
Coleman, W. P. to Sarah Bowman 11-3-1870 G
Coleman, W. S. to M. A. Norwood 9-30-1858 Sh
Coleman, Walter Archer to Massey Lavinia Pennell 10-30-1849 (11-2-1849) T
Coleman, Walter to F. A. (Mrs.) Jones 6-21-1864 Sh
Coleman, Walter to Martha A. (Mrs.) Keeling 8-12-1852 Sh
Coleman, William to Elizabeth Lafavour 3-5-1839 Hn
Coleman, Winston to Kate Ware 4-24-1873 (no return) Hy
Coleman, Wm. A. to Margarett Norman 1-13-1847 Cr
Coles, Robert I. to Eva A. King 8-6-1866 O
Colew?, Thomas W. to Martha J. Allen 11-13-1849 Hn
Coley, J. F. M. to Adeline Rose 1-8-1852 (1-11-1852) Sh
Coley, James A. to Adaline Bowden 5-12-1850 Hn
Coley, James C. to Pantha Wagster 1-6-1864 G
Coley, Jas. to Nancy Garner 4-14-1840 Be
Coley, John W. to Viola Benton 1-9-1843 Be
Coley, John to Minervy Cole 2-8-1845 Be
Coley, Thomas W. to Adeline Ross 1-20-1850 Hn
Coley, Thos. to Ann M. Stokes 3-31-1841 (4-1-1841) G
Coley, William to Queen V. Bishop 5-15-1869 G
Colier, Thos. to Sarah Jane Melton 7-19-1843 Be
Collam, Tim to Hetty Collam 5-11-1852 Sh
Collans, Thos. to Anne Maria Whalin 5-5-1862 Sh
Colley, A. T. to Martha A. Barton 12-6-1841 Hn
Colley, G. W. to Mary D. Jennings 1-25-1869 L
Colley, R. B. to Nannie Hubbard 5-22-1879 L
Colley, W. A. to Martha K. Parrish 6-6-1865 Hn
Colley, W. J. to S. E. Landrum 1-20-1879 (1-22-1879) L
Collier (Hollier), Jas. T. to Agness (Mrs.) Enloe 1-7-1860 (1-9-1860) Sh
Collier, A. H. to L. F. Jones 12-14-1865 O
Collier, Anthony to Chaney Adams 12-25-1868 (no return) Hy
Collier, Carter C. to Louisa Neelly 3-4-1824 Hr
Collier, D. W. to M. E. Maury 4-27-1865 F
Collier, Dacton F. to Adeline H. Lawrence 11-25-1859 (11-27-1860) We
Collier, Frank to M. A. Ragsdale 12-4-1873 (1-1-1874) O

Collier, H. W. to F. W. Martin 10-11-1859 We
Collier, Haywood to Sallie Wiley 12-5-1873 Hy
Collier, J. L. to Sarah A. Elliot 1-8-1859 (1-9-1859) Sh
Collier, Jeff to Judy Maclin 12-26-1872 (no return) Hy
Collier, John to Caroline Lindsey 8-2-1852 Be
Collier, Joseph to Narcissa Caraway 5-27-1859 (5-28-1859) T
Collier, Joseph to Narcissa Carraway 5-27-1859 (5-28-1859) T
Collier, Joshua to Lucinda Howard 9-18-1869 Hy
Collier, Randal to Rosetta Collier 6-29-1866 (no return) Hy
Collier, Robert P. to Mary E. Feezor 5-29-1845 T
Collier, Robert to Sarah Alexander 12-16-1868 (no return) Hy
Collier, Robt. to Narcissa Thomas 11-28-1878 Hy
Collier, Telemicus H. to Sarah Cobb 10-10-1849 (10-11-1849) Hr
Collier, Thomas to Nancy Jane Hodge 9-2-1852 Be
Collier, W. A. to Amdy Williams 8-6-1844 Cr
Collier, William to Pennie Robbins 1-7-1872 Hy
Collier, William, jr. to Sarah Robertson 3-10-1831 (3-13-1831) Ma
Collier, Wm. to Malinda Jordan 9-21-1869 (no return) F B
Collilns, Robert to Elizar Reich 2-26-1859 (2-27-1859) O
Collingsworth, James M. to Martha H. Sawrie 11-20-1855 (11-22-1855) Ma
Collins, A. B. to Virginia A. Grandee 4-14-1863 Sh
Collins, Andrew to Annie Miller 5-21-1874 T
Collins, Bryce A. to Priscilla W. Collins 9-26-1848 Sh
Collins, C. A. to Sarah Hurt 12-19-1860 (no return) Cr
Collins, Columbus J. to E. J. Brundredge 1-6-1853 Hn
Collins, Daniel to Sarah A. Tucker 8-23-1865 (8-28-1865) O
Collins, E. E. to C. E. Collins 12-24-1868 (maybe 12-29) G
Collins, E. R. to Parlee Clayton 4-28-1863 (4-30-1863) F
Collins, Edward to M. T. Stanley 12-25-1867 O
Collins, Elisha to Jane Walker 1-7-1863 (1-11-1863) Sh
Collins, Ephraim L. to Elizabeth Newhouse 8-19-1861 O
Collins, F. A. to E. C. Hicks 1-27-1879 Dy
Collins, Franklin E. to Susan E. (Mrs.) Coats 6-26-1869 (6-27-1869) Ma
Collins, George W. to Mattie E. Kirby 12-14-1870 (12-15-1870) Ma
Collins, George to Bridget Griffin 4-24-1854 (4-30-1854) Sh
Collins, H. G. D. to C. A. Thompson 11-19-1870 (no return) Hy
Collins, H. M. to Mary A. Gates 12-25-1866 Hn
Collins, Henry D. to Matilda Anderson 7-7-1823 7-15-1823 Ma
Collins, J. R. to T. M. (Mrs.) Owens 2-26-1885 (3-1-1885) L
Collins, J. to S. C. Wilson 3-4-1866 G
Collins, James A. to Sallie Bivens 12-6-1866 Ma
Collins, James T. to Nancy Phillips 9-30-1850 Cr
Collins, James to Mary Mooney 7-26-1851 (7-27-1851) Sh
Collins, James to Mary Parham 5-11-1851 O
Collins, John B. to Isabella J. Gregory 2-10-1862 (no return) Hy
Collins, John B. to Ruth Ledsinger 3-9-1843 Cr
Collins, John F. to Susan L. Warren 12-26-1844 Hn
Collins, John G. to Geraldine Ellison 2-5-1857 Hn
Collins, John H. to Susan P. Byars 3-2-1859 Hn
Collins, John J. to Julia A. Stewart 3-3-1866 (3-8-1866) Ma
Collins, John J. to Mary Ann Moore 7-31-1838 Sh
Collins, John O. to Margaret Jarrett 1-24-1859 Cr
Collins, John W. to Jane Imes 11-22-1838 Sh
Collins, John W. to Lucinda Oldham 3-1-1825 Sh
Collins, John W. to Sarah Litsinger 3-9-1854 Cr
Collins, John to Anna Miller 6-15-1874 Hy
Collins, John to Ellen O'Donnell 2-25-1854 (2-27-1854) Sh
Collins, John to Lucy Shaw 5-22-1883 L
Collins, John to Marina Young 5-31-1879 (6-8-1879) L
Collins, John to Nancy C. L.? King 8-2-1865 (8-4-1865) Cr
Collins, John to Rebecca L. Bird 9-28-1850 Cr
Collins, Joseph F. to Louisa E. Crowder 11-22-1855 (no return) Hn
Collins, Joseph N. B. to Perlina M. Warrick 7-28-1857 Be
Collins, L. D. to Mary E. Hood 1-22-1855 Cr
Collins, Leroy to Frances L. Murphy 12-24-1860 (12-25-1860) O
Collins, Leroy to Louisa Simmons 12-23-1861 (12-25-1861) O
Collins, Lerry to Eveline M. Murphy 1-8-1853 G
Collins, Lewis P. to Mary Ann Davidson 9-17-1856 Be
Collins, Marian to Susan Sorrel 6-14-1867 (6-18-1867) L
Collins, N. D. to Martha A. Taliaferro 1-15-1865 G
Collins, Oscar F. to M. E. Thompson 3-20-1867 (3-28-1867) Ma
Collins, Patrick to Ann P. Maloney 11-9-1859 (11-10-1859) Sh
Collins, Patrick to Bridget Riley 8-26-1851 Sh
Collins, Patrick to Margaret Croghan 4-12-1854 Sh
Collins, Peter A. to Ann Tims 1-18-1842 Hr
Collins, Peter H. to Lucy C. Jackson 9-30-1852 Cr
Collins, Richard D. to N. A. Aycock 2-21-1861 Hn
Collins, Robert S. to Mary J. Penick no date (1838-1852) Hn
Collins, Robert to Elizur Reid 2-26-1859 (2-27-1859) O
Collins, S. C. to Sarah Dockens 10-30-1872 Dy
Collins, S. S. to H. T. Smith 7-19-1855 Cr
Collins, Saml. to Sallie Goodman 12-24-1874 (12-25-1874) T
Collins, Samuel L. to Eliza E. Burrow 8-19-1856 Cr
Collins, Samuel to Maria J. Knight 12-5-1851 Sh
Collins, Simon A. to Sallie Yarbrough 9-12-1870 Ma
Collins, Solomon to Nancy Let 11-10-1848 Cr
Collins, Thomas F. to Loucy Ramsey 12-27-1866 (no return) Cr
Collins, Thomas J. to Armasa King 1-11-1841 (1-13-1841)] Hr
Collins, Thomas to Margaret Allen 1-24-1849 Sh
Collins, Thomas to Martha Cook 9-6-1858 We
Collins, Thomas to Mary R. Wilkins 9-29-1867 Be
Collins, Thos. L. to Sarah Fort 6-15-1847 Hr
Collins, W. I. to Nancy Young 2-3-1867 G
Collins, W. L. to E. M. Clay 2-15-1860 Cr
Collins, W. R. to M. L. Diggs 11-8-1855 Hn
Collins, William to Bridget Hartigan (Hantigan?) 10-30-1853 Sh
Collins, William to Francis Laws 1-18-1878 Hy
Collins, William to Josephine H. Berry 4-5-1861 (4-8-1861) Sh
Collins, Wm. B. to Mary J. McFadden 12-9-1849 Hn
Collins, Wm. C. to Jane Almond 12-29-1856 Cr
Collins, Zepheniah to Nancy Williams 4-9-1850 Be
Collinsworth, George P. to Amanda Rose 9-6-1873 T
Collinsworth, Pinkney to Hannah Pierson 1-24-1868 (no return) L B
Colly, A. G. to Mary Chunn 11-27-1843 We
Colly, James N. to Martha E. Overby 8-25-1858 We
Colman, Henry to Harriet Coward 12-23-1867 (12-27-1867) T
Colridge, Henry to Mary Sawyer 2-28-1868 (no return) L B
Coltart, Ed to Fony Owen 6-3-1866 Hy
Coltart, R. W. to Alice Owen 9-6-1865 (no return) Hy
Colter, Geor. C. to Mary Malone 1-4-1845 F
Colter, Geor. C. to Mary Malone 12-20-1844 (no return) F
Colter, Sims to Fannie Stokeley 3-2-1870 Hy
Coltharp, James N. to Caroline Parham 9-24-1846 We
Coltyn, Edward to Mary Sullivan 4-5-1856 (4-6-1856) Sh
Colvard, Pleasant to Jane Bailey 6-28-1826 (6-29-1826) Hr
Colvett, James to Emmy Bennett 5-24-1864 (5-25-1864) Cr
Colvin, Charner B. to Mahala Shelton 12-21-1876 (12-25-1876) Dy
Colvin, J. S. to Jesse Humphrey 9-25-1878 (9-26-1878) Dy
Colvitt, John T. to Obedience J. A. J. Smith 12-2-1867 G
Colvitt, W. C. to P. F. Miller no date (8-6-1873) Cr
Colwell, Alfonzo to Elvira Tyas 4-22-1878 (no return) L B
Colwell, E. M. to T. E. Carso 1-1-1871? (1-1-1872) L
Colwell, J. G. to S. E. Slacey (Stacey?) 9-11-1876 (9-12-1876) L
Colwell, J. L. to Nettie Quinn 1-30-1878 (1-31-1878) L
Colwell, James to Elizabeth F. Culbreath 5-4-1860 (5-5-1860) T
Colwell, Sad to Mattie Lake 3-25-1882 L
Coty, James to Sarah Hopkikns 12-20-1834 Hr
Colyear, Henry to Lidia Dixon 1-5-1828 (1-6-1828) G
Comas, Peter to Alice Boland 1-29-1853 Sh
Combes, Charles A. to Caraline Traylor 1-26-1848 (1-27-1848) F
Combs, Alfred to May Ann Rasons 9-24-1838 (9-25-1838) Ma
Combs, Collins to Neely Tabscott 9-30-1873 Hy
Combs, Dan to Fannie King 3-4-1868 (no return) Hy
Combs, David to Evaline Stevens 3-2-1869 T
Combs, Edward to Lucindy J. Williams 1-31-1843 Cr
Combs, G. N. to Cordelia Gordon 11-26-1860 Be
Combs, J. M. to Nancy P. Phillips 11-13-1863 (no return) Hn
Combs, James H. to Martha E. Hinant 12-18-1856 Be
Combs, Nick to Catherine Rodgers 12-17-1837 (12-20-1837) O
Combs, Peter to Mattie Ingram 10-10-1871 (10-14-1871) Ma
Combs, W. A. to E. P. Hudson 1-1-1863 Be
Combs, W. J. to Sarah E. Baker 3-15-1869 (no return) Dy
Combs, William to Louisa Granby 3-22-1847 (3-25-1847) Hr
Comer, E. A. to E. J. Walters 9-20-1863 Hn
Comer, Elijah to Mary Wood 10-25-1837 Hr
Comer, Henry M. to Lucy E. Daniel 10-25-1842 Hr
Comer, James to Liza Jane Thomas 8-5-1867 (8-9-1867) F B
Comer, John A. to Lucy A. Gresham 12-26-1866 Hn
Comer, John F. to Hester A. Good 2-9-1860 Hy
Comer, Wm. C. C. to Wincey C. Richardson 11-14-1860 (11-15-1860) Hr
Comes, Henry to A. S. Gee 1-1-1873 (1-2-1873) Cr
Compton, B. A. to A. L. Wilks 12-5-1877 Hy
Compton, David R. to Tabitha Lax 8-8-1853 (8-10-1853) Hr
Compton, Eli R. to Mildred Ann Clark 8-13-1840 F
Compton, Eli to E. J. Penick 2-18-1867 (2-19-1867) Cr
Compton, J. B. to Ann E. Brantley 1-31-1854 (2-2-1854) Ma
Compton, Jackson to Martha B. Estis 9-7-1867 (9-12-1867) L B
Compton, Joe to Rebecca Taylor 12-8-1884 (12-9-1884) L
Compton, John A. to Salina Anderson 3-19-1861 (no return) Cr
Compton, R. F. to Mary Payne 11-25-1851 Sh
Compton, Robert M. to Rebecca Moore 11-26-1840 Ma
Compton, W. H. to Ella W. Duglass 10-17-1870 Hy
Compton, William A. to Miria L. Wilson 1-5-1853 Ma
Compton, William H. to Mary Yates 5-21-1860 (no return) Hn
Comrie?, James to Susan Boggess 6-13-1867 Dy
Comsay, C. to Tennessee Potts 4-30-1865 Hn
Comstock, W. R. to Catharine Mingea 9-9-1862 Sh
Con?, Pompey to Harriet Carter 8-22-1872 L
Conagan, Isaac H. to Sarah Bond 12-28-1870 (no return) Hy
Conaley, George to Rochoanna Green 1-30-1875 (1-31-1875) L B
Conboy, Thomas to Hannah Shehan 4-25-1863 Sh
Conder, D. L. to Mary E. Byron (Byrum?) 12-27-1852 (12-28-1852) Sh
Conder, James to Margaret F. Long 1-10-1854 Sh
Conder, Robert L. to Mary A. Byrum 1-6-1858 (1-7-1858) Sh

Condon, Thomas to Mary Holihan 12-29-1857 Sh
Condray, William F.? to Catharine Humphry 3-10-1866 (3-11-1866) Cr
Condrey, Benjamin to Martha J. Bates 12-31-1864 (no return) L
Condrey, Thomas S. to Elizabeth Prescott 8-10-1867 (8-11-1867) L
Condry, Benj. F. to Martha J. Bates 12-31-1864 (1-11-1865) L
Condry, John M. to Sarah Jane Brown 7-31-1861 (8-2-1861) L
Condry, Thomas S. to Juan G. Hutcherson 7-27-1871 L
Cone, G. W. to Sallie O. Teal (O'Teal?) 12-13-1858 (12-15-1858) Sh
Conelly, Alfred to Emeline Harmon 12-26-1874 (12-27-1874) T
Conemer, Hilliary to Martha Ann Henderson 11-25-1839 Cr
Coneway, James to Lydia Farthing 9-2-1858 G
Conger, D. J. to Martha J. Kelly 2-28-1860 Sh
Conger, John S. to Harriet Caroline Hampton 5-20-1861 Ma
Conger, Philander D. W. to Eliza Jane Chambers 12-14-1842 (12-15-1842) Ma
Conish, John to Polly Simmons 7-2-1870 F B
Conklin, W. A. to Gennie S. Hooper 1-15-1883 (1-17-1883) L
Conlee, Harrison to Mary P. Penn 1-2-1858 G
Conlee, Henderson to Mary A. Tyson 3-7-1828 (3-13-1828) G
Conlee, Henderson to Sarah Williams 12-30-1835 Hr
Conlee, Madison to Sarah Rigsly 12-9-1839 (12-11-1839) G
Conlee, O. to Juley A. Richardson 5-29-1837 (6-1-1837) G
Conlee, Orvill to July A. Richardson 5-29-1839 G
Conlee, Russell to Mary Ann King 8-15-1833 (8-16-1833) G
Conley, A. B. to Mattie J. Mitchell 12-23-1868 G
Conley, D. W. to Maggie Thompson 12-30-1875 (1-1-1876) L
Conley, Elijah to Almira Knaff 8-18-1846 Sh
Conley, F. J. to Mahala Bryant 4-1-1858 G
Conley, Franklin to Martha M. Webb 12-30-1869 Cr
Conley, H. M. to Nancy F. White 3-5-1861 Be
Conley, Harrison J. to Nancy J. Ferless 1-17-1856 G
Conley, J. W. to M. A. W. Rie 8-15-1882 (no return) L
Conley, Joseph to Agnes Conley 7-30-1868 G B
Conley, M. M. to Adaline E. Butler 12-22-1869 G
Conley, Peter to Maggie Allen 12-22-1868 Sh
Conley, Sydney to Ardenia West 9-18-1860 Sh
Conley, T. G. to S. E. Pounds 3-10-1867 G
Conley, Tobbert F. to Cordelia J. Green 10-9-1858 G
Conley, W. H. to Nancy T. Joliet 3-1-1880 (3-14-1880) L
Conly, John to Rissa Bowls 1-12-1876 (no return) Hy
Conn, J. L. to Nancy B. Malone 2-24-1849 (2-25-1849) F
Conn, Robert W. to Caroline Duke 2-17-1842 (2-24-1842) F
Conn, Robt. to J. A. Milliner 1-14-1868 (1-15-1868) O
Conn, William to Adaline Moore 2-23-1839 G
Connally, John to Bridget Coyne 6-28-1861 (7-1-1861) Sh
Connally, Patrick to Catharine Hynes 9-17-1864 (9-18-1864) Sh
Connally, Thomas to Margaret Nenan 1-21-1864 Sh
Connel, J. C. to Emily Stout 2-12-1855 (no return) We
Connel, Peter M. to Nancy Williams 3-19-1845 (3-25-1845) G
Connell, A. J. to M. F. Warren 10-5-1868 (no return) F
Connell, Alex to Mary Smith 5-27-1871 (5-28-1871) Dy
Connell, Austin to Amanda Mulherin 2-22-1872 (2-23-1872) Dy
Connell, Austin to Nannie Light 10-6-1880 Dy
Connell, D. to Louiza Philips 1-4-1858 (1-7-1858) G
Connell, David to Martha Pell 11-25-1875 Dy
Connell, Harvey W. to Jane Patey 11-30-1864 Hn
Connell, Henry to Ada Harris 5-18-1876 (no return) Dy
Connell, Hiram D. to Ann E. Lawrence 8-21-1848 Sh
Connell, J. W. to Martha J. Pate 10-27-1868 G
Connell, Jack to Helen Light 5-4-1875 (5-5-1875) Dy
Connell, Jack to Hetta Williams 12-2-1869 (no return) Dy
Connell, James A. to Emly A. Baker 1-22-1851 (1-23-1851) G
Connell, James R. to Martha Jane Blan 1-15-1843 Ma
Connell, James W. to Nancy Mullens 12-21-1857 (12-22-1857) G
Connell, James to Rebecka Roach 7-25-1826 (6-26-1826) G
Connell, Joe to Mary Ware 12-27-1866 (no return) Hy
Connell, John F. to Jane Light 2-17-1871 (2-18-1871) Dy B
Connell, John H. to Selah Ann M. Smith 3-14-1864 (no return) Cr
Connell, John H. to Selahann M. Smith 3-14-1864 (no return) Cr
Connell, John L. to Cenith F. Mayfield 6-1-1857 (6-2-1857) G
Connell, John to Bridget Lyons 1-19-1861 (1-20-1861) Sh
Connell, John to Ellen Mitchell 8-25-1864 Sh
Connell, John to Mary Bates 5-29-1837 (not executed) G
Connell, Michal to Elizabeth Maher 5-7-1862 Sh
Connell, Patrick to Ellen Maroonery 11-20-1851 Sh
Connell, Patrick to Johanna Welch 5-12-1859 Sh
Connell, Peter to Noon? Tucker 8-9-1877 Dy
Connell, Thomas to Sarah A. Hill 2-28-1861 G
Connell, W. E. to Mary E. Gold 11-11-1871 (11-12-1871) Dy
Connell, William M. to Margaret Ann Holt 10-5-1853 (10-6-1853) G
Connell, William W. to Elizabeth R. Thedford 12-27-1843 (12-28-1843) G
Connell, William W. to Sarah Littleton 8-6-1861 We
Connell, William to Polly Sandford 10-16-1834 (10-23-1834) G
Connell, William to Susan A. Wheeler 9-26-1867 G
Connell, Wm. to Louisa E. White 7-15-1841 Sh
Connelly, John to Mollie Washington 11-6-1875 L
Connelly, Patrick to Bridget Mealy 10-25-1862 Sh
Connelly, Peter to Julia Gilland 5-21-1862 Sh

Conner, Andrew to Nancy Chapman 6-21-1845 (6-24-1845) Ma
Conner, C. J. to R. A. Suddeth 12-24-1855 (12-25-1855) Sh
Conner, C. to Louiza Nevils 4-5-1858 (4-6-1858) G
Conner, Conway to Mary Nelson 1-26-1883 (no return) L
Conner, Conway to Vickey Emmerson 12-17-1885 (12-18-1885) L
Conner, Daniel to Chany Wardlaw 1-26-1867 L B
Conner, David to Margaret Pennington 5-27-1861 Sh
Conner, Francis L. to Hannah M. Martin 2-10-1840 (2-13-1840) G
Conner, George to Alice Brinder 5-8-1869 Cr
Conner, Henry to Eveline Bryant 12-16-1845 (12-18-1845) Ma
Conner, Isham to Anna Walker 3-17-1850 We
Conner, J. T. to Sarah Lucinda Lee 2-8-1871 Ma
Conner, J. W. to Lutisha Brister 2-1-1847 (2-2-1847) F
Conner, Jackson to Julia Ann Griggs 5-25-1867 G
Conner, James O. to Margaret Miles 6-11-1848 Sh
Conner, James to Leonora Drisel 8-6-1854 Sh
Conner, Jeff to M. Hadly 1-4-1872 T
Conner, John to Katie Cornegys 12-18-1878 Hy
Conner, John to Margaret Donahue 1-7-1863 Sh
Conner, John to Mary Payne 9-26-1848 L
Conner, John to Zabra Parker 2-23-1831 Ma
Conner, Major to Mildron Dickerson 1-9-1869 (no return) Hy
Conner, Martin to Henretta Walker 12-31-1874 Hy
Conner, Martin to Henrietta Peake 9-21-1877 Hy
Conner, Patrick to Ellen Kelly 5-18-1857 Sh
Conner, Patrick to Mary Lynch 4-21-1855 (4-22-1855) Sh
Conner, S. W. to P. A. Thomas 11-24-1864 G
Conner, Samuel to Rebecca Parker 1-30-1829 Ma
Conner, Stephen to Mariah Bledsoe 9-21-1867 G
Conner, W. to Ellen Blackwood 11-2-1875 (no return) Dy
Conner, Walter to Martha Caroline Collens 4-13-1870 (4-15-1870) L
Conner, Wash to Amanda Young 12-26-1866 (12-27-1866) F B
Conner, William J. to Sarah P. Southerland 6-5-1838 Hn
Conners, Daniel to Bridget McNairy 8-1-1862 (8-3-1862) Sh
Conness, John to Mrs. Brown 9-8-1869 (9-9-1869) Dy
Conney (Cowrey?), Henry to Dora Jackson 8-18-1881 L
Connor, Benjamin S. to Martha Bishop 11-18-1869 O
Connor, Edward to Eliza Murray 9-1-1860 (9-2-1860) Sh
Connor, John Thomas to Sarah Frances Valentine 12-22-1856 (12-23-1856) Ma
Connor, John to Lucy A. Verser 12-1-1856 (12-17-1856) Ma
Connor, Joseph F. to Mary J. Volentine 12-12-1868 Ma
Connor, Laurence to Annie McManus (McManns?) 7-6-1863 Sh
Connor, Lewis to Mollie Brooks 12-13-1872 (4-24-1873) T
Connors, Daniel to Margaret Dwyer 11-27-1861 Sh
Considine, M. K. to M. A. Considine 6-3-1864 G
Considine, M. R. to M. A. E. Quinn 12-2-1858 (12-3-1858) G
Convill, William B. to Judia Bates 5-11-1833 G
Conway, Patrick to Mary Dunn 10-13-1864 Sh
Conway, B. B. to Rachel Stephens 4-19-1849 Hn
Conway, Eugene to Johanna Ryan 4-23-1848 Sh
Conway, James to Mary McCarty 9-16-1854 (9-17-1854) Sh
Conway, John W. to Elizabaeth Winn 11-4-1841 F
Conway, John W. to Martha J. Elder no date (with Dec 1847) F
Conway, John to Mary McMahan 11-1-1860 Sh
Conway, Maurice to Ellen McNamara 10-20-1849 Sh
Conway, Michael to Rebecca Borough 2-12-1840 (2-18-1840) L
Conway, Patrick to Maria Glancy 11-16-1857 Sh
Conway, Thomas H. to Nancy M. McCorkle 8-9-1854 Hn
Conway, Thos. H. to Catherine Conners 1-13-1863 Sh
Conwell, William B. to Ann Dickey 2-26-1844 G
Conyers, B. L. to Sarah Kendall 3-30-1848 Hn
Conyers, James M. to Martha Johnson 10-2-1843 Hn
Conyers, John to Mary Phillips 4-14-1853 Cr
Conyers, M. T. to L. McFadden 11-12-1850 Hn
Conyers, William H. to Adaline Bowden 2-3-1858 Hn
Conyers, Zachariah M. to Louisa E. Potts 11-7-1857 Hn
Coock, Joseph to Martha Johnson 10-1-1860 (no return) Hy
Coodey, Edward to Catharine Rainer 5-28-1829 Hr
Coody, W. R. to C. A. Ray 11-14-1853 (no return) F
Cook, A. M. to Mary M. Palmer 12-2-1850 We
Cook, Albert to Lydia Brown 3-2-1852 We
Cook, Alexander to Eliza Ann Witt 12-24-1840 (12-26-1840) G
Cook, Antony S. to Mollie F. Parker 12-21-1868 G
Cook, Atlas to Mary Trimble ?-13-1852 We
Cook, Austin to Louisa McQuinn 12-26-1857 Sh
Cook, Austin to Lucinda Harris 12-13-1851 Sh
Cook, Austin to Mary Allen 3-16-1861 Sh
Cook, Cornelius to Recy Garner 11-10-1844 We
Cook, D.C. to Victoria Morris 5-25-1873 Hy
Cook, E. N. to H. C. Carrigan 2-26-1856 (2-27-1856) L
Cook, Edward L. to Donie M. Nunn 8-27-1878 (8-28-1878) Dy
Cook, Edward N. to Nancy A. Borum 10-8-1849 (no return) L
Cook, Edward R. to Salinda K. Hawks 10-15-1845 (no return) We
Cook, Elias G. B. to Celia Johnson 10-26-1840 We
Cook, Elias to Sibella A. Darby 5-22-1843 (5-24-1843) Ma
Cook, Elisha to Leamma Stephens 9-25-1859 O
Cook, Francis M. to Permelia E. Walden 8-8-1872 Hy

Cook, Geo. Washington to Sophia C. Flowers 12-21-1851 (not executed) T
Cook, George I. to Luizer C. Walker 2-9-1868 G
Cook, George W. to Banina L. Doxey 1-10-1852 Sh
Cook, George W. to Sallie J. Love 7-11-1856 Sh
Cook, George W. to Sopha Blair 12-16-1872 (12-19-1872) Cr
Cook, George to Margarette E. Comes 10-12-1859 (10-13-1859) G
Cook, Henry to Elizabeth Yates 10-19-1849 (11-8-1849) G
Cook, Henry to Jane Pritchard 1-1-1839 T
Cook, Hugh L. to Martha B. Mims 12-17-1847 Sh
Cook, J. C. to M. J. Skallings 1-26-1880 (1-29-1880) L
Cook, J. H. to Selena C. Moore 9-21-1845 We
Cook, J. R. to Mattie Cunningham 3-2-1876 Dy
Cook, James C. to Nancy C. Rice 8-29-1861 (no return) Hy
Cook, James D. to Nancy Atwell 1-8-1850 (1-9-1850) Hr
Cook, James M. to Louisa Jane Alkins 5-11-1856 We
Cook, James M. to Martha J. Moore 12-29-1855 We
Cook, James M. to Mary Elvira Darnell 10-12-1841 (10-13-1841) Ma
Cook, James R. to Juday m. Finch 8-21-1855 We
Cook, James T. to M. A. Hearn 12-23-1869 G
Cook, James to Judah Brown Hynes 11-14-1832 Sh
Cook, James to Margaret Hicks 2-8-1853 G
Cook, James to Martha J. Farrell 1-3-1863 Sh
Cook, James to Mary J. McLemore 10-5-1869 (10-7-1869) Cr
Cook, Jas. H. to Harriet V. Deakin 11-14-1856 (11-19-1856) T
Cook, Jefferson to Jane Dorris 5-20-1834 O
Cook, Jesse to Margaret Ralls 12-26-1832 O
Cook, Jim, jr. to Sylva Raynor 3-23-1867 Hy
Cook, Jno. D. to Emily Damron 9-2-1850 We
Cook, John P. to Nancy C. Stanley 10-17-1867 Hy
Cook, John S. to Tennessee Huddleston 8-2-1841 Sh
Cook, John to Jane Dozier 7-23-1862 (7-24-1862) Dy
Cook, John to R. E. Davis 4-14-1869 G
Cook, John to Zellah Stephens 8-27-1865 G
Cook, Joseph W. to Anna Wimberley 1-19-1867 Hn
Cook, Josiah F. to Mary E. Altman 1-22-1868 G
Cook, Josiah to Temperance Dollohite 8-9-1860 (8-14-1860) Cr
Cook, L. D. to Frances E. McKinney 1-16-1865 (1-17-1865) Cr
Cook, L. J. to Sarah C. Barksdale 1-18-1858 G
Cook, Lemuel J. to Elizabeth S. Holland 10-8-1860 G
Cook, Leroy to Olive W. Farguson 1-22-1840 Hr
Cook, M. B. to Lucy Ann Jones 1-24-1828 Ma
Cook, M. K. to Maggie A. Buchanan 4-13-1864 (4-14-1864) Sh
Cook, Mack R. to Emaline Russ 12-13-1831 G
Cook, Major F. to Lucy Tucker 4-28-1880 Dy
Cook, Marion to Nancy S. Watson 10-16-1861 (no return) We
Cook, Milos C. to Martha Ann Bumpass 1-16-1842 Ma
Cook, Milton to Sophie Ellington 7-28-1838 (7-29-1838) Ma
Cook, Morgan B. to Mary E. Haynes 5-31-1850 Sh
Cook, Moses P. to Elizabeth Horton 3-14-1854 O
Cook, Ned to Victoria Taylor 8-1-1868 T
Cook, Needham H. to Mary A. Bolin 12-4-1855 (12-9-1855) G
Cook, P. W. to Sarah J. Lewis 8-23-1848 Cr
Cook, Pleasant W. to Nancy Ann Robinson 8-4-1848 Cr
Cook, R. A. to Sarah Murphy 12-23-1872 (12-24-1872) O
Cook, R. G.? to Irene E. Dougherty 9-10-1867 (no return) Cr
Cook, R. H. to N. B. Carraway 8-16-1851 (no return) F
Cook, Robert F. to Catherine L. Doty 8-6-1840 Sh
Cook, Robert to Bridgett Mahan 8-2-1853 Sh
Cook, Rolan T. to Allis Hinson 1-18-1858 (1-21-1858) G
Cook, Samuel J. to Nancy E. McCoy 3-14-1859 (3-18-1859) G
Cook, Shim to Emelin Parrish 2-19-1867 (2-21-1867) Ma
Cook, Solomon to Martha A. Hurt 2-25-1861 Dy
Cook, T. H. to Neettie Teat 6-13-1874 (6-14-1874) Dy
Cook, T. J. to N. J. Watkins 11-5-1867 (no return) F
Cook, Thomas to M. E. Cook 10-28-1866 Hy
Cook, Thos. H. to L. C. Barnes 1-10-1850 Cr
Cook, Toler to Parthena Fowlkes 1-24-1874 Dy
Cook, W. A. to Juda C. Ashford 7-18-1883 (7-19-1883) L
Cook, W. D. to Ollie Hill 12-25-1884 (12-30-1884) L
Cook, W. E. to Talithia Pittman (Pellman?) 3-2-1877 (3-4-1877) L
Cook, W. G. to Callie Curlin 5-25-1880 L
Cook, W. H. to F. L. Tucker 10-12-1865 Hy
Cook, W. L. B. to L. J. Ayres 2-12-1856 We
Cook, W. N. to Delilah A. Lacy 11-22-1866 G
Cook, William P. to Mary A. Ray 1-27-1864 Mn
Cook, William T. to Ann Babb 3-6-1864 Mn
Cook, William to Martha E. Comes 3-26-1862 G
Cook, William to Mollie E. Brown 9-9-1871 (9-12-1871) Dy
Cook, William to Sarah J. Holloway 3-2-1867 (3-3-1867) Cr
Cook, Willis to Allice Coffman 3-19-1870 (no return) F B
Cook, Wm. D. S. to Ellen V. Glover 9-8-1861 G
Cook, Wm. J. to Susan J. Bondurant 10-24-1844 (no return) We
Cook?, A. to Sarah Johnson 7-4-1842 F
Cooke, Geo. W. to Mary Ann Owens 5-28-1849 (no return) Hn
Cooke, Green B. to Eliz. Booth 1-22-1857 G
Cooke, J. J. to Mary E. Love 7-17-1842 Hn
Cooke, Joseph G. to Virginia C. Carter 10-26-1870 Hy

Cooke, Maxwell to Elizabeth Thompson 9-26-1837 (9-28-1837) O
Cooke, William M. to Jennette R. Owen 5-22-1859 Hn
Cooker, Samuel J to Lethie Albright 1-20-1870 (no return) Hy
Cooksey, James to Isbele Waldrup 6-15-1832 Hr
Cooksey, Vincent to Elizabeth Terry 9-28-1842 (9-29-1842) Hr
Cooley, Frances to H. F. Stockard 10-23-1856 We
Cooley, Jerome B. to Idotha Smith 2-25-1846 O
Cooley, John J. to Lucy J. Hendrix 12-31-1860 (12-30-1861) We
Cooley, John W. to Rebecca Jane Hatley 6-27-1864 Be
Cooley, Joshua to Jane Smith 6-29-1860 (6-30-1860) O
Coolidge, John A. to Ella A. bell 12-23-1864 (12-28-1864) Sh
Cooly, Robert W. to Martha Adaline Melton 6-6-1852 Be
Coon, George A. to Julia P. Smith 12-9-1874 Dy
Coon, James to Matilda Fullen 3-1-1848 (3-2-1848) L
Cooney, James T. to Emma J. Bowles 1-7-1854 Hn
Cooney, John to Martha Carr 8-11-1857 Sh
Coonrod, Frank to Babe Williams 2-22-1882 (2-23-1882) L
Coonrod, Pink to Elizabeth Loftin 3-17-1875 (no return) L
Coonts, Jas. W. to Susan C. Byrns? 10-15-1856 (10-16-1857?) T
Coop, Alfred to Caroline Watson 10-27-1845 (10-29-1845) L
Coop, W. A. H. to M. M. Agee 1-7-1871 (1-10-1871) Dy
Cooper, Aaron to Ellen House 4-8-1875 Hy
Cooper, Abram to Martha E. Shoemate 4-16-1867 (no return) Hy
Cooper, Adolphus to Kate Gift 5-14-1864 Sh
Cooper, Albert to Bell McConnell 10-30-1872 (11-1-1872) T
Cooper, Alexander to Rebecca Brown 9-24-1827 (8-25-1827) G
Cooper, Anthony to Amanda Johnson 9-21-1870 G B
Cooper, Asberry to Amanda Shuran 3-30-1873 Hy
Cooper, B. H. to Clarissa F. Wilkinson 1-3-1861 (1-7-1861) Hr
Cooper, B. J. to Susan Ann House 7-24-1855 G
Cooper, Benj. A. to Elvira Crockett 8-20-1850 (8-22-1850) G
Cooper, Benj. F. to M. A. Belch 11-25-1856 G
Cooper, Benjamin to Casa Ames 4-26-1855 G
Cooper, Blount to Elizabeth Freeman 9-5-1839 Hn
Cooper, C. W. to Mary Moss 5-27-1855 Be
Cooper, Charley to Emanuel Pinkston 6-25-1840 Cr
Cooper, Christopher S. to Susan M. Porter 3-30-1850 (3-31-1850) G
Cooper, Christopher to Mary E. Webb 1-12-1860 (1-13-1860) G
Cooper, Colemon to Lucy Culbreath 6-18-1870 T
Cooper, Cove to Elizabeth Thomas 11-3-1839 Hn
Cooper, Culpepper to Frances Freeman 4-3-1848 Cr
Cooper, Daniel B. to Rebecca E. Haltom 11-20-1866 (11-21-1866) Ma
Cooper, Derry to Mary Grimes 11-23-1870 (11-27-1870) T
Cooper, E. to Mary Baker 11-4-1861 (11-7-1861) L
Cooper, Edmond to Frances A. Holmes 5-28-1851 (5-29-1851) Sh
Cooper, Edmund to Mary E. Stephens 10-22-1844 Hr
Cooper, Edward to Mary Young 12-27-1855 Cr
Cooper, Ephraim to Eliza Davis 5-3-1849 (5-4-1849) G
Cooper, G. G. to Mary E. Mills 7-27-1875 (7-29-1875) Dy
Cooper, Garrett to Judith Ann Kent 8-18-1849 (8-22-1849) T
Cooper, George Levy to Margarette A. Riley 3-11-1865 G
Cooper, George W. to Mary A. Horton 11-12-1866 (11-13-1866) Ma
Cooper, George to Bridget (Mrs.) Rourke 11-30-1864 Sh
Cooper, George to Matilda Bremaker 4-24-1852 (4-25-1852) Sh
Cooper, Henry A. to Mary Boage 10-1-1854 G
Cooper, Henry to Bertha Givin 8-22-1843 We
Cooper, Henry to Catharine Moore 2-11-1846 (2-12-1846) G
Cooper, Henry to Cealey Cooper 3-25-1846 Cr
Cooper, Hugh J. to Lucinda A. Fisher? 10-5?-1853 (no return) F
Cooper, Hugh to Penelope Word 3-22-1843 (3-23-1843) G
Cooper, Isham to Nancy Cooper 4-21-1847 (no return) Hn
Cooper, J. C. to Emily Young 4-1-1856 G
Cooper, J. E. to D. J. Chapman 3-9-1868 (3-12-1868) Dy
Cooper, J. J. to Virginia Kirkland 12-22-1857 (1-7-1858) Hr
Cooper, J. N. to L. J. Robertson 7-27-1874 (7-29-1874) T
Cooper, J. N. to Margaret E. Fanner 11-16-1859 (11-17-1859) Ma
Cooper, J. P. to Caroline Graham 1-22-1863 Be
Cooper, J. W. to A. Porter 9-2-1847 Hn
Cooper, J. W. to Malinda C. Fowler 12-19-1846 We
Cooper, Jacob to Jane Dolin 1-1-1839 Cr
Cooper, Jacob to Martha Brackins 8-26-1866 Be
Cooper, James A. to Angelina Hargate 1-28-1858 L
Cooper, James F. to Eveline Beaton 1-6-1858 Be
Cooper, James H. to Rebeccah C. Barnett 3-23-1865 Dy
Cooper, James H. to Susan Southern 6-28-1870 Dy
Cooper, James L. to Delphina E. Wilson 12-7-1861 Ma
Cooper, James L. to M. A. Whitley 5-21-1867 (5-23-1867) T
Cooper, James P. to Martha Blanton 1-27-1864 Be
Cooper, James W. to Rebecca J. Turner 11-18-1860 Hn
Cooper, James W. to Sarah E. Bell 6-12-1870 G
Cooper, James to Mary A. E. Jones 4-5-1855 Hr
Cooper, Jepther to Martha T. Young 10-28-1852 Cr
Cooper, Joel to W. M. Allen 8-13-1865 G
Cooper, John C. to Virginia Allen 8-10-1852 Hn
Cooper, John H. to Lydia Keith 9-21-1857 (9-23-1857) O
Cooper, John H. to Mary Ann Stagner 9-23-1846 Be
Cooper, John N. to Eliza Davis 3-3-1848 (3-5-1848) G

Cooper, John to Eliza Glover 1-24-1868 (1-25-1871?) T
Cooper, John to Elizabeth Frey 12-18-1854 (12-21-1854) Sh
Cooper, John to Jane Bennett 4-2-1860 (4-6-1860) Cr
Cooper, John to Jane Littleton 12-16-1865 (12-18-1865) O
Cooper, John to Josephine Rowland 1-11-1872 Cr
Cooper, John to Josey Bond 12-23-1870 Hy
Cooper, John to Mahuldy Halmark 4-29-1846 Cr
Cooper, John to Martha Jane Phillips 8-1-1849 Hn
Cooper, John to Winney Wright 8-28-1833 Hr
Cooper, Joseph H. to Kaziah T. Owen 3-15-1867 (3-16-1867) Ma
Cooper, Joseph J. to Elizabet L. Gladney 11-20-1845 Ma
Cooper, Joseph M. to Elizabeth Ross 3-6-1844 Cr
Cooper, Joseph M. to Mary Bohanan 5-27-1857 We
Cooper, Joseph W. to Elizabeth J. Moore 12-1-1842 G
Cooper, Joseph to Jane Dunigan 1-30-1855 G
Cooper, Joseph to Jane Phipps 11-20-1865 (11-31?-1866?) Cr
Cooper, Joseph to Winnaford Joyce 7-23-1858 Sh
Cooper, Josiah to Nancy Jane Sane 5-3-1854 G
Cooper, Kindred A. to Nancy M. Dougal 3-10-1852 We
Cooper, L. P. to Nancy E. Tarpley 3-1-1867 Hy
Cooper, Louis C. to Clementine Baker 1-28-1861 Hn
Cooper, M. T. to Mary E. Owen 4-17-1856 Sh
Cooper, Mansel to Malinda Sexton 4-25-1844 (5-28-1844) T
Cooper, Mordecai to Caroline Guthore 2-11-1860 Hn
Cooper, P. M. to M. W. Woods 6-30-1880 (7-1-1880) L
Cooper, P. W. to Sallie Ray 11-20-1875 (11-24-1875) Dy
Cooper, Peyton to Paralee Seat 11-22-1868 G B
Cooper, Pinkney to Frances Bennett 4-21-1856 We
Cooper, R. E. to N. C. Tyree 12-24-1860 G
Cooper, Rachael to Martha Walker 10-16-1839 Be
Cooper, Redding to Elizabeth Fowler 10-31-1838 Hn
Cooper, Richard F. to Mary E. Burdaux 2-9-1839 (2-10-1839) F
Cooper, Richard to Minerva Peete 2-21-1867 (2-23-1867) T
Cooper, Robert to Elizabeth Pierce 2-28-1865 Hn
Cooper, Robert to Leanah Moore 11-18-1861 T
Cooper, Rufus to Lucy Read 10-1-1869 Hy
Cooper, Rufus to Malinda Batchelor 1-24-1877 Hy
Cooper, S. C. to M. A. Bradley 1-16-1855 Hn
Cooper, Sam to Georgeanna Thevis 9-21-1876 Hy
Cooper, Saml. to America Gibson 3-6-1869 (3-9-1869) T
Cooper, Sidney to Eliza Jones 3-24-1835 Hr
Cooper, Silas to Nancy Duncan 2-13-1840 Cr
Cooper, Solomon E. to Emily H. Blalock 12-23-1861 (12-26-1861) Hr
Cooper, Solomon to Elizabeth Ball 7-13-1852 G
Cooper, T. D. to Lucinda J. Debruce 1-6-1858 Be
Cooper, T. H. to R. E. Taylor 10-14-1868 Cr
Cooper, T. T. to E. A. Ozier 7-12-1867 (no return) Cr
Cooper, Thaddeus D. to Sarah Jane Strayhorn 10-12-1859 Ma
Cooper, Thomas P. to Eliza Campbell 6-12-1853 O
Cooper, Thos. C. to Mary E. Eason 12-28-1866 Hy
Cooper, W. F. to Margaret E. Murphy 7-4-1870 (7-5-1870) Cr
Cooper, W. R. to Martha Brown 5-7-1870 (no return) Hy
Cooper, W. S. to Martha Utley 5-22-1865 (no return) Cr
Cooper, Whitnel L. to Arkansas J. Kendall 6-16-1858 Hn
Cooper, Whitson to Elizabeth Cook 9-13-1856 (9-14-1856) G
Cooper, William D. to Susan T. Bishop 1-19-1833 (1-20-1833) Hr
Cooper, William H. to Lucrita A. Anderson 12-14-1838 Ma
Cooper, William H. to Virginia Tucker 4-30-1860 (no return) We
Cooper, William J. to Emma Snores 2-25-1884 L
Cooper, William J. to Sarah J. Grayham 7-17-1866 Be
Cooper, William R. to Sarah A. Burnett 10-29-1857 Hn
Cooper, William to Elizabeth A. Garrison 11-12-1861 (no return) We
Cooper, William to Elvira Brooks 10-18-1838 Hn
Cooper, William to Hariett Littleton 4-15-1867 Hn B
Cooper, William to Henrietta Emaline Adams 4-1-1857 O
Cooper, William to Mary Bradley 3-9-1880 L
Cooper, William to Rebecca A. Greer 1-20-1867 Be
Cooper, Willingham to Nancy Brinkey 6-18-1839 (6-20-1839) F
Cooper, Wilson to Magdalana Handcock 16-8-1843 G
Cooper, Wilson to Mary C. Weaver 9-12-1853 (9-15-1853) Ma
Cooper, Wise A. to S. Urilda Shaw 9-5-1866 G
Cooper, Wm. B. to S. S. Pickens 8-28-1870 G
Cooper, Wm. F. to Amanda Parker 9-17-1862 (9-18-1862) Cr
Cooper, Wm. F. to Sarah Jane Jenkins 1-28-1849 Hn
Cooper, Wm. to Martha A. Barker 10-7-1868 (10-8-1868) Dy
Cooper, Wm. to Mima Cooper 9-10-1843 We
Cooper, ___ Addison to Margaret Murphy 5-22-1843 T
Cooper, sr., A. J. to Sallie Turner 6-20-1869 G
Coor, Charley to Levina Morris 6-20-1843 (6-22-1843) Hr
Coor, Chas. A. to Eviline Rhodes 8-10-1854 (8-11-1854) Hr
Coor, Willie to Frances J. Smith 5-2-1836 (5-5-1836) Hr
Coover, M. H. to Anna J. Davis 7-4-1862 Sh
Cope, Caleb jr. to Martha(Maletha?) J. Davis 7-1-1856 (7-2-1856) Hr
Cope, D. J. to M. E. Fields 8-1-1869 O
Cope, James C. to Nancy J. Patterson 2-21-1861 (no return) Hn
Cope, Samuel to Elizabeth C. Garner 1-7-1841 Hn
Cope, W. H. to H. E. Hendricks 8-12-1872 (no return) Dy

Copeland, Allen to Lizzie Mitchell 10-12-1872 (no return) Dy
Copeland, Charles E. to Eliza Reese 11-23-1841 (no return) F
Copeland, F. N. to E. V. Woodson 7-15-1842 Hn
Copeland, Harry to Harriet Doak 1-7-1874 (no return) Dy
Copeland, J. to Louisa C. Butler 12-18-1855 Sh
Copeland, James to L. A. Boaz 8-24-1854 (8-25-1854) G
Copeland, John to Mollie Copeland 5-8-1877 Dy
Copeland, William L. to Mary E. J. Dick 3-19-1853 Ma
Copeland, William to Hannah McBee 1-26-1825 (2-27-1825) Hr
Copeling, Millington to Nancy J. Skipper 10-11-1860 G
Copher, J. H. to L. A. Stamps 10-4-1868 T
Copher, Wm. M. to Hannah E. Brashers 3-5-1861 (no return) Hy
Copland, Dempsey to Matilda Byrn 11-17-1828 Ma
Copland, Isaac to Nelley A. Powell 12-23-1867 (12-31-1868?) T
Coppadge, G. J. to Mary J. Bishop 1-7-1856 (1-10-1856) Hr
Coppage, John J. to Mary M. Barnet 2-5-1845 Sh
Coppage, P. B. to Chester A. Thompson 3-1-1870 G
Coppedge, Andrew to Jennie Campbell 1-25-1872 Hy
Coppedge, J. J. to Ella Lundy 2-18-1874 (no return) Hy
Coppedge, James A. to Martha F. McSanland 5-15-1864 (no return) Hy
Coppedge, John to Mary A. Alexander 8-29-1855 (9-4-1855) Ma
Coppedge, S. N. to L. G. Clancy 4-19-1869 (no return) Hy
Coppedge, T. C. to F. A. (Mrs.) Powell 6-4-1866 (no return) Hy
Coppedge, William A. to Mary A. Armstrong 9-21-1844 (9-?-1844) T
Coppidge, James A. to Susan Kerr 3-12-1866 F
Corbet, John to S. H. Packard 10-5-1858 T
Corbet, Stephen M. to Martha A. Tipton 7-27?-1864 7-13-1864 O
Corbett, Reding to Elizabeth Winford 7-31-1841 Sh
Corbett, Thomas to Margaret Feenay 2-15-1859 (2-20-1859) Sh
Corbin, H. M. to E. J. Key 9-28-1863 (10-15-1863) O
Corbit, Daniel to Jennie McDaniel 12-2-1861 (12-19-1861) Sh
Corbit, Edwin to Nancy Starkey 7-3-1849 Sh
Corbitt, A. T. to Par Rushing 4-11-1839 Be
Corbitt, Daniel V. to Mahala W. Seldon 2-24-1853 Sh
Corbitt, Daniel to Elizabeth Meriweather 6-1-1862 Sh
Corbitt, David to Martha Kingston 12-19-1843 Sh
Corbitt, Edward H. to Rachel J. Mayes 5-22-1848 Sh
Corbitt, Edward V. to Mary A. Patterson 1-16-1852 (1-29-1852) Sh
Corbitt, George C. to Ella V. Hafflabower 11-17-1869 (11-18-1869) Ma
Corbitt, James E. to Mary Kingston 12-26-1841 Sh
Corbitt, L. V. to Amanda Alexander 5-7-1861 (5-9-1861) Sh
Corbitt, Meradeth to Margret Doherty 2-23-1853 Be
Corbitt, Newton to Mary Gibson 8-18-1842 Sh
Corbitt, T. A. to Viola Utley 2-17-1858 Be
Corbitt, William J. to Lucinda W. Crank 10-1-1852 (10-2-1852) G
Corbitt, Wm. to Mary Jane Wilkerson 1-23-1847 Sh
Corckett?, Samuel to Amy Barker 9-10-1846 Be
Corcy, William R. to Carlotta Smith 10-14-1863 Hn
Corder, Joseph to F. J. Bell 6-29-1872 (6-30-1872) T
Corder, William to Nancy Jolly 4-25-1861 Cr
Cordes, H. A. to Clara Cordes 12-7-1864 Sh
Cordle, Thomas R. to Sarah Moore 3-1-1855 Hr
Cordts, George W. to Emmer C. Warren 1-15-1878 Hy
Core, Reubin to Lucinda Core 7-21-1872 Hy
Corgett, John B. to Sarah A. Adams 11-8-1860 (no return) Hn
Corkburn, David R. to Mary Ann H. Robertson 3-12-1853 G
Corlan, J. H. D. to Hellen Rochell 4-30-1840 Cr
Corley, Catlet to Mary Rial 6-25-1840 Hn
Corley, Daniel to Sarah Noone 1-6-1854 (1-7-1854) Sh
Corley, J. W. to Lucy Holland 10-2-1860 G
Corley, James C. to Pantha Wagster 1-6-1864 G
Corley, John to Elizabeth Hudson 12-29-1834 (12-30-1834) Hr
Corley, N. C. to Mary Smith 8-27-1867 G
Corley, N. H. to Martha L. Lamb 6-23-1871 (6-27-1871) Dy
Corley, Nasthaniel H. to Nancy S. Cooper 10-27-1846 (11-28-1846) G
Corley, R. J. to Mary Cassa A. Hunt 10-27-1857 (10-28-1857) G
Corley, Thomas to Mary Flowers 12-27-1841 (1-4-1842) G
Corley, William E. to Amanda Ray 5-5-1855 Hn
Cormer, S. W. to P. A. Thomas 11-24-1864 G
Cornelius, A. L. to Laura A. Davis 6-30-1862 Sh
Cornelius, Aratus T. to Julia A. Pettit 2-17-1862 (2-18-1862) Sh
Cornelius, William to Patsy Bolling 1-21-1834 Hr
Cornell, Francis to Margaret Echard 6-22-1853 Sh
Cornell, George to Mary N. Robinson 12-25-1848 Sh
Cornell, Wm. to Livina Colman 11-26-1850 We
Corr, William to Catharine Donsho 7-27-1861 Sh
Correll, A. N. to Fredica Russ 3-24-1864 Sh
Correll, Joseph to Catharine Cox 8-28-1857 We
Correy, James, jr. to Catharine H. Walker 1-29-1857 Sh
Corrington, Addison to Judia Whitley 7-10-1831 (8-9-1831) G
Corthan, O. B. to Martha A. Cowthen 10-8-1854 G
Cortner, John to Jane Hays 7-5-1824 (7-7-1824) Hr
Cortney, Joseph H. to Adaline Tilghman 6-30-1864 G
Corum, Archabald O. to Elizabeth White 2-19-1839 O
Corum, Archibald O. to Mary L. Sanford 12-11-1849 O
Corum, Archibald O. to Mary T. Sandford 12-11-1849 O
Corum, John B. to Linda Catharine Hubert 3-22-1857 O

Corum, John to Harriett Hale 12-30-1843 (1-4-1844) O
Corum, M. W. to Catharine Hale 2-17-1851 (2-18-1851) O
Corum, Robert to Amanda I. Huddleston 11-12-1863 (11-13-1863) O
Corum, Tilman D. to Matilda A. Maxwell 11-19-1847 (11-21-1847) Ma
Corum, W. H. to E. R. Harris 9-4-1875 (9-6-1875) O
Corwin, M. V. to Margaret O'Brian 4-20-1864 Sh
Cos, Harmon to Narcissa E. Hicks 7-8-1852 Be
Coseton, John H. to Elizabeth Gooldsby 1-30-1845 (no return) We
Cosgrove, Patrick to Elizabeth Lyne 4-2-1853 Sh
Cosley, sr., C. W. to Jane Gullett 12-2-1857 G
Coss, George W. S. to Elizabeth A. Cook 3-25-1858 We
Cossett, F. D. to Martha L. Moore 6-7-1855 (no return) F
Cossitt, F. G. to Sarah Frances Taylor 8-29-1861 (8-30-1861) Hr
Costello, M. C. to Ellen Doyle 2-4-1858 Sh
Costello, Martin to Ellen Cody 3-7-1860 Sh
Costello, Uriah to Elizabeth Shipman 11-15-1826 (11-16-1826) Hr
Costen, S. T. to Kate White 2-16-1861 (2-18-1861) Sh
Costilow, Wm. to Ellen Doudel 8-14-1860 Sh
Costin, John H. to Emily Ezell 11-20-1862 Hn
Costler, William to Elizabeth Belote 3-26-1838 Sh
Costler, William to Jane M. Wilson 11-26-1843 (12-3-1843) G
Costta, Gunbatista to Madalina Chunnia 7-12-1860 Sh
Cotham, Thomas to Mary Pitts 2-21-1869 (no return) Dy
Cotheran, Henry to Hannah Flower 1-13-1866 T
Cotherane, Jos. to Sallie Minor 1-5-1866 (1-27-1866) T
Cotherum, Richmond to Jane Walk 12-7-1869 (12-8-1869) T
Cothran, Dick to Loveann Bumphass 12-25-1873 T
Cothran, Erasmus R. to Rosanna Shinault 1-10-1838 (1-11-1838) Hr
Cothran, Esquire to Sallie Edwards 2-20-1873 (2-21-1873) T
Cothran, James R. to Francis C. Lankford 12-13-1864 (12-14-1864) L
Cothran, James to Elmira Butler 12-18-1843 (12-21-1843) T
Cothran, Jesse S. to Ann Rebecca Howard 11-14-1840 (11-19-1840) T
Cothran, John S. to Mary J. McCombs 12-19-1853 (no return) F
Cothran, Levi to Martha A. Parnell 4-3-1861 (4-4-1861) Dy
Cothran, Thomas A. to Nancy V. Carter 12-16-1868 (12-17-1868) L
Cotner, G. W. to Camelus Ne____? 9-24-1855 (no return) Hn
Cotner, Joel to Polly Ann Chilcut 10-14-1838 Hn
Cotten, Jason to Fannie Cotten 12-26-1868 T
Cotten, Lee to Milly Jones 7-2-1872 (7-13-1872) T
Cotten, Robinson J. to Mary Eunice Outterbridge 12-6-1865 (12-14-1865) L
Cotter (Cotton?), William to Margaret Brodie (Brodice) 8-20-1850 Sh
Cotter, Alex to Marin D. Bond 2-20-1872 (no return) Hy
Cotter, David to Becky Boyd 12-21-1878 Hy
Cotter, Joe to Rachel Curren 3-13-1873 (no return) Hy
Cotter, Shedric to Ella Bond 12-31-1878 Hy
Cotter, Thos. N. to Tobitha J. Cotter 1-11-1848 (1-12-1848) F
Cotter, Wm. to Emma Cobb 2-5-1871 Hy
Cotter, jr., H. W. to Mary Johnson 6-5-1867 (6-6-1867) Ma
Cotterill, John to J. C. Harrell 8-28-1863 Sh
Cottingham, James to Virginia D. Gully 1-25-1866 Be
Cottingham, T. to E. Watson 6-10-1841 Be
Cottingham, William to Jemima Rushing 11-2-1843 Be
Cotton, H. P. (Dr.) to Ella V. Smith 10-4-1870 (10-5-1870) Ma
Cotton, Henry W. to Julia Ann Gornet? 6-28-1869 T
Cotton, Henry Washington to Julia Ann Graham 6-28-1869 (7-1-1869) T
Cotton, J. C. C. to Amanda E. Webb 11-6-1862 G
Cotton, J. M. to Ardell Mitchelson 8-14-1866 T
Cotton, J. N. to Sophronia E. Mitchell 3-29-1870 (no return) Cr
Cotton, J. N. to Sophronia E. Mitchell 7-25-1870 Cr
Cotton, James Hooper to Ann Elizabeth Purvis 4-2-1853 (4-4-1853) T
Cotton, John to D. A. (Mrs.) Brogden 12-29-1863 (12-31-1863) Dy
Cotton, N. H. to Emma Fletcher 3-12-1864 Sh
Cotton, N. W. K. to Clay King 7-20-1878 Hy
Cotton, Nelson to Sarah Dunlap 11-24-1879 (no return) L
Cotton, Tom to Sarah Saunders 2-10-1872 (2-11-1872) T
Cotton, W. H. to Elizabeth Sanderson 4-5-1871 (4-11-1871) Dy
Cotton, Wm. P. to Lucinda J. Grist 3-2-1864 (3-8-1864) Sh
Couch, George to Bridget Buckley 1-6-1862 Sh
Couch, Levi to Sarah C. Shafter 12-1-1849 (no return) F
Couch, Robert to Lucinda Thompson 12-24-1872 Dy
Couch, S. H. to Elvira J. Baird 1-27-1858 G
Couch, Saml. to Rebecca Needham 12-1-1847 Hr
Couch, William to June E. Brumley 12-31-1859 Sh
Coughlin, Daniel to Ellen Silvers 6-18-1862 (6-19-1862) Sh
Coulter, Allen to Louisa Bounds 9-18-1854 (no return) F
Coulter, James A. to Martha A. ____ 9-19-1855 (no return) F
Coulter, Nathl. A. to Elizabeth M. Canaday 11-30-1853 O
Coulter, S. F. to E. F. Coulter 11-22-1859 (11-23-1859) Sh
Coulter, William to Tamar Newnan? 12-27-1869 (12-28-1869) Cr
Council, Benjamin to Martha Boothe 1-2-1845 Hn
Council, E. E. to Margaret J. Barnhill 11-8-1863 Hn
Council, Elisha E. to Emily L. Barnhill 12-21-1865 Hn
Council, Matthew to Jane Snider 9-4-1847 Hn
Council, Milford to Mary Hansel 12-9-1856 Hn
Counsel, William H. to Cynthia Frazer 5-13-1830 Ma
Counsel, WilliamH. to Cinthia W. Rucker 1-10-1832 Hr
Counsell, Elijah W. to Mary J Grainger 1-14-1857 Hn

Counts, James to Rose Burnett 11-?-1868 (11-22-1868) Cr
Counts, Robert to Susan C. Greer 2-16-1852 G
Counts, William to Elizabeth Ann Davidson 7-12-1836 (7-13-1836) G
Courts, Iverson to Rilly Oakley 7-9-1867 Hn B
Courts, Thos. D. to Mary A. Paschall 5-17-1846 Hn
Cousar, J. F.? to S. E. Campbell 5-9-1870 (5-10-1870) T
Cousins, James D. to Sarah J. Smith 12-9-1869 (no return) L
Cousins, Jas. D. to Mary Stephens 3-26-1858 (4-3-1858) G
Cousins, N. M. to Frances E. Carnal 7-28-1863 (7-29-1863) L
Covdy?, A. J. to Nancy Harris 10-15-1874 T
Covey, James J. to S. C. Morrison 11-21-1865 (11-26-1865) F
Covey, John E. G. to Jane Hamrick 11-13-1865 (no return) F
Covington, Ab to Caroline Savage 8-3-1876 Hy
Covington, Albert to Harriet Weams 2-20-1873 Hy
Covington, B. B. to Georgie B. West 12-22-1880 L
Covington, Caleb H. to Nancy E. Shane 12-16-1850 (12-17-1850) G
Covington, Caroline to Agnes Wilson 9-16-1869 (9-18-1869) Cr
Covington, D. A. to Mary Horton 11-25-1841 Cr
Covington, David L. to Emily Green 9-18-1853 Cr
Covington, E. H. to Mary Ellen McVay 5-19-1864 Hn
Covington, Edmond? to Nancy Matthews 12-5-1854 (12-17-1855?) O
Covington, Edward to Sarah S. Childress 2-22-1868 (2-24-1868) L
Covington, Edward to Vicey Patterson 5-18-1859 Ma
Covington, George to Rachel Taylor 12-25-1877 Hy
Covington, H. W. to A. E. Moore 12-26-1871 Hy
Covington, Henry B. to Martha Fryor 5-12-1863 Hn
Covington, I. W. to Penelope Gilbert 10-15-1860 (no return) We
Covington, J. A. to Mariah Ross 1-10-1856 (no return) We
Covington, J. A. to Mary McMinn 8-11-1868 G
Covington, J. D. to Nancy A. Dowell 1-2-1849 Cr
Covington, J. R. to A. E. Davis 6-7-1857 We
Covington, J. S. to Elizabeth Johnson 1-23-1853 Cr
Covington, James to Nanny Watkins 11-17-1846 Hn
Covington, John A. M. to Melvina Davis 6-11-1857 T
Covington, John A. to Virginia A. Harris 2-26-1866 (2-27-1866) F
Covington, John M. to Charity Johnson 12-17-1838 (12-20-1838) Hr
Covington, Joseph A. to Edney J. Adcock 8-11-1866 (8-12-1866) Ma
Covington, L. C. to Mary A. Guin 1-8-1856 We
Covington, L. C. to Rebecca T. Mathis 3-12-1857 We
Covington, Madison to Jeroline Cody 1-26-1870 Cr
Covington, Miles to Rachel A. Berryhill 6-19-1853 Hn
Covington, R. W. to Elizabeth Cope 3-29-1857 Hn
Covington, Thomas to Alice Dinwiddie 1-27-1866 F
Covington, W. F. to Fannie Mullin 1-27-1872 Hy
Covington, W. W. to Mary A. Moore 11-20-1873 Hy
Covington, William P. to Sallie E. Manley 8-9-1860 Hn
Covington, William to Nancy L. Lyon 12-7-1853 (12-8-1853) G
Cowan, A. F. to Rebecca Bull 10-22-1845 F
Cowan, Benjamin S. to Margaret E. Skiles 12-15-1853 G
Cowan, D. P. to Luzenia Bull 3-11-1851 F
Cowan, David to Nancy Davis 11-7-1846 (11-8-1846) Hr
Cowan, George to Amanda Hargrove 12-16-1853 Hr
Cowan, Harvey to Lucy Blanton 12-21-1867 Hn
Cowan, Henderson to Lucy Fields 2-14-1874 T
Cowan, Isaac F. to Mary Branch 11-29-1848 G
Cowan, J. M. to Bettie Braden 8-1-1883 (8-2-1883) L
Cowan, J. S. to P. J. Witherspoon 2-27-1868 Hy
Cowan, Jno. to Ann M. Brown 11-2-1853 (11-3-1853) Sh
Cowan, John S. R. to E. A. C. Thompson 2-8-1869 (2-10-1869) F
Cowan, John S. to Nancy H. Bond 1-9-1861 Hn
Cowan, John to Willie A. Fitsgerald 8-17-1867 (8-18-1867) F
Cowan, Lewis to Maria Thompson 9-18-1872 T
Cowan, Moses to Levina Pool 6-13-1844 F
Cowan, Patrick to Mary V. Gillespie 1-14-1862 Sh
Cowan, Robert C. to Susan Irabella 8-5-1862 (no return) Hy
Cowan, S. W. to Minerva Massey 12-19-1837 Sh
Cowan, Thomas to Mary A. Clayton 9-25-1853 Hn
Cowan?, Thomas to Leanna Moore 5-5-1842 (5-12-1842) T
Coward, Anthony B. to Mary Wooten 12-14-1841 (12-15-1841) T
Coward, Cal to Harriet Moffit 12-30-1874 (12-31-1874) T
Coward, Henry to Louisa Chamber 11-17-1865 (11-18-1865) T
Coward, William S. to Mary N. Hall 10-10-1865 (10-11-1865) T
Coward, William to Agness E. Shaw 6-7-1845 (6-12-1845) L
Coward, William to Angeline Thomas 1-7-1874 (1-8-1874) T B
Cowell, Albert Z. to Martha Boughcom(Bawcum) 9-20-1865 Be
Cowell, B. T. to Z. A. Robertson 7-10-1879 (no return) Dy
Cowell, Benjamin Francis to Ellen Cockream 9-27-1861 (9-30-1861) Sh
Cowell, Berry to Martha Ellen Cole 12-5-1844 Be
Cowell, Bryant to Mary Robinson 5-20-1848 (5-21-1848) L
Cowell, C. H. to Frances G. T. Baucum 10-21-1868 Be
Cowell, Charles T. to Adra A. A. Holland 10-5-1865 Be
Cowell, Charles to Harriett J. Pope 11-19-1840 Be
Cowell, E. G. to A. M. Brown 10-2-1866 Be
Cowell, J. S. to S. E. Byler 1-7-1879 (1-8-1879) L
Cowell, Jos. to Mazy Jordan 1-14-1841 Be
Cowell, Joseph to Mary Jordon 10-9-1847 Be
Cowell, Lewis M. to Manerva C. Howe 4-11-1860 Be

Cowell, W. H. to M. E. Jones 2-26-1872 Dy
Cowen, Benjamin F. to Nancy N. Hutchions 5-26-1847 G
Cowen, Henry F. to Margarett Wrenn 7-21-1847 (7-22-1847) G
Cowen, W. F. to L. A. Jones 12-20-1871 T
Cowgile (Cowgill), James to Violetta Givens 8-25-1837 Sh
Cowgill, Abner to Caroline Gray 8-3-1854 Sh
Cowgill, Henry W. to Elizabeth C. Job 6-11-1856 Sh
Cowgill, Henry W. to Mary E. Wales 4-19-1862 (4-20-1862) Sh
Cowgill, James W. to Mary Berry 9-13-1843 Sh
Cowgill, James W. to Sarah M. Rankin 12-13-1853 (12-14-1853) Sh
Cowgill, James to Susan Branch 1-17-1845 Sh
Cowgill, John to Louisa Anderson 5-31-1842 Sh
Cowgill, Thomas J. to Josephine King 7-21-1853 Sh
Cowgill, William A. to Louisa Jones 6-25-1848 Sh
Cowles, H. to Martha Howard 12-31-1874 Dy
Cowles, Henry to Lucinda Fowlkes 7-17-1869 (no return) Dy
Cowley, E. A. to Margaret Chandler 6-24-1862 O
Cowser, Thos. to Margaret A. Faulkner 12-24-1866 (12-25-1866) T
Cowser?, Prichard to Elizabeth A. Wright 3-25-1843 T
Cowsert, Samuel S. to Virginia A. Tyson 1-25-1856 (1-27-1856) O
Cox, A. A. to Susan Roach 11-12-1855 Sh
Cox, A. E. to Laura Ellis 9-22-1884 (9-23-1884) L
Cox, Abram to Polly Rook 10-24-1830 (11-3-1830) Hr
Cox, Acuff to Caroline Terry 3-28-1867 Hn
Cox, Albert to Ellen Davis 1-30-1869 (no return) Hy
Cox, Alexander to Elizabeth Fox 8-31-1831 (9-8-1831) G
Cox, Alexander to Mary E. Shoemake 3-29-1875 L
Cox, Alfred to Sarah Bishop 9-11-1839 (9-12-1839) Hr
Cox, Allen to Lillie Ann Hudspeth 3-11-1833 Hr
Cox, Allen to Mary Ann Parker 10-15-1858 (10-3?-1858) Hr
Cox, Andy to Caroline Wesson 11-4-1845 Sh
Cox, Asa to Martha Ann Street 12-2-1841 Hn
Cox, Asa to Nancy Harris 12-21-1835 (12-22-1835) Hr
Cox, B. F. to J. A. Butler 6-8-1867 (6-23-1867) Cr
Cox, Bernard to Sallie Mosley 12-27-1866 (1-12-1867) F B
Cox, Bryant to Cornelia Bailey 10-17-1851 (10-23-1851) Hr
Cox, Cader to Edny Bishop 12-16-1835 (12-17-1835) Hr
Cox, Caleb to Elizabeth Hicks 8-4-1832 (8-9-1832) Hr
Cox, Charles J. to Charlotte Horn 4-24-1844 (4-25-1844) Hr
Cox, Cunningham to Mary Galloway 12-30-1834 (1-2-1835) Hr
Cox, D. F. to Jena Vanhook 9-25-1864 Hn
Cox, David to Lydia A. Rodgers 1-16-1850 Cr
Cox, David to Sallie Thompson 11-16-1876 Hy
Cox, Davy to Sarah Sparkman 12-19-1867 (no return) Hy
Cox, Dempsey to Elvira Bradford 11-14-1866 (11-15-1866) Ma
Cox, Eli to E. C. Pope 3-9-1852 We
Cox, Eli to Elizabeth Young 4-19-1847 (4-20-1840 Hr
Cox, Eli to Jane Parkes 10-1-1832 (10-?-1832) Hr
Cox, Eli to Precilla W. Brown 8-2-1848 Hr
Cox, Eli to Virtuous? C. Grant 8-2-1836 Hr
Cox, F. H. to M. E. Jeffres 11-4-1868 Hy
Cox, Franklin to Eliz. Burns 11-13-1871 T
Cox, Gambrill to Marian Turner 9-13-1830 (9-16-1830) Ma
Cox, George W. to Gracey A. Hensley 3-5-1867 (no return) Hy
Cox, George W. to Mary Johnson 6-23-1855 (6-26-1855) T
Cox, George to Luan F. Bowden 10-21-1847 Hn
Cox, Gova to Sarah? Palmer 6-12-1855 Hn
Cox, Green B. to Mary P. Williams 2-6-1845 Cr
Cox, H. C. to Mary Ann Roper 10-24-1866 (10-25-1866) Cr
Cox, Herman to Martha J. Mullinicks 1-20-1858 Be
Cox, Hiram to Louisa Ford 3-16-1860 Cr
Cox, Isaac to Frances Finney 6-23-1866 F B
Cox, Isian to Mebelda Hardion 4-2-1850 Cr
Cox, J. A. to Bhethsheba? White 12-17-1872 (12-19-1872) Cr
Cox, J. D. to Josephine Grinstead 7-14-1846 Hn
Cox, J. F. to Emma C. Chambers 4-19-1870 (4-21-1870) F
Cox, J. P. to M. Ann Whippell 4-21-1870 (4-24-1870) O
Cox, J. T. to Elvine Case 2-24-1858 We
Cox, J. W. B. to S. A. Roland 12-25-1867 O
Cox, J. W. to M. M. Grimes 2-5-1857 We
Cox, J. W. to M. M. Rogers 3-23-1868 G
Cox, J. W. to Mary P. Matheny 1-24-1870 (1-27-1870) Cr
Cox, Jack to Sina Garrison 5-1-1869 (no return) Dy
Cox, Jackson to Frances Moon 1-11-1868 Hy
Cox, Jacob to Elizabeth Herne? 2-27-1834 Hr
Cox, James E. to Mary F. Furgason 2-16-1864 G
Cox, James M. to Amanda M. Edney 10-28-1856 (10-31-1856) Sh
Cox, James to Harriet Kilpatrick 5-19-1855 Hr
Cox, James to Rebecca Caldwell 12-20-1867 (no return) Hy
Cox, Jas. A. to Margaret W. Collingsworth 12-16-1850 (12-19-1850) G
Cox, Jas. A. to Rebecca Caldwell 12-15-1868 (12-16-1868) F
Cox, Jenkins to Mary A. Butler 12-22-1848 Sh
Cox, Jesse K. to Mary M. Moore 9-14-1865 Hy
Cox, Jesse to Zilpha Boyt 7-14-1832 (7-?-1832) Hr
Cox, John A. to Precilla Lowry 9-3-1857 Hn
Cox, John Allen to Martha Horne 12-13-1847 (12-17-1847) Hr
Cox, John B. to Amanda M. Reynolds 5-23-1843 (5-25-1843) Hr

Cox, John Henry to Mary Wallis 9-24-1870 (9-28-1870) L
Cox, John N. to Ann P. Isbell 10-5-1865 Mn
Cox, John to Bridget O'Malow 1-13-1861 Sh
Cox, John to L. J. Jones 1-22-1868 O
Cox, John to Lou Carrington 12-28-1880 (12-29-1880) L B
Cox, John to Martha A. Hickman 11-5-1857 Cr
Cox, John to Mary M. Pankey 8-11-1852 (8-12-1852) Hr
Cox, John to Susan Dyre 3-1-1874 O
Cox, Johnathan to Elizabeth Macon 10-31-1850 (11-7-1850) Hr
Cox, Joseph to Sally Rogers 12-19-1837 (12-21-1837) Hr
Cox, Kinchen to Olive Adams 12-22-1867 Be
Cox, Levon H. to Tela Mebane 6-30-1866 (7-15-1866) F B
Cox, Lewis C. to Martha Parthenia Sewell 11-16-1867 (11-27-1867) Ma
Cox, Lewis L. to Mary E. Young 11-10-1869 (11-11-1869) Ma
Cox, M. M. to Sallie E. Winsett 1-10-1867 Hn
Cox, Marshall W. to Nancy Gately 11-21-1840 (11-26-1840) Hr
Cox, Moses E. to Mary Campbell 3-20-1849 L
Cox, Moses to Nancy Eally 9-28-1841 Cr
Cox, N. J. to M. E. Dishough 11-12-1860 Hr
Cox, Nat. to Sally Harris 7-24-1855 Be
Cox, Nelson to Margaret A. Leslie 4-4-1844 Cr
Cox, Newton to Rosella Lowery 6-16-1860 (6-24-1860) Cr
Cox, P. G. to Mary Ann Brinkley 11-13-1839 Ma
Cox, Robert F. to Sarah G. Guinn 10-8-1865 Hy
Cox, Robert H. to Tabitha L. Watkins 10-19-1866 (10-21-1866) Ma
Cox, Samuel (James?) to Elizabeth Counts 7-1-1836 Sh
Cox, Samuel to Cilia Diggs 9-26-1839 Cr
Cox, Shadrich to Barbary Messer 9-6-1849 Be
Cox, Sharod to Nancy Roper 10-12-1840 Cr
Cox, Simpson to Armenta Byars 11-12-1845 Hn
Cox, T. W. to Mollie Johnson 11-4-1867 (11-5-1867) F
Cox, Thomas to Sophronia W. Farned 1-18-1858 (1-19-1858) Hr
Cox, W. A. to Almira Newberne 12-13-1877 Hy
Cox, W. A. to Susan A. Bowers 2-22-1872 Hy
Cox, W. B. to Catharine Denton 1-2-1860 Hr
Cox, W. H. to Louisa Ezell 3-28-1865 (3-30-1865) Cr
Cox, W. J. to Martha A. Barr 12-8-1868 Be
Cox, W. P. to L. V. King 12-23-1873 (12-25-1873) O
Cox, William G. to Martha Jane Lamber 4-25-1853 (5-5-1853) Hr
Cox, William H. to Eudora Whitesides 10-23-1866 Ma
Cox, William H. to Johanna A. Belton 3-2-1885 (3-3-1885) L
Cox, William Henry to Martha E. Shoemake 6-24-1873 L
Cox, William T. to Eliza J. Redick 3-13-1849 G
Cox, William T. to Emeline McKnight 2-23-1852 (7-24-1852) Sh
Cox, William to Elizabeth J. Glidewell 8-3-1846 Ma
Cox, William to Mandy Bolton 11-9-1875 Hy
Cox, William to Mary Bane 3-18-1852 (3-21-1852) Sh
Cox, William to Mattie Coleman 7-22-1871 Hy
Cox, William to Susan Holmes 9-23-1842 (no return) Hn
Cox, Willis to M. H. Hartsfield 1-8-1851 Hn
Cox, Wm. J. to Lorina Bruce 7-19-1846 Be
Coxe, Asa to Sophia W. Barton 7-22-1852 Hn
Coyle, A. to Rebecca Park 8-21-1850 O
Cozart, Broadie H. to Mary Jane Lightfoot 3-8-1838 (no return) Hn
Cozart, Gilbert to Amanda J. Fuller 12-2-1867 (12-3-1867) Dy
Cozart, Gilbert to Mary Kirby 1-1-1845 (1-7-1845) Ma
Cozart, Hubbard to Lucy Robbins 7-23-1866 (7-24-1866) Ma
Cozart, J. to S. E. D. Wilkinson 10-2-1871 (10-3-1871) Dy
Cozart, James B. to Irene Brown 9-5-1871 Ma
Cozart, Jasper to Susan Harris 1-13-1866 Dy
Cozart, John L. to Celia Enocks 12-23-1869 (12-26-1869) Cr
Cozart, Joshua M. to Julia Frances Marlow 2-13-1858 (2-17-1858) Ma
Cozby, Jacob A. to Mary Ann Cearly 2-17-1847 Hr
Cozby, James L. to Rebecca Womack 2-21-1839 (2-25-1839) Hr
Cozby, John to Violett O. Ozburn? 11-30-1846 (12-1-1846) Hr
Cozby, Mathew to Jane Hutson 6-12-1833 (6-15-1833) Hr
Cozby, Robert A. to Sarah Carley 12-17-1847 (12-28-1847) Hr
Cozby, Robert to Elizabeth Murdaugh 8-5-1835 Hr
Cozby, William to Mary N. Montgomery 5-5-1866 T
Cozort, Madison to Emelina Marlow 12-29-1847 (12-30-1847) Ma
Cozort, R. R. to Lilian J. Moore 11-14-1872 Hy
Cozzart, Robert W. to Catharine F. Powell 12-2-1859 (12-8-1859) G
Crab, John to Mary Gresam 2-28-1840 Be
Crab, John to Mary J. Walker 3-29-1873 (3-30-1873) Cr
Crabb, H. W. to Elisa Ann King 11-29-1868 Be
Crabb, Isaiah to Mary Hammons 2-23-1839 (2-26-1839) F
Crabb, J.(T?) W. to K. Curtis 2-4-1842 Be
Crabb, Wm. to Polly Baggett 8-6-1844 Be
Crabbe, Joseph to Mary J. Galloway 5-16-1861 Sh
Crabtree, J. E. to Margaret Allen 1-19-1858 (no return) We
Crabtree, Samuel M. to Isabell S. A. Patton 12-6-1843 Cr
Crabtree, Samuel to Barthema Thacker 7-6-1844 (no return) F
Craddock, John R. to Louisa E. Nappier 6-5-1845 Hr
Craddock, Joseph to Nancy Moon 11-16-1843 Hn
Craddock, R. W. to Mary E. Carey 7-28-1866 O
Craddock, Thos. J. to Susan T. Collinsworth 2-14-1852 (2-17-1852) G
Craddock, William M. to Catharine E. Jones 11-1-1852 (11-3-1852) G

Cradick, James to Done? Johnson 10-3-1869 G
Craft, Archibald to Jane E. Renolds 11-19-1838 Hr
Craft, John S. to Abigale L. Thompson 12-18-1833 Sh
Craft, Robert K. to Virginia C. Bettis 9-9-1856 (9-10-1856) Sh
Craft, Samuel to Penny Thompson 10-30-1833 Sh
Crafton, Daniel W. to Mary Bradford 11-22-1826 G
Crafton, J. D. to C. M. Ware 6-3-1862 (no return) Hy
Crafton, J. to Sarah J. Gillham 8-26-1859 Sh
Crafton, James W. to C. C. Moody 2-20-1856 G
Crafton, James W. to Sarah J. Roe 4-3-1854 G
Crafton, John B. to Elizabeth Haguewood 7-23-1839 (7-25-1839) G
Crafton, John to Dulla Pearce 8-14-1871 (8-17-1871) Cr
Crafton, R. L. to Mary E. Purdy 6-18-1866 (6-22-1866) Dy
Crafton, Thomas to Emily Underwood 5-23-1868 G B
Crafton, William S. to Frances C. Alexander 12-18-1852 (12-19-1852) O
Crafton, William to Candis Lawrence 9-5-1867 G
Crafton, William to Hester Ann Dial 3-27-1830 (4-1-1830) G
Crage, John to Carline Cassells 11-20-1847 (11-21-1847) G
Craig, Alfred to Aggny? Maclin 12-14-1867 (12-21-1867) T
Craig, Anderson to Harriet Fullen 6-8-1854 L
Craig, Andrew to Jane E. Lambeth 3-17-1845 (3-18-1845) Hr
Craig, Arsa to Matilda Lea 12-16-1838 Cr
Craig, B. F. to R. E. Dunlap 1-31-1849 (2-1-1849) F
Craig, C. S. to M. W. Simmons 10-14-1866 Hn
Craig, C. T. to Maranda Presson 6-5-1862 Be
Craig, Charles to Mary E. Shearman 8-28-1856 (no return) L
Craig, Charles to Susan F. Presson 12-13-1849 Be
Craig, Daniel M. to Nancy E. Nokes 12-23-1848 (12-24-1848) F
Craig, David M. to Elizabeth Hart 11-26-1860 Dy
Craig, Eli to Tennessee Bond 3-10-1870 G B
Craig, Francis Marion to Parnina H. Norvell 12-6-1859 Ma
Craig, Houston to Thersey Ann Beasley 2-8-1865 L
Craig, Huston to Mary A. Whitson 8-16-1869 L
Craig, J. D. to S. M. P. Blackwood 10-21-1871 (10-25-1871) T
Craig, J. L. to Miza Hamill 12-24-1884 L
Craig, J. O. to E. E. Bell 3-26-1877 (3-28-1877) Dy
Craig, J. Q. to S. S. Bowen 9-17-1866 Dy
Craig, James A. to Caroline Travis 8-14-1860 Hn
Craig, James S. P. to Harriet Rebecca Hood 11-24-1855 (11-25-1855) O
Craig, James to Mary Garrett 1-8-1867 (1-13-1867) Dy
Craig, Jasper W. to Lucretia C. Tatum 8-8-1850 G
Craig, John M. to Martha Baker 1-21-1850 O
Craig, John P. to Mary Hamilton 12-10-1860 O
Craig, John to Isabella Pierce 5-3-1869 G
Craig, John to Martha D. McCraw 6-26-1866 (6-28-1866) T
Craig, John to Mary Roach 3-15-1864 (3-16-1864) Cr
Craig, John to May Roach 3-15-1865 (no return) Cr
Craig, John to Sarah Margaret Delashmet 8-2-1871 (8-3-1871) T
Craig, Joseph to Peggy A. Reynolds 7-8-1862 (7-10-1862) O
Craig, L. N. to Anna Carter 3-24-1874 F
Craig, Luther Johnson to Mary R. McGuin? (McGuire?) 9-6-1871 L
Craig, R. H. to Susan A. Presson 4-26-1868 Be
Craig, Saml. S. to Jennie T. Wright 3-13-1862 T
Craig, Saml. to Ophelia Stone 4-3-1871 Ma
Craig, Samuel A. to Julia E. Allen 3-4-1853 Hn
Craig, Samuel to Jane W. Gould 10-13-1839 Hn
Craig, Samuel to Martha Smith 9-20-1862 (9-21-1862) Ma
Craig, Thos. to Sarah Allen 3-17-1843 Be
Craige, Samuel to Carroline Alvis 2-16-1839 G
Craige, William B. to Amanda Berry 7-13-1846 (7-15-1846) G
Crain, G. B. to Susie Clyatt 3-4-1884 (3-5-1884) L
Crain, Giles B. to Caroline Fulgum 2-15-1832 (2-16-1832) Hr
Crain, Isaac F. to Sarah Keathley 9-9-1842 (10-1-1842) O
Crain, Jeremiah S. to Rachael Wallace 2-5-1829 Ma
Crain, Joshua to Jane E. Shelby 7-29-1847 Sh
Crain, Lemuel to Eliza Roy 12-31-1855 (1-1-1856) Sh
Crain, Stephen to Elezabeth Collinsworth 11-18-1828 Ma
Crain, Thomas to Sally Hopper 8-31-1829 Hr
Crain, Whitmill to Catherine Cameron 7-14-1855 (7-15-1855) Sh
Crain, Whitmill to Lucy C. Ware 11-11-1847 Sh
Crain, William to Drucilla Fowler 5-24-1830 Hr
Crain, William to Narcissa L. Brooks 1-26-1837 Sh
Crain, Wm. to Mary A. Thompson 6-20-1843 Hr
Cramnatt, Valentine M. to Sucett Busbee? 5-26-1860 Hn
Crampley, T. R. to Sarah Williams 8-24-1874 (8-25-1874) Dy
Cranbury, Isaac to Bettie Sasser 3-7-1868 (3-8-1871?) T
Crandel, E. R. to Caro Russell 2-22-1873 (2-25-1873) L
Crane, Christopher C. to Mary L. Wilkins 11-3-1860 (11-4-1860) Cr
Crane, E. W. to Julia A. Manning 12-12-1884 L
Crane, Howell P. to Mary Campbell 8-8-1850 F
Crane, Josiah W. to Rebecca Bramblett 8-8-1845 (8-10-1845) O
Crane, Lemuel to Cornelia Ann Hine 7-8-1851 Sh
Crane, T. B. to E. H. Howel 1-16-1867 O
Crane, W. H. to Bettie McKani 10-19-1874 (no return) Dy
Crane, William to Rachel Crawford 3-19-1846 Sh
Cranford, J. F. to Susan E. Braden 11-26-1867 (12-1-1867) F
Crank, James A. to Sarah Howard 1-28-1851 G
Crank, John D. to Elenor M. Runalds 2-3-1844 (2-7-1844) G
Crank, William G. to Zada P. Wright 12-17-1846 (12-19-1846) G
Crank, William to Mary Thompson 11-28-1853 (12-1-1853) G
Crass, Elijah to Nancy Bishop 3-24-1844 (no return) Hn
Crass, S. S. to M. E. Willson 6-11-1865 Hn
Crassett, Henry T. to Amand Garrisson 8-7-1860 (no return) We
Crate, H. L. to Jennie Walls 3-14-1872 Hy
Crates, Wm. J. to Lucy A. Bishop 4-29-1861 (5-1-1861) Hr
Cravans, Hanson to Martha Wagster 12-27-1845 We
Craven, Lacy? to Matilda C. Blackshar 12-31-1854 (1-3-1855) O
Craven, Sam'l. to Rebecca Jane King 1-19-1853 (1-20-1853) O
Cravens, Jack to Georgiana Watson 12-8-1869 G B
Cravens, James L. to M. M. Wofford 10-16-1860 Hn
Cravens, Robert M. to Elizabeth F. Wofford 2-3-1843 (no return) Hn
Cravesn, Hugh to Zelpha A. Walker 10-7-1867 O
Cravin, John W. to Amanda J. Barr 12-31-1844 Cr
Cravin, John W. to Amanda M. Enochs 2-25-1849 Cr
Cravins, G. M. to Emeline Parks 11-26-1857 We
Cravins, John B. to Mary A. Allen 4-14-1859 We
Craw, Jas. A.? to Emeline Jones 3-23-1864 (no return) Dy
Crawford (Cranford), Joseph L. to Mary S. Phipps 1-9-1840 Sh
Crawford, Alexander to Harriett Shackleford 4-8-1828 Hr
Crawford, Andrew J. to Evelina G. A. Heath 9-17-1853 (9-19-1853) O
Crawford, Ashly R. to Elizabeth J. Ward 2-26-1848 (3-2-1848) Hr
Crawford, B. A. to S. F. Pegram 10-29-1857 We
Crawford, Bennett to S. E. Petty 3-9-1851 Cr
Crawford, Edwin to Jane Reagan 2-24-1824 (2-26-1824) Hr
Crawford, Elisha J. to Sarah Elizabeth White 8-7-1866 Ma
Crawford, Evan to Nancy Bright 10-26-1825 O
Crawford, Franklin to Ann L. Eathan 3-2-1840 (3-5-1840) F
Crawford, G. A. to E. Marshall 8-11-1868 F
Crawford, G. C. to Tennessee Ogles 2-1-1870 G
Crawford, G. W. to Margaret Carter (Sartin) 1-1-1858 O
Crawford, George to John A. Irvin 9-14-1867 (9-15-1867) F B
Crawford, Henry to T. A. Martin 2-28-1865 Hn
Crawford, Isaac W. to Sarah Lillard 8-10-1846 (8-12-1846) Hr
Crawford, Isaac to Manerva A. Mathis 3-9-1867 Hn B
Crawford, J. B. to Sarah A. Wall 4-20-1859 (4-20?-1859) F
Crawford, J. D. to M. E. Shackleton 1-19-1876 Dy
Crawford, J. F. to Mary Ann Dixon 11-13-1867 Hy
Crawford, J. I. to N. P. Rogers 8-4-1861 G
Crawford, J. J. to Margarette P. McKnight 9-19-1844 (no return) F
Crawford, J. T. to L. D. Young 12-20-1869 (12-22-1869) Cr
Crawford, J. W. to M. A. Barnett 2-11-1866 (2-12-1866) Dy
Crawford, James B. to Cyntha A. Williams 6-7-1852 Hr
Crawford, James C. to Eliza A. Been? 11-29-1849 Hn
Crawford, James L. to Eliza J. Pickins 2-6-1867 (2-7-1867) F
Crawford, James M. to Nancy J. Reno 2-4-1851 (2-6-1851) Sh
Crawford, James to Ann McGrath 5-20-1854 (5-21-1854) Sh
Crawford, James to Mary Ann Tackett 2-20-1861 (2-21-1861) Hr
Crawford, James to Rosanna Russell 10-3-1854 Sh
Crawford, Jerry to Abby Forest 2-2-1867 F B
Crawford, John C. to Caroline Alston 10-8-1839 Sh
Crawford, John F. to Clotilda Jones 6-21-1838 Ma
Crawford, John H. to Amanda M. Hampton 8-31-1869 G
Crawford, John H. to Marza Nix 2-13-1850 Hn
Crawford, John H. to Narcissa Blankenship 3-6-1854 (3-10-1854) G
Crawford, John R. to Amanda Powell 1-12-1850 (1-24-1850) Hr
Crawford, John S. to Sarah C. Thurmond 5-27-1863 (5-28-1863) L
Crawford, John W. W. to Virginia F. Bateman 8-29-1857 (8-1?-1857) Ma
Crawford, John W. to Mary Jane Owens 1-17-1856 We
Crawford, John to Lucy Green 1-6-1874 (no return) Hy
Crawford, John to Nancy Kuykendall 3-9-1867 Hn
Crawford, Joseph B. to Pricilla Cloar 1-31-1851 Hn
Crawford, Joseph to Texana V. Martin 1-8-1857 Sh
Crawford, M. A. to S. C. Stubbs 1-6-1868 (1-9-1868) Cr
Crawford, Mark to Isabella L. Job 9-1-1857 Sh
Crawford, Matthews to Cornelia Wainwright 12-29-1868 F B
Crawford, P. D. to M. A. Newby 10-10-1866 (10-11-1866) F
Crawford, Peter P. to Margret Hudson 8-22-1845 Hr
Crawford, Pitser M. to Ellen E. Ray 2-6-1860 (2-9-1860) Hr
Crawford, R. R. to Caroline Soloman 4-22-1867 Hy
Crawford, Raiford to Nancy Coor 7-1-1839 (7-15-1839) Hr
Crawford, Richard to Alice Ragland 1-17-1878 Hy
Crawford, Robert R. to Sarah A. Counts 1-12-1859 Hn
Crawford, Robert to Martha Butler 10-19-1869 (10-24-1869) Cr
Crawford, Rufus P. to Jane Milisse McCrory 10-2-1848 (10-4-1848) Hr
Crawford, Russell J. to Nancy G. Neely 11-5-1827 Hr
Crawford, Russell P. to Ruan J. Warford 5-7-1858 (5-11-1858) Hr
Crawford, Samuel B. to Evelina Willis 12-11-1845 Hn
Crawford, Samuel to Charlotte Palmer 12-27-1866 Hn B
Crawford, Simon to Ada Walker 7-16-1870 (no return) F B
Crawford, Stephen to Margaret Moore 12-29-1868 F B
Crawford, Thomas A. to S. Young 10-18-1852 Hn
Crawford, Thomas F. to Sarah A. Burns 12-24-1857 Cr
Crawford, Thomas W. to Florentine Beasley 2-17-1847 Hn
Crawford, Thos. C. to Eliza P. Marshall 2-9-1871 T

Crawford, V. R. to Winford Solan 4-30-1863 Sh
Crawford, W. H. to M. F. Currie 11-28-1866 Hy
Crawford, W. M. to Sarah F. Browning 12-3-1867 Cr
Crawford, W. R. to Amy C. Wood 12-20-1859 (12-21-1859) Hr
Crawford, W. T. to Sarah Cursey 11-22-1862 (12-4-1862) F
Crawford, William J. to Nancy G. Anderson 12-9-1860 Hn
Crawford, William L. to Elizabeth Cloar 4-23-1851 Hn
Crawford, William M. to Julia Young 3-13-1866 Hn
Crawford, William to Alsey Haynes 12-25-1867 (no return) Hn B
Crawford, William to Frances Mathis 12-29-1860 G
Crawford, William to Martha A. B. Vinson 11-3-1853 Hr
Crawford, William to Mary E. Jackson 4-26-1862 (no return) Hn
Crawford, Wm. A. to Mary A. Carroll 12-5-1854 Cr
Crawford, Wm. F. to Martha Ann Ward 5-10-1845 (5-22-1845) Hr
Crawley, Isaac to Mary Cothran 2-8-1873 (2-9-1873) T
Crawley, John to Eliza Redman 5-22-1853 Sh
Crawley, William to Mary A. Thomason 1-4-1844 Hn
Crawly, ___ to Martha A. Gouldsby 10-12-1841 (no return) Hn
Craws, Peter to Alsey Griffin 1-5-1878 (no return) Hy
Crayne, Daniel to Feriby Thornton 3-12-1842 (3-20-1842) O
Crdier, H. C. to M. A. Steel 12-26-1871 (no return) Cr
Creath, James A. to Nancy J. Amonett 2-1-1843 Sh
Creath, Thos. B. to Mary E. Jones 10-25-1849 Sh
Creed, M. V. to Unicy Cox 6-27-1859 O
Creed, Sanford T. to Mary L. Stephins 3-20-1848 (3-24-1848) O
Creekmore, Christopher to Polly Hamilton 11-3-1825 (11-4-1825) O
Creel, Nathaniel to Mary Flowers 8-7-1850 (8-8-1850) G
Creighton, Daniel to Mary Ann Murray 6-26-1858 (6-27-1858) Sh
Creighton, John C. to Julia O'Connors 10-11-1856 Sh
Cremus, Joe to Ellen Jarrett 4-6-1872 Hy
Crenshaw, A. B. to Elizabeth Mitchell 1-31-1861 G
Crenshaw, Azariah L. to Mary E. Magness 8-31-1846 (9-2-1846) F
Crenshaw, B. F. to A. W. Calhoun 9-10-1873 O
Crenshaw, C. C. to Rachael Dodson 12-14-1858 (12-15-1858) Sh
Crenshaw, C. to Catharine Waller 2-18-1874 T B
Crenshaw, Carr to Julia Baker 9-11-1845 Sh
Crenshaw, Charles to Indiana S. Wamack 10-29-1855 (10-30-1855) Sh
Crenshaw, Charles to Sarah Smith 5-6-1836 Sh
Crenshaw, Chas. to Emily V. McDaniel 5-5-1825 Sh
Crenshaw, Dabney to Hepsey (Hessy?) Branch 2-6-1845 Sh
Crenshaw, David K. to Clara A. Jackson 10-19-1853 (10-20-1853) T
Crenshaw, David to Sarah Branch 8-9-1841 Sh
Crenshaw, F. B. to M. L. Webber 7-11-1859 (7-13-1859) F
Crenshaw, F. M. to Virginia E. Crenshaw 3-21-1864 (3-28-1864) Sh
Crenshaw, Franklln (Dr.) to Kitty Branch 12-12-1849 Sh
Crenshaw, Henry to Martha Ann Overall 7-11-1869 G B
Crenshaw, J. M. to Mary A. McNees 2-9-1850 (2-10-1850) F
Crenshaw, James C. to Cleresy H. Brevard 2-11-1859 (2-13-1859) O
Crenshaw, Jesse to Jane Ross 2-24-1845 We
Crenshaw, Joe to Ella Harbor 8-8-1885 (no return) L
Crenshaw, Joel to Elizabeth (Mrs.) Moldan 11-27-1836 Sh
Crenshaw, John H. to Ida Frances Eddings 11-6-1866 (11-7-1866) F
Crenshaw, Josephus to Elizabeth J. Hendron 1-28-1850 T
Crenshaw, L. C. to L. C. Tomlin 5-16-1867 F
Crenshaw, L. C. to Paulina A. Overall 9-8-1869 G
Crenshaw, L. C. to Sallie Jane Boswell 8-18-1866 (no return) F
Crenshaw, Lewis C. to Martha W. Wyatt 10-13-1852 (10-14-1852) G
Crenshaw, M. L. to Martha C. Martin 12-13-1849 (no return) F
Crenshaw, N. B. to Mary T. Albright 5-24-1864 (5-26-1864) Sh
Crenshaw, N. M. to Elizabeth Boothe 1-20-1849 (1-24-1849) Hr
Crenshaw, Ned to L. A. Trosdale 9-8-1874 T
Crenshaw, W. B. to Phereby G. Ross 1-13-1853 (1-26-1853) Sh
Crenshaw, W. J. to Sallie J. Montgomery 12-3-1877 (12-4-1877) Dy
Crenshaw, William to Letha Burrow 1-4-1870 (1-5-1870) Cr
Crenshaw, Wm. A. to Lucy H. Crenshaw 12-17-1844 Sh
Crenshaw, Wm. B. to Elizabeth S. Mickelberry 11-4-1845 Sh
Crenshaw, Yeatman to Amanda Crenshaw 2-24-1870 T
Creps (Cress?), James M. to Mary E. Springfield 11-14-1871 Ma
Cresap, James W. to Jo Ann Puckett 11-10-1857 (11-19-1857) O
Cresaso, Thos. to Elizabeth Hall 1-7-1846 Cr
Cress, Christopher to Pamelia Waldrop 10-7-1838 Hn
Cress, Jonathan to Sarah Dees 9-2-1854 (no return) We
Cress, William D. to Martha Edmundson 1-6-1846 Hn
Creswell, W. H. to Sarah A. Duff no date (1860-1870) G
Crewel, Shepard to Lina Campbell 1-22-1874 Hy
Crewell, Charles to Sinay Maynard 12-22-1869 L
Crewes, Walter C. to Mary Jane Pearman 10-24-1860 (no return) Cr
Crews, A. F. to Georgiana Moss 7-28-1863 (no return) We
Crews, A. H. to Mary E. Hopkins 12-28-1858 G
Crews, A. J. to Lillie King 1-7-1869 G
Crews, Ambrose H. to Mary Ann Nichols 9-12-1850 Hn
Crews, Ambrose H. to Sarah Long 11-18-1874 (no return) Hn
Crews, Beverly J. to Fanny Melton 7-30-1870 (8-7-1870) Cr
Crews, C. to Jennie Baugh 9-21-1864 (9-22-1864) Sh
Crews, Corneleus J. to Elizabeth A. Crews 3-4-1860 We
Crews, David A. to Sarah Brewer 8-8-1858 Cr
Crews, David H. to Nancy Jones 9-7-1842 Cr
Crews, David to Sarah Chandley 7-24-1844 Cr
Crews, Elijah P. to Martha A. Francisco 9-8-1866 Hn
Crews, Elisha to Arabella Toleson 6-20-1844 Cr
Crews, Eppy to Syrena Carter 2-9-1837 Hr
Crews, G. P. to Prudence Roe 6-3-1861 G
Crews, Green to Nicie Rice 8-28-1871 (8-31-1871) Cr
Crews, Henry to Jane Dowdy 1-31-1848 Cr
Crews, Isaac T. to Elizabeth A. F. Tisdale 11-5-1853 (11-7-1853) Hr
Crews, Isaac to Rhodiann Myrick 8-7-1856 Hn
Crews, J. A. to Mattie Bond 8-8-1866 G
Crews, J. C. M. to Eliza J. Canon 9-19-1866 (no return) Cr
Crews, J. F. to Bell Doherty 7-11-1865 Be
Crews, James A. to Emily Crews 12-20-1859 Hn
Crews, James to Harrett Flowers 12-23-1843 (12-26-1843) G
Crews, James to Mary Pope 11-5-1849 (11-8-1849) G
Crews, Jiff to Anna Vaughan 3-7-1870 G B
Crews, John L. to Catherine Lathrick 2-4-1856 Ma
Crews, John W. to Catharine Nannie 11-4-1865 (11-5-1865) Cr
Crews, John to Elizabeth Wright 10-31-1832 (11-1-1832) G
Crews, John to Mary Jane Tisdale 12-31-1849 (1-10-1850) Hr
Crews, John to Mary Massey 12-20-1839 Cr
Crews, John to Sarrah Edmundston 8-14-1838 G
Crews, Jonathan to Elizabeth Bumpass 9-26-1827 Hr
Crews, Peter R. to Mary Adams 8-30-1854 Hr
Crews, Scotland S. to Julia A. Mathes 10-5-1846 Cr
Crews, Thomas A. to Julia Watson 3-14-1855 (3-15-1855) Ma
Crews, Thomas to Jane Swiney 10-25-1838 Cr
Crews, Thos. to Annie Chandler 5-2-1844 Cr
Crews, William S. to Elizabeth A. McWherter 12-7-1852 G
Crews, William to Lucy Baylep 12-11-1857 We
Crews, William to Malinda Owen 11-18-1847 Hn
Crews, William to P. Pope 1-19-1857 G
Crews, William to Sarah F. Parish 12-15-1858 Hn
Crews, Wm. H. to Arpy? Tisdale 2-7-1855 (2-8-1855) Hr
Cribbs, Asville P. to Sarah E. Johns 4-28-1863 G
Cribbs, Asville P. to Sarah E. Johns 4-28-1863 (no return) Cr
Cribbs, C. G. to Milinda Thomas 11-15-1864 G
Cribbs, Cullen to Sarah Hancock 10-20-1852 G
Cribbs, Daniel P. to Martha J. Stone 12-23-1845 Cr
Cribbs, Dr. ? to Nancy Harbour 8-11-1831 G
Cribbs, E. G. to R. J. Sawyer 11-18-1869 (11-19-1869) Dy
Cribbs, Gilbert to Nancy Martin 12-22-1824 (12-23-1824) G
Cribbs, J. H. to C. C. Wilkins 11-11-1868 Dy
Cribbs, J. W. to Josephine McIntosh 10-9-1878 Dy
Cribbs, J. W. to Maggie A. McIntosh 11-16-1875 (11-18-1875) Dy
Cribbs, James Porter to Sarah J. Clark 10-11-1867 (or 10-16) G
Cribbs, John Y. to Mary Jane Andrews 8-27-1855 (9-4-1855) G
Cribbs, John to Nancy Harbor 1-18-1828 (2-19-1828) G
Cribbs, Johnston to Sary Bane 9-7-1824 (9-9-1824) G
Cribbs, William to Elizabeth York 10-1-1830 G
Cribbs, William to Jane Harbour 6-16-1826 G
Cribbs, Wm. T. C. to Susan K. Stone 9-12-1843 Cr
Crichfield, Henry to Nancy Russell 2-5-1852 (2-15-1852) L
Crichfield, Richard to Martha A. Slayton 1-21-1868 Dy
Crichlow, Frank to Harriet Dunwoody 12-27-1869 (no return) Hy
Crichlow, H. S. to Sarah Klyce 11-22-1870 Hy
Criddie, Alexander G. to Mary A. N. Whitfield 10-?-1843 Hn
Criddle, Jerry to Laura Henry 12-25-1869 (6-25-1871) F B
Crider, A. I. to Artell Hampton 6-16-1853 Cr
Crider, Daniel B. to Eliza H. Rigsby 5-26-1838 (5-27-1838) G
Crider, G. C. to Mary E. Probusaugh? 10-2-1871 (10-?-1871) T
Crider, George W. to Marg Brush 2-15-1842 Hn
Crider, Henry to Frances E. Webb 1-31-1850 Cr
Crider, James C. to Jane E. Weathers 2-13-1845 Cr
Crider, John D. to Delia A. Hilliard 2-9-1865 (no return) Cr
Crider, John D. to Martha Walters 9-5-1850 Cr
Crider, Milton H. to Mary E. Freeman 1-16-1864 (no return) Cr
Crider, Milton H. to Mary E. Freeman 1-26-1864 (no return) Cr
Crider, R. H. to Mary L. Mitchell 3-6-1869 (3-7-1869) Cr
Crider, Richarad H. to Margarett White 7-25-1854 Cr
Crider, Samuel J. to Mary Yates 2-28-1835 (2-29?-1835) G
Crider, T. E. to Arcisa Spivey 9-11-1860 G
Crider, Thos. B. to Nancy Word 1-19-1843 Cr
Criggar, J. V. to Nancy H. Malett 4-5-1863 O
Crigler, James to Henrietta Kirk 11-22-1869 G B
Crihfield, Artha F. to Harriet Denie? 11-28-1860 (11-28-1861?) L
Crihfield, Benjamin Franklin F. to Mary Frances Standlin? 6-29-1857 (7-10-1857) L
Crihfield, Cyrus to Sarah E. Pillow 4-15-1861 (4-17-1861) L
Crihfield, E. J. to Mary Ann Garlin 7-13-1875 L
Crihfield, E. J. to O. A. Pipkins 2-12-1884 (2-14-1884) L
Crihfield, Elias J. to Mary E. St. John 10-21-1861 L
Crihfield, J. H. to Frances Eviline Harris 10-30-1883 (11-1-1883) L
Crihfield, J.(T?) F. to Martha L. Saint John 8-23-1864 (8-25-1864) L
Crihfield, R. P. to Martha P. Pennington 2-12-1872 L
Crihfield, Richard to Nancy Spivey 9-11-1855 L
Crihfield, Richard to Sarah Ann Battle 11-24-1863 (11-25-1863) L

Crihfield, William H. to Louisa Perkins 11-16-1866 (11-23-1866) L
Crihfield, William H. to Parmelia C. Saint John 2-11-1859 (2-16-1859) L
Criner, Robert L. to Martha Gunter 12-28-1835 Hr
Crisap, H. M. to Agness Wyatt 11-13-1873 O
Crisenberry, Robert W. to Martha J. Roberts 1-5-1862 Hn
Crisip, Plesant to Rebecca J. Lee 10-8-1862 Mn
Crisp, Benj. A. to Marinda Garrison 2-16-1870 (2-17-1870) Dy
Crisp, C. L. to S. J. Hendren 11-30-1880 (12-1-1880) L
Crisp, Charles A. to Nancy Crisp 4-7-1842 Hr
Crisp, Clinton to Mary Cheshier 9-28-1854 Hr
Crisp, Daniel J. to Sallie E. Frazier 12-13-1869 (12-15-1869) F
Crisp, Green to Eliza Wooden 11-11-1864 Sh
Crisp, Hiram C. to Martha Bates 10-20-1842 Hr
Crisp, J. E. to M. T. Mote 1-20-1874 (1-21-1874) Dy
Crisp, J. E. to R. A. Boatright 10-13-1869 (no return) Dy
Crisp, Lemuel M. to Ann J. Norton 1-1-1857 Hr
Crisp, Moses P. to Angeline B. Lawhorn 9-18-1855 Hr
Crisp, Tilman A. to Rebecca Couch 4-8-1848 (4-9-1848) Hr
Crissenberry, John B. to Jane Swor 10-4-1838 (no return) Hn
Crissman, James H. to Elizabeth A. Harder 11-26-1851 (11-27-1851) G
Crissup, Pleasent to Rebecca J. Lee 11-19-1862 Mn
Criswell, Wm. H. to Sarah Elizabeth Taylor 1-18-1868 G
Critenden, A. to Elizabeth Callicott 11-16-1848 Hn
Critendon, Phil to Eliza Bond 6-2-1878 Hy
Critendon, Philip to Misouri Merriwether 4-28-1871 Hy
Crittenden, Charley to Mary E. Callicott 12-24-1839 Hn
Crittenden, D. S. to Susan C. Younger 1-22-1861 We
Crittenden, Hezekiah to Mary J. Blythe 12-10-1846 Hn
Crittenden, James F. to Sarah Boyt 9-22-1860 (no return) We
Crittenden, Shelby to Sarah A. Goode 11-9-1839 Hn
Crittenden, Wm. H. to Ann E. Collins 1-3-1843 Hr
Crittendon, A. J. to Emma Allen 10-14-1875 L B
Crittendon, Blak to A. E. Stanley 11-14-1874 O
Crittendon, Charles to Matilda Abington 1-22-1855 (1-23-1855) O
Crittendon, Harvey S. to Mary A. Cobb 1-26-1853 Ma
Crittendon, S. T. to Narcissey J. Abington 3-18-1852 O
Croach, J. H. to M. T. Pickard 11-16-1867 O
Crobum?, T. J. to C. A. Hogan 4-27-1854 Cr
Crocker, A. G. to Irmandy S. Baker 2-6-1860 (2-7-1860) G
Crocker, A. P. to Abcesla? Step 11-17-1870 G
Crocker, A. P. to L. E. McCaslin 5-10-1864 G
Crocker, Allen J. to Mary J. Swinney 6-10-1854 Cr
Crocker, B. H. to Martha Howard 2-28-1861 G
Crocker, D. B. to Mary C. Watson 2-25-1869 Hy
Crocker, Duke to Susn A. Riley 11-6-1867 (no return) Hn
Crocker, E. H. to Susan Walker 12-26-1836 (1-5-1837) G
Crocker, Edward E. to Jane P. Newberry 7-10-1862 We
Crocker, Edwin H. to Centha Riley 12-5-1842 (12-6-1842) G
Crocker, Francis M. to Liddy Gilliland 8-9-1837 (8-13-1837) G
Crocker, G. W. to Nancy M. Cunningham 5-17-1866 G
Crocker, J. B. to Irene M. Haynes 5-28-1884 (5-29-1884) L
Crocker, J. Y. to Elizabeth Gallaher 7-7-1868 (no return) Dy
Crocker, James M. to Subra Ann Condry 1-27-1853 L
Crocker, James to Amanda M. Morphis 6-20-1846 (6-21-1846) Hr
Crocker, James to Louisa Condray 1-25-1865 (2-26-1865) L
Crocker, Joseph to Barsheba Lucey 12-20-1842 (12-21-1842) L
Crocker, Mark to Mourning Hammons 7-7-1856 (7-10-1856) G
Crocker, N. A. to Sarah Williams 5-11-1868 G
Crocker, Rufus to Martha Walker 3-11-1848 (3-16-1848) G
Crocker, W. H. to Sarah Thetford 5-8-1862 G
Crocker, W. S. to E. W. Barker 3-23-1857 G
Crocker, William L. to Patience W. Hancock 8-31-1848 G
Crocker, William S. to Melinda Nichols 8-28-1855 G
Crocker, Wm. H. to M. J. Reager 10-11-1860 G
Crocket, John N. to Serena Braden 7-16-1866 (7-19-1866) L
Crockett, A. L. to Francis Rumney 10-26-1850 Cr
Crockett, D. M. to Elizabeth Bottoms 12-17-1856 (12-18-1856) G
Crockett, E. B. to Mary Jane Meacham 1-30-1850 O
Crockett, George W. to Elizabeth Wilks 4-15-1839 (4-16-1839) G
Crockett, Hillman to Anna Webster 2-22-1883 (2-24-1883) L
Crockett, Houston to Adaline Browning 12-23-1885 (12-24-1885) L
Crockett, Hugh H. to Sarah E. Eaves 1-30-1861 (1-31-1861) O
Crockett, I. J. to F. M. Alexander 7-14-1866 O
Crockett, J. G. to Lois Anderson 3-3-1885 (3-4-1885) L
Crockett, J. M. to Catherine W. Polk 1-14-1837 (1-17-1837) O
Crockett, James E. to L. E. Philipis 8-13-1847 O
Crockett, John M. to Emily Patterson 7-15-1859 (7-17-1859) G
Crockett, John W. to Dicy Jane Wilson 1-12-1854 O
Crockett, John W. to Mary Mastisa 8-31-1833 G
Crockett, John to Gracey Crockett 12-20-1843 O
Crockett, John to Louisa McAlister 9-23-1846 (9-24-1846) O
Crockett, John to Mary Patterson 10-15-1833 (10-17-1833) O
Crockett, Joseph to Lula Sumerow 1-3-1880 (1-6-1880) L
Crockett, Nathan to Francis Thomas 9-30-1845 (no return) We
Crockett, R. H. to Mary B. Lewis 4-8-1856 Sh
Crockett, R. H. to Sarah F. Lewis 11-10-1853 Sh
Crockett, Reuben T. to Anabeck Williams 3-1-1845 (3-2-1845) O
Crockett, Robert P. to Matilda Porter 10-16-1841 (10-21-1841) G
Crockett, Robert to Rebecca J. Wicker 7-16-1851 O
Crockett, Samuel to Mary A. Pace 8-6-1866 G
Crockett, Samuel to Sidney C. Higdon 2-12-1845 Be
Crockett, Silas C. to Emily Wheeler 12-11-1852 (12-14-1852) O
Crockett, Stephen to Matilda Preyer 12-29-1869 (12-30-1869) L
Crockett, William T. to Mary E. Crockett 1-22-1862 We
Crockett, William to Clorence Boytt 3-18-1830 (3-25-1830) G
Crockett, Wm. G. to Elizer Smith 10-26-1841 Cr
Crockett, Wm. to Jane Chambers 1-12-1867 (1-13-1867) O
Crockett, Z. T. to Nancy H. Ellis 9-19-1867 Be
Crofford, William H. to Hannah E. Williams 5-19-1845 (5-20-1845) Hr
Crofford, ___ to Louisa A. Simon? 6-19-1864 (6-21-1864) T
Croft, Nathaniel to Mary Ann Williams 1-5-1860 Hn
Croft, Samuel to M. A. B. Campbell 6-16-1864 (6-19-1864) Sh
Croft, William to Asita Gamlin 2-15-1846 Hn
Croly, Leroy to Saphronia Drake 4-8-1855 We
Cromes, William to Sally Montgomery 6-23-1830 (6-30-1830) G
Cromm, Joseph to Julia A. E. Stewart 10-13-1856 (10-15-1856) Ma
Cromwell, John F. to Martha C. Richards 11-24-1857 Sh
Cromwell, O. B. to M. C. Kennon 4-20-1867 (4-21-1867) F
Cronan, James to Sophronia Taylor 10-11-1853 (10-13-1853) O
Crone, Augustus to M. Heidel 9-26-1864 (9-27-1864) Sh
Cronin, C. to Deborah Keane 3-5-1859 (3-6-1859) Sh
Cronin, Jerry to Catherine Garvey 8-8-1863 Sh
Cronin, Jerry to Mary Feney 5-1-1863 Sh
Crook, A. H. to Matilda E. Wakefield 10-24-1871 (10-25-1871) L
Crook, G. M. to Mary J. Averett 5-2-1854 (no return) F
Crook, G. M. to S. E. Crooms 3-5-1868 Hy
Crook, J. W. to Lucy E. Masey 10-3-1853 Sh
Crook, James A. to Mary E. Moore 1-4-1870 (no return) L
Crook, James A. to Virginia Ida Webb 2-21-1876 (2-24-1876) L
Crook, James B. to Martha J. Southern 7-?-1844 F
Crook, James to Jane Fowler 2-15-1883 L
Crook, John to Alice McClish 1-9-1886 (1-10-1886) L
Crook, Jonathan W. to Sally B. Haughton 10-2-1855 (10-3-1855) Ma
Crook, N. B. to Mary Hill 10-2-1860 We
Crook, Peter A. to Emely M. Simmons 9-17-1853 (no return) F
Crook, W. C. to Millie Glimp 1-6-1869 (1-?-1869) L
Crook, Wm. F. to Amanda Pattilo 6-25-1849 (no return) F
Crooke, C. R. to Mary Jane Richards 7-20-1858 We
Croom, Benjamin F. to Susan Davis 12-12-1862 (12-13-1862) Ma
Croom, Isaac N. to Mary F. Mays 5-19-1856 Ma
Croom, Isaac to Elizabeth Stier 7-22-1840 (8-13-1840) Ma
Croom, James to Mary Southall 10-19-1854 Ma
Croom, John to Narcissa Downing 8-27-1842 (8-28-1842) Ma
Croom, Richard R. to Mary F. Meadows 4-21-1857 (4-29-1857) Ma
Croom, William H. to Virginia A. Anderson 2-26-1856 (2-27-1856) Ma
Croom, William to Caroline Carrington 6-24-1840 (7-8-1840) Ma
Croom, Wm. to Sarah M. Pipkin 3-3-1863 Sh
Crooms, George to Mariah Moore 1-24-1867 (1-25-1867) F B
Crooms, Thomas to Emma E. Avery 10-15-1859 (no return) Hy
Croose, John to Eliza Emiline Collens 5-10-1870 (5-11-1870) L
Crop, J. D. to Lucy D. Ellis 9-5-1859 (9-6-1859) Sh
Cropno, D. A. to M. V. Mitchell 1-4-1869 (no return) Hy
Cropper, Lovel E. to Lucinder (Mrs.) Stafford 12-30-1864 Sh
Crosbey, Thos. R. to Elizabeth M. West 11-28-1854 (11-29-1854) G
Crosbie, Thomas to Elizabeth Reed 5-12-1862 Sh
Crosby, George to Cara C. Branish 12-6-1862 (12-7-1862) Sh
Crosby, Saml. to Henrietta Grimes 12-28-1868 T
Crosby, Solomon to Sarah Ann (Mrs.) Warmack 9-1-1860 (9-4-1860) Sh
Crosby, T. J. to Johanna Cammerdy 1-20-1862 (1-22-1862) Sh
Crosby, Thomas to Elizabeth Reed 5-12-1862 Sh
Crosby, W. H. to Lucy S. Barnwell 11-4-1860 Sh
Crosby, William to Mary Elizabeth Parkinson 4-15-1839 Ma
Crosland, John to Martha Nervell 9-8-1847 Cr
Cross, Andrew J. to Dolly Parr 7-19-1840 Sh
Cross, Elijah W. to Martha E. Irwin 11-9-1842 (11-10-1842) Hr
Cross, Elijah to Dicy Miller 5-31-1838 F
Cross, Freeman to Martha Baley 8-24-1841 G
Cross, Freeman to Nancy Patterson 6-19-1837 (6-20-1837) G
Cross, I.W. to Jessie M. Olmsted 7-12-1849 Sh
Cross, Isaac to Cinda Gray 2-3-1877 (no return) Hy
Cross, Isam to Arena Fletcher 1-31-1867 (1-8?-1867) F B
Cross, J. M. to Lavina C. Lorance 12-20-1869 (12-23-1869) Cr
Cross, Jacob to Julia Braswell 1-28-1870 (no return) F B
Cross, Jessee to Margaret Lipscomb 6-6-1842 (no return) F
Cross, Joe to Elizabeth Shore 12-20-1867 (12-22-1867) F B
Cross, John H. to Mary C. Hutchings 11-30-1848 Ma
Cross, Marcellus A. to America Crow 1-15-1868 Dy
Cross, Milton P. to Mary Moore 3-1-1841 (3-3-1841) Hr
Cross, Robert T. to Hepsebeth Runkle 1-19-1837 Sh
Cross, Sam to Mariah Shaw 8-9-1866 (no return) F B
Cross, Thos. R. to Eliza Bridges 2-13-1856 Cr
Cross, W. G. to Emily Knight 4-6-1875? (4-8-1875) O
Cross, William to Eliza Ann Hobbs 10-23-1837 (10-24-1837) Hr
Cross, Wm. T. to Sarah A. Crowder 9-15-1855 Hr

Cross, Wm. to Caratt Carver 1-13-1857 Cr
Crossett, A. T. to M. A. F. Pearman 2-17-1866 (2-20-1866) Cr
Crossett, Earls to Mary E. Cannon 1-13-1857 Cr
Crossett, Henry T. to M. Barns 12-21-1841 Cr
Crossett, J. B. to M. A. Pearman 1-8-1864 (no return) Cr
Crossett, J. B. to M. A. Pearmon 1-8-1864 (no return) Cr
Crossett, J. G. to Frances J. Watkins 1-18-1854 (no return) F
Crossett, John D. to Harriet F. McClaren 11-25-1868 (11-26-1868) F
Crossett, Joseph J. to Elizabeth A. Goodwin 12-26-1846 (1-14-1847) F
Crossett, Wm. A. to Catherine Burns 3-20-1845 Cr
Crossland, Edwin to Mary Adaline Hess 3-2-1847 G
Crossland, F. Wm. to Ann (Mrs.) Douglass 2-25-1858 Sh
Crossno, Allen D. to Frances E. Presson 7-16-1851 Be
Crossno, Allen D. to Sarah Presson 8-19-1847 Be
Crossno, C. H. to Frances J. Wyatt 10-22-1863 Be
Crossno, James to Crissa Nisler 6-10-1845 Be
Crossno, John to Mary Madary 10-16-1853 Be
Crossnoe, W. C. to Mary Jane Evans 12-13-1870 (no return) Dy
Crosson (Crossor?), M. to Eliza Wilks (Whitker) 4-20-1854 Sh
Crosswell, J. R. to Sarah A. Foust 10-24-1866 Hn
Crosthwait, E. J. to Ann Eliza Henry 10-2_-1859 (10-23-1859) L
Crotty, Thomas to Nora Fannassay 2-11-1861 (2-12-1861) Sh
Crotty, William to Bridget Keefe 4-24-1858 (4-25-1858) Sh
Crouch, A. D. to Adaline Ray 7-28-1859 Hn
Crouch, Edward Radford to RAchel Miller 8-12-1844 (8-15-1844) T
Crouch, Francis M. to Jennie R. Lourie 10-2-1859 Hn
Crouch, George W. W. to Serilda Ann Jones 5-7-1860 (5-8-1860) T
Crouch, Isaac to Isobel Deyson (Dyson) 1-27-1825 Sh
Crouch, James E. to Emily A. Stokes 1-14-1846 (2-24-1846) T
Crouch, John Hendin? to Ann Elizabeth Hurt? 3-7-1853 (3-8-1853) T
Crouch, John J. to Mary Neel 10-1-1847 F
Crouch, John R. to Frances E. Watts 1-8-1843 Sh
Crouch, Obadiah to Nancy J. Volentine 11-4-1860 Hn
Crouch, Richard H. to Nancy H. Abernathy 11-30-1837 Sh
Crouch, Thomas to Louisa Miller 4-9-1846 (no return) Hn
Crouch, W. R. to Susan Phelps 2-1-1863 Hn
Crouch, Willia Anthony to Catharine Murphy Stokes 4-12-1845 (4-15-1845) T
Crouch, William A. to Margaret Jane Hall 10-18-1854 Sh
Crouch, William to Mary Crockett 2-1-1853 (2-3-1853) O
Crouse, Jesse to Amanda L. Mills 11-5-1847 (11-7-1847) Hr
Crouse, John to Sarah Carver? 5-17-1849 Hr
Crouse, Joseph to Harriett Mills 6-22-1843 Hr
Crow, A. J. to M. C. King 10-14-1872 Dy
Crow, Calvin to Mary Cunningham 4-7-1851 (4-10-1851) O
Crow, Edward to Elizabeth Hopkins 12-22-1842 Cr
Crow, Hiram (of Illinois) to Harriet Davis 9-19-1862 Ma
Crow, Hiram J. to Harriet Davis 9-23-1862 Mn
Crow, J. A. to S. J. Hanna 1-16-1869 (1-20-1869) Cr
Crow, J.W. to Minerva Mahern(Mahan) 2-20-1832 (2-21-1832) Hr
Crow, James A. L. to N. P. Mills 10-24-1866 (10-25-1866) Dy
Crow, Jas. W. to Susan Taylor 3-17-1851 O
Crow, John to Isabel Henry 9-22-1829 Hr
Crow, R. M. to Eliza A. Morril 2-10-1862 (2-12-1862) Hr
Crow, R. S. to Harriet Gleaves 1-17-1872 (1-18-1872) Dy
Crow, R. S. to Mary Ann Ellis 11-28-1870 (11-29-1870) Dy
Crow, Robert to Ellen Donahoe 8-17-1848 Sh
Crow, W. R. G. to M. A. Hall 1-7-1867 (1-8-1867) Dy
Crow, W. R. to Eliza McBride 1-12-1870 (1-13-1870) Dy
Crow, William L. to Janetta Speer 5-26-1854 Sh
Crow, William M. to Martha Macon 8-20-1865 Mn
Crow, William to Adaline Carroll 7-18-1850 Sh
Crow, William to Martha C. Jones 1-29-1858 Sh
Crowder, G. W. to L. P. McLeod 10-19-1881 L
Crowder, Hardy to Mary C. Blythe 7-27-1841 Hn
Crowder, Jas. M. to Harriet Johnson 9-4-1849 (9-5-1849) F
Crowder, John to Bell Harrell 1-25-1874 Hy
Crowder, John to Harriet Crowder 10-31-1868 (11-14-1868) F B
Crowder, Joseph to R. Ann (Mrs.) Koonce 12-19-1865 Hy
Crowder, L. B. to Susan G. Baker 12-30-1859 G
Crowder, R. A. to L. A. Bridgwater 1-11-1859 (not endorsed) F
Crowder, Starling to Lilly Conner 12-30-1868 G B
Crowder?, T. M. D. to Hannah A. Vaughn 8-11-1861 Hn
Crowder, T. W. to Mary F. Reeves 8-12-1865 F
Crowder, W. A. to A. M. McNaim 5-22-1871 (no return) Hy
Crowder, William E. to Harrel Baker 1-8-1853 G
Crowe, Patrick to Mary Slew 9-8-1860 (9-9-1860) Sh
Crowel, John to Susanna D. Ivy 2-5-1840 Hn
Crowel, Peter F. to Senna A. (Mrs.) Deaton 7-1-1867 Ma
Crowell, Alfred to Harriett Slocum 6-14-1849 Ma
Crowell, John to Luvilla Holt 1-2-1862 Sh
Crowell, Norman to Margaret Adams 9-14-1853 (9-15-1853) Ma
Crowell, Samuel to Elizabeth Pearce 5-13-1852 (5-18-1852) Ma
Crowley, Armstead to Harriett Taylor 1-17-1871 (no return) Hy
Crowley, Caleb B. to Eliza Gullett 4-28-1849 Cr
Crowley, John to Hanora Adams 12-14-1858 (12-16-1858) Sh
Crowley, John to Patience Jones 2-26-1848 Sh
Crowley, Samuel to Elizabeth E. White 4-23-1851 (4-24-1851) Hr

Crowley, Strong to Olvizara? Nuckolls 6-24-1839 Hr
Crowly, Matthew to Rosusey Fine Parker 12-16-1843 (12-17-1843) Hr
Crownover, W. V. to Mary Ann Harden 1-6-1863 Mn
Cruchfield, Steven to Menervia Woodson 12-31-1869 Hy
Cruchfield, W. C. to Sallie Parrott 10-30-1867 (no return) Hy
Crudup, John to Permelia Mitchell 11-26-1858 (12-9-1858) O
Cruise, Elijah E. to Mervia King 11-1-1853 Cr
Cruise, James H. to Martha M. Barnes 6-15-1865 G
Cruise, James to Hester Ann White 3-2-1844 (3-6-1844) Hr
Cruise, Lemuel W. to Milinda Jones 10-1-1833 Hr
Cruise, Robert to Mary Johnson 12-11-1855 We
Crum, Elias to Fainy Kenedy 2-15-1831 Hr
Crumb, J. T. to H. E. Wilson 1-18-1871 (1-19-1871) Cr
Crummey, William to Katharine Toben 2-8-1858 Sh
Crump, John P. to Catharine Penhouse 8-19-1846 Sh
Crump, Marcus V. to Mollie R. Clarke 4-16-1873 Hy
Crump, R. O. to M. A. Greaves 12-8-1875 L
Crumpley, O. B. to Synthia A. Fleming 7-10-1856 Sh
Crunch, G. W. F. to F. A. Smith 4-27-1852 (no return) F
Crunk, John to Louise May 5-24-1826 Hr
Cruse, Samuel to Nancy Turner 2-9-1857 We
Cruse, Simon to Margaret A. V. Smith 12-24-1878 Hy
Cruse, Simon to Siller Brown 12-29-1874 Hy
Cruse, Thomas to Annie Harper 7-7-1865 (7-10-1865) Cr
Cruse, W. M. to Jennie Farris 10-23-1874 O
Cruse, William to Rebecca Road 8-2-1833 (8-7-1833) Hr
Cruse, Wm. R. to Penecea A. Osteen 3-5-1858 We
Crutcher, C. B. to Fannie Horton 3-30-1875 (4-7-1875) L
Crutcher, W. M. to Bettie L. Clark 11-18-1882 L
Crutchfield, C. B. to H. S. Wade 6-12-1855 Hn
Crutchfield, C. B. to Mary E. Vandyck 10-13-1852 Hn
Crutchfield, George K. to Mary Valentine 1-25-1845 (no return) We
Crutchfield, Isaiah to Amanda Ellis 3-11-1845 (no return) Hn
Crutchfield, James H. to Isabella Rogers 9-21-1848 Cr
Crutchfield, James to Milly Horton 12-16-1845 Cr
Crutchfield, John A. to Lucinda M. Hinson 9-26-1856 Cr
Crutchfield, John to Mary G. Travis 12-31-1840 Hn
Crutchfield, N. F. to S. A. Julian 12-6-1866 (no return) Hn
Crutchfield, P. D. to Emma J. Jeter 1-16-1873 Hy
Crutchfield, Thomas to Ann Pickens 10-21-1849 Hn
Crutchfield, Thomas to Mary Owens 4-25-1863 Mn
Crutchfield, Wm. to Sary Ann Pate 12-15-1858 We
Cubbins, Brown to Alsey Footts 5-16-1869 G B
Cubbins, John to Martha Brown 12-16-1845 Sh
Cubbins, Thomas to E. Brookshire 3-13-1848 Sh
Cubuss?, Frank to Fannie Mason 11-20-1875 (no return) Hy
Cudd, F. N. to Caroline Smith 8-24-1870 G
Cudd, Simeon to Sarah Ann Pollard 1-11-1849 G
Cuff, Charles P. to Malinda England 3-30-1854 Be
Cuff, David S. to Malissa Jane Florence 10-13-1868 Be
Cuff, F. A. to Sarah Sykes 12-23-1845 Be
Cuff, Wm. M. to Nancy Jane Parker 1-26-1865 Be
Culberhouse, William to E. A. Jones 9-12-1852 Hn
Culberson, John to Frances Hasten 11-22-1841 Hn
Culberson, King to Ellen Lightle 1-7-1868 (2-9-1868) F B
Culberson, Wm. M. to Mary C. Dunagin 8-5-1862 (8-6-1862) O
Culberson, Wm. to Susan Hall 3-31-1862 (4-1-1862) O
Culbertson, Henry to Malinda Bradford 1-29-1841 (1-31-1841) O
Culbertson, Josiah to Hannah Briers 1-7-1842 (1-9-1842) O
Culbreath, Cowell? to Eliza Clewellyn Smith 8-3-1841 (8-5-1841) T
Culbreath, Henry to Janie Ann Roil 3-31-1870 (4-1-1870) T
Culbreath, Huel D. to Sarah M. Moore 1-3-1868 (no return) F
Culbreath, J. J. to Annie Caldwell 8-24-1878 (no return) Hy
Culbreath, J.R. to S. M. A. Davis 6-20-1874 T
Culbreath, Jack to Sallie Miller 1-16-1872 Hy
Culbreath, James Jefferson to Susan Eliz. Slaughter 1-20-1851 (1-23-1851) T
Culbreath, Jas. M. to G. A. Simms 3-25-1868 (3-26-1868) F
Culbreath, William to Sarah Christmas Power 4-23-1849 (4-26-1849) T
Culbreth, C. F. to Marry Ann Bever? 6-26-1840 F
Culbreth, James J. to Mary E. Stewart 1-22-1844 (1-?-1844) T
Culbreth, John to Elizabeth Hughes no date (12-28?-1838) F
Culee?, John to Lucinda Patterson 2-12-1867 (2-13-1867) Cr
Culigan, Richard to Mary Connerey 8-22-1861 Sh
Culipher, G. W. to Cicily D. Parker 12-14-1867 (no return) Hy
Cullam, Wm. J. to Susan D. Delashmet 12-13-1869 (12-14-1869) T
Cullan, Bartholomew to Bridget Brannon 6-25-1859 (6-26-1859) Sh
Cullem, Edward to M. S. Foulks 9-22-1871 (9-23-1871) O
Cullen, Bryan to Ann Laughlan 8-14-1852 (9-13-1852) Sh
Cullen, E. D. to Amanda C. House 11-20-1856 Hn
Cullen, Z. C. to Julia C. Davidson 8-27-1860 (8-28-1860) T
Cullens, J. D. to Luler Harper 10-28-1868 T
Culley, G. T. to S. S. White 3-10-1867 G
Culligan, Patrick to Alice Powers 7-14-1862 Sh
Culligan, Thomas to Ellen Hays 1-7-1856 Sh
Cullim, William H. to Isadora Harper 12-21-1871 T
Cullipher, Goerge W. to Rebecca C. Harper 2-13-1866 Hy
Cullipher, J. G. to Mary M. Carlton 12-16-1867 G

Cullison?, Mathew to Adeline Pyles 10-26-1867 (11-4-1867) T
Cullom, A. J. to Sarah Durham 5-8-1850 (no return) F
Cullum, B. H. to Martha A. Portis 11-?-1853 (no return) F
Cullum, Hugh A. to Nancy J. Alexander 11-17-1854 (no return) F
Cullum, Marcus H. to Elizabeth Jane Davis 1-27-1845 T
Cullum, Mathew M. to Cinetia M. Childes 1-26-1848 (no return) F
Cullum, William E. to Mary A. Porter 7-20-1848 (no return) F
Culp, Cleiborn to Susan Bobbitt 9-27-1869 (10-2-1869) F B
Culp, Eli to Juli Ann Hendley 12-27-1842 (no return) F
Culp, Jack to Mattie Gregory 10-25-1870 (10-26-1870) Cr B
Culp, Judson A. to Elizabeth L. Norman 12-13-1850 (12-15-1850) F
Culp, L. T. to Cassie Jones 12-19-1870 (12-22-1870) F
Culp, Leroy to Alzora Gofourth 2-29-1844 F
Culp, Peter to Levicy C. Smith 10-20-1867 Hy
Culp, Robert to Martha Phillips 1-12-1866 (1-15-1866) F B
Culp, T. I. to L. I. Buchanan 1-24-1867 O
Culpeper, J. B. to Louisa Ivey 10-8-1849 (10-10-1849) F
Culpepper, C. J. to Sarah J. Merrill 1-24-1865 Hn
Culpepper, C. L. to Elizabeth Tucker 1-31-1856 Hn
Culpepper, Calvin to Lizzie Ann Warr 7-2-1870 (no return) F
Culpepper, Henry to Gracey Mebane 12-28-1870 (12-29-1870) F B
Culpepper, James W. to Eliza Scott 2-11-1863 Hn
Culpepper, Joseph to Mehaly Beavers? 5-30-1844 (no return) Hn
Culpepper, Thomas B. to Sarah Ann Dortch 4-16-1857 Hn
Culver, W. G. to Prudence Wormster 4-25-1850 Sh
Culverhouse, George T. to Mary A. Reynolds 1-3-1861 Hn
Culvert, John L. to Nancy J. Taylor 2-20-1859 We
Culwell, C. H. to Martha A. Bradshaw 5-3-1869 F
Cumings, John W. to Lucinda C. Clack 7-20-1861 (7-21-1861) O
Cumings, William to Agelina Fewtrill 1-26-1853 (1-27-1853) Hr
Cummings, David to Charlotte I. Shutts (Shults) 11-13-1850 Sh
Cummings, Elias D. to Martha A. Cummings 9-22-1873 (9-23-1873) Dy
Cummings, Jacob to Sidney Alexander 5-19-1866 (8-11-1866) F B
Cummings, John F. to Sarah E. Horner 12-13-1860 O
Cummings, John W. to Francis Caudle 11-11-1863 (11-12-1863) O
Cummings, John to Rachell Kenady 3-15-1834 (3-16-1834) G
Cummings, Jordan Y. to Mary E. Collins 2-24-1845 Sh
Cummings, Matthew to Ann Dunn 11-13-1858 Sh
Cummings, William H. to Mary Ann French 1-17-1856 Be
Cummings, William W. to Margaret E. Madden 9-14-1857 Sh
Cummins (Currin), Isaac D. to Cynthia Brooks 12-22-1848 Sh
Cummins, David Hays to Emma Holmes 8-14-1843 T
Cummins, Hiram F. to Eliza J. Stevens 3-19-1844 Hn
Cummins, Hiram F. to Susan M. Courts 8-7-1858 Hn
Cummins, John to Lucinda Kelley 3-24-1851 (4-3-1851) T
Cummins, Nicholas to Ellen (Mrs.) Davis 10-14-1864 Sh
Cummins, William to Bridget Quindlin 4-24-1855 (4-27-1855) Sh
Cuneo, Frank to A. Muskeo (Muscheo?) 8-13-1863 Sh
Cuneo, Joseph to Rosenia Wildberger 9-3-1860 Sh
Cuningham, Add to Parlee Striblin 1-14-1873 Cr
Cuningham, Charles to Clary Walker 12-29-1871 (11-30-1871) Cr B
Cuningham, D. C. to Mary E. Webster 3-12-1857 We
Cuningham, Daniel to Caroline Anthony 12-23-1875 (no return) Hy
Cuningham, Dick to Fannie Anthony 1-2-1872 Hy
Cuningham, J. J. to Josephine Leach 1-31-1871 (2-2-1871) Cr
Cuningham, Nelson to Amanda Britt 1-7-1873 (no return) Cr B
Cunliff, H. C. to Priscilla Reed 11-28-1860 (11-29-1860) F
Cunningham, A. C.? to Joanna? Nelson 3-4-1867 (no return) L B
Cunningham, Allen F. to Nancy Cox 2-14-1848 G
Cunningham, Andrew to Martha S. (Mrs.) Donly 4-12-1864 Sh
Cunningham, Anson A. R. to Sarah Hubert 6-17-1830 O
Cunningham, Benj. F. to Sarah F. Clark 7-19-1855 Cr
Cunningham, Booker to Amy Watkins 6-7-1838 (no return) Hn
Cunningham, Charles M. to Jane Legate 7-6-1844 (7-10-1844) O
Cunningham, Charles M. to Louisa M. McElyea 12-24-1855 (12-25-1855) O
Cunningham, Charles M. to Mary Pauline Jones 2-5-1848 (2-6-1848) O
Cunningham, Columbus to Leah Reeves 5-19-1855 (5-24-1855) O
Cunningham, Cornelius to Amanda Caldwell 12-16-1868 (12-17-1868) Cr
Cunningham, D. F. to Amanda M. Moore 9-10-1862 G
Cunningham, D. W. C. to Martha Robinson 1-5-1856 Cr
Cunningham, Daniel to Elizabeth Burris 5-7-1863 Sh
Cunningham, E. J. to Susan Rowe 8-4-1847 Be
Cunningham, Eliphus to Derinda A. Osbourne 11-11-1856 (12-1-1856) O
Cunningham, Francis M. to Elizabeth E. Hyslap 5-28-1856 Sh
Cunningham, Geo. C. to Mary Frances Nesbitt 11-17-1868 G
Cunningham, George W. to Martha Hubert 7-9-1829 O
Cunningham, Greenberry to Nancy Martin 5-12-1853 G
Cunningham, Hillard to Joella Braden 11-21-1883 (11-1?-1883) L
Cunningham, Hugh R. to Margaret C. Jones 5-13-1851 Hn
Cunningham, Isaac to Martha A. Pitts 6-23-1866 (6-24-1866) L
Cunningham, J. B. to F. A. Alexander 1-25-1882 (1-26-1882) L
Cunningham, J. D. to Susan Bivins 10-12-1868 G
Cunningham, J. L. to Ellen Greer 12-17-1868 (12-24-1868) Dy
Cunningham, J. N. to R. E. Hogg 7-8-1880 (7-11-1880) L
Cunningham, James H. to Lackey Ann Askew 9-26-1853 G
Cunningham, James M. to Meniza Joyce 7-24-1850 G
Cunningham, James to Catharine Robertson 11-29-1837 (11-30-1837) G
Cunningham, James to Ellen P. Sheehan 4-29-1862 (4-30-1862) Sh
Cunningham, Jas. B. to Mary W. Wilie 9-7-1869 (9-9-1869) Ma
Cunningham, Jas. C. to Emily E. William 2-14-1861 (no return) Hy
Cunningham, Jas. M. to Stacy Jamima Young Garrett 4-29-1858 Sh
Cunningham, Jno. A. to Polly Taylor 9-10-1861 (no return) Dy
Cunningham, John A. to Mary Hampton 10-27-1845 (12-28-1845) G
Cunningham, John D. to Nancy A. Garrison 9-18-1864 O
Cunningham, John R. to Amanda H. Malone 9-18-1855 Cr
Cunningham, John to Betsey Rice 10-25-1882 L
Cunningham, John to Em Eliza Tyus 11-24-1875 (no return) Hy
Cunningham, John to Mary Ward 12-27-1869 (12-28-1869) F B
Cunningham, John to Sarah A. Walther 12-27-1846 Hn
Cunningham, Lee to Malinda R. Stephens 10-22-1868 G
Cunningham, Matthew to Mary McMahon 5-15-1860 Sh
Cunningham, Michael to Johanna Connors 7-9-1859 (7-17-1859) Sh
Cunningham, Michael to Mary Grady 11-15-1861 (11-18-1861) Sh
Cunningham, Miles C. to Matilda J. Webster 3-9-1854 Hn
Cunningham, Moses W. to Elizabeth J. Crihfield 11-23-1868 (11-25-1868) L
Cunningham, Patrick to Hannora Maha (Malia?) 2-18-1862 Sh
Cunningham, Patrick to Mary Welsh 11-25-1856 Sh
Cunningham, Peter to Mary Burns 6-28-1853 Sh
Cunningham, R. H. to Winnie Sexton 2-26-1882 (2-28-1882) L
Cunningham, Saml. to Lizzie Moore 7-9-1870 G B
Cunningham, Samul. to Julia A. Driskell 11-19-1844 (11-20-1844) G
Cunningham, Shad to Eliza Guinn 12-31-1869 Cr
Cunningham, Tho. to Elizabeth Scalion 1-8-1846 F
Cunningham, Thomas to Louizer Lacy 8-4-1868 G
Cunningham, Thos. J. to Mary J. Carter 2-23-1863 (2-26-1863) Cr
Cunningham, Thos. J. to Mary J. Carter 2-25-1863 Cr
Cunningham, Thos. to Lucy Crafton 7-24-1850 (7-25-1850) G
Cunningham, Timothy to Bridget (Mrs.) Nash 6-25-1855 Sh
Cunningham, W. H. to Sarah J. Holt 1-20-1868 G
Cunningham, W. L. to Elen Cunningham 9-6-1858 G
Cunningham, W. L. to Malissa Jane Cunningham 5-7-1870 G
Cunningham, W. M. to Nancy C. Allen 2-2-1848 G
Cunningham, William C. to Rutha C. Wright 9-12-1844 G
Cunningham, William P. to Eliza Ann Legate 6-15-1841 (6-18-1841) O
Cunningham, William R. to Ellen Cates 3-4-1867 (no return) L
Cunningham, William to Betty Whitehead 11-7-1848 G
Cunningham, Wm. F. to Mary Robinson 10-1-1860 (10-2-1860) Cr
Cunningham, Wm. R. to Elizabeth F. (Mrs.) Deberry 6-30-1859 Ma
Cup, Elijah to Caroline C. Alexander 12-29-1846 Ma
Cup, Stephen to Cornelia A. Caviness 8-30-1850 (9-1-1850) Hr
Cup, Wesley to Martha Jane Odom 6-25-1857 T
Cup, William to Eliza Ann Adams 10-21-1869 (10-22-1869) T
Cupello, Giaconio to Teresa Martina 8-4-1859 (8-5-1859) Sh
Cupp, Thos. F. to Fanny Taylor 1-20-1869 G
Cupples, Thomas J. to Nancy C. Sanders 6-19-1868 (7-5-1868) Ma
Cupples, Thomas to Elizabeth Sipes 2-?-1848 (3-1-1848) Ma
Curbey, R. C. to Catherine Chappell 10-22-1860 (10-29-1860) O
Curbey?, John L. to Rebecca Pillow 5-25-1863 (no return) Hn
Curby, John W. to Emma James 7-23-1874 Dy
Curby, John W. to Paralee Powers 8-8-1876 (8-9-1876) Dy
Curby, Thomas to Pina Whitley 11-22-1838 T
Curd, Columbus to Elizabeth Wiseman 11-1-1864 Hn
Curd, Edward L. to Rosa J. Mahan 12-31-1838 Hn
Curd, Edward to Arena Crenshaw 9-11-1838 Hn
Curl, Dempsey E. to Mary M. Higgs 12-4-1858 (12-5-1858) Hr
Curl, Jesse B. to Mandy Wade 2-20-1847 (3-10-1847) F
Curl, Jesse B. to Margaret Ann Mathews 11-20-1843 (11-28-1843) F
Curlen, Phillip to Mary Haggard 2-26-1863 (2-10?-1863) Sh
Curley, James to Sarah Bailey 7-31-1878 (8-1-1878) L
Curley, Wm. to Lydia Wilson 9-27-1840 T
Curley?, Henry to Lizzie Vandyck 8-25-1865 (no return) Hn
Curlin, B. F. to P. W. Elvington 7-11-1868 (no return) Hy
Curlin, E. C. to Ann B. Verhine 1-12-1866 L
Curlin, J. H. to M. E. Kirksey 10-6-1885 (10-7-1885) L
Curlin, J. T. to Jane E. Garrett 2-7-1872 L
Curlin, J. W. to M. J. Dickerson 4-12-1871 (no return) Hy
Curlin, James M. to Sarah L. Traylor 4-10-1861 T
Curlin, Jesse J. to Elizabeth Williamson 11-3-1852 (11-7-1852) O
Curlin, Thomas J. to Ann Renfroe 2-4-1858 Sh
Curlin, Thomas R. to Elizabeth Seven 5-19-185? (with 1851) O
Curlin, William H. to Curlin Miles 7-27-1842 Ma
Curlin, Z. H. to N. E. L. Whitfield 9-21-1859 Sh
Curn, Patrick to Mary O'Donnell 4-27-1861 Sh
Curran, A. to Lucy Bostick 1-20-1883 (1-24-1883) L
Curran, Henry to Nancy Anderson 10-13-1866 Hy
Curran, James to Mary Ann Heickmott 4-9-1861 Sh
Curran, Michael to Rebecca Duncan 10-4-1853 (10-5-1853) Sh
Curray, Mack to Caroline Finney 12-17-1870 F B
Currey, Algermon S. to Martha A. Nimmo 4-20-1842 (4-21-1842) G
Currey, Ephraim to Ritter Elder 3-15-1870 G B
Currey, James to Emma Bumpass 8-28-1880 (8-29-1880) Dy
Currhey, William to Elizabeth Christman 1-27-1849 Sh
Currie, Alex to Anna Furguson 2-8-1877 Hy
Currie, Alexander to Loutisia Perry 1-4-1877 (no return) Hy

Currie, Alfred to Sue Parker 11-15-1871 Hy
Currie, Arthur to Milly Ann Coltart 7-16-1881 L B
Currie, Bob to Cathern Sweet 12-29-1871 (no return) Hy
Currie, Branch to Harriet Burtie 5-30-1874 Hy
Currie, Clay to Julia Bond 5-5-1877 Hy
Currie, Crockett to Jane Davis 5-16-1878 (no return) Hy
Currie, George to Susan Scott 11-3-1866 Hy
Currie, George to Susan Thomas (not executed) Hy
Currie, Green to Hatta Sparkman 12-13-1877 Hy
Currie, Harry to Ella Currie 12-12-1870 (no return) Hy
Currie, J. B. to Alice Currie 2-6-1882 L
Currie, J. M. to Jennie Lewis 7-11-1885 (7-12-1885) L
Currie, J. M. to M. A. Best 11-19-1878 (11-21-1878) L
Currie, Jesse to Jane R. Gladney 10-29-1860 Ma
Currie, John Henry to Ann Jacocks 10-23-1878 Hy
Currie, John Henry to Lucinda Currie 1-21-1866 Hy
Currie, John to Alice Sutten 5-25-1872 (no return) Hy
Currie, John to Martha Thompson 12-30-1866 Hy
Currie, John to Mit Easeley 6-23-1875 (no return) Hy
Currie, M. to Queen Peebles 12-18-1878 Hy
Currie, Marshall to Georgia Anderson 12-31-1867 Hy
Currie, N. A. to Sue Anthony 12-11-1866 Hy
Currie, Newton to Mattie (Mollie?) P. Tally 8-6-1866 (8-8-1866) L
Currie, Primus to Vickie Rice 7-12-1868 Hy
Currie, Robert to Nancy Boyd 10-31-1877 (no return) Hy
Currie, Saml. to Cintha Hurt 12-16-1873 Hy
Currie, Sandy to Fanny Haywood 12-19-1873 Hy
Currie, Shelby S. to C. O. Coltart 11-28-1873 Hy
Currie, W. T. to Araminta H. Ivie 12-18-1860 (12-20-1860) F
Currie, Washington to Eva Vaulx 5-30-1878 L
Currie, Washington to Mary S. Taylor 9-6-1853 (9-13-1853) Ma
Currie, William M. to Amanda E. Davenport 11-6-1856 (no return) L
Currie, William to Amanda Buck 12-25-1866 Hy
Currier, Nathaniel to Martha N. Manley 1-18-1842 Hn
Currin, A. D. to Maggie Mance 5-22-1880 (5-23-1880) L
Currin, Alfred to Ellen Young 10-31-1866 F B
Currin, Andrew to Ellen Soward 9-1-1885 (no return) L
Currin, Arthur to Cherry Jordon 1-2-1871 (1-8-1871) L
Currin, Henry to Edney Rose 10-20-1872 Hy
Currin, Henry to Julia Hinton 4-5-1879 (4-6-1879) L B
Currin, Jacob to Ann Jordan 2-15-1867 (no return) L B
Currin, John McKairy to Sarah J. Currin 1-17-1876 (1-19-1876) L
Currin, Madison to Lucy Lee 2-17-1879 (2-20-1879) L
Currin, Marshall to Jennie Smith 2-12-1874 (no return) Hy
Currin, Montgomery to Hardina Lee 2-2-1880 (2-4-1880) L
Currin, Price to Delia Bradford 7-6-1885 (7-12-1885) L
Currin, W. D. to Nancy A. Campbell 8-7-1854 (8-14-1854) Hr
Currin, Willis to Allice Clark 12-3-1870 (12-12-1870) L
Curry, Anderson to Jane Bird 9-28-1867 Hy
Curry, Andrew to Margaret Nowel 6-4-1832 Sh
Curry, Buck to Mattie Henderson 9-10-1881 (9-24-1881) L
Curry, Charles to Margaret Tyson 3-19-1873 Hy
Curry, James to Ellen Clifford 7-18-1857 Sh
Curry, Phillip to Amanda Harris 8-21-1867 O
Curry, S. M. to Barbara Buchanan 11-27-1867 O
Curry, Turner to Alice Shaw 3-21-1875 Hy
Curry, W. S. to Alice Coppage 2-11-1868 (no return) Hy
Curry, Webster to Molly Harbert 3-24-1874 Hy
Curry, William to Margaret A. Baxter 10-26-1865 Mn
Curso?, Isham to Diana Holloway 11-1-1872 (no return) L
Curtice, Joseph to Manie Mayo 6-30-1825 G
Curtin, Peter to Martha Turner 12-23-1880 L
Curtis(Carter?), Green B. to Martha J. McMahan 1-11-1848 (1-12-1848) Hr
Curtis, Andrew J. to Sarah J. Scales 1-25-1870 T
Curtis, B. F. to Elizabeth Ann Hoppee 7-6-1868 G
Curtis, Calvin J. to Anjanet Jackson 8-20-1842 (8-21-1842) G
Curtis, Charles to Priscilla Clark 7-29-1866 Hn B
Curtis, Edward to Lucinda Mahon 1-25-1830 (2-4-1830) G
Curtis, Golden to Moria Shaw 11-3-1877 Hy
Curtis, Green B. to Louisa J. Allen 8-23-1841 Hr
Curtis, Humphrey to Elizabeth Grice 12-26-1838 G
Curtis, J. S. to E. M. Tucker 9-3-1860 (no return) Hy
Curtis, J. W. to E. A. Harget 4-13-1865 (no return) L
Curtis, J. to Isabella W. McNutt 9-29-1857 Hn
Curtis, James H. to Harriet A. Slater 9-25-1862 (9-26-1862) L
Curtis, James to Penelope Griffee 12-27-1831 (12-27-1831) G
Curtis, Jas. H. to Martha Stegall 1-7-1846 Sh
Curtis, John F. to Ailsy Eaton 4-28-1855 (5-1-1855) Hr
Curtis, John M. to Nancy Eaton 6-23-1855 (6-25-1855) Hr
Curtis, John W. to E. A. Hargett 4-13-1865 (4-16-1865) L
Curtis, John to Mary J. Howard 12-24-1840 G
Curtis, John to Sylla J. Vaughan 12-15-1853 Hn
Curtis, Joshua to Lucy Ann Hogg 5-15-1848 Be
Curtis, N. G. to Sarah A. Nelson 12-5-1855 (no return) F
Curtis, Nedrick to Elizabeth Crihfield 3-15-1855 (3-17-1855) L
Curtis, Noah to Mary Bran 9-28-1836 (9-29-1836) G
Curtis, Sampson to Charlotte Grayor 7-4-1831 (7-5-1835) G

Curtis, Samuel H. to Esther Ann Margaret Powers 8-2-1853 (8-3-1853) L
Curtis, Samuel to Louisa Massy 6-19-1855 Be
Curtis, Thomas to Mary E. Caple 6-24-1852 G
Curtis, W. E. to Mary A. Pitts 7-30-1869 (no return) Dy
Curtis, W. S. to J. A. Coley 3-13-1857 (no return) We
Curtis, William E. to Harriett Looney 2-19-1861 Hn
Curtis, William R. to Elizabeth Lamb 2-19-1868 (2-20-1868) L
Curtis, William to Caroline Armstrong 3-6-1861 Dy
Curtis, William to Sarah Coley 12-16-1868 Hn
Curtiss, Horace H. to Mary L. Sypert 8-31-1853 Ma
Curtner, Calvin to Ellen Dodd 9-17-1855 (9-20-1855) O
Curtner, Williamson to Virginia J. Hewlett 2-21-1853 (3-1-1853) O
Cusack, Patrick to Ellen Pendergass 4-16-1860 Sh
Cushing, Richard to Margaret Cook 4-14-1863 G
Cusick, Michael to Mary Wallace 3-4-1863 Sh
Cusick, Patrick to Hannah Kelly 2-17-1862 Sh
Cuson, D. H. to S. J. Flowers 10-15-1867 G
Cussip, Pleasant to Lucenday Harris 6-9-1840 Cr
Custer, John Cox to Margaret Jane Moore 12-3-1850 (12-8-1850) T
Cuthbertson, Thomas M. to Philpina Jarman 4-1-1824 (4-3-1824) Hr
Cutler, A. P. to Virginia P. Matthews 2-28-1874 (3-1-1874) O
Cutler, J. J. G. to Eliza J. McDaniel 10-26-1847 (11-9-1847) G
Cyer, Sullavan to Nancy Sweat ?-?-1861? Mn
Cyle, Edward to Sarah McMillin 4-16-1863 Sh
Cyrus, David to Mary McLour 12-17-1851 (12-19-1851) G

Dabb, Richard to Betsy Harper 6-22-1826 Hr
Dabbs, C. H. to S. S. Hunt 12-5-1834 Hr
Dabney, Walter D. to Lucy H. Sappington 11-19-1829 Sh
Dacus, Alexander to Rebecca Starnes 8-15-1850 (8-18-1850) T
Dacus, D. D. to S. A. M. Johnson 10-30-1860 (11-2-1860) F
Dacus, H. C. to L. A. Huffman 11-7-1874 (11-10-1874) T
Dacus, Henry Jackson to Hester Ann Hamilton Rigsby 1-20-1852 (1-22-1852) T
Dacus, Joseph A. to Elizabeth C. Upchurch 7-25-1866 (7-26-1866) T
Dacus, S. to Parthena Taylor 2-15-1852 We
Dacus, Wm. A. to Margaret Johnson 12-23-1845 Sh
Dado, Giovanni to Guiseppa A. Fransioli 7-6-1870 Ma
Dagan, Martin to Mary Armstrong 6-6-1860 Sh
Dailey, Anthony to Lucinda Ury 7-27-1866 O
Dailey, John R. to Emilie Reiney 10-23-1862 Sh
Daily, Thomas to Hannah Hays 10-24-1861 Ma
Daimod, James to Mary Mack 4-16-1853 (4-24-1853) Sh
Dair, David to Nany E. Estas 7-7-1845 (7-17-1845) G
Daiz, John to B. Rumgk? 9-4-1855 W
Dalby, Thomas D. to Martha Hickerson 1-8-1836 Sh
Dale, Anderson to Elizabeth Stone 1-9-1830 Hr
Dale, Henry to Celia F. McCormick 8-13-1860 Sh
Dale, John W. to Emily S. Taylor 8-10-1856 Hn
Dale, Michael to Elizabeth Horten 1-19-1863 Sh
Dale, William E. to Catherine Fuller 3-9-1852 Hn
Daley, Nathan to Elizabeth Swindle 10-15-1846 G
Daley, Wm. J. to Tennie B. Matthews 2-28-1868 (no return) F
Dalin, John to Julia Boner 5-17-1867 T
Dallas, Aaron to Martha Thornton 12-21-1871 (no return) L
Dallas, John to Charity Broncell? 12-23-1873 L B
Dallas, Tom to Jennie Scott 9-29-1877 (no return) L B
Dallas, William to Teresy? Chapman 3-21-1869 G B
Dallis, Thomas to Docid Glaze 12-19-1870 (12-29-1871?) L
Dalton, Carson R. to Mary V. M. Upshaw 1-21-1857 Sh
Dalton, Charles to Mary Jane Barnes 1-5-1848 Be
Dalton, D. L. to Mary Ann Wilkins 8-23-1849 (8-28-1849) Hr
Dalton, Daniel H. to Catharine Crider 12-23-1867 (12-24-1867) Cr
Dalton, Isham to Mary Whitfield 7-8-1856 G
Dalton, J. T. to Jane (Mrs.) Foster 4-27-1872 (4-28-1872) Dy
Dalton, James B. to Nancy Jane Hendrix 7-13-1851 Hn
Dalton, John C. to Martha A. Bryant 1-9-1862 Sh
Dalton, John M. to Frances A. Dalton 3-6-1849 Hn
Dalton, Joseph M. to Mary Jane Whittington 10-13-1842 Ma
Dalton, R. L. to P. Rebecca Tarpley 1-29-1862 Sh
Dalton, Reuben to Catharine Bard 1-12-1857 O
Dalton, T. P. to Nancy J. Woodson 1-5-1860 Sh
Dalton, W. D. to Frances R. Hood 6-14-1879 (no return) Dy
Dalton, W. F. to Sarah Grogan 4-6-1859 Hn
Daly, Cornelius to Eliza Kelly 7-13-1850 Sh
Daly, Michael to Mary O'Brien 7-12-1851 (7-20-1851) Sh
Daly, Thomas B. to Martha A. Abernathy 12-12-1844 Sh
Daly, W. L. to Louisa C. Nesbitt 2-12-1863 Sh
Dameren, Samuel to Margaret Lamsden 4-16-1854 We
Dameren, Samuel to Margaret Lunsden 4-16-1854 We
Dameron, G. W. to Nancy E. Vowell 12-19-1855 We
Dammond?, Armstead to Jenny Wingo 2-1-1870 (2-2-1870) Cr
Damon?, Noah to Amanda L. Scott 11-14-1849 (11-15-1849) Hr
Damren, James W. to N. A. Fletcher 5-12-1859 We
Damron, John T. to Louisa M. Colsharp 12-21-1858 We
Damron, John W. to Mary Hetherington 12-21-1853 O
Damron, Saml. to Margrett Lawson 4-16-1854 We

Damron, Thomas S. to Clara Jane Fisher 3-8-1851 (3-12-1851) F
Damson?, George to Mary Ann Low? 5-19-1836 (5-22-1836) Hr
Danaher, Mike to Adelia P. Kennedy 7-20-1866 (7-25-1866) F
Danaher, Thomas to Bridget Handley 4-12-1862 Sh
Danal, Henery to Lotty Johnson 3-23-1829 (2-9?-1829) Ma
Danbury, Jno. D. to Emma Frain 10-24-1846 Sh
Danbury, John D. to Sarah G. Long 5-3-1855 Sh
Dance, B. P. to C. C. Thomas 10-16-1866 Hy
Dance, J. E. to S. G. Pyland 9-6-1870 Hy
Dance, J. R. to Sallie E. Dodson 11-1-1865 G
Dance, Tom to Edna Vaughan 2-1-1868 G B
Dancer, John to Frances E. Combs 7-25-1844 Be
Dancer, W. J. to Ann Burchett 12-24-1865 Mn
Dancey, Henry to Eddy Jackson 2-24-1873 (no return) Hy
Dancey, Watt to Amanda Dickerson 1-30-1877 (no return) Hy
Danchower, F. to Mary Williams 10-13-1866 O
Dancy, Mose to Malinda Woods 5-22-1873 Hy
Dancy, Moses to Patsey McCool 12-28-1871 Hy
Danderage, Edward to Elizabeth Spivery 1-3-1870 (no return) Hy
Dandridge, Baker to Manerva Wilks 8-26-1865 F
Dandrige, George W. to Penelope C. Smith 1-1-1856 Sh
Dane, G. B. to Martha J. Twyford 5-5-1853 Sh
Dane, Joseph to Martha E. Forrest 9-17-1868 (no return) Cr
Dane, Noah to Mary Blair 11-1-1841 (11-10-1841) F
Daneri, A. to Margaret Riely (rylett) 8-17-1855 (8-19-1855) Sh
Daneri, Austin to Mary McCue 8-11-1853 (8-21-1853) Sh
Daneri, Giovanni (John) to Mary Genokio 1-3-1860 (1-8-1860) Sh
Danforth, Wm. R. to Alabama T. Thomas 10-14-1858 (no return) Cr
Dangerfield, Jo to Julia Virginia Curtis 7-2-1880 (7-12-1880) L B
Daniel (David?), John H. to Caroline R. Jones 11-16-1853 Sh
Daniel, Alexander to Caroline Emerson 12-29-1855 (no return) F
Daniel, Aurelius to Ellen Fulton 1-15-1856 We
Daniel, Byrd to Betty Griggs 5-3-1873 (5-4-1873) T
Daniel, C. P. to M. C. Martin 9-27-1854 Hn
Daniel, E. B. to Larisa A. W. Maley 6-8-1858 T
Daniel, Edwin to Herbenia Gardner 12-19-1846 Sh
Daniel, Enoch L. to Susan L. Rayner 2-20-1850 Sh
Daniel, Enoch to Molli Loving (Lowry) 12-10-1874 O
Daniel, F. P. to Anastasia Haton 2-2-1856 (no return) Hn
Daniel, Felix to Jenny Drake 4-2-1874 Hy
Daniel, Felix to Jenny Morgan 1-24-1874 Hy
Daniel, Felix to Mary Bright 3-30-1876 (no return) Hy
Daniel, Fredrick to Ida Jones 7-31-1855 (8-1-1855) Sh
Daniel, G. W. to L. C. Aldridge 12-26-1864 (1-2-1864?) T
Daniel, Granberry to Nancy Ann Pool 8-16-1842 Ma
Daniel, Isaac M. to Mary E. Jackson 12-10-1857 (12-13-1857) Hr
Daniel, J. B. to Cornelia W. Hall 12-20-1865 T
Daniel, J. L. to M. Alice Sinclair 11-25-1869 (11-30-1869) Dy
Daniel, J. M. to Elizabeth Graham 5-25-1861 Mn
Daniel, J. M. to Martha A. Smith 1-21-1864 Sh
Daniel, J. W. to Julia E. Sanders 1-13-1873 (no return) Hy
Daniel, J. W. to N. J. Timms 12-15-1874 Dy
Daniel, James W. to Helen Ross 8-5-1850 (8-8-1850) Ma
Daniel, James to Frances Jane Cole 7-14-1850 Hn
Daniel, James to Margaret Thetford 8-16-1875 (8-18-1875) Dy
Daniel, Jno. M. to Nancy J. Muray 11-21-1860 F
Daniel, John B. to Visa Ann Davis 1-24-1852 (1-26-1852) Hr
Daniel, John M. to Permelia Onley 5-14-1850 Sh
Daniel, John N. to Lucy Perkins 12-28-1858 Hn
Daniel, John to Louisa Faircloth 6-13-1841 Hn
Daniel, John to Martha Jefferson 1-2-1869 (no return) F B
Daniel, Joseph to Nancy J. Moore 9-19-1847 Cr
Daniel, Lafayette to Nancy Vail 8-3-1847 Hn
Daniel, R. H. to Rutelia Miller 1-22-1867 F
Daniel, R. L. to Jane Myrick 6-30-1860 (7-3-1860) Hr
Daniel, Ralph W. to America T. Anderson 11-25-1854 (12-10-1854) Ma
Daniel, Rufus to Ellen E. Gennan 1-15-1856 Sh
Daniel, Samuel to Jula Ann Burrow 4-30-1873 (5-1-1873) Cr B
Daniel, Samuel to Julia Anne Ozment 4-2-1849 Sh
Daniel, Silas to Cinthia Shaw 1-15-1874 Hy
Daniel, Solmon to Laura Tyson 12-3-1871 Hy
Daniel, Spencer P. to Celia Ann Rice 12-31-1845 (1-8-1846) F
Daniel, T. M. to Sarah Lambert 2-18-1853 (2-23-1853) Sh
Daniel, Thomas M. to Mary Louisa James 8-28-1849 (9-6-1849) T
Daniel, Thomas to Margaret Patterson 2-14-1876 Dy
Daniel, W. H. (Rev.) to Amanda J. Easley 1-20-1876 (no return) Hy
Daniel, W. H. to Mary L. Dougherty 7-15-1860 (7-17-1860) Hr
Daniel, Walter E. to Sarah Atkenson 7-6-1838 G
Daniel, William J. to Mary E. Brannon 12-2-1847 (no return) Hn
Daniel, jr., William H. to Katherine Foster 1-31-1866 Hn
Daniels, C. C. to Ellen Webb 1-23-1867 (1-24-1867) F
Daniels, Isaac M. to Elizabeth Ann Hardy? 4-3-1852 (4-4-1852) Hr
Daniels, J. M. to Sarah Maley 1-31-1871 (2-2-1871) T
Daniels, Reuben to Mary (Mrs.) Patterson 5-30-1864 (6-4-1864) Sh
Danner, Bristow to Eliza Bell 1-19-1870 G B
Danner, Isaac to Miranda Sanders 5-12-1866 G
Danner, L. G. to Maggie Reeves 7-30-1869 G

Danner, Levi G. to Charlotte C. Harlan 6-23-1845 G
Danniel, Byrd to Bettie Grigg 5-3-1873 T
Danniel, J. B. to Carolin W. Hall 12-20-1865 T
Danniel, James A. to Martha M. Baker 12-13-1867 (12-15-1867) T
Danniel, Mosel C. to Ann E. Baker 12-13-1867 (12-15-1867) T
Dannil, James W. B. to Frances Owen 1-29-1868 T
Dano, Elihu W. to Harriet Davidson 10-4-1864 G
Dantrell, John Hall to Isabella T. Crawford 6-12-1852 Cr
Darbey, James D. to Janie F. Roberts 1-28-1839 (1-29-1839) F
Darbey, John W. to V(irginia) Reace? (Page?) 12-9-1863 Sh
Darby, Hume H. to Harriett Taylor 12-7-1838 Cr
Darby, Joseph to Ann Moncreiff 9-21-1844 (9-22-1844) F
Darby, Joseph to Druciller Moncreef 11-7-1838 (11-15-1838) F
Darby, William R. to Clancy D. Roberts 1-12-1841 F
Darden, A. H. to Eliza Goodwin 7-30-1869 (8-1-1869) F
Darden, J. W. to Sarah J. Preston 1-7-1855 (no return) F
Darden, James H. to Jennie Massey 12-9-1872 (12-12-1872) Dy
Darden, Joshua to Nancy Witt Reeves 11-23-1865 (11-28-1865) F
Darden, W. B. to Jane Murray 12-25-1872 (12-26-1872) Dy
Dariac (Dauriae?), Augustin to Mary Burne 11-17-1855 (11-18-1855) Sh
Dark, Joe to Lula Manley 10-29-1885 L
Darley, Charley to Louisa A. Griffin 12-4-1876 L
Darling, Andrew to Ann Mitchell 10-20-1860 (10-21-1861) We
Darling, J. S. to Margaret Philliips 1-27-1855 F
Darling, William A. to Martha J. Galaway 11-11-1857 We
Darnal, John to Mary A. Moore 11-11-1857 (11-8?-1857) O
Darnald, John to Milley Sammons 4-29-1843 (5-1-1843) G
Darnall, Daniel to Vilet Kirk 12-27-1870 (12-29-1870) Cr B
Darnall, Henry to Mary McWherter 10-12-1831 O
Darnall, J. W. to M. I. Easterwood 3-2-1863 (3-3-1863) O
Darnall, J. to S. A. Thompson 2-15-1867 Hn
Darnall, Jesse A. to Mattie E. Askew 12-15-1868 Ma
Darnall, Joseph to Dilly A. Pigg 3-5-1847 O
Darnall, Nicholas M. to Margaret Bell 8-29-1865 (no return) Cr
Darnall, William H. to Martha Diggs 5-18-1858 Hn
Darnel, Henry to Virginia Wright 9-4-1834 O
Darnel, John B. to Georgia Ann Watson 8-2-1850 O
Darnell, Adam N. to Lovicy Ann Robinson 9-29-1842 Cr
Darnell, G. W. to Josephine Ellis 2-12-1859 O
Darnell, G. W. to Mary E. Gardner 11-12-1852 We
Darnell, J. D. to Elizabeth S. Gernerson 7-4-1852 Cr
Darnell, J. W. to E.. Nored 5-12-1853 Hn
Darnell, John to Adaline Barhum 3-27-1848 (no return) Cr
Darnell, John to Martha Matthews 7-13-1861 Hr
Darnell, Joseph to Dilly A. Pig 3-5-1851 O
Darnell, N. M. to Nancy C. H. Darnell 4-3-1855 Cr
Darnell, N. to Keziah Clemons 3-25-1860 Cr
Darnell, Sanford M. to Ann R. Poyner 11-18-1851 Hn
Darnell, Thomas L. to Jeanette Upchurch 3-5-1848 Hn
Darnell, Thomas L. to Nancy Jane Turbeville 9-3-1857 Hn
Darnell, Thomas M. to Elizabeth R. Pratt 11-16-1861 Mn
Darnell, Thos. L. to Elizabeth Morgan 6-16-1844 Cr
Darnell, Wm. to Caroline A. Williams 2-3-1848 Cr
Darnold, William M. to Delila Waldrop 2-19-1848 (2-21-1848) G
Darr, Henry to Miriam Nicks 5-28-1840 (5-31-1840) Ma
Darr, J. A. to Frances E. Blankenship 10-11-1861 G
Darr, John to Angie C. Ervin 7-25-1839 Ma
Darr, Levi to Rosa Ann Herrington 10-27-1852 G
Darvin, David to Aden Evans ?-16-1873 (12-16-1873) O
Dashiell, Richard R. to Eliza Jane Taylor 1-10-1850 (1-15-1850) Ma
Dashill, W. Bond to Mary Anna Jones 9-28-1871 Ma
Daughby, Reuben to Elizabeth Williams 9-9-1839 Ma
Daugherty, James L. to Harriet L. Thetford 6-23-1859 (6-26-1859) O
Daugherty, John P. to Sarah Jane Poe 4-20-1853 Hn
Daugherty, Wm. S. to Elizabeth Atkinson 1-9-1846 (1-11-1846) Hr
Daughety, Nathan to Mollie Jane Price 8-3-1867 (no return) F
Daughirda, Richard to B. P. Turner 8-29-1861 We
Daughtrey, Major H. to Mary Maddon 3-8-1846 Sh
Daughtry, W. W. to Sarah J. Easly 11-12-1855 (11-15-1855) Sh
Daughtry, William M. to Mary E. Bagby 4-7-1877 (4-8-1877) L
Daulton, Reuben to Sarah Baugh 4-15-1863 Sh
Daum, Louis to Julia Hannig 2-4-1860 Sh
Dausson, Johnathan to Alee Kelly 11-14-1832 (11-15-1832) G
Davenport, Charles to Susan E. Richardson 12-17-1873 (12-18-1873) Dy
Davenport, D. B. to Emily S. Wingo 3-27-1861 G
Davenport, David to Maria Amanda Starnes 4-25-1849 (4-26-1849) T
Davenport, David to Mary A. Evins 3-30-1861 (3-31-1861) L
Davenport, George W. to Nancy Fisher 1-?-1841 (no return) Cr
Davenport, James H. to Susan Jane Baker 9-11-1860 (9-13-1860) Ma
Davenport, John C. to Elizabeth Coates 3-26-1833 Sh
Davenport, Marcus L. to Mary E. Martin 12-24-1857 (no return) L
Davenport, Richd. to Margaret King 8-31-1867 (9-13-1867) Dy
Davenport, Thomas to Martha Braden 5-27-1843 (6-1-1843) L
Davenport, ____ to Margarett Mitchell 12-15-1838 (12-17-1838) Ma
Davent, C. to C. R. Green 12-23-1867
David (Dawe-Daniel), Joseph N. to Manerva Vesey 11-5-1853 (11-6-1853) Sh
David, And. F. to Margarette W. Boon? 5-20-1844 (5-22-1844) F

David, D. C. to M. A. Patterson 6-22-1858 Sh
David, Edward to Catherine Williams 2-19-1837 Sh
David, Eldridge to Emily Landford 1-31-1872 (2-1-1872) Dy
David, Felix Robertson to Nancy McKenon 1-25-1842 (1-26-1842) T
David, Geo. W. to Sarah Paschal 12-9-1845 (12-10-1845) F
David, J. W. to Ruth Ann Kitchum 7-4-1870 (7-7-1870) T
David, John E. to Elizabeth Cress 10-10-1855 We
David, T. R. to Mary Land 7-14-1870 (7-17-1870) F
David, Timothy K. to Mary H. Humphreys 10-14-1840 (10-22-1841?) F
David, Wm. G. to M. A. Jackson 12-27-1868 (12-28-1868) Cr
Davidson, A. A. to Cornelia E. Overall 6-5-1860 (6-6-1860) G
Davidson, A. M. to Elizabeth Waldrop 10-17-1856 (10-18-1856) G
Davidson, A. P. to N. T. Boon 11-6-1862 G
Davidson, A. S. to Meriah E. Landin 5-5-1838 G
Davidson, Abner L. to Howell A. Little 12-18-1862 G
Davidson, Alexander L. to Mila Melissa Taylor 2-11-1836 O
Davidson, Alfred F. to Mary J. Moore 6-20-1844 G
Davidson, Anderson to Jane Considine 12-25-1866 G
Davidson, Andrew M. to Mahulda Fisher 11-13-1844 Ma
Davidson, Benjamin to Sarah J. Nicholson 1-10-1855 Sh
Davidson, C. C. to Susan P. M. Bailey 7-13-1834 O
Davidson, E. G. to Mary W. Armour 11-19-1856 (11-20-1856) Sh
Davidson, Ephraim E. to Susan Hamilton 1-28-1846 Cr
Davidson, G. B. to Lou L. Morris 12-17-1884 L
Davidson, G. N. to W. H. Lawrence 6-15-1870 G
Davidson, George S. to Martha R. Averett 12-30-1867 (12-31-1867) Dy
Davidson, George W. to Frances C. Davis 4-13-1867 (4-14-1867) L
Davidson, George W. to Lucy Fitzpatrick 10-3-1868 (10-4-1868) L
Davidson, George W. to Matilda A. Carnes 8-9-1860 Be
Davidson, Henry C. to Nancy C. Davidson 3-17-1867 G
Davidson, Henry J. F. to Louisa F. Patterson 7-26-1860 We
Davidson, J. F. to Elizabeth J. Cash 1-3-1871 (1-5-1871) Ma
Davidson, J. P. to Tennie W. Kerby 10-18-1870 Hy
Davidson, J. W. C. to E. A. (Mrs.) Puckett 2-3-1869 G
Davidson, J. W. C. to Louizer Baker 12-8-1866 G
Davidson, Jack to Eliza Titus 5-7-1857 Sh B
Davidson, Jack to Mary Hardin 5-29-1866 (6-30-1866) Dy
Davidson, James C. to Barbary Fletcher 2-2-1848 G
Davidson, James to Matilda Baulkum 10-18-1866 G
Davidson, Jesse to Martha Gunter 1-16-1842 Hn
Davidson, John D. to Narcissa Gailard 1-30-1836 G
Davidson, John D. to Zella Mainor 9-20-1835 G
Davidson, John F. to Mary C. Meacham 6-25-1861 O
Davidson, John W. to Frances Montgomery 10-18-1838 G
Davidson, John to Nancy Davis 12-17-1863 G
Davidson, John to Susan C. Smith 7-26-1853 G
Davidson, Joseph to Rebecca Price 6-15-1853 Be
Davidson, Josephus to Arabella Inman 12-28-1853 O
Davidson, K. B. to E. E. Pennington 10-13-1875 L
Davidson, M. V. to R. E. Patton 10-24-1866 Dy
Davidson, Miles L. to Dicy Pate 1-30-1840 G
Davidson, Minor B. to Eleanor K. Moore 1-4-1842 T
Davidson, Obadiah W. to Judith Carroll 4-30-1867 G
Davidson, Olediah to Lucinda K. Carlton 10-8-1851 Sh
Davidson, R. J. to Margaret J. Williams 3-5-1867 (3-6-1867) L
Davidson, R. J. to Margaret Raines 2-19-1884 (2-20-1884) L
Davidson, R. L. to Martha C. Conley 1-22-1863 G
Davidson, Richmond to Elizabeth Maner 12-25-1844 Cr
Davidson, Robert B. to Mary Hendricks 12-24-1838 G
Davidson, S. F. to Susan V. Holder 12-12-1866 G
Davidson, S. F. to Susan V. Mosley 6-18-1863 G
Davidson, S. M. to Catherine Len (Lew? Low?) 5-14-1859 (5-15-1859) Sh
Davidson, S. R. to Malvira F. Barnes 10-20-1855 Sh
Davidson, S. W. to N. N. Everett 4-5-1873 (no return) L
Davidson, Samuel H. to Catharine Warrick 6-21-1851 Be
Davidson, Samuel M. to Allezarah A. Thomas 12-2-1852 G
Davidson, Thomas A. to Marget C. Edmonds 7-22-1829 O
Davidson, Thomas B. to Katharine Emery 9-14-1848 G
Davidson, Thomas C. to Amanda Hart 3-27-1865 Hn
Davidson, Thomas P. to Sallie L. (Mrs.) Chamberlin 11-7-1855 (11-9-1855) Sh
Davidson, Thos. to Sarah Dumis 12-2-1874 T
Davidson, W. A. to Elizabeth Crouse 6-13-1861 Mn
Davidson, W. A. to Martha R. Parrish 6-23-1868 O
Davidson, W. C. to Margaret J. Lorance 9-27-1860 G
Davidson, W. C. to Mary S. Mosley 2-14-1860 G
Davidson, W. J. to M. A. McDearmon 12-7-1852 Hn
Davidson, W. L. to Emily E. Renfro 8-9-1864 G
Davidson, W. M. to M. M. McKey 4-29-1865 G
Davidson, W. T. to Martha E. Marsh 12-28-1869 (12-30-1869) T
Davidson, W. W. to Analizer Misers 3-15-1863 Be
Davidson, W. W. to E. E. Tally 8-15-1861 (8-20-1861) Sh
Davidson, W. W. to Kate J. James 3-29-1855 (4-18-1855) Sh
Davidson, William A. to Harriett L. B. Cerley 2-2-1860 Hn
Davidson, William M. to Mary J. Mosley 10-13-1856 G
Davidson, William O. to Elizabeth J. Rankins 11-9-1843 G
Davidson, William T. B. to Margaret McAdams 7-12-1862 We
Davidson, William to Allia? Canady 11-7-1867 G

Davidson, William to Elizabeth Golden 3-20-1852 Sh
Davidson, William to Emely Ballance 12-3-1845 G
Davidson, William to Mehala Rhea 7-20-1834 Sh
Davidson, Wilson L. to Nancy Barton 10-18-1837 (10-19-1837) G
Davidson, Wm. H. to Malisa Jane Barker 7-10-1845 Be
Davidson, Wm. J. to Dorraty Bobbitt 8-30-1838 G
Davidson, thomas to Lucinda Tims 11-2-1847 (11-3-1847) T
Davie, Ben to Eliza Williams 2-17-1866 Hy
Davie, Edward to Sarah A. Vincent 1-14-1869 (1-21-1869) Ma *
Davie, Geo. Edward to Frances A. McConico 10-10-1877 Hy
Davie, James A. L. to Addie H. Burrow 12-15-1860 (12-16-1860) Ma
Davie, James B. to Cornelia J. Davie 7-21-1853 Ma
Davie, James M. to E. T. Henry 10-11-1860 O
Davie, Joseph H. to Margarett J. Parrish 2-22-1859 We
Davie, Nelson to Rebecca (Mrs.) Medlin 1-8-1862 (1-9-1862) Ma
Davie, W. S. to Katie E. Hall 9-29-1874 (9-30-1874) T
Davie, William A. W. to Mildred A. Woolfolk 4-5-1869 (4-7-1869) Ma
Davie, William A. to Jane B. Davis 11-8-1841 Ma
Davies, L. E. to Fannie E. Vaughan 11-27-1860 (11-28-1860) Sh
Davis, A. J. to Letia Russell 5-14-1884 L
Davis, A. J. to Susan J. Richey 1-6-1869 (1-7-1869) F
Davis, A. M. to Ellen V. Harbin 5-14-1861 (5-21-1861) Hr
Davis, A. W. to Amanda W. Wester 9-8-1852 Sh
Davis, A. to H. E. Fite 3-18-1871 (4-11-1871) Cr
Davis, Adam to Frances Baker 9-13-1855 G
Davis, Albert A. to Anne? Ragan Olds 2-26-1842 Ma
Davis, Alex. to Anthus Carter 6-26-1845 Cr
Davis, Alexander to Nancy Jane Jackson 2-3-1845 We
Davis, Alexander to Susanah J. Brooks 11-26-1856 Sh
Davis, Allison to Pheoba Harrison 8-5-1851 (8-7-1851) Sh
Davis, Andrew to Sarah Alingny? Linsey 7-23-1836 Hr
Davis, Andrew to Sarah Needham 8-15-1830 Sh
Davis, Asa M. to S. J. Hall 5-17-1873 (5-18-1873) Dy
Davis, B. F. to M. A. Hutchinson 1-12-1867 (1-13-1867) O
Davis, Benj. W. to Mary Jane Grace 2-24-1847 Hr
Davis, Benjamin to Catherine Jones 9-1-1831 Hr
Davis, Benjamin to Sarah E. Dodd 12-19-1845 (12-23-1845) F
Davis, Benjn. to Mary Rachels 8-27-1850 (8-29-1850) F
Davis, Berry A. to Eliza J. Black 6-18-1853 (7-19-1853) Ma
Davis, Berry H. to Mary Jackson 11-2-1853 Cr
Davis, Bill to Catherine Henly 11-19-1875 (no return) Hy
Davis, Bill to Ella Howell 4-1-1871 Hy
Davis, Bill to Ellen Fields 8-19-1875 Hy
Davis, Bluford L. to Elizabeth Boswell 2-16-1858 (2-17-1858) Sh
Davis, Bryant to Nancy A. J. Rose 12-24-1855 (12-26-1855) Hr
Davis, Calvin to Nancy C. Blasingame 1-17-1872 (1-18-1872) T
Davis, Cato to Mary B. Lawson 2-13-1857 (2-18-1857) O
Davis, Charles R. to Laura T. Taylor 3-24-1856 Sh
Davis, Charles to Charlotte Hanie 12-31-1840 G
Davis, Charlie H. to Millie Bostick 9-15-1884 L
Davis, Craven A. to Lucy C. Haynes 6-15-1831 Ma
Davis, Cyrus T. to Sarah M. Davis 10-24-1850 Sh
Davis, Cyrus to Olivia Rucker 4-8-1844 (4-9-1844) Hr
Davis, D. A. to C. D. Mason 10-25-1865 (10-26-1865) T
Davis, D. J. to Elizabeth Matlock 4-19-1849 (no return) Cr
Davis, Daniel to Josie Hamilton 8-16-1878 (8-21-1878) Dy
Davis, David P. to Lizzie Calloway 5-8-1867 Ma
Davis, David P. to M. Cloar 3-6-1861 (3-7-1861) O
Davis, David to Beluchery Hawkins 8-1-1848 (8-2-1848) O
Davis, David to Elizabeth Bradford 12-8-1842 (12-11-1842) O
Davis, David to Jane Wright 11-30-1867 G B
Davis, David to Mary Lackey 6-14-1838 F
Davis, Davie to Cordie Kindle 4-16-1873 (4-17-1873) T
Davis, Dorsey to Nancy Nowell 3-21-1843 Ma
Davis, E. B. to Sallie P. Loving 2-6-1860 (2-7-1860) F
Davis, E. G. to Mary J. Nicholson 8-26-1868 (no return) L
Davis, E. J. to Sarah Ann Walker 1-9-1862 Sh
Davis, Ed to Frances Sanford 7-5-1881 L B
Davis, Ed to Maggie Bradford 1-7-1866 Hy
Davis, Edmond M. to Elizabeth Gills 9-9-1877 O
Davis, Edmund M. to Susan D. Palmer 10-8-1853 Sh
Davis, Edward O. to Amanda M. Sparks 3-20-1851 O
Davis, Edward to Louise Tamey? no date (with 12-1874) T
Davis, Edward to Mary Ann Ellington 12-21-1838 (12-25-1838) Ma
Davis, Elbert E. to Elizabeth Moody 8-25-1854 Hn
Davis, Elias to Sarah Thompson 3-15-1840 Be
Davis, Elihu W. to Harriet Davidson 10-4-1864 G
Davis, Elijah to Jane Alexander 11-29-1824 G
Davis, Ellis to Parthenia E. Lawrence 9-22-1870 G
Davis, Emanuel to Elizabeth Price 11-23-1848 G
Davis, Ephraim to Emily H. Higgs 12-27-1843 We
Davis, Eton to Lucy Williams 9-6-1855 Hn
Davis, F. F. to Anna Yarbro 7-15-1874 T
Davis, F. M. to M. J. M. Berry 8-17-1864 (8-18-1864) Cr
Davis, F. M. to Mary Glenn 12-1-1856 (12-2-1856) Ma
Davis, F. M. to S. M. Walker 3-22-1866 G
Davis, F. M. to Sarah J. Montgomery 10-30-1859 We

Davis, Fed to Julia Ann Pewett 5-2-1867 (no return) F B
Davis, Fed to Lucy Henly 12-24-1877 Hy
Davis, Francis E. to Jane E. Steel 5-10-1842 (no return) F
Davis, Fredk. to Isabella M. Alexander 8-26-1842 (8-31-1842) F
Davis, G. B. to Sophia McCoy 9-15-1859 Sh
Davis, G. C. to Sarah N. Callicott 2-24-1859 (3-1-1859) O
Davis, G. H. to Elizabeth A. Brooks 1-4-1854 (no return) F
Davis, G. W. to Anna Childress 7-16-1870 (7-17-1870) F
Davis, Gabriel to Harriet Bond 12-10-1871 Hy
Davis, Geo. W. to Mary Rose Powell 10-26-1841 Sh
Davis, Geo. to Mary A. Polk 11-19-1842 (11-17?-1842) F
Davis, George W. to Eliza Grainger 1-21-1847 Hn
Davis, George W. to Melinda Crockett 8-17-1855 O
Davis, George to Cena M. Black 11-2-1844 (11-4-1844) Hr
Davis, George to Mattie Hite 1-19-1880 (no return) L
Davis, George to Miss Sarah Spears 1-12-1852 (1-14-1852) Hr
Davis, George to Neely Butcher 11-30-1875 (no return) Hy
Davis, German W. to Cela A. Maxwell 4-16-1858 (4-18-1858) Hr
Davis, H. S. to S. S. Learned 2-4-1863 We
Davis, H. W. to Martha P. Holland 3-17-1864 Be
Davis, H. W. to Peggie A. Holland 11-7-1850 Be
Davis, Harrison to Elizabeth Grider 6-30-1837 O
Davis, Henry A. to Allis Cherry 1-22-1868 L B
Davis, Henry C. to Amanda Young 8-20-1860 We
Davis, Henry C. to Lucy C. Nuttall 6-30-1858 (7-1-1858) Ma
Davis, Henry Clay to Lucey Field 9-22-1874 T
Davis, Henry N. to Mary A. Webber 5-5-1857 Sh
Davis, Henry W. to Martha M. Holmes 12-25-1844 Ma
Davis, Henry to Emma Young 1-4-1873 Hy
Davis, Henry to Frances Ellis 1-2-1867 (no return) Hy
Davis, Henry to Lucinda Piper 5-28-1844 Hr
Davis, Henry to S. A. (Mrs.) Jackson 11-24-1843 Sh
Davis, Hezekiah J. to Rebecca J. Boyt 7-16-1842 (7-20-1842) G
Davis, Hezekiah to Salenah Hood 9-2-1850 O
Davis, Hiram to Millie Roberts 11-2-1876 Hy
Davis, Hiram to Sally Lowery 7-5-1828 G
Davis, Hughie to Elizabeth Jones 10-7-1830 (10-14-1830) Hr
Davis, I. N. to Nancy E. Barnett 2-20-1863 (2-23-1863) Dy
Davis, Irvin to Ann M. Baugh 11-15-1852 Sh
Davis, Irvin to Ellen Snell 1-11-1860 Sh
Davis, Isaac L. to Ruth L. Waddle 12-26-1847 Sh
Davis, Isham F. to Sarah Jane Gordon 11-15-1848 G
Davis, J. B. to J. A. McLeary 7-23-1863 G
Davis, J. C. to E. J. Bayliss 4-17-1860 (4-18-1860) Sh
Davis, J. C. to Margaret White 11-17-1874 Hy
Davis, J. C. to Martha L. Lay 8-16-1880 (8-17-1880) L B
Davis, J. D. to F. E. Stevens 1-15-1866 (1-16-1866) F
Davis, J. E. to Ettie Northcross 11-21-1860 G
Davis, J. F. to S. O. Duncan 2-9-1885 L
Davis, J. G. to Sarah A. Milton 10-27-1861 G
Davis, J. G. to T. J. Cole 11-5-1870 G
Davis, J. H. to Emily D. Rollins 2-28-1870 (2-29?-1870) Cr
Davis, J. H. to M. J. Harlan 6-6-1882 (6-7-1882) L
Davis, J. H. to N. J. Freeman 10-5-1874 (10-6-1874) Dy
Davis, J. L. to Susan Lovett 10-1-1866 (10-10-1866) Dy
Davis, J. M. to Josephine Bowen 1-1-1866 (1-4-1866) F
Davis, J. M. to Parolle Cole 1-10-1856? (1-10-1857) G
Davis, J. R. to Mary A. Morris 10-29-1866 O
Davis, J. T. to Nannie Davis 12-27-1879 (12-28-1879) L
Davis, J. W. to J. A. Swayne 1-9-1879 Dy
Davis, J. W. to Lizzie Cowan 7-26-1884 (7-28-1884) L
Davis, J. W. to Nancy Jane Mayfield 12-12-1859 (12-13-1859) T
Davis, J. W. to Sarah Bransett 12-27-1874 Hy
Davis, J.E. to Christinea Shoaf 11-25-1874 T
Davis, Jacob M to Caroline Jones 3-2-1866 (5-30-1866) T
Davis, Jacob to Mary A. Ables 2-21-1859 (2-23-1859) Hr
Davis, Jacob to Maryetta Burrel 12-17-1873 (12-20-1873) T
Davis, James A. to Christiana Chandler 7-6-1867 (7-7-1867) Dy
Davis, James B. to Penelope A. Little 12-18-1854 Sh
Davis, James C. to Jane Allen 1-16-1855 (no return) F
Davis, James D. to Mary Jane Smith 12-14-1834 Sh
Davis, James E. to Nancy Elizabeth Russell 12-12-1859 Ma
Davis, James F. to Melinda Marsh 10-23-1866 (10-24-1866) T
Davis, James F. to Sarah Bragg 3-30-1869 G
Davis, James H. to Amanda Simmons 9-1-1870 (9-24-1870) Ma
Davis, James H. to Clarrasy Ann Connell 10-26-1853 (10-27-1853) G
Davis, James H. to Parisett Tate 2-8-1861 Cr
Davis, James H. to Perlina Chipman 4-9-1853 Ma
Davis, James I. to Amanda J. Lewis 9-25-1837 Sh
Davis, James L. to Lucy Davis 6-26-1848 (6-29-1848) Ma
Davis, James M. to Margaret E. Fulbright 2-9-1858 Ma
Davis, James R. to Manda H. Smith 3-22-1855 G
Davis, James R. to Mary E. Jones 9-10-1850 Cr
Davis, James T. to Artemissa Bright 5-16-1867 Be
Davis, James T. to Martha P. Shipman 7-19-1868 G
Davis, James W. to Mary Ellison 2-11-1864 Hn
Davis, James to Anne Johnson 3-22-1873 (3-23-1873) L B

Davis, James to Eliza Warrick 5-8-1851 Be
Davis, James to Elizabeth Jones 2-19-1838 (2-28-1838) O
Davis, James to Elizabeth Nowlen 10-16-1862 O
Davis, James to Elizabeth Stanley 4-12-1858 (4-14-1858) O
Davis, James to Elizabeth Williams 3-4-1828 O
Davis, James to Jane Kerwsell (Kernell?) 6-9-1853 Sh
Davis, James to L. A. Teams 12-9-1865 (12-10-1865) F
Davis, James to Lavina Moore 11-18-1840 (11-19-1840) F
Davis, James to Rebecca A. Yarbrough 2-11-1852 G
Davis, James to Rebecca Dalton 3-13-1839 O
Davis, James to Sarah Bowles 7-26-1858 (no return) Hn
Davis, James to Sarah Montgomery 12-6-1843 Sh
Davis, James to Vicy Castill 8-25-1856 (no return) Hn
Davis, January to Elmira Golding 11-26-1878 L B
Davis, Jarman W. to Sarah J. Flenn 1-5-1858 Hr
Davis, Jas. C. to Frances Steel 5-22-1870 Hy
Davis, Jerome to Catharine Bobbitt 9-16-1870 (9-18-1870) F B
Davis, Jesse to Elizabeth Rowden 11-17-1866 (11-18-1866) Dy
Davis, Jesse to Jane Webb 4-9-1856 Cr
Davis, Jesse to Priscilla Kennedy 6-5-1828 (6-14?-1828) Hr
Davis, Jno. C. to Nelly Cerly 11-28-1849 Hr
Davis, Joe to Tennessee Johnson 9-30-1871 (10-9-1871) Cr B
Davis, John A. to Nellie Bond 3-8-1871 Hy
Davis, John B. to Sarah Simpson 10-12-1846 (10-15-1846) T
Davis, John C. to Ann Swanner 6-25-1879 (6-28-1879) Dy
Davis, John C. to Martha A. Roach 1-27-1847 (1-28-1847) G
Davis, John C. to Mary L. Rose (Rorex?) 6-9-1855 Sh
Davis, John Calhoon to Nannie Wilborn 1-5-1854 (no return) F
Davis, John D. to Charlotta Canaday 7-9-1851 (7-10-1851) G
Davis, John D. to Martha Couch 10-3-1849 (no return) Cr
Davis, John E. G. to Mary J. Russey 8-13-1840 Hr
Davis, John E. to Asenith Ward 10-12-1868 (10-14-1868) Dy
Davis, John E. to Eliza Pettigrew 3-14-1868 (3-15-1868) Ma
Davis, John E. to Kiziah Aldridge 11-29-1865 Mn
Davis, John F. to Mary E. Davis 12-22-1865 L
Davis, John H. to Sarah Smith 1-16-1851 Sh
Davis, John J. to Elizabeth Barton 9-27-1847 Ma
Davis, John L. to Ann Farris 1-10-1860 Cr
Davis, John L. to Elizabeth N. Baker 8-25-1840 O
Davis, John L. to Lucy Ann Thomas 12-2-1844 (12-20-1844) F
Davis, John M. to Caralin Martin 6-25-1859 We
Davis, John M. to Fanny J. Zerico 1-26-1859 G
Davis, John M. to Martha A. F. Jones 11-27-1824 Hr
Davis, John Wesley to Martha E. Davis 3-9-1870 (3-10-1870) F
Davis, John to Ann Miller 9-29-1866 (no return) Hy
Davis, John to Caroline (Mrs.) Jackson 4-29-1871 (4-20?-1871) Ma
Davis, John to Emeline Gay 4-9-1870 (4-12-1870) F
Davis, John to Fanny Hester 4-2-1865 (4-9-1865) Cr
Davis, John to Hollen Dougherty 8-13-1836 Hr
Davis, John to Jane Poe 2-7-1850 Be
Davis, John to Jenny Seward 8-17-1870 G B
Davis, John to Julia Margall 7-26-1873 (7-27-1873) Dy B
Davis, John to Julia Mayall 7-26-1873 (no return) Dy B
Davis, John to Levinia Westbrook 12-29-1846 (12-31-1846) F
Davis, John to Louisa Ragsdale 4-15-1854 (4-18-1854) G
Davis, John to Margaret Richmond 7-3-1867 (7-4-1867) Dy
Davis, John to Martha Hudson 7-17-1846 Hr
Davis, John to Martha J. Basham 2-11-1860 (2-15-1860) O
Davis, John to Mary Ann Dodd 2-10-1857 (2-11-1857) L
Davis, John to Mattie F. Nichols 2-5-1864 Sh
Davis, John to Rachael Ann Bone 8-30-1846 O
Davis, John to Sarah Phifer 12-25-1853 Be
Davis, Jonathan Calvin to Martha Jane McCain 9-13-1854 T
Davis, Jonathan to Caroline Pearce 4-18-1859 G
Davis, Jose to Celia Dockins 9-3-1847 O
Davis, Joseph M. to Mary R. Jones 5-11-1859 We
Davis, Joseph M. to Theodocia M. Wright 12-19-1839 O
Davis, Joseph R. to Lydia C. Nevill 7-5-1865 G
Davis, Joseph to Ann Hinson 8-31-1867 Hn B
Davis, Joseph to Cely Perry 7-4-1870 G B
Davis, Joseph to Patsey Cloar 5-26-1842 O
Davis, Josiah to Annie B. Dalton 11-13-1855 Cr
Davis, Josiah to Melinda Sexton 4-23-1838 (no return) Hn
Davis, Julius to Emma Mason 3-3-1883 L
Davis, King G. W. to Louisa Hutson 1-1-1856 (1-25-1856) G
Davis, L. B. to M. J. Childers 4-22-1863 (4-23-1863) O
Davis, L. C. to A. N. Stanley 2-8-1871 (4-9-1871) O
Davis, L. L. to Martha C. White 3-4-1854 Sh
Davis, L. L.(S?) to Scyntha Hale 7-10-1836 O
Davis, Laudin to Frances McLinn 5-5-1871 T
Davis, Lee to Phillis Ledsinger 1-25-1877 (no return) Dy
Davis, Lewis to Eleanor E. Edmonds 2-16-1832 O
Davis, Lewis to Julia Barbee 12-29-1872 Hy
Davis, Lewis to Mattie Rawlings 12-23-1874 Hy
Davis, Lonis to Mary Marr 12-23-1876 Hy
Davis, M. L. to Sarah Walton 1-19-1854 (no return) F
Davis, Marion to Elizabeth Brent 4-20-1865 Dy

Davis, Martin to Elizabeth T. Drake 10-3-1853 Ma
Davis, Maxvill to Mary Ann Harrison 4-24-1844 Sh
Davis, Nathan L. to Martha J. Warren 10-7-1869 Dy
Davis, Nelson T. to Fannie Justice 4-8-1872 (4-10-1872) Dy
Davis, Nelson to Nanie West 9-10-1876 Hy
Davis, O. W. to Eliza J. Carter 10-29-1842 (no return) Hn
Davis, Perry Jas. to Sarah C. Lucus 6-24-1841 Cr
Davis, Peter to Millie Spivey 12-23-1871 Hy
Davis, Pink to Caroline Gage 11-26-1870 (11-21?-1870) F
Davis, Pleasant R. to Sarah J. Manley 9-18-1861 (9-19-1861) Ma
Davis, Porter to Perimila Thorn 2-2-1859 Cr
Davis, R. D. to Mary C. Sullivan 12-18-1875 Hy
Davis, R. H. to A. F. Groome 12-18-1862 Mn
Davis, R. H. to Amanda F. Croom 12-17-1863 (11?-17-1862?) Ma
Davis, R. H. to Isabel L. Sellers 12-11-1868 (12-15-1868) Cr
Davis, R. N. to Belle J. McClellan 12-15-1859 O
Davis, R. T. to Lurana C. Lassiter 1-10-1870 (no return) L
Davis, R. W. to Susan R. Alexander 1-15-1859 (1-20-1859) G
Davis, Ralph to Adaline Harris 3-19-1869 (no return) Cr
Davis, Reuben to Ann C. Moody 12-17-1870 (12-25-1870) Dy
Davis, Richard M. to Sarah Vantrice 12-20-1842 (12-29-1842) Ma
Davis, Richard to Aramenta Davis 11-20-1855 O
Davis, Richard to Emaline Sanders 1-8-1870 (1-9-1870) T
Davis, Richard to Emily Lewallian 6-9-1842 Sh
Davis, Robert H. to Sarah R. Allen 12-10-1837 O
Davis, Robert to Ann E. Cardwell? 12-13-1858 (12-14-1858) O
Davis, Robert to Bethen Lack 2-16-1864 G
Davis, Robert to Mary Matthewson 11-9-1867 (no return) Hn
Davis, Robert to Nancy Ware 10-1-1870 (no return) Hy
Davis, Rubin to Siller Davis 11-5-1874 (11-8-1874) T
Davis, Ruf. to M. Morris 2-26-1872 O
Davis, S. H. to W. S. Petty 4-7-1860 (4-9-1860) O
Davis, S. L. to M. Harrington 12-9-1863 Sh
Davis, S. M. to Mary McClaren 1-28-1853 (no return) F
Davis, S. R. to Sarah Foster 1-28-1862 (1-29-1862) Hr
Davis, Sam to Julia Butler 11-24-1880 (11-25-1880) L B
Davis, Samuel Clark to Mary Daniel Davis 10-7-1850 Ma
Davis, Samuel H. to Gabriella Jane Lane 9-3-1847 O
Davis, Samuel H. to Laney Bramblett 11-19-1838 O
Davis, Samuel H. to Martha A. Allison 9-19-1840 (9-24-1840) O
Davis, Samuel to Nancey Hanly 4-5-1861 T
Davis, Sandy to Easter Levy 10-6-1867 G B
Davis, Seth B. to Myra A. Davis 3-2-1870 (3-3-1870) L
Davis, Shadrick to Fanny Edwards 5-27-1866 G
Davis, Sherman to Susie Miller 12-26-1883 (12-28-1883) L
Davis, Sherwood R. to Mary Jane Smith 4-2-1870 (4-3-1870) Ma
Davis, Silvain to Paulien Payole 6-16-1864 Sh
Davis, Snowden H. to Mary E. Joyce 10-21-1850 Ma
Davis, Stephen B. to Mary E. Terry 5-16-1864 G
Davis, Stevens to Adalin Hall 1-7-1865 (6-10-1865) T
Davis, T. B. to Frances Nettles 6-21-1860 G
Davis, T. W. to Fannie Scallions 12-25-1871 (12-26-1871) L
Davis, Thomas B. to Lucy A. P. Agee 12-29-1851 G
Davis, Thomas H. to Manervie J. Jones 9-8-1857 We
Davis, Thomas H. to Rosetta Jones 1-11-1848 O
Davis, Thomas to Ann Dickson 11-17-1868 G
Davis, Thomas to Elizabeth Rogers 10-14-1826 (11-20-1826) Hr
Davis, Thornton to Aggie Carter 2-16-1832 O
Davis, Thos. G. to Sarah Newsom (Mewsom) 8-31-1840 Sh
Davis, Uriah to Delia A. Hummil 8-16-1851 L
Davis, V. A. to Jane Whitehorn 3-14-1837 H
Davis, W. A. to Louisa V. Proctor 11-22-1873 (11-27-1873) T
Davis, W. A. to S. N. Parrish 2-1-1866 G
Davis, W. C. to Namie? Sullivan 3-12-1866 (3-15-1866) T
Davis, W. E. to Tabitha White 4-16-1864 (4-17-1864) Sh
Davis, W. H. to Jane Turner 12-29-1868 G B
Davis, W. H. to Louisa E. Selph 12-13-1849 L
Davis, W. H. to Susan Lane 1-19-1871 T
Davis, W. J. to Sarah Jane Reed 11-27-1866 (11-28-1866) Dy
Davis, W. K. to Sarah Ann Lee 10-15-1857 (no return) Cr
Davis, W. M. to M. J. Diggs 4-13-1867 (no return) Hn
Davis, W. P. to Mary Wethington 9-27-1869 (9-28-1869) Dy
Davis, W. S. to M. J. Hampton 5-16-1874 (5-19-1874) Dy
Davis, W. T. M. to Nancy D. Alexander 1-5-1849 Sh
Davis, W. T. to Permilia Snow 9-27-1865 (9-28-1865) F
Davis, W. T. to Susn Marchant 10-15-1868 Dy
Davis, Wade H. to Sarah J. W. Young 12-17-1866 (12-27-1866) L
Davis, Washington to Elizabeth Lowry 2-6-1838 Hn
Davis, Wesley B. to Louisa Frost 4-30-1840 G
Davis, Wesley to Esther Harris 8-21-1869 (8-13?-1869) F B
Davis, William A. to Martha A. Gargarius 11-27-1860 We
Davis, William H. to Delila Chipman 12-7-1840 Ma
Davis, William H. to Frances M. Kinney 7-23-1857 T
Davis, William H. to Jane Rutledge 12-6-1848 Sh
Davis, William J. to Elizabeth Fletcher 8-9-1856 (8-13-1856) G
Davis, William J. to Elizabeth Terrell 3-20-1841 Ma
Davis, William J. to Sarah Ann E. Terrell 9-1-1841 (9-2-1841) Ma

Davis, William M. to N. A. Rentfro 8-25-1859 G
Davis, William O. to Sarah Jane Miller 3-11-1869 Cr
Davis, William P. to Leander Jane Murrell 3-12-1853 (3-15-1853) Ma
Davis, William to Amandy Vaughan 1-8-1862 G
Davis, William to Caroline Buise 10-28-1842 T
Davis, William to Charlotte Whittaker 9-13-1872 O
Davis, William to Isabel Elrod 12-31-1865 Hy
Davis, William to Martha Peal 4-21-1860 (4-22-1860) O
Davis, William to Martha Pollock 10-2-1855 O
Davis, William to N L. Cary 6-7-1865 G
Davis, William to Rutha Beck 12-3-1868 G
Davis, Willie to Polly Tedford 8-14-1830 (8-16-1830) Hr
Davis, Willis to Caroline Treadaway 10-24-1874 (10-25-1874) T
Davis, Willis to Elizabeth M. Duncan 8-2-1845 (8-3-1845) Hr
Davis, Wm. Carroll to Sarah Adiline Davis 9-4-1854 (9-6-1854) T
Davis, Wm. D. to E. P. Thompson 8-13-1863 O
Davis, Wm. D. to Sarah Shaw 2-20-1856 Cr
Davis, Wm. H. to Elmira Jones 4-25-1866 (4-28-1866) F B
Davis, Wm. N. to N. E. H. Moore 4-17-1864 (4-19-1864) O
Davis, Wm. T. M. to Sarah S. Vasser 3-20-1844 Sh
Davis, Wm. to Mary Jackson 12-17-1846 We
Davis, Wm. to Nancy Kingston 7-23-1846 We
Davis, Wm. to Rachael Keith 12-4-1867 G
Davis, Wm. to Sarah Ann Rachel 10-7-1850 (no return) F
Davis, Zachariah to Rosanna Shinault 5-22-1824 Hr
Davis, jr., John to Eliza Jane Davis 12-18-1856 (no return) F
Davisky, Joven to Caroline Hamilton 9-1-1859 (9-1859) O
Davison, J. C. to Elizabeth Gregory 10-5-1850 F
Davison, J. C. to J. A. R. Whitehead 9-25-1848 (9-28-1848) F
Davison, Jesse to Catharine Kelton 11-18-1845 We
Daviss, John to Araminta Eveline Harp 3-4-1845
Davy, John C. to Angirary? Eddins 4-18-1843 F
Davy, John T. to Mary E. Johnson 8-29-1870 G
Davy, Manuel to Mary Read 9-16-1865 (no return) Hy
Davys, John H. to Margaret (Mrs.) Long 11-12-1864 Sh
Dawes, Starkey to Martha J. Herron 6-19-1869 (6-20-1869) Cr
Dawlton, Jno. W. to Mary J. Hardin 12-19-1867 Hn
Daws, William to Martha Todd 12-16-1840 (12-17-1840) Ma
Dawson(Damson), Stephen H. to M. J. King 1-20-1845 Hr
Dawson, David to Lila Brooks 12-3-1870 F B
Dawson, Flemming G. to Rebecca W. Porter 10-31-1843 Hn
Dawson, Hiram to Nancy Johnston 8-29-1829 (8-30-1829) G
Dawson, Isaac B. to Joanna C. Oliver 8-8-1861 We
Dawson, Isaac to Pemelia Lane Lowry 5-1-1829 O
Dawson, J. H. to Emma Eldridge 10-11-1853 Sh
Dawson, J. S. to J. H. P Brown 11-20-1850 H
Dawson, Jackson to Nancy E. Quinley 10-30-1841 (11-3-1841) Ma
Dawson, James C. to Sarah Brown 1-7-1839 (1-8-1839) Hr
Dawson, James L. to Martha Low 2-18-1843 Hr
Dawson, James O. to Barbara B. Johnson 1-9-1839 (1-11-1839) Hr
Dawson, James to Julia Senter (Smith?) 10-13-1866 G
Dawson, James to Lydia Lawrence 1-30-1856 Ma
Dawson, James to Martha Lawrence 4-12-1854 Ma
Dawson, Jessee F. to Martha A. Mills 1-18-1871 (1-19-1871) T
Dawson, John L. to Mary Hunter 2-2-1866 (2-4-1866) F
Dawson, John M. to E. A. Martin 1-10-1870 G
Dawson, John to Christianna G. Smith 12-19-1838 (12-20-1838) Hr
Dawson, Johnithan to Tennessee Sexton 6-10-1847 (6-15-1847) G
Dawson, L. G. to Mary E. Baker 5-24-1871 (5-25-1871) Ma
Dawson, Lem to Isabelle Laurie 2-20-1866 Hn
Dawson, Moses A. to Ouida C. Alexander 4-30-1847 Hn
Dawson, Nickodemus to Ida Burnett 8-13-1870 G B
Dawson, Perry to Mary Jane Cox 10-14-1872 (10-16-1872) T
Dawson, Richard to Martha Smith 9-15-1842 (9-16-1842) Ma
Dawson, Robert to Margaret Jones 1-12-1871 (no return) F B
Dawson, W. D. to Rosa Ann Jane Mills 12-?-1869 (12-19-1869) T
Dawson, W. F. to Christina Fogg 11-8-1869 G
Dawson, W. F. to M. M. Bonds 10-10-1865 G
Dawson, William C. to Eliza M. Williams 11-27-1854 Sh
Dawson, William C. to Florence King 7-22-1869 Hy
Dawson, William to Elizabeth J. Quinley 2-12-1849 Ma
Dawtry, Bryant T. to Catherine Morgan 5-22-1844 G
Dawtry, Sean to Elizabeth S. Crockett 11-20-1849 G
Day, A. J. F. to S. M. Northcross 5-8-1861 G
Day, A. S. to Eliza D. Lewis 11-9-1854 (no return) F
Day, Anderson to Elizabeth Maclin 1-23-1877 (no return) Hy
Day, Billy to Ellen Finney 12-31-1866 (1-5-1867) F B
Day, George W. to Elizabeth C. Weatherly 10-28-1856 (10-30-1856) Ma
Day, George W. to Mary E. Jones 10-12-1848 (10-15-1848) Ma
Day, George to Martha E. Lyons 1-25-1854 G
Day, H. T. to Jane Collum 11-1-1855 Sh
Day, Isaac to Martha Jane Gilkey 10-20-1859 Sh
Day, James H. to Eliza J. Deight 1-22-1849 O
Day, James O. to Margaret Baskem 12-30-1865 Mn
Day, James to Albina Gill 3-6-1873 (no return) Hy
Day, James to Angaline Crosslin 11-14-1850 We
Day, James to Maurina Currie 2-10-1870 (no return) Hy

Day, James to Tennessee Gunter 3-26-1855 We
Day, John H. to Bythenia A. Goodman 8-15-1868 G
Day, John H., jr. to Margaret A. Coleman 8-29-1850 Ma
Day, John P. to Leonora Johnson 1-17-1870 (1-19-1870) Ma
Day, Joseph to Mary A. Barnett 5-3-1845 Hn
Day, Lemuel to Mary Gowen 7-21-1849 (7-26-1849) Ma
Day, Lemuel to Sarah Smith 9-12-1871 (9-13-1871) Dy
Day, Phil to Mollie Allen 12-25-1871 Hy
Day, Richard G. to Julia V. Armstead 12-19-1856 Hr
Day, Riland to Lucey Tarry 4-15-1867 (4-27-1867) T
Day, Thomas D. to Lucinda R. Sturdevant 3-4-1868 Ma
Day, W. C. to Amanda McMurry 1-15-1867 (1-16-1867) O
Day, W. G. to Frances Patton 12-7-1853 (no return) F
Day, Wiley G. to Judith F. Lee 1-25-1846 Sh
Day, William P. to Sarilda F. Giles 9-25-1856 (9-28-1856) Sh
Day, William Parker to Susanna Hopper 4-8-1845 Ma
Dazey, J. N. to Emma Evans 12-3-1869 (12-8-1869) F
De La Hay, James J. to Mary Jane Spivey 3-17-1841 Sh
DeAragan, R. T. to E. V. Dyer 6-21-1854 (no return) F
DeBerry, Wm. H. to Polly Hendricks 6-23-1828 (6-24-1828) Hr
DeBow, Grant A. to Jennie Busby 8-20-1861 We
DeBow, R. G. to M. V. Grissom 12-14-1868 (12-15-1868) F
DeBruce, A. B. to Rebecca C. Davidson 5-18-1864 Sh
DeBruce, Archibald B. to Mary E. McFadden 9-9-1866 Hn
DeGraffenreid, Ben to Margaret Cole 10-2-1868 F B
DeGraffenried, London to Charity Ashe 1-8-1866 (1-13-1866) F B
DeGraffenried, M. F. to Francis F. Stith 4-15-1861 (4-16-1861) Sh
DeVoto, Anthony to Susan D. Kelts 10-31-1863 Sh
DeVries, Gerrit to Rosa Fisher 8-12-1872 (9-1-1872) T
DeWalt, George Anderson to Matilda Green 3-28-1868 (4-5-1868) L
Deadrick, M. D. to Jane R. Park 5-19-1857 Ma
Deadrick, William Pitt to Rachel J. Hays 5-9-1855 Ma
Deakins, Henry to Matilda Champion 8-27-1866 (8-28-1866) T
Deakins, John Henry to Eliza M. Lamb 9-19-1849 (9-20-1849) T
Deal, Bassel to Margery Pettijohn 11-22-1845 O
Deal, Joseph to Sallie Howell 8-16-1866 Dy
Dean, Clark (Charles?) to Jane _____ 10-10-1868 G B
Dean, George W. to Frances J. Conyers 12-20-1860 (no return) Hy
Dean, George to Eddie Mitchell 2-24-1886 (no return) L
Dean, H. A. to S. E. Douglass 10-3-1872 (no return) Dy
Dean, Hardy to Jane Young 2-11-1843 (2-14-1843) Ma
Dean, Henry H. to Frances E. Abbington 5-18-1846 (5-22-1846) F
Dean, Henry H. to Laura Hudson 1-23-1854 (1-26-1854) Ma *
Dean, Henry to C. J. Apperson 12-24-1863 (12-30-1863) Sh
Dean, James to Louisa (Mrs.) Miller 9-21-1863 Sh
Dean, John A. to Mary Parker 2-25-1848 (3-2-1848) Ma
Dean, John H. to Rebecca Miller 1-12-1857 (1-14-1857) G
Dean, Robert C. to Sarah J. Prewitt 3-8-1849 Sh
Dean, Sam to Alice Wyse 1-13-1871 (no return) Hy
Dean, W. B. to M. S. Putman 8-5-1870 (8-7-1870) T
Dean, W. Jasper to Martha E. Bradford 10-25-1859 (11-2-1859) Hr
Dean, W. M. to M. E. Stallings 3-6-1878 (3-7-1878) Dy
Dean, W. R. to Elizabeth Dunn 2-19-1859 (2-20-1859) Hr
Deans, Daniel to Martha Evans 10-20-1851 (10-21-1851) Sh
Deardolph, S. R. to Mary E. Kent 10-6-1854 (no return) F
Dearing, John to Sarah Eliza Clark 1-7-18557 T
Dearing, Joseph to Iva Ann Winn 6-24-1856 T
Dearman, William M. to S. E. Barnet 3-22-1865 Hn
Dearmon, William to Isabela Henry 8-18-1863 (no return) Dy
Dearmond, J. B. to S. H. Mize 11-3-1859 Sh
Dearmond, John S. to Margaret R. Davis 12-30-1852 Sh
Dearmond, William W. to Elizabeth Grisharber 11-5-1856 (11-13-1856) Sh
Dearmore, John C. to Berneta R. Golden 7-19-1848 (7-20-1848) Ma
Dearmore, John to Susan P. Hart 12-14-1846 (12-15-1846) Ma
Dearmore, Ned to Judy Tucker 2-8-1877 Dy
Dearmore, William J. to Vicey Ann Gaskins 2-20-1850 (2-21-1850) Ma
Dearmore, Wm. J. to Sarah Ann Johnson 10-4-1871 (10-5-1871) Ma
Dearth, Andrew J. to Jennie Carter 8-26-1862 (8-27-1862) Sh
Deason, Benjamin to Elizabeth Sawyer 9-21-1842 (9-22-1842) L
Deason, Jas. J. to Mary A. Allmond 3-8-1863 Hn
Deason, John to Olive Hall 10-30-1828 Hr
Deason, L. to Angeline Gabrel 5-17-1870 (5-19-1870) Dy
Deason, Samuel to Hester Piles 11-1-1834 Hn
Deason, Samuel to Minerva Chism 7-9-1853 L
Deason, William to Elizabeth Stuckey 3-16-1848 L
Deater, Frederick W. to Sally Yates 3-14-1839 (no return) Hn
Deaton, George W. to Catharine I. Dubois 1-7-1835 Hr
Deaton, John to Jane Clemmons 1-23-1863 Mn
Deaton, M. M. to Agnes P. A. Anderson 10-1-1851 Hr
Deaton, Philip to Delila Wilson 3-2-1836 (3-6-1836) Hr
Deaton, Sampson to L. A. Dickinson 2-22-1854 (2-23-1854) F
Deaton, Thomas T. to Martha Watson 12-7-1867 Be
Deaton, Wm. W. to Martha J. Nance 9-20-1863 Be
Deats, F. W. to Ann Rogers 11-24-1840 (no return) Hn
Deberry, Austin to Penny Devitt 11-11-1876 Hy
Deberry, Calvin to Henrietta Taylor 12-27-1877 Hy
Deberry, Drury to Rebecca Baker 11-20-1858 (11-23-1858) Ma

Deberry, John H. to Edith E. Rogers 11-27-1867 (11-28-1867) Ma
Deberry, John H. to Louisa R. Fulgham 11-25-1856 Ma
Deberry, Joseph to Jane Lee 8-5-1868 (no return) Dy
Deberry, Joseph to Jane Williams 11-25-1876 Hy
Deberry, Matthias to Ann Ingram 11-3-1847 Ma
Deberry, Milton L. to M. J. Boon 1-25-1867 (1-31-1867) Ma
Deberry, Sam to Louisa Hunter 1-24-1878 Hy
Deberry, Sam to Mariah Powell 12-18-1874 (no return) Hy
Deberry, W. W. to M. A. Hanes 4-11-1865 O
Deberry, William W. to Eliza I. Hudson 1-4-1839 Ma
Deboard, John to Jemima Davidson 11-5-1859 Sh
Deborn, Hugh to Bettie Lenox 7-17-1856 We
Debow, G. A. to Annie Sharp 10-6-1860 Sh
Debow, Hugh to Mira Tucker 12-25-1861 (12-26-1862?) O
Debow, S. C. to S. E. Blake 9-?-1863 (9-24-1863) O
Debow, Samuel C. to Henrietta C. Applegate 1-19-1859 O
Deck, Chas. to Catherine Carr 3-20-1845 We
Decker, Balthasar to Caroline R. Bechtold 2-7-1860 Sh
Dedjamatt, John B. to Matilda A. Chandler 5-25-1858 (no return) L
Dedmen, Yett to Martha E. Mathews 2-28-1858 Cr
Dedrick, Home? to Lidia A. Wooten 12-24-1866 (12-27-1866) T
Deeds, Robert C. to Nancy A. Ford 9-17-1850 Hn
Deeds, Rufus M. to Analiza Malone 3-12-1864 (3-13-1864) Sh
Deel, Boswell to Nancy Sowell 9-26-1860 (5-21-1861) O
Deena, Albe Roy to Derinda McDaniel 12-10-1840 Sh
Deener, J. J. to S. A. Gober 11-12-1851 (no return) F
Deener, John to Lucinda Wade 1-7-1869 (no return) F B
Deener, R. H. to Virginia W. Porter 2-27-1869 (2-28-1869) F
Deener, Thos. W. to Susanah M. Galeor 11-20-1848 (11-23-1848) F
Deer, John F. to Josephine F. Brashers 1-22-1868 (1-28-1868) Cr
Dees, Bryant to Hulda Smothers 3-9-1843 Cr
Dees, James S. to Sally Haskell 6-16-1842 Hn
Deeson?, Abraham to Mahaly Davis 12-18-1826 Hr
Deets, Alfred to Amanda S. Turner 9-15-1846 Hn
Deets, Bryan D. to Kiddy A. Cate 9-17-1867 Hn
Deets, John T. to Ester Peel 8-13-1840 Hn
Defoy, Jesstromer to Mary A. Barker 10-18-1851 (no return) Cr
Degernett, Edwin to Dora Edwards 2-18-1878 (2-21-1878) Hy
Degraffenreid, Jesse to Lucy Douglass 12-22-1866 (12-27-1866) F B
Degraffenreid, Nathan to Judy Springfield 12-25-1866 (12-27-1866) F B
Degraffinreid, J. H. to M. V. Douglass 4-9-1874 (4-12-1874) O
Dehanan, Young M. to Elizabeth Brogdon 7-21-1849 (no return) Cr
Delaney, John B. to Annenter McClure 1-20-1840 (no return) Cr
Delaney, McCord to Mary J. Phillips 6-20-1859 Cr
Delaney, N. E. to Nancy J. Edge 3-4-1863 Be
Delaney, Thomas to Bridget McVan 5-1-1860 (5-2-1860) Sh
Delaney, William to Maria Fitzmorris 2-18-1871 Ma
Delaney, Wm. B. to Elizabeth Bell 12-1-1852 Cr
Delaney, Wm. B. to Winiford Owens 10-20-1847 Cr
Delany, J. M. to Sally Patten 12-6-1865 Cr
Delap, Jim to Alsey Patterson 8-11-1866 (8-12-1866) F B
Delashmeit, Joseph G. to Julia E. Morrison 7-1-1865 T
Delashmet, Chas. to Mildred Davidson 11-18-1867 (11-21-1867) T
Delashmet, George W. to Verlinske B. Turnage 12-7-1867 (12-10-1867) T
Delashmet, William to Margaret C. Turnage 12-1-1840 (12-2-1840) T
Delashmet, Wm. to Mary Walker 2-14-1855 (2-15-1855) T
Delashmit, M. L. to Miss L. G. Turnage 12-16-1874 (12-17-1874) T
Delashmut, M. L. to V. C. Jenkins 10-14-1871 (10-19-1871) T
Delass, Hugh to Mollie H. Moore 7-6-1868 (7-7-1868) Ma
Deleny, R. A. to Susan Morris 12-20-1860 (12-23-1860) Cr
Delf, John to Elizabeth Pierce 12-30-1872 Dy
Delf, John to Sarah A. Bland 6-14-1869 Dy
Dell, F. M. to L. A. E. Bibbs 6-15-1859 Cr
Dellender, Enoch to Margaret Balley 10-8-1857 We
Delless, John Fred to Eve Smith 12-26-1871 L
Deloach, A. J. to Virginia L. Ellis 5-18-1880 (5-20-1880) L
Deloach, Arthur to Elizabeth Jane Davis 11-3-1846 Ma
Deloach, J. to N. E. Burtis 9-4-1882 (9-5-1882) L
Deloach, John to Katie E. Dickie 3-14-1871 Ma
Deloach, Loyd W. to Margaret Allen 6-16-1846 Sh
Deloach, Silas to Jane M. Hicks 1-14-1857 (1-15-1857) Ma
Deloach, W. T. to E. E. Stamps 11-23-1880 (11-26-1880) L
Deloach, William T. to Eliza Perry 9-9-1850 Ma
Delph, Daniel to Margarett Bratton 11-10-1831 G
Delph, David to Greeny McFarland 1-23-1829 (1-24-1829) Ma
Delph, John W. to Margaret A. McKelley 3-25-1862 Dy
Delph, Philip to Matilda Barnwell 8-4-1856 Ma
Delph, Philip to Susannah Pierce 8-2-1879 (8-3-1879) Dy
Delph, Phillip to Adeline Sawyer 9-18-1866 Dy
Delviney, Turner to Sidney E. Adams 3-8-1860 Sh
Demar, Luby? to Martha Ann Young 12-20-1873 T
Dement, James B. to Martha Caroline Mustin 9-29-1852 (10-7-1852) Sh
Dement, James T. to Gingeanna Alford 3-17-1852 G
Dement, John S. to Rachael C. Smith 12-22-1853 (12-23-1853) G
Dement, William T. to Martha Ann Clark 12-8-1853 (12-9-1853) O
Dement, Zachariah to Martha Smith 12-3-1857 O
Dement, Zachariah to Mary J. Spears 5-11-1862 G

Demerald, A. to Rhoda C. Jenning 8-1-1851 (8-9-1851) L
Demery, J. J. to Julia Ann Kirby 7-6-1883 (7-8-1883) L
Deming, J. W. to Mary C. Bradford 2-3-1860 Hr
Deming, J. W. to Nancy Jones 12-15-1845 (12-23-1845) Hr
Deming, Wilie to Harriet Ann Jones 10-18-1853 Hr
Demmond (McDemmond?), Syd M. to Maggie Clark 10-28-1864 Sh
Demmons, Thomas to Laura Ann Crane 5-25-1861 Sh
Demorse, Martin to Mattie Outlaw 8-11-1870 L
Demoss, Barnett S. to Mary A. P. Bryant 10-3-1852 Cr
Demoss, Claborn to Francis Anthony 2-4-1871 (2-5-1871) L
Demoss, H. B. to Mary E. Null 1-3-1855 (no return) Cr
Demoss, H. C. to Lavina H. Edwards 11-28-1866 (11-29-1866) Cr
Demoss, J. W. to Alvira Thetford 12-27-1860 G
Demoss, J. W. to Katherine Gibson 11-21-1855 Cr
Demoss, James E. to Frances Hazel 11-26-1880 (11-28-1880) L B
Demoss, James to Narcissa E. Wilson 3-18-1847 Cr
Demoss, S. T. to M. J. Greenwood 9-15-1852 Cr
Demoss, S. T. to Sarah A. McGartary 12-26-1855 Cr
Demoss, Sampson P. to Martha Greenwood 4-26-1859 Cr
Demoss, Sampson to Jane Null 3-14-1842 (no return) Cr
Demoss, William to Martha Turner 8-12-1875 (8-13-1875) L
Dempsa, Hiram to Elmira McDon 8-27-1868 Dy
Dempsey, Henry C. to Elizabeth Nipp 11-26-1861 O
Dempsey, Herman to Malissa Webb 11-2-1850 We
Dempsey, Hiram to Loreza Barnett 2-21-1866 O
Dempster, John to Mary Cannon 5-19-1852 (5-20-1852) Sh
Demsey, Stephen to Rosa White 7-24-1866 G
Demunbrie, Spencer to Ellen Watson 12-7-1848 Sh
Demyers, Jas. H. to Sarah Oliver 1-12-1876 (1-13-1876) O
Denaway, Samuel H. to Martha P. Collinsworth 12-15-1861 G
Denegan, John to Margaret Moran 6-1-1861 Sh
Denegri, Stefano to Catherine Custan 4-1-1850 Sh
Dener, John to Barbery Hub 5-8-1856 Sh
Denger (Denzer?), Charles to Sarah Mcgee 5-8-1851 (5-9-1851) Sh
Dengo, Mitchell to Nancy Hicks 9-18-1852 Sh
Denhower, Franklin to Nancy Garner 5-12-1846 Sh
Denino, James to Emily Dickison (Dickerson) 3-16-1842 Sh
Denis, W. J. to Sarah Jane Boyd 1-1-1864 Mn
Dennegan, John to Ann Conray 5-9-1864 Sh
Denney, David to Susanah Glascow 11-15-1864 (11-16-1864) O
Denney, Frank to Sallie Hill 12-25-1871 (no return) Cr
Denney, John W. to Eliza Birdsong 7-18-1850 Sh
Denney, Joseph to Jane Obene 2-18-1862 Sh
Denney, S. A. to S. E. Munns? 9-11-1876 (9-17-1876) Dy
Denney, William to Eliza M. Rogers 7-12-1847 (7-18-1847) F
Denney, Zachariah F. to Necy A. McBride 9-23-1867 O
Dennie, David to Bettie A. Byrn 11-7-1866 L
Dennie, John to Ann Chism 10-14-1882 (10-15-1882) L
Dennie, John to Martha Jane Nail 2-17-1855 (2-18-1855) L
Dennie, Martin to Mary McCure 8-11-1853 Sh
Dennie, Thomas to M. S. Arwood 3-5-1873 L
Dennies, Wheetly to Hester A. Minter 6-18-1855 (6-24-1855) Hr
Denning, A. D. to Eliza Wallace 10-7-1866 Hn
Denning, James H. to Mary M. Crittendon 5-6-1860 We
Denning, John F. to Ann M. Smith 8-13-1863 We
Denning, John to Mary Ann Patterson 11-30-1842 Hn
Denning, William to Mary Ann Klutts 1-2-1846 (no return) We
Dennis (Dicus), Samuel to Sarah McLean 1-29-1848 Sh
Dennis, Adolphus G. to Elizabeth E. Minter 4-20-1849 Hr
Dennis, Alexander to Easter Webb 10-14-1871 T
Dennis, Alexander to Josephin Cockrill 1-14-1869 (1-18-1869) T
Dennis, Benj. C. to A. E. Vanhorn 7-14-1885 (7-15-1885) Sh
Dennis, Charles to Pamelia Jane Smith 4-17-1854 (4-18-1854) Hr
Dennis, Giles to Ruth Tatom 6-1-1868 (no return) F B
Dennis, J. W. to Mary E. Bowman 3-22-1862 G
Dennis, John to Amanda Sanders 5-21-1878 L
Dennis, R. N. to M. A. Gurgett 10-25-1879 (10-26-1879) Dy
Dennis, Richard H. to Martha W. Pulley 9-1-1869 G
Dennis, Stephen to Margaret Ball 6-23-1850 (no return) Hn
Dennis, Stephen to Polly Ann Tuggle 4-8-1842 Hn
Dennis, W. M. to Catherine Palmer 12-28-1847 Cr
Denniston, James S. to Mary Ann Bounds 10-23-1844 F
Denniston, Jesse A. to Eliza E. Westerman 5-9-1856 (5-10-1856) O
Denny, B. A. to Martha Utley? 10-15-1866 (10-17-1866) Cr
Denny, Henry to Catherine Hargate 6-24-1854 (6-25-1854) L
Denny, Henry to Lucinda Hodge 5-17-1849 L
Denny, James to Ibby Dickerson 2-13-1853 Cr
Denny, John H. to Huldy C. Hannea 1-25-1846 Cr
Denny, Robert to Louisa Lyons 11-24-1836 (11-25-1836) Hr
Denny, Zach T. (D.?) to Mary J. Brown 11-28-1865 G
Densford, James O. to Caroline Clements 4-2-1862 (4-3-1862) T
Densford, William B. to Mary Bryant Dehart 10-13-1849 (10-14-1849) T
Dent, G. W. to Mollie W. Burris 10-11-1869 (10-12-1869) Cr
Dent, Henry G. to Sarah L. Gayle 10-30-1851 Sh
Dent, Jordan to Syntha Holt 12-28-1871 G
Dent, S. W. to Lucy F. S. Cole 1-3-1860 We
Dent, Thos. E. to Eliza Angeline Davis 11-3-1857 We

Denton, A. A. to M. J. Curtiss 1-1-1884 L
Denton, C. B. to F. E. Meter 11-16-1875 (11-18-1875) L
Denton, Henry F. to Frances C. Gibson 12-29-1868 (12-31-1868) L
Denton, James R. to Emily C. McCaig 12-6-1862 Ma
Denton, James to Mahilda Baucum 8-4-1864 G
Denton, Joe to Salenia Long 1-18-1873 (no return) Cr B
Denton, Joseph to Lucinda Stallings 4-2-1849 F
Denwiddie, A. M. to S. F. Grady 1-5-1869 G
Denwiddle, Alex M. to Nancy F. Chrisp 7-17-1847 (7-20-1847) G
Deraberry, P. M. to Susan C. Carper 9-18-1857 (10-2-1857) Hr
Derham, Thomas P. to Elvirah F. Waggoner 12-24-1845 (no return) We
Derington, James H. to Sarah J. Bundage 12-26-1843 Hn
Derington, Robert P. to Mary M. Myrick 5-14-1851 Hn
Derrington, Fielding W. to Nancy C. Harper 10-?-1849 Hn
Derrington, James J. to Margaret E. Brockwell 1-8-1860 Hn
Derryberry, Andrew to Cynthia Gilliam 4-8-1853 Ma
Derryberry, E. H. to Charlott Shipman 8-?-1860 (8-14-1860) Cr
Derryberry, W. A. to A. Z. Hooker 4-12-1863 Mn
Derryberry, William J. to Narcissa Weathers 7-19-1869 Ma
Derybery, E. W. to M.A. Shipman 1-8-1868 (1-9-1868) Cr
Desan, George to Lucy McDaniel 8-30-1821 Sh
Deshaser, Thomas to Elizabeth Laughlan 10-27-1851 O
Deshaser, Thomas to Zelpha Laughlan 11-26-1850 O
Deshaze, Edmund to Elizabeth Jourdan 6-19-1837 (6-20-1837) Hr
Deshong, James Y. to Lucenda C. Fielder 8-30-1853 (9-15-1853) G
Deshong, William W. to Mollie E. Enloe 6-8-1869 (6-10-1869) Cr
Deshony, L. F. to B. L. Thompson 10-28-1872 (10-29-1872) Cr
Desmond, D. Y. to Bridget (Mrs.) Quinn 11-3-1863 Sh
Desmond, Jeremiah to Jane Day 3-24-1859 G
Desobry, Louis to Kate Talbot 7-23-1859 (7-24-1859) Sh
Deson, Clark C. to Elizabeth Mila 11-27-1844 (11-28-1844) T
Deson, James to Jane Surcene? 5-18-1852 Hn
Devaughn, James to Mariah Winn 11-1-1873 (11-5-1873) T
Devenport, Adam to Jennie Walton 10-24-1864 Sh
Devenport, John R. to Anna E. Dairden 10-24-1867 F
Devenport, John to Amanda Goodric 5-14-1870 (5-17-1870) Dy
Devenport, W. J. to Susan J. Sutherland 3-28-1870 (3-29-1870) F
Devenport, William S. to Mary Jane Hatfield 11-27-1848 (11-28-1848) Hr
Devenport, Wm. J. to M. L. Surpit 2-13-1849 (2-14-1849) F
Devereux, William H. to Ann E. Williams 11-18-1852 (no return) F
Devine, Alfred to Paralle Whitehorn 8-19-1868 (8-21-1868) Cr
Devine, Guss to Nancy Claybourn 7-18-1867 Hy
Devine, John to Mary Ferrel 1-16-1864 Sh
Devinney, Charley to Patience Walker 8-4-1841 Sh
Devinney, J. L. to A. J. Forsythe 1-2-1878 (1-3-1878) L
Devinney, William to Analiza Walker 8-28-1842 Sh
Devinport, George W. to Naoma Cowell 11-28-1843 Be
Devinport?, Hiram G. to Mary R. Abernatha 11-23-1846 (11-26-1846) Hr
Devitt, William to Ann Conner 1-29-1852 Sh
Devore, James T. to Eliza F. Mason 9-7-1866 (9-9-1866) Ma
Devote, Peter to Louisa Brignole 3-9-1860 Sh
Dew, A. W. to Mary Carr 10-26-1828 Sh
Dew, George to Martha Newman 9-13-1876 L
Dew, R. J. to Amanda Ferris 1-8-1868 Sh
Dew, Thomas J. to N. L. Redding 10-22-1872 Dy
Dew, Warren W. to Elizabeth Baker 2-18-1867 (3-12-1867) Ma
Dew, William Willie to Lucy N. Morgan 8-28-1846 O
Dew, William W. to Mary Ann Anderson 1-5-1859 Ma
Dew?, Joseph I. to Martha Greenleaf 7-23-1831 (7-24-1831) Hr
Dewalt, D. D. to Cyntha Ann Livingston 9-4-1868 L
Dewalt, David C. to Eliza Halliburton 1-14-1881 L
Dewalt, David to Fannie A. Wood 4-1-1885 (4-2-1885) L
Dewalt, G. W. to Mattie Ann Nelson 4-1-1879 (4-4-1879) L
Dewalt, Henry to Fannie Green 1-15-1875 (1-19-1875) L B
Dewalt, James to Nannie Clark 11-13-1880 (11-19-1880) L
Dewalt, Lee to Lucy Thompson 12-18-1878 L
Dewalt, Peter to Eliza Osbourne 1-4-1886 L
Dewalt, Presley to Tama Dewalt 10-15-1883 L
Dewalt, Samuel to Luanna Gilliland 2-18-1871 (2-19-1871) L
Dewalt, William to Julia Lake 12-30-1868 (12-31-1868) L B
Dewberry, Andrew to Rhosha McFarlan 5-3-1859 Ma
Dewberry, Jessee to Frances S. Cotton 6-2-1860 (6-3-1860) G
Dewberry, John to Louisa R. Draper 7-12-1856 (7-13-1856) G
Dewees, S. A. to Jones Glass 11-2-1874 (11-4-1874) T
Dewey, Thos. to Nancy Gibson 3-4-1840 Cr
Dewhit, Samuel to Sintha J. Norman 10-8-1846 Cr
Dewhit, T. to Martha A. Fuller 7-28-1853 Cr
Dewhitt, Thomas to D. M. Williams 12-31-1866 (1-1-1867) Cr
Dewitt, Aaron to Millie Williams 6-28-1884 L
Dewitt, Jack to Ellen Taylor 12-26-1870 (12-27-1870) F B
Dewitt, Jno. B. to Sarah A. Alls (Able) 11-15-1848 Sh
Dewitt?, John to Nora Woods 8-30-1877 (crossed out) Dy
Dewoody, William L. to Jane M. Pharr 8-27-1851 Sh
Dews, G. W. to Nannie Lane 9-29-1867 Hy
Dezern, J. C. to Josephine Mccoy 8-5-1875 Hy
Deziel, Edward to Laura McClelland 12-20-1876 L
Dial, Abraham S. to Anna Beaver 5-2-1835 G

Dial, James M. to Hanabell M. Alexander no date G
Dial, John A. to Sarah E. Temple 3-3-1855 (no return) L
Dial, W. K. to Emily Mobley 1-17-1865 G
Dial, William K. to Rachal Mobley 12-30-1846 G
Dial, Wm. T. to Lucinda C. Jackson 1-19-1857 (1-20-1857) Hr
Dible, Joseph to Catherine Pates 7-19-1877 Hy
Dibrell, Geo. W. to Elizabeth Hall 4-4-1850 We
Dick, Benjamin H. to Nancy S. Bynum 1-25-1861 We
Dick, James to Mary Brush 9-10-1840 Hn
Dick, James to Mary Finch 1-22-1841 (1-27-1841) F
Dick, Joseph to Martha Lee 9-26-1862 Hn
Dick, M. L. to M. E. Key 11-2-1863 Hn
Dick, Sam to Ester Jones? 1-5-1869 T
Dickason, Eli to Margaret Basinger 2-4-1836 G
Dickason, John to Mary Harris 10-25-1851 (no return) F
Dickens, Anthony to Charity Williams 12-23-1872 T
Dickens, Edmund to Catherine Burton 12-25-1838 Ma
Dickens, Geo. to Missouri Alston 12-23-1872 (12-25-1872) T
Dickens, Mathew to Martha A. Clifft 10-31-1857 (11-3-1857) Hr
Dickens, Nelson to Adaline Hardin 2-8-1872 Hy
Dickens, Samuel to Josephine Botton (Bolton?) 1-22-1856 (1-23-1856) Sh
Dickens, Thomas to Mary M. Stewart 6-2-1830 Ma
Dickens, Thos. to Mary F. Lowrance 10-3-1855 (no return) Cr
Dickens, W. H. D. to Emeline Smith 1-12-1868 (1-2-1868) T
Dickens, William to Louisa Botton (Bolton?) 1-17-1859 Sh
Dickenson, G. L. to L. M. House 12-21-1875 (12-23-1875) O
Dickenson, Hiram to Sarah E. Williamls 4-13-1863 (4-14-1863) O
Dickerson, A. W. to Emmer Fitzgerill 2-14-1872 T
Dickerson, Almeron to Susanna Wilkerson 5-24-1829 Hr
Dickerson, Demsey to Sarah Glowson 1-5-1856 (no return) Cr
Dickerson, Frank to Nancy Walker 4-16-1872 Hy
Dickerson, George to Mollie Gilham 1-19-1872 T
Dickerson, James W. to Unicy Lee 2-11-1861 G
Dickerson, James to Emiline Parham 10-6-1853 We
Dickerson, John W. to L. M. Wright 6-25-1855 (7-4-1855) G
Dickerson, Jordan to Charlotte Herrod 5-26-1866 F B
Dickerson, Lewis to Zelpha Howell 8-26-1845 G
Dickerson, M. L. to Caroline Porter 8-10-1859 (no return) Hy
Dickerson, Robt. to Mary Cotton 6-22-1867 (6-23-1867) T
Dickerson, Thomas W. to Hannah C. Cunningham 5-23-1837 (5-24-1837) O
Dickerson, Thomas to Emmer Ford 1-8-1873 T
Dickerson, W. C. to R. A. Alexander 2-9-1865 G
Dickerson, W. E. to Nanie L. Gains 12-21-1865 L
Dickerson, W. M. to Lottie T. Hanley 1-26-1858 T
Dickerson, W. T. to M. E. Haye 12-10-1867 G
Dickerson, William to Jessie Heathcott 9-3-1849 Hn
Dickerson, William to Louisa House 12-29-1870 (no return) Hy
Dickerson, William to Mahala Barnhill 3-5-1844 (3-7-1844) O
Dickerson, William to Rhoda Vantreese 11-19-1864 (11-20-1864) Ma
Dickerson, Wilson to ____ Hubert 8-9-1828 O
Dickery?, Joseph to Mary J. Brown 2-15-1858 (2-16-1858) T
Dickey, A. J. to Ann Cawthon 4-12-1870 G
Dickey, Anderson to Joana Hale 10-29-1842 G
Dickey, D. C. to E. A. Allison 3-16-1860 G
Dickey, D. C. to Elizabeth Ann Mathews 9-29-1857 Be
Dickey, D. L. to N. A. Thomas 2-13-1861 G
Dickey, Daniel P. to Ruena Smith 8-29-1843 Ma
Dickey, David to Anna Nelson 3-23-1829 G
Dickey, Gaml.? C. to Catherine E. Smith 4-3-1871 (4-20-1871) T
Dickey, George W. to Margarett Fulerton 1-8-1831 G
Dickey, H. L. to Esther A. Calhoun 4-20-1864 O
Dickey, H. M. to E. B. Wilkes 9-24-1878 Hy
Dickey, H. M. to F. J. Templeton 12-8-1869 (12-10-1869) Dy
Dickey, J. D. to Jesse C. Simmons 9-19-1865 (9-20-1865) O
Dickey, J. F. to M. H. Archibald 12-8-1869 (12-9-1869) Dy
Dickey, J. L. to E. A. Holt 12-29-1868 G
Dickey, James L. to Louisa R. Trice 11-20-1850 Sh
Dickey, James L. to Winnie Nelson 11-23-1837 Sh
Dickey, James to E. J. Faulk 9-25-1851 O
Dickey, James to Margaret Moore 12-25-1861 T
Dickey, Jas. to Fannie C. Moore 5-12-1869 T
Dickey, Jerry to Tennessee Alison 10-16-1873 Hy
Dickey, John L. to Sarah A. Hatch 10-16-1855 Cr
Dickey, John W. to M. F. King 12-7-1857 (12-10-1857) Sh
Dickey, M. A. to M. W. Barnet 1-30-1854 (1-31-1854) G
Dickey, M. H. to Jennie Zarecor? 9-29-1875 (no return) Dy
Dickey, N. A. to Sarah C. Kelton 12-5-1857 G
Dickey, R. C. to N. E. Kennady 10-10-1872 Dy
Dickey, R. W. to Millie Stallcup 11-23-1871 Dy
Dickey, S. G. to M. J. Garrison 11-1-1859 (11-8-1859) O
Dickey, W. C. to M. H. Martin 12-18-1866 O
Dickey, W. C. to M. J. Radford 10-25-1879 (10-26-1879) Dy
Dickie, Burgis to Cornelius Alison 12-28-1876 Hy
Dickie, Isaac E. to Saluda J. Haynes 9-25-1848 Ma
Dickie, John to Lucy Davis 11-1-1851 (11-2-1851) Ma
Dickie, Wm. H. to Mary Wyett 9-14-1856 Cr
Dickins, Jno. R. to Mary S. Hunt 2-21-1842 (2-22-1842) Hr

Dickins, Reuben C. to Elizabeth Price 3-20-1852 (3-25-1852) G
Dickins, Robert to Mary Dickey 9-16-1846 (10-10-1846) G
Dickins, Samuel to Virginia Hunt 2-21-1842 (2-22-1842) Hr
Dickins, Thomas C. to Margaret Jane Roberts 1-14-1854 (1-17-1854) G
Dickins, Thos. to Louisa Knewland 12-24-1867 (no return) Hy
Dickins, William T. to Martha B. Wallace 2-26-1845 (2-27-1845) G
Dickinson, Benj. to Winny Goodwin 12-19-1866 (1-16-1867) F B
Dickinson, Benjamin F. to Amanda E. Hudson 3-26-1857 Ma
Dickinson, Bernard P. to Carrie F. Rogers 1-28-1869 (no return) F
Dickinson, C. R. to P. A. Lowery 12-12-1867 (12-15-1867) F B
Dickinson, Edwin D. to Cornelia A. Neal 4-21-1841 F
Dickinson, H. H. to Allie Currie 11-17-1875 (no return) Hy
Dickinson, J. H. to Susan E. Dickson 7-24-1869 (8-4-1869) Cr
Dickinson, James M. to Mary Ann Moore 7-16-1857 Hn
Dickinson, John A. to Eliza F. Brummett 12-20-1865 Hy
Dickinson, John J. to Rebecca Clark 12-10-1860 Hy
Dickinson, Jos. E. to Ema J. Rose 11-24-1873 Hy
Dickinson, Kirk to Frances Moore 7-16-1870 F B
Dickinson, Robert M. to Martha W. Hobbs 12-4-1844 (12-5-1844) Ma
Dickinson, Rufus W. to Charlotte Edmonson 1-20-1845 Ma
Dickinson, Sam to Dinah Dickinson 12-25-1866 (no return) F B
Dickinson, Sam to Violet Carpenter 5-1-1869 (5-3-1869) F B
Dickinson, Shadrack to Mary E. Old 1-24-1843 (1-25-1843) F
Dickinson, W. B. to E. (Mrs.) Algen 3-24-1870 G
Dickinson, Wesley to Nancy Williamson 3-16-1867 F B
Dickinson, William E. to Nannie M. Bates 6-12-1874 (6-16-1874) L
Dickinson, William to Caroline Moore 3-11-1858 (3-12-1858) Ma
Dickinson, William to Margaret Reed 4-4-1829 Ma
Dickinson, William to Mary Ann Beaty 12-25-1852 (12-26-1852) Ma
Dickinson, Willie B. to Wilnoth C. (Mrs.) Tarver 8-2-1871 (8-3-1871) Ma
Dickinson, Willis to Mary Tatum 12-26-1868 F B
Dickinson, Wm. D. to Lydia E. Burford 11-13-1867 (no return) Hy
Dickinson, Wm. to Virginia Williams 12-27-1865 (12-28-1865) F B
Dickinson, jr., Charles B. to Clara F. Vivier 10-15-1861 Sh
Dickinson, jr., Ed to Bettie J. Shaw 12-17-1868 F
Dickinson, jr., Marcus L. to Clarissa Pritchett 6-3-1856 Sh
Dickinson, sr., Edwin to Mary Lucette Rivers 12-27-1870 F B
Dickson, A. F. to Laura A. McCutchen 11-26-1866 (no return) Dy
Dickson, Alexander to Sarah Stallings 11-7-1828 Ma
Dickson, Andrew to Sarah Stribbling 1-9-1870 G B
Dickson, B. to Charity Coker 4-10-1838 Ma
Dickson, Ben to Adaline Caldwell 6-3-1871 (6-5-1871) T
Dickson, Charles S. to Lucetta Bernard 9-1-1846 (9-2-1846) T
Dickson, Charles Strong to Margaret Leventen Hill 1-31-1849 (2-1-1849) T
Dickson, Christopher W. to Henrietta S. Barrett 12-7-1846 T
Dickson, David B. to Margaret (Mrs.) Taylor 8-25-1845 (8-26-1845) G
Dickson, Ed to Sallie Rose 3-21-1872 T
Dickson, Edward to Sarah Pugh 11-30-1842 (12-1-1842) Hr
Dickson, G. W. to Mary E. Belote 8-3-1858 Sh
Dickson, George W. to Alley E. Holford 10-15-1850 (10-17-1850) G
Dickson, Henry R. to Elizabeth S. Alford 10-22-1867 G
Dickson, Henry to Frankey Machaum(Michum) 7-4-1827 (7-5-1827) Hr
Dickson, Henry to Mary J. Partee 6-14-1869 (no return) Hy
Dickson, Henry to Sarah Rogers 5-28-1869 G B
Dickson, J. M. to N. A. Hendrix 8-11-1862 Mn
Dickson, Jacob to Louisa Whiley 3-13-1868 (3-15-1868) Ma
Dickson, James A. to Jane L. Sevier 1-29-1849 Cr
Dickson, James F. to Rachel S.? Payne 11-22-1865 (11-23-1865) T
Dickson, James M. to Martha E. Flowers 7-12-1855 G
Dickson, James to Leon Williamls 6-17-1859 (6-18-1859) O
Dickson, James to Ory Ann Calhoun 3-23-1863 O
Dickson, John M. to Elizabeth S. W. Scates 12-21-1843 Cr
Dickson, John M. to Emma A. Patterson 12-18-1866 (12-20-1866) Cr
Dickson, John S. to Mary L. Overall 9-11-1862 G
Dickson, John to Martha McGee 4-9-1867 G
Dickson, John to Mary Stegall 2-13-1845 Cr
Dickson, John to Rachel Litus 7-20-1867 T
Dickson, Joseph A. to Mary C. McCain 9-15-1855 T
Dickson, Joseph to Emelina C. Jones 1-5-1849 (1-8-1849) Ma
Dickson, Joseph to Minnie Fry 4-11-1881 (4-17-1881) L B
Dickson, Levie to Rebecca Hansbrough 2-22-1846 (no return) Cr
Dickson, Minus to Aleatha J. Williams 10-24-1849 (no return) Cr
Dickson, Nathanial to Martha A. Kirksey 8-24-1837 G
Dickson, Newton to Mary Elder 2-28-1850 T
Dickson, Noah to Nancy Wilson 12-16-1847 Ma
Dickson, Patrick to Parnesia? Ann Miles 12-29-1854 (12-31-1854) O
Dickson, Pinkny to A. E. Harris 10-22-1851 (no return) F
Dickson, R. D. to Mary Ann Coble 10-5-1861 (10-6-1861) Cr
Dickson, R. S. to Martha S. Conley 12-22-1862 (12-23-1862?) G
Dickson, Richard D. to Mary Ann Coble 10-?-1861 (10-6-1861) Cr
Dickson, Robert T. to Emily A. Berry 9-22-1858 G
Dickson, Saml. Dunn to Sarah Isabella McQuiston 10-9-1850 T
Dickson, Samuel to Matilda Neal 12-23-1867 G
Dickson, Thos. to Rebecca Glosson 8-18-1854 (no return) Cr
Dickson, Tobias to Dollie Poke 3-1-1868 Hy
Dickson, W. H. to E. Thornton 7-16-1855 Sh
Dickson, W. P. to Arbella White 10-13-1870 F B

Dickson, W. W. W. to Jane Williams 4-1-1852 We
Dickson, William P. to Sarah J. Brightwell 10-22-1857 G
Dickson, William to Fannie Eggleston 12-14-1876 L
Dickson, William to Francis Watts 12-31-1845 We
Dickson, William to Tabitha Chisum 9-20-1827 Ma
Dickson, Willis to Dicy McCleary 1-3-1867 G
Dickson, Wm. to S. M. McSpadden 12-4-1852 (no return) Cr
Dicus?, Robert Lessley to Sarah Wilkins 6-21-1853 T
Diemer, Wm. T. to Pauline Lefort 6-5-1849 Sh
Dies, A. P. to Eliza Murphy 10-17-1861 (10-18-1861) Sh
Diffee, William to Nancy Morrison 5-31-1864 Sh
Diggers, William to Huleah? Penn 6-13-1851 (6-15-1851) Sh
Diggins, William to E. M. Staton 2-27-1866 G
Diggs, Benjamin H. to Sarah P. Freeman 4-12-1860 Hn
Diggs, David to Esther A. Atkinson 8-6-1874 O
Diggs, Dudley to Tamey Richerson 1-13-1857 Ma
Diggs, Elisha to Nancy Wright 6-28-1848 Hn
Diggs, George T. to Angeline Upchurch 1-10-1861 Hn
Diggs, Harris to Martha E. Looney 10-30-1860 Hn
Diggs, Harry to Nora W. Call 12-28-1865 Hn
Diggs, J. W. to A. J. Patterson 9-22-1852 Hn
Diggs, J. W. to Lucretia Diggs 8-27-1867 Hn
Diggs, J. W. to Mary Parr 2-12-1878 (2-13-1878) Dy
Diggs, James E. to Sidney M. Seawright 8-8-1860 Hn
Diggs, Michael to Martha Martin 5-30-1838 Cr
Diggs, P. J. to Margaret Alexander 8-20-1863 Hn
Diggs, Riley to Nancy Clarke 12-10-1846 Hn
Diggs, Riley to Sarah Clarke 7-27-1852 Hn
Diggs, Thomas F. to Mary F. Haynes 10-3-1860 (no return) Cr
Diggs, W. C. to S. T. Provine 1-6-1853 Hn
Diggs, W. M. to Elizabeth Blake 1-15-1866 Cr
Diggs, William H. to Lucretia Owens 4-19-1855 Hn
Dilda, W. D. to Mary V. Pruitt 10-20-1863 (10-25-1863) Cr
Dilda, Wm. D. to Mary V. Pruit 10-20-1864 Cr
Dilday, Charles to Winney Diggs 8-5-1869 Cr
Dilday, George W. to Tennessee ___ 12-30-1852 (no return) Cr
Dilday, Henry J. to Sarah C. Capps 5-6-1861 (5-12-1861) Cr
Dilday, James H. to R. A. Laycook 1-18-1855 Cr
Dilday, William D. to Mary V. Pruitt 10-20-1863 (no return) Cr
Dilday, Wm. B. to Hannah Lett 3-23-1841 Cr
Dildia, Jesse to Mariah Mathews 12-29-1847 (1-4-1848) F
Dill, A. W. to Sarah M. Kee 10-25-1860 Cr
Dill, Benjamin F. to Caroline A. Walker 4-1-1841 Sh
Dill, Caswell P. to Sarah H. Asken 3-27-1846 Cr
Dill, J. B. to L. V. Laycook 2-13-1873 Cr
Dill, J. B. to Sara Johnson 1-13-1857 Hr
Dill, J. F. to Axcy Johnson 12-30-1855 Cr
Dill, J. M. to Fannie Griffies 1-22-1854 Cr
Dill, James to Mary J. Willis 3-27-1874 (11-29-1874) T
Dill, Jerrimiah H. to Anney Roach 2-28-1841 G
Dill, John H. to Margaret V. Wells 8-8-1866 (8-3?-1866) L
Dill, John to Blanche Reese 7-13-1845 (no return) L
Dill, John to Carroline Malone 12-28-1841 (12-29-1841) G
Dill, John to Eda Smith 7-5-1836 (7-7-1836) G
Dill, John to Minny E. Henson 3-7-1856 (3-9-1856) Hr
Dill, Leroy R. to Rurey Mynor 8-4-1843 G
Dill, Noah W. to Paty (Patsy) P. Gibson 5-29-1850 Sh
Dill, T. J. to N. C. (Mrs.) Barham 4-9-1860 Cr
Dill, W. A. to Zelpha Wilson 12-22-1857 We
Dill, William A. to Melinda J. Holley 10-2-1851 O
Dill, Zebulm to Polly Fox 6-14-1827 (6-25-1827) G
Dillahinty, William H. to Amanda A. Walton 12-17-1866 (12-18-1866) T
Dillahunty, Francis M. to Susan E. Carter 3-16-1843 (no return) Hn
Dillahunty, Green D. to Susan C. Wall 11-20-1839 Hn
Dillahunty, John to Catharine F. Biles 9-27-1842 (no return) Hn
Dillahunty, William L. to Matilda McCorkle 1-1-1838 Hn
Dillaney, John to Eliza White 6-24-1868 L
Dillard, Allen to Lucretia Lynch 5-11-1831 (5-15-1831) Hr
Dillard, Gabriel to Arrena Vails 12-26-1837 Hn
Dillard, Isaac to Mary Ann E. Tipton 3-26-1832 Ma
Dillard, James to Juda Bullard 1-4-1869 Hy
Dillard, Joseph to Margaret Milsaps 12-24-1840 L
Dillard, Miles A. to Lucinda O. Burrow 7-28-1854 (no return) F
Dillard, Owen to Sarah Dillard 7-13-1833 (7-14-1833) Hr
Dillard, Owen to Sarah Ewing 1-7-1828 (1-8-1828) Hr
Dillard, Robert M. to Mary Ann Skaggs 5-13-1847 Hn
Dillard, W. A. to A. T. Dupree 8-10-1861 (no return) Hy
Dillard, W. A. to M. L. Taliaferro 4-1-1879 (4-2-1879) L
Dillard, William N. to Martha Ann Walker 8-22-1837 (8-24-1837) G
Dillard, Willis to Martha L. Dillard 9-3-1834 Hr
Dillehay, J. W. to Elizabeth (Mrs.) Atkinson 12-21-1864 (12-22-1864) Sh
Dillehunt, J. H. to A. E. Chappell 11-13-1862 O
Dillen, Levin to Martha J. Pritchett 5-16-1857 Sh
Dillender, John O. to Angeline Randolph 2-24-1864 Dy
Dillian, John G. to Elizabeth Williams 12-18-1856 Be
Dilliard, Benjamin to Louisa L. Holland 5-25-1858 Be
Dilliard, H. B. to Matilda Goodwin 7-4-1851 (7-6-1851) F

Dilliard, Henry M. to Lizzie W. Lucas 1-20-1859 F
Dilliard, Henry to Jennie Mosley 12-27-1866 (1-2-1867) F B
Dilliard, John to Elizabeth Childress 1-13-1829 (1-15-1829) Ma
Dilliard, L. D. to Rachel E. Osborne 11-19-1868 F
Dilliard, Thomas J. W. to Susan J. Bromly 12-19-1866 F
Dilliard, Wm. H. to Mary G. Parker 12-6-1849 (no return) Cr
Dillinger, Adam to Susan Jones 11-10-1859 We
Dillingham, Thomas to Amanda Dunlap 8-5-1870 Dy
Dillingham, Wm. to Elizabeth Glenn 10-10-1878 Dy
Dillion, J. H. to M. R. Melton 8-16-1866 Be
Dillions, James to Sarah A. Black 6-6-1870 (6-9-1870) L
Dillon, G. N. to Sarah E. Rowland 2-3-1868 (2-5-1868) Cr
Dillon, J. H. to Manerva Holland 4-7-1870 (no return) Dy
Dillon, James to Mariah Bell 3-23-1874 (3-24-1874) Dy
Dillon, James to Mary A. (Mrs.) Walker 1-15-1868 G
Dillon, John to Mary Purcill 5-5-1863 Sh
Dillon, Richard to Jane E. Shaw 2-20-1867 T
Dillon, William to Martha Condon 6-19-1862 Sh
Dilts, David to Margaret A. Green 8-1-1863 (8-3-1863) Sh
Dimond (Dearwood), James A. to Elizabeth M. Hancock 6-8-1859 Sh
Dinkins, James B. to Louiza J. Lawrence 11-26-1846 Hn
Dinkuns, B. F. to Mary Jane Fodge 1-1-1863 Hn
Dinney (Denney), John to Margaret Adams 11-27-1850 Sh
Dinney, Charles to Margaret Evetts 7-7-1853 Sh
Dinnie?, John to Ellen O'Brien 2-5-1853 (2-6-1853) Sh
Dinning, Elisha to Caroline Parker 12-4-1858 (no return) We
Dinny, Solomon to Nancy Howell 7-15-1846 (7-16-1846) G
Dinwiddie, Andrew to Mary A. Gillum 3-5-1844 Hn
Dinwiddie, J. R. D. to Sarah L. Gordon 2-22-1860 Cr
Dinwiddie, Jackson to Susan Norvell 8-4-1870 Cr
Dinwiddie, James B. to Martha P. Curtis 8-6-1867 Hn
Dinwiddie, James F. to Mary S. Dinwiddie 3-28-1860 Hn
Dinwiddie, James T. to Adaline Anderson 12-30-1845 Hn
Dinwiddie, James to Martha M. Moore 6-21-1853 Cr
Dinwiddie, Joseph to Victoria Guinn 12-29-1868 (1-2-1869) Cr
Dinwiddie, M. S. to Ann Sparks 11-2-1863 (11-5-1863) Cr
Dinwiddie, Newton A. to Charlotte M. Dillahunty 12-26-1839 Hn
Dinwiddie, P. M. to Catharine Bowers 10-11-1852 G
Dinwiddie, Preston to Tabitha Sneed 12-25-1865 (no return) Hn
Dinwiddie, Rafe to Mary Gorden 1-15-18?? (1-27-1870) Cr
Dinwiddie, S. A. to B. A. Province 8-29-1871 (8-31-1871) Cr
Dinwiddie, Thomas H. to Nancy H. Nowlin 2-12-1846 Hn
Dinwiddie, W. A. to Lula Cooper 6-18-1872 (no return) Cr
Dinwiddie, W. M. to Molly A. Higgs 9-11-1860 We
Dinwiddie, W. N. to Ann Foster 12-5-1854 Hn
Dinwiddie, William to H. R. Dillahunty 2-20-1845 Hn
Dinwiddie, Wm. I. to Lucy E. Gilliam 9-13-1838 Cr
Dinwiddy, Jno. H. to Francis M. Bobbett 7-1-1840 G
Dinwoody, Thomas Washington to Fidelia James 5-19-1842 T
Dircks, Oscar to Mary Oliver 9-9-1880 (9-12-1880) L
Dirwin, Houston to Anica Gause 10-14-1869 L
Disen, Virgin to Silly Woods 11-26-1871 Hy
Dishough, Isaac R. to Nancy Bostwick 12-15-1841 (12-16-1841) Hr
Dishourgh, Sam to Rebecca Ann Whitton 8-10-1844 (8-13-1844) F
Diskill, Joseph Y. to Elizabeth Williamson 9-28-1837 G
Dismukes, Elijah to Harriet Fisher 12-22-1874 (12-31-1874) L
Dismukes, G. W. to Agness Hannah 12-10-1867 (12-11-1867) Cr
Dismukes, John W. to Frances E. Bray 11-24-1866 (11-27-1866) Ma
Dismukes, Stephen C. to Mary Jane Grubb 6-2-1856 (no return) Hn
Dismukes, Wm. A. to Maggie Davis 8-20-1870 (8-21-1870) Ma
Dison, Tabner to Georgian Cobb 1-4-1872 Hy
Ditto, W. C. to A. C. Shoemate 12-15-1869 Hy
Ditto, W. N. to Mary R. Saunders 10-9-1866 (10-11-1866) Dy
Dixen, Sam to Sallie Young 2-17-1872 Hy
Dixon (Dickerson), R. M. to L. T. McGee 2-4-1873 Hy
Dixon, A. C. to K. S. Bridgewater 10-13-1879 (10-15-1879) L
Dixon, David B. to Salley Tincle 12-8-1824 (12-9-1824) G
Dixon, Edward to Martha Pugh 7-21-1841 (7-22-1841) Hr
Dixon, J. C. to M. J. McCommon 1-1-1861 Hr
Dixon, J. F. to H. H. Cook 4-28-1861 We
Dixon, James A. to E. T. Simmons 1-11-1871 Hy
Dixon, Jesse to Margaret A. Ferrill 2-19-1879 (2-20-1879) Dy
Dixon, John H. to R. E. Devenport 2-5-1870 (2-10-1870) F
Dixon, John to Sarah C. Brown 2-1-1853 (2-2-1853) Sh
Dixon, Linnear to Sarah Dillard 9-10-1836 Hr
Dixon, Nicholson G. to Sarah C. Ross 8-5-1858 Ma
Dixon, O. B. to Billie Hinds 12-11-1878 Dy
Dixon, Robert to Scilla Shaw 2-4-1867 Hy
Dixon, Robt. B. to Emily M. Wright 9-?-1850 Cr
Dixon, Wesley to Nancy E. McGlothlin 10-12-1853 Ma
Dixon, Wm. to Cela Shepperd 12-21-1875 (no return) Hy
Dixson, Chas. D. to Sarah Kendall 8-19-1839 (no return) Hn
Dixson, Lemuel Montague to Eliza C. Robinson 7-24-1851 Sh
Doak, Henry to Serinda Green 5-27-1869 G B
Doak, Isaac to Julia Ann Copeland 9-27-1877 Dy
Doak, John to Florence Fowlkes 3-3-1880 Dy
Doak, Robt. L. to Lucy A. Smith 1-20-1862 (no return) Dy

Dobbin, William to Ellen Goonley 4-2-1861 Sh
Dobbins, Richard S. to Harriett Leiper 1-14-1841 Hn
Dobbins, Samuel C. to America Crutchfield 12-30-1851 Hn
Dobbs, H. H. to Frances Didman 8-17-1852 Cr
Dobbs, W. J. F. to Amanda J. Winburn 11-4-1869 Dy
Dobbs, W. J. F. to Maria (Amanda?) T. Kelley 3-3-1873 Dy
Doble, Michael to Elenora L. Winfield 1-29-1870 Ma
Dobson, J. E. to N. M. McGuire 1-3-1865 T
Dobson, John to Susannah Sisk 3-22-1853 Sh
Doby, G. J. to E. J. Clyatt 10-11-1880 (10-17-1880) L
Dockins, John to Milly Ann Dockins 6-17-18514 Cr
Dockins, Lewis to Elizabeth Kinman 1-31-1855 (1-29?-1855) O
Dodd, A. G. to Sarah F. Fielder 1-2-1854 (1-3-1854) G
Dodd, Allen to Elizabeth Morris 12-21-1840 (no return) Cr
Dodd, Benj. Franklin to Martha Roberson 3-16-1869 L
Dodd, Benjamin to Mary C. Burkett 4-25-1860 (4-26-1860) Cr
Dodd, Boland to Levina Redding 10-28-1841 Ma
Dodd, Charles to Puss Ingram 10-1-1869 G B
Dodd, Chesley to Margaret Parish 10-7-1858 Cr
Dodd, Chesley to Rebecca Hinnant 9-3-1860 Be
Dodd, Daniel to Mila A. Evans 6-17-1851 Be
Dodd, David to Fatne-Fabney (Mrs.) Gregory 4-12-1833 Sh
Dodd, Doctor to Jane Hill 9-22-1867 L
Dodd, Isaac Green to Sarah Ann Scalions 4-30-1870 (no return) Dy
Dodd, J. M. to E. P. Surratt 10-13-1864 Mn
Dodd, J. M. to Margaret F. Wilson 3-4-1864 Sh
Dodd, J. W. to H. J. Tyson 10-4-1869 G
Dodd, James A. to Margaret A. Davis 1-7-1853 (1-11-1853) Ma
Dodd, James A. to Mary J. Pounds 3-25-1869 Dy
Dodd, James M. to Precilla L. Wade 11-5-1846 G
Dodd, John F. to Elizabeth Robertson 8-2-1862 (8-3-1862) Dy
Dodd, John R. to Roena J. Currie 2-12-1867 Ma
Dodd, John to Frances Gholson 8-16-1853 (8-?-1853) Ma
Dodd, John to Mollie Rutherford 11-9-1871 Ma
Dodd, W. R. to P. E. Hook 10-10-1868 Dy
Dodd, William R. to Caroline White 10-30-1861 Dy
Dodd, Wm. M. to Dirinda Johnson 12-21-1856 Cr
Dodds, G. C. to Melica M. Glover 4-12-1853 O
Dodds, G. C. to Melicia A. Glover 4-12-1850 O
Dodds, Gains C. to Eliza Jane Maddox 5-24-1852 O
Dodds, Isaac C. to Margaret L. Fisher 3-1-1848 (3-2-1848) F
Dodds, Isaac to Mary J. Allen 4-29-1845 (no return) G
Dodds, James A. to E. S. Kendrick 12-15-1839 (12-18-1839) Ma
Dodds, Joshua H. to Martha D. Freeman 5-27-1854 (no return) We
Dodds, Joshua H. to Martha D. Freemas 5-28-1854 We
Dodds, K. M. to J. C. Kemp 8-28-1861 Mn
Dodge, I. A. to Frances Weaver 12-22-1866 O
Dodge, V. B. to Susan E. Piber 9-1-1846 O
Dodson, Calvin to Nancy Allen 6-27-1855 (no return) Hn
Dodson, Charles to Jane Cain? 3-9-1867 G
Dodson, Isaac to Isabella Powell 3-6-1878 Hy
Dodson, Isham to Emily Green 12-26-1867 (12-28-1867) L B
Dodson, J. W. to M. M. Webb 8-12-1860 Be
Dodson, Jack to Rose Lemons 5-10-1871 (no return) F B
Dodson, James E. to Rebecca W. Ingram 4-7-1851 (4-9-1851) Hr
Dodson, James to Sarah E. Gibson 9-8-1846 (9-9-1846) T
Dodson, John R. to M. J. T. Wiggins 5-21-1878 (5-23-1878) Dy
Dodson, Jonah Y. to Ann Bayn 8-11-1846 (8-13-1846) G
Dodson, Lawrence B. to Elizabeth Eaton 10-9-1849 Cr
Dodson, Martin to Malinda (Mrs.) White 12-12-1872 (no return) L
Dodson, Martin to Mary Elmore 4-19-1879 (4-19-1844) L
Dodson, Reuben H. to Fanny A. Dillahunty 8-10-1852 Sh
Dodson, Robert J. to E. F. Cole 11-8-1858 (11-18-1858) G
Dodson, Robert J. to Emely J. Nobles 5-9-1846 (5-14-1846) G
Dodson, Robert T. to Mary P. Flynt 12-31-1849 (1-8-1850) Hr
Dodson, Thomas to Martha Ann Patton 10-21-1844 (10-23-1844) F
Dodson, Wadkins D. to Jarusa A. Blakemore 6-15-1847 (6-17-1847) G
Dodson, Watkins H. to Sarah T. Morten 1-6-1844 (1-9-1844) G
Dodson, Wesly C. to Sarah A. Moffitt 4-16-1853 (4-19-1853) Sh
Dodson, William to Bettie West 10-10-1871 (10-11-1871) Ma
Dodson, Wm. H. to Mary A. Ashley 1-23-1860 G
Dodson, Wm. to Ophelia J. Crews 3-19-1857 (3-17?-1857) Hr
Dodson, Wm. to Susan Williams 11-23-1854 Cr
Dodson, ___thas W. to Julia A. Parham 8-11-1868 T
Doebler, Cyrus A. to Sabrina Doebler 6-7-1849 Sh
Doer?, N. L. to Prudence Smithwick 8-20-1860 (8-22-1860) Dy
Dogget, John to Emeline Lowe 12-7-1872 Hy
Doggett, John to Louisa Bond 1-3-1876 (no return) Hy
Dogwood, Richard to Georgia N. Taylor 9-27-1848 (no return) Cr
Doheny, J. W. to Margaret B. Lewis 3-27-1856 (4-9-1856) Sh
Doherty, C. to A. C. Tipton 10-15-1868 Dy
Doherty, John A. to Manervey Askew 7-4-1854 Be
Doherty, John A. to Mary W. Ramsey 6-20-1867 Be
Doherty, John to Martha A. Wright 9-15-1853 Cr
Doherty, John to Harriet Riggs 6-22-1854 Cr
Doherty, Reuben to Mary Moss 12-28-1830 Ma
Doile, Solomon to Polly Ann Norton 12-27-1847 (12-28-1847) Hr
Doile, Wm. H. to Sarah J. Brazile 10-3-1861 (no return) Hy
Dolan (Dola), Daniel to Catherine Mulheron 10-28-1845 Sh
Dolan, James to Bridgett Finn 11-14-1859 (11-15-1859) Sh
Dolan, Robert to Mary J. Dolan 12-22-1866 (12-23-1866) Cr
Dolen, James to Caroline Bond 9-16-1852 (9-30-1852) Sh
Doling, Henry to Sarah Hearn 7-31-1842 Cr
Dollar, John H. to Eliza Duffy 1-?-1847 (1-14-1847) Ma
Dollar, Lewis to Lucy J. Duffy 4-18-1854 (4-20-1854) Ma
Dollar, William W. to Auzal Inza Moore 12-15-1858 (12-16-1858) Ma
Dolle (Dobb?), Benjamin to Mary Trule (Trub?) 7-26-1855 Sh
Dollins, Andrew to Melinda Harbeson 11-1-1855 O
Dollis, Henry C. to Sarah A. Humes 6-5-1846 Cr
Dollison, Monroe to Lutetia Pillow 6-29-1882 L
Dolly, Charley to Hester Griffin 12-3-1868 Hy
Dolohay, Martin to Bridget Morisay 4-12-1858 Sh
Dolohry, John to Mary Bradley 11-28-1859 Sh
Dolson, Nashville to Martha McElever 5-26-1843 Ma
Dolton, Berry to Mary Caroline Combs 8-5-1845 Be
Dolton, John C. to Demarious Bryant 10-3-1853 (no return) F
Dominger, John to Sarah C. L. Hammond 12-12-1852 O
Dominger, John to Sary A. Wiles 4-9-1849 O
Domingus, Almus to M. D. Corum 9-4-1875 (9-6-1875) O
Domyer, Jno. to O. J. Weaver 10-9-1882 (10-10-1882) L
Donaghue, Morty to Honora Murphy 1-26-1861 (1-27-1861) Sh
Donahay, John to Ellen Mumford 1-9-1849 Sh
Donaho, E. to Mary Ann Dial 2-8-1842 (no return) L
Donaho, Harvey C. to Harriet E. Huddleston 11-23-1853 (11-25-1853) O
Donahoe, John to Mary Barrett 4-28-1844 Sh
Donahoe, Paatrick to H. Fitzpatrick 9-25-1863 Sh
Donald(son?), Tony to Martha Reed 11-30-1867 G B
Donald, James to Hellen Silsby 1-12-1871 Dy
Donald, W. H. to Elizabeth Thompson 10-1-1866 O
Donaldson, A. J. to M. J. Moody 12-6-1868 G
Donaldson, Bob to Sarah Givens 12-16-1866 G
Donaldson, Dan to Margaret Coleman 1-4-1869 G
Donaldson, Godfrey to Fannie Killan 5-25-1872 (5-26-1872) Cr B
Donaldson, Humphrey to Judith J. Davidson 11-5-1835 G
Donaldson, John B. to Sarah Fulgum 3-21-1833 Hr
Donaldson, John to Mary Vaughn 2-7-1844 (2-8-1844) G
Donaldson, Josh to Rebecca Thompson 7-12-1849 Sh
Donaldson, Joshua to Emela Jacksn 12-19-1838 (12-20-1838) G
Donaldson, R. B. to Josephine Merriwether 3-6-1860 (3-8-1860) O
Donaldson, W. J. to Sallie E. Person 1-24-1849 Sh
Donaldson, Wellington to Elizabeth A. Meriweather 2-6-1843 (2-11-1843) O
Donaldson, William to Hellena Jenings 8-17-1842 G
Donanhoner, Louis to Mary Mangin 4-5-1861 (4-7-1861) Sh
Donavan, D. J. to Mary H. Keaney 12-27-1869 (12-28-1869) Cr
Dondare, James to Catherine Galberie 5-7-1863 Sh
Donegan, Harvey to Elizer Roper 12-26-1866 G
Donehue, Martin to Mary O'Donner 4-?-1863 Sh
Donehue, Patrick to Margaret (Mrs.) Clifford 5-9-1863 Sh
Donelsen?, Wm. Jefferson to Mary Louisa Toddy 11-13-1855 (11-15-1855) T
Donelson, Alexander to Sarah C. Royester 9-30-1841 Sh
Donelson, John to Delia C. Waters 1-13-1849 (2-13-1849) Ma
Donelson, Samuel to Jane Royester 12-23-1841 Sh
Donely, John to E. A. R. Rose 6-29-1870 T
Dongan, Robert S. to Louisa S. Ritchie 2-28-1839 Hr
Donley, Joseph A. to Susan Ann Clark 6-1-1864 (6-2-1864) Sh
Donlin, Phillip A. to Susan G. Freeling 8-3-1842 (8-4-1842) Ma
Donnan, William to C. A. Satterfield 2-28-1859 Sh
Donnaway, A. W. to Nancey Carracle? 12-19-1868 (12-20-1868) T
Donnell, George to Mary Jane Daniel 2-24-1851 Hr
Donnell, John J. to Mary H. Jones 9-18-1866 (9-19-1866) Ma
Donnell, L. N. to Rebecca J. White 3-7-1838 Hn
Donnell, P. O. to Mary Myers 11-8-1859 Sh
Donnell, Thomas O. to Alice Flynn 6-15-1856 Sh
Donnely, Patrick to Ann McCormick 10-10-1854 Sh
Donoho, Murt to Mary Brown 1-7-1861 Sh
Donohoe, Jeremiah to Mary Cocklen 6-6-1864 (6-8-1864) Sh
Donohue, Cornelius to Catharine Cogan 9-14-1860 (10-14-1860) Sh
Donolon (Donalson), Patrick to Bridget Woods 7-25-1857 (7-26-1857) Sh
Donovan, James to Sarah Redy 3-1-1862 Sh
Donovan, R. to Margaret McCarty 4-23-1861 (4-24-1861) Sh
Donoven, John to Nancy E. Murphy 6-15-1862 Mn
Dooler, John to Mary Jane Maclin 3-22-1867 (no return) Hy
Dooley, Felix G. to Mary Eliza Whitsitt 5-16-1837 Sh
Dooley, John to Elizabeth Walker 1-7-1841 Hn
Dooley, Paris M. to Georgianna H. Marion 12-11-1853 Sh
Doolin, James to Sallie Spiller 12-23-1869 (12-29-1869) F B
Doomas, James D. to Mary J. Henry? 12-13-1864 Hn
Doomis, B. F. to Malinda Walker 10-16-1855 (no return) Hn
Doran, George A. to Sarah F. Myrack 11-19-1856 We
Doran, James to Minerva Ingram 5-7-1839 Hn
Doran, Lewis? to Sarah Paschall 12-12-1844 Hn
Dorand, Joseph H. to Martha L. Lee 4-7-1851 Sh
Dorch, Henry to Holly Owen 12-28-1868 (12-31-1868) T
Dorch, Henry to Zilpha Bond 12-20-1873 Hy

Dorch, Isaac to Mexico Powell 7-20-1854 Be
Dorch, Lewis to Mary G. Davis 8-29-1849 (no return) Hn
Dorch, William to Mary E. Hethpeth 10-3-1860 We
Doren, Silas to Elizabeth A. Davis 12-14-1848 Hn
Dorherty, Ephraim to Kitsey Swan Cunningham 10-9-1863 (10-11-1863) Dy
Dorin, William to Jane Styles 9-6-1841 Hn
Dorion, jr., Charles H. to Ellen C. Morrion 4-9-1857 Sh
Dority, Ephraim to Joanna Pierce 12-13-1871 Dy
Dorman, Allen to Harriet Woolly 12-5-1846 F
Dorney, John to Mary Sheay 4-14-1856 Sh
Dorney, Morris to Ellen Marony 5-21-1857 Sh
Dorrin, William to Mary A. Harris 2-14-1845 (no return) We
Dorris, E. H. to Teressa Ann Bradford 11-10-1853 Hr
Dorris, Eldrige W. to Mary M. Binkly 1-21-1846 Hr
Dorris, F. P. to Jemima C. Ward 11-29-1863 Hn
Dorris, J. G. to Ellen Haden 11-5-1855 Be
Dorris, J. G. to Frances R. Sills 2-14-1861 Hr
Dorris, J. G. to Josephine Brown 2-3-1853 Be
Dorris, Job to Rachel Travis 12-16-1866 Hn B
Dorris, N. B. to Lucretia Nuckolls 12-28-1857 Hr
Dorris, T. P. to L. Rushing 3-10-1842 Be
Dorris, W. C. to Mary Wyett 9-27-1858 (9-28-1858) O
Dorris, W. F. to Nancy P. Young 12-4-1851 Hr
Dorris, W. W. to Mary A. Diggs 2-26-1867 Hn
Dorrity, Dennis to Lidia McCain 12-1-1850 We
Dorron, Andrew to Rebecca Pascal 12-10-1840 Hn
Dorset, Irvin to Elizabeth Tucker 4-28-1865 G
Dorsett, Person K. to Nancy J. Lowry 12-28-1847 G
Dorsey, James to Joella Smith 1-14-1869 Dy
Dorsey, Jerome to Mary R. Crouch 5-10-1855 (6-12-1853?) T
Dorsey, John to P. A. Matcik 11-28-1870 Ma
Dorsey, R. W. to Kate Harris 4-16-1868 G
Dorsey, William L. to Mattie J. Loveland 5-14-1861 Cr
Dortch, Columbus to Missouri S. Moore 12-18-1840 Hn
Dortch, David S. to Martha A. Culpepper 3-9-1843 Hn
Dortch, Edmond to Martha Gloster 4-9-1866 (4-30-1866) F B
Dortch, George to Minerva Patterson 8-16-1867 (8-18-1867) F B
Dortch, John to Martha E. Moody 8-26-1848 Hn
Dortch, Thomas to Louisa M. DeBruce 8-30-1853 Hn
Dortch, William to Middy M. Lee 9-12-1848 Hn
Doskins, John S. to Mary Molly Ann Snow 2-1-1847 O
Doss, J. M. to S. A. Brigance 2-4-1880 (2-5-1880) L
Dossett, James R. to _____ Lowry 10-17-1854 G
Dossett, P. K. to D. J. Mathis 10-20-1858 G
Dotsen, David to E. L. Craig 10-1-1867 (10-2-1867) Dy
Dotson, Jame A. to Mary Hicks 9-14-1854 Cr
Dotson, John W. to Mariah Baugh 2-13-1857 (2-14-1857) Sh
Dotson, Wat to Lucy F. McBride 9-26-1867 Dy
Dotson, William H. to Mary E. Hester 3-30-1862 (no return) Cr
Doty, Gean to Rebecca Holland 8-3-1865 Hn
Doty, George to Frances Brinkley 7-3-1841 (no return) F
Doty, John to Bridget Murphey 5-15-1861 Sh
Doty, Lemuel to Susan Humphrey 6-24-1832 Sh
Doubleday, Thomas to Helen Dwyer 1-17-1856 Sh
Doublin, Wm. to Laura J. P. Greer 2-29-1844 We
Douch, W. D. to Margaret McCamy 11-30-1867 O
Dougan, Benjamin to Virginia Branden 8-14-1868 (no return) Hy
Dougan, E. W. to C. A. Hampton 11-16-1869 (11-18-1869) F
Dougan, E. W. to Virginia Hampton 10-16-1866 (11-10-1866) F
Dougan, Frank H. to Frances J. White 12-19-1877 (no return) Hy
Dougan, George to Maryan Worthen 11-27-1843 F
Dougan, John to Ritteran Harris 1-15-1845 F
Dougan, S. T. to Laura W. Leverett 3-3-1871 (no return) F
Dougherty, Archabald to Ann Raymon 12-29-1853 Sh
Dougherty, E. C. to Caroline Bloys 7-19-1849 O
Dougherty, Edward C. to E. F. Rochell 1-23-1841 (no return) Cr
Dougherty, J. L. to J. M. Bird 6-19-1865 (6-25-1865) O
Dougherty, Michael to Jane Kana 5-13-1863 Hn
Dougherty, Morris to Mary McKinney 6-9-1860 (6-11-1860) Sh
Dougherty, Robert to M. C. Quinn 8-3-1840 Cr
Dougherty, William S. to Mary Rains 6-23-1830 G
Doughitt, W. G. to V. C. G. Brannans 3-17-1864 Sh
Doughtery, Sam'l. A. to Sarah J. Bird 1-3-1860 (1-6-1860) O
Doughtry, Samuel to S. A. Ennis 2-27-1855 (2-28-1855) G
Doughty, George W. to Mary M. Dowdy 12-22-1853 Hn
Doughty, Isaac J. to Mary Turpin 8-15-1839 Hn
Doughty, Isaac J. to Nancy J. Graham 10-14-1860 Be
Doughty, James to Adaline Beaton 11-15-1866 Be
Doughty, S. A. to Nancy M. Dowdy 12-20-1854 Hn
Doughty, William to Juliett Swift 2-13-1838 (no return) Hn
Douglas(s), John to Martha S. Oliver 8-18-1861 G
Douglas, Adam to Susan Parker 6-14-1873 (6-15-1873) T
Douglas, Andrew J. to Mary L. Taylor 12-17-1866 T
Douglas, Archy Y. to Martha J. Morrow 3-31-1845 (4-1-1845) Ma
Douglas, Ben to Harriet Plummer 3-13-1878 Hy
Douglas, Calvin to Sena Ann Barnes 3-3-1853 Be
Douglas, George L. to Joanna R. Sandiford 8-31-1835 Sh

Douglas, J. H. to H. Corum 1-11-1868 O
Douglas, James M. to Parmelia T. Johnson 6-14-1853 Hn
Douglas, John E. to Sallie Pewett 2-28-1860 (no return) Hy
Douglas, John W. to Mary Carson 8-22-1845 (no return) Hn
Douglas, John to L. V. McAlister 4-15-1865 G
Douglas, John to Sarah Beasley 1-12-1853 Be
Douglas, Johnson to Hariot Bowls 2-12-1874 Hy
Douglas, Joseph to Mary Miller 1-3-1878 Hy
Douglas, Joseph to Sarah Ann Tyner 12-20-1863 Be
Douglas, Sandy to Patience Finney 8-27-1869 F B
Douglas, Silas to Martha Reed 1-6-1870 F
Douglas, Thos. A. to Susan E. Caldwell 3-27-1844 Cr
Douglas, W. H. to Anna Wynne 11-20-1861 Sh
Douglas, William L. to Amanda Paralee Williams 11-8-1855 O
Douglas, William to Harriet M. Roswell(Boswell?) 4-25-1853 Be
Douglas, Wm. P. to Jane A. Taylor 3-5-1856 (3-6-1856) O
Douglas, Z. T. to Nancy Daws 9-10-1863 Mn
Douglas, Zachariah to Katie Powell 3-23-1877 Hy
Douglass, Addison H. to Martha Adeline Robertson 2-2-1842 Hr
Douglass, Andrew Jackson to Louisa Ann Smith 12-21-1846 T
Douglass, Carroll to Hannah Levy 8-23-1867 (9-7-1867) F B
Douglass, E. C. to Marietta C. Neel 12-1-1868 (12-3-1868) F
Douglass, Eli to Susan A. Beck 9-20-1869 (no return) Cr
Douglass, Fred to Julia Hunter 1-6-1871 (no return) F B
Douglass, Green to Morean Fields 4-1-1878 (4-3-1878) Dy
Douglass, Hugh J. to Mary B. Perkins 9-7-1843 (9-8-1843) F
Douglass, J. C. to Mamie V. Hood 10-17-1877 Hy
Douglass, J. E. to Martha A. Philips 3-9-1868 (no return) Hy
Douglass, J. M. to Mary E. Yearwood 12-19-1867 Hy
Douglass, James A. to Elizabeth J. Salmon 10-26-1841 (10-27-1841) F
Douglass, James W. to Huldah G. Ware 8-3-1846 F
Douglass, James to Mary Allison 12-15-1877 (12-16-1877) L B
Douglass, Jim to Martha Morris 12-20-1865 Hy
Douglass, John T. to Evaline H. Smith 1-21-1842 T
Douglass, John to Caroline Martin 12-29-1866 (12-30-1866) F B
Douglass, John to Martha Messenger 4-9-1867 (4-13-1867) F B
Douglass, Jordan to Lucy Prewitt 12-27-1867 (1-5-1868) F B
Douglass, Joseph E. to Frances I. Stegar 2-15-1838 F
Douglass, M. F. H. to Nancy Burnett 12-26-1865 (12-31-1865) Cr
Douglass, Matt to Mittie Pewett 9-2-1866 Hy
Douglass, Raphe to Lizzie Jones 12-26-1879 Dy
Douglass, Robert to Ann Jane Taylor 12-22-1866 (12-26-1866) F B
Douglass, Robert to Emeline Franklin 4-1-1867 (no return) F B
Douglass, Swail to Ella Plummer 1-10-1876 (no return) Hy
Douglass, Thomas I. to Mary J. Elkins 4-7-1851 (4-8-1851) O
Douglass, Thomas to Amelia Ann Davis 7-4-1855 Sh
Douglass, Thomas? B. to Frances Alguire 9-3-1855 (9-4-1855) O
Douglass, Tom to Cinthia Newsome 10-17-1878 Hy
Douglass, Wm. B. to Ann E. Fleming 8-25-1866 (8-29-1866) F
Dougless, Stephan to Parthenial Roberson 1-25-1868 (no return) Hy
Doulon, Joseph T. to Mary Burnes 4-24-1857 (4-26-1857) Sh
Douseford, John T. to Amanda J. Lamb 2-17-1858 (2-18-1858) T
Doutaz, Edward to Frances Hein 10-29-1863 Hy
Douvall, John to Nancy Stricklin 5-12-1868 Hy
Dove, John to Martha Mills 8-11-1863 (no return) Dy
Dove, John to Nancy Sprouse 9-14-1830 Ma
Dover, D. T. to Melba? Lee 12-5-1862 Mn
Dover, Mansell to Maggie Kincaid 7-6-1870 (7-14-1870) F
Dover, William to Clary Richardson 1-17-1859 (1-19-1859) G
Dover?, Anthony to Josephine _____ 4-24-1873 T
Dowd, Daniel to Margaret Fenton 7-29-1862 (7-31-1862) Sh
Dowd, William to Hity Corbet 8-28-1854 We
Dowden, S. C. to S. L. C. Keaton 11-6-1869 (11-21-1869) Cr
Dowdey, Joseph to Mathaney J. Leachman 10-7-1845 O
Dowdy, Archy to Lizzie Rawlings 2-14-1868 (2-21-1868) F B
Dowdy, Armsted to Susan Henley 3-1-1852 (no return) F
Dowdy, Benj. F. to Susan Akin 2-2-1839 (no return) F
Dowdy, C. J. to Nancy A. Sanderson 3-1-1863 O
Dowdy, Henry to Angeline Marberry 5-3-1858 Hy
Dowdy, James M. to Susan P. Marpin? 12-19-1866 (no return) Hn
Dowdy, Joab to Mary Brazier 3-9-1849 Hn
Dowdy, John J. to Lucy T. Thompson 11-10-1853 Hr
Dowdy, John W. to Henrietta Bacchus 12-20-1854 Hn
Dowdy, Linsey to Fanny Culp 12-15-1870 (12-28-1870) F B
Dowdy, Martin V. to Matilda Jane Laws 5-3-1859 (5-4-1859) Hr
Dowdy, P. L. to Nancy Williams 4-7-1842 (4-13-1842) F
Dowdy, Robert to Martha A. Dial 1-1-1857 (1-8[18]-1857) Hr
Dowdy, W. K. to Jane Dial 3-19-1856 Hr
Dowdy, W. K. to Marcilla E. Dial 9-3-1860 (9-4-1860) Hr
Dowdy, William K. to Eliza C. Crawford 10-31-1855 (11-1-1855) Hr
Dowdy, William P. to Lucy E. May? 12-15-1846 (12-16-1846) Hr
Dowdy, Willis to Adeline Phillips 3-13-1869 (3-27-1869) F B
Dowell, J. P. to Nicy E. Hudson 1-18-1866 Be
Dowell, James B. to Elizabeth Hyner 9-17-1844 Be
Dowell, James to Eliza McWhirter 1-8-1857 G
Dowell, James to Martha Boyett 12-15-1851 (12-18-1851) G
Dowell, John T. to Nancy Simpson 3-13-1843 (3-15-1843) T

Grooms

Dowell, John to Marietta H. Lowery 1-29-1858 Be
Dowell, Lorenzo to Lizzie Somerville 12-25-1871 T
Dowell, Richard C. to Rebecca A. Bell 7-16-1863 Sh
Dowell, W. B. to Nancy Lowry 9-6-1847 G
Dowell, Wiley B. to Harett J. Heath 9-7-1842 G
Dowell, William to Malinda Lowry 12-30-1834 (1-1-1835) G
Dowen, Charles to Ettie Taylor 1-10-1878 Hy
Dowland, Henry J. to Mary Semantha Yeats 11-21-1870 G
Dowland, Henry to Matilda Williams 1-16-1832 (2-4-1832) G
Dowlen (Dowell), C. F. to Emily Knox 4-20-1861 Sh
Dowlen, Timothy to Sarah Mitts 1-13-1846 G
Dowlen, William W. to Mary Jane Jackson 10-8-1853 (10-18-1853) Sh
Dowling, David to Martha Cooper 5-7-1853 (5-19-1853) Ma
Dowling, Henry to Mary I. McEwen 10-9-1862 G
Dowling, Michael to Jinny Forbert 9-28-1861 (9-29-1861) Sh
Downay, Simon to Johanna Kean 9-10-1856 Sh
Downey, John W. to Eliza Riggs 2-20-1860 F
Downey, William to Margaret C. Laughlin 3-3-1837 (3-7-1837) O
Downey, William to Martha Colyer 2-24-1834 G
Downing, Alexander G. to Elizabeth McLean 1-11-1831 Ma
Downing, Am? to Fannie Shankle 1-17-1867 T
Downing, Bennett to Kate McDougal 8-25-1869 Cr
Downing, E. M. to Elizabeth A. Vaughn 6-10-1868 T
Downing, Granderson to Georgetter Adkins 5-14-1874 (4?-15-1874) T
Downing, J. J. to Jane Moore 7-6-1867 (7-11-1867) Cr
Downing, Jackson to Annie Potts 6-12-1870 Hy
Downing, James to Honora Burke 7-2-1860 (7-3-1860) Sh
Downing, John B. to Missouri A. Wynne 12-23-1857 (12-24-1857) Sh
Downing, Jonathan J. to Flora Porter 12-14-1840 Cr
Downing, Sandy Wilson to Bettie Haynes 5-13-1874 (5-14-1874) T
Downing, T. M. to Virginia M. Scott 9-10-1850 (9-11-1850) F
Downing, Washington to Sallie Montgomry 1-6-1869 (1-8-1869) T
Downs, Baltimore to Martha Johnson 12-4-1867 (12-5-1867) F B
Downs, Daniel to Julia Galvin 4-27-1864 (4-28-1864) Sh
Downs, James to Rebecca (Mrs.) Barker 3-10-1883 (6-10-1883) L
Downs, Patrick to M. O'Neal 5-16-1859 (5-18-1859) Sh
Downs, Timothy to Catherine Kane 6-8-1863 Sh
Dows, Kirby to Emanda C. Butler 5-8-1855 Cr
Dowson, Joseph to Elizabeth Fields 4-27-1863 Sh
Doxey, James to Ellenander Etherage 1-11-1838 (1-21-1838) G
Doxey, Simon to Jane Bittney 11-9-1850 (11-10-1850) G
Doxey, Wilson to Martha Biggs 12-17-1847 G
Doyerl?, Wylie to Martha F. Hudson 2-11-1840 (2-13-1840) F
Doyl, John to Martha Robbins 5-7-1867 Hy
Doyle, David C. to Julia L. Houston 11-15-1849 Sh
Doyle, F. M. to Catie Cook 2-9-1875 Hy
Doyle, Frank to Celia Tiernan 11-15-1864 Sh
Doyle, Geo. W. to Sarah T. Cosby 9-29-1860 (9-30-1860) Hr
Doyle, Green to Franky Dickerson 12-28-1866 Dy
Doyle, Hickerson L. to Rachael Summers 8-13-1841 (8-18-1841) Ma
Doyle, J. E. to Mary A. Oakey 2-4-1863 (2-10-1863) Sh
Doyle, J. G. to L. F. Neal 10-16-1870 G
Doyle, J. H. to Josephine Booth 12-24-1883 (12-26-1883) L
Doyle, J. R. to Mary Ann Stone 1-18-1860 (1-20-1860) Hr
Doyle, John F. to Ella A. Weakley 9-17-1861 (9-18-1861) Dy
Doyle, M. E. to Catherine Rowen 4-30-1854 Sh
Doyle, M. to Sarah Polk 12-16-1851 Sh
Doyle, Matthew to Mary Ann Inman 12-9-1843 (12-17-1843) Hr
Doyle, Michael to Catharine Welch 1-13-1859 (1-14-1859) Sh
Doyle, Patrick to Julia Gibbons 8-16-1854 Sh
Doyle, Patrick to Margaret Wright 3-15-1859 Sh
Doyle, R. E. to M. S. Ray 11-25-1876 (11-26-1876) L
Doyle, Robert E. to Ella Ashmore 8-1-1873 (8-3-1873) L
Doyle, Saml. J. to Jerusha A. Sexton 1-7-1860 (1-10-1860) Hr
Doyle, William Carroll to Lucy Jennie L. Lauderdale 7-25-1860 (no return) Dy
Doyle, Zachariah B. to Margaret M. White 11-11-1868 (11-12-1868) T
Dozer, Philip to Lener Doxey 3-31-1841 (4-1-1841) G
Dozer, William to Edney Ann Simmons 7-3-1838 (7-12-1838) G
Dozey, Zach to Susan Jane Smith 8-5-1879 (8-7-1879) Dy
Dozier, D. C. to L. F. Baker 7-13-1866 (7-15-1866) Dy
Dozier, G. W. to Zylpha Warren 2-18-1873 (2-19-1873) Dy
Dozier, H. C. to L. C. Smith 8-31-1866 G
Dozier, H. H. to M. S. Arnett 2-5-1873 (2-6-1873) Dy
Dozier, I. N. to Luvisa P. Baker 9-20-1859 (9-22-1859) G
Dozier, Isaac N. to S. J. Roberson 9-23-1856 G
Dozier, J. J. to Rachel R. Dickey 10-23-1862 G
Dozier, J. N. to C. M. Hurt 12-7-1864 G
Dozier, M. H. to Mary Ann Harris 5-19-1860 (5-20-1860) Sh
Dozier, P. L. to L. J. Wright 7-30-1864 O
Dozier, V. to Mary Williams 3-1-1854 (no return) F
Dozier, W. A. to M. C. Shepherd 2-19-1867 G
Dozier, W. B. to Lucy R. Duncan 2-7-1868 G
Draffin, John H. to Parthinia Baldock 10-9-1855 Sh
Draffin, John to Margaret S. Craig 2-24-1855 T
Drake, Bennet to Labertha Madders 1-5-1858 (1-6-1858) Ma
Drake, E. J. to T. T. Wakefield 8-17-1875 L
Drake, Elijah J. to Martha Hancock 11-29-1871 L

Drake, George to Esabella Gilbert 9-2-1868 (9-3-1868) Cr
Drake, Granville to Lucy A. Bell 3-19-1873 Cr B
Drake, Green to Molly Drake 9-8-1866 Hy
Drake, Gus to Sarah Jacocks 7-7-1877 Hy
Drake, Haywood to Edmonia Williams 9-24-1874 Hy
Drake, J. P. to M. L. Ricks 5-17-1875 Hy
Drake, J. R. to S. H. Inman 11-27-1857 (11-28-1857) Sh
Drake, Jack to Fanny Harris 2-24-1875 Hy
Drake, Jim to Fannie Graves 1-20-1871 Hy
Drake, John G. to Isabell Jane Shaw 2-13-1867 Hy
Drake, John to Burdie Rice 2-13-1872 (no return) Hy
Drake, John to Mary Cox 1-15-1861 Sh
Drake, John to Nancy Clark 2-23-1867 (no return) Hy
Drake, John to Sophronia Hardin 10-16-1848 (3-10-1850) Ma
Drake, Oliver to Mattie Bryant 12-25-1873 Hy
Drake, Sam to Lucy Spike 8-19-1868 (no return) F B
Drake, Samuel B. to Margaret Hughes 4-28-1846 Hn
Drake, Simon to Nancy Newbern 8-7-1872 (no return) Hy
Drake, Thomas H. to Louise Miller 11-12-1867 Ma
Drake, W. B. to Bettie A. Burk 1-15-1873 L
Drake, W. J. to Mollie C. Chism 8-8-1883 (8-9-1883) L
Drake, William J. (Dr.) to Mary Jane Walker 5-3-1859 Ma
Drake, Willis to Nancy Read 12-28-1869 (no return) Hy
Drake, Wm. B. to Lydia R. Thomas 7-1-1871 (7-2-1871) Ma
Drane, Robt. W. to M. F. Fowlkes 12-2-1874 (no return) Dy
Drane?, Prit to Rachel Polk 12-3-1868 (12-4-1868) T
Dranna, William to Polly Lorance 5-29-1838 Hr
Draper, Alfred to Annie Bright 5-3-1871 (5-4-1871) O B
Draper, D. W. to M. E. Turner 1-12-1870 G
Draper, Elijah to Matilda M. Mills 2-21-1857 (2-25-1857) L
Draper, Robert H. to Julia E. Jackson 3-3-1855 (no return) F
Draper, S. P. to E. L. White 9-16-1866 G
Draper, Walter Scott to Mollie I. Parks 11-24-1870 Dy
Drappin, Robt. H. to Elisabeth Wright 7-17-1856 T
Drappin, W. F. to Amelia Ann Hays 10-7-1856 T
Drappin, Wm. M. M. to Margaret A. Tarbish 5-13-1856 (5-14-1856) T
Drennan, Lewis to Annie E. Allen 6-7-1869 (no return) Hy
Drennon, J. C. to M. A. Thomas 9-28-1869 Hy
Drennon, M. to Julia Ann Strayhorn 12-17-1861 (12-22-1861) T
Dressell, Fred to Virginia Carter 5-14-1878 Hy
Dreums?, William to Cordia Woods 5-10-1873 T
Drew, Andrew W. to Rebecca J. Miller 3-25-1852 Sh
Drew, George M. to Jackie E. Ruff 9-12-1846 (no return) Cr
Drew, John O. to Rosana Leace 1-14-1852 Sh
Drewery, Richard to Tusa Chambers 3-29-1869 (3-31-1869) O
Drewery, L. N. to C. T. McAdoo 8-2-1871 (8-3-1871) Cr
Drewry, Egbert W. to Elizabeth A. Galey 11-10-1846 We
Drewry, James M. to A. C. Jackson 6-1-1853 Hn
Drewry, John F. to Frances B. Swift 9-10-1845 Hn
Drewry, R. H. to Ann M. Crowder 4-5-1858 W
Drewry, Richard C. to Mary M. Harold 1-10-1861 We
Drewry, S. G. to Caroline Stout 12-14-1843 (no return) We
Dreyfus, S. to Jennetta Cohen 11-26-1861 Sh
Dreyfus, Samuel to Charlotte Dunheiser 11-24-1855 Sh
Drigers, James H. to S. I. Semore 1-18-1843 (no return) Cr
Driggers, Thomas A. to Adah Honey 8-30-1843 (8-31-1843) F
Driggers, Wm. J. to Eliza C. Ross 11-23-1854 Ma
Driggs, George to Salma Collins 1-5-1845 Cr
Driggs, Williard to Demetius Stanford 4-18-1839 Cr
Drinkard, Francis P. to Penelope J. Berry 12-11-1855 (12-13-1855) G
Drinkard, Robt. to Cordelia P. Bricheen 9-22-1853 Cr
Drinker, B. to Harriett E. Cloys 1-4-1866 Hn
Driscol, Henry to Mary Higgin 12-27-1866 (12-28-1866) Dy
Driskell, Cornelius to Winneford Ryan 9-18-1858 (9-19-1858) Sh
Driskell, Ferney G. to Ann E. Mayfield 2-16-1841 (3-1-1841) G
Driskell, James B. to Mary D. Pierce 9-16-1848 (no return) Cr
Driskell, William Henry to Eliza Jane Cates 6-11-1863 Sh
Driskill, J. S. to Sarah J. Flowers 3-14-1859 We
Driskill, William R. to Sopha W. Laughter 10-24-1842 (12-15-1842) G
Driver, James D. to Sarah L. Gillespie 11-21-1860 L
Driver, Simon dP. to Annie E. Melugin 10-18-1869 (10-19-1869) T
Driver, Wody to Betty Ross 5-13-1871 (5-15-1871) T
Drover?, Oliver M. to Eliza Jane Merrell 4-16-1845 Hn
Druffin, John to Mary L. Craig 11-19-1851 T
Drummon, J. M. to Nannie Ledbetter 2-10-1870 Dy
Drummon, J. W. jr. to M. L. Roberts 6-2-1873 (6-4-1873) T
Drummon, Michael to Bridget Redden 8-18-1857 Sh
Drummond, Andrew to Jane C. Scales 4-10-1845 Sh
Drummond, W. F. to M. I. Armstrong 12-26-1851 Cr
Drummonds, J. H. to Louisa Hayley 10-30-1867 Cr
Drummonds, James W. to Elizabeth Lindsay 2-15-1858 Cr
Drummonds, James to Arminta H. Leach 1-4-1862 (1-5-1862) T
Drummonds, S. K. to Elizabeth A. Wright 2-22-1871 (2-23-1871) T
Drummonds, S. M. to Ida F. Finley 12-21-1870 Dy
Drummonds, Thos. W. to M. E. Lynes 7-8-1852 Cr
Drummons, James to Nancy Walker 1-15-1842 (1-16-1842) T
Drummons, Mack to Elizabeth Moore 12-4-1843 (12-13-1843) T

Drummons, Robert M. to Laura Hunt 8-4-1865 (8-5-1865) T
Drumwright, C. C. to Anna E. Davis 10-21-1873 (10-22-1873) L
Drumwright, H. S. to Ellen M. Blankenship 11-30-1874 (12-2-1874) L
Drumwright, R. C. to Susan M. Lloyed 1-15-1872 (1-17-1872) L
Drumwright, W. T. to Laura A. Turner 12-9-1874 L
Drury, William C. to Anna P. Flemming 5-26-1852 O
Druse?, A. W. to Alva Miller 1-24-1871 (1-25-1871) T
Dryden, Jonathan B. to Nancy F. Allison 5-12-1836 (5-13-1836) G
Drysdale, Robt. to Eliza W. Paine 7-30-1849 (8-2-1849) F
DuBose, C. C. to Lucy A. Freeman 2-16-1860 Sh
DuRoss, B. F. to Millie Drennon 12-18-1872 (no return) Hy
Dubb, James H. to Martha E. Cook 5-6-1856 We
Duberry, Wistley to Mary Lewis 10-15-1847 (10-17-1847) F
Dublen, J. H. to M. E. Cook 5-2-1856 (no return) We
Dublin, W. J. to C. C. Roads 11-22-1854 We
Dubois, J. G. to A. E. Cooper 10-9-1845 (10-10-1845) Hr
Dubois, John to Christiana Guinn 10-14-1847 Hn
Dubois, William Archer to Elvira Chenault 4-14-1863 (4-15-1863) Sh
Dubose, A. B. C. to Camilla F. Dunn 11-19-1833 Sh
Ducast, A. F. to Rebecca Ann Oliphant 2-2-1859 (2-3-1859) T
Ducker, Churchwell B. to Mary Roberson 11-7-1860 (11-8-1860) Ma
Duckle, George to Barbara Frick 10-28-1858 Sh
Duckworth, Alex. to Isabella J. Drake 3-7-1860 (no return) Hy
Duckworth, Calvin to Priss Newburn 2-27-1877 Hy
Duckworth, James to Rachel Wise 2-9-1876 (2-10-1876) Dy
Duckworth, John B. to Julia Ann Holland 1-18-1875 Dy
Duckworth, William L. to T. P. Capelle 12-24-1867 L
Dudley, A. C. to Elizabeth J. Grimes 5-12-1859 We
Dudley, Alexander to Evelina Tanner 2-28-1854 (3-1-1854) Ma
Dudley, Elzey to Amanda Lansden 7-17-1869 (no return) Cr
Dudley, H. W. to Clara Searcey 8-10-1875 Dy
Dudley, James G. to Nannie J. Wagster 7-26-1854 (no return) Cr
Dudley, Jno. to Lively Bell 11-29-1840 Be
Dudley, John D. to M. J. Cook 4-30-1878 Dy
Dudley, John L. to Susan E. Blair 11-10-1868 Hy
Dudley, John to Elizabeth Coleman 4-11-1871 (4-15-1871) Cr
Dudley, Lisbon to Adaline Austin 4-28-1878 Hy
Dudley, Richard to Catherine Pate 7-18-1872 Cr B
Dudley, W. W. to Mary A. J. Cansen 6-6-1854 We
Dudley, W. W. to Mary A. J. Copin 6-3-1854 (no return) We
Dudney, Eli to Martha Bennett 8-4-1840 Cr
Dudney, J. T. to Elenora Bailey 11-4-1867 (11-6-1867) F
Dueast, A. F. to Rabecca Olipshaw 2-22-1859 (2-3?-1859) T
Dueast, William to M. Adline Budget 10-12-1857 (10-16-1857) T
Duese?, W. M. to E. S. Belote 6-24-1857 Hr
Duff(e)y, Jephthan to Prudence Hamilton 7-25-1864 G
Duffee, Marion to Nancy Caroline Poston 11-11-1865 (no return) Dy
Duffer, H. G. to N. L. Simmons 1-26-1871 (1-29-1871) Cr
Dufferin, Henry to Margaret Loghlen 5-21-1864 (5-23-1864) Sh
Duffey, John S. to Margaret King 2-12-1852 Ma
Duffey, Joseph W. to Emma Vail 7-?-1871 (7-28-1871) Ma
Duffey, Patrick M. to Patsey Duffey 10-27-1862 (10-28-1862) Ma
Duffey, Samuel to Eady King 10-22-1862 (10-23-1862) Ma
Duffey, Samuel to Mary C. Dollar 7-4-1854 Ma
Duffie, Barney to Mariah Glover 12-25-1849 O
Duffie, William A. to Keady King 12-17-1846 (12-20-1846) Ma
Duffiel, Landdon to Jane Hunter 5-10-1873 (5-11-1873) L B
Duffin, Cullen M. to Tabitha Brizendine 3-19-1840 Hn
Duffy, Daniel to Bridget Brown 11-10-1863 Sh
Duffy, Henry to Margaret Latty 10-22-1839 (10-24-1839) G
Duffy, James to Martha Duffy 10-17-1865 G
Duffy, John to Ann Garvin 10-20-1848 Sh
Duffy, Patrick M. to Sirena Owen 9-19-1844 Ma
Duffy, R. H. to Mary Webb 4-15-1863 Sh
Duffy, Simeon to Arcena Owens 7-31-1845 Ma
Duffy, Simeon to Letitia Owens 12-12-1866 Ma
Duffy, Thomas to Ellen Callaghan 4-30-1853 (5-1-1853) Sh
Duffy, Wm. F. to Mary E. Herndon 10-14-1871 (10-18-1871) Ma
Dugan, G. M. to Mary A. David 2-2-1857 Hr
Dugan, Jno. to Martha Oldem 6-10-1857 Sh
Dugan, John to Sarah M. Johnson 1-9-1851 (1-14-1851) G
Dugan, Lams (Larns?) to Margaret Bradshaw 4-11-1863 Sh
Dugan, Thomas to Mary Kelly 7-16-1863 Sh
Dugard, James A. to Josephine Butcher 5-31-1843 Sh
Duggan, Edmond to Johanna Burks (Burke) 11-20-1849 Sh
Duggan, Wm. S. to Emily A. Crihfield 10-13-1857 (10-15-1857) L
Duger, A. A. to Amanda M. Rowe 12-7-1854 He
Dugger, Jesse P. to Phebe A. Aulford 5-14-1845 (5-15-1845) Hr
Dugger, S. B. to Armenia B. Luckey 2-17-1867 Hn
Dugget, Mack to Caladonia Baptist 1-21-1871 T
Duggins, James to Jennie Walker 4-30-1870 G
Duggins, P. H. to Adeline Cartwright 10-28-1848 (not executed) Sh
Duggins, P. H. to Harriett O. Manley 1-24-1854 (no return) F
Dugin, Patrick to Margaret Costilo 10-18-1854 Sh
Duglas, John to Tamer Stepp 10-19-1843 Be
Duglas, Thomas to Drucilla Howe 12-4-1863 Be
Duglass, David to Mary Pain 5-30-1868 (5-31-1868) L B

Duglass, David to Missouri Henning 12-23-1870 (no return) L
Duidlinger, John to Sophia Hatchell 12-22-1851 (12-26-1851) Sh
Duke, Alex to Nancy Jones (not executed) Hy
Duke, Alexander to Eliza Hay 8-2-1877 Hy
Duke, Alexander to Ellen Williams 12-4-1869 (12-5-1869) Cr
Duke, Anthony to E. C. Lack 12-11-1866 (no return) Dy
Duke, Benj. F. to Miriah M. Morris 2-5-1857 Cr
Duke, D. M. to Mary L. Bass 12-20-1854 We
Duke, Edmund F. to Elizabeth A. Price 5-18-1849 (5-20-1849) Hr
Duke, Geo. W. to Louisanna C. Rogers 12-10-1849 Sh
Duke, George to Martha J. Henderson 2-7-1865 Dy
Duke, James M. to Tempy R. Williams 1-28-1854 (no return) F
Duke, James to Jane Williamson 2-28-1870 G
Duke, John F. to Mattie H. (Mrs.) Beall 12-23-1867 G
Duke, John T. to Sarah T. Taliafero 7-22-1860 G
Duke, John to Martha Boyd 12-28-1870 T
Duke, M. J. to H. J. Stockard 10-27-1859 We
Duke, R. T. to Emma C. Anderson 2-20-1861 Sh
Duke, Robert to Alice Money 9-27-1877 Hy
Duke, Robert to Mary Carey 9-10-1860 Sh
Duke, T. A. to Susan Y. Woods 7-15-1868 Cr
Duke, William to Elizabeth A. House 9-29-1841 Hn
Duke, William to Melvina F. House 3-19-1851 Hn
Dukes, RLobert B. to Jane Edwards 6-30-1847 (7-1-1847) Hr
Dulin, George W. to Margaret Oakes 11-8-1858 (11-14-1858) O
Dulin, J. H. to L. A. Anderson 3-14-1866 (3-15-1866) F
Dulin, John to Joanna Whalin 9-17-1852 (9-18-1852) Sh
Dumas, A. W. to Margaret E. King 1-27-1869 T
Dumas, Dick to Rilla Ann Riley 8-14-1867 Hn
Dumas, Henry to Evaline Wilkins 1-10-1867 Hn B
Dumas, John to Alice Jones 10-2-1873 (10-4-1873) Dy
Dumas, Matthew to Josephine Smith 2-16-1874 Dy
Dumas, William to Bettie Edwards (Edmonds?) 1-22-1866 G
Dunagan, Allen to Rebecca Twigg 5-15-1847 (5-16-1847) G
Dunagan, John to Nancy Harrison 4-21-1863 Sh
Dunagan, John to Sally Davidson 11-11-1830 G
Dunagan, William to Nancy Lange 6-14-1863 G
Dunaho, Richard A. to Louisa Granbery 4-3-1848 (4-5-1848) F
Dunahoe, Calvin H. to America Fish 3-4-1856 (3-6-1856) Hr
Dunavan, John to Sallie L. Vaughan 3-29-1870 (no return) Hy
Dunavan, Peter to Matilda Doyle 8-15-1867 Dy
Dunavant, A. R. to M. J. Sanders 3-24-1861 G
Dunavant, Alonzo to Mary E. Mitchell 11-28-1853 (11-30-1853) L
Dunavant, Fernando to Lizzie Bradshaw 2-10-1870 (no return) Dy
Dunavant, J. B. to H. N. Hampton 6-25-1883 L
Dunavant, J. F. to A. E. Jordan 7-26-1881 (7-27-1881) L
Dunavant, James F., jr. to Martha A. Caldwell 10-8-1853 (no return) L
Dunavant, Jim to Charlotte Fitzpatrick 12-9-1867 (no return) L B
Dunavant, John W. to Sarah A. V. Hafford 12-19-1859 (12-21-1859) L
Dunavant, Leonard to Narcissa E. Mitchell 12-28-1853 L
Dunavant, Louis to Mary Fowlkes 4-28-1869 (no return) Dy
Dunavant, O. R. to S. E. Barfield 2-10-1875 (2-11-1875) L
Dunavant, W. A. to Josie Forsythe 12-7-1883 (12-10-1883) L
Dunaway, Alexander to Sarah A. Keller? 12-24-1876 L
Dunaway, J. E. to M. A. Moore 2-4-1865 (2-7-1865) L
Dunaway, John to Sarah Colverd 7-14-1828 (7-17-1828) Hr
Dunaway, L. H. to Elizabeth Sawrie 2-28-1866 (3-6-1866) Dy
Dunaway, S. H. to Mattie A. Dickinson 11-5-1866 L
Dunaway, William H. to Frances E. Raines 9-1-1866 (9-6-1866) Ma
Dunbar, Henry D. to Louisa Teague 12-4-1860 (12-6-1860) Sh
Duncan, A. M. to Nancy Emily McBride 3-12-1856 (3-13-1856) T
Duncan, A. W. to Elizabeth Jane Dallas 7-3-1854 Sh
Duncan, Albert D. to Mary D. Jarman 8-5-1831 (8-10?-1831) Hr
Duncan, Benjamin F. to Susan C. Harrison 9-14-1857 (9-16-1857) Sh
Duncan, Benjamin to Mary R. Cobb 6-15-1838 Sh
Duncan, C. A. to Sallie Andrews 12-14-1870 F
Duncan, Calvin W. to Emeline Peter 11-12-1866 Hn
Duncan, Charles Cannough to Frances S. Elston 5-3-1856 (5-4-1856) O
Duncan, Crawford A. to Elizabeth Harvey 4-11-1838 Hr
Duncan, E. D. to Maria M. Gabbert 12-31-1856 (1-1-1857) Sh
Duncan, E. G. to Mary Ann Little 6-14-1855 (6-15-1855) Hr
Duncan, E. H. to . H. Kennally 9-20-1866 Hn
Duncan, E. S. to Siddy J. Springfield 9-5-1859 (9-6-1859) Hr
Duncan, Elijah G. to Jane Null 1-5-1829 Hr
Duncan, George K. to Annie M. Lamphier-McLauphier? 3-1-1854 Sh
Duncan, George W. to Mary E. Pearson 11-22-1852 (11-25-1852) Ma
Duncan, Henry C. to Martha Blankenship 8-17-1836 O
Duncan, Henry W. to Margaret M. Ruddle 1-2-1849 (1-3-1849) Hr
Duncan, Henry W. to Mary Burlesson 10-24-1827 (10-27-1827) Hr
Duncan, J. A. to S. E. Olds 8-26-1880 L
Duncan, J. F. to N. Shermaster 1-8-1862 Sh
Duncan, J. R. to Matilda A. Parker 9-1-1860 Hn
Duncan, J. S. to Manerva Kennedy 11-14-1869 G
Duncan, James N. to Emily Luter 10-18-1854 Cr
Duncan, James to Parthenia Adaline Tull 4-8-1879 L
Duncan, James to Sinah P. Hannis 7-7-1831 Hr
Duncan, Jephinah R. to Eliza A. Mainard 9-26-1838 (no return) Cr

Duncan, Jesse to Sophronia Reid 2-2-1850 (2-13-1850) Ma
Duncan, John B. Ash to Malvina B. Bell 10-11-1862 (no return) Hy
Duncan, John F. to Margaret Brotherton 10-20-1828 Hr
Duncan, John L. to Charlotte J. McCullough 2-18-1873 (2-20-1873) T
Duncan, John L. to Nannie Muirhead 11-5-1877 (11-7-1877) Dy
Duncan, John R. to Mary A. Midgett 12-21-1881 (12-22-1881) L
Duncan, John to Elizabeth Nichols 2-22-1858 (3-1-1858) O
Duncan, John to Georgia Bell Bass 10-13-1862 O
Duncan, John to Leah Brummet 10-2-1828 G
Duncan, John to Lucenda Reeves 4-3-1839 (4-4-1839) Ma
Duncan, John to Malinda Duncan 2-17-1830 (2-18-1830) Hr
Duncan, Jon A. to Sarah K. Waddy 12-26-1860 G
Duncan, Jonathan to Elizabeth Bowden 1-3-1858 Hn
Duncan, Joseph to Mary Andonon 11-7-1839 Ma
Duncan, Joshua to Frances Maleer 4-1-1858 Hn
Duncan, L. P. to M. E. Woolard 6-21-1862 O
Duncan, Levi P. to Margaret Vance 6-8-1841 (6-9-1841) O
Duncan, Lewis to Jane Brown 1-4-1853 Ma
Duncan, N. E. to Mattie Hupley 11-19-1864 (11-20-1864) Sh
Duncan, P. W. to Susannah Fox 12-7-1857 (12-8-1857) O
Duncan, Peter S. to Susan E. Harrison 9-30-1847 Ma
Duncan, Robert to P. Jane Gully 4-10-1854 Be
Duncan, S. K. to S. P. Lenord 10-7-1850 (10-15-1850) G
Duncan, Samuel to Mary James Smith 12-27-1855 Hr
Duncan, Stephen to Amy E. Dickey 3-3-1856 (3-4-1856) G
Duncan, Stephen to T. E. Dickey 9-6-1859 G
Duncan, Tandy P. to Lucy Davis 4-19-1839 O
Duncan, Thomas J. to Emily J. Peay 4-17-1858 (no return) Hn
Duncan, Thomas L. to Mary Carter 8-6-1853 Sh
Duncan, Thomas L. to Sarah Prader 3-4-1852 Sh
Duncan, Thomas L. to Susan Brotherton 6-11-1829 (6-21-1829) Hr
Duncan, Thomas L. to Susan Rosson 6-6-1854 (12-5-1854) Hr
Duncan, Thomas R. to Irene E. Walker 4-24-1861 Sh
Duncan, Tillman to Eveline Turner 7-27-1874 T
Duncan, Cullen to Eveline Turner 7-27-1874 T
Duncan, W. L. to V. H. Blankenship 9-26-1884 L
Duncan, Wen. D. L. to Anna M. Lovelace 9-26-1867 Dy
Duncan, William C. to Mary Jane Anthony 12-17-1849 Hr
Duncan, William H. to Mary M. Fletcher 8-20-1846 Sh
Duncan, William M. to Francis Allen 9-3-1839 (10-3-1839) O
Duncan, William W. to Thursa A. Lenard 8-23-1852 (8-28-1852) G
Duncan, William to Lula Walpole 7-26-1880 L
Duncan, Wm. A. to Mary B. Adams 9-27-1867 (10-1-1867) Ma
Duncan, Wm. B. to Phelora McAdoo 4-4-1854 Cr
Duncan, Wm. C. to Elizabeth J. Wiley 7-17-1861 (7-18-1861) Hr
Duncan, Wm. R. to Mary Ann Brown 8-29-1844 Sh
Duncan, Wm. to Martha Vaughn 10-31-1845 (no return) Cr
Dundon, John to Bridget O'Dare 2-17-1863 Sh
Dunefee, A. O. to Laura A. Taylor 9-30-1874 O
Dunevant, Flem to Ann Eliza Smith 12-16-1876 (12-21-1876) Dy
Dunevant, John to Mariah Whitson 12-12-1871 (12-13-1871) Dy
Dunevant, Robert to Calidonia Somers 2-28-1875 Hy
Dunevent, Fernando to Letitia Grimm 5-19-1875 (5-20-1875) Dy
Dunham, Benj. F. to Sarah J. Reynolds 11-26-1862 (11-27-1862) L
Dunham, Joseph Henry to Sarah Carolin Cotten 12-12-1848 T
Dunigan, F. M. to Exsey Jones 12-17-1868 G
Dunivant, L. W. to S. A. Gaines 12-24-1872 L
Dunivant, W. P. to Lida Crockett 12-29-1883 (1-1-1884) L
Dunkan, F. W. to Martha Lemmons? 8-10-1862 Hn
Dunkin, Frank to Martha Haselette 12-23-1867 (12-28-1867) F B
Dunkin, Stephen to Malinda Lett 12-24-1866 (12-27-1866) Cr
Dunkins, Robert L. to Martha Gooldsby 2-3-1860 We
Dunkum, R. A. to D. Ellen Bowers 2-25-1854 (no return) F
Dunlap, Allen Leroy to Nancy Butram 8-16-1848 (8-17-1848) G
Dunlap, Benjamin to Louisa Dunlap 4-5-1840 Hn
Dunlap, C. C. to Mary Blair 3-19-1868 Hy
Dunlap, C. D. to S. V. Ragland 7-6-1853 Sh
Dunlap, Ebenezar to Mary L. Harbour 4-20-1829 (4-21-1829) G
Dunlap, Ephraim to Elizabeth C. Hamblen 9-10-1846 Hn
Dunlap, George W. to Nancy T. Leander 11-19-1856 Cr
Dunlap, George to Rainer Parr 10-14-1878 (10-16-1878) L B
Dunlap, H. A. to L. O. Wyatt 11-1-1871 Hy
Dunlap, Henry to Ann Blackwell 10-25-1871 T
Dunlap, Henry to Ann Kemp 12-24-1866 Hn B
Dunlap, Henry to Elizabeth Taylor 12-17-1866 (12-20-1866) Ma
Dunlap, Henry to L. A. Dortch 10-19-1866 Hn
Dunlap, J. H. to M. J. Bell 11-13-1855 Hn
Dunlap, J. P. to Mary M. Parker 1-12-1865 Hn
Dunlap, J. P. to R. J. Bradley 12-14-1865 Hn
Dunlap, James J. to Margaret J. Arn 9-19-1851 Hn
Dunlap, James M. to Elizabeth Carter 12-11-1848 (12-14-1848) Ma
Dunlap, James T. to Jane B. Tharpe 10-25-1838 (no return) Hn
Dunlap, John E. to Elizabeth A. Taylor 10-16-1858 (no return) We
Dunlap, John M. to Louisa Kee 7-29-1859 (8-2-1859) G
Dunlap, John M. to Louisa M. Ledsinger 1-3-1856 T
Dunlap, John M. to Mary L. Moore 1-17-1854 (1-19-1854) G
Dunlap, John W. to Malinda E. Parker 9-3-1850 Hn
Dunlap, Moses to Susannah Sales 11-8-1879 (11-9-1879) L B

Dunlap, N. H. to Mary J. Lake 1-20-1861 Hr
Dunlap, N. J. to E. J. Perkins 2-3-1872 (2-5-1872) Cr
Dunlap, Preston to Margaret Dunlap 3-12-1845 Hn
Dunlap, R. W. to Emma E. Daugherty 12-18-1876 (12-24-1876) Dy
Dunlap, Samuel H. to E. S. S. Forest 11-30-1857 Cr
Dunlap, Samuel to Ama Mitchell 3-27-1867 (no return) F B
Dunlap, Samuel to Elizabeth Shearon 10-30-1848 (10-31-1848) L
Dunlap, Samuel to Matilda Cela Ann Sellars 9-14-1848 G
Dunlap, Silas to Frances Bugg 1-28-1841 G
Dunlap, Thomas to Mary Whitchard 8-28-1856 G
Dunlap, William L. to Malinda Stephenson 4-28-1869 (5-4-1869) L
Dunlap, William M. to Rebecca E. Allison 12-2-1844 (12-3-1844) G
Dunlap, William to Edie Thomas 12-30-1869 G B
Dunlap, William to Harriet Taylor 10-20-1856 Ma
Dunlap, William to Mary Scott 4-23-1846 G
Dunlap, Wm. A. to G. A. B. Gambles 8-28-1870 G
Dunlap, Wm. to Sarah Gohlson 8-9-1867 (8-11-1867) F B
Dunley, William H. to Parmelia E. Gunlege 7-11-1844 Hn
Dunlop, Moses to Nancy Moore 9-10-1846 We
Dunlop, P. L. to Nancy Bragg 12-2-1857 We
Dunlop, T. B. M. to Sarah J. Crittendon 11-16-1852 We
Dunlop, Wm. A. to Elizabeth McCain 3-14-1850 We
Dunn, A. F. to Mary Ann Needham 10-23-1870 G
Dunn, A. J. to Elizabeth Young 10-7-1853 (10-9-1853) Hr
Dunn, Alexander to Annie (Mrs.) Irwin 8-8-1864 Sh
Dunn, Andrew J. to Mary Anne Anderson 6-16-1846 Sh
Dunn, Bartholomew to Catharine Whittier Bond 5-27-1834 (5-29-1834) Hr
Dunn, Benjamin A. to Caroline L. Jones 3-14-1843 Hn
Dunn, Benjamin to Mary Midgett 8-10-1842 Hn
Dunn, Benjamin to Sarah Hill 2-26-1838 Hn
Dunn, Bernard to Elizabeth Hughs 10-25-1856 (10-26-1856) Sh
Dunn, C. R. to Mary Ivey 4-6-1878 (4-7-1878) Dy
Dunn, Cornelius to Catharine Cassody 10-5-1851 Sh
Dunn, Cullen to Abbe Boyte 3-8-1833 Hn
Dunn, Cyrus to Margaret Linton 11-12-1870 (11-15-1870) Dy
Dunn, David to Margaret Malory (Malany?) 9-18-1852 (9-20-1852) Sh
Dunn, David to Sarah B. Hawkins 4-24-1834 Sh
Dunn, Dudley to Paulina S. Perkins 6-22-1833 Sh
Dunn, E. M. to Ann E. Aaron 2-7-1849 (no return) F
Dunn, Elam to Lucy A. Eskridge 12-24-1859 We
Dunn, G. A. to E. V. Riley 12-14-1874 (12-15-1874) T
Dunn, G. M. to Margaret R. Dunn 12-23-1855 Hn
Dunn, G. W. to M. E. Phillips 4-10-1864 Hn
Dunn, George G. to Minerva A. Walton 9-3-1856 G
Dunn, George W. to Anne Peeler 10-4-1859 Hn
Dunn, James M. to Mary J. Fowler 5-5-1848 Hn
Dunn, James W. to D. A. Dunn 10-25-1851 (no return) Hn
Dunn, James to Della Pierce 7-26-1871 (7-28-1871) Ma
Dunn, James to Emeline Asbury 2-28-1848 (no return) L
Dunn, James to Mary E. Capehart 9-14-1857 Sh
Dunn, Jas. E. to L. J. Britt 12-11-1872 Hy
Dunn, Jno. C. to Penelope Hughes 8-29-1850 Sh
Dunn, John C. to Mary Ann Raney 5-29-1856 T
Dunn, John M. to Caroline Martin 5-10-1861 (no return) Hn
Dunn, John R. to Elizabeth Campbell 10-7-1847 Hr
Dunn, John R. to Sarah Ann Smith 8-6-1854 Hn
Dunn, John to Ann Lally (Lolly?) 12-8-1852 Hn
Dunn, John to Ardella Freeland 4-5-1864 (4-7-1864) Cr
Dunn, John to Ella Tucker 4-25-1878 Hy
Dunn, John to Flora Herring 12-4-1872 Hy
Dunn, Martin to Sarah Welsh 3-13-1849 Hn
Dunn, Maxwell to Jane Brandon 4-23-184_ (no return) Hn
Dunn, Samuel J. to Mary M. Vaden 12-22-1837 Sh
Dunn, Samuel M. to Mary Thedford 9-19-1879 (9-30-1879) Dy
Dunn, Thomas W. to Mariah Stewart 11-26-1855 (no return) Hn
Dunn, Thomas to Mary Cain 4-24-1852 (4-25-1852) H
Dunn, Thos. J. to Perleva Lankford 8-11-1842 Cr
Dunn, William H. to Sarah Lawrence 11-10-1853 Sh
Dunn, William to Hannah Mathis 10-24-1859 Hr
Dunn, William to Margaret Cook 2-14-1851 (2-16-1851) Hr
Dunn, Wm. M. to Emily P. Collins 1-11-1848 Sh
Dunnagin, John to Ann Conray 1-9-1864 (1-10-1864) Sh
Dunnavant, James to Sarah Ann Johnson 7-29-1877 Hy
Dunnavant, W. D. to Mary Perkins 5-30-1869 Hy
Dunnaway, John A. to Rachael Bryant 7-30-1846 Ma
Dunnegan, Lee to Nancy C. Barron (Barrow?) 12-30-1863 G
Dunnegin, W. L. to Bettie E. Haymes 12-8-1867 Hn
Dunnigan, George to Rebecca Binford 10-30-1868 (no return) Dy
Dunnigan, Jeremiah to Nannie Bowen 12-22-1869 (no return) Dy
Dunnigan, W. T. to N. C. Arnold 8-23-1865 G
Dunning, Andrew to Nancy Blalock 5-29-1861 We
Dunning, Charles W. to Ellen O. Dashiell 1-3-1863 Sh
Dunning, David to Ann B. Williams 6-11-1847 Hn
Dunning, George to Elizabeth Gardner 10-20-1824 O
Dunning, Jackson to Nancy Williams 1-11-1838 (1-18-1838) G
Dunning, John K. to Mary L. Woodard 8-28-1864 (no return) Cr
Dunning, L. to Eliza Moore 9-7-1842 Hn

Dunning, Noah to Nancy A. Bearden 3-1-1840 Sh
Dunnway, Robert P. to Mahilda G. York 12-28-1847 (12-30-1847) Ma
Dunome, Washington to Edy Ellis 3-21-1839 Hn
Dunphy, Mike to Ida Herring 7-15-1874 Hy
Dunscomb, S. H. to Marietta C. Elder 11-15-1854 Sh
Dunwood, Regis to Fredonia Olivia Freeman 2-16-1853 (2-17-1853) T
Dupre, C. A. to Martha E. Finley 11-27-1865 Dy
Dupree, A. E. to Lizzie R. Moore 6-4-1880 (6-6-1880) L
Dupree, A. M. to M. Z. Turner 12-31-1879 (1-1-1880) L
Dupree, Bartlett C. to Melisa V. Shelton 2-17-1869 (2-18-1869) L
Dupree, Calvin to Mary Jane Sangster 3-14-1872 Hy
Dupree, D. R. to Elizabeth Borum 5-3-1848 (no return) L
Dupree, D. R. to Frances E. Stanley 1-24-1861 (no return) Hy
Dupree, George F. to Sallie E. Astin 12-12-1868 (12-17-1868) F
Dupree, J. C. to Lou E. Wood 11-15-1881 L
Dupree, James W. to Adaline A. Lloyd 9-18-1871 L
Dupree, James W. to Hattie Larrimore 10-24-1883 L
Dupree, Manley to Eliza A. Ricks 12-17-1867 (12-18-1867) L
Dupree, Ned to Jennie King 1-27-1874 He
Dupree, Peter M. to Rebeca M. Washington 11-21-1840 (11-25-1840) F
Dupree, T. M. to Cornelia Cornelius 2-8-1854 Sh
Dupree, Thomas L. to Mary V. Price 12-12-1876 (12-13-1876) L
Dupree, Warren to Julia Perkins 12-26-1866 Hy
Dupree, William C. to Addie F. Henry 12-30-1885 L
Dupree, Wm. W. to Sarah F. Nolen 6-12-1861 Hy
Duprees, A. to Texana Stokely 12-22-1868 (no return) Hy
Duprey, Starke to Rosa B. Abington 2-15-1838 L
Dupriest, Protestant P. to Narcissa Bridges 8-9-1850 (8-11-1850) Ma
Dupuy, A. L. to Julia M. Williams 10-14-1856 (11-18-1856) Sh
Dupuy, James W. to Mary B. Webber 9-26-1849 Sh
Dupuy, Starke to Sarah Jane Webber 7-6-1846 Sh
Durant, John W. to Caroline V. Sherrod 11-2-1844 T
Durden, Edmond to Sarah Sarrett 3-2-1856 Be
Durden, H. G. to Mary E. Presson 7-9-1868 Be
Durden, J. J. to Martha Browning 7-2-1849 Be
Durden, J. J> to Margaret Arnold 7-29-1855 Be
Durden, John to Jane Donald 12-27-1877 Dy
Durden, Stephen to Eliza J. Rhodes 6-19-1867 (no return) Hn
Durden, W. D. to Louisa Presson 6-10-1868 Be
Durden, Wiley to Mary E. Tucker 11-14-1870 (11-15-1870) F
Durden, William to Jane Bryant 11-30-1854 (12-3-1854) Hr
Durham, Bryant to Lucinda Durham 12-18-1850 (12-19-1850) L
Durham, Denis to Sarah Jane Harper 1-31-1851 Sh
Durham, Dennis to Sarah Harper 2-5-1851 (2-7-1851) Sh
Durham, George W. to S. J. Stovall 10-25-1858 (10-31-1858) Sh
Durham, H. C. to Mary F. Manley 12-12-1865 (12-13-1865) F
Durham, J. M. to E. P. Tansil 5-14-1855 (no return) We
Durham, Jim to Eliza Hood 12-26-1866 (12-27-1866) F B
Durham, John M. to Trilucia Robertson 1-23-1845 F
Durham, John to Elizer Sneed 4-9-1840 Hy
Durham, Lindsley to Lucy W. Holmes 9-17-1839 (no return) L
Durham, Manly to Martha J. Davenport 2-11-1858 L
Durham, Ready to Rachael A. Hines 11-6-1873 (no return) Hy
Durham, Samuel M. to Mary J. Brady 1-27-1852 (no return) F
Durham, Stephen C. to Martha Ingram 1-29-1842 (2-3-1842) F
Durham, Thomas C. to Mary C. Davis 11-10-1864 (no return) L
Durham, Wm. W. to Bettie Henderson 12-21-1869 Ma
Durivage?, Oliver E. to J. Cordelia Dyher 4-7-1853 (4-14-1853) Sh
Durley, George W. to Eliza A. Hunt 4-9-1834 G
Durley, W. F. to M. M. Holmes 1-11-1870 G
Durley, W. H. to E. M. Ing 8-16-1866 G
Durley, William to Sarah A. Hall 2-15-1848 G
Durrett, Robert D. to Martha H. Polk 11-8-1841 F
Durrett, Wm. R. to Nancy A. McCord 8-16-1870 Ma
Durrum, Henry M to Anny Martin 10-5-1824 Hr
Durrum, James to Kisiah Chesser 3-8-1858 Sh
Durrum, T. L. to M. J. McFadden 10-21-1862 F
Dusmuke, James A. to Octavia A. Vick 11-16-1854 Ma
Duttlinger, M. to S. Gantert 1-23-1858 Sh
Duval, Benjamin T. to Mary E. Evans 4-14-1845 Sh
Duval, Francis A. to Mary E. A. Mabson 7-7-1857 Sh
Duval, Francis A. to Mary H. Spooner 5-3-1853 (5-5-1853) Sh
Duval, W. J. to Ann E. Irby 2-23-1861 (3-7-1861) Sh
Duvall, B. F. to A. J. Akins 12-27-1874 Hy
Duvall, Chas. to Elizabeth Wehman 6-28-1875 O
Duvall, Joseph S. to Mary E. Marr 11-18-1873 Hy
Duvall, T. J. to Harriett J. Irwin 3-17-1851 (no return) F
Dwyer, John to Nancy A. Gurley 11-30-1860 (no return) L
Dwyer, Patrick to Kate Faran 8-17-1859 Sh
Dwyer, William to Mary Smith 2-24-1859 (2-25-1859) Sh
Dyal?, Greenberry to Nancy M. Wilson 6-13-1836 Hr
Dyall, William B. to Hannah H. Darnald 8-12-1847 G
Dyall, William C. to Mary E. Scott 3-26-1864 Sh
Dye, Benjamin B. to Nancy Lane 1-31-1843 (2-2-1843) F
Dyer, B. P. to Emily Hosey 10-4-1879 (10-7-1879) Dy
Dyer, B. P. to N. J. Lasiter 10-25-1876 (10-26-1876) Dy
Dyer, Beverly L. to Sarah R. Branch 10-27-1852 (no return) F

Dyer, Billy to Mary Wortham 8-9-1869 T
Dyer, Clarence to Penny Henderson 2-12-1875 (no return) Hy
Dyer, J. H. to J. E. Surcey 7-18-1865 (7-19-1865) L
Dyer, John E. to Emely Wilson 7-24-1861 (7-25-1861) O
Dyer, John E. to Francis Nullers? 11-19-1863 O
Dyer, John W. to Virginia Wellar 1-29-1849 (1-30-1849) F
Dyer, John to Lucinda Moore 11-30-1840 Hy
Dyer, M. B. to D. E. Smith 4-26-1859 (4-28-1859) F
Dyer, Marion M. to Elizabeth E. Hosley 7-26-1851 G
Dyer, Moses to Caroline Kendall 2-16-1847 Hn
Dyer, Moses to Frances Edmund 2-7-1850 Hy
Dyer, Scott to Margaret A. E. Gannin 9-8-1853 Sh
Dyer, Stephen to L. Melinda Watson 10-5-1848 Ma
Dyer, Thomas H. to Nancy Conley 3-12-1855 Be
Dyer, W. A. to M. E. Luten 12-29-1870 (1-1-1871) O
Dyer, W. H. H. to M. C. Holmes 8-23-1870 (8-24-1870) Cr
Dyer, William E. to Sarah A. Brittenhaus 4-12-1853 Sh
Dyke, Thomas B. to Peggy Rogers 1-26-1838 (1-8?-1838) Hr
Dysart, John Young to Mollie M. Robinson 11-15-1869 (11-16-1869) Ma
Dysart, W. H. H. to M. C. Holmes 8-23-1870 (8-24-1870) Cr
Dyson, Hezekiah to Mary Clark 2-14-1860 (3-18-1860) Hr
Dyson, Isaac to F. Clements 12-5-1871 T
Dyson, Isaac to F. Clements 12-5-1871 (1-6-1872) T
Dyson, Jack to Ellen Wortham 8-28-1859 T
Dyson, Jacob to Mary Elam 5-21-1866 (5-22-1866) T
Dyson, James H. to Angeline J. L. Seat 9-29-1834 (10-10-1834) G
Dyson, Jonas to Eliza Jackson 12-27-1870 (12-28-1870) T
Dyson, Peyton jr. to Harriet A. Green 7-16-1870 (7-17-1870) T
Dyson, Peyton to Mary Ann Bradford 10-11-1872 (10-26-1872) T
Dyson, William to Sue Murphey 3-31-1873 (4-1-1873) T

Eader, W. H. to Eliza Kelly 12-6-1860 Sh
Eadleman, James A. to Margaret Jane Turner 3-17-1870 G
Eady, Hiram to Martha Lane 5-29-1868 Dy
Eagan, Andrew M. to Martha Ann Maroney 9-2-1856 Ma
Eagan, James to Ellen Hannigan 5-5-1863 Sh
Eagan, Thomas to Ellen Dwyer 5-27-1859 Sh
Eakin, William N. to Mary M. Miller 9-17-1864 Sh
Ealand, Samuel to Elizabeth Kendell 12-18-1856 Sh
Ealey, William A. to Lucy Jane Carpenter 7-20-1852 (no return) F
Ealom, Jackson to Catharine Piles 7-24-1854 Sh
Ealver?, Moak? to Alice Williams 12-27-1869 T
Ealy, Joseph A. to Livey ann Hays 9-12-1867 Hn
Ealy, Sam to Sarah Dickenson 12-29-1868 (12-30-1868) F B
Eans (Evans), Charles to Betsie (Mrs.) Brown 1-18-1860 Sh
Eaphland, E. C. to J. L. Williams 5-12-1850 (5-16-1850) O
Eaphland, Elija G. to Mary Williams 10-9-1849 O
Earl, John K. to Martha B. Stafford 10-7-1863 (10-8-1863) F
Earl, Turner to Caroline Stewart 9-9-1870 (no return) F B
Earle, Thomas H. to Sallie J. (Mrs.) Clemons 6-3-1873 Dy
Earley, W. E. to E. A. Shofner 4-9-1873 (4-10-1873) Dy
Earls, Elisha to Harriet Burns 9-12-1858 Cr
Earls, M. to Polly P. Capps ?-?-1840 Cr
Early, Asbury to Nancy Rooks 11-16-1869 (no return) Dy
Earnhart, Daniel to Sarah M. Holland 10-17-1855 (no return) F
Earnhart, G. W. to Mary E. Scott 11-13-1867 (11-14-1867) F
Earp, Gipson to Ammy Burns? 12-11-1851 Be
Earp, Little B. to Frances Ann C. Hinant 4-9-1855 Be
Earp, Wm. to Hester Nowell 10-24-1864 Be
Earwood, Joseph W. to Sarah E. Delancey 9-18-1867 (9-22-1867) T
Easborn, J. K. to Bettie G. Jones 9-26-1865 G
Easley, Charley to Lavinia Walker 2-9-1867 Hy
Easley, Dewitt to Frances M. Dobson 9-28-18857 Hn
Easley, Isham to Eliza King 11-16-1876 Hy
Easley, J. D. to Mary J. Pickard 2-13-1860 (2-14-1860) T
Easley, James W. to Fanny Taylor 2-27-1877 Hy
Easley, John T. to Belinda Rumbly 4-29-1838 (no return) Hn
Easley, William to Margrit Carlton 2-4-1867 Hy
Easly, Wm. H. to Nannie Sanders 11-25-1877 Hy
Easom, John to Matilda Alsop 8-20-1851 (8-24-1851) Hr
Eason, A. to Annie W. Mobley 1-2-1872 Dy
Eason, Alexander to Sarah M. West 5-11-1857 (5-20-1857) L
Eason, F. F. to Elizabeth Cox 12-20-1853 Cr
Eason, G. T. to Lucy A. Reddick 12-2-1871 (no return) Hy
Eason, James to Lucinda Pendergrast 6-11-1856 Ma
Eason, John S. to Sarah J. Asprog 12-24-1861 G
Eason, Mills to Eliza Robinson 2-12-1863 (no return) Hy
Eason, Thomas to Ann Eliza Falden 8-31-1853 Ma
Eason, W. C. to Mary Sorrell 1-1-1873 Dy
Eason, William to Sallie A. Norville 9-27-1869 Hy
East, B. G. to Elizabeth Tanner 10-29-1861 Mn
East, Joseph to Rebecca Miligan 2-6-1838 F
Eastawood, James to Eunice Norrid 2-29-1828 O
Eastep, Walter to Harriet Reed 6-10-1862 Sh
Easter, Jackville R. to America Whitaker 6-27-1833 (6-30-1833) Hr
Easter, Thos. to Rebecca A. Milton 8-11-1846 Cr
Easteridge, Larken to Susannah Millen 12-27-1828 O
Easters, Jesse C. to Sarah A. Barnhart 8-6-1866 (8-7-1866) Cr

Easterwood, Elisha to Nancy Sellers 12-27-1837 G
Easterwood, F. A. to Malinda Lee 8-26-1862 O
Easterwood, H. I. to Mary Ann F. Rodgers 12-6-1849 G
Easterwood, J. W. to S. C. Robertson 3-2-1863 (3-3-1863) O
Easterwood, W. L. to Adiline Cunningham 12-16-1868 G
Easterwood, William C. to Sylvina Jones 1-10-1856 G
Easterwood, William to Nancy Keas 5-13-1852 (5-17-1852) G
Easterwood, Wilson S. to Mary P. Reeves 4-14-1858 G
Easterwood, Wm. W. to Susan Lee 12-30-1844 (12-31-1844) Hr
Eastham, E. P. to C. M. Foster 11-28-1860 Sh
Eastham, James S. to Antoinette A. Graves 10-11-1852 (no return) F
Eastham, Thomas C. to Nancy M. Bateman 5-1-1851 (5-8-1851) Sh
Eastlack, Joseph M. to Caroline Carroll 2-5-1844 Hr
Eastman, Americus to Eliza R. Marlatt 5-19-1859 Sh
Eastman, Charles F. to Elizabeth Colbert 7-28-1834 (7-29-1834) Hr
Eastman, James W. to Sarah J. Arnold 9-24-1856 (9-25-1856) Sh
Eastridge, Cleft to Parilee Mosier 8-21-1838 (8-23-1838) O
Eastridge, J. B. to Josephine Bridges 9-23-1865 (9-24-1865) O
Eastridge, John to Hannah Bridges 7-30-1857 O
Eastridge, Tulley to Betsey Moses 2-25-1828 O
Easum(Eastham?), H. O. to Elizabeth Robinson 3-29-1848 Hr
Eatherly, J. R. to Amanda King Reynolds 1-27-1879 (1-29-1879) Dy
Eaton(Caton), Eli to Delila Butram 10-26-1839 Hr
Eaton, Abraham to Susan Williams 1-18-1847 (no return) F
Eaton, Aleck to Louisa Hart 2-15-1867 T
Eaton, D. W. to R. P. Pollock 11-5-1869 F
Eaton, David W. to Amanda Newman 10-9-1855 Hr
Eaton, Isaac to Emmer Shepard 4-10-1871 T
Eaton, J. L. to Mary J. Cearley 2-8-1862 Hr
Eaton, Joe to Phoebe Coachman 1-5-1880 L
Eaton, John sr. to Sarah C. Johnson 9-13-1858 (9-14-1858) Hr
Eaton, Robert to Lu Morgan 11-23-1869 T
Eaton, W. H. to A. C. Carey 5-10-1860 G
Eaton, Willis to Leonah Jones 2-4-1869 F B
Eaton, Wm. to Nancy J. Freels 9-21-1860 (9-23-1860) Hr
Eavans, Charly to Ellen Mullins 6-30-1873 (no return) L
Eaves, David to Susan F. Keinman 9-1-1855 (9-2-1855) O
Eaves, Stephen W. to Rutha Crockett 10-21-1844 (no return) We
Eaves, W. B. to A. Ramsey 3-17-1866 Hn
Eaves, William B. to Elizabeth Ramsey 10-20-1859 Hn
Eaves, William D. to Elizabeth Hall 2-7-1861 Hn
Eaves, Wm. D. G. to Mary Arnold 12-30-1852 Hn
Eazel, Anderson to Sarah McGhe 9-6-1856 Sh
Ebeler, Ernst (Ernest) to Eliza Fuchs 7-19-1862 (7-20-1862) Sh
Eblin, Griffin to Lydia V. McFarlan 5-12-1863 (no return) We
Echerle, Florentin to Kate Fye 2-23-1864 Sh
Echols, D. H. to Caroline J. Holt 1-8-1861 Sh
Echols, J. B. to R. Candace Lane 1-19-1876 Dy
Echols, J. W. to M. F. Smith 12-26-1876 (12-27-1876) Dy
Echols, Joseph W. to Malissie A. Mobley 11-8-1870 (11-9-1870) Dy
Echols, N. to R. J. Bowen 1-27-1877 (1-28-1877) Dy
Eckert, Henry to Elizabeth Powley 6-28-1862 (6-29-1862) Sh
Eckerty (Eckerly?), G. A. to Mary S. Brillmayer 4-21-1862 (4-24-1862) Sh
Eckford, Becton to Mollie Warmack 12-12-1866 T
Eckford, W. W. to Annie Warmath 12-12-1865 T
Eckles, James R. to Elizabeth J. Whitworth 4-20-1859 (4-21-1859) Sh
Eckles, Joseph T. to Caroline Thompson 12-13-1841 Sh
Eckley, Henry to Martha A. Finch 6-10-1846 Sh
Eckold, Robert W. to Elizabeth Woodward 10-19-1847 Sh
Eddings, E. B. to Mary F. Cobb 1-24-1870 O
Eddings, James to Frances Caldwell 11-18-1866 G
Eddington, Edmund J. to Catherine Denmark 8-24-1852 (8-25-1852) Ma
Eddins, B. H. to Susan E. Cole 10-12-1842 Sh
Eddins, Jas. A. to Caroline C. Hooker 12-10-1850 (12-11-1850) F
Eddins, John M. to Martha A. D. Standley 12-22-1841 (12-23-1841) F
Eddins, John to Mary Munn 12-13-1846 F
Eddins, Lewis L. to Elizabeth Lacy 3-27-1832 Ma
Eddins, Monroe to Mahala Reddick 9-8-1866 (no return) F B
Eddins, Washington to Caroline Given 1-24-1857 (1-28-1857) Ma
Eddins, Washington to Elizabeth Bynum 5-12-1846 (5-22-1846) F
Eddins, William T. to Burchis Warnick 1-23-1854 (1-24-1854) Sh
Eddins, Wm. L. to Elizabeth A. Norris 6-12-1850 Sh
Eddins, Wm. M. to Martha (T?) Dodson 11-27-1850 Sh
Eddleman, J. F. to Sarah W. Leonard 3-13-1866 G
Eddlemon, F. J. G. to Susan F. Adams 3-3-1856 (3-6-1856) Hr
Edenton, Jas. C. to H. C. Moore 11-21-1868 (11-24-1868) F
Edgar, Elisha M. to Nancy E. Weeks 12-27-1864 Hn
Edgar, Elisha M. to Nancy Little 8-26-1840 Hn
Edgar, Lewis C. to Mary E. Staten? 9-17-1863? Hn
Edgar, R. T. to Martha A. Lucas 6-29-1865 Hn
Edgar, Thomas M. to Mary C. Lucas 6-27-1858 Hn
Edgar, William N. to Sarah A. Mixon 11-29-1849 Sh
Edge, George to Frances Douglass 1-23-1878 (no return) Dy
Edgerly, John M. to Mary Keaven 10-16-1857 (10-18-1857) Sh
Edgerly, Jos. H. to Mary Gregory 6-23-1857 (6-24-1857) Sh
Edgington, Francis M. to Elmira Suttlemire 6-1-1864 Sh
Edings, Thomas P. to Allice A. Tucker 10-15-1859 (10-18-1859) T

Edington, C. D. to Rebecca Medlin 12-8-1840 Ma
Edington, G. W. to Malinda RRushing 12-2-1856 Be
Edington, J. F. to Priscilla C. Herrin 3-3-1861 Be
Edington, James F. to Eliza Jane Baker 10-1-1866? Be
Edington, James F. to Priscilla C. Herron 3-3-1861 Be
Edington, T. S. to Mary Ann Ward 6-26-1862 Be
Edington, W. B. to Lucinda Ward 3-24-1862 Be
Edington, Wylie B. to Elizabeth S. Ward 2-23-1852 Be
Edminston, John B. to Susan Kennon 12-1-1842 Hn
Edmonds, Charles to Samanthy Pollock 12-13-1869 (12-16-1869) F
Edmonds, Jerry to Mary Parker 12-25-1874 T
Edmonds, Nathan to Malinda R. Graves 3-30-1844 Sh
Edmonds, Robert to Samuel Key 10-2-1838 O
Edmonds, Thomas K. to Mary Ragsdale 5-9-1867 G
Edmonds, William H. to Elizabeth Jones 11-5-1854 Hn
Edmonds, William W. to Mary Ann T. Ross 12-22-1836 (12-23-1836) O
Edmonds, Williams to Mary A. Henby 8-3-1854 We
Edmondson, J. B. to I. E. Wade 2-27-1866 G
Edmondson, J. F. to Elva Cathey 10-23-1870 T
Edmondson, James H. to Mary E. Titus 2-9-1853 Sh
Edmondson, John L. to Sarah E. Lowrance 3-19-1867 G
Edmondson, William R. to Amanda F. Isrial 3-14-1846 (3-17-1846) G
Edmondson, William to Sarah Ridgway 11-8-1827 O
Edmonson, Edmond A. to Sarah A. Murrell 3-20-1866 Ma
Edmonson, G. B. to L. E. Williams 3-3-1874 O
Edmonson, Hiram to Mary E. Wilkinson 11-15-1857 O
Edmonson, J. A. to Mary F. A. Read 10-20-1870 G
Edmonson, John to Milly Stephens 10-16-1839 L
Edmonson, Robert to Mary Clark 1-5-1833 (1-8-1833) G
Edmonson, W. B. to W. A. Edmonson 9-21-1854 Sh
Edmonson, William to Nancy L. Leech 12-2-1833 Hr
Edmonston, J. Harvey to Mattie J. London 6-20-1855 (6-21-1855) O
Edmonston, W. M. to S. E. Boon 3-31-1868 G
Edmunds, Alexander to Nancy Hartsfield 11-19-1839 Hn
Edmunds, Calvin C. to Susan Hudson 11-21-1850 Hn
Edmunds, James M. to Argen Milstead 2-8-1855 Hn
Edmunds, P. B. to Angeline Crowder 8-5-1855 Hn - Preston B.
Edmunds, Preston W. to Helen Hartsfield 9-17-1840 Hn
Edmunds, Sterling H. to R. S. Jolley 12-28-1858 We
Edmunds, William H. to Elizabeth James 12-14-1842 Hn
Edmunds, Zack to Harriet H. Hill 11-19-1833 Sh
Edmunds, ___ to Mollie Coleman 3-7-1867 Hn
Edmundson, Allen to Sarah L. Halford 4-4-1842 (4-6-1842) G
Edmundson, D. M. to Lavanda Shaw 9-15-1832 (9-18-1832) Hr
Edmundson, James M. to Sarah M. Graddy 3-4-1856 (3-5-1856) G
Edmundson, John to Mulindy Trosper 8-25-1838 (8-30-1838) L
Edmundson, Robert to Nancy Edmundson 1-11-1839 (1-14-1839) G
Edmundson, Thompson to Mary A. Trosper 9-14-1857 G
Edmundson, William R. to Sentha L. N. McWhirter 3-11-1845 G
Edmundson, jr., William to Elizabeth J. Burgan 8-20-1842 (8-21-1842) G
Edmundston, Robert P. to Delila Short 1-7-1839 (1-13-1839) G
Edney, Allen to Eliza Fumbank 9-23-1869 (no return) Dy
Edney, B. F. to Martha A. Bizzle 1-29-1866 (no return) Dy
Edney, Francis to Nancy Bowling 4-23-1835 G
Edney, Henry to Frances Perkins 10-8-1873 Hy
Edney, John D. to Nancy W. Childress 11-2-1861 L
Edney, John to Fannie Langston 12-22-1869 Hy
Edney, S. H. M. W. to Amanda Williamson 12-24-1853 Sh
Edney, S. W. to Amanda Williamson 1-7-1854 Sh
Ednsley, J. N. to Louisa Ann Blakeley 1-13-1863 Hn
Edringtar, Thadius S. to Sarah E. Holloman 12-18-1858 (12-19-1858) O
Edson, John D. to Mattie E. A. Gibson 8-15-1864 Sh
Edward, Anderson to Ellen Young 2-18-1868 T
Edward, Barnabas to Mary J. Tigret 11-9-1853 G
Edward, James W. to Sarah J. Cashar 2-6-1851 G
Edward, Robert to Mary Timms 2-15-1830 Ma
Edward, William to Mary A. Wethington 10-5-1852 (10-6-1852) G
Edwards, A. C. to Tabitha A. Williams 11-8-1871 Cr
Edwards, A. O. to Emily Nelson 4-27-1842 Sh
Edwards, Albert B. to Martha Jane Kirby 12-27-1876 Hy
Edwards, Alfred M. to Luesa Vaughan 12-1-1859 We
Edwards, Amos A. to Mary Elizabeth Stephenson 8-5-1850 (8-6-1850) Hr
Edwards, Anderson to Elizabeth Wilson 4-22-1841 Ma
Edwards, Anderson to Nancy Watkins 8-9-1860 (no return) Cr
Edwards, Andrew A. to S(e)cily Fawbin? 7-2-1832 O
Edwards, Andrew Jackson to S. J. Ledbetter 11-11-1878 (11-12-1878) L
Edwards, Aulston to Susan Ott 7-17-1850 O
Edwards, Austin to Biddey Haley 8-28-1846 O
Edwards, B. B. to Hugh Elgria Sutton 10-24-1860 (no return) We
Edwards, Barnabas to Martha (Mrs.) Faulkner 11-9-1872 (11-10-1872) Dy
Edwards, Ben F. to Ellen B. Stevens 12-18-1872 Hy
Edwards, Benj. J. to Martha R. Stephenson 10-28-1854 (10-29-1854) Hr
Edwards, Benjamin to Elizabeth Smith 10-6-1827 G
Edwards, Benjamin to Elizabeth Smith 10-6-1828 (10-14-1828) G
Edwards, Bradford to Martha H. Waddy 7-14-1855 (7-15-1855) G
Edwards, C. T. to Hariet G. Peeples 1-16-1856 We
Edwards, C. W. to Charlott D. Smith 10-21-1856 G

Edwards, Caswell to Emily Trousdale 1-7-1867 F B
Edwards, Charles Philip to Elizabeth A. Smith 9-11-1859 Sh
Edwards, Charley to Nancy Palmer 10-14-1870 Hy
Edwards, Charlie to Sarah Jane Tilman 9-15-1879 L
Edwards, Claiborne to Susan Dukes 12-17-1877 (no return) Hy
Edwards, Clayburn to Caroline Rice 2-16-1869 (2-17-1869) L
Edwards, Columbus to Augusta Leath 3-12-1868 G
Edwards, David K. to Mary Jane Crawford 4-30-1853 (5-1-1853) Hr
Edwards, Drewery to Lucy Stokes 9-30-1841 Cr
Edwards, Eli to Louise E. Cochrain 5-3-1831 (5-5-1831) O
Edwards, Erasmus Darwin to Charlotte Dowdy 8-27-1844 T
Edwards, Frank to Nancy Adams 12-24-1869 (12-30-1869) Cr
Edwards, Franklin H. to Mary Elizabeth Wright 12-7-1853 O
Edwards, G. R. to Susan L. Courtney 2-1-1864 (2-3-1864) Dy
Edwards, G. W. to Frances P. Wilson 10-15-1866 (10-16-1866) Cr
Edwards, George F. to A. J. Banister 1-5-1864 G
Edwards, George M. to M. V. Darnall 11-26-1859 (11-29-1859) O
Edwards, H. L. to M. E. Trantham 10-23-1875 (10-24-1875) O
Edwards, H. W. to Mary E. Fields 2-9-1867 G
Edwards, Harbert H. to Nancy C. Webb 11-10-1853 (11-13-1853) Hr
Edwards, Harbert to Martha Carns 2-5-1844 (2-13-1844) G
Edwards, Harry to Celia Wright 8-4-1870 (8-11-1870) F B
Edwards, Henry to Louisa Granberry 6-1-1866 (6-3-1866) F B
Edwards, Henry to Mary Ann Goodman 8-28-1848 Hn
Edwards, Herbert to Sarah Love 1-12-1848 (1-13-1848) G
Edwards, Isaiah to Nancy M. George 9-1-1856 Hy
Edwards, J. F. to Mary A. Terry 11-30-1843 (no return) Hn
Edwards, J. F. to O. L. A. Akers 1-7-1871 (1-8-1871) Cr
Edwards, J. J. to Margaret E. Wortham 1-13-1858 (1-14-1858) Sh
Edwards, J. M. to M. S. Hughs 12-26-1871 Hy
Edwards, Jacob L. to Sally Boydston 2-7-1824 (2-8-1824) Hr
Edwards, James A. to Lucy A. Crosby 2-10-1863 G
Edwards, James A. to Mary Ann Carter 11-28-1860 Hn
Edwards, James A. to Nancy Murphy 5-30-1848 (6-1-1848) Hr
Edwards, James B. to Elisa Virginia Wilkinson 10-29-1827 (10-30-1827) Hr
Edwards, James J. to Barbara Nanny 9-27-1845 Ma
Edwards, James J. to Mary C. Anderson 10-17-1844 Ma
Edwards, James M. to Mary A. E. Acuff 3-18-1872 (3-21-1872) L
Edwards, James M. to Rebecca Milstead 11-23-1861 (no return) Hn
Edwards, James W. to Jane Cole 8-9-1849 G
Edwards, James W. to Pocahontas Tansel 3-12-1866 Dy
Edwards, James to Elizabeth Edwards 11-5-1849 (11-8-1849) Hr
Edwards, James to Sarah Graves 10-31-1877 Hy
Edwards, Jas. M. to Emily C. Ross 2-26-1852 We
Edwards, Jas. W. to Mary F. Jones 1-17-1871 Cr
Edwards, Jas. to Eliza J. Simmons 12-18-1843 Hr
Edwards, Jesse to Catherine Glidwell 10-25-1856 Ma
Edwards, Jesse to Elizabeth Butler 3-10-1867 G
Edwards, Jesse to Lucinda Williamson 7-1-1840 Sh
Edwards, John H. to Lucinda F. Lipe 9-14-1871 Cr
Edwards, John H. to Sarah S. Edwards 12-25-1861 We
Edwards, John M. to Mary Jones 12-13-1876 Hy
Edwards, John S. to Eliza Ann Allen 1-30-1860 Sh
Edwards, John W. to Mary Femins? 5-10-1861 T
Edwards, John W. to Susannah Jones 4-3-1860 Hn
Edwards, John to Ann Hill 12-13-1858 Sh
Edwards, John to Celier Graves 10-31-1877 Hy
Edwards, John to Elvina Venable 1-3-1848 Hn
Edwards, John to M. J. Bratton 9-22-1856 G
Edwards, John to Margaret Wesson 1-14-1847 Sh
Edwards, John to Mary Bayne 7-25-1828 G
Edwards, John to Mary White 4-2-1874 Hy
Edwards, John to Sarah Tims 7-8-1839 (7-10-1839) Ma
Edwards, Joseph B. to Sarah T. Hodges 11-6-1865 (11-15-1865) F
Edwards, Joseph L. to Martha Finney 10-23-1844 F
Edwards, Joseph R. to Jane Tune 9-17-1849 (9-19-1849) O
Edwards, Joseph R. to Lucinda Scott 1-2-1833 O
Edwards, Joseph R. to Nancy J. Curlin 6-21-1855 (6-22-1855) O
Edwards, Joseph to Martha E. Norvell 11-29-1843 Ma
Edwards, Julius to Mary A. E. Dungan 11-6-1852 (11-11-1852) Ma
Edwards, Justin H. to Sarah J. White 11-19-1860 (no return) Hy
Edwards, Justin L. to Mary Vann 3-14-1832 Ma
Edwards, L. M. to Martha A. Bretton 6-9-1870 (6-12-1870) Ma
Edwards, Leander D. to Harriet Hill 12-8-1866 (12-9-1866) Ma
Edwards, Lewis to Laura Harris 5-11-1867 (no return) Hy
Edwards, Lewis to Sarah Ragland 3-9-1868 (3-21-1868) F B
Edwards, Lewis to Tennessee Alexander 3-18-1873 Hy
Edwards, Luke M. to Elizabeth Parker 5-24-1833 G
Edwards, Marion to Mary Ann Shofner 3-16-1864 Cr
Edwards, Marion to Maryann Henderson 3-16-1864 (no return) Cr
Edwards, Marklin to Mary Matilda Berry 1-12-1848 Sh
Edwards, Martin to Matilda Jane King 8-12-1866 G
Edwards, Matthew to Amanda Henderson 8-16-1873 (8-21-1873) L B
Edwards, Matthew to Martha Woods 10-24-1850 Sh
Edwards, Miles D. to Neely D. Stokes 9-1-1852 Cr
Edwards, N. A. to S. J. Hall 12-21-1864 (no return) Dy
Edwards, N. G. to Sallie McFall 11-1-1871 O

Edwards, Nathaniel J. to Mary F. Spellings 10-6-1865 (10-8-1865) Cr
Edwards, Nathaniel M. to Sarah L. Hicks 11-21-1848 Hn
Edwards, O. T. to Anna E. Dickinson 1-30-1867 F
Edwards, Owen H. to Sarah A. Thomas 12-19-1859 (12-20-1859) O
Edwards, Paul to Tena Taylor 6-17-1871 (no return) Hy
Edwards, R. A. to Mary A. Hale 12-11-1855 (12-12-1855) Ma
Edwards, Richard A. to Susan Wildar 8-11-1842 G
Edwards, Richard to Indy Macklin 12-20-1867 T
Edwards, S. M. to C. C. Crawford 10-23-1865 (10-24-1865) F
Edwards, S. W. to Marsha A. Dickins 3-5-1856 Cr
Edwards, Samuel H. to Alice W. Cook 12-3-1867 Ma
Edwards, Silas W. to Sarah E. Thomas 12-3-1857 Ma
Edwards, Silas to Mary Freeman 11-18-1853 (11-24-1853) G
Edwards, Spencer to Sarah Jane Hanning 6-19-1850 Cr
Edwards, T. C. (Dr.) to Narcissa H. Bond 3-2-1876 (no return) Hy
Edwards, Thomas C. to Mary J. Hicks 7-24-1841 Hn
Edwards, Thomas to Eliza Ann Antridge 1-2-1863 (12-19-1863?) Sh
Edwards, Thomas to Mary Robertson 11-26-1835 G
Edwards, Thos. E. to Sarah Yates 9-26-1852 Hn
Edwards, Thos. J. to Pricilla B. Brewer 2-6-1865 (2-7-1865) Dy
Edwards, Vinson to Amanda A. Harris 12-4-1866 (12-5-1866) Ma
Edwards, W. A. to M. E. Verhine? 11-24-1842 (10?-29-1842) O
Edwards, W. A. to Nancy T. Ware 1-24-1854 Cr
Edwards, W. H. to Ada Robinson 2-10-1863 Sh
Edwards, W. J. to Jane T. Lapley 1-13-1867 Hy
Edwards, W. W. to Mattie McDavid 9-14-1870 Dy
Edwards, William A. to Cornelia B. Durham 12-28-1868 (12-31-1868) F
Edwards, William A. to Sarah M. Pearce 2-26-1861 We
Edwards, William B. to Alice G. Tucker 1-28-1867 Ma
Edwards, William C. to Jane Karns 4-3-1843 (5-3-1843) G
Edwards, William H. to Catherine Barrier 7-3-1866 Ma
Edwards, William H. to Lucinda Wilson 1-28-1846 Ma
Edwards, William H. to Mary Ann Epperson 3-22-1854 (3-3?-1854) Ma
Edwards, William J. to Julia F. Roberson 9-24-1879 (9-25-1879) L
Edwards, William J. to _____ 12-8-1866 (12-11-1866) Cr
Edwards, William T. to Elizabeth H. Henry 9-27-1860 We
Edwards, William T. to Malvina Birmingham 5-9-1844 Ma
Edwards, William to Ann Martin 7-23-1866 G
Edwards, William to Cardelia Luckado 8-21-1868 T
Edwards, William to Eliza Williams 12-16-1834 Sh
Edwards, William to Georga Ann Martin 4-17-1867 G
Edwards, William to Margaret Drewry 2-15-1850 Hn
Edwards, William to Martha C. Wynn 7-21-1846 (7-23-1846) G
Edwards, William to Mary Sherod 11-7-1859 (no return) Hy
Edwards, William to Nancy A. Swift 7-29-1870 (8-1-1870) Dy
Edwards, Wm. J. to Margery Algea 2-2-1843 G
Edwards, Wm. M. to Harriett A. Landrum 5-26-1866 O
Edwards, Wm. N. to Jane Jolnes 8-24-1852 Sh
Edwards, Wm. N. to Martha P. Trobough 8-20-1861 (8-22-1861) Sh
Edwards, Wm. to Cassy Haywood 12-17-1846 Cr
Edwards, Wm. to Mary Robinson 11-2-1858 Cr
Edwin, W. M. to Mary V. Lewis 10-26-1849 (10-30-1849) F
Egan, John to Elizabeth Suckett 1-6-1855 (no return) F
Egans, Daniel to Eliza Johnson 9-30-1870 (10-11-1870) L
Egleston, James to Mariah Bostick 12-13-1876 (12-14-1876) L
Egner, Henry to Annie Harphan 11-7-1863 Sh
Ehrhard, Gabriel to Bettie A. Wyatt 12-15-1871 (no return) L
Ehrlick, Lewis to Jane Young 11-14-1859 Sh
Ehrman, Isaac to Cecelia Wearthemier 2-25-1863 Sh
Eilert, Louis F. to Louise Bake 7-6-1858 Sh
Eisenmayer, John to Elizabeth Oeder 5-9-1859 Sh
Eisenschmidt, Bernard to Marinda Mellan 9-27-1842 Sh
Eison, Alexander to Mary Lea 1-7-1875 L B
Eison, Allen to Louensia Young 1-16-1871 (1-17-1871) L
Eison, Allen to Mitt Parr 2-13-1879 L B
Eison, Brooks to Eva Hooper 3-29-1879 (3-30-1879) L
Eison, Charles to Lizzie McDearmon 3-11-1879 (3-12-1879) L B
Eison, F. W. to Astasia Jones 6-13-1867 G
Eison, Howard to Jane Rucker 9-3-1873 (no return) L B
Eison, Howard to Janie Rucker 9-3-1873 (9-4-1873) L
Eison, James to Matilda F. Parr 12-29-1874 L
Eison, Lawson to Delor? Young 1-22-1874 L
Eison, Parry to Addie Soward 4-3-1879 (4-4-1879) L B
Eison, R. to Eliza J. Brim 8-2-1876 (8-3-1876) L
Eison, Wesley to Ailsey Young 1-8-1880 L
Eitel, Jacob F. to Ann Walker 1-12-1843 Sh
Eitel, Willis M. to Sarah E. Bennett 7-3-1855 (7-11-1855) Sh
Eitel, Wm. H. to Charlotte Gester 4-2-1846 Sh
Eitle, W. M. to Mary Ozier 1-13-1869 F
Ekle, William to Frances Cunningham 8-28-1862 Mn
Elam, D. B. to Mollie A. Benson 1-25-1873 (1-29-1873) T
Elam, Geo. to Rachel Cotton 7-2-1870 T
Elam, George to Eunice Norrid 12-17-1827 O
Elam, Jefferson to Margaret Tennant 1-21-1852 (1-25-1852) T
Elam, John D. to Martha Ann Sykes 12-8-1845 Ma
Elam, John to Rebecca Kirby 11-24-1866 (11-29-1866) Ma
Elam, Joseph to Catherine Jones 10-6-1841 G

Elam, Mark to Elizabeth Maberry? 1-10-1855 (no return) F
Elam, Mills to Jane Yancey 5-16-1870 G B
Elam, Robert to Cordelia Wood 3-29-1858 (4-1-1858) T
Elam, S. A. to F. O. Reeves 8-18-1859 G
Elam, Thomas to Jane Aden 4-23-1863 G
Elam, W. A. to Eliza E. Simmons 4-7-1853 G
Elam, Washington to Anny Smith 7-29-1867 G B
Elam, William F. to Eliza Barton 1-7-1868 G
Elam, William to Elizer Martin 3-16-1870 G B
Elbertson, Tobert to S. Cothran 2-8-1838 F
Elbowe, Gross to Mary C. Bowden 9-14-1865 (9-17-1865) Cr
Elcan, A. L. to Bettie T. Swayne 11-3-1869 (11-4-1869) T
Elcan, Alfred to Sarah Maclin 12-29-1876 Hy
Elcan, Cyrus to Martha Bledsoe 10-10-1870 (10-29-1870) F B
Elcan, Felix to Ruth Collier 1-26-1876 (no return) Hy
Elcan, H. H. to Martha A. Hunt 7-10-1865 T
Elcan, Henry L. to Mary H. Kennon 9-1-1865 (9-7-1865) T
Elcan, Junius H. to Heurin C. Carter 3-2-1865 T
Elcan, Junius H. to Heurin? C. Carter 3-2-1865 (3-7-1865) T
Elcan, N. H. to Virginia E. Clements 7-4-1859 (7-6-1859) T
Elcan, Preston to May Bennet? 11-11-1871 T
Elder, Benj. F. to Margaret V. Hamilton 7-21-1853 G
Elder, Benj. F. to Fannie Dickason 3-4-1872 T
Elder, Benjamin F. to Louisa Davie 12-6-1858 Ma
Elder, C. A. to S. Belle Bright 6-2-1861 G
Elder, Claiborn to Mary Ann Foster 4-29-1840 (5-3-1840) O
Elder, E. N. to R. M. Carthel 9-5-1866 G
Elder, Franklin to Sarah Ann Jackson 3-28-1857 (3-31-1857) L
Elder, G. L. to Susan J. Thomas 5-14-1863 Mn
Elder, G. W. to Meliara J. Hanna 2-17-1859 G
Elder, Henry to Amanda Harper 12-27-1869 G B
Elder, J. M. to Eliza E. Hughes 1-6-1871 (1-12-1871) F
Elder, J. M. to S. A. Dickason 1-15-1861 F
Elder, John A. to Anna Ellis 9-28-1880 (9-29-1880) L
Elder, John H. to Sally Hickey 2-2-1826 G
Elder, John H. to Sally Hickey 2-2-1828 G
Elder, John to Nancy Burress 4-27-1842 T
Elder, John to Ruth A. Haislip 1-10-1846 (1-11-1846) O
Elder, Joseph to Emily Mildred Talley 7-2-1849 (7-5-1849) T
Elder, Munroe B. to Lucy A. Baber 11-2-1837 G
Elder, P. G. to Mary S. Price 3-16-1862 Mn
Elder, Patrick H. to Sarahann Driver 7-17-1844 (7-18-1844) F
Elder, Phill to Ellen Rucker 3-29-1875 (no return) Hy
Elder, R. F. to L. E. Patten 1-1-1866 (1-7-1866) Cr
Elder, W. F. to Martha E. Middleton 12-17-1883 (12-18-1883) L
Elder, William D. to Sarah Jane Wilson 1-28-1857 (1-29-1857) O
Elder, William E. to Almira Carthel 12-24-1851 G
Elder, William to Eliza Harper 3-4-1829 (3-7-1829) G
Elder, William to Louiza Schrigs? 7-6-1861 (7-9-1861) T
Elder, William to Sarah F. Ramsey 7-23-1834 G
Elder, Wm. Franklin to Lorania C. Elder 8-18-1851 (8-19-1851) T
Elder, jr., James to Mary F. Haislip 10-25-1853 (10-26-1853) O
Eldler, John to Virginia Henderson 1-3-1855 (1-4-1855) O
Eldridg, William S. to Rebecca E. Witt 12-24-1856 (12-25-1856) G
Eldridge, Alfred to Mildred T. (Mrs.) Crump 4-13-1844 Sh
Eldridge, O. H. to Sarah E. Overly 10-13-1860 Hn
Eldridge, Wesley to Catharin Woodley 7-1-1869 T
Eldridge, Wm. M. to Mary F. Delashment 1-23-1865 T
Elem, Richard to Julia Strayhorn 7-26-1872 (no return) Cr
Elender, Wm. F. to Delora Reden 10-8-1850 Hn
Elerson, Green? B. to Susannah Glenn 11-18-1845 (11-20-1845) Hr
Elgin, Frank to Julia Marris 10-1-1870 (10-2-1870) Cr
Elgin, John to Mary Mitchell 10-18-1844 F
Elgin, John to Nancy O. Hughes 3-24-1839 (3-25-1839) Hr
Elgin, Robert to Mary A. Norment 3-19-1827 (3-21-1827) Hr
Eli, Joseph to Penelope High 3-26-1844 Hn
Elicker, B. F. to S. F. Poiner 1-25-1866 Hn
Eliff, Josiah A. to Roseann Page 12-24-1862 Mn
Elinder, E. B. to Elizabeth Louder 2-12-1851 Cr
Elington, E. to Jane Thomas Ellington 5-8-1848 (5-9-1848) F
Elington, Ephraim to E. M. Curtis 10-25-1871 (no return) Hy
Eliott, J. M. B. to Rety Dunn 3-10-1864 Hn
Eliott, John J. to Sarah C. Petty 9-1-1840 (9-2-1840) F
Elison, Larance to Lonezar Clark 9-26-1870 (10-9-1870) Cr
Elison, Wm. to Ann J. Dunlap 1-27-1868 (1-30-1868) T
Elkin, Winston to Eliza Collier 2-13-1867 (no return) Hy
Elkins, Hiram to Ann Haislip 3-9-1844 (3-10-1844) O
Elkins, Hiram to Margaret Henson 12-24-1850 (12-29-1850) Hr
Elkins, J. M. to Polly J. Butler 10-11-1871 (10-12-1871) Cr
Elkins, J. W. to Eliza Ann Hogue 12-27-1860 Hn
Elkins, James to Luceney E. Drake 7-22-1841 (no return) Cr
Elkins, John W. to Elizabeth Ross 2-6-1855 Hn
Elkins, John to Winny McFadden 11-21-1842 Hn
Elkins, Louis to Rachael Davis 7-1-1840 (7-2-1840) Ma
Elkins, Merrell W. to Mary S. G. Baucum 9-25-1859 Hn
Elkins, Merrell to Mary Grisham 1-6-1851 Hn
Elkins, Miles to Caroline Coor(Coon) 7-31-1838 (8-2-1838) Hr
Elkins, Reuben to Nannie Jones 7-4-1868 (7-5-1868) O B
Elks, F. to P. Reecks? 3-22-1860 Hr
Elks, N. E. to Dolly A. Mitchard 9-18-1865 O
Elks, William B. to Sarah Jane Holliday 7-16-1850 (7-21-1850) Hr
Ellam (Elam?), Isaac to Sarah H. Henry 2-7-1850 Hn
Ellam, Jno. C. to Alice J. Harley 11-20-1871 T
Elledge, J. T. to M. Cherry 5-26-1861 (4?-26-1860?) O
Elledge, J. T. to Mandy Cherry 4-26-1860 O
Elledge, Joseph to E. A. Hollis 1-5-1858 Sh
Ellender, B. F. to N. C. King 9-15-1860 (9-16-1860) Cr
Ellenton, William H. to Nancy B. Lane 9-22-1855 (10-4-1855) Ma
Ellerman, Henry to Elizabeth Harrison 8-6-1864 (8-8-1864) Sh
Elliett, F. W. (or James) to Lucinda Josalin 4-25-1864 Sh
Elliett, John to Mary Ballard 3-5-1866 (3-8-1866) T
Elliff, A. O. to Mary E. Horn 11-19-1865 Mn
Elliff, A. O. to Nancy 'A. Elliff 12-17-1861 Mn
Elliner, W. H. to Caroline Lowall 10-22-1854 We
Ellington, Chasteen to Mary M. Mathis 9-17-1845 (9-18-1845) Ma
Ellington, Dempney to Sarah E. Davis 5-28-1861 (5-30-1861) Ma
Ellington, John to Elizabeth Williams 5-17-1838 (5-18-1838) Ma
Ellington, Newton to Mary Richards 10-9-1866 (10-11-1866) Ma
Ellington, Pascal A. to Sidney S. Hall 1-29-1860 G
Ellington, Phil to Mariah Neil 2-16-1867 F B
Ellington, Richard to Ruthy Watson 12-19-1835 (12-22-1835) G
Ellington, Winston to Emily Johnson 8-22-1868 (8-25-1868) Ma
Ellington, Winston to Mary Jane Young 6-6-1859 (6-8-1859) Ma
Ellington, Wm. R. to Rowena Williams 9-21-1869 (9-29-1869) Ma
Ellinor, Frederick C. to Mary Ann Moore 12-30-1838 Cr
Elliot, George to Martha Garret 5-26-1863 Sh
Elliot, Joseph to Margaret A. Wright 9-2-1849 Sh
Elliot, Thomas W. to Elizabeth Andrews 4-5-1871 Ma
Elliot, Wm. C. to Emma J. Williams 12-17-1870 (12-22-1870) F
Elliott, A. J. to Martha Deane 5-7-1857 Sh
Elliott, A. S. Pasco to Lucinda Snow 12-19-1844 F
Elliott, Andrew C. to Alphia Johnson 10-18-1828 (10-19-1828) Hr
Elliott, Andrew J. to Mary Clark 1-30-1847 (2-3-1847) G
Elliott, Bertrande E. to Lucretia Bolton 5-26-1838 Sh
Elliott, E. F. to Elizabeth (Mrs.) Joslin 3-24-1864 Sh
Elliott, Flanders to Martha Goodloe 3-6-1871 (3-11-1871) F B
Elliott, Francis to Sarah M. Alexander 1-2-1843 (1-5-1843) G
Elliott, Henry J. to Mary F. Webb 2-5-1868 Ma
Elliott, Henry to Valensa Smith 1-7-1840 Hn
Elliott, James E. to Julia L. Browning 12-26-1877 Hy
Elliott, John D. to Cornelia C. Turner 9-9-1856 (9-10-1856) Sh
Elliott, John W. to Elvira (Mrs.) Quinn 1-28-1864 Sh
Elliott, Lewis to Rachall Manley 1-8-1846 Sh
Elliott, R. T. to M. A. Rowlet 4-20-1856 We
Elliott, Riley to Adeline Williams 2-27-1845 (no return) We
Elliott, William H. to Frances E. Hill 8-19-1830 Sh
Elliott, William to Arabella F. A. Jenkins 10-1-1853 We
Elliott, William to Elizabeth Thompson 9-12-1850 (9-17-1850) Sh
Elliott, William to Hannah A. Miller 1-23-1855 Sh
Elliott, Wm. to Mary Jane Hanks 11-30-1864 (no return) Dy
Elliott, Zachariah to Louis Clark 4-3-1838 Hn
Ellis, A. J. to Harriet Mahan 8-17-1866 (no return) Hy
Ellis, A. J. to R. A. Pace 12-18-1876 (12-21-1876) Dy
Ellis, Alga to Cyntha C. Arnold 11-19-1873 L
Ellis, B. F. to Elizabeth Peterson 1-27-1863 L
Ellis, B. F. to Sallie F. Whitson 2-17-1886 L
Ellis, Ben to Eveline Meeler 2-14-1874 (2-15-1874) T
Ellis, Bob to Mary Bradford 9-26-1877 Hy
Ellis, C. A. to S. A. Atkinson 12-15-1884 (12-24-1884) L
Ellis, C. W. to Julia Coleman 1-27-1875 (1-28-1875) Dy
Ellis, David to Jane James 6-13-1854 Sh
Ellis, E. S. to M. E. Miller 1-17-1872 (1-18-1872) T
Ellis, Edward to Mattie Woods 4-17-1872 (4-18-1872) Dy
Ellis, F. G. to C. J. Nixon 3-2-1863 (3-4-1863) Dy
Ellis, F. G. to Eliza J. Mills 12-1-1866 (12-2-1866) Dy
Ellis, Frank W. to Mary L. Ellis 8-5-1880 L
Ellis, G. R. to Mary Ann (Mrs.) McGee 3-6-1868 G
Ellis, George to Martha Goodwinn 2-12-1855 (2-14-1855) Sh
Ellis, Griffin to Harriet Elliot 1-5-1866 (1-27-1866) T
Ellis, Hayden to Susan E. Pate 2-6-1856 We
Ellis, Henry J. to Martha F. King 8-27-1860 We
Ellis, Isaac to Lue Dickson 1-1-1873 O
Ellis, J. K. P. to Amanda Smith 3-20-1866 G
Ellis, J. N. to Rebecca A. Hamilton 8-26-1868 (8-27-1868) Dy
Ellis, J. S. to Mollie Legett 3-25-1872 L
Ellis, J. T. to M. L. Ellis 2-2-1874 (2-3-1874) Dy
Ellis, J. W. to M. J. Hamilton 2-15-1870 (2-16-1870) Dy
Ellis, JSames M. to Cornelia Nixon 5-12-1827 Hr
Ellis, James P. to Nancy Harrison 12-27-1869 (no return) L
Ellis, James R. to Louisa Jane Wootten 3-9-1853 O
Ellis, James to Euphobia Wade 11-16-1847 Hn
Ellis, James to Margaret Faris 5-19-1852 (no return) Hn
Ellis, James to Mary E. Clark 3-17-1851 L
Ellis, James to Sarah L. A. Jennings 9-30-1852 G

Ellis, John A. to Etna Wallace 11-28-1850 Sh
Ellis, John A. to Harriet G. Wallace 9-8-1855 (9-10-1855) Sh
Ellis, John O. to Auvenia Tennessee Coursey 5-7-1856 (5-8-1856) O
Ellis, John to Elizabeth Hastings 4-1-1855 Hn
Ellis, John to Julia Nolan 3-27-1857 Sh
Ellis, John to R. Griffin 5-7-1849 Sh
Ellis, Jonas to Harriet Athony 7-26-1867 (8-8-1867) L B
Ellis, Joseph F. to Emma E. Davis 3-16-1852 (no return) F
Ellis, Matthew Houston to Mary Elizabeth Lucas 6-25-1861 Sh
Ellis, Nathl. D. to Elizabeth Adams 12-3-1833 (12-5-1833) Hr
Ellis, P. S. to Lucy J. Beloat 10-6-1864 Sh
Ellis, R. D. to Nancy J. Hobs 6-3-1863 Sh
Ellis, Robert L. to Mary E. Cross 1-6-1849 Sh
Ellis, Robert M. to Sarah Ann Peterson 3-26-1862 (no return) Hy
Ellis, Robert to Ida Hitt 12-5-1883 (12-6-1883) L
Ellis, Robet M. to Mary Moore 7-17-1880 (7-18-1880) L
Ellis, Rufus to Julia A. Brewer 10-24-1858 Hn
Ellis, Rufus to Louisa E. Greer 12-18-1852 Hn
Ellis, S. to Martha J. Shoemaker 1-25-1871 (1-26-1871) F
Ellis, Theophilis to Sarah Alvianson? 2-21-1840 Hn
Ellis, Theophilus to Mary Lewis 5-24-1848 Hn
Ellis, Thomas T. to Martha E. Crouch 3-9-1842 Sh
Ellis, W. A. to Annie W. Lanier 12-19-1865 (no return) Cr
Ellis, W. A. to Mollie Crowder 9-13-1869 (9-15-1869) F
Ellis, W. H. to Isadora Blakemore 1-28-1868 G
Ellis, W. S. to Sarah E. Parker 5-4-1853 Hn
Ellis, W. W. to Dolly Ann King 11-4-1864 Be
Ellis, William to Louisa A. Varnell 7-17-1842 Sh
Ellis, William to Pheobe Bishop 5-30-1875 Hy
Ellis, William to Susan Hunter 12-21-1857 O
Ellis, William to Susan Hunter 3-25-1858 O
Ellison, Absalom to Sarah Lemons 3-6-1839 Hn
Ellison, John C. to Francis J. Riggs 3-19-1864 O
Ellison, John to Dorothy H. Teague 2-20-1843 (2-21-1843) Hr
Ellison, Timothy to Elizabeth Lackey 7-18-1839 Hr
Ellison, William to Caroline Beechamp 6-7-1842 (no return) Hn
Ellison, Zachariah to Martha Ann Kelley 11-3-1842 Sh
Elliss, James T. to M. J. Smith 4-25-1865 (_-26-1865) O
Ellsberry, B. L. to Mattie V Parnell 10-31-1870 (no return) Cr
Ellsberry, E. M. to L. W. Barlow 7-12-1864 (7-13-1864) Cr
Elmore, A. M. to E. J. (Mrs.) Gaines 12-27-1871 Hy
Elmore, Edward to Caroline Boswell 1-31-1843 Be
Elmore, F. M. to Elen B. Cole 1-15-1856 Be
Elmore, Henry C. to Nancy E. Hale 10-9-1863 Be
Elmore, Hugh to Mary Barrett 10-23-1863 (10-25-1863) Cr
Elmore, Hugh to Mary Barrett 10-23-1864 (no return) Cr
Elmore, J. W. to Georgeanna Robinson 11-27-1850 (11-28-1850) Hr
Elmore, Jas. T. to Lurany J. Brewer 12-20-1856 Be
Elmore, Jesse W. to Sarah Ann Lynch 10-10-1844 Be
Elmore, John B. (R.?) to Louisa F. Smith 3-13-1861 (3-14-1861) Sh
Elmore, John E. to Mary P. Cole 11-1-1861 Be
Elmore, John M. to Maryann Cottingham 3-9-1843 Be
Elmore, Newton C. to Nancy A. Rushing 12-20-1866 Be
Elmore, Richard Thomas to Martha Jane Brooks 12-9-1841 T
Elmore, Robert H. to Drucilla Ward 2-25-1863 Cr
Elmore, Robert H. to Drucilla Ward 2-25-1863 (2-27-1863) Cr
Elmore, Rufus to Mary M. Covington 12-23-1875 L
Elmore, Thomas G. to Ann Burns 4-28-1834 Hr
Elmore, W. T. to Pricilla A. White 7-16-1862 (no return) Hy
Elmore, William E. to Julia F. Cannon 7-18-1840 T
Elmore, Wm. P. to Elizabeth A. Lynch 2-12-1853 Be
Elmore, Wm. to Mary Hart 6-3-1863 Dy
Elms, Amos to Rebecca Johnson 7-9-1840 (no return) F
Elrod, J. G. to Nancy (Mrs.) Germany 11-5-1867 G
Elrod, J. J. to Martha Jones 8-4-1860 (no return) Hy
Elrod, James to Caroline D. Long 3-15-1855 Ma
Elrod, John to Martha J. O'Daniel 7-1-7-1862 G
Elrod, S. T. to Martha Robbins 9-15-1877 Hy
Elrod, S. T. to Mary Epps 6-9-1860 (no return) Hy
Elrod, Solomon to Sally Avry 1-26-1860 (no return) Hy
Elrod, Sterling to Julia Witherington 6-3-1869 G B
Elrod, W. P. to E. A. O'dannel 5-6-1870 G
Elrod, W. P. to Phoebe J. Hamilton 1-19-1866 G
Elsberry, E. M. to Nancy E. Scoby 9-7-1846 Cr
Elsberry, Isaac to Elizabeth Drake 6-28-1830 Ma
Elsberry, Isaac to Sally Delaney 1-31-1843 Cr
Elsten, Milton to Margaret Miller 2-15-1858 Ma
Elverton, Harrison A. to Martha Gidcomb 7-16-1873 L
Ely, Wesley to Elizabeth Anderson 11-1-1836 (11-2-1836) G
Elzan, James C.? to Clarinda E.? Cribbs 7-28-1860 (7-31-1860) Cr
Elzey, Andrew J. to Mary T. Colwell 9-4-1867 (9-5-1867) L
Elzey, William C. to Roda G. Reynolds 10-24-1867 L
Emberson, W. H. to Caroline Davis 9-6-1847 (9-9-1847) F
Embrey, Rubin A. to Jane Townsend 3-7-1835 Hr
Embrey, S. H. to Jessie B. Tanner 10-24-1874 (no return) Hy
Emerson, B. R. to Malinda Alexander 1-16-1862 Hn
Emerson, Balaam to Alice Huggins 10-25-1876 (no return) Dy

Emerson, D. B. to Nancy E. Alexander 12-13-1866 (no return) Hn
Emerson, Edwin S. to Julia A. Ryan 4-7-1851 Sh
Emerson, Elisha to Susan Ann Bush 1-2-1849 Hn
Emerson, J. H. to Nancy Puckett 9-24-1845 We
Emerson, J. W. to Mary Porter 12-21-1871 Hy
Emerson, John to Bettie New 12-2-1871 (12-3-1871) L
Emerson, Marian to Mary Stone 7-4-1867 (7-7-1867) Ma
Emery, John to Celyam Jones 6-5-1842 Hn
Emery, Michael to Elizabeth Williams 4-29-1855 Hn
Emery, Mikel to Elizabeth Snider 7-17-1847 (no return) Hn
Emery, S. E. to Sarah Ann Upchurch 12-28-1864 Hn
Emery, William to Mary Hart 2-28-1836 (no return) Hn
Emgel, Fred to Fredericka Rosa Ludenback 3-8-1858 (3-10-1858) Sh
Emison, Benjamin to Mary H. Permator 11-20-1854 (11-22-1854) Ma
Emison, R. to Elizabeth Bray 2-9-1856 Hn
Emison, William to Bedy Richard 12-27-1850 (1-2-1851) Ma
Emmerson, George W. to Tanizen E. Bush 12-29-1853 Hn
Emmerson, Jacob to Lanny Bush 1-4-1844 Hn
Emmerson, John S. to Susannah R. Hampton 4-25-1857 O
Emmett, Thomas to Mattie Tims 7-22-1871 Hy
Emmons, E. to Nancy Adams 1-28-1863 Mn
Emmons, J. H. to Rebecca G. Brown 1-12-1865 Mn
Emmons, Nickson to Rebecca Jones 12-31-1862 Mn
Emory, Jarvis to Eliza Ann Armstrong 6-26-1841 Hn
Enboe?, Thomas E. to Rebeca A. Spillings 9-6-1865 (9-8-1865) Cr
Enderson, C. C. to Emmiline E. Bathune 8-25-1867 Hy
Engele, Antone to Mary Gatz 11-4-1864 Sh
Engelhercher, Henry to Mary Dillinger 9-18-1855 Sh
Engell, F. to Crestine Lung 3-6-1860 (3-7-1860) Sh
England, A. J. to Sarah Roberson 6-13-1867 Be
England, B. A. to F. C. Saunders 12-2-1859 (12-6-1859) F
England, Daniel to Louisa Ann James 8-2-1847 (8-3-1847) G
England, J. C. to Martha Farrow 1-25-1856 Be
England, Joseph to Martha Walker 1-21-1828 G
England, Robt. to Mary Ash 5-29-1867 (no return) Hy
England, William F. to Elizabeth C. Walker 12-20-1848 Hn
England, William to Polly Walker 2-28-1827 G
Englihs, J. B. to Martha E. Prince 11-27-1858 T
English, Arche to Mary McCommack 9-23-1868 (9-24-1868) T
English, Barney to Winney Burke 8-8-1855 Sh
English, Charles B. to Jacka Ann Edwards 11-22-1858 (11-24-1858) Sh
English, James G. to Margaret J. Cowan 2-11-1850 (2-12-1850) G
English, James P. to Ann J. Willis 10-?-1863 O
English, James to Nancy Chilcutt 7-28-1844 Hn
English, John A. to Parthena E. Gordon 9-5-1833 Sh
English, Richard W. to Bridgett Burke 12-1-1845 Sh
English, Stephen to Drucilla R. Tredwell 1-9-1841 Sh
English, Thomas C. to Delia L. Potter 2-15-1853 (3-1-1853) Sh
English, William to Margaret Gorman 4-4-1853 Sh
English, William to Mary J. Compton 7-8-1857 Hn
Enis, Saml. to Cathanne(Catharine) Gray 2-18-1858 Hr
Enleo, Abraham to Sarah Pate 7-12-1836 (1-12-1836?) O
Enloe, Abraham B. to M. E. Hutchinson 5-1-1856 O
Enloe, Benj. B. to Nancy Blairs 9-27-1840 Cr
Enloe, Samuel to Susan Burrow 11-2-1868 (11-8-1868) Cr
Enlow, Joel S. to Mary Winters 4-23-1825 O
Enlow, John C. to Mary E. Hipps 9-17-1846 L
Ennis, G. R. to Parlee Littleton 8-7-1862 (8-11-1862) O
Ennis, Peter D. to Mary C. Thompson 2-8-1871 (2-9-1871) T
Enoch, Henry to Eliza Jones 7-18-1868 (7-19-1868) Dy
Enoch, W. S. to Rachel E. S. Graves 7-31-1867 (8-1-1867) Dy
Enochs, Edmond to Angeline Wynne 8-19-1870 (no return) Dy
Enochs, F. A. to Catharine R. Scott 8-30-1869 (9-16-1869) T
Enochs, G. F. to Sarah Read 9-28-1848 (no return) Cr
Enochs, G. V. to Elizabeth Reed 9-11-1865 (9-12-1865) Cr
Enochs, G. V. to Winny Read 12-28-1869 (12-30-1869) Cr
Enochs, Isaac S. to Susan A. Moore 8-2-1854 Cr
Enochs, Isaac to Susan Kirk 11-25-1851 (no return) Cr
Enochs, J. W. to Eliza A. Fuller 2-20-1861 Dy
Enochs, M. P. to Hellen Vaughan 9-22-1874 Dy
Enochs, Saml. to Jennie Bell 12-27-1871 (12-28-1871) Dy
Enochs, Samuel to Lucinda Ledsinger 3-20-1873 Dy
Enochs, Washington C. to Pairlee Patton 10-9-1856 Cr
Enochs, Wm. to Sarah Brown 11-22-1855 Cr
Enocks, R. N. to M. N. Wright 12-17-1872 Cr
Enquehart?, Charles to Pherobe Rochell 12-28-1848 Hn
Enscow, Jas. C. to Mary Ann Fedrick 4-27-1863 L
Ensley, R. G. to Amanda Starnes 10-23-1869 (10-24-1869) T
Enwright, Jeremiah to Johanna Mayher 7-21-1860 (7-22-1860) Sh
Eperson, R. F. to O. C. Farmer 10-24-1868 (10-25-1868) T
Epley, A. J. to Amanda Brown 1-6-1868 G
Epley, Solomon to Christine Owens 7-23-1865 G
Epperson, Benj. F. to Martha W. Dumanet 11-13-1861 (11-17-1861) Ma
Epperson, Issac A. to Leticia Shelton 6-6-1843 Sh
Epperson, Jos. to Ara Powell 12-17-1868 Hy
Epperson, Richard Morning to Julia C. Jackson 5-27-1843 (5-30-1843) T
Epperson, Samuel to Elizabeth H. Hill 11-18-1844 Ma

Eppinger, Louis to Margaretha Wittman 4-25-1861 Ma
Epps, H. L. to Helen Eagan 11-1-1869 (11-2-1869) F
Epps, J. P. to Nancy E. Crooms 1-25-1866 Hy
Epps, Spencer to Nancy Marsh 1-4-1848 (1-5-1848) Ma
Epps, William to Elizabeth R. James 11-25-1848 Sh
Erbridge, Jas. R. to E. E. Parrish 12-9-1852 We
Erck, Charles to Amelia Longbein 3-2-1858 Sh
Erickson, Francis to Tempe. S. Bryant 1-28-1851 F
Erman, H. S. to Louisa Livingston 9-3-1862 Sh
Erman, J. B. to Mary Jane Vernon 5-1-1879 (5-4-1879) L
Error, Turner to Margaret Mason 8-30-1867 (8-31-1867) F B
Erskine, Alexander to Augusta White 12-12-1861 Sh
Erskine, John to Margarett McDermott 2-11-1861 Sh
Ervel, John to Ann M. Davis 7-1-1865 (7-2-1865) O
Erven, William C. to Margarett Eveline Mills 2-6-1847 (2-7-1847) Hr
Ervin, Albert to Mary Sangster 6-13-1867 Hy
Ervin, George to Mary E. Hogan 9-28-1848 (9-29-1848) F
Ervin, Joe to Winny Pender 4-7-1875 Hy
Ervin, Richard to Mollie Lake 1-3-1874 (1-4-1874) L B
Ervin, Robert to Mary A. E. Price 2-5-1848 (2-10-1840) G
Ervin, Theophilus to Jane Dillard 1-22-1861 Hr
Ervin, William C. to Ann T. L. Bell 7-12-1855 (7-15-1855) Hr
Ervin, William to Lucinda Burleson 7-23-1835 Hr
Ervin, William to Narcissa Wilbourne 12-16-1833 (12-17-1833) G
Ervin, Wm. C. to Catharine W. Parker 5-19-1841 Hr
Ervine, Henry to Mary J. Griffin 11-10-1859 O
Ervine, Mathew to Nancy Hargis 10-22-1830 Sh
Ervins, Prince to Dosia Alexander 11-12-1868 (no return) Hy
Erwin (Ervin), Robert to Elizabeth Haley 9-23-1853 (9-25-1853) O
Erwin, Albert P. to Anna Harrison 12-16-1861 Sh
Erwin, Alexander P. to Elizabeth A. Moody 1-9-1858 Hn
Erwin, George to Margarett Campell 2-5-1849 (2-26-1849) O
Erwin, Hiram to Elizabeth Jones 2-8-1836 (or 2-6-1836) Sh
Erwin, J. D. to Louisa Brown 6-29-1863 Mn
Erwin, John D. to Susan Land 9-29-1847 (9-30-1847) T
Erwin, John P. to Nancy Wilson 12-24-1866 (12-25-1866) T
Erwin, Lafayett to Rebecca A. Littlejohn 2-27-1864 Mn
Erwin, R. P. to R. T. Bowden 6-8-1874 T
Erwin, Robert M. to Nancy Caroline Moore 9-12-1867 (no return) L
Erwin, Robert P. to Mildred C. Bowden 9-2-1867 (9-5-1867) T
Erwin, T. A. to Mary E. Moody 5-6-1866 Hn
Erwin, Tandy W. to Aurelia J. Rice 12-12-1860 Sh
Erwin, Troy B. to Lucinda Wardlowe 12-14-1862 Mn
Erwin, William G. to E. J. Compton 11-11-1846 Hn
Erwin, William T. to Elizabeth M. Read 11-25-1869 T
Erwin, William to Narcissa Wilborn 10-15-1831 (10-18-1831) G
Erwin, Wm. D. to Julia Densford 6-4-1866 (6-12-1866) T
Erwood, J. W. to L. A. Anderson 5-25-1869 (no return) Hy
Erwood, W. S. to M. E. Proctor 1-8-1872 (1-9-1872) T
Eschew, Elisha to Arbella Ramsey 10-5-1863 G
Escue, I. M. to L. J. Humphreys 12-15-1878 Hy
Escue, William to Matilda Fennell 2-9-1873 Hy
Escue, Wm. A. to Texanna F. Moore 12-28-1876 Hy
Esery, Joab to Elizabeth McCloud 5-11-1830 O
Eses, Joseph to Clady L. Toleson 12-10-1845 Cr
Eskew(Askew?), Nathan Berry to Mary Brown 3-6-1849 Hr
Eskew, Alford to Orphy Dority(Daugherty?) 3-9-1846 (3-11-1846) Hr
Eskew, D. J. to Julits E. Lives? 1-31-1857 (no return) Cr
Eskew, Hance S. to Martha C. Fish 12-?-1861 (12-22-1861) Cr
Eskew, J. M. to A. J. Dildy 11-1-1870 Cr
Eskew, J. W. to M. J. Larance 11-15-1871 (11-16-1871) Cr
Eskew, Jesse to Sarah Kennon 12-2-1850 (no return) Cr
Eskew, John to Elizabeth Eskew 11-10-1844 Cr
Eskew, John to Mary J. Robinson 7-26-1856 Cr
Eskew, Samuel to Martha Cannon 11-7-1844 Cr
Eskew, Thomas to M. E. Collins 12-6-1858 (no return) Cr
Eskew, William to Polly Eskew 4-7-1873 (8-8-1873) O
Eskew?, Enoch to Sarah Ann Crawford 4-22-1847 (4-18?-1847) Hr
Eskridge, Ben N. to Mary Payne 9-19-1858 We
Eskridge, Benjamin to Catharine Francis 8-9-1863 We
Eskridge, Samuel J. to Laura A. Thompson 2-26-1862 We
Eskridge, Thos. to Penelolpe Smith 4-7-1849 F
Eskridge, Will to Charlotte McClain 5-3-1857 We
Eskue?, Enoch to Mary Matilda Ross 7-29-1841 Hr
Espey, F. C. to May Tinsley 1-20-1875 (1-22-1875) Dy
Espy, J. T. to Rhody J. Pinkston 7-24-1865 Dy
Espy, R. R. to Hilly (Mrs.) Brandon 9-23-1863 (no return) Dy
Espy, Robert G. to Catherine Ward 11-18-1846 (11-19-1846) L
Espy, Robert to Mary E. Butler 2-28-1868 Hy
Espy, Samuel to Mariah Harris 2-25-1875 (2-26-1875) L B
Esry, Isaac to Nancy King 3-8-1851 (4-7-1851) O
Estes, A. C. to Nora P. Mann 11-6-1872 Hy
Estes, A. F. to Virginia Algee 9-29-1868 (10-1-1868) Cr
Estes, A. J. to M. A. Johnson 9-24-1870 (9-26-1870) O
Estes, Adam to Doney Hazel 4-18-1883 (4-18-1883) L
Estes, Adam to Lou King 12-23-1869 (no return) L
Estes, Albert M. to Arabella Cates 10-19-1869 Ma

Estes, Alx. to Harriet Cage 5-26-1870 Hy
Estes, Andrew J. to Julian Lambert 1-30-1850 (1-31-1850) Hr
Estes, Asa to Minerva Long 11-29-1827 Hr
Estes, Bedford M. to Sarah Jane Johnston 4-24-1854 (5-4-1854) Ma
Estes, Bob to Amy Dupree 8-13-1867 (no return) Hy
Estes, Bob to Harriet Parks 1-27-1875 L B
Estes, Daniel to Millie Thornton 12-15-1877 Hy
Estes, Elbridge to Sallie Dennie 12-18-1885 (12-20-1885) L
Estes, Erwin to Sarah Waller 9-9-1861 Hr
Estes, F. M. to S. F. Phillips 10-13-1875 Dy
Estes, Green to Cora Claiborne 12-17-1867 Hy
Estes, Harrison to Mollie Wardlaw 9-26-1885 (9-30-1885) L
Estes, Henry W. to Rosa Ann Duet 7-6-1847 Hr
Estes, Henry to Caroline Wilson (not executed) Hy
Estes, J. A. to M. C. Mathis 9-3-1860 G
Estes, J. H. to Julia Ingram 1-18-1869 G
Estes, Jacob to Francis Currie 6-29-1878 (no return) Hy
Estes, Jesse to J. E. Bass 12-28-1869 Hy
Estes, Joel H. to Martha H. Mann 2-24-1862 (no return) Hy
Estes, John to Aliry Kilzer 7-3-1865 G
Estes, John to Eliza Minor 7-15-1876 Hy
Estes, John to Martha Ellen Cates 1-6-1882 (1-10-1882) L
Estes, Joshua to Martha Carley 6-8-1838 (6-10-1838) Hr
Estes, Joshua to Martha Wood 3-25-1843 (3-26-1843) Hr
Estes, Louis P. to Lilly Moore 10-30-1875 (no return) Hy
Estes, M. C. to Lucinda Hamilton 12-24-1843 Hn
Estes, Major to Rhoda Wood 10-23-1845 Hr
Estes, Moreau P. to Catharin Sherrod 11-27-1867 T
Estes, Nimrod to Charlotte Walker 6-1-1841 (1-3-1842) Ma
Estes, P. N. to Nancy Sweeton 10-3-1861 Hr
Estes, Reubin to Martha J. Lambert 1-6-1846 (1-6-1846) Hr
Estes, Richard to Telia Fitzpatrick 12-9-1878 (12-30-1878) L
Estes, Steven to Caroline Reeves 1-5-1867 (no return) Hy
Estes, Thomas to Bettie Nelson 2-17-1869 (2-18-1869) L
Estes, Thos.H. to Emma Powell 10-20-1869 Hy
Estes, W. T. to M. E. Mathis 9-29-1856 G
Estes, Washington to Emma Currie 5-11-1871 Hy
Estes, Wesley to Lidia A. Deaton 7-24-1865 Mn
Estes, William A. to Cintha W. Bridges 1-23-1839 (1-24-1839) G
Estes, Wm. to Bell Cooper 3-8-1870 (no return) Hy
Estes, Wm. to Louisa Thompson 1-21-1870 (no return) Hy
Estill, Milton to Louisa Boulton 4-12-1833 Sh
Estill, Thomas S. to Cynthia Underwood 8-22-1824 Sh
Estis, J. A. to Mary Taylor 12-22-1868 G
Estis, R. S. to Rosa A. Estis 7-21-1868 G
Estis, York to Jane Pickett 12-22-1870 Hy
Estress, John W. to Marinda M. Day 11-29-1866 Hn
Estridge, B. G. to Jane Reeves 5-6-1848 O
Estridge, B. G. to Jane Reeves 5-6-1848 (5-7-1848) O
Estridge, Carter to Agga Snider 9-6-1837 (9-7-1837) O
Estridge, Jerry to Junetta Hamer 4-30-1868 (5-10-1868) F B
Estridge, Saml. J. to H. M. Thompson 6-14-1852 We
Estus, John to Ursley Malone 1-15-1845 Be
Estus, M. H. to Ann Estus 6-5-1872 L B
Estus, T. J. to Virginia Lawson 4-23-1875 L
Etchison, W. R. to Dovey Ennis 10-3-1853 (10-6-1853) G
Etharage, James A. to Jane Strawbridge 12-26-1844 Hn
Etherage, J. to Mary Perry 1-31-1857 (no return) Hn
Etherage, James T. to Martha A. Perry 1-25-1851 (no return) Hn
Etherage, William to Lucy Willaford 10-14-1849 Hn
Etherby (Etherley?), Henry O. to Matilda Donaldson 2-27-1851 (2-26?-1851) Sh
Etheridge, A. C. to Lucy J. Williams 10-15-1867 Hy
Etheridge, Emerson to Fanny A. Bell 10-17-1849 We
Etheridge, Gordius F. to Sarah Christian 4-27-1847 Sh
Etheridge, J. H. to W. C. Sweaney 10-8-1863 O
Etheridge, J. H. to W. C. Sweaney 10-8-1863 (no return) Cr
Etheridge, John C. to Mattie Britt 12-3-1873 (no return) Hy
Etheridge, John to Mary West 6-1-1841 (6-3-1841) G
Etheridge, John to Rachael Ann Hall 12-11-1848 G
Etheridge, Joseph J. to Centha Vickers 8-24-1837 G
Etheridge, Thomas J. to Sarah M. Coleman 6-6-1859 Hn
Etheridge, Thomas to Lucretia Briley 4-21-1853 Sh
Etheridge, Tom H. to Elizabeth A. C. Rogers 12-25-1843 We
Etheridge, Tony to Molly Robinson 3-21-1874 Hn
Etheridge, W. F. to G. M. Williams 1-4-1866 Hn
Etheridge, Willis to Justin T. Jenkins 10-24-1844 We
Etherly, Joseph to Mary L. Rose 4-15-1868 (4-18-1868) T
Ethridge, Crockett to Eliza Pearce 12-26-1852 Hn
Ethridge, J. H. to W. C. Serconas 10-8-1864 Cr
Ethridge, James P. to S. A. Williams 4-26-1873 (4-27-1873) Dy
Ethridge, Jerrod J. to Mary A. Smith 10-1-1847 (10-3-1847) Hn
Ethridge, Joel to Nancy McCuiston 2-1-1840 (no return) Hn
Ethridge, Mark to Mary J. E. Beny 8-9-1856 (8-14-1856) G
Ethridge, T. J. to Margaret Webb 12-13-1866 Hn
Ethridge, William F. to Mary A. Carter 7-18-1863 (no return) Hn
Ethridge, Willis to Lucy Braswell 12-19-1845 Sh
Etta, John to Annie Palmer 12-23-1874 Hy

Etter, Jacob to Lizzie Sutton 12-18-1872 Hy
Eubanks, Henry to C. Harris 7-11-1845 Cr
Eubanks, Henry to Ellen Harris 6-24-1852 Cr
Eubanks, J. T. to Mary E. McGowan 12-20-1858 (12-24-1858) Hr
Eubanks, R. B. to S. J. Boswell 3-10-1870 Cr
Eudaily, M. W. to Laura E. Simmons 6-30-1869 (no return) Dy
Eudaily, William to Louisa Colvin 2-10-1868 (no return) Dy
Eudaley, James T. to Mary B. Mays 11-19-1862 Dy
Eudaly, Clement to Harrit Eudaly 4-1-1844 (4-2-1844) G
Eudaly, Jo to Jane Beaumont 1-5-1867 Dy
Evans, Absolam Hendricks to Eliza Janie Dawson 10-8-1853 (10-9-1853) T
Evans, Absolum H. to Martha Kelley 6-30-1847 (7-1-1847) T
Evans, Ambrose L. to Callie Webb 12-10-1867 L
Evans, Anderson to Elizabeth A. Rust 1-6-1861 We
Evans, B. F. to S. E. Ward 1-4-1868 O
Evans, Benjamin W. to M. D. C. Whyte 3-19-1839 (3-21-1839) F
Evans, Benjamin to Mary Burford 12-31-1842 (1-3-1843) O
Evans, Benjamin to Sarah Caldwell 7-2-1860 (7-8-1860) O
Evans, Charles E. to Alice Bond 1-17-1878 L
Evans, Charles to Mary Corbitt 11-13-1856 Be
Evans, Daniel to Elizabeth Andrews 9-28-1852 (9-30-1852) G
Evans, David C. to Lucanda E. Tatum 10-27-1850 (10-31-1850) G
Evans, David to Caroline Ware 9-22-1866 Hy
Evans, David to Elizabeth Donnell 2-6-1843 (2-9-1843) Hr
Evans, David to Malinda Nelson 12-14-1839 (12-24-1839) F
Evans, David to Mary Ann Elkins 12-24-1861 (12-26-1861) Hr
Evans, Dudley to Mary A. Prewett 4-16-1845 Cr
Evans, E. L. to Evaline H. Degraffenreid 10-6-1841 (no return) F
Evans, E. T. to Clorina Quillen 10-27-1868 Be
Evans, Edward F. to Mary E. Quillin 11-4-1856 Be
Evans, Eli F. to Rebecca F. Jones 2-8-1870 (no return) Hy
Evans, Ellis to Sely Culpepper 7-30-1863 Be
Evans, Ely to Mary A. Joslin 7-17-1833 (7-18-1833) G
Evans, Ephraim to Lucy Westmoreland 2-1-1871 (2-6-1871) F B
Evans, G. C. to Virginia A. Cross 2-7-1857 (2-12-1857) Hr
Evans, George to Eliza Littleton 4-17-1840 O
Evans, George to Mary McIntyre 9-6-1841 T
Evans, George to Tennessee Baskins 1-4-1870 (1-6-1870) T
Evans, H. C. to Barbara Cook (Kisk) 4-9-1848 Sh
Evans, H. L. to Charity A. Evans 7-26-1859 (7-1859) O
Evans, Hanibell to Silvy Cotter 11-20-1868 Hy
Evans, Henry to Martha Scallions 8-16-1867 (9-18-1867) Dy
Evans, Henry to Mary Deason? 12-4-1839 Hr
Evans, Henry to Senia Wright 2-25-1868 (no return) Dy
Evans, Howel to Mariah Wilson 1-4-1876 (no return) Hy
Evans, Isaac D. to Martha R. Cargit 10-20-1849 (no return) F
Evans, J. B. to E. B. Hill 3-11-1868 G
Evans, J. B. to Terese Moore 3-15-1864 (3-17-1864) Sh
Evans, J. D. to Amanda E. Smith 1-18-1870 (no return) Hy
Evans, J. H. D. to Annie C. A. (Mrs.) Peirce 9-24-1870 (9-25-1870) Ma
Evans, J. H. to Anna Barfield 1-4-1882 L
Evans, J. H. to Elizabeth H. Pickens 10-9-1862 Mn
Evans, J. N. to N. J. Davis 3-10-1863 (3-12-1863) Dy
Evans, J. S. to Ellen Stansberry 9-18-1855 (no return) F
Evans, J. W. to Dillie Hatch 4-23-1872 (no return) Cr
Evans, J. W. to Nancy Brigens 1-10-1871 Cr
Evans, J. to Susan Phifer 9-20-1864 Be
Evans, James A. to Elizabeth Corbitt 1-23-1851 Be
Evans, James S. to Cornelia F. Trotter 1-28-1851 (1-29-1851) F
Evans, James to E. Hunter 8-12-1871 (no return) Hy
Evans, James to E. Lowden 5-4-1869 G
Evans, James to Eliza Dickson 2-7-1872 (2-8-1872) O
Evans, James to Lavinia Barber 1-15-1868 Hy
Evans, James to Matilda Ward 1-6-1869 Dy
Evans, Jeremiah to Matilda Simpson 11-27-1852 (11-30-1852) L
Evans, Jerry to Angeline Johnson 8-19-1872 (8-5-1873) T
Evans, Jerry to Kate Brown 12-31-1885 L
Evans, Joel T. to Ann L. Robinson 11-6-1856 G
Evans, Joel T. to Lou A. McDonal 12-9-1867 (12-10-1867) Ma
Evans, John E. to Mary E. Wedington 3-31-1851 O
Evans, John J. to Nancy F. Jackson 12-31-1867 Ma
Evans, John L. to L. J. Cargil 12-28-1849 (no return) F
Evans, John S. to Dorritt Lloyd 12-3-1881 (12-7-1881) L
Evans, John to Frances J. Hewey 8-29-1866 (9-2-1866) Cr
Evans, John to Lidia Birdwell 2-21-1853 Cr
Evans, John to Lydia Simms 8-15-1869 G
Evans, John to Mariah G. Swink 7-16-1839 Ma
Evans, John to Rebecca Puckett 4-1-1841 G
Evans, John to Rose Payne 12-21-1867 (12-26-1867) T
Evans, John to Tabitha Ritchie 6-26-1867 F
Evans, Joseph F. to Narcissa P. Smoot 11-23-1853 Cr
Evans, Joseph H. to Sarah T. Duncan 4-21-1868 (4-23-1868) Dy
Evans, Joseph S. to Nancy Baldridge 5-15-1847 (no return) F
Evans, Josiah A. to Mary Elizabeth Anderson 3-26-1854 Be
Evans, L. H. to Sarah Reese 9-1-1874 (9-2-1874) Dy
Evans, L. to Susan E. Barker 10-17-1866 G
Evans, Levi to Martha A. Williams 7-14-1858 G
Evans, Levi to Martha Loller 9-15-1859 G
Evans, Levy to Elizabeth Elder? 9-23-1867 L
Evans, Lewis G. to Jantha Virginia Griffin 5-20-1859 Sh
Evans, Nathan to Rebecca Johnson 12-23-1856 G
Evans, Nelson to Sarah E. Gately 1-3-1870 Cr
Evans, Peter W. to M. A. (Mrs.) Evans 10-4-1860 Sh
Evans, Plummer to Frances Reeves 1-21-1869 F B
Evans, R. J. to Sarah Hawes 2-26-1866 (no return) Hn
Evans, R. L. to Elizabeth P. Allen? 10-13-1847 (11-12-1847) F
Evans, R. R. to Margaret Wilson 2-13-1861 (2-15-1861) Sh
Evans, Robert to Mary Elizabeth Johnston 9-28-1867 Ma
Evans, Sam to Puss Mitchell 12-25-1868 (12-26-1868) F B
Evans, Serel to Minerva Wilson 8-31-1833 (?-19-183-) Hr
Evans, Sidney to Eugenia Lee 12-11-1873 (no return) Hy
Evans, Silas to Ann Brown 2-10-1869 (2-11-1869) O
Evans, Squire to Mary Green 2-11-1870 G
Evans, Sugars T. to Mary H. Willard 12-20-1848 (12-28-1848) L
Evans, T. J. to M. A. Norvel 2-1-1866 Hy
Evans, T. N. to Sarah L. Salisberry 9-28-1868 (10-1-1868) L
Evans, T. W. to C. F. Carroll 8-24-1869 Dy
Evans, Thomas S. to Marthaann Neal 1-30-1841 (2-18-1841) F
Evans, Thos. H. to Ann Benson 4-25-1822 Sh
Evans, W. H. to Mary A. Jackson 3-20-1856 Sh
Evans, W. R. to Elizabeth Stevens 12-27-1865 (12-28-1865) T
Evans, W. T. to Sarah Carroll 12-27-1869 (12-29-1869) Dy
Evans, W. to Carilla E. Lowden 2-15-1867 G
Evans, Wade H. to D. A. Lloyd 4-13-1859 L
Evans, Wallace to Harriet F. Raybern 8-6-1864 (no return) Dy
Evans, Wesley to Julia E. Trimble 5-17-1861 O
Evans, William to Maria Mary Lewis 2-3-1846 (2-5-1846) F
Evans, Willis W. to Elizabeth Medlin 3-19-1845 (3-23-1845) Ma
Evans, Wm. H. to C. A. Clark 11-9-1871 Hy
Evans, Wm. H. to Carolin M. Forbbs 4-28-1846 F
Evans, Wm. H. to Mary Davis 10-4-1859 (10-6-1859) Hr
Evans, Wm. Henry to Anna Minger 2-3-1878 Hy
Evans, Wm. J. to Sarah H. Vaughn 5-15-1851 Sh
Evens, Thomas to Nancy A. Marsh 9-13-1848 (9-14-1848) Hr
Evens, Thos. P. to Narcissa D. Pierce 9-16-1848 (no return) Cr
Evens, William Henry to Susan Young 2-11-1851 (2-13-1851) Hr
Everett, Benjamin F. to Mary J. Jetton 5-5-1852 (5-6-1852) G
Everett, E. G. to M. S. Bucy 12-10-1846 We
Everett, Isham to Harriet Wingo 4-28-1870 (5-1-1871?) Cr
Everett, J. E. to E. C. Matheny 4-26-1867 (5-2-1868?) Cr
Everett, J. K. to Margaret Morgan 1-1-1867 (not executed?) Cr
Everett, James A. K. M. to Margaret Williams 11-13-1860 Hr
Everett, Thomas to Molly Henderson 12-24-1869 (12-25-1869) Cr
Everett, William to Emaly Caroline 1-14-1851 (1-16-1851) O
Everett, William to Emily Caroline Taylor 1-14-1851 (1-16-1851) O
Everett, Wm. B. to S. A. Everett 12-7-1860 Cr
Everett?, William B. to Sarah A. Everitt 12-7-1860 (12-13-1860) Cr
Everight, Thomas E. to Ann Hubbs 5-4-1846 (5-20-1846) O
Everman, Lewis to Margaret B. E. Green 3-27-1849 (no return) Cr
Everson, Arnold B. to Mary Hester 2-22-1848 Sh
Evert, C. J. to Caroline Pate 12-28-1855 (no return) Cr
Evert, Joshua to Mary Farr 8-9-1849 O
Everton, John to Nelly Sutton 2-1-1863 Mn
Evetts, James to Margaret Hayes 12-23-1846 Sh
Evetts, John H. to Margaret Stocks 4-18-1837 Sh
Evetts, Thomas F. to Mary Jane Cole 10-19-1834 Sh
Evins, Abner A. to Hester A. Patterson 2-15-1848 G
Evins, John to Mary Tally 7-27-1844 (7-29-1844) G *
Evins, Ned to Duencia Taylor 4-28-1870 (5-20-1870) L
Evritt, F. W. to Martha F. Myers no date (with 12-1861) T
Ewart, James to Sarah E. Starnes 6-30-1857 T
Ewell, Harry to Julia Ewell 5-12-1870 (5-15-1870) F B
Ewell, John to Amanda Crawford 1-2-1854 (1-7-1854) T
Ewell, Joseph D. to Mattie J. Flemming 1-8-1868 Ma
Ewell, P. D. to Bella C. Falls 11-12-1863 (11-17-1863) F
Ewell, P. D. to Mollie A. Chaffin 8-5-1867 F
Ewell, R. H. D. to ElizabethS. Sheppard 11-2-1843 Hr
Ewell, Silas to Lou Branscomb 2-24-1868 (2-29-1868) F B
Ewell, Thomas W. to Lundy Andrews 10-12-1853 (10-18-1853) Ma
Ewell, Thos. A. to Estell Turner 2-9-1870 (2-10-1870) F B
Ewell, Wm. B. to Margaret M. Brown 4-2-1855 Ma
Ewing (McEwing?), Judson to Catherine Bohean 1-20-1864 (1-21-1864) Sh
Ewing, A. P. to Jane Latham 10-31-1881 (11-2-1881) L
Ewing, Newton A. to Nancy N. Lorant 12-15-1829 Hr
Ewing, Samuel to Mary (Mrs.) Clark 3-24-1855 (3-25-1855) Sh
Ewing, Samuel to Sarah Gage 12-3-1852 (12-4-1851?) Sh
Ewing, Tom to Lizzie Wills 12-23-1866 (12-29-1865?) F B
Ewing, William M. to Elizabeth Caroline Currie 4-29-1857 Ma
Ewing, William to Judy Gwynn 12-23-1866 (12-29-1865?) F B
Ewing, Zebina C. to Maria Tittleton 3-18-1850 (3-?-1850) Ma
Exum, E. G. to L. Henderson 11-6-1860 F
Exum, Franklin to Parthena J. Mayfield 12-26-1859 G
Exum, John to Jane Young 4-15-1840 (4-16-1840) F
Exum, Joseph W. to Julia A. Wilson 9-18-1867 (9-19-1867) Ma

Exum, Washington T. to Margaret C. Watson 12-11-1854 (12-13-1854) Ma
Exum, Wm. C. to M. J. Exum 9-17-1859 (9-20-1859) F
Eykes, Martin to Margaret Wendell 9-18-1861 Sh
Eyrich, George C. to Virginia P. Frain 12-30-1864 Sh
Ezell, B. to Addie Williamson 9-21-1870 (9-22-1870) Cr
Ezell, Benj. to Susan Tirill 2-2-1858 Cr
Ezell, Fielding A. to Martha C. Hall 7-28-1859 We
Ezell, J. H. to Mary E. Denning 6-24-1865 (no return) Hn
Ezell, James H. to Rebecca Elizabeth Key 12-28-1858 Ma
Ezell, James M. to Martha Whitehorn 11-7-1847 (no return) Cr
Ezell, Robert G. to S. J. McDonald 3-16-1858 Cr
Ezell, S. W. to Vianna E. Dent 6-29-1859 We
Ezell, Thos. to Mary Johnson 10-24-1855 Cr
Ezell, Uriah M. to Sarah E. Chipman 6-28-1865 (6-29-1865) O
Ezell, W. I. to M. A. H. Stribbling 5-27-1858 Cr
Ezell, Wm. to Fannie Freeman 5-1-1862 G
Ezell, Zachius to Peggy Smith no date (with Dec 1837) O
Ezen (Izen), J. to Sarah Fenster (Feuster?) 10-18-1864 Sh
Ezzell, B. G. to Elizabeth J. Allen 5-12-1847 Hn
Ezzell, B. G. to Ella Loving 5-4-1872 (5-5-1872) Cr
Ezzell, D. S. to Lenora M. Roach 12-31-1872 (1-1-1873) Cr
Ezzell, J. to Elizabeth E. White 7-17-1860 (no return) Cr
Ezzell, Mason to Sophiah L. Milner 7-27-1854 We
Ezzell, Parham to Margaret Barr 3-20-1838 (no return) Hn
Ezzell, Plase to Mary Pattison 5-19-1873 (5-29-1873) Cr B
Ezzell, Robert G. to Frances M. Elam 6-28-1855 We

Faby, Green to Sarah Tucker 5-8-1831 Sh
Facen, Richmund to Ann Coleman 7-8-1875 L
Fackler, C. W. to Hattie A. Watkins 1-15-1859 Hr
Fackler, Calvin M. to Anna (Amona?) S. Kirk 1-10-1853 (1-12-1853) Sh
Fadly, John M. to Jane McWilliams 10-17-1847 Sh
Fagan, Charles to Mary Nolan 7-26-1863 (7-27-1863) Sh
Fagan, M. L. to Mollie Spaine 10-28-1867 Hn
Fagan, Thomas to Martha A. Wren 12-15-1868 G
Fagan, W. M. to Mary (Mrs.) Goddard 2-23-1863 Sh
Fain, C. B. S. to Gillee Derrinda Braden 12-1-1863 (12-2-1863) L
Fain, G. L. to M. A. Lauren 12-20-1855 Hn
Fain, Hiram to Sarah R. Pety 4-5-1842 F
Fain, J. D. R. to Melvina A. Stewart 8-8-1860 G
Fain, R. S. to Bettie Smith 1-17-1872 Dy
Fain, Thomas H. to Laura Fuller 3-19-1878 (3-29-1878) Dy
Fair, Edward to Mary Jane Fair 4-16-1849 (4-17-1849) G
Fair, William A. to Virginia Swift 1-7-1847 Hn
Fairbourn, James to Martha M. Phillips 4-2-1863 Sh
Faircloth, James to S. E. Hutchison 1-6-1867 G
Faires, W. J. to E. C. Pickard 4-28-1857 T
Fairless, D. H. to Elizabeth Varner 12-28-1865 G
Fairless, Norfleet to Mary A. Rooks 11-26-1840 Ma
Faison, Wm. to Temperance Crawford 2-2-1846 (2-5-1846) Hr
Falkenburg, L. to Sophia Heiman 12-16-1856 Sh
Falker, Elijah to Bettie A. Scott 2-13-1872 Cr
Falker, William to Mary F. Davidson 5-1-1880 (5-2-1880) L
Falkner, H. to Sarah Ann Bull 1-8-1868 (no return) Dy
Falkner, James W. to Hellen M. Hancock 2-25-1861 (2-26-1861) Sh
Falkner, John to Pamelia Gwin 11-30-1850 F
Falkner, William to Elizabeth McLeod 5-18-1869 (5-23-1869) L
Fall, Gilberth to Frances D. Menice? 11-26-1839 F
Fallin, James R. to Lucy A. Slaughter 1-18-1871 T
Fallin, John W. to Sallie Hill 1-7-1874 T
Fallon, Chas. W. to Sarah E. Tally 10-6-1840 T
Fallon, Patrick to Elizabeth Ford 4-26-1843 Sh
Falls, Frank G. to Bettie A. Evans 2-24-1871 (3-1-1871) F
Falls, Gilbreath to Laronia McKinney 2-8-1859 (2-9-1859) Sh
Falls, H. H. to Seragh Jane Scott 10-27-1852 (10-28-1852) Hr
Falls, John to Lucy F. Finch 5-13-1862 (5-14-1862) F
Falwell, H. C. to H. L. Williams 3-21-1859 Sh
Falwell, Samuel to T. T. (Z? Z?) Messick 9-27-1859 (9-28-1859) Sh
Fanasy, Richard to Hannora Ryne (Ryan?) 5-20-1852 Sh
Fannasey, Timothy to Johannah Hustigan 7-29-1862 (8-3-1862) Sh
Fanner, Patrick to Ann Oliver 12-29-1854 G
Fanon, John to Louisa Martin 1-5-1856 (1-10-1856) G
Fant, B. S. to Sarah T. Walker 4-25-1849 Sh
Fanville, Jno. F. to M. Callie Wilson 2-22-1869 Ma
Faquin, F. to L. Magermus 6-11-1864 Sh
Farabee, B. F. to Emma Blair 1-30-1861 (1-31-1861) Sh
Farabough, Thomas R. to Sarah Ward 12-16-1846 Hn
Faray?, Gideon to Jane Medley 2-11-1867 (2-12-1867) Cr
Fare, John C. to Mary Jane Box 12-6-1864 (12-25-1864) O
Farherne (Farberne?), James to Martha A. Philips 9-20-1863 Sh
Faribee, John R. to Carrie L. Marshall 12-24-1858 F
Farington, Wm. to Fanny Bond 8-17-1867 (no return) Hy
Faris, Anderson to Eliza C. Reaves 7-29-1840 (7-30?-1840) Hr
Faris, Ezekiel to Martha Moore 10-18-1841 Ma
Faris, Jas. McWherter to Martha V. Harris 2-4-1856 T
Faris, Jesse Thomas to Elvira Lake 10-23-1848 (10-24-1848) T
Faris, Moses B. to Nancy Savage 10-26-1842 (10-28-1842) Hr

Faris, Thomas H. to Nancy J. Davis 2-12-1863 (no return) Cr
Faris, Washington to Hariett McCarley 12-16-1850 (12-18-1850) F
Farley, J. B. to Nannie Fleming 12-7-1860 (12-18-1860) Sh
Farley, J. M. to Virginia Thorpe 12-29-1870 (no return) F
Farley, Joseph J. to Rebeca Tatum 11-20-1840 (11-26-1840) F
Farley, Sterling to Lucinda F. Stone 7-7-1847 F
Farley, Thomas to Martha Tatum 10-6-1843 (10-10-1843) F
Farley, William H. to Emily Miller 9-22-1842 Hn
Farley, William W. to Mary Jane Redd 4-17-1851 (4-20-1851) Hr
Farley, William to Julia Baw 12-15-1854 (no return) F
Farley, William to Manerva Ann Stone 10-4-1848 (no return) F
Farmer, A. J. to Tenny Hall 12-25-1867 Be
Farmer, Aleck to Sarah Norman 6-28-1868 G B
Farmer, Anderson C. to Mary A. Lawrence 1-4-1840 Hn
Farmer, B. A. to Elizabeteh Sanders 7-31-1870 G
Farmer, B. F. to Effa Brewer 6-5-1866 Be
Farmer, B. W. to Pheeba A. Montgomery 10-23-1855 We
Farmer, B. to Sarah J. Cox 5-13-1861 Hn
Farmer, Benj. F. to Emily J. Parrish 11-6-1865 Dy
Farmer, Colin M. to Sallie F. Etheridge 4-14-1856 Sh
Farmer, F. to Thursby Baskin 6-25-1829 (6-27-1829) O
Farmer, Frank to Angeline Coltart 5-22-1874 Hy
Farmer, Franklin M. to Elizabeth Dean 9-15-1860 (no return) Hy
Farmer, G. W. to Elizabeth Holland 12-13-1843 Be
Farmer, George W. to Canzada Hall 12-26-1861 Be
Farmer, George W. to Kate Neutzel 12-24-1862 Sh
Farmer, H. J. to M. J. Gills 10-1-1862 O
Farmer, H. M. to Ann J. Hesler 7-13-1849 (7-17-1849) F
Farmer, Harry (Henry) M. to Mary Ann Price 4-27-1871 F
Farmer, Henry K. to Amand L. Wiseman 9-21-1867 (9-24-1867) T
Farmer, Hiram to Anna Willingham 1-9-1844 We
Farmer, Hiram to Mary Morrell 5-18-1846 We
Farmer, Huy M. to Rebeca C. Lorrence 11-2-1840 (no return) F
Farmer, J. C. to M. E. Hall 1-21-1866 Be
Farmer, J. C. to S. E. Salisbury 11-6-1876 (11-8-1876) Dy
Farmer, J. S. to Mary J. Cross 10-16-1858 We
Farmer, J. to M. Davidson 3-11-1842 Be
Farmer, Jackson to Temperance Melton 2-18-1843 Be
Farmer, James K. to Elizabeth Ralph 7-30-1841 (8-3-1841) T
Farmer, James M. to Ellen Moore 9-7-1865 (no return) Hy
Farmer, Jesse to Jane Ballard 4-20-1867 Be
Farmer, John D. to Charlotte T. Melten (Mitten?) 1-4-1856 (no return) We
Farmer, John D. to Lucinda Frost 6-26-1856 We
Farmer, John H. to Martha Jane Mc_____ 11-27-1854 Be
Farmer, John H. to Sabra Ann Lusk 6-27-1862 (6-28-1862) L
Farmer, John L. to F. E. Thurman 12-5-1872 Hy
Farmer, John to Martha Melton 12-8-1867 Be
Farmer, John to Mary Glancy 12-26-1859 Sh
Farmer, L. to Sarah L. Whitfield 12-21-1860 (12-24-1860) Sh
Farmer, M. P. G. to Martha A. E. Farmer 2-17-1872 (2-18-1872) L
Farmer, R. P. to M. A. E. Palmer 11-24-1859 We
Farmer, S. L. to Virginia Teams 1-28-1864 Sh
Farmer, Samuel to Susan Watt 9-14-1846 Ma
Farmer, Squire to Edmonia Taylor 6-22-1875 (no return) Hy
Farmer, Thomas M. to Sarah J. Lovelace 11-11-1857 We
Farmer, Uel H. to Ann Butterworth 10-10-1839 F
Farmer, W. to Harriet Benson (Burrows?) 6-1-1851 Sh
Farmer, Wm. F. to C. F. Hurley 1-30-1871 (2-14-1871) F
Farmon, Grant to Caroline Winters 5-25-1832 Sh
Farned, Wm. M. to Tabitha A. Floyd 11-12-1857 (11-15-1857) Hr
Farnsworth, H. A. to Laura White 10-7-1856 O
Farnsworth, H. F. to C. M. Palmer 11-3-1843 Sh
Farr, James H. to Catsey Bramblet 9-21-1836 O
Farr, James H. to Martha Nichols 9-19-1844 O
Farr, John E. to Olive Hodges 10-31-1831 O
Farr, W. H. (Wm. C.) to Melissa A. Massey 9-7-1862 G
Farrar, Asa Thomas to Maranda F. House 6-27-1852 Be
Farrar, Geo. W. to Virginia E. Flippin 11-5-1866 (11-7-1866) F
Farrar, J. S. to R. Harris 1-21-1861 (1-23-1861) F
Farrel (Famel?), James to Teresa Hughes 4-22-1851 (4-24-1851) Sh
Farrell, Daniel S. to Malisa Hall 11-17-1851 (no return) F
Farrell, James to Sarah Warren 8-4-1866 (no return) F
Farrell, Joseph to Ann Campbell 4-16-1856 F
Farren, Edward to Bridget Burnes 6-3-1862 Sh
Farrer, J. T. to Martha S. Farrer 7-21-1851 (7-24-1851) F
Farrer, Madison to Elizabeth F. Crutchfield 8-3--1853 Be
Farrer, Thos. J. to Zany Ann Benson 12-14-1844 (12-19-1844) F
Farrier, J. M. to M. A. McCollum 2-10-1860 (2-12-1860) O
Farrington, Andrew H. to Areadna Ray 7-15-1845 F
Farrington, Jonathan T. to Elizabeth Anderson 8-24-1847 Sh
Farrington, Robert to Tenny Bond 3-16-1872 F
Farrington, Tom to Nancy Bond 7-29-1872 (no return) Hy
Farrington, Wm. to Hannah Maclin 11-5-1869 Hy
Farrior, J. M. to M. A. McCollum 2-10-1860 (2-11-1860) O
Farris, Austin to Mary E. Bryant 6-9-1853 Sh
Farris, Dandrage to Tabby Trent 12-1-1868 (12-27-1868) F B
Farris, E. D. to Mollie M. Denning 9-4-1867 (9-5-1867) O

Farris, Edward D. to Martha C. Dickey 6-10-1852 O
Farris, Isaac N. to Jane Hogin (Hogue) 6-27-1849 O
Farris, Isaac N. to Jane Hogue 6-27-1849 O
Farris, Isaac N. to Mariah E. White 1-9-1854 O
Farris, James M. to Louisa Gammons 4-29-1867 (no return) Dy
Farris, James S. to Frances Bayne 2-9-1835 Sh
Farris, James W. to Willey Ann Stovall 2-11-1862 (2-11?-1862) O
Farris, James to Cynthia P. Hanly 11-8-1834 Sh
Farris, James to Eighty Scott 5-15-1848 Hr
Farris, John to Nancy Allen 12-12-1850 Hn
Farris, Joseph H. to Dosha W. Mooton 11-9-1842 O
Farris, Joseph to Lucinda Lane 6-30-1838 (7-3-1838) O
Farris, Oliver B. to Frances E. Townsend 12-29-1865 (12-31-1865) T
Farris, Thomas I. to Nancy E. Turner 11-9-1866 (11-10-1866) O
Farris, Thos. H. to Nancy J. Davis 2-12-1850 Cr
Farris, Thos. J. to Sarah T. Steward 12-23-1856 (12-25-1856) Hr
Farris, W. H. to E. A. Smith 2-3-1868 (2-5-1868) F
Farris, W. H. to G. M. Garrison 5-14-1866 O
Farris, W. N. to Mary Ann Johnson 10-4-1838 Hr
Farris, William A. to Martha G. Berry 5-30-1861 (no return) Hn
Farris, William to Elizabeth Crawford 7-3-1848 G
Farrow, A. M. to Cynthia May 12-13-1862 (no return) Hy
Farrow, Alfred G. to Isabel Pafford 3-14-1847 Be
Farrow, Allen C. to Malissa L. Mitchell 1-20-1867 Be
Farrow, Elisha to Caroline Benson 1-23-1858 (1-24-1858) G
Farrow, Henry M. to Caroline Miller 11-8-1868 Be
Farrow, J. J. to Mary J. Howell 2-1-1866 (no return) Hy
Farrow, J. M. to Elizabeth S. Rodgers 3-21-1853 Sh
Farrow, James to Lucy Crow 12-28-1870 (12-29-1870) Dy
Farrow, Wiley E. to Elliott Boyd 3-23-1843 Sh
Farrow, Wm. to Mary Goodridge 10-11-1869 (no return) Hy
Farthing, S. B. to Rebecca McGran 9-1-1854 (9-2-1854) G
Farthing, Solsly to Elizabeth Ross 9-25-1843 (9-26-1843) G
Farzin, John to Nancy Thomas 7-25-1840 Hn
Fasmyre, Augustus C. to Margaret J. Shaw 12-19-1848 Ma
Fassett, Joseph to Catherine L. Fisher 11-10-1852 (11-12-1854?) L
Fasthing, Salesbury to Martha Haley 12-14-1830 (12-29-1830) G
Fathey, Augustus B. to Mary Kemp 12-9-1858 Hn
Faucett, James A. to Eliza J. Stewart 6-2-1858 (6-6-1858) Ma
Faucett, John M. to Sarah Ann Cox 3-26-1853 (3-29-1853) Hr
Faucett, John T. to Ann Cullen 7-4-1842 (no return) L
Faucett, Josiah T. to Malinda Huddleston 5-13-1853 (5-17-1853) Hr
Faucett, William R. to Martha J. Burrus 5-7-1870 (5-8-1870) Ma
Faulk, Allen to Aggy Robinson 5-7-1869 T
Faulk, Allin to Aggy Robinson 5-7-1868 T
Faulk, J. B. to Lizzie D. Thomas 10-23-1867 O
Faulk, J. C. to Margaret M. Whiteside 8-27-1863 (8-27-___) O
Faulk, James to Charlott Adkins 1-2-1872 T
Faulk, James to Emily L. Baker 10-31-1844 Sh
Faulk, James to Henrietta Power 10-28-1843 (11-2-1843) T
Faulk, Jessee to Julia Crenshaw 12-20-1865 T
Faulk, John to Samantha Hendrix? 6-22-1850 F
Faulk, Johnathan B. to Margaret J. Grant 11-24-1874 (11-25-1874) T
Faulk, S. W. to Emma Shenault 10-19-1872 (10-24-1872) T
Faulkland, Johnson to Mary Nany Mahon 2-14-1838 Ma
Faulkner, Amos to Martha Warpole 12-21-1863 (no return) Dy
Faulkner, C. C. to Mary Phillips 10-23-1874 (no return) Hy
Faulkner, E. H. to Elizabeth Permenter 9-1-1860 (no return) Hy
Faulkner, G. H to Frances Marshall 7-7-1859 (no return) Hy
Faulkner, Jas. J. to Mary E. Moore 10-7-1856 T
Faulkner, John J. to Martha A. McCain 11-25-1867 (11-26-1867) T
Faulkner, John J> to Jane Strain 11-8-1871 (11-9-1871) T
Faulkner, John to Amanda C. Marlow 9-25-1850 (9-26-1850) Ma
Faulkner, John to Martha Frances Franklin 3-24-1854 (3-29-1854) T
Faulkner, Lafayette to Cornelia O. Boland 4-3-1862 Dy
Faulkner, M. M. to Cornelia A. Williams 12-26-1867 L
Faulkner, M. M. to Susan Ann Soward 11-2-1854 (11-8-1854) L
Faulkner, T. L. to Mary A. E. Kelley 10-7-1873 (10-9-1873) T
Faulkner, Wm. to Harriet Whitmore 7-2-1867 Hy
Faulks, Edmond to Sarah Bevel 12-4-1861 G
Fausett, David to Margaret Stockinger 4-27-1862 (4-30-1862) F
Fausett, William T. to Sarah A. Murrell 12-24-1850 Hr
Faust, William J. to Mary E. Swaim 3-5-1863 We
Fautner, David to Lavenia Gammons 8-16-1864 (no return) Dy
Fawcett, David A. to Mary Anne E. Barbee 11-6-1844 Sh
Fawcett, Wm. E. to Ardenia F. Grace 7-26-1859 Hr
Fawlk, Jonathan to Louisa Cothran 1-17-1848 (1-20-1848) F
Faxon, William to Amelia Young 1-2-1874 Hy
Fay, James A. to Susan A. Johnson 2-5-1859 We
Fay, W. C. to Texana Crawford 5-19-1864 Sh
Fayers, William to Mina De'lieu 12-14-1859 Hn
Fayette, Joseph Deman to Elizabeth Carter 2-10-1844 Hn
Fazzi, Henry to Mary Riley 7-26-1862 Sh
Feagan, Thomas H. to Martha I.? Gray 11-14-1843 (11-15-1843) Hr
Fealy, Frank to Augusta Lowe 10-5-1861 (11-24-1861) Sh
Featherston, C. R. to S. E. Moore 9-30-1875 (no return) Dy
Featherston, Daniel M. to Sarah A. House 10-11-1860 We

Featherston, Henry D. to Amanda L. Lusk 5-12-1862 (no return) Cr
Featherston, James to Laney George 9-7-1854 G
Featherston, John W. to Tabitha C. Conlee 12-6-1855 G
Featherston, Lewis H. to Lavinia Felts 10-15-1856 (10-16-1856) Sh
Featherston, W. D. to S. A. Oneal 12-20-1865 (no return) Dy
Featherston, William J. to Willy Corley 1-8-1845 (1-9-1845) G
Featherstone, T. J. to Arabella E. Wingo 12-10-1869 T
Feazur, Ephriam to Matilda Jones 6-15-1867 (6-16-1867) T
Fedrick, W. W. to Paralee White 5-5-1863 (5-6-1863) Dy
Fee, Charles D. (Capt.) to Julia L. Childress 9-26-1863 (9-27-1863) Sh
Fee, G. D. to Frances A. Murrell 8-8-1847 Sh
Feeley, Daniel to Rutha Caton 5-28-1850 Hr
Feely, Hugh to Bridget Garvin 5-31-1856 (6-22-1856) Sh
Feely, Thomas J. to Cynthia J. Childress 10-3-1868 (10-25-1868) L
Feeman, T. S. to Susan Thomas 2-12-1850 G
Feezor, E. A. to Elizabeth C. Cooper 11-27-1867 (11-28-1867) T
Feezor, O. S. to M. C. Huffman 2-23-1874 T
Feezor, Otho S. to Mary Elizabeth Clark 12-21-1854 T
Feezor, Peter L. to Sarah A. E. Yount 7-27-1854 T
Feezor, Smith M. to Purlina M Tennant 3-5-1849 (3-8-1849) T
Feezor, Smith Miller to Peggy Owen 6-18-1846 T
Feezor, William Henry to Dora Bledsoe 10-17-1867 T
Fef___?, Alexander to Barbara A. M. Swift 5-4-1843 Hn
Feild, R. S. to Anna H. Lemaster 10-28-1857 Sh
Feild, Rosco to Emma A. Ecklin 1-5-1861 Sh
Felix, F. to Kate Bauert 10-24-1860 Sh
Fellosby, Pallen to Pathanna Mitchell 8-27-1850 We
Fellow, Robert G. to Elizabeth H. Haynie 1-18-1848 Sh
Fellow, William to Martha Birdwell 10-16-1841 (10-17-1841) F
Fellow, William to Penny Spurlin 6-3-1831 (6-12-1831) Hr
Fellow, Wm. M. to Jane Eckolds 10-12-1841 Sh
Fellows, Joseph J. to Sarah Robinson 2-6-1847 (not executed) T
Felsenthal, Emanuel to Carrie Auker 1-15-1873 Hy
Felsenthal, Joseph to Rachael Felsenthal 6-17-1862 (no return) Hy
Felt, T. D. to E. A. Caldwell 2-29-1848 Hn
Felts, A. P. to D. P. Hardister 4-16-1866 (4-25-1866) Cr
Felts, Charles R. to Jennie A. Powers 11-4-1862 (no return) We
Felts, George A. to Ann Eliza Whipple 1-26-1857 (1-29-1857) O
Felts, James M. to Amanda C. Price 3-11-1862 Cr
Felts, Joseph D. to Zely A. Ward 1-6-1862 (no return) We
Felts, Joseph W. to Addie T. Hardister 8-31-1865 (no return) Cr
Felts, Thomas W. to Ann M. Jackson 11-30-1864 Hn
Felts, W. W. to H.(A?) E. Henning 2-22-1870? (2-23-1871) L
Felts, William to Laura V. Strong 10-31-1854 (11-2-1854) G
Femister, William W. to Lenora Smith 1-14-1864 Sh
Femzer, William to Nellie Mays 12-7-1872 Dy
Fenegan, James Peter to Anne Maria Bernard Atwell 6-5-1861 Sh
Fenel, A. to Abba Saunders 7-7-1883 (7-8-1883) L
Fenesy, Pat to Bridgit Byrne 5-29-1851 Sh
Fenex, William to Sarah Sinclair 1-25-1843 Hn
Fenlen?, Allen to Sarah L. Hardie 9-5-1870 (9-6-1870) Dy
Fenn, J. I. to Josie Smith 2-7-1872 Dy
Fennel, Charles Fox to Sallie F. Hartsfield 11-22-1859 (11-23-1859) Hr
Fennel, W. D. to Rebecca Burdon 12-16-1868 (no return) Hy
Fennell, J. M. to Alice Green 11-27-1880 (11-28-1881?) L
Fennell, John to Minerva Townsend 5-21-1870 (5-22-1870) Ma
Fennell, Joseph to L. J. Sanders 9-17-1872? Hy
Fennell, Robert to Nettie Wilkins 1-7-1875 Hy
Fenner, John M. to Eunice B. Hugh 7-25-1844 Ma
Fenner, John s. to I. Virginia Day 2-27-1867 Ma
Fenner, Joseph F. to Mary M. Gossett 8-31-1852 (8-30?-1852) Hr
Fenner, Richard H. to Fanny E. Rogers 8-29-1853 (8-30-1853) Ma
Fenner, Richard J. to Marianna Johnson 3-23-1841 (3-24-1841) Ma
Fenner, Robert to Ann M. Jones 7-23-1828 Ma
Fenner, Thomas B. to Hannah Jane Pettus 7-22-1853 (7-26-1853) Ma
Fennesy, Richard to Mary Keting 1-22-1852 L
Fentern, John H. to Mary Ann Higgins 12-28-1857 (12-29-1857) Sh
Fenton, John H. to Sarah Anne Ellis 3-19-1845 Sh
Fenton, Robt. W. to Sarah J. Shaw 2-20-1867 (2-21-1867) T
Fenton, Robt. W. to Sarah J. Shaw 2-26-1867 (2-27-1867) T
Fentress, George W. to Mary E. Nedry 7-30-1857 O
Fentress, J. N. to Margarett J. Hilliard 10-6-1867 O
Fentress, James to Mary T. Perkins 8-24-1859 Hr
Fentress, John R. to Anne E. Fitzhugh 6-15-1848 Hr
Fentriss, George W. to Matilda Louisa Winters 12-13-1827 O
Feran, Hugh to Margaret Callahan 2-8-1860 (2-12-1860) Sh
Ferbury, Phillip to Malissa Jackson 10-12-1867 (10-13-1867) T
Fergarson, Lazerus to Sarah A. Grady 3-9-1853 (3-10-1853) G
Fergason, Felix G. to Darthala Byrn 10-10-1854 (10-11-1854) L
Fergason, Fillmore to Mary Tyus 2-14-1878 Hy
Fergason, Tom J. to Catharine McKinnon 8-7-1860 (no return) Hy
Fergerson, A. A. to Nancy M. Cooper 3-9-1865 G
Ferguson, A. T. to Lavina Dunevant 9-18-1879 Dy
Ferguson, Allen to McUla Cole 11-14-1831 G
Ferguson, Andrew J. to Lizzie DeKine 3-26-1879 L B
Ferguson, Barnett to Lucinda Woods 9-21-1826 G
Ferguson, Charles W. to Jane C. Dunn 12-2-1869 Ma

Ferguson, Emery A. to Louisa C. Nantz 6-17-1847 L
Ferguson, F. W. to Margaret Lawrence 2-4-1837 Hr
Ferguson, Fillmore to Maggie Gauldin 9-29-1875 Dy
Ferguson, Frank to Jane S.? Fletcher 5-1-1865 (5-4-1865) Dy
Ferguson, George M. to Martha F. Tomlinson 12-24-1867 L
Ferguson, George M. to Menerva A. Strickland 10-24-1861 L
Ferguson, J. Bell to Leila G. Trimble (Tamble?) 11-30-1882 L
Ferguson, J. L. to E. J. Bailey 11-29-1850 Hr
Ferguson, J. T. to F. E. Camp 10-17-1861 (10-22-1861) Hr
Ferguson, Jack to Mary Light 6-27-1866 Dy
Ferguson, James L. to Telitha C. Hood 11-28-1855 (11-29-1855) Hr
Ferguson, Jefferson C. to Mary (Lucy?) A. Whitworth 2-4-1852 (2-5-1852) Sh
Ferguson, Jo Green to M. J. Pate 11-30-1870 (nor return) Dy
Ferguson, Joe to Susan Campbell 3-5-1868 (3-7-1868) L B
Ferguson, John Henry to Cornelia Flippin 2-4-1880 (no return) L
Ferguson, John to Ellen Hatfield 2-22-1849 Sh
Ferguson, John to Rebecca Stone 11-23-1849 Sh
Ferguson, Joseph to Elizabeth Hale 11-21-1844 Sh
Ferguson, King to Alsie Isham 8-4-1883 (8-5-1883) L
Ferguson, Lee to Margaret Mays 8-10-1874 Dy
Ferguson, Lee to Mary Fields 10-24-1876 Dy
Ferguson, Robert to Argeanta Rebecca Stephens 8-2-1848 Ma
Ferguson, Robert to Fannie Nixon 12-20-1882 (no return) L
Ferguson, Robt. H. to Palmira Spence 10-7-1863 Dy
Ferguson, T. J. to A. E. Dixon 9-12-1861 (10-21-1861) Hr
Ferguson, Thomas to Asena Collins 8-22-1839 Hn
Ferguson, Thomas to Martha J. Strickland 10-26-1853 (10-27-1853) L
Ferguson, W. W. to Susan C. Locke 12-21-1854 (12-23-1855?) Sh
Ferguson, Will F. to Marietta Howell 11-27-1854 (11-29-1854) Hr
Ferguson, William D. to Elizabeth Petty 4-19-1858 Sh
Ferguson, William J. to Tempy Chronister 1-18-1833 (1-20-1833) G
Ferguson, William to Maryan Cole 8-26-1829 G
Ferrel, Charles M. to Laura L. Bowden 9-27-1864 (9-28-1864) Sh
Ferrel, John to Elizabeth Hughes 5-2-1846 (no return) F
Ferrel, Thomas to Susan Bullard 3-6-1850 L
Ferrell, Alfred to Susan A. Richardson 1-5-1843 G
Ferrell, C. H. to Lavinia R. Scates 4-7-1864 G
Ferrell, C. W. to Tempy Ann Hudson 2-9-1846 F
Ferrell, George P. to Sarah H. Birk 5-22-1864 G
Ferrell, Harbert to Judy Daniel 2-22-1841 (3-2-1841) Ma
Ferrell, Harry to Mollie Smith 7-7-1868 G B
Ferrell, Hubbard to Mary R. Flanikin 5-26-1855 (5-31-1855) T
Ferrell, J. M> to Sarah H. Sawyer 12-15-1870 Dy
Ferrell, James B. to Catherine Ross 12-23-1850 (12-26-1850) Ma
Ferrell, James to Dosha Riploge 6-21-1851 (7-24-1851) Hr
Ferrell, John B. to Malinda Gaddy 8-28-1856 Hr
Ferrell, John C. to Mary J. Shelby 11-8-1858 (11-11-1858) G
Ferrell, John P. to Susanah J. Vaughan 5-4-1864 G
Ferrell, John to Jane Gilmore 2-6-1848 Sh
Ferrell, John to Sarah Duvaughn 5-21-1862 G
Ferrell, Major to Mary J. Turner 1-24-1843 G
Ferrell, N. P. to M. N. Waller 10-2-1854 (no return) F
Ferrell, S. A. to Mary J. Steen 2-18-1865 (no return) Dy
Ferrell, Samuel to Mary E. Wyatt 9-17-1851 G
Ferrell, Thomas B. to Sophronia Walker 4-14-1859 O
Ferrell, W. H. to L. C. Stallins 3-1-1866 G
Ferrell, William H. to Ann Grissom 12-15-1855 (12-16-1855) G
Ferrell, Wilson to Nancy Wood 11-11-1847 Sh
Ferrell, Wm. B. to Catharine Marsh 11-17-1851 (11-19-1851) Hr
Ferrell, Woodring to Sarah M. Howard 11-24-1866 (11-25-18??) O
Ferril, Dimeon to Tibatha Wood 1-28-1841 Sh
Ferrill, Charles to Lucy Foster 12-24-1873 (12-25-1873) Dy
Ferrill, D. P. to M. F. Wilkins 2-22-1866 Dy
Ferrill, J. D. to Mary Jane Floyd 7-3-1866 (7-5-1866) Dy
Ferrill, Thomas C. to Addie Walker 1-11-1866 Dy
Ferrill, Thomas to Nancy Rogers 10-7-1853 Hr
Ferrill, William M. to Mary Lackey 12-20-1876 (no return) Hy
Ferris, George C. to Abagal A. Bowman 10-24-1844 G
Fesmire, Thomas to Lenora (Mrs.) Winslow 10-6-1869 (10-14-1869) Ma
Fetherston, Charles E. to Jane Young 12-4-1852 G
Feucht, Simon to Julia Bowers 4-18-1864 Sh
Feuqua, James L. to Mary L. Stewart 10-22-1861 G
Fewell, Benj. C. to Thevizah Merritt 7-12-1841 (7-13-1841) G
Fewell, William to F. M. Barron 1-17-1848 (1-18-1848) F
Fewell, WilliamH. to Mary E. West 2-8-1844 (2-9-1844) Hr
Field, Alex. to Eliza J. Brown 10-15-1842 (no return) F
Field, Billam? to Mahaly Williamson 12-4-1830 H
Field, Caleb to Lucy Ann Bragg 12-27-1872 (1-1-1873) T
Field, J. G. to Ann Eliza Caples 10-23-1865 (10-26-1865) F
Field, James M. to Frances Z. McKinnie 8-11-1855 (8-12-1855) Hr
Field, John to Eliza Ann Walker 4-18-1863 (4-19-1863) Sh
Field, Robert to Fanny Jordan 9-17-1870 (no return) F B
Field, Scipio to Amelia Brodnax 9-6-1872 (no return) Hy
Field, Silas F. to Jane M. Talbot 4-24-1854 (4-25-1854) Ma
Field, Sip to Luvenia Owens?! 11-15-1869 (11-15-1869) T
Field, Thos. A. to Matilda H. Harrison 10-31-1859 (11-1-1859) G
Field, William to Catharine McLorie 7-11-1852 O

Field, William to Laura Green 12-27-1870 T
Fielder, Boston to Malinda Johnson 12-21-1868 (12-30-1868) Dy
Fielder, J. J. to Caron Ann Turpin 9-1-1838 (9-4-1838) G
Fielder, James to Everett May 2-28-1874 (3-1-1874) Dy
Fielder, Jim to Sarah Edwards 5-14-1880 (5-16-1880) Dy
Fielder, John J. to Rebecca J. Mays 2-12-1835 (2-19-1385) G
Fielder, R. J. to S. F. Goodwin 12-19-1869 G
Fielder, Wm. P. S. to L. B. Williams 9-13-1838 G
Fielders, Samuel H. to Susan Maria Davis 8-5-1848 O
Fielding, Henry to Elizabeth How 2-16-1859 Sh
Fields, A. J. to Elizabeth Johnson 2-11-1869 Be
Fields, A. J. to Perneta A. Mullin 12-4-1867 Cr
Fields, Abe to Susan James 3-31-1871 Hy
Fields, Absalem to Sarah A. Berton 8-26-1859 (8-29-1859) O
Fields, Benj. to Chaney Fields 2-11-1871 (no return) Hy
Fields, Benjamin F. to Elizabeth Guinn 10-31-1858 O
Fields, Beverly to Alsey Cose 11-5-1870 (no return) Hy
Fields, D. R. to Susan Pierce 9-14-1865 Dy
Fields, Daniel B. to Isabella Watts 11-3-1857 G
Fields, David to Sarah A. Fitz 12-12-1869 Hy
Fields, Davy to Hester Webb 6-15-1867 (6-18-1867) T
Fields, Elisha? to E. McAdoo 10-3-1850 Cr
Fields, Frank to Fanny Fergerson 2-4-1876 (no return) Hy
Fields, Franklin to Elizabeth Dickson 12-25-1855 Cr
Fields, Green B. to Lucinda Wren 1-2-1851 Cr
Fields, H. Y. to Sarah J. Robertson 7-11-1859 Cr
Fields, Hansford A. to Lavinia Susan Roachell 1-17-1849 (1-24-1849) G
Fields, Harrison to Almarinda Olive 12-25-1860 Hn
Fields, Henry to Louisa Clay 1-10-1866 (1-13-1866) Dy
Fields, Henry to Margret V. Barret 8-9-1865 T
Fields, Isham to Henrietta Boyssian 11-28-1843 (11-29-1843) F
Fields, J. H. to Rebecca F. Senter 9-8-1861 G
Fields, J. J. to M. J. Blackburn 11-4-1871 O
Fields, J. L. to Emily J. Peeples 10-4-1854 We
Fields, J. T. to Lucy S. Jennings 11-8-1876 Dy
Fields, J. to J. Carnes 8-30-1842 Be
Fields, Jack to Anna L. Macklin 12-26-1868 (1-20-1870) T
Fields, Jack to Rose Fields 12-24-1866 (12-29-1866) F B
Fields, James H. G. to Sarah W. Bransford 2-16-1858 (2-18-1858) O
Fields, James H. to Nancy J. Trout 10-31-1842 G
Fields, James M. to Katharine James 9-18-1848 (9-27-1848) O
Fields, James W. to Manda C. McAmy 1-12-1853 Cr
Fields, James W. to Margaret Ramsey 6-18-1838 Hr
Fields, Jefferson G. to Fannie A. Smithwick 9-16-1863 (9-17-1863) Sh
Fields, Jefferson M. to Diena M. L. Hunter 1-8-1851 (1-9-1851) Hr
Fields, John B. to Delila Givens 1-9-1880 (1-11-1880) L
Fields, John B. to Lucy L. Williamson 1-3-1868 (1-9-1868) F
Fields, John G. to Mary A. F. Fields 11-2-1843 We
Fields, Jordan to Nancy Joiner 11-14-1872 (11-15-1872) T
Fields, Joseph to Lucy Culberhouse 8-26-1855 Hn
Fields, Lewis to Ann Huffman 12-31-1868 (1-3-1869) Cr
Fields, M. A. to Martha A. Sherrell 7-13-1872 (no return) Cr
Fields, Michael to Elizabeth Moore 11-28-1839 Hn
Fields, N. A. to Emmeline Wise 8-28-1879 (8-29-1879) L
Fields, N. A. to Juntly Chism 5-29-1861 (5-30-1861) L
Fields, N. A. to Lucy M. Fields 6-9-1843 We
Fields, Nathaniel to Olive Lee 8-14-1861 (8-15-1861) O
Fields, Peter G. to Emely V. Jetton 9-30-1845 G
Fields, R. N. P. to M. C. Cochrow 8-29-1852 We
Fields, R. to M. Wilson 1-28-1864 G
Fields, Rawley to Lucinda Holland 11-10-1869 (not executed) F B*
Fields, Richard to Jane Parker 8-28-1869 (no return) F B
Fields, Robert A. to Matilda Jarrott 11-9-1859 (no return) Hy
Fields, Samuel S. to Mary A. Penick 12-15-1859 Hn
Fields, Samuel V. to Martha J. Pinson 11-28-1865 (no return) Cr
Fields, Smith to Nancy Rodgers 8-20-1856 T
Fields, Solomon to Rose Wilkes 7-4-1868 G B
Fields, T. F. to Mary L. Fox 3-17-1864 (3-21-1864) O
Fields, W. J. to Margaret D. Rothrock 5-6-1864 (5-7-1864) Cr
Fields, W. L. to Elizabeth A. Moseley 2-16-1857 (2-19-1857) L
Fields, W. R. to Eliza Jones (Janes) 11-4-1860 We
Fields, W. S. to Mary Robinson 3-10-1873 (3-28-1873) L
Fields, W. T. to M. A. Walton 12-22-1869 G
Fields, William B. to Mary M. Fields 3-26-1849 (3-27-1849) G
Fields, William H. to Elizabeth C. Crutchfield 12-21-1864 (12-22-1864) Cr
Fields, William N. J. to Sallie A. Flowers 3-4-1852 Sh
Fields, Wm. D. to Elizabeth Hail 11-7-1842 (11-8-1842) G
Fife, R. S. to Ann H. Greer 3-9-1860 (3-11-1860) Sh
Fifer, Parmenias to Sarah N. London 1-3-1860 Ma
Fifer, Parnemus to Jane Walker 2-20-1844 (2-21-1844) G
Fifer, William to Carissa R. Edwards 4-7-1848 G
Figgins, Joseph M. to Harriet V. Cassel 2-16-1867 (2-22-1867) F
Fight, E. W. to Annie E. Pennington 12-23-1865 T
Fike, A. to Sarah Jane Kennedy 3-16-1857 Sh
Fike, H. F. C. to Emelie M. C. Meier 10-31-1869 (11-1-1860) Sh
Filaboe, Peter to Caroline Bonner 2-17-1851 Sh
Finch, A. C. to S. A. Gardner 11-17-1859 (11-18-1859) F

Finch, A. M. to Elizabeth A. Garrison 10-4-1849 O
Finch, Adam to Elizabeth P. Warren 12-30-1856 We
Finch, B. to S. A. Pickens no date (1864 or 65?) F
Finch, Boldin to Lively Pitchford 5-23-1829 G
Finch, C. M. to Lida Medlin 1-13-1876 (no return) Hy
Finch, Caswell to Nancy G. Beever 10-20-1852 Cr
Finch, Daniel M. to G. Eckles 9-3-1862 (9-16-1862) O
Finch, David W. to Theodocia Eckley 9-3-1862 O
Finch, Edmond to Melissa J. Pinkston 10-25-1869 (10-28-1869) Cr
Finch, Elmer to Mary M. Hern 8-12-1858 Cr
Finch, G. W. to Callie Moss 10-19-1871 (10-22-1871) O
Finch, George A. to Mary Badgett 12-31-1864 Dy
Finch, Green to Frances Nowell 8-29-1856 Cr
Finch, Henry C. to Lucinda Hicks 8-31-1870 (9-1-1870) Cr
Finch, Henry to Clarissa Williams 1-29-1838 (no return) Hn
Finch, Irvin to Mary Ann Horton 1-21-1841 Cr
Finch, Irvin to Susan M. Jordon 12-2-1843 (12-3-1843) Ma
Finch, Isham to Martha Beiver 10-12-1856 Cr
Finch, J. B. to P. A. Cooper 11-30-1851 Cr
Finch, James W. to N. M. Ellis 10-31-1849 Hn
Finch, John H. to Emily L. Finch 12-26-1844 We
Finch, John W. to Lucy? J. Botts 9-16-1849 F
Finch, John W. to Nancy R. Davis 10-21-1846 O
Finch, Nelson to Mary A. Moore 6-12-1845 Cr
Finch, Thomas A. to Cintha Bowman 5-24-1841 (no return) Hn
Finch, W. A. to Martha J. Smith 11-12-1849 (11-14-1849) Hr
Finch, William A. to Martha M. Cook 7-13-1857 We
Finch, Wright to L. A. Mallory 12-21-1847 Hn
Fincher, Alexander to Sarah Ann Harden 6-2-1877 (6-3-1877) L
Findle, Hiram to Emiline Connell 11-19-1869 (no return) Dy
Finely, Jesse I. to Eliza H. Lamb 1-1-1839 Sh
Fingenbeim, Charles to Mary Goodpaster 5-1-1838 Sh
Finger, Andrew L. to Mary S. Haynes 12-15-1843 (12-20-1843) Ma
Finger, J. H. to Nancy P. McFall 10-29-1865 Mn
Fink, George W. to Elizabeth Welsh 2-28-1849 Sh
Fink, John to Louisa Sundheim 5-19-1856 Sh
Finlay, Arthur F. to Julia Ann Moore 5-16-1831 Sh
Finley, A. R. to Martha Swor 10-12-1841 (no return) Hn
Finley, Albert to Candas M. Roaney 2-3-1864 (no return) Cr
Finley, Allen to Jane Weakly 12-7-1865 Dy
Finley, J. Buck to Donie Peery 1-13-1874 Dy
Finley, J. W. to Lorina Stewart 10-6-1857 (no return) Cr
Finley, Jacob to Nancy Parker 11-14-1826 Hr
Finley, James R. to Sarah E. Campbell 6-19-1842 Hn
Finley, James W. to D. E. Braiden 8-8-1859 Sh
Finley, James to Martha Rolin 5-12-1863 O
Finley, John B. to Elizabeth Lamb 11-1-1845 Sh
Finley, John W. to M. A. Bell 11-30-1857 Cr
Finley, John W. to Martha C. Bishop 8-13-1862 Mn
Finley, John to Elizabeth Stewart 2-12-1845 Cr
Finley, John to Elvira Berry 4-1-1838 (no return) Cr
Finley, Newton to Martha C. Jenkins 2-17-1863 (no return) Cr
Finley, Richard to Obedience Parker 11-24-1836 Hr
Finley, Robert F. to Nancy Aiken 11-16-1835 (11-18-1835) G
Finley, Samuel P. to Elizabeth B. Gibbon 12-1-1830 Sh
Finley, Thomas to Mary Fields 1-25-1844 Cr
Finley, Thos. to Elizabeth Ruff 12-16-1846 (no return) Cr
Finley, W. B. to Mattie E. James 12-29-1877 (12-30-1877) Dy
Finley, William A. J. to Mary M. Alsup 7-31-1861 (8-1-1861) Sh
Finley, William H. to Rachel E. Powers 6-13-1848 Hn
Finley, William to Jane Brown 4-23-1870 (no return) F B
Finley, William to Paralee A. Redden 12-31-1869 (1-5-1870) Cr
Finley, Wm. to Lucindy Freeman 4-6-1856 Cr
Finley, Wm. to Mary Freeman 4-28-1853 Cr
Finn, Matias to Christiana Whlmena. Hafarman 6-18-1849 Sh
Finne, Franz H. to Paulina Rebsamen 6-23-1858 Sh
Finney, B. C. to Mary Bass 1-23-1856 (1-24-1856) O
Finney, B. D. to Elizabeth J. Jernigan 5-18-1846 (5-26-1846) F
Finney, Moses to Rose Cloyd 3-14-1870 (no return) F
Finney, Richd. F. to Martha Ann Finney 1-5-1839 (1-6-1839) F
Finney, T. C. to Pamella A. Baker 11-2-1859 (11-3-1859) Sh
Finney, W. P. to Martha J. Finney 9-28-1849 (9-10?-1849) F
Finnie, John G. to Susan T. Johnston 4-10-1849 Sh
Finny, A. B. to H. W. Burt 10-29-1854 (no return) F
Fioke (Hicke?), Augusta to Elizabeth Harvey 8-27-1851 Sh
Firth, Richard M. to Martha F. Adams 2-18-1841 F
Firth, T. J. to S. J. Branch 8-28-1868 (9-9-1868) F
Firth, W. S. to Maggie G. Leach 3-1-1870 (3-2-1870) F
Firth, Wm. T. to Martha E. Smith 11-15-1859 (12-13-1859) F
Fischer, Adolph to Berta Heig 8-28-1854 Sh
Fischer, Jacob to Bertha Fyrick 6-20-1859 Sh
Fiser, Willis A. to Offa Ridgeway 1-3-1841 Hn
Fish, Edwin to Mary J. Cozby 8-13-1855 Hr
Fish, Edwin to Mary M. Woodard 2-21-1850 Cr
Fish, James W. to Frances Crammer? 4-22-1873 (4-27-1873) Dy
Fish, James to Olivia C. Parker   Hr
Fish, John to Centhia Hicks 9-24-1844 (9-26-1844) Hr

Fisher, A. J. to N. J. Stroud 10-7-1874 (10-8-1874) T
Fisher, Allen to Judy Fowlkes 5-13-1874 (5-15-1874) Dy
Fisher, Armstead H. to Harriet N. Turner 12-12-1857 (12-15-1857) L
Fisher, Bob to _rinia Halliburton 2-22-1877 L B
Fisher, Bolling S. to Ann E. Moorer 11-29-1856 (no return) L
Fisher, C. E. to S. E. Blankinship 6-23-1870 G
Fisher, Charles J.? to Martha W. Smith 12-3-1868 (12-9-1868) T
Fisher, Edward to Mary Ann Risley 12-7-1855 Sh
Fisher, Eldridge L. to Sarah E. Hicox 9-21-1857 Ma
Fisher, Feldman to Mary Ryan 9-5-1860 Sh
Fisher, Fre. Phillman to Catherine Brown 4-28-1863 Sh
Fisher, George M. to Martha E. Thomas 12-14-1837 G
Fisher, George M. to Mary E. Jones 2-4-1858 G
Fisher, George W. to Sarah Underwood 5-5-1855 Cr
Fisher, Henry Jefferson to Frances Barker 11-4-1857 O
Fisher, Henry to Josephine Fisher 3-10-1868 (no return) F B
Fisher, Ike to Silvia Lloyd 1-7-1878 L
Fisher, Isaac to Lizzie Jones 11-18-1874 Hy
Fisher, J. H. to Bettie A. Matthews 5-7-1866 (5-9-1866) F
Fisher, J. P. to Mary F. Valentine 1-16-1867 G
Fisher, J. W. to Julia A. Rose 4-16-1878 Hy
Fisher, James to Jane Quinn 8-5-1847 Cr
Fisher, John H. to May Grigory 1-27-1841 G
Fisher, John to Eliza Hetirzir 10-15-1862 (10-16-1862) Sh
Fisher, John to Emiline Owen 5-19-1869 (5-23-1869) L
Fisher, Joseph C. to Elizabeth Person 10-2-1849 Sh
Fisher, Lacey to Margaret Nutson 1-22-1870 (no return) F B
Fisher, Louis to Emaline Dickens 3-20-1866 (3-24-1866) T
Fisher, P. A. to Rachel C. Jones 8-28-1866 G
Fisher, Pleasant to Sarah Etheredge 11-15-1833 (11-16-1833) G
Fisher, Richard to Prudence James 11-7-1870 G
Fisher, Richd. W. to Mattie A. Gattis 12-8-1866 (12-11-1866) Ma
Fisher, Shirley to Mary Sanford 2-14-1874 (2-15-1874) T
Fisher, Thomas A. to Annie M. Bryan 4-10-1858 Sh
Fisher, Thomas E. to Sarah (Mrs.) Strouse 10-21-1873 (10-22-1873) L
Fisher, Thomas to Jennie Dougherty 4-1-1864 (4-5-1864) Sh
Fisher, Thomas to Mary Barker 11-12-1856 (11-13-1856) G
Fisher, Thomas to Nora Mann? 9-25-1869 (9-26-1869) L
Fisher, Thos. E. to M. E. (Mrs.) Maury? 9-1-1866 (9-2-1866) Dy
Fisher, Thos. E. to Nancy Jane Andrews 5-17-1862 (5-18-1862) L
Fisher, Thos. to Mary Carter 10-17-1868 (10-24-1868) L B
Fisher, W. H. to Bettie Davenport 7-22-1871 T
Fisher, W. O. to Arvazena Hall (Stanley) 9-19-1869 G
Fisher, William Dunham to Sophia Cotten Flowers 1-19-1852 (1-20-1852) T
Fisher, William O. to Eliza Jane Jones 12-30-1851 G
Fisher, William to Elizabeth Hardlage 4-13-1854 (4-24-1854) Sh
Fisher, William to Isabella Green? (Gwin) 1-25-1873 (no return) L B
Fisher, William to Isabella J. Baucum 10-3-1852 Hn
Fisher, Wm. P. to Maria B. Peacock 4-17-1839 Sh
Fisk, Fred B. to Lucy Jane Leake 5-25-1857 (5-27-1857) Sh
Fisk, James F. to Martha Bagwell 7-9-1863 O
Fisk, Martin to Susan Persons 3-30-1834 Sh
Fisk, Samuel W. to Penniah Dodds 3-6-1854 (no return) F
Fitch, A. W. to Margaret Ellis 4-17-1845 (no return) Hn
Fitch, Anderson W. to Lucinda Hamilton 11-22-1856 (no return) Hn
Fitch, James to June Clendenin 5-3-1838 Hn
Fitch, John J. to Clarinda Callahan 12-28-1854 Hr
Fitch, William H. to Louisianne Buchanan 2-13-1860 Hn
Fitch, William to Isabla? Neel 11-27-1874 T
Fitch, Young to Margaret Brown 11-25-1865 F B
Fitch, jr., W. H. to Eleanora Underwood 10-3-1857 (10-6-1857) Sh
Fitchugh, Wash to Lucinda Rawlings 1-8-1867 (1-12-1867) F B
Fite, David L. to Ellen Banks 10-14-1857 (10-15-1857) T
Fite, John R. to H. E. Wallace 5-27-1863 G
Fite, John R. to Mary E. Wallace 10-23-1852 (10-24-1852) G
Fite, Mosses to Elizabeth Lytaker 8-27-1827 (9-6-1827) G
Fite, Thomas J. to Elizabeth F. (Mrs.) Jackson 9-2-1856 Cr
Fite, William C. to Sarah A. F. Hogg 10-14-1841 G
Fithugh, James W. to Penny A. McDaniel 1-11-1871 Hy
Fithugh, Thomas to Fannie Crisp 11-26-1871 Hy
FitsJerrel, Jeremiah to Ann McNamara 1-7-1873 (1-28-1873) Cr
Fitts, William H. to Mary Edwards 1-8-1852 (no return) F
Fitz (Fith?), James A. to Mariah L. Edwards 9-4-1843 (9-6-1843) Ma
Fitz, Clement P. to Caroline E. Williamson 9-3-1849 (10-3-1849) Ma
Fitz, Gipson S. to Lou Cummings 12-30-1873 Hy
FitzGerald, Martin to Mary Ryan 7-17-1854 Sh
FitzPatrick, John to Ellen Carter 7-13-1860 (7-15-1860) Sh
Fitze, George to Caroline Smith 3-15-1873 T
Fitzgerald, Alfred to Easter Carthel 4-21-1866 G
Fitzgerald, B. F. to Mary T. Hobson 3-13-1850 G
Fitzgerald, Bob to Mary Smith 1-1-1868 G B
Fitzgerald, Clinton to Jemina Hopper 3-9-1833 (3-19-1833) Hr
Fitzgerald, Edward to Martha Hawkins 8-27-1856 Hn
Fitzgerald, George to Corella Brown 7-26-1880 (no return) Dy
Fitzgerald, Henry to Sarah W. Bill 7-23-1850 Sh
Fitzgerald, Houston to Sallie Mitchell 1-22-1856 G
Fitzgerald, J. W. to Venie Bolding 1-1-1879 Hy

Fitzgerald, John W. to Ann Lusk 6-19-1874 L
Fitzgerald, Martin to Joana Kennedy 7-17-1852 (7-18-1852) Sh
Fitzgerald, Michael to Mary Eagan 11-5-1861 Sh
Fitzgerald, O. G. to Lucy P. Freeman 3-24-1868 G
Fitzgerald, Pleasant to Mary Porter 10-25-1866 Hn
Fitzgerald, R. D. to O. Hartsfield 3-7-1860 G
Fitzgerald, Thomas to Bridget Griffin 2-27-1860 Sh
Fitzgerald, Thomas to Caroline Hooks 10-11-1853 (10-12-1853) T
Fitzgerald, Thos. to Ellen Wadner 11-27-1869 Hy
Fitzgerald, Thos. to Mary Bayby 12-11-1872 (12-12-1872) Cr B
Fitzgerald, W. L. to Mary Fields 1-7-1880 (1-8-1880) L
Fitzgerald, William to Eliza Brannon 1-18-1864 (1-19-1864) Sh
Fitzgerald, Willis to Martha Lockard 4-18-1876 L
Fitzgerald, ____ to ____ Adams 9-5-1838 (no return) F
Fitzgibbon, Thomas to Maggie Burke 9-5-1863 Hy
Fitzgibbons, Michael to Ann Graham 10-18-1857 Sh
Fitzhugh, B. B. to Jane E. Brannon 12-25-1862 Dy
Fitzhugh, Bryant to Annariah Delph 3-26-1879 Dy
Fitzhugh, Bryant to Sallie Pate 11-18-1867 Dy
Fitzhugh, Ezekiel to Martha J. Ford 1-20-1852 (1-21-1852) Ma
Fitzhugh, Jno. W. to Bettie H. Glenn 1-2-1869 Ma
Fitzhugh, John W. to Mintha Bryan 2-2-1829 Ma
Fitzhugh, John to Sarah V. McCoy 10-20-1875 Dy
Fitzhugh, L. P. to E. J. McFarlin 10-8-1879 (10-9-1879) Dy
Fitzhugh, T. H. to Mary Davis 8-12-1868 Dy
Fitzhugh, T. J. to Lou McCoy 2-28-1877 (2-29?-1877) Dy
Fitzhugh, W. C. to J. M. Evans 1-9-1878 (1-10-1878) Dy
Fitzhugh, W. C. to Mary J. Follis 9-29-1869 (9-30-1869) Dy
Fitzpatrick, Billy to Mollie Pierce 4-30-1883 (not used) L
Fitzpatrick, Caz to Mollie Braden 6-14-1873 (no return) L B
Fitzpatrick, Charlie to Jane Johnson 4-27-1885 L
Fitzpatrick, David to Lou Gause 2-2-1876 (no return) L
Fitzpatrick, David to Pamelia B. Hargrove 11-14-1847 (11-18-1847) L
Fitzpatrick, Dennis to Cilla Henning 2-5-1885 (no return) L
Fitzpatrick, Ephraim to Henny Ann Fitzpatrick 12-29-1875 L B
Fitzpatrick, Ephraim to Winney Hawkins 12-23-1867 (12-24-1867) L
Fitzpatrick, Fred to Violet Casey 5-24-1876 L B
Fitzpatrick, George to Emily Fitzpatrick 9-10-1868 (9-20-1868) L B
Fitzpatrick, Granville to Ellen Bridly 1-26-1842 (1-27-1842) F
Fitzpatrick, Green to Lila Parker 11-14-1868 (11-4?-1868) L
Fitzpatrick, Ham to Nancy Green 2-11-1880 (2-12-1880) L B
Fitzpatrick, Harrison L. to Hester Ann Turner 12-12-1871 (12-13-1871) L
Fitzpatrick, John B. to Sue P. Raynr 11-14-1867 Hy
Fitzpatrick, John to Martha Baxter? 11-14-1877 (12-6-1877) L
Fitzpatrick, John to Mary Babb 9-17-1865 Mn
Fitzpatrick, Merrick to Nellie Thornton 12-15-1885 (12-17-1885) L
Fitzpatrick, Michael to Hannah Crow 7-22-1862 Sh
Fitzpatrick, Mike to Margaret McGlauthron 11-29-1877 (12-16-1877) L
Fitzpatrick, Nathan to Elizabeth Maclin 11-12-1869 (11-13-1869) L
Fitzpatrick, Samuel to Susanah Bradly 11-2-1840 (11-5-1840) F
Fitzpatrick, Thomas to Kizziah Ann Green 12-19-1870 (12-30-1870) L
Fitzpatrick, W. H. to Alice E. Anthony 7-18-1876 (7-19-1876) L
Fitzpatrick, Walker to Sallie Ann Harper 11-30-1872 L B
Fitzpatrick, Wash to Amanda Burks 4-2-1881 (4-4-1881) L B
Fitzpatrick, Wright to Catherine Demow 9-23-1880 L
Fiveash, John to Sarah Jones 12-16-1845 Sh
Fizer, Ed to Jane Muzier? 4-5-1876 Dy
Fizer, Edward to Fannie Tipton 7-23-1874 (no return) Dy
Fizer, Green to Alice Prichard 2-24-1875 (2-26-1875) Dy B
Fizer, S. H. to Mollie E. Tharpe 2-4-1867? (no return) Hn
Flack, Caleb to Martha Murray 3-11-1874 Dy
Flack, J. E. to A. M. Isbell 12-27-1867 (12-28-1867) O
Flack, J. Y. to Margaret Bruce 5-25-1874 (5-26-1874) Dy
Flack, P. J. to L. M. Wynne 12-17-1872 Dy
Flag (Flager), John to Sarah Jane High 10-15-1862 (10-16-1862) Sh
Flag, Bob to Caroline Chilton 12-23-1871 (no return) Hy
Flag, Wm. to Nancy Evans 1-20-1871 Hy
Flagg, Eliot to Jane Rosewater 1-14-1860 Hy
Flagg, George W. to Elizabeth Brockwell 7-5-1858 (no return) Hn
Flaharty, Patrick to Ellen McLoughlin 8-1-1851 Sh
Flaherty, James to Caroline Tomlinson 8-31-1846 (9-1-1846) Ma
Flaherty, Patrick to Bridget Delaney 9-2-1858 Sh
Flahive, John to Ann Holihan 8-20-1860 Sh
Flake, Amsey to Mary Hall 4-27-1848 (no return) Hn
Flake, Andrew to Edy Hampton 1-8-1872 (no return) Cr B
Flake, James to Winnie Kee 12-19-1872 (no return) Cr
Flake, Wm. to Espran Burnett 2-18-1865 (2-21-1865) Cr
Flanagan, Morris to Cecila Monahan 4-23-1858 Sh
Flanakin, C. W. to Eliza J. Smith 1-23-1858 (2-4-1858) T
Flanakin, Robert J. to Nancy Griffith 9-9-1867 T
Flanarey, Peter to Mary Conners 7-25-1857 (8-2-1857) Sh
Flanigan, John D. to Martha F. Rodgers 3-13-1867 T
Flanigan, Martin to Mary Connell 2-8-1864 Sh
Flanigan, R. J. to Laura Jones 8-26-1874 (8-27-1874) T
Flanigan, R. J. to Mary Ann Harri 5-14-1864 Sh
Flanigan, Z. A. to Marth Ford 2-13-1867 (2-15-1867) T
Flannagan, John J. to Susan F. Hamilton 11-4-1868 G
Flannery, R. W. to Louisa St. C. Cullen 12-10-1858 Sh
Flargan?, Wm. to Elizabeth Conerly 4-29-1851 (4-?-1851) L
Flasher, John to Martha Hall 12-29-1860 Sh
Flatt, Henry M. to Penicia A. Morton 11-14-1862 Mn
Fleet, James M. to Susan Prewett 6-14-1843 Hr
Fleet, John J. to Emeline Mullikin 1-9-1847 Hr
Fleet, Wilie D. to Sarah Knox Barkley 12-24-1850 (12-25-1850) Hr
Fleet, Wm. C. to Caroline Ham 12-15-1842 Hr
Fleetwood, Stark to Polly Reeves 7-21-1824 Sh
Fleetwood, Starkey to Martha Ann Gunter 7-22-1854 Sh
Fleetwood, York to Pefrina Wilson 5-6-1871 (no return) Hy
Fleltcher, John to Mary A. Word 9-26-1859 (9-27-1859) O
Fleming, A. H. to Amanda Harns 5-29-1859 Hn
Fleming, A. M. to Elizabeth Hensley 2-7-1868 (no return) Hy
Fleming, A. T. to Matilda Ellison 2-12-1853 Sh
Fleming, A. to P. (Mrs.) Stull 9-16-1866 G
Fleming, Abe to Ann Walker 10-25-1873 Hy
Fleming, Alphus H. to Caroline P. Browning 12-26-1854 Hn
Fleming, Benjamin F. to Augusta Stratton 11-2-1853 Sh
Fleming, Cecil to Emma Williams 1-29-1870 (1-31-1870) Ma
Fleming, Charles K. to Sarah J. Cobb 12-12-1865 Hy
Fleming, Downey to M. E. Fleming 12-25-1871 T
Fleming, Edmund to Ann P. Armstrong 9-11-1848 (no return) Hn
Fleming, Emmet to Nancy Taylor 9-28-1872 (no return) Hy
Fleming, Erasmus A. to Jamima J. Hopper 6-24-1852 G
Fleming, Everett B. to Cynthia Ann Harris 6-25-1845 Sh
Fleming, Henry S. to Judy A. Glover 5-22-1854 (no return) Cr
Fleming, J. R. to M. O. Mitchell 2-5-1868 G
Fleming, James H. to Annalizar Waggener 3-4-1860 We
Fleming, James O. to Elizabeth C. Brown 2-3-1851 (2-4-1851) Hr
Fleming, James R. to Julia L. Doyle 12-22-1860 (12-24-1860) Sh
Fleming, Joseph to Sarah Core 9-16-1854 (9-21-1854) Hr
Fleming, Napolian to Cynthia M. Bledsoe 12-11-1868 T
Fleming, Simon to Mollie Sutton 12-25-1869 Hy
Fleming, Thomas to Gracie Taliaferro 1-17-1878 Hy
Fleming, Thomas to Rachael C. Kirkman 2-12-1859 (2-19-1858?) Hr
Fleming, Thomas to Sally Ann Glisson 11-21-1854 (11-22-1854) Sh
Fleming, William C. to Artilla Davis 7-26-1847 (7-26-1847) O
Fleming, William to Nancy Bedwell 5-25-1859 (5-29-1859) Ma
Fleming, Wm. C. to A. C. Glover 2-22-1864 (2-24-1864) O
Fleming, Z. T. to Ema E. Croom 12-28-1873 Hy
Fleming, Zackriah to Sarah Avery 11-13-1860 (no return) Hy
Flemmen, Offee to Jane Campbell 11-19-1874 Hy
Flemming, Alexander to Catherine Harris 3-10-1846 Sh
Flemming, B. W. to M. M. Moultrie 5-25-1867 O
Flemming, Cornelius to Milly Tibbs 12-22-1875 (no return) Hy
Flemming, D. C. to Polly Williams 10-13-1844 Be
Flemming, Edwin B. to Nancy J. Smith 1-8-1851 Sh
Flemming, F. to S. L. Feezor 10-12-1870 (10-13-1870) T
Flemming, Franklin to Mary Ann Pinkett 12-21-1831 Sh
Flemming, J. M. to Hanna? Martin 2-8-1870 T
Flemming, John to Winny Johnston 4-11-1849 (4-12-1849) F
Flemming, Lemuel H. to Penelope Bazdel 2-23-1853 Sh
Flemming, Robert C. to Mary Thompson 4-3-1838 Cr
Flemming, Robert to Nancy Torrence 2-21-1859 (2-23-1859) F
Flemming, W. A. to Mary J. Elliott 5-31-1859 (6-8-1859) F
Flemming, Wm. Cannon to Laura Ann Kenney 4-13-1854 (4-15-1854) T
Flemmings, G. S. to M. N. Phillips 12-7-1864 (not endorsed) F
Flerms?, L. to Elisabeth Ticon 7-7-1856 T
Fleschbert, William to Martha E. (Mrs.?) Caldwell 10-24-1863 (11-17-1863) Sh
Fletcher, A. J. to Martha Jones 7-28-1858 G
Fletcher, A. J. to Nancy P. Hooker 9-11-1863 Sh
Fletcher, Abner J. to Martha J. Johnson 6-17-1868 G
Fletcher, Abner J. to Mary J. Wilkes 12-10-1849 (12-12-1849) G
Fletcher, Asberry to Martha Sanders 4-6-1866 (4-10-1866) F B
Fletcher, Benjamin to A. E. Foster 8-21-1863 Hn
Fletcher, Edward F. to Ann Boulton 7-14-1862 (7-16-1862) Sh B
Fletcher, Elijah to Nancy Hatler 4-1-1845 (no return) We
Fletcher, Ephraim to Delithia Sherman 1-17-1866 Hy
Fletcher, Ephran P. to Bettie Turnage 5-27-1867 (6-2-1867) T
Fletcher, Felix to Eliza Smith 11-19-1869 (no return) F B
Fletcher, G. Edwards to Jane Bedford 9-21-1824 L
Fletcher, G. W. to Mollie G. Hill 2-15-1873 (2-16-1873) Cr
Fletcher, G. W. to Sarah E. Woodward 3-23-1855 (no return) Cr
Fletcher, G. W. to Sarah F. Dowdy 3-4-1841 (no return) F
Fletcher, George to Sarah Winders 3-7-1849 Sh
Fletcher, Henry M. to Mary F. Daniel 9-22-1848 Hn
Fletcher, Henry to Caroline Piolate 8-8-1843 G
Fletcher, Henry to Mary Wilkins 7-17-1834 G
Fletcher, Henry to Susan Alexander 10-25-1842 Sh
Fletcher, Isaac L. to Sarah J. Johnson 4-1-1856 (4-2-1856) G
Fletcher, J. B. to Sarah E. Acock 8-4-1873 (8-7-1873) T
Fletcher, J. F. to Metilda F. Butram 6-13-1860 G
Fletcher, J. M. to Elizabeth Henderson 10-7-1846 Sh
Fletcher, J. T. to Mitilda F. Beckam? 6-13-1860 G
Fletcher, James J. to Sallie F. Adams 1-31-1878 Hy
Fletcher, James R. to Delia J. Copeland 8-9-1856 (8-14-1856) G

Fletcher, Jessee to Sally Ann Cornelius 11-17-1838 (11-18-1838) Hr
Fletcher, Jno. H. to Susanna Howard 10-19-1854 Sh
Fletcher, John T. to Caroline Compton 1-7-1840 (1-16-1840) Ma
Fletcher, John to Adaline Rowlan 1-11-1859 Cr
Fletcher, John to Polly Mills 5-17-1854 (5-21-1854) O
Fletcher, Joseph to Rebecka Forrester 9-8-1829 (9-10-1829) G
Fletcher, M. to S. T. Ivey 12-14-1864 (12-18-1864) T
Fletcher, Martin L. to Mary E. Fleshart 11-25-1847 Sh
Fletcher, Moses to Mary Ann Maddocks 10-12-1852 (10-14-1852) T
Fletcher, Reuben to Elizabeth Baysinger 9-21-1831 (9-22-1831) G
Fletcher, Richard to M. A. E. Hall 12-20-1865 (12-24-1865) Dy
Fletcher, Richard to Rozeny Hooks 6-28-1858 (6-29-1858) O
Fletcher, Robert to Jane Wilson 12-5-1855 Sh
Fletcher, Simon to Mary E. Dortch 1-25-1870 (1-26-1870) F B
Fletcher, T. E. to S. M. Davis 8-30-1871 O
Fletcher, Thomas to Elizabeth Miller 11-17-1835 (11-18-1835) G
Fletcher, Thomas to Lucratis Whitley 3-19-1835 G
Fletcher, Thomas to Sarah Lewis 11-27-1830 (12-2-1830) G
Fletcher, W. A. to Elizabeth Forester 9-4-1866 G
Fletcher, William C. to Susan T. Carpenter 1-20-1852 (1-21-1852) O
Fletcher, William to Emily Claiburne 1-15-1868 T
Fletcher, William to Louisa Allen 1-19-1871 (1-22-1871) T
Fletcher, William to Margaret Griffee 4-28-1831 (5-3-1831) G
Fletcher, William to Nancy Fisher 7-14-1830 G
Fletcher, Wm. D. to Elizabeth E. Montgomery 12-12-1870 Ma
Fletcher, Wm. P. to Mary S. Wright 1-26-1843 Cr
Flewellen, Isaiah to Ada Crocker 12-24-1874 L B
Fliedner, George to Louisa Buerklin 1-16-1854 Sh
Flin, Isaiah to Rhoda Teague 12-31-1828 Hr
Flin, John C. to Susan F. McGuire 8-12-1856 (8-13-1856) Ma
Flinn, Connor to Catharine Leslie 9-19-1862 Sh
Flinn, John J. to Annie Clenton 12-5-1867 Hy
Flinn, John to Mary Colligan 11-24-1863 Sh
Flinn, Philip to Cloa Hillard 7-30-1840 G
Flinn, William W. to Mary L. Neely (Nooby?) 7-9-1855 (7-11-1855) Sh
Flinn, William to Mary Hughes 6-9-1860 (6-10-1860) Sh
Flinter, Stewart to Charity T. Thompson 5-31-1832 (6-3-1832) G
Flippen, Thomas to Mary Hatchett 1-4-1865 G
Flippin, Albert R. to Charlott Roachell 9-19-1849 (no return) Cr
Flippin, Allen to Martha A. Holt 8-3-1862 G
Flippin, Benj. M. to Eliza Jane Caldwell 7-22-1838 L
Flippin, Booker to Jantha Brewer 1-7-1870 (no return) F B
Flippin, E. E. to Emma Conger 7-1-1871 (7-3-1871) Ma *
Flippin, G. W. to M. M. Cribbs 4-11-1867 G
Flippin, H. M. to P. J. Belew 11-11-1866 G
Flippin, H. S. to Martha Quinn 1-6-1866 (no return) Cr
Flippin, J. A. to Bettie E. Ddupree 4-11-1864 (4-16-1864) F
Flippin, J. B. to Alice Baird 12-30-1869 G
Flippin, Jabes H. to Patience A. Holt 5-19-1860 (5-21-1860) G
Flippin, James A. to Manirva White 10-24-1846 (10-28-1846) G
Flippin, Jno. L. to Sarah A. Bryant 2-3-1838 G
Flippin, John R. to Mildred A. Nelson 5-2-1871 Hy
Flippin, Joseph T. to Elizabeth Hancock 2-12-1842 (2-17-1842) G
Flippin, M. B. to J. R. Ward 4-7-1866 (4-8-1866) Cr
Flippin, T. J. to Betty N. Word 2-24-1864 (2-25-1864) F
Flippin, Thos. A. to Hanah Belew 12-20-1840 G
Flippin, Thos. A. to Jane A. Patton 2-27-1852 We
Flippin, W. H. to Martha A. Hall 6-14-1864 (6-17-1864) L
Flippin, William J. to Elizabeth Palmore 12-13-1848 (12-21-1848) G
Flippo, Hugh to Lucy H. Thompson 7-27-1867 O
Flippo, Rob't A. to Elizabeth Wallis 7-17-1867 (7-25-1867) O
Flora, Richard to Rebecca H. (N.) Stafford 3-1-1854 O
Flora, William to Nancy Ellis 1-26-1858 Sh
Flora, William to Sarah E. White 4-28-1859 Sh
Flornce, J. B. to Cintha Greer 10-16-1862 We
Flourney, Thomas to Lucy Rice 8-9-1860 Sh
Flower, Andrew Davis to Dicy A. Covinton 2-19-1869 T
Flowers, A. B. to Margarette Wright 7-30-1862 G
Flowers, Alfred to Martha Patterson 12-26-1845 (12-28-1845) G
Flowers, Allen to Elizabeth J. Sims 11-23-1853 (11-24-1853) G
Flowers, Andrew D. to D. A. Carrington 2-19-1869 (2-20-1869) T
Flowers, B. L. to E. L. Haliburten 1-10-1866 G
Flowers, B. S. to Mary F. Ferress 8-25-1859 G
Flowers, Blakers to Malinda Carey 10-19-1858 G
Flowers, Briant to Susan Strauther 8-4-1836 (8-14-1836) G
Flowers, Burnell to Mary A. Flowers 1-21-1860 (1-22-1860) G
Flowers, Calvin to Lucenda Boyett 3-11-1851 (3-14-1851) G
Flowers, Calvin to Martha Wollard 3-21-1859 (3-22-1859) G
Flowers, Calvin to Nancy R. Wiggs 11-3-1864 G
Flowers, Calvin to Susan C. Crews 5-17-1845 (5-22-1845) G
Flowers, David to Charrity Keathly 1-31-1846 (2-1-1846) G
Flowers, David to Eveline Flowers 11-8-1869 G
Flowers, David to Nancy Keathly 6-15-1843 (6-18-1843) G
Flowers, Edmund K. to Susan Lyons 2-7-1848 G
Flowers, Elihu to Susan E. Canada 2-6-1867 G
Flowers, Enoch to Nancy E. Whitley 12-30-1853 (1-1-1854) Sh
Flowers, Green G. to Sarah A. Gordon 12-11-1866 Be

Flowers, Henry L. to Sarah M. Porter 2-14-1865 G
Flowers, Henry to Mary T. Halliburton 9-20-1836 G
Flowers, Henry to Nancy J. Howell 11-18-1866 G
Flowers, Hilary J. to Susan F. Evens 10-18-1870 G
Flowers, Hillorry to Nancy Thetford 4-4-1835 (4-5-1835) G
Flowers, Ickabad to Jane Partridge 12-21-1833 Hr
Flowers, Isaac H. to Martha F. Crenshaw 8-21-1866 G
Flowers, Isaac L. to Martha F. Carey 8-14-1860 G
Flowers, J. H. to R. H. Rice 11-13-1860 T
Flowers, J. T. to S. J. Orms 4-6-1865 G
Flowers, Jacob C. to Elizabeth A. House 2-3-1852 (2-5-1852) G
Flowers, Jacob to Adaline Wilson 1-10-1867 G
Flowers, Jacob to Margaret Thedford 5-21-1836 (5-?-1836) G
Flowers, James C. to Sarah L. Burkett 11-9-1854 Be
Flowers, James H. to Nancy E. Hargett 8-31-1876 O
Flowers, James to Elizabeth Caraway 5-3-1868 G
Flowers, Jessee to Dibby E. Robertson 11-19-1839 (11-29-1839) G
Flowers, Jessee to Sarah Halford 9-18-1845 G
Flowers, John B. to Margaret A. E. Condor 1-13-1863 (no return) Dy
Flowers, John W. to Elizabeth Flowers 9-29-1835 G
Flowers, John to Delila McNeely 9-4-1877 (9-5-1877) O
Flowers, John to Margaret Gregory 9-1-1832 G
Flowers, John to Matilda Porter 12-6-1856 (12-7-1856) G
Flowers, John to Parzada Borrin 5-24-1838 G
Flowers, Joseph to Martha Tyus 1-26-1875 Hy
Flowers, Leoma to Mary A. E. Wright 10-5-1842 (10-6-1842) G
Flowers, Leoma to Nanny Hobbs 12-27-1849 G
Flowers, Lewis to Elizabeth Pigues 12-19-1868 G B
Flowers, M. E. to S. J. Oliphant 5-21-1865 G
Flowers, M. M. to M. F. Snell 9-29-1870 G
Flowers, Mark D. to Lena Guthery 9-28-1864 (10-2-1864) Sh
Flowers, Martin to Sarah Ann Jameson 7-26-1844 Sh
Flowers, Matt W. to Lucinda Young 4-16-1842 (4-17-1842) G
Flowers, Michael to Zady M. Mitchel 12-27-1841 (12-28-1841) G
Flowers, R. B. to Martha Tiner 8-19-1866 G
Flowers, S. W. to Sarah Jane Porter 5-25-1864 G
Flowers, T. J. to L. M. Carrol 3-11-1863 G
Flowers, Thomas J. to Louisa Cathey 9-12-1860 G
Flowers, Thomas to Catherine Graddy 11-29-1841 (11-30-1841) G
Flowers, Thos. to Carroline Warren 2-24-1860 (2-26-1860) G
Flowers, W. A. to S. M. Sorrell 3-19-1867 Dy
Flowers, W. M. to Calista C. Flowers 1-17-1865 G
Flowers, W. M. to M. E. Bonds 9-29-1867 G
Flowers, W. P. to Mary E. Cummins 5-8-1871 T
Flowers, Wile to Margaret Crockett 3-22-1830 (3-25-1830) G
Flowers, Wm. D. to Eliza A. Autry 3-12-1856 Cr
Floyd (Flora), William to Elizabeth W. Woods 8-6-1845 Sh
Floyd, Calvin S. to Elizabeth F. Sisco 10-16-1850 (10-17-1850) F
Floyd, George to Mary F. Trigg 1-31-1855 We
Floyd, Henry to Susan A. Wright 12-23-1854 (12-24-1854) Sh
Floyd, James to Caroline R. Rawlings 12-21-1865 (12-24-1865) F
Floyd, John A. to Susan L. Wright 10-12-1861 (10-20-1861) Dy
Floyd, John C. to Nelly McNeely 12-29-1839 (12-2-1840) Hr
Floyd, John W. to B. M. Clarke 7-19-1859 (7-24-1859) O
Floyd, Madison to Mary Prim 2-17-1846 Hn
Floyd, Miles to Frances Smith 11-30-1865 Dy
Floyd, Thomas W. to Polly Campbell 9-19-1820 Sh
Floyd, Thomas to Nancy Reynolds 2-29-1840 (3-4-1840) Hr
Floyd, Thomas to Sarah Horn 9-11-1838 (9-13-1838) Hr
Floyd, William F. to Mary E. Tyson 1-16-1854 G
Floyd, William H. to Mary E. Howley 8-14-1867 (8-15-1867) L
Floyd, William J. to Edna J. Brownlow 8-8-1846 (no return) F
Floyd, William to Mary A. E. Farris 7-8-1847 Sh
Floyed, R. W. to Mary Catharine Walker 4-13-1852 (no return) F
Fly, Benjamin F. to Mary J. E. Mooring 1-17-1846 (1-21-1846) Ma
Fly, Christopher C. to Amanda M. Doak 3-6-1841 (3-7-1841) Ma
Fly, Flavius to Luvina M. Day 11-9-1852 (11-12-1852) Ma
Fly, G. W. to C. Williams 9-6-1865 G
Fly, H. M. to Sue Roe 3-3-1870 G
Fly, Hannibal to Jenny McDearmon 1-14-1869 G G
Fly, J. C. to Ancie Shaw 12-20-1865 G
Fly, J. C. to M. R. Shelton 6-30-1869 G
Fly, J. H. to Vannie Green 11-27-1866 G
Fly, James C. to Malissa A. Jacobs 9-25-1865 (10-3-1865) Cr
Fly, Jim to Dicy Ingram 2-1-1869 G
Fly, John L. to Mary J. McDaniel 9-25-1847 (12-3-1847) G
Fly, John L. to Sarah A. Davie 12-19-1853 (12-21-1853) Ma
Fly, John to Eliza Ann Tyson 4-23-1830 Ma
Fly, John to Mary F. Lile 11-29-1831 G
Fly, M. D. to Amelda L. Beard 1-16-1861 Sh
Fly, M. D. to Annie McDonald 1-20-1869 G
Fly, M. to Elizabeth A. Smith 5-6-1847 Cr
Fly, Micajah to Frances Senter 9-15-1846 (9-17-1846) G
Fly, S. C. to Nancy M. Hix 12-11-1866 G
Fly, Spencer to Rhoda E. Hale 12-26-1867 G B
Fly, Valse to Sally Word (Ward?) 2-28-1869 G B
Fly, W. A. to Martha E. Hale 11-14-1860 G

Fly, Wm. D. to Sarah L. Lite 10-30-1838 (11-1-1838) G
Flynn, John to Ellen Marcy 2-3-1854 (2-5-1854) Sh
Flynn, Patrick to Mary Ragan 4-13-1861 (4-14-1861) Sh
Fobbs, John to Elizabeth Nowlin 6-19-1843 (no return) Hn
Fodge, George to Catherine B. Denton 1-4-1865 (no return) Hn
Fodge, H. to Saphronia Williams 2-4-1865 (no return) Hn
Fodge, John to Nancy Bowden 11-18-1842 Hn
Fodge, Samuel to America Malear 7-19-1852 Hn
Fodge, William to Nancy Banks 6-27-1844 Hn
Fogarty, Wm. H. to Minerva C. Dawson 9-10-1866 (9-11-1866) Ma
Fogg, Francis A. to Archebia Ann Swan 12-17-1839 (12-20-1839) Ma
Fogg, John D. to Leonora A. Haynie 9-4-1860 Sh
Fogg, Joseph A. to Eliz. R. Dickinson 10-9-1860 Ma
Fogg, Wm. W. to Eliza Smith 12-23-1847 Sh
Folan (Tolan?), John to Margaret Mahon 7-7-1860 (7-15-1860) Sh
Folets?, Alpha J. to Martha H. Wardlaw 6-24-1857 L
Foley (Haley?Holey?), Edward to Margaret McNama 3-4-1851 Sh
Foley, Andrew to Annie Davis 10-14-1874 (10-15-1874) T
Foley, Barthly to E. Kennedy 10-28-1863 Sh
Foley, Benjamin F. to Mary H. Brown 12-22-1853 Sh
Foley, C. A. to Mary Foley 4-4-1855 Sh
Foley, Daniel to Mary Dalsy 9-25-1847 Sh
Foley, Jas. N. to Harriett C. Hart 1-5-1843 Sh
Foley, John to Mary Barron 8-21-1858 (8-22-1858) Sh
Foley, Michael to Margaret Crimmans 4-24-1861 (4-28-1861) Sh
Foley, Michael to Mary Flanikin 1-6-1857 (1-7-1857) Sh
Foley, Morris to Margaret Killeen 4-13-1860 (4-15-1860) Sh
Foley, Thomas to Ann Kennedy 10-22-1861 Sh
Foley, Thomas to Mary Brennan 6-19-1860 Sh
Folger, Benjamin F. to S. C. Tarpley 1-1-1858 Sh
Folkner, Francis C. to Nancy T. Willingham 11-10-1855 (no return) F
Folks, D. L. to Sarah A. Hart 6-10-1855 Hn
Folks, Sherwood to Elizabeth Chamberlin 4-11-1858 Cr
Folks, T. H. to J. A. Ferrell 2-18-1874 (2-19-1874) O
Folks, W. E. to Mary E. Warrington 7-8-1852 Sh
Follis, Francis A. to Lucinda P. Jones 10-23-1860 (10-25-1860) Ma
Follis, Miles H. to Mary Andrews 7-23-1853 G
Follis, Thomas H. to Elizabeth A. Jones 12-21-1859 (12-22-1859) Ma
Follis, W. J. to Julia Peel 10-31-1871 Dy
Folson, Daniel to Eliza A. McDaniel 8-26-1869 (no return) Dy
Folts, Harrison G. to Mary Jane White 6-7-1841 Hr
Folts, Henry to Narciss Bond 4?-18-1868 (no return) L B
Folts, J. C. to Sophronia E. Poston 12-23-1844 Hr
Folwell, William Marsh to Nannie Phillips 11-22-1854 Sh
Folz, T. to Sarah Wolff 8-29-1856 Sh
Fondille, W. G. to M. A. Coggins 12-14-1867 Ma
Fondren, George to Emiline Arnold 9-29-1870 Hy
Fondville, Graves to Mollie M. Ball 8-4-1870 G
Fontaine, Noland to Jennie W. Eanes 4-18-1864 (4-21-1864) Sh
Fonville, Andrew to Kizzie Brooks 1-23-1872 (no return) L
Fonville, Edward to Elizabeth Thompson 5-6-1848 (5-9-1848) O
Fonville, Edwin to Ann Jane Bush 12-12-1831 G
Fonville, John to F. G. Thomas 1-8-1863 (1-12-1863) Dy
Fonville, W. W. to Martha J. Jarvis 1-14-1859 G
Fonville, William A. to Martha Fletcher 9-7-1833 G
Fooshee, T. V. to G. A. Whitten 6-24-1868 G
Foote, T. H. to Mary A. Pickens 11-23-1869 (11-25-1869) F
Forbers, H. J. to Fred E. Bagley 8-31-1861 (9-5-1861) Hr
Forbes, Francis M. to Lucinda Aulsup 7-2-1870 (7-4-1870) F
Forbes, Hamilton F. to Elizabeth Rogers 6-15-1843 Hn
Forbes, Henry T. to Fannie G. Webb 9-12-1855 (no return) F
Forbes, Ira W. to Lydia Boyd 11-19-1864 Sh
Forbes, James to Tiressa Spoon 9-9-1876 (9-15-1876) Dy
Forbess, A. B. to Sarah And. Airs 9-4-1848 (9-27-1848) F
Forbess, A. L. to S. A. Easly 1-8-1872 T
Forbess, C. A. to A. R. F. Wilks 3-25-1858 Cr
Forbess, James to Sarah Laycock 8-7-1845 Cr
Forbess, John C. to Mary W. Howell 5-23-1845 (5-25-1845) T
Forbess, John W. to Martha S. Watson 11-11-1856 Cr
Forbess, Samuel to Rhoda Duveast 12-18-1854 (12-26-1854) T
Forbess, Solomon R. to Sarah P. Turnage 1-26-1870 (1-27-1870) T
Forbess, T. J. to J. A. Miller 12-21-1870 (12-22-1870) T
Forbess, Thomas to Louvina A. McBride 7-16-1866 (7-18-1866) T
Forbess, Wm. C. to Lucy A. Strickland 11-10-1852 Cr
Forbis, Arthur to Martha A. L. Dollar 7-19-1847 (7-20-1847) Ma
Forbis, John to Julian Childress 12-5-1832 H
Forbiss, A. L. to P. Ann McCraw 12-6-1859 (9-8-1859) T
Forbiss, James B. to C. H. Houston 2-25-1859 (2-28-1859) T
Forbiss, James P. to Clerisa H. Houston 2-25-1859 (2-28-1859) T
Forbiss, L. A. to Penelopee Ann McCraw 12-6-1859 T
Forbus, B. T. to L. Ann Bennett 10-26-1871 G
Forbush, Overton to Martha M. Moore 10-6-1834 (10-10-1834) Hr
Force, Chas. O. to Amanda Force 11-24-1884 (11-26-1884) L
Force, John to Amanda Click 4-12-1879 (4-13-1879) L
Force, L. M. to Sarah E. Lincoln 6-11-1880 (6-13-1880) L
Force, Saml. F. to Mary E. Bolt 7-15-1879 (no return) L
Ford, Aaron to Fanny Wright 2-14-1880 (2-18-1880) L

Ford, Augustin P. to Pearcy Ann Lee 8-9-1849 Hr
Ford, B. A. to Martha J. Maxwell 9-17-1850 Hn
Ford, B. C. to C. C. Williams 5-29-1862 Sh
Ford, Charles to Angeline Wright 2-13-1867 Dy
Ford, David to Eliza Addams 7-22-1846 (no return) L
Ford, David to Sarah Caroline Thurmond 7-4-1859 (7-6-1859) L
Ford, David to Sarah F. Pitts 12-4-1846 L
Ford, David to Sarah H. Pitts 2-20-1846 (no return) L
Ford, David to Sarah Salisbury 1-5-1858 (1-6-1858) L
Ford, Edward C. to Elizabeth Bagley 8-30-1845 (9-25-1845) F
Ford, Epraim D. to Susan Baker 3-22-1838 (no return) Hn
Ford, George W. to Nancy Walker 7-18-1829 Sh
Ford, Isaiah to Paulina Burton 1-22-1879 (1-23-1879) L
Ford, J. A. to L. P. Watson 2-3-1873 (2-5-1873) T
Ford, J. P. to S. J. Fleming 11-26-1867 G
Ford, J. W. to Mary F. Pyland 8-28-1866 G
Ford, Jacob to Sally McMullins 10-16-1839 (no return) Cr
Ford, James H. to Harriet O. Goodman 12-16-1867 (no return) Hy
Ford, James to Eliza Earl (Carl?) 6-24-1864 (6-23?-1864) Sh
Ford, James to Linton B. Scruggs 11-11-1836 Sh
Ford, James to Nancy J. Witherspoon 10-7-1866 Hn
Ford, Jefferson to Polly Cain 6-31?-1828 (7-3-1828) Hr
Ford, Jerre to Minerva Walton 1-20-1870 T
Ford, John C. to Jane C. Roberson no date (with 1861) T
Ford, John F. to Margarett E. Williams 10-13-1828 Hr
Ford, John F. to Martha J. McAlister 11-6-1854 (11-13-1854) G
Ford, John T. to Celia Cox 4-28-1845 Cr
Ford, John to Betsy Ann Lauderdale 4-14-1866 T
Ford, John to Nancy Oldham 3-29-1827 Sh
Ford, John to Vilet Hall 9-28-1829 (9-29-1829) G
Ford, Johnson to Sarah T. Soap 12-19-1842 (no return) F
Ford, Josiah S. to Huldy Jones 12-18-1846 (12-20-1846) G
Ford, Larkin H. to June Jones 11-1-1843 Hn
Ford, Loyd to Amanda M. Scruggs 11-22-1837 Sh
Ford, Nathan W. to Malinda Lowry 2-14-1853 (3-3-1853) G
Ford, Nimrod to Ann T. Williams 8-28-1830 Sh
Ford, P. to Margarett A. Kensey 6-18-1858 (6-20-1858) G
Ford, Peter to Elizabeth Williams 1-3-1852 (1-7-1852) Ma
Ford, Powell to Mary E. Anderson 3-10-1854 (3-13-1854) L
Ford, R. S. to S. L. Delancey 2-23-1874 (2-26-1874) T
Ford, Robert P. to Martha A. Day 1-23-1850 (1-25-1850) Ma
Ford, Robert to Mary Murphy 10-8-1836 Hr
Ford, Solomon D. to Nancy (Mrs.) Wilkins 11-30-1860 Ma
Ford, Sterling B. to Martha W. Parker 3-29-1849 G
Ford, T. J. to Susan A. Vaughn 2-17-1858 G
Ford, Thomas J. to Julia A. E. McCaslin 10-30-1860 G
Ford, Thomas to Alice Burke 12-16-1845 Sh
Ford, Thomas to Elizabeth Pittman 8-16-1858 Sh
Ford, Thos. to _____ 4-3-1867 (no return) Hy
Ford, Tom to Caroline Tops 8-30-1870 (no return) Hy
Ford, W. P. to Susan J. McCaslin 1-23-1861 G
Ford, William R. to Mary E. Ellis 11-1-1843 Hn
Ford, William to Margaret Valentine 7-14-1852 We
Ford, William to Martha Magee 12-7-1840 Hr
Ford, William to Mary Henley 2-10-1854 Sh
Ford, Wm. Thos. to Dorcus Melissa Thompson 1-28-1851 T
Fore, Peter to Mary Gunter 1-10-1849 Sh
Forehana, Solomon to Telitha Ammons 11-29-1837 Hr
Forehand, Eli to Margaret Weaks 2-17-1829 Ma
Forem, J. A. to M. E. Lowry 1-11-1865 G
Foreman, John J. to Arabella Armstrong 9-14-1855 (9-17-1855) Sh
Foreman, John to Pamina Higginbottom 11-23-1842 Ma
Foren, Alex to Sarah Stiller 7-5-1834 G
Foren, George W. to Elizabeth Webb 2-9-1850 (2-13-1850) G
Foren, John to Sarah J. Cooper 1-1-1866 G
Foren, Moses to Ciely Reagan 4-27-1824 (4-29-1824) Hr
Foren, William to Arreana Griffin 5-9-1836 (5-10-1836) G
Foreshee, John to M. C. House 5-28-1867 Dy
Forest, Benjamin to Susan Ann Townsend 3-17-1851 Be
Forest, Calvin to Rebecca Clayborn 5-3-1845 Be
Forest, F. M. to Lany Adams 12-5-1853 Be
Forest, H. to Susan Alsup 12-5-1856 Be
Forest, James H. to America Thompson 1-15-1851 Cr
Forest, John H. to Sarah A. Cole 2-2-1865 Be
Forest, John J. to Elizabeth Buchanan 6-22-1863 Be
Forest, John W. to Nancy Farmer 12-31-1860 (1-1-1861) Sh
Forest, Levi W. to Lydia Smothers 1-10-1854 Be
Forest, Mark to Rebecca Pollard 1-24-1829 (1-31-1829) G
Forest, Moses to Fanny Tucker 12-4-1868 (no return) Hy
Forest, Watson to Sarah Crafton 11-?-1834 G
Forest, Wm. D. to Mary Bilerly 6-21-1854 Cr
Forest, Wm. F. to Margaret C. Allen 9-23-1871 (9-24-1871) Cr
Forester, C. B. to Frances E. Arnold 4-7-1870 G
Forester, David to Caroline Forister 3-15-1840 Be
Forester, Dillard to Malinda Cantrell 5-28-1831 (6-17-1831) G
Forester, James to Mary A. McKinney 8-5-1835 (8-15-1835) G
Forester, John to Nancy Rochell 6-26-1840 (no return) Cr

Forester, Jonah to Amanda Reans 1-7-1858 We
Forester, Josiah to Celia Morris 7-7-1845 Be
Forester, William to Mary Rualdo 12-31-1830 (1-10-1831) G
Foresyth, T. D. to F. A. B. Pearce 1-15-1873 Cr
Forgey, A. J. to Samantha Glover 10-26-1853 Sh
Forgey, Henry to Jane M. Bond 10-8-1852 Sh
Forhand, Hardyman to Phildes Burns 6-4-1846 Be
Forisher, Thomas V. to Marian A. Leetch 6-9-1864 Dy
Forister, Hardin G. to Catherine Quarles 7-3-1835 Sh
Forley, Timothy to Margaret Callahan 5-1-1858 (5-2-1858) Sh
Forren, William to Elizabeth Vaughn 11-16-1843 G
Forrest, Aron to Lidy Cobb 12-26-1877 Hy
Forrest, Balis to Martha Townsend 11-21-1844 Be
Forrest, Benj. F. to Mary E. Bibb 11-11-1871 (11-12-1871) T
Forrest, C. to Sarah J. White 12-23-1866 Hn
Forrest, Dock to Tempe Simmons 2-22-1866 (no return) F B
Forrest, Francis M. to Sarah Jane Short 9-25-1851 Be
Forrest, Harrison to Mary McKennan 1-7-1870 (no return) Hy
Forrest, James N. to Roena H. Pearce 2-23-1851 Be
Forrest, John G. to Martha H. Stubblefield 9-25-1865 (no return) Hn
Forrest, Light to Fannie Transon 2-2-1877 Hy
Forrest, Matthew Bishop to Polly Edwards 8-8-1850 Cr
Forrest, Peter to Millie Horton 1-11-1878 (no return) Hy
Forrest, Robt. to Ella Bryant 2-26-1873 Hy
Forrest, S. B. to Sarah N. Wateridge 11-21-1869 Hy
Forrest, Samuel B. to Mary C. McDonald 1-17-1852 Ma
Forrest, Samuel L. to Elizabeth Harter 2-7-1850 Hn
Forrest, Turner to Mollie Grey 1-26-1867 Hy
Forrest, W. H. to H. Maxwell 7-9-1864 Sh
Forrest, William to Jane Cruse 4-7-1858 Hn
Forrest, Wm. L. to Eliza J. Turner 5-10-1845 (no return) Cr
Forrest, Wm. S. to Ann Chumney 9-23-1864 (9-25-1864) O
Forrester, Charles to Kizza Sellers 10-23-1839 G
Forrester, J. F. to Eliza Ann Oliver 12-21-1864 Sh
Forrester, Van to Louisa Poole 5-3-1852 (5-6-1852) Sh
Forrester, William F. to Martha J. Rocheld 10-23-1844 (10-24-1844) Ma
Forristed, Henry to Mahaley Cantrell 1-21-1854 (1-22-1854) G
Fors, Sherwood to Louisa L. Pinson 6-28-1846 Cr
Forshee, F. N. to Nancy Evans 5-13-1866 Dy
Forsyth, Benj. Franklin to Mary Paralee Shivers 8-22-1871 (8-23-1871) Ma
Forsyth, John W. to Pheby Jane Helm 1-23-1869 (1-28-1869) L
Forsyth, Joseph to Elizabeth M. Sherrill 11-13-1866 (11-15-1866) T
Forsyth, S. A. to Lucinda Brackin 12-28-1872 (1-7-1873) Dy
Forsyth, Thomas to E. G. Murphy 11-12-1863 Mn
Forsyth, W. S. to H. H. Johnson 6-11-1873 (6-15-1873) Dy
Forsythe, Edward to Isabella Tayler 7-13-1865 G
Forsythe, Isham L. to Nancy E. Brasher 9-5-1873 (9-7-1873) L
Forsythe, Robert to Frances Hawkins ?-?-1862? Mn
Forsythe, P. W. to S. M. Fisher 1-29-1866 G
Forsythe, S. L. to E. J. Watson 2-24-1855 (2-25-1855) Sh
Forsythe, T. J. to Sibetta Lewis 11-11-1871 (no return) Hy
Fort, David W. to Adeline D. Goode 12-6?-1841 (no return) F
Fort, Hilliard to Marabeth Rayden 2-19-1857 Cr
Forte, Elias to Nancy Simmons 10-13-1825 (10-15-1825) Hr
Fortenberry, Malv. D. to Ann Eliza Lanier 4-11-1867 Hy
Fortenberry, Wm. J. to Annisy Allen 8-10-1842 (8-11-1842) Hr
Fortner, Benjamin to Elizabeth A. Bryant 12-15-1847 (12-21-1847) Hr
Fortner, David to Mary Jackson 9-10-1859 (9-11-1859) Hr
Fortner, Efel D. to Margaret Nabers 6-23-1838 (7-1-1838) Hr
Fortner, G. W. to V. F. Hendren 4-4-1876 (no return) Hy
Fortner, George W. to Martha Elizabeth Anthony 12-22-1852 (12-23-1852) Hr
Fortner, James H. to Safronia Evaline Burkhart 8-27-1846 (9-3-1846) T
Fortner, James M. to Frances J. Cross 2-5-1850 (2-10-1850) Hr
Fortner, John F. to Emmia L. Ellis 8-14-1875 T
Fortner, Joseph E. to Lucy E. McKnight 12-17-1850 Ma
Fortner, Joseph E. to Mary E. Taylor 10-12-1853 (10-13-1853) L
Fortner, L. D. to Ada R. Griffith 7-30-1883 (7-31-1883) L
Fortner, Lewis D. to Martha A. Taylor 12-16-1854 (no return) F
Fortner, M. B. to Susie Davidson 9-16-1884 (no return) L
Fortner, Robert F. F. to Margaret Baker 12-29-1846 Sh
Fortner, Robert T. to Martha Mickelberry 3-29-1851 (3-30-1851) T
Fortner, Robt. J. to Elizabeth Grantham 8-6-1856 (8-7-1856) Hr
Fortner, Sample A. to Nancy (Jane) Rankin 1-9-1858 (2-11-1858) Hr
Fortner, William A. to Sallie E. Myers 12-17-1866 (12-16?-1866) T
Fortson, George to Winney Granberry 4-27-1869 (no return) F B
Fortune, E. F. to Frances Johnson 11-17-1855 (11-6?-1855) Hr
Fortune, Frank to Ann Liza Yarbro 11-21-1867 G
Fortune, James V. to Mary E. Thompson 8-4-1856 (8-7-1856) Hr
Fortune, NiNicholass to Racheal Pascal 4-30-1834 Hr
Fortune, William to Elizabeth A. F. Gill 1-25-1842 G
Fortune, Wm. N. to Susan E. Stewart 5-15-1861 Hr
Forwell, Oscar O. to Sarah Ann Coker 7-30-1859 Ma
Fossett, Burkie A. to Jane D. Hays 8-23-1867 (8-25-1867) Ma
Foster, A. C. to Catharine J. Brooks 12-23-1844 We
Foster, A. D. S. to Elizabeth J. Punch 4-26-1856 (4-27-1856) Hr
Foster, A. G. to Elizabeth Campbell 4-27-1853 (no return) F
Foster, A. J. to Elizabeth Eason 7-29-1865 (8-1-1865) Dy

Foster, Amos to Eliza Parks 9-30-1826 (10-3?-1826) Hr
Foster, Andrew P. to Sibly Johnston 2-17-1838 (2-21-1838) G
Foster, Antonio J. to Catherine (Mrs.) Lewis 11-20-1864 Sh
Foster, Boston to Allie Jeans 8-11-1874 Hy
Foster, Braddock to Marcilla C. Brown 2-11-1860 (2-14-1860) Hr
Foster, Bryant to Nancy Ann Tilmon 12-2-1841 Hr
Foster, C. A. to F. D. Weston 12-4-1838 (1-22-1839) F
Foster, Charles to Mary Roth 6-15-1860 Sh
Foster, Clabourn to Priscilla Owen 10-8-1825 O
Foster, D. C. to Mary A. McGehee 1-8-1852 Hn
Foster, D. to Paralee Harrison 9-21-1867 G
Foster, Daniel D. to Martha S Lemings 12-17-1860 (12-27-1860) Hr
Foster, Dave to Eliza Walker 12-16-1876 (12-24-1876) Dy
Foster, E. J. to S. J. Weeks 12-17-1860 Sh
Foster, Elijah to Mary McCall 9-6-1838 Hn
Foster, G. M. to S. F. Caton 6-29-1865 (no return) Hn
Foster, Hamilton to Nancy Chandler 12-27-1847 (12-28-1847) G
Foster, Henry to Mary Ann Call (Cole) 3-7-1859 Sh
Foster, Henry to Sarah Walker 12-11-1880 (12-17-1880) Dy
Foster, J. A. to Martha J. Dortch 5-26-1867 Hn
Foster, J. W. to R. A. Dockins 8-29-1866 G
Foster, J. W. to Sarah C. George 12-11-1865 (12-31-1865) Cr
Foster, J.A. to A. S. Kennedy 12-20-1866 G
Foster, Jack to Angeline Ware 4-27-1866 (no return) Hy
Foster, Jacob to Eliza Doyle 1-7-1868 Dy
Foster, Jacob to Martha Maggard 9-7-1870 (no return) Dy
Foster, James A. to Elizabeth Ashley 4-21-1861 Hn
Foster, James A. to Montie Ferguson 5-11-1875 Dy
Foster, James C. to Maryann Roe 1-25-1843 (2-2-1843) F
Foster, James Marlon to Sarah Jane De Armond 8-27-1857 Sh
Foster, James P. to Margaret A. Hailey 10-4-1849 G
Foster, James to Eliza Jane Bellamy 1-3-1853 Sh
Foster, James to Laura Mebane 10-28-1868 (no return) F B
Foster, James to Patsey Whitley 11-15-1870 T
Foster, Joel to Margaret Nixon 9-22-1829 Hr
Foster, John C. to Martha A. Cole 8-30-1843 (8-31-1843) G
Foster, John C. to Samira C. Craven 12-22-1854 (12-24-1854) Hr
Foster, John D. to Parale M. E. Webb 12-22-1852 L
Foster, John W. to Matilda Fletcher 11-22-1841 (11-23-1841) G
Foster, John to Frances A. McKee 1-6-1851 (1-7-1851) Hr
Foster, John to Sarah Ann Simpkin 5-5-1830 (5-6-1830) Hr
Foster, Joseph A. to Malissa H. Canada 11-8-1859 G
Foster, L. J. to V. L. Mitchell 11-12-1874 (11-15-1874) O
Foster, L. W. to Elizabeth Wilkinson 12-28-1852 Hr
Foster, Lee to Manerva Harris 12-24-1872 (12-26-1872) Cr B
Foster, Louis to Mary Divine 8-24-1864 Sh
Foster, Murry W. to Mary P. Caples 1-6-1855 (1-7-1855) G
Foster, Orlando P. to Ella Wood 4-11-1860 (no return) Hn
Foster, P. W. C. to Manda C. Winn 2-21-1858 G
Foster, Peter G. to Hannah S. Willett 3-16-1853 Hn
Foster, Pleasant H. to Mary J. Parker 8-2-1860 Hn
Foster, R. M. to Belle Fields 1-19-1881 L
Foster, Robert A. to Mary Ann Stevens 10-19-1843 Hn
Foster, Robert G. to Sarah C. Nance 12-20-1857 Hn
Foster, Robert L. to Lucy M. Crank 5-6-1852 (no return) F
Foster, Robert Thompson to Louisa A. P. Hill 12-20-1847 (12-23-1847) T
Foster, Robert W. to Sarah M. Willett 3-24-1845 Hn
Foster, Robert to Milly Ann Lynch 10-6-1866 Ma
Foster, Robt. Thompson to Louisa Townsend 12-1-1851 (12-4-1851) T
Foster, Samuel C. to Rutha Crockett 10-14-1845 We
Foster, Samuel L. to Elizabeth Harter 2-7-1850 Hn
Foster, Thomas H. to Mary Keating 4-30-1865 (no return) Hn
Foster, Thomas J. to Louisa F. Alrich? 12-18-1866 (12-19-1866) Cr
Foster, Thomas to Margarett Neal 8-31-1835 O
Foster, Thomas to Sarah E. McRee 7-5-1860 O
Foster, Thomas to Susan Ezell 5-17-1855 (no return) We
Foster, Thomas to Susan Ezzell 5-17-1856 (no return) We
Foster, W. B. to Eliza Rogers 5-1-1851 Hr
Foster, W. B. to Martha Somers 8-31-1860 (9-2-1860) Hr
Foster, W. D. to Hester Mangrum 3-18-1863 O
Foster, W. H. to M. L. Maclin 12-10-1872 (12-11-1872) L
Foster, W. H. to Mary A. Belch 12-27-1867 G
Foster, W. H. to R. E. (Mrs.) George 5-30-1867 G
Foster, W. H. to Sue Lannom 9-10-1866 G
Foster, W. L. to Frances M. Gilbert 10-22-1856 We
Foster, Wildon to Barbery B. Barber 9-11-1838 Ma
Foster, William B. to Ann Rogers 5-1-1835 (5-14-1835) Hr
Foster, William B. to Susan G. Donaldson 3-5-1849 G
Foster, William G. to Nannie Johnson 8-15-1859 (no return) We
Foster, William J. to Lavina J. Craven 12-27-1854 (12-28-1854) Hr
Foster, William to C. A. Ross 1-2-1870 G
Foster, William to Jane Gay 11-18-1844 We
Foster, William to Mary Donne (Donna?) 11-23-1864 (11-24-1864) Sh
Foster, William to Phoebe Moores 11-27-1856 O
Fouch, Ed to Elizabeth Hancock 11-25-1867 G B
Fouler, P. T. M. to Malinda Wilson 4-1-1846 We
Foulkes, Charley to Phillip Pierce 10-30-1880 (10-31-1880) Dy

Foulks, N. G. to Mary Barnett 8-20-1865 (8-20-___) O
Foulks, N. G. to Sarah Barnett 7-5-1876 (7-6-1876) O
Foulks, W. F. to H. A. Turner 1-15-1874 O
Fountain, William to Clara A. Parker 3-31-1859 (4-5-1859) Sh
Fouse (Foust), Henry to Morton Eliza 8-21-1875 (no return) Hy
Foust, Abin to Harriet Taliaferro 1-1-1867 Hy
Foust, Daniel to Hannah Sawyer 4-16-1872 Dy
Foust, Elija to Ann M. Davison 11-17-1857 Hn
Foust, Elijah to Mary Calloway 3-1-1849 Hn
Foust, George to Malinda A. Brown 1-15-1842 Hn
Foust, H. D. to A. M. Terry 1-22-1852 Hn
Foust, Jacob to Mary Ann Dunlap 11-15-1846 Hn
Foust, Jesse to Martha Rial 6-27-1838 Hn
Foust, Mik to Viney Stewart 3-5-1868 Dy
Foust, Peter to Sarah Ryals 10-21-1840 We
Foust, William to Sarah Palmer 12-20-1854 Hn
Foust, Wm. to Catherine Sawyer 10-23-1867 (no return) Dy
Fouster, B. R. to Eliza Holt 2-11-1857 G
Foutch, James A. to Louisa Lee 5-5-1846 Hn
Foutch, John to Emily Braden 6-9-1855 (6-10-1855) G
Foutch, William V. to Martha Attman 2-12-1852 G
Fouth, John F. to Rebecca L. Seahorn 3-30-1867 Ma
Fowler, Abram to Margaret Wyatt 12-25-1856 Sh
Fowler, Adam to Eliza Patterson 11-25-1865 (4-14-1866) Cr
Fowler, Andrew to Louisa Green 12-8-1880 L
Fowler, C. C. to Elmyra Williams 3-9-1881 L
Fowler, C. S. to H. A. Smith 1-10-1856 We
Fowler, Calvin C. to Elizabeth A. Dunn 1-31-1850 Hn
Fowler, Cezar to Emma Ware 1-18-1875 Hy
Fowler, Daniel N. to Mary S. Strengths 8-1-1877 Hy
Fowler, Dixon G. to Geraldine Porter 10-20-1859 Hn
Fowler, Francis F. to Caroline M. Fleming 1-7-1841 Sh
Fowler, G. W. to Mary F. Legate 1-10-1856 Be
Fowler, George W. to Hannah Roberts 11-19-1854 Hn
Fowler, George W. to Miamma A. Roach 2-5-1855 We
Fowler, George to Ann E. Hall 2-11-1867 (2-17-1867) T
Fowler, H. W. to Elizabeth Patterson 10-5-1854 We
Fowler, Hardy to Sarah Dockings 3-15-1839 (3-20-1839) G
Fowler, Isaac to Rebecca Cooper 10-21-1843 (10-24-1843) G
Fowler, Isaac to Sabra Cooper 3-17-1840 G
Fowler, J. C. H. to Jane Darnell 11-1-1850 Hr
Fowler, J. C. H. to Jane Darnell 7-14-1853 Hn
Fowler, J. C. to Rachael Ann Guise 6-3-1864 Sh
Fowler, James A. to Martha A. Tuberville 12-22-1858 We
Fowler, James E. to L. C. Harris 3-1-1848 Hn
Fowler, James F. to Fereby Stone 2-7-1839 Cr
Fowler, James W. to Lucy A. Wilson 12-12-1855 We
Fowler, James to E. J. See 2-22-1853 Hn
Fowler, Jesse to Elizabeth Banks 6-20-1850 Hn
Fowler, Jno. T. to Eliza Young 2-28-1871 Ma
Fowler, John Fell to Clarisa Aldridge 9-14-1868 T
Fowler, John W. to Louisa Oldham 9-12-1840 Sh
Fowler, John W. to R. Eagle 1-6-1858 Sh
Fowler, John to Bettie Rhodes 3-13-1873 T
Fowler, Joseph B. to Martha E. Jarrett? 10-21-1861 (no return) Cr
Fowler, Joseph to Eliza Shaw 2-25-1869 (2-26-1869) F B
Fowler, Mason to Sarah E. Middleton 11-30-1861 Mn
Fowler, R. T. to Sallie E. Sparks 2-4-1867 (2-14-1867) Cr
Fowler, Robert L. to M. Adella Cheek 3-4-1879 L
Fowler, Samuel to Sarah Ann Puckett 11-2-1851 Hn
Fowler, T. H. to Rachel Husted 10-16-1854 (no return) We
Fowler, Thomas J. to Sarah A. Sadler 11-13-1856 We
Fowler, W. H. to Emma (Mrs.) Frazier 7-11-1874 (7-12-1874) Dy
Fowler, William H. to Nancy C. Payne 12-26-1846 (12-27-1847?) F
Fowler, William J. to C. H. Duncan 8-25-1853 Hn
Fowler, William L. to Kessiah Adams 9-15-1837 Sh
Fowler, William S. to Elizabeth Langford 8-16-1852 Hn
Fowler, William S. to Martha Ann McCaslin 7-15-1850 (7-17-1850) G
Fowler, William to Elizabeth M. Lester 6-22-1846 Hn
Fowler, Winifred to Mary Spencer 11-6-1844 Hn
Fowler?, Simon to Ellen Ridgeway 12-28-1868 (12-29-1868) O
Fowlk, Joseph to Elizabeth Millikin 12-6-1842 Sh
Fowlkes, Albert to Martha Southern 12-28-1866 Dy
Fowlkes, Base to Easter Neely 12-12-1871 (12-13-1871 Dy
Fowlkes, Benj. to Dora Brooks 4-1-1870 (4-3-1870) T
Fowlkes, Calvin to Martha Saichern? 10-9-1876 Dy
Fowlkes, Daniel to Caroline Crow 10-11-1877 Dy
Fowlkes, David to Jane Fumbank 9-8-1866 (no return) Dy
Fowlkes, Frank to Eliza Vinson 11-27-1875 Dy
Fowlkes, G. A. to Z. F. Ledsinger 4-4-1865 (4-6-1865) Dy
Fowlkes, Geo. to Jane Corley 1-6-1876 (1-13-1876) Dy
Fowlkes, Green to Amanda Sigrary? 2-14-1880 (2-16-1880) Dy
Fowlkes, Green to Lucy Parker 11-18-1870 Dy B
Fowlkes, H. A. to Z. F. Fowlkes 10-29-1874 Dy
Fowlkes, Isaac to Tennessee Light 4-17-1877 Dy
Fowlkes, J. A. to A. O. Ledsinger 6-3-1869 Dy
Fowlkes, James to Lucy Smith 12-1-1870 Dy B

Fowlkes, Jeptha L. to Mary C. King 5-30-1850 Sh
Fowlkes, Jeptha to Sarah Lamb 10-26-1852 Sh
Fowlkes, Jeptha to Sidney G. Lamb 6-11-1842 Sh
Fowlkes, Jerry to Lucinda Ferguson 10-4-1873 Dy
Fowlkes, Jerry to Mary Connell 11-28-1867 Dy
Fowlkes, Jery to Lou Barnett 3-28-1876 (no return) Dy
Fowlkes, Jo to Lucinda Foster 9-22-1877 (9-25-1877) Dy
Fowlkes, John to Laura Copeland 12-29-1880 (12-30-1880) Dy
Fowlkes, Lewis to Rhoda Haskins 7-8-1871 (no return) Dy
Fowlkes, Louis to Candice Fuller 2-6-1878 (2-7-1878) Dy
Fowlkes, Manson to Eliza Davis 7-11-1878 Dy
Fowlkes, Matt to Judy Chitwood 12-22-1866 (12-24-1866) Dy
Fowlkes, Mose to Adaline Wallae 9-4-1876 Dy
Fowlkes, Parsha L. to Scrappie E. Light 11-12-1874 Dy
Fowlkes, Taylor to Nancy Smith 8-14-1868 (8-16-1868) Dy
Fowlkes, William to America Ferguson 6-29-1871 Dy
Fowlkes, jr., William P. to Sarah E. Connell 6-15-1863 Dy
Fowlks, Boss to Mollie Woods 9-25-1879 Dy
Fowlks, Martin to Joanna Wyatt 8-28-1879 Dy
Fox, Alen to Jane Hall 4-11-1828 G
Fox, Alexander to Sarah A. Mitts 10-20-1853 (10-24-1853) G
Fox, Allen to Mary Ann Reed 11-23-1848 G
Fox, C. H. to Lizzie Brock 1-13-1875 Hy
Fox, Daniel to Mary Frick 2-11-1843 Sh
Fox, Daniel to Matilda Ingram 10-18-1848 (10-19-1848) G
Fox, Daniel to Sarah A. Fox 2-21-1856 We
Fox, David C. to Tennessee Reed 3-16-1869 G
Fox, Edward to Mary Morris 5-2-1837 (6-8-1837) G
Fox, Enoch to Darcus Fox 7-15-1845 G
Fox, George to Sarah Fuller 2-17-1873 (no return) L
Fox, Gideon to Susan Martin 2-8-1856 O
Fox, H. G. to Sarah A. Lee 3-11-1852 Sh
Fox, Henry C. to Emily F. Gates 3-17-1862 (3-20-1862) F
Fox, Jackson to Dilly Morris 10-27-1838 G
Fox, John O. to Alsey M. Beck 5-6-1850 (5-8-1850) G
Fox, John to Lavinia F. McNair 6-8-1869 G
Fox, John to Susan Monroe 12-27-1866 Hn
Fox, John(son?) M. to S. Johns 2-3-1869 G
Fox, Johnston to Nany Ingram 6-13-1843 G
Fox, Joseph W. to Mary A. Hampton 2-9-1869 G
Fox, Paton to Catharine Murphey 3-5-1830 (3-18-1830) G
Fox, Thomas J. to _____ 1-23-1882 (no return) L B
Fox, William L. to Mary J. Hamilton 4-21-1852 (4-27-1852) Ma
Fox, William to Margaret Maroney 12-13-1862 Sh
Fox, William to Susan Ann Morris 12-15-1846 (12-20-1846) G
Foy, B. F. to Rachel E. Champin 6-28-1848 Hn
Foy, J. H. to Elizabeth C. Matthews 1-11-1854 (1-11-1855?) Sh
Foy, M. T. to Hannah Ellis 10-22-1865 Mn
Fradle?, Alex. W. to Emly McGuire 5-18-1854 T
Fraizar, Ephran to Matilda Jones 6-15-1865 T
Fraley, Phillip to Laura Campbell 12-30-1869 (1-7-1870) T
France, B. F. to Ragner Bell 1-26-1858 Cr
Frances, E. T. to Mary A. Parish 12-9-1854 We
Franchey, L. M. to S. _. Richardson 4-29-1876 L
Francis, A. E. to Nancy Ann Dorhorty 8-1-1846 We
Francis, General M. to Margaret D. Harris 6-23-1866 (6-24-1866) Ma
Francis, John M. to Mary Ann Morgan 6-19-1858 We
Francis, Moses D. to Harriett Chandler 8-20-1845 Hn
Francis, Nathan to Catherine Drake 1-29-1859 Ma
Francis, Nathan to Cynthia McVey 5-1-1848 Ma
Francis, Oliver to Rebecca Mangrum 2-14-1842 (2-16-1842) F
Francis, Stephen to Mary Gammill 10-6-1863 Sh
Francis, W. H. to L. A. Myers 8-8-1866 (8-9-1866) T
Francis, William L. to Susan Winters 11-29-1861 We
Francisco, Peter to Maria L. Rowe 1-24-1861 Be
Francisco, William to Rebeca Monroe 11-21-1861 (no return) Cr
Frank, John to Caroline Mannet 4-25-1848 Sh
Frank, John to Rebecca Long 1-22-1880 (1-25-1880) L
Frank, W. H. to F. J. Robertson 5-30-1859 F
Franklin, Alexander to Charlotte Doss 12-30-1866 (1-1-1866?) F B
Franklin, August Munroe to Caroline Lloyd 10-31-1868 (11-1-1868) L B
Franklin, B. D. to Mary Ann Stephenson 9-22-1844 We
Franklin, Ben to Sarah Parilee 4-30-1866 Hy
Franklin, Benj. to Mary White 3-19-1851 (no return) Cr
Franklin, Beverly to Ann Maria Nevils 5-26-1848 (no return) L
Franklin, C. M. to M. E. Thurmond 10-22-1859 (10-27-1859) Hr
Franklin, Cornelius to Becky Shaw 12-25-1867 F B
Franklin, D. C. to N. B. Van Eaton 10-20-1879 (10-21-1879) Dy
Franklin, Fleming to Mary E. Johnston 2-3-1860 (no return) Hy
Franklin, George to Kittie Woods 12-26-1871 Hy
Franklin, Henry D. to Anna B. Sherwood 12-8-1869 (12-9-1869) Ma
Franklin, Henry to R. Jane Allen 1-22-1870 (1-27-1870) F B
Franklin, J. L. to Mattia Bell 4-9-1863 Mn
Franklin, James F. to Eliza A. Anderson 4-26-1858 (4-27-1858) Ma
Franklin, Jesse B. to May C. Wilson 11-10-1845 Hr
Franklin, Jessee D. to Amelia L.(S?) Thurmond 1-25-1849 (1-30-1849) Hr
Franklin, John J. to Eliza J. Banks 1-15-1868 Dy

Franklin, John N. to Nancy Hardy 2-8-1852 Ma
Franklin, Joseph P. to Elizabeth W. Browder 1-24-1865 Mn
Franklin, Josiah to Virginia Cox 4-2-1860 (no return) Hy
Franklin, Logan to Sarah Jane Beassee 5-20-1857 O
Franklin, M. B. to Nancy H. Brown 8-18-1850 O
Franklin, Meshack to J. P. Wilborne 4-26-1866 (5-2-1866) F
Franklin, Monroe to Mary Green 4-6-1867 (4-20-1867) L B
Franklin, Robert A. to Livinia Jane Wilson 6-29-1842 Hr
Franklin, Robert H. to Susan Frances Ross 12-8-1853 O
Franklin, Robert to Elizabeth Page 8-19-1828 G
Franklin, Stephen to Mary E. Smith 11-1-1864 (10?-1-1864) Sh B
Franklin, T. H. to R. A. King 11-9-1869 (11-10-1869) Dy
Franklin, Thomas D. to Mary L. C. Moodey 5-3-1845 (5-7-1845) F
Franklin, Thomas to Augusta Parr 7-21-1877 (7-22-1877) L B
Franklin, Thomas to Catherine Little 9-30-1850 Hn
Franklin, Thomas to Ellen Duncan 9-23-1867 (9-24-1867) Cr
Franklin, William C. to Saryan Crowson 9-22-1847 O
Franklin, William to Caroline Stephens 10-28-1847 Hn
Franklin, William to Hannah Mebane 12-27-1867 (no return) L
Franklin, Wm. E. to Willie Wilkinson 2-7-1871 (2-8-1871) F
Franklin, Wm. to Lucy Baldwin 1-1-1869 (1-2-1869) F B
Franks, Peter to Julia Pace 1-26-1864 Sh
Fransiola, Felix to Amana (Amena) Fegan 8-3-1850 Sh
Fransiolo, Joseph to Susan Coward 6-16-1863 Sh
Fransisco, John W. to Lydia J. Taylor 11-24-1857 Cr
Fraser, George W. to L. V. Nelson 1-17-1860 (1-18-1860) Sh
Fraser, Henry to Jennie Pattillo 1-2-1867 F B
Fraser, John to Frances Swift 2-21-1867 (no return) F B
Fraser, M. G. to Harriet Wortham 2-20-1867 F
Fraser, R. C. to Mollie Graham 9-5-1866 (9-6-1866) F
Fraser, Silo to Berlin Dickinson 1-3-1868 (no return) F B
Fraser, Washington C. to Elizabeth H. Champion 1-16-1836 Sh
Fraser, Wm. L. to Hattie E. Fraser 6-8-1865 F
Frasier, Bob to Viney Cross 9-6-1867 Hy
Frasier, Sam to Mary Fitzpatrick 12-22-1876 L
Frasure (Frazier), J. L. to M. E. Florence 12-18-1862 Be
Frayser, John R. to Pauline A. P. Brown 11-22-1837 Sh
Frazer, Mark M. to Louisa Blessing 9-11-1845 (12-6-1845) F
Frazer, Milton G. to Mary H. Harvey 2-11-1854 (no return) F
Frazier (Fracre), William to Adelia McDunn 3-5-1851 Sh
Frazier, A. M. to E. E. Spence 12-27-1866 Be
Frazier, A.(W.?) A. to Nancy E. Cantrel 3-27-1865 G
Frazier, Charles to Matilda Smith 8-21-1869 (8-23-1869) T
Frazier, Daniel G. to Betsey J. Hill 2-3-1846 (2-25-1846) F
Frazier, Daniel W. to Perlina C. Morriss 12-1-1843 (11?-16-1843) F
Frazier, Daniel to Martha J. Owens 11-20-1861 (no return) Hn
Frazier, Daniel to Sarah Ann Upchurch 9-2-1838 G
Frazier, David W. to Bernetta Looney 5-14-1857 Hn
Frazier, Ephraim to Emma Stephenson 2-1-1868 (2-2-1868) Dy
Frazier, G. B. to Lanith White 11-13-1855 (no return) F
Frazier, Isaac G. to Elizabeth Hiflin 12-22-1857 We
Frazier, J. W. to Beulah Fitzpatrick 3-1-1880 (3-2-1880) L
Frazier, James M. C. to Nancy Templeton 8-18-1863 (no return) We
Frazier, James to Polly Tibbs 12-25-1870 Hy
Frazier, John M. to George Henrietta Rawls 12-5-1864 (12-12-1864) Sh
Frazier, Levi D. to Jane Wimberley 3-14-1848 Hn
Frazier, O. C. to Mary M. Welch 11-24-1872 Hy
Frazier, Phillip A. to Sarah A. Hart 8-18-1863 (no return) We
Frazier, S. F. to R. C. McCoy 12-19-1867 G
Frazier, Samuel W. to Izelah J. Gibson 9-8-1863 G
Frazier, Stephen to Nancy Hancock 10-25-1843 G
Frazier, Thos. J. to Drucilla Rogers 9-10-1850 We
Frazier, Thos. J. to Mary J. Williamson 5-28-1867 Dy
Frazier, Troy to Mary Jane Colburn 9-2-1852 G
Frazier, William B. to Clarissa Babb 1-14-1846 Hn
Frazier, William M. to Judith Arun 10-10-1839 (could be 1849) Hn
Frazier?, Henry to Emily McIntosh 3-24-1870 (3-30-1870) T
Frazure, Jeremiah to Louiza E. Wall 11-13-1851 (no return) F
Frederick, H.K. to Nancy A. Thompson 9-22-1860 (9-23-1860) Hr
Freear, E.H. to Lucey A. Towls 4-29-1853 (no return) F
Freed, Wm. P. to Amanda L. Cloud 9-22-1871 (9-28-1871) O
Freedman, Ephram Hart to Parlee Curtis 2-9-1866 (no return) Dy
Freel, S. J. to Rosetta Ann Healey 2-5-1863 Hn
Freeland, A. D. to Margaret Buchanan 9-3-1854 Hn
Freeland, Alphonzo to Martha E. Dill 11-15-1865 (11-16-1865) Cr
Freeland, George W. to T. P. Pickler 8-27-1869 (8-29-1869) Cr
Freeland, James to Elizabeth Carrington 8-2-1847 (no return) Cr
Freeland, Joseph J. to Margaret J. Johnston 11-15-1870 (11-22-1870) F
Freeland, Robert D. to Keziah E. Simpson 10-23-1867 (no return) Hn
Freeland, Robert D. to Sarah J. Acuff 10-6-1859 Hn
Freeland, Thomas J. to Eliza A. Steely 12-18-1853 Hn
Freeland, Will A. to Martha E. Stigall 11-11-1853 Hn
Freelin, John N. to Nanc S. Pickler 12-7-1867 (12-15-1867) Cr
Freels, Beverly to E. J. Halmark 4-5-1841 Cr
Freeman, Aaron to Elizabeth S. Thomas 1-18-1853 Hr
Freeman, Aaron to Polly Kindrick 8-23-1853 (8-24-1853) Hr
Freeman, Albert to Lizzie Fisher 1-28-1864 Sh

Freeman, Andy to Dolly Hull (Hall?) 7-5-1870 G B
Freeman, Asberry M. to Susan C. Howard 6-26-1858 (6-30-1858) G
Freeman, Asberry to M. W. Murry 12-7-1850 (1-7-1851) O
Freeman, Binkley to Eady Harriss 4-17-1839 (4-18-1839) F
Freeman, Charles C. to Eliza Pace 1-16-1860 T
Freeman, Charles Christopher to Prefom? Mathis? 7-17-1843 (8-18-1843) T
Freeman, Charles to Allis Anderson 11-15-1845 (11-18-1845) Hr
Freeman, Charles to Melinda Morris 8-28-1843 (8-29-1843) H
Freeman, Claiborn A. to Mary Phillips 2-3-1845 (4-2-1845) G
Freeman, Clark to Harriet Core 5-2-1843 (5-5-1843) Hr
Freeman, D. A. to Beda A. Bowers 8-18-1854 We
Freeman, D. A. to N. T. Neely 9-2-1871 (9-3-1871) Dy
Freeman, Daniel to Mary A. Cocke 4-23-1870 (4-28-1870) F B
Freeman, David S. to Mary E. Page 6-10-1847 Hn
Freeman, E. A. to Margarett Turner 12-20-1855 We
Freeman, E. C. to Elizabeth King 1-18-1854 Cr
Freeman, Ed to Martha Freeman 11-5-1866 G
Freeman, Edmund A. to Nancy E. Hamilton 11-4-1847 (12-3-1847) G
Freeman, Eli J. to Mary Angeline Livington 8-24-1857 (8-25-1857) O
Freeman, Francis M. to America Cochrum 9-26-1849 Hn
Freeman, G. W. to Martha Allen 10-15-1854 (no return) F
Freeman, Gaston G. B. to Mary Ann Smithwick 7-6-1843 (7-7-1843) Ma
Freeman, George W. to Samantha L. Graves 1-17-1859 Ma
Freeman, George to Polly Poore 7-9-1846 (no return) Hn
Freeman, Green to Rachel Nutt 11-7-1839 Sh
Freeman, H. F. to S. A. Darden 12-15-1862 (12-17-1862) F
Freeman, Hardy to Eunice E. McGee 10-4-1866 G
Freeman, Henry to Nancy Lett 1-2-1867 F
Freeman, J. N. to Susan Hambleton 10-8-1870 (10-9-1870) Cr
Freeman, J. P. to Parilee Burnham 12-23-1873 Dy
Freeman, J. Y. to Helen Bowden 1-24-1866 Hn
Freeman, James C. to Mollie L. Curtis 11-16-1870 Hy
Freeman, James E. to Portia J. Allen 4-7-1858 Hn
Freeman, James L. to Martha Nance 2-27-1848 Hn
Freeman, James to Frances Alexander 3-15-1838 Hn
Freeman, John A. to Mary E. Lane 8-25-1866 (8-28-1866) T
Freeman, John G. to Elvira E. Coburn 2-7-1842 (2-8-1842) Hr
Freeman, John H. to Anna Bell Elder 9-20-1866 G
Freeman, John Haml. to Ada Noel Green 11-1-1871 Hy
Freeman, John P. to Elizabeth Curtis 6-3-1844 T
Freeman, John W. to A. F. Clements 1-23-1855 We
Freeman, John to Liney(Siney) Scott 4-4-1831 (4-14-1831) Hr
Freeman, Jose. B. to Virginia Caruthers 10-25-1849 Ma
Freeman, Joseph O. to Indiana Parsons 5-14-1859 (5-16-1859) T
Freeman, Kinchin to Rutha Murchean 6-11-1834 G
Freeman, King to Clara Mebane 12-24-1868 (12-25-1868) F B
Freeman, Macon H. to Margaret T. Julin 10-18-1854 We
Freeman, Major to Darancy Flowers 3-21-1869 G B
Freeman, Nathan to Mariah Surratt 6-4-1864 Mn
Freeman, R. F. to Nancy A. F. Brown 12-5-1876 Dy
Freeman, R. W. to Mary Ellis 9-2-1876 (8?-3-1876) O
Freeman, Richard W. to Margaret Ann Nedry 9-8-1855 (9-14-1855) O
Freeman, Richard to Margaret Nevils 5-6-1836 Sh
Freeman, Robert to Sallie Cothern 9-5-1870 (9-7-1870) Dy
Freeman, Samuel to Martha Mitchell 1-6-1876 O B
Freeman, T. E. to Mary V. Waters 11-7-1866 Cr
Freeman, Thomas J. to Martha L. Raines 7-28-1852 G
Freeman, Thomas W. to Cynthia W. Freeman 11-18-1851 G
Freeman, Thos. W. to Frances Freeman 7-20-1854 G
Freeman, W. H. to Frances Jane Snow 10-8-1850 Sh
Freeman, W. H. to Harriet J. Braden 11-4-1865 (11-5-1865) F
Freeman, W. W. to Mary F. Fitzgerald 9-29-1859 G
Freeman, Warren to Tabitha Bullock 11-19-1854 Hn
Freeman, William R. to Louisa (Mrs.) Belton 10-12-1861 (10-13-1861) Ma
Freeman, William to Candace Eggleston 10-27-1880 L B
Freeman, William to Mary Muirhead 1-20-1831 G
Freeman, William to Maryana Patterson 1-17-1870 (1-18-1870) T
Freeman, William to Sarah Word 7-30-1840 G
Freeman, Wm. A. to Elizabeth Harper 3-20-1845 (no return) We
Freeman, Wm. W. to Elizabeth J. Fitzgerald 7-4-1856 G
Freeman, Zachariah to Agnes A. Bowers 11-15-1853 G
Freemon, John to Caroline Finney 12-24-1846 Be
Freenson, Jas. to Brittannia Bond 6-1-1868 G
Freeth, George to Ann Eliza Malone 1-9-1863 (1-10-1863) F
Freezer, Benjamin to Eliza Jane Vinson 1-24-1862 (no return) Hn
Freiberg, Isaac to Charlotte Neuburger 2-1-1864 Sh
Frence, Jeff to Ednie Gilliam 11-24-1878 Hy
French, A. M. to Nancy Martin 10-26-1844 Cr
French, Asa to Nancy L. Martin 8-5-1845 (no return) Cr
French, C. J. to Martha M. E. Gamons 10-7-1873 (10-8-1873) O
French, C. W. to Ann Lee 10-20-1862 (no return) Hn
French, Coleman J. to Martha L. Arington 11-15-1860 (11-20-1860) Cr
French, Cullen to Caroline Lee 1-2-1845 Hn
French, Dillion to Christy Hastin 7-28-1846 Cr
French, G. D. to M. L. Bowers ?-6-1873 (9-7-1873) O
French, George to Annie Nelson 9-15-1873 Hy
French, H. B. to Martha E. Bush 10-17-1867 Hn

French, J. A. to Sarah Lowry 10-5-1865 Hn
French, J. B. to Phebee Vester 9-10-1854 Be
French, J. F. to Eula Virginia Rinehart 2-5-1863 Hn
French, J. G. to Mary Robey 10-20-1868 Cr
French, Jackson to Mary Lindsey 8-25-1843 Cr
French, James to Isabella Marton 10-19-1856 Hn
French, James to Julina Green 11-3-1846 Cr
French, James to Mary Ann Lanthrop 7-23-1845 F
French, Jesse P. to Mary B. Groom 1-6-1870 Cr
French, John A. to Elizabeth Bomar 8-6-1848 Hn
French, John H. to L. Virginia Smith 1-11-1853 (1-12-1853) Sh
French, John W. to Latitica A. Cox 7-21-1866 (7-22-1866) Cr
French, John to Elizabeth Smith 8-3-1839 (8-4-1839) O
French, L. L. to Amand Garrett 2-16-1871 Cr
French, L. N. to Milly Carter 10-7-1867 Cr
French, Morgan G. to T. E. Push 3-24-1849 Hn
French, Rich to Mary Frances Moore 8-21-1845 Cr
French, Robt. H. to Mary E. Taylor 12-16-1867 (12-17-1867) Ma
French, Samuel C. to Mary J. French 12-31-1859 Hn
French, T. H. to Martha Swinney 1-17-1872 (no return) Cr
French, William A. to Mary M. McMackins 9-12-1865 (9-14-1865) Cr
French, William J. to Myranda F. Munson 1-15-1852 Hn
French, William M. to Sarah J. Easley 1-1-1874 T
French, William to Sallie Swinney 8-10-1871 Cr
French, Wm. Carroll to Mary A. Branch 9-17-1854 Cr
Frensley, James D. to Martha J. Young 10-8-1851 Hn
Frey, Joseph to Mary Magdalina Frey 6-3-1863 (6-6-1863) Sh
Frey, Samuel to Amanda A. Davis 11-1-1852 (11-2-1852) Sh
Friar?, Thomas to Ann McCullough 1-28-1853 Hn
Frick, Henry to Maria C. Shaller 10-10-1842 Sh
Frick, Jno. G. to Rosina Byers 6-30-1849 Sh
Frick, Nicholas to Denah Acabe (Aecker) 2-12-1847 Sh
Friel, Daniel to Mary Ann Richarson 4-2-1870 (9-29-1872?) T
Friel, Fred to F. Frietag 1-5-1856 (1-6-1856) Sh
Frields, William to Susan F. French 6-25-1857 We
Friemmer, Andrew to Martha A. Taylor 4-21-1866 (4-26-1866) Ma
Friend, D. H. to H. E. Friend 7-21-1873 (7-23-1873) L
Friend, David H. to Sarah H. Flannagan 12-29-1848 (1-25-1849) L
Friend, Jacob to Julia Levy (Luy-Sey?) 10-8-1855 (10-8-1854?) Sh
Frierson, Benjamin to Margarett Thompson 12-24-1870 (no return) F B
Frierson, John S. to Harriet N. McCormick 2-5-1855 (2-8-1855) T
Frierson, M. B. to Cassandra P. Shanks 9-28-1848 Sh
Frierson, Richard to Mattie Jeffreys 1-12-1881 L B
Frinch, W. M. to M. C. Row 2-10-1865 (3-12-1865) Cr
Frink, M. N. to S. J. Harper 12-19-1866 Hy
Frisby, Thomas to Louisa Newby 7-2-1857 Sh
Fritz, B. to Elizabeth Ludwig 2-27-1852 Sh
Fritz, F. to Sarah Mills 11-15-1853 (11-18-1853) O
Frogan, Monrow to Catharine Cox 8-15-1857 We
Frosh, Emanuel to Emily Culwell 2-17-1872 (2-18-1872) Dy
Frosh, Manuel? to Rebecca Smith 3-2-1878 (3-3-1878) Dy
Frost, A. M. to Alice McGarg 12-16-1878 (12-18-1878) Dy
Frost, Allen to Lue (Sue) Johnson 1-25-1867 (no return) Hy
Frost, B. T. to L. F. McCollum 3-4-1872 (3-5-1872) Cr
Frost, J. E. to Tennessee Oliver 11-11-1858 Sh
Frost, James A. to Edwina Moore 1-12-1857 Cr
Frost, L. M. to Lucinda Coble 11-6-1855 (no return) Hn
Frost, Stephen to D. M. Kirby 3-29-1858 Sh
Frost, W. C. to Mahala A. Newton 11-14-1855 We
Frost, Wade H. to Mary E. Page 11-14-1854 (11-15-1854) O
Frost, William D. to Martha L. Brown 9-13-1854 O
Frost, Wilson to Margaret Byrn 11-18-1867 Dy
Frothschild, Joseph to Ellen Van Campen 9-18-1866 (9-20-1866) F
Frutay (Friday), John to Joanna Keller 8-10-1861 (8-11-1861) Sh
Fry, Alex to Bora Walker 5-4-1880 (no return) L
Fry, Alexander to Eliza E. Coachman 8-27-1867 (8-?-1867) L B
Fry, Anderson to Cynthia P. Prince 6-1-1870 (6-9-1870) T
Fry, Andrew to Mahala Wheeless 11-13-1879 L
Fry, Henry to Mary Luellen Livingston 8-22-1874 (8-23-1874) T
Fry, J. D. to Martha McDaniel 9-4-1851 Be
Fry, James B. to Minerva Murphy 9-15-1857 (no return) Cr
Fry, John A. to Mary E. J. Weaver 5-?-1863 Mn
Fry, John to Martha French 8-7-1875 (no return) Hy
Fry, Joseph H. to Nancy H. Wesson 8-31-1853 (9-1-1853) G
Fry, R. D. to Elizabeth McLemore 6-13-1860 (6-14-1860) Cr
Fry, Samuel B. to Clara Armstrong 12-21-1853 (no return) Cr
Fry, Samuel M. to Lucy Ann Ward 12-23-1848 (12-26-1848) Ma
Fry, Thomas to Jennie McAlexander 1-31-1871 Ma
Fryar, M. B. to Elizabeth Gilliam 5-22-1866 G
Frye?, Shadrach Sl. to Elizabeth Burns 6-28-1834 (7-3-1834) Hr
Fryer, B. N. to M. A. Weakley 11-28-1864 (11-29-1864) Dy
Fryer, W. S. to Lucy R. Comer 10-25-1859 Hn
Fuchs, V. D. to Victerine Kline 9-4-1863 Sh
Fudge, George W. to Prudence L. Jones 4-7-1864 Sh
Fudge, William J. to Susan Humphreys 8-23-1839 L
Fuel, Benjamin to Rachel McMahon 11-20-1828 (1-9-1829) G
Fuel, Robin to Martha Johnston 10-20-1841 G

Fuell, Benjamin to Mahala Merritt 10-2-1844 G
Fuell, John P. B. to Mary Nunn 1-30-1843 (2-2-1843) G
Fugate, James to Virginia Conyers 1-21-1865 (1-22-1865) Dy
Fulbright, Alpha to Nancy Caruthers 12-31-1840 Ma
Fulbright, David L. to Missouri Harrison 11-12-1866 (11-14-1866) Ma
Fulbright, Jacob to Mary Nail 1-4-1830 (1-6-1830) Ma
Fulbright, Jacob to Mary Nail 1-4-1831 Ma
Fulcher, James to Elizabeth Lamb 5-21-1858 Hn
Fulcher, Joseph to Sarah E. Browning 3-18-1867 (3-19-1867) Ma
Fulford, John J. to Jane Hall 4-6-1844 Sh
Fulgham, Pearce to Hester A. Hines 3-3-1832 (3-6-1832) Hr
Fulgham, William to Elizabeth Seat 3-13-1828 G
Fulgham, Wm. to Martha Donnelson 3-10-1831 (3-16-1831) Hr
Fulghum, A. L. to Mary M. Senter 12-9-1867 (12-10-1868?) G
Fulghum, Augustus A. to V. M. (Mrs.) Gilchrist 6-6-1862 G
Fulghum, Benjamin R. to Merinda Crawford 6-22-1840 (6-25-1840) Hr
Fulghum, E. R. to I. C. J. Hamilton 9-5-1861 G
Fulghum, Raiford to Susan Craig 11-26-1836 (11-27-1836) Hr
Fulghum, William R. to Susan V. Blakemore 12-14-1857 (12-16-1857) G
Fulkerson, J. A. to Lizzie Goosby 2-13-1877 (2-14-1877) L
Fulkerson, J. A. to Nancy Lockard 2-22-1872 L
Fulkerson, James A. to Sallie Maynard 9-27-1878 L
Fulkerson, James R. to Harriet Tucker 7-30-1852 (8-5-1852) L
Fulkerson, P. D. to Annie E. Miller 8-29-1883 L
Fulkerson, R. S. to Annis L. Chronister 9-11-1884 L
Fulkerson, W. A. to Laura Spry 2-20-1877 (no return) L
Fulks, Albert A. to Elizabeth Hanston 10-1-1850 (no return) Cr
Fulks, Andrew to Peggie Reid 3-8-1869 (no return) F
Fulks, J. A. to Elizabeth Barrow 8-4-1859 (no return) Cr
Fulks, John D. to Rebecca Houston 9-10-1845 Cr
Fulks, Nathan F. to Mary E. Ward 1-31-1846 (1-31-1846) O
Fullen, A. J. to Viney Smith 5-12-1838 (5-17-1838) L
Fullen, A. M. to M. J. Meacham 10-31-1878 L
Fullen, Alexander to Emma Tyas 12-25-1876 (by 1-1-1877) L
Fullen, George to Susan Turner 12-27-1877 L
Fullen, J. W. to N. L. Meacham 12-22-1875 L
Fullen, John to Sarah Ann Fleming 12-12-1844 L
Fullen, P. J. to Cintha R. Steward 10-12-1871 L
Fullen, P. J. to Milly H. Harred 12-21-1867 (12-22-1867) L
Fullen, Pleasant to M. A. Roberson 1-13-1864 L
Fullen, Washington to Mary Jordan 6-6-1864 Sh
Fuller (Fulton), Joseph to Sarah Ederington 1-3-1832 Sh
Fuller, Albert to Nancy Pender 1-6-1875 (no return) Hy
Fuller, Arthur to Levina Moore 12-5-1836 (12-6-1836) G
Fuller, D. E. to M. F. Tarrant 9-8-1869 (9-9-1869) Dy
Fuller, David to Matilda J. Clark 4-21-1866 (no return) F
Fuller, E. R. to D. M. Ward 8-26-1862 Mn
Fuller, Ellison P. to Mary B. Thompson 9-6-1843 (9-7-1843) L
Fuller, G. R. to Emma Dickey 12-22-1873 (12-23-1873) Dy
Fuller, Geo. B. to E. J. McGinnis 9-14-1863 (9-17-1863) Dy
Fuller, Henry F. to Kate Duncan 1-24-1859 Sh
Fuller, Horace to Mary Parker 3-29-1884 (3-30-1886?) L
Fuller, J. B. to Mary E. Darnall 11-16-1867 (11-17-1867) Cr
Fuller, J. R. to M. J. Kyle 1-25-1871 (1-26-1871) Cr
Fuller, J. W. to S. A. Crisp 9-7-1868 (9-8-1868) Dy
Fuller, James T. to Lucyann Trezvant 7-25-1848 (no return) F
Fuller, James to Sylvia Bradford 2-18-1877 Hy
Fuller, John M. to Elizabeth Milliken 10-24-1849 Hn
Fuller, John T. to Mollie J. Justis 1-17-1877 Dy
Fuller, John W. to Ann P. Bridges 4-26-1833 Sh
Fuller, John to Ailsy Bass 12-17-1878 (no return) Hy
Fuller, John to Candis Haily 12-22-1853 (no return) F
Fuller, John to Mary F. Battle 4-3-1873 Dy
Fuller, Robert to Martha Duglas 10-31-1867 (12-5-1867) Dy
Fuller, Sam A. to Sarah C. White 10-21-1859 We
Fuller, Spencer to Mary Partee 10-9-1878 (10-10-1878) L B
Fuller, Spivy to Letha Dickson 3-12-1832 G
Fuller, Turner J. to Susan Tate 7-1-1841 Ma
Fuller, W. A. to Bettie C. Justis 1-17-1877 Dy
Fuller, William H. to Elizabeth B. George 12-29-1844 T
Fuller, Wm. H. to N. Catharine Totty 7-9-1855 (7-19-1855) T
Fullerton, A. J. to Nancy J. Reed 9-22-1868 Dy
Fullerton, David to Julina Barr 6-6-1854 Be
Fullerton, H. F. (T.?) to A. E. Powell 6-3-1868 G
Fullerton, Hugh A. to Elizabeth H. Reed 3-13-1837 (3-16-1837) G
Fullerton, James M. to Sophronia Price 9-8-1870 Ma
Fullerton, John S. to Rachal L. Thomas l7-24-1838 (7-26-1838) G
Fullerton, John to Martha Cooper 7-10-1866 (7-12-1866) Ma
Fullerton, Leander to Nancy Grissom 4-28-1844 Be
Fullerton, WilliamB. to Jane Allen 12-21-1851 Be
Fulps, William N. to Amanda M. Ayers 2-21-1854 Hr
Fultin, Charles W. to Mary A. McFarland 6-7-1848 (6-?-1848) T
Fulton, Eliphlet G. to Eliza A. Davidson 7-21-1845 Hr
Fulton, James to Matilda C. Fleming 9-10-1856 (9-11-1856) Sh
Fulton, Joseph H. to Linie Taylor 11-4-1874 Hy
Fumbank, George to Martha Clark 3-1-1867 (3-2-1867) Dy
Fumbanks, A. G. to Elizabeth F. Neely 12-4-1866 Dy

Fumbanks, Allen to Lowella Allen 7-5-1879 (7-6-1879) Dy
Fumbanks, C. J. to Harriet Sawyer 2-1-1879 (2-2-1879) Dy
Fumbanks, Jack to Sarah Becket 2-10-1869 (no return) Dy
Funderbunk, W. J. to Martha E. Smart 4-13-1869 (4-15-1869) Ma
Funk, Daniel W. to Ann Eliza McClane (McCana) 5-16-1850 Sh
Funke, William to Margeret Schad 2-3-1851 Sh
Fuqua, David to Elizabeth E. Palmer 6-24-1844 (no return) Cr
Fuqua, Grand to Hannah Clay 12-13-1868 G B
Fuqua, J. H. to Elizabeth A. Tucker 12-13-1869 (12-15-1869) Cr
Fuqua, J. W. to M. L. Coleman 3-2-1868 (3-4-1868) Cr
Fuqua, Jacob to Frances Knuckles 8-5-1872 Cr
Fuqua, James P. to Martha Norman 11-25-1853 Cr
Fuqua, John T. to Martha Hurt 10-21-1867 (no return) Cr
Fuqua, Joseph H. to Martha Ann Palmer 8-27-1840 Cr
Fuqua, Samuel R. to Milly Vick 2-26-1853 G
Fuqua, Stephen to Caroline Gentry 2-4-1834 G
Fuqua, W. J. to L. Cooper 9-10-1864 (9-12-1864) Cr
Fuqua, Walter S. to Ann Pate 5-20-1863 Cr
Fuqua, Walter S. to Ann Pate 5-20-1863 (no return) Cr
Fuqua, Walter S. to Susan Morris 11-17-1868 (11-18-1868) Cr
Fuqua, William to Martha E. Dean 12-29-1840 (12-31-1840) G
Fuqua, Wm. Y. to Matilda Walker 7-25-1840 (no return) Cr
Fuquah, Wm. to Hattie McFadden 10-13-1877 (10-15-1877) O B
Fuquea, Samuel R. to Mary Lemmons 12-6-1841 (12-9-1841) G
Furgarson, Barnet to Mariah Orms 9-12-1841 (9-13-1841) G
Furgarson, Joel to Sarah Peal 1-1-1845 (1-2-1845) G
Furgarson, Joseph W. to Sophia L. Blanton 6-9-1858 G
Furgarson, Thomas to Winaford Peal 11-17-1845 (11-20-1845) G
Furgason, Benjamin F. to Elisabeth L. Daniel 12-6-1848 (no return) F
Furgason, R. B. to Tennessee Chipman 2-14-1877 L
Furgason, Will O. to Lavender D. Edmonson 10-12-1838 (10-14-1838) Hr
Furgeon, Anthony to Mollie Cozart 6-21-1868 Hy
Furgerson, A. D. to Martha J. Farr 1-19-1865 G
Furgerson, D. to Susan Rily 5-7-1866 O
Furgerson, Hardy to Clarisa Roberson 11-17-1870 Hy
Furgerson, Harris J. to Sarah P. Crafton 8-18-1855 (8-19-1855) G
Furgerson, James J. to Margaret Jane Owen 10-10-1855 (10-11-1855) T
Furgerson, John D. to M. N. Taylor 4-25-1865 G
Furgerson, John W. to Rebecca C. Stanly 8-19-1856 (8-20-1856) Ma
Furgerson, John to M. L. (Mrs.) Tyus 1-28-1873 Hy
Furgerson, L. D. to Mary Robinson 12-31-1867 G
Furgerson, M. G. to M. C. Riley 7-25-1864 (7-27-1864) L
Furgerson, Saml. D. to Mary E. Byrn 6-26-1860 (6-27-1860) L
Furgerson, T. L. to J. R. Bentley 2-23-1867 (2-24-1867) L
Furguson, A. D. to M. W. Harrison 2-9-1869 G
Furguson, Isaac to Cyntha Wilson 2-1-1844 Hn
Furguson, James J. to Martha J. Owen 1-15-1867 (1-22-1867) T
Furguson, James to Sarah Rankstead 5-18-1844 Sh
Furguson, Joel to Sarah M. Flint 2-6-1834 (2-11-1834) Hr
Furguson, Lewis to Elizabeth Newman 2-10-1843 Sh
Furguson, S. N. to H. M. Fisher 1-12-1876 L
Furlong, William to Allice Bird 4-29-1873 (no return) Cr
Furlong, William to Christian Baird (Bird) 12-20-1849 O
Furr, James A. to Fanny Ballard 11-5-1870 (11-10-1870) F
Furr, Levi to Nancy Hynant 4-28-1867 Be
Fussell, J. J. to M. E. Fields 4-22-1867 Cr
Fussell, James W. to Sarah C. Johnson 11-18-1857 Be
Fussell, Jasen W. to Sarah Cook 3-5-1867 (3-7-1867) Ma
Fussell, William N. to Martha Jane King 9-11-1866 (9-13-1866) Ma
Fussell, William to Susan Dockins 3-31-1830 Ma
Fussell, Wm. N. to Hannah Josephine Cook 7-23-1868 G
Fussell, Wyatt to Mary Elizabeth Maddox 4-20-1842 (4-21-1842) Ma
Futerell, N. to Amanda Valenten 1-14-1858 We
Futhey, James to Margaret J. Kilpatrick 11-17-1869 (11-18-1869) T
Futrel, Isaac to Nancy Alford 3-23-1843 (3-30-1843) Hr
Futrell, Berry to Elizabeth Saul 7-25-1853 (7-28-1853) Hr
Futrell, Isaac to Sarah A. Stewart 2-4-1839 (2-5-1839) Hr
Futrell, James G. to Martha Ann Lewis 9-3-1866 (9-5-1866) Ma
Futrell, John S. to Elizabeth Stewart 11-25-1841 Hn
Futrell, Wilie to Sarah Chandler 7-7-1855 Hr
Futrell, William S. to Elizabeth Young 8-29-1849 Hn
Fuzzell, James A. to Martha Clark 4-24-1858 We
Fuzzell, John F. to Sarah Arrington 12-3-1857 Cr
Fuzzell, Nathaniel to Martha Nelson 7-31-1841 Hn
Fuzzell, W. A. to Caroline Johnson 4-7-1864 Be
Fuzzell, W. G. to N. W. Jackson 8-5-1865 (8-6-1865) O
Fuzzle, Thos. H. to Amanda Nunn 8-1-1861 Dy
Fyker, Moses to Elizabeth Colman 1-31-1870 (no return) Dy

Gabbie (Gallbie?), Robt. M. to Margarett J. Allen 1-27-1845 (1-28-1845) F
Gabley, John to Eveline Booth 4-17-1852 (no return) F
Gabriel, M. to Matilda Moses 10-22-1863 Sh
Gacy, John to L. P. Murrin 11-24-1867 T
Gadd, D. F. to Mary Ann E. Powell 12-9-1857 Hr
Gaddy, S. Robinson to Elizabeth Hinson 12-18-1848 Sh
Gaddy, Wm. H. to Hannah M. Phillips 1-29-1861 Hr
Gadis(Galdis-Galdy), A. F. to Josephine Scallions 12-23-1876 (12-24-1876) L

Gadlin, Taylor to Mary Weddington 2-7-1868 G B
Gadwell, William R. to Martha Ann McLain 1-20-1852 Hn
Gafford, Michael to Sarah St. Clair 8-4-1838 Sh
Gage, Alfred to Elizabeth Doland 4-5-1843 (4-9-1843) G
Gage, David to Martha A. Pinion 12-24-1844 G
Gage, E. R. to Sarah M. Roper 8-28-1859 O
Gage, John to Elizabeth Massey 9-28-1854 Sh
Gage, Milford to Martha Cooper 1-27-1842 G
Gage, William A. to Clara E. Morgan 8-30-1864 (9-1-1864) Sh
Gague, William to Jane Mariah White 11-3-1849 (11-4-1849) G
Gailey, Daniel C. to Martha A. Stout 12-23-1862 We
Gailey, John W. to Martha J. Perry 9-25-1862 We
Gaily, Clinton to Mary Howard 7-9-1855 (7-12-1855) G
Gainer, Asa M. to Eliza A. Dunlap 12-22-1842 Hn
Gaines, A. M. to Ednie J. Coleman 10-28-1865 (10-31-1865) L
Gaines, Alexander to Synthia Tivool? 9-4-1872 T
Gaines, Edmond to Lelia E. Bentley 3-1-1884 L
Gaines, H. G. to N. A. Simpson 1-3-1881 (1-4-1881) L
Gaines, Harrison to Adalin Read 1-15-1872 (1-18-1872) T
Gaines, Ira to Narisa M. Bloodworth 3-25-1845 L
Gaines, Jesse T. to Mary E. Brown 7-7-1869 (7-28-1869) L
Gaines, John L. to Amelia A. Boyd 3-24-1874 L
Gaines, John R. to Elizabeth A. Lacy 8-12-1861 (8-13-1861) L
Gaines, John T. to Jane Dickerson 4-7-1859 (4-13-1859) L
Gaines, L. W. to Elizabeth F. Simpson 8-31-1875 (9-1-1875) L
Gaines, R. B. to K. G. Borum? 12-25-1879 (12-26-1879) L
Gaines, R. J.(I?) to Vester Haynes 12-1-1885 L
Gaines, Richard F. to Amanda M. L. Key 6-9-1840 Sh
Gaines, Robert to Mollie Williams 9-6-1879 L
Gaines, S. L. to Fanny Stone 10-4-1882 (10-5-1882) L
Gaines, S. L. to Sarah C. Clark 7-5-1860 (7-8-1860) L
Gaines, S. M. to Harriet E. Bates 5-3-1859 (5-4-1859) L
Gaines, Thomas T. to Sue A. Bandy 2-27-1873 T
Gaines, Wade to Hannah Smith 4-16-1874 (4-23-1874) T
Gaines, Zachariah to Tennessee V Haynes 9-7-1869 L
Gains, J. Tucker to M. V. Barfield 6-21-1882 L
Gains, Jeff to Harriett Taylor 2-17-1872 Hy
Gains, John T. to Sarah A. Alexander 10-23-1865 (10-24-1865) L
Gains, Richard F. to Rebecca A. G. Dewalt 9-18-1866 (9-20-1866) L
Gains, S. L. to P. F. Alsbrook 11-14-1865 (no return) L
Gains?, Demos to Louisa Montgomery 9-29-1843 We
Gaise, Frank to Emily Sadler 4-4-1867 (4-6-1867) T
Gaisman, J. to Sarah Kaufman 3-8-1864 T
Gaither, Andrew to Louisa Futhey 12-20-1870 T
Gaither, E. to Emily T. Guy 3-14-1864 (3-15-1864) F
Gaither, Ham to Bettie Cobbs 2-1-1870 F B
Gaither, Henry to Caroline Hudson 12-28-1869 F B
Gaither, Saml. E. to Martha A. Roberts 3-31-1871 (4-4-1871) F
Gaither, Thomas to Elizabeth M. Spenser 1-20-1839 (1-21-1839) O
Gaither, William to Frances A. Reaves 12-12-1844 G
Galagher, James to Mary Conery 4-29-1858 (5-13-1858) Sh
Galamore, Tilman to Harriett Moton 2-5-1842 Hn
Galard, David C. to Sarah Ann Warren 9-4-1850 (9-5-1850) G
Galbreath, B. A. to Eliza A. Lewis 11-13-1861 G
Galbreath, D. to Haddie A. Orne 7-7-1858 (7-8-1858) Sh
Galbreath, John to Susan Renfro 1-11-1860 Hn
Galbreath, W. W. to Ann Traylor 5-6-1867 (5-7-1867) T
Galbreth, James H. to Lucinda C. Lasseter 2-5-1866 (2-18-1866) T
Gale, Thomas C. to Mary H. Coller? 1-31-1861 Hn
Gale, Thomas to Melina Owen 12-18-1867 (no return) Hy
Gale, Thos. to Idea Stanley 9-9-1867 (no return) Hy
Gales, James A. to Martha J. Taylor 1-8-1863 We
Galey, Clinton to Lucinda Cunningham 12-19-1842 G
Galey, Rouland H. to Ann C. Bowers 10-23-1845 We
Gallagher, Hugh to Mary O'Hara 10-29-1855 Sh
Gallagher, James to Martha Young 8-6-1862 Sh
Gallagher, James to Mary Macklin 4-23-1867 (not executed) F
Gallagher, James to Tennessee Sullivan 1-4-1870 (1-6-1869?) F
Gallagher, John to Catharine Finan 3-28-1857 (3-29-1857) Sh
Gallagher, John to Teressa Lalon 2-10-1850 Sh
Gallagher, P. C. to Mary Gallagher 12-1-1844 Sh
Gallaher, L. to Elizabeth Garrison 10-25-1860 (no return) Dy
Gallaher, Patrick to Hannah Henneley 11-7-1857 (11-8-1857) Sh
Gallaher, William to Eliza Ann Hill 4-26-1851 (4-29-1851) O
Gallaspie, Steaven to Chainey Burnett 2-6-1878 Hy
Gallavin, Jerry to Mary Sullivan 6-30-1860 (7-4-1860) Sh
Gallaway, James to Vina McClish 1-17-1872 (no return) Hy
Gallaway, Joseph to Emily Hopkins 1-24-1855 Ma
Gallege, John J. to Elizabeth Frances Folks 12-23-1868 G
Gallemore, J. W. to Margaret Throgmorton 1-28-1864 Hn
Galliger, Mickeal to Cathern Gillen 8-24-1862 Sh
Galliher, W. T. to M. J. Hinson 2-6-1872 (2-9-1872) Dy
Gallimore, George W. to Mary E. Perkins 8-15-1870 (8-16-1870) Cr
Gallimore, Larkin J. to Mary Throgmorton 10-22-1846 Hn
Gallimore, Larkin J. to Sarah A. Berry 11-8-1853 Cr
Gallimore, Richard to Jane Throgmorton 1-15-1855 Hn
Gallimore, Richard to Martha Perry 2-27-1850 (no return) Hn

Gallimore, Samuel J. to Sarah J. Overcast 8-24-1861 Hn
Gallimore, William M. to Minerva Vaughn 9-30-1851 Hn
Gallimore, William to Sarah J. Andrew 10-25-1851 Hn
Gallimore, Wm. to M. R. Alexander 12-5-1846 (no return) Cr
Gallin, Franklin B. to Lenora J. Williamson 2-16-1853 (no return) Cr
Galling(Gatling?), Enoch S. to Elizabeth Champion 9-2-1845 Hr
Gallion, Eldridge J. to Susan C. Patterson 3-10-1863 Hn
Gallion, William W. to Elizabeth Baker 12-22-1853 G
Gallivan, Richard to Ellen O'Brien 1-13-1856 Sh
Galloway, Austin to Betsy Ann Taylor 10-26-1875 (no return) Hy
Galloway, C. B. to Anna O'Bryan 1-4-1861 Sh
Galloway, C. B. to Lottie E. Ostuhhout 10-22-1861 (10-23-1861) Sh
Galloway, C. G. to Tennessee H. Robins 10-8-1850 Sh
Galloway, Enoch to Lucretia J. Edwards 2-2-1855 (no return) F
Galloway, N. W. to Susan H. Harris 5-1-1871 (5-2-1871) F
Galloway, R. W. to Rebecca A. Nely 12-19-1866 O
Galloway, Richd. E. to Martha H. Exum 5-14-1849 (no return) F
Galloway, Robert M. to Harriett B. Robbins 11-29-1843 Sh
Galloway, Robert W. to Melinda Boyd 3-24-1852 O
Galloway, Robert to Martha McCrory 8-7-1839 (8-8-1839) Hr
Galloway, William to Henrietta Wynne 7-14-1864 Sh
Galloway, William to Rebecca Cox 12-20-1837 (12-21-1837) Hr
Gally, D. B. to Leonora S. O'Brien 6-11-1861 Hr
Galvin, Jeremiah to Katherine Breen 4-10-1863 Sh
Gambell, John to Rebecka Hopkins 7-21-1829 G
Gambell, M. F. to S. J. Wheeler 12-23-1874 (12-24-1874) O
Gambill, J. G. to Martha A. Jones 1-31-1867 G
Gambill, Thomas J. to Mary F. Cunningham 1-16-1868 G
Gamble, Andrew Jackson to Sarah Eliza Robertson 1-6-1852 (1-7-1852) Hr
Gamble, Ephraim B. to Winaford Gray 12-6-1853 Hr
Gamble, Harmon to Dicey Jackson 12-13-1846 Hn
Gamble, James to D. K. Bond 3-3-1844 Hn
Gamble, Richard K. to Tallulah Hening 3-14-1873 Hy
Gamble, Thomas M. to Martha Tipton 11-23-1849 (11-29-1849) O
Gamble, William to Martha Holder 3-10-1851 (3-13-1851) Hr
Gambley, Guin (Given) to Mary Taylor 9-3-1844 We
Gamel, William H. to Charity C. Ward 5-16-1855 L
Gamel, William S. to Sarah Jane Tanner 2-27-1849 (3-1-1849) O
Gamewell, Francis to Martha J. Jackson 5-17-1849 Ma
Gamlin, John S. to Frances J. Upchurch 6-10-1865 Hn
Gammen?, Theodore to Angeline Wardlaw 2-2-1867 L B
Gammill, Robert to Martha A. Davis 2-1-1864 Hn
Gammon, Jas. to Fatitia Gammon 5-15-1863 (5-17-1863) Dy
Gammon, John R. to Helen V. Moore 11-12-1866 (11-13-1866) Dy
Gammon, W. C. to M. S. Turner 12-28-1867 O
Gammon, William R. to Sandal Bryant 1-27-1846 (1-28-1846) G
Gammons, Frank E. to Nancy A. Gammons 4-29-1867 (no return) Dy
Gammons, Jack to Sarah A. Lattimore 1-13-1868 Dy
Gammons, Jack to Sarah A. Patterson 3-13-1868 (1?-14-1868) Dy
Gammons, Samuel N. to R. M. F. Williams 2-17-1858 (no return) Hn
Gamp, Conrad to Antonia Hoffman 12-6-1862 (12-8-1862) Sh
Ganaway, Allen to Sarah Dodd 1-13-1870 G
Ganaway, Samuel G. to Margarett Gholson 10-12-1843 Ma
Ganden, Charles R. to Nannie E. West 3-30-1860 Sh
Gandolph, Gerome to Ellen Carnes 1-19-1853 Sh
Ganen, Martin to Julia Brenen 6-10-1862 (7-8-1862) Sh
Gann, J. C. to Emeline Dickens? 1-17-1866 (no return) Hn
Gann, J. S. to Martha A. Brice 6-19-1870 Hy
Gann, John to Cynthia A. Hallmark 8-14-1862 Mn
Gann, John to Sarah Johnson 8-13-1857 Sh
Gannaway, Nilson to Rosette Belle 7-6-1876 Dy
Gannon, A. J. to Maggie E. Whitson 9-24-1868 G
Gannon, Edward to Mary Murphey 6-7-1852 (6-13-1852) Sh
Gannon, Thomas to Mary Shaughnessy 2-26-1860 Sh
Gannon, W. C. to Amanda Brown 12-6-1871 (12-7-1871) Dy
Gans, Isaac M. to Charlotte Macourse 10-10-1859 Sh
Gant, Berry to Mollie Robertson 2-6-1883 (2-7-1883) L
Gant, Ed to Mira Warren 3-1-1871 (3-3-1871) F B
Gant, Edward to Martha Jordan 8-22-1868 (no return) F B
Gant, H. C. to M. L. McKinzie 10-11-1864 G
Gant, J. W. to S. S. Keller 12-23-1852 Sh
Gant, John H. to Martha L. Owen 10-8-1843 Sh
Gant, John J. to Eliza E. Waits 12-22-1875 (12-23-1875) Dy
Gant, William H. to Keziah A. Durley 3-22-1842 G
Gant, William to Nancy (Mrs.) Holland 12-7-1843 G
Gant, Wm. J. to Catharine Parish 3-16-1870 F
Ganthenheim, Christian to Rebecca A. McCenley 2-11-1853 Sh
Gantlett, E. T. to Mary Hogue 3-24-1847 O
Gantlett, Wm. R. to Ellen Harris 5-20-1864 (5-26-1864) O
Gantlett?, Wm. to Ellen Hern 5-25-1841 (no return) Cr
Gantling, Briggs to Frances Wills 1-12-1839 (1-15-1839) F
Garagnon, H. to Fredericka Neff 11-19-1863 Sh
Garcelon, John to R. Whitaker 5-25-1859 (5-29-1859) Sh
Garden, J. F. to Mary A. Ozier 8-15-1859 (no return) Cr
Gardener, David A. to M. J. Bledsoe 1-11-1866 T
Gardiner, Edmund L. to Susan Ann Adams 5-20-1844 Sh
Gardner, C. M. to Mary Broger 2-21-1851 (no return) Cr

Gardner, Calvin to Elizabeth A. Delph 2-26-1856 (2-27-1856) Ma
Gardner, Collin to Edney Roper 6-29-1872 O
Gardner, David A. to J. A. Payne 2-15-1870 (2-16-1870) Dy
Gardner, David to Ella Campbell 12-31-1883 (1-1-1884) L
Gardner, David to Martha A. Thomason 4-8-1840 G
Gardner, F. M. to Luseetta Brady 10-1-1866 O
Gardner, Fielding C. to Caroline Williamson 5-21-1839 (5-25-1839) F
Gardner, G. S. to Martha F. Hamilton 2-12-1863 G
Gardner, Geor. to Hanah Coleman 6-10-1871 Cr
Gardner, George J. to Hannah L. Sexton 11-4-1856 (11-6-1856) L
Gardner, George L. to Amandy Morris 3-18-1866 G
Gardner, Harmon to Caroline Kendrick 1-18-1838 Hn
Gardner, Henry to Lydia Gardner 11-11-1843 (11-16-1843) Hr
Gardner, J. A. to Mary Williams 12-1-1882 (12-3-1882) L
Gardner, J. H. to Nancy L. Hamilton 11-27-1860 (11-28-1860) Cr
Gardner, J. H. to Nancy L. Hamilton 11-27-1863 (no return) Cr
Gardner, J. J. to Margarette Hopkins 10-9-1854 G
Gardner, J. M. to Presella L. Jones 3-4-1846 We
Gardner, James D. to Matilda Kendrick 3-17-1838 Hn
Gardner, James M. to Catherine Widner 1-27-1877 (no return) Hy
Gardner, James M. to Martha J. Webster 5-13-1869 (5-17-1869) F
Gardner, James N. to Ann J. Jones 11-26-1856 Cr
Gardner, James R. to Melissa Abington 10-24-1854 O
Gardner, James W. to Caroline M. Clay 3-31-1862 (4-1-1862) Ma
Gardner, James W. to Jane Holt 2-2-1841 (3-1-1841) G
Gardner, James W. to Maranda J. Shaw 8-12-1846 G
Gardner, James to Linda Guile 6-8-1848 Hn
Gardner, Jesse F. to Corddia C. West 9-10-1868 G
Gardner, Jesse G. to Harriet Hale 9-9-1852 We
Gardner, John A. to Martha E. Bondurant 11-6-1850 We
Gardner, John E. to Jane McGee 9-27-1838 F
Gardner, John M. to Sarah A. Lovone 1-18-1855 Cr
Gardner, John R. to Sarah E. Alexander 3-30-1861 Ma
Gardner, Jonathan to Ann Mariah Franklin 1-27-1862 (no return) L
Gardner, Jonathan to Caroline Laney 10-5-1847 (10-30-1847) L
Gardner, Joseph Lewis to Louisa Lavinia Prewett 2-1-1846 T
Gardner, Limpulas to Nancy Powers 12-25-1850 We
Gardner, Moses to Milla Stidham 9-13-1867 (no return) F B
Gardner, Neil M. to Lavinia B. Hardgrove 6-18-1857 (6-23-1857) Ma
Gardner, Randel to Amy Jones 12-9-1872 (no return) Hy
Gardner, Robert to Ellen Glass 5-29-1877 (5-31-1877) O
Gardner, S. M. to Nancy J. Harper 5-30-1866 O
Gardner, Stephenas to Sarah E. Shoemaker 9-4-1862 (9-11-1862) L
Gardner, Swinson? to Louisa Henry 4-13-1843 (4-15-1843) T
Gardner, T. C. to Ann Benton 10-9-1862 (not endorsed) F
Gardner, Thomas J. to Sarah G. Lawhorn 5-4-1847 (5-?-1847) Hr
Gardner, Thos. J> to Lucy J. Crisp 6-14-1843 Hr
Gardner, Thos. to Miss Anders 1-17-1850 We
Gardner, W. A. to Martha E. Kee 11-6-1858 Cr
Gardner, W. L. to Julia A. Hill 11-26-1863 G
Gardner, W. P. to A. P. Boyd 9-19-1858 Cr
Gardner, W. R. to Emeline Vaughan 6-11-1861 (6-13-1861) Cr
Gardner, W. S. to A. M. Thomas 7-20-1843 Dy
Gardner, W. S. to Mollie A. Wiles 5-16-1873 (no return) Cr
Gardner, Washington to Mary M. Jackson 7-14-1852 Hn
Gardner, William F. to Jane Elizabeth Haltom 6-4-1855 Ma
Gardner, William M. to Martha Killingsworth 3-24-1847 (3-?-1847) T
Gardner, William R. to Catharine S. Porter 11-26-1866 (12-2-1866) Cr
Gardner, William to Elizabeth J. Burditt 10-14-1860 G
Gardner, William to Jane F. Welch 5-23-1844 G
Gardner, Wiloly to Elizabeth McFarland 12-1-1852 (12-2-1852) G
Gardner, Wm. T. to Elizabeth Bell 10-9-1861 (no return) L
Gardner, Wm. to Bettie Parrish 11-12-1867 (11-13-1867) Dy
Gargett, James H. to Mary A. W. Lockard 9-25-1862 (no return) L
Gargus, Robt. to Laney Jones 5-24-1846 We
Garibalde, Joseph to M. Rodgers 11-7-1857 (11-8-1857) Sh
Garison, Monrow to Tilda Craighead 9-16-1876 (9-17-1876) L B
Garland, Ed A. to Nannie J. Williams 10-19-1859 Sh
Garland, James L. to Mary Ann Ferrell 8-29-1863 (9-1-1863) L
Garland, John C. M. to Ann Eliza F. O. Perry 9-5-1854 Ma
Garland, John C. to Mary C. Slaughter 4-21-1868 T
Garland, Reubin F. to Susan Ann Elizabeth Greer 7-25-1853 (7-26-1853) Hr
Garland, Thomas L. to Julia C. Crenshaw 2-23-1865 T
Garland, William W. to Eliza A. Exum 1-13-1841 (1-15-1841) Ma
Garland, William W. to Mary E. McKnight 12-18-1854 (12-19-1854) Ma
Garmany, Henry to Lotty Jordan 12-26-1866 G
Garmany, Hugh to Nancy Mann 3-18-1861 G
Garmany?, Henry to Rose Morris 9-14-1871 O
Garnell, William I. to S. J. Tanner 2-29-1849 G
Garner (Gasner?), John to M. J. Howell 7-26-1870 G
Garner, B. F. to Edney S. Hamilton 1-15-1872 (1-16-1872) Cr
Garner, B. to Mary Jane Carr 7-14-1863 G
Garner, Bethnell to M. J. Ellington 10-18-1864 Dy
Garner, Brice A. to Susan Anderson 12-16-1840 Hr
Garner, F. L. to Martha A. King 10-19-1846 (no return) Cr
Garner, J. A. to Parlee Long 12-1-1876 Hy
Garner, J. T. to Mary A. Brown 7-13-1856 Cr

Garner, Jacob B. to Mary E. Jennings 10-28-1857 We
Garner, James to Elizabth Parker 11-15-1849 Be
Garner, John A. to Eliza G. McAlexander 5-4-1850 (5-16-1850) Hr
Garner, John A. to Frances E. Thompson 6-29-1852 Hr
Garner, John T. to Rebecca Dillard 8-29-1832 (8-30-1832) Hr
Garner, John to Elizabeth Cupp 1-19-1843 Be
Garner, John to Isabelle Chumbly 7-25-1846 (no return) Hn
Garner, R. G. L. to Elizabeth Diggs 2-7-1842 Hn
Garner, S. C. to Matilda A. Moliter 9-22-1858 (9-23-1858) Sh
Garner, Sam to Jenny Harris 12-28-1874 Hy
Garner, William S. to Charlotte Rhodes 9-10-1835 Sh
Garner, William to Mintee Diggs 11-4-1860 (not endorsed) Cr
Garner, William to Nancy Richardson 6-2-1835 Hr
Garner, Wm. F. to Nancy R. Rogers 6-10-1861 (not endorsed) Cr
Garner, Wm. H. to Sarah A. Moore 9-7-1865 L
Garnett, Jno. H. to Mary F. Rutledge 12-15-1868 F
Garrash, John to Mary Johnson 3-14-1869 Be
Garret, Isaac to Sarah A. Morris 4-10-1867 Dy
Garret, Isham to Jane Henderson 3-8-1867 (3-9-1867) T
Garret, J. J. to E. J. McCormack 12-17-1872 T
Garret, Robert F. to Mary M. Hamilton 1-23-1871 (1-25-1871) T
Garrett, Alfred D. to Tennessee Freeling 1-23-1849 (1-24-1849) Ma
Garrett, Alse to Fanie (Mrs.) Smith 9-12-1866 (9-13-1866) Dy
Garrett, Andrew O. to Sarah C. Williams 12-14-1859 We
Garrett, Arvell to Susan Alexander 4-4-1838 (4-5-1838) Ma
Garrett, Ashvill to Susan B. Alexander 11-25-1857 We
Garrett, Benj. G. to M. A. Collins 12-25-1856 Sh
Garrett, D. C. to F. E. Percifull 1-25-1874 Hy
Garrett, D. J. to Josephine Blyler 2-11-1878 (2-13-1878) L
Garrett, E. R. to M. L. Applewhite 2-1-1873 Dy
Garrett, Geo. G. to Margaret E. Green 11-6-1850 (no return) Cr
Garrett, Geo. W. to Eliza Horton 9-16-1848 (no return) Cr
Garrett, Geor. B. to Mollie L. Dickason 6-3-1872 (6-5-1872) Cr
Garrett, Henry S. to Susan J. Perkins 8-2-1867 (8-4-1867) L
Garrett, J. H. to J. A. F. Harman 9-21-1871 Cr
Garrett, J. T. to M. M. Miller 11-18-1877 Hy
Garrett, J. T. to Sally Hamrick 12-31-1866 (no return) F
Garrett, Jacob to Mary Polk 9-12-1829 (10-3-1829) H
Garrett, James I. to Hattie Ferguson 1-26-1878 (1-29-1878) L
Garrett, James N. to Margaret Hellix 12-11-1866 O
Garrett, James P. G. to Martha Ann Sanderson 1-3-1867 Ma
Garrett, James to Sarah Nolan 1-27-1843 Ma
Garrett, John D. to Eliza Jane Clayton 5-23-1863 (5-31-1863) Sh
Garrett, John M. to Mary Corlern 9-10-1863 Mn
Garrett, John to Caroline Churchwell 12-1-1854 Sh
Garrett, John to Frances E.? Rhodes 5-16-1865 (5-17-1865) T
Garrett, John to Martha J. Kneeland 10-19-1867 (no return) Hy
Garrett, Joseph to Frances Bradley 8-22-1855 Cr
Garrett, Kenneth to Louisa C. Patrick 8-1-1853 (8-2-1853) Sh
Garrett, Martin R. to Adelaide Marshall 2-15-1849 Sh
Garrett, Matthew D. to Joycy Ann Wilkinson 3-6-1843 Hr
Garrett, Moses to Mary Burns 4-16-1879 L
Garrett, R. C. to Sarah A. Rhodes 5-1-1848 (5-3-1848) F
Garrett, Rufus K. to Sarah E. Luckey 1-21-1851 (1-22-1851) F
Garrett, Samuel I. to Eliza Rickman 2-7-1842 (2-8-1842) Ma
Garrett, Samuel J. to Sarah Jane Caldwell 1-14-1878 (1-16-1878) L
Garrett, Simon to Elizabeth Dudley 10-3-1849 (no return) Cr
Garrett, Thomas H. to Martha Jane Brown 10-29-1856 Ma
Garrett, Thomas H. to Susan B. Henderson 11-30-1859 (12-1-1859) Ma
Garrett, Thomas S. to Elizabeth Jane Mitchell 12-19-1848 (12-21-1848) Hr
Garrett, Turner to Martha A. Fletcher 11-26-1860 (11-27-1860) Hr
Garrett, Vincent to Mary Fonner 2-6-1841 Ma
Garrett, W. R. to Mary E. Green 9-23-1862 (9-25-1862) Cr
Garrett, Wesley to Callie Briley 12-21-1872 Hy
Garrett, Wesley to Ellen Cobb 10-31-1878 Hy
Garrett, William C. to Lina Reynolds 4-3-1844 (5-17-1844) Ma
Garrett, William H. to Lucinda L. Pennington 5-28-1870 (no return) L
Garrett, William to Electy C. Pyland 12-30-1854 (12-31-1854) G
Garrett, William to Mary Jane Lee 1-20-1883 (1-21-1883) L
Garrett, Wm. H. to Lidia E. Bromley 9-23-1849 Be
Garrison, A. C. to Mary L. McAlister 3-9-1852 O
Garrison, A. J. to J. E. Scates 12-12-1859 (12-13-1859) O
Garrison, Archibald C. to Minerva Sinkler 2-18-1858 O
Garrison, B. P. to Isabella Seymour 4-4-1864 F
Garrison, Benjamin to Pheby Crockett 8-31-1864 (9-1-1864) O
Garrison, Currie to Mag Holt (Hast?) 7-24-1875 (7-25-1875) L
Garrison, Ezekiel to Viney Nichols 3-6-1845 O
Garrison, J. F. to S. J. Tilghman 2-18-1867 G
Garrison, J. R. to A. B. Fisher 4-10-1858 Sh
Garrison, James L. to Lucy Ann Ivey 8-31-1847 (no return) F
Garrison, James V. to Susannah Baker 12-14-1846 (no return) F
Garrison, John T. to Mary H. Cleaves 5-7-1863 F
Garrison, Laban J. to Ann M. Reynolds 10-8-1857 (10-15-1857) L
Garrison, Levi to Jane Spivey 8-12-1871 Hy
Garrison, M. to Marinda Howell 6-24-1869 (6-30-1869) F
Garrison, Matthew M. to Ann Eveline Van Atty 7-24-1849 (7-26-1849) G
Garrison, Moses to Elzira Grifin 10-30-1865 Cr

Garrison, N. N. to N. F. Worel 9-15-1867 O
Garrison, P. C. to Mary Butler 12-27-1840 Cr
Garrison, Phillip to Catherine Bright 8-6-18688 O B
Garrison, W. B. to Sarah E. Bryan 3-1-1836 Sh
Garrison, W. G. to _____ Worel ?-?-1867 (with 9-1867) O
Garrison, William B. to Belinda Shipman 12-2-1826 (12-7-1826) Hr
Garrott, Thomas M. to C. J. Chipman 11-13-1875 (11-14-1875) L
Garth, H. E. to Alice D. Jones 4-25-1859 (4-26-1859) Sh
Garthur, Albert to Elizabeth Williams 10-15-1839 Hn
Gartman, Henry E. to Virginia J. Gibbins 2-14-1850 Sh
Gartman, Jacob to Cornelia E. Gilbins 6-4-1856 (6-5-1856) Sh
Garvey, Patrick to Bridget King 11-27-1861 (11-28-1861) Sh
Garvin, H. to Mary Eddins 7-27-1863 (8-11-1863) F
Garvin, J. G. to M. T. Burnett 9-6-1862 (9-9-1862) F
Garvin, John A. to Albenia T. Culp 12-11-1866 (12-13-1866) F
Garvins, _____ to Nancy A. Wills 3-24-1850 Sh
Garwood, George to Nancy Bobbitt 2-28-1869 G B
Gary, Albert to Taldona Loving 2-1-1877 Hy
Gary, Thomas to Johanna Kennedy 3-17-1863 Sh
Gaska, John to Charlotte Hillsman 5-3-1849 Sh
Gaskin, Mc to Louisa Benton 7-22-1848 O
Gaskin, Roy to L. C. Hardican 3-5-1873 (3-10-1873) Dy
Gaskins, Amos L. to Rebecca Arnold 6-18-1860 We
Gaskins, Enoch to Perlina W. Dearmore 9-17-1849 Ma
Gaskins, Enoch to Susan Scott 12-10-1867 (12-24-1867) Ma
Gaskins, George to Fannie Dixon 8-15-1878 (no return) Hy
Gaskins, J. R. to J. A. Wood 5-15-1858 Cr
Gaskins, Mac to Louisa Benton 7-22-1848 (7-23-1848) O
Gaskins, Mc to Louisa Burton 7-22-1848 (7-23-1848) O
Gaskins, Thomas G. to Matilda Raines 7-16-1858 (7-18-1858) Ma
Gaskins, Thomas to Delila Rains 1-16-1833 (12-16-1833) G
Gaskins, Thos. to Delila Rains 11-16-1832 G
Gaskins, Thos. to Jane Gutner 10-5-1857 We
Gastin, Cyrus to Margaret Rust 12-31-1867 G B
Gaston, Chas. A. to Jennie Campbell 6-18-1867 (6-20-1867) F
Gaston, Daniel M. to Minerva Grant 12-22-1866 (12-23-1866) Ma
Gaston, Z. T. to Martha Rogers 10-29-1866 (10-30-1866) Ma
Gately, Henry to Martha B. Wallingsford 3-7-1836 G
Gately, James M. to Lumisa Howell 9-22-1857 (10-1-1857) Ma
Gately, James M. to Mary Jane Lovill 11-9-1852 (12-22-1852) Ma
Gately, John W. to Nancy McCleur 7-3-1846 (7-7-1846) G
Gately, Robert to Biney Parks 2-1-1859 F
Gatens, P. to H. Cunningham 4-26-1864 Sh
Gates, Benjamin F. to Mary J. Westen 12-22-1859 We
Gates, Benjamin F. to Narcissa M. (Mrs.) Stone 5-4-1859 Ma
Gates, Benjamin to Mary King 1-9-1841 Sh
Gates, David A? to Sarah L. Hervell? 11-9-1850 Hr
Gates, Egbert H. to Cynthia Ann Allen 5-31-1838 Hn
Gates, James F. to Emiline Webster 12-15-1846 Hn
Gates, Jno. H. to Mattie V. Yancy 12-2-1867 (12-6-1867) F
Gates, John H. to Eliza M. C. Avent 11-23-1852 (11-25-1852) Hr
Gates, John to Mary A. Benge 8-29-1840 (9-3-1840) F
Gates, Martin to Christiana Bender 5-11-1860 (1-12-1860) Sh
Gates, Person to Elizabeth Oliver 1-8-1857 We
Gates, Peter F. to Mary Jones 9-27-1838 Hn
Gates, Robert to Callie J. Jester 10-29-1867 Ma
Gates, William to Martha Acuff 4-24-1878 (4-26-1878) L
Gatevam, William G. to C. S. Magee 12-27-1852 We
Gatewood, Bazzell to Mary A. L. Owen 12-22-1858 We
Gatewood, H. to S. M. Beckley 5-14-1856 We
Gatewood, John R. to Nancy McDonald 11-3-1840 (11-15-1840) Hr
Gatewood, Osborn to Mary Ann Westbrook 2-15-1848 Sh
Gatewood, Wm. to Martha E. Simms 8-1-1858 Hr
Gatewood, Wm. to Rhoda Winn 10-17-1866 (10-20-1866) T
Gatland, Thomas T. to Manerva F. Vinson 12-8-1866 (no return) Cr
Gatland, Wm. to Angelin Box 8-21-1842 Cr
Gatlin, Andrew S. to Jane West 10-22-1836 Hr
Gatlin, Elias to Mary Marshal 3-16-1866 Hy
Gatlin, John A. to Isabella Woodson 9-17-1854 Hr
Gatlin, John A. to Lucy Ann Cross 9-26-1849 (9-27-1849) Hr
Gatlin, John A. to Nancy E. McDaniel 5-19-1855 (5-27-1855) Hr
Gatlin, Riley to Martha C. Shelly 4-26-1835 (4-29-1835) Hr
Gatlin, Stephen to Chelly Branch 12-16-1840 (12-17-1840) Ma
Gatlin, Stephen to Priscilla Box 10-14-1867 (10-15-1867) Cr
Gatling, Richard B. to Sarah E. Granberry 7-8-1844 (7-9-1844) F
Gattas, George to Sarah Ann Boswell 4-27-1843 Ma
Gatti, J. B. to Alice C. howard 5-26-1853 (6-5-1853) Sh
Gattis, George Carson to Amanda Harris Davis 6-11-1853 Ma
Gattis, William L. to Mary A. Davis 12-21-1847 (12-22-1847) Ma
Gatty, George to Martha A. Manning 8-16-1853 (no return) Cr
Gauden, W. A. to Elizabeth Brandon 11-5-1873 Hy
Gauger, Daniel to Sarah E. Lyon 4-11-1843 G
Gaugh, Eleazar to Maria J. Powell 8-2-1856 (8-3-1856) Hr
Gaugh, Eleazar to Sarah E. Adams 6-25-1861 Hr
Gaulden, J. W. to M. A. Jones 12-20-1864 (12-21-1864) Dy
Gaulden, M. D. to Mollie Capell 9-29-1875 (9-30-1875) Dy
Gaulden, Roland to Malissa Palmer 4-3-1878 (no return) Dy

Gaulden, Roland to Margaret Pierce 3-4-1876 (4-12-1876) Dy B
Gauldin, Willis to Lou Webb 1-21-1870 (1-31-1870) Dy
Gaunt, Alfred to Louisa Byrn 11-6-1875 L
Gaunt, Joseph to Mary A. Simister 6-6-1854 Sh
Gaus (Gans), Irvin to Sarah Estis 1-27-1869 Hy
Gause, Abner to Margaret Jinkins 12-20-1873 (12-21-1873) L B
Gause, B. C. to Cora Scott 9-28-1869 Hy
Gause, B. C. to Harriet A. Moorer 12-25-1860 L
Gause, Bailey to Fannie Weston 1-20-1881 (no return) L B
Gause, Bailey to Frances Scott 2-28-1874 (no return) Hy
Gause, F. B. to Mattie L. Rice 11-12-1867 (11-15-1868?) L
Gause, Green to Sallie Newton 12-15-1874 (12-16-1874) L
Gause, Henry to Joanna Byars 1-29-1881 (1-30-1881) L
Gause, John P. to Hattie W. Allen 5-22-1867 L
Gause, Peter to Anna Edwards 12-22-1870 Hy
Gause, Sampson to Nancy Outlaw 10-24-1878 (no return) L B
Gause, Silas to Lula Westbrook 10-28-1880 L B
Gause, Steven to Lizzie Watkins 12-26-1867 Hy
Gause, William to Cherry Tyus 3-27-1874 (no return) Hy
Gauspobe, John H. to Martha Kennedy 8-24-1847 Sh
Gavens, Charles N. to N. S. Brown 2-5-1863 Sh
Gawley, Donald to Elizabeth Ford 9-8-1860 (9-9-1860) Sh
Gay, A. T. (Capt.) to Emma Jetton 12-31-1867 G
Gay, Alexander to Elizabeth Guin (Green?) 1-25-1873 (no return) L B
Gay, B. F. to Marselia Bass 5-21-1857 (5-24-1857) Hr
Gay, Columbus F. to Nancy J. Dickerson 6-22-1867 T
Gay, Edwin to Margaret McKay 4-3-1829 Hr
Gay, Edwin to Margarette Jones 7-19-1855 (11-11-1855) Hr
Gay, Elbert to Martha Ross 10-20-1838 (no return) Hn
Gay, Elbert to Mary Ann Nickols 11-19-1850 We
Gay, Gary to Elizabeth Overall 5-9-1831 (5-10-1831) Hr
Gay, Gary to Minerva Wells(Wills?) 1-29-1850 (1-31-1850) Hr
Gay, John H. to Margaret Y. Biles 12-19-1831 Hr
Gay, John L. to Martha C. Mayo 1-15-1844 We
Gay, John to Elizabeth Sanderson 12-23-1839 Sh
Gay, Lemmon B. to Margaret Cox 12-22-1852 (12-29-1852) Hr
Gay, Lemon to Eliza Wilkerson 1-2-1834 Hr
Gay, Richard to Nancy Oldham 11-28-1850 G
Gay, Thomas to Emma Spiller 11-22-1884 (11-23-1884) L
Gay, Thomas to Mahala Bone 6-25-1829 O
Gay, William to E. M. E.? Mays 11-2-1865 G
Gayford, Alfred B. to Alice Taylor 8-25-1854 Hr
Gayl, Edmond to Flora Wilson 11-28-1869 Hy
Gaylaor, E. M. to E. M. Albright 12-29-1875 (no return) Hy
Gayle, P. S. to Sarah E. Brown 11-17-1867 Hy
Gayle, Thomas C. to Mary Ann Eckford 3-5-1857 Sh
Gayler, Atheriah to Catherine Tiger? 12-3-1834 Hr
Gayler, Stephen S. to Polly Ann Murphy 12-14-1839 (12-19-1839) Hr
Gaylor, William to Jane Moore 1-10-1872 O
Gaylord, J. W. to Sallie A. Hauser 2-7-1869 G
Gaza, Joshua to Elendar A. Phelan 5-5-1842 G
Gazzam, Charles W. to Clementina Lea 11-29-1827 Hr
Gear, George J. to Sue F. King 11-27-1860 Sh
Gearing, John G. to Martha Jane Casey 2-6-1856 Be
Geary, Edward to Mary Geary 1-14-1862 Sh
Geary, Thomas to Julia McKevor 7-8-1855 Sh
Gee, D. W. to J. C. Merritt 12-11-1866 Cr
Gee, Geo. W. to Sarah Lambert 3-10-1852 (3-11-1852) Hr
Gee, George H. to Nancy P. Adkin 3-14-1844 Cr
Gee, James A. to Sarah M. Parkenson 1-11-1854 Cr
Gee, James P. to Matilda C. Demoss 8-6-1861 (8-7-1861) Cr
Gee, James to Nancy Casey 12-18-1847 (12-19-1847) Hr
Gee, Nathan to Diannah Mayfield 11-23-1853 (11-24-1853) Hr
Gee, Philip E. to Adeline M. Simmonds 9-14-1866 (no return) Hn
Gee, Robert to Sarah Bowling 7-29-1835 Sh
Gee, Robert to Susan Dillihunty 6-15-1859 (6-?-1859) T
Gee, Smith H. to Sarah Beckham 12-12-1835 G
Gegg, Paul to Annie W. Knowles 12-23-1858 Sh
Gehe, Louis to Joanna Lienhardt 4-16-1853 (4-17-1853) Sh
Gehen, John B. to Louisa Chapman 12-13-1859 (12-15-1859) T
Gehen, John B. to Louisiana Chapman 12-13-1859 (12-15-1859) T
Geiger, Martin to Laura Ganionhil 11-18-1854 (11-19-1854) Sh
Geist, Theodore to Elizabeth Sherrill 9-3-1858 Sh
Gelby, R. C. to Dollie Younger 8-13-1866 (no return) Cr
Geleun, W. L. to Angeline Jones 7-1-1858 We
Gemwell, Thos. W. to Mary A. Parks 4-1-1845 Sh
Gennett, R. H. to Susan R. Reid 3-15-1851 Sh
Gennette, Lewis to Hannah Shrieger 6-13-1859 (6-19-1859) Sh
Gentry, C. C. to M. C. Lassiter 12-24-1866 G
Gentry, Charles C. to Elizabeth McFarland 12-14-1863 Dy
Gentry, Dock to Susan Lake 3-21-1874 (no return) Dy
Gentry, Frank to Katie Dougherty 7-20-1865 (no return) Dy
Gentry, John G. to Martha A. A. Young 3-7-1861 Dy
Gentry, John to Mary Key 8-22-1865 (8-23-1865) Dy
Gentry, Napoleon to Narcissa H. Butler 7-1-1868 (7-2-1868) Ma
Gentry, Robert to Emily Rhodes 9-29-1851 (9-30-1851) Hr
Gentry, William to Lavina Scallion 1-9-1836 (1-10-1836) G

Gentry, Wm. L. to Mary Outhouse 6-10-1858 We
Geoghegan, John to Emma Carroll 12-31-1860 Sh
Geoghegan, John to Mary McDaniel 6-30-1856 (7-1-1856) Hr
George, Benjamin to Saphronia Huggins 12-25-1864 G
George, Brinkley to Elizabeth Kingston 2-8-1846 We
George, Caswell E. to Elizabeth Gay 5-2-1855 G
George, Caswell E. to Mary T. Bass 8-25-1846 (8-26-1846) G
George, G. H. to Susan E. Fergerson 2-24-1855 Cr
George, Grief to Martha Henry 5-17-1849 Sh
George, H. F. to Martha Nip 1-1-1861 O
George, J. B. to Arenia Wallice 4-28-1860 Cr
George, J. B. to Sarah Ann E. Bets 3-30-1858 O
George, James T. to Mahala A. Baker 2-12-1845 G
George, John C. to Margaret C. Forbess 12-19-1870 (12-22-1870) T
George, John H. to Margaret Henderson 1-24-1845 (no return) F
George, Martin S. to Martha E. Revely 11-30-1857 (12-3-1857) Ma
George, R. to Loucinda C. Capelinger 4-8-1868 Be
George, W. H. to Amanda Davis 8-10-1850 Cr
George, W. R. to Sally Whittington 3-7-1864 (3-10-1864) O
George, Wilson to Mary Conner 6-30-1864 (7-1-1864) Sh
Gerfee?, James to Mary Williams 12-1-1840 Cr
Gerlinger, Jacob to Ellen Sheppard 10-21-1862 Sh
German, Kingsberry to Liley Denny 4-1-1856 (4-11-1856) Ma
Germon, William H. to Tennessee M. Rosenburn 12-12-1853 Ma
Gerred?, Hugh to Easter Adams 3-15-1853 T
Gerren, G. to M. A. Herren 1-26-1837 Be
Gerrico, Henry to Mary Loving 11-27-1867 O
Gerris, G. N. to Mary A. Beck 9-18-1856 We
Gerritt, William to Ann Butterworth 6-1-1867 (no return) Dy
Gerson, Benjamin to Mary Levy 10-11-1847 Sh
Gess, Charles R. to Eddie Emerson 12-7-1874 (12-8-1874) L
Geter (Jeter), J. B. to Frances M. Bruce 8-13-1865 Hy
Gettys, Samuel S. to Sarah Grant 6-8-1857 (6-9-1857) Sh
Geugel, John to Anna Schottlin 9-12-1856 Sh
Geurin, James to Elizabeth Walters 12-24-1867 Hn
Gevert, Henry to Ann (Mrs.) Ford 8-16-1864 Sh
Geyer, J. to M. J. Hawkins 7-23-1853 (no return) F
Geylard, Thomas to Polly Seratt 8-1-1828 (8-3-1828) G
Ghann?, T. B. to Nancy Ann Burnham 9-18-1866 (9-19-1866) Dy
Gholson, Thomas to Catherine D. McLemore 9-16-1841 Sh
Gholson, William T. to Sarah Hart 4-9-1831 Sh
Gholston, James M. to Sarah S. Hicks 4-17-1858 (4-20-1858) O
Gibb, John C. to Penelope Barker 10-1-1850 Cr
Gibbens, William R. to Catherine Randolf 8-19-1863 Sh
Gibbins, William to Polly Ann McGehee 4-21-1842 Sh
Gibbon, James T. to Lamira R. Burns 8-21-1861 (8-22-1861) Cr
Gibbons, A. B. to S. C. Moore 2-13-1863 (no return) Cr
Gibbons, M. J. to Mary Green 4-16-1861 Sh
Gibbons, S. T. C. to Nancy A. Richardson 12-15-1869 (12-16-1869) Cr
Gibbs, A. F. to Elizabeth J. Ward 1-8-1850 Sh
Gibbs, A. F. to Isabella Andrews 5-21-1844 Sh
Gibbs, Alfred to Violet Clements 3-23-1872 (3-31-1872) T
Gibbs, Charles N. to Matilda E. Vaulx 6-5-1850 Ma
Gibbs, Cyrus to Emer Harrison 2-15-1867 (2-16-1867) T
Gibbs, Felix G. to Martha Kendrick 1-10-1845 Ma
Gibbs, G. Couper to Elizabeth Elcon 4-9-1847 Sh
Gibbs, George to Verena Tenfel 7-23-1858 We
Gibbs, James to Martha Hopkins 3-27-1869 (no return) Dy
Gibbs, Jesse A. to Victoria A. Cutler 12-13-1859 We
Gibbs, John A. to Caroline Blythe 1-21-1851 Hn
Gibbs, John C. to Permelia F. Gallion 9-8-1862 Hr
Gibbs, P. A. to Mary J. Crutchfiel 2-14-1855 We
Gibbs, R. B. to A. C. Carter 12-7-1860 (11-9-1860) Dy
Gibbs, Turner R. to Monan Milton 3-20-1844 (4-3-1844) G
Gibbs, Turner R. to Nancy Borran 11-30-1839 (12-1-1839) G
Gibbs, Walter to Louisa Neal 2-27-1875 (2-28-1875) Dy
Gibbs, William H. to Rosanna James 2-27-1867 Be
Gibbs, William to Martha P. Blythe 12-5-1841 Hn
Gibbson, William to Mary Holland 1-17-1851 (1-20-1851) Sh
Gibson, A. D. to Mary R. Richards 11-21-1860 Sh
Gibson, A. H. to A. G. Roney 11-1-1879 (11-5-1879) Dy
Gibson, A. R. to M. J. Voss 12-18-1883 (12-19-1883) L
Gibson, A. to Mary A. Vickers 6-17-1854 We
Gibson, Allen to Sarline Edmondson 12-22-1864 G
Gibson, Alvert to Marry Williams 6-19-1873 Cr
Gibson, Anderson to Elizabeth Rodgers 7-30-1841 (8-3-1841) G
Gibson, Andrew J. to Jennie D. Ware 1-22-1867 (no return) Hy
Gibson, Archibald to Frances M. Quisenberry 6-5-1838 (no return) Hn
Gibson, Archibald to Jane Rogers 11-13-1844 Hr
Gibson, B. F. to Martha G. Stubbs 11-15-1863 (no return) Cr
Gibson, Daniel P. to Sarah Gauntlett 3-6-1860 G
Gibson, David L. to Annie C. Dunbar 12-22-1859 Sh
Gibson, David to Louisa Derryberry 12-6-1859 Mn
Gibson, Elijah to Catherine Price 2-15-1843 Sh
Gibson, Elijah to Elizabeth Bas 12-5-1839 Sh
Gibson, Elijah to Lucretia Ann Boothe 9-11-1848 (9-14-1848) T

Gibson, George S. to Nancy Henson 1-27-1828 (1-29-1828) Hr
Gibson, George W. to Sarah F. King 9-4-1862 Hn
Gibson, George to Claway? Smith 4-29-1868 T
Gibson, George to Fenton Mitchell 1-16-1843 Sh
Gibson, George to Lavanda Binkley 4-11-1866 (no return) Dy
Gibson, George to Margaret Harper 12-8-1825 O
Gibson, Gideon to Martha Hicks 9-9-1862 Be
Gibson, H. A. to Margaret Carter 8-9-1865 Mn
Gibson, Harberd to Emma Bradshaw 12-7-1880 Dy
Gibson, Hiel to Sarah Henson 12-23-1846 (12-24-1846) Hr
Gibson, I. B. to Mary D. Taylor 9-28-1865 O
Gibson, I. Y. to Anna R. Moore 9-9-1851 Sh
Gibson, Irvin to Martha Hatley 11-1-1866 Be
Gibson, Irvin to Martha Lewis 6-17-1840 G
Gibson, Isaac Z. to Catherine Van Pelt 6-10-1846 Sh
Gibson, J. N. to Victoria J. March 6-3-1868 F
Gibson, J. T. to Lou Curtis 10-24-1883 (10-25-1883) L
Gibson, J. Z. to Mary Able 10-6-1847 Sh
Gibson, James H. to Alley Edmondson 2-17-1844 (2-18-1844) G
Gibson, James H. to Ann F. Wright 7-15-1850 (7-23-1850) G
Gibson, James Knox to Rosa C. Somervel 11-20-1866 (no return) Hy
Gibson, James M. to Fanlee A. McCrackin 3-21-1863 (no return) Cr
Gibson, James M. to Paula A. McCracken 3-24-1863 Cr
Gibson, James to Elizabeth Battle 11-22-1837 (11-23-1837) G
Gibson, James to Elizabeth Bird 9-20-1854 O
Gibson, James to Martha R. Richardson 12-22-1847 (12-23-1847) G
Gibson, Jeff to Carry Morgan 2-22-1872 (no return) Hy
Gibson, Jeremiah to Polly Mainard 7-23-1838 (no return) Cr
Gibson, John S. to Tibitha Taylor 10-14-1848 (no return) Cr
Gibson, John to Mary Sutherland 12-22-1858 Cr
Gibson, John to Polly Ann Simmons 2-3-1862 (2-6-1862) Dy
Gibson, Jordan to Mary Ann Johnson 2-18-1863 Sh
Gibson, Joseph to Mary Nanney 11-11-1847 Hn
Gibson, Matthew T. to Mima Brown 5-27-1870 (5-28-1870) F B
Gibson, Nathaniel to Harriet L. Ownby 8-20-1857 Cr
Gibson, Orvid to Sallie E. Sugg 2-19-1870? (3-16-1869?) L
Gibson, Porter to Sarah J. Bainey 5-8-1863 (5-17-1863) Cr
Gibson, Richard P. to Amanda Thompson 8-17-1867 (no return) Dy
Gibson, Samuel B. to A. W. Wrigs 11-2-1841 Sh
Gibson, Smith to Rebecca A. Dortch 12-27-1860 Hn
Gibson, Stephen to Cela A. Highfield 5-28-1856 (5-29-1856) Hr
Gibson, Stephen to Mary Henson 11-1-1836 Hr
Gibson, Stephen to Mary M. Massey 6-21-1857 Be
Gibson, Thomas J. to Melissa Phillips 12-22-1851 (no return) Cr
Gibson, Thomas R. to Jane Winford 11-22-1840 Sh
Gibson, W. C. to Mary C. Griffin 11-29-1853 Cr
Gibson, William H. to M. C. Cooper 5-23-1872 (no return) Dy
Gibson, William P. to Ariminta R. Belotte 11-29-1852 (12-16-1852) Hr
Gibson, William to Elizabeth Hill 4-28-1850 (5-3-1850) O
Gibson, William to Isabella Sanders 7-21-1841 (7-22-1841) F
Gibson, William to Mary Read 5-8-1871 T
Gibson, William to Nancy Gwinn 8-17-1847 G
Gibson, William to Sarah Edmundson 10-20-1838 (10-21-1838) G
Gibson, William to Sarah Harrison 7-18-1853 (7-21-1853) O
Gibson, William to Susan V. Parris 2-28-1861 (3-7-1861) Hr
Gibson, Wyley P. to Ann Dilelay? 3-12-1861 Cr
Gibson, Z. T. to Margarett E. Stubblefield 11-9-1867 G
Gidcomb, James Willis to Louisa Augusta Thompson 7-14-1870 L
Gidcomb, Noah to Jane Baker 7-?-1857 (no return) L
Gidcumb, Sampson to Pelina Lucy 7-14-1849 (7-15-1849) L
Giddens, W. K. to Rebecca Luceford 1-26-1872 Hy
Gideon, Alsman to Mary J. Houton 8-1-1859 (no return) Hy
Gideon, Francis to Rosey Russell 12-30-1839 O
Gieser, Johan to Celia Heer 9-27-1860 Hy
Giffin, George W. to H. H. Oliver 7-9-1861 (7-11-1861) O
Giffin, Samuel Y. to Mary T. Smith 2-13-1838 O
Gifford, Levi to Martha Montgomery 9-15-1864 Sh
Gifford, R. L. to Ann E. Draper 7-26-1856 (7-27-1856) Sh
Gift, Hinson to Mary A. Greenlaw 12-8-1836 Sh
Gift, James to Elizabeth Douglas 5-14-1835 Sh
Gift, Robert H. to Sarah J. Sigler 12-22-1858 (12-23-1858) Sh
Gift, Robert to Lavinie Choate 8-13-1833 Sh
Gift, William A. to Mary E. Jeter 9-21-1848 Sh
Gilbert, A. G. to Adelia Wall 6-23-1861 Hn
Gilbert, Albert to Patient Clemons 5-18-1875 O
Gilbert, Benj. to Eliza Allen 10-28-1857 Cr
Gilbert, Benjamin P. to Mary L. Jouett 5-5-1846 (no return) Hn
Gilbert, Benjamin to Julia Danks 5-2-1846 Sh
Gilbert, Calvin to Myra Drake 11-30-1878 Hy
Gilbert, Edmund to Harriet Jones 12-20-1865 Hn
Gilbert, G. J. to Sarah J. Birmingham 9-16-1872 Cr
Gilbert, J. H. to Liza Beazley 11-4-1866 Be
Gilbert, J. M. to Sallie W. Porter 12-28-1858 Hy
Gilbert, J. W. to Manerva Allen 6-27-1867 Hn
Gilbert, James M. to Carrie Whitten 5-18-1869 Cr
Gilbert, James M. to Susan Isabella Jones 8-9-1857 Hn
Gilbert, James Z. to Charlotte D. Caruthers 12-11-1845 Cr

Gilbert, James Z. to Elizabeth New 12-27-1838 Cr
Gilbert, Joel H. to Susan J. Osboron 3-4-1862 O
Gilbert, John to Mariah Wiggins 1-9-1871 Cr B
Gilbert, Joseph to Emeline Gilbert 1-21-1871 (no return) Cr B
Gilbert, M. R. to S. E. Boyd 5-5-1852 We
Gilbert, Martin R. to Elizabeth H. Foster 12-1-1842 Hn
Gilbert, Martin to Elizabeth Wingo 1-4-1871 (1-5-1871) Cr
Gilbert, Ned to Ellen Nelson 7-14-1867 Hy
Gilbert, P. B. to A. M. Griswell 12-16-1866 O
Gilbert, Peter to Sarah Young 11-30-1878 Hy
Gilbert, Robert to Ellen Gilbert 2-18-1870 (2-20-1870) Cr
Gilbert, Robertson G. to Nancy Fance? 7-26-1873 (no return) L
Gilbert, Sylvester to Margaret White 5-2-1863 Sh
Gilbert, Thos. to Narcisa Wiggins 1-9-1871 Cr B
Gilbert, W. H. to Mary J. Boyd 1-22-1876 L
Gilbert, William to Ellen Carpenter 4-16-1867 (not executed) F B
Gilbert, Wilson R. to Mary Jane Griffin 11-10-1871 (11-12-1871) Ma
Gilbert, Wm. C. to Mary E. Gwin 7-17-1848 (no return) Cr
Gilbreath, Andrew to Martha E. Presson 6-29-1860 Be
Gilbreath, George to Madaline Wiseman 8-8-1852 Be
Gilbreth, James to Mary Blaylock 1-12-1871 Cr
Gilchrist, Lucion B. to Valiria M. Wright 1-26-1848 G
Gilchrist, Robert J. to Drucilla Culp 7-10-1832 G
Gilcust, John A. to Ann Somers 9-4-1860 We
Gildon, Stephen to Ida Dewalt 7-11-1884 (7-13-1884) L
Gile, Alfred E. to Catharine A. Frollie 7-28-1864 (7-29-1864) Sh
Giles, Archibald to Martha A. Green 3-10-1848 (no return) Cr
Giles, C. G. to Margaret McKinney 3-28-1868 (3-29-1868) Cr
Giles, George to Betsy J. Busick 2-7-1858 Cr
Giles, J. G. to Mary Dodd 8-31-1857 We
Giles, James J. to Margaret E. Edward 12-2-1850 G
Giles, James to Hannah W. Caldwell 8-31-1843 Hn
Giles, John William to Susan Connell 10-27-1866 (10-28-1866) Ma
Giles, L. G. to Sarah C. Williams 11-12-1872 G
Giles, Melville to Betty Allen 12-23-1879 (12-24-1879) L B
Giles, N. C. to Susan C. Tarply 11-7-1860 Cr
Giles, Ned to Emeline Hunter 12-12-1868 (12-19-1868) F B
Giles, R. M. to Eliza C. Spicer 10-17-1848 G
Giles, T. L. to Lenora C. Lock 3-7-1853 (no return) F
Giles, Thomas to Julia Mullins 12-31-1874 L
Giles, Thomas to Rebecca Pettus 12-7-1876 L B
Giles, Varner to Jane Vaughn 7-14-1867 Hn
Giles, Wm. H. to Margaret H. Hatchett 10-19-1843 (no return) Cr
Gilfillan, James to Elizabeth Hardy 12-6-1857 (12-7-1857) Sh
Gilford, Elias to Caroline Lane 11-25-1870 (no return) F B
Gilkey, James T. to Sarah L. Crafter 1-11-1870 (1-13-1870) Cr
Gilkey, Robert C. to Mary C. Williamson 1-27-1852 Cr
Gilkey, S. B. to L. D. King 7-2-1863 (no return) Cr
Gill, B. F. to Cordelia Bryant 12-25-1876 (1-4-1877) O
Gill, David to Rebeccah Fly 10-12-1840 Ma
Gill, George W. to Lucy D. Pruitt 6-17-1844 G
Gill, H. W. to Mary W. (Mrs.) Ferrill 10-30-1866 G
Gill, Henry C. to Lizzie Edwards 10-12-1863 G
Gill, J. C. to Candace Lile 10-13-1847 (no return) F
Gill, James C. to Martha Curtis 3-24-1856 Sh
Gill, James T. to Prudence T. Hopper 1-8-1850 (1-19-1850) Ma
Gill, James to Patient Jacocks 2-18-1871 Hy
Gill, John M. to Lucy Pearce 5-10-1845 Sh
Gill, John P. to Elizabeth W. Pruitt 9-15-1848 G
Gill, N. O. to Martha P. Stephens 10-13-1870 G
Gill, Patrick to Elizabeth Ragan 10-17-1859 Sh
Gill, Robert L. to Martha A. Brookins 3-2-1876 (no return) Hy
Gill, Robert to Eliza M. Goodman 9-16-1857 G
Gill, Robert to Eliza M. Goodman 9-16-1857 (9-21-1857) G
Gill, Robert to Elizabeth Frances Allen 1-21-1867 (1-22-1867) Ma
Gill, T. N. to S. J. Jostling 3-12-1870 (3-13-1870) Dy
Gill, Tom to Annie Taylor 12-1-1873 Hy
Gill, Tom to Ellen Rogers 8-27-1870 Hy
Gill, William F. to Olly Ann McDowell 10-10-1853 (10-12-1853) G
Gill, William to Lucinda Statham 4-6-1853 (4-6-185?) O
Gillam, A. P. to E. O. Neal 1-19-1858 Hr
Gillam, William to Caroline Guinn 5-23-1857 (no return) We
Gillaspie, John P. to Sarah C. Gainor 5-19-1859 Hn
Gillaspie, Leroy C. to Tempy S. Johnson 10-29-1852 (10-30-1852) Ma
Gillaspie, Mathew to Mary Cozby 8-29-1835 Hr
Gillaspie, Robert to Margaret Elizabeth M Jones 11-15-1851 Sh
Gillem, Jerry to Emeline Woodson 9-25-1878 Hy
Gillem, John W. to Polly Coldwell 5-29-1868 (no return) Hy
Gillespie, Andrew J. to Julia ann Wright 2-12-1844 (2-13-1844) F
Gillespie, B. F. to Lucinda Horne 12-25-1848 G
Gillespie, Davis to Martha Ann Morris 6-17-1848 (no return) F
Gillespie, J. L. to Ovilla Smith 9-6-1880 (9-8-1880) L
Gillespie, J. W. to Catharine (Mrs.) Bond 10-8-1858 (10-12-1858) Sh
Gillespie, James B. to Anessa J. Johnson 3-8-1866 G
Gillespie, James E. to Jennie Luten 4-13-1869 (4-14-1869) L
Gillespie, James L. to Elizabeth Gordon 7-11-1842 (7-14-1842) O
Gillespie, James W. to Jane E. Taurman 1-11-1845 Sh

Gillespie, Jesse W. to Sarah C. Harris 9-23-1845 Sh
Gillespie, John A. to Benthie? L. Cole 2-5-1861 G
Gillespie, Johns to Florence Frazer 7-2-1872 Hy
Gillespie, Jonathan (James?) P. to Mary A. E. Keller 8-25-1869 (9-1-1869) L
Gillespie, Josephus to Sarah J. Bridges 3-29-1868 G B
Gillespie, L. C. to Eloise C. Conner 12-2-1868 Hy
Gillespie, L. K. to Bettie C. Ralston 2-12-1867 G
Gillespie, Moses to Manerva A. (Mrs.) Jones 3-18-1864 Sh
Gillespie, Robert to Mary E. Gillespie 2-6-1864 Sh
Gillespie, William H. to Martha A. Comer 5-22-1854 Hn
Gillespie, William to Rebeca Allen 8-7-1845 (8-8-1845) T
Gillet, Amasa to Rebecca McCord 1-9-1844 (1-11-1844) Hr
Gilliam, A. P. to S. A. Hicks 9-9-1867 (no return) Hy
Gilliam, Dell to Ann Fly 1-1-1874 Dy
Gilliam, James B. to Lucy K. Ritchey 1-18-1870 (1-20-1870) F
Gilliam, James M. to Elizabeth F. Hall 6-3-1852 (no return) F
Gilliam, James M. to Margarett A. Wall 1-16-1843 (1-17-1843) F
Gilliam, John A. to Mary Curtis 1-22-1853 (no return) F
Gilliam, John E. to Martha Ann Gilliam 11-19-1866 (11-20-1866) Ma
Gilliam, Mason to Olive Hopkins 2-27-1854 (2-28-1854) Ma
Gilliam, R. M. to N. J. Adams 10-20-1857 Be
Gilliam, Sandford W. to Mary M. Barnett 2-15-1861 (5-15-1861) Ma
Gilliam, Thomas M. to Martha H. Wilkinson 9-16-1857 (10-17-1857) Sh
Gilliam, Thomas P. to Sarah High 12-23-1847 Hn
Gilliam, William R. to Jane Kirkland 10-7-1858 Hn
Gilliam, William to Eliza Ryan 11-23-1878 Hy
Gilliam, William to Mary S. Newberry 1-10-1860 (no return) We
Gilliam, Wm. A. to Emma D. Holloway 2-17-1869 F
Gillikin, James to Amacivil Duncan 2-17-1844 Ma
Gillikins, James to Lotty L. Duncan 5-27-1850 Ma
Gilliland, Aron J. to Narcissa C. Paris 8-31-1853 (9-2-1853) G
Gilliland, B. F. to Minty Ann Stokes 1-1-1868 (no return) L
Gilliland, B. F. to Sarah L. Hubbard 2-4-1876 L
Gilliland, Benjamin F. to Eliza Cartwright 1-15-1872 (no return) L
Gilliland, J. A. to Ann Shain 10-26-1865 G
Gilliland, J. C. to Sarah J. Roberson 8-30-1862 G
Gilliland, John to Tabitha Nicholas 7-16-1841 (7-14?-1841) O
Gilliland, Joseph to Bettie Jordan 2-17-1869 (no return) Ma
Gilliland, Joseph to Margaret M. Robinson 2-7-1848 Ma
Gilliland, Major to Fanny Williams 9-23-1869 (no return) L B
Gilliland, W. F. to Victoria Smith 2-19-1865 G
Gilliland, William to Katharine Hubbert 12-23-1846 O
Gilliland, William to Lousa Glass 1-25-1877 L
Gilliland, Wm. to Anna Willis 8-8-1845 Be
Gillis, Arch to Frances Hicks 4-18-1839 Cr
Gillis, I. D. to R. A. Calhoun 12-7-1866 (12-9-18??) O
Gillis, John to Emily Auston 12-6-1843 Sh
Gillis, John to Nancy Kemp 12-21-1843 Cr
Gillis, Owen to Rebecca Chambers 3-27-1842 Cr
Gillispie, Leroy C. to Mary J. Tyson 10-28-1845 (11-1-1845) Ma
Gillispie, Robert N. to Mary E. Fry 11-12-1845 Ma
Gillispie, Thomas J. to Mary E. Henning 7-15-1851 (7-16-1851) Sh
Gillispie, William to Olivia Gillispie 12-28-1853 Be
Gillon?, Tillmon to Nancy Wingo 10-7-1850 (no return) Cr
Gillooly, John to Sarah M. Green 7-26-1866 Hn
Gillooly?, John to Margaret Flynn 4-13-1857 Hn
Gills, James R. to Nancy S. Gills 9-28-1844 (10-29-1844) O
Gills, James to Martha Louisa Gills 5-12-1858 O
Gills, John to Mary J. Myres 7-21-1862 (7-25-1862) O
Gills, W. P. to Sarah F. Hester 12-30-1868 O
Gills, William to Luandy Statum 4-6-1848 O
Gillum, Peter to Rosena Powell 11-4-1875 (no return) Hy
Gillum, William P. to Lucinda Owens 11-2-1827 G
Gilman, James S. to Martha Meeks 4-10-1857 (4-16-1857) Hr
Gilmore, Jerome B. to Emma L. Danbury 5-6-1854 Sh
Gilmore, John S. to Angeline A. Graham 8-28-1860 Hr
Gilmore, Peter C. to Elizabeth West 11-14-1829 Sh
Gilmore, Richard to Louisa Faughton? 1-9-1837 (1-15-1837) Hr
Gilmore, William to Louisa Hudson 4-16-1851 Sh
Gilroy, James to Susan Lucentia Melton 3-22-1865 Hn
Gilson, William to Floranna Peterson 7-4-1837 Sh
Gilstrap, Edmund to Mary Crow 4-4-1844 N
Giltner, Jacob A. to Mary H. Madding 5-23-1849 Sh
Gingry, Jacob to Elizabeth Caruth 3-23-1861 (3-26-1861) L
Gingry, Thos. to Julia Ann Wright 1-27-1867 (no return) L B
Ginzburger, Augustus to Rosa Slager 6-11-1864 Sh
Gipson, A. D. to Amanda M. Harder 9-13-1866 Hn
Gipson, Clinton to Sarah Smoot 2-21-1864 Hn
Gipson, Thomas to Mary E. Hughes 11-22-1857 Hn
Girley, Lewis to Nancy Bird 6-16-1844 Cr
Gist, Chas. to Lucy Bailey 9-28-1869 (9-29-1869) T
Gist, John P. to Hulda Sherrill 5-7-1840 Cr
Gitchell, Ezra to Charlana Adcock 7-9-1870 (7-10-1870) L
Given, James H. to America? Carney? 8-30-1857 (9-1-1858) L
Given, Peleg K. to Nancy E. Hutchison 1-21-1861 (no return) L
Given, Samuel A. to Kate Hearring 2-22-1871 L
Given, jr., Samuel A. to Catherine Morris 4-6-1846 (4-9-1846) L

Givens, Alexander to Delila Jane Russell 9-2-1850 Hn
Givens, George N. to Nancy Key 1-19-1848 (no return) Hn
Givens, James to Mary Jane Ermand 12-19-1881 (12-28-1881) L
Givens, James to Sallie Coggchall 3-26-1883 (3-29-1883) L
Givens, John A. to Sallie I. Murchison 11-4-1871 (11-6-1871) Ma
Givens, John J. to Martha O. Dennis 11-29-1854 (11-29-1854) Hr
Givens, Robert H. to Lucinda Hill 8-9-1831 Ma
Givens, Robert H. to Rachel (Mrs.) Dodd 12-13-1867 Ma
Givens, Samuel D. to Susan A. Morton 5-5-1842 G
Givin, James Lycurgus to Sarah Clark 11-11-1843 (11-?-1843) T
Givin, John to Sally Adams 12-5-1864 (no return) Cr
Givins, William W. to Mary Ann Hoffman 1-28-1861 Hn
Gladish, A. M. to L. K. Buslen 7-13-1862 Mn
Gladney, John A. to Catherine Davis 3-27-1869 (4-1-1869) Ma
Gladney, Samuel to Ann Trousdale 3-13-1829 Ma
Glakin?, John D. to Martha T. Rodger no date (with 1867) T
Glancey, Martin to Catharine Sweeney 10-13-1851 (10-17-1851) Sh
Glancy, John to Bridgett Higgins 5-10-1851 (5-11-1851) Sh
Glasco, John to Rebeca Taylor 1-15-1855 We
Glascock, Edmund J. to Cassa A. Varner 1-11-1853 G
Glascock, Jones to Sarah Phelan 1-24-1844 G
Glascock, Peter to Carroline Butler 2-12-1842 (2-15-1842) G
Glascock, Scarlet M. to Jane Trosper 9-15-1838 (9-16-1838) G
Glascock, Scarlet M. to Nancy Long 3-7-1842 (3-10-1842) G
Glascock, Spenson to Nany Glascock 10-14-1844 G
Glasgo, W. J. to Sarah A. Denny 8-13-1862 (8-14-1862) O
Glasgoe, Jesse to Emily C. Roffe 8-30-1846 (no return) We
Glasgoe, Joseph D. to Mary Ann Smith 10-14-1845 (no return) We
Glasgow, G. to Minerva Childress 11-30-1830 Hr
Glasgow, Isaac to Martha Moore 1-11-1867 (1-19-1867) F B
Glasgow, J. G. to Mexico Baker 11-23-1866 Hn
Glasgow, Jas. W. to Mary Jane Fisher 10-25-1837 (10-26-1837) G
Glasgow, John M. to Martha C. Fields 10-19-1858 G
Glass, Bob to Kitty Beard 8-26-1871 O B
Glass, Charles to Harriet Cook 12-25-1869 (12-28-1869) T
Glass, D. L. to Matilda J. Roe 8-31-1859 (9-1-1859) T
Glass, Dudley to Mary Gillam 4-15-1855 We
Glass, George to Mariah Hays 8-14-1867 (8-15-1867) L
Glass, Henry to Minnie Gabbert 8-18-1858 Sh
Glass, Hiram D. to Jennie H. Palmer 10-8-1872 L
Glass, Isaac to Elizabeth Pool 9-11-1848 (9-14-1848) Hr
Glass, J. C. N. to Lucy Ann Roe 11-11-1858 F
Glass, James H. to Nancy L.(S.) Davis 1-18-1858 (1-21-1858) Hr
Glass, James Knox Polk to Barbara Luticia Billings 12-8-1859 T
Glass, James S. to Jane Vickers 4-29-1843 (5-4-1843) Hr
Glass, John E. to Susan A. Norvell 11-2-1859 (11-3-1859) Ma
Glass, John H. to Virginia C. Taliaferro 12-18-1850 G
Glass, John to Mary Branson 11-15-1853 (11-16-1853) G
Glass, Josiah to Elizabeth Adams 11-1-1841 (11-2-1841) L
Glass, Mathew A. to Nancy Ann Putnam 12-22-1831 G
Glass, P. T. to S. T. Barbie 12-18-1868 Hy
Glass, Peter to Betsey Grant 10-8-1869 (10-9-1869) T
Glass, Peter to Lucinda White 1-8-1874 Hy
Glass, Pressley to Sarah C. Partee 12-20-1848 L
Glass, Prince to Ann Chipman 1-4-1873 (1-5-1873) L B
Glass, Prince to Jennie Fitzpatrick 11-6-1879 L
Glass, Promise to Lula Brown 12-30-1885 L
Glass, Robert to Jane E. Miller 3-29-1836 Sh
Glass, S. F. P. to N. J. Hightower 12-20-1871 (12-21-1871) T
Glass, Thomas E. to Sallie Thomas 5-3-1871 Hy
Glass, Thomas to Susan Parker 3-18-1842 Hn
Glass, William A. to Margarette E. Faucett 10-29-1845 (10-30-1845) Ma
Glass, William G. to M. A. Allen 3-27-1851 Hn
Glass, William M. to Sarah Ann Alford 8-13-1863 L
Glassco, J. M. to C. C. Bidix 2-25-1869 G
Glasscock, George to Caroline Oldham 5-12-1836 Sh
Glasscock, J. W. to Mary Elizabeth Hardy 3-3-1870 G
Glassgo, John Henry to Claricy Williams 8-18-1884 (no return) L
Glassgow, W. J. to Rebecca Lovit 10-10-1871 (10-12-1871) Dy
Glawson, Alexander to Angeline Barnhart 1-7-1847 Cr
Glaze, A. C. to R. E. Colbert 12-16-1872 (12-19-1872) L
Gleason, Alford to Mary Gilles 2-1-1847 (2-3-1847) O
Gleason, Alfred to Betheny Severe 7-22-1828 Ma
Gleason, John E. to Henritta A. Vaden 7-14-1859 G
Gleason, John to Catharine McCarty 5-16-1858 Sh
Gleason, Josiah to Mary C. Reeves 12-14-1850 O
Gleason, Richd. to Louisa Fowlkes 12-29-1880 (not executed) Dy
Gleason, Samuel L. to Sarah C. Griffin 10-11-1870 (no return) Dy
Gleason, Timothy to Martha B. Sanders 3-5-1849 (3-13-1849) G
Gleason, W. T. to C. C. Grady 12-25-1866 G
Gleason, William B. to Isabella Taylor 12-16-1850 O
Gleaves, J. M. to Tennessee Wright 12-21-1876 Dy
Gleaves, W. D. to Martha Blair 12-16-1874 Dy
Gleaves, Z. T. to H. D. Whittenton 12-20-1871 (12-21-1871) Dy
Gleaves, Z. T. to M. W. Burnham 12-24-1874 Dy
Gleen (Glenn?), John C. to Sarah E. Coleman 10-19-1870 G
Gleeson, S. S. to S. A. Kennedy 11-5-1869 G

Glen, David to Margarett Bookart 9-4-1834 Hr
Glenn, Christopher to Cynthia C. Kilpatrick 12-4-1848 Ma
Glenn, Edward to Amanda Allen 9-28-1867 (9-29-1867) T
Glenn, Foster to Mariah Donaldson 6-8-1867 G
Glenn, Frank to Celia Winn 4-20-1876 L B
Glenn, Geo. T. to Mollie G. Crandle 2-18-1873 Hy
Glenn, J. A. to A. V. Gaines 1-20-1874 L
Glenn, J. E. to A. I. Marr 10-29-1869 (no return) Hy
Glenn, J. H. to Laura J. Gaines 1-5-1875 (1-6-1875) L
Glenn, James A. to Henrietta M. Pitts 11-18-1852 L
Glenn, James L. to Martha Pace 6-18-1861 (6-23-1861) Hr
Glenn, James R. to Elizabeth M. Hunter 4-3-1854 (4-5-1854) Ma
Glenn, Jas. G. to Lucy Eugenie Hunt 10-5-1868 (10-6-1868) Ma
Glenn, John J. to Eliza F. Templeton 3-19-1860 We
Glenn, John to Betsy Newhouse 12-15-1869 G B
Glenn, John to Eliza Jane Griffin 10-25-1845 (10-28-1845) F
Glenn, Lawson to Jane Baker 12-27-1847 (12-30-1847) Ma
Glenn, Lewis to Priscilla Brown 8-9-1836 Hr
Glenn, R., jr. to Frances M. Peak 10-29-1846 Sh
Glenn, Randle to Febby Mann 11-7-1874 (no return) Hy
Glenn, Richard to Permelia Bates 7-19-1853 Ma
Glenn, S. P. to V. E. Averett 1-28-1868 Hy
Glenn, Solomon to Nancy Anderson 4-19-1852 (4-25-1852) Ma
Glenn, T. B. to J. Layne 11-15-1884 (11-16-1886?) L
Glenn, W. A. to I. G. Lea 12-23-1868 (no return) Hy
Glenn, W. H. to Addie Lloyd 1-17-1883 L
Glenn, W. L. to Ann Treese 7-26-1859 (7-28-1859) Hr
Glenn, W. R. to Mary M. Graves 12-13-1870 (12-14-1870) L
Glenn, W. S. to Fannie Johnson 10-19-1859 (10-20-1859) Sh
Glenn, William A. to Hannah J. Kilpatrick 1-21-1867 Ma
Glenn, William to Mary Diew (Dieu) 1-18-1871 Hy
Glenn, Wm. B. to Susan M. Hawkins 4-9-1844 We
Glenney, John J. to Martha F. Baker 5-20-1875 (5-23-1875) L
Glesson, Patrick to Sarah Brown 9-6-1843 G
Glidell, James to Polly Reynolds 9-23-1856 Hr
Glidewell, Anderson to Mary Biddy 4-13-1835 Hr
Glidewell, Jerry T. to Annie Starkey 12-24-1867 (12-25-1867) Ma
Glidewell, Jesse to Polly King 11-7-1842 (11-8-1842) Hr
Glidewell, Matthew to Ann Edwards 4-6-1857 (4-8-1857) Ma
Glidewell, Nash to Susan Tims 8-22-1838 (8-23-1838) Ma
Glidewell, Robt. to Eliza Jane King 8-5-1845 (8-10-1845) Hr
Glidewell, T. H. to Catharine Bender 11-12-1855 Ma
Glidewell, W. L. to Amandy Ellis 12-7-1869 (12-8-1869) Dy
Glidewell, William W. to Jane Cozby 9-10-1851 (9-28-1851) Hr
Glidewell, William to Sarah Tims 12-17-1840 Ma
Glidewell, Wm. to Susana Timens 11-6-1861 (11-7-1861) T
Glidwell, Jesse to Jane Sims 8-7-1841 (8-8-1841) Ma
Glidwell, Nineviah to Matilda Cox 7-21-1847 (7-22-1847) Ma
Glidwell, Samuel to Nancy Dill 2-6-1835 (2-8-1835) G
Glidwell, Thomas to Jane Sims 11-4-1840 Ma
Glidwell, Timothy to Caroline Edwards 5-27-1867 G
Glidwell, Timothy to Mary Ann Timms 8-18-1853 Hr
Glimp, David C. to Annitta Brogdon 1-11-1858 (1-12-1858) G
Glimp, Henry B. to Mary Read 2-4-1865 G
Glimp, Henry to Susan E. Huckabee 5-4-1857 (no return) L
Glimp, J. W. to V. B. Haynes 12-11-1882 (12-12-1882) L
Glimp, John A. to Tennessee E. Haynes 7-24-1866 (?-28?-1866) L
Glimp, John T. to Rebecca Griggs 2-11-1885 L
Glimp, L. C. to S. L. Smith 3-24-1881 (3-25-1881) L
Glimp, T. W. to L. E. Brogdon 10-9-1882 (10-12-1882) L
Glimp, jr., John A. to Elmira A. Braden 9-23-1876 (9-24-1876) L
Glindcauf, Herman to Catherine Frenk 9-18-18?? Sh
Glisson, Abraham to Martha M. Ellington 1-18-1858 G
Glisson, Abraham to Rebecca Flowers 7-23-1863 G
Glisson, Daniel to Docia M. Sims 2-18-1851 (2-20-1851) G
Glisson, Daniel to Mitty Willis 1-3-1867 Hn
Glisson, Dennis to Arena Moore 10-22-1838 (no return) Hn
Glisson, Everett to Metilda Long 6-1-1858 G
Glisson, George W. to Harrett Flowers 1-10-1852 G
Glisson, J. A. to R. A. Crockett 8-19-1867 O
Glisson, J. D. M. to Adline Todd 11-26-1865 Hn
Glisson, J. D. to Fannie Thurmond 12-23-1876 (1-4-1877) Dy
Glisson, James to Elizabeth Nedry 6-25-1855 (6-28-1855) O
Glisson, James to Elvira E. Kimbel 9-18-1861 Hn
Glisson, Marshall B. to Martha M. Flowers 11-26-1855 (11-29-1855) G
Glisson, R. H. to Catharine Hawkins 4-25-1854 (4-27-1854) Sh
Glisson, Stephen H. to Nancy Hall 6-22-1852 G
Glisson, W. B. to Amanda Byrd 11-6-1871 O
Glisson, W. B. to R. E. Stewart 1-22-1861 Sh
Glisson, W. H. to Nancy Perry 12-30-1867 (no return) Hn
Glisson, William Haygood to Hepsey Eliza Jones 7-27-1852 O
Glisson, Yancy D. to Sarah C. Bryant 9-10-1855 (9-12-1855) G
Glosson, A. F. to M. C. Bennett 3-7-1872 Cr
Glosson, H. N. to P. C. Keenan 1-11-1868 Cr
Glosson, James to Anna Boswell 12-22-1869 (12-23-1869) Cr
Glosson, Wm. to Julia Cox 6-30-1846 Cr
Glover, A. T. to Elizabeth Whitesell 8-5-1859 (no return) We

Glover, Alexander to Mary Jane Killian 4-28-1850 O
Glover, Anderson to Martha Moxley 4-10-1867 O
Glover, Andrew to Mary Benson 5-11-1867 O
Glover, C. C. to Eliza N. Shaw 4-29-1854 (no return) F
Glover, C. P. to Mary C. Norrid 2-5-1861 (2-6-1861) O
Glover, F. M. to Louiza McKelvy 12-28-1858 (12-30-1858) G
Glover, Francis M. to Louisa Patton 5-7-1854 (no return) Cr
Glover, G. A. to Jennie Smith 4-9-1872 (4-10-1872) O
Glover, H. G. to Lidda Stafford 6-25-1846 (no return) Cr
Glover, H. L. to Amanda Hickman 1-19-1865 O
Glover, Heran to Martha A. Chappel 10-12-1857 We
Glover, Hiram to P. A. Matheny 4-27-1844 (no return) Cr
Glover, J. B. to Mary J. Robinson 8-28-1853 Cr
Glover, J. W. to F. S. Jenkins 2-24-1853 Hn
Glover, J. W. to Rebecca Perry 7-8-1868 (7-9-1868) F
Glover, James G. to Jennetta W. Caldwell 3-14-1855 (3-15-1855) O
Glover, Jasper L. to Henrietta M. Gray 1-24-1866 O
Glover, Jesse T. to Alabama S. Snider 3-17-1867 Hn
Glover, John M. to Martha Ann Mosier 8-29-1854 (9-7-1854) O
Glover, John O. to Susan A. Piercy 3-7-1850 (3-8-1850) Ma
Glover, John to Elenor Hodges 12-29-1840 O
Glover, John to Elizabeth W. Kirby 1-5-1845 (1-8-1846) Ma
Glover, John to Mary Rachels 3-4-1834 G
Glover, John to Sylvia Allen 8-22-1848 Ma
Glover, Joseph L. to Lucy B. Vaughan 9-26-1843 Sh
Glover, Marquis L. to Obedience Allen 11-20-1838 (no return) Hn
Glover, P. T. to Elizabeth M. Waller 1-2-1867 O
Glover, Samuel to Miram S. Anderson 9-8-1858 (9-9-1858) Ma
Glover, Thomas W. to Susan Sullens 7-27-1841 Hn
Glover, Wilie A. to Lee G. Southall 12-5-1863 (12-13-1863) F
Glover, William to Jane Brockwell 12-28-1852 Hn
Glynne, Larry to Mary Pursley 11-20-1861 (11-29-1861) Sh
Goad, Henry to Mary M. Sewall 12-23-1841 Ma
Goad, James M. to M. J. Riggs 7-22-1856 (7-23-1856) Hr
Goad, John A. to Elizabeth Beaver 9-17-1852 (9-22-1852) Hr
Goad, John H. to M. J. Young 12-17-1874 T
Goad, John to Lucinda Piercy 8-17-1838 Ma
Goad, Malden Y. to Elizabeth Pierce 2-22-1841 (3-14-1841) Ma
Goad, Morris to Polly Ward 3-25-1830 Ma
Goar, Columbus to Sarah Ralls 12-21-1854 We
Goatley, A. J. to M. J. Baley 7-14-1860 (7-17-1860) Dy
Gober, Daniel, jr. to Rosella C. McDavitt 3-27-1849 Sh
Gober, James A. to Eliza H. Watters 8-6-1845 (8-7-1845) F
Gober, M. A. to M. A. Penn 11-24-1865 (11-29-1865) F
Goble, S. P. to M. J. Hutcherson 1-23-1882 (1-24-1882) L
Godby, James M. to Susanah E. Williams 9-14-1852 (no return) F
Godby, Wilson J. to _____ 7-19-1849 (no return) F
Godfrey, Solomon to Dicey (Mrs.) Davis 12-18-1860 Ma
Godfreyson, Charles to Siny E. Jackson 10-12-1854 Sh
Godsey, G. B. to C. B. Teater 11-22-1867 O
Godsey, James to Lucinda Haskins 1-19-1853 Sh
Godsey, T. J. to M. A. Carter 10-9-1865 O
Godsey, William to Mary Jane Davidson 1-18-1854 (1-19-1854) Sh
Godwin, John R. to Mary F. Mullins 11-15-1859 Sh
Godwin, Thomas to Johanna Kelly 8-29-1861 Sh
Godwin, Williailm to Lovanna Bundy 6-14-1862 (6-15-1862) O
Goethals, John to Louisa Barth 1-10-1861 Sh
Goff, Aurelius L. to Martha M. Daniels 8-2-1849 Sh
Goff, J. W. to Johanna M. Byler 3-9-1883 L
Goff, Jessee T. to Elizabeth Sexton 4-11-1848 Hr
Goff, Thomas W. to Vilott Amanda Henderson 12-26-1836 (12-29-1836) G
Goff, William H. E. to Elizabeth A. Hays 1-28-1874 L
Goforth, Alfred to Mary C. Cowell 9-27-1860 Dy
Goforth, Alfred to Sarah J. Smith 4-27-1858 (5-12-1858) L
Goforth, Andrew C. to Sarah A. Holland 9-3-1857 Be
Goforth, Calvin to Celia Dickson 2-4-1854 (2-5-1854) Ma
Goforth, H. M. to Mary Carper 6-20-1859 (6-23-1859) Hr
Goforth, J. C. to Jiffy R. Trobough 1-3-1866 (1-1?-1866) T
Goforth, James C. to Mira Jane Thompson 4-20-1860 L
Goforth, James to Mary Watson 9-8-1882 L
Goforth, Jeff to Amanda Smith 8-5-1879 (8-7-1879) Dy
Goforth, John to Nancy Owen 1-19-1867 T
Goforth, John to Nancy Owen 1-19-1867 (1-20-1867) T
Goforth, Josiah to Eliza Whitlock 1-7-1850 (1-16-1850) T
Goforth, Josiah to Louisa B. Bently 1-1-1873 (1-2-1873) T
Goforth, Russell to Susan R. Myres 3-16-1859 T
Goforth, Samuel J. to Martha E. F. Hendricks 10-31-1853 Hr
Goforth, Thomas J. to Rhoda Nice Caroline Staggs 6-6-1868 (6-7-1868) L
Goforth, W. H. to Elizabeth Gurly 12-8-1854 Hr
Goforth, William to Mary Jane Dickson 1-28-1854 (1-31-1854) Ma
Goforth, Wm. to Mary Carven 12-2-1865 (12-3-1865) O
Goforth, Zachariah to Charity King 6-2-1855 Be
Gogchell, Nora (Nord?) to Jennie Cole 4-17-1877 (4-18-1877) L
Goins, C. A. to Sarah F. B. Elder 3-17-1843 (no return) F
Golay, E. J. to F. E. (Mrs.) Miller 11-24-1857 Sh
Gold, J. M. to Missouri Pierce 7-24-1872 Dy
Gold, P. B. L. to Martha J. Bkaer 7-16-1845 Hn

Grooms

Golden, David A. to Elizabeth C. Totten 12-11-1847 (12-13-1847) O
Golden, David to Matilda C. Watts 12-31-1845 We
Golden, James H. to Charlatta A. Golden 1-14-1861 We
Golden, James O. to Martha Tucker 1-9-1859 Hn
Golden, John to Eliza Moorman 1-28-1869 (1-30-1869) F B
Golden, John to Jane Stewart 12-27-1845 Ma
Golden, R. T. to L. Evaline Wallan 8-22-1866 (8-23-1866) Dy
Golden, Samule D. to Nancy A. Smart 2-21-1860 We
Golden, William to Lucinda Fisher 8-14-1845 Ma
Goldin, J. W. to Susan A. Miller 2-21-1856 (no return) Hn
Golding, Henry to Susan Fisher 2-8-1876 L
Golding, John to Julia Lindsey 8-9-1859 L
Golding, Richard to Henrietta Roberts 11-4-1872 L
Golding, Travis G. to Mollie Harris 1-15-1874 L
Goldsby, Edwin A. to Helena Waddington 2-3-1847 Hn
Goldsby, S. J. to Lucinda Bolten 10-1-1860 Sh
Goldsby, T. T. to Mary Harrison 11-29-1861 Sh
Goldsby, T. T., jr. to Frances E. Wynn 12-12-1849 Sh
Goldsby, W. T. to Martha K. Thomas 10-22-1851 Sh
Goldsmith, D. P. to Margaret O'Brien 4-7-1860 (4-16-1860) Sh
Goldsmith, David to Bridget Breining 2-11-1854 (2-12-1854) Sh
Goldsmith, Jas. to Mary Ann Hughes 4-27-1843 Sh
Goldsmith, Moses to Leona Herch 3-27-1872 Hy
Golin, George to Rebecca Tatum 8-27-1869 (no return) F B
Golston, Geo. to Amanda? Smith 12-15-1866 (12-16-1866) T
Gonnelly, Martin to Ellen Kelly 7-14-1860 (7-15-1860) Sh
Gooch, Alfred B. to Eleanor Watson 5-19-1841 Ma
Gooch, Alfred to Lucinda Abbott 9-20-1869 (9-21-1869) Cr
Gooch, Allen G. to Mary E. Smith 4-27-1852 (4-28-1852) Ma
Gooch, Bennet to Polley Ann Brogden 8-5-1841 G
Gooch, Charles Y. to Eliza E. Mebane 10-31-1846 Cr
Gooch, G. R. to Nancy Todd 7-26-1865 (7-27-1865) Dy
Gooch, Henry A. to Lucinda S. Cobb 1-30-1861 (1-31-1861) Dy
Gooch, James C. to Delia White 2-22-1869 (2-28-1869) Ma
Gooch, James C. to Sarah J. Davis 8-28-1848 (no return) Cr
Gooch, John B. to Charlotte Ann McCalla 1-11-1870 T
Gooch, John T. to Sarah Ann Rutherford 3-2-1865 Mn
Gooch, Littleton O. to Mary E. Pugh 3-16-1869 (3-17-1869) Cr
Gooch, Nicholas to Sarah E. F. Jones 9-6-1845 Mn
Gooch, Priestley to Elizabeth Cozart 8-13-1870 (8-14-1870) Cr
Gooch, R. P. to Gilla A. Jones 1-25-1854 Cr
Gooch, Sam to Frances Marrows 4-13-1873 Hy
Gooch, W. B. T. to Mary E. Brown 10-22-1864 Mn
Gooch, W. H. to Marissa Sawyer 12-20-1869 Dy
Gooch, W. L. to Nancy Rogin 10-18-1869 (10-20-1869) Cr
Gooch, Wm. H. to Indian McAuley 2-10-1841 Cr
Gooch, Wm. L. to Sarah H. Taylor 12-10-1844 Cr
Good, John H. to Charlotte Hubert 9-15-1836 O
Good, John P. to Elizabeth Hightower 4-21-1873 (5-1-1873) T
Good, Reps to Harriet Crawley 3-14-1876 (no return) Hy
Good, Thomas G. to Hester Perry 4-28-1850 Hn
Goode, Daniel to Nola Johnson 6-11-1869 (no return) F B
Goode, J. A. V. to Elizabeth F. Murphey 11-30-1853 (no return) F
Goode, James to Maria Hare 12-24-1866 (no return) F
Goode, John L. (D?) to Elizabeth (Mrs.) Landriss 11-18-1864 Sh
Goode, Reps to Sue Coleman 3-3-1872 Hy
Goode, Thomas J. to Sarah M. Corlern 9-10-1863 Mn
Goode, W. E. to Amanda Taylor 11-16-1873 Hy
Goode, William to Elizabeth Sibley 9-25-1855 Sh
Goode, Wm. P. to Lucinda Baker 12-27-1870 F B
Goodell, Austin to Mary Ann Newsom 6-15-1855 (6-21-1855) Ma
Goodell, Lorenza to Laura C. Clark 8-24-1847 Ma
Gooden, Bartlett to Jamima Spencer 7-20-1847 (7-27-1847) G
Gooden, Gus to Lucy Ann Morris 11-5-1869 (11-6-1869) F B
Gooden, H. C. to Malvina Wilson 12-20-1855 (no return) Hn
Gooden, Jas. to Ellen Green 12-1-1869 (12-1-1869) T
Gooden, Ned to Susan Hart 12-30-1869 (12-31-1869) F B
Gooden, William W. to Rebecca C. Humphris 3-8-1837 (3-12-1837) G
Goodin, Augustus B. to Martha J. Ward 10-3-1848 (10-5-1848) Ma
Goodin, Henry to Martha E. Lovell 11-18-1857 Cr
Goodin, John W. to Martha J. Jones 5-6-1859 Hn
Goodin, John to Tabitha Ramsay 4-5-1852 Hn
Goodin, Sidney W. to Alsey J. Robins 4-12-1857 Hn
Goodin, Thomas to Susan Cunningham 5-2-1870 (no return) Cr
Goodlett, J. B. to S. R. Greer 10-6-1851 (no return) Cr
Goodlett, Job H. to Henrietta F. Stratton 6-15-1848 Sh
Goodlett, John H. to Mildred C. Rogers 10-28-1856 (10-29-1856) Ma
Goodloe, A. H. to Mary W. Cunningham 9-27-1871 Dy
Goodloe, Alexander H. to Mary E. Cunningham 12-21-1863 (no return) Cr
Goodloe, Aqula J. to Margarett A. Jones 12-23-1843 (12-27-1843) G
Goodloe, Frank to Sally Williams 2-9-1870 G
Goodloe, G. W. to Emily W. Jones 12-29-1852 (no return) F
Goodloe, I. M. C. to A. ?. Thomas 1-1-1855 G
Goodloe, M. H. to H. E. Thacker 9-5-1870 (no return) Dy
Goodlow, Andrew J. to Margarett Ann Jones 8-17-1843 Ma
Goodlow, C. A. to Sallie P. Ward 5-14-1868 (5-16-1868) Dy
Goodlow, James to P. Burns 2-4-1869 Cr

Goodlow, Robert H. to Nancy Baldridge 12-9-1834 G
Goodman, A. R. to L. J. Burns 12-27-1860 (no return) Cr
Goodman, Albert to Cathrine Ralph 4-11-1872 T
Goodman, Alfred H. to Mary E. Murphy 10-29-1866 T
Goodman, Calvin to Marian Bibee 3-4-1840 Sh
Goodman, David C. to Lucy F. Johnson 1-9-1858 (1-12-1858) G
Goodman, F. G. to Dilila P. Woodson 12-15-1836 (12-28-1836) G
Goodman, F. G. to Maria N. Robinson 12-17-1862 (11-26-1861?) G
Goodman, Isham to Anner Smith 11-28-1868 T
Goodman, J. T. to M. M. Halfacre 3-13-1882 (3-15-1882) L
Goodman, James M. to Parlee Demoss 4-18-1849 (no return) Cr
Goodman, Jerry to Patsy Walker 7-16-1878 (no return) Hy
Goodman, Jesse to Luizer Bellow 10-25-1869 G
Goodman, John F. to Elizabeth J. Crump 8-9-1854 (no return) F
Goodman, John J. to Sarah A. Jones 11-3-1859 G
Goodman, Joseph to Babette Rieper 7-23-1863 Sh
Goodman, Kelley to Mary Smith 11-3-1866 (11-4-1866) T
Goodman, Marshall to Mary Dallas 5-18-1864 (5-26-1864) O
Goodman, Marshall to Mary J. Carey 4-17-1855 (4-19-1855) O
Goodman, Monroe to Ann Baskerville 12-29-1866 F B
Goodman, O. B. to Mary E. Bell 10-19-1860 (no return) Dy
Goodman, R. G. to Eleanor H. Roulker? 8-7-1866 T
Goodman, R. G. to S.B. Murphey 11-18-1869 T
Goodman, R. H. to Mary C. Vick 11-14-1866 G
Goodman, Rufus to Clarisa Ann Johnson 12-19-1866 T
Goodman, Samuel A. to Martha A. Ingraham 12-1-1856 (12-4-1856) G
Goodman, Samuel to Mary Jane Ellis 1-31-1850 Sh
Goodman, Selim to Lizzie Bryant 2-29-1868 G B
Goodman, Spencer to Donna Smith 3-29-1871 (4-4-1871) T
Goodman, Thomas to Mollie M. Ladd 3-24-1864 Sh
Goodman, W. H. to Louisa Stanley 10-16-1880 (10-25-1880) L
Goodman, Will to Martha Burnett 9-23-1871 (no return) Hy
Goodman, William B. to Susan Hargate 12-18-1859 L
Goodman, William L. to Jane Coop 6-30-1831 G
Goodman, William V. to Ellen C. Clark 9-26-1865 T
Goodman, William to Ann Hardister 7-27-1831 (7-28-1831) G
Goodman, William to Lou Allison 8-3-1872? (7-28-1872?) L B
Goodman, jr., William to Martha A. McMinn 2-17-1835 (2-19-1835) G
Goodner, S. S. to Martha S. Wells 2-10-1864 (2-11-1864) Sh
Goodner, Sardis S. to M. A. Gregory 12-22-1856 (12-23-1856) Sh
Goodram, Washington to Louisa Yarbro 11-20-1867 (11-21-1867) T
Goodrich, Edmond W. to Susan E. Harcey 9-3-1839 T
Goodrich, Edward H. to Nancy R. Rollins 6-2-1866 (6-3-1866) Ma
Goodrich, G. P. to Martha A. Barnett 7-28-1854 (8-?-1854) Ma
Goodrich, Gedion to Rebecca Vier 1-24-1846 (1-27-1846) G
Goodrich, Gideon to Adalin Vaden 10-18-1855 We
Goodrich, Gideon to Nancy Baird 2-13-1862 G
Goodrich, James H. to M. Thompson 7-6-1870 Dy
Goodrich, John C. to Eliza Harris 3-27-1844 (3-28-1844) Ma
Goodrich, John C. to Elisha Walker 7-11-1848 Sh
Goodrich, John to Sarah F. Skepper 12-27-1864 (no return) Dy
Goodrich, Malcolm H. to Emily B. Roane 2-11-1852 (2-12-1852) Ma
Goodrich, Stephen B. to Caroline Luckey 7-24-1858 (7-29-1858) Ma
Goodridge, Matthew N. to Rebecca Mason 2-12-1848 (2-17-1848) Ma
Goodrum, William to Caroline Elizabeth Townsend 7-12-1849 T
Goodrun, Wm. to Fanny Fisher 4-1-1869 (4-27-1869) Cr
Goodwin, Edmund C. to May E. Whitson 9-28-1848 (no return) Hn
Goodwin, Elam to Elizabeth A. House 9-18-1850 G
Goodwin, Green B. to Elizabeth P. Eliott 7-7-1849 (7-8-1849) G
Goodwin, J. A. to L. J. Hall 11-24-1866 (11-24-18??) O
Goodwin, J. H. to Callie Covington 11-18-1867 Hn
Goodwin, J. H. to Lizzie V. Goodwin 1-26-1869 (1-28-1869) Dy
Goodwin, James to Ann Smith 6-20-1870 T
Goodwin, John C. to Nina C. White 12-13-1854 (12-14-1854) Sh
Goodwin, John F. to Sarah Johnson 11-22-1847 (11-24-1847) L
Goodwin, John to Martha Saunders(Launders?) 3-22-1828 Hr
Goodwin, Marion to Louisa Evans 12-7-1853 Ma
Goodwin, W. T. to E. C. Howell? 1-10-1870 (1-12-1870) Dy
Goodwin, Washington to Harriet Bobbitt 12-9-1869 (12-16-1869) F B
Goodwin, William to Laury Ann Williams 7-26-1831 Ma
Goodwyn, R. D. to Sallie A. Buntyn 1-5-1854 Sh
Goodyear, D. F. to Hannah F. Barker 1-2-1860 (1-3-1860) Sh
Gookin, Eugene E. to Mary E. Cowell 1-7-1874 Hy
Gookin, Sam'l L. to Jane P. Stanton 9-25-1845 Sh
Gooldin, Warren to Elmira Goodwin 11-25-1859 Sh
Gooldsby, J. M. to Gilly C. Winston 1-8-1857 We
Goolsby, Elias A. to Margaret B. McDaniel 2-22-1845 (no return) We
Goolsby, Elvin A. to Nancy Terry 7-2-1839 Hn
Goolsby, Isaac to Mary Reddick 1-20-1862 Be
Goolsby, Miles W. to Sarah Brooks 6-6-1834 Sh
Goolsby, Miles to Mary Ann Harrell 8-15-1837 Sh
Goosby, Melancthou to Fanny Nowell 11-23-1867 Hy
Gordan, George to Hannah Moore 10-16-1867 (10-19-1867) F B
Gordan, James F. to Julia E. Barksdale 12-31-1853 (1-1-1853) G
Gordan, Jessee to Elizabeth Perry 11-9-1870 Dy
Gorden, George to Amanda Boyd 8-23-1872 (8-20?-1872) T
Gorden, P. W. to Nancy J. Smith 1-1-1866 Cr

Gordin, Samuel to Mary Ann Graves 11-6-1838 (12-3-1838) Ma
Gordon, Allen R. to Elizabeth Moore 11-3-1867 Hy
Gordon, Bennett G. to Martha L. Baker 4-24-1850 Hn
Gordon, Bernard G. to Lucy F. Randal 12-18-1839 Cr
Gordon, Charles C. to Sarah English 4-30-1831 Sh
Gordon, Charles R. to Elizabeth Ruddle 4-11-1855 (4-12-1855) Hr
Gordon, David to Sarah Usher 3-21-1827 G
Gordon, Geo. L. to Isabella Gooch 10-11-1858 Cr
Gordon, George W. to Emma B. Mann 1-17-1876 (no return) Hy
Gordon, Isaac to Virginia Waller 4-25-1875 Hy
Gordon, J. K. to Mary High 1-22-1865 Hn
Gordon, J. P. to Caroline Moore 11-1-1866 Hy
Gordon, Jackson to Kandis Gordon 4-5-1869 Cr
Gordon, Jacob F. to Julia Ozier 1-13-1853 (no return) Cr
Gordon, Jacob to Margaret Mitchell 1-20-1870 T
Gordon, Jesse B. to Josephine C. Hays 1-9-1871 Ma
Gordon, Jesse to Susan Gambrell 2-14-1844 (no return) F
Gordon, John A. to M. A. Stewart 2-15-1872 Hy
Gordon, John H. to Joanna A. Preston 12-19-1861 Ma
Gordon, John K. to Mary E. Prewett 1-1-1861 Hr
Gordon, John T. to L. F. Flowers 12-5-1867 G
Gordon, Joseph to Mary Allen 6-12-1839 Sh
Gordon, Julius C. to Sarah Jane Hooton 3-9-1860 (no return) Hy
Gordon, Levi to Mary Ann Smith 10-19-1858 Cr
Gordon, Louis to Harriet Hampton 3-21-1872 (no return) Cr
Gordon, M. to Martha J. Dinwiddie 8-26-1840 Cr
Gordon, Nathaniel to Ann H. Aston 4-22-1838 F
Gordon, Robert S. to Mary J. E. Allbright 10-9-1854 G
Gordon, Robert W. to Sarah Lowell 1-7-1848 (1-20-1848) Ma
Gordon, Robert to Lizzie Richardson 5-8-1872 G
Gordon, Solomon to Candis Grishom 9-14-1846 (9-17-1846) T
Gordon, T. C. to Kate Latta? 6-24-1879 (6-25-1879) Dy
Gordon, Watson to Delia Barker 9-15-1858 (9-16-1858) G
Gordon, William J. to Harriet Tennessee Roach 11-2-1860 (11-5-1860) Ma
Gordon, Wm. F. to Mattie L. Moore 12-1-1869 Hy
Gordon, Wm. G. to Lucy M. Davidson 6-26-1862 Be
Gore, Blewford to M. Copland 10-21-183_ (with 1837) O
Gore, Charles to Mary A. Rusk 4-5-1838 Hn
Gore, Isaac D. to Margaret Walls 3-24-1859 Hn
Gore, Isaac D. to Sarah Alexander 6-14-1838 Hn
Gore, Isaac to Caroline Stagner 7-3-1839 Hn
Gore, J. J. to S. J. Jones 3-10-1863 (3-11-1863) O
Gore, James M. to M. H. Morris 10-30-1866 (11-2-1865?) F
Gore, John to Polley Calhoun 10-28-1828 O
Gore, Thomas M. to Sarah E. Haynes (Harris) 11-15-1854 O
Gore, Thomas to Sarah Box 1-8-1840 (1-9-1840) Hr
Gore, William T. to Adaline Glover 3-16-1852 O
Gorene, Edward to Emma Tilman 12-25-1867 G B
Gorin, jr., Franklin to Sallie A. Nicholson 1-19-1861 (1-21-1861) Sh
Gorin?, George W. to Frances Jane Sweney 4-19-1842 (5-2-1842) T
Gorley, James to Cloah Payne 8-9-1844 (8-11-1844) O
Gorman, J. J. to Ellen Albright 8-20-1861 (8-21-1861) Cr
Gorman, Jim to Hannah Jackson 10-8-1870 (no return) Hy
Gorman, John to Ellen Dawyer 5-14-1863
Gorman, John to Margaret Flenn? 7-20-1849 Sh
Gorman, John to Mary Noland 10-26-1852 Sh
Gorman, John to Rose O'Hara 1-18-1857 Sh
Gorman, William to Joana Hanly 6-14-1860 (6-25-1860) Sh
Gormon, Parish A. to A. E. Mallory 9-6-1848 (9-12-1848) F
Gorsuch, W. K. to Lizzie Gibson 2-1-1870 G
Gorton?, Edward J. to Jane Powell 12-15-1840 (no return) Cr
Gosey, Mark to Nancy Diggins 12-28-1834 (12-30-1834) G
Goss, Andrew to Sarah Ann Dallas 1-29-1850 Sh
Goss, David to Ellen C. Ternas 9-6-1873 (9-11-1873) T
Goss, David to Nancy J. Quinby 7-12-1859 T
Goss, H. A. to Christiana Hill 12-31-1857 Sh
Goss, John A. to Eliz. H. Isbell 12-30-1859 (1-1-1860) Sh
Goss, John A. to Nancy Catharin Fleming 2-4-1857 T
Goss, John to Lillie F. Darlin 12-30-1868 (no return) F
Goss, William W. to Sarah A. Hutchinson 12-22-1847 (12-25-1847) T
Gossett, A. R. to Nancy Jane Midleton 4-18-1858 Be
Gossett, A. T. to Cornelia W. Pope 1-14-1871 (1-17-1871) F
Gossett, Abraham to Mary Swindle 4-25-1856 Be
Gossett, Abram to Sarah Hatley 4-2-1848 Be
Gossett, Andrew to Rody E. Muldan 12-26-1831 Hr
Gossett, Burrell to Evalina M. Roundtree 1-28-1840 G
Gossett, Burrell to Margaret C. Gwin 5-13-1839 (no return) Cr
Gossett, D. A. to Elizabeth E. Utley 1-7-1869 Be
Gossett, Hail to Ellen Woods 5-7-1870 (5-8-1870) Cr
Gossett, Hambleton to Nancy Colier 4-20-1847 Be
Gossett, Harvy M. to Elizabeth Roberts 9-15-1841 Hr
Gossett, James J. to Louisa Thompson 12-10-1858 Be
Gossett, James L. to Priscilla Thompson 3-29-1829 Hr
Gossett, John Allen to Martha A. C. Mullinicks 8-29-1852 Be
Gossett, John to Frances C. Hatley 1-15-1840 Hr
Gossett, V. D. to Mary N.? Hatley 3-21-1825 (3-24-1825) Hr
Gossett, Wesley R. to Candis Brown 7-22-1846 (7-23-1846) G

Gossett, Wm. to Catharine Warrick 12-24-1863 Be
Gotchalk, Julius to Therisee Longbein 7-14-1862 (7-15-1862) Sh
Gother, Julius to Cary Kauzler 12-26-1868 G
Gouch, Granvell to Louise Adkerson 10-24-1861 (10-27-1861) O
Gough, Richard S. to Marie Meriweather 9-1-1847 Sh
Gough, Ruffin to Catherine McBride 4-19-1846 Cr
Gough, William R. to Rizpah E. White 10-28-1844 O
Gould, John W. to Laura V. Napier 10-17-1853 Hr
Gourdlock, Milton to Ann Scott 9-4-1869 F B
Gourgues, Theophile to Salina Isler 5-10-1860 Sh
Govan, Daniel C. to Mary F. Otey 12-20-1853 Sh
Gowan, Drury to Fanny Hall 1-17-1853 (1-19-1853) G
Gowan, M. N. to Pinckney A. McCoy 1-2-1877 (1-4-1877) Dy
Gowan, Pleasant A. to Mary A. E. Harris 7-30-1849 Ma
Gowan, R. M. to Mary Jane McFarlen 11-24-1854 (11-27-1854) G
Gowan, Thomas F. to Susan F. Debnam 10-3-1867 G
Gowan, William J. to Dicey McFarland 8-21-1851 G
Gowen, David C. H. to Pricilla H. Fuller 10-26-1854 Cr
Gowen, Wm. C. to Evaline Wood 1-14-1839 (no return) Cr
Goyer, C. W. to Laura Harpon 7-3-1849 Sh
Goyer, William to Marina F. Rutland 8-19-1852 Sh
Goza, David M. to Elizabet M. Howell 2-14-1867 G
Goza, Edmond M. to L. A. Brown 2-11-1864 G
Grable, Felix G. to Mary J. Young 5-12-1848 Hn
Grable, Samuel A. to Sarah T. Watkins 3-28-1862 (4-4-1862) F
Grace, Abel to R. C. Harvey 10-20-1849 (10-28-1849) F
Grace, J. C. to Sallie Chrisman 2-8-1877 Dy
Grace, J. M. to Ruth Fawcett 3-8-1859 Hr
Grace, James H. to Lucy Ann Taylor 11-17-1852 (11-18-1852) G
Grace, Jesse G. to Phebe Gately 8-31-1830 (9-2-1830) Ma
Grace, Robt. to Elsie Palmer 5-23-1877 (5-24-1877) Dy
Grace, W. C. to E. J. Gardner 12-22-1868 G
Grace, William Gillom to Eliz. Caroline Rebec Cullum 1-13-1846 T
Grace, Wm. A. to Martha A. E. Davis 5-1-1855 T
Gracey, J. H. to Sarah Collier 11-16-1864 (11-21-1864) Sh
Gracy, Abram to Julia Pender 11-21-1878 Hy
Gracy, J. Barnett to Margaret J. Calhoun 12-9-1868 (12-10-1868) T
Gracy, W. N. to S. E. Lusk 5-23-1881 (no return) L
Graddy, J. F. to L. E. C. Folks 8-9-1858 (8-12-1858) G
Graddy, Samuel to Martha A. Briant 1-31-1855 (2-1-1855) G
Graddy, Travis F. to Mary Ann Keathley 2-21-1854 (2-23-1854) G
Grader, G. W. to Mary E. Klinck (3-11-1856) Sh
Grady, D. J. to M. J. Penny 1-25-1866 G
Grady, Jesse to Sally Elder 6-13-1828 G
Grady, John W. to Sarah L. Lucker 10-8-1862 G
Grady, Marcus L. to Sarah L. Hartsfield 11-2-1852 (11-3-1852) G
Grady, Mark to Lucinda E. Phillips 1-28-1861 (no return) We
Grady, Michael to Mary Cleary 7-23-1855 Sh
Grady, Micheal? to Ellen Sullivan 12-2-1862 Sh
Grady, R. D. to P. R. Freeman 11-23-1869 G
Grady, Rigdon to Nancy Gleason 8-1-1836 (8-19-1836) G
Grady, Robert R. to Margarett A. Ragan 5-31-1855 (6-9-1855) G
Grady, T. C. to E. J. (Mrs.) Petty 2-8-1864 Sh
Grady, Thomas to Eliza Cormick 1-8-1857 Sh
Grady, W. J. to Sarah A. Penny 1-25-1866 G
Grady, Willis L. A. to Delila Mobley 2-23-1854 (3-13-1854) G
Grady, Willis to Armantha A. Bledsoe 2-14-1856 G
Grafford, George W. to Minerva M. Mosly 11-26-1840 Ma
Grafton, Paul C. to Margarett A. Davis 6-22-1854 (6-23-1854) G
Gragg, J. B. to Susam McMullen 7-20-1857 (7-22-1857) Sh
Graham, A. J. to S. A. Herring 6-14-1863 O
Graham, A. K. to Eva Marshall 1-15-1866 (no return) F
Graham, Alex to Maria Barbee 1-23-1873 Hy
Graham, Anthony to Mary C. Smith 2-2-1870 (2-3-1870) Ma
Graham, Barnett to Amanda Dorfeville 2-6-1843 Sh
Graham, Barnett to Sarah C. Carr 10-10-1850 Sh
Graham, Ben to Elva Foust 11-28-1878 Dy
Graham, Beverly to Henrietta Winbush 12-24-1883 (12-27-1883) L
Graham, Charles P. to Bathsheba Culpepper 12-12-1846 (no return) Hn
Graham, Charles to Sarah Mathis 2-9-1860 Hn
Graham, Elihue G. to Evelina Willouby 8-24-1850 (8-25-1850) Hr
Graham, Elija to Eliza C. Pankey 2-27-1850 (2-28-1850) Hr
Graham, Elijah to Nancy Maynard 12-11-1854 We
Graham, Erasmus to Almira Wright 3-9-1847 (not exec.) O
Graham, Frank to Ellen Haynes 2-24-1868 (no return) Hy
Graham, George B. to Mary E. O'Brien 1-30-1861 (1-3?-1861) Sh
Graham, George to Mary Halliburton 4-18-1868 G
Graham, Harrison to Frances Washington 1-2-1871 (1-4-1871) F
Graham, Henry to Permelia Gray 2-19-1874 Hy
Graham, J. W. to Kate McDonald 8-17-1863 Sh
Graham, James C. to Jane Ballard 1-16-1841 (1-20-1841) F
Graham, James C. to Lacky M. Blythe 12-15-1835 Sh
Graham, James M. to Rebecca Spivey 7-15-1881 (no return) L B
Graham, James M. to Weney Deck 10-8-1871 We
Graham, James S. to Frances A. Bickerstaff 9-4-1839 Sh
Graham, James to Elizabeth West 1-6-1876 L B
Graham, James to Octave S. Patterson 7-17-1855 Sh

Graham, Jehu to Mary A. D. Smalman 6-26-1851 F
Graham, Jo L. to Nancy L. Kerr 11-6-1860 (11-27-1860) Hr
Graham, John C. to Lucinda E. Coburn 1-18-1851 (1-27-1851) Hr
Graham, John K. to Jane Conyers 12-20-1847 (no return) Hn
Graham, John K. to P. C. Guinn 12-5-1864 (no return) Hn
Graham, John M. to Betsy Brantley 5-5-1826 (5-20-1826) Hr
Graham, John W. to Allice Bugg 6-26-1867 (6-27-1867) Cr
Graham, John to Celia Ann Rice 11-18-1876 Hy
Graham, John to Christiana Brown 3-9-1847 (3-11-1847) O
Graham, John to Ella Young 7-4-1874 (no return) Hy
Graham, John to S. E. (Mrs.?) Wilson 10-27-1863 Sh
Graham, Joseph to Sarah Kimbrough 11-4-1828 Sh
Graham, Ned to arion Dickason 11-26-1869 (11-27-1869) T
Graham, Nimrod to Mary Jane Macon 8-17-1851 Hr
Graham, O. C. to E. C. Harpool 6-14-1863 O
Graham, Paschal to Mary Martin 11-27-1844 Sh
Graham, Robert M. to Mary Ann Melton 10-14-1846 Be
Graham, Saml. R. to Elizabeth Roberts 10-22-1866 (10-23-1866) Cr
Graham, Samuel to Sarah F. Bryen 3-18-1855 We
Graham, T. J. to Winnie E. McFarland 10-31-1874 Dy
Graham, Thomas G. to Mary Parker 2-8-1838 Hr
Graham, Thomas to Isabella Jane Miller 3-2-1863 Sh
Graham, W. A. H. to Cornelia E. Davis 2-14-1861 Sh
Graham, W. H. to E. J. Hilliard 6-21-1864 Sh
Graham, William A. to Lizzie A. Speed 8-29-1862 (no return) Hy
Graham, Wm. E. M. to Nancy C. Payne 8-16-1843 Hr
Graham, Wm. J. to Lucy Ann Peacock 8-7-1851 O
Grainger, Alfred M. to Mary Ann Watkins 7-26-1854 Hn
Grainger, George W. to Ellen C. Fuller 12-1-1859 Hn
Grainger, John E. to Edy Snider 2-7-1841 Hn
Grainger, Richard A. to Lively Grainger 1-2-1861 Hn
Grainger, William to Sarah Gibson 7-19-1838 Hn
Grammar, P. H. W. to Mary A. Harper 12-24-1853 (no return) F
Grammar, W. H. to Mattie Jones 8-2-1882 L
Grammer, William to Amanda Walker 8-2-1861 (8-4-1861) Sh
Granade, Wm. R. to Mary J. Cole 12-11-1865 (12-14-1865) Cr
Granberry, Dudley to Mary J. Ketchum 10-24-1868 (no return) F B
Granberry, Everett to Margaret Granberry 10-23-1869 (10-24-1869) F B
Granberry, G. B. to M. E. Wheeler 3-21-1862 Sh
Granberry, J. H. to L. J. Brown 4-9-1866 (4-11-1866) F
Granberry, J. L. to Sallie T. Williamson 10-9-1865 (10-12-1865) F
Granberry, Jackson to Lucy A. Taylor 1-18-1868 (1-26-1868) F B
Granberry, John to Lydia Williams 12-25-1866 (12-27-1866) F B
Granberry, Milton to Luvenia Granberry 1-18-1868 (1-26-1868) F B
Granbury, Gabril to A. Vertun? 12-28-1869 (12-30-1869) T
Grandee, James to Victoria Chancelor 2-16-1882 (2-19-1882) L
Granger, John G. to Sarha L. (Mrs.) Vault 10-14-1867 (10-15-1867) Ma
Grant, Alston to Rebecca Hodges 1-7?-1834 Hr
Grant, Archibald to Mary C. Page 12-19-1864 (no return) Cr
Grant, B. F. to Margaret Williams 4-29-1874 Hy
Grant, Ben F. to Sarah E. Duckworth 12-28-1859 (no return) Hy
Grant, Elijah to Charlotte Biggs 2-10-1871 (2-15-1871) F B
Grant, H. T. to Maggie E. Ledsinger 9-2-1873 Hy
Grant, James F. to Eliza Jane Bailey 12-25-1870 (12-28-1870) Ma
Grant, John W. to Elizabeth J. Day 9-25-1850 Ma
Grant, John W. to Salome Ramsey 1-17-1842 Sh
Grant, John to Charlotte Prentiss 1-10-1863 Sh
Grant, John to Evaline F. Collins 6-7-1848 Hn
Grant, Jorden to Mariah Stokeley 2-22-1872 (no return) Hy
Grant, Levin D. to Mary Virginia Ashby 12-19-1861 Sh
Grant, Lewis to Mary E. Jones 3-3-1858 Sh
Grant, Nathan to Matilda Morrow 11-1-1838 Cr
Grant, R. D. to Polly Branch 6-23-1849 F
Grant, T. I. to M. M. Singleton 4-22-1866 (4-22-1865?) O
Grant, William A. to Sarah F. Smith 7-14-1862 Mn
Grant, William M. to Mary L. Noel 2-11-1852 Sh
Grant, Wm. P. to Julia M. Anderson 11-7-1871 (11-8-1871) T
Grant, Wm. to L. W. Johnston 12-31-1866 Hy
Grantham, Alvin to Mary Ann Carter 12-25-1849 Hr
Grantham, Chalkley to Abegill Grantham 5-29-1841 (5-31-1841) Hr
Grantham, G. W. to Elizabeth Flemming 6-30-1858 (7-4-1858) Hr
Grantham, James to Sarah Jane Hale 4-17-1850 (4-24-1850) Hr
Grantham, Joel to Mehala Musgrave 1-1-1829 Hr
Grantham, Josiah to Marry A. Harris? 11-3-1859 Hr
Grantham, Lewis to Martha L. Fortner 10-11-1853 Hr
Grantham, Moses H. to Mary J. Bailey 5-18-1860 Hr
Grantham, Richd. to Emily E. Goad 12-5-1844 (12-12-1844) Hr
Grantham, Scion to Betsy(Elizabeth) Rogers 9-29-1838 (10-3-1838) Hr
Grantham, Sion to Clarky Grant 8-31-1833 (9-1-1833) Hr
Grantham, Thomas R. to Mary A. Bizzell 12-16-1857 (12-17-1857) Hr
Grantham, Thomas to Edy Ann Cole 6-23-1841 Hr
Grantham, William to Malinda Bell 8-30-1849 Hr
Grantham, Z. T. to Sarah A. Chambers 3-5-1862 Mn
Granthan, Solomon to Emily Sacer(Sasser) 9-8-1838 (9-9-1838) Hr
Granville, Amos to Tibitha C. Furgeson 9-6-1859 G
Grattum, Lewis to Sarah Coats 3-3-1842 T
Graus, Calvin to Mary L. Lea 2-11-1859 Ma

Grave, Andrew to Nancy Duffee 10-30-1840 (11-5-1840) G
Grave, George E. to Elizabeth Adams 10-25-1829 (11-5-1829) Hr
Graves, A. P. to Amelia A. W. Eastham 12-4-1852 (no return) F
Graves, Aquiller P. to Arbella G. Fitzgerald 10-23-1846 Hn
Graves, Bird to Belden Dark 10-30-1884 L
Graves, Dick to Fannie Estis 1-26-1870 (no return) Hy
Graves, Eddie to Sarah J. Hale 12-11-1873 L
Graves, Edward D. to Mollie Wharton 12-31-1879 (1-1-1880) L B
Graves, Edwin A. to I. M. H. Jordan 8-2-1864 (8-10-1864) L
Graves, Elijah W. to Kezirah Perry 7-7-1845 Hr
Graves, G. M. to Lizzie Purdy 12-16-1855 Cr
Graves, G. to Malinda Torrence 9-22-1849 (11-27-1849) F
Graves, George W. S. to Eliza H. Enoch 7-31-1867 (8-1-1867) Dy
Graves, George W. to Manerva Hamilton 6-6-1861 Cr
Graves, George W. to Minerva Hamilton 6-?-1861 (6-6-1861) Cr
Graves, George to Janie Henderson 8-5-1867 (8-6-1867) T
Graves, Henry to Elizabeth Smith 4-23-1864 Be
Graves, Henry to Harriett Emily Jolly 7-5-1840 Cr
Graves, Henry to Rose Bailey 10-29-1869 Hy
Graves, Howell F. to Hetha Brumage 11-9-1848 (no return) Cr
Graves, Hudson C. to Adaline S. Turner 2-22-1844 (2-26-1844) Ma
Graves, Isaac to Emma Rogers 12-22-1870 Hy
Graves, J. E. to Sue H. Coleman 3-8-1875 Hy
Graves, J. F. to Virginia M. McGee 12-15-1860 (12-23-1860) Sh
Graves, J. M. to Tabitha A. Wood 9-16-1874 L
Graves, J. R. to Juda Koonce 1-3-1877 L
Graves, James H. to M. Jennie Park 7-20-1868 (7-21-1868) Ma
Graves, James R. to Louisa J. Snider 7-31-1856 Ma
Graves, James S. to Susan Chilton 10-17-1859 (no return) Cr
Graves, James to Ann Boon 9-21-1857 (9-22-1857) Ma
Graves, John D. to Mary J. Walker 10-18-1853 Hn
Graves, John H. to Sarah J. Thompson 11-8-1867 (11-10-1867) Ma
Graves, John M. to Sophia C. Maddox 4-3-1851 Sh
Graves, John to Bulia Hart 12-20-1882 L
Graves, Joseph S. to Ann Brown 3-29-1852 G
Graves, Joseph to Sarah ANn Edwards 11-7-1844 (11-14-1844) F
Graves, Lance to Lavina McCoy 1-18-1842 L
Graves, Lewis to C. C. Arbuckle 12-6-1849 (no return) F
Graves, Lewis to Mary E. Estis 1-18-1872 (no return) Hy
Graves, Mat to Menervia Grammar 5-17-1871 (no return) Hy
Graves, McDonald to Sarah A. Couch 7-11-1859 Cr
Graves, Miles to Emily J. Cotner 9-27-1853 Hn
Graves, Moses C. to Susan P. Crabb 8-22-1852 Be
Graves, Nathaniel H. to Sarah A. Porter 8-1-1859 G
Graves, Patterson to Misoura Ann Hardin 12-17-1853 Ma
Graves, R. J. to M. J. Sutton 10-23-1865 (no return) Hy
Graves, Reuben to Josie R. Chapman 5-4-1876 (no return) Hy
Graves, Richard T. to Mary Jane Thompson 10-30-1845 Hn
Graves, Richard to Ida Currie 1-4-1876 Hy
Graves, Richd. to Lucy Henning 8-5-1876 (no return) Hy
Graves, Robert B. to Josephine Murray 2-9-1870 (2-10-1870) Cr
Graves, Samuel to Rosella Fitzpatrick 1-7-1879 L B
Graves, Sive to Flora A. Tyus 3-10-1870 Hy
Graves, Solm. O. to Elizabeth Perkins 9-5-1853 (no return) F
Graves, Stephen to Becca Turner 12-30-1874 (no return) L B
Graves, Tarlton H. to Frances M. Fly 1-27-1844 (1-30-1844) Ma
Graves, Tarlton H. to Virginia M. Oliver 8-3-1858 (9-7-1858) Ma
Graves, Thomas H. to Martha J. Johnston 2-16-1871 L
Graves, Thomas J. to Artelia J. Wills 1-28-1840 (1-30-1840) F
Graves, Thomas M. to Emily _____ 1-29-1844 (2-1-1844) Ma
Graves, W. W. to Julia A. Phillips 12-25-1850 F
Graves, Walter C. to Elizabeth Black 1-1-1846 Cr
Graves, Washington to Mary E. Branch 12-17-1876 Hy
Graves, Wilborn B. to Elizabeth P. Hamilton 9-22-1858 Cr
Graves, Wilborn H. to Sopherina H. Weathers 7-18-1854 Cr
Graves, Wilbron H. to Elizabeth P. Hamilton 9-22-1858 Cr
Graves, William A. to Nancy M. Barnett 9-7-1867 (9-12-1867) Ma
Graves, William L. to Mary Jane Turner 12-27-1854 (12-28-1854) Ma
Graves, William M. to Jane Watson 12-3-1838 Ma
Graves, William M. to Martha C. Robertson 3-7-1877 (no return) L
Graves, William to Shemima McInteref 1-30-1849 F
Gravett, Obediah to Mary L. Ruffin 12-22-1856 (12-24-1856) Cr
Gravette, William D. to Minerva Fitz 12-30-1847 (12-31-1847) Ma
Gravitt, Obidiah to Sarah F. Edwards 12-22-1845 Ma
Gravy, Aux? W. to Miss Jane Finty? 3-13-1869 (3-17-1869) T
Gray, Alexander to Mary (Mrs.?) Reed 2-10-1864 (2-11-1864) Sh
Gray, Alfred W. to Elizabeth Laney 4-12-1854 (4-19-1854) Hr
Gray, Alfred W. to Susan Gamble 8-26-1851 (8-27-1851) Hr
Gray, Armstead to Alace Avery 6-28-1872 T
Gray, C. Y. to Josephine Martin 12-9-1863 O
Gray, Campbell D. to Sarah T. Gardner 10-19-1856 We
Gray, Charles H. to Mary B. O'Conner 2-6-1869 Cr
Gray, Claiborne to Mary Jane Bowls 9-22-1866 (no return) F B
Gray, D. L. to C. A. Foster 1-27-1846 Sh
Gray, Daniel to Mary A. Glass 1-29-1848 (2-1-1848) Hr
Gray, David to Elen Parr 8-17-1866 O
Gray, David to Elizabeth Selph 2-17-1855 (2-18-1855) O

Gray, David to Jane Jones 3-5-1849 (3-8-1849) O
Gray, David to Rachel McKinsey 11-27-1839 (12-1-1839) O
Gray, Eli to Casander A. Massey 12-27-1849 Sh
Gray, Frazier to Mary Williams 10-17-1839 Hn
Gray, Geor. C. to Harriet Parham 1-22-1845 F
Gray, George to Casandra Rutherford 1-10-1833 Hr
Gray, George to Charlotte Doll 5-18-1860 Sh
Gray, George to Loutesia Tipton 1-23-1877 Hy
Gray, H. P. to Sally Hutchison 2-12-1868 Hy
Gray, H. to Hariett Roberson 1-30-1851 F
Gray, Henry to Angeline Stovall 7-14-1872 (7-15-1872) O
Gray, Henry to Anner Walter 2-6-1877 Hy
Gray, Hiram V. to Mahaley Swinney 10-24-1840 Hn
Gray, Hugh A. to Martha E. Haily 10-26-1857 Hr
Gray, J. I. L. to H. J. Park 12-22-1863 (12-23-1863) O
Gray, J. J. to C. J. McCracken 11-2-1870 (11-4-1870) Dy
Gray, J. L. to Martha Ann Redding 11-22-1865 (11-23-1865) Dy
Gray, J. W. to Mallie Keathley 2-15-1870 G
Gray, James A. to Louisa Dickin 3-27-1863 O
Gray, James M. to Louisa F. Beasley 4-17-1839 (4-18-1839) F
Gray, James M. to Mary Grantham 9-5-1850 (9-8-1850) Hr
Gray, James M. to Mary W. Mizell 1-2-1862 (no return) Hn
Gray, James M. to Sarah K. Bradford 7-23-1846 Hn
Gray, James N. to Elizabeth M. Williams 3-7-1857 (3-12-1857) Sh
Gray, James P. to Phetama Phillips 1-31-1843 (2-7-1843) Hr
Gray, James to Elizabeth P. Moon 1-16-1835 Sh
Gray, Jesse to Caroline Mooring 12-25-1847 Ma
Gray, Jesse to Minerva Jenkins 3-20-1832 Hr
Gray, Jim to Ann Eliza Winchester 10-17-1877 (10-20-1877) Dy
Gray, John D. to Harriet Jane Laster 11-24-1864 O
Gray, John E. to Rowena Wardlaw 9-7-1856 (9-18-1856) L
Gray, John Lenoir to Mary Goforth 8-10-1852 T
Gray, John M. to Sarah E. Parish 1-18-1849 Sh
Gray, John to Caroline Fields 2-17-1869 (2-18-1869) Cr
Gray, John to Marilda Hysmith 11-20-1864 Mn
Gray, John to Mary A. B. Haines 3-17-1847 Sh
Gray, John to Mary Jane Gunter 5-26-1862 Sh
Gray, John to Nancy J. Chamber 1-15-1844 We
Gray, John to T. E. Fields 1-21-1871 (1-24-1871) Cr
Gray, Joseph Y. to Mary Wortham 8-19-1840 (9-22-1840) F
Gray, Lee to Amanda Howard 2-18-1840 (2-19-1840) O
Gray, Lee to Amanda Howard 2-18-1846 O
Gray, Lee to M. J. Creg 12-17-1872 O
Gray, Lee to Nancy Howard 2-27-1848 (2-29-1848) O
Gray, Louis to Laura Smith 12-10-1870 T
Gray, M. F. to M. D. Byrns 10-27-1883 (10-29-1883) L
Gray, Phineous to Synthia A. Rowland 1-28-1870 (2-1-1870) Cr
Gray, Robt. to Rebecca Brown 7-21-1870 (7-22-1870) F B
Gray, Sidney to Nancy Ann Cozart 2-10-1842 Ma
Gray, Tho. Evans to Mary Kulbeth 9-16-1851 (9-17-1851) T
Gray, Thomas D. to Mary A. Harvey 7-13-1838 Hr
Gray, Thomas D. to Nancy Gamble 12-23-1848 Hr
Gray, Thomas to Maria Mabene 5-4-1872 T
Gray, Thos. J. to Sallie E. Brown 11-23-1867 (11-24-1867) T
Gray, W. B. W. to P. P. Bigham 3-5-1867 (no return) Cr
Gray, W. C. (Rev.) to Maggie Trent 5-11-1863 (5-20-1863) F
Gray, W. G. to F. M. Kerr 1-21-1871 Cr
Gray, William Henry to Morning Sherman 10-6-1869 Hy
Gray, William M. to Susan M. Cradle 12-13-1838 Hn
Gray, William to Ann Wilson 8-22-1853 (8-23-1853) G
Gray, William to Lucy A. Gambell 2-7-1839 Hr
Gray, William to Nancy C. Newton 2-27-1854 We
Gray, William to Susan Boyd 10-6-1860 (10-7-1860) Ma
Gray, Willis to Alice Curren 12-24-1875 L B
Gray, Young E. to Eliza E. Galoway 9-28-1846 We
Gray, Young to Eleanor McKee 12-23-1830 Sh
Gray, Young to Nancy Owen 10-21-1851 (10-23-1851) T
Gray, Young to Susan Lanster 9-16-1847 Sh
Grayham, J. B. to Levina Herndon 10-22-1865 Be
Grayham, Jessee to Mary Walker 5-5-1873 (7-4-1873) T
Grayham, Lewis to Martha Hodge 9-22-1869 G B
Grayham, Olliver C. to Mary Jane Watson 5-22-1859 O
Grayham, R. A. to Jane Pierce 10-13-1859 (no return) Cr
Grayham, William J. to Virginia H. Polsgrove 7-25-1858 O
Grayson, Armstead to Frankie Jones 7-4-1876 Dy
Grayson, Armstead to Liza Stricklin 4-2-1867 Dy
Grayson, Lamuel F. to Willie Miller 12-30-1868 (12-31-1868) Ma
Greable, S. A. to Susan E. Avery 10-25-1866 Hy
Grear, G. N. to M. D. Caldwell 1-19-1876 L
Grear, Tom to Easter Johnson 8-2-1867 (no return) F B
Greathouse, John F. to Charlotte Crawford 1-28-1868 (1-30-1868) Ma
Greathouse, William to Mary A. Johnston 2-7-1850 Sh
Greaves, B. B. to Georgia Pugh 5-9-1875 L
Greaves, E. B. to Annie M. Wills 4-11-1861 Hy
Greaves, G. P. to Mary J. Paris 1-14-1879 L
Greaves, Joe to Hannah Jero__ 12-25-1867 (12-26-1867) L B
Greaves, Robert to Dollie Polk 1-9-1878 (no return) Hy
Greaves, Thomas to Mollie Winrow 12-20-1876 (no return) L
Greaves, William F. to Mary Alice Gause 5-29-1866 (6-6-1866) L
Greaves, Wily to Lucinda Bond 4-1-1877 Hy
Greaves, Wm. to Callie Perry 2-21-1879 Hy
Greear, William to Elizabeth Sayers 7-26-1855 We
Greely, Thomas to Catharine Niland 10-18-1859 Sh
Green (Guin-Given?), Benjamin H. to Mary A. Gregory 10-24-1853 (10-25-1853) L
Green (Guin-Given?), George A. to Sarah A. Gause 10-25-1853 (10-27-1853) L
Green(Greer?), Benjamin H. to Mary E. McGill 9-17-1862 Be
Green, A. A. to Laura Lake 5-9-1860 (no return) Hy
Green, A. H. to Nancy J. Atkinson 1-15-1855 (1-18-1855) Hr
Green, A. M. to M. C. Graves 3-7-1867 (3-11-1867) Cr
Green, A. M. to Mary J. Hufstettler 6-22-1874 (6-23-1874) Dy
Green, Abram to Emma Lovelace 11-16-1868 (no return) L B
Green, Abram to Lou Pinson 8-24-1883 (8-30-1883) L
Green, Ad to Mary L. Taylor 12-29-1875 (no return) Hy
Green, Albert to Jane Bragg 9-1-1870 G B
Green, Allen to Eveline Lee 9-13-1853 (9-16-1853) G
Green, Alonzo O. to Mary (Mrs.) Mitchell 3-15-1867 (3-17-1867) Ma
Green, Ambrose E. to Ann Henry Ford 10-3-1868 (10-8-1868) F
Green, Anderson to Anjaline Henderson 8-2-1877 Hy
Green, Anderson to Winny Fisher 12-17-1881 (12-18-1881) L B
Green, Andrew J. to Ann Moore 2-2-1870 Hy
Green, Andrew to Bell Fisher 3-13-1876 (3-16-1876) L
Green, Armstead to Francy McMigins 12-26-1867 (12-28-1867) L B
Green, Armstead to Lizzie Green 2-1-1875 L
Green, Armsted to Dilsey Perry 12-16-1875 Hy
Green, Asa W. to Sally (Mrs.) Dodson 8-24-1827 Sh
Green, Asaph to Feribe Sawyers 1-2-1826 Sh
Green, Ben to Jennie Morgan 10-25-1876 (no return) L B
Green, Ben to Mattie Moss 1-3-1873 (1-5-1873) L B
Green, Bob to Luvena Reddick 2-1-1870 (no return) Dy
Green, Bowling to Emily Abston 2-6-1873 (no return) Hy
Green, Carter to Charlotte Green 6-16-1866 (no return) F B
Green, Charlie to Milley Bailey 9-9-1876 (no return) L B
Green, Claiborne to Laura Lake 9-18-1879 L
Green, D. H. to Ada Haskiel 12-19-1882 (12-20-1882) L
Green, D. J. to M. M. Matheny 4-23-1869 (4-25-1869) Cr
Green, D. L. to E. M. Summers 12-22-1873 Dy
Green, David C. to Louisa B. Yates 11-14-1866 (11-15-1866) O
Green, David C. to Sarah E. Shelton 11-1-1858 (11-3-1858) Sh
Green, David to Amanda Stainbuck 2-28-1878 (no return) Hy
Green, David to Amanda Williams 12-21-1866 (12-22-1866) Dy
Green, David to Maria Stainback 11-27-1866 (12-2-1866) F B
Green, E. H. to Ellen J. Kirk 9-6-1860 Dy
Green, Edmund to Lemory Word 9-25-1845 G
Green, Edward (Edmund?) P. to Anna Painer 6-20-1830 Sh
Green, Edward Holister to Catharine Clamentine Hall 7-17-1851 T
Green, F. L. to Frances J. Gallimore 9-16-1865 (9-20-1865) Cr
Green, F. T. to L. L. Fuller 1-16-1856 (no return) Hn
Green, Fayett to Frances Green 4-7-1873 O
Green, Fed to Mollie Patton 10-8-1872 (10-10-1872) L
Green, Fras. M. to Mary Catherine Field 11-15-1853 (11-16-1853) T
Green, G. R. to M. J. Bragg 12-12-1877 (12-13-1877) L
Green, G.? J. to M. A. Slaughter 10-22-1866 (10-25-1866) F
Green, Galen E. to Mattie D. McRee 11-7-1864 (11-9-1864) Sh
Green, Garland F. to Lydia McCulloch 7-16-1868 G B
Green, Geo. R. to Martha J. Monroe 5-27-1846 (no return) F
Green, George to Ann Deener 11-14-1868 (11-15-1868) F B
Green, George to Burney Oughton 2-26-1880 (no return) L B
Green, Gilbert to Eliza Martin 11-8-1839 Cr
Green, Goodwin to Malinda C. Russell 7-16-1846 (7-28-1846) Ma
Green, Hamilton J. to Lucy A. Davis 11-19-1850 (11-21-1850) F
Green, Harry to Catherine Fraser 3-20-1866 (3-28-1866) F B
Green, Harry to Genny Smith 10-9-1868 Hy
Green, Henry D. to India M. Swift 12-21-1859 (12-22-1859) F
Green, Henry to Bettie Jerry 11-25-1869 Hy
Green, Henry to Celia Bond 2-11-1866 (no return) Hy
Green, Henry to May Mentlow 10-13-1875 (no return) Hy
Green, Henry to Sarah Dolton 1-6-1852 Be
Green, Hiram to Jenny (Mrs.) Casteel 11-23-1864 Sh
Green, Ira N. to Rebecca Jackson 10-7-1840 (10-13-1840) F
Green, Isaac to Loula Davis 12-8-1876 (no return) Hy
Green, Isaac to Margaret Frances McBroom 5-27-1869 (5-30-1869) L
Green, J. A. to Ellen Arnold 2-20-1873 (2-23-1873) L
Green, J. A. to Rosa Davis 12-6-1881 (12-7-1881) L
Green, J. D. R. to Elizabeth Liles 4-16-1864 Cr
Green, J. D. to J. J. Robertson 12-23-1862 (12-30-1862) F
Green, J. M.(N?) to Mary Kearns 7-8-1863 Sh
Green, J. R. to N. W. Stewart 8-6-1861 Mn
Green, J. R. to S. J. Blankenship 11-24-1866 (11-25-1866) Dy
Green, Jackson to Ida Whibby (Whitby?) 2-28-1880 (3-3-1880) L
Green, Jackson to _____ to 3-12-1869 (no return) Hy
Green, James C. to S. E. Hedden 11-18-1862 (11-19-1862) Dy
Green, James C. to Sarah Neely 10-18-1860 Cr
Green, James F. to Bettie Barbee 2-14-1866 Hy

Green, James F. to Virginia A. Hare 10-14-1848 (10-18-1848) F
Green, James H. to Agnes Lorance 11-14-1866 (11-16-1866) Cr
Green, James Lewis to Mary Frances Holloway 2-20-1871 (no return) Hy
Green, James R. to F. J. White 12-6-1875 (12-7-1875) Dy
Green, James T. to E. S. Shackleton 6-26-1875 (6-27-1875) Dy
Green, James to Alice Evans 1-28-1874 (no return) Hy
Green, James to Caroline Harrison 10-5-1867 Be
Green, James to Mirah L. Jones 4-23-1849 (no return) Cr
Green, James to Sarah Branch 11-15-1850 O
Green, Jesse A. to Sophia E. Scobey 8-1-1877 Dy
Green, Jesse to Tempa Williams 3-1-1839 Cr
Green, Jim to Rosa Pitts 3-3-1868 (3-?-1868) L B
Green, Joel J. to Elizabeth Ann Wilson 5-1-1867 (5-2-1867) L
Green, Joel J. to Mary Harris 8-13-1878 (8-15-1878) L
Green, John A. to Emma F. Morrow 2-15-1857 Hn
Green, John Bell to Hester Mann 11-1-1884 L
Green, John C. to Allsey M. Edwards 11-23-1856 Cr
Green, John C. to Mary E. Taylor 7-15-1850 Cr
Green, John H. to F. M. Quinn 1-19-1869 (1-22-1869) Cr
Green, John N. to M. E. Green 11-11-1875 Dy
Green, John P. to Martha Moody 1-23-1857 Hn
Green, John Uriah to Mary Jane Sanford 4-7-1853 T
Green, John Uriah to Sallie Ann Green 3-29-1865 (3-30-1865) T
Green, John W. to E. E. Utley 6-9-1868 G
Green, John to Eliza Alexander 11-17-1875 (no return) Hy
Green, John to Frances Nixon 12-4-1870 Hy
Green, John to Julia Ann Stanley 5-20-1857 (5-24-1857) O
Green, John to Kittie Ann Conner 2-2-1884 (no return) L
Green, John to Margaret Cardle 9-26-1855 Sh
Green, John to Mollie McKee 1-2-1869 (1-3-1869) Dy
Green, John to Priscilla Jones 12-24-1878 (12-26-1878) L B
Green, Jones to Lucy Winrow 3-24-1874 (3-26-1874) L B
Green, Joseph Allen to Elizabeth Frances Newman 3-4-1845 T
Green, Joseph M. to Martha Humphrey 10-11-1852 Ma
Green, June to Harriett Boyce 11-9-1870 (11-11-1870) T
Green, King to Jane Sudberry 1-1-1878 Dy
Green, Lafayett to Nancy Bradford 10-25-1854 G
Green, Lea to Bettie Nunn 8-17-1869 Hy
Green, Leander W. to Martha Jenkins 3-14-1857 Cr
Green, Lee to Amanda Walker 2-12-1870 (2-25-1870) F B
Green, M. J. to A. L. Blackwell 10-1-1872 (10-2-1872) T
Green, M. J. to Mary Harigan 6-8-1861 Sh
Green, Marcus C. to Sarah Ann Sanford 3-23-1848 T
Green, Marshall to Sophronia Craig 3-18-1876 (no return) Hy
Green, Martin A. to Jamima E. McNeil 12-3-1872 Dy
Green, Mashack to Nancy M. Meacham 7-27-1861 (7-30-1861) O
Green, Mike to Mary T. Flower 12-8-1868 (12-26-1868) T
Green, Moses F. to Armate Manier no date (not married) Cr
Green, Neptune to Mary Green 3-27-1878 L
Green, Noah to M. J. Cribbs 12-1-1874 Dy
Green, Noah to S. E. (Mrs.) Starrett 3-13-1873 Dy
Green, Paul to Maria Fogerty 4-13-1850 Sh
Green, Peter to Mary Susan Rice 12-24-1885 L
Green, Peter to Phoebe Ann Taylor 1-20-1876 (no return) Hy
Green, Philip to Jennie Halliburton 7-31-1879 L
Green, R. Moses to Mary F. Owen 11-25-1854 (no return) F
Green, R. S. to Evelina Alston 2-16-1885 (2-18-1885) L
Green, R. T. to Celia A. Dillon 2-5-1874 Dy
Green, R. W. to Kate Fisher 12-19-1879 (12-21-1879) L
Green, R. to Phoebe Calhoun 12-15-1866 (3-30-1867) T
Green, Richard W. to Harriet H. Scott 5-8-1839 (5-15-1839) F
Green, Richard to Adaline Miller 11-9-1872 T
Green, Richard to Burtie Parker 3-20-1873 Hy
Green, Richard to Laura Hill 3-2-1872 (3-5-1872) T
Green, Richard to Martha L. Fain 10-1-1859 L
Green, Richard to Nancy Miller 4-18-1874 T
Green, Robert H. to Victoria G. Taliaferro 4-23-1866 Ma
Green, Robert J. to Lucy J. Cole 6-7-1853 (6-8-1853) Sh
Green, Robert M. to Rachel L. McBride 9-7-1867 T
Green, Robert to Susan Peete 3-22-1869 (3-?-1869) T
Green, S. A. to Nancy L. Lawrence 7-1-1867 O
Green, S. P. to Kate Aubry Somerville 10-13-1869 (10-20-1869) T
Green, S. P. to S. L. Payne 7-21-1862 (no return) Hy
Green, S. T. to Jennie Lynn 12-24-1872 O
Green, Samuel to Elizabeth Wright 3-13-1859 Hn
Green, Samuel to Rice Townsend 6-15-1872 (no return) L
Green, Samuel to Snophia Stewart 3-15-1877 Hy
Green, Sandy to Henryetta Tyus 11-6-1875 (no return) Hy
Green, Sherwood to Lucy K. Macon 6-30-1837 (7-3-1837) Hr
Green, Simon W. to Melvinia Clements 6-23-1862 F
Green, Soleman to Ellen Young 1-27-1873 (1-28-1873) L
Green, Solomon to Mary Witt 3-2-1872 (not executed) L B
Green, Solomon to Sarah B. Degraffenreid 10-30-1848 (no return) F
Green, T. A. to Elizabeth Jourdon 12-30-1847 (no return) Cr
Green, T. F. to Sidney Fulton 6-20-1861 Mn
Green, T. L. to G. V. Green 9-3-1870 (9-4-1870) Cr
Green, T. W. to Catherine T. Somervill 10-26-1869 (10-27-1869) T

Green, Thomas R. to Mary J. Pinson 5-15-1857 Cr
Green, Thomas T. to S. E. Balling 9-23-1861 (9-24-1861) Sh
Green, Thomas W. to Kate McDonnel 8-13-1864 (8-15-1864) Sh
Green, Thomas to Malissa Jordan 6-12-1868 (no return) L B
Green, Thomas to Margaret Young 10-18-1869 (no return) Dy
Green, Thos. to Charity Strange 2-18-1873 (3-25-1873) T
Green, Thos. to Mary Warmack 4-1-1877 Hy
Green, W. C. to E. M. Borum 11-15-1884 (11-16-1884) L
Green, W. G. to P. B. Clemace 5-12-1858 Cr
Green, W. J. to Caroline Couch 6-18-1854 Cr
Green, Washington to Elizabeth Fraser 2-13-1869 (2-17-1869) F B
Green, Washington to Jane Outlin 8-8-1871 (no return) L B
Green, Washington to Julia Caldwell 1-12-1877 Hy
Green, Washington to Susan White 3-17-1884 (3-22-1884) L
Green, Wesley to Caroline Tayler 12-30-1871 Hy
Green, William C. to Sarah Jane Miller 7-29-1863 Sh
Green, William E. to Emily S. Jordan 11-4-1845 (11-5-1845) F
Green, William E. to Mary E. Jordan 10-9-1843 (10-11-1843) F
Green, William F. to Emaline Marberry 7-18-1839 (no return) Hn
Green, William S. to Viola L. Chaffin 12-20-1870 (no return) F
Green, William to Mary Cooksey 1-14-1847 Hr
Green, William to Minnie Scott 2-20-1871 L B
Green, Willis M. to Catharine Wirt 3-15-1838 F
Green, Willis to Lena Green 10-15-1875 (no return) Hy
Green, Wm. H. to Szieber? C. T. Martin 1-21-1862 (no return) Cr
Green, Wm. J. to Elizabeth Bullington 7-28-1844 Cr
Green, Wm. to Elizabeth Roberts 2-27-1849 (no return) Cr
Green, Wm. to Joanna O'Leary 3-17-1849 Sh
Green, dJohn to Elizabeth Jorden 9-16-1838 (9-18-1838) Hr
Greenberg, Jacob to Rose Weiskopf 8-7-1862 Sh
Greenberry, John to Hester Wright 10-7-1867 (no return) F B
Greenbery, John F. to Mary c. Mitchell 1-4-1851 (1-6-1851) F
Greene, Austin to Elsa Turbeville 12-26-1867 Hn B
Greene, Edward to Emma Tilman 12-25-1867 G B
Greene, Moses F. to Nancy C. Myers 1-19-1857 Hn
Greene, Nathaniel to Rebecca Hubbs 2-17-1853 Hn
Greene, William to Kitty Northcross 1-13-1870 G B
Greener, Nicholas to Martha Whitaker 2-22-1862 (2-23-1862) Ma
Greenfield, C. F. to L. A. Cox 9-26-1870 (9-27-1870) Cr
Greenlaw, Anguss to Ellenorah E. Bayless 7-13-1844 (7-14-1844) F
Greenlaw, B. S. to Susan Sawyer 2-9-1831 Sh
Greenlaw, John O. to Sarah E. Wickham 6-5-1839 Sh
Greenlaw, William B. to Mozella Bonds 3-14-1832 Sh
Greenlaw, William B. to Narcisa L. Tate 8-1-1838 Sh
Greenlee, Abram to Julia Hilliard 7-25-1870 F B
Greenly, William to Zilpha Warren 10-12-1834 (10-15-1834) Hr
Greenwald, Leopold to Johanna Cloch 5-25-1861 (no return) Hy
Greenwalt, Joseph to Eliza Haas 3-9-1864 Sh
Greenway, William W. to Elisabeth M. Young 5-2-1848 F
Greenway, Wm. W. to Mary A. E. Rhodes 9-5-1850 F
Greenwood, Allen J. to Mary J. (P.) Thompson 2-14-1850 O
Greenwood, J. to Lucinda Merrewither 3-25-1873 Hy
Greenwood, Jordan to Lucinda Witherspoon 3-25-1873 Hy
Greenwood, Malcom H. to Elizabeth C. Boney 6-29-1838 (7-1-1838) Hr
Greer (Grier?), N. D. to E. J. Thomas 2-1-1866 G
Greer, Asa to Biga Jolley 5-17-1854 (no return) We
Greer, Asa to Biga Jolly 5-17-1854 We
Greer, Benjamin F. to Jane Black 6-12-1851 Be
Greer, Brison to Sarah Ann Bowden 11-8-1867 Hn
Greer, C. W. to Sarah Patterson 1-13-1874 (1-18-1874) Dy
Greer, Carroll to Mandy Bane 2-8-1840 Be
Greer, Charles to Ellen Currie 7-5-1869 (7-17-1869) F B
Greer, Creed F. to Martha Sears 8-8-1866 Hn
Greer, Creed T. to Sarah Cate 7-15-1843 (no return) Hn
Greer, David A. to Elizabeth Bethay 5-28-1851 Be
Greer, Francis M. to Mahaly A. Hudson 2-14-1867 Be
Greer, Franklin to Sarah A. Haynes 10-11-1862 (10-12-1862) Dy
Greer, G. W. to Jane Bush 10-5-1854 Be
Greer, Gabriel to Julya Ann Dozier 8-18-1867 G B
Greer, George to Amy Luter 4-3-1869 (4-4-1869) Cr
Greer, George to Katharine Winkle 12-16-1848 Be
Greer, George to Rhoda Ball 5-15-1869 G B
Greer, H. W. to Susan J. Wilson 7-30-1856 (7-31-1856) G
Greer, Henry to Laura A. Fitzgerald 5-1-1855 Hn
Greer, Isaac to Anne Peters 10-30-1867 G B
Greer, J. C. N. to D. C. Wilson 4-20-1867 G
Greer, J. F. to Sallie Dodson 12-30-1868 G
Greer, J. J. H. to Mary A. Goode 7-9-1860 Hr
Greer, J. R. to Mary C. Madden 10-11-1857 Be
Greer, James A. to Jemima Rushing 8-5-1847 Be
Greer, James F. to Mary E. Tice 2-18-1869 Be
Greer, James M. to Minerva Hansey 2-10-1846 Cr
Greer, James N. to Henrietta Askew 9-13-1858 Ma
Greer, James to Catharine Kee 7-25-1839 Be
Greer, James to Eliza Hunt 3-20-1845 Cr
Greer, James to Julia Ann Harris 10-21-1849 Be
Greer, James to Mandy Cross 4-3-1853 Be

Greer, James to Mary Cole 4-25-1839 Be
Greer, James to Sarah Ann Ward 7-11-1852 Be
Greer, Jason to Eliza Jane Patrick 9-12-1851 (9-14-1851) G
Greer, Jefferson to Sarah E. Jones 6-30-1851 (7-3-1851) Sh
Greer, Jno. C. A. to Margarett C. Oliphant 6-5-1858 (6-8-1858) G
Greer, John A. to Jane F. Bryant 10-24-1855 (11-4-1855) G
Greer, John A. to Louisa Ingram 5-21-1859 (5-22-1859) Ma
Greer, John T. to S. J. Dillahunty 3-5-1867 Hn
Greer, John to Nancy McDaniel 6-10-1839 Be
Greer, Jordan to Maca Young 8-24-1870 Hy
Greer, Joseph A. to B. D. Caroline Rushing 7-3-1854 Be
Greer, P. E. to Nancy Mitchael 7-3-1854 (7-4-1854) Hr
Greer, P. to Sarah Owens 8-1-1848 O
Greer, Robert to Mary Taylor 3-8-1859 Sh
Greer, Robt. E. R. to Mary J. Johnson 11-5-1867 (11-7-1867) F
Greer, Rowland to Susan Anthony 1-19-1849 (2-6-1849) G
Greer, S. A. to Sarah Jane Woods 9-16-1868 (9-17-1868) Dy
Greer, Samuel S. to Harrett Carl 11-3-1853 G
Greer, Thomas D. to Kissiah E. Leary 8-27-1838 Sh
Greer, Thomas to Rachel Baldwin 1-7-1875 Hy
Greer, Thos. M to Mary Reid 1-1-1846 Ma
Greer, W. B. to Nancy E. Sullivan 12-2-1866 Hn
Greer, W. H. to W. M. Palmer 9-3-1865 Hn
Greer, W. J. to Elizabeth McRed 5-11-1843 Be
Greer, W. L. to Nancy D. Rushing 3-1-1860 Be
Greer, William H. to Sarah Ann Wise 7-2-1850 Ma
Greer, William to H. G. C. Bondurant 12-30-1845 Hn
Greer, Wm. H. to Julia Ann Nance 12-30-1849 Be
Greer, Wm. W. to Mazy Jane Cole 12-24-1866 Be
Greer, Zachariah to Abigale E. Wren 12-20-1851 (12-23-1851) G
Gregg, Charles C. to Mary Hines 2-12-1838 Hr
Gregg, J. C. to Catharine Frey 1-21-1860 (1-22-1860) Sh
Gregg, William H. to E. Stocks 10-28-1854 (10-29-1854) Sh
Gregory, B. S. to Fannie Anthony 12-19-1861 L
Gregory, C. H. to Bettie Murphy 12-20-1882 L
Gregory, Francis M. to Mary A. McNabb 8-25-1842 Sh
Gregory, Harvy to Harriet Ezell 2-20-1869 Cr
Gregory, J. F. to Mary A. Williams 3-20-1868 G
Gregory, J. P. to F. A. Powell 10-27-1875 (no return) Hy
Gregory, J. T. to M. L. McCorkle 5-24-1864 (5-25-1864) Dy
Gregory, James T. to Sarah ANn Hodges 8-5-1852 Sh
Gregory, James T. to Sarah E. Morriss 8-3-1861 Sh
Gregory, James to Elisabeth Beal 7-5-1852 Sh
Gregory, John H. to Eliza Brooks 11-3-1846 (11-6-1846) Ma
Gregory, John to Bettie Baldridge 12-15-1867 G
Gregory, Joseph M. to Bettie Stovall 4-18-1854 Sh
Gregory, Joseph P. to Pinkie L. Finch 9-10-1873 Hy
Gregory, Lewis to Neoma Duncan 9-18-1841 Ma
Gregory, Majer to Susan Wood 7-29-1871 (no return) Hy
Gregory, Major to Rebecca Caroline Huskey 12-28-1845 Sh
Gregory, Malachi to Elizabeth Staton 7-28-1842 Sh
Gregory, Nathan to Mary Jane Bland 1-19-1843 Sh
Gregory, Peyton to Parlee Hooks 12-24-1869 (no return) Cr
Gregory, Robt. C. to Sarah Jane Martin 12-9-1851 (no return) F
Gregory, Sam to Lucinda Jeter 11-16-1869 (no return) Hy
Gregory, Samuel P. to Ann E. Jones 9-3-1851 (9-4-1851) Sh
Gregory, T. F. to Mary Glass 6-11-1885 L
Gregory, Thomas to Sarah Jane Gregory 10-13-1870 (10-14-1870) T
Gregory, Thomas to Winney Gooch 1-11-1843 G
Gregory, Tillman to Parmelia Shivers 9-24-1838 Sh
Gregory, Tillman to Sarah Dudley 9-28-1845 Cr
Gregory, W. H. to Mollie Johnson 10-6-1865 (no return) Cr
Gregory, William L. to Mary Jane Duncan 3-18-1852 Ma
Gregory, Wm. C. to Mary C. Grier 2-27-1865 (3-1-1865) Dy
Gregson, P. E. to M. S. Milam 5-4-1871 Dy
Grehan, J. R. to Mary F. Groves 6-25-1861 Sh
Greminger, Konrad to Magdelina Meshly 12-20-1854 (12-28-1854) Sh
Grenade, Luther to Betty Covington 12-25-1865 (no return) Hn
Grenade?, John M. to Sally E. Osborne 7-8-1863 We
Greppin (Griffin?), James to Margaret Meehan 4-4-1861 Sh
Gresham, Benjamin M. to Mary A. Hays 2-17-1853 Hn
Gresham, George to Centhia Jane Younger 2-18-1863 Hn
Gresham, W. H. to Sarah E. Jones 12-26-1860 Sh
Gressom, Jerome B. to Sarahann Teague 7-16-1844 (no return) F
Grey, Ephraine L. to Artelia Y. Acres 3-29-1854 (3-30-1854) Ma
Grice, Jesse G. to Bathis Hart 11-14-1827 Hr
Grice, William to Elizabeth Ringgold 11-30-1843 G
Grider, Anderson to Christiana Fritz 9-7-1852 Sh
Grider, B. H. to Rebecca C. Worrell 1-28-1845 F
Grider, John S. to Mattie F. Seat (Seah?) 12-27-1860 Sh
Grider, Tobias to Mary B. Worrell 1-5?-1839 F
Grider, W. H. to Rachel H. Maddox 1-21-1857 Sh
Grier, A. M. to Frances E. Becton 2-11-1852 (2-12-1852) G
Grier, Elijah to Vina Hicks 3-20-1854 G
Grier, Jacob T. to Elizabeth H. Wyatt 1-26-1842 (1-27-1842) G
Grier, James P. to Parmelia A. Moore 3-19-1844 G
Grier, Quincy M. to M. J. Bobbett 8-26-1848 G
Grier, William to Anne Manor 12-16-1863 G
Grieshaber, Anthony to Elizabeth Coffield 3-22-1849 Sh
Grieshaber, Joseph to Caroline Rehkoff 3-1-1853 (3-2-1853) Sh
Grif (Griss?), George to Zilphia Williams 12-29-1840 L
Grifen, Michael to Mary Holland 9-15-1864 (9-16-1864) Sh
Griffe, James to Elizabeth Reaves 7-10-1855 Cr
Griffee, William to Nancy C. Flanakin 1-11-1860 T
Griffen, George W. to Mary Jane Durham 4-8-1862 Sh
Griffet, James J. to E. Baldridge 1-20-1852 We
Griffeth, Jessee to Norciss Vaughan 11-11-1868 (11-12-1868) L
Griffey, Charles to Heneretta C. Wilks 10-10-1849 G
Griffey, John H. to Sarah E. Jenno 1-24-1861 Sh
Griffie, Richard to Sarah F. Foster 2-13-1860 (no return) We
Griffin, A. B. to M. M. Macke? 8-7-1871 (8-8-1871) T
Griffin, Andrew J. to Mary E. Furgarson 6-7-1851 (7-8-1851) G
Griffin, B. P. to H. A. C. Lile 10-5-1860 (10-18-1860) F
Griffin, Benjamin to Winney Birdson 2-8-1847 F
Griffin, Chas. F. to Sarah F. Smith 12-27-1871 (1-25-1872) T
Griffin, D. G. to M. J. Smith 9-14-1860 (no return) Hy
Griffin, Daniel to Ann Haren 7-8-1863 Sh
Griffin, Douglass to Joanna Williams 5-23-1867 Hy
Griffin, Durell to Maria Rosser 11-3-1870 (11-8-1870) F
Griffin, Edward J. to Gertie Jacobs 4-18-1868 (4-20-1868) Ma
Griffin, Elijah to Margaret Cherry 2-1-1858 (2-2-1858) Sh
Griffin, F. M. to Susan C. Patterson 2-12-1859 (2-15-1859) G
Griffin, F. P. to Sue E. Ellis 12-1-1878 Hy
Griffin, Francis M. to Margaret E. Pickins 12-24-1847 (12-28-1847) F
Griffin, Franklin H. to Catharine Hopper 1-24-1855 O
Griffin, G. W. to Eliza J. Spurlock 12-21-1852 (no return) F
Griffin, George W. to Mary A. Brown 6-17-1856 Sh
Griffin, Gus to Margaret Boals 2-24-1869 (2-25-1869) F B
Griffin, H. to Catharine White 10-9-1860 Sh
Griffin, Henry to Louisa Griffin 12-27-1866 Dy
Griffin, I. P. to Susan C. Campbell 12-31-1866 (no return) Hy
Griffin, Isaac to Milly Mitchell 1-20-1870 T
Griffin, J. A. to Alice Leath 5-1-1861 G
Griffin, J. R. to L. J. Watson 9-3-1872 (9-5-1872) Dy
Griffin, J. W. to Maggie Carrell 7-7-1875 (no return) L
Griffin, James C. to Clotilda Lay 6-25-1851 F
Griffin, James H. to Z. A. Thomas 1-6-1851 (no return) F
Griffin, James R. to Martha Ann James 8-9-1848 (8-10-1848) Hr
Griffin, James T. to Carrie A. Cravens 2-21-1865 Hn
Griffin, James to Eliza Beasley 2-8-1875 L
Griffin, James to Sarah Nipper 7-13-1843 Ma
Griffin, James to Tabitha J. McFarland 3-7-1849 Hn
Griffin, Jehocakin to Alsey Cartwright 5-28-1862 (no return) Hy
Griffin, Jerome to Caroline Thomas 8-22-1835 (8-23-1835) G
Griffin, John B. to L. A. Strickland 12-27-1870 (12-28-1870) L
Griffin, John H. to E(ddy?) E. Bentley 9-17-1867 (9-20-1867) L
Griffin, John R. to M. L. Lucas 9-3-1867 (no return) Dy
Griffin, John S. to Susan E. Furgarson 9-22-1853 (9-23-1853) G
Griffin, John W. to Amelia J. Morison 12-30-1848 (12-31-1848) F
Griffin, John to Fanny Parks 9-15-1841 Cr
Griffin, John to Isabella Coffey 5-2-1840 (5-3-1840) F
Griffin, John to Letty Butler 9-16-1871 (9-21-1871) T
Griffin, John to Mary Cary 8-9-1862 (8-10-1862) Sh
Griffin, John to Mary Griffin 7-7-1871 Hn
Griffin, John to Mary Penelope Evans 2-10-1844 Sh
Griffin, John to Polly Evalene Vincent 6-24-1851 O
Griffin, Jonathan B. to Virginia W. Petigrue 12-30-1852 Hr
Griffin, Joshua J. to Sarah S. Wilkins 11-13-1851 G
Griffin, Leander to Rowana Moore 7-12-1858 (no return) L
Griffin, Lovick J. to Martha J. Bell 7-2-1861 (no return) Hy
Griffin, Michael to Mahala Sweeton 4-19-1860 Hr
Griffin, Michael to Margaret Mescar 1-28-1860 (1-30-1860) Sh
Griffin, Miles B. to Peggy Caplinger 8-9-1842 Hn
Griffin, Morris to Frances Suggs 12-20-1882 (no return) L
Griffin, Morris to Nancy Kelless 7-2-1872 (no return) L
Griffin, Morrison to Martha Cryant? 12-4-1858 Cr
Griffin, Patrick to Margaret Nealon 1-18-1862 (1-20-1862) Sh
Griffin, Robert to Caty Loving 2-4-1867 (no return) F B
Griffin, Robert to Pearcy Herring 2-2-1843 Sh
Griffin, Stanley to Polly Clements 4-28-1834 (5-1-1834) G
Griffin, T. E. to D. A. Morgan 1-23-1878 (1-24-1878) Dy
Griffin, T. J. to Mary J. Franklin 12-28-1875 (no return) Hy
Griffin, Thomas to Rebecca Dunlap 11-10-1867 G
Griffin, Thos. J. to Elizabeth V. Garrett 12-20-1870 (no return) Dy
Griffin, W. J. to Elizabeth Warren 11-7-1866 Dy
Griffin, W. N. to Nancy Wood 10-16-1864 (no return) Hn
Griffin, William E. to Mary Ann Crenshaw 9-11-1846 (9-18-1846) F
Griffin, William T. to Mary Ann Rollins 12-21-1866 (12-23-1866) Ma
Griffin, William to Delila Baley 9-12-1838 Ma
Griffin, William to Elizabeth Burks 3-21-1864 Cr
Griffin, William to Julia A. D. Taylor 6-4-1853 (6-7-1853) O
Griffin, William to Mary (Mrs.) Eason 12-12-1837 Sh
Griffin, William to Mary Ann Williamson 2-12-1844 Sh
Griffin, William to Mary Malaughney 7-7-1860 (7-8-1860) Sh

Griffin, Wm. L. to Mary L. Jones 10-14-1868 (10-15-1868) F
Griffing, J. C. to Martha L. Hart 11-14-1850 Sh
Griffing, James B. to Francis M. Grant 2-5-1851 Sh
Griffing, William A. to Amelia W. Boher 1-17-1855 Sh
Griffith, Allen to E. J. Care 10-31-1837 (11-2-1837) G
Griffith, Bennet S. to Roxey S. V. Reynolds 2-16-1870 Hy
Griffith, C. G. to Martha H. Smith 12-13-1858 (12-15-1858) T
Griffith, Charles G. to Indiana M. Burkhart 11-12-1866 (11-13-1866) T
Griffith, David to Ann Morrow 11-9-1868 (11-13-1868) F B
Griffith, Hiram S. to Nancy G. Haynes 5-14-1848 Sh
Griffith, Isham to Louisanna Matheny 2-3-1862 We
Griffith, James to Ann Purser 2-6-1854 Sh
Griffith, John to Rosesetty Rhods 11-23-1858 We
Griffith, Lewis to Eliza Childers 7-25-1859 Sh
Griffith, W. A. to Martha E. Work 11-17-1867 Hy
Griffith, W. B. to M. E. Kirksey 3-30-1880 (3-31-1880) L
Griffith, William to Amanda E. Matheny 5-20-1860 We
Griffith, Wm. H. to Sarah E. McGuire 10-20-1860 (10-21-1860) T
Grifford, Robert to Frances E. Fausett 12-3-1851 (no return) F
Griffy, Benjamin G. to Amanda M. Hurt 1-25-1873 (1-26-1873) O
Grigby, John E. to Jullia A. Crichlow 2-25-1869 Hy
Grigg, Charlie to Martha Jarrett 7-5-1872 (no return) Hy
Grigg, David to Creasy Friar 2-12-1880 (no return) L
Grigg, J. L. to Manerva C. Wade 1-26-1858 T
Grigg, John D. to Lidia C. Neal 3-19-1860 Hn
Grigg, John to Rose Holloway 12-28-1866 (no return) Hy
Grigg, Wiley H. to Frances A. Neill 10-5-1854 Hn
Griggs, Berry to Edney C. Whitson 3-2-1859 (3-3-1859) L
Griggs, Berry to Frances Johnson 1-28-1864 L
Griggs, H. C. to Elizabeth Murphy 9-9-1854 (9-13-1854) Hr
Griggs, Henry to Ada Allison 12-15-1884 (12-?-1884) L
Griggs, J. B. to M. A. Burns 8-2-1879 (8-3-1879) L
Griggs, L. W. to E. M. Matthews 8-22-1882 (8-23-1882) L
Griggs, R. B. to Sarah A. Todd 1-27-1867 G
Griggs, Robert to Mahala Shearman 2-6-1866 L
Griggs, Thos. to Elizabeth Fields 10-26-1850 (10-27-1850) L
Griggs, William M. to Elizabeth A. Riddle 1-31-1849 (2-1-1849) Hr
Griggs, William to Martha Barnes (Baines?) 1-23-1865 (1-24-1865) L
Griggs, jr., Wiley to Virginia Dyre 6-26-1866 L
Grigsby, John to H. F. (Mrs.) Maver 5-2-1861 Sh
Grigsby, Robert to Lizzie Buck 10-8-1868 (no return) Dy
Grigsby, W. H. to Nancy Ann McCullough 11-16-1872 (11-19-1872) T
Grigsby, William T. to Emma Bright 5-31-1854 G
Grilesby, George to Rachel Garrett 10-20-1855 Cr
Grills, A. J. to L. E. Gregory 11-14-1871 Dy
Grimes, George F. to Pattie E. Grimes 2-25-1873 (2-26-1873) T
Grimes, H. A. to Alice McLeod 12-25-1882 (12-26-1882) L
Grimes, H. F. to Nannie Bradshaw 12-15-1877 (12-19-1877) Dy
Grimes, Henry to Mary A. Owens 10-14-1860 G
Grimes, Mack to Caroline Roberson 9-9-1877 Hy
Grimes, N. W. to C. A. French 1-17-1861 (1-20-1861) T
Grimes, W. C. to Eliza Orr 4-22-1873 (4-23-1873) T
Grimes, W. H. to Sarah Roffe 2-23-1860 We
Grimes, William to Martha J. Jones 2-6-1846 Ma
Grimes, Wm. M. to Mary E. Short 7-9-1862 G
Grimes, Wm. W. to Mary E. Koonce 7-27-1870 (7-28-1870) L
Grimm, Amos to Ann Turnage 4-7-1877 (4-9-1877) Dy
Grimm, Amos to Ella Wynne 1-3-1874 Dy
Grimm, Edmund to Amanda Douglass 2-19-1873 (2-20-1873) Dy
Grimm, Elijah to Bettie Grimm 1-10-1876 (1-12-1876) Dy
Grimm, Gay to Mourning Grimm 9-26-1877 (no return) Dy
Grimm, Guy to Sallie Fields 3-18-1873 (3-19-1873) Dy
Grimm, Harry to Harriet Tucker 1-3-1872 (1-4-1872) Dy
Grimm, Harry to Martha Harris 6-30-1876 Dy
Grimm, Jessup? to Nancy Evans 11-14-1877 Dy
Grimm, Ned to Bettie Doyle 12-21-1878 (12-25-1878) Dy B
Grimmer, Thomas W. to Elmarine Jones 5-19-1840 Hn
Grimmet, Charles to Cynthia C. Ross 8-27-1860 (8-28-1860) Hr
Grisamore, A. G. to Hester A. Freeman 6-15-1852 Sh
Grisham, G. R. to Mary P. Whitaker 2-16-1867 Hn
Grisham, George R. to Barbara J. Upchurch 3-16-1848 (no return) Hn
Grisham, George W. to Teletha (Mrs.) Furgarson 12-31-1844 (1-1-1845) G
Grisham, J. C. to Mary F. Byram 2-20-1874 Hy
Grisham, James to Thiaza Autry 5-8-1830 (5-15-1830) Hr
Grisham, W. H. to Frances J. Maupin 12-19-1866 (no return) Hn
Grisham, William to Stacy Bounds 10-31-1845 (no return) F
Grissam, John A. to Mary C. Beasley 8-13-1863 (no return) Hn
Grissom, Enons J. to Elizabeth Campbell 7-4-1846 (7-9-1846) Hr
Grissom, F. H. to Elizabeth McMackin 7-16-1873 (7-17-1873) Cr
Grissom, Hugh R. to Julia Ann Litton 10-1-1856 O
Grissom, John C. to Elizer A. Belch 5-5-1867 G
Grissom, John W. to Mary Outlaw 11-15-1869 (11-16-1869) F
Grissom, John to Elizabeth Nease 9-9-1868 (9-17-1868) Cr
Grissom, Lafayett to N. V. White 10-29-1856 G
Grissom, William T. to Hester S. Jones 2-17-1861 We
Grissom, Willis B. to Margrette E. Cash 10-3-1854 G
Grissom, Willis to Ann Bell 6-17-1865 G

Grist, E. to Arsenia Ringold 8-1-1866 G
Griswold, Charles A. to Mary A. Grant 11-22-1858 Sh
Grizard, Robert W. to Missouri A. Wells 1-1-1866 Hy
Grizzard, Charles B. to Mary E. Crockett 12-17-1861 (12-18-1861) Cr
Grizzard, Charles B. to Mary E. Crockett 12-19-1861 Cr
Grizzard, Dennis to Parlie McNeill 2-6-1872 Cr B
Grizzard, Hulon? W. to Mary E. Flack 11-20-1860 (11-21-1860) Cr
Grizzard, James A. to Mary Alice Courts 10-24-1866 Hn
Grizzard, Jno. to Martha W. Lundy 7-17-1848 Sh
Grizzard, Mark to Henrietta Turnage 3-10-1873 (3-13-1873) T
Grizzard, R. E. to Clemagart Marshall 12-8-1869 G
Grizzard, W. B. to Irene? McNeill 1-19-1871 Cr
Grizzle, R. R. to Susan A. Hood 10-3-1868 (10-7-1868) F
Grizzurd?, Walter B. to Anna Courts 9-7-1858 Hn
Grogan, J. P. to Margaret E. Riley 10-29-1849 (no return) Cr
Grogan, John to Jane Fitts 12-24-1857 Hn
Grogan, John to Mary Welch 11-22-1856 (11-23-1856) Sh
Grogan, Joseph W. to Eliza C. Pritchard 1-12-1869 (1-13-1869) Cr
Grogan, Michal to Mary Gibbons 9-22-1862 Cr
Grogan, Nathan H. to Lila Ragland 5-21-1869 Cr
Grogan, Rice to Mary Lucus 9-9-1841 Cr
Grogan, W. C. to E. A. McKenny 11-14-1855 (no return) Hn
Grogan, Wm. B. to Mary Hopper 1-9-1873 Cr
Groghan, F. M. to Mary Turner 7-4-1874 (7-5-1874) L
Groms, J. M. to W. E. Carlton 12-20-1852 We
Groom, F. Samuel to Elizabeth Baldwin 11-5-1855 (no return) Hn
Groom, J. W. to Sarah H. Rowland 12-1-1860 (12-2-1860) Cr
Groom, James H. to Harriett Richie 12-17-1855 We
Groom, James L. to Elizabeth S. Chandler 7-5-1862 (7-11-1862) Cr
Groom, Leroy T. to Mary C. Baldwin 9-27-1857 Hn
Groom, Thomas to Sarah A. Crichfield 1-19-1878 (1-23-1878) Dy
Groom, Thos. W. to Mary F. Groom 3-1-1871 Cr
Groom?, James L. to Nancy Chandler 3-20-1868 Cr
Grooms, Almus to Jane V. London 1-24-1872 (1-25-1872) Cr
Grooms, J. M. to Elizabeth Rowland 2-19-1866 Cr
Grooms, James L. to Mary J. Hammett 2-9-1848 Cr
Grooms, James P. to Martha L. Spears 1-11-1863 We
Grooms, James W. to Sarah H. Rowland 2-22-1870 Cr
Grooms, James to Jane Green 10-14-1846 Cr
Grooms, John to Betsy Kimbrough 5-22-1830 Sh
Grooms, Lewis to Elizabeth Imes (Innes) 6-5-1838 Sh
Grooms, Moses to Mary Ann Herron 12-24-1850 Sh
Grooms, Richard to Margaret Saint 3-5-1863 Sh
Grooms, Richard to Mary Imes 7-13-1847 Sh
Grooms, Right M. to Eliza Ray 3-12-1852 We
Grooms, Samuel to Elizabeth Scott 2-11-1854 Hn
Grooms, Thomas to Elizabeth Cobb 11-14-1855 Hn
Grooms, Thomas to Mary E. Green 12-13-1869 (12-14-1869) Cr
Grooms, Thos. to Marilda Jane Russian 9-5-1867 G
Grooms, Wm. H. to Nancy M. Green 11-18-1850 (no return) Cr
Gross, B. to Nancy Lindsey 3-25-1856 Be
Gross, Barnabas to Margaret Ann Atchison 7-17-1860 Be
Gross, Charles L. to Sophia Loeb 2-9-1864 Sh
Gross, J. E. to Ester A. Roark 11-16-1854 Cr
Gross, J. F. to Rackey Lindsey 8-10-1865 Be
Gross, James to Sarah Lathan 1-10-1855 (1-11-1855) T
Gross, John to Joice Hunley 2-16-1841 (2-17-1841) T
Gross, John to Leana Moore 5-30-1865 Cr
Gross, Peter to Louisa (Mrs.) Armstrong 12-24-1862 Sh
Gross, Peter to Sarah Bunce 12-31-1861 L
Gross, Thomas to Nancy J. Innis 4-7-1870 T
Gross, William to Caroline Lankford 10-8-1857 Be
Groth, Henrich to Anna M. Freeman 5-20-1882 (no return) L
Grove, Henry J. to Deliah Copeland 12-27-1864 (12-29-1864) Sh
Grove, James H. to Jane H. Harris 1-29-1850 (1-31-1850) Hr
Grove, John L. to Margaret Thompson 1-2-1860 (1-24-1860) Hr
Grove, William B. to Emeline C. Rivers 12-22-1831 (12-23-1831) Hr
Groves, George to Rebecca Wise 6-5-1844 Hn
Groves, P. W. to Mary A. Swift 11-13-1863 (11-18-1863) Dy
Groves, William R. to Mary Martha Malery 7-1-1848 (7-2-1848) Hr
Groves, William R. to Nicey McCarver 11-17-1858 Ma
Grubb, Elijah H. to Vina Oakley 1-29-1863 We
Grubbs, James to Mary Faris 8-24-1846 Sh
Grubbs, John B. to Sarah C. Salmon 12-17-1857 Hn
Grubbs, Thomas W. to Polly Steward 7-17-1838 Sh
Grubbs, Thomas to Mary Gallop 1-13-1845 (1-23-1845) Ma
Gruben, Frank to Mary Fink 6-19-1855 Sh
Gruber (Gruten), Francis to Barbara Faben (Fater-Faber) 3-18-1850 Sh
Gruber, Jacob to Elizabeth Jane Miles 5-5-1846 Sh
Gruber, M. W. to Mary E. Carper 8-9-1859 (7?-1-1859) Hr
Gruff (Graff), Ignatius to Emily L. Brookshire 12-14-1848 Sh
Grugett, M. L. to M. E. Vails 12-16-1874 Dy
Grugett?, A. J. to M. A. Wherry 1-15-1874 Dy
Grun?, James C. to M. E. Neely 10-14-1864 Cr
Grunade, Harvey W. to Nancy C. Swan 12-10-1830 (12-15-1830) Ma
Grundy, Henderson to Patience Hammon 2-20-1869 (2-12?-1869) F B
Grundy, J. T. to Mattie Sparks 7-26-1871 Cr B

Grundy, James P. H. to Eliza G. Hogg 5-13-1828 G
Guardner, Pleasant to Jane Read 8-31-1838 (no return) F
Guarrant, Robert D. to L. A. Exum 8-26-1847 (no return) F
Guernant, Geo. B. to Mariella Woodson 10-27-1852 (10-28-1852) Sh
Guess, A. P. to Alabama L. Gardner 8-31-1856 We
Guest, Jesse to Betsy Price 2-14-1879 (3-3-1879) L B
Guevokowsky, Augustus to Louisa Paty 4-7-1857 Sh
Guffey, John to Elizabeth S. Burns 8-3-1868 (8-4-1868) Cr
Guffey, John to Malinda Williams 12-28-1835 Hr
Guffie, John to Julian Ellinor 4-2-1838 Hn
Gufford, Thomas to Nelty G. Jones 5-5-1844 Hn
Guill, J. J. to Lavinia C. Moody 12-7-1865 Hn
Guill, Jasper to Elizabeth Steel 11-19-1857 Hn
Guill, John H. to Provie E. Phillips 6-3-1868 (6-4-1868) Dy
Guilmord, H. to Louisa Doutaz 6-11-1864 Sh
Guin, Danl. M. to Olivia Ricks 9-13-1832 Hr
Guinn, James E. to Mary E. Bucy 11-29-1866 Hn
Guinn, James F. to Mary Davis 6-21-1862 (6-22-1862) Ma
Guinn, Jesse to Jane Jackson 1-1-1879 (1-2-1879) Dy
Guinn, John A. to Mariah J. Mathis 4-14-1858 (no return) Hn
Guinn, John B. to Nancy H. Winsett 1-12-1859 Hn
Guinn, Manoah B. to Martha P. Green 8-6-1857 (8-7-1857) O
Guinn, T. P. to Nancy Harris 6-26-1858 O
Guinn, W. M. to Liza Hawkins 1-4-1860 Hn
Guinn, W. M. to Sarah Eliza Petree 9-23-1864 (no return) Hn
Guinn, Wesley M. to Sarah E. Petree 2-17-1867 Hn
Guinn, William C. to Harrett Skipper 5-16-1846 (5-17-1846) G
Guinn, William to Elizabeth Jones 6-9-1860 (6-10-1860) O
Guion, H. L. to Margaret J. Lemaster 10-20-1841 Sh
Guion, Henry L. to Mary Ann McMillan 12-18-1838 Ma
Guiteau, Benjamin F. to Josephine E. Moore 11-7-1864 (11-8-1864) Sh
Gulledge, Thos. L. to Elizabeth J. Roach 10-14-1845 (no return) Cr
Gulledge, William to Sarah Lax 12-26-1842 (no return) Hn
Gullege, Joseph to Mary Hedge 5-19-1857 (no return) Cr
Gullender?, John C. to Racheal Davis 1-18-1835 Hn
Gullespie, John C. to Sarah W. Knight 12-6-1866 O
Gullett, G. T. to N. E. Borum 8-10-1874 L
Gullett, George T. to Louisa J. Neighbors 4-5-1866 L
Gullett, J. D. to Mollie F. Blakemore 4-10-1867 G
Gullett, John D. to Nannie M. Burford 3-8-1861 G
Gullett, John to Burford Nannie M. 3-4-1861 (no return) Hy
Gullett, Lenke H. to Rebecca Stephenson 10-9-1847 (10-14-1847) O
Gullett, Luke H. to Ruth Wade 1-7-1854 (1-8-1854) O
Gully, D. B. to Emaline Bruce 3-12-1854 Be
Gully, D. B. to Virginia Williams 1-6-1858 Be
Gully, James R. to Mary Ann Gossett 3-6-1853 Be
Gum, C. C. to Mary A. Hastings 1-8-1848 Hn
Gunham, Joseph to Sarah Williams 11-7-1857 (11-8-1857) O
Gunn, Bernard to Anna Fitzgerald 6-20-1861 (6-22-1861) Sh
Gunn, George W. to Geraldine H. Ann Sexton 3-2-1857 Sh
Gunn, John to Catharine Sexton 11-24-1855 (11-26-1855) Sh
Gunn, Levi to Violett Parker 9-19-1867 G
Gunnis, W. R. to Josephine Redford 3-6-1861 Sh
Gunnon, Samuel to Caroline Hendricks 3-19-1861 Sh
Gunson, John to Nancy Hamby 9-8-1853 (9-10-1853) O
Gunter, Claiborne to Elizabeth Flemming 8-23-1850 Sh
Gunter, Claiburne to Martha Caroline Dallas 10-26-1850 Sh
Gunter, Elias to Jane Prince 2-11-1856 We
Gunter, Isaac M. to Sophia J. Revel 11-12-1862 G
Gunter, J. W. to Martha E. Russell 8-20-1862 (no return) Cr
Gunter, James M. to Elender Jones 4-7-1828 (4-13-1828) Hr
Gunter, James to Lizzie E. Petit 5-18-1872 (5-22-1872) T
Gunter, Jesse to Eliza Powell 12-30-1846 Hn
Gunter, John to Christianna Kelley 9-16-1841 Hn
Gunti, Urs. to Filo Mina Walter 1-31-1860 Sh
Guon, H. L. to Annie Smith 4-14-1857 Sh
Gurat, James to Sarah Edwards 2-2-1839 Hn
Guren, Jacob S. to Melvina Bayless 12-10-1862 (no return) Hn
Gurganes, Abram to Mary Burrow 1-31-1859 (2-2-1859) G
Gurganus, James to Nancy M. Furgerson 7-12-1854 G
Gurley, Alfred to Zilpha C. Walker 3-1-1857 O
Gurley, H. to America W. Tyler 5-28-1840 G
Gurley, James H. to Frances E. Robertson 7-29-1848 (8-1-1848) Hr
Gurley, John R. to Susan P. Gregory 12-22-1856 (12-23-1856) Sh
Gurley, Lewis to Rachel Walker 12-14-1851 (12-24-1851) O
Gurley, Oliver G. to Eliza H. Stevenson 2-28-1856 Ma
Gurley, William H. to Polina C. George 11-12-1840 (11-18-1840) T
Gustan, E. to Agnus S. Fox 8-8-1865 (no return) Cr
Guter, Joseph W. to Lucy Ann Ritchie 9-2-1860 We
Gutheridge, James B. to Mary Jane Marberry 4-30-1846 Hn
Gutherie, Robert to Colorado Harris 11-4-1854 (11-5-1854) T
Guthery (Gutlege), Fredrick to Susan Schuffisser 1-21-1850 Sh
Guthery, Henry to Martha E. Barber 3-14-1865 (3-16-1865) O
Guthery, John W. to Susan Medkeff 2-22-1858 (no return) We
Guthery, W. E. to E. Beasley 2-27-1841 Be
Guthra, William J. to Elizabeth James 1-24-1842 (5-16-1842) F
Guthrey, G. A. to Roseanah McAutry 2-16-1863 (2-19-1863) O

Guthrey, Walker to Naoma Sharp 7-26-1848 O
Guthridge, John W. to Louisa Spivey 12-25-1834 Sh
Guthrie, Andrew to Mary Ann Taylor 4-12-1843 Ma
Guthrie, Daniel to Nancy Rainey 1-17-1848 (1-18-1848) Hr
Guthrie, Frederick C. to Sarah S. Autrey 2-27-1856 (2-28-1856) O
Guthrie, George H. to Mary Stone 1-16-1844 Cr
Guthrie, John to Etzira Evans 12-7-1869 Hy
Guthrie, Lea to Dona Wallace 3-5-1860 Sh
Guthrie, Orin to Eliza Davis 1-23-1829 Hr
Guthrie, R. A. to Martha Guy 9-25-1860 We
Guthrie, R. E. to M. J. Williamson 9-9-1851 Cr
Guthrie, Robert to Amanda Harrison 11-26-1855 (11-29-1855) T
Guthrie, Robert to Amanda J. Whitlock 10-4-1845 Hn
Guthrie, W. H. to Amanda Hitower 6-17-1871 (6-22-1871) T
Guthrie, William F. to Esther J. Lemonds 6-6-1858 Hn
Guthrie, William F. to Mary A. Guthrie 11-28-1852 Hn
Guthrie, William H. to Permelia J. Lackey 10-6-1853 Ma
Guthrie, jr., D. J. to Joanna Moss 11-21-1867 Hy
Guthry, Henry to Mary A. Mosier 1-16-1867 (1-17-1867) O
Guthry, Orrin to Nancy Boyd 1-20-1827 (1-21-1827) Hr
Guy, G. A. to M. F. Guy 3-20-1867 O
Guy, H. P. to C. A. Tomlinson 8-9-1854 (no return) F
Guy, H. P. to Martha L. J. Rogers 1-4-1865 F
Guy, H. W. to Susan Patrick 6-8-1881 (6-10-1881) L
Guy, Henry to Mary Williams 7-5-1870 (7-17-1870) F
Guy, James A. to Elizabeth Faust 2-1-1832 (2-7-1832) O
Guy, James to Sallie Webb 2-8-1870 G
Guy, John J. to Sarah Eliza Adams 5-7-1856 (5-22-1856) O
Guy, John L. to Elizabeth Craig 1-9-1862 O
Guy, John L. to Margaret E. Whiteside 8-26-1840 (8-27-1840) O
Guy, John L. to Margaret Whiteside 8-26-1840 (8-27-1840) O
Guy, John L. to Sarah Slider 11-15-1865 O
Guy, John to E. J. Tomlinson 7-3-1849 (7-11-1849) F
Guy, Nathaniel to Jane Nabors 11-4-1871 (11-5-1871) Ma
Guy, Nathaniel to Mary Ann Nabors 4-10-1869 (4-15-1869) Ma
Guy, William B. to Elizabeth Taylor 11-8-1851 (11-13-1851) O
Guy, William R. to Malinda J. Bird 3-13-1851 O
Guynn, G. W. to Mary Elizabeth Litton 9-15-1853 O
Guynn, Hugh R. to Julia Ann Litton 10-1-1856 O
Gwaltney, D. M. to Sarah C. Holland 5-13-1861 (no return) Dy
Gwaltney, J. H. to Nancy P. Wilson 6-19-1858 (6-20-1858) O
Gwaltney, W. T. to Stacy A. R. Fuller 4-28-1869 (no return) Dy
Gwaltney, William L. to Nancy J. Miller 6-14-1858 (6-17-1858) O
Gwin, James to Isabella S. Bobbitt 1-10-1853 (no return) F
Gwin, John E. to Nannie M. Brannock 9-10-1852 (no return) Cr
Gwin, W. M. to Mary J. Bell 12-19-1855 Cr
Gwin, Wm. H. to Louise E. Setters 12-18-1854 Cr
Gwinn, John E. to Medora Alice Persons 1-6-1868 (1-8-1868) Cr
Gwinn, Pearse to Betsey Gordan 12-23-1871 (no return) Cr B
Gwinn, Pearson to Amanda J. Temples 6-8-1863 Mn
Gwyn, Albert to Lavenia Brewster 12-23-1866 (12-27-1866) F B
Gwyn, Elijah to Mary Wilkerson 12-28-1868 (12-5?-1868) F B
Gwyn, H. L. to America J. Poor 2-4-1865 (2-6-1865) F
Gwyn, Hugh A. to Sally G. Dickinson 6-7-1852 (6-9-1852) Hr
Gwyn, R. R. to Elizabeth A. Smith 12-19-1842 Cr
Gwyn, R. R. to Mary C. Dickinson 11-1-1854 (11-9-1854) Hr
Gwyn, Richd. R. to S. E. Butterworth 11-10-1859 (11-15-1859) F
Gwynn, Henry C. to Julia L. Rich 6-25-1866 (6-28-1866) F
Gwynn, Henry C. to Susan Roberts 12-18-1865 (12-20-1865) F
Gwynn, James to Georgia Ann Jones 7-13-1866 (7-28-1866) F B
Gwynn, James to Viney Crawford 3-21-1870 (3-31-1870) F
Gwynn, N. to Susan Wilkerson 8-10-1866 (8-12-1866) F B
Gwynn, S. J. to S. M. Gwynn 1-28-1866 (1-30-1866) F
Gwynne, A. D. to Eliza A. Henderson 9-7-1859 Sh

Haas, Z. to Lizzie Dalton 4-8-1869 Ma
Hack, F. to May Devine 2-15-1859 Sh
Hack, John N. to Agatha Duttlingar 6-5-1854 Sh
Hacket, George W. to Susan E. Rogers 11-8-1845 (11-18-1845) F
Hackett, James to Bridget Flaherty 5-11-1861 Sh
Hackett, John to Mary Keilher 9-24-1864 Sh
Hacklin, Neverson to Susan Broadnax 12-26-1867 F B
Hackney, Joseph D. to Malinda Pirtle 11-15-1852 Hr
Hadbeck, R. A. to Nancy Sayles 2-1-1859 (no return) Cr
Hadden, John to Attie F. Welch 12-17-1868 G
Haddley, R. V. to Lyda A. Lancaster 7-27-1855 (7-30-1856) We
Haddon, James to Elizabeth Kollinsworth 1-25-1867 Ma
Haddoway, James F. to Isabela Murchison 4-23-1842 (4-24-1842) Ma
Haden (Haiden), Jacob M. to Elizabeth Bolling 9-2-1846 Sh
Haden, G. W. to Permelia J. Henderson 4-11-1866 G
Haden, J. S. to Isabella Armour 1-4-1844 (no return) F
Haden, R. M. to Laura J. Paulson 6-23-1869 (6-24-1869) F
Hadin, George W. to Rebecca Gee 11-6-1844 G
Hadley, Ike to Jenney Monroe 12-4-1865 (12-9-1865) F B
Hadley, L. P. to P. J. Starrett 3-11-1859 O
Hadson, E. to Susanna Golden 8-16-1842 (8-18-1842) Ma
Hadway, Jacob D. to Eliza Heistan 3-27-1849 Sh

Haegan (Haagan), Samuel F. to Margaret Beck (Berk) 11-23-1849 Sh
Haenar, Joseph to Nannie C. Taylor 4-2-1862 Sh
Haeslip, Johnathan J. to Suta A. Middleton 12-3-1855 (12-4-1855) G
Hafford, Bob to Martha Yancy 12-19-1878 Hy
Hafford, Coleman to Nannie Mitchell 11-5-1867 L
Hafford, F. T. to Mary F. Wright 6-18-1864 (6-19-1864) L
Hafford, John D. to Mirah J. Tucker 11-17-1868 L
Hafford, John to _____ 3-5-1831 Ma
Hafford, L. C. to Mary F. Prichard 9-14-1876 Dy
Hafford, W. D. F. to Mary Belle Palmer 3-8-1859 F
Hafford, William to Mary O. Bentley 9-17-1867 (9-20-1867) L
Hafley, James M. to Mary C. Burrough 2-1-1870 Ma
Haflin, Francis M. to Laura E. Henry 4-12-1866? (with 1862) Cr
Hafter, Charles W. to Martha E. Hafter 4-16-1872 T
Hagar, Benj. F. to Eliza J. Boothe 1-15-1855 (no return) L
Hagar, Beverly D. to Caroline Dalson 12-5-1857 Sh
Hagar, John A. to Emily Clay 1-29-1848 (1-30-1848) L
Hagar, Sterling A. to Mary Jane Huckabe 1-11-1847 (1-13-1847) L
Hagerty, Richard to Sallie Davis 8-3-1877 (no return) Hy
Haggard, James L. to Emily Smith 1-16-1839 (no return) Cr
Haggard, John to Nancy E. Cashow 3-7-1865 Mn
Hagler, Blount to Nancy Hagler 5-21-1866 Hn
Hagler, Cash to Sallie Hagler 5-20-1866 Hn
Hagler, Edmund J. to Martha A. Giner 8-26-1842 Hn
Hagler, Felix B. to Perneta H. Routon 1-19-1841 Hn
Hagler, J. J. to A. P. Hicks 12-27-1865 Hn
Hagler, Joel to Mary Neece 2-1-1854 Hn
Hagler, Lewis to Tennessee Puckett 12-13-1866 Hn B
Hagler, Manuel to M. y Williams 1-22-1867 Hn B
Hagler, Moses to Fan:.y Penick 12-27-1866 Hn B
Hagler, Richard T. to Mary M. Thomas 12-13-1859 We
Hagler, Robert to Sarah Rice 12-17-1868 (12-18-1868) Cr
Hagler, William L. to Caroline T. Gregson 2-21-1865 Hn
Hagler, William to Patty Foster 3-29-1863 Hn
Hagood, John M. C. to Parmelia M. McFarland 3-17-1842 Hn
Hahn, Emanuel to Rosa Hymen 4-7-1854 Sh
Hail, George W. to Cynthia Meadows 11-9-1830 O
Hail, John to Emeline J. Hail 2-4-1841 (2-7-1841) G
Hail, Shadrich to Amanda Brown 8-2-1837 (8-3-1837) Hr
Hail, Thomas to Elizabeth Luster 12-25-1832 (12-30-1832) G
Hail, W. J. to Margaret A. M. Boon 1-12-1870 (no return) Hy
Haile(Hails?), Fleming to Silphia Williams 5-25-1829 (5-1?-1829?) Hr
Hailey, Benjamin to Martha L. Bush 12-28-1854 Hn
Hailey, C. H. to Caroline Penny 5-18-1870 Ma
Hailey, Gastin to Margaret J. Todd 12-14-1859 (12-15-1859) Hr
Hailey, J. F. to Bettie Boone 2-1-1870 G
Hailey, J. M. to E. Jenken 10-5-1865 G
Hailey, James E. to Eliza Ann Inman 2-17-1857 O
Hailey, James H. to Margaret Irwin 3-11-1869 F
Hailey, James L. to Lidia S. McKee 10-22-1865 Mn
Hailey, John to Elizabeth Davis 12-24-1854 O
Hailey, L. S. to Elizabeth Sanders 12-22-1847 (no return) F
Hailey, R. L. to Rebecca J. Watt 10-21-1869 G
Hailey, Robt. to Frances McAdoo 3-29-1870 G
Hailey, S. B. to Lizzie (Mrs.) Young 12-2-1869 G
Hailey, S. B. to Martha J. Mullins 10-8-1863 G
Hailey, Thomas J. to Hannah W. Vaden 10-28-1858 G
Haily, G. W. to Carilile Osberne 11-29-1860 Be
Haily, John t. to Nancy Jones 12-23-1841 Hn
Haily, William to Mahaley Rushin 7-26-1841 (7-29-1841) G
Haines, John A. to Catharan E. Dale 10-15-1870 (10-16-1870) T
Haines, Samuel A. H. to Sallie J. Plott 3-18-1862 (3-20-1862) Sh
Hainey, Peter to Frances Jones 7-13-1862 We
Hainline, Benjamin R. to Nancy Chesher 7-27-1847 (7-29-1847) Hr
Hainline, Benjamin to Marcella Frances Drake 6-13-1857 (6-16-1857) Hr
Hainline, Jacob to Mary Jane D. Muse 12-26-1839 (1-16-1840) Hr
Hains, Armstead to Nancy Currie 12-23-1870 Hy
Hains, James B. to Martha Arnold 9-29-1852 Sh
Hains, James T. to Mary C. Gentry 12-14-1831 G
Hair, S. W. to M. C. Clouch 10-11-1861 Mn
Hairsten, J. N. to Jennie F. Adair 2-27-1861 Sh
Haise, Wesley M. to Mary Arington 10-2-1856 Cr
Haislip, G. H. to Martha J. Brown 1-22-1877 (1-24-1877) L
Haislip, G. M. D. to Nancy M. Beasley 9-18-1866 O
Haislip, G. W. to M. E. Duncan 7-4-1861 O
Haislip, George W. to Elizabeth Allen 7-21-1834 O
Haislip, Jonathan to R. R. Culbertson 9-3-1846 O
Haislip, L. to L. P. Brown 10-14-1867 (10-15-1867) O
Haislip, Laborne to Jincy Ann Pittman 12-9-1871 (12-10-1871) L
Haislip, William to Mary A. Malone 12-10-1847 (12-14-1847) G
Haislip, William to Mary Ann Holoman 10-24-1866 L
Haislip, William to Tabitha Allen 2-29-1832 (4-7-1832) O
Haist, David to Rebecca Varner 8-10-1843 G
Halaway, Henry to Ann Eliza Twisdale 12-26-1859 T
Halay, W. to E. Bremer 11-19-1841 Be
Halberstadt, August to Hulda Busse 4-27-1861 Sh
Halbert, R. W. to Anna G. Goff 11-17-1864 Sh

Halcomb, Benj. to Eugenia Moore 6-8-1871 (no return) Hy
Halcomb, Nevell to Jennett F. Moore 6-8-1871 (no return) Hy
Halcombe, James to Isora E. Moore 12-11-1872 Hy
Hale (Hail), John B. to Salley A. Madry 12-29-1829 Sh
Hale (Hail), Richard J. to Mary E. Madry 8-5-1820 Sh
Hale (Hak), Christian to Barbara Grider 12-21-1849 Sh
Hale, Alexander to Martha Sanders 7-22-1831 (7-?-1831) Hr
Hale, Bernard to Emma Brewer 12-20-1867 (12-28-1867) F B
Hale, C. C. to Martha A. Carr 1-19-1861 Sh
Hale, Daniel to Ellen Bradshaw 2-12-1880 Dy
Hale, E. W. to Martha Jordian 11-23-1839 (11-28-1839) G
Hale, G. W. to Ruth Jourdan 8-30-1864 (9-1-1864) L
Hale, H. C. to Rebecca T. Porter 10-14-1864 (10-16-1864) Cr
Hale, Henry to Isabella Bell 9-25-1878 (10-16-1879?) L B
Hale, Henry to Sarah Ann Sartor 1-26-1853 G
Hale, James B. to Mary E. Savage 10-18-1851 (10-30-1851) Hr
Hale, James G. to Catherine Horten 12-20-1857 We
Hale, James J. to Mary C. Sedberry 6-23-1855 Cr
Hale, James R. to Isabella Corum 11-16-1845 (11-18-1845) O
Hale, Jo. S. to Ida M. Keller 2-2-1882 L
Hale, John B. to Mary Corum 11-11-1851 (11-12-1851) O
Hale, John C. to Pamelia W. Wardlaw 1-27-1847 (1-28-1847) L
Hale, John T. to Martha A. L. Boon 9-1-1861 G
Hale, John to Rebecca Gibson 5-30-1839 Cr
Hale, Joseph J. J. to Manerva J. Walker 8-15-1849 (8-16-1849) G
Hale, Joseph P. to Susan Chandler 4-24-1850 G
Hale, Julius to Winie C. Harland 10-7-1858 G
Hale, Madison to Martha Cribbs 9-25-1855 (9-27-1855) G
Hale, N. L. to Margaret C. Sims 3-21-1858 We
Hale, Nathaniel M. to Martha C. Robinson 2-2-1865 G
Hale, Ornal to Ann Green (Gunn?) 4-4-1874 (no return) L B
Hale, R. A. to S. F. Phillips 7-14-1858 We
Hale, Robert to Amandy C. Goodloe 7-29-1856 G
Hale, Robert to Fannie Gooch 9-23-1842 Cr
Hale, Robert to Mattie Crockett 1-15-1876 (2-17-1876) L
Hale, S. H. to Emily Cunningham 8-6-1865 G
Hale, W. B. to Mary M. Pritchard 2-14-1861 G
Hale, W. E. to E. J. Waddle 12-2-1866 G
Hale, W. F. to Mary Petty 4-21-1863 Mn
Hale, W. H. to Mary Ann Wade 11-21-1848 Hn
Hale, William C. to Lucy L. Parker 3-23-1843 (3-26-1843) G
Hale, William J. to Frances A. McKelvey 10-18-1856 (10-21-1856) G
Hale, Wilson Y. to Tennessee Collins 10-22-1855 (10-23-1855) O
Hale, Wilson Y. to Vandelia R. Barham 12-11-1844 O
Hale, Wm. C. to Jame Oglesby 3-16-1848 Sh
Haleman, S. R. to Martha P. Walker 4-13-1854 Hn
Hales, Henry to Mary F. Gallien 9-22-1852 G
Haley, Alex to Chany Bond 4-11-1878 Hy
Haley, Benjamin to Biddey Stroud 12-18-1839 (12-19-1839) O
Haley, D. S. to Mary J. Hilliard 2-15-1853 (no return) F
Haley, David L. to Jane Hicks 2-17-1830 (2-12-1830) G
Haley, E. P. M. C. to Minerva J. Lankford 6-8-1851 Hn
Haley, Edward to Jane C. Hart 1-5-1859 Hn
Haley, Edward to Jans Hardister 9-17-1833 (9-19-1833) G
Haley, Franklin to Tabitha J. Cox 9-4-1858 (9-5-1858) Hr
Haley, George W. to Harriet E. Threadgill 9-20-1867 (no return) Cr
Haley, George to Purnetta A. Berry 3-20-1852 (3-25-1852) G
Haley, H. S. to Nancy E. Cocke 12-16-1867 (no return) Cr
Haley, Henry to Sarah Smith 12-27-1872 T
Haley, James A. to Martha S. Anderson 12-30-1868 Be
Haley, James to Johanna McCarty 11-27-1858 (11-28-1858) Sh
Haley, James to Martha J. Kelly 10-2-1849 (no return) F
Haley, James to Mary Ann Cogan 1-8-1864 (1-10-1864) Sh
Haley, John A. to Elizabeth Kirsey 2-14-1831 G
Haley, John W. to Eliza Jane Mooring 4-1-1850 (4-4-1850) Ma
Haley, John W. to Susan E. Haley 12-15-1858 (12-16-1858) G
Haley, John to Sarah A. Carroll 3-2-1859 (3-3-1859) O
Haley, Joseph to Dora McLemore 10-5-1869 (10-7-1869) Cr
Haley, R. K. to Nancy E. Ballard 11-26-1861 Be
Haley, Robt. A. to Mary E. Harrell 10-17-1860 Dy
Haley, S. F. to M. S. Fielder 10-26-1867 (no return) Dy
Haley, Sterling B. to Elizabeth Massey 12-25-1832 G
Haley, Sterling to Nancy Foster 1-27-1851 (1-30-1851) G
Haley, Thomas to Catharine Carow 8-4-1854 (8-6-1854) Sh
Haley, William to Amanda Bushart 11-11-1854 Hn
Halfacre, Ben to Lucinde Golding 4-4-1867 (no return) L B
Halfacre, Benjamin to Charlotte Tanner 11-20-1884 L
Halfacre, George to Bettie Richardson 12-4-1876 L
Halfacre, J. F. to N. C. Tucker 1-2-1883 (1-3-1883) L
Halfacre, William to Sarah Clay 10-27-1870 L
Halford, J. R. to E. C. Cary 2-21-1861 G
Halford, James M. to Rebecca E. Kimbro 2-9-1847 G
Halford, Jas. M. to Eliza A. H. Burton 10-30-1837 (10-31-1837) G
Halford, John E. to Rebecca M. Rigsby 3-1-1841 (3-9-1841) G
Halford, Joseph W. to Elizabeth M. Smally 12-19-1840 (12-23-1840) G
Halford, N. W. to M. L. Butram 3-8-1866 G
Halford, William M. to Frances M. Wilks 10-1-1842 (10-2-1842) G

Haliburton, Benj. E. to Sallie C. Nixon 10-15-1861 (10-16-1861) L
Haliburton, D. F. to S. A. Flowers 2-25-1865 G
Haliburton, Epps to Harriett Coltart 2-24-1868 Hy
Hall(Hale), D. W. to Catharine Childress 6-19-1837 (6-20-1837) Hr
Hall, A. A. to M. C. Morris 6-30-1870 G
Hall, A. B. to Mary Ann Wersham 3-27-1885 (no return) L
Hall, A. C. to Mariah L. Clark 5-8-1846 T
Hall, A. F. to R. F. Leonard 1-9-1878 (1-10-1878) Dy
Hall, A. G. to Adaline Givens 2-24-1852 (no return) Hn
Hall, A. J. to Jane Finch 8-16-1873 (8-18-1873) Dy
Hall, A. M. to Parthenia Wilburn 3-28-1866 Hn
Hall, A. R. to Melvina George 12-13-1870 (12-15-1870) Cr
Hall, Aga to Bashaby Melton 9-21-1841 Be
Hall, Albert A. to Dorthey E. Whitaker 11-6-1826 (11-14-1826) Hr
Hall, Alex to Dilcey Douglas 2-14-1866 T
Hall, Alexander to Mary E. Gobble 12-20-1858 (12-29-1858) O
Hall, Alfred to Elizabeth Ramsey 9-27-1862 O
Hall, Alfred to Matilda McDonald 3-6-1849 (no return) Hn
Hall, Allen C. to Mollie E. Howard 3-22-1864 (no return) Cr
Hall, Andrew J. to Sue M. Taylor 5-16-1866 Ma
Hall, Andrew to Butie Jackson 10-31-1842 Hn
Hall, Andrew to Lucretia Matheny 6-17-1851 (no return) Hn
Hall, Andy to Frances Smith 6-6-1873 (6-14-1873) T
Hall, Andy to Rebecca Patterson 10-20-1858 G B
Hall, Arnold to Melinda Hardy 11-15-1866 (no return) Hy
Hall, Benjamin M. to Martha A. Sumerow 12-5-1860 (no return) L
Hall, Benjamin W. to Minerva E. J. Cavitt 10-4-1841 (no return) Hn
Hall, Bennett G. to Mary E. Randolph 1-20-1845 (1-21-1845) G
Hall, Billy to Mary Robertson 4-1-1867 (4-3-1867) T
Hall, Burton to Jane Cherry 11-30-1844 G
Hall, Calvin to E. W. Cherry 5-21-1840 Be
Hall, Caswell P. to Tennessee Thompson 2-17-1849 (2-22-1849) G
Hall, Charles K. to Maria B. (Mrs.) Sannoner 8-3-1864 Sh
Hall, Charles to Susannah Shoemaker 11-17-1869 G
Hall, Claudius B. to Mary Eliza Flowers 4-11-1859 (4-13-1859) Ma
Hall, Coleman to Amanda Yarbro 10-15-1873 (10-16-1873) T
Hall, D. B. to Sarah E. Avery 9-11-1858 G
Hall, David to Nancy Morris 5-7-1860 (4?-8-1860) G
Hall, Dennis to Margaret Dickinson 9-7-1867 (9-8-1867) F B
Hall, E. A. G. to Elizabeth J. Wood 1-15-1873 (1-16-1873) Cr
Hall, E. H. to R. Ramispuger 3-14-1850 Hn
Hall, E. M. to Cornelia Faulkner 11-28-1882 (11-29-1882) L
Hall, E. W. to Elizabeth Cates 10-25-1851 (no return) Cr
Hall, Edward D. to Hetty (Mrs.) Madry 5-17-1828 Sh
Hall, Edward to Mary Ann Perry 9-3-1857 Hn
Hall, Edward to Sidney Haynes 10-18-1840 Cr
Hall, Elias S. to Amanda L. Flowers 8-23-1860 G
Hall, Erastus D. to Fannie O. Carrigan 7-15-1873 L
Hall, F. W. to Elizabeth C. Duncan 8-14-1855 (8-15-1855) G
Hall, Farris to Elizabeth Williams 1-16-1874 T
Hall, Felix Josiah to Sarah Ann Elizabeth Williams 12-13-1856 (12-14-1856) Ma
Hall, Frank to Mary Catten 6?-15-1867 (6-16-1867) T
Hall, Geo. W. to Laura] Sherril 12-29-1865 (1-3-1866) T
Hall, George H. to Margarett Thompson 9-13-1834 Hr
Hall, George M. to Mary J. E. Hailey 1-11-1858 (no return) Cr
Hall, George W. to Martha N.? Fletcher 2-14-1864 G
Hall, George to Feebe Calhoun 10-29-1870 T
Hall, Green to Eliza Jane Blankenship 10-30-1840 (11-4-1840) G
Hall, H. W. to Josephine Brooks 10-2-1860 We
Hall, Henry W. to Martha B. Lavier 5-15-1867 (5-16-1867) F
Hall, Henry to Caroline Green 1-7-1869 T
Hall, Henry to Lean Atkins 1-15-1877 (no return) Dy
Hall, Henry to Martha Williams 3-25-1870 (no return) Dy
Hall, Hinton to Richard Jane Sneed 1-20-1842 Dy
Hall, Hiriam to Sarah M. Holderfield 7-26-1843 (7-27-1843) Ma
Hall, Isaac to Nancy Willingham 9-21-1864 Sh
Hall, J. B. to L. D. Hannings 10-28-1858 We
Hall, J. C. to E. B. Crider 12-17-1872 (12-18-1872) Cr
Hall, J. C. to Mary Jane DeMent 4-14-1862 Sh
Hall, J. F. to C. E. Ligon 2-4-1873 (2-9-1873) T
Hall, J. H. to Ellen Scates 2-8-1855 We
Hall, J. L. to S. J. Davis 5-9-1878 (5-12-1878) Dy
Hall, J. M. to Susan C. Minton 7-10-1861 (6-11-1861) Dy
Hall, J. R. to C. A. Russ no date (with Mar 1866) Cr
Hall, J. S. to E. F. Smith 12-7-1868 (12-8-1868) Dy
Hall, J. W. to Caroline _____ 1-15-1850 O
Hall, J. W. to E. L. Featherston 3-8-1870 (no return) Dy
Hall, J. W. to L. McFarland 12-9-1867 (12-11-1868?) G
Hall, J. W. to Matilda J. Curtis 12-15-1873 (12-18-1873) Dy
Hall, J.R. to Mary J. Cristenberry 11-16-1868 (no return) Hy
Hall, Jackson to Caroline Palmer 1-3-1839 Cr
Hall, James A. to Martha E. McClary 4-4-1843 Cr
Hall, James Dup___ to Adelade Rachel Henning 10-5-1870 L
Hall, James F. to Charlotte Henson 4-22-1860 Sh
Hall, James G. to Elizabeth Thetford 2-8-1834 (2-16-1834) G
Hall, James H. M. to A. K. Rhodes 4-22-1838 F
Hall, James H. to Adalade Bradshaw 12-14-1864 (12-15-1864) Dy

Hall, James H. to Mary Ann Lee 3-12-1842 (no return) Hn
Hall, James Iredell to Sarah Irene Lemmon 12-26-1849 (12-27-1849) T
Hall, James J. to Mary E. Hall 1-2-1866 T
Hall, James M. to Mary Ann Gibson 11-26-1846 Cr
Hall, James N. to Ellen Morgan 4-4-1860 Ma
Hall, James R. to Mary F. Green 11-17-1868 (11-18-1868) Dy
Hall, James T. to Louisa M. Standley 1-20-1861 G
Hall, James T. to Rhoda Ethridge 4-18-1849 (4-19-1849) G
Hall, James W. to Eliza B. Carnes 3-16-1840 Hr
Hall, James to Julia Ann Smith 1-29-1872 (no return) Dy
Hall, James to Lucy High? 2-11-1846 (no return) Hn
Hall, Jas. J. to Mary E. Hall 1-2-1866 T
Hall, Jeames to Martha J. Osteen 1-22-1878 L
Hall, Joe to M. Larrimoore 12-17-1874 T
Hall, Joel to Sarah Ann Elizabeth Ogbourne (Oghowin) 5-20-1845 Sh
Hall, John B. to Eliza Clinton 9-27-1828 Ma
Hall, John G. to Ermine Munford 5-29-1872 T
Hall, John Green to Patti W. Rose 12-21-1871 T
Hall, John H. to Mary Sneed 1-4-1854 Cr
Hall, John I. to Susan Purcell 4-9-1845 Hn
Hall, John J. to Margaret J. Sharp 3-15-1841 (3-18-1841) T
Hall, John N. to Hollen Applewight Green 3-5-1842 (3-8-1842) T
Hall, John P. to Columbia E. Laster 4-11-1877 (4-12-1877) Dy
Hall, John R. to Harriett Bell 9-26-1845 (no return) Hn
Hall, John R. to Nancy C. Holmes 4-23-1868 G
Hall, John W. to Lucy A. Givens 12-21-1853 Hn
Hall, John to Annette Williamson 6-23-1866 F B
Hall, John to Harriett J A. Maupin 8-16-1860 Hn
Hall, John to Sarah Massey 9-12-1857 Be
Hall, John to Susan Buckley 5-16-1844 T
Hall, Josiah to Martha S. Flake 6-28-1849 (no return) Hn
Hall, Josiah to Mary Jane Laney 4-22-1854 (4-23-1854) Hr
Hall, Julius M. to Mulindy Cole 3-28-1838 G
Hall, Julius to Parthena Holland 2-23-1844 G
Hall, Laban to A. P. Carr 12-21-1857 Hr
Hall, Leroy to Mary Wright 6-21-1876 Hy
Hall, Lewis W. to Mattie W. Cochrane 3-5-1868 Ma
Hall, Lycurgus to Sarah E. Curlin 11-1-1872 (11-27-1872) O
Hall, M. A. to Lovey A. Turner 1-25-1869 (no return) Dy
Hall, M. W. to Mary A. E. Barnes? 5-27-1858 (6-10-1858) Hr
Hall, M. W. to Nancy T. Hadden 4-27-1861 (4-29-1861) Hr
Hall, Mack to Mollie Bowers 9-1-1877 Hy
Hall, Martain to Elizabeth Williams 10-8-1870 T
Hall, Melford to Rebecca Curtis 4-29-1832 Ma
Hall, Perry M. to Margaret Litsinger 1-21-1847 Cr
Hall, Peter E. to Elizabeth E. Fry 8-16-1860 T
Hall, Peyton to Sophronia Tweedle 12-29-1874 (12-28?-1874) T
Hall, Prescott to Martha W. Powell 11-21-1849 Hn
Hall, R. J. to L. C. J. Smith 2-26-1881 (2-3-1881) L
Hall, R. S. to A. E. Stitt 11-10-1858 (11-11-1858) T
Hall, R. W. to Martha C. Thomas 1-10-1843 Hn
Hall, Richard to Rutha Hopkins 10-21-1841 G
Hall, Robert F. to Alcy Brener Eliz. Brinkley 1-21-1868 Be
Hall, Robert H. to A. S. Rust 4-18-1864 (4-20-1864) Cr
Hall, Robt. P. to Mary M. Autry 11-7-1871 (11-8-1871) Cr
Hall, S. R. to Marion M. Lowe 4-19-1856 (4-20-1856) Sh
Hall, Seth to Mary J. Courtley 5-18-1864 Dy
Hall, Sidney to Elizabeth Smith 4-4-1870 (4-10-1870) T
Hall, Simeon? to Bettie Campbell 8-16-1881 L
Hall, Solomon S. to Lenora J. Thetford 3-25-1868 (no return) Dy
Hall, Spencer to M. C. (Mrs.) Givens 8-2-1866 G
Hall, T. W. to E. I. McMelon 8-25-1866 O
Hall, T. W. to Margaret E. Dickey 1-22-1868 (no return) Dy
Hall, Thomas E. to Sarah Killet 2-16-1871 Dy
Hall, Thomas E. to Susan Clark 3-22-1848 Hn
Hall, Thomas L. to C. E. Guiheni? (Gresham?) 8-29-1877 L
Hall, Thomas P. to Martha E. Orgain 2-11-1840 Hn
Hall, Thomas? to 'Amanda? Sanford 1-20-1869 (1-21-1869) T
Hall, Thos. J. to Betsy Brown 1-21-1857 Cr
Hall, Travis E. to Elenor M. Turner 9-27-1850 G
Hall, W. A. to Caifa? Frances Akin 2-5-1869 (no return) Dy
Hall, W. A. to M. E. King 2-11-1867 (2-12-1867) Cr
Hall, W. H. to L. C. Brewer 1-29-1877 (no return) Dy
Hall, W. J. to Nancy Pearce 4-16-1868 G
Hall, W. L. to Susan R. Hansel? 2-14-1852 (no return) F
Hall, W. M. to Emma Matthews 2-3-1875 O
Hall, W. M. to Jane Reynolds 8-1-1871 (8-2-1871) Dy
Hall, W. R. to M. A. Bradley 12-1-1857 G
Hall, W. R. to Mattie Farmer 9-23-1862 G
Hall, W. S. to Mary J. Hill 12-12-1855 We
Hall, W. S. to S. J. Nelson 12-19-1861 Hr
Hall, Warren to Rebecca Hampton 11-10-1877 (no return) Dy
Hall, Wash to Catharine Anderson 3-2-1874 T
Hall, Wells W. to Frances Salsberry 1-27-1865 (1-28-1865) Dy
Hall, Will to Sally Mitchell 1-31-1855 Hn
Hall, William F. to Julia Jones 12-21-1859 Sh
Hall, William F. to Sarah A. Raffity 4-9-1840 (no return) Hn

Hall, William H. to Elizabeth Arnold 8-4-1861 G
Hall, William H. to Virginia A. Joleff 4-16-1847 G
Hall, William J. to Eliza W. Collier 7-9-1850 (7-10-1850) T
Hall, William L. to Armelia Patton 12-11-1847 (12-23-1847) F
Hall, William M. to Laura McFadden 11-31-1865 G
Hall, William Minor to Sarah Rebecca Holmes 8-7-1849 (8-8-1849) T
Hall, William W. to Mary C. Koen 8-13-1861 (8-14-1861) Sh
Hall, William to Levisa Duncan (Dilbeck) 11-4-1840 O
Hall, William to Lidia Hall 1-5-1829 G
Hall, William to Lizzie Wood 10-13-1882 (10-16-1882) L
Hall, William to Nancy Elmiria? Barker 5-7-1842 (5-8-1842) Hr
Hall, William to Sarah E. Fly 12-31-1838 Ma
Hall, William to Sarah Halton 2-27-1830 (3-20-1831?) Ma
Hall, Willis W. to S. A. E. Kellow 9-30-1868 G
Hall, Wm. R. to Harriett A.? Brinley 1-19-1861 (1-24-1861) Cr
Hall, Wm. to Gracy Hanlin 12-30-1871 T
Hall, Wm. to Martha Sherill 10-14-1865 (2?-14-1865) T
Hall, Wm. to Martha Sherril 10-14-1865 T
Hallaran, Michael to Margaret Gorman 1-18-1854 (1-19-1854) Sh
Hallaway, James K. to Margarett Gregory 7-31-1857 We
Haller, D. C. to Alice Crook 4-11-1857 Sh
Halleran, William to Bridget Masco 5-14-1860 (5-15-1860) Sh
Halley, Creed P. to Mary W. (Mrs.) Spencer 7-18-1839 F
Halliburton, Albert to Isadora Lucas 12-18-1884 (12-19-1884) L
Halliburton, Auther to Selinia Currin 10-13-1871 Hy
Halliburton, Ben to Eliza Henning 2-5-1885 (no return) L
Halliburton, Bill to Eliza Green 10-9-1877 (10-10-1877) L
Halliburton, Daniel G. to Martha Leggett 1-18-1871 (1-19-1871) L
Halliburton, David to Babe Allen 12-28-1882 L
Halliburton, Elias to Martha J. Walker 4-2-1875 (no return) Hy
Halliburton, George Washington to Mollie Boyd (Bond?) 1-11-1873 (1-13-1873) L B
Halliburton, Haskins to Anna Greer 2-27-1873 Hy
Halliburton, Henry to Jane Scott 2-14-1874 L B
Halliburton, Isaac to Bettie Gause 12-18-1872 (no return) L B
Halliburton, J. E. to Sada Halliburton 1-31-1882 (2-2-1882) L
Halliburton, James to Isabella Horton 1-30-1886 (2-4-1886) L
Halliburton, John T. to Mary J. Rush 8-2-1875 (8-3-1875) L
Halliburton, John W. to Cordelia Parr 12-22-1884 (12-24-1884) L
Halliburton, John to Matilda Parks 9-26-1869 G B
Halliburton, Lindsey to Mollie Lee 1-6-1886 (no return) L
Halliburton, Martin to Edney Flowers 10-23-1841 (10-26-1841) G
Halliburton, Paul M. to Tabitha A. Thompson 10-28-1857 L
Halliburton, R. H. to Lou Taylor 8-31-1870 (9-1-1870) Dy
Halliburton, Robert to Hannah Nixon 12-24-1885 (12-28-1885) L
Halliburton, S. G. to Mary V. Hann 12-26-1868 (no return) Hy
Halliburton, Tinsly W. to Mary K. Davis 2-23-1843 Ma
Halliburton, Ute S. to Ann Travis 7-23-1855 G
Halliburton, W. A. to Mary E. Nixon 10-20-1868 (10-21-1868) L
Halliburton, W. R. to Jennie Boyd 2-9-1874 (2-10-1874) L
Halliburton, Wesley to Julia Dangerfield 5-15-1884 L
Halliburton, William to Mary F. Allen 11-19-1856 G
Halliburton, Wm. to Ann McKinnie 5-5-1877 (no return) Hy
Halliburton, Wyatt to Laura Bradford 6-2-1877 (6-7-1877) L
Hallies, C. A. to T. A. Ross 7-7-1858 We
Halliman, Granville to Isabella Reynolds 8-2-1854 Hn
Halliwell, James to Lucinda Reams 8-18-1857 (8-19-1857) Sh
Hallmark, John D. to Elizabeth S. J. Norwood 11-1-1850 Cr
Hallmark, John to Sarah Ann Barnes 9-24-1865 Be
Hallmark, Lewis to Rachel Hale 12-6-1843 Be
Hallmark, W. G. to Martha J. Barnes 3-6-1872 (no return) Cr
Halloway, Saml. F. to Harriett Ford 11-9-1847 F
Hallows, Robert to Sally Bevan 12-13-1860 Sh
Hallum, Abner J. to Martha L. J. Cody 12-23-1851 Hn
Hallum, Charles to Mary Fergason 7-31-1845 Sh
Hallum, James to Manerva Mathews 8-24-1845 Sh
Hallum, John to Virginia W. Snead 11-26-1853 Sh
Hallum, Morris to Sudie Ray 8-26-1879 (8-28-1879) Dy
Hallum, Relix Grundy to Patsey Safroney Quinaly 10-22-1846 (10-26-1846) T
Hallum, William to Ellen Queen Ann Hill 5-10-1855 Sh
Hallum, Wm. D. to Ardelia Barham 1-3-1851 Cr
Hallums, James to Susan Walker 3-29-1861 Sh
Hally, D. T. P. to Margaret A. Revell 8-1-1856 (8-5-1856) Sh
Hally, Edward W. to Catharine Fitzgibbon 9-13-1859 Sh
Hally, Michael to Mary O'Neal 6-18-1863 Sh
Hally, P. C. to Margaret C. Brown 5-18-1853 (5-31-1853) Sh
Hallyburton, John T. to Virginia H. Keller 1-26-1858 (2-3-1858) L
Halmark, Miles to Jane Norman 2-7-1839 (no return) Cr
Halpin, Michael to Catharine Riley 5-2-1857 (5-3-1857) Sh
Halstead, Thos. J. to Eliza Ann Allen 9-2-1855 Hn
Haltom, B. F. to Elizabeth Barrett 9-24-1856 Hr
Haltom, Benj. F. to Julian Suggs 12-15-1855 (12-19-1855) Hr
Haltom, Benjamin F. to Nancy Blair 10-30-1850 (10-31-1850) Ma
Haltom, Edmund to Sarah Francis Davis 12-17-1856 (12-18-1856) Ma
Haltom, Ezekiel to Rebecca Moore 12-10-1855 (12-18-1855) Ma
Haltom, John S. to Susan E. Young 9-24-1853 (10-6-1853) Ma
Haltom, N. P. to Martha J. Henson 10-10-1861 (10-13-1861) Hr

Haltom, William B. to Catherine Johnson 3-3-1853 Ma
Haltom, William G. to Mary Ann Wrenn 2-19-1839 Ma
Halton, Eli to Nancy J. Garrett 11-10-1856 (11-12-1856) Hr
Haly, Calvin A. to Charlotte Gentry 7-2-1864 Sh
Haly, William to Nancy Vann 1-27-1845 Hn
Ham (Haines?), Thomas I. to Martha Fisher 2-1-1838 F
Ham, David F. to Harriett A. Moore 7-11-1840 (7-17-1840) Hr
Ham, Edward S. to Sarah Pate 3-16-1847 O
Ham, G. B. to Elizabeth Keithly 1-2-1866 O
Ham, G. W. to Martha P. Fisher 1-4-1841 (1-7-1841) F
Ham, James M. to R. C. Farley 3-9-1850 (no return) F
Ham, James to Mary Crafton 10-18-1851 (10-21-1851) G
Ham, Mansfield to Julia Ann Clayton 9-24-1836 Sh
Ham, William to Maria Moore 12-3-1850 (12-4-1850) Hr
Ham, Willie to Susan S. Moore 5-1-1844 (5-2-1844) Hr
Hamack, Thomas to Margratt Warren 4-26-1838 (4-28-1838) G
Hamalton, Joseph S. to Julia Ann (Mrs.) Lemmons 11-1-1852 Sh
Hamberger, Hosea to Arcada Brewer 4-1-1857 Be
Hamberlin, Thomas A. to Margaret V. Taylor 3-17-1864 Sh
Hamblin, Benjamin to Susannah Newton 12-18-1831 (12-23-1831) Hr
Hamblin, Jackson to Mary E. Harris 7-25-1861 We
Hamblin, William to Elizabeth Croslin 7-23-1824 Hr
Hambrick, F. M. to Tabitha Fowlkes 11-15-1866 (no return) Dy
Hamby, J. H. to M. A. Loyd 5-24-1873 (5-25-1873) T
Hamby, Robert J. to Louisa V. Cooke 3-5-1838 Hn
Hamby, Sam to Luada Johnston 11-13-1870 G
Hamel, James W. to Sarah C. Davis 11-27-1872 Cr
Hamell, W. H. to R. A. Bell 1-20-1869 Hy
Hamelton, William to Narcissa Caroline Smitheal 9-11-1867 T
Hamer, A. M. to Laura J. Hardison 11-29-1858 Hr
Hamer, A. M. to Sarah Ann Janes 12-2-1854 (12-5-1854) Hr
Hamer, Milton J. to Mary Ann Shepperd 11-7-1838 (11-8-1838) Hr
Hamer, P. O. to Mary J. Moss 1-18-1854 Hr
Hamer, Thomas to Sarah Mask 11-10-1856 (11-19-1856) Hr
Hamer, W. R. to Caroline Hall 7-25-1854 Be
Hamerick, Saml. to Juliana Wright 3-13-1847 (3-16-1847) F
Hamerle, William to Christiana Fricke 4-21-1851 Sh
Hames, C. F. to Martha E. Bryant 2-27-1844 G
Hamet, Sam'l. to Mary C. Myeyrs 8-7-1858 (8-8-1858) O
Hamett, Andy to M. A. Pearce 4-17-1872 (no return) Cr B
Hamil, A. B. A. to Mary Lindsey 7-18-1867 L
Hamil, A. to Isabella Lott 12-26-1882 L
Hamil, A. to N. E. Brown 3-21-1877 (3-22-1877) L
Hamil, John A. to Frances M. Chambers 12-18-1867 (no return) Hy
Hamil, R. L. to Lucinda E. McGavock 4-17-1862 (no return) Hy
Hamilton, A. B. to M. J. Hare 2-6-1871 (2-7-1871) Dy
Hamilton, A. I. to Laura Naylen 1-1-1867 (1-3-1867) O
Hamilton, Alexander to Emily Huddleston 10-16-1852 (10-17-1852) Hr
Hamilton, Ben to Lucy Lockhart 2-21-1881 (2-24-1881) L
Hamilton, Clay to Mary Camden 8-15-1869 G B
Hamilton, David W. to Prudance Newhouse 12-14-1846 (12-15-1846) G
Hamilton, E. E. to Ann Eliza Poyner 1-7-1858 Hn
Hamilton, E. E. to Tennessee Poyner 5-9-1854 Hn
Hamilton, Frank B. to Dinebia Walsh 11-18-1869 Ma
Hamilton, George F. to Martha McLoad 11-17-1853 (no return) F
Hamilton, George to Mollie Isbell 6-11-1868 (6-13-1868) O B
Hamilton, Gilbert to Frances J. Cooper 9-17-1868 G B
Hamilton, H. C. to R. A. Browder 10-2-1863 (10-4-1863) O
Hamilton, H. M. to M. C. Hamilton 7-16-1855 (7-17-1855) G
Hamilton, Henry to Eliza Hayley? 1-18-1871 T
Hamilton, Henry to Polina S. Phillips 11-26-1859 We
Hamilton, Ishmael to Mary Williams 9-11-1838 (9-13-1838) O
Hamilton, J. A. to Mary Ann Nail 9-16-1837 (9-19-1837) Hr
Hamilton, J. H. to M. A. McCoy 11-13-1866 G
Hamilton, J. J. to V. A. Pitts 1-22-1879 (1-23-1879) Dy
Hamilton, J. R. B. to Martha L. S. Carroll 2-11-1854 (no return) Cr
Hamilton, J. R. to H. J. Bird 2-23-1869 (2-25-1869) T
Hamilton, James B. to Annie L. Fisher 10-24-1867 T
Hamilton, James F. to Louisa Moore 4-15-1853 (4-21-1853) O
Hamilton, James G. to Mary Jane Kirk 7-22-1869 Cr
Hamilton, James M. to Sarah Sweatt 8-15-1853 Hn
Hamilton, James N. to Zepharum Milstead 9-5-1862 Hn
Hamilton, James to Elizabeth Breeding 1-2-1830 M
Hamilton, James to Maria Cross 7-29-1882 (7-30-1881) L
Hamilton, James to Mary Mills 7-19-1845 (7-20-1845) Hr
Hamilton, James to Nancy Burney 10-6-1856 Hr
Hamilton, John W. to Elizabeth J. Jones 9-20-1852 (9-21-1852) O
Hamilton, John to Elly Williamson 3-11-1842 Cr
Hamilton, John to Nancy Grantham 9-24-1842 (9-25-1842) Hr
Hamilton, Joseph R. to Mary Smith 6-20-1838 Sh
Hamilton, Joseph to Mailha J. Rogers 10-26-1848 Cr
Hamilton, Joseph to Margarett McClary 8-3-1830 G
Hamilton, L. W. to M. R. Byrd 2-15-1870 (2-20-1870) T
Hamilton, M. C. to Mollie F. Moore 12-18-1876 (12-21-1876) Dy
Hamilton, O. E. to M. E. Rhodes 10-26-1868 (10-29-1868) T
Hamilton, P. S. to Marizila Tosh 12-6-1858 Cr
Hamilton, Perry to Emiline Kirk 12-30-1867 G B

Hamilton, Pete to Mary Hooper 12-30-1872 Cr B
Hamilton, Peyton S. to Jennett McCullock 1-13-1849 (1-23-1849) Ma
Hamilton, Phillip to Catherine Roney 11-29-1836 (11-29-1836) O
Hamilton, Randle to Frances Spurling 12-11-1833 Hr
Hamilton, Ransom to Jane Singleton 7-2-1870 (no return) Dy
Hamilton, Smith to Adeline Parks 5-30-1860 (5-31-1860) G
Hamilton, Thomas to Hannah Henning 3-12-1864 (3-16-1864) Cr
Hamilton, Thomas to Hannah Henning 3-12-1864 (no return) Cr
Hamilton, Thomas to Izora Overton 4-30-1884 (5-6-1884) L
Hamilton, Thomas to Margaret Evans 12-30-1873 (1-1-1874) T
Hamilton, Thomas to Martha Montgomery 5-16-1857 (5-18-1857) T
Hamilton, Thomas to Mary Cole 8-19-1869 Hy
Hamilton, Thomas to Ruthy Steel 11-29-1828 (12-4-1828) Hr
Hamilton, Tom to Dilsy Perkins 9-17-1870 (no return) Hy
Hamilton, W. H. to Elizabeth Wheatley 7-30-1867 Be
Hamilton, W. N. to E. J. Clement 1-3-1865 G
Hamilton, W. R. to Mary E. Moore 7-21-1861 Mn
Hamilton, W. S. to N. A. Parks 2-20-1867 G
Hamilton, Washington E. to Ellen R. McClary 4-11-1838 Cr
Hamilton, William P. to Sarah J. Stewart 11-1-1858 (11-3-1858) Ma
Hamilton, William to Cynthia Casinger 11-12-1838 Hn
Hamilton, William to Martha E. Quisenberry 1-21-1858 (no return) Hn
Hamilton, William to Narcissa Jane Wilks 7-27-1835 Hr
Hamlet, Henry to Amarilla Chitwood 4-14-1866 (no return) Dy
Hamlet, James W. to Mary Jane Broom 5-8-1840 (5-14-1840) F
Hamlett, Christopher to Louisianna Mooney 1-2-1867 (1-6-1867) Ma
Hamlett, J. N. to Laura G. Campbell 1-11-1858 (1-13-1858) Sh
Hamlett, Joseph S. to Margaret E. McNeill 9-11-1854 (9-12-1854) Ma
Hamliln, Job to Elizabeth Davis 2-13-1840 O
Hamlin, Charles to Ann E. Ridley 1-1-1860 Hn
Hamlin, Elija to Sarah J. Dennington 11-30-1859 (12-1-1859) O
Hamlin, James to Lucinda Kilian 2-23-1839 (3-17-1839) O
Hamlin, John F. to Cornelia Ann Carnes 6-24-1858 (6-28-1858) Sh
Hamlin, John F. to Judith A. Quinichet 5-17-1839 Sh
Hamlin, John to Nancy Bennet 9-8-1828 (9-9-1828) Hr
Hamlin, William to Lydia Ann Brown 7-10-1847 (7-18-1847) Hr
Hamlin, William to Lydia Ann Kinard 12-7-1846 Hr
Hamlin, William to Martha J. (Mrs.) Clark 12-21-1858 Sh
Hamm, B. F. to Mary W. Smith 9-5-1861 Mn
Hammar, B. E. to Annie Z. Trumball 10-29-1860 (10-30-1860) Sh
Hammer, John to Julia Ann Hickman 3-31-1845 O
Hammers, Joel to Lydia Tims 8-31-1846 (9-3-1846) Hr
Hammers, John F. to Josephine Wilkins 1-24-1871 T
Hammers, John to Nancy Tims 5-22-1867 T
Hammers, Raleigh to Mary Ann White 7-4-1859 (7-5-1859) Ma
Hammersly, Charles H. to Julie Copperthwaite 7-18-1864 (7-24-1864) Sh
Hammet, Ruben to Elizabeth N. Parker 8-7-1837 Hr
Hammett, Elijah to Elizabeth McKinney 8-2-1838 O
Hammett, James to Lielia Baker 7-22-1862 (no return) Cr
Hammett, John W. to Martha Jane Brewer 10-15-1856 (no return) Cr
Hammett, William N. to Lidia J. Robeson 11-16-1865 Cr
Hamming, Joseph to Virginia Noel 10-11-1840 (no return) Hn
Hammock, Charlie to Lula Blakely 1-11-1886 L
Hammock, J. W. to Frances Freeman 11-5-1880 (11-7-1880) L
Hammon, Hiram to Mary Patterson 10-4-1828 O
Hammon, Isaac to Elizabeth King 11-2-1830 Hr
Hammon, William to Phalba M. Harris 2-28-1867 Ma
Hammond, Andrew to Elizabeth Hoge 1-16-1855 Sh
Hammond, Franklin W. to Susan C. Noles 12-21-1853 (12-22-1853) O
Hammond, H. L. to Syntha A. Wrenn 6-29-1866 G
Hammond, J. C. to Tex Ann Harrison 8-9-1866 G
Hammond, James H. to Eliza J. Rideout 1-17-1861 (1-20-1861) F
Hammond, James M. to Julia (Mrs.) Harrison 7-8-1866 G
Hammond, James M. to Rebecca Marcum 10-27-1848 (10-29-1848) F
Hammond, Lemuel B. to Elizabeth Davis 11-2-1860 Mn
Hammond, Miles M. to Margaret A. Simonton 5-9-1853 Ma
Hammond, Nathaniel to Thiresa Blackman 2-21-1854 (2-28-1854) O
Hammond, S. J. to Amanda J. Flowers 12-14-1866 G
Hammond, Sam E. to Bettie Raiford 11-8-1864 Sh
Hammond, W. C. to Susan Joice 6-5-1857 Sh
Hammond, W. H. to Nancy C. Blackman 10-8-1856 O
Hammond, William to Elsey Hearn 9-13-1845 (9-14-1845) Ma
Hammond, Wm. N. to Nancy K. McKelva 1-5-1852 (1-8-1852) G
Hammonds, C. C. to N. M. Auslian 11-3-1860 G
Hammonds, E. D. to Elizabeth Thomas 9-24-1859 Hr
Hammonds, James M. to Nancy Pratt 9-1-1852 Hn
Hammonds, John B. to M. A. Kidwell? 12-19-1867 (12-20-1868?) G
Hammonds, John W. to Mary A. Bailey 11-20-1850 Hn
Hammonds, Uriah J. to Mary E. Bobbett 3-27-1864 G
Hammonds, William W. to Sarah C. Thompson 1-2-1850 (1-3-1850) Ma
Hammons, Edward D. to Elizabeth C. Roberts 10-7-1870 (10-9-1870) F
Hammons, James M. to Kittura Foxwell 12-16-1847 Ma
Hammons, John to Margaret E. Richardson 8-8-1853 G
Hammons, L. B. to Caroline Simmons 3-2-1854 (no return) F
Hammons, Steaphan to Alice Ross 3-1-1878 Hy
Hammons, Thomas D. to Lucinda Thomas 12-19-1837 Hr
Hammons, William H. to Mary Jane Mashburn 2-26-1853 (2-27-1853) Hr

Hammons, Wm. to Lucy Able 7-3-1838 F
Hammons, Young J. to Susan E. McCaslin 1-15-1851 (1-16-1851) G
Hammontree, Samuel to Martha E. Sigler 11-13-1858 (11-16-1858) Sh
Hamner, A. B. to M. A. V. Hooker 8-31-1857 (9-10-1857) Sh
Hamner, A. M. to Mary E. Webber 11-2-1854 Sh
Hamner, Constantine S. to Martha J. Cockrill 8-18-1857 (8-19-1857) Ma
Hamner, G. W. to Eunity Carroll 6-19-1838 (6-24-1838) O
Hamner, H. F. to Caledonia M. Scales 12-23-1834 Sh
Hamner, James A. to Mary T. Hooker 1-19-1858 Sh
Hamner, William B. to Mary E. Rodgers 2-21-1854 (2-23-1854) Sh
Hamon, Nuton A. to Martha J. Leonard 9-7-1852 (no return) F
Hamons, Andrew to Lizzy Brooks 12-30-1873 Hy
Hampe, Henry G. to Josephine Vollmer 5-28-1860 (5-29-1860) Sh
Hampton, Albert to Sarah Jane Pritchett 4-16-1870 (4-17-1870) Dy
Hampton, Andrew B. to Rebecca Upstead 12-30-1855 Cr
Hampton, B. J. to Susan Snider 11-14-1854 Hn
Hampton, Charles to Elizabeth (Mrs.) Smith 11-3-1866 G
Hampton, David M. to Mattie J. Perry 12-19-1866 (12-20-1866) Ma
Hampton, E. S. to Elizabeth Brinkley 5-13-1852 Cr
Hampton, Edmund H. to Nancy Farris 7-26-1843 (7-27-1843) O
Hampton, Haywood to Eliza J. Robertson 1-4-1862 (1-5-1862) Cr
Hampton, Henry A. to Nancy E. Wood 7-17-1869 (7-18-1869) Cr
Hampton, J. E. to Melony? Umpstead 3-11-1856 Cr
Hampton, J. H. to R. C. Klyce 11-6-1871 (no return) Hy
Hampton, J. L. to Bettie J. Stewart 2-26-1869 (no return) Dy
Hampton, J. T. to Paulina Oberley 2-5-1842 (no return) F
Hampton, J. W. to H. McAvoy 9-30-1847 F
Hampton, James G. to Pricilla Davis 2-25-1845 Cr
Hampton, James W. to Sarah E. Haislip 11-22-1860 O
Hampton, James to Fannie Brinkley 12-29-1842 Cr
Hampton, James to Mary Mount 1-31-1867 G
Hampton, John A. to Frances Brigham 4-13-1850 (no return) Hn
Hampton, John A. to Nancy Ritch? 6-25-1864 Hn
Hampton, John P. to Catharine Stewart 8-23-1869 (8-26-1869) F
Hampton, Jonathan T. to Betsy Dunning 1-14-1847 Hn
Hampton, Jonathan to Eliza Rhoads 1-4-1853 Hn
Hampton, Joseph to Cassandra Ann Meadows 1-5-1842 (no return) Cr
Hampton, N. C. to R. P. Medlock 9-18-1846 Hr
Hampton, N. W. to Loucinda C. Hatch 8-24-1858 Cr
Hampton, Noah D. to Mary June Nichols 5-20-1844 (no return) Hn
Hampton, Thomas D. to Mary C. Williams 12-23-1861 (12-25-1861) O
Hampton, Thomas J. to Caty Parson 12-23-1841 Cr
Hampton, Thomas to Dolly Wilson 3-29-1848 (3-31-1848) G
Hampton, W. H. to Alice Vinson 12-25-1872 Dy
Hampton, W. L. to Louisa Jackson 7-1-1867 (7-2-1867) Dy
Hampton, Wade to Martha Johnson 1-29-1877 Dy
Hampton, Wiley A. I. to Ponta Rigsby 1-29-1856 Cr
Hampton, Wilford F. to Mary Catharine Woods 7-30-1860 (10-1-1860) O
Hampton, William F. to Fancy Christopher 2-1-1863 Hn
Hampton, William R. to Mary Gately 2-?-1866 (2-26-1866) Cr
Hampton, William to Eliza Pickett 10-21-1865 (no return) Cr
Hampton, William to Sarah Knott 2-15-1847 (2-16-1847) G
Hampton, Wm. N. to S. A. J. Ozier 6-1-1854 Cr
Hampton, Wm. S. to Elizabeth L. J. Eskew 11-21-1852 Cr
Hampton, Wm. S. to Lucenda E. McCalister 3-14-1850 (no return) Cr
Hamrick, William to Marey E. F. Coby 12-14-1859 F
Hamson, Lorenzo D. to Mary D. Jones 2-22-1866 G
Hamton, T. L. to Cincinnati Anthony 8-25-1869 Dy
Hamure?, Alexander to Agnes Harper 12-17-1850 Hn
Hanagan, John to Elizabeth Hurt 7-30-1857 Sh
Hanburg, T. E. to R. A. McCauley 2-12-1862 (2-16-1862) Sh
Hancock, A. H. to Elizabeth P. Lankford 10-6-1867 Hn
Hancock, A. S. to Sarah J. Ball 1-11-1841 (1-12-1841) F
Hancock, Abraham to Rebecca Butram 3-10-1858 G
Hancock, Abram to Leander Caroline Jones 3-19-1851 (3-20-1851) G
Hancock, Benjamin L. to Rebecca A. C. Lowry 7-28-1877 (7-29-1877) L
Hancock, E. H. to Irena M. Crocker 6-27-1846 (7-2-1846) F
Hancock, Fountain E. to Eliza Winborn 2-28-1885 (3-1-1885) L
Hancock, George to Nancy Ann Hall 12-19-1874 (12-20-1874) L
Hancock, Green B. to Rebecca R. Chandler 2-16-1859 L
Hancock, Harrison N. to Maria Collins 11-1-1855 O
Hancock, J. C. to A. P. Galloway 3-14-1859 (3-28-1859) F
Hancock, J. H. to Polly A. Hutchinson 11-17-1866 O
Hancock, J. L. to Mary Monroe 1-4-1881 L
Hancock, J. W. to W. A. Miller 1-2-1878 (no return) L
Hancock, James G. to Amanda M. Dugger 3-9-1863 (no return) Hn
Hancock, James to Louisa Young 10-18-1855 Hn
Hancock, James to Mary Foster 12-23-1862 (12-25-1862) O
Hancock, Joseph C. to Z. M. Trice 11-13-1844 We
Hancock, N. S. to Catharine McCrary 8-23-1856 (8-28-1856) G
Hancock, S. T. to Fousanna W. Jetton 9-27-1868 G
Hancock, Thomas H. to Sarah Usher 2-9-1848 (2-10-1848) Hr
Hancock, Thos. H. to Elmira J. Anderson 2-24-1859 Hr
Hancock, W. F. to Catharine M. Mask 9-10-1855 (9-13-1855) Hr
Hancock, W. G. to D. F. Tidwell 6-27-1863 O
Hand, B. B. to Nancy Lahal? ?-4-1862 Be
Hand, Richard to Hattie Duncans 7-3-1878 (no return) Dy

Handley, F. M. to G. C. Dollern 8-17-1867 (8-18-1867) O
Handly, John to Visy Ham 11-29-1842 Ma
Handsbrough, William C. to Tabitha Jones 10-17-1841 Hn
Hane, Samuel S. to Mary F. Warbrittan 10-7-1865 (10-8-1865) Cr
Haneline, Perry to Harriet Brown 5-5-1841 Hn
Hanes, Henry to Susan Killgore 2-26-1863 O
Hanes, Jonathan L. to Nancy Calhoon 2-13-1840 (2-16-1840) O
Haney, Benjamin to Thursday Matilda Littrull? 7-14-1849 (9-7-1849) Hr
Haney, David to Lydia Vanpelt 10-1-1869 (10-2-1869) F B
Haney, Henry P. to Rachel R. Indman? 10-12-1854 Hn
Haney, John to Letitia Brannon 12-13-1841 (no return) Hn
Haney, Lindsey to Eliz R. Futill 8-12-1839 (8-13-1839) Hr
Hanin, Oliver to Polly Crawford 2-6-1845 Sh
Hanis, Martin L. to June Mitchell 12-16-1845 Hr
Hank, Hansford to Susan Foster 1-7-1829 (1-11-1829) Hr
Hankins, Dewey H. to Judy A. Sewel 11-7-1846 Hn
Hankins, Henry H. to Frances A. Sherman 9-23-1843 (9-28-1843) Ma
Hankins, John H. to Julia A. Steelman 11-28-1860 Sh
Hankins, John H. to Nancy Ann Cameron 7-15-1857 (7-16-1857) Sh
Hankins, Samuel to Nancy Compton 10-28-1846 (no return) Hn
Hankins, Thos. D. to Ruth G. Casey 1-7-1860 (1-8-1860) Hr
Hankins, W. D. to Satira Savage 6-1-1861 (6-2-1861) Hr
Hankison?, Thomas to Martha King 6-29-1852 (7-1-1852) T
Hanks, Allen to Elizabeth Wolverton 1-23-1833 (1-24-1833) Hr
Hanks, Hugh T. to Eliza G. Rice 3-17-1865 (3-18-1865) T
Hanks, J. E. (C.?) to Frances M. Noel 10-6-1870 G
Hanks, William to Mary C. Gibson 7-30-1864 Sh
Hanley, J. D. to Martha B. Stubelfield 3-30-1857 We
Hanley, James G. to Frances W. Adams 5-24-1842 (5-25-1842) T
Hanley, John to Catherine Johnson 12-23-1856 (no return) We
Hanley, Michael to Catherine McDonough 2-12-1850 Sh
Hanly, Gabriel W. to Mahala Swor 6-27-1843 Hn
Hanna, Charles F. to Julia A. McNeill 8-10-1848 Cr
Hanna, H. M. to Elizabeth C. Null 11-23-1843 Cr
Hanna, Henry to Bridget Dennegan 5-26-1862 (5-27-1862) Sh
Hanna, James to Nancy Stewart 4-9-1842 Hr
Hanna, John E. to Mary O. Faussett 1-10-1867 T
Hanna, John M. to Magaret A. J. Berryhill 4-3-1844 We
Hanna, N. W. to E. C. Hanna 12-22-1864 (1-1-1865) Cr
Hanna, Thomas to Juli Roe 1-3-1870 G B
Hannagin, John to Mary Stapleton 8-23-1851 (8-24-1851) Sh
Hannah, Alexander to Martha Wooten 1-22-1846 Cr
Hannah, Elijah to Ellen Swayne 1-6-1871 Cr B
Hannah, J. M. to M. P. Mason 2-14-1866 G
Hannah, J. S. to Cornelia Welch 12-19-1865 Mn
Hannah, James, jr. to Mattie W. Thompson 11-10-1857 Sh
Hannah, John D. to Sarah J. Blakemore 7-6-1826 G
Hannah, John to Betsy Moses 3-4-1871 (no return) Hy
Hannah, William to May Huffman 11-20-1838 Sh
Hannan, B. Desha to Mary J. Loftin 2-8-1849 Hr
Hanner, Abner J. to Mary E. Wylie 1-3-1857 T
Hannigan, Thomas to Ann Morgan 2-21-1852 Sh
Hannings, Solomon to Eveline Green 12-2-1868 (12-6-1868) Cr
Hannis, David S. to Charlotte Caraway 12-26-1849 Hr
Hannis, Samuel to Mary Taylor 4-10-1824 (4-11-1824) Hr
Hannis, William D. to Tabitha D. Carricker 7-15-1848 (7-20-1848) Hr
Hannon, Patrick to Bridget Lanney 1-27-1851 Sh
Hansard, James to Lydia Allen 6-23-1849 (6-24-1849) Hr
Hansard, William M. to Polly Kinnaird 1-17-1833 Sh
Hansbro, H. J. to M. C. Weatherford 2-4-1861 (2-7-1861) Cr
Hansbrough, D. J. to M. E. Warren 11-5-1867 (11-7-1867) O
Hansbrough, J. N. to Millard A. Terry 12-14-1857 Cr
Hansel, John J. to Nancy E. Ross 3-8-1860 Be
Hansel, William J. to Elizabeth Gibson 2-16-1860 Hn
Hansel, William to Zelpha A. Bell 11-4-1852 Be
Hansell, Nehemiah M. to Elizabeth C. Barnhill 8-31-1848 Sh
Hansford, G. W. to R. E. McCarver 4-10-1856 (4-16-1856) Hr
Hanson, G. A. to Mary A. Magivney 6-17-1856 Sh
Hanson, John P. to Harriet Ryan 9-29-1864 Sh
Hanson, Stephen to Jerusha A. G. Sanderson 10-14-1839 Sh
Hanson, Thomas to Sarah Ann Hardison 9-4-1856 Cr
Hanswait, Henry to Ida C. St. Clair 10-8-1864 Sh
Hapgood, Thomas to Mary F. Saxton 4-20-1867 Ma
Happek, Itzig to Yittel Gensburger 5-3-1856 Sh
Har, Wm. to Mary Woods 5-12-1865 (6-1-1865) Cr
Haragan, James to Catherine Clifford 10-1-1864 (10-4-1864) Sh
Haralson, D. G. to Amanda Mansfield 6-2-1860 O
Haralson, J. H. to Lena Weaver 12-20-1877 Hy
Haralson, R. W. to S. C. Barcroft 12-15-1870 Hy
Haralston, James R. to M. P. Jones 1-5-1858 Sh
Harber, George to Eliza E. James 11-7-1863 (no return) L
Harber, John H. to Rachel L. Dickison 9-26-1859 Ma
Harberson, John D. to Ann H. Chambers 10-8-1839 Sh
Harbert, Arther to Louanna Bell 1-23-1871 Hy
Harbert, Arther to Mary Ling 10-12-1871 Hy
Harbert, Booker to Martha Newborn 11-21-1873 Hy
Harbert, C. W. to Neppie R. Bond 12-5-1859 (no return) Hy

Harbert, Haywood to Edmonia Oldham 2-6-1869 Hy
Harbert, James H. to Harriet J. Gregory 1-24-1859 (1-27-1859) Ma
Harbert, Stephen to Nancy Vincent 7-20-1840 (7-23-1840) Ma
Harbin, John N. to M. F. Cornwell 4-7-1862 (4-8-1862) Ma
Harbison, George to Lavina Bryant 11-13-1875 (11-14-1875) Dy
Harbor, Thos. G. to Malinda Lemons 8-23-1854 (8-24-1854) G
Harbor, William A. to Frances C. Cromes 6-4-1853 G
Harbour, Elisha T. to Martha Lawrence 8-22-1868 (8-26-1868) Ma
Harbour, George A. to Eliza Dean 4-28-1851 (4-29-1851) G
Harbour, Jacob to Peggy Childress 5-8-1827 (5-10-1827) G
Harbour, John to Ella Hardin 2-27-1880 (2-29-1880) L
Harbson, J. W. to Martha Ann Harris 10-1-1865 G
Harbson, Jas. H. to Eliza J. Stegall 7-1-1850 (7-9-1850) F
Harburger, William to Stacy J. Y. Garrett 8-6-1859 (8-7-1859) Sh
Harbut, Thomas C. to Tempee Hutchison 5-11-1870 Ma
Harbut, William to Mary Waddell 12-30-1829 (12-31-1829) Ma
Harcourt, T. C. to Bethenia Ann Dunlap 1-15-1862 Hn
Hardage, Andrew J. to Jane Spencer 7-24-1839 Ma
Hardage, John B. to Malinda Dean 11-6-1837 Hr
Hardage, Joseph A. to Sarah Sanford 2-10-1846 Ma
Hardaway, Ishmael N. to Nancy E. Philips 1-12-1853 Sh
Hardcastle, John to Sarah Moon(Moore) 6-26-1830 Hr
Hardee, George to Elizabeth (Mrs.) Walker 5-23-1868 (5-24-1868) Ma
Hardeman, J. B. to Nancy Jane Smith 6-30-1863 Mn
Hardeman, John M. to Mary Hardeman 5-13-1828 Hr
Hardeman, John O. to Jane H. Gray 9-6-1853 (9-7-1853) Sh
Hardeman, Samuel to Malinda Stagner 8-27-1857 Be
Harden, Alexander to Flora Thompson 1-28-1841 Hn
Harden, Allen to Lucy Midgett 9-30-1871 Hy
Harden, Hampton to Bettie Hurdle 1-?-1871 Hy
Harden, Himon to Tilde Haliburton 1-1-1877 Hy
Harden, James M. to Martha Jane Meter 2-20-1862 (2-21-1862) L
Harden, James to Rody (Mrs.) Brogden 2-28-1872 (2-29-1872) L
Harden, Jefferson to Nancy E. Dixon 2-1-1862 (no return) L
Harden, John C. to Louisa M. Moore 1-22-1846 Cr
Harden, Joseph to Susan Jobe 2-3-1845 Hn
Harden, Lewis to Susan Smith 10-30-1873 Hy
Harden, Moses to ____ Jabasford? 12-15-1842 Ma
Harden, Robert to Lucinda Walker 2-3-1857 Be
Harden, William to Sarah Capps 7-1-1851 Be
Hardenbrook, Ransom to C. B. Black 1-5-1859 (1-6-1859) Sh
Harder, George M. to Mildred Hoskins no date (with Oct 1842) G
Harder, Henry to Ellen Ames 6-30-1853 Sh
Harder, J. L. to B. J. Umsted 10-5-1858 G
Harder, James to Mary Crawford 10-11-1838 Hn
Harder, Joseph to Virginia Short 1-22-1838 Hn
Hardester, Elisha to Mary Jane Smith 6-18-1839 (no return) Cr
Hardester, Henry to Jane Stone 11-25-1833 (11-27-1833) G
Hardgrave, Felix R. to Susan E. Bonner 2-28-1852 (3-2-1852) Ma
Hardgraves, Francis to Ann Green 5-25-1830 Ma
Hardican, J. E. to Mary F. Williams 8-17-1869 (no return) Dy
Hardie, J. A. to Elizabeth (Mrs.) McWhirter 3-14-1869 G
Hardin, A. J. to M. Hargus 3-24-1846 We
Hardin, Elijah to Elizabeth Sayles 5-5-1852 Be
Hardin, Gabriel to Mary E. Dickson 6-5-1858 (6-6-1858) Ma
Hardin, George W. to Eliza J. Bells 1-26-1852 (1-29-1852) G
Hardin, George W. to Sarah A. E. Harris 6-11-1838 (no return) F
Hardin, Hiram to Cynthia Estill 10-29-1838 Sh
Hardin, J. G. to S. A. Hollis 5-9-1878 (5-12-1878) Dy
Hardin, James to Susan Capps 2-13-1867 (2-14-1867) L
Hardin, John C. to Elly Jane Robinson 1-2-1858 Hr
Hardin, John H. to Martha A. Bridgewater 7-26-1849 (7-31-1849) F
Hardin, John to Mollie Parker 2-12-1869 (no return) Dy
Hardin, Joseph D. to Nancy Israel 10-22-1850 (10-23-1850) G
Hardin, Joshua to Lucy E. M. J. Woodson 6-15-1848 Hr
Hardin, Martin L. to Helen C. Harriss 6-22-1846 (6-25-1846) Hr
Hardin, Moses J. to Lucinda Newsom 1-11-1858 (1-12-1858) Ma
Hardin, Moses T. to Sarah C. Newsom 9-22-1846 Ma
Hardin, Richard to Frances Moore 4-29-1843 (4-30-1843) Ma
Hardin, S. V. to Nancy J. (I?) Rawling (Bowling) 8-29-1831 Sh
Hardin, William S. to Parthenia Meadows 5-7-1853 (5-10-1853) Ma
Harding, Augustus to Dollie Irwin 11-8-1869 (no return) F B
Harding, George L. to Lou Deloach 12-12-1866 (12-20-1866) Ma
Harding, Gilbert to Lavitha E. Conyors 10-28-1865 Hn
Harding, J. R. to L. M. Young 9-12-1865 Hn
Harding, Jno. Mesina to Frances Eliza Coward 12-22-1855 (1-2-1856) T
Harding, John A. to Susannah Clanton 2-26-1867 (2-28-1867) Ma
Harding, Joshua to Eliza Oquin 2-7-1857 Ma
Harding, Nicholas D. to Nancy M. Todd 12-18-1866 (12-20-1866) Ma
Harding, Thomas P. to Minerva J. Starkey 12-4-1850 Sh
Harding, Wiley to Temperance Wyblood (Hyblood) 9-12-1837 Sh
Hardison, Asa J. to Martha Land 3-18-1858 Hr
Hardison, J. H. to M. L. Miller 8-29-1876 (8-31-1876) Dy
Hardison, William B. to N. A. C. White 3-18-1851 (3-19-1851) Hr
Hardison, William to Emma Ross 3-5-1871 Hy
Hardridge, Wm. to Martha Cain 12-24-1831 (12-?-1831) Hr
Hardwick, Robert C. to Margaret C. Moon(Moore?) 2-28-1850 (2-7?-1850) Hr

Hardwicke, Lawriston to Mollie R. Taylor 2-1-1871 (2-2-1871) Ma
Hardy, Austin to Henrietta Barnes no date (not executed) Hy
Hardy, Benjamin T. to Missouri E. Murrell 4-17-1853 (4-21-1853) Ma
Hardy, Calvin J. to Julianna Wooddard 11-24-1830 Ma
Hardy, Davy to Rosanna Crewer 12-21-1867 F B
Hardy, George to Dilly Grundy 12-28-1867 (no return) F B
Hardy, George to Jane Jones 3-16-1867 (3-19-1867) F B
Hardy, George to Mary Ann Fletcher 5-18-1868 (no return) F B
Hardy, Henderson M. to Mary E. Grizzard 11-21-1872 Hy
Hardy, Henry B. to Harriett Avery 10-31-1854 Hn
Hardy, Henry H. to Melvina Moss 10-21-1846 L
Hardy, Henry R. to Annie M. Ledbetter 11-12-1867 (11-13-1867) L
Hardy, Henry to Wenney A. Sharp 1-15-1867 G
Hardy, Hillary to Hattie Evans 9-11-1880 (9-16-1880) L
Hardy, Jasper N. to Elizabeth M. Kelton 1-4-1854 (1-5-1854) G
Hardy, Mark to Sarah A. Smith 8-22-1868 (8-23-1868) Ma
Hardy, R. N. to ____ Shepherd 7-19-1852 Cr
Hardy, Rufus S. to Isabela Jane McDowell 9-9-1847 Hr
Hardy, Thomas M. to Frances C. Hicks 11-30-1878 (12-3-1878) L
Hardy, Thomas M. to Rebecca Jane Carson 12-28-1870 (12-29-1870) L
Hardy, W. A. to H. H. Aikin 12-13-1873 Hy
Hardy, Wash to Martha Brown 3-20-1870 Hy
Hardy, Will to Catherine Wilson 12-15-1880 (12-16-1880) L B
Hardy, William to Mary Beckum 12-18-1851 O
Hardy, William to Sally Ann Williams 2-1-1847 (2-4-1847) Hr
Hardy, Wm. H. to Sarah T. Woodfin 9-18-1877 O
Hare, David to Lucy G. Ware 3-26-1840 Sh
Hare, Frank to Amanda Mebane 10-1-1870 (10-4-1870) F B
Hare, Jacob to Margarett E. Neal 10-31-1853 (no return) F
Hare, John A. to Mary B. Ware 12-17-1839 Sh
Hare, Paten to Charity Carroll 11-16-1869 (no return) F B
Hare, Starkey S. to Ann T. J. Ware 8-15-1846 (8-18-1846) F
Hare, Starky S. to Eda A. Brown 2-14-1859 (2-22-1859) F
Hare, Thomas P. to Oliver B. Turbeville 1-10-1848 (1-13-1848) F
Hare, William to Mary Henry 6-11-1853 (6-12-1853) Sh
Harehaw, S. M. to Sarah S. Bogue 9-1-1860 Hr
Harel, William H. to Eliza A. Sumer 10-16-1861 Hn
Harelson, I. H. to Mary E. Tyser 2-24-1872 (2-25-1872) O
Harelson, Joseph T. to Fransis? Jane Watts 6-7-1828 Ma
Harendon, Hankins E. to Virginia A. Miller 9-3-1839 F
Hares, Nathan to Leana Wright 1-4-1854 Sh
Harget, A. B. to Louisa Keathly 1-1-1840 Y
Harget, Alfred T. to Mary E. Ward 10-5-1857 (10-13-1857) O
Harget, Lewis H. to M. M. Leonard 12-24-1862 G
Hargett, A. B. to Louisa Keithley 1-1-1849 O
Hargett, Daniel F. to Rebecca M. Hargett 8-3-1842 (8-4-1842) O
Hargett, H. H. to Aneliza Cook 11-26-1871 Hy
Hargett, J. A. to M. J. Rint 1-9-1866 O
Hargett, J.F. to Mary E. Howard 9-3-1879 L
Hargett, Joseph F. to Mary Ann Ledbetter 7-19-1862 (9-25-1862) L
Hargett, Joseph F. to Mary Ann Ledbetter 7-29-1862 (7-?-1862) L
Hargett, L. W. to N. M. McNeely 1-9-1866 O
Hargett, Thos. to Mary E. Word 7-5-1867 (no return) Hy
Hargett, William A. to Martha J. Harrison 5-2-1871 (5-4-1871) L
Hargis, J. W. L. to Augustine L. Hargis 12-22-1841 (12-23-1841) F
Hargis, John G. to Lucy Ann Taylor 6-24-1840 (6-25-1840) Ma
Hargis, Richard to Louisa Whitworth 12-23-1857 Ma
Hargis, Shadrock to Nancy Cockraham 12-17-1829 Sh
Hargis, Thomas G. to Mary E. Bryant 12-1-1860 (12-2-1860) O
Hargiss, J. A. to Theresse C. Bennett 1-3-1850 Sh
Hargiss, James A. to Amanda L. Barnes 6-11-1852 (no return) F
Hargiss, Marion S. to Tranquilla E. Lester 5-30-1846 (6-10-1846) F
Hargrove, Jacob to Mariah Oldham 9-15-1866 Hy
Hargrove, John T. to B. L. Fitzpatrick 9-29-1881 L
Hargrove, John T. to Eliza Ann McLean 11-22-1848 Hn
Hargrove, L. M. to Nancy Farriss 11-14-1857 (11-16-1857) Hr
Hargrove, R. W. to Caroline C. Loving 10-15-1860 (10-16-1860) F
Hargrove, W. B. to Adelaid Ware 1-15-1873 Hy
Hargrove, W. T. to Vicia Walls 8-11-1866 O
Hargrove, William to Mary Bond 3-14-1868 T
Hargroves, Jackson to Ann Johnson 8-2-1839 (9-2-1839) Hr
Hargroves, John A. to Isabella Medlock 11-19-1845 (no return) Hn
Hargroves, John to Sarah Burton 12-28-1856 Hn
Hargus, Henry to Louisa Hampton 1-27-1869 (1-29-1869) Cr
Hargus, Washington B. to Elizabeth J. Bradberry 5-16-1844 (5-17-1844) F
Harhen, Michael to Mary Flaherty 11-24-1853 Hy
Harigan, Cunelius to Anna Megher 8-20-1864 (8-21-1864) Sh
Haring, J. W. D. to Nancy Moss 3-26-1850 (3-28-1850) F
Haris, James to Nannie Doherity 9-26-1870 (9-28-1870) Cr
Harison, Benjamin C. to Mary Mayo 1-23-1850 Sh
Hark, M. J. to Mary G. Wood 11-8-1877 Dy
Harkins, Aaron W. to Ann Frances Shelton 2-4-1856 Ma
Harkins, Hugh to Jane Myrick 2-3-1847 Hr
Harkins, James C. to Lurany Ann Campbell 12-17-1845 (12-18-1845) Ma
Harklervad, Daniel to Ann Bettes 2-10-1830 Sh
Harkus, Richard to Nancy Clark 7-2-1867 (no return) Hn B
Harlan, Calvin H. to Delphia M. Lankford 1-24-1872 L

Harlan, Jack to Ann Hicks 8-30-1867 G B
Harland, Isaiah to Mandy Carter 2-12-1866 G
Harland, Jack to Charity Bradford 11-2-1868 G B
Harlen, Samuel A. to Bridget Broun 4-22-1863 Sh
Harley, George C. to Martha C. Stone 12-8-1845 G
Harley, George C. to Martha J. Blair 2-8-1844 G
Harley, John to Menerva Shipman 1-5-1829 (1-8-1829) Hr
Harley, Thomas to Martha R. A. Beard 7-2-1849 (7-11-1849) Hr
Harlin(Hardin?), Ellis to Synthia Sweeton 8-14-1826 (8-15-1826) Hr
Harlin, Isaac to Eliza J. Patterson 5-25-1863 (5-27-1863) Cr
Harlin, Isaac to Eliza Jane Patterson 5-25-1863 Cr
Harling, R. E. to Sophia S. Linden 10-17-1856 Cr
Harlon, Wyatte to Julia Ann Tuning?(Luning?) 9-19-1850 Hr
Harlow, James to Mary E. McGuire 9-16-1848 (9-18-1848) Hr
Harman, Alexander to Mary Jane Rowe 12-6-1843 Hn
Harman, Willis R. to Nancy Ward 10-12-1862 We
Harmen, Wm. L. to M. E. Jackson 1-10-1861 G
Harmes, Raymond B. to Nancy Starnes 9-29-1846 Sh
Harmon, A. C. to Sarah E. Aiken 8-30-1870 (8-31-1870) Dy
Harmon, Abraham to Betsy Ann Rogers 3-8-1828 O
Harmon, Ambrose to Mary Ann Sparks 11-12-1839 Cr
Harmon, B. H. to Lizzie Davis 11-5-1867 (11-7-1867) Dy
Harmon, John H. to Elizabeth Davidson 12-17-1867 (12-18-1867) Dy
Harmon, John S. to Nancy Cook 1-20-1858 We
Harmon, John to Tabitha Hill 7-3-1860 Hn
Harmon, Josiah to Eliza Cook 7-26-1856 We
Harmon, Lewis O. to Jane White 6-11-1868 O
Harmon, Stewart to Fanny Freeman 10-19-1867 Hy
Harmon, W. W. to Blunett Jeffrys 9-28-1865 G
Harmon?, John to Nancy Mills 2-17-1871 G
Harnesberry, Elijah to Mariah C. Bushart 2-8-1853 Hn
Harness, W. P. to W. A. Green 10-23-1869 Cr
Harns, Willie T. to Nancy Ann Replogle 2-18-1845 Ma
Harold, G. G. to Lucinda Reynolds 2-12-1869 (no return) Dy
Harper, Abram to Susan G. Buchannon 11-10-1864 (no return) Cr
Harper, Alfred M. to Lucy A. Tucker 11-5-1867 (no return) Dy
Harper, Andrew to Marthantha Clary 1-30-1856 We
Harper, Archibald H. to Martha P. Miller 11-4-1871 Ma
Harper, Assa to Elimly J. Albright 1-20-1848 Cr
Harper, Benj. N. D. to Hardinia J. Hatchett 1-8-1849 (1-9-1849) G
Harper, Benjamin K. to Margaret E. Smith 1-31-1838 (2-1-1838) O
Harper, Benjamin to Almeda F. Garrett 12-24-1860 (12-27-1860) G
Harper, Benjamin to Elizabeth Adams 11-1-1842 O
Harper, Blaney to Elizabeth Griffy 9-3-1832 (9-12-1832) G
Harper, Blaney to Winneford Toller 1-7-1832 G
Harper, Charles to Leana Mann 8-27-1881 L B
Harper, D. H. to M. A. (Mrs.) Brooks 5-14-1864 Sh
Harper, Danl. to Mary D. Jones 10-14-1825 Hr
Harper, David to Matilda McAlister 7-20-1866 O
Harper, E. F. to Julia Wilder 1-5-1861 Sh
Harper, E. to Mary Ann Kyle 1-14-1851 (no return) F
Harper, Edgar to Carrie E. Lockard 2-4-1885 (2-21-1885) L
Harper, Edgar to M. E. Matthews 12-16-1881 (no return) L
Harper, Edgar to Martha Ann York 10-29-1872 (10-30-1872) L
Harper, Epperson W. to Nancy C. Williams 8-25-1832 (8-30-1832) G
Harper, G. W. to Mrs. Thedford 7-22-1874 (no return) Dy
Harper, George A. to Mary Norton 6-1-1861 Sh
Harper, George to Lucy Dobson 12-13-1868 G B
Harper, Gwinn to Narcissus Graves 8-9-1851 Cr
Harper, Gwinn to Sarah Benton 5-16-1844 Cr
Harper, H. T. to Harriet A. McKinney 1-24-1870 (1-26-1870) Cr
Harper, Henry D. to Eliza J. Underwood 11-28-1842 G
Harper, Henry D. to Ruth Irwin 1-22-1851 G
Harper, J. A. to E. J. Gilkey 3-4-1869 (3-7-1869) Cr
Harper, J. A. to Frances Rich 9-3-1850 (no return) F
Harper, J. J. to Mattie J. Goodloe 2-20-1867 G
Harper, J. P. to Mary A. Cullepher 9-30-1868 G
Harper, J. W. to Famie Rudder 10-16-1878 Dy
Harper, Jack to Susan Jones 2-7-1870 T
Harper, James B. to Margaret E. Marshall 2-26-1839 O
Harper, James B. to Susan F. Maupin 11-8-1849 O
Harper, James Franklin to Elizabeth Susannah Johnston 4-3-1844 (4-4-1844) T
Harper, James M. to Nancy W. Williams 3-17-1858 Be
Harper, James T. to Elizabeth Shelton 12-7-1868 (12-10-1868) Ma
Harper, James to Catharine Wood 12-1-1857 (12-12-1857) Sh
Harper, James to Maggie Smith 11-29-1873 Hy
Harper, James to Mary Ann Burt 12-21-1838 Sh
Harper, John to Caroline Caldwell 4-6-1849 O
Harper, John to Cassie Halliburton 12-24-1880 (12-31-1881?) L
Harper, John to Eliza Ann Allbright 5-30-1844 Cr
Harper, John to Lucinda R. Stovall 9-28-1843 O
Harper, John to Nancy Perkins 8-4-1840 Cr
Harper, John to Perina Crewes 5-7-1849 (no return) Cr
Harper, Joseph to Harriett V. Thomas 10-16-1864 O
Harper, Joseph to Sarah A. Blackwell 1-31-1861 S
Harper, Lewis W. to Mary Gresham 9-2-1850 (9-4-1850) F
Harper, Moses D. to Mary Ann Hood 4-20-1839 (4-23-1839) O

Harper, Moses to Ruth Box 2-14-1843 (2-15-1843) Hr
Harper, Nat to Gertrude R. Maxwell 12-28-1867 (1-8-1868) F
Harper, Parriss? to Hanna Alexander 3-13-1869 (3-14-1869) T
Harper, Patrick to Sally Jackson 1-5-1841 (1-10-1841) Ma
Harper, Peter to Jincy Shaw 1-20-1877 Hy
Harper, Quincy A. to America J. McAdoo 2-13-1866 Cr
Harper, R. M. to Sallie B. Walls 1-22-1878 Hy
Harper, Richard to Louisa E. Green 9-4-1854 G
Harper, Robert B. to Martha McQLuiston 9-9-1847 T
Harper, Robert B. to Mary M. Hart 9-12-1864 (9-13-1864) F
Harper, Robert P. to Martha H. McClerkin 5-17-1841 (5-18-1841) T
Harper, Robert to Martha T. Presson 5-16-1858 Be
Harper, Robt. L. to Mary Frazier 11-19-1860 (11-27-1860) Dy
Harper, Ruffin to Emma Hinton 11-8-1873 L B
Harper, S. W. to M. E. Martin 12-19-1865 G
Harper, Saml. W. to Ora Barksdale 9-15-1867 G
Harper, Samuel B. to Ann S. Jones 12-27-1827 (1-1-1828) Hr
Harper, Samuel L. to E. J. Maupin 1-10-1848 O
Harper, T. L. to Sullie E. Sullivan 12-27-1869 Hy
Harper, T. P. to A. E. Green 12-3-1866 O
Harper, Thomas M. to Sophia Wilson 6-9-1857 (6-10-1857) Sh
Harper, W. A. to Julia Stanford 4-28-1849 (no return) Cr
Harper, W. A. to Lucy H. Rich 11-11-1853 (no return) F
Harper, W. A. to Mary Hicks 12-31-1844 Cr
Harper, W. S. to Louizer Ellen Harper 4-17-1868 G
Harper, William B. to Elizabeth Hood 11-25-1847 O
Harper, William B. to Mary A. Copeland 4-3-1851 (no return) Hn
Harper, William D. to Martha E. Wiggs 2-13-1845 (2-27-1845) Ma
Harper, William H. to Margaretta A. T. Caruthers 11-19-1847 T
Harper, Wm. J. to Mollie R. Wall 12-31-1874 (no return) Hy
Harper, Wm. to Elizabeth Drummonds 9-17-1847 (no return) Cr
Harpole, Abram H. to Elvira M. Reden 10-19-1860 (10-21-1860) Ma
Harpole, Albert C. to Martha Cloys 3-24-1849 (4-11-1849) O
Harpole, D. to Sallie R. Hammond 3-19-1868 G
Harpole, George D. to Eliza A. Dodd 8-4-1868 (8-6-1868) Dy
Harpole, J. F. to Virginia Hunter 10-21-1874 (10-22-1874) O
Harpole, J. T. to M. A. Paschal 6-23-1872 (9-26-1872) O
Harpole, John A. to Elviry Jackson 6-23-1841 (6-29-1841) G
Harpole, John A. to Martha J. Reasons 6-10-1866 G
Harpole, John A. to Sarah H. Harpole 1-3-1855 (1-9-1855) G
Harpole, John M. to Emily A. Rankin 7-15-1851 (7-16-1851) O
Harpole, S. C. to Martha H. Williams 11-12-1860 G
Harpole, Sollomon W. to Malinda Sellers 12-27-1842 O
Harpole, Solomon C. to Elizabeth McMahon 1-6-1838 G
Harpole, Solomon P. to Sarah Jane Harpole 2-4-1868 G
Harpole, W. H. to Isabella Hawkins 1-30-1872 G
Harpole, William B. to Mary Ann Lindsly 1-2-1841 (1-7-1841) G
Harpole, Wilson P. to Milly B. Fowler 2-23-1850 (2-26-1850) G
Harpoll, S. C. to Elizabeth McMahon 1-6-1837 (3-1-1837) G
Harpool, J. M. to E. P. Graham 10-2-1862 (10-5-1862) O
Harrel, A. D. to Margaret Egnew 8-5-1856 We
Harrel, E. B. to Susan Wickham 10-22-1846 Sh
Harrel, John S. to Sarah E. Strong 4-1-1861 (4-9-1861) Sh
Harrel, R. N. to E. Dillahunty 11-6-1865 (11-15-1865) T
Harrel, W. J. to Callie V. Griffin 9-14-1869 (no return) F
Harrell (Howell?), Charles W. to Mahala C. Beasley 11-17-1858 (no return) L
Harrell(Howell?), Joab to Anide May 1-11-1834 (1-13-1834) Hr
Harrell(Howell?), Thomas C. to Elizabeth E. Howell? 10-13-1846 Hr
Harrell, A. T. to Ida M. Ferguson 12-23-1867 Dy
Harrell, Alfus C. to A. A. Anderson 1-9-1854 Cr
Harrell, Asburry to Sarah Blain 12-13-1866 (no return) F
Harrell, Benj. to Rebeca A. Griffith 11-8-1854 (no return) We
Harrell, C. T. to Mary A. Garwood 7-26-1853 Cr
Harrell, D. A. to S. F. Webber 3-7-1855 (3-14-1855) Sh
Harrell, David to B. Carter 3-2-1838 F
Harrell, Dossey to Lucy E. Tucker 12-22-1862 (12-23-1862) Dy
Harrell, J. C. to Fanney Mitchell 3-16-1859 F
Harrell, J. K. P. to Sue Doyle 6-16-1868 (no return) Dy
Harrell, James M. to Cassandra C. Allen 1-17-1853 Sh
Harrell, James R. to Sarah I. Glisson 8-9-1838 Sh
Harrell, James W. to Nancy Jane Pace 8-20-1855 (8-21-1855) Hr
Harrell, John G. to Sarah McDaniel 12-5-1839 Sh
Harrell, Joseph B. to L. A. Dellahunty 11-17-1868 (11-18-1868) T
Harrell, Joseph to Malinda J. Goodman 7-22-1861 (no return) Dy
Harrell, Knight? to Malinda Beckett 2-23-1878 (no return) Dy
Harrell, Lemmel D. to Maria C. Vaughan 10-10-1844 Sh
Harrell, Levi to Jenny Crawford 10-6-1866 (10-8-1866) F B
Harrell, Milton to Sarah A. Crouch 11-20-1838 Sh
Harrell, Pett to Lear Hurt 9-27-1871 (9-28-1871) Cr B
Harrell, Poke to Sarah Jones 3-12-1872 (no return) Cr B
Harrell, R. G. to Sue Bell 12-19-1866 (12-20-1866) Dy
Harrell, Samuel to Mary Bowden 7-21-1846 Sh
Harrell, Thomas to Betsy Taylor 11-19-1838 Hr
Harrell, Thomas to Luan Pipkin 5-15-1848 (5-18-1848) Ma
Harrell, W. A. to Martha A. McDaniel 2-8-1860 (2-16-1860) Sh
Harrell, W. M. to Tenney C. Swinney 7-27-1872 (7-28-1872) Cr
Harrell, W. S. to Nancy Caroline Braden 10-19-1871 (10-26-1871) L

Harrell, William G. L. to Elizabeth Sturdivant 1-16-1850 (1-17-1850) Ma
Harrell, William to Tabitha Pierce 10-20-1846 (10-29-1846) Ma
Harrell? (Howell?), S. Flutcher to R. P. Morriss 12-28-1872 (12-29-1872) L
Harrelson, Daniel I. to Susan E. Wilson 5-4-___ (5-6-1855) O
Harrelson, William P. to Eliza C. Dueley 10-18-1860 Cr
Harri, William H. to Elizabeth A. McGehee 6-27-1859 We
Harrigan, John to Margaret M. Garret 7-29-1861 (7-30-1861) Sh
Harrill, Charles to Sophia J. Blakemore 2-20-1847 Sh
Harriman, Jos. to Elizabeth R. Vinson 9-17-1859 (9-18-1859) Hr
Harriman, Stephen to Parrylee Ellen Harty 9-6-1858 (9-12-1858) Hr
Harriman, Wm. H. to Sarah E. (Mrs.) Christenberry 7-17-1868 Ma
Harrington, Hardy to Elizabeth Strain 7-28-1840 G
Harrington, Mathias to Nancy Grant 4-1-1856 Ma
Harrington, Rewben J. to L. A. Neal 11-28-1876 (11-29-1876) Dy
Harrington, Saml. J. to Elizabeth N. Jarman 1-28-1846 (1-30-1846) Hr
Harrington, Thomas M. to Elizabeth Cooper 12-17-1863 Sh
Harrion, W. J. to Rosean C. Cavitt 9-10-1854 We
Harris, A. G. B. to M. A. E. Blair 9-14-1866 (9-16-1866) F
Harris, A. G. to Mary E. Coldwell 7-16-1867 G
Harris, A. J. to E. A. Feezor 10-2-1865 (10-3-1865) T
Harris, A. to B. Marks 12-18-1858 Sh
Harris, A. to Matilda Morrison 1-4-1869 (1-8-1869) T
Harris, Addison J. to Eliza L. Hutley 8-4-1836 Sh
Harris, Aleck to Lotty Sims 7-9-1868 G B
Harris, Alex to Emma Light 2-19-1880 (no return) Dy
Harris, Alford W. to Mary Lucinda Sale 2-24-1846 (no return) F
Harris, Alford to Amanda Morgan 10-11-1849 O
Harris, Alfred B. to Nancy Thedford 12-6-1843 (12-7-1843) G
Harris, Alfred F. to Rachel Webb 1-5-1850 (no return) Cr
Harris, Alfred to Enia R____ ? 10-14-1859 (no return) Cr
Harris, Alfred to Susan Spinster 1-7-1840 Cr
Harris, Amanuel to Catharine Brown 12-10-1873 (12-11-1873) T
Harris, Anderson B. to Eliza Turlington 12-4-1845 Sh
Harris, Andrew to Bettie Gauldin 9-30-1868 Dy
Harris, Archibald R. to Sarah R. Estridge 2-12-1848 Ma
Harris, Arthur to Martha F. Browder 10-26-1862 Mn
Harris, Austin to Nellie Shaw 10-25-1870 (10-30-1870) F B
Harris, B. F. to Martha J. Penn 1-24-1859 G
Harris, B. to Amanda Young 1-29-1886 (1-31-1886) L
Harris, Benjamin F. to Sarah E. Penn 3-20-1844 G
Harris, Benjamin to Elizabeth Nowell 7-9-1858 (7-15-1858) Ma
Harris, Bob to Drusilla Smith 12-15-1871 T
Harris, Burrel to Ema? Lawson 2-4-1874 (2-14-1874) L B
Harris, C. (Dr.) to Ellen C. Allen 12-15-1842 Ma
Harris, C. (Dr.) to Mary S. Johnson 8-23-1845 (8-25-1845) Ma
Harris, C. C. to Mollie E. Towns 12-25-1865 (no return) Cr
Harris, C. H. to Minerva Jones 12-2-1865 (12-3-1865) F B
Harris, C. R. to Columbia W. McGregor 1-4-1865 T
Harris, Caleb T. to Mary E. Rodgers 2-3-1869 (2-24-1869) F
Harris, Calvin to Jane Hughleette 6-18-1870 T
Harris, Charles to Ann Young 1-22-1870 (2-13-1870) Cr
Harris, Charles to Mary Rodgers 7-17-1856 Hn
Harris, Christopher C. to Frances Ann Whittington 2-10-1848 (2-14-1848) Ma
Harris, Crock to Martha McCrory 2-22-1876 (2-24-1876) L
Harris, Curtis to Sarah J. Cothran 5-27-1854 (no return) F
Harris, Cyrus P. to Julia Looney 7-8-1851 Hn
Harris, D. C. to Susan Umsted 11-20-1854 (11-21-1854) G
Harris, Dallas to Elizabeth J. Ball 1-12-1866 G
Harris, Dallis to Betty J. Ball 1-8-1867 G
Harris, Daniel to Martha Jane Atkins 10-27-1866 (10-28-1866) Ma
Harris, Daniel to Sarah Ruff 2-5-1842 Ma
Harris, David D. to Martha Burns 11-20-1843 Sh
Harris, David to Elizabeth Earneast 11-8-1828 Ma
Harris, Duke H. to Mary Brown 10-30-1824 M
Harris, E. G. to M. E. Jordan 10-15-1879 (10-21-1879) Dy
Harris, E. G. to Mariah Drake 2-13-1855 (2-14-1855) Ma
Harris, Edward R. to Lucy S. Williams 5-14-1861 Sh
Harris, Edward Thomas to Elizabeth Ann Williams 1-6-1849 (1-7-1849) T
Harris, Edward to C. J. Carnell 1-10-1872 (1-17-1872) L
Harris, Edwrd to Sarah Laycook 8-19-1840 (no return) Cr
Harris, Eleazar to Martha Hutchinson 4-15-1833 O
Harris, Eli C. to Charity Renfro 6-30-1853 (no return) Cr
Harris, Eli to Elizabeth Owen 12-13-1832 Hr
Harris, Eli to Susan N. McKinnie 7-22-1848 (7-27-1848) Hr
Harris, Elisha W. to Sarah B. Payton 11-19-1846 (11-24-1846) F
Harris, Eugene T. to Eva L. Porter 2-6-1866 Hn
Harris, F. M. to Nancy J. Huffman 4-3-1871 (4-4-1871) T
Harris, F. P. to Sarah A. E. Leverett 8-7-1867 F
Harris, Foster B. to Elizabeth Akin 6-8-1836 Sh
Harris, Foster B. to Nancy Irwin 11-30-1837 Sh
Harris, Frank to Silvy Coldwell 12-31-1868 Hy
Harris, Frederic L. to Sarah Doughty 4-29-1863 G
Harris, G. P. to Mary C. Chisum 5-16-1860 (5-23-1860) Hr
Harris, G. W. to Mariah Moffatt 5-19-1866 O
Harris, George M. to Eliza Ann Dewitt 6-19-1838 Hn
Harris, George W. to Martha W. Lake 5-7-1836 Hr
Harris, George W. to Nancy H. Smith 10-19-1839 Ma

Harris, George to Alice Tucker 7-15-1878 Hy
Harris, George to Helen Britt 9-26-1872 Cr B
Harris, Gillum to Sarah Parker 9-2-1834 Hr
Harris, Granville to Nora Holmes 12-22-1880 (12-23-1880) Dy
Harris, H. D. to Octavia Taylor 5-21-1868 Hy
Harris, H. L. to Eviline F. Austin 10-24-1859 (no return) We
Harris, H. L. to Martha H. Chambers 1-1-1867 O
Harris, H. to Martha Jane Williams 7-30-1851 (no return) F
Harris, Haywood F. to Elizabeth H. Wood 7-31-1848 (no return) Cr
Harris, Haywood F. to Louisa J. Butler 3-2-1863 Cr
Harris, Haywood F. to Louisa J. Butler 3-2-1863 (no return) Cr
Harris, Henry L. to J. W. McGuier 12-23-1874 T
Harris, Henry to Elizabeth R. Barker 4-15-1848 (4-18-1848) Ma
Harris, Henry to Hannah Stienbow 12-13-1873 (no return) Hy
Harris, Henry to Juda E. Jamison 7-9-1870 (no return) Cr
Harris, Henry to Julia Braden 3-8-1867 (3-9-1867) F
Harris, Henry to Lou Rieves 8-15-1867 (8-17-1867) F B
Harris, Henry to Rose Boyd 3-23-1867 (3-30-1867) F B
Harris, Howell to Nancy Bosher 6-1-1853 Sh
Harris, Hughlut to Lucy Boswell 2-16-1870 (2-22-1870) T
Harris, I. G. to Martha Travis 7-6-1843 Hn
Harris, Ira to Permelia Winston 5-5-1874 (5-6-1874) T
Harris, Isaac A. to Jennie Tucker 12-24-1873 (12-25-1873) Dy
Harris, Isaac P. L. to Mary Jane Tooley 3-5-1857 O
Harris, Isaac R. to Elizabeth Turner 6-18-1850 Hr
Harris, Isaac W. to Sarah A. LaBone 4-2-1853 Sh
Harris, Isaac to Peggy Graves 9-9-1869 Hy
Harris, Isaac to Sarah Ross 3-19-1839 (no return) Cr
Harris, Isham B. to Lucy R. Watkins 9-15-1859 Hn
Harris, J. C. to Sarah M. Anderson 8-10-1865 O
Harris, J. N. to Annie E. Somerville 1-18-1869 T
Harris, J. N. to Leah Meredith 1-12-1869 G
Harris, J. P. to Bettie Coulter 10-3-1869 G
Harris, J. R. to Mary F. Winbourne 12-15-1869 F
Harris, J. T. to Minerva J. Dunlap 4-1-1868 G
Harris, J. W. to Elizabeth McGregor 7-15-1851 T
Harris, James B. to Martha J. Arnold 9-29-1852 Sh
Harris, James B. to Mary Ann Robb 4-22-1835 M
Harris, James C. to Mary A. Nevill 3-17?-1857 (3-12-1857) O
Harris, James E. to Mary H. Drake 11-7-1857 (11-10-1857) Ma
Harris, James G. to Mary Boyde 12-26-1830 Ma
Harris, James I. to Mary Ella Bayne 6-7-1879 L
Harris, James R. to Lucinda Webb 8-13-1854 Hn
Harris, James T. to Maria L. Martin 4-11-1856 Sh
Harris, James W. to A. C. Morris 2-16-1855 Cr
Harris, James W. to Isabella M. Murchison 11-16-1858 (11-18-1858) Ma
Harris, James to Elizabeth Cross 3-3-1855 Ma
Harris, James to Martha Fenler? 12-15-1834 Hr
Harris, James to Nancy Ann Campbell 9-22-1877 (9-23-1877) Dy B
Harris, James to Parthena Parker 3-5-1874 Dy
Harris, Jas. A. to Elizabeth O. Tucker 12-15-1866 (12-6?-1866) T
Harris, Jas. B. to Matilda Thompson 7-29-1847 Sh
Harris, Jas. O. to Mary L. Adams 1-3-1853 T
Harris, Jeptha V. to Emma F. Cobb 12-28-1869 Ma
Harris, Jerimiah to Catharine King 3-22-1836 Hr
Harris, Jerry to Charity Allen 5-13-1871 Hy
Harris, Jesse L. to Sarah Bayne 8-20-1856 (8-21-1856) Sh
Harris, Jesse to Martha Jones 7-18-1868 Dy
Harris, Jesse to Mary Gillim 9-7-1856 We
Harris, Jesse to Sarah Ross 10-14-1843 (no return) Hn
Harris, Jim to Millie Mitchell 11-1-1879 F
Harris, Jno. R. to Elizabeth Outlaw 5-8-1869 Hy
Harris, Jno. W. to Eliza Ann McCaig 12-16-1869 Ma
Harris, Joe to Caroline Garvin 5-9-1866 F B
Harris, Joel A. to Milly B. Cherry 11-8-1848 Be
Harris, John B. to Mary Biskirk 12-30-1856 (12-31-1856) L
Harris, John C. to Mittie E. Drave 10-18-1866 (no return) Dy
Harris, John C. to Sarilla Thompson 10-17-1827 (10-18-1827) Hr
Harris, John H. L. to Clarissa Mainard 7-10-1839 (no return) Cr
Harris, John M. to Angaline Smith 10-25-1872 (10-27-1872) T
Harris, John M. to Mary D. Adams 2-26-1862 Mn
Harris, John N. to Margaret O. Kile 4-19-1870 (4-21-1870) Ma
Harris, John P. to Marina T. Bell 4-1-1856 (4-2-1856) O
Harris, John W. to E. C. Young 4-3-1871 (5-2-1871) F
Harris, John W. to Emma C. Goodwin 1-4-1870 (1-5-1870) Ma
Harris, John W. to Frances Wilburn 1-12-1854 Hn
Harris, John W. to M. E. (Mrs.) Sappington 11-10-1869 G
Harris, John W. to Mary Almund 1-8-1854 Hn
Harris, John Woods to Mollie E. Christmas 6-29-1858 Sh
Harris, John to Easter Richards 6-27-1866 T
Harris, John to Elizabeth Keeling 8-29-1843 Cr
Harris, John to Jane Sulivan 7-10-1854 (7-18-1854) Hr
Harris, John to Jane, jr. Goodrich 4-6-1849 (4-17-1849) Ma
Harris, John to Lucrita New 8-15-1865 Hr
Harris, John to Luverny I. Evans 1-10-1867 O
Harris, John to Mary Biskirk 12-30-1856 (no return) L
Harris, John to Mary E. Jones 10-23-1856 O

Harris, John to Nancy Prince 11-25-1853 Be
Harris, John to Sarah Taylor 9-19-1877 Hy
Harris, Jonathan A. to C. I. W. Harris 9-29-1853 O
Harris, Jordan to Jane Douglass 9-2-1876 (9-3-1876) Dy
Harris, Joseph S. to Mary R. Bain? 11-11-1850 (11-12-1850) T
Harris, Joseph to Fanny _____ 4-18-1835 Sh B
Harris, Joseph to Jane Askew 5-15-1869 (no return) F B
Harris, Joseph to Melissa Stallings 7-11-1869 G B
Harris, Joseph to Sarah A. Murphey 9-1-1869 (9-9-1869) T
Harris, Joshua to Martha Smith 2-10-1845 Cr
Harris, Joyner to Sophia Cotter 3-9-1873 Hy
Harris, Julius C. to Martha Ann King 2-28-1859 (3-3-1859) Ma
Harris, Julius C. to Susan C. Smith 11-18-1852 Ma
Harris, L. S. to Allice Jenkins 7-29-1874 L
Harris, Laburn W. to Mary Ann Halcrom 10-31-1833 Sh
Harris, Levin Hill to Clara R. Humphreys 11-15-1871 (11-22-1871) Ma
Harris, Levy to Ellen Burton 1-18-1874 Hy
Harris, Lewis M. to Rebecca Park 1-5-1857 O
Harris, Lewis to Mary Jane Cotheran 3-6-1872 (3-7-1872) T
Harris, Loami to Frances K. Bonds 11-13-1854 (11-14-1854) Hr
Harris, M. B. (Dr.) to Elizabeth Clark 11-16-1861 (11-19-1861) Cr
Harris, M. T. to Mary E. Vincent 2-9-1858 We
Harris, M. V. B. to Susan A. Downing 5-5-1871 T
Harris, Marshall to Phebe A. Medlin 12-26-1871 (no return) Hy
Harris, Moses to Silvia Glass 7-17-1869 (7-18-1869) T
Harris, Nathan to Rebecca Gill 3-28-1860 Sh
Harris, Nathanl. to Elizabeth Starling 7-23-1850 (no return) F
Harris, Nelson to Priscilla Jones 12-29-1870 F B
Harris, Newel W. to Sally P. Whitmore 10-4-1852 (no return) F
Harris, Newit to Malsey Harris 2-14-1853 (no return) F
Harris, Newitt to Sallie M. Newsom 10-24-1867 F
Harris, Newton J. to Catherine C. Copeland 1-7-1861 Ma
Harris, Nic to Ellen Ware 7-11-1878 (no return) Hy
Harris, Orange to Amanda Marshall 12-9-1868 (1-3-1869) F B
Harris, Orange to Frances Carpenter 11-21-1885 L
Harris, Orris to Lucille W. Price 8-30-1858 Hr
Harris, Osborn to Mary Ann Carlisle 1-10-1847 Sh
Harris, Overton to Eliza Cumings 2-23-1867 (3-2-1867) F B
Harris, Paul T. to Tempie A. Yarbrough 11-12-1866 (11-15-1866) Ma
Harris, R. D. to L. M. Haskins 12-21-1869 (no return) Dy
Harris, R. E. to Mary J. Winfred 12-8-1869 (12-9-1869) Dy
Harris, R. S. to Elizabeth C. Whitworth 3-21-1855 We
Harris, R. S. to Lucy E. Travis 8-30-1854 We
Harris, R. to Eliza Palmore 5-18-1871 (5-21-1871) Dy
Harris, Reuben to S. E. C. Gardner 5-5-1851 (no return) F
Harris, Richard D. to Narcissa Bowman 10-20-1846 G
Harris, Richard to Susan Thornton 1-30-1877 (1-31-1877) Dy
Harris, Richardson to Frances King 12-31-1868 (1-1-1869) Cr
Harris, Robert C. to Nancy J. Williams 9-28-1857 (9-23?-1857) O
Harris, Robert to Harriet Ramsey 8-9-1869 G R
Harris, Robert to Minerva Fussell 8-6-1846 (8-20-1846) Ma
Harris, Robt. L. to Mary J. Wood 1-18-1873 (1-19-1873) Cr
Harris, Roland R. to Julia A. Bowers 10-18-1860 W
Harris, Rowland G. to Margaret Benson 11-23-1859 (11-24-1859) Ma
Harris, S. C. to A. P. Clay 10-30-1867 T
Harris, Samuel B. to Exy(Elizabeth) S. Elkins 1-14-1834 (1-14-1834) Hr
Harris, Samuel S. to Sarah A. C. Dodd 6-11-1840 O
Harris, Samuel to Dolloy Thom 8-16-1838 Ma
Harris, Samuel to Rebecca Crank 1-9-1870 G B
Harris, Shepard to Ellen Oldham 12-19-1883 (12-20-1883) L
Harris, Sidon to Harriet Sanders 11-28-1866 Hy
Harris, Spencer M. A. G. W. to Sarah M. Thedford 2-28-1842 G
Harris, Sterling to Mary Isabella Forbs 3-25-1851 (no return) F
Harris, T. B. to H. M. Jones 12-13-1859 (12-14-1859) F
Harris, T. G. to Mary L. Quinn 1-7-1850 Cr
Harris, T. H. to Mary E. Murphey 10-24-1874 (10-5?-1874) T
Harris, T. J. to Frances Michaels 1-4-1877 Dy
Harris, T. J. to Mary Briant 4-26-1867 (no return) Cr
Harris, T. H. L. to Cathrine Robinson 2-1-1850 Cr
Harris, T. P. to Lucy Martin 5-13-1863 (5-14-1863) F
Harris, Tex to Ellen Parker 9-29-1870 (10-1-1870) Dy
Harris, Thomas D. to Ann E. Haltom 12-15-1860 Hr
Harris, Thomas H. to Nancy J. Harris 3-12-1848 Hn
Harris, Thomas L. to Fannie W. Ray 10-19-1859 (10-26-1859) Hr
Harris, Thomas T. to Mary F. Jones 11-26-1856 Cr
Harris, Thomas W. to Caroline Burford 8-21-1843 (no return) F
Harris, Thomas W. to Caroline E. Overton 1-21-1852 We
Harris, Thomas W. to Mary E. Turley 3-24-1842 Ma
Harris, Thomas to Lucinda Cheshier 10-17-1838 (10-18-1838) Hr
Harris, Thomas to Margaret Willoughby 12-3-1835 H
Harris, Thomas to Mary Stovall 12-6-1842 (12-7-1842) F
Harris, Thomas to _____ 8-24-1866 (no return) Dy
Harris, Thos. L. to Lucy A. Hobbs 8-9-1852 Cr
Harris, Thos. to Margaret A. Clark 8-17-1854 Hr
Harris, Tom to Isbella McFarland (McFail?) 2-14-1868 (no return) L
Harris, Turner J. to Ann E. V. Bates 4-1-1854 (4-2-1854) Hr
Harris, Turner to Ary Ann Mitchel 6-11-1847 (6-17-1847) F

Harris, Tyler to Mitty McGregor 1-3-1867 T
Harris, Vanburen to Martha A. Chapmana 4-12-1859 O
Harris, Victor M. to C. J. Transou 7-6-1858 (7-7-1858) Ma
Harris, W. D. to Cyntha Duncen 1-18-1868 (1-22-1868) Dy
Harris, W. D. to S. E. Mathena 4-18-1867 O
Harris, W. H. to Sarah P.? Parsons 11-8-1869 (11-9-1869) Cr
Harris, W. T. to Caladonia Cooper 2-7-1874 T
Harris, W. W. to Mary B. Bowen 5-18-1870 (no return) Hy
Harris, Wesley to Amanda Farris 3-18-1854 (no return) F
Harris, Wesley to Emma Harper 1-27-1879 (no return) L B
Harris, Wesley to Rebecca Reeves 3-11-1869 F
Harris, West to Elvira Moorefield 3-5-1860 (no return) Hn
Harris, Whitson A. to Mary E. Winston 1-24-1848 (1-28-1848) F
Harris, Wilkerson to Emeline Jones 12-24-1866 (12-27-1866) F B
Harris, William F. to Jane Bolin 6-1-1849 Sh
Harris, William G. to Mary Huffman 1-7-1867 (1-13-1867) T
Harris, William H. to Amanda McFarland 12-7-1859 (12-8-1859) G
Harris, William S. S. to Anjeletta Meadows 7-3-1831 (7-4-1831) O
Harris, William to Abigail Tipton 3-25-1850 O
Harris, William to Catharine Oxford 6-10-1852 Be
Harris, William to Elizabeth P. Lewis 3-24-1867 Be
Harris, William to Sarah A. Hicks 12-21-1869 Be
Harris, Willie S. to Caroline Roberts 4-17-1841 Ma
Harris, Wm. C. to Lucinda J. Demming 1-21-1850 (1-22-1850) F
Harris, Wm. F. to Martha E. McSpadden 7-16-1844 F
Harris, Wm. F. to Mary S. Mickleberry 10-28-1823 Sh
Harris, Wm. H. to Mary E. Haskins 12-14-1870 Ma
Harris, Wm. Henry to Ellen Evans 11-17-1866 (no return) Hy
Harris, Wm. L. to Jennie Williams 5-7-1870 Ma
Harris, Wm. P. to Tabitha Cain 11-27-1868 (12-3-1868) Ma
Harris, Wm. T. to Mary A. Woods 11-8-1854 Cr
Harris, Wm. W. to Mary C. Cribbs 12-23-1848 (no return) Cr
Harris, Wm. to Lizzie Paul 2-19-1876 (4-15-1876) Dy
Harris, Zack to Susan Turner 6-20-1869 G B
Harris, jr., Henry to Betsy R. Cole 12-26-1868 (no return) Hy
Harris, jr., J. W. to Mary Goode 9-12-1865 (9-13-1865) F
Harris?, Nathl. to Elizabeth Starling 7-25-1850 (no return) F
Harrison (Hanna?), James M. to Mary A. Wilson 10-29-1848 L
Harrison, A. C. to E. J. McKnight 12-15-1875 (12-17-1875) Dy
Harrison, Albert to Mariah Williams 2-13-1869 G B
Harrison, Alf to Randa Louiville 7-1-1871 (no return) Hy
Harrison, Andrew H. to Eliza J. Graves 9-9-1845 (9-11-1845) Ma
Harrison, B. F. to Julia A. Brigaman 12-1-1857 Cr
Harrison, Benjamin S. to Mary E. Miller 4-28-1868 (4-30-1868) L
Harrison, C. M. to J. A. Ford 9-9-1866 G
Harrison, Calvin M. to Mary A. E. Rentfro 7-15-1846 (7-16-1846) G
Harrison, Cris R. to Sarah R. Adams 4-22-1845 Hr
Harrison, D. W. to Elizabeth Rogers 2-23-1856 (2-24-1856) G
Harrison, Daniel to Tabitha Abbott 6-14-1838 Sh
Harrison, David to Elizabeth Forsyth 10-1-1840 (10-4-1840) Hr
Harrison, David to Sarah Gibbs 5-8-1873 (no return) Hy
Harrison, E. W. to Sarah E. McCully 9-18-1854 (no return) F
Harrison, Elisha to A. J. E. Hunt 5-13-1868 G
Harrison, Francis M. to Mary Ann Cole 8-13-1852 (8-14-1852) Hr
Harrison, Francis M. to Musidora Graves 8-10-1853 Ma
Harrison, G. P. to Julia A. Nichols 12-29-1869 Hy
Harrison, Geo. T. to E. F. Mooring 4-21-1866 (4-22-1866) Ma
Harrison, George E. to Ann Paulock 4-7-1847 (4-14-1847) O
Harrison, George S. to Mary Elvina M. Bishop 4-27-1838 (5-10-1838) Ma
Harrison, George W. to Mary Ann Hicks 2-20-1866 Be
Harrison, Grant Z. to Angaline Riley 5-13-1847 G
Harrison, H. J. to Mary Ann Sley 8-5-1856 Sh
Harrison, Harmon to Rebecca J. Doyle 12-21-1858 (12-22-1858) Hr
Harrison, Henry H. to Martha J. Pickler 9-27-1863 Be
Harrison, Henry L. to Frances C. Dunevant 12-3-1878 (12-4-1878) Dy
Harrison, Henry T. to Emma F. Barber 3-19-1855 Sh
Harrison, Henry to Margaret Semons 9-1-1870 G
Harrison, Henry to Sarah Elizabeth Walker 1-2-1842 (1-3-1842) T
Harrison, Herman to Mary Pattison 10-4-1828 (9-18-1828?) O
Harrison, Isaac to Mary Ann Smith 7-8-1854 (7-9-1854) Sh
Harrison, J. C. to Virginia F. Johns 12-20-1859 G
Harrison, J. H. to Amy Maclin 1-2-1878 Hy
Harrison, J. H. to L. E. Parker 7-28-1875 (7-29-1875) Dy
Harrison, J. P. to V. E. Abbot 5-30-1870 G
Harrison, J. W. to M. R. McAliIley 2-26-1879 (2-29-1879) Dy
Harrison, J. W. to Pelina N. Ford 6-26-1857 (6-28-1857) G
Harrison, James C. to Margaret Cole 8-13-1852 (9-19-1852) Hr
Harrison, James D. to Margarett Cooper 12-5-1843 (12-12-1843) G
Harrison, James Hutson to Alvira Cheshier 4-1-1844 (4-2-1844) Hr
Harrison, James P. to Lucinda P. Saggs? 11-23-1860 Hn
Harrison, James to Alleline Adams 5-7-1846 (5-10-1846) G
Harrison, James to Fannie A. Campbell 12-21-1869 (12-23-1869) Ma
Harrison, James to Luzene Saunders 10-27-1858 Hn
Harrison, Jno. E. to O. E. Murphey 8-13-1838 (no return) F
Harrison, Joe to Rosa Warren 12-27-1865 (12-30-1865) F B
Harrison, Joel W. to Elizabeth J. McWherter 11-12-1844 G
Harrison, Joel W. to Elviry A. Hutchens 4-4-1843 (4-13-1843) G

Harrison, John B. to Elizabeth McGee 10-27-1842 Hr
Harrison, John E. to Nancy Jane Wilkins 5-17-1853 (5-?-1853) T
Harrison, John T. to Nannie Givens 5-6-1867 (5-16-1867) Ma
Harrison, John W. to Manervia Ann Dial 7-23-1844 (7-24-1844) Hr
Harrison, John Y. to Judy F. Gibbs 12-23-1845 (12-25-1845) G
Harrison, John to Martha Moore 7-6-1867 F B
Harrison, John to Mary Frances Nelson 8-27-1873 (8-28-1873) L
Harrison, Joseph H. to C. A. Short 9-23-1847 G
Harrison, Joseph to Martha Peal 10-1-1845 (10-2-1845) G
Harrison, Joseph to Narcissa Vire 5-15-1866 (5-16-1866) Dy
Harrison, Kinsey to Mary Ruth Morgan 11-1-1839 (11-7-1839) Ma
Harrison, L. M. to Sarah Jane Craig 10-15-1857 (10-18-1857) Hr
Harrison, L. R. to Martha (Mrs.) McMahon 12-6-1854 Ma
Harrison, Landon to Clara Brown 12-12-1868 F
Harrison, Lawrence to Bridget Mangin 4-14-1857 Sh
Harrison, Lyttleton to Fannie Meux 8-17-1876 Hy
Harrison, Lyttleton to Lucy Fields 1-29-1878 Hy
Harrison, M. B. to Sarah E. Goforth 1-19-1870 T
Harrison, M. to Mary Tittle 4-13-1847 Be
Harrison, Mat to Ava Walker 12-29-1868 G B
Harrison, Medley to Mary L. Noel 3-2-1850 (no return) Hn
Harrison, N. F. to Eliza J. Nealy 2-10-1859 (2-16-1859) Sh
Harrison, R. H. to Mattie V. Towell? 5-5-1856 T
Harrison, Richard H. to Lucy G. Bishop 7-15-1852 Ma
Harrison, Robert to Nancy Duboyce 3-1-1830 (3-2-1830) Hr
Harrison, Robt. to Mary Wilkins 3-17-1867 G B
Harrison, Samuel F. to Pelina L. Rodgers 11-26-1853 (11-29-1853) Sh
Harrison, Seith to Mary C. Wade 12-4-1856 G
Harrison, Thomas B. to Eliza J. Meacham 4-6-1864 (4-7-1864) L
Harrison, Thomas to Hannah Bailey 5-24-1842 Sh
Harrison, Thomas to Rachael Lunsford 1-30-1850 (2-3-1850) L
Harrison, W. H. to Angeline Beaver 1-25-1878 (1-27-1878) Dy
Harrison, W. H. to Jane Williams 10-14-1862 Dy
Harrison, W. T. to J. W. Miller 1-4-1881 (no return) L
Harrison, William Henry to Elizabeth Winney Stevens 11-22-1845 T
Harrison, William N. to Nancy C. McGee 9-16-1846 Ma
Harrison, William R. to Sarah J. Short 1-19-1858 G
Harrison, William to Elizabeth R. Pounds 8-1-1842 (8-3-1842) G
Harrison, William to Melinda Ragsdale 2-18-1832 (1-23-1832) Ma
Harrison, William to Virginia L. Trezevant 8-16-1870 Ma
Harrison, William to Winnie Howard 11-21-1870 G
Harrison, Wm. H. to Mariah J. Smith 4-3-1868 (4-4-1868) T
Harrison, Wm. H. to Martha Faulkner 10-26-1870 (10-27-1870) Dy
Harrison, Wm. J. to Sarah A. T. Ellington 10-4-1849 F
Harrison, Wm. M. to America C. Wade 9-27-1852 G
Harrison, Wm. M. to Margaret E. Neely 12-15-1847 Sh
Harrison, Wm. R. to Milley Forsythe 4-29-1840 (4-30-1840) Hr
Harrison, Wm. to Polly Irvin 2-18-1830 Hr
Harrison, Zachariah to Manerva Daniel 1-31-1857 (2-5-1857) T
Harrison?, John M. to Martha A. Reeves 2-28-1853 (3-1-1853) O
Harriss, Benjamin A. to Rebecca Pirtle 12-27-1837 (12-28-1837) Hr
Harriss, Eli to Martha M. Forbuss 2-25-1846 (2-26-1846) Hr
Harriss, J. B. to Mary E. Rogers 10-12-1857 (11-8-1857) Hr
Harriss, J. C. to Rhody Frasier? 1-6-1845 (1-8-1845) F
Harriss, James H. to Isabella Adams 10-28-1847 Hr
Harriss, Jesse to Percilla Simmons 9-20-1856 (10-1[7]-1856) Hr
Harriss, Robert to Irena Simpson 11-10-1877 (11-11-1877) L B
Harriss, Sandin to Mary (Mrs.) Lay 10-24-1882 (10-26-1882) L
Harriss, West to E. J. Clinton 10-29-1857 Hr
Harriss, West to Mary Ann Palmer? 11-25-1846 (11-26-1846) Hr
Harrisson, Thomas R. to Darthul Lewis 4-8-1830 (4-15-1830) G
Harrity, Fredrick to Nancy Nunn 1-31-1878 (no return) Hy
Harroe, James B. to Mary C. Johnson 11-25-1860 We
Harrol, Benjamin F. to Ann Douglas 4-10-1835 Sh
Harrol, Warner to Maria Phillips 11-9-1833 Sh
Harroldson, John to Mary E. Minnis 2-7-1849 Sh
Harroldson, Silas to Sarah Williams 9-28-1829 Sh
Harrolson, Major to Lucinda Dawson 3-31-1832 Sh
Harron, William to Sarah C. Hubbard 7-24-1839 G
Harsten (Hasting), W. L. to Sarah E. Rose 3-4-1871 (no return) Hy
Harston, D. W. to N. C. Wilson 12-29-1860 Ma
Harston, Henry to Susan Brant 10-13-1846 (10-14-1846) Ma
Harston, J. Polk to Bettie Lackie 11-28-1868 Ma
Harston, Jarrod to Susan M. Fitzhugh 10-21-1871 Ma
Harston, Marmaduke Y. to Clara A. Worley 12-30-1845 (1-1-1846) Ma
Hart, A. S. to Mary E. Corley 1-3-1855 (3-30-1855) G
Hart, Aaron to Caroline Crisenberry 3-16-1843 Hn
Hart, Aaron to Sarah S. Chrisenberry 5-8-1860 Hn
Hart, Allen to Juvel Loving 12-23-1866 Hy
Hart, Andrew M. to Violet J. Taylor 6-12-1843 (6-13-1843) Ma
Hart, Andrew to Sarah C. Turner 4-16-1860 Dy
Hart, Andrew to Sarah Jane Ferrell 10-11-1870 (10-12-1870) Dy
Hart, Anthony to Julia Murray 5-8-1852 (5-9-1852) Sh
Hart, Benjamin to Martha L. Locke 5-12-1862 Sh
Hart, Calvin D. to Eleaner J. (Mrs.) Shar 1-17-1863 (1-18-1863) Sh
Hart, Calvin V. to Sadie E. Alexander 2-20-1871 (2-22-1871) Ma
Hart, Charles Henry to Ann Faris 1-31-1844 (2-8-1844) T

Hart, Charles V. to Julia A. R. Tanner 3-30-1861 (3-31-1861) Sh
Hart, Charles V. to Mary E. Tauner 3-27-1858 Sh
Hart, Charles to Lucy Hart 7-25-1882 L
Hart, David to Masouri Woods 9-3-1846 We
Hart, F. P. to Ula Durham 12-5-1877 L
Hart, George to Lizzie Mann 11-30-1876 Hy
Hart, H. C. to D. L. Pope 2-15-1876 Dy
Hart, J. A. to A. E. Williams 8-10-1875 L
Hart, J. B. to Lola M. Strickland 12-16-1885 L
Hart, J. L. to Drusilla Ballard 10-22-1863 Hn
Hart, Jack to India Shirley 8-18-1867 Hy
Hart, James A. to Jane Allen 4-29-1845 Cr
Hart, James A. to Lurinda B. Brown 5-27-1856 Sh
Hart, James M. to Ann King 7-28-1854 Ma *
Hart, James M. to Daley Marsh 5-31-1848 Hn
Hart, James N. to Martha S. Mayo 11-22-1869 Ma
Hart, James to Mary B. Locke 6-27-1850 Sh
Hart, James to Nancy Robinson 1-20-1839 (2-7-1839) O
Hart, John to Elizabeth Brundage 10-10-1844 Hn
Hart, John to Elizabeth Clanton 12-20-1869 (12-22-1869) Ma
Hart, John to Lizzie Hampton 3-7-1871 Cr B
Hart, John to Tilia Patterson 8-31-1870 (no return) Cr
Hart, Jordon to Lizzie Smith 5-28-1870 T
Hart, Josephus to Mollie Langford 7-13-1868 (no return) Hy
Hart, Martin to Mary O'Conner 6-19-1849 Sh
Hart, Milton J. to Parilee Patterson 11-19-1860 (11-20-1860) Cr
Hart, Milton to Parilee Patterson 11-19-1860 Cr
Hart, N. H. to N. T. Alexander 1-23-1859 Hn
Hart, P. W. to Nancy A. Thurmond 9-11-1873 Dy
Hart, Patrick to Ellen O'Neill 6-9-1860 (6-10-1860) Sh
Hart, R. L. to L. M. Johnson 5-10-1861 (no return) Cr
Hart, Robert D. to Ellen May 10-1-1862 (10-?-1862) Ma
Hart, S. A. to Susan Smith 7-31-1855 (no return) F
Hart, S. M. to M. J. Moore 3-11-1866
Hart, S. M. to N. J. Strayhorn 2-29-187? Hy
Hart, Spencer Thomas to Martha Caroline Hoffler 6-1-1844 (6-6-1844) T
Hart, Stephen to Frances Sturdivant 7-28-1847 Hn
Hart, Thomas to Jane Bauchman 3-4-1847 Hn
Hart, Thos. W. to Julia F. Wise 3-30-1868 (no return) Hy
Hart, W. L. to Sallie Holt 10-16-1865 (10-17-1865) F
Hart, William C. to Eleanor C. Davis 1-28-1850 T
Hart, William J. to Mary Rickman 12-3-1866 (no return) Hn
Hart, William W. to Elizabeth M. Johnson 1-5-1857 (1-6-1857) Ma
Hart, William to Eliza Meadows 3-31-1841 Hn
Hart, William to Mary Milstead 12-25-1854 Hn
Hart, jr., Benjamin to Hester A. Johnston 11-17-1874 L
Harte, John M. to Nancy V. Edwards 4-3-1856 (no return) We
Harte, Thomas G. to Ruth P. McWherter 11-11-1857 We
Hartfield, M. F. to Hariet L. Max 1-3-1870 (1-5-1870) T
Hartgraves, Andrew to Mary Johnson 7-14-1841 Sh
Hartie, John to Caroline Hurst 6-2-1860 Sh
Hartis, Andrew S. to Josaphin Marshall 10-31-1851 (no return) F
Hartlage, William to Emma Ullman 9-3-1864 Sh
Hartley, Albert J. to Margaret Cook 12-11-1856 (12-10?-1856) Sh
Hartley, George to Clary Owens 8-7-1845 (no return) We
Hartley, Joseph to Frances Jones 12-28-1875 Hy
Hartley, Joseph to Mary Spillers 10-8-1881 (10-9-1881) L
Hartley, Nathan F. to Rhoda Jane Tubbs 4-1-1857 Sh
Hartman, Jacob to Mary (Mrs.) Balmer 8-8-1863 (8-9-1863) Sh
Hartman, W. B.? to Mary A. Norman 10-1-1860 (10-2-1860) Cr
Hartman, Wm. to Sarah Massey 6-7-1857 Cr
Harton, John W. to Nannie Wheeler 7-31-1869 (8-1-1869) Dy
Harton, John to Catherine B. McKnight 6-8-1843 Ma
Harton, M. L. to Lula Landis 12-4-1877 Dy
Hartsfield, Benjamin F. to Nancy Ann Leach 8-8-1855 T
Hartsfield, Berry to Tempa Banks 2-16-1867 G B
Hartsfield, Jacob to Martha F. Hartsfield 1-3-1873 (1-5-1873) T
Hartsfield, James to Abigail Williams 8-16-1849 T
Hartsfield, John C. to Catharine E. Truman 10-3-1853 (10-4-1853) G
Hartsfield, M. H. to M. F. Myers 9-29-1866 (9-30-1866) T
Hartsfield, Marcus H. to Susan Myers 11-30-1853 (12-1-1853) T
Hartsfield, Marcus Henry to Emily Leach 12-26-1849 T
Hartsfield, Simeon B. to Elizabeth Crawford 11-15-1856 (no return) Hn
Hartsfield, Simeon B. to Malinda Crawford 12-21-1841 (no return) Hn
Hartsfield, W. A. J. to Rebecca Ewell 3-5-1857 T
Hartsfield, William S. to Caroline S. Lane 1-5-1857 (1-6-1857) G
Hartung, J. E. to Elizabeth Steiner 11-20-1854 Sh
Hartwell, N. W. to Sarah Snow 4-4-1844 Sh
Harty, Jacob to Alsy Eaton 9-26-1845 (10-1-1845) Hr
Harty, John R. to Juda E. Scoggins 8-16-1855 Hr
Harty, Peter to Ellen (Mrs.) Reddyn 2-10-1864 (2-9?-1864) Sh
Hartz, Mathias to Christina Allison 12-23-1854 (12-25-1854) Sh
Hartz, Peter to Barbara Rush 11-27-1861 Sh
Hartzfield, W. G. to M. E. Cummings 3-18-1861 Sh
Harvard(Howard?), James W. to Winneford C. Moore 2-3-1842 Hr
Harvell, Allen to Amanda? S.? Rhodes 11-28-1867 T
Harvell, L. C. to Puss Giles 3-7-1865 (3-8-1865) Dy
Harvell, W. R. to Mary Williams 9-7-1874 (9-9-1874) T
Harver, Wilk to Betty Maclin 3-2-1874 (no return) Hy
Harvey, A. I. to Nancy Adams 12-25-1844 Cr
Harvey, Abner to Minney(Winney) W. Duncan 2-12-1836 (1?-17?-1836) Hr
Harvey, Albert G. to Martha G. Joyner 5-16-1848 Hr
Harvey, B. R. to Mary E. Sheffield 1-13-1845 Sh
Harvey, Blunt to Sarah E. Sullivan 3-4-1868 (3-10-1868) F
Harvey, F. F. to M. J. Roach 1-5-1857 (no return) Cr
Harvey, Franklin S. to Sarah A. Gallion 1-11-1855 G
Harvey, George to Ella Brown 9-22-1877 (9-28-1877) L
Harvey, H. to Sarah Quinn 1-2-1843 (no return) Hr
Harvey, James M. to Margret Murphy 4-14-1845 Hr
Harvey, James to Annie Archey 1-4-1860 O
Harvey, Jeff to Margaret Halleburton 1-28-1871 (no return) L
Harvey, Jesse S. to Mary A. Hamlett 8-14-1855 (8-15-1855) Hr
Harvey, Jesse to Nancy Rodgers 11-10-1866 (11-20-1866) F
Harvey, John to Kate Johnson 6-30-1863 Sh
Harvey, Lot to Nancy Boyd 3-23-1866 (4-1-1866) F B
Harvey, Marcus D. to Rebeca C. Burford 4-8-1839 (4-9-1839) F
Harvey, Oney S. to Elizabeth C. Murphy 12-29-1847 (12-30-1847) Hr
Harvey, R. H. (Dr.) to Mary J. Rogers 6-16-1869 F
Harvey, R. K. to Josephine Wilson 4-11-1857 (no return) We
Harvey, Richd. H. to Della Ann Harrison? 12-19-1848 F
Harvey, Samuel to Sarah Vaught 8-1-1844 (8-20-1844) Hr
Harvey, Stephen to Manerva Green 11-22-1876 L
Harvey, Stephen to Mollie Bond 10-19-1871 Hy
Harvey, T. J. to Sallie Earle 12-30-1878 (12-31-1878) Dy
Harvey, Thomas to Jane Cartwright 5-20-1859 (5-22-1859) Hr
Harvey, W. B. to J. C. Rhodes 3-31-1869 (no return) F
Harvey, W. M. to Alice C. Farrell 8-1-1860 (8-2-1860) Sh
Harvey, William H. to Mary R. Penn 11-15-1849 Hr
Harvey, William to Jane Elliot 11-28-1883 (12-1-1883) L
Harvey, William to Lucy Seay 5-8-1828 Sh
Harvey, William to Sarah A. Keel 4-24-1863 G
Harville, J. H. to Nancy A. English 10-16-1867 (10-17-1867) O
Harville, T. Z. to Nancy N. Morgan 12-3-1867 O
Harvy, G. M. to Slomy L. Elrod 11-4-1867 (no return) Hy
Harvy, James L. to Elizabeth A. Walker 11-14-1842 (11-15-1842) F
Harvy, T. K. to M. A. Leech 2-3-1866 (2-5-1866) Cr
Harvy, Wm. to M. P. Ellis 8-17-1864 O
Harwell, Abner to Martha F. Craig 5-28-1867 Dy
Harwell, Buckner to Mary J. Ross 10-2-1867 (10-3-1867) F
Harwell, Buckner to Rose Ann Hamlett 7-8-1840 (7-9-1840) F
Harwell, H. L. to Elizabeth Snow 12-21-1875 (12-22-1875) Dy
Harwell, James S. to Lucy Ann Harvey 2-15-1844 Sh
Harwell, L. C. to Sallie M. Martin 10-21-1872 (no return) Hy
Harwell, Neal S. to Virginia Moore 1-17-1871 (1-18-1871) Dy
Harwell, Thomas to Elizabeth W. Eddins 1-17-1848 (1-20-1848) F
Harwell, W. F. to Rosina Wells 11-15-1865 (11-21-1865) F
Harwell, W. F. to Sally Malory 3-17-1865 (3-21-1865) Dy
Harwell, W. P. to Mary P. Smith 1-1-1874 Hy
Harwood, James A. to Virlinda C. Beazley 7-22-1834 G
Harwood, jr., R. D. to ___ E. Pybas 6-3-1861 G
Hasbey, Burwell S. to Rebecca M. Eddins 1-13-1840 (1-14-1840) F
Haselet, James A. to Darcus Branch 9-21-1867 (no return) F B
Hashler, D. M. B. to Jane Locke 10-11-1854 (no return) F
Hask, Philipp to Mary Keim 5-20-1858 Sh
Haskell, John to Ama Crowder 11-26-1871 Hy
Haskell, William T. to Sarah J. Porter 2-7-1838 Hn
Haskill, J. F. to M. E. Dodd 12-20-1869 (no return) L
Haskill, J. F. to R. J. McDearman 1-7-1869 (not executed) L
Haskin, Lafayette to Lucinda Harris 12-30-1878 (1-18-1879) Dy
Haskins, A. B. (Dr.) to M. A. Tucker 5-19-1873 (no return) Dy
Haskins, A. L. to Edmonia Fortune 12-23-1869 Hy
Haskins, Alex to Eliza Daugherty 3-15-1877 (no return) Dy
Haskins, Ben to Lucinda Lanier 12-25-1877 (12-26-1877) Dy
Haskins, Calvin to Mary Young 12-22-1866 (12-24-1866) F B
Haskins, Crred B. to Nancy Johnson 12-26-1848 (12-27-1848) Ma
Haskins, Haf to Fannie Prichard 8-16-1873 (8-17-1873) Dy
Haskins, Henry to Emma Ledsinger 9-24-1872 (9-26-1872) Dy
Haskins, J. B. to M. J. Draper 8-8-1860 G
Haskins, J. C. to Ann E. Douglass 11-12-1866 (11-13-1866) Dy
Haskins, James V. to Elisabeth Smith 11-30-1857 (12-10-1857) Hr
Haskins, James V. to Margaret Meaxey 7-19-1865 Ma
Haskins, R. C. to M. A. Snodgrass 10-26-1862 Hn
Haskins, Richard to Martha Harris 8-19-1874 (8-20-1874) Dy
Haskins, Sam to Amelia Swift 4-30-1874 (5-1-1874) Dy
Haskins, Wash to Jessie Hightower 4-3-1873 Hy
Haslerigg, A. J. to Mary Futurell 10-30-1860 (11-1-1861) We
Haslewood, John R. to Martha L. Barger 3-11-1859 We
Hassal, James to Mary King 8-31-1840 Hr
Hassell, Daniel to Monah Thomas 1-23-1856 (1-24-1856) G
Hassell, David to Susanah A. Butler 12-6-1854 G
Hassell, George E. to Narcissa E. Butler 10-6-1855 (10-7-1855) G
Hassell, George E. to Rachel E. Bryan 12-3-1865 G
Hassell, John to Elizabeth Jones 5-1-1855 G
Hassell, John to Emma January 12-18-1860 G

Hassett, John to Margaret Harrington 6-30-1862 Sh
Hast, Josiah to Duicy (Drucy?) Brown 8-24-1850 L
Haste, H. T. to S. J. Powell 5-25-1865 G
Haste, Jacob to Fanny Wilkins 1-8-1867 G
Haste, W. H. to Martha J. Hendrix 10-26-1865 G
Hasten, John C. to Dinah Francisco 11-23-1854 Be
Hasten, William D. to Mahaly E. T. Francisco 3-11-1852 Be
Hasteto, Isaac to Martha Thom 3-3-1842 Ma
Hastin, John to Charity Bond 3-3-1841 (no return) Hn
Hasting, J. T. to E. E. Fortner 11-12-1874 L
Hastings, F. W. to Mary Jane Pearce 12-28-1856 Hn
Hastings, Henry W. to Sarah A. Ward 1-3-1855 Hn
Hastings, Henry to Lucy Lacy 7-6-1867 T
Hastings, J. E. to Charlotte J. Key 11-2-1863 Hn
Hastings, James C. to Mary E. Wright 2-26-1863 Hn
Hastings, James H. to Mary A. Smith 10-12-1853 Hn
Hastings, James P. to Mary E. Stanfield 2-13-1850 Hn
Hastings, John T. to Elizabeth G. Norred 12-12-1860 Hn
Hastings, Joseph M. to Mary Gregston 4-17-1850 Hn
Hastings, Lawrence G. to Nancy M. Winsett 11-23-1860 Hn
Hastings, Samuel M. to Martha A. Biles 5-18-1853 Hn
Hastings, Samuel M. to Sarah Ann McGowan 1-17-1858 Hn
Hastings, Simpson to Susan A. Fortner 8-21-1844 (8-?-1844) T
Hastings, Thomas M. to Catharine Horn 10-16-1845 Hn
Hastings, W. R. to Rebecca F. Morton 7-17-1861 Mn
Hastings, William G. to Elvira A. Hagler 10-10-1852 Hn
Hastings, ____ to S. A. Wimberly 11-19-1866 Hn
Haston, James N. to Elizabeth J. Mathews 3-27-1856 Be
Hasty, William to Hester Ann Cole 8-27-1855 O
Hatch, B. D. to Funtrey? Williams 8-?-1861 (no return) Cr
Hatch, E. R. to Jane Grooms 6-28-1841 T
Hatch, Geo. T. to Ridley J. Mitchell 1-16-1872 (no return) Cr
Hatch, Granvil L. to Winnie C. Suggs 4-7-1873 (4-9-1873) Cr
Hatch, Harry J. to Milly Kirk 2-12-1861 (no return) Cr
Hatch, Henry to Sarah Wilson 9-21-1858 (9-23-1858) Hr
Hatch, J. W. to Elizabeth Griggs 12-16-1846 Cr
Hatch, James A. to Lucinda Suggs 4-5-1861 (no return) Cr
Hatch, Thomas F. to Samantha A. Newton 8-1-1866 (8-2-1866) L
Hatch, Thomas H. to Mary Jane McFarland 10-20-1867 Hn
Hatch, W. S. to M. A. E. Hall 9-19-1869 G
Hatchel, E. L. to Martha Wilson 9-6-1871 (9-12-1871) T
Hatcher, Augustus to Elizabeth Thomas 1-11-1868 (1-12-1868) F B
Hatcher, Charles S. to Mary A. Robbins 9-6-1838 Sh
Hatcher, David M. W. to Francis Estes 11-20-1862 We
Hatcher, Henry to Lucy Fletcher 6-26-1851 G
Hatcher, J. W. to S. P. Lete 2-3-1869 L
Hatcher, James G. to M. E. J. Hellis 2-28-1850 We
Hatcher, James L. to Nancy Wilson 5-15-1852 O
Hatcher, James L. to Nancy Randolph no date (with Oct 1837) O
Hatcher, Richard H. to Harriet H. Marr 4-4-1853 O
Hatcher, W. T. to C. L. Hardy 10-5-1865 Hn
Hatchett, A. to S. A. (Mrs.) Best 3-10-1863 (3-11-1863) Sh
Hatchett, Edwards G. to Ester W. Carter 7-12-1839 Cr
Hatchett, Samuel W. to Susan M. Scrape 10-21-1852 G
Hatfield, James to Aphra Byford? 11-29-1870 (12-1-1870) L
Hatfield, John to Milly Byford 11-7-1870 L
Hatfield, William to Sarah Pryor 9-9-1870 (9-11-1870) L
Hatfield, Wm. to Ellen Smith 12-17-1847 Sh
Hathaway, J. J. to Anna M. Newton 2-3-1871 (2-14-1871) L
Hathaway, James H. to Emily McIver 12-30-1862 (no return) Hy
Hathaway, Joseph F. to Lucinda Christian 5-18-1848 Sh
Hathaway, Kinchen to Susan Cozart 12-5-1859 (12-8-1859) Ma
Hathaway, Ralph to Eviline H. Carlton 10-15-1856 Sh
Hathaway, Richard K. to Permelia Ann Emerson 8-23-1870 (9-11-1870) L
Hathaway, Theopolus to Lucy Anna West 11-7-1853 Sh
Hathcock, William to Mary Evans 1-8-1857 Sh
Hathcock, Wm. H. to Frances R. McKinnon 9-3-1867 Hy
Hathorne, George to Letsey Moten 12-29-1865 (no return) Hy
Hathway, James A. to Martha F. Holland 11-27-1862 (11-30-1862) Dy
Hatler, Franklin M. to Elizabeth Bass 12-16-1861 We
Hatler, H. M. to Sarah Ann Martin 9-26-1849 Hn
Hatler, John to Rachel Haskins 1-28-1856 (no return) Hn
Hatler, Samuel to Jane Hatler 9-18-1860 We
Hatley, Alsey W. to Mary A. Hatley 2-7-1865 Be
Hatley, Edward to Polly Ann Gossett 9-21-1845 Be
Hatley, Eli to Susan Merrick 11-24-1839 Be
Hatley, Green to Martha L. Bohanon 3-9-1848 Be
Hatley, Hardy to Paralee Baggett 1-2-1853 Be
Hatley, Hardy to Rebecca Harden 12-28-1856 Be
Hatley, Jackson to Elizabeth Ann Tedder 3-27-1845 Be
Hatley, Luke to Augustine Nichols 10-27-1863 Be
Hatley, Mark A. to Mary C. Thompson 2-14-1867 Be
Hatley, P. H. to Persilla Morris 1-10-1869 Be
Hatley, Richard to Mary Reagan 1-5-1825 (1-9-1825) Hr
Hatley, Thomas to P. E. Phifer 12-25-1867 Be
Hatley, Wesley to Anna M. Tedder 3-14-1850 Be
Hatley, William to Elizabeth Jane Smith 2-8-1844 Be
Hatley, Wyly to Rebecca Nichols 3-8-1861 Be
Hatton, Joshua C. to Lucinda Morgan no date Ma
Hauck, John C. to Louisa Albert 10-24-1860 (10-25-1860) Sh
Hauck, Thomas L. to Sarah Miller 7-4-1863 (7-5-1863) O
Hauf, Joseph to Roselia Beer 1-24-1854 (no return) F
Haughey, Alex to Jinnie Scott 12-23-1874 Hy
Haughton, A. G. to Mollie Bennett 3-2-1869 G
Haughton, George to Harriett Barrett 9-14-1840 (9-15-1840) Ma
Haughton, J. C. to Nancy Taylor 1-19-1831 O
Haughton, Lemuel B. to P. E. Geyle 5-8-1860 (5-9-1860) Ma
Haughton, Willis to Mary D. Ellington 10-23-1867 (10-24-1867) Ma
Haulton, Elisha to Amanda Roark 6-25-1850 (6-28-1850) Hr
Haun, Robert F. to Malinda F. Williamson 5-24-1870 G
Haurer, Peter to F. Mathies 6-27-1859 Sh
Haven, Alexander to Unity P. Fowler 1-6-1840 Sh
Havens, R. W. to Cornelia Ulmo 11-24-1858 Sh
Havercamp, Harmon to Isabella A. M. Montgomery 2-5-1867 F
Haviall, J. L. to Anabell Sanling 7-10-1865 (7-11-1865) O
Hawes, Luyton C. to America Shrote 10-6-1851 Hn
Hawes, Wyatt to Elizabeth Gurat? 2-28-1839 Hn
Hawk, Ephreham to Judy Shelton 12-16-1871 (12-17-1871) T
Hawk, George W. to Martha L. Porter 9-21-1853 Cr
Hawkes, J. S. to Adrienne Swift 11-21-1878 Dy
Hawkins, A. G. to Susan E. Prince 11-10-1869 (11-11-1869) Cr
Hawkins, Albert to Lear Whitelaw 12-23-1877 (no return) Hy
Hawkins, Anderson to Susan Whillis 6-30-1844 Cr
Hawkins, Ashton to Sarah A. Lilly 9-15-1847 (no return) Hn
Hawkins, B. F. to Mary L. Blanton 9-8-1862 O
Hawkins, B. H. to Lucy E. Vaughan 2-4-1840 Sh
Hawkins, Bray to Sarah King 4-16-1840 Hr
Hawkins, Camillus to Joe Ann Cole 11-9-1868 (11-12-1868) Cr
Hawkins, Carroll to Jinnie Bell 4-14-1872 (no return) Cr B
Hawkins, E. E. to Harriet L. Ferguson 2-12-1867 (2-13-1867) Dy
Hawkins, G. B. to Sallie A. Worrell 1-17-1866 F
Hawkins, G. W. to A. A. Ferguson 10-6-1868 (no return) Dy
Hawkins, Harvey to Elizabeth Reaves 1-20-1831 Sh
Hawkins, Isaac R. to Ellen Ott 3-29-1843 Cr
Hawkins, J. J. to E. R. Bond 8-2-1864 (no return) Hy
Hawkins, J. W. to Willie Baxter 12-3-1878 (12-4-1878) L
Hawkins, James L. to Sarah Vaughan 12-21-1837 Sh
Hawkins, James W. to Mary E. Kinsolving 8-22-1857 Hn
Hawkins, James to M. Haskins 12-26-1855 (no return) Hn
Hawkins, Joe to Caroline Priest 12-30-1871 (no return) Cr B
Hawkins, John C. to Persia M. Porter 5-27-1863 Cr
Hawkins, John N. to E. Hill 11-11-1844 Hn
Hawkins, John S. to Sarah Dean 1-17-1846 Sh
Hawkins, John to Sarah M. Owen 5-14-1833 Sh
Hawkins, Joseph R. to Ellen Cochran 9-19-1860 We
Hawkins, Joseph to Sarah Randolph 6-27-1847 Sh
Hawkins, L. B. to Julia Taylor 3-5-1860 (no return) Hy
Hawkins, L. L. to Rebeca W. Caldwell 10-2-1861 Cr
Hawkins, Levi to Lucy Bledsoe 11-26-1871 Cr B
Hawkins, Mathew S. to Sarah A. L. Kennedy 2-7-1859 G
Hawkins, Matt to Henrietta Tyus 2-19-1878 (no return) Hy
Hawkins, Matthew to Rhoda Jarrett 1-27-1885 (1-29-1885) L
Hawkins, Moses A. to Pelina C. Hatchett 9-11-1861 G
Hawkins, Moses B. to A. U. M. S. Word 10-16-1844 G
Hawkins, Moses B. to Nancy Lattie 7-29-1835 (8-2-1835) G
Hawkins, Ralph to Susan Jane Erwin 9-14-1861 (9-16-1861) Hr
Hawkins, Ransom to Martha Jane (Mrs.) Howard 3-18-1856 Sh
Hawkins, Richard to Margaret Cox 12-20-1874 Hy
Hawkins, Richard to Silvy Halliburton 4-4-1874 (4-5-1874) L B
Hawkins, S. E. to Mary A. Butler 6-21-1864 (6-22-1864) Sh
Hawkins, S. H. to ____ Dinkins 5-6-1868 T
Hawkins, S. P. to Sarah A. Hardin 4-5-1870 (4-6-1870) Dy
Hawkins, Saml. B. to Mary A. Crawford 7-23-1846 Sh
Hawkins, Samuel B. to Mary I. Dunkin 6-2-1842 Sh
Hawkins, Samuel J. to Mildred E. Trotter 5-15-1855 Sh
Hawkins, Samuel W. to Hester? B. Gardner 3-20-1867 Cr
Hawkins, Silas to Jane Utley 2-14-1868 G B
Hawkins, Thomas R. to Charity Powell 12-4-1844 Sh
Hawkins, Thomas to Fannie Lake 1-20-1875 (no return) Hy
Hawkins, Thomas to Orphy Huddleston 7-28-1841 Sh
Hawkins, W. H. H. to Susan E. Underwood 3-6-1861 O
Hawkins, W. H. to Mary E. Blackwell 10-7-1868 (10-9-1868) Cr
Hawkins, William B. to Malvina Jobe 3-4-1858 Sh
Hawkins, William D. to Anna Guthery 9-28-1864 (10-2-1864) Sh
Hawkins, William R. to Martha McGill 10-11-1855 Sh
Hawks, D. J. to Eveline Keath 12-5-1853 G
Hawks, J. D. to Elizabeth Westbrooks 12-30-1857 We
Hawks, J. G. to Sabina J. Smith 10-5-1858 We
Hawks, John to Margaret Price 2-28-1857 We
Hawley, A. to Eliza J. Comb 12-19-1865 Be
Hawley, Jos. H. to Susan C. Brown 9-28-1843 Sh
Hawley, R. M. to Laura Brown 1-14-1869 Be
Hawley, R. M. to Sarah Carter 12-12-1857 Be
Hawley, R. M> to Fendee Forehand 8-4-1856 Be

Hawley, W. S. to Margaret F. Shoemaker 2-9-1871 (2-24-1871) F
Hawson, D. H. to Nancy C. Oliver 11-15-1833 Sh
Hawson, George H. to Mary A. White 2-11-1869 Ma
Hawthorn, John G. to Mary (Mrs.) Payne 6-24-1841 Sh
Hawthorn, John W. to Sarah Ann Oliver 2-15-1842 Sh
Hawthorn, R. H. to E. Gillispie 12-24-1847 Be
Hawthorne, John to Nancy (Mrs.) Beasley 11-16-1864 Sh
Hawze, W. D. to Bettie J. Adkins 6-18-1874 (6-25-1874) T
Hay, Abrom to Elizabeth Winberg 10-14-1866 (no return) Cr
Hay, Allen to Mollie Walker 5-23-1878 Hy
Hay, Benjamin to Amanda A. Hester 5-19-1865 (5-21-1865) O
Hay, G. T. to Rebecca J. Murray 3-9-1874 (3-11-1874) Dy
Hay, H. D. to Mary Bell 7-19-1871 (7-20-1871) Dy
Hay, Henderson to Matilda Wyatt 11-15-1877 Hy
Hay, Henry S. to Lucinda Humphrey 12-24-1863 Sh
Hay, Jacob H. to Sophia J. Lainer 12-27-1854 G
Hay, Jeremiah to Ibby M. J. Harbour 3-20-1848 G
Hay, John B. to Margaret E. Coop 1-7-1846 G
Hay, John H. to Frances E. Taylor 9-13-1867 (no return) Dy
Hay, Martin to Catharine Kine 6-24-1858 Sh
Hay, Moses to Luciller Wood 12-10-1870 (12-11-1870) T
Hay, W. B. to Emily Shaw 2-22-1875 (no return) Hy
Hay, William H. to Mary Dunn 6-27-1838 (no return) Hn
Hay, Wm. B. to Lucy Blye 3-23-1871 Hy
Hayce, Isaac to Silva Hayce 5-6-1866 G
Hayden, Daniel to Maggie Payne 9-21-1869 (9-24-1869) T
Hayes, Alex F. to Sidney Walls 11-18-1852 Sh
Hayes, Alexander to Susan Moore 10-17-1855 Cr
Hayes, Frank to Camilea Mitchell 11-18-1884 (11-19-1884) L
Hayes, Freeman to Lizzie Curtis 3-3-1877 Hy
Hayes, G. W. to Mary E. Jones 9-25-1871 (9-26-1871) O
Hayes, Henry to Ann Daves 3-19-1862 O
Hayes, Henry to Mary Finnigen 5-27-1856 Sh
Hayes, James F. to Rosetta E. Crain 3-22-1876 (3-26-1876) L
Hayes, James M. to Sarah J. Crutchfield 10-24-1844 Cr
Hayes, Jno. W. (Dr.) to Lue Moore 10-9-1872 Hy
Hayes, John to Ellen Corcoran 3-18-1863 Sh
Hayes, John to Mary Webb 11-6-1833 Sh
Hayes, Patrick to Nancy Ford 3-10-1841 Sh
Hayes, Pinkey R. to Carcilla M. Palmer 11-1-1859 Hn
Hayes, W. H. to Sue M. Moore 10-17-1872 Hy
Hayes, Will R. (Dr.) to Sallie Fakes 12-18-1878 Dy
Haygood, James P. to Sarah G. McFarland 8-17-1847 Hn
Haygood, James to Mary L. Austin 12-5-1857 (no return) We
Hayley, Benjamin to Mariah T. Fleming 11-24-1846 (11-25-1846) Ma
Hayley, George to Harriet (Mrs.) Hayley 8-15-1871 (8-17-1871) Ma
Hayley, James T. to Nancy E. Tomlin 11-6-1856 Ma
Hayley, James to Mary E. Moxley 1-23-1869 (1-24-1869) Ma
Hayley, John B. to Margaret A. Tomlin 6-23-1860 (6-27-1860) Ma
Hayley, John to Laura Ann Fowler 11-9-1842 Ma
Hayley, S. M. to Evalin Poindexter 3-21-1871 (no return) Cr
Hayley, S. S. to Mollie A. Mills 12-5-1865 (12-14-1865) Cr
Hayley, Wm. H. to Louisa McKinney 1-28-1857 Cr
Haylon, U. R. to Susan Coleman 12-24-1867 O
Haymes, David E. to Elizabeth V. Young 12-23-1864 Hn
Haymes, Manuel to Lucy Russell 5-19-1866 (no return) Hn
Hayne, John to Margaret Miller 8-3-1858 Sh
Hayne, Wm. F. to Jane E. Waldron 4-13-1844 Sh
Haynes, A. B. to Lizzie Buntyn 12-31-1859 (1-1-1860) Sh
Haynes, A. F. to Missouri J. Williams 8-27-1868 (no return) L
Haynes, A. J. to Sarah Oliver 10-19-1869 (10-20-1869) L
Haynes, A. L. to Minerva J. Ledbetter 4-12-1879 (4-20-1879) L
Haynes, Andrew J. to Mellissa Patton 1-26-1852 (no return) Cr
Haynes, Charles H. to Susan E. Cates 1-26-1870 (1-27-1870) Cr
Haynes, Charles to Eliza Rogers 7-25-1838 (no return) Cr
Haynes, Clifton J. to Berta Bailey 9-7-1878 Hy
Haynes, Clifton J. to Mary E. Greaves 11-18-1859 (no return) Hy
Haynes, David A. to Martha E. Jones 3-6-1851 Hn
Haynes, David to Martha Glover 4-1-1847 Hn
Haynes, Elridge to Mary Putman 9-8-1842 Cr
Haynes, Elvin to Ann E. Wall 3-15-1867 Hn B
Haynes, H. G. to P. J. Petty 2-7-1856 (no return) Hn
Haynes, Harbert H. to Sarah E. Roberson 9-21-1843 Ma
Haynes, Henry to Jane Dinwiddie 1-27-1867 Hn B
Haynes, Henry to Matilda Butler 1-2-1828 (1-3-1828) Ma
Haynes, Isaac C. to Ann E. Cunningham 12-17-1853 (12-20-1853) G
Haynes, Isaac N. to Mary T. McKee 8-20-1873 (8-21-1873) Dy
Haynes, J. G. to E. V. Ledbetter 5-4-1885 (5-5-1885) L
Haynes, J. J. to Annie Fortner 12-13-1882 L
Haynes, James A. to Ann E. Candler 9-20-1849 Sh
Haynes, James F. to Elizabeth Stone 2-21-1865 (no return) L
Haynes, James T. to Anna E. Haynes 9-22-1858 Hn
Haynes, John A. to Selina Hamblin 7-3-1837 O
Haynes, John E. to Mary E. Youngblood 1-11-1845 (1-12-1845) L
Haynes, John G. to Laura Croom 2-16-1870 (2-17-1870) Ma
Haynes, Jonatan to Mary D. Glover 1-7-1841 (1-7-1842?) O
Haynes, Joseph D. to Julia Strawn 11-20-1860 (11-21-1860) Dy

Haynes, Joseph N. to Margaret E. Davis 6-15-1831 Ma
Haynes, Mc. W. to S. L. Wakefield 10-15-1877 (10-18-1877) L
Haynes, Numan to Susanah Jones 10-10-1838 G
Haynes, Richard to Harriett Haynes 9-30-1865 (no return) Hn
Haynes, Richels D. to Mary A. Huffman 7-15-1858 Cr
Haynes, Sal W. to Nancy Rumley 11-14-1872 Cr
Haynes, Sam'l. L. to D. C. Houry 1-18-1859 (1-19-1859) O
Haynes, Samuel C. to Mary D. C. Harry 1-18-1859 O
Haynes, Samuel R. to Clara C. Gaines 11-28-1867 (no return) L
Haynes, Samuel to Maria Murrell 12-24-1878 (no return) Hy
Haynes, Solaman to Bettie Walton 12-11-1866 (12-13-1866) T
Haynes, Solomon to Lizzie Clark 12-9-1874 T
Haynes, Thomas Y. to Fanny A. Pickett 12-21-1869 (12-22-1869) Cr
Haynes, W. G. to S. E. Ledbetter 5-26-1873 (5-27-1873) L
Haynes, W. W. to Eliza C. Haynes 5-3-1870 Dy
Haynes, W. W. to Melissa J. Scoby 11-19-1866 (no return) Dy
Haynes, W. W. to P. A. Scoby 12-30-1869 (no return) Dy
Haynes, William D. to Susan E. Barham 1-23-1861 Hn
Haynes, William J. to Martha Hendrix 9-20-1879 L
Haynes, William R. to Emily Walters 8-25-1848 Hn
Haynes, Wm. to Christian Nordon 3-28-1841 Cr
Haynie, Daniel to M. L. Suggs 3-15-1852 Sh
Haynie, David E. to Maggie Saddler 1-10-1871 (1-11-1871) T
Haynie, George W. to Martha A. Delashmet 5-29-1852 (5-30-1852) T
Haynie, Jesse R. to Paulina S. Walker 8-13-1850 T
Haynie, John L. to Mary G. Sadler 12-19-1872 T
Haynie, L. P. to Eliza J. Henning 12-7-1867 (no return) L
Haynie, Thomas J. to Susan J. Douglas 12-31-1866 (1-1-1867) T
Hayns, Franklin to Elizabeth Bryant 9-1-1846 (8-29-1846) G
Hayns, James S. to Ann Holder 10-22-1842 (10-25-1842) G
Hayns, Rye to Sallie Williams 1-2-1871 Cr B
Hays, A. J. to Laura M. Kirtland 6-18-1861 (6-20-1861) Sh
Hays, Absolom F. to Jane E. Agee 1-24-1855 G
Hays, Amos to M. J. (Mrs.) Pullen 8-25-1868 G
Hays, Andrew J. to Elizabeth M. Walker 4-17-1855 (4-18-1855) Sh
Hays, Andrew J. to Sarah Brock 9-11-1841 (10-12-1841) Hr
Hays, Benjamin to Tennessee Newson 12-22-1847 Ma
Hays, Blackmon B. to Ursula P. Raines 11-30-1859 Ma
Hays, Booker to Sarah Cole 5-11-1871 (5-27-1871) F B
Hays, Boon to K. (Mrs.) Frazier 11-19-1844 Sh
Hays, Callin to Elizabeth York 12-25-1847 (12-28-1847) Ma
Hays, Charles W. to Frances Gooch 11-4-1842 Cr
Hays, George E. to Isabella Ellison 7-9-1849 Sh
Hays, H. G. to Martha Russell 10-3-1854 Hn
Hays, H. M. to Nancy Koonce 12-9-1856 (12-10-1856) Sh
Hays, H. Scruggs to Elizabeth J. Cozby 6-4-1856 (6-5-1856) Hr
Hays, Hannibal to Mary Francis Bosvell 7-4-1863 Sh
Hays, Henderson to Bettie Reynolds 4-24-1884 L
Hays, Henderson to Hanner Drake 2-16-1870 Hy
Hays, Henry G. to Mary E. Biles 2-15-1847 (no return) Hn
Hays, Henry to Mary Wells 10-25-1860 Sh
Hays, Hugh D. to Ann M. Hawkins 7-17-1837 (7-18-1837) G
Hays, Isaac to Eliza Kennedy 11-19-1832 (11-22-1832) Hr
Hays, J. G. to Melissa I. Skiles 12-30-1869 O
Hays, J. M. to Mary Ann Reed 5-19-1859 Sh
Hays, J. W. to Elizabeth Sharp 9-26-1870 (9-27-1870) T
Hays, James B. to Elvira Wilson 12-22-1858 Hn
Hays, James C. to Martha Ann House 5-1-1839 Hn
Hays, James C. to Mary Jane Maxwell 5-4-1847 (no return) Hn
Hays, James E. to Elizabeth F. Williams 7-14-1866 O
Hays, James E. to Martha Ann Bell 8-18-1853 G
Hays, James H. to Amanda E. Penn 2-27-1844 Hn
Hays, James J. to E. H. Fulks 10-11-1866 G
Hays, James M. to Nannie J. Brooks 11-9-1868 (11-12-1868) Ma
Hays, James W. to Mary M. Cowans 6-2-1844 Hn
Hays, James to June Ward 8-6-1859 Hn
Hays, James to Mary Ann Finey 4-13-1837 (4-15-1837) G
Hays, James to Pernita A. Caplinger 7-9-1863 Hn
Hays, James to Sarah Jackson 10-13-1880 (10-14-1880) L
Hays, Jessee J. to Epsey M. Butler 9-25-1845 G
Hays, Jno. P. A. to E. C. Vincent 12-17-1846 We
Hays, Joab E. to R. J. Philips 1-6-1852 O
Hays, John A. to Julian Miller 3-16-1842 (3-17-1842) G
Hays, John B. to Sally M. Craig 2-5-1827 (2-8-1827) G
Hays, John F. to Sarah E. Ingram 12-22-1847 (12-23-1847) G
Hays, John to Amanda D. Darnel 1-10-1867 O
Hays, John to Rebecca Brown 10-10-1826 Sh
Hays, Joseph to Martha Jones 12-24-1840 L
Hays, Larkin to Giley Kernay? 12-17-1829 Hr
Hays, Lewis De. C. to Sally A. M. Aldridge 1-25-1853 (1-27-1853) Sh
Hays, M. L. to Julia A. Harrison 11-11-1854 (11-12-1854) G
Hays, Middleton to Sallie P. Caruthers 12-16-1868 Ma
Hays, N. R. to Mary Gilbert 2-5-1845 Sh
Hays, Robert J. to Callie S. Jinkins 11-17-1862 We
Hays, Robert to Eliza Hart 6-4-1827 (6-7-1827) Hr
Hays, Robert to Maria Vaughn 8-4-1876 Hy
Hays, Samuel E. to Hannah Scott 2-6-1835 Hr *

Hays, Samuel E. to Hannah Scott 2-6-1836 (2-11-1836) Hr
Hays, Samuel to Elizabeth Rynder 6-8-1857 (6-9-1857) O
Hays, Thos. to Nannie Gay 1-4-1871 T
Hays, W. P. to M. C. Daugherty 6-25-1879 (6-27-1879) Dy
Hays, W. R. (Dr.) to Louella Chamblin 12-9-1874 Dy
Hays, W. W. C. to S. J. Koonce 3-26-1856 (3-28-1856) Sh
Hays, William E. to Rebecca McGehee 3-7-1839 Hn
Hays, William F. to Elizabeth S. Bradley 11-30-1853 O
Hays, William H. to Sarah Smith 11-22-1853 Hn
Hays, Wm. B. to Mary C. Jackson 11-9-1868 (11-12-1868) Ma
Hays, Wm. G. to Nancy Henson 3-7-1833 Hr
Hays, Wm. L. to Mary E. Peel 8-11-1867 Hy
Hayse, James to Lucy Ann Wood 11-20-1856 Hn
Hayse, Joseph N. to Lena Jane Williams 8-10-1870 L
Hayward, Charles A. to Currilla A. Patrick 4-10-1862 Sh
Haywood, B. Z. to Elizabeth M. Rowe 1-21-1868 (1-28-1868) Cr
Haywood, E. W. to Mary A. Linch 11-10-1871 Cr
Haywood, E. W. to Rowann Rust 3-24-1869 Cr
Haywood, Ed to Agness Read 4-9-1869 (no return) Hy
Haywood, Egbert to Sarah Johnson 5-7-1828 (5-10-1828) Hr
Haywood, Henry H. to Marth Williams 11-14-1866 (11-18-1866) Cr
Haywood, J. C. to L. R. Autry 6-21-1867 (6-23-1867) Cr
Haywood, James to L. A. Rust 4-28-1844 Hr
Haywood, John C. to Cardilea A. King 11-22-1866 (11-24-1866) Cr
Haywood, John to Caroline Bateman 1-3-1839 Cr
Haywood, Jones? R. to Winfred Brinkly 1-19-1861 (1-27-1861) Cr
Haywood, Joshiah? to Martha Haywood 5-26-1842 Cr
Haywood, Lewis to Clarissa Hall 6-16-1867 T
Haywood, Partain to Fannie Taylor 5-25-1846 (no return) Cr
Haywood, Robt. W. to Mary Jane Read 4-4-1861 (no return) Hy
Haywood, S. A. to Florenza A. Trousdale 11-3-1866 (no return) Hn
Haywood, W. T. to Eliza J. Pruett 12-7-1865 (12-10-1865) Cr
Haywood, Whitley A. to Zelvey E. Taylor 11-1-1866 Cr
Haywood, William R. to Sarah A. Walker 9-1-1852 G
Haywood, William to Eliza Jones 3-27-1836 Hr
Haywood, Willis to Maria Jane Taylor 8-26-1866 Hy
Hazel, Mack to Donia Turbin 12-4-1880 (12-5-1880) L B
Hazell, William to Isabella Bush 1-8-1879 (1-9-1879) L
Hazelwood, Joseph F. to Malinda Raines 6-6-1849 (6-7-1849) G
Hazelwood, Nathaniel to Mary A. Doty 1-27-1833 Sh
Hazle, Jackson to Kissey Mineard 11-24-1874 Hy
Hazlegrove, George H. to Cary Alsop 12-18-1847 (12-23-1847) Hr
Hazlewood, B. F. to Eliza B. Sharp 7-4-1860 G
Hazlewood, G. W. L. to Nancy G. Moore 7-29-1862 (7-31-1862) O
Hazlewood, J. D. to Julia S. Irby 12-8-1866 F
Hazlewood, James T. to M. F. Bennett 12-30-1866 G
Hazlewood, Joshua to Catharine Tate 5-27-1826 (6-7?-1826) Hr
Hazlewood, Randolph to Malinda D. Digg 8-12-1839 (8-13-1839) Ma
Hazlewood, W. T. to B. J. Hazlewood 12-19-1865 (12-20-1865) F
Hazlewood, W. W. to Louisa Pankey 3-15-1862 O
Hazlewood, William R. to Susan M. Cassels 9-13-1848 (9-14-1848) G
Hazlewood, William to Caroline T. Gill 2-11-1856 Ma
Hazlewood, William to Mary Ann Tate 5-29-1827 Hr
Hazzard (Haggard?), John R. to Milley W. Posey 12-1-1858 L
Head, Absalom to Rhoda Holland 5-13-1854 (5-14-1854) L
Head, Benjamin W. to Sarah E. McWherter 4-16-1861 We
Head, E. J. to Elizabeth Roberts 8-21-1845 W
Head, Henry to Elizabeth S. Beazley 1-13-1838 (1-24-1838) G
Head, Horace to Catharine M. St. Clair 3-6-1855 O
Head, Horace to Marey B. Brown no date (with Oct 1837) O
Head, Jacob to Delila Williams 2-6-1846 Hn
Head, John T. to Mary A. Galard 6-22-1854 G
Head, John to Sarah A. L. Robertson 1-6-1842 Sh
Head, M. R. to Catherine Cops 3-12-1856 (3-13-1856) G
Head, Madison to Melinda Underwood 3-13-1833 Sh
Head, William to Pincky Holland 4-17-1854 (4-16?-1854) L
Headen, H. H. to B. A. Green 2-19-1866 G
Heady, John T. to Matilda Pool 10-3-1850 Sh
Heaggins, James to Isabaline Owens 2-11-1871 (no return) F B
Heald, Zeke to Jane Harris 2-16-1860 (2-17-1860) O
Healey, James to M. A. Cogan 1-8-1864 Sh
Healy, Daniel to Hannah Nash 4-7-1860 (4-14-1860) Sh
Healy, Michael to Mary Ann White 2-4-1856 Sh
Heany, Nelson H. to Mary Conelly 10-18-1838 Sh
Heard, C. B. to Mary E. Jones 8-29-1859 (8-30-1859) G
Heard, Franklin C. to Lucy Hunt Taylor 12-15-1874 Hy
Hearing, M. E. to M. R. Wilson 1-7-1864 Sh
Hearn, A. H. to Eliza Cocke 11-5-1862 G
Hearn, James to Elizabeth Carey 3-12-1856 O
Hearn, John W. to Jearn Hearn 12-9-1854 (12-10-1854) Ma
Hearn, M. E. to S. R. Grier 3-22-1868 G
Hearn, Noah G. to Minerva Hartgrave 1-15-1839 Ma
Hearn, Oren A. to Frances F. Hunter 12-9-1859 (12-11-1859) Ma
Hearn, W. G. to J. A. Trout 6-5-1873 Dy
Hearn, W. H. to Nancy Fonville 10-24-1859 G
Hearn, W. N. to Elizabeth Hudson 12-21-1846 Ma
Hearn, Whitman H. to Aurelia Harris 1-11-1847 Ma

Hearring, W. E. to Madorah E. Sumrow 7-15-1876 (7-16-1876) L
Heas, James R. to Gabella Lankford 9-1-1841 Ma
Heasenburg, John W. to Davy Theresa Alexander 6-13-1854 (6-15-1854) Ma
Heaslet, Abraham to Anna Deener 12-3-1869 (no return) F B
Heaslet, Fielding to Blanch Ann Dobbs 12-2-1869 (no return) F B
Heaslet, James A. to Emily Philpott 5-3-1827 Hr
Heaslet, Robert to Mary Deener 11-29-1869 (no return) F B
Heaslett, Adam to Emily Shackleford 11-15-1867 (no return) F B
Heaslett, Jesse to Easter Blaine 9-27-1871? (SB 1870?) F B
Heaslett, Mitchell to Mary Grider 1-11-1870 (no return) F B
Heatcock, Ruebin to Julia Ann Hopkins 5-22-1838 Hr
Heath, A. J. to Melissa H. Kirk 11-15-1869 (11-16-1869) Dy
Heath, Chapel to P. A. Legate 1-24-1864 Mn
Heath, Danl. W. to Martha V. Kirk 12-21-1864 (12-22-1864) Dy
Heath, Enoch to Joan Hughes 1-13-1863 We
Heath, Harry S. to Eliza J. Campbell 7-12-1859 G
Heath, James W. to Ellen Davey 12-16-1857 (12-17-1857) Sh
Heath, Levi T. to Deller M. Self 4-6-1863 (4-8-1863) Dy
Heath, Marcus to Salina James 7-22-1834 Sh
Heath, O. to Martha Manning 8-17-1867 (8-18-1867) Dy
Heath, Richard to Elizabeth Cole 12-20-1834 G
Heath, Thomas I. to Mary Cason 5-28-1838 (5-21?-1838) Ma
Heath, William H. to Susan A. Campbell 10-3-1853 (11-17-1853) G
Heath, Willis J. to Almarinda E. Campbell 10-7-1860 G
Heath, Wm. L. to Elizabeth Williams 1-1-1860 (no return) Hy
Heath, Z. W. to Bettie Yancy 1-26-1869 (1-27-1869) F
Heathcock, A. J. to Julia McDaniel 1-13-1878 Hy
Heathcock, John to Harriet Donel 1-14-1835 (1-15-1835) Ma
Heathcock, N. J. to Martha V. Horton 4-30-1867 G
Heathcock, Nelson to Zedie Ray 1-8-1871 Hy
Heathcock, R. P. to Norciss C. McLeod 9-28-1869 (9-29-1869) L
Heathcot, John G. to Phebe Fuller 4-4-1865 (4-5-1865) L
Heathcot, John to Elizabeth Irby 7-28-1846 (no return) Hn
Heathcot, John to Martha Miller 3-1-1849 Hn
Heathscot, John to A. McMayhan 9-7-1856 We
Heathscott, George to Frances Moss 11-27-1856 We
Heathscott, James to Emily C. Jolly 9-29-1856 We
Heathscott, Richard to Mary J. Williams 7-25-1856 We
Heckiman, John W. to Martha J. S. Adams 10-27-1856 Cr
Heckle, David to M. E. Allen 3-22-1854 (3-23-1854) Sh
Heckle, Fredrick to Elizabeth Stoll 11-1-1859 (11-2-1859) Sh
Heckon?, James L. to Harriet E. Webb 12-20-1858 Hr
Heddin, A. C. to M. F. Fields 5-27-1869 (no return) Dy
Heddin, Elias to Sarah E. Lyon 8-3-1866 (8-7-1866) Dy
Heddin, S. A. to Mollie L. Wright 10-5-1869 (no return) Dy
Hedge, B. F. to Martha A. Bevill 2-10-1855 Hn
Hedge, James J. to Nancy C. McCord 12-14-1848 Hn
Hedge, John W. to Permiley F. Smith 4-4-1856 Cr
Hedge, John to Margaret E. Thomason 3-11-1857 Cr
Hedge, Samuel to Eliza Autry 7-20-1845 Cr
Hedgecock, Elisha to Amanda Grier 1-10-1863 G
Hedgecock, J. H. to Mary F. Mount 9-29-1859 G
Hedgecock, J. W. to M. F. Quinn 7-2-1866 (no return) Cr
Hedgecock, John N. (W.?) to Louisa Mount no date (with Jul 1864) G
Hedgecock, Joshua A. to Melinda A. McKelvy 11-10-1860 G
Hedgecock, W. E. to Caroline V. Mount 11-26-1868 G
Hedgepath, Arthur J. to Ann Eliza Howard 8-20-1846 Ma
Hedgepeth, Jo. (Dr.) to Mary A. Campbell 9-28-1872 (9-29-1872) L
Hedgepeth, ___ to Sally Robinson 11-18-1852 F
Hedgepith, J. C. to Nancy E. Taylor 3-27-1855 We
Heester, Jacob to Tennessee Miller 5-11-1861 Sh
Hefley, H. W. to Sarah Bradford 7-31-1860 G
Hefley, T. W. to America Meritt 12-30-1867 G B
Heflin, H. L. to Mary J. Maxwell 12-28-1867 (1-8-1868) F
Heflin, Micajah to Elizabeth Jackson 9-12-1838 Hn
Hegarty, James to Mary Butler 11-23-1864 (11-24-1864) Sh
Hegel, William to Matilda Fike 9-22-1860 Sh
Heidel, George to Rosina Frick 7-19-1856 Sh
Heidel, W. H. to Catherine Meyer 1-15-1855 (1-16-1855) Sh
Heidelberg, Frederick to Magdalena Brenner 5-31-1864 Sh
Hein, Peter to Evelin Wechtenhausen 5-8-1845 Sh
Heinrich, John J. T. to Mary W. Creamer 1-15-1861 (1-22-1861) Sh
Heinrich, P. H. to Ernestine Walser 11-15-1859 (11-16-1859) Sh
Heinzer, Charles A. to Mary Hoffman 3-28-1863 (3-31-1863) Sh
Heiskell, Anderson to Martha Jane Taylor 2-6-1878 Hy
Heiskell, James H. to Mary M. Crihfield 7-22-1851 (7-23-1851) L
Heiskell, John F. to Effy Ball 9-14-1852 (9-16-1852) L
Heiskell, John F. to Louisa Angelina Nearns 6-28-1857 (6-29-1857) L
Heiss, Thomas to Matilda Clandolt (Claudett) 2-27-1850 Sh
Helbing, Adolphus to Ida A. Handworker 8-8-1856 (8-12-1856) Sh
Helen, William M. to Nancy Espy 3-20-1862 Dy
Helfer, Meyer to Adaline Hathaway 10-17-1848 Sh
Helfley, Henry W. to Eliza James 2-5-1847 G
Hellard, George C. to Lucendia Arnold 11-4-1850 G
Hellard, George R. to Caroline V. Brown 6-1-1857 (6-2-1857) Ma
Hellenk, Frederick to Martina Boos 12-6-1856 Sh
Hellons, Wm. to Mary Williams 3-9-1867 O

Hellums, Henry to Amanda Bone 3-22-1873 (3-29-1873) Dy
Hellums, M. to N. Spence 7-12-1862 (no return) Hn
Helm, Alex to Candis White 11-8-1884 L
Helm, Brice E. to Ann Bradford 2-13-1872 Hy
Helm, Columbus to Ann Harris 2-9-1877 L B
Helm, John to Jane Barnes 1-3-1883 (1-4-1883) L
Helm, John to Tennessee Curren 1-7-1875 L B
Helm, Saml. to Laura Dillahenty 2-24-1872 T
Helm, William M. to Elizabeth A. Durham 3-11-1872 (3-12-1872) L
Helm, William M. to Violet G. Lackey 2-4-1861 L
Helman, Leon to Regina Oppenheimer 5-24-1858 Sh
Helmes, Thomas to Mary Jane Green 12-6-1853 Be
Helms, John to Sarah Presson 2-20-1848 Be
Helms, Morris to Sarah L. McElyea 8-22-1866 O
Hemly, Thos. to F. A. Thomas 12-23-1851 (no return) F
Hemp, Bill to Lusten Fisher 1-5-1869 (not executed) T
Hemp, Henderson to M. J. Dyer no date (with 12-1874) T
Hemp, Jim to Annie Johnson 12-24-1874 T
Hemphill, Wm. to Jane Smith 12-20-1871 T
Hemson, W. J. to F. M. Edwards 11-27-1865 (11-28-1865) F
Henderson, A. A. to Agnes P. Murray 1-20-1841 Cr
Henderson, Alfred L. to Elizabeth Lewis 1-24-1835 Sh
Henderson, Alfred to Ann Covington 12-8-1869 (12-9-1869) Cr
Henderson, Ambros to Mollie Wheler 3-25-1871 (no return) Hy
Henderson, Bennett to Kezziah Moon 5-5-1843 Hn
Henderson, Bennett to Mary Ann Kinman 10-20-1855 (11-1-1855) O
Henderson, Bennette to Lucinda Anderson 4-14-1847 (4-15-1847) O
Henderson, Brum to R. F. Brevard 8-30-1866 O
Henderson, Calvin to Ela Patterson 3-18-1842 Ma
Henderson, Daniel to Vianna C. Watson 10-31-1859 Sh
Henderson, David to Frances Bateman 9-18-1871 (9-20-1871) T
Henderson, E. A. to M. F. (Mrs.) Callahan 8-31-1874 (no return) Dy
Henderson, Elam D. to Martha Jane Bryant 10-27-1856 (10-29-1856) Ma
Henderson, F. H. to Julia A. Covington 12-11-1844 (no return) Cr
Henderson, Frank to Vina Lee 12-30-1869 Hy
Henderson, G. G. to Mary House 2-2-1868 Hy
Henderson, Gabriel A. to Nancy J. Newton 8-15-1855 (8-16-1855) Ma
Henderson, George C. to Mary Glass 3-9-1843 Hn
Henderson, George to Julia Williamson 12-27-1869 F B
Henderson, George to Mariah Chambers 11-24-1871 O
Henderson, Hugh C. to Mary S. Maddox 4-28-1852 Ma
Henderson, J. W. to Frances Poff 2-20-1867 (2-21-1867) T
Henderson, J. W. to Martha A. Reville 12-28-1865 Hy
Henderson, Jackson R. to Ann Eliza McPherson 4-30-1846 (no return) F
Henderson, James M. to Edline Wright 9-19-1838 Cr
Henderson, James R. to Matilda S. Stokes 11-18-1869 Hy
Henderson, James W. to Delphia R. Morton 12-28-1859 Hn
Henderson, James to Ann Harvell 12-25-1866 (12-26-1866) F B
Henderson, James to Dilcey Winston 9-15-1873 (9-16-1873) L
Henderson, James to Eleira? Drake 2-3-1868 (2-6-1868) Cr
Henderson, James to Elizabeth Ross 5-14-1861 (5-15-1861) O
Henderson, James to Jane Willson 4-21-1870 (4-23-1870) T
Henderson, James to Julia Springfield 11-12-1875 (no return) Hy
Henderson, James to Martha A. Brigance 4-9-1861 (not executed) O
Henderson, James to Nancy A. Vinson 8-14-1855 (8-16-1855) Ma
Henderson, Jas. to S. A. Mosier 4-17-1867 O
Henderson, John J. to Dolly Ann Walker 9-9-1860 Hn
Henderson, John O. to Elizabeth Pearce 6-30-1850 (6-6?-1850) G
Henderson, John to Altonetta Echols 3-17-1866 (3-22-1866) Dy
Henderson, John to Nancy Glass 10-18-1842 Hn
Henderson, Jorden to Susan Wilson 11-9-1866 T
Henderson, Joseph to Elizabeth Cocke 6-11-1839 Sh
Henderson, Joseph to Mary Ann Steeley 6-19-1841 (no return) Hn
Henderson, Joseph to Virginia Guthrie 12-19-1848 (12-21-1848) O
Henderson, March to Easther Haynes 5-27-1856 Hn
Henderson, Mark C. to Mary Ann Hogsett 2-6-1867 (2-7-1867) Ma
Henderson, Mark C. to Tenie J. Nesbitt 12-29-1870 (12-30-1870) Ma
Henderson, Milton A. to Elizabeth C. Sewell 11-9-1854 Hn
Henderson, Nathaniel to Susan Patterson 11-1-1859 (11-2-1859) Ma
Henderson, Pleasant to Emily V. Mays 1-30-1841 (2-3-1841) F
Henderson, Pleasant to Fanny Gray 12-27-1877 Hy
Henderson, Prince to Clary Henderson 12-13-1870 (12-12?-1870) Cr B
Henderson, Robert F. to Mary J. Allison 5-2-1870 (5-4-1870) Ma
Henderson, Robert H. to Nancy Maddox 5-3-1855 Ma
Henderson, Robt. to Fillis DeGraffenreid 10-3-1868 (10-4-1868) F B
Henderson, Rufus to Julia Frost 9-7-1867 (9-12-1867) Dy
Henderson, Rufus to Malvina Tumage 3-16-1871 (3-19-1871) Dy
Henderson, S. C. to Mary Hudspeth 7-4-1848 Hn
Henderson, Samuel C. to Martha McCraey 1-12-1856 (1-17-1856) G
Henderson, Samuel to Jennie Smith 2-22-1883 (3-10-1883) L
Henderson, Samuel to Mary Jane Bailey 5-31-1849 Hn
Henderson, Scott to Margaret Thomas 10-29-1874 L
Henderson, T. J. to Earnestine Rodgers 12-23-1870 (12-25-1870) Dy
Henderson, Tho. B. to Sarah J. Honnell 9-1-1846 (9-3-1846) F
Henderson, Thomas to Ann Eliza Lancaster 7-25-1848 Ma
Henderson, Thomas to Marion Patterson 11-2-1852 Ma
Henderson, Thomas to Sallie Craighead 12-21-1876 Hy

Henderson, Tobias C. to Eunicy Haralson 12-10-1823 Ma
Henderson, W. H. to S. F. B. Green 5-25-1862 Mn
Henderson, W. to Elvira A. Williams 2-3-1842 Sh
Henderson, William F. to Mary P. McCorry 11-8-1847 Ma
Henderson, William J. to Margarett E. Rosemond 12-17-1850 Ma
Henderson, William L. to Harriet Bishop 6-1-1841 (no return) Hn
Henderson, William T. to Donia C. Hogsett 12-2-1867 Ma
Henderson, William to Elizabeth West 3-6-1845 G
Henderson, William to Nancy J. Arnold 2-25-1852 G
Henderson, William to Willie Turpin 3-1-1876 (no return) Hy
Henderson, Wm. H. to Sarah W. Mays 5-8-1843 (no return) Hn
Henderson, Wm. Lafayette to Margaret J. Steele 8-31-1864 Sh
Henderson, Wm. R. to Permelia J. Anderson 7-13-1853 (7-14-1853) O
Henderson, Wyatt to Kitty Rogers 11-1-1867 (11-2-1867) F B
Henderson, Yancy to Patsy Wood 2-26-1870 (no return) Dy
Hendley, Leonard W. to Syrena McDanile 12-10-1839 Hr
Hendly, Joseph to Susan Patridge 2-24-1839 Hr
Hendon, Dock to Cloe Haskins 7-30-1870 F B
Hendren (Henden), Wm. to Anna C. Smith 6-1-1840 Sh
Hendren, J. F. to Janie Voss 10-31-1882 (11-1-1882) L
Hendren, J. H. to Isabella Cornelius 1-13-1874 (no return) Hy
Hendren, T. O. to Eva A. Crisp 12-18-1880 (12-20-1880) L
Hendren, W. G. to P. E. Garrett 8-25-1869 Hy
Hendrick, B. G. to Martha A. Old 5-30-1842 (no return) F
Hendrick, Bernard G. to Sarah P. Higenbothem 2-19-1851 (no return) F
Hendrick, Daniel R. to Sarah Fields 3-29-1839 G
Hendrick, Daniel R. to Sarah Fields 3-29-1839 (4-2-1839) G
Hendrick, Dennis to Mary Joyce 4-12-1856 (4-13-1856) Sh
Hendrick, Ezekiel to Nancy McCluer 2-4-1830 Sh
Hendrick, W. E. to Mary Katzenback 12-24-1860 (12-25-1860) Sh
Hendrick, William to Rachael Coope 11-7-1835 (11-12-1835) G
Hendrick, Wm. J. to Lucina T. Anderson 12-31-1849 (1-1-1850) F
Hendricks, A. C. to S. A. Lambert 9-21-1875 (9-30-1875) Dy
Hendricks, George W. to Amanda S. A. Hood 2-10-1864 (no return) Dy
Hendricks, H. C. to Tempe Bean 12-8-1873 (12-9-1873) Dy
Hendricks, J. B. to S. M. Shepherd 3-7-1866 Hn
Hendricks, J. S. to Pattie H. Cason 10-23-1866 Hn
Hendricks, James to Elizabeth A. Dalton 5-27-1851 Hn
Hendricks, Jerimiah E. to Jane R. McMillan 7-9-1845 Sh
Hendricks, John B. to Mary Elizabeth Morgan 10-20-1828 (10-25-1828) Hr
Hendricks, John M. to Mary Black 12-20-1848 Ma
Hendricks, L. L. to Abarilla Upchurch 11-1-1859 Hn
Hendricks, M. R. to Sallie Pierce 3-23-1874 (3-24-1874) Dy
Hendricks, Thomas R. to Sarah F. Harman 11-19-1858 Hn
Hendricks, W. H. to Mary M. Headden 7-24-1877 Dy
Hendricks, Wm. L. to Mary I. Turrentine 9-16-1869 G
Hendrickson, Charles R. to Mary J. Alexander 1-3-1855 Sh
Hendrix, E. A. to R. J. Burch 5-30-1875 Hy
Hendrix, Gilbert W. to Sarah J. Colly 8-21-1861 We
Hendrix, Richard to Sarah C. Cox 12-12-1864 Mn
Hendrix, Thomas J. to Mary M. McPherson 5-26-1877 L
Hendrix, W. B. to Catherine Hollands 5-6-1863 Mn
Hendrix, W. H. to Lucy A. Doak 4-16-1879 (4-17-1879) Dy
Hendrix, W. M. to Mary E. (Mrs.) Hight 7-5-1865 G
Hendron, J. A. to Katie L. Given 7-20-1885 L
Hendron, John W. C. to Susan M. Williams 2-1-1841 (2-3-1841) Ma
Hendron, M. F. to Plura A. Pennington 12-22-1885 (no return) L
Hendron, O. T. to Agnes Gregory 11-28-1842 F
Hendron, T. W. to O. J. Patten 2-5-1867 Hy
Hendy, John to Louisa Volmer 12-10-1864 (12-11-1864) Sh
Henesee, John to Bridget O'Hern 7-5-1847 Sh
Henesy (Hanasay), Thomas to Mary Mara 8-8-1849 Sh
Hengholt, B. H. to Mary Schrader 5-20-1862 Sh
Heniley, Thomas to ann Rededenton 6-5-1858 Sh
Henley (Hurley?), T. W. to Maria L. Neal 2-24-1855 Sh
Henley, A. N. to Martha E. Howell 8-15-1850 Sh
Henley, C. S. to E. M. Byars 1-8-1878 Hy
Henley, Elijah D. to Lucinda Hubbard 11-11-1846 F
Henley, Henrique to Mary Byars 4-11-1876 Hy
Henley, Hugh to Sarah Byrum 10-26-1871 Hy
Henley, Isaac A. to Christina Bryant 1-28-1848 (no return) F
Henley, Isaac P. to Manda C. Ellison 12-8-1842 F
Henley, J. B. D. to Delia Chapman 12-16-1869 Hy
Henley, J. S. to Mary M. Kirkland 12-13-1866 Hn
Henley, Jackson to Alice Beard 12-14-1882 (12-15-1882) L
Henley, James A. to Ann (Mrs.) Dillahunt 12-19-1877 Dy
Henley, Jasper to Emily Cleaver 1-8-1870 (no return) Cr
Henley, John B. D. to Mary R. Briggs 10-9-1849 (no return) L
Henley, L. F. to Sarah J. Cook 11-14-1871 (11-16-1871) L
Henley, Morris to Maggie Fleming 12-6-1876 Hy
Henley, Nelson to Minnie Bond 11-20-1871 (no return) Hy
Henley, Newton to Martha Todd 1-11-1872 Cr
Henley, R. L. to Eliza A. Stailey 5-1-1858 Sh
Henley, R. W. to Emily P. Watkins 11-12-1870 (no return) Hy
Henley, Richard to Martha Peveyhouse 2-13-1865 (no return) L
Henley, Richardson W. to Julia A. E. Carrigan 12-1-1841 (12-2-1841) L
Henley, Saml. F. to Amanda C. Carrigan 3-4-1846 (3-5-1846) L

Henley, Scott to Lucy A. Watkins 2-1-1871 Hy
Henley, Thomas W. W. to Mariah P. Throgmorton 11-6-1844 Hn
Henley, W. S. to Heloise V. Mitchell 7-12-1878 (7-15-1878) L
Henley, William H. to Mariah Cowan 9-9-1840 F
Henley, William to Elizabeth Terry 10-6-1853 (10-7-1853) Hr
Henley, Wm. H. to Sarah E. Henley 11-9-1868 (11-11-1868) F
Henley, Wmson. to Nancey Green 3-10-1845 F
Henley, jr., Elijah to Pantha Grissum 9-28-1843 F
Henly, A. L. to Elmira J. Anderson 4-18-1867 Hy
Henly, Olison to Lucy Read 1-22-1876 (no return) Hy
Henly, Ollenson to Ellen Jarratt 9-22-1878 Hy
Henly, William to Rebecca Cooksey 11-19-1834 (11-20-1834) Hr
Henly, William to Susan Wynn 5-27-1847 O
Henly, Zackary A.? to Nancy Hays 10-13-1855 (10-14-1855) T
Henneger, John C. to Minna Fika 10-14-1858 Sh
Hennessey, Thomas to Ellen Lundergin 5-19-1860 (5-20-1860) Sh
Henniger, F. to Louisa Koler 6-10-1856 Sh
Henniger, Henry to Johane Michels 1-13-1852 Sh
Henniger, John A. F. to Mary Bungner 8-2-1862 (8-3-1862) Sh
Henniker, Henry to Catharine Isele 3-3-1851 Sh
Henning, Albert to Caroline Price 3-25-1876 L
Henning, Arch to Easter Mann 6-26-1875 L
Henning, George to Emma Barbee 8-20-1877 L
Henning, Henry to Eliza Sweat 10-19-1877 (10-?-1877) L
Henning, Henry to Harriet Hayes 12-14-1882 (no return) L
Henning, J. H. to Emma Halliburton 12-6-1884 (12-10-1884) L
Henning, James to Cassy Currin 12-9-1885 L
Henning, John D. to Elizabeth A. Brookshire 12-12-1859 Ma
Henning, John to Lucy Ward 2-13-1878 L B
Henning, John to Sallie Bell Young 12-23-1885 (12-24-1885) L
Henning, John to Sarah T. Loftin 3-3-1851 Sh
Henning, Lewis to Hannah Warren 8-5-1839 (no return) Hn
Henning, Lit to Rosa Young 1-15-1879 (no return) L
Henning, Phil to Taylor Barbee 1-19-1881 L B
Henning, Richard G. to Lurannia Hill 10-11-1831 Ma
Henning, Richard to Lucy A. Lackey 1-17-1861 (no return) L
Henning, S. H. to Lee Moore 12-11-1880 (12-12-1881?) L B
Henning, Thomas to Amanda Palmer 11-10-1871 (11-12-1871) L
Henning, Thomas to Eliza Halliburton 12-16-1872 (no return) L
Henning, William H. to Martha Ann Davis 10-15-1839 Ma
Henning, William to Lucinda Thompson 2-26-1879 L
Hennissee, John to Allice Moorer 2-7-1872 (2-8-1872) L
Henpler (Henssler?), Lewis to Sarah Ann Lee 8-8-1851 Sh
Henrich (Henry), Frederick to Caroline Wacasen 1-23-1842 Sh
Henrichs, John to Caroline Bland 5-1-9-1860 Sh
Henrick, H. to Sallie Bender 8-22-1860 Sh
Henry(Heniny), A. J. to Anna Hughes 9-28-1829 Hr
Henry, A. B. to Martha A. Hendren 4-25-1867 (4-26-1867) L
Henry, A. W. to Martha A. Foster 11-22-1865 Dy
Henry, C. W. to Mrs. S. B. Wilkerson 11-28-1851 (12-10-1851) Hr
Henry, Charles W. to Mary K. Newby 1-5-1863 (no return) Hy
Henry, Charley to Lydie Jones 3-9-1876 (no return) Hy
Henry, David W. to Ashley? W. Pate 7-29-1861 (no return) Cr
Henry, F. A. to Mary B. Porter 1-8-1883 L
Henry, George W. to Nancy R. Kindrick 2-17-1855 (2-21-1855) Hr
Henry, J. H. to Rebecca Lumley 1-1-1872 (1-4-1872) Dy
Henry, James O. to Martha E. Hendron 9-26-1855 T
Henry, James S. to Frances L. Doomas? 11-12-1838 Hn
Henry, James W. D. to Lizzie Heit (Hart) 2-8-1867 (2-12-1867) F
Henry, James to Joanna Shannon 10-18-1859 Sh
Henry, James to Martha Crabb 8-29-1844 Be
Henry, James to Sarah Yancy 3-10-1846 Sh
Henry, John A. to A. E. (Mrs.) Funk 5-14-1861 Sh
Henry, John G. to Estelia Worthan 2-18-1840 (2-20-1840) F
Henry, John L. to Martha Ross 11-5-1840 Ma
Henry, John M. to Mary A. Pursley 12-13-1859 (12-18-1859) O
Henry, John P. to Caroline S. Sharp 2-18-1858 G
Henry, John P. to Mary Sharp 5-10-1842 (5-11-1842) G
Henry, John T. to Isabella Nelms 6-21-1855 O
Henry, Johnathan to July Strother 4-15-1836 (4-17-1836) G
Henry, M. P. to Venina Owens 11-5-1862 Mn
Henry, Malcolm to Mary Smothers 2-8-1846 Cr
Henry, Osborn to Mary Taylor 3-8-1845 Hn
Henry, Philip to Phoebe Roark 5-26-1850 Sh
Henry, R. H. to Ann M. Crowder 4-5-1858 We
Henry, R. to Creacy Stephens 8-3-1869 L
Henry, Richard to Rilda Carpenter 5-29-1869 (no return) F B
Henry, Robert to Elizabeth Anderson 4-13-1848 Sh
Henry, Samuel C. to Eleanor Haislip 3-14-1844 O
Henry, Samuel to Roda Ross 4-12-1830 (4-13-1830) G
Henry, Samuel to Susanna Jackson 10-28-1828 (11-19-1828) O
Henry, Spence to Isabella House 12-24-1867 Hn B
Henry, T. M. to Sarah J. Estes 5-17-1863 Mn
Henry, Thomas J. to Martha Perry 3-25-1858 We
Henry, Thomas to Bridget Cox 5-27-1861 Sh
Henry, Thomas to Roberta D. Alexander 3-3-1859 Hr
Henry, W. B. to Josephine Holder 11-15-1863 G
Henry, W. R. to Victory Oliver 4-16-1865 Hn
Henry, Wade to Mary Margaret Giles 10-30-1849 (11-1-1849) T
Henry, Walker to Drusilla Dirk 10-22-1881 (10-23-1881) L
Henry, Walker to Margaret Ann Howard 7-28-1880 (not executed) L
Henry, William E. to Amanda A. Willson 4-18-1848 Hn
Henry, William E. to Eliza A. Frazier 2-5-1846 Hn
Henry, William H. to M. J. Lemmons 3-31-1860 (4-1-1860) Sh
Henry, William to Martha Ann Asberry 12-13-1853 (12-15-1853) O
Henry, William to Martha J. Davis 8-20-1872 (8-21-1872) L
Henry, William to Mary E. Rutledge 12-25-1856 (12-20?-1856) Ma
Henry, William to Melissa Allison 1-17-1848 Be
Henry, William to Neicie Hawthorne 12-16-1863 Sh
Henry, William to Rachel Poyner 3-13-1855 Hn
Henry, Wm. F. to Mary F. McClanahan 12-9-1868 Ma
Henry, Wm. to Ellen Burns 9-26-1857 Cr
Henry?, William B. to Mary Garrett 4-7-1847 Hr
Henshaw, Samuel to Jane M. Wynne 7-20-1857 (7-21-1857) Sh
Henslee, Enoch to Maranda Box 1-6-1859 (5-29-1859) Hr
Henslee, John J. to Mary E. Pierce 3-6-1868 (no return) Cr
Hensler, J. T. to M. F. Lipe 9-1-1870 Cr
Hensley, Christopher to Sarah Jane Rogers 11-4-1864 Sh
Hensley, George W. to Margaret Crawford 6-7-1843 (6-13-1843) Hr
Hensley, Henry to Louisa Massey 11-5-1863 Sh
Hensley, John H. to Susan L. Parten 5-12-1858 G
Hensley, John to Amelia Ann Morris 4-8-1858 Ma
Hensley, John to Rachel Poole 1-23-1858 Sh
Hensly, Martin to Rachel M. C. Thrasher 1-22-1846 (1-23-1846) Hr
Henson, Andrew T. to Margaret E. Babb 1-28-1850 (1-29-1850) Hr
Henson, Daniel to Mary J. Ross 10-19-1860 Hr
Henson, George to Mary E. Carley 1-24-1861 Hr
Henson, Giles to Sarah Reynolds 3-29-1845 Hn
Henson, Isaac to Susan Brown 1-15-1870 (1-16-1870) Dy
Henson, Jesse to Sarah Sperling 3-7-1827 (3-14-1827) Hr
Henson, John sr. to Charlotte Patterson 3-28-1859 (3-29-1859) Hr
Henson, John to Arrena Odum 10-21-1848 (10-22-1848) Hr
Henson, John to Polly Phillips 12-19-1856 Hr
Henson, Joseph J. to Sarah C. Rogers 2-22-1851 (3-5-1851) Hr
Henson, Saml. to Susan King 10-17-1838 (10-18-1838) Hr
Henson, Samuel to Lotty Cozby 9-21-1849 (9-23-1849) Hr
Henson, W. A. to Cassie A. Hearn 2-14-1870 G
Henson, Will to Elizabeth Jones 2-21-1835 Hr
Henson, Wm. to Talitha Pipkins 6-2-1856 Hr
Hentz, Henry to Jennie Hazle 12-25-1885 (12-27-1885) L
Hentz, Henry to Jenny Hazle 10-27-1881 (10-28-1881) L
Hentz, John to Fannie Barbee 5-26-1881 L B
Henwood, B. F. to Caroline Baker 12-12-1879 (12-12-1880?) L
Herald, James to Isa Stroud 12-29-1833 O
Herber, John G. to Elizabeth Katterman (Kattman) 10-17-1849 Sh
Herbers, John D. to Catharine Kateman (Kattman) 10-7-1850 Sh
Herbert, J. A. to R. T. Kirby 11-17-1860 (no return) Hy
Herbert, O. E. (Dr.) to L. Alice Harbut 3-25-1867 G
Herbert, Wm. T. to Martha Ann Latham 3-11-1871 (3-15-1871) Ma
Heren, W. O. to Mary Hudson 1-8-1864 Be
Herendon, J. S. to M. A. Quimby 11-24-1878 Hy
Herin, Isaac C. to Manda A. McRee 7-20-1861 (7-21-1861) O
Hering, Daniel W. to Mahalah Lamb 12-6-1847 (12-22-1847) T
Herly, Thomas N. to Mary E. Jones 3-12-1848 F
Herman, J. J. to Vickey T. Ross 5-25-1861 O
Hermon, J. N. to Delila A. Bushart 11-12-1867 Hn
Hermon, N. S. to Eliza H. Poe 10-16-1853 Hn
Hern, G. W. to Nancy C. Williams 12-3-1851 (no return) Cr
Hern, Haywood to Martha J. McSwain 3-22-1857 Cr
Hern, Joe T. to Mary A. Rowland 6-20-1843 Cr
Hern, John C. to Polly A. Rowland 1-21-1847 Cr
Hern, Stephen to Emley Stafford 8-5-1844 (8-8-1844) F
Herndon, Anderson to Mary Grissom 10-21-1858 G
Herndon, B. R. to S. A. Sadler 11-24-1849 Hr
Herndon, Daniel B. to Kathorine Phifer 3-19-1844 Be
Herndon, David to Isabella Vester 9-3-1850 Be
Herndon, Jerome to Mollie Gallant 12-28-1867 (1-2-1868) Ma
Herndon, John S. to Elizabeth A. Wall 11-5-1862 (11-6-1862) F
Herndon, John S. to Mary E. Dodson 1-18-1854 (no return) F
Herndon, John to Matilda Herndon 8-27-1848 Be
Herndon, Madison F. to R. E. C. Thomason 4-22-1854 G
Herndon, R. H. to F. H. Peak 12-24-1854 (no return) F
Herndon, Thomas H. to Sarah J. Kent 5-17-1865 F
Herndon, Thomas to Louisa Thetford 4-20-1853 G
Herndon, W. L. to Eliza A. McDaniel 4-16-1863 Be
Herndon, Wm. C. to Elizabeth J. Sallie 12-28-1867 (1-1-1868) Ma
Herndon, Wm. H. to Margaret Y. Martin 2-20-1841 H
Herndon, Wm. M. to Martha Howard 12-5-1856 (no return) F
Herny (Haney), Patrick to Wineford Beirns 5-6-1858 (5-9-1858) Sh
Herod, James to Sarah Bullard 3-14-1866 O
Herod, John H. to Louisa Mirack 4-2-1834 G
Heron, George W. to Emily Milworth 10-23-1862 (10-25-1862) O
Herrell, Columbus to Penny Herrell 10-23-1868 Cr
Herrell, Humphrey to Julia Lankford 8-19-1871 Cr B

Herrell, Wm. to Nancy Lewis 8-5-1857 (8-11-1857) Hr
Herren, Clabourn to Frances A. Byrn 11-6-1865 Be
Herren, Thomas B. to Fredonia A. Lockhart 10-28-1866 Be
Herren, William O. to Mary Lynch 7-13-1862 Hy
Herrick, Alonzo to Sarah Reeder 12-23-1868 (12-24-1868) F
Herridge, John W. to Rosa Graham 10-20-1866 Ma
Herriman, Stephen to Nancy Welch 1-25-1851 (1-26-1851) Hr
Herrin (Hening), Joel S. to Louisa Jane Gillispie 1-7-1840 Sh
Herrin, Allen to Martha Wiseman 8-7-1855 Be
Herrin, C. M. to Martha McRae 1-26-1869 Be
Herrin, Gilbert E. to America C. Clarke 11-12-1844 (no return) Hn
Herrin, P. G. to N. Herrin 3-18-1842 Be
Herrin, Richmond to Martha C. Pace 10-4-1872 (10-6-1872) Dy
Herrin, Samuel to Phoeby Thompson 9-26-1866 (no return) Dy
Herring, Andrew to Mary E. Neighbours 7-4-1866 L
Herring, C. F. to Perlina Best 9-16-1872 (not executed) L
Herring, Chas. F. to C. L. Sumerow 10-27-1875 Dy
Herring, Claudius to Sarah A. G. Dickson 2-7-1842 (2-9-1842) O
Herring, Edwin to Dorcus Wherry 12-23-1834 Sh
Herring, J. F. to M. A. Crosthwaite 11-24-1879 (11-25-1879) L
Herring, James W. to Elizabeth Susan Jones 7-10-1854 (7-12-1854) Sh
Herring, James to Alice Jackson 8-31-1872 (9-1-1872) O
Herring, Jno. to Mary J. Lea 3-24-1860 (no return) Hy
Herring, Joel to Eliza Stewart 1-22-1856 (1-2_-1856) Sh
Herring, John to Maggie Scalling 12-16-1863 Sh
Herring, Lewis to E. Witherington 8-15-1844 Sh
Herring, M. K. to Martha M. Bond 3-23-1848 Sh
Herring, Marshal to Shelley Robertson 15-18-1858 T
Herring, Marshall to Emily Ann Griffen 8-10-1848 Sh
Herring, R. G. to J. C. Rawls 4-1-1868 Hy
Herring, Richard G. to Emma A. Compton 12-5-1877 Hy
Herring, Stephen B. to Rebecca Jane Gillispie 1-2-1845 Sh
Herring, William S. to Cordelia Gehan 10-23-1849 (10-24-1848?) T
Herring, sr., Lewis to Mildred M. Essex 2-1-1851 Sh
Herringdon, A. B. to Matilda Brewer 3-1-1840 Sh
Herrington, Anderson to Leila Ward 1-14-1882 L B
Herrington, D. J. to Sarah E. Harris 1-27-1842 (2-2-1842) F
Herron, A. H. to Mary Featherston 2-6-1838 F
Herron, Abner C. to Nancy Herron 9-3-1849 Be
Herron, Andrew to Phebe Emily Hargis 1-10-1833 Sh
Herron, Benjamin to Laura Smith 3-23-1869 (3-24-1869) Cr
Herron, Beverly to Elizabeth Cole 7-29-1849 Be
Herron, D. L. to Harriet A. Bridgers 2-16-1859 Sh
Herron, Francis to C. Lanier 10-15-1850 Cr
Herron, Hardy to Esther Strayhorn 1-19-1869 (1-21-1869) Cr
Herron, Harrison to Sallie A. V. Shore 10-7-1867 (10-17-1867) F
Herron, James to Easter Moore 3-12-1873 (3-13-1873) Cr B
Herron, James to Lydia Gray 1-29-1839 Ma
Herron, James to Martha McKee 1-12-1860 Sh
Herron, Jno. to Sallie Baird 8-5-1868 (8-6-1868) F B
Herron, John S. to Lucy Burford 10-14-1854 (no return) F
Herron, John T. to Eliza Broom 3-22-1838 F
Herron, John to Anna Powell 6-4-1874 (no return) Hy
Herron, Joseph to Mary Borden 3-21-1876 Dy
Herron, Levi B. to Nancy Wilmoth Hutchison 12-29-1858 (12-30-1858) Ma
Herron, Lewis to Roxana Green 2-1-1879 (2-2-1879) L
Herron, Ned to Virtue Heaslet 3-5-1870 (3-6-1870) F
Herron, Needham H. to Nellie Carolton 12-27-1870 (12-28-1870) T
Herron, S. J. to Louisa W. Wilson 2-28-1869 G
Herron, Smith A. to Emily Burrow 10-3-1859 (no return) Cr
Herron, W. G. to Callie Webb 1-15-1868 (1-16-1868) F
Herron, William R. to Nancy Stone 3-14-1844 Be
Herryman, Joseph to Louisa Jane Harty 11-10-1842 Hr
Hershaw, Daniel to Rebecca Emerson 3-4-1850 (3-7-1850) Ma
Hertsfield, Franklin to M. E. Davis 2-12-1872 (2-13-1872) T
Hervey(Harvey?), Thomas R. to Lucinda Jones 5-29-1848 (6-1-1848) Hr
Hervey, Calvin M. to Temperance H. Williams 12-14-1841 Hr
Herzog, George to Sarah Outlaw 9-10-1865 Mn
Heskett, John C. to Mary Lane 10-11-1867 (10-12-1867) O
Heslip, L. R. to G. D. Scot (Scat?) 11-16-1860 Sh
Hess, A. J. to Emma Buchanan 3-1-1870 G
Hess, D. Antoine to Ester L. Joiner 10-26-1862 Mn
Hess, George to Kitty Regan 12-31-1868 G
Hess, Henry to Pricilla Hamlin 11-10-1873 Hy
Hess, James A. W. to Louiza Webb 12-8-1831 G
Hess, N. J. to R. E. Dayton 12-10-1870 (12-13-1870) F
Hess, Neilson J. to Catharine H. Hill 7-2-1840 G
Hess, Nelson I. to Adeline Northcut 2-27-1830 (2-28-1830) G
Hess, Preston to Rebecca Butler 10-28-1859 O
Hess, Robt. to Parthenia Bond 11-14-1872 Hy
Hess, jr., Nelson I. (Dr.) to Sarah E. Joyce 1-31-1865 G
Hess, jr., Nelson I. to Ida R. Seay 11-16-1867 (11-20-1867) Ma
Hessey, Luther to Uginia Walker 1-7-1868 Hy
Hession, Andy to Mary Riley 7-28-1855 Sh
Hester, B. F. to Roda Harpole 12-16-1875 O
Hester, E. L. to Susan Dunevant 8-23-1884 (8-24-1884) L
Hester, Francis to Catharine Sanders 6-16-1856 (6-19-1856) Sh

Hester, H. G. to T. C. Roffe 2-22-1863 We
Hester, Henry to Adaline Dunlap 1-10-1843 Hn
Hester, J. B. to Frances K.(R?) Ford 3-19-1835 Sh
Hester, James T. to Susan J. Aiken 9-5-1860 Dy
Hester, James to Mahala Lewis 12-25-1865 F B
Hester, James to Sarena E. Emmerson 11-23-1853 Hn
Hester, John B. to Armanda M. White 4-16-1835 Sh
Hester, John B. to Elizabeth C. White 6-24-1854 Sh
Hester, John H. to Mary E. Sykes 12-28-1869 Ma
Hester, John W. to E. S. Brame 1-7-1841 F
Hester, John W. to Mary J. Harris 12-12-1854 (no return) F
Hester, John to Harriet Turner 3-3-1842 (no return) Hn
Hester, Joseph to Saletha Gardner 9-11-1871 (9-12-1871) Cr
Hester, Lacy J. to Lucy J. Hester 4-26-1858 Cr
Hester, P. W. to M. C. Harper 8-6-1865 Cr
Hester, Robert H. to Judah Anderson 9-30-1846 Hr
Hester, Thomas to Mary Gay 9-30-1850 Hr
Hester, W. B. to Mary Hale 3-20-1860 Cr
Hester, W. H. to Mary T. Kennon 10-10-1856 We
Hester, William F. to Emeline Frence 10-29-1866 (no return) Hn
Hester, William H. to Sinia E. Wall 4-3-1841 (4-5-1841) F
Hester, Wyatt to Eliza B. Jones 12-2-1823 (12-4-1823) Hr
Hesther, James D. to S. A. Breene? 6-28-1842 (7-14-1842) F
Hetawer, William to O. Smith 4-29-1867 (4-13?-1867) T
Hethcock, John to Ellen Watson 9-15-1863 Sh
Hethcock, William to Eudora E. Sanford 9-14-1858 (9-16-1858) G
Hetherington, Claborn to Susan E. Temple 2-23-1850 O
Heuer, Anton Freadarich to Sophia Van Demark 2-14-1851 Sh
Heughan, W. W. to Mattie Landrum 7-27-1877 (8-2-1877) Dy
Heuly, Theoplius? to Lucy J. Bridges 7-10-1853 Cr
Hewatt, John M. to Nancy Miller 5-30-1857 Sh
Hewatt, Richard A. to Mahala J. Ke(e)llan 1-3-1854 (1-5-1854) O
Hewett, Peter to Ann E. Williams 2-24-1862 Sh
Hewett, Thomas R. F. to Mary Choate 11-11-1859 Sh
Hewett, W. H. to M. A. Norton 5-17-1858 (5-20-1858) Hr
Hewin, Asa to Catharine J. Huddleston 5-2-1853 (no return) F
Hewit, Hazael to Malinda Sensemon 12-22-1849 (12-25-1849) Ma
Hewit, James to Sarah Tanner 3-1-1858 Sh
Hewitt, Samuel to Martha Upchurch 5-2-1828 (5-4-1828) O
Hewlet, John C. to Sallie A. Mitchell 2-2-1866 (2-8-1866) F
Hewlett, Thomas P. to Agatha Owens 6-14-1824 O
Hewlin, Matthew to Malinda C. Roach 3-29-1851 O
Heyes, Henry Grinshaw to Mary Elizabeth Motley 1-27-1862 Sh
Heyward, jr., T. S. to Louisa Watkins 4-17-1860 Sh
Hezekieh, Henry E. to Irene E. Stickley 4-17-1849 Sh
Hiant, J. M. to Emily Burns 3-17-1853 Be
Hibbitt, James to Louiza Harris 10-31-1882 (11-2-1882) L
Hibbitt, John D. to Ellen Whitby 1-21-1862 Sh
Hibbs, Isaac to Deliah Sanders 12-27-1843 We
Hichcock, G. W. to E. A. Dickerson 2-22-1850 We
Hickerson, Moses to Jane C. Johnson 7-12-1838 Sh
Hickerson, Thomas to Eliza Jane Green 12-29-1869 T
Hickey, James to Mary Heely (Keeley?) 9-14-1850 Sh
Hickey, Michael to Margaret Gorman 5-30-1847 Sh
Hickey, Patrick to Margaret N. Mehan 11-28-1859 Sh
Hickey, Richard to Catherine Toomey 11-24-1845 Sh
Hickey, Timothy to Catharine Creighton 5-23-1856 (5-24-1856) Sh
Hickine, Hughey to Mary Hill 6-23-1860 T
Hicklin, W. M. to N. Snider 10-4-1866 Hn
Hickman, Asa Oliver to S. E. Elder 7-4-1850 O
Hickman, Henry W. to Mary Louisa Howard 3-5-1855 (3-8-1855) O
Hickman, Henry to Sissie Forest 12-4-1868 (no return) Hy
Hickman, J. H. to S. A. E. Jenkins 12-28-1855 (no return) Hn
Hickman, J. R. to A. E. Gullet 1-11-1869 (1-14-1869) Cr
Hickman, James F. to Lucinda McAlexander 11-26-1839 Cr
Hickman, James F. to Ursul M. Mathis 5-23-1866 (5-3?-1866) Cr
Hickman, Jesse to Sarah A. Herron 2-12-1857 Cr
Hickman, Jessie to Elizabeth Carter 11-22-1842 Cr
Hickman, John A. to Eliza (Mrs.) Dillard 9-10?-1864 (9-9-1864) Sh
Hickman, John D. to Rachel Haley 8-22-1844 O
Hickman, T. S. to Margaret Glover 1-7-1856 (1-9-1856) O
Hickman, Thomas to Margrett K. Ross 3-9-1847 (4-8-1847) Hr
Hickman, William L. to Ma Henry 4-4-1837 O
Hickman, William to Sarah Robertson 5-14-1850 G
Hickman, Wyatt to Mary A. Thompson 2-16-1838 (2-20-1838) Hr
Hickox, James L. to Nannie E. Turner 11-6-1867 Hy
Hicks, A. B. to Lucinda Leuter 11-6-1856 Cr
Hicks, A. G. to Matti Buchanan 8-31-1864 G
Hicks, A. J. to Martha J. Melton 10-27-1855 (no return) Hn
Hicks, A. R. to Peggy Wade 12-25-1873 T
Hicks, Albert to Caroline Jones 5-7-1864 Sh B
Hicks, Ashley to Elsa Hicks 8-12-1854 (8-?-1854) G
Hicks, Austin to Rebecca Bowen 12-31-1872 Dy
Hicks, Austin to Vina Holdsbrooks 7-11-1844 Hn
Hicks, B. C. to Margaret N. Pouchen 7-16-1861 Mn
Hicks, Benjamin M. to Mary C. McClellan 10-26-1847 (10-28-1847) Ma
Hicks, Bushrod to Eveline Upton 6-7-1843 Hn

Hicks, C. H. to Luch sH. Ingram 10-6-1848 Hr
Hicks, Charles to Nancy Ann Gray 11-18-1856 (11-29-1856) Sh
Hicks, Chas. H. to Virginia Trip? 12-27-1870 Hy
Hicks, Claborn to Martha Cooper 12-10-1843 Be
Hicks, Daniel to Harriet King 5-1-1871 Ma
Hicks, Edwin A. to Lucresha? Dickens 9-8-1831 Ma
Hicks, Erasmus F. to Alice Jelks 3-16-1858 (3-17-1858) Ma
Hicks, Felix to Caroline Burton 1-19-1869 L
Hicks, G. R. to S. C. Lawson 12-21-1864 O
Hicks, George B. to Eliza J. McClellan 10-9-1849 (10-10-1849) Ma
Hicks, George to Mary Buckley 5-8-1858 (5-9-1858) Sh
Hicks, George to Susan Tubbs 12-25-1866 We
Hicks, Gideon to Ann R. Deloach 12-19-1860 (12-20-1860) Ma
Hicks, Glenn to Eliza Currie 10-14-1873 Hy
Hicks, Green B. to Sally Hicks 3-26-1844 (3-28-1844) Hr
Hicks, Hardy to Mary Byler 11-3-1853 L
Hicks, Harrison to Anabella Wade 12-2-1850 Hn
Hicks, Henry C. to Kitty Ann Asburn 12-10-1855 (12-11-1855) G
Hicks, Henry to Margaret Young 7-29-1844 Sh
Hicks, Irvin to Elizabeth Robertson 2-22-1878 (2-23-1878) Dy
Hicks, Irvin to Henrietta Robertson 8-25-1877 (no return) Dy
Hicks, J. B. to Amanda Whit 3-6-1861 Mn
Hicks, J. N. to Mary A. Nelson 2-7-1866 (2-8-1866) F
Hicks, J. R. to Isabella Abbott 10-24-1866 Be
Hicks, J. T. to Sarah E. Carter 9-21-1848 Sh
Hicks, J. to Ida Skillern 9-3-1872 Hy
Hicks, J. to Sarah Wiseman 1-8-1839 Be
Hicks, Jacob to S. Smith 1-31-1861 Be
Hicks, Jacob to Sarah Reed 9-2-1852 G
Hicks, James N. to Luizer C. Grimes 2-6-1870 G
Hicks, James W. to Nancy S. Taylor 10-17-1860 (10-18-1860) Ma
Hicks, James to Clara A. Kee 2-2-1865 Be
Hicks, James to Elizabeth Jenkins 10-11-1852 (10-13-1852) Ma
Hicks, James to Susanah C. Sanford 8-15-1832 (8-16-1832) G
Hicks, Jesse to Martha J. Brogdon 2-24-1862 Be
Hicks, Jesse to Parthina Williams 1-9-1867 (1-10-1867) Dy
Hicks, Jessee H. to Susan M. McCrory 2-14-1861 (no return) Hy
Hicks, Jiles to Caroline Taylor 10-20-1875 (no return) Hy
Hicks, Jno. F. to Nancy J. White 10-19-1846 We
Hicks, Jo to Louisa Wynne 3-2-1867 Dy
Hicks, Jobe to Elizabeth McAlelly 12-14-1833 (12-19-1833) G
Hicks, Jobe to Vergency S. Hagler 2-24-1847 Hn
Hicks, John F. to Nancy White 10-22-1846 We
Hicks, John F. to Sarah W. Harbert 12-5-1853 (12-6-1853) Ma
Hicks, John J. to Elizabeth Lett 9-10-1856 Cr
Hicks, John J. to Martha oliver 4-27-1848 (no return) Cr
Hicks, John M. to Emily M. Berton 1-31-1850 Hn
Hicks, John M. to Marietta E. Olin 5-14-1862 Sh
Hicks, John M. to Susan F. Jackson 3-12-1863 G
Hicks, John R. to Elizabeth E. Taylor 12-19-1854 (12-21-1854) Ma
Hicks, John R. to Fannie T. Duncan 9-18-1866 (9-19-1866) Ma
Hicks, John T. to M. E. Robertson 12-28-1859 Hr
Hicks, John W. to Elizabeth Bledsoe 2-18-1867 G
Hicks, John W. to Kittie D. Pugh 11-15-1874 Hy
Hicks, John W. to Martha E. Andrews 2-26-1868 (2-27-1868) F
Hicks, John W. to Winney P. Vanhook 2-23-1865 Hn
Hicks, John to Elizabeth Williams 6-4-1867 Hy
Hicks, John to Nancy Garwood 1-26-1870 G
Hicks, John to Rebecca Hatley 5-5-1867 Be
Hicks, John to Susan White 8-16-1855 Be
Hicks, Johnson to Jane Dement 12-27-1866 G
Hicks, Johnson to Jane Sinclair 1-21-1868 G B
Hicks, Joseiah to Polly Paine 5-16-1829 Sh
Hicks, Joseph to Rebecca E. Russom 3-1-1863 Mn
Hicks, Kenneth G. to Cynthia A. Gill 9-28-1858 (9-29-1858) Ma
Hicks, Marville to Annie B. Bennett 7-21-1850 Be
Hicks, Michael H. to Elizabeth J. Fields 6-16-1840 G
Hicks, Michael to Betsy Claiburne 3-6-1869 T
Hicks, Monroe to Amanda Dillingham 10-10-1878 (no return) Dy
Hicks, N. B. to Exes Jane Mauldin 2-29-1840 (3-12-1840) Hr
Hicks, Nathaniel S. to Mary Leeper 2-24-1863 Hn
Hicks, Nonod to Amanda J. Walls 4-24-1855 (4-26-1855) G
Hicks, Peter Juchoore? to Temperance Lucintha Clark 6-20-1850 (7-3-1850) T
Hicks, R. B. to Rosa L. Andrews 12-19-1866 (no return) F
Hicks, Ransom Burns to Lydia C. Withers 10-8-1861 (10-9-1861) Ma
Hicks, Reding to Alvinia Hicks 7-25-1854 (7-26-1854) G
Hicks, Riley to Martha Flowers 4-9-1871 Hy
Hicks, S. M. to Sarah McRee 5-12-1864 O
Hicks, S. P. to Marinda Lee 10-25-1865 G
Hicks, Samuel to Maranda S. Mayfield 9-15-1858 (9-16-1858) G
Hicks, Samuel to Margarette Shain 1-5-1856 (1-8-1856) G
Hicks, Samuel to Rebecca George 4-26-1857 Cr
Hicks, Shephard B. to Parmelia T. Watt 8-15-1848 (8-20-1848) Ma
Hicks, Silas M. to Martha J. Hastings 3-24-1853 (no return) Hn
Hicks, Silas M. to Mary Kitchen(s) 1-9-1854 (1-10-1854) O
Hicks, Solman D. to Martha A. Colman 8-5-1858 We
Hicks, Stephen P. to Ellen E. Lasiter 4-11-1850 (no return) Hn

Hicks, T. H. to Lucy A. Hawkins 1-1-1867 (no return) Hy
Hicks, T. M. to M. C. Hartsville 4-4-1874 (4-8-1874) O
Hicks, Thomas L. to Mary Ann Rates 6-7-1860 Be
Hicks, Thos. J. to Rebecca Jane Casey 12-22-1856 (12-23-1856) Hr
Hicks, Thos. to Lucinda Simmons 7-3-1856 Cr
Hicks, W. G. to Eliza A. Swinney 10-8-1857 Hn
Hicks, W. H. to Sarah V. Childress 12-30-1862 (12-31-1862) L
Hicks, W. R. to Lancy Clifton 11-30-1862 Mn
Hicks, W. W. B. to Mary A. Ray 12-30-1857 Hr
Hicks, Wesley W. to Louisa E. McCord 8-27-1854 Hn
Hicks, Wiley M. to Caroline Smith 12-24-1866 (12-25-1866) Dy
Hicks, William C. to Margarett McAlelly 1-29-1846 G
Hicks, William K. to Paralee Bridges 9-6-1860 Hn
Hicks, William M. to Maranda P. C. Glasgow 3-20-1862 We
Hicks, William M. to Mary C. Newton 6-26-1856 We
Hicks, William R. to Mahala C. McCord 4-3-1861 (no return) Hn
Hicks, William R. to Martha Page 2-16-1854 L
Hicks, William to Harriet Whitten 12-29-1873 T
Hicks, William to Lucinda Parsons 6-9-1859 Hn
Hicks, William to Mary Cox 3-14-1828 (3-18-1828) Hr
Hicks, William to R. M. Worthy 3-20-1870 G
Hicks, Williamson to Livey Franklin 2-26-1863 (no return) Hn
Hicks, Williamson to Mahala Head 5-28-1859 (5-29-1859) O
Hicks, Willis to Elizabeth Williams 8-15-1855 Cr
Hicks, Winfield S. to Nancy Jane English 3-1-1854 (3-28-1854) G
Hicks, Wm. J. to Julia A. Thomas 9-28-1858 (no return) L
Hicks, Wm. S. to Sarah Ann Hollinsworth 3-31-1864 Be
Hicks, Wm. to Margaret Boston 10-17-1857 Cr
Hicks, Wm. to Martha A. Lightie 3-12-1859 (3-18-1859) F
Hicky, Bartley to Margaret Gardner 3-23-1871 (4-2-1871) L
Hiett, N. B. to Milly Arnold 10-20-1869 L
Hifield, F. to Mollie McNilly 6-17-1874 T
Hifiley, Henry to Mary C. White 10-14-1847 Cr
Hiflin, George H. to Mary F. Robertson 11-28-1854 (no return) F
Higbee, Adam to Ella Woods 12-25-1868 (12-26-1868) F B
Higbee, H. H. to Annie Cowden 11-30-1863 Sh
Higden, William H. to Almira E. Fly 6-21-1858 (6-22-1858) Ma
Higdon, John to Harriet L. May 2-16-1868 G
Higdon, John to Mary E. Sexton 5-19-1847 Cr
Higdon, M. H. to Mattie McCrackin 2-14-1874 (2-18-1874) Dy
Higdon, T. to L.F. Kilberth 2-26-1863 Be
Higdon, Thomas to Dolly Thompson 3-14-1839 Be
Higdon, Thomas to Jane Mullin 11-7-1866 Cr
Higdon, W. T. to Sarah Rowe 5-27-1867 (5-29-1867) Cr
Higdon, William to Mary E. Whitehead 2-28-1861 Be
Higgason, J. T. to Frances Hurt 1-13-1868 (1-15-1868) Dy
Higgenbottom, George E. to Mary Moody 1-14-1834 Sh
Higgenbottom, William to Sarah Warren 11-9-1836 Sh
Higgens, Wesley N. to Lucinda Sanders 12-24-1848 Sh
Higgins, J. B. to L. J. Campbell 12-14-1869 G
Higgins, James N. to Emeline Wilkins 8-2-1839 (8-4-1839) G
Higgins, John to Ann Yancy 1-25-1873 Hy
Higgins, John to Catharine Cassady 5-21-1857 Sh
Higgins, John to Dicey Turner 8-28-1869 Hy
Higgins, Thomas to Ann McAnally 3-16-1852 (4-19-1852) Sh
Higgins, W. P. to Martha E. Watson 1-12-1868 Hy
Higgins, W. W. to Nancy A. Moore 11-15-1864 (11-16-1864) Sh
Higgins, Wesley to Louisa Loyle 6-19-1860 Sh
Higgs, Isham to Barbary Foust 1-9-1840 (no return) F
Higgs, Jonathan to Mary H. Adams 7-25-1844 We
Higgs, Levy to P. Parmer 6-10-1852 We
Higgs, Reuben to Rebecca Mangum 11-6-1844 (11-10-1844) Hr
Higgs, Stephen to M. Robbins 1-2-1856 (no return) Hn
Higgs, T. J. to Martha E. M. Fuqua 1-22-1870 (1-27-1870) Cr
Higgs, Theophelus to Margaret B. Chears 1-24-1856 (1-31-1856) Hr
Higgs, Thomas to Margret Rosson 12-30-1845 We
Higgs, Thompson H. to Martha A. Paschal 7-17-1862 (no return) We
Higgs, W. L. to Margaret Freeman 2-27-1855 We
Higgs, Wm. to Virginia A. Jenkins 1-6-1846 (no return) We
High, David G. to Lucy Ann Todd 3-1-1859 We
High, David G. to Mary J. Todd 11-18-1855 We
High, James to Ann Adeline Brown 9-8-1838 (9-10-1838) Hr
High, James to Mary J. Holliday 12-19-1863 Hn
High, Jno. W. to Sarah Eliz. Simmons 9-11-1850 F
High, John to Elizabeth F. Chappell 3-22-1855 We
High, John to Rowan Boothe 8-4-1859 Hn
High, M. to Matilda P. Vaughn 1-11-1851 (1-16-1851) F
High, S. M. to Margaret N. Webster 10-9-1854 (10-10-1854) Sh
High, William T. to Elizabeth H. Thompson 12-28-1853 (12-29-1853) Sh
High, William to Ann Eliza Hester 8-8-1837 Hr
Highams, John to Lizzie Williams 6-21-1860 Hr
Highfield, Bennett to Margrett Johnson 12-29-1846 (12-31-1846) Hr
Highfield, Hezekiah to Tempe Rook 9-17-1829 Hr
Highfield, Jerimiah to Malinda Nabers 11-10-1851 (11-11-1851) Hr
Highfield, William R. to Tennie L. Ashby 12-25-1871 Hr
Highfill, James to Martha Jackson 4-22-1833 (4-25-1833) Hr
Highfill, Thomas to Isabella Hartsfield 9-10-1850 Hn

Highfill, William H. to Celia A. Patterson 9-11-1852 (9-19-1852) Hr
Hight, Jas. D. to Mary E. Watson 12-23-1858 G
Hightower, Henry to Silla Jeffreys 12-28-1873 Hy
Hightower, John H. to Malissa J. Glass 1-30-1869 (2-4-1869) T
Hightower, Stephen to Mary Ann New? 12-19-1836 Hr
Hightower, William S. to Martha D. Palmer 4-28-1866 (5-14-1866) Cr
Hilams?, Charles to Alice Brown 3-23-1870 Hy
Hilderbrand, Benj. to Susan Robertson 3-28-1833 Sh
Hilderbrand, Henry K. to Mary Virginia Robinson 5-19-1869 Ma
Hill, A. B. to Harriet Thompson 1-23-1865 (1-24-1865) T
Hill, A. G. to Elizabeth Reed 11-23-1847 Cr
Hill, Albert G. to Martha J. Gooch 1-31-1839 (no return) Cr
Hill, Alfred to Martha Parrish 9-7-1870 (9-18-1870) F B
Hill, Allen to G. A. J. Powell 5-6-1861 (5-9-1861) Sh
Hill, Allen to Malinda Wilson 1-25-1840 Ma
Hill, Alvadas to Mary Bowlen 8-13-1839 G
Hill, Arthur E. to Elizabeth Edmond 3-28-1834 O
Hill, Batt to Susan Read 12-15-1867 Hy
Hill, Ben to Bettie Campbell 1-26-1876 (no return) Hy
Hill, Ben to Patience Harris 8-29-1868 (8-30-1868) F B
Hill, Benj. M. to Mary Howell(Harrell) 8-9-1833 (8-15-1833) Hr
Hill, Benjamin W. to Elizabeth Twiford 7-7-1850 Sh
Hill, Bird to Louisa Eddings 6-12-1830 (6-15-1830) Ma
Hill, Bryant to Ann Galaway 9-24-1869 (9-25-1869) T
Hill, Byrd to Levinia R. Butler 10-21-1852 Ma
Hill, C. H. to F. E. Burnes 12-12-1861 Mn
Hill, Charles A. to Mary Elizabeth Nelson 5-14-1839 (5-16-1839) Ma
Hill, Charles H. to Sarah Y. Cockrill 10-28-1840 (10-29-1840) T
Hill, Charles O. to M. J. B. Bigham 1-13-1842 Cr
Hill, Charles to Emily Sanders 12-17-1869 (no return) F B
Hill, Charles to Nancy Person 5-17-1848 Sh
Hill, Charley to E. J. Atkins 8-25-1873 (no return) Dy
Hill, Daniel to Sallie Cotton 6-8-1872 (6-9-1872) T
Hill, David to Ellen Beavers 7-13-1867 (7-14-1867) Cr
Hill, Dorstal to Ellen Billings 9-10-1869 T
Hill, E. W. to Martha Steveson 9-5-1870 (9-7-1870) T
Hill, Ed to Tabby Jones 8-5-1874 (no return) Hy
Hill, Edmond to Caroline Green 1-20-1873 Hy
Hill, F. P. to Mary J. Kelton 1-16-1866 G
Hill, F. W. to L. S. Hall 12-12-1872 T
Hill, Francis to Sarah J. Culp 12-2-1850 (12-3-1850) F
Hill, G. C. to Wrady Kathey 12-31-1855 (no return) Hn
Hill, George W. to Fanny C. Bledsoe 2-20-1867 Cr
Hill, George W. to Sarah E. Fuller 11-13-1866 (11-15-1866) Dy
Hill, George to Louisana Mitchell 12-28-1848 Ma
Hill, Gilbert to Eliza Dyson 10-5-1871 (10-6-1871) T
Hill, Green L. to Louisa F. Cock 6-19-1861 (6-27-1861) Ma
Hill, H. M. to Nancy Raney 5-28-1864 (no return) Cr
Hill, Henry C. to Belle Christ 2-4-1867 G
Hill, Henry to Mattie Whitworth 12-14-1870 (12-15-1870) T
Hill, I. H. to S. I. Boone 12-27-1865 O
Hill, Ira M. to Mary T. Johnson 4-3-1849 Sh
Hill, Ira to Angeline Jones 12-17-1872 Hy
Hill, Isaac S. to Mary Wright 6-10-1867 (6-11-1867) T
Hill, Isaac to Martha A. Matheny 2-1-1863 Be
Hill, J. A. to M. C. Everett 9-17-1866 (9-18-1866) Cr
Hill, J. C. to Mary J. Worrell 5-14-1870 (5-15-1870) Cr
Hill, J. G. to Ann Bessent 12-24-1873 Dy
Hill, J. H. to Margaret J. Wood 3-12-1866 T
Hill, J. M. to M. J. Simms 3-27-1875 (3-28-1875) L
Hill, J. R. to Mary E. Hall 1-1-1873 (1-2-1873) Cr
Hill, J. T. C. to Maggie Bradshaw 2-27-1867 G
Hill, J. T. to Mattie E. Senter 12-22-1868 G
Hill, J. T. to Sarah M. Jordan 1-13-1869 Be
Hill, J. W. to J. T.? Bledsoe 2-11-1871 (2-12-1871) Cr
Hill, J. W. to Sarah C. Baskins 1-12-1869 T
Hill, Jackson to Mary Ann Williams 5-30-1848 Sh
Hill, Jacob to Laura Noel 2-24-1869 (3-2-1869) Ma
Hill, James A. to Eliza J. Lauderdale 7-31-1867 (9-1-1867) T
Hill, James C. to Mary Ann Diggs 12-29-1842 (no return) Hn
Hill, James C. to Z. T. Farrington 2-6-1867 T
Hill, James D. to Minnie C. Laycock 2-4-1875 Cr
Hill, James K. to Nancy S. Smith 5-12-1840 (5-13-1840) Hr
Hill, James L. to Sarah L. C. Moran 11-14-1846 Sh
Hill, James M. to Martha J. Nelson 11-13-1866 (11-16-1866) T
Hill, James M> to Salina M. Davis 12-27-1859 (12-28-1859) T
Hill, James N. to Julia L. Kelton 2-2-1854 G
Hill, James R. to Angeline Ray 10-17-1867 (no return) Hn
Hill, James to Delitha Thedford 1-13-1857 G
Hill, James to Ella Richardson 3-2-1870 Hy
Hill, James to Jane Hays 11-3-1869 (no return) L
Hill, James to Mahala Williams 1-14-1879 (1-16-1879) Dy
Hill, James to Martha Moore 6-5-1863 Mn
Hill, James to Musie Dora Harrison 12-22-1870 L
Hill, James to Texana Crafton 11-4-1867 G B
Hill, Jessee to Millie Moody 12-5-1870 (12-8-1870) F B
Hill, Jessee to Rachael Hartsfield 12-5-1860 T

Hill, Jno. C. F. to Mary Owen 12-8-1837 Hr
Hill, Jobe to Louisa Stanford 8-28-1869 (9-1-1869) Cr B
Hill, John C. to Terry J. Lowrence 12-24-1852 Cr
Hill, John F. to Sarah A. McClain 5-26-1859 Hn
Hill, John G. to Martha A. Beard 11-4-1862 We
Hill, John H. to Jane Hancock 1-22-1876 (1-28-1876) L
Hill, John H. to Mary E. Long 6-16-1873 (no return) Hy
Hill, John H. to Nancy C. Brown 9-23-1853 (no return) F
Hill, John N. to Cynthia Carroll 1-21-1847 Hn
Hill, John N. to Julia A. Holmes 2-19-1866 (2-20-1866) T
Hill, John R. to Julia A. Nevills 6-13-1850 Sh
Hill, John S. to Mariah E. Davidson 1-26-1843 G
Hill, John W. to Margaret Ellen Kyle 3-28-1867 Ma
Hill, John W. to Martha F. Jones 12-6-1856 (12-7-1856) G
Hill, John to Emma Keneday 6-4-1868 G
Hill, John to Jinnie Briant 7-24-1869 (7-29-1869) Cr
Hill, John to Lusina Alston 11-9-1866 (11-10-1866) T
Hill, Jordan to Callie Vaulx 12-22-1866 (no return) Hy
Hill, Joseph A. to Rachel C. Pulliam 6-6-1859 (6-7-1859) F
Hill, Joseph W. to Tabitha N. Newhouse 12-29-1845 Hn
Hill, Joseph to Minnie Green 12-20-1871 (no return) Cr
Hill, Josiah A. to Nancy Seymore 2-13-1845 (no return) Cr
Hill, Josiah M. to Lucinda Caldwell 3-6-1843 (3-7-1843) Hr
Hill, LaFayette to Elizabeth Catharine Haynie 10-13-1847 T
Hill, LaFayette to Seraphina C. Tipton 11-15-1855 T
Hill, Leonidas J. to Ann R. Eddins 2-27-1856 Ma
Hill, Lewberry to Syntha Pickler 8-25-1844 Be
Hill, Lewis to Elizabeth Webb 12-13-1843 Sh
Hill, Lewis to Lucy Ann Haynes 9-25-1867 Hn
Hill, Lewis to Margaret Jackson 12-16-1848 (12-17-1848) Hr
Hill, Lion to Mary Cook 9-9-1831 (9-13-1831) O
Hill, Louis to Mahulda Porter 5-19-1880 (5-20-1880) Dy
Hill, M. P. to Jane Shepherd 11-14-1854 Sh
Hill, M. P. to Lucinda Black 2-18-1850 Hn
Hill, Mike to Silvia Adkins 10-13-1874 (10-14-1874) T
Hill, Napoleon to Mary M. Wood 7-7-1858 (7-8-1858) Hr
Hill, Nathan G. to Sarah E. Montgomery 4-11-1855 Cr
Hill, Nathan to Mary Mason 12-24-1869 F B
Hill, P. C. to S. A. Short (Sharp?) 9-1-1866 G
Hill, P. E. to Mary G. Bodkin 8-16-1866 G
Hill, Pelly to Mary Winn 12-24-1873 (12-25-1873) T
Hill, Perry to Selia Wooden 11-16-1875 (11-18-1875) L
Hill, Peter to Hanna Bledsoe 2-7-1867 T
Hill, Pleasant to Martha Reynolds 6-1-1833 (6-4-1833) G
Hill, R. D. to Martha E. C. Anderson 12-28-1865 G
Hill, R. J. to Martha F. Enochs 10-7-1872 (10-9-1872) Cr
Hill, R. S. to Frances C. Craig 9-13-1862 (9-14-1862) F
Hill, R. T. to M. L. Griffin 12-21-1870 (12-22-1870) Dy
Hill, Richard C. to Mary Ann Crews 11-27-1849 (11-29-1849) Hr
Hill, Richard H. to J. A. Parker 12-12-1853 Sh
Hill, Robert A. to Martha Walker 1-10-1848 L
Hill, Robert C. to Rebecca F. Dodd 3-27-1866 (3-29-1866) Cr
Hill, Robert N. to Betty A. Maxey 9-10-1856 Ma
Hill, Robert to Ida Taylor 12-27-1877 Hy
Hill, Rufus C. to Tennessee Yow 12-3-1865 Hn
Hill, Rufus to Elizabeth Shepard 12-16-1870 (12-17-1870) T
Hill, Rufus to Henrietta Short 1-12-1876 (no return) Hy
Hill, Sam to Frances Potter 3-24-1866 Hy
Hill, Samuel B. to Sarah A. Alexander 11-21-1839 Hn
Hill, Samuel J. to Sarah E. Sexton 12-28-1862 G
Hill, Sevie C. to Manervia E. Gailey 6-24-1860 We
Hill, Sidney to Eliza Ann Hill 12-27-1854 (12-27-1854) O
Hill, Smith H. to Newoma Harvey 1-13-1844 Hr
Hill, Sparrel to Annie Elder 10-20-1864 G
Hill, Stephen J. to Susan E. Carithers 2-18-1858 O
Hill, T. J. to Margaret Stephens 6-1-1862 Mn
Hill, Thomas F. to Emma McFadden 6-30-1869 G
Hill, Thomas G. to Sarah A. Smith 2-7-1848 (2-8-1848) Hr
Hill, Thomas J. to Amanda J. Johnson 3-21-1870 T
Hill, Thomas J. to Lucretia Jane Smith 4-16-1869 (4-18-1869) T
Hill, Thomas J. to Mary R. Kennelly 7-20-1839 (no return) L
Hill, W. E. H. to M. J. Simmons 12-12-1870 (12-15-1870) T
Hill, W. H. to Elizabeth Williams 12-27-1845 (12-28-1845) F
Hill, W. H. to Mary F. Evans 2-1-1868 (no return) F
Hill, W. V. to Martha A. Oliphant 10-11-1858 (10-13-1858) G
Hill, W. V. to R. R. Rooks 1-4-1868 Hy
Hill, W. V. to S. L. Oliphant 7-31-1862 G
Hill, W. to Emaline Smith 10-16-1873 T B
Hill, William A. to Mary A. Blankenship 12-14-1863 (12-15-1863) Dy
Hill, William B. to Ellen Clackston 6-18-1833 O
Hill, William B. to Matilda W. Person 1-19-1843 Sh
Hill, William E. to Sarah A. Manly 2-14-1855 Hn
Hill, William F. to Joanna Powers 12-19-1870 L
Hill, William F. to Mary Diggs 5-9-1850 F
Hill, William Green to Martha Ann Jameson 12-7-1848 Hn
Hill, William J. to Edy Turner 2-27-1843 Hr
Hill, William Kenan to Emily B. Pleasant 6-12-1855 Sh

Hill, William P. to Elizabeth M. Ellison 12-10-1840 Hn
Hill, William W. S. to Sarah J. Nevills 10-31-1849 Sh
Hill, William to Lottie Briley 7-7-1872 Hy
Hill, William to Mahala Mathias 4-10-1862 (no return) L
Hill, William to Polly Taylor 5-18-1866 (5-19-1866) F B
Hill, William to Samantha A. Crockett 6-13-1863 (no return) We
Hill, Wm. B. (Rev.) to Virginia J. Laughy 10-30-1851 (no return) F
Hill, Wm. C. to Merandra C. Hill 12-22-1841 Cr
Hill, Wm. H. to Elizabeth Seymore 8-23-1847 Cr
Hill, Wm. Henry to Martha Burton McGrogan 2-8-1859 T
Hill, Wm. P. to Louiza M. Null 2-24-1866 Cr
Hillard, Robert to Mary Hooper 5-7-1864 O M
Hillhouse, Benjamin M. to Rachel Norton 12-20-1833 Hr
Hilliard, A. B. to T. C. McAdoo 12-20-1854 Cr
Hilliard, A. T. to Jennie R. Tuckniss 12-1-1866 (12-2-1866) F
Hilliard, Albert to Emily Holliday 1-8-1857 Cr
Hilliard, Albert to Phillis Jefferson 3-20-1869 (3-24-1869) F B
Hilliard, C. to C. Rogers 9-11-1850 Cr
Hilliard, Charney to Blanch Pollerd 2-4-1871 (2-12-1871) F B
Hilliard, D. B. to M. B. Burford 12-14-1875 (no return) Hy
Hilliard, D. M. to Catharine B. Sommers 10-19-1859 We
Hilliard, David B. to Martha Ann Blair 2-2-1846 (2-5-1846) F
Hilliard, Frank to Orrenia Brandon 8-1-1872 (8-4-1872) Cr
Hilliard, Henry E. to Sallie Anna Old 7-18-1860 F
Hilliard, J. P. to C. S. Tripp 3-24-1866 (3-29-1866) F
Hilliard, J. T. Z. to Mary V. Trotter 9-24-1860 (9-25-1860) F
Hilliard, J. W. T. to Mary A. Chambers 12-6-1854 (no return) F
Hilliard, J. W. T. to Nancy A. Willis 9-16-1854 (no return) F
Hilliard, John P. to Rebecca Watson 3-5-1863 We
Hilliard, John to Mary Lafloor 9-16-1855 Cr
Hilliard, Joseph to Elizabeth Jones 10-15-1873 (10-16-1873) O
Hilliard, Joseph to Mary Dabbs 1-31-1855 O
Hilliard, Michell G. to Elizabeth Craig 6-7-1838 F
Hilliard, N. R. to Alberta H. Stewart 8-30-1859 (no return) Hy
Hilliard, N. S. to Elizabeth Evans 12-29-1865 (1-3-1866) F
Hilliard, W. A.? to Elizabeth D. Chambers 2-1-1847 (2-4-1847) F
Hilliard, W. E. to M. L. Taylor 3-6-1872 (3-7-1872) Cr
Hilliard, W. H. to E. C. Haley 10-5-1866 (10-7-1866) F
Hilliard, Walter A. to Ann Furber 10-25-1854 (10-30-1854) Sh *
Hilliard, Wiley H. to Caroline C. Johnson 10-30-1856 Cr
Hilliard, William to Virginia C. Buckley 5-29-1860 We
Hilliard, Wm. B. to Manda E. Norwell 2-23-1854 Cr
Hilliard, Wm. D. to Martha A. E. McKasey 5-28-1856 (no return) Cr
Hilliard, Wm. to Armento Williams 9-27-1849 Cr
Hillis, J. B. to Mollie S. Allison 2-1-1858 (2-2-1858) Sh
Hillis, J. I. to Catherine P. Winston 9-17-1856 We
Hillis, William to Lucy Choate 5-12-1831 Sh
Hillman, James to Avie Wellington 2-12-1870 (no return) Hy
Hillsman, Beverly E. to Miriah A. N. Mathis 9-2-1858 Cr
Hillsman, Norvell to Sally Hillsman 8-29-1868 (no return) Cr
Hillsman, Stephen to Ann Stanford 12-20-1871 (12-21-1871) Cr
Hillsman, William to Betsy Ross 11-29-1869 (no return) Cr
Hilson, Bernhart to Lydia Ann George 6-2-1838 Sh
Hilton, T. B. to Mary M. Evans 12-15-1866 (12-17-1866) O
Hiltz, Morris to Louisa Genberger 3-9-1863 Sh
Himbrough, George to Rebecka E. Crockett 2-25-1839 (2-26-1839) G
Himey, Elijah Robert to Margaret Ann Smith 8-20-1857 T
Himmaugh, C. C. to M. E. Hooton 8-15-1871 (no return) Hy
Hinant, Hillsbury to Rebecca Hatly 1-4-1855 Be
Hinchee (Hinchen?), John Wm. to Virginia J. Waynesburg 8-20-1853 (8-21-1853) Sh
Hinchey, John B. to Rebecca Rice 7-24-1849 Hn
Hinchey, Joshua C. to Mary J. Waller 12-1-1850 Hn
Hinchey, W. B. to Hixey Myrick 7-27-1842 Hn
Hindes, William W. to Brown A. Brown 3-28-1868 (4-16-1868) L
Hindman, Alexander to Elizabeth McClerkin 3-26-1860 (3-29-1860) T
Hindman, David to Lousella Wolen 2-26-1870 T
Hindman, James G. to Sarah J. Linn 2-1-1858 (2-2-1858) T
Hindman, Jos. to Emeline S. Townsend 2-2-1870 T
Hindricks, Robert B. to Sarah J. Warmack 3-24-1858 Hn
Hinds, A. J. to Emily C. Gidcomb 8-25-1874 (8-26-1874) L
Hinds, James to Jane Baker 1-22-1859 (1-28-1859) L
Hinds, Josiah to Mary M. Hardy 1-23-1860 Sh
Hine?, William to Jane Band 12-1-1852 T
Hineman, D. G. to M. A. Stockinger 2-9-1859 F
Hines (Hynes), Jesse to Catharine Gillis (Giles) 4-22-1841 O
Hines, Benj. to Susanna Hill 3-1-1869 (no return) Hy
Hines, Britton to Martha Cotton 1-27-1855 Sh
Hines, Burl to Jennett Powell 10-1-1866 Hy
Hines, D. G. to Nancy E. Warren 12-24-1855 (1-2-1856) G
Hines, D. L. to O. D. Kelsoe 11-22-1869 (no return) Hy
Hines, Ellet to Emeline Mebane 12-27-1870 (12-30-1870) F B
Hines, F. T. to Rebecca Garner 9-19-1870 (9-21-1870) Dy
Hines, Henderson to Emily Walker 12-29-1870 (no return) Hy
Hines, Henry to Izena Shelton 8-24-1872 (no return) L B
Hines, J. L. (Dr.) to Fanny Furrah 7-1-1859 (7-5-1859) Sh
Hines, James W. to Caroline Carter 2-23-1847 Hr

Hines, James to Hannah Matilda Beaton 12-27-1848 (12-28-1848) Hr
Hines, James to Mary Beaden 12-21-1860 (1-1-1861) Hr
Hines, Jas. M. to Amanda M. Moore 6-2-1861 Hy
Hines, John D. to Lucinda Griffin 12-12-1850 Sh
Hines, John D. to Mary Ann Mires 9-4-1844 Sh
Hines, John to Jane Guthrie 1-15-1872 (no return) Cr B
Hines, John to Mary Downes 8-8-1858 Sh
Hines, John to Rachel Hines 8-1-1872 (no return) Hy
Hines, Parker to Kizzy Harper 6-4-1881 (no return) L
Hines, Richard to M. A. (Mrs.) Cage 8-9-1870 Ma
Hines, Sherrod to Mary Ann Chapman 9-9-1844 (9-?-1844) Hr
Hines, Solomon to Malinda White 7-23-1836 (7-28-1836) G
Hines, Thomas J. to Mary Hignight 2-29-1836 G
Hines, Thomas to Mary Ann Thompson 11-17-1846 (11-19-1846) Hr
Hines, Turner W. to Mary J. Griffin 7-20-1847 Sh
Hines, W. A. to M. E. (Mrs.) Carrigan 10-17-1881 (10-18-1881) L
Hines, W. B. to M. C. (Mrs.) Harrel 11-4-1864 (11-10-1864) Sh
Hines, W. S. to Frankie (Mrs.) Hall 2-12-1873 Dy
Hines, W. W. to Virginia Gaines 5-15-1856 Cr
Hines, Walker to Anna Walker 10-5-1871 Hy
Hines, Watkins to Hannah Jones 12-26-1872 Hy
Hines, William B. to Lucinda Miers 4-22-1850 Sh
Hines, William to Mary Ann Byrum 10-31-1849 L
Hines, Zephaniah to Sarah Kelly 2-10-1841 (2-11-1841) Hr
Hinesly, Elias to Parthena Gailor 2-29-1873 Hy
Hinnant, John C. to Sarah Swindle 1-20-1850 Be
Hinnon, Tim to Martha Raydon 1-8-1878 (1-10-1878) L
Hinsen, J. B. to Lucretia A. Webb 11-17-1840 G
Hinshaw, Addison to Calidona B. Martin 1-9-1844 F
Hinshaw, Pleasant to Margarett A. Martin 11-6-1841 (11-7-1841) F
Hinson, Hiram to Elizabeth Cardin 5-20-1845 (no return) Hn
Hinson, James W. to Sarah Horton 1-4-1860 G
Hinson, John G. to Narcessus Compton 8-15-1838 F
Hinson, John to Martha Savage 4-16-1849 Ma
Hinson, W. H. to J. P. Atkins 9-27-1867 G
Hinson, William F. to Amanda Finley 8-11-1838 (no return) Hn
Hinson, William to Malvina Compton 11-10-1838 (11-11-1838) F
Hinson, lHiram G. to Martha J. Reagan 9-28-1846 (9-30-1846) Hr
Hint?, James Osburn to Ann Eliza Pilkington 12-9-1851 (12-10-1851) T
Hintom, Edwin H. to Sarah A. Alsabrooks 12-20-1843 G
Hinton, Alex G. to Mary E. Hinton 4-23-1849 (4-25-1849) L
Hinton, Charlie to Emma Harris 3-15-1884 (3-16-1884) L
Hinton, E. H. to Sallie Hicks 6-6-1866 L
Hinton, Edwin H. to Lucy Ann Wright 1-26-1842 (1-27-1842) L
Hinton, R. L. to S. B. Montrose 8-22-1860 Dy
Hinton, Ransom to Margaret Henderson 4-28-1871 (5-1-1871) L
Hinton, Reuben to Margaret Epprs 4-4-1861 (no return) Hy
Hipp, Haulditch to Catherine Sawyer 10-5-1859 (no return) L
Hipp, Henry to Lucinda Wood 12-7-1867 L B
Hipp, James S. to Francis Elizabeth Wilson 9-10-1872 (9-11-1872) L
Hipp, James S. to Mary C. Barns (Bunn-Burris?) 8-1-1860 (8-2-1860) L
Hipp, N. J. to E. L. Barnes 4-30-1873 (5-1-1873) L
Hipp, William to Caroline Biles 7-7-1873 (7-9-1873) L B
Hirlson, Benjamin to Martha A. Reed 10-26-1863 O
Hirsh, Aaron to Amelia Blockmann 6-16-1852 (6-17-1852) Sh
Hirshberg, David to Clarice Block 2-28-1876 Hy
Hisaw, David to Sentha J. Pope 9-2-1844 G
Hisaw, George M. to Sarah S. McWilliams no date Cr
Hisaw, Sampson to Sarah Smith 4-10-1845 (no return) Cr
Hise, W. H. to Elizabeth Ladd 9-4-1874 (9-6-1874) T
Hitchcock, Ira B. to Perdilia (Permelia) Minton 8-22-1847 Sh
Hitchings, C. A. J. to Molly A. Hill 6-23-1855 (6-24-1855) Sh
Hite, Christopher to Mary Care 2-21-1837 G
Hite, Francis to Mary Ingram 4-26-1853 (no return) F
Hite, Richard C. to Adaline Adams 12-24-1849 Sh
Hite, William H. to Mary S. Alton 12-23-1841 Sh
Hitt, J. M. to M. C. Allen 12-19-1865 (no return) Hn
Hix, C. W. to Dicy J. Bryant 1-17-1865 G
Hix, C. W. to Louisa C. Hunt 3-9-1860 (3-11-1860) G
Hix, Henry Clay to Nancy Ann Skipper 10-31-1864 G
Hix, J. J. to Polly Ann Foster 4-25-1863 (4-26-1863) O
Hix, James M. to E. E. Kee 8-23-1866 (no return) Cr
Hix, James Y. to Martha H. P. Sanders 11-10-1856 (11-11-1856) G
Hix, John to Susan Parrish 9-25-1850 G
Hix, Merrit D. to Elizabeth Holloway 9-14-1853 (no return) F
Hizer, Jasper to Mary Ray 2-23-1857 (2-26-1857) Hr
Hoad, David to R. Caroline Williams 7-2-1859 (7-3-1859) Ma
Hoag, Lewis to Teresa Rappenchen 2-28-1855 Cr
Hoalms, Titus to Mary O. J. Thurmond 10-18-1862 (no return) Hn
Hoard, William to Nancy Willis 10-15-1827 Ma
Hobbs, Emmett to Katie Guinn 1-1-1879 (1-15-1879) Dy
Hobbs, Ezekiel B. W. to Feriby F. Williams 10-16-1848 (10-17-1848) Ma
Hobbs, Ezekiel B. W. to Perlina Cock 4-14-1862 (4-17-1862) Ma
Hobbs, Francis M. to Susan Hickey 8-23-1865 F
Hobbs, James U. to Utha Overman 2-26-1842 (2-28-1842) G
Hobbs, John M. to Susan L. McCullough 8-18-1874 (8-20-1874) T
Hobbs, John to Madelena Johnson 7-12-1843 (7-13-1843) Ma

Hobbs, John to Susan Spencer 1-9-1850 (1-10-1850) G
Hobbs, Nathaniel to Jane Hutchins 9-23-1851 Sh
Hobbs, William to Mary Orrell 10-4-1838 Hn
Hobbs, William to Sally H. Knight 2-2-1835 G
Hobby, S. M. to Mary Trevathan 6-16-1867 Hn
Hobday, B. P. to M. E. Kent 2-29-1876 (3-1-1876) Dy
Hobday, S. M. to Nettie Boone 10-21-1873 Dy
Hobday, T. M. to M. E. Kirk 12-18-1876 (12-19-1876) Dy
Hobday, W. R. to M. C. Hicks 11-25-1874 Dy
Hobgood, Joseph F. to Virginia Laird 11-23-1857 (11-24-1857) Sh
Hobgood, Solomon H. to Elizabeth C. Carr 7-19-1853 (7-25-1853) G
Hobs, Edward to Sarah V. Mayes 6-5-1862 Hn
Hobson, A. to S. E. Wilson 12-13-1881 (12-14-1881) L
Hobson, J. N. B. to Margaret Pankey 2-13-1860 Hr
Hobson, Marshall to Mollie J. Hunt 5-7-1867 Hn
Hobson, W. H. to Temperance J. Sullivan 4-27-1840 (5-2-1850) F
Hobson, W. O. to Nancy E. Wood 4-18-1874 (4-19-1874) Dy
Hochersberger, Frederick to Eliza Hoffman 1-27-1842 Sh
Hock, Fredrick to F. Correll 10-1-1858 (9?-4-1858) Sh
Hockaday, Nathaniel J. to Pricella J. Sanderford 9-7-1847 G
Hockard, James to Jane E. Lowry 7-2-1850 We
Hocke, Joseph William to Mary Fitzgerald 10-20-1860 (10-21-1860) Sh
Hocker, Parkerson to Nancy McKeehan 5-7-1861 Sh
Hockersmith, W. to Martha L. (Mrs.) Pace 9-14-1866 G
Hodge, A. J. to Lucy F. Morris 10-9-1844 (10-13-1844) O
Hodge, Ambrose to Dolly Aikin 10-1-1835 Sh
Hodge, David T. to Margaret J. Kelly 8-28-1848 (8-31-1848) Ma
Hodge, Ed to Peggy Ann Graham 1-15-1878 Hy
Hodge, H. C. to Barbara F. Via 1-22-1878 (1-24-1878) Dy
Hodge, Henry to Susan Carter 6-23-1845 Hn
Hodge, James M. to M. J. Lipe 8-14-1863 (no return) Cr
Hodge, James M. to Martha J. Lipe no date (with Aug 1863) Cr
Hodge, James R. to Florida Ann Stoker 7-4-1872 (no return) Cr
Hodge, James R. to Mary A. Holmes 7-28-1866 (7-29-1866) Cr
Hodge, James R. to Sarah A. Rodgers 12-16-1853 Cr
Hodge, James R. to Virginia A. Beasley 6-13-1854 (no return) F
Hodge, James to Martha Stokes 5-14-1843 Cr
Hodge, James to Polly Edwards 4-26-1838 Cr
Hodge, Jasper to Sarah J. Neese 12-27-1867 Hn
Hodge, John W. to Sophrina E. Parks 4-29-1846 Cr
Hodge, M. D. to Salina Parrish 12-31-1872 (1-1-1873) Dy
Hodge, Samuel to Margaret J. Allison 12-18-1838 G
Hodge, Samuel to Sally D. Brown 8-12-1843 (no return) F
Hodge, Thomas to Anna Maclin 3-20-1869 (no return) F B
Hodge, W. W. to Emma (Emily?) F. Rodgers 1-21-1858 Sh
Hodge, Wm. A. to Sarah L. Lanier 10-17-1876 Dy
Hodgeman, Stephen A. to Ann E. Douglass 6-28-1855 (6-29-1855) Sh
Hodges, Able to Susan Chapman 7-12-1836 Hr
Hodges, Amasa to Isabel Walston 10-24-1850 Sh
Hodges, Andrew J. to Martha Morphus 1-23-1839 G
Hodges, C. B. to Dorcas Newport 7-13-1848 Hn
Hodges, C. B. to Sallie P. Harpole 11-18-1873 (11-20-1873) O
Hodges, David to Rebecca Hale 6-28-1839 Hn
Hodges, Drury to Selina (Selma) Crane 11-19-1837 Sh
Hodges, Edward to Basney? Hodges 12-9-1863 (no return) Hn
Hodges, J. A. to Augustie Cherry 1-18-1870 (no return) Hy
Hodges, J. W. to F. A. Berry 4-12-1860 Sh
Hodges, J. W. to F. W. Arnold 11-2-1865 G
Hodges, James T. to Elizabeth Rogers 12-26-1848 (1-4-1849) Hr
Hodges, James to Ann Hargate 5-6-1858 (5-8-1858) L
Hodges, James to Elizabeth Epperson 8-7-1843 Sh
Hodges, Jno. W. to Virginia Hamblet 12-2-1867 (12-11-1867) F
Hodges, John H. to Jemina Aikens 9-5-1835 Sh
Hodges, John T. to Ann E. Coates 1-9-1850 (1-11-1850) Hr
Hodges, John T. to Mahala Bailey 3-11-1836 Hr
Hodges, Jonathan to Winney E. Ammons 1-4-1851 (1-16-1851) Hr
Hodges, Josiah to Martha Waggoner 5-2-1844 Ma
Hodges, Josiah to Mary Patton 7-10-1839 Ma
Hodges, Mark to L. Annie Fogg 2-5-1867 Hn
Hodges, R. R. to Cynthia P. Ward 5-24-1862 (no return) Hy
Hodges, R. R. to Elizabeth Ward 10-14-1867 G
Hodges, W. K. to D. E. C. Krouth 6-10-1860 (6-14-1860) F
Hodges, William to Cassandra Epperson 8-7-1847 Sh
Hodges, William to Eliza Jane Stephenson 12-13-1841 Hr
Hodman, Daniel to Elmira J. Hoskins 1-20-1850 (no return) F
Hoedy (Hardy?), David to Rebecca Jones 1-1-1851 Sh
Hoeg, John to Sarah C. Harvey 12-28-1843 Sh
Hoeser, Jonas to Sirena Hart 10-28-1854 (11-2-1854) G
Hoesey, Samuel to Sellah Coleman 4-13-1867 G
Hoffler, Charles Webster to Martha Agnes Walker 8-7-1849 T
Hoffler, Nathaniel C. to Elizabeth Jane Tinnen 12-12-1853 (12-13-1853) T
Hoffman, Charles to Fredericka (Mrs.) Killesinsky 6-18-1846 Sh
Hoffman, Christian to Roana Heathcott 3-9-1843 Sh
Hoffman, Daniel H. to Elizabeth Rutherford 6-30-1847 Sh
Hoffman, Fredrick to Margrett Wunderlich 10-11-1862 Sh
Hoffman, John P. to Elvina Leblance 11-20-1858 Sh
Hoffman, John P. to Rose Scmutz? 7-9-1853 Sh

Hoffman, John to Jeanette Leonard 9-10-1869 G
Hofsi, Martin to M. Mear 11-3-1862 Sh
Hogan, Atlas M. to Sarah J. E. Stevenson 8-1-1866 Ma
Hogan, Calumbus to Eliza Polk 12-1-1869 (12-2-1869) T
Hogan, Columbus to Joanah Howard 9-11-1871 T
Hogan, Daniel W. to Pryam Miller 9-19-1866 O
Hogan, George W. to Eleanor J. Verhine 1-27-1856 (1-29-1856) O
Hogan, Granville H. to Mary Jane Taylor 7-23-1845 (7-24-1845) F
Hogan, H. H. to M. S. Spradlin 9-29-1876 (9-30-1876) O
Hogan, Henry E. to Mary Jane Brim 6-25-1870 (6-26-1870) L
Hogan, Hugh to Catharine Lahoff 1-7-1862 Sh
Hogan, Isaah to Mary I. Fox 12-24-1866 O
Hogan, Isiah to Sarah Johnson 12-20-1849 Ma
Hogan, J. B. to Ella M. Hewitt 12-6-1877 (no return) Hy
Hogan, J. M. to J. T. Doherty 7-11-1867 Be
Hogan, James F. to Seeny Box 1-8-1845 O
Hogan, James to Elizabeth Grishum 4-28-1854 (5-2-1854) G
Hogan, John H. to Nancy E. Brown 9-27-1870 (9-28-1870) Ma
Hogan, John to Amanda Howard 6-21-1854 L
Hogan, S. E. to Nancy Ramsey 9-21-1843 F
Hogan, Thomas to Margaret McCabe 10-29-1846 Sh
Hogan, Thomas to Margaret McNamara 2-25-1849 Sh
Hogan, William C. to Levina Massy 1-26-1842 (1-27-1842) F
Hogan, William to Elizabeth Johnson 10-8-1866 (10-11-1866) Ma
Hogans, Caswell to Jane Johnson 8-3-1845 Ma
Hogg, A. J. to Sarah O. Smith 10-25-1864 Be
Hogg, A. J. to _____ 3-12-1864 (3-13-1864) L
Hogg, Calvin to Eliza B. Foust 1-3-1860 We
Hogg, J. W. to N. L. Emery 1-9-1866 Hn
Hogg, James H. to Susan M. Baggett 8-25-1853 Be
Hogg, John B. to Berlinda Turner 3-28-1839 G
Hogg, John P. to Mary E. Ledbetter 11-11-1865 (11-12-1865) L
Hogg, John W. to Sarah A. Emery 12-29-1852 Hn
Hogg, Joseph to Elizabeth Harris 3-3-1867 Be
Hogg, Samuel to Emily Lacy 4-17-1854 Hn
Hogg, Starky to Lucinda Jane Goforth 9-9-1846 Be
Hogg, Sterling B. to Elizabeth Murphy 12-12-1831 G
Hogg, William to Sarah Baggett 9-9-1846 Be
Hogge, Archibald to Mary Anderson 12-18-1833 O
Hogge, James B. to Mary L. Harper 10-9-1833 O
Hogger, F. C. to S. J. Cooper 1-7-1869 Hy
Hoggins, Robert Cecil to Mary Belle Brown 8-2-1866 Hn
Hogie, Frank to Edmonia Whitelaw 7-7-1866 Hy
Hogsett, Charles to Jamima C. Sharp 3-18-1846 Ma
Hogsett, William G. to Margaret S. McKinley 8-22-1842 (8-24-1842) L
Hogshead, James E. to Marietta H. Prewitt 11-3-1841 Ma
Hogue (Hogan), William to Nancy Garrison 3-27-1849 O
Hogue, A. N. to Sophia M. Ward 8-17-1859 O
Hogue, Archibald C. to Sarah Hayes 7-21-1855 (7-26-1855) O
Hogue, George to Elizur Jones 2-26-1847 (3-5-1847) O
Hogue, J. A. to M. E. Wallace 1-3-1861 (1-4-1861) Hr
Hogue, Jeptha to Martha Maria Hunt 2-24-1847 (2-25-1847) T
Hogue, John B. to Jane D. Robinson 3-26-1840 O
Hogue, John B. to Malinda H. Farris 1-23-1843 O
Hogue, Samuel A. to Mary F. Smith 3-22-1851 (3-27-1851) Hr
Hogue, Samuel G. to Elizabeth J. Hobbs 2-12-1861 G
Hogue, Willis A. to Ann Salina Davis 10-1-1855 (10-2-1855) O
Hogue, Willis A. to Caroline Powell 10-11-1849 O
Hogue, Willis G. to Martha Jane Meacham 3-16-1854 O
Hogue, Wilson R. to Elizabeth B. Hutchinson 4-12-1848 (4-20-1848) O
Hoke, Michael Wesley to Mary Ann Roton 10-21-1851 T
Holabaugh, David to Elizabeth Ann Winders 12-9-1841 Sh
Holaday, R. to Josephine Brevard 12-28-1870 Cr
Holaman, William H. to Sarah J. Wright 11-20-1843 (11-26-1843) G
Holamon, William H. to Sarah J. Wright 11-20-1843 G
Holan, Edward to Sarah Ann Eagan 10-7-1856 Sh
Holaway, Henry to Anne Nolen 7-6-1878 (7-7-1878) L
Holbrook, A. B. to Nancy J. Gutherie 11-7-1869 Hy
Holbrook, F. M. to Buena Vista Hill 5-6-1868 G
Holbrook, J. T. to E. M. Wade ?-?-1861? Mn
Holbrook, Martin B. to Julia Brown 9-9-1858 Sh
Holcomb, Beverly L. to Eugenia D. V. Hunt 6-25-1829 (7-2-1829) Hr
Holcomb, Frankling to Artesia Harris 12-28-1875 (no return) Hy
Holcomb, H. B. to Martha A. Smith 10-3-1867 Hn
Holcomb, Henry to Margaret J. Harris 1-2-1834 Sh
Holcomb, Hosey to Mary Brooten 9-4-1841 G
Holcomb, John T. to Nancy E. Ramsey 3-28-1854 Hn
Holcomb, John to A. E. Whitten 12-17-1874 Hy
Holcomb, John to Elizabeth Jane Barnhart 2-27-1834 Sh
Holcomb, John to Lizzie Bradford 12-16-1882 (12-20-1882) L
Holcomb, P. to Martilla _____ 8-28-1851 (no return) G
Holcomb, Phillips to Sarah B. Harlean 10-27-1836 (11-25-1836) G
Holcomb, Powell to Versia Watson 1-19-1881 L
Holcomb, Thomas to Virginia A. Wright 1-22-1862 G
Holcomb, Thurman to Bettie Crowder 12-23-1874 Hy
Holcomb, W. M. to Ellena J. Clark 6-28-1868 G
Holcum, Stephen to Sarah Baldwin 11-14-1850 Hn

Holden, B. J. to Mary Ann Herron 12-24-1848 Be
Holden, George to Lucinda Atkinson 12-20-1869 (12-23-1869) F B
Holden, John to Ann Eliza Wilkins 12-11-1841 F
Holden, Soloman to Mary J. Paschal 12-10-1869 (12-12-1869) L
Holden, ____ G. to Mary Ann Vancleave 12-18-1851 Hn
Holder, Daniel to Martha (Mrs.) Simpson 5-9-1843 G
Holder, G. W. to Frances Ann Dyer 6-30-1851 O
Holder, J. F. to Jamsey Rankin 8-12-1862 (8-18-1862) Sh
Holder, James F. to Elizabeth A. Miller 1-17-1867 G
Holder, Jas. S. to Emeline Farr 2-1-1855 G
Holder, John to Nancy Gray 1-30-1854 (2-2-1854) Hr
Holder, M. D. to Polly Ray 9-11-1847 (9-14-1847) G
Holder, Marion to Louiza V. Goodman 1-2-1860 (1-5-1860) G
Holder, Thomas to Mahaly A. Allen 3-28-1861 G
Holder, William to Jane Mosley 8-6-1861 Be
Holdsbrooks, James M. to Sarah Ann Rushing 6-28-1853 Be
Holdsworth, William to Minnie Dean 11-21-1870 Ma
Holehen, E. to Honarie Malourney 10-11-1859 (10-16-1859) Sh
Holeman, Marcus to Peletha Curtis 3-30-1838 G
Holeman, Otis H. to Lizzie C. Wynn 9-15-1857 Sh
Holeman, jr., Thomas to R. F. Walker 1-9-1860 (1-10-1860) Sh
Holford, John W. to Fannie N. Crews 3-14-1859 (3-15-1859) Hr
Holford, L. W. to L. A. Latimer 11-23-1865 O
Holford, William to Martha Ann Minerva Sylvester 12-22-1840 (12-24-1840) Hr
Holiday, George to Eliza Walker 11-19-1873 Hy
Holiday, James F. to Sarah C. Haley 10-17-1854 Hn
Holiday, T. M. to Martha Rogers 1-24-1871 (1-25-1871) F
Holion, John to Martha Ward 9-6-1839 (no return) Cr
Hollad, Benjamin to Mary T. Allen 12-1-1831 Hr
Holladay, Harvey B. to Elizabeth Nichols 9-28-1845 Hn
Holladay, Henry to Agnes Nichol 1-24-1849 Hn
Holladay, John F. to Jane Marberry 10-10-1846 Hn
Holladay, Sanders to Leona Holloman 5-23-1869 G B
Holladay, Steven C. to Emaline Crider 1-16-1844 (no return) Cr
Hollady, Jeremiah to Elizabeth Smith 6-5-1847 (6-13-1847) Hr
Hollamon, John W. to Nancy McClelland 12-28-1838 L
Hollan, Lemual W. to Carroline Pettus 1-11-1841 (1-14-1841) G
Holland, Abraham to Mary King 3-7-1874 (3-8-1874) L
Holland, B. H. to Nancy E. Bottoms 11-5-1854 (11-6-1854) G
Holland, B. M. to M. A. Collins 7-8-1842 Be
Holland, B. N. to Georgiann Quilling (Quillen) 10-23-1866 Be
Holland, Bethel to Paralee Sykes 9-27-1857 Be
Holland, Britten H. to Martha J. Gant 10-2-1843 (12-7-1843) G
Holland, Caleb to Nancy Bird 3-25-1867 (4-6-1867) T
Holland, Charles to Nancy Taylor 8-24-1832 Hr
Holland, Charley to Mary Hodge 8-30-1838 Hr
Holland, Daniel to D. Ann Wilson 11-7-1850 Be
Holland, Daniel to Eliza Loyd 3-21-1848 Be
Holland, Edmund to Hawkins Hall 9-17-1838 G
Holland, Enos to Elizabeth Bond 11-13-1853 Hn
Holland, F.? M. to Caroline Holinsworth 11-1-1862 Be
Holland, Frank to Nancy Arnold 10-9-1869 G
Holland, G. W. to Susan Austin 12-25-1865 (12-27-1865) Dy
Holland, Gaih to Mary L. Bledsoe 12-4-1854 G
Holland, George W. to Amanda Susan Fowler 1-31-1858 Be
Holland, George to Mary Dunn 2-24-1874 T
Holland, George to Milly Herron 8-1-1868 (8-2-1868) Cr
Holland, Gilbert to Frances Bryan 8-15-1856 Be
Holland, Isah to Eliza Flowers 8-27-1839 G
Holland, J. C. to S. A. Humphreys 10-20-1858 Sh
Holland, J. K. P. to Ellen Ferrill 8-19-1869 Dy
Holland, J. W. N. to Margaret Boswell 11-7-1869 G
Holland, James to Ruth Ann Kenady 1-14-1865 (1-15-1865) Dy
Holland, Jefferson to Nancy Rose 1-26-1847 (1-27-1847) G
Holland, John A. to Eliza E. Robinson 5-27-1861 G
Holland, John A. to Elmyra Berry 1-1-1867 G
Holland, John G. to Penelope C. Presson 1-4-1854 Be
Holland, John S. to Jane J. (Mrs.) Norvell 2-21-1869 G
Holland, John S. to Trythana Watt 2-16-1869 G
Holland, John T. to Elizabeth P. Fowler 8-29-1865 Be
Holland, John W. to Mary E. Keathley 12-2-1869 G
Holland, John to Amanda Matthews 4-9-1861 Hr
Holland, John to Emily Jane Locke 6-11-1844 T
Holland, John to Jullia Ellis 4-1-1859 Hr
Holland, John to Rebecca C. Jones 12-1-1865 Be
Holland, LaFayette to E. A. Worship (Bishop?) 12-21-1878 (12-24-1878) Dy
Holland, Lewis to Polly Pafford 6-11-1839 Be
Holland, Marion to Emaline Arnold 9-19-1867 Be
Holland, Modecai to Harriet A. Luther 12-7-1842 Hn
Holland, Needham to Ann E. Donaldson 12-7-1839 (12-19-1839) G
Holland, Nicholas to Elizabeth Ballowe 1-8-1852 Be
Holland, Phillip to Anney (Mrs.) Casey 2-8-1844 (2-13-1844) G
Holland, Preston to Sarah H. Cole 10-1-1838 (10-2-1838) G
Holland, Pridgen to Roxana Melton 5-5-1851 Be
Holland, Robert to Mary Turner 11-6-1867 T
Holland, Thomas to Mary Ann Wilson 11-23-1852 (no return) F
Holland, W. F. to M. J. King 11-18-1867 (11-19-1867) Dy
Holland, W. J. to Kisann Prichard 2-1-1865 (2-2-1865) Dy
Holland, W. P. to Nancy Box 8-29-1864 Be
Holland, W. T. to Tennessee Rollins 12-29-1879 (1-1-1880) L
Holland, W. W. to Mary Collier 1-27-1856 Be
Holland, Wesley to Rebecca Cooke 12-10-1846 Hn
Holland, William R. to Nancy J. Brewer 10-30-1863 Be
Holland, William W.(H?) to Martha J.(H?) Wakefield 12-16-1851 (12-18-1851) L
Holland, Wm. M. to Lucy Jane Thogmorton? 2-22-1858 Be
Hollander, Bernard to Margaret Beck 3-7-1860 (3-8-1860) Sh
Hollandsworth, George to Mary Rena Moore 1-16-1868 Be
Hollandsworth, T. to Polly Lewis 11-30-1840 Be
Hollaway, Isaac to Liley Vaulx 5-31-1869 Hy
Hollaway, James P. to Sarah Ozment 4-20-1854 (4-24-1854) Hr
Hollaway, Samuel to Mariah Harris 8-25-1845 G
Hollaway, Simon to Mary E. Lewis 3-2-1873 Hy
Hollaway, T. A. to Mary Ann Milum 1-4-1872 (no return) Cr
Hollaway, Wm. to Emaline Hedge 12-11-1844 Cr
Hollaway, Wm. to Sallie Ann Moore 9-9-1857 (9-21-1857) T
Holleman, Joe to Cornelia Poor 12-26-1866 (12-27-1866) F B
Hollen, WM. to Annie King 1-4-1878 (no return) Hy
Hollenbeck, J. H. to Mary M. Smith 12-1-1857 (12-7-1857) Sh
Hollerday, William to Sarah Elizabeth High 9-28-1862 Hn
Hollerman, J. H. B. to Mary E. Randol 3-19-1874 L
Holley, Calvin J. to Sarah Ann Rogers 10-9-1830 (10-10-1830) Hr
Holley, Green to Ellen Wiley 10-22-1872 Hy
Holley, Henry to Frances L. Winters 1-28-1848 Sh
Holley, John D. to Avy Core 4-20-1833 Hr
Holley, Nathan to Alsey Carlene Ray 6-9-1852 Hn
Holley, William to Ann Willheight 4-20-1833 Hr
Hollice, James to Frances Hammons 12-15-1863 (12-17-1863) F
Holliday, Andrew J. to Mary A. McCrewry 12-30-1857 Hr
Holliday, C. L. to Lucy Bayles 3-20-1867 (3-21-1867) Cr
Holliday, George W. to Julia A. Williams 8-6-1847 (8-15-1847) F
Holliday, Henry to Jane Warren 8-8-1838 Hn
Holliday, James F. to Caroline Haley 3-6-1854 (no return) Hn
Holliday, Jasper to Paralee M. Elliott 6-16-1852 Ma
Holliday, Jeremiah to Mary W. White 8-28-1827 (8-31-1827) Hr
Holliday, John to Eveline Armstrong 3-12-1848 (no return) F
Holliday, Martin to Catharine Sims 8-8-1859 (8-9-1859) Hr
Holliday, Martin to Nancy Etheridge 8-17-1838 Hn
Holliday, William H. to Deborah Murry 1-27-1838 Hn
Holliday, William W. to Lavicy Lovin 12-9-1847 Ma
Holliday, Zachariah to Ann Dearmore 3-21-1846 (4-2-1846) Ma
Holliman, Anthony to Mattie White 12-26-1877 Hy
Hollin, James M. to Martha G. Smith 1-30-1856 Cr
Hollin, John S. to Harriet Winder 5-11-1866 (5-12-1866) F B
Hollinger, A. J. to Oney Young 4-22-1863 Sh
Hollinghead, Thomas to Sallie Sumner 1-21-1875 Hy
Hollingshead, James to Josie Summers 7-16-1875 (no return) Hy
Hollingsworth, H. G. to Mary L. Sarrett 11-21-1849 Be
Hollingsworth, L. H. to M. J. Palmer 1-31-1877 (2-1-1877) Dy
Hollingsworth, Robert to Mary Simmons 4-3-1859 Hn
Hollinsworth, Henry H. to Fannie B. Thetford 5-13-1876 (5-14-1876) Dy
Hollinsworth, Isaac to Elizabeth Looper 5-4-1848 Be
Hollinsworth, Jarrett to Minerva H. McAlfee 10-7-1848 Ma
Hollinsworth, Robert to Martha J. Dowdy 11-4-1845 Hn
Hollinsworth, Samuel to Elizbeth King 7-23-1845 Hn
Hollinsworth, Thomas to Mariah Arnold 11-1-1855 Be
Hollinsworth, William to J. C. Davis 2-2-1854 Be
Hollir, Lewis to Elizabeth Williams 5-5-1859 (no return) Hy
Hollis, Alfred to Chanie Light 12-5-1878 (no return) Dy
Hollis, E. P. to Elizabeth H. Thompson 9-6-1859 We
Hollis, H. T. to Faney E. Gillaspie 10-25-1854 We
Hollis, J. .W. to Lecia A. Boon 11-1862 O
Hollis, Jno. W. to Mary Jane Woolley 8-15-1868 (8-16-1868) F
Hollis, Thos. J. to Patsy Garrett 11-16-1867 (11-17-1867) F
Holloman, Joseph to Mary Jane Dunavant 6-18-1844 (6-20-1844) L
Holloman, Joseph to Mary Underwood 9-14-1848 G
Holloman, L. J. to Eliza L. Hodge 12-15-1869 G
Holloman, Lucilius A. to Sarah F. Culley 6-13-1869 G
Holloman, Malachi to Matilda Patterson 8-5-1857 Ma
Holloman, N. to S. M. Boyett 3-17-1851 O
Holloman, Thomas H. to Allice A. Zaricor 11-7-1866 O
Holloman, William to M. J. Bradford 7-1-1851 (no return) Hn
Holloman, William to Margaret A. Hutchins 2-12-1857 O
Holloman, William to Melvina Harris 1-7-1863 (1-?-1863) Ma
Hollomon, J. W. to Jennie Jones 1-27-1874 (1-29-1874) O
Hollomon, Thos. to Winny Taylor 4-5-1843 Be
Hollomon, W. H. to Martha Arnold 11-14-1867 Be
Holloway, ----- to _____ Bell 3-1-1858 O
Holloway, D. T. to Jane Cothran 7-16-1866 (7-18-1866) F
Holloway, David T. to Adaline L. Sharp 7-24-1855 T
Holloway, David to Emily Bell 9-23-1857 O
Holloway, Frank to Hanna Mason 1-10-1872 (1-15-1872) T
Holloway, Geo. G. to Zilpha Branch 10-18-1851 (10-21-1851) Sh
Holloway, Henry to Ann Nolen 7-9-1878 (no return) Hy

Holloway, J. J. to Mary Brumley 10-27-1849 (10-28-1849) F
Holloway, James F. to Nancy T. Marshall 1-27-1859 Ma
Holloway, James P. to M. Pryor Dixon 8-24-1861 Hr
Holloway, Jim to Marhea Read 1-20-1870 (no return) Hy
Holloway, John C. to Savanah Pinkley 4-1-1841 Cr
Holloway, John J. to Mary Ann (Mrs.) Shumate 3-11-1868 G
Holloway, John to Margaret E. Blasengame 1-25-1863 Mn
Holloway, John to Rebeca Bryles 1-8-1841 F
Holloway, M. C. to Elizabeth Jane Henley 11-20-1845 F
Holloway, Marshall to Texanna Jones 1-23-1878 Hy
Holloway, Nathan to Mary A. Thompson 9-24-1861 Hr
Holloway, Q. T. to Mary J. England 10-12-1852 (no return) F
Holloway, Richard to M. J. Bell 3-1-1856 O
Holloway, Richard to Mary Jane Bell 3-1-1851 O
Holloway, Robt. to Nellie Nixon 1-12-1859 (no return) Hy
Holloway, Sam to Frances Mann 12-24-1870 Hy
Holloway, Smith to Mandy Henly 8-21-1876 (no return) Hy
Holloway, T. O. to C. A. Baird 2-21-1867 Hy
Holloway, W. B. to Mary Jane Low 12-25-1856 Sh
Holloway, W. H. to Mattie J. Wordlow 12-26-1871 (no return) Hy
Holloway, W. to Permelia Knight 8-22-1837 Be
Holloway, William C. to Virginia Roland 11-17-1858 (12-1-1858) Ma
Hollowell, George to Margarett Roberts 10-23-1864 (10-26-1866?) Cr
Hollowell, Hinkly to Sarah H. Tate 12-27-1855 Cr
Hollowell, James M. to Martha J. Smith 1-30-1856 Cr
Hollowell, John A. to Jamiah Rust 1-12-1852 (no return) Cr
Hollowell, John to Hester Dyer 12-25-1869 (12-26-1869) O
Hollowell, M. D. to Dixie E. Graves 12-21-1868 (no return) F
Hollowell, S. H. to Nancy Brinkley 1-8-1866 (no return) Cr
Hollowell, S. S. to Laura Culpepper 2-16-1869 (2-18-1869) F
Hollowell, Wm. G. (Gibson Co.) to Marianna Fitts 8-3-1870 (8-4-1870) Ma
Holly, Henry to Mary S. Poiner 9-10-1838 (9-11-1838) Hr
Holly, Hoyle to Sophia Flake 5-12-1835 Hr
Holly, Marion J. to Malinda F. Thompson 12-9-1869 Ma
Holly, Nicholas to Martha Ann Lamb 6-9-1852 Hn
Hollyfield, Thomas M. to Nancy J. Morris 3-29-1844 We
Holman, George to Lou Shaw 5-2-1878 (no return) Hy
Holman, Mark to Charlotte E. Burnset 9-10-1846 (9-17-1846) F
Holman, R. S. to Rebecca Jones 3-9-1880 (3-17-1880) L
Holmark, George to Mary Ann Cole 3-20-1863 Be
Holmes, A. C. to Mary L. Wall 5-1-1873 Cr
Holmes, A. H. to Nancy J. Green 10-19-1866 (10-21-1866) Cr
Holmes, Abraham to Chany Baldwin 2-14-1878 Hy
Holmes, Benjamin to Margaret E. Bone 11-4-1840 (11-5-1840) G
Holmes, Charles to Emily McGill 10-7-1830 Ma
Holmes, Eli B. to Louisa Robertson 11-8-1857 Be
Holmes, G. M. to I. J. Green 12-23-1867 (12-25-1867) Cr
Holmes, G. to C. M. Harvey 1-2-1843 (no return) Cr
Holmes, Gabriel to Lenore Neal 10-12-1841 Hn
Holmes, Gabriel to Martha Lee 12-27-1838 Hn
Holmes, Geo. D. to Sallie E. Munford 1-18-1866 T
Holmes, George C. to A. Fannie Jones 11-26-1853 (11-27-1853) Sh
Holmes, George L. to Sue M. Curtis 6-28-1860 (6-29-1860) Sh
Holmes, George Q. to Elizabeth J. Woodall 12-29-1842 Cr
Holmes, George to Ann Eliza Rice 7-27-1847 (7-?-1847) T
Holmes, Isaac M. to E. F. Stone 11-30-1867 G
Holmes, Isaiah to Jane Winsett 12-26-1871 Hn
Holmes, J. A. to M. M. Durham 2-21-1878 L
Holmes, J. R. to Frances Brandon 5-28-1873 Cr
Holmes, James C. to Martha W. Miller 2-11-1856 (2-13-1856) G
Holmes, James to Lucinda Aycres 11-1-1841 (no return) Hn
Holmes, James to Mary A. Howard 7-15-1864 Sh
Holmes, John F. to M. J. Holmes 11-26-1872 Cr
Holmes, John R. to Eliza A. D. McAlexander 7-2-1839 Cr
Holmes, John to Eliza Ann Estes 1-17-1880 (1-18-1880) L
Holmes, John to Elizabeth Singleton 9-3-1832 (9-20-1832) G
Holmes, L. (Dr.) to Sallie F. Herron 12-8-1857 (12-9-1857) Sh
Holmes, Levy to Sarah Davis 12-27-1869 (1-1-1870) F B
Holmes, M. J. to Margaret F. Gray 3-9-1858 (3-10-1858) Sh
Holmes, Meredith to Sarah H. Stokes 5-25-1838 F
Holmes, Needham to Orlena Hurst 10-29-1861 Mn
Holmes, P. E. to Martha Pound 2-6-1837 (2-9-1837) G
Holmes, R. E. to S. E. Baldridge 7-3-1858 (7-8-1858) G
Holmes, Robt. to Liddie Patton 4-15-1863 G
Holmes, Saml. A. to Frances Ann Bragg 12-17-1851 T
Holmes, Samuel H. to G. A. Morphis 5-16-1844 Hn
Holmes, Samuel to Mary Gullege 9-1-1848 (no return) Cr
Holmes, Thos. R. to Elizabeth Cleavis 1-30-1844 L
Holmes, Turner P. to Cherry A. Hicks 8-30-1854 Ma
Holmes, W. H. to V. A. Quinn 9-8-1871 (9-9-1871) Cr
Holmes, W. to Mary E. Temple 5-22-1849 O
Holmes, William H. to Canzey Burgan 12-17-1850 G
Holmes, William H. to Elizabeth Forgey 3-26-1846 Sh
Holmes, William H. to Ellenor Dozier 12-10-1855 (12-11-1855) G
Holmes, William H. to Mary Jane Thomas 9-14-1841 G
Holmes, William K. to Susan E. Thompson 11-13-1845 Ma
Holmes, Wm. to Eliza Hartfield 2-26-1869 (no return) Hy

Holmgrist, Augustus to Rebecca Brashears 8-6-1870 (no return) Cr
Holms, David to Mary Jackson 9-8-1874 T
Holoman, John W. to Margarett A. Garrison 11-7-1866 O
Holoman, John to Sarah Willson 3-29-1865 Be
Holoman, Thomas to Allice Williams 12-18-1878 Hy
Holoman, William J. to Ann Andrews 11-27-1869 (no return) L
Holomon, Elijah to Margret Parker 2-17-1853 Be
Holomon, Harmon to Mary Ann Benton 8-20-1852 Be
Holoway, Henry to A. E. Twisdale 12-26-1859 (12-28-1859) T
Holoway, I. H. P. to L. M. Chumney 8-1-1865 (8-2-1865) O
Holoway, Mitchell to Julia Ann Read 11-11-1869 Hy
Holowell, George to Elender Allen 1-1-1851 Be
Holowell, L.(C?) W. to C. J. Fisher 3-21-1864 Sh
Holowell, Stephen to Sarah J. Baber 12-9-1852 Be
Holst, J. C. to Ellen F. Brooks 6-27-1855 (7-2-1855) Sh
Holst, Morritz to Magdaline Maschle 4-24-1861 Sh
Holt, A. G. to Martha J. Wall 10-28-1847 (no return) F
Holt, Carroll to Mary Connell 5-13-1837 (5-25-1837) G
Holt, Carter to Margaret Dors 1-6-1868 (no return) F B
Holt, Daniel to Nancy (Mrs.) Heath 8-6-1850 (8-9-1850) O
Holt, Daniel to Nancy Heath 8-6-1850 (8-9-1850) O
Holt, David to Nancy Shane 4-13-1846 (4-16-1846) G
Holt, Frank to Melinda Campbell 11-25-1880 L B
Holt, Freeman to Hannah Chambers 11-6-1869 (12-4-1869) F B
Holt, H. H. to Martha Stone 1-22-1860 We
Holt, Harrison to Elizabeth A. Waltrop 7-14-1842 (7-17-1842) G
Holt, Harvey to Rebecca Conner 7-28-1846 (7-30-1846) Ma
Holt, Herrod to Sarah Gilland 12-28-1833 (1-2-1834) G
Holt, J. C. to M. C. Templeton 4-3-1865 (4-5-1865) Dy
Holt, James H. to E. J. Blankinship 9-1-1859 (9-2-1859) G
Holt, James M. to Mary A. Martin 1-25-1847 (1-28-1847) G
Holt, James to Eveline Black 5-10-1852 (5-14-1852) Sh
Holt, James to Mary Martin 4-9-1860 Sh
Holt, Jas. T. to L. Butler 4-10-1860 G
Holt, Jerry to Margaret Murry 1-31-1874 L B
Holt, John A. to A. Isabella Redford 11-7-1860 (11-8-1860) Sh
Holt, John F. to Catharine M. Markham 3-1-1860 Sh
Holt, John F. to Louisa George 1-31-1853 (2-3-1853) Sh
Holt, John M. to Partenia J. Umstead 11-1-1848 (11-2-1848) G
Holt, John M. to Vashtine Martin 2-5-1864 G
Holt, John N. to E. J. Morris 5-5-1847 Sh
Holt, Joseph B. to Mary Ross 10-24-1862 G
Holt, Labon to Elizabeth Ann Batt 5-25-1842 F
Holt, Leander C. to Elizabeth Severe 10-14-1830 Ma
Holt, M. B. to S. C. English 3-16-1867 G
Holt, M. M. to Artula Ross 9-21-1862 G
Holt, Moses to Lourana Moser 9-13-1869 Ma
Holt, Murphy G. to Jane Welsh 12-28-1843 (1-4-1844) Ma
Holt, N. (Niel) B. to Mary J. Gregory 11-3-1836 Sh
Holt, N. J. to Margarett Holt 7-28-1866 G
Holt, Neil Alexander to Sabrina E. Adams 8-8-1848 (8-10-1848) G
Holt, Perrey to Mildred A. Jones 9-12-1842 (9-13-1842) G
Holt, Peter to Ann Elizabeth Dawson 10-20-1856 (10-21-1856) Sh
Holt, Peter to Catherine Quinlan 7-21-1862 Sh
Holt, Preston to Emily Capps 8-13-1857 We
Holt, Preston to Honey Thetford 8-23-1833 (8-25-1833) G
Holt, R. L. to Sallie E. Wingo 8-29-1871 (9-3-1871) Cr
Holt, Thomas to Dilly Marley 7-31-1885 (8-1-1885) L
Holt, Thomas to Sarah Ann Maddox 10-4-1842 Hn
Holt, V. A. to Mary O. Parker 3-4-1869 G
Holt, Wesly to Nancy C. Lawson 3-23-1858 We
Holt, Wilie to Ann Ramey 8-14-1839 Hn
Holt, William to Martha J. Dotson 11-29-1861 We
Holton, James to Mary Wilson 5-7-1841 (5-8-1841) T
Holtsford, Asa P. to Jane Fry 8-23-1855 Ma
Holtzclaw, Ezra to Manerva S. Grisham 12-8-1852 (no return) F
Holyfield, James L. to Louisa A. Hightower 1-14-1863 Mn
Holyfield, S. B. to Caroline Guise 2-6-1861 (1?-10-1861) Hr
Holyfield, Wm. R. to Elizabeth C. Ayers 7-8-1839 Hr
Holzleisber, Geo. to Mary Koch 3-4-1861 Sh
Homan, A. to N. J. Bringle 12-11-1869 (12-12-1869) T
Homan, George to Adaline Walker 8-8-1867 (8-9-1867) T
Home, James to Susanah Stevens 9-25-1857 T
Home, Josiah to Susan M. Thomas 10-16-1848 (10-18-1848) T
Hon, John A. to Martha A. Kirkman 11-27-1869 Hy
Hon, R. C. to Caroline E. Hatsell 5-7-1860 (no return) Hy
Honborn, Washington to Manda I. Hood 11-16-1855 Cr
Hone, Hugh to Eliza Henderson 8-1-1852 Sh
Hone, Hugh to Hannah Butler 10-21-1861 Sh
Honea, Thos. J. to Martha Curlee 1-28-1855 T
Honey, H. A. to Narcissa Johnson 7-29-1845 Cr
Honey, Henry O. to Lucinda Dilday 11-7-1839 Cr
Honey, John to Mary Ann Lynch 2-15-1847 (2-21-1847) F
Honey, Lilborn to Mary L. Hudson 9-5-1866 (9-9-1866) O
Honey, R. F. to M. A. Parker 8-26-1859 (no return) Cr
Honey, Silas B. to E. M. Shain 9-28-1843 Sh
Honey, Thomas to Unis Null 12-31-1845 (no return) Cr

Honey, Wm. G. to Martha L. Davis 10-10-1838 Cr
Honeycut, Jacob to Martha Smith 12-7-1859 (12-8-1859) O
Honeycutt, Hiram H. to Rachael (Miss) Gray 8-19-1862 O
Honeycutt, James to Jane Bramblett 4-18-1858 O
Honley, Geo. to A.a C. Dilliard 3-15-1866 F
Hood, A. M. to M. J. Reams 2-3-1864 (not endorsed) F
Hood, Adrian to Beckey Wade 7-10-1868 (no return) F B
Hood, Allen to Nancy Guy 7-18-1843 (7-20-1843) O
Hood, C. H. to L. C. Campbell 9-14-1864 O
Hood, Danl. B. to Margaret Ann Davis 9-8-1857 (9-10-1857) Hr
Hood, Elijah to Martha Zaracor 5-12-1866 O
Hood, George W. to Mary Bennett 2-23-1841 F
Hood, Hugh W. to Alafare? West 12-24-1861 O
Hood, J. A. to Emma Be.. Weaver 11-1-1877 Hy
Hood, J. W. to Anne E. Wright 9-9-1868 G
Hood, J. W. to M. A. Sexton 11-17-1860 (11-18-1860) Hr
Hood, James A. to Nannie Vincent 7-26-1884 (7-27-1884) L
Hood, James to E. J. Clampit 1-3-1842 (1-13-1842) F
Hood, Jno. A. to Angeline Ray 3-10-1860 (3-13-1860) F
Hood, Job to Eliza I. Frasier 9-18-1845 O
Hood, John R. to Susan E. Ferguson 12-24-1855 Hr
Hood, John to Eliza Wicker 12-13-1865 O
Hood, Josiah to Jane M. Baker 12-17-1845 (12-18-1845) O
Hood, Josiah to Elizabeth Jones 2-23-1860 O
Hood, L. D. to Ciney Carter 10-6-1840 (10-27-1840) F
Hood, M. W. to Nancy Smith 2-24-1877 (2-25-1877) Dy
Hood, Martin S. to Mollie A. Linire (Lynne?) 6-1-1874 L
Hood, Mathew to Mary Duberry 10-3-1853 (no return) F
Hood, Matt to Martha Wray 12-27-1867 (12-31-1867) F B
Hood, Monroe to Levenna Neal 9-19-1861 O
Hood, Richard to Eliza (Mrs.) Williams 1-6-1858 (1-7-1858) Sh
Hood, Richard to Martha Ann Lewis 3-17-1851 (no return) F
Hood, Robert T. to Adelia (Mrs.) Murphey 4-25-1859 Sh
Hood, Robert to Esther A. Ferguson 7-31-1849 H
Hood, Robert to Pollie (Mrs.) Corbitt 11-29-1856 (11-30-1856) Sh
Hood, Robertson to Catharine Teage? 10-10-1848 F
Hood, Saml. H. to Nancy J. Jamison 12-22-1853 O
Hood, W. H. to M. I. Collins 3-13-1865 O
Hood, W. H. to M. J. Collins 3-13-1865 O
Hood, W. H. to M. S. Telford 3-3-1862 (3-5-1862) Dy
Hood, William to Ann Vales 4-22-1858 Sh
Hood, William to Sarah Patterson 11-26-1848 L
Hooey, Daniel T. to Ellen Smith 7-9-1869 (7-11-1869) F
Hoofman, Benjamin to Mary A. F. Brogden 4-26-1843 Hn
Hoofman, Charles D. to Emily Hays 11-18-1857 Hn
Hoofman, Chas. D. to Nancy C. McCord 8-7-1851 Hn
Hoofman, Jacob Y. to Frances E. McCord 1-29-1852 Hn
Hoofman, S. to M. Hoppman 7-19-1852 We
Hoofman, Solomon to Martha Ann Reynolds 1-10-1849 Hn
Hoofman, Thomas to Elizabeth Bunton 3-7-1844 We
Hooker, Elias H. to Elizabeth Ward 12-21-1845 (no return) Cr
Hooker, Frank to Ellen Currie 1-31-1883 (1-29?-1883) L
Hooker, Henry to Catharine Robinson 10-5-1853 G
Hooker, Henry to Malicia Moore 2-10-1841 Hn
Hooker, Joseph to Malisa Pride 9-29-1864 Sh
Hooker, R. J. to Sarah E. Voss 3-9-1863 (3-10-1863) L
Hooker, R. M. to A. E. Denton 1-28-1865 (1-29-1865) Cr
Hooker, S. J. to Mary G. Gwyn 12-8-1866 (no return) F
Hooker, Samuel to Ann Barrett 3-19-1867 G
Hooker, Thos. to Sarah Cunningham 1-13-1866 (1-21-1866) Cr
Hooker, W. G. to Mary Jane Rogers 1-7-1855 Sh
Hooker, Wm. to Jane Brown 1-3-1849 (no return) F
Hooks, A. D. to Octavia Branch 10-19-1865 (10-24-1865) T
Hooks, Charles F. to Hatty Claibon 2-24-1867 Hy
Hooks, George to Nancy Brown 1-16-1870 Hy
Hooks, J. A. to Sarah E. Neeley 12-18-1871 (12-21-1871) Dy
Hooks, Jno. Henry to Mildred N. Compton 12-12-1867 (no return) F
Hooks, Lewis to Betsy Chrisman 3-4-1867 Dy
Hooks, M. C. to Drusilla A. Bond 11-22-1858 (11-25-1858) Sh
Hooks, Robert D. to Charlotte N. Fulgham 3-16-1828 (3-18-1828) Hr
Hooks, Robt. B. to Laura J. McIntosh 12-12-1867 (12-15-1867) F
Hooks, Thomas to Mattie Sharp 4-11-1869 Hy
Hooper, A. H. to Ardelia Reynolds 8-27-1873 (8-28-1873) L
Hooper, A. Lewis to Philibene Krenkle 12-26-1856 Sh
Hooper, Absalom A. to Mary Rundell 6-10-1845 Sh
Hooper, Benj. F. to Lauryan Hooper 1-18-1843 (no return) F
Hooper, C. S. to Mary V. Brogdon 3-17-1874 (3-19-1874) L
Hooper, Calvin S. to Narcissa Pillow 1-19-1859 (1-20-1859) L
Hooper, D. J. to Mary A. Jemison 8-13-1866 Be
Hooper, Daniel to Catharine Hamilton 3-10-1853 O
Hooper, David to Sarah M. Agnew 2-28-1854 (3-11-1854) O
Hooper, Eli T. to Mildred E. Claiborne 2-10-1877 Hy
Hooper, Ennis to Sarah Ann Davenport 6-8-1853 (7-29-1853) O
Hooper, F. M. to Malvina A. Patterson 1-21-1861 (1-22-1861) Hr
Hooper, Franklin to L. A. Bounds 2-8-1838 F
Hooper, G. W. to Mary A. Powers 12-8-1858 We
Hooper, Isaac to Dulcena Wheatly 6-2-1856 Be

Hooper, Jack to Elvira Cogbell 6-15-1870 (no return) F B
Hooper, James M. to L. A. Harper 1-26-1861 (no return) Hy
Hooper, Jeremiah to Eleonor Gilmore 12-30-1841 Hr
Hooper, Jeremiah to Mary Murley 12-18-1846 (12-20-1846) Hr
Hooper, John to Cathanne Patterson 2-10-1858 Hr
Hooper, Joseph W. to Francis S. E. Jones 12-22-1852 Sh
Hooper, Joseph to Louisa Hart 8-22-1843 Hn
Hooper, Joseph to Tempe Bonds 12-10-1873 (12-16-1873) T
Hooper, Robt. to Jennie Brown 5-28-1872 Hy
Hooper, William F. to Martha Ann Curtis 7-14-1852 (no return) L
Hooper, Wm. W. to C. A. Marlar 2-19-1845 Hr
Hooper, Wm. W. to Martha Marler 8-7-1843 Hr
Hooten, Jesse to Jane Heidleburg 2-13-1843 (2-14-1843) Ma
Hooten, Joseph W. to Julia Ann Blair 12-15-1870 Hy
Hooton, John T. to Callie Hensley 2-16-1876 (no return) Hy
Hoover, Andrew to Nancy King 9-8-1843 O
Hoover, H. B. to Anna H. Newhouse 12-22-1835 (12-29-1835) G
Hoover, H. J. to Caroline Morgan 7-13-1864 Sh
Hoover, Washington to Martha Iverson 4-25-1876 Hy
Hope, Adam S. to Margaret A. Harris 6-28-1855 Hn
Hope, Edward E. to Margaret A. Bird 2-4-1851 (2-5-1851) O
Hope, James A. to Elizabeth Robertson 8-19-1852 (8-22-1852) O
Hope, James to Louisa H. Williams 10-24-1860 Sh
Hope, Pleasant M. to Josie Curd 10-4-1859 Hn
Hope, W. L. to E. C. Martin 11-4-1858 Hn
Hope, Wm. M. to E. J. David 4-19-1854 (no return) F
Hopkins, Cullen P. to Mollie E. Casey 6-7-1867 (6-12-1867) Ma
Hopkins, E. T. to Martha J. Clark 8-31-1847 Cr
Hopkins, G. M. to Mary Carne 12-22-1863 G
Hopkins, Gilbert to Drucilla Andrews 3-9-1859 (3-10-1859) Ma
Hopkins, Isham to Adeline Bangster 2-27-1883 (3-1-1883) L
Hopkins, J. F. to Sarah A. Claeber? 1-9-1855 We
Hopkins, James F. to Jemima Gibson 3-25-1868 Cr
Hopkins, James T. to Mary C. Smith 4-5-1860 (no return) Hy
Hopkins, John D. to Annie Culbreath 10-2-1871 (10-5-1871) T
Hopkins, John E. to Judith E. A. Martin 6-30-1838 Hr
Hopkins, John E. to Sarah G. Darnell? 9-7-1847 (9-9-1847) Hr
Hopkins, Joseph to Mary Owen 12-21-1867 (no return) Hy
Hopkins, Josiah to Rhoda A. Owens 3-22-1859 (3-26-1859) O
Hopkins, Logan to Josephine Brock 11-16-1857 Ma
Hopkins, Robert L. to Martha Cantrell 7-28-1854 We
Hopkins, Sam to Di Smith 2-4-1868 Hy
Hopkins, Thomas H. to Mary Petty 8-19-1855 Cr
Hopkirk, Adam to Rebecca Earls 5-4-1847 Sh
Hopper, A. K. to Mary E. Combs 8-27-1857 G
Hopper, A. M. to P. A. Browning 11-25-1871 (no return) Cr
Hopper, A. W. to Sarah A. Davis 12-24-1867 G
Hopper, Barzilla to Nancy L. Piercey 4-22-1844 Ma
Hopper, Barzillai to Sarah A. W. Jones 5-24-1859 (5-25-1859) Hr
Hopper, Daniel to Lucinda Burres 10-4-1838 Ma
Hopper, Duncan to Eliza McRea 12-11-1869 (12-12-1869) Cr
Hopper, Elmore C. to Mary E. Wilson 7-18-1855 (7-19-1855) G
Hopper, J. T. to M. M. Williams 5-22-1871 (no return) Cr
Hopper, James E. to Catherine Tanner 1-30-1841 Ma
Hopper, James M. to Susan M. Carpenter 11-16-1855 (11-20-1855) Ma
Hopper, John P. to W. M. Bennett 11-16-1857 Cr
Hopper, John W. to America Melissa Mobley 2-5-1868 Hy
Hopper, John to Matilda J. West 11-6-1851 Sh
Hopper, N. M. to Mary I. Forsythe 9-22-1859 (9-23-1859) G
Hopper, P. L. to P. W. Mitchell 3-20-1866 G
Hopper, Pleasant W. to Lucinda A. Berry 11-26-1855 (11-28-1855) G
Hopper, Ransom E. to Fannie Sharrock 11-1-1866 Ma
Hopper, T. P. to Missouri Mobley 8-30-1870 G
Hopper, Turley to Margaret Carrothers 9-22-1852 (9-23-1852) Ma
Hopper, William P. to Elizabeth Perry 1-4-1845 Ma
Hoppers, John to R. C. Nabrady 8-1-1843 Sh
Hoppers, Thos. D. to Mariah Frances (Mrs) Hoppers 8-26-1868 (8-27-1868) Ma
Hopson, Joseph to Martha M. Barndell 1-6-1843 (no return) Hn
Hopson, Nathan J. to Jane A. James 4-7-1846 Hn
Hopson, V. to Edny Brown 1-30-1860 (no return) L
Hopton, Abner to Susan M. Porter 1-20-1847 Sh
Horan (Horne), William to Ellen Finley 10-10-1863 Sh
Horbin, George C. to Juliet M. Grant 5-18-1853 Sh
Hord, A. S. to Rebecca Simpson 7-8-1861 O
Hord, Allen S. to Jane McWherter 3-5-1851 (3-6-1851) O
Hord, Thomas P. to Nancy M. Farris 11-1-1841 (11-7-1841) O
Hord, William H. to Mary Jane McKenzie 1-23-1839 O
Hordon?, Joseph to Parthanan Kirby 9-22-1851 (no return) Cr
Horlacker, Frederick to Gertrude Snyder 6-7-1852 (6-8-1852) Sh
Horn, Anderson to Sarah Horn 3-18-1846 Ma
Horn, Cannon to Mary C. Gooch 12-23-1872 (12-24-1872) Cr
Horn, Dempsy to Mariah Williams 4-21-1871 (no return) Hy
Horn, J. G. to Elizabeth Fisher 6-3-1857 Sh
Horn, J. J. to Malvina A. Suggs 1-11-1867 (1-13-1867) Cr
Horn, James B. to Martha Griffen 8-18-1842 Sh
Horn, Joel to Mary E. Montgomery 12-23-1840 Cr
Horn, John to Mary A. Huey 5-17-1843 Cr

Horn, John to Penina Thompson 2-27-1853 Be
Horn, Josiah L. to Sarah M. Baisinger 9-15-1847 G
Horn, O. A. to M. J. Perkins 2-17-1866 (no return) Hn
Horn, Ripley S. to Harriet Myrick 10-10-1854 Hn
Horn, S. to Mary Ann R. Green 5-18-1870 Cr
Horn, Sidney to Roan Hampton 4-24-1852 Cr
Horn, Thomas to Angile Montgomery 12-25-1858 Cr
Horn, Vincent to Mary Settles 3-7-1843 Be
Horn, Willie to Hulda Stacy 3-16-1843 Cr
Horn, Willis to Sarah Mullins 7-7-1856 (7-13-1856) Hr
Hornbeak, Elijah E. to Mary F. Taylor 4-2-1863 (no return) We
Hornbuckle, William to Mary Jane Corley 2-5-1864 (5-30-1864) Cr
Hornbuckle, Wm. to Mary A. Harness 12-27-1858 Cr
Hornbuckle, Wm. to Mary Jane Corley 2-5-1864 (no return) Cr
Horne, J. B. to Mary Jane Berry 8-2-1860 Sh
Horne, Matthew to Martha Chamberlain 3-19-8150 (3-21-1850) Ma
Horne, Simeon to Ann M. Cowan 4-27-1841 T
Horne, Simeon to Sarah C. Bettis 10-10-1848 Sh
Horne, Thomas C. to Jane Jones 12-15-1854 (12-20-1854) Sh
Horne, Thomas G. to Mary Rogers 8-24-1837 Sh
Horne, Thos. C. to Eliza Miller 10-5-1870 (10-10-1870) T
Horne, William to Jane Griffin 5-2-1837 Sh
Horner, B. B. to Susan Newby 2-16-1850 (2-20-1850) F
Hornesby, A. G. to Elizabeth Price 2-29-1860 (3-1-1860) Hr
Hornesby, Kimbro E. to May C. Bradford 1-2-1860 Hr
Horning?, Samuel K. to Nancy C. Wright 9-21-1842 T
Hornsbury, John to Sarena Pearce 4-14-1862 (no return) Hn
Hornsby, Felix to Mary E. Walker 12-1-1863 Sh
Hornsby, Kimbro to Martha Ann Sebastian 4-6-1833 Hr
Horseley, John R. to Sarah M. Smith 9-10-1855 (9-11-1855) Sh
Horsley, Rowland to Amanda Reinhardt 12-1-1835 Sh
Horsted?, Tipton to Lively Beck 1-29-1849 Hn
Horster, William to Mary Gerlach 4-17-1860 Sh
Horten, G. W. to E. M. Cathy Hulday 8-8-1855 We
Horten, John to Eliza Mills 2-17-1858 We
Horton, A. to M. Amanda Todd 11-26-1874 Dy
Horton, Alex to Ella Harris 6-6-1874 (6-11-1874) Dy B
Horton, Calhoun to Tricy Farrow 7-30-1850 Be
Horton, David to Elizabeth Norville 7-16-1870 Hy
Horton, Hiram to Elizabeth Adams 9-12-1871 Cr
Horton, J. L. to Mary E. Palmer 7-29-1871 Cr
Horton, John to Cy McLister 4-25-1866 T
Horton, John to Mary Jane Cooper 12-18-1848 Ma
Horton, Needham to Mary Folwell 5-1-1840 (5-6-1840) F
Horton, Thomas A. to Matilda C. Craig 12-6-1868 Be
Horton, Thomas to Annie Fowlkes 1-13-1874 (1-14-1874) Dy
Horton, W. C. to R. C. Butler 3-11-1872 Cr
Horton, W. H. to Mollie E. Scruggs 2-2-1860 Sh
Horton, William to Rebecca Thompson 12-24-1834 (12-26-1834) Hr
Horton, Wm. to Caroline Pippens 2-12-1867 Be
Horton, Wm. to Mariah Menzies 9-14-1868 (9-17-1868) Dy
Horton?, James M. to Mary Cox 8-?-1861 (8-15-1861) Cr
Hosea, James J. to Martha C. Basinger 10-31-1860 G
Hoskins, Dodson to Julia Davis 7-24-1856 G
Hoskins, John to Tericey Elender Boling 12-25-1849 Sh
Hoskins, W. M. to Mary Reed 1-17-1874 (1-18-1874) Dy
Hoskins, William to Mary Moore 8-5-1852 G
Hosse, Martin to M. Mear 6-?-? (after 1850) Sh
Hostetter, Elias J. to M. A. Hubbard 3-21-1861 Mn
Hotchkiss, E. B. to Mildred M. Cobb 12-16-1858 Sh
Hotter, Johan to Catharine Heniger 9-18-1854 Sh
Houck, James to Susan E. McGowan 9-20-1858 (9-22-1858) Sh
Houghs, Samuel to Nancy Gleason 8-19-1838 G
Houghton, Burkett L. to Margaret E. Askew 1-17-1853 (1-18-1853) Ma
Houghton, Seaborn J. to Lydia Nixon 2-2-1885 (2-3-1885) L
Houk, B. F. to Isabella Beaver 4-20-1867 (4-21-1867) F
Houk, Lysander to Nannie Whitelaw 5-6-1860 (no return) Hy
Houlsouser, Howard to Sarah Walk 12-29-1858 (12-28?-1858) T
Houn, S. K. P. to Martha Jane Berry 7-28-1864 G
Houpt, H. to Sarah E. Borum 2-14-1863 (2-15-1863) L
Housden, Henry to Nancy J. Freeland 11-23-1861 (no return) Hn
Housden, Samuel to Emily R. Freeland 2-12-1858 Hn
Housden, William to Martha Smith 11-12-1851 Hn
House, Alexander M. to Sarah J. Shane 12-17-1855 (12-20-1855) G
House, Ambros to A. L. Bolin 2-9-1858 G
House, Archibald B. to Eliza Wilks 11-21-1840 Hr
House, B. F. to Florence L. Thornton 7-18-1876 Hy
House, Benj. to Nancy Humphrey 1-11-1849 (no return) Cr
House, C. G. to Millie R. Johnson 10-3-1871 (no return) Hy
House, Charles to Mary Jones 12-2-1870 (no return) Hy
House, Chesley to Martha Ann Kinny 11-26-1860 (no return) Hy
House, David to Jane House 12-22-1843 Hr
House, George to Elizabeth Crow 6-24-1845 (6-26-1845) O
House, Gus to Amanda Watkins 12-27-1877 Hy
House, Harvey to Nancy Crawford 3-20-1872 Hy
House, Hiram to Dice Broaden 7-10-1867 (no return) Hy
House, Hiram to Kissire Fleming 8-18-1877 Hy

House, Isham to Reubecca Scott 1-25-1844 We
House, J. A. to Julian Seward 11-15-1838 F
House, J. S. to Susan A. Nickelson 1-16-1868 Hy
House, J. W. to Susan E. West 1-7-1869 G
House, James D. to Mary Jane Farrow 8-27-1850 Be
House, James G. to Susan F. Hudson 12-5-1866 (12-6-1866) Ma
House, James J. to Elizabeth Lemmonds 10-5-1839 (10-15-1839) O
House, James to Emily Weldon 12-23-1866 Hn B
House, James to Mary House 11-5-1869 (11-11-1869) F B
House, James to Mary M. Prichard 4-16-1867 (no return) Dy
House, Jared to Eron Strother 12-27-1848 Sh
House, John P. to Mahaly Bonds 10-20-1847 Be
House, John to Eliza Kelsoe 5-28-1861 (no return) Hy
House, John to Elizabeth A. Wilkes 10-15-1860 Hr
House, John to Mary Edwards 9-7-1848 (no return) Cr
House, John to Nancy Campbell 1-21-1867 (1-22-1867) Cr
House, Joseph to Sarah Jane Wilson 11-22-1838 Cr
House, M. T. to T. C. Martin 11-2-1870 G
House, Mathew W. to Adalin Evans 12-12-1848 (no return) Cr
House, Moses A. to Mary Ann Petis 2-17-1834 G
House, Paten to Jane Jarnigan 12-10-1864 (12-11-1864) Sh
House, S. J. to Josephine Campbell 9-9-1876 (9-10-1876) Dy
House, Samuel J. to Elnore A. Tynes 1-9-1871 (1-10-1871) Cr
House, Simon to Eliza Hyer 10-29-1842 (no return) Hn
House, Thomas F. to Sarah Farrow 1-1-1852 Be
House, Timothy T. to Sarah Jane Minter 9-12-1853 Hr
House, W. B. to A. E. Wade 7-26-1854 G
House, W. T. to Rebecca Brown 3-8-1874 Hy
House, William H. to Mary Snipes 4-17-1845 Hn
House, William R. to Emily Jane Dodson no dates (with Dec 1845) F
House, William to Mary Henry 10-13-1867 Hn B
House, William to Mary Rhine 11-5-1869 (11-11-1869) F B
House?, David C. to Letitia F. Hazlewood no date (with Dec 1852) F
House?, Hugh to George Perry 6-1-1869 (6-2-1869) T
Houseman, John G. to Phoebe Timms 2-27-1838 Hn
Houseman, W. B. to Emeline Baker 4-11-1876 (4-23-1876) L
Houseman, W. B. to Kisie H. Rushen 8-28-1869 (9-1-1869) L
Houser, Anthony to Lucinda Shores 11-27-1858 (12-1-1858) O
Houser, Harman J. to Mary B. Felts 10-9-1873 (10-10-1873) O
Houser, Harmon J. to Sarah Ann James 8-5-1848 (8-7-1848) O
Houser, Jonas to Elizabeth Long 1-5-1830 (2-4-1830) O
Houser, Lewis to Adaline Holloway 12-21-1852 (12-22-1852) O
Houser, Noah B. to Rebecca L. Long 8-13-1840 O
Housman, G. W. to Martha L. Ingram 11-27-1867 (12-1-1867) Cr
Houston, Barrett to Sarah Houston 4-22-1866 G
Houston, Benjamin to Henrietta O. Wilkins 10-27-1845 (10-29-1845) F
Houston, Charlie to Lettie Cross 12-27-1870 (12-29-1870) F B
Houston, Chas. B. to Emma Buckner 9-22-1869 Ma
Houston, Felix to Cynthia Gillespie 6-6-1832 Hr
Houston, George to Elizabeth Linville 6-11-1852 Cr
Houston, H. M. to Emma L. Wilson 7-9-1868 T
Houston, James G. to Jane E. Davis 8-10-1848 Sh
Houston, James M. to Mary Lou Tomlin 2-16-1870 Ma
Houston, James to Susan Frances Toney 8-16-1843 Sh
Houston, Joe to Sarah Leopard 2-28-1867 G
Houston, John W. to Amanda M. Carson 6-14-1880 (6-17-1880) L
Houston, John to Isabella Spickernagle 1-29-1846 Sh
Houston, John to Sophia Davis 3-10-1885 (3-15-1885) L
Houston, Jordan A. to Amanda J. Scarborough 11-14-1859 (11-15-1859) Ma
Houston, R. S. to Irena E. Michie 4-15-1863 Mn
Houston, William B. to Harriet Jane Stellman 10-4-1842 Sh
Houston, William H. to Elizabeth Glover 3-17-1866 (3-18-1866) Cr
Houston, Willis to Roan Bailey 1-17-1859 (1-19-1859) F
Houston, Wm. to Charlotte Dudley 4-4-1843 (no return) Cr
Houze, Williamson to Mary T. Bledsoe 5-31-1853 Sh
Howal, C. R. to Margaret Hargis 10-24-1851 We
Howan, John to Christena Switzer 10-25-1862 Sh
Howard, A. W. to Martha Gray 4-1-1847 (4-5-1847) O
Howard, Alexander to Frances A. Lea 1-30-1838 (no return) L
Howard, Alfred W. to Lydia Ann Perkins 11-21-1856 (11-23-1856) O
Howard, Andrew J. to Susan S. Ham? 7-23-1850 (7-24-1850) Hr
Howard, B. T. to Emeline E. Kendall 1-1-1853 Hn
Howard, Barnett A. to Sarah J. James 8-14-1851 Hn
Howard, Benjamin A. to Mollie C. Johnson 7-4-1860 Cr
Howard, Benjamin F. to Elizabeth Muse 1-31-1830 Ma
Howard, Benjamine F. to Elizabeth Muse 1-31-1831 Ma
Howard, Booker to Sallie Harris 4-2-1873 (3?-2-1873) Dy
Howard, Charles F. to Mary Nolan 4-16-1863 Ma
Howard, Collumbus to Mary Vaughan 1-29-1869 (2-8-1869) L
Howard, D. F. to H. E. Bridges 5-31-1871 (6-1-1871) L
Howard, Dock to Amanda Clark 1-10-1870 (no return) Dy
Howard, E. W. to Lucind Husky 3-16-1869 (no return) L
Howard, Eli to Centha Ann Melton 12-14-1838 (12-20-1838) G
Howard, Elijah to Maria Bailey 3-7-1867 Hn B
Howard, Elleson to Jane Hawkins 12-25-1839 G
Howard, Elsey to Mary Jane Luallen 8-29-1871 (8-30-1871) L
Howard, Francis M. to Mary N. Birdsong 10-9-1866 Ma

Howard, G. G. to Polly Jane Gray 7-11-1866 (7-12-1866) O
Howard, Geo. C. to Eliz. J. Crenshaw 10-28-1851 (10-29-1851) T
Howard, George to Martha J. Henshaw 8-28-1854 Sh
Howard, Hartwell to Marry Holman 5-17-1829 Hr
Howard, Hasting P. to Sarah E. Renshaw 3-11-1859 Hn
Howard, Henry to Cynthia McKnight 7-6-1854 Sh
Howard, Henson to Eliza E. Walker 7-30-1838 G
Howard, Hiram to Sarah Boswell 9-28-1872 (9-29-1872) T
Howard, J. H. to S. E. Myers 5-10-1871 (5-11-1871) T
Howard, Jack to Caroline Gordon 2-27-1871 Cr
Howard, James G. to Isabella C. Clements 1-23-1861 We
Howard, James M. to Roberta F. Williamson 2-4-1845 Sh
Howard, James to Mahaly Clark 12-27-1870 (no return) Cr B
Howard, James to Mahulda Howell 2-25-1847 Sh
Howard, James to Nancy Hurley 2-1-1870 Dy
Howard, Jessee to Lizzie Whitehead 4-28-1869 Hy
Howard, John W. to Sarah E. Roach 12-11-1855 Cr
Howard, John to Adaline Helms 1-30-1869 (1-31-1869) Cr
Howard, John to Martha Allen 4-11-1871 Cr B
Howard, Joseph T. to Isabella Gordon 3-2-1869 (3-4-1869) Ma
Howard, Joseph to Martha Vaughan 2-22-1868 (2-23-1868) L
Howard, Joseph to Mary J. Harland 9-9-1859 (9-11-1859) G
Howard, L. S. to L. A. Younger 7-8-1867 (7-10-1867) Cr
Howard, L. W. to S. B. Porter 1-18-1882 (1-19-1882) L
Howard, Leonard K. to Martha S. Crittenden 7-29-1858 Hn
Howard, Lucius P. to Julia A. Davis 12-18-1853 Hn
Howard, M. N. to Nancy Rentfrow 6-7-1877 L
Howard, M. S. to A. E. Morphis 12-9-1841 Hn
Howard, Monroe to Elizabeth Evans 6-21-1879 (6-25-1879) L
Howard, N. C. to Mattie E. Love 1-30-1865 (no return) Cr
Howard, N. P. to Mattie A. Love 5-6-1866 We
Howard, Nat to Lyddia Reeves 12-25-1869 (12-31-1869) F B
Howard, Patrick to Mary Redden 10-6-1857 Sh
Howard, Peola? to Mary Butler 12-22-1842 (12-?-1842) T
Howard, Permanis to Mildred Mitchell 1-1-1851 Hr
Howard, Polk to Josephine Sanders 12-22-1876 (1-24-1877) Dy
Howard, Polk to Kisa Walker 1-26-1870 (no return) Dy
Howard, Polk to Millie Harris 12-26-1872 Dy
Howard, R. W. to Alice Newman 11-27-1878 (11-28-1880?) L
Howard, Richard to Ann Browning 7-28-1866 Hn B
Howard, Rufus to Harriet Gillun 5-25-1867 T
Howard, S. M. to Margarett Mecham 1-8-1867 (1-9-1867) O
Howard, Samuel to Sarah A. Wright 12-29-1868 (12-30-1868) F B
Howard, Solaman to Kate Valley 3-20-1867 (3-21-1867) T
Howard, Stephen S. to Mary Jane Wright 12-9-1863 (no return) Dy
Howard, Stephen to Mary A. Howard 4-21-1860 (4-24-1860) Dy
Howard, T. D. to E. J. Kirksey 3-1-1879 (3-2-1879) L
Howard, T. M. to M. M. Williams 1-19-1878 (1-20-1878) L
Howard, Thomas A. to Susan Powell 7-16-1850 Hn
Howard, Thomas C. to Mary J. Vaughan 4-28-1852 T
Howard, Thomas to Mary Biford 9-29-1871 L
Howard, Thomas to Mollie Connell 6-3-1871 (6-4-1871) Dy
Howard, W. T. to Amelia Hungerford 7-10-1858 (7-12-1858) Sh
Howard, Wardlaw to Mary Polk 12-29-1834 Hr
Howard, Wesley to Malinda Fowlkes 5-26-1871 (5-25?-1871) Dy
Howard, William H. to Margaret Wilson 2-2-1842 (2-4-1842) L
Howard, William O. to Martha A. Sallee 8-30-1854 Hn
Howard, William P. to Elizabeth Hammond 4-23-1856 Ma
Howard, William P. to Mary K. Hammond 4-24-1869 Ma
Howard, William to Amanda J. Thomas 1-10-1872 (no return) Cr
Howard, William to Sarah Ann Arnold 12-24-1840 Sh
Howard, Wm. B. to America Hayns 12-27-1839 (12-29-1839) G
Howarton, W. R. D. to Sarah L. Lea 10-26-1854 (10-29-1854) G
Howcott, B. to Sue A. (Mrs.) Speckernagle 10-31-1860 Sh
Howe, Azilvin to Manervy C. Barker 7-23-1848 Be
Howe, Dennis to Nancy Thomason 2-18-1868 Be
Howe, Emsley to Candice Cole 12-30-1839 Be
Howe, J. S. to Abba Jones 6-22-1866 (6-24-1866) Dy
Howe, Matthew to Frances Chapel 9-26-1867 O
Howe, Newton to Frances M. Massengill 12-26-1867 Be
Howe, Z. B. to Mary F. Malin 10-15-1869 Be
Howe, Zebadee to Rachele Thomason 1-23-1848 Be
Howel, C. B. to Sarah N. Cherry 7-2-1866 O
Howel, John to Susan Hooker 7-4-1846 Sh
Howel, K. David to Nancy Smith 7-22-1853 Sh
Howell, A. J. to Elizabeth Ragsdale 5-6-1861 We
Howell, A. W. to Elvie G. Yancey 10-1-1878 (10-2-1878) Dy
Howell, Alexander to Susan S. Wiggs 8-3-1854 Ma
Howell, Andrew B. to Mary Rutledge 11-28-1840 Sh
Howell, Caleb to Ann M. Hobbs 6-24-1839 (6-27-1839) G
Howell, Caleb to Henrietta Beckom 8-26-1868 G
Howell, Canady to Margaret A. McDaniel 10-26-1847 Sh
Howell, Charles C. to Frances E. Carpenter 12-21-1847 (12-23-1847) F
Howell, Chas. to Martha Johnson 9-25-1844 Sh
Howell, David C. to Nancy Jane Jones 12-12-1851 (12-18-1851) Hr
Howell, David to Frances Reynolds 12-29-1884 (12-30-1884) L
Howell, Eli Blackburn to Cytnha A. King 12-2-1869 G
Howell, G. G. to Caroline Isom 8-8-1863 (8-9-1863) T
Howell, George S. to Agnis M. Bankhead 4-24-1841 (4-30-1841) F
Howell, Green M. to Sarah Porter 1-5-1856? (1-5-1857) G
Howell, Henry to Elizabeth Tatum 4-21-1851 (5-1-1851) G
Howell, Henry to Elizabeth Woolard 3-25-1863 G
Howell, Henry to Jane Stanton 3-30-1878 (no return) Hy
Howell, J. B. to Mattie Wilson 9-17-1873 Hy
Howell, J. B. to S. A. Latimer 11-27-1865 O
Howell, J. I. to Sallie Bond 11-26-1872 T
Howell, James to Elizabeth A. Roundtree 7-10-1833 (7-14-1833) Hr
Howell, James to Nanny Hill 7-26-1865 L
Howell, Jethro to Elizabeth Needham 8-17-1840 (8-18-1840) G
Howell, Jethro to Mary Ann Wear 2-28-1871 (3-1-1871) O
Howell, Joel C. to Ann J. Carpenter 9-13-1851 (no return) F
Howell, John C. to Mattie E. Smith 12-24-1877 L
Howell, John R. to Merilla H. Johnson 6-3-1840 (6-4-1840) Hr
Howell, John T. to Mary P. Pierce 8-19-1867 Dy
Howell, John W. to Amanda C. Dozier 9-30-1862 G
Howell, John W. to Jennie (Mrs.) Bevill 11-30-1867 (12-1-1867) Ma
Howell, John to Keziah Corbett 6-23-1857 (6-30-1857) O
Howell, K. P. to Nancy Farris 7-25-1859 Hr
Howell, Major to Sallie Woodard 7-28-1853 G
Howell, Malvin to Mollie Owen 8-16-1868 Hy
Howell, Melvin to Sophronia Davis 1-17-1873 (no return) Hy
Howell, R. W. to Winefred Fulgham 2-15-1835 (2-26-1835) Hr
Howell, Robert to Tempy Flowers 4-21-1841 (5-13-1841) G
Howell, Rufus R. to Elizabeth Brown 11-19-1850 (11-24-1850) Hr
Howell, S. U. to Sallie E. Hensler 10-4-1857 Ma
Howell, Samuel to M. E. Clark 7-18-1874 (7-19-1874) O
Howell, Samuel to Nannie Bennett 5-20-1877 Hy
Howell, Spencer to Anna Codry 6-10-1875 Hy
Howell, Sterling to Elizabeth Davis 6-9-1842 (6-11-1842) O
Howell, Thomas N. to Sarah Putman 10-10-1859 (no return) Cr
Howell, Thomas to Margaret Ray 11-22-1859 (11-25-1859) Ma
Howell, Thos. C. D. to Sarah Stewart 6-15-1835 G
Howell, W. C. to R. T. Craig 10-1-1867 (10-2-1867) Dy
Howell, W. H. to Frances Perry 9-3-1869 (9-5-1869) Dy
Howell, W. H. to S. C. Duncan 5-28-1873 (5-29-1873) T
Howell, W. L. to Mary E. Dozier 10-3-1867 G
Howell, W. N. to Sallie Peal 3-29-1876 (no return) Hy
Howell, W. R. to Nancy Brown 5-19-1842 Hr
Howell, Washington to Sarah Taylor 8-18-1877 Hy
Howell, William to Jane Stallings 9-6-1864 (9-7-1864) Sh
Howell, Wm. H. to Amanda M. Hooper 11-29-1861 Hr
Howell, Wm. N. to Florence D. Dennis 12-20-1879 (12-21-1879) L
Howell, Wm. P. to Mary L. Estes 7-5-1858 (7-8-1858) Hr
Howell, Wm. to Dollie Pierce 5-24-1869 Dy
Howell, Wm. to Elizabeth J. Sneathen 6-14-1843 O
Howell, Woodward to Exeline Tyson 11-3-1840 O
Howell?, Dvid to Marian Willis 8-17-1861 (no return) Dy
Howerd, George to Malinda Smith 8-17-1872 T
Howerton, W. R. D. to Nancy A. Barber 8-3-1867 (8-4-1867) L
Howerton, William to Missouri C. Barron 11-23-1866 (11-25-1866) Ma
Howitt, Isaac to Mary C. Shelton 12-19-1854 We
Howl?, R. A. to Caroline Jones 10-1-1864 Hn
Howlett, Green C. to Virginia Harp 9-15-1842 (9-13?-1842) Ma
Howlett, William P. to Lucinda Patterson 10-1-1866 (10-2-1866) Ma
Howlett, William R. to Ann Eliza Dickson 10-7-1843 (10-12-1843) Ma
Howling, John to Maria Powell 11-29-1877 Hy
Howsar, Lippman jr. to Caroline Yarbro 8-27-1867 (8-29-1867) T
Howse, Lewis C. to Mollie E. Hazlewood 11-9-1866 (11-14-1866) F
Hoy (Houg), Patrick to Margaret Luby 4-23-1855 Sh
Hoy, Abram to Nancy Bond 9-16-1867 Be
Hoyle, Allen to Fannie V. Keefe 12-18-1856 Sh
Hoyle, Robert to Adline Ware 2-25-1869 (no return) Hy
Hrris, G. B. to Bettie Hannah 7-25-1868 (7-27-1868) Cr
Hubbard, Albard H. to Rachel Davis 12-29-1874 Hy
Hubbard, Benjamin H. to Mary Richardson 1-30-1834 G
Hubbard, Champ to Helen Walker 10-4-1869 F B
Hubbard, Davis M. to Nancy Hamilton 12-3-1867 G
Hubbard, E. J. to Elizabeth M. Durham 7-15-1844 (no return) F
Hubbard, Ezekial to Sarah G. Wesson 12-19-1838 Sh
Hubbard, Frank to Indiana Cleave 8-27-1870 (no return) F B
Hubbard, Freman to Nancy Jane High 9-11-1850 (9-12-1850) F
Hubbard, G. J. to Mary Campbell 2-16-1848 (no return) Hn
Hubbard, George N. to Martha Jane Jones 12-31-1862 (no return) Hy
Hubbard, George W. to Mahala Span 3-31-1863 (no return) We
Hubbard, H. H. to Felecana Arnold 10-5-1857 We
Hubbard, Isaac B. to Mary Ann Pirtle 1-3-1849 Hr
Hubbard, Isaac N. to Ailsy Warren 6-1-1849 (6-3-1849) Hr
Hubbard, Isham to Angelina L. Hall 6-20-1847 Sh
Hubbard, J. L. to Z. L. Dickson 6-28-1865 (6-29-1865) O
Hubbard, James to Sarah Francis Rowson 11-6-1873 L B
Hubbard, John B. to Mary Frances S. Dyer 3-7-1829 (3-8-1829) L
Hubbard, John C. to Clementine Harris 10-24-1837 G
Hubbard, Samuel R. to J. Mila Lowter 5-1-1861 G
Hubbard, William J. to Margaret E. Newley 2-6-1877 L

Hubbard, Wm. W. to Aurelia A. Wheeler 6-29-1850 We
Hubbard?, Charles to Nancy Williams 11-18-1856 O
Hubbert, James F. to Elizabeth Bose 7-11-1843 O
Hubbs, J. C. to Eliza White 10-6-1853 Be
Hubbs, John F. to M. E. Bloodwood 9-26-1863 (9-27-1863) O
Hubbs, John S. to Eliza Ann McGill 9-9-1847 Be
Hubbs, T. J. to Sutha McElwain 11-28-1839 Be
Hubbs, William H. to Charlotte Curlin 12-19-1848 O
Hubbs, William T. to Mary Ann Ross 2-20-1851 O
Huber, John to Margaret C. Cox 6-22-1859 Sh
Hubert, B. W. to Rusia Davis 12-28-1851 O
Hubert, Westley to Elizabeth London 1-31-1860 O
Hubner?, Martin to Mary Ford 7-3-1841 Hn
Huchins, Merite to Elizabeth Crossett 11-4-1850 (11-7-1850) F
Huckabee, John to Susan Boyd 3-3-1834 (3-6-1834) G
Huckaby, R. J. to C. Boulten 3-12-1867 G
Huckaby, R. J. to Martha Thom 12-23-1869 G
Huckby, Wm. T. to Sarah Glasscock 11-22-1836 (11-23-1836) G
Huddleson, Thos. Z. to Elizabeth K. Cobb 12-29-1865 (12-30-1865) O
Huddleston, David M. to Catharine Huddleston 11-26-1855 Hr
Huddleston, David to Margaret Hammon 5-4-1842 (5-5-1842) Ma
Huddleston, Fielding to Temperance Farrell 10-29-1842 Sh
Huddleston, I. F. to Mary Braden 3-7-1861 Mn
Huddleston, M. H. to Elizabeth D. Corum 8-27-1863 (8-28-1863) O
Huddleston, Nelson to Charlotte Wilson 10-8-1849 (10-10-1849) Hr
Huddleston, P. M. to Martha Arun? 8-25-1842 Hn
Huddleston, Pleasant to Cytnha Huddleston 8-18-1844 Hn
Huddleston, William H. to Mahala Huddleston 3-27-1850 Hr
Huddleston, William W. to Martha Rice 2-20-1838 Hn
Huddleston, William W. to Sarah Pryer 3-1-1863 (no return) Hn
Hudgen, Robert to Silvia Pigel 12-26-1872 Cr B
Hudgens, Abram to M. E. Arun 10-16-1855 (no return) Hn
Hudgens, James to Martha Young 12-8-1840 Hn
Hudgens, John to Delila Glover 3-17-1851 Hn
Hudgens, John to Lucinda Williams 11-30-1848 Hn
Hudgens, Moses to Martha Coulter 4-13-1867 (no return) Hn B
Hudgens, Moses to Mary Henderson 8-11-1864 (no return) Hn
Hudgens, T. F. to G. L. Thompson 8-26-1879 (8-27-1879) L
Hudgens, Thomas to Elizabeth Gibson 7-10-1849 Hn
Hudgens, William W. to Emily Hunt 1-31-1858 Hn
Hudgens, William to Sarah E. Arun 10-11-1858 Hn
Hudgens, Wm. to Sarah Fowlkes 5-22-1880 Dy
Hudleston, Samuel W. to Mary A. Morrison 9-3-1872 T
Hudnell, George M. to Indiana D. McCabe 4-4-1855 Sh
Hudson, A. F. to S. E. Clark 12-24-1853 (no return) F
Hudson, A. J. B. to Rebecca Greer 6-12-1858 Be
Hudson, A. J. to Angeline Busbee 12-24-1863 Hn
Hudson, A. M. to Mary Scarborough 3-26-1846 We
Hudson, Aron to Asena Reddick 9-19-1847 Hn
Hudson, E. D. to Martha A. Jones 5-8-1877 (5-14-1877) Dy
Hudson, F. H. to Sallie Thetford 2-23-1869 G
Hudson, F. L. to Mary S. S. Gay 12-7-1859 F
Hudson, Felix G. to Frances R. Combs 11-14-1867 Be
Hudson, Francis E. to Eugenia V. Lovelace 2-13-1856 (2-14-1856) Ma
Hudson, G. G. to Martha Gillaspie 12-26-1860 (12-3?-1860) F
Hudson, G. W. to Susan Cox 12-17-1859 (12-15?-1859) Hr
Hudson, George to Harriet Manly 1-26-1869 (1-27-1869) Ma
Hudson, Giles G. to Martha J. S. Hammons 7-1-1853 (7-3-1853) Hr
Hudson, Glanson to Polly Johnson 3-25-1866 Hy
Hudson, H. P. to Hannah F. Dickinson 10-8-1878 (no return) Hy
Hudson, Henry H. to Mary E. Hudson 1-25-1866 (1-30-1866) T
Hudson, Henry to Sarah Frisbee 10-22-1860 Cr
Hudson, Isaac to Susan Williams 12-30-1868 (12-31-1868) F B
Hudson, J. C. to Sarah A. Dowell 2-5-1860 Be
Hudson, J. H. to Elizabeth C. Wygal 3-11-1868 Be
Hudson, J. H. to S. M. Arnett 2-14-1867 Be
Hudson, J. H. to V. V. Williams 9-9-1856 O
Hudson, J. N. to S. E. Corum 2-20-1871 O
Hudson, J. U. to Parmelia C. R. Hagler 4-10-1850 Hn
Hudson, J. W. to Annie L. Coop 11-13-1868 G
Hudson, James A. to E. M. Musgrave 5-25-1859 (no return) Hy
Hudson, James A. to Nancy Jane Gillespie 2-6-1840 Sh
Hudson, James C. to Emily J. Collier 12-9-1850 Ma
Hudson, James P. to Hesperan A. Perry 7-8-1867 Ma
Hudson, James R. to Elizabeth Nance 8-9-1853 Be
Hudson, Jarman to Mary Ann Rogers 12-17-1842 (12-20-1842) Hr
Hudson, Joel to Liza Jane Taylor 9-17-1867 Hn
Hudson, John A. to Celeste C. Patrick 11-6-1854 (11-7-1854) Sh
Hudson, John B. to Mary L. Crockett 1-29-1861 O
Hudson, John H. to Louisa C. Wright 1-31-1848 (2-3-1848) Ma
Hudson, John W. to Ann Branch Perkinson 9-27-1841 (9-28-1841) T
Hudson, John to Ellen Smith 11-27-1830 (12-2-1831) Hr
Hudson, John to Elmira Childress 4-10-1850 Hn
Hudson, John to Lotty Hagler 9-8-1850 Hn B
Hudson, John to Mary S. Price 9-4-1845 Hr
Hudson, Jonathan to Louiza Pratt 2-2-1863 Hn
Hudson, Joseph D. to Frances C. Hunt 7-30-1861 G
Hudson, Joseph W. to Leona F. Johnson 12-8-1868 Be
Hudson, Joseph to Sarah Moulder 2-13-1830 Ma
Hudson, Joshua to Mary Ross 1-12-1842 (1-19-1842) Hr
Hudson, Lawrence T. to Adeliza Fulbright 12-21-1846 (12-22-1846) Ma
Hudson, Mack to Matilda Mabin 4-18-1867 (no return) F B
Hudson, Marion E. to Emily Treadwell 12-7-1842 Sh
Hudson, P. T. to Mary E. Perkins 5-9-1866 F
Hudson, P. W. to Susan A. Lowry 10-21-1860 Be
Hudson, S. M. to Mary L. Board 4-28-1857 O
Hudson, Thomas D. to Rebecca F. Roark 2-9-1854 (2-21-1854) Hr
Hudson, Thomas to Betty Evans 1-5-1867 (no return) Dy
Hudson, Thomas to Maria Bailey 3-7-1867 Hn B
Hudson, Thomas to Ritta Avery 6-6-1867 G B
Hudson, Thos. W. to Elizabeth C. McKinnie 5-7-1846 Hr
Hudson, W. H. to Mary M. Wygul 12-27-1864 Be
Hudson, Washington to Lucinda Rutherford 8-19-1836 (9-16-1836) Hr
Hudson, Washington to Patsey Moore 7-8-1869 G B
Hudson, William A. to Mary A. Henderson 10-5-1841 Ma
Hudson, William L. to Nancy C. Litrell 7-11-1853 (7-13-1853) Hr
Hudson, William T. to Tappan Marsh 1-28-1840 (2-12-1840) F
Hudson, William c. to Sarah Ann Elizabeth Barns 12-10-1850 Sh
Hudson, Wm. C. to Lucy E. Humphrey 3-31-1845 Hr
Hudson, Wm. F. to Margaret A. Hardage 11-17-1870 Ma
Hudson, Zack to Mary Thetford 3-16-1863 G
Hudsons, Richard to Charlottie Dawson 8-18-1875 O
Hudspeth, A. J. to Sarah H. Beasley 3-28-1858 We
Hudspeth, George to Catharine Hart 1-25-1847 Hn
Hudspeth, James W. to Margaret Holly 12-21-1859 Hn
Hudspeth, James to Mary Clack 4-11-1839 O
Hudspeth, John C. to Nancy E. Cocke 8-30-1834 Hr
Hudspeth, John J. to Amarylla Jackson 5-5-1847 Hn
Hudspeth, John J. to Elenor Bedford 3-15-1840 O
Hudspeth, John W. to Martha J. Holly 6-1-1855 Hn
Hudspeth, R. S. to Elizabeth Slayton 12-25-1867 (12-26-1867) Dy
Hudspeth, R. S. to Mary E. Lipscomb 8-11-1870 G
Hudspeth, Samuel M. to Marthaann M. Long 4-19-1840 (6-19-1840) F
Hudspeth, Seaton to Agnis Winn 10-17-1848 (10-19-1848) F
Hudspeth, Seten to Agnis Winn 10-17-1848 F
Hudspeth, William H. to Lucy E. Ballard 9-19-1860 Hn
Hudspeth, William to Agnes Hancock 7-26-1838 Hn
Hudspeth, William to Ester Ann Northern 11-2-1846 Hn
Hue, Benj. to Margrett Betts 9-8-1845 (9-10-1845) G
Hues, Jesse to Delinda Newman 8-3-1872 (8-7-1872) L
Huet, Michael to Catherine Hogan 3-5-1849 Sh
Huey, J. K. (Dr.) to Sally James 4-7-1869 Dy
Huff, H. A. to E. N. Butram 10-2-1870 G
Huff, J. M. to Elizabeth Cox 12-9-1850 We
Huff, James to Margarett Babb 7-7-1850 O
Huff, James to Mary (Mrs.) Ray 6-17-1861 O
Huff, William F. to Susan J. Bevill 4-14-1847 Hn
Huffman, Daniel to Francis Holson (Wolson) 10-31-1839 (11-3-1839) O
Huffman, David to Aseny (Ammy) Brown 8-23-1836 Sh
Huffman, Flranklin to Eve Ann Bungle 1-29-1846 O
Huffman, Franklin to Hester Ann Dacus 10-3-1859 (10-4-1859) T
Huffman, G. A. to Catharine F. Morrisett 1-8-1872 (1-9-1872) T
Huffman, G. L. to Ellen Shankle 11-20-1871 (11-21-1871) T
Huffman, George to L. A. E. Clark 12-23-1858 O
Huffman, Isiah to Louiza E. Wall 8-23-1849 Cr
Huffman, J. L. to Martha B. Knight 8-28-1861 (8-29-1861) O
Huffman, Jacob to Matilda Miller 6-12-1836 O
Huffman, James to Elizabeth Braswell? 12-22-1846 Sh
Huffman, James to Lucy Dill 11-7-1866 (11-8-1866) Cr
Huffman, James to Nancy Thompson 11-12-1857 T
Huffman, John H. to Mary E. May 2-4-1841 Cr
Huffman, John R. L. to Fanny C. Hackney 12-20-1869 (12-23-1869) F
Huffman, John to Sarah Dudney 9-20-1842 Cr
Huffman, Joshua to Cathrine E. Beavers 5-9-1847 Cr
Huffman, L. M. to Mary E. Cunningham 2-3-1870 Cr
Huffman, Shofner to Susanna Nelson 11-10-1847 Cr
Huffman, T. A. to Mary A. Medearis 10-6-1861 Cr
Huffman, Vance to Sarah Wright 3-26-1857 (3-27-1857) Hr
Huffman, W. C. to Amanda Guinn 11-30-1873 (12-2-1874?) T
Huffman, W. M. G. to Jane J. Osborn 10-8-1847 Cr
Huffman, William to Frances Johnson 9-4-1865 F
Huffman, Wm. A. to Julia A. C. Banks 11-29-1854 (12-1-1854) T
Huffstutter, Adam to Syntha Ann Stover 3-15-1859 (3-17-1859) O
Huffstutter, George to Jane Cramer 4-2-1849 (4-5-1849) O
Huffstutter, James K. to Marry Ann Call 12-11-1863 O
Hufman, William to Sarah Firrell 6-27-1854 N
Hufner, George to Rodah Adams 11-19-1830 Ma
Hufstutter, Adam to Clara J. Stroud 12-22-1851 (12-23-1851) O
Hufstutter, William to Mary Elizabeth Keith 3-17-1857 (3-18-1857) O
Hug, Cristean to Augusta (Mrs.) Vagts 12-3-1864 (12-4-1864) Sh
Hugely, Wm. to Lucy A. Parnell 2-19-1866 (2-20-1866) Dy
Hugg, E. B. to Lavicia Lane 4-13-1869 (4-15-1869) F
Huggan, Thomas to Ann E. Workman 11-12-1857 We
Huggans, J. M. to Louisa Howard 9-25-1856 We

Huggard, Byds to Elbena Morris 11-16-1857 We
Huggard, J. M. to J. Easterwood 10-22-1870 G
Huggins, Benjamin M. to Nancy P. Covington 2-12-1857 Hn
Huggins, Iveson to Harriet Clary 2-16-1841 (no return) Hr
Huggins, John to Elizabeth A. McBlancett 9-24-1865 Mn
Huggins, S. F. to Hannah E. Caruth 2-11-1855 (2-13-1855) L
Huggins, W. M. to Nancy Jane West 12-24-1856 Hn
Hughes, A. F. to Lottie Dawson 7-12-1876 Hy
Hughes, Alexander L. to Jane Park 4-2-1851 (4-3-1851) Hr
Hughes, Alfred to Tennessee Bell Cook 12-27-1877 (12-30-1877) L B
Hughes, B. F. to Sarah Ann Stamps 2-9-1876 (no return) Hy
Hughes, C. T. to Teresa Russell 3-13-1851 Hn
Hughes, Cornelius to Rebecca Ann Beck 6-23-1857 O
Hughes, Edward to Mary Sharp 8-13-1861 L
Hughes, Elijah Collins to Martha M. Reddit 10-11-1859 Sh
Hughes, F. M. C. to Catherine Collins 4-9-1867 (4-11-1867) F
Hughes, F. M. to M. E. Stewart 1-30-1863 Sh
Hughes, Fountain E. to Lucy E. Finch 11-12-1863 Dy
Hughes, G. L. to _____ 3-18-1867 (3-22-1867) O
Hughes, G. W. to Fanny Quimby 7-24-1876 (no return) Hy
Hughes, George G. to Sally H. Hill 5-8-1860 (5-9-1860) Ma
Hughes, George to Gray Boswell 6-18-1867 (no return) F B
Hughes, Harvey to Evalina Pantillie? Couch 5-15-1843 T
Hughes, Hiram to Hannah Bledsoe 9-29-1874 T
Hughes, J. F. to Virginia Stamps 1-9-1877 Hy
Hughes, J. H. W. to Ellen Baucum 6-12-1854 (no return) F
Hughes, J. N. to Eliza Foster 6-27-1853 Hn
Hughes, J. P. to Indianna E. Nolley 8-3-1854 (8-6-1854) Sh
Hughes, J. W. to S. J. Clayton 11-29-1866 (11-30-1865?) F
Hughes, James A. to I. M. Forsythe 12-21-1862 Mn
Hughes, James B. to Sophronia Blan 12-27-1856 (1-1-1857) G
Hughes, James E. to Nancy Woods 11-22-1865 O
Hughes, James R. to Mattie Aden 12-13-1866 Hn
Hughes, Jas. H. to Malinda Hooton 2-12-1863 Hy
Hughes, Jesse A. to Manerva A. Chaney 9-2-1868 (9-6-1868) Cr
Hughes, Jesse to Mary Bradley 7-7-1840 (7-9-1840) F
Hughes, Jessee M. to Fidelia A. Fausett 9-10-1852 (no return) F
Hughes, John A. to Nancy Haney 2-9-1869 (2-11-1869) F B
Hughes, John C. to Samantha E. Hubbard 3-3-1857 Hr
Hughes, John to Amanda James 3-6-1869 G B
Hughes, Joseph to Milly David 12-18-1849 (no return) F
Hughes, P. T. to Kate? McDonough 8-5-1860 Sh
Hughes, Patrick to Elizabeth Caslin 5-5-1858 (6-6-1858) Sh
Hughes, R. E. to Sallie Ann Wade 12-18-1868 (12-20-1868) F
Hughes, Sam to Paula? McBride 5-20-1874 T
Hughes, Saml. Henry to Henrietta Stewart 7-15-1850 (7-16-1850) T
Hughes, Samuel D. to Holy B. Mobly 7-8-1867 (7-10-1867) L
Hughes, Silas to Matilda Rushen 11-17-1852 (no return) F
Hughes, Silas to Minta E. Davis 7-11-1863 (7-22-1863) F
Hughes, T. N. to Mary P. Gilliam 2-18-1868 (2-27-1868) F
Hughes, Thomas B. to Nancy L. McLeroy 7-14-1860 (no return) Hy
Hughes, W. L. to Mary E. Houston 12-27-1852 (12-29-1852) Sh
Hughes, W. P. to Sarah M. Upshaw 3-2-1861 (3-4-1861) O
Hughes, W. R. (Dr.) to Elizabeth J. Overall 11-15-1870 G
Hughes, W. S. to Irene Cheek 7-24-1855 (7-25-1855) Sh
Hughes, William F. to Mary E. Boyd 8-10-1844 Hr
Hughes, William R. to Mary Ann Goodall 10-28-1868 (10-29-1868) Ma
Hughes, William W. to Elizabeth Hubbard 3-14-1853 (3-17-1853) O
Hughes, William to Caroline Patterson 12-28-1840 Ma
Hughes, William to Lou Turner 12-21-1868 (12-23-1868) L
Hughes, William to Louisa Joyner jr. 5-18-1854 O
Hughes, William to Nelly(Ellen) Cox 9-28-1829 (10-2-1829) Hr
Hughes, Wm. to Catharin Allen 8-26-1850 (9-1-1850) F
Hughes, Wm. to Frances Tilman 10-23-1873 T
Hughey, A. H. to A. H. Chears 12-24-1855 (no return) Hn
Hughey, A. J. to Elizabeth Brown 11-20-1849 Hn
Hughey, Jacob to Jane Journagan 8-28-1839 (8-29-1839) Hr
Hughey, Wm. to Mary J. Gordon 10-22-1857 (no return) Cr
Hughlet, Thomas to Caroline Dorris 5-18-1836 (6-2-1836) O
Hughlett, Fed to Rebecca Brown 3-5-1873 (3-6-1873) T
Hughlett, Thomas T. to Parthenia Kinney 7-30-1856 O
Hughlett, W. W. to Margarete D. L Pate 9-12-1867 (no return) We
Hughlette, Adkin to Marth Hill 12-28-1866 (12-29-1865) T
Hughs (Hugger), Joseph to Lucinda Barden 1-5-1847 Sh
Hughs, Alexander to Elizabeth Stamps 9-18-1855 (9-20-1855) G
Hughs, John to Roda Moore 3-30-1868 (no return) Hy
Hughs, L. to Hannah R. Stilwell 12-10-1868 G
Hughs, S. H. to Sarah A. Horton 2-9-1865 G
Hughs, William to Mary Emma Horgot 1-18-1870 Hy
Hughsand, Jessee to Almanda J. Daugherty 2-20-1863 Mn
Huguley, Saml. E. to Lucy E. Scoby 12-13-1864 (12-14-1864) Dy
Huie, James W. to Martha J. Hankins 2-19-1860 Hn
Huie, Noah to Louisa Chappell 8-24-1856 Hn
Huie?, Joseph G. to Frances C. Franklin 7-28-1868 (7-29-1868) Dy
Hulbert, William R. to Annie Broadnax 7-29-1864 Sh
Hulen, James M. to Delany Durham 10-27-1847 Sh
Huline, William T. to Margarett Prescott 3-27-1838 (3-29-1838) L

Huling, Thomas B. to Sarah Meaghar (Menghar) 9-17-1828 Sh
Hull (Hall?), Sip to Jane Berry 12-30-1869 F B
Hull, Calvin B. to Elizabeth Skinner 3-22-1842 Hn
Hull, David to Isabella Matthews 12-5-1842 (12-13-1842) Hr
Hull, J. F. to Elizabeth W. Murphy 3-2-1843 Hr
Hull, James Francis to Nancy Jane Catherine Webb 8-12-1868 G
Hull, John D. to Mary A. Reams 12-14-1868 Be
Hull, Sip to Jane Green 12-29-1865 (1-30-1865) F B
Hull, Spencer to Catharine Murphy 5-19-1866 (8-11-1866) F B
Hulsey, Andrew I. to Lovey Francis 9-7-1842 Sh
Hulsey, W. J. to R. J. Rains 1-8-1862 Mn
Hults, G. F. to Eliza Pierce 8-22-1855 (8-23-1855) Sh
Hum, Matthew to Mary Reece 11-11-1858 We
Human, J. to J. N. Currie 12-18-1878 L
Human, Solomon to Nancy P. Porter 12-17-1833 G
Humble, Abraham to Jane Addams 12-13-1838 L
Humble, Andrew to Angeline Owen 6-7-1873 (6-8-1873) Cr B
Humble, Carroll to Jinnie Steele 6-20-1868 (6-21-1868) Cr
Humble, George W. to Caroline Pinson 12-22-1853 G
Humble, James to Mary K. Balentine 8-8-1845 (8-9-1845) G
Humble, William to Frances Stone 5-25-1841 (5-26-1841) Ma
Humble, Willie to Ann Overton 6-8-1840 Ma
Humbles, J. L. to V. A. Kinley 12-18-1872 (12-19-1872) Dy
Hume, Enoch to Cordelia Burks 9-30-1869 L
Hume, Willis to Minerva Aiken 7-11-1857 (7-12-1857) Sh
Humes, J. A. to Ella Schoolcraft? 12-31-1870 (1-1-1871) Dy
Humingway, C. F. to C. M. Sofge 10-25-1858 (11-25-1858) Sh
Humphrey, David to Mary Ann Thrift 11-21-1842 Hr
Humphrey, David to Susan Bowland 8-24-1866 Cr
Humphrey, Doy to Mary Humphrey 12-30-1857 Cr
Humphrey, E. O. to Julia A. Bunting 12-18-1852 (12-30-1852) Hr
Humphrey, Elsey to Harriet M. Kelly 12-12-1844 F
Humphrey, Francis U. to Minerva Coats 1-10-1855 Hn
Humphrey, George W. to Melissa A. Newsom 11-14-1859 (11-17-1859) Sh
Humphrey, Isaac T. to Mary Jane Tilson 6-28-1845 Sh
Humphrey, J. A. to R. M. Moore 9-4-1860 (9-5-1860) F
Humphrey, James F. to Angerona Warr 8-16-1852 H
Humphrey, James H. to Martha C. Black 4-6-1848 (no return) Cr
Humphrey, James to Phebe C. Myers 10-17-1855 We
Humphrey, Jesse to Nancy Brown 11-24-1848 F
Humphrey, Joseph to Julia A. Wilson 8-19-1859 (no return) Cr
Humphrey, Louisa to Bethenea C. Collins 7-20-1853 Cr
Humphrey, M. C. to Sallie J. Hall 3-15-1858 (3-17-1858) Hr
Humphrey, Thomas to Mary Taylor 12-25-1869 (12-26-1869) F B
Humphrey, Wiliam G. to Mary Todd 2-1-1844 Ma
Humphrey, Wm. to Mary M. Giles 9-10-1851 (no return) Cr
Humphreys, Abner to Lucinda Key 3-28-1844 Hn
Humphreys, Absolum T. J. to Mary E. Smith 10-7-1844 (10-24-1844) T
Humphreys, Asa to Elizabeth C. Coats 1-11-1853 Hn
Humphreys, Ben. P. to Mary E. Jones 4-23-1873 Hy
Humphreys, Collin to Emma Isbell 4-18-1867 F B
Humphreys, Daniel to Caroline Caldwell 9-16-1867 Hn
Humphreys, H. to Sarah Ann Coats 11-7-1848 Hn
Humphreys, Ira to Mary Ann Mathis 10-14-1854 Hn
Humphreys, J. F. to Sallie E. Baxter 12-18-1860 F
Humphreys, James G. to Jane Young 5-6-1861 Hn
Humphreys, James H. to Ann E. Ward 10-6-1857 (10-7-1857) Sh
Humphreys, James M. to Winifred B. Drew 12-29-1851 (12-30-1851) Sh
Humphreys, James to Ann Cooney 12-30-1854 Sh
Humphreys, John C. to Sanaol Fort Battle 2-14-1842 Sh
Humphreys, Lemual J. to Mollie J. Hart 1-10-1870 (1-12-1870) Ma
Humphreys, Perry W. to Susan A. Knapp 12-18-1848 Sh
Humphreys, Sol. B. to Melissa C. Carlton 9-24-1862 (no return) Hy
Humphreys, Thomas A. to Frances L. Hodges 6-22-1845 Sh
Humphreys, Thomas to Millie Haskins 2-10-1874 (2-12-1874) Dy
Humphreys, W. D. to Catherine Davis 9-1-1862 (no return) Hn
Humphreys, W. H. to Ann E. Freeman no date (1838-1852) Hn
Humphreys, William R.? to Sophia E. Stricklin 3-2-1852 (3-3-1852) L
Humphreys, Wm. T. to Margaret R. Wall 11-2-1850 (no return) F
Humphries, Benjn. to Sarah E. Duval 7-15-1858 (7-18-1858) Sh
Humphries, Ezekial to Mary McKenzie 8-27-1837 Hr
Humphries, George W. to Elizabeth Bannon 11-25-1851 Sh
Humphries, Henley to Mary D. Hendrix 8-21-1864 Hn
Humphrys, J. M. to Matilda Rhodes 4-14-1857 (4-20-1857) Sh
Hundley, Calvin C. to Emily J. Jones 5-27-1861 (5-29-1861) Hr
Hundley, E. D. Y. to Sealia Ann Hudson 7-16-1849 (7-17-1849) G
Hundley, James to Gilla Fuller 10-23-1849 (10-25-1849) Ma
Hundley, John H. to Elizabeth Anderson 11-26-1860 (11-27-1860) Ma
Hundley, John to Martha P. Craig 5-13-1844 Sh
Hundly, Wm. H. to Fannie W. Page 5-23-1859 (5-24-1859) F
Hungerazo?, Robert to Caroline R. Reibert 3-25-1863 Sh
Hunley, C. to Margaret Acock 12-10-1854 We
Hunley, James H. to Laura Pinson 10-25-1872 T
Hunnel, Peter to Mary Savage 1-21-1836 Hr
Hunnell, Moses to Maranda Martin 10-8-1838 (10-18-1838) Hr
Hunphreys, Bryant to Pritena Hardwick 4-16-1839 (5-1-1839) Hr
Hunsaker, O. F. to Julia Staples 7-10-1860 Sh

Hunsucker, A. to Louisa Ross 3-11-1869 (3-23-1869) F
Hunt, A. to Emeline Legett 3-14-1859 (3-15-1859) G
Hunt, Absolem D. to Fannie M. Guthrie 1-1-1868 (1-2-1868) Ma
Hunt, Albert to Mary A. Henry 12-23-1866 G
Hunt, Anderson to Mary Cooper 11-21-1860 (11-22-1868) T
Hunt, Avery to Maria L. Thompson 7-4-1844 Ma
Hunt, Avery to Sarah C. Dickens 12-18-1841 (12-23-1841) Ma
Hunt, B. F. to Elizabeth Cook 10-29-1831 (11-3-1831) Hr
Hunt, Charles W. to Lucy Ann Ruffin 9-2-1834 Hr
Hunt, Christofer to Catharine Burrel 2-22-1868 T
Hunt, Daniel to Sarah Thurmond 3-21-1833 (3-26-1833) Hr
Hunt, Dempsy to Patience Whitly 11-18-1865 (12-10-1865) T
Hunt, Douglass R. to Mary E. Polk 4-3-1846 (4-8-1846) F
Hunt, E. N. to Sarah M. Lowe 5-22-1857 (6-4-1857) Hr
Hunt, Elisha R. to Mary Ann Price 10-11-1842 (10-13-1842) Ma
Hunt, Fenton Edward to Mary Eliza Black 12-16-1878 Hy
Hunt, George E. to Eliza M. Hannah 4-9-1856 (4-10-1856) Sh
Hunt, George W. to Sarah E. Hays 1-3-1869 G
Hunt, Henry G. to Jane W. Allen 8-24-1846 (8-25-1846) G
Hunt, Hukbald? D. to Sallie M. Wilson 12-21-1848 F
Hunt, Isaac J. to Phebe Shotwell 12-21-1848 Hn
Hunt, Isaac to Ann Parks 12-24-1867 (12-26-1867) F B
Hunt, James B. to Frances J. Burton 12-7-1872 (12-12-1872) T
Hunt, James T. to Matilda W. Gant 7-8-1834 Ma
Hunt, James W. to Elvira Freeman 3-4-1857 Hn
Hunt, James W. to Nancy Ann Greenwood 4-19-1843 (4-20-1843) Hr
Hunt, James to Henritta Hall 6-17-1871 F
Hunt, James to Mary Irvine 1-31-1830 Sh
Hunt, Jesse M. to Elizabeth Jane Harrel 9-8-1847 Sh
Hunt, Jessee to Sallie Foreman 12-29-1866 T
Hunt, John A. to Fannie T. Watkins 5-15-1860 Sh
Hunt, John F. to Louisa J. Alexander 6-1-1868 (6-3-1868) Ma
Hunt, John H. to Nancy E. Bass 9-8-1867 G
Hunt, John M. to Mary P. Bond 10-11-1866 G
Hunt, John S. to Catharine Simpson 1-16-1849 (1-17-1849) Hr
Hunt, John W. to Virginia E. Marton 1-13-1842 (1-20-1842) F
Hunt, Matthew to Sarah Fletcher 1-7-1862 G
Hunt, Milton to Neadis Isis Phelps 9-27-1847 (9-30-1847) T
Hunt, Robert to Margaret E. Matthews 4-28-1857 (4-29-1857) Ma
Hunt, Simeon to Elizabeth Upchurch 5-25-1856 Hn
Hunt, Tennessee to Nellie Springfield 12-31-1868 (1-2-1869) F B
Hunt, Thomas J. to Susan Mendinall 12-3-1834 Sh
Hunt, Thomas W. to Judith P. Mosly 5-20-1841 Sh
Hunt, Thomas to Anna Wilson 6-15-1866 Be
Hunt, Thomas to Laura McGaughy 3-19-1874 Dy
Hunt, Thompson to Penelope Whichard 2-18-1856 (2-21-1856) G
Hunt, W. M. to Charlotte Lynn 5-25-1853 Hn
Hunt, W. M. to E. L. Neal 7-3-1867 G
Hunt, W. R. to Ann Ward 8-28-1843 (no return) Cr
Hunt, W. R. to Sarah E. Driver (Dineve) 2-12-1850 Sh
Hunt, W. T. to Dora King 12-15-1869 Hy
Hunt, W. W. to Eliza A. Lane 1-16-1861 G
Hunt, William C. to Henerotta T. Hopkins 1-21-1845 (1-23-1845) G
Hunt, William H. to Elizabeth F. Dickens 8-2-1830 Ma
Hunt, William H. to Eugenia Lafayette Jackson 12-22-1846 Ma
Hunt, William H. to Flora White 3-17-1857 G
Hunt, William H. to Margaret Connell 1-14-1860 (no return) We
Hunt, William H. to Orleana T. Eppes 4-23-1860 (4-24-1860) Ma
Hunt, William T. to Carolin Petty 7-1-1844 (no return) F
Hunt, William to Elizar Kirby 12-23-1869 Hy
Hunt, William to Manerva White 6-21-1869 Cr
Hunt, William to Martha Turner 3-26-1850 (3-28-1850) G
Hunt, William to R. P. Oakley 9-18-1878 (9-19-1878) Dy
Hunt, Wilson D. to Jamima E. Durley 11-14-1838 (11-16-1838) G
Hunt, Wm. R. to Mary L. Marsh 2-7-1871 (2-9-1871) T
Hunt, Wm. to Susan White 2-6-1869 (no return) Hy
Hunter, A. D.? to Elizabeth A. Alexander 1-4-1866 T
Hunter, A. J. to Ann M. House 1-16-1851 (1-22-1851) F
Hunter, Ag? D. to Clarinda A. Weaver? 10-19-1841 (10-21-1841) T
Hunter, Amos to Margaret Loving 12-27-1865 Hy
Hunter, Andy to Vina Bluford 1-10-1871 (no return) F B
Hunter, C. W. to Martha Forest? 7-24-1845 Hn
Hunter, G. H. to R. Y. Allen 2-15-1872 Cr
Hunter, Geo. J. to Drucilla V. Champ 10-16-1850 Hr
Hunter, Geo. T. to Ann Eliza Broom 11-2-1846 (11-5-1846) F
Hunter, Green to Adelade Mann 11-3-1868 (no return) Hy
Hunter, Green to Anna Spivey 12-28-1871 Hy
Hunter, Grundy to Ellen Hill 8-22-1870 G B
Hunter, Henry W. to Anna Stalcup 11-7-1831 G
Hunter, Henry to Anna Stacup 11-7-1830 G
Hunter, Henry to Annie Rogers 12-26-1868 Hy
Hunter, Isaiah to America Thomas 2-4-1869 Cr
Hunter, J. F. to M. A. Shelton 10-28-1875 Dy
Hunter, J. H. to Mollie E. Gause 4-29-1861 (no return) Hy
Hunter, J. S. (Dr.) to N. S. Harlow 10-12-1872 (10-16-1872) L
Hunter, J. T. to S. F. Weaver 11-9-1876 Hy
Hunter, James to Orelia Ann Allen 5-20-1870 (5-21-1870) F B
Hunter, John D. to J. L. Brown 5-30-1870 (no return) F
Hunter, John H. to Elizabeth Miller 4-3-1844 Hn
Hunter, John J. to Eleanor Hogden 1-28-1836 Sh
Hunter, John W. to A. W. Wortham 6-6-1860 Sh
Hunter, John to Delilah Glimp 12-7-1880 (12-8-1880) L
Hunter, John to Ellen L. Thasee 11-9-1843 Ma
Hunter, John to Kate (Mrs.) Osborne 11-14-1864 Sh
Hunter, John to Nancy Futhey 2-13-1820 T
Hunter, John to Nancy J. Eastland 1-2-1860 Sh
Hunter, John to Sarah Fields 5-19-1850 (6-19-1850) Hr
Hunter, Marshall to Margaret Jones 6-21-1867 (7-13-1867) F B
Hunter, Marvin to Nancy Ann Hunter 4-3-1869 (4-18-1869) F B
Hunter, Nelson to Nancy J. Williams 2-13-1868 (no return) F B
Hunter, P. H. to Ann E. Mitchell 9-2-1865 O
Hunter, Price (Prince?) to Lucy Halfacre 12-16-1871 (12-17-1871) L
Hunter, R. H. to Ida Hill 2-17-1886 (2-25-1886) L
Hunter, S. A. to Caroline Shaw? 9-22-1877 (9-23-1877) L
Hunter, Samuel to Clarinda Wicker 2-28-1850 Hn
Hunter, Shepherd to Jane Cox 1-30-1873 (no return) Hy
Hunter, Sims to Chaney Palmer 1-24-1867 (no return) Hy
Hunter, W. A. to Margaret A. Gause 4-30-1861 (no return) Hy
Hunter, Warren to Diana Strain 1-6-1870 (no return) L
Hunter, William M. to Elizabeth Glimp 2-26-1867 (2-27-1867) L
Hunter, William T. to Z. S. Pate 11-18-1872 (11-19-1872) Dy
Hunter, William to Winna Frances Glimp 11-6-1856 L
Hunter, Wm. C. to Nancy C. Bull 5-19-1847 (5-20-1847) F
Huntsman, Adam to Elizabeth Todd 6-13-1829 (6-14-1829) Ma
Huntsman, Alexander to Matilda Atkins 10-11-1849 Ma
Huntsman, C. I. to Elizabeth Edward 2-10-1844 Ma
Huntsman, George T. to Anna M. Henry 12-17-1857 Sh
Huntsman, Samuel to Mary Horton 10-3-1840 Ma
Huntsman, William to Eliza Banks 1-19-1829 Sh
Hurbert, A. to Catharine Kelly 6-18-1861 Sh
Hurd, James R. to Amanda Hamilton 11-2-1869 (11-4-1869) Dy
Hurdle, William to Ellen Rice 12-13-1882 (12-14-1882) L
Hurey, Thos. G. to Mary E. Sharp 8-9-1853 Cr
Hurley, Andrew B. to Eliza E. Womac 6-6-1848 (6-8-1848) F
Hurley, Aron L. to Martha Baird 10-20-1856 L
Hurley, B. F. to Frances Scott 12-8-1863 Mn
Hurley, George W. to Mary L. W. (Mrs.) Boyd (Becton?) 11-2-1858 Ma
Hurley, John to Mary Gunter 12-28-1835 Hr
Hurley, John to Sarah Forsythe 1-4-1869 F
Hurley, Moses to Martha Burrow 2-10-1846 (2-12-1846) G
Hurley, W. M. to Mattie J. Salliers 8-15-1874 (8-16-1874) T
Hurly, John to Gerusha Adams 11-26-1839 (11-28-1839) F
Hurn, W. G. to Mary W. Whitten 8-22-1865 G
Hursh, H. H. to E. J. Prewitt 1-23-1862 (1-28-1862) Hr
Hurst, E. V. to Mary S. Irvin 9-24-1861 Mn
Hurst, Henry to Amanda Preston 1-11-1850 Hr
Hurst, Lewis (Lt.) to Fredonia Childress 8-11-1863 (8-13-1863) Sh
Hurst, Shevarts to Matilda Upton 10-31-1842 (10-4?-1842) Ma
Hurt, Adam to Jane Clay 5-14-1870 (5-15-1870) Cr
Hurt, Berry to Sopha Collins 10-12-1867 Cr
Hurt, Charles A. to Leonia W. Wright 2-27-1884 L
Hurt, Charles J. F. to Elizabeth Pryor 1-17-1854 Hn
Hurt, Daniel to Dilsey Blackwell 10-27-1872 (11-2-1872) Cr B
Hurt, David to Louisa E. Jordian 3-6-1845 G
Hurt, Geo. T. to Mollie E. Hooper 2-20-1873 Dy
Hurt, George T. to Mary E. McKnight 7-28-1874 Dy
Hurt, George W. to Addie E. Wright 12-14-1877 (12-16-1877) L
Hurt, George W. to Eliza C. Jordan 12-3-1866 (12-5-1866) L
Hurt, Granville C. to Martha A. Harris 8-2-1839 Cr
Hurt, Henry I. to Lucretia Bell 10-24-1870 Dy B
Hurt, Jacob to Emma Somervell 12-8-1866 (12-9-1866) T
Hurt, Jno. W. to Jane Ellender 1-19-1850 We
Hurt, John A. to Julia A. Clark 9-12-1850 G
Hurt, John J. to Margaret Marberry 10-5-1856 Hn
Hurt, John J. to Martha A. Pryer 2-3-1845 (no return) Hn
Hurt, John R. to Sarah E. Chappell 6-20-1860 (6-21-1860) Ma
Hurt, John Z. to Caroline Craig 12-4-1865 (12-6-1865) T
Hurt, John to Emily Alexander 6-10-1859 Cr
Hurt, L. A. to Annie Clay 6-28-1870 (6-30-1870) Cr
Hurt, Philemon to Mary J. Cunningham 3-8-1852 (3-10-1852) G
Hurt, R. M. to Martha E. (Mrs.) Woods 4-24-1860 Cr
Hurt, Robert H. to Susan A. Deberry 6-1-1843 (6-3-1843) Ma
Hurt, Samuel B. to Julia M. L. Desmond? 7-2-1842 (7-16-1842) T
Hurt, Samuel S. to Margaret A. Jones 12-22-1863 (12-21?-1863) T
Hurt, W. W. to Leona Hurt 12-27-1884 (12-28-1884) L
Hurt, William G. to Mary D. Porter 5-12-1860 Ma
Hurt, William to D. G. Wilson 12-6-1855 Hn
Hurt, William to Margaret Stone 3-25-1860 G
Hurt, Wm. to Mary Woods 5-12-1865 (no return) Cr
Husbands, William to Susannah M. Thompson 4-16-1847 (4-22-1847) G
Huskett, Joseph G. to Lucinda Cantrell 8-9-1846 We
Huskey, Thomas to Sarah Ward 6-15-1835 W
Husky, William L. to Martha J. Johnson 7-12-1853 Sh
Husten, Jordan to Martha Hobbs 4-22-1865 (5-25-1865) O

Hustin, James to Emma Garrett 10-17-1868 (no return) Hy
Huston, Calvin to Milley R. Richerson 7-2-1873 T
Huston, James to Harrett C. Delnice 7-7-1850 Be
Huston, R. B. to M. E. Spinger 8-6-1877 L
Hutchens, C. S. to Mary Tinkle 11-6-1855 (11-6-1855) G
Hutchens, John B. to Angeline R. Alexander 1-19-1858 Hn
Hutchens, Lewis to Elizabeth Bedwell 8-21-1859 Hn
Hutchens, Reuben M. to Lucinda S. Gately 5-27-1849 Hn
Hutchens, Tucker to Sarah Stan 12-12-1839 (12-22-1839) G
Hutchens, W. D. (Capt.) to Jennie L. (Mrs.) Freleigh 12-5-1863 (12-6-1863) Sh
Hutchenson, John to Kitty Parker 5-30-1866 Hn B
Hutcher, William to Louizer Welch 9-22-1867 G
Hutcherson, Enoch P. to Rody F. Lierd 9-9-1871 (9-10-1871) L
Hutcherson, F. E. to Lora Kissell 7-7-1880 (no return) L
Hutcherson, G. W. to Sarah E. Webb (West?) 10-12-1871 (10-13-1871) L
Hutcherson, J. P. to Mary Laird 4-14-1876 (4-16-1876) L
Hutcherson, James B. to Matilda Wakefield 9-15-1841 (9-16-1841) L
Hutcherson, James S. to Susan B. Childress 7-3-1858 (no return) L
Hutcherson, John V. to Susan E. Shutts 7-11-1861 Mn
Hutcherson, Lewis J. to R. J. Carson 12-3-18879 (12-3-1880?) L
Hutcherson, Lewis S. to Camantha J. Harber 9-16-1845 G
Hutcherson, Richard B. to Mira Jourden 12-21-1835 (12-22-1835) G
Hutcherson, Saml. W. to Nancy Ray 12-27-1873 (12-31-1873) T
Hutcherson, Saml. to Jane Baker 3-4-1850 (3-7-1850) Ma
Hutcherson, W. J. to Martha A. Vernon 11-22-1875 (no return) L
Hutcherson, William to Jane C. Williams 2-26-1855 (3-1-1855) L
Hutcheson, A. J. to Emily Foss 1-8-1868 (1-9-1868) L
Hutcheson, Aaron to Mary Richardson 8-31-1866 T
Hutcheson, Asa to Ann Vaughn 11-16-1843 We
Hutcheson, Charles W. to Agnes A. B. B. Baugh 2-27-1841 (3-4-1841) Hr
Hutcheson, Daniel to Eliza Hillsman 6-28-1870 (6-30-1870) Cr
Hutcheson, Jackson to Martha Hutcheson 3-18-1844 L
Hutcheson, James M. to Lucinda McElmayee 9-14-1858 (9-16-1858) O
Hutcheson, John to E. R. Brooks 2-16-1839 Hn
Hutcheson, Lewis to Emiline Huckeby 11-19-1842 (11-20-1842) L
Hutcheson, Lou J. to Aggy Nelson 1-16-1868 (no return) L B
Hutcheson, William to Margaret M. Pittman 6-18-1867 (6-19-1867) L
Hutchings, Bruce to Mariah Cardwell 1-21-1861 O
Hutchings, C. C. to Martha S. Boykin 8-30-1856 Ma
Hutchings, Christopher to Louisa Edwards 3-16-1829 Ma
Hutchings, Horace H. to Susan A. (Mrs.) Vann 6-22-1858 Ma
Hutchings, W. E. to Celia Jordan 12-25-1863 G
Hutchins, C.? M. to Tabitha Watson 1-22-1868 Cr
Hutchins, E. H. to N. A. Barnheart 8-2-1839 Be
Hutchins, E. W. to Elizabeth (Mrs.) Sparkman 3-13-1867 G
Hutchins, Erasmus J. to Sarah A. L. Lowery 7-7-1866 (7-8-1866) Cr
Hutchins, Isaac R. to Martha T. Allen 1-15-1872 (no return) Cr
Hutchins, James to Iredell Jones 4-2-1849 G
Hutchins, John to Caroline M. James 4-7-1833 (5-12-1833) G
Hutchins, John to Samantha James 5-7-1833 G
Hutchins, Lewis to Lucinda Bell 9-30-1865 (10-1-1865) F
Hutchins, Nathaniel M. to Martha A. Apleton 12-16-1847 (12-18-1847) F
Hutchins, Robert to Mary York 8-6-1868 Cr
Hutchins, W. C. to Hariet J. Towery 4-4-1868 (4-6-1868) Cr
Hutchins, Wm. P. to Tonser Wheeler 11-3-1866 (11-4-1866) F
Hutchinson, Benj. to Mary J. Nixon 10-18-1866 Hy
Hutchinson, Ewell C. to Sarah Jane Foster 7-28-1855
Hutchinson, Guilford J. to Sue V. Bates 12-18-1866 (no return) L
Hutchinson, J. R. P. to Martha Huffstutter 12-15-1865 O
Hutchinson, James to Louisa Turner 12-15-1856 (12-16-1856) O
Hutchinson, John P. to Ellen Thacker 8-5-1867 (8-6-1867) T
Hutchinson, John to Nancy Lovin 2-23-1851 (2-24-1851) O
Hutchinson, Joseph to Nancy Hendde 1-15-1867 (1-16-1867) O
Hutchinson, R. B. to Mary Clark 2-10-1845 (no return) Cr
Hutchinson, Samuel M. to Susan A. Waddle 2-14-1850 Sh
Hutchinson, Thomas to S. J. Hillsman 2-23-1860 Cr
Hutchinson, William H. to Mary Ellen Ray 5-3-1856 (5-4-1856) O
Hutchinson, William M. to Mary S. Baker 12-15-1869 G
Hutchinson, William Walker to Sarah Goss 4-12-1844 (4-15-1844) T
Hutchinson, William to Eliza (Mrs.) Massengale 12-14-1861 (12-15-1861) O
Hutchison, A. D. to Tennie Pewett 12-19-1868 Hy
Hutchison, Alfred to Sarah Thomas 4-2-1849 L
Hutchison, Alfred to Susan Mosley 4-25-1861 (?-2 -1861) L
Hutchison, Cyrus W. to Harriet Smith 12-16-1849 T
Hutchison, J. H. to Elizabeth Dowdy 6-1-1864 Be
Hutchison, J. K. to Isabella Garrison 8-20-1867 F
Hutchison, Jessee to Clary Davis 11-6-1855 Be
Hutchison, John Leroy to Mary Frances Ray 2-24-1853 T
Hutchison, John to Martha Pinkston 12-1-1871 (no return) Cr
Hutchison, Joseph to L. J. Lallier(Sallier?) 2-21-1857 (2-22-1857) Hr
Hutchison, Lewis to Jane Hufstutte 4-19-1865 O
Hutchison, P. P. to L. J. Thompson 1-26-1870 G
Hutchison, William I. to Elizabeth May 5-25-1830 Ma
Hutchison, William to Henrietta Hipp 11-25-1872 (11-26-1872) L
Hutchison, Willis to Martha A. Prewett 3-17-1861 Be
Hutchison, Wm. to Mollie Jackson 6-5-1865 (6-8-1865) O
Hutson, Andy to Mary Pratt 2-12-1862 Hn

Hutson, Henry to Margarett E. J. Craig 1-8-1848 O
Hutson, James A. to Sarah Rhoda F. Craig 12-24-1848 O
Hutson, John W. to Polly Harrisson 9-17-1828 (9-30-1828) G
Hutson, Joseph to Julia A. Hoskins 5-3-1856 (5-4-1856) G
Hutson, Richard D. to Permelia Dillenham 10-10-1828 Hr
Hutson, William C. to Mattie Williamson 1-9-1877 (1-10-1877) Dy
Hutson, William to Fanny A. Grisham? 10-28-1847 Hn
Hutt, John to Mary Harriett Field 12-8-1831 Sh
Hutton, Samuel to Caroline Tyson 4-4-1850 Sh
Huzza, Columbus C. to Elizabeth Wyatt 10-14-1858 O
Hyatt, A. V. to Martha A. McNight 4-27-1867 (4-28-1867) Cr
Hyde, Henry J. to Mary E. Wood 1-9-1872 L
Hyde, Jerome B. to Sally A. Raines 4-24-1860 (4-26-1860) Ma
Hyde, Jonah to Catherine Turner 1-6-1870 G B
Hyde, Reubin to Martha Linn 11-8-1848 Sh
Hyde, W. B. to Margaret A. Kinnon 12-29-1866 (12-30-1866) F
Hyer, William D. to Wilmoth B. Woodson 5-7-1840 Hn
Hyland, William to Johanna Barron 7-10-1858 Sh
Hynds, Benjamin D. to S. E. Tuck 1-15-1862 We
Hynds, Francis P. to A. S. Taylor 11-14-1861 We
Hynes, John to Matilda Wildan 10-20-1859 (no return) Cr
Hynson, Augustus to Nannie Fleming 10-11-1853 Sh
Hyott, Stephen W. to Sariah Meriah Mitchell 11-1-1846 Be
Hyte, George to Venie Ivey 8-19-1866 Hy

Iams, William M. to Martha P. Adair 2-18-1859 (2-24-1859) Sh
Ibos, Bertrand to Cyrian Tieran 1-8-1855 Sh
Iby, Richard to Hepsabeth Caple 2-22-1841 (2-24-1841) F
Idleberger, John to Millie O'Daniel 5-20-1866 G
Ikard, A. T. to Mary E. Lindsay 1-1-1869 (1-5-1869) T
Iler, I. T. to Mary I. Olfin 10-9-1866 O
Iler, John T. to Julia Ann Forrest 12-26-1852 Hn
Imes, R. D. to Margaret Schultz 3-29-1850 Sh
Imes, William to Paulina Grooms 7-1-1838 Sh
Indman, Jesse to Elizabeth Weaks 10-19-1854 Hn
Indseth, Ole to Elizabeth Clusen 8-11-1862 Sh
Ing, E. W. to Mary A. Dunlap 12-19-1865 G
Ing, Eli W. to Nancy E. Thomas 3-18-1853 (2?-20-1853) G
Ing, Isaac A. to Mary Tucker 6-8-1866 G
Ing, J. M. to M. E. Durley 11-26-1860 G
Ing, John to Susan A. (Mrs.) Woolfkill 11-17-1863 Sh
Ing, John to Susan Knox 9-15-1855 (no return) F
Ing, R. B. to Fanny Woodsen 12-2-1866 G
Ing, R. W. to Ellen Galloway 12-3-1856 (no return) F
Ingalls, William to Jennie Pyle 12-8-1864 Sh
Ingate, Fredrick to Judith M. Pope 7-3-1855 (7-4-1855) Sh
Ingelass (Ingles), Balthasar to Bridgett Mize (Musse) 2-28-1842 Sh
Ingle, Franklyn to Caroline Threlkill 11-7-1862 Mn
Ingle, J. A. to E. J. Holmes 11-20-1868 (11-22-1868) Cr
Inglish, John to Samantha Williams 4-19-1863 Mn
Ingraham, Thomas J. to Nancy J. Powell 11-5-1855 (11-14-1855) G
Ingram, A. C. to China Green 8-18-1846 Cr
Ingram, Chapman to Rebecca Mays 4-14-1866 G
Ingram, Clemons to Catharine C. Breaden 3-9-1854 Sh
Ingram, Daniel to Ann Elisa Overton 10-16-1878 Hy
Ingram, David to Josephine Roberson 8-30-1882 (8-31-1882) L B
Ingram, Hendleton to Charlotte Dowell 12-10-1831 G
Ingram, James F. to Charity Springfield 6-29-1850 (6-30-1850) Hr
Ingram, James H. to Zaoda Alice Clark 1-12-1867 (no return) Hn
Ingram, James to Adaline Reece 4-4-1873 (4-5-1873) T
Ingram, James to Milly Bond 1-5-1876 (no return) Hy
Ingram, Jno. B. to Rachel Cole 11-14-1869 Hy
Ingram, John to Louisa Logan 9-18-1873 T
Ingram, John to Mary Hyett 7-17-1851 (7-20-1851) Sh
Ingram, Jordan to Lucy Haynes 6-19-1873 Hy
Ingram, Needham to Jane Simpson 12-18-1830 (12-23-1830) Hr
Ingram, Richard to Naomi A. Ashley 2-28-1856 Sh
Ingram, Ruben S. to Julia A. Mays 2-19-1850 G
Ingram, Samuel P. to Rebecca Scott 11-6-1841 (11-12-1841) Hr
Ingram, Samuel to Eliza Caplinger 2-28-1844 Hn
Ingram, Samuel to Sarah A. Reed 8-28-1860 G
Ingram, Thomas M. to Mary T. S. Jones 10-30-1850 (11-14-1850) Hr
Ingram, Thos. D. to M. J. Fletcher 11-13-1866 (11-14-1866) Cr
Ingram, W. C. to Sallie C. Gravette 1-25-1869 G
Ingram, Washington to Mary Parker 12-13-1869 (12-26-18689) F B
Ingram, William D. to Ann E. Woodruff 1-3-1854 G
Ingram, William to Jane Hays 8-11-1847 (11-11-1847) G
Ingram, Willis J. to Elenor E. Bourman 11-7-1844 (11-12-1844) G
Ingram, Wilson to Rebecca Ingram 12-4-1878 (no return) Hy
Ingram, Wm. M. to Allice M. Stainback 10-21-1867 (10-24-1867) F
Ingram, Wm. P. to Martha Harris 6-4-1849 (6-5-1849) F
Ingrim, M. H. to A. A. Moody 2-28-1861 Sh
Ings?, James to L. B. Epps 12-12-1874 T
Inman, D. M. to Ann E. Milsted 1-24-1860 Sh
Inman, D. R. to Christianna Chandler 1-7-1864 Mn
Inman, G. W. to E. A. Duncan 6-5-1855 Hn
Inman, George W. to Caroline Guill 10-5-1859 Hn

Inman, John F. to Martha Buchannan 11-11-1858 O
Inman, John to Eliza Jane Hale 7-14-1852 (7-16-1852) O
Inman, Nicholas F. to Margaret Jane Sinkler 1-2-1857 O
Inman, Rufus to Matilda Laum (Launy, Lawry?) 12-21-1854 L
Inman, Sam'l to Elizabeth Taylor 7-3-1852 (7-8-1852) Sh
Inman, T. R. to R. A. Boone 8-3-1865 O
Innes, Wm. W. to Martha A. Weed 8-9-1848 L
Innman, William S. to Mary E. Walton 9-28-1847 L
Inns, Charles to Rody Pitts 12-17-1870 Hy
Insco, J. W. to Julia A. Grimes 11-4-1861 (no return) We
Irbey, Silas C. to Jane C. House 12-15-1846 (12-22-1846) F
Irbey, W. L. to Bettie Rodgers 9-26-1866 T
Irby, Benjamin to Henrietta F. Anderson 10-15-1853 (10-18-1853) Sh
Irby, Edmond to Virginia A. Lundy 5-23-1853 Sh
Irby, Edward to Elizabeth R. Trigg 4-1-1859 (4-5-1859) Sh
Irby, Edward to Martha Harper 3-12-1851 (3-13-1851) Sh
Irby, Henderson A. to Nancy S. Gibson 4-10-1846 Sh
Irby, J. P. to Nancy J. York 1-16-1871 (no return) F
Irby, James H. to Mary J. Hicks 3-28-1860 Be
Irby, Jefferson to Lucinda Lee 7-31-1843 (no return) Hn
Irby, Silas R. to Nancy M. Irby 3-12-1847 (no return) F
Irion, John P. to Bettie Walters 1-21-1864 G
Irion, Thomas to Delila F. Baldwin 5-6-1851 Hr
Irion, William to Frances White 1-7-1851 (1-16-1851) Hr
Irion, Wm. M. to Mary A. Glasgow 3-19-1851 (3-20-1851) Sh
Irons, Cenica to Lucy Baltin 4-24-1877 Hy
Irons, George to Fanny Outerbridge 8-16-1867 Hy
Irons, Sam to _____ 8-7-1866 G
Irvin, B. D. to Agnes Moran 11-5-1856 We
Irvin, Daniel to Martha M. McGhee 7-22-1845 G
Irvin, James B. to Elizabeth White 12-14-1835 (12-15-1835) Hr
Irvin, James C. to Sarah Herryman 2-4-1836 Hr
Irvin, John S. to Eliza L. Beach 10-4-1866 Hn
Irvin, John to Susan Gidcum 9-1-1863 (no return) L
Irvin, Saml. to Susan W. Rainey 10-2-1837 (10-12-1837) Hr
Irvin, Samuel to Agnes King 1-13-1844 (1-14-1844) F
Irvin, Scott to Eady Haliburton 3-2-1875 Hy
Irvin, Simeon T. to Elizabeth L. Bates 1-28-1851 (1-29-1851) O
Irvin?, A. H. to M. J. Irvin 2-11-1860 T
Irvine, F. W. to Clemintine B. Carnes 11-16-1850 (12-18-1850) Hr
Irvine, Frank to Margarett White 2-26-1866 (no return) Cr
Irvine, R. N. to Nannie S. Winston 4-20-1853 We
Irvine, William to Sarah N. Via 3-27-1865 G
Irvine, Wm. to Mary Carr 5-11-1820 Sh
Ivy?, James H. to Martha E. Garrison 4-12-1844 (no return) F
Irwin, A. O. to Mary E. Griffith 1-15-1859 (1-20-1859) Sh
Irwin, Andrew to Margaret L. Chamberlin 8-31-1840 Sh
Irwin, Grandison to Octavia McNeill 11-10-1868 (11-11-1868) F B
Irwin, Green? L. to Cordelia L. Poiner 12-18-1844 Hr
Irwin, Hiram to Sarah Spears 11-30-1837 Sh
Irwin, James to Mary E. Farley 8-8-1857 (8-9-1857) Sh
Irwin, Jesse H. to Elizabeth Foster 7-20-1861 (7-22-1861) Hr
Irwin, Jesse R. to Margarett M. Miller 9-14-1844 (no return) F
Irwin, L. N. to Nettia West 2-1-1866 F
Irwin, Larkin H. to Martha J. Fargurgson 12-29-1853 G
Irwin, Randal M. to Augusta Trice 11-16-1854 Sh
Irwin, Samuel L. to A. M. Roach 5-24-1855 Sh
Irwin, Samuel L. to Sarah L. Roach 4-29-1847 F
Irwin, Thomas J. to Mary C. Pucket 4-23-1841 F
Irwin, Thomas J. to Nancy C. Mathis 2-5-1845 Hn
Irwin, Thos. to Mary McFee 11-12-1860 Sh
Irwin, William to Nancy Alexander 3-30-1841 (4-1-1841) F
Irwin, Wm. M. to Ruth Jones 6-24-1837 (6-26-1837) G
Isaacs, M. to Elizabeth Raphaelsky 9-20-1862 Sh
Isbell, Beverly to Sue Chaffin 9-26-1867 F B
Isbell, Daniel to Roanna Holloway 7-9-1870 F B
Isbell, George C. to Sally C. Branhama 11-3-1859 (11-10-1859) O
Isbell, Joe to Betty Clay 8-22-1876 L
Isbell, Johnson to Elizabeth H. Sloan 12-24-1834 (12-26-1834) G
Isbell, Johnson to Emilia Duncan 10-15-1827 Hr
Isbell, L. M. to Henrietta Goss 2-12-1859 (2-15-1859) Sh
Isbell, Nathaniel S. to Ally Hicks 11-4-1846 (11-9-1846) Hr
Isbell, R. H. to Elizabeth Hamm 4-24-1841 (4-29-1841) Hr
Isbell, Thomas D. to Frances E. Holyfield 11-10-1838 (11-13-1838) Hr
Isbell, Wm. to Mollie W. Kirby 3-4-1868 (3-5-1868) O
Isham (Eison), James to Kezia A. Green 3-3-1884 L
Isham, Byrd to Lue Soward 12-16-1885 (12-17-1885) L
Isham, Elijah to Charlotte Able 4-8-1847 (4-9-1847) F
Isham, Elijah to Mary L. Anderson 12-6-1841 Sh
Isham, G. A. to Sarah Simmons 1-8-1870 (1-13-1870) F
Isham, Sanders to Sarah C. Harrell (Howell?) 1-8-1873 (1-9-1873) L
Isla, William to Bell Sandeford 10-25-1866 G
Isler, John P. to R. R. Merriwether 12-7-1852 (12-21-1852) O
Isler, William B. to Margarett Meriwether 9-22-1847 (10-21-1847) O
Isnarde, Edward Sebastian to Stephanie Lambert 6-22-1861 Sh
Isom, John to Elisa Thomas 9-3-1828 Hr
Isom, W. C. to Mary A. E. Bennett 12-23-1851 (12-24-1851) Sh

Isom, W. C. to P. E. Appleberry 7-20-1864 (7-24-1864) F
Isom, William to Malissa Jones 4-23-1874 (4-24-1874) L B
Israel, John to Della Jeolson 5-7-1853 Cr
Ivans, Joseph to Mariah Robertson 7-1-1829 Sh
Ivens, Jerry to July Jones 7-31-1874 (8-1-1874) O
Ivers, Edward to Mary Hudgins 2-15-1862 Sh
Iverson, Captain to Dicey McNeal 7-14-1866 (7-15-1866) F B
Ivey, A. V. to Philadelphia F. Cooper 5-1-1847 (5-2-1847) F
Ivey, Enoch G. to Elizabeth O. Wade 8-15-1844 G
Ivey, Henry to Caroline Read 10-31-1871 Hy
Ivey, J. H. to Catharine O'Larry 7-2-1864 (7-11-1864) Sh
Ivey, Joseph to Mary Weddle 2-3-1877 Hy
Ivey, R. L. to Mary L. Barren 7-11-1865 F
Ivey, Robert D. to Mary E. Wade 11-19-1861 G
Ivey, Turner to Naomi Pender 7-31-1872 Hy
Ivie, Benjamin to Elizar Bishop 10-10-1859 We
Ivie, George W. to Mary N. Johnson 2-11-1867 (2-13-1867) Dy
Ivie, J. F. to Lucy F. Anderson 2-2-1865 Hn
Ivie, W. W. to Anna E. Moore 8-1-1866 G
Ivie, Washington to Elizabeth Mitchell 12-7-1846 (no return) F
Ivins, John to M. Cantrell 9-17-1845 We
Ivy, A. J. to Nannie J. Thompson 1-21-1867 (1-24-1867) F
Ivy, Benjamin W. to Mary C. House 7-12-1859 We
Ivy, Dawson to Rose Barbee 12-25-1866 (no return) Hy
Ivy, Isaac N. to Adella Jones 7-25-1882 (no return) L
Ivy, J. R. to Emily Brady 11-4-1866 G
Ivy, James to Carolina Souward 12-28-1842 Sh
Ivy, James to Rosanna Crowell 2-5-1840 Hn
Ivy, T. J. to Ana Sims 12-30-1876 (1-1-1877) L
Ivy, William H. to Ann D. Moore 7-22-1837 G
Ivy, Wyott to Nora Holloway 2-9-1870 (2-10-1870) F B
Izard, F. J. to Sarah E. Whittaker 5-2-1854 (no return) F

Jack, Daniel B. to Martha R. Ward 1-21-1871 (1-24-1871) F
Jack, Jas. A. to Nancy Wallice 2-10-1857 G
Jack, John N. to Winey Harrisson 9-1-1831 (9-4-1831) G
Jack, John S. to Ann A. Gage 2-10-1857 (2-11-1857) G
Jack, Samuel to M. A. Butler 2-16-1864 (2-17-1864) Sh
Jack, William C. to Malinda Glasscock 9-24-1831 (10-2-1831) G
Jack, William M. to Jane Cooper 11-15-1852 G
Jack, William to Eugenia Butler 2-16-1854 Sh
Jack, Wm. to Elizabeth W. Beckham 6-26-1868 (7-5-1868) F
Jackson, A. C. to Rosenah C. Outlaw 4-29-1862 Sh
Jackson, Aaron to Emeline Motley 1-13-1842 G
Jackson, Aaron to Willie Carlisle 3-14-1861 Sh
Jackson, Abram to Anna Molena 8-6-1874 O
Jackson, Andrew to Amy Shephard 3-13-1869 (3-15-1869) F
Jackson, Andrew to Ann Donelson 8-18-1867 G B
Jackson, Andrew to Annie Rayner 1-5-1869 Hy
Jackson, Andrew to Charity Martin 3-21-1878 Dy
Jackson, Andrew to Fannie Burnes 8-3-1871 (8-4-1871) T
Jackson, Andrew to Jane Allen 7-6-1850 (7-10-1850) Hr
Jackson, Andrew to Mary Ann Alexander 12-23-1867 (12-25-1867) T
Jackson, Andrew to Mary Jane Parmer 4-15-1852 We
Jackson, Andrew to Matilda Tisdale 12-27-1845 (9?-30-1845) Hr
Jackson, Andrew to Milly Freeman 10-3-1867 G B
Jackson, Andrew to Molly Rimpson(Simpson?) 7-5-1879 (7-10-1879) L
Jackson, Andrew to Sarah Shofner 2-25-1870 (2-26-1870) Cr
Jackson, Andrew to Sophia Smith 10-12-1870 Dy
Jackson, Andrew to Tempy Etheridge 11-7-1861 Mn
Jackson, Andy to Bettie Mayo 7-3-1868 (7-4-1868) F B
Jackson, Andy to E. Pearce 5-3-1870 G B
Jackson, Anthony to Rebecca A. Swor 9-29-1853 Hn
Jackson, Bedford to Lukky Williams 12-27-1869 T
Jackson, Bob E. to Sophia S. Marshall 3-17-1845 (no return) F
Jackson, C. B. to Elizabeth Freeman 12-13-1873 O
Jackson, C. L. to Lucy V. Rhoades 8-9-1869 (no return) Hy
Jackson, Calvin to Elizabeth A. Jeffers 1-22-1863 Mn
Jackson, Calvin to Martha Patridge 3-23-1852 Hr
Jackson, Calvin to Sarah Bass 10-22-1832 (10-31-1832) G
Jackson, Carroll to Sarah E. Roseman 10-27-1858 (10-28-1858) G
Jackson, Charles J. to Mary Sheen 7-16-1860 Sh
Jackson, Charles to Candis Nesbitt 1-28-1870 G B
Jackson, Charles to Evaline James 11-23-1877 (11-24-1877) Dy
Jackson, Charley to Mariah Boyd 3-16-1875 (3-17-1875) O
Jackson, Cincinnatus to Mary E. Alsobrook 5-27-1841 Sh
Jackson, D. H. to Mattie Glisson 3-28-1874 (4-12-1874) O
Jackson, Daniel N. to Ann E. Hall 11-3-1849 Sh
Jackson, Daniel to Mary Alexander 12-26-1872 T
Jackson, David R.? to Louisa E. McClinsley 4-10-1848 (4-13-1848) F
Jackson, David to Rachal Paine 11-15-1842 (11-17-1842) G
Jackson, Dennis to Julia Ann Porter 7-2-1869 (no return) F B
Jackson, Dickson to Tibatha Rasberry 11-5-1836 G
Jackson, E. J. to Martha S. Walter 12-3-1868 Cr
Jackson, E. to Ann E. Pinson 10-24-1867 Hn
Jackson, Ed to Jane Fox 7-28-1875 (7-29-1875) Dy
Jackson, Edmond S. to Rebecca B. Cothran 11-30-1866 (12-4-1866) F

Jackson, Edmund to Elizabeth Morton 4-4-1855 Hn
Jackson, Edward to Margaret Howell 1-2-1868 Hy
Jackson, Eli to Margarett James 2-22-1838 (2-27-1838) G
Jackson, Elias to Marion W. Hess 10-9-1854 (10-11-1854) G
Jackson, Elisha to Jane Williams 4-17-1872 (4-18-1872) Dy
Jackson, Elisha to Martha Gauldin 12-25-1871 (no return) Dy
Jackson, F. M. to M. J. Throgmorton (no date) (with 1866) O
Jackson, Frederick S. to Susa C. Malone 5-17-1841 (5-20-1841) F
Jackson, G. W. to Jane Wilkins 6-10-1876 (6-11-1876) Dy
Jackson, Gabriel to Susan Willis 11-20-1841 (11-23-1841) F
Jackson, Geo. W. to Clara A. Vaughan 1-7-1847 (1-14-1847) F
Jackson, Geo. W. to Kate O'Larry 1-26-1864 Sh
Jackson, George W. to C. C. Wynn 8-3-1853 Hn
Jackson, George W. to Eliza J. Kirk 4-27-1866 O
Jackson, George W. to Sarah Upchurch 11-1-1854 Hn
Jackson, George to Celie Campbell 7-5-1876 Hy
Jackson, George to Elizabeth A. Pilkinton 7-14-1861 We
Jackson, George to Fannie Parks 12-5-1874 Hy
Jackson, George to Mary Ann Herron 9-20-1860 Dy
Jackson, Halcum to Sarah F. Sherfield 8-16-1856 (8-14?-1856) O
Jackson, Hardin to Mary Ditto 2-29-1866 Hy
Jackson, Harmon O. to Cinderralla Hunnell 11-30-1833 (12-4-1833) Hr
Jackson, Harmon to Elizabeth Brannon 12-28-1853 (12-29-1853) Hr
Jackson, Harvey to Cornelia Bryant 2-6-1844 G
Jackson, Henry G. to Aramenta Malone 11-19-1838 Sh
Jackson, Henry to Elizabeth Moon(Moor) 8-2-1832 Hr
Jackson, Henry to Emma Rice 4-28-1871 Hy
Jackson, Henry to Louisa Blake 5-28-1869 (5-29-1869) Cr
Jackson, Henry to Patience Bolling 3-17-1866 (3-21-1866) F B
Jackson, Henry to Priscilla Davis 10-16-1867 (no return) L
Jackson, Howell E. to Sophia Molloy 5-31-1859 Sh *
Jackson, Isaac to Ann Kingm 2-14-1864 O
Jackson, Isaac to Betsy Brooks(Polk?) 10-22-1828 (10-29-1828) Hr
Jackson, Isaac to Margaret Herron 4-28-1860 (4-29-1860) Dy
Jackson, J. A. to M. A. Williams 5-1-1866 (5-3-1866) O
Jackson, J. D. to Elizabeth Wasden 8-6-1864 Sh
Jackson, J. D. to Paralee Brant 2-8-1871 (2-10-1871) Dy
Jackson, J. M. to Annie White 4-29-1868 (no return) Dy
Jackson, J. M. to Hettie Bunks 5-29-1863 (6-2-1863) Dy
Jackson, J. R. to Donie Yates 10-3-1870 (no return) Dy
Jackson, J. W. to C. A. Strouse 12-12-1865 (12-16-1865) Cr
Jackson, J. W. to Queen E. Ethridge 8-21-1862 Hn
Jackson, J. to Mary Taylor 5-16-1872 (7-24-1872) T
Jackson, Jack G. to M. E. (Mrs.) Towns 12-1-1868 G
Jackson, James A. to Barbra Cantwell? 11-26-1845 (11-27-1845) Hr
Jackson, James A. to Judy Ann Bowles 1-11-1841 Hn
Jackson, James C. to Tommy Colmer 12-11-1869 (12-14-1869) T
Jackson, James D. to Susan F. Williams 1-19-1860 G
Jackson, James F. to Mary Ann Perutes? 7-12-1848 (no return) Hn
Jackson, James L. to Mary C. Stockard 12-5-1861 G
Jackson, James M. to Lydia Candace Jackson 8-12-1870 G
Jackson, James M. to Mary M. Glidwell 5-5-1856 (5-13-1856) Hr
Jackson, James N. to Sarah E. Tims 2-15-1848 Hr
Jackson, James T. to Elizabeth Gather 4-18-1845 G
Jackson, James T. to Malinda Jane Gregg 12-6-1857 Sh
Jackson, James W. to Mary A. Davis 9-2-1861 O
Jackson, James to Artilia Ann Foster 6-22-1853 Cr
Jackson, James to Harriett Buck 9-3-1855 Cr
Jackson, James to Honell M. Bush 9-3-1856 Cr
Jackson, James to Louisa Anderson 11-21-1861 Mn
Jackson, James to Mary Rains 9-14-1850 Sh
Jackson, James to Nancy Cary 4-26-1848 (4-27-1848) O
Jackson, James to Nancy J. Finley 12-9-1863 Hn
Jackson, James to Pennelope Williams 7-12-1860 We
Jackson, Jerry to Elizabeth Golding 8-29-1868 (8-30-1868) L B
Jackson, Jesse A. to Mary E. Lambe 12-24-1845 Sh
Jackson, Jesse B. to Elizabeth Milstead 8-3-1856 Hn
Jackson, Jobe to Ledla? Rosanna Bell 9-6-1850 Cr
Jackson, John A. to Mary A. Dodson 9?-17-1853 (no return) F
Jackson, John B. to Elizabeth A. Nelson 1-27-1855 Cr
Jackson, John F. to Elizabeth Cox 12-23-1840 Hn
Jackson, John W. to Julia C. Young 1-12-1867 (1-13-1867) T
Jackson, John to Evaline Statham 3-11-1865 (3-13-1865) O
Jackson, John to Fanny Gambell 4-18-1845 (4-25-1845) Hr
Jackson, John to Lenorah Pardue 5-30-1861 O
Jackson, John to Lucenda Elder 11-21-1831 G
Jackson, John to Nancy Hill 8-11-1851 Hr
Jackson, John to Susan Ann Porter 4-6-1867 (4-14-1867) F B
Jackson, Jones to Elizabeth Butler 11-6-1845 Cr
Jackson, Jordan to Ann Brown 1-21-1843 Hy
Jackson, Joseph A. to Bettie W. Campbell 12-7-1868 (12-8-1868) L
Jackson, Joseph to Mary Morrow 1-13-1845 F
Jackson, L. H. to Emeline Walker 7-21-1856 Hy
Jackson, L. H. to T. C. Leath 1-11-1873 (1-12-1873) Dy
Jackson, Lyman to Alcy Blakemore 5-5-1866 G
Jackson, M. L. to Priscilla J. Hammon 3-11-1850 F
Jackson, Mark to Priscilla Moore 9-14-1841 (no return) Hn

Jackson, N. G. to Frances Wallis 12-24-1855 G
Jackson, Needham to Hannah Casy 1-25-1834 (1-26-1834) Hr
Jackson, P. H. to Edna K. Bullington 2-9-1869 G
Jackson, P. H. to Eliza W. Shane 1-3-1859 (1-4-1859) G
Jackson, P. H. to Eugenia Jackson 2-7-1870 (2-9-1870) L
Jackson, Peter Simpson to Mary Eliz. McBride 12-3-1855 (12-6-1855) T
Jackson, R. J. to Nancy Robins 11-14-1878 Hy
Jackson, R. K. to Amanda J. Dodd 4-16-1857 We
Jackson, Rev. G. W. to Henrietta Ross 1-16-1872 Hy
Jackson, Richard C. to Mary A. Birmingham 6-22-1861 (6-23-1861) O
Jackson, Robert D. to Melinda King 10-5-1835 Hr
Jackson, Robert H. to Sarah E. Nobles 9-1-1867 Hy
Jackson, Robert to Catherine Tincle 1-14-1837 (1-15-1837) G
Jackson, Robert to Levica Hall 9-6-1853 Be
Jackson, Robert to Nancy Winsett 11-8-1860 Sh
Jackson, Robert to S. E. Croutch 2-4-1866 Hn
Jackson, Robert to Sarah Jane White 10-21-1866 Hy
Jackson, Robert to Sarah Stuckey 6-10-1864 (12-23-1864) L
Jackson, Robt. T. to Mary J. Bruce 7-28-1845 (7-30-1845) F
Jackson, Robt. to Margaret Wyatt 8-27-1839 Be
Jackson, Ruffin to Hanna Johnson 12-?-1866 T
Jackson, Ruffin to Laura Taylor 11-11-1871 T
Jackson, S. A. to Margaret Cooper 11-7-1857 Cr
Jackson, S. A. to Molly Brown 4-12-1866 (5-13-1866) O
Jackson, S. K. to Susan P. Howell 12-14-1870 (12-15-1870) Dy
Jackson, S. N.? to Edna C. Diggs 11-29-1865 Hn
Jackson, Sam to Cary Holmes 3-18-1869 F B
Jackson, Samuel D. to Elizabeth P. Taylor no date (1838-1852) Hn
Jackson, Samuel H. to Mary Jane Price 11-6-1850 O
Jackson, Samuel T. to Clementine T. Covington 1-13-1859 We
Jackson, T. H. to Sophia R. D. Frierson 8-11-1851 (8-12-1851) Sh
Jackson, T. M. to E. F. Bishop 12-16-1849 Cr
Jackson, T. M. to L. J. Fuller 12-19-1874 (12-20-1874) Dy
Jackson, T. W. to S. J. Dial 8-24-1865 G
Jackson, Thomas B. to Ellen Hart 8-10-1852 Hn
Jackson, Thomas C. to Clarinda Hunter 12-11-1858 Hn
Jackson, Thomas N. to Mary Walker 2-16-1841 Hn
Jackson, Thomas P. to Elizabeth Allman 3-5-1856 Hn
Jackson, Thomas P. to Sarah Allman 1-16-1846 Hn
Jackson, Thomas to Harriet Polk 10-17-1874 (10-28-1874) T
Jackson, Thomas to June Wynn 11-14-1850 Hn
Jackson, Thos. D. to Susan Coleman 1-15-1857 O
Jackson, Thos. S. to Mary Harris 5-26-1845 (no return) F
Jackson, W. B. to Eliza Ann Philips 5-23-1869 Hy
Jackson, W. H. to A. E. Bricken 6-24-1861 Mn
Jackson, W. H. to Elizabeth Allen 3-10-1864 Sh
Jackson, W. H. to Lillie (Mrs.) Thompson 2-7-1864 Sh
Jackson, W. Harrison to Harriet Ivey 9-22-1867 Hy
Jackson, W. J. to L. V. Reeves 7-7-1865 O
Jackson, W. T. to Susan H. Crowder 10-7-1867 (10-10-1867) Cr
Jackson, William A. to Mary E. Roberts 1-18-1863 Hn
Jackson, William B. to Rachel E. Horne 12-18-1849 (12-20-1849) T
Jackson, William E. to Mary A. Umstard 8-12-1846 G
Jackson, William F. to Mary A. Walker 6-22-1853 (6-23-1853) G
Jackson, William F. to Mary Dickinson 6-8-1863 G
Jackson, William H. to Louiza Foster 12-26-1855 (12-27-1855) G
Jackson, William J. to Elizabeth Wynn 3-1-1849 Hn
Jackson, William to Ann Logan 4-22-1852 Sh
Jackson, William to Candis Dial 2-15-1866 G
Jackson, William to M. C. Fuller 2-15-1865 (2-16-1865) Dy
Jackson, William to Margaret A. Shivers 12-18-1849 Sh
Jackson, William to Margaret Somervill 12-29-1866 (12-31-1867?) T
Jackson, William to Mariah Parks 11-16-1872 (11-18-1872) Dy
Jackson, William to Mary Smith 2-6-1867 F B
Jackson, William to Nancy Enix? 5-12-1858 Hn
Jackson, William to P. A. Baker 9-5-1846 (no return) Hn
Jackson, William to Polly A. Lacy 1-6-1837 (1-10-1837) G
Jackson, Wm. H. to Mary E. Letsinger 11-13-1849 Cr
Jackson, Wm. to Jane Morgan 4-19-1848 Sh
Jackson, Zachy G. to Sarah J. Fite 12-16-1856 (12-18-1856) G
Jacob, John Wesley to Nancy hopper 4-8-1850 Cr
Jacob, William P. to Margrett D. Little 5-27-1840 (6-25-1840) G
Jacobi, J. C. to Amanda Pollock 1-9-1855 (1-11-1855) Sh
Jacobs, A. W. to Susan Birdwell 12-9-1869 G
Jacobs, Caleb to Charlotte Taylor 12-24-1866 (12-25-1866) T
Jacobs, Charles W. to Kate P. Bond 1-1-1878 Hy
Jacobs, F. W. to Ellen Clark 6-8-1864 (6-9-1864) Sh
Jacobs, Green to Mary Ann H. Wallingsford 10-21-1834 (10-23-1834) G
Jacobs, Henry to Jane Dillard 5-14-1826 (5-15-1826) Hr
Jacobs, Henry to Mary Fortune 10-11-1854 (10-12-1854) Hr
Jacobs, Hugh to E. C. Reeves 10-8-1862 O
Jacobs, James M. to Martha Anderson 12-13-1843 (12-14-1843) Hr
Jacobs, James M. to Parmelia Harris 12-2-1858 (12-8-1858) Hr
Jacobs, John C. to Mary S. Sherrod 5-9-1859 (5-10-1859) T
Jacobs, John J. to Julia Ann Jordan 12-12-1859 (12-15-1859) Hr
Jacobs, John to Martha Lewis 12-9-1829 (12-10-1829) Hr
Jacobs, M. to M. F. Butler 1-1-1867 G

Jacobs, Newton D. to Louisa V. Childress 11-23-1870 G
Jacobs, Robert to Susan E. Hendrix 1-21-1863 (1-22-1863) O
Jacobs, Rufus P. to Susan E. Thum 3-5-1866 (3-7-1866) L
Jacobs, Solomon to Olive Crawford 1-30-1838 (2-1-1838) Hr
Jacobs, W. E. to Sally Butler 12-22-1869 G
Jacobs, W. G. to Mollie O. Childress 10-4-1866 G
Jacobs, W. W. to B. C. Jones 3-9-1859 Sh
Jacobs, William R. to Jinnetta A. Fortune 12-10-1855 (12-13-1855) Hr
Jacobs, William R. to Martha Whitaker 12-17-1849 (12-20-1849) Hr
Jacobs, William to Sarah Bass 8-4-1824 Hr
Jacocks, J. T. to Julia A. Brummett 3-13-1875 (no return) Hy
Jacocks, Jesse to Tamar Taylor 2-24-1875 Hy
Jacocks, Martin to Marthy Jane Taylor 1-18-1877 Hy
Jacocks, Thos. to Susan Green 1-3-1878 (no return) Hy
Jahuka, John to Lettie King 4-25-1859 Sh
Jaines, Benj. B. to Amanda Weed 9-26-1853 Sh
Jamerson (Gimmerson), J. G. W. to Sarah Baker 3-14-1848 (3-21-1848) O
Jamerson, B. B. to Mary Tayler 4-15-1861 (4-17-1861) Cr
Jamerson, R. B. to Mary Taylor 4-15-1861 (4-17-1861) Cr
James (Johns?), James to Elizabeth Johnson 1-29-1853 L
James, Allen C. to Nancy Rains 7-29-1850 (8-1-1850) G
James, Allen to Della Watkins 12-15-1868 G
James, B. C. to L. C. Hurley 1-23-1862 Mn
James, B. F. to Elizabeth Hollingsworth 10-18-1856 (10-19-1856) Sh
James, Benjamin F. to Ellen Smith 9-24-1852 (9-28-1852) G
James, Buckhanan to Jula Ann Poyner 12-20-1845 (12-23-1845) Hr
James, C. P. to Dilly Polk 9-17-1849 (no return) F
James, D. Glasgow to Louisa G. Ball 4-18-1855 Sh
James, D. J. to Sarah Fillingham 6-24-1851 Sh
James, David C. to Mollie Gillis 1-16-1867 Dy
James, David H. to Margaret H. Cox 2-12-1849 (2-13-1849) G
James, Elias to Amelia Crowder 1-14-1869 (1-16-1869) F B
James, F. M. to H. A. O. Daniel 7-2-1858 G
James, Geo. W. to Matilda J. Creighton 5-12-1851 (5-14-1851) Sh
James, H. W. to S. E. Jeanes 6-18-1863 Mn
James, Henry F. to Caledonia Pope 1-?-1864 (1-15-1864) Sh
James, Henry F. to Matilda Lee 9-30-1824 Sh
James, Henry to Martha J. Whitfield 5-26-1862 Sh
James, Holland Y. to H. C. Waldrup 1-23-1847 (no return) Hn
James, Isaac to Affey A. Slaydon 6-29-1858 G
James, Isham to Lethe E. Golden 8-24-1868 (no return) Dy
James, J. M. to E. P. Reed 4-11-1871 (4-12-1871) Dy
James, J. P. to Fannie S. Dodd 8-18-1863 L
James, J. P. to S. P. Gilliam 3-15-1866 G
James, J. W. to B. A. Taylor 9-25-1857 (no return) We
James, James B. to Francis Patterson 5-5-1862 (5-10-1862) Sh
James, James D. to Artemicia Robertson 1-12-1840 Hn
James, James to Mahala Upchurch 6-2-1851 Hn
James, Jenning? to Fanny Nash 1-22-1867 (1-20?-1867) Dy
James, Jessie to Harriet C. Travis 10-8-1847 Hn
James, Jim to Margaret Taylor 7-4-1873 T
James, John D. to Kate Wheatley 5-18-1863 (5-21-1863) Sh
James, John L. to Mary Atkinson 5-19-1867 G
James, John M. to Eliza J. Lankford 4-15-1877 Dy
James, John S. to Martha S. Futrell 11-29-1838 Hn
James, John T. to Parile Cathery 9-3-1857 We
James, John W. to Lucenda D. McWherter 12-6-1837 G
James, John W. to Mary N. Bradford 9-28-1859 G
James, John to A. E. Hayes 12-22-1870 (no return) Hy
James, John to Fannie Burnes (Burrus) 3-26-1874 O
James, John to Martha Bailey 12-14-1868 (12-17-1868) F
James, John to Nancy Ann Pennington 6-22-1878 (6-23-1878) Dy
James, John to Rachel Ferguson 1-4-1844 Sh
James, Joseph B. to Massey Lavinia Pennell 5-18-1849 (not executed) T
James, Joseph B. to Sarah T. Scott 9-6-1849 Sh
James, Joseph to Mary Mathis 6-13-1866 G
James, Lewis to Louisa Mays 1-22-1868 G B
James, Madison to Adelphi A. Lankford 12-25-1869 (12-26-1869) Dy
James, Milton to Nancy Wilson 5-11-1861 (5-12-1861) O
James, Nathan to Jane Smith 6-30-1869 G
James, Perley to Lucinda Parish 5-11-1846 T
James, Perley? to Sarah Eliz. Roberts 10-25-1852 (10-31-1852) T
James, R. A. to S. J. Curtis 7-10-1878 L
James, R. C. to Elizabeth Broadway 6-17-1857 We
James, Reason I. to Martha J. Pratt 6-9-1861 G
James, Robert B. to Mary C. James 8-19-1855 G
James, Robert N. to Martha A. M. James 12-9-1850 G
James, Robert R. to C. S. Thomas 10-19-1874 (10-21-1874) T
James, Solomon to Sukey Egglestin 12-27-1867 (12-30-1867) L B
James, Thomas E. to Adaline Hellard 3-31-1868 G
James, Thomas to Annie James 12-31-1860 (1-1-1861) Sh
James, Thomas to Jamie (Jennie?) Neeley 2-2-1876 (2-4-1876) L B
James, Thomas to Jane G. Lacy 11-1-1836 Hr
James, Thomas to Louisa A. A. Miller 9-18-1855 (9-19-1855) Sh
James, Thomas to Margaret R. Dunlap 7-11-1843 (7-13-1843) G
James, Thomas to Maria L. Krafft 3-4-1858 Sh
James, Thompson to Amanda Gill 10-16-1840 (no return) F

James, William A. to Sarah Woods 1-17-1866 Hn
James, William G. to Barbary J. Harpoll 1-4-1843 (1-5-1843) G
James, William M. to Fredonia Underwood 10-29-1851 Sh
James, William to Mary Mallery 5-7-1844 (5-21-1844) Hr
James, William to Sarah Barker 1-5-1836 Hr
James, William to Sarah E. Williams 3-13-1843 Hr
James, William to Susan Gilland 1-6-1863 (1-7-1863) Sh
James, Wm. B. to Frances Lea 11-30-1836 Hr
James, Wm. to Elizabeth Hurley 5-18-1863 (5-20-1863) Dy
Jameson, C. G. to Margaret Connell 11-4-1861 Hn
Jameson, C. K. to Adaline Taylor 2-24-1863 (no return) Cr
Jameson, Geo. W. to Sarah E. Pearce 7-27-1842 Sh
Jameson, James Harris to Mary Caroline Black 6-30-1846 T
Jameson, Jefferso to Rebecca Ann Turner? 12-13-1862 (no return) Hn
Jamey?, Geo. W. to Mary Bobett 4-12-1873 (4-16-1873) Dy
Jamison, A. T. to E. B. Williams 3-13-1869 (3-14-1869) Cr
Jamison, Alge to Harriet Peoples 12-13-1871 (no return) Cr
Jamison, C. K. to Adaline Taylor 2-24-1863 (no return) Cr
Jamison, J. L. to Sallie Dillahunty 12-15-1874 T
Jamison, James H. to Martha E. Farmer 4-23-1857 T
Jamison, Jarrett to Hanah Mathis 12-30-1869 G B
Jamison, Jordan to Gabella Ann Roberts 1-13-1870 T
Jamison, Jorden to Martha Hammett 7-6-1870 (7-10-1870) Cr
Jamison, Lewis C. to Rebecca J. Williams 1-29-1867 G
Jamison, Robert G. to Elizabet Ellen Smith 10-21-1869 T
Jamison, Robert to M. E. Johnson 11-14-1866 (11-15-1866) Cr
Jamison, Samuel to Martha A. (Mrs.) Goodman 10-11-1866 G
Jamison, Samuel to Mary A. Taylor 11-17-1853 Cr
Jamison, Thomas A. to Amanda Hill 4-3-1858 Cr
Jamison, William M. to Phoebe Ann Hunt 10-5-1855 (no return) Hn
Jamison?, George to Pamelia Trayler 10-20-1855 (10-25-1855) T
Janagin, Jeremiah to Mary Robinson 12-28-1847 Cr
Janell, J. Lewis to M. M. Booker 2-1-1858 G
Janes, Andrew F. to Martha Keith 5-15-1861 (5-16-1861) Hr
Janes, B. R. to Mary J. Eaves 1-3-1860 (1-4-1860) O
Janes, Benjamin S. to Elvira Jones 1-15-1859 We
Janes, Daniel W. to Elizabeth E. Bowden 12-19-1844 Hn
Janes, Elisha to Elizabeth Kenedy 6-17-1844 (no return) We
Janes, Levi to Lodusky Milan 7-22-1859 (no return) Hn
Janes, Miles B. to Sarah J. Thompson 9-24-1846 Hn
Janes, T. F. M. to Mary E. Valentine 3-18-1858 Hn
Janes, Thomas to Mary C. Dalton 9-4-1855 Hn
Jansen, Lewis to Caroline Newman 8-5-1853 (8-6-1853) O
January, W. H. to Carie L. Scales 5-14-1867 G
Japan, Stephen to Emily J. Tansil 9-19-1862 O
Jarel, John to Julia Armstrong 3-17-1845 Cr
Jarman, John to Martha Koonce 2-18-1840 Sh
Jarmon, Richard B. to Tebitha H. Kilpatrick 12-19-1829 (12-24-1829) Hr
Jarmon, Robert F. to Rosanna S. Jarmon 11-14-1845 (11-18-1845) Hr
Jarnigan, James to Jane Philips 10-21-1851 Hr
Jarratt, J. F. to P. J. Graves 1-16-1864 (no return) Cr
Jarratt, John A. to Harriet Neely 5-7-1857 Hr
Jarratt, William to Hannah Harris 11-11-1869 Hy
Jarrell, Calvin Z. to Isabella Thompson 1-12-1858 Be
Jarrell, John Q. to M. L. Loyd 11-25-1869 G
Jarrell, Melvin to Venia Allen 12-30-1875 (no return) L B
Jarrell, W. D. to Lamira Combs 3-6-1860 Be
Jarrell, William R. to Louisa Cash 12-22-1857 Hn
Jarrell, William to Lydia C. Sled 3-2-1854 Hn
Jarrett, Arch to Charlotte Campbell 12-19-1875 Hy
Jarrett, Babe to Ann Peebles 5-4-1870 Hy
Jarrett, Baily to Harriet Tugwell 4-3-1869 Hy
Jarrett, Clark to Mary Shaw 1-3-1885 (1-8-1885) L
Jarrett, David P. to Jane Newsom 4-10-1839 (no return) F
Jarrett, Gaston to Sarah H. Proctor 1-13-1876 (no return) Hy
Jarrett, Isham to Margaret Greaves 11-10-1878 Hy
Jarrett, J. T. to Nancy E. Smith 7-30-1857 Cr
Jarrett, J. T. to P. J. Graves 1-16-1864 (1-17-1864) Cr
Jarrett, J. W. to Mary Thompson 2-20-1872 (2-21-1871?) L
Jarrett, J. W. to Susan E. G. Lundal 12-10-1838 (12-12-1838) F
Jarrett, Jacob to Ellen Owen 9-6-1873 Hy
Jarrett, Jim to Mandy Bradford 2-1-1875 Hy
Jarrett, Jno. to Lyde L. Moore 2-7-1872 Hy
Jarrett, John A. to Jane C. Durrett 11-30-1842 (12-1-1842) Hr
Jarrett, John to Bet Tyus 2-5-1868 Hy
Jarrett, Jonathan to Curly Humphries 9-14-1845 Cr
Jarrett, Jordan to Hattie Thompson 1-25-1877 Hy
Jarrett, Nelson to Ellen Read 1-13-1866 Hy
Jarrett, Randell to Cordelia Minor 3-7-1874 Hy
Jarrett, Robert to Harriett Minor 4-21-1871 Hy
Jarrett, S. L. to M. A. Kelley 6-4-1873 Cr
Jarrett, W. S. to Bettie Talleferro 12-24-1878 Hy
Jarrett, Wm. D. to Mary Lacy 12-22-1871 (12-23-1871) Cr
Jarried, A. C. to Martha Kemp 4-17-1852 Cr
Jarrott, Lem to Nancy Humphrey 7-7-1841 Cr
Jarvis, David W. to Alley M. Edmundson 7-2-1844 (7-4-1844) G
Jarvis, George W. to Eliza Taylor 3-20-1855 (3-29-1855) O

Grooms

Jarvis, John E. to Adeline E. Petty 1-5-1864 G
Jarvis, Phillip D. to Anna J. Campbell 11-15-1870 G
Jarvis, Regis to Parella Yarbrough 1-5-1836 Hr
Javan, H. Maddox to Sary E. Turk 4-21-1852 O
Jay, M. S. to Elisabeth Lowrey 1-21-1861 (2-17-1861) Sh
Jaycocks, J. T. to A. S. Bettis 4-25-1866 (no return) Dy
Jayroe, Henry to Maria Hurdle 5-22-1873 (no return) L B
Jayroe, Henry to Mary Ann Oldham 6-24-1882 L
Jean, Francis A. to Hannah A. Brant 9-16-___ (9-17-1857) L
Jeanes, Bassel to Jane C. Griffith 3-6-1870 (5-9-1870) T
Jeanes, J. L. to Nancy E. Robinson 3-6-1865 Mn
Jefferds, J. Manly to M. J. Larisson 12-15-1859 (12-19-1859) Sh
Jefferies, John M. to Isabella Harrison 1-19-1871 Hy
Jefferies, W. P. to Jennie Rooks 1-17-1872 Hy
Jeffers, Sina to Prudy Pibus 12-25-1873 Hy
Jeffers, Wilson J. to Laura Bell Majors 9-14-1863 Sh
Jefferson, Adam to Susan Farrar 12-19-1866 (no return) F B
Jefferson, Andy to Ruthy Hilliard 8-17-1869 (8-18-1869) F B
Jefferson, John to Leana Marshall 1-28-1871 (no return) F B
Jefferson, Redman to Jennie A. Barnes 10-8-1871 Hy
Jefferson, Redmond to Eliza White 4-18-1872 (4-22-1872) Dy
Jefferson, Redmond to Susan Coker 10-13-1874 Hy
Jefferson, W. H. to Sai Coker 7-8-1877 Hy
Jeffres, George to Ella Allison 3-8-1875 (no return) Hy
Jeffress, Wm. B. to Nancy C. Dodds 11-21-1846 (no return) We
Jeffrey, Joseph to Mary E. Hooper 9-1-1863 L
Jeffreys, Edward to Penelope Simmons 4-8-1835 (4-13-1835) G
Jeffreys, George to Angeline Joyner 12-29-1875 (no return) Hy
Jeffries, Frank to Puss Mann 8-2-1878 (no return) Hy
Jeffries, G. C. to Sallie L. Richardson 10-4-1877 Hy
Jeffries, Jacob to Lou Bowers 2-23-1878 (2-24-1878) L
Jeffries, James A. to Mary J. T. Posey 1-21-1867 L
Jeffries, John E. to Martha Capps 12-9-1840 F
Jeffries, John to Estell Henley 1-26-1875 (1-27-1875) L
Jeffries, Robt. to Fannie Desberry 11-23-1876 L
Jeffries, W. R. to Mary M. Bradford 11-30-1876 L
Jeggetts, Francis W. to Mary A. Carr 9-11-1855 Sh
Jehl, Charles to M. E. Oakley 7-8-1861 G
Jelks, Cisero to Harriet Mayfield 12-26-1871 Hy
Jelks, George to Cherry Manning 5-8-1873 (no return) Hy
Jelks, John A. to Elizth. Guarrant 11-25-1844 (no return) F
Jelks, Peter to Tilda Bradford 8-14-1873 (no return) Hy
Jelks, Solomon to Eliza Moody 10-26-1869 (no return) Dy
Jelks, Solomon to Katy Maclin 7-4-1873 (no return) Hy
Jelts, Anthony to Ellen Greaves 8-18-1880 (8-20-1880) L
Jelts, Gilbert to Chany Roberson 7-21-1867 Hy
Jemerson, James M. S. to Mary Jane Ayres 10-4-1838 F
Jemison, G. W. to E. A. Wicker 3-21-1866 O
Jenkins (Jennings?), William B. to Lucinda Rush (Rust?) 9-23-1854 (9-24-1854) L
Jenkins, A. B. to Martha Bickel 3-12-1864 Sh
Jenkins, A. R. (or R. A.) to Syrenie E. Stuckey 10-6-1869 L
Jenkins, Abraham to Luncinda Price 11-9-1840 (11-12-1840) F
Jenkins, Absolom D. to Lovey Martin 8-31-1850 Sh
Jenkins, Ben to Celia Ward 3-25-1880 L B
Jenkins, Benjamin to Elizabeth Given? 3-26-1873 (3-28-1873) L B
Jenkins, C. T. to Ellen S. Jacobs 2-12-1879 F
Jenkins, Charley to Amanda Spencer 9-28-1871 Hy
Jenkins, Columbus to Harriet Smith 11-11-1873 (11-12-1873) T
Jenkins, Columbus to Mattie Smith 11-21-1884 (11-30-1884) L
Jenkins, D. P. to L. A. Scott 1-21-1861 (1-24-1861) Cr
Jenkins, Daniel C. to Mary E. Custer 12-20-1859 (no return) We
Jenkins, David P. to Mildred A. Elum 1-9-1844 (1-11-1844) G
Jenkins, Ed D. to Mary Pickett 9-23-1844 (9-26-1844) F
Jenkins, Elisha to Margaret Fullerton 12-28-1870 (12-29-1870) Dy
Jenkins, Henry S. to Fanny J. McDougle 5-22-1859 We
Jenkins, Henry to Mary Whitesell 12-29-1843 (no return) We
Jenkins, J. A. to Addie Brummett 12-6-1870 (no return) Hy
Jenkins, J. G. to Mary Brown 12-19-1851 Cr
Jenkins, J. L. to A. M. Prewett 12-24-1860 Hr
Jenkins, James D. to Margaret E. Davis 12-18-1856 Hn
Jenkins, James G. to Eleanor Terry 8-9-1830 Hr
Jenkins, James L. to M. E. Blain 11-6-1865 (no return) F
Jenkins, James M. to Mary J. Meadows 8-5-1862 (8-7-1862) L
Jenkins, James R. to Frances A. Williams 11-13-1866 L
Jenkins, James to Nancy J. Harlow 4-4-1855 Hn
Jenkins, John N. to Susan Fulgham 9-5-1826 Hr
Jenkins, John W. to Martha Ann Pentecost 2-13-1845 We
Jenkins, John W. to Mary E. Lindsey 9-17-1872 (9-19-1872) T
Jenkins, John W. to Nancy Ann McMackens 10-4-1869 (10-28-1869) Cr
Jenkins, John to Nancy Reaves 7-26-1846 Hn
Jenkins, John to Rebecca Ballard 1-12-1849 Sh
Jenkins, Jos. A. to Mildred A. Halliburton 12-10-1879 L
Jenkins, Joseph F. M. to Elizabeth Bradshaw 1-21-1866 Hn
Jenkins, Joseph to Sarah Lee 1-2-1865 (no return) Cr
Jenkins, R. G. to Ma_ L. Buckner 4-10-1876 (4-11-1876) L
Jenkins, S. D. to E. M. Roberson 11-26-1873 L
Jenkins, S. D. to Mary E. Bates (Batey?) 10-5-1864 (10-6-1864) L
Jenkins, Silas to Selah Ann Newton 4-29-1849 Hn
Jenkins, Thomas to Mary A. C. Hernden? 11-30-1851 Hn
Jenkins, Thomas to Caroline S. C. Roberts 12-6-1841 (12-15-1841) Hr
Jenkins, Thomas to Sarah Smith 1-28-1857 Hn
Jenkins, Tom to Elizer Ward (Wood?) 7-24-1866 G
Jenkins, W. C. to E. L. Blain 3-3-1868 (3-5-1868) F
Jenkins, W. H. to Roena M. Meeks 5-2-1853 (5-10-1853) Hr
Jenkins, W. J. to M. F. Smith 5-24-1880 (5-25-1880) L
Jenkins, W. W. to S. E. R. Jenkins 2-10-1867 Cr
Jenkins, William E. to Lucinda J. Martin 8-21-1859 Hn
Jenkins, William P. to Nancy Boothe 6-22-1838 Hn
Jenkins, Wm. C. to Penelope Sumner 12-21-1840 F
Jenkins, Wm. D. to E. E. Carter 2-6-1845 Cr
Jenkins, Young to Elizabeth Childers 9-2-1861 Hn
Jenne, Stephen to Louisa Simpson 10-11-1856 O
Jenning, Joseph H. to Margaret Higgins 2-5-1860 We
Jennings (Jinnans?), Joseph to Josephine Larrison 2-13-1873 (2-22-1873) L B
Jennings, Aaron to Caroline Dunlap 1-17-1885 (1-18-1885) L
Jennings, Alford to Jane (Mrs.) Bills 2-23-1864 (2-27-1864) Sh
Jennings, Azariah to Safronia E. Smith 7-30-1856 L
Jennings, Charles R. to Cermanthia Ann Stewart 6-10-1869 (6-16-1869) L
Jennings, D. F. to S. A. Barfield 2-11-1878 L
Jennings, D. H. to S. J. Norman 7-26-1884 (7-29-1884) L
Jennings, E. H. to Rachel Halliburton 6-12-1873 (no return) L B
Jennings, G. B. to Sarah Ann Maynard 12-6-1865 (12-7-1865) L
Jennings, G. B. to Tabitha A. Boydston 8-?-1862 L
Jennings, G. C. to Mary A. J. Dotson (Watson?) 2-3-1873 (2-12-1873) L
Jennings, Green B. to Mary E. Curtis 8-7-1852 (8-8-1852) L
Jennings, Green B. to Talitha A. Boydston 8-5-1862 (no return) L
Jennings, Green to Susan L. Brantly 11-1-1882 (11-2-1882) L
Jennings, J. B. to Laura Jackson 10-23-1868 (no return) Dy
Jennings, J. R. D. to Joella Ray 6-9-1877 (6-14-1877) L
Jennings, Joseph to Josephine L. Espary 2-12-1879 L
Jennings, Richard C. to Rachel E. Carson 7-17-1868 (7-19-1868) L
Jennings, Robert J. to Harriet T. Anderson 5-17-1843 Sh
Jennings, Royal to Sarah C. Smith 11-20-1856 L
Jennings, S. A. to E. O. Cherry 6-7-1855 O
Jennings, Thomas to Catherine Grady 9-21-1863 Sh
Jennings, Thomas to Eliza Ann Maynard 7-18-1883 L
Jennings, Thomas to Sophronia J. Cook 4-20-1881 L
Jennings, Thos. to Talitha Lusk 9-18-1849 (9-19-1849) L
Jennings, W. J. to Julia G. Bradford 8-24-1868 (8-25-1868) Dy
Jennings, W. R. to M. E. Moore 1-15-1877 (1-16-1877) L
Jennings, William J. to Sarah J. Donaldson 2-9-1845 G
Jennings, Wm. to Martha Nearn 10-22-1840 L
Jenny, I. I. to Bregreta Iringlas 3-9-1844 Sh
Jentry, Samuel S. to Syntha A. Dotson 9-2-1861 (no return) We
Jerden(Jordan), W. N. to Rody Holland 8-16-1865 Be
Jericho, William to Margaret Snyder 10-24-1860 (10-25-1860) Sh
Jerman, Jefferson to Mary McKinsey 2-3-1826 (2-7-1826) Hr
Jernagun, William J. to Eliza Clark 12-20-1847 G
Jernigan, David J. to Martha J. Caraway 9-30-1844 (no return) F
Jernigan, James to Margaret A. Howell 2-27-1854 (3-2-1854) Hr
Jernigan, Thomas P. to Elizabeth R. Randle 4-4-1846 F
Jernigan, Thos. W. to Elizabeth J. Jones 3-31-1853 G
Jernigan, William C. to Mary Ann Taylor 8-16-1849 (8-19-1849) Hr
Jernigan, William H. to Dicy Moore 10-10-1840 Hr
Jernigan, Wrigdon to Martha Howard(Howell?) 1-28-1848 Hr
Jernigans, Wm. A. to Colistia A. White 6-14-1845 Sh
Jessen, J. to N. J. Paxton 10-22-1859 (10-25-1859) Sh
Jester, Andrew J. to Elizabeth M. Madison 9-16-1851 (9-17-1851) G
Jester, Charles B. to Mariah P. Sanders 8-5-1845 G
Jester, Joseph to Margart Layne 4-15-1871 (4-30-1871) L
Jeter, Albert G. to Sintha Comberford 6-9-1847 (no return) F
Jeter, Benj. W. to Sarah M. Busey 4-13-1868 (4-16-1868) L
Jeter, C. W. to Catherine A. Mann 11-14-1859 (no return) Hy
Jeter, Charles W. to Martha Garvin 12-28-1848 Sh
Jeter, Esquer to Harriet Wallace 12-1-1872 Hy
Jeter, J. E. to Mattie A. Lay 10-8-1866 Hy
Jeter, J. H. to Susannah U. Adams 7-21-1865 (no return) Hy
Jeter, James E. to Nannie Johnson 12-6-1869 (no return) Hy
Jeter, Jessee to C. M. Mitchell 12-2-1849 Hr
Jeter, Robert E. to F. Jones 2-20-1850 We
Jeter, Robert E. to Lucy A. Young 12-12-1856 We
Jeter, Squire to Amanda Woodson 8-19-1870 (no return) Hy
Jett, David to Hester Walker 1-30-1872 (no return) L B
Jett, John to Lucy Taylor 10-17-1871 Hy
Jett, Milton to Caroline Taylor 8-16-1867 Hy
Jett, Milton to Henrietta Taylor 5-26-1866 (6-2-1871?) T
Jett, Milton to Mollie Freeman 12-24-1869 Hy
Jett, T. H. R. to M. C. Utley 12-7-1844 Be
Jett, William R. to Angelina M. Vaden 5-26-1847 Sh
Jetten, Ed to Sallie Claybrook 2-18-1871 (no return) Hy
Jetton, C. A. W. to Nannie C. Allen 12-19-1878 Hy
Jetton, Daniel E. to Jestina Yates 7-22-1844 G
Jetton, Daniel E. to Martha McGee 7-9-1862 G

Jetton, I. N. to Fannie Cozart 1-12-1870 (no return) Hy
Jetton, Isaac L. to Lucreatia R. Sinclair 10-27-1853 G
Jetton, Jerry to Emiline Rucker 6-30-1866 (no return) Hy
Jetton, Lewis to Emily Buck 9-18-1871 Hy
Jetton, R. H. to S. A. Moore 10-18-1871 Hy
Jetton, R. L. to L. B. Lovett 9-2-1879 (9-10-1879) Dy
Jetton, R. N. to N. L. Boyett 10-13-1873 (10-16-1873) O
Jetton, William A. to Sallie C. Warren 11-23-1874 (11-24-1874) Dy
Jewell, James H. to Sarah M. Park 1-5-1850 (1-6-1850) Hr
Jewett, William F. to Sarah J. Vaughan 9-1-1842 Hn
Jimason, J. S. to Harriet M. Davis 10-16-1856 Sh
Jimerson, James G. to Elizabeth J. Oneal 10-3-1861 Mn
Jimerson?, James K. to Isabella Wicker 4-28-1857 O
Jimeson, S. to H. M. Ingram 12-1-1864 G
Jimmerson, James M. to Susan A. Dean 11-26-1873 (12-3-1873) T
Jimmerson, William to Mary Hubbard 7-5-1848 O
Jinkens, Isaac to Elizabeth Titus 5-4-1843 Sh
Jinkins, John M. to Arrena Mitchell 7-11-1861 We
Jinkins, John to Nancy Jackson 5-15-1847 Be
Jinkins, Lavander to Mary E. Barnes 1-27-1858 (1-28-1858) Sh
Jinkins, Levi to Mary Ann Nelson 5-19-1841 Sh
Jinkins, W. P. C. to Mary E. Brawner 5-10-1861 We
Job, C. M. to Margery E. Drown 6-2-1845 (no return) We
Job, C. M. to Margery E. Drown 6-2-1846 We
Job, P. D. to Mary C. Parks 3-12-1858 (3-16-1858) Hr
Job, Pleasant to Nancy Townsend 5-17-1832 Sh
Jobe, Benjamin N. to Julia N. Pillow 11-24-1863 Hn
Jobe, Benjamin to Julia A. Pillow 12-23-1863 (no return) Hn
Jobe, Henry C. to Amarintha Hudson 2-22-1858 (2-24-1858) Hr
Jobe, James T. to Maria Kirby 3-14-1867 Hn
Jobe, James to Milly A. Nored 3-19-1846 Hn
Jobe, Robert M. to Levina Rankin 1-12-1845 Hn
Jobe, Samuel M. to Fany J. Gayle 5-2-1855 (5-3-1855) Sh
Jobes, W. H. to Mary J. Vaughan 10-17-1874 (10-18-1874) Dy
Jobes, Wm. to Lucindy Priest 5-25-1848 Cr
Joeggy, Jno. Joseph to Henena R. Brogany? 2-3-1845 Sh
John, Bernard J. to Rica M. Kaufemann 4-21-1850 Sh
John, Jacob Peter to Mary E. Green 3-30-1852 We
John, Madison G. to Elizabeth V. Bullen 3-16-1843 O
Johnakin, J. N. to Mary Conner 11-8-1858 (11-9-1858) O
Johnes, Nathan to Martha Bernard 7-20-1867 T
Johns(t)on, John A. to Elizabeth Henderson 5-9-1848 O
Johns, B. F. to Eliza J. Williams 3-3-1863 G
Johns, C. F. to Sarah J. Fisher 10-11-1860 O
Johns, I. H. to Lula Stewart 1-10-1885 (1-11-1885) L
Johns, Jacob W. to Portia Ann E. Young 8-19-1868 G
Johns, James to M. Mitchum 5-10-1872 (5-12-1872) Cr B
Johns, R. D. to C. S. Argo 12-17-1872 (12-19-1872) Cr
Johns, R. W. to R. C. Hall 10-9-1866 G
Johns, S. B. to A. P. Keltner 12-22-1873 (12-23-1873) L
Johns, W. F. to Holen E. Dyer 1859 O
Johns, W. H. to Emily J. Mount 4-1-1861 G
Johnson, A. H. to Mary J. Abbott 11-15-1858 G
Johnson, A. J. to Mary A. Hood 4-15-1846 Cr
Johnson, A. J. to V. J. Nicholson 12-23-1865 (12-26-1865) F
Johnson, A. S. (Rev.) to Mattie J. Lucas 12-13-1875 (no return) L
Johnson, A. W. to R. A. Hasaway (Hataway?) 8-22-1866 G
Johnson, Aden to Matilda Ann Smith 10-1-1842 (10-6-1842) F
Johnson, Albert H. to Ceznshin P. Rop (Ross?) 12-12-1858 We
Johnson, Albert to Cynthia Cloyd 7-23-1870 (7-29-1870) F B
Johnson, Albert to M. J. Parker 12-25-1878 (12-26-1878) Dy
Johnson, Albert to Manerva Mann 12-25-1868 Hy
Johnson, Alex to Elen Orr 11-28-1865 (11-29-1865) Cr
Johnson, Alex to Fanny Estes 2-13-1879 L
Johnson, Alex to Lizzie Sherrill 6-19-1869 (6-20-1869) T
Johnson, Alexander to Melvina Brinkley 7-14-1846 We
Johnson, Alfred to Jane Bryant 5-31-1870 G
Johnson, Alfred to Lettie McClane 6-15-1867 (no return) F B
Johnson, Allen C. to Drusilla C. Walls 9-2-1857 Hn
Johnson, Allen jr. to Sarah J. McKinney 9-20-1871 (9-21-1871) Cr
Johnson, Allen to Clarissa Wynne 1-4-1873 (no return) Dy
Johnson, Alson Y. to Lucinda Swift 7-19-1846 Be
Johnson, Anderson to F. Lawson 1-9-1851 Hn
Johnson, Andrew J. to T. E. Broyle 12-23-1875 (no return) Hy
Johnson, Andrew to Alice Murray 1-10-1877 (1-11-1877) Dy
Johnson, Andrew to Annie Smith 7-12-1873 (7-13-1873) Dy
Johnson, Andrew to Charlotte Hurst 4-16-1868 G B
Johnson, Andrew to Lavenia Worsham 12-28-1869 (12-9?-1869) F B
Johnson, Andrew to Mariah Smith 2-5-1876 (no return) Hy
Johnson, Andrew to Nancy Conley 9-20-1883 (9-24-1883) L
Johnson, Andrew to Rosanna McNeel 7-3-1868 (7-4-1868) F B
Johnson, Andrew to Sela Evans 1-15-1878 Hy
Johnson, Anthony O. to Olive L. Collin 1-16-1850 Cr
Johnson, B. A. to Sarah J. Kerley 10-9-1860 Dy
Johnson, B. F. to Nancy Robinson 10-18-1859 (no return) Hy
Johnson, B. S. to Elizabeth F. Wood 4-19-1846 Sh
Johnson, B. W. to Mary A. Smith 9-31?-1854 Cr

Johnson, Ben to Elizabeth Casin 6-6-1878 (6-8-1878) L
Johnson, Ben to Henry Ann Fitzpatrick 1-16-1883 (no return) L
Johnson, Ben to Noel Taylor 1-1-1876 (no return) Hy
Johnson, Ben to Sarah Winters 12-23-1875 (no return) Hy
Johnson, Benj. F. to Louisa E. Gwin 10-12-1858 Cr
Johnson, Benjamin G. to Mary A. Clark 8-7-1847 (9-12-1847) Hr
Johnson, Berry to Nancy Read 6-10-1834 (6-12-1834) Hr
Johnson, Beverly to Lily Maclin 7-26-1867 (7-27-1867) T
Johnson, Beverly to Sophia Maclin 12-24-1869 (12-27-1869) T
Johnson, Bodley to Eliza B. Hampton 11-23-1846 (11-24-1846) F
Johnson, Bryant to Elizabeth Fish 5-9-1849 (5-17-1849) Hr
Johnson, Bryant to Susan J. Bell 1-9-1861 G
Johnson, C. A. to C. V. Gray 12-1-1874 T
Johnson, C. A. to M. W. Caskey 12-31-1870 (1-5-1871) T
Johnson, C. G. to A. C. King 7-2-1866 (7-3-1866) Dy
Johnson, C. G. to Mollie Pugh 2-2-1875 Dy
Johnson, C. to Mary Ann Oliver 2-26-1839 Cr
Johnson, Case to Wiry? Mabon 2-13-1870 (no return) Cr
Johnson, Cezar to Rhoda Simmons 2-8-1871 Hy
Johnson, Charles C. to Letitia Daley 5-5-1860 (5-6-1860) Sh
Johnson, Charles C. to Rose Bradford 9-23-1876 Hy
Johnson, Charles M. to Mary A. Pittman 1-24-1853 (1-27-1853) G
Johnson, Charles to Jane Roberson 12-23-1865 Mn
Johnson, Charlie to Lucinda Miligan 5-5-1884 (5-9-1884) L
Johnson, Claboarn to Martha Hood 10-7-1841 Cr
Johnson, Claiborne to Elizabeth Stewart 10-8-1834 Sh
Johnson, D. C. to N. M. Ostean 8-30-1862 (9-3-1862) O
Johnson, D. H. to Lizzie House 1-15-1863 Sh
Johnson, D. S. to Harriet Miller 9-8-1864 (9-9-1864) Sh
Johnson, Daniel to Sarah A. Watkins 2-11-1871 (2-16-1871) F B
Johnson, David B. to Margaret E. White 1-2-1855 F
Johnson, David H. to Elizabeth P. Allen 8-?-1842 (not endorsed) F
Johnson, David H. to Sarah A. Carraway 11-26-1845 (11-27-1845) F
Johnson, David T. to Sallie A. Christian 10-22-1849 Sh
Johnson, Dennis to Eliza Hoas 12-29-1875 (no return) L
Johnson, Dick to Henrietta Mathewson 12-23-1872 (12-27-1872) Cr B
Johnson, Dick to Mariah Rivers 2-9-1867 (2-10-1867) F B
Johnson, Dick to Mary Garmany 12-27-1866 G
Johnson, Drew to Mattie Lucas 12-20-1872 Hy
Johnson, E. G. to Mary J. Outerbridge 12-31-1851 (1-1-1852) L
Johnson, E. L. to C. A. Reasens? 7-15-1846 Hr
Johnson, E. R. to Fannie Eudaly 12-22-1875 Dy
Johnson, E. to Elzira Whittenton 8-2-1869 (12-28-1869) Dy
Johnson, Edmond to Sarah Ann (Mrs.) Robertson 7-13-1868 G B
Johnson, Eli to M. W. Frith 12-23-1868 (12-24-1868) Dy
Johnson, Elias to Frances Pearce 12-25-1860 (12-2?-1860) L
Johnson, Elisha T. to Catharine Downey 12-24-1844 F
Johnson, Emanuel to Dicy Johnson 3-31-1866 G
Johnson, F. A. to Martha E. Meeks 12-11-1865 Mn
Johnson, F. A. to Nora Rice 4-4-1885 (4-8-1885) L
Johnson, F. M. to Jane Caps 4-30-1855 Sh
Johnson, F. P. to Lacy J. Mitchel 7-15-1844 (no return) We
Johnson, Fields H. to Harriett E. Davis 3-6-1861 (3-7-1861) Hy
Johnson, Francis M. to Myra V. P. Fielder 9-8-1863 (no return) Dy
Johnson, Francis to Abby Foley 4-29-1843 Sh
Johnson, Frank to Ann Phillips 2-22-1867 (2-24-1867) F B
Johnson, Frank to Celia Bond 1-21-1877 Hy
Johnson, Frank to Louisa Oldham (not issued) Hy
Johnson, Frank to Louiza Oldham 8-13-1868 (8-15-1868) L
Johnson, Frank to Salina Marshall 12-30-1874 T
Johnson, Freeman to Laura Hawkins 8-5-1870 (no return) Cr
Johnson, Freeman to Sally Hammond 12-28-1866 G
Johnson, G. L. to Nancy C. Lewis 11-27-1865 (11-28-1865) L
Johnson, G. T. to N. E. Crawford 11-27-1865 (11-30-1865) F
Johnson, G. W. S. to Mary Stidham 1-8-1845 (1-9-1845) F
Johnson, Gaines to Sarah Dortch 1-2-1869 F B
Johnson, Geo. T. to Fannie Hurt 11-29-1877 Dy
Johnson, Geo. to Leathy Washington 12-12-1872 Hy
Johnson, Geo. to Sue Byars 11-29-1872 Hy
Johnson, George A. to A. E. Buckner ?-?-1841 Cr
Johnson, George Anderson to Jane Hall 5-5-1873 T
Johnson, George F. to Jane Johnson 7-6-1844 (no return) F
Johnson, George W. to Mary A. Chambers 11-30-1870 Cr
Johnson, George to Alice Young 11-12-1874 L B
Johnson, George to Emma Light 9-16-1870 Dy
Johnson, George to Ernesta? Bledsoe 4-6-1867 (4-7-1867) T
Johnson, George to Martha Rush 5-18-1853 T
Johnson, George to Mary E. Huzzy 7-17-1852 O
Johnson, George to Susan Arnold 3-30-1850 Hn
Johnson, Grant to Lina Ann Mask 10-30-1868 (no return) F B
Johnson, Green B. to Martha C. Orrell? 8-26-1857 Hr
Johnson, Guid to Maze Jones 8-23-1877 O
Johnson, Gustaf to Julia Allison 7-28-1858 Sh
Johnson, H. C. to Mary F. Ward 10-6-1858 We
Johnson, H. N. to Nancy A. White 10-15-1866 (no return) Dy
Johnson, H. W. to Charlotte A. Christie 1-30-1869 (no return) Dy
Johnson, H. W. to Mattie J. Ledbetter 1-3-1864 Sh

Johnson, Harvy to Ellen Carpenter 3-17-1869 (3-19-1869) F B
Johnson, Haywood to Cintha Blunt 2-27-1873 Hy
Johnson, Henry A.(L?) to Martha A. Brandon 11-4-1846 Sh
Johnson, Henry R. to Mary T. Oliver 10-13-1858 Cr
Johnson, Henry W. to Mattie J. Ledbetter 1-1-1864 (1-3-1864) Sh
Johnson, Henry to Amanda Harrell 1-28-1868 (no return) Hy
Johnson, Henry to Bettie Warren 12-24-1869 (no return) F B
Johnson, Henry to Margaret Poors 2-12-1852 Sh
Johnson, Henry to Margaret S. Rogers 3-16-1876 (no return) Hy
Johnson, Henry to Martha Jane Stephens 9-20-1853 (9-21-1853) G
Johnson, Henry to Mary Ann Coates 1-3-1857 (1-4-1857) Hy
Johnson, Henry to Mary L. Adams 12-13-1876 (no return) Hy
Johnson, Henry to Mein? Smith 11-30-1878 (12-1-1878) Dy
Johnson, Henry to Mollie Elcan 1-1-1872 Hy
Johnson, Henry, sr. to Annie E. Grove 12-20-1871 Hy
Johnson, Hiram to Bettie Easley 6-22-1871 (no return) Hy
Johnson, Horace to Fanny Johnson 9-2-1874 Hy
Johnson, Ira to Lewis? Terrell 8-24-1839 Hn
Johnson, Isaac N. to Mahala J. Childress 3-9-1876 L
Johnson, Isaac to Della McElwee 12-22-1877 Hy
Johnson, Isaac to Martha A. Clifton 4-22-1841 Sh
Johnson, Isaac to Martha Beard 1-19-1872 (1-20-1872) Dy
Johnson, Isham to Mary Ferguson 2-6-1833 (2-7-1833) G
Johnson, J. A. to Mary Williams 1-13-1873 (1-16-1873) T
Johnson, J. B. to Mahala Haskins 1-9-1866 Hn
Johnson, J. E. to Susan J. Massey 4-26-1859 We
Johnson, J. F. to Agnes Cain 7-6-1865 Be
Johnson, J. F. to Susan F. Bledsoe 8-20-1866 G
Johnson, J. H. to Arabella W. Winston 8-10-1862 We
Johnson, J. H. to Elizabeth Stewart 6-17-1878 Dy
Johnson, J. H. to Emma Curtis 12-20-1879 (12-23-1879) L B
Johnson, J. H. to Sarah Prewitt 1-4-1849 Hr
Johnson, J. I. to Fannie F. Harris 2-7-1866 (2-8-1866) F
Johnson, J. J. to M. A. White 12-2-1868 (12-3-1868) Dy
Johnson, J. M. to Betty B. Smithwick 1-24-1881 (1-25-1881) L
Johnson, J. M. to H. M. Oliver 12-27-1871 (no return) Cr
Johnson, J. M. to Julia N. Lemmons 2-14-1867 (no return) Cr
Johnson, J. M. to Margaret H. Williamson 1-10-1849 (1-11-1849) F
Johnson, J. N. to Susanna Swain 11-7-1861 Mn
Johnson, J. R. to Mary V. Crowder 12-1-1869 (12-8-1869) F
Johnson, J. S. to M. A. Wright 12-28-1864 O
Johnson, J. T. to Tobitha Barham 11-16-1866 (11-18-1866) Cr
Johnson, J. W. to Margaret C. Davis 11-15-1855 (no return) Hn
Johnson, J. W. to Martha Dawson 1-16-1846 Cr
Johnson, J. W. to Mattie McFarland 4-16-1870 (no return) Hy
Johnson, J. W. to S. J. (Mrs.) Fletcher 4-27-1870 G
Johnson, J. William to Sue W. Haynes 5-14-1856 Hn
Johnson, Jack to Harriet Turner 12-26-1867 Hy
Johnson, Jake to Artemecia Haselett 1-18-1868 (no return) F B
Johnson, James A. to Elizabeth Bledsoe 11-2-1856 Cr
Johnson, James A. to Emma Cook 8-26-1863 (8-27-1863) Cr
Johnson, James A. to Sarah A. Davis 10-30-1860 Cr
Johnson, James E. to Nancy Cherry 9-16-1854 (9-19-1854) O
Johnson, James H. to Emline Cole 9-18-1839 Be
Johnson, James H. to F. M. Cogbill 12-5-1852 (no return) F
Johnson, James J. to Mary F. McCollum 3-3-1862 Mn
Johnson, James M. to Elizabeth J. Lay 8-28-1864 (9-4-1864) Cr
Johnson, James M. to Elizabeth J. Lay no date Cr
Johnson, James M. to Mary A. Murphy 4-26-1849 Cr
Johnson, James P. to Eliza Hilliard 1-1-1849 Cr
Johnson, James W. to Elizabeth McDonald 3-8-1859 Sh
Johnson, James to Amanda Wyrick 12-4-1875 Dy
Johnson, James to Eliza Fowlkes 10-5-1880 Dy
Johnson, James to Elizabeth Waldran 7-17-1854 Sh
Johnson, James to Harriet Lowry 6-4-1864 (6-19-1864) L
Johnson, James to Julia Alvis 9-15-1869 G B
Johnson, James to Lizzie Pierson 8-13-1879 (8-15-1879) L B
Johnson, James to Mallasie Montgomery 9-12-1839 Cr
Johnson, James to Mandy Rightsdale 12-16-1867 F B
Johnson, James to Mariah Ash ow 12-30-1870 L
Johnson, James to Martha Louisa Brown 7-3-1880 (no return) L
Johnson, James to Mary Eliza Aydlote 10-29-1857 Sh
Johnson, James to Mary J. Reed 6-12-1867 (6-13-1867) Cr
Johnson, James to Mary Messenger 4-13-1871 (4-16-1871) F B
Johnson, James to Melvina Crisp 8-22-1829 (8-23-1829) Hr
Johnson, James to Mollie Williams 12-28-1878 (no return) L B
Johnson, James to Susan A. Key 3-27-1849 (4-12-1849) L
Johnson, James to Susan Read 12-7-1841 Cr
Johnson, James to V. Coldwell 2-14-1885 L
Johnson, Jas. K. to Rosa West 1-8-1867 (no return) F
Johnson, Jeff to Sallie Ivy 2-15-1868 (2-16-1868) F B
Johnson, Jerry to Dovy Sims 8-24-1871 Hy
Johnson, Jess J. to Martha J. Valentine 12-8-1859 We
Johnson, Jesse M. to Elizabeth A. Sullivan 8-6-1860 (8-8-1860) Sh
Johnson, Jessee to P. Howe 10-25-1855 Be
Johnson, Jim to Sarah A. Carroll 3-12-1867 G
Johnson, Joel to James Devenport 3-13-1846 Be

Johnson, John A. to Elvira A. Wilson 1-28-1863 (no return) Dy
Johnson, John A. to Mary Pitts 1-25-1849 Cr
Johnson, John C. to M. A. E. Fisher 6-9-1856 (6-11-1856) Sh
Johnson, John G. to Rebecca Wilkins 2-23-1852 (2-24-1852) Hr
Johnson, John G. to Susan A. Powell 11-21-1862 (11-22-1862) L
Johnson, John Gregory to Tina Bet Roberson 1-20-1877 (not certified) L
Johnson, John H. to Charity Moore 5-16-1860 Hr
Johnson, John J. to Mary P. Gordon 12-?-1859 (no return) Hy
Johnson, John M. to Margaret Philips 8-27-1849 (8-29-1849) Hr
Johnson, John M. to Rebecca McCollum 5-24-1837 (5-?-1837) Sh
Johnson, John O. to Amanda Branch 12-8-1859 G
Johnson, John P. to Eliza Ann Griffee 10-11-1869 (no return) Hy
Johnson, John P. to Elizar J. Reddick 1-4-1860 We
Johnson, John P. to Emma Bigham 7-23-1866 (no return) Cr
Johnson, John P. to Jnnu? Ratliff 5-7-1845 (5-14-1845) Hr
Johnson, John P. to Lucy A. Caldwell 7-1-1868 G
Johnson, John S. to Manerva A. Hope 10-1-1851 (no return) F
Johnson, John W. to Frances Marchbanks 12-28-1863 Be
Johnson, John W. to Penny Moore 9-21-1873 Hy
Johnson, John to Amanda Akin 12-26-1855 Sh
Johnson, John to Amanda Norvell 8-21-1868 Hy
Johnson, John to Catharine Flanagan 12-1-1858 Sh
Johnson, John to Celia Baker 8-16-1869 G
Johnson, John to Elizabeth Jones 12-15-1826 (1-6-1827) Hr
Johnson, John to Fanny Lane? 7-17-1844 Cr
Johnson, John to Kate Scally 4-20-1864 (4-23-1864) Sh
Johnson, John to Lucinda Flowers 10-29-1870 F B
Johnson, John to Mary Allen 12-12-1841 Cr
Johnson, John to Mary Starks 1-2-1872 Hy
Johnson, John to Rose Claibun? 1-28-1867 (1-30-1867) T
Johnson, John to Sarah Mitchell 2-20-1856 Hr
Johnson, John to Susan Wilks 3-3-1849 Cr
Johnson, John to Winnie Smith 3-1-1871 (3-2-1871) T
Johnson, John? to Charlotte Lea 9-8-1871 (9-12-1871) L
Johnson, Jordan to Charlotte Hinton 1-1-1879 (1-2-1879) L B
Johnson, Jordan to Louisa Lowry 12-28-1869 Hy
Johnson, Jordan to Mary Thompson 10-25-1883 L
Johnson, Joseph A. to M. C. McLeod 9-?-1857 Cr
Johnson, Joseph to Agnes A. Elliott 1-31-1870 (2-4-1870) F
Johnson, Joseph to Cintha Browne 2-3-1845 (2-4-1845) F
Johnson, Joseph to H. A. Fish 11-19-1859 (11-20-1859) Hr
Johnson, Joseph to Martha Jones 7-8-1872 Hy
Johnson, Joseph to Opelia Shepherd 2-14-1872 (2-15-1872) O
Johnson, Joseph to Sally Sutton 1-3-1868 (no return) Hy
Johnson, Joshua to Altha Birdsong 10-28-1851 (11-5-1851) Hr
Johnson, Joshua to Altha Birdsong 9-9-1847 L
Johnson, Julias to Sarah A. Dilliard 9-25-1865 (9-26-1865) F
Johnson, Kit to Mary Maclin 9-4-1879 (9-6-1879) L
Johnson, L. D. to Nancy R. Hood 7-5-1846 Cr
Johnson, L. W. to C. A. Matherson 11-30-1875 (no return) Hy
Johnson, Lee to Harriet Crichlow 11-25-1880 (11-26-1880) L B
Johnson, Levi to Mary Maclin 4-21-1872 Hy
Johnson, Lewis to Mary Morris 2-10-1873 (2-13-1873) O
Johnson, Luke to Glora Porter 2-18-1882 (2-21-1882) L
Johnson, Luke to Rose Hinton 11-15-1871 (11-16-1871) L B
Johnson, M. H. to J. M. Wrather 11-6-1864 G
Johnson, M. J. to Sarah A. Torian 1-7-1861 (1-8-1861) Sh
Johnson, M. W. to Emeline Singleton 11-12-1869 (11-18-1869) Cr
Johnson, Mack to Alice Canida 3-20-1873 Hy
Johnson, Mack to Mareno Wilson 2-12-1868 (2-15-1868) F B
Johnson, Madison to Mary M. Brown 12-12-1866 (12-13-1866) O
Johnson, Manuel to Bobry Jones 4-1-1869 (no return) Hy
Johnson, Marion to Louisa Jones 4-19-1866 O
Johnson, Marion to Mary Penick 7-21-1869 Be
Johnson, Martin H. to Penellop Morris 11-28-1839 (no return) L
Johnson, Martin T. to Susan E. Adams 8-14-1865 (8-15-1865) T
Johnson, Martin to Mary Jones 6-15-1828 (6-19-1828) Hr
Johnson, Matt to Tennessee Hunter 5-25-1878 (no return) Hy
Johnson, Matt to Zilpha Bond 11-6-1875 (no return) Hy
Johnson, Matthew to Amanda Castellaw 12-29-1866 (no return) Hy
Johnson, Meredith to Mary Ann Grogan 3-11-1852 Be
Johnson, Meredith to Mary Whittington 1-16-1848 Hr
Johnson, Michael to Mary A. Holloway 3-30-1857 Hr
Johnson, Milton H. to America J. Thomas 8-30-1834 (9-2-1834) G
Johnson, Mingo to Mariah Tucker Moore 1-19-1872 (1-20-1872) T
Johnson, Moses to Jone? Reaves 1-4-1871 T
Johnson, N. K. to Kiziah Brush 12-15-1849 (12-16-1849) Hr
Johnson, N.(A.?) W. to Rebecca F. Crow 7-22-1860 Be
Johnson, Nathan to Eleanor E. Nealy 5-23-1861 (6-2-1861) Hr
Johnson, Nathan to Margaret S. Neely 11-30-1854 L
Johnson, Nathan to Rosella Collier 2-8-1878 Hy
Johnson, Newton to P. A. Tarry? 9-8-1849 (no return) F
Johnson, O. H. P. to Melissa A. Stricklin 7-7-1857 (7-8-1857) Hr
Johnson, P. B. to Eliza Elin Pinson 11-7-1874 (11-8-1874) T
Johnson, P. G. to Mary A. Williamson 10-5-1862 G
Johnson, P. H. to Minerva Cantrell 9-15-1846 We
Johnson, Parker to Joanna Walker 1-3-1880 (1-4-1880) L

Johnson, Patrick to Julie Glancy 9-24-1866 (9-28-1866) Cr
Johnson, Peter S. to Jane Maclin 1-15-1870 Hy
Johnson, Peter to Mary Wells 1-12-1874 T
Johnson, Peter to Mollie Nelson 12-24-1871 Hy
Johnson, R. Fenner to Lizzie W. Flowers 5-20-1868 (5-21-1868) T
Johnson, R. J. to Agness Bryant 10-26-1861 (10-27-1861) Cr
Johnson, R. J. to M. D. Doyle 1-6-1868 (1-7-1868) F
Johnson, R. R. to Anna Douglas 6-30-1866 (no return) Dy
Johnson, Raney (Romeo?) to Sarah Lee 12-26-1885 (12-27-1885) L
Johnson, Richard T. to Ellen Walker 10-8-1849 Sh
Johnson, Richard to Sarah E. Brotherton 7-1-1868 (7-19-1868) Dy
Johnson, Ro. Taylor to Adeline Taylor 12-29-1875 (no return) Hy
Johnson, Robert F. to Sarah Taylor 6-13-1864 (no return) Hy
Johnson, Robert J. to Frances Tucker 12-29-1852 L
Johnson, Robert N. to Frances C. Parker 12-29-1873 (1-1-1874) L
Johnson, Robert to Laura Cunningham 12-23-1868 (no return) Hy
Johnson, Robt. to Allice Baw 12-3-1867 (no return) F
Johnson, Rolling H. to Mariah Davis 12-15-1851 (no return) F
Johnson, S. to Oma Neal 3-20-1863 Be
Johnson, S. E. to Ann E. Green 5-30-1859 T
Johnson, S. E. to E. F. McFarlin 12-27-1866 G
Johnson, S. F. to Martha Collins 1-3-1873 (1-5-1873) Dy
Johnson, S. H. to Malinda E. Rauls 7-28-1868 (7-30-1868) Dy
Johnson, S. L. to Angeline Morris 11-28-1876 (11-29-1876) Dy
Johnson, S. T. to Bettie Street 5-30-1879 (no return) Dy
Johnson, S. T. to S. J. Rust 5-31-1867 (6-2-1867) Cr
Johnson, Sam to Martha Whittenton 6-3-1869 (no return) Dy
Johnson, Saml. P. C. to Lucy Ellen Smith 2-5-1844 T
Johnson, Samuel A. to Lide McLemore 11-16-1873 Hy
Johnson, Samuel to Harriet W. Erwin 6-12-1839 F
Johnson, Samuel to Joana Walters 1-9-1857 We
Johnson, Samuel to Melvina Ginn 8-6-1863 Mn
Johnson, Sandy to Minerva Boyd 8-10-1866 Hy
Johnson, Sherrod to Mary E. Fuller 12-29-1869 (12-30-1869) Dy
Johnson, Sidney A. to Manerva C. Traywick 9-26-1866 (10-4-1866) Cr
Johnson, Sidney to Belison Sauls 2-19-1852 (no return) Hn
Johnson, Silas to Ellen Timms 12-21-1864 (12-22-1864) T
Johnson, Silas to Nancy Ann York 12-21-1852 (12-25-1852) Sh
Johnson, Solomon to Matilda Johnson 12-28-1870 (no return) L
Johnson, Spencer to Kittie Alley 4-12-1868 (no return) F B
Johnson, Stephen B. to Nancy Jane Jones 4-27-1847 (4-30-1847) T
Johnson, Stephen to D. Jones 2-16-1841 Cr
Johnson, T. A. to Susan A. Jones 11-13-1851 Hn
Johnson, T. B. to M. S. Smith 11-9-1847 Cr
Johnson, T. B. to Margaret Marr 5-17-1866 Hy
Johnson, T. B. to Marion B. Cox 6-15-1856 (6-16-1856) Sh
Johnson, T. C. to Rebecca Mann 1-9-1867 G
Johnson, Terry to Annice? Easley 3-24-1873 Hy
Johnson, Thomas D. to Nancy Appleberry 7-1-1854 (7-20-1854) Sh
Johnson, Thomas M. to Sarah C. Voss 12-23-1862 (no return) L
Johnson, Thomas to Artelia Light 9-9-1875 Dy
Johnson, Thomas to Churney Caruthers 9-11-1873 T
Johnson, Thomas to Hattie Hay 11-13-1877 Hy
Johnson, Thomas to Will Rayner 11-11-1874 (no return) Hy
Johnson, Thos. H. to Amanda M. Potter 12-21-1867 (12-22-1867) Dy
Johnson, Thos. J. to Malinda Bradshaw 5-7-1846 We
Johnson, Thos. to Sallie Rivers 6-12-1867 F
Johnson, Tillman to Centha Wray 7-8-1856 (no return) We
Johnson, Tom to Alice Sumner 1-12-1871 (no return) F B
Johnson, Tom to Eliza Whittington 2-19-1868 (no return) Dy
Johnson, Tom to Elvira Thomas 6-8-1867 Hy
Johnson, Vincent to Pataline McMurry 2-20-1867 (no return) F
Johnson, W. A. to M. M. Ellige 11-14-1865 (11-15-1865) O
Johnson, W. C. M. to Melissa Putnam 11-27-1854 Sh
Johnson, W. C. to C. A. Ellis 3-7-1872 (3-12-1872) L
Johnson, W. C. to Martha G. Thompson 6-1-1867 (6-2-1867) F
Johnson, W. D. to Frances G. Jenkins 11-27-1878 L
Johnson, W. H. to Sallie Mays 12-31-1858 Sh
Johnson, W. J. to Mary C. Gill 3-12-1870 (3-13-1870) Cr
Johnson, W. L. to Matilda E. Davis 3-9-1858 Cr
Johnson, W. M. to Polk Lanier 1-1-1872 (no return) Dy
Johnson, W. P. to Melvina E. Bibb 12-21-1869 (12-24-1869) Cr
Johnson, W. R. to Annie E. Plummer 1-21-1869 F
Johnson, W. R. to Ellen Tyson 9-15-1860 (9-20-1860) Sh
Johnson, Walker to Mary Jane Atchison 10-13-1867 G B
Johnson, Washington to Elizabeth Williams 4-17-1856 L
Johnson, Washington to Ellen Palmer 7-23-1868 (no return) Cr
Johnson, Washington to Laura Mayo 12-30-1869 F B
Johnson, Washington to Virginia Balderson 4-20-1867 (4-21-1867) L
Johnson, Wesley J. to Dicey Hopper 3-10-1864 (no return) L
Johnson, Wiley J. to Dicey Hopper 3-10-1864 (3-12-1864) Cr
Johnson, William A. to Amanda J. Heathcock 11-9-1870 (11-10-1870) F
Johnson, William A. to Mary Chapman 10-23-1860 Hy
Johnson, William A. to Mary N. Heinman 5-9-1857 (5-10-1857) O
Johnson, William A. to Mary Walpole 8-31-1839 (no return) L
Johnson, William D. to Rebecca J. Pearce 3-27-1864 G
Johnson, William H. to Susan A. Hudson 7-28-1842 F

Johnson, William P. to Jane Parks 11-24-1857 (11-26-1857) Hr
Johnson, William R. to Ellen Holland 10-6-1864 Sh
Johnson, William S. to Molly Perkins 7-17-1868 (no return) Cr
Johnson, William to Ann Childress 3-29-1841 (4-1-1841) Hr
Johnson, William to Bettie Taylor 5-20-1869 T
Johnson, William to Elenora A. Caldwell 10-18-1869 G B
Johnson, William to Elizabeth McDonald 12-2-1852 Sh
Johnson, William to Emily J. Poindexter 3-20-1869 F B
Johnson, William to Fanny Allen 8-17-1869 F B
Johnson, William to Harriet Blakemore 5-10-1868 G B
Johnson, William to Henrietta Zetta Williams 10-17-1881 (10-20-1881) L B
Johnson, William to Lavinia Sanderlin 1-13-1851 (1-15-1851) Sh
Johnson, William to Lela Nowlin 11-20-1846 We
Johnson, William to Lucinda E. Mathis 3-2-1859 (3-3-1859) G
Johnson, William to Manda Currie 12-29-1875 (no return) Hy
Johnson, William to Margaret Stafford 8-1-1870 (8-2-1870) F
Johnson, William to Margarett V. Tate 5-25-1848 (5-31-1848) F
Johnson, William to Martha A. Brown 9-14-1850 (9-18-1850) G
Johnson, William to Martha Morgan 4-28-1871 (no return) F B
Johnson, William to Perlina Barnes 12-25-1872 (12-26-1872) O
Johnson, William to Sarah Bratton 9-18-1855 Hn
Johnson, William to Susan Grooms 9-28-1836 Sh
Johnson, Willis to Georga Harris 12-17-1873 T
Johnson, Wm. A. to Jerusha B. Hanson (Harson) 11-19-1846 Sh
Johnson, Wm. B. to Elizabeth E. Cenuse 12-23-1858 We
Johnson, Wm. C. to Frances M. Barker 10-7-1848 Sh
Johnson, Wm. C. to Frances Moon(Moore?) 6-1-1846 (6-11-1846) Hr
Johnson, Wm. C. to Mary Green 12-30-1874 Hy
Johnson, Wm. C. to Susan Smith 7-24-1845 Cr
Johnson, Wm. H. C. to Ripsey Steadham 12-17-1838 (12-20-1838) F
Johnson, Wm. H. to Julian B. Ballard 12-2-1852 Be
Johnson, Wm. L. R. to Anna D. Avant 8-22-1861 Hr
Johnson, Wm. M. to Margaret J. Johnson 1-4-1862 (1-5-1862) Hr
Johnson, Wm. R. to Sarah Winford 2-14-1833 Sh
Johnson, Wm. to Eliza H. May 9-1-1840 Cr
Johnson, Wm. to Frances Johnson 9-5-1846 Cr
Johnson, Wm. to Laura J. Dunnavant 12-16-1877 Hy
Johnson, Wm. to Louisa Martin 4-25-1844 Cr
Johnson, Wm. to Lucindy Ann Williams 11-11-1845 Cr
Johnson, Wm. to Margaret Currie 1-23-1873 Hy
Johnson, Wm. to Narcissa Newman 12-20-1868 Be
Johnson, Wm. to Penny Ann Nellums 3-14-1839 F
Johnson, Wm. to Sophia H. Britt 11-18-1857 Cr
Johnson, Wm. to Susan A. Alexander 2-15-1847 (2-16-1847) F
Johnson, Wylie A. to Nancy Curlin 10-13-1856 O
Johnson, ___ to Nancy Stephens 4-4-1877 (not executed) L
Johnston, Ben W. to Harriett H. Hood 10-11-1855 (no return) F
Johnston, Bill to Cama Pates (Dates?) 11-11-1876 (11-12-1876) L
Johnston, C. W. to Mollie E. Fowlkes 12-5-1859 Sh
Johnston, Dickson M. to Martha J. Willson 10-3-1847 Hn
Johnston, Edmon M. to Sarah Ann Banks 11-9-1843 Hn
Johnston, Edward to Martha Chadwick 8-9-1860 (8-12-1860) Cr
Johnston, Ferlacky J. to Pernicia Johnson 3-14-1841 Hn
Johnston, G. W. to Martha J. Foster 10-9-1845 Hn
Johnston, Haden to Charlotte Riddle 4-24-1850 (no return) F
Johnston, J. F. to Pettie Light 1-27-1869 (1-28-1869) Dy
Johnston, J. H. to E. W. G. Bowers 10-14-1868 (10-25-1868) F
Johnston, J. H. to S. A. Edwards 12-1-1866 (12-5-1866) F
Johnston, J. R. to A. R. Larimore 1-8-1878 L
Johnston, Jam. A. to Juliann Carr 10-14-1846 Hn
Johnston, James A. to Anabel Moore 12-3-1879 (12-4-1879) L
Johnston, James E. to Eliza L. Gunter 11-26-1861 Sh
Johnston, James to Henrietta Bridgewater 11-15-1865 (11-16-1865) F
Johnston, James to Kitty Burton 10-30-1882 (11-17-1882) L
Johnston, Joe to Maggie Jordan 9-25-1884 (no return) L
Johnston, John A. to Mattie L. Wilson 7-25-1866 L
Johnston, John C. to Nancy R. Harper 12-31-1844 O
Johnston, John R. to Eleanor A. Nolly 11-15-1865 (11-22-1865) F
Johnston, John to Delila Oar 10-25-1850 (10-27-1850) O
Johnston, John to Mary A. Oakes 11-29-1845 (1-10-1846) O
Johnston, L. T. to Bettie Hendron 1-22-1884 L
Johnston, M. E. to Matilda N. Bram 8-17-1848 Be
Johnston, R. R. to Jane (Mrs.) Davis 1-10-1863 Sh
Johnston, Robert C. to Margaret J. Smith 1-30-1842 Hn
Johnston, Samuel G. to Mary A. Malone 1-22-1851 Hn
Johnston, Samuel Mc. to Mary Litton 4-23-1849 O
Johnston, Shep to Dilly A. Randolph 4-21-1884 (4-22-1884) L
Johnston, T. L. to Mary W. Dunavant 12-18-1877 (12-19-1877) L
Johnston, T. R. to Mary Stacy 7-8-1851 O
Johnston, Thomas B. to Kucy J. Merton 2-12-1846 Hn
Johnston, Thomas L. to Sallie M. Dunavant? 1-28-1873 (1-29-1873) L
Johnston, Thos. to Martha Pope 4-9-1839 (4-11-1839) G
Johnston, W. R. to E. Edmondson 1-2-1866 G
Johnston, Washington to Christina Nelson 1-12-1869 (1-19-1869) T
Johnston, Wilis to Mary Peerson 1-18-1868 (1-19-1868) L B
Johnston, William A. to Amanda R. Seat 1-5-1859 G
Johnston, William to Elizabeth Deason 9-9-1849 Sh

Johnston, Wm. to Nancy Williams 6-9-1866 (6-12-1866) T
Joilet, Alford to Nancie Burch 3-30-1874 (4-2-1874) L
Joiner, Henry to Nancy S. Cleaver 7-18-1854 (no return) Hn
Joiner, James M. to Mary E. Williams 9-17-1860 (9-18-1860) Cr
Joiner, John G. to ____ E. Horn 3-1-1864 (3-2-1864) T
Joiner, Moses to Mary Reed 6-9-1841 Cr
Joiner, N. C. to Nancy T. Pugh 11-5-1867 Cr
Joiner, Richard to Sarah Jane Young 10-30-1848 (11-21-1848) O
Joiner, Rufus S. to Eliza S. Baird 4-15-1845 Sh
Joiner, Thomas S. E. to Mary Fuller 9-15-1837 Sh
Joiner, Thos. S. E. to Cynthia McNutt 10-21-1842 Sh
Jolley, C. M. to Mollie Golding 8-2-1877 L
Jolley, James to Mary A. Heathscott 9-26-1855 We
Jolly, James to Charlotte Fry 3-30-1854 Cr
Jolly, Johns W. to Emma J. Fry 10-1-1861 Cr
Jolly, Joseph M. to Louisa Armstrong 1-5-1842 Cr
Jolly, William to Eliza Wood 12-23-1841 Sh
Jone, Ned to Rosa Bennett 1-6-1867 G
Jone, W. R. to Martha J. Vaughan 11-20-1867 G
Jones (Janes), Levi to R. C. Dickerson 10-17-1863 O
Jones (Janes), Thos. S. to Nancy Autry 11-9-1846 (11-12-1846) O
Jones, A. B. to Louisanna I. Anderson 2-22-1839 Sh
Jones, A. B. to Mary E. Neesbit 11-23-1839 (11-27-1839) F
Jones, A. G. to Sarah E. Alford 12-5-1869 G
Jones, A. I. to A. C. Martin 12-24-1859 We
Jones, A. R. to Amanda Alford 11-3-1864 G
Jones, Aaron to Flora Lockhart 4-25-1866 (no return) F B
Jones, Abraham to Matilda Hale 10-4-1834 (10-7-1834) Hr
Jones, Abram A. S. to Margaret Perkins 10-27-1858 (10-1858) O
Jones, Abram to Abigail Graham 5-28-1855 We
Jones, Abram to Angeline Peebles 12-25-1867 Hy
Jones, Abram to Mary Wilson 12-28-1865 Hy
Jones, Albert T. to B. F. McBride 2-19-1854 Hn
Jones, Albert to Myra Douglas 5-17-1867 (5-18-1867) Dy
Jones, Albert to Sallie Harris 10-10-1877 (no return) Hy
Jones, Albert to Sarah Snow 8-13-1860 (no return) Dy
Jones, Alex to Fannie Wyatt 1-2-1872 Hy
Jones, Alexander M. to Matilda W. Bass 12-18-1850 G
Jones, Alexander to Jane Whitman 11-30-1843 T
Jones, Alfonza S. to Callie Burton 12-18-1862 We
Jones, Alford to Happy Hartsugg 6-30-1853 Cr
Jones, Alford to Mary Green 10-14-1870 (no return) L
Jones, Alfred S. to Sarah D. Plummer 11-28-1855 Sh
Jones, Alfred to Lee Harvey 2-26-1870 (12-28-1870) F B
Jones, Allen to Elizabeth Minerva Cole 2-15-1836 (2-23-1836) O
Jones, Allen to Malissa Jackson 5-10-1873 T B
Jones, Allen? B. to Wynaford Laird 9-12-1853 (9-14-1853) L
Jones, Alx. to Moriah Mann 5-4-1872 (no return) Hy
Jones, Ander J. to Nancy J. Adams 12-16-1852 Cr
Jones, Anderson to Caroline Simpson? 12-23-1876 (12-26-1876) L
Jones, Anderson to Eliza Newbill 9-28-1869 (9-30-1869) Cr
Jones, Anderson to Emma Crow 1-2-1879 Dy
Jones, Anderson to Rilla Jane Miller 3-30-1876 Dy
Jones, Andrew to Frances Wray 7-9-1870 H
Jones, Anthony to Amelia Rose 7-29-1873 (8-14-1873) T
Jones, Arch to Harrett Rutledge 12-15-1876 Hy
Jones, Arther B. to Eliza C. Swift 12-14-1852 (no return) F
Jones, Atlas B. to Mary F. Cheairs 2-7-1853 (3-10-1853) Hr
Jones, B. A. to S. A. Williamson 1-7-1867 (no return) Cr
Jones, B. F. to Sarah A. Moore 9-21-1847 Cr
Jones, B. F. to Sarah C. Foster 1-25-1858 G
Jones, B. H.? to M. J. Mitchell 1-1-1868 (1-2-1868) Cr
Jones, B. M. to Afphie Eskeridge 11-3-1866 G
Jones, B. S. to Mary E. Roy 11-29-1871 (12-3-1871) O
Jones, Bartlet to Bettie Neal (Taylor) 4-3-1869 Hy
Jones, Batie to Malissy Tates 3-28-1878 L
Jones, Ben to Darcus Flippin 11-3-1866 (11-4-1866) F B
Jones, Ben to Hannah Baird 2-22-1867 (2-23-1867) F B
Jones, Ben to Margaret White 1-11-1871 T
Jones, Benj. to Isabella Powell 12-24-1868 Hy
Jones, Bill to Charlotte Chapman 1-3-1870 G B
Jones, Billy to Bet Taylor 2-1-1868 Hy
Jones, Billy to Ellen White 6-4-1872 Hy
Jones, Booker to Susan J. Green 3-12-1860 T
Jones, Brother M. to Susan A. Green 3-12-1860 (3-20-1860) T
Jones, Buckner to Jane Cozby 2-28-1829 Hr
Jones, Bucy to Mary Griffin 1-11-1876 (no return) Hy
Jones, Burril to Caroline Cole 1-11-1867 Dy
Jones, Butten to Nancy Lacy 8-13-1860 Dy
Jones, C. B. to Francis Henry 10-23-1856 We
Jones, C. D. to S. E. Sanford 8-18-1869 (8-19-1869) Dy
Jones, C. H. to Mary Frances Nelson 5-14-1867 Hy
Jones, C. R. to Jane Gullett 8-5-1844 Cr
Jones, C. T. to Amanda Wright 1-7-1855 Cr
Jones, Ca_y to Mary Grooms 1-4-1851 (1-5-1851) Sh
Jones, Calven to Betcy Ann Baker 2-16-1865 (no return) Dy
Jones, Calvin S. to Margaret L. Martin 12-7-1868 G

Jones, Calvin to M. E. Powers 3-8-1870 Dy
Jones, Calvin to Mary E. Hampton 11-6-1856 Cr
Jones, Calvin to Mary Hampton 12-2-1847 Cr
Jones, Calvin to Susan Taylor 8-15-1860 (8-16-1860) Cr
Jones, Charles E. to Sarah Bryant 6-9-1860 O
Jones, Charles E. to Sarah Bryant 6-?-1860 (6-10-1860) O
Jones, Charles G. to Camilla Porter 10-9-1865 (10-11-1865) F
Jones, Charles K. to Frances E. Parr 2-19-1850 (2-20-1850) L
Jones, Charles to Callie Turner 10-21-1874 T
Jones, Charles to Casandra Reddick 10-13-1866 (no return) F B
Jones, Charles to Elizabeth Jane Knapp 1-11-1844 Sh
Jones, Charley to Julia Lucas 12-20-1872 Hy
Jones, Charley to Malinda Buford 12-27-1869 (12-30-1869) F B
Jones, Church to Lizzie Stokely 2-10-1876 (no return) Hy
Jones, Cladius C. to Lucinda G. Bailey 9-1-1834 Hr
Jones, Cooper B. to Eliza A. Harpoll 10-7-1837 (10-10-1837) G
Jones, Cooper B. to Emay K. Reddin 5-27-1847 G
Jones, Crawford to Sarah A. Jones 1-16-1855 (1-17-1855) G
Jones, Crawford to Tempa F. Jones 10-23-1850 (10-24-1850) G
Jones, Cuthbert H. to L. P. Thompson 1-3-1849 Hn
Jones, D. B. to Mary Barnes 11-3-1851 O
Jones, D. L. to Mary J. Carter 12-28-1859 (12-29-1859) T
Jones, D. M. to Jane F. Walker 11-8-1866 Hn
Jones, D. T. to K. C. Neal 3-28-1867 Hn
Jones, D. T. to L. A. Stewart 8-11-1869 (8-13-1869) F
Jones, D. W. to Mary A. Mohundrow(Omohundro) 9-22-1867 Hn
Jones, Danel to Sally Buckner 9-7-1867 (no return) Hy
Jones, Daniel H. to Edmonia Fitzpatrick 6-3-1865 (6-6-1865) L
Jones, Daniel to Elizabeth J. Bowden 4-10-1848 Hn
Jones, Daniel to Eveline Teague 1-1-1867 F B
Jones, David B. to Mary Barnes 11-3-1851 (12-3-1851) O
Jones, David B. to Minerva A. Ladd 10-27-1860 (10-28-1860) Hr
Jones, David H. to Sarah F. White 1-16-1863 (no return) Dy
Jones, David P. to Malinda E. Carter 3-28-1839 Cr
Jones, David to Emiline House 3-30-1867 G B
Jones, David to Julia Ann McGinnis 12-15-1866 (12-22-1866) Dy
Jones, David to Malinda Caledonia Boone 10-24-1857 (10-25-1857) O
Jones, David to Mariah Craighead 4-14-1874 Hy
Jones, David to Mary (Mrs.) Bender 9-12-1864 Sh
Jones, David to Mary M. F. Heskett 12-14-1865 O
Jones, David to Tibitha Martin 1-5-1852 G
Jones, Dred to Corie Taliaferro 1-20-1870 (no return) Hy
Jones, E. J. V. to Sallie Applewhite 1-23-1878 Dy
Jones, E. J. to Bettie Griggs 12-22-1885 (12-23-1885) L
Jones, E. T. to D. N. Manning 5-10-1857 Cr
Jones, E. W. to Mary J. Pryor 5-14-1857 Hn
Jones, Ed to Mary Partee 11-16-1882 L
Jones, Edmund to Harriet Campbell 5-21-1868 (5-23-1868) F B
Jones, Edward L. to Sarah A. Carter 3-4-1843 (no return) Hn
Jones, Edward R. to Martha A. Montgomery 12-11-1844 G
Jones, Edward to Julian Cowherd 4-12-1836 Sh
Jones, Eli to Minerva Walker 3-14-1856 (3-18-1856) G
Jones, Elihu to Emeline Gorgass 8-9-1854 Hn
Jones, Elij. S. to Polly P. Hubert 1-8-1833 (2-8-1833) O
Jones, Elijah to Nancy Mathews 1-1-1855 (1-10-1855) G
Jones, Emanuel M. to Kate McMurray 3-17-1862 Sh
Jones, Emri to Alice Parker 1-25-1883 L
Jones, Etheldred to Anne Childress 10-7-1862 (10-8-1862) Dy
Jones, Ezekiel to Caroline Dunlap 7-11-1882 L
Jones, F. J. to S. R. Wilkins 2-13-1856 (no return) Hn
Jones, F. R. to Alline O. Gilliam 12-14-1876 Hy
Jones, Fayette to Tempy Williamson 12-25-1866 (12-29-1866) F B
Jones, Felix to Mollie Jordan 10-12-1870 Hy
Jones, Finis E. to Lelila Jones 6-25-1859 Hn
Jones, Fonzey to Elizabeth Walls 9-16-1850 (9-17-1850) G
Jones, Forrest to Mary E. Stokeland 1-29-1883 L
Jones, Frank to Chaney Black 2-3-1871 (5-20-1871) F B
Jones, Frank to Sarah Mann 1-5-1873 Hy
Jones, Frederick W. to Mary E. Rittenberry 2-1-1849 O
Jones, Frederick W. to Mary E. Rittenberry 2-1-1849 (2-26-1849) O
Jones, G. A. to Susan A. Kerby 11-22-1868 (12-10-1868) Cr
Jones, G. F. to N. E. Stults 1-25-1876 (1-26-1876) Dy
Jones, G. L. to M. J. McArthur 11-7-1852 Cr
Jones, G. W. D. to Annie B. House 10-6-1872? Hy
Jones, G. W. to Mary Jane Smith 6-10-1861 (6-11-1861) T
Jones, G.? J. to Amanda J. Billings 1-1-1863 T
Jones, Gaston L. to Elizabeth Davis 3-14-1855 (2?-14-1855) O
Jones, George A. to Nannie I. Mathews 5-20-1869 G
Jones, George S. to Ann T. Kirkland 5-13-1868 (5-17-1868) Cr
Jones, George S. to Fannie Stanly 12-19-1867 (no return) Cr
Jones, George W. to Laura Jenkins 2-21-1855 We
Jones, George W. to Louisa J. Merrell 9-18-1856 Cr
Jones, George W. to Martha C. Means 6-30-1853 Sh
Jones, George W. to Mary Jane Tyler 12-7-1852 (12-9-1852) G
Jones, George W. to Sallie Swain 9-21-1871 Dy
Jones, George to Annie Rafferty 9-24-1860 Sh
Jones, George to Leer Moore 4-17-1871 T

Jones, George to Roberta Maclan 7-20-1867 (no return) Hy
Jones, Gilbert to Mary J. (Mrs.) Fowlkes 10-19-1864 Sh
Jones, Gilliam to Eliza Armstrong 12-30-1867 (12-31-1867) F B
Jones, Gip to Molba? Patterson 2-28-1871 (3-2-1871) Cr
Jones, Granville to Lizzie Bradford 9-8-1870 (no return) Dy
Jones, Green to Lou Ely 12-30-1868 F B
Jones, Green to Mary Harris 1-1-1874 T
Jones, Guilbord to Malvina E. Horton 10-1-1861 Sh
Jones, Guy S. to Susan C. Terrill 1-6-1838 (1-9-1838) O
Jones, H. B. to Martha A. Crickmure 11-13-1878 Hy
Jones, H. F. to Ellen Whitelaw 2-18-1869 Hy
Jones, H. G. to Martha A. Luter 12-7-1865 Hn
Jones, H. L. to M. E. Miller 4-14-1865 Hn
Jones, H. Y. to Martha Mosley 7-30-1868 G
Jones, Harrison to Mattie Flowers 5-2-1884 (5-5-1884) L
Jones, Henry A. to Mary Lee Fitzpatrick 10-31-1859 (11-1-1859) L
Jones, Henry H. to Luiza J. Dunn 11-8-1849 Hn
Jones, Henry M. to Lydia Ann Kenneday 8-30-1843 (9-2-1843) Hr
Jones, Henry T. to Mary A. Moore 2-6-1866 (2-8-1866) Cr
Jones, Henry T. to Nancy G. Anderson 3-6-1855 (3-8-1855) Sh
Jones, Henry to Adaline Harrell 6-2-1866 (no return) F B
Jones, Henry to Adaline Upchurch 7-14-1872 (7-15-1872) T
Jones, Henry to Aregon Parham 8-22-1867 (no return) F B
Jones, Henry to Arnetta Tuggle 3-13-1874 Hy
Jones, Henry to Eliza Jourdan 7-8-18__ (maybe 1870) G B
Jones, Henry to Elizabeth Browning 6-2-1833 Sh
Jones, Henry to Emeline Smith 11-26-1869 T
Jones, Henry to Emily Ann Hoggard 7-28-1852 We
Jones, Henry to Eveline Mitchell 12-28-1870 F B
Jones, Henry to Lucy Ward 3-2-1842 Hn
Jones, Henry to Mary K. Dudley 9-2-1873 Dy
Jones, Henry to Mattie Rogers 12-4-1873 (no return) Hy
Jones, Henry to Retta Horton 10-14-1876 (10-15-1876) Dy
Jones, Henry to Winnie Eison 3-18-1868 (3-22-1868) L B
Jones, Hiram B. to Ann King 1-31-1867 (2-1-1867) F
Jones, Hiram M. to Mary Jane Morris 2-3-1845 (no return) F
Jones, Ike to Millie Bradford 2-8-1878 Hy
Jones, Irvin to Harriet Starns 11-7-1877 (11-8-1877) L
Jones, Isaac C. to Frances A. Anderson 2-26-1851 (2-27-1851) Sh
Jones, Isaac to Angeline Bell 10-17-1885 (10-18-1885) L
Jones, Isaac to Charity E. Burrow 8-15-1844 Cr
Jones, Isaac to Jane Jones 10-7-1848 Hn
Jones, Isaac to Nancy Baskerville 12-28-1866 (12-29-1866) F B
Jones, Isaac to Nannie B. Saunders 5-11-1861 (5-12-1861) Sh
Jones, Isaiah to Elizabeth F. Barnres 4-10-1855 (4-12-1855) O
Jones, Isaiah to Lucinda Morris 1-28-1874 Hy
Jones, J. A. to Martha A. Norton 8-24-1858 Hr
Jones, J. A. to Mary E. Cleek 2-20-1871 (2-26-1873) Dy
Jones, J. A. to Sarah Bullard 10-14-1869 Dy
Jones, J. A. to Sophia A. Young 11-5-1867 (no return) Hn
Jones, J. B. to E. F. Norman 12-4-1883 L
Jones, J. C. to Frances Hurt 2-19-1872 Cr
Jones, J. C. to Mary F. Freeman 11-5-1868 Hy
Jones, J. Calvin to Mary Louisa Kirk 7-20-1858 (7-21-1858) Sh
Jones, J. D. to Sally V. Burris 11-20-1861 (11-21-1861) O
Jones, J. D. to Zenovia C. Stanfield 6-10-1871 (no return) Hy
Jones, J. E. to Ema Read 3-4-1874 Hy
Jones, J. H. to Florrence Cole 6-25-1867 (6-30-1867) T
Jones, J. H. to Mary A. Goode 9-21-1857 Sh
Jones, J. H. to Virginia Ward 8-20-1877 (8-21-1877) L
Jones, J. J. to A. C. Cullum 1-4-1871 (1-5-1871) T
Jones, J. J. to Eugenia Rickman 1-26-1874 (1-28-1874) O
Jones, J. J. to Malissa Olive 9-17-1866 (9-20-1866) O
Jones, J. K. to Martha J. Chandler 12-24-1873 Hy
Jones, J. M. to A. M. Bruce 10-27-1859 We
Jones, J. M. to C. E. Goodin 12-11-1866 Hn
Jones, J. M. to Lizzie Cook ?-19-1878 (with Nov 1878) Dy
Jones, J. M. to Susan Peevey 2-4-1861 (2-5-1861) L
Jones, J. N. to Louisa J. Bond 11-25-1852 Sh
Jones, J. P. to Katie Yearwood 5-1-1869 (5-4-1869) Dy
Jones, J. R. to Mary A. Leach 10-27-1866 (no return) Cr
Jones, J. R. to S. V. Hiatt 1-3-1867 Cr
Jones, J. S. to Mary E. Cherry 2-2-1875 (no return) Hy
Jones, J. V. to Emma V. Word 12-11-1867 (no return) F
Jones, J. W. to Amanda Gregory 7-4-1844 Sh
Jones, J. W. to Jane Manning 4-10-1861 (4-11-1861) Dy
Jones, J. W. to Marietta Melton 12-22-1869 (no return) L
Jones, J. W. to N. N.(Mrs.) McClure 6-10-1866 G
Jones, J. W. to Phebee M. Holland 10-28-1856 Be
Jones, J. W. to Tempy A. Baily 5-14-1868 (5-15-1868) Dy
Jones, J. to Mary Stokes 1-17-1859 Sh
Jones, Jack to Cora Green 5-29-1873 Hy
Jones, Jack to Emmaline Owen 11-20-1870 Hy
Jones, Jack to Louisa Pulliam 4-14-1866 (4-22-1866) F B
Jones, Jack to Phillie Starks 11-18-1878 Hy
Jones, Jack to Priscilla Purdle 11-13-1875 (no return) Dy
Jones, Jacob to Margaret Compton 12-17-1872 (12-22-1872) T

Jones, James B. to Rachal A. Tate 9-22-1846 (10-10-1846) G
Jones, James C. to Christena Feezor 12-24-1849 T
Jones, James D. to Jane Crittendon 8-22-1850 (no return) Hn
Jones, James E. to Abiger C. Rodgers 2-2-1853 Cr
Jones, James E. to M. E. Rodgers 12-19-1855 Cr
Jones, James G. to Martha Fay 8-16-1862 Sh
Jones, James G. to Nancy J. Killebrew 1-21-1845 We
Jones, James H. to Mary A. London 2-6-1862 (2-11-1862) O
Jones, James H. to Susan Wells 1-1-1850 Hr
Jones, James I. to Iola Clay 11-15-1869 (11-17-1869) F
Jones, James L. to Ella H. French 5-17-1884 (5-18-1884) L
Jones, James M. to Elizabeth Jones 9-10-1860 (9-13-1860) O
Jones, James M. to Jane James 12-16-1841 Hr
Jones, James M. to Lettie Hays 9-24-1872 (11-24-1872) T
Jones, James M. to M. E. Browning 10-7-1859 G
Jones, James M. to Nancy McClain 12-8-1857 Hn
Jones, James M. to Rebecca Casey 3-18-1835 Hr
Jones, James R. to Louiza C. Tate 7-1-1850 (7-4-1850) G
Jones, James S. to Eliza Chance 1-12-1857 (no return) Hn
Jones, James W. to Calista L. Bruff 3-22-1865 G
Jones, James W. to Clemency Jane Jones 10-2-1851 Hr
Jones, James W. to Martha A. E. Dockins 2-17-1859 O
Jones, James r. to Elizabeth S. Haines 7-13-1853 Hn
Jones, James to Charlotte Flora 11-29-1853 (11-30-1853) O
Jones, James to Elizabeth Walker 3-8-1856 (3-9-1856) G
Jones, James to Ella Shaw 12-12-1878 Hy
Jones, James to Florence Harris 5-13-1874 T
Jones, James to Gracey Maclin 12-7-1874 T
Jones, James to Hannah Cambell 10-13-1866 (no return) Dy
Jones, James to Louisa Hurt 12-19-1871 (no return) Cr B
Jones, James to Lutisha Jorden 1-3-1878 Hy
Jones, James to Martha Ward 9-2-1870 (9-6-1870) Dy
Jones, James to Mary B. Gardon 1-24-1840 F
Jones, James to Matilda Harrold 1-2-1856 Sh
Jones, James to Rosetta Coleman 3-1-1869 (no return) L B
Jones, James to Winaford Duncan 10-5-1848 (11-7-1848) Hr
Jones, Jarrette to Marget C. Farmer 2-21-1829 (2-22-1829) O
Jones, Jarvis to Elizabeth Jones 11-20-1851 O
Jones, Jas. a. to M. H. Harpool 12-12-1871 (12-14-1871) O
Jones, Jasper M. to Mary E. Lawrence 10-27-1850 Hn
Jones, Jasper to Chaney Adams 8-19-1872 Hy
Jones, Jasper to Frances Rainer 8-29-1867 (9-23-1867) F B
Jones, Jasper to Josephine Douglas 3-8-1877 Hy
Jones, Jeff to Emily J. Macklin 12-26-1878 Hy
Jones, Jeremiah J. to F. J. Allen 2-11-1863 (2-12-1863) O
Jones, Jeremiah to S. W. Harrold 2-20-1867 (no return) Dy
Jones, Jerry to Minda McKinley 10-29-1870 F B
Jones, Jesse to Leida Millard 5-11-1874 Hy
Jones, Jesse to Rodia Cook 10-18-1831 Sh
Jones, Jesse to Unetta? E. Carruth? 8-13-1847 (8-15-1847) Hr
Jones, Jim to Martha Taylor 6-20-1868 Hy
Jones, Jim to Sally Taylor 11-19-1875 (no return) Hy
Jones, Jno. C. to Sarah E. Allen 1-7-1869 Hy
Jones, Jno. Henry to Harriett A. M. Keel 12-28-1862 Sh
Jones, Jo to Agg Fowlkes 5-8-1869 (no return) Dy
Jones, Joe F. to Lucy M. Bishop 6-4-1846 Cr
Jones, Joel to Elizabeth Cheny 2-23-1864 (no return) Dy
Jones, John A. to Mary Ann Townsend 8-5-1840 (8-9-1840) Hr
Jones, John B. to Cyntha C. Jones 3-5-1850 Sh
Jones, John C. to Martha J. Crawford 12-28-1858 (12-29-1858) G
Jones, John C. to Sarah A. McCollum 5-12-1857 Cr
Jones, John G. to Frances Jane Williams 2-21-1843 Sh
Jones, John G. to Margaret T. Dunavant 6-1-1846 (6-9-1846) L
Jones, John H. to Elizabeth Scales 1-28-1846 Sh
Jones, John H. to Frances C. Moudy 12-2-1845 (12-7-1845) G
Jones, John H. to Lanah Vaughn 12-7-1857 Hn
Jones, John H. to Lucy Ann Hazelwood 7-1-1847 Sh
Jones, John H. to Mary E. Patrick 1-13-1851 (1-14-1851) Sh
Jones, John H. to Rebecca H. Rawls 3-7-1860 (no return) Hy
Jones, John H. to Sarah E. Thorn 7-5-1866 Cr
Jones, John Henry to Sallie Bond 9-14-1869 (no return) Hy
Jones, John J. to Jane Wallace 10-27-1861 (no return) Hy
Jones, John K. to Jacksey M. Bondurant 10-3-1843 We
Jones, John L. to M. A. Walton 7-21-1864 (7-23-1864) Cr
Jones, John Lewis to Winnie Young 11-20-1883 (11-21-1883) L
Jones, John M. to Mary J. Perry 10-19-1844 Cr
Jones, John R. to Adaline Caraway 1-7-1856 (1-9-1856) O
Jones, John R. to Martha Ann Doak 7-5-1839 Cr
Jones, John R. to Sarah Carter 1-2-1851 Sh
Jones, John S. to Martha A. Ramsey 7-31-1849 Sh
Jones, John T. to Martha J. Clark 6-9-1873 (no return) Cr
Jones, John T. to Martha Swindle 4-13-1836 Hr
Jones, John T. to Narcissa Cathey 11-9-1848 (no return) F
Jones, John T. to Savana T. E. Pascal 1-19-1874 (1-21-1874) L
Jones, John W. to Elizabeth (Mrs.) Bland 11-16-1847 Sh
Jones, John W. to Matilda J. Burns 10-20-1859 Cr
Jones, John to Amy Meriweather 3-2-1867? (3-3-1867) F B

Jones, John to Betty Murrell 1-11-1870 (2-9-1870) F B
Jones, John to Bridgett Bartley 5-20-1854 Sh
Jones, John to Eliza Nelson 12-27-1869 (no return) L
Jones, John to Fannie Eggleston 4-7-1874 L
Jones, John to Judy Clay 10-4-1869 (10-9-1869) Cr
Jones, John to Jurncia Stone 10-25-1847 (11-15-1847) O
Jones, John to Lizzie Currie 12-12-1876 Hy
Jones, John to Lucinda Bates 12-26-1835 Hr
Jones, John to Malinda Williams 1-12-1837 Hr
Jones, John to Margaret Robertson 9-6-1867 Dy
Jones, John to Martha Talley 4-13-1831 (4-14-1831) O
Jones, John to Mary Brown 3-16-1867 (3-17-1867) F B
Jones, John to Mary Jones 12-28-1866 (12-29-1866) F B
Jones, John to Polly Ann Martin 10-26-1826 Hr
Jones, John to Rachel A. Crippin 5-12-1860 (5-13-1860) F
Jones, John to Rebecca King 12-5-1865 Hn
Jones, John to Sallie Palmer 12-24-1870 (no return) Hy
Jones, John to Sarah Price 7-26-1844 (7-28-1844) O
Jones, John to Sarah Stanley 12-27-1864 (12-29-1864) O
Jones, Jonathan J. to Elizabeth Harris 2-19-1855 (2-21-1855) Sh
Jones, Jonathan to Kitty Reaves 10-13-1844 Cr
Jones, Jonothan to Evelina Brown 7-15-1825 Hr
Jones, Jordan to Patsy Anthony 5-27-1871 (no return) Hy
Jones, Jordon to Lue Rice 12-23-1870 (no return) Hy
Jones, Joseph R. to Elizabeth Pendergrass 6-29-1839 (7-10-1839) O
Jones, Joseph to Jamima Beard 12-6-1841 G
Jones, Joseph to Lilly Kee 12-8-1868 (12-12-1868) F B
Jones, Joseph to Margaret E. Milam 11-19-1853 (no return) Hn
Jones, Joseph to Sarah A. Reynolds 11-8-1858 Hn
Jones, Joshua J. to Sarah W. Freeman 10-23-1843 F
Jones, Joshua L. to Mary A. Busby 5-25-1847 Hn
Jones, Julius to Rhoda Ward 9-28-1843 Hn
Jones, Kennie to Liza Bond 11-7-1869 Hy
Jones, L. A. to Mary A. Coppedge 2-7-1877 Hy
Jones, L. F. to Amanda (Mrs.) Johnson 1-23-1867 G
Jones, L. M. jr. to S. E. Webb 1-7-1873 (no return) Cr
Jones, L. P. to Ioda B. Williams 1-11-1864 (1-13-1864) Sh
Jones, L. P. to Sallie Owen 1-17-1861 F
Jones, L. R. to M. J. Campbell 10-20-1879 (10-21-1879) Dy
Jones, L. W. to Charity C. Woods 10-1-1850 Cr
Jones, LaFayette to Susan Ann Dunn 3-16-1832 Sh
Jones, Larkin P. to Mary E. Hodges 8-9-1838 F
Jones, Lee to Anna (Mrs.) Chrisp 9-8-1867 G B
Jones, Lemuel to Elisabeth Young 8-6-1846 Hr
Jones, Leolen to Susan Dixon 12-10-1857 Hr
Jones, Leroy to Marier Green 12-28-1865 T
Jones, Levi to Rachel C. Dickerson 10-17-1864 O
Jones, Lewis to Ally Gooddin 1-27-1868 (1-30-1868) T
Jones, Lewis to Henrietter Parr 1-11-1874 L B
Jones, Lewis to Mag Williamson 4-24-1867 (no return) F B
Jones, Logan to Ann Higgason 3-19-1866 (no return) F B
Jones, Lorenzo D. to Sarah Laney 1-13-1861 We
Jones, Lou to Alice Simmons 12-26-1870 F B
Jones, Louallen to Eliza V. Bordman 12-20-1844 (12-22-1844) Hr
Jones, Louis to Margaret Pippin 3-15-1871 (3-20-1871) F
Jones, M. A. to Sarah Morris 1-8-1850 F
Jones, M. D. to Ann E. Jones 9-?-1860 (no return) Hy
Jones, M. H. to Martha E. Baugh 2-10-1857 We
Jones, Malachi to Martha J. Ballard 1-30-1851 Hn
Jones, Manuel to Jane Bullock 1-27-1866 (no return) F B
Jones, Marcus to Adaline Bobo 9-9-1846 Sh
Jones, Marcus to Mary E. Porter 11-27-1848 Sh
Jones, Marion D. to Frances A. Wallace 2-23-1863 (no return) Hy
Jones, Marion to Ider C. Boyd 10-22-1856 T
Jones, Marsellis to Frances Cane 10-6-1869 Cr
Jones, Marshall B. to Eliza J. Griffin 12-15-1870 F
Jones, Martin B. to Kissiah C. Sloan 2-25-1841 (2-26-1841) G
Jones, Martinn to Parthena Williams 9-22-1866 O
Jones, Mathias to Anna Grumbleby 11-22-1860 Sh
Jones, Milton C. to Sarah A. Underwood 6-19-1865 Hn
Jones, Milton to Nancy Johnson 12-26-1878 Hy
Jones, Monroe to Jans Eison 6-10-1874 (6-11-1874) L B
Jones, Monroe to Puss Booker 10-30-1870 G
Jones, Monroe to Vena Pearce 12-28-1869 (no return) Dy
Jones, Montezuma to A. E. Wood 10-11-1849 Hr
Jones, Montgomery to Frances J. Brickeem 12-5-1865 Mn
Jones, Morgan to Jane Eley 7-13-1867 (7-14-1867) F B
Jones, Moses E. to Lucinda C. Cook 1-25-1856 Cr
Jones, Moses N. to Elisabeth Magby 3-7-1838 (3-11-1838) Hr
Jones, Moses to Jennetta Stafford 1-2-1869 (1-3-1869) Cr
Jones, N. B. to Sarah Farris 1-5-1837 G
Jones, Napoleon to Roxie King 2-28-1878 Hy
Jones, Nash to Fanny Clark no date (1-1-1867) Dy
Jones, Nash to Matilda Scroggins 7-24-1875 (7-25-1875) Dy B
Jones, Nate to Sally Farmer 7-1-1866 Hn B
Jones, Nathan to Mary Mosely 9-12-1869 G B
Jones, Nathaniel P. to Polly E. Jones 4-27-1839 Hn
Jones, Nathaniel to Malind J. Buck 7-8-1862 Sh
Jones, Ned to Emeline Davidson 10-29-1869 G B
Jones, Ned to Emeline Turnley 1-11-1868 F B
Jones, Nepoleon to Hanah Brooks 11-30-1872 (no return) Hy
Jones, Nicholas to Mary Coleman 11-13-1871 T
Jones, Norman W. to Susan Reaves 7-25-1848 Sh
Jones, O. A. to Susan J. Johnson 1-28-1868 (1-29-1868) Dy
Jones, Orange to Harriett Peet 12-23-1878 Hy
Jones, Oswell F. to Julia A. Gwyn 10-31-1838 (11-1-1838) F
Jones, P. B. to Anna L. David 1-10-1872 Hy
Jones, P. T. to Minerva Ann Moore 6-20-1851 (6-23-1851) Sh
Jones, P. to Sarah M. Tinkle 4-13-1854 G
Jones, Paul S. to Martha C. Armstrong 12-23-1847 Hn
Jones, Paul T. to Jane M. Wood 2-26-1849 (3-1-1849) Hr
Jones, Paul to Charlotte Lea 7-8-1881 (7-24-1881) L
Jones, Paul to Laura Baker 10-16-1876 (no return) Hy
Jones, Peter to Ann Hale 12-27-1871 O
Jones, Phil to Henrietta Wilkins 1-29-1871 (no return) Hy
Jones, Phillip R. to Mary Jane White 9-22-1841 (10-5-1841) Hr
Jones, Phillip to Nettie Proctor 11-18-1870 G B
Jones, Polk to Louisa Fowlkes 7-6-1867 (7-7-1867) Dy
Jones, R. D. to John P. Wade 9-20-1854 G
Jones, R. D. to Mary Reeves 2-28-1856 (3-5-1856) Hr
Jones, R. S. to Martha J. Guinn 11-17-1867 Hn
Jones, R. W. to Tennessee Williams 1-22-1866 (1-25-1866) Cr
Jones, Ralph to Louizer Montgomery 6-1-1866 G
Jones, Ransom H. to Nancy E. Peeples 1-28-1858 Hn
Jones, Reddick to Catharine Baker 5-16-1861 Dy
Jones, Richard B. to Martha A. Ward 6-17-1866 G
Jones, Richard H. to Jane Humphreys 11-30-1851 Hn
Jones, Richard James to Ellen Conway Rose 1-7-1850 (1-10-1850) T
Jones, Richard L. to Mattie J. King 11-15-1859 (11-17-1859) Sh
Jones, Richard to Adaline Baxter 7-18-1870 (8-1-1870) Dy
Jones, Richard to Harriett Adkison 9-21-1867 (no return) Cr
Jones, Richard to Mary Whalon 6-3-1869 (no return) Hy
Jones, Richard to Sallie Davis 3-6-1871 F B
Jones, Robert Alexander to Nancy J. Haynes 7-31-1856 Hr
Jones, Robert B. to Mary A. Cantwell 2-25-1858 We
Jones, Robert B. to Mary Jeans 3-11-1861 T
Jones, Robert E. to Nancy J. Johnson 8-8-1858 Cr
Jones, Robert M. to Martha Fletcher 12-31-1861 G
Jones, Robert M. to Susan Malrina Felphs 4-9-1861 Sh
Jones, Robert P. to Martha J. Trought 12-24-1849 Cr
Jones, Robert W. to Mary Ann Fletcher 8-9-1852 (8-10-1852) G
Jones, Robert to Matilda Luster 8-12-1844 (8-13-1844) G
Jones, Robert to Melinda Yewing(Ewing) 4-2-1827 (4-5-1827) Hr
Jones, Robert to Priscilla Bishop 10-17-1868 (10-18-1868) F B
Jones, Robt. T. to E. I. House 12-28-1862 G
Jones, Robt. to Lou Jackson 4-24-1877 (no return) Dy
Jones, Rupert to Roda Pierce 10-14-1870 Dy
Jones, Russel to Harriet Ealy 8-7-1869 (8-9-1869) F B
Jones, S. C. to Mary Walsh 10-11-1864 Mn
Jones, S. L. W. to Parthina McDonald 7-27-1859 Cr
Jones, S. M. to F. A. House 11-10-1860 (no return) Hy
Jones, S. P. to Sarah A. Harper 12-22-1845 Sh
Jones, S. W. to M. S. Smith 5-12-1866 Hn
Jones, S. to Sarah Webster 10-16-1851 Hn
Jones, Sam to Callie Adams 9-13-1870 (9-15-1870) Cr B
Jones, Sam to Ellen Bradford 11-5-1877 (11-9-1877) L
Jones, Sam to Laura Skiles 2-15-1872 Hy
Jones, Sam to Mariah Bell 12-29-1879 (no return) Dy
Jones, Sam to Mary Kilpatrick 9-14-1872 T
Jones, Sam. B. to M. E. Maclin 4-2-1866 (no return) Hy
Jones, Saml. to Gracey Flurnoy 12-28-1870 F B
Jones, Saml. to Mary Parsons 9-8-1857 T
Jones, Saml. to Susan A. Stewart 9-9-1867 (not endorsed) F
Jones, Sampson to Evaline Watkins 1-14-1869 Hy
Jones, Samuel A. to Mary Jane Vaden 11-5-1853 G
Jones, Samuel D. to Julia Ann Allen 1-5-1843 Hr
Jones, Samuel J. to Louisa A. Harris 10-26-1869 (no return) Dy
Jones, Samuel to Ellen (Mrs.) McGowen 12-21-1863 Sh
Jones, Samuel to Mary F. Martin 4-11-1860 Hn
Jones, Samuel to N. J. Farris 9-27-1862 Mn
Jones, Scott to Julia Purson (Pierson?) 12-25-1873 L B
Jones, Sevraves to Isabel Scobey 1-29-1873 (1-30-1873) Dy
Jones, Shedrick to Lillie Byars 11-18-1873 Hy
Jones, Shelby to Crisey Hightower 11-11-1867 Hn B
Jones, Sherred to Mary Ramsey 11-12-1846 Sh
Jones, Silas P. to Mary J. Galion 10-13-1841 Cr
Jones, Simon to Eliza Jones 12-26-1868 Hy
Jones, Simon to Kissie Lee 12-23-1879 (12-29-1879) L
Jones, Solomon to Martha Pryor 5-11-1871 (5-14-1871) L
Jones, Solomon to Mary A. Atkins 4-11-1867 (no return) Hn
Jones, Solomon to _____ Puett 1-21-1868 Hy
Jones, Sommerset P. to Celia Hill 2-16-1871 Hy
Jones, Sommerset P. to Feeby Jones 10-1-1866 (no return) Hy
Jones, Spencer to Dafney Coleman 8-23-1866 (8-26-1866) T

Jones, Spencer to Lucy Hornsby 9-7-1842 (9-8-1842) O
Jones, Spencer to Vina Younger 1-31-1871 (2-2-1871) Cr
Jones, Stephen B. to Elizabeth C. Roberts 9-9-1839 Hr
Jones, Stephen B. to Martha M. J. Pointer 1-20-1862 We
Jones, Stephen B. to Melissa J. Holland 3-1-1863 G
Jones, Stephen jr. to Margaret Fitzgerald 9-19-1832 (9-27-1832) Hr
Jones, Stephen to Barbery Glisson 2-6-1852 G
Jones, Stephen to Honera Connelly 4-20-1861 Sh
Jones, Stephen to Rebecca A. Thompson 4-27-1855 (5-7-1855) Sh
Jones, Stephen to Surany? Matthews 11-11-1836 (11-13-1836) Hr
Jones, Stynax to Mary Sevier 8-28-1873 Hy
Jones, Sylis J. to Malinda Rhodes 3-24-1859 Cr
Jones, Sylvester to Betty Ann E. Martin 12-19-1850 F
Jones, T. B. to M. D. Graves 5-21-1862 Hn
Jones, T. E. to Harriet L. McCarter 1-13-1866 Cr
Jones, T. J. to R. A. Jarrett 7-22-1871 (7-23-1871) Cr
Jones, T. P. to Vina Neal 7-31-1866 Hn
Jones, T. to M. A. Smawley 4-10-1842 Be
Jones, Tazewell M. to Winney Humphreys 2-5-1852 Hn
Jones, Thomas C. to Mary C. Irons 5-17-1837 Hr
Jones, Thomas D. to Elizabeth Pounds 8-14-1865 G
Jones, Thomas E. to Amanda M. Randall 9-30-1861 (10-1-1861) Cr
Jones, Thomas E. to Nancy S. Cunningham 12-15-1850 Hn
Jones, Thomas G. to Sophia W. Woods 1-15-1838 (1-18-1838) G
Jones, Thomas J. to Amanda M. Long 3-16-1844 (6-24-1844) O
Jones, Thomas J. to Sarah J. McConnell 11-1-1866 Hn
Jones, Thomas L. to Emeline Thomas 1-10-1854 G
Jones, Thomas M. to Mary Davis 2-29-1840 (3-1-1840) O
Jones, Thomas R. to Celia A. Malone 1-19-1856 (no return) Hn
Jones, Thomas S. to Nancy Autry 11-9-1845 (11-12-1845) O
Jones, Thomas W. to Elizabeth E. Mitchell 7-12-1848 (7-13-1848) G
Jones, Thomas to Agnes Wilson 4-27-1866 Hy
Jones, Thomas to Chainey Howard 10-3-1874 T
Jones, Thomas to Chrischania Chunn 9-15-1842 Hn
Jones, Thomas to Eliza Becket 12-25-1879 (12-26-1879) Dy
Jones, Thomas to Elizabeth A. D. Childers 1-4-1855 Sh
Jones, Thomas to Francis L. Allen 1-30-1860 (1-31-1860) O
Jones, Thomas to Mary B. Kimble 9-21-1842 Sh
Jones, Thomas to Mollie Fowlkes 1-13-1876 Dy
Jones, Thomas to Sally P. Sparkes 7-7-1853 (no return) F
Jones, Thomas to Virginia C. Davis 5-17-1849 Hn
Jones, Thos. W. to Cordelia Williamson 5-29-1866 F
Jones, Thos. to Winny Pender 9-3-1867 (no return) Hy
Jones, Tignell to Mary E. Lankford 3-8-1861 Hr
Jones, Tobe to Fannie Clark 1-9-1878 (1-10-1878) Dy
Jones, Tom to Matilda Jelks 6-30-1870 Hy
Jones, Tony to Mary Jones 5-26-1867 Hy
Jones, W. A. to Elizabeth W. Hess 2-16-1857 G
Jones, W. B. to E. Jones 1-17-1868 O
Jones, W. B. to Martha J. Forgey 5-11-1861 (5-15-1861) Sh
Jones, W. C. to Pruda A. Barn 1-3-1860 (1-4-1860) G
Jones, W. C. to Sarah B. Childress 7-27-1854 We
Jones, W. D. to J. A. Porter 11-6-1861 Cr
Jones, W. F. to D. E. Davis 12-17-1868 (1-7-1869) T
Jones, W. F. to Julia A. Anderson 3-2-1864 F
Jones, W. F. to V. C. David 12-17-1868 (12-3-1869?) T
Jones, W. G. to Eliza J. Crawford 6-18-1864 Hn
Jones, W. H. to Katie C. James 12-22-1874 (12-23-1874) Dy
Jones, W. H. to M. E. Clark 11-13-1865 (no return) Hy
Jones, W. H. to S. J. Robbins 10-10-1878 Hy
Jones, W. J. to Elizabeth Key 1-23-1865 Hn
Jones, W. J. to Sarah Crider 8-4-1857 Hn
Jones, W. J. to Sarah E. Loyd 12-31-1866 G
Jones, W. J. to Tilda Larrison 12-16-1874 (12-17-1874) L B
Jones, W. L. to Elizabeth Anthony 12-22-1869 (12-23-1869) Dy
Jones, W. L. to Lizzie Pace 9-19-1877 (9-20-1877) Dy
Jones, W. N. to Charlotta Ellis 12-15-1870 Dy
Jones, W. to Jane Moore 12-15-1849 Sh
Jones, Waimon to Permelia Demara 9-4-1874 (9-5-1874) L
Jones, Walker to Jane Stone 1-1-1845 (1-3-1845) O
Jones, Walter to Mary Leeman 1-8-1870 G B
Jones, Wash to Peggy Brown 5-2-1867 (5-5-1867) F B
Jones, Washington E. to Sarah A. Ramsey 7-18-1854 (7-19-1854) G
Jones, Wes to Harriett Matthews 1-2-1868 (1-3-1868) F B
Jones, Wesley F. to Mary A. Wilkins 10-28-1847 G
Jones, Wesley to Elizabeth Wells 12-31-1873 T
Jones, Wesley to Frances Maclin 12-21-1869 T
Jones, Wesley to Laura Glover 2-24-1876 (no return) Hy
Jones, Wiley B. to Isabella I. Harrison 11-20-1867 Hy
Jones, Wiley to Laura Dickinson 5-4-1870 (5-7-1870) F B
Jones, Wilie to Minnerva A. Estes 9-21-1849 (9-23-1849) Hr
Jones, Wilie to Sarah Holliday 12-26-1837 Hr
Jones, Will M. to Mary S. Dent 3-6-1854 Hn
Jones, William A. to Cynthia West 8-21-1838 Sh
Jones, William A. to Eliza L. King 12-23-1849 Sh
Jones, William A. to Martha L. Featherston 12-1-1842 Sh
Jones, William A. to Susan E. Kirk 1-24-1855 Sh

Jones, William B. to Mary C. Jones 11-3-1842 (11-10-1842) G
Jones, William B. to Parthena Parish 1-15-1846 O
Jones, William Carnall to Nancy Ann Lankford 12-22-1847 (no return) L
Jones, William D. to Amanda J. Canaday 12-20-1852 G
Jones, William E. to Fanny M. Kirkland 9-3-185 (9-6-1855) Hr
Jones, William H. to Jane Carter 2-7-1843 Hn
Jones, William H. to Mary B. Oliver 6-6-1855 (no return) F
Jones, William H. to Mary E. George 8-25-1863 O
Jones, William H. to Mary J. Horne 12-19-1853 (12-21-1853) Sh
Jones, William H. to N.E. Brumley 3-5-1860 Sh
Jones, William H. to Nancy A. Pulley 8-2-1856 (8-7-1856) Sh
Jones, William J. to Minervia Campbell 6-8-1848 (6-11-1848) Hr
Jones, William L. to Mary C. Joyner 12-7-1843 Hr
Jones, William M. to Harrett Brickhouse 4-16-1846 (4-26-1846) G
Jones, William M. to Rebecca Pentecost 12-23-1856 (12-25-1856) O
Jones, William S. to Mary G. Balen 10-19-1841 (no return) Hn
Jones, William T. to Nancy Kesiah Hartsfield 10-24-1864 (no return) Hn
Jones, William W. to Elizabeth H. Swearingen 2-5-1850 Hn
Jones, William to Eliza Jones 3-20-1867 (no return) Hy
Jones, William to Elizabeth Newbill 3-7-1866 (no return) Cr
Jones, William to Elizabeth P. Milner 6-15-1854 We
Jones, William to Kate Coleman 10-11-1877 Hy
Jones, William to Martha A. Wilbanks 12-28-1860 (1-1-1861) Hr
Jones, William to Mary (Mrs.) Vernon 10-12-1867 G B
Jones, William to Mary A. Givings 10-6-1853 Sh
Jones, William to Mary E. Cavinar 7-12-1850 (7-14-1850) Hr
Jones, William to Mary E. Vaughan 4-24-1860 (no return) We
Jones, William to Mary Elkin 9-7-1868 (9-10-1868) T
Jones, William to Nancy Ann Carroll 7-6-1861 Mn
Jones, William to Neomi Robertson 4-19-1838 (4-26-1838) Hr
Jones, William to Sarah Black 7-12-1872 (no return) Hy
Jones, William to Sarah H. Hornsby 11-29-1839 (12-3-1839) O
Jones, William to Sarah Young 12-29-1825 G
Jones, William to Susie Jones 12-10-1873 Hy
Jones, Willis to Jane Taylor 9-?-1863 O
Jones, Wilson to Polly Herrin 10-25-1847 (10-26-1847) O
Jones, Wm. A. to Mary Jane Granbery 3-2-1848 F
Jones, Wm. A. to Sophia Montgomery 6-18-1843 Cr
Jones, Wm. A. to Truly Humphrey 5-27-1852 Cr
Jones, Wm. B. to Delelah Short 4-25-1846 (4-30-1846) Hr
Jones, Wm. C. to Rebecca A. Harris 9-23-1858 Cr
Jones, Wm. D. to Rebecca M. Crockett 2-13-1866 (2-14-1866) O
Jones, Wm. E. to J. B. James 11-27-1871 (no return) Cr
Jones, Wm. E. to Mrs. Underhill 12-16-1859 Sh
Jones, Wm. F. to Mary E. Cleere 9-2-1845 (9-4-1845) F
Jones, Wm. H. to Ann Adams 10-26-1842 (11-3-1842) Hr
Jones, Wm. M. to Anthior Weed 9-13-1846 Sh
Jones, Wm. N. to Sarah Speer 5-29-1837 (5-30-1837) G
Jones, Wm. R. to Emily R. Chambers 5-19-1864 O
Jones, Wm. S. to Aillvice? Slaughter 12-31-1839 F
Jones, Wm. T. to Emily R. Chance 2-20-1860 Cr
Jones, Wm. T. to Louisa J. McAuley 1-26-1857 Cr
Jones, Wm. T. to Sarah Comer 12-5-1855 Hr
Jones, Wm. W. to Susan E. Chitman 8-7-1857 (8-16-1857) G
Jones, Wm. to Ann Gause 1-23-1866 Hy
Jones, Wm. to Frankey Taylor 9-20-1867 (9-21-1867) F B
Jones, Wm. to Manurva Roberts 8-13-1839 (8-22-1839) G
Jones, Wm. to Martha Randal 1-8-1869 (1-16-1869) F B
Jones, Wm. to Mary Test? 9-8-1850 We
Jones, Wm. to Susan Springfield 1-23-1869 (no return) F B
Jones, sr., William H. to Mary E. Key 9-15-1873 L
Jones?, John W. to Elizabeth Ann Luton 3-14-1857 O
Jones?, Wm. B. to Mary H. Ring 9-30-1864 O
Jonstone, B. F. to Jane Thomas 9-8-1877 O
Joodard, James A. to Martha M. Walker 3-13-1861 T
Joplin, Aaron to Nancy Jane Edwards 10-20-1870 L
Joplin, Aaron to Sarah Daniel 3-27-1880 (3-29-1880) L
Jordan, Albert to Alabama Faulk 12-21-1867 (12-22-1867) T
Jordan, Alex to Caledonia Wright 9-19-1885 (9-20-1885) L B
Jordan, Arch to Belle Reid 2-23-1869 G
Jordan, Bill to Katy Holland 12-23-1869 G B
Jordan, Burrell to Bettie A. Holmes 1-11-1871 (1-12-1871) F
Jordan, Callis to Nielli Light 12-16-1874 (12-17-1874) Dy B
Jordan, Charles W. to Callie B. Boswell 12-10-1866 (12-12-1866) F
Jordan, Dandridge M. to Susanah R. Johnson 9-25-1852 (no return) F
Jordan, Dave to Martha Eison 1-22-1878 (1-24-1878) L
Jordan, David to Elizabeth M. Hight 1-14-1852 G
Jordan, E. E. to E. L. Yancy 10-1-1879 (10-2-1879) L
Jordan, E. F. to M. H. Rogers 11-13-1840 Be
Jordan, Edward T. to Ann S. Green 10-27-1846 (10-28-1846) F
Jordan, F. M. to Sarah E. Howard 1-30-1867? Hn
Jordan, G. S. to S. F. Cole 10-29-1860 Sh
Jordan, George to Sarah J. McFadden 7-29-1867 (8-7-1867) F
Jordan, Green to Betsy Yancy 1-31-1870 G B
Jordan, George to Margarett Jordan 8-3-1869 G B
Jordan, Harry to Hannah Davis 7-26-1877 (7-27-1877) O
Jordan, Henry to Leanor Gause 2-28-1868 (no return) Dy

Jordan, Horace G. to Sophia L. Taliaferro 9-28-1866 Hy
Jordan, Howell T. to Mary H. Windrow 12-15-1857 (no return) L
Jordan, Howell to E. Currie 2-24-1886 (2-25-1886) L
Jordan, J. B. to C. Hurt 8-18-1874 (8-23-1874) L
Jordan, James to Rachel McQuiston 6-1-1866 (6-3-1866) T
Jordan, Jim to Emily Harris 1-26-1878 (1-31-1878) L B
Jordan, Joe to Nancy White 3-17-1869 (3-18-1869) L
Jordan, John M. to Celea A. Woodard 1-1-1853 (1-2-1853) G
Jordan, John W. to Margery E. Neely 10-7-1842 (12-12-1842) F
Jordan, John to Eller Green 10-9-1867 (10-12-1867) L B
Jordan, John to M. Whitehead 12-11-1847 (12-16-1847) F
Jordan, John to Maggie Jones 10-18-1870 (no return) F B
Jordan, John to Mary Ledsinger 5-14-1878 (5-15-1878) Dy
Jordan, Joseph to Martha Ennis 1-21-1880 (1-23-1880) L
Jordan, Joseph to Mary J. E. S. Nobles 11-24-1857 L
Jordan, Joseph to Sarah Pea? 1-8-1879 (1-9-1879) L
Jordan, Josh to Angeline Briant 8-1-1871 Cr B
Jordan, M. R. to M. Merrick 5-15-1842 Be
Jordan, Mack to Lucy Williams 4-24-1869 (4-29-1869) F B
Jordan, Mike to Amanda Clark 12-27-1870 (12-29-1870) Cr B
Jordan, N. J. to Josey Howard? 10-4-1877 (10-5-1877) L
Jordan, Nat to Mary King 2-12-1873 Hy
Jordan, Peter to Frances Wirt 2-20-1869 (3-21-1869) F B
Jordan, Peter to Maria Caldwell 3-11-1885 (3-12-1885) L
Jordan, Philip to Sarah Jordan 1-22-1873 L
Jordan, R. C. to F. M. Newton 1-15-1879 (1-16-1879) L
Jordan, R. E. to Rena Right (Wright?) 5-18-1876 (6-4-1876) L
Jordan, R. to N. C. McLeod 8-11-1840 Be
Jordan, Richard to Julia Bradford 2-8-1870 (no return) L
Jordan, Samuel to Moriah Maclin 11-5-1872 Hy
Jordan, Samuel to ____ ____ 8-10-1867 (no return) L B
Jordan, Stephen J. to Mary A. Nunn 10-17-1860 G
Jordan, Thomas A. to Elizabeth B. Gause 11-9-1859 (11-11-1859) L
Jordan, Thomas to Gracey Davis 11-25-1869 (no return) L
Jordan, Tom to Betsy Poindexter 1-4-1869 F B
Jordan, W. W. to F. E. Pierce 12-4-1871 Dy
Jordan, W. W. to Susan F. Hawthorn 12-6-1855 Be
Jordan, William J. to Ella M. Dunavant 11-25-1871 (11-26-1871) L
Jordan, William S. to Susan Pursley 11-9-1863 O
Jordan, Wm. C. to Juliand Lester 12-23-1839 (12-24-1839) F
Jordan, Wm. to Nannie Hudson 3-26-1880 Dy
Jordeen?, Jesse J. H. to Julie A. McLune? 4-2-1866 (no return) Cr
Jorden, Benjamin to Susan M. Harget 12-28-1865 Hy
Jorden, Joseph to Harriet Young 10-29-1867 (10-30-1867) T
Jordian, John L. to Martha N. Harlan 8-8-1843? (9-12-1844) G
Jordian, Thomas C. to Martha Ann Williams 10-16-1839 (10-17-1839) G
Jordian, Thos. W. to Idortha S. A. Seat 3-8-1841 (3-11-1841) G
Jordon, Alvin to Lucy Ann Poe 9-14-1845 Be
Jordon, E. F. to Lucy A. Bevill 3-14-861 Cr
Jordon, Evans to Margarett Tolbert 4-27-1847 Be
Jordon, Henry to Rebecca Cole 4-11-1847 Be
Jordon, James to Lucinda Robertson 1-20-1846 Hr
Jordon, M. D. L. to Martha Hillsman 11-8-1858 Cr
Jordon, Rightmon to Amanda Pearce 7-30-1843 Be
Jordon, Saml. B. to Eliza W. Hilliard 1-31-1849 F
Jordon, Thomas to Harriet Snow 4-9-1870 (4-23-1870) L
Jordon, William R. to Sarah Jane Crocket 12-?-1871 (12-11-1871) L
Joseph, Henry to Nellie Robison 5-29-1867 T
Joslin, Willis to Mary Dorset 11-8-1845 G
Joslyn, John to Joysy W. Thomas 11-15-1833 (11-21-1833) Hr
Josslyn, Silas M. to Elizabeth A. Thomas 9-10-1833 (9-19-1833) Hr
Jost, Jacob to Dalmedia Booth 6-22-1871 Hy
Jourdan, Alvin to Sarah Barker 10-12-1850 O
Jourdan, Alvin to Sarah Barker 10-12-1850 (10-13-1850) O
Jourdan, C. P. to Zilphy Cherry 10-26-1847 (10-28-1847) Hr
Jourdan, James S. to Wincy Macon 1-3-1848 (1-6-1848) Hr
Jourdan, James to Sarah A. Wittenborough 5-12-1842 Hn
Jourden, Joseph J. to Mary F. Norden 1-9-1868 Be
Jourdon, Thos. W. to Martha Clark 4-21-1845 Cr
Journey, James C. to Mary Godsey 10-8-1848 O
Jouvenat, E. to Minnie Morris 1-15-1862 Hr
Jowien, Herman to Sophia Meier 3-13-1861 Sh
Joy, Christopher G. to Ellen D. Nappier 12-22-1842 Hr
Joyce, Archibald to Louisa Denny 1-1-1838 Hr
Joyce, Hardin to Mary Smalley 4-16-1838 (4-19-1838?) Hr
Joyce, J. H. to E. C. Carlton 12-6-1866 G
Joyce, John to Mary Glancy 11-29-1862 Sh
Joyce, Michael to Mary Jane Conner 1-19-1861 (1-22-1861) Sh
Joyce, Patrick to Margaret McCail 7-10-1863 Sh
Joyce, Richard to Margaret Ann Watson 1-31-1863 Sh
Joyce, Robert to Meinga? Pollard 11-16-1839 Cr
Joyce, Thomas to Ann (Mrs.) McDonough 11-19-1862 Sh
Joyce, W. W. to A. M. Ford 1-3-1849 Sh
Joyce, Wm. T. (Capt.) to Alcina A. (Mrs.) Hume 3-30-1838 Sh
Joyner, Anthony to Helen Taliaferro 2-1-1877 Hy
Joyner, E. Marshall to Lucy J. Morris 2-27-1866 (3-1-1866) Cr
Joyner, E.? C. to Amdan F. Dunn 8-9-1867 (no return) Hn

Joyner, H. H. to Ann H. Drummons 11-5-1866 (11-6-1866) T
Joyner, Henry to Jenkins Thomason 2-8-1850 (no return) Hn
Joyner, J. R. to S. A. Janes 11-5-1860 (11-8-1860) Hr
Joyner, J. to P. P. Hall 1-19-1875 Hy
Joyner, Jacob to Elizabeth J. Small 3-13-1851 Sh
Joyner, Jacob to Weschina A. Neville 11-26-1861 (11-28-1861) Sh
Joyner, John to Elvina Shepard 5-29-1850 Hn
Joyner, Jonathan to Bettie S. Royster 4-19-1851 (5-6-1851) Sh
Joyner, Jonathan to Mary Jane Crews 4-14-1858 (4-20-1858) Hr
Joyner, Joshua to Lucinda A. Robertson 7-28-1842 Cr
Joyner, Mathew to Mary Ann Nutt? 7-3-1837 (7-4-1837) Hr
Joyner, N. L. to C. W. King 7-6-1865 Cr
Joyner, Nick G. to Martha E. Sellers 2-7-1866 (2-8-1866) Cr
Joyner, R. H. to Ellen P. Bell 11-28-1865 O
Joyner, R. M. to Annie E. S. McMurry 5-1-1870 Hy
Joyner, Robert to Sarah Price 12-28-1868 (12-3-1869?) T
Joyner, Turner B. to Elizabeth A. Dunnegin 9-24-1853 (9-25-1853) O
Joyner, Washington to Sarah Ann Forbess 7-21-1868 (7-23-1868) T
Joyner, William to Jane Vance 12-30-1861 (1-1-1862) Sh
Joyner, William to Mary E. Thomson 11-12-1844 Sh
Joyner, Wm. H. to Sarah A. Robinson 9-26-1848 Cr
Joyner, Wm. Henry to Mary E. Forbess 2-27-1866 (3-1-1866) T
Joynier, W. D. to Susan A. Mills 12-1-1868 Hy
Jukes, Thomas S. to Emma M. Syfert 2-16-1863 Sh
Julian, T. A. to M. J. Kelser 10-20-1874 O
Julin, Elijah J. to Sarah F. Sommers 8-5-1860 We
Julin, James to Sarah J. Wainscot 5-28-1855 We
Julius, Louis to Amanda Allen 10-25-1881 (10-25-1882?) L B
Justice, Allen A. to Nancy A. M. Burney 9-28-1853 G
Justice, Daniel to Frances A. Webb 2-16-1856 (2-17-1856) Hr
Justice, John W. to Lucy W. Shearin 12-23-1858 G
Justice, Louis to Martha Dickinson 8-28-1869 (10-17-1869) F B
Justice, Samuel H. to Arlesa Yarbrough 3-16-1853 (3-17-1853) Hr
Justice, William A. to Susan H. Felts 1-5-1854 Hr
Justice, William to Mary Margaret Kimey 12-20-1856 (12-23-1856) T
Justice, Wm. M. to Bethuenia P. Rogers 12-25-1861 (1-1-1862) Hr

Kahn, Simon to Sarah Kahn 1-8-1850 Sh
Kail, Hiram to Mary A. Tyler 1-17-1866 Hy
Kail, Ivey to Sarepta J. Daniel 4-26-1871 (no return) Hy
Kail, J. F. to M. J. Revelle 1-14-1873 Hy
Kail, Joseph to Eliza L. Baker 1-20-1860 (1-24-1860) Sh
Kail, R. E. to N. J. Revelle 12-21-1872 (no return) Hy
Kain, William to Elizabeth Moss 5-2-1866 (5-3-1866) Cr
Kaine, Thomas to Rosa Maguire 8-14-1852 (8-15-1852) Sh
Kaiser, John to Rowenna Huffman 1-5-1854 Sh
Kaler, John W. to Amelia A. Martin 11-26-1841 Hn
Kaley, John to Bridget Bryan 4-26-1851 (4-28-1851) Sh
Kammerer, Charles to Mary Kinzler 7-30-1857 Sh
Kane, James to Julia Russell 3-2-1864 Sh
Kane, Thomas to Nancy Lillis 6-23-1862 (6-24-1862) Sh
Kaplinger, John to Mary Culpeper 1-12-1860 Be
Kappel, John to Catharine Wittig 1-31-1853 Sh
Karnes, Abraham to Martha McKelvy 2-27-1843 (2-28-1843) G
Karnes, Absalom to Rebeca Brogden 11-15-1869 G
Karnes, John to Cynthia Sainford 7-21-1851 (7-23-1851) G
Karnes, William F. to Levina Hicks 1-24-1867 G
Karr, David to Isabell C. Cobb 12-6-1838 Sh
Karr, J. W. to Lizzie C. Wray 1-3-1853 (no return) F
Karting, Martin to Eliza Shehan 6-2-1860 (6-4-1860) Sh
Kates, William to Ginny Hart 7-23-1868 (no return) Cr
Kathy, John to Martha Pain 4-5-1855 Cr
Kattman, Henry to Fanny Marrick 2-10-1855 (2-17-1855) Sh
Katzenmeier, Jacob to Mary Yearger 5-31-1847 Sh
Kaufman, David to Anna Emanuel 7-20-1850 Sh
Kaufman, H. to Caroline Wolf 10-30-1854 (10-31-1854) Sh
Kaufman, Herman to Amalia Leinkauf 2-23-1864 Sh
Kaufman, Moses to Jeanette Keahn 10-14-1861 Sh
Kaufmann, Louis to Ernestine Brummer 5-21-1858 Sh
Kaughman, Joe to Barbara Smith 1-22-1880 (1-25-1880) L
Kavanaugh, Jas. P. to Mary F. Beasly 3-7-1863 (no return) Hy
Kawinkel, Charles to Elionie Shnieder 12-3-1852 Sh
Kay, C. N. to Nancy A. Tague 2-8-1872 Dy
Keal, James D. to Mary B. Holmes 8-28-1856 Cr
Keal, Jesse to R. C. Spears 12-20-1866 G
Kealey, Andrew to Julia Cartay 6-20-1857 (6-21-1857) Sh
Kealthley, Weston to Elizabeth Pate 11-14-1853 G
Kean (Keon), Thos. H. to Helen Slade 7-21-1846 Hr
Kean, Frederick W. to Rachel North 7-8-1873 (not executed) L *
Keane, John O. to Mary Ellis 10-25-1860 (10-28-1860) Cr
Keane, Thomas to Catharine Dolan 1-21-1860 (1-22-1860) Sh
Keaner, Augustus to Amelia L. Wetli 2-3-1849 Sh
Keaner, Christopher to Barbara Hechelman 2-3-1849 Sh
Kearney, J. K. to Florence A. Drewry 12-27-1869 (12-28-1869) Cr
Kearney, Philip I.? to Sarah Ramsey 1-6-1829 Hr
Kearney, Wm. H. H. to Emeline Turner 3-20-1866 (3-22-1866) Ma
Kearns, Patrick to Naomi Vincent 3-26-1856 Sh

Keath, James R. to Luisa C. Ward 10-17-1846 (9?-18-1846) G
Keath, John to Hannah R. Hollan 1-29-1838 (1-31-1838) G
Keath, Joseph D. to Sarah A. Prichard 11-13-1874 (11-14-1874) Dy
Keathley, Calvin to Eliza Jane Gleason 2-21-1843 (2-?-1843) O
Keathley, G. W. to A. J. Keathley 1-10-1868 (could be 1-8) G
Keathley, J. G. to Hepsey Ann Branch 12-1-1851 G
Keathley, Jeremiah to Sarah A. O'Daniel 12-25-1858 (12-26-1858) G
Keathley, John G. to Elizabeth Bowder 2-1-1851 G
Keathley, Johnathan to Sarah Houston 12-28-1859 (12-29-1859) T
Keathly, Archalus to Sarrah Branch 5-28-1840 (5-31-1840) G
Keathly, Archelus to Margaret Linton 1-1-1853 G
Keathly, Branch to Manirva Burnes 5-27-1850 G
Keathly, Elisha to Hepsy A. Grady 5-23-1854 (5-25-1854) G
Keathly, Marshall B. to Mary F. Wilson 11-25-1854 G
Keating, J. M. to Elizabeth Browning 4-27-1857 Cr
Keating, James R. to Sarah A. Mitchell 11-26-1846 Cr
Keating, N. J. to Dicy Cooper 2-2-1846 (no return) Cr
Keating, Wm. to Mary A. Piper 2-18-1850 Cr
Keatley, Henry S. to Mary A. Pyle 10-18-1854 Sh
Keaton, C. L. to Sarah E. Fuqua 8-4-1868 (no return) Cr
Keaton, Edmd. to Catharine Houlehan 5-8-1852 (5-9-1852) Sh
Keaton, G. H. to Jane Arnold 11-2-1857 G
Keaton, J. P. to Amanda Larimore 2-25-1868 T
Keaton, J. W. to Mollie A. Keaton 1-30-1873 (1-31-1873) Cr
Keaton, James A. to R. J. Browning 12-29-1855 Cr
Keaton, James W. to Rebecca Webb 12-14-1859 (12-24-1859) Ma
Keaton, James to Martha N. Leach 12-29-1851 Cr
Keck, E. to Mattie J. Felts 1-27-1864 Sh
Kee, Charles to Mary J. Cox 4-14-1849 Cr
Kee, G. W. to L. F. Laycock 10-27-1872 Cr
Kee, Hol. to Eliza Dean 11-16-1840 Be
Kee, Holoway to Susan E. Edwards 1-27-1867 Be
Kee, Isaac to Lydia Sullivan 3-30-1844 F
Kee, J. W. to Martha Caffrey 9-29-1860 Cr
Kee, James L. to Adaline Adams 9-4-1865 (9-6-1865) F
Kee, Janes to Clery? A. Suggs 11-10-1860 (11-17-1860) Cr
Kee, John H. to Elizabeth Knowls 11-7-1867 G
Kee, John J. to Martha E. Gillispie 1-26-1868 Be
Kee, Lewis K. to M. L. V. Forsheer 8-6-1873 (8-7-1873) Cr
Kee, Milton B. to Savanah Hicks 6-16-1866 (6-17-1866) Cr
Kee, Robert to Florida Dunn 8-7-1867 F B
Kee, T. J. to Cairo A. Barfield 2-11-1878 (2-13-1878) L
Kee, T. J. to Elizabeth Allen 3-2-1863 Be
Kee, Th. to C. Hale 4-21-1840 Be
Kee, Thomas L. to Susan E. Pritchard 8-12-1868 (8-13-1868) Cr
Kee, W. R. to C. A. Walker 8-10-1862 Be
Kee, Wm. to Mary Dill 6-7-1855 Cr
Keeble, J. W. to Binga H. Powell 9-10-1855 (no return) F
Keeble, James R. to Mary E. Robertson 11-23-1862 Hy
Keech, Horace M. to Indiana E. Norton 1-6-1862 Sh
Keefe, Thomas to Catharine McGuire 5-12-1850 Sh
Keefe, William to Bridget Toben 11-25-1855 Sh
Keefe, Willington to Catherine Stricklin 3-20-1868 Ma
Keegin, John to Catharine Hoolihan 10-25-1859 Sh
Keel, E. T. to Martha C. Bledsoe 5-14-1864 (5-16-1864) Sh
Keel, Ezekiel T. to Louisa C. Grace (Groce) 2-17-1842 Sh
Keel, Henry to Queen Yancy 1-8-1876 (no return) Hy
Keel, L. B. to A. T. (F?) Spellings 8-11-1870 G
Keel, William J. to Martha C. Briggins 4-10-1862 Sh
Keelen, Floridore A. to Margaret Ann Neely 7-15-1856 (7-16-1856) Ma
Keelen, Floridore A. to Mary I. Williamson 4-8-1861 Ma
Keelin, Percy to Martha J. Parnell 6-9-1853 Cr
Keeling, David H. to Nannie Hoskins 4-16-1852 (5-4-1852) Sh
Keely, Edmund to Louise A. Battle 10-12-1853 G
Keely, Thomas to J. Carbery 11-13-1863 Sh
Keen, Wm. J. to Mary E. R. Wilson 11-9-1848 Sh
Keenan, G. M. to A. V. Fulghum 12-15-1869 G
Keenan, Michel to Pemela S. H. Hamilton 6-18-1845 (6-19-1845) G
Keenan, W. P. to Sallie Hicks 4-18-1878 (4-19-1878) Dy
Keene, M. L. to M. E. Hult? 12-16-1874 T
Keenen, Edward to Mary Killfinin 8-13-1864 (8-14-1864) Sh
Keenon, John to Mary Hollins no date (with 1861) Be
Keer, John to Puss Taylor 3-4-1868 (3-7-1868) F B
Keese, Geo. W. to Harriett A. Purkins 7-26-1847 Sh
Keim, George to Elizabeth C. Trezevant 4-24-1856 Sh *
Keim, Mathias to Catharine Scherer 1-6-1860 (1-7-1860) Sh
Keinman, Moses H. to Mary M. Eaves 9-1-1855 (9-2-1855) O
Keirman, Thomas to Ann Fergerson 4-10-1869 (4-17-1869) Cr
Keisacker, F. T. to Margaret A. Seaier 3-1-1853 Sh
Keiser, George F. to Prudence Jackson 1-1-1831 O
Keith, A. D. to M. O. Stockton 9-14-1854 Hr
Keith, John to Polly Robertson 11-11-1837 G
Keith, Josiah to Susan Burton 2-13-1857 (2-16-1857) O
Keith, Lewis to Mary Haller 12-6-1854 Sh
Keith, Micajah to Susan Replogle 5-19-1832 Ma
Keith, William to Johanna Kennedy 10-20-1863 Sh
Keith, William to Mollie Steward 11-27-1869 Ma

Kelch, Philip J. to Martha Watkins 8-20-1859 (no return) L
Keliher, John to Mary Doyle 8-25-1862 Sh
Kell, Pennell to Elizabeth Scallarn 12-23-1829 (12-24-1829) G
Kellar, George W. to Kate Barber 12-21-1870 Ma
Kellar, Solomon to Mary Roberson 2-20-1873 Hy
Kellebrew, James F. to Sharlott E. Turner 2-21-1858 We
Keller, A. H. P. to M. E. E. Wood 9-22-1875 L
Keller, Alfred E. to Louisa Linn 11-7-1848 Sh
Keller, Alfred E. to Martha Louise Simm 11-7-1848 Sh
Keller, Charles W. to Mary Elizabeth Rippins 3-12-1863 Sh
Keller, E. to S. E. Chambers 5-19-1880 L
Keller, George to Louisa Baumgardner 4-11-1860 (4-12-1860) Sh
Keller, H. M. to Helen M. Decker 12-14-1859 (12-15-1859) Sh
Keller, H. P. to Fanny E. Davis 12-16-1879 L
Keller, Hiram W. to Roberta C. E. Burks 12-18-1860 (12-19-1860) L
Keller, Isaac W. to Nancy Ellen Twyford 12-4-1856 (3-18-1857) Sh
Keller, J. F. to Tenny Dunivant 9-25-1873 Hy
Keller, Jefferson to Rosella Jennings 11-23-1876 (not certified) L
Keller, Joseph to Elizabeth Baumgartner 5-22-1845 Sh
Keller, Robert to _____ 12-26-1868 L
Kellett, Ethelbert to Evaline Brent 12-25-1866 (12-27-1866) Dy
Kelley, A. A. to C. A. Kelley 11-1-1874 G
Kelley, A. J. to M. F. Baker 9-14-1859 T
Kelley, Albert Ambrose to Martha Jane Roberts 10-27-1855 (10-29-1855) T
Kelley, David to Rebecca Bell 9-1-1866 G
Kelley, Edmond to Ela Ann Williams 7-5-1838 F
Kelley, G. W. to Susan A. Andrews 12-10-1856 We
Kelley, Isaac N. to Paulina Jordan 12-18-1848 (12-24-1848) T
Kelley, J. F. to H. A. Burns 8-2-1879 (8-3-1879) L
Kelley, James to Pheriba Lancaster 2-14-1856 Sh
Kelley, John M. to Jane H. Parish 7-20-1867 O
Kelley, John to Mary Ward 6-11-1862 (no return) Hn
Kelley, John to Sophia Caroline Johnson 11-5-1864 Sh
Kelley, John to Susan Moore 11-25-1876 (11-26-1876) L
Kelley, John to Susan N. Powell 2-6-1871 (2-7-1871) L
Kelley, Joseph to Lavina Thompson 6-13-1833 G
Kelley, M. H. to S. E. Hood 12-26-1867 F
Kelley, Munro to Nancy Shankle 8-12-1873 T
Kelley, Nathana to Mary Ann Crockett 10-16-1862 O
Kelley, Oliver P. to Julia Ann Hartsfield 7-14-1847 T
Kelley, P. G. to D. A. Kelley 12-14-1870 (12-15-1870) T
Kelley, Philip to Joanna Neill 8-6-1855 (8-7-1855) Sh
Kelley, Tho. Jefferson to Mary Jane McMinns 7-20-1850 T
Kelley, Thomas to Ann Branan 5-19-1862 Sh
Kelley, Thomas to Mary O'Conner 8-22-1870 (8-23-1870) Ma
Kelley, V. H. to R. J. H. Lewis 1-4-1871 Cr
Kelley, Vincent P. to S. J. Upchurch 12-30-1858 T
Kelley, Vincent P. to Sarah J. Upchurch 12-30-1858 T
Kelley, W. C. to J. E. Holmes 9-5-1867 L
Kelley, W. O. to Lucella Elder 10-1-1867 G
Kelley, Washington to Alamerana Skeggs 8-16-1842 Sh
Kelley, Wesley to Penelope A. Brashear 5-13-1869 C
Kelling, George to Matilda Alberson 11-28-1849 Hn
Kellis, Henry to Nicey Jones 3-28-1867 (no return) L B
Kellough, Samuel to Elizabeth P. Allison 4-16-1840 G
Kelloum, W. H. to J. E. Hines 10-13-1879 (no return) L
Kellow, A. A. to Janettie A. Parrish 12-27-1876 Dy
Kellow, James to O. D. Moore 8-8-1876 (8-9-1876) Dy
Kellow, John W. to Sallie Echols 11-22-1877 Dy
Kellow, Samel J. to L. C. Saunders 10-29-1874 Dy
Kellow, Samuel to Mary J. Patterson 12-26-1867 G
Kellow, Thomas H. to Nancy You 1-20-1875 (1-21-1875) Dy
Kelly, A. M. to Margaret J. McConnell 12-18-1863 (no return) Hn
Kelly, Aaron to Phebe Trigg 11-27-1872 (12-16-1873?) T
Kelly, Alfred M. to Martha Henley 4-7-1843 G
Kelly, Alfred to Malinda Shelby 2-16-1835 Hr
Kelly, Alfred to Martha Boswell 3-9-1847 (no return) F
Kelly, Alfred to Tabitha Jackson 6-2-1842 Hn
Kelly, Augustus to Martha P. Williams 7-20-1846 (7-23-1846) F
Kelly, Barnett to Bridget King 11-26-1857 Sh
Kelly, C. L. to E. R. Bomer 4-11-1856 Hn
Kelly, Cornelius to Julia Fitzpatrick 8-25-1860 (8-26-1860) Sh
Kelly, Daniel G. to Susan E. Field 4-3-1843 (4-5-1843) Hr
Kelly, Dennis to Johanna Coffee 1-22-1861 (1-23-1861) Sh
Kelly, E. H. to Annie Gridly 11-20-1866 (no return) Hy
Kelly, E. Mis? to Martha A. Pool 12-27-1865 Dy
Kelly, Elisha to Trusiana C. Creasy 2-7-1864 Be
Kelly, George to Mary E. Fisher 10-25-1849 F
Kelly, Henry to Martha A. F. Robb 12-21-1852 G
Kelly, Hugh to Bridget Coggen 4-16-1860 Sh
Kelly, Isaac to Sarah Osteen 12-6-1846 We
Kelly, J. B. to Maggie Locke 2-16-1874 T
Kelly, J. M. to Malinda J. Baskins 1-21-1861 (1-23-1861) T
Kelly, J. M. to Z. L. Tosh 12-19-1872 Cr
Kelly, J. W. to M. E. Louis 1-2-1873 Cr
Kelly, James C. to Louisa W. Nowlin 11-15-1846 (11-19-1846) F
Kelly, James F. to Susan M. Cole 2-20-1855 Ma

Kelly, James M. to Mary Ann Parker 2-12-1853 Sh
Kelly, James to Ellen Gray 10-12-1852 Sh
Kelly, James to Lucy Boswell 4-19-1849 Cr
Kelly, James to Nancy C. Jackson 6-28-1828 Ma
Kelly, James to Susan McCarver 9-16-1846 Ma
Kelly, John C. to E. A. Johnson 4-30-1861 Be
Kelly, John H. to Mary Sawyer 10-15-1859 Sh
Kelly, John Z. to Nancy Tosh 1-10-1866 Cr
Kelly, John to Alice (Mrs.) Kernan 7-28-1855 (8-5-1855) Sh
Kelly, John to Hannah Doran 1-7-1857 Sh
Kelly, John to Lousanna Phillips 3-11-1854 (3-12-1854) T
Kelly, John to Marinda Pain 2-22-1834 Hr
Kelly, John to T. Glass 10-24-1874 (10-29-1874) T
Kelly, Joseph to Ellen Harrison 4-1-1857 Sh
Kelly, M. to Ellen Higgin 5-15-1856 Sh
Kelly, Michael to Amanda Winsett 2-25-1857 Hn
Kelly, Michael to Ann Doyle 8-19-1863 Sh
Kelly, Michael to Bridget Crimen 6-16-1856 (6-17-1856) Sh
Kelly, Michael to E. Galloway 11-16-1863 Sh
Kelly, Michael to Elizabeth Walker 6-2-1863 Sh
Kelly, Michael to Ellen Bargan (Hargan?) 3-31-1861 Sh
Kelly, Michael to Maria McNorton (Norton?) 10-4-1853 Sh
Kelly, Miles to Winney Jane Jones 5-2-1864 (no return) Hn
Kelly, Nathan to Salina Ellis 9-16-1862 O
Kelly, P. C. to Mary Killian 5-19-1852 (5-20-1852) Sh
Kelly, Patrick to Hannora Burke 7-21-1864 (8-17-1864) Sh
Kelly, Patrick to Jane Woods 9-30-1859 (10-2-1859) Sh
Kelly, Patrick to Mary Mannigan 1-19-1856 (1-20-1856) Sh
Kelly, Patrick to R. L. Merrick 2-27-1849
Kelly, Peter to Ellen Burke 12-26-1858 Sh
Kelly, Richard to Lavinia Perry 1-31-1859 Hn
Kelly, S. B. to Elizabeth Clayton 2-3-1846 Sh
Kelly, Saml. to Charlotte Harmon(Hannon) 12-16-1833 Hr
Kelly, Samuel A. to Sarah A. McDonald 2-24-1857 Cr
Kelly, Stephen to Emarline Pritchard 7-23-1846 Cr
Kelly, Thomas J. to Mary Jane McMins 12-3-1850 Sh
Kelly, Thomas to Mary Hanly 8-2-1862 Sh
Kelly, Thomas to Mary O'Brien 3-23-1854 Sh
Kelly, Thos. H. to Mary A. E. Jordon 12-9-1847 Be
Kelly, W. A. to Martha Haynes 12-15-1866 (12-17-18??) O
Kelly, Wesley to Rachel Giles 3-30-1858 Cr
Kelly, William to Bridget Fitzpatrick 5-2-1859 Sh
Kelly, Willsen to Mary E. Spear 1-18-1860 We
Kelly, Wm. J. to Emily Wilson 1-19-1850 Cr
Kelly, Wm. to Martha Wetherley 2-9-1846 We
Kelough, Joseph to Allis Donegan 4-23-1867 O
Kelsall, Thomas to Belvadora Wilson 5-24-1859 (5-25-1859) Sh
Kelsey (Kilsey), Thomas T. to Emily J. Gill 5-29-1850 Sh
Kelsey, Samuel A. to Rhoda Ann Hicks 7-25-1848 Hn
Kelso, F. N. to Mary A. Crawford 3-5-1873 (3-6-1873) Dy
Kelso, J. J. to M. E. Ford 10-18-1870 (no return) Hy
Kelso, James to Martha Jane Jamison 8-11-1856 Hn
Kelso, Robert to Emmaline Killebrew 1-6-1844 (no return) Hn
Kelsoe, John to Sarah E. Sims 1-1-1868 Hn
Keltner, E. M. to Sarah L. Haynes 12-17-1879 L
Keltner, G. H. to L. A. Belton 5-12-1875 L
Keltner, H. H. to Delilah E. Marell 2-9-1859 Sh
Keltner, J. A. to M. E. Keltner 2-27-1886 (3-1-1886) L
Keltner, J. G. to Sophronia E. Osteen 10-14-1874 (10-15-1874) L
Keltner, James S. to Priscilla Jennings 7-29-1844 (8-1-1844) L
Keltner, John L. to M. E. (Mrs.) Thompson 11-7-1883 (11-8-1883) L
Keltner, John to Lissa Wells 1-21-1871 (no return) Hy
Keltner, Mc. to Lucy Ann Ball 12-31-1866 (1-1-1867) L
Keltner, W. F. to M. F. Byler 6-22-1882 (6-28-1882) L
Kelton, B. F. to Catharine McLaurin 1-25-1866 G
Kelton, Benj. F. to Sarah A. Hardy 1-11-1854 (1-12-1854) G
Kelton, R. A. to Sarah L. Man 10-7-1866 G
Kelton, Robert to Elizabeth Norrod 8-6-1856 (8-13-1856) G
Kelton, Samuel H. to Harriet Britton 9-27-1866 G
Kelton, William S. to Hester Ann Rucker 6-1-1859 G
Kelton, William to Ann Ridgeway 8-26-1844 (no return) We
Kelton, William to Louisa Simpson 3-17-1859 We
Kelton, Wilson to Tenny Johnson 6-22-___ (with 1870) G
Kemmitt, Edward to A. J. Clore 11-3-1869 G
Kemp, A. B. to Martha A. Carter 12-27-1854 Cr
Kemp, B. W. to Nancy Hatchett 9-27-1849 Cr
Kemp, Basey D. to Mahulda A. Williams 3-17-1869 Cr
Kemp, E. D. to Harriet A. Clonch 7-13-1862 Mn
Kemp, F. A. to Elizabeth Ward 8-23-1846 We
Kemp, N. L. to A. A. Williams 6-18-1863 Mn
Kemp, Pleasant G. to P___less Albright 5-12-1857 Cr
Kemp, S. M. to R. Thornton 4-8-1857 We
Kemp, Silas M. to Mary Ann Patterson 10-14-1844 (no return) We
Kemp, Silas N. to Nancy Ann Baker 3-28-1850 We
Kemp, Thomas to Rebecca Shutts 8-14-1861 Mn
Kemph, Michael to G. Caroline Carter 7-10-1854 (7-11-1854) Sh
Kenaday, Abron to Lucy Hall 8-28-1837 (9-21-1837) G

Kenaday, David J. to Eliza W. Harris 3-8-1838 Ma
Kenady, Allen to Martha Gibson 6-20-1849 Hn
Kenady, J. C. to Jane Todd 1-13-1846 We
Kenady, James M. to Letta C. Tinkle 9-5-1855 G
Kenady, Lawson W. to Araminta E. Lamb 8-1-1866 Hn
Kenahan (Kernehan), Robert to Elizabeth Jane Thomas 12-19-1844 Sh
Kendal, Thomas to C. C. Burton 11-12-1860 We
Kendall, A. L. to Martha Gurley 11-30-1851 O
Kendall, Benjamin to Geraldine P. Presnell 7-4-1857 Hn
Kendall, Benjamin to Martha A. Russell 2-5-1854 Hn
Kendall, Charles to Jane Kendall 7-28-1867 Hn B
Kendall, David to Elizabeth J. Lee 11-29-1849 Hn
Kendall, Edward E. to Mary Ann McElyea 10-14-1858 O
Kendall, Isaac to Mary J. Wilson ?-24-1844 (2-29-1844) F
Kendall, J. L. to Martha Gurley 11-30-1857 O
Kendall, James to Martha Wynn 10-1-1856 Hn
Kendall, James to S. C. Warren 10-29-1844 Hn
Kendall, John F. to Martha F. Kendall 8-31-1865 Hn
Kendall, John F. to Nancy Rumbly 4-29-1855 Hn
Kendall, Martin to Judith Kendall 4-6-1867 Hn B
Kendall, Norris to Harriet L. James 11-17-1862 Sh
Kendall, Peter to Selena B. Taylor 8-17-1857 Sh
Kendall, Robert S. to Mary Ann Taylor 9-1-1859 O
Kendall, Samuel P. to Elizabeth Easley 3-11-1855 Hn
Kendall, Samuel to Jane N. Davis 12-9-1838 Hn
Kendall, Thomas J. to Martha E. Caldwell 5-2?-1853 Hn
Kendall, W. D. to Ada Crawford 1-1-1868
Kendall, W. R. to Lydia Wheaton Harrison 12-27-1869 Ma
Kendall, William to Rilley Ann Rumbley 7-15-1847 Hn
Kendall, Wilson to Eliza Copeland 4-30-1843 Hn
Kendel, William Clark to Martha Ann Eliza Barry? 3-11-1841 Hr
Kendell, W. F. to M. C. Carroll 9-27-1854 We
Kendrich, John B. to Drucilla Fanning 12-4-1833 Sh
Kendrick, James to Elizabeth Russell 3-12-1856 Ma
Kendrick, Lewis to Gracy Neel 10-19-1867 (11-6-1867) F B
Kendrick, Nathaniel to Margaret Coble (Colte) 7-26-1840 Sh
Kendrick, Robt. to Ann Notgrass 5-7-1846 (no return) F
Kendrick, W. A. to Aley M. Russell 12-28-1859 Ma
Kendrick, Wright to Lucy C. Ortin 10-28-1863 Sh
Keneday, Joshua to Mary Jane Ledbetter 3-19-1877 L
Kenedy, P. G. to Charlotte Crossnoe 6-27-1869 Be
Kenedy, Vinson to Sarah (Mrs.) Bell 4-21-1841 (no return) F
Keneley, L. B. to M. A. Burks 12-21-1881 (12-22-1881) L
Keneo, John to Mary Maschio 7-12-1860 (7-15-1860) Sh
Kenley, J. A. to Sarah C. Lankford 9-3-1878 (9-4-1878) Dy
Kenna, John to Margaret O'Neill 10-25-1860 Sh
Kennaday, M. A. to Nancy Barnett 8-14-1866 (8-16-1866) Cr
Kennady, Henry to Mary Ann Biggs 1-18-1854 (1-24-1854) G
Kennady, Nelson to Laura J. Simmons 9-18-1839 Hn
Kennady, Rob't Q. to M. E. Simmons 3-5-1867 O
Kennan, James to Bridget Doyle 2-14-1859 Sh
Kenneday, Henry to Susannah Mainor 8-12-1835 G
Kenneday, Samuel D. to Isabella Mews 1-2-1840 Ma
Kennedy, Francis to Emma Holaman 6-15-1876 (6-16-1876) L
Kennedy, Irvin to Selina Meshow? 6-26-1834 Hr
Kennedy, J. L. to Ellen H. Gilbert 10-1-1850 Sh
Kennedy, James to Katharine Jones 3-5-1827 (3-8-1827) G
Kennedy, James to Margaret Anden 7-17-1862 (7-27-1862) Sh
Kennedy, James to Margaret Donavan 5-4-1857 Sh
Kennedy, Jas. to Sarah Barton 7-17-1850 Sh
Kennedy, John A. to Sarah A. Hefley 10-28-1858 (10-30-1858) Ma
Kennedy, John to A. B. Dunn 12-4-1872 T
Kennedy, John to Ailsy E. Boyte 8-21-1839 (8-29-1839) Hr
Kennedy, John to Mary A. E. Brooks 3-19-1867 O
Kennedy, John to Sallie E. Crutcher 12-5-1866 (12-10-1866) Sh
Kennedy, John to Thrulina Bland 3-18-1832 Sh
Kennedy, Louis to Martha Hughlett 12-27-1865 T
Kennedy, Martin to Mary Smith 8-8-1853 Hn
Kennedy, Michael to Mary Gallagan (Garragan?) 10-18-1859 Sh
Kennedy, Patrick to Catharine Burke 11-5-1855 Sh
Kennedy, Riley S. to Sarah Ann Hargas 9-17-1842 (9-21-1842) F
Kennedy, Robert to Sarrah Ward 7-12-1865 G
Kennedy, Saunders to Polly Box 4-14-1827 (4-19-1827) Hr
Kennedy, Thomas to Margaret Coffy 5-28-1862 Sh
Kennedy, William A. to Isabella Butler 6-18-1840 Sh
Kennedy, William to A. K. Tull 12-22-1871 (12-24-1880?) L
Kennedy, William to Maaranda A. Tull 3-16-1875 (3-18-1875) L
Kennedy, William to Mary Blackburn 9-9-1868 G
Kennedy, William to Susan A. Gunter 12-24-1857 Sh
Kennelly, T. R. to Margaret Mizels 3-10-1851 L
Kennelly?, Richard to Mary Ann Newman 4-29-1856 (4-30-1856) L
Kenner, James to Nancy Chipman 4-1-1852 (4-3-1852) Ma
Kenner, Thos. W. to Emily Bailey 3-17-1868 (3-18-1868) Ma
Kenneth, P. G. to L. R. Richards 1-4-1858 Sh
Kenney (Kelley?), Abraham to Fannie Lea 5-24-1873 (5-29-1873) L B
Kenney, John to Sarah M. Wells 5-21-1857 Hr
Kenney, Michael to Alice Callahan 5-14-1853 Sh

Kenney, Thomas to Ann Sammons 4-11-1840 Hr
Kennon, George W. to Jemimah (Samanth?)J. Thompson 9-1-1849 (9-5-1849) L
Kennon, John to Harritt A. Carter 12-20-1870 (12-21-1870) Cr
Kennon, Nelson to Tempy Frazier 4-15-1871 (4-17-1871) F
Kennon, Thos. W. to Tennessee C. Carpenter 9-26-18686 (9-27-1866) F
Kennon, William B. to Susan A. Moore 9-14-1866 (no return) Cr
Kennon, William to Eliza Kennon 12-17-1840 Hn
Kennon, William to Elizabeth Joplin 10-11-1859 Hn
Kennon, Wm. B. to Amanda M. Bigham 5-18-1854 Cr
Kenny, George to Lucinda Tucker 1-11-1834 (1-13-1834) Hr
Kensler, Joseph to Margaret Mohr 4-30-1858 Sh
Kent, J. B. to Fannie Morgan 9-23-1865 T
Kent, James W. to M. M. Prichard 2-5-1879 (2-6-1879) Dy
Kent, John R. to Sarah W. Echols 11-26-1829 Sh
Kent, Prince to Bittie Jordan 9-16-1872 (9-21-1872) L
Kent, Thos. B. to Sarah McGregor 1-13-1866 T
Kent, William to Arene Hay 12-23-1873 Hy
Kent, Wm. Alexr. to Rachel Gray 11-29-1851 (12-3-1851) T
Kent, Wm. to Siney King 10-12-1870 (no return) Hy
Kently (Kietley?), Francis to Martha T. Conwell (Cornwell?) 6-12-1851 Sh
Kents, Wm. J. to Margaret E. Cotton 12-18-1852 (12-21-1852) T
Keny, David C. to Mary King 2-22-1858 We
Keough, Timothy to Mary Kane 9-6-1862 Sh
Kephart, Simon W. to Margaret Subber 4-5-1831 Sh
Kepler, Heinrich to Frances Fahnisihon 10-11-1852 Sh
Kerby (Kelby), Patrick to Julia Lucett 5-12-1863 Sh
Kerby, B. F. to Julian Saunders 4-11-1876 (4-23-1876) L
Kerby, F. M. to Margaret J. Hord 3-29-1862 (3-30-1863?) Cr
Kerby, Geo. W. to Mary Clark 12-27-1850 (no return) Hn
Kerby, Henry to Letty Ann Reynolds 3-19-1846 L
Kerby, J. W. to Rhoda Ellis 2-13-1872 (2-14-1871?) L
Kerby, Joseph T. to Rocinda Carter 12-19-1868 (12-23-1868) Cr
Kerby, Martin W. to Mary Ann Bennet 7-2-1857 Ma
Kerby, Smith C. to M. J. Pate 5-5-1860 O
Kerby, Smith to Carson E. Asburry 12-17-1866 (12-18-18??) O
Kerin, Thomas B. to Prudy M. (Mrs.) Crews 7-1-1868 G
Kerkendall, Abner to Maria Duff 12-8-1829 (9-30-1830) Hr
Kerkpatrick, J. S. to C. D. Gray 12-6-1873 T
Kerly, James A. to Mary Jane Cloyd 8-9-1860 (8-12-1860) Cr
Kern, Lewis to Caroline Block 5-18-1848 Sh
Kern, Thomas to Elizabeth Jenkins 5-24-1841 (5-26-1841) T
Kernan, John T. to M. J. Mitchell 8-20-1874 O
Kernan, M. T. to Laura A. Pope 5-28-1872 (no return) Cr
Kernes (Korns), Patrick H. to Margaret Collins 11-3-1845 Sh
Kerney, Dennis to Bridget Condon 10-18-1859 (10-23-1859) Sh
Kerniham, Lawrence to Nancy A. Rodgers 7-29-1868 (no return) F B
Kerns, William M. to Martha S. Webb 11-17-1856 (11-18-1856) G
Kerr, Addison to Lucy Ann Williams 4-11-1850 M
Kerr, Andrew H. to Mary J. C. Ward 3-3-1846 Sh
Kerr, Augustus to Henrietta Baxter 7-6-1868 (7-18-1868) L
Kerr, B. F. to Martha Weaver 2-25-1863 Mn
Kerr, J. H. to S. L. Bowen 2-12-1861 (2-13-1861) Sh
Kerr, J. R. to Mary J. Alexander 11-10-1847 F
Kerr, Jerry to Mary J. Green 2-19-1877 (not executed) L B
Kerr, Joseph to Jane Beasley 3-7-1871 (3-8-1871) Dy
Kerr, M. W. to Sarah E. McGee 11-22-1869 G
Kerr, Miles Wade to Elisabeth Nancy Wilbanks 4-22-1865 T
Kerr, Pinkney to Martha Eastwood 10-29-1869 (11-7-1869) L
Kerr, Samel M. to Rebecca O. Williams 12-21-1850 (12-25-1850) F
Kerr, Thomas to Issabella Treese 10-17-1854 (10-18-1854) Hr
Kerr, W. C. to Ema C. Hall 6-29-1854 G
Kerr, W. F. to P. P. Sharp 12-18-1867 G
Kerr, W. J. to Amanda M. Townes 12-17-1867 (12-19-1867) Cr
Kerr, WM. to Kate Stevens 4-6-1869 (no return) Dy
Kerr, William Henry to Julia Gordon Law 10-17-1859 (10-18-1859) Sh
Kerr, William to Louisa G. Mitchell 7-8-1837 (7-13-1837) Hr
Kerr, Wm. A. to Elizabeth Murray 3-1-1861 Hy
Kerr, Yoring F. to Louisa M. J. Hampton 11-19-1850 Cr
Kerrman, Simon to Philomene Fuchs 11-27-1856 (11-29-1856) Sh
Kersey, D. T. J. to C. H. Calhoun 3-5-1861 O
Kersey, H. T. to S. J. Williams 11-4-1860 O
Kersey, Hall to Rebecca Buckley 12-1-1863 (12-3-1863) F
Kersey, John D. to Martha P. Boucher 9-15-1853 G
Kersey, Thomas to Nancy C. Payne 12-29-1844 Sh
Kesfel (Kessel?), Augustus to Anna Folmer 10-1-1855 Sh
Kessler, John to Caroline Walker 1-2-1862 Sh
Kesterson, J. H. to E. J. Bagwell 6-10-1865 (6-14-1865) O
Kesterson, J. H. to Mary Green 9-6-1854 We
Kesterson, J. P. to L. C. Norris? 8-21-1859 Hn
Kesterson, John to Ann H. Hardaway 5-13-1847 Sh
Kesterson, John to Belinda Dorsey 2-1-1827 (2-?-1827) Hr
Keston, Julius to Mary S. Pruit 8-24-1854 Sh
Ketcham, James to Jane Garrison 10-4-1848 F
Ketchum, Frank to Rosella Rainer 10-28-1868 (no return) F B
Ketchum, L. to Annie C. Bradford 4-15-1858 Sh
Ketchum, Wm. to Hannah Buryhill 2-7-1846 We

Ketchum, Wm. to Sarah Ward 8-2-1846 We
Kettering, J. T. to Mary Fitzgerald 12-29-1859 (1-1-1860) Sh
Kettle, Josiah to M. M. B. Watson 5-14-1846 L
Kettman, Henry to Lizette Koney 11-14-1856 (11-16-1856) Sh
Key (Kay), Paul C. to Eleanora Peace (Pearce) 7-13-1846 Sh
Key, C. to Omy Sykes 8-30-1841 Be
Key, Carroll J. to Susan A. Davis 10-27-1859 Hn
Key, F. J. to M. J. Rogers 2-20-1868 G
Key, Garland to Frances Lynn 4-11-1839 Hn
Key, Hiram C. to Elizabeth A. Box 10-4-1841 (10-7-1841) O
Key, J. H. to N. ____ 2-?-1860 (no return) Cr
Key, J. H. to Nancy Pondell 2-21-1860 Cr
Key, J. L. to Sophia Cox 11-21-1865 Hn
Key, James B. to Leeann E. Pickens 5-14-1856 Hr
Key, James M. to Elizabeth M. Brown 9-4-1854 (9-12-1854) Sh
Key, James M. to Mary W. Scruggs 7-14-1836 Sh
Key, John G. to R. E. Young 11-10-1868 (11-12-1868) Ma
Key, John L. to Emily Maxwell 2-8-1848 Hn
Key, John L. to Lucinda Tyson 3-18-1862 Hn
Key, John S. to Melinda Humphrey 4-7-1853 Cr
Key, John T. to Hester Pool 12-29-1834 Sh
Key, John to Mary Feely 5-31-1856 (6-15-1856) O
Key, John to Mary J. Colvett 12-26-1866 (12-27-1866) Cr
Key, L. C. to Catharine F. Brown 10-5-1865 O
Key, M. to Elizabeth Murphy 8-2-1859 Cr
Key, Martin B. to Vilet Puckett 2-8-1853 (2-10-1853) Ma
Key, Martin to Mary L. Wood 4-3-1842 Sh
Key, Napolian B. to Louiza Wade 10-24-1872 O
Key, Richard to Martha Morgan 3-20-1865 (3-22-1865) Cr
Key, Richard to Minnie Cox 11-25-1856 Cr
Key, Robert T. to Amanda Worsham 3-25-1869 Cr
Key, Tandy to Eliza Thacker 12-4-1830 Sh
Key, Thomas P. to Margarett Hailey 1-23-1863 G
Key, W. C. to Mary F. Dortch 1-25-1867 Hn
Key, W. F. B. C. to S. J. A. Riley 2-21-1855 (2-?-1855) Sh
Key, W. H. to M. F. Ward 6-28-1865 (no return) Hn
Key, William H. to Sarah E. Marchbanks 4-19-1860 Be
Key, William O. to Sarah Ann Key 12-23-1852 Hn
Key, William to Huldey R. Vaughn 12-21-1844 (12-22-1844) O
Key, William to Louiza S. Chamberlain 1-31-1861 Dy
Keyor?, Francis C. to Hetty Shinel 9-21-1841 (no return) F
Keys, David G. to Mary A. Farr 8-24-1858 (8-26-1858) G
Keys, Edom to Matilda Ridley 6-14-1868 G
Keys, James to Mary E. Gordon 12-10-1856 G
Keys, Jas. N. to Eliza J. Gordon 3-27-1858 (3-28-1858) G
Keywood, L. D. to Jane R. Brinkley 3-7-1855 (no return) F
Khyle, W. H. to M. A. Pride 10-2-1867 O
Kible (Kibbe?), Beverly to Bridget Quirk 11-3-1854 Sh
Kidd, Handy to Arrabella Murray 12-31-1884 L
Kidd, I. I. to E. H. Ginn 5-14-1866 O
Kidd, W. T. to Elizabeth Wallace 12-31-1878 (1-1-1879) Dy
Kidd, William A. to Sarah E. Barnes 6-19-1851 (no return) F
Kidd, William to Jennet Wilson 1-2-1866 (1-10-1866) T
Kiernam, Byran to Alice McCraith 3-2-1851 F
Kiernam, Owen to Bridget Daly 5-23-1858 Sh
Kiernan, Braxton W. to Harret? Comer 11-20-1845 Hr
Kierolf, A. S. to Susan Harman 5-22-1852 Sh
Kiger, E. J. to Eliza C. Simpson 12-24-1874 Dy
Kilberth, Squire to Jane Ash 12-12-1837 Be
Kilbreath, Geo. to Martha Short 2-5-1839 Be
Kilbreath, James to Mary Sanders 3-1-1855 Be
Kile, G. W. to Melvina Steele 12-6-1869 Cr
Kile, Jack to Caroline Patterson 12-31-1869 (1-1-1870) Cr
Kilgore, John W. to Henrietta Newman 10-19-1844 (no return) We
Killabru, G. C. to Lenore Callicott 10-7-1850 (no return) Hn
Killbreath, James to Martha Jones 1-13-1845 O
Killebrew, J. D. to Mary J. Henderson 12-24-1844 We
Killebrew, Kinchen to Susan Pentecost 9-9-1862 We
Killebrew, Levi to Frances S. Blake 11-16-1866 Hn
Killebrew, Samuel to Fannie Bradford 2-14-1872 Hy
Killebrew, Thomas L. to Martha A. Kennedy 12-19-1865 Hn
Killen, Ducan to Adaline McAlexander 3-31-1844 Cr
Killey, Wilson to L. Hicks 3-16-1848 Cr
Killgore, Alonza to Paulina F. Alexander 4-19-1867 Hn
Killgore, G. W. C. to Susan M. Parham 5-4-1866 Hn
Killgore, J. W. to M. A. Killgore 1-25-1863 We
Killick, T. J. to Sarah St. John 11-8-1884 (11-9-1884) L
Killick, Thomas J. to H. R. Heade 12-17-1870 (12-22-1870) L
Killien, Burrell to Kissandria Cafrey 7-6-1842 (7-7-1842) O
Killien, John to Christena Snider 8-1-1839 (8-4-1839) O
Killim, Samuel to Nelly Gofford 3-10-1853 Be
Killingsworth, Edward J. to Mary C. Christain 3-25-1855 Cr
Killingsworth, Morris to Elizabeth Clark 1-31-1844 (1-?-1844) T
Killion, Henry to M. E. Lowrance 2-14-1866 O
Killman, Henry to Frances Hooper 6-20-1846 (6-21-1846) Hr
Killong, Wm. H. to S. E. Watson 10-8-1856 Cr
Killough, John to Sarah Jones 10-12-1830 Hr

Grooms

Killough, Melton A. to Mary H. Pate 2-16-1841 Cr
Killough, Samuel D. to Mary A. Evans 9-22-1845 Cr
Killow, W. T. to Fanny (Mrs.) Nesbitt 12-4-1866 G
Killyon, J. D. to Nancy Ann Glover 8-21-1866 Hn
Kilpatrick, Andrew to Sarah Wilkins 8-16-1842 (8-18-1842) Ma
Kilpatrick, Chas. to Emalin Hanna 2-22-1872 T
Kilpatrick, Ebenezer to Cynthia M. Latta 1-13-1858 Sh
Kilpatrick, George to Lucy Bickers 3-15-1856 Ma
Kilpatrick, John W. to Frances S. Buster 11-17-1869 T
Kilpatrick, Needham to Laura Morrison 6-3-1869 (6-4-1869) T
Kilpatrick, Needhan to Martha Hughlett 9-28-1872 T
Kilpatrick, Wm. W. to Caroline Allen 2-20-1864 Sh
Kiltennor, John to Marthy Bryant 12-26-1876 Hy
Kilzar, Elijah to Mary Pruitt 10-31-1841 (not executed) G
Kilzer, George to Malinda Jane Owens 8-8-1867 G
Kilzer, James B. to Sarah J. Adcock 2-1-1855 G
Kilzer, Jno. A. to Sarah Jane Kilzer 7-26-1867 G
Kilzer, John to A. H. Baily 9-16-1866 G
Kilzer, Jordan to Mary J. McCutchen 10-26-1860 G
Kilzer, Jordan to Nancy Estes 3-23-1863 G
Kilzier (Rilzier?), J. B. to Mary A. Brogdon 2-8-1871 (no return) L
Kilzoe, Elijah to Margaret King 2-20-1845 (2-23-1845) G
Kim, James to Sarah Jane West 1-30-1864 Sh
Kim, Lewis to Catherine Prince 3-15-1858 Sh
Kimball, Lunsford L. to Frances D. Maroney 12-28-1829 (12-29-1829) Hr
Kimbel, John to Nancy Wharton 8-12-1836 Sh
Kimbell, Riley to Angeline Cloe 2-10-1852 (2-12-1852) Sh
Kimber, Joshua to Mary Blackamore 10-10-1851 (10-12-1851) Hr
Kimberlin, S. A. to Susan Rowland 10-26-1875 (10-27-1875) O
Kimble, A. L. to Eliza A. Martin 9-8-1879 L
Kimble, Alexander to Paralee Watt 2-8-1850 Ma
Kimble, James to Mary A. V. Traub 5-24-1838 Sh
Kimble, W. R. to Mary Gleason 10-21-1852 Hn
Kimble, William H. to Mary G. Tyus 11-30-1842 Sh
Kimbo, J. B. to A. M. F. Frazar? 10-12-1852 Sh
Kimbrel, Francis M. to T. Arnold 1-15-1860 We
Kimbrell, A. H. to M. A. Cock 12-3-1867 Ma
Kimbro, Azariah L. to Fannie Vincent 12-22-1864 Sh
Kimbro, John to Elizabeth Page 2-28-1848 G
Kimbro, John to Sarah P. Bellew 8-12-1837 G
Kimbro, R. P. to S. A. (Mrs.) Overall 2-7-1867 G
Kimbro, William R. to Rachael E. Reed 7-16-1858 (7-17-1858) T
Kimbrough, A. G. to Willie Pettus 4-12-1876 Hy
Kimbrough, A. H. to Susan Wood 1-19-1865 Be
Kimbrough, Albert to Virginia Smith 5-1-1843 Hr
Kimbrough, Buckley to Martha Kimbrough 7-24-1825 Sh
Kimbrough, Henry to Sally Collins 12-29-1876 Hy
Kimbrough, James to Mary E. Freeman 4-6-1842 Sh
Kimbrough, Nat M. to Fannie S. Hunt 5-20-1867 (5-22-1867) T
Kimbrough, Thomas T. to Eliza Jane Gunter 11-25-1833 Sh
Kimpel, Crockett to Martha R. Glisson 8-29-1861 Hn
Kincaid, David G. to Polly Bradley 12-26-1829 Sh
Kincaid, James P. to Lizzie West 3-3-1874 (3-4-1874) T
Kincaid, Jefferson to Rachael Holloman 10-5-1870 G B
Kincaid, Sidney to Sallie Murphy 10-1-1874 T
Kincaid, THomsa L. to Charlotte Caonia Reid 9-2-1856 (9-3-1856) Ma
Kincaid, William M. to Drucilla Layne 12-24-1829 Sh
Kincaid, Wm. S. to Ann Fry 5-23-1871 Ma
Kincannon, James L. to Mary Roberts 4-13-1861 (4-15-1861) Sh
Kincey, Henry to Elizabeth Peel 12-17-1860 G
Kincey, Samuel to Adaline Billingsley 11-27-1848 G
Kinchey?, Woodson to Celia McArver 5-8-1828 Hr
Kindred, John H. to M. K. Vincent 12-17-1857 We
Kindria, Joseph C. to Jane Hawkins 6-4-1834 O
Kindrick, James to Julia May 5-6-1844 (5-7-1844) Ma
Kindrick, James to Mary Crabtree 4-13-1838 F
Kindrick, Johna? to Nancy M. McKenzie 12-18-1862 Mn
Kindrick, Saml. to Amelia Davis 10-17-1846 (no return) F
Kindrick, Saml. to Elizabeth Anderson 5-18-1872 (5-19-1872) T
Kindrick, William H. to Nancy M. Henry 2-17-1853? (2-21-1855) Hr
Kiney, William A. to Mary S. Wiseman 2-29-1860 T
King, A. G. to Lucy Gibson 3-2-1863 (3-3-1863) O
King, A. J. to C. E. Barton 11-6-1860 G
King, A. J. to Clara Ann Moore 12-9-1854 (12-6?-1854) Hr
King, A. L. C. to Harriet C. Parham 12-3-1844 We
King, A. W. to Isabella Towns 8-29-1851 (no return) Hn
King, A. to M. Boon? 11-2-1870 G
King, Abraham to Elizabeth Bloys 4-17-1830 (4-18-1830) G
King, Alen to Malinda Bratton 3-4-1833 G
King, Alex M. to Matilda Johnson 12-14-1864 (12-15-1864) Sh
King, Alfred to Frances Worley 3-28-1829 Ma
King, Alfred to Mary L. King 11-27-1839 (11-28-1839) Ma
King, Alfred to Sarah Anderson 8-10-1871 Cr
King, Alphius to Mary Boswell 12-10-1850 G
King, Alx. to Winny Bond 1-27-1868 (no return) Hy
King, Amos G. to Samantha E. Dill 12-19-1857 Cr
King, Anderson to Jane Gilmore 1-4-1849 (1-7-1849) Hr

King, Andrew J. to Sarah L. Jackson 1-27-1868 (1-30-1868) Ma
King, Andrew Thomas to Alpha Jane Parris 3-7-1852 (3-9-1852) Hr
King, Anthony to Dinkey Ridley 8-8-1879 (8-14-1879) L B
King, Augustus W. to Abegail McClay 12-4-1826 (12-5-1826) G
King, Austin A. to Nancy Roberts 5-12-1828 (5-13-1828) G
King, B. J. to Nannie Birmingham 6-12-1871 (no return) Hy
King, B. N. to Martha Childress 8-17-1857 (8-18-1857) O
King, Barney to Laney Whittington 9-29-1856 (10-16-1856) Ma
King, Benassa to Sarah A. Flowers 10-12-1847 G
King, Benjamin W. to Mary C. Wilson 7-5-1861 (7-6-1861) O
King, Benjamin to Sarah Gooch 9-20-1871 Cr B
King, Bundy to Jane Bradford 8-22-1869 Cr
King, Calvin to F. Eubanks 2-12-1864 (2-14-1864) Cr
King, Charles F. to Angelina Steale (Steate) 4-13-1841 Sh
King, Charles F. to Lucy Bettis 9-20-1842 Sh
King, Charles P. to Ann M. Taylor 11-14-1855 (11-15-1855) Sh
King, Charles to Adaline Walker 8-15-1884 L
King, Charles to Julia Read 7-28-1866 (no return) Hy
King, Charly to Elen Ferguson 2-23-1878 Hy
King, Chesley to Catherine Keeling 1-1-1846 Cr
King, Clinton to Martha T. Read 12-23-1841 Cr
King, Clinton to Mary J. Moore 10-24-1871 (10-25-1871) Cr
King, D. C. to Mary Harris 2-6-1869 (2-8-1869) F
King, D. C. to N. L. Reeves 7-16-1867 G
King, David to Virginia Garrison 11-29-1875 (12-2-1875) O
King, E. D. to Nancy R. Parham 1-20-1845 (no return) We
King, E. G. to S. A. Hopper 5-28-1866 G
King, Elisha L. to Mary Jane Howell 1-25-1870 G
King, Enoch to Leah? Ragan 3-14-1837 (3-15-1837) Hr
King, Enoch to Mary Womack 6-12-1841 Hr
King, Erasmus to Evalina Head? 9-6-1873 (9-14-1873) L
King, F. to Susanna Dugan 3-4-1861 (3-5-1861) Sh
King, Frank to Sharlett Sangster 1-2-1872 Hy
King, Franklin to Lucy A. Hathorn 6-28-1874 Hy
King, George D. to Roena P. Conger 9-11-1860 Ma
King, George W. to Amanda F. Hammond 2-24-1869 (2-25-1869) Ma
King, George to Mary Elizabeth Irwin 4-8-1869 F
King, Gillard to Malissa Hendly 2-3-1836 Hr
King, Haliard to Polly Jarnigan 11-25-1856 Hr
King, Hamner to Sarah C. Wilson 9-6-1858 (9-8-1858) Ma
King, Henry A. to Susan Goodloe 10-23-1854 (10-29-1854) G
King, Henry to Callie Reed 7-17-1873 Hy
King, Henry to Issie Anderson 2-16-1873 Hy
King, Henry to Mary E. Williams 10-12-1864 (10-14-1864) L
King, Henry to Sarah W. Crafton 3-19-1842 (3-24-1842) G
King, Hubbard to Julina C. Lemonds 12-23-1852 Hn
King, Hugh S. to Angelina Jackson 3-26-1850 Ma
King, Isaac to Viney Potter 10-25-1865 Hy
King, J. A. to Julyie E. Jones 12-31-1856 Cr
King, J. C. to Eveline Sugs 2-20-1866 (2-25-1866) Cr
King, J. D. to Amanda Taylor 1-5-1856 (1-6-1856) G
King, J. F. to G. A. Bishop 12-3-1878 (12-4-1878) Dy
King, J. G. to Maggie A. Scott 10-22-1866 (10-4?-1866) F
King, J. H. to Nancy Valliant 4-4-1859 (4-7-1859) O
King, J. M. to Cynthia Griffin 10-12-1865 Dy
King, J. M. to Mary Rice 4-7-1881 (no return) L
King, J. M. to Mattie H. Harper 1-2-1862 G
King, J. M. to Preciller Cantrell 1-3-1871 (1-4-1871) Cr
King, J. M. to Sarah L. Hampton 3-21-1868 (3-22-1868) Cr
King, J. M. to Sarah T. Henry 12-26-1860 (12-29-1860) O
King, J. P. to A. G. White 12-18-1878 Dy
King, J. P. to M. J. Peoples 11-8-1859 (11-9-1859) G
King, J. Q. to T. A. Nichols 2-15-1866 G
King, J. R. to M. J. Maxwell 7-30-1873 (7-31-1873) Cr
King, J. S. to Florence E. Sanders 11-20-1873 Hy
King, J. T. to M. J. McFarland 3-24-1874 Dy
King, J. V. to C. E. Thomas 2-19-1861 (3-5-1861) O
King, J. W. to L. A. Tarrant 7-9-1878 (7-10-1878) Dy
King, J. W. to Martha Jackson 9-28-1842 Hn
King, J. W. to Mary A. Jones 1-1-1873 (1-2-1873) Cr
King, J. W. to Mary E. Joyner 11-19-1866 (11-20-1866) Cr
King, J. W. to Nancy E. Sugg 12-3-1868 (12-6-1868) Cr
King, Jackson to Margaret Crews 11-19-1856 Hr
King, James A. to Martha An Robertson 3-6-1848 (3-16-1848) F
King, James C. to Susan E. Jones 12-22-1866 (12-24-1866) Cr
King, James H. to Elizabeth Henry? 2-3-1848 N
King, James H. to Rebecca J. Walker 7-21-1849 (7-25-1849) G
King, James M. to Catharine Pickard 2-5-1844 (2-6-1844) O
King, James W. to Harriet R. Thomas 8-11-1853 Sh
King, James W. to Mary F. Walker 1-15-1857 (1-18-1857) Ma
King, James William to Susan Caroline Hector 7-13-1843 Sh
King, James to Edney Perry 12-13-1874 Hy
King, James to Emly Hall 8-23-1877 Hy
King, James to Jane Hamner 11-2-1839 (11-3-1839) Ma
King, James to Lucinda Sawyer 7-29-1880 Dy
King, James to Martha G. Malone 6-5-1851 Cr
King, James to Mary Willson 10-23-1862 (no return) We

King, James to Mercina Rochella 11-15-1847 Ma
King, Jesse to Matilda Anderson 12-6-1827 Ma
King, Jesse to Rachael Osment 9-28-1859 Hr
King, Jesse to Sarah Jane Savage 7-5-1841 (7-6-1841) Hr
King, Jessee M. to Mattie C. Owen 10-31-1885 (11-1-1885) L
King, Jethro to Roberta (Mrs.) Thurmond 4-30-1879 Dy
King, Jim to Alice Shaw 1-15-1874 Hy
King, Jno. Franklin to Naomie Jane Graves 5-23-1868 (5-26-1868) Ma
King, Joberry to Bethinia B. Naylor 10-26-1852 (10-27-1852) Hr
King, John A. to Mary Hale 12-19-1850 G
King, John E. to Grizzy Ann R. Todd 5-23-1861 Hn
King, John L. to E. A. Thomas 1-6-1842 Hn
King, John M. to Mahala Tull 1-16-1874 (1-19-1874) L
King, John M. to Sarah J. Freeland 12-30-1845 Cr
King, John M. to Sarah Neely 8-14-1855 Be
King, John R. to Docia McLeary 10-4-1827 G
King, John R. to Elizabeth B. Butler 4-18-1870 (4-19-1870) Cr
King, John Vincent to Susan Jane Neville 1-31-1856 (2-7-1856) Ma
King, John W. to Mary Parsons 11-5-1869 (11-9-1869) Cr
King, John W. to Nancy B. White 7-9-1846 We
King, John to Ellen Boran 7-19-1864 Sh
King, John to Juliana Vassor (Vapor?) 9-23-1840 (9-24-1840) L
King, Jonathan to Lucretia Huey (Henry) 4-14-1849 O
King, Joseph A. to Elizabeth White 1-24-1850 We
King, Joseph A. to Sarah Ann Smith 2-1-1845 We
King, Joseph C. to Elizabeth J. Boaz 10-24-1861 We
King, Joseph to A. M. Whitehurst 1-8-1874 Hy
King, Joseph to Isabella Moore 6-26-1856 We
King, Josiah W. to May L. B. Mitchell 12-12-1840 Ma
King, Josiah to Jane A. Causly (Causby?) 12-7-1849 (no return) L
King, L. B. to Melisa Ann Weedin 6-18-1844 Hr
King, Lafayett to Clara Suggs 12-2-1881 (12-15-1881) L B
King, Lucas to Lucy Moore 12-21-1881 (no return) L B
King, M. B. to Juliet Harris 6-16-1846 Hn
King, M. C. to Mattie McMurry 10-13-1856 (10-15-1856) Sh
King, M. L. to L. A. Tarrant 7-18-1876 (no return) Dy
King, Michael to Nancy Ward 9-6-1828 Ma
King, Monroe to Sarah Leslie 11-12-1867 Be
King, Napoleon to Jane Weaver 7-26-1854 (7-27-1854) Sh
King, Napoleon to Jane Wilson 7-22-1857 Sh
King, Newton W. to Cynthia C. Roe 10-15-1868 (10-18-1868) T
King, O. to Frances Whitelaw 12-28-1875 (no return) Hy
King, Patrick to Winnie (Nannie) McElroy 3-4-1850 Sh
King, Peter C. to Mary T. Bates 9-27-1861 (no return) We
King, Peter to Martha B. Valliant 2-19-1855 (2-20-1855) O
King, Phillip to Emaly Furgarson 3-18-1846 Cr
King, Phillip to Jane Powell 12-10-1878 (12-11-1878) Dy
King, Porter B. to Mary Eliza Norvell 6-23-1857 (6-24-1857) Ma
King, Presley to Luisa Haywood 12-8-1865 (12-10-1865) Cr
King, Presley to Ridley Hampton 11-28-1849 Cr
King, Priesty to Eliza Montgomery 5-2-1844 Cr
King, Quinton C. to Francis E. Riley 3-27-1861 We
King, R. L. to Nannie Smith 3-27-1878 Hy
King, Rewbin to Pollie Cantroll 8-5-1871 (8-6-1871) Cr
King, Rice to Nancy Mayberry 7-4-1853 Be
King, Richard to Elizabeth Hicks 4-2-1867 Hn
King, Robert B. to Virginia Stilsy 4-28-1857 Cr
King, Robert to Susanah Hastin 5-20-1840 (no return) Hn
King, Rufus E. to Ketsey Flowers 12-17-1853 (12-24-1853) G
King, Rufus F. to Mary W. Harrison 1-12-1852 G
King, Rufus to Elizabeth Hartsfield 8-21-1860 Hn
King, Rufus to M. S. Brimingham 12-3-1874 Dy
King, Rufus to Mary Ann Stillman
King, S. C. to Liza F. Rideout 6-16-1857 (6-17-1857) Sh
King, S. H. to M. E. Cavitt 9-3-1878 (9-4-1878) Dy
King, S. S. to Amanda Holloway 3-31-1859 Hy
King, Samuel N. to Mary A. Neese 12-19-1860 Hn
King, Samuel to Nancy Thomas 10-20-1861 Hn
King, Sidney to Nirva Bruce 1-29-1876 (no return) Hy
King, Soloman to Nancy Pearyear 6-16-1870 (11-20-1870) L
King, Stephen to Allice Shaw 1-19-1876 (no return) Hy
King, Stephen to Mary Eliza Dickson 11-14-1848 G
King, Thad to Harriet Lankford 12-20-1877 Hy
King, Thomas B. to Susan J. Heistand 8-9-1860 Sh
King, Thomas J. L. to Laura J. McGee 9-16-1856 (9-17-1856) Sh
King, Thomas J. to Margaret Cole 2-26-1861 Sh
King, Thomas L. to Martha E. Peoples 12-11-1860 G
King, Thomas S. to Willie B. Ripley 9-11-1877 (9-12-1877) Dy
King, Thomas W. to Martha Hector 6-25-1831 (6-30-1831) G
King, Thomas to Caroline Suggs 2-20-1864 (2-22-1864) Cr
King, Thomas to Dolly Morris 4-29-1845 Be
King, Thomas to Elizabeth Butler 6-12-1824 Hr
King, Thomas to Elizabeth Robinson 11-14-1851 Cr
King, Thomas to Katherine New 9-22-1853 Cr
King, Thomas to Sarah Watson 12-16-1857 Be
King, Thos. to Sucky Hammett 2-15-1844 Cr
King, Tom to Emma Bond 12-28-1878 Hy

King, V. to M. J. Barker 7-3-1870 G
King, Vinson to Lioty(Sioty?) Crouse 7-5-1847 Hr
King, W. A. to Mary J. Stidham 1-13-1868 (1-14-1868) F
King, W. E. to Margaret A. Choate 11-2-1865 (11-5-1865) Cr
King, W. P. to Ann Roberson 12-16-1872 (12-17-1872) Cr
King, W. P. to Martha J. Parish 11-3-1868 (11-4-1868) Cr
King, W. R. to A. B. Cole 11-23-1872 (11-24-1872) Dy
King, W. T. to S. A. Wassey 10-17-1871 (10-19-1871) F
King, W. T. to Saluda J. King 6-24-1869 Dy
King, Warney to Harriet Lane 3-5-1874 Hy
King, Wash to Lotta Coleman 7-10-1875 (7-4?-1875) Dy
King, Wash to _____ no dates (with Sep 1875) Dy
King, Wesley S. to Mary H. Rust 12-10-1850 Sh
King, Wesley to Rebecca Ann Autry 8-1-1838 Cr
King, Wiley to Polly Austin 1-18-1849 Be
King, William I. G. to Mary Ann King 10-11-1838 Ma
King, William J. to Harriet A. Fisher 9-12-1846 (9-17-1846) F
King, William J. to Matilda A. Swor 1-22-1861 Hn
King, William T. to Nancy Williams 4-10-1861 Dy
King, William to Amanda Roberts 10-27-1879 Dy
King, William to Caroline Reed 12-14-1860 (12-19-1860) Cr
King, William to Emily Jackson 7-2-1861 (7-3-1861) Ma
King, William to Mary E. Young 11-9-1855 Sh
King, William to Mollie Rucker 11-21-1875 (no return) L
King, William to Parmealia Martin 2-16-1830 Ma
King, William to Rebecca A. Bowen 12-17-1860 (12-18-1860) Dy
King, William to Theodocia White 10-1-1846 (10-15-1846) O
King, Williamson to Louisa Johnson 1-9-1834 Sh
King, Wilson to Eviline Rhodes 5-11-1865 (5-14-1865) Cr
King, Wilson to Nancy S. Killie 1-5-1852 Cr
King, Wm. M. to Sarah E. Noel 5-15-1860 (no return) Hy
King, Wm. S. to Nancy J. Hammond 1-4-1870 (1-5-1870) Ma
King, Wm. to Henrietta Currie 12-11-1878 Hy
King, Wm. to Mary Jane Cox 1-21-1853 Cr
King, Wm. to Tempy Taylor 10-17-1877 Hy
Kinghin, David to Mary A. Conley 5-8-1851 Sh
Kingkade, Asa to Riller Ray 10-21-1867 (10-30-1867) T
Kingkaid, Robert to Harriet M. Robertson 1-1-1866 (no return) Dy
Kingman, A. D. to Mary A. Donaldson 4-21-1849 (4-28-1849) O
Kingston, John to Leathia P. Johnson 2-4-1854 (2-5-1854) G
Kingston, T. N. to Louisa Gales 11-15-1854 W
Kinion, Albert to Emaline Wess 3-1-1863 Mn
Kinkead, David to Caroline Sanders 3-27-1868 (3-29-1868) L
Kinley, John to Lucinda Harbour 3-17-1831 G
Kinman, Moses H. to Amanda E. Hall 5-3-1866 O
Kinnard, George to Lyda Brown 2-25-1840 (2-26-1840) Hr
Kinnard, James P. to Manerva Ann Harland 8-10-1832 (8-13-1832) Hr
Kinnard, James to Margaret Norris 11-10-1841 Hr
Kinnard, Samuel to Rebecca Sutton 12-10-1873 (no return) Hy
Kinney, Buck to Ellen Currin 5-13-1881 (5-15-1881) L B
Kinney, G. L. to Mary E. Smith 12-16-1873 (12-17-1873) T
Kinney, J. C. to Sarah E. Walton 2-20-1873 T
Kinney, James J. to Mary E. Wilson 10-27-1862 (no return) Hy
Kinney, James K. to Sophronia Yarbro 1-24-1861 T
Kinney, Jesse to Frances J. Goren 11-23-1859 (11-24-1859) T
Kinney, Lewis F. to Nesia A. Bledsow 6-15-1864 (6-16-1864) O
Kinney, Michael W. to Carolina Klinch 2-10-1852 (2-14-1852) Sh
Kinney, Thomas to Albertine Smith 5-25-1846 T
Kinney, Thomas to Emeline Smith 9-26-1855 T
Kinney, Wm. A. to M. E. Wiseman 2-29-1860 T
Kinney, Wm. A. to Mary E. Wiseman 2-29-1860 T
Kinney, Wm. to Sarah Lucas 3-22-1877 Hy
Kinny, George T. to Msaggie W. Kerr 12-23-1873 (12-24-1873) T
Kinny, Jessee to Perlina Best 12-30-1873 (12-31-1873) T
Kinseule, Patrick to Ann Foley 2-21-1862 (2-23-1862) Sh
Kinsey, Felix G. to Mary J. Jones 2-11-1850 (2-15-1850) G
Kinsey, James to Mary Baldridge 12-14-1864 (12-15-1864) O
Kinsey, Joseph J. to Lura A. McDaniel 5-26-1851 (5-27-1851) G
Kinsey, Peter H. to Mary E. Peel 3-19-1850 (3-27-1850) G
Kinsey, Samuel to Sarah Bruce 1-1-1849 (1-2-1849) G
Kinsley, Jacob L. to M. J. Ross 12-7-1864 O
Kinton, Chapman to Susan F. Graddy 1-24-1857 G
Kipp, John to Mary Bailey 3-8-1862 Hn
Kirby, Alvis to Martha D. Bennett 12-4-1854 (12-5-1854) Ma
Kirby, Archable W. to Provy Lucas 3-21-1844 Cr
Kirby, Berry to Mary McVey 8-24-1870 (8-25-1870) Cr
Kirby, D. W. to Ruth A. Carter 12-11-1869 (12-12-1869) Cr
Kirby, David to Nancy Ross 10-29-1846 Cr
Kirby, Dennis to Ann Leach 3-10-1850 Sh
Kirby, Habon to Mary Sowell 1-3-1849 Ma
Kirby, Henderson to Eliza Childress 4-26-1848 (4-27-1848) Ma
Kirby, Henrey to Parthana Hall 7-22-1848 Cr
Kirby, Henry to Martha Littleton 1-21-1861 (no return) L
Kirby, Henry to Sarah Long 1-22-1850 Cr
Kirby, Herod to Elizabeth Dickinson 12-27-1853 Ma
Kirby, J. A. to Nancy Holmes 1-30-1848 Cr
Kirby, James A. to Rebecca Jane Hall 12-21-1853 (12-22-1853) Ma

Grooms

Kirby, James F. to Mary A. Mizzle 7-16-1853 (7-20-1853) L
Kirby, Jesse to Nancy M. Bennett 2-24-1846 Ma
Kirby, Joseph C. to Nancy A. Murphy 5-15-1862 (5-18-1862) Cr
Kirby, Joseph to Mary Smith 12-14-1871 (12-15-1871) Cr
Kirby, Lowrence to Catharine McCarty 3-17-1862 Sh
Kirby, Nathan S. to Susan C. Taylor 3-27-1848 Sh
Kirby, R. W. to Sue Wells 1-8-1868 Hy
Kirby, Richard W. to Lydia Bevill 11-12-1870 (11-13-1870) Ma
Kirby, Robt. to Puss Drake 9-25-1870 Hy
Kirby, William W. to Martha Parrish 10-30-1855 O
Kircheval, Alexander W. to Kate E. Wards 10-24-1863 (10-25-1863) Sh
Kirckner, C. F. to Alice Wellon 7-19-1854 Sh
Kirk, A. H. to Sarah J. Wright 10-3-1867 Dy
Kirk, Alex to Elenna Hampton 12-24-1844 Cr
Kirk, Allen to Cornelia Mebane 9-6-1866 (no return) F B
Kirk, Anderson to Julia Ann Brown 8-20-1853 (8-25-1853) O
Kirk, Archibald to Elizabeth Roarke 6-12-1851 (6-14-1851) Sh
Kirk, D. R. to Guentiller Thomas 10-8-1851 Be
Kirk, Dick to Mariah Bradford 1-1-1879 (1-2-1879) Dy
Kirk, George M. to Nancy Sassems 8-9-1826 (8-10-1826) Hr
Kirk, George to Polly A. Sims 10-23-1871 Dy
Kirk, Henry T. to M. L. Fuqua 3-19-1878 Dy
Kirk, Henry to Margaret Ellis 8-21-1867 (8-22-1867) Dy
Kirk, Hulypus to Patsey Pealey 1-23-1842 Cr
Kirk, J. M. to A. E. Roberts 9-16-1869 Cr
Kirk, J. W. to Nancy Perry 10-29-1859 (11-2-1859) O
Kirk, James Y. to Sarah Elizabeth? 11-9-1868 Ma
Kirk, James to C. Neatherland 1-20-1847 Cr
Kirk, John P. to Luisa J. Kilbreath 2-27-1863 Be
Kirk, Nathan to Mary Jane Warbritton 1-24-1870 (1-29-1870) Cr
Kirk, Nathen to Elizabeth Warbritton 12-4-1850 Cr
Kirk, P. T. to S. E. Shoffner 8-13-1866 (8-14-1866) Dy
Kirk, Robert M. to Amy M. Underwood 10-14-1858 (no return) Hn
Kirk, Samuel M. to Mary E. Boykin 9-5-1843 Ma
Kirk, Thomas F. to Mary Wenderoth 8-21-1852 (8-22-1852) Sh
Kirk, Thomas to Caroline Brock 9-26-1861 O
Kirk, Thomas to Caroline McKenzie 9-7-1861 O
Kirk, Thomas to Leander Wright 1-13-1855 Sh
Kirk, William Addison to Mary Strawn 10-24-1848 (11-1-1848) T
Kirk, William M. to Mary A. Henderson 12-6-1842 Hn
Kirk, William to Sally Roark 4-21-1850 Sh
Kirk, William to T. E. Sanders 10-18-1875 Dy
Kirk, Wm. J. to Elizabeth A. Fly 11-2-1854 Cr
Kirkendall, George to Louisa Marbry 2-20-1867 Hn B
Kirkendall, J. E. to Mary A. McClain 12-8-1855 (no return) Hn
Kirkendall, John C. to Melinda Steelman 2-16-1832 Sh
Kirkland, Andrew J. to Louiza N. Martin 7-2-1859 Hn
Kirkland, David to Elizabeth Haynes 3-31-1853 (4-7-1853) Sh
Kirkland, David to Margaret A. Henshaw 7-6-1846 (7-12-1846) F
Kirkland, E. W. to Sarah A. Turner 3-24-1867 G
Kirkland, George W. to Margaret Birdah? 10-23-1839 Hn
Kirkland, Harrison to Elizabeth Jackson 12-3-1862 (no return) Hn
Kirkland, Harrison to Manerva McFadden 2-18-1841 Hn
Kirkland, Harrison to Mary McFadden 6-27-1854 Hn
Kirkland, Henry to Mahala Jeffries 1-24-1870 (1-25-1870) F
Kirkland, J. F. to S. M. Wood 10-26-1869 Hy
Kirkland, J. P. to H. E. Nabors 11-21-1864 (11-23-1864) Sh
Kirkland, James H. to Mary Davis 1-21-1857 Sh
Kirkland, John W. to Sarah Ann Jones 1-1-1855 (1-4-1855) Hr
Kirkland, Joseph B. to Nancy J. Blaylock 1-9-1858 (1-13-1858) Hr
Kirkland, P. H. to Amanda E. Ray 9-30-1866 Hn
Kirkland, S. P. to Martha Butler 1-2-1860 (1-4-1860) T
Kirkland, Thomas B. to Harriet S. J. Parker 10-23-1867 Hn
Kirkland, Thomas to Nancy Peacock 11-29-1847 Hn
Kirklin, Richard W. to Nancy Hurt 1-18-1838 (no return) Hn
Kirkman, Jesse to Sophia Gray 10-27-1871 (10-28-1871) T
Kirkman, Robert S. to Lemiza Shaw 12-30-1844 (1-2-1845) G
Kirkman, T. P. to Nancy Mayfield 12-21-1868 G
Kirkpatrick, G. W. to Caroline Golding 12-7-1851 L
Kirkpatrick, Henry to Mattie Savage 8-30-1875 (9-?-1875) L
Kirkpatrick, Henry to Tranquilla Robertson 8-22-1843 Ma
Kirkpatrick, James S. to Manerva E. Meadows 4-11-1864 Dy
Kirkpatrick, Jno. Alex to Caroline McClish 10-9-1848 Ma
Kirkpatrick, John A. to Harriet F. Horton 7-29-1863 (8-2-1863) Dy
Kirkpatrick, John W. to Jennie H. Scott 12-15-1879 L
Kirkpatrick, John to Jane Walker 7-30-1849 (8-14-1849) T
Kirkpatrick, John to Rebecca J. Dinwiddie 9-17-1842 (9-21-1842) G
Kirkpatrick, R. Y. to Carni Litton 7-31-1854 (no return) F
Kirkpatrick, Thomas N. to Margarett A. Howell 1-9-1840 Cr
Kirkpatrick, Thomas to S. R. Scott 3-7-1871 L
Kirkpatrick, W. J. to Sarah J. Stackerd 5-10-1854 (no return) F
Kirkpatrick, Wm. P. to Susan A. Harrell 1-29-1840 Cr
Kirksey, Abraham to Elizabeth Boon 6-28-1832 G
Kirksey, John to Eliza Etheridge 10-12-1846 (no return) We
Kirksey, John to Slalie Green 12-27-1869 F B
Kirksey, Young to Mary E. C. Asher 8-27-1832 G

Kirkwood, Jas. H. to Amanda Mowdy 9-28-1843 We
Kirkwood, John to Mary C. Dubois 3-14-1856 (no return) Hn
Kirley, William E. to Sallie J. Crowder 10-14-1850 Hn
Kirsch (Hirsch?), Samuel to Rosale Elb 10-11-1856 Sh
Kirsey, Alexander to Elenora E. Hankins 12-14-1858 (12-16-1858) Sh
Kirth, Nickolas to Elizabeth Kinsler 7-19-1855 Sh
Kirtland, Richd. Mc. to Martha Firth 8-24-1863 F
Kirtland, S. P. to Martha J. Butler no dates (with 1860) T
Kirts, James to Margaret Adkins 3-20-1865 T
Kirwan, Thomas to Kate Rigney 1-22-1861 (1-31-1861) Sh
Kiser, John J. to Mary Gilfil 3-30-1861 (3-31-1861) Sh
Kissell, Benjamin to Martha E. Dunham 5-17-1879 (5-18-1879) L
Kitcham, J. W. to Nancy Ward 12-16-1854 (no return) We
Kitchem, Levi to Georgeann Walker 1-19-1844 F
Kitchen(s), William to Harriett Bumpass 2-9-1854 O
Kitchen, Wallace to George A. Strong 3-27-1869 (3-30-1869) T
Kitchens, Campbell to Mary Ann Russell 7-3-1861 (7-10-1861) O
Kitsoe, Andrew to Catharine Callenden 10-18-1851 Sh
Kitson, Andrew to Mary Geary 6-15-1851 Hn
Kittell, Amma? to Mahola? Freeman 2-22-1831 Ma
Kizer, David to Temperance Yarbrough 2-9-1848 Cr
Kizer, Francis C. to Martha Abels 2-1-1842 F
Kizer, James H. to Margaret Avrett 3-6-1864 Mn
Kizer, W. F. to H. (Mrs.) Jones 10-5-1870 Ma
Klee, William T. to Sally C___ 2-3-1871 (3-5-1871) O
Kleisley (Kleuthy), Coleman to Odeiss (Odeispes) ___ 7-18-1849 Sh
Klenk, Frederick to Mary Spencer 1-3-1853 Ma
Klinck, Hayne J. to Margaret A. Robertson 8-11-1856 (8-14-1856) Sh
Klink, Thomas to Amelia Best 9-21-1852 Sh
Klinke, Augustus to W. Benger 7-14-1857 Sh
Klophel, C. G. B. to Elizabeth (Mrs.) Ball 7-8-1885 (7-12-1885) L
Klutt, Ephram to Mary Tucker 11-27-1850 (no return) Hn
Klutts, Caldwell to Milly Moon 4-9-1843 Hn
Klutts, D. A. to Amy Maness 10-30-1878 (10-31-1878) L
Klutts, J. A. to G. A. Maness 5-1-1877 (no return) L
Klutts, John to Margaret A. Ezell 9-18-1849 Hn
Klutts, Lawson A. to C. A. Klutts 12-13-1861 (no return) Hn
Klutts, R. C. to S. C. Maness 5-14-1879 L
Klutts, Robert to Martha Hyer? 12-15-1845 (no return) Hn
Klutts, Samuel C. to Christian E. Ezell 5-9-1858 Hn
Klutts, Tobeas to Martha T. Day 10-12-1857 (no return) We
Klyce, Andrew J. to Mary E. Hammon 6-24-1841 G
Klyce, Duke to Mary E. Epperson 6-8-1844 (6-12-1844) G
Klyce, J. M. to Lola Wright 12-22-1884 (12-23-1884) L
Klyce, James M. to M. C. Keiroff 4-24-1859 Hy
Klyce, William H. to Mattie H. Tyus 10-15-1863 (no return) Hy
Klyce, Willis to Harriet Moore 8-28-1872 Hy
Knapp, Geo. W. to Lewisey Leggett 5-18-1843 Sh
Knapp, J. F. to Mary C. Bradford 7-20-1858 Sh
Kney, Charles to J. Hidle 11-11-1862 Sh
Knight, Burriss to Malinda Arnold 12-30-1844 We
Knight, Calvin to Mary Jane Clack 7-3-1868 (7-5-1868) O
Knight, Daniel to Elizabeth Browning 4-15-1852 We
Knight, Elijah to Mary E. Knight 2-8-1863 Mn
Knight, F. M. to Rebeca A. Dacus 11-22-1860 T
Knight, Henry to Sarah Jarrett 9-11-1844 (9-12-1844) Hr
Knight, JSames A. to Margaret Elam 11-13-1866 T
Knight, James W. to Lucy D. Roberts 1-6-1861 We
Knight, James to Lavinia Starnes 12-1-1852 L
Knight, James to Mary E. Ezell 3-1-1865 Mn
Knight, John H. A. to Jane C. Fillmore 7-26-1844 (no return) We
Knight, John M. to Mattie E. Stewart 6-10-1869 (no return) L
Knight, Jos. T. to SophiaH. Cheairs 12-11-1860 Hr
Knight, Joseph to Elizabeth Barwell 1-12-1869 (1-13-1869) T
Knight, R. K. to V. R. Aughey 7-8-1854 Sh
Knight, Robert F. to Frances E. Robison 5-25-1869 Cr
Knight, S. C. to Susan Simpson 2-20-1855 (2-21-1855) Hr
Knight, W. (Dr.) to Minerva Victoria Kelly 11-7-1859 (11-17-1859) Sh
Knight, W. L. to Amanda E. Michaels 12-26-1872 (no return) Dy
Knight, W. M. to Emily S. Roberts 11-16-1847 (11-17-1847) F
Knight, W. P. to Elvira S. J. Dodd 9-10-1866 (9-11-1866) Dy
Knight, Woodson to Harriet Ellison 5-16-1870 T
Knolton, Horrace C. to Mary A. Stone 8-15-1848 (8-17-1848) Hr
Knot, Ormond to Mandana Adams 3-24-1842 Sh
Knott, Caleb S. to Sarah Polk 9-5-1863 Sh
Knott, Henry to Camilla Martin 2-6-1849 (2-7-1849) G
Knott, J. J. to Elizabeth Ford 10-29-1857 G
Knott, James B. to Henrietta J. Janes 6-15-1860 We
Knott, Jas. W. (Rev.) to Sally W. Miller 5-27-1849 F
Knott, John to Arie F. Connell 1-17-1854 G
Knott, Marcellas to Meranda Yarbrough 3-17-1860 Hr
Knott, Sydney S. to Rachael Murdough 1-10-1861 Hr
Knott, William G. to Artilla Holt 10-10-1854 (10-11-1854) G
Knott, William L. to Martha J. Murdaugh 1-19-1858 Hr
Knoulen, Kinchin to Mary Johnson 6-10-1852 We
Knowles, William J. to Mary E. Butler 6-12-1875 (6-13-1875) Dy
Knowlton, L. to Melissa Blackwell 6-15-1869 (6-16-1869) Dy

Knox, Absolem to Sarah Ann Higgins 4-13-1833 (4-14-1833) G
Knox, Andrew J. to Tabitha G. Brevard 10-15-1852 (10-17-1852) O
Knox, E. Pheaton P. to Sarah J. Henderson 3-28-1838 Cr
Knox, Henry to Sallie Sparks 12-11-1878 Hy
Knox, James F. to Martha F. Blankenship 9-8-1858 (9-9-1858) G
Knox, James R. to Jame L. Hamilton 9-18-1839 Cr
Knox, John B. to Jennetta L. McFarland 3-7-1848 (3-?-1848) T
Knox, John Bray to Amanda Williams 8-8-1851 (8-17-1851) T
Knox, John W. to Adelia (Mrs.) Hobum 5-11-1863 Sh
Knox, John to Ellen Bell 12-4-1839 (12-5-1839) G
Knox, Jordan to Sarah Grist 11-4-1848 (11-5-1848) G
Knox, Milton H. to Emily Teague 12-30-1843 (no return) F
Knox, R. L. to Fannie C. Steger 1-29-1866 (1-31-1866) F
Knox, R. M. to Dicy Culbreath 7-1-1868 (7-2-1868) T
Knox, Robert to Catharine Kirk 11-30-1823 (11-31?-1823) Hr
Knox, Robert to Elizabet Hins (Hines) 2-6-1841 Sh
Knox, Samuel to Louisa Marshall 3-27-1869 F B
Knox, W. S. to Mahala Parks 3-17-1866 (3-18-1866) F
Knox, William B. to Rachael S. Donelson 11-28-1860 Sh
Knox, William S. to Frances A. E. Hale 8-24-1847 (no return) F
Koch (Cook?), Henri to Bettie Finn 12-8-1857 Sh
Koch, M. to Anna Henigar 4-25-1859 Sh
Koen, Benjamin F. to Margaret M. Ragan 10-7-1839 F
Koen, J. W. to Josie Graves 12-4-1878 Hy
Koen, Robert B. to Bulah J. Bledsoe 4-17-1856 Cr
Koen, Thos. H. to Cloie Owen 3-5-1864 Sh
Koerper, F. to Louisa Beck 12-27-1855 Sh
Koffman, J. J. to R. R. Motley 10-6-1867 G
Koffod, Tyos to Elizabeth Brown 12-5-1860 Sh
Kohl (Cole?), Christopher to Sopha Shuman 4-9-1863 Sh
Kohnmann?, John to Ida McKenzie 12-4-1878 Dy
Kohoe, John to Sally Sperling 3-4-1845 Sh
Kolb, Sebastian to Eliza Motto 11-13-1860 Sh
Koller, Jos. to Mary M. Steinhammer 12-31-1860 (1-1-1861) Sh
Konegay, William B. to Jane S. Boggs 2-25-1845 O
Koonce, Henry J. to Sarah E. Wiley 1-30-1855 (1-31-1855) Sh
Koonce, J. W. to M. E. J. McMullin 4-8-1874 (4-9-1874) T
Koonce, James M. to Margaret E. West 7-22-1868 (7-26-1868) L
Koonce, John W. to Matilda M. McMullins 12-23-1867 T
Koonce, John to Sarah Jenkins 9-17-1852 L
Koonce, Lewis to Elizabeth Farn (Fain?) 4-18-1853 (4-19-1853) L
Koonce, Peter to L. A. Jones 4-20-1874 Hy
Koonce, R. M. to S. E. Cotner 1-12-1871 F
Koonce, Robt. J. to Martha A. Warner 9-17-1851 (9-30-1851) Sh
Koonce, T. J. to Catherine Perkins 12-26-1866 (12-27-1866) L
Koonce, Thomas L. to Wineford Pittman? 3-26-1873 L
Kooper, Frederick to Louisa Beck 12-27-1855 Sh
Koser, Frank to Evaline Knox 8-27-1857 Sh
Kraft, Romnald to Akafa Kraft 4-24-1856 Sh
Kramer, Moses to Katherine O'Bryan 11-13-1843 Sh
Krauss, Christian to Elizabeth Cox 10-29-1855 Sh
Kreher, John to Catharine Reasin 1-28-1860 (1-30-1860) Sh
Krider, John to Elizabeth McConnell 10-3-1851 (no return) F
Krits, Franklin to Louisa McFerrin 9-3-1866 (no return) Hy
Krocker, Friedrich to L. Hoetterbar 5-11-1863 Sh
Krokroska, M. N. to Hanorah McDonnell 5-4-1864 Sh
Kruse, Benjamin to Margaret Green 3-26-1859 (3-27-1859) Sh
Kruze, Wm. to Margaret Ingling 10-20-1853 (10-21-1853) Sh
Kuger, Charles to Johanna Burke 2-13-1863 Sh
Kummisink, T. to Clementina Thomas 3-1-1859 Sh
Kunckel, Joseph to Bettie Davis 4-23-1863 Sh
Kunholz, Charles to Mollie Giles 11-1-1859 Sh
Kunkle, Conrad to Martha Parker 5-21-1857 Sh
Kurkendall, Sam'l to M. E. Cossett 5-24-1864 Sh
Kurr, Newton to Miry Wiseman 7-22-1859 Be
Kurts, John to L. A. Lock 12-21-1858 T
Kurts?, Martin Harvey to Ellen Ann White 9-24-1853 (9-28-1853) T
Kuttenberg, Henry to Kate Shweitzer 7-8-1863 Sh
Kuykendall, John R. to M. C. McClain 9-13-1863 Hn
Kuykendall, R. L. to Charatza Kyle 2-10-1862 (2-11-1862) O
Kuykendall, Robert to Harriet Hargrove 10-5-1841 (no return) Hn
Kyle, Dallis to Ann Murrell 12-26-1870 (no return) F B
Kyle, Dr. T. A. to Mattie G. Adams 7-2-1860 (7-3-1860) T
Kyle, E. R. to Angeline Butler 5-17-1866 (5-13-1866) Cr
Kyle, Erastus J. to Oney Williams 7-17-1839 Cr
Kyle, Gale H. to Helen M. Perry 7-25-1843 Ma
Kyle, L. C. to M. C. King 2-6-1873 Cr
Kyle, Patrick to Margaret Coyne 9-12-1857 (9-13-1857) Sh
Kyle, R. G. to _____ Crittenden 2-18-1858 We
Kyle, Robt. to Elizabeth Martin Tull(Taber?) 12-16-1835 Hr
Kyle, Samuel B. to Josie M. Astin 12-12-1868 (12-17-1868) F

LaBone, William to Sarah Ann Tyler 12-2-1844 Sh
LaVoc, George to Martha Sarah Kindred 2-28-1856 O
Labesque, Barthelemey to Amanda Halbrook 6-17-1862 Sh
Lacefield, D. N. to Milley A. Lockman 2-3-1863 Mn
Lacefield, Martin V. to Rebecca Lineberry 4-18-1861 Hr

Lacewell, Daniel to F. Pollock 9-21-1850 O
Lacewell, Jefferson to Catharine Young 12-24-1858 (12-26-1858) O
Lacewell, Joseph to Jane Hale 3-4-1877 O
Lacewell, Joseph to Nancy Clark 12-31-1843 (no return) We
Lacewell, Miles to Elizabeth Collins 8-24-1867 O
Lacewell, Wm. to N. A. Pannell 6-7-1875 O
Lacewell?, Peter to B. A. Alexander 7-1-1852 (no return) Hn
Lacey, David S. to Martha R. Gullett 5-17-1844 L
Lacey, Francis S. to Elizabeth A. Wilkins 7-9-1862 Dy
Lacey, James A. to Dillie C. Moody 1-24-1878 Hy
Lacey, Jos. B. to Sally Benson 10-13-1866 (10-17-1866) F
Lacey, Joseph H. to Jane Howard 6-25-1833 (6-26-1833) Hr
Lacey, Joseph P. to Nancy Churchwell 6-24-1840 Cr
Lacey, Wm. L. to Amandy J. Reader 8-14-1845 Cr
Lackey, B. F. to Agnes F. Lynn 3-11-1880 L
Lackey, Benjamin F. to Clementine Lawson 1-4-1854 (1-5-1854) Hr
Lackey, Ephraim A. to Nancy T. Lawson 5-13-1854 (5-14[18]-1854) Hr
Lackey, James A. to Rebecca Richardson 3-10-1842 L
Lackey, John to Florida McVey 11-22-1853 (11-23-1853) Hr
Lackey, W. K. to Eddie Wardlaw 12-8-1881 L
Lackey, W. O. to Julia M. Jeffries 11-6-1879 L
Lackie, James A. to Sarah A. Jackson 2-29-1868 Ma
Lackie, Theodore to Elizabeth Steele 12-27-1836 (12-28-1836) Hr
Lackie, Thos. to Elizabth. Lackie 12-9-1849 (12-11-1849) F
Lacky, Alexander A. to Harriet Robertson 3-9-1830 (3-25-1830) Ma
Laconier, J. W. to M. C. Enoch 9-14-1874 O
Lacroix, Jacob to Josephine Wetter 11-4-1861 (1-9-1862) Sh
Lacy, Beverly to Clara Broom 12-28-1868 F B
Lacy, Daniel S. to Mary A. Williams 4-14-1858 (4-15-1858) Ma
Lacy, David to Sarah P. Hill 8-10-1842 Ma
Lacy, G. W. to Margaret Lee 9-26-1878 (10-6-1878) L B
Lacy, Harvey to Elizabeth Wood 12-11-1849 Hn
Lacy, Isaac to Lucinda H. Christman 2-7-1843 (2-9-1843) F
Lacy, J. C. to S. A. Gidcomb 4-21-1877 (4-22-1887) L
Lacy, James to Anna Hill 12-14-1850 Ma
Lacy, James to Judah Edwards 4-26-1848 F
Lacy, Jno. S. to Sally M. Lawrence 12-1-1868 (12-2-1868) Ma
Lacy, John B. to Ann B. Smith 12-15-1853 (12-16-1853) Hr
Lacy, John D. to Ellen Thacker 3-12-1870 Hy
Lacy, John D. to Sarah McAllister 9-1-1854 (9-3-1854) G
Lacy, John M. to Ella C. Herron 11-20-1872 (11-21-1872) Cr
Lacy, Josiah L. to Alsey Jane Johnson 12-5-1843 Ma
Lacy, Levey to Penelope E. Bryant 7-10-1848 (7-12-1848) Ma
Lacy, Stephen to Catharine Dowing 2-?-1838 F
Lacy, Stephen to Sarah Ann Eastman 9-16-1847 Sh
Lacy, Thomas to Mary A. Madden 12-23-1857 (12-28-1857) Sh
Lacy, Thos. to Eliza Ann Hill 10-25-1841 (10-28-1841) Ma
Lacy, W. B. to M. J. Jenkins 9-18-1867 (9-19-1867) Dy
Lacy, W. D. to M. J. Ross 1-26-1884 (1-27-1884) L
Lacy, W. S. B. to Ritter K. Snowden 4-4-1866 (4-5-1866) Cr
Lacy, William P. to Elizabeth Latham 9-13-1858 Ma
Lacy, William P. to Elizabeth Smithwich 7-19-1853 (7-21-1853) Ma
Lacy, William P. to Martha Johnson 10-1-1854 (1-12-1854) L
Lacy, William P. to Mary E. Brown 7-15-1867 (7-18-1867) Ma
Lacy, William R. to Ann Eliza B. Lawrence 12-17-1867 (12-18-1867) Ma
Lacy, William to Cassander J. Matthews 1-7-1852 (no return) L
Lad, Edward to Mary T. Kimble 10-6-1866 (not executed) Ma
Ladd, T. M. to Susan Roberts 9-7-1845 We
Ladd, Wm. H. to Mary Turnbull 5-16-1855 Sh
Laddamare, Hugh to Lidda Brunsull? 1-10-1867 (1-13-1867) Cr
Ladyman, Henry L. to Elizabeth Holland 8-5-1852 We
Ladyman, Joseph to Susanna Gains 11-17-1845 (no return) We
Laflore, J. T. to A. C. Ruff 8-17-1859 Cr
Lafon, Frederick to Margaret Martin 3-2-1843 Hn
Lagomargino, Carlo to Gerolima Trabucco 4-10-1858 (4-11-1858) Sh
Laham, Thos. to Elizabeth Crawford 2-14-1848 L
Lain (Lion?), Henry to Caroline Freeman 10-17-1860 G
Lain, Cannon H. to F. W. Chrisp 10-3-1854 G
Lain, J. A. to Lucinda W. Flowers 1-9-1868 G
Lain, John W. to Feliste Breatt 2-13-1846 Sh
Lain, Joseph L. to Martha C. Berryman 8-22-1860 (9-2-1860) We
Lain, M. D. to Elizabeth Bowers 11-29-1860 We
Lain, Patrick to Elizabeth Kennedy 4-12-1846 Sh
Lain, Wm. to Harriett Jeffries 2-15-1870 (no return) Hy
Laine, J. B. to M. A. Zeller 10-9-1859 Sh
Laine, J. M. to Jane Karr 2-16-1846 (2-17-1846) F
Lainn?, Isaac to Mary Ann Orwell 1-19-1847 T
Laird, David to Eliza Glascoe 9-30-1858 Hn
Laird, James L. to Laurah J. Roberts 9-22-1860 (9-3?-1860) O
Laird, James to Catheran Conner 12-19-1866 T
Laird, Luther to Jane M. Oswald 11-19-1851 (11-20-1851) Sh
Lake, Alexander to Rachel Henning 1-22-1868 (no return) L B
Lake, Allen Debow to Indiana Crenshaw 11-15-1848 (11-16-1848) T
Lake, Anthony to Bettie Rogers 12-24-1878 Hy
Lake, Armistead to Mary Green 7-1-1867? T
Lake, Daniel T. to Elizabeth A. Ivey 4-4-1861 T
Lake, Daniel T. to Virginia Culbreath 1-11-1855 T

Lake, Daniel to Dianna Nelson 3-2-1871 L
Lake, E. M. to Texanna Poe 10-2-1875 (10-7-1875) L
Lake, Henry to Harriett Tibbs 10-6-1876 Hy
Lake, Henry to Rebecca Maclin 4-20-1871 L
Lake, James C. to Mary Ann Siler 11-25-1857 (11-26-1857) T
Lake, Jerry to Jane Green? 12-31-1873 (no return) L B
Lake, Jerry to Nicy Henning 4-22-1871 L
Lake, Joseph E. to L.? A. Nabors 12-29-1845 Hr
Lake, Joseph E. to Laura H. Alexander 11-7-1860 (11-8-1860) Hr
Lake, Levin to Maggie E. Williams 10-28-1864 (10-29-1864) F
Lake, M. H. to M. F. Moore 12-20-1856 (12-23-1856) Hr
Lake, Milton F. to Lucinda Braden 5-21-1843 L
Lake, Nathan to Lueser Clark 3-4-1867? Hy
Lake, Ned to Aquilla Alston 3-11-1868 (3-13-1868) L B
Lake, Richard to Mary Jane McLarty 12-19-1853 (12-22-1853) Hr
Lake, Robert H. to Mary M. Sanders 9-8-1828 Ma
Lake, Wiley R. to Patience Turner 2-2-1859 Hn
Lake, Wm. Henry to Catharine M. Bailey 5-22-1854 (5-23-1854) Sh
Lakey, James H. to Elvira E. Addington 9-8-1860 Hr
Lakey, James H. to Sarah Lakey 1-15-1851 F
Lakey, William to Jane Cordle 3-9-1856 Hr
Lalusan?, J. S. to Martha A. Cross 7-7-1849 (not endorsed) F
Laman, Thomas to Mahulda A. Hathaway 12-14-1867 (12-18-1867) Ma
Lamar, Andrew to Sarah Easley 8-1-1867 (8-2-1867) T
Lamar, Frank to Mary Harrison 8-1-1867 (8-2-1867) T
Lamar, J. D. W. to Martha A. L. Babb 1-14-1869 G
Lamar, Samuel to Lucy Story 2-25-1826 (2-26-1826) O
Lamar, Thos. W. to Isadora Brooks 5-8-1867 G
Lamar, W. F. to Margaret V. Linton 11-12-1870 (11-15-1870) Dy
Lamar, W. F. to Mendie Eady 11-12-1870 (11-15-1870) Dy
Lamarr, W. F. to Rachel Aronhart 8-18-1866 Dy
Lamb, B. B. to Elizabeth J. Thompson 11-22-1865 (no return) Hn
Lamb, Benjamin F. to Elizabeth Adams 2-21-1848 (2-22-1848) L
Lamb, Benjamin F. to Sophronia Brogdon 4-23-1853 Hn
Lamb, Calvin to Martha Ellen Crawford 8-20-1870 G
Lamb, David to Ann Dunn 7-21-1843 Hn
Lamb, Elijah to Nancy Lamb 8-25-1847 Hn
Lamb, Elisha to Elizabeth Jamison 8-17-1847 Hn
Lamb, Enos to Frances Parish 2-5-1849 T
Lamb, H. to Sarah Manness 4-12-1864 Sh
Lamb, Henry to Mary Palmer 8-15-1866 Hn B
Lamb, Hugh to Isabella Ware 2-21-1874 (no return) Hy
Lamb, J. F. to M. V. Skeggs 7-17-1866 Hy
Lamb, J. P. to Clementine Sweat 12-14-1843 (no return) Hn
Lamb, James M. to Martha O. Masey 4-21-1854 We
Lamb, James P. to Anna J. Willie 12-12-1859 Hn
Lamb, James to Fannie E. Cox 1-14-1863 Sh
Lamb, James to Virginia Ray 12-5-1854 (no return) Hn
Lamb, Janus to Martha O. Matty (O'Matty) 4-21-1854 We
Lamb, John G. to Letha E. Glover 7-21-1841 Hn
Lamb, John W. P. to Elizabeth Horten 3-25-1863 (no return) We
Lamb, John to Getteller Barton 3-30-1875 Hy
Lamb, Joseph to Martha Potts 4-20-1841 Hn
Lamb, L. B. to Martha V. Douglas 12-16-1865 (12-19-1865) F
Lamb, Martin D. to Virginia C. McClain 1-12-1854 Hn
Lamb, Paschal to Sarah C. Osborne 1-18-1837 Sh
Lamb, Richard to Elizabeth Pirtle 1-7-1828 (1-8-1828) Hr
Lamb, Spencer H. to Estella Avery 11-8-1849 Sh
Lamb, Thomas to Elizabeth M. Potts 7-21-1847 Hn
Lamb, W. T. to M. A. F. Cook 11-22-1851 (no return) F
Lamb, W.I. to Lucinda Waldrup 8-13-1858 We
Lamb, Washington to Harriet Flemming 10-27-1851 Hn
Lamb, William to Mary H. Jenkins 10-20-1853 Hn
Lamberson, Thomas to Jane Jones 5-5-1847 Sh
Lambert, A. J. to M. H. Armstrong 3-29-1879 (4-1-1879) Dy
Lambert, Franklin to Rachel Sewell 11-15-1855 Ma
Lambert, Grandonfield to Martha Estis 9-14-1839 (9-15-1839) Ma
Lambert, J. J. to S. A. M. Norville 1-4-1870 (no return) Hy
Lambert, J. S. to Fannie C. Crawford 2-24-1879 (2-25-1879) Dy
Lambert, James to Willey Gee 9-15-1859 Hr
Lambert, Jehu to Mincy Jane Huddleston 9-15-1854 (9-18-1854) Hr
Lambert, John J. to Ailsy O. Harris 7-19-1848 Hr
Lambert, John J. to Mary Jane Cox 7-12-1858 (7-14-1858) Hr
Lambert, John to Alice Cunningham 3-11-1870 (3-13-1870) Cr
Lambert, John to Mary Hammers (Hanners) 10-13-1842 Sh
Lambert, John to Sarah Whitaker 12-17-1862 Mn
Lambert, Joseph to Louisa Arnold 10-10-1863 Sh
Lambert, Leonard to Sally Kerby 2-5-1829 Hr
Lambert, Orrin to Chatarine Kearley 3-13-1832 Hr
Lambert, Saml. H. to Martha C. Crews 4-14-1858 (4-15-1858) Hr
Lambert, Saml. to Martha Barnett 1-11-1826 (1-12-1826) Hr
Lambert, Samuel D. to Sophia H. Wiggins 2-9-1864 O
Lambert, Thomas to Susan A. Ellis 5-12-1863 (5-17-1863) Dy
Lambeth, A. G. to Sarah Jane Williams 3-11-1850 (3-21-1850) Hr
Lambeth, Alfred M. to Carolin E. Campbell 4-8-1835 (4-16-1835) Hr
Lambeth, F. to M. J. Pankey 8-16-1856 (8-17-1856) Hr
Lambeth, N. W. to Mary A. Sanford 7-10-1865 (7-12-1865) F

Lambkin?, J. W. to Sarah C. Terry 3-26-1850 Hn
Lambkins, J. to Susan Ann Davis 8-8-1873 (8-9-1873) T
Lamkin, Robert to Louisa Chapman 4-14-1874 T
Lamkin, Thomas H. to Bettie McCraw 4-1-1869 Hr
Lamkin, William to Mary Glen 4-4-1840 Hr
Lamkins, A. D. to Mary Ann M. Jones 5-30-1864 Hn
Lammond, Thomas to Laura Heflin 11-16-1869 (11-17-1869) Cr
Lammons, James to Milly Dial 4-2-1828 (4-3-1828) G
Lamoine, Francis to Mary A. Humbles 11-12-1858 (11-17-1858) G
Lamon, J. F. to N. J. McLeod 1-29-1877 L
Lamphier, James S. to Virginia Woodward 7-15-1845 Sh
Lampkin, Archer to Mary Vaughan 6-4-1870 T
Lampkins, A. H. to M. A. Byars 9-11-1863 Hn
Lampkins, Alexander to Emily J. Byars 2-6-1850 Hn
Lampkins, G. B. to Martha F. Smithey 10-6-1863 Hn
Lampkins, M. S. to Theresa A. Somers 10-31-1861 (no return) Hn
Lampkins, Robert to Permelia Fry 2-8-1856 (no return) Hn
Lampley, Asberry to Sarah Thomas 4-20-1851 Hn
Lampley, John to Ruth _____ 11-12-1846 Hn
Lanbinck, Izer to Cheesa J. Traywick 11-10-1852 Cr
Lancaster, A. J. to Fanny Weithington 7-3-1867 Hy
Lancaster, B. F. to T. A. Bynum 12-14-1876 O
Lancaster, Benj. to Clary A. Williams 12-19-1868 Hy
Lancaster, Edwin R. to Susan R. Connally 9-2-1850 Ma
Lancaster, G. E. to Elizabeth Martin 2-25-1863 G
Lancaster, Henry to Sarah A. Coleman 12-26-1844 (12-29-1844) O
Lancaster, J. B. to M. Hadley 7-10-1855 We
Lancaster, J. K. P. to M. E. Board 3-6-1872 (3-7-1872) O
Lancaster, Jno. B. to Lucy V. Leake 7-22-1852 Sh
Lancaster, John L. to Christiana E. Snider 10-30-1855 (10-31-1855) Ma
Lancaster, Wm. D. to F. A. Ward 11-25-1864 O
Lancaster, Wm. to E. A. Leake 6-6-1846 Sh
Land (Laird), William T. to Margaret Ann Bain 12-23-1847 Sh
Land, Charls to E. C. Branham 1-14-1869 Hy
Land, Elihu T. to Margarete Wherry 7-2-1833 Sh
Land, James M. to Mary Miller 3-15-1872 (3-17-1872) L
Land, James R. to Martha Halser 12-26-1835 Sh
Land, James T. to Mary A. Crawford 8-8-1852 (no return) F
Land, John to Mary Anne Johnson 11-12-1850 Sh
Land, P. B. to Margaret Ann Scott 5-11-1848 Sh
Land, Silas to Sarah Henry 5-17-1849 Sh
Land, W. A. to Isabella Buckley 11-8-1858 (11-9-1858) Sh
Land, W. L. to Eveline Buckley 2-11-1861 (2-13-1861) Sh
Land, William T. to Mahuldy Ramsey 7-25-1827 (7-26-1827) Hr
Landadal, Wm.H. to Mary Susan Ausbon 3-21-1872 T
Landen, Harvey to E. T. Chapman 1-27-1847 Sh
Landen, James to Emma H. Fairfax 12-17-1869 T
Landen, John J. to Jane Elander 2-24-1852 We
Lander, Augustus to Rosa Delkie 7-28-1858 Sh
Landers, A. to S. A. Brantley 7-3-1866 O
Landers, Robt. A. to Mary E. Anderson 12-17-1869 Ma
Landers, W. G. to N. J. Bradley 12-31-1875 (no return) Hy
Landers, William T. to Sarah J. Wood 12-17-1869 (12-19-1869) Ma
Landerstedt, John to Anna Ereka Norquist 9-6-1873 T
Landis, Benjamin to Jane N. Nimmo 3-13-1850 G
Landis, Jim to Luizer Lannom 2-9-1868 G B
Landis, John to Lucy Ann Trousdale 2-28-1850 Hn
Landis, William D. to Mary E. Trousdale 4-24-1856 Hn
Landon, Hinson to Sally Vanhog 11-11-1861 G
Landragan, Richard to Mary Rule 11-21-1859 Sh
Landran, Robert to Lucresa Wilson 4-28-1831 G
Landreth, W. F. to M. P. Clay 4-8-1863 (4-30-1863) F
Landrum, A. R. to Nancy Biggs 10-5-1854 G
Landrum, Benjamin T. to Matilda C. Snow 6-18-1852 (6-20-1852) O
Landrum, Benjamin to Mary E. Allison 6-25-1846 O
Landrum, Henry to Susan Landrum 6-28-1844 (no return) We
Landrum, Hiram to Susan Dowell 4-26-1872 (5-10-1872) Dy
Landrum, James E. to Susan A. Tidwell 4-232-1859 (4-24-1859) O
Landrum, James W. to Sarah D. McConnell 2-13-1861 G
Landrum, Jason to Sarah Bullard 7-19-1854 O
Landrum, John H. to Mary A. E. Mangrum 9-16-1859 We
Landrum, John to Bettie Burch 3-7-1877 (3-8-1877) Dy
Landrum, Joseph to Anna Edwards 1-5-1861 (5-21-1861) O
Landrum, Joseph to Lurane Parker 12-18-1855 (1-11-1856) O
Landrum, L. T. to Callie Guthrie 6-3-1872 (6-5-1872) Cr
Landrum, Samuel to Mary E. Guthrie 8-3-1863 (8-6-1863) O
Landrum, Samuel to Volumnia W. Lawson 2-21-1853 O
Landrum, Shepherd to Rebecca Hamet 11-9-1848 O
Landrum, Shepphard to Nancy Jane Matheny 4-20-1857 (4-27-1857) O
Landrum, Thomas J. to Mary E. Tidwell 4-21-1859 O
Landrum, Thomas T. to Nancy E. Dunnegan 10-6-1864 O
Landrum, Thomas to Malinda Young 3-1-1850 (3-3-1850) O
Landrum, Thomas to Permilia (Pernelia) Carey 11-11-1854 (11-14-1854) O
Landrum, W. E. to M. A. Newbill 12-3-1870 (12-6-1870) Cr
Landrum, W. H. to Em C. Rogers 3-6-1862 G
Landrum, W. P. to Indiana Welch 12-3-1856 We
Landrum, William L. to Matilda Snow 6-25-1849 O

Grooms

Landrum, William to E. J. Busby 8-2-1871 O
Landrum, William to Emeline Rolen 8-12-1858 (8-13-1858) O
Landrum, William to Jane Ray 6-27-1844 We
Landrum, Wm. to Charlotte Landrum 10-22-1844 We
Lane, Abner G. to Mary R. Wade 3-3-1853 G
Lane, Absalem to Matilda Brown 7-10-1837 (7-15-1837) Hr
Lane, Albert to Rosetta Boyd 11-21-1872 T
Lane, Allen to Eliza J. Williams 6-18-1868 Be
Lane, B. F. to Georgia E. Oliphant 6-4-1868 G
Lane, Brandon to Tennie Bumpass 1-14-1871 (1-15-1871) Ma
Lane, C. P. to Ann Maclin 1-23-1874 (no return) Hy
Lane, Cullud to Elizabeth Loving 1-6-1841 (2-16-1841) Ma
Lane, Daniel to Harriet Morris 6-8-1867 (no return) F B
Lane, Drury to Sarah Grooms 1-17-1839 Sh
Lane, Felix D. to Leah Phillips 8-11-1847 F
Lane, Geo. T. to Martha A. Pridy 7-14-1851 Sh
Lane, George W. to Sarah P. Killet 9-3-1863 Dy
Lane, George g. to Sarah Reese 10-12-1832 Sh
Lane, Gilbert to Elizabeth Whitteker 7-16-1853 (7-17-1853) O
Lane, Henry to Elizabeth E. Ward 4-7-1846 O
Lane, J. B. to M. C. James 10-21-1860 Hn
Lane, J. C. to Martha A. Gray 12-15-1858 (12-16-1858) Sh
Lane, J. D. to Polly Murray 8-6-1857 (8-20-1857) Hr
Lane, J. G. to Elizabeth Williams 5-8-1841 O
Lane, J. J. to Elizabeth Dodd 5-1-1867 G
Lane, J. J. to M. E. Pierce 10-15-1868 G
Lane, J. L. to H. L. Blankinship 1-31-1866 (2-10-1866) O
Lane, James J. to Seney Williams 10-1-1840 O
Lane, Jane E. to P. E. Edwards 3-12-1872 Dy
Lane, John Jay to Alice Hubbard 2-28-1859 (3-2-1859) Ma
Lane, John P. to Hepzhibad Watkins 12-17-1844 (12-19-1844) Ma
Lane, John T. to Mary L. Hampton 1-30-1872 Dy
Lane, Lawson to Margaret Wright 1-26-1870 T
Lane, M. C. to E. W. Harris 1-25-1858 (1-27-1858) G
Lane, Monroe to Amanda Forrest 4-8-1869 Cr
Lane, Patrick to Joana McMahan 8-7-1854 Sh
Lane, Philip B. to Margaret Scott 7-10-1846 Sh
Lane, Ross to Anna Cherry 8-18-1879 (no return) L B
Lane, S. B. to Catherine Roberson 11-25-1867 (11-26-1867) L
Lane, Sampson to Sarah E. Wilburn 9-7-1854 (no return) F
Lane, Samuel to Martha Chrisp 12-22-1852 (12-23-1852) G
Lane, T. B. to Lucy E. Ferrill 11-18-1878 (11-20-1878) Dy
Lane, T. D. to Mrs. L. J. Herrell 12-17-1873 T
Lane, Thomas C. to Christinna Turnage 3-4-1852 (3-8-1852) Ma
Lane, Thomas F. to Allia G. Woodfolk 11-11-1871 (11-12-1871) Ma
Lane, W. G. to Hannah Gilliam 12-14-1864 G
Lane, W. P. to Mary A. Connell 1-5-1871 Dy
Lane, William to Cyntha P. Sales 8-13-1841 (8-26-1841) G
Lane, William to Isabella Baley 12-21-1840 (12-23-1840) G
Lane, Willis H. to Elizabeth Wynn 9-3-1847 O
Lane, Willis H. to Susan Thomas 6-29-1841 G
Lane, Willis W. to Margaret Harris 4-1-1861 (4-3-1861) O
Lanear, J. H. to M. E. Christian 12-18-1866 (12-20-1866) Cr
Lanery (Lavery?), John P. to Eleanor Whitworthy 12-23-1849 (12-24-1849) L
Laney, Calvert to Sarah Anderson 1-19-1846 Ma
Laney, Culbert M. to Elizabeth Dick 5-5-1828 Ma
Laney, John A. to Laura E. Cox 9-12-1871 (9-14-1871) Ma
Laney, John P. to Susas S. Hutcherson 6-28-1871 (6-29-1871) L
Laney, Jonathan to Delila Turner 5-23-1828 Ma
Laney?, John P. to Mahala E. Mathias 8-18-1862 (8-20-1862) L
Lang, John to Augusta Burke 5-5-1858 Sh
Lang, Wm. to Jane Garvey (Gancy) 3-6-1849 Sh
Langan, Michael to Eliza Miller 10-20-1845 Sh
Langbein, Herman to Caroline Lutz 12-2-1854 Sh
Langdon, J. J. to Margaret Davenport 10-19-1866 (10-28-1866) F
Langdon, Wm. R. to S. Downy 12-29-1869 F
Langford, Abram B. to Rebecca V. Carter 5-16-1860 (5-17-1860) Ma
Langford, Andrew B. to Cora C. Conger 8-14-1866 (8-15-1866) Ma
Langford, Elias to Nancy C. Piercy 3-6-1850 (3-8-1850) Ma
Langford, H. to S. L. Autry 7-8-1867 O
Langford, James E. to Mary Elizabeth Rust 10-11-1848 (10-18-1848) G
Langford, John W. to Sarah R. Tate 12-17-1849 (12-18-1849) G
Langford, Joseph E. to Judia H. Butts 1-2-1860 (1-4-1860) Ma
Langford, Littleberry to Adeline Nichol 2-1-1855 (2-4-1855) Ma
Langford, W. B. to Bettie Ewell 7-26-1870 Ma
Langford, Willis J. to Sidna A. Morris 2-28-1874 (3-1-1874) O
Langford, Willis to Elizabeth Herrington 9-24-1850 (9-25-1850) Ma
Langham (Langhorn, ___ to Nancy Saunders 4-2-1829 Sh
Langham, A. J. to Jane Brown 2-7-1842 (no return) F
Langham, Edward to P. D. Woodall 11-26-1868 Hy
Langham, Lemuel to Susan Jane Laughter 1-1-1846 (no return) F
Langley, B. F. to Mary E. Alford 5-30-1871 L
Langley, B. Frank to Jennie Pitts 12-17-1874 L
Langley, James to Martha J. Shelton 4-2-1860 (4-5-1860) L
Langley, John to Ann Deason 11-27-1839 (11-28-1839) L
Langley, M. N. to Martha Jane Price 5-23-1846 (no return) L
Langley, Matthew M. to Martha Ann Meadows 4-12-1848 (no return) L

Langley, W. R. to Sarah A. Williams 3-7-1866 G
Langley, William W. B. to Merica Hawkins 7-16-1831 (7-17-1831) G
Langley, William W. B. to Amanda M. Cochrun 8-4-1861 We
Langley, William to Priscilla Winfrey 12-30-1868 (12-31-1868) F B
Langley, Wm. A. to Elizabeth Andrews 3-16-1865 (no return) L
Langly, Henry W. to Hannah Roberts 11-27-1867 Hn
Langly, Wm. B. to Cornelia A. Smith 3-12?-1842 (no return) F
Langstaff, Alfred A. to Sallie A. McCall 11-13-1871 (11-15-1871) T
Langster, George to Amanda Robertson 3-9-1856 (4-9-1856) Hr
Langston, Calvin to Martha Dawkins 2-2-1839 Ma
Langston, George R. to Winney Elkins 5-21-1841 (5-26-1841) Hr
Langston, John C. to Sarah McGraw 11-8-1841 Ma
Langston, Major to Susan Croom 1-10-1843 Ma
Langston, Mark to Pheraby B. Pyle 4-4-1854 Sh
Langston, W. H. to Elen C. Kelsey 5-27-1850 Hr
Langston, William to Tobitha Thomas 6-18-1825 (6-19-1825) Hr
Langston, Wm. to Martha A. Shepherd 11-28-1849 (11-29-1849) L
Langum, A. J. to Vernelia Scott 12-21-1844 (no return) F
Lanham, James F. to L. L. Lockridge 8-1-1861 We
Lanhann, W. R. to Elizabeth L. Baird 1-31-1855 (2-1-1855) G
Lanier, Aaron to Mary Ward 9-26-1866 (no return) Dy
Lanier, Bill to Louisa Taylor 3-2-1866 (no return) Hy
Lanier, Charley to Gertrude Jones 11-8-1877 Hy
Lanier, Charlie to Ellen Beard 11-28-1872 Hy
Lanier, Frank to Laura Burch 1-19-1878 (1-20-1878) Dy
Lanier, H. H. to Martha E. Hay 12-23-1869 G
Lanier, J. D. to M. B. Chalk 12-24-1874 Hy
Lanier, J. S. to Nancy J. Avery 7-10-1867 Hy
Lanier, J. to Mary J. Echols 7-24-1867 Dy
Lanier, James C. to Jane Ann Cosby 5-16-1854 (5-17-1854) T
Lanier, James to Lizzie Taylor 3-13-1873 Hy
Lanier, Jno. C. to MaryL. Howcott 12-15-1852 Sh
Lanier, John A. to Sarah Cox 12-15-1856 (12-18-1856) Hr
Lanier, John C. to Eliza A. Robinson 10-6-1853 Ma
Lanier, John to Delia Ann Nelson 12-6-1873 T
Lanier, Kenneth B. to Janie Frances Farmer? 1-13-1856 (1-31-1856) T
Lanier, L. P. to Cynthia Pruitt 1-1-1868 (1-2-1868) Dy
Lanier, O. E. to Mary E. Pope 10-28-1867 (10-29-1867) Dy
Lanier, Porter to Mary F. Powell 12-17-1867 Ma
Lanier, Robert F. to Elizabeth M. Lanier 12-29-1846 Sh
Lanier, S. J. to A. W. Vowel 4-12-1858 (no return) We
Lanier, Tecumseh to Nannie Lockhart 10-27-1874 Dy
Lanier, Tom to Adaline Graves 8-27-1878 (no return) L B
Lanier, W. S. to E. V. Avery 8-18-1869 Hy
Lanier, William to Lucy Pierson 9-5-1870 (9-22-1870) L
Lanigan, Dan to Bridget Mugovan 4-4-1861 Sh
Lankford, A. R. to M. E. Wiley 10-2-1865 Hn
Lankford, Champ to Martha Frith 2-13-1872 (2-14-1872) Dy
Lankford, Charles F. to Alice Barfield 2-25-1880 L
Lankford, D. M. to Ann E. Reed 1-14-1847 Cr
Lankford, D. M. to M. C. Coble 4-9-1867 (4-10-1867) Cr
Lankford, H. D. to Siby T. Hamilton 7-20-1867 G
Lankford, H. W. to M. C. Carter 1-17-1854 Hn
Lankford, Harris to Sallie Calhoun 3-14-1867 Hn B
Lankford, J. W. to Roxana Jeffries 5-2-1877 Hy
Lankford, James N. to Manda Dickson 2-12-1856 Cr
Lankford, Jessee to Caroline Nichols 5-16-1852 Be
Lankford, John D. to Anna Burks 2-15-1879 (2-19-1879) L
Lankford, John D. to Harriet S. Warren 6-8-1848 (6-11-1848) L
Lankford, M. P. to Susan W. Barfield 12-10-1851 (12-11-1851) L
Lankford, Nicholas L. to Sarah Willson 11-29-1831 L
Lankford, Peter L. to Mary E. Thum 12-11-1865 (12-13-1865) L
Lankford, Smith to Anna E. Oliver 9-10-1872 (9-11-1872) Cr
Lankford, Thomas W. to E. J. Rodgers 1-24-1851 Cr
Lankford, W. B. to Callie Burks 12-7-1880 (12-8-1880) L
Lankford, W. J. to M. A. Adams 1-24-1883 L
Lankston, William to Frances Tyson 10-25-1872 O
Lannum, Richard to Marinda F. Harrison 1-10-1866 G
Lannum, Wm. D. to Molly Harrell 11-28-1864 (no return) Cr
Lanom, David to Parlea Hess 4-7-1870 G B
Lanom, John R. to Martha Gillespie 12-5-1860 G
Lanon, E. H. to M. J. Sims 2-5-1868 Hy
Lansdell, A. C. to Cornelia Hadley 6-4-1860 (no return) Hy
Lanton, Albert Gallatin to Mary Amanda Turnage 12-16-1843 (12-22-1843) T
Lapier, William to Harriet Henderson 12-16-1873 Hy
Lappet, John Jesse to Mary Bass 4-13-1871 (no return) F B
Larallette, A. S. to Louisa J. McMannus 12-31-1850 Sh
Laraner, Jacob to Susannah Gage 9-19-1831 (9-?-1831) Hr
Lard, J. M. to Mary Ann Johnston 5-2-1855 We
Lard, W. L. to Tabitha King 5-3-1855 We
Laremore, A. to Sina McBride 8-1-1872 (8-4-1872) T
Laremore, Aderson to Mary Hutton 2-27-1869 (3-4-1869) T
Largent, W. H. to Lucy A. Averett 11-26-1860 (12-5-1860) F
Largent, Wm. H. to Sarah J. Dinkins 2-12-1855 (no return) F
Larimore, Hana? Miller to Catharine Howard 5-31-1853 T
Larimore, Pleasant K. to Sarah George 5-18-1847 (5-20-1847) T
Lark, Peter to Rosetta Harris 1-18-1872 (1-20-1872) T

Larkin (Larker?), Michael to Lucinda Blankenship 1-4-1869 G
Larkin, James to Annie Burns 12-21-1860 (12-22-1860) Sh
Larkin, John to Johanna Murphy 8-6-1859 (8-8-1859) Sh
Larkin?, James R. to Elizabeth A. Cabe 9-10-1846 (no return) Hn
Larkins, J. H. to Huldah Lee 7-29-1885 (7-30-1885) L
Larrabee, E. R. to Julia A. Guynn 9-27-1866 O
Larrantree, Augustus to Mary C. Ager 4-22-1856 Sh
Larrell, S. A. to Elizabeth Trease 2-21-1863 Mn
Larrison, Harriss to Eveline Lea 6-29-1876 (6-30-1876) L
Larrison, Henry to Sarah Wright 10-20-1885 (10-21-1885) L
Larrison, Newton to Jane Freeman 2-1-1886 L
Larue, John C. to Elizabeth Gooch 12-30-1865 Mn
Lary, John to Mary E. Barfield 9-3-1873 L
Lary, John to Nancy E. (Mrs.) Tiner 5-1-1863 (5-5-1863) O
Lary, John to Sarah I. Martin 1-12-1875 (no return) Hy
Lasater, J. C. to A. P. Wagster 12-2-1858 We
Lasater, J. C. to M. E. Dyer 7-28-1873 (7-31-1873) Dy
Lasater, Miles to Leddy Joiner 3-18-1844 (no return) Hn
Lasater, William H. to Nancy Hart 5-31-1857 Hn
Lashby, James to Sarah Ann Bond 10-16-1849 Sh
Lashlee, A. to L. Brown 9-20-1866 G
Lashlee, Burrell to Jerline Ballard 11-26-1847 Be
Lashlee, Geo. A. to Ann Brown 4-14-1853 Be
Lashlee, Horace to Lua Wyly 9-15-1867 Be
Lashlee, Hugh to Mary Elizabeth Hartley 8-11-1869 Be
Lashlee, James C. to Martha Boswell 7-6-1851 Be
Lashlee, John P. to Martha A. Roberson 12-26-1864 Be
Lashlee, John T. to Jane Wood 1-23-1850 Be
Lashlee, L. to S. C. Claxton 4-29-1842 Be
Lashlee, Peyton to Elizabeth Capps 3-6-1846 Be
Lashley, James to Mary Ann Ward 8-17-1840 F
Lashley, R. to Rodey A. Williams 3-12-1867 Hn
Lasiter, E. D. to Sarah I. Phelps 9-2-1858 We
Lasley, Craig N. to Mary L. Henderson 12-18-1850 O
Lasly, John H. to Isabella N. Baldridge 12-30-1844 (1-1-1845) G
Lassater, Loyd to Jane Hall 3-14-1867 (3-17-1867) T
Lasseter, T. C. to Susan J. Mathews 8-4-1864 Mn
Lassiter, H. L. to Clemintine Wright 2-28-1857 (3-5-1857) Hr
Lassiter, Isaac to Parilee F. Maxwell 12-7-1858 Hn
Lassiter, J. R. to Sarah Winsett 6-26-1866 (no return) Hn
Lassiter, Jas. M. to Catherine Jones 7-?-1836 (7-28-1836) G
Lassiter, Jesse W. to Emily E. Douglass 2-6-1871 (2-7-1871) Ma
Lassiter, Jesse to Emla Hammons 11-11-1840 F
Lassiter, Joe to Candace Jetton 3-13-1869 G B
Lassiter, M. A. to Lenord Clements 12-17-1872 (12-19-1872) T
Lassiter, N. T. to M. A. Evans 1-10-1866 Dy
Lassiter, Silas to Caroline Webb 9-8-1860 (9-9-1860) Ma
Lassiter, Silas to Emily Kerksey 1-1-1857 (1-2-1857) Ma
Lassiter, Silas to Minerva Copeland 1-12-1855 (1-16-1855) Ma
Lassiter, William to Elizabeth Duffey 4-3-1852 (4-7-1852) Ma
Lasslie, Prince to Matilda McRony 6-3-1876 O B
Lasswell, Joseph to Lydia A. Cooley 7-22-1860 We
Laster, Calvin to Virginia Pervis 6-25-1866 (no return) Hy
Laster, Elias to Mary W. Johnson 11-1-1854 O
Laster, H. to Susan King 6-23-1863 Cr
Laster, J. A. to R. J. Taylor 1-9-1869 (no return) Dy
Laster, J. P. to Susan E. King 1-24-1863 (1-25-1863) Cr
Laster, Josiah to Lavina Gamble 1-8-1833 O
Laster, Louis to Mary Gamble 6-29-1830 (6-30-1830) O
Laster, Wesley to Mrs. Hulda Steward 1-2-1854 Hr
Latapie?, Eugene to Mary E. Bowles 10-17-1853 Hn
Latermend?, Saml. to Mary E. Buckley 7-7-1852 We
Latham, Amos to Mary C. E. Toddy 12-2-1861 L
Latham, Amos to Rebecca Golding 4-12-1849 (4-15-1849) L
Latham, E. P. to Rebecca Casey 8-14-1860 L
Latham, Elhanon W. to Mahala Crihfield 5-30-1852 L
Latham, H. R. to Nancy Manning 12-13-1872 (12-14-1872) L
Latham, J. H. W. to Pattie Brown 12-13-1870 Hy
Latham, J. H. to Mollie J. Johnson 5-27-1875 Hy
Latham, John D. to Martha L. Butcher 3-18-1863 We
Latham, Leander to Mary Hill 2-18-1852 (2-19-1852) G
Latham, R. Wilson to Parthena Butler 6-1-1872 (6-2-1872) Cr
Latham, T. J. to Mollie H. Wooldridge 3-6-1861 (3-7-1861) Sh
Latham, Thomas J. to Sarah Frances Martin 8-23-1853 We
Latham, William H. to Malinda Moore 10-31-1871 Ma
Latham, William H. to Mollie H. Haynes 11-24-1870 (12-1-1870) Ma
Latham, William to Sarah F. Davis 7-21-1856 (7-24-1856) Ma
Latham, Wm. to Prudence Jones 7-3-1860 Sh
Lathrop, Daniel to Mary West 6-22-1864 We
Latimer, J. L. S. to Henretta Ann Moppin 1-1-1861 O
Latimer, J. T. to Fanny C. Wright 10-17-1867 Be
Latimer, Jacob to Margaret C. Dunlap 5-15-1845 Hn
Latimer, James R. to Sarah F. Summersett 5-12-1862 (5-15-1862) O
Latimer, T. J. to M. T. Ramsey 3-4-1868 O
Latimer, William to Eda Reiney 8-30-1870 G
Latimer, William to Nancy E. Latimer 10-6-1855 (10-17-1855) O
Latour, T. B. to M. E. Hutcherson 1-15-1878 (1-16-1878) L
Latour, T. B. to Mary H. Munns 7-4-1885 (7-5-1885) L
Latta, Charles T. to Martha J. Coleman 12-28-1859 G
Latta, Harvey M. to Charlott H. Alsabrooks 10-16-1834 G
Latta, James to Martha J. Harrison 12-7-1846 (12-8-1846) G
Latta, John M. to Margaret M. Cochran 2-8-1848 Sh
Latta, Matthew F. to Margaret A. Ozier 9-8-1852 Ma
Latta, William to Pameta Throgmorton 11-6-1842 Hn
Lattimer, John to Addie Wills 11-8-1876 Hy
Latum, N. R. to Charlotta J. Boothe 10-2-1860 G
Laudaman, James B. to Frances Marial 11-5-1850 (11-7-1850) F
Lauderdale, B. W. to Mary C. Taylor 3-13-1860 Sh
Lauderdale, E. B. to Leonora Cobb 12-30-1871 (1-1-1872) Dy
Lauderdale, Henry to Parelee Johnson 11-12-1874 T
Lauderdale, J. M. to Rebecca Wright 5-4-1869 Dy
Lauderdale, James H. to Roasina Hatch 6-2-1841 T
Lauderdale, John W. to Queen Tipton 11-3-1870 Dy
Lauderdale, Josiah H. to Clara H. Lauderdale 4-4-1866 (4-4-1865?) T
Lauderdale, Lymas to Susan Yarbro 12-18-1872 T
Lauderdale, Thos. S. to L. J. Tipton 1-30-1861 T
Lauderdale, Wesley H. to Agnes Truitt 3-26-1869 (4-4-1869) T
Lauderdale, William to Alcy Walk 5-24-1867 (5-26-1867) T
Laughhon, Aden to Dacare Moore 6-21-1825 Hr
Laughlin, David to Sallie (Mrs.) Wilson 3-23-1863 (3-25-1863) Sh
Laughlin, William to Sarah J. Hughes 9-7-1861 Mn
Laurence, H. M. to Jane Brashers 4-20-1867 (4-21-1867) Cr
Laurence, James H. to Marie Brown 6-9-1824 T
Laurence, James to Sarah Huling 12-19-1838 Sh
Laurence, William to Eliza S. Brown 11-22-1821 Sh
Laurence, William to Frances Armour 11-4-1847 Sh
Laurie, James to Angeline Bowles 1-20-1854 We
Laurison, Toby to Anna Taylor 9-8-1877 (9-12-1877) L B
Lavallette, Albert T. to Louisa J. McManus 12-31-1850 Sh
Lavell, Isaac to Alvin A. Pace 8-21-1874 (9-8-1874) T
Lavell, Patrick to Manerva Ann Williams 12-12-1859 (12-13-1859) T
Lavell, Thomas to Sarah Ann Baskins 11-27-1869 (12-2-1869) T
Lavender, Joseph to Elizabeth Outlaw 4-28-1852 (no return) F
Lavezzo, M. to Rosa Seniago 4-16-1860 (4-22-1860) Sh
Lavigne, Francois to Annie Heffernan 8-14-1862 Sh
Lavines, Gus to Harriett Rogers 1-10-1878 Hy
Lavrenz, Peter to Lisetta Ruttlemager 2-28-1855 (3-1-1855) Sh
Law, Geo. W. to Louisa Kee 2-27-1873 Dy
Law, L. J. to N. L. Crafton 2-21-1869 G
Law, Umphrey to Dinkie Turnage 4-16-1872 (4-18-1872) Dy
Lawhorn, Albert H. to Clarisa? Caraway 4-5-1845 (4-24-1845) Hr
Lawhorn, Isaac to Jane Shaw 1-3-1872 (no return) Cr
Lawler, Christopher to Sarah Tobin 10-10-1860 Sh
Lawler, John S. to Susan Jones 1-27-1838 Sh
Lawler, Lafayette to Martha Hicks 10-6-1867 Be
Lawler, Michael to Ann Cull 7-23-1855 Sh
Lawler, Walter to Mary Lunay 7-12-1856 (7-13-1856) Sh
Lawless, B. F. to Malvina Akers 2-26-1867 G
Lawless, John to Norah Nugent 7-9-1844 Sh
Lawrance, A. to Jane King 10-10-1854 O
Lawrance, Alexander to Mary A. Huffman 4-15-1852 Cr
Lawrance, Charles J. to Charlott Cantrol 11-3-1842 G
Lawrance, Eli J. to Lidda Lowder 4-25-1844 Cr
Lawrance, Elisha to J. S. Blair 2-5-1846 Cr
Lawrance, George M. D. to Rebecca Smith 1-23-1844 G
Lawrance, John W. to Eliza Butler 4-2-1849 Cr
Lawrence, Abraham to Martha Pickens 2-17-1837 Hr
Lawrence, Adam C. to Martha F. Mason 4-22-1876 (4-23-1876) O
Lawrence, C. B. to Maggie Summerow 12-23-1884 (12-24-1885?) L
Lawrence, Cuthbert B. to Sarah B. Hedge 1-1-1856 (no return) Hn
Lawrence, Elias to Adaline Hill 11-30-1851 Hn
Lawrence, Elias to Sarah Davis 12-3-1840 (12-8-1840) Ma
Lawrence, Elisha to Jane Piercy 12-26-1848 Ma
Lawrence, George W. to Martha Griffin 7-27-1852 G
Lawrence, H. C. to Sarah Harrison 2-20-1850 Hn
Lawrence, Hiram C. to Martha J. Bradly 3-15-1859 Hn
Lawrence, James A. to Amanda Blackshire 11-20-1850 Hn
Lawrence, James H. to A. Johnston 6-14-1852 Hn
Lawrence, James H. to Frizzy A. Todd 12-8-1846 (12-9-1846) Ma
Lawrence, John G. to Nancy Parale Key 11-14-1869 Cr
Lawrence, John W. to Annis Wilson 12-14-1841 (12-21-1841) F
Lawrence, Leander D. to Sarah Wallace 12-13-1845 (12-15-1845) G
Lawrence, M. C. to W. E. Ward 1-18-1865 Hn
Lawrence, Manson to Lavinia Loyd 12-28-1867 G B
Lawrence, Monroe to Lizzie Fisher 1-4-1886 (1-7-1886) L
Lawrence, Monroe to Mary Ellen Carter 10-4-1877 (no return) L B
Lawrence, N. L. to Harriet S. Watkins 5-31-1855 Sh
Lawrence, R. J. to Susanah Haynes 3-23-1845 Be
Lawrence, R. S. to Lida A. Stailey 3-17-1859 Sh
Lawrence, Sawnee to Zilpha L. Taylor 10-22-1868 Ma
Lawrence, T. A. to M. C. Jones 9-13-1863 Hn
Lawrence, Thomas R. B. to Malinda (Mrs.) Rawlings 4-14-1885 (no return) L
Lawrence, Thomas to Mollie Scott 8-9-1870 G B
Lawrence, William L. to Symantha C. Word 3-9-1859 G

Lawrence, William to Nancy W. George 4-11-1826 (4-12-1862) Hr
Lawrence, Wm. H. to Lucinda Monroe no date (with 10-1867) Cr
Lawrence?, Wm. Alen to Amanda Minerva McBride 3-12-1856 (3-13-1856) T
Lawrens, Jobe P. to Mary S. Miskelly 3-1-1865 (3-2-1865) L
Lawrison, York to Docia Conner 5-25-1871 L
Lawry, James to Abagail Faulkner 6-27-1859 (6-28-1859) Ma
Laws, Allen B. to Rachel Magee 6-5-1852 Sh
Laws, George W. to Angelina Baker 9-13-1850 Ma
Laws, Homer to C. Terry 2-4-1873 (2-10-1873) O
Laws, Wesley to Susan Williamson 9-23-1856 Cr
Laws, Wm. Riley to Martha Elizabeth Hall 6-3-1861 Sh
Lawsen, James T. to Mary A. Thornsbrough 1-20-1858 We
Lawso, Will S. to Nancy S. Atkins 11-30-1846 Hn
Lawson, E. A. to Mary Jones 8-12-1867 O
Lawson, James to Delila Barnhill 2-11-1868 Be
Lawson, Jno. M. to Mary Bolden 5-21-1856 (5-22-1856) Hr
Lawson, S. P. to M. E. Woods 12-12-1866 O
Lawson, Tom to Aggie Alston 11-20-1871 (11-23-1871) T
Lawson, W. H. to M. E. Dickey 4-9-1865 G
Lawson, W. S. to Margaret E. Jones 7-19-1864 Sh
Lawson, William A. to Lucy B. Page 11-6-1852 (11-10-1852) O
Lawton?, Mathew M. to M. E. Penson 1?-30-1868 T
Lax, Benjamin to Nancy V. Gates 3-2-1846 (3-5-1846) Hr
Lax, Berryman to Georgiana Adams 12-27-1852 Hr
Lax, J. L. to Eliza Cook 12-7-1859 Hr
Lax, J. to E. W. Burton 11-7-1865 Hr
Lax, Joel to Elizabeth W. Cook 6-8-1838 Hn
Lax, Joel to Luvinia P. Clarke 3-31-1841 (no return) Hn
Lax, John A. to Elizabeth H. Meade 10-9-1859 Hn
Lax, John jr. to Ann Usher 2-26-1849 (2-27-1849) Hr
Lax, R. M. to Mary E. Shinault 12-26-1854 (12-28-1854) Hr
Lax, Timothy to Mary H. Crews 12-17-1852 (12-19-1852) Hr
Lax, William C. to Elizabeth Shaw 6-22-1848 Hn
Lax, William C. to Maria Chilcutt 8-3-1865 Hn
Laxton, J. J. to Nancy J. McBride 2-2-1870 (2-3-1870) T
Lay, Elisha to Elizabeth Ingram 9-16-1839 (no return) F
Lay, Elisha to Helen Palmer 4-17-1861 (4-18-1861) Sh
Lay, J. A. to Georgia Andrews 11-30-1859 (12-2-1859) Hr
Lay, James to Rebecca Carnes 2-21-1832 (2-23-1832) Hr
Lay, Mose to Martha Lockey 12-25-1871 Hy
Laycock, Francis M. to Mary J. Forluss 7-28-1860 (7-29-1860) Cr
Laycock, John S. to |illy E. Wilks 12-2-1866 Cr
Laycook, Henderson to Hallie Thonton 11-8-1853 Cr
Laycook, John C. to N. C. Dill 12-31-1868 Cr
Laycook, John to Mina Haris 12-6-1843 Cr
Laycook, Wm. J. to Mary M. Harris 1-31-1849 Cr
Laymare, Julius to Martha E. Crain 9-10-1857 Sh
Laymon, Absolum B. to Mary R. Crossby 5-27-1848 (5-31-1848) G
Laymon, Isaac to Mahalia Webb 11-22-1842 G
Laymon, John to Elizabeth Stuart 11-24-1836 G
Laymon, William to Emily E. Kelton 7-9-1857 G
Laymon, William to Mary Ann Mathis 3-9-1850 (3-10-1850) G
Laymond, Raysdon to Rebecca Younger 9-20-1848 Cr
Layn, William W. to Mary Jane Wadley 3-10-1856 (3-16-1856) Ma
Layne, T. W. to Mary E. McClintock 12-21-1881 (12-22-1881) L
Layne, William M. to Sarah Davis 12-14-1859 (no return) Hy
Layne, William T. to Mary (Mrs.) Tansil 12-16-1874 (12-25-1874) L
Layton, D. A. to S. A. Harland 8-3-1861 G
Layton, W. R. to Amanda E. Hunter 7-2-1863 Mn
Lazenby, Wm. to Nora Baxter 11-20-1869 (11-25-1869) F
LeCoq, A. H. to M. A. L. P. Scrogin 5-14-1857 Sh
LeCoq, Charles A. to Mary H. Joyner 3-20-1861 Sh
LeCoq, Charles A. to Susan A. Rudisill 9-15-1852 Sh
LeRoy, Robert to Ellen Farrer 7-20-1857 Sh
Lea, A. W. C. to Martha Jane Price 7-16-1847 L
Lea, Cesa to Mattie Suggs 1-30-1869 Hy
Lea, Dock to Harriet Coachman 12-31-1872 Hy
Lea, E. W. to Elizabeth Haynes 3-4-1850 (3-7-1850) Ma
Lea, Frank to Annie Taylor 7-15-1871 Hy
Lea, Haywood to Nancy Shilcutt 12-26-1871 Hy
Lea, Henry to Sarah Ann Hardin 4-17-1845 Sh
Lea, Isiah to Helen Sorrell 12-27-1862 (1-3-1863) Dy
Lea, J. M. to Mollie J. Brown 9-26-1868 (no return) Hy
Lea, Jackson to Cornelia Rhodes 8-6-1868 (no return) Hy
Lea, Jake to Annie Barnett 7-27-1877 (7-29-1877) L B
Lea, James to Clarisa Morris 9-8-1828 (9-9-1828) Hr
Lea, Jerman W. to Mary Cooper 6-29-1843 (7-4-1843) G
Lea, John F. to Mary A. McClish 5-14-1855 (5-16-1855) Ma
Lea, John G. to Nancy J. Fulbright 5-17-1854 (5-?-1854) Ma
Lea, John M. to Elizabeth Overton 5-1-1845 Sh
Lea, John to Eliza Alexander 9-7-1846 (no return) We
Lea, Lewis to Elizabeth Leathus 3-17-1874 (3-18-1874) L B
Lea, Lindsey to Sally Ann New 3-12-1828 Hr
Lea, Lorenzo (Rev.) to Fannie (Mrs.) Cobb 3-29-1858 (3-30-1858) Ma
Lea, Nash to America Byus 4-17-1867 (no return) Hy
Lea, Phil to Sallie Woods 11-19-1881 L B
Lea, Robert F. to Sarah Ann White 12-24-1850 G

Lea, Robert to Lucy Hinton 1-6-1875 (1-7-1875) L B
Lea, Sam to Emaly Bond 1-4-1869 Hy
Lea, Sam to Maggie McIntosh 1-7-1871 Hy
Lea, Sam to Margarett Boner 12-27-1875 (no return) Hy
Lea, Solomon P. to Molie B. Chapman 3-23-1861 (3-28-1861) L
Lea, W. H. to Missouri Nolan 12-5-1883 (12-6-1884) L
Lea, William to Caldonia Dunaway 7-13-1878 (no return) L
Lea, William to Eliza Shelton 7-18-1866 Hy
Lea, William to Sallie Bostic 1-22-1872 (1-23-1872) L
Lea, William to Sarah Price 5-16-1863 Mn
Lea, Wm. Harrison to Martha E. Brown 6-14-1852 (no return) F
Lea, Wm. C. to Mollie J. Nolen 12-29-1859 Hy
Lea, Wm. to Mary Odom 11-14-1877 Hy
Lea, Zack to Celia Ann Snoddy 1-14-1870 G B
Lea, r. C. to Mary P. Mitchell 12-6-1847 (12-23-1847) F
Leach, A. G. to Fannie A. Lockhart 1-14-1868 (1-15-1868) F
Leach, Abner to Amanda A. Brooks 12-10-1850 Cr
Leach, Asa to Emily Matilda Brown 11-28-1854 T
Leach, Gideon to Mary J. Blackwell 2-8-1840 Sh
Leach, J. F. to J. M. McCollum 1-?-1867 (1-15-1867) Cr
Leach, J. N. to Maggie Dewease 12-18-1874 (12-22-1874) T
Leach, J. W. to S. C. House 12-27-1870 (12-28-1870) Cr
Leach, James Madison to Louisa Rutherford 7-17-1849 T
Leach, James to Eliza Cannon 6-24-1854 (6-26-1854) T
Leach, John D. to Mary Jane Vawter 12-11-1852 Cr
Leach, John L. to Amanda F. Lockhart 2-19-1866 (2-21-1866) F
Leach, John R. to Elizabeth B. Hart 12-17-1857 Cr
Leach, John to Armenta Brown 4-8-1855 (4-14-1855) T
Leach, Joseph D. to Amanda C. Cribbs 10-19-1859 (10-20-1859) G
Leach, Lindsey J. to Eliza M. Wilson 8-19-1841 Cr
Leach, Robert P. to Lucinda Hooker 1-11-1854 Cr
Leach, Santrel F. to Margaret J. Horton 11-20-1858 Cr
Leach, Smith to Rachel Brooks 12-14-1842 Cr
Leach, Smith to Rebecca S. Smith 6-13-1854 Cr
Leach, Thomas W. to Delila M. Burrow 1-31-1866 (2-1-1866) Cr
Leach, Thos. A. to Mollie A. Hurt 10-27-1865 Cr
Leach, Thos. to Rebecca P. Jones 5-12-1853 Sh
Leach, W. H. to Mary Prichard 1-14-1852 (1-15-1852) Sh
Leach, W. J. to M. W. Ballew 3-31-1865 (no return) Cr
Leach, Wm. G. to Amanda Reader 1-19-1856 Cr
Leach, Wm. H. to Catharine E. Scott 12-10-1860 T
Leach, Wm. P. to Mary M. Culp 12-2-1846 Cr
Leach, Wm. to Elizabeth Briggs 1-22-1856 Sh
Leachman, C. to Caldonia Bradford 4-3-1874 (no return) Hy
Leacy, John to Ann Mann (Marr) 5-15-1849 Sh
Leadford, A. to Sarah King 5-11-1861 Mn
Leak, David to Adaline Turner 11-2-1869 G
Leak, William N. to Naomi F. Ruth 1-26-1878 (1-30-1878) L
Leake, E. M. to Catharine T. Watkins 3-20-1844 (no return) F
Leake, Edwd. C. to Polly L. Little 6-23-1857 Sh
Leake, G. W. to Malvina Tennessee London (Landon?) 7-20-1869 G
Leake, Lemuel to Eveline London 3-30-1849 (4-1-1849) Ma
Leake, Thos. H. to Martha Ann Hicks 7-14-1846 Ma
Leake, Virginius to Martha A. Field 10-2-1849 L
Leap, Frederick to Mary Casen 11-21-1854 (11-23-1854) O
Leap, George to Martha Cason 10-25-1857 O
Leap, N. to Sarah A. Taylor 11-1-1873 (11-2-1873) O
Leapord, James S. to Margaret Bradshaw 10-6-1865 Mn
Leary, Daniel to Mary Downs 7-4-1857 (7-5-1857) Sh
Leary, John to Ann Marr? 5-1-1849 Sh
Leary, Martin to Mary Leonard 5-30-1857 Sh
Leary, Michael to Mary Rhelahan 5-21-1860 Sh
Leath, Bruce to Emma Bower 1-8-1872 Hy
Leath, Daniel to Rachel Lawson 9-18-1863 Mn
Leath, G. A. to Leona J. McMackin 12-1-1874 (12-2-1874) Dy
Leath, J. M. to Elizabeth Barker 7-7-1868 G
Leath, J. Z. to Emiline Parker 8-16-1872 (8-22-1872) Dy
Leath, James T. to Laura W. White 12-2-1862 Sh
Leath, P. M. to Vallie M. Leath 7-12-1855 Sh
Leath, jr., J. T. to Rebecca E. Hamilton 7-19-1855 Hn
Leathe, J. B. to Mary Buchanan 11-21-1867 O
Leathers, Geo. M. to Margaret C. Lany 7-24-1860 Hr
Leathers, Reubin to Elizabeth Roach 7-28-1852 Hr
Leathers, William to Amanda Robinson 6-21-1844 Ma
Leaveque, C. to Ann Tooke 7-3-1847 Sh
Leavy, Robt. to Hannah Dickinson 10-17-1868 (10-18-1868) F B
Lebdor, Henry to Elizabeth Gibbons 4-8-1850 T
Leck, John to Rosina Uninger 9-29-1854 Sh
Lecorner, Wm. to Georgia Ann Roach 4-1-1874 (4-2-1874) O
Ledbetter, A. M. V. to Mary Brown 9-8-1867 G
Ledbetter, Alfred to Martha F. Meadows 9-11-1860 L
Ledbetter, Henry to Alice A. Hutstette 9-7-1850 Sh
Ledbetter, Henry to Sarah Smith 9-9-1873 (9-10-1873) L
Ledbetter, Isaac J. to Nancy H. Singleton 12-22-1862 L
Ledbetter, J. M. to Jane (Mrs.) Bradford 10-2-1872 Dy
Ledbetter, J. W. to Louiza V. Fields 7-19-1862 L
Ledbetter, J. W. to S. L. Finley 3-27-1873 (no return) Dy

Ledbetter, James R. to Martha Weaver 11-3-1841 Ma
Ledbetter, James R. to Sarah J. Ledbetter 5-30-1853 L
Ledbetter, James W. to Lucy J. Barlow 11-17-1864 Mn
Ledbetter, James to Nina Ann Mosier 7-10-1842 Hn
Ledbetter, Jesse to Elizabeth Bowman 5-27-1842 (6-2-1842) L
Ledbetter, John C. to Mary E. Johnson 11-27-1852 (11-28-1852) Ma
Ledbetter, John L. to Martha R. Moore 11-21-1846 (11-22-1846) L
Ledbetter, John W. to Harriett S. Suggs 1-3-1844 Hn
Ledbetter, Riley C. to Rebecca E. Coldwell 5-25-1871 L
Ledbetter, Roland to Mariah S. Bowman 12-3-1839 L
Ledbetter, Rolen to Mary Ann Meadows 9-11-1860 L
Ledbetter, S. W. to Minerva Shearer 7-25-1850 L
Ledbetter, S. W. to Susan H. Wesson 5-19-1848 Sh
Ledbetter, Samuel to Emily Thompson 12-13-1843 Sh
Ledbetter, Thomas to Lenora Magary 4-4-1872 (no return) Dy
Ledbetter, W. A. to S. J. Norris 9-19-1885 (9-20-1885) L
Ledbetter, William R. to Martha ANn Bishop 10-4-1864 Mn
Ledbetter, Wm. R. to Nancy C. Acuff 12-8-1855 (12-11-1855) L
Ledger, Geo. H. to Mary F. Dowdy 2-26-1851 F
Ledsinger, Boss to Alice Fowlkes 4-26-1876 (4-27-1876) Dy B
Ledsinger, J. Z. to M. J. Johnson 12-2-1868 (no return) Dy
Ledsinger, John to Matta Stewart 12-31-1872 (1-1-1873) Dy
Ledsinger, Thomas F. to Mary Louisa Ferguson 9-27-1865 Dy
Ledwith, Michl. to Anon Atkinson 12-20-1852 Sh
Lee, A. D. to Amanda Jane Long 4-5-1865 Mn
Lee, A. to Rebecca Haney 4-26-1858 Be
Lee, Armstead to Rachel Fitzpatarick 11-22-1883 L
Lee, Berry to Mary Rogers 10-7-1845 (10-9-1845) F
Lee, C. E. to Lydia A. Timms 8-27-1874 T
Lee, C. W. to Mary Redin 1-21-1847 Hn
Lee, Calvin L. to Jane Cook 12-13-1852 Cr
Lee, Calvin to Darcey? E. Pankey 9-3-1858 (9-5-1858) O
Lee, Calvin to Dorcias E. Pankey 9-5-1858 O
Lee, David to S. S. Wilbanks 10-31-1861 We
Lee, Duncan C. to Amanda J. Caplinger 9-27-1857 Hn
Lee, Ephraim J. to Mary C. E. York 6-1-1858 Ma
Lee, Felix W. to Elizabeth Howard 2-12-1839 F
Lee, Francis Marion to Mary A. Henry 10-9-1848 (10-12-1848) T
Lee, Franklin W. to Amanda M. Marberry 5-19-1850 Hn
Lee, Geo. to Martha Thurmond 12-17-1873 Hy
Lee, George A. to H. F. N. E. Hays 10-3-1850 Hn
Lee, George W. to Lucinda Umstead 6-1-1846 (6-3-1846) G
Lee, Henderson to Ella Halliburton 6-14-1878 (6-15-1878) L B
Lee, Henry C. to Sarah Woods 7-27-1851 Hn
Lee, Henry to Marth M. Williams 10-11-1854 (no return) F
Lee, Henry to Susan M. Massey 10-8-1849 Sh
Lee, Hugh W. to Mary P. Jordan 2-5-1868 (2-6-1868) L
Lee, Hugh W. to Sarah S. Hafford 12-8-1885 (12-9-1858) L
Lee, Isaac S. to Laura L. Shankle 6-29-1880 L
Lee, J. B. to M. F. Wheeless 12-24-1881 (no return) L
Lee, J. J. A. to Martha E. Dement 3-20-1851 G
Lee, J. J. H. to Malvina sims Scott 12-2-1847 Sh
Lee, J. P. to Rebecca Ann Wainscott 10-23-1864 Hn
Lee, J. W. to Mary J. Lemons 10-2-1865 (10-3-1865) Cr
Lee, Jacob to Fannie Mitchell 12-28-1885 (12-29-1885) L
Lee, James H. to Sarah A. Williams 3-2-1846 (no return) Hn
Lee, James T. to Malinda Chilcut 4-19-1842 Hn
Lee, James to Mariah McIntire 3-14-1864 Sh
Lee, James to Mary Simmons 2-8-1842 F
Lee, James to Sarah Hood 12-14-1848 Cr
Lee, James to Tennessee Gainer 7-26-1838 Hn
Lee, Jeremiah to Sarah Murphy 2-2-1841 (2-4-1841) Hr
Lee, Joe to Georgia Lee 9-13-1880 (9-14-1880) L B
Lee, John C. to Avena B. Deen 5-30-1866 O
Lee, John F. to Nancy C. Upchurch 1-1-1852 Hn
Lee, John J. to Marting S. Dement 8-3-1846 G
Lee, John W. to Catharine T. Perry 3-5-1855 (3-7-1855) Hr
Lee, John W. to Hulda E. Mashburn 12-22-1846 (12-23-1846) Hr
Lee, John to Harrett Cook 8-21-1856 T
Lee, John to Mary Cooper 2-21-1879 (2-23-1879) L
Lee, John to N. A. Gillespie 9-14-1862 G
Lee, John to Nancy Hay 4-19-1873 T
Lee, John to Nancy J. Farris 4-19-1863 Mn
Lee, John to Purnesa Lamb 5-2-1833 Sh
Lee, John to Susan E. Williams 6-1-1867 (6-3-1867) Dy
Lee, Joshua C. to H. V. Shumate 12-1-1853 Ma
Lee, L. M. to E. J. Smiley 3-5-1863 Hn
Lee, L. M. to Rebecca Mige 11-6-1855 We
Lee, Lewis to Frances Struther 12-31-1869 Hy
Lee, Nathan to Alice T. Parr 11-22-1884 (3-6-1885) L
Lee, Nathan to Josie Lee 3-28-1882 (3-29-1882) L
Lee, Nelson to Amanda Lea 12-17-1872 Hy
Lee, Patrick to Hannora Moriarty 2-22-1862 (2-23-1862) Sh
Lee, Robt. to Mary Morris 1-5-1866 (1-6-1866) F B
Lee, Samuel to Matilda Robinson 8-1-1858 Hn
Lee, Scott to Henretta Robertson 12-24-1874 Hy
Lee, Scott to Susan Graham 10-16-1880 L
Lee, Thomas F. to Susan G. Williamson 7-10-1855 (7-11-1855) Sh
Lee, Thomas H. to Elizabeth A. Webb 9-16-1853 Ma
Lee, Thomas V. to Adeline Tubbs 8-22-1854 Mn
Lee, Thomas to Easter Turner 12-30-1873 (12-3?-1873) T
Lee, Thomas to Harriett Allen 10-6-1877 (no return) Hy
Lee, W. A. to Lucy E. Taylor 10-15-1859 (10-16-1859) G
Lee, W. A. to Mollie E. Davis 8-5-1868 (8-5-1870?) G
Lee, W. H. to M. A. Woodson 4-14-1878 Hy
Lee, W. T. to M. F. Warford 5-14-1873 (5-15-1873) O
Lee, W. T. to S. E. D. Tucker 8-7-1870 G
Lee, Wallace to Louvinia Nixon 1-22-1884 L
Lee, William B. to Laura L. Butler? 11-8-1869 (no return) L
Lee, William C. to T. Gatewood 12-6-1858 We
Lee, William E. to Elizabeth J. Roberts 12-27-1865 O
Lee, William R. to Lucinda Allman 6-25-1846 Hn
Lee, William S. to Martha E. Jackson 2-23-1867 (2-27-1867) Cr
Lee, William to Juliann Howell 11-13-1846 Hn
Lee, William to Mary J. Swift 2-12-1864 (no return) Hn
Lee, William to Sarah Wilson 10-26-1860 (10-28-1860) Hr
Lee, William to Venie Stuart 1-9-1873 Hy
Lee, Wm. D. to Louisa P. Harris 5-7-1844 Cr
Lee, Wm. T. to Martha A. Ussery 11-16-1860 Hr
Lee, Wm. to Eliza Tyus 12-12-1877 Hy
Lee, Z. to Sarah F. Brumager 11-2-1865 Be
Lee?, Joel to Melissa Ann Linsey 11-15-1837 Hr
Leech, A. to Elizabeth (Mrs.) Branch 10-8-1861 Cr
Leech, Aliner to Elizabeth Branch 10-1-1861 (10-8-1861) Cr
Leech, Charles H. to Mary G. A. Allen 11-28-1867 T
Leech, James B. to Nancy Jane Crowel 12-12-1868 (12-15-1868) Cr
Leech, T. D. to Hiley? Bryant 10-6-1861 G
Leech, Thomas A. to Malissa A. Hurt no date (10-31-1865) Cr
Leechman, Lafayett to Fannie Yancy 10-22-1871 Hy
Leecray, Louis to Caroline Leinhart 11-15-1854 Sh
Leehy, Edward to Ellen Tangany 10-24-1859 Sh
Leek, Bolivar to Elizabeth Crews 6-4-1860 (6-5-1860) Cr
Leen, David to Honora Shehan 4-5-1856 (4-6-1856) Sh
Leeper, Guy to Lizzie J. Hurt 1-6-1869 Ma
Leeper, Hugh to Holly Wardlaw 8-3-1843 L
Leet, John to Sarah Borden? 12-14-1860 (12-16-1860) L
Leeton, William to Elizabeth Cole 12-18-1832 (12-23-1832) G
Leewright, R. B. to Louisa A. Davis 5-11-1859 (5-12-1859) Sh
Lefever, Lewis to Sarah C. Alexander 1-9-1844 Hn
Lefevre, Amanuel to Louisa J. Stinson 1-27-1850 Hn
Lefevre, John to Avarilla Ballard 1-6-1863 Hn
Leflore, S. P. to Julia Crosswell 10-20-1869 (10-21-1869) Cr
Leftwich, Isaac to Frances Dunn 12-24-1870 T
Leftwick, A. L. to Mary F. Jones 3-4-1861 Sh
Legan, Thomas W. to Arnetta T. Hudgens 12-22-1864 Hn
Legate, James to Martha Holland 9-30-1855 Be
Legate, Jefferson H. to Gemima N. Baker 3-30-1842 O
Legate, John H. to Eliza Jane Combs 6-2-1855 (6-3-1855) O
Legate, John T. R. to Isabella J. Reeves 2-25-1842 (2-28-1842) O
Legate, Joseph H. to Martha Ann Stockdale 5-8-1853 Be
Legate, William L. to Sarah M. Buchanan 9-21-1859 (9-22-1859) O
Legate, William to Sarah Robinson 4-7-1827 Hr
Legett, John D. to Sarah L. Peterson 10-23-1871 (no return) L
Leggatte, Samuel C. to Elizabeth Watson 12-28-1833 G
Leggett, Francis M. to Nancy Ann Emerson 8-7-1867 (8-11-1867) Ma
Leggett, Francis W. to Octavia I. Gwyn 10-26-1848 Sh
Leggett, J. B. to Melissa J. Breece 2-21-1870 (2-23-1870) Dy
Leggett, James to Rachel Carley 2-15-1844 Hr
Leggett, Josiah to Sarah Preer 10-13-1857 Sh
Leggett, W. T. to Emma Cavnar 2-27-1875 Hy
Leggett, William S. to Mary Jane Ames 11-27-1845 Hr
Leggit, Noah to Sarah P. Echols 7-11-1862 (7-13-1862) Dy
Legins, Samuel to Winnie Neal 9-8-1870 L
Legion, Albert H. to Elizabeth Bell 2-1-1858 G
Legion, Geo. W. to E. D. Hall 3-15-1858 (3-31-1858) G
Legon, Benj. H.? to Ann C. (Mrs.) White 5-11-1855 (no return) F
Lehman, J. H. to Caroline Strauss 9-18-1856 Sh
Leigh, James D. to Emeritter Smith 3-13-1867 (3-14-1867) Cr
Leigh, Richard to Mary E. Greene 3-30-1859 Cr
Leigh, W. J. D. to M. T. Fly 11-25-1868 G
Leigs, Wm. to M. T. Strang 12-18-1860 (12-19-1860) Sh
Leip, Nicholas to Mary Collins 2-12-1850 O
Leird, John to Mary Webb 2-13-1869 (2-14-1869) L
Leird, L. D. to S. M. Welch 9-10-1871 L
Leird, Samuel to Sarah Jane Boydston 2-29-1860 L
Leird, William to Nancy J. Condry 4-8-1858 L
Leland, Benjamin E. to Margaret Pendleton 12-5-1850 Sh
Lelievre, Francois to Sarah (Mrs.) Black 12-31-1864 Sh
Lemaire, H. A. to Luisa Townsend 7-9-1863 Be
Lemaster, N. F. to Olivia A. Rauling 10-21-1857 Sh
Lemes?, Charles to Cylvia Gibbs 5-26-1866 (5-27-1866) T
Lemmon, Jas. W. to Miss M. B. Jones 2-5-1866 (2-8-1866) T
Lemmond, Thomas M. to Lucretia E. Kingcade 4-23-1853 (4-26-1853) G
Lemmons, A. H. to Mary White 2-11-1867 (2-12-1867) Cr

Lemmons, Joel G. to Margaret M. Adams 1-5-1842 G
Lemmons, Thomas to Margaret H. Hardican 3-3-1862 (3-4-1862) Dy
Lemmons, William to Elizabeth Evert 8-9-1849 O
Lemmons, Wm. A. to Juliana Craige 12-24-1838 G
Lemmons, Wm. to Jane Hogsett 4-26-1845 (4-27-1845) L
Lemond, J. W. to Mary A. Hopper 3-3-1867 G
Lemonds, George C. to Mary W. Williams 10-16-1867 Hn
Lemonds, Granville to Martha C. Dale 10-22-1861 (no return) Hn
Lemonds, John L. to Margaret E. McCorkle 10-4-1865 Hn
Lemons (Clemons), Wm. to Louisiana Paste 5-11-1864 Sh
Lemons, Andrew J. to Mary Cassels 12-7-1862 G
Lemons, C. P. to Susan J. Buford 5-5-1840 (5-7-1840) F
Lemons, Calvin to Nancy E. Allen 11-27-1858 Hn
Lemons, Daniel to Margaret Yancy 11-5-1860 (no return) Hy
Lemons, Ed to Eliza Fields 1-6-1871 (no return) F B
Lemons, H. A. to Mary Jane Gooch 4-20-1864 Mn
Lemons, H. C. to N. S. White 12-7-1871 (no return) Cr
Lemons, Hircutus W. to Delita F. Forest 7-1-1858 Cr
Lemons, Isaac to Lucinda Gibson 3-31-1839 Hn
Lemons, J. M. to E. F. Hardican 2-8-1870 (no return) Dy
Lemons, J. W. to Nancy A. Howell 1-20-1857 (1-21-1857) G
Lemons, James to Mary Stanford 3-20-1842 Cr
Lemons, Marion A. to Mary E. Childers 12-30-1867 Dy
Lemons, Saml. O. to Mollie M. Williams 9-18-1871 (9-21-1871) T
Lemons, Thomas M. to Mary E. Curtis 1-30-1861 G
Lemons, W. C. to L. F. White 4-4-1872 G
Lemons, William to Elizabeth Evert 8-9-1849 O
Lemore, Charles M. to Sarah A. McFarlan 8-29-1849 Cr
Lemoutoy, C. G. to SaHa? Hadol 6-17-1862 We
Lenaghan, Henry to Maria Quinn 7-3-1852 (7-5-1852) Sh
Lenard, Wm. to Charlott Chaffin 7-20-1867 (7-27-1867) F B
Lendsy, John to Amanda F. House 11-29-1856 Cr
Lenek?, Asa? to Elizabeth Jane Brown 2-19-1853 T
Lenien, Soloman J. to Frances Vowell 6-25-1854 We
Lennard, William N. to Lucy N. Polk 4-18-1827 Hr
Lenoir, W. F. to Harriett E. Osborn 7-6-1858 (7-7-1858) Sh
Lenord, Joseph to Mehaley Hamett 1-29-1842 Cr
Lenow, J. to Frances Broom 1-7-1845 (1-9-1845) F
Lenow, James to Indiana H. Leake 6-9-1842 Sh
Lenox, Jesse S. to Ann E. Wilkins 9-29-1854 (10-4-1854) O
Leon, Richard M. to M. L. Sober 8-29-1850 We
Leonard, Arch to Susan Rice 6-5-1883 L
Leonard, Arvy to Matilda Nickels 2-7-1853 Be
Leonard, Chas. E. to Mary Lewis 1-10-1851 (1-11-1851) Sh
Leonard, D. H. to M. A. Wallice 10-5-1863 G
Leonard, David to Ellen Dwyer 4-14-1860 (4-15-1860) Sh
Leonard, Edward to Johanna English 12-5-1859 Sh
Leonard, Jno. W. to Martha E. Inman 2-6-1871 Ma
Leonard, Lawrence to Mary Buckley 11-22-1856 (11-23-1856) Sh
Leonard, Michael to Sarah M. White 8-26-1836 Sh
Leonard, Peter to Margaret Grear (Green?) 3-30-1853 (3-31-1853) Sh
Leonard, Stephen to Ellen Welch 2-4-1854 (2-6-1854) Sh
Leonard, Thomas to Martha Ann Brown 4-13-1848 Sh
Leonard, William to Sary Dickey 2-5-1831 (2-10-1831) G
Leonly?, Henry to Mary E. Howell 4-20-1867 (4-22-1867) Dy
Leopard (Leopan), John H. to Mary M. Sharp 12-18-1843 We
Leowenstein, Elias to Babethe Wolfe 1-20-1864 Sh
Lepperd, Samuel to Susan Joinor 9-15-1842 G
Leroy, John T. to Elizabeth J. A. F. Goswick 11-29-1853 (12-1-1853) Sh
Lesenberry, Wm. H. to Mary A. M. Wilden 12-24-1847 Cr
Leskey, Jo. M. to E. E. Carter 6-29-1858 We
Leslee, Harvy to Elizabeth King 12-30-1866 Be
Lesley, James to Harriett Johnson 2-15-1850 Cr
Leslie, H. to M. A. Johnson 10-24-1844 Cr
Leslie, James to Elizabeth Ann Atkins 8-18-1832 (8-19-1832) Hr
Leslie, S. G. to T. H. Bevill 11-26-1872 (11-27-1872) Cr
Lesner, A. V. to Nancy Caroline Derriggon 4-15-1858 Cr
Lesslie, James to M. J. McAuley 9-6-1871 (9-7-1871) Cr
Lester, Edward to Margaret Costello 9-28-1848 Sh
Lester, John E. to Frances A. Shore 12-2-1843 (12-3-1843) Hr
Lester, John M. to Elizabeth Anderson 7-2-1838 (7-19-1838) Ma
Lester, Philip K. to Mary Ann Rogers 12-1-1855 (12-2-1855) Sh
Lester, Richard N. to Amanda Wright 2-20-1839 G
Lester, S. H. P. to Amanda Pierce 6-14-1875 (no return) Dy
Lester, Stephen J. to Ann J. Woods 2-7-1838 F
Lester, U. W. to Mariah Gill 9-16-1864 Sh
Lester, Winfrey A. to Alsey Russell 8-7-1841 (8-8-1841) O
Lestrange, Michael to Bridget Holend 8-19-1859 Sh
Letsinger, John M. to M. C. Gillis 11-2-1849 Cr
Letsinger, Wm. T. to Elizabeth Collins 11-5-1849 Cr
Lett, A. L. to E. C. Abbott 1-28-1850 (1-31-1850) G
Lett, A. L. to M. A. Baker 11-22-1856 G
Lett, Broady to Caroline Ball 11-19-1866 G
Lett, George W. to Elizabeth Collins 11-5-1849 Cr
Lett, J. L. to Mary N. Ware 8-26-1868 Hy
Lett, John H. to Elizabeth Wood 10-12-1852 G
Lett, John W. to Janiah Lett 11-20-1848 Cr

Lett, John W. to Nancy Lett 3-7-1854 Cr
Leveque, Jean (John) to Antoinette Rhodes 7-16-1853 (7-20-1853) Sh
Leverett, Joseph T. to Marthena Harris 11-26-1870 (11-27-1870) F
Leverett, Wm. to Mary A. Littlefield 6-11-1851 (6-12-1851) Sh
Levett, Frank to Mattie Mebane 2-4-1870 (no return) F B
Levey, Archibald C. to Christina Jane Overall 1-9-1840 G
Levi, Ernest to Mary Rieser 12-9-1856 Sh
Levi, Saml. to Sarah Gensberger 12-15-1852 Sh
Levi, Wilson to Eliza Malone 1-11-1843 (no return) Hn
Levisay, D. T. to Salina Crawford 1-11-1842 (no return) F
Levister, John C. to Nancy Wash 12-25-1862 We
Levto?, Authen J. to Lavinia Orr 2-9-1869 T
Levy, A. S. to Fannie Emanuel 12-21-1853 Sh
Levy, E. A. to C. L. Crawford 7-17-1858 (7-19-1858) G
Levy, Emanuel to Celina Seebis (Seckis) 7-22-1850 Sh
Levy, Enoch W. to Elizabeth Edwards 10-11-1842 (10-13-1842) Ma
Levy, Green to Julia Carter 10-19-1867 (10-20-1867) F B
Levy, Joseph to Catharine Vincent 5-18-1859 (5-19-1859) Sh
Levy, King to Isabell Rhea 12-29-1868 (1-16-1869) F B
Levy, Lewis to Phebe Fite 7-15-1835 G
Lewellen, George to Mahala J. Roberts 8-1-1861 T
Lewellen, James to Matilda Wiett 2-2-1866 G
Lewellen, Robert J. to Frances Moore 9-4-1850 Ma
Lewellen, Robt. to Charlotte Davis 12-24-1878 Hy
Lewellen, W. B. to Mary Anderson 1-30-1871 (2-1-1871) Ma
Lewelling, A. J. to L. P. Childress 2-25-1873 (2-27-1873) Dy
Lewelling, J. N. to M. F. Boatwright 2-25-1873 (2-27-1873) Dy
Lewellyn, Marion to Elizabeth Foster 3-4-1860 Sh
Lewellyn, T. E. to Sarah Slayton 3-6-1876 (3-8-1876) Dy
Lewellyng, John E. to Mary A. Henry 1-1-1868 (1-15-1868) L
Lewers, W. J. to M. C. Caraway 1-15-1856 L
Lewis, A. E. to E. F. Crews 7-16-1856 Hr
Lewis, Aaron R. to Matilda Ballard 1-30-1854 (no return) Hn
Lewis, Abram to Amanda Overton 12-17-1849 (1-20-1849) Hr
Lewis, Amos F. to Sabina E. Culpeper 6-17-1845 Be
Lewis, Andrew Jackson to Lavica Parker Morrow 2-25-1859 (3-1-1859) Ma
Lewis, Anthony to Sally Stanley 9-21-1824 L
Lewis, B. R. to Mary W. Jones 6-10-1855 Hn
Lewis, Benj. P. to Caroline R. Doyle 4-4-1874 (4-5-1874) L
Lewis, Benjamin E. to Sophronia A. Fulghum 8-23-1854 (8-25-1854) Ma
Lewis, Benjamin M. to Mary Hastings 1-2-1851 Hn
Lewis, Benjamin to M. E. Turbeville 1-28-1856 (no return) Hn
Lewis, Benjamin to Mary Nelson 11-2-1856 Ma
Lewis, Benjn. R. to Sabella Allen 7-19-1852 Sh
Lewis, C. R. to Mollie J. Thornley 12-27-1882 (12-28-1882) L
Lewis, Calvin to Elizabeth Smith 11-17-1844 Be
Lewis, Charles S. to Jane Hurt 2-14-1843 (no return) Hn
Lewis, Clark to Melissa W. McClanahan 4-24-1831 Sh
Lewis, Corbin to Willie Dangerfield 5-27-1874 (no return) L
Lewis, David to Isabella Walker 12-3-1859 Sh
Lewis, E. B. to Bettie Ann Turner 11-7-1867 (no return) Hn
Lewis, E. B. to Virginia A. Willis 5-27-1861 Sh
Lewis, Edmond to Laura Donelson 9-2-1868 (no return) F B
Lewis, Edward to Mary Oldham 7-22-1841 Sh
Lewis, Emmett J. to Lou E. Deberry 11-26-1864 (11-27-1864) O
Lewis, Ephram G. to Mary J. Brooks 3-8-1863 We
Lewis, Francis M. to Matilda Missouro 12-22-1859 Sh
Lewis, Frank C. to Dola Garner 3-26-1884 L
Lewis, Frank to Fannie Taylor 3-15-1873 T
Lewis, Frank to Martha A. Outlaw 12-3-1870 (no return) Hy
Lewis, G. A. to Lucinda Lewis 12-7-1871 Hy
Lewis, G. B. to S. J. Cooke 2-19-1867 Hy
Lewis, G. W. to D. P. Swor 1-15-1845 Hn
Lewis, G. W. to E. J. Drinkard 10-30-1866 G
Lewis, G. to Sarah Oatsball(Oatsvall?) 9-19-1843 Be
Lewis, H. C. to Susan Lewis 12-24-1871 Hy
Lewis, H. H. to Sophia A. McQuinn 9-24-1862 Mn
Lewis, H. Walter to Lucy Winfield 8-9-1870 (8-10-1870) F
Lewis, Henry to Jane Anderson 11-28-1870 Hy
Lewis, Henry to Kitty Mathews 2-5-1870 G B
Lewis, Henry to Lucrecia Loney 1-20-1840 (12?-27-1840) F
Lewis, Henry to Mary Prince 6-7-1846 Be
Lewis, Isaac to Malinda Baxter 12-21-1867 (12-24-1867) F B
Lewis, J. F. to E. A. Glover 12-2-1871 (no return) Cr
Lewis, J. L. to Mary A. Patrick 6-29-1869 G
Lewis, J. P. to Catherine Crave (Crans) 10-31-1837 Sh
Lewis, J. R. to T. A. Vester 5-22-1861 Mn
Lewis, J. W. P. to Elizabeth Hutchison 4-6-1856 Be
Lewis, Jacob to Nancy H. Hastings 2-2-1852 Hn
Lewis, James A. to Elizabeth Kitchen 4-9-1850 (4-10-1850) O
Lewis, James M. to Jemima J. Gately 10-25-1853 Ma
Lewis, James M. to Nancy R. L. Wood 11-9-1843 Cr
Lewis, James N. to Nancy W. Whitsen 2-17-1859 We
Lewis, James W. to Nancy Jackson 11-14-1878 (11-17-1878) Dy
Lewis, James to Edney Reasons 8-31-1841 G
Lewis, James to Fanny H. Sample 5-10-1842 (5-12-1842) F
Lewis, James to Kitty Parker 11-2-1878 (11-3-1878) L B

Lewis, James to L. Stevens 11-16-1864 (11-17-1864) T
Lewis, James to Susan Smith 4-16-1873 (4-17-1873) L B
Lewis, Jerry to Addie Redditt 9-11-1880 (9-12-1880) Dy
Lewis, Jesse H. to Mary E. Hardy 12-30-1848 Ma
Lewis, Job A. to Ann B. Thompson 3-14-1842 Sh
Lewis, Joel B. to Martha M. Davidson 11-19-1846 G
Lewis, John C. to Lelia Jennings 12-21-1885 (12-29-1885) L
Lewis, John C. to Louisa Wright 1-1-1846 Hy
Lewis, John E. to Eliza (Mrs.) Shelton 11-21-1864 Sh
Lewis, John E. to Sarah E. Farrow 3-17-1860 (no return) Hy
Lewis, John N. to Frances C. Leake 8-29-1833 Sh
Lewis, John N. to Kerron R. Rice 3-16-1846 (no return) F
Lewis, John T. to Olivia J. Rogers 7-27-1857 (7-29-1857) Ma
Lewis, John to Mary Smith 9-30-1855 Be
Lewis, John to Melissa Vanhook 9-19-1853 Hn
Lewis, John to Susan Ogin(Agin) 8-25-1856 Hr
Lewis, Larkin A. to Rachel J. Kennon 12-24-1849 Cr
Lewis, Lenord to Nancey Cage 11-25-1876 L
Lewis, Leonard to Adeline Brown 7-23-1869 (7-24-1869) F B
Lewis, Lilbourn A. to Sarah C. Mereweather 1-22-1866 (2-16-1866) O
Lewis, M. R. to M. E. King 9-10-1875 (9-12-1875) Dy
Lewis, Mark to Harriet Hunter 1-1-1869 (1-2-1869) F B
Lewis, McDonald to Sarah Hall Beman 9-9-1855 Hn
Lewis, N. L. to M. A. Cooper 11-11-1853 Hn
Lewis, Nathan to Emily C. Capps 8-16-1845 (no return) F
Lewis, Obadiah to Malinda Malone 10-23-1828 (10-23-1828) G
Lewis, Owen to Laura Hill 1-12-1867 (1-13-1867) F B
Lewis, Patrick H. to Sarah G. Jones 11-2-1850 Hn
Lewis, Peter to Mary McGrath 10-1-1853 (10-20-1853) Sh
Lewis, Phil to Becky Forrest 10-15-1875 Hy
Lewis, Quincy H. to Mary Jane Smothers 5-8-1867 (no return) Hy
Lewis, Ransom to Jenny Taylor 4-4-1868 (4-5-1868) F B
Lewis, Richard to Eliza J. Forrest 1-28-1868 (1-30-1868) Cr
Lewis, Richard to Nancy Vester 4-2-1863 Mn
Lewis, Roberson to Lucretia Weston 9-2-1855 Hn
Lewis, Robert A. to Mary W. Tyler 1-22-1855 (1-23-1855) O
Lewis, Robert J. to Mary L. White 8-12-1857 O
Lewis, Robert N. to Elizabeth C. Fisher 8-2-1844 (8-6-1844) O
Lewis, Robertson to Sarah Duke 8-20-1848 Be
Lewis, Robt. to Annie Hunt 6-2-1876 (no return) Hy
Lewis, S. D. to Mary J. Braden 12-3-1877 (12-6-1878?) L
Lewis, S. S. to Laura A. Houston 5-5-1846 Sh
Lewis, S. to Mary Villner 2-28-1863 Sh
Lewis, Samuel to Mollie E. Trout 8-6-1862 G
Lewis, T. H. to M. M. Jackson 11-2-1865 G
Lewis, T. P. to Mary Jane Grady 4-27-1853 (4-28-1853) Sh
Lewis, Tavner to Lucindia Jordan 1-3-1853 (1-5-1853) Hr
Lewis, Thomas J. to Sarah Ann Best 5-14-1831 Sh
Lewis, Thomas to Emily Burres 4-18-1843 Hn
Lewis, Thomas to Manda Dentenac 8-15-1867 T
Lewis, Thomas to Tabitha Ballard 7-29-1841 Hn
Lewis, Tom to Kitty Witt 2-1-1868 (2-2-1868) F B
Lewis, William A. to Elizabeth (Mrs.) Fortner 3-19-1870 (3-24-1870) Ma
Lewis, William J. to Mary F. Barfield 9-24-1864 (9-25-1864) L
Lewis, William R. to Sarah A. Warmoth 3-17-1852 (3-18-1852) Ma
Lewis, William W. to Lecy Lampley 5-5-1842 Hn
Lewis, William to Annis Hefron 7-2-1836 Sh
Lewis, William to Armanda Prince 8-17-1854 Be
Lewis, William to Ella Brown 8-28-1869 (8-29-1869) F B
Lewis, Willis E. to Lucretia Dizen 3-12-1829 Hr
Lewis, Wm. C. to Maurina Harrell 7-27-1843 Sh
Lewis, Wm. C. to N. A. Kenady 1-22-1846 We
Lewis, Zack to Charlotte Newsom 12-10-1868 (12-11-1868) F B
Leyde, Willis to Sarah C. Jones 9-18-1865 (9-19-1865) O
Liabar, August to Rose Langenbacher 6-7-1855 Sh
Libo, Mike to Sarah Baker 11-20-1876 (no return) L
Liddle, J. M. C. to Sarah V. Mitchell 1-1-1846 We
Liddleton, David to Lucinda Ridge 12-29-1843 We
Liddy, Michiel to Catherine Keef 2-24-1852 Sh
Lide, O. H. to L. C. Morrison 12-18-1849 Sh
Lidrow, Reuben to Margaret A. Nobles 10-4-1849 G
Lidy, Andrew to Sarah M. Reynolds 8-1-1831 (8-2-1831) Hr
Lienhardt, Charles to Genevieve Wetzel 2-7-1850 Sh
Lieper, J. C. to Melvina F. Lovelace 1-8-1854 Hn
Lieuallen, Willy to Catherine Pane 10-12-1830 Ma
Lifsey, Thomas R. to Susan Bennett 1-12-1858 Le
Liftey, Thos. to Mary M. Williams 10-17-1853 Cr
Liggate, John to Elizabeth Johnson 3-22-1847 Sh
Liggett, Hampton to Emeline Harris 11-21-1838 (11-25-1838) Ma
Liggett, Joseph to Elizabeth Cannon 6-2-1845 (6-4-1845) G
Liggett, Samuel C. to Levina Bird 1-8-1849 G
Liggett, William S. to M. R. Cearce 2-19-1872 (2-21-1872) Dy
Liggett, Wm. S. to Elizabeth Savage 12-18-1841 (12-26-1841) Hr
Liggin, Daniel to Ellen Dunvegard? 1-26-1867 (no return) Dy
Liggon, J. B. to S. P. Randle 8-31-1847 Hn
Liggon, William to Lorey A. Baker 6-2-1848 Hn
Ligh, Elilen to Martha Umphrey 11-26-1856 Cr

Light, Hiram to Nancy Matthews 4-2-1874 Dy
Light, James to Harriet Williams 12-16-1875 Dy
Light, Joel A. to Susan M. Yancey 9-21-1852 (9-26-1852) G
Light, Joel E. to Mollie James 12-12-1878 Dy
Light, Liss to Winnie Joyner 5-6-1875 Dy
Light, Randle to Susan Spence 8-11-1866 Dy
Lightfoot, B. D. to Martha M. Burkett 11-14-1877 (11-15-1877) Dy
Lightfoot, B. H. to Catherine Mix? 11-23-1843 Hn
Lightfoot, Joel F. to Catharine C. Gallagher 2-15-1846 Sh
Lightfoot, John to Margaret Hardin 8-31-1841 Hn
Lightfoot, M. A. to M. A. Scobey 11-4-1875 (no return) Dy
Lightfoot, Moses to Serena Miller 10-25-1870 (no return) F B
Lightfoot, Oliver to Arrena Bond 12-24-1885 L
Lightfoot, Peter to Henrietta Wright 11-29-1864 Sh B
Lightforte, Robert L. to Ellen R. Montgomery 7-23-1851 (7-24-1851) Hr
Lightle, John C. to Jane C. Steadham 12-20-1864 (12-22-1864) F
Ligon, Benj. Haskins to Elizabeth E. Weller 12-30-1846 (12-31-1846) T
Ligon, Benjamin H. to Louisa Adaline Owen 11-22-1841 (11-26-1841) T
Ligon, George to Margaret Finney 9-3-1869 F B
Ligon, Henry B. to Mary Jane Wood 1-4-1848 (1-5-1848) T
Ligon, John to Sarah Hill 1-5-1868 G
Ligon, Newton M. to E. T. Henderson 12-22-1852 Sh
Ligon, Owen to Ellen Whitt 12-27-1866 F B
Ligon, Silas P. to Eliza H. M. Roberts 2-14-1852 Sh
Ligon, Washington to Mary Smith 1-17-1874 (1-4?-1874) T
Ligon, William H. to Martha Wood 9-12-1842 (9-20-1842) T
Ligon, William to Ann White 3-15-1867 (3-17-1867) F B
Ligtner, Daniel to Mary Nash 5-29-1850 Be
Lile, John W. to Mary Jane Doak 5-27-1843 Ma
Liles, Anderson to Elizabeth A. Martin 9-3-1851 Cr
Liles, Andrew to Sarah Carver 4-13-1858 Cr
Liles, D. (Rev.) to M. E. A. Wingo 10-6-1855 Cr
Liles, David A. to July Ann Chandler 8-7-1866 (8-8-1866) Cr
Liles, Henry to Martha Herron 12-9-1869 Cr
Liles, Mitchell to Parlee Garson 7-30-1856 Cr
Liles, Sherwood L. to Elizabeth Phelps 7-3-1866 (12-27-1866) Cr
Lillard, J. T. to Mattie J. Powell 4-8-1876 (no return) Hy
Lillard, James F. to Mattie E. Kimbrel 5-13-1876 (5-14-1876) Dy
Lillard, James M. to Nancy Campbell 10-26-1841 (10-27-1841) Hr
Lillard, John H. to Martha Jenkins 5-11-1858 (no return) We
Lillard, Washington to Eliza Wade 11-6-1873 Dy
Lilley, John S. to Martha Ann Wynn 2-9-1855 (2-13-1855) O
Lilly, J. B. to T. A. Perry 8-7-1870 Hy
Lilly, John to Mary J. Riley 5-8-1860 (5-10-1860) Sh
Lilly, Patrick to Margaret O'Gorman 9-1-1860 (9-2-1860) Sh
Lilly, Thomas F. to Polly Upchurch 12-4-1845 Hn
Limbarger, David Henry to Sarah Adeline Green 3-1-1865 T
Limbarger, John to Caroline M. Aynesworth 8-25-1841 (8-29-1841) F
Linahan, Charles to Bridget Scott 10-25-1856 (10-26-1856) Sh
Linch, Ansil to Frances Horn 7-13-1863 Cr
Lincoln, Elijah to Elizabeth Hickman 3-22-1852 (3-23-1852) Sh
Lindamond, James W. to T. C. Blythe 12-13-1854 Hn
Linden, Robt to Bettie Greenfield 12-28-1874 T
Linder, J. P. to Mary C. Linder 10-13-1877 (10-14-1877) O
Lindley, James to Susan Pippin 7-30-1866 (7-31-1866) F
Lindsay, Jesse B. to Delilah Harris 8-3-1843 T
Lindsay, William to Rebecca Hethcock 8-15-1866 Hy
Lindsey, A. Dupont to Monticeli (Mrs.) Bishop 2-2-1863 Sh
Lindsey, A. W. to Louisa C. Morris 1-15-1858 Be
Lindsey, D___ to Roxalina Wynn 1-25-1857 Be
Lindsey, E. M. to Mary E. Allen 12-24-1863 Hy
Lindsey, George to Martha Swindle 12-10-1865 Hn
Lindsey, Hubbard L. to Elizabeth F. Warmack 3-16-1864 Be
Lindsey, J. B. to Nancy E. Pierce 11-12-1857 Be
Lindsey, J. W. to Francis A. McLeod 12-31-1867 L
Lindsey, James C. to America J. Rushing 9-3-1860 Be
Lindsey, Jesse T. to Delila Lindsey 8-29-1843 (9-5-1843) F
Lindsey, John H. to Mary L. Walker 12-26-1877 Hy
Lindsey, John T. to Jane M. Turner 12-18-1836 Sh
Lindsey, Martin to Angeline Potts 10-16-1858 Hn
Lindsey, N. M. to Mary E. Trobough 2-28-1862 T
Lindsey, Norris M. to Rebecca E. Dial 9-11-1852 (9-14-1852) L
Lindsey, R. D. to Julia A. Williamson 10-29-1861 (no return) We
Lindsey, Robert S. to Ella Tomlin 10-24-1866 Ma
Lindsey, Thomas J. to Nancy E. Vanpelt 12-21-1859 (no return) Hy
Lindsey, W. H. to Lucinda A. Akers 12-7-1860 Hy
Lindsey, Washington to Lucy Moody 1-16-1868 Be
Lindsey, Wm. to Anna Moore 1-20-1842 Cr
Lindsy, W. H. to Delila Harris 10-22-1839 F
Linebarger, John to Rachael C. Campbell 12-19-1860 (12-25-1860) Hr
Linebarger, Wm. C. to Mary E. Tatum 11-21-1865 (11-22-1865) F
Lingo, James T. to D. A. Greenwood 9-11-1860 (9-13-1860) Cr
Lingo, James T.? to D. A. Greenwood 9-11-1860 (9-13-1860) Cr
Link, Albert to Leanna Lanier 1-23-1873 Hy
Link, Andrew to Caroline Wills 12-26-1866 Hy
Link, Edmond to Vina Taylor 1-25-1873 Hy
Link, Oliver to Ellen Oldham 12-25-1878 Hy

Link, Wm. J. to Amanda (Mrs.) Ware 12-12-1866 Hy
Linn, C. B. to Mandeville Bridges 10-18-1856 Hn
Linn, Charles B. to Elizabeth C. Parker 12-24-1858 Hn
Linn, Charles to Louiza A. Phin 10-21-1858 Hn
Linn, Reuben to Nancy Erwin 5-13-1838 Hn
Linnell, Alfred to Jane Graham 2-11-1860 (2-12-1860) Sh
Linnell, Alfred to Mefrinda? Bullard 8-30-1862 (9-11-1862) Dy
Linny, Samuel B. M. to Mary J. Tompkins 5-13-1839 Cr
Linsey, W. J. to Harriet Spain 11-22-1871 (no return) Cr
Linson, James T. to Mary Elliott 1-21-1857 (1-22-1857) L
Lintchicum, John H. to Margarett L. Goodrich 8-19-1841 Ma
Linton, Alison to Eliza C. Anderson 3-17-1842 (no return) Hn
Linton, B. O. to Mary Moncrief 1-9-1866 Hn
Linton, J. B. to M. E. Self 7-13-1874 Hy
Linton, John to Nancy M. Bowden 1-2-1855 Hn
Linton, Joshua to Elizabeth Clark 2-25-1846 (no return) Hn
Linton, Madison to Aletha F. Waller 10-10-1855 Hn
Linton, Samuel P. to Eliza Ann Little 10-10-1854 (10-12-1854) G
Linton, Samuel to Reamy Bowden 3-1-1848 Hn
Linton, Thomas J. to Susan Bowden 2-20-1850 (no return) Hn
Linton, W. H. to Parthenia J. Atchison 12-2-1860 G
Linvell, Worley to Racheal Pugh 3-23-1829 Hr
Linville, Aaron J. to Delilah S. Lax 1-5-1857 Hn
Linyard, W. K. to Cornelia C. Franson 5-20-1875 Hy
Lipard, C. T. to Nancy E. Sharp 7-2-1850 (7-7-1850) O
Lipart, C. T. to Nancy Sharp 7-2-1850 (7-7-1850) O
Lipe, Aaron to Sealeana F. Pinson 8-25-1841 Cr
Lipe, George to Ann Jordan 4-25-1871 (4-27-1871) Cr
Lipe, J. W. to Mary E. Hodge 11-30-1872 (12-1-1872) Cr
Lipe, James to Mary A. Grooms 11-12-1846 Cr
Lipford, James E. to Jane Harralston 10-19-1848 Sh
Lippard, C. T. to Winney Sidney Burton 8-31-1857 O
Lipperd, Henry to W. Knoeppel 5-1-1855 Sh
Lipscomb, G. B. to Sallie F. Brooks 11-10-1856 Sh
Lipscomb, Geo. R. to Mary R. Branch 2-21-1870 (2-22-1870) F
Lipscomb, George A. to Catharine G. Yancey 9-4-1847 (no return) F
Lipscomb, George A. to Priscilla S. Simmons 12-25-1854 (no return) F
Lipscomb, J. A. to Anna Shirley 12-29-1868 (12-31-1868) F
Lipscomb, Rob. B. to Willie C. Moorer 11-10-1883 (11-13-1883) L
Lipscomb, W. P. to Mary Pullen 2-4-1868 (2-26-1868) F
Lipscomb, W. P. to N. E. (Mrs.) McNamee 2-15-1870 (3-2-1870) F
Lipscomb, Willis to A. C. Dublin 3-23-1856 We
Lipsey, E. J. to Eliza J. Dalton 3-29-1864 Sh
Lipsey, Robert to Nancy Gibson 12-8-1824 Sh
Lircher, Edward Edwin to Esther Magee 5-24-1858 Sh
Lissenberry, M. E. to E. T. Johnson 2-1-1873 (no return) Cr
Lissey, John B. to Caroline Tucker 5-3-1860 Cr
List, Thomas to Mary Shanklin 3-3-1830 O
Listen, L. B. to S. B. Field 12-22-1870 O
Liston, John to Martha Howard 11-12-1847 Cr
Liston, John to Sarah Pettyjohn 4-18-1842 (no return) Hn
Liston, Michael to Mary Swinney 6-17-1856 Sh
Liston, Samuel S. to Margarett T. Stewart 5-27-1856 Cr
Literal, Marcus L. to Amanda Billings 10-17-1870 (10-18-1870) L
Littan, Francis to Margaret Spalding 3-20-1869 (3-21-1869) L
Litten, Isham to Sindy Foster 4-23-1874 (4-25-1874) T
Litteral, James to Caroline Robson 10-27-1843 Hr
Little, A. G. to Martha F. Chapple 7-4-1857 Cr
Little, A. J. to M. J. Walker 5-14-1864 (no return) Cr
Little, Adam to Ellen Duncan 7-30-1870 (7-31-1870) Cr
Little, Alexander G. to Lucy Stone 3-22-1853 G
Little, Allen to Louisa Reese 7-6-1847 Ma
Little, Ara T. to Mary Tombs 1-25-1859 Cr
Little, Austin P. to Fannie Barksdale 5-14-1863 (no return) Cr
Little, Charles J. to Manirvy Connell 3-21-1867 G
Little, David L. to Angeline Presson 12-12-1852 Be
Little, David to Sarah McGarett 1-28-1836 (2-2-1836) G
Little, David to Willy Clark 8-7-1868 (8-12-1868) Cr
Little, E. S. to Nancy Davis 10-9-1858 (10-12-1858) Hr
Little, Fair M. to Sally Staton 10-13-1829 (10-22-1829) G
Little, G. M. to M. A. Merrett 12-7-1872 (12-8-1872) Cr
Little, George A. to Martha F. Hammer 4-28-1843 Sh
Little, George W. to Lucy Ann Tucker 11-?1-1844 (no return) Hn
Little, Harry to Elizabeth Routon 2-10-1860 Be
Little, Harvy T. to Nancy C. Williams 1-12-1867 (1-13-1867) Cr
Little, Howell to Mary E. Butler 11-12-1840 G
Little, Isaac N. to Frances Gillum 10-3-1849 Hn
Little, Isaac N. to Margaret Ann Smith 2-20-1862 Hn
Little, James H. to Elizabeth F. Elmore 2-11-1861 (2-13-1861) L
Little, James L. to Hester Ann Rodgers 2-18-1852 Cr
Little, James T. to Nancy E. Delk 6-16-1857 (6-18-1857) Hr
Little, James to Eliza Pankey 8-11-1852 (8-12-1852) Hr
Little, James to Mary Ann Hogsett 6-17-1846 (6-18-1846) L
Little, James to Nancy L. Johnson 11-24-1857 (11-25-1857) Hr
Little, John A. to Mary J. Singleton 10-10-1839 Hr
Little, John D. to Elizabeth Bain 2-5-1829 (2-17-1829) G
Little, John W. to Mary J. Duncan 12-17-1856 (12-18-1856) Hr

Little, John Wesley to Eliza Caroline Craven 9-2-1854 (9-3-1854) Hr
Little, John to Eliza Coody(Cody) 10-9-1834 Hr
Little, Joshua to Jane Jackson 9-15-1834 (9-18-1834) G
Little, Miles W. to Elizabeth A. Presson 2-15-1867 Be
Little, Oscar to Parmelia Sutherlin 1-29-1857 Cr
Little, Samuel to Lucy Ann Murray 3-30-1834 Sh
Little, Samuel to Maggie Thorn (Thom?) 2-15-1859 (2-16-1859) Sh
Little, Thomas I. to Sarah Roberts 5-22-1860 We
Little, Thomas to Ana Liza Rual? 12-26-1861 We
Little, Thomas to Sarah J. Cunningham 3-11-1863 Cr
Little, Thomas to Sarah J. Cunningham 3-11-1863 (no return) Cr
Little, W. R. to M. E. Palmore 2-22-1863 (no return) Hy
Little, William B. to Barbary L. Holt 5-6-1863 G
Little, William H. to Mary Temple 7-12-1847 Ma
Little, William to Mary Williams 4-7-1866 (4-15-1866) Cr
Little, Wm. W. to Mary Elizabeth Hamner 2-23-1843 Sh
Little, Wm. to Amanda C. Hase? 10-6-1840 F
Little, Wm. to Delph Stokes 9-28-1854 Cr
Littlefield, Andrew to Elizabeth Bellew 8-17-1837 (8-20-1837) G
Littlefield, Ben to B. M. McGarity 6-11-1836 (6-?-1836) G
Littlefield, James A. to Ann Baird 8-4-1846 Sh
Littlefield, James W. to Julia Holt 2-6-1868 G
Littlefield, Robert to Sarah Jane Hurt 11-8-1843 Sh
Littlejohn, Charles to Malinda Arant 3-31-1840 Hn
Littlejohn, Joseph B. to Ann M. (Mrs.) Sneed 1-9-1843 (1-10-1843) F
Littlejohn, S. S. to M. J. Shenault 12-18-1865 Mn
Littlejohn, William to Eliza Ann Chisolm 9-10-1833 (9-11-1833) Hr
Littlejohn, Willie J. to Margaret H. Chesolm 1-18-1843 F
Littlepage, Powhattan B. to Mary Jane Dearmore 4-20-1841 Ma
Littleton, A. T. to Susan E. Choate 3-6-1845 Sh
Littleton, David L. R. to Lucy Thomas 1-15-1857 We
Littleton, David R. to Martha Dunning 7-17-1860 We
Littleton, Hubbart to Marey Hampton 7-2-1834 O
Littleton, John to Jane Allen 12-7-1852 (1-30-1853) O
Littleton, Naman to Nancy M. Reeves 4-11-1860 (4-12-1860) O
Littleton, W. J. to M. L. Aikins 9-29-1879 (9-30-1879) L
Littleton, William R. to Sarah Stewart 12-6-1860 Hn
Littleton, William to Edie Thompson 12-29-1870 (no return) F B
Litton, F. M. to L. C. Guynn 12-26-1859 (12-27-1859) O
Litton, John to Sarah Crowder 1-15-1856 (1-17-1856) O
Litton, William to Rebecca Gilbert 12-20-1866 Be
Littrell, Eli to Mary M. Barton(Baston?) 5-29-1846 (6-2-1846) Hr
Littrell, Shelton to Bashiba Sims 12-29-1849 (12-30-1849) Hr
Lively, D. C. to M. E. Hall 1-8-1868 (1-9-1868) Dy
Lively, Garland to Martha J. Reynolds 1-29-1866 (no return) Dy
Livingston, Andrew J. to Mary Page 1-25-1840 (1-29-1840) O
Livingston, Francis M. to Dorithey Sale 3-20-1848 (3-?-1848) G
Livingston, Henry J. to Tempe J. Somerville 11-28-1872 Hy
Livingston, James L. to Ann W. Carlton 12-12-1860 (no return) Hy
Livingston, James M. to Mary A. Oaks 8-23-1851 (8-24-1851) O
Livingston, M. to Rebecca Owensbey 12-1-1863 (no return) Hy
Livingston, Mark to Mary J. Jarret 2-17-1860 (2-18-1860) Cr
Livingston, Marshal to Cyntha Ann Churchwell 11-28-1860 (no return) L
Livingston, Nat to Lou Mann 9-25-1878 (9-25-1879?) L B
Livingston, Nat to Moriah Burnett 12-28-1871 Hy
Livingston, Thomas O. to Laira A. T. Jordan 2-2-1869 (2-3-1869) L
Livingston, William C. to Eliza J. Johnson 5-8-1848 (5-9-1848) G
Llewelling, Adam T. to Rachel Cronk? 1-13-1856 T
Lloyd, A. B. to Martha J. Johnson 12-19-1868 (12-22-1868) F
Lloyd, A. J. to Anna Dunn 10-16-1884 L
Lloyd, C. H. to S. N. J. Bentley 11-7-1874 (11-11-1874) L
Lloyd, Clarence E. to Sallie A. Nixon 10-31-1882 (11-2-1882) L
Lloyd, Claudius B. to Artelia B. Lloyd? 12-2-1873 (12-?-1873) L
Lloyd, E. C. to Emma L. Evans 1-5-1883 (1-10-1883) L
Lloyd, Geo. M. to Mary T. Manson 2-13-1860 (2-15-1860) Hr
Lloyd, Henry A. to Myra L. Nixon 3-9-1860 (3-12-1860) L
Lloyd, John Wesley to Emily Scott 12-23-1881 (12-24-1881) L
Lloyd, Joseph J. to Elizabeth Raines 10-20-1845 Ma
Lloyd, Joseph to Caroline Halliburton 12-3-1870 (12-4-1870) L B
Lloyd, T. B. to Anna E. McMullin 12-25-1865 (1-1-1866) F
Lloyd, W. A. to Ada M. Nixon 12-12-1881 (12-14-1881) L
Lloyed, Dewees C. to Cyntha A. Hunter 1-15-1872 (1-17-1872) L
Lobdale, Manuel to Margaret Graves 5-21-1870 (5-22-1870) L
Lochart, Elijah to Elizabeth J. Matheny 8-9-1849 Be
Lock (Lack?), John to Fanny Bradford 8-6-1867 (8-7-1869?) G
Lock, B. F. to Sarah Smith 3-1-1860 T
Lock, F. A. to Lucy M. Wesson 3-12-1853 (no return) F
Lock, G. W. to Mary E. Brewer 11-8-1865 G
Lock, John Wesley to Nancy Light 7-29-1868 (7-30-1868) Dy
Lockard, George W. to Frances R. Richardson 12-16-1856 L
Lockard, Henry to Rebecca Sanders 11-5-1881 L
Lockard, John Leroy to Ellen Fitzgerald 5-29-1871 (5-30-1871) L
Lockard, John to Mary Ledbetter 7-15-1841 L
Lockard, Leroy F. to Mary Johnson 8-3-1846 (8-4-1846) L
Lockard, Leroy F. to Nancy Woods 9-11-1839 (9-13-1839) L
Lockard, Miles N. to Williammetta Davis 11-20-1860 Hr
Lockard, Moses P. to Martha Fields 10-4-1848 L

Lockard, N. S. to Frances Cox 12-10-1884 L
Lockard, Tho. E. to Nancy C. Fields 8-31-1848 L
Lockard, Thomas E. to Alice Osteen 9-9-1878 (9-11-1878) L
Lockard, W. T. to Elizabeth Baker 3-19-1863 (no return) L
Lockard, William W. to Sarah E. Anderson 11-7-1853 (11-10-1853) Ma
Locke, Ben F. to Sarah Smith 3-1-1860 (3-3-1860) T
Locke, Charles C. to Martha D. Hill 11-22-1832 Sh
Locke, Gardiner B. to Mary Jane Prescott 7-10-1836 Sh
Locke, George to Leah F. Rhodes 6-10-1868 (6-11-1868) Ma
Locke, J. W. to Sarah F. Bell 5-17-1860 (no return) Hy
Locke, Jas. Monroe to Lorina Kurts 1-2-1856 T
Locke, Joseph L. to Charity M. Warren 12-5-1832 Sh
Locke, Richard to Sallie L. Rodgers 10-18-1866 G
Locke, Rollin J. to Mary McIntosh 11-30-1848 Ma
Locke, Thomas D. to Susan E. F. A. McCrary 11-29-1860 We
Locket, Wm. to Catharine Ryne (no date) Hy
Lockett, F. H. to Susan Smith 6-2-1847 (no return) F
Lockett, Jessee to Rebecca A. Sloss 3-4-1861 (3-17-1861) T
Lockett, Johnson to Rosetta Reives 7-1-1867 (no return) Hy
Lockett, Thos. P. to Georgiana Jones 5-8-1854 Sh
Lockett, Zachariah to Elizabeth C. Stewart 2-2-1846 Hr
Lockhart, Adam to Ann Scott 5-25-1861 (5-26-1861) Hr
Lockhart, J. S. to Cora I. Massey 12-10-1873 (12-11-1873) Dy
Lockhart, James to M. A. Pickett 2-7-1859 (6-20-1859) Hr
Lockhart, S. H. to Mollie E. Adams 6-30-1862 (not endorsed) F
Lockhart, T. J. to Lavina Husband 7-1-1875 (no return) Dy
Lockhart, W. M. to Margrie McGowan 6-19-1882 (no return) L
Lockhart, Will to Elizabeth Scott 12-23-1837 Hr
Lockhart, William to Nancy Musick 10-23-1828 O
Lockheart, Jasper to Lucy Glaze 7-1-1875 (7-7-1875) L
Lockheart, L. H. to Mattie E. Leach 10-27-1870 (no return) F
Locklear, Eli to Eliza Kimbrile 6-12-1836 Sh
Locust, Wm. to Charity Rice 2-11-1870 (no return) Hy
Lodvig, Frederick to Margaret Smith 9-29-1851 Sh
Lodwick, E. B. to Rhoda R. Gates 1-19-1847 Sh
Loeb, Lehman to Wanda Bergman 9-12-1864 Sh
Loffman, John to Martha Burge 4-4-1844 We
Lofland, David to Elizabeth Tisdale 4-7-1824 Hr
Lofland, Wm. O. to Emily Clark 10-29-1846 We
Loflin, Thomas R. to Frankie J. Wallace 5-28-1866 G
Loften, Jessa to Margaret Fruman? 1-27-1874 (1-29-1874) L
Loftin, George Burwell to Teresa M. Bedford 4-29-1831 (5-4-1831) Ma
Loftin, William C. to Ann Joiner 9-1-1852 (9-2-1852) Sh
Loftin, William to Sarah Johnson 12-8-1852 Ma
Logan, Benjamin B. to Scyntha Clack 5-31-1838 (6-7-1838) O
Logan, Charley to Claricy Buchinm? 1-29-1875 (1-30-1875) L B
Logan, Charley to Julia Bailey 7-18-1882 (7-23-1882) L
Logan, Henry D. to Frances Hubert 1-24-1828 (1-26-1828) O
Logan, James J. to Nancy P. Bell 7-3-1841 G
Logan, John to Louisa Peterson 3-7-1833 Sh
Logan, N. D. to Mary Carter 1-20-1846 O
Logan, Robert to Ann Haly 3-18-1840 Sh
Logan, W. P. to Ada F. Griffin 2-13-1860 (2-14-1860) F
Logan, W. R. M. to Georgia Ann Reatherford 12-28-1859 T
Logan, William to Manerva Matheny 3-12-1861 (3-14-1861) Dy
Logan, Young Thomas to Phebe Renick (Reynick) 2-28-1835 Sh
Logue, F. M. to Eliza Spain 12-15-1869 (12-22-1869) Cr
Logue, Geo. P. to F. B. (Mrs.) Davis 8-26-1858 Sh
Logwood, Thos. H. to Mary S. Driver 11-1-1855 Sh
Loil, Wesley to Catherine Johnson 12-7-1845 Sh
Lokey, J. P. to Mary Ann Farriss 9-27-1854 Hr
Lomas, Moses to Aga Bruce? 2-25-1845 (no return) Hn
Lomax, William B. to Evaline Rust 7-11-1859 We
Lonalgan, Michael to Johanna Costello 9-30-1856 Sh
Londa, York to Liza Wade 7-13-1867 F B
London, William to Mary E. McFarland 2-7-1865 (no return) Hy
Londrith, Pliney B. to Helen M. Zellner 6-21-1859 (6-23-1859) F
Lone (Love?), Orlin B. to Louisa A. Borman (Bauman?) 1-7-1853 (1-8-1853) Sh
Long, A. C. to A. Elizabeth Riley 8-18-1862 Sh
Long, Albert to Mary M. Cothan 2-3-1868 (no return) Dy
Long, Augustus to Margaret Srogent (Scogin) 12-4-1849 Sh
Long, Benj. C. to Margaret Ann King 5-28-1868 Ma
Long, Breten to Nancy Walker 2-14-1850 W
Long, D. L. to Callie Pyland 10-14-1882 (10-15-1882) L
Long, Drue to Eliza Earmon 9-14-1875 L
Long, Ed to Mary J. Shirley 9-8-1870 (no return) Hy
Long, G. W. to Nancy Fletcher 1-10-1855 G
Long, George H. to Elizabeth C. Whitesides 9-1-1842 O
Long, Green Berry to Minerva Millen 7-24-1843 (11-27-1843) Ma
Long, H. Carroll to Mary Pryor 3-4-1852 We
Long, H. J. to Sallie McIlwaine 5-22-1871 (5-23-1871) T
Long, H. W. to Fannie Temple 3-2-1871 Hy
Long, Henry to Martha Pate 9-8-1838 (9-11-1838) G
Long, I. T. C. to Margarett Jones 12-7-1866 O
Long, J. W. S. to Elizah Smith 8-29-1838 (8-30-1838) F
Long, Jacob to Mary D? Moore 5-1-1839 (5-2-1839) O

Long, James (Jonas) to Jane Crawley 11-18-1845 Sh
Long, James H. to Addie V. Brooks 1-22-1867 Ma
Long, James to Sarah Owens 8-23-1843 (8-24-1843) L
Long, John A. to Lovenia Hervey 12-20-1848 Hr
Long, John B. to Eliza J. Hardage 12-7-1847 (12-?-1847) Ma
Long, John H. to Nancy H. McFarland 2-3-1853 Hn
Long, John to Polly Walker 3-8-1865 (3-10-1865) Cr
Long, John to Susan Herring 4-26-1854 (4-27-1854) Sh
Long, Maurice to Mary Linkelake 6-18-1859 Hy
Long, N. P. to Sarah L. Thurmond 1-26-1866 (1-27-1866) L
Long, Ned to Amanda Belew 11-25-1877 Hy
Long, Nicholas to Margarett J. Rhea 7-12-1848 F
Long, Nicholas to Sarah Humphrey 9-10-1844 F
Long, Peter to Lucy Darr 12-9-1840 T
Long, Pleasant M. to Rachel Ann Erwood 9-20-1873 (9-21-1873) T
Long, Reese R. to Phebe Fletcher 8-31-1853 G
Long, S. S. to M. Cuningham 8-21-1872 (no return) Cr B
Long, Sam to Sarah C. White 8-21-1861 T
Long, Saml. D. to Margaret Ann Dodson 2-9-1846 (2-12-1846) F
Long, Shelton to B. A. Scott 10-8-   (with 1870) G
Long, Tho. H. to Nancy J. Beaty 11-17-1859 (11-18-1859) Hr
Long, Thos. J. to Mary Denngtin? 3-14-1844 We
Long, Virgil to Laura L. Beavers 9-1-1866 (9-6-1866) T
Long, William to Celia Kerr 6-16-1845 Ma
Long, William to Margaret Fravel 2-26-1862 Sh
Long, Wm. H. to Bettie Fossett 12-25-1869 (12-20?-1869) Ma
Long, Wm. H. to Bettie M. Hunt 11-30-1868 (12-8-1868) F
Long, Wm. R. to Eliza Stone 1-22-1839 Cr
Long, Wm.J. to Casey M. Gray 10-18-1849 Sh
Longhorn, James L. to Margarett M. Gladney 11-22-1842 Ma
Longly, Franklin to Nancy A. Stephenson 8-29-1851 (9-1-1851) O
Longly, Silas to Elizabeth Stroud 6-5-1830 (6-14-1830) O
Longmire, Wm. Martin to Martha Ann Walters no date Ma
Longworth, Brigus to T. E. Smith 10-28-1866 G
Longworth, H. A. to Julia A. Grier 4-2-1860 (4-5-1860) G
Lonigan, Thomas to Mary Lonigan 6-16-1849 L
Lonnergan, Wm. to Margaret Carney 10-13-1856 Sh
Looby, Michael to Mary Brown 5-29-1852 (5-30-1852) Sh
Look, N. L. to Susan C. Thomas 2-19-1862 Sh
Loomis, Alfred to Caroline Gibson 3-11-1844 Hn
Looney, B. H. to America Griffin 1-17-1870 (1-18-1870) Cr
Looney, Charles to Mary Walsh 11-23-1861 (11-24-1861) Sh
Looney, David to Mary Roland 7-1-1845 Sh
Looney, E. J. to Esperann Pearce 12-28-1844 We
Looney, Frank M. to Anna G. Goff 9-16-1859 Sh
Looney, G. G. to Rose Ann Deloach 6-26-1838 (no return) F
Looney, J. C. to Elizabeth Patterson 1-7-1864 N
Looney, J. F. to E. C. Henderson 12-19-1865 Cr
Looney, John C. to Mary F. Hagler 8-26-1860 We
Looney, Jonathan to Tennessee Hays 11-16-1864 Hn
Looney, Peter to Mary E. Bruce 10-5-1865 Hn
Looney, Robt. to Jane Smith 9-11-1844 (no return) We
Looney, William S. to Maria Pritchett 12-20-1853 Hn
Looper, Sherwood to Mary F. Hale 9-5-1850 Be
Looton(Tuoton?), Henry to Sarah Thornton 3-19-1858 (3-21-1858) Hr
Loovell, David to Martha Sulfrick 3-3-1859 (3-9-1859) T
Lorance, A. H,. to Sally Maxwell 7-26-1848 (7-27-1848) Hr
Lorance, J. A. to A. E. Butler 9-15-1865 G
Lorance, J. A. to L. H. Lusk 1-11-1867 (1-16-1867) Cr
Lorance, Levi W. to Martha Glover 2-5-1839 Cr
Lorance, Samuel L. to Mary M. C. Reed 1-30-1840 (2-2-1840) G
Lorance, W. J. to Nancy West 12-24-1863 G
Lores, J. to R. Branans 5-29-1842 Be
Lott, A. H. to Emma Harrison 12-24-1881 (12-25-1881) L
Lott, J. E. to N. P. Booth 11-10-1869 Hy
Lott, S. W. to Louisa Jones 4-6-1875 (no return) Hy
Lott, T. N. to M. W. Burnham 2-15-1882 (no return) L
Lott, William to Julia A. Dillard 12-29-1855 (1-1-1856) Sh
Lotter (Sotter?), John to Terrace Lenn (Senn?) 12-30-1854 Sh
Louch, Henry to Nancy Honey 12-23-1843 (12-24-1843) L
Loud(Land), W. H. to A. E. Purnell 12-14-1858 (12-16-1858) Hr
Louder, Morris to Fannie Fowlkes 1-30-1879 Dy
Loudermilk, Jacob to Jane S. Rogers 10-23-1838 Hr
Louds, John W. to Nancy E. Rhodes 1-18-1842 Cr
Lough (Laugh), John to Margaret Devlin 4-17-1844 Sh
Loughman, Michael to Joana Hartizen 4-23-1852 Sh
Louis, Jacob to Mary Levy 1-16-1861 Sh
Louisen, Allen to Mariah English 9-7-1866 (9-9-1866) T
Lounder, T. R. to Julia A. Britt 10-3-1854 Cr
Louney, Michael to Ann Barry 1-10-1856 Sh
Lounsford, Levi to S. R. Bargan 12-24-1868 Hy
Lourance, William M. to Sardinia E. Arnold 5-26-1855 (5-27-1855) G
Lourance, Zophar to Eliza M. Lourance 4-15-1835 Hr
Lourence, David E. to Virginia F. Rodgers 8-12-1857 Sh
Lourence, Thomas B. to Sarah H. Medearis 11-15-1834 (11-16-1834) G
Lourniggan, W. C. to Sally Strickland 10-14-1862 Be
Louther, Harvy to Mary Katharine Carns 12-22-1844 Be

Lovallette, Albert Talmedge to Sallie Cornelia Day 10-6-1855 (10-9-1855) Ma
Love, A. G. to Rosy Patton 11-22-1870 (11-24-1870) Cr
Love, A. L. to Alice Harrison 12-12-1870 (12-15-1870) Dy
Love, A. R. to Elizabeth L. Gant 9-9-1856 G
Love, Albert G. to Mira Jordan 6-24-1839 (7-3-1839) G
Love, Alonzo F. to Emma Haughton 4-25-1871 Ma *
Love, C. A. to Ella Barnett 8-2-1870 G
Love, C. R. to E. Cartwright 1-3-1850 We
Love, Charles H. to Allie D. Alsobrooks 12-17-1880 (12-21-1880) L
Love, Charles to Mary G. Smith 9-22-1839 Sh
Love, Frank to Jane Gardner 7-16-1868 G B
Love, George to Ada Chaney 12-24-1884 (12-25-1884) L
Love, George to Louisa Bailey 12-27-1876 (no return) L B
Love, J. P. to Elizabeth J. Wiley 3-22-1855 (no return) F
Love, J. R. to Mollie A. Calhoun 7-28-1863 Hn
Love, J. W. to Amanda (Mrs.) Willard 7-5-1869 G
Love, James B. to Martha McCissick 9-24-1848 Hn
Love, James C. to Annah Curd 8-14-1856 Sh
Love, James M. to Terrison A. Braden 5-31-1828 Ma
Love, Jas. C. to Mary A. Teague 12-24-1855 Hr
Love, Jas. M. to Margaret Coleman 12-15-1867 Hy
Love, Jas. P. to Sallie P. Brock 12-19-1868 (1-13-1869) F
Love, John B. to Sarah Ann Bruton 6-13-1848 (6-14-1848) Ma
Love, John D. to M. L. Dillahunty 9-7-1848 (no return) Hn
Love, John M. to Elizabeth Acree 10-12-1869 (10-14-1869) Ma
Love, John W. to M. E. A. Jackson 12-4-1867 (11?-20-1867) G
Love, John W. to Martha M. Wharton 8-3-1831 Ma
Love, John W. to Sarah O. King 12-23-1862 Dy
Love, Joseph B. to Rebecca McLeroy 12-12-1828 Ma
Love, Lemuel to Mary A. Thomas 2-26-1840 (2-27-1840) G
Love, R. B. to M. D. Barnet 9-18-1860 G
Love, R. B. to Sophia Robinson 11-17-1851 Cr
Love, S. J. to Mary S. Vawters 1-4-1859 Cr
Love, Samuel to D. Crutchfield 11-18-1852 Hn
Love, Samuel to Cretia Powell 11-25-1866 Hn
Love, Thomas W. to Virginia Warren 12-16-1858 Hn
Love, William K. to Emily B. Jones 3-14-1840 (3-17-1840) Ma
Love, William K. to Louisiana L. Jones 4-21-1836 G
Love, Wm. C. to Catharine Smith 7-3-1838 G
Love, Wm. E. to Martha E. Christian 12-8-1853 Cr
Love, Wm. R. to R. J. Bell 9-17-1859 (9-18-1859) F
Loveene?, Henry M. to Irena R. Pickard 7-2-1872 (7-4-1872) T
Loveing, James to Margaret Travis 7-17-1836 O
Lovel (Lorel?), David to Eliza Pendleton 2-9-1852 (2-12-1852) Sh
Lovel, James to Didama Campbell 12-7-1872 (12-8-1872) Dy
Lovel, Jas. to Mary Hatcher 1-2-1847 Sh
Lovelace, C. D. to Amanda Lea 5-30-1850 We
Lovelace, Charles B. to Nannie J. Yelverton 11-14-1877 Hy
Lovelace, Elijah to Helen Walker 12-16-1884 (12-17-1884) L
Lovelace, H. H. to Emma Foster 5-1-1861 G
Lovelace, J. G. to A. B. Bonds 1-24-1871 (1-25-1871) Dy
Lovelace, J. S. to Ellen Sullivan 12-20-1869 G
Lovelace, James P. to Nancy J. Beasly 11-19-1885 (no return) L
Lovelace, James R. to Adaline M. Lovelace 9-5-1858 We
Lovelace, Joseph to Nancy H. Temple 5-26-1857 (no return) L
Lovelace, L. M. to Mary E. Styers 3-6-1865 L
Lovelace, Nelson to Rhoda E. Fitzpatrick 12-29-1875 L B
Lovelace, S. B. to L. F. Sturdevant 12-21-1881 (12-22-1881) L
Lovelace, Thos. J. to Mary Ann Todd 10-9-1843 We
Lovelace, Thos. to Genett Gaither 11-9-1865 F
Lovelace, Wilson to Emma Light 7-10-1880 (7-11-1880) Dy
Lovelace, Wm. O. to Lureny Sanford 12-26-1853 (1-11-1854) Ma
Lovelady, John to Elizabeth Campbell 7-15-1839 F
Lovelady, T. H. to S. L. Moore 9-28-1854 (no return) F
Loveless, J. S. to L. C. Bi_gart 8-16-1866 G
Loveless, James S. to Martha J. Roberson 12-15-1856 (12-16-1856) G
Loveless, P. C. to Mollie G. Deshong 12-27-1865 (12-28-1865) Cr
Loveless, William E. to Josephine Cogbell 9-20-1848 (9-27-1848) F
Lovell, John M. to Rebecca Watt 5-26-1852 G
Lovell, Pat? to Frances Baskin 12-23-1867 (12-24-1867) T
Lovell, W. M. to Sullie Stanly 2-24-1868 Hy
Lovens, A. P. to Minerva Stublefield 9-22-1867 Hn
Lovett, John to Mary Ann Vantrip 11-17-1847 (11-18-1847) O
Lovill, Wm. to Sinia Scritchfield 6-2-1848 Sh
Lovin, Austin to Mary J. Horn 1-24-1872 Cr
Lovin, John J. to Margaret Ann Dennis 10-23-1854 Sh
Loving, A. J. to Lucy H. Moody 4-25-1870 (no return) Hy
Loving, A. W. to Sallie Black 10-21-1857 (10-22-1857) Sh
Loving, Aaron to Lizzie Whitelaw 5-13-1876 Hy
Loving, Andrew to S. A. Whitelaw 1-28-1869 Hy
Loving, B. F. to Mattie E. Gowan 1-26-1885 (1-28-1885) L
Loving, Bob to Queen Hay 12-29-1869 Hy
Loving, Charles to Kitty Taliaferro 2-16-1866 Hy
Loving, D. M. to J. A. Simpson 2-28-1868 (no return) Dy
Loving, Dallas to Ellen Rogers 12-28-1869 Hy
Loving, Dalles to Emma Lea 12-27-1872 Hy
Loving, E. L. to Tennie C. H. Gowan 3-9-1885 (3-10-1885) L

Loving, Francis to Susan T. Rayn 11-28-1839 (no return) F
Loving, Henry to Sarah Barker 9-8-1847 O
Loving, Jim to Fannie Hare 1-15-1868 F B
Loving, Jim to Poke Taylor 11-15-1870 (no return) Hy
Loving, John S. to Julia A. S. Sales 4-25-1849 Sh
Loving, Josephus to Edwanna? Alston 1-21-1840 (1-22-1840) F
Loving, Josephus to Mary C. Allen 4-5-1854 Sh
Loving, Luke to Julia Carter 4-10-1877 Hy
Loving, Thomas A. to Maria Renfrow 11-8-1873 Hy
Loving, William to Amanda M. Zerrico 12-27-1842 (12-28-1842) G
Lovitt, George W. to Nancy Porter 11-22-1852 (11-23-1852) G
Lovless, George to Nancy A. Taylor 6-20-1853 (6-22-1853) L
Low (Law), Thomas to Viola L. Deloach 3-28-1848 Sh
Low, Ellis to Nancy Young 2-7-1831 Ma
Low, Ezekiel E. to Mary A. L. Aitkin 9-3-1847 (9-5-1847) Hr
Low, John B. to Catharine K. Fleming 7-19-1856 (7-20-1856) Sh
Low, Saml. to Bettie Wright 1-1-1868 (no return) F B
Low, W. H. to Emily H. Garrett 8-13-1859 (8-14-1859) Sh
Low, W. L. to Sarah C. Hawkins 2-23-1850 (2-26-1850) Hr
Lowary, Henry to Julia Ann Dowell 3-5-1838 (3-8-1838) G
Lowden, John to Margarett Jester 3-1-1841 Ma
Lowder, Lewis to Charlotte Sharpe 1-25-1839 Cr
Lowder, Thos. C. to Martha A. Cross 6-24-1847 Cr
Lowder, Wm. J. to Mary Ann K. Bell 2-16-1864 (no return) Cr
Lowder, Wm. J. to Maryann K. Bell 2-16-1864 Cr
Lowdermilk, James W. to Lucinda C. Faucett 5-7-1870 (5-8-1870) Ma
Lowe, Charles to Mary Witt 12-24-1874 (12-27-1874) L B
Lowe, Granville C. to Sarah M. Bevill 12-22-1859 Ma
Lowe, Isaac W. to M. E. Michell 9-4-1872 (9-8-1872) Dy
Lowe, Isaac to Margaret Pitchard 3-10-1843 (3-12-1843) L
Lowe, Marvila to Belle J. Roberts 2-25-1878 (2-27-1878) Dy
Lowe, Samuel to Ellen Herrin 5-10?-1868 T
Lowe, Sherwood to Hannah Matthis 1-24-1831 Hr
Lowe, W. J. to M. F. Harris 12-5-1867 G
Lowe, Willis to Cle. Hill 12-22-1870 T
Lowerence, F. P. to R. C. Raines 3-8-1858 G
Lowery, E. M. to Luretta Williams 4-4-1839 Hn
Lowery, Elijah to Wincy Yarbrough 7-18-1839 Hn
Lowery, Jacob to Mary Owens 4-26-1830 (4-27-1830) Hr
Lowery, John N. to Martha A. Burgess 8-2-1842 Hn
Lowery, Robert W. to Rebecca J. Barnes 1-22-1851 Hn
Lowery, Robert to Esther Price 10-15-1828 Ma
Lowery, Thomas to Sarah Richie 12-14-1853 (no return) F
Lowery, W. M. to Lean Bruff 8-23-1863 G
Lowery, William to Deena Young 11-26-1856 We
Lowery, William to Mary A. McClain 4-9-1857 We
Lowill (Lovel?), W. (Wm.) to Mary Jane Gates 1-6-1863 Sh
Lowland, Wm. A. to Elizabeth Walker 12-21-1863 (12-22-1863) Sh
Lowrance, Abram C. to Nina C. Bridges 2-4-1855 Cr
Lowrance, Danil W. to Nancy J. Maxwell 9-29-1845 (10-11?-1845) Hr
Lowrance, E. B. to L. A. Jackson 12-21-1869 G
Lowrance, J. K. to A. C. Cherry 5-28-1860 G
Lowrance, John H. to M. A. E. Reed 11-15-1863 Dy
Lowrance, Levi W. to Elizabeth Eckols 10-28-1841 Sh
Lowrance, Levi to Frances A. Rogers 10-7-1847 Sh
Lowrance, Ned to Fanny Lowrance 6-8-1870 G
Lowrance, W. G. to Martha A. Lowrance 8-22-1869 G
Lowrance, Wm. D. to Virginia E. Watson 1-5-1870 G
Lowrey, Arthur to Nancy A. Coleman 2-28-1848 (no return) Hn
Lowrey, E. V. to Mary Phillips ?-?-1862? Mn
Lowrey, Elijah M. to Virginia E. Butler 2-24-1870 (2-25-1870) Cr
Lowrey, George to Caroline Harvey 8-18-1866 (not endorsed) F B
Lowrey, James H. to Holly Hendley 11-17-1850 We
Lowrey, John to Mary E. York 2-27-1875 (2-28-1875) L
Lowrey, Kenneth P. to Mariah P. Lowery 2-4-1858 Hn
Lowrey, W. H. to Ennis Rowland 12-31-1872 (1-1-1873) Cr
Lowrince, Jasper F. to Polly Ann Midiant 11-27-1839 Cr
Lowry, Allen to Fanny Mann 7-9-1867 Hy
Lowry, Allen to Matilda Newborn 2-25-1876 (no return) Hy
Lowry, Allen to Vina Musgrave 3-13-1873 Hy
Lowry, Charley to Elmira Brown 9-29-1876 (10-1-1876) L
Lowry, D. S. to Elizabeth Cravans 9-4-1844 We
Lowry, G. W. to Lemony Spate 3-22-1865 Hn
Lowry, H. P. to Rada E. Bell 10-17-1855 (no return) Hn
Lowry, H. W. to Mary Brigance 4-16-1857 Hn
Lowry, Henry to Jane Bodkin 10-3-1855 (10-4-1855) G
Lowry, Isaac B. to Sarah Jones 5-4-1863 Mn
Lowry, Isaac to Susan W. Lowry 12-16-1841 Sh
Lowry, J. J. to Rebecca French 2-21-1864 Hn
Lowry, J. P. to Sarah A. Poor 7-17-1860 (7-19-1860) T
Lowry, J. P. to Martha A. French 10-24-1867 Hn
Lowry, J. T. to O. E. Allen 5-26-1846 Sh
Lowry, James R. to Winnie J. B. Lowry 4-17-1859 Hn
Lowry, James to Elizabeth F. Lea 11-18-1846 We
Lowry, James to Elizabeth King 4-5-1860 Hn
Lowry, James to Elizabeth Lea 11-16-1846 We
Lowry, Jesse H. to Eddie C. Cox 10-30-1851 Cr

Lowry, Jesse P. to Frances B. Lilly 1-5-1838 (no return) Hn
Lowry, John B. to Mary Tidwell 2-21-1835 (4-27-1835) G
Lowry, John J. to Richard (SB Rachel) Lindsy 11-27-1845 Be
Lowry, John M. to Elizabeth Jane Monroe 8-6-1840 Cr
Lowry, John M. to T. A. Cofield 7-11-1844 Hn
Lowry, John to Ann C. (Mrs.) Moore 5-20-1868 (5-28-1868) L
Lowry, John to Mary Wilcox 2-1-1824 Sh
Lowry, Johnathan to Evaline Smith 7-9-1844 Hn
Lowry, Joseph M. to Matilda Dial 4-18-1845 (4-19-1845) L
Lowry, Orange to Mary J. Winters 5-28-1858 Hn
Lowry, Robert O. to Nancy B. (Mrs.) Hardgraves 1-19-1867 (1-20-1867) Ma
Lowry, Robert to Elizabeth Alexander 8-22-1859 Hn
Lowry, Robert to Orlina Jane Petty 12-29-1855 (1-5-1856) T
Lowry, Samuel to Rebecca J. James 12-27-1847 G
Lowry, Stephen W. to Mary J. Ward 8-25-1856 (8-26-1856) G
Lowry, Thomas W. to Sarah A. Staton 4-28-1858 Hn
Lowry, W. H. to Mary Brewer 4-13-1864 Be
Lowry, William C. to Margaret A. Dowdy 4-25-1861 Hn
Lowry, William C. to Nancy W. J. Doughty 4-15-1857 Hn
Lowry, Wm. to Elinora Abington 3-25-1839 (4-3-1839) F
Lowry?, William T. to Susan B. Cunningham 1-16-1846 Hn
Lowther?, William to Smiley J. Ethridge 12-17-1850 Hn
Loyd, Alfred to Nancy Taylor 12-25-1838 Hn
Loyd, Andrew J. to Adaline G. Delashmet 1-16-1872 (1-17-1872) T
Loyd, J. W. to E. A. Reasons 11-2-1865 G
Loyd, Jackson to Sarah Coker 3-26-1846 F
Loyd, John to Amanda Walk 10-19-1869 T
Loyd, Josiah to Alice Blackman 6-1-1867 G B
Loyd, Thomas E. to Caledonia Roberts 1-13-1857 We
Loyd, Thomas to Polly Nutt 11-22-1837 Sh
Loyd, W. A. to Elvira Hudson 12-19-1866 G
Loyd, W. A. to M. J.? Hannah 12-12-1866 (12-13-1866) T
Loyd, Wilson to Sarah A. Rodgers 2-16-1859 (2-22-1859) Sh
Luallen, J. W. to S. C. Groom 3-12-1852 We
Lubbren, Gustave to Mary Welch 3-6-1860 Sh
Lucade, Isaac J. to Mahala Forbess 12-16-1843 (12-20-1843) Hr
Lucado, E. P. to Margret Simonton 6-28-1856 (7-11-1856) T
Lucas, A. D. to Cynthia Daryberry 9-29-1864 Hn
Lucas, Anderson to Susan Sterling 4-17-1850 (4-18-1850) F
Lucas, B. H. to Mattie O. Simms 10-2-1865 (10-3-1865) F
Lucas, Booker to Anna Driver 9-27-1879 L
Lucas, F. (Dr.) to Martha T. Huce 12-12-1849 G
Lucas, Fielding A. to Sarah P. Walker 9-15-1841 Sh
Lucas, G. J. to Lurann Elllis 7-27-1861 (7-28-1861) L
Lucas, Granville to Martha Blackwood 12-24-1870 (12-25-1870) F B
Lucas, Ichabold M. to Jackan Turpin 1-18-1845 (no return) F
Lucas, Isaac to Lucy A. Weshl (West?) 4-10-1867 (4-11-1867) L
Lucas, J. A. to Bettie J. Adams 2-8-1872 (2-13-1872) Dy
Lucas, J. B. to Josie Bain 11-20-1878 Hy
Lucas, J. M. to Julia C. Everett 12-21-1875 (12-23-1875) Dy
Lucas, James H. to Aneliza Braddy 8-20-1851 8-21-1851) Sh
Lucas, James P. to Delia Lane 7-25-1885 (7-26-1885) L
Lucas, James Y. to Mary E. Lanier 12-25-1847 (no return) F
Lucas, James to Fanny Paris 5-24-1877 Hy
Lucas, John to Synthia Trap 6-23-1850 Sh
Lucas, Lemuel T. to Missouri J. Lanier 11-6-1867 (no return) Dy
Lucas, Mike to Sophia Ann Wells 4-5-1869 (4-6-1869) F
Lucas, Mitchell to Becky Rainey 12-22-1877 (12-23-1877) L
Lucas, Robert to Lillie McClish 6-5-1884 L
Lucas, Thomas to Mollie Bush 12-23-1868 (no return) L
Lucas, Tom to Ellen De Moore (Morse?) 3-19-1873 (3-20-1873) L B
Lucas, W. R. to Mary F. Thompson 12-14-1859 Sh
Lucas, William to Sarah Dun 4-27-1855 Sh
Lucas, Wm. D. to Martha A. P. Scoggins 7-12-1851 (7-13-1851) Sh
Lucas, Wm. A. to Martha A. Alston 7-23-1851 L
Lucey, Amos H. to Mary Booker 8-10-1865 Hn
Lucey, Denis to Mary Real 1-20-1855 (1-21-1855) Sh
Luck, Alen R. to Sarah C. Tilman 11-26-1849 (12-5-1849) F
Luck, J. S. to Lucy Clear 11-5-1869 (11-9-1869) F
Luckada, P. P. to Martha Ann Appleberry 1-21-1851 (2-5-1851) Sh
Luckado, Edward P. to Jane W. Irby 6-23-1845 F
Luckado, Wilson to Grissey Slauson 6-20-1853 (no return) F
Luckado, Wilson to Mary Dubois 2-3-1835 Hr
Luckey, George E. to Elizaeth Ore 9-3-1854 Hn
Luckey, Joseph to Susan Baker 12-24-1845 (12-27-1845) Ma
Luckey, Samuel R. to Victoria J. Wilgerson 2-16-1856 (no return) Hn
Luckey, Samuel to Holland P. Dillard 10-15-1838 (10-16-1838) Ma
Lucky, John F. to Susannah Baker 8-16-1847 (8-26-1847) Hr
Lucus, Dallis to Mariah Wells 1-19-1876 (1-20-1876) L B
Lucus, Francis M. to Mary P. Porter 7-1-1872 (no return) L
Lucus, George H. to Sarah E. Underwood 2-1-1876 L
Lucus, John W. to Nancy E. Lierd 6-16-1870 (6-26-1870) L
Lucus, John to Martha Salmons 2-28-1841 Cr
Lucy, G. W. to Mary E. Coldwell 1-24-1855 Hn
Lucy, L. P. to N. O. Horton 11-12-1875 (11-4?-1875) L
Lucy, W. H. to Ada M. Smith 6-28-1883 L
Ludi, L. to Paulina Prince 10-3-1856 Sh
Ludwick, John to Lavina Cox 7-17-1865 T
Ludwig, Conrad to Antonia Hert 8-4-1855 Sh
Lugoria, James to Nancy Grace 5-24-1858 Sh
Luke (Luker?), John A. to Matilda A. Heathcock 12-30-1868 G
Luker, Daniel to Malinda Rutledge 10-27-1856 (10-29-1856) O
Luker, Daniel to Melinda Rutledge 10-27-1854 (10-29-1854) O
Luker, Jerome P. to Elizabeth F. Moore 2-25-1859 O
Luker, Joseph to Mary A. Jones 3-20-1860 O
Lumbrick, James P. to Nancy Martin 8-9-1842 Hn
Lumbrick, William M. to Mary Ross 10-22-1858 Hn
Lumkins, Anderson to Isabella Kennedy 9-14-1850 (9-15-1850) Sh
Lumley, J. P. to Sarah Cavnar 1-31-1859 Hr
Lumley, N. M. to Martha Jane Whirley 12-12-1864 Sh *
Lumly, Wm. E. to Paralee Swanner 4-9-1872 (no return) Hy
Lumpkins, George W. to Margarett Goad 8-2-1848 (8-3-1848) Ma
Lumpkins, John F. to Narciss Wheatley 9-13-1869 L
Lumpkins, R. C. to Nancy Ann Mager 3-21-1861 Mn
Lumpkins, R. F. to Milly Whitley 5-2-1867 G
Lumpkins, Thomas W. to M. A. M. Johnston 1-7-1861 (1-10-1861) Sh
Lumpkins, W. F. to Martha Berry 2-4-1861 (2-5-1861) Dy
Lunamand, Andrew to Elizabeth Stringer 4-10-1858 (4-11-1858) Sh
Lunday, James M. to Mary A. Dunlap 8-28-1856 Cr
Lunday, Wm. B. F. to Frances Springer 5-9-1847 Cr
Lundergan, Richard to Mary Solon 4-19-1856 (4-20-1856) Sh
Lundsford, Aruous E. to Elizabeth D. Glimp 2-14-1866 L
Lundsford, Green C. to Maria L. Thompson 1-8-1866 (1-16-1866) L
Lundy, Balam to Zilpha Giffrey 3-9-1867 (3-12-1867) T
Lundy, Joshua? C. to Sophia W. Simmons 8-4-1845 (8-5-1845) F
Lunnon, Hinson to Elizabeth Mitchell 11-27-1843 Ma
Lunsford, A. B. to Margaret Ann Brimm 1-12-1863 (no return) L
Lunsford, A. D. to America Nixon 5-23-1839 Hr
Lunsford, Alfred L. to Frances L. Jones 12-20-1843 (12-21-1843) Ma
Lunsford, Burtis to Mary Ann Young 5-27-1843 (6-8-1843) Ma
Lunsford, C. H. to Huldy Woods 3-20-1869 (3-29-1869) L
Lunsford, George A. to Susan Wilson 2-19-1861 Ma
Lunsford, George W. to Mary Jane Smith 1-9-1867 (no return) L
Lunsford, Harason to Sarah Evans 1-8-1870 (no return) L
Lunsford, Henry H. to Emily J. Manley 10-10-1863 (no return) L
Lunsford, L. J. to Demeris Taylor 5-1-1869 (5-2-1869) L
Lunsford, O. G. to M. L. Shoemake 2-13-1880 (2-16-1880) L
Lunsford, P. W. to Martha Smith 4-3-1878 (4-7-1878) L
Lunsford, Pleasant to Caroline Chism 5-14-1857 L
Lunsford, S. T. to Frances Ray 5-18-1869 (no return) Dy
Lunsford, Thomas to Mary C. Nixon 10-19-1847 (12-24-1847) Hr
Lunsford, W. E. to A. L. Davis 2-14-1877 Dy
Lunsford, W. E. to M. E. Davis 1-22-1879 (1-23-1879) Dy
Lunsford, William to Cordelia J. Osteen 9-11-1852 (9-12-1852) L
Lunsford, William to Maria Rine 1-12-1837 (1-22-1837) Hr
Lunsford, Wyatt to Amy M. Moore 8-6-1846 L
Luntsford, J. A. to P. A. Crow 12-24-1875 (no return) Dy
Luper, Cullen to Nancy Tedder 2-28-1853 Be
Luper, John to L. Malin 2-7?-1865 Be
Lupo, William to Mary Tedder 11-21-1865 Be
Lurence, James C. to Lowtica? Leigh 12-19-1867 Cr
Lurgan, Patrick to Ann Brackin 9-6-1861 (9-7-1861) Sh
Luron, Daniel to Susan Andrews 3-18-1840 (3-19-1840) Ma
Lurry, Thomas to Martha F. Little 2-17-1855 (2-27-1855) Sh
Lurry, Thomas to Sarah Allen 12-17-1844 Sh
Lusby (Lisby), Pleasant to Mary Ann Piles 3-17-1845 Sh
Lusby, James L. to Elizabeth Baker 12-16-1841 (12-23-1841) F
Lusby, Pleasant to Elizabeth Breeding 1-30-1829 Sh
Luscombe, F. M. to Mary Avery 3-24-1849 L
Luscumbe, Frank W. to Georgia Stevens 9-10-1872 Dy
Lush, John D. to Fannie Haines 12-11-1860 (12-13-1860) Cr
Lusk, G. A. to Jennie Steele 11-30-1881 L
Lusk, George H. to Elizabeth Jennings 9-19-1849 (9-20-1849) L
Lusk, James M. to Malvina Joiner 1-12-1871 Ma
Lusk, James M. to Nancy E. Ledbetter 4-29-1854 (4-31-1854) L
Lusk, John H. to Henrietta A. Hinton 6-28-1866 L
Lusk, John to Mary E. Logan 9-7-1864 Sh
Lusk, Joseph to Minerva S. Bell 7-23-1833 (7-24-1833) Hr
Lusk, R. H. to Laura A. Harlan 12-2-1867 L
Lusk, Richard N. to Louinda M. Willis 12-2-1872 (12-3-1872) L
Lusk, Samuel B. to Permelia T. Dickey 2-4-1840 Sh
Lusk, W. E. to _. J. Caten 12-28-1860 }
Luskey, Wm. to Martha J. Reynolds 11-26-1856 Cr
Luster, Barton to Caralin Pearce 3-3-1868 (3-4-1868) T
Luster, George to Sarah Tate 12-25-1865 Mn
Luster, George to Martha Francess Barnett 12-17-1846 (12-20-1846) O
Luster, Henry to Marcindy Brook 3-12-1867 (3-15-1867) F B
Luster, John W. to Penina Williams 8-3-1853 O
Luster, Stafford to Susan Dearmore 6-19-1860 Dy
Luten, Meredith W. to Margaret E. Chance 10-12-1858 Hn
Luter, Axlanda to Della Eason 1-24-1855 Cr
Lutes, James T. to Mary A. Murphey 7-8-1864 (7-9-1864) Sh
Luton, John R. to Louisa C. Harper 9-5-1867 (no return) Hy
Luton, Sterling to Emma J. Nelson 2-25-1873 (2-26-1873) L

Grooms

Luton, W. S. to S. A. Parker 12-11-1876 (12-12-1876) O
Lutsinger, G. L. to Rebecca Everett 11-26-1870 (11-27-1870) Cr
Luttrell, John W. to E. V. Thompson 1-20-1857 (1-22-1857) Hr
Luttrell, Silas to Rachel M. Hartfield 9-25-1867 (9-26-1867) T
Luvin (Loving?), Goolsberry to Elizabeth Lynn 2-25-1839 Hn
Lux(Sax?), Benj. to Mary Hendricks 3-13-1860 (3-14-1860) Hr
Lyell, Travis to Elizabeth Ragsdale 2-25-1855 Hn
Lyer?, James to Mary Wilson 1-18-1836 Hr
Lykes, J. E. to Mary Mathis 11-9-1877 (11-11-1877) O
Lyle, Sam W. to Mattie B. Curtis 11-21-1871 (no return) Hy
Lyles, A. S. to Francis A. Roberts 2-3-1866 (2-4-1866) O
Lyles, Dennis M. to Nancy E. Foltz 7-21-1840 Hr
Lyles, James L. to Sarah Linsey 10-18-1837 (11-25-1837) O
Lyles, N.L. to Josephine Jones 4-7-1873 (4-10-1873) T
Lyles, Reding to Sarah Ann Hinant 12-9-1852 Be
Lyles, W. W. to Martha E. Hunsucker 1-30-1867 F
Lynch, Anderson to Maegret? Russell 12-6-1868 Be
Lynch, Charles P. to Martha E. Butler 7-31-1849 Sh
Lynch, Clyde to Sally Hatley 1-25-1832 Be CC
Lynch, David to Emily Montcrief 10-30-1853 (no return) F
Lynch, Dennis to Ellen Moriarty 4-21-1860 (4-22-1860) Sh
Lynch, Edward to Mary Burke 8-7-1850 Sh
Lynch, G. R. to Rosa A. Edwards 12-4-1874 (12-6-1874) O
Lynch, Isaac J. to Hester Ann Douglass 11-1-1853 O
Lynch, J. N. M. to Margaret J. Kencall 5-4-1853 Hn
Lynch, James to Bridget Costello 12-2-1862 Sh
Lynch, James H. to Martha M. Evans 7-2-1846 G
Lynch, Jeremiah D. to Johanna Conway 1-26-1858 (1-27-1858) Sh
Lynch, John to America J. Ramsey 12-24-1855 (1-20-1856) Sh
Lynch, John to Mary N. Bledsoe 12-3-1844 (12-4-1844) G
Lynch, Moses to Selena C. (Mrs.) Sutherland 12-31-1839 F
Lynch, R. W. to Mary Webb 6-3-1854 (no return) F
Lynch, Samuel C. to Mary Jane Swan 1-7-1846 Ma
Lynch, Smedley to Tempe Williams 3-21-1855 Sh
Lynch, Walter to Ann Farley 8-21-1848 Sh
Lynch, William W. to Artena Northcut 9-1-1852 G
Lynch, William to Olive (Olvid) G. Lurry 12-23-1845 Sh
Lynch, Wm. W. to Mary Brockwell 9-20-1877 O
Lyne, James A. to Nellie P. Mart 10-12-1873 Hy
Lynn, Benson F. to Maryann Garrett 12-20-1840 F
Lynn, Charles to Esther V.? Kerr 7-18-1841 (6?-22-1841) F
Lynn, Charles to Henry Orr 1-4-1869 (1-5-1869) F
Lynn, H. M. to Henrietta B. Polk no date (with 5-1860) Sh
Lynn, Henry to Susanna Morrison 7-3-1869 T
Lynn, Hugh M. to Martha S. Simpson 4-9-1862 T
Lynn, J. W. to M. E. McCain 6-2-1869 (6-3-1869) T
Lynn, James O. to Margaret W. Caskey 12-31-1870 (1-2-1871) T
Lynn, James to Eliza Truit 1-26-1859 Sh
Lynn, Mathew to Elizabeth C. Higgs 6-14-1862 We
Lynn, Robert to Luticia Scott 3-17-1852 Sh
Lynn, Sidney to Amanda McDowell 12-24-1866 (12-25-1866) F B
Lynn, Spencer to Rena Parish 3-3-1870 (3-6-1870) L
Lynn, William E. to Carrie M. Lewis 12-2-1880 L
Lynn, William E. to M. F. E. Byrn 7-8-1869 L
Lynn, Wm. H. to Mary Parks 9-16-1858 We
Lynn, lJ. P. to R. Shaw 1-9-1871 (1-10-1871) T
Lynn?, J. A. to Bettie Heffman 12-31-1870 F
Lynne, T. N. to E. A. Wherry 1-16-1860 (1-18-1860) Sh
Lynton, Silas S. to Sarah Burnum 9-15-1840 (no return) Hn
Lyon, J. R. to A. E. Vandike 3-5-1868 Hy
Lyon, J. W. to Sarah J. Baker 12-25-1855 (12-27-1856?) We
Lyon, John to Louisa N. Massy 12-14-1853 G
Lyon, John to Nancy A. Lyons 5-6-1861 (5-9-1861) Dy
Lyon, John to R. I. Lyons 3-19-1866 (3-22-1866) O
Lyon, Richard B to Virginia F. Phillips 10-10-1849 (10-11-1849) G
Lyon, Richd. T.k to Phafama Elizabeth Hale 12-21-1854 (12-27-1854) Hr
Lyon, Saml. W. to Mary Jane Boyce 3-24-1857 (3-25-1857) Sh
Lyon, Thomas to Adeline Sewell 6-20-1870 (7-3-1870) Ma
Lyon, Wade W. to Mary Reid 11-2-1869 Ma
Lyon, William J. to Niecy Carroll 4-17-1861 Ma
Lyon, William T. to Rebecca King 1-1-1842 (1-3-1842) Ma
Lyon, William W. to Mary Douglass 7-20-1858 Hn
Lyones, Jeremiah to Ellen Lynch 8-25-1863 Sh
Lyons, Ben to Lessie? Johnson 11-27-1867 T
Lyons, Bob to Casire Holms 1-12-1869 Hy
Lyons, John Lewis to Sarah Allen Baskins 1-2-1868 G
Lyons, Lewis to Sarah Peres 12-1-1862 Sh
Lyons, Michael to Ellen Ragan 11-12-1861 Sh
Lyons, Patrick J. to Mary Jones 11-26-1868 F
Lyons, Patrick to Bridgett Ryan 9-11-1859 Sh
Lyons, Perry to Nancy Ellison 7-31-1865 (8-2-1865) O
Lyons, Robert S. to Minerva Oakes 1-17-1842 Hr
Lytaker, Finas to Elizabeth Stanley 3-3-1834 (3-6-1834) G
Lytle, Gardner to Mary Elizabeth Lewis 11-12-1867 (11-13-1867) Ma
Lytle, Oscar to Betheny Ray 1-5-1869 (no return) L
Lytlee, John J. to Susannah J. Culp 9-11-1851 (no return) Cr

M____, John to Elizabeth Coleman 3-18-1856 Hn
Maas, Ferdinand to Rosena Dudling 12-24-1862 Sh
Maberry, James to Fanny Walker 2-9-1867 (2-16-1867) F B
Maberry, James to Frances McFarland 2-25-1873 Hy
Maberry, Joseph to Docia Wright 9-26-1847 O
Mabery, Henry to Elizabeth Colier 3-11-1850 Be
Mabery, Wm. to Jane Douglas 10-16-1849 Hy
Mabin, Dempsie to Harriet Porter 4-28-1868 (no return) F B
Mabin, Essex to Susan Douglas 1-10-1878 Hy
Mabin, Jessee to Etmonia Hays 10-11-1877 Hy
Mabin, John to Matilda Ferguson 3-15-1879 Dy
Mabin, Wiley to Malissa Mabin 5-3-1867 (6-3-1867) F B
Mabrey, John to Gracy Britt 4-13-1849 Cr
Mabrey, William A. to Rozillia Gause 3-16-1868 (3-19-1868) L
Mabson, Samuel to Martha C. Carter 10-26-1859 Hn
Maburn, George to Bammer Pool 9-7-1871 (9-9-1871) T
Mabury, Alfred to Caroline Smally 10-21-1847 Be
MacNiel, Mac to Mary Winston 5-9-1877 (5-10-1877) L
Macafee, Geo. to Junior Trotman 1-3-1869 Dy
Macbeth, Thos. to Molly A. Pearson 4-15-1864 (4-17-1864) Sh
Mace, John W. C. to Rebecca McCoy 7-16-1850 (7-18-1850) Hr
Mack, Barney to Araminta Wallace 10-27-1860 Cr
Mack, Pat to Kate Hill 10-29-1870 Hy
Mackado, Calvin to Nancy Stallins 5-16-1871 T
Mackecy, R. E. to S. E. Leach 2-8-1856 Cr
Mackey, Aleck to Fanny Rains 11-30-1870 (12-1-1870) F
Mackey, Cyrus to Molly Moseley 12-26-1868 (12-29-1868) F B
Mackey, R. F. to E. R. Carithers 10-24-1864 (10-26-1864) O
Mackey, Thomas D. to Lydia Richardson 1-9-1867 G
Mackleroy, Micajah to Elvira Myrick 10-7-1834 L
Macklin, Andrew to Amanda Jett? 10-23-1865 (10-29-1865) T
Macklin, Benjamin to Roxanna S. Neely 4-11-1853 (4-13-1853) Sh
Macklin, Bob to Ann Smith 5-13-1869 T
Macklin, Hannibal to Catherine Shaw 5-3-1869 G B
Macklin, James to Eliza White 12-27-1877 Hy
Macklin, Jefferson to Mariah James 10-21-1851 Hr
Macklin, John to Mary Walker 11-12-1874 Hy
Macklin, Joshua to Polly A. Tucker 12-24-1870 (no return) F B
Macklin, Paul to Eudora Taylor 6-21-1867 T
Macklin, Robert to Fathy Williamson 1-29-1866 T
Mackling, Anderson to Edy Davidson 10-17-1868 G B
Macky, John to Ann O'Hara 3-29-1856 (3-30-1856) Sh
Maclin, Albert to Vergun Taylor 12-24-1869 T
Maclin, Bevly to Henrietta Broadnax 2-20-1869 (2-23-1869) F B
Maclin, Charles to Raciel Vance 7-21-1877 (7-27-1877) L B
Maclin, Charley to Lucy Tappscott 2-27-1873 (3-1-1873) L B
Maclin, Dick to Bettie Hooper 2-3-1866 Hy
Maclin, Edmond to Agnes Somerville 9-23-1871 Hy
Maclin, George to Louisa Maclin 4-8-1870 T
Maclin, Harvey to 'Bettie Taylor 1-14-1868 T
Maclin, Henry to Hester Carter 1-11-1877 Hy
Maclin, J. N. to Florence Brodnax 5-24-1869 (5-30-1869) F
Maclin, J. W. to Mary J. Brodnax 6-17-1861 (6-19-1861) F
Maclin, James S. to Louisa H. Read 8-3-1864 (no return) Hy
Maclin, Jerry to Bettie Maclin 12-23-1866 (no return) F B
Maclin, Jerry to Mary Currie 3-21-1869 Hy
Maclin, John H. to Nellie King 3-19-1870 Hy
Maclin, John Junius to Mary Maclin 12-20-1878 Hy
Maclin, John to Allice Lacy 3-25-1874 (no return) Hy
Maclin, John to Martha Owen 12-22-1871 Hy
Maclin, Lackfield to Sallie D. Alston 12-30-1871 (1-3-1875?) T
Maclin, Lewis to Mariah Sutton 9-11-1869 Hy
Maclin, Littleton to Amanda Nelson 12-14-1878 Hy
Maclin, Major William to Louiza Jane Mitchell 1-29-1868 (2-1-1868) L B
Maclin, Nelson to Milly Hardin 12-31-1867 G
Maclin, Rasmus to Lemon Buford 12-23-1869 F B
Maclin, Reubin to Biner Nelson 9-30-1871 (no return) Hy
Maclin, Rueben to Mary Oldham 2-25-1884 (2-27-1884) L
Maclin, Sam to Caroline Watkins 6-8-1872 (6-9-1872) L B
Maclin, Samuel to A. Marshall 9-30-1871 (10-6-1871) T
Maclin, Smith to Mattie Lacey 1-25-1871 T
Maclin, W. T. to M. E. Harrelle 9-1-1868 Hy
Maclin, W. to M. A. Bailey 6-10-1877 Hy
Maclin, Warner to Charity Berry 11-11-1871 (11-12-1871) L
Maclin, Washington to Mary Rhodes 1-19-1868 (1-20-1868) T
Maclin, William P. to Jane C. Donaldson 8-5-1846 (8-6-1846) G
Maclin, William to Easter Maclin 2-27-1874 Hy
Maclin, William to Vina Jarrett 11-21-1868 Hy
Maclin, Willie to Nellie Jackson 11-11-1874 T
Maclin, Willis Green to Mary Emma Currie 10-20-1878 Hy
Maclin, Wm. to Looky Plummer 12-20-1871 T
Maclin, Zeek to Malinda Armstrong 12-22-1871 (no return) Hy
Macon, A. G. to Elizabeth Rucker 12-22-1863 (12-23-1864?) L
Macon, Arthur to Nancy Davis 4-21-1865 (4-22-1865) L
Macon, Bailey to Martha Ann Fortune 11-25-1846 (11-26-1846) Hr
Macon, David to Elizabeth Jacobs 11-20-1848 (11-23-1848) Hr
Macon, Henry to Loueser House 9-15-1867 Hy

Macon, Isaiah to Eldiss Cox 3-1-1844 Hr
Macon, John T. to Mary B. Fitzhugh 7-21-1842 Hr
Macon, Thomas J. to Easther Hubert 2-1-1834 O
Macon, W. H. to Mary Walker 9-28-1871 Dy
Macon, W. H. to Nancy E. Davis 12-26-1864 (no return) L
Macon, W. L. to M. A. Bain 11-29-1871 Hy
Macon, Whitson to Jane Maria Jourden 2-7-1849 (2-8-1849) Hr
Macon, Willia to Eleanor H. Somerville 12-25-1843 T
Madaras, Eno Real to Elizabeth Goodman 7-2-1840 G
Madden, George A. to Rosmond Hawley 4-11-1867 Be
Madden, James to Eliza Kelly 3-5-1859 (3-6-1859) Sh
Madden, John M. to Sarah Herren 3-21-1865 Be
Madden, John W. to Caroline Dalson 6-27-1859 (7-4-1859) Sh
Madden, John to Catharine Lynch 4-9-1858 Sh
Madden, Michael to Mary Mahar 1-23-1856 Sh
Madden, Samuel H. to Rebecca A. Greer 12-21-1853 Be
Madden, Thomas B. to Louisa J. Collins 9-23-1851 Be
Madden, Thomas B. to Nancy Jane McDonel 10-28-1863 Be
Madden, Thomas to Francis A. Nipp 6-9-1860 (6-10-1860) O
Madden, Thomas to Margaret Dunn 1-6-1856 Sh
Maddin, Calvin D. to Martha Hollemon 6-10-1847 F
Madding, C. D. to Mary L. Turlington 6-1-1845 Sh
Madding, David to Lucretia Taylor 12-20-1869 (12-28-1869) F B
Madding, Richard to Mary Duke 12-23-1870 (no return) Dy B
Maddox, Frank to Julia Carpenter 1-13-1869 (1-14-1869) F
Maddox, Henry S. to Fannie R. Anderson 1-10-1860 Sh
Maddox, Javan H. to Sarah E. Turk 4-21-1852 O
Maddox, Jesse to Sarah White 10-30-1848 Sh
Maddox, Jessee T. to Ellen Eston 9-4-1852 (9-9-1852) Sh
Maddox, John A. to C. L. Curtis 7-26-1867 (no return) Hy
Maddox, John R. to Mary A. Pentecost 5-4-1855 We
Maddox, Nathan to Louisa J. Holden 1-19-1858 Hn
Maddox, S. C. to Sarah E. Bolton 11-1-1859 Sh
Maddox, William E. to Margaret S. Kent 12-19-1848 Sh
Maddox, William J. to Mary Jane Altman 10-27-1856 (10-19?-1856) Ma
Maddox, William to Fanny Goff 11-2-1846 (11-4-1846) Hr
Maddox, William to Susan Mullikin 12-11-1849 Hr
Maddrey, Elmore to Mollie Prichard 12-12-1877 (12-13-1877) Dy
Maddrey, Isaac to Malinda Foust 12-21-1868 (no return) Dy
Maddrey, Ricahrd to Adaline Crow 12-18-1866 (12-25-1866) Dy
Madigan, P. to Bridget Green 11-5-1863 Sh
Madison, Baily to Pheba McCaslin 5-6-1828 (5-22-1828) Ma
Madison, James to Lucy Foster 11-13-1871 (no return) Cr B
Madison, James to Patsey Thompson 2-1-1867 (2-16-1867) F B
Madison, R. to L. A. Dalton 2-17-1862 (2-18-1862) Sh
Madison, Richard to Sarah Chavers 9-30-1841 G
Madison, Robert to Elizabeth Holder 12-10-1841 (12-16-1841) G
Madox, L. C. to M. A. Tittsworth 7-25-1860 O
Madra, John to Rebecca A. McGill 6-11-1862 Be
Maender, Fr. to M. Duttlinger 10-3-1859 (10-4-1859) Sh
Magalon, Joseph Jonah Batiste to Mary Regoult 7-25-1848 Sh
Magee, Andrew M. to Nancy E. Stewart 10-16-1866 O
Magee, B. F. to Susan E. Price 9-1-1852 (no return) F
Magee, D. S. to Nancy O. More 10-24-1844 We
Magee, Henry to Lily Green 10-23-1873 (12-16-1873) T
Magee, Leroy P. to Delila E. Sample 9-16-1851 (10-7-1851) O
Mager, William G. to Elmira McKalip 10-19-1861 Mn
Magerney, Eugene to Mary Smith 5-31-1840 Sh
Magevney, Michaell to Mary W. (Mrs.) Gallagher 12-29-1857 Sh
Maggard, George to Isabella Doyle 8-26-1869 (no return) Dy
Maggard, Jerry to Louisa Foster 7-14-1869 (no return) Dy
Maggard, John to Lucy Wood 12-29-1875 (1-2-1876) Dy
Maggard, Sandy to Lou Parr 1-12-1878 Dy
Maginnis, James L. to Mary E. Wandell 1-29-1862 (1-30-1862) Sh
Maginty, Pat to Catherine Cox 5-8-1863 Sh
Magrave, Nicholas to Ellen Slattery 5-12-1855 Sh
Maguire, Thos. to Pheobe Stoddard 4-19-1853 (5-1-1853) Sh
Maha, Michael to Ann Taylor 1-11-1858 (1-20-1858) Sh
Mahaffy, James G. to Mary Ann Taylor 3-26-1838 Ma
Mahaffy, James T. to Mary L. Campbell 6-3-1849 Sh
Mahan (Maher), Wm. to Julia Whalings 7-17-1850 Sh
Mahan, Allen to Bette Doak 1-4-1871 (no return) Dy
Mahan, Jessee to Callie Cameron 12-28-1877 Hy
Mahan, John to Bridget Gilhouly 2-1-1856 (2-3-1856) Sh
Mahan, L. M. to Elizabeth Meacham 9-13-1865 (9-14-1865) O
Mahan, Milton to Millie Autry 12-30-1870 Hy
Mahan, T. A. to S. E. J. Howard 11-30-1859 Hn
Mahan, Tom to Amy Brown 12-13-1873 Hy
Maher, Mathew to Alice Finnessey 6-23-1856 Sh
Maher, William to Catherine Malone 5-9-1846 Sh
Mahler, F. A. to Louisa Keller 10-10-1860 Sh
Mahler, Frank to Caroline Boke 5-25-1858 Sh
Mahn, James to Ann Shields 9-8-1852 Sh
Mahon, Dallas to Alice Walker 1-28-1868 (2-10-1868) Dy
Mahon, F. E. to E. L. Perry 12-3-1864 (12-13-1864) Dy
Mahon, George T. to Mary H. Kirkpatrick 2-7-1848 (2-?-1848) Ma
Mahon, Howel H. to Matilda C. Holder 12-30-1850 (12-31-1850) G

Mahon, Michael to Maggie Rand 11-5-1867 Hy
Mahon, P. J. to Mary Dippel 5-26-1862 (7-4-1862) Sh
Mahon, Robert H. to Annie V. Blakemon 12-14-1865 G
Mahone, Wm. to Julia Puryear 2-14-1868 (2-15-1868) L B
Mahoney, Cain to Mary McGlathlen 3-25-1860 We
Mahoney, Pat to Ellen Lenshan 10-20-1864 Sh
Mahoney, Thomas to Johanna O'Brien 9-15-1856 Sh
Mahoney, Wm. to Ann Stapleton 8-17-1861 (8-18-1861) Sh
Maiar, Baptiste to Hannah Macon 8-21-1856 Sh
Maiar, Conrad to Catharine Walder 9-27-1858 Sh
Maiers, John to Ellen Lynch 2-3-1863 Sh
Mailey, Anderson to Lavicey Ann Wood 3-16-1848 T
Mailey, Henry J. to Nancy Jane Tucker 1-23-1851 T
Mailey, Henry James to Sarah Ann Eliz. Richardson 5-16-1843 (5-18-1843) T
Mailey, James O. to Julia Ann L. Wiseman 3-27-1853 T
Mailey?, John to Angeline Jane Morents? 4-5-1843 (4-6-1843) T
Mainard, A. M. to Mary R. Young 6-9-1868 O
Mainard, Gideon W. to Dovey Smith 8-21-1837 (8-31-1837) G
Mainard, Israel E. to Rutha A. Petty 8-7-1866 Cr
Mainard, John to Lucy Ann Wood 4-23-1854 Hn
Mainor, Nathan I. to Fannie H. May 2-10-1868 (2-12-1868) Ma
Mainor, William to Martha A. Edwards 10-8-1847 G
Maior, Frank to Louisa C. (Mrs.) George 5-10-1858 Sh
Majors, Marshall D. to Ida Landrum 4-1-1878 (4-7-1878) L
Malady, J. D. to Sophia Darnall 12-2-1862 (12-3-1862) O
Malam, Lennard to Mary Shinault 12-28-1839 (12-29-1839) Hr
Malcomb, W. M. to Casamie White 3-4-1866 Hn
Malear, G. W. to Mary E. Rogers 1-20-1866 (3-4-1866) Cr
Maley, James S. to Fannie C. Turner 12-31-1866 (1-1-1867) T
Malick (Moelch), Louis to Mary France 1-27-1848 Sh
Malin, James to Charlotte L. Melton 11-21-1859 We
Malin, John A. to Susann E. J. Hudson 12-3-1868 Be
Maline, Geo. to Betsy Bowling 1-20-1872 Hy
Mallard, Jefferson V.? to Didama Jackson 2-10-1841 F
Mallory, Alonzo C. to Eliza W. James 4-23-1851 (4-24-1851) Sh
Mallory, E. W. to Maria W. Penn 12-2-1858 Sh
Mallory, Eugene W. to Martha E. English 10-2-1851 Sh
Mallory, James B. to Eliza Branch 10-27-1830 Ma
Mallory, Wm. M. to Victoria Laney 10-26-1870 (10-28-1870) Ma
Maloan, Andrew to Margaret E. Gleeson 12-27-1846 We
Maloan, R. W. to Mary Robertson 10-28-1857 We
Malona, John to Harriet Brunston 2-19-1845 Sh
Malone, A. W. to Elizabeth (Mrs.) Coten 12-20-1866 Hy
Malone, Alex to Phebe Ann Brodway 10-13-1865 T
Malone, Anderson to Clara Bond 8-5-1873 Hy
Malone, Andrew to Roxannah Kernodle 8-18-1862 Mn
Malone, B. to Emily Ellison 9-16-1847 (no return) F
Malone, Benjamin to Nancy Dill 4-25-1845 Hr
Malone, C. to Fannie Twisdale 1-3-1870 T
Malone, Calvin to Nancy A. Lewis 1-8-1839 F
Malone, Chancy to Sarah P. Rudd 6-10-1852 Hn
Malone, Daniel to Melisa Plunk 8-5-1862 Mn
Malone, David to R. A. Pinson 11-21-1850 Cr
Malone, Elisha G. to Margaret White 6-24-1858 (6-27-1858) O
Malone, Gabriel to Lucinda Hays 1-11-1839 (1-6?-1839) Hr
Malone, George J. to Martha J. Tucker 10-8-1859 (no return) Hn
Malone, George to Louisa Cheek 10-18-1859 Sh
Malone, Gilbert D. T. to Louisa C. Guy 10-17-1848 (10-25-1848) Hr
Malone, Harrison to Martha Smith 11-8-1872 T
Malone, Harrison to Narcissa Plunk 5-7-1861 Mn
Malone, Harry to Gracia A. Martin 1-9-1867 G
Malone, Henry to Nancy Morris 4-15-1838 Cr
Malone, Isaac M. to Nancy A. Wright 8-31-1858 Cr
Malone, J. H. to Sarah Jane McClain 8-30-1865 Hn
Malone, James N. to Louisa C. Lodgins 4-28-1865 (4-29-1865) Cr
Malone, Jefferson to Bell (Mrs.) Lane ?-?-1863 (with Aug 1863) Cr
Malone, Jefferson to R. J. Lewis 5-26-1851 Hn
Malone, John M. to Virginia Morton 12-10-1867 Hy
Malone, John to Maria Burke 2-6-1855 Sh
Malone, Jordan to Elizabeth Green 1-16-1878 (1-28-1878) L
Malone, Jordan to Mollie Taylor 3-11-1880 (no return) L
Malone, L. H. to E. C. Turner 10-4-1867 (10-6-1867) Cr
Malone, L. H. to Mary Jones 7-29-1851 F
Malone, Leonard to Ann Pullam 8-18-1849 (9-1-1849) Hr
Malone, Louis to Maria Middlebrooks 12-27-1867 (12-28-1867) F B
Malone, N. M. to Emaline Lewis 1-4-1857 Cr
Malone, Polk to Maggie Patton 11-7-1872 (no return) Hy
Malone, R. H. to Mary C. Cassett? 10-2-1849 (10-3-1849) F
Malone, Samuel to Elizabeth Philips 12-12-1835 (12-17-1835) G
Malone, Taylor to Mary Thompson 2-28-1870 (3-2-1870) F
Malone, Tho. to Piny E. Ozier 12-16-1846 (12-17-1846) F
Malone, Thomas to Mary Rogers 5-2-1858 Sh
Malone, Van to Susan Monroe 1-22-1865 Hn
Malone, Vinson to Emily Ellis ?-?-1850 Cr
Malone, W. B. to Ella K. Burlen 1-6-1869 Hy
Malone, W. C. to E. M. Gardner 7-20-1850 (8-8-1850) F
Malone, W. P. to Mary A. Jacobs 5-21-1870 (5-22-1870) T

Malone, William G. to Sarah V. Battle 2-26-1836 Sh
Malone, William to Mary C. Riggs 12-8-1862 F
Malone, Wm. H. to M. F. Cummings 7-3-1861 (7-4-1861) Sh
Maloney, Edward to Bridget Fannigan 1-18-1862 (1-19-1862) Sh
Maloney, Elbert S. to Mary Isabella Wylie 9-24-1855 (10-8-1855) O
Maloney, James C. to Clory Ann Willis 8-12-1852 Sh
Maloney, Patrick to Ann McMahan 9-9-1848 Sh
Maloney, Patrick to Mary Forks 6-23-1866 Hy
Maloney, Peter to Ellen Noland 9-12-1859 Sh
Maloney, T. B. to F. T. Farris 7-21-1859 O
Malorkney, John to Mary Mahan 5-22-1853 Sh
Malow, Joseph to Louisa Strayhorn 7-25-1854 Sh
Malton, Joseph to Eliza Morten 12-23-1862 (12-24-1862) Sh
Maly, Thos. to Mary Farrell 10-3-1864 (10-4-1864) Sh
Mamier?, Tom to Felicia Day 5-19-1866 (8-11-1866) F B
Man, Wm. to Emaline Liloe? 10-10-1857 Cr
Manahan, Patrick to Mary Lacy 3-31-1857 Sh
Manard, James O. to Louisa Harris 2-1-1847 Cr
Manard, John to Mary Ann Huston 3-8-1846 Be
Manard, Micajah to Nelly Shous? 1-30-1853 Hn
Manard, Robert S. to Mary W. J. Hill 12-7-1854 Hn
Manasco, Charles to Jane Macafee 1-10-1866 T
Manasco, J. R. to Mary Payne 9-24-1861 (9-27-1861) T
Manasco, James to Emily Webb 6-21-1859 (6-23-1859) T
Manasco, James to Mary M. Kitchen 6-30-1860 (7-7-1860) T
Manasco, Jeremiah to Mary Jane Flanakin 7-6-1857 T
Manasco, Jerry to Eugenie P. Moore 2-27-1871 (3-1-1871) T
Manasco, Joel R. to Mary M. Boothe 12-20-1859 (12-21-1859) T
Manasco, John to Senith Elizabeth Maston 4-22-1874 (4-23-1874) T
Manasco, Pleasto to Lucy C. Kitchen 6-30-1860 (7-5-1860) T
Manasco, Plesant to Josephine Crofford 6-19-1867 (6-18?-1867) T
Manasco, Plesant to S. A. Crofford 5-6-1870 (5-8-1870) T
Manasker, Plesant to V. T. Slass 11-2-1868 (11-4-1868) T
Manasker, George Washington to Mary Jane Walker 12-19-1848 (12-7?-1848) T
Mancenier, Martin to Honone Geary 6-21-1851 (6-22-1851) Sh
Mandenall, Elisha to Mary A. Donaldson 1-2-1844 G
Maneer (Manees), James to Julia T. Shore 4-8-1850 Sh
Manees, Z. H. to Minerva L. Brown 6-2-1853 Sh
Maner, Stephen B. to Cynthia A. Patrick 1-1-1858 (1-10-1858) G
Maness, F. P. to Susanah Nicholdson 6-8-1872 (6-9-1872) L
Maness, H. A. to M. J. Jennings 6-24-1874 L
Maness, J. P. to Lucy J. Clayton 9-3-1862 Mn
Maness, J.M. to M. A. Perry 7-9-1873 L
Maney, Alexander to Auze Lewis 12-21-1871 Hy
Mangan, Timothy to Mary Leonard 2-19-1849 Sh
Mange, Clark to Sela Harris 11-20-1869 (12-6-1869) L
Mangrum, A. D. to Nancy Church 9-12-1862 G
Mangrum, James H. to Mahaley McCoy 4-6-1858 (4-8-1858) G
Mangrum, James J. to Sarah E. Meter 8-19-1867 (8-20-1867) Dy
Mangrum, Robert to Amanday Rowly 11-16-1867 (no return) Dy
Mangrum, W. H. to Mattie J. Gibson 1-16-1866 Dy
Mangrum, W. J. to Mollie L. Bentley 12-9-1873 (12-10-1873) L
Mangrum, W. P. to Amanda E. Aldridge 1-27-1857 (1-29-1857) Hr
Mangrum, Wiley P. to Nancy Glisson 3-9-1857 (3-10-1857) O
Mangum, Owen to Hannah Conner 2-27-1871 (2-28-1871) F B
Mangum, Willey (Wiley) to Elizabeth Hall 1-12-1830 Sh
Manifee, Mansfield to Ann Ross 9-1-1869 (no return) F B
Maning, Joseph to Elizabeth Keller 2-12-1871 Hy
Maning, W. P. to S. P. Cole 8-4-1842 Be
Manley, David S. to Frances McMahan 1-15-1862 (1-16-1862) Sh
Manley, F. C. to E. A. Buford 12-22-1869 F
Manley, Green R. to Nancy S. Crafford 12-23-1841 G
Manley, Green to Luentia Alexander 1-2-1856 (no return) Hn
Manley, J. B. to Jacksey B. T. Dunn 11-14-1850 Hn
Manley, John F. to Mary Castelaw 4-1-1865 (no return) L
Manley, John F. to Mollie Isham 11-14-1874 (11-15-1874) L
Manley, John to Catherine Harber 9-7-1853 (9-8-1853) G
Manley, John to Mary Moran 9-5-1863 Hy
Manley, Joseph B. to Susan F. Randle 6-23-1847 (no return) Hn
Manley, Michael to Margaret Graham 10-25-1856 (10-26-1856) Sh
Manley, N. A. to Sarah P. Edwards 12-10-1861 Hn
Manley, Patrick to Mary Leiden 2-26-1856 Sh
Manley, R. to Catharine Downey 12-27-183? (3-9-1840) F
Manley, Richard to Margaret G. Durham 9-6-1854 (no return) F
Manley, Richd. M. to Ann E. Davis 8-5-1846 F
Manley, Theof J. to Mary Manley 5-4-1847 F
Manley, William B. to Eliza J. Johnson 10-21-1850 Ma
Manley, William C. to Mary Caton 10-29-1857 Hn
Manley, William C. to Rachel Ann Moody 1-21-1855 Hn
Manley, William W. to Lydia A. Johnson 6-15-1860 (6-17-1860) Ma
Manley, William to Missourie Crane 9-11-1877 (9-12-1877) L
Manley?, Thomas A. to Parmelia R. Hagler 12-1-1859 Hn
Manly, Grundy to Jane Dinwiddie 2-21-1866 Hn
Manly, Hamlin S. to Susan E. Elam 12-20-1843 (no return) We
Manly, I. N. to E. Randle 10-18-1838 (no return) Hn
Manly, John to Matilda Diggs 1-20-1842 Hn

Manly, Miles to Emily McCalister 10-19-1867 (10-20-1867) Dy
Manly, Peter H. to Martha A. E. Gray 9-12-1860 Hn
Manly, T. J. to Mary E. (Mrs.) Jackson 2-23-1867 F
Manly, William to Milly Ann Morphis 11-6-1841 (11-14-1841) Ma
Mann, Adifears to Sarah Peate 1-16-1869 Hy
Mann, Allen to Becca Tucker 10-28-1874 Hy
Mann, Amos to Dilcy Purkins 1-14-1872 Hy
Mann, Andrew J. to Rachel Johnson 1-31-1870 (no return) Hy
Mann, Asa O. to Sue T. Read 5-7-1878 Hy
Mann, Austin to Ann (Mrs.) Tanner 10-22-1867 L
Mann, Austin to Ann Tanner 10-19-1867 (no return) Hy
Mann, Austin to Jennie Williams 2-4-1880 (2-5-1880) L
Mann, B. A. to Jane Huston 11-10-1866 (no return) Hy
Mann, Buck to Ann Whitelaw 12-28-1865 (no return) Hy
Mann, Buck to Nancy Coachman 1-25-1879 L B
Mann, Buck to Rachal Bayns 1-5-1878 Hy
Mann, Buck to Rose Holloway 1-23-1873 Hy
Mann, C. G. to Julie E. Mann 5-19-1860 (5-20-1860) Cr
Mann, Charles to Lizzie Barbee 1-2-1878 Hy
Mann, Coleman to Virginia Taylor 3-25-1877 Hy
Mann, Cornelius to Toerzer Henly 10-12-1876 Hy
Mann, Crocket to Lucy Walker 1-31-1872 Hy
Mann, Daniel W. to Sarah A. L. Carter 11-3-1874 (11-4-1874) L
Mann, Daniel to Lavenia Bailey 10-23-1875 (no return) Hy
Mann, Dave to Tidy Rayner 1-30-1869 Hy
Mann, David to Elizabeth Tharpe 12-23-1856 Hy
Mann, David to Lizzie Taylor 2-2-1872 (no return) Hy
Mann, Ed to Sarah Johnson 12-26-1868 Hy
Mann, Frank to Barbie Owen 3-21-1868 (no return) Hy
Mann, George to Ann Johnson 4-2-1870 Hy
Mann, George to Elizabeth Angus 1-4-1869 (1-10-1869) T
Mann, George to Emmer Jackson 10-28-1877 Hy
Mann, Hiram to Henrietta Whitaker 7-10-1869 (no return) Hy
Mann, Hiram to Mollie L. Rice 11-2-1857 (11-4-1857) L
Mann, J. J. to E. H. Neal 11-3-1858 (11-9-1858) Sh
Mann, J. W. to N. C. Edmerson 3-23-1872 (3-24-1872) Cr
Mann, Jack to Mariah Nowell 11-25-1866 Hy
Mann, James A. to Fannie W. Hall 1-2-1869 (1-6-1869) F
Mann, James H. to Georgianna Taylor 10-11-1865 Hy
Mann, James to Arrinda Hopgood 12-7-1876 Hy
Mann, James to Rachel Smith 6-21-1867 G B
Mann, Joel to Maria J. Tuggle 4-19-1860 (no return) Hy
Mann, John G. to Harriet Ann Long 6-27-1860 (6-28-1860) Ma
Mann, John J. to Mary A. Core 2-4-1863 (no return) Hy
Mann, John T. to Martha A. Clark 12-1-1854 Hn
Mann, John to Rebecca Seay 2-6-1851 Sh
Mann, John to Sarah Reed 12-26-1865 (no return) Hy
Mann, Johnathan to Mary Langlie 3-28-1872 (no return) Cr
Mann, Jonas to Bell Buck 10-29-1875 (no return) Hy
Mann, Jos. T. to Sarah E. Tomlin 4-22-1850 Ma
Mann, Joseph B. to Nancy E. Norman 9-28-1852 L
Mann, Matt to Harriet Pender 9-13-1866 Hy
Mann, Mug to Jane Lenier 1-8-1868 Hy
Mann, Omma to Mary Shaw 2-26-1868 (no return) Hy
Mann, P. H. to Annie L. Estes 12-6-1859 (no return) Hy
Mann, Patee to Louisa Mann 10-1-1871 Hy
Mann, Pleasant to Judy Bradford 11-10-1866 (no return) Hy
Mann, R. T. to Delila Jane Womble 10-18-1875 (no return) Hy
Mann, R. V. to Roberta Taylor 12-20-1865 Hy
Mann, Reuben to Judy Belle Edwards 12-23-1875 (no return) Hy
Mann, Reuben to Lizzie Batcheler 12-25-1874 Hy
Mann, Richard to Bettie Grimm 2-8-1876 (no return) Dy
Mann, Richard to Frances Barbee 12-21-1870 Hy
Mann, Richard to H. A. Taylor 12-10-1867 Hy
Mann, Robert to Emma A. Tanner 11-1-1871 Hy
Mann, Robert to Susan J. Connell 9-15-1871 (9-20-1871) Cr
Mann, Robert to Susan Walker 7-29-1844 (7-31-1844) Ma
Mann, Robt. to Melissa Jane Farmer 2-28-1868 G B
Mann, S. D. to Rosanna J. Kemp 10-30-1860 Hy
Mann, Squire to Sallie Nelson 7-14-1867 Hy
Mann, Thad to Alice Bradford 12-11-1873 Hy
Mann, Thos. J. to Dicey H. Mann 8-7-1862 Cr
Mann, Wallace to Lucy Shaw 1-28-1874 Hy
Mann, William A. to Mary F. Nelson 8-10-1870 (8-11-1870) Cr
Mann, William H. to Saphona Vinney 4-10-1851 (4-11-1851) G
Mann, William L. to Ann E. Carver 1-12-1870 Cr
Mann, William to Caroline (mrs.) Singleton 7-19-1873 (7-20-1873) Dy
Mann, William to Mollie Gwinn 4-9-1884 (no return) L
Mann, Willis to Sarah Taylor 9-10-1842 (9-11-1842) Ma
Mann, Wm. H. to B. A. Gallery 4-4-1863 Sh
Mann, Zeb to Caroline Baynes 1-15-1870 Hy
Manney, Jerry to Ida Murray 4-1-1881 (4-2-1881) L B
Mannien, John to Martha E. Young 8-30-1871 (no return) Hy
Manning, A. to Sarah Jane Williams 2-14-1852 (no return) F
Manning, D. M. to Harriett W. Haines 3-23-1859 Cr
Manning, David W. to Ellen J. Willingham 12-19-1860 We
Manning, E. K. to M. P. (Mrs.) Shipman 12-14-1872 (12-15-1872) Dy

Manning, J. M. to Emily M. Green 7-10-1871 (7-12-1871) Cr
Manning, Jacob C. to Henrietta T. Bowers 6-5-1848 Sh
Manning, James Monroe to Lucinda Sanderson 2-3-1871 (2-5-1871) L
Manning, James W. to Martha W. Smith no date (with Oct 1852) F
Manning, James to Elizabeth Moore 7-23-1850 Cr
Manning, John A. to Mary A. E. Baker 1-9-1862 Sh
Manning, John M. to Martha H. Vaughn 2-17-1844 (2-18-1844) O
Manning, John N. to Martha J. Stalls? 1-3-1851 Hn
Manning, John R. to Mary S. Hansil 12-23-1851 (no return) F
Manning, John to Elizabeth Jacobs 7-20-1843 Hn
Manning, Kenneth to Mary B. Knox 2-13-1856 We
Manning, Michael to Bridget Dorgon 11-30-1860 Sh
Manning, Michael to Martha Phelps 5-20-1861 (no return) Hn
Manning, Michael to Mary A. Waddell 4-15-1858 Hn
Manning, Ned to Josephine Perry 7-11-1865 (7-17-1865) Dy
Manning, Patrick to Margaret Givins 12-23-1854 (12-26-1854) Sh
Manning, Patrick to Mary Hogan 8-18-1855 Sh
Manning, R. T. to R. B. Pearson 10-28-1868 Hy
Manning, Thomas B. to Mattie E. McLemore 4-13-1870 (4-24-1870) Cr
Manning, Wiley D. to Mary J. Reynolds 2-1-1862 (2-2-1862) L
Manning, Wiley D. to Nancy Manning 2-14-1859 L
Manning, Wilie D. to Martha Jennings 6-20-1859 (6-29-1859) L
Manning, Willis W. to Elizas J. Ross 11-1-1860 We
Manning, Wm. A. to Delia Wilson 2-26-1856 Sh
Manning, Wm. T. to Mary E. Sanders 3-19-1856 Sh
Mannix, Patrick to Bridget Ryan 11-7-1858 Sh
Mannon, J. H. to C. Clement 6-19-1856
Mannon, Joseph L. to Lydia J. Alsup 5-2-1862 Be
Mannon, Matthew to Jane Clement 12-2-1860 Be
Manns, S. B. to Rhody Lowery 10-5-1865 G
Manny?, Robt. to Elizabeth Massey 3-27-1859 Cr
Manor, John to M. J. Lamb 12-26-1866 G
Manor, William to Malisa Weaks 12-12-1868 (12-17-1868) L
Manscoe, Wm. C. to Alice M. Barnett 7-23-1853 (7-24-1853) Sh
Mansfield, Grasty to Abby Andrews 9-19-1832 (9-25-1832) O
Mansfield, Grasty to Polly Stoker 2-7-1839 O
Mansfield, James to Fanny Hooth 9-8-1864 Hn
Mansfield, John to Elizabeth Wade 5-5-1845 Hn
Mansfield, Wm. to Sarah E. Osteen 10-14-1858 We
Manson, Robert P. to Sarah Gaddis 12-26-1877 Hy
Manual, George to Margaret Wood 10-18-1872 (10-19-1872) T
Manual, Mark to Mary A. McCraw 11-12-1865 Mn
Manual, Robert T. to Nancy A. Simmons 9-23-1860 We
Manuel, Alexander to Martha J. Rogers 4-21-1864 (4-23-1864) Cr
Manuel, Benjamin E. to Julia Marks 11-8-1846 Hn
Manuel, H. K. to Victoria Owen 3-15-1869 (3-16-1869) Cr
Manuel, Rob. T. to Frances Duberry 12-6-1845 (12-7-1845) F
Manuell, John C. to Polly Townsend 12-18-1827 Hr
Manus (Meincus), Wm. H. to Frances Brown 7-18-1843 Sh
Maphey, Stephen to Eliza Grant 6-6-1838 Ma
Maples, Josiah to Mary A. Marshall 10-1-1853 (no return) F
Mar, Joseph to Mary Kelly 12-16-1858 Sh
Marberry, John to Ann E. Green 6-6-1838 Hn
Marberry, John to Caroline A. Biles 11-11-1841 Hn
Marberry, John to Frances Dalton 7-27-1850 Hn
Marberry, John to Mahuldah Cook 12-2-1855 Be
Marberry, Pleasant M. to Oney McClure 5-25-1856 Hn
Marberry, Pleasant to Maria Caldwell 11-5-1840 Hn
Marberry, William to Adeline Boothe 8-24-1856 (no return) Hn
Marberry, William to Susan M. Eson 3-16-1842 O
Marbery, P. H. to M. E. Harper 12-26-1867 O
Marbry, Benjamin to Mary Pierce 1-11-1868 Be
Marbry, Isaac F. to L. J. Rowe 9-5-1867 Be
Marbry, John to Susan Burkley 10-9-1850 Be
Marbury, B. F. to Margaret Yelvington 9-20-1868 Hy
Marbury, P. H. to Martha B. Gregory 9-20-1868 Hy
Marbury, Robert to Sarah C. White 12-6-1866 Hy
Marbury, W. C. to Mary S. Barnett 5-11-1872 T
Marcela, Gerard to Victoria Tribbe 1-6-1863 Sh
March, Daniel O. to Emeline Hopper 4-6-1852 Ma
March, Obediah to Elizabeth Beavers 10-29-1850 (10-30-1850) Hr
March, William D. to Ann E. Nance 6-11-1862 G
Marchant, J. W. to M. J. Rawles 2-9-1876 Dy
Marchant, Jerry to Lizzie Fowlkes 7-6-1867 Dy
Marchbanks, A. to M. C. Utley 12-21-1842 Be
Marchbanks, Giles to Mary Lewis 10-11-1831 G
Marchbanks, John L. to Jane Stewart 4-8-1852 Be
Marchbanks, John to Cathrine Boswell 1-27-1859 Cr
Marchbanks, T. E. to Parile Prock 3-1-1863 Be
Marchbanks, Thomas E. to Martha C. Cole 7-2-1858 Be
Marchbanks, Thomas to Elizabeth L. D. Nunnery 1-5-1864 Be
Marchbanks, Thomas to Jane Fowler no date (with 1861) Be
Marchbanks, Thos. to Jane Fowler 12-5-1860 Be
Marchbanks, William R. to Washington Ann Yates 10-3-1854 Be
Marchbanks, Wm. to Edy Ann Stewart 1-30-1853 Be
Marckmolter, M. to Mary E. Clay 3-14-1859 Sh
Marcom, J. G. to _____ _____ 12-28-1859 Hy

Marcum, F. to Nancy J. Glasscock 9-6-1868 G
Marcum, Hiram to Cassie E. O___s 12-25-1861 G
Marcum, J. to Margaret L. Brown 1-12-1868 G
Marcum, Jas. to Elizabeth F. Sherell 3-30-1858 G
Marcum, Jefferson to Lucretia A. E. Brent 7-1-1858 G
Marcum, Jefferson to Surmanthilus E. Ward 9-21-1850 (9-22-1850) G
Marcum, John to Agnes Douglass 7-29-1851 Sh
Marcum, John to Catherine S. Mosely 11-17-1840 Sh
Marcum, Mathew to Mary S. Huckaby 12-28-1859 G
Marcum, Wiley J. to Mary S. Christie 10-22-1867 Dy
Marcus, James T. to Susanah Mayo 10-10-1850 (not endorsed) We
Marcus, James to C. P. Mayo 11-13-1860 We
Marcus, John to Elizabeth Mayo 11-26-1845 We
Marcus, Richard to Frances Priest 12-13-1855 We
Margan, Asa to Ellen Smith 10-28-1865 T
Margrave, J. C. to Julia A. Little 1-7-1869 Hy
Margraves, J. D. to Lotta Bridger 11-2-1869 Hy
Mariner, Edward Joseph to Mary Frances Lamb 3-8-1850 (3-11-1850) T
Marion, Francis N. to E. V. Bardon 12-9-1864 Sh
Maris, William to Jane L. McGowan 12-1-1841 (12-2-1841) Hr
Mark, Jesse to Kate (Mrs.) Williams 6-25-1870 (6-26-1870) Ma
Markey, John to Ann O'Haig 3-29-1856 Sh
Markham, Henry to Fanny Russell 2-21-1864 Hn
Markham, J. M. to Elizabeth F. Clayton 6-5-1860 Be
Markham, James H. to Matilda R. Bentley 9-19-1847 Sh
Markham, Jesse E. to Mary Anne Grainger 11-2-1854 Hn
Markham, Samuel R. to Susan R. Parker 5-1-1867 Hy
Markham, Squire to Rebecca Snider 4-5-1840 Hn
Markham, Sydney to Columbia A. Bell 1-6-1851 (1-8-1851) Sh
Markham, Thomas W. to Indianna P. Booker 5-28-1846 T
Markham, Thos. to Louisa Claiburne 2-1-1866 (2-7-1866) T
Markham, W. D. to M. J. Warrick 8-14-1848 Be
Markham, W. J. L. to Sarah McClure 11-12-1863 Hn
Markham, Wilie to Mary McCoy 11-5-1849 (11-8-1849) G
Markham, William to Lucinda Burress 1-26-1840 Hn
Markham?, J.? W.? to Sophia? Moss? 11-26-1862 T
Marks, Ezell to H. M. Shelton 1-16-1849 Hn
Marks, James A. to Margarett C. Russell 6-19-1845 Ma
Marks, M. D. to Betty Blumenthal 7-22-1856 Sh
Marks, Soloman to Dora Rothgarber 4-20-1860 Sh
Marksman, Dormick to Mary Quinn 5-16-1860 (5-17-1860) Sh
Markum, J. H. to Mary Bay 7-14-1862 (7-15-1862) Sh
Marlar, Jesse to Cynthia Smith 8-15-1846 (no return) F
Marlar, W. T. to Prudence A. Davis 12-7-1848 Sh
Marler, James to Mary Casey 8-1-1838 Hr
Marler, John C. to Eliza S.? Thrift 1-1-1841 (1-5-1841) F
Marler, Silas to Margaret Kerr 7-4-1842 Hr
Marler, Simpson L. to Caroline Yeates 3-4-1841 F
Marler, Stephen to Elizabeth Hooper 4-6-1839 Hr
Marler, Thomas J. to Sarah Devenport 8-12-1838 F
Marley, Ben to Beate Barnett 5-16-1877 (no return) L
Marley, Francis to Henrietta Thornton 11-27-1860 (no return) L
Marley, Isaac to Louiza Harris 12-19-1868 (no return) L
Marley, Jerry to Harriet Beard 2-7-1878 (2-28-1878) L
Marley, Joseph to Mary E. Edwards 9-20-1853 (9-22-1853) Ma
Marley, Josiah C. to Narcissa H. Clay 10-17-1870 L
Marley, Young F. to Lizzie C. Verser 5-19-1857 (5-20-1857) Ma
Marlow, James to Martha Hammell 11-12-1857 (11-13-1857) O
Marlow, Reuben S. to Ann Sturdevant 1-30-1870 G
Marlow, Thomas to Elizabeth Pollock 8-14-1852 (8-19-1852) O
Marlow, W. H. to Adalaide McCulloch 11-20-1877 Dy
Marlow, William E. to Judith Davis 6-26-1833 Sh
Marlow, William H. to Mahulda Cozart 12-25-1852 (12-26-1852) Ma
Marlow, William to Josephine Mitchell 9-2-1853 (9-6-1853) O
Maro (Mary), Rady to Annie Dougherty 5-29-1863 Sh
Maroney, James T. to Hannah Halton 8-24-1854 Ma
Maroney, Middleton to Sarah C. Johnson 11-25-1858 Sh
Maroney, Patrick to Eliza Tangnay 10-22-1859 (10-23-1859) Sh
Maroney, Timothy to Catharine Cullen 6-9-1860 (6-10-1860) Sh
Marony, W. H. to M. E. Tomlinson 11-16-1876 (11-20-1876) O
Marr, Albert to Mary Lilly 7-12-1882 L
Marr, G. W. L. to Lucinda P. Brown 8-5-1841 (8-8-1841) O
Marr, Hugh to P. Ellis 6-29-1848 Hn
Marr, John W. to Permelia Mathis 5-4-1858 G
Marr, John to Nancy R. Mills (Miles) 7-18-1846 O
Marr, Richard P. to Sophia B. Warner 5-13-1846 We
Marr, Robert A. to Mary F. Lavallett 4-6-1850 Sh
Marr, Robert to Julia Green 5-6-1870 (no return) Hy
Marr, Sam to Caroline Estes 10-23-1869 Hy
Marr, William D. to Susan Jane Dick 6-13-1857 Hn
Marrer, Timothy to Anora Garren 12-3-1853 Sh
Marriot, Wm. H. to Lucy Spencer 12-12-1860 Sh
Marrow, Gourius to Lucy Read 3-12-1871 Hy
Marrs, John W. to Elizabeth Welch 12-17-1842 (12-18-1842) Hr
Marrs, Robert J. to R. E. Hannis? 3-9-1848 Hr
Marrs, William to Jane Fodge 10-23-1858 Hn
Marrs, Wm. to Martha Vaughn 5-9-1846 (5-10-1846) Hr

Marsden, James to Mary V. Williams 5-23-1842 (5-24-1842) F
Marsh, Bird to Harriet Dunn 12-28-1852 (no return) F
Marsh, Charles to Catharine McKnight 12-22-1843 Sh
Marsh, David to Kitty Ing 12-14-1861 (12-15-1861) Sh
Marsh, Henry to Hannah Cain 9-17-1828 (9-18-1828) Hr
Marsh, Hiram to Jane Martin 2-11-1839 (2-14-1839) Hr
Marsh, James M. to Sarah Jane Whitford 12-20-1859 Hr
Marsh, James S. to Jane Murphy 1-12-1846 (1-25-1846) Hr
Marsh, James W. to Mary C. Richardson 7-30-1847 (8-1-1847) Ma
Marsh, John M. to Harriott Isom 6-27-1839 Ma
Marsh, Joshua B. to Sarah Butler 4-3-1848 Ma
Marsh, Munford S. to Caroline Jones 11-13-1829 (11-17-1829) Hr
Marsh, P. G. to Ellen Piercy 7-17-1861 (7-18-1861) Sh
Marsh, R. A. to Elizabeth Norment 2-5-1844 (2-6-1844) Hr
Marsh, Saml. J. to Martha V. Acock 12-22-1874 (12-23-1874) T
Marsh, Saml. J. to Permelia Long 6-20-1859 (6-21-1859) T
Marsh, Silas M. W. to Elizabeth J. Willoughby 11-8-1842 Hr
Marsh, Thomas P. to Mary A. V. Toone 12-26-1842 (12-29-1842) Ma
Marsh, William C. to Sarah J. Bass 1-19-1860 (6?-19-1860) T
Marsh, Wm. Carroll to Mary Valentia Davidson 12-21-1853 (12-22-1853) T
Marshal, Peter to Frances Blackwell 1-13-1872 (1-21-1872) L
Marshall, A. to Julia Ward (Word?) 1-2-1866 G
Marshall, Archibald to Ellen Moore 10-13-1854 (11-1-1854) T
Marshall, Augustus to Charity H. Joiner 7-4-1860 Hn
Marshall, C. K. to Emma Fitch 3-27-1856 Sh
Marshall, Charles to Martha Ann Prince 2-10-1857 Hn
Marshall, Clarence to Lucinda Knox 12-20-1870 (12-22-1870) F B
Marshall, D. B. to M. M. McCaw 1-9-1868 O
Marshall, D.? to Susan A. Pearman 1-5-1863 (1-7-1863) Cr
Marshall, Daniel G. to Rebecca C. Burford 4-13-1839 (4-19-1839) O
Marshall, E. (C?) to H. A. McCluer 4-6-1864 (4-7-1864) Sh
Marshall, J. J. to Anna Hopton 9-12-1859 Hr
Marshall, James A. to Martha Ann Mariah Marshall 5-5-1836 (5-17-1836) O
Marshall, James C. to Margaret Futhey 3-22-1852 Sh
Marshall, James H. to Sarah J. Avant 11-6-1854 (11-15-1854) Hr
Marshall, James M. to Elizabeth N. Blanchett 5-8-1859 Hn
Marshall, Jas. A. to Nancy A. Wright 1-9-1860 (1-10-1860) O
Marshall, Jefferson to Elizabeth Ware 9-3-1844 Sh
Marshall, John A. to Mary M. Waldran 5-6-1844 Sh
Marshall, John Q. to Nancy McBride 12-1-1852 G
Marshall, John T. Z. to L. R. McClannohan 11-26-1867 (11-28-1867) T
Marshall, Joseph to Bettie Smith 10-12-1867 G
Marshall, L. P. to T. C. Culbreth 9-28-1870 T
Marshall, Liz to Tempy Knox 4-6-1871 (4-7-1871) F B
Marshall, M. D. to Susan A. Pearman 1-5-1863 (no return) Cr
Marshall, M. M. to Mary L. Stevens 2-24-1879 Dy
Marshall, Marcus L. to Judah Ann Boyles 9-15-1845 Sh
Marshall, Mathias (Metellus) to Ann Wareham 5-18-1863 (5-19-1863) Sh
Marshall, Moses S. to Mary E. Cloar 1-17-1853 (1-20-1853) O
Marshall, Newt to Emma Morgan 3-13-1871 (4-5-1871) F B
Marshall, Richard H. to Melissa Whitaker 11-11-1856 (11-12-1856) O
Marshall, T. H. to A. R. (Mrs.) Seat 11-2-1867 (not executed) G
Marshall, T. H. to Martha Ann Pate 2-23-1869 G
Marshall, T. J. to M. F. Bonner 9-24-1874 Hy
Marshall, William C. to Bettie Anderson 5-3-1870 Ma
Marshall, William J. to Sarah Thompson 5-31-1847 (4?-?-1847) T
Marshall, Wm. N. to S. M. R. Harris 12-11-1854 Cr
Marshall, Wm. to Carnea Culbeath? 11-15-1865 (11-16-1865) T
Marshall, Wm. to Eliza J. Sampson 8-6-1844 Cr
Marshall, Wm. to Nancy Carver? 12-24-1850 Cr
Marshall, jr., Robert to Martha Wilkes 11-12-1857 Sh
Marshner, Berthold (Capt.) to Mary Ann Keller 12-4-1862 Sh
Martain, Albert to Mary Janice Dickerson 7-12-1871 (7-21?-1872?) T
Martain, Allen to Ellen Owen 2-25-1869 T
Martain, Nathan to Mariah Jones 1-25-1873 (1-28-1873) T
Marteen, J. C. to Martha Ann Wren 8-22-1865 Hn
Martin, A. T. to Nancy J. Moore 1-16-1845 Cr
Martin, A. W. M. to D. M. A. Spain 8-7-1871 Cr
Martin, Alfred to Fannie Rhodes 9-5-1868 (9-6-1868) F B
Martin, Allen to Angeline McMackens 12-25-1868 (12-27-1868) Cr
Martin, Allen to Matilda Elizabeth Owens 9-15-1868 T
Martin, Amos to Nancy E. Raoch 11-18-1839 Cr
Martin, Andy to Nancy E. Warmick 7-28?-1840 Hn
Martin, Arin to Larcind E. King 7-6-1857 Cr
Martin, Austin to Catherine Ramsay 12-18-1838 Hn
Martin, Benjamin P. to Elizabeth A. Hartsfield 4-5-1860 Hn
Martin, Beverly to Senid _____ 5-27-1864 Sh B
Martin, Buckham to Adeline Claiburn 1-6-1868 (1-11-1868) T
Martin, C. H. to Sarah Burns 7-22-1861 (7-24-1861) Cr
Martin, C. L. to Malissa P. Ryland 1-14-1865 L
Martin, C. R. to Nettie Windle 11-2-1863 Sh
Martin, C. W. to S. E. Penn 11-16-1865 G
Martin, Caswell H. to Elizabeth A. Jackson 1-29-1857 O
Martin, Charles L. to Malissa F. Pyland? 1-14-1865 L
Martin, Clark to Nancy W. Carson 2-13-1858 (2-15-1858) L
Martin, David T. to Elizabeth T. Ware 1-21-1850 Cr
Martin, David W. to Mary E. Coffman 12-20-1865 (no return) Hy

Martin, Drury to Elizabeth Dunnegan 11-4-1829 (11-?-1829) G
Martin, Edward J. to Dora Crisp 1-14-1869 (1-19-1869) Ma *
Martin, Edwin W. to T. A. Thompson 7-3-1857 Cr
Martin, Eli to Ellen L. Williams 4-27-1878 (no return) L
Martin, Elijah to Nancy E. Moore 2-25-1857 We
Martin, Emanuel Jackson to Victoria Robinson 9-10-1870 G
Martin, G. W. to S. M. Kimbrough 11-19-1870 (no return) Hy
Martin, Geo. W. to Eleanor C. Brown 12-11-1849 F
Martin, Geo. W. to Eliza G. Gunter 7-24-1850 Sh
Martin, George H. to Maria O. Thompson 2-3-1868 (no return) Hy
Martin, George H. to Martha E. Gowan 11-14-1868 (11-12?-1868) Cr
Martin, George M. to Mahaley J. Oliver 5-17-1848 Hn
Martin, George W. to Mary Neal 12-14-1867 (no return) Hy
Martin, George W. to Mattie L. Williams 5-23-1878 Hy
Martin, George to Caroline Hunter 12-29-1869 (no return) F B
Martin, Green to Mary Delashment 1-8-1850 (1-10-1850) O
Martin, Green to Mary Delshment 1-8-1850 (1-10-1850) O
Martin, H. B. to Ruth Talbot 3-25-1862 Sh
Martin, H. H. to Louisa Russell 2-1-1844 Cr
Martin, H. P. to E. J. Freeman 6-19-1869 (6-20-1869) Cr
Martin, Henry to Caroline Puckett 8-17-1866 Hn
Martin, Henry to Fannie Lewis 10-28-1877 Hy
Martin, Hudson to Mary Rieley 10-14-1864 (10-15-1864) Sh
Martin, I. B. to M. L. Weaver 12-17-1868 Hy
Martin, I. H. to Lucinda Hogan 12-27-1865 O
Martin, J. M. to Eliza J. Worrell 12-26-1863 (1-17-1864) F
Martin, J. M. to Frances W. Carroll 11-22-1873 (11-26-1873) Dy
Martin, J. W. to S. E. Hunter 1-20-1860 (1-1860) O
Martin, James C. to Susan Strickland 2-27-1869 (2-28-1869) F B
Martin, James D. to Maggie Liles 11-5-1856 Cr
Martin, James D. to Mary Baxter 12-20-1849 Cr
Martin, James E. to Nancy E. Ray 2-1-1877 Hy
Martin, James E. to Rebecca E. Wickham 6-3-1839 Sh
Martin, James F. to Martha M. Martin (11-21-1866) Cr
Martin, James G. D. to Matilda Prewett 11-8-1849 Cr
Martin, James H. to Violet L. Carr 9-11-1836 (9-13-1836) G
Martin, James M. to Margaret Worrell 9-16-1854 (9-21-1854) Hr
Martin, James M. to Mary S. Cox 8-14-1861 (8-15-1861) Cr
Martin, James N. to Morning P. Evans 9-23-1847 O
Martin, James Norfleet to Parthenia Ann Melisa Cox 7-8-1844 T
Martin, James P. to Mary E. Davis 3-20-1861 Hn
Martin, James to Elizabeth Grissom 9-9-1865 (9-10-1865) O
Martin, James to Margaret Keathley 1-8-1861 G
Martin, James to Mary Ann Verible 1-23-1828 Ma
Martin, James to Mary Jones 9-25-1869 (no return) F B
Martin, James to Rocinda C_____ 6-6-1850 O
Martin, James to Sirtha Brown 7-28-1858 Cr
Martin, Jas. D. to Lizze McMahon 8-3-1864 Sh
Martin, Jas. J. to Sallie E. Street 9-14-1864 Sh
Martin, Jas. M. to Sarah J. Sasser 2-16-1853 (no return) F
Martin, Jno. A. to Alice Armour 11-20-1855 (11-21-1855) Sh
Martin, Jno. H. to D. Stanley 9-12-1870 (no return) Hy
Martin, Jno. L. to Maggie Nichols 5-23-1866 Dy
Martin, John A. to Elizabeth Prince 1-28-1843 Cr
Martin, John D. to Charlotte Algea 12-27-1854 Cr
Martin, John D. to Sarah Dickens 1-10-1830 Ma
Martin, John G. to H. R. E. Taylor 5-23-1859 (5-25-1859) F
Martin, John G. to Nancy M. Jordon 3-29-1854 Cr
Martin, John H. to Emma A. Lee 1-27-1885 (1-29-1885) L
Martin, John J. to Eliza Jane Cox 4-1-1844 T
Martin, John J. to Susana E. Rowe 10-12-1858 Cr
Martin, John S. to Mary F. Black 3-8-1870 Ma
Martin, John T. to Eliza V. Williams 2-14-1870 (2-18-1870) L
Martin, John W. H. to Mary J. Province 10-16-1866 (no return) Hn
Martin, John W. to Kisey E.? Boren 2-26-1867 L
Martin, John W. to Lucy A. E. Puckett 12-4-1856 Hn
Martin, John W. to M. J. Hill 11-25-1873 (11-15-1873?) T
Martin, John W. to Mary Ann Briscoe 9-5-1864 Hn
Martin, John to Elizabeth Holt 11-19-1847 (11-21-1847) G
Martin, John to Elizabeth Hope 12-6-1842 Hn
Martin, John to Jane Box 1-15-1823 Sh
Martin, John to Lucretia Torbet 3-6-1842 Hn
Martin, John to Mary E. Robison 2-2-1869 G
Martin, L. L. to M. J. Lewis 8-5-1868 Cr
Martin, Lee to Flora Banks 10-15-1869 G B
Martin, Louis R. to Elizabeth A. Currie 5-6-1869 L
Martin, M. S. to Fannie R. Jordan 3-9-1869 (3-11-1869) Cr
Martin, Marion L. to Susan J. Harnes 7-11-1861 G
Martin, Michael B. to Malinda Cooper 10-20-1849 (10-21-1849) T
Martin, Michael B. to Susan Godbey 9-14-1846 (no return) F
Martin, Moses P. to Lucy Ann Palmor 11-22-1848 F
Martin, Newton H. to Matilda D. Pinson 2-20-1865 (2-25-1865) Cr
Martin, O. E. to K. F. McGregor 2-10-1874 T
Martin, Patrick to Bridget (Mrs.) Caldon 11-7-1864 (11-28-1864) Sh
Martin, Peter to Jane Haynie 10-20-1866 (10-21-1866) T
Martin, Poleman to Elizabeth Dillard 8-16-1836 (8-17-1836) Hr
Martin, Reuben to Tabitha J. Hardidge 9-7-1850 O

Martin, Reuben to Tabitha T. Hardridge 9-7-1850 (9-9-1850) O
Martin, Rhodham to Jane Hix 9-28-1840 (9-30-1840) G *
Martin, Richard M. S. to Medora Va. Posey 6-16-1870 L
Martin, Richard to Nancy Trentham 10-30-1872 (10-31-1872) T
Martin, Richd. to Neely Tibbs 12-28-1871 Hy
Martin, S. J. B. to Nancy A. Vincent 12-2-1846 (12-9-1846) O
Martin, Sam to Mariah Harmen 12-21-1870 (no return) Hy
Martin, Sam. to Caldonia Bradford 10-16-1872 Hy
Martin, Saml. B. to Ardis Meredith 2-17-1846 (no return) F
Martin, Saml. G. to Mary E. (Mrs.) Wallace 12-2-1861 (12-5-1861) Sh
Martin, Samuel F. to Nancy A. Shepherd 10-15-1840 Cr
Martin, Samuel J. B. to Elisa Levington 9-23-1838 O
Martin, Samuel to Lovely Ulcer (Alcey) 7-13-1843 Sh
Martin, Samuel to Margaret Oliver 4-20-1853 G
Martin, Sidney to E. F. Hill 8-24-1872 (8-25-1872) T
Martin, T. P. to E. A. Blankenship 12-30-1865 G
Martin, T. P. to Maggie Mitchell 10-9-1874 (10-10-1874) T
Martin, Thomas A. to Lou Ann Malone 12-4-1860 Hn
Martin, Thomas A. to Mary Ann Martin 10-26-1838 Cr
Martin, Thomas B. to Susanna Tompkins 3-29-1829 Sh
Martin, Thomas W. to Martha Henderson 9-3-1849 (9-4-1849) O
Martin, Thomas to Isabela Lafers 8-30-1854 We
Martin, Thos. to Sarah A. Greenwell 3-26-1860 G
Martin, Turner J. to Dycy? Anderson 12-31-1839 Hr
Martin, W. A. to M. F. Anderson 11-21-1874 Hy
Martin, W. A. to Mary C. Lamb 9-5-1859 (9-6-1859) T
Martin, W. C. to Susan V. Puckett 11-30-1863 (no return) Hn
Martin, W. James to Mary Funderburk 3-4-1868 (3-8-1868) Ma
Martin, W. T. to Eveline Olive 10-5-1865 Hy
Martin, Wiley to Sarah P. Horton 8-23-1838 Cr
Martin, William B. to M. A. Mathis 1-26-1864 Hn
Martin, William C. to Nannie J. Durham 1-15-1879 L
Martin, William H. to E. J. Hagler 1-16-1848 Hn
Martin, William H. to Martha Jane Edwards 4-18-1844 Hn
Martin, William H. to Rosa A. Edwards 1-10-1848 (1-11-1848) F
Martin, William M. to Lauretta E. Aden 11-6-1857 Hn
Martin, William S. to Lucretia A. Holland 8-23-1855 G
Martin, William to Angeline Turner 12-25-1815 We
Martin, William to C. Cummins 8-3-1865 Be
Martin, William to Frances E. Odum 3-21-1855 Hn
Martin, William to Harriet Johnson 12-5-1869 G B
Martin, William to May Kenady 10-17-1861 Hn
Martin, William to Rebecca Dunn 12-27-1873 (12-28-1873) T
Martin, William to Sarah Frances Ferrill 11-11-1871 (11-12-1871) L
Martin, William to Susan Ward 12-7-1847 Hn
Martin, Wm. H. H. to Martha J. Crockett 8-14-1862 O
Martin, Wm. P. to Mary A. Rogers 12-15-1860 (not endorsed) Cr
Martin, Wm. to Martha R. Breedmon 6-3-1868 T
Martin, Zebulon to Lucinda Shoemake 12-23-1850 (12-24-1850) L
Martin, _____ to JSane Dosson 5-26-1863 (5-28-1863) T
Martindale, Thomas J. to Martha Averett 7-8-1833 Hr
Martindale, William to Rispha Williams 5-19-1830 (5-21-1830) Hr
Marx, John to Catharine Young 11-21-1859 Hn
Maser, Wm. M. to Mary Ann Parker 9-27-1855 T
Masey, D. P. to Sarah E. McIntire 9-22-1861 Mn
Masey, John to Eliza Ann Lowry 10-16-1843 (no return) We
Masfield, W. H. to Nancy A. Baldridge 12-26-1860 We
Mashburn, Alfred to May Davis 4-19-1847 Hr
Mashburn, Hardy to Barbara Brown 1-9-1836 (1-10-1836) Hr
Mashburn, John A. to Sarah Ann Hunter 3-13-1854 (3-16-1854) Hr
Mashburn, Lewis to Vasty Mashburn 2-6-1839 (2-7-1839) Hr
Mashburn, Moses J. to Vashti Cox 4-7-1828 (4-10-1828) Hr
Mashburn, William C. to Mary Ann Webb 11-30-1849 (12-5-1849) Hr
Mask, Hamilton to Amandy P. Whitmon 12-13-1847 (12-14-1847) Hr
Mask, James M. to Elizabeth J. McKinnie 12-29-1851 (12-31-1852) Hr
Mask, Jesse to Adeline Hammond 5-16-1855 Ma
Masman?, John to Temperance Raines 4-28-1853 Hn
Mason, Abner W. to Catherine Piercy 1-9-1850 Hn
Mason, Abner W. to Elizabeth Crosby 3-7-1853 (3-8-1853) G
Mason, Asa to Elizabeth Caven? 1-16-1840 Hn
Mason, Chas. G. to Emma Young 1-22-1866 (1-24-1866) F
Mason, Cubie to Cora Green 8-4-1866 (no return) Hy
Mason, Daniel J. to Nancy King 9-12-1852 Cr
Mason, Daniel to Lucy Buttner? 11-20-1872 T
Mason, David B. to Martha Ann Hickman 10-6-1837 (10-10-1837) G
Mason, David G. to Cynthia Dockins 7-3-1849 Ma
Mason, F. G. to H. A. Atkins 12-13-1865 (12-14-1865) Dy
Mason, Frank to Eveline May 12-24-1868 (12-27-1868) F B
Mason, G. W. to Amanda Baker 11-17-1864 Mn
Mason, H. J. to Fannie Gannon 11-7-1871 (11-9-1871) Dy
Mason, Henry to Jane Edwards 3-12-1877 Dy
Mason, Isaac H. to Mary A. E. Cox 9-21-1846 (9-24-1846) Ma
Mason, J. W. to E. S. Phillips 10-16-1855 (10-17-1855) Sh
Mason, J. W. to Tiercy Lizzie Cox 1-19-1870 Hy
Mason, James A. to Ann E. Person 5-15-1871 (5-16-1871) Ma
Mason, James R. to Amanda Ashby 9-8-1858 Hn
Mason, James to Mary F. Funches 2-23-1875 (2-24-1875) L

Mason, John H. to M. P. Wilkins 12-25-1853 Sh
Mason, John J. to Lucinda Weaver 1-21-1833 Sh
Mason, John P. to Alsey Foster 12-26-1833 O
Mason, John to Adaline L. Britt 12-9-1843 (12-?-1843) T
Mason, John to Elizabeth Corburn? 12-1-1834 (12-2-1834) Hr
Mason, John to Mattie Ella Young 10-23-1880 (10-24-1880) L
Mason, Joseph D. to Eliza Bigelow 9-17-1844 (9-18-1844) Ma
Mason, Joseph J. T. to Anne Marie McCowel 11-23-1845 Sh
Mason, Levi W. to Louisa C. Baker 1-1-1858 (1-5-1858) Ma
Mason, M. W. to Mary Ketler 11-19-1853 (11-20-1853) Sh
Mason, Micajah to Anna Wasson 3-25-1841 Hn
Mason, Micajah to Martha N. Blue 9-22-1847 Sh
Mason, Nickolas to Martha Williams 12-24-1868 (12-26-1868) F B
Mason, Richard to Alice B. Greenlaw 9-24-1832 Sh
Mason, Richard to Behethland C. Jones 10-7-1847 Sh
Mason, Richard to Dyanna Paschall 3-12-1862 We
Mason, Robert E. to Josephine M. Neal 5-16-1854 (no return) F
Mason, Robert W. to Martha C. Herron 3-30-1859 (3-31-1859) Ma
Mason, Robt. to Frances Brewer 2-7-1868 (2-9-1868) F
Mason, Rufus M. to Eunica A. Doake 10-5-1850 Ma
Mason, Stephen to Easter Miller 2-21-1871 (2-26-1871) F B
Mason, Thomas C. to Elizabeth M. Williams 12-30-1839 Hn
Mason, Thomas to Victoria McGaughey 12-27-1876 (12-28-1876) Dy
Mason, W. H. to Elizabeth Stevens 2-25-1870 (2-27-1870) T
Mason, William B. to Aquilla Ann Brown 8-4-1841 Ma
Mason, William H. to Melvina McDearman 3-9-1869 (3-14-1869) L
Mason, Wm. H. to Laura Hudgens 6-19-1871 (6-22-1871) Ma
Mason, Wm. S. to M. E. Dixon 8-11-1873 (no return) Hy
Mason, Wm. to Rose Ann Harris 12-26-1867 (12-29-1867) F B
Mason, Wyatt to Rebecca (Mrs.) Farris 6-9-1866 G
Mason?, J. A. to Laura Harris 10-26-1871 (10-27-1871) T
Masons, John P. to Rebecca Goodman 5-19-1847 (5-20-1847) O
Massengale, Wm. B. to Louisa V. Harrison 1-4-1872 O
Massengill, A. to Thursey Dilion 12-3-1865 Be
Massengill, Sidney M. to Mary F. Martin 2-4-1864 Mn
Massey, A. J. to Lilly Ann Prince 2-3-1871 T
Massey, Allen N. to Nancy A. N. Shaw 1-23-1867 Ma
Massey, Andrew to Susan Boyett 12-3-1844 (12-4-1844) Ma
Massey, D. B. to Mary Darden 12-16-1850 (no return) F
Massey, Drury to Elender Haynes 10-21-1844 L
Massey, Duncan to Mary Olsabrooks 5-12-1838 (5-17-1838) G
Massey, F. A. to Lucy A. McCauley 3?-13-1850 (no return) F
Massey, H. C. to Martha J. Osborne 12-26-1853 Sh
Massey, Henry C. to Sarah Ann Thomson 11-14-1842 Sh
Massey, J. C. to Sarah P. Bledsoe 2-14-1854 Sh
Massey, J. R. to P. C. Pinson 2-25-1870 (2-28-1870) Cr
Massey, James C. to Jane Lockhart 3-7-1861 L
Massey, James M. to Mary T. Santiford 9-11-1838 Sh
Massey, James S. to M. A. Johnson 5-10-1860 Dy
Massey, James Y. to Mary King 2-13-1855 Cr
Massey, James to Virenna Shepherd 12-17-1868 (12-18-1868) Cr
Massey, Jeremiah to July Ann Kemp 7-5-1838 Sh
Massey, Jeremiah to Mary L. Hickerson 8-15-1849 Sh
Massey, Joel C. to Drucilla E. Sanderford 8-30-1849 Sh
Massey, Joel to Mary Allen 8-13-1840 Sh
Massey, John W. to M. E. Walker 3-1-1879 (3-5-1879) Dy
Massey, John to Judiath S. Rogers 4-22-1871 (4-26-1871) Cr
Massey, John to M. F. Burkham 3-25-1847 O
Massey, Joseph M. to Narcissa Wood 4-13-1869 G
Massey, Joseph to Eliza Borren 2-4-1830 Ma
Massey, Joseph to Nancy Herring 5-25-1843 Sh
Massey, L. H. to S. J. Brown 6-9-1848 O
Massey, Mansfield to Elender Bright 5-23-1850 Be
Massey, Richard to Rebecca Boyd 2-13-1841 Ma
Massey, Thomas J. to Sarah A. M. Gwyn 9-5-1866 (7?-11-1866) F
Massey, Thos. D. to H. F. Bateman 4-17-1858 Sh
Massey, W. H. H. to Mary E. Russel 9-26-1870 (9-28-1870) Cr
Massey, W. R. to F. M. King 12-31-1865 G
Massey, W. R. to Mollie J. Howard 11-18-1869 G
Massey, Wiley B. to Isabella R. Montgomery 2-10-1847 G
Massey, William Henry to Mary Elizabeth Adams 2-16-1859 (2-17-1859) Ma
Massey, William to Martha Talley 3-21-1861 G
Massey, William to Ruth George 6-14-1855 G
Massey, Wm. H. to Mary E. Copeland 1-13-1855 (1-16-1855) Ma
Massey, Wm. N. to Nancy D. Piercy 1-27-1856 Cr
Massey, Wm. to Louisa Simmons 11-15-1857 Cr
Massey, Wm. to Missouri Jones 11-11-1868 (11-14-1868) F B
Massey, jr., Jeremiah to Elizabeth Hill 3-16-1842 Sh
Master, William to Hester Ann Cole 8-27-1855 (8-30-1855) O
Masters, William to Narcissa J. Walker 3-26-1863 O
Masterson, G. W. to Docia (Doria?) A. Morgan 5-5-1851 Sh
Masterson, Hugh E. to Rosalee Paddock 12-30-1854 Sh
Mastin, Jno. E. to Mary E. Atkinson 10-20-1848 (10-26-1848) Hr
Mateer, P. R. to Laura E. Jones 9-17-1856 W
Mates, Peter to S. S. Frizzele 1-22-1852 We
Mathall, Alex to Martha Taylor 2-14-1872 Hy
Mathena, James M. to Mary E. Cooper 3-28-1863 (4-1-1863) O

Grooms

Matheney, Chas. B. to Julia A. Brizendine 9-11-1864 Hn
Matheney, David C. to Kissiah Pierce 3-5-1846 Hn
Matheney, Isaac B. to Margaret J. Hancock 3-10-1858 Hn
Matheney, J. J. to Martha E. Gainer 2-7-1848 Hn
Matheney, J. P. to Luraney High 1-27-1854 Hn
Matheney, James H. to Louisa Pierce 11-7-1844 Hn
Matheney, James W. to Patience E. Todd 3-28-1858 Hn
Matheney, John to Mary Bedford 12-17-1828 (12-18-1828) O
Matheney, Wiley C. to Sarah Ann Hewlett 7-9-1855 (8-7-1855) O
Matheny, J. L. G. to Margaret A. Alexander 6-2-1844 We
Matheny, J. L. to A. L. Wilson 4-12-1863 Be
Matheny, James M. to Elizabeth Baxter 8-25-1859 We
Matheny, James W. to Judith L. Craft 2-23-1870 (no return) Cr
Matheny, John to Lucy J. Brinkley 12-21-1862 We
Matheny, John to Mary Johnson 1-10-1856 We
Matheny, Jonathan to Elizabeth Oakley 3-6-1862 (no return) We
Matheny, Louis to Nancy Patterson 8-17-1861 (8-31-1861) Dy
Matheny, Luke to M. E. Dockins 3-9-1867 O
Matheny, W. A. to P. A. Tucker 9-29-1868 (10-1-1868) Cr
Matheny, W. R. to Malissa A. McMerter 8-12-1866 Be
Matherson, David A. to Emma O. Whitehurst 3-13-1878 Hy
Mathes, H. K. to Anna Green 1-16-1875 (1-17-1875) O
Mathes, Luke C. to Elizabeth Norton 12-19-1866 O
Mathes, W C. to Sarah P. Bigham 12-19-1847 Cr
Mathess, Milton A. to Celesta LaRouge 4-13-1869 (no return) Hy
Mathew, B. C. P. to Elizabeth P. Pankey 11-14-1838 (11-15-1838) O
Mathew, J. N. to M. E. White 12-4-1862 (12-5-1862) O
Mathew, James S. to Louisa Willson 11-18-1862 We
Mathews (Mathis?), Larkin M. to Susan S. Bedford 1-2-1873 L
Mathews, Andrew to Judy Pender 12-14-1875 (no return) Hy
Mathews, Aretny to Jane Stedham 4-2-1849 (5-3-1849) F
Mathews, Barney to Mary A. E. Gablin 3-5-1841 (3-9-1841) F
Mathews, Ben to Emeline Mathews 12-17-1874 T
Mathews, Bird L. to Ellen M. Pennel 6-3-1861 (6-5-1861) T
Mathews, Calaway to Sarah A. Phelan 10-21-1850 (10-?-1850) G
Mathews, Colbert to Jane Lovewell 2-2-1824 G
Mathews, Daniel to Rebecca Seles? 3-6-1856 Cr
Mathews, David to Femby Hope 7-29-1860 Sh
Mathews, David to Nancy Russell 1-18-1856 Be
Mathews, Edward J. to Rhoda N. Comwell? 12-6-1859 Hr
Mathews, George W. to Sarah Jane Winfrey 11-6-1843 Sh
Mathews, George to Martha Hart 8-26-1867 (8-29-1867) Ma
Mathews, Granville to Mary Marsh 12-17-1840 (12-19-1840) Ma
Mathews, Haywood to Ann Sanders 9-30-1865 O
Mathews, Henry to Victoria Boyd 3-3-1877 (no return) Hy
Mathews, J. P. to Elizabeth Newton 1-28-1846 (no return) We
Mathews, James M. to Emily F. Williams 12-16-1865 (12-18-1865) Dy
Mathews, James N. to Nancy S. Stoker 3-24-1850 O
Mathews, Jeptha to Sarah Davie 4-20-1830 Hr
Mathews, Jeptha to Sarah Davis 4-20-1831 (4-21-1831) Hr
Mathews, John G. to Mary J. O'Neill 1-25-1854 Cr
Mathews, John G. to Sarah J. Strong 12-23-1850 T
Mathews, John H. to Sarah A. B. Allen 3-21-1839 F
Mathews, John S. to Permelia Gibson 1-25-1858 Be
Mathews, John to Celia Shackleford 3-23-1867 (no return) F B
Mathews, John to Mary G. Pender 3-11-1863 (no return) Hy
Mathews, Miles to Nancy Woods 1-16-1871 (1-19-1871) Dy B
Mathews, Mussintyre? Sloane to Mary Frances Houston? 11-10-1842 T
Mathews, Quincy J. to Elizabeth Lewellen 3-11-1862 Cr
Mathews, R. J. to Mary Ashcraft 4-4-1864 (4-6-1864) Sh
Mathews, Robert S. to Nancy L. Hart 10-29-1866 (10-30-1866) Ma
Mathews, S. H. to M. A. Taliaferro 11-25-1868 Hy
Mathews, S. W. to N. Cagbills 2-20-1868 Hy
Mathews, Seth L. to A. M. Kee 10-29-1857 Cr
Mathews, Thomas to Elzady Lightner 8-2-1855 Be
Mathews, Valentine I. to Nancy Barnhill 6-8-1850 (6-12-1850) O
Mathews, William to Lucy A. Pickett 10-28-1877 L
Mathews, Wilson F. to Sarah E. A. Patten 7-7-1846 We
Mathewson, J. P. to Marianna Currier 11-20-1866 Hn
Mathis, A. I. J. to Martha J. Rust 1-10-1855 G
Mathis, Allen to Martha Haynes 12-23-1866 Hn B
Mathis, B. S. to Cornelia A. Tucker 11-8-1866 Hn
Mathis, Ben to Mary Mathis 1-13-1870 G B
Mathis, Cyrus E. to Wilmouth J. Wat 10-30-1844 Ma
Mathis, Dalles to Mary Douglass 12-11-1869 (no return) Hy
Mathis, Daniel to Fanny Tunstull 1-11-1868 Hy
Mathis, David to Laura C. McDaniel 2-8-1849 (no return) Hn
Mathis, David to Maggie Houghton 2-13-1873 Hy
Mathis, E. S. to C. A. Jordon 9-4-1860 G
Mathis, Edwin to Patsey Sparkman 12-13-1830 (12-14-1830) G
Mathis, Elisha to Mahulda Sanders 8-22-1853 G
Mathis, Ellis to Catherine Robinson 9-11-1867 G B
Mathis, F. M. to Nancy N. Garvin 9-14-1860 Sh
Mathis, Garret L. to Elizabeth Thomas 9-19-1838 Hn
Mathis, Henry to Mary Farris 8-8-1871 (no return) Hy
Mathis, Isaac C. to Lucy C. Smith 11-4-1856 (11-5-1856) G
Mathis, Isaac to Metilda S. Dowland 5-22-1860 G

Mathis, Isaiah M. to Sarah Jane Wimberley 2-3-1847 Hn
Mathis, Isaiah to Angeline D. Poyner 10-15-1850 Hn
Mathis, Ivey B. to Susan A. R. Petty 12-9-1846 Cr
Mathis, J. D. to Martha J. Nawl? 3-10-1863 Hn
Mathis, J. to Elmyra Alexander 12-14-1843 Hn
Mathis, Jackson to Mary Crockett 10-15-1834 (10-16-1834) G
Mathis, Jacob T. to Sarah C. Oliver 7-10-1852 (7-12-1852) G
Mathis, Jacob to Caroline (Mrs.) Drake 7-13-1853 (7-16-1853) G
Mathis, James B. to Sarah A. Brisendine 9-15-1850 Hn
Mathis, James C. to Flora J. McNeel 8-30-1860 G
Mathis, James C. to Lucy J. Olaver 11-29-1847 (12-2-1847) G
Mathis, James D. to Susan M. Weaver 1-3-1862 G
Mathis, James M. to M. M. Alexander 3-25-1839 Hn
Mathis, James M. to Pamela Ann Brizendine 10-11-1857 Hn
Mathis, James W. to Sarah Jane Roach 6-19-1869 Ma
Mathis, James W. to Tennie E. Mitchell 9-5-1867 T
Mathis, James to Catharine J. Warren 2-17-1851 (2-22-1851) G
Mathis, James to Martha Emiline Morris 1-10-1850 L
Mathis, John D. to Mary J. Drake 2-6-1854 (2-7-1854) G
Mathis, John to Mary Jane Stewart 10-26-1841 Hn
Mathis, John to Sarah A. Alexander 10-13-1839 Hn
Mathis, John to Sarah J. Bevill 12-14-1843 Hn
Mathis, Joseph A. W. to Eliza E. Rone 2-14-1848 G
Mathis, Joseph to Ellender Fowler 3-22-1841 (3-30-1841) G
Mathis, Josiah to Jane Warmick 5-28-1839 Hn
Mathis, L. C. to Betsy (Mrs.) Norton 3-4-1867 G
Mathis, Lebanon D. to Margarette Scott 4-18-1841 G
Mathis, Leonard to Martha R. Martin 12-27-1864 Hn
Mathis, Lorenzo D. to Jane Simpson 7-18-1868 (7-19-1868) Ma
Mathis, Lorenzo D. to Martha A. E. Eathridge 3-15-1853 G
Mathis, Luke Seay to Persilla C. Siske 8-2-1864 G
Mathis, M. M. to Sarah Isabell Brogdon 1-18-1863 Hn
Mathis, M. R. to Margaret Biggart 10-20-1866 (10-21-1866) Cr
Mathis, Major to Mary House 6-8-1867 G
Mathis, Robt. N. to Susan H. Combs 2-18-1867 (2-20-1867) Ma
Mathis, Robt. to Sallie Reaves 12-25-1873 Hy
Mathis, Rufus D. to Nancy C. Edwards 11-8-1856 (11-17-1856) G
Mathis, S. S. to Elizabeth Patterson 10-18-1861 G
Mathis, S. W. to Margaret Seaton 4-23-1861 Hn
Mathis, Samuel W. to Mary Ann Alexander 10-28-1841 Hn
Mathis, T. M. to Mattie E. Miller 12-14-1871 Hy
Mathis, Thomas to Martha Jane Ennis 12-21-1865 G
Mathis, Thomas to Nancy A. Brizandine 9-5-1852 Hn
Mathis, V. S. to Nancy Barnhill 6-8-1850 O
Mathis, W. H. to Amanda L. Pennie 12-4-1872 (12-8-1872) L
Mathis, W. H. to Eliza Jane Brizendine 10-25-1866 G
Mathis, W. H. to Elizabeth Jones 12-24-1860 G
Mathis, W. H. to Frances Elizabeth Curtis 9-22-1877 (9-23-1877) L
Mathis, W. H. to Mary A. Jordan 6-8-1865 G
Mathis, William H. to Nancy E. Shearman 12-16-1865 (12-17-1865) L
Mathis, William T. to Elizabeth A. Scott 7-12-1848 (7-16-1848) G
Mathis, William T. to Martha J. Brizendine 8-10-1856 Hn
Mathis, William to Ann Noel 10-16-1861 G
Mathis, William to Martha Ann Harber 9-16-1836 (9-18-1836) G
Mathis, Willis H. to Caledonia J. Norton 2-2-1860 G
Mathis, Wm. E. to Sarah E. Clements 5-26-1862 G
Matkins, L. D. to Mary Mason 1-21-1848 (no return) F
Matlock, A. J. to Caroline N. Robins 10-8-1850 Sh
Matlock, Brinkley to Sarah A. E. Wilkins 12-20-1866 G
Matlock, Henry to Charlotte E. Wilkins 12-31-1855 (1-1-1855?) Ma
Matlock, James to Sarah A. E. Brown 1-25-1858 (1-27-1858) O
Matlock, John W. to E. B. Flowers 10-18-1848 Be
Matlock?, Simpson to Lucy M. Asberry 8-18-1858 (8-19-1858) O
Matmass, Madison to Victoria Green 12-14-1870 (12-18-1870) F B
Matney, Giles to Lottie Boyd 11-30-1871 Hy
Mattern, Jacob H. to Martha (Mrs.) Dewberry 11-5-1864 (11-7-1864) Sh
Matthews, Aaron to Catherine McDowell 12-26-1870 (no return) F B
Matthews, Abner S. to Mary C. Alexander 5-10-1842 (5-19-1842) Hr
Matthews, Amos Jay to Mary Tipton 10-29-1846 (11-?-1846) T
Matthews, Charles to Betsy J. Miller 7-28-1856 Hr
Matthews, David F. to Caroline Howard 5-27-1835 (5-28-1835) G
Matthews, Edward D. to Louisa S. Barham 4-26-1865 G
Matthews, Edward to Mattie A. Smith 4-13-1859 (4-14-1859) Ma
Matthews, George D. to Parmelia Cantrell 4-22-1857 (4-23-1857) O
Matthews, George to Harriet Ealy 4-8-1871 (4-3?-1871) F B
Matthews, George to Lucy McCully 9-4-1868 (no return) F B
Matthews, Gilbert to Melvina Garrison 8-10-1853 (8-11-1853) O
Matthews, Henry to Mary Humphreys 3-22-1870 (3-18?-1870) F B
Matthews, James S. to Effie P. McDowell 11-17-1866 (11-20-1866) F
Matthews, James to A. M. Parrish 7-14-1840 (7-16-1840) Ma
Matthews, James to Sarah Titus 10-8-1866 T
Matthews, James to Susan Malinda? Nedry 2-9-1857 O
Matthews, Joe to Louisa Williamson 9-5-1868 (9-6-1868) F B
Matthews, John A. to Ann E. Hannings 11-13-1861 (no return) We
Matthews, John G. to B. M. Hill 12-18-1872 T
Matthews, John H. to Bettie Robinson 12-29-1869 Ma *
Matthews, John J. to Mary A. Bostick 9-2-1847 Ma

Matthews, John P. to Malinda Ray 2-27-1867 G
Matthews, John R. to Margaret Jones 12-19-1853 (12-22-1853) Sh
Matthews, John W. to Eliza R. Alexander 1-23-1839 Hr
Matthews, Joseph B. to Horpolacy? McGehee 3-3-1843 Hr
Matthews, Joseph E. to Nancy McCaslin 5-15-1835 (5-19-1835) G
Matthews, Joseph R. to Martha Tinker 2-9-1868 Be
Matthews, Joseph R. to Mary E. Richardson 3-4-1867 Hy
Matthews, Joseph W. to Sarah Hatley 1-1-1829 Hr
Matthews, M. W. to Sallie E. Patton 11-3-1883 (11-4-1883) L
Matthews, Richmond to Laura Taylor 12-24-1868 (12-28-1868) F B
Matthews, Rob't S. to Sallie J. Bynum 1-3-1868 O
Matthews, Samuel J. to Martha E. Richarson 12-7-1868 (12-8-1868) Ma
Matthews, Samuel to Alcy Carter 7-5-1846 (8-30-1846) O
Matthews, Silas to C. A. Moore 9-19-1867 (no return) Dy
Matthews, Stephens to Elizabeth McKinney 3-9-1836 Sh
Matthews, Thomas to Catherine Jones 1-19-1866 (1-27-1866) F B
Matthews, Wash to Gracy Maxwell 1-2-1868 (1-3-1868) F B
Matthews, William P. to Mary S. M. Stoker 10-22-1854 O
Matthews, William to Lelia Winfrey 10-27-1865 (10-28-1865) F B
Matthewson, John J. to Mary F. Brown 11-10-1846 Hn
Matthies (Mathias), Thos. to Eliza A. (Mrs.) Higgins 8-1-1863 Sh
Matthis, B. L. to V.? F. Byrd 2-21-1866 (2-22-1866) T
Matthis, Wm. B. to Martha Ann M. Fowler 6-3-1834 Hr
Mattice, W. H. to E. G. Malone 7-19-1873 T
Mattox, H. C. to L. J. Officer 3-15-1862 Sh
Mattress, Thomas to Alice Wells 7-16-1881 (7-17-1881) L
Matty, J. J. to J. M. Cullom 12-17-1859 (12-20-1859) F
Mauldin, C. J. to Sarah F. Whitaker 9-13-1859 (no return) Hy
Mauldin, James C. to Martha Ann Lile? 11-30-1842 (12-1-1842) Hr
Mauldin, William P. to Susans Bryans 5-14-1827 Ma
Maupin, James H. to Hariett E. Harper 8-22-1850 O
Maupin, John to Elizabeth Long 7-12-1843 O
Maupin, John to Jane Stacey 9-27-1852 (9-29-1852) O
Maupin, S. B. to Octavia Simmons 3-30-1870 G
Maurach?, Samuel to Margarett Pinket 11-2-1840 F
Maurer, Philip to Barabara Wind (Wine?) 11-22-1860 Sh
Maury, Abram to Mary Jane Hancock 8-22-1859 Hr
Maus, Jacob S. to Mary R. Hill 4-28-1848 Sh
Mauzy, John to Mary Ladd 8-21-1872 (8-25-1872) T
Mavis, Wm. to Sarah (Mrs.) Wainwright 7-17-1855 (no return) F
Max, Ed. Jeruiza? to Mary Harris 9-11-1869 (9-15-1869) T
Max, Francis M. to Elizabeth Billing 11-26-1866 (11-27-1866) T
Max, W. A. to M. J. Yarbro 8-19-1868 (8-26-1868) T
Maxey, C. F. to Nancy Johnson 2-13-1867 O
Maxey, J. B. to Louisa Boone 10-1-1859 (no return) Hy
Maxey, J. R. to Nancy Jane Elidge 1-3-1863 Sh
Maxey, Joseph H. to Elizabeth Dockins 4-12-1844 (4-16-1844) O
Maxey, Lewis to Georgeanna Forrest 5-28-1868 Hy
Maxey, O. C. to Mary A. Bradley 8-16-1865 (8-17-1865) O
Maxey, Robert to Cressy Jackson 12-21-1876 Hy
Maxey, Samuel I. to Harriet A. Westbrook 4-4-1860 We
Maxey, Thomas H. to Elvira Allison 5-26-1845 T
Maxley, William to Sarah Watson 7-13-1835 (8-6-1835) G
Maxwell, Absolum to Rutha Bland 1-9-1845 Cr
Maxwell, Alexander C. to Amanda B. Flemming ?-?-1839 Cr
Maxwell, Charles J. to Armedia A. Sharp 9-21-1852 (no return) F
Maxwell, D. D. to Elizabeth A. Smith 2-1-1842 Cr
Maxwell, E. D. to Harriet E. Beaty 1-3-1856 T
Maxwell, E. J. to Mary Elam? Archer 2-11-1856 (2-14-1856) T
Maxwell, George to Ownnie Carlton 12-24-1867 (no return) Hy
Maxwell, H. P. to Charlotte M. Morrison? 3-19-1841 F
Maxwell, Isaac D. to Mary Parker 2-10-1842 L
Maxwell, J. B. to Partheny Sanders 12-22-1852 We
Maxwell, J. H. to Betty Morgan 6-10-1880 L
Maxwell, James J. to Mary Eliza Maxwell 9-26-1867 (9-27-1867) T
Maxwell, James to Elizabeth Martin 3-28-1848 Hn
Maxwell, Jesse to Martha Claiborne 7-24-1827 G
Maxwell, Jessee to Martha Claiborne 7-24-1828 G
Maxwell, John R. to Sarah C. Drennon 1-15-1850 (1-20-1850) Hr
Maxwell, John W. to Ellen C. Poyner 10-25-1850 Hn
Maxwell, Joseph to Amanda Wood 11-28-1861 T
Maxwell, Robert P. to Tabitha S. Henry 9-24-1854 We
Maxwell, Simon to Rose Malone 7-27-1872 Hy
Maxwell, Thomas A. to Margaret Feezor 8-27-1866 (8-29-1866) T
Maxwell, W. L. to M. A. Garrett 5-10-1848 Ma
Maxwell, William C. to Sarah Hail 8-22-1832 Hr
Maxwell, William H. to Bethena Stephens 8-25-1825 Hr
Maxwell, William M. to Martha J. Howard 1-13-1848 Hn
Maxwell, William to Bridget Doyle 6-9-1860 (6-10-1860) Sh
Maxwell, William to Mary Brooks 7-15-1839 G
Maxwell, Wm. to Martha McClure 3-17-1850 We
Maxwell, York? to Patty Covington 12-25-1865 (no return) Hn
May, Ben to Dee A. Simmons 4-27-1857 Sh
May, Benjamin to Delitha Becton 10-28-1833 (10-29-1833) G
May, Charles to Fannie V. Heistand 5-21-1856 Sh
May, Charles to Kate Wilson 6-13-1859 Sh
May, Christopher C. to Martha Ann Neill 4-22-1852 (4-28-1852) Ma

May, D. D. to M. Y. Roney 2-13-1851 Cr
May, David I. to Sarah Wright 1-15-1843 Cr
May, David K. to Martha A. Watkins 9-12-1855 Sh
May, David to Mary L. Dickerson 10-22-1850 Cr
May, Elias W. to Lucy A. Golden 12-2-1846 (12-3-1846) Ma
May, Elias W. to Seleta West 7-24-1838 Ma
May, Elijah to Eliza Davis 5-3-1840 O
May, Greene B. to Mary A. bowers 1-31-1853 Cr
May, Henry to Lila Baines 1-7-1828 Hr
May, Hiram C. to Louisa J. Waldrop 7-19-1858 (7-27-1858) Hr
May, J. to Martha Park 12-26-1860 (12-27-1860) Hr
May, James H. to Eva J. Lane 9-3-1846 G
May, James S. to Nancy French 3-5-1870 Cr
May, James to Ann Edwards 1-12-1863 (no return) Cr
May, Jno. T. to Susan Middleton 9-17-1855 (9-19-1855) Sh
May, Joseph to Harriet Bonds 1-2-1854 Cr
May, K. D. to Martha A. Watkins 9-10-1855 Sh
May, M. A. to Susan W. Clark 1-20-1847 F
May, Newett N. to Sarah A. Lanier 11-3-1858 Ma
May, Oliver C. to Lucinda Richardson 4-4-1836 (4-5-1836) Hr
May, P. A.? to Amy Branch 12-7-1852 (no return) F
May, Paul to Amy Rook 1-2-1827 (1-4-1827) Hr
May, Phil to Mary Beavers 1-6-1868 (no return) F B
May, Philip M. to Caroline Dent 5-25-1830 (5-26-1830) Ma
May, Reuben M. to Sarah E. Pullum 2-15-1854 Ma
May, Reuben M. to Sarah E. Russell 3-14-1855 (3-15-1855) Ma
May, Robert M. to Mary C. Wilson 3-31-1866 Ma
May, Soloman C. to Martha R. Newson 11-20-1860 (11-21-1860) Sh
May, Thomas G. to Sarah A. Ursery 10-31-1855 (11-1-1855) Ma
May, Thomas to Eliza Bounds 1-13-1870 (1-31-1870) F B
May, W. B. to M. A. Barham 11-9-1858 Cr
May, W. L. to Paralee Terrell 8-22-1878 Hy
May, William S. to Sarah Dilday 2-10-1863 Cr
May, William to Frances Sain 9-30-1852 G
May, William to Laury E. Gibbs 3-15-1868 Be
May, William to Lucy Mooney 2-16-1871 Cr
May, William to Nancy Brown 3-3-1829 Ma
May, Wm. C. to Emily P. Mohundro 7-24-1839] (7-28-1839) Hr
May, Wm. S. to C. S. Revel 8-29-1864 (9-1-1864) Cr
May, Wm. to Pamela Tharp 12-19-1841 Sh
Mayben, Jeff to Ella Wallace 2-14-1878 (2-17-1878) L
Maybern, Ben to Margaret Purcell 5-21-1885 L
Mayberry, John to Elizabeth Wallace 11-15-1866 (11-18-1866) T
Mayberry, Samuel B. to Caroline M. H. Thomas? 1-20-1842 Cr
Mayberry, Thomas A. to Mary A. Mitchell 8-4-1849 Cr
Maydwell, C. C. to Susan M. Vanhook 4-23-1861 Sh
Maydwell, James to Sophia Harsen 12-22-1858 (12-23-1858) Sh
Maydwell, Thomas to Lucy L. Fleshhart 7-25-1859 (7-26-1859) Sh
Maye, Lucian to Nancy J. Partlow 5-31-1866 T
Mayer (Meyer?), Isaac to Josephine Noger 10-29-1863 Sh
Mayer, Edward to Mary J. Crane 11-27-1856 Sh
Mayer, R. F. to Sarah A. Roton 10-23-1862 Mn
Mayes, David N. to Mary Cloys 3-7-1855 (3-11-1855) O
Mayes, J. S. to L. J. Elam 4-1-1867 (4-2-1867) T
Mayes, Stephen to Amand Darnall 9-2-1872 (no return) Cr B
Mayfield, A. B. to Martha Ervin 8-20-1836 G
Mayfield, A. M. to N. J. R. Wright 3-13-1857 Sh
Mayfield, Allen to Eliza Whitaker 1-28-1870 Hy
Mayfield, Archibald to Mary Gee 11-1-1852 (11-2-1852) Hr
Mayfield, Archibald to Nancy Lambert 10-3-1859 Hr
Mayfield, Bailey to Nancy(Ann) Partridge 8-1-1833 (8-7-1833) Hr
Mayfield, G. W. to B. H. Morrow 9-12-1853 (9-13-1853) Ma
Mayfield, George A. to Mollie McDurmit 3-22-1869 (3-24-1869) Ma
Mayfield, Henry to Melitia Ward 12-23-1866 G
Mayfield, Isrial to Margaret Allen 10-20-1835 (10-22-1835) Hr
Mayfield, J. D. to Rachael Bland 2-16-1870 G
Mayfield, James to Mary A. Harris ?-?-1862? Mn
Mayfield, Joel to Louisa J. Champ 11-17-1854 (11-19-1854) Hr
Mayfield, John E. M. to Sythia Pate 11-10-1836 G
Mayfield, John N. to Sarah S. Boothe 1-1-1861 G
Mayfield, John S. to Martha Laughter 6-16-1836 G
Mayfield, Joseph G. to Rebecca M. Bowman 10-12-1850 (10-13-1850) G
Mayfield, Newton to Margaret Patterson 1-24-1852 G
Mayfield, Randolph to Elizabeth Thompson 11-6-1843 Hr
Mayfield, Reuben to Mancy (Mary) Aldridge 4-6-1842 Sh
Mayfield, Sam to Eliza Thompson 12-29-1870 Hy
Mayfield, Samuel F. to Nancy ___ford? 12-30-1859 Hn
Mayfield, Virgil H. to Mary D. Lane 7-3-1846 F
Mayfield, W. P. to Metilda J. Clark 10-6-1856 (10-9-1856) G
Mayfield, William S. to Kitty A. Jarrett 10-13-1843 (no return) F
Mayfield, William to Terissa Faller 10-6-1828 Hr
Maynard, A. A. to P. C. Nicholson 12-22-1885 (12-23-1885) L
Maynard, Evan to Louvina Alexander 1-1-1855 We
Maynard, J. M. to Mary E. Graham 6-28-1871 Cr
Maynard, Jerry to Lucy Lewis 12-23-1874 Hy
Maynard, John M. to P. M. Thomas 4-28-1855 (5-1-1855) Ma
Maynard, John to Eliza Meadows 4-24-1861 L

Maynard, P. T. to M. J. Hogsett 7-13-1864 (7-14-1864) L
Maynard, P. T. to Mary Jane Hoggsett 7-13-1864 (7-14-1864) L
Maynard, Samuel to Mary Jane Ritchie 7-21-1869 (7-22-1869) Cr
Maynard, Thomas to Araminta Caplinger 9-17-1858 Hn
Maynard, William to Catharine E. Ellis 4-15-1870 (4-17-1870) Cr
Maynor, John to Mary Manning 9-21-1867 (no return) Hn
Mayo, Allen to Martha Springer 7-25-1865 G
Mayo, Andrew to Martha A. Hix 5-10-1852 (5-?-1852) G
Mayo, Benj. F. to Jerleen Vaugahn 7-9-1863 We
Mayo, C. B. to Martha A. Trotter 4-1-1850 (4-9-1850) F
Mayo, Council B. to Caroline Johnson 11-8-1843 Ma
Mayo, Council B. to Sarah A. Walsh 2-1-1870 Ma
Mayo, David E. to Lucy A. Revell 2-16-1868 Hy
Mayo, F. A. to Laura Cocke 2-23-1869 (2-25-1869) F
Mayo, Fredrick to Catherine Bunton 3-5-1843 Ma
Mayo, Hardy to Sarah Givens 3-31-1853 Ma
Mayo, Henry J.W. to Maggie E. Templeton 2-24-1868 (2-26-1868) T
Mayo, J. D. to V. R. Priest 11-23-1854 We
Mayo, James to Mary A. Gramer 12-12-1854 (no return) F
Mayo, Joel to Cornelia A. Campbell 12-13-1855 Ma
Mayo, John W. to Emily A. Winston 2-2-1842 F
Mayo, Jonas to Susan Fussel 3-8-1848 (3-9-1848) Ma
Mayo, L. S. to Mary E. Terrill 12-27-1850 (12-28-1850) F
Mayo, Lucien to Mary Ann Partlow 12-21-1859 (12-22-1859) T
Mayo, M. L. to Pernica Ward 5-3-1855 (no return) We
Mayo, Remon to Ann E. Boon 1-10-1839 Ma
Mayo, William R. to Martha A. Daniel 12-26-1848 Sh
Mayo, William to Annie Stokes 2-26-1860 We
Mayo, William to Maryann E. Hart 9-22-1860 We
Mayo, Wm. M. to J. E. Anderson 12-23-1844 (12-24-1844) F
Mayor, Alexander to Justine Levy 5-9-1860 Sh
Mays, A. P. to Mary McFarland 12-22-1858 (12-23-1858) G
Mays, A. P. to N. J. Davidson 6-7-1884 (6-11-1884) L
Mays, Alfred H. to Ann E. McCoy 11-7-1859 (11-8-1859) Ma
Mays, C. B. to Sarah L. Cook 7-11-1866 (7-19-1866) Cr
Mays, D. D. to R. A. Cherry 2-5-1867 (no return) Hy
Mays, E. P. to N. J. Peery 1-24-1878 Dy
Mays, F. M. to Rebecca Shinn 9-24-1851 (no return) F
Mays, G. D. to S. E. Colvin 2-24-1870 Dy
Mays, J. M. to Nancy L. Odom 8-14-1861 Dy
Mays, James G. to Catharine Fulbright 2-7-1831 Ma
Mays, James G. to Cyrena Jane Weaver 6-24-1859 (6-28-1859) Ma
Mays, James G. to Louisa Eason 12-16-1861 (12-18-1861) Dy
Mays, James to K. T. Calhoun 11-27-1871 (11-28-1871) T
Mays, John W. H. to Julia A. Fields 1-30-1836 (1-31-1836) G
Mays, John W. to Paralee Simmons 1-23-1869 (1-25-1869) Ma
Mays, M. W. to Ann (Mrs.) Bellows 11-28-1863 Sh
Mays, N. L. to E. J. (Mrs.) North 6-27-1874 (6-28-1874) Dy
Mays, Robert J. to America J. Jacobs 12-14-1866 (12-18-1866) Cr
Mays, Stephen to Jane Marshall 12-25-1868 G B
Mays, Thos. J. to Mary J. Frazier 1-4-1879 (1-5-1879) Dy
Mays, W. J. to E. B. Patterson 10-1-1855 (10-2-1855) G
Mays, W. M. to C. E. Baxter 4-2-1883 (4-3-1883) L
Mays, W. T. to Susan B. Curtis 4-17-1867 Dy
Mays, William D. to Mary Ann Cotton 12-11-1837 Sh
Mays, William L. to Margaret E. McClellan 2-5-1851 F
Mays, William to Letta (Mrs.) Mays 7-15-1856 G
Mays, William to Nancy Burrow 9-26-1860 G
Mazic, Baptiste to Relien Felica 5-7-1862 Sh
McAba, Robert to Ann Williams 2-29-1852 We
McAbee, James to Vinetta Brown 12-17-1850 Hn
McAbee, Joseph to Sarah C. Kendall 3-2-1866 (3-6-1866) O
McAdams, B. W. to Mary E. Smith 4-6-1869 F
McAdams, Edwin J. to Mary E. Dickson 1-21-1870 (1-30-1870) Ma
McAdams, H. to Mary C. Twain 12-1-1856 Cr
McAdams, J. B. to Sarah W. Davidson 12-15-1868 G
McAdams, James to Cynthia A. Rossin 8-18-1853 Sh
McAdams, Tom to Nancy Williams 2-19-1867 (2-10-1867) T
McAdoo, A. E. to S. F. Stone 11-17-1859 (11-20-1859) G
McAdoo, Alonzo to Martha Merrett 1-13-1872 (no return) Cr
McAdoo, Austin to Margaret A. Davis 9-?-1862 (9-14-1866?) Cr
McAdoo, B. M. to F. Elizabeth Edwards 12-23-1855 Cr
McAdoo, D. L. to ___ J. (Mrs.) Crowder 10-20-1867 G
McAdoo, E. L. to Marian Ozier 2-10-1846 (2-15-1846) Ma
McAdoo, Enoch V. to Mary A. Hampton 8-6-1846 Cr
McAdoo, Enoch to Mary Thomas 9-9-1857 Cr
McAdoo, Ephraim L. to Frances Crowder 1-8-1859 (1-11-1859) Ma
McAdoo, J. R. to M. L. Britt 12-22-1868 (12-23-1868) Cr
McAdoo, Leonedas to Mary Key 12-3-1864 Cr
McAdoo, P. P. to E. A. Foster 11-25-1865 Hn
McAdoo, P. R. to Jane A. Arnett 12-17-1857 Hn
McAdoo, R. E. to Caroline Thomas 9-22-1849 Cr
McAdoo, Robert B. to Lucinda A. Robins 9-13-1860 Hn
McAdoo, Vergil to M. Atkins 12-22-1855 (no return) Hn
McAdoo, William H. to Nannie J. Duvall 12-20-1858 (12-21-1858) Ma
McAdoo, William H. to Susan A. Haynes 3-18-1856 Ma
McAdoo, Wm. to Laura Jones 2-2-1866 (2-4-1866) Cr

McAdoo, Wm. to Mahala Mathis 8-6-1864 (no return) Cr
McAfee, Asa to Margaret Jackson 12-6-1866 Ma
McAfee, G. B. to Mary Fowler 3-24-1860 Hr
McAfee, J. A. T. to Rosana Smith 9-14-1864 (9-15-1864) T
McAfee, John to Frances A. Powell 2-1-1859 G
McAfee, John to M. J. (Mrs.) Echols 5-20-1874 Dy
McAfee, William J. to Jane C. Barnett 3-16-1858 (3-25-1858) Ma
McAily, Samuel to Sally Robinson 12-28-1866 G
McAleer, James to Bridget Hickey 6-21-1861 (6-23-1861) Sh
McAlelley, George P. to Mary Ann Goodrich 12-12-1850 Ma
McAlenny, J. L. to Parthenia W. Grey 9-23-1851 (9-24-1851) Sh
McAlester, Daniel E. to Margarett A. E. Johnson 10-25-1847 (10-28-1847) G
McAlexander, Albert A. to Mary A. Kennon 1-26-1859 (1-27-1859) G
McAlexander, J. R. to S. E. Leach 2-5-1866 (2-8-1866) Cr
McAlexander, James J. to Ester M. Carter 2-11-1851 Cr
McAlexander, James to Martha Smith 2-23-1852 (2-24-1852) Ma
McAlexander, James to Winerford Johnson 8-21-1843 G
McAlexander, John J. to Sarah Ann Nichols 3-11-1847 Cr
McAlexander, John P. to Mary Caroline Coopwood 12-12-1844 Sh
McAlexander, Nelson to M. E. Hickman 3-17-1871 (3-18-1871) Cr
McAlilly, F. M. to Sarah Jane Lodgings 7-27-1858 T
McAlilly, Richard to Ann L. McLean 10-7-1856 (10-9-1856) G
McAlister, Archibald to Isabel Hayes 12-23-1853 (12-25-1853) Sh
McAlister, Charles to Martha T. Harper 2-6-1833 O
McAlister, Daniel to Nancy Shepard 1-18-1850 O
McAlister, Daniel to Nancy Shepherd 1-18-1850 O
McAlister, J. F. to M. N. Ferguson 10-17-1861 (10-28-1861) Hr
McAlister, J. Z. to M. F. Henry 2-7-1872 Dy
McAlister, James A. to Martha C. Fields 4-20-1865 G
McAlister, James A. to Susan A. Woodson 9-25-1870 G
McAlister, James to Ann (Miss) Cary 3-5-1863 O
McAlister, James to Polley Vickers 11-5-1828 Sh
McAlister, W. T. to F. E. Kenady 12-4-1868 Cr
McAlilly, Richard to Nancy McKeown 4-10-1833 (4-11-1833) G
McAllester, Thos. S. to Arreanna Pratt 11-22-1852 (11-23-1852) G
McAllexander, Jesse to Rebecah F. Hickman 2-24-1868 Cr
McAllister, G. C. to Mary A. Buryhill 10-20-1846 We
McAllister, Geo. D. to Julia C. C. Cole 7-8-1862 Ma
McAllister, J. A. to Mary Ellen Davis 12-6-1861 (12-8-1861) Sh
McAlpin, Calvin to M. A. Hamah 3-22-1862 Mn
McAlpin, Robert C. to _____ 12-31-1835 Sh
McAlwee, S. A. to Lou Perry 6-27-1878 (no return) Hy
McAnally, Hugh to Ann Gunn 1-27-1860 Sh
McAnally, Hugh to Catharine Burday 2-2-1856 (2-3-1856) Sh
McAnally, John E. to Jane Abanathy 4-18-1833 Sh
McAnally, John to Lydia Harris 1-1-1832 Sh
McAnaly, Jas. W. to Louisa Sullivan 7-21-1857 (7-22-1857) Hr
McAnelly, Alexander to Martha Flowers 2-10-1846 G
McAnley, B. S. to Mary J. Hill 12-17-1866 (12-20-1866) Cr
McAnulty, Joseph S. to Margaret Ann Woods 11-17-1842 (11-18-1842) Hr
McAnulty, Peter to Anna Norton 6-14-1853 Sh
McArdle, Henry to Margaret (Mrs.) Carroll 6-26-1858 (6-27-1858) Sh
McArnally, James R. to Emma C. Warbritton 3-11-1867 (3-13-1867) Cr
McArthur, Daniel N. to Mary Matlock 12-7-1858 Cr
McArthur, H. V. to E.L. Jones 2-25-1867 (2-27-1866?) Cr
McArthur, John B. to Kathrine Butler 8-23-1855 Cr
McArthur, W. A. to Neter T. Butler 5-1-1856 T
McAulay, J. M. to L. W. Butler 12-29-1870 Cr
McAuley, A. G. to Jane Bell 9-20-1872 (9-22-1872) Cr B
McAuley, Alexandria to Harriet Rushing 2-25-1869 Be
McAuley, Calvin to Louisa G. Flowers 1-1-1845 Be
McAuley, Daniel G. to Frances H. Dowtin 2-14-1860 Cr
McAuley, Elias to S. L. Butler 1-1-1851 Cr
McAuley, Enos to Marsha Duke 8-8-1854 Cr
McAuley, John B. to Dorothy A. Rust 8-20-1838 Cr
McAuly, E. T. to M. J. Hall 2-4-1868 (2-5-1868) Cr
McAvery, Thomas H. to Levina I. Dickson 10-3-1831 (10-4-1831) G
McAvoy, M. C. to Susan Thompson 6-30-1867 G
McBain, J. G. to Belle Arnold 12-15-1864 Sh
McBarrett, John to Elizabeth Tatum 5-14-1861 Mn
McBride, Alex to Frances Liles 2-20-1854 Cr
McBride, Alexander to Nancy Liles 11-21-1850 Cr
McBride, Alfred to Elizabeth Jane Harrell 8-29-1849 Sh
McBride, Barzilla C. to Crarisa C. Bringle 2-3-1853 T
McBride, D. J. to Sarah M. Jones 9-14-1854 Hn
McBride, D. L. to D. W. Trobough 6-16-1866 (6-20-1866) T
McBride, Daniel to Mary Bridges 11-20-1830 Sh
McBride, David to Angeline Cross 9-11-1830 (9-12-1830) G
McBride, E. R. to Elizabeth Cole 12-15-1849 (12-26-1849) Hr
McBride, E. R. to M. C. Nelson 1-4-1872 (no return) Cr
McBride, G. A. to M. C. Nelson 1-4-1872 (no return) Cr
McBride, George J. to Emma F. Fisher 1-20-1869 (1-21-1869) T
McBride, Henry to Tresa Ann L. Hood 5-30-1879 (6-1-1879) Dy
McBride, Hugh M. to Marcila A. Bunnell 10-6-1845 (10-9-1845) G
McBride, J. C. to A. S. George 11-4-1865 (11-7-1865) T
McBride, J. C. to D. R. Trobough 2-22-1869 (2-27-1869) T
McBride, J. L. to Martha L. Harrison 3-19-1855 (3-21-1855) Hr
McBride, J. W. to Harriet Dickson 1-14-1847 Sh

McBride, J. W. to Mary Jane Fisher 12-27-1854 (no return) We
McBride, James A. to Mary E. Harrison 2-28-1845 (3-6-1845) Hr
McBride, James W. to Susan A. White 9-12-1860 We
McBride, James to Mary Norton 12-15-1845 (12-18-1845) Ma
McBride, John M. to Elizabeth Sanderlin 7-19-1852 Sh
McBride, L. A. to E. F. McBride 7-18-1854 Sh
McBride, Pleasant B. to Eady Ann Cole 9-14-1857 (9-15-1857) Hr
McBride, Pleasant to Nacy C. Patterson 12-5-1854 Cr
McBride, Pleasant to Polly Ann Hardin 2-14-1841 Cr
McBride, S. R. to M. I. Brawner 8-27-1858 We
McBride, Solomon to Juley Ann Orshin? 5-20-1864 (3?-21-1864) T
McBride, Solomon to Sarah Manasco 1-5-1834 Sh
McBride, Thomas to Mary Hines 2-26-1860 Sh
McBride, W. A. to Crecy Ann McBride 7-10-1884 L
McBride, W. F. to Margaret Wayson 4-2-1877 (4-3-1877) Dy
McBride, W. R. to Katie Blanton 6-6-1877 Dy
McBride, W. W. to Mary E. Jamison 1-27-1857 (1-28-1857) T
McBride, William H. to Jane McKaughan? 8-14-1829 Hr
McBride, William Y. to Jane Ann Chambless 7-25-1852 (7-29-1852) Hr
McBride, William to Margaret Rice 2-7-1847 T
McBride, William to Sarah Thomas 9-23-1829 (9-24-1829) G
McBride, Wm. to Elizabeth Hogin 5-18-1863 (no return) We
McBroom, J. W. to Decena Guardner 1-8-1877 (1-9-1877) L
McBroom, J. W. to Stacey Ann Williams 7-23-1883 L
McBroom, Joseph C. to N. J. Blakely 7-30-1878 (7-31-1878) L
McBroom, W. F. to M. R. Raines 12-7-1867 G
McBroom, W. H. to Martha Freeman 7-28-1874 (7-30-1874) L
McBryde, Harvy to Mary Barham 1-30-1832 (1-20?-1832) Ma
McBryde, William M. to Sarah Grigsby 11-16-1847 G
McCabe, James to Hanora Dolan 7-2-1861 Sh
McCabe, John to Elizabeth Tibbadore 9-26-1885 (10-11-1885) L
McCabe, R. B. to Elizabeth Fielder 1-7-1880 (1-8-1880) L
McCabe, W. F. to Mary Sutton 11-24-1859 (no return) Hy
McCaddams, Isaak K. to Mily A. Walker 11-19-1856 We
McCaddan, Hugh to Harriett Radditt 12-30-1832 Sh
McCafflin, Laurence to Susan L. Wigg 5-5-1870 Ma
McCage, W. H. to Annie Bott 7-9-1863 Sh
McCain, Dennis to Mary Ann Prichard 8-21-1869 (8-22-1869) Cr
McCain, E. R. to Sarah Jane Wallace 6-30-1846 (no return) We
McCain, J. G. to O. C. Davis 1-26-1862 (1-29-1862) T
McCain, Jacob to Mary Shoemaker 12-14-1844 Ma
McCain, James H. to Elizabeth Manning 1-7-1860 Sh
McCain, James to Eliza Wright 3-16-1864 Sh
McCain, Jefferson to Ann Elam 8-9-1867 (8-10-1867) T
McCain, John A. to Caroline R. Wharton 4-20-1847 Hn
McCain, John J. to Nancy Bell 12-4-1856 Hn
McCain, Joseph to Margaret Leefon 3-25-1845 We
McCain, L. to Elizabeth Strong 9-23-1865 T
McCain, M. H. to R. H. Bledsoe 10-24-1850 Cr
McCain, Robert to Maria Jane Kinman 7-29-1847 O
McCain, W. S. to M. E. Thomason 10-20-1867 Hn
McCain, William N. to Tibitha Armstrong 11-9-1846 (11-11-1846) G
McCain, William to Narcissus C. McNeese 1-31-1853 (2-2-1853) Hr
McCain, Wm. N. to Elizabeth Sulivan 11-18-1846 We
McCain, Wm. Ross? to Leticia Simonton 2-13-1856 T
McCain, Wm. to Elizabeth Sulivan 11-11-1846 We
McCalab, John F. to Elizabeth C. Shipman 2-24-1848 G
McCalap, Danl. J. to Sarah Faison 1-16-1839 (1-?-1839) Hr
McCaleb, A. M. to Nancy Quick 1-13-1861 G
McCaleb, Hugh S. to Nancy Duberry 10-7-1846 (10-10-1846) G
McCaleb, James M. to Julia A. E. Bradford 7-23-1850 (7-31-1850) L
McCaleb, William F. to Frank F. Short 1-30-1845 G
McCalester, Benjamin to Lucinda Taylor 9-2-1848 Cr
McCalister, G. C. to M. A. Baryhill 10-20-1846 We
McCall, A. H. to Paralee Drew 3-25-1858 We
McCall, Alfred to Caroline Stevens 10-16-1869 T
McCall, Henry to Rebecca f. Bolin 12-29-1845 (12-30-1845) Ma
McCall, James R> to Mary A. Hooks 4-23-1846 (5-25-1846) T
McCall, James to M. Andrews 7-27-1866 (no return) F
McCall, Jas. R. to Lucy Nelson 11-29-1871 Hy
McCall, John M. to Emaline E. Spivey 8-30-1843 (8-31-1843) F
McCall, John R. to American P. Cooke 2-6-1843 Hn
McCall, John to Carena Herron 6-4-1862 Cr
McCall, Joseph A. to Mira Henry 4-21-1846 Sh
McCall, Lewis to Jane Blake 3-10-1867 Hn
McCall, M. S. to Elizabeth Driver 9-21-1871 Sh
McCall, Robert R. to Mary E. Dawson 9-16-1846 (9-20-1846) Cr
McCall, Robert to Eliza Gravault 9-2-1848 (9-3-1848) F
McCall, W. A. to Nannie Royall 10-?-1867 (10-29-1867) Cr
McCall, W. J. to W. S. Whitley 11-1-1873 (11-7-1873) T
McCall, W. T. to Janie Snead 5-20-1872 (no return) L
McCall, Will S. to Mary D. Looney 12-21-1854 Hn *
McCall, William S. to Rachel J. Crawford 6-3-1861 (no return) Cr
McCalla, James M. to Ann Eliza Irions 1-29-1842 (2-1-1842) Hr
McCalla, James W. to Isabella McClure 5-19-1831 Sh
McCalla, John L. to Mollie E. Gooch 1-3-1870 (1-4-1870) T
McCallen, Henry to Theodosia T. Blythe 11-19-1834 Sh

McCallie, R. M. to N. E. Lynn 10-5-1868 (10-6-1868) T
McCallister, A. P. to Sallie F. Pate 10-20-1869 (10-21-1869) Dy
McCallister, Aeneas to Catharine Stanley 6-6-1856 Sh
McCallister, J. W. to Nancy Lassiter 6-18-1862 Mn
McCallum, T. C. to Frankie Jayroe 10-15-1880 (10-17-1880) L
McCallum, Wm. to Ellen Taylor 10-3-1863 Sh
McCally, James B. to Mary E. Hall 2-13-1870 Cr
McCally, Robt. to Charity McCully 2-24-1850 (3-5-1850) F
McCam, George to Nancy Stevenson 10-1-1870 T
McCampbell, Thomas to Ann Colley 9-11-1866 Hn B
McCan, John to Fannie Ann Field 4-8-1870 T
McCan, John to Farrie Ann Field 4-8-1870 T
McCane, Amos to Margaret Robinson 12-25-1860 (12-27-1860) Cr
McCann, Hugh to Bridget Russell 6-8-1861 (6-9-1861) Sh
McCann, James to Willy Brewer 7-27-1841 (7-28-1841) Hr
McCann, Jefferson to Mary Randolph 4-5-1873 (4-11-1873) T
McCann, Stephen to Marian Rudder 10-29-1874 Dy
McCann, Thomas L. to Jane B. Black 8-14-1852 (8-17-1852) Hr
McCargo, Oscar to Sarah McCracken 1-22-1869 (1-28-1869) Cr
McCarley, Alexander to Elizabeth S. Ozment 12-28-1848 Hr
McCarley, Dean to Mary Barrett 8-9-1838 F
McCarley, Peter to Ann Pulliam 6-11-1868 (6-13-1868) F B
McCarley, S. T. to Elizabeth Ortry 7-26-1857 O
McCarley, W. W. to Frances I? Robertson 3-12-1859 (3-15-1859) Hr
McCarlin, William C. to Elizabeth Robinson 2-10-1862 Ma
McCarmond, A. G. to N. E. Yandell 6-16-1870 G
McCarnel, Wash. to Susan Whitehurst 10-11-1867 Hy
McCarroll, Eli to Elizabeth Cate 5-29-1873 Dy
McCarroll, H. L. to L. J. Winters 1-30-1875 (2-3-1875) Dy
McCarroll, J. A. to Eliza Dodd 12-12-1867 G
McCarroll, James to Lizzie Corvin 3-7-1873 Dy
McCarroll, John R. to Elizabeth Eddings 6-12-1830 Ma
McCarrus, John to Mary Ann Greeds 10-22-1838 Ma
McCarson, C. C. to Laura Norris 8-14-1867 (8-15-1867) F
McCarter (McCarty), George to Elizabeth Williford 9-1-1837 Sh
McCarter, D. L. to H. M. E. Carter 3-10-1873 (no return) Cr
McCarter, Geo. to Harriett Grooms 11-28-1850 Sh
McCarter, Isaac N. to Martha F. A. Bayliss 9-18-1853 Hn
McCarter, James to Elizabeth J. Lutrell 12-15-1858 (12-26-1858) Hr
McCarter, Jeremiah to Mary Jame? Glover 3-14-1854 Sh
McCarter, Tho. to Sarah Ann E. Thompson 3-4-1857 (3-5-1857) Hr
McCarthy, Patrick to Rose McGuire 11-27-1858 Sh *
McCartney, J. W. to Susan H. Grier 12-6-1868 T
McCartney, William to Nancy Irvin 5-24-1852 (5-27-1852) G
McCarty, Armenious to Amanda A. Cook 2-4-1867 G
McCarty, B. F. to Mary Ann Nall 4-17-1848 (4-18-1848) O
McCarty, Charles to Mary Rodgers 7-15-1853 Sh
McCarty, Edward to Esther Roach 12-11-1832 Sh
McCarty, George to Eliza Jones 2-8-1842 Sh
McCarty, Hugh B. to Mary Macon 4-4-1846 Hr
McCarty, J. R. to M. A. Slaughter 1-29-18686 (2-1-1866) F
McCarty, James M. to M. P. Malone 4-18-1848 Hn
McCarty, John to Polly McCulloch 9-22-1831 Sh
McCarty, Joseph to M. Stewart 4-18-1830 Sh
McCarty, Moses to Sarah Plant 8-31-1831 Hr
McCarty, Robert K. to Georgiana Mathews 12-29-1860 Sh
McCarty, Thomas to Mary Ann Halsted 9-27-1848 Sh
McCarty, Thos. to Mary Hogan 6-10-1862 Sh
McCarty, W. H. to Margaret Theessa Stailey 5-31-1861 Sh
McCarver, F. T. to Louisa E. Taylor 12-18-1866 O
McCarver, I. N. to E. Berryman 10-23-1865 O
McCarver, Isaac to Martha Glidewell 8-6-1849 Ma
McCarver, James to Eliza J. Cross 2-15-1849 Cr
McCarver, John to Rosanna Kingston 12-26-1841 Sh
McCarver, Joshua to Elizabeth Drannon 10-25-1838 (10-26-1838) Hr
McCary, Thomas to Benigna Johnson 9-19-1851 (9-21-1851) Hr
McCasburn, John C. to Elizabeth W. Cole 3-24-1846 Ma
McCaskill, James A. to F. E. Smith 12-19-1856 (no return) F
McCaskill, Wm. C. to Mary M. Ozier 10-5-1854 (no return) F
McCaskill, Wm. to F. H. Barham 4-27-1859 Cr
McCaslin, Andrew J. to Sarah F. Holt 1-27-1858 (1-28-1858) G
McCaslin, Green to Mary Holmes 11-6-1835 G
McCaslin, Jesse R. to Mary Admon 6-28-1857 Cr
McCaslin, John F. to Susan Holt 5-29-1854 (5-30-1854) G
McCaslin, John M. to Sallie Barnett 5-10-1870 Ma
McCaslin, Thomas J. to Caroline Richars? 12-18-1866 (12-19-1866) Cr
McCasling, William to Flora Holt 11-16-1850 (11-13?-1850) G
McCasling, Willis F. to Mary S. Campbell 11-15-1848 (11-16-1848) G
McCater, Isaac N. to Rebecca Dudley 3-29-1860 We
McCaughan, John to Margarett G. Allen 10-21-1854 (no return) F
McCaul, J. P. to Minnie L. Moore 12-1-1869 G
McCauley, H. C. to Sarah C. Bronn (Brown?) 12-22-1874 L
McCauley, John C. to Eliza J. Hall 11-8-1855 (11-16-1855) T
McCauley, Nelson to Margaret Foster 4-23-1874 T
McCetcham, Joseph W. to Martha H. Culbreath 1-12-1869 (1-13-1869) T
McCharen, J. A. to A. J. Green 11-9-1868 (11-11-1868) F
McCheshire, James M. to Roxanne W. Hindman 9-18-1850 T

McCheven, R. E. to M. F. Slaughter 12-3-1866 (12-5-1866) F
McClain, Eli to May J. Albritton 1-12-1867 (no return) Hn
McClain, G. W. to E. M. Godwin 10-20-1863 Hn
McClain, J. H. to Mary A. Golden 1-31-1870 (2-1-1870) T
McClain, James H. to Mary A. Templeton 1-5-1858 We
McClain, James R. to S. A. Donaway 12-29-1866 O
McClain, James R. to Sarah A. Donaway 12-29-1866 O
McClain, James to Sarah J. Cunningham 5-12-1857 O
McClain, John C. to Sharlett McAdoo 7-11-1839 Cr
McClain, M. A. to S. A. Phelps 11-10-1884 Hn
McClain, Macon to Mary A. L. Culbreth 12-27-1860 Hn
McClain, Samuel T. to Sarah J. Lamb 3-15-1848 Hn
McClain, Thomas to Ann Humphreys 11-9-1848 Hn
McClain, W. A. to Eliza I. Foreshee 11-7-1866 O
McClain, W. A. to Maggie Cummings 4-29-1862 Sh
McClain, William to Mary Pickins 12-4-1839 (12-5-1839) Hr
McClain, Wm. F. to Mary Ritchie 4-8-1835 Hr
McClain, Wm. H. to Susan J. Jourdon 2-18-1860 Cr
McClamrock, Harrison to Caroline E. Angus 12-16-1844 (12-17-1844) Ma
McClanahan, A. S. to Laura E. Caruthers 12-18-1860 Ma
McClanahan, David to Betsey McCoy 7-28-1830 (7-28-1830) Hr
McClanahan, David to Emily Fletcher 2-3-1835 R
McClanahan, F. M. to Sarah A. R. Sullivan 5-1-1860 Sh
McClanahan, Hamden to Frances W. Smallwood 6-5-1860 Hn
McClanahan, Hamden to Lucy K. Green 1-27-1851 (2-4-1851) Hr
McClanahan, Hamilton to Ann Jane Smith 11-5-1829 Hr
McClanahan, Henry to Nancy J. Patterson 2-2-1869 (2-7-1869) F B
McClanahan, Henry to Nancy Rhodes 3-31-1871 (4-1-1871) T
McClanahan, John D. to Margaret Ann Robertson 10-17-1840 (10-22-1840) T
McClanahan, S. G. to Mary E. Davis 2-20-1867 (no return) Dy
McClanahan, Samuel C. to A. M. Gilbert 10-9-1860 We
McClanahan, Samuel to Laura V. Fortune 12-28-1858 (12-29-1858) Ma
McClane, A. H. to A. P. Burton 12-20-1864 Hn
McClaren, B. D. to Eliza J. Tyus 10-20-1847 Sh
McClarren, Alexander J. to Margarett J. Fisher 2-4-1840 (2-19-1840) F
McClarty, W. W. to Laura L. Slaughter 4-7-1868 (4-12-1868) F
McClary, James to Emley James 2-3-1838 (2-8-1838) G
McClary, James to Juda A. Blair 11-13-1846 Cr
McCleary, A. C. to B. J. Hamilton 10-9-1866 G
McCleland, Jno. H. to Mary E. Humphrey 11-4-1858 (11-10-1858) Hr
McClellan, E. R. to Sallie Jones 3-7-1868 Hy
McClellan, Hugh to Catherine Seigler 8-6-1839 Sh
McClellan, James D. to Isabella C. McLean 5-12-1832 Ma
McClellan, John H. to Mary G. McAnulty 5-29-1838 Hr
McClellan, John to Paralee Mosby 11-16-1867 (1-4-1868) F B
McClellan, R. H. to Mary Allen 11-20-1873 (11-26-1873) O
McClellan, Robert N. to Elizabeth Ann Williams 11-20-1842 (12-1-1842) Ma
McClellan, Robert N. to Henrietta Briggance 5-25-1860 (5-27-1860) Ma
McClellan, Robert to Charity Miller 12-17-1874 Hy
McClellan, Samuel C. to Balsora Vann 1-14-1829 Ma
McClellan, T. D. G. to Frances E. Porter 8-29-1848 F
McClellan, Wm. Green to Nancy E. Bryant 11-14-1849 T
McClelland, J. B. to Mathena Young 7-14-1846 Hn
McClelland, James M. to Louisa Davenport 10-4-1843 (10-5-1843) L
McClelland, James to Frances Smith 9-22-1859 T
McClelland, Jefferson to Margrett Thomson 11-15-1859 (11-22-1859) Sh
McClelland, John C. to Alfarnia Saunders 1-7-1847 L
McClelland, John G. to Mary Josephine McClelland 2-10-1867 (2-20-1867) L
McClelland, John H. to L. C. Malone 8-14-1864 Sh
McClelland, John to Catherine Laney 3-6-1850 (3-7-1850) L
McClelland, Robert to Jane McClanahan 12-30-1868 G
McClelland, William S. to Margaret A. Moore 2-21-1872 (2-22-1872) L
McClelland, Williamson to Amanda Hamilton 7-12-1859 T
McClelland, Williamson to Mary Hamilton 11-28-1854 T
McClelland, Wm. to Prudence S. Hills 11-2-1858 Sh
McClemen, James to Nancy Erwin 7-19-1852 (8-2-1852) O
McClend(McLeod?), William to Mary Avent 3-21-1847 Hr
McClenden, Thomas to Nancy Caroline Moore 6-6-1870 (6-7-1870) L
McClendon, David to Susannah May 8-1-1827 (8-3-1827) Hr
McClendon, Geo. to Elizabeth McGlaughlin 12-22-1851 (12-23-1851) Hr
McClendon, Thomas E. to Elizabeth A. Dixon 6-5-1856 Hr
McClennin, Robt. F. to Euphemia Smith 2-10-1859 Hr
McClenny?, R. P. to Lucey A. Hill 3-21-1868 (3-24-1868) T
McClerkin, J. K. to I. J. Smith 3-28-1871 (3-29-1871) T
McClerkin, James D. to Annie Hill 4-19-1877 Dy
McClerkin, James to Elizabeth E. Kelley 11-8-1856 (11-11-1856) T
McClerrin, Robert to Millie Batt 12-6-1870 (no return) F B
McClerry, Thomas to Isabella Moon 12-4-1869 F B
McCleskey, B. G. to Ella S. Rogers 6-27-1866 Hy
McClesky, James to Susan A. Cawthen 7-14-1866 G
McClintock, J. M. to L. N. Harden 3-23-1862 Mn
McClintock, J. M. to Narcissa C. McKinzie 8-11-1866 (no return) Cr
McClintock, R. S. to A. C. Stephenson 12-8-1862 Mn
McClintock, W. S. to Isabella Beck 12-31-1861 Mn
McClish, Albert to Roxy Maclin 12-26-1874 Hy
McClish, Andrew J. to Martha Jnae Johnson 12-27-1856 (12-28-1856) Ma
McClish, J. A. to Mary S. Self 9-30-1871 (no return) Hy

McClish, J. to Emma Crooms 3-13-1873 (no return) Hy
McClish, Samuel to Matilda Glass 1-8-1885 L
McClish, Samuel to Rachel J. Stevens 6-9-1862 (no return) Hn
McClohm, Joseph W. to Ann Gladney 5-10-1842 (5-12-1842) Ma
McClory, lHenry to Susan Bennett 1-25-1862 Hr
McCloskey, James to Catharine Ford 5-20-1861 Sh
McCloud, Daniel to Elizabeth McFadden 8-1-1842 Hn
McCloud, David to Martha White 1-31-1870 (no return) Cr
McCloud, Jessee J. to Abigal Davis 10-15-1836 G
McCloud, John A. to M. Upchurch 8-10-1862 Hn
McCloud, Malcolm to Jane McFadden 2-1-1854 Hn
McCloud, Neill to Ann M. Sawyers 1-15-1827 Sh
McCloud, William D. to Nancy Allen 5-31-1846 Sh
McClour, Wm. C. to Sarah Ing 9-15-1839 (9-19-1839) G
McCluer, Thomas G. to Mary G. Darnold 4-30-1844 (no return) We
McCluney, S. G. to J. M. Cooper 9-5-1870 (9-13-1870) T
McClure, A. J. to Harriet A. Darnell 3-5-1856 We
McClure, Alexander to Zilpha Charles 2-6-1863 Hn
McClure, Andrew J. to Sarah Jane Owen 12-25-1857 Hn
McClure, Eli to Mary Jane Albritten 1-13-1867 Hn
McClure, Elijah to Sarah A. Span 3-18-1855 We
McClure, H. H. to Ellen Singleton 5-17-1867 (5-18-1867) Dy
McClure, J. M. to S. M. Cole 4-4-1864 (no return) Hn
McClure, J. S. to Sarah Karnes 3-21-1867 G
McClure, Jackson to Martha F. Harris 12-23-1852 (12-26-1852) Sh
McClure, James to Nancy N. Watt 9-22-1846 Ma
McClure, Jaret to Elzader Ferrell 11-4-1863 Hn
McClure, Jesse to Elizabeth Vikckery 4-25-1850 Hn
McClure, Jesse to Martha J. Malone 11-28-1861 Hn
McClure, Jonathan to Caroline Orr 6-9-1863 (no return) We
McClure, Jonathan to Elizabeth Hart 11-14-1844 Hn
McClure, Joseph to Elizabeth McBride 6-2-1829 G
McClure, Reuben to Roanna Vickery 10-28-1849 Hn
McClure, Samuel D. to Nannie Sibley 9-19-1861 Sh
McClure, W. H. to Mary H. Lyon 11-22-1860 Sh
McClure, W. N. to Sarah F. Curlee 1-27-1858 Cr
McClure, William to Epsey McClure 2-16-1845 Hn
McClure, Wm. H. to Liza Justice 11-23-1858 C
McClurere?, James B. to Susan D. Alexander 3-24-1848 (4-16-1848) F
McClusky, J. M. to P. Delany 1-5-1866 (1-6-1866) Cr
McCoard, Isaac H. to Nancy Long 11-23-1846 (11-5?-1846) F
McCole?, G. G. to Fredonia Muze 12-25-1856 W
McCollam, Thomas W. to Susan Pollard 12-29-1851 (1-8-1852) G
McCollaster, Frank to Ada Lea 2-25-1871 Hy
McColler, John to Margie Currin 2-24-1868 (7?-29-1868) L B
McColley, John M. to Maria Wheelin (Wheeler) 4-3-1837 Sh
McCollister, William H. to Elizabeth Clayton 7-31-1848 Hn
McCollom, Benjamin C. to Martha E. Leach 12-29-1868 (12-31-1868) Cr
McCollom, Jesse to Sarah Ann Howard 12-21-1868 (12-22-1868) Cr
McCollum, Allen to Mahaly Hopper 9-28-1844 Cr
McCollum, Arch to Sina Gregory 2-3-1872 (no return) Cr B
McCollum, Arch to Sinia Gregory 1-7-1870 (not endorsed) Cr
McCollum, George to Mary Williams 1-2-1866 G
McCollum, J. C. to M. C. Giles 12-28-1872 (12-29-1872) Cr
McCollum, J. H. to Mary McCaslin 9-5-1867 G
McCollum, James J. to Catharine R. Davidson 4-16-1840 O
McCollum, James to Charlott Brooton 2-11-1840 G
McCollum, James to Jane Cruse 7-12-1852 We
McCollum, Jesse to Mary M. (Mrs.) Putman 7-3-1860 (7-5-1860) Cr
McCollum, Jessy to Mary M. Putman 7-3-1860 (7-5-1860) Cr
McCollum, John C. to Maniza P. Joyce 9-9-1854 (9-14-1854) G
McCollum, John C. to Mary C. Clement 10-20-1850 Cr
McCollum, John H. to Ellen Warpooll 1-?-1867 (1-16-1867) Cr
McCollum, L. H. to Mary Ann Erwin 1-8-1863 Mn
McCollum, M. C. to Virginia J. Blankenship 8-28-1878 L
McCollum, Malcomb to Mary A. Thomas 12-8-1839 Sh
McCollum, Peter to Roxannah Estes 1-28-1854 Ma
McCollum, Robert to Martha J. Clark 2-28-1848 Cr
McCollum, S. A. to S. D. Hogue 7-21-1861 O
McCollum, Samuel to Mary Hassell 12-14-1869 (12-16-1869) Cr
McCollum, Sidney A. to Sarah J. Meadows 4-27-1846 (2-11-1847) O
McCollum, T. M. to Sarah J. Bigham 7-14-1858 Cr
McCollum, W. J. to S. C. McTintrick 2-26-1859 Cr
McColum, Allen G. to Harriet V. Crews 1-6-1868 (1-7-1868) Cr
McComack, R. S. to Malina Shaw 11-29-1841 (12-9-1841) F
McCombs, Robert J. to Fanny H. Holland 4-27-1867 G
McCombs, William to Elenor C. Taylor 1-5-1865 G
McCommon, C. W. to A. C. Stricklin 10-6-1860 (10-11-1860) Hr
McCommon, Geo. W. to Elizabeth D. Thomson 2-9-1853 (2-10-1853) Hr
McCommon, George R. to Margaret Ann Glass 10-1-1852 (10-3-1852) Hr
McCommon, Isaac N. to Elizabeth H. Rogers 6-19-1838 Hr
McCommon, James M. to Agness McClennan 1-2-1846 (1-6-1846) Hr
McCommon, Jas. (Jos.) H. to Martha M. Wells 3-9-1858 (3-10-1858) Hr
McCommon, John A. to L. C. Wafford 8-5-1857 (8-6-1857) Hr
McCommon, Joseph A. to Isabella Lamar? 7-27-1835 Hr
McCommon, Reese to Catharine Lavina Sharp 3-24-1848 (3-28-1848) Hr
McCommon, Seth Brownlee to Tebitha C. Cole 1-6-1841 (1-7-1841) Hr

Grooms

McCommon, Thos. R. to Eliza J. Ferguson 4-5-1859 (6-11-1859) Hr
McCommon, W. H. to Nancy' Caroker 12-3-1851 Hr
McCommon, W. M. to Elizabeth J. Ferguson 12-21-1857 (12-22-1857) Hr
McCommons, Stanhope? to Jula Ann Youngblood 12-29-1846 (12-31-1846) Hr
McCon, Jacob to Ruth Pierce 4-15-1873 (4-16-1873) Dy B
McConkey, Henry to Sarah Jane Greggery 10-7-1864 (10-8-1864) Sh
McConley, R. J. to Ellen Cady? 5-19-1870 Dy
McConnaway, Friday Mockrell to Ellen Haun 3-18-1868 G B
McConnel, Martin to Susan Tedleton 3-7-1859 O
McConnel, Winfrey to Jane Gibson 10-23-1866 O
McConnell, Andrew W. to Nancy Howard 10-21-1841 Hn
McConnell, C. W. to L. M. Baw 4-23-1860 (4-26-1860) F
McConnell, Francis R. to Sarah C. Hinchey 3-18-1840 Hn
McConnell, Francis to Theresa Hinchey 6-13-1838 Hn
McConnell, J. B. to R. E. Davis 2-16-1863 (2-18-1863) Sh
McConnell, J. C. to Susan E. Landrum 10-16-1861 G
McConnell, J. W. to Mary A. Landrum 6-21-1863 G
McConnell, M. to Perline D. Matheny 3-23-1859 We
McConnell, Marton to Patsey Brownlow 9-30-1841 (10-15-1841) F
McConnell, Patrick to Maria Dunn 1-28-1864 Sh
McConnell, Saml. to Mary Baker 5-23-1869 G
McConnell, William M. to Frances J. Howard 11-3-1844 Hn
McConnell, William to Amanda Knott 8-1-1844 Hn
McConnell, Winfrey B. to Martha Ann Motheral 5-17-1842 O
McConnico, W. C. to Carrie E. Livingston 1-31-1877 Hy
McCook, Wm. H. to Dorothy Ann (Mrs.) Baker 3-18-1871 (3-19-1871) Ma
McCool, Harvey to Patsy McCool 9-27-1869 Hy
McCool, Martin to Martha E. Stanley 2-5-1844 (2-7-1844) T
McCool, Wm. H. to Mary Wallace 11-29-1876 Hy
McCord, Alexander to Charlott Wright 12-2-1857 (12-3-1857) L
McCord, Asbury F. to Susan J. Huff 11-14-1858 Hn
McCord, Asbury to Emily Bevill 6-26-1856 Hn
McCord, Calvin E. to Ann E. V. Bates 3-7-1860 Hr
McCord, D. B. Y. (Rev.) to Barbara Thomas 2-5-1846 Hn
McCord, F. J. W. to Emily J. Manle3y 8-13-1863 (8-23-1863) L
McCord, H. C. to Louisa Williams 1-31-1851 Cr
McCord, H. G. to E. S. Keltner 1-14-1885 L
McCord, J.W. to N. R. Tillman 5-5-1877 (5-9-1877) L
McCord, Jacob to MarthaH. Wall 12-20-1860 Hn
McCord, James to Louisa Ingram 6-2-1850 Hn
McCord, James to Mary J. Holmes 12-29-1854 Hn
McCord, Jesse to Sallie G. Bevill 8-22-1857 Hn
McCord, John W. to Martha J. Bushart 8-14-1848 Hn
McCord, John to Sally Stokes 2-5-1846 Cr
McCord, Levi A. to Mary J. Hutchison 6-11-1874 (no return) Hy
McCord, R. H. to Sophronia Axly 11-14-1865 (11-16-1865) L
McCord, Richard H. to Elizabeth Silvertooth 7-24-1863 (no return) L
McCord, Richard H. to Frances A. Williams 1-11-1854 (1-12-1854) Hr
McCord, T. Solomon M. to Margaret Wetherly 1-3-1861 Hn
McCord, W. G. to C. J. Madden 2-2-1865 Hn
McCord, William G. to Elmina Hicks 7-12-1853 Hn
McCord, Wm. C. to Eliza Blunt 3-28-1843 Cr
McCord, Wm. N. to E. A. Rodgers 9-19-1854 Cr
McCordell, James to Ann Gilmore 4-19-1853 Sh
McCorkle, A. J. to Martha G. Pitts 7-21-1856 (7-24-1856) G
McCorkle, A. M. to Jemima S. Simms 11-3-1852 Hn
McCorkle, Blythe to Sarah M. Jones 12-13-1855 Ma
McCorkle, Cobb to Allis McNail 6-27-1870 G B
McCorkle, D. A. to E. A. Amons 8-29-1864 O
McCorkle, Eli to Adaline Roberts 12-27-1847 (12-28-1847) Ma
McCorkle, F. A. to S. J. Jackson 12-19-1867 O
McCorkle, Hiram R. A. to Margarett A. Cowan 11-14-1849 (11-?-1849) G
McCorkle, J. D. to Etherline Ellis 1-6-1879 (1-8-1879) Dy
McCorkle, J. S. to E. O. Clement 8-14-1862 (no return) We
McCorkle, J. S. to Mary C. Frazier 8-23-1871 (8-24-1871) Dy
McCorkle, James to Ellen C. Smith 6-28-1861 (6-30-1861) O
McCorkle, Jo B. to Caroline McCutchen 12-20-1871 (12-21-1871) Dy
McCorkle, John J.? to Jane Moore 4-27-1840 (5-5-1840) T
McCorkle, John M. to Jemima C. Edwards 2-3-1858 (no return) Hn
McCorkle, John M. to Margaret E. Diggs 11-18-1840 (no return) Hn
McCorkle, Robt. A. H. to Lirzah Scott 12-1-1828 (12-4-1828) G
McCormack, Charles to Sarah Bradberry 12-22-1856 (12-23-1856) Sh
McCormack, Edward to Feraby Wilson 5-26-1867 Be
McCormack, Haden to Polly Smith 2-16-1831 G
McCormack, James to Margaret English 3-20-1865 T
McCormack, John to Juda Chandler 4-24-1873 Hy
McCormack, M. C. to B. Z. Jackson 9-23-1879 (9-24-1879) Dy
McCormick, Charles to Laura M. Ayres 2-15-1860 (2-16-1860) Sh
McCormick, G. N. to Sarah S. Hindman 1-22-1861 (1-23-1861) T
McCormick, Jermiah to Anna Ryan 10-18-1868 Sh
McCormick, John P. to Julia Bunch 6-7-1853 Hn
McCormick, N. R. to Julia A. Huffman 8-29-1855 T
McCormick, Owen to Vezie Brannen 9-5-1864 T
McCormick, Thos. to Mary McDearmott 5-1-1856 Sh
McCormick, Wm. to Margaret Brennon 7-16-1863 Sh
McCorry, Henry W. to Corriana A. Henderson 12-11-1838 Ma
McCorry, Henry to L. Cole 12-16-1868 Hy

McCortney, Middleton to Charity Flinter 10-18-1833 (10-20-1833) G
McCounts, Thomas to Delia (Mrs.) Hood 1-7-1874 (1-24-1874) Dy
McCowan, Jackson to Anna Box 4-11-1835 (4-16-1835) Hr
McCowell, Thos. to Kate Miles 8-3-1864 Sh
McCoy (Coy), Barney to Ann Dover 7-15-1863 Sh
McCoy, A. J. to M. M. Morton 1-4-1869 (1-5-1869) F
McCoy, Charles to Elizabeth Morphis 12-26-1838 (12-29-1838) Ma
McCoy, Chas. David to Frances Malvina Hartsfield 12-22-1853 (SB 1852?) T
McCoy, Elisha to Mary E. Bibb 11-6-1845 L
McCoy, Ezekiel T. to Eady Mozelle Boon 10-22-1845 (10-23-1845) Ma
McCoy, J. W. to Anne McFarlin 3-20-1879 Dy
McCoy, J. W. to Caroline Wright 2-1-1862 (2-2-1862) Sh
McCoy, Jacob to Isabella Butterworth 3-18-1868 (3-19-1868) Dy
McCoy, Jacob to Miss _____ Smith 4-2-1874 Dy
McCoy, James L. to Margaretta A. Hufstettler 7-21-1874 (7-27-1874) Dy
McCoy, James to Nancy Nowell 1-5-1829 Ma
McCoy, John to Elizabeth Roy 9-24-1855 (9-31?-1855) Sh
McCoy, John to Emma Parr 3-28-1883 L
McCoy, John to Lundy? Harris 1-22-1878 (1-23-1878) Dy
McCoy, John to Martha A. Taylor 5-5-1870 (5-8-1870) Ma
McCoy, Joseph to Sarah Singleton 1-28-1832 (1-29-1832) Hr
McCoy, Mack to Josevine Needham 6-30-1866 G
McCoy, N. W. to N. J. Self 12-23-1875 Dy
McCoy, Nathan to Sarah Stevens 5-8-1880 (5-9-1880) Dy
McCoy, Newton A. to Martha E. Hunter 11-7-1855 (11-?-1855) Ma
McCoy, W. B. to M. J. Draffin 5-5-1873 T
McCoy, W. F. to Virginia H. Latham 10-19-1876 Dy
McCoy, W. W. to Alice Z. King 9-13-1871 Dy
McCoy, William F. to Mary E. Meter 7-4-1861 L
McCracken, David P. to Margaret Bloyce 1-26-1841 Cr
McCracken, J. R. to Mattie A. Brown 11-19-1866 (no return) Cr
McCracken, James to Mary A. Campbell 11-9-1840 (no return) Hn
McCracken, Jas. W. to Mary A. Sherry 5-12-1853 Sh
McCracken, John to Mary F. Haggart 1-21-1862 (1-23-1862) Dy
McCracken, Lycurgus to Susan A. Rothrock 11-10-1863 Cr
McCracken, Robert L. to Caroline Fitz 2-2-1858 Ma
McCracken, Saml. to Margaret Rogers 7-25-1868 (7-28-1868) Cr
McCracken, Samuel to Eliza Payne 11-12-1849 Cr
McCracken, William L. to Martha L. Thomas 10-22-1861 Cr
McCrackin, J. R. to A. Newbill 12-15-1864 (no return) Cr
McCraig, James C. to Mary C. Underwood 9-6-1853 (9-?-1853) G
McCraken, Robert P. to Eliza Jane Miller 9-24-1851 (9-24-1851) G
McCrary (McCrory?), S. S. B. to Elizabeth T. Hall 10-15-1868 G
McCrary, George to Sallie J. Rogers 2-15-1866 G
McCrary, Hiram to Hariat Coleman 6-20-1850 Sh
McCrary, J. H. to Harriet Wells 4-13-1867 G
McCrary, John W. to Charlotte F. Boswell 4-6-1851 Be
McCrary, William H. to Susan E. F. A. Rogers 2-24-1857 We
McCraw, Frank to Sallie Williams 1-17-1874 (1-18-1874) T
McCraw, Gabriel to Nancy Sullivan 6-29-1841 T
McCraw, Henry to Margarett Fields 1-3-1871 (no return) F B
McCraw, J. A. to F. A. E. Sanders 12-7-1870 (12-8-1870) T
McCraw, John to Margaret Johnson 9-21-1866 F
McCraw, Jonathan H. to Mary B. Jackson 10-16-1843 F
McCraw, Jonathan to Elizabeth P. Harris 1-4-1851 (no return) F
McCraw, Thomas C. to Harriet Childers 1-28-1860 T
McCraw, Thomas C. to Mary E. Freeman 2-22-1865 (2-23-1865) T
McCraw, Thomas C. to Mary Freeman 3-14-1868 T
McCraw, Thos. C. to Elizabeth McCraw 10-26-1861 T
McCrawley, Perry (Commodore) to U. Mullins 4-9-1840 Hn
McCray, M. to M. Thomas 10-26-1869 (10-28-1869) F
McCree, Clem to Cate McClellan 6-29-1867 G
McCree, Davie to Lavenia J. McAdoo 1-20-1858 Ma
McCright, O. H. to A. J. Merrill 12-4-1860 Sh
McCrillis, Lafayette to Augusta Montgomery 12-27-1865 (12-28-1865) F
McCrory, Cyrus G. to Sarah C. Bateman 10-20-1851 T
McCrory, J. C. to M. E. Hendren 1-15-1878 (1-17-1878) L
McCrory, J. M. to L. A. Lewis 4-17-1880 (4-20-1880) L
McCrory, John T. to Iren? M. Carter 4-17-1876 (4-18-1876) L
McCrutchen, Abe W. to Louisa Hill 2-2-1869 (2-3-1869) T
McCuan, W.A. to Pernethia E. Parten 10-4-1867 (no return) Hn
McCue, John to Mary McWilliams 12-8-1853 (12-10-1853) Sh
McCuie, Lewis B. to Cherlie Cage 12-1-1866 (12-14-1866) L
McCuin, Albert Gallatin to Martha Jane Simonton 7-25-1850 T
McCuiston, Allen to Eliza Davis 6-13-1852 Hn
McCuiston, William A. to Mary Ann Crabtree 12-28-1858 Hn
McCullers, J. R. to Sallie A. Curtis 10-20-1859 Sh
McCulley, John to Lizzie Palmer 2-28-1883 L
McCulley, Tom to Louisa Word 12-25-1866 (no return) F B
McCulloch, C. to Ann Raines 12-28-1866 G
McCulloch, George to Emily Wyatt 12-30-1868 G B
McCulloch, James to Elizabeth Turner 6-7-1849 Hn
McCulloch, John S. to Sarah L. Wilkins 10-28-1847 G
McCulloch, John to Catherine Hicks 10-25-1865 (10-26-1865) Dy
McCulloch, Lee to Gus Stokely 12-28-1885 (12-29-1885) L
McCulloch, M. T. to Sarah C. Carthal 12-23-1841 G
McCulloch, W. L. to C. Dozier 10-1-1866 (10-4-1866) Dy

McCullough, Alexa to Jane Walker 11-29-1851 (11-30-1851) Sh
McCullough, Alexander to Salina Bomar 11-24-1859 Hn
McCullough, Hally? to Tucy Still 12-28-1871 T
McCullough, Hiram to Peggy Connell 2-22-1872 Dy
McCullough, J. W. to Flora A. Hawkins 9-25-1869 (9-26-1869) Cr
McCullough, James to Martha Ballard 7-11-1855 (no return) F
McCullough, John to Edney Walls 7-14-1853 G
McCullough, John to Mary Tennant 4-8-1851 (4-9-1851) T
McCullough, Owen to Mariah McCullough 5-21-1866 (no return) Hn B
McCullough, Robert to Elizabeth Moore 10-29-1851 (10-30-1851) T
McCullough, Robert to Nancy Bird 7-25-1853 (7-26-1853) T
McCullough, Robert to Winney Hooker 10-15-1845 Hn
McCullough, S. J. to Susan Corder 12-3-1872 (12-5-1872) Cr
McCullough, Silas to Emily Smith 8-19-1871 T
McCullough, W. B. to Martha Ann Bomar 7-26-1865 (no return) Hn
McCullough, Wm. M. to Mary Jane (Mrs.) Howard 8-4-1857 Sh
McCully, Gabe to Lucy Woodfolk 12-24-1870 (no return) F B
McCully, J. M. to M. C. McCully 4-3-1860 (4-5-1860) F
McCully, John H. to Margaret Earl 12-6-1853 (no return) F
McCully, W. H. to Berlin Amis 11-10-1866 (11-11-1866) F
McCure, John H. to Harriet C. Alexander 11-16-1845 We
McCusker, Hugh to Louisa Swiney 2-18-1861 Sh
McCustin, Isaac to Eliza Albright 1-19-1872 Hy
McCutchan, John H. to Gilly Ray 12-24-1856 G
McCutchen, Allen to Ida Norwich 7-8-1878 (8-1-1878) Dy
McCutchen, David D. to Mary M. McDougal 4-15-1858 G
McCutchen, Frank to Margaret Porter 12-3-1873 (12-4-1873) Dy
McCutchen, H. C. to Mary C. Edwards 5-30-1846 (no return) We
McCutchen, J. Thomas to Anna Adamson 11-4-1867 (11-5-1867) Ma
McCutchen, Porter to Silla Redley 2-4-1867 Dy
McCutchen, Robert D. to Susan A. Howard 9-20-1854 Hn
McCutchen, W. T. to S. B. Harvey 7-28-1873 (7-31-1873) Dy
McCutcheon, B. F. to Elizabeth C. Johnson 10-25-1865 G
McCutcheon, George to Adaline Wyatt 10-10-1869 G B
McCutcheon, James D. (Joseph L?) to Betty Blackman 1-20-1870 G
McCutcheon, John to Margaret Moody 5-20-1847 Hn
McCutchin, William L. to Mary J. Garrison 10-29-1857 (11-3-1857) O
McDade, Bennett W. to Susan J. Davidson 2-13-1858 (2-17-1858) Ma
McDade, John to Josephine Womble 10-22-1844 F
McDade, John to Sally A. Whiteside 9-24-1859 We
McDade, Theopolous to Isabella Elsberry 4-6-1851 Cr
McDaniel, Abner to Unity Freeman 5-19-1847 Hr
McDaniel, Alexander to Mary Louisa Smith 2-8-1835 (2-12-1835) Hr
McDaniel, Alsey to Martha J. Pitt 10-17-1844 Be
McDaniel, Arman B. to Rebecah E. Canady 12-12-1848 Hn
McDaniel, B. A. to Ellen V. Harbin 4-28-1858 (5-11-1858) Hr
McDaniel, C. C. to Elizabeth C. M. Rose 5-18-1859 (5-19-1859) Hr
McDaniel, C. P. to O. B. Starrett 1-30-1875 (1-20?-1875) O
McDaniel, Cornelius to Hester Sain 12-9-1848 (12-14-1848) Hr
McDaniel, D. A. to Mary Ethridge 7-3-1854 G
McDaniel, E. to Minnie E. Smith 2-26-1874 T
McDaniel, Ephraim to Tabitha A. Odum 1-20-1867 Hn
McDaniel, G. W. to Nancy A. Wiseman 7-5-1863 Be
McDaniel, Geo. E. to Louisa W. Rainer 4-24-1861 (4-25-1861) Hr
McDaniel, Grengor to Polley Bowen 1-13-1828 Sh
McDaniel, H. C. to Kate Holman 12-29-1869 G
McDaniel, Henry to Edith A. Parker 11-26-1855 (no return) Hn
McDaniel, J. B. to S. E. Mattice? 7-19-1873 (7-23-1873) T
McDaniel, J. K. to Mary Barner 4-20-1856 We
McDaniel, J. L. to Elizabeth Baird 6-6-1861 T
McDaniel, J. R. to S. E. Moore 12-24-1865 Hy
McDaniel, J.(I) J. to Drusilla P. Harrell 12-8-1855 (12-13-1855) Sh
McDaniel, James L. to Missouri Ware 12-8-1835 Sh
McDaniel, James N. to Sarah J. Reed 1-16-1854 (1-17-1854) G
McDaniel, James to Malinda Gross 6-19-1850 Be
McDaniel, James to Meriah Cheatam 10-15-1844 Be
McDaniel, John C. to Levy Ann Fry 3-30-1854 Be
McDaniel, John M. to Mary C. Johnston 6-22-1864 G
McDaniel, John Ready to Martha McQuiston 5-5-1851 T
McDaniel, John to Sarah McKinney 9-13-1832 Sh
McDaniel, Johnson to Martha A. J. Lambert 12-22-1843 (no return) Hn
McDaniel, Joseph to Margaret Crenshaw 6-8-1826 Sh
McDaniel, Josiah to Nancy Presson 8-21-1853 G
McDaniel, Lewis T. to Mary A. Alsup 11-14-1867 Be
McDaniel, Luny to Nancy Adcock 3-6-1830 (3-11-1830) G
McDaniel, P. R. to Spicy Ellis 2-27-1849 Hn
McDaniel, Peter to Julia Maggard 8-26-1869 (no return) Dy
McDaniel, Peter to Minerva Swift 4-2-1874 Dy
McDaniel, R. E. to Sally Kimbro 6-9-1866 G
McDaniel, R. W. to E. P. Hale 11-12-1859 (11-13-1859) Sh
McDaniel, R. Z. to R. E. Wilson 1-4-1869 (1-5-1869) Dy
McDaniel, Samuel A. to Mary A. Carr 10-10-1854 G
McDaniel, W. C. to M. M. Garrison 11-13-1867 O
McDaniel, W. D. to Martha J. Richards 4-14-1862 Mn
McDaniel, Walter J. to Margaret A. W. Harrison 3-22-1850 (3-26-1850) O
McDaniel, William to Eliza Jane Hart 11-7-1857 (11-11-1857) Ma
McDanniel, E. to Lusetta Bernard 4-22-1868 T

McDanniel, William to Silva Semore 7-6-1878 (no return) Hy
McDavid, James L. to Victoria Neal 1-29-1868 (no return) Dy
McDavid, S. to Fanni A. Walsin 10-1-1867 (10-2-1867) Dy
McDaw, John to Sarah Smith 9-1-1867 (9-12-1867) T
McDearman, Creed T. to Eveline T. Chambers 10-28-1867 (10-30-1867) L
McDearman, Jas. C. to Theodora McCulloch 12-4-1867 Hy
McDearman, S. H. to Alvira S. Rucker 12-17-1870 (12-22-1870) Dy
McDearman, Wes to Tennessee Roberson 12-11-1884 (12-12-1884) L
McDearmen, W. E. to Harriet F. Tucker 7-13-1869 (7-15-1869) L
McDearmin, Smith to Minerva Dodd 12-27-1866 G
McDearmon, Barney to Margaret Flynn 4-11-1857 (no return) Hn
McDearmon, Clem C. to Rebecca A. Edwards 4-12-1863 Hn
McDearmon, Clement to Mary Darby 5-14-1854 Hn
McDearmon, Dolph to Alice Jordan 12-14-1881 (no return) L
McDearmon, G. W. to Louisa A. Chambers 8-25-1884 (8-27-1884) L
McDearmon, J. M. to S. A. Rucker 12-22-1874 (12-23-1874) Dy
McDearmon, John S. to Sarah Travis 4-2-1854 Hn
McDearmon, N. E. to M. E. Rogers 1-15-1872 (1-16-1872) Dy
McDermet, William D. to Jane Baily 4-10-1832 G
McDermot, Roddy to Mary McDermot 6-9-1857 Sh
McDonal, Milton to Ann Fulks 3-12-1872 Cr B
McDonald, Alex C. to Mary Ann Shelton 4-26-1852 Sh
McDonald, Alexander to Janie Mullen 11-20-1878 Hy
McDonald, Alexander to Rebecca Avann 9-8-1837 (9-14-1837) Hr
McDonald, C. W. (C. F.) to Elizabeth Crutchfield 11-24-1869 Hy
McDonald, Cash to Martha Haskins 1-5-1871 F B
McDonald, Charles to Addie Hays 12-3-1863 Sh
McDonald, Charles to Cornelia A. Fowlkes 4-12-1854 Sh
McDonald, David A. to Mary E. McAlexander 8-17-1852 Cr
McDonald, David to Elizabeth A. Wats 10-6-1853 Cr
McDonald, David to Jane M. Banks 12-3-1851 (12-4-1851) T
McDonald, David to Nancy E. Sullivan 12-24-1866 (12-26-1866) F
McDonald, George D. to Sarah Ann Weseney 8-11-1851 G
McDonald, George to Mollie Price 1-19-1871 Cr B
McDonald, J. J. to Elizabeth Woodruff 12-4-1860 O
McDonald, J. W. to J. R. Avery 6-24-1875 Hy
McDonald, James I. to Charity Lankford 3-2-1830 Ma
McDonald, James M. to Sarah C. Maddind 11-27-1844 (11-28-1844) Ma
McDonald, James to Catharine McDouggle 11-23-1869 (11-25-1869) T
McDonald, John H. to A. S. Caldwell 11-12-1856 Hn
McDonald, John L. to E. A. Reeves 10-20-1856 (10-22-1856) G
McDonald, John M. to Kate Davis 9-28-1864 G
McDonald, John to Mary Ann Sullivan 7-8-1852 Hr
McDonald, John to Mary E. Pettus 11-10-1857 Ma
McDonald, John to Mary Maxfield 2-14-1855 (2-15-1855) Sh
McDonald, John to Melinda Rose 6-5-1849 Sh
McDonald, John to Susan Cox 2-8-1836 Hr
McDonald, Joseph E. to Emma C. Warlick 10-3-1859 (10-6-1859) Ma
McDonald, Lewis A. to Sarah E. McKinnen 12-24-1870 (no return) Hy
McDonald, Michael to Margaret Moroharty 12-1-1855 Sh
McDonald, Mike to Mary Muskel 7-14-1862 Hn
McDonald, Peter to Reddie Horton 1-17-1878 Dy B
McDonald, Richard to Emma Algee 2-1-1872 Cr B
McDonald, Richard to Katty Sullivan 10-17-1868 F B
McDonald, Saml. D. to Emma C. (Mrs.) McDonald 11-3-1869 Ma
McDonald, T. B. to J. Goodwin 2-16-1870 G
McDonald, Taylor to Bell Isbell 1-3-1868 (1-7-1868) F B
McDonald, William A. to Frances C. Davis 3-10-1847 (3-11-1847) Hr
McDonald, William to Mary Joyce 6-20-1857 (6-21-1857) Sh
McDonnald, Luke to Margaret (Mrs.) McHala 2-6-1864 (2-7-1864) Sh
McDonnell, George to Mary Brenakin 4-14-1865 (4-17-1865) Dy
McDonnell, Luke to Margaret (Mrs.) McHala 1-26-1864 Sh
McDonnell, Michael to Margaret Moroharty 12-1-1855 Sh
McDonough, Michael to Margaret Hoban 5-16-1864 Sh
McDonough, Patrick to Mary Jane Hamelton 7-23-1859 Sh
McDougal, Calvin to T. H. Dinwiddie 4-5-1866 Cr
McDougal, James A. to Rebecca A. Burrow 9-17-1853 Cr
McDougal, James L. to Lucinda Cowan 3-22-1838 (no return) Hn
McDougal, James L. to Rachel Miller 3-19-1846 Hn
McDougal, Richard B. to Margaret Sexton 3-11-1858 We
McDougal, Sam to Dilsy Newhouse 6-22-1868 G B
McDougald, Alexander to Elanor Wade 8-8-1834 G
McDougald, Alexander to Lavinia McDonald 3-3-1870 G
McDougald, Archibald C. to Sarah E. Avery 2-5-1845 G
McDougald, Daniel to Susan N. Morton 8-13-1835 G
McDougald, Giles to Paralee Vaughan 9-22-1869 G B
McDough, George to Martha Cashen 2-1-1855 We
McDougle, James M. to Elizabeth Garner 10-22-1850 Be
McDow, J. J. to Mary A. Pullin 10-30-1865 (11-1-1865) T
McDowel, Henry to Mariah Lucas 2-23-1867 (2-26-1867) F B
McDowell, Allen to Anna Sanders 10-6-1869 F B
McDowell, Erasmus Patton to Evelina S. McNeal 4-23-1838 (4-24-1838) Hr
McDowell, George to Malissa Brooks 9-26-1868 (9-27-1868) F B
McDowell, George to Tennessee Freeman 5-27-1867 O
McDowell, Henry to Clara Johnson 10-10-1868 (no return) F B
McDowell, Henry to Winona Fleming 2-8-1864 Sh
McDowell, J. H. to M. R. E. Sandeford 11-2-1865 G

McDowell, J. W. to Susan E. Scott 9-12-1853 Cr
McDowell, James H. to Rutha Walker 4-1-1834 (4-3-1834) G
McDowell, James L. to M. S. Simons 12-1-1852 Cr
McDowell, Jos. to Anna McDowell 8-13-1866 (8-15-1866) F B
McDowell, Matthew to Sarah E. Low 3-9-1852 (3-10-1852) Sh
McDowell, Solomon to Victoria Morton 1-6-1871 (no return) F B
McDowell, W. M. to M. A. Flowers 12-1-1857 G
McDowell, W. W. to A. E. Jones 3-28-1867 G
McDowell, Wm. to Mary C. Knight 9-16-1871 (9-17-1871) Dy
McDuffie, Stephen to Cynthia A. Corbitt 12-6-1858 (12-8-1858) Sh
McDugal, James A. to Mary S. Adams 1-8-1861 (1-10-1861) Cr
McDugal, Wm. W. to Mary A. Adams 4-6-1868 (4-8-1868) Cr
McDummet, James to Charity Webb 3-16-1836 G
McDummitt, WilliamD. to Asinith Bledsoe 12-24-1839 Ma
McDurmit, Thomas J. to Emeline Bowling 1-17-1857 (1-18-1857) Ma
McDurmit, Wm. H. C. to Mary Abagail Jones 4-27-1859 Ma
McElroy, Virginius A. to Fanny Capers 10-14-1869 (10-18-1869) F
McElmore, Mat to Sallie Densford 12-12-1872 T
McElmurry, Phillip to M. L. Shaw 6-22-1870 (6-23-1870) Dy
McElroy, Brice T. to Testimony Free Love Inman 7-29-1844 (no return) L
McElroy, James to Amanda M. Measler 8-14-1851 Hn
McElroy, James to Martha McDaniel 4-23-1846 Be
McElroy, William to Elizabeth Arnold 10-29-1866 Be
McElroy, Willson B. to Milly Crews 10-15-1838 Hr
McElwain, H. F. to M. Brier 8-23-1842 Be
McElwain, Ned to Maranda Rives 2-19-1870 (2-20-1870) F B
McElwe, Dave to Celister Taylor 8-24-1877 Hy
McElwee, John W. to Cynthia J. Kirkpatrick 8-28-1847 Ma
McElwee, John W. to Cynthia J. Prendergrast 8-31-1847 Ma
McElwee, Saml. S. to Hannah Walker 1-27-1855 Ma
McElyea, A. A. to Mary Ann Tanner 11-12-1860 (11-18-1860) O
McElyea, Alexander H. to Odelia Littleton 3-29-1854 (3-31-1854) O
McElyea, Daniel F. to Jane Stigall 9-17-1861 Be
McElyea, Humphrey D. to Nancy Rice 2-25-1847 O
McElyea, James P. to Sintha Jones 7-16-1838 O
McElyea, John W. to Elvira B. Jones 7-29?-1839 (7-10-1839) O
McElyea, John W. to Martha Ann Smith 1-23-1850 Sh
McElyea, John W. to Miranda Killet 2-20-1853 (2-24-1853) O
McElyea, John W. to Nancy Perkins 6-22-1855 (6-24-1855) O
McElyea, L. T. to M. A. Helms 10-12-1863 (10-13-1863) O
McElyea, Samuel M. to Martha Riddle 12-29-1856 (12-30-1856) O
McElyea, Thomas J. to F. J. Gunson 3-21-1850 O
McElyea, William G. to Elizabeth Polsgrove 8-17-1856 (8-18-1856) O
McEntire, J. Y. to Mary E. McCampbell 6-20-1866 Hn
McEver, Angish to Elizabeth Fortner 7-14-1860 (no return) Hy
McEwen, Christopher E. to Narcissa F. Newsom 5-26-1828 Ma
McEwen, F.L. W. to Wineford Avery 8-7-1829 (8-20-1829) G
McEwen, Green B. Y. to Sarah A. Arbuckle 11-25-1845 G
McEwen, Hugh to Holly Scarbrough 7-25-1843 Cr
McEwen, J. A. to Nancy Duggor 12-4-1865 G
McEwen, J. D. to S. C. Johnson 12-26-1872 Cr
McEwen, Jas. A. G. to L. S. Crawford 6-19-1855 (6-20-1855) G
McEwen, John Francis to Sarah E. Osbourn 9-9-1878 (9-11-1878) L
McEwen, Joseph F. to Jane Stone 10-27-1867 G
McEwen, R. M. to M. E. Norris 10-6-1859 Sh
McEwen, T. B. to Annie M. Owen 7-25-1857 Sh
McEwen, W. M. to Mary A. M. Stone 11-6-1867 G
McEwin, John to Nancy H. Olahan 2-15-1838 Ma
McEwin, Robt. McComb to Elvira Moore 11-15-1850 T
McFadden, Andrew J. to Nancy Lewis 7-11-1848 Hn
McFadden, Benjamin W. to Margaret A. Sturdivant 9-23-1866 Hn
McFadden, J. H. to Sabina E. Lewis 3-5-1850 Hn
McFadden, J. M. to Fannie Sharp 11-4-1863 (11-5-1863) F
McFadden, James to Catherine Clark 2-4-1869 (2-9-1869) Ma
McFadden, Jno. to Sarah E. Watson 1-8-1857 F
McFadden, John M. to Mary M. Morrison 11-27-1844 (no return) F
McFadden, John to Margaret McDaniel 3-18-1841 Hn
McFadden, N. C. to Miss Mollie McFadden 11-29-1862 T
McFadden, N. H. to J. D. Watts 11-27-1873 T
McFadden, Peter to Anna Suggs 11-24-1877 (no return) L
McFadden, Peter to Harriet West? 3-8-1867 (no return) L B
McFadden, R. W. to Alvina Cole 8-8-1849 Hn
McFadden, Robert L. to Margaret L. Hill 7-24-1866 T
McFadden, Thomas to Ruth Watson 11-10-1838 F
McFadden, William to Margaret Seawright 3-23-1854 (no return) Hn
McFadden, William to Sarah Clementine Booth 10-29-1857 Hn
McFall, Alexander R. to Wine Bane 1-5-1830 (1-7-1830) G
McFall, John A. to Hannah Brown 8-9-1828 (8-10-1828) Hr
McFarlan, A. C. to Rebecca J. Cawhon 7-14-1865 (7-16-1865) Dy
McFarlan, A. S. to N. E. Harris 1-15-1867 F
McFarland, Andrew to Catherine Wilson 11-28-1829 (11-29-1829) O
McFarland, Andrew to Phebe Caldwell 8-31-1854 O
McFarland, C. F. to Angeline Hart 9-11-1867 Hn
McFarland, Charles to Cattie West 9-30-1875 (10-17-1875) L B
McFarland, D. F. to Mary L. Jacobs 8-3-1854 O
McFarland, E. J. to Karen C. Bunch 1-8-1846 Hn
McFarland, Edward to Louisiana Moule 5-10-1843 Sh

McFarland, Felix to Martha A. Douglass 6-28-1842 F
McFarland, George to Sara Ragland 11-27-1865 (12-30-1865) F B
McFarland, Henry T. to Malissa C. Sloan 7-21-1854 (7-23-1854) G
McFarland, Henry to Angeline Poindexter 5-11-1868 (5-16-1868) F B
McFarland, Isham to Easter Steward 12-18-1870 Hy
McFarland, J. F. to Nancy Rumley 1-6-1872 Dy
McFarland, James P. to E. J. L. Coward 2-3-1859 Hn
McFarland, James to C. M. Williams 1-15-1857 O
McFarland, James to Rebecca Jordon 8-22-1845 Be
McFarland, John B. to A. S. Cooke 3-4-1845 Hn
McFarland, John J. to Sarah A. Burch 8-29-1859 (8-30-1859) G
McFarland, John J. to Tennessee L. Bevens 10-3-1862 G
McFarland, John Joseph to Mary Isabella Shelby 1-5-1847 Sh
McFarland, John to Cassandra Berry 4-17-1852 (4-21-1852) G
McFarland, John to Martha Bohanon 5-29-1859 Hn
McFarland, Mat to Em Currie 1-3-1868 Hy
McFarland, Moses to Lucinda Burch 8-1-1860 G
McFarland, Radford to Mahaly Lowry 2-3-1834 (2-4-1834) G
McFarland, Reuben Fletcher to Helen Goheen 9-30-1850 (10-2-1850) T
McFarland, Tho. D. to Mary Bass 10-7-1850 (10-9-1850) T
McFarland, W. H. to Nannie Jones 12-18-1869 G
McFarland, W. H. to Tabitha J. Kirkland 7-10-1867 Hn
McFarland, W. J. to J. P. Norvell 12-18-1870 Hy
McFarland, W. R. to Emily Jackson 9-24-1865 Hn
McFarland, W. to Dodeski Ann Merritt 8-6-1869 G
McFarland, William A. to Amantha Dunlap 2-8-1838 Hn
McFarland, William H. to Sarah E. McFadden 12-26-1863 Hn
McFarland, William J. to Paralee F. King 10-29-1850 Ma
McFarland, William J. to Parthenia A. E. Dungan 2-23-1856 (12-25-1856) Ma
McFarland, William to Lucinda Jacobs 9-18-1838 G
McFarland, William to Mary Lucretia Harrison 12-6-1854 O
McFarlane, Doctor Wesley to Costinza Missouri Harris 12-18-1844 (12-19-1844) T
McFarlane, John W. to Peggy Ann Bettis 12-13-1866 (12-26-1866) Dy
McFarlen, J. J. to Narcissa T. Coleman 12-27-1854 G
McFarlen, Jas. A. to Jane Moore 12-21-1854 G
McFarlen, John to Mmary Smithwick 11-25-1843 Ma
McFarlen, John to Polly Welch 8-18-1843 G
McFarlin, Dennis to Hepsy Ann Robinson 8-5-1852 Ma
McFarlin, F. M. to M. A. Caudle 1-29-1863 O
McFarlin, Henry to Angelina Belton 7-27-1850 (7-28-1850) Ma
McFarlin, J. G. to Mary F. Holt 12-1-1870 G
McFarlin, J. N. to Mollie Jones 12-20-1866 G
McFarlin, J. W. to Belle Williams 3-20-1879 Dy
McFarlin, James V. to America C. Poindexter 7-5-1859 (7-7-1859) Ma
McFarlin, Joseph to Susan King 4-15-1861 (4-16-1861) Ma
McFarlin, Robert J. to Elizabeth Ann Beard 10-21-1858 Hn
McFarlin, T. M. to M. A. Caudle 1-29-1863 (1-31-1863) O
McFarlin, W. M. A. to Elizabeth Ramsey 8-30-1859 Cr
McFarlin, Washington to Armitty Brogden 1-8-1858 (6-23-1858) Ma
McFarlin, Wm. to Charity McLin? 11-5-1850 Cr
McFeadden (McFadden), M. to Ellen Kennelly 1-17-1861 Sh
McFerren, William M. to Nancy M. Walker 11-20-1852 (no return) F
McFerrin, Addison to Mary Hamilton 7-23-1869 (no return) F B
McFerrin, John H. to Tommie Matthews 1-24-1866 (1-31-1866) F
McFerrin, Ned to Sidney Jones 1-4-1868 (1-7-1868) F B
McFerson, A. G. to Drusillar Brewer 9-4-1855 Be
McGallary, Turner to Fannie Douglass 10-3-1878 Hy
McGann, Charles to Elizabeth Weaver 11-30-1870 Hy
McGarg, Henry to Lou Frost 1-14-1879 (no return) Dy
McGarg, Peter to Rachel Nash 3-7-1878 (3-7-1878) Dy
McGarrity, James to Mattie Anderson 11-2-1874 (11-3-1874) L
McGaugh, W. M. to Martha E. Brown 8-1-1867 O
McGaugh, Wm. to M. C. Bransford 6-24-1865 O
McGaughey, George to Jane Lanier 2-21-1873 (4-21-1873) Dy
McGaughey, John R. to Martha H. Williams 12-21-1870 (12-22-1870) L
McGaughey, Richd. H. to Mary A. Richardson 9-1-1845 (no return) L
McGaughey, William L. to Margt. J. Alston 9-21-1869 (no return) L
McGavoc, Ned to Cheney (Mrs.) Ellington 1-28-1868 G B
McGavock, David H. to Willie E. Harding 5-23-1850 Sh
McGee, A. C. to Margarette Jane Bogle 5-25-1854 (5-26-1854) G
McGee, A. to Jane Smith 12-5-1860 (12-6-1861) We
McGee, George to Jane Mays 1-23-1870 G B
McGee, Gideon G. to Julia Ann Maley 8-23-1857 T
McGee, Giles to Martha Ridge 12-17-1861 Sh
McGee, H. M. P. to Prudence Barham 11-15-1853 Cr
McGee, Harison to Delaney Rose 12-12-1848 Cr
McGee, Henry to Manirva Davis 9-3-1868 G B
McGee, Henry to Margaret M. C. Martin 11-21-1846 (11-3?-1846) G
McGee, Henry to Martha Fleming 11-21-1854 G
McGee, J. L. (Dr.) to S. J. Johnson 3-12-1868 G
McGee, J. P. to Jennie C. Elder 2-22-1866 G
McGee, James A. to Elizabeth H. Gillespie 11-8-1854 (11-9-1854) G
McGee, James A. to Mrs. Nancy M. Keenan 5-16-1860 T
McGee, James H. to Mary Amos 5-16-1869 G
McGee, James W. to Martha Bradshaw 3-7-1843 Hn
McGee, James W. to Nancy Tennessee Detta 9-10-1862 (no return) Hy

McGee, James to Mary Rose 12-9-1854 Sh
McGee, James to Nancy T. Ditto 12-23-1861 (no return) Hy
McGee, Jerry to Betsey Baley 12-31-1828 G
McGee, Jno. H. to Rachel Estes 11-11-1868 Ma
McGee, John H. to Mary M. Mercer 8-18-1856 (8-19-1856) Hr
McGee, John to Kitsy Elam 9-27-1872 (10-16-1872) T
McGee, John to Nancy Cachman 11-21-1868 L
McGee, Joseph L. to Emma Osborn 5-16-1865 G
McGee, L. B. to Nancy A. Rash 12-3-1863 O
McGee, R. G. to Mary Jane McGee 12-12-1839 (no return) F
McGee, Richard to Eliza E. Scrape 2-19-1846 G
McGee, T. L. to Sallie E. McKinnie 4-10-1858 (4-22-1858) Hr
McGee, Thomas B. to M. E. A. Strong 12-19-1877 Hy
McGee, Thos. to Sarah Moore 8-?-1842 (no return) F
McGee, Tilman to Patienc Maley 1-17-1868 T
McGee, W. C. to S. E. Scrope 4-25-1861 G
McGee, W. H. to Jane A. Lock 9-7-1857 Cr
McGee, W. J. to W. M. Tomlinson 12-2-1855 Be
McGee, W. T. to Louisa J. Dickson 12-6-1875 (no return) Hy
McGee, William H. to Mary M. Wiles 5-21-1855 G
McGee, William to Louisa Martin 6-22-1833 (6-23-1833) Hr
McGee, Wm. to Mary Ann Kerly 1-21-1833 Hr
McGee, Wylie W. to M. J. Carroll 12-10-1857 (1-19-1858) O
McGehe, William to Rutha Hall 3-13-1849 G
McGehee, A. F. to Margaret Jane Ward 11-27-1854 (11-28-1854) Hr
McGehee, Abner C. to Susan Chandler 11-11-1849 Hn
McGehee, Beverly to Margaret McCavley 12-29-1866 Hn B
McGehee, E. D. to N. J. Paschall 2-5-1867 Hn
McGehee, Elijah A. C. to Sarah J. Frazier 10-18-1860 Hn
McGehee, F. A. C. to A. B. Williams 8-27-1855 Hn
McGehee, Fountain to Cyntha Thompson 1-13-1839 (1-24-1839) F
McGehee, Fountain to Cynthia Thompson 1-13-1839 (no return) F
McGehee, J. J. to P. A. McDearmon 1-2-1854 (no return) Hn
McGehee, James E. to Martha Kelly 12-29-1841 G
McGehee, John B. to Lucy Paschall 2-26-1845 Hn
McGehee, John C. to Mary Hays Shelby 7-4-1848 Sh
McGehee, John J. to Eliza A. McGehee 5-28-1846 Hn
McGehee, John O. to Rachael C. Trigg 2-14-1850 Sh
McGehee, John T. to Mary J. Davis 9-4-1871 O
McGehee, John W. to Louiza F. Rowe 2-27-1851 Hn
McGehee, Milton N. to Anna Hooper 7-9-1846 We
McGehee, Richard to Julia Edwards 12-30-1866 Hn B
McGehee, William H. to Louisa P. Wilson 8-20-1849 Hn
McGehee, William J. to Rebecca Key 1-21-1855 Hn
McGehee, William W. to Susan T. Looney 9-23-1854 Hn
McGenley, Benjamin R. to Mary (Mrs.) Carl 1-4-1864 Sh
McGevany, John to Susan McClabahan 10-30-1838 (11-1-1838) Ma
McGhee, Benjamin to Lively Rushing 8-22-1846 Ma
McGhee, John Wesley to Cara Nipper 9-23-1856 Ma
McGhee, N. W. to Eliza Stephens 7-19-1843 Sh
McGill, A. to Lissey Gibson 10-28-1869 Be
McGill, Anderson to Eliza A. M. Phillips 3-11-1841 Cr
McGill, Anderson to Sarah Collier 12-24-1845 Cr
McGill, D. to J. C. Malone 8-16-1860 Be
McGill, David to Mary Ann Watson 4-9-1844 Be
McGill, Henry to Mary Caraway 4-23-1862 Be
McGill, J. to D. Rushing 9-22-1841 Be
McGill, James A. to Perina J. Mizzell 10-16-1869 (10-20-1869) Cr
McGill, James to Elizabeth Mitchell 5-16-1847 Be
McGill, James to Julian Bond 9-27-1853 Be
McGill, James to Martha Whitehorn 11-1-1847 Cr
McGill, John jr. to Mary Jane Ward 9-17-1848 Be
McGill, John to Mary Crossno 12-30-1865 Be
McGill, Marion to Elizabeth Tubbs 12-28-1853 Be
McGill, Thomas J. to Eliza Ann Jackson 7-23-1866 Be
McGill, Thomas to Caroline H. Connelly 2-2-1862 Ma *
McGill, Thomas to Elizabeth J. Greer 3-9-1853 Be
McGill, Thomas to Laury Ozier 3-4-1841 Cr
McGill, Thomas to Minta Wesson 1-15-1856 Be
McGill, W. to D. M. Greer 6-5-1839 Be
McGill, Wm. A. to Sallie K. McKnight 3-9-1867 Ma
McGill, Wm. to Beady Watson 8-8-1860 Be
McGinley, B. R. to Ada E. Cook 10-6-1857 Sh
McGinnis, A. B. to Demaris E. Brown 10-11-1851 (10-12-1851) Sh
McGinnis, David to Martha Ward 8-29-1860 (8-31-1860) O
McGinnis, Dennis to Rosah Black 4-30-1868 (no return) F B
McGinnis, Eli to Anne Baird 3-27-1868 G B
McGinnis, J. R. to Mary E. Boyd 12-21-1862 (1-1-1863) F
McGinnis, James W. to Nanny H. Dunagin 5-9-1866 O
McGinnis, Thomas J. to Marandy H. Horten 7-10-1865 G
McGinnis, Thomas J. to Mary E(liza) Gammon 1-24-1866 (1-25-1866) Dy
McGinnis, Thos. J. to Margarette _____ 3-12-1863 G
McGinsey, Daniel (David?) to Rachel Lewis 12-21-1872 (12-22-1872) L B
McGinty, James R. to Harriet L. Browning (Bronning) 6-18-8161 (7-1-1861) Sh
McGirnsey, C. P. to Lucinda M. Neely 12-8-1852 Sh
McGlohon, J. T. to Mary Pierce 7-9-1863 Be
McGlon, George to E. Jane Doherty 5-11-1852 Be

McGlothin, J. L. to Henrietta M. Fonvill 2-26-1856 We
McGlothin, James to Margaret M. M. Moore 10-7-1860 (no return) L
McGlothlin, Ephraim to Margaret J. Crane 3-12-1857 Hr
McGlothlin, John to Eunice Keller 11-2-1826 (11-4-1826) Hr
McGlothlin, Wm. R. to Henrietta Thornton 1-6-1862 Hr
McGowan, Alexander to Margaret T. Odell 5-7-1845 Sh
McGowan, Andrew to Elizabeth Williams 8-4-1866 (8-7-1866) T
McGowan, Andrew to Martha Baker 7-21-1882 (7-24-1882) L
McGowan, J. G. to Ann E. Ferri 9-26-1866 (9-27-1866) Ma
McGowan, James E. to Mary Frances Holloway 1-19-1855 (1-30-1855) Sh
McGowan, James E. to Willy Ann Lucado 9-23-1850 (no return) F
McGowan, James G. to Mary E. Oliphant 10-16-1860 G
McGowan, John to Mary Hennesy 8-20-1850 Sh
McGowan, Joseph to Cordelia Joyce 11-7-1854 T
McGowan, Richard to Malvina H. Childress 8-7-1841 (8-8-1841) Ma
McGowan, Richard to Mary McFarland 11-21-1842 Ma
McGowan, W. B. to Alice A. Waddy 9-5-1867 Hn
McGowan, William P. to Margaret E. Leeper 2-18-1841 Hn
McGowen, Evanda to Mary J. Burrow 8-16-1854 Cr
McGowen, James to Ellen Burns? 7-27-1854 Sh
McGowen, James to Ester Tucker 7-30-1831 Sh
McGowen, T. H. to Sarah Burrow 8-16-1854 Cr
McGown (McGowern), James to Ann McGowan 3-20-1856 Sh
McGran, Daniel to Elizabeth Ingram 4-26-1858 (4-27-1858) G
McGrath, Edward to Mary Caley 1-26-1861 (1-27-1861) Sh
McGrath, J. D. to Annie F. Byram 11-23-1874 (11-25-1874) T
McGrath, John to Catharine Fogerty 8-10-1853 Sh
McGrath, John to Matilda Sweeney 4-23-1861 Sh
McGrath, Michael to Mary Maranan 1-10-1860 (1-11-1860) Sh
McGrath, Patrick to Ann Campfield 1-5-1846 Sh
McGrath, Patrick to Elener (Mrs.?) McDroit 7-30-1864 Sh
McGrath, Phillip to Margarett Cook 7-29-1851 Sh
McGraves, Stephen to Adaline McAdoo 5-6-1846 G
McGraw, A. A. to Sallie Reynolds 12-31-1872 Dy
McGraw, Elhennan to Mary Rogers 10-31-1844 Hr
McGraw, James to Julia Sweeney 11-16-1845 Sh
McGraw, Jno. H. to Elizabeth Sanders 8-12-1845 Hr
McGraw, John to Cathrine Wallace 8-8-1847 Cr
McGregor, Alexander to Mary Jane 3-15-1849 Sh
McGregor, Frank to Sallie Bledsoe 2-19-1873 (2-20-1873) T
McGregor, Rob Roy to Ada B. Martin 6-10-1867 (7-6-1867) F
McGrory, Edward to Margaret Dorough 5-1-1860 Sh
McGuair (Mcguire), D. A. to Josie P. Hale (Hall?) 2-12-1879 L
McGuffin, W. H. to S. A. Wilkins 9-4-1860 G
McGuinn (McGrinn?), John to Ellen McCormick 10-21-1861 Sh
McGuire, Alfred to Louisa J. Hartsfield 2-12-1842 (2-15-1842) T
McGuire, Anderson to Susanah Soward 12-22-1868 L
McGuire, D. W. S. to Sarah T. Andrew 9-14-1858 We
McGuire, George W. to Martha Jane Eddins 11-11-1856 Ma
McGuire, George to Elizabeth McKay 1-5-1836 Hr
McGuire, James A. to Priscilla E. Beasley 10-5-1871 L
McGuire, James Y. to Elizabeth W. Turner 8-11-1845 (8-12-1845) Hr
McGuire, James to Jane Hendren 11-22-1878 Dy
McGuire, John Y. to Harret? Scoot 10-13-1845 (10-14-1845) Hr
McGuire, Joseph J. to Lovey F. Walter 6-20-1858 Cr
McGuire, M. D. L. to Ann F. Temmens 10-28-1860 We
McGuire, M. L. J. to D. Acree 6-30-1861 We
McGuire, Obediah to Eliza Whitson 88-7-1846 (8-13-1846) T
McGuire, Thomas to Fanny Griffin 12-5-1866 G
McGuire, William B. to Sarah Matilda Blankinship 9-23-1874 L
McGuire, William F. to Sarah M. Stephens 4-7-1858 T
McGuirk, John to Louisa A. Mahaffy 5-24-1853 (no return) F
McGuiver, John to Del Cash 3-15-1870 T
McGuiver, Wm. M. to Nealy Barnet 5-21-1866 (5-22-1866) T
McGuiver?, Harry to Sarah A. Steele 10-29-1869 (11-13-1869) T
McHale, James to Salvina? M. Davis 12-27-1859 T
McHamy, Jacob to Elvira Berry 6-27-1840 (no return) Hn
McHaney, Lafayette to Nancy C. Thorn 10-2-1860 G
McHenry, DeSoto B. to Donna M. Greenlaw 6-12-1862 (6-16-1862) Sh
McHenry, H. A. to Nancy C. Richer 10-15-1856 G
McHenry, Henry A. to Cyntha M. McRee 11-4-1852 G
McHenry, Jesse to Annie (Mrs.) Field 11-24-1864 Sh
McHood, J. R. to Norah J. Reece 9-5-1872 Cr
McHood, James to D. Robertson 1-1-1866 Cr
McHood, James to Mary L. Robinson 12-2-1843 Cr
McHugh, Daniel to Mary Looney 9-19-1859 Sh
McHughs, Moses to Sarah Jane Lightner 3-26-1845 Be
McIlleavy, M. C. to Martha Jenkins 1-25-1856 (no return) Hn
McIlwain, Ephraim to Maggie J. Cozart 12-4-1866 (12-5-1866) Ma
McInnes, John to Sarah Doragh 10-8-1860 Sh
McIntire, James to Eveline Edwards 7-20-1877 (7-22-1877) L
McIntosh, Andrew J. to Louisa Crow 6-28-1852 (7-1-1852) O
McIntosh, D. F. to Mary M. Parks 12-2-1865 G
McIntosh, J. G. to Margarett Holt 8-11-1867 G
McIntosh, James S. to Miss Lucy Walk 4-9-1862 T
McIntosh, James S. to Susan Smith 9-14-1867 (9-15-1867) T
McIntosh, James to A. V. Gillespie 12-15-1869 G

Grooms

McIntosh, Jas. S. to Lucy A. Walk 7-21-1866 T
McIntosh, Jesse to Mary Maloney 10-16-1850 O
McIntosh, Jesse to Mary Nolan Davis 10-16-1850 O
McIntosh, Jesse to Milissa Jane Thompson 8-10-1841 (9-22-1841) O
McIntosh, Jno. B. to Martha Campbell 12-25-1868 (12-27-1868) Dy
McIntosh, John B. to Margaret Ann Twilla 1-24-1878 Dy
McIntosh, John to Elizabeth Burton 12-13-1838 Hr
McIntosh, John to Hannah E. Hart 3-6-1839 (3-7-1839) Ma
McIntosh, John to Susana Boreing 11-11-1826 G
McIntosh, Roderick A. to Mary Brown 6-3-1828 Ma
McIntosh, William to Minnoy? Smith 7-29-1865 Sh
McInturf, Ephaim to Sarah Williams 2-12-1874 Hy
McIntyre, J. W. to M. E. Vernon 8-21-1878 (no return) L
McIntyre, J. W. to Sarah J. Stamps 6-28-1879 (6-29-1879) L
McIntyre, James to Mary Cooper 3-20-1843 (3-23-1843) T
McIntyre, Michael to Bridget Manoney 7-9-1860 Sh
McIntyre, Thos. to Matilda Clay 7-3-1872 (7-4-1872) T
McIntyre, W. C. to Candia Johnson 2-21-1855 (2-25-1855) Hr
McIrby, P. to H. M. Thompson 11-3-1858 (11-4-1858) Sh
McIver, Alexander to Martha C. Poe 12-8-1830 Ma
McIver, Daniel to Virginia B. Harrison 1-10-1843 (1-11-1843) Ma
McIver, Donald to Matilda McClary 3-14-1828 G
McIver, James A. to Sarah Jane Ledbetter 10-22-1853 (10-28-1853) L
McIver, John to Manirva F. Byrn 11-9-1854 L
McJones, Ira M. to Sarah M. Garland 8-22-1839 Ma
McKalip, Andrew M. to Narcissa Koffman 5-23-1854 (5-24-1854) Hr
McKamey, John C. to Elizabeth A. Polly 4-9-1859 (4-14-1859) O
McKamy, John C. to Martha Lilly 11-27-1863 (11-29-1863) O
McKamy, William D. to Elizabeth C. Buchanan 8-29-1852 (9-2-1852) O
McKamy, Wm. D. to Elvary J. Calhoun 9-28-1866 O
McKane, Samuel to Nancy C. Webb 10-9-1865 G
McKarley, James to Elizabeth Oxbury 1-2-1835 Sh
McKaughan, John S. to Rachel B. Taylor 1-21-1848 (1-23-1848) Hr
McKay, Angus to E. Strange 1-14-1864 Sh
McKay, H. M. to Juliet M. Clark 3-10-1856 Sh
McKay, Henry T. to Fanny McKay 1-3-1854 (1-4-1854) Sh
McKay, John to Fanny Black 9-5-1839 Sh
McKay, Richard F. to Eliza R. Carithers 10-20-1864 O
McKay, Robert H. to Maria Louisa Truehart 4-10-1857 (4-13-1857) Sh
McKean, J. C. to Nancy A. Wilkinson 11-3-1830 Hr
McKee (McRee), W. B. to Sophia A. Weaver 10-10-1850 Sh
McKee, A. H. to C. A. Jones 12-1-1867 (no return) Dy
McKee, J. F. to S. C. Bizzell 7-11-1885 (7-12-1885) L
McKee, James R. to Elizabeth Wilson 5-10-1838 O
McKee, James to Lucinda Whitby 11-7-1848 (11-24-1848) Hr
McKee, Jno. to Elizabeth Estill 10-18-1837 Sh
McKee, John W. to Sophia C. Castell 3-11-1863 Sh
McKee, John to Diana C. Goodwin 9-20-1832 Hr
McKee, John to Elizabeth Fleming 9-5-1850 Sh
McKee, John to Louisa Foster 12-22-1856 (12-23-1856) Hr
McKee, John to Zelphi A. E. McKinne 12-12-1848 (12-16-1848) Hr
McKee, R. A. to Samarimus (Sue) Roycroft 1-8-1867 (1-10-1867) Dy
McKee, William to Adelia Gregory 12-31-1844 Sh
McKee, Wm. H. to Lemisa R. Birdsong 9-12-1871 (9-13-1871) Ma
McKeehan, Nathan to Eliza J. Stephenson 6-25-1859 (6-26-1859) Sh
McKeever, James J. to Charlotte Gwynne 2-24-1859 (2-28-1859) Sh
McKehan, Wm. to Nancy M. Lasiter 5-28-1860 (5-30-1860) Sh
McKelsey, John C. to Julia A. (Mrs.) Henning 1-30-1861 (no return) Cr
McKelvey, Dennis to Catharine Riley (McKelroy?) 7-17-1858 Sh
McKelvey, James G. to M. L. Shane 8-30-1860 G
McKelvey, John W. to Polly J. Coats 12-20-1851 (12-22-1851) G
McKelvie, William J. to Mary C. Ward 10-5-1861 Be
McKelvin, Meredith to Margaret Poyner 8-15-1850 Hn
McKelvy, D. F. to R. J. Hedgecock 9-11-1843 G
McKelvy, Hugh to Rebecca Paschal 1-3-1860 Hn
McKelvy, J. W. to Elizabeth E. Holt 2-1-1870 G
McKelvy, Jasper N. to Nancy A. Presson 11-14-1867 Be
McKelvy, Mathew to Sarah Pafford 7-7-1836 Be
McKelvy, T. S. to Rebecca E. Howard 11-22-1858 (11-25-1858) G
McKendree, W. C. to Mattie Loving 1-8-1866 (1-9-1866) F
McKendrick, John W. to Martha Felts 9-7-1852 (9-9-1852) G
McKenna, Robert to Martha M. White 11-9-1861 Sh
McKenna, William J. to Rosa Ann Williams 10-11-1848 (10-12-1848) Ma
McKennee, Thomas to R. M. Reynolds 2-2-1852 (2-8-1852) L
McKennie, Jonathan to Semon Cozby 3-31-1836 Hr
McKennon, Miller to Frances Wynne 5-20-1876 Hy
McKennon, John a. to Sarah C. Fowler (Fonter?) 3-29-1871 (3-30-1871) L
McKenny, Young to Mary D. Carlton 3-3-1849 Cr
McKensie, G. S. to Jane Covington 10-8-1856 Hn
McKentosh, John A. to Nancy A. McKentosh 8-6-1842 (8-7-1842) G
McKenzie, D. M. to Ada B. Love 12-4-1869 (12-7-1869) Dy
McKenzie, Gilbert to Easther F. Pitt 2-10-1846 Be
McKenzie, Homer to Hattie F. Love 12-12-1870 (12-17-1870) Dy
McKenzie, Homer to L. D. Love 11-26-1877 Dy
McKenzie, J. A. to N. L. Darnall 6-16-1864 (6-19-1864) O
McKenzie, J. M. to M. L. Coleman 3-5-1842 Cr
McKenzie, John to Arelia David 5-10-1861 (7-8-1861) T
McKenzie, John to Mary M. Woods 12-28-1865 Mn
McKenzie, Louis to Molly Jones 7-3-1878 (no return) Hy
McKenzie, Malcomb to Mary Pierce 12-24-1854 Be
McKenzie, W. L. to E. Jane Pearce 3-16-1848 Be
McKenzie, Wm. to Maria Fennessey-Hennessey 5-24-1861 Sh
McKeon, James to Ann Dolan 1-7-855 Sh
McKeon, Thomas to Mary Hughes 9-24-1845 Sh
McKeown, James to W. Drummond 2-8-1869 (2-10-1869) T
McKey, A. to Nancy M. Russell 8-14-1857 Cr
McKey, James W. to Sarah Jane Moore 9-28-1857 (10-1-1857) Ma
McKey, John to Julia C. Moore 4-4-1838 Sh
McKey, Richard L. to Francis N. Caruthers 10-18-1860 O
McKey, T. B. to S. E. W. Rogers 9-18-1861 (9?-29-1861) Hr
McKey, William to Kezier? Sellers 10-18-1847 (10-19-1847) Hr
McKibben, Jas. to Anne Marie Crockett 6-10-1844 Sh
McKiel, James J. to Bettie W. Klyce 7-20-1875 Hy
McKilvy, William C. to Manerva Tate 12-10-1842 (1-22-1842?) G
McKimon, Loftin to Elizabeth Sherman 3-4-1850 Ma
McKindry, Frank to Ella Parks 12-20-1870 (no return) F B
McKiney, J. H. to Caladonia J. Darnell 9-17-1861 (9-23-1861) Cr
McKiney, J. H. to Mary L. Evans 11-2-1865 (11-5-1865) Cr
McKiney, John C. to Mary E. McCaslin 12-17-1866 (12-18-1867?) Cr
McKiney, John a. to Martha Ann Edwards 1-16-1867 L
McKing, John J. to M. E. Britton 1-27-1866 (2-1-1866) Cr
McKinie, Samuel Martin to Sarah Anders 9-4-1855 (9-6-1855) Hr
McKinley, Andy to Kitty Williams 1-17-1871 F B
McKinley, H. B. to Salina Alender? 11-26-1850 (12-3-1850) F
McKinley, J. H. to Sarah A. McClarty 12-31-1851 (12-18?-1851) Hr
McKinne, J. R. to Mary E. Kennedy 2-18-1856 (2-21-1856) Hr
McKinney, A. G. to Unis T. Evans 10-10-1855 Cr
McKinney, Alexander to Malvina Whitfield 7-9-1846 Sh
McKinney, Anderson to Mary A. Scott 3-28-1854 Cr
McKinney, Byrd to Rebecca Pinson 1-16-1859 Hn
McKinney, C. S. to Ada F. Pierson 2-20-1872 L
McKinney, D. V. to Minerva Kerley 10-30-1862 Dy
McKinney, Eacle to Sarah Hicks 2-6-1851 Cr
McKinney, Elijah to Lou Bradford 8-16-1871 Hy
McKinney, Henry to Sinith Ann Williams 6-5-1873 Hy
McKinney, J. R. to Sallie Johnson 2-20-1867 (2-22-1867) Cr
McKinney, J. T. to Virginia B. Burns 6-20-1881 (no return) L
McKinney, James to Margaret Bivins 12-29-1842 Sh
McKinney, John H. to Frances A. Edward 12-8-1842 Cr
McKinney, Jonathan to Martha A. E. Crihfield 8-16-1859 (8-17-1859) L
McKinney, Jonathan to Martha Jane Reynolds 1-25-1851 (2-2-1851) L
McKinney, Joseph to Mary Lancaster 2-5-1846 Hn
McKinney, Martin to Ann Ryan 1-25-1862 (1-28-1862) Sh
McKinney, N. M. to Susan E. Lacy 2-6-1865 F
McKinney, Perry to Mary McNeill 8-5-1867 (8-10-1867) F B
McKinney, Robert to Lucinda Reynolds 9-30-1828 Sh
McKinney, Samuel to Lucy A. Sanders 8-15-1854 (no return) F
McKinney, T. C. to E. V. Terry 6-27-1868 (7-1-1868) Cr
McKinney, William J. to Elizabeth T. (Mrs.) Davis 8-9-1858 (8-10-1858) Ma
McKinnie, Arthur to Harriet D. Lee 3-23-1833 (3-26-1833) Hr
McKinnie, Beverly R. to Zarina Williams 3-24-1839 (3-28-1839) Hr
McKinnie, John R. to Susan F. Crawford 2-11-1830 (2-16-1830) Hr
McKinnie, John to Elizabeth C. Reaves 3-8-1841 (3-11-1841) Hr
McKinnie, John to Mary H. Johnson 12-2-1830 Sh
McKinnie, Michial to Julia McKinnie 11-13-1832 (11-22-1832) Hr
McKinnie, Saml. M. to Jane Martin 2-28-1848 (3-2-1848) Hr
McKinnie, William W. to Billa E. Hammons 12-18-1855 (12-26-1855) Hr
McKinnie, William to Susannah McKinnie 3-15-1826 (3-16-1826) Hr
McKinnie, Wm. P. to Lucy Moon(Moore?) 10-5-1846 (10-6-1846) Hr
McKinnie, Wm. P. to Sarah F. Crawford 12-1-1832 (12-5-1832) Hr
McKinnon, J. A. to S. E. Chalk 7-30-1862 (no return) Hy
McKinnon, Neal to Mary Revell 8-19-1859 (no return) Hy
McKiny, Candour to Margaret C. Morton 11-20-1844 (no return) F
McKinny, Jeff to Sinda Henning 6-5-1885 (6-26-1885) L
McKinny, Joseph to Sarah Hollingsworth 8-26-1830 Sh
McKinny, Roland to Maria Jones 12-28-1853 Sh
McKinny, W. W. to Mary J. Delaney 8-3-1872 (8-4-1872) T
McKinstry, J. W. to E. W. West 2-24-1860 Sh
McKinstry, W. P. to P. E. Parrott 11-16-1869 (11-17-1869) F
McKinstry, Wm. to Eliza Ann Davis 12-16-1858 T
McKinza, Asa to Matilda Condra 2-17-1828 Hr
McKinzie, T. D. to S. E. Travis 10-20-1868 (10-22-1868) Cr
McKirby, Abraham to Sally McDaniel 1-11-1830 (1-19-1830) G
McKisick, Wm. H. to Matilda Lee 12-24-1867 F B
McKissick, Alfred to Catherine Carter 2-19-1839 Hn
McKissick, R. J. to Ellen Somers 10-6-1858 (10-7-1858) Hr
McKizzick, Jno. W. to Sarah Thompson 12-14-1850 Hr
McKneely, Thos. to Leathen Fuller 11-21-1836 (12-1-1836) G
McKnight, A. A. to J. A. Wilson 2-25-1856 (2-28-1856) G
McKnight, David M. to Martha M. Jimeson 9-4-1861 Sh
McKnight, Franklin to Eliza M. Buckley 11-7-1843 (11-14-1843) F
McKnight, G. W. to Marsha Clark 1-15-1859 Cr
McKnight, Hamilton J. to Margaret K. Black 11-2-1847 Ma
McKnight, J. H. to Elizabeth Boyett 3-19-1863 O

McKnight, James A. to Louisana Hess 10-31-1831 (11-3-1831) G
McKnight, James M. to Mary Robley 1-18-1845 Ma
McKnight, James P. to M. E. Ward 1-6-1863 (1-14-1863) O
McKnight, James to Susan M. Jones 5-5-1841 (5-6-1841) F
McKnight, Jas. A. to Rachael E. McDaniel 12-9-1858 G
McKnight, John B. to Louisa Stewart 8-10-1842 Sh
McKnight, John D. to Victoria A. Williams 3-9-1867 (3-14-1867) T
McKnight, John J. to Ellendor L. Thomas 2-21-1837 G
McKnight, Joseph H. to Nancy C. Fisher 1-24-1859 (2-1-1859) G
McKnight, Joseph to Frances Beckett 1-29-1872 (1-30-1872) Dy
McKnight, Joseph to Jane McCarley 12-7-1839 (12-10-1839) F
McKnight, Joseph to T. E. McKnight 1-31-1854 G
McKnight, Leander to Tempy Westbrooks 12-13-1879 (no return) L
McKnight, Leonidas to Jannett S. Maxwell 2-7-1848 Sh
McKnight, Luther D. to Mary E. Bland 6-14-1843 Sh
McKnight, Moses to Caroline C. Flynt 6-12-1852 Hr
McKnight, Richard T. to Catherine Reeves 12-31-1844 (1-2-1845) Ma
McKnight, Robert F. to Mary Jane Bradford 4-7-1859 Ma
McKnight, Robert M. to Louisanna E. Reeves 4-13-1839 Ma
McKnight, S. A. to Susan M. Kelly 2-28-1865 (3-1-1865) Dy
McKnight, Sam A. to Sarah T. Enochs 10-27-1873 (10-28-1873) Dy
McKnight, Samuel W. to Mary Louisa Sweeny 4-10-1856 Ma
McKnight, Silas M. to Margaret W. Craig 9-21-1828 (9-25-1828) G
McKnight, Thos. R. to Margart A. Howell 12-12-1850 (no return) F
McKnight, W. H. to Lina C. Warren 1-13-1868 G
McKnight, William F. to Mary E. Lester 4-15-1856 Ma
McKnight, William I. to Rebecca J. Mathews 10-13-1828 (11-13-1828) G
McKnight, William N. to Lucy A. McDavid 1-16-1864 (1-17-1864) Dy
McKoy, John C. to Irena McDonald 9-7-1852 (9-9-1852) Ma
McLagan?, W. R. to Josephine Blume 11-3-1863 (no return) L
McLain, Francis to Jane Sexton 7-25-1866 (8-20-1866) T
McLain, John H. to Louisa Webb 1-5-1860 (no return) We
McLain, John to Elizabeth Curley? 12-13-1837 Hr
McLain, W. A. to Ronanah C. D. Thomas 3-1-1855 G
McLain, William T. to Martha Hart 1-5-1860 We
McLain, William to Parthena A. M. Butler 8-9-1861 (8-10-1861) T
McLane, Daniel to Mary N. W. Avery 4-1-1845 (4-3-1845) G
McLane, Jeshua to Caroline Marberry 10-10-1850 Hn
McLary, John B. to Francis H. King 6-27-1829 L
McLary, Samuel to Jane Isabella McKnight 11-18-1834 (11-20-1834) G
McLaughlin, John to Nancy White 10-11-1854 (10-12-1854) T
McLaughlin, Liberty H. to Margarett Murray 6-16-1862 (6-19-1862) Sh
McLaughlin, Martin to Rusia Jones 3-22-1863 Sh
McLaughlin, Michael to Margaret Burke 8-22-1863 Sh
McLaughlin, Pat to Elizabeth McDermot 12-7-1860 Sh
McLaughlin, Pat;rcik to Mary Whalan 10-25-1842 Sh
McLaughlin, Patrick to Ann McDermat 7-28-1858 (5?-28-1858) Sh
McLaughlin, R. W. to H. E. McDill 5-25-1871 (5-30-1871) T
McLaughlin, Ray to N. E. Perminter 7-7-1851 F
McLaughlin, Thomas to Rachel McLaughlin 2-21-1824 (2-24-1824) Hr
McLaughlin, W. R. to Mary E. McClerkin 3-7-1874 (3-18?-1874) T
McLaughlin, W. V. to Nancy A. Taylor 5-29-1864 Mn
McLean, Arch. to Lucy Ferguson 10-6-1839 Sh
McLean, Charles P. to Mariah J. Mathis 12-24-1840 G
McLean, Daniel to E. A. Palston 12-17-1851 Cr
McLean, Ed to Ann Walker 9-5-1884 (9-6-1884) L
McLean, W. A. to Nancy J. Skyles 3-29-1866 G
McLean, William J. to Elizabeth A. (Mrs.) Bartis 7-3-1848 (7-4-1848) F
McLeary, John to Laura Lynch 6-14-1864 G
McLeary, Joseph to Ellen Gravitt 12-13-1866 G
McLeary, Robert R. to Pauline A. Bell 9-18-1849 Sh
McLeary, S. M. to S. C. Warren 1-8-1867 G
McLeary, Saml. D. to Sarah A. Weller 10-11-1841 (10-?-1841) T
McLeary, W. T. to Amanda E. Pugh 9-14-1854 (10-3-1854) Hr
McLeary?, James Allen to Mary S. Weller 7-17-1855 (7-18-1855) T
McLelland, Billy to Lizzy Graham 12-23-1875 (no return) Hy
McLemon, Major to Jane Haynes 7-28-1866 Hy
McLemore, A. to Margaret L. McMillan 1-20-1866 (no return) Hy
McLemore, Abraham to Sally Erwin 5-4-1823 (5-8-1827) G
McLemore, Edwin to Elizabeth Baker 1-28-1845 Sh
McLemore, Egbert to Martha J. Camp 9-20-1865 G
McLemore, Frank to Darcus Smith 12-12-1870 (12-15-1870) T
McLemore, J. K. P. to Margaret C. Jackson 10-11-1870 G
McLemore, Joseph to M. C. Graves 3-22-1883 (no return) L
McLemore, King to Lizzy Herron 4-16-1870 (4-17-1870) Cr
McLemore, Nat. to Ann Webb 7-16-1867 G
McLemore, Robert N. to Mary Ann Eliza Boykin 9-1-1855 (9-5-1855) Ma
McLemore, S. B. to Ann McCall 4-5-1858 Sh
McLemore, Sugars to Mary J. Taylor 7-28-1862 (no return) Cr
McLemore, Wm. S. to Oregon N. Teague 12-21-1861 (12-24-1861) Hr
McLemore, jr., John C. to Sallie T. Lane 6-24-1857 (6-25-1857) Sh
McLennen, Daniel to Emer H. Adkins 12-23-1865 (12-26-1865) T
McLennon, John to Susanna M. C. Adkins 1-24-1850 T
McLenon (McClean), J. to Matilda Freeman 6-29-1869 (no return) Hy
McLeod, Daniel to Jennie Hudson 7-26-1871 (no return) Hy
McLeod, H. D. to S. E. Lay 12-11-1878 Hy
McLeod, John P. to Anna E. Spence 5-1-1878 Hy

McLeod, John to Ann McDougald 8-20-1839 G
McLeod, Neil to Mariah L. Pope 9-10-1844 L
McLeod, R. D. to Mary E. Friend 7-19-1873 (7-29-1873) L
McLeod, Robert D. to Sallie A. Hood 1-30-1878 Hy
McLeod, William M. to Sarah Bostick 6-7-1841 (7-29-1841) Hr
McLeon, J. N. to Sallie E. Horman 3-13-1862 Sh
McLeroy, John to Mary Jane Caplinger 10-2-1856 Be
McLester, Z. L. to Ann M. Scott 2-15-1859 Hn
McLeughlin, Michael to Bridget Rovers 8-15-1863 Sh
McLevee, N. H. to O. M. Bibbs 3-7-1867 Cr
McLewain, R. G. to Laura L. Pullen 11-18-1858 (11-23-1858) T
McLeyea, W. L. to Polly K. George 7-3-1863 O
McLillie, James to Martha Jane C. Richardson 8-7-1871 (8-8-1871) T
McLin, J. D. to M. A. Green 11-25-1866 G
McLin, Patrick to Goodlow Taylor 9-5-1867 (no return) Hy
McLin, W. H. to M. M. (Mrs.) Goganus 10-9-1866 G
McLinn, William to Rebecca McDougold 12-18-1843 (12-21-1843) G
McLintock, Jas. L. to R. B. McCormick 5-6-1867 T
McLish, Joseph B. to Sarah B. Currie 11-14-1859 (no return) Hy
McLister, John C. to Mary Adaline Allen 11-21-1855 (11-22-1855) T
McLode, James to Mary M. Crowder 8-22-1865 Hy
McLoid, Wm. D. to M. E. McCully 11-23-1854 Cr
McLoughland, John to Mary A. Strong 12-8-1860 (12-12-1860) T
McLune, Zachariah to Amy Parting 1-5-1859 We
McLure, D. H. to Louisa Patterson 7-7-1852 Cr
McLure, Martin V. to Martha Merrell 12-14-1859 We
McLure, William I. to Elizabeth J. Somers 11-25-1860 We
McLuster, J. C. to E. C. Faussette 7-10-1873 (7-11-1873) T
McMAckin, James W. to Sarah J. Driver 10-14-1866 Hn
McMack, James to Josephine Browder 4-27-1858 Be
McMackin, Andrew to Lucinda McMackin 10-9-1867 (10-10-1867) Cr
McMackin, David to Amanda Ruff 12-24-1866 Cr
McMackin, David to Minter Lee Rodgers 2-10-1846 Cr
McMackin, David to Sarah E. Driver 9-11-1859 Hn
McMackin, Edward to Harriet Finch 2-2-1841 Cr
McMackin, James to Elizabeth Grooms 8-8-1858 Cr
McMackin, James to Elizabeth Porterfield 12-17-1843 Cr
McMackin, M. to Lucinda Lipe 12-27-1843 Cr
McMackin, W. J. to L(ucy) E(mma) Saulsberry 8-19-1873 (8-21-1873) L
McMackin, Wm. to Harriet William 2-26-1843 Cr
McMackins, David to Susan R. Lowery 3-18-1863 (3-19-1863) Cr
McMackins, E. A. to F. P. Smith 1-5-1872 (1-7-1872) Cr
McMackins, L. F. to Randy J. Rust 12-23-1869 (12-29-1869) Cr
McMahan, Andrew to Lucenda Ruff 5-4-1840 Ma
McMahan, C. C. to Sarah Tate 1-31-1857 (2-1-1857) Sh
McMahan, George H. to Harriet A. Johnson 8-26-1863 We
McMahan, J. G. to F. J. Harrell 9-26-1855 (9-27-1855) Ma
McMahan, Jno. to Fanny Hendricks 3-3-1848 Sh
McMahan, John to Lotty Golden 7-7-1851 (7-10-1851) Hr
McMahan, Robt. B. to Martha Steagall 5-13-1846 (5-17-1846) Hr
McMahan, Wm. S. to Antonia Saunders 12-20-1855 Sh
McMahen, Jno. S. to A. L. Stewart 11-10-1860 (no return) Hy
McMahen, R. C. to E. B. Masebach 11-20-1871 (no return) Hy
McMahon, Daniel to Catharine Waters 9-7-1861 (9-9-1861) Sh
McMahon, James A. to Nancy A. Gaines 11-23-1869 (11-25-1869) L
McMahon, John to Margaret Quinlan 10-28-1861 Sh
McMahon, John to Mary McMahon 7-28-1857 Sh
McMahon, Patrick to Mary McNerney 7-25-1863 Sh
McMahon, T. J. to M. C. Cameron 2-14-1878 Hy
McMahon, Thomas J. to Frucy Hays 9-28-1831 Ma
McMahon, Timothy to Anne Jennings 12-2-1861 (12-3-1861) Sh
McMallen, Thomas to Sarah E. Laxton? 1-26-1870 (1-27-1870)] T
McMaster, Saml. T. to Nancy Elizabeth Black 10-4-1858 Ma
McMaster, Thos. J. to Lidy E. Spencer 1-12-1869 Ma
McMasters, W. D. to P. P. Parks 11-4-1861 Ma
McMellon, Duncan to Rebecca Ewing 11-21-1840 Ma
McMichael, John W. to Margaret E. Sheridan 11-19-1854 Hn
McMichael, Joseph to Penesa Podge 4-9-1851 Hn
McMicken, John to Mary Bledsoe 12-26-1867 T
McMilan, Daniel to Louisa Williams 1-16-1858 Cr
McMillan, Archibald to Julia A. F. Young 10-23-1856 (10-26-1856) Ma
McMillan, Edward A. to Drucilla White 7-28-1841 T
McMillan, James Howard to Nancy Jackson 3-22-1842 Hr
McMillan, James to Mary Jane Marlow 2-26-1850 Ma
McMillan, John H. to Mary Ann Speh 10-9-1871 (10-10-1871) Ma
McMillan, Joshua to Nancy M. McMillan 8-1-1839 (8-7-1839) Ma
McMillan, Neil to A. Combs 2-27-1868 G
McMillan, Robert D. to Minerva Anderson 10-13-1836 Hr
McMillan, Valentine to Elizabeth Downing 1-25-1843 (1-27-1843) Ma
McMillan, Wm. to Jane Beavers 4-4-1843 Ma
McMillen, Alex to Ann Higgins 1-15-1852 (1-16-1852) Sh
McMillen, James to A. (Mrs.) Jones 10-31-1871 O
McMillen, T. J. to C. R. Scott 9-10-1859 (10-10-1859) Hr
McMillian, Duncan to Sarah A. Butler 12-19-1850 Cr
McMillin, Addison to Mary Harris 5-18-1830 Hr
McMillin, Wm. to Clementine C. Williamson 2-2-1869 Ma
McMillon, J. M. to Mary Hart 12-15-1849 (12-18-1849) F

McMinn, J. N. to S. A. Coleman 2-26-1866 (3-1-1864?) G
McMinn, James M. to Elizabeth A. Foutch 1-30-1870 G
McMinn, John W. to Sarah J. McKelvy 9-25-1866 G
McMinn, Samuel to Elizabeth Lyon 1-23-1843 (1-25-1843) G
McMinn, William to Matilda Wallingford 2-29-1844 G
McMorris, Howard to Fannie Nelms 5-26-1877 O B
McMullen, C. M. to Lucinda McMullen 8-29-1853 (8-30-1853) Sh
McMullen, J. W. to Wilmoth G. Jones 8-24-1857 (8-25-1857) Sh
McMullen, Michael to Alice McGrigan 10-28-1846 Sh
McMullen, Nathan to Malinda Richardson 5-7-1827 (5-15-1827) G
McMullen, Stuart to Martha W. Jones 10-4-1869 (10-6-1869) F
McMullen, Wm. P. to Georgia Lloyd 4-20-1868 (4-22-1868) F
McMullin, Eli to Harriett Davidson 12-22-1832 (12-27-1832) G
McMullin, J. W. to Cornelia Wilkerson 12-23-1858 Cr
McMullin, John to Mary Morrison 3-17-1857 (3-18-1857) Sh
McMullin, Luther to Harriet N. Orr 2-13-1854 Sh
McMullin, Silas W. to Sarah Adaline McKeasy 12-31-1845 F
McMullin, Wm. R. to Frances Agee 3-19-1840 F
McMullins, Albert T. to Joannah Boles 6-6-1859 (6-9-1859) Ma
McMurray, H. to Sarah G. Freeland 6-24-1849 Hn
McMurray, Logan to Lilly Mays 2-2-1870 G B
McMurray, T. J. to Martha P. Hon 1-15-1868 Hy
McMurrey, Wm. to Annie Loveland 1-4-1864 Sh
McMurry, I. E. to Amanda Carethers 12-7-1866 O
McMurry, J. A. to Fannie P. Markham 11-28-1867 Hy
McMurry, J. F. P. to Salie E. Speight 2-1-1877 Hy
McMurry, J. F. to A. M. Thomas 12-2-1869 Hy
McMurry, J. W. to Judy Bell Faris 2-27-1878 Hy
McMurry, John F. to Martha J. McGaugh 9-22-1864 O
McMurry, Melvin to Mary Jane McKnight 10-15-1865 Mn
McMurry, Robert A. to Nancy Richardson 11-3-1860 (no return) Hy
McMurry, Sam'l W. to R. M. Tucker 4-16-1872 (4-18-1872) O
McMurry, Silas to Lucy Smith 10-22-1870 (10-23-1870) O
McNab, E. B. to Elizabeth (Mrs.) Paterson 11-2-1864) Sh
McNab, Ewing Y. to Mahaley Nelson 4-20-1839 Sh
McNabb, Ezekiel to Martha Ann Bryan 3-16-1833 Sh
McNabb, Green S. to Frances Wright 5-27-1854 Hn
McNabb, Wm. to Maria Jones 6-24-1845 Sh
McNail, Henry to Nancy Wyatt 8-1-1869 G B
McNail, Robt. H. to Susan L. McCorkle 11-23-1869 G
McNail, Thomas A. to Emily Jane Herron 11-5-1855 (11-7-1855) Ma
McNair, Evander to Mary J. McBride 11-23-1860 (11-27-1860) T
McNair, Hector to Eliza Parker 2-14-1852 (2-15-1852) T
McNair, James E. to Patience E. Flippin 1-18-1862 G
McNair, John to Zena Manaskie 7-15-1847 Sh
McNair, Neil to Mary F. Bronson 2-16-1860 (2-22-1860) Sh
McNair, W. H. to Martha Carter 2-25-1860 T
McNair, Wiley P. to Nancy Ann Flippin 6-21-1868 G
McNaire?, Saml. to Martha A. Paten 5-3-1867 F
McNairn, John to Margaret Harris 11-5-1874 (11-6-1874) L
McNairy, George to Lavinia Wright 8-8-1879 (8-10-1879) L B
McNairy, George to Mittie Parr 3-11-1878 (not executed) L
McNally, John to Mary Flaherty 4-21-1858 (4-22-1858) Sh
McNama, John to Isabella D. Adams 2-17-1841 (2-18-1841) F
McNamara, Daniel to Ann Green 10-17-1858 Sh
McNamara, James to Catharine McMahan 11-5-1860 Sh
McNamara, James to Catherine Dowds 4-1-1864 (4-3-1864) Sh
McNamara, John to Elizabeth Maguire 6-9-1852 (6-10-1852) Sh
McNamara, John to Hannah Mishel (Miskel?) 7-30-1853 (7-31-1853) Sh
McNamara, John to Mary Daly 3-17-1860 Sh
McNamara, Michael to Ann Kitchen 8-10-1848 Sh
McNamara, Michael to Ann Rogan 7-30-1843 Sh
McNamara, Michael to Margaret McNamee 5-9-1859 (5-12-1859) Sh
McNamara, Tim to Jane (Mrs.) Cunningham 12-31-1864 Sh
McNamarer, Michael to Ann Green 4-27-1864 Sh
McNamee, Charles to Emily Finch 1-11-1849 (no return) F
McNamee, Charles to Mary Kedd 1-27-1840 (no return) F
McNamee, Chas. to Eliz. Bryant 6-21-1845 (no return) F
McNamee, Michael to Catherine Buckley 12-27-1843 Sh
McNamee, W. F. to Fannie M. Freeman 11-2-1866 (11-7-1866) F
McNar, Z. H. to Martha Carter 2-25-1860 T
McNary, Isaac to Sallie Ford 5-21-1868 (5-27-1868) F B
McNary, Willis to Frances Carothers 6-13-1866 (6-15-1866) T
McNary, Wm. to Caroline Montgomery 2-3-1870 (2-5-1870) F B
McNatt, L. R. to Mahala Powell 11-24-1862 Mn
McNeal, Andrew to Mattie McGill 11-1-1873 T
McNeal, Ezekiel P. to Ann Williams 1-22-1835 Hr
McNeal, Isham G. to Jacinda? Gamewell 9-6-1867 (9-14-1869?) T
McNeal, John H. to Elizabeth Rogers 9-21-1850 Ma
McNeal, John S. to Lucy A. Townsend 11-23-1857 (11-26-1857) T
McNeal, Nathan W. to Elizabeth H. Covington 12-15-1858 Cr
McNeal, Thomas C. to Lucy Randol 2-21-1861 G
McNeal, William W. to Elizabeth W. Berry 11-26-1844 Hr
McNear, A. F. to F. V. Horne 11-12-1856 Hy
McNeeley, A. H. to Essey Keathley 7-2-1839 (7-18-1839) O
McNeeley, James to Nancy Keathley 12-6-1841 (12-11-1841) O
McNeeley, Richard C. to Delilah Woods 11-6-1865 O

McNeeley, T. F. to Nancy E. Woods 8-5-1866 G
McNeeley, William W. to Nancy E. Reeves 2-24-1843 (3-2-1843) O
McNeell, A. C. to Mary E. Baker 7-28-1862 (7-29-1863?) Dy
McNeely, A. H. to Martha Rogers 7-21-1853 O
McNeely, A. T. to L. P. McNeely 11-4?-1865 (11-3-1865) O
McNeely, James B. to Sarah S. Bradberry 3-19-1586 (3-20-1856) Ma
McNeely, John W. to Sarah E. Baxter 3-6-1838 Sh
McNeely, John to Hester Brown 1-17-1843 Hr
McNeely, John to Manervy Taylor 10-29-1844 O
McNeely, Joseph B. to Margaret McNeely 1-6-1855 (1-10-1855) Sh
McNeely, Joseph to Rebecca Strong 1-7-1841 Sh
McNeely, Louis to Mary A. Holmes 1-31-1854 (2-1-1854) Ma
McNeely, Samuel to Margaret Houston 6-12-1841 (could be 1842) Sh
McNeely, Thomas W. to Sarah Shipman 3-31-1860 (4-1-1860) O
McNeely, Wm. C. to Rhoda C. Morton 1-1-1869 (no return) F
McNees, Richard H. to Nancy H. Johnson 9-24-1828 (9-25-1828) Hr
McNees, Robert L. to Lucy F. Arbuckle 11-6-1854 (no return) F
McNeil, A. C. to Sarah W. Muray 3-8-1854 Cr
McNeil, Buck to Martha Jones 1-6-1866 (1-14-1866) F B
McNeil, Henry to Martha Jones 12-28-1865 (1-14-1866) F B
McNeil, Horace to Caroline McNeil 3-17-1866 (8-26-1866) F B
McNeil, John to Tabitha E. Person 6-16-1835 Sh
McNeill, Abraham to Patience Randle 1-20-1871 (1-22-1871) Cr B
McNeill, Alfred to Emma Gaines 4-20-1870 (4-21-1870) Cr
McNeill, George to Cora Palmer 11-6-1867 Hn
McNeill, Green to Milly Derden 12-31-1866 (1-6-1867) F B
McNeill, J. A. to Kate E. Austin 1-9-1865 (1-10-1865) F
McNeill, J. H. to Minerva Armstrong 7-20-1859 (7-21-1859) Sh
McNeill, J. R. to M. P. Perry 12-16-1862 (12-24-1862) F
McNeill, James H. to Appless P. Sledge 4-17-1855 F
McNeill, John A. to Mary M. Powell 2-6-1871 (no return) Hy
McNeill, John C. to Ann Polk 5-10-1859 (6-15-1859) Hr
McNeill, Jordan to Rose Reeves 11-9-1867 (no return) F B
McNeill, N. to Eliza Moss 8-23-1840 Be
McNeill, Simon to Mary E. Perry 12-9-1867 (12-16-1867) F
McNeill, Thos. A. to Rachel M. Coldwell 8-11-1862 (no return) Cr
McNelis, Michael to Sarah Frances Dodson 3-9-1869 (3-21-1869) F
McNiel, Archey to Sarah Robison 3-2-1872 Hy
McNiel, Henry to Jane Griffin 10-9-1855 Be
McNight, Aaron to Josephine Maclin 2-9-1876 (no return) Hy
McNight, Wm. D. to Nancy Manansco 6-21-1844 Sh
McNutt, S. F. to Ann White 1-5-1848 (1-11-1848) Hr
McNutt, Thomas to Kinah Caldwell 10-5-1851 Hn
McNutt, Thomas to L. A. Clayton 1-1-1856 (no return) Hn
McNutty, Michal to Evaline E. Davis 12-23-1839 (12-24-1839) G
McNutty, Phillip to M. Spivey 4-13-1863 Mn
McO'Conner, ___ to Lucinda A. Medlock 5-19-1867 Hn
McPartlin (McWarlin), John to Mary Higgins 1-10-1863 Sh
McPherson, A. G. to Jane Sullivan 3-3-1861 Be
McPherson, C. to Lidia Ann Ackers (Akers) 10-30-1862 Be
McPherson, Enoch to R. J. Christie 8-16-1866 Dy
McPherson, John to Abigail Scripson? 2-8-1834 Hr
McPherson, Miles to Elmyra Brown 10-11-1882 (10-29-1882) L
McPherson, Rob't to Sophia H. Lambert 11-19-1867 O
McPherson, Rufus Thomas to Mary Martha Callehan 1-10-1872 L
McPherson, Samuel to Bettie Thompson 12-15-1875 L
McPherson, Samuel to Mollie Denton 9-26-1881 (9-23?-1881) L
McPherson, Stephen to Frances C. Belew 3-17-1849 (3-16?-1849) G
McPherson, W. L. to Artemicia Byrum 7-15-1878 (7-17-1878) L
McPherson, William to Jane Buford 2-27-1871 (3-4-1871) F B
McPortland, Owen to Ann McKinney 4-4-1864 (4-5-1864) Sh
McQuary, William to Darcus E. Bell 8-14-1871 (no return) Hy
McQuerter, David Hemphill to Nancy Jane Wham? 5-6-1853 T
McQuillan, John to Catherine O'Harra 8-17-1862 Sh
McQuin, Patrick to Louine Sanderlin 10-8-1855 Sh
McQuinig, Daniel to Nancy McDaniel 12-17-1839 Be
McQuire, J. M. to Rebecca E. Crawford 1-14-1859 Cr
McQuirter, Chas. E. to A. E. Scott 2-10-1867 F
McQuirter, George M. to Margaret Douglas 10-20-1869 (no return) F B
McQuistian, Louis to Nancy McLain 9-16-1865 T
McQuistin, David H. to Margaret Wright 4-8-1843 (4-11-1843) T
McQuistin, Wm. to Jane W. Allen 2-24-1845 (2-25-1845) F
McQuiston, Alexander J. to Margaret G. McCain 12-16-1845 T
McQuiston, Andrew to Sally Gillespie 11-13-1856 Sh
McQuiston, D. H. to Mary Ann Mcquiston 8-31-1870 T
McQuiston, H. W. to M. A. McDier? 2-26-1870 (3-1-1870) T
McQuiston, Thomas to Sallie Robinson 12-19-1870 (12-24-1871?) T
McQuiston, William H. to Sarah Wilson 9-26-1855 T
McQuiston, William sr. to Eliza Ann Baird 7-23-1844 (7-25-1844) T
McQurter, George to Chany Sprout 2-5-1853 Hn
McRae, Alexander C. to Luan Brown 1-1-1868 Be
McRae, Dandridge to Angelina W. Lewis 12-7-1854 (1-10-1855) Sh
McRae, John L. to Mahala Jane Alsup 4-24-1860 Be
McRae, W. H. to Lydia J. McBride 1-13-1869 Be
McReaves(Reaves?), W. to Edmonia T. Neece 4-7-1859 (4-9-1859) Hr
McRee, C. W. to Emma H. Johnson 10-11-1869 (10-12-1869) F
McRee, D. W. to Mary S. Dewitt 12-27-1860 O

McRee, David to E. T. (Mrs.) McKinney 11-11-1868 G
McRee, F. M. to Minnie Crockett 11-13-1867 O
McRee, James H. to Francis Bundy 10-28-1863 O
McRee, James H. to Sarah Ann Brown 5-5-1857 O
McRee, John B. to Jane Trout 8-13-1863 G
McRee, John W. to Sophia C. Casteel 3-11-1863 Sh
McRee, William to Sarah Ann Nipp 6-23-1857 O
McReynolds, L. D. to Jennie Jordan 9-4-1869 (9-6-1869) L
McRoe, James to Olivia Day 10-10-1842 Ma
McShane, P. to Mary Shadwick 11-7-1868 (11-8-1868) Cr
McShared, Rufus to Ann E. Spier 6-27-1862 L
McSharp, John to Elizabeth Trout 1-9-1846 (1-12-1846) G
McShaw, John to Nancy Brown 12-5-1870 (no return) F
McSheyn, Charles to Hannah McKinney 12-6-1866 Dy
McSmith, John to Kate M. Kelly 1-1-1861 We
McSmith, John to Sarah J. Stell 3-4-1853 Sh
McSpadden, Wm. B. to Caroline Bayne 4-13-1848 Sh
McSwain, David E. to Mariah J. Forest 9-13-1853 Cr
McSwain, William A. to Louisa Ann Justice 9-24-1852 (9-26-1852) Hr
McSwine, John to Ann W. Bailey 2-19-1852 (no return) F
McVay, A. O. to Nancy J. Campbell 1-13-1846 Hn
McVay, A. to Narsissa Ringer 10-20-1864 Sh
McVay, Basel to Cladus Laughter 9-25-1847 F
McVay, Hugh to Sophia Davidson 9-13-1827 Sh
McVay, John to Margaret Johnson 11-18-1848 (no return) F
McVay, Jourdan W. to Martha C. Brown 11-16-1843 (no return) Hn
McVey, Argile to J. H. (Mrs.?) Armour 12-19-1859 Sh
McVey, James to Mary E. Taylor 6-29-1867 Hn
McVey, John F. to Alice R. Kirby 6-13-1865 (6-14-1865) O
McVey, Reuben to Jane Pemberton 6-6-1844 (6-11-1844) Ma
McVey, William to Adaline Smith 6-12-1867 (6-25-1867) F
McWest, Mercer to Martha A. Bazemore 7-6-1853 (7-7-1853) Sh
McWherter, George D. to Gina Webb 3-4-1863 We
McWherter, Jas. S. to Mary Patterson 12-20-1845 (12-21-1845) G
McWherter, John to Mary A. Old 12-17-1860 We
McWherter, John to Ruth Clayton 3-5-1829 (3-6-1829) O
McWherter, Stephen M. to Tabathy Webb 11-9-1852 We
McWherter, Wm. P. to Lucy Ann Beckley 1-12-1859 We
McWherter, ___ to Jane Farris 4-22-1830 G
McWhirter, Charles E. to Sarah J. Kennedy 9-27-1854 (9-28-1854) G
McWhirter, James B. to Paulina L. McWworth 2-15-1832 Hr
McWhirter, John C. to Sarah S. Barton 9-29-1869 G
McWhirter, William M. to Martha A. V. Parker 7-17-1844 (7-18-1844) G
McWhorter, H. C. to Elizabeth Odam 10-18-1863 G
McWhored, J. S. to Mary S. Caraway 1-2-1860 G
McWhorter, James M. to Elizabeth I. Kirby 1-14-1857 (1-17-1857) O
McWhorter, Jeremiah to Martha Boon 10-1-1835 G
McWhorter, John C. to Mary E. Swink 1-22-1865 O
McWhorter, Reuben to Elizabeth Wright 12-13-1832 O
McWilliams, A. R. to Virginia M. Gayle 2-26-1856 Sh
McWilliams, James to Margaret Vanhook 1-2-1832 Sh
McWilliams, James to Rhody Murphy 5-25-1847 (5-27-1840 Hr
McWilliams, John to Elender Burrow 11-12-1846 O
McWilliams, P. B. to Joanna Caskey 1-20-1869 (1-21-1869) T
McWilliams, Robert R. to Mary Moore 2-29-1839 Ma
Mcdurmott, W. J. to Susan Taylor 7-13-1869 (no return) Hy
Mchelby, James W. to Harriett Burrow 12-8-1854 Cr
Mcllister, J. K. to Nancy Johnson 3-29-1868 G
Meacham, Abram to Caroline Kelly 1-4-1869 (1-10-1869) F B
Meacham, George to Louisa Norvell 9-1-1880 L
Meacham, Henry Banks to Mary Ann Robinson 12-11-1854 (12-?-1854) Sh
Meacham, Henry J. to Sarah L. Foster 12-10-1883 (12-11-1883) L
Meacham, J. B. to R. E. Wood 2-16-1886 L
Meacham, J. E. to S. M. Ellis 9-5-1884 (9-7-1884) L
Meacham, J. P. C. to Mary L. Pollard 12-16-1874 L
Meacham, James E. to Sarah E. Lunsford 11-27-1878 (11-28-1878) L
Meacham, James H. to Millie Pleasants 2-22-1837 O
Meacham, Jesse M. to Mary F. Wardlaw 10-3-1855 (10-4-1855) L
Meacham, Jesse to Margaret Edmonds 6-15-1830 (6-16-1830) O
Meacham, Jessee to Ellen J. Brown 1-7-1861 L
Meacham, R. B. to Sallie Parish 5-22-1884 L
Meacham, Thomas E. to Eliza J. Shoemake 9-14-1854 L
Meacham, William Henry to Jane Whitson 7-30-1857 (no return) L
Mead, Benjamin F. to Sarah J. Simpson 8-16-1847 (8-17-1847) O
Mead, J. H. to Millie E. Bailey 6-10-1871 (6-11-1871) Dy
Meade, Patrick to Elizabeth Ryan 10-8-1854 Sh
Meader, James A. to Alvira L. Kingsbury 3-8-1855 (3-10-1855) Sh
Meador, Andrew J. to Sarah Ann Swindle 12-25-1860 Hr
Meador, J. V. to S. A. Jennings 9-6-1880 (9-7-1880) L
Meador, W. J. to S. A. (Mrs.) Carroll 12-10-1867 Cr
Meadors, W. J. to Mary Jennings 1-19-1886 (1-20-1886) L
Meadow, C. F. to J. A. McClain 3-31-1867 Hn
Meadow, J. N. to T. B. Thompson 1-1-1878 (1-2-1878) L
Meadow, Wm. M. to Mary A. Smith 7-25-1864 (7-26-1864) O
Meadows, A. J. to A. Holmes 7-16-1883 L
Meadows, A. J. to Marietta Henley 3-17-1866 (3-20-1866) L
Meadows, Foster to Eliza Wingo 12-24-1870 (12-27-1870) Cr

Meadows, J. G. to S. E. Jones 10-10-1870 (no return) Dy
Meadows, J. N. to Mary E. Ledbetter 2-22-1869 (2-29?-1869) L
Meadows, J. T. to Mollie J. Savage 12-18-1883 (12-19-1883) L
Meadows, John M. to America Thompson 11-26-1861 We
Meadows, John W. to Francis H. Chism 5-18-1842 (5-19-1842) L
Meadows, Jonas B. to Catharine Wilborn 5-11-1848 O
Meadows, Nathan to Lucy Carroll 8-23-1848 (8-10-1848) G
Meadows, S. C. to M. L. Mallory 12-22-1870 (no return) Dy
Meadows, Solomon G. to Amanda E. Webb 11-17-1852 L
Meadows, Thomas J. to Mary Kemp 3-30-1859 We
Meadows, William D. to Margaret E. Elmore 3-14-1885 (3-15-1885) L
Meadows, William to Sarah Beckett 1-15-1873 (1-16-1873) Dy
Meak, John M. to Jane Burrow 10-24-1848 (no return) F
Meaks, James R. to Elizabeth Upchurch 1-4-1848 Hn
Meals, Daniel J. to Martha H. Morrow 12-6-1843 (12-7-1843) Ma
Meals, Geo. W. to Malesa Morrow 9-26-1840 Cr
Meals, John M. to Elizabeth E. Morrow 12-3-1846 (12-24-1846) Ma
Meals, John M. to Margaret E. (Mrs.) Caruthers 1-19-1867 (1-22-1867) Ma
Meals, Levi M. to Martha H. Murphy 1-31-1854 Cr
Meals, Wm. M. to Julia A. Pearcy 7-22-1865 (7-25-1866?) Cr
Meals?, L. H. to M. J. Flake 1-6-1873 Cr
Means, Billy to Mary Edmonson 11-3-1858 Sh
Means, James H. to Mary Hutcheson 11-15-1862 Mn
Means, James P. to Malinda Neece 8-7-1848 (8-8-1848) Hr
Means, John H. to Sarah A. Grant 4-15-1847 Sh
Means, Thomas M. to Ann E. Boley 10-4?-1853 (no return) F
Means, Thos. M. to Rachel Henderson 4-27-1843 Sh
Means, W. B. to Sophia Phoebus 10-28-1847 Sh
Mears, John G. to Eliza McGuise 12-24-1856 (1-1-1857) T
Mears, John G. to Frances M. Tucker 6-18-1860 (6-29-1860) T
Mears, William P. to Amy Bowles 1-17-1848 (1-?-1848) T
Mears, William to Elzabeth Delashmet 11-21-1848 (11-22-1848) T
Measells, J. W. to Martha C. Norman 5-27-1867 (5-29-1867) L
Measle, Jno. M. to Martha N. White 7-9-1873 Hy
Measles, Gilbert to Elizabeth Toby 2-12-1835 Sh
Measles, John to Polly Busby 7-31-1830 Sh
Measles, Timothy m. to Mary Ann Norman 5-27-1861 L
Measles, William to Elizabeth Clayton 2-8-1835 Sh
Meath, Patrick to Catherine Kennedy 11-20-1845 Sh
Meazles, John L. to Elizabeth Hadnott 1-9-1830 Sh
Mebane, Baker to Edmonia Wigglesworth 12-29-1870 (no return) F B
Mebane, Dave to Nannie Pittman 2-20-1871 (2-21-1871) F
Mebane, Freeman to Chaney Jordan 6-4-1869 (6-5-1869) F B
Mebane, Harris B. to Martha J. Fields 1-11-1854 Cr
Mebane, J. G. to L. J. Gooch 2-4-1868 (2-5-1868) Cr
Mebane, J. W. to Sarah E. Morrow 7-24-1851 Cr
Mebane, W. E. to Louisa Eason 1-29-1867 (1-30-1867) Cr
Mebene, Sidny A. to Tennessee R. Briggance 2-12-1861 Cr
Medanis, John W. to Jacky C. Simpson 11-9-1842 L
Medards, R. A. to C. M. I. Yates 9-24-1860 (10-2-1861?) G
Medaris, S. to A. E. Dyer 1-6-1855 (1-7-1855) O
Medaris, Salathiel to Nancy Jane Osburn 11-21-1851 (11-23-1851) O
Medaris, Salathiel to Sarah Eliza Holloman 2-3-1854 O
Medders, Lewis to Tempey Jackson 12-13-1831 Ma
Medford, Jonathan to Isabella Wilson 4-20-1871 F
Medines, Joll B. to Mary H. Butler 10-27-1848 Cr
Medlen, T. G. to Matelada Tompkins 10-26-1871 (no return) We
Medley, James A. to Matilda P. Lochridge 6-2-1851 (6-5-1851) F
Medlin, Bradley to Susan Rains 10-14-1840 Ma
Medlin, Briant to Emily Finch 9-1-1845 We
Medlin, G. B. to Sarah A. Brown 5-15-1859 Hy
Medlin, G. M. to Eliza Tompkins 11-16-1859 We
Medlin, George C. to Jane Knight 1-20-1852 (1-21-1852) Ma
Medlin, George to Jane McBride 1-17-1850 Cr
Medlin, Herny? to Elizabeth Grazum 2-16-1860 We
Medlin, J. P. to Lovey A. French 11-11-1864 (11-12-1864) Cr
Medlin, J. R. to Arcada Marberry 3-29-1852 Hn
Medlin, Jack to Flora Drake 9-11-1872 Hy
Medlin, James H. to Rebecca M. McWilliams 10-9-1847 (10-13-1847) Ma
Medlin, James L. to Susan A. Holyfield 4-16-1850 Ma
Medlin, James M. to Catherine Burrow 12-18-1850 Ma
Medlin, James T. to Evelin Allen 6-15-1872 (no return) Cr
Medlin, James to Catharine Allen 4-22-1865 (4-23-1865) Cr
Medlin, Jno. T. to Nancy A. Jones 4-12-1871 (4-13-1871) Ma
Medlin, Moses to Dilly William 8-14-1867 (3-10-1870) Ma
Medlin, Petser to Mary R. Perkins 11-3-1853 Ma *
Medlin, Samuel H. to Mary Catherine Cate 8-1-1865 Hn
Medlin, Wiley to Emily Jones 9-9-1868 (9-10-1868) Ma
Medling, Andrew J. to Mary Betts 9-22-1870 G
Medling, Joseph L. to Elizabeth R. Bradberry 5-11-1838 (5-17-1838) Ma
Medlock, John S. to Louiza M. Fowell 12-31-1854 (no return) Hn
Medlock, Thomas to Mary J. Stinson 7-30-1838 Hr
Medom?, James to Jane Pritchett 2-17-1849 Sh
Meek(Merk), John E. to Catharine Hughes 5-7-1838 (5-10-1838) Hr
Meek, A. W. to Elizabeth Herralston 8-2-1858 Sh
Meek, A. W. to Elizabeth T. Tanner 12-27-1849 Sh
Meek, Elmore to Sarah Vanalsin 12-19-1846 Sh

Meek, J. F. to Rebecca A. Graves 2-5-1862 Mn
Meek, J. G. to Ardenia A. Blankenship 10-22-1860 G
Meek, Jefferson L. to Mary E. F. Meek 11-11-1862 G
Meek, Rufus to Mary T. McCloud 7-25-1853 (7-26-1853) Sh
Meek, Thomas H. to Mary E. Davidson 8-19-1852 G
Meek, William M. to Margarette T. Rooks 8-21-1861 G
Meeke, T. A. to Sally A. Jones 5-7-1876 Hy
Meeker, Moses to Margaret Ann Parker 11-21-1848 Sh
Meeks, Elias W. to Mattie H. Hofford 2-8-1872 (2-13-1872) L
Meeks, J. H. to Mary A. Merandy 1-14-1868 Dy
Meeks, Josephus to Elizabeth May 8-13-1838 (8-19-1838) Hr
Meers, Thomas to Eliza Cochran 5-11-1861 (5-12-1861) Sh
Meigs, A. L. to Catharine E. Kirkpatrick 6-11-1855 (no return) F
Meiler (Wiler), Philip to Cecilia App 12-23-1862 Sh
Meinrath, J. J. to Phoebe F. Choate 12-1-1853 Sh
Meisenhimmer, Jacob W. to Hetty Slough 12-25-1835 Sh
Meley, Jesse W. to Mary A. Gray 12-24-1867 G
Meliam, Benjamin F. to Nancy O. Pickins 10-13-1851 (no return) F
Melier, Wm. to Nancy L. Sparks 11-10-1846 Cr
Mellersh, Francis to Charlotte Augustus Leach 6-4-1855 Sh
Mellersh, George to Elizabeth D. James 11-24-1858 Sh
Mellworth, John to Emily Briant 6-23-1860 O
Melone, Patrick to Mary Rine 11-8-1862 Sh
Melson, M. A. to Anna E. Jackson 10-14-1864 (11-10-1864) Sh
Melton, A. H. to Elizabeth Pafford 9-14-1865 Be
Melton, Alvy to Mary Ann Melton 5-19-1853 Be
Melton, Beverly to Rebecca Radford 10-8-1864 Be
Melton, Braxton to Catharine McCraw 12-29-1869 (no return) F B
Melton, Coonrod J. to Lucritia Holland 4-10-1844 Be
Melton, David to Elizabeth Holland 8-23-1849 Be
Melton, E. W. to Serrilda Manuel 8-2-1872 (8-3-1872) Cr
Melton, Elijah W. to Lidia Pinkston 11-26-1864 Be
Melton, Elijah to Aney Ross 8-17-1843 Cr
Melton, Eltheldred to Crecy Holms 11-21-1865 Be
Melton, Etheldredge to Sintha Melton 6-25-1839 Be
Melton, Henry to Mary M. Montgomery 7-17-1850 (7-18-1850) F
Melton, Hiram to Rebecca Garman 8-28-1861 Mn
Melton, J. C. to M. A. McRea 12-12-1839 Be
Melton, J. C. to Pernicy H. Snider 12-11-1866 Hn
Melton, J. D. to lAmanda Bellew 9-19-1861 Be
Melton, J. F. L. to A. C. Bruer? 8-11-1841 Be
Melton, J. M. to Mary M. Ferguson 11-23-1865 Mn
Melton, James H. to Sarah A. Willson 3-16-1853 (no return) F
Melton, James P. to Susan R. Renfro 12-5-1866 Hn
Melton, James to Julia Herndon 9-12-1867
Melton, John A. to Sarah A. ___ 12-27-1863 G
Melton, John to Isabel Benton 1-17-1855 Be
Melton, John to Mary Ann Parker 1-10-1861 Be
Melton, Joseph to Susanah Hall 1-18-1850 Be
Melton, L. F. to Rebecca A. Finger 11-3-1865 Mn
Melton, M. A. to Louella Ethridge 9-9-1866 Hn
Melton, M. M. to Sophia Lock (Lack?) 9-25-1865 G
Melton, Monroe to Malissa Lock (Lack?) 8-24-1863 G
Melton, Pinkney H. to Eviline Pinkston 6-22-1861 Be
Melton, R. R. H. to M. L. Bradford 9-5-1866? (9-8-1867) Cr
Melton, Robert to Penelope Pate 7-30-1840 (8-30-1840) G
Melton, S. to Elizabeth Harris 10-4-1866 Hn
Melton, T. J. to Margaret T. Brown 12-18-1865 Mn
Melton, Thos. H. to Elizabeth Bargo 8-23-1846 We
Melton, W. T. J. to Mily A. Reader 12-27-1867 (12-28-1867) Cr
Melton, W. W. to America Given 5-25-1866 (5-27-1866) L
Melton, Wiley C. to Rebecca J. Mannon 2-24-1853 Be
Melton, William M. to Martha A. Julin 9-23-1860 We
Melton, William to Rachel Holland 12-5-1855 Be
Melugin, T. M. to C. V. Stewart 12-11-1862 F
Menasco?, John to Permelia Jane McClellan 3-8-1852 T
Mench?, ___ to Amanda Anderson 2-12-1849 (no return) F
Menden(h)all, W. S. to Louisa Potts 5-9-1864 (5-12-1864) Sh
Mendenall, F. to Sarah E. Barnhill 1-21-1858 Sh
Mendenall, J. G. to Sarah Ann Carr 7-3-1850 Sh
Mendeth?, David to Artis Y. Capp 12-28-1840 (no return) F
Meneece, J. T. to A. G. Walker 4-18-1872 O
Menees, Isaac to Emaline Gore 5-30-1831 O
Menefee, W. O. to Martha E. Calhoun 11-14-1860 (11-15-1860) T
Menes, Jacob C. to Rachael A. Hartsfield 7-3-1858 T
Menetree, Frank to Clementine Louit 5-27-1863 Mn
Menifee, R. S. to Elizabeth A. Hubbard 12-1-1859 Hn
Menken, Peter to Bettie McFadden 7-23-1874 (7-24-1874) T
Menley, James to Dora Molley 7-9-1863 Sh
Menschel, Frank to Annie Brugger 12-23-1859 (12-24-1859) Sh
Menzies, David to Mary F. Burton 10-31-1872 (no return) Dy
Menzies, George to Ann Buchanan 12-19-1865 (12-22-1865) Dy
Menzies, Isaac to Parthena Parker 10-24-1872 (9?-24-1872) Dy
Menzies, R. G. to Sarah F. Hall 7-18-1853 Hr
Mercer, Abner B. to Nancy Ann Robinson 4-12-1850 (4-16-1850) Hr
Mercer, Dennis to Pevy Sykes 7-5-1843 Be
Mercer, Isaac B. to Sarah D. Alexander 8-13-1849 (no return) F

Mercer, James P. to Marieller Burton 5-12-1855 (no return) F
Mercer, Joseph A. to Rebecca L. Robinson 2-20-1860 (2-23-1860) Hr
Mercer, Joseph S. to Mary Notby 8-13-1849 (no return) F
Mercer, T. C. to R. Boggs 2-2-1873 Hy
Mercer, Thomas B. to Catherine Chism 12-4-1838 Ma
Merchant, James to Nancy Little 6-26-1847 (no return) Hn
Merchant, John to Catherine McCorkle 12-20-1849 Hn
Meredith, J. S. to Mildred Wesson 7-19-1871 (7-25-1871) Dy
Meredith, James to Sarah Wimberly 2-1-1866 Hn
Meredith, John to Annis Beck 12-20-1853 Hn
Meredith, Simpson to Amanda Lemon 11-13-1867 Dy
Merell, John to Martha Claton 3-31-1865 Hn
Mereto, A. to Mary Nagle 12-27-1854 Sh
Mereto, Joseph to Rosa Devota 11-20-1858 (11-28-1858) Sh
Meritt, William to Catherine Grant 9-9-1848 Hn
Meriweather, Harm. to Lucy Stott 8-10-1866 Hy
Meriwether, D. J. to H. L. Williamson 4-2-1860 (4-4-1860) F
Meriwether, James G. to Lizzie Deberry 1-24-1871 (1-25-1871) Ma
Meriwether, James to Sarah B. Dunn 2-8-1840 Ma
Meriwether, Matt D. to Lydia A. Johnson 11-14-1860 (11-15-1860) Ma
Meriwether, Minor to Elizabeth E. Avery 1-5-1852 Sh
Meriwether, Thomas M. to Elvira Edmonston 7-16-1845 Ma
Meriwether, W. O. to Mary A. E. Exum 8-29-1854 (8-30-1854) Sh
Meriwether, William H. to Rebecca F. Deberry 12-15-1838 Ma
Merlin, William to Edy Jackson 2-13-1827 Hr
Meroney, William to Charity Peake 11-9-1830 Ma
Merrell, Andrew to Sarah G. Harrell? 12-24-1851 Cr
Merrell, George to Marg. Willson 12-18-1863 We
Merrell, James D. to Syntha Jarrell 2-22-1852 Cr
Merrell, John G. to Frances M. Merrill 2-19-1863 Hn
Merrell, W. P. to Elizabeth J. West 4-6-1863 We
Merrett, Anderson H. to Mary Jarrett 6-10-1847 Cr
Merrett, J. C. to A.? Williams 4-4-1849 Cr
Merrett, J. C. to Arytine Holms 4-28-1873 Cr
Merrett, J. C. to Parilla Jarrett 7-30-1869 (8-1-1869) Cr
Merrett, J.H. to M. W. Gee 1-17-1871 (1-20-1871) Cr
Merrett, John C. to Ester C. Jones 2-26-1860 Cr
Merrett, Riley N. to SarahJ. Rumley 3-23-1847 Cr
Merrick, James C. to Nancy Thompson 4-17-1839 (4-21-1839) F
Merrick, W. M. to N. A. Adams 4-29-1866 G
Merrill, Burgis to Sallie Shaw 1-20-1864 (1-7?-1864) T
Merrill, D. A. to Mary Miller 12-29-1856 T
Merrill, Ewing to Ann Reeves 8-2-1843 (no return) Hn
Merrill, John G. to Pressy Ann McKinney 2-7-1849 Hn
Merrill, William to Minereva M. Crutchin-McCrutchin 12-16-1834 Sh
Merriman, C. G. to M. L. White 8-21-1855 (8-22-1855) Sh
Merriman, Theodore to Lizzie Etheridge 6-4-1865 (no return) Hn
Merritt, Daniel to E. Norton 2-2-1863 Sh
Merritt, Hadley to Kezziah Finly? 1-16-1861 Cr
Merritt, J. C. to Nancy Merritt 4-28-1866 (4-29-1866) Cr
Merritt, Lucian to Sarah Durden 1-20-1867 Be
Merriweather, Henry W. to Virginia T. Herndon 9-8-1858 Sh
Merriwether, David J. to Elizabeth Tarver 10-31-1849 Ma
Merriwether, Henry to Amelia Young 5-2-1868 Hy
Merriwether, James to Martha Hunter 11-4-1843 (no return) F
Merriwether, James to Mary Alice Hicks 12-12-1878 Hy
Merriwether, Jesse to Eliza Coe 12-28-1865 (12-29-1865) F B
Merriwether, Peter to Victoria Pate 10-30-1878 L B
Merriwether, Synan to Bita Tatum 1-11-1873 (no return) L
Merriwether, William D. to Sarah J. Donaldson 4-9-1860 (4-10-1860) O
Merriwether, Wm. P. to Judie A. Henning 12-20-1859 (12-21-1860) Ma
Mertimer (Mortimer?), Robert to Kate Kesterson 4-10-1863 (4-12-1863) Sh
Merton, Robert C. to Manessa Story 10-13-1855 (no return) Hn
Merweather, Francis A. to Eliza J. Hardy 3-2-1853 (no return) F
Merygin?, William P. to Sally Rodgers 10-16-1866 (no return) Dy
Mesham(Mesbow?), John to Hannah Marsh 12-5-1834 Hr
Mesley, Wm. to Jane Ward 9-12-1858 We
Mesmer, Charles to Catherina Bower(s) 5-18-1863 Sh
Mesmer, Charles to Catherina Bowers 5-28-1863 Sh
Messick, Jefferson to Fedelia Stewart 6-26-1831 Sh
Messinger, Geo. W. to Ann Mereto 1-9-1857 Sh
Metcalf, Jno. C. to Tennessee Nichols 3-28-1855 (3-29-1855) Sh
Metcalf, John A. to Fannie Williamson 3-3-1858 (3-7-1858) Ma
Meter, Benjamin F. to Mollie E. Gibson 1-8-1873 (1-9-1873) L
Meter, Daniel J. to F. C. Thurmond 8-12-1874 (8-13-1874) L
Metheney, John W. to Delila Williams 4-21-1858 Hn
Metheney, Lewis G. to Lourana E. Snider 2-1-1863 Hn
Metheny, Eli S. to Quixanna Jones 8-31-1871 (9-3-1871) Cr
Metheny, James T. to Susan Fields 6-22-1853 Hn
Metheny, Lewis J. to Mary J. Clement 1-5-1854 Be
Mets (Mils?), John T. to Mary A. Dowland 4-15-1861 G
Mettler, Martin to Louisa Fink 2-10-1860 Sh
Meux, Booker to Rachael Maclin 12-30-1865 (no return) Hy
Meux, Charles to Louisa Kimbrough 1-24-1878 Hy
Meux, Samuel to Permelia Fields 1-4-1877 Hy
Meux, Thomas R. to Molly E. Davis 6-3-1874 Hy
Mewborn, James C. to Mary L. McFerrin 11-2-1867 (11-7-1867) F

Mewborn, Joseph L. to Mary Mathews 11-16-1866 (11-20-1866) F
Mewborn, Joshua W. to Mattie Lou McFerrin 11-2-1867 (11-7-1867) F
Mewborn, William to Caroline Dupree 1-3-1871 (no return) F B
Meyer, Franklin to Mary Ann Fantom 11-30-1861 Sh
Meyers, Louis P. to Callie D. Bigham 6-3-1872 (6-6-1872) Cr
Meyers, W. B. to Amanda Burnell 8-31-1848 Sh
Mich, Boyna to Cathrine Bryant 5-13-1858 Cr
Michael, David M. to Mary Fodge 12-31-1854 Hn
Michael, John to Ann Lovelace 11-17-1840 (no return) Hn
Michael, T. J. to A. E. Banister 9-29-1870 G
Michael, W. R. to Stacy Mullins 10-30-1854 (10-31-1854) G
Michaiett, T. J. to Francis A. Ingram 10-27-1855 Cr
Michal, Thomas to Mary Roberts 1-13-1852 We
Michals, Nathan to Mary Ann Thompson 12-8-1840 Cr
Michel, Arval to Sarah E. Bibb 7-18-1845 Cr
Michell, Crawford to Olive Pate 1-22-1867 (1-24-1867) Dy
Michell, James B. to Florence H. Henly 10-18-1876 L
Michell, N. J. to Louisa Pugh 12-2-1869 (12-5-1869) Dy
Michell, R. H. to M. F. Hall 8-5-1868 (no return) Dy
Michell, Richard to Ellen Haynes 12-12-1876 (no return) L
Michell, Robert to Nancy Harrell(Howell?) 8-5-1828 (4?-6-1828) Hr
Michell, Thos. C. to Lizzie Bell 5-11-1867 (no return) Dy
Michie, John to Almira Pulliam 4-9-1866 F B
Michum, Saml. A. to Mary W. Person (Pirson) 2-2-1854 (2-8-1854) Sh
Michum, Thomas A. to Alice Bilbery 12-3-1856 Cr
Michum, William to Mary F. Pennington 10-21-1874 (10-22-1874) L
Mickens, Nat to Mary (Mrs.) McCain 5-23-1861 (5-28-1861) Ma
Mickleberry, J. S. to Mary Cothram 11-30-1841 (12-2-1841) F
Mickleberry, James to Arineth Harris 10-28-1823 Sh
Mickleberry, John A. to Harriett W. Bond 7-8-1824 Sh
Mickleberry, R. A. to S. J. Reid 1-7-1857 (1-8-1857) Sh
Mickleberry, Robert Y. to Emeline D. Harris 10-23-1823 Sh
Mickum, John to Mariah Williamson 9-18-1847 Ma
Midchiff, William to M. C. Griffin 5-23-1850 We
Middaugh, M. H. to E. R. Hoffman 8-5-1856 Sh
Middlebrook, Albert to Mary Bourne 9-20-1875 (no return) Hy
Middlebrook, J. S. to Mary C. Hicks 3-7-1872 Hy
Middlebrook, Lewis to Peggie Nelson 12-21-1874 (no return) Hy
Middlebrooks, Robt. to Isadore Green 1-3-1868 (no return) Hy
Middlehook, James to Lucy Arnold 3-5-1867 F
Middleten, Alford to Judith Lacewell 7-4-1858 We
Middleton, Hugh to Nancy Starky 2-29-1828 L
Middleton, J. S. to Sophronia Land 1-24-1883 (1-25-1883) L
Middleton, John T. to Rosanna Pulliam 6-14-1858 Hr
Middleton, Saml. to Tempa Gocher 2-8-1860 Hr
Middleton, Thomas J. to Minerva Alsup 1-17-1846 Sh
Middleton, Vincent to Martha E. Dodson 7-14-1855 (no return) F
Middlewest, John D. to Melissa D. Looney 12-21-1848 Hn
Midgett, Alexander to Jennie Nunn 12-13-1868 Hy
Midgett, Ashley to Mary E. Knight 5-6-1850 (5-8-1850) Ma
Midgett, E. R. to Martha (Mrs.) Tucker 10-19-1867 (no return) Hy
Midgett, J. H. to Nancy J. Evans 5-10-1860 (no return) Hy
Midgett, M. B. to M. A. Johnson 11-24-1869 (no return) Hy
Midgett, Math to Prissilla Johnson 12-1-1871 Hy
Midgett, Micajah to Retha C. Lefever 1-9-1844 Hn
Midgett, Nicholas L. to Nancy O. (C.?) Smith 7-19-1868 G
Midgett, R. M. to J. A. J. Cox 2-12-1880 L
Midgett, Sam to Georgianna Taylor 6-12-1875 (no return) Hy
Midgett, T. H. to S. J. Russ 11-24-1869 (no return) Hy
Midgett, W. M. to Margarett E. Midgett 12-27-1882 (12-28-1882) L
Midkeff, Robert to Elizabeth Henderson 5-9-1856 We
Midkiff, G. W. to Sarah Fowler 9-7-1856 We
Midlebrooks, William S. to Mary V. Lacy 12-25-1849 Hr
Midlin, G. M. to T. S. Henley 6-17-1870 (6-19-1870) Cr
Midyett, Nicholas L. to Louisa A. McIver 11-1-1856 (11-2-1856) Ma
Midyitt, M. to Elizabeth Young 11-30-1854 We
Miers, George Milo to Ellen E. Hurley 1-6-1862 Sh
Miers, Wm. T. to Mary Witherspoon 6-30-1844 Sh
Mifflay, Acan to Sarah Long 11-11-1865 Mn
Mifflin, Armstrong to Louisa Blunt 8-30-1845 G
Mifflin, C. C. to Ellen James 1-8-1870 (1-9-1870) Dy
Mifflin, Caswell C. to Catherine Glisson 1-21-1871 (1-22-1871) Dy
Miflin, Caswell to Tabitha Ray 1-21-1847 G
Migen, M. J. to Farina J. Neely 11-5-1856 Cr
Migliozzo, Paul to Josephine Fransioli 7-26-1854 Sh
Mikel, Thomas to Martha Podge 2-6-1849 Hn
Milam, B. T. to Elizabeth Bowden 9-16-1848 Hn
Milam, B. to Eliza White 1-7-1879 (no return) Dy
Milam, G. S. to Nancy J. Wallace 3-15-1865 Dy
Milam, Harry to Betsy Curtis 2-10-1866 Hn
Milam, J. T. W. to L. J. Wilkinson 7-15-1862 (no return) Hy
Milam, James B. to Mary E. Alexander 5-15-1867 Hn
Milam, James W. to Mary Ann Curtis 10-9-1849 (no return) Hn
Milam, John T. W. to Sophia Carter 6-27-1844 Hn
Milam, Joseph G. to Susan L. Stubbs 9-3-1870 (no return) Cr
Milam, S. E. to M. E. Featherston 12-4-1873 Dy
Milam, S. _ to E. J. Allen 12-13-1852 Hn

Milam, T. H. to Lucy Lucas 3-11-1885 (3-12-1885) L
Milam, T. M. to Kitty L. Perkins 12-20-1865 (12-27-1865) F
Milam, T. R. to Mary June Mitchell 8-23-1844 Hn
Milam, Thomas R. to Lugenia Jones 9-13-1850 Hn
Milam, W. A. to E. M. Walker 10-17-1866 G
Milam, W. L. to E. C. Kinnie 12-20-1870 Hy
Milan, Claudius L. to Mary E. Attkisson 6-24-1868 (6-25-1868) Ma
Milan, R. L. to Martha A. Massey 12-23-1848 Cr
Milan, W. B. to Mary Christian 3-23-1844 Cr
Milbern, H. H. to Margarett Snow 4-12-1865 (4-14-1865) O
Milegan, John to Ann Brickene 7-30-1864 O
Miles, Benjamin C. to Mary Jane Johnson 6-12-1877 Hy
Miles, D. M. C. to Jane M. McCoyen? 9-13-1828 Hr
Miles, Dorsey to Nancy Appleby 12-14-1839 Sh
Miles, Everett G. to Mariah F. Smith 1-13-1846 O
Miles, G. S. to Charlotte Voorheis 4-21-1855 (5-1-1855) O
Miles, Guy S. to Martha A. Tylor 4-12-1840 Sh
Miles, Isaac to Fanny Lovin 12-16-1866 G
Miles, J. M. to Tennessee Norton 8-27-1862 O
Miles, James R. to Saluda Sawen 11-23-1858 We
Miles, John R. to Ollive Koen 10-8-1841 Sh
Miles, Patrick to Celia Ann (Mrs.) Young 6-9-1868 G
Miles, Thomas W. to Martha R. W. Guthery 4-18-1855 We
Miles, William C. to Leah Reaves 12-24-1829 Sh
Miles, Wm. C. to A. J. Steaphenson 2-14-1865 O
Mill, Fred Augustus to Easter Jane Taylor 7-24-1867 (7-25-1867) T
Millane, Daniel to Julia Pennelton 9-21-1863 Sh
Millard, Clarence to Leah Elizabeth Grimes 5-25-1863 Sh
Millard, Francis B. to Margreth McKanna 8-6-1864 (8-7-1864) Sh
Millard, George to Bell Williams 11-12-1873 (11-13-1873) Dy
Millard, John to Jane Butler 9-12-1867 G B
Millem, Francis M. to Cordelia M. Lovelace 8-21-1868 (9-?-1868) L
Millen, Henry to Ann Yarbro 11-19-1868 T
Miller (Minton?), J. T. to Eliza Turner 8-24-1869 L
Miller (see Weller)
Miller, A. C. to Bell Leigh 4-24-1865 (5-25-1865) O
Miller, A. H. to F. M. Elenor 9-25-1872 (9-26-1872) Cr
Miller, A. W. to Sarah Whaler 10-4-1864 Sh
Miller, A. to Caledonia Ray 6-20-1885 L
Miller, Abel C. to Virginia L. Pritchet 1-13-1859 Hn
Miller, Abraham to Sarah E. Miller 9-5-1857 (9-8-1857) O
Miller, Adolph to Mary Schraeder 1-5-1858 (1-9-1858) Sh
Miller, Albert S. to Esther A. Wallace 4-15-1840 Sh
Miller, Alexander K. to Rebecca A. Wollard 12-20-1837 Sh
Miller, Anderson to Mary Ann Simmons 12-28-1868 F B
Miller, Andrew J. to Elizabeth Ellen Duncan 6-20-1866 Ma
Miller, Andrew J. to Julia Ann Jones 12-29-1869 Hy
Miller, Austin to Adeline Moore 3-1-1873 Hy
Miller, Austin to Mary Jane McNeal 10-22-1849 (10-23-1849) Hr
Miller, B. F. to Mary Smith 11-12-1867 O
Miller, Benjin F. to Eliza Smiley 7-27-1844 Sh
Miller, Carroll J. to Sarah J. Carpenter 12-27-1869 (no return) L
Miller, Caswell to Mary V. Stoddard 11-11-1831 G
Miller, Charles A. to J. E. Gill 1-2-1867 G
Miller, Charles F. to Margaret J. Turner 5-6-1873 L
Miller, Charles J. to Emma M. Jansen 12-3-1851 Hr
Miller, Charles to Frances Willis 11-17-1866 G
Miller, Charley to M. A. Pitner 7-27-1869 Hy
Miller, Christopher to Mennie Hall 4-7-1868 G
Miller, Christopher to Sarah Crocker 11-21-1869 G
Miller, Daniel L. to Margaret Reinhardt 3-28-1848 Sh
Miller, Daniel to Margaret Harwell 12-30-1868 (12-31-1868) Dy
Miller, David to P. F. Taylor 9-2-1856 (no return) We
Miller, E. D. to Caroline Farrer 10-3-1860 Be
Miller, Edmund to Tenie Ferror 12-17-1878 Hy
Miller, Elbert to Susan Stagner 8-23-1857 Hn
Miller, Eli to Helen Miller 1-4-1876 (no return) Hy
Miller, Elias to Helana S. Frayer 1-22-1846 G
Miller, Eullen M. to Sarah A. Russell 2-28-1849 Cr
Miller, F. P. to M. D. Hill 12-15-1880 (no return) L
Miller, Franklin to Susan Gleaves 6-5-1852 (6-6-1852) O
Miller, Fred Marion to Nancy S. Smith 11-4-1850 (11-6-1850) T
Miller, Fred to Catherine M. Withare (Withers) 5-27-1847 Sh
Miller, G. C. to L. L. Mcguire 12-9-1879 (12-10-1879) L
Miller, G. C. to Mary A. Bowers 8-9-1860 O
Miller, G. F. to A. E. Wilkes 1-30-1867 Hy
Miller, G. H. to Martha J. Gause 12-19-1864 (12-21-1864) L
Miller, G. K. to Jane Barton 6-29-1859 (7-1-1859) Sh
Miller, Geo. C. to Hesiltine Horton 12-14-1864 Sh
Miller, George W. to Eliza Glidewell 8-4-1846 (8-5-1846) Ma
Miller, George W. to Elizabeth Monroe? 3-9-1841 (3-10-1841) T
Miller, George W. to Mary J. Hargett 2-26-1861 (no return) Hy
Miller, George to Mary H. M. Byrn 9-7-1843 (no return) L
Miller, George to Rachell Biggs 4-7-1847 Sh
Miller, Gothilf to Catharine Leaser 3-18-1861 Sh
Miller, H. G. to Lizzie S. Hart 12-7-1859 F
Miller, H. P. to Julia (Mrs.) Davison 6-17-1861 Sh

Miller, Haden to Emma Bledsoe 2-11-1871 (no return) F B
Miller, Harry to Anny Douglas 12-25-1873 Hy
Miller, Haywood to Eliza Ann Cartwright 6-3-1869 (no return) F B
Miller, Henry H. to Amanda Cunningham 7-30-1864 Sh
Miller, Henry to Emma Cross 1-4-1870 (no return) F B
Miller, Henry to Rhoda Oliver 12-31-1854 Hn
Miller, Howard to Letha Hargis 6-20-1844 Sh
Miller, Isaac M. to Martha P. Wright 7-25-1855 (7-26-1855) T
Miller, Isaac to Almina Cheney 2-6-1877 (2-8-1877) L
Miller, Isaac to Fanny Lovin 12-16-1866 G
Miller, Isaac to Mary Chambers 11-4-1841 Cr
Miller, Isaac to Sarah Farris 6-11-1853 Ma
Miller, Isaac to Winney Ingram 9-17-1828 (9-21-1828) Ma
Miller, Isom to Adeline Barken 12-22-1869 F B
Miller, J. B. to Mary A. (Mrs.) Bradford 10-16-1854 Sh
Miller, J. C. to Margaret Howard 12-7-1881 L
Miller, J. E. to M. E. Hays 11-26-1860 Hn
Miller, J. M. to E. E. Flowers 7-29-1860 G
Miller, J. M. to Eliza C. Reynolds 7-12-1879 (no return) L
Miller, J. S. to Jane Norris 4-3-1869 (4-4-1869) L
Miller, J. S. to N. E. Robertson 10-20-1869 Hy
Miller, J. T. to Elizabeth Lackey 8-10-1871 Hy
Miller, J. T. to M. F. Foster 12-23-1880 L
Miller, J. W. N. to Manerva A. Dillon 4-23-1867 Be
Miller, J. W. to Caroline Jenkins 12-14-1860 (no return) Hy
Miller, J. W. to E. F. Thompson 7-21-1874 (no return) L
Miller, J. W. to Virginia Hubbard 9-10-1860 (no return) Hy
Miller, Jack to Mary Dodson 3-30-1867 Hy
Miller, Jacob Hillman to Amanda Malvina Clark 12-21-1853 (12-22-1853) T
Miller, Jacob to Margaret E. Montgomery 8-13-1844 Sh
Miller, Jacob to Mary D. Sales 3-26-1860 Sh
Miller, James C. to Gabriella Davis 1-24-1861 Dy
Miller, James L. to Sophia Darnell 3-2-1854 Hr
Miller, James M. to Evelina Reese 12-24-1844 (no return) F
Miller, James R. to A. Jackson 1-11-1865 (1-12-1865) T
Miller, James R. to Milly Wheatly 11-25-1863 O
Miller, James to Caroline Henderson 12-27-1866 (no return) Dy
Miller, James to Dovie Hoart 6-4-1876 Hy
Miller, Jan L. to Mariah Buck 7-15-1851 (no return) F
Miller, Jasper to Flora Strain 7-24-1877 (7-25-1877) L
Miller, Joel to Sally Baley 3-26-1828 G
Miller, John A. to Polly A. Parish 10-24-1858 Cr
Miller, John B. to Anna C.(S?) Borchedt 12-31-1863 (1-2-1864) Sh
Miller, John B. to Catherine T. Latham 10-24-1844 L
Miller, John C. to Nancy E. Pfleuger? 1-27-1858 Hn
Miller, John C. to Nancy J. Flatt 7-8-1867 O
Miller, John F. to Eliza M. Miller 10-26-1869 T
Miller, John F. to Laura A. Payne 4-11-1871 (4-12-1871) T
Miller, John H. to Jane Phillips 2-26-1842 (3-1-1842) G
Miller, John H. to Nancy Hays 9-21-1842 (10-13-1842) O
Miller, John N. to Catharine Schafner (Chofner) 10-1-1855 (10-2-1855) Sh
Miller, John Q. to Mary J Upton 5-12-1860 (5-13-1860) O
Miller, John T. to Nancy Long 4-20-1867 (4-19-1868?) L
Miller, John to America Ezell 6-14-1846 We
Miller, John to Josephine Stagner 2-17-1865 (no return) Hn
Miller, John to Louis Haskin 11-7-1867 Dy
Miller, John to Mary Ann Sinkler 9-27-1847 (9-28-1847) O
Miller, John to Nancy E. Parker 4-22-1866 Hn
Miller, John to Nancy Roberson 1-23-1840 L
Miller, John to Sally Kelly 2-18-1846 Ma
Miller, John to Sarah Chisum 11-3-1827 Ma
Miller, Joseph E. to Sarah E. Montgomery 3-7-1866 (3-8-1866) Dy
Miller, Joseph F. to Sarah F. Caruthers 4-13-1857 (4-16-1857) O
Miller, Joshua M. to Elizabeth Ann Mailey 7-28-1845 (8-1-1845) T
Miller, Joshua N. to Nancy Ann Murphy 7-8-1847 T
Miller, Joshua to Sarah Sperry 3-26-1849 Sh
Miller, Josiah D. to Emily Adaline Swindle 9-14-1853 (9-15-1853) Hr
Miller, L. B. to Sibby Branson 10-3-1861 G
Miller, Lee to Fannie Rhodes 1-9-1873 T
Miller, Levi D. to Tabitha Dodd 1-22-1858 (1-27-1858) Hr
Miller, Lewis W. to ary Robinson 5-13-1844 (5-17-1844) T
Miller, Lewis to Mary Jane Trip 12-25-1867 (12-28-1867) F B
Miller, M. to Annie Brown 11-9-1885 (11-10-1885) L
Miller, Markas to Mary Hedigs (Hediger) 8-22-1846 Sh
Miller, Marshall J. to Eudora R. Barry 8-15-1846 Sh
Miller, Martin V. to Mary J. Gardner 4-17-1860 Hr
Miller, Nathan to Sarah E. Flowers 11-23-1868 G B
Miller, Nathaniel to Evalina L. Glidwell 8-27-1856 Ma
Miller, Nowes to Louisa Heidleburg 10-11-1842 (10-12-1842) Ma
Miller, Oliver R. to Julia M. Young 12-31-1856 Sh
Miller, Pearson to Sarah Fodge 1-27-1846 (no return) Hn
Miller, Peter to Nancy Short 8-28-1867 (no return) Hy
Miller, Peyton to Dinah Miller 3-27-1874 Hy
Miller, Peyton to Nancy Short 3-22-1873 Hy
Miller, Pitser to Sarah Ann Stevens 12-19-1834 (12-21-1834) Hr
Miller, R. F. to Ada Barnes 8-6-1879 (8-10-1879) L
Miller, R. F. to M. C. Widner 3-1-1870 (no return) Hy
Miller, Richd. to Mildred Exum 8-30-1867 (8-31-1867) F B
Miller, Robert C. to Rebecca Angeline Moultrie 10-1-1853 O
Miller, Robert C. to Rebecca S. J. Lee 10-14-1853 (no return) Hn
Miller, Robert to Becky Clabrooks 9-18-1877 Hy
Miller, Robert to Elizabeth Acuff 6-25-1875 (6-27-1875) L
Miller, Robert to Harriet R. McCreight 9-5-1848 (9-7-1848) T
Miller, Robert to Sallie Patrick 12-22-1869 F B
Miller, Rolin to Martha Rider 10-14-1846 (10-15-1846) Ma
Miller, S. A. to Lucinda Rhea 8-28-1849 F
Miller, S. A. to M. C. Mathis 1-24-1867 Cr
Miller, S. B. to Eliza Phaland 4-4-1849 H
Miller, S. C. to Alice Meadows 12-24-1879 (12-24-1880?) L
Miller, Saml. to C. F. Warren 8-9-1852 Cr
Miller, Samphord A. to Annie E. McCool 1-24-1878 Hy
Miller, Samuel B. to Eliza Ann Foster 2-19-1842 (2-27-1842) T
Miller, Samuel to Nancy E. Easterwood 4-17-1854 (4-20-1854) G
Miller, Silas to Sina Hill 6-27-1869 Hy
Miller, Simon to Caroline Newsom 8-26-1868 (no return) Hy
Miller, Spencer to Charlotte Lloyd 1-27-1883 (12?-26?-1883) L
Miller, Stephen to Harriett Garland 2-27-1838 Ma
Miller, Stephen to Louisa Jane Gladney 9-28-1849 (10-2-1849) Ma
Miller, T. W. to Elizabeth Sheppard 7-16-1859 (7-17-1859) Sh
Miller, Thomas E. to Sarah Jane Allen 7-5-1855 Hn
Miller, Thomas to Annie Mitchel 2-8-1877 (2-11-1877) L
Miller, Thomas to Caroline Griggs 2-5-1870 (no return) L
Miller, Thomas to Martha A. Tweedy 1-14-1826 (1-16-1826) Ma
Miller, Vann to Nancy Thurman 4-20-1854 Ma
Miller, W. F. to L. I. Williams 5-4-1867 O
Miller, W. G. to Eliza Huffman 12-9-1856 (12-11-1856) T
Miller, W. H. to P. McAllister 7-21-1868 G
Miller, W. M. to Caroline Rickoff (Riekoff) 5-31-1854 Sh
Miller, W. R. to Amanda M. Byrn 3-26-1874 L
Miller, W. W. to Mary A. Young 10-26-1844 Sh
Miller, Willam to Caroline Brake 10-15-1857 Hn
Miller, William E. to Mary Ann Chipman 9-4-1867 (10-6-1867) L
Miller, William H. to Martha Conner 7-11-1837 Hr
Miller, William J. to Mary Jane Turner 3-9-1852 (no return) F
Miller, William M. to Loueza A. Houser 11-25-1863 O
Miller, William N. to Lucy A. Whitman 2-7-1859 (2-8-1859) Sh
Miller, William P. to Mary M. Forest 10-5-1858 (10-6-1858) T
Miller, William P. to Sarah Ann Ray 2-12-1858 (no return) Hn
Miller, William to Eliza Haney (Harvey) 5-2-1840 Sh
Miller, William to Louisa Brown 10-31-1837 Sh
Miller, William to Lucinda Osburn 12-26-1867 Hn B
Miller, William to Miledge Read 2-5-1874 Hy
Miller, William to Octavo Rolph 10-1-1870 (10-2-1870) L
Miller, William to Susan Taylor 2-25-1871 (no return) F B
Miller, Willie B. to Louisa E. Pope 5-19-1845 Sh
Miller, Wilson to Lucinda S. Halfacre 3-3-1886 L
Miller, Wilson to Mary E. Gardner 12-21-1847 (12-30-1847) F
Miller, Wm. D. K. to Mary E. Floyd 1-22-1859 Sh
Miller, Wm. E. to Laura W. Thompson 12-9-1856 (12-17-1856) Sh
Miller, Wm. H. to Mary Ann Myers 2-13-1856 Sh
Miller, Wm. S. to S. A. Benton 2-3-1867 G
Miller, Wm. T. to Adaline Clark 1-13-1859 T
Miller, Wm. to Martha Hawkins 4-1-1858 Cr
Milligan, Harvey N. to Addie C. Hutcherson 11-16-1870 Ma
Milligan, John to Mary Halbrooks 5-7-1856 (5-8-1856) Sh
Milligan, Lewis J. to Mary E. Bogle 10-1-1860 (10-4-1860) Cr
Milliken, G. M. to E. C. Powell 2-8-1849 Hn
Milliken, L. H. to Livinia Moody 7-5-1841 T
Milliken, Samuel to Ann H. Campbell 6-18-1855 (no return) L
Milliken, W. A. to Mary Humphreys 2-3-1870 F
Milliken, William M. to Gilley Ann Hartsfield 1-2-1845 Hn
Millikin, John to Sarah Williams 2-20-1854 (no return) L
Millikin, Leonard H. to Mary Levinia Moody 7-5?-1841 Hr
Milliner, D. S. to E. T. Clark 11-13-1871 (11-15-1871) O
Milliner, L. D. to Amanda J. Hudston 9-15-1871 (9-17-1871) O
Milliner, Robert to Lockey Bright 3-19-1853 (3-23-1853) O
Milling, John to Lucinda E. Kincaide 5-11-1869 Ma
Millirons, George to Frances E. Doddridge 4-23-1838 F
Mills, A. E. to Nancy J. Rice 7-26-1851 O
Mills, Andrew J. to Frances Morris 8-27-1850 (8-29-1850) Hr
Mills, Andrew to Miranda A. Harris 12-17-1853 Ma
Mills, B. D. to E. J. Lenea? 10-7-1871 (10-9-1871) Cr
Mills, Benj. F. to Jane D. Vevely 8-8-1866 (8-16-1866) Ma
Mills, Curtis to Marta Jane Holloway 1-27-1848 (no return) F
Mills, Elvy to Nancy Carley 9-11-1841 (9-12-1841) Hr
Mills, Felix to Gertrude Owen 9-2-1867 (no return) L B
Mills, G. W. to C. J. Adams 12-14-1871 (no return) Cr
Mills, G. W. to M. E. McCracken 5-22-1869 (no return) Dy
Mills, G. W. to Nannie Read 1-9-1877 (1-10-1877) Dy
Mills, Green to M. E. Hicks 12-28-1857 (12-29-1857) Sh
Mills, Henry M. to Sarah Ann King 7-25-1849 Hr
Mills, Humphrey to Margaret Houston 12-29-1832 (12-30-1832) Hr
Mills, Isaac to Maria Long 12-8-1827 Hr
Mills, J. C. to Mary B. Doggett 9-28-1863 Sh

Mills, J. C. to Mary E. Solomon 9-2-1872 (9-6-1872) T
Mills, J. C. to Mary J. McKenny 5-6-1868 (5-7-1868) T
Mills, J. Dix to Emily T. Lucken 9-9-1858 (9-23-1858) Sh
Mills, J. F. to Bettie King 9-29-1871 (10-3-1871) Dy
Mills, J. J. to P. F. Moody 8-19-1872 (8-21-1872) Dy
Mills, J. R. to Eliza Butler 2-21-1870 G
Mills, J. W. to Margarett L. Gibbons 9-18-1865 (9-20-1865) Cr
Mills, James B. to Martha Vinson 1-24-1856 (1-26-1856) Hr
Mills, James R. to Martha E. Garner 3-5-1872 (3-7-1872) Dy
Mills, James to Anny Johnson 8-30-1866 T
Mills, James to Nancy? Jones 12-7-1836 (12-8-1836) Hr
Mills, John A. to Prudence (Mrs.) Williamson 12-12-1876 (12-14-1876) Dy
Mills, John A. to Temperance Bessent? 1-1-1867 Dy
Mills, John F. to Caledonia C. Brevard 12-19-1853 (12-21-1853) O
Mills, John S. to Drusilla R. Kersey 6-22-1858 O
Mills, John S. to Margaret A. Manwell 9-23-1860 We
Mills, John to Cinthey Williamson 10-14-1847 F
Mills, John to Dianah Bond 8-21-1832 (8-24-1832) Hr
Mills, John to Lucy Butler 12-4-1852 (12-9-1852) Ma
Mills, Jonathan to Martha Simpson 12-28-1878 (12-29-1878) Dy
Mills, Jonathan to Nancy ann Wiggington 12-7-1864 Sh
Mills, Lewis E. to Emily L. White 2-2-1859 (2-3-1859) G
Mills, Marion to Ellen Harris 5-25-1868 (5-26-1868) Ma
Mills, Napolean B. to Mary Marlow 12-25-1856 O
Mills, Nat. A. to Almedia C. Ellis 11-6-1866 (11-7-1866) Dy
Mills, Nathaniel to J. E. Edwards 12-30-1873 Dy
Mills, S. C. to M. A. Burrow 1-27-1873 Cr
Mills, Saml. J. to Mary E. Mills 8-28-1865 T
Mills, Sample to Bethenia Henry 11-24-1851 (11-27-1851) Hr
Mills, Tandy P. to Fanny A. Ramey 11-5-1851 (11-6-1851) O
Mills, Thomas to Annie Tilman 3-27-1880 (3-28-1880) L
Mills, Thomas to Nancy Dickens 2-4-1830 Sh
Mills, W. R. to N. S. Steward 11-1-1859 (11-3-1859) Hr
Mills, W. W. to Sarah F. Threadgill 11-18-1865 (no return) Cr
Mills, Walter to Nancy Prewett 12-25-1849 Cr
Mills, William to Felicia Dangerfield 12-24-1869 L
Mills, Wm. Y. to Mary Rodgers 8-16-1841 (8-17-1841) Hr
Millsaps, Darmond to Parle Vickery 7-29-1841 L
Millsted, George C. to Frances E. Mullens 5-3-1849 Hr
Millsted, James A. to Martha J. Wells 10-10-1872 (10-13-1872) L
Milner, G. B. to M. A. Alexander 9-8-1874 (9-9-1874) O
Milner, H. C. to Mary A. Jeffres 11-1-1854 We
Milner, R. H. to Sarah Walker 11-26-1860 O
Milner, Saml. T. to Sophia Mosley 12-27-1849 We
Milner, Travis L. to Elizabeth Barber 5-24-1838 (5-27-1838) O
Milner, W. M. to Aletha J. Warren 12-29-1859 O
Milsap, George to Elizabeth Vickory 5-29-1839 L
Milsap, Thomas to Elizabeth Alread 3-31-1839 L
Milstead, John to Mary A. Sweat 7-17-1844 Hn
Milten, Adam to Sarah E. Cashen 7-30-1859 We
Milten, William Charles to Margaret E. Rothemer 10-23-1863 Sh
Milton, Abraham B. to Julia McDearmont 6-24-1870 (6-26-1870) L
Milton, Frank to Ann L. Smith 12-27-1865 F
Milton, Jesse J. to Temptha Ann Gardner 11-8-1844 We
Milton, John to Salina Tripp 3-10-1857 Sh
Milton, Tilghman to Harrett Moore 12-2-1844 (12-3-1844) G
Milton, Wm. to T. Boswell 1-28-1858 Cr
Milum, H. S. to S. Frances Williams 10-28-1861 Sh
Milum, John W. to Tennessee J. Hooper 2-18-1866 Hn
Minard, J. A. to Rebecca Harris 11-25-1845 Cr
Minehan, Michael to Catharine McCarty 11-1-1855 (11-4-1855) Sh
Miner, Peter to Margaret F. Davis 10-5-1861 (10-9-1861) Sh
Ming, Samuel P. to Mary E. Andrews 1-17-1843 Sh
Mingea, Nathaniel to Catharine Vincent 4-6-1858 Sh
Minor, A. C. to Sallie Ferguson 5-31-1855 Sh
Minor, Allen to Peggy Southerland 1-3-1849 (no return) F
Minor, Jas. Shelton to Bettie Freeman 1-4-1869 (1-8-1869) F B
Minson, William to Elvira T. Woollum 5-24-1847 (no return) F
Minter, Franklin to Lucinda Ham 1-19-1847 Hr
Minter, George W. to Louisa T. Warr 2-13-1849 (2-14-1849) Hr
Minter, George W. to Martha R. Allen 11-28-1853 Hr
Minton, A. J. to Angeline Rankin 6-23-1863 Mn
Minton, G. W. to Margaret E. Robinett 5-29-1858 Sh
Minton, John L. to Louisa Crofford 2-6-1855 Sh
Minton, Joseph to Cytha Hines 5-19-1836 Hr
Minton, Joseph to Malvina C. Giles 5-8-1856 Sh
Minton, R. F. to Mary Needham 1-13-1867 G
Minton, R. R. to Ansonetta M. Mitchell 2-28-1869 G
Minton, Simon H. to Rhody Wilson 12-25-1831 Sh
Minton, Theodrick to Mary Reed 12-16-1843 G
Minton, W. L. to I. J. McMillan 8-18-1848 (8-23-1848) F
Mires, Wilson to Eliza Henderson 1-27-1838 Sh
Miron?, Alonza to Emma Currie 1-11-1872 Hy
Misenheimer, Hampton C. to Emily Cummings 3-4-1848 (3-9-1848) Hr
Misenheimer, Henry B. to Elizabeth I. White 10-25-1838 Sh
Misenheimer, Henry B. to Nancy B. McAnulty 3-2-1837 (3-7-1837) Hr
Miskelly, E. to Martha A. Pool 12-27-1865 (12-30-1865) Dy

Misskelly, P(arse) A(lphonse) to Mary Pennington 7-22-1867 (no return) L
Mitchel, Allen to Harriett Young 2-1-1878 Hy
Mitchel, B. F. to Mary D. Searcy 5-19-1866 (5-25-1866) T
Mitchel, Ben to Eliza Jane Elder 3-31-1873 (4-3-1873) T
Mitchel, C. C. to Elizabeth Earp 4-4-1858 Be
Mitchel, Charley to Catherine Tucker 12-24-1868 (12-26-1868) F B
Mitchel, H. H. to Louisa Hicks 12-19-1852 Be
Mitchel, Henry C. to Malinda Strickland 4-20-1843 Be
Mitchel, J. T. to Caroline Farrar 2-24-1857 Be
Mitchel, James to Sarah Ann McGee 2-8-1831 (2-10-1831) Hr
Mitchel, Jerome to Nancy Hester 8-1-1849 (no return) F
Mitchel, Jerry to Fanny Wilson 2-1-1867 (2-16-1867) F B
Mitchel, Jerry to Martha McCutchin 10-23-1872 (10-24-1872) Cr
Mitchel, P. R. to L. Harris 1-30-1872 (1-31-1872) T
Mitchel, Reubin to Jane Edwards 3-15-1849 Be
Mitchel, Thomas to Sarah P. Hill 3-30-1867 (3-31-1867) Cr
Mitchel, W. P. to Sarah F. Summers 7-?-1862 Be
Mitchell, A. F. to Sarah Ann Philips 12-18-1844 (12-19-1844) Hr
Mitchell, A. H. to Susan F. Fortner 12-2-1872 (12-5-1872) L
Mitchell, A. J. to Jane Hilliard 12-19-1848 Cr
Mitchell, Ahi (Ase) to Louisa Hoskins 8-31-1848 Sh
Mitchell, Alex to Caroline Radford 1-25-1869 (no return) Dy
Mitchell, Alexander to Sabry Fuller 9-21-1878 (9-?-1878) L B
Mitchell, Alvay J. to Eliza A. Cox 1-15-1855 (no return) F
Mitchell, Ambrose B. to Mary Ann Walton 11-16-1843 (no return) Hn
Mitchell, Ambrose B. to Wilmath P. Sparks 8-18-1858 Cr
Mitchell, B. H. to Finetta Prichard 10-19-1876 Dy
Mitchell, Ben to Louisa Simpkins 5-13-1870 (5-15-1870) F B
Mitchell, Benj. to Sarah? (Mrs.) Griffin 8-20-1839 (9-3?-1839) F
Mitchell, Billy to Mollie Jones 12-15-1870 (12-30-1870) F B
Mitchell, Carroll to Anna Glenn 11-15-1871 Hy
Mitchell, Charles G. to Elizabeth Blackwell 8-21-1838 F
Mitchell, Charles to Mary A. Hubbard 3-23-1837 Sh
Mitchell, Clem to Texanna Heaslett 12-25-1868 (no return) F B
Mitchell, D. W. to Martha S. Taylor 3-15-1869 (3-9?-1869) L
Mitchell, David to Ann (Mrs.) Brewer 12-5-1865 Hy
Mitchell, Dewit C. to Martha J. Jordan 12-3-1866 (12-5-1866) L
Mitchell, E. J. to N. A. Howard 7-5-1852 We
Mitchell, Elisha to Eliza Parker 9-29-1862 Mn
Mitchell, F. M. to Mary E. Mitchell 2-10-1867 Be
Mitchell, Freeman to Ruth Cloys 3-21-1849 (3-22-1849) O
Mitchell, G. T. to Demetra E. Hartsfields 1-15-1861 G
Mitchell, G. W. to Winney H. Berry 3-3-1864 Mn
Mitchell, George W. to Martha Carrahan 11-22-1834 (11-23-1834) G
Mitchell, George to Rosa Williams 8-9-1871 (8-10-1871) T
Mitchell, George to Susan Sergant 1-26-1874 Hy
Mitchell, H. H. to Louise H. Ingram 5-10-1875 Hy
Mitchell, H. H. to M. C. Walker 12-12-1860 (12-13-1860) F
Mitchell, H. H. to V. C. Walker 12-30-1866 (1-3-1866) F
Mitchell, Henry P. to Harriett Philpot 12-21-1848 Sh
Mitchell, Henry to Henrietta Powell 10-19-1877 (10-21-1877) Dy B
Mitchell, Henry to Margarite McKee 12-26-1846 Sh
Mitchell, Henry to V. C. Meek 7-12-1863 Mn
Mitchell, Houston to Martha V. Whitmore 11-30-1853 Hr
Mitchell, I. S. to Sarah Wilson 5-14-1829 Sh
Mitchell, Isaac C. to Mary A. Reed 1-5-1847 (1-7-1847) G
Mitchell, J. C. to Julia A. Reed 7-13-1866 G
Mitchell, J. D. to Martha Ann Grier 4-5-1848 (4-6-1848) G
Mitchell, J. D. to Unis Hodges 10-1-1868 Hy
Mitchell, J. H. to Annie Jennings 8-26-1874 L
Mitchell, J. H. to Martha Hobsen 9-12-1870 (9-13-1870) Dy
Mitchell, J. H. to Nannie Davis 10-10-1881 L
Mitchell, J. L. to M. J. Parker 10-1-1877 (10-2-1877) L
Mitchell, J. N. to Martha Williams 7-27-1861 Sh
Mitchell, J. R. H. to Mary C. Dalton 6-11-1846 Cr
Mitchell, J. R. to Frances Brown 2-11-1866 Hn
Mitchell, J. R. to M. L. O. Morton 2-11-1877 Hy
Mitchell, J. R.? to Sarah A. Ray? 12-6-1860 Cr
Mitchell, J. T. to Lucinda Allford 7-1-1862 (7-3-1862) L
Mitchell, J. W. to M. A. Huffstutter 12-25-1867 O
Mitchell, J. W. to Mary L. Gardner 1-21-1868 (1-22-1868) Cr
Mitchell, Jacob W. to Margaret E. Burnes 11-10-1874 (no return) L
Mitchell, James Buford to Annie E. Robinson 1-13-1880 (1-14-1880) L
Mitchell, James D. to Mary Baxter 12-20-1849 Cr
Mitchell, James L. to Cecelia B. Dunavant 2-2-1852 L
Mitchell, James M. to Elizabeth Henson 11-17-1858 (11-20-1858) Hr
Mitchell, James N. to Mary Philips 12-16-1862 Hn
Mitchell, James T. to Mary J. Renn (Penn?) 11-23-1866 G
Mitchell, James T. to Mexico Hays 11-27-1844 We
Mitchell, James to Ferriby Bomar 10-8-1865 Hn
Mitchell, James to Louisa Fuller 2-17-1878 Hy
Mitchell, James to Mary Vaught 9-12-1835 Hr
Mitchell, James to Sarah M. Bloodworth 7-21-1842 Sh
Mitchell, Jno. M. to Olivia Ann Hornesby 2-25-1857 (2-26-1857) Hr
Mitchell, Jno. to Matilda Hester 3-1-1842 Sh
Mitchell, Jo to Annie Young 11-23-1878 (11-24-1878) L
Mitchell, John D. to Ellen M. Arnold 3-15-1854 Sh

Mitchell, John E. to Carrie Davis 10-14-1877 Hy
Mitchell, John H. to Elizabeth A. Bell 3-9-1861 (3-10-1861) Sh
Mitchell, John H. to Lucy A. Harrell 5-13-1862 (5-21-1862) F
Mitchell, John H. to Lucy A. Harrell 5-13-1862 (not endorsed) F
Mitchell, John H. to Martha A. Ivie 12-13-1854 (no return) F
Mitchell, John H. to Matilda Jane Carter 4-19-1869 (no return) L
Mitchell, John Henry to Rebecca Williams 9-22-1871 (9-24-1871) L
Mitchell, John J. to Parilee A. Peden 1-5-1860 Hn
Mitchell, John Robert to Ellen Custard 12-11-1867 Hn
Mitchell, John W. C. to Mary Farmer 7-31-1844 We
Mitchell, John to Catherine J. Williams 9-1-1859 (no return) L
Mitchell, John to Dorcas Wyatt 9-12-1858 We
Mitchell, John to Eliza Jane Birdsong 3-23-1848 Hr
Mitchell, John to Ella Parker 2-15-1872 Hy
Mitchell, John to P. A. Smith 10-27-1863 (10-28-1863) L
Mitchell, John to Verdona C. Bennett 2-20-1853 Cr
Mitchell, Johnathan H. to Susan A. Beloat 12-26-1854 Sh
Mitchell, Jonathan P. to Mary E. Notgrass 3-4-1839 (3-13-1839) F
Mitchell, Joseph J. to M. C. McCorkle 1-17-1848 Hn
Mitchell, Joseph to Esper An T. Mann 11-12-1870 (11-13-1870) Cr
Mitchell, Joseph to Margaret Edmison 2-8-1869 (no return) Cr
Mitchell, Joshua Thomas to Mary Evans 8-16-1847 (8-17-1847) T
Mitchell, L. B. to Louissanna Hardgrave 6-24-1839 (6-26-1839) Ma
Mitchell, L. M. to C. B. Duncan 2-23-1860 (4-3-1860) O
Mitchell, Luther N. to Darcas Bruison 8-5-1848 Ma
Mitchell, M. P. to Cornelia Jackson 8-22-1861 Hr
Mitchell, Mac McCay to May E. Williamson 10-26-1867 (10-29-1867) F B
Mitchell, Mark to Margaret Lattimer 9-13-1853 Ma
Mitchell, Matthew J. to Virginia Fourshee 1-11-1857 We
Mitchell, Maurice to Mary Miller 9-5-1849 (9-9-1849) T
Mitchell, Moses D. to Mary L. Read 5-2-1869 Hy
Mitchell, Moses to Caroline Hawkins 12-19-1873 T
Mitchell, Moses to Emma Senter 2-4-1863 G
Mitchell, Munroe to Amanda Williams 12-27-1870 (12-28-1870) F B
Mitchell, N. J. to Mollie J. Johnson 12-26-1855 (12-27-1855) L
Mitchell, Nathan M. to Martha C. McCommon 9-17-1842 (9-22-1842) Hr
Mitchell, Nathan to Callie Holt 4-13-1869 (4-14-1869) Cr
Mitchell, Nelson to Nancy Pond 2-3-1840 (2-6-1840) F
Mitchell, P. R. to Margaret Vanderver 1-4-1873 (1-5-1873) T
Mitchell, Peter to Harriet Griffin 1-6-1874 (1-7-1874) Dy
Mitchell, Peter to Susan Boyd 1-8-1869 (1-9-1869) F B
Mitchell, Phillip to Ann H. Patteson 9-17-1867 (9-25-1867) F B
Mitchell, R. H. to Justianna Nelson 9-22-1861 Hr
Mitchell, R. L. to Eliza Hysan 1-2-1856 We
Mitchell, R. L. to Sarah A. W. Palmer 12-25-1849 Sh
Mitchell, R. W. to J. E. M. Turney 2-10-1875 (2-19-1875) Dy
Mitchell, R. W. to Nancy Jane Grier 7-22-1841 (7-29-1841) G
Mitchell, R. to Harriet Earp 1-4-1863 Be
Mitchell, Randle to Talitha Hopkins 5-12-1866 O
Mitchell, Richard to Nancy Turner 11-20-1846 (no return) Hn
Mitchell, Rubin to Alcy Jane Earp 1-30-1867 Be
Mitchell, Saml. D. to Malina Tinnan 9-5-1855 (9-8-1855) T
Mitchell, Shepard to Julia Nash 12-29-1875 (12-30-1875) Dy
Mitchell, Stephen to Emarine Watts 1-27-1855 O
Mitchell, T. J. to Mollie Adams 12-21-1875 (12-22-1875) L
Mitchell, Thomas C. to Rebecca Killingsworth 1-11-1842 G
Mitchell, Thomas J. to Martha J. Jenkins 3-27-1856 We
Mitchell, Thomas J. to Nancy E. Scoggins 12-16-1858 (12-17-1858) Hr
Mitchell, Thos. to Elizabeth Hopkins 6-14?-1851 (6-2?-1851) Sh
Mitchell, Tom to Bettie Burnett 3-12-1870? Hy
Mitchell, W. B. to Annie E. Pattison 1-6-1859 Sh
Mitchell, W. B. to Sallie Merrell 6-4-1857 Sh
Mitchell, W. E. to Martha Walton 9-21-1864 O
Mitchell, W. F. to Mary J. Hollowell 12-19-1853 (no return) F
Mitchell, W. H. to Mary A. Westbrook 2-4-1878 (1?-6-1878) L
Mitchell, W. H. to Nancy H. Babb 3-4-1864 Mn
Mitchell, W. M. P. to Mollie C. Hunt (Hurt?) 8-20-1872 (8-25-1872) L
Mitchell, W. R. to Mary V. Kidd 1-26-1878 (1-28-1878) Dy
Mitchell, Waid to Nancy B____? 5-11-1857 Cr
Mitchell, Wash P. to Hariet Dixon 10-2-1844 Cr
Mitchell, William to Angeline Morris 9-5-1868 (9-6-1868) Cr
Mitchell, William to Jane Stockley 5-27-1872 (6-14-1872) T
Mitchell, William to Melvan P. Jackson 12-12-1853 (1-4-1854) O
Mitchell, William to Mollie Nesitt 2-4-1869 Cr
Mitchell, William to Viola Moslyew 12-28-1864 Be
Mitchell, Willis to Cornelia Fuller 11-29-1876 L B
Mitchell, Wm. F. to Bettie A. Cocke 8-22-1860 (8-28-1860) F
Mitchell, Wm. M. to Margaret A. Knox 1-22-1840 Cr
Mitchell, Wm. N. to Margarett Tyson 12-5-1837 G
Mitchell, Wm. S. to Winford Laycock 6-3-1846 Cr
Mitchell, Wm. to Ann M. Tipping 7-25-1864 (7-27-1864) Sh
Mitchell, Wm. to Julia King 3-8-1877 Hy
Mitchell, Wm. to Martha A. Lowry 10-15-1860 Sh
Mitchell, Z. S. A. to Fanny E. Porter 3-27-1867 G
Mitchum, A. B. to E. A. Hillsman 11-30-1842 Cr
Mitchum, Harvy to Hellen Patterson 6-1-1866 (6-7-1866) Cr
Mitchum, J. M. to M. A. Newbill 2-9-1871 (no return) Cr
Mitchum, James to Caroline E. Webb 12-1-1857 Cr
Mitchum, Jesse to Mary A. Holmes 6-11-1840 Cr
Mitchum, Lewis F. to Elizabeth Hart 2-17-1840 Cr
Mitchum, Nelson to Marsha Scates 12-5-1870 (no return) Cr
Mitchum, W. E. to Jennie (Mrs.) Sandford 12-13-1866 G
Mitchum, W. E. to Mattie A. Cunningham 6-5-1869 G
Mitt, J. D. to Virginia T. McWherter 5-13-1858 We
Mix, Jack to Fannie Ray 5-21-1875 Hy
Mixon, John to Mary Mason 7-3-1828 G
Mixon, Samuel B. to Harriett Joslin 9-27-1832 G
Mize, Edwin to Visena Alsbrook 10-3-1837 Sh
Mize, James H. to Mary James 8-13-1857 We
Mizell, A. J. to Amanda J. Rogers 11-28-1867 (1-6-1868) Cr
Mizell, Craton to Martha Ann Miller 8-23-1857 Hn
Mizell, James L. to Mary C. Christopher 7-1-1861 We
Mizell, Wm. to Camolia Moss 5-16-1850 Be
Mo(o)re, James to Oma Chounce (Chance?) 4-6-1876 L
Moalett, George A. to Milly Matthews 5-3-1857 O
Mobley, Alexander H. to Saloda Richardson 12-23-1852 G
Mobley, Alexander to Dorithy Frances Vaden 2-1-1849 G
Mobley, Allen to Mary E. W. Crawley 11-29-1852 (12-7-1852) G
Mobley, James to Eveline F. Brown 1-15-1856 G
Mobley, Johnathan to Mary A. Robinson 10-26-1846 (10-28-1846) G
Mobley, Levi to Elmira Hammonds 11-24-1866 G
Mobley, R. A. to Victoria Ellis 11-26-1868 (no return) L
Mobley, Rufus to M. H. Brown 2-24-1867 G
Mobley, Turner to Sally G. Haynes 2-15-1854 G
Mobley, William to Dorethy Harrisson 12-29-1851 G
Mobley, William to Hawkins Bledsoe 11-12-1840 G
Mobly, Jacob to Sarah H. Ward 1-12-1860 Hy
Mobly, Licurgus L. to Manervia Kilmer 7-8-1867 (7-10-1867) L
Mobly, William to Mary E. Vaughn 10-2-1852 O
Modlin, J. C. to M. J. Compton 3-4-1865 (3-5-1865) Cr
Modlin, J. F. to Bettie Currie 7-18-1867 Hy
Modlin, J. H. to M. A. Winters 2-16-1875 (2-17-1875) Dy
Modlin, J. H. to T. S. McCarroll 2-16-1875 (2-17-1875) Dy
Moffat, John to Catharine Murray 5-22-1852 Sh
Moffatt, Augustus D. to Nancy Jane McClurkin 2-6-1850 T
Moffatt, E. to Alla Simmons 11-9-1864 Hn
Moffatt, Frank L. to Mollie M. T. Herndon 1-27-1870 F
Moffatt, James to Emily M. (Mrs.) Davis 9-28-1864 Sh
Moffatt, Thomas B. to N. A. Hamelton 2-20-1861 O
Moffatt, Wm. S. to Martha Jane Wilson 4-16-1856 (4-17-1856) T
Moffet, J. C. to M. E. Simonton 9-20-1870 T
Moffett, Chas. Christopher to Margaret Jane Bonner 10-27-1855 (10-30-1855) T
Moffett, David to Martha L. Strong 10-23-1867 (10-24-1867) T
Moffett, James S. to Martha J. Williamson 5-14-1860 O
Moffitt, H. E. to Belle McClain 7-1-1875 Hy
Moffitt, John to Mary C. Caviness 2-21-1853 (2-22-1853) Hr
Mohan, James to Ann Murry 5-15-1861 (5-16-1861) Cr
Mohler, Bonifaz to Josephine Tenz (Terry?) 8-23-1859 Sh
Mohundrow, E. C. to May E. Hill 1-13-1867 Hn
Moise, Arther to Fannie Jones 1-27-1871 (no return) Hy
Moize, Alfred to Bettie Moore 12-16-1867 (12-19-1867) Ma
Moize, Lafayette to May Ann King 7-4-1850 (7-10-1850) Ma
Molett, Wm. to Luvenia ------ 10-12-1865 O
Molin, Benjamin to Edna F. Fowler 5-3-1858 We
Molin, John to Sookey Kee 8-8-1860 Be
Moliter, C. F. to Martha Hallaburton 3-6-1857 (3-8-1857) Hr
Moliter, Jos. F. to M. L. James 3-5-1861 (3-7-1861) Sh
Moloughbury, Thos. to Joana Ryan 10-18-1851 (10-19-1851) Sh
Molton, Henry F. to Harriet A. Alexander 11-27-1855 Hn
Monaghan, James to Catharine Conway 5-31-1858 Sh
Monan, Joshua to Mary Ann Harris 7-6-1831 G
Moncreef, Samuel to Elizabeth Haveway 1-1-1839 F
Monger, John to America Henry 2-26-1869 G B
Monroe, A. L. to Elizabeth Vinson 2-17-1869 (2-18-1869) O
Monroe, Frank to Ella Fenner 11-24-1869 Ma
Monroe, Frank to Lizzabella Nolen 1-27-1876 L B
Monroe, Geo. W. to Lucy Malone 2-1-1855 Cr
Monroe, George F. to Elizabeth M. Williams 12-24-1873 (1-5-1874) T
Monroe, Henry to Mollie J. Shepard 6-18-1869 (6-20-1869) F
Monroe, James W. to Mary Elizabeth Ferrill 9-14-1853 (9-16-1853) O
Monroe, Josiah A. to Indiana Deakins 3-23-1852 (3-25-1852) T
Monroe, P. D. to Fanny Gibson 11-4-1868 Hy
Monroe, Randolph J. to Leticia E. Tauman 7-15-1848 Sh
Monroe, Thomas R. to Margaret Ann McLane 8-20-1857 Hn
Monroe, W. H. to Christian Parmer 2-28-1850 Hr
Monroe, William to Pearcy Westbrook 11-8-1852 Hr
Monroe, Wm. to Rebecca Monroe 7-22-1857 Cr
Monrow, John to Elizabeth D. Boydston 4-1-1861 (4-3-1861) L
Montague, A. W. to Hittie Hearring 11-29-1875 L
Montague, Rhodes to Suck Anderson 2-3-1868 (2-9-1868) F B
Montague, Thomas to Fanny Stewart 2-26-1870 (2-27-1870) F B
Montague, W. H. to Nellie Blaydes 12-31-1868 Hy
Montague, Young to Martha A. (Mrs.) Batt 5-25-1848 F

Montcries, Abram to Mary N. Clayton 2-21-1860 (2-23-1860) Sh
Montcuff, Sanders to Martha Hamblet 8-2-1844 (8-4-1844) F
Monteverde, Angelo to Caroline Brigniola 1-21-1863 Sh
Montgoery, Ross to Charlotte Coleman 8-23-1866 (8-26-1866) T
Montgomery, A. J. to J. F. Flanakin 5-7-1868 T
Montgomery, A. J. to Mary Joyce 2-5-1866 (2-8-1866) T
Montgomery, A. R. to Frances M. Hall 12-14-1864 (no return) Dy
Montgomery, Alexander A. to Margaret Hamilton 12-29-1856 (12-30-1856) T
Montgomery, Anda M. C. to Elizabeth Montgomery 9-9-1840 (9-10-1840) F
Montgomery, Andrew to Lucinda Mears 5-19-1849 (5-20-1849) T
Montgomery, Clay. to Mattie Poston 1-8-1874 Hy
Montgomery, David J. to Tennessee Mitchell 9-8-1842 Sh
Montgomery, Edmond to Milly Ann Golding 3-15-1871 L
Montgomery, George W. to M. E. Carter 1-3-1870 (1-5-1870) Cr
Montgomery, Green to Alice Robertson 12-30-1865 (no return) Dy
Montgomery, Hugh A. to Tabitha E. Hopper 2-21-1848 (2-23-1848) Ma
Montgomery, Hugh to Mariah Williams 12-6-1843 (12-7-1843) Ma
Montgomery, Hugh to Mary M. Newsom 8-8-1839 F
Montgomery, J. C. to P. B. Finch 4-6-1852 We
Montgomery, J. D. to Sarah D. Davis 3-7-1860 (3-8-1860) Sh
Montgomery, J. D. to Susie E. Williams 11-15-1869 (11-18-1869) F
Montgomery, J. L. to Mollie B. Fry 10-18-1870 (10-19-1870) Cr
Montgomery, J. M. to Jane White 11-3-1834 (11-4-1834) Hr
Montgomery, J. R. to Martha E. Peake 11-14-1844 Sh
Montgomery, Jackson to Martha T. Wright 10-6-1838 (10-8-1838) F
Montgomery, James G. to Rebecca Robinson 9-16-1841 Ma
Montgomery, James to Mahaly McKezick 12-17-1836 G
Montgomery, Jas. to Susan L. Manley 11-5-1850 F
Montgomery, Jess to Rebeca Crow 7-1-1867 Cr
Montgomery, John to Augustina Umpstead 4-12-1849 Cr
Montgomery, John M. to Ann C. Locke 1-15-1861 G
Montgomery, John W. to Unity Phillips 8-23-1863 We
Montgomery, John to Elden Welden 1-9-1843 Sh
Montgomery, Jonathan to Zeulah Fry 10-4-1842 Cr
Montgomery, L. R. to Thulina Knox 1-21-1840 Sh
Montgomery, Leroy to Cassandria Yeary? 1-30-1827 Hr
Montgomery, Peter to Mary (Mrs.) McGraw 9-23-1863 Sh
Montgomery, R. G. to Alice Roberson 1-4-1866 Hy
Montgomery, Richard J. to Mary A. McDougal 2-18-1850 Cr
Montgomery, Robt. to Frances Oliver 11-4-1866 Hy
Montgomery, Rufus W. to H. C. Vowell 2-26-1863 (no return) We
Montgomery, S. J. to L. A. Neely 1-13-1869 Cr
Montgomery, S. M. to M. J. Long 3-8-1855 (no return) F
Montgomery, Samuel W. to Malisa E. Strickland 1-7-1848 (1-9-1848) Hr
Montgomery, T. D. to Laura Ward 10-7-1866 (10-30-1866) G
Montgomery, T. W. to Martha (Mrs.) Mosely 8-12-1866 G
Montgomery, W. B. to M.L. Spain 2-8-1873 (2-9-1873) Cr
Montgomery, W. J. to Anna A. Cassett 2-25-1860 (5-2-1860) F
Montgomery, W. S. to Selina Bland 4-3-1856 (4-4-1856) Sh
Montgomery, William to Jane H. Boyd 3-12-1852 (3-16-1852) Ma
Montgomery, Wm. H. to Levice Wirt 4-7-1831 Sh
Montgomery, Wm. J. to Artemisa Farmer 7-29-1855 We
Montgomery, Wm. L. to Julia F. Coulter 1-9-1855 (1-11-1855) Sh
Montgomery, Wm. L. to Mary A. Jones 1-9-1845 Sh
Montgomery, Wm. to Emeline C. Robeson 1-28-1864 (2-1-1864) Cr
Montgomery, Wm. to Emeline C. Robeson 1-29-1864 (no return) Cr
Montgomery, Wm. to Mailsey Jane Trousdale no date (with 11-1874) T
Montinues, A. A. to M. Gooch 3-2-1854 Cr
Moock, Zaclok to Baslette Block 11-14-1849 Sh
Moody, Allen to Ann Marley 2-19-1840 O
Moody, Allen to Jane Wyatt 4-26-1843 O
Moody, C. C. to M. F. Harper 2-21-1861 (no return) Hy
Moody, Charles to Sellah Jones 4-14-1867 G
Moody, Clemments to Joanah Yeates 9-13-1849 Be
Moody, Daniel to Emeline Davis 10-20-1872 Hy
Moody, Daniel to Hannah Taylor 12-24-1865 Hy
Moody, David T. to Eleanor Midgett 12-19-1848 (12-20-1848) Ma
Moody, Ed to Mollie Williams 8-20-1877 (8-30-1877) L B
Moody, Edward J. to Mary R. Lilly 12-1-1859 Hn
Moody, Eli A. to Sallie Yarington 12-10-1870 (12-11-1870) Dy
Moody, Eli to Frances Finch 7-18-1849 Hn
Moody, Elijah N. to Sarah H. Steele 9-19-1860 Hn
Moody, Elijah W. to Rebecca Chilcutt 11-4-1857 Hn
Moody, G. H. to S. J. Johnson 9-20-1849 F
Moody, Giles F. to Eliza C. Staggs 10-2-1867 (no return) Dy
Moody, Green H. to Eliza D. Johnson 3-1-1848 (3-2-1848) F
Moody, J. N. to Nancy Weldon 8-22-1862 (no return) Hn
Moody, James A. to Elizabeth A. McCuiston 7-21-1860 Hn
Moody, James A. to Lucy A. Whitehead 1-24-1866 Hy
Moody, John A. to Minerva Branch 6-11-1860 (6-13-1860) F
Moody, Joseph E. to Anna M. Laurence 6-14-1849 (6-15-1849) F
Moody, L. P. to Sarah C. Bennett 10-28-1866 Hn
Moody, Lewis to Elizabeth Stroud 4-26-1855 (no return) Hn
Moody, Lewis to Malinda Gleen 9-27-1869 G B
Moody, M. M. to Ann A. Irons 5-26-1866 (no return) Hn B
Moody, Nathaniel to Tracey Ferguson 6-14-1831 Sh
Moody, Richd. E. to Eliza J. Cocke 1-20-1849 (1-24-1849) F

Moody, Samuel R. to Susan F. Lowry 9-2-1866 Hn
Moody, Samuel to Sarah Mankins 8-31-1857 Hn
Moody, Thomas J. to Mary Provow 10-24-1849 Hn
Moody, Thomas L.(Q?) to Nelly Hannah 3-9-1830 Sh
Moody, Thomas to Nancy Higganbottom 6-12-1836 Sh
Moody, Timothy S. to Mary M. King 9-2-1857 Hn
Moody, W. A. to Tabithy Brooks 6-27-1869 G
Moody, West to Adeline Veazey 5-20-1866 Hn B
Moody, William M. to Elizabeth Key 1-25-1855 Hn
Moody, William to Rachel Henry 12-31-1857 Hn
Moody, Wilson H. to M. E. Moore 2-6-1873 Hy
Moon(Moore?), Wm. H. to Virginia Doxey 4-27-1846 (4-28-1846) Hr
Moon, Bartley to Lucy Wilson 12-12-1867 G B
Moon, Calvin S. to Sarah A. Kennedy 3-26-1861 Hn
Moon, Isaac W. to Gilly A. Goldsby 10-19-1848 Sh
Moon, Jacob N. to Harrett M. Rembert 2-26-1844 Sh
Moon, John W. to Elizabeth Vickery ?-8-1845 Hn
Moon, John to Harriet Yancey 4-20-1866 G
Moon, T. J. to Amanda J. Hale 2-8-1866 (2-15-1866) G
Moon, Thomas to Milley Robbins 10-28-1851 O
Moon, Vicent to Sarah P. Haston 7-3-1839 (7-9-1839) Ma
Moon, Wilson to Ann Covington 9-19-1842 Ma
Moone, Levin B. to Elizabeth Williams 12-13-1828 (12-18-1828) Hr
Mooney, Daniel to Nancy C. Bayer 9-9-1844 We
Mooney, James R. to Sarah T. Simmons 10-12-1868 (no return) Hn
Mooney, Joseph M. to Julia Ann Dunn 1-13-1850 Hn
Mooney, Thomas to Dolly Paschall 1-25-1839 Hn
Mooney, William C. to P. Alexander 9-11-1844 Hn
Moor(e), Charles to Mary Bowles 12-20-1827 Sh
Moor, J. B. to Julina Pierce 1-11-1857 Be
Moor, S. H. to Susan C. Shelton 12-30-1878 (1-1-1879) Dy
Moor, Wm. to Leitia Davis 3-2-1856 Be
Moor-?, George to Chlorina H. Quillen 4-19-1864 Be
Moore, A. E. to B. J. Harris 12-24-1872 (12-25-1872) Dy
Moore, A. G. to Martha E. Parker 12-17-1856 We
Moore, A. N. to Elizabeth Sargent 6-7-1879 (no return) Dy
Moore, A. W. to Indiana M. Cabler 8-16-1838 F
Moore, Abner to Mary Ann Anderson 6-21-1842 (6-22-1842) Hr
Moore, Abner to Rebecca Black 1-2-1854 (1-3-1854) Hr
Moore, Abriham to Deliah Strayhorn 3-10-1873 (3-13-1873) Cr B
Moore, Alex to Mahala Ivory 3-11-1882 (3-12-1882) L
Moore, Alexr. to CAthrine Jordan 4-4-1870 (no return) L B
Moore, Alfred P. to Eliza Jane Ferrill 10-19-1870 (10-20-1870) Ma
Moore, Alfred W. to Jane McFarland 5-23-1850 Cr
Moore, Alfred to Julia Ann Brown 12-30-1847 Cr
Moore, Alfred to Martha Jane Lanier 9-29-1842 L
Moore, Alfred to Nancy E. Macklin 1-4-1867 G
Moore, Alfred to Nancy Eliz. Ellen Smith 1-23-1849 (1-30-1849) Hr
Moore, Allen to Delana A. Cooper 1-1-1865 G
Moore, Alphard to Mary Ann Armes 6-29-1865 G
Moore, Alphus P. to Temperance Brooks 12-24-1841 (12-30-1841) Ma
Moore, Amos to Vicy Musgrays 12-24-1868 Hy
Moore, Andrew J. to Rachel Shull 6-8-1836 H
Moore, Andrew to Adline M. Anderson 3-9-1846 (3-10-1846) Hr
Moore, Arthur to Mildred E. Farmer 12-28-1847 G
Moore, Azariah to Nancy S. Nolen 12-31-1860 (1-1-1861) O
Moore, Azariah to Susan Smith 9-7-1869 G
Moore, Ben to Lucinda Donaldson 12-22-1869 (12-23-1870?) G B
Moore, Benjamin F. to Mary Ann Watson 2-9-1869 (2-11-1869) F
Moore, Benjamin to Betsy Jane Bradford 2-8-1868 (2-10-1868) Cr
Moore, Berny to Maria Tuggle 10-6-1866 (no return) Hy
Moore, C. P. to Mattie W. White 11-30-1874 O
Moore, C. to Mary J. Spires 1-12-1860 Be
Moore, Calloway B. to Martha F. Dandridge 3-11-1846 Sh
Moore, Carroll to Vira Gilbert 12-25-1871 (no return) Cr B
Moore, Caswell J. to Levy White 3-2-1846 (3-8-1846) G
Moore, Charles S. to Mary E. Wallis 5-26-1867 G
Moore, Charles to Louisa Vancamp 1-26-1860 Sh
Moore, Charles to Mary Tennessee Lawrence 12-25-1867 G B
Moore, Charles to Minnie Romans 6-13-1885 (6-14-1885) L
Moore, Charley to Mollie Light 12-25-1877 (12-27-1877) Dy
Moore, Covey to Amanda Dixon 12-1-1873 (12-3-1873) T
Moore, Curtis to Frances Robertson 2-10-1845 (2-13-1845) Hr
Moore, D. A. to L. A. Alexander 1-10-1869 Hy
Moore, D. M. to Amelia G. Garrett 12-14-1854 Sh
Moore, D. S. to Jane Henry 9-11-1869 Hy
Moore, Daniel to Mollie King 7-6-1872 (no return) Hy
Moore, Danl. to Mary E. Wardford 2-16-1876 (no return) Hy
Moore, David A. to Luiza F. Thurmond 5-15-1863 (5-16-1863) L
Moore, David Fletcher to Susan Ann Sullivan 9-17-1844 (9-19-1844) T
Moore, David S. to R. A. Robinson 11-22-1854 (11-23-1854) Hr
Moore, David Sidney to Melisa Roberson 1-2-1866 L
Moore, David to Ann Dowdy 11-1-1852 (no return) F
Moore, David to Elizabeth Sanders 6-20-1868 (6-25-1868) L
Moore, David to Mahaley Neel 10-12-1832 O
Moore, David to Margaret Clements 9-19-1849 Cr
Moore, E. W. to Martha E. Wherry 1-13-1853 (1-18-1853) G

Moore, Edmond to Hannah Shane 3-22-1867 G
Moore, Elex. to Elizabeth Moore 9-3-1840 Cr
Moore, Eli to Adeline M. Jacobs 7-16-1839 (7-18-1839) Hr
Moore, Eli to Anna Miller 2-26-1830 Ma
Moore, Elias to Jackey Ann Perry 2-4-1850 (2-5-1850) Hr
Moore, Elihuge to Mandy Hutchison 8-30-1860 (no return) Hy
Moore, Elisha to Charlotta J. Waldrop 3-25-1857 Hy
Moore, Elwood to Mary H. King 9-25-1861 (9-29-1861) Cr
Moore, Euphrates to Samantha C. Clement 3-3-1860 Hn
Moore, Ezekial to Polly Ann Kirby 3-1-1871 L
Moore, Ezekial to Sarah New 2-13-1869 (no return) L
Moore, F. B. to Elizabeth Bruce 7-26-1866 (no return) Hn
Moore, F. C. to L. J. Williamson 2-11-1879 (2-12-1879) Dy
Moore, F. M. to G. A. Kesbitt 3-24-1866 (3-29-1866) Cr
Moore, Frank to Eliza Fowlkes 1-6-1872 Dy
Moore, Frank to Nancy Beard 12-11-1878 Dy
Moore, Frank to Sarah Halliburton 8-7-1873 L B
Moore, G. D. to N. A. Rodgers 1-23-1867 Cr
Moore, G. W. to Jane F. Nicholdson 10-6-1858 (10-7-1858) G
Moore, G. W. to M. A. Castle 3-23-1865 (3-27-1865) O
Moore, Geo. W. to Mary A. Crutchfield 1-2-1839 Hn
Moore, Geo. to Lendora Byrne 4-12-1864 Sh
Moore, George B. to Mary Jackson 12-30-1859 Ma
Moore, George C. to Mahala Cathey 10-21-1852 G
Moore, George E. to Elizabeth Kennon (Kenmore?) 9-1-1849 (9-5-1849) L
Moore, George E. to Matilda E. Vaiden 1-2-1872 (1-3-1871?) L
Moore, George S. to Ann Jones 2-3-1869 (2-4-1869) Cr
Moore, George T. to Mary A. C. King 12-4-1848 (no return) Hn
Moore, George W. to Ann Louiza J. Gardner 2-22-1849 G
Moore, George W. to Christian S. Jones 2-2-1843 G
Moore, George W. to Eliza J. Hoozer 12-23-1847 (12-30-1847) G
Moore, George W. to Martha J. Gorden 1-4-1870 Hy
Moore, George W. to Sallie R. Jones 3-19-1868 Ma
Moore, George to Ama Smith 12-25-1872 (12-26-1872) Cr B
Moore, George to Mariah Killabrew 4-28-1866 Hn B
Moore, George to Sallie Moore 6-19-1875 Hy
Moore, Gillam J. to Mollie H. Perry 11-15-1871 Ma
Moore, Green B. to Lydia Holyfield 1-26-1847 Ma
Moore, Green to Mary Kind 1-17-1855 Ma
Moore, Henry D. to Avy Deal 4-13-1842 (no return) Hn
Moore, Henry H. to Elizabeth Moore 12-17-1861 (no return) Hy
Moore, Henry H. to Mattie R. Hood 12-17-1874 Hy
Moore, Henry N. to Sarah P. Rogers 11-14-1868 Cr
Moore, Henry W. to Izora Stokely 10-2-1873 Hy
Moore, Henry to Ann Taylor 11-4-1866 Hy
Moore, Henry to Emily Carter 8-3-1872 (no return) Hy
Moore, Henry to Harriet Fitzgerald 1-8-1870 G B
Moore, Henry to Lucinda Pile 6-25-1869 T
Moore, Henry to Martha J. Hannah 5-15-1855 (5-16-1855) T
Moore, Henry to Susan Eison 3-30-1880 (4-1-1880) L
Moore, Heywood to Lue Gibson 2-10-1872 Hy
Moore, Hezekiah to Elizabeth Abernathy 10-10-1861 Cr
Moore, Hugh D. to Mary Ann Thompson 6-20-1844 F
Moore, Hugh to Nancy Hunter 6-8-1837 Sh
Moore, Hugh to Octavia D. Anderson 8-11-1859 (8-14-1859) Hr
Moore, Ichabud to Mary E. Cooper 10-1-1845 G
Moore, Ira to Harriett Braswell 1-10-1847 Sh
Moore, Ira to Sallie Scott 5-24-1859 Sh
Moore, Isaac to Casey Lee Flower 7-12-1834 (7-17-1834) Hr
Moore, Isham to Ellen Newborne 3-12-1869 Hy
Moore, Isral C. to Nancy A. Burkhart 8-1-1838 G
Moore, J. A. to M. E. Thompson 1-14-1868 (1-15-1868) Dy
Moore, J. A. to M. J. McCain 12-3-1866 (12-4-1866) T
Moore, J. B. to L. D. Yancy 2-5-1868 (1?-11-1868) Cr
Moore, J. B. to Mary V. Brown 10-23-1867 (10-24-1867) F
Moore, J. Dennis to Mary Townes 5-4-1866 (5-6-1866) Cr
Moore, J. G. to S. (Mrs.) Randolph 11-28-1864 Sh
Moore, J. H. to Edny M. McFarland 4-20-1864 G
Moore, J. H. to M. L. Borum 11-1-1877 L
Moore, J. H. to Martha A. Redmon 10-9-1864 Mn
Moore, J. H. to N. C. Jones 7-12-1863 G
Moore, J. I. to Mattie P. Boydston 2-16-1881 (no return) L
Moore, J. M. to Mollie Mallory 1-6-1868 (1-8-1868) Dy
Moore, J. M. to Sarah E. Cates 10-1-1870 (no return) Hy
Moore, J. S. to Cathie Cook 11-29-1877 Dy
Moore, J. S. to Elizabeth Price 9-11-1855 We
Moore, J. S. to Lizzie Shahon ?-?-1867 (4-28-1867) Dy
Moore, J. S. to Susan L. O'Brien 10-25-1859 Hr
Moore, J. W. E. to Mary M. Wood 12-8-1874 Hy
Moore, J. W. to M. C. Boydston 11-12-1884 L
Moore, J. W. to S. F. Adams 12-1-1874 (12-2-1874) T
Moore, Jack to Caroline Coppadge 12-25-1868 Hy
Moore, Jack to Margaret Wyatt 4-6-1880 (4-8-1880) Dy
Moore, James (Jno.) W. to Mary C. Schabel 1-12-1867 (no return) Hy
Moore, James A. to Margaret E. Wilson 5-14-1864 (5-16-1864) T
Moore, James A. to Mary L. Learns 10-19-1863 Sh
Moore, James C. to Minerva Rumley 1-25-1846 Cr

Moore, James Chalmers to Sarah Ann Cousar? 11-5-1842 (11-8-1842) T
Moore, James E. to Emma D. Ward 4-6-1866 Hy
Moore, James F. to Nancy A. F. Beaman? 2-1-1852 Hn
Moore, James H. to Charlotte F. Carsine 4-20-1846 Cr
Moore, James J. to Susan H. Lundy 8-3-1853 Sh
Moore, James M. to Jane Ellis 2-26-1856 (3-2-1856) O
Moore, James M. to Letitia F. Hearn 10-5-1860 (10-9-1860) Ma
Moore, James R. to Mary E. Page 9-18-1859 Hn
Moore, James S. to Elizabeth Turnham (Turnbow) 6-21-1831 (7-23-1831) O
Moore, James Thomas to Ella C. Vaughn 7-11-1874 (7-12-1874) L
Moore, James V. to Mary Campbell 9-18-1865 (9-19-1865) T
Moore, James W. to Elizabeth Bird 12-23-1848 Sh
Moore, James to Elinord Turbeville 9-28-1857 Hn
Moore, James to Elizabeth McIree 12-21-1848 Sh
Moore, James to Hannah Mitchell 2-18-1869 F B
Moore, James to Henrietta Simms 1-29-1866 (2-4-1866) F
Moore, James to Judician Ann Scates 12-14-1845 Cr
Moore, James to Martha Ward 1-8-1861 Hn
Moore, James to Penelope Underwood 9-4-1856 We
Moore, James to Sarrah E. Rowland 10-6-1870 Cr
Moore, James to _____ _____ 4-1-1872 (4-10-1872) L B
Moore, Jas. H. to Adra Scott 6-18-1859 (6-19-1859) O
Moore, Jasper to Birda Penick 12-20-1869 (no return) L
Moore, Jasper to Catheran Phillips 3-1-1867 (3-16-1867) T
Moore, Jefferson to A. M. Pate 12-26-1868 (no return) Dy
Moore, Jesse to Alsse Spring? 11-26-1858 Cr
Moore, Jno. M. J. to Martha A. Duke 8-8-1867 G
Moore, Jo to Susan Foster 1-21-1880 (1-22-1880) Dy
Moore, Joel to Martha C. Turnham 11-4-1844 (11-7-1844) O
Moore, John A. to Elizabeth A. Dison 1-8-1852 Hr
Moore, John A. to Mary C. Easley 10-4-1842 T
Moore, John A. to Mary Jane McCluhen 11-31-1857 (12-1-1857) T
Moore, John B. to Isabella Shelton 11-18-1847 T
Moore, John C. to Harriet C. King 4-22-1852 Cr
Moore, John C. to Lou N. Gregory 2-13-1860 (2-14-1860) Sh
Moore, John D. to S. E. Davidson 8-2-1872 (8-6-1872) T
Moore, John E. to M. E. Timmons 1-24-1866 (no return) Hy
Moore, John G. to Mary Ann Parks 9-13-1855 (9-15-1855) Hr
Moore, John G. to Rhoda A. Kelzey 4-11-1855 Cr
Moore, John H. C. to Sarah A. Gibson 10-4-1853 Hn
Moore, John H. to Martha E. McBride 3-16-1854 Cr
Moore, John H. to Mary W. Orr 11-30-1840 (12-1-1840) Hr
Moore, John L. to Fannie Irby 1-24-1862 (1-30-1862) Sh
Moore, John N. to Mary E. Dodd 1-25-1860 (1-29-1860) Sh
Moore, John P. to Elizabeth S. Harriss 12-23-1843 Hr
Moore, John R. to Mary A. Clay 2-26-1867 (2-28-1867) Dy
Moore, John R. to sarah B. Smith 8-16-1859 Cr
Moore, John S. to Jane Courtney 12-10-1841 Hn
Moore, John S. to Lutitia E. Chaney 12-19-1866 Hy
Moore, John T. to Arabella Pope 12-28-1867 Ma
Moore, John V. to Frances P. Colly 12-10-1856 We
Moore, John W. to Fannie Cunningham 3-4-1876 (3-5-1876) L
Moore, John W. to Georgeanna Sanders 8-20-1873 Hy
Moore, John W. to L. V. Farris 11-6-1865 (11-7-1865) F
Moore, John W. to Sobina Yates 10-29-1835 (10-29-1835) G
Moore, John to Abigale Freeland 12-31-1845 Cr
Moore, John to Catherine Wright 11-12-1869 T
Moore, John to Emeline Turnham 7-13-1859 O
Moore, John to Martha M. Nelson 7-9-1845 Sh
Moore, John to Mary Davidson 2-27-1884 L
Moore, John to Mary Ann Clark 1-20-1885 L
Moore, John to Nancy Carson 12-7-1854 Cr
Moore, John to Nannie Hicks 1-6-1876 (no return) Hy
Moore, John to Salina E. Allen 10-7-1853 (10-13-1853) G
Moore, John to Sallie Elam 12-27-1872 Hy
Moore, John, sr. to Eliza P. Chambers 12-21-1864 (12-22-1864) L
Moore, Johnson to Violet McNeill 5-25-1870 (5-28-1870) F B
Moore, Jordan A. to Ann Cary 4-16-1868 (4-23-1868) L
Moore, Jordan to Latitia Howard 8-13-1866 (no return) Dy
Moore, Jos. C. to Mary A. Murray 5-1-1853 Sh
Moore, Joseph W. to Julia A. Moore 8-10-1852 Hn
Moore, Joseph to Eliza Gilbert 9-25-1868 (9-27-1868) Cr
Moore, Josiah N. to Milley E. Crawley 1-29-1863 We
Moore, Josiah to Lucy Smith 6-10-1831 G
Moore, June to Mary Taylor 1-27-1877 Hy
Moore, L. D. to Elizabeth Brown 9-13-1867 (9-15-1867) Dy
Moore, L. M. to A. A. (Mrs.) Eastham 5-5-1864 (5-9-1864) Sh
Moore, Ladd to Sarah Gooden 5-12-1853 (5-14-1853) O
Moore, Larkin L. to Charlott Palmore 11-17-1840 G
Moore, Leonard to Susan Dillard 5-25-1827 Ma
Moore, Lewis to Jane Anderson 8-5-1839 (8-7-1839) Hr
Moore, Lewis to Parilee Wilkinson 12-20-1853 (12-21-1853) Hr
Moore, Littleton to Susannah Hays 11-12-1869 (11-13-1869) F B
Moore, Lodwick(Ridwick) to Mary Ann Turner 10-18-1848 (10-19-1848) Hr
Moore, Lum? Tho. to Octavia Shepherd 12-19-1855 (12-20-1855) T
Moore, M. C. to Sarah G. Roberts 1-8-1853 Hn
Moore, M. V. to M. J. Hubart 4-20-1876 (4-23-1876) O

Moore, Marian to Margaret McMullen 1-22-1852 G
Moore, Martin to Jane Jefferson 1-18-1868 (no return) F B
Moore, Martin to Martha Sammons 3-6-1841 (3-11-1841) Hr
Moore, Masias J. to Elena Williams 9-9-1834 (9-10-1834) Hr
Moore, Melvil A. to Mary L. Moore 11-17-1869 (11-18-1869) T
Moore, Miller to Belle Fowlkes 9-15-1877 Dy
Moore, Morris to Mary Jones Brown 8-29-1853 (9-7-1853) Sh
Moore, Moses to Ann F. Carrington 1-25-1840 (1-29-1840) Ma
Moore, N. K. to N. V. McDaniel 12-25-1860 G
Moore, N. M. to Tenness King 12-3-1866 (11?-6-1866) Cr
Moore, N. S. to Mary C. Alexander 11-28-1866 (no return) L
Moore, N. S. to Mollie E. Smith 12-14-1880 L
Moore, N. to M. Calhoun 12-22-1874 (12-24-1874) T
Moore, Nathan to Elizabeth C. Brown 9-4-1848 Ma
Moore, Nathaniel B. to Sarah Campbell 7-25-1837 (7-31-1837) Hr
Moore, Nathaniel S. to Susan Ray 2-3-1858 (2-4-1858) L
Moore, Nathaniel to Hellen M. Spurier 7-4-1859 (7-5-1859) G
Moore, Nathaniel to Julia Adams 5-17-1831 Sh
Moore, Nathaniel to Louisa Bray 8-7-1841 G
Moore, Nathaniel to Martha Minton (Winton) 9-18-1838 Sh
Moore, Needham to Sapponia Cox 7-29-1843 (7-31-1843) G
Moore, Neely to El Justice 10-11-1855 Cr
Moore, Nelson to Charity McNeal 10-14-1871 (no return) Hy
Moore, Nelson to Mira Estis 3-16-1872 (no return) Hy
Moore, Nick to Nancy Smith 10-28-1880 Dy
Moore, Peter S. to Elizabeth Harrison 10-1-1846 Sh
Moore, Peter to Margaret Hill 3-30-1862 Mn
Moore, Peyton to Maria Farley 12-30-1865 (12-31-1865) F B
Moore, Pierce to Margaret Tipton 2-25-1871 (2-26-1871) Dy
Moore, Pierce to Rebecca Horton 9-20-1873 Dy
Moore, R. A. to S. A. Johnson 6-5-1851 Hn
Moore, R. G. to Mary J. Hutson 10-26-1854 G
Moore, R. G. to Roxanna F. Williams 2-9-1864 (3-10-1864) Cr
Moore, R. G. to Roxanna F. Williams 2-9-1864 (no return) Cr
Moore, R. J. to Azalee H. Williams 10-25-1868 G
Moore, R. M. to Bettie L. McClellan 2-2-1860 F
Moore, R. P. to Mary M. Hubbard 10-25-1831 (10-27-1831) Hr
Moore, R. R. to Mary Elizabeth Forrest 12-5-1874 (12-8-1874) T
Moore, R. W. to Elizabeth Pullam 4-3-1863 O
Moore, Ral to Fannie Wall 12-1-1871 Hy
Moore, Raleigh to Sarah J. Nelson 9-22-1852 Ma
Moore, Randolph to Mary B. Mills 11-15-1849 O
Moore, Richard B. to Lou J. Goodwin 11-10-1870 (11-24-1870) Cr
Moore, Richard C. to Pearle M. Billings 9-6-1860 Sh
Moore, Richard to C. Gooch 4-3-1838 Cr
Moore, Richard to Ibby Whitehead 7-15-1865 (no return) Hy
Moore, Richard to Polly Guinn 10-31-1861 Hn
Moore, Robert B. to Martha Ann Carson 4-17-1867 (4-18-1867) L
Moore, Robert C. to Malisa Sanders 10-31-1848 Ma
Moore, Robert C. to Martha A. Wright 1-21-1847 Hn
Moore, Robert M. to Nancy A. Utley 12-13-1849 Cr
Moore, Robert W. to Deliah Wolverton 2-25-1864 Mn
Moore, Robert W. to Caroline R. Carter 1-13-1854 Cr
Moore, Robert Y. to Sarah E. Shepherd 1-27-1855 Cr
Moore, Robert to Wena Jeames 7-5-1861 Mn
Moore, Robt. D. to Fredonia Curtice 2-18-1863 (2-29-1863) L
Moore, Robt. to Martha Vinson 2-19-1872 (2-20-1872) Cr
Moore, Ruffin to Susan Penny 9-23-1868 G B
Moore, Russell to Mary Walker 3-20-1854 (3-21-1854) T
Moore, Russell to Nancy McDaniel 10-16-1849 Sh
Moore, S. H. to Martha J. Scoby 12-11-1865 (12-13-1865) Dy
Moore, S. P. to Rebecca A. Small 11-14-1866 (11-15-1866) Ma
Moore, S. Perry to Clara J. Williams 7-2-1864 (7-3-1864) Sh
Moore, S. W. to Jane Smith 4-22-1854 (4-27-1854) Sh
Moore, Saml. A. to Ann E. Brooksher 4-11-1855 Sh
Moore, Sampson to Hannah Shelton 12-20-1866 Hy
Moore, Samuel to Charlotte Miller (Milton) 3-11-1838 Sh
Moore, Samuel to Elizabeth Holloway 10-4-1862 Mn
Moore, Seth M. to D. M. Alexander 8-30-1865 (no return) Hy
Moore, Seth T. to Elizabeth Freeman 8-19-1850 (8-21-1850) G
Moore, Sidney A. to Joana P. Koonce 4-18-1861 (no return) Hy
Moore, Silas to Sophronia H. Lamb 12-28-1861 Hn
Moore, Stanstill to Ava Clendenin 3-21-1838 Hn
Moore, Stephen to Sarah Diffy 3-6-1840 Ma
Moore, Sydney to Martha Jane Oniel 12-14-1853 (12-15-1853) Ma
Moore, T. D. to Marg Johnson 12-30-1862 Mn
Moore, T. L. to Elender Grant 4-28-1845 Cr
Moore, Thad to Adney Chaffin 2-28-1868 (no return) F B
Moore, Thomas B. to Mary Browning 2-17-1841 Cr
Moore, Thomas C. to Sarah Jane Love 7-12-1850 Cr
Moore, Thomas D. to Sarah Crumply 2-9-1852 (2-10-1852) Hr
Moore, Thomas E. to Elizabeth J. Joy 9-17-1846 Hr
Moore, Thomas M. to Caroline R. Gorman 7-1-1851 Sh
Moore, Thomas M. to Malbily J. Robertson 7-26-1856 Cr
Moore, Thomas to Ann Elizabeth Roshel? 10-31-1859 (11-1-1859) Hr
Moore, Thomas to Josephine Payne 5-30-1859 Sh
Moore, Thomas to Mary I. Cazort 1-22-1873 Hy

Moore, Thomas to Sarah Hartwell 8-29-1850 Sh
Moore, Thomas to Sarah M. Hubbard 12-13-1848 Hr
Moore, Thomason to Emily A. Hamilton 11-13-1856 Cr
Moore, Thompson to Luenida Pillows 12-20-1866 G
Moore, Thompson to Martha E. Hill 10-5-1869 Cr
Moore, Thos. F. to Martha J. Cogbill 12-19-1870 (12-21-1870) F
Moore, Thos. H. to Lucy Brown 2-4-1839 (2-5-1839) Hr
Moore, Thos. R. to Mary E. Light 5-20-1869 Dy
Moore, Thos. to Amanda (Mrs.) Tuff 3-3-1864 (3-6-1864) Sh
Moore, Thos. to Susan C. Echols 10-24-1863 Sh
Moore, Toney to Carrie Smith 3-26-1874 (3-28-1874) Dy
Moore, Turner to Callie Steward 12-24-1868 (no return) Hy
Moore, Vincent S. to Elizabeth Hooker 5-2-1843 Hn
Moore, W. A. to Carolyn Webb 10-15-1857 O
Moore, W. A. to Dicey Ann Dickens 1-11-1860 (1-12-1860) Hr
Moore, W. A. to Virginia Lewis 2-4-1878 (no return) Hy
Moore, W. C. to Harriett Bledsoe 12-3-1860 (12-6-1860) Cr
Moore, W. D. to Eva J. Mann 4-28-1875 Hy
Moore, W. E. to S. A. Read 11-30-1868 G
Moore, W. H. to C. G. Holifield 5-4-1861 O
Moore, W. M. to C. A. Smith 10-11-1882 L
Moore, W. S. to E. C. Jacobs 1-16-1863 Mn
Moore, W. S. to M. E. Yancy 10-29-1868 G
Moore, W. T. to Emma Hardister 11-23-1874 Hy
Moore, W. T. to M. J. Conklin 12-12-1876 (no return) L
Moore, W. T. to Mattie Brown 5-23-1869 Hy
Moore, W. W. to Elizabeth Watt 11-6-1854 (11-?-1854) G
Moore, W. to Matilda Stewart 11-25-1852 Sh
Moore, Watkins to Linington Jones 2-2-1843 G
Moore, Wesley to Elizabeth Pettard 10-21-1846 Cr
Moore, William A. to Epsey Ann Bradbury 1-15-1846 Ma
Moore, William B. to Elizabeth J. Thompson 3-29-1832 (4-1-1832) G
Moore, William B. to Piercy Bradberry 1-5-1828 (3-3-1828) G
Moore, William C. to Jane B. West 12-31-1838 Sh
Moore, William G. to Mary E. Moore 12-21-1853 Hr
Moore, William G. to Nancy Smith 9-3-1832 G
Moore, William I. to Nancy L. Childress 6-10-1874 (no return) L
Moore, William J. to Mary Ann Byrn 12-2-1857 L
Moore, William N. to Mary Ann Riggs 10-16-1850 (10-22-1850) Hr
Moore, William R. to Maria Stewart 12-22-1847 (12-23-1847) Ma
Moore, William R. to Martha A. Gibson 10-6-1855 (no return) Hn
Moore, William S. to Eliza Ann Harget 6-17-1854 (6-22-1854) O
Moore, William W. to Mary Ann Mayfield 10-4-1864 G
Moore, William to Almarinda Bennett 10-7-1850 Hr
Moore, William to Amanda Cole 9-1-1862 (no return) Hy
Moore, William to Betsy Boaz 6-1-1867 G B
Moore, William to E. A. Dickson 7-5-1848 O
Moore, William to Georgia Ann Mitchell 10-15-1868 (10-17-1868) F B
Moore, William to Jane Williams 9-12-1853 (9-22-1853) G
Moore, William to Margaret M. McMaccan 7-19-1862 (7-20-1862) L
Moore, William to Sarah H. Walker 7-4-1838 (7-5-1838) O
Moore, Wilson to Rebecca Quinley 1-22-1849 (2-3-1849) Ma
Moore, Wm. A. to Susan Kerr 7-28-1849 (7-29-1849) F
Moore, Wm. A. to Susannah Bates 12-14-1842 (12-17-1842) Hr
Moore, Wm. B. to Eliza J. Smith 3-4-1838 Cr
Moore, Wm. C. to C. Martin 3-18-1841 Cr
Moore, Wm. I. to Isabella Edwards 8-27-1858 Cr
Moore, Wm. L. to Mary C. Abington 12-7-1846 (12-9-1846) F
Moore, Wm. L. to Mary L. Roberts 1-29-1850 Cr
Moore, Wm. M. to Mary Hartgraves 12-14-1852 Sh
Moore, Wm. P. to Sidney E. Barnett 4-13-1858 Cr
Moore, Wm. W. to Harriett R. Smith 7-8-1854 Cr
Moore, Wm. W. to S. E. Kellow 11-11-1874 (11-12-1874) Dy
Moore, Wm. to Amy Watkins 10-30-1868 (10-31-1868) F B
Moore, Wm. to Ann Moore 2-1-1841 Cr
Moore, Wm. to Emalina Liles 10-7-1856 Cr
Moore, Wm. to Salina A. Lanksley (Tanksley) 1-19-1863 Sh
Moore, Wm. to Sarah Barnhart 2-19-1840 Cr
Moore, Yancy to Kathrine Martin 12-20-1850 Cr
Moore, Zack to Eliza Simms 8-22-1877 (8-23-1877) L
Moore?, jr., Cooper to Millie Pitts 9-5-1867 G B
Moore?, John to Amanda Moore 11-9-1869 Hy
Moorehead, Joseph H. to Susan Ann Lawson 5-26-1857 (5-28-1857) O
Mooreman, Robert A. to Martha A. Morgan 5-31-1838 Sh
Moorer, H. B. to Mary E. Henning 12-14-1875 (12-15-1875) L
Moorer, Isaac to Nellie Compton 6-4-1883 (no return) L
Moorer, John to Adeline Anthony 1-7-1885 L
Moorer, L. C. to Louise Anthony 9-22-1874 (9-23-1874) L
Moorer, Thomas to Ann Walker 12-29-1870 (no return) L
Moorer, William H. to Fannie A. Henning 11-16-1879 L
Moorhead, James M. to Ellen V. Howlett 1-30-1862 Sh
Mooring, H. L. to A. B. Butler 2-27-1854 (3-2-1854) Ma
Mooring, H. W. to Mary J. Patterson 10-11-1841 Cr
Mooring, Henry L. to Catherine Hastings 1-4-1858 Ma
Mooring, John A. to Charlotte Mary Connell 12-20-1860 (12-21-1860) Ma
Mooring, John C. to Eliza Jane Christian 3-9-1850 (3-12-1850) Ma
Mooring, John W. to Sophia P. Jones 1-15-1858 (1-18-1858) Ma

Moorman, Hiram C. to Frances J. Armstrong 1-27-1870 F
Moorman, Randal to Louisa Marshall 4-12-1869 F B
Moorney, M. B. to Amanda Cottam 1-28-1864 (1-29-1864) Dy
Mootre, Sam to Mary Ann Murrell 4-29-1870 (5-1-1870) F B
Mootry, Henry to Sue Mason 4-8-1881 L B
Mootry, Phil to Mollie Bush 12-12-1883 (12-13-1883) L
Mop?, B. V. to Elizabeth Williams 12-7-1858 We
Moppin, Harrison to Mary Blackwell 6-1-1868 (no return) Cr
Moran, Geo. W. to Angeline McDaniel 3-28-1860 (3-29-1860) Hr
Moran, Henry L. to Martha T. Sandiford 12-6-1836 Sh
Moran, James to Mary Kelly 6-15-1863 Sh
Moran, John F. to Millissa A. Gibbons 4-28-1842 Sh
Moran, M. Y. to Mary A. Herndon 1-24-1849 (1-26-1849) F
More, Edward to Eliza Tickell 5-30?-1840 (5-5-1840) O
Morean, Jno. F. to Melissa A. Gibbins 4-28-1842 Sh
Morefield, John to Rebecca E. Rose 7-9-1870 (7-10-1870) F
Morehead, Henderson to Silvia Henning 8-18-1877 (8-19-1877) L
Morehead, John Walter to Harriet Anderson Rice? 7-12-1843 (7-18-1843) T
Morehead, Wm. T. to Harriet L. Rudisill 12-24-1857 Sh
Moreland, John W. to Mary B. Duprey 10-10-1852 Sh
Morelli, Sebastian to Maria Arrata 4-12-1856 (4-13-1856) Sh
Morfield, Martin to Bethany C. Jones 4-27-1839 Hn
Morgan, Albert to Rachel P. Shaver 12-31-1856 Cr
Morgan, Albert to Sallie Tipton 7-26-1866 T
Morgan, Alfred to Roanne Gooch 12-18-1850 Cr
Morgan, Allen F. to Kate G. Bowers 6-10-1861 (6-12-1861) Sh
Morgan, Allen W. to Jane P. Hearn 3-18-1859 Hn
Morgan, Anthony to Mattie Howard 2-7-1882 L
Morgan, Arch to Mary Hill 3-15-1867 (7-4-1867) T
Morgan, B. C. to Louisa Williams 2-27-1853 Be
Morgan, Ben to Sallie Robbs? 7-17-1871 T
Morgan, Benjamin R. to J. Ann Lemons 12-17-1857 Hn
Morgan, Benjamin to Mahala A. Cannon 11-28-1860 Cr
Morgan, C. to Jane Wills 8-27-1844 Be
Morgan, Calvin J. to Mary M. Stanford 7-3-1853 Cr
Morgan, Carter to Julia A. Tate 4-5-1867 (no return) F B
Morgan, Charles to Menerva Morgan 6-21-1846 Cr
Morgan, Daniel to Callie Stevens 1-20-1878 Hy
Morgan, Dick to Narcissey Jones 10-16-1874 Hy
Morgan, E. D. F. to Clara F. Krafft 3-2-1860 (3-3-1860) Sh
Morgan, E. W. to Susan Gatland 12-15-1862 (12-16-1862) Cr
Morgan, Edward to Mary A. Neely 1-22-1860 Cr
Morgan, Edwin James to Martha Hill Stone 8-10-1852 (8-11-1852) T
Morgan, Emmet T. to Sarah A. Wilson 7-27-1858 (8-10-1858) Ma
Morgan, Ephraim to Indy Tipton 1-11-1866 T
Morgan, Felix G. to Mary Mathis 10-15-1861 Cr
Morgan, Frank M. to M. A. Lany 9-29-1868 Hy
Morgan, G. H. to M. L. Coleman 12-29-1866 (12-20-1866) Cr
Morgan, G. W. to Elizabeth Bobo 3-9-1847 Sh
Morgan, George to Baker Wallace 11-11-1882 (11-16-1882) L
Morgan, George to Martha Hines 1-2-1877 (1-4-1877) L
Morgan, Henry A. to P. R. Morrow 3-5-1868 G
Morgan, Henry H. to Nancy Flewellen 7-13-1838 Cr
Morgan, Henry to Lucinda Tate 8-17-1883 L
Morgan, Henry to Mary Jane Nettles 6-24-1867 (7-25-1867) Dy
Morgan, Ike to Ella Jones 12-30-1879 (12-31-1879) L B
Morgan, Isaac to Katie Dallas 7-3-1871 L
Morgan, J. B. to L. A. Dougherty 11-23-1857 (11-24-1857) Sh
Morgan, J. R. to C. Dillion no date (with 1861) Be
Morgan, J. T. to C. P. Patterson 10-30-1869 (11-3-1869) T
Morgan, James E. to Nancy Bass 4-16-1844 (4-24-1844) F
Morgan, James W. to Margaret Cross 12-5-1843 Hn
Morgan, James to C. C. Dobson 12-20-1870 (12-22-1870) T
Morgan, Jerie to Martha Bledsoe 12-30-1865 T
Morgan, Jerre to Martha Bledsoe 12-30-1865 T
Morgan, Jerry to Martha Bledsoe 12-30-1867 (12-30-1866?) T
Morgan, Jerry to Minerva Johnson 4-16-1876 Hy
Morgan, Jerry to Myema Wilson 11-5-1877 Hy
Morgan, Jerry to Nancy C. Bradford 12-25-1873 Hy
Morgan, Jessee B. to Eliza Waller 1-17-1850 G
Morgan, Joe to Ditha Sutherland 9-12-1867 F
Morgan, Joe to Priscilla Isbell 12-15-1883 (12-18-1883) L
Morgan, John H. to A. Jernigan 3-27-1842 (3-31-1842) F
Morgan, John H. to Martha Davis 4-23-1868 Hy
Morgan, John H. to Mary C. Hays 8-12-1865 (8-13-1865) O
Morgan, John J. to Martha Shaver 11-8-1855 Cr
Morgan, John M. to Louisa A. Russell 2-8-1858 O
Morgan, John P. to Frances R. Allen 4-24-1866 T
Morgan, John P. to Mary Ann Caldwell 1-16-1849 O
Morgan, John to Issabella Edmonds 8-8-1839 Hn
Morgan, John to Luan Westmoreland 10-17-1870 (10-18-1870) L
Morgan, John to Martha Ross 1-8-1839 Sh
Morgan, John to Susana A. Bysinger 4-23-1835 G
Morgan, Joseph to Emma Moss 1-20-1872 (1-21-1872) Cr
Morgan, Julias to Julia Lea 1-4-1871 (no return) L
Morgan, L. M. to Mary M. Tate 2-13-1867 O
Morgan, M. B. Vurrant to Rosanna Weble 5-28-1860 Hn

Morgan, Milton R. to Mary Jane Johnson 11-17-1847 (11-18-1847) G
Morgan, Monroe to Violet Shaw 12-5-1878 Hy
Morgan, Nathan to Martha Shaw 12-8-1853 Cr
Morgan, Nelson to Annie Caldwell 1-2-1871 Hy
Morgan, Pleasant G. to Mary P. Mathis 8-1-1866 (8-2-1866) Cr
Morgan, Ralph to Caroline Younger 12-16-1868 (12-17-1868) Cr
Morgan, Robt. to Harriet Givens 8-20-1870 T
Morgan, Saml. W. to Elizabeth D. Rivers 3-13-1832 Sh
Morgan, Samuel to Nancy ____ ? 9-18-1839 Hn
Morgan, St. Clair M. to Maria P. Pope 5-4-1854 Sh
Morgan, T. B. to Martha F. Ellenor Allen 10-28-1839 Cr
Morgan, T. T. to Bettie Sampson 1-3-1872 (no return) Cr
Morgan, Thomas C. to Love Oneal 6-11-1842 G
Morgan, Thomas Jefferson to Sarah A. Barnes 12-15-1855 (12-18-1855) Ma
Morgan, Thomas P. to Amanda M. Jones 11-2-1850 (11-3-1850) Ma
Morgan, Thomas S. to Nancy J. Dale 1-12-1858 Hn
Morgan, Thos. to Elizabeth Pritchard 11-11-1848 Cr
Morgan, W. T. to Nannie E. Morrison 12-11-1874 T
Morgan, W. W. to Nancy Messiniah Robins 7-5-1856 (7-6-1856) O
Morgan, Waler Brice to Martha L. Nettles 7-8-1874 Hy
Morgan, Wiley to Martha Bowling 9-16-1870 (9-21-1870) F B
Morgan, William A. to Ann E. Courts 6-23-1839 Hn
Morgan, William F. to Nancy Miller 6-24-1872 L
Morgan, William N. to Elisabeth A. Bolling 10-24-1848 (11-1-1848) F
Morgan, William N. to Elizabeth Butler 9-11-1828 Ma
Morgan, Willie A. to Frances E. Williams 4-26-1850 Hn
Morgan, Wm. B. to Lucy Ann Parham 12-27-1855 We
Morgenroth, Falk to Mina Monheimer 2-15-1856 Sh
Moriarty, Daniel to Fanny Mahony 7-11-1857 (7-12-1857) Sh
Moriarty, Thomas to Mary Jane Watson 12-27-1866 Be
Morighan (Molhan), Thomas to Bridget Doyle 2-20-1863 Sh
Morris, Dick to Lucy Tyus 3-9-1872 Hy
Moris, John H. to Malinda Mosier 2-12-1876 O
Moris, Stephen E. to Tabitha Dysen 4-25-1842 Sh
Morison, Amos to Jane Allison 6-8-1848 Sh
Morison, Thomas to Parthena Spencer 7-12-1838 Sh
Morison?, John to Lucisa N. Phelps 8-12-1856 (8-14-1856) T
Morland, Charles to Libby Ellen Watson 5-18-1867 (5-21-1867) L
Morland, Jack to Judy McClish 6-4-1866 (no return) Hy
Mormoner, Peter to Mary Ann Propst 7-10-1852 Sh
Moroney, N. to Elizabeth C. Hardin 11-15-1852 (?-2-1852) Sh
Moroney, Patrick to Bridgett Quinn 7-14-1845 Sh
Morphis, Alsy to Sarah Steward 2-13-1835 Hr
Morphis, George to Elizabeth Mauldin 1-10-1842 (1-11-1842) Ma
Morphis, George to Mary Roberts 1-6-1849 Ma
Morphis, James to Jackah Veazey 2-22-1838 Hn
Morphis, John B. to Eliza J. Shelton 11-26-1855 (11-28-1855) Hr
Morphis, Solomon to Mary Sanders 11-21-1846 Ma
Morphis, T. J. to S. J. Miller 11-8-1863 Mn
Morphis, W. J. to B. P. Foust 5-10-1865 Hn
Morphis, William A. to Jane Almond 8-31-1843 Hn
Morphys, J. L. to Mary J. Tannehill 6-27-1855 (7-5-1855) Hr
Morrasett, J. R. to Martha Ann Huffman 1-8-1872 (1-9-1872) T
Morrassey, Thomas to Ann Dwyer 2-1-1862 (2-9-1862) Sh
Morrell, Walter to Susan Mays (Hays?) 10-12-1867 (no return) L B
Morrill, Jno. to Ann V. Adams 7-25-1846 Sh
Morrill, John M. to Georgiana H. Lea 4-23-1855 Ma
Morris, A. J. to S. D. King 7-1-1878 (7-2-1878) Dy
Morris, Alex to Elizabeth Hooper 2-22-1858 (2-24-1858) Hr
Morris, Allen to Almeda Foster 6-12-1868 G
Morris, Answell F. to Elizabeth Jan Doren 10-14-1857 Hn
Morris, Armstead G. to Elizabeth E. Davison 1-15-1839 Cr
Morris, B. S. to S. E. Webb 12-4-1879 L
Morris, Benj. F. to Mary F. Taylor 5-1-1848 Sh
Morris, Charles to Martha Ann Mathis 10-26-1849 (10-28-1849) G
Morris, Charly to Rachel Wilder 8-19-1868 (no return) Hy
Morris, D. C. to Elizabeth Reams 4-2-1859 (4-3-1859) F
Morris, D. G. to Mary A. Carraway 2-3-1866 (2-8-1866) F
Morris, D. J. to T. L. Wagster 1-21-1865 (1-23-1865) O
Morris, D. to Nancy C. Grimes 9-15-1852 We
Morris, Daniel R. to Mary M. C. A. Hawkins 5-27-1856 Hn
Morris, Dudley to Mary Graham 2-4-1874 (2-5-1874) O
Morris, Edward to Delila Fox 9-5-1866 G
Morris, Edwin K. to Kate K. Morris 8-4-1863 (no return) We
Morris, Elisha to Catharine Rodger 6-28-1848 (6-29-1848) F
Morris, Ely to Martha T. Butler 5-1-1856 Cr
Morris, Frank to Clorie Morris 12-30-1872 O
Morris, Freeman to Nancy J. Mayo 12-6-1850 (12-7-1850) F
Morris, G. T. to Sarah J. White 3-14-1866 G
Morris, G. W. to H. M. Granberry 3-26-1855 (no return) F
Morris, George B. C. to Elizabeth Ann Nairon 10-13-1863 (no return) Hn
Morris, Green to Sarah Payne 11-26-1870 Hy
Morris, Henry T. to Mary S. McGehee 10-5-1854 Hn
Morris, Henry to Julia Young 12-23-1838 Hn
Morris, Henry to Lidia Gantlett 11-11-1852 (9?-19-1852) O
Morris, Henry to Lydia Gantlet 11-11-1854 (11-19-1854) O
Morris, Henry to Zurie Johnson 12-28-1867 (1-3-1868) F B

Morris, Hezekiah to Margaret Freeman 2-21-1843 Hr
Morris, Hilbert to Betsy Hafford 7-26-1878 (7-28-1878) L
Morris, Holloway to Sarah E. Taylor 9-2-1854 (9-3-1854) Sh
Morris, Isaac P. L. to Mary Jane Tulley 3-5-1857 O
Morris, Isarah to Sarah A. Barbrey Leigh 11-3-1866 Cr
Morris, Israel to Ann Squires 7-4-1841 Sh
Morris, J. F. to Mary Jenkins 2-4-1875 L
Morris, J. H. to H. S. Johnson 4-14-1859 We
Morris, J. K. to Cora A. Vanpelt 10-25-1869 (11-26-1869) F
Morris, J. K> to N. Bell 8-23-1842 Be
Morris, J. L. to M. J. Stewart 1-8-1879 L
Morris, J. M. to Loiza Sulivan 3-11-1866 Hy
Morris, J. T. to Harriet Phillips 3-27-1860 O
Morris, J. W. to A. J. King 9-23-1873 (9-24-1873) Dy
Morris, J. W. to M. T. Reaves 4-14-1879 (4-18-1879) Dy
Morris, J. W. to Rebeca Boyd 6-15-1855 (no return) F
Morris, James B. to Margarett Henley 2-16-1841 (2-18-1841) F
Morris, James B. to Mary M. Gainer 2-4-1847 Hn
Morris, James F. to Catherine Frields 10-28-1858 We
Morris, James M. to Dean? Wrightsell 3-24-1842 F
Morris, James N. to Mary A. Legon 2-12-1859 (no return) We
Morris, James N. to Mary Ann Nubb (Nutt?) 10-20-1854 (10-22-1854) Sh
Morris, James W. to Lucy Granberry 2-5-1845 (2-6-1845) F
Morris, James W. to Lydia T. Wilbanks 2-6-1856 We
Morris, James to Elizabeth Blane 12-9-1856 We
Morris, James to Rebecca Ford 1-1-1829 (1-7-1829) G
Morris, James to Rebecca Ford 1-15-1830 G
Morris, James to Sarah Steelman 11-19-1855 (11-20-1855) Sh
Morris, Jesse M. to Polly Sullivan 4-6-1850 (4-7-1850) F
Morris, Jesse to Roda A. P. Turner 12-3-1855 We
Morris, Jessee to Elizabeth Sullivan 12-30-1869 Hy
Morris, Jessie W. to Nancy E. Landrum 11-5-1850 We
Morris, John B. to Catharine Wintercast 12-24-1860 (12-25-1860) Sh
Morris, John B. to Parthenia Stewart 5-4-1854 Ma
Morris, John C. to Sallie Brown 2-25-1870 (no return) F B
Morris, John F. to Priscilla Ellis 4-22-1862 Be
Morris, John J. to Mary Wyett 2-16-1853 Cr
Morris, John L. to Mary E. E. Sansberry 1-29-1873 L
Morris, John R. to Nancy Ann (Mrs.) Hillis 1-27-1836 Sh
Morris, John to Elizabeth Holman 9-23-1845 Hn
Morris, John to Loucinda A. Turner 6-21-1854 Cr
Morris, John to Martha J. Hamilton 3-16-1868 (3-17-1868) F
Morris, Joseph to Nancy Edward 1-25-1854 (1-26-1854) G
Morris, L. H. to Minerva Hall 12-19-1860 F
Morris, Lafayett to Lucinda Holt 12-30-1847 (12-31-1847) G
Morris, Lenard W. to Rebecca W. Bell 4-26-1849 F
Morris, Lovett to Susan J. Rea 4-25-1866 (4-29-1866) F
Morris, M. B. to Prudence Bomar 1-11-1848 (no return) Hn
Morris, M. M. to Louisa Robeson 3-31-1865 (4-6-1865) Cr
Morris, M. V. to S. M. Capps 10-3-1859 Cr
Morris, March to Margaret Williams 1-2-1868 (1-5-1868) F B
Morris, Milton to L. A. Jones 3-6-1871 (no return) Cr
Morris, Moses to Harriet Gilhan 1-1-1871? (1-1-1872) T
Morris, N. C. to F. M. Weakes 5-7-1861 Be
Morris, N. M. to Martha Ann Robinson 1-22-1864 Cr
Morris, N. M. to Martha Ann Robinson 1-22-1864 (no return) Cr
Morris, Nathan to Margaret Barlow 7-23-1862 Cr
Morris, O. L. to Letha A. Pearce 4-6-1860 (4-8-1860) G
Morris, Oliver T. to Jane Morris 5-2-1854 (5-21-1854) G
Morris, Oliver to Polly Read 2-27-1875 Hy
Morris, Pateric to Cyntha Thompson 12-25-1869 O
Morris, Primos to Harriett Hill 1-21-1871 Hy
Morris, Ransom to Ella Turner 1-20-1873 Hy
Morris, Richard to Margaret R. A. Duke 4-15-1858 Cr
Morris, Rob't P. to Willie Ann Mott 7-3-1877 (7-4-1877) O
Morris, Robert D. to Mary M. Glover 12-3-1850 (12-5-1850) Ma
Morris, Robert H. to Sarah Elizabeth Davis 6-10-1852 Hr
Morris, Robert J. to Elizabeth S. Harrell 1-30-1855 (2-1-185_) Sh
Morris, Robert J. to Susanna L. Osborne 9-29-1849 (10-1-1849) T
Morris, Robert to Charlotte Mendenall 5-24-1841 Sh
Morris, Robert to Nancy M. Green 10-6-1857 (10-8-1857) Sh
Morris, Robert to Sarah Ann Arnold 7-10-1850 Be
Morris, S. J. to J. L. Cook 1-16-1860 Cr
Morris, S. W. to E. E. Horten 6-5-1866 G
Morris, S. to Mary A. Foushee 3-6-1860 We
Morris, Scott to Carry Gorden 12-21-1876 Hy
Morris, Scott to Ela Taylor 1-1-1874 Hy
Morris, Simion to Elvyra Thomason 12-20-1845 (12-23-1845) F
Morris, Solomon to Margaret S. McDaniell 3-7-1859 (no return) We
Morris, Thomas A. to Amanda Hackney 11-7-1862 (11-9-1862) F
Morris, Thomas J. to Louisa Stewart 2-26-1862 (2-27-1862) Cr
Morris, Thomas J. to Sallie E. Shepard 4-?-1871 (5-1-1871) T
Morris, Thomas to A. E. J. Wheeler 6-13-1858 We
Morris, Thomas to Sally Scott 8-12-1839 Cr
Morris, W. E. to Sarah E. Lockhart 7-25-1864 Be
Morris, W. H. H. to Mary J. C. Reddin 7-18-1867 (7-17?-1867) Dy
Morris, W. H. to Martha J. Williams 7-1-1862 G
Morris, W. J. to Agnes Guy 3-11-1867 (3-12-1867) O
Morris, W. J. to Fannie F. Shore 11-30-1859 (12-4-1859) F
Morris, W. T. to Kiziah L. Estes 1-17-1863 Mn
Morris, Wilie B. to Rebecca E. Rodgers 5-12-1851 (5-14-1851) F
Morris, William C. to Susan J. Horn 10-27-1844 Hn
Morris, William H. to Louisa Jackson 1-25-1859 Ma
Morris, William H. to Mary Baird 8-6-1840 (8-13-1840) G
Morris, William L. to Sarah J. Hatchcock 11-25-1862 (no return) Hy
Morris, William to Drucilla McDade 3-16-1840 (3-19-1840) F
Morris, William to Elizabeth Herington 12-27-1843 (12-28-1843) F
Morris, William to Jane Moncreeff 11-5-1838 (11-7-1838) F
Morris, William to Mary Banks 4-21-1838 (no return) Hn
Morris, William to Sabrinah Jane Blunt 4-12-1858 (4-14-1858) Hr
Morris, Willis to Eliza Knight 12-29-1845 (1-1-1846) F
Morris, Wm. (Esq.) to Emily Carter 5-12-1857 Cr
Morris, Wm. C. to Sarah C. Haywood 9-28-1850 Cr
Morris, Wm. H. to Mary A. Lane 8-18-1849 Cr
Morris, Wm. M. to Harriett Atkerson 1-30-1859 We
Morris, Wm. Wilson to Sarah Jane Clark 1-31-1866 T
Morris, Z. N. to N. B. Hallet 2-19-1866 (2-20-1866) Dy
Morris?, W. P. to Judy? Whitehead 11-23-1849 F
Morrison, Adli S. to Mary Bartlett 10-16-1833 (10-17-1833) Hr
Morrison, Alexander to Adaline Lynn 3-16-1869 (3-17-1869) T
Morrison, Archie to Sarah Jane Barnes 12-23-1872 (12-25-1873) T
Morrison, Charles to Amelia M. Jackson 2-9-1855 (2-11-1855) Sh
Morrison, Chas. to Mary Edmonds 2-29-1864 Sh
Morrison, Ezra T. to Sophria W. Griffin 1-3-1842 (1-6-1842) F
Morrison, F. M. to M. E. Andrews 10-24-1857 (no return) We
Morrison, Geo. to Mary Hall 12-2-1865 T
Morrison, Heb. C. to Miss M. E. Hill 3-28-1861 T
Morrison, Hiram to Betsey Saunders 5-20-1825 Sh
Morrison, Hugh to Lucinda Arnett 12-22-1869 (12-23-1869) T
Morrison, Hyram to Delphy Purgson (Penguson) 7-10-1831 Sh
Morrison, Isaac to Adeline B. Mitchell 1-8-1849 T
Morrison, James A. to Matilda A. Kimbro 9-17-1853 G
Morrison, James A. to Matilda M. Kimbro 11-3-1853 G
Morrison, John H. to Mary E. McHugh 5-28-1862 Sh
Morrison, John W. to Elizabeth J. Herring (Henning?) 1-28-1851 Sh
Morrison, L. L. to Lyda McLean 10-18-1856 (no return) We
Morrison, R. G. to Susanah C. Brown 9-27-1857 We
Morrison, R. K. to Elizabeth Bailey 3-13-1866 F
Morrison, T. M. to Mary E. Mears 6-18-1861 (6-19-1861) T
Morrison, Thomas to Mary Jane Dove 6-11-1863 Dy
Morrison, Thomas to Sarah Clementine Monroe 3-6-1844 (3-7-1844) T
Morrison, William to Catharine Stalls 5-16-1850 Sh
Morriss, A. J. to Ann J. Hill 5-2-1865 Be
Morriss, J. T. to Mary Taylor 8-27-1864 Mn
Morriss, John P. to Catharine Bowls 11-29-1863 Be
Morriss, Robert to Altetha E. Nixon 6-21-1841 (6-29-1841) Hr
Morrissey, Mauris to Margaret (Mrs.) Donnell 9-25-1858 (9-26-1858) Sh
Morrisy, Thos. to Margaret Coin 9-19-1856 Sh
Morroe, J. W. to Mary G. Walton 12-2-1873 (12-3-1870?) O
Morrow, Abraham to Harriet Guinn 11-24-1857 (11-25-1857) O
Morrow, Alfred to Louiza Hart 12-23-1867 (12-24-1867) F B
Morrow, E. L. to Eliza A. Cathcart 11-18-1867 G
Morrow, Elijah to Susan Ray 7-23-1853 (7-24-1853) G
Morrow, Geo. N. to Darthula V. Price 3-23-1856 (4-1-1856) Hr
Morrow, George to Millie Ann Morrow 8-20-1868 (8-27-1868) F B
Morrow, George to Sarah Pickard 8-19-1856 O
Morrow, George to Susan E. Mathews 6-16-1862 (6-18-1862) O
Morrow, Ike to Lou Boyd 12-8-1868 (no return) F B
Morrow, J. W. to Frances G. Morrow 11-26-1850 (11-27-1850) F
Morrow, James W. to Susan F. Williams 5-4-1858 (5-13-1858) O
Morrow, John T. to Margarett F. Marsh 9-9-1854 Hr
Morrow, John W. to Mary Ray 5-24-1853 (6-1-1853) G
Morrow, John to Cynthia Ann Polsgrove 4-9-1857 O
Morrow, Joshua to Chaney Shaw 4-28-1871 (5-1-1871) F
Morrow, Josiah A. to Mildred N. Champion 9-3-1849 (9-6-1849) T
Morrow, Josiah A. to Sarah E. Wilson 7-8-1847 T
Morrow, M. S. to S. E. Kindell 5-14-1863 (no return) We
Morrow, Mastion to Amanda Bowen 12-29-1863 Mn
Morrow, Newton to Sarah J. Morrow 12-22-1866 O
Morrow, S. D. to T. O. Davenport 11-8-1882 L
Morrow, Saml. R. to Melinda C. Gillespie 1-24-1842 (1-27-1842) Hr
Morrow, Samuel J. to S. J. (Mrs.) Edwards 2-6-1868 Ma
Morrow, Samuel J. to Sarah F. McKnight 1-27-1852 Ma
Morrow, Samuel J. to Sarah J. Tucker 10-1-1860 (10-10-1860) Dy
Morrow, Simon F. to Silvesta A. Booth 1-18-1865 Hn
Morrow, Simon to Donie Holt 9-27-1870 F B
Morrow, Thomas to George Anna Wright 4-15-1869 F B
Morrow, Thomas to Savannah Foster 12-16-1865 Hn
Morrow, Thomas to Susannah Clifft 11-29-1830 (11-30-1830) Hr
Morrow, Thomas to Winsey Foster 9-16-1838 (9-22-1838) Hr
Morrow, Tom to Maria Jones 1-7-1867 (1-10-1867) F B
Morrow, W. B. to Martha J. Smith 7-17-1855 (7-19-1855) Hr
Morrow, W. S. to Susan J. Garrison 3-4-1864 G
Morrow, William L. to Elizabeth Jane Craddock 11-21-1867 G

Morrow, William to Charity? Fargason 1-3-1837 Hr
Morrow, William to Maria Sanford 1-3-1879 L B
Morrow, William to Sarah A. Glenn 11-11-1854 (12-10-1854) O
Morrow?, Willis to Nancy Trobough 10-8-1873 T
Morse, David to Martha Wright 5-28-1857 Hn
Morse, Elihu to Sarah E. Weatherford 12-13-1865 (12-14-1865) T
Morse, John to Louisa Brooks 11-17-1852 Hn
Morse, Thos. to Sarah Meacham 2-11-1841 Ma
Morse?, Thomas J. to Paulina S. Pierce 9-23-1838 Hn
Morterson?, James H. to Rebecca J. Massey 2-20-1843 (3-15-1843) T
Mortimer, Robt. to Kate Kesterson 4-10-1863 Hn
Morton, Albert to Mary A. Moody 1-1-1868 (1-27-1868) F B
Morton, Daniel G. to Nancy J. Sweatt 11-20-1856 Hn
Morton, George to Lou Hagan 3-30-1876 (no return) Hy
Morton, Henderson to Lucy Jones 11-16-1867 G B
Morton, Horace to Maria Kerr 12-28-1868 (1-3-1869) F B
Morton, Howard to Arcenia Hays 5-10-1868 Hy
Morton, Howard to Jenetta Jones 5-24-1875 Hy
Morton, James to M. A. Campbell 10-21-1869 (no return) Hy
Morton, John M. to Narcissa M. Stewart 2-6-1841 F
Morton, John V. to Sarah E. Scott 4-27-1853 G
Morton, John W. to R. V. Yarbroh 3-21-1865 (3-22-1865) T
Morton, John Z. to Polly (Mrs.) Harwell 11-12-1862 (not endorsed) F
Morton, John Z. to Polly Harwell 11-12-1862 (not endorsed) F
Morton, John to Lydia Ann Blackburn 1-13-1870 (1-18-1870) F B
Morton, Joseph A. to Mollie E. Barden 12-18-1877 Hy
Morton, Joseph to Jane C. Alexander 11-10-1847 (11-11-1847) F
Morton, Mahlon R. to Margaret B. Allen 2-14-1848 Sh
Morton, Nicholas to Ellen Wilson 4-3-1851 Sh
Morton, Richard to Bell Cooper 11-18-1873 Hy
Morton, Thomas to Roxanna M. Daniel 8-1-1865 Mn
Morton, W. F. to F. Williams 5-9-1849 Hn
Morton, W. J. to Mary M. McClanahan 11-30-1865 Hy
Morton, William C. to Elizabeth Gallimore 1-7-1851 Hn
Morton, William C. to Mary A. M. E. Shackleford 11-13-1856 Hn
Morton, William to Mary A. Moore 2-7-1855 (2-8-1855) Sh
Morton, Wm. T. to Mollie E. Fancher 5-8-1871 (5-9-1871) Ma
Mosby, Britton to Lydia Ann Mosby 7-15-1870 (no return) F B
Mosby, Dewitt C. to Virginia A. Booker 11-19-1841 (11-20-1841) F
Mosby, Joseph H. to Maria L. McLean 11-31-1835 (SB 11-30?) Sh
Mosby, L. V. to Mazeppa E. Holland 12-2-1864 Sh
Mosby, Saml. to Sarah S. Leake 7-20-1846 Sh
Mosby, Samuel to Susan H. Hunt 5-31-1843 Sh
Moseley, Burwell S. to Lucy C. J. Stanley 2-16-1846 (2-19-1846) F
Moseley, H. W. to Elizabeth J. Burk 10-10-1865 G
Moseley, Hillory W. to M. A. Martha Flowers 1-20-1849 (1-24-1849) G
Moseley, I. N. to Mattie Foster 8-15-1867 G
Moseley, J. M. to E. E. Shelton 8-5-1874 (no return) Dy
Moseley, Joe to Mary Green 8-26-1866 G
Moseley, John G. to America Melton 12-25-1868 (12-26-1869?) L
Moseley, Robt. to Sarah Ann Alexander 5-26-1869 G
Moseley, Thomas to Mary Morgan 11-7-1881 (11-10-1881) L B
Moseley, W. F. to Mattie Rollins 5-7-1884 (5-10-1884) L
Moseley, W. H. to Sarah J. Knight 5-5-1870 Dy
Moseley, William T. to Nancy Flowers 7-1-1852 (7-6-1852) G
Moseley, Wm. T. to Susan Blankenship 8-24-1853 L
Mosely, Archer to Mary Mifflin 5-9-1874 (5-10-1874) Dy
Mosely, G. B. to Mary J. Earls 5-20-1858 We
Mosely, G. B. to Sarah J. Flowers 3-21-1841 (3-28-1841) G
Mosely, John B. to Martha E. Leak 11-5-1846 Sh
Mosely, John E. to Mary Worrels 9-30-1869 (no return) Dy
Mosely, Walter to Lizzie Boswell 1-11-1873 (no return) Hy
Moser, George W. to Mary P. Howard 1-2-1860 (1-1860) O
Moser, J. R. to Martha Cloar 4-15-1861 (4-18-1861) O
Moser, John to Malinda Davis 2-20-1843 (2-26-1843) O
Moser, John to Maticia? J. Ray 8-13-1859 (1-29-1860) O
Moser, Joseph to Sarah Ann Davis 3-2-1854 (3-3-1854) O
Moses, Albert to Parthenia Freeman 3-16-1867 Hy
Moses, James to Rebecca R. Ware 12-20-1865 Hy
Moses, James to Martha Jane Smith 4-23-1853 (4-25-1853) O
Moses, John to Tempa Smith 8-12-1869 (no return) Hy
Moses, R. Y. to Tex Nicholson 11-18-1875 (no return) Hy
Moses, Richard to Nancy Williams 4-4-1873 Hy
Mosier, Daniel to Elizabeth C. Blount 9-19-1849 (9-20-1849) O
Mosier, J. L. to M. J. Glover 3-23-1863 O
Mosier, John to Mary Mosier 8-4-1866 (8-5-18??) O
Mosier, John to Polly Davis 7-2-1831 O
Mosier, Joseph to Nancy Davis 11-24-1836 O
Mosier, Leonard to Emila Killian 5-26-1840 (5-27-1840) O
Mosier, Samuel to Sarah Davis 4-6-1831 O
Mosley, Benj. A. to Mildred A. Parrish 10-7-1867 (10-16-1867) T
Mosley, E. G. to A. J. Mosley 7-27-1854 We
Mosley, G. W. to Elizabeth Goff 2-8-1879 (2-12-1879) L
Mosley, George W. to Nancy Ann C. Nevels 3-27-1867? (4-4-1868?) L
Mosley, Hartwell to Nancy C. Ward 12-15-1858 G
Mosley, J. B. to Elizabeth Whitworth 1-19-1865 (1-21-1865) L
Mosley, J. B. to Malinda Jane Gatey 10-15-1862 (no return) L

Mosley, J. G. to Caroline Etheridge 4-14-1879 (4-17-1879) L
Mosley, John E. to Miss Milner 12-29-1849 We
Mosley, M. E. to Sarah J. Short 1-18-1858 G
Mosley, Moses E. to Martha C. Bryant 2-22-1858 G
Mosley, Peterson to Sarah Ann Thornton 9-11-1838 F
Mosley, Robert to Carline A. Dolohite 1-31-1856 We
Mosley, Thomas F. to Mary Harrison 5-29-1871 Ma
Mosley, Thos. F. to Sarah King 1-4-1870 Ma
Mosley, William T. to Martha F. Lockard 2-21-1867 (no return) L
Mosley, William to Mary S. Salemon 8-26-1845 (9-11-1845) G
Mosly, Joseph R. to Cornelia R. Booker 5-26-1847 Sh
Moss (Mop?), B. A. to E. M. Exum 4-17-1860 (4-19-1860) Sh
Moss, Alexander to Betsey Dickens 1-6-1831 Sh
Moss, Benjamin to Isabel Moody 3-28-1838 Hn
Moss, Eli S. to Lucinda McMackins 3-28-1870 (3-31-1870) Cr
Moss, Ephraim to Caroline Stephens 8-29-1862 (8-31-1862) O
Moss, Ephram to Nancy Jones 9-22-1864 (9-27-1864) O
Moss, G. W. to V. S. P. Bryant 2-24-1869 Hy
Moss, Hudson W. to Cary H. Massee 6-22-1837 G
Moss, J. A. to Virginia H. Fuqua 1-18-1865 Cr
Moss, J. S. to Elizabeth Dean 11-30-1868 G
Moss, J. W. to Caroline Inman 6-29-1862 Hn
Moss, James H. to Emma T. Gordan 1-18-1869 (1-20-1869) Ma
Moss, James R. to Mary E. Blackburn 9-25-1844 (9-26-1844) F
Moss, James R. to Mary E. Blackburn no dates (with Feb 1844) F
Moss, James W. to Arminta Ross 2-5-1845 F
Moss, James W. to Mary E. Permenter 12-11-1865 (no return) Hy
Moss, Jeremiah to Narcissa S. Major 12-20-1860 We
Moss, Jno. to Sarah J. Brooks 10-13-1857 (10-14-1857) Hr
Moss, John H. to Mahala Shelton 1-27-1863 (1-29-1863) Dy
Moss, John H. to Nancy Franklin 6-5-1839 F
Moss, Joseph M. to Polly Ann Owen 2-11-1847 Hn
Moss, Josephus to Harriet Vincent 11-18-1843 (no return) We
Moss, Levi to Temple Maclin 11-16-1869 (no return) Hy
Moss, Mason to Sophia C. Webb 7-3-1858 (7-4-1858) T
Moss, W. E. to Nancy A. Allen 8-12-1864 (no return) Cr
Moss, W. F. to Mary E. Bryant 12-14-1869 (no return) Hy
Moss, William D. to Eliza Phillips 9-14-1882 L
Moss, William D. to Fanney Moore 1-19-1867 (no return) L B
Moss, William H. to Jane Lavinia Taylor 12-16-1852 O
Mossman, John Stafford to Mary E. Holliday 5-1-1867 Hn
Mossman, John to Mary Gresham 1-15-1840 Hn
Mote, James C. to Mary Ann Taylor 9-12-1845 Ma
Moten, James to Susan Burrow 8-5-1871 (8-13-1871) Cr
Moten, Jerry to Bettie Angus 5-6-1867 (5-7-1867) T
Moten, W. H. to M. A. Fleming 7-16-1867 (7-18-1867) T
Mothershed, John to Mary Barnes 9-23-1844 Be
Mothershed, Wm. to Ann Elizabeth Pierce 6-15-1856 Be
Motin, F. G. N. to Ann Archer 5-31-1858 T
Motley, J. S. to S. J. Luckado 12-17-1866 (12-19-1866) F
Motley, John to Sarah Jane Wacker 10-21-1839 (no return) F
Motley, Nelson to Fannie Peacock 3-4-1875 (3-5-1875) Dy
Motley, William to Missouri F. Lynch 8-30-1851 (9-7-1851) G
Motley, Wm. M. to Margaret E. Woodard 3-10-1867 G
Moton, John W. to R. V. Yarbroh 3-21-1865 T
Mott, James to Louiza Cheers 10-12-1858 Hn
Mott, Jeff to Rebecca Graves 8-11-1872 O
Mott, John to Elizabeth Fort 3-7-1827 Hr
Mott, Peter M. to Lucy F. Morris 9-6-1849 O
Moultrie, J. L. to Rebecca Miller 11-26-1863 (11-27-1863) O
Moultrie, John L. to Harriett M. Watson 12-16-1854 (12-17-1854) O
Moultrie, John L. to Levisa Barker 4-18-1838 (4-26-1838) O
Moultrie, John L. to Nancy Cashion 4-16-1853 (4-19-1853) O
Moultrie, Moses B. to Rebecca Summers (Inman?) 5-24-1847 (5-25-1847) O
Moultrie, W. L. to Nanie M. Johnson 3-30-1866 O
Moultrie, William to Mary Carroll 5-17-1838 (5-27-1838) O
Mounce, Granville V. to Elizabeth T. West 9-19-1865 (10-12-1865) L
Mount, C. R. to Mary J. Patterson 5-29-1861 (could be Apr) G
Mount, H. N. to Catherine Salisbury 10-18-1866 Dy
Mount, J. M. to Sarah A. Flippin 12-2-1863 G
Mount, Robert to Sarrah Hampton 9-19-1867 G
Mount, Samuel C. to Margaret Wyant 6-23-1852 Sh
Mount, Samuel to Frances Flippin 9-27-1854 G
Mount, Wesley P. to Melinda P. Williams 6-9-1860 (6-17-1860) G
Mount, Wm. T. to Mary Elizabeth Hedgecock 7-28-1870 G
Mourning, Wm. to Margaret Core 1-7-1875 (no return) Hy
Moutrie, R. C. to Frances P. Wilson 11-16-1866 O
Mowhorn, Gilbert to Mary Jane Adams 6-5-1869 (6?-1-1869) F B
Moxey, Geo. A. to S. P. Winfrey 9-18-1866 (9-19-1866) Ma
Moxley, George H. to Martha Watson 7-16-1832 O
Moxley, Joseph W. to Sophia A. Rogers 11-10-1868 (11-11-1868) Ma
Moxley, W. C. to Martha Cruse 11-17-1863 O
Moylan, Michael to Mary Daly 1-18-1854 (1-19-1854) Sh
Mudings, Henry to Polly Taylor 5-2-1867 Hy
Muehler, Frederick N. to Sarah H. Taylor 1-20-1844 T
Muirhead, Enoch to Martha Simons 4-21-1831 G
Muirhill, Michael to Catharine Hardigan 2-20-1860 Sh

Mulcahy, Edwd. to Mary Solon 10-13-1850 Sh
Mulcahy, James to Ellen Murphy 6-13-1857 Sh
Mulcahy, Joseph to Margaret Kennedy 2-13-1858 (2-14-1858) Sh
Mulcahy, William to Margaret Newgent 5-2-1857 (5-3-1857) Sh
Mulcaley, Thomas to Alice Rohern 6-9-1860 (6-10-1860) Sh
Muldrow, Israel to C. L. Pate 11-19-1877 (11-20-1877) O B
Mulhaupt, F. H. to Caroline Krenkel 11-2-1858 Sh
Mulherin, Frank to Jane Moore 4-6-1880 (no return) Dy
Mulherin, Joseph H. to Hellen M. Durran 5-30-1869 Hy
Mulherin, Samuel H. to Robecca? J. Skillern 8-2-1860 Ma
Mulherin, Tom to Mollie Bryant 12-8-1880 (12-9-1880) Dy
Mulherin, William to Nancy Harris 4-22-1875 Dy
Mulherin, Wm. to Fannie Connell 10-22-1868 Dy
Mulherren, C. T. to Bettie Durham 1-24-1866 (no return) Hy
Mulherrin, Oliver to Sarah Ruffin 2-28-1876 L
Mulherrin, Sam H. to Eliza W. Thomas 12-5-1865 Hy
Mulherron, Charles to Ann C. Durham 12-12-1849 (12-13-1849) Hr
Mulherron, Charles to Nancy H. Goodman 2-7-1861 (no return) Hy
Mulholland, Edward to Rachel Vaughn 6-2-1864 Sh
Mulikin, Zeddack to Pernecy Noland 2-23-1839 (2-28?-1839) Hr
Mull, James to Cilla Murry 5-4-1872 (no return) Cr B
Mullany, Michael to Mary Collins 4-28-1862 Sh
Mullekin, Levi to Nancy Shickles 12-29-1846 Hr
Mullen, Ben to Ann Burden 12-28-1876 L
Mullen, Bud (Bird) to Lucretia Jones 8-30-1823 Sh
Mullen, Edward to Catharine Conlin 5-3-1859 Sh
Mullen, J. W. to W. L. Tate 8-2-1854 (8-3-1854) Hr
Mullen, James to Maria Sheeley 5-15-1863 Sh
Mullen, Wm. G. to Amanda I. Stewart 11-2-1866 O
Mullens, James M. to Delpha Jones 5-28-1873 T
Mullens, Silas to Mary Fox 9-7-1858 (9-8-1858) G
Mullens, Thomas to Ferroby Demoss 8-31-1853 G
Muller (Miller), Charles to Catharine Milltenberger 7-20-1860 Sh
Muller, Charles to Dorothea Bender 1-19-1858 Sh
Muller, Chris. to Lucy McCook (or Cook?) 10-22-1860 (10-23-1860) Sh
Muller, F. G. to Gertnie Tenfel 10-20-1858 Sh
Muller, L. F. to Catherine (Mrs.) Heidle 4-22-1862 (4-24-1862) Sh
Mullera, James to Mary McManaman 8-26-1861 Sh
Mullhall, James to Jane Nuckolls 12-28-1843 Hr
Mullhollan, N. M. to Mary W. Bradey 2-22-1848 (2-24-1848) L
Mullican, Aquilla to Sarah Jane Parker 5-17-1853 Hr
Mulligan, L. J. to M. L. J. Branch 12-23-1872 (12-24-1872) Cr
Mulligan, Michael to Lizzy Mohon 4-15-1861 Sh
Mullikin, W. H. to Mildard M. Rush 12-16-1868 L
Mullin, Benjamin to Molly Williams 3-22-1873 Hy
Mullin, James E. to Jane A. Tillman? 10-13-1858 Cr
Mullin, James to Jane Malone 7-1-1861 (7-7-1861) Cr
Mullin, Richard Q. to Sarah E. Vawter 10-11-1855 Cr
Mullin, Thomas to Rebecca Rumley 2-23-1861 (2-24-1861) O
Mullinicks, J. H. to M. A. Foreham 8-27-1840 Hr
Mullinicks, J. H. to Pheby Gossett 3-12-1850 Be
Mullinix, Plesat (Pleasant) W. to Martha Ann Smith 8-18-1847 Be
Mullins, A. E. to Lucinda M. Bush 6-4-1857 Sh
Mullins, Alexander to Rebecca Nelson 11-21-1870 (11-22-1870) Ma
Mullins, Charles H. to Permelia Olen Stone 12-19-1868 (12-20-1868) L
Mullins, Edward A. to Eliza A. Summers 12-10-1849 Ma
Mullins, H. R. to Mary J. Glenn 2-9-1864 (2-16-1864) O
Mullins, Harvey to Sarah C. Barnett 9-11-1866 (9-12-1866) Ma
Mullins, Howard K. to Betty C. Murphy 11-7-1855 O
Mullins, Jesse V. to America W. Oaks 8-29-1860 (8-31-1860) T
Mullins, Lewis J. to Mary E. Bogle 10-?-1860 (10-4-1860) Cr
Mullins, Paul to Ferdy A. Young 9-12-1859 (9-14-1859) G
Mullins, Thomas G. to Hannah T. Wiggins 9-10-1862 (9-11-1862) Ma
Mullins, W. W. to Evaline Smith 3-30-1864 Be
Mullins, Wm. to Lucy A. Bustard 3-12-1857 Sh
Mulloy, Patrick to Sarah Wallace 2-21-1850 Sh
Mulvehill, Thomas E. to Ellen Conners 2-15-1867 (no return) Hn
Muncrief, Austin to Caroline Hudspeth 11-3-1845 (11-2?-1845) F
Muncrief, David to Margaret Rudisill 3-15-1858 (3-24-1858) Sh
Muncrief, N. M. to S. A. Neely 1-12-1864 Sh
Muncrief, S. W. to Maria A. Stockton 2-13-1851 (2-19-1851) Sh
Muncrief, Wm. to Mary Adaline Sanderlin 1-15-1858 (1-17-1858) Sh
Mundin, John to Sarah Bryant 7-15-1844 Hr
Mundinger, C. to S. M. Stewart 7-26-1864 (7-28-1864) Sh
Munford, Adam to Hipsy Lockheart 4-14-1871 (5-13-1871) L
Munford, Amos to Millie Parmele 9-4-1862 Sh
Munford, James to Hattie Klyce 9-18-1873 Hy
Munford, Theophilus to M. E. A. Bayliss 12-22-1846 Sh
Mungel, Anderson to Martha Cobb 6-22-1878 (no return) Hy
Munly, George to Martha Ware 12-7-1876 Hy
Munn, John S. to Sarah Jane Jones 7-26-1849 Hr
Munn, John to May Ann Langford 5-20-1841 Ma
Munn, William to Sarah Lovitt 11-13-1839 Ma
Munn?, Samuel D. to A. B. Edwards 1-29-1852 Hn
Munns, Alexander to Martha Ann Chamberlain 5-28-1828 Ma
Munroe, Albert to Sarah Kinney 12-28-1870 F B
Munroe, John L. to Nancy E. Malone 1-7-1858? Hn

Muns, George W. to Mary A. (Mrs.) Merchant 12-22-1863 Dy
Muns, Loveitt R. to Martha Jane Langston 2-26-1845 Sh
Muns, Loveitte R. to Eliza Westbrook 1-2-1848 Sh
Munson, Newton to Orpha L. (Mrs.) Martin 6-5-1845 Sh
Munson, T. P. to Martha Ann Hill 10-8-1855 Hn
Muntz, Daniel to Lydia Wycoff 1-7-1825 Hr
Murchison, D. P. to Hilean Ann Herron 10-14-1868 (10-16-1868) F
Murchison, Henry C. to Mary A. E. Strauchn 5-31-1871 (no return) Hy
Murchison, J. A. to L. C. Benson 1-27-1873 (1-29-1873) T
Murchison, John R. to Susan (Mrs.) Trice 10-4-1869 (10-5-1869) Ma
Murchison, John to Hanah Ramsy 8-3-1829 (8-9-1829) Hy
Murchison, Micado to Jane E. Hood 2-4-1841 (3-15-1841) T
Murchison, Murdoch M. to Rhoda Vance 11-7-1852 Ma
Murchison, W. A. to U. C. Cason 11-16-1847 Ma
Murdaugh(Mordough), Samuel to Hannah Cearly 11-30-1848 Hr
Murdaugh, James to Lavanda Brooks 6-2-1859 Hr
Murdaugh, John to Mary Leggett 2-12-1840 Hr
Murdaugh, John to Matilda C. Binkley 1-1-1842 (1-2-1842) Hr
Murdaugh, L. B. to Martha C. Hillhouse 12-1-1853 Hr
Murdaugh, Robert to Sarah Leggett 10-6-1840 Hr
Murdoch, A. R. (Lt.) to Alice Ella Dudley 4-3-1864 Sh
Murdoch, W. Henry to Frances Case 9-22-1863 Sh
Murdock, A. J. to Mary Moore 11-20-1849 G
Murdough, J. C. to Mary Elizabeth Pratt 11-23-1867 G
Murley, Hamilton to Frances Jackson 12-9-1857 Hr
Murley, Hamilton to Jane Mills 2-4-1839 (2-7-1839) Hr
Murley, William H. to Nancy Brown 7-24-1848 (7-26-1848) Hr
Murphee, David D. to Mary C. Ward 9-23-1867 Cr
Murphey (Umphrey), Henry to Martha Blythe 2-29-1844 Sh
Murphey, A. B. to Teresa House 3-20-1875 Hy
Murphey, A. W. to Julia Ann Ewell 12-20-1869 (12-21-1869) T
Murphey, Alexander to Mary Yount 1-12-1874 (1-13-1874) T
Murphey, George W. to Martha Jane Eaves 4-22-1866 Hn
Murphey, Henry Stephen to Sarah Young Lucas 3-14-1849 (3-15-1849) L
Murphey, James to Mary Gaul 1-8-1859 (1-10-1859) Sh
Murphey, Jery to Effarilla Pearson 5-25-1872 (5-26-1872) Cr B
Murphey, John E. to Rosa Ann Coats 2-7-1872 (2-8-1872) T
Murphey, Jonas to Nancy Stevens 11-1-1871 (11-2-1871) Dy
Murphey, Michael to Bridget Lavin 8-15-1861 Sh
Murphey, Michael to Margaret Brown 10-10-1859 Sh
Murphey, R. H. to Martha L. Marshall 9-30-1865 T
Murphey, Rob't S. to Annie L. Morris 7-26-1877 O
Murphey, W. H. to M. B. Malone 1-17-1870 T
Murphey, W. N. to Eliza J. Grayham 1-19-1859 (no return) We
Murphey, William G. to Kathleen Cochran 12-9-1861 We
Murphey, Wm. T. to Lizzie M. Haley 7-25-1859 Sh
Murphey, Wm. to Eliza Neal 9-29-1839 (10-3-1839) F
Murphrey, Thos.B. to Harriett H. Carroll 8-4-1832 G
Murphy, Alex to Frances E. Hartsfield 2-7-1859 (2-10-1857) T
Murphy, Alexr. W. to Mary Jane Campbell 2-5-1851 T
Murphy, Andrew L. to Elizabeth Brenard 12-10-1828 (12-11-1828) Hr
Murphy, Benjamin W. to Martha M. Crafton 8-25-1835 (8-27-1835) G
Murphy, Charles to Emily Harvey 12-29-1828 (1-1-1829) Hr
Murphy, Charles to Sarah J. Howard 3-4-1852 Hr
Murphy, Edward to Mary Fitzgerald 2-22-1862 (2-25-1862) Sh
Murphy, Eli to Rebecca Tuttle 7-4-1826 (7-5-1826) Hr
Murphy, Ethan A. to Mary Broiles 2-25-1828 (4-5-1828) Hr
Murphy, Francis to Mary Murphy 11-22-1862 O
Murphy, Henry to Susan O'Conner 4-8-1868 Cr
Murphy, Hugh S. to Martha R. Hogan 11-13-1843 (11-14-1843) O
Murphy, J. B. to P. A. F. Young 12-31-1859 (1-4-1860) F
Murphy, James to Eliza O. Wornick 7-26-1872 (no return) Hy
Murphy, James to Elizabeth Hervey 10-31-1843 (11-2-1843) Hr
Murphy, James to Harriet Atchison 12-23-1869 G B
Murphy, Jehu? to Selina? Nesbit 12-10-1829 Hr
Murphy, John A. to Lorena Parker 2-12-1853 Cr
Murphy, John C. to Sarah E. Freeman 9-30-1868 Ma
Murphy, John R. to Elizabeth B. Stewart 9-14-1868 (9-20-1868) Cr
Murphy, John W. to M. A. Haynie 5-11-1869 T
Murphy, John to Eliza Wood 8-11-1847 L
Murphy, John to Mary Nugent 5-4-1853 (5-5-1853) Sh
Murphy, Joseph W. to Mary Johnson 3-22-1860 Cr
Murphy, L. E. to Mary J. Hood 10-6-1868 (10-7-1868) F
Murphy, N. B. to Kate (Mrs.) Smith 6-19-1869 (6-22-1869) L
Murphy, Newt to Emily Palmer 1-22-1876 (no return) Hy
Murphy, Robt. J. to Martha Jane Seay 11-6-1852 (11-7-1852) T
Murphy, Simon Q. to M. C. Foster 9-21-1859 We
Murphy, Socrates L. to Jerata Henderson Madew (Maden?) 10-7-1864 (11-24-1864) Sh
Murphy, Theodore to Jane Dunegan 4-7-1870 G
Murphy, Thomas to Nancy Rossel 7-26-1863 Be
Murphy, Tilmon to Sarah C. Smithwick 10-6-1845 Hr
Murphy, Tilson to Martha A. Ross 6-24-1870 (6-25-1870) Cr
Murphy, Timothy to Mary Brannan (Brennan?) 8-4-1854 (8-6-1854) Sh
Murphy, W. M. to M. M. Honner? 9-23-1872 (9-26-1872) L
Murphy, Walter M. to Martha A. F. Smith 1-10-1844 (1-11-1844) Hr
Murphy, William to Caroline Boatman 6-13-1863 Mn

Murphy, William to Charlotte Brown 11-13-1843 (11-15-1843) Hr
Murphy, William to Rebecca Adams 5-9-1838 G
Murphy, Wm. A. to Nancy E. Burton 11-2-1855 (11-4-1855) Sh
Murrah, Samuel F. to Julia A. Griffin 4-22-1848 Sh
Murray, A. H. to Mary E. Evans 12-20-1871 Hy
Murray, Charles B. to Margaret A. Hawthorn 5-5-1836 Sh
Murray, Christopher to Mary Dolan 9-9-1861 (9-15-1861) Sh
Murray, G. W. to Josephine Beck 3-22-1854 Sh
Murray, Henry to Elizabeth Simpson 3-25-1857 Sh
Murray, I. W. to M. A. Thomas 3-12-1867 Hy
Murray, J. F. to E. S. Hammel 12-20-1870 (12-22-1870) Dy
Murray, James H. to Mary G. Wray 1-21-1846 F
Murray, James M. to Anna Warren 12-22-1870 F
Murray, James to C. Moore 1-8-1844 (no return) Hn
Murray, James to Ellen Monroney 1-21-1861 Sh
Murray, Jeffrey to Margaret Mooney 5-11-1855 (5-13-1855) Sh
Murray, John C. to Amand J. Wessen 12-19-1860 (12-20-1860) Dy
Murray, John L. to Adaline Neely 8-28-1869 (8-29-1869) Cr
Murray, John W. to Lizzie Harshaw 5-4-1864 Sh
Murray, Patrick to Margaret Carey 4-12-1861 Sh
Murray, Peter to Catharine Fox 1-30-1860 Sh
Murray, Richard to Susan J. Teroging 1-25-1839 Hn
Murray, Thomas M. to Evaline Carrel 6-30-1874 (7-1-1874) Dy
Murray, Thomas to Elizabeth McCulloch 10-29-1862 (no return) Hy
Murray, Thomas to Gracy McLure 2-11-1874 Hy
Murray, Thomas to Mary Pucket 5-7-1860 Sh
Murray, W. D. to A. E. Surratt 3-28-1861 Mn
Murray, W. H. to Martha E. Pinnon 11-23-1876 Dy
Murray, W. H. H. to Mary E. Burnham 10-10-1865 (10-11-1865) Dy
Murray, W. N. to M. S. Hodge 12-17-1873 Dy
Murray, W. W. to Mary Henry Strange 1-4-1869 Cr
Murrell, Alexander C. to Lavinia Swink 9-9-1871 (9-13-1871) Ma
Murrell, B. F. to Mary Bondurant 6-?-1842 (no return) F
Murrell, Benj. F. to Mary J. Witt 10-6-1855 (no return) We
Murrell, Charley to Jane Askew 12-31-1869 (no return) F B
Murrell, Charley to Mima Minor 4-25-1870 (7-17-1870) F B
Murrell, G. P. to Martha A. Beedles 2-10-1857 We
Murrell, J. B. to J. A. McCorkle 7-18-1858 Hn
Murrell, J. M. to Nancy N.? Smotherman 10-3-1867 Hn
Murrell, J. Q. to M. A. Williamson 8-30-1859 (8-31-1859) F
Murrell, J. T. to A. V. Cartwright 9-27-1852 (no return) F
Murrell, J. W. to Judia A. Carroll 1-18-1869 (no return) F
Murrell, Joe to Agnis Sawyer 3-30-1867 F B
Murrell, John B. to Jane Davis 11-27-1845 Hn
Murrell, Kelly to Betsy Palmer 8-16-1873 (8-21-1873) Dy
Murrell, Millard to Catharine Williams 3-1-1870 (9-?-1870) F B
Murrell, Robert to Josephine Sayers 2-12-1870 (no return) F B
Murrell, Robertson to Cynthia Thompson 1-21-1867 (1-22-1867) F B
Murrell, Thomas R. to Mattie M. Farrar 11-2-1876 Hy
Murrell, William to Nancy Mitchell 10-19-1829 Hr
Murrill, John to Alithia Campbell 11-5-1850 Ma
Murrin, James to L. P. Weathington 2-11-1860 T
Murrphey?, W. H. to M. E. Duncan 1-13-1877 (1-14-1877) L
Murry, Fountain to Jennie Bingham 8-10-1867 (8-13-1867) Ma
Murry, James B. to Eliza Anne Wright 6-16-1842 Sh
Murry, John to Dorathy Bowlin 3-23-1846 Hr
Murry, Michael to Ellen White 11-12-1856 Sh
Murry, Peter to Jinnie Jamison 6-24-1872 (no return) Cr B
Murry, Pleasant to Mariah Coffman 1-3-1870 (no return) F B
Murry, R. C. to Arnilla Moore 1-15-1865 Mn
Murry, Wm. to Lucinda A. Ward 6-22-1843 We
Murtaugh, Thomas to Susan Reeves 2-9-1869 (2-11-1869) Ma
Muse, C. A. to F. A. Jackson 10-17-1862 Mn
Muse, George A. to Elizabeth Cain 5-25-1830 Ma
Muse, H. C. to A. H. Forbus 11-2-1854 We
Muse, James M. to Eugenia A. Brooks 11-13-1868 Ma
Muse, Thomas C. to Elizabeth C. Collier 9-5-1855 (9-12-1855) Ma
Musgrave, Berny to Mary A. McDearman 11-6-1884 L
Musgrave, Calvin to Maria Walden 7-21-1830 (7-29-1830) Hr
Musgrave, J. H. to Betha J. Forrest 11-24-1875 (no return) Hy
Musgrave, Pinkney A. to Susannah H. Singleton 9-6-1867 (9-8-1867) L
Musgrave, Thomas to Sarah Maxwell 2-13-1828 Hr
Musgraves, Dock to Ann Wiley 11-23-1872 Hy
Musgraves, J. S. to Mollie E. Cameron 1-20-1869 (no return) Hy
Musgraves, Jacob to Fannie Shaw 12-28-1873 Hy
Musgrove, Alex to Jama Jordan 8-3-1869 (8-5-1869) L B
Musgrove, Jacob to Maria Jane Johnson 11-16-1878 Hy
Muskum, J. H. to Mary Bay 7-14-1862 Sh
Musley, Daniel to Nancy Logan 8-30-1828 Ma
Mussy, D. G. to Martha Henly 3-14-1849 (no return) F
Mustin, H. G. to Lucinda T. Massey 1-13-1859 (1-16-1859) Sh
Mustin, J. W. to Martha Welsh 1-8-1852 Sh
Mustin, Samuel to Elizabeth McLeland 11-1-1859 (11-2-1859) Sh
Mutemas?, Berry to Cornelia A. Carloss 2-3-1871 (2-8-1871) F B
Mutton?, Henry to Rachal Scott 10-17-1876 Hy
Muyrhead, George P. to Elizabeth Vaughn 7-12-1837 G
Muzzall, A. M. to Lucinda Purvis 11-23-1842 Hn

Muzzall, J. T. to Martha Webb 11-7-1854 Hn
Muzzall, N. G. to P. C. Compton 1-2-1871 (1-5-1871) Cr
Muzzall, O. E. to Adaline Hightower 11-6-1851 Hn
Muzzall, Peter to Liddie Ann Peeples 1-8-1867 Hn
Muzzall, Stephen W. to A. E. Lowry 6-24-1858 Hn
Muzzle, Orlanda E. to Martha H. Hastings 11-13-1850 Hn
Mydyett, Jesse to Adaline T. Mitchell 10-24-1833 G
Myer, Henry S. to Susan Cathey 4-22-1861 Cr
Myers, Alfred A. to Sarah E. Maley 9-13-1855 T
Myers, Andrew to Sarah C. Tidwell 6-6-1850 Sh
Myers, B. to Martha Petty 12-26-1849 Hn
Myers, Charles to Elisa Nelson 2-4-1853 Sh
Myers, Charles to Mary Summers 9-19-1867 G
Myers, Charlie to Sally Dunlap 9-25-1867 Hn B
Myers, David to Jane C. Hudson 4-24-1852 (no return) F
Myers, David to Louisa Legate 12-3-1855 O
Myers, Frank to Mary S. Taylor 11-13-1868 (11-15-1868) F
Myers, H. A. to Mary A. Bird 8-18-1867 Be
Myers, Henry to Caleder Pinkins 2-18-1875 Hy
Myers, J. B. to Elizabeth Underwood 1-17-1854 Hn
Myers, J. W. to Hellen Smith 4-2-1874 T
Myers, Jacob to Catherine Miller 1-27-1846 Sh
Myers, James to Lurena Baker 10-5-1854 We
Myers, Jas. to S. J. Buchanan 2-5-1867 O
Myers, John Carr to Frances Jane Wiseman? 2-25-1858 T
Myers, John L. to Pheraby Raybourn 4-25-1858 Be
Myers, John to Anna F. Gibson 3-6-1854 (3-21-1854) Sh
Myers, John to Charlotte House 12-5-1848 (12-6-1848) Hr
Myers, John to Sophia Myers 10-28-1853 Sh
Myers, Michael to Jane Cunningham 2-10-1855 (2-11-1855) Sh
Myers, Moses to Missouria A. Cooper 12-12-1864 (12-13-1864) Cr
Myers, P. B. to Elizabeth F. Ramsey 11-21-1864 (11-22-1864) Sh
Myers, Phillip to Virinda C. Swayne 9-7-1862 (9-8-1862) Cr
Myers, Robert E. to Elizabeth C. Cooper 2-11-1863 Cr
Myers, Robert E. to Elizabeth Cooper 2-11-1863 Cr
Myers, Rufus Wsh. to Evaline Grace 1-18-1853 T
Myers, S. O. to Mary A. Mask 8-18-1852 Hr
Myers, Thomas to Fanny Raybourn 12-11-1856 Be
Myers, Thomas to Louisa J. Maly 8-17-1869 T
Myers, W. N. to W. P. Larimore 2-18-1873 (2-20-1873) T
Myers, William T. to Artimissa Dial 9-25-1850 Hn
Myers, William to Martha Hutchins 11-10-1869 (11-11-1869) F B
Myers, sDaniel M. to Martha C. Hartsfield 12-28-1843 T
Myett, W. R. G. to Annie Anderson 2-17-1872 (2-18-1872) Dy
Myles, Patrick to Margaret Morrison 7-27-1862 (7-29-1862) Sh
Mynatt, Thomas B. to M. H. Van Pelt 12-10-1846 Sh
Myrack, W. D. to Elizabeth Vancleave 3-22-1867 (3-24-1867) Cr
Myres, A. A. to Martha Goforth 2-22-1860 T
Myres, W. I. to M. J. (Mrs.) Morris 9-25-1866 O
Myric, Samuel to Nancy Dowdy 5-10-1867 Hy
Myric, William to Reubecca Brand 12-27-1843 We
Myrick, Alfred to Adelia Crawford 5-18-1844 (5-19-1844) Hr
Myrick, Charles to Sarah Alexander 4-14-1850 Hr
Myrick, Edward M. to Lucretia Harris 10-14-1840 (10-15-1840) Hr
Myrick, Edward M. to Susan E. Moore 6-24-1844 Hr
Myrick, Franklin A. D. to Fannie C. Osgood 10-28-1864 Sh
Myrick, George W. to Clara Anne Scruggs 4-14-1844 Sh
Myrick, George W. to Julia Ann Berry 8-11-1868 (8-12-1868) Cr
Myrick, Gwin D. to Eliza Blackwell 9-10-1844 Hn
Myrick, H. D. to Ann Vastine Wiley 12-24-1865 (no return) Hn
Myrick, James to Elland Rhoads 10-6-1840 Hn
Myrick, John M. to Mary A. Glover 9-6-1860 Sh
Myrick, John W. to Louiza Palmer 3-18-1852 Hn
Myrick, Moses to Nanney Rodgers 5-24-1842 Hn
Myrick, Wesley to Dorcas Myrick 10-7-1834 G
Myrick, William H. to Lucy A. Harrison 2-24-1855 (2-26-1855) Sh
Myrick, William T. to Annie E. Lea 4-3-1866 L
Myrick, William to Jane Thompson 5-24-1842 (5-31-1842) Hr
Myrick, Wm. E. to Charity K. Legate 10-9-1853 Be
Mysell (Mizell), Thomas A. to Llisa J. Presson 6-28-1863 Be
Myzell, R. W. to Susan Mahaly Rowe 4-14-1867 Be

Nabers, Perry to Frances Brantly 1-21-1826 Hr
Nabers, Robert to Prudence Foster 11-21-1829 Hr
Nabors, Andrew to Martha Barnett 2-8-1864 Sh B
Nabors, Joseph to Malinda Garrett 8-2-1838 Hr
Nagel, John to Elizabeth Hifs (Hiss?) 8-30-1851 Sh
Nail, Julon to Abigail J. Brown 11-13-1842 O
Nail, R. B. to Mary E. Fortum 3-19-1868 Hy
Nail, William R. to Sarah R. Coop 11-25-1850 (12-4-1850) G
Nailing, Due to Nelley Ford 8-19-1876 O
Nailing, John N. to Elizabeth Smith 10-15-1845 We
Nailing, Joseph W. to Tenie Harrison 5-28-1868 (5-8?-1868) O
Naill, John Jesse to Martha A. Berry 12-25-1856 Cr
Naill, John to Kittie Williams 11-30-1870 (no return) Hy
Nailling, Edward to M. A. Jones 2-27-1860 (2-29-1860) O
Nailor, Joshua D. to Mary Ann Burkhead 1-21-1857 Hr

Nairy, Thos. to Mary O'Day 9-11-1863 Sh
Nale, A. J. to Emily C. Hagard 2-12-1855 (2-14-1855) G
Nale, Henry C. to Rachael C. Salsberry 7-29-1865 (8-?-1865) L
Nale, J. H. to Mary L. Collins 6-15-1864 (6-16-1864) Sh
Nale, Joseph to Ester (Easter) Rhea 2-19-1831 Sh
Nall, James F. to Esther Cunningham 9-17-1856 (10-2-1856) O
Nall, Robert C. to Drucilla Whittaker 9-8-1857 O
Nall, Robert C. to Mary A. Tippett 8-25-1859 Sh
Nallig, R. F. to Ellin Marlen 9-24-1857 We
Nance, Franklin to Martha J. Wagster 2-23-1854 Hn
Nance, Green to Mary A. Dick 12-30-1858 Hn
Nance, Houston to Crecy Collins 5-21-1866 Hn B
Nance, J. A. to Elenora Kensey 1-26-1866 G
Nance, J. K. to N. Bram 3-1-1841 Be
Nance, J. K. to Olly Rushing 3-28-1841 Be
Nance, Jacob to Fanny Runnells 10-31-1878 Hy
Nance, James A. to Elizabeth J. Thompson 4-11-1850 Hn
Nance, James R. to Mathia Morton 12-27-1841 Cr
Nance, John M. to Louiza Malone 4-10-1867 Hn
Nance, John W. to Amanda Blythe 11-14-1844 Hn
Nance, John to Elizabeth Ward 10-25-1865 Hn
Nance, John to Polly Pointer 7-23-1862 (no return) Hn
Nance, Joseph W. to Susan F. Greene 11-1-1863 Hn
Nance, Lemuel B. to Nancy Rebecca Bell 5-15-1855 O
Nance, Lemuel to Mary Runalds 10-7-1845 (10-11-1845) G
Nance, Martin V. to Mary Davidson 9-6-1858 (9-9-1858) G
Nance, Nelson to Susana Boyd 8-5-1868 (8-6-1868) F B
Nance, P. H. to Martha T. Davis 10-5-1864 (10-9-1864) Cr
Nance, P.L. to Diana Wilburn 10-12-1865 Hn
Nance, Peter R. to Martha A. Wilson 2-24-1846 Hn
Nance, Peter S. to M. J. Lindsey 2-11-1849 Be
Nance, Reuben B. to Mary E. Biles 12-18-1845 Hn
Nance, Richard M. to Caroline Finch 8-8-1867 Hn
Nance, Richard S. to Eliza A. Williams 5-10-1863 Be
Nance, Richard to Elender Herron 7-6-1843 Be
Nance, S. B. to Nancy J. Harrison 9-5-1850 G
Nance, T. M. to Mary J. Williams 2-11-1875 Hy
Nance, Thomas S. to Mary A. Wilson 10-19-1854 Hn
Nance, Thomas S. to Nancy S. Ward 5-26-1859 Hn
Nance, Thomas S. to T. C. Ward 8-13-1864 (no return) Hn
Nance, W. F. to Mary A. Hill 10-16-1854 Hn
Nance, Wesley B. to Mary A. Hill 2-5-1845 Hn
Nance, William to Eliza Ann Yow 11-18-1846 Hn
Nance, William to Tiny McClish 3-1-1876 (no return) Hy
Nance, Wilson to Hager Spence 2-11-1876 L
Nanney, Addison to Mourning Norton 1-29-1852 Ma
Nanney, Charles B. to Sela B. Paschal 12-3-1862 We
Nanney, William J. to Susan A. Pachall 12-16-1860 We
Nanny, Hugh to Elizabeth R. Hart 11-26-1853 (11-29-1853) Ma
Nanny, James W. to Margarett Nail 6-21-1840 (6-22-1840) Ma
Nanse, Thomas to Louisa Crosby 9-17-1850 (no return) L
Nants, Peter R. to Malinda Farris 3-5-1844 O
Nany, Tomes to Emaline Bunn 2-14-1842 Cr
Naper, Nathan to Eliza Evans 5-25-1882 (6-10-1882) L B
Napier, Walter to Virginia Maley 11-23-1872 (11-24-1872) T
Napper, Nathan to Mattie Dallis 2-28-1876 (3-2-1876) L
Nappier, George F. to Mary Pricilla Green 11-29-1849 Hr
Naremore, Joseph to Malinda Tubbs 1-31-1867 Be
Naron, John C. to Malissa A. Dixon 12-18-1838 Hn
Nash, A. to Letha Murry 7-19-1840 Be
Nash, Allen to Lucy Knapp 9-19-1837 Sh
Nash, Andrew to Sarah Pettit 12-17-1870 (12-18-1870) F B
Nash, Anthony to Mary Powers 12-3-1860 Sh
Nash, Bryant to Anna Davis 5-27-1867 Hy
Nash, C. T. to Fannie S. Lovelace 5-27-1867 (5-30-1867) Dy
Nash, D. A. to Julian King 5-25-1852 Be
Nash, Geo. to Tennessee Jelks 2-23-1880 (2-25-1880) Dy
Nash, George to Violet Forrest 12-6-1867 (no return) Hy
Nash, Henry to Jenny Butler 12-25-1873 Hy
Nash, Isaac to Martha Pane 9-22-1851 (no return) F
Nash, Isaiah to Adaline Hunt 8-26-1866 G
Nash, J. C. to Hannah D. Wilkinson 6-10-1863 O
Nash, J. N. to Emily Nash 8-7-1865 (8-8-1865) Dy
Nash, J. Z. to Newty L. Cobb 1-30-1869 (1-31-1869) Cr
Nash, John R. to Amanda Miller 11-14-1877 (11-15-1877) Dy
Nash, John to Martha E. Dent 10-31-1847 (11-1-1847) Ma
Nash, John to Mary Jane Anderson 7-23-1858 G
Nash, John to Victoria J. Luckey 8-3-1863 (no return) Hn
Nash, Joseph to Amanda Gills 2-12-1873 O
Nash, Luke to Alice Porter 10-8-1877 (10-9-1877) Dy
Nash, Michael to Bridget McCabe 11-12-1847 Sh
Nash, R. R. to Emma McDavid 10-11-1860 Dy
Nash, Richard A. to Martha Allen 12-29-1853 Hn
Nash, Stephen to Elizabeth J. Doughty 2-23-1848 (no return) Hn
Nash, Thos. (Dr.) to Harriet McDavid 10-22-1868 Dy
Nash, W. B. to Ann Stallings 1-7-1867 (no return) Dy
Nash, W. F. to Merandy G. Morley 7-9-1868 (no return) Dy

Nash, William to Frances Re(a)dman 11-8-1834 O
Nash, William to Julina Melton 3-7-1848 Be
Nash, Zachariah to Martha J. Ligen 9-17-1865 Hn
Nat, Wiley to Nancy Garrett 12-31-1877 Hy
Nathan, Julius to Hanna Ehrman 5-21-1864 (5-24-1864) Sh
Nation, Wm. E. to Mary Ann Read 3-22-1843 (no return) F
Naylor, Wm. A. to Lidia Blair 12-18-1855 (12-20-1855) Hr
Naylor, Wm. to Mary Agnes Conner 1-2-1864 Sh
Nayns?, Thomas B. to D. A. Allen 5-24-1862 Hn
Neabor, James to Mary C. Rushing 2-17-1852 Be
Neagle, John to Margaret A. Daughry 3-7-1853 Ma
Neal, A. J. to Elizabeth H. Griffin 10-15-1852 (no return) F
Neal, A. M. to F. D. Wortham 2-13-1873 Hy
Neal, Albert to Emily Walker 3-20-1871 (no return) F B
Neal, Alfred to Elizabeth Polk 9-16-1829 (10-3-1829) Hr
Neal, Anderson to Margaret Crawford 1-9-1869 (1-10-1869) F B
Neal, B. F. to Z. A. Carter 12-15-1870 Dy
Neal, Benjamin to Jemima Neal 5-22-1866 G
Neal, Benjamin to Susan Wood 11-21-1846 (11-23-1846) Ma
Neal, Charles to Martha Buchanan 11-3-1869 G B
Neal, D. B. to M. M. Ridens 10-5-1871 Dy
Neal, D. C. to Anna Marks 6-26-1867 Ma
Neal, Dempsey C. to Mary Ann Reavis 11-13-1856 Ma
Neal, Duncal to Elizabeth Blakely 9-19-1862 Mn
Neal, George W. to Martha G. Prince 9-8-1852 Be
Neal, George to Margaret Jeter 11-11-1870 (no return) Hy
Neal, Isaac to Sarah Green Ayres 7-9-1858 (7-11-1858) O
Neal, J. B. to James Harris 4-7-1879 Dy
Neal, J. B. to Josephine Boles 2-25-1871 (2-26-1871) Cr
Neal, J. M. to Julia F. Hudgens 4-29-1867 (no return) Hn
Neal, J. M. to Lucy T. Smith 10-5-1869 Hy
Neal, J. T. to Catherine Pittman 3-28-1866 Hy
Neal, J. W. to M. A. Herall 6-22-1865 O
Neal, James A. T. to Josie Ferril 10-14-1874 (10-19-1874) Dy
Neal, James M. to Mary Smith 9-28-1838 (9-30-1838) F
Neal, James to Elizabeth Watson 7-31-1855 (8-3-1855) O
Neal, John C. to Mary A. Smith 1-14-1847 (no return) Hn
Neal, John M. to Lucinda A. Hudson 11-23-1841 (11-25-1841) Ma
Neal, John to Phillis Bond 1-20-1872 Hy
Neal, Joseph R. to Margaret Armour 10-31-1854 (11-9-1854) O
Neal, Meredith H. to Harrit Spencer 12-4-1845 F
Neal, Newton to Mary Brown 10-4-1858 Ma
Neal, R. B. to M. W. Land 1-27-1868 (1-28-1868) F
Neal, Rice to Caroline Reddick 12-23-1865 (12-25-1865) F B
Neal, Richard M. to Rachael A. Hutchinson 10-3-1851 (10-5-1851) O
Neal, Richard M. to Rachel A. Hutchinson 10-3-1851 (10-5-1851) O
Neal, S. G. to M. C. Harrell 12-13-1859 O
Neal, Samuel to Elizabeth Richards 4-13-1841 T
Neal, Samuel to Jane Traywick 5-18-1869 (5-20-1869) Cr
Neal, T. S. to Sallie E. Reddick 2-22-1869 (2-24-1869) F
Neal, Thomas S. to Lucky J. McLannahan 10-16-1860 (no return) Hy
Neal, V. R. to Rusiah A. Sanders ?-?-1862? Mn
Neal, William to M. F. Poore 12-22-1856 (no return) F
Neal, William to Mildred Crenshaw 10-28-1830 Sh
Neal, Wm. H. to Winiford S. Carraway 7-3-1852 (no return) F
Neal, Wm. L. to Kate R. McKinney 6-29-1866 (7-3-1866) F
Neal, Wm. to Martha Warford 1-25-1858 Hr
Neal, Wyatt to Lucy Layne 11-14-1885 (12-13-1885)
Neale, Abraham to Harriet Lampley 1-19-1857 Hn
Neale, John to Caroline Bateman 1-14-1836 Sh
Neale, William F. to Harriet Blalock 3-26-1855? (no return) Hn
Nealen? (Nealy), Timothy to Bridget Hollahan 6-5-1860 Sh
Nealey, Allen to Mary Jane Roark 12-2-1844 T
Nealey, W. J. H. to Candis M. Moore 1-2-1849 (no return) F
Nealey, Wm. to A. Hall 12-18-1874 (12-19-1874) T
Nealy, John to Caroline Roberts 4-24-1870 G
Nearin, E. L. to Elizabeth Leathers 2-21-1845 (2-23-1845) Hr
Nearn, Benjamin to Theresa Thomas 10-3-1843 (10-8-1843) L
Nearn, Joseph B. to Sophronia Jane Newman 11-10-1847 (no return) L
Nearn, M. L. to Viginia Soward 11-23-1866 (11-26-1866) L
Nearn, William W. to Effe Jane Haskell 7-23-1843 L
Nearn?, J. D. to Mary J. Bolin 6-5-1869 (6-9-1869) Dy
Neary, William F. to Mary McNeely 1-24-1861 (1-26-1861) O
Nease, G. H. to Arcenoe Barnett 7-18-1871 Cr
Nease, Henry to Sarah Dolen 8-19-1838 Cr
Neasier, David to Lucy Kirk 8-18-1853 Cr
Neathery, Samuel to Elizabeth C. Johnson 3-21-1839 Sh
Neber, Simpson to Mary McGill 6-3-1855 Be
Neblett, D. M. to Anna E. McFarland 12-11-1868 (no return) Hy
Neddie, Geo to Vina Douglass 5-16-1874 Hy
Neding, Alfred to Telitha Hodges 6-15-1829 G
Nedry, John to Letta Reeves 3-5-1838 O
Nedry, William to Nancy Boyt 8-23-1836 (8-25-1836) G
Nee, Joseph to Matilda J. Hosea 1-12-1859 G
Needham, Bensom to Mary E. Cooper 10-4-1860 G
Needham, Charles to Amanda Scott 10-30-1861 (no return) Hn
Needham, Enoch to Mary J. Tucker 1-31-1861 G

Needham, Franklin to Mirna Tilghman 10-13-1846 (10-5?-1846) G
Needham, H. T. to E. A. Tyson 1-8-1859 (1-9-1859) G
Needham, J. W. to Margarette Tillman 1-1-1861 G
Needham, James to Mary E. Oliver 3-5-1865 G
Needham, Jeramiah to Racheal Spalding 10-23-1827 Hr
Needham, Jessee to Semilda A. Barton 4-3-1854 (4-6-1854) G
Needham, John to Margaret Donohoo 10-24-1867 T
Needham, John to Mary(Polly) Lea 1-31-1835 (2-?-1835) Hr
Needham, Jones to Hannah Newell 2-3-1867 G
Needham, Lewis to Matty Oglesby 6-6-1829 G
Needham, Lewis to Matty Olgesby 6-6-1831 G
Needham, Miles W. to Martha E. Younger 1-22-1863 Mn
Needham, Rosell to Elizabeth E. Ramsey 10-26-1836 Hr
Needham, Silas to Milisa Moore 12-23-1866 G
Needham, Solomon to Rebecca Dillard 12-3-1834 (12-4-1834) Hr
Needham, Solomon to Sarah King 4-28-1831 Sh
Needham, Thomas to Mary Brady 1-12-1856 (1-13-1856) Sh
Needham, Washington to Elizabeth E. Tilghman 1-14-1847 G
Needham, William to Patsy Needham 4-17-1832 (4-19-1832) Hr
Needham, William to Sarah M. Ruddle 9-10-1836 Hr
Needham, Wm. to Jane Foster 3-23-1867 O
Neel, Drew to Mary Gillespie 10-20-1869 (10-21-1869) F B
Neel, G. W. to Minerva Fitzgerald 11-12-1856 (11-13-1856) Sh
Neel, J. L. (Dr.) to A. S. T. Belote 9-22-1855 Sh
Neel, James M. to Elizabeth O. Patton 11-22-1841 (11-23-1841) F
Neel, John F. to Margaret C. Morrison 10-18-1842 F
Neel, John F. to Martha A. Lemmonds 2-18-1843 (2-19-1843) O
Neel, John T. to Rebecca Snider 12-5-1839 (12-12-1839) O
Neel, John to Ella Madore 12-28-1869 (no return) F B
Neel, Jurdon to Oma Jackson 1-4-1871 (no return) F B
Neel, R. K. to Emma H. Robertson 11-25-1865 (11-29-1865) F
Neel, Saml. M. to Mary J. Watkins 11-28-1865 O
Neel, Thomas S. to Margaret Ann Henderson 6-1-1857 Sh
Neel, Thos. J. to Francis J. (Mrs.) McCarty 6-12-1863 Sh
Neel, Wilson H. to Martha A. Oakley 3-1-1852 (3-3-1852) Sh
Neel, Wm. A. to Permilla Ann Nixon 6-1-1847 Hr
Neel, Wm. H. to Amelia J. Scott 2-23-1856 (2-28-1856) Sh
Neeley, A. to Martha M. Blair 1-23-1848 Cr
Neeley, Jas. to Lizzie Hill 3-14-1874 T
Neeley, M. W. to Elizabeth Dodd 6-5-1873 Dy
Neeley, Richard to Rachell Biggs 4-14-1849 (4-15-1849) F
Neeley, Taylor to Amanda Koonce 11-26-1874 T
Neely, A. B. to Rachel Reynolds 12-31-1840 L
Neely, A. H. to Marry Anderson 3-25-1847 Cr
Neely, A. R. to Martha J. Kirk 1-5-1853 Hr
Neely, A. S. J.? to Martha A. Algee 5-23-1860 (no return) Cr
Neely, C. C. to S. M. Brown 12-28-1865 Cr
Neely, C. F. to M. E. Doyle 9-27-1859 (10-6-1859) F
Neely, David A. to Irena Kemp 12-18-1844 Cr
Neely, Elmore to Caroline J. Perritt 9-13-1857 Cr
Neely, Hiram S. to Sarah J. Rinds 8-7-1856 O
Neely, I. P. to Olive Case 12-6-1866 O
Neely, J. A. to Allice C. Kyle 2-6-1871 (2-8-1871) F
Neely, J. A. to Belle Irby 12-18-1868 (12-23-1868) F
Neely, J. D. to Margaret Cates 9-5-1865 O
Neely, J. J. to Fanny M. Stephens 5-11-1848 Hr
Neely, James A. L. to Lucretia Lear? 4-1-1833 (4-14-1833) Hr
Neely, James L. to Elizabeth C. Lynn 9-24-1857 (9-29-1857) Sh
Neely, James M. to Mary E. Hester 10-25-1865 Cr
Neely, James S. to L. T. Brown 11-29-1871 (11-30-1871) Dy
Neely, Jno. M. to Clarissa Hunt 7-9-1833 (7-23-1833) Hr
Neely, John B. to R. H. Brown 3-26-1864 Cr
Neely, John J. to Maria(Mana) Marsh 7-1-1858 Hr
Neely, John K. to Rebecca T. Glass 11-29-1858 (11-30-1858) Hr
Neely, John N. to Minirva Anderson 1-28-1833 Hr
Neely, Johns R. to Margarett A. L. Wells 10-29-1845 (10-31-1845) Ma
Neely, Moses S. to Julia E. Newbern 10-25-1859 (10-30-1859) Ma
Neely, Phillip J. to M. J. Smith 12-19-1859 (12-22-1859) Hr
Neely, R. A. (Rev.) to Sadie Currie 4-16-1868 Hy
Neely, R. J. to Mary Hull 4-2-1851 Hr
Neely, Richard to Patty Rice 10-7-1882 L
Neely, Robert C. to Nancy (sen.) Williamson 9-14-1858 Ma
Neely, Robert M. to Martha E. McClish 10-12-1859 Ma
Neely, Rufus P. to Elizabeth Lea 5-16-1829 (5-19-1829) Hr
Neely, S. J. to Elizabeth S. Cobb 12-1-1866 (12-4-1866) Dy
Neely, Samuel F. to Tirzah Caldwell 11-14-1837 (11-16-1837) Hr
Neely, Samuel to Archelius Ann (Mrs.) Fogg 6-29-1858 (7-1-1858) Ma
Neely, Samuel to Malissa J. Hamilton 2-4-1858 Cr
Neely, Samuel to Mary E. J. White 1-2-1841 (1-7-1841) G
Neely, T. G. to P. A. Sorrell 2-20-1866 Dy
Neely, Thomas I. to Charity Springfield 1-29-1840 Ma
Neely, Thomas I. to Susan M. Teagart 7-31-1838 (8-4-1838) Ma
Neely, Thomas to Annie Humphrey 8-5-1862 (no return) Cr
Neely, Thomas to Mary Lemmons 5-25-1843 Cr
Neely, W. C. to Eliza D. Karr 10-31-1857 Sh
Neely, William C. to Caroline Meacham 4-2-1852 (2-5-1852?) Ma
Neely, William T. to Leonora Doyle 1-3-1867 (1-9-1867) F
Neely, Wm. A. to Susan F. Tate 2-3-1862 (2-9-1862) O
Neenan, Patric to Nancy E. Jenkins 9-21-1861 Cr
Neep, Francis J. to Mary (Mrs.) Mack 1-14-1864 Sh
Neesbit, Wm. H. to Catharine Herington 12-27-1843 (12-28-1843) F
Neese, Alfred to Bettie Roberts 12-19-1860 Hn
Neese, C. M. to Manerva Hagler 9-30-1856 Hn
Neeves (Nevis), Daniel to Elizabeth Odam 1-18-1831 Sh
Neeves, Danl. to Maria Evans 5-5-1832 Sh
Neff, Sixtus to Bernardin Brass 9-25-1856 Sh
Neff, Wm. D. to Mary Ann Inman 12-27-1869 (12-29-1869) Ma
Negel, Dedrick to Barbara Deuser 2-18-1858 Sh
Neif, Henry to Frederica Heidel 5-31-1852 (6-3-1852) Sh
Neighbor, M. to Elizabeth Wilson 11-28-1864 Be
Neighbors, D. L. to S. E. Shelton 3-25-1874 (3-25-1875?) L
Neighbors, Elija to Anna E. Haywood 11-5-1855 Cr
Neighbors, Mathias to Mary Ann Davidson 8-13-1847 Be
Neighbors, William R. to Fannie N. Hearring 1-31-1866 (2-1-1866) L
Neighbours, Harvey to Nancy A. E. Brecheen 11-27-1860 Cr
Neighbours, W. R. to Ellen F. Kenneday? 8-29-1877 L
Neil, J. R. to Mary Elizabeth Horton 9-25-1877 Dy
Neil, John to Pernisia Hays 11-26-1832 Hr
Neil, Robert B. to Jane Young 6-29-1861 Sh
Neil, Sidney R. to Angeline Cresswell 3-12-1879 Dy
Neil, W. A. to Fannie Wood 2-14-1861 Sh
Neil, W. F. to Martha Northcutt 8-4-1867 G
Neild, Thomas to Ann Tarr 9-17-1859 Sh
Neill, A. J. to Emily Sheridan 12-8-1865 Hn
Neill, Gilbreth to Hibernia A. Person 12-8-1869 Ma
Neill, James Q. to Catharine Williamson 1-3-1855 Sh
Neill, William M. to Jane B. Hughes 8-11-1831 Ma
Neill, William R. to Harriet M. Neill 5-2-1866 Hn
Neilson, A. D. to Martha Durrett 3-19-1851 Hr
Neilson, Alexander G. to Eugenia Polk 7-18-1827 Hr
Neilson, Hugh D. to Aly Jones 3-7-1833 G
Neilson, Hugh D. to ____ (Mrs.) Brassfield 2-4-1830 G
Neilson, Jos. H. to Martha E. Hardy 5-26-1859 Hr
Neilson, Joseph D. to Pattie Hurt 4-30-1867 (5-1-1867) Ma
Neise, Thomas to M. M. Tatum 11-15-1862 Mn
Nelems, John to Mary kSLusan McBride 6-19-1847 (6-21-1847) Hr
Neliuse, Arnold to Sophia Engle 3-13-1856 Sh
Nell, Chas. K. to Margaret Choate 12-7-1864 Sh
Nellums(Nelms), William to Rachel Brooks 8-1-1840 (8-4-1840) Hr
Nelms (Helms), F. D. to Elizabeth Williams 5-28-1841 (5-27?-1841) O
Nelms, A. C. to Sophronia O. Tedford 11-20-1843 (11-22-1843) Hr
Nelms, A. J. to Sarah E. Whitesides 11-10-1863 (11-12-1863) O
Nelms, H. F. to Mary E. Pinkston 3-5-1870 (3-6-1870) T
Nelms, Madison to Emily Rhodes 9-14-1853 (9-15-1853) Hr
Nelms, Richard to Louisa Jane Crow 6-20-1836 (7-21-1836) O
Nelms, Saml. to Martha Stephens 6-12-1838 (6-26-1838) Hr
Nelms, William M. to Mary Pryor 4-3-1854 O
Nelms, Wm. R. to U. L. Clement 2-9-1860 Hr
Neloms, Charley to Sarah Mann 12-23-1875 (no return) Hy
Nelson, A. J. to Amanda J. Johnson 2-13-1856 (2-14-1856) Hr
Nelson, Albert to Cordelia Estis 6-6-1872 Hy
Nelson, Alex to Pamiel? Taylor 4-28-1866 T
Nelson, Alexander to Nancy McMillin 8-31-1856 Cr
Nelson, Alf to Hettie Wright 2-3-1881 L B
Nelson, Andrew J. to Eliza Jane Braden 12-15-1851 (12-18-1851) L
Nelson, B. F. to Rachel Churchill 1-30-1849 F
Nelson, Barnabas to Mary Dawson 12-15-1834 (12-18-1834) Hr
Nelson, Beverly C. to Robutte Ann Orell 7-27-1858 We
Nelson, Braetin to Lucinda Childress 8-28-1834 (9-3-1834) Hr
Nelson, C. H. (Dr.) to Jane Smith 8-29-1860 Sh
Nelson, Charles H. to Louisa Walls 10-14-1856 Ma
Nelson, Charles I. to Mary Radford 12-17-1844 Sh
Nelson, Charles to Emily B. Rooks 9-9-1869 Ma
Nelson, F. M. to L. M. T. Smith 11-22-1877 (11-25-1877) Dy
Nelson, G. L. to C. L. Green 11-3-1846 Cr
Nelson, George W. to Mariah P. Bond 10-24-1866 Be
Nelson, George to Francis Fitzpatrick 2-2-1878 (no return) L
Nelson, Henry to Fannie Linston 12-20-1875 (no return) Hy
Nelson, Hugh F. to Love Ann Bomar 1-12-1860 Hn
Nelson, Isaac to Burtie Anderson 12-10-1868 Hy
Nelson, J. H. to Lucy Lewis 9-30-1879 (9-23?-1879) L B
Nelson, J. L. to E. C. McLeod 11-6-1878 L
Nelson, James C. to M. J. K. ____ 3-20-1860 (3-22-1860) T
Nelson, James C. to Marth J. Kilpatrick 3-22-1860 T
Nelson, James C. to Martha Helperin? 3-20-1860 T
Nelson, James H. to Christina Thompson 10-31-1859 (11-1-1859) Ma
Nelson, James H. to Sideous I. Johnson 11-1-1842 (11-3-1842) Ma
Nelson, James W. to Lucie A. C. Wilkerson 10-22-1866 L
Nelson, Jarrett to Rebecca Thompson 12-21-1846 Ma
Nelson, Jno. to Laura Winchester 8-15-1844 Sh
Nelson, Joe to Susan Coltart 12-30-1865 Hy
Nelson, John J. to Narcissa H. Partee 9-26-1849 L
Nelson, John P. S. to Mary Ann Barnett 5-24-1870 (5-26-1870) Ma
Nelson, John W. to Mary E. Royester 5-26-1842 Sh

Nelson, John to Caldonia Young 2-5-1866 Hy
Nelson, John to Edy Ware 10-20-1866 (no return) Hy
Nelson, John to Jane Matthews 9-7-1840 (9-17-1840) Hr
Nelson, John to Mary Jane Nelson 8-20-1859 (8-21-1859) Ma
Nelson, John to Mary M. Gillespie 11-20-1851 L
Nelson, John to Mary McFarlin 2-14-1846 Ma
Nelson, Jonathan A. to Margaret Moore 8-17-1846 (8-18-1846) T
Nelson, L. to Lou Tyas 12-24-1883 (12-26-1883) L
Nelson, Lewis to Arner Shaw 3-19-1870 Hy
Nelson, Lewis to Mattie Halliburton 4-4-1873? (4-5-1874) L B
Nelson, M. W. to C. V. Ellington 4-18-1854 (no return) F
Nelson, Noah to Ann Elizabeth Johnson 9-24-1850 (9-25-1850) Ma
Nelson, R. M. to Georga Carter 5-7-1872 (5-8-1872) T
Nelson, Ras to Mollie Jackson 6-6-1874 (no return) Hy
Nelson, Richard to Hannah Nelson 1-6-1875 Hy
Nelson, Robert to Maria Nusom 3-19-1873 Hy
Nelson, S. H. to Syrena Mathis 8-29-1867 G
Nelson, Sam to Francis Anderson 3-13-1869 Hy
Nelson, Samul S. to Sophronia L. Linsdey 11-18-1848 (no return) F
Nelson, Stitts M. to Susan Ann Allen 2-26-1835 Sh
Nelson, Taylor to Mary Stokeley 11-6-1871 Hy
Nelson, Thomas C. to Margaret Harris 3-16-1846 Sh
Nelson, Thomas to Ann Partee 1-22-1878 Hy
Nelson, Thomas to Betty McFarland 1-3-1877 Hy
Nelson, Thomas to Matilda Strickland 5-3-1866 (no return) Hy
Nelson, Thomas to Mollie McDearmon 12-3-1885 L
Nelson, Tom to Betty Wade 6-13-1868 G B
Nelson, W. G. to Sarah J. Hutton 7-11-1850 O
Nelson, W. H. to Charity Ann Brashier 1-21-1878 (1-22-1878) Dy
Nelson, W. T. to Anna M. Deberry 12-20-1870 (12-21-1870) Ma
Nelson, Washington to Henrietta Pierce 5-21-1885 L
Nelson, William E. to Aggy M. Harrison 12-28-1875 L
Nelson, William H. to Alice Matthews 12-5-1867 (12-8-1867) Ma
Nelson, William H. to Elizabeth S. McAfee 11-22-1856 (12-1-1856) Ma
Nelson, William H. to Martha A. Ray 3-5-1859 (3-9-1859) G
Nelson, William H. to Nancy Buffalo 3-19-1866 (not executed) Ma
Nelson, William S. to Sarah H. Bird 11-23-1867 (11-24-1867) Cr
Nelson, William W. to Mahaly Broyles 5-10-1826 (not endorsed) Hr
Nelson, Wm. A. to Eliza Eagan 8-11-1862 Sh
Nelson, Wm. L. to Mary Bland 3-5-1860 (3-7-1860) F
Nelson, Wm. W. to E. A. McClarran 1-28-1842 (2-10-1842) F
Nelson, Wm. to Lucy Ann Nelson 1-22-1870 (no return) Hy
Nelson, ___ to Martha Cooper 11-16-1858 Cr
Nelson, jr., John to Ruth C. McAfee 12-22-1845 Ma
Nenningar, Seraphim to Nancy Godsey 10-19-1853 Sh
Neron?, Rainy to Matilda Gann 11-21-1871 T
Nesbett, B. H. to Martha Pinson 1-6-1852 Cr
Nesbett, B. H. to Mary J. Pinson 9-27-1848 Cr
Nesbett, Ed to Sarah E. Dolron 1-25-1871 (1-26-1871) Cr
Nesbett, Fed to Sarah Barker 10-20-1870 Cr B
Nesbit, William D. to Margaret L. Morgan 5-19-1848 Sh
Nesbitt, Andrew B. to Rebecca Horn 3-2-1840 Sh
Nesbitt, Andrew to Mary Ann Shoffner 2-19-1870 (2-20-1870) Cr
Nesbitt, Jerry to Harriett Milam 2-3-1873 (2-6-1873) Cr B
Nesbitt, John A. to Susan Haselett 5-18-1867 (no return) F B
Nesbitt, N.? B. to S. F. Mebane 2-27-1867 Cr
Nesbitt, R. N. to Martha R. Thomas 1-3-1855 (no return) F
Nesbitt, S. S. to Sarah Harris 12-26-1864 (12-27-1864) Cr
Nesbitt, Sidney B. to Jinnie Mitchell 9-12-1872 Cr B
Nesbitt, Thomas J. to Sophia E. Swink 4-20-1870 (4-21-1870) Ma
Nesbitt, Toney to Silvey Strayhorn 2-27-1869 Cr
Nesbitt, W. L. to Malissa J. Robertson 2-13-1861 G
Ness, Charles J. H. to Parmenta (Mrs.) Whitby 9-30-1856 (10-1-1856) Sh
Netherly, A. J. to E. J. Cruce 6-8-1875 (6-9-1875) O
Nettle, George to Eliza Taylor 12-22-1877 Hy
Nettles, George to Edmonia Blakemore 2-8-1877 Hy
Nettles, George to Eliza Ford 8-21-1872 Hy
Nettles, Heavry to Nancy Welch 9-9-1834 (9-10-1834) G
Nettles, R. H. to L. P. Ramsey 12-16-1866 F
Nettles, T. J. to Martha W. Applewhite 8-5-1869 Dy
Netzel?, Lorenze to Hannah Liedenstone 12-24-1845 Sh
Neuborn, James to Beller Currie 4-18-1868 Hy
Neuell?, George to C. L. Gilbert 11-8-1858 Hn
Neuman?, William C. to Sarah H. McFadden 6-3-1866 Hn
Neumyer, Lewis to Elizabeth Whealan 10-24-1859 Sh
Neuton, Thos. P. to Isabella Cole 7-20-1864 Sh
Nevell, Albert G. to M. R. McKinney 8-28-1854 (no return) F
Nevels, Virgil to Minnie Harper 2-8-1871 Hy
Nevil, Corsy O. D. to Martha J. Motley 10-11-1861 (10-13-1861) L
Nevil, Jesse to Priscilla Steager 11-15-1869 (11-18-1869) F B
Nevil, John W. P. to Eliza F. Williams 8-19-1869 G
Nevill, Andrew J. to Elizabeth Craft 2-9-1846 (2-11?-1846) Hr
Nevill, David W. to Sarah F. Thedford 10-20-1871 (10-22-1871) Ma
Nevill, Edward W. to Elizabeth Ann Peoples 12-22-1840 Cr
Nevill, James D. to Nancy A. Davidson 12-22-1866 (12-23-1866) Ma
Nevill, Matthew to Emily Morton 10-27-1847 Sh
Nevill, Soloman to Nancy Patterson 10-12-1840 Cr

Nevill, W. B. to Emily Manning 12-20-1869 (12-23-1869) Cr
Neville, Burrel B. to Syntha C. Reddit 5-24-1853 Sh
Neville, Cain to Laura Strickland 9-7-1867 F B
Neville, Wm. B. to C. H. Aston 2-3-1851 (2-11-1851) F
Nevils, George M. to Ive Ann Deming 2-11-1871 (2-12-1871) T
Nevils, John C. to Elizabeth Hutchison 4-19-1849 L
Nevils, Joseph A. to Melissa Catherine Baker 7-3-1861 (7-4-1861) Sh
Nevils, Parish G. to Nancy A. Wilson 5-5-1850 Sh
Nevin, W. N. to M. J. Holt 7-19-1866 G
New, Curtis B. to Harriet Clifton 9-25-1854 (9-28-1854) O
New, G. B. to Eliza Simmons 5-1-1830 (5-2-1830) Hr
New, John R. to Madona Ann Warren 11-26-1864 (11-27-1864) Sh
New, JohnH. to Elizabeth Darnell 3-8-1848 Cr
New, Joseph to Willie Reviere 3-23-1880 L
New, L. M. to Ellen Stiger 8-18-1859 Sh
New, Nathan to Elizabeth Goodman 1-1-1838 Hr
New, W. D. to H. D. Wilson 3-15-1863 Mn
New, W. D. to Nannie Wheatley 11-20-1880 (11-21-1880) L
New, William to Sally Ann Craft 9-21-1846 (9-22-1846) Hr
Newbern, D. J. to Catharine L. Ramsy 11-18-1850 (11-19-1850) Hr
Newbern, Darius D. to Elizabeth A. Hill 3-25-1850 Ma
Newbern, George W. to Louisa C. Hill 8-10-1852 Ma
Newbern, Henry to Rosa Bond 4-5-1871 L
Newbern, James R. to Ana H. Bond 7-23-1878 (no return) Hy
Newbern, Peter to Mary B. Lewis 1-8-1885 L
Newbern, Sandy to Manerva Sawyer 8-19-1874 L B
Newbern, William J. to Polly (Mrs.) Underwood, sr. 5-2-1844 G
Newbern, William Y. to Lavinia J. Wilson 3-16-1840 Hr
Newbern, William Y. to Sarah B. Jeffrys 7-2-1840 (7-7-1840) Ma
Newbern, William Y. to Winiford J. Holland 9-16-1861 (no return) Hy
Newbern, Wm. W. to Anna L. Mewbern 6-20-1860 F
Newberry, Isaac J. to Elizabeth J. Crawley 9-4-1863 (no return) We
Newberry, M. C.? to Gatsy H. Smith 7-20-1842 F
Newberry, Samuel to Nancy W. Trantham 9-25-1844 (no return) We
Newbery, Thos. M. to Elizabeth Snow 7-13-1857 Sh
Newbery, Wm. to Nancy Terrell 10-6-1845 (no return) We
Newbill, Abraham to Martha J. Mitchell 9-2-1858 Cr
Newbill, John A. to Sarah Pearce 12-8-1869 (12-9-1869) Cr
Newbill, John G. to Catherine Birat 4-18-1844 Cr
Newbill, N. T. to Caroline E. Sweany 6-23-1866 (no return) Cr
Newbill, Nathaniel to Nancy Popkins 7-26-1866 (no return) Cr
Newbill, R. A. to Bettie S. Upton 8-26-1868 Cr
Newbill, Richard to Allice Harper 12-28-1872 (12-24?-1872) Cr
Newbill, W. G. to M. M. Brown 11-30-1872 (no return) Cr
Newbill, Wm. to Emily Harper 12-4-1863 (no return) Cr
Newborn, Daniel to Sophie Davis 1-31-1869 Hy
Newborn, E. W. to Mary Ann Webb 3-23-1869 F
Newborn, T. R. to Frances McCoy 7-23-1876 Hy
Newborn, Tom to Mariah White 12-27-1870 Hy
Newborne, Henry to Maria Currie 3-26-1869 Hy
Newburn, Bloom. to Martha Boyd 12-19-1872 (no return) Hy
Newburn, Ell to Sallie Potter 12-21-1871 (no return) Hy
Newburn, John to Fannie Cox 12-29-1871 Hy
Newby, J. W. to G. A. Crossett 11-13-1867 (11-14-1867) F
Newby, Oswill to Orabella Strayhorn 12-18-1841 (12-22-1841) Ma
Newby, R. W. to Nancy Jane Branch 10-27-1852 (no return) F
Newell, David to Elizabeth A. V. Brown 11-4-1861 Sh
Newell, Elum F. to Rutha Palmer 12-29-1843 G
Newell, Joseph to Maria Davis 2-12-1846 G
Newell, N. R. to Martha Arnold 1-31-1867 G
Newell, R. A. to Mollie Jones 1-7-1867 (no return) Cr
Newell, R. N. to ___ C. McKeen 6-17-1865 G
Newell, W. J. to Louisa C. Keel 4-30-1863 Sh
Newgent, W. G. to Martha Runnells 10-10-1860 O
Newgent, William G. to Arabella E. Harpole 4-19-1853 (4-20-1853) O
Newhiski, Valentine to Mary Jakubs 9-7-1852 Sh
Newhouse, Anthony to Silva Bradford 1-13-1867 G
Newhouse, Benjamin to Martha Ann Simmons 3-31-1856 O
Newhouse, Benjamin to Susanah Pully 8-10-1829 (8-13-1829) Hr
Newhouse, Francis M. to Martha F. M. Roe 1-13-1858 (1-14-1858) G
Newhouse, James to Elizabeth Chapple 4-12-1873 (4-13-1873) O
Newhouse, John to Mary Simmons 9-10-1861 O
Newhouse, John to Mary Simmons 9-11-1861 O
Newhouse, Joseph to Luiza Martin 2-7-1853 (2-10-1853) O
Newhouse, Samuel to Charlotte Jordan 12-29-1871 O
Newhouse, Thos. O. to Frances L. Bryant 1-1-1857 (1-2-1857) G
Newhouse, W. W. to Mary E. Frazier 12-31-1861 G
Newhouse, William to Elizabeth Hawkins 9-15-1861 (12-25-1861) O
Newland, Chas. T. to Martha A. Hudson 3-24-1860 (4-3-1860) Hr
Newland, Henson G. to Margaret Campbell 8-21-1839 (8-22-1839) Hr
Newland, Joseph K. to Jane Campbell 11-2-1846 (11-4-1846) Hr
Newland, Joseph K. to Sarah S. Crocker 10-28-1858 (11-10-1858) Hr
Newland, S. H. to Martha Skipper 2-20-1850 (no return) L
Newland, William to Jane Stone 2-1-1845 (2-6-1845) Hr
Newlett?, William D. to Elnora Purslay 11-8-1865 (11-11-1865) Cr
Newman, Benjamin to Rebecca Fenster 2-20-1862 Sh
Newman, David to Pernicy McFadden 2-28-1839 Hn

Newman, Dawson D. to Isabella Clemintine King 12-15-1843 (12-21-1843) Ma
Newman, Elias to Caroline Oliver 3-13-1847 (3-16-1847) O
Newman, Felix G. to Lavina Arnold 1-7-1842 (no return) L
Newman, Frances to Cynthia Malone 4-19-1849 L
Newman, Frank to Melviny Bonds 8-26-18__ (probably 1870) G B
Newman, Hollis F. to Martha M. Phillips 7-25-1854 (no return) L
Newman, J. D. to Mattie Cox 12-5-1878 L
Newman, James to Mary Turner 7-18-1849 Sh
Newman, John C. to Martha Littlefield 8-13-1846 Sh
Newman, John Wesley to Martha R. Raney 1-19-1874 (1-20-1874) L
Newman, Meier to Berthie Platt 5-18-1864 Hn
Newman, Patrick to Nancy E. Jenkins 9-21-1861 Cr
Newman, Pomp to Eliza Stafford 5-6-1867 (5-30-1867) T
Newman, R. H. to Winey Benson 11-9-1862 Mn
Newman, Thos. to Josephine Randolph 5-10-1856 (5-11-1856) Sh
Newman, W. G. to Lucrecia? Ellis 2-16-1876 L
Newman, Wallace to Eliza White 10-30-1844 Ma
Newman, Walter to Nancy Nevill 2-1-1855 Sh
Newman, William Green to Eliza White 8-13-1870 (8-14-1870) L
Newman, William W. to Margaret E. Raines 12-8-1857 (12-10-1857) Ma
Newman, William to Mary Forwerk 1-3-1856 (1-5-1856) Sh
Newman, Wm. C. to Mary A. Pinkston 8-6-1861 (8-9-1861) Cr
Newmon, John to Mary A. Renfrow 7-2-1872 (7-4-1872) L
Newnam, J. W. to Martha C. Knowles 12-5-1877 (12-6-1877) Dy
Newport, J. Columbus to Matilda Ethridge 12-4-1859 Hn
Newport, James C. to Martha A. Hendricks 3-30-1849 Hn
Newport, Mordecai to Dorcus Gooch 12-8-1842 Hn
Newsom, A. K. to Savanah Key 8-12-1868 G
Newsom, Andrew J. to Elizabeth B. Smith 10-21-1865 (no return) F
Newsom, Andrew to Sarah M. C. Johnson 10-13-1851 (no return) F
Newsom, Charles to Sidney Miller 11-18-1870 Hy
Newsom, George to La Askew 6-8-1867 F B
Newsom, H. E. to E. H. Turner 4-18-1861 Mn
Newsom, H. S. to Elizabeth Ann Parks 1-6-1862 (1-7-1862) Sh
Newsom, Hance to Elizabeth Dorsett 6-30-1862 G
Newsom, Henry to Susan (Mrs.) Jones 7-6-1863 (7-7-1863) Sh
Newsom, Isaac to Kate Perry 1-25-1872 Hy
Newsom, J. J. to Lucy Worsham 7-12-1860 Sh
Newsom, J. T. to Shelley Knox 12-26-1872 T
Newsom, James A. to Nancy M. Kittrell 9-14-1854 (9-19-1854) Ma
Newsom, James E. to Mary Q. McKnight 8-29-1854 Ma
Newsom, Jenkins to Eliza A. Bond 4-17-1850 Ma
Newsom, Jerry to Minerva Jeter 2-12-1878 (no return) Hy
Newsom, John F. to M. E. Smith 8-6-1860 Hr
Newsom, John F. to Susan Epperson 5-4-1853 Ma
Newsom, John W. to Elizabeth Ann Meadows 3-6-1855 (3-7-1855) Ma
Newsom, John to Margaret Akin 5-24-1842 Sh
Newsom, John to Martha Ann Henson 4-25-1854 Sh
Newsom, Lemuel to Nancy Crowder 2-25-1832 (2-28-1832) Ma
Newsom, Lemuel to Nancy E. Harris 1-4-1856 Sh
Newsom, M. to Nancy Wilson 5-3-1860 Sh
Newsom, Montreal to Nancy M. Patterson 6-4-1857 Sh
Newsom, Robert N. to Nancy (Mrs.) Ross 2-16-1867 (2-17-1867) Ma
Newsom, Robert to Narcissus Harris 10-15-1850 Ma
Newsom, Thomas to Clarissa Johnson 4-25-1837 Sh
Newsom, Thomas to Rachael Walker 5-30-1844 Sh
Newsom, Thomas to Tabitha Huttleson 8-5-1839 Sh
Newsom, Wilson to Clarrissa Walker 1-2-1878 Hy
Newsom, Wm. A. to Eva E. Jones 9-2-1864 Sh
Newsom, Wm. R. to Tryphenia Newsom 2-25-1868 (2-26-1868) F
Newsome, Thomas J. to Susan A. Howse 11-14-1866 Hy
Newsome, William to Mary W. Griffith 6-18-1864 G
Newson, G. R. to Mary L. Nailing 2-14-1855 O
Newson, James M. to Eliza Stocks 1-21-1834 Sh
Newson, John to Martha Mathis 2-10-1845 Ma
Newson, Patrick to Arabella C. Owens 9-19-1860 (9-20-1860) Cr
Newson, Thomas H. to Lucy A. Bowslon? 12-1-1865 (12-4-1865) Cr
Newson, Wm. R. to Missouri A. Roach 7-5-1859 Cr
Newten, G. W. to Sarah E. Cress 9-7-1854 We
Newten, Joseph to Rutha A. Francis 9-10-1859 We
Newten, Marion to Jennie Sandlin 3-3-1871 (no return) Hy
Newter, Dennis to Celemanda Mahon 10-31-1853 (11-1-1853) G
Newto, R.? M. to Mary M. Linton 12-19-1866 Hn
Newton, Albert G. to Lucy Clark 7-18-1858 We
Newton, B. F. to Eliza Jane Fowler 5-7-1857 We
Newton, Benjamin F. to Susan A. Taylor 12-23-1862 We
Newton, Charles F. to C. D. Brinkley 9-5-1872 (9-8-1872) T
Newton, Daniel C. to Susan E. Hawkins 9-5-1866 L
Newton, F. A. to Annie Davis 12-16-1878 (12-17-1878) Dy
Newton, Henry to Elizabeth W. Shelton 5-22-1852 Ma
Newton, Isaac to Martha Ann Jennings 1-19-1863 Sh
Newton, James W. to R. J. Lewis 11-9-1846 (no return) We
Newton, James to Cynthia I. Cashion 3-26-1845 We
Newton, John B. to Nannie D. Massengill 7-4-1874 (7-3-1874) O
Newton, John to Mary E. L. Nely 1-21-1858 We
Newton, John to Sarah Box 9-9-1839 (9-12-1839) O
Newton, Lytle to Martha Exum 3-20-1871 Ma
Newton, Lytle to Martha Wright 1-7-1858 Ma
Newton, Nichelous to Alcy Dotson 10-7-1839 (10-10-1839) O
Newton, Nicholas to Polly Boon 1-4-1845 O
Newton, R. G. to Josie H. West 2-26-1878 (2-27-1878) L
Newton, R. W. to W. M. Johnson 7-29-1867 O
Newton, Robert to Sarah Moorer 9-22-1873 (9-5?-1873) L B
Newton, Robt. E. to Sarah Margaret Hanes 12-10-1867 Ma
Newton, S. to Martha Dunning 12-14-1848 (no return) Hn
Newton, Thomas P. to Catherine E. Campbell 4-21-1862 (4-22-1862) Sh
Newton, Thos. P. to Nancy Long 3-28-1865 O
Newton, W. B. to Tabitha Appleberry 3-18-1856 Sh
Newton, W. P. to Caldonia Hooten 10-17-1877 Hy
Newton, William C. to Mary Ann Carroll 8-14-1851 (no return) Hn
Newton, William F. to Jane Appleberry 11-18-1847 Sh
Newton, William H. to Caroline Lovelace 1-10-1871 Ma
Newton, William M. H. to Hester Lea 1-4-1824 Hr
Newton, William to Matheny Taylor 8-4-1834 O
Newton, Wm. B. to Sarah C. Cheney 12-28-1844 (1-3-1845) L
Newton, Wm. Chas. to Margaret E. Rothemer 10-23-1863 Sh
Newton, Wm. T. to Clarinda Davis 12-1-1845 (no return) We
Niblet, Emanuel to ___ Johnson 3-23-1873 Hy
Niblett, Manuel to Julia A. Lockett 7-4-1867 Hy
Niceler, John N. to Elizabeth Ann Crossnoe 10-5-1852 Be
Nicely, James to Mary E. Wells 5-11-1864 O
Nichelson, Miles to Edy Davis 12-25-1868 Hy
Nichloas, John W. to Abigail Weatherlan 5-3-1860 We
Nichol, Moses to Deevy Wagsted 5-25-1860 (no return) Dy
Nicholas, C. to Eliza E. Strother 10-21-1871 (10-22-1871) Dy
Nicholas, Charles Henry to Sarah Ann Woode 6-18-1870 (6-19-1870) L
Nicholas, J. R. to Rebecca M. Paschall 11-1-1860 Ma
Nicholas, Jacob to Malinda Anne Billings 8-7-1845 L
Nicholas, John to Anjalene Martin 4-30-1854 We
Nicholas, John to Anjalin Minten 4-3-1854 We
Nicholas, P. H. to Mary Ann Keltner 10-14-1866 L
Nicholas, Thomas A. to Cordelia F. Keltner 3-14-1868 (3-16-1868) L
Nicholas, Thomas O. to L. A. Perry 12-26-1849 Hn
Nicholas, William to Nancy Jones 10-4-1845 (10-9-1845) O
Nicholasson, Obed to Elizabeth A. Donaldson 1-26-1837 (1-?-1837) G
Nichold, Henry to Mary Ann Parrish 5-7-1851 (5-8-1851) G
Nicholdson, James I. to Elizabeth Gibson 7-17-1846 O
Nicholls, Nathan to Cass Ann Cayton 2-25-1846 (2-26-1846) G
Nichols, A. R. to Sarah Jane Burrow 5-26-1865 (no return) Cr
Nichols, Alanson to Mary J. Goosby 3-27-1864 Be
Nichols, Alford to S. E. Gately 3-2-1859 Cr
Nichols, Alfred T. to Martha Shackleton 4-26-1870 (4-27-1870) Dy
Nichols, Andrew J. to Mary M. Shroat 5-19-1858 Hn
Nichols, B. T. to S. R. Haskins 9-26-1865 Hn
Nichols, Calvin to Ann E. Hollomon 1-1-1845 (1-5-1845) O
Nichols, Charles H. to Laura E. Brantley 6-26-1878 L
Nichols, Daniel W. to Mary T. House 11-9-1868 (11-12-1868) Cr
Nichols, Daniel to Mary C. Pierce 2-2-1849 Cr
Nichols, Dick to Sarah Laurison 1-30-1880 (2-1-1880) L B
Nichols, George W. to Ann Wallons 5-26-1853 Sh
Nichols, Gilbert to Martha Ragsdale 11-14-1853 (11-15-1853) O
Nichols, Henry H. to Sylvania James 1-3-1834 Sh
Nichols, Henry to Elizabeth Parish 6-2-1850 Cr
Nichols, Irvin to Jane Watt 2-2-1830 Ma
Nichols, Isaac W. to Beedy C. Greer 12-26-1867 Be
Nichols, Isaac to Nancy M. Brooks 8-20-1854 Be
Nichols, James T. to Frances Odom 6-4-1879 Dy
Nichols, James W. to Sarah E. Antwine 1-9-1868 (1-12-1868) Dy
Nichols, James to Eliza Ann Deason 7-19-1846 T
Nichols, John M. to Angeline F. Nance 9-1-1855 (no return) Hn
Nichols, John W. to Margaret E. Cook 1-22-1850 (1-23-1850) G
Nichols, John to Lucinda Pipins 3-25-1857 O
Nichols, Jonathan to Amanda Shackleton 4-28-1866 (no return) Dy
Nichols, Jonathan to Susan Hargett 6-21-1848 (6-22-1848) O
Nichols, Joshua W. to Minerva Ann Barton 10-6-1841 (10-7-1841) Ma
Nichols, Lane to Tabitha Elizabeth Waldron 8-23-1868 G
Nichols, Mathew to Darcas Adkins 10-24-1854 (no return) F
Nichols, Mathias to Martha Conley 12-4-1862 Be
Nichols, Richard to Laura Gause 10-10-1885 (10-11-1885) L
Nichols, Robt. H. to Rhoda Long 2-19-1870 (2-20-1870) Ma
Nichols, S. to Luisa Alston 3-21-1862 Be
Nichols, W. A. to Dora Klyce 12-28-1869 Hy
Nichols, W. A. to M. F. Klyce 11-23-1865 O
Nichols, W. M. to M. A. Miller 1-11-1865 (2-6-1865) T
Nichols, William H. to Mary E. Metheny 10-13-1853 Be
Nichols, William W. to Milly Allison 5-16-1849 (5-17-1849) Ma
Nichols, William W. to Susan A. Shuford 10-16-1862 (10-22-1862) Ma
Nichols, Wm. J. to Mary A. Taylor 11-13-1846 Cr
Nichols, ___ G. to Sephronia W. Jones 10-21-1857 Hn
Nicholson, Archibald M. to Esther Hobb 2-25-1856 (2-26-1856) Ma
Nicholson, D. S. to Lucy C. Baxter 12-17-1868 F
Nicholson, David S. to Senia A. Harbert 2-1-1859 Ma
Nicholson, Frank to Lucy Fearse 12-23-1869 (no return) Hy
Nicholson, G. R. to Flora A. Jones 1-30-1868 Hy

Nicholson, George C. to Arcada Young 10-23-1835 Sh
Nicholson, George to Eliza Harbut 4-12-1874 Hy
Nicholson, Henry to Mollie Mays 3-2-1867 G
Nicholson, J. D. to Margaret Cartrell 7-2-1864 Sh
Nicholson, J. Talbot to Elisabeth Hathaway 8-23-1852 Sh
Nicholson, James E.? to Mrs. Mary A. Petty 10-21-1874 T
Nicholson, James H. to Eleanor G. House 3-11-1876 (no return) Hy
Nicholson, James to Jane Whitley 1-5-1837 Hr
Nicholson, John W. to Tabitha Trusty 1-29-1845 Sh
Nicholson, Joseph to Evaline Carter 6-24-1871 (no return) Hy
Nicholson, Nathaniel to Mary Nicholson 9-8-1827 (9-12-1827) Hr
Nicholson, Obed to Elizabeth Rodgers 9-30-1852 Sh
Nicholson, Robert W. to Laurie J. Allison 6-9-1861 Hn
Nicholson, Robt. to Hannah W. Walker 3-30-1854 Sh
Nicholson, W. T. to J. A. Mays 5-23-1860 G
Nicholson, Wm. B. to Martha A. Grayson 9-3-1849 Sh
Nicholson, Wyatt to T. C. Wright 12-3-1847 (12-15-1847) F
Nicklas, Dupont to Eliza (Mrs.) Williams 5-1-1863 Sh
Nickleson, Albert to Kate Harbert 2-28-1878 Hy
Nickleson, W. D. to Martha A. Goodman 11-15-1865 T
Nickols, Henry to Frances Cocke 1-3-1867 (no return) F B
Nickols, J. J. to Rosa A. Pearcy 9-28-1880 (9-29-1880) L
Nickolson, Henry to Rosanna Warran 9-26-1868 (no return) F B
Nicks, B. J. to Margaret Oneal 1-16-1862 Mn
Nickson, Wm. to Lizy Taylor 3-10-1869 Hy
Nicler, Albert to H. S. Aurenchine 6-26-1873 (no return) Cr
Nicols, N. G. to S. W. Gills 1-11-1868 O
Niel, Benjamin to Weltha Medling 5-11-1838 (5-17-1838) Ma
Niemeyer, William to Louisa Dyer 12-3-1853 Sh
Nietschke(Dietrike?), J.(P?) kD. to Harriet Alvorde 2-4-1851 Hr
Night, Ben M. to Josephine Clark 12-30-1866 (no return) Dy
Night, Peter to Ann Currie 12-26-1868 Hy
Night, Presly to Mary Cruise 10-5-1870 (10-6-1870) Cr
Night, W. M. to Emily S. Roberts 11-16-1847 (11-17-1847) F
Nimmo, Hyram to Marsha L. Cochram 10-28-1845 Hn
Nimrod, James N. to Anna Dick 2-2-1839 Cr
Nipper, Wm. G. to Lucy Burrow 12-16-1848 O
Niseler, Alexander to Frances E. Manning 12-5-1858 Hn
Nisler, Aaron H. to Susan E. Nisler 4-11-1867 Be
Nisler, D. N. to E. Pearce 5-1-1840 Be
Nisler, Henry to Lucinda Crosno 7-25-1839 Be
Nivell, Nicholas to Mary M. Watt 2-2-1842 (2-3-1842) Ma
Nivins, W. H. to Mary J. Barker 10-26-1869 Be
Nix, Asa to Margaret Scott 11-28-1863 Sh
Nix, Charles to Elizabeth Carmack 7-21-1853 O
Nix, Charles to Lockey Tanner 4-22-1836 O
Nix, Charles to Mary L. Crider 5-28-1846 O
Nix, Jesse to Sarah Snow 7-21-1847 O
Nix, John N. to Martha B. Jimmerson 8-30-1865 (8-31-1865) O
Nix, John to Elizabeth Phillips 1-1-1861 O
Nix, Jonathan to Milley McElrey 10-5-1844 (10-9-1844) O
Nix, Mark to Elphidel Harvey 10-24-1839 Hn
Nix, Martin to Amanda Crider 1-8-1853 (1-9-1853) O
Nix, Riley F. to Mary A. Alexader 10-17-1838 Hn
Nix, Robert to Nancy Jane Hood 9-23-1857 O
Nix, T. J. to Margaret E. Alexander 2-23-1853 Hn
Nix, Wiley to Nancy Pamphlett 2-3-1847 O
Nix, William to E. S. Hodges 7-16-1867 (7-17-1867) O
Nixen, Joshua to E. S. Stephens 1-23-1856 (no return) Hn
Nixon, D. C. to Catharine Jones 4-7-1864 Dy
Nixon, Elliote H. to Mary Lunsford 5-1-1837 Hr
Nixon, Granville to Annice Allen 1-17-1853 (2-8-1853) Hr
Nixon, Isaac to Jane Crissman 5-27-1847 Sh
Nixon, J. B. to Mattie J. Williams 11-17-1881 L
Nixon, J. H. to Cornelia F. Borum 1-2-1878 L
Nixon, James B. to Mary E. Blackwell 4-16-1861 (4-17-1861) L
Nixon, James D. to Sarah S. Ford 8-19-1847 Hn
Nixon, John R. to Ann J. Lovelace 6-6-1859 L
Nixon, John to Bettie Isbell 3-19-1879 L B
Nixon, Jonathan J. to Elizabeth C. Lloyd 6-17-1858 (6-18-1858) L
Nixon, Lewis to Mary Allice Halliburton 12-17-1874 L
Nixon, Lindsey M. to Nancy Ann Harper 8-22-1845 (8-28-1845) Hr
Nixon, Nathan to Polly Outlaw 12-10-1870 Hy
Nixon, Tas to Any Hobbs 8-9-1873 Hy
Nixon, Thomas F. to Arenia Lunsford 5-30-1868 (no return) Dy
Nixon, Wallace to Delila Bloodworth 9-7-1869 (no return) L
Nixon, Wallace to Ellen Henderson 12-27-1883 L
Nixon, William C. to Mary R. Jordan 9-26-1865 L
Nixon, William to Martha E. Johnson 5-3-1838 Hn
Nixon, Wm. to Mollie Read 12-24-1867 Hy
Nobb, D. W. to M. J. Holloway 2-20-1855 (no return) F
Nober, John A. to Eliza G. C. Rushing 7-18-1850 Be
Noble(s), Franklin W. to Mary Ann Bowling 12-12-1853 O
Noble, Joe to Sarah Capell 2-8-1886 (2-9-1886) L
Noble, Martin to Mary Scruggs 3-12-1840 Sh
Noble, William to Morning Sheoril 5-11-1866 Hy
Noble, Wm. O. to Mary P. Plummer 2-2-1864 Sh

Noble, Wm. O. to Mary Plummer 10-5-1864 (10-6-1864) Sh
Nobles, Abner W. to A. M. Johnson 1-26-1875 (1-27-1875) L
Nobles, Abner to Mary E. Enlow 4-14-1858 (no return) L
Nobles, Absolum W. to Nancy Vanog 12-2-1846 G
Nobles, George to Mary E. Wiseman 7-18-1866 (7-19-1866) T
Nobles, Harrell to Sarah Wheatly 9-15-1853 Be
Nobles, Harvie to Celia Hill 8- -1847 Be
Nobles, John S. to Margaret M. Denney 4-28-1856 O
Nobles, John to Nancy A. Wood 11-25-1857 Be
Nobles, John to Sally Diggins 10-14-1831 G
Nobles, John to Sarah Jane Short 9-4-1853 Be
Nobles, Joshua to Sarah J. Dickson 4-10-1848 G
Nobles, Nathaniel to Margaret E. Griffy 10-5-1846 (10-6-1846) G
Nobles, Prier W. to Mary Craddock 7-18-1849 G
Nobles, Simon to Mary Ann Benton 3-20-1856 Be
Nobles, William A. to Elizabeth P. Mann 12-11-1847 (12-14-1847) Ma
Nobles, William H. to Annis Johnson 4-4-1844 Ma
Nobles, William to Amanda Starnes 1-27-1853 L
Noblin, William H. to Nancy Huntsman 7-10-1856 (no return) We
Noblin, William S. to Charlotte A. Garner 5-5-1858 Sh
Noe, Bennett to Rachel Burnett 9-3-1870 (9-4-1870) Dy
Noe, John A. to Sarah C. May 11-14-1860 (no return) Hy
Noel, H. D. to Almedy Walls 17-18-1865 G
Noel, Jess G. to Mary Jane Willson 5-19-1850 Hn
Noel, John to Rebecca Tolbert 4-26-1845 (4-27-1845) F
Noel, Robert F. to Rody Ann Dunagan 10-30-1861 G
Noel, Thos. W. to Nancy G. Sexton 2-26-1859 (2-27-1859) G
Noell, Chas. P. to Fannie S. Green 9-23-1873 (9-24-1873) T
Noell, James H. to Eliza J. Dill 12-20-1865 Cr
Noell, Jerry G. to Harrett T. Preist 4-23-1856 Cr
Noell, Washington L. to Brunetta Thomas 9-29-1840 Cr
Noell, Washington to Sarah Thomas 8-21-1838 Cr
Noell, William C. to Martha A. McEwen 9-8-1840 (no return) Hn
Noen, M. G. to Malissa Ann King 4-12-1866 L
Noger, Maximilian to Annie Cunif 1-13-1862 Sh
Nokes, E. to Martha Evans 11-10-1864 (11-10-1865?) Sh
Nokes, P. H. to Jane Craine 9-10-1862 (9-14-1862) Sh
Nolan, Henry to Wilhemina Knoffle 5-1-1860 (5-5-1860) Sh
Nolan, James to Ellen Dwyer 8-24-1863 Sh
Nolan, Joseph to Ellen Culnan 4-4-1863 Sh
Nolan, Thomas to Mary Landress 7-26-1863 Sh
Nolen (Noles), John D. to Mary Oliver 12-18-1847 O
Nolen, B. C. to Mattie Wilson 10-18-1870 (no return) Hy
Nolen, B. R. to Susan Webb 11-4-1850 (11-6-1850) O
Nolen, Benjamin to Nancy Jones 5-30-1850 Be
Nolen, Columbus L. to E. E. Wright 3-9-1874 Dy
Nolen, David to _____ 1-30-1847 Ma
Nolen, Geo. M.(W.?) to Mary J. Graves 8-3-1859 Hr
Nolen, H. C. to Mary Whitelaw 11-11-1863 (no return) Hy
Nolen, James A. to Leeana Timms 12-17-1853 (12-18-1853) Ma
Nolen, Thomas to Lurena Parker 1-31-1885 (no return) L
Nolen, William to Eliza Smith 11-29-1875 L B
Nolen, William to Ellen Lewis 1-21-1873 (1-23-1873) L B
Nolen, Wm. to M. E. Nelson 12-8-1870 Hy
Nolen, Z. C. jr. to Emma King 1-29-1878 Hy
Nolen, Z. C. to Eliza King 2-9-1871 Hy
Nolen, Z. C. to Ella Brontly 8-17-1859 (no return) Hy
Nolin, James M. to Sophronia Hatton 8-16-1842 Ma
Nolin, Thos. to Mary McElroy 8-27-1842 F
Nolly, G. W. to Elizabeth Hilliard 11-3-1862 (not endorsed) F
Nolly, Henry to Tilda Rowlett 7-19-1867 (7-20-1867) F B
Nolly, Ike to Jenny Rives 1-15-1870 (1-19-1870) F B
Nolly, Josiah to Lucy Redford 2-15-1849 Sh
Nolly, Josiah to Manervy Owen 11-28-1848 (not executed) Sh
Nolly, William H. to Mary J. Simmons 10-13-1868 (10-14-1868) F
Nomandin, Louis A. to Catharine McDonald 1-2-1860 Sh
Nonnent, Wm. M. to T. S. Jamson 1-7-1849 (no return) F
Noonan, Michael to Mary Buckly 11-3-1853 (11-6-1853) Sh
Nooner, John P. to Ibby Reynolds 11-15-1832 Hr
Nooner, Nathan to Elizabeth Gates 8-28-1828 Hr
Nooner, Wm. L. to L. J. (Mrs.) Taylor 11-18-1869 (11-21-1869) Ma
Nooner, Wm. S. to Melinda E. Harkey 10-18-1858 We
Nooning, Patrick to Rebecca Young 12-20-1865 Mn
Nordin, Alexander to Elizabeth Dodd 2-16-1828 (2-17-1828) Hr
Nordon, Elias to Louisa Bryant 5-21-1850 Cr
Nordon, H. W. to Elizabeth Herndon 4-21-1847 Cr
Nordon, John D. to Lucy A. Allen 10-3-1853 Cr
Nordon, Wm. G. to Mary E. Cate 1-9-1853 Cr
Nored, Hyman to Elizabeth J. Jackson 1-1-1857 Hn
Nored, James to Sally Wynn 1-24-1867 Hn
Nored, W. D. to Caroline Caldwell 3-8-1855 Hn
Nored, William C. to Mary A. E. Wright 2-28-1856 (no return) Hn
Norid, W. L. to Amy Culberson 3-5-1860 O
Norman, A. J. to Henrietta Hansen 5-19-1852 Hr
Norman, Abner S. to Fannie Maddox 11-14-1857 (11-15-1857) Sh
Norman, Abraham to Jane Anyon 10-29-1857 Sh
Norman, Albert? S. to Eliza J. Stinson 10-29-1845 (10-30-1845) Hr

Grooms

Norman, Cord to Lucinda Smith 7-15-1857 (7-19-1857) L
Norman, D. L. to C. Benton 5-29-1842 Be
Norman, Daniel W. to Mary A. Dorset 11-17-1846 G
Norman, G. B. to Louisa Underwood 4-14-1857 (no return) We
Norman, G. W. to Bedie A. Parham 10-28-1859 We
Norman, George W. to Charlotte Jackson 4-30-1860 Dy
Norman, H. O. to Emma L. Tatum 4-13-1860 (4-15-1860) F
Norman, Henry to Rebecca (Mrs.) Caldwell 7-17-1858 (7-18-1858) Ma
Norman, James T. to Sarah E. Carlton 10-14-1867 (10-15-1868?) L
Norman, John B. to Fanny Ragland 10-31-1865 (11-1-1865) Cr
Norman, John W. to Kisiah Williams 1-12-1875 (1-13-1875) L
Norman, Kinard to Janella? Jones 7-1-1845 Hr
Norman, Marion to Annie Jackson 5-5-1871 (no return) Hy
Norman, Morgan P. to Martha Hoke 11-28-1842 Sh
Norman, Nathaniel P. to Sarah C. Alleson 12-22-1851 G
Norman, R. T. D. to Charlotte Davis 10-28-1869 Dy
Norman, R. T. D. to Mexico Barrett 1-27-1876 (1-28-1876) Dy
Norman, Robert J. to Mary Elizabeth Self 12-12-1849 G
Norman, Robert to Louiza C. Davis 8-20-1851 (8-21-1851) G
Norman, Sanford to Dicy Yelverton 10-20-1868 (no return) Hy
Norman, William W. to Mary J. Stone 5-16-1860 (5-20-1860) L
Norman, Wm. P. to Esther Culp 7-14-1849 F
Norment, Ben E. to Maggie Craig 9-7-1868 (no return) Dy
Norment, J. J. to M. F. Payne 11-5-1869 (no return) Hy
Norment, Magor to Julia Connell 4-29-1880 Dy
Norment, Robt. W. to Sallie J. White 11-25-1867 (11-28-1867) F
Normont, John S. to Nancy S. Burford 7-27-1847 (7-28-1847) F
Norred, Aaron L. to Margaret J. McFarland 8-20-1857 Hn
Norred, Benjamin to M. A. J. Hopkins 8-24-1853 Hn
Norred, Hyman to Malinda Hart 3-10-1863 Hn
Norred, Richard to Lucy A. Upchurch 2-4-1848 Hn
Norrey, James to Lucy aNN Corbit 12-1-1846 Sh
Norrid, A. J. to Zelly Bethell 3-21-1848 (3-28-1848) O
Norrid, Abraham E. to Mary Ann West 8-18-1846 (8-25-1846) G
Norrid, Bassell to Elizabeth Reed 1-27-1842 O
Norrid, Jeremiah to Susan M. Nedry 3-25-1839 O
Norrid, W. C. to Sarah McNeely 8-11-1866 O
Norrid, William C. to Barberly Taylor 7-29-1850 O
Norrid, William C. to Barberry Taylor 8-12-1850 Hn
Norrid, William Carroll to Martha Bramblett 6-26-1836 O
Norris, A. J. to Amanda Dennie 8-19-1869 (no return) L
Norris, Andrew J. to Francis E. McKinnie 8-25-1871 (8-27-1871) L
Norris, B. F. to Jane E. Sanders 5-8-1861 L
Norris, Calvin to Ajesty Smith 4-18-1839 Hr
Norris, David to Elizabeth M. Leath 8-31-1868 (9-2-1868) F
Norris, J. J. to Amanda Burbins 5-2-1864 Sh
Norris, J. W. to A. N. C. Jane Lunsford 3-24-1857 L
Norris, John D. to Julia Ann Gillette 6-17-1843 Sh
Norris, Samuel to Renis (Romia) Weaver 8-26-1854 (8-27-1854) Sh
Norris, Sanford B. to Betsey Lindsey 9-8-1829 (9-10-1829) O
Norris, Stephen M. to C. C. Law 2-3-1857 (2-16-1857) Sh
Norris, W. S. to S. T. C. Drake 1-29-1870 (no return) Hy
Norrow, Benjamin to Margaret Norrow 12-5-1842 (12-7-1842) Ma
Norsworthy, J. W. to D. J. Prichard 12-18-1878 (12-19-1878) Dy
Norten, John to Bridget McNamara 3-6-1859 Sh
North, David to L. J. Maclarby 12-25-1862 Mn
North, Green to Ella Skipper 10-7-1867 L
North, J. T. to Nancy Privett 8-18-1877 (8-19-1877) Dy
North, Jesse C. to Eliza Neal 5-27-1868 Dy
North, Joseph T. to Leitha Jane Brent 9-1-1862 (9-2-1862) Dy
North, P. M. to Mary Farris 4-29-1862 Mn
North, Richard to Eliza Reaves 5-28-1840 Cr
North, W. L. E. to E. A. Turner 8-6-1869 (no return) Hy
Northcross, J. W. to Leanorah Irwin 11-16-1865 G
Northcross, Jeff to Rozanna Bowers 11-7-1869 G B
Northcross, Wyatt to Nancy Moore 8-10-1867 G B
Northcut, William J. to Elizabeth F. Spain 7-16-1868 Cr
Northcutt, William C. to Mahaly Billingsly 2-13-1834 G
Northern, Eli to M. J. P. Tuggle 12-3-1846 Hn
Northern, J. J. W. to Mary A. White 10-23-1859 We
Northern, Jno. M. to Mahetable Ballintine 1-9-1837 (1-17-1837) G
Northern, P. E. to Mary F. Maclin 3-4-1874 (3-5-1874) T
Northern, Philip to Mary Vinson 12-4-1841 Ma
Northing, Allen to Martha Edwards 8-3-1842 Cr
Northway, H. K. to Susan E. Parkes 10-14-1852 (no return) F
Norton, Aaron to Sarah Fentress 2-17-1857 O
Norton, Alexander to Cardine Canaday 1-15-1853 (1-16-1853) G
Norton, Benjamin L. to Jane Prewitt 10-6-1841 (10-7-1841) Ma
Norton, Edward to Ann Short 9-27-1833 Hr
Norton, George J. to Mary A. Elizabeth Branch 11-11-1857 (11-12-1857) Ma
Norton, Hugh G. to Eliza J. Lacey 7-4-1840 Hr
Norton, I. W. to T. E. Goodlore 10-9-1865 O
Norton, Isaac J. to Sarah Nabers 7-11-1837 Hr
Norton, Jacob A. to Rachael March 6-28-1845 (7-1-1845) Ma
Norton, Jacob N. to Elizabeth Curley(Carley?) 12-22-1838 (12-25-1838) Hr
Norton, Jacob T. to Sarah M. Boyd 3-16-1847 Cr
Norton, James H. to Malvina Mills 12-8-1856 (12-9-1856) Ma

Norton, James H. to Martha Smith 6-21-1866 (6-22-1866) Ma
Norton, James W. to Nancy Highfield 1-26-1853 (2-2-1853) Hr
Norton, John K. to Nancy M. Vaughn 12-14-1859 Hn
Norton, John W. to Louisa Carrington 7-23-1849 Ma
Norton, John to Hannah Shehee 7-4-1863 Sh
Norton, Josephus to Tennessee Oakes 9-10-1853 (9-11-1853) O
Norton, M. P. to R. F. Davidson 1-27-1869 (1-28-1869) F
Norton, Messer to Margarett Cosby 1-6-1829 Hr
Norton, Norman to Elizabeth Innis 9-19-1853 (9-21-1853) G
Norton, Peter K. to Catherine Baker 1-9-1839 (1-10-1839) Hr
Norton, Stephen A. to Sarah E. Pulliam 12-8-1847 Hn
Norton, Thomas J. to Nancy E. Dunlap 8-10-1857 (no return) L
Norton, Thomas M. to Minerva Mills 9-15-1860 (9-17-1860) Ma
Norton, William to Sophia Short 9-25-1832 Hr
Norton, Wm. Campbell to Estella Ann Pinson 9-7-1852 T
Norton, _____ to Eliza Jane Owen 12-16-1851 Hn
Norval, Alex to Polly Clay 1-2-1866 Hy
Norvell, D. B. to Alvira T. Nave 10-24-1869 Hy
Norvell, Enos to Mary Williams 10-3-1855 (10-4-1855) G
Norvell, John C. to Lucy Stevens 2-10-1871 (no return) Hy
Norvell, Milton D. to Nancy J. Hickman 7-10-1849 Ma
Norvell, R. H. to A. M. Brown 4-13-1875 Hy
Norvell, Robt. D. to M. A. Hawtin 12-20-1871 (no return) Hy
Norvell, Thos. E. to V. E. Jones 9-14-1864 Sh
Norvell, W. H. to M. L. Whitaker 6-19-1869 Hy
Norvell, William R. to Esther E. Anderson 10-17-1844 Ma
Norvil, J. C. to M. J. Cates 3-25-1866 Hy
Norvill, J. S. to Margaret J. Taylor 12-7-1867 (12-11-186_) G
Norvill, L. K. to Martha Kiersey (Kinsey?) 9-1-1867 G
Norvill, Thos. H. to C. R. S. Nicholson 11-11-1868 Hy
Norville, Jack to Susan A. Conley 3-6-1870 Hy
Norwood, James R. to Elstuly Jones 1-17-1856 Cr
Norwood, John H. to Eveline V. Fredericks 6-5-1860 (6-7-1860) Ma
Norwood, John to Matilda O'Neal 9-16-1830 Ma
Norwood, Lewis to Adaline Brackins 3-11-1845 Cr
Norwood, Lewis to Mary A. (Mrs.) Brooks 7-20-1860 (7-22-1860) Cr
Norwood, S. M. to Mary J. Peak 5-7-1857 Sh
Norwood, Samuel L. to Eliza Robinson 3-27-1867 Ma
Norwood, Thos. to Elizabeth Pinkston 1-2-1866 Cr
Norwood, William to Anna Moorer 3-8-1877 L B
Norwood, Wm. to Allie O'Neal 10-11-1845 Cr
Notgrass, J. R. to Ardela Anderson no dates (not executed) Hy
Notgrass, J. R. to Becy S. Thomas 12-21-1871 Hy
Notgrass, John W. to Sarah E. Ross 3-22-1852 (no return) F
Notgrass, Thos. to Delina Cook 5-10-1845 (5-13-1845) F B
Nowel, Tom to Amanda Mosby 9-24-1868 (9-27-1868) F B
Nowel, W. C. to Mary E. Tate 1-15-1866 (1-17-1866) T
Nowell, A. J. to Sarah Ann Merrick 10-17-1847 Be
Nowell, Barnabas to Nancy Bell 3-19-1831 Ma
Nowell, Dempsey to Elizabeth Barnett 10-29-1866 (10-30-1866) Ma
Nowell, Dempsey to Harriet Pearcy 7-1-1828 Ma
Nowell, Jacob W. to Martha J. Robinson 6-27-1860 (no return) Hy
Nowell, James H. to Frances J. Jackson 2-8-1854 (2-9-1854) G
Nowell, James to Cath Baggett 10-12-1847 Be
Nowell, James to Marthene Cox 11-1-1849 Be
Nowell, James to Mary Ann Gully 3-26-1865 Be
Nowell, John A. to C. P. Green 1-20-1858 G
Nowell, Laten to Sarah J. Kirk 9-7-1854 Be
Nowell, Smith to Moriah Robertson 3-2-1867 Hy
Nowell, W. C. to H. M. Johnson 11-30-1859 G
Nowell, Wm. R. to Harriett A. McMackins 8-17-1858 Cr
Nowlan, John to Ellen Toola 5-27-1850 Sh
Nowlan, Patrick to Johanna Breen 1-7-1857 Sh
Nowlin, Briant to Mollie Denton 11-27-1871 (no return) Cr
Nowlin, D. R. to Mary W. Chambers 6-14-1853 Hn
Nowlin, G. W. to Mary A. Yonger 1-5-1867 (no return) Cr
Nowlin, J. A. to M. A. Penn 11-3-1868 G
Nowlin, James C. to Anlize Johnson 12-22-1837 (12-24-1837) Hr
Nowlin, Stephen to Ruth F. McGehe 2-15-1842 Hr
Nowlin, Wade H. to Emma Henderson 10-17-1870 (10-20-1870) Cr
Nowlin, William D. to Caroline E. Glass 1-29-1862 (no return) We
Nubbs, E. C. to V. A. McDaniel 12-11-1860 Be
Nuckells, Starling Norman McKinza 5-1-1832 (5-8?-1832) Hr
Nuckolls, Richard to Lucinda D. Lillard 3-15-1855 Hr
Nuckolls, William jr. to Eliza Polk 9-5-1850 Hr
Nugent, E. B. to E. C. Scott 11-28-1865 Hy
Nugent, John to Mary Ann Salisbury 3-20-1848 (3-21-1848) L
Nugent, Thomas to Joanna Shea 6-7-1855 Sh
Nugent, W. G. to Martha Rumeley 9-10-1860 (9-15-1860) O
Null, Abner to Susan Mullins 12-21-1846 (12-24-1846) Hr
Null, John to Elizabeth Rosson 3-22-1845 (3-23-1845) Hr
Null, M. D. to Francis J. Demoss 1-12-1846 Cr
Null, M. H. to Emolen Strayhorn 10-7-1853 Cr
Null, R. G. to Eliza D. Demoss 1-7-1847 Cr
Null, Wm. A. to Amanda Wilson 3-20-1845 Cr
Nunery, Samuel to Minerva Akin 3-10-1840 Cr
Nunn, Abram to L. Noel 12-27-1865 Hy

Nunn, Alfred to Elizabeth Robinson 12-23-1867 (12-26-1868?) G B
Nunn, Alfred to Martha Cook 12-28-1868 G B
Nunn, Andrew J. to Mary E. Pitts 12-10-1860 (no return) L
Nunn, B. H. to Adaline Baker 11-14-1850 Sh
Nunn, Bill to Eliza Leath 12-9-1869 G
Nunn, D. A. to Tennessee Whitehead 6-20-1871 Hy
Nunn, David A. to E. R. Young 9-29-1873 (9-30-1873) L
Nunn, Isaac C. to Maria M. Redick 12-20-1866 (no return) Dy
Nunn, J. H. to Mary J. Perry 10-16-1871 (10-17-1871) Dy
Nunn, J. N. to Margaret C. Jacock 1-30-1867 (1-31-1867) Dy
Nunn, James H. to Eleanor A. Burke 11-1-1851 (11-4-1851) L
Nunn, Joel to Sarah L. Elder 4-13-1864 G
Nunn, John C. W. to Mary A. E. Porter 9-4-1854 (9-5-1854) G
Nunn, Joseph to Julia Perry 12-28-1867 (no return) Dy
Nunn, Oscar to Bettie Noel 6-20-1869 Hy
Nunn, Solomon to Betsy Manix 12-20-1878 Hy
Nunn, Solomon to Louisa Tweety 1-4-1871 (no return) Hy
Nunn, Thomas to Anna A. Collins 10-9-1866 Hn
Nunn, William R. to Sarah Davidson 9-6-1858 (9-9-1858) G
Nunn, Wm. F. to Mary Murray 10-25-1870 (10-26-1870) Dy
Nunnelly, James S. to Parthenia Hitchcok 8-6-1852 (8-15-1852) Hr
Nunnery, J. to Fredonia Davis 9-6-1860 Be
Nunnery, James to Sarah Ann Pearce 7-20-1847 Be
Nunnery, John to Sarah McKinney 11-12-1842 Cr
Nunnery, Kinchen to Phebey J. Dillian 5-15-1858 Be
Nunnery, N. to E. Ann Thomason 9-6-1847 Be
Nunnery, Nathaniel to Frances Brewer 10-31-1860 (11-10-1860) Cr
Nunnery, Nehemiah to Roena C. Swindle 7-30-1850 Be
Nunnery, W. J. to Eliza Ann Watkins 3-22-1853 (3-24-1853) Sh
Nuss, Michael to Christiana Nagal 5-23-1856 Sh
Nusston, Nelson to Sina Adelina Matahis 6-22-1854 G
Nutt, H. J. to M. A. Holt 10-21-1866 G
Nutt, Robert to Cynthia Ramsey 12-25-1831 Sh
Nutt?, James C. to Mary Jackson 1-23-1851 (no return) Hn
Nutter, Henry P. to Sallie McQueen 9-24-1861 (10-8-1861) Sh

O'Bannian, D. B. to Mary Ann Grammar 7-17-1852 (7-18-1852) Sh
O'Brian, Joseph W. to Amanda M. Walker 3-16-1847 (4-19-1847) F
O'Brien (O'Bion), James to Mary McManhon 8-20-1862 Sh
O'Brien, David to Catharine Pindergast 9-21-1857 Sh
O'Brien, James to Johanna Sheehan 7-11-1859 Sh
O'Brien, John to Bridget Magrath 10-17-1855 Sh
O'Brien, John to Mary Carmody 11-20-1858 (11-2_-1858) Sh
O'Brien, Michael to Ellen Doyle 11-22-1856 (11-23-1856) Sh
O'Brien, Wm. to Julia Patterson 2-22-1861 Sh
O'Bryan, J. C. to Susan Joyner 2-15-1863 (2-16-1863) O
O'Connell, Daniel to Mary O'Conner 2-2-1863 Sh
O'Conner, Danniel to Mary Ann O'Conner 3-21-1853 O
O'Conner, James to Mary A. Connelly 8-25-1860 (8-26-1860) Sh
O'Conner, James to Mary L. O'Brien 8-3-1864 Sh
O'Conner, John to Mary P. Wilson 4-22-1845 Cr
O'Conner, Timothy to Mary Dunahon 8-17-1855 Sh
O'Conner, William to Mary Jacob 8-13-1859 Sh
O'Connor, James to Mary Brisolari 2-5-1861 Sh
O'Connor, Thos.(Jas?) (Maj.) H to Laura E. Biscoe 4-8-1863 Sh
O'Connor, Wm. to Mary Ruff 7-16-1859 Sh
O'Conor, Mulucky? to Mary O'Bryan 6-7-1871 (6-8-1871) T
O'Daniel, Wm. to Eliza T. Brooks 12-23-1846 (no return) F
O'Donald, Jeremiah to Judy Butler 7-25-1857 (7-26-1857) Sh
O'Donald, Michael to Bridget Burnet 4-30-1864 (5-1-1864) Sh
O'Donell, Thos. to Catherine Monohan 2-2-1863 Sh
O'Donnell, Edward to Margaret Louby 7-14-1858 (7-15-1858) Sh
O'Donnell, James to Catharine Carune 4-19-1852 Sh
O'Donnell, Thomas to Ellen Hanley 9-7-1860 Sh
O'Donnell, Thos. to Catharine Carter 4-4-1861 (4-7-1861) Sh
O'Hallan, Thomas to Mary Carter 2-13-1858 (2-15-1858) Sh
O'Hara, Michael to Rose O'Hara 12-24-1853 (12-28-1853) Sh
O'Hern (O'Herron), Mike to Nora O'Donnon 2-4-1861 Sh
O'Hern, William to Ellen Hennisey 6-10-1855 Sh
O'Herron, William to Ellen O'Herron 2-11-1860 (not executed) Sh
O'Herron, Wm. to Mary Lynch 7-13-1862 Sh
O'Huie, Pat to Sarah Gill 4-29-1861 Sh
O'Kane, A. A. to Milissia A. Gibson 8-8-1873 (9-3-1873) Cr
O'Keeffe, Patrick to Elizabeth Travis 11-27-1859 Sh
O'Kelley, James P. to Rebecca Jane Thorp 9-25-1843 (10-3-1843) F
O'Kelly, J. P. to Tempy Wall 8-18-1859 (8-21-1859) F
O'Kelly, Lewis J. to Nancy B. Herron 9-5-1866 (9-9-1866) F
O'Leary, Williamson Coleman to Laura Anna (Mrs.) Burns 11-5-1864 (11-6-1864) Sh
O'Lery, Michael to Julia Deving (Deviney) 1-25-1864 (1-28-1864) Sh
O'Mahony, John P. to Mary Nolan 2-2-1862 (2-3-1862) Sh
O'Mahony, John to Mary Barnett 5-21-1868 (5-23-1868) T
O'Malley, M. J. C. to F. E. Williams 3-7-1870 (3-8-1870) Cr
O'Meley, Edward to Bridget Henley 5-30-1858 Sh
O'Neal, Absolum H. to Rebecca Jane Dickey 12-12-1848 G
O'Neal, Daniel to Mary Cuningham 10-20-1862 Sh
O'Neal, Emerson to Z. A. McGowoan 2-11-1857 Sh

O'Neal, Joseph F. to Mary Ann Petree 4-16-1853 O
O'Neal, William to Olivia Wallace 12-31-1878 (1-2-1879) L B
O'Neal, Wm. to Elizabeth Vincent 5-17-1845 Cr
O'Neil, Benj. to Sarah Ross 4-20-1845 Cr
O'Neil, Jos. to Virginia Garland 4-12-1856 (4-13-1856) Sh
O'Neil, Patrick to Catharine Landregan 2-5-1853 (2-7-1853) Sh
O'Neil, Robert to Cordelia J. Oliver 1-22-1839 Cr
O'Neill, Samuel M. to Mary Bigham 11-1-1869 Cr
O'Quinn, A. M. to Annetta Harris 2-3-1866 (2-6-1866) F
O'Quinn, James E. to Mary Freeman 7-13-1853 (7-14-1853) Sh
OGuin, John to Eliza Madden 8-26-1857 Be
OKelly, L. J. to Malvina Herron 8-19-1862 (8-23-1862) F
O'Brian, W. to Ann Keefe 1-25-1853 Sh
O'Connar?, Lawrence to Elvira Medlock 9-29-1861 Hn
O'Connel, Edward to Elender Hill 10-24-1840 (10-25-1840) O
O'Daniel, B. F. to Etta Ward 3-31-1874 (4-1-1874) O
O'Daniel, F. M. (Dr.) to Myra L. Nesbett 8-31-1870 G
O'Daniel, Giles to Polly Eliza Sims 8-15-1855 G
O'Daniel, J. to Susan H. Alexander 3-16-1864 Hn
O'Daniel, John to Met Wade 4-28-1869 G B
O'Daniel, Joseph to Martha Cole 9-11-1863 Hn
O'Daniel, Robert T. to Frances E. Davis 12-22-1858 (12-28-1858) G
O'Daniel, Stephen to Elizabeth Gordon 7- -1863 G
O'Daniel, W. B. to S. L. Ellington 10-20-1866 O
O'Daniel, William W. to Martha Baldwin 10-12-1858 Hn
O'Hanlon, Robert T. to Lucretia Doeller 9-5-1850 Sh
O'Hannen (O'Harver), Benjamin to Sarah Stainback 7-26-1847 Sh
O'Hare, Michael to Margaret Supples 4-20-1840 Sh
O'Kelly, Willis S. to Lucy Cock 12-17-1850 (no return) F
O'Laughlin, Terrence to Anne Grant 2-7-1848 Sh
O'Leary, Jeremiah to Nancy Ann Somerfield Gain? 10-18-1870 (10-29-1870) L
O'Neal, Alfred to Molly Mays 1-1-1870 G B
O'Neal, Henry F. to Altrecy Lasiter 2-25-1856 (no return) Hn
O'Neal, John W. to Jane K. Motheral 6-25-1840 O
O'Neal, John to Harriet Harland 12-13-1866 G
O'Neal, Johnson to Louisa I. McGowan 2-25-1847 Sh
O'Neil, Ruffin to Rachel Levy 11-10-1867 G B
O'Neill, W. C. to L. L. Woollen 10-25-1870 (10-26-1870) Cr
O'Neill, William to Fanny Bivins 10-7-1881 (10-9-1881) L B
O'Steen, William to Lucretia Dillard 2-11-1829 Ma
Oakes, John to Winney Fowler 2-10-1832 G
Oakes, William J. to Margaret E. Lyons 4-11-1859 Ma
Oakford, William S. to Mary E. McLaurine 3-15-1848 G
Oakley, Ben Jamin to Perry? Warren 8-12-1867 (no return) Dy
Oakley, E. to Mary F. Furgerson 3-23-1853 (3-24-1853) Sh
Oakley, Henry to Elizabeth Dorhorty 3-21-1845 (no return) We
Oakley, J. W. H. to Mary A. Shackleton 10-24-1871 (10-25-1871) Dy
Oakley, James K. P. to Mary J. H. Barron 6-27-1860 Ma
Oakley, John T. to Mary Jane Watson 4-13-1864 Sh
Oakley, John to Eliza Gibbs 12-7-1858 We
Oakley, M. C. to Mary A. L. Sanders 11-21-1859 (11-23-1859) G
Oakley, McFarlen to Jane S. White 5-19-1858 (5-20-1858) G
Oakley, Thos. C. to Abigail Roach 4-7-1852 Sh
Oakley, W. B. to M. L. Crain 12-12-1874 (12-14-1874) O
Oakley, William to Eliza A. Brewer 11-25-1871 (no return) Dy
Oakly, James A. to Lucy A. Morgan 7-30-1863 We
Oakly, Richard to Ellen Draw 1-29-1875 (1-31-1875) Dy B
Oaks, John to Missouri Goodrich 7-9-1873 Dy
Oaks, Joseph W. to Frances Johnson 11-20-1857 O
Oates, J. A. to Mollie C. Baker 2-18-1871 (no return) F
Oates, John H. to Sarah McFadden 9-24-1851 (no return) F
Oates, John T. to Mary Eliza Elrod 5-7-1856 (5-8-1856) Ma
Oates, Oliver to Virginia O. Wellborn 3-22-1855 Sh
Oates, Thomas J. to Eliza Stevens 6-8-1846 T
Oates, Wm. C. to Fanny S. Guy 10-11-1859 (10-12-1859) Hr
Oates, Wyatt to Caroline Edwards 11-24-1858 (11-25-1858) Ma
Oats, Stephen K. to Celia J. Crittenden 5-11-1867 (5-16-1867) F
Oats, Wm. J. to Mary Maxwell 11-21-1844 F
Oatsfall, Jordan to Elizabeth McLain 2-5-1844 Hr
Oatsvall, Green to Sarah C. Hatley 3-7-1868 Be
Obar, Robed to Mary Weaver 1-12-1832 Ma
Obenchain, J. T. to Ella J. Hicks 6-8-1868 Ma
Oberst, A. J. to Parmelia C. Laird 1-8-1861 Sh
Oberst, J. F. W. to Catherine E. Cook 5-3-1858 Sh
Obrian, Henry to Jane McNeely 11-28-1856 Sh
Obrien, James to Hanorah Welsh 7-9-1862 (7-12-1862) Sh
Obrien, William to Martha Loyd 1-29-1867 (1-31-1867) T
Odam, Caleb to Elizabeth C. Butler 8-30-1853 (8-31-1853) Ma
Odam, John H. to Louisa E. Carwile 12-25-1842 Sh
Odam, John W. to Betsey Patterson 8-7-1821 Sh
Odam, Ransom to Rebecca Robertson 11-11-1830 (11-15-1830) Ma
Odam, William H. to Martha Jane Williams 12-16-1848 (12-20-1848) T
Odancer?, George D. to Margaret L. Alexander 11-14-1850 Hn
Odel, Albert M. to Almira Williams 9-17-1846 (no return) Dy
Odell, J. W. to E. C. Wind 8-6-1875 (no return) L
Odell, Stephen to Mary Sangster 12-23-1865 Hy
Odell, Terry to Sally Davis 10-25-1831 G

Odle, M. E. to Mary Cashian 9-19-1859 We
Odle, R. to L. Tippet 12-12-1842 Be
Odle, Wm. A. to Melissa C. Renfro 11-1-1869 Dy
Odom, A. to B. A. Harrison 3-6-1866 G
Odom, B. V. to Nancy A. Land 8-7-1860 (8-8-1860) O
Odom, B. W. to Caroline E. Brown 12-26-1856 We
Odom, Burrel to Meriah Goodman 11-25-1844 Be
Odom, Demous to Elizabeth Lyles 3-1-1863 Mn
Odom, J. S. to Mollie Odom 8-25-1869 G
Odom, Riley to Martha Rinkle 4-5-1864 Mn
Odom, S. J. to Sarrah F. Foster 9-20-1865 G
Odom, William to Sally Young 10-16-1862 Be
Odonald, John to Sarah Haynes 12-26-1860 (no return) Hy
Odum, Theophila W. to Mary Dill 12-7-1857 (no return) We
Offenshine, John to Mary J. Pace 4-14-1869 (4-15-1869) Cr
Offill, Elza to Fannie Wilkins 11-17-1874 O
Ogara, Martin to Elizabeth Overton 10-15-1868 G
Ogburn, Josiah to Mary L. Hyne 2-7-1845 Be
Ogelsbie, Elisha to Sarah Jane Applewhite 12-2-1838 O
Ogle, Jesse to Mary A. Marks 11-10-1855 (11-19-1855) Sh
Ogles, Joh to Fouzanna McGinnis 4-7-1868 G
Ogles, John L. to Malinda R. I. Smith 6-19-1852 (6-20-1852) G
Oglesby, Elisha to Polly Morgan 12-8-1829 (12-10-1829) G
Oglesby, Henry E. to Mary T. Fleming 10-13-1866 O
Oglesby, James S. to Mary E. Henderson 9-3-1851 Sh
Oglesby, John to Annie Wilson 11-4-1867 (11-5-1867) T
Oglesby, William C. to Mary E. Anderson 11-7-1859 (11-9-1859) Sh
Ogwain, J. R. to Mary E. Herrin 9-14-1868 Be
Ohanlon, John to Kate Lynch 11-4-1869 Ma
Ohara, John E. to Henrietta Williams 12-3-1861 (12-5-1861) Ma
Ohern (Ahern), Matthew to Ellen Green? (Gunn?) 1-21-1859 (1-23-1859) Sh
Ohern, William to Julian Murphy 4-18-1857 (4-19-1857) Sh
Ohern, William to Mary Ohern 9-20-1857 Sh
Oishei, Joseph to Theresa Wildt 4-22-1858 Sh
Okelly, L. J. to Melvina Herren 8-19-1862 (not endorsed) F
Okley, M. to S. A. Michan 7-30-1854 We
Old, Jere to Elizabeth (Mrs.) Parden (Rarden?) 11-18-1863 Sh
Old, Patrick H. A. to Mahala I. I. Davis 2-27-1845 We
Old, W. C. to Mary J. Crawford 2-4-1863 F
Old, William A. to Cecilia Beverly Darby 1-30-1847 (2-?-1847) T
Old, William A. to Martha A. Deaner 9-30-1845 (no return) F
Old, William Mct. to Martha M. McMurry 6-18-1860 O
Oldenberge, C. to Susanna Stander 6-22-1859 Sh
Oldham, Algernon S. to Drucilla F. Partee 7-9-1856 (no return) L
Oldham, Beverly to Cherry Currin 1-18-1883 (1-19-1883) L
Oldham, C. C. to Lucinda C. Milner 12-17-1846 We
Oldham, Chas. Thos. to E. J. Walker 3-18-1842 T
Oldham, E. R. to Mattie L. Bacon 12-5-1876 (12-6-1876) L
Oldham, Ebeneze to Elizabeth Jackson 12-11-1827 Ma
Oldham, Elias to Nany Bruton 1-8-1831 Sh
Oldham, George to Joanna Scott no dates (not executed) Hy
Oldham, Grandison to Mary Wilson 12-28-1871 Hy
Oldham, Green Lea to Mila (Milla) Gay 2-17-1839 Sh
Oldham, James to Cora Richardson 2-4-1874 L
Oldham, James to Eliza M. Paxton 4-21-1853 Sh
Oldham, James to Lydia Fryers 7-7-1877 (7-21-1877) L B
Oldham, Jim to Rachel Baynes 2-6-1873 Hy
Oldham, Joel to Margaret Bishop 4-26-1853 Sh
Oldham, John to Missouri E. Willis 9-27-1856 (9-28-1856) Sh
Oldham, Ned to Phillis Williams 12-26-1866 (12-28-1866) F B
Oldham, Robert H. to Laura E. Partee 1-8-1851 L
Oldham, Robert H. to Lucy A. Palmer 1-24-1877 L
Oldham, Samuel to Lizzibella Hooker 10-24-1877 (10-25-1877) L
Oldham, Shack to Susan Goin 3-16-1880 Dy
Oldham, Tapley to Fanny Paxton 1-20-1853 Sh
Oldham, Tapley to Susan W. Geter 8-18-1857 Sh
Oldham, Travis to Cherry Brooks 12-15-1866 (no return) Dy
Oldham, William to Cinda Bond 2-22-1877 Hy
Oldham, William to Emiline Vincent 1-10-1855 We
Oldham, William to Martha Burton 2-14-1883 L
Oldham, Willis to Mariah Ross 9-5-1869 Hy
Olds, A. C. to Elizabeth Cowell 4-4-1853 (no return) L
Olds, Andrew to Harriet Cooper 12-24-1867 (12-31-1867) F B
Olds, Arthur to Effi Crichfield 12-23-1840 (12-24-1840) L
Olds, Arthur to Mary Davis 4-24-1849 (4-26-1849) L
Olds, C. M. to V. E. Cheek 3-5-1884 (3-6-1884) L
Olds, Daniel to Sarah Sherly] 9-11-1824 Hr
Olds, Gideon to Rachel A. Cowell 1-2-1861 L
Olds, Gideon to Sarah A. Cowell 1-25-1857 (no return) L
Olds, J. T. to J. P. Only 2-16-1878 (2-19-1878) Dy
Olds, John Thomas to Sophronia Ellen Garner 1-14-1873 (1-15-1873) L
Olds, Mat to Ella Hayes 6-11-1869 (6-12-1869) F B
Olds, R. A. to Mary E. Stokes 1-25-1878 (1-28-1878) L
Olds, Thomas C. to Gatsy Ann Spivey 9-22-1847 L
Olds, Thomas C. to Jane Crihfield 6-22-1842 (6-23-1842) L
Olds, William W. to Fannie T. Marcum 11-16-1876 (11-29-1876) Dy
Olds, Zack to Nancy Brewer 12-28-1870 F B

Oliphant, Richard to Sarah Ann Hoskins 9-1-1848 Sh
Oliphant, Robert to Cynthia Chester 8-14-1845 Sh
Olivar, George to Judat Campbell ?-?-1861? Mn
Olivar, Lewis to Amanda Hines 12-4-1872 Hy
Olive, Ashley to Caroline Berry 1-28-1841 Hn
Olive, Cornelius M. to Sarah E. Moore 11-18-1860 Hn
Olive, Harvest to Mattie M. J. Stanford 4-12-1858 Cr
Olive, Henry to Anne Brown 12-19-1874 (12-20-1874) T
Olive, Howell to Ann Lyon 2-13-1839 Hn
Olive, I. N. to Paralee Byas? 10-2-1864 Hn
Olive, J. W. to Mattie Ann Jackson 10-31-1878 Dy
Olive, James M. to Parthana Dacus 8-11-1857 We
Olive, James R. to Elmira B. Waller 11-14-1854 (11-15-1854) Sh
Olive, James to Elizabeth Flake 9-9-1865 (9-13-1866?) Cr
Olive, Leroy to Martha Kendall 2-22-1860 Hn
Olive, S. W. to N. H. Elliot 3-3-1859 We
Olive, Samuel to Russie P. Watson 2-20-1860 Hn
Olive, W. W. to Josephine Janes 4-23-1867 Hn
Oliver, A. B. to Sarah Taylor 8-13-1854 Hn
Oliver, A. G. to Susan Smith 7-23-1840 Hn
Oliver, A. M. to M. J. Carr 8-9-1870 G
Oliver, Alexander to Mary E. Mann 12-7-1866 G
Oliver, Allen F. to Mary C. Crittenton 1-2-1856 (1-3-1856) Ma
Oliver, Allen to Mary W. Fowlkes 8-28-1848 (9-1-1848) O
Oliver, Allen to Susan A. G. Herring 9-18-1854 (9-20-1854) O
Oliver, Alvin J. to Tennessee Boulten 9-24-1868 G
Oliver, Burrell to Charity Carter 2-24-1843 Cr
Oliver, Calvin F. to Ann Riggs 10-18-1860 We
Oliver, Elijah to Eliza Jones 7-28-1846 Sh
Oliver, G. W. to Frances C. Wilson 8-17-1865 Mn
Oliver, George S. to Martha A. Belote 1-20-1854 Sh
Oliver, Harry to S. E. Cook 7-13-1863 (7-19-1863) O
Oliver, Henry P. to Becky D. Vaughn 6-3-1858 We
Oliver, Henry S. to Mary Ann Nolin 4-18-1847 Hn
Oliver, Isaac S. to Martha Jane Brunson 11-8-1848 G
Oliver, Isaac to Louizer Branson 5-16-1869 G
Oliver, J. M. to Tabitha E. Haynes 5-5-1866 (5-9-1866) Cr
Oliver, J. R. A. D. to Mary Adams 11-24-1842 Cr
Oliver, J. R. to Sada Ward 11-5-1872 (11-6-1872) O
Oliver, J. S. to J. H. Todd 12-15-1867 Hn
Oliver, J. W. to Martha Elam 3-27-1866 G
Oliver, Jackson C. to Piety A. Berry 10-26-1865 Hn
Oliver, James G. to Mattie Hays 5-7-1868 Ma
Oliver, James I. to Luisa E. Sanders 9-18-1869 (no return) Hy
Oliver, James M. to Mary A. Moody 11-1855 Hn
Oliver, James R. to C. H. Roper 9-4-1865 O
Oliver, James W. A. to Martha J. E. Sheridan 3-28-1866 Hn
Oliver, James to Alethea Roberts 11-5-1850 Hr
Oliver, James to Deliah Fowlkes 12-27-1871 (12-28-1871) Dy
Oliver, James to Mary Williams 12-9-1866 G
Oliver, Joe to Mandy Beavers 12-3-1868 (12-5-1868) F B
Oliver, John C. to Angeline Chapman 4-2-1832 (4-3-1832) Ma
Oliver, John C. to Sarah A. T. Berrycroft 6-2-1855 Ma
Oliver, John J. to Harriett R. Day 6-2-1853 (6-3-1853) Ma
Oliver, John W. to Sarah E. Chilcutt 12-5-1860 Hn
Oliver, John W. to Susan E. Haley 12-15-1858 G
Oliver, John to Eliza Jane Webb 11-26-1853 Hr
Oliver, John to Elizabeth Wood 9-24-1838 Ma
Oliver, John to Lacy Baily 6-16-1853 G
Oliver, John to M. Casy 9-10-1831 Hr
Oliver, John to Rebecca F. Connally 9-17-1850 (9-18-1850) Ma
Oliver, L. L.(F.?) to Mary Jane Prewett 2-24-1870 G
Oliver, M. B. to N. E. Jones 2-4-1867 G
Oliver, Malechi to Minerva Hodge 11-30-1830 (12-2-1830) Ma
Oliver, Moses C. to Rebecca A. Steele 5-20-1866 Hn
Oliver, Moses to Sarah Linton 9-27-1854 (9-28-1854) G
Oliver, Pleasant to Artemesia Cloud 11-5-1836 Hr
Oliver, R. H. to Mary C. Parks 7-23-1855 Sh
Oliver, Richard to Martha Moffett 8-14-1839 F
Oliver, Robert L. P. to Sarah Ann Brunson 10-25-1848 G
Oliver, Robert to Mima Bemis 4-8-1866 Hy
Oliver, Robt A. to Lydia Nutt 12-21-1843 Cr
Oliver, Ruebin W. to Elizabeth W. Wilson 2-3-1836 Hr
Oliver, S. J. to Martha A. Fallin 3-31-1853 Cr
Oliver, Shelton to Elizabeth J. Crisp 6-26-1850 (6-25?-1850) Hr
Oliver, T. J. to Adelia C. Ridley 10-17-1866 (10-18-1866) Cr
Oliver, T. J. to M. A. Scott 1-8-1861 G
Oliver, Thomas to Elizabeth Price 4-21-1859 We
Oliver, Thomas to Martha R.(P?) Crews? 1-14-1840 Hr
Oliver, W. C. to S. V. Jackson 12-12-1865 G
Oliver, W. T. to Martha A. Thredgill 12-2-1867 (12-4-1867) Cr
Oliver, William J. to Rebecca M. Follis 3-12-1853 (3-17-1853) Ma
Oliver, William to Arsena King 10-21-1846 (10-22-1846) Hr
Oliver, William M. J. Norton 8-5-1844 (no return) Hn
Oliver, William to Martha Watson 4-3-1862 G
Oliver, William to Mary Hall 9-26-1861 (no return) We
Oliver, William to Sarah Todd 4-4-1846 (4-5-1846) Ma

Oliver, Wilson to Susan A. Adams 2-16-1843 Cr
Oliver, Wm. B. to Pruda Chappel 9-17-1839 (9-19-1839) F
Oliver, Wm. to L. A. Purkins 3-9-1872 Hy
Olliver, James to Harriet Omohundros 12-26-1839 (12-31-1839) L
Olmstead, George to Mary Ellen Dougherty 3-20-1882 L
Omara, Jerry to Ofilia Davis 1-8-1867 T
Omesly?, T. H. to Lucy J. Franklin 2-12-1849 (no return) F
Oneal, Francis M. to Anna Clark 2-28-1871 (3-1-1871) Ma
Oneal, Harvey D. to Menerva Rone 12-9-1868 (12-13-1868) Ma
Oneal, James H. to Rachel McCorkle 5-16-1859 Ma
Oneal, Nathaniel C. to Susie A. Warren 9-22-1879 (no return) Dy
Oneal, Samuel to Mary Greggory 11-4-1839 (1-1-1840) G
Oneal, With T. to M. E. Parker 1-7-1868 Ma
Oneil, J. A. to Mattie Younger 2-28-1871 Cr
Onion, C. Howard to M. A. Branch 10-31-1871 Hy
Onley, John to Mary Alsobrook (Ashbrook) 8-29-1847 Sh
Onley, Robert D. to Jane Kincade 12-23-1847 (no return) Hn
Onsman, Wm. to Nancy Throgmartin 9-6-1865 (9-7-1865) O
Oquinn, E. A. to Mattie Gay 7-28-1874 (7-30-1874) Dy
Oral, Samuel to Holley Morris 5-2-1842 Cr
Ore, George A. to Malinda Williams 1-5-1846 (no return) Hn
Ore, Joseph A. to Virginia Frizzell 1-1-1846 (no return) We
Orey, Robert to Mary Terrell 6-28-1863 Hn
Orgain, Edmond J. to Sarah J. Kimball 2-5-1850 (2-7-1850) Ma
Organ, Charles H. to Lissidia Winchester 3-22-1860 Sh
Organ, James to Emely F. James 2-22-1853 (3-1-1853) G
Organ, Thomas L. to Elizabeth J. Trotter 10-1-1844 (10-9-1844) F
Orily, Wm. J. to Manda L. Pinkston 2-18-1863 Be
Ormann, James L. to Carolin Bryles 1-9-1843 (1-16-1843) F
Ormon, Jacob to Elizabeth Jones 3-19-1838 F
Ornsby, Henry to Ellin McDormot 3-28-1864 Sh
Orr, A. B. to Nancy Lovett 10-14-1843 (10-15-1843) G
Orr, Alexander B. to Epsa Needham 7-12-1862 G
Orr, Allen to Tennessee Cole 12-28-1868 (1-3-1869) F B
Orr, B. P. to Leanor E. Wilson 12-5?-1859 Hn
Orr, C. M. to Jane D. Wilson 11-2-1866 (no return) Hn
Orr, C. P. to Jane D. Paschall 12-31-1844 Hn
Orr, David to M. G. Malone 5-18-1855 We
Orr, Eleazer P. to Jane Lovett 8-6-1851 G
Orr, G. W. to Ann Sparks 11-23-1857 Sh
Orr, J. P. to Sarah Jan Paschall 9-27-1866 Hn
Orr, James H. to Amanda C. Greer 9-26-1859 G
Orr, James H. to Sally s. Brown 10-6-1857 (no return) Hn
Orr, James to Emily Evans 11-1-1854 (11-2-1854) Sh
Orr, James to Sarah Glass 2-24-1869 (2-25-1869) T
Orr, Jesse P. to Louisa Lamb 6-2-1858 Hn
Orr, John K. to Susan J. Alexander 1-7-1836 Sh
Orr, John R. to Elizabeth Morrow 9-10-1857 (9-15-1857) O
Orr, John W. to Catherine C. Nicholas 11-26-1851 Hn
Orr, John to Margarett Falkner 10-18-1865 Cr
Orr, Jones K. to Sarah Ann Young 5-15-1835 (5-21-1835) Hr
Orr, Robert D. to Susan P. Russell 7-21-1852 Cr
Orr, Robt. to Lizzie Best 12-2-1853 Sh
Orr, Samuel G. to Catherine Rogers 3-11-1850 Hn
Orr, Samuel G. to Frances E. Willson 11-17-1845 Hn
Orr, Samuel to Lucy Ann Perry 1-24-1857 Hn
Orr, Stephen B. to Permelia M. Waldrop 11-11-1849 Hn
Orr, Thomas to M. J. Johnson 1-13-1870 Cr
Orr, W. E. to Mary A. Bobbet 2-12-1865 G
Orrell, J. C. to Elizabeth Kain 12-10-1862 (12-11-1862) F
Orrell, Robert to Margaret Rachels 1-27-1856 We
Orrell, Wm. Joseph to Laura Catherine Marrs 12-17-1868 G
Orsburn, Franklin to Lucinda L. Haislip 9-5-1850 O
Orsburn, J. E. to Nancy J. Hollomon 10-19-1849 O
Orsburn, W. P. to Elizabeth A. Oldham 3-12-1861 O
Orsidy (Orsnly), Andrew to Elizabeth Lieb (Lish) 11-6-1849 Sh
Orterbridge, William to Matilda J. Wright 12-19-1873 (12-20-1873) L B
Orton, D. W. to Louisa H. Farrar 1-30-1868 G
Orton, Robert W. to Sarah Cochran 8-9-1838 F
Ortry, James to Mary A. McCarty 12-2-1857 O
Orverby, R. M. to N. J. Goad 9-21-1872 (9-22-1872) O
Osben, Daniel to Mary C. Sipes 12-26-1853 (12-27-1853) Ma
Osborn, Charles to Ann Bowling 2-21-1870 (no return) Hy
Osborn, Enoch to Ida Evans 12-24-1869 (12-26-1869) Dy
Osborn, J. F. to Nannie B. Sinclair 10-1-1867 (no return) Dy
Osborn, J. M. to Ann E. Gates 11-19-1868 (no return) L
Osborn, J. T. to Slatyra J. Adams 12-12-1865 (12-13-1865) L
Osborn, James W. to Mariah Jane Vauen? 1-3-1865 (no return) Hn
Osborn, Jesse to Sarah Robinson 7-14-1836 Sh
Osborn, L. P. to Jane (Mrs.) Scags 10-6-1864 (10-11-1864) Sh
Osborn, Levi P. to Cornelia M. Gregory 7-24-1848 (7-27-1848) F
Osborn, Thomas A. to Mary T. Woodfin 2-17-1853 Hr
Osborn, Thomas to Elvira Kelly 1-13-1835 Sh
Osborn, W. F. to Sarah C. Rice 3-18-1863 (no return) Hy
Osborn, William A. to Mattie Allen 11-13-1867 Hn
Osborne, C. F. to Addie Bigham 2-4-1868 (2-5-1868) Cr
Osborne, E. H. to Bettie Crisp 7-20-1870 Hy

Osborne, E. H. to Cynthia Crisp 6-24-1850 Hr
Osborne, Isaac to Augustina Hargiss 9-16-1851 (no return) F
Osborne, J. H. to Ada Weatherford 11-7-1833 Hr
Osborne, R. H. to Hettie Paschal 8-3-1881 L
Osborne, T. B. to Cal Goodloe 6-26-1867 O
Osborne, T. C. to Tempy Eital 8-16-1849 Sh
Osborne, Thomas A. to Sidney Jane Carruth 12-22-1858 Hr
Osborne, W. H. to Mary Ann Wells 6-17-1879 (6-18-1879) L
Osborne, W. W. to Margaret V. Adams 1-26-1865 (1-31-1865) F
Osbourn, James W. to Martha M. Hogue 9-17-1856 (10-2-1856) O
Osbourn, James to Sarah Scott 9-7-1856 O
Osbourn, Pleasant to Elizabeth Matthews 2-7-1858 O
Osburn, John B. to Sarah Calhoun 5-25-1853 O
Osburn, John H. to Elizabeth A. Hatler 4-29-1860 We
Osburn, John P. to Nancy Robertson 4-13-1854 Hn
Osburn, McCamy W. to Caroline Ponder 5-5-1846 Be
Osburn, Perry to Sarah Gregson 2-13-1840 Sh
Osburn, Robert T. to Mary A. Cate 3-20-1860 We
Osburn, T. G. to Adriadna Irvin 1-10-1870 (1-11-1870) Ma
Osgen, William to Mary Ann Vanzandt 12-26-1842 (12-27-1842) Ma
Osier, Samuel C. to Maunda Coble 8-19-1851 (no return) F
Oslin, J. W. to F. E. Wesson 12-20-1871 (12-21-1871) Dy
Osment, B. C. to R. A. Hudgpith 9-12-1855 We
Osment, Daniel to Sarah McCearly] 12-26-1846 (12-27-1846) Hr
Osteen, G. B. to L. J. Thompson 3-28-1883 L
Osteen, Hardy to Elizabeth Lunsford 8-12-1846 L
Osteen, Isaac N. to Nancy M. Bethell 4-9-1859 (4-11-1859) O
Osteen, J. L. to Amanda F. A. Lunsford 7-26-1855 L
Osteen, J. L. to Amanda F. Lunsford 3-19-1856 (no return) L
Osteen, J. R. to M. E. Best 1-27-1880 L
Osteen, James J. to Priscilla Keltner 7-31-1860 L
Osteen, James Jose to Malinda Bowman 3-5-1838 (3-8-1838) L
Osteen, James R. to Martha Ann Austin 12-19-1859 L
Osteen, W. R. to Martha J. Harris 2-22-1875 (2-23-1875) L
Osteen, William R. to Celia A. Lunsford 8-11-1852 (no return) L
Osten, Homer to Elizabeth Sawyers 7-27-1834 Sh
Ostmann, Theodore to Minnie Ruschhaupt 4-4-1860 (4-9-1860) Sh
Oswald, Thomas M. to Jane Barclay 7-6-1842 Sh
Oswell, William to Mary A. Ricks 5-22-1845 Hr
Otey, John to Margaret Maloney 4-16-1858 Sh
Otman, Mike to Edda Fahrigheon *12-27-1855* Sh
Ottenheimer, Louis to Fanny Schwartz 10-15-1853 (10-18-1853) Sh
Otterbridge, Stephen to Katie Green 12-9-1875 (no return) L B
Ottmans, Weije F. to Elizabeth (Mrs.) Boschamp 8-3-1863 Sh
Oumage?, James W. to Mary Manaslk? no date (with 1868) T
Ourie?, John H. to Mary M. Blake 6-5-1851 Hn
Ousler, George L. to Thena Jane Cox 8-13-1850 (8-14-1850) G
Outerbridge, Esaw to Vira Estis 4-28-1870 Hy
Outerbridge, Stephen to Marina Patterson 8-19-1845 Ma
Outhouse, Israel F. to Alsey D. Orr 10-10-1843 We
Outhouse, Peter to Mary Doolinger 11-21-1850 We
Outland, Edmond to Elenora Montgomery 10-10-1866 (10-11-1866) Ma
Outland, Eli to Eliza Ann Lindsey 12-20-1853 Be
Outland, Thomas to Martha A. Parker 1-6-1858 (no return) Hn
Outlaw, A. J. to Harriet A. Williams 12-28-1859 (no return) Hy
Outlaw, Alonzo to Rachel Harris 12-20-1877 Hy
Outlaw, Geo. W. to Roena C. Linley 3-10-1860 (no return) Hy
Outlaw, Henry to Mollie Sullivan 12-27-1884 (12-28-1884) L
Outlaw, J. C. to M. H. Mills 12-29-1851 O
Outlaw, Joe to Cena Crowder 11-17-1871 Hy
Outlaw, Lenson to Mariah Johnson 12-4-1871 (no return) Hy
Outlaw, M. R. T. to Martha E. Outlaw 9-24-1830 O
Outlaw, Samuel to Martha West 10-18-1877 Hy
Outlaw, Turner to Cornelia Hicks 11-9-1878 Hy
Outlaw, Turner to Edmonia Oldham 3-27-1870 Hy
Outlaw, W. M. to Ellen Phillips 1-22-1885 (1-23-1885) L
Outlaw, York to Alice Brown 12-20-1873 Hy
Overall, A. M. to Amanda Jane Williams 11-15-1869 (11-16-1869) T
Overall, Albert L. to Ellen V. Bowers 4-27-1868 (4-28-1868) T
Overall, E. D. to Martha A. Ramsay 9-23-1863 G
Overall, Ed to Sallie Hemphill 1-31-1871 (2-1-1871) T
Overall, Gabriel to Mary Knox 7-22-1866 G
Overall, George W. to Aggie J. Bowers 9-24-1867 T
Overall, Jake to Augustine Ball 12-24-1869 G B
Overall, James P. to Mary Owen 1-22-1867 (1-23-1867) T
Overall, John to Ellen Wyatt 10-6-1870 G
Overall, Nathaniel M. to Perlina Rhodes 11-25-1845 (11-27-1845) O
Overall, R. B. to Caphronia Ramsay 10-19-1870 G
Overall, W. J. to Clementine Hutcherson 2-28-1860 G
Overby, Harbert to S. Vincent 11-17-1846 (no return) We
Overcast, Thomas D. to Henrietta Nixon 1-19-1860 Hn
Overstreet, William F. to Susan Doherty 11-3-1867 Be
Overton, A. G. to Susie J. Hon 10-22-1873 Hy
Overton, Absalom to Malinda Harrell? 1-18-1845 (1-23-1845) Hr
Overton, Albert to Lou Robertson 12-28-1872 (12-31-1872) Dy
Overton, Albert to Sallie King 12-25-1874 Dy
Overton, Archibald to Sarah E. Anderson 8-16-1859 (8-17-1859) Hr

Grooms

Overton, Arter (Arthur?) to Mahala Peters 10-31-1844 Sh
Overton, B. W. to Mattie Reece 12-16-1867 (12-17-1867) F
Overton, Benjamin to Phoebe McMillan 9-24-1834 Sh
Overton, Bradley to Susan F. M. Murry 10-22-1873 Hy
Overton, Charles to Maria L. Crutchfield 10-25-1866 Hy
Overton, Charles to Martha J. Chambers 5-2-1873 (no return) Hy
Overton, D. H. to M. A. Groom 2-12-1852 We
Overton, E. D. to Angeline Parker 11-14-1845 Sh
Overton, Elija to Jane Monton 4-4-1846 (4-5-1846) Hr
Overton, Elijah to Lucy Taylor 2-19-1838 Hr
Overton, Francis M. to Nancy Jane Baker 8-13-1866 Ma
Overton, Henry to Lucy McGowan 11-19-1867 (11-23-1867) F B
Overton, James A. to Eliza A. Willingham 7-4-1843 We
Overton, John M. to Parthenia Chambers 7-27-1867 (no return) Hy
Overton, Redic (Reddick) to Polly Greggory 1-20-1832 Sh
Overton, Richard to Elizabeth Mathews 12-18-1866 G
Overton, S. W. to Sarah O. Williams 2-25-1855 We
Overton, Scott to amanda Talley 12-21-1874 (12-30-1874) Dy B
Overton, Thomas A. to M. K. Drewry 1-15-1860 We
Overton, Thomas A. to Mary J. Patton 1-7-1858 Cr
Overton, Thomas G. to Rozina Gwinn 12-17-1840 F
Overton, Thomas to Permelia Patterson 10-5-1869 Ma
Overton, Westley to Livinda Alexander 4-6-1839 Hn
Overton, William E. to Tennie Hon 9-10-1873 Hy
Overton, William J. to Sarah E. Jennings 6-20-1861 (no return) Hy
Overton, William to Virginia Childers 5-16-1861 We
Overton, Willis to Mary I. Clark 11-28-1842 Ma
Overton, Wilson to Chaney Williams 12-31-1872 Hy
Overton, Wm. A. to Sarah Ann Herald 11-26-1843 We
Overton, Wm. to Mary J. Mashburn 9-30-1856 (10-2-1856) Hr
Owen, A. M. to L. A. Upchurch 1-15-1862 T
Owen, Alfred B. to Margaret Jane Billings 5-22-1844 T
Owen, Alfred B. to Matilda Elizabeth Wiseman 3-15-1849 T
Owen, Alfred W. to Mary A. Rice 10-30-1865 (11-2-1865) T
Owen, Benjamin J. F. to Tennessee C. Rogers 12-27-1861 (12-29-1861) Sh
Owen, Benjamin to Virginia Carnell 1-1-1850 (1-3-1850) L
Owen, Blunt H. to Rebecca West 2-11-1830 Sh
Owen, Charles C. to Sarah E. Lancaster 12-6-1855 (no return) F
Owen, Christopher to Mary Elizabeth Wiles 10-6-1855 (10-24-1855) Sh
Owen, Clay to Nanie Flag 3-7-1877 Hy
Owen, Cornelius to Emiline Ware 9-29-1876 Hy
Owen, Cornelius to Nancy Williams 12-29-1869 Hy
Owen, D. W. to Martha D. Howard 12-13-1859 (12-14-1859) O
Owen, David B. to Rhoeba S. Shaw 1-6-1868 (1-7-1868) Ma
Owen, David to Catherine Vasser 12-27-1842 Sh
Owen, David to Margaret English 3-9-1866 T
Owen, Edward to Betsy Jane Hightower 3-4-1871 (3-5-1871) Ma
Owen, Ezekiel B. to Adelia P. Payne 9-29-1832 Sh
Owen, G. R. to S. C. Bell 12-13-1865 Hn
Owen, George to Milly Ann Golding 5-22-1876 (5-23-1876) L
Owen, H. S. to Nancy Hicks 3-21-1846 Hr
Owen, Henry to Maggie Sweet 6-12-1872 (no return) Hy
Owen, Henry to Martha S. Tate 3-27-1856 Sh
Owen, Howard to Sarah Baugus 12-25-1845 Sh
Owen, Howard to Virginia Foster 1-14-1857 Sh
Owen, Isaac W. to S. Evolin Fortner 3-24-1862 T
Owen, Isaac to Clora Burns 3-30-1871 Hy
Owen, J. A. to Namie Smith 12-4-1866 T
Owen, J. H. to Louisa C. Oldham 10-19-1880 L
Owen, J. R. to S. E. Cawthou 10-19-1870 (10-20-1870) Cr
Owen, J. T. to Elizabeth Brown 10-10-1856 We
Owen, J. U. to Cora Henderson 10-23-1877 Hy
Owen, J. W. to Hennorah Boyle 2-3-1848 Hr
Owen, James B. to Sarah J. Bell 10-10-1859 (no return) Hy
Owen, James C. to Martha Hall 8-13-1850 Hn
Owen, James H. to Jetty F. Ralph 4-16-1857 T
Owen, James to Jane R. Smith 11-5-1838 (no return) F
Owen, Jas. to Tempy Wade 1-2-1874 O
Owen, Jefrey to Manerva Southall 2-19-1876 (no return) Hy
Owen, John G. to Etta Wright 1-7-1877 Hy
Owen, John to Laura Bond 10-10-1872 (no return) Hy
Owen, John to Malinda Sawyer? 12-26-1868 (12-27-1868) T
Owen, John to Martha A. Gore 1-17-1860 (1-18-1860) O
Owen, Jos. R. to Milly Las? 1-23-1869 (1-24-1869) T
Owen, Joseph A. to Jane (Mrs.) Scott 2-3-1857 (2-4-1857) Sh
Owen, N. L. to Ann R. Allen 5-7-1855 (no return) F
Owen, Nathaniel to Martha E. Boswell 10-4-1871 (10-5-1871) Cr
Owen, Parsons to Mary Harper 4-28-1874 Hy
Owen, Peter to Mary Sweeney 1-5-1867 (1-6-1867) T
Owen, R. M. to Nancy A. Melton 3-14-1867 Hn
Owen, Ralph to Caroline Wilson 12-22-1865 Hy
Owen, Ransom W. to Lovis Covington 10-10-1843 (no return) Hn
Owen, Richard B. to Sarah F. Walton 12-18-1867 T
Owen, Robert D. to Willie S. Fisher 12-1-1866 (12-2-1866) L
Owen, Robert H. to Susanah Whitson 2-16-1859 T
Owen, Robert H. to Susanah Whitson 7-16-1859 T
Owen, Russell to Caroline Pickett 12-21-1871 Hy

Owen, S. Y. to Mary E. Brown 1-21-1869 (1-23-1869) T
Owen, Saml. S. to E. F. Sanders 5-22-1860 (5-23-1860) Sh
Owen, T. P. to Fannie Chapman 1-4-1868 (no return) Hy
Owen, Thomas C. to Sarah Ann Morris 12-9-1852 We
Owen, Thomas P. to Martha E. Chapman 11-18-1877 Hy
Owen, Westley to Tabitha C. Trantham 9-27-1848 Hn
Owen, William J. to Camile Jane Johnson 1-10-1859 (1-12-1859) L
Owen, William L. to N. E. Gurley 5-3-1856 (5-4-1856) Sh
Owen, William W. to Elizabeth Roberts 11-28-1850 Sh
Owen, William to Harriett A. West 2-12-1829 Sh
Owen, William to Mary Elizabeth Carnal 11-6-1847 (11-7-1848?) L
Owen?, Josiah to Delina C. Brogdon 7-15-1858 (no return) Hn
Owen?, P. R. to S. C. Cauthern 1-13-1868 (1-16-1868) Cr
Owenby, Cahl P. to Orpha J. Malcar 12-13-1866 Cr
Owenby, E. P. to Martha E. Joiner 1-?-1867 (1-23-1867) Cr
Owenby, J. G. to Ida Chandler 12-17-1872 (12-18-1872) Cr
Owenby, J. J. to Jane Cooper 9-7-1857 Cr
Owenby, W. D. to Dilla Huffman 8-14-1867 (8-15-1867) Cr
Owenby, Wm. W. to Mary E. Dickson 11-4-1846 Cr
Owenes, George to Mary Goure 7-24-1852 We
Owens, Alfred Z. to Arabella McAllister 1-19-1854 Cr
Owens, Benj. to Mary R. Harris(Hanis?) 5-29-1839 (6-1-1839) Hr
Owens, Benjamin to Elizabeth Taggart 11-3-1830 Hr
Owens, David O. to Martha E. Lay 8-23-1854 (no return) F
Owens, Enoch to Winney Smith 11-20-1864 Mn
Owens, Ezekiel to Juliann Wilkes 10-11-1847 (10-12-1847) Hr
Owens, Felix to Permelia H. Plant 1-12-1839 (1-15-1839) F
Owens, George to Bitha McFerrin 2-15-1871 (no return) F B
Owens, George to Mary Clare 7-6-1864 Mn
Owens, George to Sarah J. Morgan 11-29-1871 (11-30-1871) Cr B
Owens, Harrington to Malinda M. Hamner 10-4-1855 Sh
Owens, Harrington to Louisa M. Harman 9-21-1855 Sh
Owens, Henry to Caroline Rogers 4-29-1867 Hy
Owens, J. J. to Mary Turner 11-11-1876 (11-14-1876) Dy
Owens, J. W. to M. S. F. Onstead 12-16-1861 Mn
Owens, J. W. to Martha E. Swink 11-21-1867 G
Owens, James E. to Caroline Scarborough 11-17-1856 Hn
Owens, James H. to Mary H. Wallace 11-15-1855 (no return) Hn
Owens, James P. to Mary E. Wagster 7-13-1866 G
Owens, John B. to Mary A. Corbett 12-30-1847 Hn
Owens, John Thomas to Mary Conalty 11-12-1853 Sh
Owens, John to Delila Kean 2-16-1856 Sh
Owens, John to Ellen Bradshaw 12-31-1873 T
Owens, John to Sarah Terrill 11-30-1882 (12-1-1882) L
Owens, L. P. to Sarah A. SSummers 3-16-1858 We
Owens, Leonard to Amanda Barnes 9-23-1854 (10-10-1854) Ma
Owens, Robert A. to Mary M. Wimberley 2-24-1859 Hn
Owens, Robert to Verna Spellings 1-8-1857 Cr
Owens, Samuel A. to F. A. Cawthon 4-23-1866 (4-26-1866) Cr
Owens, Samuel L. to Polly Carter 3-18-1829 (3-22-1829) Hr
Owens, Thomas H. to Jennie Lee Baker 4-16-1866 (4-25-1866) F
Owens, William C. to Elizabeth Jane Blythe 4-21-1860 (4-22-1860) Ma
Owens, William C. to Susan E. Barham 7-19-1860 (no return) Hn
Owens, William M. to Sarah Phelps 2-21-1856 Hn
Owens, Winfrey to Sophia Duff 2-14-1827 (2-18-1827) Hr
Owens, Wm. H. to Louisa Vails 12-29-1842 (12-30-1842) Hr
Owings, R. A. to Rachel E. Holman 9-9-1865 (9-12-1865) F
Owls, Marion to Rebecca Porter 2-19-1866 (no return) Hn
Ownby, C. R. to N. H. Cannon 10-9-1868 (10-11-1868) Cr
Ownby, Milton B. to Mary E. Todd 12-30-1858 Hn
Ownby, Thomas to Ann Whitworth 1-19-1848 Cr
Oxford, James to Susana Roberson 5-?-1861 Be
Oxford, John to Martha M. Barns 12-25-1851 Be
Ozier, C. J. to Luella A. McFadden 3-17-1860 F
Ozier, George to Sally Wade 1-25-1871 (1-26-1871) F B
Ozier, J. R. to N. A. Moore 3-21-1871 T
Ozier, James H. to E. A. Tate 11-25-1862 Cr
Ozier, James W. to Narcissa H. Hamilton 10-15-1867 (no return) Cr
Ozier, Levi to Martha E. Taylor 11-5-1870 (11-6-1870) Cr
Ozier, Loid to E. Allen 1-12-1846 Be
Ozier, Loyd to Jane Bobitt 11-7-1861 (no return) Cr
Ozier, M. D. to Sarah O. Tucker 10-2-1855 (10-4-1855) Ma
Ozier, Rubin to Elizabeth Nutt 5-21-1859 Cr
Ozier, Saml. M. to Annie Cook 9-26-1866 Ma
Ozier, W. C. to Sarah C. Elder 1-2-1863 F
Ozier, Willie to Winney C. Bostick 12-1-1843 F
Ozment, N. M. to Mary A. M. King 2-1-1860 (2-2-1860) Hr
Ozment, Robert B. to Fanny G. Hudson 4-23-1853 (5-1-1853) G
Ozment, Varnum to Emily V. Henderson 5-10-1847 (no return) F
Ozwell(Oswald), Edward to Abedian Sanders 10-15-1856 Hr

P---?, Ansel to Sarah Ann Hicks 8-29-1844 Hn
Pace, A. L. to Elizabeth McKee 8-10-1868 (8-11-1868) Dy
Pace, A. R. to Lucy McCullough 8-20-1875 (8-22-1875) Dy
Pace, B. F. to S. S. Scobey 11-1-1879 (11-4-1879) Dy
Pace, Benj. Franklin to Lowrana? Webb 1-26-1856 (1-29-1856) T
Pace, G. W. to Emma A. Nicolson 7-25-1867 Hy

Pace, H. J. to M. F. Weatherington 12-9-1874 (12-10-1874) Dy
Pace, J. B. to S. F. Baucum 2-12-1873 Hy
Pace, J. C. to M. E. Haynes 12-24-1867 G
Pace, J. D. to Fannie Shofner 10-30-1867 Dy
Pace, J. D. to Henrietta Sherwood 11-29-1871 Dy
Pace, J. P. to Susan A. Ware 2-15-1866 (no return) Cr
Pace, J. T. to L. E. Smith 7-22-1873 (7-24-1873) Dy
Pace, Jo. D. to T. A. Scoby 9-7-1869 (9-8-1869) Dy
Pace, John C. to Louisianna C. Smith 2-25-1847 (3-?-1847) T
Pace, Kinchin to Mary Magdalin Hoke 5-6-1851 T
Pace, M. R. to S. E. Hamilton 12-17-1878 (12-19-1878) Dy
Pace, R. R. to H. I. Taylor 7-25-1865 O
Pace, R. R. to J. A. Martin 6-2-1860 O
Pace, W. C. to Rebeccah Cook 4-26-1865 Dy
Pace, W. H. to Mary Ann Leathers 9-16-1835 Hr
Pace, W. J. to Elizabeth Boswell 10-5-1857 (10-16-1857) T
Pace, W. T. to Miley Halum 9-18-1866 (9-20-1866) Dy
Pace, W. T. to Stacy S. Strawn 12-29-1865 (12-30-1865) Dy
Pace, Wicke H. to Matilda W. Kirk 10-26-1836 Hr
Pace, William F. to Rosalind A. Roberts 11-19-1854 Be
Pace, William to Mary Osborne 11-18-1848 Be
Paden, William to Jane H. McCanla 4-27-1840 T
Padgett, C. M. to Catherine Connell 6-26-1862 Sh
Padgett, Wesley to Clarissa McQueen 9-16-1856 Sh
Padin, D. M. to Susan E. Settle 7-19-1849 F
Pafford, Cooper to Martha Pafford 6-20-1852 Be
Pafford, David to Katharine Melton 11-28-1846 Be
Pafford, Elcany to Lucinda Mitchel 7-5-1857 Be
Pafford, Henry to Sarah Redeck 9-23-1851 Be
Pafford, James to Francis Arnold 11-16-1842 Be
Pafford, James to Penelope Vester 6-12-1843 Be
Pafford, John to Louisa Arnold 10-22-1851 Be
Pafford, John to Sarah Patience Melton 11-30-1866 Be
Pafford, Lewis to Paralee Madden 5-26-1856 Be
Pafford, Randle to Martha Jane Frazier 3-24-1867 Be
Pafford, Randoll to Martha C. Benton 10-22-1863 Be
Pafford, Robert C. to Elmina J. Cuff 9-24-1865 Be
Pafford, T. W. to Mary E. Cuff 5-13-1868 Be
Pafford, Thomas W. to Lany Hall 10-18-1849 Be
Pafford, Timothy to Manervy Riddick 9-15-1853 Be
Pafford, W. C. to Amy Parker 11-1-1840 Be
Pafford, Wm. M. to Martha J. Melton 8-31-1861 Be
Pagan, Edwin A. to Martha J. Blocker 1-18-1848 Sh
Page, Alfred to Bettie A. Myers 7-24-1871 (7-26-1871) T
Page, Asbury to Harriet Moor 10-20-1867 Hy
Page, Birch to Hannah Adkins 4-1-1874 (4-2-1874) O
Page, D. K. to Fannie Johnson 8-5-1859 (no return) Cr
Page, George to Sue (Lue) Tyus 4-4-1868 (no return) Hy
Page, Iverson W. to Sarah D. Puckett 8-12-1841 Hn
Page, James L. to Jane Henly 11-18-1866 Hn
Page, James M. to Sarah E. Neely 5-18-1860 (5-20-1860) L
Page, James R. to Frances M. Dilday 1-20-1853 Cr
Page, Jesse W, jr. to Fannie Taylor 11-12-1858 Sh
Page, Jno. F. to M. Eleanor Doyle 3-1-1860 Sh
Page, John P. to Lucinda Washbourne 11-26-1846 Hn
Page, Joseph to Betsy Henry 11-11-1866 Hn B
Page, Lawrence to Artemisia Ann Montgomery 2-1-1851 (2-6-1851) T
Page, Leander B. to Mary M. White 10-2-1851 (10-3-1851) O
Page, N. D. to J. A. Graddy 12-25-1883 L
Page, Norvell A. to Mary E. Douglas 11-26-1850 Hn
Page, Richard H. to Sarah Hutcherson 1-23-1856 G
Page, Saml. N. (Dr.) to Narcissa S. Roberts 3-7-1869 G
Page, Samuel J. to Minerva J. Underwood 5-22-1858 We
Page, William to Everline Myers 7-5-1866 T
Page, Wily E. H. to Caroline Blake 8-10-1861 (no return) Cr
Page, Wm. A. to Mary E. Isbell 12-16-1865 (12-19-1865) O
Page, Wm. C. to Elizabeth Welch 10-8-1832 (10-9-1832) G
Paget, Calvin to Phebe J. Welch 5-16-1849 Sh
Pagie, Lott to Susan Williamson 3-29-1871 F B
Pahal, Levi to Mary Jane Garner 1-2-1863 Be
Pailey, John C. to Sarah B. Shelton 3-24-1866 (3-26-1866) Ma
Pain, Isaiah to A. F. Suttles 12-16-1839 Be
Pain, Phil to Fanny Kent 8-25-1870 T
Pain, Richard to Sophia Anderson 7-1-1872 (7-4-1872) L B
Pain, Sam C. to S. S. Cloud 4-29-1861 Sh
Paine, Blueford to Jenny Hunter 12-28-1868 F B
Paine, Bob to Nealy Koonce 11-18-1869 Hy
Paine, Constantine to Susan A. Person 7-8-1856 (7-10-1856) Sh
Paine, James A. to Mary P. Poston 7-11-1856 Hr
Paine, John M. to Margaret A. Porter 11-1-1869 F B
Paine, Johnson to Flora Lockhart 1-28-1869 (1-30-1869) F B
Paine, L. to Hannah A. Neely 2-10-1859 (2-16-1859) Sh
Paine, S. L. to Frances M. Croomes 1-28-1868 (no return) Hy
Paine, Thomas N. to Marzell Welch 2-1-1843 G
Paisley, John R. to Margaret Weatherly 9-17-1857 (9-29-1857) Ma
Paisley, M. J. to Wm. A. Wilson 2-2-1854 Ma
Paliner?, Isaiah to Nancy Tranthum 5-31-1838 Hn

Palmer, Benjamin to T. Adams 9-24-1852 Hn
Palmer, Brandon to Susan Williams 1-2-1867 (no return) Hy
Palmer, D. D. to F. A. Moore 3-7-1866 G
Palmer, David E. to Ann E. Tucker 1-27-1852 (no return) F
Palmer, E. A. to Anna P. McRany? 10-22-1856 Hn
Palmer, E. B. to Tennessee B. Carrington 1-24-1861 Cr
Palmer, E. Clark to Elizabeth J. Clark 4-9-1861 (4-10-1861) Dy
Palmer, E. Washington to Mary A. Rowland 3-17-1863 Hn
Palmer, Edward H. to Margaret N. Diggs 5-4-1858 Hn
Palmer, Edwin to Helen Gribbin 1-1-1852 Sh
Palmer, Geo. to Mary E. Price 5-19-1864 Sh
Palmer, George to Salina Tyus 4-10-1869 (no return) Hy
Palmer, Green to Harriet Forbess 8-13-1851 Cr
Palmer, Harvey to Harriett Butler 1-13-1872 (1-14-1872) Cr
Palmer, Henry to Emma Jones 1-9-1873 Hy
Palmer, Henry to P. A. Sadler 3-23-1867 (3-30-1867) T
Palmer, Henry to Tilda Thompson 1-3-1868 (1-11-1868) F B
Palmer, Hesekiah L. to Lucinda Isbel 1-13-1850 Sh
Palmer, J. H. to Permelia W. Clark 11-23-1863 (no return) Cr
Palmer, J. M. to H. E. Green 2-4-1866 Hn
Palmer, J. R. to Ellen Grace 10-5-1876 (10-7-1876) Dy
Palmer, J. T. C. to Tennie Stone 11-17-1876 (12-19-1876) Dy
Palmer, J. T. to Darcas S. Swan 10-31-1839 (11-6-1839) F
Palmer, J. T. to S. T. Bird 7-30-1864 Hn
Palmer, J. W. to B. B. Crutchfield 2-11-1863 (no return) Hn
Palmer, James F. to Mary J. Allen 2-24-1866 (2-26-1866) Cr
Palmer, James F. to Nancy E. Martin 8-2-1856 Cr
Palmer, James H. to Eliza Wood 1-27-1859 Hn
Palmer, James H. to Sarah J. Hall 12-20-1841 Cr
Palmer, James I. to Mary J. Evans 1-8-1842 (1-11-1842) O
Palmer, James Madison to Lucinda Caroline Cate 4-19-1865 Hn
Palmer, James to Jane Workman 2-16-1855 (no return) We
Palmer, James to Mandy Meagin 12-12-1874 (no return) Hy
Palmer, Jas. H. to Mary Ann Eliza Moon(Moore) 11-23-1844 (12-24-1844) Hr
Palmer, Jesse W. to Martha J. Ross 11-14-1867 (11-17-1867) Cr
Palmer, Jesse to Matilda M. Parsons 4-15-1843 (4-16-1843) T
Palmer, Jessie to Mollie Jones 6-22-1871 Cr
Palmer, John H. to Martha J. Winsett 8-25-1860 (no return) Hn
Palmer, John K. to Mary Ward 10-11-1843 Hn
Palmer, John L. to Nancy E. Kirby 12-14-1850 Cr
Palmer, John M. to Ellender Bustle 12-7-1855 (no return) We
Palmer, John W. to Margory Johnson 8-12-1845 We
Palmer, John to Elizaeth C. Hubbs 2-8-1845 O
Palmer, John to Polly Deen 12-11-1843 Cr
Palmer, Joseph M. to Martha J. Faust 6-28-1865 (no return) Hn
Palmer, L. to E. J. Catron 1-28-1868 (1-29-1868) O
Palmer, Lea to Fronnie E. Crider 12-15-1853 Cr
Palmer, Levin to Lettie Shofner 12-20-1869 (1-10-1870) Cr
Palmer, Ludson to Rachel Cox 12-20-1866 Hn B
Palmer, Nash to Mittie Sherley 11-26-1874 Hy
Palmer, Nelson to Jane Byrn 3-12-1869 (3-13-1869) L
Palmer, Nelson to Moriah Byrn 1-18-1873 L
Palmer, Reubin to Ortry Sanders 12-12-1867 F B
Palmer, Robert S. to S. J. Hutcherson 12-16-1862 (no return) We
Palmer, S. D. to Emeline Medlin 11-17-1857 Cr
Palmer, Stephen to Rachel (Mrs.) Newsom 8-19-1857 Sh
Palmer, Thomas M. to Adeline Browning 1-7-1863 Mn
Palmer, Thomas M. to Elmira J. Edwards 1-23-1861 Hn
Palmer, Thomas W. to S. J. Walker 2-15-1861 We
Palmer, Tilman to Margarett J. Blair 12-20-1866 Cr
Palmer, Tom to Sarah Willams 1-7-1867 (no return) Hy
Palmer, W. A. to M. A. Belew 10-27-1868 (10-28-1868) Cr
Palmer, W. G. to Sarah A. Spoon 1-14-1870 (1-16-1870) Cr
Palmer, W. H. to Mary A. Green 11-1-1871 Cr
Palmer, W. L. to E. P. Jackson 4-21-1863 Hn
Palmer, Will H. to Matilda C. Palmer 10-30-1850 Hn
Palmer, William H. to Eliza Poe 2-5-1845 Hn
Palmer, William H. to Harriet G. Hicks 9-18-1848 Hn
Palmer, William H. to Mary A. Adams 9-15-1856 Hn
Palmer, William Henderson to Mary J. Palmer 3-3-1849 (no return) Hn
Palmer, William K. to Sarah J. Milliken 5-12-1853 Hn
Palmer, William R. to Lucy W. Jenkins 12-4-1862 We
Palmer, William R. to Martha E. Williams 5-2-1861 (no return) We
Palmer, William Russel to Elizabeth (Mrs.) Becton 3-1-1855 (3-4-1855) Sh
Palmer, William to Nancy Kendall 12-4-1845 Hn
Palmer, Wm. F. to Nancy B. Hubbard 6-9-1840 Hr
Palmer, ____ to Sarah Jane Farabough 1-31-1849 Hn
Palmere, James W. to Susanah Aiken 8-31-1868 (9-1-1868) Dy
Palmo, J. B. to Margaret McAnally 1-15-1855 (1-16-1855) Sh
Palmore, Beng. to Frances E. Little 5-16-1863 (no return) Dy
Palmore, C. C. to S. J. Christian 9-11-1876 Dy
Palmore, C. S. to Sarah (Mrs.) Trigg 3-3-1858 (3-10-1858) Sh
Palmore, J. S. to Sarah E. Isbell 6-20-1849 (6-29-1849) F
Palmore, M. M. to Nancy Ann Warren 7-25-1871 (no return) Dy
Palmore, Thomas to Jane Kelly 3-5-1851 (3-6-1851) G
Pamberger, Moses to Caroline Lune 6-5-1843 Sh
Pamper?, J. C. to Susan A. Farmer 3-14-1868 (no return) Hy

Pandry, John R. to Phoeba Beddo 9-23-1869 Ma
Panel, George P. to Sarah A. Berry 3-28-1871 O
Panesi, A. to Eliza Magehee 11-5-1856 Sh
Pankey, J. L. to Florence Richardson 5-19-1867 G
Pankey, John E. to Sarah J. Snellings 8-20-1869 (8-21-1869) F
Pankey, John to Martha Carter 10-17-1832 O
Pankey, Joseph M. to Julia Morris 12-23-1863 (12-24-1863) O
Pankey, Luther N. to Susan E. Cottrell 3-9-1864 Hn
Pankey, M. D. to Harriet Cross 2-20-1860 Hr
Pankey, Robert to Eliza J. Reece 10-14-1859 O
Pankey, William to Sarah Jones 7-11-1832 (7-12-1832) O
Pankey, Wilson N. to Louisa Cheisher 12-16-1844 (12-17-1844) Hr
Panky, James P. to Delelah Davis 11-29-1845 (11-30-1845) Hr
Panky, Robert to Eliza J. Reece 10-14-1860 O
Pannell, E. M. to Martha Stone 5-16-1860 Hr
Pannell, Elihu S. to Martha J. Garrett 8-24-1859 Hr
Parchman, J. R. to Ella C. River 1-8-1883 (1-9-1883) L
Parchman, James to Alice Sutton 2-21-1877 Hy
Parchman, Judel? (J. W.?) to Elizabeth Stedham 10-6-1838 (10-8-1838) F
Pardew, Thomas J. to Lydia T. Cassell 12-3-1866 (12-4-1866) F
Pardue, James H. to Elizabeth Tanner 3-26-1856 (3-27-1856) O
Pardue, James T. to Elizabeth J. Maloney 1-14-1856 (1-17-1856) O
Pardue, Joseph A. to Susan L. Jackson 6-6-1859 (6-10-1859) O
Pardue, Joseph J. to Elizabeth C. (Mrs.) Moore 5-6-1861 (5-7-1861) Ma
Pare, William to Rebecca Dean 12-12-1837 Hr
Paremore, Daniel W. to Mary Thomas Stafford 8-8-1871 T
Parent, Cornelius to Tennessee F. Sampson 4-28-1862 (5-1-1862) O
Parham, Alfred to Mary Jane Hill 4-11-1867 (5-12-1867) F B
Parham, Allen to Virginia A. Brooks 6-21-1858 We
Parham, Avery to H. C. Chappell 1-28-1852 We
Parham, Ben to Jenny Hendly 7-6-1868 (7-10-1868) F B
Parham, C. R. to Eliza J. Foster 12-23-1844 We
Parham, Cradock R. to Matilda J. Thomas 3-27-1849 O
Parham, E. G. to Sarah J. Bean 2-11-1862 Hr
Parham, Henry to Vicey Emmerson 1-27-1883 (2-16-1883) L
Parham, J. H. to Sutecall M. Powers 2-6-1858 (no return) We
Parham, James H. to Susan Deck 7-16-1845 We
Parham, Jesse T. to Mary Jane Adderton 1-17-1857 (1-19-1857) Ma
Parham, John L. to Lucinda A. Runkle 10-17-1832 Sh
Parham, Jos. D. to Missouri A. J. C. Wilkerson 3-26-1851 (no return) F
Parham, L. G. to Louiza Smith 5-27-1871 (6-7-1871) Cr
Parham, Nathaniel to Sarah Ward 12-11-1846 (no return) Hn
Parham, Nelson to E. Parilee Phelps 2-2-1867 Hn B
Parham, R. S. to Annie C. Williamson 2-23-1853 (no return) F
Parham, R. S. to Priscilla B. Williamson 11-25-1854 (no return) F
Parham, Rich'd H., jr. to Ora C. Trezevant 2-2-1858 (2-3-1858) Sh
Parham, Sikes to Patsy Graves 4-18-1866 (6-16-1866) F B
Parham, Thomas E. to Margaret E. Ward 12-7-1852 Hn
Parham, William E. to Margaret Drake 12-28-1844 We
Parham, Williamson H. to Sarah Kendrick 12-23-1847 F
Parham, Wm. R. to M. E. Lanier 2-20-1860 (2-22-1860) F
Parham, jr., Jno. to Anna Harwell 12-18-1860 (12-19-1860) F
Parier, James to Frances Smith 3-15-1874 Hy
Paris, Henry S. to Alsey Edwards 10-14-1858 G
Paris, W. M. to Susie Harris 11-5-1873 L
Paris, William L. to Elizabeth Chandler 4-5-1858 (4-8-1858) G
Paris, Wm. to Lucsicia Harlim 4-25-1843 Sh
Parish, A. H. to Catherine (Mrs.) Malone 2-18-1867 (no return) F
Parish, Asberry H. to Catharine Malone 2-28-1867 (3-1-1867) F
Parish, Bawdy to Margot Rodgers 1-6-1841 Cr
Parish, Benjamin F. to Elizabeth C. Alexander 10-6-1859 (no return) Hn
Parish, Charles to Frances O. L. McCullock 8-29-1831 G
Parish, Claborn to Judith Butler 2-7-1839 Cr
Parish, Claborn to Louisa McAuley 7-18-1859 Cr
Parish, David M. to Indiana Morrow 11-5-1866 (11-7-1866) L
Parish, David M. to Sarah Ann Deakins 2-12-1853 (2-16-1853) T
Parish, E. F. to S.? M. Clark 3-14-1872 Cr
Parish, Elcaner to Harriet Smelage 6-10-1844 We
Parish, Elijah to Rianna Kates 12-18-1865 Cr
Parish, G. F. to Sarah A. Miller 9-17-1872 (9-19-1872) Cr
Parish, Geo. J. to Mary J. Pate 1-27-1859 We
Parish, George to Martha Wallace 2-14-1844 Cr
Parish, J. J. to L. A. House 12-27-1866 G
Parish, J. R. to Mary Jane Herendon 3-18-1858 Hr
Parish, Joel Currin to Paulina A. Lamb 2-18-1849 (2-22-1849) T
Parish, Lewis C. to Isabella Wynn 6-5-1848 (6-11-1848) O
Parish, M. T. to Mary D. Clements 12-2-1856 G
Parish, Thornton to Mary Jamison 8-12-1870 (8-13-1870) T
Parish, Wm. to Elizabeth Burton 1-12-1854 Cr
Park(s), Comadore P. to Martha J. Maupin 12-11-1854 (12-13-1854) O
Park, C. W. M. to J. A. Armer 1-3-1861 (1-11-1861) O
Park, C. W. to S. H. Wilson 2-4-1867 O
Park, Charles to Leira Beaver 10-23-1858 Cr
Park, D. E. to A. E. Goad 4-19-1865 (5-21-1865) O
Park, Dugan to Martha Jane Yopp 10-26-1858 (11-3-1858) Hr
Park, Eli to Darcus Cholwell 2-26-1840 (3-10-1840) Hr
Park, George W. to Elizabeth J. Bowland 11-3-1860 (11-4-1860) Cr

Park, H. O. to Susan F. Duncan 3-30-1861 (4-5-1861) Cr
Park, J. B. to Harriet B. Bone 11-22-1846 Sh
Park, J. C. to Elizabeth Self 2-1-1847 Be
Park, Jacob to Cassanda Moody 1-3-1866 (no return) F B
Park, James A. to Aneliza T. Jones 10-12-1858 (10-__-1858) O
Park, James A. to M. F. Crawford 1-3-1856 Hr
Park, James P. to Amada Horton 3-1-1861 (no return) Cr
Park, James P. to Amanda Eason 2-8-1851 Cr
Park, James to Millie Warrell 2-12-1860 Cr
Park, John C. to Nancy Brasfield 8-26-1869 G
Park, John H. to Flenda Finch 2-9-1861 (2-10-1861) Cr
Park, John M. to Mary Rankin 12-16-1848 (12-21-1848) Hr
Park, John N. to Elizabeth Park 11-21-1851 Cr
Park, John to Adline Shelley 1-16-1855 Cr
Park, John to C. Martina Gallagher 7-7-1852 Sh
Park, Joseph L. to Sarah J. Coleman 12-7-1863 Hn
Park, Levi to Jane E. Devenport 12-7-1846 (12-8-1846) Hr
Park, Pearson M. to Elizabeth Teater 10-17-1857 (10-20-1857) O
Park, Robert to Amanda M. H. Caldwell 12-8-1857 O
Park, Robert to Margaret Jane Hogan 10-6-1841 (10-7-1841) Hr
Park, Robert to Rhoda Abraham 3-13-1843 (4-2-1843) Hr
Park, Samuel to Mary Ann Pitman 1-29-1848 (1-31-1848) Hr
Park, Samuel to Mary Long 1-29-1834 Hr
Park, Smith to Juliza F. A. Miller 10-26-1841 G
Park, Squire F. to Mary M. Craig 10-15-1854 (10-23-1855) O
Park, Syrus to Elizabeth Caldwell 11-16-1838 Hr
Park, T. H. to E. T. Douglas 9-10-1867 O
Park, T.C. to Mary A. Campbell 3-24-1849 (4-5-1849) Hr
Park, Thomas C. to Carrie Scott 12-5-1857 (12-8-1857) Hr
Park, W. B. to Martha M. Cliff 10-25-1878 (10-27-1878) Dy
Park, William to Rebecca Cocke 10-18-1838 Sh
Park, Wm. A. to Mary A. Boswell 10-10-1852 Cr
Parke, James to Nancy Shelley 2-27-1840 Cr
Parke, Richard to Mary Jane McGrew 12-1-1856 (12-2-1856) Sh
Parke, Wm. to Sarah E. Dowdy 2-13-1851 (no return) F
Parker, A. J. to M. E. Condrey 12-22-1879 (12-24-1879) L
Parker, A. P. to M. F. Howard 5-30-1871 (5-31-1871) T
Parker, Abraham to Martha Ann Bearden 1-27-1840 Sh
Parker, Albert to Mary Layne 3-10-1881 L B
Parker, Albert to Mattie Halliburton 12-28-1874 (12-31-1874) L B
Parker, Albert to Mattie Helum 12-24-1875 (no return) Hy
Parker, Albert to Virginia Ann Young 11-12-1870 (11-22-1870) L
Parker, Aleck to Mary Witt 6-7-1877 L
Parker, Alexander to Ellen Macey 3-18-1857 Sh
Parker, Anderson to Elizabeth Stone 6-13-1838 Cr
Parker, Andrew to Mary Jane Ford 9-4-1868 (no return) L
Parker, Anthony to Godey A. Alston 1-25-1868 L B
Parker, Asa to Lodoriska Hays 2-14-1834 (2-15-1834) Hr
Parker, Benjamin to Emaline Standley 6-7-1851 (6-8-1851) O
Parker, Benjamin to Emeline Webb 9-8-1870 (9-11-1870) L
Parker, Benjamin to Jemima Peterson 7-13-1842 Sh
Parker, Benjamin to Tempie Isam 1-6-1827 (1-7-1827) Hr
Parker, Carroll S. to Elizabeth A. L. McWhirter 3-2-1843 G
Parker, Claibon to Joanna Taylor 11-26-1873 Hy
Parker, Clayburn to Emma Taylor 12-5-1868 (no return) Hy
Parker, D. C. to Mary Jane Webb 11-27-1860 (11-28-1860) Hr
Parker, Dan to Lou Beaumont 2-19-1869 (no return) Dy
Parker, Daniel E. to Robin T. Hart 11-12-1856 Cr
Parker, David H. to Mariah T. D. Reeves 5-24-1853 Ma
Parker, Dempsey to L. Baley 12-16-1839 Ma
Parker, Dennis to Fanny Harris 12-28-1868 (no return) Dy
Parker, E. C. to Mary King 3-12-1856 Sh
Parker, E. W. to Luizer Haynes 10-7-1865 G
Parker, Edmund to Mary Holt 2-17-1880 L
Parker, Ellis to Caldonia Dunivant 12-27-1870 (12-28-1870) L
Parker, Ewell to Molly Easly 7-21-1873 Hy
Parker, F. A. to Jullia (Mrs.) Smith 5-13-1869 (5-16-1869) F
Parker, Felix to Mary O. Gibson 6-22-1826 G
Parker, Francis M. to Martha Brown 8-22-1862 We
Parker, Francis to Mary N. Ornell 4-5-1860 We
Parker, Frank to Caroline Green 12-1-1877? Hy
Parker, Frnaklin J. to Eliza Dis? 6-17-1871 (6-18-1871) Ma
Parker, Frunler to Nancy Ann Semons 10-14-1848 (10-15-1848) G
Parker, G. W. to Mary A. Robison 1-13-1868 (1-14-1868) Cr
Parker, Gamaliel to Rebecca Boyd 1-28-1829 (1-29-1829) Hr
Parker, Garnet to Frances Williams 10-4-1854 Sh
Parker, Geo. L. to Cornelia L. Lundy 12-8-1855 Sh
Parker, George W. to Lew Jurance 3-16-1844 Hn
Parker, George to Ann Clark 3-2-1860 Sh
Parker, George to Betetie Clay 6-5-1875 L B
Parker, George to Fanny Gallagher 5-4-1853 (5-9-1853) Sh
Parker, Giles to Elizabeth Isam 10-29-1828 Hr
Parker, Green W. to Catharine Meadows 11-17-1852 O
Parker, Green W. to Elizabeth A. Allison 5-5-1845 O
Parker, H. L. to Nelly Scott 1-14-1874 (no return) Hy
Parker, Hanks to Nicie Blaydes 2-4-1871 (no return) F B
Parker, Henry F. to Margaret Jane McKnight 9-10-1859 (9-11-1859) Ma

Parker, Henry to Matilda McCalop 12-20-1843 G
Parker, Hiram to Belle Emma Yancey 12-18-1868 F B
Parker, Hosia to Elizabeth Strong 9-7-1847 G
Parker, Irwin to Catharine Howell 2-8-1847 G
Parker, Isaac D. to Sarah L. Huntsman 12-27-1845 (12-28-1845) Ma
Parker, Isaac L. to Mary M. Soward 9-8-1860 (9-10-1860) L
Parker, Isaac S. to H. A. Warner 10-29-1850 Sh
Parker, Isaac to Annie Isum 10-25-1827 (11-18-1827) Hr
Parker, Isaac to Susan Moore 12-15-1831 G
Parker, Isham I. to Mary Ann Ford 12-6-1849 G
Parker, Isham to Ann Goodman 6-19-1868 G
Parker, Isreal to Alice Keller 12-24-1875 (not executed) L
Parker, J. A. J. to Jane Clary 10-7-1858 Hr
Parker, J. D. to Nancy A. Richard 11-30-1876 Dy
Parker, J. G. to Ann F. Etheridge 9-29-1858 We
Parker, J. H. to M. J. C. White 12-20-1862 (12-21-1862) Sh
Parker, J. J. to M. Barker 12-2-1857 G
Parker, J. R. to Mary E. Brooks 5-13-1863 (no return) We
Parker, J. W. to Mary Ann Goss 12-5-1850 O
Parker, Jack to Mary Ferguson 1-10-1880 (1-18-1880) Dy
Parker, Jacob to Elizabeth H. Glover 9-22-1850 Ma
Parker, James A. to E. C. Johnson 4-25-1872 Dy
Parker, James C. to Delila Ann Daniel 9-24-1855 (10-1-1855) Sh
Parker, James F. to Fanney V. Arnn 2-2-1865 Hn
Parker, James H. to Evaline G. Myrick 1-7-1847 Hn
Parker, James P. to Eliza F. Green 1-4-1868 (1-5-1868) T
Parker, James R. to Mary An Petty (Perry?) 12-18-1848 F
Parker, James to Charity Walker 11-19-1873 Hy
Parker, James to Ema Ridley 3-9-1876 L B
Parker, James to Judia Bell 1-10-1867 Hy
Parker, James to M. Charles 7-23-1849 Hn
Parker, James to Marth J. Carr 3-31-1843 T
Parker, James to Rebecca Barton 2-11-1851 Hn
Parker, Jesse R. to Emmaline Bibb 4-6-1843 Hn
Parker, Jesse to Elizabeth Gregory 1-30-1841 Hr
Parker, Jessee to Elizabeth Brewer 2-22-1855 Be
Parker, Jessee to Elizabeth Clark 8-27-1856 We
Parker, Joel to Ann L.(T?) Moore 3-18-1835 Hr
Parker, John A. to Sarah Angelina Smith 8-18-1847 (8-19-1847) L
Parker, John F. to Ann Kemes 3-28-1856 We
Parker, John F. to Martha A. Smith 4-4-1860 (no return) We
Parker, John G. to Anne Ray 7-25-1850 Hr
Parker, John H. to Jennie McDaniel 12-6-1877 Hy
Parker, John H. to L. A. Crafton 3-13-1865 G
Parker, John H. to Lue E. Hood 10-8-1868 Hy
Parker, John H. to Mahala Phelan 1-22-1855 G
Parker, John H. to Margaret Craton? 5-28-1833 (6-9?-1833) Hr
Parker, John L. to Fanny Pamphlett 5-6-1853 G
Parker, John L. to Sophia Green 9-10-1833 Hr
Parker, John M. to Mary E. Albright 12-22-1846 Sh
Parker, John R. to Mary McCartry 10-11-1841 (no return) F
Parker, John T. to Martha Ray 10-29-1856 (10-30-1856) Hr
Parker, John to E. Burkett 7-29-1872 (7-31-1872) Dy
Parker, Joseph R. to Rebecca T. Thomas 2-13-1860 F
Parker, Joseph to Nancy Nobles 2-24-1831 G
Parker, K. H. to A. B. McKinnon 11-15-1877 Hy
Parker, L. P. to Catharine Landrum 7-15-1850 O
Parker, Lemel J. W. to Rebeca H. Dupew 11-21-1840 (11-25-1840) F
Parker, Light N. to Mary Ann Pinon 1-31-1856 O
Parker, Light to Lurana Roland 8-17-1849 (8-22-1849) O
Parker, M. S. to Mary Ann Wheatley 5-22-1863 Be
Parker, Madison to Frances C. Cross 12-27-1847 (12-30-1847) F
Parker, Manuel to Susan Vinson 12-25-1869 (no return) Cr
Parker, Marian F. to Vanleer S. Walker 1-11-1854 (1-12-1854) G
Parker, Marion to Melinda Hutchison 3-31-1842 (4-1-1842) L
Parker, Mat to Emma Tapscott 1-12-1872 (no return) Hy
Parker, Matthew to Ellen Tanner 3-31-1861 Sh
Parker, Nathan to Huldy Durley 7-18-1833 G
Parker, Nathan to Rodena Clark 3-6-1863 Mn
Parker, Neid? to Hannah Jones 7-29-1876 Dy B
Parker, Norah to Beccy Halliburton 4-4-1877 (4-5-1877) L
Parker, O. B. to Martha Williams 10-5-1840 (10-6-1840) F
Parker, P. F. to Mollie M. Mason 10-17-1864 (10-18-1864) F
Parker, Payton L. to Eliza Jacobs 8-12-1840 (8-13-1840) Hr
Parker, Payton to Emily Stephenson 6-17-1844 Hr
Parker, Pleasant to Fannie Byars 12-21-1876 Hy
Parker, Priesley E. to Joanna F. Murphy 12-7-1853 Cr
Parker, R. A. jr. to Sarah Jane Flowers 5-24-1858 (5-25-1858) T
Parker, R. B. to Mary J. Richards 12-27-1871 (12-28-1871) Dy
Parker, R. C. to E. Cottingham 12-12-1847 Be
Parker, R. M. to M. E. Campbell 12-22-1879 (12-23-1879) L
Parker, Richard to Hannah Rice 8-12-1882 L
Parker, Robert S. to Anna Crockett 11-5-1842 (11-6-1842) O
Parker, Robert to Tennessee Smith 12-17-1879 (no return) Dy
Parker, Samuel to Sally Payne 4-12-1838 Sh
Parker, Solomon to Jane Harris 8-16-1868 Hy
Parker, Sylvester G. to Louisa F. Jones 9-10-1851 (9-11-1851) Hr
Parker, T. R. to Elizabeth Davis 7-2-1846 Cr
Parker, Thomas B. to Mary Ann Northern 10-17-1856 O
Parker, Thomas H. to Catharine P. Elliott 4-2-1846 G
Parker, Thomas W. to Elizabeth Tuck 10-21-1858 We
Parker, Thomas to Mary J. Cotton 7-28-1853 Be
Parker, Thomas to Pamillia Ann Rook 8-12-1846 (8-16-1846) Hr
Parker, Thompson A. to Maniva A. Crause 11-28-1848 (11-30-1848) Ma
Parker, Thos. to Harriet Daniel 8-1-1868 (8-3-1868) T
Parker, Tom to Sarah Johnson 4-17-1869 (no return) Dy
Parker, Turner to Polly Johnson 9-27-1842 Cr
Parker, W. E. to Almeta Farris 11-2-1875 (no return) Hy
Parker, W. E. to Mattie Chapman 5-7-1867 F
Parker, W. J. to Buelah B. Henry 3-23-1885 L
Parker, W. M. to Harriett Payne 1-4-1838 Sh
Parker, Wesley to S. E. Perry 3-8-1862 G
Parker, Wiliston to Jemima Wynn 9-3-1847 O
Parker, Will to Mary Thomas 5-7-1836 Hr
Parker, William H. to Juliam Boone 1-5-1840 (1-7-1840) Ma
Parker, William J. to Barbra Billings 1-27-1850 Hn
Parker, William to Frances M. Courts 3-12-1839 (no return) Hn
Parker, William to Sally Nerren 3-26-1829 Ma
Parker, William to Winnie L. Falanigan? 6-22-1871 T
Parker, Wm. C. to Mary E. Scott 6-14-1861 Hr
Parker, Wm. M. to Sarah Maynard 2-25-1866 G
Parker, Wm. to Elizabeth Goodin 7-22-1846 Sh
Parker, Wm. to Nancy Butler 12-15-1842 Cr
Parker, Wm. to Nancy Pafford 11-10-1842 Be
Parkerson, W. D. to Catherine Louther 5-8-1849 Hn
Parkes, William H. to Sarah Wrightsell 11-9-1841 (11-11-1841) F
Parkin, Washington to Harriet Boet 9-15-1842 (9-16-1842) Ma
Parkinson, G. M. to Corsicana? Swift 12-8-1863 (no return) Cr
Parkison, R. H. to Nancy Smith 1-20-1858 Be
Parkman, B. W. to Sue Smith 7-9-1874 O
Parkman, D. A. to S. E. Gallop 2-12-1863 O
Parks, A. G. to Sarah H. Peplow 5-29-1858 Sh
Parks, Andrew S. to M. E. Harris 7-8-1868 (no return) Dy
Parks, Andrew to F. R. Stinnett 4-13-1875 (4-15-1875) Dy
Parks, B. R. to S. A. Douglass 12-24-1872 (12-25-1872) Dy
Parks, Benjamin R. to Millie A. Young 4-17-1880 (4-26-1880) L
Parks, Chas. to Dilsa Rawlings 9-13-1867 (no return) F B
Parks, Chas. to Elvira Whitson 12-26-1867 G B
Parks, Eli to Clarinda Callahan 5-11-1859 (5-15-1859) Hr
Parks, Ephraim to A. A. Leming 5-15-1861 Hr
Parks, Estorn to Ellen Burrow 1-21-1867 G
Parks, Geo. W. to Mary Tubbs 6-8-1854 Be
Parks, Green to Ellen Wardlaw 10-4-1871? (no return) L B
Parks, Green to Martha Brown 11-26-1873 (11-27-1873) Dy
Parks, Henry to Adaline Fullerton 6-24-1852 Be
Parks, James to Anne A. Kiser 1-2-1845 Hr
Parks, James to Emily Worrell 10-12-1859 Cr
Parks, James to Malinda J. Harrold 7-29-1867 (no return) Dy
Parks, Jesse to Canda Jones 5-17-1867 (5-18-1867) Dy
Parks, John B. to Sarah A. Foster 2-2-1856 (2-5-1856) Hr
Parks, John F. to E. V. Saunders 12-27-1859 G
Parks, John T. to Margaret ann Swor 5-25-1863 Hn
Parks, John to Catherine Lyle 1-13-1847 Sh
Parks, John to Mary C. Kennedy 8-30-1854 Sh
Parks, John to Neoma N. Windows 1-14-1841 Sh
Parks, Joseph B. to Elisabeth M. Trowbridge 5-22-1852 (5-23-1852) Sh
Parks, Lewis to Esther Bone 7-20-1867 G B
Parks, Moses to Mary A. Culp 12-2-1850 (12-3-1850) F
Parks, Oliver to Judy Steger 1-29-1870 (2-22-1870) F B
Parks, R. N. to Mattie M. Stewart 2-13-1860 (2-16-1860) F
Parks, Richard to Amy Henry 10-28-1867 Ma B
Parks, Richard to Milly Jones 2-1-1867 (2-2-1867) Dy
Parks, Robert N. to Mary Ann Stewart 1-31-1842 (2-2-1842) Hr
Parks, Robert Thomas to Mary Elizabeth Grissom 6-17-1860 G
Parks, Robert to Elvira Dowdy 12-29-1868 (12-31-1868) F B
Parks, Sam to Martha Jones 6-8-1867 (6-9-1867) Dy
Parks, Sam to Mary Parks 11-20-1877 (11-23-1877) Dy
Parks, Smith to Ruth Starrert 5-1-1866 O
Parks, Thomas to Elizabeth Grissom 6-27-1860 G
Parks, Toney to Martha Griffin 12-17-1879 (12-18-1879) Dy
Parks, William r. to Emily Permelia Coleman 8-7-1863 Hn
Parks, William to Susan Carlton 1-17-1860 We
Parks, Wm. P. to Lavinia Jeffries 3-31-1858 O
Parks, jr. 2nd, H. to M. E. Menzies 10-27-1873 (10-28-1873) Dy
Parks, jr., Hamilton to Manie G. Webb 10-5-1878 (10-7-1878) Dy
Parlow, Isaac to Nancy J. Day 2-8-1868 (2-13-1868) Ma
Parlow, Nathan to Arlesia Yarbrough 8-15-1870 (8-18-1870) Ma
Parmenter, J. H. to Belle Matheney 2-19-1876 (2-20-1876) Dy
Parmer, Francis to Mariah Herron 1-16-1844 Ma
Parmer, J. C. to Sarah Ann Grove 9-29-1847 Hr
Parmer, John to Elizabeth May 1-7-1841 Ma
Parmer, Munroe to Becky Suton 2-18-1867 Hy
Parmour, John to Minerva Downs 11-26-1836 (11-27-1836) Hr
Parn (Parm-Parir), Thomas P. to Martha Sevier 10-15-1850 We

Grooms

Parnel, Jeremiah to Mary Davis 12-23-1873 O
Parnell, H. R. to M. E. Wray 12-19-1868 (12-20-1868) Cr
Parnell, H. R. to S. E. Boyd 9-20-1858 Cr
Parnell, J. B. to Sarah Davis 11-13-1867 (11-14-1867) Dy
Parnell, J. H. to S. A. Foggerson 9-8-1860 (9-11-1860) Dy
Parnell, James C. to Rebecca Wright 4-12-1873 (4-13-1873) Dy
Parnell, James to Martha Jones 9-29-1869 (9-30-1869) Cr
Parnell, John A. to Martha Dodson 12-26-1877 Cr
Parnell, Osaah to Martha M. Brechum 3-6-1855 Cr
Parnell, R. E. to Amelia C. Jones 10-28-1868 (no return) Dy
Parnell, S. D. to G. W. James 12-19-1870 (12-21-1870) Cr
Parnell, T. F. to R. L. Hamilton 11-30-1869 (12-3-1869) Dy
Parnell, Wiley B. to L. J. Jones 4-19-1873 (4-20-1873) Dy
Parnell, Wiley M. to Harriet J. Jones 10-24-1860 Cr
Parnell, Wm. to Mary Crudup 1-7-1867 (1-10-1867) Dy
Parr, Allen to Martha Jones 12-8-1840 G
Parr, Andrew to Dicy Jones 1-27-1869 (1-28-1869) L
Parr, Ben to Luella Fowlkes 3-22-1877 Dy
Parr, Cary to Sarah W. Smith 10-4-1838 Sh
Parr, Columbus R. to Alice Bugg 8-22-1866 Dy
Parr, Edmond to Eliza Young 12-23-1867 (12-26-1868?) L B
Parr, Gantry to Fannie Foster 10-16-1879 Dy
Parr, Henry to Nancy Stephens 4-4-1877 (4-3?-1877) L B
Parr, J. W. to Mariah P. Pendleton 4-1-1865 (4-2-1865) L
Parr, James W. to Caledonia T. Burk 4-4-1853 (4-9-1853) L
Parr, James to Anna Bostick 10-13-1881 (10-16-1881) L B
Parr, James to Rena Caroline Davis 11-4-1833 (11-5-1833) Hr
Parr, Joel to Isabella Porter 9-8-1840 Sh
Parr, Julian to Josephine Soward 12-23-1875 Dy
Parr, Lewis to Jane Embry 8-14-1880 (no return) L
Parr, Lewis to Lizzie Gray 5-18-1884 L
Parr, N. J. H. to Eliza Wright 1-25-1865 G
Parr, Noah to Rosannah McKnight 12-27-1880 (12-30-1880) Dy
Parr, Richard to Pennie Sumerow 12-23-1871 (12-26-1871) L B
Parr, Stanton to Susan Pharr 12-19-1868 (no return) L B
Parr, Thomas J. to Isabella W. Edmonds 5-3-1858 (5-4-1858) O
Parr, Woodson to Jane Pewett 12-23-1867 (no return) L B
Parran, Thomas A. to Maria C. Wood 11-2-1848 Hr
Parran, Thomas D. to Ann Carr 2-29-1828 Sh
Parratt, Charles A. to Amanda M. Willsen 12-12-1858 We
Parratt, Geo. W. to Emily F. Boswell 10-6-1848 (10-12-1848) F
Parret, James H. to Martha Jane Gibson 10-21-1854 We
Parriatt, Lewis G. to Susan E. Willson 10-5-1861 (no return) We
Parris, A. E. to Anna L. Walker 7-2-1863 (7-3-1863) O
Parris, Charley to Mattie Smith 10-24-1885 (10-25-1885) L
Parris, Henry to Elizabeth Johnson 9-15-1849 (9-27-1849) Hr
Parris, Nuggy to Alsey Haselette 12-23-1867 (no return) F B
Parrish, George to Elizabeth Wallace 11-3-1863 Cr
Parrish, Green to Julianna Lock 11-30-1825 Hr
Parrish, Henderson to Elizabeth Waggener 12-3-1857 We
Parrish, Henry to Sarah Ann Marshall 8-2-1847 F
Parrish, Isaac to Parthena Lucas 3-9-1876 (no return) Hy
Parrish, J. J. P.(B.?) to R. F. Coleman 1-11-1870 G
Parrish, James B. to Margaret J. Hassell 8-20-1868 (no return) Dy
Parrish, James H. D. to Rebecca Payne 8-3-1860 We
Parrish, James M. to Matilda Henderson 4-25-1845 We
Parrish, James N. to Lucy V. Lanier 12-9-1868 (12-16-1868) Ma
Parrish, John A. S. to Mildred M. Childress 2-8-1841 (2-11-1841) Ma
Parrish, John Y. to S. A. Shanklin 12-23-1861 (no return) We
Parrish, John to Arminta Umstead 8-7-1845 Cr
Parrish, John to Ednay Jackson 7-14-1856 (no return) We
Parrish, Joseph to Eliza Goins 10-24-1872 O
Parrish, Lawson to Mary Harrison 5-20-1873 (5-25-1873) Dy
Parrish, M. R. to Mary A. Cook 12-10-1856 Sh
Parrish, Mark to Elizabeth Brinkly 6-27-1866 (no return) Cr
Parrish, S. G. to Mary M. Brann 5-23-1858 We
Parrish, Samuel to Mary Umstead 9-5-1848 Cr
Parrish, Syron? to Eliza J. Montgomery 12-10-1866 (12-13-1866) Cr
Parrish, Thomas H. to Martha L. Manley 8-3-1847 (8-8-1847) F
Parrish, V. C. to L. M. Shanklin 7-16-1857 We
Parrot, Ethan H. to Mary H. Grant 12-3-1855 (12-24-1855) Ma
Parrot, John H. to Sibbey Ellis 8-15-1850 (8-18-1850) T
Parrot, Norflet F. to Ellen Copeland 5-12-1856 Ma
Parrot, Washington to Mary Spurlock 12-17-1846 Ma
Parrot, William H. to Louisa Duncan 12-22-1841 (12-23-1841) Ma
Parrot, Wm. to Elizabeth Knight 6-27-1858 T
Parrott, Albert G. to Mary Matilda Rainer 10-4-1849 (10-18-1849) Hr
Parrott, Irwin to Lucinda Waller 3-4-1846 (3-5-1846) F
Parrott, J. to Margaret E. (Mrs.) Waller 12-11-1854 (no return) F
Parry, James to Angeline Caldwell 12-15-1874 Hy
Parsley, M. H. to L. A. Mathis 2-3-1872 (no return) L
Parsons, G. W. to Adelia Joiner 10-18-1853 Sh
Parsons, George to Gennetta Birthwright 2-13-1861 (2-14-1861) O
Parsons, Henry to Julia Phelps 10-10-1857 Cr
Parsons, J. B. to Mary Smith 6-9-1866 (6-10-1866) T
Parsons, J. P. to Cornelia Jones 9-15-1878 Hy
Parsons, J.B. to Margaret Scales 3-13-1872 T
Parsons, Jas. L. to Bridget Haden 6-17-1854 Sh
Parsons, John B. to Mary Martin Lyles 9-30-1853 (10-2-1853) T
Parsons, Joseph to Mary Jane Fox 1-3-1869 G
Parsons, Lawson to Mary Adams 8-9-1865 Mn
Parsons, Plesant K. to Elizabeth Jane Bibbs 10-29-1845 Cr
Parsons, Shad to Elizabeth Prichard 8-27-1845 Cr
Parsons, Thomas to Laura Ann Edwards 8-16-1850 (8-20-1850) T
Parsons, Thos. to Lowina A. Parsons 2-15-1857 Cr
Parsons, Vinson to Mary A. Woods 7-10-1855 Cr
Parsons, Wesley to Luizer Fox 1-1-1867 G
Partee, B. F. to S. J. Palmer 5-1-1872 L
Partee, B. L. to M. C. Wade 12-21-1853 G
Partee, Church to Lucretia Byrn 2-24-1877 L
Partee, Henry to Dora Mann 3-2-1870 (no return) Hy
Partee, Hiram to Lilly Mays 10-24-1854 (10-25-1854) G
Partee, Jesse D. to Ann E. Higgins 8-15-1835 (8-16-1835) G
Partee, Joseph H. to Eliza Ann Harber 11-20-1869 (11-21-1869) L
Partee, Madison to Vina Byrn 12-8-1860 L B
Partee, Natan to Callie Patterson 12-23-1882 (12-26-1882) L
Partee, Richard A. to Hannah Bradshaw 11-4-1883 L
Partee, Robert to Nancy Clay 12-30-1865 (no return) Hy
Partee, Robert to Nancy Clay 2-10-1866 Hy
Partee, Shavers to Catherine McKenzie 5-5-1870 G B
Partee, Tobe to Caroline Gray 1-5-1870 (no return) L
Partee, William A. to Susan Conner 12-18-1856 L
Partee, William to Amelia Byrns 11-27-1869 (11-29-1869) L B
Partee, Wm. to Kattie Haynes 10-12-1869 Hy
Partete, Richd. T. to Manerva F. Rollins 9-24-1861 (9-29-1861) Cr
Partiel, William H. to Nancy Biggs 6-29-1852 (6-30-1852) G
Partin, Lodwick to Lucy Ann Johnson 6-10-1856 (6-11-1856) Sh
Partin, Lodwick to M. S. Warburton 6-9-1855 Sh
Partlow, William D. to Adelener H. Bowling 9-4-1831 (9-29-1831) Hr
Parton, Thomas H. to Malissa A. Seay 7-7-1867 Hn
Parton, William to Jane Douglass 1-25-1842 (1-27-1842) O
Partridge, Edward to Martha (Mrs.) Ezell 7-19-1866 G
Pary, Malone to Lucy J. Bridges 8-31-1866 (9-2-1866) Cr
Pascal, Ridman to Fannie Wily 5-6-1872 O
Paschal, Aquila to Margaret Paschal 4-20-1842 Hn
Paschal, Cleopas to Virginia E. Malone 10-18-1867 (no return) Hn
Paschal, Elisha M. to Elizabeth M. Moore 9-10-1862 We
Paschal, G. W. to Frances A. Bullock 8-10-1854 We
Paschal, George W. to Jerusha Wilson 10-1-1839 (no return) Hn
Paschal, Green H. to Nancy J. Barton 10-13-1867 Hn
Paschal, Henry A. to Wealthy Worthington 3-9-1839 Hn
Paschal, J. D. to Esther Murphy 6-12-1871 (1-12-1871?) O
Paschal, James T. to Elizabeth P. Wilson 8-10-1866 G
Paschal, James to Phebe Hunt 5-20-1862 (no return) Hn
Paschal, John to Susan R. Dickson 8-17-1865 Mn
Paschal, R. A. to Nacy (Nancy?) Adkins 11-15-1838 F
Paschal, Velarious J. to Margret A. Addison 12-10-1869 (12-12-1869) L
Paschal, William to Sarah Ridgeway 10-10-1839 Hn
Paschal, ____ to Jane Paschal 10-22-1845 Hn
Paschall, Alfred to Mary Nance 4-?-1845 Hn
Paschall, Calvin to Nancy Nichols 9-18-1858 Hn
Paschall, David to Frances Wilson 8-23-1846 Hn
Paschall, E. P. to E. W. Brisendine 12-29-1864 Hn
Paschall, E. to Martha Wilson 3-13-1867 Hn
Paschall, Elisha to Elizabeth E. Martin 9-28-1854 Hn
Paschall, Elisha to Louisa Taylor 9-22-1856 Hn
Paschall, James A. to Rebecca E. Nichols 10-15-1867 (no return) Hn
Paschall, James to Senie F. Rogers 11-16-1859 We
Paschall, John D. to Malinda J. Nance 10-9-1859 Hn
Paschall, John F. to Clementine Reynolds 12-8-1852 Hn
Paschall, L. D. L. to Olive E. Stevens 1-21-1866 (no return) Hn
Paschall, Samuel to Elvina Martin 8-17-1851 Hn
Paschall, Samuel to Nancy W. Spann 11-14-1839 Hn
Paschall, Stephen to Rebecca Spence 6-19-1838 Hn
Paschall, W. H. to Luiza Humphreys 11-8-1866 Hn
Paschall, William Geo. W. to Mary Ann Johnson 1-25-1849 Hn
Paschel, Eli to Margaret Thompson 2-3-1831 Sh
Paschell, P. P. to Ruth Wood 8-16-1855 We
Paschell, W. B. to Mary A. Alexander 2-11-1856 We
Paskel, Andrew to Agnes Cardwell 12-28-1872 (no return) Hy
Paskell, B. F. to Lucy J. West 3-12-1863 Hn
Pasmose, William to Fanny Kendrick 1-10-1843 (1-12-1843) Ma
Pass, Fanteleroy to Susan Rice 2-25-1845 Sh
Pass, Washington G. to Caroline M. Couch 9-17-1843 Sh
Passmore, James H. to Lucy E. Massey 1-2-1855 Ma
Passmore, Moody to Ann Eliza Searcy 11-2-1854 Ma
Pate, A. F. to M. J. Hudspeth 8-24-1856 We
Pate, B. to Mary C. Philips 10-6-1862 (no return) Hy
Pate, Benajah to Polly Long 10-22-1829 O
Pate, F. H. to Emma G. Fletcher 5-15-1869 (5-17-1869) Cr
Pate, G. W. to Sallie Adams 1-12-1876 Dy
Pate, Geo. to Mary C. Philips 10-6-1862 (no return) Hy
Pate, Geo. W. to Gyaura? Saunders 10-28-1874 T
Pate, George B. to Bridget Street 8-24-1845 L

Pate, George to Sally Delph 10-3-1864 (no return) Dy
Pate, J. B. to Julia A. Coleman 10-7-1872 (10-8-1872) O
Pate, J. D. to S. V. Turner 10-8-1867 (10-10-1867) Cr
Pate, J. K. to S. V. Pate 2-27-1873 (3-2-1873) Cr
Pate, J. M. to Mollie Cauthorn 9-29-1875 (9-30-1875) Dy
Pate, J. M. to Nancy Ridgeway 2-27-1870 G
Pate, Jacob M. to Julia A. Bryant 2-19-1856 (2-20-1856) G
Pate, James A. to Sarah R. Franklin 11-14-1868 (11-15-1868) L
Pate, James M. to Martha Jane Gantlett 3-10-1857 (3-11-1857) O
Pate, James to Unia Avery 2-13-1843 G
Pate, John C. to M.E. Hurley 8-3-1872 (no return) Dy
Pate, John R. to Clarissa Glisson 9-19-1850 (9-22-1850) G
Pate, Joseph to Nancy Glasscock 6-22-1836 G
Pate, M. D. L. to H. C. Snell 7-21-1874 (7-22-1874) Dy
Pate, M. D. to Elizabeth M. Shelton 12-16-1869 Dy
Pate, M. D. to Mary Cosby 1-10-1867 G
Pate, P. M. to Manerva C. Mahar 1-7-1856 Sh
Pate, R. S. to E. J. Clark 9-7-1856 We
Pate, Richard L. to Altaquory Thomas 3-10-1840 Cr
Pate, S. S. to Elizabeth Huff 10-24-1854 We
Pate, Samuel to Hannah Gee 8-25-1870 (8-28-1870) O
Pate, T. J. to A. A. Glascock 8-6-1863 G
Pate, T. M. to M. E. Curtis 1-2-1878 Dy
Pate, T. W. to E. B. Pate 8-2-1876 O
Pate, Thomas G. to Mary Butler 8-3-1831 Ma
Pate, Thomas N. to Mary (Mrs.) Shikle 12-5-1870 O
Pate, W. F. to An Keathley 4-25-1870 G
Pate, W. H. to Sallie Crockett 4-12-1871 Dy
Pate, W. N. to Mary F. Selvidge 10-9-1867 G
Pate, William H. to Mary Ann Jones 5-26-1857 O
Pate, William to Barbay Boyte 10-8-1834 Hr
Pate, William to Jinnetta Irvin 6-23-1836 Hr
Paterson, G. F. to Sallie Boden 6-4-1865 Hn
Patiller, Hartwell to Arabella Presley 1-27-1868 Ma
Patillo, J. E. to Martha E. C. Simons 9-11-1850 (9-11-1850) F
Patison, Henry to Lavina Oneal 2-24-1838 (3-1-1838) G
Paton, James W. to Nancy Estes 2-10-1867 Hy
Patric, J. J. to Mary Dial 12-28-1864 Hn
Patric, W. M. to M. J. Wylie 7-30-1861 G
Patrick, Andrew J. to Susan B. Harpool 11-2-1846 Ma
Patrick, Andrew to Frances H. Weaver 12-29-1862 (12-30-1862) Ma
Patrick, Andrew to Susannah B. Harpole 12-7-1846 G
Patrick, B. to Annie E. Eastland 8-23-1864 Sh
Patrick, Benjamin to Anna C. Ledbetter 9-5-1847 Sh
Patrick, David to D. J. Evans 12-24-1867 G
Patrick, G. W. to Sarah F. Davis 12-14-1867 (12-23-1867) Dy
Patrick, Geo. C. to Susan C. Templeton 7-29-1856 (7-31-1856) Sh
Patrick, George W. to Irabella C. Cherry 3-19-1849 Ma
Patrick, Jack to Maggie Clemms 11-24-1880 (11-25-1880) L
Patrick, Jessee A. to Nancy J. Pounds 1-8-1852 G
Patrick, John H. to Elizabeth F. Houston 1-1-1869 (no return) F
Patrick, John M. to Elizabeth Wiseman 12-24-1866 Be
Patrick, John Wesley to Martha Ann Hurley 7-13-1854 (8-17-1854) Sh
Patrick, Joseph B. to Sarah Strong 8-28-1845 Sh
Patrick, Manian to Mary L. Mede Alford 6-21-1838 (6-26-1838) Hr
Patrick, Nathan to Lucinda McCaslin 10-10-1859 (10-11-1859) G
Patrick, Page H. to Annie C. Patrick 1-23-1861 (1-24-1861) Dy
Patrick, Robert M. to Mary Frances Hargett 4-28-1868 (4?-7-1868) L
Patrick, Thos. G. to Sarah J. Joyner 8-1-1844 (8-8-1844) Hr
Patrick, Z. H. to M. S. Curl 6-20-1842 (no return) F
Patridge, B. F. to S. A. V. Kernodle 1-5-1867 Mn
Patrum, A. to Mary F. Peel 1-17-1862 Hn
Patson, Wm. to Jettie Robinson 3-8-1853 Cr
Patten, Benj. F. to Margaret S. Barker 9-30-1857 We
Patten, Jessee to Lizzie Waggoner 10-12-1867 (10-13-1867) T
Patten, John R. to Elizabeth J. Dunn 11-2-1857 T
Patten, John to Mariah Brown 10-17-1874 T
Patten, Robert to Malissa Bond 12-14-1874 Hy
Patten, Thos. J. to E. J. Crabtree 1-19-1858 (no return) We
Patten?, George to Mary Jemison 10-8-1855 (no return) Hn
Patterso, John F. to Minerva Davis 11-11-1856 G
Patterson, A. H. to Frances A. Wilder 10-3-1864 (no return) Cr
Patterson, Alexander to Martha Craig 7-28-1858 Ma
Patterson, Alexander to Mary Lowery 9-5-1862 Mn
Patterson, Alford to Jane Partee 4-19-1882 (4-27-1882) L B
Patterson, Andrew J. to Clary Ann Richardson 1-5-1833 G
Patterson, Asa to Matilda Herse 5-3-1852 Ma
Patterson, Bernard M. to Martha E. Bosley 10-25-1848 Sh
Patterson, Bernard M. to Temperance P. Battle 10-21-1849 Sh
Patterson, Berry to Lucenda Gibson 6-13-1837 G
Patterson, Billy to Jane Ingram 3-2-1870 G B
Patterson, Billy to Mary Spivy 10-23-1874 Hy
Patterson, Burrell to Matilda Payne 8-16-1869 G
Patterson, Burrell to Pricilla Boun 7-9-1836 G
Patterson, C. J. to M. E. Gentry 9-21-1865 G
Patterson, Caswell C. to Susan A. Swindell 10-10-1861 G
Patterson, Charley to Cela Graves 12-2-1872 Hy

Patterson, Colen M. to Laura L. Williams 11-26-1868 Ma
Patterson, David to Nancy Amanda Kincaid 9-30-1857 (10-1-1857) Ma
Patterson, Davis to Amanda Brim 12-30-1868 L
Patterson, Dolphin to Eleanor Martin 12-23-1831 Sh
Patterson, Edmund to Caroline Sims 12-15-1884 (12-16-1884) L
Patterson, F. M. to M. F. Liston 12-23-1868 Cr
Patterson, Freeman to Martha Raines 11-30-1850 (12-3-1850) Ma
Patterson, Freeman to Susan Ellen Margrave 9-22-1855 (9-23-1855) Ma
Patterson, G. M. to Julia M. Keefe 12-18-1856 (1-1-1857) Sh
Patterson, George W. to Adeline Potts 9-20-1877 (9-23-1877) L
Patterson, George W. to Mary Johnson 8-16-1838 F
Patterson, George to Annis Travis 5-17-1866 Hn B
Patterson, George to Charity Lane 11-27-1852 Ma
Patterson, George to Pasley Hutcherson 3-16-1858 L
Patterson, Henry to Debu Travis 5-20-1866 Hn B
Patterson, Henry to Queenie? Ferrill 12-18-1879 (12-25-1879) Dy
Patterson, J. B. to T. E. Wells 7-2-1881 (7-3-1881) L
Patterson, J. H. to Mary W. Hale 3-6-1855 Cr
Patterson, J. N. to Emily Stuart 10-3-1861 (no return) Hn
Patterson, J. R. to Frances A. Gibbons 11-4-1844 Sh
Patterson, James A. to Susan G. Dudley 6-12-1852 Cr
Patterson, James B. to Martha E. Selvidge 8-30-1865 G
Patterson, James B. to Nancy Jane Gray 8?-22-1859 (8-23-1859) Hr
Patterson, James C. to Ann Brogdon 3-10-1859 Hn
Patterson, James C. to Mary F. Veazey 9-5-1846 Hn
Patterson, James M. to Dionico M. Oneal 1-15-1848 (1-18-1848) G
Patterson, James S. to Nancy C. Newton 9-5-1844 Hn
Patterson, James W. to Jane P. Russell 11-13-1845 Hn
Patterson, James to Jane Adkinson 5-11-1857 (5-18-1857) O
Patterson, James to Josephine Alsten 6-18-1869 G
Patterson, James to Mary Matthews 2-11-1856 (2-12-1856) O
Patterson, James to Mary Nash 10-24-1859 Sh
Patterson, John H. to Lucinda Young 1-20-1860 Cr
Patterson, John Matthew to Martha Hutcheson 3-29-1844 (3-31-1844) L
Patterson, John to Cely Kimbrough 3-19-1835 Hn
Patterson, John to Louiza Walton 9-12-1851 (no return) Hn
Patterson, John to Nancy Stewart 3-15-1874 Hy
Patterson, Joseph to Mary Jane Morphis 12-13-1845 Ma
Patterson, K. K. to N. J. Burrow 10-9-1861 Mn
Patterson, L. W. to Elizabeth Estes 8-22-1861 Mn
Patterson, P. M. to H. F. Hurt 10-11-1854 Cr
Patterson, P. P. to Hannah M. Britenham 7-30-1839 G
Patterson, R. A. to Emily S. Norville 12-30-1867 G
Patterson, R. G. to Cynthia A. Lowe 4-11-1851 (4-15-1851) Hr
Patterson, Raiford C. to Unicy? Miller 10-29-1842 (11-2-1842) Hr
Patterson, Robert to Julia Jones 12-6-1866 F B
Patterson, Robt. T. to Sarah N. Daly 4-24-1870 G
Patterson, S. A. to M. A. Looney 1-18-1865 (no return) Hn
Patterson, S. G. to S. V. Aldridge 3-16-1863 Mn
Patterson, Samuel J. to Lucinda Haislip 11-1-1852 (11-2-1852) Ma
Patterson, Samuel to Emily L. Faulk 8-10-1847 Sh
Patterson, Samuel to Mrs. Malissa Beverly 1-13-1870 T
Patterson, Smith to Catharine Humphrey 1-19-1844 (not endorsed) F
Patterson, Stokeney to Rebecca W. French 9-25-1856 Sh
Patterson, T. M. to L. C. Ward 1-4-1870 (1-5-1870) Dy
Patterson, Thomas J. to Mary Ann Stewart 2-16-1867 Hn
Patterson, Thomas to Mary F. Cate 5-14-1857 Hn
Patterson, Thomas to Mary Lynton 12-31-1839 Hn
Patterson, Thos. F. to Anna W. Holmes 10-25-1866 T
Patterson, W. A. to Eliza Stone 9-30-1841 Cr
Patterson, W. G. to Emma Elder 8-22-1863 G
Patterson, W. M. to M. B. Chester 1-6-1858 Sh
Patterson, W. R. to C. A. Johnson 12-23-1867 (no return) Dy
Patterson, Warren to Mary Kimbrough 4-8-1836 Sh
Patterson, Warren to Mary L. Odom 7-12-1840 Sh
Patterson, William C. to Annis Taylor 10-17-1854 G
Patterson, William C. to Mary J. Cravins 10-3-1855 We
Patterson, William L. to Sarah F. Lankford 3-10-1863 Hn
Patterson, William to Mary Patterson 12-29-1845 (1-7-1846) G
Patterson, William to Mary Sexton 3-13-1839 (3-14-1839) G
Patterson, William to Sarah Gandey 12-30-1844 Sh
Patterson, Wm. C. to Livina Gregory 6-8-1864 Cr
Patterson, Wm. to Felias Perkins 7-14-1867 Hy
Patterson, Wm. to Lucy Baily 3-5-1873 (no return) Hy
Patterson, Wm. to Lucy Springfield 11-11-1869 F B
Patterson, Wm. to Susan Sparks 10-7-1857 Hr
Pattillo, John E. to Harriet (Mrs.) Stafford 2-12-1870 (2-13-1870) F
Patton, A. H. to M. H. Patton 11-27-1845 Cr
Patton, Abraham to Elizabeth Woods 11-6-1826 G
Patton, Alexr. J. to Rebecca Hancock 1-1-1868 (1-2-1868) L
Patton, Carroll to Dorrah Pettus 1-21-1871 O
Patton, David to Elizabeth Cook 7-28-1830 (7-29-1830) G
Patton, David to Susan Moore 2-4-1863 (2-5-1863) L
Patton, G. G. B. to Alcenia A. Rawles 1-9-1861 (no return) Dy
Patton, G. W. to Susan M. McAlister 7-5-1860 G
Patton, George to Rhoda Ann McWhorter 2-26-1831 (2-27-1831) G
Patton, Isaac S. to Mary A. Dickson 9-13-1848 F

Patton, J. H. to M. E. Fox 1-23-1869 (1-26-1869) Cr
Patton, James M. to Emily N. Kerr 1-19-1848 F
Patton, James N. to Margaret Patton 5-9-1861 (no return) Hy
Patton, James V. to Eleanor Shaw 3-15-1832 Sh
Patton, John B. to Levinia E. Thompson 2-22-1842 (2-23-1842) G
Patton, John to Nancy Marley 1-1-1868 (1-4-1868) L B
Patton, Monro to Millie Clemons 9-5-1870 (no return) Cr
Patton, Newton C. to Martha C. Yancey 6-23-1848 G
Patton, Pryus to Lucy Rowder 2-23-1867 (3-11-1867) F B
Patton, Thomas M. to Molly Terry 12-18-1866 (no return) Cr
Patton, W. H. to S. E. Morris 7-20-1870 (no return) Hy
Patton, Wade M. to Mattie Douglas 11-15-1876 Hy
Patton, William to Reen Allice Hale 5-2-1859 (5-3-1859) G
Patton, Wm. E. to Agnes A. Starr 1-27-1840 (1-28-1840) F
Patty, R. C. to Ella Campbell 11-8-1869 (11-11-1869) F
Paty, D. L. to Lou A. Glass 1-15-1867 (no return) Hn
Pauf, A. J. to Dilla Albright 3-12-1873 Hy
Paul, James A. to Della Westbrook 9-13-1866 L
Paul, John H. to Elvira Wilson 11-29-1853 (no return) Hn
Paul, M. H. to Catharine B. Casey 10-21-1850 (10-22-1850) Hr
Paul, Sherod S. to Mary Miller 6-19-1838 (6-21-1838) G
Paul, Travis to Charlotte Box 9-9-1834 (9-17-1834) Hr
Paul, Wiley to Mariah McGarg 12-30-1878 (no return) Dy
Paulett, William to Sarah Sherman 2-15-1864 Hn
Paulson, Geor. to Mary B. Adams 4-17-1845 F
Paxter, R. E. to Mary Jane Garvin 5-14-1859 (5-15-1859) Sh
Paxton, M. B. to Elizabeth Garvin 2-18-1862 Sh
Pay, William R. to Alfred Sarah Smitoe 9-16-1839 Ma
Payne, A. J. to E. E. Payne 2-12-1877 Hy
Payne, A. J. to Lucy J. Croom 1-11-1866 Hy
Payne, Alfred to Maria Dodson 7-19-1858 (7-20-1858) Sh
Payne, B. P. to S. A. B. Shelton 8-17-1866 Dy
Payne, Banyan to Melinda A. Thompson 6-15-1835 Sh
Payne, Culbertson B. to Jane Henley 11-27-1828 Sh
Payne, Daniel Wiley to Cora Dickson 11-12-1867 (11-14-1867) T
Payne, Daniel to Elizabeth ANn Myers 9-3-1849 T
Payne, David to Hannah Jane Archey 9-4-1854 O
Payne, Duke to Louisa Philips 10-19-1871 (no return) Hy
Payne, Fielding A. to Lucy Jane Hooker 7-31-1849 Sh
Payne, Friday to Cassa Harris 2-5-1870 T
Payne, G. B. to Sarah Ann Webb 12-4-1869 (12-22-1869) F
Payne, G. W. to Sarah Fina McCoy 3-22-1860 F
Payne, Gilbert to Josephine Adkins 12-24-1868 (12-26-1868) T
Payne, Guilford W. to Angeline Brinkley 3-26-1846 Hn
Payne, Hamilton C. to Sarah Fields 10-31-1848 Sh
Payne, Henry to Nancy Alston 7-5-1873 (7-6-1873) T
Payne, Hyram to Mirilda Hamilton 3-1-1832 Sh
Payne, Isaac to Jennie Gant 10-9-1874 T
Payne, Isaac to Louisa Brooks 1-26-1867 (2-2-1867) T
Payne, Isaac to Mary Yarbro 4-17-1869 (6-9-1869) T
Payne, J. W. to M. J. Smith 2-20-1871 (3-7-1871) T
Payne, J. W. to M. Williams 1-26-1863 Sh
Payne, James to Fanney Kirsey 2-6-1865 O
Payne, James to Frances Jane Gorin 12-17-1850 T
Payne, Jesse to Louisa McDaniel 2-25-1832 Sh
Payne, Jim to Celia Patterson 12-18-1875 (no return) Hy
Payne, John Booker to Sarah L. Foster 12-2-1863 (12-3-1863) T
Payne, John L. to Mary Fannie McGregor 2-6-1861 (2-7-1861) T
Payne, John to J. C. Malone 2-6-1866 Hy
Payne, John to Mary Jane Wells 5-29-1858 (5-30-1858) O
Payne, Jordan to Pernetta Joiner 1-23-1835 Sh
Payne, Joseph G. to Summerfield Roberson 4-19-1859 L
Payne, R. A. (Col.) to Calley (Miss) Miles 9-27-1864 (9-28-1864) O
Payne, R. A. to Cally Miles 9-7-1864 O
Payne, Rich D. L. to Martha Bundrige 1-24-1845 We
Payne, Richard T. to Elizabeth W. Rodgers 5-1-1854 (5-6-1854) T
Payne, Richard to Johanna O'Brien 11-14-1857 (11-15-1857) Sh
Payne, Robert B. to Martha M. Rogers 8-15-1859 Cr
Payne, Robert to Mary J. McGowan 11-30-1857 Sh
Payne, Saml. to Sallie McClelland 2-17-1866 T
Payne, Sehern to Martha Ann Ross 1-27-1845 (no return) We
Payne, Thomas N. to Susan Dickson 7-30-1866 G
Payne, V. L. to S. M. Barton 5-17-1873 (5-20-1873) T
Payne, W. H. to Lou Chatman 11-23-1876 Dy
Payne, W. S. to M. E. Sherrod 12-24-1877 (12-25-1877) Dy
Payne, Wiley to Elizabeth Adkins 2-4-1841 T
Payne, Wiley to L. E. Crim 10-25-1871 Hy
Payne, William H. to Lucy A. Loving 3-3-1840 Hn
Payne, William to M. F. Davis 9-6-1865 (9-7-1865) T
Payne?, John to Phoebe Oliver 4-11-1850 Hn
Paynter, Henry H. to Henrietta Mary Hafercamp 11-11-1841 Sh
Payton?, Lewis to Carusa Coffman 12-31-1873 T
Peace, William B. to Lydia A. Hail 7-11-1849 G
Peace, Wm. H. to Sophena A. Butler 1-15-1857 Cr
Peach, C. W. to Jennie Couch 3-17-1863 Sh
Peach, Henderson to Elizabeth Chapman 1-2-1844 (1-4-1844) Ma
Peach, Henry S. to Eliza Williams 3-21-1863 (3-29-1863) Sh

Peacock, Council M. to Ann Brock 1-14-1857 (1-15-1857) O
Peacock, E. J. to M. E. Garrison 10-10-1867 Hy
Peacock, George to Mariah Talley 3-24-1870 (no return) Dy
Peacock, J. S. to Maryann White 1-26-1841 Be
Peacock, Jim to Clarasa Bunnell 2-13-1868 (2-19-1868) Dy
Peacock, John to Sarah J. Watkins 2-1-1851 Sh
Peacock, R. W. to Martha Davie 4-21-1860 (no return) Hy
Peacock, R. W. to Mary J. Woodson 8-4-1852 G
Peacock, Robert H. to Mary Ann Baker 12-1-1868 (12-2-1868) L
Peacock, Thomas to Mary C. Smith 12-17-1840 Sh
Peacock, Wilson N. to Martha C. Napier 2-17-1846 (2-18-1846) Hr
Peagio, John to C. Bacigalupo 4-22-1854 (4-24-1854) Sh
Peak, Booker to Leacy Ellis 11-21-1844 Hn
Peak, Booker to Riddy? Hastings 11-7-1848 Hn
Peak, Burrett A. to Elizabeth Rowe 1-27-1847 Hn
Peak, Champ to Puss Harris 12-11-1876 (no return) Dy
Peak, Robert C. to Catherine Rowe 1-29-1846 Hn
Peak, Thomas H. to Mary Short 8-16-1843 Hn
Peak, William D.? to Matilda Short 2-7-1844 Hn
Peal, E. L. to Milley Davis 1-24-1849 Hn
Pealer, Ezariah to Sarah C. McClemore 7-5-1856 Cr
Pealer, Sameul H. to Louiza McCord 8-1-1843 Cr
Pearce, A. C. (Dr.) to Mattie E. Barham 12-8-1866 (12-11-1866) Cr
Pearce, Anderson to Margaret Mosely 4-4-1869 G B
Pearce, Andrew to Anna Warren 12-25-1868 (no return) F B
Pearce, Augustus to Paulina C. Pattilo 1-9-1851 Sh
Pearce, D. M. to Margarette McDaniel 3-17-1861 G
Pearce, D. to E. Beavers 3-4-1841 Be
Pearce, George W. to Luella Doyle 10-1-1879 L
Pearce, George to Ella Sawyer 11-23-1878 (11-23-1879) L B
Pearce, H. C. to Sallie Williams 11-15-1870 Hy
Pearce, Isaac to S. A. Browning 1-9-1871 (1-12-1871) Cr B
Pearce, J. C. to Harriett Thompson 12-18-1866 (12-20-1866) Cr
Pearce, J. R. to Maggie Rosser 12-3-1866 (12-5-1866) F
Pearce, James H. to Mary E. Hail 10-21-1851 (10-22-1851) G
Pearce, Jas. to Martha M. Connell 5-31-1858 G
Pearce, Jim to Cresia Alexander 3-21-1868 F B
Pearce, John A. to Lucy Ann Smith 2-5-1870 (2-10-1870) F
Pearce, John C. to Mary M. Whitworth 8-11-1861 We
Pearce, John K. to Jane E. Nesbitt 1-22-1844 (1-23-1844) G
Pearce, John W. to Lila McNeil 10-24-1851 Be
Pearce, Latent to Any (Mrs.) Pickler 8-20-1860 (8-24-1860) Cr
Pearce, Leander to Laretha Rogers 10-14-1846 G
Pearce, Levi to Susan Blount 5-15-1844 (5-16-1844) Hr
Pearce, M. C. to Julia A. Humphrey 9-29-1860 Hr
Pearce, Martin to Eliza Pickens 8-14-1869 (8-15-1869) Ma
Pearce, N. to R. Townsend 11-25-1841 Be
Pearce, Nelson to Ester Ann Mitchel 12-20-1849 Be
Pearce, R. N. to M. E. Coley 2-15-1866 G
Pearce, Reuben to Lucretia Hutson 10-23-1851 Hn
Pearce, Robert to Mary J. Snow 4-8-1849 Hn
Pearce, Ruben to Elizabeth Mobly 5-13-1827 (5-16-1827) G
Pearce, Stephen to Rebecca Cook 7-18-1853 G
Pearce, Stephen to Sarah Ann Holaday 7-19-1848 Hn
Pearce, Thomas to Catharine Mitchell 12-30-1847 Sh
Pearce, Thomas to Jane McAda 8-29-1830 Sh
Pearce, Thomas to Mary Jones 9-9-1871 (9-10-1871) Ma
Pearce, W. C. to Susan E. Plant 11-30-1866 (12-5-1866) F
Pearce, W. F. to Mary J. Noah 1-17-1867 O
Pearce, W. R. to Mary J. Potts 10-13-1860 (10-16-1860) Sh
Pearce, W. R. to Susan A. Claxton 10-24-1860 G
Pearce, W. S. to Tennessee Branch 11-28-1862 (12-2-1862) F
Pearce, Wiley to Lizzie CArter 3-6-1885 L
Pearce, William R. to Amanda E. Woodson 6-1-1859 (6-2-1859) G
Pearce, William T. to Susan Catherine Hayley 3-9-1857 (3-10-1857) Ma
Pearce, William to Jacsabena Moss 1-24-1860 G
Pearce, Wm. M. to M. M. Rome 1-4-1862 Cr
Pearce, Wm. M. to Emily Mizell 3-19-1846 Be
Pearcy, James B. to Martha E. Hicks 12-4-1849 Ma
Pearcy, John J. to Nancy May 11-25-1857 (2-5-1857?) Ma
Pearcy, Ruben to Martha Pendergrass 1-26-1859 Cr
Pearcy, Thomas to Axalina Rook 7-30-1830 (7-31-1830) Ma
Pearcy, William to Lucy Powell 9-4-1836 Sh
Pearsall, E. J. to J. E. Williams 5-14-1850 (5-16-1850) F
Pearson, Alfred to Leathy Turnley 10-19-1867 F B
Pearson, Andrew to Martha Weddle 1-13-1872 Hy
Pearson, Antina to Lucinda Duglas 6-14-1872 (no return) Cr B
Pearson, Farris to Emma Brown 12-6-1877 (no return) Hy
Pearson, G. H. to Lucindy Rains 11-5-1840 Hn
Pearson, Henry J. to Martha (Mrs.) Hamilton 8-8-1867 Ma
Pearson, Henry to M. B. Griffith 6-20-1865 (6-21-1865) O
Pearson, Isaac J. to Lannie Lewis 9-24-1870 (10-6-1870) F B
Pearson, J. B. to M. C. Randle 3-4-1868 G
Pearson, J. D. to A. L. McGee 12-23-1874 (no return) Hy
Pearson, J. M. to Mary E. Haynee 12-18-1860 Sh
Pearson, J. W. to Alice E. Lee 2-24-1886 (2-25-1886) L
Pearson, James A. to Mary V. Pearson 12-18-1860 (no return) L

Pearson, James H. to Cornelia Arndt 5-7-1861 Sh
Pearson, James to Nancy Walker 3-28-1869 G B
Pearson, John D. to Conelia Holland 12-15-1851 (no return) F
Pearson, John E. to Mary D. Wilkes 11-7-1852 (11-10-1852) Ma
Pearson, John R. to Margaret L. Lansdon 10-20-1840 F
Pearson, John R. to Mary W. Cooper 9-14-1854 (no return) F
Pearson, John S. to Fanny Manies 10-25-1855 Sh
Pearson, John to Eviline Parker 1-25-1865 (1-26-1865) Cr
Pearson, Moses to Mary M. Dobkins 1-31-1855 Sh
Pearson, Peter to L. E. Milon 10-6-1866 (10-11-1866) Cr
Pearson, Read to Lucy Wilson 8-31-1878 Hy
Pearson, Samuel C. to Perny English 7-4-1841 Hn
Pearson, Shadrick to Eliza Liffsy 9-19-1864 (9-21-1864) Cr
Pearson, Thomas J. to Nannie Temple 2-20-1869 (2-24-1869) Ma
Pearson, Thos. to Maney Coleman 9-25-1874 Hy
Pearson, William to Susie Chilton 3-27-1884 L
Pearson, Wm. to Carolina E. Stiger 3-13-1841 (no return) F
Peary, F. K. to H. H. Hopkins 2-22-1837 G
Peat, Robert to Harriet Adams 10-19-1866 (no return) Hy
Pebles, Thomas to Clarissa Roberts 10-5-1850 Hr
Peck, J. F. to Lizzie Cocks 7-11-1860 (no return) Hy
Peck, James C. to Lucinda P. Wolverton 12-3-1864 (12-4-1864) Sh
Peck, Tristam B. to Laura E. Miller 11-24-1862 Mn
Peck, William to Sarah Cox 2-19-1861 G
Peck, Wm. to Mary Brooks 2-6-1849 Sh
Pecks, Joseph to Honey Thedford 12-25-1832 G
Pedigo, Levi E. to Molonia A. V. Whitson 12-23-1867 (12-24-1868) L
Pedigrew, Wm. to Froney Autry 2-23-1850 Cr
Peeble, T. A. to M. A. Nobels 9-16-1841 Be
Peebles, Alfred to Emily Hammons 9-28-1870 F B
Peebles, Bolin to Mary E. Lundy 2-19-1846 Sh
Peebles, Cipio to Ann Thomas 12-23-1867 (no return) Hy
Peebles, E. D. to Nannie Whitaker 4-27-1859 (4-28-1859) F
Peebles, George to Mollie Tyas 1-21-1884 (1-23-1884) L
Peebles, Henry to Hannah Stewart 12-11-1878 Hy
Peebles, J. N. to C. N. Ward 3-15-1859 We
Peebles, J. N. to E. J. Miller 2-23-1856 (2-26-1856) G
Peebles, James W. to Anna B. Read 11-24-1869 T
Peebles, James to Leathy R. Wallace 11-9-1848 (no return) Hn
Peebles, John Jarrett to Mary C. Haynie 2-24-1852 T
Peebles, John N. to Ann C. Upton 5-12-1853 Hn
Peebles, John N. to Palina Matheny 7-20-1861 (no return) Hn
Peebles, Lewis R. to Susan A. Kirby 12-5-1859 (no return) Hy
Peebles, S. R. to Sarah E. Kirby 9-22-1859 (no return) Hy
Peebles, Scipio to Silvey Sturdivant 4-7-1866 (no return) Hy
Peebles, Wm. R. to Nancy McWilliams 12-22-1842 Sh
Peek, James to Susan Potts 5-1-1835 Hr
Peek, John S. to Ann E. Soults 11-27-1862 Sh
Peek, T. D. to H. M. Hart 3-5-1873 (3-6-1873) Dy
Peeks, W. M. to Lou Clarke 12-15-1878 Hy
Peel, Bryant to Elizabeth D. Cate 11-17-1847 (no return) Hn
Peel, Elijah to Ann James 12-?-1843 (no return) Hn
Peel, J. A. to Sarrah A. Yates 3-19-1865 G
Peel, J. P. to N. M. McHood 2-12-1872 (2-14-1872) Cr
Peel, James M. to Martha F. Bland 12-31-1851 (1-8-1852) Sh
Peel, James to Martha Weaver 11-27-1828 Ma
Peel, John F. to Martha R. Roberson 7-6-1854 Hn
Peel, M. C. to Elizabeth Allen 6-10-1845 Sh
Peel, N. J. to Mary E. Scarlett 1-12-1871 (1-13-1871) Cr
Peel, Thomas J. to Mary Jane Griffin 1-6-1874 (1-7-1874) Dy
Peel, W. Riley to M. M. Treadaway 2-22-1873 (2-25-1873) Dy
Peeler, B. F. to Nancy McKenzie 1-14-1869 Be
Peeler, Samuel to Emily Johnson 8-4-1857 Cr
Peeler, Stephen A. to Sarah A. Morris 12-22-1866 (12-25-1866) F
Peeler, W. L. to Ann E. McGuire 12-19-1865 T
Peeler, Willis to Anna Lee Williams 3-13-1874 (3-4?-1874) T
Peeples, Alfred H. to Cincinattia Paschall 9-16-1860 We
Peeples, Benjamin F. to Bettie C. Wilkins 4-2-1867 Hn
Peeples, J. B. to Nancy C. Barham 3-1-1862 Mn
Peeples, John R. to Mary A. Murphey 7-17-1866 O
Peeples, Nathan to Selina Seaborn 9-13-1867 (9-15-1867) Ma
Peeples, Samuel to Mariah Wheeler 8-8-1861 We
Peeples, William W. to Mildred C. Nimmo 6-16-1853 G
Peeples, Wm. C. to Harriet McAdoo 10-26-1863 (no return) Cr
Peers, Jas. M. to Mary E. Pledge 3-28-1855 (4-2-1855) Hr
Peers, V. C. to Sarah L. Dupuy 10-23-1855 (no return) F
Peery, A. B. to S. M. C. Gillis 4-4-1871 (4-6-1871) Dy
Peery, Arcabald to Ann Peery 5-5-1844 We
Peery, B. P. to Pamela R. Para 12-17-1866 Dy
Peery, Jerome B. to C. B. Greenwood 5-8-1869 (no return) Dy
Peery, W. A. to L. F. Rust 4-11-1855 We
Peery, W. A. to Sarah Colevitt 3-16-1875 Dy
Peery, W. A. to V. A. Jones 1-31-1872 Dy
Peete, Austin to V. Ann Miller 1-14-1877 T
Peete, Ed to Jennie Maclin 12-26-1870 T
Peete, Edwin Robert to Jane Eleanor Taylor 10-21-1851 (10-22-1851) T
Peete, Ferry to Ann Peete 12-23-1865 (12-25-1865) T

Peete, Handy to Caroline Lewis 12-26-1878 Hy
Peete, Horace to Rose Tucker 4-13-1872 Hy
Peete, Joe to Tempie Allen 2-9-1871 Hy
Peete, John S. to Ann E. Whitley 10-21-1844 T
Peete, Joseph to Lucendy Gause 8-14-1872 Hy
Peete, Joseph to Martha Davis 4-19-1871 (no return) Hy
Peete, Joseph to Sallie M. Whitley 10-3-1864 (10-5-1864) T
Peete, Nelson to Mary Bailey 3-29-1883 L
Peete, Phillips to Mary Lucy Taylor 6-5-1867 (6-8-1867) T
Peete, Sam to Margaret Winfield 12-10-1874 Hy
Peete, West to Bettie Clement 12-25-1873 T
Pegees, Jacob to Martha Williamson 4-18-1867 F B
Pegram, Francis V. to Elizabeth M. Williams 10-11-1863 We
Pegram, R. W. to Mary E. Brown 9-10-1847 F
Pegram, R. W. to Victoria Belote 1-2-1860 F
Pegram, Samuel G. to Harriett G. Jones 7-25-1836 (7-27-1836) Hr
Pegram, Thomas S. to Juby F. Morgan 12-20-1862 (no return) Hn
Pegues, Asbury to Mary E. Hewitt 1-27-1843 (2-1-1843) Ma
Pegues, Oliver H. to Ann Eliza Alston 1-9-1829 Ma
Pelworth, Henry to Jane Hutchens 2-19-1845 Sh
Pemberter, Joshua L. to Sarah M. Irvin 11-12-1850 (11-13-1850) G
Pemberton, Andrew J. to Lucinia J. Morris 5-22-1856 Hn
Pemberton, Henry W. to Mary M. Wallace 3-21-1853 (3-22-1853) G
Pemberton, J. M. to Jerldean Tison 8-11-1864 (no return) Hn
Pemberton, James M. to Caroline Dinkins 12-1-1857 Hn
Pemberton, John A. to Sarah C. Harrison 6-17-1846 Ma
Pemberton, Lewis to Bess Alexander 7-1-1840 Hn
Pemberton, Lewis to Harriet Swen? 1-8-1846 Hn
Pemberton, Lewis to Sarah S. Yoiung 11-6-1849 Hn
Pence, Jesse to Rebecca Hoke 6-22-1839 (6-23-1839) Hr
Pender, Joseph W. to Tralucia L. Durham 4-1-1847 F
Pender, Manuel to Martha Carter 6-5-1871 (no return) Hy
Pender, R. to Ferdelia Anderson 10-23-1859 Hy
Pender, T. W. to Elizabeth Mathis 5-10-1870 Hy
Pender, Thomas to Harriet Cotter 4-13-1874 Hy
Pender, William to Rendy Johnson 2-2-1875 Hy
Pender, Wm. R. to Mildred N. Neil 7-1-1867 Hy
Pender, Wm. to Sarah Bond 9-16-1869 (no return) Hy
Pendergrass, J. W. to Elizabeth Kirly 3-27-1872 Cr
Pendergrass, Wm. to Mary Halcomb 5-20-1853 (no return) Cr
Pendergrast, Edward (Capt.) to Mary Wardlow 7-25-1862 Ma
Pendergrast, Samuel R. N. to Synthia Jane Kirkpatrick 12-6-1843 Ma
Pendergrast, Vincent L. to Nancy Williams 11-13-1866 (11-14-1866) Ma
Pendigrass, William to Mary Murphy 1-27-1866 (1-28-1866) Cr
Pendleton, E. B. to Lucy Rogers 10-12-1869 Dy
Pendleton, N. P. to E. J. Gibbs 10-30-1858 (11-3-1858) Sh
Pendleton, William to Viney Moore 2-18-1869 (2-20-1869) F B
Penegar, Joseph to Elizabeth A. Mosely 12-17-1846 We
Penick, E. W. to E. A. Patterson 9-15-1853 Hn
Penick, E. W. to Mary J. Rowland 11-11-1858 Cr
Penick, Elijah W. to Susan A. McDaniel 12-4-1845 Hn
Penick, J. J. to L. H. Laster 10-19-1865 Hn
Penick, J. O. to A. T. Greer 8-19-1865 L
Penick, Jacob M. to C. A. Johnson 5-21-1845 Hn
Penick, James to Vandalia Henderson 10-25-1865 Hn
Penick, James to W. J. Morphis 10-26-1865 Hn
Penick, Jno. W. to Susanna C. Miller 8-10-1859 F
Penick, W. E. to Delia A. Holman 12-12-1870 (12-14-1870) F
Penington, W. T. to Narcissa Williams 3-24-1871 Hy
Penn, A. C. to Gilly A. Rigsbee 3-10-1858 (3-11-1858) G
Penn, A. C. to Lavina Kelton no date (with Jul 1841) G
Penn, Flavius J. to Jennie E. Turner 9-4-1864 G
Penn, G. H. C.(G.?) to S. A. Clements 10-10-1866 G
Penn, G. T. to Mary E. Mitchel 6-22-1864 G
Penn, George S. to Eliza Ellen Conner 2-15-1854 G
Penn, Henry to Frances Hunt 3-23-1870 G B
Penn, J. F. to Matilda Odle 2-13-1867 G
Penn, J. W. to Anne Eliza Campbell 5-14-1868 G
Penn, J. W. to Collie M. Stedwell 5-16-1860 (5-17-1860) G
Penn, Jacob F. to Margrett Odle 5-21-1838 G
Penn, James L. to Martha Williamson 6-4-1851 F
Penn, James L. to Nannie B. Balch 4-25-1848 Sh
Penn, James to Mary Vincent 2-25-1828 (2-28-1828) Ma
Penn, Josiah F. to Frances A. (Mrs.) Wade 11-7-1850 G
Penn, Martin to Susan McLeary 5-20-1866 G
Penn, Pinkney R. to Frances O. Alexander 8-30-1851 (8-29?-1851) G
Penn, W. C. to Eliza E. Bryant 4-12-1854 G
Penn, W. C. to Olivia F. Jackson 8-22-1872 L
Penn, William C. to Texie C. Boyce 10-21-1862 Ma
Pennel, George W. to Sarah E. Crouch 1-14-1846 (1-15-1846) T
Pennel, Thomas D. to Sarah E. Cultin 12-16-1858 (12-23-1858) T
Pennel, Thos. D. to Sarah F. Farriss 8-10-1861 (8-14-1861) T
Pennell, Francis Marion to Sarah Ann Timms? 1-1-1851 (1-4-1851) T
Penneuter, Neal to Charlotte Bowling 5-19-1870 Hy
Penney, James to Mary L. Pluckrose 3-2-1863 Sh
Penney, James to Pheby Hailey 7-2-1842 (7-3-1842) G
Penney, Luther to Harriett B. Wilson 11-10-1839 Sh

Pennick, ____ to Emily Wimberly 5-28-1843 Hn
Pennington, Abel to Mary Hurt 3-14-1841 Hr
Pennington, Archibald to Melissa Cooksey 11-16-1833 (11-17-1833) Hr
Pennington, B. F. to Rebecca B. Tillman 1-11-1853 (no return) F
Pennington, David A. to E. C. Flippin 12-7-1867 (no return) L
Pennington, E. J. to Emily J. Manley 6-5-1869 (6-6-1869) L
Pennington, Edwin to Sarah Clift 12-16-1844 (12-19-1844) F
Pennington, G. W. to S. E. Voss 12-2-1874 (12-5-1875) L
Pennington, J. R. to M. M. Garrett 1-28-1879 (1-29-1879) L
Pennington, J. V. W. to J. E. Howard 12-6-1883 L
Pennington, J. W. to S. E. Howard 1-10-1882 (1-11-1882) L
Pennington, John C. to W. Martha Pewett 12-24-1868 (12-25-1868) L
Pennington, John M. to Abby Mills 12-28-1831 (12-29-1831) Hr
Pennington, John W. to Mary Jane Hair 2-18-1863 Mn
Pennington, John to Harriet Whit 12-13-1862 (12-14-1862) Dy
Pennington, John to Martha Hammond 8-16-1842 (8-18-1842) Ma
Pennington, John to Mary E. Bedwell 1-23-1861 (no return) Hy
Pennington, Marcus J. to Bethany Eason 9-4-1842 (9-20-1842) F
Pennington, Marcus J. to Hetty Sherrel 9-4-1834 Sh
Pennington, N. A. to M. J. Baker 10-9-1865 G
Pennington, R. H. to Sarah E. V. Crihfield 12-25-1872 L
Pennington, W. Y. to Julia M. Dennie 4-30-1874 L
Pennington, William D. to Mollie Blankenship 11-8-1871 L
Pennix, Amos to Hester Estis 3-6-1872 (no return) Hy
Penny, Lewis to Margarette L. Tucker 2-11-1856 (2-13-1856) G
Penny, W. W. to Frances L. Day 12-11-1861 G
Penson, Wm. L. to Mary C. Price 1-2-1844 Cr
Pentacost, Jefferson to Martha Fileds 2-11-1851 Hn
Pentecost, George to Mary Furlong 1-27-1855 (2-1-1855) O
Pentecost, John to F. Beaman 8-24-1853 Hn
Pentecost, John to Nancy A. E. W. Daniel 3-17-1860 Hn
Pentecost, Monterville to Louisa Jane Canaday 12-23-1856 Hn
Pentecost, William to Sarah Kilpatrick 12-29-1846 Ma
Peoples, Nathan B. to Mollie J. Prather 3-28-1861 Hn
Peoples, Nathan M. to Mary L. Williams 2-12-1851 (no return) F
Peoples, Nathan M. to Mary S. Williams 11-19-1850 (license lost) F
Peoples, Wm. C. to Sarah Ann Woods 11-26-1839 Cr
Pepkins, John D. to Louisa Dickins 9-23-1851 G
Peplow, Robert to Fanny Burke 12-15-1864 Sh
Pepper, Ervin to Sarah A. Ward 3-24-1844 Cr
Pepper, Geo. F. to Silviann Workman 6-3-1851 Sh
Pepper, Harry to Jennetta Teague 12-17-1867 G
Pepper, Timothy S. to Susan M. Taylor 12-10-1872 L
Percell, Henry to Fannie Smith 11-28-1868 (no return) L
Percell, Wm. to Martha Edwards 5-31-1840 Cr
Percell, Wm. to Neely Phillips 12-29-1844 Cr
Perciful, James T. to Allie Bickers 12-24-1868 (1-4-1869) Ma
Perciful, John to Mary Thompson 11-11-1856 Ma
Perciful, William to Elizabeth Glenn 3-16-1854 Ma
Percifull, Andrew to E. J. White 12-4-1879 L
Percifull, Andrew to Virginia Mallory 9-25-1855 Ma
Percival, J. F. to Josie Tansill 12-27-1881 (12-28-1881) L
Percival, Thomas to Sarah Glidwell 11-27-1840 Ma
Percy, G. C. to Dorcus Massey 5-10-1855 Cr
Perdue, James H. to Mary A. Lucre 8-4-1866 O
Pergreson, William to Alba McPherson 5-29-1845 Sh
Peritz, Isaac to Amelia Solomon 7-5-1853 (7-6-1853) Sh
Perkins, A. J. to America A. Gilespie 5-24-1854 Be
Perkins, A. M. to Jane Williams 10-3-1866 (10-4-1866) Dy
Perkins, Abner to Martha Aikens 4-30-1874 Dy
Perkins, Adam to Ann Russell 10-4-1862 Hn
Perkins, Adam to Mary Odom 12-9-1861 (no return) We
Perkins, Bob to Chaney Henderson 6-12-1864 (6-14-1864) Sh *
Perkins, Charles to Mary Gilbert 4-10-1874 (no return) Hy
Perkins, Cornelius to Marthena Burton 10-26-1858 O
Perkins, D. C. to Lidia Williams 2-4-1841 Be
Perkins, D. T. to Jemima Byram 10-31-1872 Hy
Perkins, David L. to Eliza Watson 12-20-1852 (no return) F
Perkins, David to Mary Mann 1-11-1883 L
Perkins, David to Sophia McElwee 8-15-1872 (no return) Hy
Perkins, E. D. M. to Elizabeth J. Sanders 3-31-1863 Mn
Perkins, E. L. to Anna Pierce 12-21-1854 (12-23-1854) Sh
Perkins, E. to Mary Moses 1-23-1864 Be
Perkins, Ephraim to Milly J. Holmes 11-7-1854 Be
Perkins, G. W. to E. L. Herne 7-13-1847 (7-15-1847) O
Perkins, George G. to Adeline Reeves 10-8-1845 (10-9-1845) Ma
Perkins, J. G. to Elizabeth Lewis 2-8-1866 Hn
Perkins, J. H. to Fannie V. Chitts 10-3-1867 F
Perkins, Jacob A. to Mary L. Braden 6-7-1879 (6-8-1879) L
Perkins, Jacob to Mary Salaake? Anderson 10-11-1831 (10-12-1831) Ma
Perkins, James C. to Sarah Gibson 2-11-1863 Mn
Perkins, James M. to M. A. Murphey 10-27-1856 We
Perkins, James to Martha Lasiter 9-29-1863 Hn
Perkins, Jesse C. to Charity A. Herald 2-7-1853 (3-1-1853) O
Perkins, Jesse L. to Mary F. Garrett 2-8-1858 (no return) L
Perkins, Jesse L. to Mary Frances Garrott 2-8-1858 L
Perkins, Jim to Mony Tuggle 8-8-1867 Hy

Perkins, Jno. A. to Jane Hotchkiss 7-12-1848 Sh
Perkins, John H. to Sarah Jane Cooper 12-28-1848 Be
Perkins, John P. to Amie Wiggle 8-9-1865 Mn
Perkins, John P. to Lizzie Armour 6-29-1858 (6-30-1858) Sh
Perkins, John W. to Margaret C. Cates 4-5-1862 (4-9-1862) L
Perkins, Josephus to Eleathia J. McKnight 1-24-1852 Ma
Perkins, Littleton H. to Lou Boyd 3-1-1871 F
Perkins, N. T. to Pocahuntus Estes 1-29-1868 Hy
Perkins, Newton C. to Sallie H. Todd 11-13-1861 Sh
Perkins, Peter to Mary Henry Hodge 1-20-1841 Hr
Perkins, R. T. to Belle Baird 8-8-1870 F
Perkins, Rufus to ____ Rouch 2-10-1860 Hr
Perkins, Saml. to Bettie Brown 11-14-1878 Hy
Perkins, Ulysses S. to Mary A. Stanley 1-15-1850 Cr
Perkins, W. H. to S. B. Sedbury 10-4-1869 G
Perkins, W. K. to Parthena Herrin 3-26-1839 Be
Perkins, W. P. to Lucinda Sutton 3-12-1863 Mn
Perkins, W. T. to E. L. Hamilton 1-8-1863 Mn
Perkins, William M. to Lockey Ann Henderson 5-13-1841 Sh
Perkins, William to Sarah Heron 7-30-1856 (8-2-1856) O
Perkins, Williams to Sary Brown 7-10-1827 (7-12-1827) Hr
Perkins, Wm. R. to M. G. Sykes 11-30-1847 Be
Perkins, Wm. W. to Emily E. Haynes 1-13-1850 Cr
Permenter, Braton to Elizabeth Jernigan 2-21-1849 (2-22-1849) G
Permenter, John to Mary Huggins 12-19-1844 (no return) We
Permenter, Ruffin to Mary Blurton 9-24-1866 (9-25-1866) Ma
Perminter, G. W. to Sallie A. McMillen 12-31-1868 Hy
Perminter, Henry to Adaline Rhodes 9-20-1867 (9-22-1867) Cr
Perminter, James to Nany Smith 2-19-1846 G
Perrago, C. E. to Sallie Willie 7-31-1870 Hy
Perrett, Johnson to Martha E. Hardy 10-16-1872 Cr
Perrin, Edwin O. to Rachel Stanton 4-4-1850 Sh
Perritt, Johnson to Mitilda Carver 10-5-1854 Cr
Perritt, William to Nancy Ann Rushing 9-2-1849 Be
Perron, Benjamin R. to Emery Guin 1-2-1844 (1-9-1844) Ma
Perry, A. to Ann A. Smith 1-8-1873 (1-9-1873) L
Perry, Abraham to Mary Crook 11-19-1844 F
Perry, Alexander S. to Elizabeth A. Gailey 5-6-1863 We
Perry, Andrew to Ellen Hilliard 1-19-1871 (1-21-1871) F B
Perry, Anthony to Bell McCutchen 3-14-1868 Dy
Perry, Asa to Lyda Smith 2-2-1843 (2-4-1843) G
Perry, Austin to Polly Nicholas 6-7-1847 (no return) Hn
Perry, B. J. to Canellis E. Moore 11-21-1867 (11-22-1867) Cr
Perry, Barham to Rowena Eliza Williams 8-27-1869 (9-1-1869) Ma
Perry, Benj. W. to Sarah Moss 7-19-1827 G
Perry, Benjamin W. to Elizabeth Dick 12-22-1854 Ma
Perry, Benjamin to Maria Crowder 1-1-1866 (1-7-1866) F B
Perry, Charles to Lavinia Vaughan 1-31-1850 Hn
Perry, Charley to Judy McGee 10-8-1852 Cr
Perry, Commodore to U. Mullins 4-9-1840 Hn
Perry, Craig to Millie Whitson 1-17-1877 Dy
Perry, Daniel to Martha Price 2-5-1845 Cr
Perry, Dr. A. to Miss Emma C. Day 11-12-1860 (11-13-1860) T
Perry, Edmund B. to Eliza J. Shaw 1-2-1869 (1-6-1869) F
Perry, Elijah to Martha Hall 6-17-1852 (no return) Hn
Perry, Elvis to Amanda Hopper 10-6-1870 Cr
Perry, Felix to Annie L. Justice 3-15-1842 Cr
Perry, Foster to Sarah Ann Griffith 12-9-1857 (12-10-1857) Ma
Perry, Francis to Elizabeth Pollard 12-3-1827 (12-6-1827) G
Perry, Francis to Nany Glidewell 7-23-1842 (7-26-1842) G
Perry, Francis to Rebecca Reed 1-24-1848 (1-25-1848) G
Perry, Franklin to L. J. Strahorn 12-23-1867 Dy
Perry, Frieland to Ellen Shelton 7-28-1869 G B
Perry, G. W. to Elizabeth Campbell 8-8-1874 (8-17-1874) T
Perry, George to Spanzy? Jane Randolph 1-15-1849 G
Perry, Gideon to Nancy Smith 4-5-1857 We
Perry, H. T. to Margaret C. Allen 6-18-1866 (no return) Hn
Perry, Henry C. to I. Etta Parker 9-5-1870 (9-7-1870) Dy
Perry, Henry H. to Martha V. Powell 5-25-1860 (no return) Hy
Perry, Herbert to Mary M. Howlett 11-27-1848 (11-30-1848) Ma
Perry, Isaih S. to Louisa W. Goldsby 4-5-1842 Sh
Perry, J. L. to M. C. McCrorry 8-5-1866 Hn
Perry, J. M. to A. J. Vaughn 12-23-1857 We
Perry, J. to Mary J. Ketchum 12-16-1850 (not endorsed) We
Perry, James G. to Mary S. Kyle 11-20-1851 Ma
Perry, James H. to E. A. Ellington 12-4-1871 (12-6-1871) Dy
Perry, James L. to Lucy T. D. Johnson 9-12-1847 Sh
Perry, James Turner to Lou Morgan 12-17-1866 (12-20-1866) Ma
Perry, James W. to Mary Hunter 12-22-1838 Ma
Perry, James to Mahaly Rogers 8-23-1849 Hn
Perry, James to Mary A. Kerr 12-11-1850 (no return) F
Perry, James to Mary Baker 10-24-1857 (10-25-1857) Sh
Perry, James to Sarah Wallice 6-24-1862 (6-25-1862) G
Perry, Jarrett to Elizabeth Gamer 1-5-1858 G
Perry, Jesse to E. M. Hopper 9-1-1870 Cr
Perry, John J. to Julia A. Dailey 12-29-1860 F
Perry, John to E. A. Webb 1-31-1850 F

Perry, John to Elzira Cheney 2-15-1882 (3-15-1882) L
Perry, John to Laisa J. Hall 10-12-1865 Hn
Perry, John to Malvina Latimer 9-2-1859 (9-14-1859) O
Perry, John to Penelope Holiday 12-23-1852 (12-24-1852) Hr
Perry, John to Sarah Reed 12-9-1857 G
Perry, John to Zilla Ann Davenport 8-27-1844 We
Perry, John to Zoda Council 5-7-1867 Hn
Perry, Josephus S. to Mary Reynolds 10-11-1859 (10-12-1859) G
Perry, Laburn to Martha (Mrs.) Collinsworth 11-10-1869 (11-11-1869) Ma
Perry, Lewis to Jane Newell 2-18-1843 (2-23-1843) G
Perry, M. to S. P. Day 2-6-1866 T
Perry, Merlin to Elizabeth Boon 9-12-1843 (9-21-1843) Ma
Perry, Merlin to Sarah Ann Stone 12-5-1854 Ma
Perry, Nathaniel to Fidelia E. Williams 12-31-1868 Ma
Perry, Nazerith to Mary Catherine L. McCommon 11-10-1853 Hr
Perry, Nicholas to Nancy Miller 9-18-1849 (9-20-1849) Ma
Perry, Polk to Mary Glisson 4-4-1867 Hn
Perry, Richard to Susan Sheppard 12-17-1879 (12-18-1879) L B
Perry, Robert H. to Sarah A. Haynes 12-24-1849 (12-25-1849) Ma
Perry, Sam to Ellen Nusom 3-29-1867 (no return) Hy
Perry, Saml. A. to America Webb 10-5-1846 (no return) F
Perry, Solomon to Fanny Gatlin 1-4-1871 (1-5-1871) F B
Perry, Stephen to Adaline Nance 10-11-1838 Hn
Perry, T. S. to Harriet Denning 11-18-1843 We
Perry, Thomas to Marey E. Smullin 12-3-1864 (12-5-1864) O
Perry, Turner to Julion Blackard 8-7-1844 Ma
Perry, W. C. to Elizabeth J. McElyen (McElzin) 5-11-1858 We
Perry, W. F. to Alminda N. J. Giles 12-7-1852 (12-9-1852) G
Perry, W. F. to Charity Chapman 5-17-1858 (5-18-1858) Hr
Perry, Wiley to Priscilla N. Carroll 5-7-1860 (5-9-1860) Ma
Perry, William S. to Prudence N. Perry 1-19-1848 (1-20-1848) Hr
Perry, William to Mary Edwards 2-19-1870 Ma
Perry, William to Nancy Holloway 2-25-1851 (2-27-1851) F
Perry, William to Rose Thorp 3-3-1875 (no return) Hy
Perry, Wm. A. to Frances M. Bromly 11-25-1852 Sh
Perry?, D. J. to S. E. McKorey 3-27-1867 Hn
Perrygo, C. E. to Fannie Thacker 4-10-1869 Hy
Perryman, John D. to Mary W. Napier 6-3-1843 (6-4-1843) Hr
Perryman, John to Mary Allen 1-20-1846 Ma
Perse, Loverance J. D. to Nancy Rodgers 6-29-1843 Cr
Perser, Wm. to Caroline Burrow 8-16-1849 (no return) F
Persey, Ruben to Martha Cox 9-26-1856 Hn
Person, Amos S. to Matilda Reddett 12-15-1847 Sh
Person, B. Alexr. to Elenore Epperson 5-9-1866 Ma
Person, Benjamin B. to Susan E. Green 10-20-1842 Ma
Person, E. H. to Mary Crenshaw 7-7-1836 Sh
Person, J. R. to Harriet E. Biggs 2-13-1858 (2-22-1858) Sh
Person, James L. to Emily Polk 11-23-1858 (11-24-1858) Sh
Person, John B. to Susan Ann Gardiner 6-11-1851 Sh
Person, R. F. to J. L. Giles 2-23-1858 (2-24-1858) Sh
Person, Thos. I. to L. M. Donald 9-20-1842 (9-29-1842) Ma
Person, W. C. to M. A. Sanford 3-8-1876 L
Person, W. E. to Mary C. Green 2-19-1862 T
Person, William to Mary J. Armour 11-6-1860 (11-7-1860) Sh
Person, William to Winny Manley 12-29-1871 L
Person, Willis to Polly Ann Craige 4-30-1864 (5-4-1864) F
Persons, Cato to Henrietta Thompson 2-6-1866 Hn
Persons, James T. to Mary L. Moore 11-4-1851 (11-5-1851) Sh
Pertle, James G. to Theny P. Wood 10-23-1845 We
Pervis, Allen W. to Angeline Roach 5-19-1842 Cr
Pervis, George to Elizabeth Seate(Scott?) 6-29-1838 Hr
Perwit?, James Willis to Amanda J. Bashears 9-6-1868 (9-7-1868) T
Pery, L. M. to Isabella S. Welch 1-3-1861 (no return) We
Pery, Soleman to Margaret A. Garham 8-3-1848 We
Peryear, J. S. to T. J. Keltner 1-6-1872 L
Pete, Joe to Polly Boyd 12-30-1874 Hy
Pete, Napolion to Cathran Day 3-26-1866 (3-31-1866) T
Peterbock, Jack to Eliza Castles 1-15-1869 (1-16-1869) F B
Peters, Charles H. to Sarah J. Carrington 9-24-1866 (9-25-1866) Ma
Peters, Daniel to Elizabeth Taylor 5-17-1868 G
Peters, E. L. to Elizabeth Burton 4-18-1850 (no return) F
Peters, Edward J. W. to Mary Ann Sheets 3-11-1854 (3-12-1854) Hr
Peters, Edward L. to Judah Hester 6-7-1848 Hr
Peters, Edward L. to Lettrice Parker 1-27-1827 (2-1-1827) Hr
Peters, Edward L. to Rachel Murphy 6-30-1840 (7-2-1840) Hr
Peters, Ely to Peggy Stott 1-1-1867 Hy
Peters, Frederick to Emelline (Emelie) Richter (Richten) 11-29-1849 Sh
Peters, George B. to Eveline L. McDowell 7-29-1841 Hr
Peters, George B. to Narcissa Williams 5-9-1839 Hr
Peters, Jno. to Catharine Finessey 7-15-1861 (7-16-1861) Sh
Peters, Thomas to Ann Eliza Glasgow 6-15-1837 (6-22-1837) Hr
Peters, Thomas to Sarah Jane Irions 10-28-1846 Hr
Peters, William Edgar to Anna Eliza Hall 12-15-1844 Hn
Peterson, G. B. to Bettie Atkinson 4-28-1884 (4-30-1884) L
Peterson, George W. to Mirina Scaggs 12-1-1836 Sh
Peterson, Isaac S. to Jane Sissil 12-19-1885 (12-22-1885) L
Peterson, James to Harret M. Martin 1-29-1850 (no return) F

Peterson, John to Aurora Harrison 6-26-1866 Ma
Peterson, Peter to Catherine Sandage 6-1-1846 Sh
Peterson, Theodore to Johannah Jehl 2-27-1861 (2-28-1861) Sh
Peterson, W. D. to Mary L. Vaughan 6-16-1856 (6-17-1856) Sh
Peterson, W. J. to Martha Roberts 2-21-1877 (2-22-1877) L
Peterson, William D. to Martha Stewart 12-20-1842 (12-22-1842) Ma
Peterson, William to Sarah Ellis 2-12-1862 (2-13-1862) L
Peticats, Arthur E. to _____ 3-15-1852 (no return) F
Petit, Nasibet to Sarah Jones 6-27-1840 (6-28-1840) G
Petre, John F. A. to Caroline Feidlin 3-12-1853 Sh
Petree, J. W. to S. A. Winchester 1-16-1866 Hn
Pettett, James to Eliza V. Grey 1-31-1838 F
Pettey, Francis M. to Sarah ann Elliott 8-26-1848 (no return) F
Pettie, John Isaiah W. to Louisa Price 1-22-1853 Cr
Pettigrew, Alfred to Lucinda J. Hollowell 6-1-1864 Be
Pettigrew, H. A. to L. J. Gilchrist 12-31-1865 Mn
Pettigrew, J. M. to N. E. Ellis 7-27-1862 Mn
Pettigrew, Levi to Martha E. Sanders 1-2-1862 Mn
Pettigrew, Samuel to Nancy Nichols 7-17-1826 (7-18-1826) Hr
Pettigrew, Wm. R. to Sarah Elizabeth Ellington 9-18-1867 (9-20-1867) Ma
Pettijohn, John to Elizabeth Smith 2-1-1845 (2-2-1845) O
Pettijohn, Samuel to Elizabeth Coward 12-13-1837 Sh
Pettis, David to Margaret Atkins 10-4-1871 (10-5-1871) Dy
Pettis, Jack to Margaret Newhouse 1-7-1867 Sh
Pettit, James to Georgia Cooper 10-27-1857 Sh
Pettit, James to Levina Scott 8-15-1844 G
Pettit, James to Mary Jane Gray 8-3-1852 (no return) F
Pettit, John W. A. to Maria Louisa James 9-23-1849 Sh
Pettus, A. W. to Maria A. R. (Mrs) Key 8-9-1836 Sh
Pettus, Benj. R. to Ann M. Farmer 4-6-1866 (3?-7-1866) Ma
Pettus, Henry L. to Eliza A. Ruffin 9-25-1851 Hr
Pettus, Rufus to Mary Woodson 12-23-1876 Dy
Pettus, Sterling H. to Drue A. Coleman 6-20-1866 (6-21-1866) L
Pettus, William to Jane Mayo 12-30-1880 Dy
Pettus, William to Martha A. McDaniel 2-7-1845 (2-13-1845) G
Pettus, Wm. to A. E. McDaniel 12-30-1871 (1-7-1872) O
Petty, David to Caroline Hicks 4-4-1856 Cr
Petty, David to Ruth Orrell 3-21-1839 Hn
Petty, G. R. to Mary A. Herron 9-28-1842 (no return) Hn
Petty, Geo. A. to Hester Mongomery 12-10-1870 (no return) Hy
Petty, George J. to B. A. Callis 4-23-1853 Sh
Petty, George to A. Lee 8-29-1867 G B
Petty, H. C. to Nancy A. Williams 12-26-1865 (12-27-1865) Cr
Petty, Henry to Ann Whitworth 8-21-18682 Dy
Petty, Henry to Caly Dorson 1-1-1877 Hy
Petty, J. H. to Elizabeth Holeday 5-22-1861 Mn
Petty, J. N. to Cas Blanchett 1-4-1866 Hn
Petty, Jas. H. to Mary A. Goodman 5-21-1867 T
Petty, John to Elizabeth Forkam 3-20-1855 Sh
Petty, Joseph to Susan Gresham 8-29-1850 Hn
Petty, Joshua R. to Mary Jane Underwood 2-20-1850 Hn
Petty, Lewis to Jane Wallis 10-30-1855 Cr
Petty, Nathan S. to Sarah E. Prince 12-2-1850 Sh
Petty, Nathan to Fanny Poole 1-29-1859 (1-31-1859) Sh
Petty, Nathan to Nancy E. M. Tilley 10-22-1860 T
Petty, Pinkney J. to Emaline Russell 10-18-1857 Cr
Petty, Ralph to Rebecca Parker 7-3-1859 Hn
Petty, T. F. to Elizabeth A. Hendrix 8-29-1861 Hn
Petty, Thomas F. to Susan Cope 1-3-1861 (no return) Hn
Petty, Wyatt to Sarah Williams 9-15-1838 Hn
Pettyjohn, A. J. to F. A. Jordan 9-13-1864 (9-14-1864) Cr
Pettyjohn, H. to Martha H. Busby 5-1-1864 Hn
Pettyjohn, Isaac to Martha J. Furlong 10-26-1859 We
Pettyjohn, Isaac to Mary Jane Perry 2-13-1845 We
Pettyjohn, James L. to Mary F. Foust 10-31-1855 Hn
Pettyjohn, Thomas H. to Sarah F. Hudson 11-20-1855 Hn
Pettyjohn, Thomas to Eliza Hudson 11-22-1855 (no return) Hn
Pevahouse, M. J. G. to Nancy J. Keer 6-24-1856 (6-25-1856) Hr
Pevehouse, M. M. M. to Martha E. Hipp 3-22-1855 (no return) L
Pew, John to Catherine Manerva Pew 11-21-1850 Hr
Pew, John to Elosie? Vail 7-28-1869 (7-30-1869) Dy
Pew, Wm. C. to Elizabeth Ann Williams 10-8-1838 (10-14-1838) Hr
Pewbeck, B. W. to A. E. Robinson 1-7-1857 Cr
Pewett, David to Eliza Witherson 12-21-1875 (no return) Hy
Pewett, Ennis to Elsie Ballard 1-13-1867 Hy
Pewett, Isham to Bullock Tennie 1-19-1869 Hy
Pewett, J. to Martha W. Vale 5-23-1860 (5-24-1860) L
Pewett, John to Eliza Adams 7-25-1846 (9-26-1846) L
Pewett, Nelson to Somerville Mollie 1-21-1871 (no return) Hy
Pewett, Sam to McFarland Harriett 12-6-1877 Hy
Pewett, Sam to Miller Patsy 11-26-1870 (no return) Hy
Pewett, Thomas H. to Fannie Henkle 2-25-1869 G
Pewett, Tom J. to Mary Ann Simmons 10-27-1861 (10-29-1861) T
Pewett, Washington to Susan Voss 9-7-1859 Hy
Pewett, Wyatt to Alderson Nancy 1-2-1869 Hy
Pewit, Andrew Jackson to Jane Turner 11-11-1856 (11-4?-1856) L
Pewit, James to Jane Roberson 2-24-1877 (2-25-1877) L

Pewitt, James C. to Harriet Murren 12-23-1840 (12-24-1840) T
Pewitt, Wm. Pleasant to Virginia C. Locke 4-25-1852 T
Pews, Daniel to Charlett Trigg 7-2-1872 (7-13-1872) T
Peyton, Henry S. to Sarah B. Lawrence 12-27-1844 (no return) F
Peyton, Presley R. to Indiana H. Lennow 1-31-1854 Sh
Peyton, Thos. F. to Martha C. Woolsey 7-23-1851 (7-24-1851) Sh
Pfemfert?, Frederick to Therissa Weisener 11-10-1859 Sh
Pfisterer, Gotlieb to Theriasia Behrens 4-13-1859 (4-14-1859) Sh
Pfyfer, Melchior to Barbara Truob 5-30-1868 (6-5-1869?) Ma
Phalen, James G. to Amanda M. Spencer 10-7-1842 G
Phaling, John to Izabellar Alexander 9-20-1836 (9-?-1836) G
Pharr, Elias to Ursula M. Alexander 10-14-1847 Sh
Pharris, Wm. W. to Rutha Scott 9-1-1861 O
Pheaton, Knox E. to Sarah J. Henderson 3-28-1838 Cr
Phebus, Lankford to Brown Helen M. 9-25-1877 Hy
Phelan, B. G. to Isabella H. Holloway 4-16-1865 G
Phelan, D. S. to Eliz. P. Cail 2-4-1858 G
Phelan, David C. to Mary E. Walker 11-18-1863 G
Phelan, David S. to Celea A. Cole 7-26-1853 G
Phelan, David S. to Selay A. Hart 10-5-1840 (10-5-1840) G
Phelan, H. T. to Nancy Hendrix 1-3-1866 G
Phelan, J. M. to Elizabeth M. Taylor 12-21-1865 G
Phelan, J. W. to Ellen Watson 10-27-1875 Dy
Phelan, John to Emeline Hayes 2-1-1853 G
Phelan, Patrick to Mary Sammon 10-7-1854 (10-8-1854) Sh
Phelan, Wm. H. to Mary Spencer 10-16-1850 G
Phelin, John to Mary Dwyer 7-13-1857 Sh
Phelon, B. to Mary S. Norris 5-21-1855 Sh
Phelps, Archibald to Mary Olive 3-9-1852 Hn
Phelps, Benjamin F. to Susan A. Brummitt 8-30-1863 We
Phelps, F. M. to Anna B. Chandelor 3-29-1863 We
Phelps, Green to Harrit (Mrs.) Donald 12-26-1867 G B
Phelps, Henry to Dora Miller 4-20-1867 Hn
Phelps, J. W. to Sanders P. M. 8-6-1873 Hy
Phelps, James W. to Martha Ross 1-13-1886 (1-17-1886) L
Phelps, John F. to Sarah M. Liles 11-25-1864 (11-26-1864) Cr
Phelps, Joseph N. to Elizabeth Price 12-15-1870 (no return) Cr
Phelps, M. G. to Olive (Mrs.) White 8-5-1867 G
Phelps, Philip P. to Arkansas Overton 9-23-1848 (9-28-1848) Hr
Phelps, R. to Susan E. Malone 1-27-1869 (1-30-1869) Cr
Phelps, T. B. to Louisa E. (A.) Glass 9-18-1855 (no return) We
Phelps, Thomas A. to Martha Grissom 5-1-1859 We
Phelps, William L. to June Bohannon 4-7-1850 Hn
Phelps, William to Julia A. Davis 11-9-1852 Hn
Phelps, William to Lucy Medlin 3-9-1871 Ma
Phifer, J. to M. Farmer 4-21-1842 Be
Phifer, John to Judah Hill 4-15-1847 Be
Phifer, John to Phebee Cooly 7-27-1855 Be
Phifer, John to Sally Warrick 1-13-1848 Be
Phifer, Uriah to Ann Elizabeth Phifer 6-11-1850 Be
Phifer, Uriah to Elizabeth Sayles 7-23-1846 Be
Phigeon, Philip to Margaret Dwyer 1-26-1861 (1-27-1861) Sh
Philips, Alexander to Jordan Sarah E. 1-18-1866 Hy
Philips, Alfred D. to Margaret McLendon 12-21-1853 (12-22-1853) Hr
Philips, Alfred to Hughs Mary J. 10-10-1866 Hy
Philips, C. F. to Cyntha Ann Roberts 11-3-1853 Be
Philips, Charles J. to Ella M. Coe 1-25-1860 Sh
Philips, D. c. to Allen Martha A. 8-29-1859 Hy
Philips, Edwin P. to Elizabeth Hill 2-14-1843 Sh
Philips, George R. to Caroline Meachum 7-19-1850 (7-25-1850) Hr
Philips, Henry G. to Sarah F. Fitzgerald 3-6-1860 (3-7-1860) G
Philips, Henry to Martha A. Morgan 1-4-1863 Hn
Philips, J. B. to Lula Waggoner 12-12-1867 Be
Philips, J. F. to Sarah Drolinger 12-21-1845 We
Philips, John J. to Catherine Holsowser 8-16-1866 (8-17--1866) T
Philips, John J. to Mary Eliza Rose 6-23-1857 (6-24-1857) T
Philips, John James to Sarah Ann Rose 7-25-1849 (8-1-1849) T
Philips, Marion J. to Mary J. Smith 10-4-1855 (10-5-1855) G
Philips, Marion to Ellen Fullen 8-8-1872 (7?-3-1872) L
Philips, R. H. to Mary F. J. Bird 12-22-1856 G
Philips, Robert to Elizabeth Brooks 12-23-1842 Hn
Philips, Thos. H. to Elizabeth Steel 7-29-1843 We
Philips, W. J. to Mary Jane McWherter 7-19-1852 We
Philips, Westley G. to Sarah A. Ward 11-18-1863 Hn
Philips, William to Jane Wiggins 8-23-1856 Hr
Philley, Calvin to Lucretia Hanley 7-18-1827 (7-22-1827) Hr
Philley, Miles to Mary Stinson 6-4-1838 Hr
Phillip, Andrew to Eliza Williams 8-31-1837 Sh
Phillips, A. F. to Lucy kA. Rogers 11-18-1871 T
Phillips, A. G. to Sarah Wolf 2-15-1857 Cr
Phillips, A. M. to Aubanett Green 10-7-1867 (10-10-1867) T
Phillips, Albert P. to Louisa Mullins 1-3-1853 (1-6-1853) G
Phillips, Albert to Elizabeth Chapman 12-7-1863 G
Phillips, Alexander to Lucy Rolands 1-13-1877 G
Phillips, Alfred to Davis Emaline 2-14-1876 (no return) Hy
Phillips, Alfred to Hair Fanny 12-30-187? Hy
Phillips, Andrew J. to Margaret M. Fleming 10-12-1857 (10-14-1857) Sh

Phillips, Andrew to Eliza Ford 2-27-1870 G
Phillips, Archibald to Mary G. Thurston 12-11-1844 Hn
Phillips, Atlas to Caroline Bishop 8-15-1848 Ma
Phillips, Benj. to S. C. Thomason 5-17-1860 G
Phillips, Benjamin Taylor to Sarah E. Hampton 12-8-1866 (12-12-1866) Cr
Phillips, Benjamin to Ann I. Thomason 3-11-1858 O
Phillips, Benjamin to R. M. Grier 2-11-1866 G
Phillips, Bill to Susana Strickland 4-20-1867 F B
Phillips, Charles to Emily A. Freeman 11-13-1848 Ma
Phillips, Charles to M. L. Hays 12-8-1859 O
Phillips, Charles to Malissa Atkison 8-27-1869 Cr
Phillips, Cullen to Elizabeth Burton 3-31-1842 Hn
Phillips, David T. to Malvina Duffey 4-17-1869 (4-25-1869) Ma
Phillips, David T. to Malvina Duffey 5-7-1866 (not executed) Ma
Phillips, David to Amanda Little 7-3-1864 Cr
Phillips, Elbert L. to Nancy Faulkner 12-23-1852 Cr
Phillips, Francis to Elizabeth Bird 9-2-1845 Cr
Phillips, Frank to Caroline Hicks 11-6-1869 (no return) F B
Phillips, Franklin to ____ Huffman 9-15-1857 Cr
Phillips, George R. to Margaret Tosh 11-10-1853 Cr
Phillips, George to Bowers Susan 1-17-1875 Hy
Phillips, George to Caroline Faulk 1-1-1874 (1-2-1874) T
Phillips, George to Elizabeth Anderson 2-21-1839 Sh
Phillips, George to Malinda Enochs 8-23-1879 (no return) Dy
Phillips, H. H. to H. A. H. Miller 1-15-1866 Dy
Phillips, H. M. to Rachel C. Edwards 9-24-1870 (no return) Dy
Phillips, Harrison to Emily McKendrick 3-4-1828 G
Phillips, Harrison to Fielder Sarah J. 12-5-1872 (no return) Hy
Phillips, Harrison to Mattie Goforth 12-28-1880 (12-29-1881?) L
Phillips, Isaac R. to Susan Terry 9-29-1844 Sh
Phillips, J. P. to C. (Mrs.) Barden 12-11-1856 (12-17-1856) Sh
Phillips, J. W. to A. A. Ramsey 11-9-1865 G
Phillips, J. W. to Nancy E. Parks 3-23-1861 We
Phillips, J. W. to Susan S. Stokes 10-7-1852 Cr
Phillips, Jacob to Elizabeth Lewis 12-26-1874 (no return) L B
Phillips, James G. to Nancy Ezale 4-11-1855 Cr
Phillips, James Munroe to Sally Makey 12-23-1868 (12-24-1868) F B
Phillips, James O. to Allee M. Edmundson 12-20-1841 (12-21-1841) G
Phillips, James W. to Rebecca E. Hannis 6-9-1849 (6-10-1849) Hr
Phillips, James to Celestia Jones 11-9-1867 F B
Phillips, James to Harriett Sherrell 8-6-1853 (no return) F
Phillips, James to Jane Fisher 12-3-1844 Cr
Phillips, James to Martha Ann Hampton 2-17-1866 Cr
Phillips, James to Sarah J. McLin 7-20-1863 G
Phillips, Jas. M. to Martha A. Roberts 6-4-1859 (6-5-1859) Hr
Phillips, Jasper to Julia Hawkins 6-22-1872 (no return) Cr B
Phillips, Jesse R. to Nannie J. Watkins 12-2-1869 (12-7-1869) Ma
Phillips, Joab to Mary Elizabeth Sandlin 11-24-1857 O
Phillips, John B. to Mary Brinkley 5-27-1860 Sh
Phillips, John F. to Elizabeth Sinclear 9-9-1845 G
Phillips, John H. to Naomi C. Davenport 4-24-1854 (no return) L
Phillips, John L. to Nancy (Mrs.) Polk 8-11-1882 (8-12-1882) L
Phillips, John M. to Jane L. Harris 6-7-1855 Ma
Phillips, John P. to M. P. Phillips 12-31-1866 Hn
Phillips, John P. to Sarahann Abernathy 10-28-1841 (no return) F
Phillips, John R. to Teressa (?) Shelton 1-6-1850 Sh
Phillips, John to Lucindy McAlister 4-5-1852 Cr
Phillips, Joseph T. to Octavia H.? Jones 12-18-1860 (12-19-1860) Ma
Phillips, Joseph W. to Catherine R. Holden 1-21-1868 (1-22-1868) F
Phillips, Joseph to Nannie McCaslin 1-13-1870 G
Phillips, Lagrand P. to M. F. (Mrs.) Rowland 8-25-1860 (8-26-1860) Cr
Phillips, Levin to Jane Murphy 3-8-1845 Be
Phillips, Lewis N. to E. J. Barnhart 1-9-1858 Cr
Phillips, Monroe to Green Lucy 6-30-1877 Hy
Phillips, N. G. to Permelia A. Holiday 12-20-1855 Cr
Phillips, Nathan to Catharine Breeden 8-21-1856 Hr
Phillips, Pinkney P. to Mary E. Glisson 12-12-1837 (12-15-1837) O
Phillips, R. D. to Sarah A. Carter 12-16-1862 (no return) Cr
Phillips, Richard M. to Melinda J. Ossman? 12-28-1865 Hn
Phillips, Richard to Elizabeth Pinson 12-27-1850 O
Phillips, Richard to Maria Jordan 10-21-1882 L
Phillips, Riley to Catherine C. Smith 2-16-1860 Cr
Phillips, Robert C. to Nancy A. Finley 6-14-1848 Cr
Phillips, Robert S. to Charley M. Powell 11-20-1855 (no return) F
Phillips, Robert to Elizabeth Youth 12-15-1864 O
Phillips, Robert to Rebecca P. Powell 1-7-1842 (no return) Hn
Phillips, Rush to Nancy Clemm 1-3-1866 (1-10-1867) Dy
Phillips, S. P. to Mary A. Patterson 1-23-1850 F
Phillips, Sam to Nancy Warford 1-31-1870 (2-1-1870) F B
Phillips, Sam to Roberta Allen 2-28-1866 (3-10-1866) F B
Phillips, Samel to Elizabeth Birdsong 12-26-1839 (no return) F
Phillips, Samuel W. to Elizabeth Taylor 12-13-1832 Sh
Phillips, Stephen to M. A. Buchanan 2-20-1872 (2-22-1872) O
Phillips, Swain D. to Elizabeth Boon 11-4-1846 Cr
Phillips, T. L. to I. T. Warren 8-26-1865 O
Phillips, Thomas C. to Mary A. Chance 12-31-1860 (or 1859?) We
Phillips, Thomas to Mary Mills 12-11-1860 O

Phillips, Thos. H. to Ellen K. McGinnis 10-5-1854 Sh
Phillips, W. A. to Mary E. Hall 11-21-1860 G
Phillips, William A. to Amanda F. Newsom 1-26-1858 (1-27-1858) Ma
Phillips, William to Huldy Brinkley 4-16-1842 (4-17-1842) Ma
Phillips, William to Mourning E. Pritchard 9-11-1860 Cr
Phillips, Wm. M. to Julia A. Breedon 8-20-1859 (8-21-1859) Hr
Phillips, Wm. to Nancy Carter 7-18-1844 Cr
Phillips, Wm. to Winney Purser 8-9-1838 Sh
Philly, Calvin to Sarah Ann Stephenson 12-25-1838 Hr
Philmott, J. A. to Anna Newcomb 9-30-1864 Sh
Philpot, John to Mary Alexander 3-14-1831 (3-15-1831) Hr
Philpott, Edward to Mary Ann Taylor 4-25-1829 Hr
Phipps, E. D. to Caroline Ezell 7-17-1860 (no return) Cr
Phips, W. B. to M. E. Blackburn 3-27-1872 O
Phoebus, Thomas to S. P. Brown 4-7-1828 Sh
Physick, Harry S. to Martha A. Wright 1-19-1863 Sh
Pickard, John to B. A. Royer 10-13-1874 (10-22-1874) L
Pickard, John to Rebecca A. Johnson 10-6-1885 (10-8-1885) L
Pickard, L. P. to A. J. Tucker 12-16-1865 (12-20-___) O
Pickard, L. P. to Matilda A. Huges 2-23-1846 We
Pickard, Lee to Julia Ann Wright 8-20-1849 O
Pickard, Lee to Julia Ann Wright 8-28-1847 O
Pickard, Thomas to Ardelia Pickard 1-9-1872 (1-14-1872) L
Pickard, Travis to Harriett Doran 12-21-1867 (no return) Hn
Pickard, William to Mary Parr 2-28-1848 (2-29-1848) O
Pickel, Robert to Sarah Winfred 12-22-1840 Sh
Pickens, A. G. to Elizabeth F. Batt 1-17-1842 (1-19-1842) F
Pickens, C. L. to A. E. Shorter 3-4-1858 Sh
Pickens, Jas. M. to Jane Singleton 1-24-1853 (no return) F
Pickens, Jas. S. to Mary Exum 6-3-1849 F
Pickens, Owen to Elizabeth (Mrs.) Howell 4-26-1871 Ma
Pickens, Robt. T. to Mary W. Pearson 3-14-1870 (3-15-1870) F
Pickens, Samuel W. to Tennessee Brown 8-14-1871 L
Pickens, Thos. R. to Mary J. Jones 11-5-1857 G
Pickens, W. Y. to Rosalean Bynum 12-18-1877 O
Pickerell, L. M. to Mary Lemon 4-25-1844 Sh
Pickett, Captain to Judy Henning 3-2-1882 L
Pickett, Ceasar to Bettie Blackwell 1-16-1875 L B
Pickett, James C. to Rebecca Ann Wright 11-28-1864 Sh
Pickett, James to Belle Williams 12-25-1878 L B
Pickett, Robert to J. Elizabeth Fitzpatrick 12-15-1857 (12-16-1857) L
Pickett, W. R. to Mary E. Benton 1-14-1862 Cr
Pickett, Wm. G. to Sussie T. Holt 2-8-1864 Sh
Pickings, Christopher C. to Mary Harris 1-31-1840 Hn
Pickins, A. L. to Martha Stedham 12-21-1842 (12-22-1842) F
Pickins, J. F. to L. J. Zellner 11-15-1852 (no return) F
Pickins, J. M. to Harrett J. Churchhill 10-11-1852 (no return) F
Pickins, W. H. to Susan E. Stanly 9-29-1849 (9-30-1849) F
Pickler, Carroll J. to Louisa Butler 9-5-1854 Cr
Pickler, Carroll J. to Martha D. Hicks 8-10-1854 Cr
Pickler, David to Sinther Percell 3-12-1840 Cr
Pickler, George W. to Sarah E. Nelson 7-16-1859 Cr
Pickler, J. M. to Margaret Rowland 12-29-1866 (12-31-1867?) Cr
Pickler, James David to Annie Palmer 2-12-1854 Cr
Pickler, Jesse to Lucy Butler 8-2-1865 (8-3-1865) Cr
Pickler, John H. to Sallie spears 7-11-1871 (no return) Cr
Pickler, John to Sally Young 7-4-1867 Be
Pickler, William to Isabel Hollomon 6-18-1865 Be
Pidgeon, Christopher to Mary Coleman 1-6-1862 Sh
Pieper, George to Mary Jane Gordon 5-15-1856 O
Pierce, A. G. to Jane Hawk 5-2-1866 (5-3-1866) Dy
Pierce, A. J. to A. C. A. Walker 1-6-1864 Dy
Pierce, A. J. to T. J. Westbrook 12-11-1869 (12-12-1869) Dy
Pierce, A. to Middey Thompson 2-25-1856 (no return) Hn
Pierce, Ansel W. to Catharine Fowler 12-29-1853 Be
Pierce, Archie to Elizabeth Lea 11-6-1872 (no return) L
Pierce, B. R. L. to Susan E. Jordan 1-29-1857 Be
Pierce, Ben to Letitia Clark 12-27-1877 Dy
Pierce, Clement to Mary Brogden 12-30-1852 Ma
Pierce, Dick to Manda Wardlaw 4-14-1883 L
Pierce, E. A. to Milly F. Bullock 12-11-1865 Be
Pierce, E. N. to Catharine Strother 6-26-1855 (6-27-1855) G
Pierce, Ethelbert L. to Ella Walls 11-21-1867 Be
Pierce, Felix to Casander Duncan 2-6-1860 (2-21-1860) O
Pierce, G. B. to S. T. Husbands 9-18-1874 (9-20-1874) Dy
Pierce, George P. to H. E. C. Cribbs 1-23-1868 (no return) Dy
Pierce, H. R. to Nancy J. Stockdale 10-10-1857 Be
Pierce, Henry M. to Elizabeth Pettus 12-12-1851 (12-16-1851) G
Pierce, Henry to Nancy Ann Enoch 9-15-1869 (no return) Dy
Pierce, Isaac W. to Arena W. Pierce 1-5-1856 Be
Pierce, J. A. J. to Sarah A. Feagan 3-3-1858 Sh
Pierce, J. F. to Ozella Stevenson 3-2-1875 Dy
Pierce, J. H. to A. E. Tuley 1-29-1861 (2-1-1861) O
Pierce, J. H. to D. E. Pope 1-19-1876 (no return) Dy
Pierce, J. R. to Sarah E. Burgess 3-11-1866 Be
Pierce, James M. to Luticia Nowell 2-21-1854 Be
Pierce, James P. to Nancy Caroline McKenzie 12-4-1867 Be

Pierce, James to Mollie Herrin 10-25-1871 (10-26-1871) T
Pierce, Jefferson to Ann Smith 8-27-1868 Dy
Pierce, Joel to Nancy Choate 12-28-1854 Sh
Pierce, John A. to Elizabeth Burns 9-4-1849 Cr
Pierce, John A. to Sarah A. Brewer 11-28-1867 Be
Pierce, John J. to Martha R. Hill 10-19-1847 Hn
Pierce, John M. to Ella N. Stevens 4-29-1876 (4-30-1876) Dy
Pierce, John W. to Susan J. Conley 12-5-1848 G
Pierce, John to Mary L. Moore 5-8-1841 T
Pierce, Josiah to Haley Goodwin 11-5-1836 (11-7-1836) Hr
Pierce, L. A. to Sarah J. Forest 6-16-1858 Be
Pierce, L. D. to Rebecca Boyd 9-3-1850 Cr
Pierce, Martin to M. A. Tisdale 12-5-1871 (no return) Dy
Pierce, Martin to Mary E. Moore 4-20-1867 (4-21-1867) Cr
Pierce, N. S. to Mary E. Arnold 8-4-1855 (8-7-1855) G
Pierce, Pinckney S. to Mary Davis 1-26-1853 Cr
Pierce, R. A. to A. E. Mathews 12-28-1869 (12-30-1869) O
Pierce, R. C. to Margrett E. Askew 2-26-1847 Cr
Pierce, R. C. to Mary Simmons 11-6-1848 (no return) Cr
Pierce, R. M. to Nancy Barlow 8-22-1855 (8-23-1855) G
Pierce, Richard to Ann Joplin 8-9-1854 Hn
Pierce, Rily to Fannie Coker 1-1-1873 (12-2-1873) Dy
Pierce, S. J. to Bulah Steele 1-26-1882 L
Pierce, Sam to Angaline Wynne 3-30-1867 (4-1-1867) Dy
Pierce, Sam to Sarah E. McKnight 10-18-1871 (no return) Dy
Pierce, Samuel C. to Rebecca C. Hunt 1-23-1854 (1-24-1854) G
Pierce, Samuel M. to Mary Adams 4-2-1846 Cr
Pierce, Stephen to Dora B. Leech 12-30-1869 (no return) Dy
Pierce, Suger D. to Kizear Forest 8-21-1848 Cr
Pierce, T. J. to L. E. Harper 1-23-1872 (1-24-1872) Dy
Pierce, Thomas to Alcey Lustre 1-12-1844 (1-14-1844) O
Pierce, Thomas to Martha S. Medlin 1-4-1856 (1-6-1856) Ma
Pierce, Thomas to Rebecca Richards 12-27-1853 (12-29-1853) Ma
Pierce, Uriah to Judy Chandler 4-26-1833 (4-30-1833) Hr
Pierce, W. M. to Milly N. Gilbert 4-5-1866 Be
Pierce, W. W. to M. W. Irwin 11-25-1862 (11-26-1862) F
Pierce, Warrin to Jane Phillips 12-24-1869 (12-27-1869) O
Pierce, William T. to Martha E. Brown 9-8-1859 Hn
Pierce, William to Margaret Stegall 9-9-1862 Dy
Pierce, William to Mary Cooper 1-4-1865 Be
Pierce, Wm. T. to Mary F. Throgmorton 1-24-1867 Be
Piercey, James to Eliza J. Workman 4-22-1863 We
Piercy, Cader to Jane Lawrence 7-19-1845 (7-20-1845) Ma
Piercy, Everett G. to Axelina Whiteside 7-28-1847 (7-29-1847) Ma
Piercy, George W. to Becky Jane Baker 5-26-1856 Ma
Piercy, Miles Wilson to Susan Jane Boals 8-2-1869 Ma
Piercy, W. T. to Sarah Parker 11-5-1868 Dy
Piercy, William H. to Margaret Mason 3-7-1849 (3-8-1849) Ma
Pierone, Simone to Mary Costi 9-19-1864 Sh
Pierre, Dupay to Nancy Snowden 9-7-1859 Sh
Pierson, Atwood to M. L. Jones 2-18-1880 L
Pierson, Blair to E. E. Jones 2-18-1880 L
Pierson, Buck to Laura Johnston 2-11-1880 L B
Pierson, Calvin to Ellen Palmer 1-9-1869 (1-10-1869) L
Pierson, Charles to Mona Rucker 12-26-1867 (no return) L B
Pierson, Daniel to Mary Hafford 12-28-1869 (no return) L
Pierson, E. F. to Margaret E. Robinson 7-30-1863 Sh
Pierson, Jake to Mollie Cornell 12-27-1872 (1-11-1873) L B
Pierson, John F. to Susan E. Lee 1-29-1849 L
Pierson, John to Frances Eggleston 10-1-1880 (10-2-1880) L B
Pierson, Scot to Emma Hite 2-16-1883 (2-17-1883) L
Pierson, Sylar to Lucy Parr 4-5-1870 (5-1-1870) L
Pierucci, Ansel to Fredricka Horn 12-24-1860 Sh
Piffin, Henry A. to Margaret A. Kilpatrick 9-18-1866 Ma
Piger, Nathan to Mollie Green 6-26-1869 (6-27-1869) Cr
Pigg, John C. to Mary Cook 10-6-1838 Hn
Pigg, John to Salina Darnall 1-20-1834 O
Piggue, Elizah to Zora Montgomery 7-14-1871 (7-15-1871) Cr
Pigue, James B. to Yarbrough Margaret 2-11-1877 Hy
Pigue, N. W. to Lexanah Patterson 12-27-1855 G
Pigue, Spencer to Sopha Williams 7-5-1868 G B
Pike, David to Rogers Sarah E. 12-26-1877 Hy
Pike, Harry to Cotter Minerva 2-16-1867 Hy
Pike, James D. to Malinda R. Jarrett 8-22-1872 Dy
Pile, S. C. to M. J. McElyea 9-21-1866 (9-23-1866) Dy
Piles, Hiram to Elizabeth Wright 12-30-1833 (1-3?-1834) Hr
Piles, James M. to Minerva M. Pipkin 4-3-1861 (4-4-1861) Hr
Piles, Lennard to Martha McIver 10-6-1827 (10-?-1827) Hr
Piles, S. B. to Elizabeth (Mrs.) Curtus? 1-7-1873 (1-9-1873) L
Pilkington, Saml. Woodfin to Elizabeth Ann Faris? 12-3-1851 T
Piller, W. H. to Nancy M. Caraway 12-22-1856 (no return) F
Pillow, Alexander H. to Mary F. Gunter 9-3-1845 Sh
Pillow, Allen to Milly Somerow 1-7-1868 (no return) L B
Pillow, Ben F. to Sarah A. Eison 5-12-1869 (5-14-1869) L
Pillow, Benjamin F. to Susan McFadden 6-23-1861 Hn
Pillow, Davy to Peggy Young 7-7-1877 (7-8-1877) L
Pillow, Frank to Amanda Rogers 9-12-1878 Dy

Pillow, Granville T. to Amelia E. Parker 4-23-1850 Hn
Pillow, Henry C. to Josephine O. Jones 7-1-1852 L
Pillow, James W. to Ellen Gillum 9-13-1855 (no return) Hn
Pillow, John B. to Mary P. Jobe 6-1-1841 Hn
Pillow, John H. to Fannie S. Eyson (Eison) 9-2_-1866 (9-22-1866) L
Pillow, Peter to Amanda Powell 10-2-1871 Dy
Pillow, Peter to Fannie Bell 9-12-1876 (no return) Dy
Pillow, Scott to Eliza Jane Doak 2-8-1877 Dy
Pillow, William J. to Cyntha W. Crowder 10-22-1854 Hn
Pillow, William P. to Martha H.? Chambers 5-22-1843 (5-23-1843) L
Pillow, Willis A. to Elizabeth McFadden 10-5-1854 (no return) Hn
Pillow, Wm. P. to Elizabeth C. Eison 5-12-1869 (5-14-1869) L
Pinckley, A. A. to M. L. Rose 7-12-1872 (no return) Cr
Pinckley, Andrew to Susan F. Comer 12-18-1869 (12-19-1869) Cr
Pinckley, R. K. to Elizabeth Lawrance 10-13-1865 (10-15-1865) Cr
Pinckley, Scott to Burnetta Springer 3-29-1869 (3-31-1869) Cr
Pinckley, Simpson to Araminta B. Moore 3-9-1870 (3-10-1870) Cr
Pinckston, Green C. to N. A. Morris 4-15-1872 (no return) Cr
Pinckston, Napoleon B. to Matilda Killbreath 12-31-1869 (1-4-1870) Cr
Pinder, Edmond to Ellen O'Donald 11-3-1859 Sh
Piner, William to Mary Ella Nixon 8-2-1883 L
Pingston, Therling to Susan Gibson 3-18-1847 Hn
Pinion, Felix to Lucinda Doak 9-27-1879 (9-29-1879) Dy
Pinion, Solomon to Anny Brunson 7-21-1838 G
Pinkard, William A. to Sarah Whitney 6-20-1855 (6-21-1855) Sh
Pinkerton, P. C. to Mary C. Warren 10-16-1859 We
Pinkley, Clark to Ann F. Harris 8-19-1852 Cr
Pinkley, John to Sarah E. Allman 12-26-1858 Cr
Pinkley, Silas to Mary Lawrence 3-16-1843 Cr
Pinkley, Wm. to Mary F. Hardy 12-29-1858 Cr
Pinkney, James K. to Frances B. Waddle 3-2-1845 Cr
Pinkston, Elija to Hanna C. Uptengrow 10-24-1855 Cr
Pinkston, G. C. to Anna J. Hunter 2-8-1871 T
Pinkston, George Croghan to Eliz. Ann Whitlock 3-19-1850 T
Pinkston, Green B. to Nancy C. Smothers 5-20-1857 Cr
Pinkston, J. D. to Manerva Butler 4-29-1870 (5-7-1870) Cr
Pinkstol, Jackson to Jane Miller 8-26-1871 (8-29-1871) T
Pinkston, John to Nancy Freeman 2-12-1857 We
Pinkston, John to Phidy Ross 2-21-1841 Cr
Pinkston, S. to A. Brackins 7-28-1841 Cr
Pinkstone, Wm. P. to Julia A. Newnan 6-23-1865 (6-25-1865) Cr
Pinner, J. W. to Margaret J. Draffin 1-3-1874 (1-15-1874) T
Pinner, Joseph C. to Missouri Todd 4-20-1870 Dy
Pinner, Sterling Harris to Margaret Forbus 12-22-1845 T
Pinner, Sterling to Eliza Yunt 12-31-1847 (1-7-1848) T
Pinnon, Nathaniel to Elizabeth Jane Langston 4-28-1854 (5-24-1854) O
Pinon, William to Polly Ann Worlds 2-17-1852 (2-18-1852) O
Pinson, Archibald to Mary Culbreath 1-11-1841 (1-?-1841) T
Pinson, David to Sarah Pickler ?-?-1860 Cr
Pinson, Isaac to Eliza Shofner 11-7-1864 (11-8-1864) Cr
Pinson, J. H. to Mary T. Luter 1-4-1859 Cr
Pinson, J. M. to Henrita Cobb 1-13-1859 Cr
Pinson, J. W. to Mollie Clement 9-23-1872 T
Pinson, James to Elizabeth Tolbert 12-24-1855 Cr
Pinson, Joseph to Nancy A. Coble 11-11-1840 Sh
Pinson, Lewis to Curtis Nelia 10-1-1876 Hy
Pinson, Lewis to Miller Colie 12-3-1867 (no return) Hy
Pinson, R. C. to Sarah E. Beasley 12-28-1858 Hn
Pinson, S. A. to Rebecca Beasley 10-11-1854 (no return) Hn
Pinson, Smith to Anilee Keen 8-29-1867 Hn
Pinson, T. J. to Ann E. Beasley 12-4-1854 Hn
Pinson, Thomas W. to Martha Massey 10-24-1860 (10-25-1860) Cr
Pinson, W. L. to Martha C. Loveall 11-2-1870 (11-6-1870) Cr
Pioneer, Jacob to Harriett Smith 3-16-1836 Sh
Piper, Erasmus to Martha T. Green 8-9-1860 Cr
Piper, Wm. R. to Susan Moore 12-2-1852 Cr
Pipkin, A. J. to Cropno Mary E. 6-28-1865 Hy
Pipkin, Burton (Dr.) to Mary Chitmun 5-16-1855 Ma
Pipkin, David B. to Elizabeth M. Yarbrough 9-28-1853 (9-29-1853) Hr
Pipkin, Francis M. to Pipkin Delphina 1-27-1863 (no return) Hy
Pipkin, Hinton J. to Sarah Jane Norris 5-23-1840 (5-28-1840) Hr
Pipkin, J. F. to Beulah Roy 11-21-1881 (11-23-1881) L
Pipkin, J. W. to Fannie Bethune 3-26-1884 (3-27-1884) L
Pipkin, James A. to Rebecca F. Perkins 2-24-1868 L
Pipkin, Jesse to Sally Piles 1-4-1828 (1-6-1828) Hr
Pipkin, John A. to Neety Jane Pugh 1-16-1848 Hr
Pipkin, John W. to Marnetta Ferrelll 2-3-1875 (2-4-1875) L
Pipkin, John W. to Stamps Paralee 12-21-1873 Hy
Pipkin, Jonas S. to Susan C. Dockins 10-10-1850 (10-13-1850) G
Pipkin, Kinion to Treasy Cogial 10-24-1828 (10-27-1828) Ma
Pipkin, Lewis C. to Elizabeth Bowman 9-9-1828 Ma
Pipkin, W. M. to Mary Keathley 2-17-1857 Sh
Pipkin, William M. to Harriett Wilhington 2-1-1859 (2-3-1859) G
Pipkin, William to Gila Ann Newman 1-17-1855 (1-21-1855) Hr
Pipkin, jr., L. W. to Sallie Ann West 10-21-1865 G
Pipkin, sr., L. W. to Sarah Ann West 11-2-1865 G
Pipkins, Charles R. to Caroline J. Akin 9-10-1879 L

Pipkins, Chesley P. to Margaret Chipman 5-18-1854 Ma
Pipkins, David B. to Elizabeth Poyner 4-15-1848 (4-16-1848) Hr
Pipkins, H. P. to Harrell Sarah J. 8-30-1870 Hy
Pipkins, Hughs to Mary E. Steadman 9-25-1855 (10-10-1855) Ma
Pipkins, Isaac M. to Manervy D. Lewis 12-13-1860 We
Pipkins, J. H. to Margaret A. Pope 7-16-1870 (7-17-1870) F
Pipkins, John D. to Margaret E. (Mrs.) Replogle 8-22-1870 G
Pipkins, L. W. to Mary J. Toombs 6-6-1869 G
Pipkins, Needham to Henrietta Newton 12-8-1834 Hr
Pipkins, Stephen L. to Maria Jane Piles 2-20-1861 Hr
Pipkins, W. H. to Nancy H. Pipkins 3-13-1869 (no return) L
Pipkins, William to Louisa A. Patridge 1-16-1863 Mn
Pippin, Benjamin to Ann Kendrick 10-30-1861 T
Pippin, Elisah to Emma Clayton 3-16-1869 (3-18-1869) F
Pippin, James to Sina Hill 7-27-1851 Be
Pippin, Joseph to Eliza Pullman 11-5-1838 (11-?-1839?) F
Pippins, H. S. to Bettie Kindreck 9-6-1869 (9-7-1869) F
Pirce, Rubin to Susan Volentine 4-15-1839 (4-17-1839) G
Pirdle, Ephraim to Charlotte Burford 12-25-1868 (12-28-1868) F B
Pirkins, Ransom to Lea Dony 12-29-1870 Hy
Pirtle, Benjamin W. to Harriett E. Dubois 12-29-1837 (1-4-1838) Hr
Pirtle, Benjamin W. to Sarah Jane Leathers 9-16-1839 Hr
Pirtle, Isaac W. to Sarah E. Toone 11-12-1844 (11-14-1844) Hr
Pirtle, Isaac to Eunisa Cunningham 12-13-1828 Hr
Pirtle, Jacob T. to Agness Overton 10-4-1852 (10-9-1852) Hr
Pirtle, James to E. A. Priest? 5-5-1847 Hr
Pirtle, John A. to Mary B. Champion 8-19-1831 (8-24-1831) Hr
Pirtle, John B. to Susan Priest 5-6-1850 (5-8-1850) Hr
Pirtle, Lewis to Susannah? Jackson 10-8-1846 (10-13-1846) Hr
Pirtle, Martin to Martha Jane Duboise 12-20-1833 (12-25-1833) Hr
Pirtle, Peter B. to Mary E. Paschall 9-21-1858 We
Pirtle, Peter B. to Sarah J. Brandon 12-22-1847 (12-23-1847) Hr
Pirtle, Robert J. to Rebecca J. Toone 12-20-1848 (12-21-1848) Hr
Pirtle, Robert to Elizabeth Bennett 9-19-1833 Hr
Pirtle, Robert to Mary Jane Taggart 3-13-1830 (3-17-1830) Hr
Pirtle, William W. to Lucy Jane Robinson 5-14-1850 (5-16-1850) Hr
Pistol, John T. to Lavinia Ann Frizzell 10-23-1855 (10-24-1855) O
Pitan, Calvin to Margaret L. Hubbard 3-30-1881 L
Pitchford, John to Caroline Hutchison 6-23-1854 (no return) L
Pitman, Ethelana to Elmina Jacobs 9-27-1829 Hr
Pitman, Henry M. to Mary J. Kerr 6-30-1849 (no return) F
Pitman, J. W. to Elizabeth McDaniel 3-22-1846 We
Pitman, John to Matilda Somers 9-13-1872 O
Pitman, L. W. to M. A. Holmes 3-31-1869 (4-1-1869) Cr
Pitman, R. W. to M. E. Rives 10-29-1866 (10-31-1866) F
Pitmon, S. to Sarah A. J. (Mrs.) Bell 5-15-1841 (no return) F
Pitner, C. P. to Bridger C. A. 12-10-1876 Hy
Pitner, H. M. to Little M. A. 11-4-1869 Hy
Pitner, R. M. to Robertson Elizabeth 11-24-1870 Hy
Pits, William to Nancy A. Dunaway 11-3-1865 O
Pitt, Anderson to Omy Deener 8-31-1867 F B
Pitt, Levi H. to Frances C. Ferrill 9-30-1868 (no return) Dy
Pitt, Marion to Amanda Fuller 9-2-1867 Dy
Pitt, Thomas to Harriett Brewer 11-5-1867 Be
Pittenger, J. J. W. to Malinda Harreld 4-27-1867 G
Pittman, A. W. C. to L. Jane Duncan 10-21-1872 (10-24-1872) T
Pittman, Abell to Sarah A. Colleth 7-13-1860 (no return) Dy
Pittman, Edwin to Emily M. Terry 9-4-1864 G
Pittman, Henry C. to Sarah M. Yeargain 12-8-1852 (12-9-1852) G
Pittman, J. A. W. to Tericy Gilliland 11-29-1853 (12-1-1853) G
Pittman, J. H. to Smothers M. A. 9-21-1865 Hy
Pittman, J. W. to Bettie M. Richards 3-2-1864 Sh
Pittman, Jacob to Martha J. Shelly 10-30-1845 Ma
Pittman, James B. to Helen S. Cozart 3-24-1869 (3-25-1869) Ma *
Pittman, John to Mrs. Watkins 4-15-1851 Sh
Pittman, L. G. H. to Leuvenia M. Pittman 11-16-1847 (11-18-1847) G
Pittman, R. F. to Brezel Sallie A. 1-23-1867 Hy
Pittman, T. H. to Revelle S. F. 12-26-1872 Hy
Pittman, Thomas to Mary Jane Gowan 10-24-1882 L
Pittman, W. J. to Hendren M. f. 10-4-1866 Hy
Pittman, William to Mary J. Bettis 2-5-1850 Sh
Pittner, James to Charles Mary 7-26-1871 (no return) Hy
Pitts, A. C. to Mattie Myers 11-20-1883 L
Pitts, A. J. to Mollie Roberson 10-27-1883 (10-28-1883) L
Pitts, Andrew J. to Mary Adelaide Blankenship 9-5-1876 (9-6-1876) Dy
Pitts, Billy to Fluviana Brimm 12-11-1878 L
Pitts, Cary to McCulle Leann 1-5-1878 Hy
Pitts, E. K. to M. M. Baily 8-21-1865 G
Pitts, H. T. to Nancy Brimm 3-5-1877 (3-6-1877) L
Pitts, Henry T. to Elizabeth F. Gains 1-23-1866 (1-25-1866) L
Pitts, Henry T. to Mary J. Whitson 9-24-1857 L
Pitts, Imri S. to Lucy Ann Tennessee Rives 11-12-1872 (no return) L
Pitts, James W. to Susan S. Gaines 6-10-1852 L
Pitts, Jerry to Fanny Fowlkes 2-2-1867 Dy
Pitts, John W. to Mary A. Blankenship 6-24-1873 (no return) Dy
Pitts, John to Sarah Patterson 9-3-1855 (9-4-1855) G
Pitts, Lafayette to Mabel Jones 12-11-1867 (12-12-1867) Dy

Pitts, Marion to Susan Elizabeth Trim (Grim) 2-13-1858 O
Pitts, Matthew to Mary Jane Richer 2-18-1861 G
Pitts, Nelson to Julia Frazier 4-10-1873 L B
Pitts, Nelson to Sallie Currin 1-19-1880 (1-20-1880) L
Pitts, Richard S. to Drucinda E. Young 12-18-1855 Ma
Pitts, Robert to Belle Parr 6-12-1880 (6-13-1880) L B
Pitts, Theo. to Ann Freeman 5-10-1864 (5-12-1864) Dy
Pitts, W. A. to Caroline Smith 10-23-1860 Dy
Pitts, William J. to Lucy E. Williams 9-3-1866 (9-4-1866) L
Pitts, William J. to Mary J. Burk 12-20-1848 L
Pitts, William to Olly Kemp 10-9-1873 L B
Plank, Chas. J. to Susan Ellison 4-16-1861 Sh
Plank, James to Lucinda Taber 10-9-1833 Hr
Plant, Christopher H. to Susan N. Ramsey 11-17-1845 (12-2-1845) F
Plant, Mad to Mary A. Cargell 3-14-1853 (no return) F
Plant, S. M. to Ellen Elizabeth Stony 7-19-1851 (no return) F
Plant, William to Emily W. Sitler 6-20-1843 (no return) F
Platt, D. to Elizabeth Campbell 5-21-1856 Dy
Plattenburg, George to Josephine Howard 9-15-1855 (no return) F
Plaxco, W. R. to Lucy Hawkins 10-25-1860 Sh
Plaxter, Wm. S. to Margarett J. McKinstrey 1-13-1852 (no return) F
Pleasant, Caldwell to Louisa Hogue 6-2-1842 O
Pleasant, Edmend to Gimima Bayer 10-20-1859 We
Pleasant, Rancey to Adaline E. Shores 3-16-1852 O
Pleasant, Saml. L. to Sarah C. Griffin 10-11-1870 (no return) Dy
Pleasant, W. M. to Elizabeth Miles 9-11-1858 We
Pledge, Lemuel M. to Mary W. Dodd 12-23-1826 (12-24-1826) Hr
Pledge, William A. to Elvira J. Yancy 10-27-1849 (11-1-1849) F
Pleitz, Edward to Juliana Hornberger 6-15-1857 Sh
Plemons, James A. to Rebecca T. Weaver 8-20-1854 Hn
Plemons, T. H. to Nancy H. Ross 10-14-1852 Hn
Plumer, Junias to Bobo Jennie 12-12-1870 (no return) Hy
Plumer, Nathan F. to Eliza D. Stockinger 10-26-1846 (11-5-1846) F
Plummer, F. S. to Johnson Mollie 1-9-1871 (no return) Hy
Plummer, Henry to Sutton Easter 5-22-1871 Hy
Plummer, Horace to Taylor Lucy 1-4-1875 (no return) Hy
Plummer, J. R. to Lizzie Bigham 7-14-1869 (no return) Cr
Plummer, Joseph E., jr. to Mary K. Henderson 4-11-1853 Sh
Plummer, Lovelace to Plummer Martha 9-28-1867 Hy
Plummer, Marcus to Catherine Hays 7-24-1839 Sh
Plummer, N. F. to Rachel Alexander 8-12-1834 Sh
Plummer, T. L. to Emma Kellow 12-13-1876 (12-14-1876) Dy
Plummer, William to Fields Arelia 12-26-1877 Hy
Plummer, William to Vaulx Malissa 12-23-1878 Hy
Plunk, Michael to Martha A. Hulett 11-26-1850 (12-2-1850) O
Plunkett, Achilles to Elizabeth A. Walker 12-1-1836 Sh
Plyland, William to Malissa Crockett 3-21-1853 G
Poarch, J. M. to M. A. Kent 2-29-1876 (3-1-1876) Dy
Poe, Green to Jane Walker 8-6-1844 Be
Poe, Joseph P. to Nancy Jones 10-?-1851 (no return) Hn
Poe, M. G. to Mary F. Buckley 8-6-1849 Hn
Poe, William H. to Fanny Powell 11-4-1879 L
Pogue, D. M. to Martha J. Pollock 6-17-1865 (6-18-1865) L
Pohel, Christian to Angeline M. Moore 12-27-1865 Mn
Pohl, Theodore to Mary Limberg 10-30-1860 Sh
Poindexter, Bob to Lutetia Clark 9-16-1867 (9-21-1867) F B
Poindexter, C. C. to Ella A. Shelton 11-15-1873 (11-18-1873) T
Poindexter, C. C. to Virginia Clifton 1-24-1870 (1-25-1870) F
Poindexter, Christopher C. to Anna Harris 4-24-1871 (5-5-1871) F
Poindexter, David to Dionca Ann Garner 4-2-1842 (4-7-1842) Ma
Poindexter, Geo. to Mat Tucker 1-1-1868 (1-2-1868) F B
Poindexter, Louis H. to Sarah E. Clifton 1-23-1871 (1-25-1871) F
Poindexter, R. J. to Mary S. Adcock 6-5-1867 G
Poindexter, Raleigh W. to Winnifred L. Hilliard 9-7-1846 (no return) F
Poindexter, Rolla to Sarah Wells 12-12-1854 (no return) F
Poindexter, T. H. to Hattie V. Farrar 12-6-1866 (12-12-1866) F
Poindexter, Thomal C. to Ann E. Cole 9-20-1847 F
Poindexter, Thos. H. to Sallie B. Hunt? 11-16-1872 (11-20-1872) T
Poindexter, W. G. to Dora O. Hunt 11-16-1872 (11-20-1872) T
Poindexter, William J. to Martha L. McFarlen 2-15-1858 (2-17-1858) G
Poindexter, William to Eveline McFoslin 1-1-1855 (1-2-1855) G
Poindexter, Wm. H. to Grizzard Ann M. 9-8-1872 Hy
Poindexter, Wm. to Clara Tucker 8-10-1866 (8-12-1866) F B
Poitevent, Stephen J. to Catharine Johnson 2-13-1861 Sh
Poland, James to Pittman Sarah Ann 5-23-1867 (no return) Hy
Poling, J. H. to Ozment Elizabeth 7-31-1861 (no return) Hy
Polk(Pack), Thomas to Ann Morrow 12-18-1833 Hr
Polk, Alexander to Elizabeth Jackson 6-17-1829 Hr
Polk, Britton to Sally Henderson 12-25-1866 (12-26-1866) F B
Polk, Charles G. to Mary Ann Massey 12-27-1838 Sh
Polk, Charles P. to Ellen M. Fitzhugh 10-7-1835 Hr
Polk, Colins to Clark Martha 1-25-1872 Hy
Polk, Edman to McClish Ailsey 12-29-1874 Hy
Polk, Edwin to Octavia R. Jones 7-29-1846 (7-30-1846) Hr
Polk, Enzkial W. to Martha Jane Clay 6-22-1840 (6-23-1840) Ma
Polk, George to Eliza Jane Marshall 7-25-1837 O
Polk, Headly to Hetta Eliza Sebastin 6-3-1845 Hr

Polk, Horace M. to Ophelia J. Bills 6-15-1843 (6-20-1843) Hr
Polk, Jackson J. to Elvira T. Boles 2-21-1835 (2-24-1835) Hr
Polk, James K. to Mollie Moore 12-27-1867 (12-26?-1867) Dy
Polk, Jas. to E. A. Harper 5-14-1867 O
Polk, John to June Hisaw 12-24-1844 (12-25-1844) G
Polk, John to Sarah Croose 1-16-1830 (1-17-1830) Hr
Polk, Johnathan to Agness Anderson 8-4-1851 Hr
Polk, Marshall T. to Evilina M. Bills 1-10-1856 Hr
Polk, Osco to Adaline Nelson 1-18-1868 F B
Polk, Robert to Laura McNeill 4-11-1867 (4-20-1867) F B
Polk, Saml. to Eldora Cotherun 1-5-1870 T
Polk, Tho. R. to Lucy N. Cocke 6-11-1846 (6-24-1846) F
Polk, Thomas R. to Carolina L. Smith 12-15-1841 F
Polk, Thomas W. to Sarah E. Brady 10-11-1838 (10-12-1838) Hr
Polk, Thos. R. to Bettie Kean 2-27-1862 (3-12-1862) F
Polk, Walley to Carney Amanda 2-2-1873 Hy
Polk, William to Elizabeth J. Bradford 10-24-1850 Hr
Polk, William to Susan Harper 4-3-1856 Hr
Polk, Wm. J. to Maggie Q. Coopwood 4-28-1860 Sh
Polk, Wm. to Mary C. Thomas 7-23-1839 (7-30-1839) F
Poll, John H. to Margaret Hassell 1-18-1842 G
Pollan, John to Mary Harpe 11-13-1827 Ma
Pollard, Edward T. to Moody F. Raggin 10-3-1871 (10-4-1871) Ma
Pollard, Ezikeal to Elizabeth Watson 12-29-1871 L
Pollard, Howel T. to Emily A. Tripp 9-14-1844 Sh
Pollard, Isaac to Maniza Legate 11-24-1832 (11-28-1832) G
Pollard, James C. to Allice Gray 11-30-1850 F
Pollard, John L. to Lucy E. Weatherford 11-18-1867 (11-19-1867) T
Pollard, John L. to Mary Buck 2-6-1850 Sh
Pollard, Otha C. to Nancy Rowntree 12-24-1845 (12-25-1845) G
Pollard, Stephen to Ann Stephens 2-24-1828 G
Pollard, Wallis to Macilda E. Cunningham 4-22-1870 (4-24-1870) Cr
Pollock, Andrew to Nancy Snow 3-15-1847 O
Pollock, David C. to Sarah Jane Sisco 1-4-1858 (1-7-1858) O
Pollock, George to Mary A. Murphy 6-28-1842 O
Pollock, James H. to Sarah E. Davis 1-4-1849 O
Pollock, Julius A. to Kate Boone 9-20-1864 O
Pollock, Robert H. to M. H. Ward 7-17-1850 O
Pollum, Edward C. to Elizabeth Park 7-27-1850 O
Polly, A. J. to Mary A. Cranford 7-9-1864 (7-11-1864) O
Polly, Andrew J. to Sarah Owen (Orren) 9-19-1854 (9-21-1854) O
Polly, H. A. to Frances J. (Mrs.) Bramlett 11-18-1867 O
Polsgrove, A. S. to M. M. Whitlock 9-28-1865 O
Polsgrove, Alfred T. to Elizabeth Beadles 2-22-1857 O
Polsgrove, George M. to Nancy D. Sammons 7-10-1849 O
Polsgrove, George M. to Nancy M. Sammon 11-24-1855 (11-27-1855) O
Polsgrove, Henry to Louisa Graham 8-9-1861 (8-11-1861) O
Polsgrove, James to Lucinda Beedles 5-29-1856 We
Polsgrove, W. H. to Mary A. Walker 11-23-1871 O
Polsson, William to Harriet A. Jones 2-20-1862 We
Polston, J. R. to C. L. Rodgers 10-31-1878 (no return) Dy
Polston, J. W. to Polley Worlds? 12-22-1866 (12-23-1866) Cr
Polston, James E. to S. J. Kelly 12-20-1866 Dy
Polston, James E. to Susan C. Ray? 6-26-1860 Dy
Polston, James E. to V. C. (Mrs.) Speed 5-9-1883 (5-17-1883) L
Pomeroy, H. B. to Sallie Ann Reed 1-21-1879 (1-22-1879) Dy
Ponder, R. T. to Sarah E. Parker 10-19-1872 (10-24-1872) Dy
Pondexter, John S. to Anna L. Bronaugh 2-3-1852 (2-4-1852) Sh
Pool, Alex'r R. to Mary J. Timberman 7-1-1852 O
Pool, Alfred to Mary A. Benson 3-15-1855 Ma
Pool, Alfred to Mary Karr 9-15-1843 (9-17-1843) Ma
Pool, Armstead P. to Martha E. Langford 8-17-1848 Ma
Pool, B. F. to Nancy McClure 1-20-1856 Sh
Pool, E. F. to Amanda Jenkins 10-1-1857 We
Pool, G. M. to Mary L. Clayton 5-14-1866 (5-16-1866) F
Pool, G. W. to Elizabeth M. Key 7-13-1836 Sh
Pool, George W. to Ann C. (Miss) Ezell 7-23-1862 (7-27-1862) O
Pool, Hezekiah to Elizabeth Ashbey 4-9-1864 (no return) Hn
Pool, Isaac to Margaret Hanley 10-3-1835 Sh
Pool, James H. to Matilda Fararow 10-12-1848 Sh
Pool, James to Elizabeth Stofle 6-9-1859 Hn
Pool, James to Louisa T. Sanders 1-28-1867 F
Pool, James to Nancy Neely 1-1-1830 Hr
Pool, John G. to Mary J. J. Pool 1-21-1861 (1-23-1861) Sh
Pool, John L. to Deborah M. Sloan 10-11-1839 (10-17-1839) F
Pool, John W. to Sarah A. Morris 6-1-1872 T
Pool, John to Jane Miller 1-29-1868 T
Pool, John to Mary E. Kelley 6-1-1848 Sh
Pool, John to Mary E. Robertson 5-12-1870 T
Pool, John to Mary Helen Baldock 12-26-1854 (12-28-1854) T
Pool, Joseph to Frances A. E. Miller 2-6-1861 L
Pool, Joshua to Eliza A. Kernel 3-22-1848 Cr
Pool, M. L. to Margaret F. Cates 6-2-1857 We
Pool, R. H. to C. A. Henslee 7-14-1858 (no return) Hn
Pool, Robert A. to Mary Hammon 2-10-1869 T
Pool, Robert A. to Susan A. Laws 7-11-1850 Sh
Pool, S. C. to Day Martha E. 2-25-1869 Hy

Pool, Sanders to Mary J. Neely 4-6-1855 Sh
Pool, Whitson to Caroline Phillips 11-21-1848 G
Pool, William J. to Louisa M. Lasater 2-28-1861 We
Pool, William to Mary E. Lea 8-21-1849 (8-23-1849) Ma
Pool, Wm. to Mary E. Gray 5-8-1854 (5-9-1854) T
Poole, Henry to Neely Fawcett 1-15-1881 L
Poole, Sanders to Sarah McCargo 6-10-1852 Sh
Poole, Wade U. to Martha J. Pritchard 8-17-1852 Cr
Poor, Edwin H. to A. S. Boals 3-21-1867 F
Pope, Alse L. to Malinda Huffine 11-28-1877 (11-29-1877) Dy
Pope, Andrew R. to Mary A. Murrell 9-2-1865 (9-10-1865) F
Pope, Archibal to Darcus Porter 3-19-1856 (3-20-1856) G
Pope, Benjamin to Sarah Boyd 6-15-1867 (6-23-1867) L B
Pope, Bryant to R. J. Martin 2-23-1858 G
Pope, Daniel T. to Newby Alice 1-4-1866 Hy
Pope, Daniel to Bradford Eliza 5-16-1867 Hy
Pope, Drew H. to Nannie M. Buster 9-11-1850 (9-18-1850) Sh
Pope, E. P. to A. L. McCorkle 11-5-1873 (11-6-1873) Dy
Pope, E. W. to Meriah Prichett 1-10-1842 Cr
Pope, Elijah to Adaline Dudley 1-20-1846 We
Pope, Ezekeal to Emily Paschell 11-12-1857 (no return) We
Pope, Ezekiel to Martha A. Vermilion 9-27-1861 We
Pope, H. T. to Sarah C. Huffine 12-4-1878 (no return) Dy
Pope, H. to Jane Terry 3-17-1852 Cr
Pope, Henry B. to Mary A. Castellaw 1-31-1856 L
Pope, J. A. to Lucy F. Dozier 12-23-1868 Dy
Pope, J. M. to J. L. Gooding 1-19-1878 (1-20-1878) Dy
Pope, James D. to Elizabeth Doak 8-20-1873 (no return) Dy
Pope, John A. to Louisa A. Exum 12-6-1852 (no return) F
Pope, John C. to Nancy E. Lunsford 4-19-1879 (4-20-1879) L
Pope, John W. to Haskey Dennis 4-30-1837 G
Pope, John W. to Nancy Blair 4-14-1863 (4-15-1863) Cr
Pope, John W. to Nancy Blair 4-14-1864 (no return) Cr
Pope, John Wesley to Martha Ann Carroll 9-11-1867 (no return) Dy
Pope, John to Clara Adela Chambliss 1-5-1857 (1-8-1857) Sh
Pope, John to Lethia Sope 12-15-1842 (no return) F
Pope, John to Mary McDowell 11-7-1870 (11-14-1870) F
Pope, John to Sarah Hall 12-21-1878 (no return) Dy
Pope, Joseph A. to Eliza Ann Bridges 7-8-1844 Be
Pope, Joseph to Sophronia Estes 5-17-1859 (5-18-1859) Ma
Pope, L. H. to Jane Masser 10-8-1840 Be
Pope, Madison to Julia F. McClaran 4-6-1858 Sh
Pope, Oswald to Sallie P. Dubose 4-30-1856 Sh
Pope, Robert to Elizabeth Smith 5-16-1834 G
Pope, S. B. to Mary E. Martin 4-28-1860 (5-1-1860) G
Pope, S. N. J. to Martha Jones 7-19-1861 (no return) Cr
Pope, Solomon to Mary Higgs 12-7-1855 We
Pope, T. W. to Pracht A. O. 12-5-1877 Hy
Pope, Thadeus to Mary Elizabeth Stribling 12-13-1853 Ma
Pope, W. H. to Harriett Perkins 2-28-1866 (3-1-1866) Cr
Pope, W. H. to M. Jane Maynard 9-21-1870 (9-22-1870) Cr
Pope, Wiley to Mollie Cook 10-27-1874 Dy
Pope, William to Ann Strayhorn 8-20-1838 (8-25-1838) Ma
Pope, William to Elizabeth Dickey 2-8-1841 Ma
Pope, William to Elvira M. (Mrs.) Byrd 12-12-1859 Ma
Poplen, William to Sarah Whitworth 10-11-1841 Hn
Porch, S. M. to M. E. Buchanan 9-21-1867 O
Porch, William to Francis Wooldridge 12-6-1859 (no return) We
Porte (Parte), P. O. to Mary L. Biffell 7-16-1854 We
Porte, John N. to Nelly B. Taylor 12-31-1855 (1-1-1855?) G
Porteet, J. H. to Sarah Jane Loving 12-13-1862 (12-17-1862) Sh
Porteous, Thos. P. to Martha Lancaster 4-7-1863 Sh
Porter, A. A. to N. M. Ivy 10-25-1865 (11-6-1865) T
Porter, Abraham to Nannie Bost 10-21-1876 L
Porter, Alex to Harriet Boyd 1-4-1872 (1-15-1872) T
Porter, Alfred to Mariah Williams 6-9-1866 (10-13-1866) G
Porter, Andrew A. to Martha A. Taylor 10-17-1846 (10-22-1846) F
Porter, Andrew to Polly Howell 1-2-1837 (1-17-1837) G
Porter, Arnold to Honora O'Rian 9-11-1860 Sh
Porter, Axum to Sarah Dobbin 12-27-1867 F B
Porter, B. T. to M. A. T. (Mrs.) Clement 1-18-1872 Dy
Porter, Benj. to Ann L. Thurmond 3-30-1843 L
Porter, Benjamin J. to Callie Virginia DeLoach 1-15-1867 (1-16-1867) L
Porter, Cezar to Martha A. Travis 5-15-1866 Hn B
Porter, Charles to Cary Baley 2-11-1832 (3-8-1832) G
Porter, D. G. to Nancy E. Spain 12-10-1868 (12-11-1868) Cr
Porter, D. H. to Louisa Drake 3-7-1851 (3-9-1851) Hr
Porter, D. T. to M. A. (Mrs.) Meacham 2-3-1858 (2-4-1858) Sh
Porter, Danil to Parthena Nash 11-30-1870 (12-3-1870) Dy
Porter, David B. to Lucinda Golden 8-7-1848 (8-?-1848) Ma
Porter, David B. to Susan M. A. Moore 1-3-1843 G
Porter, David M. to Susan B. Newby 1-24-1850 Sh
Porter, E. H. to Bettie W. Porter 10-3-1861 Sh
Porter, Felix F. to Hariet A. Loving 11-29-1859 Hn
Porter, G. S. to A. C. Lee 3-12-1861 O
Porter, Gardner to Jenny Springfield 12-1-1869 (no return) F B
Porter, Geo. C. to Bond Mollie P. 11-1-1870 Hy

Porter, George M. to Elizabeth A. Crawford 1-4-1839 Hn
Porter, Harry to Sarah Provine 5-28-1866 Hn
Porter, Henry to Hant Gudzer 9-30-1871 (10-1-1871) L B
Porter, Hershall S. to Martha A. Person 6-14-1853 Sh
Porter, J. G. to M. E. Thornton 2-12-1866 G
Porter, J. J. to Elizabeth Reaves 1-17-1871 (1-18-1871) Cr
Porter, J. J. to K. E. Matthews 9-24-1866 G
Porter, J. M. to M. P. Thompson 10-17-1859 (10-18-1859) G
Porter, J. R. to Easter J. Jones 12-6-1866 (12-5?-1866) Cr
Porter, J. W. to Harriet A. Southerel 8-29-1868 (8-30-1868) Cr
Porter, J. W. to Nannie Bryant 8-2-1873 (no return) Cr
Porter, James D., jr. to Susan A. Dunlap 6-18-1851 Hn
Porter, James D., sr. to H. J. Dawson 12-18-1850 Hn
Porter, James H. to Jane A. Harris 7-25-1848 Sh
Porter, James R. to Catharina Gregory 9-4-1851 G
Porter, James W. to Laura E. Miller 10-27-1870 G
Porter, James to Sarah J. Craddock 10-14-1833 (12-16-1833) G
Porter, Jas. J. to Margaret C. Moore 2-25-1873 (2-26-1873) Cr
Porter, Jeff to Mary Williams 5-3-1870 (no return) F B
Porter, Jeramiah to Ora Lea 1-29-1874 (1-29-1875) L B
Porter, Jesse W. to S. S. Hilliard 7-10-1855 We
Porter, Jim to Lucas Beatie 12-28-1870 Hy
Porter, John C. to Susan Ellen 12-6-1837 G
Porter, John M. to Rebecca Fuller 12-20-1830 Sh
Porter, John M. to Sarah Rose 2-15-1848 Hr
Porter, John to Lotta Henderson 3-18-1873 (no return) Dy
Porter, John to Lucy Bradford 12-28-1878 (12-31-1879) L B
Porter, Josiah to Judith D. Clark 10-14-1846 Hn
Porter, Limus to Susan Nash 12-28-1872 (2-2-1873) Dy
Porter, Manuel to Susan Jane Porter 5-21-1866 (no return) Hn
Porter, N. B. to M. B. Bomar 1-25-1866 Hn
Porter, Perry to Martha Porter 2-14-1870 (2-15-1870) Cr
Porter, Ricks to Mary G. Berry 9-9-1841 Cr
Porter, Robert A. to Mary M. Arnold 10-5-1853 (10-6-1853) G
Porter, Robert S. to Felicia Anthony 10-9-1861 (10-10-1861) L
Porter, Sam to Sinda Johnson 1-7-1880 (1-13-1880) L B
Porter, Sidney J. to Malinda Fletcher 3-2-1843 (3-9-1843) G
Porter, Sidney to Hester A. Weaver 7-31-1870 G
Porter, Spencer to Nancy Ford 1-17-1866 (1-20-1866) F B
Porter, Sydney to E. L. Flowers 12-9-1866 G
Porter, Thomas R. to Harriett R. Smith 9-27-1858 Cr
Porter, Tobe to Julia Atkins 4-17-1867 (no return) Hn B
Porter, W. A. to Adaline Rosen 3-20-1867 G
Porter, W. A. to E. J. Hickman 9-5-1870 (9-8-1870) Cr
Porter, W. L. to Eliza Brighton 3-1-1861 Sh
Porter, W. N. to Fannie P. Sharber 8-1-1870 Dy
Porter, Wash to Pennie Doyle 11-4-1875 Dy
Porter, Will W. to Ella E. Tharpe 10-24-1864 Hn
Porter, William to Mary Wilson 12-7-1856 Hr
Porter, William to Susannah Rose 5-19-1841 (5-20-1841) Hr
Porter, Wm. G. to Mary A. Stubblefield 2-5-1850 We
Porter, Wm. H. to Nancy Wells 4-2-1858 (4-4-1858) Sh
Porter, Wm. L. to Mary A. Bower 3-21-1861 Sh
Porterfield, James H. to Nancy Rowland 10-31-1843 Cr
Portis, Benjn. H. W. to Equilla Bieber 6-20-1842 (6-?-1842) Hr
Portis, Clinton D. to Sarah A. Portis 10-20-1849 G
Portis, E. D. to Amanda F. Everett 1-27-1853 (no return) F
Portis, Frank to Lucinda Nixon 12-13-1873 (12-14-1873) L
Portis, John C. to Lucy A. Averett 11-23-1855 (no return) F
Portis, W. N. to Annie J. Lee 5-12-1860 (5-16-1860) F
Portis, Wm. N. to Mattie B. Lee 11-1-1869 (11-3-1869) F
Posey, Albert W. to Frances B. Smith 4-20-1859 L
Posey, Albert W. to Susan H. Boyd 12-21-1843 L
Posey, Emmerson to Vina Murry 3-5-1877 (3-7-1877) L B
Posey, Horace to R. A. McDowell 11-10-1870 (1-14-1871) T
Posey, John to Maggie Maris 12-23-1885 (12-24-1885) L
Posey, Rob't A. to Octavia C. Cresswell 11-8-1872 O
Posey, Thomas N. to S. J. Keller 2-27-1872 (2-28-1872) L
Posey, William P. to Mary E. Lackey 1-20-1848 (1-20-1847?) L
Poss, Henry to P. Adlerbaum 1-26-1864 Sh
Possie, Perry to Todd Elizabeth 2-7-1878 Hy
Posten, John to Mary Moncrief 7-10-1854 (no return) F
Posten, N. H. to Agness J. Obanion 12-8-1858 (12-9-1858) Sh
Posten?, Noah H. to Louisa J. Eskridge 3-2-1854 (no return) F
Postlethwaite, John T. to Ann Eliza Cooper 1-15-1857 Hn
Postlethwaite, John to Rebecca W. Blanton 2-15-1866 Hn
Poston, George N. to Eliza E. Murrell 2-15-1848 Sh
Poston, J. W. to Sarah E. Compton 10-20-1863 (10-21-1863) F
Poston, James A. to Williams Mattie E. 3-5-1873 Hy
Poston, John A. to Rebeca R. Locke 10-13-1864 Sh
Poston, John H. to Williams Mollie J. 12-6-1877 Hy
Poston, Samuel A. to Charity Whitehead 1-11-1855 Sh
Poston, W. F. to Duffer Jennie 11-2-1872 (no return) Hy
Poston, Wm. K. to Mary L. Park 4-13-1843 Sh
Poteete, Wm. Andrew to Mary Susan Gowan 5-28-1870 (5-29-1870) Ma
Poter, P. O. to H. H. Mizell 2-20-1862 We
Poterfield, Matthew A. to Mary Davis 10-4-1838 Hr

Potter, Elias M. to Prudence Keeser 5-16-1842 (5-18-1842) O
Potter, G. W. to E. E. Godsey 9-15-1866 (9-16-1866) O
Potter, Gustavus to H. M. Minster 12-9-1863
Potter, J. H. C. to E. J. Tomlinson 1-10-1882 (1-11-1883) L
Potter, John S. to Jane Stark 4-7-1852 (4-8-1852) Sh
Potter, Silas M. to Olive S. Wilson 4-15-1869 (no return) L
Potter, T. M. to Sevier M. C. 10-18-1870 Hy
Potter, W. E. to S. C. Nichols 10-8-1867 (10-9-1867) Dy
Potter, William S. to Caroline Gire 1-26-1861 We
Potter, William to Owen Margaret 11-24-1875 (no return) Hy
Potts, Allen K. to Martha Ann Linsey 10-26-1858 (no return) Hn
Potts, Charles to Jane S. Bordley 9-1-1840 (9-10-1840) F
Potts, Ellison T. to Isabella C. Hill 1-20-1846 Hn
Potts, Ellison T. to Judy F. Roberts 9-19-1857 (9-20-1857) Ma
Potts, G. H. to Starns Mary Ann 4-3-1866 Hy
Potts, H. W. to Malissa A. Fields 11-22-1865 Hn
Potts, John to Sarah A. Wright 12-24-1850 (no return) Hn
Potts, Joseph to Emma Renshaw 1-31-1839 Hn
Potts, Noah to Marietta Goode 8-23-1867 (8-24-1867) F B
Potts, R. W. to Fennel R. A. 6-2-1870 Hy
Potts, Tho. J. to Lucy Lanier 9-18-1865 (9-20-1865) F
Potts, Thomas M. to Delina Massey 2-4-1850 Hn
Potts, Wilie to A. J. Jimmerson 10-9-1850 (no return) Hn
Potts, Wm. H. to Rebecca H. Gilmore 11-25-1848 Sh
Potts, Zachariah Taylor to Nancy Jane McClaren 6-26-1870 G
Potts?, C. F. to M. A. Comsay? 5-30-1865 Hn
Pouge?, John to Susan An Williams 12-22-1849 (12-23-1849) F
Poulson, Martin to Mary Barnett 7-2-1850 Sh
Pouncy, Rufus D. to Catherine C. Bynum 7-15-1860 We
Pound, David W. to Mary A. Jones 7-23-1844 (7-25-1844) O
Pound, Hiram to Jane Page 9-2-1828 (9-4-1828) O
Pounds, Andrew J. to Hannah Pruitt 7-2-1855 (7-5-1855) G
Pounds, Andrew J. to Rebecca Haislip 12-7-1860 Ma
Pounds, Daniel to Sarah Oakley 1-4-1860 We
Pounds, James M. to Nancy Sherron 2-2-1846 (2-4-1846) G
Pounds, John H. to Christiana E. Morris 12-24-1866 (12-25-1866) Cr
Pounds, John H. to Mary Johnston 3-7-1859 (3-15-1859) G
Pounds, John T. to Mary J. Mason 7-5-1859 (7-7-1859) Ma
Pounds, N. N. to Amanda McKelvy 9-21-1862 G
Pounds, Thomas L. to Eliz J. Connell 2-29-1848 G
Pounds, William to Margret Davis 9-24-1860 G
Powden, Hooper J. to Lydia A. F. Messick 3-6-1851 (3-5?-1851) G
Powel, Alfred W. to Mary W. Harrington 10-2-1828 Ma
Powel, D. H. to Lear M. Antwine 12-6-1860 Sh
Powel, Grant to Adaline Tatum 9-7-1870 (no return) L
Powel, I. W. to A. E. Pleasant 3-20-1866 (3-22-1866) O
Powel, John G. to Elizabeth (Mrs.) White 12-9-1863 Sh
Powel, Josiah to Louiza Pearce 8-30-1864 G
Powel, McNeal to Jane Bryan 8-25-1831 Sh
Powel, Wm. R. to Margaret P. Beaton 5-28-1851 Be
Powell, A. M. to Hill O. A. L. 9-23-1872 (no return) Hy
Powell, A. P. to Josephine Wilkins 1-14-1874 (no return) Dy
Powell, A. P. to Martha E. Hancock 10-19-1862 G
Powell, Albert to Sarah Curtis 1-1-1851 L
Powell, Alfred P. to Trangnella A. McGee 4-1-1859 Ma
Powell, Allen to Nancy E. Frazier 12-28-1869 G
Powell, Amos J. to Hathaway Emma F. 7-27-1870 (no return) Hy
Powell, Austin to Short Polly 11-21-1868 Hy
Powell, B. A. to Mary Jane Pierce 10-24-1867 Dy
Powell, B. A. to Sallie E. Nelson 2-28-1866 (3-1-1866) F
Powell, B. C. to Helen Olive 1-20-1848 Hn
Powell, Benjamin J. to Elizabeth B. Davis 2-2-1848 Ma
Powell, Carter to Gilliam Lidda 5-25-1871 Hy
Powell, Charles to Martha Davis 9-23-1842 O
Powell, Charlie M. to Sarah A. Cavitt 2-10-1859 We
Powell, Dayerous to Elizabeth Lee 7-3-1855 We
Powell, G. W. to Coleman Mary C. 6-18-1874 (no return) Hy
Powell, G. W. to N. H. Vick 11-14-1866 G
Powell, Geo. to Powell Leacy 9-18-1871 Hy
Powell, George W. to Emma Powell 11-23-1878 (11-27-1878) L
Powell, George to Williams Eliz 12-31-1867 Hy
Powell, Govan to Collier Jennie 6-14-1876 (no return) Hy
Powell, Henry B. to Lizzy L. Dunkin 11-11-1856 Sh
Powell, Henry C. to Margaret A. Howard 12-2-1857 Hn
Powell, Henry to Maria Williams 1-22-1841 Sh
Powell, J. B. to Jones Lavinia 12-23-1861 (no return) Hy
Powell, J. D. to Fannie E. Cobb 12-20-1882 L
Powell, J. D. to Martha A. Dunivant 3-15-1864 (3-16-1864) Dy
Powell, J. M. to Johnson Martha Ann 12-6-1865 Hy
Powell, J. W. to Martha Brown 12-16-1858 Cr
Powell, J. W. to Rebecca Spears 9-22-1862 G
Powell, Jack to Fanny Nicholson 12-23-1869 G B
Powell, James A. to Pate Jane 5-16-1866 Hy
Powell, James B. to Pochahontas Davis 1-21-1854 (1-22-1854) O
Powell, James H. to Smith Julia F. 8-25-1861 (no return) Hy
Powell, James M. to J. A. A. S. Willard 5-24-1851 (5-28-1851) L
Powell, James R. to Melia F. A.? Darby 10-8-1850 O

Powell, James R. to Sarah Dalton 3-10-1845 O
Powell, James W. to Arminta H. Harper 11-15-1860 O
Powell, James to Eliza Ivie 12-11-1866 (12-13-1866) F
Powell, James to Mirth Y. Hayes 8-27-1856 Cr
Powell, James to Sarah A. Foust 1-2-1852 (no return) Hn
Powell, John A. to Elizabeth Carly 11-17-1858 Cr
Powell, John W. to McNiel Mary C. 9-13-1866 Hy
Powell, John W. to Mollie Randol 9-27-1862 G
Powell, John to Annis Rawlings 12-17-1869 (no return) F B
Powell, John to Elizabeth Pruden 10-4-1847 (10-5-1847) Ma
Powell, John to Mary Reason 7-19-1847 (7-27-1847) Hr
Powell, Joshua E. to Hassie M. Morris 1-5-1860 Hn
Powell, Joshua H. to Ann E. Coffey 11-13-1866 L
Powell, L.(D?) H. to Mollie Dunnegan 8-11-1869 G
Powell, Lemuel to Elizabeth Porter 3-25-1851 (3-27-1851) Hr
Powell, Lewis to Rebecca Mitchell 12-26-1866 (12-27-1866) Dy
Powell, Mordica to Emily M. Chaney 7-29-1836 Sh
Powell, Naum to Harriet Cobb 5-18-1857 (5-19-1857) Ma
Powell, Needham J. to Nancy M. Webb 11-24-1849 (11-27-1849) Hr
Powell, Nixon to Prudy Clark 3-10-1868 G B
Powell, Nuton to Jones Louisa 1-4-1871 (no return) Hy
Powell, Peyton to Ann H. Fowler 6-23-1835 Hr
Powell, Prince to Missy Peery 8-23-1869 (no return) Dy
Powell, R. H. to E. J. Gadd 1-10-1860 (1-11-1860) Hr
Powell, R. P. to M. Michaels 5-4-1872 (5-5-1872) Dy
Powell, R. P. to R. W. Bradshaw 3-16-1861 Dy
Powell, Richard D. to Rebecca A. Bell 7-16-1863 Sh
Powell, Richard E. to Mary Gay 10-15-1836 (10-20-1836) Hr
Powell, Richd. to Sutton Adaline 6-17-1871 Hy
Powell, Rufus W. to Margaret R.? Baxter 2-6-1850 F
Powell, Stephen M. to Mildred E. Shelton 11-7-1859 (11-8-1859) Ma
Powell, T. C. to S. C. Sample 5-1-1854 (5-3-1854) O
Powell, Taylor to Miller Marthy 10-10-1876 Hy
Powell, Thomas J. to Mary L. Dunlap 12-16-1864 Hn
Powell, Thomas M. to Elizabeth Wardlow 12-24-1861 Mn
Powell, Thomas to Frances Wynne 1-8-1880 Dy
Powell, Tobe to Elizabeth Crow 10-22-1879 (10-23-1879) Dy
Powell, W. A. to S. C. Shores 1-24-1868 O
Powell, W. H. to Ann Bowman 10-13-1863 Hn
Powell, W. J. to E. S. Rooks 11-22-1866 (11-25-1866) Dy
Powell, W. R. B. to Nancy M. Johnson 10-23-1857 (11-5-1857) Hr
Powell, W. S. to Cole Theodocia 11-24-1873 (no return) Hy
Powell, W. T. to Mary (Mrs.) Bradshaw 1-8-1867 Dy
Powell, Washington to Rachel Manning 1-22-1867 G
Powell, Wiley to Elizabeth Allen 5-28-1823 Sh
Powell, William B. to Elvira S. Weddington 8-24-1852 Hn
Powell, William D. to Narcissa J. Henderson 12-3-1861 Dy
Powell, William H. to V. H. Guesent 12-13-1859 (12-14-1859) Sh
Powell, William R. to Elizabeth C. Smith 11-21-1849 Hn
Powell, William to Sarah Green 12-8-1868 G
Powell, Wm. A. to Martha Jane Ewen 12-24-1864 (12-25-1864) Sh
Powell, Wm. C. to Pearcey Winford 1-1-1861 (no return) Hy
Powelson, Simon to Jane Bickers 9-18-1863 F
Power, John to Eliza Goldsmith 3-25-1864 Sh
Power, Stephen F. to Maria S. Baskwell 9-13-1838 (SB 1839) Hr
Power, Stephen F. to Maria S. Baskwell 9-13-1839 (9-26-1839) Hr
Power, Wm. to Mary E. Kelly 11-?-1853 (no return) F
Powers, Anthony to Bridget Cursie 6-12-1861 Sh
Powers, Anthony to Mary Nash 1-7-1860 (1-8-1860) Sh
Powers, Benj. F. to Martha C. Whitney 10-7-1850 (10-6?-1850) F
Powers, Benj. F. to Sarah J. Elam 7-28-1856 Sh
Powers, C. L. to Lucy Willitt 10-1-1861 Sh
Powers, Chas. L. to Lucy L. Small 1-28-1857 Sh
Powers, David W. to Nany Howell 2-16-1843 (2-20-1843) G
Powers, Donaldson to Jennie Wintiser 2-20-1879 L
Powers, Doxey to Thomas Junior 11-21-1870 (no return) Hy
Powers, Edward to Sarah A. Bingham 9-6-1854 Sh
Powers, Ephraim to Martha Robertson 10-7-1862 Dy
Powers, Ephraim to Mary Ann Waters 8-7-1876 (8-9-1876) Dy
Powers, Frances Carter to Charlotte Penick 3-25-1875 (3-28-1875) L
Powers, G. W. to F. A. Findley 7-22-1852 Hn
Powers, James to Lizzy Jane Yates 2-23-1859 Hn
Powers, James to Sarena Butler 10-28-1845 We
Powers, John A. to Elizabeth Steel 10-2-1858 We
Powers, John C. to Bridget McEwen 9-18-1862 Sh
Powers, John T. to M. A. Reid 5-4-1858 Sh
Powers, John to Ann Conners 5-18-1861 (5-20-1861) Sh
Powers, John to M. C. Hicks 10-21-1856 We
Powers, Joseph J. to Helen J. Mulholland 7-21-1862 (7-22-1862) Sh
Powers, L. T. to Elizabeth Knight 1-15-1848 (1-17-1848) F
Powers, Michael to Mary Ann Bayne (Bain) 2-5-1848 Sh
Powers, N. G. to Martha P. Henning 8-30-1851 Sh
Powers, Patrick to Mary Gillis 6-15-1863 Sh
Powers, Richard to Berthy A. Smith 9-?-1844 (no return) Hn
Powers, Samuel to Mary Boles 11-26-1825 Sh
Powers, Stephen to Catharine Mitchell 5-19-1864 Sh

Powers, W. A. to M. A. L. Babb 8-13-1884 (8-14-1884) L
Powers, W. H. to Bettie Fry 6-21-1875 (6-22-1875) O
Powers, William to Amelia Cheek 9-2-1849 Sh
Powers, William to Elizabeth Fodge 1-28-1846 Hn
Poyner, George T. to Myra A. Luter 3-15-1865 Hn
Poyner, J. W. to M. Williams 1-26-1863 (1-28-1863) Sh
Poyner, James to Marinda T. Crowder 12-2-1847 Hn
Poyner, John H. to Nancy Ann Milliken 9-15-1859 Hn
Poyner, Lemuel to Elizabeth Smith 11-14-1840 (11-15-1840) Hr
Poyner, Samuel T. to Susan F. Crowder 6-23-1853 Hn
Poyner, Thomas W. to Sophia Arabella Bumpass 4-24-1866 Hn
Poyner, Thomas to Elizabeth Futrell 3-29-1853 Hn
Poyner, W. D. to Amanda M. F. Bumpass 4-14-1853 Hn
Poyner, William W. to Mary A. E. Forest 10-22-1850 Hn
Poynter, L. D. to D. F. Bowden 12-8-1845 Hn
Poynter, William B. to Paralee Newton 12-27-1848 (no return) Hn
Prast?, J. A. to M. F. Jackson 7-12-1847 Hr
Prat, W. to S. C. Belew 9-13-1870 Cr
Prater, G. W. to L. P. Lambdin 10-5-1845 (no return) Hn
Prater, R. M. to Louisa Trim 9-12-1868 (9-15-1868) T
Prater, Robert A. to E. C. Rogers 5-5-1847 O
Prather, Thomas to Charlotte Ann Applegate 1-17-1848 (1-18-1848) O
Pratt, Charles to Emma Redick 9-24-1880 (9-25-1880) L B
Pratt, G. W. to P. S. Case 3-8-1860 Sh
Pratt, G. W. to S. A. Tippett 1-22-1863 Be
Pratt, George L. to Margaret R. McCallister 12-11-1848 (12-14-1848) G
Pratt, Isaac to Gilly Brown 10-31-1867 G B
Pratt, James S. to Sarah J. McCartney 3-8-1858 (3-9-1858) G
Pratt, John M. to Sarah V. Smith 10-24-1854 (10-26-1854) G
Pratt, Moses E. to Mary Jane Oliver 9-9-1871 (9-10-1871) Ma
Pratt, Moses E. to Mary M. McCabe 12-23-1867 (12-24-1867) Ma
Pratt, Nelson T. to Anne Dudley 6-18-1879 (6-19-1879) Dy
Pratt, W. T. to Hannah Bryant 10-17-1860 G
Pratt, William T. to Susannah James 12-15-1864 G
Preesler, J. S. to Dodd Roeana T. 12-23-1877 Hy
Prehit, Fredrick to Jane Brown 1-18-1867 T
Prescott, Daniel to Anna M. Carver 5-18-1828 Hr
Prescott, Ephraim to Mays Lucy A. 1-11-1870 (no return) Hy
Prescott, Henry to Harrison Mary 11-29-1860 (no return) Hy
Prescott, J. D. to N. E. Boling 10-23-1882 L
Prescott, James to Ann B. Bennett 2-9-1857 Be
Prescott, James to Mahala Braden 8-16-1843 (8-17-1843) L
Prescott, John to Martha Thomas 3-10-1845 (3-18-1845) L
Prescott, Josiah to Electa Bobbitt 10-20-1831 Sh
Prescott, Oscar F. to Ann R. Plummer 7-25-1844 Sh
Prescott, Oscar F. to Mary Davis 2-14-1855 Sh
Prescott, William to Bell Louiza J. 1-2-1861 (no return) Hy
Presley, Cavert to Nancy Howard 7-4-1876 (7-5-1876) L
Presley, Denning to Emily (Mrs.) Pole 2-8-1868 Ma
Pressley, Noel M. to Ellen Wilkins 5-29-1861 (5-30-1861) O
Presson, B. F. to Elizabeth A. Cole 12-10-1863 Be
Presson, Christopher C. to Ellen Little 8-29-1852 Cr
Presson, David C. to Mary Bivins 8-19-1856 Be
Presson, Ellis T. to Katharine Rushing 3-14-1850 Be
Presson, H. T. to Lucinda E. P. Presson 12-18-1860 Be
Presson, Isaac M. to Laviny C. Hale 6-10-1865 Be
Presson, Isaac N. to Martha C. Cole 1-29-1867 Be
Presson, J. A. to Louina Stigall 6-26-1853 Be
Presson, J. to Polly Presson 6-5-1842 Be
Presson, James F. N. to Eady Matilda Helms 3-31-1867 Be
Presson, James F. to Syntha Holland 12-21-1846 Be
Presson, Jas. H. to Malinda L. Presson 6-28-1868 Be
Presson, John B. to Patience C. Presson 7-11-1861 Be
Presson, John T. to Nancy Greer 1-2-1844 Be
Presson, John Toomar to Mahaly Presson 8-7-1866 Be
Presson, John to A. P. Cole 6-10-1863 Be
Presson, Matthew to Sarah Waters 8-27-1865 Be
Presson, N. David to Sarah A. Pickler 3-8-1860 Cr
Presson, N. W. to Lidda Liles 11-29-1849 Cr
Presson, R. A. to M. E. Turner 10-9-1871 (no return) Cr
Presson, Samuel M. to Mary Frances Greer 1-13-1862 Be
Presson, Samuel to Elender K. Bruce 12-1-1853 Be
Presson, T. H. H. to Elizabeth Liles 12-?-1861 (12-15-1861) Cr
Presson, T. H. W. to Elizabeth Tiles 12-13-1861 (12-15-1861) Cr
Presson, Theophilus to Mary Cole 4-16-1868]
Presson, Thomas H. to Lucinda Presson 11-30-1867 Be
Presson, Thomas J. to Louisa J. Greer 12-23-1851 Be
Presson, Thomas N. to Angeline Herron 10-15-1845 Be
Presson, Thos. H. to Lesa Ann Greer 9-29-1868 Be
Presson, Wm. F. to Eda Presson 1-31-1844 Be
Presson, Wm. H. to Matilda Presson 3-22-1847 Be
Presson, Wm. P. to Sarah Wiseman 12-15-1850 Be
Presson, Wm. W. to Martha S. Greer 11-1-1866 Be
Prestidge, George to Mollie Scott 7-21-1870 L
Preston, C. W. to Sarah E. Taylor 12-19-1849 (12-22-1849) F
Preston, Ross to Susan Wilcocks 4-16-1877 (9-12-1877) O B
Preston, Walter E. to Fannie Middleton Hays 3-9-1858 (3-10-1858) Ma

Preston, William to Louisa Parker 3-19-1851 Hn
Preswood, Cullen to Eliza Ann Robert 2-28-1863 (3-1-1863) Sh
Previtt, N. H. to Mary J. Perkins 3-?-1852 (no return) F
Previtt, William to Martha A. Thomas 7-14-1855 (7-16-1855) L
Prewet, W. R. to Jamima Winberry 10-11-1871 (10-12-1871) Dy
Prewett, A. N. to Caroline Bunting 11-15-1858 (11-18-1858) Hr
Prewett, A. O. to Luvenia Bailey 2-16-1859 (2-17-1859) Hr
Prewett, Albert to R. Dill 12-31-1846 Cr
Prewett, Daniel M. to Nancy Davis 6-6-1838 (6-12-1838) Hr
Prewett, J. H. to Martha E. Hill 12-18-1858 (12-22-1858) Hr
Prewett, J. N. to Elizabeth Walker 12-8-1871 (no return) Cr
Prewett, J. T. to I. E. Jackson 9-20-1870 G
Prewett, James W. to Mary A. Hanis(Harris?) 1-21-1848 (1-25-1848) Hr
Prewett, James to Eliza J. Martin 1-16-1844 Cr
Prewett, James to Elizabeth A. McLioud 11-10-1853 Cr
Prewett, James to Paralee Bishop 12-18-1869 (12-19-1869) O
Prewett, John M. to Elizabeth H. Russell 11-30-1859 Ma
Prewett, John to Elizabeth A. Hampton 12-22-1846 Cr
Prewett, Robt. E. to Dicy Ann Robinson 10-31-1868 (11-3-1868) Ma
Prewett, S. L. to M.F. Bass 9-29-1860 (10-24-1860) Hr
Prewett, T. N. to Mary E. Harris 1-4-1860 (1-5-1860) Hr
Prewett, Thomas H. to Fannie Henkle 2-25-1869 G
Prewett, W. H. to Martha A. Evans 10-19-1860 Hr
Prewett, W. J. to F. A. Kennan 9-15-1870 G
Prewett, W. T. to Martha A. Holt 11-3-1842 Sh
Prewett, William to Temperance Burch (Bunge) 8-10-1837 Sh
Prewett,, W. F. to Mollie E. Culbreath 12-15-1874 T
Prewit, Levi to Mary Landers 11-15-1851 Hn
Prewitt, Berry to Phoeba A. Jones 12-24-1867 (no return) F B
Prewitt, Crawford to Margrat G. Griffin 10-25-1836 (10-28-1836) G
Prewitt, John P. F. to Malinda C. Brown 9-20-1843 H
Prewitt, Mastin to Polly Standly 2-26-1838 (2-27-1838) Hr
Prewitt, Mathew Thomas to Rebecca Ann Glass 4-10-1848 (4-11-1848) Hr
Prewitt, Milton W. to Lucy V. Gates 12-9-1867 (12-10-1867) F
Prewitt, Milton W. to Mariah W. Prewitt 8-9-1847 (8-12-1847) Hr
Prewitt, W. F. to Nancy Ann Cole 11-25-1846 Be
Price, A. C. to E. D. Williams 12-28-1845 We
Price, A. H. to Mary Ann Chambers 10-9-1848 (10-23-1848) F
Price, Alfred to Sarah Brent 3-5-1835 (no return) Hn
Price, Allen to Paralee Russell 8-14-1861 Be
Price, Andrew J. to Feliciana Alytt? 3-23-1843 Sh
Price, Anthony to Dicy Mosby 2-15-1867 (2-16-1867) F B
Price, Arthur to Emeline Maris 12-29-1866 F B
Price, Benj. C. to Sonora Byrn 12-17-1866 (12-19-1866) L
Price, Benjamin F. to Martha A. Wilsonn 11-17-1847 Sh
Price, Benjamin to Elizabeth Hernard 2-13-1842 Cr
Price, Bevely to Mary Hailey 3-29-1847 (4-7-1847) G
Price, Bob to Milly Swan 10-27-1854 (1-2-1855) Sh
Price, Campbell to Sophronia Hicks 2-9-1867 (2-10-1867) Ma
Price, Cartwright to Emily Akin 9-7-1848 Sh
Price, Chatman to Lillie Cherry 11-25-1885 (11-29-1885) L
Price, D. S. to E. C. Buchanan 12-18-1862 Mn
Price, David S. to Mary A. Redwin 1-25-1849 Sh
Price, Doc to Eliza Tucker 12-29-1870 (no return) Dy
Price, Edwin H. to Maria A. Ruffin 4-27-1836 (4-29-1836) Hr
Price, Elijah (Memphis TN) to Mary S. Swink 4-17-1853 Ma
Price, F. M. to M. A. Boon 1-17-1870 (1-19-1870) Dy
Price, Geo. W. to Margaret L. Hopper 12-24-1869 Ma
Price, George H. to Mary E. Mathis 10-22-1851 G
Price, George W. to Gatson Ann S. Anderson 12-17-1849 (12-20-1849) G
Price, George to Margaret J. Hornbeak 3-27-1861 We
Price, H. J. to Caroline V. Saffarrans 1-16-1860 Sh
Price, Hammond E. to Dixie E. Strickland 10-13-1884 (10-16-1884) L
Price, Henry J. to Augusta B. Trice 6-2-1859 Sh
Price, Henry to Caroline Maddox 8-23-1867 (8-24-1867) F B
Price, Henry to Mary Paterson 4-10-1869 (4-11-1869) L
Price, J. K. to Mary Jane Branch 2-5-1873 O
Price, J. W. to Louisa Crow 5-21-1857 We
Price, J. Y. to Martha J. Ballard 2-14-1878 (no return) L
Price, James A. to Martha E. West 1-17-1854 (1-18-1854) G
Price, James H. to Helen P. Potts 12-15-1868 (12-16-1868) Ma
Price, James M. to Atlanta E. Coats 2-3-1851 (2-2?-1851) G
Price, James W. to Elizabeth R. Toone 4-28-1852 (4-29-1852) Hr
Price, James to Betty Sparks 9-16-1869 (9-18-1869) Cr
Price, James to Nancy Campbell 6-26-1848 G
Price, James to Sarah F. Stidam 12-14-1868 (12-16-1868) F
Price, James to Susan Swim? 12-2-1866 Hn
Price, Jerry to Fanny Q. Wemby 2-18-1867 Hn
Price, Jessee to Sarah J. West 9-9-1844 (9-12-1844) G
Price, Jim to Ann Smith 5-4-1867 G B
Price, John F. to Euphania Wadlington 1-19-1870 Ma
Price, John G. to Jane Klutts 2-17-1856 We
Price, John J. to Elizabeth Bailey 8-7-1858 Sh
Price, John R. to Edy Brogdon 10-5-1857 G
Price, John R. to Mary Ann Brewer 8-25-1854 Be
Price, John W. to Sarah E. James 5-9-1860 (5-15-1860) T
Price, John to Martha B. Reagan 8-1-1853 (8-15-1853) Hr

Price, John to Mary J. M. Sawyers 9-20-1827 Sh
Price, John to Rebecca Ann Taylor 3-30-1854 Ma
Price, Joseph to Emma Francis Samuels 5-4-1874 (5-5-1874) L
Price, Joseph to Lou L. Lankford 7-9-1879 L
Price, Joshua to Eloner Leadbetter 12-3-1838 Ma
Price, Masha? to Matilda Brigum 9-2-1828 Ma
Price, Meshack to Sarah Whitamore(Whitaman?) 4-9-1857 L
Price, Michael to Elizabeth Brown 8-17-1837 Hr
Price, Mothen? R. to Frances G. Bounds 12-17-1849 (no return) F
Price, N. B. to Mollie E. Millikin 6-9-1868 (6-10-1868) F
Price, Nathaniel M. to Harrell McKnight 10-2-1843 (10-5-1843) Ma
Price, Newt to Martha Bradley 4-20-1867 Hn
Price, Peter to Willie Ann Williamson 2-4-1871 (no return) F B
Price, Richard B. to Sarah R. Edwards 10-9-1855 O
Price, Richard M. to Susan Ann Duffer 11-13-1869 (11-14-1869) Ma
Price, Right to Sarah Russell 9-1-1860 Be
Price, Robert to Nancy Pipkins 11-22-1862 Mn
Price, Sam to Camelia Hobson 1-5-1867 (1-6-1867) F B
Price, Samuel to Nancy Luten 11-16-1867 L
Price, Silas to Clark Anna 5-7-1878 Hy
Price, Stephen J. to Louisa Price 10-17-1857 L
Price, T. C. to Mollie E. Bell 2-17-1859 Cr
Price, Thomas M. to Sarah E. Marshall 3-5-1845 O
Price, Thomas to Elizabeth Privett 3-15-1855 (3-16-1855) L
Price, Thos. H. to Elizabeth F. Allen 1-12-1859 Cr
Price, Thos. M. to Sarah E. Marshall 3-3-1846 O
Price, W. F. to Mary C. Breedon 3-21-1861 Hr
Price, W. H. to Fannie L. Spain 1-18-1872 O
Price, W. H. to M. E. Adamson 1-8-1868 G
Price, Weight to Sally Corsort 1-11-1830 (1-17-1830) Ma
Price, William B. to Sally Carey 6-25-1846 Sh
Price, William E. to Mary L. Featherstone 12-21-1858 (no return) We
Price, William F. B. to Susan C. Durham 1-14-1858 L
Price, William M. to Minerva Teague 7-17-1846 (7-23-1846) F
Price, William W. to Nancy C. Robison 12-8-1841 (12-9-1841) Ma
Price, William to Bettie Christman 10-15-1868 Ma
Price, William to Julia Covington 10-24-1883 (10-30-1883) L
Price, William to Maria Hess 12-31-1838 (1-2-1839) G
Price, William to Mary Covington 6-28-1882 (no return) L
Price, William to Sherron Anna 9-7-1877 Hy
Price, Wm. A. to Virginia E. Wilson 2-1-1848 Sh
Price, Wm. E. to Mary L. Fetherstone 12-23-1858 We
Price, Wm. J. to Martha Alsop 10-25-1850 Be
Price, Wm. M. to Frances Humphrey 2-26-1855 (no return) F
Price, Wm. to Rener Calhoun 4-11-1874 (4-8?-1874) T B
Price, Zechariah W. to Caroline Brewer 2-7-1851 Be
Price?, John to M. Ramsay 3-3-1846 Hn
Price?, O. to Sarah Jane Neal 12-16-1852 Hn
Prichard, A. A. to Ella E. Chaffin 9-23-1868 F
Prichard, B. R. to J. A. Brewer 12-27-1877 Dy
Prichard, Ben F. to Mary E. Hampton 12-21-1872 (no return) Dy
Prichard, E. S. to Julia Moore 1-25-1859 F
Prichard, F. R. to M. E. Mitchell 8-25-1885 (8-26-1885) L
Prichard, G. W. to Sarah A. Prichard 9-7-1868 (no return) Dy
Prichard, Green to Amanda Wyatt 11-29-1877 Dy
Prichard, J. M. to Bettie Mitchell 2-12-1878 (2-13-1878) L
Prichard, J. R. to A. J. Davis 8-9-1869 (8-10-1869) Dy
Prichard, J. R. to H. (M.?)J. Hall 3-2-1878 (3-7-1878) Dy
Prichard, James to Julia Owens 11-30-1840 Sh
Prichard, Jerry to Laura Wyatt 4-2-1877 (4-5-1877) Dy
Prichard, John R. to Sarah E. Williams 12-24-1864 (12-25-1864) Dy
Prichard, John to Paralee Dunevant 12-27-1877 Dy
Prichard, Martin to Rosannah Dillard 9-1-1869 (no return) Dy
Prichard, Newton R. to Sarah S. Redding 1-1-1865 Dy
Prichard, Richard to Anna E. Deloach 11-21-1854 (11-22-1854) Sh
Prichard, S. D. to Elizabeth Straine 12-5-1864 (12-7-1864) Dy
Prichard, W. E. to Alice Brewer 9-18-1878 (9-19-1878) Dy
Prichard, W. H. to Mattie Savage 12-18-1878 (12-24-1878) Dy
Prichard, W. J. to Rosa Lee Ledbetter 2-13-1878 Dy
Priddy, George L. to Jane Conner 3-1-1870 (3-3-1870) Ma
Priddy, H. Leigh to C. D. Cole 10-29-1866 (10-31-1866) F
Priddy, Jas. P. to Elizabeth Netherly 11-19-1846 Sh
Priddy, William to Pietty Pearce 3-4-1847 Sh
Pride, Edward D. to Louisiana Nabers 7-16-1832 Sh
Pride, Jesse P. to Emily Margaret Hudspeth 11-24-1855 (11-26-1857) O
Pride, W. W. to M. J. Wyatt 12-21-1867 O
Prideman, Elihu to Mary Johnson 9-25-1862 Mn
Pridogh, George to Mary Littletown 4-17-1845 Cr
Pridy, Watson to Sally Cook 7-5-1831 (7-6-1831) G
Prier, Bill to Rebecca Moore 2-12-1874 (2-13-1874) T
Priest, Benj. F. to Mary L. A. Jackson 1-31-1855 (2-1-1855) Hr
Priest, Franklin to Mary Watson 2-18-1847 Cr
Priest, Hiram H. to Martha S. Griffin 1-20-1860 (no return) We
Priest, John to Lucy B. (Mrs.) Cogbill 12-22-1863 Sh
Priest, Joseph to Jane Haites 12-10-1850 Cr
Priest, Milton to Louisa Grizzard 9-8-1858 Cr
Priest, R. W. to E. J. Stewart 12-9-1852 Sh

Priest, Thomas to Harriet Priest 7-9-1860 (7-10-1860) Ma
Priest, Wm. C. to Helen Sloan 7-2-1860 (7-4-1860) Hr
Primble, Joe to Varnor Jane 3-21-1871 (no return) Hy
Primm?, C. H. to Martha Craft 8-16-1863 (10-4-1863) Sh
Prince, Frank to Nannie Edwards 12-15-1872 Cr B
Prince, George H. to Martha J. Carison 5-4-1846 (no return) Cr
Prince, George H. to Susan T. Hays 9-19-1839 Cr
Prince, James to Martha Ann Wood 10-23-1845 Be
Prince, Jason to Rebecca J. Wilkerson 12-22-1863 Hn
Prince, Jeffersn to Martha Fields 9-5-1855 Hn
Prince, John G. to Cherry L. Earp 1-13-1850 Be
Prince, John S. to Zilpha Ann Prince 10-13-1860 (no return) Hn
Prince, John Y. to Cyntha V. Hudson 5-8-1862 (5-11-1862) T
Prince, John to Elizabeth Osborn ?-?-1837 Be
Prince, John to Nancy Combs 9-15-1853 Be
Prince, Morgan H. to Sarah E. Prince 9-5-1855 (no return) Hn
Prince, Samuel to Margaret Hawkins 12-25-1868 (12-30-1868) Cr
Prince, Thomas E. to Mary E. Merrick 11-10-1850 Be
Prince, Tom to Laura Williamson 8-3-1867 (no return) F B
Prince, William J. to Tillie A. E. Daniel 4-6-1867 (4-9-1867) T
Prince, William to Susan Matheny 11-16-1860 (11-20-1861) We
Prince, Wm. Jasper to Ruby Elmira Gregory 9-12-1860 (9-13-1860) T
Pringle, J. A. to L. A. Baines 9-30-1867
Pringle, James S. to Mary A. Wood 4-4-1868 (4-5-1868) L
Prior, Belfield W. to Elizabeth Theridge 12-21-1848 Sh
Prior, Jno. to Lucinda Smith 10-21-1846 We
Pritchard, B. S. to Manda Phillips 2-16-1860 Cr
Pritchard, Bemin to Nancy C. Key 12-26-1869 Cr
Pritchard, Dudly to Edin Cox 2-6-1841 Cr
Pritchard, H. M. to Sallie Ann McClame 8-12-1873 Cr
Pritchard, Isaac to Amatha Bennett 10-24-1848 Cr
Pritchard, J. P. to Elizabeth Cook 10-13-1855 Cr
Pritchard, Jason to Frances E. Hanfred? 3-24-1866? (3-25-1868) Cr
Pritchard, John H. to Louisa Bledsoe 10-27-1851 Cr
Pritchard, Jonathan to C. M. Thomas 5-4-1867 (5-8-1867) Cr
Pritchard, Pleasant W. to M. T. Holmes 2-1-1844 Cr
Pritchard, William to Issabel Brandon 10-14-1867 (10-15-1867) Cr
Pritchard, Wm. to Gatty _____ 8-25-1853 L
Pritchett, George P. to Mary McDearmon 8-1-1847 Hn
Pritchett, J. W. to Mary S. Martin 5-20-1869 Cr
Pritchett, James W. to M. S. Cooper 9-6-1862 (no return) Hn
Pritchett, John to Elizabeth A. Yates 1-6-1859 Hn
Pritchett, M. E. to Susan A. Bazdel 1-19-1852 Sh
Pritchett, N. C. to Susannah Lumley 2-20-1879 Dy
Pritchett, Thos. J. to Louisa Milam 2-4-1863 (2-5-1863) Dy
Pritchett, Wm. to Lucinda Traynor 6-7-1838 G
Privett, Riley to Minerva P. (Mrs.) Howard 10-31-1865 Dy
Privett, W. R. to Nancy C. Fultcher 4-17-1875 (4-20-1875) Dy
Privett, William F. to Martha M. Laxton 8-31-1843 Ma
Privett, William to Eliza Price 3-16-1855 (no return) L
Privett, William to Martha A. Burnett 12-19-1862 (12-25-1862) Dy
Prock, William to Mayville Wallace 8-12-1861 (8-13-1861) Dy
Proctor, Dave to Margaret Straten 12-26-1867 G B
Proctor, J. M. to Jennie Shipman 7-28-1869 G
Proctor, John C. to Ann Ray 2-20-1864 Mn
Proctor, Joseph M. to Joanna L. Scott 10-26-1868 F
Proctor, Paul S. to Nancy Marcum 10-23-1850 (11-26-1850) G
Propst, A. G. to Sarah A. Cunningham 11-3-1867 G
Proudfit, W. P. to Laura N. Harris 11-24-1852 Sh
Province, W. H. to Mary E. Harris 12-17-1850 Cr
Province, William N. to Lydia P. Harris 2-13-1840 O
Provine, Andrew M to Sarah A. Munrow? 4-24-1851 Hn
Provine, James M. to Mary Jane Hendrix 7-31-1864 Hn
Provine, James M. to Sarah A. P. Wren 10-15-1846 Sh
Provine, John C. to Mary E. Warmick 10-25-1866 Hn
Provine, John to Delilco Lannom 1-9-1861 (no return) Hn
Provow, Edward L. to Elizabeth A. Smith 12-18-1858 Hn
Provow, James A. to Druciller A. Parker 11-6-1862 Hn
Provow, William F. to Lucy Ann Sears 10-25-1850 Hn
Pruden, R. A. to Mary Jane Swanson 7-31-1855 Sh
Pruete, James C. to Emblem Ham 9-23-1839 (9-26-1839) Hr
Pruett, Alfred to Sarah Canada 10-5-1846 (10-7-1846) G
Pruett, Ferrell to Mary S. Rowe 12-6-1870 (12-8-1870) Cr
Pruett, James W. to Nancy Dilday 8-9-1865 (8-10-1865) Cr
Pruett, James to B. L. King 3-8-1871 Cr
Pruett, John to J. Chambers 2-7-1871 Cr
Pruett, John to Rebecca Nail 2-7-1831 (2-9-1831) Hr
Pruett, Robert M. to Nancy C. Rowe 10-2-1865 (10-8-1865) Cr
Pruett, Stephen to Elizabeth Breeding 4-19-1827 Hr
Pruett, Willis N. to Elizabeth Tucker 12-18-1851 Hr
Pruit, Ren to Eathea M. B. Summers 5-17-1849 G
Pruitt, Harris B. to Elizabeth Motly 7-30-1845 (7-31-1845) G
Pruitt, John to Rossan Champain 8-8-1829 (8-9-1829) G
Pruitt, Martin to Nancy I. Nipp 7-20-1865 O
Pryer, E. D. to Sarah Burton 5-4-1848 Hn
Pryer, Henry to A. A. Hamilton 8-2-1852 (8-3-1852) O
Pryer, Isaac to Mariah Burchet 4-26-1870 T

Pryer, John to Nancy D. Wicker 12-24-1852 O
Pryor, David C. to Emma McKissick 11-2-1841 Sh
Pryor, Henry to A. A. Hamilton 8-2-1852 (8-3-1852) O
Pryor, Henry to Elizabeth Pate 10-21-1829 (10-22-1829) O
Pryor, Henry to Sarah Houe 5-19-1859 O
Pryor, Isaiah A. to Martha A. Turbeville 5-23-1855 Hn
Pryor, John L. to Lucinda Smith 10-19-1846 We
Pryor, John L. to N. J. Julin 10-29-1858 We
Pryor, John P. to Eliza P. Long 9-19-1845 Ma
Pryor, William B. to Nancy Williams 6-19-1860 Hn
Pryor, William Oscar to Laura Elizabeth Bernard 1-6-1850 T
Ptts, James M. to Rosanna Parks 10-8-1859 Sh
Pucket, Merion to Harbert Manervia 1-22-1872 Hy
Puckett, J. C. to E. A. Guill 1-24-1856 (no return) Hn
Puckett, J. E. to Sarah A. Clifton 12-23-1858 Hr
Puckett, J. H. to Cassa Cook 5-26-1874 (5-27-1874) L
Puckett, James C. to Nancy J. McLain 1-6-1863 We
Puckett, James to Love Barnett 9-30-1861 Sh
Puckett, John S. to Mary Ann Bushart 9-23-1851 Hn
Puckett, John to Margaret Shankle 12-20-1858 (no return) Hn
Puckett, N. W. to E. Miller 10-16-1867 Hn
Puckett, Peter P. to Margaret T. Delf 10-8-1849 (10-9-1849) Ma
Puckett, S. W. to Nancy Edgar 11-12-1865 Hn
Puckett, Socrates to Catharine O'Sallee 8-29-1856 Hn
Puckett, Wiley to Amanda Wheeler 7-6-1847 O
Pugh, A. L. to Ada Duncan 4-12-1871 (4-13-1871) L
Pugh, Andrew Jackson to Dovist? Ann Eatus 1-22-1852 Hr
Pugh, Bass to Mahala Wardlaw 5-2-1885 L
Pugh, D. M. to Elizabeth Little 1-2-1861 G
Pugh, Davis J. to Susan F. Nichols 9-6-1867 (9-11-1867) Cr
Pugh, Henry R. to Frances J. Beatty 4-20-1842 Sh
Pugh, J. L. to Bell Swanner 12-11-1877 (12-12-1877) Dy
Pugh, James R. to Charity M. Low 1-20-1840 (1-24-1840) Hr
Pugh, James T. to Eliza B. Whitmore 8-21-1835 (8-27-1835) Hr
Pugh, James T. to Salina Darnell 9-28-1853 (9-29-1853) Hr
Pugh, James to Elizabeth Ryster 12-5-1853 (12-8-1853) G
Pugh, James to Mira Vinton 3-22-1861 (3-23-1861) R
Pugh, Jesse to Zelpha Dickson 5-26-1842 (5-27-1842) Ma
Pugh, Joel M. to Catharine Williams 1-22-1879 (1-23-1879) Dy
Pugh, Joel to Martha James 8-24-1863 (8-25-1863) Dy
Pugh, John to Mary Carnes 8-29-1867 (9-6-1867) F B
Pugh, N. T. to Martha A. Billings 10-19-1867 (10-20-1867) T
Pugh, Nelson to Spivey Caroline 12-8-1871 Hy
Pugh, Patrick H. to Mary Jane Carson 11-17-1853 (no return) L
Pugh, S. A. to L. M. Curtis 12-21-1865 (12-22-1865) L
Pugh, S. A. to Mary A. Adams 5-22-1869 (5-29-1869) L
Pugh, T. M. to Nanna Cavnaugh 8-1-1872 (8-4-1872) T
Pugh, W. C. to Frances Jamess 10-25-1860 G
Pugh, Walter C. to Tensy E. Kee 11-13-1860 (11-14-1860) Cr
Pugh, William to Melvina C. Wilson 9-6-1858 (9-8-1858) G
Pugh, Willoughby to Martha Kerr 10-8-1840 Ma
Puiett, Dudly to Jeter Fannie 1-24-1878 Hy
Pullen, E. J. to E. J. Stokes 11-10-1853 H
Pullen, William A. to Susan A. Thomas 2-20-1868 T
Pulliam, A. B. to E. V. Pettit 6-4-1862 F
Pulliam, Benjamin T. to Angeline Corum 3-26-1842 (3-27-1842) O
Pulliam, Bob to Easter Skipper 12-31-1867 (1-4-1868) F B
Pulliam, Campbell to Mina Thornton 12-18-1865 (12-26-1865) F B
Pulliam, Clem to Martha Atkinson 12-30-1852 Hr
Pulliam, D. K. to Mary E. Farley 2-5-1867 (no return) F
Pulliam, J. J. to Lucy F. Burton 4-24-1850 F
Pulliam, John to Sophia Gray 12-20-1868 (12-28-1868) F B
Pulliam, Joseph O. to Lucy A. Edwards 11-26-1855 (11-27-1855) Sh
Pulliam, Mark P. to Cynthia A. (Mrs.) Crawford 11-19-1864 (11-24-1864) Sh
Pulliam, R. C. to Mary Stafford 8-20-1847 O
Pulliam, Tilman P. to Martha J. Hinson 12-20-1854 Hr
Pulliam, W. B. to Martha J. Leonard 11-10-1856 Sh
Pulliam, Zeb to Lucinda Thornton 1-22-1866 (2-28-1866) F B
Pullian, Joseph to Mahala Casey 12-13-1877 (12-30-1877) O B
Pullin, Aaron to Mary Sadler 11-26-1865 (11-6?-1865) T
Pullin, Edmond to Mollie Borum 11-19-1872 T
Pullin, John B. to Christina E. Roan 10-30-1865 (10-31-1865) T
Pullin, Richard to N. A. Wooten 2-4-1867 (2-15-1867) T
Pullin, William to Amanda Ann Johnson 3-5-1868 T
Pullion, John N. to Jane F. C. Davis 9-3-1860 Hn
Pullum, Lossum to Shelton Judy 2-10-1876 (no return) Hy
Pullum, Vachel W. to Martha M. Murphy 11-11-1848 (11-16-1848) Hr
Pully, Thomas W. to Sarah Ann Taylor 11-28-1847 Be
Pulmigino, Pietro to Anny Corles 7-5-1861 (7-7-1861) Sh
Pump, Maier to Lizatte Straus 5-22-1859 Sh
Punch, Mathew L. to Elizabeth Reagan 10-11-1838 (10-12-1838) Hr
Purcell, Jesse D. to Mary Elizabeth Norville 9-8-1846 O
Purcell, Robt. to Margaret Echols 9-20-1879 Dy B
Purchais, James to Viola Houseman 7-11-1874 (7-12-1874) O
Purdee, Hiram to Frances E. Presgrove 11-17-1863 (no return) Dy
Purdy, George R. to Sarah D. Carmon 10-9-1845 (no return) We
Purham, Peter to Boyd Helen 8-15-1872 Hy

Pursell, H. T. to E. E. Fowlkes 12-9-1873 Dy
Pursell, Isaac to Eliza Mauldin 5-25-1867 Dy
Pursell, Joel H. to Serena Isibella Mahan 11-3-1862 (11-4-1862) Dy
Purser, F. M. to Nancy E. Carlton 1-12-1853 (1-13-1853) Sh
Purser, F. M. to Sarah A. Carlton 12-20-1860 Sh
Pursley, Arnett to Blanchie Chitwood 11-24-1874 (11-25-1874) Dy
Purty, Tom to Martha Turner 2-8-1868 L B
Purvis, J. E. to Sallie L. Robertson 9-1-1885 (9-2-1885) L
Purvis, K. S. to M. A. Bryan 10-4-1869 G
Purvis, K. S. to Philips Mary 6-26-1877 (no return) Hy
Purvis, Storkie to Wincie Bramblett 12-28-1830 (1-30-1831) O
Purvis, Wm. to Martha Akins 1-16-1856 Cr
Puryear, Stephen to Eliza Jones 5-9-1885 (5-10-1885) L
Puryear, Wesley to Sallie Brim 4-16-1885 (4-18-1885) L
Puryear, Wm. to Sarah Burns 9-7-1848 Sh
Puryer?, William to Almyra Culla 5-2-1842 Hn
Pustell, John to Elizabeth F. Gore 1-1-1846 Sh
Putman, H. G. to F. A. Lovelace 1-23-1870 (1-25-1871) Dy
Putman, I. H. to Margarett Ervin 10-16-1866 (10-17-1866) O
Putman, James A. to Susan Kluats 5-19-1857 Hn
Putman, John to Mary Little 7-21-1842 Cr
Putman, Newton to Lucy Bledsoe 3-19-1868 G
Putman, Wm. to Martha Overton 11-24-1852 Cr
Putnam, J. M. B. to Martha B. Taylor 9-13-1867 G
Putney, David E. to Elizabeth Harris 9-25-1831 (9-27-1831) Hr
Putzel, M. L. to Mina Levy 12-31-1861 Sh
Pybas, J. C. to A. M. Clark 5-2-1870 (5-3-1870) Ma
Pybus, Adolphus to Ware Emma 10-26-1876 Hy
Pye, James H. to Lavinia E. (Mrs) Tilden 7-4-1850 Sh
Pyland, Abner F. to Lovie E. N. Anderson 10-6-1869 L
Pyland, J. A. to Mary E. J. McEwen 9-6-1854 L
Pyland, J. F. to S. C. M. Agee 9-30-1867 (no return) Dy
Pyland, J. H. to C. A. Mathis 9-29-1870 G
Pyland, J. W. to Disey E. Reddick 8-13-1860 (8-17-1860) Dy
Pyland, John Henry to Susan J. M. Rucker 11-27-1867 L
Pyland, W. F. to Mary E. Lacy 1-19-1880 (1-20-1880) L
Pyland, W. J. to Anna E. Bobbitt 8-13-1868 G
Pylant, Francis M. to Mary A. Collins 7-11-1849 (7-12-1849) Hr
Pyles, Francis M. to Cynthia Thompson 9-7-1854 Ma
Pyles, J. F. to Mollie Gammons 2-17-1875 (2-18-1875) Dy
Pyles, Overton to Loty Robinson 2-19-1833 (2-?-1833) Hr
Pyles, Wade H. to Susan I. Moores 6-23-1855 (6-24-1855) O
Pyron, James to Elizabeth Tally 5-5-1825 O
Pyron, L. H. to Martha Ferguson 12-22-1846 Sh
Pyron, L. H. to Martha U. Vaughan 11-6-1861 Sh

Qualls, Davy to Lucy Douglas 2-20-1869 F B
Quarles, G. L. to Rebecca M. Hatford 4-7-1863 G
Quarmby, Jos. to Elizabeth F. Booth 8-8-1860 Sh
Quarmby, Thomas to Ann (Mrs.) Graham 3-23-1852 Sh
Queen, Geo. W. to Caroline W. Griffin 1-31-1859 F
Quick, Elijah to Sarah Moss 6-17-1837 (6-?-1837) G
Quick, Kenneth to Mary E. Anthony 9-16-1867 G
Quigley, J. T. to Ruth W. Rawlings 10-3-1861 Sh
Quigley, James to Mary Burk 2-19-1857 (2-22-1857) Sh
Quillen, Allen to Jame P. Birdwell 7-10-1845 Cr
Quillen, David to Clavina Hall 10-28-1841 Cr
Quillen, E. N. to Mary Pahol 9-28-1865 Be
Quillen, J. M. to Sarah J. Newman 9-15-1865 Be
Quillin, David to Ann Browning 2-7-1851 Be
Quillin, E. N. to Sarah Spence 11-14-1867 Be
Quillin, W. A. to Lacy J. Pierce 7-22-1855 Be
Quimby, Jonas to Uniun McLaughlin 4-9-1848 Sh
Quimmly, John Allen to Harriet Jane Eliz. Faris 9-26-1853 (9-27-1853) T
Quin, James L. to Elizabeth L. Jones 9-23-1873 (9-25-1873) T
Quin, John K. to Maranda F. Ward 9-9-1853 (9-13-1853) L
Quin, Patrick to Mary Doyle 4-26-1855 Sh
Quinan, Robert E. to Augusta L. Huggins 4-7-1855 Sh
Quinan, Robt. E. to Nancy Pierce 10-2-1861 Sh
Quinlan, Dennis to Ellen Kennedy 1-28-1854 (1-29-1854) Sh
Quinlan, Dennis to Ellen McMahon 10-26-1861 (10-27-1861) Sh
Quinlan, John to Sarah Keshan 11-14-1853 Sh
Quinlan, Rody (Rodny) to Ellen Burke 6-29-1847 Sh
Quinlen, Daniel to Ellen Ryan 6-2-1855 (6-3-1855) Sh
Quinlen, Dennis to Alice Burks (Burke) 5-20-1850 Sh
Quinley, David M. to Exalina Lawrence 2-12-1850 Ma
Quinley, Richard B. to Jane A. Biggers 12-23-1848 (12-25-1848) Ma
Quinlin, Michl. to Ellen McNairy 4-30-1860 Sh
Quinly, David M. to Sylvia L. Moore 6-29-1846 Ma
Quinly, Wm. C. to Martha J. Dawson 9-3-1842 (9-4-1842) Ma
Quinn, G. W. to Virginia Griffin 9-21-1853 (no return) F
Quinn, J. T. to Frenetta Honey 10-18-1854 (no return) Cr
Quinn, J. T. to M. E. Meadows 11-29-1881 (no return) L
Quinn, J. W. to Mary Moore 9-10-1860 (9-11-1860) Sh
Quinn, James A. to Louisa Joice Travis 5-29-1847 Cr
Quinn, James W. to Mary Cross 11-1-1858 (11-2-1858) Sh
Quinn, James to Ann Comboy 6-7-1860 Sh

Quinn, John to Mary J. Walker 3-12-1861 Be
Quinn, Joseph to Cary Argo 6-17-1847 Cr
Quinn, Lawson to Nancy Smith 4-12-1861 (no return) Cr
Quinn, Mathew to Martha York 1-2-1841 G
Quinn, Mitchell to Frances Hutchison 3-6-1871 (no return) Cr
Quinn, Patrick to Mary Ann Dougherty 10-24-1857 (10-25-1857) Sh
Quinn, Robert to Jane A. Harris 5-14-1852 (no return) F
Quinn, S. R. to Emaline Harvey 11-21-1842 (no return) Cr
Quinn, Thos. to Bridget McCade 5-24-1862 (5-25-1862) Sh
Quinn, William P. to Martha Jackson 2-24-1864 (no return) Cr
Quinn, Willie B. to Louisa Harvey 5-10-1843 Cr
Quinn, Wm. P. to Martha Jackson 2-24-1864 (2-26-1864) Cr
Quinn, Zachariah to Susan Pierce 5-9-1867 Dy
Quinn, Zacheriah to Martha J. Chambers 1-7-1873 (1-8-1873) L
Quinton, Washington to Elizabeth Schultz 12-1-1840 Hn
Quisick, John to Johana McDonald 6-17-1855 Sh

Raborn, John to Jane Crocker 5-21-1861 Mn
Rachel, Thomas D. to Maryan Davis 1-8-1848 F
Rachels, Nathan to Sarah Weaver 8-19-1852 T
Rachels, Silas L. to Demaras Wallden 8-25-1859 We
Rackley, James to Rila McDermitt 11-24-1832 G
Rackley, John to Elizabeth Guess 1-3-1839 G
Rackly, James to Elizabeth Cole 5-5-1832 G
Rackly, W. Henderson to Synthia Deason 10-31-1847 L
Radford, David to Elizabeth Cole 3-5-1866 (no return) Hn
Radford, Henry to Nancy J. Nelson 10-8-1861 (no return) Hn
Radford, Henry to Nancy Williams 9-22-1847 Hn
Radford, James to Hannah C. Sanders 12-9-1858 (1-15-1859) O
Radford, Jethro S. to Eliza Ann Cruse 10-23-1856 Hn
Radford, John to Mary Sullivan 2-25-1855 Hn
Radford, O. J. to W. D. Moore 8-2-1871 (8-22-1871) Dy
Radford, W. P. to Sarah Pikston 12-22-1857 Be
Radford, Wm. L. to Frances C. Lawrence 10-23-1855 Sh
Rafe, J. W. to Martha A. Galleway 3-18-1847 (3-26-1847) F
Raferty, William to Margaret L. Owen 12-4-1845 Hn
Raffalty, Thomas to Mary jane Dolen 5-9-1861 Sh
Raffo, D. to Bridget O'Neil 4-5-1856 (4-6-1856) Be
Rafter, Alexander M. to Elizabeth R. Luckett 6-17-1854 (6-21-1854) Sh
Ragan (Logan), C. A. to N. M. Whippell 3-19-1868 (3-21-1868) O
Ragan, Alexander to Anna R. McCrory 9-3-1861 Ma
Ragan, B. W. to Sarah C. McDonald 3-3-1857 G
Ragan, Bennet to Susan Yancy 4-17-1838 (4-19-1838) G
Ragan, C. E. to Susan J. Mitchell 12-6-1865 G
Ragan, J. H. to Mary W. Hartsfield 3-14-1855 (3-15-1855) G
Ragan, J. W. to M. E. Williams 9-11-1863 G
Ragan, John to Julia Ann Payne 12-2-1852 (12-9-1852) O
Ragan, John to Mary Hess 2-21-1867 G
Ragan, Louie to Angeline Steuler 4-24-1863 (4-26-1863) Sh
Ragan, Nathaniel to Mary Vincent 2-9-1842 (2-10-1842) Hr
Ragan, Richard to Mary Neal(e) 10-25-1848 O
Ragan, Thomas J. to Alpha Howard 12-24-1863 G
Ragan, William B. to Nancy C. Rutherford 9-3-1847 (9-5-1847) Hr
Ragan, William F. to Barbara E. Pryor 2-15-1854 (2-16-1854) O
Ragan, William to Permelia Hynnell 12-9-1837 Hr
Ragan, Wm. B. to Martha Ann Hanniss 11-10-1838 (11-15-1838) Hr
Ragen?, James P. to L. A. Hagen 1-11-1856 (no return) Hn
Ragens, W. J. to N. E. White 10-5-1868 (10-8-1868) T
Raggio, John to Barbara Rock 2-7-1859 Sh
Ragland, Burrel to Eliza Mebane 12-29-1869 (12-9?-1869) F B
Ragland, Evan L. to Cecile L. Galleher 9-18-1844 (9-24-1844) O
Ragland, F. B. to Calender Mary A. 9-5-1865 (no return) Hy
Ragland, J. B. to H. R. W. Upshaw 4-28-1860 (5-1-1860) Sh
Ragland, John T. to H. J. Williamson 2-14-1861 Cr
Ragland, John to Betsy Watkins 12-28-1865 (12-30-1865) F B
Ragland, M. E. to McCool Alice E. 11-25-1862 Hy
Ragland, Milton E. to McCool Mary E. 4-19-1869 (no return) Hy
Ragland, Shed to Polk Ella 2-12-1874 Hy
Ragland, W. H. to Lenora Williamson 4-27-1870 (4-28-1870) Cr
Ragsdale, Alexander to Valery Miller 10-12-1843 Ma
Ragsdale, Edward to Eliza A. L. Whitmore 8-20-1855 (no return) F
Ragsdale, Herbert A. to Nancy Arnold 7-29-1837 (8-1-1837) G
Ragsdale, J. R. to Susan Bludworth 9-13-1867 O
Ragsdale, John A. to Nancy J. Grissam 9-15-1858 (9-16-1858) O
Ragsdale, John H. to Mary F. Jones 7-28-1852 (5?-30-1852) G
Ragsdale, Lewis B. to Nancy B. Eskridge 11-15-1846 We
Ragsdale, Samuel to Sarah A. Anderson 12-23-1873 (12-24-1873) O
Ragsdale, William J. to Susan Davis 8-14-1847 (8-17-1847) Ma
Ragsdale, William to Paulina M. Pleasants 10-18-1847 (10-20-1847) F
Raiford, Morris to Ann Boyte 12-12-1837 (1-4-1838) Hr
Raiford, Needham to Rachel Sanders 8-13-1841 Hr
Railford, Thos. W. to Sarah C. Barbee 9-26-1846 Sh
Rails, Wm. to Caroline (Mrs.) Cowgil 12-30-1863 Sh
Raima, Jonathan to Sarah Grider 8-24-1832 G
Rain, Cornelius to Martha Ann Field 4-11-1838 (4-12-1838) Hr
Rainer, Chas. to Elizabeth Stringlin 2-6-1854 Sh
Rainer, Eli to Eliza C. Sexton 1-18-1854 (1-19-1854) Hr
Rainer, Joel to Polly Wellins 9-27-1837 Hr
Rainer, Joseph S. to Zilpha Greenlee 12-18-1851 (12-19-1851) Hr
Rainer, Joseph Sutton to Sarah Mainer 3-22-1842 (10-?-1842) T
Rainer, P. M. to Arkansas Phelps 8-7-1858 (8-8-1858) Hr
Rainer, Pitser R. to Martha J. Kelly 12-10-1850 (12-19-1850) Hr
Raines, Alex W. to A. C. Crawford 11-17-1868 G
Raines, Erasmus B. to Mary Ann Dunlap 12-19-1854 (12-20-1854) G
Raines, G. L. to F. W. Barfield 1-21-1873 L
Raines, H. H. to Annis Camp 8-30-1865 G
Raines, Harvey L. to Jennie M. Elam 10-23-1867 G
Raines, J. G. to Tennessee Boyd 11-23-1868 G
Raines, J. H. to Elizabeth J. Magee 9-25-1863 Mn
Raines, Joel S. to Elizabeth Yarbrough 8-27-1832 Hr
Raines, John H. to Eliza A. Bunting 12-22-1849 (12-23-1849) Hr
Raines, Marcus to H. C. Braswell 10-8-1861 Sh
Raines, Marshall to Emeline Chessher 4-8-1847 Hr
Raines, R. P. to Rebecca J. Rice 8-1-1867 Hn
Raines, Robert E. to Elizabeth C. Hill 12-9-1868 G
Raines, Robert L. to Mary L. Blackwood 9-7-1865 Hn
Raines, Saml. L. to Mary Ford 1-15-1856 Sh
Raines, Thomas to Elizabeth Peck 10-29-1851 (10-30-1851) Hr
Rainey, A. L. to Anderson A. H. 10-12-1871 Hy
Rainey, Adison L. to Rutledge Sarah J. 9-16-1859 (no return) Hy
Rainey, Alfred M. to Elizabeth J. Birdsong 7-11-1855 (7-12-1855) Hr
Rainey, D. P. to Caroline Carricker 5-1-1848 (5-16-1848) Hr
Rainey, Enos to Amanda C. Norrington 7-7-1865 (7-15-1865) Dy
Rainey, H. A. to Maggie E. Moore 7-17-1872 Hy
Rainey, J. B. to Sarah C. Pryor 4-9-1857 Hn
Rainey, James A. to Elizabeth Anthony 5-19-1858 L
Rainey, James H. to Martha J.? Burch 12-21-1867 (12-24-1867) Cr
Rainey, James O. to Mary E. Jones 3-16-1852 Hr
Rainey, James W. to Sarah E. Hendren 8-16-1866 L
Rainey, James to Nancy S. Carricker 8-23-1852 (8-26-1852) Hr
Rainey, John M. to Martha C. Rives? 7-22-1873 (7-23-1873) Dy
Rainey, John W. to Mary Jamima Lockard 5-28-1868 L
Rainey, John to Rachiel Clark 3-23-1843 Be
Rainey, Josiah F. to Tempy M. Irwin 9-9-1839 (9-10-1839) F
Rainey, Louis L. to N. A. Jones 6-29-1854 Hn
Rainey, Peter to Mary Garrett 6-10-1846 Ma
Rainey, R. M. to Nannie Chitwood 10-16-1873 Dy
Rainey, Robert A. to Martha Peoples 8-23-1838 Cr
Rainey, Robert G. to Amanda J. Henry 8-24-1861 (8-25-1861) L
Rainey, Samuel to Edie Dix 8-12-1865 F
Rainey, Stephen Henry to Margaret Milissa Cloyd 8-26-1848 (8-29-1848) Hr
Rainey, Thos. C. to Mary A. Beaty 12-20-1869 Ma
Rainey, W. F. to Cinthy Hatch 6-9-1852 Cr
Rainey, William C. to Rebecca Bell 9-27-1858 (9-29-1858) L
Rainey, William D. to Mary J. Hefley 7-18-1859 (7-20-1859) Ma
Rainey, William T. to Talibhta C. McCommons 10-17-1848 (10-19-1848) Hr
Rainey, Williamson B. to Matilda Dean 11-5-1841 (11-7-1841) Hr
Rainey, Williamson E. to Rebecca Duberry 3-21-1843 Hr
Rains, Acy to Rebecca McMahan 1-15-1833 G
Rains, Albert A. to Susan P. Graves 12-22-1859 Ma
Rains, Albert L. to Mantora F. Davis 10-13-1870 G
Rains, B. H. to E. H. Ivey 3-20-1863 G
Rains, Edmond W. to Elizabeth Lattie 11-15-1828 (11-18-1828) G
Rains, Elijah to Martha Armstrong 11-30-1850 (12-3-1850) G
Rains, Elisha to Elizabeth F. Hathaway 10-10-1862 (10-23-1862) Ma
Rains, Elisha to Emely V. Armstrong 12-9-1852 G
Rains, G. L. to Harriet Lankford 12-7-1869 (no return) L
Rains, George R. to Jane Yarbrough 9-1-1836 Hr
Rains, Hiram P. to Sallie Bishop 1-27-1870 G
Rains, J. C. to Amanda Rains 3-4-1863 Mn
Rains, J. W. to Mary J. Huie 2-11-1864 Hn
Rains, John to Drusilla Stevens 5-9-1836 Sh
Rains, Stephen to Clary Daugherty 5-15-1830 (5-20-1830) G
Rains, Stephen to Elda McGee 11-2-1839 Ma
Rains, Stephen to Unicy Perminter 7-6-1841 (no return) Hn
Rains, Thomas to Margaret Roberson 10-7-1859 Hn
Rains, W. N. to Mary A. Mager 6-6-1862 Mn
Rains, William H. to Elizabeth Bledsoe 8-20-1839 (8-22-1839) G
Rains, William J. to Sarah E. Beavors 4-8-1864 Hr
Rains, Wm. H. to Eliza J. Tidwell 8-1-1848 (no return) F
Rains, Wm. McD. to Clemintine M. Gossett 12-9-1840 (12-10-1840) Hr
Rainy, Henry G. to June Riley 6-23-1846 (6-25-1846) Hr
Rainy, James to Elmedia Hielderbrand 8-3-1830 Ma
Rainy?, Wm. T. to Sarah A. Mashburn 9-4-1846 Hr
Rall, Samuel H. to Geraldine Almond 3-19-1863 Hn
Rall, W. B. to S. A. (Mrs.) Price 5-1-1855 (5-2-1855) Sh
Ralls, J. L. to Elizabeth Hall 9-5-1865 (9-7-1865) Dy
Ralls, James to Nancy Allen 6-28-1846 Hr
Ralph, A. G. to Mary A. Beavers 1-2-1860 (not endorsed) F
Ralph, Absolum C. to Martha E. Waller 7-28-1852 (no return) F
Ralph, Alfred H. to Orlenia McCraw 8-6-1855 (8-16-1855) T
Ralph, Canter B. to Margaret M. Grant 9-12-1855 T
Ralph, Hiram H. to Eleanor W. Owen 12-8-1846 (12-10-1846) T
Ralph, Isaac to Lucindia McCarver 1-6-1842 Hr

Ralph, James W. to Lucinda E. Johnson 8-5-1854 (8-27-1854) T
Ralph, John Ligon to Malvina Sylvester 9-24-1851 T
Ralph, Robert H. to Margaret F. Maley 2-17-1870 (2-20-1870) T
Ralph, Robert H. to Nancy E. Delashmit 8-8-1871 (8-10-1871) T
Ralph, T. J. to Elizabeth M. Barns 2-5-1839 Sh
Ralph, Thoas to Mary Ann Brown? 12-2-1843 T
Ralph, William to Elizabeth Dagling 11-7-1866 (11-8-1867?) T
Ralph, William to Grizzy Ann Branch 8-4-1841 W
Ralston, David C. to Elizabeth C. Winston 10-24-1849 Sh
Ralston, James to Sarah Ann Jones 10-27-1859 Sh
Ralston, John to Lucy T. McDaniel 8-29-1822 Sh
Ramage, H. C. to Nancy A. Holmes 2-?-1863 G
Ramage, James R. to Caroline Ramsey 11-2-1864 (11-3-1864) Sh
Ramage, Josiah to Margaret McIver 9-9-1831 (9-15-1831) Hr
Rambo (Ramber), John to Phebe Berry 9-2-1846 Sh
Rambo, James A. to Susan Pennington 4-25-1861 Dy
Rambo, Matt to Nancy R. A. Lacy 10-16-1866 (10-20-1866) Dy
Rambo, S. G. to Rebecca F. Saunders 2-24-1863 (2-26-1863) Dy
Rambout, jr., G. V. to Susan A. Apperson 3-5-1860 (3-6-1860) Sh
Rambury (Bambury?), Richard to Bridget Harrington 4-28-1864 Sh
Ramsay, Nathan to Sarah Sexton 2-10-1859 Hn
Ramsay, William J. to Sarah J. Barbee 2-21-1864 (no return) Hn
Ramsay, William J. to Sarah J. Beahm 3-8-1864 Hn
Ramsey, Alexander to Lucinda Caplinger 12-16-1858 Hn
Ramsey, Alexander to Margaret Norris 10-26-1864 (10-27-1864) Sh
Ramsey, Alexander to Sarah Black 12-?-1843 (12-22-1843) Hr
Ramsey, Allen to Margaret Huggins 12-31-1845 We
Ramsey, C. W. to Nancy Porterfield 3-13-1861 (3-14-1861) Sh
Ramsey, Daniel to Jane Burrow 4-30-1846 Cr
Ramsey, G. H. to Emma S. (L.?) Blake 12-20-1860 G
Ramsey, George to Mary Alston 6-10-1867 (6-11-1867) Ma
Ramsey, Green H. to Lavenia (Mrs.) Arnold 11-1-1869 Ma
Ramsey, H. B. to Elizabeth A. Thompson 11-7-1846 Sh
Ramsey, I. W. to M. I. Buchanan 10-22-1866 O
Ramsey, J. W. to V. M. Hand (Hard?) 1-3-1866 G
Ramsey, James H. to Ann E. Farley 9-4-1855 (9-6-1855) Sh
Ramsey, James H. to Mary Ann Shadwick 3-5-1848 Hn
Ramsey, James S. to Mary C. Kendrick 4-4-1848 Hn
Ramsey, Jesse B. to Sarah McKinney 12-20-1847 Sh
Ramsey, John to Ellen McFerren 6-9-1869 T
Ramsey, Nathaniel P. to Judith D. Waddy 4-26-1863 G
Ramsey, P. H. to Darthula Koonce 11-24-1852 F
Ramsey, R. B. to Lucy A. E. Lain 2-17-1860 (2-19-1860) Sh
Ramsey, R. N. to M. A. Biggs 5-30-1865 G
Ramsey, R. W. to Lucy J. Lankford 10-16-1860 (10-15?-1860) Cr
Ramsey, Ralph H. to Mary Bryant 10-14-1830 Sh
Ramsey, T. J. to Martha A. Nettles 9-30-1856 G
Ramsey, T. J. to Sallie J. Newall 3-18-1862 F
Ramsey, Thomas B. to Elizabeth A. Newsom 10-10-1854 Hr
Ramsey, Thomas T.? to Virginia Mathews 7-29?-1858 (7-30-1858) Hr
Ramsey, W. C. to Sarah Jane Brigman 2-25-1861 (2-26-1861) Hr
Ramsey, W. D. to Mollie A. Robinson 3-13-1867 Sh
Ramsey, William to Olive P. Patrick 1-16-1830 (1-17-1830) Hr
Ramsey, Wm. B. to Mary W. Manley 2-25-1862 Be
Ramsey, Wm. B. to Sarah Moncreif 10-17-1854 (no return) F
Ranale, E. H. to S. H. Alexander 12-14-186? Hn
Randal (Randle), George to Sarah Ann Paterick (Patrick) 1-8-1845 Sh
Randal, Alexander to Bettie Heaslett 3-27-1869 (no return) F B
Randal, John to Mary Quinn 7-15-1847 Sh
Randall, Cedric B. to Mary A. (Mrs.) Philips 11-27-1864 Sh
Randall, Sanford to Sarah Owen 11-15-1878 (11-21-1878) L B
Randel (Randle), Peter T. to Joanna McKinney (McKinna) 7-15-1849 Sh
Randle (Randal), William to Elizabeth Knox 2-2-1848 Sh
Randle, A. N. to H. G. Carothers 9-10-1846 Hn
Randle, Coleby to Elizabeth Sexton 5-2-1851 Hn
Randle, E. G. to Amanda Rodgers 3-9-1843 Cr
Randle, Edmund to Harriet Lee 1-4-1845 (no return) Hn
Randle, Elbert to Harriet Hughes 10-20-1847 Hn
Randle, H. S. to Annie C. Williams 1-19-1869 G
Randle, James M. to J. M. Hays 12-1-1855 (no return) Hn
Randle, James R. to Margaret A. Daniel 9-27-1854 Hn
Randle, John B. to Elizabeth Moncrief 12-10-1853 (no return) F
Randle, John H. to Susan Caruthers 11-6-1845 (no return) Hn
Randle, Maston to Caroline Mayberry 4-11-1865 (4-12-1865) Cr
Randle, N.? P. to U. R. Lilly 8-5-1866 Hn
Randle, Richard W. to Lillian A. Cnanon 11-23-1841 (no return) Hn
Randle, W. G. to Sarah E. Kendal 1-29-1857 Hn
Randle, W. T. to Sarah Randall 1-6-1862 (1-16-1862) Sh
Randle, William to Elizabeth Paterick (Patrick) 9-27-1843 Sh
Rando, Carmelo to Carmela Gabriele 1-10-1856 Ma
Randolph, E. W. to F. M. Dowell 5-2-1855 (5-3-1855) Sh
Randolph, E.A. to Elleanor G. Riddle 10-3-1854 Hr
Randolph, J. H. to Lou Craig 8-9-1871 (no return) Dy
Randolph, James F. to Melinda Doud 3-10-1848 G
Randolph, James F. to Parmelia Williams 10-8-1859 Ma
Randolph, James L. to Rebecca A. Meek 6-30-1861 Mn
Randolph, John W. to Rutha Ann Baskwell 3-16-1853 Hr

Randolph, John to Betty Alston 7-28-1871 (7-18?-1871) T
Randolph, John to Fannie Dickson 5-15-1867 (5-18-1867) T
Randolph, Johnb to Mary _____ 5-20-1869 T
Randolph, R. H. to Larue Giles 5-27-1863 (5-29-1863) Sh
Randolph, Richard B. B. to Elizabeth Perry 1-4-1842 Hr
Randolph, Richard B. B. to Elizabeth Perry 5-6-1844 (5-30-1844) Hr
Randolph, Thos. to Permelia W.(A?) Murphy 10-7-1864 (10-11-1864) Sh
Randolph, Willis to Emma Batchelor 5-18-1877 Hy
Randolph, Willis to Mary Ann Nobles 4-20-1883 (4-23-1883) L
Raner, Henry to Mollie Mathes 7-25-1885 (7-29-1885) L
Ranes, David to Susan Gaskins 2-11-1858 We
Raney (Roney-Ramy?), Henry P. to Mary A. Scott 6-2-1852 L
Raney, Francis M. to Nancy Finley 7-5-1849 (no return) Cr
Raney, J. J. to Vick Miller 3-26-1871 Hy
Raney, John W. to Mary E. Griggs 6-25-1870 (6-26-1870) L
Raney, Robert G. to Terry Butler 11-18-1843 Ma
Raney, S. M. to Nannie M. Senter 12-8-1869 G
Raney, T. C. to Elizabeth Hatch 11-21-1854 Cr
Raney, William R. to C. A. Coltharp 9-6-1839 (9-9-1839) F
Ranka, Joseph T. to Eliza Allen 9-16-1849 Sh
Ranken, Allen D. to Mary M. Arnold 11-6-1854 (no return) We
Ranken, Allen D. to Mary M. Arnold 11-7-1855 We
Rankens, Marcus to H. C. Braswell 10-8-1861 (10-10-1861) Sh
Rankin, Andrew to Katy Byrn 3-18-1876 (3-19-1876) L B
Rankin, B. B. to Sophronia Williams 12-31-1860 Ma
Rankin, James J. to Margaret G. Rolong 1-2-1856 Hr
Rankin, James to Charlotte A. Davis 1-6-1868 (1-7-1868) Dy
Rankin, Joseph T. to Kitty Dobbs 11-10-1854 (11-12-1854) Ma
Rankin, Joseph to Lee Holloway 2-15-1870 (2-17-1870) F
Rankin, M. J. to M. E. Whittenton 1-30-1867 (2-3-1867) Dy
Rankin, Perry to Hannah Williams 5-25-1872 Hy
Rankin, Robert to Mary Cedona Terril 7-3-1844 G
Rankin, Robt. A. to Tabitha A. Legat 10-10-1837 G
Rankin, Robt. J. to Sarah F. Goforth 4-11-1859 (4-17-1859) Hr
Rankin, Samuel to Mercilla Goodman 9-18-1832 G
Rankin, William H. to Emily A. Herring 12-31-1849 (1-1-1850) O
Rankins, E. G. to Elizabeth Roberson 11-11-1856 (11-26-1856) G
Rankins, James S. to Martha J. Cauthran? 9-17-1861 We
Ranlin, J. S. to Mattie E. McCool 1-13-1869 (no return) Hy
Ranser, Henry to Nancy Sudberry 1-3-1866 (1-20-1867) Dy
Rapelje, Daniel S. to Naoma R. Edmonson 11-22-1859 O
Rapler?, John A. to Mary H. Evans 6-7-1849 Hn
Rapoleand, Lewis to Eliza Tibbs 1-10-1876 (no return) Hy
Rapp, G. W. to Amanda Wilson 5-9-1859 Sh
Rappner, J. G. to M. Novacovich 11-9-1863 Sh
Rasberry, Allen to Elizabeth Weatherford 10-18-1847 (10-19-1847) G
Rasberry, G. W. to Nancy Boatright 12-3-1868 (12-9-1868) Dy
Rasberry, Willis to Mary Pethel 1-3-1867 Be
Rasbury, Asa to Sarah Jackson 7-18-1849 Be
Rasbury, Joseph F. to Jeannette Whitby 3-31-1886 (4-4-1886) L
Rasbury, L. G. to Frances A. Winters 11-7-1862 Dy
Rascoe, Marcus S. to Mary Pierce 9-17-1858 Hn
Rash, James to M. Winfreys 2-29-1864 O
Rash, Thomas H. (A.) to Marcella J. Leake 8-30-1837 Sh
Raspbury, John H. to Minevery J. Cole 3-28-1843 Be
Rast, W. N. to S. D. Dearen 7-24-1862 Mn
Rateree, A. C. to Emily M. Guill 9-13-1866 Hn
Rateree, J. R. to Mary M. Rowlett 11-29-1866 Hn
Ratlieff, Alfred to Mary H. Park 9-25-1866 O
Ratliff, Robt. H. to Ida Lowery 10-18-1875 (no return) Hy
Ratten, William M. to Nancy Kremer(Creamer) 4-1-1835 (4-5-1835) Hr
Ratteree, Asa C. to Mary J. Steele 12-27-1860 Hn
Ratteree, James to Carmelia Burton 6-16-1840 (no return) Hn
Ratzall, Charles to Sarah Chitwood 11-7-1861 Sh
Raub, A. A. to Ernestine McClure 5-2-1864 Sh
Raulston, George H. to Lucy A. Nailling 7-4-1843 We
Raulston, George H. to Lucy Gaines 9-2-1856 Cr
Raulstone, Jas. G. to M. J. Tipton 8-8-1864 O
Rauson, Wm. H. to Pheby Morgan 11-10-1845 (no return) We
Ravenall, A. to Miss R. S. Kimbro 1-7-1861 (1-8-1861) T
Ravenall, Alfred to Mary Boulton 6-18-1862 (5?-19-1862) Sh
Rawles, W. F. to P. Toombs 8-27-1872 Dy
Rawles, W. F. to S. L. Bloar 1-22-1870 (1-23-1870) Dy
Rawlings, J. J. to Mary A. Gift 8-3-1848 Sh
Rawlings, J. J. to Sophia H. Lowrey 11-2-1854 Sh
Rawlings, Jackson C. to Jane C. McKay 5-9-1849 Sh
Rawlings, Joseph J. to Lucinda M. Brown 3-10-1840 Sh
Rawlings, Reuben to Eliza Harris 4-24-1871 (4-25-1871) F B
Rawlings, Thomas J. to Ariminta Daniel 2-12-1837 Sh
Rawlings, Thomas to Jane M. Jones 1-29-1855 (2-1-1855) Ma
Rawlings, Thos. J. to Almira J. Wickham 6-29-1848 Sh
Rawlings, Wm. A. to Nancy M. May 4-30-1849 (5-2-1849) F
Rawlins, Danl. to Betty Walker 12-31-1872 Hy
Rawlins, John W. to Mary F. Coleman 6-26-1860 G
Rawls, A. A. to C. F. Rawls 2-5-1878 Hy
Rawls, E. H. to Martha Ann Tuck 10-23-1860 We
Rawls, John W. to Issabella J. Brown 11-21-1842 O

Rawls, R. H. to Cordelia Wolff 2-11-1869 Cr
Rawls, W. L. to S. A. Bowers 12-19-1876 (2-21-1876) L
Rawlstone, John to Mary E. Steele 12-9-1860 We
Raworth, D. B. to Mollie L. Read 3-16-1870 Hy
Raworth, E. A., jr. to Helen E. Holloway 9-16-1869 Hy
Ray, A. F. to Sarah A. Ellis 1-6-1863 (1-8-1863) Dy
Ray, A. F. to Savannah E. Poteet 6-22-1877 (6-24-1877) Dy
Ray, A. L. to Nancy E. Walker 11-5-1860 (11-6-1860) Dy
Ray, Abel C. to Elizabeth A. Massey 12-21-1854 L
Ray, Alexander to Pemetea C. Weaver 6-22-1854 G
Ray, Alfred to Adaline Armstrong 6-9-1841 G
Ray, Alfred to Saphronia Little 11-25-1862 G
Ray, Alpia G. to Catharine Carter 11-4-1847 (12-1-1847) G
Ray, B. F. to Emily Nelson 4-1-1874 (4-5-1874) L
Ray, Barrum R. to Caroline M. Alexander 8-26-1841 Hn
Ray, Benj. F. to Ann Smith 5-26-1860 (no return) L
Ray, Bony to Lelia Morgan 1-8-1877 Hy
Ray, D. H. to Catharine Conway 4-22-1855 Sh
Ray, Eli to Eliza Newsom 12-15-1866 (12-16-1866) Ma
Ray, Eli to Sarah Vickers 8-13-1856 G
Ray, Elisha B. to Mary Susan Lake 1-27-1852 (1-28-1852) T
Ray, F. M. to Martha Hurt 10-4-1847 Cr
Ray, Francis M. to Margaret E. Petty 10-31-1867 Hn
Ray, Franklin to Susan Nix 9-21-1849 Hn
Ray, George to Frances Burrow? 11-7-1833 Hr
Ray, J. S. to S. A. Cole 12-29-1875 Dy
Ray, James A. to Docia A. Reid 6-7-1867 O
Ray, James C. to Addie Smith 12-21-1870 (12-22-1870) Ma
Ray, James C. to Lucinda Wade 2-2-1842 Hn
Ray, James D. to Melissa A. Morris 9-29-1855 (9-30-1855) G
Ray, James M. to Alice A. Caldwell 6-4-1861 Hn
Ray, James M. to D. A. Burnwat 5-4-1858 (5-6-1858) G
Ray, James M. to Matilda Delk 3-12-1859 (3-13-1859) Hr
Ray, James M. to Sarah F. Jones 8-1-1867 Hn
Ray, James R. to Malisa P. Speight 2-1-1877 Hy
Ray, James W. to Luvica W. David 8-6-1860 (8-8-1860) Cr
Ray, James W. to Sintha Morrow 8-16-1852 (8-17-1852) G
Ray, James to Eliza Jane Harmon 12-2-1860 Hn
Ray, James to Margaret Moore 7-25-1863 (no return) L
Ray, James to Tempy D. Kirkland 12-29-1862 (no return) Hn
Ray, Jesse to Emily J. Hill 11-20-1856 (no return) We
Ray, John F. to Amada E. Goza 7-13-1863 G
Ray, John F. to Martha F. Tucker 8-5-1862 (8-19-1862) Dy
Ray, John S. to Mary Swor 1-8-1846 Hn
Ray, John W. to Margarett E. Elnor 1-16-1859 (no return) We
Ray, John to Eliza Aldridge 9-13-1879 (9-14-1879) L
Ray, Joseph to Marinaan Laster 8-29-1871 (8-30-1871) Dy
Ray, L. B. to M. P. Lucy 12-26-1876 L
Ray, L. P. to Harriet A. Walls 12-25-1865 G
Ray, L. P. to Mollie Cannon 12-18-1872 (12-19-1872) Cr
Ray, Lemuel L. to Elmira Kemp 5-4-1834 Hr
Ray, Martin V. to Elizabeth Riley 9-20-1866 G
Ray, Milton to Pheby Furgarson 7-26-1839 G
Ray, Moses to Susan Caroline Rosson 11-17-1836 Hr
Ray, Nathan to Emaline Bledsoe 2-6-1838 (not endorsed) G
Ray, Nathan to Mary Hill 12-28-1850 (not endorsed) We
Ray, R. C. to Mary Ann E. Thompson 3-28-1866 Hn
Ray, R. K. to Elizabeth Hart 12-25-1867 (no return) Hn
Ray, Richard to Alderana Jane Brown 5-22-1848 Sh
Ray, Richard to Sallie (Mrs.) Mitchell 1-17-1867 G
Ray, Saml. to Martha J. Gray 7-16-1870 (7-17-1870) T
Ray, Samuel J. to Henrietta T. Clark 9-22-1857 Hn
Ray, Samuel to Amelia C. Wilson 12-19-1860 (12-10?-1861?) Hr
Ray, Samuel to Caroline Johnson 9-22-1844 Hy
Ray, Samuel to Oney Rogers 11-27-1833 (11-29-1833) Hr
Ray, Simpson to Catherine Hansbrough 11-7-1838 Hn
Ray, Solomon to Anne Hutcherson 3-25-1868 G B
Ray, T. F. to M. E. Pope 1-7-1869 Dy
Ray, Thomas A. to Elizabeth F. Biggs 11-10-1858 G
Ray, Thomas J. to Rosenia R. Martin 11-21-1856 Hn
Ray, Thomas W. to Caroline Key 10-13-1858 Hn
Ray, Thomas to Martha Richardso 3-29-1863 Hn
Ray, Thomas to Mary Flowers 10-9-1861 (10-12-1861) Dy
Ray, Thomas to Mary Morgan 2-13-1847 (2-14-1847) G
Ray, W. A. to Malissa Searcy 8-14-1861 Hn
Ray, Washington F. to Elizabeth Holden 12-21-1841 Hn
Ray, William C. to Mary E. Austin 11-28-1855 L
Ray, William F. to Ruth Davis 5-18-1850 O
Ray, William to Laura M. Alexander 12-14-1846 (12-22-1846) F
Ray, Wm. G. to Bettie A. Melia 11-15-1852 (11-18-1852) T
Rayborn, William N. to Melissa Brandon 5-27-1841 Hn
Rayboun (Rayborn), J. E. to Rachal M. Tomkins 10-16-1844 (no return) We
Rayburn, G. B. to Sally Nichols 11-2-1854 Be
Rayburn, Mc to Nancy A. Arnold 8-29-1849 O
Rayburn, W. H. to Tabitha Grainger 4-12-1853 Hn
Rayder, John J. to Laura Wright 4-14-1863 G
Raye, John to Mary L. Lyons 6-27-1864 Sh

Raynard, Joseph S. to Martha J. Minton 12-10-1833 (12-17-1833) Hr
Rayner, Austin to Leanna Lea 12-26-1870 (no return) Hy
Rayner, Bob to Penny Bond 3-24-1866 (no return) Hy
Rayner, Eli to Maryann C. Jones 8-18-1841 (no return) F
Rayner, J. R. to Sarah Jane Watson 4-9-1863 Sh
Rayner, Jacob to Fillis Gill 1-25-1870 (no return) Hy
Rayner, Joe to Maria Joyner 12-2-1875 (no return) Hy
Rayner, Kenneth to S. T. Read 12-24-1867 Hy
Raynor, Hill to Rose Gardner 12-24-1869 (no return) F B
Raynor, Lawrence to Elizabeth Coats 9-4-1861 (9-5-1861) T
Rayond, Archer to Bettie Harris 10-2-1869 T
Rea, Abraham K. to Elizabeth Jane Davis 3-18-1841 Sh
Rea, Andrew J. to Elizabeth Winstead 12-10-1850 We
Rea, H. W. to M. A. Boggs 1-14-1872 Hy
Rea, John H. to Ann Twyford 11-14-1843 Sh
Reach, John W. to Catharine D. Strong 2-2-1857 (2-3-1857) G
Reacouik, John B. to Amanda J. Claybern 2-15-1859 We
Read, Abner N. to Mary A. F. Boyett 8-26-1848 O
Read, Alfred T. to Laura E. Oldham 7-24-1867 Hy
Read, Andy to Cornelia Mann 8-7-1869 Hy
Read, Antney to Lou Ricks 12-2-1871 Hy
Read, Asa to Cenia Crowder 1-30-1867 (no return) Hy
Read, Benjamin to Martha Anderson 9-6-1842 (9-8-1842) Ma
Read, Bob to Nancy Henning 5-19-1870 Hy
Read, Bob to Sue Dunlap 9-25-1873 Hy
Read, Bradford to Rebecca Burns 12-7-1833 Hr
Read, Charles L. to Mary S. Taylor 7-20-1852 (no return) F
Read, Dave to Martilda Outlaw 12-9-1877 Hy
Read, Douglass to Mary Read 12-15-1869 (no return) Hy
Read, Edward J. to Elizabeth L. Conner 5-17-1859 L
Read, Edward to Laura Newborn 2-23-1876 (no return) Hy
Read, Evans to Mary Johnson 1-4-1873 (1-6-1873) T
Read, F. T. to A. E. Pace 12-18-1871 (12-20-1871) T
Read, Felix to Margaret F. Blaydes 6-20-1868 L
Read, Francis H. to Rachel B. Bratton 10-20-1853 Hn
Read, Garland J. to Mary J. Hanna 3-11-1851 Cr
Read, George W. to Adeline Plumer 5-19-1874 Hy
Read, Greenbury to Nancy Ann Agnes E. Lowry 12-11-1846 (12-12-1846) L
Read, H.C. to Eveline Lott 4-27-1875 (no return) Hy
Read, Harvey to M. A. Moore 1-11-1869 Hy
Read, Haywood to Ella Morten 1-15-1874 Hy
Read, Henry to Ann Taylor 12-16-1866 Hy
Read, Henry to Dicy Perkins 3-15-1876 (no return) Hy
Read, Henry to Mary J. Hendron 10-31-1868 Hy
Read, Henry to Rebecca Hazle 2-1-1876 (2-4-1876) L B
Read, Howel L. to Irene Boyd 11-18-1873 Hy
Read, Howel to Jane Newborn 3-13-1872 (no return) Hy
Read, Howell to Albertie Dixon 3-2-1871 Hy
Read, Isaac to Delia A. Burks 1-14-1886 (1-17-1886) L
Read, Isaac to Sarah A. Carpenter 12-24-1878 Hy
Read, J. A. to Katy Maclin 12-20-1873 Hy
Read, Jake to Mariah Parham 1-17-1872 Hy
Read, James M. to Nancy E. Stanly 7-12-1878 (no return) Hy
Read, James to Catharine Vantrice 11-24-1828 (11-27-1828) Hr
Read, James to Dolly J. Hollaway 2-29-1872 Hy
Read, James to Elizabeth Caroline Berryhill 11-23-1843 We
Read, James to Mary Tyson 3-15-1877 Hy
Read, James to Mollie Whitelaw 9-20-1872 Hy
Read, Jim to Annie Shaw 4-18-1869 Hy
Read, Jim to Molly Branch 8-20-1875 (no return) Hy
Read, John C. to Kate Louis French 5-7-1873 Hy
Read, John R. to Martha Ann Trawick 10-28-1845 Cr
Read, John T. to N. J. Read 12-30-1869 T
Read, John to Charine Jones 12-23-1846 Hy
Read, Lewis V. to Elizabeth Wethen 11-27-1867 (11-28-1867) Dy
Read, Mansfield to Fanny Maclin 12-30-1865 (no return) Hy
Read, Mike to Harritt Vaulx 5-16-1869 Hy
Read, Moses to Emmer Currey 11-10-1867 Hy
Read, Moses to Tillie Bond 4-1-1884 L
Read, Ned to Callie Ruffin 12-3-1874 L B
Read, Nicholas to Mary Maclin 3-21-1870 Hy
Read, Peter to Jane Miller 7-7-1866 T
Read, Peter to Laura White 11-28-1872 (no return) L B
Read, Peter to Sallie Wills 12-17-1865 Hy
Read, R. N. to S. A. Moore 9-22-1838 (no return) F
Read, Robert J. to Nancy J. Enochs 12-24-1846 Cr
Read, Robert to Eliza Whitelaw 8-4-1878 Hy
Read, Robert to Etta Fields 7-2-1881 L
Read, Robert to Lucinda Norwood 5-29-1827 Hr
Read, Robert to Nancy Williams 10-4-1855 We
Read, Robin to Agnes Taylor 9-8-1867 Hy
Read, Rogers to Bety Easly 3-11-1875 Hy
Read, Royal to Sarah Read 11-25-1865 (no return) Hy
Read, Saml. W. to Virginia A. Nolly 1-26-1853 Sh
Read, Sandy to Isabella Austin 8-17-1878 Hy
Read, Sandy to Lou Clark 10-28-1875 (no return) Hy
Read, Scott to Frances Jarrett 1-17-1876 (no return) Hy

Read, Scott to Nancy Read 9-8-1866 Hy
Read, Sidney to Agnes Haywood 4-20-1872 Hy
Read, Thomas to Catharine B. Green 11-11-1847 Sh
Read, Thos. J. to Rosanna Blade 1-1-1866 Hy
Read, Tom to Lucy Maclin 2-4-1872 Hy
Read, W. H. to Nannie Mills 12-20-1877 Dy
Read, Washington to Sarah Pool 11-28-1828 (11-30-1828) Hr
Read, Wiley to Ann Davis 12-26-1867 Hy
Read, William to Sarah Wethford 10-4-1848 (no return) L
Readen, Eatley to Adaline Smith 8-?-1859 Cr
Readen, Wm. to Mandy Bowling 4-17-1869 (no return) Hy
Reader, James K. to Rutha Rose 2-1-1849 (no return) Cr
Reader, James R. to Tyresee Smith 12-1-1856 Cr
Reader, Philip to Frances Henning 3-13-1858 (no return) L
Reader, T. T. to Ellen J. Moore 1-9-1851 Cr
Reading, Edward M. to Inez Norvell 2-18-1862 Sh
Ready, Jonathan to Ellen G. Turlington 8-4-1853 Sh
Ready, Thos. J. to Duann W. Warford 9-18-1855 (no return) F
Reagan, Charles to Lucinda Webster 6-16-1827 Hr
Reagan, Jessee to Polly Welch 12-20-1838 Hr
Reagan, Jim to Lucy White 5-25-1877 (5-27-1877) Dy
Reagan, John to Jane Davis 9-19-1833 Hr
Reagan, W. L.(S.?) to S. A. J. Yates 10-2-1860 G
Reager, James S. to Elizabeth Tinkle 9-21-1869 G
Reager, John P. to Ellen M. Edmundson 2-12-1853 (2-17-1853) G
Reames, G. H. to Mollie E. Hood 12-11-1867 (12-12-1867) F
Reames, Henry J. to Mary T. Baker 1-29-1842 (2-1-1842) F
Reames, J. B. to Sue Johnson 12-11-1867 (12-12-1867) F
Reams, Joshua M. to Artela F. Davis 12-2-1868 (12-4-1868) Ma
Reams, R. W. to Sarah A. Carter 7-12-1849 F
Reams, jr., M. J. to Bettie E. Hood 11-3-1870 F
Reans, John to Ellen Davis 3-21-1869 Hy
Reardon, John to Ellen Ryan 4-4-1853 Sh
Reason, John to Mary Solles 8-10-1842 (8-11-1842) G
Reason, William to Levina Tatom 7-7-1838 (7-9-1838) G
Reasoner, W. R. to Rachel M. Flowers 3-12-1853 Sh
Reasons, Calvin B. to Lavina Reasons 2-2-1848 G
Reasons, George F. to I.(D.?) A. Berry 8-10-1870 G
Reasons, J. C. to Susan Connell 10-18-1879 (10-19-1879) Dy
Reasons, M. C. to Margaret Wheeler 2-9-1878 Dy
Reasons, M. G. to M. A. Wheeler 11-17-1877 (11-21-1877) Dy
Reatherford, William to Martha Parkes 6-27-1863 (6-28-1863) O
Reaves, Amos to Ardenia Wilson 12-26-1873 (12-27-1873) L
Reaves, David to Elizabeth Tipler 12-28-1840 (12-31-1840) Hr
Reaves, Edmund to Charlotte McKinnie 2-17-1838 Hr
Reaves, Elijah to Elizabeth Ashbrooks 5-13-1830 (5-19-1830) O
Reaves, Felix F. to Louisa S. Utley 7-16-1846 Be
Reaves, Geo. W. to Eliza Wyly 10-7-1847 Be
Reaves, George M. to Elizabeth Balentine 3-13-1858 We
Reaves, J. N. to R. J. McCullough 10-18-1870 (10-19-1870) Cr
Reaves, John H. to Susan Baker 5-26-1856 Ma
Reaves, John to Elizabeth Meriwether 10-21-1841 Sh
Reaves, John to Rebecca W. Thompson 1-13-1869 Be
Reaves, Lewis to Rebecca Hulon 10-18-1821 Sh
Reaves, Maulden to Mary Neeley 11-12-1829 Ma
Reaves, Nathan to Isabella L. Anderson 8-6-1850 Sh
Reaves, R. R. to Sarah Herron 12-4-1844 Cr
Reaves, R. to Caroline Duberry 6-8-1862 G
Reaves, Samuel to Elizabeth Purvace 1-6-1830 (1-7-1830) O
Reaves, W. B. to E. C. Carother 3-29-1866 (4-5-1866) T
Reaves, William to Nancy Carooth 12-23-1850 Hr
Reaves, Wm. P. to Betsy Bradley 6-14-1827 Sh
Reaves, Wm. to Lydia Crisp 5-14-1844 Hr
Reavis, Ashbey to Ann Mildred Mallory 12-21-1846 (12-24-1846) Hr
Reavis, Elijah R. to Emily F. Sims 1-22-1862 We
Reavis, Isaac C. to Jane C. Cassilman 11-3-1861 We
Reavis, Isaac C. to Julia F. Everett 12-27-1860 (no return) 'e
Reavis, James M. to M. E. Janes 1-25-1864 We
Reavis, James M. to Margaret A. Brown 2-13-1862 Ma
Reavis, James to Mary F. Foster 4-10-1863 O
Rebman, Joseph to Elizabeth Ludwig 2-16-1856 Sh
Reborri, Joseph to Cecilia Arata 2-13-1858 (2-15-1858) Sh
Reckord (Keckord?), Walter H. to Jane Goss 11-23-1864 Sh
Rector, Alex P. to Clarkey Ann Williams 5-21-1870 (5-22-1870) Ma
Rector, John to Mahala Scott 1-18-1875 (1-19-1875) L
Red, Jesse to Rosanna Pool 12-30-1869 (no return) F B
Redd, Jesse to Martha A. Sumner 3-8-1859 (3-13-1859) F
Redd, W. J. to Mollie E. Montgomery 1-19-1861 (1-24-1861) Hr
Reddeck, Joseph to Elizabeth Harris 11-28-1869 Hy
Redden, A. L. to Mary E. Throgmorton 4-7-1862 (no return) Hn
Redden, Charles G. to Martha Davis 6-6-1848 Hn
Redden, G. W. to Mary Trimm? 9-?-1874 (9-22-1874) T
Redden, H. J. to M. C. Britt 7-24-1872 (no return) Cr
Redden, Lewis to Elizabeth Mofield 9-20-1846 Hn
Redden, N. E. to K. E. Clark 3-3-1842 Be
Redden, Samuel to Arrency Dunham 10-28-1826 (10-29-1826) O
Reddick, A. J. to M. A. Brewer 10-16-1869 (10-19-1869) Dy

Reddick, Alfred to Delila Freeman 2-2-1869 (no return) Dy
Reddick, Alfred to Martha A. Ferguson 2-10-1866 (no return) Dy
Reddick, Benj. F. to Laura A. Cleaves 1-27-1840 F
Reddick, Benj. F. to Armenia Mansfield 1-30-1866 (1-31-1866) Dy
Reddick, Calvin to Isabella Powell 12-22-1868 (no return) Hy
Reddick, D. to Martha W. Harmon 3-13-1852 (no return) F
Reddick, E. to L. McNiel 10-10-1841 Be
Reddick, Edward G. to Harriet Ann Mayo 3-13-1846 (3-18-1846) F
Reddick, Francis to Amanda Reddick 3-9-1864 Dy
Reddick, Franklin to Levica Ann Harris 3-10-1860 (no return) Hy
Reddick, Franklin to Mary Lewis 9-11-1860 (no return) Hy
Reddick, George to Harrit Maclin 12-31-1870 (1-2-1871) T
Reddick, Henry to Mary Donnily 1-15-1869 (no return) F B
Reddick, J. K. P. to L. F. Stalling 12-19-1866 (12-20-1866) Dy
Reddick, J. L. to M. F. Brewer 11-28-1866 (11-29-1866) Dy
Reddick, Jessie to Bettie Nunn 2-15-1868 Dy
Reddick, L. W. to Elizabeth Pentecost 4-5-1859 (no return) We
Reddick, Lewis W. to Hannar A. Ward 10-6-1862 We
Reddick, M. L. to N. J. Moon 10-8-1854 We
Reddick, M. V. B. to Harriet Stallings 10-26-1860 (10-27-1860) Dy
Reddick, Martin to Martha Garner 11-25-1860 Be
Reddick, Richard to Ritta Lanier 12-7-1868 (no return) Dy
Reddick, Robert to Sally M. Smith 1-17-1838 Sh
Reddick, T. T. to Mary J. Farmer 3-30-1864 (no return) Dy
Reddick, Thomas to Matilda Brown 3-16-1867 (3-18-1867) F B
Reddin, Harmon to Elizabeth Witherlington 12-28-1839 Ma
Reddin, William A. to Josephine Allen 1-16-1866 (1-18-1866) Cr
Redding, David to Martha Browder 11-24-1861 Mn
Redding, Forney W. to Martha Ann Ralph 8-2-1851 (no return) F
Redding, George W. to Mary Payne 12-16-1869 (12-23-1869) F
Redding, Sidney to Elizabeth Galloway 12-6-1853 (no return) F
Redding, T. W. to Martha Jane Nash 12-5-1877 (12-6-1877) Dy
Redding, William H. to Mary Murdough 5-4-1863 (no return) Dy
Reddington, Marton to Ann Eliza Finnerty 8-2-1862 (8-10-1862) Sh
Reddit, LaFayette to Sarah Jane Dunnegin 1-5-1854 O
Redditt, G. W. to Nancy S. Belote 7-25-1855 (7-26-1855) Sh
Redditt, George W. to Malinda J. Roberts 11-6-1866 (11-8-1866) T
Redditt, John to Adeline Young 1-9-1839 Sh
Redditt, Sam to May F. Thompson 12-21-1848 Sh
Redditt, William to Caroline Slate 12-24-1845 Sh
Redditt, Wm. R. to Caroline Williams 1-28-1862 Sh
Redford, James to Louisa Cannon 5-9-1856 (5-10-1856) G
Redick, Humphrey to Frances Bolen 12-27-1864 (12-29-1864) Dy
Redick, J. H. to Louisa Jackson 1-10-1869 Be
Redick, James D. to Mary A. Grooms 7-2-1846 We
Redick, John B. to Sarah E. Harvel 1-17-1854 Cr
Redicks, J. D. to M. A. Grooms 6-24-1846 We
Redman, Alfred to Margt. Currin 12-18-1867 (12-22-1867) L B
Redman, R. W. to Narcissa A. Dowdy 9-18-1864 Hn
Redmon, S. W. to Emeline F. Brassfield 2-2-1860 G
Redmon, William to Malvina Moore 10-11-1862 Mn
Redmond, M. A. to Mary Boswell 1-12-1848 F
Redmond, William to Letty Mays 6-27-1868 G B
Redrick, George to Amy L. McLin 8-19-1867 Hy
Redus, J. M. to Mary Jane Polk 10-22-1859 (10-25-1859) Sh
Redus, S. D. to Mary A. Patten 2-20-1858 Sh
Ree, William C. to William J. Arnold 1-19-1853 G
Reeble, James R. to Mary E. Banks 10-8-1856 G
Reece, Henry Temp to Susan Lane Little 1-5-1865 (1-7-1865) Dy
Reece, James R. to Latrissa Fullerton 2-2-1856 Sh
Reece, James S. to Narcissa A. Phipps 5-7-1867 (no return) Cr
Reece, John to Susan E. Travis 1-26-1867 (1-30-1867) Cr
Reece, Merritt to Susan McCulloch 10-12-1867 G
Reece, Samuel P. to Mary E. King 1-7-1861 (1-9-1861) Cr
Reece, Yarnall to Susan A. Sample 7-3-1849 (7-4-1849) O
Reed, A. N. to S. Tyson 11-23-1850 O
Reed, Alexander to Caroline Crumpton 8-3-1861 Sh
Reed, Allen to Frances M. Crider 8-8-1839 G
Reed, Arch to Lucy Ann Spencer 8-29-1873 (8-30-1873) L B
Reed, C. C. to M. J. Watson 11-25-1875 O
Reed, C. H. to Emma Redman 2-16-1864 Sh
Reed, C. L. to Martha Reed 9-11-1866 (9-19-1866) T
Reed, Charles T. to Catherine J. Wilson 7-31-1842 Hn
Reed, Clark to Nancy Connell 1-25-18?3 G
Reed, David S. to Emma E. Blalock 12-19-1863 (12-24-1863) F
Reed, David to Harriet Riley 11-15-1853 O
Reed, Ephraim to Winney Ann Swift 1-7-1869 (2-4-1869) F B
Reed, Finiss to Lugina Hopkins 7-28-1831 (8-4-1831) Hr
Reed, Geo. to Eliza A. Brenish 11-17-1863 (11-19-1863) Sh
Reed, George to Elizabeth Taylor 12-31-1853 G
Reed, George to Lucy Battle 12-2-1869 (no return) F B
Reed, Green to Telitha Ball (Batt?) 12-31-1868 G B
Reed, H. A. to Martha A. Hendricks 7-15-1878 (no return) Dy
Reed, H. to M. J. Green 1-3-1872 Hy
Reed, H. R. to Paralie McCarroll 10-12-1853 Be
Reed, Henry F. to Sarah A. Trout 12-19-1846 (1-6-1847) G
Reed, J. M. to M. E. Chambers 2-11-1874 (2-25-1874) O

Reed, J. N. to Betsy Whitley 3-22-1868 G
Reed, J. Shelby to Ann Laura Reed 2-12-1859 Sh
Reed, J.M. to A. P. White 2-26-1867 G
Reed, James A. to Martha J. Taylor 12-20-1854 (12-24-1854) Sh
Reed, James P. to Sarah Patterson 3-7-1831 (3-?-1831) G
Reed, James S. to Sarah Jane Smith 1-21-1850 G
Reed, James S. to Sarah Jane Smith 7-16-1850 G
Reed, James Y. to Mary J. Jones 3-23-1861 Hr
Reed, Jas. H. to Martha C. Prince 4-22-1865 Be
Reed, Jessee to Frances Kelly 7-7-1856 (7-21-1856) G
Reed, John H. to Louisa Kevit 7-26-1836 Hy
Reed, John N. to D. E. Middleton 1-13-1858 (1-17-1858) G
Reed, John R. to Mary C. McIver 3-18-1841 (3-19-1841) Ma
Reed, John Y. to Martha Ayres 2-18-1840 Hr
Reed, John to Elizabeth Truett(Pruett) 3-18-1828 Hr
Reed, John to Narcisa Rust 10-1-1857 We
Reed, Jonathan to Sintha A. Wallace 10-23-1860 Hn
Reed, M. L. to Margaret J. Bundy 8-22-1860 O
Reed, Maltimore to Nancy Marant 12-29-1868 Hy
Reed, Mose to Dora Gibson 3-29-1883 (4-1-1883) L
Reed, Neal to George Ann Bond 6-12-1874 (no return) Hy
Reed, Pinkney to Cyntha Barker 5-9-1855 (no return) F
Reed, R. F. to Caroline M. Johnson 11-17-1840 Cr
Reed, R. M. to M. L. McBride 12-9-1874 Dy
Reed, Robert D. to Mary A. Peoples 7-31-1855 (no return) Hn
Reed, Robert H. to Eliza Bell 11-14-1848 G
Reed, Rufus F. to Mary E. Barker 12-9-1857 (12-10-1857) G
Reed, Rufus to Elizabeth Herrin 7-4-1863 (7-5-1863) O
Reed, S. A. to Margaret E. Brewer 12-27-1865 Dy
Reed, Samuel H. to Ellen C. Bell 2-22-1848 (2-24-1848) G
Reed, Samuel to Amanda M. Coffman 12-24-1851 Hn
Reed, Samuel to Elizabeth Parks 8-6-1831 G
Reed, Samuel to Margaret H. Cox 11-3-1853 G
Reed, Solomon to Delila F. English 11-10-1841 G
Reed, Thomas B. to Laura A. Cooper 11-30-1858 Sh
Reed, Thomas to Mollie Winston 2-10-1867 G
Reed, Thomas to Nancy Morris 11-11-1850 We
Reed, W. M. to Mary C. White 1-1-1851 Sh
Reed, Washington C. to Mary A. Barton 9-14-1866 Cr
Reed, William C. to Elizabeth Carruth 7-12-1841 Ma
Reed, William F. to Cynthia E. Tilghman 3-14-1866 G
Reed, William to Kesia Thomas 3-15-1843 (3-16-1843) G
Reed, William to Margaret Whicker 5-30-1870 G
Reed, Wm. E. to Cresy Maclin 7-17-1872 Hy
Reed, Wm. to Martha C. Young 6-24-1858 We
Reed, Zelman to Mazana Applewhite 3-30-1857 (3-31-1857) Sh
Reeden, Jacob to Mary Ann Davis 4-11-1842 Hn
Reeder, John M. to Harriett E. Mosley 5-9-1850 Sh
Reeder, Martin to Sarah Cate 4-18-1855 Hn
Reeder, Micajah to Mary Jane Culp 10-29-1847 Hn
Reeder, Phillip to Mary N. Bass 1-13-1851 (1-14-1851) Sh
Reedon, Samuel to Mahala Reedon 1-9-1862 Hr
Reef, J. M. to E. McNeil 11-25-1847 Be
Rees, John to Lotta Busby 11-30-1856 We
Reese, Calvin M. to Mary M. Fields 9-22-1849 (10-3-1849) G
Reese, Dewitt A. to Elizabeth J. Blakemore 9-5-1854 G
Reese, Hullam J. to Esther Jones 1-22-1845 Sh
Reese, James M. to Louisa Adams 1-11-1847 Hn
Reese, James N. to A. E. Berry 8-31-1854 G
Reese, Zachariah to Malinda Starr 10-13-1841 (10-15-1841) T
Reeser, T. M. to S. E. Carter 12-23-1861 (12-27-1861) Hr
Reeves, A. F. to Louisa Loller 5-2-1854 Sh
Reeves, Alpheus W. to Mary A. Shanahan 4-22-1852 Sh
Reeves, Benjamin to Jane Shields 12-27-1869 (12-30-1869) F B
Reeves, Bethell to Harriet Jane McNeely 1-15-1844 O
Reeves, Charles W. to Mary Elizabeth Nelson 12-7-1869 Ma
Reeves, D. S. to Mary S. Reeves 9-12-1867 O
Reeves, Frederick L. to Patience F. M. P. Exum 2-3-1857 (2-4-1857) O
Reeves, George W. to Fanny Smith 12-19-1842 (12-22-1842) O
Reeves, George W. to Mary Ann Carter 9-15-1856 (9-23-1856) Ma
Reeves, George to Jane Hughes 1-26-1857 (1-29-1857) O
Reeves, Henry W. to Elizabeth J. McCorkle 12-19-1861 Dy
Reeves, Henry to Eliza Owen 6-6-1868 E B
Reeves, Hiram G. to Easter A. Hubbard 1-6-1852 O
Reeves, J. M> to Elizabeth Ussery 12-17-1860 (12-19-1860) Hr
Reeves, Jacob J. R. to Mary Ann McCollough 12-7-1855 Ma
Reeves, James B. to Rebecca Buchanan 12-25-1851 O
Reeves, Joel W. to America Ann Crenshaw 1-14-1850 (1-15-1850) Ma
Reeves, John J. to S. M. Davese 1-5-1859 O
Reeves, John M. to Charlott Ballance 1-15-1841 (1-17-1841) G
Reeves, John to Lucy Ann Harrison 10-31-1855 Be
Reeves, P. J. to R. J. Martin 1-3-1863 (1-4-1863) F
Reeves, P. M. to J. A. Ford 8-13-1856 G
Reeves, Peter S. to Nancy Rooker 11-12-1835 G
Reeves, Robert S. to Luroney B. Parker 1-18-1847 (1-21-1847) Ma
Reeves, S. D. to Sallie J. Walker 11-12-1866 G
Reeves, S. H. to A. J. Miles 1-17-1868 (1-19-1868) O

Reeves, Solomon to Lottie A. Miller 5-7-1868 (5-15-1868) F B
Reeves, Thomas C. J. to Nancy W. Holmes 4-14-1853 (no return) F
Reeves, Thomas F. to Catharine S. Cunningham 12-24-1839 (12-25-1839) O
Reeves, Thomas to Rosa Botto 4-30-1859 Sh
Reeves, Urius to Martha Boyt 4-11-1833 (4-13-1833) O
Reeves, W. C. to Julia Hefley 11-2-1847 Cr
Reeves, W. C. to Mary McCarley 12-21-1852 (no return) F
Reeves, W. H. to P. G. Danner 3-1-1859 G
Reeves, William A. to Elizabeth Jane Mayfield 8-26-1854 (8-27-1854) O
Reeves, William C. to Mary C. Brown 11-17-1842 (11-22-1842) O
Reeves, William D. to Susan Garrison 1-6-1845 (1-7-1845) O
Reeves, William to Mary Ann Shelly 9-18-1843 Hn
Reeves, William to Sarah Farris 4-3-1835 (4-7-1835) Hr
Reeves, Willis G. to Mary J. Latta 11-6-1854 (11-8-1854) Hr
Reeves, Willis L. to Mary Robinson 9-19-1846 (9-24-1846) G
Reffington, John S. to Mary A. Lauderdale 11-18-1868 Dy
Regan, Cornelius to Ellen Cartege? (Cortiez?) 2-20-1853 Sh
Regan, Patrick to Ellen Powers 2-22-1851 Sh
Regas (Ragan), Levine to Angeline Sluter 4-24-1863 Sh
Rehkoff, Ernest to Caroline Neiching 3-8-1853 (3-9-1853) Sh
Rehkopt, Henry to Lina Maier 4-5-1860 Sh
Reich, I. T. to Louisa Faulk 10-1-1863 O
Reid, A. to Mary J. Roach 11-20-1838 F
Reid, Archibald to Adelia Atterberry 3-6-1855 O
Reid, Augustus C. to Laura Taylor 3-1-1869 (3-3-1869) Ma
Reid, Booker to Hanner Jones 3-10-1874 T
Reid, D. W. to Eliza J. Timmins 12-20-1858 (12-21-1858) Sh
Reid, David to Sarah F. Williamson 10-3-1849 (10-10-1849) Ma
Reid, James G. to Mattie Wharton 11-6-1866 (11-8-1866) Ma
Reid, Jno. B. to Wallace L. Neal 2-3-1859 (2-8-1859) F
Reid, Jno. D. to Susan L. Flemming 1-1-1866 T
Reid, John A. to Mollie J. Davie 10-30-1878 Hy
Reid, John C. to Jane M. Taylor 4-19-1845 Sh
Reid, John H. to Mary Ann Carpenter 2-1-1858 (2-4-1858) O
Reid, John S. to Bettie Stafford 9-28-1869 G
Reid, John to Lide A. Greer 10-1-1867 (10-2-1867) Ma
Reid, John to Matilda Montgomery 11-14-1863 Sh
Reid, Robt. A. to A. W. Mahan 12-13-1853 Sh
Reid, T. J. to Kate M. Neal 1-15-1868 (1-22-1868) F
Reid, Thomas A. to Laura Hutchison 11-16-1869 (11-18-1869) Ma
Reid, Thomas to Rachel Price 3-9-1834 Sh
Reid, W. C. to Analine Bentley no date (with Jun 1855) F
Reiley (Riley), Edward to Ellen Cannon 9-24-1860 Sh
Reiley, Mat to Ann Brown 1-6-1852 Sh
Reilley, Barney to Mary McGrath 5-21-1864 Sh
Reinach, A. R. to Elise (Elize?) May 1-5-1858 Sh
Reinhardt, F. W. to Ellen Daly 1-24-1856 Sh
Reinhardt, Wilhelm to Fredericka Imboone 5-26-1856 (5-27-1856) Sh
Reister, J. L. to Ada E. Lockwood 12-7-1858 Sh
Reives, Alfred to Telia Patterson 9-7-1872 Cr B
Rembert, L__levin C. to Mary E. Ragland 7-6-1853 Sh
Rembert, S. S. to Ann Duncan 2-3-1840 Sh
Remlen, Wm. to Christine Schoesser 2-4-1861 Sh
Remson, Robert to Anna Morgan 1-17-1873 (1-19-1873) L B
Ren, John to Ann (Mrs.) Shehan 7-2-1864 (7-6-1864) Sh
Renalds, G. B. to N. C. Anderson 2-27-1873 Hy
Rene, jr., James to Sarah Crosby 6-7-1845 (6-9-1845) Ma
Renoew, I.L.. to Margaret A. (Mrs.) Howell 9-9-1870 Ma
Renfro, Henry to Tempy Mitchell 4-2-1867 G
Renfro, J. A. to Mary E. Gardner 1-4-1866 Hn
Renfro, William J. to Alabama S. Byars 10-27-1863 Hn
Renfroe, Jno. S. to H. C. Worrell 12-22-1868 (12-23-1868) F
Renfroe, John to Jincy Wilborn 3-11-1845 Cr
Renfroe, M. S. to Amanda Dougan 1-25-1860 (1-26-1860) F
Renfrow, J. W. to Jullia A. Smith 10-10-1865 G
Renick, William H. to Marguerite Logan 3-19-1834 Sh
Renkert, Andrew to Lizzie Lampricht 1-30-1860 (2-2-1860) Sh
Renkert, Andrew to Ottilia Handwerker 9-24-1863 Sh
Rennolds, Edwin E. to Margaret C. Cox 1-11-1866 Hn
Reno, Benj. to Jane E. Duvalt 8-24-1869 Hy
Renshaw, J. S. to S. E. Smith 10-12-1871 L
Renshaw, James P. to Catherine P. Hill 10-8-1854 Hn
Renshaw, John to Easter Anderson 5-21-1842 (5-24-1842) Ma
Renshaw, John to Hannorah Hogan 9-28-1857 Sh
Rentfro, J. D. to Sarah McKeown 1-22-1857 G
Rentfro, Jasper N. to Emily Bunn 3-16-1853 G
Rentfro, John A. to S. E. McCaleb 7-25-1848 G
Rentfro, Joseph D. to Sarah Dial 6-24-1835 G
Replogle, Benjamin to Sally Ann Duncan 9-19-1854 (9-21-1854) Ma
Replogle, Henry V. to Margarette E. Sharp 1-13-1857 (1-14-1857) G
Replogle, P. M. to Mary L. House 1-17-1856 (1-20-1856) G
Rest, Charles to Mary Teresa Hendricks 1-12-1863 Sh
Reuther, Edward to Mary Campbell 7-6-1859 (7-7-1859) Sh
Reutter, John to Verona Grot 8-25-1849 Sh
Revel, Benjamin M. to Jennie Philips 7-10-1863 G
Revel, Ezekiel to Louisa Mathews 3-5-1868 G
Revel, Newton S. to Mary B. Hammonds 11-23-1855 (11-25-1855) G

Reves, J.R. to Ann Carns? 2-15-1848 Be
Revis, Hilliard to Fannie Williamson 1-11-1868 (1-12-1868) F B
Revis, L. B. to Margaret Mathis 7-5-1873 (7-6-1873) L
Revis, R. H. to F. A. Pitts 11-28-1876 (11-29-1876) L
Revis, Wm. M. to Louisa White 12-12-1850 We
Reycroft, W. T. to Eliza Pope 6-8-1870 (10-5-1870) Dy
Reynold, Daniel to Manerva B. E. Bledsoe 8-23-1853 G
Reynold, Green to Sarah Wallace 3-13-1850 L
Reynolds, Amos C. to Rebeccah Parker 1-16-1838 Hr
Reynolds, B. R. to Octavia L. Thurman 9-21-1882 (9-24-1882) L
Reynolds, C. C. to Malissa W. Aaron 8-5-1857 Hn
Reynolds, D. H. to Mattie Knight 8-23-1873 (8-24-1873) Dy
Reynolds, Daniel to Jane Childress 2-5-1846 L
Reynolds, Dodson to Elizer Jane Ball 12-24-1865 G
Reynolds, E. B. to Jemima E. Chism 9-29-1840 L
Reynolds, Elhanon to Tabitha Bethsheares 3-11-1868 Hy
Reynolds, G. W. to Idella Walker 3-6-1876 (3-8-1876) Dy
Reynolds, George W. to Sarah Laster 2-21-1857 Hn
Reynolds, H. P. to M. S. Jacobs 12-13-1870 (no return) Cr
Reynolds, Henry H. to A.? J. Perkins 1-25-1862 (no return) Hn
Reynolds, Henry to Lucinda Kirby 9-17-1845 (9-19-1845) L
Reynolds, Henry to Mima Brown 3-31-1871 (4-2-1871) Cr
Reynolds, Henry to Missouri Read 10-18-1841 L
Reynolds, Henry to Nancy Sanders 9-27-1849 L
Reynolds, Isaac to Lucinda Paine 4-11-1874 (4-12-1874) Dy
Reynolds, J. D. to Amanda J. King 3-30-1875 (4-1-1875) Dy
Reynolds, J. M. to Mary Perritt? 5-15-1869 (5-16-1869) Cr
Reynolds, J. S. to Emanda Rayburn 5-14-1869 Be
Reynolds, J. W. to Bettie Shankle 9-26-1878 (9-27-1878) Dy
Reynolds, J. W. to Elmina Cope 9-19-1863 (9-28-1863) Dy
Reynolds, James M. to Elizabeth Ann V. Reynolds 2-18-1864 Cr
Reynolds, James M. to Elizabeth ann V. Reynolds 2-18-1864 (no return) Cr
Reynolds, James T. to S. W. Owens 6-1-1877 (6-2-1877) L
Reynolds, James W. to Susan A. E. Pate 7-23-1857 L
Reynolds, Joel J. to Sarah Cockram 11-27-1834 Hr
Reynolds, John C. to Martha Mashburn 5-29-1847 Hr
Reynolds, John K. to Nancy M. Carr 8-19-1869 G
Reynolds, John M. to Martha Lasiter 8-29-1855 (no return) Hn
Reynolds, John R. to Emeline Yeargan 7-31-1870 G
Reynolds, John R. to Martha E. England 5-26-1852 G
Reynolds, John W. to Margaret C. Blair 12-3-1859 Hr
Reynolds, John to Caroline Dodd 6-15-1863 Dy
Reynolds, John to Catharine Pierce 9-7-1857 O
Reynolds, John to Jane Wallice 12-2-1859 (12-3-1859) G
Reynolds, John to Kiziah J. Forrest 9-19-1865 Mn
Reynolds, John to Malissa Cole 6-15-1853 (6-16-1853) G
Reynolds, John to Mary Butler 2-11-1862 G
Reynolds, John to Mary S. Lowey? 12-13-1866 Hn
Reynolds, John to Miry Wiseman 3-31-1861 Be
Reynolds, John to Sarah McGraw 4-22-1844 Hn
Reynolds, John to Sophona McDonald 5-21-1861 (no return) L
Reynolds, Joseph to Ann Halliburton 1-6-1875 (1-7-1875) Dy
Reynolds, Joseph to Mary C. Sheridan 5-8-1849 Hn
Reynolds, Lawson M. to Naomi E. Tacker 8-14-1861 Mn
Reynolds, Lewis L. to Aminisa M. Brogdon 7-28-1858 (7-29-1858) G
Reynolds, Marion to Jemimia Walton 7-31-1854 (8-2-1854) L
Reynolds, Newnham to Julia Ruff 3-9-1859 Hr
Reynolds, Norman to Mary Elizabeth Darby 6-26-1850 T
Reynolds, R. B. to P. L. Williams 5-14-1870 (5-15-1870) Cr
Reynolds, R. to D. A. McIntyre 1-3-1865 Mn
Reynolds, Reynold to Betsey F. Bowen 11-6-1828 Sh
Reynolds, Richard G. to Nancy Hargett 12-4-1841 (12-5-1841) O
Reynolds, Robert B. to Sarah Ann Bohannon 2-4-1857 Hn
Reynolds, Silas to Nancy Thornton 7-22-1831 Sh
Reynolds, Simon to Dolly Billips 2-8-1854 G
Reynolds, T. B. to Fannie E. Toof 5-25-1857 Sh
Reynolds, T. P. to M. L. Ward 9-6-1865 G
Reynolds, Thomas to Amanda Hurly 6-19-1863 L
Reynolds, Thomas to Penny Wallice 3-7-1861 G
Reynolds, Thomas to S. E. Melton 10-8-1868 G
Reynolds, Thos. J. to Eliza King 10-26-1872 (10-27-1872) Dy
Reynolds, Thurene E. to Mary Ann C. Rankin 12-14-1840 Hr
Reynolds, W. H. to M. A. C. Brogdon 9-28-1847 Hn
Reynolds, W. T. to M. J. Garner 6-22-1861 (8-1-1861) Cr
Reynolds, Watson to Birtie (Bettie?) Morris 6-24-1874 (no return) L
Reynolds, William E. to Permelia C. Ward 9-9-1853 (9-13-1853) L
Reynolds, William to Rebecca Farmer 12-4-1858 (12-5-1858) G
Reynolds, William to Tabitha Cookburn? 11-4-1830 Hr
Reynolds, Wm. C. to Amanda Sloss 1-13-1857 (1-22-1857) T
Reynolds, Wm. J. to Mary Jane Litte 2-5-1862 (no return) Dy
Reynolds, Z. T. to Sadie Hall 1-7-1879 (1-9-1879) Dy
Rezins, N. B. to M. A. Allison 10-28-1875 L
Rhea, Benjamin T. to Isabel Bray 11-5-1854 Hn
Rhea, E. D. to Fannie C. Blackwell 9-17-1885 L
Rhea, J. W. to Italie G. Porter 4-12-1860 Sh
Rhea, James to Rebecca Bracken 3-30-1867 (no return) F B
Rhea, John to E. L. Rhea 12-22-1840 F

Rhea, Joseph to Racheal Kelly 8-15-1835 (8-16-1835) Hr
Rhea, M. to Addie A. Tucker 12-14-1870 F
Rhea, Wm. A. to Harriet Gilbert 9-7-1861 (9-8-1861) Sh
Rhea, Wm. A. to Mollie R. Irvin 2-11-1869 F
Rhea, jr., Matthew to H. H. (Mrs.) Boyd 9-15-1859 F
Rhegness, W. E. to Virginia Huddleston 7-14-1867 G
Rhine, Amos D. L. to Afferilla Sanders 9-22-1856 L
Rhine, John D. to Emily Derriberry 3-26-1860 (no return) We
Rhoades, Frank to Eliza Whitelow 3-21-1868 (no return) Hy
Rhoades, Netanial to Laura Dean 11-13-1864 (11-15-1864) Sh
Rhoades, Thos. to Catherine Studard 1-27-1872 Hy
Rhoads, Andrew to Jane Bowen (Brown) 7-15-1838 Sh
Rhoads, Andrew to Jane Bowen 7-13-1838 Sh
Rhoads, James H. to Mary E. Massey 11-30-1870 (12-1-1870) Cr
Rhoads, Jessy to Sue Russell 3-24-1872 Hy
Rhoads, John A. to Mary Dodd 12-23-1857 (12-24-1857) O
Rhoads, John W. to Nancy Crutchfield 8-16-1838 (no return) Hn
Rhoads, W. B. to Sarah Sampson 10-27-1870 Cr
Rhodes, Alexander to Elizabeth Smith 8-19-1869 T
Rhodes, Alexander to Malviny Harris 6-10-1862 We
Rhodes, Alexander to Margaret Armor 7-17-1835 Hr
Rhodes, Bartlett to Sarah Perry 3-25-1850 Hn
Rhodes, Bob to Jane Williamson 1-15-1868 (1-16-1868) F B
Rhodes, C. F.(L?) to M. L. Gaines 11-20-1876 (11-21-876) L
Rhodes, Cicero to Susan Bolt 11-25-1850 (11-28-1850) Hr
Rhodes, Clink to Emma Mathis 12-25-1871 (12-26-1871) T
Rhodes, Daniel Mordecai to Mary Jane Townsend 8-11-1846 (8-?-1846) T
Rhodes, Daniel to M. B. Myrick 7-10-1845 Hn
Rhodes, Daniel to Malvina Mebane 3-19-1866 (3-22-1866) F B
Rhodes, David H. to Phebe Myrick 9-23-1860 Hn
Rhodes, David to Emily Sexton 3-11-1841 Cr
Rhodes, F. M. to Nancy Rumley 5-24-1843 Cr
Rhodes, Francis M. to Sarah A. Simpson 12-28-1853 Cr
Rhodes, Gilbert to Tilpha A. Brown 5-2-1857 Hr
Rhodes, Henry to Rena Ward 11-13-1868 (11-16-1868) F B
Rhodes, Henry to Sarah Coffy 1-12-1867 (not executed) F B
Rhodes, Isaac to Maria Jackson 12-16-1874 T
Rhodes, Isaac to Rena Lake 12-10-1868 T
Rhodes, J. C. to Margaret Fleming 1-23-1861 (1-24-1861) T
Rhodes, James Cicero to Sarah ANn Townsend 7-23-1844 (7-?-1844) T
Rhodes, James H. to Mary Cox 3-12-1832 Hr
Rhodes, James H. to Nancy Ann Rose 5-23-1844 (6-2-1844) Hr
Rhodes, James to Henrietta Howard 4-28-1868 (5-2-1868) T
Rhodes, James to Jane Algee 1-19-1843 Cr
Rhodes, James to Mary A. P. Morgan 6-26-1838 F
Rhodes, Jim to Malinda Walker 1-14-1870 G B
Rhodes, John F. to Rachael Chisum 7-19-1839 (7-29-1839) Hr
Rhodes, John W. to Lydice Mathews 10-10-1849 Cr
Rhodes, John to Hannah Hall 9-25-1880 (no return) L B
Rhodes, John to Nancy Brown 8-13-1851 Hr
Rhodes, Joseph C. C. to Nancy C. Laycock 1-5-1870 Cr
Rhodes, L. A. to Cornelia M. Boardman 9-21-1864 (9-27-1864) Sh
Rhodes, M. S. to H. J. Patton 12-11-1847 (12-23-1847) F
Rhodes, Mansfield to Martha Ann Trusdale 11-6-1869 (11-7-1869) T
Rhodes, Marien to Margarett Saddler 12-21-1858 We
Rhodes, Martin to Ann Cruis 12-21-1867 (12-22-1867) F B
Rhodes, N. O. to Kate Rodgers 12-7-1864 Sh
Rhodes, Osborn to Hannah Johnston 9-12-1867 (9-22-1867) T
Rhodes, Pleasant to Malinda Brooks 2-17-1852 (2-19-1852) Hr
Rhodes, R. D. to Eliza Williams 2-11-1847 Cr
Rhodes, R. J. to Mattie T. Nevill 4-9-1866 (4-15-1866) F
Rhodes, Robert E. to E. H. Lancaster 4-8-1839 (4-9-1839) ?
Rhodes, Saml. to Elizabeth Williamson 10-27-1866 (12-1-1866) T
Rhodes, Saml. to Grace Somervill 9-30-1869 T
Rhodes, Simon to Sarah Williamson 1-15-1868 (1-16-1868) F B
Rhodes, Solomon A. to Henrietta B. Bradshaw 12-21-1846 (12-23-1846) T
Rhodes, Thornton to M. C. F. P. Elles 5-22-1861 Mn
Rhodes, Thornton to Nancy Leach 10-4-1851 (10-5-1851) T
Rhodes, Vernon to Sarah M. Moody 7-22-1845 (7-23-1845) F
Rhodes, W. H. to Martha Huie? 2-11-1864 Hn
Rhodes, Westley to Harriet R. Rollan 12-27-1855 Hr
Rhodes, Will W. to Lavicy Smith 4-4-1839 (4-10-1839) Hr
Rhodes, Willis to Mary Taylor 8-30-1870 T
Rhodes, Wilson B. to Nancy Bumbley 11-10-1861 (11-17-1861) Cr
Rhodes, Wilson B. to Nancy Rumly 11-16-1861 (11-11?-1861) Cr
Rhodes, Z. B. to Tabitha Matthew 5-18-1843 Hn
Rhodes, Z. T. to Lucinda Benton 2-19-1869 (2-23-1869) Cr
Rhodgers, L. M. to M. E. Hilliard 4-5-1869 (4-9-1869) F
Rial, T. J. to Clarkie Ruff 12-29-1868 (12-30-1868) Cr
Ribsy, Samuel to Mary Capps 3-17-1859 Cr
Rice, Abram to Narissa C. Bevill 3-23-1846 Hn
Rice, Alston G. to Mary Sheridan 4-18-1860 Sh
Rice, Amasa to Rebecca Hodges 4-23-1836 Hr
Rice, C. C. to Margaret Johnson 7-26-1854 Sh
Rice, C. C. to M. J. Dearmond 11-3-1859 Sh
Rice, C. G. to Eliza E. House 12-8-1863 (no return) Hy
Rice, C. H. to Ella Capers 12-19-1870 (12-20-1870) F

Rice, C. S. O. to Lucy Q. Estes 8-29-1865 (no return) Hy
Rice, C. W. to Millie Griggs 8-14-1875 (8-15-1875) L
Rice, Calvin to Milly Sasser 9-4-1867 L
Rice, Charley to Mary Hut 8-10-1877 (8-11-1877) L B
Rice, Columbus to Lucinda Compton 12-18-1872 (no return) L B
Rice, Cyrus C. to Martha V. Feezor 1-30-1859 T
Rice, D. F. to Margaret L. Fletcher 4-3-1866 G
Rice, Daniel to Eliza J. Williams 4-25-1877 (4-26-1877) L B
Rice, Daniel to Fann Eskus (Estus?) 4-5-1872 (4-10-1872) L B
Rice, David John to Challie A. Gause 1-19-1867 L
Rice, E. L. to Mollie P. Fletcher 2-6-1871 (no return) Cr
Rice, Edward E. to Bridget Grant 10-8-1860 (10-9-1860) Sh
Rice, Frank T. to Martha V. Tally 11-6-1865 (11-9-1865) L
Rice, Frank to Hannah Lee 2-7-1877 Hy
Rice, Freeman to Ellen Austin 3-26-1878 L B
Rice, G. A. to Lizzie Cophir 11-24-1867 Hy
Rice, G. H. to Julia Elling 2-13-1878 (2-14-1878) L
Rice, Henry to Elizabeth Simmons 11-27-1868 (no return) Hy
Rice, Henry to Lucinda Carter 6-19-1869 G B
Rice, J. D. to Holloway Susana J. 11-3-1873 (no return) Hy
Rice, J. D. to Mary J. Caldwell 7-22-1879 (7-23-1879) L
Rice, J. J. to Sallie A. Calhoun 12-6-1866 T
Rice, J. M. to Mary Skelly (Kelly?) 2-24-1859 Sh
Rice, J. R. to Millie Rice 7-22-1882 (7-23-1882) L
Rice, Jacob to Melia Warren 3-2-1867 G
Rice, Jake to Lamb Ingram 9-6-1869 G B
Rice, James C. to Sallie Wormik 1-5-1872 (1-10-1872) T
Rice, James to Jane Plunkett 2-4-1856 Sh
Rice, James to Nancy Beck 1-11-1844 Hn
Rice, James to Sarah Massey 4-17-1852 Cr
Rice, Jenkins to Mary Easter Russell 3-24-1875 (4-2-1875) L B
Rice, John J. to Alice Faust 6-11-1859 (6-12-1859) Sh
Rice, John S. to Helen Walker 8-5-1856 Be
Rice, John W. to Charity Taylor 12-31-1859 (no return) Hy
Rice, John to Belle Shoulong 9-30-1881 (10-13-1881) L
Rice, John to Mary C. Arwood 9-22-1869 (no return) L
Rice, Joseph to Cally Vine 12-?-1878 Hy
Rice, Joseph to Tempe Hunt 1-3-1866? (1-5-1867) T
Rice, Joshua to Mary Luckey 11-17-1868 G B
Rice, L. L. to Katie Turner 2-28-1885 (3-1-1885) L
Rice, Lewis to Amanda Bailey 8-26-1873 Hy
Rice, Lewis to Emma Richardson 8-3-1875 (no return) Hy
Rice, Lewis to Manda Bryant 10-7-1872 (no return) Hy
Rice, Miles to Luella Jones 12-31-1868 F B
Rice, N. L. to Nancy A. Green 3-27-1868 (3-29-1868) Cr
Rice, Nathaniel E. to Jennie Massey 4-3-1848 Cr
Rice, Newton J. to Elizabeth J. Ingram 2-19-1852 Hn
Rice, Peter to Sela Rice 1-14-1868 Hy
Rice, R. W. to Mary VanBuren 10-9-1862 (no return) Hy
Rice, Richard to Emma (Mrs.) Henning 1-28-1886 L
Rice, Richard to Sue Rice 11-5-1874 L B
Rice, Robert A. to Martha J. McBride 1-?-1867 (1-16-1867) T
Rice, Robert to Caroline Rice 3-19-1873 (3-20-1873) L B
Rice, Robt. A. to Mary A. Austin 12-17-1871 (12-19-1871) T
Rice, Rufus W. to Adelia E. Harbert 4-5-1853 Ma
Rice, S. Mc. to V. A. Neighbours 9-13-1872 (9-8?-1872) L
Rice, Shedrach to Sarah Potter 3-19-1870 (3-24-1870) L B
Rice, Smart to Sallie Smith 3-22-1871 L
Rice, T. A. to Ninah V. Green (Gause) 10-23-1871 (10-25-1871) L
Rice, T. F. to Sallie E. Borum 8-17-1869 (8-19-1869) L
Rice, T. J. to M. A. Bowen 6-17-1876 (6-20-1876) Dy
Rice, T. J. to N. P. Bowen 4-6-1868 (4-9-1868) Dy
Rice, Thomas to Lurana Tatum 6-8-1867 (6-9-1867) L B
Rice, Thomas to Mary Stitt 9-26-1873 (10-6-1873) T
Rice, Tisha to Elizath? Johnson 12-2-1871 (no return) L
Rice, W. C. to F. E. Llewellyn 12-27-1879 (12-28-1879) L
Rice, William Daniel to Mary Ann Roberts 7-26-1847 (7-?-1847) T
Rice, Wm. J. to Eliza E. Griffith 12-21-1868 (12-22-1868) T
Rice, Wm. O. to Deborah Smith 11-15-1860 (11-18-1860) Sh
Rice, Wm. T. to Sarah Hay 8-25-1859 (no return) Hy
Rice?, E. M. to F. A. L. Lucus 6-2-1850 We
Rich, C. W. to Elenor L. Alexander 8-22-1854 (no return) F
Rich, Chas. W. to Mary E. Bounds 12-3-1844 (no return) F
Rich, Duncan T. to Elizabeth S. Bennett 9-2-1861 (9-3-1861) Hr
Rich, F. G. to A. E. M. Coleman 8-4-1859 G
Rich, James K. Polk to Amanda M. Bunn 2-18-1868 (no return) L
Rich, John to Malinda Bevill 2-23-1842 Hn
Rich, Joseph to Eliza Jane Grissom 12-23-1844 (12-25-1844) F
Rich, Nathan G. to Martha H. Berry 10-15-1866 (10-17-1866) Cr
Rich, Thomas to Mattie Lilley 9-8-1877 (9-9-1877) L
Richa, Zack M. to Susan H. Thompson 4-14-1852 (no return) We
Richard, Alfred to Jane Tumage 1-14-1871 T
Richard, Wm. B. to Minerva McAllister 9-26-1858 Cr
Richardet, W. B. to Laura E. Curtis 6-9-1863 Sh
Richards, B. T. to Sylvester Forte 10-3-1836 (10-4-1836) Hr
Richards, F. H. to Elizabeth Richards 2-23-1857 Sh
Richards, J. G. to Hellen Spurriers 2-11-1879 Dy

Richards, James B. to Holtan Moore 9-18-1866 (9-20-1866) Ma
Richards, Jesse to Margaret Hannery 5-13-1863 Sh
Richards, John C. to Rebecca Parker 12-12-1838 Hy
Richards, John to Mary Ann Springer 3-18-1863 Mn
Richards, Orrange to Caroline Tanner 10-29-1867 (10-30-1867) F B
Richards, Redmond to Manerva Pierce 10-9-1850 (10-10-1850) Ma
Richards, Robert E. to Valeria Winchester 8-15-1856 (8-16-1856) Sh
Richards, S. M. to Caroline Williamson 2-24-1873 (no return) Dy
Richards, Saml. R. to Mary J. Willett 9-15-1858 Sh
Richards, Solomon to Maria Johnson 11-21-1871 T
Richards, W. M. to Martha Bradbery 10-12-1854 We
Richards, W. P. to Virginia Scates 9-24-1873 (9-25-1873) O
Richards, Walter to Lucinda E. Wallace 10-7-1845 Sh
Richards, William M. to Margaret Bradberry 1-14-1861 (no return) We
Richardson, Bob to Rose Capell 12-4-1873 Hy
Richardson, C. A. S. to Mary F. Woods 12-21-1857 (12-24-1857) Sh
Richardson, C. G. to Jennie Lucket 12-18-1851 Sh
Richardson, C. W. to Frances Hooker 7-14-1848 Sh
Richardson, C. W. to Mary Eliza Trotter 2-17-1845 (no return) F
Richardson, Daniel to Mary Jane Kelly 10-29-1866 (no return) Hy
Richardson, Dick to Susan Veneer 5-9-1874 T
Richardson, E. G. to Elizabeth Dalton 5-2-1856 Cr
Richardson, E. G. to Rebecca J. Terrell 8-1-1863 (8-2-1863) O
Richardson, E. to Susanna Wormick 11-29-1866 T
Richardson, Elam to Bazilla Jane Davis 1-11-1853 Ma
Richardson, G. W. to H. A. P. Morris 12-3-1874 L
Richardson, Geo. W. to Mary Carr 6-8-1871 (6-11-1871) Ma
Richardson, Geo. W. to Sarah F. Hattom 12-10-1866 Ma
Richardson, George to Margaret C. Rogers 9-4-1873 (9-14-1873) T
Richardson, Goodman to Rebecca Cupples 7-14-1849 Ma
Richardson, H. H. to Mary E. Porter 1-30-1844 Hy
Richardson, Harrison to Moriah Green 10-4-1872 (no return) Hy
Richardson, Henry to Elizabeth Killy 2-20-1868 (2-25-1868) T
Richardson, Henry to Lizzie Wray 3-11-1871 (3-14-1871) F B
Richardson, Hiram to Mattie Shad 12-15-1869 (12-16-1869) Cr
Richardson, J. E. to E. S. Newton 1-26-1874 (1-27-1874) O
Richardson, J. H. to F. C. Dillon 12-20-1862 (12-25-1862) O
Richardson, J. H. to Harriet Vancleave 7-22-1846 Hn
Richardson, J. J. to M. E. Powell 12-9-1874 Hy
Richardson, J. M. to S. J. Gentry 12-21-1864 O
Richardson, J. M. to Sarah C. Jennings 9-7-1864 (9-8-1864) L
Richardson, J. W. to S. R. Koonce 1-1-1874 L
Richardson, J. W. to Sarah Singleton 1-8-1856 (1-9-1856) L
Richardson, J. to Nancy C. Hill 1-7-1860 T
Richardson, James A. to Evelina L. Clay 10-9-1837 (10-19-1837) G
Richardson, James M. to Catharine Jones 4-4-1855 (4-10-1855) Hr
Richardson, James T. to Mary L. Brightwell 12-29-1845 (1-1-1846) G
Richardson, Jasper to Malenda Knight 3-8-1857 We
Richardson, Jno. L. to Martha (Mrs.) Chives? 10-14-1844 (10-17-1844) F
Richardson, John to Elizabeth Cearly 9-26-1869 (9-27-1869) Dy
Richardson, John to Malina Clemmit 11-27-1874 T
Richardson, John to Mary Jane Ward 6-26-1867 (no return) Dy
Richardson, John to Nancy Jones 8-20-1868 (no return) Dy
Richardson, John to Sarah Mathews 11-21-1839 G
Richardson, Jordon W. to Amanda Jones 11-27-1848 (11-28-1848) L
Richardson, Jos. S. to Martha A. McDavid 1-6-1864 (no return) Dy
Richardson, Joseph to Margaret Wilhelm 2-8-1862 Mn
Richardson, Leander M. to Mary B. Rader 10-17-1846 G
Richardson, M. T. to S. T. Culbreath 7-16-1872 (7-20-1872) T
Richardson, Malcom to Emma Owen 11-20-1867 Hy
Richardson, Matthew to Martha R. Moody 10-27-1856 Hn
Richardson, N. P. to Susan O. Cole 9-8-1855 (9-9-1855) G
Richardson, Ned to Sallie Gainer 5-8-1872 T
Richardson, Peter to Annie Taliaferro 1-3-1869 Hy
Richardson, R. H. to T. S. Maxwell 1-23-1873 Hy
Richardson, Richard to Martha Coleman 12-27-1877 Hy
Richardson, Robert to Ailsey Green 3-19-1880 (3-20-1880) L
Richardson, Robert to Ann Eliza Saunders 8-8-1868 (8-9-1868) Dy
Richardson, Saml. to Cary Rice 5-2-1846 (5-3-1846) F
Richardson, Samuel to Lucretia Paralee Latham 11-19-1855 Ma
Richardson, Samuel to Lucy Ezzell 9-27-1848 Hn
Richardson, Shed to Ann Tool 9-5-1871 T
Richardson, Simeon to Mary Wilson 5-8-1874 T
Richardson, Solaman to Susan Roberts 7-18-1874 (7-22-1874) T
Richardson, Stephen to Laura Little 1-2-1871 (1-12-1871) F B
Richardson, T. J. to M. E. Finley 3-6-1873 (3-5?-1873) Dy
Richardson, T. M. to Permelia Brauner 6-24-1863 (no return) We
Richardson, Thomas G. to Dilly A. Busby 12-7-1852 Hn
Richardson, Thomas T. to Mary J. Baker 3-7-1857 We
Richardson, Thomas to Elizabeth Nicholls 10-30-1841 (10-31-1841) Hr
Richardson, Thos. T. to Mary J. Baker 2-28-1857 (no return) We
Richardson, Tony to Anny Ferguson 3-13-1880 (3-14-1880) L B
Richardson, W. B. to Martha Ione Williams 10-1-1842 (10-6-1842) Ma
Richardson, W. G. to W. F. Towns 11-26-1872 (11-27-1872) Cr
Richardson, W. H. to Eva M. Alston 8-31-1868 (9-2-1868) T
Richardson, W. J. to Clora R. (Mrs.) Wilson 9-6-1864 Sh
Richardson, W. L. to Amanda J. McMurry 4-11-1860 (no return) Hy

Richardson, Wade W. to Mary M. Barksdale 6-15-1854 Cr
Richardson, Washington to Edney Bennett 1-28-1862 Mn
Richardson, William to Amelia Ann Lewis 10-8-1863 Mn
Richardson, William to Malinda Gibson 12-18-1851 Be
Richardson, William to Melvinia Littlejohn 1-4-1873 T
Richardson, Willie C. to Virginia C. Gibbons 11-29-1871 (11-30-1871) Cr
Richardson, Willis to Lydia A. Noromore? 2-15-1844 Hn
Richardson, Wm. A. to Sarah C. Nixon 11-12-1876 Hy
Richardson, Wm. B. to E. C. Rainey 8-9-1864 (8-12-1864) Cr
Richardson, Wm. to Adaline Dickinson 5-26-1866 F B
Richardson, Wm. to Levina Fuller 4-9-1873 Cr B
Richardson, Wm. to Louisa (Mrs.) Fulton 10-15-1864 Sh
Richardson, Yimri? to Elizabeth Williams 5-26-1848 (5-22?-1848) Hr
Richardson, Zachiriah to Lucinda Kesterson 10-6-1832 (10-?-1832) Hr
Richars, William to Nancy Williams 8-15-1842 Ma
Riche, David R. to Nancy E. Vermillion 10-13-1861 We
Riche, Jessee to Elizabeth Alston 4-29-1868 (5-21-1868) T
Richee, Thos. G. to Mary J. Kinsey 1-26-1856 (1-29-1856) G
Richerson, Bedford to Mittie King 1-12-1870 Hy
Richerson, Caleb W. to Eliza F. Gober 7-12-1839 (7-18-1839) F
Richerson, Patrick to Polly Hunt 1-13-1866 T
Richey, A. G. to Louving Gaitley 11-29-1869 (11-26?-1869) F
Richey, James R. to Tennessee J. Baker 8-11-1852 (no return) F
Richey, James to Gennett Humphrey 4-18-1840 (4-19-1840) F
Richey, John H. to Mary Throgmorton 1-28-1838 (no return) Hn
Richey, John M. to Lucy A. Sanders 1-6-1856 (1-9-1859) F
Richey, Robert to Margaret Kephart 12-25-1838 Sh
Richey, Y. W. to Rutha Jane Baker 7-21-1852 (no return) F
Richie, G. W. to Susan C. Cross 1-9-1867 (1-11-1867) Dy
Richie, Henry to Menton Baker 8-13-1843 We
Richie, Isaac P. to Nancy Murphy 7-29-1834 (7-30-1834) Hr
Richie, Jas. L. to Martha Humphrey 1-19-1850 (1-20-1850) F
Richie, W. T. to Josephine Baker 10-10-1855 (no return) F
Richison, Davy to Harriet Lester 12-31-1865 (1-4-1868) F B
Richman, J. W. to Mary E. Merrith 6-22-1859 Cr
Richmon, George O. to Martha H. Morton 10-28-1839 (10-29-1839) G
Richmond, B. to Adamie (Mrs.) Selby 5-21-1851 (6-9-1851) Sh
Richmond, Ben to Silva Coppedge 6-18-1869 (6-20-1869) F B
Richmond, D. A. to Martha A. Whicker 10-15-1867 G
Richmond, D. A. to Tennessee S.(L?) Penn 12-6-1860 G
Richmond, Esekel P. to Matilda Moore 7-31-1848 (4?-3-1848) F
Richmond, Ezekiel to Margaret Alexander 2-16-1832 Hr
Richmond, Frank to Elvira Bradshaw 9-19-1864 (no return) Dy
Richmond, J. H. C. to Sarah T. Bashears 8-7-1865 (8-8-1865) T
Richmond, John to Sarah A. Roberson 9-28-1870 (no return) Hy
Richmond, Marion to Amanda Chism 12-30-1873 Hy
Richmond, Monroe to Minerva McCurley 1-5-1880 (1-6-1880) L
Richmond, Monroe to Queen Loving 2-17-1883 (2-20-1883) L
Richmond, Sebastian P. to Amanda R. Owen 10-5-1833 O
Richy, John to Louisa Bennett 2-3-1846 (2-5-1846) F
Rickenbacker, Frank to Mary Aff 5-11-1848 Sh
Rickett, Thomas to Caroline Harris 1-7-1870 (1-8-1870) F B
Ricketts, H. L. to Georgiana Wethers 6-5-1880 (6-6-1880) L
Ricketts, Robert N. to Martha Ann Holt 6-25-1844 Sh
Rickman, J. B. to Mary A. Harper 1-3-1867 (no return) Hn
Rickman, Marcus to Nancy E. Wilkinson 8-21-1841 (8-23-1841) Ma
Rickman, Robert F. to Ann Caplinger 5-8-1866 (5-9-1866) L
Ricks(Riggs), John H. to Rebecca Colbert 5-2-1829 (5-7-1829) Hr
Ricks, E. M. to Mary C. White 6-19-1872 (no return) Hy
Ricks, Edmund M. to Sally M. Hubbard 2-23-1863 (no return) Hy
Ricks, R. W. to Ann E. English 12-16-1854 (12-21-1854) Sh
Ricks, Robert F. to Mary E. Tadlock 12-12-1864 (12-13-1864) L
Rickter, John to Amana Coltart 3-1-1869 (3-5-1869) L B
Riddick, J. H. to Lucy McFoster 12-25-1860 Sh
Riddle, Barnett to Lydia Short 1-28-1864 O
Riddle, George to Harriett Mitchell 9-10-1849 O
Riddle, George to Jane Bloyce 10-22-1857 O
Riddle, John to Ann Watson 10-25-1853 O
Riddle, Samuel to Jane Rittenberry 7-2-1858 (9-5-1858) O
Riddle, Samuel to Lucy Rittenburg 3-4-1861 (5-21-1861) O
Riddle, Wilie J.? to Ruth Bowers 7-29-1833 (8-8-1833) Hr
Riden, Konrad to Elizabeth Kathmund? 12-6-1852 Sh
Riden, Thomas B. to Nancy J. Fields 7-27-1847 O
Riden, Thomas to Sarah Patrick 7-2-1839 Ma
Ridens, Jefferson M. to Mary Lane 9-21-1862 Dy
Rideout, John to Martha S. Williams 11-29-1852 Sh
Rideout, Johnson to Rody Mitchell 12-9-1872 (12-13-1872) L B
Rideout, Richard to Mollie Fields 12-28-1867 (no return) F B
Rider, David F. to Elizabeth Ann Kiley 6-20-1845 O
Rider, Louis to Emsey Hollyfield 7-12-1839 (7-2?-1839) Ma
Rider, Robert L to Katharine Fields 6-30-1847 O
Rider, T. R. to S. E. Hamlin 5-1-1864 Hn
Ridge, Samuel W. to Martha Pulla(Pully) 7-17-1829 Hr
Ridgeway, Alexander to Misanies Crabtree 7-22-1829 (7-23-1829) O
Ridgeway, David L. to Mary (May) R. Stuckley (Starkey) 3-27-1849 Sh
Ridgeway, J. G. to Mary A. Clayton 1-27-1857 We
Ridgeway, James to Eliza Martin 2-18-1840 Hn

Ridgeway, Joseph B. to Mary E. Bedlock 12-25-1860 Hn
Ridgeway, Lafayette to Sarah E. Cunningham 2-17-1859 Hn
Ridgeway, Richard H. to Malissa Wilson 3-28-1851 (4-1-1851) G
Ridgeway, Richard to Delila Ann Kincaid 1-5-1829 (1-8-1829) O
Ridgeway, S. F. to Mary Ann Ridgeway 12-19-1866 (no return) Hn
Ridgeway, S. H. to Elizabeth Hart 11-12-1854 We
Ridgeway, Samuel C. to Louisa Anna Ridgeway 2-11-1840 Hn
Ridgeway, William W. to Mary M. Jenkins 11-18-1858 Hn
Ridgeway, William to Nancy Warren 11-8-1827 O
Ridgeway, William to Sarey Glason 4-3-1830 G
Ridgeway, Wm. A. to Anjaline Keneda 5-7-1846 (no return) We
Ridgeway, Z. T. to Jonah A. Shotwell 11-8-1871 O
Ridgway, A. C. to Louisa Glisson 12-29-1861 G
Ridgway, Alex C. to Elizabeth Serratt 6-17-1837 (6-18-1837) G
Ridgway, Alex C. to Elizabeth Serratt 6-17-1839 G
Ridgway, B. F. to Eugenia C. Ray 9-20-1862 (no return) Hn
Ridgway, G. W. to Jane Lewis 8-5-1845 We
Ridings, James Crayton to Rachel Elizabeth Taylor 8-18-1867 G
Ridings, R. W. to Elmasand Rust 12-7-1856 Cr
Ridings, William to Mollie Blackwell 8-30-1871 (no return) Hy
Ridley, C. H. to N. L. Oliver 3-7-1870 (3-9-1870) Cr
Ridley, Charles L. to Hettie B. Fitzpatrick 11-6-1869 (no return) L
Ridley, Frank to Josee A. Shivers 11-24-1869 Hy
Ridley, Henry A. to Mary E. Smith 9-15-1853 (no return) F
Ridley, Jack to Sally Kendall 12-14-1867 Hn B
Ridley, Julius to Frances Sparks 12-31-1868 (1-7-1869) Cr
Ridley, R. R. to Mary C. Walker 9-10-1851 (no return) F
Ridley, Robt. to Charity Haynes 12-22-1870 (12-29-1870) Cr B
Ridley, Thomas J. to Sarah L. Smith 6-9-1852 (no return) F
Ridley, Willie to Sallie Cole 1-11-1871 (1-12-1871) Cr
Ridol, J. W. to C. M. Rodgers 9-5-1864 (9-7-1864) Sh
Ridout, James W. to Mary E. Beloate 3-31-1841 Sh
Ridout, John to Lucy Williams 12-26-1837 Sh
Riebert, August to Ellen Uric 12-31-1855 Sh
Ries, Frederick to Josephine Schuldheis 11-21-1862 (11-22-1862) Sh
Rieves, J. W. to C. A. Haze? 5-29-1872 Cr
Rig, Samuel M. to Margarette G. Mathews 9-9-1852 Cr
Rigby, William B. to Caroline E. King 6-7-1854 (no return) Hn
Riggans, J. R. to Mary Bynum 12-7-1854 We
Riggans, J. V. to Sina Abernatha 12-7-1855 (in question) We
Riggin, Bedford to Martha Bird? 3-4-1846 (maybe 1845) Hn
Riggin, John A. to Sarah C. Brooks 11-2-1871 Hy
Riggins, Henry to Lucy Green 10-9-1872 Cr
Riggs, J. M. to Mary Q. Haynes 12-27-1869 (12-29-1869) Cr
Riggs, James to Mary K. Gibbins 2-6-1845 Sh
Riggs, John W. to E. A. Gibson 12-26-1867 F
Riggs, John W. to Mary C. Guthrie 11-8-1856 (11-9-1856) Hr
Riggs, Josiah to Rebecca Dunlap 1-23-1843 (1-24-1843) F
Riggs, N. C. to Julia Ann Highfield 2-7-1867 H
Riggs, Reubin M. to Louisa I.? Delk 12-18-1850 (12-24-1850) Hr
Riggs, Thos. to Eliza J. Parish 5-29-1867 (5-30-1867) F
Riggs, Thos. to Polly Davis 12-13-1853 (no return) F
Right (Kight), H. J. to Sarah Heathcock 9-22-1869 Hy
Right, J. A. to Mary A. Cook 11-5-1846 We
Right, Rafe to Ellen Miller 8-10-1867 Hy
Rigsbee, J. W. to Mary Procton 2-16-1873 Hy
Rigsbee, James E. to H. L. Cole 11-13-1856 G
Rigsby, D. L. to Sarah Lammond 12-5-1868 (12-7-1868) Cr
Rigsby, James A. to Elizabeth Parker 8-9-1854 Cr
Rigsby, John H. to Lucy Palmer 11-26-1867 Hn
Rigsby, Moses M. to Hanna R. Phelps 8-12-1862 (no return) Cr
Rigsby, Samuel J. to Harriett A. Alley 11-21-1867 Hn
Rigsly, John A. to Lee Ann Webb 4-2-1841 (4-6-1841) G
Riley, Barney to Mary McGrath 5-21-1864 (5-24-1864) Sh
Riley, Bernrnd to Ellen Carroll 2-14-1862 (2-18-1862) H
Riley, Bernard to Maryk Ingram 2-1-1855 Hn
Riley, Bernard to Susan Williams 8-13-1846 Hn
Riley, Charles to Jane Mink 1-22-1861 Hn
Riley, Conner to Margaret A. Clark 9-1-1864 (9-4-1864) O
Riley, Daniel J. to Milly Benson 7-10-1847 (7-11-1847) G
Riley, Edward to Annie Burke 10-29-1864 Sh
Riley, Francis to Martha Dickerson 4-25-1860 (4-29-1860) Sh
Riley, Francis to Martha Golden 6-25-1845 Sh
Riley, J. A. to Elizabeth Biddix 7-18-1863 (7-19-1863) O
Riley, J. W. to E. P. Kallis 2-26-1868 G
Riley, James A. to Arabella W. Foster 11-18-1866 Hn
Riley, James G. to V. L. Shankle 1-1-1866 T
Riley, James to Martha Allison 7-23-1844 Sh
Riley, Jesse to Delia A. Stamps 11-2-1859 (11-3-1859) Sh
Riley, John C. to Lavinia Miller 6-10-1876 (no return) Hy
Riley, John F. to Elizabeth Axsom 8-3-1859 (8-7-1859) Sh
Riley, John W. to M. C. Reaves 1-16-1860 O
Riley, John to Angeline Gray 5-27-1862 O
Riley, John to Ella Butt (Britt) 9-30-1874 Hy
Riley, John to Kittie Anderson 9-5-1869 Hy
Riley, John to Sarah Ann Forsythe 4-2-1855 (4-5-1855) L
Riley, Joseph to Rebecca Lonsberry 8-24-1839 Hr

Riley, Michael H. to Mary E. Creighton 5-30-1857 Sh
Riley, Nelson to Rhoda Jackson 4-6-1866 G
Riley, Owen to Julia Burke 4-25-1861 Sh
Riley, Pat to Mary Kelly 4-21-1860 (4-22-1869) Sh
Riley, Patrick to Bridget Kelly 4-13-1860 Sh
Riley, Solomon to Jane Wallis 6-21-1855 O
Riley, Stacey to Lizzie Hicks 8-13-1874 O B
Riley, T. J. to Elizabeth V. Frazier 11-18-1868 Be
Riley, W. H. to Sarah Phillips 9-8-1859 O
Riley, Washington to Emiline J. Roberts 12-23-1854 (12-24-1854) G
Riley, William to Elizabeth Morris 3-24-1858 Sh
Riley, William to Mary Orms 10-14-1841 G
Riley, Wm. C. to Lavinia Rugg 2-12-1855 (2-14-1855) Sh
Riley, Wm. to Nelly Ann Harris 10-1-1869 (10-3-1869) F B
Rily, James to Sarah Griffith 3-10-1858 We
Rimmer, J. H. to Sarah E. Riley 1-10-1864 Mn
Rinehart, A. W. to Sarah E. Thompson 3-24-1877 (no return) Hy
Riner, Charles to Amelia Man 10-4-1859 (10-5-1859) Sh
Ring, B. A. to Mary C. Flowers 7-19-1860 G
Ring, W. R. to Matilda C. Corner 3-25-1861 (3-29-1861) O
Ring, William to Catherine Baldridge 8-13-1836 (8-18-1836) O
Ringer, G. W. to Sallie Robirson? 5-2-1885 (5-3-1885) L
Ringgold, Bryant to Mary A. Nobles 12-28-1837 G
Ringgold, James to Elizabeth Easterwood 10-11-1842 (10-14-1842) G
Ringgold, John to Mary Harrison 11-30-1843 (12-12-1843) G
Ringly, Cornelius to Margaret O. Ward 5-8-1851 Sh
Ringwald, Lewis to Mary Kreider 1-25-1859 Sh
Ringwald, W. to Amelia Frest (French-Frech) 4-4-1850 Sh
Ringwald, Wm. to J. F. Margeram 4-6-1864 Sh
Ringwold, John to Caroline Unninger 8-9-1858 Sh
Rinklin, Andrew to Christine Matmiller 5-9-1859 (5-10-1859) F
Rinks, E. E. to Sarah Paschal 11-6-1864 Mn
Rinks, E. S. to M. T. Ray 12-14-1862 Mn
Rinn, Henrick to Catharine Croupe 6-10-1851 (6-10-1850?) Sh
Riorden, Matthew to Winifer Dunn 5-24-1856 (5-25-1856) Sh
Ripley, J. M. to S. J. Simons 1-24-1876 (1-26-1876) Dy
Ripley, W. P. to Mary E. Roper 2-24-1872 (2-25-1872) Dy
Ripley, William P. to Biddy (Mrs.) Bond 11-28-1860 Ma
Ripley, William P. to M. D. Dickinson 9-18-1849 (9-20-1849) Ma
Rison, E. R. to Nancy Poyner 7-25-1849 Hn
Rison, J. V. to Elizabeth Provine 12-6-1853 Hn
Rison, J. V. to Julia W. Cherry 6-26-1856 Hn
Rison, M. H. to Mary E. Moon 2-16-1859 Hn
Rison, Marcelius N. to Susan A. Freeman 2-13-1840 Hn
Ritchey, John to Sarah Love 4-23-1836 Hr
Ritchey, Samuel H. to Martha E. Hall 4-6-1848 Cr
Ritchie, J. M. to O. E. Shinault 12-1-1866 (12-4-1866) F
Ritchie, W. W. to Katharine J. Butler 8-24-1858 Sh
Ritchy, James G. to James? Smithdorch 1-15-1841 Ma
Rittenberry, Charles to Mary Ann Andrews 2-11-1868 G
Rittenburgh, Wm. to Elizabeth Ballard 8-11-1859 (8-12-1859) Sh
Rittenhouse, Daniel Gillman to Elisabeth Flemming 9-22-1864 Sh
Ritter, Everett R. to Rebecca Autry 9-7-1840 Cr
Ritter, Everett to Anna Goodwin 5-15-1828 (5-20-1828) Hr
Ritter, Isham to M. Marler 3-3-1845 Hr
Ritter, James to Elzy Burns 12-13-1861 (12-15-1861) Cr
Ritus (Retus), Albert G. to Mary Baugus? 7-6-1836 Sh
Rivers, Archile to Rosietta Patterson 9-24-1870 F B
Rivers, Dick to Jane Rivers 2-19-1870 F B
Rivers, Dick to Martha Ann Patterson 2-12-1870 (2-13-1870) F B
Rivers, Sandy to Jane Murphy 12-24-1868 (not executed) F B
Rivers, Tom to Julia Pender 3-1-1871 Hy
Rivers, Wallace to Eliza Jane Patterson 1-19-1871 F B
Rivers, Wiley to Julia Williamson 1-24-1871 (2-2-1871) F B
Rives (Reeves), N. F. to M. L. Hargett 10-24-1866 Hy
Rives, Christopher to Mary Ann Shelton 7-12-1838 F
Rives, D. N. to A. A. Ligon 11-22-1877 Hy
Rives, E. D. B. to L. A. Williams 12-27-1854 (no return) F
Rives, Evans to Rachel Dickinson 2-20-1869 F B
Rives, Grandison to Henrietta Brown 12-25-1867 (12-26-1867) F B
Rives, Henry A. to Mary Ann Taylor 11-22-1838 F
Rives, Jack to Lydia Ewell 11-19-1866 (11-20-1866) F B
Rives, John F. to Mary E. Bailey 5-14-1874 Hy
Rives, John G. to Florence M. Harris 5-10-1864 Sh
Rives, R. B. to Lucy Ann Rodrey 1-18-1855 Sh
Rives, Richard H. to Eulah H. Thomas 11-15-1873 (11-18-1873) T
Rives, Richard to Catharine Poindexter 9-25-1869 F B
Rives, Robert to Margaret Harvell 12-25-1866 F B
Rives, Saml. to M. J. King 5-31-1866 O
Rives, W. M. to Sally A. Rives 9-17-1838 F
Rives, William A. to L. A. Scale 11-17-1851 (no return) F
Rives, William C. to Lucy T. Ferress 12-16-1839 (12-17-1839) F
Rives, William to Evelina Dickenson 1-3-1839 F
RoJoux, Marcus to Mina Bauer 8-27-1855 (8-28-1855) Sh
Roach(Roark?), William to Lucy Gregory 7-17-1844 Hr
Roach, A. J. to Martha J. Jones 11-23-1852 G
Roach, Abner C. to Sally Thedford 10-24-1827 G

Roach, Admiral G. to Mary A. C. Tedford 10-21-1868 (10-22-1868) Ma
Roach, Amos to Louisa Parson 9-25-1849 Cr
Roach, Amos to Matilda Brandon 7-31-1845 Cr
Roach, Amos to Nellie Scott 3-15-1842 Cr
Roach, Benjamin to Polly T. Bradberry 9-11-1833 (9-12-1833) G
Roach, C. L. to Margaret E. Williamson 12-18-1863 Hn
Roach, Cincematus to Lethia Bruff 8-25-1835 G
Roach, Eaton to Elizabeth Baber 2-18-1849 Be
Roach, Edward to Mary Riggs 11-10-1830 Hr
Roach, Elisha to Henrietta Newborn 11-19-1873 Hy
Roach, J. C. to L. E. Younger 5-20-1872 (5-21-1872) Cr
Roach, J. F. to Abigale Overton 10-23-1854 (10-26-1854) Hr
Roach, J. F. to Martha A. Thomas 6-7-1858 Hr
Roach, J. J. A. to Saluda A. Wilson 11-15-1858 (11-24-1858) G
Roach, J. R. to L. L. Wheeler 12-10-1862 (12-4?-1862) O
Roach, James M. B. to Eliza J. Wedington 7-14-1853 Cr
Roach, James M. to Martha Abernathy 1-18-1843 Sh
Roach, John A. to Eliza J. Starkey 8-13-1867 (8-16-1867) Ma
Roach, John R. to Melvena Massters 8-12-1858 O
Roach, John W. to Mary A. Welch 3-29-1844 (no return) We
Roach, John to Ellen Lonargan 11-1-1856 (11-3-1856) Sh
Roach, John to Nancy Morgan 1-15-1828 (1-17-1828) G
Roach, Kit to Adeline Granberry 8-19-1870 (no return) F B
Roach, Kit to Harriet Alexander 12-7-1866 (12-8-1866) F B
Roach, Manly to Analiza Jordan 1-1-1852 Be
Roach, Robert M. to Lucy Wagoner 11-27-1866 Hn
Roach, S. D. to Lucy D. Flowers 1-18-1860 (1-19-1860) Sh
Roach, S. R. to S. A. Givens 11-26-1874 Hy
Roach, Samuel to Emily Barnett 11-12-1863 O
Roach, Silas to Nannie Parker 12-25-1873 Hy
Roach, Stephen J. to Almira Bradberry 2-4-1830 (3-11-1830) G
Roach, Stephen to Elizabeth Bane 2-27-1826 G
Roach, T.? to Mary Winters 1-21-1862 Cr
Roach, W. H. to Alice Lansdon 9-23-1867 (10-1-1867) Cr
Roach, W. T. to E. J. Morrow 7-8-1863 Mn
Roache, David to Bridget Kennedy 4-12-1856 (4-13-1856) Sh
Roachel, Thomas G. to Mary J. Bogal 6-28-1865 G
Roades, Ashley to Nancy C. Boyt 5-30-1846 (5-31-1846) Hr
Roads, Danl. to Sarah E. Thompson 4-6-1863 (4-8-1863) Dy
Roads, Jno. W. to Mary A. Welch 4-3-1844 We
Roan, John to Ann Tennessee Etheridge 8-30-1868 G
Roane, Albert to Mrs. Salina Walker 7-19-1867 (7-21-1867) T
Roane, C. P. to Rebecca B. Washburn 5-26-1857 (5-27-1857) Sh
Roane, Henry to L. E. A. (Mrs.) Parker 11-12-1850 (11-16-1850) G
Roane, Lucas to Elmira Caraway 11-6-1869 (11-7-1869) F B
Roane, Sterling S. to Mary Sharp 4-28-1841 (4-27?-1841) T
Roane, Thos. W. to Mary Hillen Somervill 11-13-1858 (11-17-1858) T
Roark, Amos C. to Manerva A. Philips 10-11-1858 (10-12-1858) Sh
Roark, Aulsey D. to Jane McWilliams 12-29-1845 (1-1-1846) Ma
Roark, James to Lucy Boswell 2-18-1828 Sh
Roark, James to P. C. Briggins 4-4-1850 Sh
Roark, John to Mary Murphy 2-14-1843 (2-15-1843) Hr
Roark, Samuel to Mary Jane Alexander 9-18-1841 Sh
Roark, W. D. to Rienia Brandon 7-23-1872 (no return) Cr
Roark, William to Elizabeth B. Shepherd 12-27-1832 Hr
Roark, Wm. C. to Harriett Malone 10-15-1845 Cr
Roaz, E. H. to Sarah P. Gateley 1-11-1865 (1-14-1865) Cr
Robards, E. C. to Sarah M. Walker 4-16-1867 Ma
Robards, Henry M. to Mary E. Harris 5-28-1867 (5-29-1867) F
Robards, Howell R. to Margaret Camp 5-9-1848 Sh
Robards, James to Lucinda Clark 10-18-1884 (10-19-1884) L
Robards, W. J. to Margaret Alexander 5-20-1848 Sh
Robb, J. V. to Nancy C. Jacobbs 9-4-1869 T
Robb, James to Patience Bradley 8-16-1848 Ma
Robb, John to Eliza Kay 12-1-1827 Hr
Robb, Washington G. to Julia Ann Thompson 12-11-1833 (12-12-1833) Hr
Robbins, A. M. to F. B. Dunlap 1-2-1873 Hy
Robbins, A. M. to Sarah Garrett 1-19-1871 (no return) Hy
Robbins, Augustus R. to Sophorina J. Orr 3-10-1869 Hy
Robbins, Elijah to Milly Moody 2-18-1828 G
Robbins, Elisha to Ada Gideons 12-6-1871 (no return) Hy
Robbins, Elliot to Mary Caroline (Mrs.) Robbins 12-28-1858 Sh
Robbins, H. H. to Fanny Jiles 9-14-1874 Hy
Robbins, J. S. to E. J. Featherston 10-31-1877 (no return) Dy
Robbins, J. to Missouri E. Morten 1-20-1864 Sh
Robbins, James M. to Mattie V. Munns 12-13-1871 Hy
Robbins, James to M. E. Lunceford 11-25-1870 (no return) Hy
Robbins, John D. to Susan Weatherspoon 11-2-1829 (11-3-1829) G
Robbins, Joseph to Nancy Rodey 1-9-1832 (1-12-1832) G
Robbins, M. A. to Margaret E. Turner 1-5-1876 Dy
Robbins, Moss (Moses?) to Elizer Stone 3-15-1869 G B
Robbins, Oscar R. to M. L. Stith 10-11-1869 (10-12-1869) Dy
Robbins, S. C. to Frances S. Lankford 11-17-1877 (11-18-1877) Dy
Robbins, Sylvester to Marian Tarleton 3-5-1879 (3-6-1879) Dy
Robbins, Thomas E. to Jane Miller 8-28-1882 L
Robbins, William to Jincy Phillips 8-21-1838 (8-23-1838) O
Robbins, William to Piercy Glisson 2-25-1843 (2-?-1843) O

Robbins, Wm. S. to Zilphia Harrison 11-22-1859 (no return) Hy
Robers, Richd. to Manerva J. Phillips 2-20-1870 Hy
Roberson, Abram W. to Sarah M. Pettyjohn 3-5-1857 Hn
Roberson, Alexander to Isabella Henderson 4-5-1859 Sh
Roberson, Alonzo R. to Lucy Simmons 12-17-1876 Hy
Roberson, B. F. to M. A. Langley 2-3-1880 (2-5-1880) L
Roberson, Ben to Ader Williamson 11-25-1869 Hy
Roberson, Coleman to Sarah Ann Stray 4-20-1850 (4-21-1850) G
Roberson, Cullen to Agnes Watkins 12-23-1857 Hn
Roberson, E. G. to Nancy E. Blackburn 12-25-1858 (12-28-1858) G
Roberson, Elijah to Callie McBride 5-13-1885 (5-17-1885) L
Roberson, Elijah to Mary Moreland 6-1-1858 Sh
Roberson, George to Ellen Roper 10-12-1866 G
Roberson, George to Margarette Steel 4-11-1861 G
Roberson, Gus to Ella Owen 3-20-1878 (3-21-1878) L
Roberson, Hayward to Sarah Ann Jones 7-14-1867 Hy
Roberson, Henry to Martha Brimm 7-12-1866 (no return) Hy
Roberson, Hugh to Rebecca Rollins 7-21-1838 Cr
Roberson, J. M. to S. J. Wilson 10-3-1852 Hn
Roberson, J. N. to M. H. Fullerton 1-9-1867 G
Roberson, J. T. to L. A. Pennington 9-15-1879 L
Roberson, Jack to Susan Bynum 12-15-1876 Hy
Roberson, James D. to L. E. Corbet 11-24-1869 (11-25-1869) T
Roberson, James E. to Eliza M. Randall 5-17-1853 Sh
Roberson, James H. to Nancy T. Salmon 12-1-1847 F
Roberson, James M. to Nancy E. West 10-19-1863 G
Roberson, James M. to Sarah F. Venable 3-31-1859 Hn
Roberson, James to Elizabeth Spann 11-6-1864 Hn
Roberson, James to Mary Rieves 8-26-1840 Cr
Roberson, James to Mary Rieves 8-26-1840 (no return) Cr
Roberson, James to S. C. Stout 7-10-1858 We
Roberson, Joel Thomas to Louisa Fullen 6-25-1856 L
Roberson, John D. to A. A. Kellar 11-27-1883 (11-28-1883) L
Roberson, John D. to Elizabeth J. Barron 9-22-1843 (9-28-1843) Ma
Roberson, John M. to Elizabeth Brigham 1-2-1850 Ma
Roberson, Lewis to Mary Bell Sawyer 4-7-1870 L
Roberson, Monroe to Alice Whitmore 5-13-1885 (no return) L
Roberson, Philly to Adaliza Montgomery 6-13-1850 Cr
Roberson, Robert D. to Emma R. Keller 12-22-1879 (12-24-1879) L
Roberson, Silvestis to July Ann Jordan 11-23-1870 (12-1-1870) Cr
Roberson, Stephen to Melinda Pewett 3-23-1867 Hy
Roberson, T. H. B. to Nancy G. Stiggall 12-30-1857 (12-31-1857) G
Roberson, Thomas J. to Mary Sanders 6-8-1882 (no return) L
Roberson, Thomas R. to Malissa L. Jeans 12-10-1865 Mn
Roberson, W. E. to Martha J. Luton 7-11-1868 (no return) L
Roberson, William M. to Barshebn? E. Blackwell 12-22-1859 G B
Roberson, William M. to Mary E. Durham 1-13-1874 L
Roberson, William to Martha Moore 8-27-1861 (8-30-1861) L
Roberson, Wm. R. to Sarah F. Butler 11-27-1872 Cr
Roberson, Wm. to Martha Cook 1-16-1845 Cr
Roberson, henry to Sarah L. Blackmon 10-5-1859 (11-6-1859) G
Roberts, A. D. to N. J. Hudspeth 5-18-1856 We
Roberts, A. W. to Sarah Jones 6-6-1865 (no return) Hy
Roberts, Amos to Eliza Shaver 8-26-1868 Cr
Roberts, Andrue to Ellen Eaves 12-17-1846 We
Roberts, B. to Susan H. Alexander 1-8-1850 Sh
Roberts, Benjamin F. to Levica A. Moberry 7-31-1857 We
Roberts, C. N. to Flora Oliver 8-29-1857 G
Roberts, Calvin to Mary White 12-29-1866 (12-31-1866) F B
Roberts, Charles N. to Flora Oliver 9-11-1857 (9-10?-1857) Ma
Roberts, Clem to Susanna Evans 12-13-1876 Hy
Roberts, Columbus W. to Malinda E. Thomas 7-19-1860 Hn
Roberts, David E. to Margaret Andrews 8-15-1861 Ma
Roberts, Duncan to Rebecca Burton Smith 12-1-1856 Cr
Roberts, F. M. C. to Martha Fowler 4-6-1847 Hn
Roberts, Fantry to Martha J. Petty 12-12-1867 Cr
Roberts, Francis M. to A. W. Parrish 1-30-1861 We
Roberts, G. T. to Martha Cherry 11-8-1865 (11-9-1865) O
Roberts, G. W. to S. C. Moore 9-4-1855 (no return) Hn
Roberts, George N. to Luzana C. Bevill 10-16-1869 (10-17-1869) Cr
Roberts, George to Mary Currie 10-15-1874 Hy
Roberts, George to Mary Macklin 12-19-1867 T
Roberts, George to Parthenia Weston 10-25-1852 Hn
Roberts, George to Sarah Winn 8-25-1845 O
Roberts, George to Susan Bailey 4-25-1844 Hn
Roberts, Goin to Alice Read 7-15-1879 (7-16-1879) L
Roberts, Hammet to Susan A. Vaughan 1-23-1867 G
Roberts, Harvey A. to Isabella Roberts 4-3-1855 Ma
Roberts, Henry D. to Mildred A. Compton 6-3-1853 (no return) F
Roberts, Henry M. to Clarissa Ann Ammons 5-16-1846 (5-17-1846) Hr
Roberts, Henry S. to Rebecca Barnes 4-22-1861 Hn
Roberts, Hilliary to Sylla Coleman 1-3-1878 Hy
Roberts, Isaac S. to Martha Ann Williams 2-4-1863 Hn
Roberts, Isaac W. to Maryland Upchurch 6-18-1857 Hy
Roberts, Isham B. to Susan E. Horne 9-18-1848 (9-19-1848) T
Roberts, J. H. to Martha L. Roberts 9-7-1865 G
Roberts, J. M. to L. B. McCollum 8-10-1872 (8-13-1872) Cr
Roberts, J. M. to Mary M. Thomason 8-23-1864 (8-24-1864) Cr
Roberts, J. R. to America Sweet 10-26-1869 Hy
Roberts, J. to M. A. Burgett 2-6-1860 (2-7-1860) O
Roberts, Jacob F. to Margaret M. McBride 11-27-1849 Sh
Roberts, James A. to Martha M. Martin 2-23-1857 (no return) Hn
Roberts, James H. to Lucy Ann Gregg 9-3-1838 (no return) F
Roberts, James M. to Elizabeth Fleming 5-21-1856 (5-24-1856) G
Roberts, James M. to Louisa J. Sanders 8-2-1858 (8-3-1858) O
Roberts, James W. to Elizabeth Appleberry 2-22-1869 (2-24-1869) T
Roberts, James to Adeline Boles 7-19-1863 We
Roberts, James to Emes Carr 2-21-1868 (no return) Hy
Roberts, James to Margaret Rodgers 3-3-1858 Cr
Roberts, John F. to Virginia C. Johnson 11-24-1869 G
Roberts, John L. to Rebecca Saveley 11-11-1858 We
Roberts, John N. to Harriet A. Roberts 5-19-1871 (5-21-1871) Cr
Roberts, John T. to Sarah J. McBride 3-15-1853 Sh
Roberts, John to Mollie Stull 5-20-1876 (5-21-1876) L
Roberts, John to Rachel Mills 5-17-1855 O
Roberts, Joseph A. to Elizabeth A. Lewis 12-20-1859 We
Roberts, Joseph F. to Dinkie Hassell 3-3-1875 Dy
Roberts, Joseph L. to Mary Susan Davis 12-8-1852 (12-9-1852) T
Roberts, Joseph to Julia Harden 10-20-1877 (10-25-1877) L B
Roberts, Josiah to Sarah A. Fielder 12-6-1860 We
Roberts, L. B. to Martha Simpson 2-16-1845 Hn
Roberts, Lewis to Susan Clayton 2-21-1842 Sh
Roberts, Louis? M. to Martha Jane Rawls 4-3-1848 (no return) F
Roberts, Lytle B. to Louisa Mills 2-8-1844 Hr
Roberts, M. E. to Sarah E. Gilbert 8-7-1847 Sh
Roberts, M. to Fannie Clements 8-17-1867 (8-18-1867) T
Roberts, Mark to Melinda Autry 11-2-1856 Cr
Roberts, Miles J. to Nancy C. Green 9-6-1860 (9-19-1860) Cr
Roberts, Nathan to Mary P. Rosser(Roper) 10-20-1831 Hr
Roberts, Nelson to Milla Smith 1-18-1868 F B
Roberts, Obadiah to Matty Edwards 1-12-1826 O
Roberts, Osbourne to Nannie Spivey 12-1-1881 L B
Roberts, P. R. to Elizabeth Jones 10-18-1860 Sh
Roberts, Prestly H. to Margaret R. David 9-14-1853 Hr
Roberts, R. F. to Matilda Smith 9-8-1842 O
Roberts, Reuben D. to Calpernia Brogdon 1-20-1855 Hn
Roberts, Richard W. to Jane Marchbanks 8-29-1852 Be
Roberts, Robert C. to Julia Miller 1-24-1861 Dy
Roberts, Rufus to Susan Lea 2-22-1882 L
Roberts, Ryland to Martha J. Key 11-3-1849 Hn
Roberts, S. W. to Elizabeth A. Parish 9-17-1861 (9-18-1861) Cr
Roberts, S.(L) B. to Catharine Waller 10-4-1850 Hr
Roberts, Samuel A. to Ann I. Arnold 4-22-1854 G
Roberts, Samuel B. to Eliza Jane French 3-19-1843 Hn
Roberts, Samuel to Elizabeth Daniel 2-25-1848 Be
Roberts, Samuel to Lucinda Roach 3-15-1852 (3-22-1852) T
Roberts, Schuylar H. to Missiniah G. Pass (Parr) 5-11-1841 Sh
Roberts, Schyler to Mary Keener 8-7-1849 Sh
Roberts, Suel to Clarisee I. Holeman 1-17-1872 Hy
Roberts, T. A. to M. A. C. Alexander 12-29-1860 G
Roberts, Thomas D. to Naomi Roberts 12-21-1837 Sh
Roberts, Thomas Wesley to Frances Betcy Bays 9-10-1857 (9-11-1857) T
Roberts, W. C. to M. J. (Mrs.) Roberts 2-4-1863 Sh
Roberts, W. J> to Mary A. Clements 11-6-1865 (12-5-1865) T
Roberts, W. V. to Elizabeth Palmer 2-14-1859 (2-15-1859) Sh
Roberts, William C. to Emely J. Rutledge 9-29-1849 (10-4-1849) G
Roberts, William D. to Martha Brown 12-7-1843 Hn
Roberts, William E. to Elvira Strother 12-24-1869 (no return) Dy
Roberts, William F. to Sarah Parker 8-10-1862 We
Roberts, William W. to Sibby Hamilton 10-2-1851 G
Roberts, William to Amea? E. Rogers 1-2-1862 (no return) Cr
Roberts, William to Anna E. Rogers 1-1-1862 (1-2-1862) Cr
Roberts, William to Anna Rogers 12-31-1861 (1-1-1862) Cr
Roberts, William to Arky Burton 12-8-1844 Be
Roberts, William to Bell F. Coffman 11-19-1873 (no return) Hy
Roberts, William to Kizziah Lampkins 10-16-1851 (10-16-1851) Hr
Roberts, William to Mary Mellish 2-17-1862 Sh
Roberts, William to Nancy Ewell 1-22-1869 (1-24-1869) F B
Roberts, William to Nancy Mizell 10-23-1853 Hn
Roberts, Willis to Artemissa Butler 12-8-1869 (12-9-1869) Cr
Roberts, Wm. F. to Amanda M. Vails 12-12-1839 Hr
Roberts, Wm. Jas. to Lucinda Webb 4-11-1855 T
Roberts, Zachariah H. to Sarah Fly 8-2-1830 Ma
Roberts, Zachariah to Mary Morris 6-3-1855 O
Robertson, A. R. to Mattie Brown 3-8-1867 L
Robertson, A. T. to Martha Jane Vaden 10-27-1845 (11-2-1845) Hr
Robertson, Albert to Venia Williams 10-5-1878 (10-6-1878) L
Robertson, Alexander C. to Mary Eliza Vaulx 11-11-1852 Ma
Robertson, Alexander M. to Meedy Goodwin 7-29-1852 G
Robertson, Alfred C. to Mary Bickerstaff 10-12-1838 (10-16-1838) F
Robertson, Allen to Eliza Jarrett 7-30-1871 Hy
Robertson, Andrew J. to Talitha Womack 4-7-1839 Be
Robertson, B. F. to Alice Chisholm 12-27-1885 (12-30-1885) L
Robertson, Battle to Martha Willis 9-29-1830 Ma

Robertson, Bill to Eliza Somervill 12-16-1865 (12-25-1865) T
Robertson, Bob to Biddy Leaf 2-4-1869 G B
Robertson, Caleb A. to Martha McCutchan 9-17-1849 (9-19-1849) G
Robertson, Charles S. to Lucinda E. Ayers 5-12-1852 (6-12-1852) Hr
Robertson, Charles to S. E. Grier 9-20-1876 Dy
Robertson, Christopher to Nancy E. Taylo 11-1-1854 (11-2-1854) Hr
Robertson, D. A. to Mary G. Ledbetter 9-19-1866 (9-20-1866) Dy
Robertson, D. P. to Louisa Ray 5-10-1848 Hn
Robertson, Edmond to Rhoda Graves 4-27-1872 (no return) Hy
Robertson, Edward to Harriett A. Barne? 4-4-1839 Hr
Robertson, Elijah to Mary (Mrs.) Moreland 6-1-1858 (6-9-1858) Sh
Robertson, Elisha to Elizabeth Woodward 5-24-1860 Hr
Robertson, F. M. to A. E. Erwin 1-10-1852 (no return) F
Robertson, Frank to Joanah Howard 7-31-1868 (8-1-1868) T
Robertson, G. F. to Mary A. Webb 11-11-1855 We
Robertson, G. W. to Marry F. Winfield 2-10-1845 F
Robertson, G. W. to Mary Bull 1-22-1853 (no return) F
Robertson, G. W. to Virginia Neely 7-19-1865 (7-20-1865) Dy
Robertson, George to Elizabeth Robins 8-5-1845 Be
Robertson, George to Harriet Baw 8-22-1867 (no return) F B
Robertson, Green to Elvira Jones 1-27-1869 (1-28-1869) F B
Robertson, Harrison to Tennie Hooper 12-25-1872 (12-26-1872) Dy
Robertson, Henry L. to Mary C. McAuley 12-14-1865 Be
Robertson, Henry to Nannie Studivan 3-2-1870 (3-7-1870) F B
Robertson, I. P. to Elizabeth Williams 1-20-1866 O
Robertson, I. W. to Frances Cummings 12-19-1866 (12-20-1866) O
Robertson, J. B. to J. B. Drake 11-20-1861 (no return) Hy
Robertson, J. D. to Katherine Peel 11-3-1852 Hn
Robertson, J. F. to Isabella Claybrooks 8-6-1868 Hy
Robertson, J. F. to N. A. Dickerson 7-14-1868 Hy
Robertson, J. M. C. to Elizabeth Watson 8-1-1832 (8-2-1832) Hr
Robertson, J. M. to E. A. Lane 12-24-1878 (12-26-1878) Dy
Robertson, J. P. to Neer Barton 9-8-1857 We
Robertson, J. R. to Alice C. Ray 8-28-1849 Hn
Robertson, J. V. to G. A. Powell 3-15-1866 Hn
Robertson, J. W. to Pheby Peterson 8-26-1861 (8-27-1861) Dy
Robertson, James to Ann E. Richardson 9-29-1869 (9-30-1869) Dy
Robertson, James to Eliza A. U. Gailey 12-26-1855 (no return) We
Robertson, James to Minerva Rushing 10-27-1841 (10-28-1841) Ma
Robertson, James to Sarah Ann Stafford 5-31-1838 Hr
Robertson, Jefferson to Elizabeth Trout 12-28-1840 (12-31-1841) G
Robertson, Jerimiah W. to Mary Jane Patton 2-11-1854 (2-19-1854) Hr
Robertson, Joel B. to Nancy E. Joiner 7-21-1853 Hn
Robertson, John C. to Mary Jane Clark 4-23-1868 G
Robertson, John D. to Elizabeth Braden 1-12-1848 L
Robertson, John F. to Nancy Johnson 7-31-1827 Hr
Robertson, John H. to Julia Ann Cooper 9-15-1853 (9-17-1853) G
Robertson, John H. to Vina Cornelius 11-4-1832 (11-6-1832) Hr
Robertson, John N. to Martha Banks 9-28-1850 Hn
Robertson, John W. to Harriet Peterson 1-26-1864 (1-29-1864) Dy
Robertson, John to Bell Mays 3-23-1830 Ma
Robertson, John to Mary R. Mayfield 2-5-1836 G
Robertson, Jonah to Amy Saunders 8-25-1830 Ma
Robertson, Jonas to Elizabeth Chisum 8-6-1828 (8-7-1828) Hr
Robertson, Joseph J. to Fatis C. Howell 4-12-1845 (4-15-1845) F
Robertson, Joseph R. to Mary A. Craig 6-26-1840 (7-7-1840) Hr
Robertson, Joshua to Nancy Hogg 9-17-1845 Be
Robertson, Josiah S. to Pernetta E. Williams 9-28-1867 (9-29-1867) Ma
Robertson, L. A. to Malvina Stokes 12-22-1862 (12-23-1862) Dy
Robertson, L. to Mollie Wise 12-30-1882 (12-31-1883) L
Robertson, Lafayette to Mary Crenshaw 12-28-1868 T
Robertson, Lewis to Ann Eliza Hunter 11-5-1866 (no return) Hy
Robertson, Loyd to Lucy Jane Taylor 12-28-1868 T
Robertson, Lycurgus to Virginia A. Parnell 12-25-1857 Sh
Robertson, M. A. to L. P. Brake 1-16-1852 Hn
Robertson, M. L. to Mary Jane Hill 2-25-1842 (3-3-1842) F
Robertson, Moses to Cinda Jelks 12-26-1868 (no return) Hy
Robertson, N. L. to M. J. Montgomery 12-2-1871 (12-3-1871) Dy
Robertson, Pleasant to Elizabeth Bunds 3-18-1842 Hn
Robertson, Rawlings to Martia McCarley 7-9-1846 F
Robertson, Richard to Sarah Griffin 11-24-1838 (11-25-1838) G
Robertson, Robert F. to Amanda M. Harriss 6-11-1855 L
Robertson, Robert to Mary Edwards 11-26-1865 Hy
Robertson, S. R. to E. F. Richie 10-23-1856 (no return) We
Robertson, S. S. to M. E. Sledge 8-15-1855 Ma
Robertson, Sam to Mary Ozier 1-30-1869 (2-6-1869) F B
Robertson, T. L. to Elizabeth Wells 6-16-1859 Hy
Robertson, T. M. to Sarah A. Witherspoon 9-29-1842 Hn
Robertson, Theophulis S. to A. C. Dial 5-24-1847 (5-30-1847) Hr
Robertson, Thomas H. to Elizabeth Fowler? 12-17-1857 Hn
Robertson, Thomas J. to Delila A. Caviness 11-11-1854 (11-12-1854) Hr
Robertson, Thomas to Emily Holliway 4-25-1855 (4-28-1855) Hr
Robertson, Thos. H. to Mary Jane Gurley 1-28-1848 (2-2-1848) F
Robertson, Thos. L. to Ida Sanders 10-28-1853 Sh
Robertson, W. F. to J. A. Jopling 5-22-1883 (5-23-1883) L
Robertson, W. N. to Louisa Hardison 1-15-1879 (1-16-1879) Dy
Robertson, Walter to Rebecca Hill 6-15-1824 (6-17-1824) Hr
Robertson, William C. to Elizabeth Danner 12-17-1853 (12-22-1853) G
Robertson, William H. to Mary Caroline Moore 5-5-1858 (5-8-1858) L
Robertson, William H. to Nancy C. Ward 1-31-1858 Hn
Robertson, William Henry to Nancy Ellis 9-16-1871 (9-17-1871) L
Robertson, William Jarrett to Luizer Welch 7-12-18__ (probably 1865) G
Robertson, William P. to Louanna Harris 9-3-1867 (9-4-1867) Ma
Robertson, William to Elizabeth Askew 4-2-1857 (4-5-1857) O
Robertson, William to Jestin Rust 12-9-1827 G
Robertson, William to Julia Taylor 4-21-1870 (no return) Hy
Robertson, William to Prutie Watson 12-23-1869 Hy
Robertson, William to Sallie Blanten 10-4-1866 G
Robertson, Willis to Easter Wardlaw 4-1-1885 (4-2-1885) L
Robertson, Wm. C. to Eliza J. Montgomery 11-28-1838 G
Robertson, Wm. C. to Martha A. Cooper 10-28-1840 (10-29-1840) G
Robertson, Wm. D. to Catherine E. Swindle 1-6-1848 Be
Robertson, Wm. R. to Jane C. Dial 12-26-1844 (12-28-1844) Hr
Robertson, Wynham to Judith M. Pope 9-22-1847 Sh
Robeson, Hugh B. to Caroline Duckworth? 12-28-1830 Ma
Robeson, John M. to M. E. Swindle 8-23-1855 Be
Robeson, Nathan P. to Elizabeth Ann Parrow 11-14-1851 Be
Robey, Benedict S. to Lucy M. Watkins 3-3-1867 Hn
Robin, Joset R. to Emily Mandiville 4-20-1852 Cr
Robinett, Cyrus W. to Susan Smith 12-20-1853 (12-22-1853) Sh
Robinett, W. B. to Sarah Ann Hanegin 5-9-1846 (5-12-1846) T
Robins, C. A. to Mary E. Lindsey 4-13-1856 Be
Robins, Columbus to Ruth V. F. Whitethorne 8-3-1857 (8-4-1857) O
Robins, Edward to Lotta Ray 1-16-1843 G
Robins, Elisha to Louisa Chism 3-2-1872 L
Robins, Evans S. to Sarah Ann E. Brannon 2-5-1860 Hn
Robins, J. G. to Elizabeth Brannom 2-19-1865 (no return) Hn
Robins, John A. to Alice Beasley 3-25-1860 L
Robins, John W. to Tomsella Culbreath 5-30-1855 Hn
Robins, Joseph to Nancy Rody 1-9-1831 G
Robins, M. N. C. to H. L. Grant 12-13-1867 (12-16-1867) Cr
Robins, S. F. to Mary E. Laton 10-8-1862 Mn
Robins, W. S. to Angeline Cooper 10-23-1871 L
Robins, William N. to Elizabeth J. Weatherley 12-1-1858 Hn
Robins, William to Jane King 12-17-1840 F
Robins, Wm. B. to Matilda C. Lindsey 4-27-1843 Be
Robinson, A. C. to Marion Kennie 1-30-1860 Sh
Robinson, A. C. to Martha Revel (Reid) 5-13-1849 Sh
Robinson, A. M. to Ella Baldridge 4-12-1864 (4-13-1864) O
Robinson, Abel to C. Hunt 12-2-1867 G B
Robinson, Albert to Molly Spencer 8-28-1876 (no return) Hy
Robinson, Alfred to Nancy Haflen? 1-2-1847 Hn
Robinson, Alfred to Nancy Weaver? 7-23-1831 Hr
Robinson, Anderson to _____ Haywood 10-21-1866 (10-23-1866) Cr
Robinson, Andrew to Ann Wood 9-7-1866 (9-16-1866) T
Robinson, Andrew to Susan Uptergrove 3-13-1853 Cr
Robinson, Asa to Frances Cozby 12-29-1833 Hr
Robinson, Austin to Catherine Hamer 1-2-1868 (1-5-1868) F B
Robinson, Benjamin M. to Rebecca C. Williams 9-8-1856 O
Robinson, Bob to Anna Rainey 2-25-1869 G B
Robinson, Charles N. to Mary Bemas 6-11-1851 Sh
Robinson, D. B. to Nancy P. Liles 11-4-1852 Cr
Robinson, Daniel to Caroline Sharp 1-15-1868 G B
Robinson, Darius to Eliza J. Usher 1-17-1843 Hr
Robinson, Ed to Frances Jones 12-24-1870 (no return) F B
Robinson, Edward to Hellen E. Vernon 2-9-1850 (2-19-1850) Hr
Robinson, Elijah to Frances E. McAdoo 12-8-1858 (12-12-1858) Ma
Robinson, Elipha Z. to Nancy Jane Dodson 4-21-1857 (4-26-1857) Ma
Robinson, Elisha to Barbara Chisum 1-5-1830 (1-7-1830) Hr
Robinson, F. B. to M. J. Erwin 3-24-1858 (3-25-1858) Sh
Robinson, F. M. to Susan E. Luster 12-29-1853 (12-29-1853) Ma
Robinson, G. M. to Harriett Trawick 11-20-1851 Cr
Robinson, G. W. to Amelia Overall 8-30-1865 G
Robinson, G. W. to Mary T. Thetford 1-27-1870 G
Robinson, G. W. to Pamoni? A. Gooch 2-15-1855 Cr
Robinson, Geo. to Elizabeth Smith 2-28-1844 G
Robinson, Geo. to Louisiana Duncan 2-18-1863 Sh
Robinson, George to Ann E. Hamby 8-2-1870 G
Robinson, H. A. to Elizabeth Umphrey 9-28-1855 Cr
Robinson, H. B. to Adaline (Mrs.) Rochester 2-18-1864 Sh B
Robinson, Harry to Lucy Macklin 8-24-1877 Hy
Robinson, Harry to Rosett Tatum 3-30-1867 G B
Robinson, Henry A. to Margaret Light 4-5-1876 (4-6-1876) Dy
Robinson, Henry T. to Susannah Crouch 6-17-1845 Sh
Robinson, Hugh B. to Arabella Herndon 8-8-1868 (9-3-1868) Ma
Robinson, Hugh B. to Caroline R. Miller 5-3-1855 G
Robinson, Hugh B. to Sarah M. Tigrett 12-19-1838 Ma
Robinson, Hugh to Nancy Jacobs 10-31-1858 Cr
Robinson, Isom to Lucinda Furgerson 1-17-1871 (2-4-1871) Cr B
Robinson, J. A. to Augusta A. Burns 12-10-1857 Cr
Robinson, J. K. to Drewhannah Holden 7-20-1865 Hn
Robinson, J. N. to F. J. Johnson 12-17-1860 (no return) Hy
Robinson, J. W. to E. D. Donaldson 12-4-1860 G
Robinson, J. to Martha Jeno (Jene) 1-27-1863 Sh

Robinson, Jack to Hannah Somervell 12-8-1866 (12-9-1866) T
Robinson, James D. to Jane A. Fletcher 10-7-1850 Cr
Robinson, James H. to Mary Alice Ramsey 2-20-1868 G
Robinson, James H. to Sarah E. Wilson 1-24-1848 (1-25-1848) Hr
Robinson, James J. to Frances M. Cornnell 3-15-1853 Cr
Robinson, James L. to Almira M. Fletcher 11-4-1846 Cr
Robinson, James L. to Catherine E. Brooks 3-4-1859 Ma
Robinson, James P. to Anna Bell Sutton 12-30-1868 (1-19-1869) Ma
Robinson, James W. to Mary C. A. Canaday 7-17-1851 G
Robinson, James to Margarett Frazier 12-17-1851 (12-18-1851) O
Robinson, James to Mary Ann Burt 8-18-1832 Hr
Robinson, James to Mary Frazier 12-24-1857 O
Robinson, James to Nancy Vernon 3-26-1860 Hr
Robinson, James to Topsie Anthony 1-23-1877 Hy
Robinson, Jerry to Elizabeth Logan 1-12-1872 (1-17-1872) T
Robinson, Jesse S. to Mary A. Salisbury 2-20-1867 Dy
Robinson, Jessee to Emily Smith 12-8-1876 Hy
Robinson, Jno. B. to E. Douglass 3-26-1851 (no return) F
Robinson, John C. to Elizabeth J. Turner 12-23-1848 (12-26-1848) Hr
Robinson, John E. to Caroline Roe 10-11-1869 (10-14-1869) Ma
Robinson, John G. to Susan J. Jackson 4-9-1849 Cr
Robinson, John H. to Elizabeth Traftor 12-25-1849 (12-27-1849) G
Robinson, John K. to Jane? Faulk 10-28-1841 T
Robinson, John R. to Louisa E. Vinson 1-24-1843 Cr
Robinson, John T. to Pamelia J. Nelson 9-14-1841 Sh
Robinson, John W. to Callie Abney 12-19-1867 G
Robinson, John W. to Martha Burrus 11-22-1842 (11-23-1842) Ma
Robinson, John W. to Mary Jane Stray 1-7-1869 G B
Robinson, John to Clementine Mitchell 7-7-1867 Be
Robinson, John to Jane Vail 1-22-1848 (1-23-1848) Ma
Robinson, John to Levisa Grantham 8-28-1826 (8-28-1826) Hr
Robinson, John to Molly Thompson 11-7-1864 Sh
Robinson, John to S. J. Mynett 9-22-1867 G
Robinson, Jonathan A. to Amanda A. Young 11-13-1845 Cr
Robinson, Lewis to Mary Ward 10-21-1848 G
Robinson, Luke to Rebecca Mickel 3-1-1858 (3-2-1858) Sh
Robinson, M. T. to Mary Brown 11-12-1852 Sh
Robinson, Martin to Mary Revel 9-24-1846 Sh
Robinson, Moses to Martha Clements 10-17-1871 T
Robinson, Nicholas to Sophia Valzine Kersey 11-20-1870 G
Robinson, Oliver to Martha Ragland 2-17-1866 F B
Robinson, Patrick F. to Louisa I. Ayers 11-29-1850 (11-30-1850) Hr
Robinson, Paul to Becky Morris 8-5-1873 (no return) Hy
Robinson, Pleasant to Elizabeth Montgomery 12-21-1835 Hr
Robinson, R. W. to Delila Averett 8-22-1833 Hr
Robinson, R. W. to M. A. Lewis 3-1-1859 (3-13-1859) Hr
Robinson, Robert W. to Mary Hall 5-10-1831 Hr
Robinson, S. H. to Caroline Montgomery 8-20-1854 Cr
Robinson, S. M. to I. A. Dunlap 3-27-1859 O
Robinson, Saml. B. to Sophrona J. Goodin 12-14-1848 (12-20-1848) F
Robinson, Saml. B. to Susan Tanner? 5-23-1860 (5-24-1860) Sh
Robinson, Samuel A. to L. E. Martin 2-2-1870 (2-13-1870) Cr
Robinson, Samuel M. to Elcy Jane Guy 9-4-1839 (9-5-1839) O
Robinson, Samuel to Rhoda A. Tippett 1-6-1851 Be
Robinson, Thos. L. to Ida Sanders? 10-28-1863 (10-29-1863) Sh
Robinson, Thos. W. to Mary Louisa Woodard 10-20-1853 G
Robinson, Thos. to F. L. Vaughn 2-2-1852 Cr
Robinson, W. D. to Julia A. Jones 10-8-1851 Cr
Robinson, W. J. to Jennie Hill 12-14-1867 G
Robinson, Wade to Tennessee Jackson 7-27-1867 O
Robinson, William P. to Mary E. Williamson 4-30-1850 (5-1-1850) Ma
Robinson, William P. to Malinda Crockett 11-24-1847 O
Robinson, William S. to Josephine Wagster 10-8-1867 (10-10-1867) Ma
Robinson, William to Isabella Patterson 6-10-1844 Sh
Robinson, William to Jane Gregory 4-17-1830 We
Robinson, William to Virginia Taylor 12-8-1845 (12-17-1845) T
Robinson, Wm. B. to Laura B. Pettie 3-8-1870 (3-10-1870) T
Robinson, Wm. C. to _____ 6-26-1867 Ma
Robinson, Wm. E. to Virginia Bunting 10-14-1859 (10-18-1859) Hr
Robinson, Wm. J. to Mary A. Beasley 1-16-1847 Cr
Robinson, Wm. J. to Mary E. McKennon 9-3-1844 Cr
Robinson, Wm. to Betsy Grear 12-29-1877 Hy
Robinson, Wm. to Beverly Burrow 9-15-1844 Cr
Robinson, Wm. to Cornelia F. Rainey 1-8-1861 Sh
Robinson, Wm. to Eliza E. James 2-17-1860 F
Robinson, Wm. to Puty Rust 1-7-1855 Cr
Robinson, Wyly J. to Winey F. Michell 9-29-1860 Be
Robinson, Zach to Bell Hardin 1-8-1874 Hy
Robison, G. T. to Sarah Bridges 2-14-1870 (2-15-1870) Cr
Robison, J. D. to Elizabeth Brim 2-16-1854 Cr
Robison, Jacob to Louisa Anderson 5-23-1867 (no return) Cr
Robison, James A. to Mary Elizabeth Jeno 10-15-1861 Sh
Robison, James W. to Mary E. Ethridge 3-9-1840 Hn
Robison, John E. to Elizabeth Mercer 1-13-1852 Hr
Robison, John L. to Catherine Burson 11-29-1862 Ma
Robison, L. C. to Everline King 12-5-1871 (no return) Cr
Robison, L. C. to Mary Loving 4-22-1866 (no return) Cr
Robison, Nelson to Massely? Browning 10-4-1870 (10-6-1870) Cr
Robison, Peyton L. to Mary M. W. Chapman 12-22-1858 L
Robley, Charles B. to Nancy (Mrs.) Staton 3-31-1870 Ma
Robley, John H. to Catharine Oswald 12-16-1858 Hr
Robley, John R. to Ellen B. Black 12-25-1852 (12-28-1852) Ma
Robson, Ira S. to Mary M. Snow 11-12-1870 (11-13-1870) F
Rocco, B. to Rose Mariane 9-1-1860 (9-3-1860) Sh
Rocco, Henry to Theresa Conner 6-29-1859 Sh
Rocco, Lazzario to Columbia Boggiana 8-20-1860 Sh
Roche, Michael to Mary Roche 1-21-1858 Sh
Rochell, J. J. to Amanda J. Cloid 1-15-1873 (no return) Cr
Rochell, James A. to Nancy A. King 12-11-1843 We
Rochell, John S. to Agnes A. Stone 11-29-1854 Ma
Rochell, N. A. to Sarah F. Burnett 8-29-1861 (no return) Hy
Rochell, N. W. to Mary S. Parker 12-8-1858 Cr
Rochell, N. W. to T. C. Ward 1-18-1841 Cr
Rochelle, J. S. to Sarah Jane Jolly 3-27-1848 (3-29-1848) F
Rochelle, T. J. to V. E. Cain 1-6-1869 G
Rockholt, J. H. to Ella Jones 12-21-1859 Sh
Rockliff, Madison to Elizabeth Rushing 7-12-1863 Mn
Rocksey, Gidion to Rebecca Rogers 7-22-1841 Ma
Rode, Adam to Miss Mary Ann Townsend 5-20-1874 T
Rodenhizer, John to Emilina Davis 8-21-1858 (8-22-1858) Ma
Rodery (Roding), Benjamin to Elizabeth Webb 1-17-1844 (no return) We
Rodery?, Calvin B. to Charlotte Brizendine 2-2-1848 Hn
Rodgers, Abner L. to Anna L. Sutton 9-1-1851 (9-2-1851) L
Rodgers, Amariah to Mary E. Pattillo 10-9-1844 Sh
Rodgers, Andrew to Harriett Perry 7-20-1847 Cr
Rodgers, Benjamin L. to Nancy M. Fisher 11-16-1830
Rodgers, Beverly A. to Lizzie D. Allison 8-9-1868 (no return) F
Rodgers, C. W. to L. A. Patrick 12-8-1875 (12-9-1875) Dy
Rodgers, Clement N. to Elizabeth E. Teel 2-6-1850 Sh
Rodgers, Daniel P. to Ellen Pinson no date (1838-1859) Cr
Rodgers, David J. to Martha Rowland 1-11-1855 Cr
Rodgers, E. A. J. to E. A. Lytle 11-22-1851 Cr
Rodgers, E. M. to Dianna Boyd 11-25-1841 Cr
Rodgers, Edmund S. to Mary Allen 4-18-1840 F
Rodgers, Eli W. to Linday Green 12-9-1841 Cr
Rodgers, Elijah to Dorothy T. Bratton 5-1-1851 Cr
Rodgers, Elisha to Martha A. Harvey 12-11-1854 Cr
Rodgers, G. W. to Lydia A. Houston 12-20-1855 Cr
Rodgers, Geo. W. to Mary Jane Chambers 2-16-1863 L
Rodgers, Green B. to Sealy Fields 3-24-1848 Cr
Rodgers, Hugh S. to Delia Brogdon 1-1-1839 Hn
Rodgers, Hugh to Sarah Ray 2-6-1835 Sh
Rodgers, J. M. to Dumbilla Polston 8-14-1876 (8-15-1876) Dy
Rodgers, J. M. to M. J. Shirrin 10-12-1867 G
Rodgers, J. N. to M. A. Parham 4-15-1880 (4-16-1880) L
Rodgers, J. R. to E. Y.? Rodgers no date (with Aug 1866) Cr
Rodgers, J. S. to A. M. Taylor 11-23-1869 (11-24-1869) Dy
Rodgers, J. W. to Martha Watson 7-22-1879 Dy
Rodgers, James F. to Martha A. Liles 12-7-1854 Cr
Rodgers, James M. to Eliza Liles ?-?-1860 Cr
Rodgers, James S. to Sarah F. Fields 1-16-1851 Cr
Rodgers, James to Mahala Murphy 12-23-1842 Sh
Rodgers, James to Polly Davis 4-14-1842 F
Rodgers, Jas. to Cornelia Harris 6-30-1849 (7-1-1849) F
Rodgers, Jeremiah T. to T. H. Covington 9-22-1841 Cr
Rodgers, John A. to Sarah L. Scott 4-21-1858 (4-22-1858) G
Rodgers, John L. to Martha A. Teal 11-22-1850 Sh
Rodgers, John P. to Catherine Wray 6-11-1862 Sh
Rodgers, John T. to Adeline McMillan 4-30-1866 (5-4-1866) Ma
Rodgers, John W. to Elizabeth A. Mann 2-16-1853 Cr
Rodgers, John W. to H. E. Cunningham 7-28-1858 Cr
Rodgers, John W. to Henrietta E. Eddings 3-15-1854 Sh
Rodgers, John to Elizabeth Jennings 3-13-1855 (3-16-1855) L
Rodgers, John to Emeline Carver 5-29-1843 O
Rodgers, John to Henrietta Wilson 10-9-1884 (10-11-1884) L
Rodgers, John to Mahala Rowe 1-10-1841 Cr
Rodgers, Joshua to Susan McMackin 12-27-1847 Cr
Rodgers, Jubille P. to Mary H. Burrow 4-15-1847 Cr
Rodgers, Martin to Ellen Welch 1-12-1858 Sh
Rodgers, Nathaniel to Mary Polk 2-23-1843 Hr
Rodgers, Peter to Judie Smith 9-27-1871 Hy
Rodgers, Phillip H. to Sarah H. Dudley 12-20-1855 Cr
Rodgers, Polk to Amanda Wood 12-27-1871 Dy
Rodgers, R. S. to Mary J. Fletcher 6-22-1850 Sh
Rodgers, Robert T. to Elizabeth A. Brown 1-31-1856 Cr
Rodgers, Robert to Corian Rowe 11-8-1839 Cr
Rodgers, Robert to Tennessee Spence 1-1-1880 Dy
Rodgers, T. L. to Malinda E. Laismer (Larimer) 10-16-1849 Sh
Rodgers, Thomas L. to Caroline Wells 2-21-1867 Be
Rodgers, V. A. to Cornelia A. Thomson 11-25-1857 Cr
Rodgers, W. E.? to Ann E. Lambert 9-21-1864 (10-25-1864) T
Rodgers, William to Amelia E. Brooks 6-26-1849 Cr
Rodgers, William to Eliza Bland 8-28-1844 Sh
Rodgers, William to Lucy Marshall 1-13-1870 G B

Rodgers, Wm. A. to Mary Tucker 7-8-1841 Cr
Rodgers, Wm. E. to Elizabeth B. Battle 5-25-1853 Sh
Rodgers, Wm. H. to Cripia N. Crawley 6-8-1859 Sh
Rodgers, Wm. J. to Mary M. Pearce 12-4-1865 (12-6-1865) F
Rodgers, Wm. M. to Elender Carver 12-28-1854 Cr
Rodgers, Wm. R. to Mary Ann Elmore 12-10-1846 Be
Rodgers, Wm. Z. to Mary L. Green 1-2-1857 Cr
Rodick, Gray to Candis Wright 1-20-1840 (1-22-1840) Ma
Rodiman, John to Mary A. Gillespie 5-2-1850 Sh
Rodrin, Anton to Allis Chalk 11-21-1870 (12-4-1870) L
Rody, John to Joanna Maher 6-9-1854 Sh
Roe, B. F. to A. S. Gillespie 6-4-1861 G
Roe, Duncan to Mary McElyea 8-15-1839 Be
Roe, Francis A. to Eliza Snyder 9-17-1849 Sh
Roe, J. G. to H. J. Robison 12-20-1866 G
Roe, J. N. to M. C. Vaughan 10-30-1860 G
Roe, James C. to Anna L. Harris 2-20-1867 (no return) Dy
Roe, John A. to Nancy Newhouse 1-10-1846 (1-15-1846) G
Roe, John to Fannie Page 8-29-1874 (8-30-1874) T
Roe, N. to Drucilla Gastings 1-7-1840 (2-2-1840) Ma
Roe, Robert A. to M. Emma Henderson 1-23-1867 (1-24-1867) Dy
Roe, Saml. to Amanda C. Wood 1-4-1869 (1-5-1869) T
Roe, Samuel to Jane Harrison 6-24-1851 (6-26-1851) T
Roe, William Joseph to Franky Jane Shankle 8-17-1867 (8-18-1867) T
Rogan, James W. to Alice L. W. Holloway 4-11-1871 (4-12-1871) F
Rogers, A. E. to Mary J. Brinkly 10-9-1865 (no return) Cr
Rogers, A. J. to M. L. Duning 12-2-1872 (12-5-1872) Cr
Rogers, A. J. to Nancy J. Vernon 3-6-1869 (3-9-1869) L
Rogers, Alex to N. T. Hill 9-24-1869 (9-28-1869) Dy
Rogers, Alexa to Mary L. Butler 1-27-1842 Cr
Rogers, Alexander to Belinda Wallis 1-29-1828 (2-2-1828) Ma
Rogers, Alexander to Martha Rogers 3-13-1875 Hy
Rogers, Allen to Frankie Lee 10-30-1869 Hy
Rogers, Archibald S. to Margaret E. Fry 7-15-1856 (7-17-1856) Ma
Rogers, Archibald S. to Nancy G. Weaver 2-20-1849 (2-22-1849) Ma
Rogers, Auston to Nancy M. Marshall 3-17-1859 Cr
Rogers, B. A. L. to J. J. Peeples 10-29-1856 We
Rogers, B. A. to Beadi L. Terrill 4-25-1859 We
Rogers, B. W. to Nancy Crews 2-7-1866 G
Rogers, Benjamin to Mary Strickland 4-23-1851 Hr
Rogers, C. A. to Mary E. Elkins 1-22-1873 (1-23-1873) Cr
Rogers, Calvin J. to Mary A. Gleeson 10-9-1845 (no return) We
Rogers, Charles to Manerva L. Taylor 1-30-1878 Hy
Rogers, Chester M. to Sarah A. Preast 10-6-1861 We
Rogers, Claton to Jane Reeves 2-9-1848 Be
Rogers, David M. to Sarah Ann McElroy 3-6-1845 Sh
Rogers, David to Carolin Fletcher 10-9-1845 (10-12-1845) Hr
Rogers, Elam to Margaret Forsheath 10-23-1844 (10-25-1844) Hr
Rogers, Elias to Ann Cooper 1-5-1851 (1-7-1851) O
Rogers, Elijah G. to Martha L. Butler 1-21-1868 (1-22-1868) Cr
Rogers, G. P. to Mary E. Rivers 7-11-1870 (7-14-1870) F
Rogers, G. W. to C. L. Bradley 1-27-1874 Dy
Rogers, G. W. to Francis Gillam 7-19-1863 We
Rogers, Geo. E. to S. A. E. Matlock 2-14-1865 (2-16-1865) O
Rogers, George C. to Ann Caroline Derrah 12-17-1840 Ma
Rogers, George H. to Mary E. Null 10-13-1863 (no return) Cr
Rogers, George H. to Mary McIntyre 2-20-1879 (2-23-1879) L
Rogers, George W. to Elizabeth W. Turnage 1-11-1841 (1-12-1841) T
Rogers, George W. to Mary Ann Medford 2-3-1840 (2-4-1840) Hr
Rogers, George to Nannie Tucker 8-7-1874 (8-12-1874) Dy
Rogers, Gid to Hettie Wood 5-3-1874 Hy
Rogers, Green Berry to Frances Webb 5-21-1834 Sh
Rogers, Green C. to Martha J. Smith 7-31-1866 (8-2-1866) Cr
Rogers, H. A. to Eliza Rose 12-7-1858 Sh
Rogers, H. H. to M. K. Hughes 2-1-1870 (2-2-1870) Ma
Rogers, H. S. to Susan A. Pickins 11-20-1867 (11-26-1867) F
Rogers, Henry J. to Malenda Highfill 12-6-1845 Hr
Rogers, Henry to Margaret Garrison 12-5-1866 (no return) Hy
Rogers, Henry to Polly Hunnell 3-3-1831 Hr
Rogers, Henry to Sarah Gause 6-9-1875 Hy
Rogers, Irvin Q. to Sophronia Baskwell 12-28-1854 Hr
Rogers, Isaac to Elsey Cook 3-22-1841 G
Rogers, Isaac to Mahala Elkins 3-18-1834 Hr
Rogers, Isaac to Polly Anne Fleming 12-26-1873 Hy
Rogers, J. A. W. G. to Mary Jane Grisson 7-31-1861 (8-1-1861) Cr
Rogers, J. F. to Sarahann M. Williams 6-16-1871 (6-18-1871) Cr
Rogers, J. H. to Nancy M. Bennett 8-19-1871 (8-20-1871) Cr
Rogers, J. S. to Jennie A. Sears 12-11-1868 (no return) Hy
Rogers, J. T. to F. A. Joiner 5-14-1864 Cr
Rogers, J. V. B. to Frances A. Clevies 2-24-1869 (2-25-1869) T
Rogers, Jack to Harriet Rogers 12-27-1865 Hy
Rogers, James H. to Harriet A. Patrick 11-24-1855 (11-28-1855) Sh
Rogers, James H. to Mary A. E. Slaton 10-1-1855 (10-4-1855) G
Rogers, James K. P. to Georgiann Litle 8-3-1869 C
Rogers, James K. to Elizaeth L. Hull? 8-8-1867 (8-9-1867) Cr
Rogers, James M. to Eliza Liles 8-27-1860 (9-7-1860) Cr
Rogers, James M. to Elizabeth S. Stone 2-26-1838 (3-13-1838) Hr

Rogers, James M. to Emila Simmons 5-21-1843 (no return) F
Rogers, James M. to Emmaline Marcum 10-1-1855 (10-4-1855) G
Rogers, James R. to Mary Ann Gilbert 8-1-1861 Mn
Rogers, James to Alice Vowell 3-3-1886 L
Rogers, Jerome to Motherlinda (Mrs.) Coster 2-5-1865 (2-7-1864) Sh
Rogers, Jerry to Julia Ann Tenant 1-29-1875 Hy
Rogers, Jno. W. to Deliah L. Hansford 10-25-1858 (10-28-1858) Hr
Rogers, Joe to Elizabeth Crafton 4-10-1869 G B
Rogers, Joel A. to Mary Holland 11-11-1857 Be
Rogers, John C. to Mary Ann Butler 4-12-1847 Ma
Rogers, John C. to Mollie Wood 10-16-1873 Hy
Rogers, John D. to Beda A. Jones 5-23-1865 (5-24-1865) Cr
Rogers, John F. to Elizabeth E. Mosely 9-26-1836 G
Rogers, John M. to Nannie Harrison 4-26-1879 (4-27-1879) Dy
Rogers, John R. to Frances Bingham 2-1-1838 Sh
Rogers, John R. to Nancy R. Reynolds 8-9-1853 Be
Rogers, John V. to Marthen Lassiter 9-25-1853 Hn
Rogers, John W. to Eliza Childress 2-23-1858 (2-25-1858) O
Rogers, John W. to Sarah A. Graham 2-16-1863 L
Rogers, John jr. to Eliza Cox 10-28-1835 (10-29-1835) Hr
Rogers, John to Jane Mills 12-10-1845 Hr
Rogers, John to Katy Botto 4-30-1859 Sh
Rogers, John to Mary Johnson 9-19-1861 Hr
Rogers, Jones (James) to Nancy Ann Grissom 9-17-1853 (9-18-1853) O
Rogers, Jubelee P. to Mary H. Burrow 4-15-1847 Ma
Rogers, Lemuel to Clarissa Eliza Bowers 9-28-1833 (10-3-1833) Hr
Rogers, Lewis M. to Emma Jones 7-8-1878 Dy
Rogers, Louis to Emma Brown 12-7-1869 (no return) F B
Rogers, Magilba to Nancy Staton 12-8-1832 G
Rogers, Monroe to Parlee Welch 8-13-1872 O
Rogers, N. J. to Sarah E. Phelps 5-15-1873 Cr
Rogers, Nathan to Emma Larrison 12-16-1874 Hy
Rogers, Nathan to Sarah Livingston 9-8-1877 (no return) Hy
Rogers, P. M. to Martha F. Blakeman 1-3-1858 We
Rogers, Peter to Julia Sanders 8-9-1875 (no return) Hy
Rogers, Phillip to Ella Scroggins 10-14-1880 Dy
Rogers, R. B. to Katie Burlison 9-22-1874 (9-23-1874) L
Rogers, Richard E. to Julia E. House 2-12-1861 G
Rogers, Richard to Mary Riprogle 10-19-1858 Hr
Rogers, Robert E. to Ann E. Harvey 10-6-1869 (10-7-1869) F
Rogers, Robert L. to Sarah Jane Haynie 1-17-1843 Ma
Rogers, Robert to Debbie Angeline Ray 6-28-1868 G
Rogers, Robert to Nancy Mann 12-31-1877 Hy
Rogers, Robt. R. to Martha W. Absent 11-9-1859 Hr
Rogers, S. J. to Mollie Allcock 9-18-1867 O
Rogers, S. James to Caroline Hudson 3-22-1858 (3-25-1858) Hr
Rogers, Saml. B. to Mary C. Yopp 2-4-1861 (2-7-1861) Hr
Rogers, Saml. W. to Mary A. Woolberton 9-29-1860 Hr
Rogers, Sampson to Elizabeth Stokes 11-7-1853 (11-15-1853) T
Rogers, Sampson to Hollis Jackson 12-8-1830 (12-9-1830) Hr
Rogers, Spier to Elizabeth Casey 10-27-1836 Hr
Rogers, Stephen to Polly Fulgham 12-8-1829 (12-10-1829) Hr
Rogers, Theophilus to Martha Wood 1-18-1836 Sh
Rogers, Thomas C. to Easter R. Peckins 8-7-1862 (8-17-1862) O
Rogers, W. A. to Mary J. Fussell 9-2-1861 (9-3-1861) Cr
Rogers, W. B. T. to Martha L. J. Rogers 9-30-1857 Sh
Rogers, W. B. to Rebecca J. Richards 1-21-1869 G
Rogers, W. H. to M. E. Simerson 10-23-1866 (10-25-1866) F
Rogers, W. J. to Amanda Williams 5-11-1865 (5-12-1865) T
Rogers, W. J. to Elizabeth Wilds 1-15-1866 (1-18-1866) F
Rogers, Walter James to Frances Ida McDearmond 12-14-1866 (12-19-1866) L
Rogers, William B. to Sarah E. Keys 10-28-1858 G
Rogers, William H. to Mary A. Wilson 7-25-1840 (7-30-1840) G
Rogers, William H. to Sarah Ann Mitchell 7-5-1836 Sh
Rogers, William R. to Nancy Robinson 5-7-1828 Hr
Rogers, William S. to Mary M. Caruthers 12-31-1840 (no return) Hn
Rogers, William to Adaline Davidson 10-17-1869 G B
Rogers, William to Calpurnia C. Peden 2-13-1851 Hn
Rogers, William to Cynthia Sherrin 4-20-1851 (6-2-1851) O
Rogers, William to Elizabeth Boswell 3-24-1853 O
Rogers, William to Eugenia Williams 1-30-1867 F
Rogers, William to Jane Dolan 9-21-1847 (9-23-1847) G
Rogers, William to Susan Mashburn 1-9-1829 Hr
Rogers, Willoughby to Sally Smith 1-4-1837 Hr
Rogers, Wm. H. to Martha Ann Walker 3-4-1853 Sh
Rogers, Wm. R. to Joisey Hanks 9-8-1827 Hr
Rogerson, W. T. to Martha Moore 1-30-1867 G
Rogerson, William to Nancy J. Palmore 9-2-1859 Hy
Rogin, James R. to Mary Ann Oakley 2-22-1849 Hn
Rohmer, Martin to Rosena Kelley 5-24-1859 (5-25-1859) Sh
Rohwer, J. H. to Maria Schweizer 12-3-1860 Sh
Roland, H. G. to Elizabeth Dunlap 8-27-1869 G
Roland, Jacob to Sarah Elizabeth Malone 10-29-1874 (10-31-1874) T
Roland, Wm. to Elizabeth Branhart 9-14-1845 Cr
Roley, James to Louisa Stacy 2-10-1848 Cr
Rolfe, A. V. B. to Martha D. McClaran 12-12-1853 (no return) F
Rolings, Wm. J. to Mary Elizabeth Massey 1-10-1843 Sh

Rolins, John W. to Sarah Humphrey 9-16-1858 Cr
Rolins, John to Caroline Condelly 11-29-1858 Cr
Rolland, W. A. to Nancy Prince 11-9-1848 Hn
Rollings, Tim to Cinthy Walker 7-5-1877 Hy
Rollins, Augustin to Elizabeth Harns 3-29-1843 Ma
Rollins, Elbert to Sarah Ann Caurdel 4-27-1857 Ma
Rollins, Enoch to Mary Brown 12-12-1838 (12-13-1838) Ma
Rollins, Gastin to Mary E. Harris 5-27-1846 (6-4-1846) Ma
Rollins, George W. to Lindia Wilson 3-21-1873 (3-23-1873) L
Rollins, George to Mary Harris 3-9-1871 T
Rollins, James H. to Mary P. Humphrey 2-10-1869 Cr
Rollins, James to Elizabeth K. Blackmon 2-21-1855 (2-25-1855) Ma
Rollins, Jesse E. to S. J. Jones 9-6-1866 G
Rollins, Jimmie to Tennessee Sawyer 8-1-1870 Dy
Rollins, William H. to Manerva F. Harris 6-1-1867 (6-2-1867) T
Rolls, Edmond E. to Sarah Caplinger 12-29-1853 Be
Rolls, Thomas A. to Emiline Stogdale(Stockdale) 8-18-1860 Be
Romaine, Abraham C. to Araminta S. Davis 1-15-1862 (1-16-1862) Sh
Rombly, John M. to Keziah Allman 6-23-1839 Hn
Romer, John to Catharine Rausher 4-11-1857 (4-13-1857) Sh
Romine, G. A. to S. J. Denington 3-9-1874 O
Romine, Thomas to Ann Sneed 9-8-1843 (no return) F
Romly, Carroll to Louisa Parker 11-6-1848 Be
Romon, Jacob to Martha Fields 4-15-1869 (no return) Hy
Ronalds, John to Patsey Smith 3-17-1838 (3-20-1838) G
Rond, Lewis B. to Elizabeth Wilson 2-12-1846 Sh
Rone, G. W. to Sarah A. Anderson 10-22-1857 Sh
Rone, John T. to Jonnie L. Blackmon 1-3-1867 (1-6-1867) Ma
Rone, John to Jacky Whitehorn 3-24-1856 Cr
Roney, Benjamin to Malinda Box 5-24-1845 (6-1-1845) O
Roney, Jr., Benjamin to Rosannah Barker 1-20-1840 (1-23-1840) O
Roney, M. F. to M. J. Finley 12-31-1862 (1-1-1863) Cr
Roney, M. F. to Nelly Bernard 10-26-1872 (10-27-1872) Cr
Roney, M. W. to Elizabeth T. Swinney 7-18-1854 Cr
Roney, T. J. to Mary C. Pinon 12-20-1867 O
Rook, Amon Y. to Martha Kearley 1-15-1840 (1-22-1840) Hr
Rook, Barney to Mary E. Nell 11-5-1865 Mn
Rook, Benjamin to Polly Smith 12-16-1829 (12-17-1829) Hr
Rook, Benjamin to Sarah A. Jones 9-3-1866 (9-4-1866) F
Rook, Grove to Biddy Huddleston 7-26-1845 (7-29-1845) Hr
Rook, James Y. to Margaret Ramage 2-27-1828 Hr
Rook, John M. to Martha K. Cheairs 1-17-1859 (1-18-1859) F
Rook, John S. to Tennessee Watson 10-2-1861 Dy
Rook, William Y. to Elizabeth Eaver 12-23-1834 Hr
Rooker, Edward T. to Mary M. Adams 4-3-1858 (4-4-1858) Ma
Rooker, George W. to Ann Eliza Holt 9-15-1856 (9-17-1856) Ma
Rooker, William J. to Susan Jane Phillips 1-3-1860 (1-5-1860) Ma
Rooks, Alexander to Arabela Johnson 9-1-1863 We
Rooks, Bailey G. to Lucy May 9-24-1840 Ma
Rooks, C. A. to Idella Sawyer 2-17-1877 (2-18-1877) L
Rooks, Emry to Sarah E. Johnson 4-17-1867 G
Rooks, F. T. to A. A. Brown 1-10-1872 (1-11-1872) Dy
Rooks, Fullington to Martha Fearless 1-30-1847 Ma
Rooks, George W. to Maggie M. Weddle 7-19-1867 G
Rooks, James D. to Mary Elizah Estes 11-24-1870 Ma
Rooks, James K. to Elizabeth A. Boles 12-31-1868 G
Rooks, Joseph to Susan F. Hutcherson 5-16-1869 Hy
Rooks, William R. to Mary F. Maynard 9-19-1863 (9-20-1862?) Ma
Rooks, William R. to Mary J. Richardson 1-21-1853 (1-23-1853) G
Roose, Jack to Doragherty Hein 4-19-1858 (4-25-1859) Sh
Root, Charles to Martha Roberts 9-27-1831 Sh
Root, E. H. to Caroline Pool 12-25-1843 Sh
Rooter, Adam to Elizabeth Bunn 7-2-1854 Be
Roper, A. L. to A. L. Lawton 10-9-1870 G
Roper, Abner to C. C. Fletcher 12-8-1874 O
Roper, G. L. to M. A. Vaughter 5-18-1868 (5-19-1868) Cr
Roper, G. L. to Margaret A. Bowden 7-13-1848 Hn
Roper, Griffin L. to Mira E. Williams 7-11-1853 (8-7-1853) G
Roper, James to Ann M. West 5-25-1848 Hr
Roper, Jediah to E. J. Massey 7-17-1848 Cr
Roper, John S.(L?) to Sarah Mask 8-23-1838 Hr
Roper, John to Celly Edwards 4-6-1847 Cr
Roper, John to Sallie Staggs 10-10-1863 (11-3-1863) Dy
Roper, Joseph to Eliza Cox 12-30-1840 F
Roper, Joshua to Nancy Stigall 6-19-1844 (6-20-1844) F
Roper, Norwood to Leanna Longmyre 8-14-1868 (8-16-1868) Cr
Roper, Samuel H. to Jane Ervine 7-11-1857 O
Roper, T. R. to Nannie S. Zarecor 10-20-1869 G
Roper, Thomas G. to Elizabeth Pritchard 7-15-1868 (7-16-1868) Cr
Rorburg, Andrew to Louisa Miller 4-28-1859 Sh
Rorie, E. B. to M. J. Breedlove 5-11-1854 Hn
Rosamon, George M. to Mary L. Reddin 10-22-1866 (10-24-1866) Ma
Roscoe, William S. to William (Miss) Abington 10-19-1846 (10-21-1846) F
Rose, Alex P. to Mary D. Gloster 1-22-1867 (1-24-1867) F
Rose, Alexander to Catharine Hone 11-5-1861 (11-6-1861) Sh
Rose, Benjamin to Zilphia Coor? 7-20-1833 Hr
Rose, C. A. to Prudie Talley 11-19-1860 (11-20-1860) Sh

Rose, D. G. to M. E. McConnell 10-12-1861 (no return) Hn
Rose, Edmond to Eliza Jones 11-24-1866 T
Rose, Edward R. to Adaline Hall 12-1-1869 (no return) Hy
Rose, Erasmus T. to Maria L. Rose 3-27-1845 Hn
Rose, Erasmus to Mary Goforth 12-20-1853 (12-21-1853) T
Rose, George to Anny Newborn 2-11-1874 (no return) Hy
Rose, Henry M. to A. C. Aycock 7-15-1866 Hn
Rose, J. A. to Alice Correll 11-9-1881 (11-14-1881) L
Rose, J. E. to Emily J. Washum 9-1-1867 Hn
Rose, J. H. to Mary J. Sullivan 10-28-1869 (10-31-1869) F
Rose, J. W. to Sarah Rogers 12-17-1856 (12-18-1856) Hr
Rose, James A. to Eliza T. Crews 3-10-1852 (3-11-1852) Hr
Rose, James M. to Lucinda M. Taylor 8-1-1871 (8-2-1871) Ma
Rose, James to Elizabeth Maxwell 4-30-1832 (5-3-1832) Hr
Rose, James to Jamy Enoch 1-10-1870 (1-11-1870) Dy
Rose, James to Mary Fannin Newman 10-28-1856 (10-29-1856) T
Rose, James to Prudence Littrell? 9-27-1848 (9-28-1848) Hr
Rose, John P. to Mary Stout 8-12-1854 (8-13-1854) Hr
Rose, John P. to Ruth Smithson 5-2-1866 Hn
Rose, John Thomas to Susan E. Phillips 2-14-1854 T
Rose, John W. to Mary M. Walton 4-21-1858 T
Rose, John W. to Minah Hipkins 9-17-1853 Cr
Rose, John W. to Urilda C. Tally 4-25-1867 Hn
Rose, John to Jane Wat 4-18-1853 (4-21-1853) Sh
Rose, John to Louisa (Mrs.) Wolf 4-11-1860 (4-17-1860) Sh
Rose, John to Mary Smith 12-30-1851 (1-1-1852) Sh
Rose, John to Sarah Gardner 1-14-1856 (1-15-1856) L
Rose, John to Sarah Thompson 7-15-1835 (7-23-1835) Hr
Rose, Kinchen L. to Jinnette C. Cherry 10-20-1853 (10-27-1853) Hr
Rose, Kincheon L. to Susan Jane Covington 6-5-1841 (6-10-1841) Hr
Rose, Kindid C. to Aurena Adams 11-13-1843 Hn
Rose, N. Augustus to Maggie Manning 11-16-1863 Sh
Rose, Robert A. to Elizabeth Ford 7-19-1869 (7-20-1869) T
Rose, S. V. to Arrena Hudgens 9-21-1856 Hn
Rose, Sam? P. to Mildred L. Boyd 4-12-1871 T
Rose, Samuel J. to Dorothy Ann Jones 5-27-1847 (5-28-1847) T
Rose, Samuel J. to Prudence Jones 8-21-1839 Sh
Rose, Thomas K. to Margaret Hudgens 9-30-1858 Hn
Rose, Thomas to Emeline Z. Brown 9-8-1856 (9-11-1856) Hr
Rose, V. L. to Tabitha W. Walker 1-14-1852 Sh
Rose, W. H. to Martha E. Hardy 3-4-1861 (3-19-1861) Cr
Rose, W. H. to Mary Jane Carr 2-4-1835 Sh
Rose, W. J. to Elizabeth Coleman 2-28-1882 (3-1-1882) L
Rose, William J. to Isabella Brooks 12-16-1867 Ma
Rose, Wm. H. to Elizabeth Freeman 8-20-1860 (8-23-1860) Hr
Rose, Z. B. to Julie E. King 1-2-1867 (no return) Cr
Roseberry, James S. to Sarah F. Comer 3-5-1857 Hn
Rosebery, Thomas to Susan M. Gardner 4-14-1866 (4-15-1866) Cr
Rosebrough, Samuel to Agnes Moncrief 1-13-1855 (1-14-1855) Sh
Roseman, George M. to Frances A. Smith 1-30-1860 (no return) Hy
Rosensteel, August to Schanett Hirsch 1-3-1867 Hy
Rosenthal, Frederick to Louisa Shidecker 1-16-1863 Sh
Rosingbun, Wm. R. to Albina Rutherford 10-21-1847 Cr
Ross(Rass-Russ), Enoch to Prudence Foster 1-14-1829 Hr
Ross, A. to A. J. O'Banion 8-4-1857 Sh
Ross, Abner to Fanny Lewis 4-28-1875 Hy
Ross, Albert to Marion Springfield 10-31-1877 Hy
Ross, Albert to Mary D. Bratton 1-15-1853 (1-18-1853) G
Ross, Albert to Polly Williams 11-4-1869 (no return) F B
Ross, Alexander to Elizabeth Colbert 1-3-1826 (1-5-1826) Hr
Ross, Alexander to Mary Bumpass 2-3-1870 Dy
Ross, Alexander to Mary W. Stone 1-16-1849 (1-18-1849) G
Ross, Alfred to Margarett Ann Bratton 10-31-1849 (11-1-1849) G
Ross, Andrew J. to Leer Smith 9-14-1837 (9-21-1837) G
Ross, Andrew to Nancy Cody 6-6-1826 (6-7-1826) Hr
Ross, Anthony to M. A. Miller 12-29-1869 (12-30-1869) T
Ross, Caleb to Harriet Robertson 3-3-1862 (3-4-1862) Dy
Ross, Caleb to Louisa Olive 9-12-1839 Hn
Ross, Charles H. to Celestia A. Henings 2-28-1853 G
Ross, Charles H. to Patience White 8-11-1839 G
Ross, Charles M. to Ellen E. Cobb 6-10-1863 Cr
Ross, Charles M. to Ellen E. Cobb 6-10-1863 (6-14-1863) Cr
Ross, Charles M. to Ellen E. Cobb 6-10-1863 (no return) Cr
Ross, Chas. M. to Lucy A. Harder 4-22-1871 (4-27-1871) Cr
Ross, Daniel A. to Elizabeth A. Wilkes 10-14-1860 (10-15-1860) Hr
Ross, Davy to Lou Taylor 12-23-1867 (12-27-1867) F B
Ross, E. C. to Martha A. M. Barker 10-12-1849 Be
Ross, E. P. to Milly J. Hopkins 8-18-1867 Hn
Ross, F. C. to Elizabeth E. Stoker 1-21-1858 We
Ross, F. M. to Harriet Overton 2-24-1862 F
Ross, Francis M. to Sarah Ann Eliza Gaddy 9-23-1851 Sh
Ross, Franklin to Elizabeth Chilcutt 3-1-1855 Hn
Ross, George to Celia Chilcutt 3-4-1858 Hn
Ross, George to Emaline Hall 2-24-1866 T
Ross, Henry to Fannie Williams 5-8-1869 (no return) F B
Ross, Highim to Sarah L. Groran 1-7-1855 Cr
Ross, Hiram W. to Nancy Burns 7-7-1828 Hr

Ross, J. Coleman to Fannie (Mrs.) Adams 1-24-1867 (1-27-1867) Ma
Ross, J. R. to Margarett McIntosh 1-2-1870 G
Ross, J. R. to Nancy E. Tucker 1-24-1856 Hn
Ross, Jackson to Fereby H. Oakly 3-5-1840 Hr
Ross, Jacob to Mariah Johnston 6-19-1825 (7-19-1825) Hr
Ross, Jacob to Martha Harris 5-13-1863 (5-16-1863) Cr
Ross, James F. to Sarah George 4-27-1841 Hr
Ross, James M. to Mary Ann Brown 9-8-1831 O
Ross, Jarratt to Eliza R. Tanner 12-13-1866 O
Ross, Jesse to S. A. L. Harwell 11-8-1865 Mn
Ross, John A. to Ferribee(Fenibee) G. Bond 11-3-1851 (11-13-1851) Sh
Ross, John A. to Nancy Wilson 2-3-1843 (2-4-1843) Hr
Ross, John J. to Ann E. Westbrook 7-3-1838 O
Ross, John M. to Rebecca E. Young 1-30-1863 Mn
Ross, John W. to Louisa E. Cross 10-8-1859 (10-12-1859) Hr
Ross, John Wm. to Melissa C. Odle 10-30-1875 (10-31-1875) Dy
Ross, John to Susan Carothers 8-8-1870 T
Ross, Joseph A. to Nancy Buchanan 3-5-1848 Be
Ross, Joseph W. to M. A. McMahon 1-5-1863 (no return) Hy
Ross, L. C. to Araminta Council 12-3-1847 Hn
Ross, LeGrand to Mollie Warren 12-18-1866 (12-19-1866) F B
Ross, Levin E. to Percilla Hail 12-29-1846 Sh
Ross, M. C. to P. A. Sulivan 9-22-1863 (11-16-1863) Dy
Ross, Melvin to Rebecca Smith 8-23-1834 (8-25-1834) G
Ross, Nathan to Ann Eliza Jones 6-10-1833 Sh
Ross, Peter B. to Rozana Overton 12-19-1849 (12-20-1849) F
Ross, Reuben to Manervia A. Vincent 11-7-1860 We
Ross, Robert to Catharine Jones 11-20-1872 Hy
Ross, Ruben M. to Mary E. Eskridge 12-15-1855 We
Ross, Ruben W. to Miram C. Wilt 11-8-1857 We
Ross, Saml. to Sally Harris 1-24-1841 Cr
Ross, Samuel H. to Sarah Ann Bond 4-14-1839 Sh
Ross, Samuel to P. A. Ross 8-13-1861 We
Ross, Stephen D. to Sarah W. Jones 2-16-1838 (2-23-1838) Ma
Ross, Thomas J. to Sarah Ann Frances Mickelberry 3-28-1844 Sh
Ross, Thomas J. to Theodocia E. Farington 5-13-1858 T
Ross, Thomas L. to Martha Wilson 2-1-1849 (2-4-1849) Hr
Ross, Thomas to Ophelia Lofton 1-3-1871 (1-15-1871) F B
Ross, Thos. to Rachael Smith 9-12-1835 (9-20-1835) G
Ross, W. C. to Martha Pruden 11-4-1864 (11-6-1864) Sh
Ross, W. F. to Willie Ann Parker 1-21-1861 (1-23-1861) Hr
Ross, W. J. to Susie Crook 9-29-1884 (10-5-1884) L
Ross, W. P. to Elizabeth J. Ford 7-4-1852 We
Ross, Warren to G. A. Mallery 11-13-1855 (no return) Hn
Ross, Wesley V.? to Nancy Walker 9-16-1838 Hr
Ross, William A. to Clarrissa E. Price 7-19-1848 (7-23-1848) G
Ross, William A. to Mary J. Bratton 9-21-1844 (9-25-1844) G
Ross, William C. to Orfrey M. Palmer 12-8-1860 (12-9-1860) Cr
Ross, William H. to Emily Terrell 12-28-1849 Hn
Ross, Wm. A. to Frances Blake 8-13-1855 Cr
Ross, Wm. B. to Catharine Elizabeth Topp 5-25-1861 Sh
Ross, Wm. B. to Mary Ann Gee 12-27-1847 Cr
Ross, Wm. B. to Susan Glisson 1-21-1848 Hr
Ross, Wm. R. to Mary A. W. Bowers 12-28-1843 We
Ross, Wm. to Sarah Short 4-11-1867 Hy
Ross?, James M. to Elizabeth Cooper 9-29-1845 Be
Rossen, Asa to Tennessee (Mrs.) Manasses 11-19-1862 Sh
Rossen, William to Elizabeth Jacob 12-22-1824 Hr
Rosser, Henry to Rebecca C. Williamson 8-15-1870 Ma
Rosser, William to Melvina Hunt 5-29-1833 Hr
Rosser, William to Tempence A. Anderson 9-7-1854 Ma
Rosser, Wm. H. to Jane Parker 8-27-1841 Hr
Rossom, W. C. to Latitia Riggs 10-17-1861 (10-11?-1861) Cr
Rosson, Abner to Lucretia Holbut? 8-26-1836 (8-25?-1836) Hr
Rosson, D. W. to Sarah A. Graves 3-14-1853 (3-16-1853) Hr
Rosson, J. H. to Elizabeth Smith 5-1-1860 Sh
Rosson, James to Deborah Crocker 1-23-1841 (1-26-1841) Hr
Rosson, John to Delina Taylor 12-7-1853 (12-8-1853) Hr
Rosson, John to Harrett Ware 10-31-1871 O
Rosson, Joseph L. to Mary Atkins 6-9-1858 (6-29-1858) Hr
Rosson, Joseph L. to Ruth Ray 2-24-1851 Hr
Rosson, John to Mary J. Bedtick 3-1-1865 G
Rosson, S. E. to Mary Whitfield 9-22-1837 Hr
Rosson, William to Polly Jobe 4-19-1826 Hr
Roswell(Boswell?), William to Malinda Step 11-1-1852 Be
Roten, Alfred to Nancy J. Smith 5-18-1861 Mn
Rothschild, M. to Mary Levi 3-26-1873 Hy
Rou__?, Benjamin C. to Nancy Burton 12-7-1843 Hn
Roulhac, Francis L. to Lucinda H. Person 4-10-1844 Sh
Roulhac, J. P. G. to Lucy E. Hawkins 12-6-1851 (12-7-1851) Sh
Roundtree, John to Franky Pitts 7-13-1872 (7-14-1872) L
Roundtree, William to Elizabeth N. Jones 12-23-1846 (12-30-1846) L
Rounthall (Ruthall), Frederick to _____ 1-17-1863 (1-18-1863) Sh
Rountree, Henry C. to Bettie Keller 1-19-1867 L B
Rountree, William T. to Rebecca Jones 7-1-1852 L
Rountree, Woodson to Rosannah L. Baird 6-18-1838 G
Rourk, Henry N. to Elizabeth Brandon 11-15-1854 Cr

Rousch, John A. to Mary Musso 1-19-1864 Sh
Rouse, Daniel to Catherine Horn 9-10-1865 Mn
Rousenbun, Alex to H. M. Scarbrough 2-5-1845 Cr
Rously, G. W. to Laura A. Ray 10-30-1875 Hy
Routly, Matthew to Amanda Stevens 12-1-1866 Dy
Routon, A. F. to Elizabeth Williams 7-11-1847 Be
Routon, John H. to Martha Wimbush 2-19-1855 Hn
Routon, John to Margaret Corum 1-17-1859 (1-19-1859) O
Routon, Philip to Sarah A. Wimbush 7-22-1858 Hn
Routon, Stephen P. to Mary C. Haymes 6-1-1858 Hn
Row, Henry to M. Pool 4-16-1868 (no return) F B
Row, Washington L. to Mary C. Stone 12-7-1842 (12-20?-1842) F
Rowark, A. W. to Margaret Tosh 2-9-1859 Cr
Rowark, W. H. to Rosaline Rudder 12-4-1867 Dy
Rowe, Allen H. to Sarah A. Vanosten Stone 12-3-1860 (12-5-1860) Sh
Rowe, E. G. to Alice B. Wood 3-29-1869 (3-30-1869) Cr
Rowe, Elisha to Narcissa Rodgers 12-22-1840 Cr
Rowe, J. D. to Olivia A. Taylor 4-9-1864 (no return) Hn
Rowe, J. W. to S. F. Butler 8-10-1872 (8-12-1872) Cr
Rowe, James C. to Ella J. Bray 10-4-1858 Hn
Rowe, John M. to Josephine J. Jordan 10-1-1868 Cr
Rowe, John W. to Elizabeth A. Martin 8-16-1855 Cr
Rowe, Thomas A. to Nancy E. Young 2-23-1853 Hn
Rowe, William M. to Nancy E. Rowe 11-28-1861 Hn
Rowe, Wm. to Mary Ann Banks 4-25-1843 Be
Rowell, R. to C. C. Neely 3-11-1857 (3-12-1857) Sh
Rowland, Alsey to Mary E. Ryan 10-19-1858 (no return) Hn
Rowland, Alvin to D. Vincent 10-12-1846 (no return) Cr
Rowland, Eben to Eliza A. Park 3-13-1866 Cr
Rowland, Ebin to Lids M. Milton 8-6-1843 Cr
Rowland, Elmer to Elizabeth Allen 1-10-1839 Cr
Rowland, G. M. to L. N. Bettis 10-9-1865 (10-10-1865) Dy
Rowland, H. P. to M. E. Chambers 7-7-1873 (7-4?-1873) L
Rowland, Isaac to Martha E. Roberts 11-17-1847 Cr
Rowland, J. T. to J. A. Bynum 4-7-1876 (3-11-1877) O
Rowland, James D. to Martha E. Gordon 1-20-1855 Cr
Rowland, John M. to Nancy A. Moore 4-25-1861 Cr
Rowland, John to Mary E. Dickerson 8-22-1850 T
Rowland, Moses to Adaline Massey 1-23-1869 (1-27-1869) Cr
Rowland, Pinkney B. to Martha E. Bailess 11-25-1865 (11-26-1865) G
Rowland, Robt. N. to Elizabeth F. McMackins 11-25-1872 (11-26-1872) Cr
Rowland, Sam to Della Cumpton 7-29-1868 (7-30-1868) Cr
Rowland, Sherrill to Margaret McMillan 12-10-1846 Cr
Rowland, T. B. to Nancy Rowland 1-24-1867 Cr
Rowland, Thomas to Mary R. Killough 6-6-1859 Cr
Rowland, Thos. L. to Anna Butler 9-18-1872 Cr
Rowland, William to Elizabeth Barnhart 12-17-1840 Cr
Rowlett, A. to Francis Guthery 10-15-1859 (no return) We
Rowlett, D. S. to Margaret Ann Eaves 6-19-1852 Hn
Rowlett, Geo. W. to Cornelia H. Coulter 3-21-1861 (3-22-1861) Sh
Rowlett, George W. to M. Powers 10-10-1852 Hn
Rowlett, J. D. to S. M. Rateree 1-14-1866 Hn
Rowlett, Jerry to Manerva Warren 5-29-1875 O
Rowlett, John R. to Eliza Garland 11-11-1841 Ma
Rowlett, John T. to Nannie M. Rust 7-31-1870 G
Rowlett, P. W. to Nancy Tompkins 1-5-1844 Sh
Rowlett, Sanford M. to Narcissa Justice 9-19-1838 (no return) Hn
Rowlett, Wm. to Jane Murphy 6-28-1848 Sh
Rowlette, William to Harriett R. Roberts 6-5-1847 Sh
Rowlin, Howard to Elvira King 7-28-1839 Cr
Rowlin, Wesley to Ann Sullivan 1-23-1840 Cr
Rowlin, William P. to Tabitha C. Baker 9-22-1849 (no return) Hn
Rowlin, Williamson to Sarah Phillys 1-23-1840 Cr
Rown, Isaac to Tempy Robins 6-5-1845 Be
Rowsey, Houston to Susan Roberson 12-4-1884 L
Rowsey, John W. to Catherine E. Fry 11-12-1861 (11-14-1861) Ma
Rowsey, W. H. to Eliana M. Sharpe 1-23-1851 Hr
Rowten, William to Arrotta Cooper 8-8-1867 Hr
Roy (Leeroy), William A. to Frances Jane Mustin 12-30-1856 (1-1-1857) Sh
Roy, John B. to Nannie J. Fletcher 5-14-1872 (5-15-1872) O
Roy, S. M. to Ellen Pipkins 12-13-1876 L
Roy, Samuel M. to Amanda Cobb 1-14-1868 L
Royal, Henry to Ann Mathis 1-13-1870 G B
Royal, William C. to Elizabeth D. Butler 8-26-1866 (8-27-1866) Cr
Royall, J. P. to Sallie Appleberry 9-27-1869 (9-30-1869) F
Royall?, E. N. to F. C. Ozier 8-15-1861 Cr
Roycroft, A. J. to Margaret Reed 9-21-1841 G
Roycroft, Calvin C. to Nancy E. Taylor 11-30-1846 (12-2-1846) F
Royer, Daniel to Polly Cockeburn 8-7-1825 Sh
Royister, John to Mary A. Brundridge 6-4-1860 We
Royster, D. R. to Evilina Joyner 11-15-1858 (11-16-1858) Sh
Royster, Fedo to Matilda Lea 2-12-1876 Hy
Royster, W. H. to M. W. E. Oneal 7-27-1869 (no return) Dy
Royston, Frank W. to Helen M. Lake 5-23-1849 Hn
Rozell, B. L. to Lizzie C. Lyon 2-26-1855 (2-27-1855) Ma
Rozelle, C. W. to Susan A. Humphrey 10-7-1840 Sh
Rubotton, J. W. to Virginia C. Smotherson? 8-25-1854 (no return) F

Ruby, J. G. to Elizabeth Hurley 12-16-1845 F
Rucise?, G. W. to R. C. Raney 2-8-1854 Cr
Rucker, Alfred C. to Mary N. Philips 11-4-1854 (11-8-1854) T
Rucker, Ambrose to Adeline Austin 1-31-1872 Hy
Rucker, Bob to Athy Redeck 9-11-1868 Hy
Rucker, C. M. to L. A. Burks 12-21-1881 (1-5-1882) L
Rucker, Cale to Denkey Soward 1-15-1885 L
Rucker, Gus to Sarah McLemore 8-9-1877 Hy
Rucker, Harry to Ella Halliburton 3-30-1878 (3-31-1878) L
Rucker, Hut to Lucy Fisher 1-21-1882 L B
Rucker, James M. to Elizabeth Bessent 7-19-1869 (7-21-1869) Dy
Rucker, James to Mary Trulove 12-23-1873 Hy
Rucker, John to Martha E. Sumerow 3-16-1857 (no return) L
Rucker, Linsey P. to Mary W. Tarver 11-15-1836 Hr
Rucker, Neil B. to A. F. McDearmon 3-13-1873 Dy
Rucker, Peter to Fannie Smith 12-10-1873 (12-14-1873) L B
Rucker, Peter to Georgiana Wortham 1-20-1879 (1-29-1879) L B
Rucker, Samuel W. to Edy Airy 4-12-1843 Hn
Rucker, W. J. K. to Elizabeth J. Chapman 11-23-1841 Hr
Rucks, Arthur to Mary M. Yerger 10-27-1851 (10-28-1851) Sh
Rudd, G. D. to Roberta Rice 12-6-1880 (12-7-1880) L
Rudd, Jack to Lue Whitelaw 3-8-1873 Hy
Rudd, James to Bettie Reece 2-26-1873 (2-27-1873) T
Rudd, Jerry to Agnes Bullock 6-19-1878 Hy
Ruddell (Buddell?), Salathial to Lucy J. Beck 9-25-1855 (9-26-1855) Sh
Ruddle, Cornelius to Sarah Emeline Graves 7-23-1849 (7-12?-1849) Ma
Ruddle, Robert K. to Dohorty J. Hankly 1-23-1849 (1-29-1849) Hr
Rude, Isaac J. to Isabellar Alexander 6-15-1854 G
Rudin, Edward to Emma Strassler 1-15-1861 Sh
Rudisill, Jonas C. to Chloe Ann Edwards 11-21-1838 Sh
Rudisill, Jonas C. to Mary Webster 10-17-1844 Sh
Rudisill, Joseph to Mary C. D. Champion 12-6-1832 Hr
Rudisill, Z. A. to Margaret Waldran 8-10-1840 Sh
Rudolph, J. E. to Malinda E. Sockette 8-13-1856 Hn
Rudolph, J. E. to Malinda E. Stockette 8-13-1856 Hn
Rudolph, James H. to M. J. Whitworth 3-30-1846 Hn
Rudy (Rodry?), Charles H. to Josephine Levi 12-24-1860 Sh
Rue, James to Mary Lovell 5-1-1855 (5-3-1855) Sh
Ruff, Bennet M. to Sarah A. Jackson 2-22-1853 (2-23-1853) Sh
Ruff, Charley to Lutitia Wynne 10-13-1866 (no return) Dy
Ruff, Charley to Penny Ledsinger 12-19-1867 Dy
Ruff, Haywood to Lizzie Fizer 1-4-1877 (1-5-1877) Dy
Ruff, Haywood to Lou Moore 9-9-1880 (no return) Dy
Ruff, James E. to Rebecca M. Hale 10-26-1847 (10-28-1847) Ma
Ruff, James G. to Catharine Lashlee 1-23-1846 Be
Ruff, John L. to Elizabeth J. Freeman 5-16-1843 Cr
Ruff, John to Martha A. Eason 8-3-1853 Cr
Ruff, R. R. to L. M. H. Eason 5-16-1851 Cr
Ruff, S. D. to Isabella Lashlee 4-12-1845 Be
Ruff, William H. to W. F. Eason 11-24-1851 Cr
Ruffian, Douglass to Lucinda Rucker 3-1-1883 L
Ruffin, Cook to Patsy Coleman 1-28-1872 Hy
Ruffin, Edmond to Sarah Chipman 12-2-1878 L B
Ruffin, James D. to Basina Ruffin 7-8-1834 (7-17-1834) Hr
Ruffin, John B. to Mary T. Anderson 3-12-1856 (3-13-1856) Ma
Ruffin, John M. to Mary B. Coleman 9-27-1846 Sh
Ruffin, John to Ada Glass 11-24-1880 L B
Ruffin, Joseph to Catherine Leggitt 12-19-1849 Sh
Ruffin, Robert J. to Melissa A. Williamson 4-24-1856 Ma
Ruffin, T. L. to Wadie A. Meacham 9-3-1885 (9-5-1885) L
Ruffin, Thomas to Jane Blanton 12-18-1854 (12-20-1854) O
Ruffin, Thos. D. to Parlee Byrn 6-27-1861 (6-30-1861) L
Ruffin, W. Brooks to Harriet Jones 3-9?-1833 Hr
Ruleman, W. J. to A. M. Sanderson 9-8-1863 Sh
Ruliford, Joe to Alice Lovelace 12-31-1881 (1-1-1882) L B
Rulkley (Bulkley?), Henry D. to Caro A. Byler 12-15-1853 Sh
Rumbly, Thomas J. to Mary Jane Radford 11-5-1857 Be
Rumbough, Geo. P. C. to Anna F. Trezevant 5-17-1859 (5-18-1859) Sh
Rumley, Allen to Z. A. Rome 1-8-1852 Cr
Rumley, Enoch to Ann W. Reed 8-18-1850 Cr
Rumley, Hiram to Elizabeth Kemp 3-3-1841 Cr
Rumley, John R. to Celia Ann E. Kendall 1-18-1866 Hn
Rumley, Joseph to Sarah Darnell 12-8-1841 Cr
Rumley, Thomas to Elizabeth ____ 2-7-1852 Cr
Rumley, Willis to Caroline Dwiggins 8-29-1854 Cr
Rummage, Geo. to Mary B. Webb 2-5-1853 Hr
Rummage, Joseph to Peggy Weaver 12-29-1825 Hr
Rummage, William to Leatha Rochell 4-13-1846 Cr
Rummen, Chesley to Lusetta Chamness 10-12-1862 Mn
Rumnell, Samuel to Margaret R. Medanis 8-19-1829 Ma
Rumsey, John to Fannie McFerrin 9-11-1878 Hy
Runaldo, William S. to Rachel Frazer 12-23-1831 (12-29-1831) G
Runalds, John R. to Selina A. Hague 2-6-1847 G
Runalds, William to Kissiah Smith 4-21-1847 (4-22-1847) G
Runkle, Samuel to Hezebeth (Hipzebeth) Blake 7-26-1831 Sh
Runnals, Martin to Mary Harvy 4-9-1870 F
Runnell, Jas. M. to Elizabeth Vaughan 8-16-1848 Sh

Runnells, Josiah to Susan Ann Thetford 6-16-1867 G
Runnels, Granville to Adelia Montgomery 4-29-1871 (5-2-1871) T
Runnels, Martin to Mary Reily 3-20-1859 Sh
Runnels, Robt. to Sarah E. McGraw 6-6-1865 G
Runnels, Sanford to Tallie Gavage? 1-22-1876 Hy
Runnels, Wm. to Eliza Dogget 5-5-1869 (5-9-1869) T
Runolds, James to Nancy Jenkins 11-2-1837 (12-7-1837) G
Runolds, Thomas to Matilda Conwell 2-24-1827 G
Runstetter, Andrew to Lizzie Smith 4-9-1860 Sh
Ruschaupt, Wm. to Dorothea Mendermann 4-21-1862 Sh
Ruse, Baher to Jane Beavers 5-23-1864 (5-27-1864) Cr
Rush, Charles S. to Elizabeth Ann Walker 3-12-1844 Sh
Rush, J. R. to E. R. West 12-22-1880 L
Rush, J. T. to S. A. Hipp 11-13-1884 (11-23-1884) L
Rush, Robert to Ann Russom 12-13-1865 Mn
Rush, Virgil E. to M. A. Reeves 10-1-1879 L
Rush, William L. to Mary E. McGaughey 10-3-1866 L
Rush, William W. to Ellen Vanbiber 12-25-1857 (12-27-1857) L
Rush, William to Margaret E. Nailor 12-2-1850 (12-12-1850) Hr
Rush, Wm. H. to Sarah A. Kershaw 6-14-1871 (6-15-1871) Ma
Rushen, Geo. W. to Mary S. Roach 8-12-1840 Cr
Rushing, Abel to Tabitha C. Presson 4-3-1850 Be
Rushing, Alfred to Rebecca S. Perkins 3-19-1851 Be
Rushing, Calvin to Mary Ann Rushing 11-15-1847 Be
Rushing, Calvin to Nancy B. Warren 3-8-1852 (no return) Hn
Rushing, David L. to Sarah A. Moore 10-17-1850 Be
Rushing, Davis C. to Mahaly Bennett 5-27-1846 Be
Rushing, F. M. to Nancy McGill 3-13-1844 Be
Rushing, Geo. W. to Martha B. Madden 2-1-1853 Be
Rushing, Geo. W. to Mary Spires 11-19-1846 Be
Rushing, George to Sarah F. Morriss 12-27-1862 Be
Rushing, James to Martha Cross 9-16-1849 Be
Rushing, Joel to Lucyan Stafford 2-19-1846 Be
Rushing, Joel to Margaret A. S. (Mrs.) Vick 2-2-1858 (2-3-1858) Ma
Rushing, John M. to Nancy E. Diggs 3-28-1861 Hn
Rushing, John W. to Tennessee Pate 9-25-1865 (9-28-1865) Cr
Rushing, John to Mary Bohannan 11-3-1854 G
Rushing, Levin to M. M. Presson 7-2-1845 Be
Rushing, Lumbus to Susan Isabella McCullough 4-5-1856 (no return) Hn
Rushing, Noah to Margaret F. Danly 7-16-1865 Hn
Rushing, Noah to Sarah A. Young 2-27-1853 Hn
Rushing, Philip to Rachel Pace 1-12-1846 Be
Rushing, R. B. to Elizabeth Warrick 3-31-1848 Be
Rushing, Robert to Elizabeth J. Hicks 2-28-1861 Be
Rushing, Robert to Sarah Ann Walters 10-17-1839 Hn
Rushing, S. T. to S. E. Garrett 2-20-1868 Hy
Rushing, Simeon B. to Callie A. Sykes 12-28-1870 (12-29-1870) Ma
Rushing, Stanly to Elizabeth McCallister 1-9-1847 Ma
Rushing, Stephen A. to Salina Jane Cook 2-18-1867 Be
Rushing, W. C. to Sophiah Rushing 1-19-1853 Be
Rusk, W. H. F. to Mary A. Hollin 10-17-1850 We
Ruskin, Steward to Amanda Friz? 1-25-1873 (1-27-1873) L B
Russel, George to Susan Smith 8-20-1869 (8-22-1869) F B
Russel, Henry to Matilda Norvell 1-7-1870 (1-8-1870) Cr
Russel, James to Sarah Busey 1-6-1872 (no return) Cr
Russel, Jno. K. to Eva L. Douglas 5-19-1869 T
Russel, W. N. to Adeline Dunn 10-24-1864 Sh
Russell(Russell), Stephen H. to Hannah Adeline Reed 9-8-1827 Hr
Russell, A. L. to Lucy C. Fields 10-5-1861 O
Russell, Alex R. to Cairo Lankford 1-4-1859 (1-6-1859) L
Russell, Alexander to Caroline Patterson 7-6-1865 Mn
Russell, Andrew C. to Catharine E. Pickett 3-16-1853 Sh
Russell, Austin to D. A. Manley 2-22-1844 Hn
Russell, Berry A. to Margret A. E. Christopher 2-18-1869 Be
Russell, C. B. to Mary F. Gattis 11-8-1859 (11-9-1859) Ma
Russell, Christinberry to Jane Macon 11-14-1849 Ma
Russell, Cornelius to Lou Crawford 8-8-1868 (no return) F B
Russell, D. L. to Eliza A. Weaks 4-14-1842 Hn
Russell, Daniel to Katie G. Pope 2-16-1876 Hy
Russell, David C. to Sarah Jones 12-4-1852 (no return) F
Russell, David H. to Saphronia C. Blake 1-?-1866 (1-11-1866) Cr
Russell, Elijah B. to Mary M. Barron 2-26-1852 G
Russell, Elisha to Jane C. F. Mason 1-9-1842 Cr
Russell, Elisha to Matilda J. Parker 7-14-1853 Cr
Russell, F. B. to Mary E. McCarmick 2-20-1868 Hy
Russell, F. to Harriet Lewis 12-19-1872 O
Russell, G. G. to Maggie Short 9-29-1860 (9-30-1860) Sh
Russell, G. L. to M. E. Altum 6-29-1865 Hn
Russell, G. S. to Mary E. Cossett 12-3-1856 Hn
Russell, George to Fanny Johnson 3-6-1873 Hy
Russell, George to Susannah Cook 7-11-1830 Ma
Russell, H. F. to Mollie J. Duckworth 10-13-1870 Hy
Russell, H. to Tempie Harris 4-25-1870 Hy
Russell, Henry to Elizabeth Smiley? 1-8-1857 Hn
Russell, I. W. to Francis C. Callis __-7-1865 (9-7-1865) O
Russell, Isaac P. to Elizabeth Alsup 8-22-1828 (9-24-1828) Hr
Russell, Isaac to Mary Owens 3-16-1875 L

Russell, J. A. to Permelia C. Nevills 8-27-1869 (8-29-1869) Cr
Russell, J. H. to Sarah Curd 10-30-1865 Hn
Russell, Jacob L. to Jane L. (Mrs.) Cook 12-26-1864 Sh
Russell, James H. to Sarah Hall 12-10-1840 Cr
Russell, James L. to Elizabeth Mullins 8-10-1829 (8-11-1829) Hr
Russell, James T. to Nancy A. Arnett 1-27-1861 Hn
Russell, James to Charity Black 3-21-1853 (3-22-1853) O
Russell, Jas. M. to Mary J. Jones 9-1-1876 O
Russell, John (Joseph?) to Lucinda McFadden 6-11-1867 G B
Russell, John A. to Martha E. Dickerson 6-18-1863 G
Russell, John C. to Amanda Sauls 1-13-1857 (1-14-1857) Hr
Russell, John H. to Ruth Casey 1-7-1829 (1-9-1829) Hr
Russell, John S. to Mariah Flowers 8-4-1846 (8-6-1846) Ma
Russell, John to Fanny Barton 6-17-1852 Sh
Russell, John to Hester Ann Mitts 7-16-1831 (7-17-1831) G
Russell, John to Mary Stackhouse 1-20-1843 Sh
Russell, John to Purlie F. Reaves 1-19-1871 Hy
Russell, John to Sarah Petty 9-12-1843 Be
Russell, John to Veria Markham 4-21-1866 Hn
Russell, Jonathan J. to Mary Wauller? 8-23-1853 Cr
Russell, Josiah to Nancy G. Ward 2-8-1845 We
Russell, Kirksey W. to Emaline E. Chapell 8-27-1839 Cr
Russell, L. M. to Lue E. Rhodes 1-2-1866 Hy
Russell, Lewis to Esther Doherty 6-1-1870 (6-5-1870) Cr
Russell, Martin to Adaline Davis 12-5-1843 O
Russell, Newton to Sarah Flagg 1-22-1876 Hy
Russell, Pink to Press Manerd 3-27-1872 Hy
Russell, R. P. to S. M. Bullock 1-31-1866 (no return) F
Russell, Robt. J. to Sarah J. Brown 8-24-1857 Hr
Russell, S. H. to M. A. Williams 9-24-1863 Mn
Russell, Saml. F. to Matilda Needham 6-18-1865 G
Russell, Sidney C. to Julia E. Patterson 12-16-1867 F
Russell, Stephen H. to Dolla Ann Dunigan 10-11-1859 (10-12-1859) G
Russell, T. H. to Emeline Webster 8-1-1836 (8-23-1836) Hr
Russell, T. P. C. to Mary Vance 7-27-1837 O
Russell, Thomas W. to Cassandra E. Lovelace 5-24-1870 (no return) L
Russell, Thomas to Nannie Aldridge 1-15-1856 Cr
Russell, Thos. to Ellen Arrington 6-8-1863 (6-11-1863) Cr
Russell, W. B. to Ellen F. Schooley 3-4-1869 (3-7-1869) T
Russell, W. J. to Margarett Dunagan 10-30-1870 G
Russell, Wilbourn to Margaret A. Russell 12-24-1846 Cr
Russell, Wiley P. to C. A. Barron 10-22-1856 G
Russell, William B. to Nancy Durham 9-22-1840 (9-24-1840) F
Russell, William H. to Sarah A. Moorefield 7-15-1852 Hn
Russell, William to Julia Ann Williams 2-17-1870 G
Russell, William to Sophia S. Sanders 2-17-1855 (2-20-1855) O
Russell, Wm. H. to Susan C. Gair 2-24-1858 (3-2-1858) Sh
Russell, Wm. to Nancy Cox 11-29-1857 Cr
Russell, jr., Jesse to Sarah E. Teague 4-22-1868 Ma
Russell?, George to Ann Fleming 12-21-1869 Hy
Russom, Henry C. to Sarah J. Byrn 9-12-1866 L
Russom, J. M. to Eliza A. Moore 12-25-1862 Mn
Russom, Jefferson to Louisa Wilson 2-12-1863 Mn
Rust, A. H. to Sarah J. Roe 9-11-1855 (9-12-1855) G
Rust, C. T. to Martha J. Ellinor 8-1-1867 (8-2-1867) Cr
Rust, Daniel to Sarah Haslip 1-21-1841 Ma
Rust, G. M. to C. J. Brigance 2-4-1858 We
Rust, George M. to Lucretia F. Mathis 1-9-1867 G
Rust, J. E. to M. E. Bethell 10-1-1867 O
Rust, J. G. to M. J. Elliner 7-27-1863 (7-27-1866?) Cr
Rust, J. R. to Mary A. Taylor 2-24-1856 Cr
Rust, J. T. to Arminta Parish 9-10-1870 (9-11-1870) Cr
Rust, James N. to Lucy A. Pemberton 9-29-1853 G
Rust, James N. to Mary J. Walker 9-5-1860 G
Rust, Jermiah T. to Mary E. Price 12-22-1859 We
Rust, John R. to Bettie (Mrs.) Giles 10-12-1867 (10-13-1867) Cr
Rust, John W. to Amanda E. Senter 3-29-1863 G
Rust, John Y. to Lucy G. Smith 2-25-1846 Cr
Rust, John Y. to M. J. Ellmor 2-27-1862 (no return) Cr
Rust, L. D. to Eliza McAuly 10-7-1850 G
Rust, L. W. to Elizabeth Evans 1-9-1856 We
Rust, Lemuel W. to Lorenia Shute 3-20-1830 Ma
Rust, O. R. to Adaline Williams 3-6-1844 Cr
Rust, Saml. W. to Marget Smort 6-16-1842 Cr
Rust, Samuel P. to Ellenor Bledsoe 11-10-1829 (11-12-1829) G
Rust, Samuel S. to Patsey Hurley 12-22-1825 (12-25-1825) G
Rust, W. R. to Elizabeth Harold 5-21-1854 We
Rust, William H. to Martha Jane Senter 9-6-1849 G
Rust, William L. to Mary E. Churchwell 12-16-1871 (no return) Cr
Rust, William V. to Malissa A. Brigance 11-25-1860 We
Rust, Wm. Benj. to Gertrude McCauley 6-29-1863 (6-30-1863) Sh
Rust, Wm. R. to Elizabeth Harrold 5-20-1854 (no return) We
Ruth, E. L. to Ella Lee Turner 11-12-1879 L
Ruth, J. V. to Nancy Ellis 6-5-1880 (6-6-1880) L
Ruth, James V. to Rebecca Ballard 6-19-1843 F
Rutherford, B. B. to Sophronia A. Reaves 9-3-1861 Hr
Rutherford, Charles to Millie Williams 11-13-1873 T

Rutherford, Dock to Martha Ware 12-18-1867 Hy
Rutherford, Ed to Alice Haynes 12-1-1871 Hy
Rutherford, Essex to Manervia Varner 1-24-1878 Hy
Rutherford, G. L. to Ann M. Betts 5-11-1842 (no return) L
Rutherford, Joel to Louisa Harrington 3-19-1846 Sh
Rutherford, John C. to Sallie Hill 12-18-1873 (12-17?-1873) T
Rutherford, John J. to Sarah D. Odam 1-30-1844 Sh
Rutherford, John R. to Polina M. Grace 4-29-1851 (4-30-1851) Hr
Rutherford, Lewis to Ellen Hill 10-21-1869 (10-22-1869) T
Rutherford, Linzy J. to Hetty Hodges 9-28-1830 (10-7-1830) Hr
Rutherford, Robt. M. to Eliza Gordon 12-13-1866 Ma
Rutherford, Thomas H. to Hettie L. Bernard 10-18-1869 (10-19-1869) T
Rutherford, William N. to Catherine T. Mitchell 4-3-1861 (4-4-1861) L
Rutherford, Wm. L. to Sarah A. Perry 11-28-1866 (11-29-1866) Ma
Rutherford, Wright H. to Artina Billingsley 11-25-1845 G
Rutlage, Wm. to Lucinda A. Bradshaw 7-9-1846 We
Rutland, Allen to Susan Bene 9-7-1841 Sh
Rutland, Harrison to Paulina Hathway 12-16-1847 Sh
Rutland, W. N. to Martha Jane Ramey 5-6-1852 (5-12-1852) Sh
Rutland, Wm. C. to Lydia A. Graham 12-11-1850 Sh
Rutledge, B. M. to Ann Shumate 12-29-1857 G
Rutledge, Benjamin to Angeline L. Burnett 10-23-1854 (10-29-1854) G
Rutledge, Charles to Caroline Ward 12-27-1841 (12-28-1841) O
Rutledge, David N. to Martha Jane Taylor 12-26-1851 G
Rutledge, David to Manurvy E. Flowers 8-27-1864 (8-28-1864) O
Rutledge, Elzey to Judith Terrell 4-6-1824 G
Rutledge, Francis M. to Martha Ann Eleston 1-19-   (12-23-1856) O
Rutledge, Francis M. to Martha Ann Elston 12-19-1850 (12-23-1850) O
Rutledge, G. T. to Mattie L. Bills 6-12-1870 G
Rutledge, James to Mary Ann Taylor 8-11-1851 (8-13-1851) G
Rutledge, John to Darcus C. Davis 9-3-1855 (9-4-1855) G
Rutledge, John to Margaret A. Baxter 1-22-1846 Sh
Rutledge, Mat to Lucy Hammons 12-31-1866 (1-8-1867) F B
Rutledge, Nathan F. to Nancy P. Davis 2-23-1858 (2-24-1858) Sh
Rutledge, Nathaniel to Elizabeth Speares 8-23-1843 (8-24-1843) F
Rutledge, Reason A. to Mary A. Davidson 12-2-1867 G
Rutledge, Reason to Lucy Jane Davidson 2-24-1859 G
Rutledge, Robert to T. J. Thetford 1-27-1858 (1-28-1858) G
Rutledge, W. R. to Martha B. Hammons 4-6-1842 F
Rutledge, W. W. to Claudia Nolen 6-4-1874 Hy
Rutledge, William to Alice Yancey 12-9-1885 (12-12-1885) L
Rutlige, David to Martha M. Dearman 12-28-1853 Sh
Rutshuan, Sebastian to Mary Hoffman 11-11-1858 Sh
Rutter, George R. to Sarah V. Tarply 7-10-1861 Sh
Rutts, E. F. (Capt.) to Mary A. Elliott 5-9-1844 Sh
Ruvers (Reevers?), B. H. to Matilda Davis 11-11-1856 Sh
Ryan, A. L. to N. F. Woodard 10-27-1877 (10-28-1877) L
Ryan, Cornelius to Bridget McAvoy 1-28-1856 Sh
Ryan, Cornelius to Mary Jane McGrath 6-16-1860 (6-17-1860) Sh
Ryan, Denis to Ann Cook 5-27-1859 (6-2-1859) Sh
Ryan, Dennis to Catharine McDonald 3-30-1861 (3-31-1861) Sh
Ryan, Dennis to Mary Griffin 1-24-1860 (1-25-1860) Sh
Ryan, J. B. to N. B. Brantley 7-25-1876 (7-28-1876) L
Ryan, James to Margaret Caina 6-3-1861 (6-4-1861) Sh
Ryan, Jeremiah to Mary Karney 4-22-1860 Sh
Ryan, John V. to Flavia Phillips 3-30-1871 (4-4-1871) T
Ryan, John to Mary Delaney 7-15-1850 Sh
Ryan, John to Mary O'Brien 1-9-1858 (1-10-1858) Sh
Ryan, John to Matilda Ann Ray 4-5-1879 (4-6-1879) L
Ryan, Lafayett to Martha Young 1-27-1874 (1-27-1875?) L
Ryan, Michael to Ann Kitchell 6-1-1853 Sh
Ryan, Michael to Joanna Madden 6-13-1853 Sh
Ryan, Patrick to Amanda Fortune 12-25-1862 Mn
Ryan, Patrick to Ellen Buckley 5-15-1858 (5-16-1858) Sh
Ryan, Rody to Bridget Doyle 6-15-1857 Sh
Ryan, Simpson S. to Lydia Taylor 5-7-1867 G
Ryan, Thomas to Catharine Cowry (or Conry) 2-25-1851 (2-27-1851) Sh
Ryan, Thomas to Ellen Finley 2-18-1854 (2-20-1854) Sh
Ryan, Thomas to Johanna Hays 4-7-1863 Sh
Ryan, Tim to Mary Shanahan 9-5-1851 (9-7-1851) Sh
Ryan, Timothy to Mary Dorsey 2-24-1852 Sh
Ryan, William to Margaret Fannessey 5-21-1857 Sh
Ryan, Wm. C. to Emily Smith 1-11-1851 (1-15-1851) L
Ryder, George W. to Louisa Hickman 6-25-1839 (6-30-1839) O
Ryder, James W. to Ediah Hickman 3-6-1843 (3-12-1843) O
Ryder, W. A. to Martha M. Jones 5-5-1860 O
Rye, John B. L. to Elizabeth A. Bush 10-15-1854 Hn
Rye, Lure to Catherine Moore 2-10-1847 Hn
Rye, Wayne to E. H. Atcheston 3-30-1856 Be
Ryker, John J. to Caraline Miller 2-10-1873 L
Ryle, W. H. to Martha Wilson 8-30-1859 Cr
Rynolds, Wm. H. to Sarah Edwards 1-9-1855 Cr

Sacket, Alexander to Elizabeth C. Snell 2-19-1852 (2-20-1852) Sh
Sackett, James M. to Mary A. Montgomery 8-8-1850 Sh
Sadberry, Jordian W. to Clayrindy May 2-16-1848 G
Sadberry, William to Hannah Jane Lorance 9-26-1843 (10-5-1843) Hr
Sadden?, Phill to Lucy Bradshaw 12-24-1869 (1-9-1870) T
Saddler, Geo. to Margaret Tharp 1-23-1869 (no return) F B
Saddler, H. W. to Margaret Deshazer 10-22-1857 We
Saddler, John L. to Nancy M. Hopkins 3-29-1859 We
Saddler, Thomas C. to Pheba E. Cook 12-2-1857 We
Sadler, B. W. to Mary E. Moore 12-26-1859 (12-29-1859) Hr
Sadler, John to Louisa C. David 7-1-1844 (7-10-1844) F
Sadler, S. R. to Judie B. Henning 12-7-1867 (no return) L
Sadler?, Rihd. to Maria Cockrill 10-7-1867 (10-13-1867) T
Safaran(Saffamans?), R. R. to C. E. Harris 12-23-1869 G
Safferans, John to M. J. Humphreys 6-21-1856 (6-23-1856) Sh
Saffoon, Geo. to Puss Ellington 12-15-1868 (12-17-1868) F
Sain (Sam?), Anderson to Rinday? Moore 12-30-1866 G
Sain (Sam?), John A. to Martha E. Thompson 5-9-1865 G
Sain, Daniel B. to Mary E. Riddle 1-13-1838 (1-14(16)-1838) Hr
Sain, Enoch to May Ann Elizabeth Panky 3-10-1847 (3-12-1847) Hr
Sain, Henry to G. A. Clacks 12-10-1851 (no return) F
Sain, James to Louisa Macon 12-19-1843 (12-21-1843) Hr
Sain, William to Frances Lathain 7-10-1838 (7-12-1838) G
Sain, lPerry to Nancy McK. Jacobs 1-6-1845 (1-7-1845) Hr
Saines, Solomon to Elizabeth Moore 2-2-1870 (2-3-1870) F B
Sainford, Samuel to Jane Strain 1-19-1847 (1-20-1847) G
Saino, L. to Josephine Fansioli 7-24-1858 (7-25-1858) Sh
Sains, John W. to Emma Gause 12-15-1885 (12-20-1885) L
Sale, Ezekiel to Elizabeth Nichols 11-14-1843 O
Sale, G. B. to Lola Wooten 11-16-1869 (11-17-1869) T
Sale, James to Eliza Hill 5-5-1870 (no return) F
Sale, John C. to Elizabeth N. Milton 11-22-1842 G
Sale, John to Louiza Chadwick 3-9-1849 (3-11-1849) G
Sale, Thomas to Susan Williams 12-19-1870 (12-25-1870) T
Sales, E. W. to M. V. Ford 6-5-1865 Be
Sales, J. L. to M. J. Algee 1-19-1861 (1-21-1861) Cr
Sales, Louis to Susan Hodge 12-27-1876 (or 12-28?) Dy
Sales, Peter to Angelina Pierce 1-10-1878 Dy
Sales, William to Rebecca Howard 12-18-1843 (12-20-1843) G
Salisbury, A. B. to Lucy Ford 10-9-1850 (10-18-1850) L
Salisbury, J. F. to M. M. Brandon 2-25-1879 (2-26-1879) Dy
Salisbury, Noah David to Sarah Ellen Moore 12-18-1883 (12-20-1883) L
Salisbury, T. E. to Frances I. Cook 8-21-1875 Hy
Salisbury, T. E. to Martha Jane Chambers 4-9-1870 (4-12-1870) L
Salisbury, William F. to Susan T. Dunaway 5-5-1863 (5-6-1863) L
Salisbury, William to Lucy Ellen Pitts 3-26-1856 (3-27-1856) L
Sallier, N. B. to Mary Avant 12-18-1844 (12-19-1844) Hr
Salmon, T. R. to Mary Giles 5-24-1843 Cr
Salmons, Wm. R. to Frances P. Butler 9-9-1841 Cr
Salter, Abraham to Julia Wade 12-24-1865 Mn
Salter, Thomas C. to Nannie B. Hubbard 8-7-1866 (8-8-1866) Ma
Saltler, J. F. to Susan R. Bason 1-30-1862 Sh
Salyton, Lewis J. to Louisa H. Featherston 11-1-1854 (11-6-1854) G
Sammons, H. A. to Henrietta C. Wilkes 11-11-1859 (11-7?-1859) Hr
Sammons, J. A. to Sue A. Sammons 8-15-1872 Hy
Sammons, J. W. to Naoma T. Wilks 12-3-1858 (12-9-1858) Hr
Sammons, John H. to Mary M. Wilkes 10-16-1854 (10-26-1854) Hr
Sammons, John to Cherry (Chessy?) Sappington 5-19-1866 G
Sammons, Wiley F. to Sarah Ann Bane 8-5-1852 G
Sammons, Wilie to Martha F. Wilkes 10-4-1850 (10-10-1850) Hr
Sammons, William to Hinna Nobles 4-10-1832 G
Sammons, William to Sarah T. Miller 8-19-1868 Hy
Sample, Hider A. D. to Nancy C. Smith 8-24-1862 (8-25-1862) O
Sample, J. H. to Elizabeth Garrett 8-8-1864 Sh
Sample, Joseph to Sally Appleton 10-7-1850 (no return) F
Sample, William to Bitsy Crain 11-26-1842 (12-1-1842) F
Sample, William to Mary Campbell 11-12-1850 (12-2-1850) O
Samples, Joseph to Margt. E. Cobb 11-9-1850 (11-10-1850) F
Sampson, Alexander to Lucy Bunton 4-21-1858 We
Sampson, Frank G. to Rebecca Wallace 2-6-1868 Dy
Sampson, Henry to Susan Holt 10-27-1866 (no return) F B
Sampson, Isaac to Mary A. Benton 9-19-1865 (9-20-1865) L
Sampson, J. K. to Sarah Butler 2-10-1848 Cr
Sampson, James W. to Juley A. Merritt 5-3-1843 Cr
Sampson, James to Susan M. Bone 8-27-1840 O
Sampson, Lewis to Mary A. Moore 11-6-1871 Hy
Sampson, Pleasant to Sarah T. Lesten 1-5-1853 Cr
Sampson, T. N. to M. L. Stewart 11-21-1857 Cr
Sampson, Wat B. to Maggie J. McGinnis 4-9-1861 Dy
Sams, Geo. to Lettie Smith 1-7-1873 O
Samuel, Ulis to Samanthy P. Rudd 7-13-1867 Hy
Samuels, J. A. to Mary F. Thompson 12-4-1874 (12-9-1874) L
Samuels, J. N. to Tabitha V. Thompson 12-18-1876 (12-21-1876) L
Samuels, John P. to Frances A. (Mrs.) Jones 11-12-1859 (11-13-1859) Sh
Samuels, John P. to Mary E. Smith 8-30-1855 Sh
Samuson?, W. R. to Nancy Knott 12-18-1862 (no return) F
Sandeford, Joseph A. to Martha T. Coleman 4-10-1835 Sh

Sander, Charles to Catharina Stroh 10-8-1861 Sh
Sanderford, Anthony to Lucy Ragan 12-29-1866 G
Sanderford, Bob to Emily Mitchell 1-1-1867 G
Sanderford, David to Clara Turnipseed 2-10-1870 G B
Sanderford, Dawson to Elizabeth Redman 4-11-1868 G B
Sanderlin, Dempsey M. to Loucretia Seward 8-22-1848 Sh
Sanderlin, Dempsey M. to Mary W. Ward 3-30-1842 Sh
Sanderlin, Ezekiel to Ann Eliza Allen 1-13-1848 Sh
Sanderlin, Ezekiel to Mary A. Jones 5-1-1834 Sh
Sanderlin, Joseph to Eveline Flemming 5-21-1845 Sh
Sanderlin, Lemuel to Mary Moody 12-24-1850 Ma
Sanderlin, M. M. to Betheland C. Jones 11-25-1849 Sh
Sanderlin, Malachi to Elizabeth A. Fleming 6-11-1844 Sh
Sanderlin, Valdura to Elvira Kirsey 6-6-1862 Hy
Sanderlin, W. M. to Elizabeth Luny (Lurry) 8-26-1841 Sh
Sanderlin, W. W. to Susan E. Seward 12-24-1850 Sh
Sanderlin, Wilson S. to Louisa C. Comer 8-29-1842 (9-1-1842) Hr
Sanders, A. A. to Rachel (Mrs.) Sanders 10-16-1864 Sh
Sanders, A. J. to Sarah A. Hood 7-9-1851 (7-11-1851) Sh
Sanders, A. M. to D. L. Sanders 2-19-1863 Mn
Sanders, A. Q. to Margaret Barnett 12-24-1868 G
Sanders, Aaron T. to Mollie F. Wells 1-18-1870 (1-19-1870) F
Sanders, Aaron to Mary M. Coop 12-27-1859 G
Sanders, Alexander P. to Mary P. Freeman 2-9-1871 L
Sanders, Andrew J. to Mary Ann E. Best 1-25-1858 L
Sanders, Andrew Jackson to Jane Hood 4-5-1843 Sh
Sanders, Andy to Matilda Ann Farr 6-26-1844 Hr
Sanders, Ben to Sallie Adams 1-16-1873 Hy
Sanders, Benj. L. to Mary Lee 8-10-1836 Sh
Sanders, Bennett to Sarah Jane Turnbow 5-24-1863 Hn
Sanders, C. W. to M. A. Gale 12-19-1871 Hy
Sanders, Cleyton D. to Rebecca Emeline Wilson 6-4-1856 (6-5-1856) O
Sanders, Dausey to Lucy C. Rox? 2-11-1846 Cr
Sanders, David H. to M. L. England 6-28-1859 (6-30-1859) F
Sanders, David to C. E. Simpson 9-30-1858 Hr
Sanders, Drewry to Lucy E. Ross 2-11-1846 Cr
Sanders, Ed to Paralee Coltart 2-16-1873 Hy
Sanders, Edmond to Nancy Lyons 12-13-1843 (12-14-1843) G
Sanders, Edward to Anne E. Hall 7-12-1841 Sh
Sanders, Elijah B. to Emmeline J. Hailey 2-2-1866 (2-6-1866) F
Sanders, Elijah to Mary J. Winn 6-30-1846 (7-1-1846) G
Sanders, Enoch to Elizabeth D. Lawrence 3-17-1839 Cr
Sanders, George W. to Elizabeth F. Yancy 8-11-1843 Sh
Sanders, George to Sarah Bassham 10-10-1864 (10-25-1864) O
Sanders, Gilford to Mahaly Sarrett 1-5-1851 Be
Sanders, Gilliad A. to Martha W. Burt 8-19-1840 Hr
Sanders, H. C. to Martha D. Huskey 3-22-1868 Hy
Sanders, Hamilton J. to Dosia Stricklin 8-4-1869 Hy
Sanders, Isaac to Rebecca Spivey 2-7-1848 (2-10-1848) L
Sanders, J. B. to Sarah Jane Epps 6-30-1841 Sh
Sanders, J. E. to L. A. Munn 1-21-1872 Cr
Sanders, J. H. to E. J. Reeves 3-6-1870 O
Sanders, J. H. to Julia E. Terrell 12-1-1872 Hy
Sanders, J. L. to Mary C. Pounds 2-9-1862 G
Sanders, J. Milton to Elvira C. Harrell 2-17-1854 Sh
Sanders, J. R. to M. E. Donell 7-14-1864 Mn
Sanders, J. W. to Elizabeth Wisson 1-31-1853 (no return) F
Sanders, J. W. to Isabeler Brown 1-18-1866 O
Sanders, J. W. to Sarah A. Ford 1-8-1867 G
Sanders, J. W. to Sarah Abbett 8-16-1857 Be
Sanders, J. W. to Susan F. Hilliard 12-11-1865 (12-12-1865) F
Sanders, James M. to Susan Wilson 4-5-1842 Sh
Sanders, James to Eliza Hall 2-4-1839 Cr
Sanders, James to Isabella Meeks(Merks?) 2-22-1838 Hr
Sanders, Jesse P. to Martha Joice 9-1-1841 Sh
Sanders, John A. to E. A. Hutchinson 10-13-1866 Hy
Sanders, John M. to Mary A. McAnley 4-10-1867 Cr
Sanders, John M. to Mary Ann Waddell 9-11-1856 Ma
Sanders, John R. to Sarah A. Johnson 11-15-1862 Hy
Sanders, John W. to Maryann Marchbanks 8-29-1847 Be
Sanders, John Wesley to Elizabeth Taylor 3-25-1841 Hr
Sanders, John to Amanda Powell 6-25-1848 Sh
Sanders, John to Caroline Middlebrook 10-19-1871 Hy
Sanders, John to Louisa Steelman 7-26-1880 L
Sanders, John to Polly Phillips 4-2-1826 Sh
Sanders, Joshua J. to Rachael Mason 12-22-1840 (12-23-1840) Ma
Sanders, Joshua to Charrity Cooper 12-28-1846 (12-31-1846) G
Sanders, Kelly to Elizabeth Pearson 3-12-1844 (no return) F
Sanders, L. L. to Amanda McCollum 12-29-1863 Mn
Sanders, L. M. to Maggie Church 7-19-1869 (7-20-1869) Dy
Sanders, Lary A. to Elizabeth J. Crawford 1-16-1849 (1-18-1849) Hr
Sanders, M. A. to S. L. Blount 1-15-1872 (1-17-1872) Cr
Sanders, Madison to Long Richardson 1-9-1870 G B
Sanders, Mathew to Mary E. Moore 7-20-1866 Hy
Sanders, Moses to Martha A. Robertson 3-11-1866 Hy
Sanders, Moses to Mattie Warpool 3-18-1872 Hy
Sanders, Nathaniel to Jane Jenkins 1-17-1866 L

Sanders, Noal W. to Mary J. Mainard 6-2-1860 Hy
Sanders, R. P. to M. A. Vaughn 10-13-1858 G
Sanders, Richard to Sarah Rogers 7-18-1840 (no return) Hn
Sanders, Smith B. to Martha E. Hawkins 3-18-1858 Cr
Sanders, Stephen to Amy Moore 10-25-1853 (10-27-1853) Hr
Sanders, Stephen to Heisey H. Simmons 1-8-1838 Hr
Sanders, Stephen to Malinda Maddrey 1-4-1877 Dy
Sanders, T. J. to Candis M. Hall 11-19-1860 (11-20-1860) Dy
Sanders, T. J. to Frances Adams 1-1-1862 Mn
Sanders, T. J. to M. E. (Mrs.) Moore 9-30-1875 (10-3-1875) Dy
Sanders, Theoophelus to Louisa J. Morgan 11-23-1852 (11-24-1852) Sh
Sanders, Thomas A. to Rhoda J. Bean 1-3-1848 Sh
Sanders, Thomas D. to M. J. Mason 1-15-1867 G
Sanders, Thomas to Margaret Birdsong 8-27-1859 (8-28-1859) Ma
Sanders, Thomas to Sarah Emily Whitehorn 4-18-1842 (4-22-1842) Hr
Sanders, Tom to Callie Whitelaw 6-2-1870 Hy
Sanders, Turman C. to Elizabeth L. McAuley 1-23-1859 Cr
Sanders, V. A. to Artimesia (Miss) Atkins 1-4-1864 Sh
Sanders, W. A. to Cinthia Forester 3-14-1879 (no return) Dy
Sanders, W. D. to Melissa C. Lane 5-12-1859 G
Sanders, W. H. to Nancy E. Grizzle 1-11-1868 (1-12-1868) F
Sanders, W. I. to Martha A. Sanders 2-4-1867 O
Sanders, W. L. to Louiza M. Pounds 1-4-1858 (1-5-___) G
Sanders, W. L. to Malissa Elder 7-14-1854 (no return) F
Sanders, Wilie to Tabith Steward 5-26-1870 L
Sanders, William F. to Mary E. Brown 8-30-1854 (no return) L
Sanders, William H. to Martha Jane Waddle 12-12-1840 (12-14-1840) Ma
Sanders, William to Caroline M. Baldwin 10-26-1865 Hn
Sanders, Wm. T. to Elizabeth Bond? 12-30-1855 Cr
Sanders, Wm. to Elmira Smith 12-21-1844 (12-22-1844) F
Sanders, Woodson J. to Mary B. Sartor 1-2-1846 (1-5-1846) G
Sanders, jr., Lindsey to Molly E. Justice 9-6-1865 Mn
Sanderson, James M. to Mary Ann Fain 1-2-1867 L
Sanderson, Overall to Eliza Lyon 4-7-1831 L
Sanderson, Robt. to Martha N. (Miss) Harrison 9-15-1864 Sh
Sandford, Geo. to Alice Miller 5-18-1878 (5-24-1878) Dy
Sandford, James to Susan Nuirhead 1-13-1877 (1-14-1877) Dy
Sandford, Jessee to Manirva Karnes 2-24-1846 (2-25-1846) G
Sandford, Richd. to Jane E. Alexander 5-17-1851 (no return) F
Sandford, Rufus to Sarah Wormack 3-10-1872 Hy
Sandford, Stephen to Mary Ann Carithers 10-27-1853 O
Sandford, Will to Laura Breasted? 12-28-1880 Dy
Sandford, William to Fannie Nash 12-26-1871 (12-27-1871) Dy
Sandige, Arch to Molly Foster 6-19-1875 Hy
Sandlin, Andrew to Amanda Fanin 2-1-1872 Hy
Sandlin, B. W. to Elizabeth Varvell 1-27-1861 (1-29-1861) O
Sandlin, E. H. to Sarah C. Vail 3-3-1870 Dy
Sandlin, Valdura to Caroline Shannon 12-17-1859 Hy
Sandlin, W. E. to Mary E. Kerbough 8-26-1879 (8-27-1879) L
Sandlin, William to Catherine Battle 7-23-1867 (7-24-1867) L
Sandling, J. H. to M. L. Kersey 7-22-1865 (7-23-1865) O
Sandrey, John to Susan Betts 1-22-1844 Ma
Sandrs, William P. to Martha J. Webb 3-16-1846 (3-17-1846) G
Sands, Bevely to Larra Love 1-28-1872 Hy
Sands, James to Jessie Marie Craft 1-13-1853 Sh
Sandsberry, John S. to Mary C. Williams 12-24-1855 L
Sane, Sampson M. to Lucyann E. Winfield 11-28-1838 (no return) F
Sanford, Bailey to Susan G. Hill 1-6-1865 T
Sanford, Ben J. to Sue M. Taylor 10-29-1873 (10-30-1873) T
Sanford, C. F. to Agnus G. Jayroe 5-11-1878 (no return) L
Sanford, David to Mary E. McGeehe 12-24-1855 (12-28-1855) G
Sanford, Edward L. to Mary F. Simmons 12-23-1857 Ma
Sanford, H. W. to Sue M. Anthony 2-1-1881 (2-2-1881) L
Sanford, James R. to Ann D. Tipton 2-9-1859 T
Sanford, John to Annie Collins 2-28-1870 (3-17-1870) L
Sanford, John to Sarah L. Williams 5-19-1867 G
Sanford, Joseph to Sarah A. Finly 11-2-1867 (11-3-1867) Dy
Sanford, Louis to Elizabeth Flemming 12-17-1865 (12-28-1865) T
Sanford, Louis to Harriet Ligon 4-17-1868 (4-18-1868) T
Sanford, M. A. to Ann E. Bowman 11-22-1865 Hn
Sanford, Marvin (Marion?) to Delia Gillespie 7-29-1870 G
Sanford, Nathan to Leeva? Caruthers 10-2-1873 T
Sanford, Nelson to Mary Somerville 3-30-1867 (3-31-1867) T
Sanford, Patrick H. to Mary C. Ball 1-5-1859 (1-6-1859) Ma
Sanford, Peter to Fany Maclin 7-2-1867 Hy
Sanford, Richard to Jane Elizabeth Alexander 5-17-1851 Hr
Sanford, Robert B. to Catherine Ann Chambers 12-23-1839 (12-24-1839) Ma
Sanford, Robert H. to Tyre Elizabeth Caruthers 1-10-1856 O
Sanford, Robert to Martha E. Conley 8-30-1852 (9-2-1852) G
Sanford, Robert to Mary E. Fisher 7-1-1869 (7-4-1869) Dy
Sanford, Saml. W. to Rozelle Tipton 12-2-1870 T
Sanford, Valerius F. to Harriet A. Norris 9-28-1859 (9-29-1859) Sh
Sanford, William A. to Sarah J. Ball 1-29-1855 Ma
Sanford, William to Bettie Douglas 1-17-1867 T
Sanford, William to Malisa Baker 9-15-1867 G
Sanford?, Saml. Crawford to Eliz. Lucretia Elmore 11-22-1855 T
Sanger, Chas. H. to Sarah E. (Miss) Editt 4-20-1864 Sh

Sangster, Buck to Fanny Richardson 4-14-1867 Hy
Sangster, Esquire to Amanda Jones 4-1-1869 Hy
Sangster, Francis M. to Mary Loulie Given 1-19-1869 (1-21-1869) L
Sangster, H. C. to Minnie Rayner 5-31-1859 Hy
Sangster, Henry to Bettie Bennett 3-18-1878 Hy
Sangster, J. W. to Margaret Hunter 1-16-1860 Hy
Sangster, John to Annie L. Williams 12-7-1885 (12-10-1885) L
Sangster, John to Nancy Taylor 9-12-1867 Hy
Sangster, Nelson to Elmonia Taliaferro 4-29-1876 Hy
Sangster, R. B. to Eliza A. Coleman 1-4-1861 Hy
Sangster, Taylor to Julia Currie 3-17-1870 Hy
Sangster, Thomas to Bertha Whitelaw 11-28-1877 Hy
Sangster, W. L. to Willie B. Anderson 11-30-1876 Hy
Sangster, Wesley to Eliza Sturdivan 4-4-1872 Hy
Sangster, William to Emma Lea 10-23-1880 (10-28-1880) L
Sanguinetti, Jack to Christian Wiebel 1-18-1855 (1-20-1855) Sh
Sanguinetti, Nicholas to Margaret Akin 2-19-1855 (2-20-1855) Sh
Sann, Rancelier to Emily L. Magit 6-19-1843 (6-21-1843) F
Sannoner, John A. to Maria B. Walker 10-31-1853 (11-2-1853) Sh
Sansberry, J. S. to Sally A. Williams 4-7-1874 L
Sapp, M. J. to Lucy F. Buckner 12-23-1884 L
Sapp, W. B. to Nannie M. White 12-2-1884 L
Sappington, Benjamin R. to Margaret S. Davis 2-13-1841 Sh
Sappington, J. B. to Nannie Martin 9-5-1869 G
Sappington, J. M. to Sue Johnston 3-8-1870 G
Sappington, J. W. S. to M. C. Wade 4-4-1858 G
Sappington, Mark B. to Eliza A. Pendleton 12-21-1832 Sh
Sappington, W. G. to Alice C. Wade 9-28-1859 G
Saratt, Washington L. to Louisa Hollingsworth 2-16-1854 Hn
Sargent, A. J. to C. A. Cummins 1-2-1856 Be
Sargent, G. W. to J. Merrill 4-5-1871 (4-9-1871) T
Sarlett, Normal to Thysby Viots 11-11-1851 Cr
Sarrell, James to Martha A. Rooks 11-18-1851 (11-21-1851) Sh
Sarrett, Charles M. to Willy A. Hall 9-27-1843 Cr
Sarrett, W. L. to Susan Ann Sarrett 4-25-1847 Be
Sarrett, William to Abigail Dougherty 10-22-1837 Hr
Sasenson(Sarrenson?), A. B. to Mary Ray 6-21-1860 (2-22-1860) Sh
Sasser, Joel S. to Epsey J. Casey 11-24-1857 (11-26-1857) H
Sasser, John to Mary Ann Chisum 6-10-1834 (6-20-1834) Hr
Sasser, William to Charlotte Rhodes 1-15-1842 (1-16-1842) Hr
Sasser, William to Litilia? Lambeth 10-11-1850 (10-13-1850) H
Saterfield, James H. to Mary L. Reynolds 7-19-1836 (7-20-1836) Hr
Satterfield, Andrew C. to Caroline Robinson 4-2-1838 (no return) F
Satterfield, Andrew to Elizabeth Campbell 10-13-1843 Hn
Satterfield, H. B. to Elizabeth M. Moody 12-24-1867 O
Satterfield, Lealin to Lucy Ann Hornsby 4-27-1841 O
Sauer, Phillip to Margaret Eberts 5-28-1861 Sh
Sauls, Burril to Jane Matthews 8-5-1829 (8-11-1829) Hr
Sauls, Calvin to Winney Johnson 10-4-1847 Ma
Sauls, David C. to Elizabeth A. Russell 1-22-1867 (1-23-1867) L
Sauls, Joseph D. to Elya(Diya) Ann Jones 9-10-1856 (9-11-1856) Hr
Sauls, Patrick to Elizabeth Waddleton 1-30-1843 (2-2-1843) Ma
Sauls, Roy to Juntia Bowden 1-23-1849 Cr
Sauls, Thomas E. to Mary J. Abernathy 2-22-1851 Cr
Sauls, William to Elizabeth C. Bunting 10-18-1849 (10-22-1849) Hr
Sauls, Wm. N. to Christina House 9-28-1854 Cr
Saulsburg, Wm. to Jane Nance 5-22-1879 Dy
Saulsbury, James to F. E. Sudberry 12-30-1871 Dy
Saunder, J. C. to Maggie Burns 2-2-1870 Dy
Saunders, Aleck to Emma Harris 8-22-1874 (9-22-1874) Dy
Saunders, Andrew to Malinda Wilson 7-1-1858 Hn
Saunders, Arden to Prudillar Philips 8-31-1859 Hn
Saunders, Benj. A. to Mary E. Butler 9-19-1860 (9-20-1860) Cr
Saunders, D. D. to Kate S. (Miss) Wheatley 3-14-1860 Sh
Saunders, Daniel L. to Charlotte Coosy Bradley 6-19-1831 Sh
Saunders, Dempsey to Ellinor Woods 2-14-1843 Hn
Saunders, E. B. to C. V. Hurt 10-10-1865 Hy
Saunders, Elisha to Elizabeth Thomas 9-2-1846 L
Saunders, F. P. to Artimissa Wyly 1-6-1845 Be
Saunders, George to Millie Daniel 3-5-1883 L
Saunders, Green to Ellen Greer 8-18-1866 G
Saunders, Hardy to Elizabeth Wilkes 7-6-1836 (8-7-1836) Hr
Saunders, Henry to Mary E. Hughs 3-19-1877 (no return) L
Saunders, Henry to Matilda A. Woodard 11-15-1880 (11-19-1880) L
Saunders, Henry to Tabitha Reynolds 5-2-1858 (5-8-1858) L
Saunders, J. W. to Sallie Kelly 11-8-1866 Be
Saunders, James to Nancy Barns 11-11-1857 Be
Saunders, Jefferson to Mary Adeline Thomas 9-17-1846 L
Saunders, Jefferson to P. A. Kinney 2-26-1886 (2-28-1886) L
Saunders, Jo. to Sarah Stanley 2-8-1869 (no return) Dy
Saunders, John A. to Polly Allen 11-2-1841 O
Saunders, John M. to Prissy Jackson 5-5-1834 (5-8-1834) G
Saunders, John T. to Mary F. Hatley 11-14-1868 Be
Saunders, John W. to Eugenia C. Eggleston 6-16-1858 L
Saunders, Murry to Lucinda Parrish 7-15-1867 (7-16-1867) Dy
Saunders, Peter A. to Frances E. Merrick 6-9-1867 Be
Saunders, Pleasant P. to Hollandberry Atkins 8-26-1846 (8-27-1846) F

Saunders, R. B. to Elizabeth Giles 10-1-1866 (10-2-1866) Dy
Saunders, R. G. to Mahala C. Shaw 2-8-1842 F
Saunders, Richman to Mary Taylor 1-7-1872 T
Saunders, S. L. to E. F. Boyd 1-9-1871 (no return) Dy
Saunders, Thomas N. to Polly Saunders 6-23-1857 Hn
Saunders, W. S. to M. A. Jenkins 8-1-1883 L
Saunders, Wilie to Tabitha Caniday 9-27-1858 Hn
Saunders, William C. to Elizabeth D. Boyd 3-18-1869 Cr
Saunders, William to Mary Israil 12-30-1830 Hr
Saunderson, J. W. to Darcus Smith 5-4-1872 (5-5-1872) Dy
Savage, Albert to Zelin Mann 12-9-1877 Hy
Savage, G. M. to Hettie McCane 10-20-1870 G
Savage, Hamilton to Amanda Wiloughby 9-3-1849 (9-6-1849) Hr
Savage, Hamilton to Rebecca Parr 2-17-1857 (2-18-1857) Hr
Savage, Henry M. to Frances Mills 1-21-1858 (1-22-1858) Hr
Savage, J. V. to Mallie Voss 5-25-1882 (no return) L
Savage, James M. to Mary Jane Westbrook 7-21-1858 (7-24-1858) Hr
Savage, James M. to N. A. Bingham 8-10-1853 Hr
Savage, Jefferson C. to Lucy Dean 1-10-1843 (1-13-1843) Hr
Savage, John D. to Sarah A. Welch 6-20-1872 (6-21-1872) L
Savage, Levin to Rebecca Rainey 8-4-1829 Hr
Savage, Marion F. to Laura Ellis 4-13-1885 (4-15-1885) L
Savage, W. B. to Julia A. F. Phillips 9-22-1860 (9-23-1860) Hr
Savage, W. L. to M. A. Wells 3-31-1874 (no return) L
Savage, Wiseman to N. Glidwell 1-26-1848 Hr
Savely, Sam D. to Julia A. Vaughn 12-8-1867 Hy
Sawers, Abell to Sarah Baraxtin 10-24-1858 We
Sawrie, R. A. to S. E. Harwell 11-4-1868 (no return) Dy
Sawtelle, Benjamin N. to Eugenia L. Reinhardt 7-5-1855 Sh
Sawyer, Calier to Mary F. Beaty 2-8-1870 Ma
Sawyer, Charles to Fanny Akin 12-26-1868 (12-28-1868) Dy
Sawyer, Charley to Martha Featherston 1-1-1874 Dy
Sawyer, Chas. to Mary Bradford 6-29-1868 Dy
Sawyer, Daniel to Rhody Williams 5-12-1866 (5-16-1866) Dy
Sawyer, Dennis F. to Joella Webb 8-15-1872 (8-16-1872) Dy
Sawyer, Elisha to A. P. Chisum 10-5-1864 L
Sawyer, George C. to Caroline M. Clay 12-14-1859 Hy
Sawyer, George C. to Mary Jones 11-16-1857 Hn
Sawyer, George to Mollie Brown 1-25-1869 (1-20?-1869) L
Sawyer, Hardy to Linda Puryear 5-19-1883 (5-20-1883) L
Sawyer, Henry to Ida Brim 12-23-1872 (12-26-1872) L
Sawyer, Joel to Elizabeth Givins 1-29-1846 Sh
Sawyer, Joel to Harriet L. State (Slate?) 7-5-1853 Sh
Sawyer, John to Frances Barnes 1-25-1869 (1-28-1869) L
Sawyer, John to Mary Ann Leroy 6-26-1871 Dy
Sawyer, Joseph to Anna Light 6-8-1870 Dy
Sawyer, Lee to Celia Brim 10-6-1881 (10-7-1881) L
Sawyer, Milton to Jane Deason 1-3-1849 (1-4-1849) L
Sawyer, Noah to Elizabeth Anderson 12-23-1867 (12-24-1867) L
Sawyer, P. M. to Josie Pillow 10-6-1876 (10-10-1876) L
Sawyer, Stephen to Martha Jane Ferrill 4-17-1873 (no return) Dy
Sawyer, Thomas J. to Charity A. (Mrs.) Wardlaw 8-16-1883 (no return) L
Sawyer, W. L. to Louiza Staples 1-8-1862 (1-9-1862) Sh
Sawyer, William to Amanda J. Chism 2-24-1842 L
Sawyer, William to Anna Mann 7-9-1881 (7-10-1881) L
Sawyer, William to Mary E. Stuckey 11-23-1854 L
Sawyer, Wm. H. to Nannie R. (Miss) Woodson 12-15-1864 Sh
Sawyer, Wm. R. to Mary Gibson 1-27-1840 G
Sawyers, Alfred A. to Eliza A. Morris 12-3-1865 Mn
Sawyers, G. to M. A. Hunnacutt 8-24-1852 We
Sawyers, Isaac O. to Martha A. Williams 5-9-1848 (5-10-1848) F
Sawyers, Joel to Sarah Bennett 9-20-1873 (9-21-1873) T
Sawyers, John G. to G. B. Nixon 1-21-1830 Sh
Sawyers, John J. to Sarah Peacock 9-27-1867 (9-28-1867) T
Sawyers, Thomas J. to Ella Pierson 1-1-1872 (1-4-1872) L B
Sawyers, Thomas to Mary Ann McCaleb 8-15-1867 G
Sawyers, W. B. to A. T. Loyed 12-26-1876 (12-28-1876) O
Sawyers, Wm. R. to Sarah H. Gibson 6-22-1836 (6-23-1836) G
Saxon, Frank to Malinda A. Speight 4-4-1875 Hy
Saxton, James W. to Eliza Ann Curtis 11-21-1844 T
Sayle, William A. to N. J. Baxter 1-23-1861 (1-24-1861) Cr
Sayles, Andrew to Nancy Newbill 10-21-1848 Cr
Sayles, J. G. to Santefee B. Coleman 7-9-1862 (no return) Cr
Sayles, James I. to Zelinda Carnall 5-7-1866 (6-28-1866) L
Sayles, John to Elizabeth Shoeterick? 3-16-1866 (3-23-1866) Cr
Sayles, John to Minerva J. Summers 12-18-1856 Cr
Sayles, Robert to Elizabeth Younger 6-20-1849 Cr
Sayles, Wm. A. to Mary Morris 2-14-1865 (2-15-1865) Cr
Sazer, Samuel to Nancy Kenley 12-29-1846 (1-5-1847) L
Sbarbaro, V. to Teresa Boro 1-9-1861 Sh
Scaggs, Ebenezer to Priscilla J. Hargis 12-26-1850 Sh
Scaggs, Moredack to Mahaly Brown 7-15-1830 Sh
Scaggs, William to Mary Dunn 10-15-1830 Sh
Scalbrough, Wm. H. to Charlott Holmes 8-9-1860 (8-11-1860) Cr
Scales, Ellis to Amanda E. Cox 1-23-1863 (1-29-1863) Cr
Scales, Henry to Rada Jackson 10-11-1868 O
Scales, J. M. A. to Virginia Whitmore 9-15-1854 (no return) F

Scales, John to Amanda Patterson 2-26-1872 (2-27-1872) Cr
Scales, S. S. to Lou Burney 11-22-1876 (no return) Dy
Scales, Thomas E. to Carrie L. Givens 4-28-1856 (4-30-1856) G
Scales, William to Judy Crews 11-17-1868 G B
Scalhurst?, Washington to O. J. Smith 11-19-1852 (no return) F
Scallion, Benj. F. to Matilda C. Berry 7-10-1846 G
Scallion, Washington to Margarett Toten 10-12-1836 (10-13-1836) G
Scallions, John to Ann E. Pewitt 8-29-1874 (8-30-1874) L
Scallions, Joseph to Martha Blessing 6-8-1847 (6-9-1847) F
Scallions, W. M. to Margaret Ann Ivy 11-13-1871 (11-14-1871) L
Scallions, W. M. to Missouri Harvell 5-17-1869 (5-18-1869) Dy
Scallorn, John to Lovina Jackson 12-20-1830 G
Scanlin, Bartholomew to Mary Devlin 4-22-1861 (4-23-1861) Sh
Scarborough, George A. to Sarah A. Mainord 5-2-1870 (5-5-1870) Ma
Scarborough, John B. to Sarah E. Swink 7-30-1856 Ma
Scarborough, John W. to Emily Chilcut 12-30-1841 Hn
Scarborough, William to Malinda Herron 4-14-1841 Ma
Scarbro, R. P. to E. P. Ross 12-3-1866 (12-5-1866) Cr
Scarbrough, A. M. to Lou E. (Miss) Jackson 9-30-1863 Sh
Scarbrough, A. to Hariet Woods 1-1-1850 (no return) Hn
Scarbrough, George S. to Margaret Jane G. White 11-10-1840 (11-12-1840) Hr
Scarbrough, James P. to Sarah Walker 12-17-1860 (no return) Hn
Scarbrough, James to Sarah (Mrs.) McBryde 4-13-1869 (4-14-1869) Ma
Scarbrough, John G. to Katie A. Malone 4-1-1872 (4-2-1872) T
Scarbrough, John Y.(Z?) to Pamelia A. Jackson 1-11-1854 (1-12-1854) Hr
Scarbrough, Joseph H. to Louisa Jane Riggins 9-21-1856 Hr
Scarbrough, L. A. to Edna E. Malone 3-21-1866 (3-22-1866) T
Scarbrough, R. F. to Martha A. Hamlin 7-5-1858 We
Scarbrough, S. F. to Lucy Chappell 7-23-1844 Cr
Scarbrough, Thomas to Adna Henderson 12-22-1860 Hn
Scarce, J. H. to Minerva Orr 9-2-1878 (9-5-1878) Dy
Scarce, R. H. to M. D. Bennett 10-2-1867 (10-3-1867) O
Scarimon?, Robt. to Lou Mullin 6-3-1867 (6-1?-1867) T
Scarlott, Norwood to Rebeca (Mrs.) Marshall 7-18-1860 Cr
Scates, Alex H. to Perneacy Payne 9-28-1842 Cr
Scates, B. F. to Nancy H. Nash 2-24-1874 O
Scates, Daniel H. to Emma J. Biggs 10-20-1858 (10-21-1858) G
Scates, E. D. to Elizabeth Harris 1-11-1859 (no return) We
Scates, Elijah A. to Martha J. Wilder 11-20-1849 Cr
Scates, Elisha to Rebecca J. Hanning 12-6-1849 Cr
Scates, Elisha to Sary E. Pingleton 11-25-1858 We
Scates, John H. to Amanda J. McEwings 1-26-1860 We
Scates, John N. to Sarah E. Reddick 9-29-1856 (no return) We
Scates, John to Amanda Patterson 3-4-1870 (no return) Cr
Scates, Lafayette to Sarah E. Wilder 11-6-1850 Cr
Scates, William T. to Sarah E. Hagg 9-17-1859 (no return) We
Scates, Wm. B. to Susan E. Dickson 3-21-1844 Cr
Scates, Wm. F. to M. A. Wray 2-28-1858 Cr
Scates, Z. B. to Lucinda Stubblefield 9-1-1861 We
Scearce, Wellington to Mary E. A. Patterson 2-15-1860 O
Schabel, George W. to Martha J. Barnett 5-23-1844 Sh
Schade, George to Lisette Schobert 10-31-1857 Sh
Schanaber (Schualer), John to Catherine Thayer 1-22-1846 Sh
Scharmahoran, J. W. C. to Laura C. Taylor 1-1-1859 (1-7-1859) Ma
Schattlin, Hermann to Rosalia Rutchmann 2-3-1860 Sh
Scheer, Hermann to Catharine Hermany 3-15-1858 (3-16-1858) Sh
Scherman, John J. to Sarah Hutchens 7-26-1850 Hn
Scheuermann, G. J. to Augusta Horne 1-25-1862 Sh
Schick, A. C. to Pauline Lauftmeister 6-14-1859 (6-16-1860) Sh
Schick, A. Charles to Elizabeth Schmidt 6-20-1860 (6-21-1860) Sh
Schiffman, S. to H. (Miss) Klein 10-29-1864 Sh
Schlemmer, Henry to Elizabeth Bradford 5-14-1862 Sh
Schlesinger, J. to Aurelia Beck 6-24-1864 Sh
Schloss, Charles to Barbetta Levy 9-13-1861 Sh
Schmeller, John to Caroline Zimmermann 11-19-1858 T
Schmely, Henry to Louisa Matilda Miles 5-15-1871 Hy
Schmidt, Casper to Elizabeth Brown 9-10-1862 Sh
Schmidt, Charles to Mary Tefft 7-20-1857 Sh
Schmidt, Conrad to Catharine Conrad 12-18-1852 Sh
Schmidt, Conrad to Ignata Stumphf 8-15-1855 (8-16-1855) Sh
Schmidt, F. W. to Rebecca Wright 7-8-1861 Sh
Schmidt, Jno. to Wilhelmina Peonse 1-15-1852 Sh
Schnaller, Jacob to Helena? Gresharber 1-28-1853 Sh
Schneider, George to Wilhemina Horn 2-8-1859 Sh
Schneider, J. Joseph to Dorothea E. Henrich 11-27-1858 Sh
Schneider, Ludwig to Catharine Taylor 2-11-1856 Sh
Schnerring, C. F. to Mary Rice 11-6-1862 Sh
Schnider, Jno. Geo. to Madeline Bargantey 4-13-1846 Sh
Schobel, James F. to Mary E. Safferrans 12-30-1852 Sh
Schofer, P. H. to Susan M. Hardy 2-10-1874 O
Schoffer (Schaffer), Sebastian to Marah H. Hardy 1-13-1874 O
Scholding, James H. to Isabela Pipes 6-13-1876 (6-14-1876) L
Schooley, James K. to Frances Eleanor Pendergrass 1-1-1850 T
Schrimsher, G. R. to Mary Williams 6-6-1858 (6-6-1858) Hr
Schrimsher, James L. to Sarah Jane Slaughter 6-1-1868 (6-20-1868) L
Schrimsher, Jasper Newton to Susan Sawyer 5-10-1862 Sh
Schroeder, Lafayette to Mary A. Pool 1-2-1853 Hn

Schuck, Magdalenor to Sneider 3-9-1858 Sh
Schulthus, F. to Caroline Zimmerman 7-2-1857 Sh
Schultz, Albert to Ottillie Kepler 12-22-1856 Sh
Schulz, W. B. to Christine Hamm--had 6-20-1863 Sh
Schurmayer, John to Carolina Doser 11-22-1860 Sh
Schuttkies, Fredrick to Johona Voges 9-5-1861 Sh
Schveizer, Gottlieb to Katherina Wissling 3-8-1862 Sh
Schwar, John M. to Anna W. Rives 9-21-1868 (9-30-1868) F
Schwartz, Ezekiel to Caroline Meyer 12-15-1848 Sh
Schwartz, Mathias to Elizabeth Goodhart 2-25-1850 Sh
Scirratt, James to Rosetta James 3-2-1862 Mn
Scisco, Wm. to Martha Moncreif 9-18-1847 (9-23-1847) F
Scisson, Brown to Sarah Hughes 12-21-1843 We
Scobey, F. E. to M. E. Smith 12-11-1878 (12-12-1878) Dy
Scobey, L. C. to Parthena Scobey 11-22-1871 (11-24-1871) Dy
Scoby, D. J. to C. R. Hugueley 5-5-1863 (5-6-1863) Dy
Scoby, James A. to Mary A. Doherty 10-26-1854 Cr
Scoby, John S. to M. M. Drake 11-23-1841 Cr
Scoby, Matthew C. to Mary A. McCrocker 6-27-1839 Cr
Scoby, W. A. to Elizah Bayley 10-25-1870 (10-26-1870) Cr
Scoby, W. B. to Margaret M. Huguely 2-8-1862 (2-12-1862) Dy
Scofield, S. to A. J. Wood 11-2-1856 We
Scoggins, James W. to Creesy Clouse 8-20-1836 Hr
Scoggins, James to Sarah A. C. Young 6-30-1855 (7-4-1855) Hr
Scoggins, John to Lydia Taylor 3-20-1837 (3-22-1837) Hr
Scoggins, Stephen to Alsy M. McClanahan 6-28-1836 (not executed?) Hr *
Scoggins, Stephen to Martha Welch 2-6-1837 (2-7-1837) Hr
Scoggins, William to Margaret E. Weir 4-5-1859 (4-6-1859) Hr
Scott, Abner T. to Elizabeth J. Roark 1-8-1870 (1-9-1870) Cr
Scott, Abner Tom to Alice Matheny 4-8-1879 Dy
Scott, Albert to Lizzie Conner 6-12-1875 L B
Scott, Aleck to Evelin Jones 8-11-1866 (8-12-1866) F B
Scott, Allen to Sallie Oliver 12-20-1871 (12-21-1871) Dy
Scott, Andrew (Anderson) to Letha (Lettie) Vincent 9-4-1849 (9-1?-1849) O
Scott, Andrew to Letha Vinson (Viner) 9-4-1849 (9-1?-1849) O
Scott, Author to Mary Wardlaw 11-18-1882 (11-20-1882) L
Scott, Ben to Gella Ragan 2-1-1869 G B
Scott, Benj. to Eliza R. Campbell 1-25-1839 (1-31-1839) F
Scott, Beverly to Emily Edwards 10-13-1880 L
Scott, Billy Barlow to Martha Ann Young 6-8-1870 (6-9-1870) L
Scott, Booker to Eliza Dickerson 12-8-1871 Hy
Scott, Cornelius to Eliza Douglass 9-28-1872 Dy
Scott, Crittendin to M. E. Bridges 2-7-1851 Cr
Scott, David to Missie Applewhite 12-17-1872 (12-18-1872) Dy
Scott, Dock to Abbie Heaslett 2-11-1871 (no return) F B
Scott, E. T. to L. A. Neal 12-23-1857 (12-25-1857) Sh
Scott, Edward C. to Elizabeth A. Kernell 5-27-1859 Sh
Scott, Elbert to Fannie Byrn 12-29-1883 L
Scott, Eli to Sarah Erwin 11-23-1835 Sh
Scott, Elisha to Elizabeth G. J. Scott 7-12-1852 (7-29-1852) G
Scott, F. T. to J. L. (Mrs.) Roberts 2-16-1861 (2-20-1861) Sh
Scott, G. A. to A. J. Hurley 2-19-1878 (2-21-1878) Dy
Scott, G. T. to M. A. Neil 5-26-1869 T
Scott, G. W. to Mary Ann Byars 12-7-1854 Hn
Scott, G. W. to Sarah H. Byars 5-15-1863 Hn
Scott, Garland to Jane Rainey 7-12-1868 G B
Scott, Gary to Inda Gay 9-29-1867 G
Scott, Geo. E. to Fannie Stevens 4-28-1874 Dy
Scott, Geo. R. to Jennie Brooke 1-4-1870 (1-6-1870) F
Scott, Geo. W. to Eloise (Miss) Barbieri 3-3-1863 (2?-3-1863) Sh
Scott, George R. to Euginia J. Hudson 10-27-1866 (10-30-1866) Ma
Scott, George R. to Hester Ann Halton 2-7-1839 (2-14-1839) Ma
Scott, George to Hannar Loving 9-20-1877 Hy
Scott, Guss to Alice Gardner 8-28-1875 O
Scott, H. C. to D. J. Gulledge 6-22-1867 (6-23-1867) Cr
Scott, H. C. to Emma Jordan 1-8-1878 (1-10-1878) Dy
Scott, Harder to Nancy C. Crouch 2-21-1838 Sh
Scott, Harrison D. to Margaret Spencer 3-6-1845 Cr
Scott, Henry F. to A. P. Ewell 8-1-1860 (8-2-1860) F
Scott, Henry to Tilda Burks 12-18-1876 (12-26-1876) L
Scott, Hiram to Nancy R. Vaughan 4-8-1831 Hr
Scott, Hubbard P. to Christian McKinnon 3-23-1843 (3-27-1843) L
Scott, Hubbard P. to Nancy Carter 6-16-1842 Hr
Scott, Hudson to Catherine Walker 4-3-1876 (no return) L B
Scott, J. B. to Mary W. F. Farris 8-11-1865 Mn
Scott, J. M. to L. V. Cocke 12-20-1869 (no return) F
Scott, J. M. to Mary Susan Little 2-2-1867 (2-4-1867) Cr
Scott, J. Madison to Lucey Blackwood 11-12-1831 Hr
Scott, J. R. to T. E. Erocker 12-14-1865 (12-21-1865) Cr
Scott, J. T. to Arbelier F. Snellings 8-6-1869 (8-8-1869) F
Scott, Jack to Jinney Fleece 8-15-1868 (8-19-1868) F B
Scott, Jack to Pinkey Page 11-13-1875 (11-14-1875) L
Scott, James E. to Rosa Brigman 7-17-1873 (7-18-1873) T
Scott, James F. to Lizzie Puckett 12-10-1864 Ma
Scott, James H. to Elizabeth T. Fuller 8-23-1854 Hn
Scott, James L. to Eliza Land 7-5-1827 Hr
Scott, James M. to Elizabeth V. Gause 4-5-1856 (4-8-1856) L

Scott, James S. to Caroline Coley 11-8-1860 Hn
Scott, James W. to Emeline Harris 12-6-1848 G
Scott, James to Frances J. Chamberlin 11-4-1870 Cr
Scott, James to Martha McDaniel 2-12-1839 Hr
Scott, James to Martha ____? 10-7-1850 Cr
Scott, James to Mary F. Johnson 6-23-1866 (no return) Cr
Scott, James to Mary Landers 6-14-1838 G
Scott, James to Vilett B. Roddy 12-8-1832 (12-10-1832) G
Scott, James to Virginia Bradberry 1-26-1853 Cr
Scott, Jasper N. N. to Julia Humphrey 12-9-1850 Cr
Scott, Jerry to Hester Mann 2-28-1870 Hy
Scott, Jerry to Lilly Mann 3-18-1877 Hy
Scott, Jerry to Vina Bradford 12-30-1865 Hy
Scott, Jerry to Vina Bradford 3-4-1866 Hy
Scott, Jesse M. to Effey J. Wilson 4-16-1832 O
Scott, Jessee to Edna F. Vandegrift 10-30-1861 (10-31-1861) Hr
Scott, Joe to Charlotte Mann 9-15-1866 Hy
Scott, Joe to Elizabeth Merrewither 7-27-1872 Hy
Scott, Joe to Rachel Maclin 12-1-1870 Hy
Scott, John A. to Dora Jarrett 10-7-1874 Hy
Scott, John A. to Rosella Childers 10-29-1877 (10-30-1877) O
Scott, John D. to Susanah C. Williams 7-1-1828 (7-3-1828) G
Scott, John Gardiner to Charlotte Edwards Browne 3-31-1864 Sh
Scott, John H. to Amelia F. Jackson 6-14-1831 (6-16-1831) O
Scott, John R. to Sarah E. Morrison 2-19-1870 G
Scott, John W. to Margarett Ann Lake 12-30-1851 (1-3-1852) Hr
Scott, John to Catharine F. McCarthy 7-21-1860 Sh
Scott, John to Densi Harris 4-23-1870 Dy
Scott, John to Elizabeth Blair 2-24-1861 G
Scott, John to Elizabeth Holmes 9-18-1847 Cr
Scott, John to Emy Gleason 1-2-1867 G
Scott, John to Fany Smith 6-19-1869 T
Scott, John to Fortna Holmes 10-2-1853 Cr
Scott, John to Maria Green 5-13-1858 Sh
Scott, John to Mariah Cooke 2-27-1871 (3-2-1871) T
Scott, John to Martha Ann Vandergrifft 7-25-1861 (7-15?-1861) Hr
Scott, John to Mary Myers 9-1-1853 Hn
Scott, Joseph to Catherine Vaughn 12-18-1878 Hy
Scott, Joseph to Eliza S. McElver 2-18-1840 Ma
Scott, Joseph to Martha Jackson 9-1-1829 (9-2-1829) O
Scott, Lewis to Annie Cason 2-15-1886 L
Scott, Lewis to Mary F. Booker (Barker) 3-2-1847 Sh
Scott, Lions C. to Martha Chafero 2-22-1838 G
Scott, Lunsford W. to Sarah D. Bridges 1-14-1843 (1-25-1843) Hr
Scott, Lycurgus to Abbey Pendleton 1-29-1838 (1-30-1838) Hr
Scott, M. C. to Sallie F. Tarley 10-31-1867 (no return) F
Scott, M. G. to Jackey Ann Willoughby 9-10-1857 Hr
Scott, Matthew G. to Sarah J. Kirby 2-15-1855 Sh
Scott, N. B. to S. D. Slate 12-14-1853 Sh
Scott, Nathaniel to Elizabeth Reynolds 11-15-1835 (11-19-1835) Hr
Scott, Nathaniel to Mary Ham 11-13-1838 (11-22-1838) Hr
Scott, Nelson to Mattie Moseley 2-5-1880 Dy
Scott, Newton C. to Harrett Mills 7-7-1841 (7-8-1841) Hr
Scott, P. L. to V. A. Humble 5-22-1879 (6-7-1879) Dy
Scott, Peter to Elizabeth Gardner 7-28-1858 (8-1-1858) T
Scott, Peter to Lucinda Stackhouse 5-15-1846 Sh
Scott, Peter to Nancy Tyson 12-26-1853 Hn
Scott, Phillip G. to Nancy A. Tidwell 11-11-1862 O
Scott, Pinkey A. to Mary Groom 10-4-1857 Hn
Scott, Preston B. to Jane E. Campbell 11-12-1861 (11-13-1861) Ma
Scott, R. Q. to Sallie J. Owen 5-21-1867 G
Scott, Reubin S. to Eliza Jane Perry 5-20-1850 (5-23-1850) Hr
Scott, Richard G. to Jane E. Miller 5-5-1835 Sh
Scott, Richard G. to Letitia Williams 10-12-1836 Sh
Scott, Richd. G. to Mary B. W. Edwards 11-2-1867 (11-5-1867) F
Scott, Robert to Joana Mara 12-23-1854 Sh
Scott, S. D. to Genetta Lampkins 11-29-1865 Hn
Scott, S. M. to Susan Tucker 3-5-1862 Hn
Scott, Sam to Caledonia Booker 2-20-1870 G B
Scott, Samel to Susan Porter 12-24-1872 (12-30-1872) Dy
Scott, Saml. T. to Elizabeth Corbitt 7-16-1849 Sh
Scott, Saml. T. to Josie P. Holmes 2-13-1872 Cr
Scott, Sammie T. to Mary E. Holmes 5-15-1856 Cr
Scott, Samuel B. to Mary Williams 12-17-1845 (12-19-1845) T
Scott, Samuel C. to Martha S. Ingram 2-9-1849 (4-10-1849) Hr
Scott, Samuel to Eliza Gillum 12-28-1855 (no return) Hn
Scott, Sandy to Alice Mills 2-5-1835 (2-6-1835) Hr
Scott, Spencer to Martha Morris 1-18-1877 Hy
Scott, Sterling B. to Mary E. Biggs 11-23-1847 G
Scott, Surs to Martha Daniel 2-16-1886 (no return) L
Scott, Sydney to Martha A. Robins 5-15-1849 Sh
Scott, T. W. to Mary Cox 11-7-1865 Mn
Scott, T. W. to Roxanna Walker 8-11-1853 (no return) F
Scott, Tho. M. to Malvina H. Murley 11-28-1849 L
Scott, Thomas F. to Virginia L. Bragg 11-2-1870 (11-3-1870) T
Scott, Thomas J. to Nancey Dancey 7-3-1861 Hy
Scott, Thomas M., jr. to V. M. Palmer 5-9-1876 L

Scott, Thomas to Mary Ann Aspy 3-12-1846 Cr
Scott, Thos. to Nancy Mullins 1-21-1856 (1-22-1856) G
Scott, Tom to Rax A. King 8-19-1869 Hy
Scott, U. W. to Susan Fuller 11-28-1846 (11-29-1846) We
Scott, V. F. to Martha H. Moran 3-27-1856 We
Scott, W. C. to Mary S. Clements 4-19-1854 (6-19-1854) We
Scott, W. E. to Emily Scirratt 9-12-1861 Mn
Scott, W. H. to Elizabeth Bargo 5-4-1846 (no return) We
Scott, W. J. to M. E. Scoby 10-25-1860 Cr
Scott, W. L. to A. M. Fernandy 7-26-1870 G
Scott, W. S. to Ann E. King 1-28-1874 (1-29-1874) Dy
Scott, W. S. to Nancy E. Milam 4-8-1868 (4-9-1868) Dy
Scott, Walter to Amanda Fowlkes 1-6-1866 (no return) Dy
Scott, Washington to Jane Ezell 10-1-1852 Hn
Scott, William D. to Amanda G. Gilchrist 6-9-1835 G
Scott, William D. to Sutelda E. Webb 4-30-1849 (4-1?-1849) G
Scott, William P. to Elizabeth A. Little 1-24-1852 G
Scott, William S. to Mary E. Harris 4-4-1861 O
Scott, William to Betsey Johnson 5-18-1877 (no return) L
Scott, William to Biddy King 9-24-1846 (9-26-1846) G
Scott, William to Eliza I. Green 10-20-1843 Ma
Scott, William to Evalina Day 3-20-1861 (3-21-1861) Hr
Scott, William to Lila Hall 4-16-1870 (4-17-1870) F B
Scott, William to Melissa Jane Black 11-20-1866 (11-22-1866) L
Scott, William to Sarah Allen 12-12-1859 (12-15-1859) Hr
Scott, William to Sarah Spencer 8-9-1862 G
Scott, Winfield to Nancy E. Pollock 12-28-1858 (1-6-1859) O
Scott, Winfrey to Polly Baulkum 2-4-1839 (2-6-1839) F
Scott, Wm. M. to Lou Read 3-18-1875 Hy
Scott, Wm. M. to Sarah O. Taylor 12-21-1844 (12-29-1844) F
Scott, Wm. to Sarah A. Bruce 3-20-1843 (3-22-1843) F
Scott, Z. to Elizabeth Gillam 10-26-1851 Hn
Scott, Zerubbable to Lucy A. Culpepper 7-17-1858 Hn
Scrape, J. W. to Amanda Cooper 9-1-1870 G
Scrape, W. H. to Eliza M. Baber 10-9-1862 G
Scrape, William C. to Frances Wyson 10-24-1844 G
Screws, E. D. to Ann E. Ballentine 10-15-1859 (10-16-1859) G
Screws, Edmund D. to Charity Castles 3-26-1846 (4-2-1846) Ma
Screws, James H. to Sarah L. Pennington 1-8-1867 G
Scritchfield, Green to Martha Kimbrough 9-1-1830 Sh
Scroggins, Giles to Nancy J. A. Shopher 1-19-1858 (1-20-1858) Hr
Scroggins, Jesse to Lissa Yarbrough 3-6-1835 (3-11-1835) Hr
Scroggins, Jesse to Nancy Hamilton 7-17-1830 (7-20-1830) Hr
Scroggins, Otey to Bettie King 9-5-1868 (no return) L B
Scruggs, Edmund R. to Fannie M. Higgason 3-18-1868 F
Scruggs, F. P. to Susan J. Murphy 7-19-1849 Hn
Scruggs, H. H. to S. F. Foster 7-15-1870 (7-18-1870) Dy
Scruggs, Jackson to Abigail A. Williams 4-12-1843 Sh
Scruggs, James to Honora Mahar 12-24-1856 Sh
Scruggs, Phineas T. to Malinda C. Hewett 5-22-1861 (5-23-1861) Ma
Scruggs, William to Mary Stewart 10-23-1845 Sh
Scruggs, Wm. to Purlee Gay 11-16-1858 Cr
Sctarz, Willem to Mary M. Rezer 5-29-1851 (6-3-1851) Sh
Scudder, John B. to Mary Ann Cox 6-23-1857 (6-24-1857) Sh
Sculley, Robt. to Anne Costello 3-5-1862 Sh
Scurry, Jacob to Mary Glass 11-8-1873 T
Scurry, Louis to Lyda Jones 1-11-1866 T
Seals, Anthony to Jane Harkins 9-27-1827 Ma
Seals, Henry to Martha Chaney 1-9-1869 G B
Seals, Thomas J. to Sarah F. Hallam 6-28-1852 (7-6-1852) O
Seals, Thomas J. to Sarah M. Watson 3-10-1856 O
Searcy, Calvin to Drucilla Green 1-24-1884 L
Searcy, Edmund to Rose Mann 1-20-1881 L
Searcy, Ellar to Kizie Osbourne 10-29-1878 (11-1-1878) L B
Searcy, Henry to Alice Daniel 10-21-1885 (10-27-1885) L
Searcy, Henry to Nancy Estes 2-2-1881 L B
Searcy, James to Eliza Gilliland 2-15-1876 (2-17-1876) L
Searcy, John to Barbrier Wolf 7-7-1856 Sh
Searcy, Major to Matilda Dotson 6-28-1867 Hy
Searcy, Robert to Susan Ann Stevens 8-3-1851 (8-10-1851) T
Searcy, Robt. to Jane M. Haskell 6-16-1857 Sh
Searcy, Thomas to Mary E. Thompson 12-30-1872 (1-1-1873) L B
Searcy, William to Allice Davis 12-22-1873 (12-24-1873) L B
Searcy, William to Eliza Talley 7-24-1875 (7-25-1875) Dy B
Searcy, William to Julia Ann Johnson 5-1-1869 (no return) Dy
Searingen, George B. to Mary M. Herron 11-28-1866 (11-29-1866) Cr
Sears, Alexander to Mary Stevens 7-31-1869 L
Sears, John to Lizzie Winingham 12-23-1876 Hy
Seat, J. G. to Lucy Latta 10-18-1871 Dy
Seat, Joseph to Carlin Freeman 8-5-1870 G
Seat, L. G. B to Virginia Ann Fly 1-5-1854 Ma
Seat, L. G. B. to Ann (Mrs.) Clark 7-11-1865 G
Seat, Lea to Ritter Lewis 12-29-1868 G B
Seat, Robert to Martha E. Gilchrist 7-7-1831 G
Seat, Robert to S. T. Glenn 2-23-1846 We
Seat, William H. to Sarah Jane Butler 8-25-1856 (8-26-1856) Ma
Seaton, E. G. to Sarah M. Ashland 1-1-1867 (no return) Hn

Seaton, Geo. to Delina Griffin 5-13-1845 (5-16-1845) F
Seaton, George W. to Heneretta Radford 8-26-1844 (8-27-1844) F
Seaton, Hiram to Eliza Huddleston 6-24-1846 (6-25-1846) Hr
Seaton, Hiram to Rhoda Read 12-10-1840 Hn
Seaton, James to Maryann Helton 12-17-1838 (12-20-1838) F
Seaton, John L. to Lucy Hart 11-17-1853 (no return) F
Seaton, W. J. to S. E. Robbins 2-8-1872 Hy
Seaton, William B. to Elizabeth Herrell? 1-4-1851 (1-5-1851) Hr
Seavers, Augustus C. to Elizabeth McLemore 12-12-1855 (12-13-1855) G
Seavers, John to Mary F. Dailey 8-21-1858 Cr
Seawright, Joseph B. to Elizabeth J. Gibson 5-3-1849 Hn
Seawright, Richard to Esther Sproul 12-21-1853 (no return) Hn
Seawright, William A. to Martha A. Jones 10-29-1862 Hn
Seawright, William A. to Mary F. McCutcheon 10-26-1852 (no return) Hn
Seawright, William A. to Sarah Aaron 12-24-1857 Hn
Seawright, William to Susan Beard 12-5-1853 (no return) Hn
Seay, Lewis to Mary McCullar 7-25-1863 Mn
Seay, Luke P. to Ann Row Hall 9-22-1831 G
Seay, Robert M. to Mary S. Davis 6-7-1856 (6-8-1856) O
Seay, Thos. J. to Mary A. Gardner 3-8-1858 (3-11-1858) We
Sebastian, Fabian S. to Catharine Buckley 5-1-1861 Sh *
Sebralla, Charles C. to Maria Benges 6-30-1858 Sh
Secrest, Jno. M. to Martha N. Parcham 1-16-1846 F
Sedberry, Miles W. to Louisa Ann Butler 2-24-1852 Cr
Sedberry, Miles W. to Martha Jamison 7-26-1858 Cr
Seddens, Marshall to Frances Simpson 11-24-1828 Hr
Seddens, William H. to Assennith Lamberth 12-20-1853 Hr
Sedwick, Salmon to Fanny P. Fly 1-22-1827 G
See, Louis to Deborah Parker 12-13-1831 G
Seehorn, William J. to Martha A. Rone 4-28-1860 (4-29-1860) Ma
Seeley, Freeman H. to Martha J. Graham 5-19-1866 (5-20-1866) Ma
Seeton, William M. to Tennessee Blair 12-9-1828 Ma
Segraves?, Jack to Ellen Ledsinger 12-27-1877 Dy
Seiber, John to Minna Schelli 5-12-1857 Sh
Seigers, Dan to Louisa (Miss) Dean 8-6-1864 Sh
Seitz, Federline to Teresa Fritz 1-7-1856 Sh
Seivers, John D. to Hannah A. Haynes 12-5-1848 (12-7-1848) Hr
Selby, Andrew J. to Amanda Morey 1-27-1861 We
Selby, Edward to Fanny Shaw 10-9-1869 (10-20-1869) F B
Self, J. A. to M. F. Drummonds 11-11-1873 (11-15-1873) Dy
Self, S. J. to Frances Gwaltney 12-5-1860 (no return) Dy
Self, William to Marina Jane Jones 2-12-1873 (2-13-1873) Dy
Self, Willoughby to Mary Self 4-2-1833 G
Selfridge, William H. to Martha Starnes 10-2-1849 (10-3-1849) T
Seligman, Joseph to Mary E. Davenport 11-25-1858 Sh
Sellars, Andrew Jackson to Sarah Amanda Alexander 1-18-1871 (1-19-1871) Ma
Sellars, Isaac to Rebecca Guise 8-27-1857 (8-28-1857) Hr
Sellars, John to Nancy Sullivan 2-2-1850 Hn
Sellars, Joseph to Susan McKinnie 3-3-1840 (3-4-1840) Hr
Sellars, Richard C. to Mariah Hampton 5-18-1846 G
Sellars, Robert to Margarett Miller 5-10-1832 G
Sellars, Thomas S. to Elizabeth Gill 2-11-1861 (2-13-1861) Sh
Sellas, Thomas to Johnita Isalm? 12-30-1847 F
Sellers, Archie to Eliza Chunn 3-11-1870 (3-12-1870) F B
Sellers, Benjamin to Martha Bennett 6-30-1848 Sh
Sellers, Burell to Elizabeth Sellers 4-30-1840 Cr
Sellers, Francis M. to Zelpha A. D. Phillips 12-14-1847 Cr
Sellers, Hardy to Sarah Scott 1-2-1840 Cr
Sellers, Isaac P. to Elizabeth Burken 3-1-1842 Cr
Sellers, J. F. to Mary E. (Miss) Hills 11-2-1858 Sh
Sellers, James to Margaret McChord 9-17-1855 Ma
Sellers, Jesse L. to Rebecca Neigbors? 8-?-1867 (8-11?-1867) Cr
Sellers, Jno. R. to Margarett Holmes 1-18-1872 (1-19-1872) Cr
Sellers, John W. to Louisa Scott 9-27-1839 Cr
Sellers, John W. to Tabatha Tosh 1-25-1853 Cr
Sellers, John to Julian Fonville 7-12-1828 (7-17-1828) G
Sellers, Joseph C. to Sarah Jane Parsons 5-25-1850 Cr
Sellers, R. C. to A. E. Crawford 1-29-1867 G
Sellers, Robert to Rebecca Fletcher 11-16-1826 G
Sellers, Robert to Rebecca Fletcher 11-6-1826 G
Sellers, Thos. B. to Virginia W. Pate 12-21-1870 (12-24-1870) O
Sellers, William R. to Elizabeth A. Hunt 11-24-1856 G
Sellers, Wm. D. to L. F. Taylor 5-24-1873 (5-25-1873) Cr
Sellers, Wm. R. to Lussella Scott 6-16-1858 Cr
Sells, A. P. to Mary E. Williams 6-23-1871 Hy
Selmons, Thos. A. to M. J. Butler 6-25-1864 (7-3-1864) Cr
Selph, Anderson P. to Sallie A Jackson 12-24-1867 (12-29-1867) Ma
Selph, D. H. to Lavinia E. Stewart 12-21-1852 Ma
Selph, James P. to Ida A. Ball 1-25-1877 Hy
Selph, Mark to Ann M. Hays 12-16-1841 G
Selph, Mark to Millia Holder 11-20-1832 G
Selvidge, Reuben to Alice Edwards 1-20-1870 G B
Selvidge, Robt. to Mary E. Tipton 6-14-1868 G
Semirello, B. to Kattie (Mrs.) Rodgers 10-8-1863 Sh
Semmes, J. M. to Mary O. (Miss) Dougherty 11-23-1857 (11-24-1857) Sh
Senn (Lenn?), Hewer to Magdaline Witman 11-18-1854 Sh
Sensing, Jno. P. to Margaret T. Bucy 9-5-1867 (9-10-1867) F

Sensing, John P. to Nancy Moore 4-24-1841 (no return) F
Sensing, William to Martha R. Drake 5-24-1847 (no return) F
Senter, A. A. to Emily F. Elam 8-17-1859 (8-18-1859) G
Senter, Alvin to Nancy Elum 1-27-1851 (2-7-1851) G
Senter, Green to Laura Transon 12-8-1869 G
Senter, James M. to Margaret E. Hess 10-14-1852 G
Senter, Moses E. to Margaret J. Elam 2-10-1840 G
Senter, N. A. to Elizabeth (Mrs.) Lawhorn 12-19-1867 G
Senter, Thomas J. to Sarah J. Fly 11-1-1848 (11-2-1848) Ma
Senter, William M. to Nancy J. Pemberton 12-5-1857 (12-6-1857) G
Senter, William T. to Anna Mitchell 2-22-1870 G
Sepune, Daniel to Nancy M. Vaughn 12-20-1841 G
Serat, Jacob to Mary A. S. Stegall 12-18-1861 Mn
Serratt, A. L. to Mary Hollinsworth 8-11-1864 Be
Sertor, T. G. to Nancy Bell 7-2-1867 G
Session, Charles to Adaline Bott 3-23-1867 (3-30-1867) F B
Session, Charles to Ann Pulliam 9-4-1868 (9-5-1868) F B
Sessom, A. D. to Mary E. Miller 10-25-1855 (10-30-1855) Sh
Sessom, Wm. C. to Margaret Smith 10-25-1855 Sh
Settle, A. G. to Amanda Fowler 8-3-1869 G
Settle, Alexander to Eliza Jane Pollock 7-30-1870 (8-5-1870) Ma
Settle, Benjamin C. to Martha N. Swinney 10-18-1848 Hn
Settle, Daniel to Lucy Horn 8-21-1848 Be
Settle, David W. to Elizabeth F. Daniel 12-28-1859 (no return) Hn
Settle, Frank to Julia Mann (Manson) 12-6-1850 Sh
Settle, Geo. Washington to Clara Johnson 1-7-1869 (no return) F B
Settle, John Calvin to Martha Ann Twisdale 6-22-1850 (6-25-1850) T
Settles, F. M. to Suentia Pool 1-28-1844 Hn
Setzer, John to Mary Moore 9-27-1872 (9-29-1872) L
Seuberth, Conrad to Amelia Jane Hight 11-22-1855 Ma
Sevier, Adam to Nancy Cook 12-5-1838 Ma
Sevier, Enoch to Rebecca M. Sullivan 1-5-1846 (1-6-1846) F
Sevier, J. B. to Mollie F. Farmer 5-20-1863 G
Sevier, James E. to Mary Fields 5-17-1871 Hy
Sevier, R. W. to Anna E. Sangster 2-23-1878 Hy
Sevier, V. B. to Mary E. Whitehad 7-10-1862 Hy
Sevier, Valentine B. to E. T. (Miss) Westbrook 6-24-1857 (6-25-1857) Sh
Sevier, William to Jane McElwee 10-29-1873 Hy
Seward, B. to Lockey Clayton 9-26-1869 G
Seward, F. M. to Susanah Rasbury 7-5-1853 Be
Seward, Frank to Adeline Turnage 2-17-1869 (2-21-1869) F B
Seward, Hinchie (Kinchie) to Elizabeth Sanderlin 12-13-1850 Sh
Seward, J. W. to M. E. Davis 9-11-1871 (no return) Dy
Seward, Phillip M. to Nancyann Myers 1-27-1840 (2-6-1840) F
Seward, Warren B. to Martha E. Burrow 7-12-1855 (7-13-1855) G
Seward, York to Julia Turner 9-20-1868 G B
Sewart, Wm. L. to Susan R. (Mrs.) Logan 12-23-1857 Sh
Sewell, A. R. to Lucy Plunk 2-27-1862 Mn
Sewell, Allworth to Nancy C. Luton 11-8-1865 Mn
Sewell, Dempsey N. to Amanda Henderson 2-1-1849 Ma
Sewell, Edward G. to Mattie J. Taylor 11-30-1859 Sh
Sewell, Jeremiah to Mary E. Roberson 2-27-1862 Mn
Sewell, Joe to Arabella Boyle 2-7-1868 (2-8-1868) F B
Sewell, Joseph H. to Marianna Hampton 5-8-1871 (5-9-1871) Ma
Sewell, M. V. to Elizabeth Ross 1-28-1864 Mn
Sewell, Marcus to Frances E. Hines 10-25-1875 (10-27-1875) Dy
Sewell, Martin to Rachel Howell 2-8-1867 (2-10-1867) Ma
Sewell, Reuben to Martha A. Johnson 9-29-1841 Ma
Sewell, Samuel to Wynne Anders 10-25-1830 (10-27-1830) G
Sewell, W. J. to Emaline Caruth 4-15-1865 Mn
Sexten, Richard to Mary Nogent 11-15-1862 Sh
Sexton, Allen to Fanny Hammonds 3-2-1859 (3-3-1859) Hr
Sexton, Andrew to Martha Butler 3-7-1850 (3-8-1850) G
Sexton, Frank to Caroline Trigg 9-18-1871 (9-25-1871) T
Sexton, H. D. to Amanda Thomason 9-13-1866 G
Sexton, Henry L. to Amanda J. Dortch 8-18-1861 Hn
Sexton, Henry M. to Lucy Jane Walston 7-4-1866 (7-5-1866) Ma
Sexton, J. R. to Mary J. Justice 9-17-1857 (9-24-1857) Hr
Sexton, James to Milberry Ellis 8-5-1839 (no return) Hn
Sexton, James to Tennessee Mathews 9-4-1838 G
Sexton, John W. to Mary W. Good 2-1-1860 G
Sexton, John to Ella McBroom 2-10-1875 (no return) L
Sexton, Lincefield to Hellen Jones 7-16-1844 (7-4?-1844) Ma
Sexton, Peter to Frances May 3-20-1843 (4-1-1843) G
Sexton, Peter to Martha Woods 9-12-1839 G
Sexton, Richd. A. to Nancy A. Hogan 3-7-1861 (3-10-1861) Hr
Sexton, Thomas to Rachael Mashburn 7-4-1855 (7-24-1855) Hr
Sexton, W. T. to Hanna Addison 11-23-1872 (11-26-1872) L
Sexton, W. W. to Eliza Ann Parker 8-15-1855 Hn
Sexton, Wilie L. to Mary E. Bledsoe 4-19-1853 G
Sexton, William W. to Emily Hewett 8-16-1867 (8-18-1867) Ma
Sexton, William to Zuby Boyd 7-17-1843 (7-18-1843) G
Seymore, Elisha S. to Julia A. Bullock 10-20-1847 F
Seymore, F. M. to Mary Belew 10-28-1869 G
Seymore, F. T. to R. G. Short 11-12-1868 Hy
Seymore, F.(T.?) W. to Emiline Jackson 9-18-1870 G
Seymore, Geo. to Mary L. McCallum 2-4-1850 Cr

Seymore, Geo. to Rachel McClintock 11-17-1863 (no return) Cr
Seymore, John K. to Ellin Barton 9-27-1842 (9-29-1842) F
Seymore, Robert C. to Mary L. Hansbrough 3-30-1857 Cr
Seymore, Thomas to Kate Scott 1-1-1862 Sh
Seymore, Thos. R. to F. Bagdale (Ragsdale?) 1-11-1855 (1-12-1855) Sh
Seymore, W. F. to Elizabeth Ann Leach 2-23-1863 (no return) Cr
Seymore, W. F. to Elizabeth Ann Leach 2-23-1863 Cr
Seymore, W. H. to Tennessee Belew 1-19-1864 G
Seymour, Billy to Eliza Holloway 12-17-1870 F B
Seymour, Emory P. to Louisianna C. (Mrs.) Duke 2-16-1864 (2-17-1864) Sh
Seymour, Henry to Candis Trousdale 12-29-1868 F B
Seymour, James A. to M. A. Wall 11-7-1854 (no return) F
Seymour, Tom to Lou Catron 1-16-1866 F B
Shackelford, David to Sarah Heaslet 4-17-1869 (no return) F B
Shackelford, Wm. W. to Celia Hays 4-8-1837 (4-9-1837) Hr
Shackleford, Charles (Dr.) to Henrietta (Mrs.?) Cogburn 1-1-1872 (1-2-1872) Dy
Shackleford, Henry to Mary Heaslitt 3-9-1867 (no return) F B
Shackleford, J. B. to H. H. (Mrs.) Hamlett 1-22-1866 G
Shackleford, Richmond N. to Martha Ann Moses 11-9-1854 Ma
Shackleford, William to Nancy Angeline Taylor 3-5-1868 G
Shackleford, Wm. to Henrietta Dickens 12-16-1868 (12-25-1868) T
Shackleford, Zachariah M. to Sophia T. Mitchell 11-10-1846 (11-12-1846) F
Shad, Levi to Vandalia Dickson 1-24-1870 (1-27-1870) Cr
Shaddinger, Nathan to Adaline Reeves 9-5-1867 F
Shaddow, Robert to M. J. Hastings 11-16-1854 Hn
Shade, Joseph to Mary Prim 3-16-1863 Hy
Shadrick, James to Eliza J. Stagner 12-24-1849 Hn
Shadwick, James to Margaret Cochrun 4-2-1856 (no return) We
Shae, Michael to Bridget Morisay 11-1-1854 Sh
Shaf, J. H. to T. A. Laremore 7-27-1874 (7-29-1874) T
Shaffer, Killian to G. Creasin 2-29?-1847 Sh
Shaffin, S. B. to M. S. Stroud 3-29-1869 (3-31-1869) Cr
Shafnor, B. D. to H. E. Thomas 8-22-1849 (no return) F
Shallow, Ben to Fannie Connell 6-19-1876 Dy
Sham, William to Luize E. Lyon 2-19-1831 (2-21-1831) G
Shanaghan, Thomas to Ann O'Hair 7-4-1859 Sh
Shane, Alexander C. to Malinda Mays 6-26-1861 Ma
Shane, George to Martha A. T. Arnold 11-16-1841 (12-6-1841) G
Shane, Jacob to Lucinda Bowles 8-11-1825 Sh
Shane, John to Clara Day 9-4-1866 Ma
Shane, S. to L. A. House 8-10-1865 G
Shane, Samuel to Rebecka Umstead 12-5-1831 G
Shane, William to Louisa E. Lyson 2-18-1831 Ma
Shane, William to Matilda A. Delph 1-24-1859 (1-27-1859) G
Shankel, William F. to Mary Hopkins 9-26-1855 Hn
Shankle, Beverly to Mary Morgan 11-1-1861 (no return) Hn
Shankle, Beverly to Nancy Sweat 1-1-1860 Hn
Shankle, Beverly to Winney McFadden 11-19-1854 (no return) Hn
Shankle, Edmund to Ann Walker 10-8-1838 (no return) Hn
Shankle, Edward to S. C. Hartsfield 6-4-1860 (6-14-1860) T
Shankle, Edward to Susan E. Ewell 9-4-1855 (9-6-1855) T
Shankle, Eli to Cynthia M. Walker 1-20-1857 Hn
Shankle, Jacob to Mary Hinds 7-20-1853 T
Shankle, James T. to Laura Mitchell 8-24-1869 (8-29-1869) T
Shankle, N. W. to M. L. Gardner 2-14-1860 Cr
Shankle, Riley to Nancy Sweat 1-27-1850 Hn
Shankle, T. D. to Melica Ann Mizell 1-6-1867 Hn
Shankle, Terrell to Elizabeth Evans 1-1-1842 T
Shankle, W. B. to Martha A. Dowell 1-20-1870 (no return) Dy
Shankle, Wilson to Sarah Wimberley 1-17-1839 Hn
Shankle, Wyatt to Ann Wainscott 2-9-1843 Hn
Shanklin, Jesse A. to Nancy S. Parrish 12-30-1857 We
Shanklin, John to Cely Holloway 6-13-1831 (6-14-1831) O
Shanklin, William C. to M. T. Mathis 3-26-1856 G
Shanly (Shanny), Pat to Bridget McGarry 1-7-1861 Sh
Shannon, David to Eveline Nesbitt 2-15-1867 G
Shannon, H. H. to C. Boyce 6-29-1863) Sh
Shannon, Moses to Milly M. Lytle 11-11-1839 (11-14-1839) Hr
Shannon, Wm. to Mary Strickland 12-9-1877 Hy
Shanon, D. H. to Jane Holmes 4-12-1863 Mn
Shanon, H. J. to Mary A. Mosley 2-20-1855 We
Shantly, Jefferson to Indiana Freeman 9-17-1866 (9-19-1866) T
Shapard, Lewis B. to Catherine G. Vaulx 7-24-1860 Ma
Shapard, W. B. to Cordelia C. Frierson 10-23-1849 Sh
Shaply, Wm. T. to Elizabeth M. Beard 4-20-1846 (4-28-1846) Hr
Shara, Zebnia to Catharine O'Brian 2-24-1851 (3-1-1851) Sh
Shares, David L. to Luisa M. Gardner 12-2-1851 We
Sharon, Albert to Arabella Shearon 8-8-1851 (8-10-1851) Hr
Sharp, A. A. to F. A. Creswell 3-19-1861 G
Sharp, Ben to PatienceAmanda Thurman 12-30-1870 Hy
Sharp, Benjamin to Lucinda Hardeson 4-15-1866 G
Sharp, Christopher Col. to Ann Jane Ligon 9-6-1854 T
Sharp, Columbus C. to Louisa Estes 12-22-1857 Ma
Sharp, Cyrum to Mary C. Baxter 1-16-1849 Ma
Sharp, Cyrus to E. C. Johnson 5-27-1856 G
Sharp, E. A. to Sarah M. V. Baker 10-26-1857 (10-27-1857) G
Sharp, Geo. W. to Lucy E. McClaran 3-25-1846 (3-26-1846) F

Sharp, George A. to Martha E. Hawse 12-14-1852 (12-15-1852) Ma
Sharp, Granderson to Mary C. Whitlock 2-4-1868 (2-5-1868) T
Sharp, Granville S. to Sarah A. Caps 5-21-1855 (5-22-1855) G
Sharp, J. S. to Lewella G. Soward 12-14-1868 (12-15-1868) L
Sharp, J. W. to E. V. C. Hockaday 10-28-1850 G
Sharp, James A. to Omey Nicholas 11-30-1841 (12-2-1841) O
Sharp, James M. to France R. (Mrs.) Boon 10-27-1868 Ma
Sharp, James R. to Mary L. Sheffield 3-12-1850 T
Sharp, James R. to Mary Siler 11-10-1858 T
Sharp, Jo. E. to Mamie Stevens 11-6-1878 (11-7-1878) Dy
Sharp, John M. to Sarah Wright 9-1-1849 (9-2-1849) O
Sharp, John to Viney Stevens 9-15-1866 (9-22-1866) T
Sharp, Joseph C. to Margarett Ann Action 6-19-1839 Ma
Sharp, Joseph C. to Sarah E. Hill 2-16-1857 (2-17-1857) Ma
Sharp, Joseph D. to Martha McLeary 2-19-1835 Sh
Sharp, Joseph G. to Martha Mizell 11-16-1843 Ma
Sharp, Joseph H. to Mary E. C. Taylor 12-22-1858 (12-26-1858) G
Sharp, Joseph to Jurasha Taylor 3-6-1839 (3-7-1839) G
Sharp, Judge to Levenia Webb 5-5-1866 G
Sharp, R. B. to Rachel M. Sawyer 11-30-1866 (12-3-1866) L
Sharp, Robt. M. to Virginia A. Pyles 10-24-1866 (10-25-1866) Ma
Sharp, S. W. to Frances J. Cowan 9-3-1851 Hn
Sharp, Saml. to Sallie Boyd 5-11-1872 (5-12-1872) T
Sharp, T. A. to Martha A. Sharp 2-24-1864 G
Sharp, Thomas to Elizabeth Millikin 10-8-1847 (10-10-1847) F
Sharp, Thomas to R. G. Taylor 12-23-1866 G
Sharp, Thomas to Sallie A. January 12-8-1866 G
Sharpe, C. C. P. to Mary Buckner 3-26-1857 Hr
Sharpe, Joseph A. F. to Martha C. Cloyed 9-24-1838 (10-2-1838) F
Sharpe, Saml. to Idotha Fulghum 6-19-1866 Ma
Sharpe, Wm. W. to Jane M. F. Meadows 12-15-1845 (12-17-1845) L
Sharps, Geo. to Elisabeth Chapman 3-22-1862 (3-27-1862) Sh
Sharrod, Richard to Milly Hains 3-4-1828 G
Shaub, William H. to Georgie Bishop 1-27-1862 (1-28-1862) L
Shaull, John to Elizabeth Paschal 8-13-1844 (8-14-1844) F
Shaver, J. M. to Sarah F. Spain 12-25-1874 (12-27-1874) O
Shavour, John C. to Sabra Madison 3-17-1841 G
Shaw, A. B. to Ellen J. McLemore (McLane) 2-1-1845 Sh
Shaw, A. D. to S. E. Sandsberry 2-11-1874 L
Shaw, A. W. to S. E. Hunter 1-29-1869 (1-30-1869) T
Shaw, Aaron to Fannie Koonce 12-5-1877 Hy
Shaw, Africa to Martha Smith 9-26-1874 Hy
Shaw, Alexander C. to Mary E. Wimberley 2-14-1860 Hn
Shaw, Alexander to Mary E. Reinhardt 2-5-1856 Sh
Shaw, Alfred to Amanda Locust 1-20-1872 Hy
Shaw, Artemas to Mary Ann Fleming 4-26-1838 Sh
Shaw, Ben to Harriet Drake 12-23-1865 Hy
Shaw, C. A. S. to Sallie N. Dickinson 4-25-1866 (4-26-1866) F
Shaw, Caswell to Charity Walker 3-3-1866 (3-5-1866) F B
Shaw, Charles J. to Malissa Webb 1-19-1848 (1-20-1848) F
Shaw, Cornelius to Bettie Patton 1-25-1883 L
Shaw, Craig N. to Parthena Aiken 9-22-1869 Dy
Shaw, D. A. to M. J. Cope 8-3-1866 (8-12-1866) Dy
Shaw, D. A. to Mollie Pierce 1-16-1872 Dy
Shaw, Daniel B. to Jane Freeman 3-20-1844 (no return) We
Shaw, Daniel E. to Martha Shaw 11-24-1865 (11-?-1865) T
Shaw, Daniel to Tabby Newsom 12-24-1877 Hy
Shaw, David to Rose Taylor 3-22-1876 Hy
Shaw, E. H. to M. J. Hicks 8-21-1877 Hy
Shaw, Elizah C. to Pearl F. Russell 8-23-1873 (8-24-1873) T
Shaw, Ephraim to Lucinda Hazle 1-2-1875 (no return) L
Shaw, F. M. to M. J. Johnson 10-14-1868 G
Shaw, F. to P. C. Burford 10-24-1850 (no return) F
Shaw, Francis M. to Elizabeth H. Willis 7-31-1856 G
Shaw, Frank to Martha Loving 12-13-1867 (no return) F B
Shaw, Frank to Sylva Galloway 10-1-1870 (10-8-1870) F B
Shaw, G. M. to Pruble Shism 12-19-1883 (12-20-1883) L
Shaw, Geo. to Ellen Bradshaw 12-22-1860 (12-25-1860) Sh
Shaw, George W. to Sarah M. Handy Sheth 9-21-1860 (9-27-1860) O
Shaw, Harry to Nancy Oldham 1-31-1878 Hy
Shaw, Heck to Dolly Carter 12-23-1870 Hy
Shaw, Henry to Fannie Greggs 12-25-1867 (12-28-1867) F B
Shaw, Henry to Lucy Jones 12-4-1879 L B
Shaw, Henry to Martha Hazel 8-14-1875 L
Shaw, Henry to Mary Shane 3-18-1867 G
Shaw, Hugh to Aberville Jane Ince 7-6-1852 G
Shaw, Hugh to Nancy Cornelius 9-26-1827 (9-28-1827) Hr
Shaw, Isaac to K. Whitley 12-22-1870 T
Shaw, J. P. to Cornelia A. Mayar 12-24-1866 (12-26-1866) Cr
Shaw, J. P. to M. C. Ledsinger 12-21-1869 Cr
Shaw, J. Q. to Pheriba Williams 7-13-1841 (7-14-1841) F
Shaw, Jack to Annie Jeffries 8-11-1877 Hy
Shaw, James A. to Mary H. Boswell 4-28-1849 (4-29-1849) Ma
Shaw, James H. to Sarah Jane Newton 10-7-1848 (no return) Hn
Shaw, James M. to Martha A. Nix 1-27-1852 Ma
Shaw, James M. to Parthenia J. Carwell 8-21-1869 (8-22-1869) Ma
Shaw, James P. to E. J. Allen 10-16-1866 G

Shaw, James to Charity Boyt 7-26-1831 (7-28-1831) Ma
Shaw, Jesse to Jane Owens 10-20-1852 Cr
Shaw, Jim to Lydia A. Williamson 2-8-1870 (2-10-1870) F B
Shaw, Jim to Polly Wills 3-28-1872 Hy
Shaw, Joe D. to Mariah Stanley 9-5-1831 G
Shaw, Joe to Mary Todd 5-28-1884 (5-31-1884) L
Shaw, Joe to Roena Holloway 12-6-1883 L
Shaw, John A. to Louisa Bledsoe 9-13-1879 (9-14-1879) Dy
Shaw, John M. to Angeline McGill 2-22-1845 (2-25-1845) Hr
Shaw, John M. to Sallie M. Anthony 8-8-1878 Hy
Shaw, John W. to Agness E. Hunter 11-1-1838 Hr
Shaw, John W. to Lizzie L. Higgason 3-3-1870 F
Shaw, John Z. to Sarah J. Neighbours 10-14-1862 Mn
Shaw, Judge to Mattie J. Clemmons 12-12-1874 (12-17-1874) Dy B
Shaw, Martin to Ann Z. Williams 8-3-1846 Ma
Shaw, Martin to Mariah I. Boyd 1-14-1839 (1-15-1839) Ma
Shaw, Nelson to Fender Jones 12-28-1868 (1-15-1869) F B
Shaw, Nelson to Maggie Brooks 2-21-1880 (2-22-1880) L B
Shaw, Nelson to Mattie Talley 1-27-1880 (no return) Dy
Shaw, Nelson to Millie Connell 9-12-1872 Dy
Shaw, Offy to Harriet Gaither 6-20-1868 (no return) F B
Shaw, Peter to Emma Wise 1-10-1878 Hy
Shaw, Peter to Lizzie Forrest 2-15-1877 Hy
Shaw, Phillip to Pennie Burl 12-5-1874 T
Shaw, R. L. to Polly Via 12-10-1874 Dy
Shaw, R. L. to Sophronia Patton 10-7-1865 (10-10-1865) F
Shaw, S. R. to E. J. Comer 12-1-1861 (12-2-1865?) Cr
Shaw, S. R. to E. J. Comer 12-?-1861 (12-2-1861) Cr
Shaw, S. to L. A. House 8-10-1865 G
Shaw, S. to M. A. Clay 4-28-1837 (5-2-1837) G
Shaw, Sam'l. M. to Eliza Ann Ray 3-16-1855 (3-18-1855) O
Shaw, Silas to Caroline Stewart 8-12-1871 Hy
Shaw, Simpson to Elizabeth D. Jones 5-30-1837 (6-?-1837) G
Shaw, Solomon H. to Caroline Douglass 4-22-1844 F
Shaw, Theophilus to Rebecca Harris 5-5-1835 Hr
Shaw, Theopulus to Elizabeth Randolph 6-5-1850 (6-6-1850) Hr
Shaw, Thomas A. to Martha Drake 11-19-1870 Hy
Shaw, Thomas J. to Orphelia A. Baldridge 2-17-1869 G
Shaw, Thomas to Caroline Koonce 10-28-1868 (10-29-1868) L
Shaw, Thomas to Joanna Macon 10-1-1869 (no return) F B
Shaw, Turner to Berter Whitelaw 3-17-1876 Hy
Shaw, Turner to Bettie Whitelaw 11-28-1878 Hy
Shaw, Vig to Annie Granberry 3-30-1871 (3-31-1871) F B
Shaw, W. L. to A. E. Johnson 12-24-1870 (12-25-1870) Dy
Shaw, William S. to Nancy S. Edgar 4-23-1840 Hn
Shaw, William to Elizabeth Thomas 1-17-1863 (1-22-1863) Dy
Shaw, William to Lucinda Neel 12-27-1870 (1-7-1871) F B
Shaw, William to Margaret E. Roe 12-18-1855 (12-19-1855) G
Shaw, William to Mary Williams 5-8-1871 (5-11-1871) T
Shaw, Wm. J. to Eliza J. Collins 8-13-1853 Cr
Shaw, Wm. J. to Mary C. Rawles 2-13-1867 Hy
Shaw, Zachariah to Cassandra Bowman 12-21-1840 (12-22-1840) G
Shaw, Zachary to Frances E. Trotter 3-20-1855 (no return) F
Shaw, Zack to Lizzie Brown 12-25-1866 (12-27-1866) F B
Shaw?, James A. to N. D. Caldwell 11-24-1866 (11-27-1866) Cr
Shawl, Alexander to Ellen Shelly 10-3-1865 Cr
Shea (Shaer), Henery to Catherine Wallace 10-7-1862 Sh
Shea, Daniel to Ellen Fight 6-29-1860 (6-30-1860) Sh
Sheahan (Sheny?), Brian to Margaret Kelly 6-15-1863 Sh
Sheahan, James A. to Adeline Able 10-20-1858 (10-21-1858) Ma
Shearer, Henry to Penelope Juen Berry 1-16-1837 (1-19-1837) G
Shearin, Belfield S. to Rebecca Rogers 11-24-1854 Hr
Shearin, Jesse B. to Jane C. Webster 2-16-1857 (2-18-1857) Hr
Shearman, John H. to Nancy E. Neal 10-3-1852 Hn
Shearman, Monroe to Nancy Wicker 1-19-1855 Hn
Shearman, Wm. B. to Martha Slater 1-14-1863 L
Shearon, B. S. to Amanda Cox 7-11-1860 (7-15-1860) Hr
Shedrick, Phillip to Elvira Curry 12-30-1877 Hy
Sheeks, Cornelius to Mary E. Guy 12-13-1830 O
Sheeks, William to Mary V. Pulliam 7-12-1842 O
Sheeks, William to Mary V. Pulliam 7-12-1842 (7-19-1842) O
Sheels, Edward to Margaret Johnson 4-12-1855 (4-1-1856?) Sh
Sheets, Geo. W. to Sarah J. Hines 12-18-1859 Hy
Sheets, Jacob F. to Anne Hines 1-20-1838 (1-23-1838) Hr
Sheets, John C. to Harriet M. Weaver 5-20-1860 Hy
Sheffield, Henry M. to Martha H. Ellington 2-25-1851 (2-26-1851) F
Sheffield, Jason B. to Leilia R. Jones 12-18-1871 (12-19-1871) O
Sheffield, John A. to Sarah A. McClellan 2-3-1857 (2-19-1857) Hr
Shehan, John to Judith Sullivan 8-7-1854 Sh
Shehan, John to Mary Sheehy 7-8-1862 (7-9-1862) Sh
Shehan, John to Sarah Daly 5-17-1862 (5-20-1862) Sh
Shekle, A. L. to H. R. Curtis 10-3-1870 (no return) Dy
Shelbun?, Marion T. to Nancy James 7-10-1840 (no return) Hn
Shelby, Cyrus F. to Sarah I. Allen 12-25-1838 Hr
Shelby, Daniel G. to Jennie E. Colhoun 10-12-1876 Hy
Shelby, G. W. to Mary T. Winn 10-13-1849 (10-16-1849) O
Shelby, Isaac L. to Sarah Babb 11-26-1849 (11-29-1849) O

Shelby, James C. to Mary A. Nichols 12-20-1858 O
Shelby, Jno. M. to Amanda F. Rudisill 4-11-1833 Sh
Shelby, M. to Gertrude Fleming 8-22-1864 Sh
Shelby, Russell B. to Andromacha Cravens 11-15-1848 Sh
Shelby, Thomas Colwell to Elizabeth Jane Lashley 3-4-1859 (3-10-1859) Sh
Shelby, Thomas S. to Elizabeth Grayham 9-29-1840 (10-1-1840) O
Shelby, Washington to Malvena Lewis 10-7-1851 Be
Shelby, Wm. F. to B. A. Brown 6-20-1865 O
Sheldon, Oney to Caroline Chamberlain 12-28-1848 Ma
Sheldton, E. Henry to Mary C. Cooper 10-3-1843 (no return) F
Shelee, Martin to Mary Cleary 2-22-1862 (2-23-1862) Sh
Shell, A. D. to Louisa Baker 6-12-1832 (6-?-1832) Hr
Shell, James B. to Harriet T. Morrison 2-18-1854 Sh
Shell, John to Olive Stephens 10-23-1845 (no return) Hn
Shell, Martin to Matilda Norris 2-24-1834 Hr
Shell, Washington L. to Martha K. D. Hicks 3-23-1865 Hn
Shell, William S. to Eliza Alexander 3-19-1847 Hn
Shell, William to Aletha Foster 2-25-1839 Hn
Shelley, James to Mollie Newson 3-15-1869 (3-15-1869) F B
Shelley, Wm. to Martha Gorman 2-1-1867 (7-6-1867) F B
Shells, Raleigh to Mary Geter 4-7-1866 (4-22-1866) F B
Shelly, Isaac L. to Elizabeth Wynn 2-20-1847 O
Shelly, James T. to Harriett Smoot 1-25-1844 Cr
Shelly, James to Martha Thompson 2-6-1854 Sh
Shelly, John D. to Palunie A. Gardner 10-30-1850 We
Shelly, John to Nancy Biebers 12-29-1852 (12-30-1852) Hr
Shelly, Thomas C. to Maria Redwine 6-14-1856 Ma
Shelton, A. W. to Elizabeth Hunter 9-7-1848 Hn
Shelton, Alfred A. to Nancy C. Smithee 11-25-1858 Sh
Shelton, Alfred to Martha Early 2-27-1867 (3-5-1867) Dy
Shelton, Bryant A. to Jennie Gaines 2-10-1871 L
Shelton, Doc to Phillis Branch 7-17-1879 (no return) Dy
Shelton, E. O. to Martha Tucker 10-8-1849 (10-17-1849) F
Shelton, Edward Y. to Melinda Jane Pollock 3-11-1848 (3-16-1848) O
Shelton, Elijah H. to Runinia Gurganus 9-29-1865 (10-1-1865) Dy
Shelton, Elijah to Mary Grimes 9-10-1866 (9-16-1866) T
Shelton, Flover to Faney G. Teppett 5-3-1852 We
Shelton, Francis A. to Matilda Crank 3-16-1854 G
Shelton, George A. to Mary Wolverton 10-27-1835 Hr
Shelton, George T. to Sarah E. Wiggs 12-20-1859 Ma
Shelton, George W. to M. J. Sawyers 10-13-1873 T
Shelton, George to Kitty Aclin 12-28-1868 Hy
Shelton, George to Sarah Gurley 9-7-1867 (9-8-1867) L
Shelton, Halewell to Caroline Snow 12-31-1850 We
Shelton, Hardy W. to Martha T. Green 12-12-1848 (12-14-1848) G
Shelton, Henry V. to Malinda Robinson 1-5-1858 Ma
Shelton, Hilliard to Martha Ann Snow 1-19-1850 We
Shelton, Isaac R. to Mary E. Smith 5-8-1855 (5-20-1855) Sh
Shelton, J. E. to H. A. McCormack 12-22-1875 Dy
Shelton, J. F. to Martha McMullen 1-22-1857 (2-5-1857) Sh
Shelton, J. H. to Susan Payne 10-12-1867 (10-13-1867) Dy
Shelton, J. M. to Martha A. Cross 8-7-1849 (8-21-1849) F
Shelton, J. V. to Julia Rice 1-10-1866 G
Shelton, J. W. to Emma Ross 2-3-1875 Hy
Shelton, J. W. to S. A. M. Gurganus 8-26-1867 Dy
Shelton, James B. to Lue Thompson 10-30-1867 (10-31-1867) T
Shelton, James to Josephina Chiles 7-2-1857 Sh
Shelton, Jesse L. to Margaret Bryant 1-31-1850 Sh
Shelton, Jno. M. to F. M. Walk 11-27-1873 T
Shelton, John A. to Mahaly Corbett 8-30-1843 Sh
Shelton, John L. to Mary Dugan 9-12-1870 Ma
Shelton, John W. to Artimissa Powell 11-2-1852 Ma
Shelton, John W. to Bettie J. Reatherford 1-30-1861 T
Shelton, Jonas C. to Frances Ann Sherrod 12-26-1866 (12-28-1866) F B
Shelton, Joseph to Mary J. McGee 7-31-1854 (8-3-1854) Sh
Shelton, Judithan C. to Lydia Powell 12-21-1859 (12-22-1859) Ma
Shelton, L. V. to M. P. Cole 5-10-1859 (5-11-1859) F
Shelton, Lemuel to Milly Dyson 8-18-1866 T
Shelton, Martin to Catherine Twyford 12-25-1849 Sh
Shelton, N. A. to Susan E. Blankenship 10-7-1866 G
Shelton, P. M. to Ann A. Clark 5-1-1855 We
Shelton, Peter to Malvina Umsted 1-21-1869 G B
Shelton, Richard to Luiza Ward 12-27-1871 (12-28-1871) T
Shelton, Richard to Mary A. Dunnaway 3-10-1854 Hn
Shelton, Robert O. to Nancy Durham 7-29-1846 (7-30-1846) L
Shelton, Robert W. to Margaret A. Harding 2-23-1858 Sh
Shelton, Robert W. to Sarah Jane Rivers 1-24-1829 Hr
Shelton, S. B. to Laura E. (Mrs.) Read 12-18-1875 (12-19-1875) L
Shelton, Saml. R. to Sallie B. Rutherford 5-4-1857 (5-5-1857) T
Shelton, Sheppard to Sarah Ann Mashburn 1-23-1849 (1-26-1849) Hr
Shelton, Stephen L. to Ann Cornelia Montgomery 8-16-1869 (8-19-1869) Ma
Shelton, T. J. to Mary E. Jeter 8-12-1873 Hy
Shelton, Thomas to Caroline S. Thomas 2-5-1840 (2-7-1840) F
Shelton, Thomas to Mary A. H. Phillips 11-30-1874 (12-2-1874) Dy
Shelton, Tom to Mary Woodfolk 12-27-1867 (no return) F B
Shelton, W. A. to Ruth E. Renfrow 7-13-1861 (7-14-1861) O
Shelton, W. E. to Sarah A. Shull 8-9-1863 Mn

Shelton, W. M. to Julia A. Redford 7-7-1852 Sh
Shelton, William C. to Mattie J. Parrish 12-17-1867 (12-19-1867) Ma
Shelton, William H. to Sarah D. Sullivan 10-13-1835 Sh
Shelton, William M. to Margaret E. Campbell 2-17-1849 Ma
Shelton, William T. to Margaret J. Stroud 3-22-1843 (3-23-1843) O
Shelton, Wm. A. to Margaret Ann Capes 10-16-1864 G
Shelton, Wm. M. to Sallie J. Duncan 10-4-1870 Ma
Shelton, Wynn to Julia Ann Tyner 11-7-1850 Ma
Shelton, jr., Tho. Jeffreys to Matilda R. Mulliken 2-22-1864 F
Sheneer, W. M. to Mary Babb 2-8-1867 G
Shepard (Sherman), E. to Pollie Wilkerson 12-25-1869 Hy
Shepard, Ananias to Adaline Warren 3-7-1872 (3-11-1872) O
Shepard, Jas. R. to Susan Steviss? 9-13-1871 T
Shepard, John J. to Callie Jackson 7-1-1878 Hy
Shepard, John W. to Sarah J. Terry 6-24-1871 O
Shepard, July to Silar Raut 4-11-1876 (4-14-1876) L
Shepard, London to Lany Rice 12-15-1869 (no return) L
Shepard, R. B. to Eliza F. Patton 3-16-1857 G
Shepard, Robt. to Amy Wood 11-4-1865 (11-6-1865) T
Shepard, T. M. to Malinda M. Champion 9-28-1867 F
Shepard, William to Elizabeth Newton 1-15-1844 Hn
Shepard, William to Sallie Gibson 6-12-1872 Hy
Sheparson, William to Deletha Riley 3-3-1856 (3-6-1856) L
Shephard, Chauncey to Jane Black 9-17-1851 (9-18-1851) Sh
Shephard, Richard L. to Eliza Jane Holmes 1-1-1849 (1-2-1849) G
Shephard, W. M. to Cora A. Roach 4-26-1872 (no return) Cr
Shepherd, A. F. to Nannie Covington 4-1-1874 Hy
Shepherd, Alexander to Elizabeth Nettles 8-26-1841 F
Shepherd, Frederick to Matilda Ann Luttrell 5-18-1844 (5-21-1844) Hr
Shepherd, George to Elizabeth Jackson 8-11-1866 O
Shepherd, Henry to Frances Carter 11-3-1877 H
Shepherd, J. W. to Ella Barcroft 12-20-1871 Hy
Shepherd, Joe to History Allen 5-19-1870 (5-21-1870) F B
Shepherd, John Y. to T. T. Mathis 4-26-1859 Cr
Shepherd, July to Katie Walker 12-4-1872 (12-5-1872) L B
Shepherd, K. M. to V. A. Sanders 12-24-1862 Mn
Shepherd, Levi to Fannie Smith 4-10-1873 (4-11-1873) Dy
Shepherd, M. P. to Julia Rodgers 3-4-1862 (3-5-1862) Sh
Shepherd, M. W. to Louisa Covington 9-30-1869 Hy
Shepherd, Thomas J. to Harriet Anderson 1-10-1833 Hr
Shepherd, W. M. to P. S. Harris 11-5-1860 (11-6-1860) Sh
Shepherd?, Melzer to Marion Radford 1-15-1851 (1-16-1851) F
Shepley, David to Sarah Jones 2-27-1878 (2-28-1878) Dy
Sheppard, Frank to Jane Read 12-6-1866 Hy
Sheppard, Isaac to Williametta Allen 2-22-1868 (no return) F B
Sheppard, J. V. to Nancy Angeline King 5-13-1852 O
Sheppard, James H. to Rebecca Johnson 10-15-1828 Hr
Sheppard, John to Martha Beton 4-29-1845 Hr
Sheppard, W. M. to Elizabeth Gardner 3-6-1865 (no return) Hn
Shepperd, George to Nicy B. Smith 11-14-1830 Ma
Shepperd, John C. to Amanda Hines 2-6-1849 (2-13-1849) Hr
Shepperd, Robt. H. to Laura H. Wood 12-29-1858 (12-30-1858) Hr
Shepperson, S. M. to LuAnn Box 12-19-1881 (12-21-1881) L
Sheridan, A. J. to A. M. M. Neal 9-30-1856 Hn
Sheridan, Adison W. to Martha A. N. Speight 2-5-1861 Hn
Sheridan, Andrew J. to Susan R. Neal 11-4-1860 Hn
Sheridan, Finis Ewing to Sarah Ann Roberts 10-3-1866 Hn
Sheridan, George W. to Maranda J. Moore 1-1-1860 Hn
Sheridan, J. A. to Mary F. Paschall 1-25-1866 Hn
Sheridan, James M. to Mary Ann Speight 12-19-1857 Hn
Sheridan, John to Julia Hays 11-28-1859 Hn
Sheridan, Thomas H. to Mary E. Neill no date (1853-1867) Hn
Sheridan, Thomas M. to Altha L. Grigg 11-24-1847 Hn
Sheridan, William R. to America J. Simmons 7-18-1847 Hn
Sherill, Hasen W. to Mary D. Anderson 11-24-1854 (11-25-1858) We
Sherill, J. G. to Mary B. Dacus 8-8-1860 T
Sherin, W. A. to Eliza Ezell 8-4-1862 (8-10-1862) O
Sherley, J. J. to Tennessee M. Wallace 11-5-1865 Mn
Sherly, James to Mary Barnes 1-7-1849 Be
Sherman, Arthur Matt. (Capt.) to Antoinette L. Stetson 6-1-1863 Sh *
Sherman, Bennett to Mary L. Lockett 11-6-1843 Sh
Sherman, Boyce E. to Martha E. Revely 10-15-1857 (10-18-1857) Ma
Sherman, David M. to Louisa J. Keel 1-12-1853 Hn
Sherman, David M. to Louisa J. Sherman 8-23-1854 (no return) Hn
Sherman, David to Elizabeth E. Adams 4-17-1859 Hn
Sherman, G. W. to Sarah E. Greenhaw 8-1-1861 Mn
Sherman, Geo. to Maggie Herbertson 12-17-1859 Sh
Sherman, Henry D. to Mary E. Hawkins 3-2-1846 Sh
Sherman, James D. to Amanda C. Tapscott 4-15-1866 Hy
Sherman, James to Amanda Whitker 2-13-1867 (2-14-1867) L
Sherman, Jim to Dorcas Weddington 2-7-1868 G B
Sherman, M. B. to Caroline Jackson 9-22-1856 Ma
Sherman, Parson M. to Rebecca J. Alsabrooks 12-18-1838 G
Sherman, Wm. T. to Catherine Thomas 12-19-1869 Hy
Sheron, Jas. H. to Emely Webb 12-7-1838 (12-11-1838) G
Sheron, Moses to Sarah A. Wells 4-14-1865 O
Sheron, Norman to C. R. Douglass 12-27-1868 Hy

Sherrard, W. H. to Tennessee Powell 11-15-1865 Hy
Sherrell, James T. to Irine Stacy 6-7-1838 Cr
Sherrell, Nelson to Annie Williams 12-11-1871 (12-14-1871) T
Sherrill, Amus to Ellen Alston 9-23-1869 (9-26-1869) T
Sherrill, Enos Alexander to Ceelin Ethalinda Hall 4-7-1845 (4-16-1845) T
Sherrill, F. J. to Lenny Fleming 11-4-1868 T
Sherrill, Francis J. to Mary E. Forsythe 11-15-1871 T
Sherrill, George Washington to Caroline Thomas 12-26-1866 (12-27-1866) T
Sherrill, George to Emma Johnson 12-25-1873 T
Sherrill, Hosea W. to Catharine M. Bledsoe 4-1-1850 (4-3-1850) T
Sherrill, Jerry to Nancy Holland 3-2-1874 T
Sherrill, Jessee to Henrietta Alston 10-14-1874 T
Sherrill, John F. to Susan M. Temple 10-12-1850 Ma
Sherrill, Samel to Elenor Eadon 11-18-1840 F
Sherrill, Wm. E. to E. E. Hall 2-8-1866 F
Sherrod, Alfred to Rosa Capers 12-27-1869 (12-30-1869) F B
Sherrod, Ben to Lizzie Williams 8-31-1867 (no return) F B
Sherrod, Felix G. to Lou Jane Davis 5-4-1868 (5-18-1868) Ma
Sherrod, G. F. to C. H. Sayers 7-2-1868 (7-8-1868) F
Sherrod, George to virginia Sawyers 2-28-1866 (3-1-1866) F
Sherrod, H. R. to Lilie C. Sayers 4-5-1869 (4-15-1869) F
Sherrod, Irvin R. to Catharine Bond 1-7-1862 Hy
Sherrod, Jno. G. to Nia Sherrod 12-26-1865 (12--29-1865) T
Sherrod, John J. to Lucinda C. Smith 5-13-1857 T
Sherrod, Joshua to Elizabeth Morgan 12-24-1866 (12-29-1866) T
Sherrod, Lumon to Emily Clements 1-5-1867 (1-6-1867) T
Sherrod, Nathaniel to Hanah Hanes 4-5-1828 G
Sherrod, Richard to Sarah Jane Taylor 6-9-1856 Ma
Sherrod, Soloman to Florence Bond 12-25-1866 T
Sherrod, Vernas? to Susan McCall 12-29-1866 T
Sherron, Aaron to Elizabeth Hailey 12-3-1838 (12-4-1838) G
Sherron, B. J. to Amanda Cox 1-7-1859 Hr
Sherron, G. W. to Sarah Becca Harrison 11-4-1859 Hr
Sherron, Joseph to Mary J. Hicks 9-25-1855 Cr
Sherron, Nathaniel K. to Elizabeth Wilson 2-13-1844 G
Sherron, Perry to Fannie Taylor 6-9-1878 Hy
Shert, Berd to Sarah Guinn 3-17-1860 (3-22-1860) O
Sherwin, Christopher to Lizzie Solomon 5-11-1861 (5-12-1861) Sh
Sherwood, John G. to D. A. Shirt (Short?) 9-1-1864 Sh
Sherwood, Leon to Martha Wilson 3-17-1862 Sh
Sherwood, M. to Mollie Peery 6-12-1869 (6-13-1869) Dy
Sherwood, William to Permelia Rumley 12-14-1871 (5-23-1871?) Cr
Sheton, John A. to Scelia A. Williams 4-22-1865 (no return) Dy
Shevlin, Daniel to Ann Burns 10-5-1861 (10-8-1861) Sh
Shew, Jacob to Fannie C. Thompson 7-27-1870 (7-28-1870) Ma
Shields, Harvey to Mollie Rogers 10-16-1870 Hy
Shields, Henry to Sophia Taylor 4-3-1872 Hy
Shields, Winny to Martha Crawford (Carthel?) 10-20-1867 G B
Shields, Wm. to Phebi Subtle 3-4-1846 (no return) We
Shiers, Charles to Mary Dillon 6-9-1858 Sh
Shifley, D. to Christina Beger 10-3-1859 Sh
Shifley, M. to Louisa Baker 5-25-1860 Sh
Shikle, A. L. to H. R. Curtis 10-3-1870 (12-5-1870) Dy
Shikle, Martin to Elizabeth Horten 4-24-1844 (no return) We
Shilcut, Isac to Bettie Sutton 1-31-1878 Hy
Shilcut?, James to Nancy Eveline Ross 12-22-1864 (no return) Hn
Shilicutt, E. C. to Charlotte Jones 12-21-1846 O
Shilling, D. N. to N. J. Shepherd 6-19-1840 Be
Shilling, J. to Feede Zimmerman 10-5-1864 Sh
Shilling, M. to V. Gisel 9-6-1855 Sh
Shilling, William A. to Sarah Rutherford 3-2-1836 (3-10-1836) Hr
Shillings, W. J. to M. S. Baugh 7-31-1866 F
Shillman, D. H. to Mollie McGowen 12-13-1871 (12-14-1871) O
Shinault, A. J. to Amanda Campbell 8-29-1850 F
Shinault, Isaac to Lucindia Ragan 12-14-1833 (12-17-1833) Hr
Shinault, Isaac to Nancy Brumley 2-2-1843 F
Shinault, Isaac to Octavia Morris 12-18-1860 (12-19-1860) Hr
Shinault, John J. to Mary M. Puckett 9-19-1861 (9-21-1861) Hr
Shinault, John W. to Caroline Pullum 1-13-1840 (1-14-1840) Hr
Shinault, John W. to Martha Cook 3-7-1856 (3-9-1856) Hr
Shinault, Walter M. to Nancy Harriss 2-26-1853 (3-2-1853) Hr
Shinault, Walter to Mary Woods 6-19-1849 (6-27-1849) Hr
Shinault, Walter to N. C. Frasier 12-6-1866 (12-2-1866) F
Shinley, Thos. to Mary Burke 4-30-1851 (5-1-1851) Sh
Shinpeck, William to Martha Carroll 12-23-1826 Hr
Ship(p), William to Minerva Williams 1-5-1832 Sh
Ship, W. L. to N. J. Arbuckle 8-4-1859 (8-10-1859) F
Ship, William to Sarah ANn Blake 5-15-1843 (no return) Hn
Shipes, Edwin P. to Sinay McCombs 9-4-1854 (9-5-1854) Ma
Shipley, Elijah to Trianna Berton 11-27-1851 Hn
Shipley, John T. to Fanny L. Ellizer 6-2-1870 (7-25-1870) F B
Shipley, Joseph to M. J. Burton 3-23-1856 Hn
Shipley, Joseph to Tabitha Ann Burton 1-19-1862 Hn
Shipley, Russell to Frances Clayton 5-21-1846 (no return) Hn
Shipman, C. P. to Minerva P. Bulter 5-26-1858 G
Shipman, Elijah D. to Mary T. Reevze 1-11-1865 (6-1-2-1865) O
Shipman, Henry A. to Clarissa Simmons 1-2-1861 G

Shipman, Jacob S. to Martha Benson 12-13-1842 G
Shipman, Jacob S. to Susan A. Darnell 9-9-1851 G
Shipman, Jacob to Elizabeth Fuller 10-29-1834 Sh
Shipman, Samuel to Betsy Pully 11-21-1828 (11-23-1828) Hr
Shipman, William to Sarah Brown 12-23-1846 Hn
Shipp, J. W. to B. S. Crenshaw 4-30-1855 (no return) F
Shipp, Tiller to Amanda Hutchinson 12-4-1852 (12-9-1852) O
Shipps, Cyrus C. to Pauline A. Newbern 12-13-1858 (12-14-1858) Ma
Shires, Squire to Emma Quamby 4-18-1859 Sh
Shirley, Benjamin J. to Martha Boman 11-29-1855 Ma
Shirley, Edmond to Nancy Goings 5-2-1878 Dy
Shirley, G. H. to Annie Saunders 1-22-1861 (1-29-1861) Sh
Shirley, John A. to Frances A. Dale 12-29-1862 Hn
Shirley, Solomon to Lue Graves 7-9-1868 Hy
Shiron, N. K. to Sarah Williams 10-10-1863 (10-11-1863) O
Shivers, J. B. F. to Nancy E. Brily 12-27-1852 (12-28-1852) Sh
Shivers, J. B. to R. A. Shivers 3-23-1875 O
Shivers, James to Mary Malina Garrison 3-27-1843 Ma
Shivers, Jesse to P. C. Shivers 10-26-1843 Sh
Shivers, Oliver to Isabella Baird 11-16-1866 (11-25-1866) F B
Shivers, P. to Elizabeth I. Watkins 2-3-1840 (2-6-1840) Ma
Shivers, R. I. P. to A. C. Shivers 9-19-1842 Sh
Shivers, Sam to Emily Williams 12-22-1869 Hy
Shivers, Shadrach to Louisa Redditt 9-24-1844 Sh
Shmid, Henry to Elizabeth Hoffman 1-12-1858 Sh
Shoal, James to Margerett Rial 7-22-1866 Be
Shoate, Isom to Elizabeth Young 9-29-1856 G
Shockley, Harrison to Margaret A. (Mrs.) McGeer 5-14-1864 (5-15-1864) Sh
Shoefer, Arma to Sally Henson 2-17-1830 (2-18-1830) Hr
Shoemake, Elisha P. to America E. Langley 12-5-1862 We
Shoemake, G. N. to Ella Green Stewart 7-2-1881 (7-3-1881) L
Shoemake, J. A. to Margaret Griggsw 2-22-1872 L
Shoemake, J. W. to E. A. Moore 5-24-1876 (5-25-1876) L
Shoemake, James to Julia Randolph 10-11-1860 L
Shoemake, James to Lucretia Griggs 1-30-1861 (no return) L
Shoemake, L. to Mary J. Moore 7-14-1849 L
Shoemake, M. to Amanda E. Tucker 6-13-1850 (6-23-1850) L
Shoemake, Robert F. to Sarah E. Elmore 10-15-1884 L
Shoemake, W. F. to Lucey McCarve 5-9-1874 L
Shoemaker, James A. to Nancy N. Hipp 9-5-1871 (9-6-1871) L
Shoemaker, James W. to Eleanor A. Hines 5-30-1848 (5-31-1848) L
Shoemaker, Linsey to Mary Jane Moore 7-24-1820 Sh
Shoemaker, William to Earry? Basford 10-30-1839 Ma
Shoemate, J. D. to Sallie N. Trail 6-21-1871 Hy
Shoemate, James to C. J. Robinson 12-3-1864 Hy
Shoer, Henery to Catherine Wallace 10-7-1862 Sh
Shofer, Calvin to Mary M. Mitchell 2-6-1854 (2-10-1854) Hr
Shofer, Frederick to Delila Weaver 11-4-1825 (11-6-1825) Hr
Shofer, John to Nancy t. Clines 8-16-1859 (8-17-1859) Hy
Shoffner, Isaac to Deliar A. Rust 9-5-1871 (9-6-1871) Cr B
Shoffner, Robert D. to E. T. Spellings 9-20-1869 (9-23-1869) Cr
Shofner, Cain to Dosha Shofner 10-9-1869 (10-10-1869) Cr
Shofner, D. J. to Jane Shofner 5-15-1861 Cr
Shofner, Daniel to Emily E. Read 8-4-1845 Cr
Shofner, R. D. to Mary E. Alger 4-4-1848 Cr
Shofner, Redden D. to Amanda May 12-6-1838 Cr
Shofner, W. P. to F. A. Hamilton 3-18-1873 (3-23-1873) Dy
Shole, Franklin to Elizabeth H. Carter 4-5-1848 Cr
Shoot, Young to Mary A. Townson 3-3-1847 Cr
Shore (Thore), Caswell to Elizabeth Snow 4-17-1837 O
Shore, Calvin to Eliza A. Cummings 10-17-1861 O
Shore, Caswell to Mahala Good 8-15-1845 (8-28-1845) O
Shore, Joseph F.(T?) to L. A. V. Hathaway 2-21-1855 Sh
Shore, Robert B. to Sarah E. Mooring 10-25-1848 Sh
Shore, Robt. B. to Olivia G. (Mrs.) Lynch 8-11-1853 Sh
Shore, T. B. to Lucy C. Callis 11-29-1865 O
Shore, Thos. W. to Sarah Jane Tharp 3-12-1842 (3-15-1842) F
Shores, John I. to Mary M. Guy 12-10-1867 O
Shores, John to Mary M. Guy 12-11-1867 O
Shores, Samuel W. to Manerva McGowen 11-24-1842 Sh
Shores, Wyly to Elizabeth Snider 3-26-1845 Be
Shorkey, James W. to Ellen E. Farrell 4-30-1863 Sh
Short, A. A. to F. A. Creswell 3-19-1861 G
Short, Alfred H. to Nancy C. Asberry 3-13-1864 (3-27-1864) O
Short, Alonzo to Ellen Williams 12-10-1874 Hy
Short, Anderson to Harriet Mason 9-15-1871 Hy
Short, Ansil A. to Susan Short 5-24-1849 Be
Short, B. F. to Jarette Patterson 11-12-1862 G
Short, Beal to Mary Turner 1-30-1872 Hy
Short, Ben to Catty Miller 10-13-1866 Hy
Short, Burrel to Martha Williams 10-3-1848 Be
Short, Byrd to Catharine Ro(w)land 6-23-1854 O
Short, C. C. to Anneta J. Blair 11-5-1845 Cr
Short, C. to Mary Allen 6-29-1863 Sh
Short, David A. to Mary A. Hill 6-16-1873 Hy
Short, Elijah to Mary Ann King 3-11-1843 (3-7?-1843) Hr
Short, G. L. to Martha A. Pope 10-8-1857 G

Short, H. M. to Francis Taylor 11-14-1860 (11-4-1861) We
Short, Hiram C. to Mary H. Gambell 6-26-1847 (6-29-1847) Hr
Short, Howell to Catharine Miller 10-24-1842 Ma
Short, Isaac to Martha Moore 1-28-1840 Cr
Short, Jack to Bettie Miller 12-30-1869 Hy
Short, Jacob H. to Cela Long 5-8-1849 Hr
Short, James H. to Elizabeth Hollyman 12-14-1847 (12-25-1847) Ma
Short, James H. to Syntha Pinkston 7-23-1851 Be
Short, John L. to Martha Knowls 11-7-1867 Be
Short, Joseph to Oliva Jones 11-13-1834 Hr
Short, Joseph to Sarah Jeter 12-27-1877 Hy
Short, Lewis to Lucy Ann Newsom 1-18-1877 Hy
Short, R. L. to Adaline Wilkison 10-15-1849 (11-25-1849) Hr
Short, Rush to Isen Vaulx 9-6-1876 Hy
Short, Thomas F. to Sarah F. Taylaor 11-2-1853 Hr
Short, Thomas S. to Mary A. Gorden 12-10-1857 Be
Short, William Riley to T. J. D. Wilson 10-5-1868 G
Shorter, Levi T. to Flora Webster 3-31-1868 (no return) Dy
Shorter, Robert to Felicia Neely 5-18-1854 Hn
Shott, Charles to Mary Kennady 5-5-1851 (5-8-1851) Hr
Shott, Hugh to Louisa McBride 2-1-1843 (2-3-1843) Hr
Shotwell, A. to Nancy Dees 10-22-1843 Hn
Shotwell, William to Rebecca Atkins 2-7-1839 Hn
Shoulders, T.(F?) S. to Amanda Bass 8-27-1863 (8-31-1863) Sh
Shoults?, Jacob to Nancy Ann Osburn 3-2-1858 Hn
Shover, Rankin to Nancey Dark 7-22-1876 (7-23-1876) L
Showin, G. W. to M. R. (Mrs.) Childress 1-22-1877 (1-25-1877) L
Shren, Herrill to Ann Besheers 5-13-1846 Sh
Shroat, John T. to Elizabeth M. Bailey 9-26-1858 Hn
Shroder (Schoder), George S. to Caroline Jaque 6-20-1853 Sh
Shropshire, W. F. to Mary L. Faulk 9-14-1865 O
Shroyer, J. R. to Mattie P. Franklin 10-23-1863 (10-25-1863) Sh
Shryack, E. A. to Lou A. Alderson 3-2-1859 (3-8-1859) F
Shuck, Francis M. to Ellen W. Baldrlidge 8-3-1877 O
Shuffey, Edward to Priscilla Cornton 12-26-1867 L B
Shuffield, John to Anne Diffy 10-10-1842 F
Shuffield, Washington D. to Ruth A. Duncan 7-31-1850 (8-1-1850) Ma
Shuffy, Ed to Jose Williams 2-9-1877 Hy
Shuford, W. S. to Ellen Grider 2-15-1851 (2-19-1851) F
Shukle, Samul to Mary Mitchell 10-11-1854 We
Shull, R. M. to R. J. Hill 4-24-1863 Mn
Shults, L. M. to Mary A. E. Cloar 11-19-1867 O
Shultz, John to Elizabeth Brown 12-29-1843 We
Shultz, Joseph H. to Eliza Duff 1-30-1833 (1-31-1833) Hr
Shurley(Shirley), James to Elizabeth Fifer(Phifer) 11-26-1865 Be
Shurley, Edward to Mariah Musgrave 12-28-1872 Dy
Shutts, D. W. to Kizziah ____ 2-21-1866 O
Siddall, Plumpton to Honora Crimmin 5-21-1859 Sh
Siddle, J. N. to Sarah A. Osburn 3-27-1853 (no return) Hn
Siddle, John to E. Steel 12-29-1840 (12-31-1840) F
Sidebottom, A. W. to Julia Ann McCormick 11-13-1867 (no return) Hn
Sidle, Joseph to Mary J. Houston 5-9-1848 Sh
Sidney, Henry to Anna Green 11-15-1879 (11-16-1879) L B
Sidney, Sam N. to Laura A. Burton 12-4-1876 (12-14-1876) Dy
Siebenman, Edward to Elizabeth Schwartz 1-14-1851 Sh
Siegal, Andrew to Louisa (Mrs.) Johns 1-30-1852 (2-3-1852) Sh
Sievert, Henrich to Louise Teimans 11-14-1864 Sh
Sigler, James J. to Sarah S. Bolton 6-22-1842 Sh
Sigler, William A. to Martha M. Carrell 9-1-1853 Sh
Sigman, W. F. to Mary E. Kimbrough 2-14-1838 Sh
Sigmon, Joel B. to Barbary R. Martin 8-2-1847 G
Signaigo, J. A. to Theresa Airolo 8-5-1858 (8-8-1858) Sh
Signiago, J. A. to Ione S. Brown 10-23-1863 (10-25-1863) Sh
Sigrest, Chas. M. to Mary Sullivan 11-21-1859 Sh
Sikes, Alex to Eliza Shirley 5-29-1869 Hy
Sikes, Dick to Maria Golden 1-30-1869 G B
Sikes, Joseph to Nancy Ross 3-3-1849 F
Sikes, M. R. to Mary Jones 3-19-1855 Sh
Sile, John W. to Mary Jane Wit 10-14-1843 (10-19-1843) G
Siler, John M. to Ann M. Hooks 2-2-1848 T
Siler, John to Mary Johnson 6-18-1830 Ma
Siler, Peter P. to H. F. Joyner 6-27-1853 Hr
Silk, John to Eliza Heiney 1-7-1861 Sh
Silliman, Michael to Bridget Deware 2-27-1859 Sh
Sills, Henry E. to Eliza Revel 12-17-1855 Sh
Sills, Isham to Milly Harris 3-1-1833 Hr
Sills, William T. to Nancy J. Taylor 8-16-1856 (8-17-1856) Hr
Silsby, Louis H. to Harriet Liller Kent 4-28-1860 (4-29-1860) Dy
Silver, Charles to Abbie Griffin 12-27-1856 (12-28-1856) Sh
Silver, Larry to Ellen Brady 4-9-1861 Sh
Silvers, John S. to Martha J. Lewellen 5-11-1858 T
Silverthorn, I. G. to Sarah F. Morgan 6-29-1863 (6-30-1863) O
Silvertooth, Jacob to Callie H. McFadden 2-14-1871 T
Silvertooth, John to Elizabeth Williams 11-14-1850 L
Silvertooth, T. E. to R. F. Byram 6-6-1881 (6-8-1881) L
Simerson, J. H. S. to N. J. Hall 12-30-1853 Sh
Simerson, John to Delilia Haskeah? 7-1-1841 F

Simes, B. F. to Elizabeth J. Williamson 5-31-1855 We
Simins, W. M. to L. F. Buchanan 5-6-1855 We
Simison, John H. to Susan Ann Watson 11-9-1847 F
Simmerson, J. H. S. to Nancy J. Hall 12-21-1853 (no return) F
Simmonds, Abram to Caroline Swor 11-2-1865 Hn
Simmonds, B. B. to Mary Massey 11-9-1863 (11-10-1863) Cr
Simmonds, James to Clara Abbott 5-7-1870 (5-8-1870) Cr
Simmons, Albert to Letty Stewart 12-24-1873 (12-25-1873) Dy
Simmons, Albert to Susan Wood 8-5-1841 O
Simmons, Allen H. to Charlotte Smart 3-1-1858 We
Simmons, Almarine to Fannie E. Franklin 11-12-1867 (11-14-1867) Ma
Simmons, Archeball to Mary Phillips 8-24-1842 Cr
Simmons, Athlin (Arthur) to Martha Gregory 2-12-1840 Sh
Simmons, Augustus A. to Mary N. Elliott 11-25-1846 (11-26-1846) F
Simmons, Augustus B. to Elizabeth Temple Allen 3-13-1866 (3-18-1866) Ma
Simmons, B. S. to Frances C. Jones 12-13-1856 (no return) Hn
Simmons, Bartlett to Tabitha Redden 1-12-1844 Hn
Simmons, Beng. to Jane Menzies 1-21-1869 Dy
Simmons, Benj. K. to Sarah A. Dennis 2-17-1868 (2-18-1868) T
Simmons, Benjamin A. to Martha O. Harriss 1-21-1861 (1-24-1861) Hr
Simmons, Berry to Melvina Foust 4-8-1875 Dy
Simmons, Carroll C. to Nancy J. Urbey 11-1-1860 (no return) We
Simmons, Caswell to Cynthia E. Barker 1-29-1859 Hn
Simmons, Charles L. to Margaret A. Roach 2-15-1844 Sh
Simmons, D. M. to Sasander Anderson 5-16?-1853 Hn
Simmons, Dan to Isabella Smith 3-17-1875 (3-18-1875) Dy
Simmons, Dave to Allice Luckey 11-10-1867 G B
Simmons, David to Elizabeth C. Nelson 10-3-1869 G
Simmons, David to Frances Simmons 10-12-1850 Cr
Simmons, E. N. to Elizabeth A. Nail 1-6-1840 Ma
Simmons, E. Z. to Maggie D. McClamick 11-23-1870 T
Simmons, Ed to Rebecca Asper 8-9-1873 (no return) Dy
Simmons, F. H. to Elizabeth Hill 1-31-1864 Mn
Simmons, F. S. to Jane Lawrence 3-17-1863 Hn
Simmons, Franklin to Lucinda Howell 9-25-1853 Hn
Simmons, Franklin to Mary A. Israel 7-22-1862 We
Simmons, G. W. to Martha Ann Prince 1-17-1864 Be
Simmons, G. W. to Martha Nutt 12-21-1854 Cr
Simmons, G. W. to Mary Sanford 10-26-1865 O
Simmons, Garrett W. to Mary A. Johnson 10-27-1848 (10-29-1848) F
Simmons, H. A. to Susan A. Williams 4-11-1860 Hn
Simmons, Harmon to Martha Potts 1-29-1844 Hn
Simmons, Harrison to Mary Francis Rainey 1-15-1868 Ma
Simmons, Henry P. to Mary C. Pinkston 4-13-1853 Cr
Simmons, J. P. to Sarah J. Craig 8-24-1854 (no return) F
Simmons, J. R. to S. E. Kirksey 10-6-1885 (10-7-1885) L
Simmons, J. to Rosea A. Franklin 5-17-1871 O
Simmons, James to Amanda Puckett 2-8-1855 O
Simmons, James to Emerline Morrison 11-28-1868 (11-30-1868) T
Simmons, James to Martha Massey 11-5-1846 Cr
Simmons, Jas. T. to Martha Thompson 10-7-1851 (no return) F
Simmons, John C. to Rebecca L. Garland 10-21-1867 (10-22-1867) Ma
Simmons, John D. to Mary J. Davis 10-12-1862 Mn
Simmons, John H. to Olivia F. Harriss 1-13-1858 Hr
Simmons, John P. to Martha E. Lock 9-30-1848 Ma
Simmons, John to Folly Ann Bragden 8-24-1864 (no return) Cr
Simmons, John to Matilda Fowler 2-28-1843 (3-1-1843) F
Simmons, John to Matilda Newhouse 2-4-1858 (2-7-1858) O
Simmons, John to Rebecca Johnson 4-30-1866 (5-2-1866) O
Simmons, John to Rosanah Staten 4-6-1856 Hn
Simmons, John P. Compton 11-13-1849 Cr
Simmons, John to Zerilda A. Jordan 1-18-1854 Sh
Simmons, L. W. to Sarah E. Drewry? 7-22-1863 We
Simmons, Lemuel D. to Amy Bacon 9-17-1842 Ma
Simmons, Levi C. to Frances Cole 1-21-1857 (1-23-1857) O
Simmons, Lucius C. to Florence Bradford 2-25-1860 (2-27-1860) L
Simmons, M. A. to Elizabeth T. Reid 1-1-1851 Sh
Simmons, Martin to Elizabeth Myers 9-16-1854 O
Simmons, Martin to Sarah S. Reeves 12-6-1861 (12-19-1861) O
Simmons, Peter to Ann Elizabeth Chester 9-7-1857 (9-10-1857) Ma
Simmons, Pleasant H. to Emely K. Dickens 3-5-1849 (3-7-1849) G
Simmons, R. G. to S. A. Chrisman 2-19-1868 G
Simmons, Richd. to Elizabeth Pate 12-11-1870 (12-15-1870) Cr B
Simmons, Rowe B. to Tannie Rice 2-5-1867 Hn
Simmons, S. A. to Fannie E. Tally 7-21-1870 (7-24-1870) Ma
Simmons, S. F. to A. E. Lawrence 12-1-1869 G
Simmons, Samuel D. to Jennie O. Howell 3-16-1858 (3-?-1858) Hr
Simmons, Samuel J. to Sophronia Green 9-9-1858 Cr
Simmons, Samuel to Martha Pope 9-7-1878 (9-17-1878) Dy
Simmons, T. J. to M. E. Lycen 8-31-1854 T
Simmons, T. M. to M. A. Cooper 6-20-1854 Be
Simmons, T. P. to Meed Ford 2-4-1865 Be
Simmons, Thomas A. to Margaret J. Hart 12-21-1848 Ma
Simmons, Thomas A. to Martha M. Gibbs 12-23-1858 Sh
Simmons, Tom to Polly Bragg 12-26-1868 (1-1-1869) T
Simmons, W. B. to Almeter Thompson 1-20-1852 (no return) F
Simmons, W. D. to Mary A. Mitchel 2-26-1858 Be

Simmons, W. D. to Rebecca Higgs 6-30-1846 Hr
Simmons, W. H. to Dicey Ridens 6-17-1869 Dy
Simmons, W. H. to M. C. Hinshaw 2-24-1860 Sh
Simmons, W. J. to Margaret A. Wilmoth 12-23-1855 We
Simmons, W. J. to Mary W. Miller 2-25-1854 (no return) F
Simmons, W. R. to S.(L.?) C. Pennington 12-18-1867 G
Simmons, W. S. to Mary Lowery 12-12-1866 Hy
Simmons, W. S. to Savannah Hastings 8-30-1879 (9-1-1879) Dy
Simmons, W. W. to Arabella C. Walker 10-23-1861 (no return) Dy
Simmons, W. W. to H. O. Bond 3-16-1860 Sh
Simmons, Washington to Jennie Banks 2-15-1867 G B
Simmons, Wesley to Manervy Pryer 1-11-1870 (1-12-1870) F B
Simmons, Westley to Hariet Upchurch 10-20-1858 Hn
Simmons, William C. to Mary Adaline Willett 11-23-1841 Hn
Simmons, William J. to Margaret E. Wilon 9-24-1861 (9-25-1861) O
Simmons, William to Elizabeth Lumbrick 8-20-1861 Hn
Simmons, William to Lucinda Norman 5-2-1861 (5-12-1861) L
Simmons, William to Martha Ann Smith 12-10-1839 Ma
Simmons, William to Sarah E. Martin 9-17-1856 Hn
Simmons, Willoby D. to Ann Hervey 3-29-1843 Hr
Simmons, Wm. to Elizabeth Prewitt 12-23-1852 T
Simmons?, Flournoy T. to Mary E. Williamson 12-12-1866 (12-13-1866) Dy
Simmonton, Charles B. to Mary A. McDill 10-15-1866 (10-16-1866) T
Simms, B. D. to T. A. Trout 2-1-1865 G
Simms, John C. to Matilda Montgomery 1-4-1841 G
Simms, William H. to Sarah A. McCracken 8-10-1847 (8-11-1847) G
Simon, J. W. to Mary Feibelman 5-21-1864 (5-24-1864) Sh
Simons, David C. to M. J. Sexton 3-5-1857 G
Simons, David C. to Mary E. Rogers 5-9-1868 (5-10-1868) Dy
Simons, David to Mary Crockett 5-24-1842 G
Simons, E. T. to Emma A. McNeil 6-6-1878 Hy
Simons, Henry J. to Margaret W. Bradley 2-5-1842 (2-23-1842) G
Simons, John B. to Mary Jane Duncan 3-5-1849 (3-6-1849) G
Simons, M. B. to Laura Miller 6-28-1862 Mn
Simons, P. S. to S. A. Robertson 3-21-1859 Sh
Simons, Samuel Darby to Nancy Emaline Harrison 7-22-1845 (7-?-1845) T
Simons, Thos. to Letitia Burnett 1-1-1867 (1-3-1867) Dy
Simons, W. B. to Lucy Forbes 4-27-1872 (4-28-1872) Dy
Simonton, Alex to Hanna Ellis 10-7-1873 (10-9-1873) T
Simonton, C. J. to N. E. Thompson 7-24-1865 (7-25-1865) T
Simonton, Christopher A. to Margaret C. Thompson 2-5-1848 (2-10-1848) T
Simonton, Christopher to artha Baird 8-31-1853 T
Simonton, Henry to Nancy McQuiston 7-3-1871 (7-4-1871) T
Simonton, John to Martha A. Miller 5-18-1847 (5-21-1847) T
Simonton, R. C. to Martha E. Wilson 9-5-1859 T
Simonton, R. R. to Mary Huffman 2-8-1870 T
Simonton, Robert to Margaret McQuiston 9-4-1855 T
Simonton, William B. to Eliza A. Miller 12-18-1866 (12-19-1866) T
Simonton?, Archibald M. to Lotty Strong 2-19-1842 (3-3-1842) T
Simpkins, B. R. to Harriet Guinn 10-2-1863 (10-5-1863) L
Simpkins, Thos. J. to Elvira Hanlin (Harlin?) 1-20-1851 (1-23-1851) Sh
Simpkins, W. D. to C. T. Chapman 2-6-1866 (2-8-1866) F
Simpson, A. S. to M. E. McMahon 10-1-1881 (10-5-1881) L
Simpson, Asher to S. C. Dollar 1-3-1871 Cr
Simpson, Christopher G. to Rebecca E. Crockett 11-29-1843 (11-30-1843) O
Simpson, Frederick to Caroline Rakob 1-23-1855 Sh
Simpson, G. B. to Malvira Grantham 9-7-1835 Hr
Simpson, G. W. to Susan Jenkins 11-29-1876 Dy
Simpson, George A. to Sallie R. Pierce 10-16-1861 Hn
Simpson, George W. to M. A. Mathews 7-29-1869 Hy
Simpson, George W. to Mary Nail 4-8-1847 (4-9-1847) G
Simpson, George to Mary Ann Dalton 1-9-1854 (1-12-1854) T
Simpson, H. N. to R. J. Davis 4-4-1871 Hy
Simpson, Harmon to Margarett Trayner 1-8-1833 (1-9-1833) G
Simpson, Harrison to L. E. F. Belew 10-24-1847 G
Simpson, Harrison to Wilmoth C. Philps 12-11-1860 Cr
Simpson, Henry N. to Nancy Jane Holderfield 7-28-1868 Ma
Simpson, Isaiah to Nelly Winscott 1-29-1866 Hn
Simpson, J. E. to R. A. Umsted 4-22-1868 G
Simpson, J. R. to G. A. Pasteur 2-19-1866 (2-20-1866) Cr
Simpson, J. S. to Mary Reece 5-15-1872 O
Simpson, James A. to Elizabeth Rowe 2-28-1854 Hn
Simpson, Jas. G. to Harriet C. Wooldridge 3-6-1861 (3-7-1861) Sh
Simpson, Jesse to Martha Ann Simpson 7-31-1872 (8-1-1872) T
Simpson, John Madison to Martha Combs 11-22-1853 (11-24-1853) Ma
Simpson, John P. to Sanai Needham 6-15-1831 Ma
Simpson, John T. to Lucy Morris 9-19-1839 Sh
Simpson, John T.(F?) to Jane Wilson 11-21-1837 Sh
Simpson, John W. to Charity Luker 7-31-1856 O
Simpson, John to J. E. Phillip 12-15-1851 Cr
Simpson, John to Matilda Topp 6-1-1867 (6-10-1867) Dy
Simpson, Levi T. to Sarah E. Atkins 3-26-1856 We
Simpson, Lowranza D. to Louisa F.? Thompson 9-14-1840 (no return) Hn
Simpson, M. A. to Sarah E. Fullerton 5-12-1877 (5-24-6-1877) Dy
Simpson, Moses to Mary Flanagan 10-11-1825 O
Simpson, Nathaniel to Elizabeth Greer 1-1-1866 Hy
Simpson, Nathaniel to Elizabeth Greer 1-3?-1866 Hy

Simpson, Needham K. to _____ _____ 12-20-1853 Hr
Simpson, Robert to Winny Roark 3-5-1849 Cr
Simpson, Samuel to Harriet Mitchell 12-11-1838 (12-12-1838) Hr
Simpson, Samuel to Rebecca McKaughn 2-1-1833 Hr
Simpson, T. F. to Lucy J. Howard 10-13-1873 (10-14-1873) Dy
Simpson, T. F. to M. J. Singleterry 9-16-1868 (9-26-1868) Dy
Simpson, T. J. to E. R. Graham 3-4-1864 Mn
Simpson, Thomas J. to Martha (Emily) Tatum (Graham) 9-22-1861 Mn
Simpson, Thomas R. F. to Evelina W. Cash 1-6-1842 F
Simpson, W. B. to Julia A. Kernodle 8-11-1861 Mn
Simpson, W. B. to Mary B. Wateredge 5-15-1878 Hy
Simpson, W. E. to Harret Walker 8-17-1875 (8-19-1875) O
Simpson, W. F. to R. E. Revel 11-8-1866 (11-9-1866) Cr
Simpson, W. H. to Jennie Chamblin 8-14-1867 (no return) Dy
Simpson, W. K. to Mary A. Henry 12-29-1869 (12-30-1869) Dy
Simpson, W. R. to A. F. (Mrs.) Murphey 11-30-1872 (11-3?-1872) Dy
Simpson, W. R. to Tempe J. Williamson 12-16-1874 Dy
Simpson, William (Willis) C. to Eliza J. Walker 4-8-1848 (4-9-1848) O
Simpson, William A. to Martha Jane McFadden 11-1-1849 Hn
Simpson, William P. to Mary Ann White 12-11-1858 (12-13-1858) T
Simpson, William to Ann Christian 2-24-1869 Be
Simpson, William to Henrietta Sellers 1-29-1861 Cr
Simpson, William to Mariah Ingram 12-12-1831 Hr
Simpson, William to Nancy A. Atkins 3-30-1856 We
Simpson, William to Nancy C. Brothers 3-16-1835 Sh
Simpson, Wm. H. to Alzira Gaines 10-7-1848 Sh
Simpson, Wm. to Frances Harper 8-15-1844 (8-20?-1844) Hr
Sims, Berry to Mariah Turner 1-31-1872 (no return) L
Sims, C. C. to Susan Tyler 7-23-1861 G
Sims, Charles to Lucinda Reeves 12-5-1868 G B
Sims, Charlie to Matilda Titus 9-14-1881 (9-15-1881) L B
Sims, Don Fernando to Mary Fleedwood? 6-22-1836 Sh
Sims, Edward to Ardell Maclin 10-12-1874 (no return) L
Sims, G. S. to K. J. (Mrs.) Tucker 11-22-1860 (11-25-1860) Sh
Sims, G. S. to Virginia A. Haynes 8-4-1852 Sh
Sims, G. W. to E. P. Wilson 1-16-1856 (1-17-1856) G
Sims, G. W. to Elizabeth Sims 6-29-1856 We
Sims, George to Manda Johnson 7-4-1869 Hy
Sims, Henry to Ailsey McCollum 8-26-1868 G B
Sims, J. C. to Mary Jane Wilson 1-31-1865 (no return) Dy
Sims, J. L. to M. A. Tucker 12-25-1869 G
Sims, J. L. to Sarah E. Hodge 10-1-1842 Sh
Sims, Jack to Lucentia Sadbury 2-10-1868 G
Sims, James A. to Mary Fellow 11-25-1840 Sh
Sims, Josephus to Rachel J. Hopper 12-28-1852 (12-29-1852) Ma
Sims, M. L. to Maaria L. Gift 6-3-1846 Sh
Sims, R. A. to Elizabeth C. Tilley 3-4-1855 We
Sims, R. H. to M. C. Pearce 1-2-1859 We
Sims, Robert W. to Nancy Mitchell 8-1-1853 (8-3-1853) Ma
Sims, Robert W. to Sarah K. King 10-10-1862 (10-23-1862) Ma
Sims, Thomas N. to Jane Reasons 8-31-1857 G
Sims, W. H. to Martha T. Tucker 5-19-1864 G
Sims, W. J. to Rachel E. Hart 10-7-1866 (no return) Hn
Sims, W. V. to P. C. Winston 4-5-1855 We
Simson, Frederick to Hannah Fricke 12-3-1856 (12-4-1856) Sh
Sinclair, Ben to Adaline Avery 9-28-1871 (no return) Dy
Sinclair, Benjamin A. to Sarah J. Gaines 11-13-1849 L
Sinclair, Daniel to Margrett M. Reynolds 3-22-1847 (3-25-1847) Hr
Sinclair, David to Rilla Boothe 10-14-1869 G B
Sinclair, Frank M. to Sadie T. (Mrs.) Sutherland 10-16-1867 L
Sinclair, George to Louella Wynne 2-11-1874 (2-12-1874) Dy
Sinclair, Hezekiah to Narcissa Whitten 12-26-1838 Hn
Sinclair, J. D. to Naomi L. Neal 9-26-1866 (9-27-1866) Dy
Sinclair, James R. to Nancy Noell 2-15-1835 (no return) Hn
Sinclair, John F. to Louisa C. Jelks 10-29-1849 (10-31-1849) Ma
Sinclair, T. H. to Martha Jane Stephenson 7-13-1847 Hr
Sinclair, William to Mary E. Reach 1-10-1859 (1-22-1859) G
Sinclear, John F. to Isabella R. Dunwoody 1-21-1841 G
Sinclear, John F. to Nancy Joyce 9-11-1843 (9-13-1843) G
Sing, W. Jefferson to M. C. Miller 5-3-1864 (5-5-1864) Sh
Singer, Samuel to Mary A. E. Smith 2-3-1859 Ma
Singh?, W. H. to Mary C. Brooks 12-13-1852 Hn
Singler, John C. to Sarah D. Francis 12-24-1870 (12-25-1870) Ma
Singleton, George to Margaret Perry 12-30-1867 (1-1-1867?) L
Singleton, J. D. to A. V. Green 12-12-1871 (12-14-1871) Cr
Singleton, John to Margaret Autry 7-27-1854 Cr
Singleton, Josiah to Ann Trusty 5-19-1853 O
Singleton, Patrick E. to Frances E. Lawrence 5-17-1855 (5-20-1855) G
Singleton, Washington to Margaret Pickard 2-28-1872 (3-9-1872) T
Singleton, William G. to Mary Jane Watson 7-17-1856 O
Singleton, William H. to Jane Norris 2-6-1868 L
Singleton, William to Elizabeth Castelaw 3-3-1856 (3-4-1856) L
Singleton, Wm. J. to Matilda C. Koonce 6-12-1860 Hy
Singly, Franklin to Rozanah Smith 5-12-1859 G
Singner (Lingner?), George to Elizabeth Campbell 1-3-1856 (1-8-1856) Sh
Sink, Jacob H. to Tobitha A. Gaither 12-2-1848 (12-6-1848) T
Sinklar, C. F. to M. A. F. Summers 11-29-1866 (11-29-18??) O

Sinklar, C. F. to M. A. T. Summers 11-29-1866 O
Sinkler, James M. to Cinderella E. S. Toombs 7-25-1856 O
Sipe, James D. to Nancy Bradley 3-11-1862 Cr
Sipes, Alfred to Mary F. Lowry 2-6-1860 Hr
Sipes, George W. to Mary A. Sewell 4-25-1861 Mn
Sipes, J. R. to Lear Mosier 3-30-1864 Mn
Sipes, Samuel R. to Elizabeth A. Lowery 12-15-1859 (12-16-1859) Hr
Sipes, William J. to Susan E. Revely 12-24-1862 (12-25-1862) Ma
Sires, Lazarus to Elizabeth E. Fouch 10-13-1857 (10-14-1857) G
Sisco, Claibourn to Martha A. Keef 2-24-1859 O
Sisco, Claibourn to Rebecca Nelms 10-5-1850 (10-8-1850) O
Sisco, J. C. to Virginia Carter 12-1-1868 (12-2-1868) F
Siscoe, G. H. to Mary Didny? 12-23-1848 (no return) F
Siscoe, John to Catharine H. McGehee 7-5-1842 (no return) F
Sissom, Andrew to Elizabeth Childress 7-5-1846 (7-6-1846) Hr
Sistruck, J. T. to M. E. Given 1-25-1882 (1-29-1882) L
Sistrunk, J. T. to Janey F. Gains 11-26-1877 (12-2-1877) L
Sitton, Isham to Sindey Foster 4-24-1874 T
Skeen, Jackson to Hanah Bowman 2-21-1872 Hy
Skelly, James to Lula Nolen 4-10-1878 (4-11-1878) L
Skelton, N. T. to V. A. Robertson 9-21-1864 Sh
Skelton, T. N. to M. J. Dean 10-13-1870 Hy
Skiles, H. M. to Frances A. Hays 12-21-1869 G
Skiles, Henry H. to Mary J. Wootten 8-30-1856 G
Skiles, Henry H. to Sarah E. Phelan 10-27-1858 (10-28-1858) G
Skiles, Jacob S. to Mary J. Little 11-18-1858 G
Skiles, James M. to Martha Fairless 1-12-1870 G
Skiles, James to Mary Lowrance 5-26-1853 G
Skiles, Juleus A. to Menurva F. Davidson 12-24-1857 G
Skiles, Marshal to Juda Reaves 2-28-1873 Hy
Skiles, Thomas W. to Jane Richardson 12-20-1858 T
Skiles, William G. to Mary W. Brown 9-26-1848 (9-27-1848) G
Skiles, William G. to Melissa Glasgow 6-18-1855 (6-19-1855) G
Skillern, Anderson S. to Temperance Springfield 1-25-1847 Ma
Skillern, Anderson to Margaret McDowell Christian 5-3-1830 Ma
Skillern, Anderson to Mary Ann Buckannon 12-1-1841 Ma
Skillern, James P. to Susan McGown 12-28-1841 Ma
Skillern, John Henry to Sallie J. Alston 11-19-1870 (11-23-1870) Ma
Skinner, Aron T. to Martha A. Markham 5-3-1863 Hn
Skinner, Bernard E. to N. E. Soape 6-13-1845 (no return) F
Skinner, E. P. to Elizabeth Murrell 11-18-1857 (11-19-1857) Hr
Skinner, Edmond to Martha Dance 12-4-1866 G
Skinner, John to Elizabeth Jones 3-10-1825 Hr
Skinner, Martin to Nancy J. Hinson 12-28-1850 (12-31-1850) Hr
Skinner, Martin to Sarah A. Davis 12-23-1859 (12-25-1859) F
Skinner, Polk to Susan Randle 6-16-1870 G B
Skipper, James to Nancy H. Grady 7-2-1863 Dy
Skipper, Jerry to Jane Johnson 12-4-1865 Dy
Skipper, Needham to Sarah Cartwright 3-14-1832 (3-?-1832) Hr
Skipper, Noah to Sarah J. Davis 5-1-1856 G
Skipper, Silas to Sofrona Hoge 5-2-1865 (5-3-1865) Dy
Skipper, Thomas to Martha A. Quinn 4-1-1846 (4-2-1846) G
Skipper, Thomas to Mary Johnson 7-4-1860 Dy
Skipper, William to Sarah Johnson 12-25-1860 Dy
Skipweth, J. C. to H. B. Chitwood 10-30-1867 (no return) Dy
Skipwith, Peyton to Mary J. Collier 3-23-1859 (3-24-1859) Sh
Slack, C. F. to Frances F. Flemming 9-8-1866 T
Slack, Samuel L. to Elizabeth I. Busted 9-6-1838 Sh
Slack, William L. to Sarah A. Johnston 8-21-1843 (8-24-1843) Ma
Slade, Wm. to Elizabeth J. Lane 6-27-1856 Sh
Slagle, A. G. to Josephine Rennalds 10-4-1870 Hy
Slate, Henry A. to Mary R. Harris 1-6-1855 (1-7-1855) Sh
Slate, James to Amanda Hallum 11-24-1858 (11-25-1858) Sh
Slate, John A. to Frances Hamblen 9-10-1838 Hn
Slate, W. R. to Caroline c. Hainie 12-7-1858 (12-9-1858) T
Slate, W. R. to S. A. Elam 11-13-1866 (11-14-1866) T
Slater, A. J. to Penelope Carson 6-17-1857 L
Slater, Charles W. to L. E. Parchman 1-11-1843 (1-12-1843) F
Slater, F. A. to J. E. Johnson 10-17-1874 (10-18-1874) Dy
Slater, Isaac to Mary Nash 2-19-1867 (3-23-1867) Dy
Slater, John W. to Nancy Sullivant 2-24-1845 (no return) F
Slater, Joseph W. to Catherine J. Douglass 4-4-1839 Sh
Slater, Joseph W. to Sarah Ware 10-5-1844 Sh
Slater, L. A. to A. B. Duncan 1-4-1864 (no return) Dy
Slater, T. L. to Lucy A. Johnson 7-10-1868 (no return) L
Slater, T. P. to Martha W. Ross 7-3-1851 (7-15-1851) Sh
Slaton, William to Nancy Nelson 8-8-1859 (8-11-1859) Ma
Slator, Edward C. to Ary C. Cole 11-27-1854 (11-28-1854) Ma *
Slaughter, Alexander to Flora Ann Skinner 11-28-1869 G B
Slaughter, Bill to C. Boston 12-28-1874 T
Slaughter, C. K. to Lutitia Langdon 11-24-1856 Sh
Slaughter, David Cannon to Susan America Ovnall? 7-15-1850 (7-?-1850) T
Slaughter, Dennis to Elvira Kinney 9-23-1851 (9-25-1851) T
Slaughter, G. W. to Frances M. Shelton 10-3-1861 Hn
Slaughter, Gabriel I. to Louisa Person 5-4-1842 Sh
Slaughter, Gabriel J. to Elizabeth Glover Fisher 3-6-1849 T
Slaughter, George M. to Frances Lindsey 10-16-1854 Hn
Slaughter, George W. to Parmelia Watkins 4-7-1844 Hn
Slaughter, James H. to Rebecca J. Edwards 3-31-1841 Hn
Slaughter, John J. to Mary J. Cross 3-8-1866 (3-11-1866) F
Slaughter, Michael to Catherine McAnulty 7-24-1846 Sh
Slaughter, Munrow to Tobitha Ana Mallard 4-21-1841 (4-25-1841) F
Slaughter, Owen to Katurah J. Kelsoe 11-24-1862 (no return) Hn
Slaughter, R. C. to S. A. Grider 12-20-1849 Sh
Slaughter, Sylvester to Lydia Chunn 6-1-1847 Hn
Slaughter, Thomas S. to Sarah Jane Crisp 5-26-1850 Hr
Slaughter, W. C. to Frances A. Sullivan 11-18-1867 (11-19-1867) F
Slaughter, Wiley to Matilda J. Simmons 12-16-1850 (12-23-1850) F
Slaughter, Wilson to Algenie? Ozier 12-21-1839 (12-26-1839) F
Slaughter, Wm. P. to P. E. Green? 5-6-1844 (5-8-1844) Hr
Slaydon, Jas. H. to Kizzy Barker 9-12-1859 (9-13-1859) G
Slaydon, William to Selva Richardson 1-2-1868 G B
Slaydon, Wm. W. to Martha E. Jackson 6-12-1856 G
Slayton, D. H. to Susan E. Hudson 11-17-1863 Hy
Slayton, Willis W. to Jane Harris 11-20-1860 Dy
Sled, John to Minerva Jarrolds 3-4-1855 Hn
Sled, William D. to Mary McLane 12-16-1856 Hn
Sledge, Robert to Sarah Gammons 3-8-1879 (3-9-1879) Dy
Sledge, William to Beckie Gammons 7-15-1879 (7-16-1879) Dy
Sledge, Willis P. to Louisa C. Fisk 12-3-1853 (12-6-1853) Sh
Sledge, Wm. H. to Ann D. McKendree 8-15-1850 (8-20-1850) F
Sleight, William W. to Elizabeth C. Ray 11-16-1862 Hn
Slider?, Edward M. to Sarah Wicker 7-23-1855 (7-26-1855) O
Slig, Charles to Elizabeth Marshall 4-14-1853 Sh
Slippy, Isaac to Catherine Myers 7-23-1850 Sh
Sloan, Alexander to Helan M. Duncan 5-16-1853 (5-18-1853) Hr
Sloan, Calvin C. to Elizabeth Davie 12-8-1869 Hy
Sloan, George F. to Mary Raines 11-21-1860 (11-22-1860) Ma
Sloan, James F. to Rebecca Sweney 12-29-1869 (1-6-1870) Cr
Sloan, James J. to Sarah N. Hill 1-1-1867 G
Sloan, John Bunyan to Nancy E. Matthews 6-25-1869 (6-27-1869) Ma
Sloan, Martin L. to Isabella L. Weakly 3-9-1868 (3-10-1868) Dy
Sloan, Martin L. to Rachael O'Daniel 12-21-1854 G
Sloan, Miles F. to Fidelia E. Mathews 9-10-1866 (9-12-1866) Ma
Sloan, Miles J. to Louisa F. Watt 11-14-1861 (11-17-1861) Ma
Sloan, Robert R. to Frances Sloan 1-5-1836 (1-6-1836) G
Sloan, Rylin B. to Nancy E. Hall 4-4-1867 G
Sloan, Samuel H. to Mary E. McKnight 5-28-1850 G
Sloan, Samuel to Hannah Dance 12-21-1841 Sh
Sloane, James to Darthula Casey 7-18-1848 (no return) F
Sloane, Joseph K. to Lucinda Walter 1-15-1852 (1-19-1852) Sh
Slocum, Ebenezer to Maria Hartwell 1-6-1842 Sh
Slocum, Thomas J. to Luzinda Walker 7-23-1857 (7-27-1857) Ma
Slone, James K. to Betsy Thompson 2-14-1843 Sh
Slone, M. A. to Elizabeth Trobaugh 12-22-1874 (12-23-1874) T
Sloss, W. C. to Catharine Morrison 4-1-1878 (4-4-1878) L
Slough, John to Elizabeth A. Holmes 11-30-1857 (12-3-1857) Sh
Slough, Moses to Mary Ann Milton 12-1-1851 Sh
Slover, J. C. to Martha A. Chapman 3-9-1855 (3-11-1855) Sh
Small, Charles to Margaret Everett 2-7-1850 Sh
Small, Henry D. to Mary Jane Cary 12-31-1845 Sh
Small, Henry to Vicey Lorimore 2-8-1872 T
Small, Joshua to Allace Smith 5-12-1873 T
Small, Peter to Rody Alexander 8-13-1867 T
Smalley, A. to Martha Finny 2-26-1860 Be
Smalley, Anderson to Susan Bone 5-30-1871 (5-31-1871) Dy
Smallwood, A. H. to W. J. Grant 7-10-1864 Mn
Smally, James H. to Sally Bell 7-10-1850 Be
Smally, Wm. H. to Martha Jones 2-20-1850 Be
Smalshwaite, George to Wilhelmina Leonard 7-3-1850 Sh
Smalwood, Jefferson to M. L. Leath 10-27-1861 Mn
Smart, Alf? to Tete Mulherin 7-3-1877 Dy
Smart, J. T. to Mary Young 5-19-1861 We
Smart, James to Julia A. E. Fortson 10-15-1861 Sh
Smart, M. W. to R. P. Warren 7-15-1879 (7-17-1879) Dy
Smart, Stephen to Sarah Ann Jennings 8-14-1843 (no return) We
Smart, W. P. to Aby A. Corgell 8-10-1854 We
Smawley, J. P. to M. E. Barns 8-27-1840 Be
Smeledge, F. M. to Martha S. Legon 9-1-1855 We
Smiddy, Peirce to L. D. McKelly 9-5-1857 (9-6-1857) Sh
Smiler?, John G. to Martha J. Baker 6-12-1859 Cr
Smiley, A. H. to Ann G. Cowan? 5-13-1846 Hn
Smiley, Lawrence to Mary Jane Beard 11-14-1850 Hn
Smily, Jackson to Mary Rumbly 10-20-1866 Hn
Smily, John to Mary M. Brundige 5-25-1854 Hn
Smith (Sith), Wm. to Fannie Mitchell 12-18-1872 Hy
Smith (Smidt), John to Harriet Jaler (Jaben) 11-23-1849 Sh
Smith (Smidtz), Fred to Roser Wetz 3-8-1858 (3-10-1858) Sh
Smith, A. F. to Lucretia E. Williams 7-18-1869 G
Smith, A. F. to M. A. Duckworth 8-7-1867 Hy
Smith, A. G. to Sallie W. Owen 9-27-1870 (9-29-1870) F
Smith, A. H. to S. H. L. Palmer 12-28-1870 Dy
Smith, A. J. to Francisia Davis 12-18-1858 (12-22-1858) Hr
Smith, A. J. to Nancy Lakey 5-23-1848 F

Smith, A. J. to Nancy M. Kirby 10-18-1838 L
Smith, A. M. to R. A. Crockett 7-12-1875 (7-13-1875) O
Smith, A. M. to Susan Leggett 12-15-1868 (no return) Dy
Smith, A. P. to Annie Maurring? 12-1-1869 T
Smith, A. P. to Martha Crihfield 11-18-1876 (11-22-1876) L
Smith, A. to Perlina J. Kelly 10-22-1856 G
Smith, Abe to Bettie Pearson 7-4-1868 (7-10-1868) F B
Smith, Absolom to Mahaly Conlee 12-22-1834 (12-25-1834) G
Smith, Adam to Hannah Mitchell 11-24-1834 Hr
Smith, Albert C. to R. V. C. Miller 12-27-1848 L
Smith, Albert to Fannie Milligan 12-25-1884 (12-30-1885) L
Smith, Albert to Jane Rose 1-18-1869 (1-19-1869) T
Smith, Albert to Leona J. Seward 7-9-1869 G B
Smith, Albert to Mary J. Heath 3-14-1863 (no return) We
Smith, Albert to Susan Jones 11-28-1854 Cr
Smith, Albert to Susan Miller 2-21-1873 (2-22-1873) T
Smith, Aleck to S. Jackson 12-13-1866 (12-16-1866) F
Smith, Alex to Jane Douglass 3-9-1871 Dy
Smith, Alex. to Mary A. Currie 12-29-1869 Hy
Smith, Alexander to Catharine Arbuckle 11-9-1843 G
Smith, Alexander to Hannah Smith 5-10-1852 T
Smith, Alexander to Martha Horton 9-24-1872 (9-25-1872) Dy
Smith, Alford to Cathrine Moran 5-27-1854 (5-28-1854) T
Smith, Alfred to P. A. C. Blackwood 3-27-1853 Hn
Smith, Allen H. to Harriet D. McKee 1-25-1870 (no return) F
Smith, Allen M. C. to Margaret Hickerson 1-6-1828 Sh
Smith, Allen to Piety Watt 7-9-1846 Sh
Smith, Almeron to Catharine Rider 12-9-1864 Sh
Smith, Amon to Isabella Snell 11-17-1852 Sh
Smith, Amos to Kissey L. Tate 3-11-1844 We
Smith, Amphias to Martha L. Jarnagin 12-16-1844 (12-19-1844) Ma
Smith, Anderson to Nancy Woods 1-30-1869 G B
Smith, Andrew J. to Martha Tedder 8-6-1846 Be
Smith, Andrew to Caroline Keller 7-3-1876 (7-4-1876) L
Smith, Andrew to Louisa Winford 4-27-1870 T
Smith, Andrew to Mary Madry 12-26-1867 Dy
Smith, Andrew to Mary Wanger 6-9-1860 (6-11-1860) Sh
Smith, Andrew to Susan A. Sawyers 7-13-1872 (no return) Dy
Smith, Anthony to Dilcey House 11-23-1869 (11-28-1869) F B
Smith, Anthony to Julian Vanburen 3-14-1877 Hy
Smith, Anthony to Wineford Lee 5-25-1835 Hr
Smith, Anton to Susanna Sulzmann 6-7-1859 (6-8-1859) Sh
Smith, Armistead to Mollie Beard 11-11-1880 Dy
Smith, Arther to Martha Warrin 5-7-1838 (5-8-1838) G
Smith, Arthur to Mary Pounds 11-10-1849 O
Smith, Augustus W. to Mary E. Yarbrough 9-29-1845 (10-2-1845) T
Smith, Augustus to Martha Fuller 10-12-1842 L
Smith, Averett to Nancy Jennings 4-11-1846 (4-12-1846) L
Smith, B. C. to Sopha A. Hatch 1-24-1872 (1-25-1872) Cr
Smith, B. F. to A. M. Notgrass 11-24-1875 (11-25-1875) L
Smith, B. F. to Julia A. Henry 2-22-1869 Dy
Smith, B. F. to Tempy E. Hilliard 6-15-1843 Cr
Smith, B. G. to Malvinia Medlin 12-2-1850 (12-1?-1850) G
Smith, B. H. to Minerater Groves 10-28-1856 Cr
Smith, B. to Catharine Archey 2-24-1850 O
Smith, Barker to Nancy J. Clark 9-9-1863 (9-10-1863) L
Smith, Barnett to Mary Bell 12-20-1834 G
Smith, Bedford to Tennessee Smith 11-7-1878 Dy
Smith, Benj. F. to Harriet Jo Smith 5-20-1868 (5-24-1868) Cr
Smith, Benjamin A. to Mary C. Blair 11-10-1852 Sh
Smith, Benjamin B. to Eveline Mahan 4-9-1840 Sh
Smith, Benjamin Franklin to Delitha Coats 12-22-1873 (12-23-1873) T
Smith, Benjamin M. to Virginia Latham 12-30-1861 (no return) We
Smith, Bill to Rose Ridley 12-21-1878 (12-22-1878) L
Smith, Bird to Jane Burnes 11-27-1839 (12-1-1839) F
Smith, Bird to Martha H. C. Nobles 2-24-1869 (2-25-1869) L
Smith, Bob to Lucy Bond 11-21-1871 Hy
Smith, Boyd to Lucy Jackson 2-3-1868 G B
Smith, Bradford to Cynthia Couts? 3-24-1842 T
Smith, Burton L. to Fannie Farrar 12-19-1868 T
Smith, Byrd to Judy McDonald 12-15-1861 L
Smith, C. A. to E. M. Johnston 9-26-1879 L
Smith, C. A. to L. F. Weatherington 2-24-1879 (2-27-1879) Dy
Smith, C. F. to Alice E. Nelson 3-1-1870 G
Smith, C. H. to M. J. Jones 9-24-1869 Dy
Smith, C. P. to Catistia J. Smith 6-13-1863 Mn
Smith, Caleb to Mary Boatright 1-13-1856 Be
Smith, Cannon to Martha J. Higgs 12-27-1857 (1-5-1858) Hr
Smith, Cannon to Nancy C. Usher 12-22-1848 (12-20?-1848) Hr
Smith, Carter to Eliza Williams 5-22-1872 (5-29-1872) O
Smith, Carter to Phebe Ann Jefferson 12-31-1866 (no return) F B
Smith, Carville to Susan Richmond 6-2-1868 G
Smith, Casper M. to Sarah Smith 2-27-1844 T
Smith, Caswell to Mary R. Ross 12-29-1863 Mn
Smith, Charles B. to Sary Bridges 3-3-1841 Cr
Smith, Charles D. to Ann L. Burnett 12-11-1829 Hr
Smith, Charles E. to Mildred E. Malone 9-20-1853 (9-22-1853) T

Smith, Charles W. to Mary Kenady 4-10-1840 (4-12-1840) G
Smith, Charles to Adaline Dodson 9-14-1866 (9-16-1866) F B
Smith, Charles to Katie Burrel 12-17-1873 T
Smith, Chas. G. to Catherine E. Smith 1-13-1870 T
Smith, Claiborn to Sarah E. Stinson 2-7-1843 Hr
Smith, Cornelius to Frances J. Wood 7-30-1860 (7-31-1860) Sh
Smith, Crawley to Ripey Watkins 1-18-1867 Hy
Smith, Curtis to Nancy J. Elleson 12-12-1854 We
Smith, Curtise C. to Elizabeth J. Richie 10-7-1862 We
Smith, Cyrus to Mary E. Rollins 8-5-1865 (8-6-1865) Cr
Smith, D. A. to T. P. Hill 12-18-1868 (12-21-1868) Dy
Smith, D. H. to Martha A. VanBuren 7-25-1861 Hy
Smith, D. H. to Mary J. Rhodes 2-6-1869 (2-7-1869) T
Smith, D. H. to Sallie O. Goodman 5-2-1871 (5-3-1871) T
Smith, D. T. to C. A. M. Willoughby 10-4-1857 Hr
Smith, D. to Rachel Paden 9-23-1871 (9-26-1871) T
Smith, Dabney to Tennessee Lunford 1-14-1873 (1-16-1873) T
Smith, Dallis to America Fowlkes 12-8-1873 (no return) Dy
Smith, Dan to Nancy Lowe 12-7-1871 (12-9-1871) T
Smith, Daniel to Bettie Walker 11-13-1869 Hy
Smith, Daniel to Irena Cunningham 12-21-1843 Be
Smith, Daniel to Lucy Johnson 1-10-1850 We
Smith, Daniel to Sarah Byrum 7-17-1849 Ma
Smith, Daniel? to Hannah Clark 11-24-1869 (11-25-1869) T
Smith, Dave to Amanda Cooper 2-23-1870 Hy
Smith, David to Jane E. Butler 10-31-1864 (4-9-1864?) Dy
Smith, David H. to Polly Smith 2-4-1841 T
Smith, David L. to Mary Ann Sargent 2-22-1848 F
Smith, David T. to Malissa G. Boon 10-1-1844 (10-3-1844) F
Smith, David to Elizabeth Wilborn 12-4-1845 Cr
Smith, David to Emily Duke 8-25-1872 Hy
Smith, David to Nancy J. Crockett 12-4-1862 We
Smith, David to Nelly Starns 12-28-1826 Sh
Smith, Dennis to Charita Walker 1-18-1871 (1-19-1871) Dy B
Smith, Dick to Angaline Fowlkes 1-26-1867 (1-27-1867) Dy
Smith, Dick to Mary A. Howard 12-24-1866 (12-29-1866) Dy
Smith, E. E. to Martha A. Taylor 9-29-1861 G
Smith, E. H. to A. J. Morris 9-30-1866 Hn
Smith, E. H. to Aramissa Wiley 2-17-1868 (2-19-1868) Cr
Smith, E. H. to Eliza W. Cater 5-5-1863 (5-6-1863) F
Smith, E. H. to Nancy C. Spratt 11-25-1830 Ma
Smith, E. J. to Jane Bailey 10-2-1867 (no return) F
Smith, E. W. to Louanna Harton 2-10-1874 (2-11-1874) Dy
Smith, Edley P. to Sarah J. Caldwell 6-2-1842 (no return) Hn
Smith, Edmond to Jane Russell 3-6-1841 Cr
Smith, Edward L. M. to Martha Ann Tennessee Lewis 7-18-1860 (7-19-1860) Ma
Smith, Edward L. to Sarah V. Hathaway 2-5-1852 Sh
Smith, Edward W. to Sarah J. Beech 6-19-1855 Hn
Smith, Edward to Frances Lemmons 6-7-1867 (6-9-1867) Cr
Smith, Edwin W. to M. (Miss) Bramlett 6-30-1862 (6-31-1862) O
Smith, Eli to Dolly H. Moffitt 12-12-1831 (12-15-1831) Hr
Smith, Eli to Jennie Lewis 11-14-1871 (11-15-1871) Ma
Smith, Eli to Lucy A. (Mrs.) Midgett 9-27-1866 Hy
Smith, Elias to Alsey Elkins 11-16-1846 (5-23-1847) Hr
Smith, Elias to Mary Jane Farrow 6-5-1868 T
Smith, Elija to Martha E. Pace 12-19-1854 Ma
Smith, Elijah to H. F. Morgan 3-2-1866 (3-4-1866) Dy
Smith, Emmitt E. to Mary H. Wortham 9-13-1873 Hy
Smith, Ephm. to Allice Smith 1-2-1868 T
Smith, Ephraim Hall to Susan Elizabeth Collier 10-16-1851 T
Smith, Ephraim to Susan Shepperd 1-29-1876 Hy
Smith, Erwin to Susannah Oglesby 5-19-1832 G
Smith, Etheldred L. to Rebecca Ann Fenner 12-17-1856 Ma
Smith, Everett to Margrett Newell 9-17-1837 G
Smith, Evin J. to P. F. (Mrs.) Miller 12-4-1866 O
Smith, F. L. to M. J. Cheek 9-5-1871 (9-6-1871) T
Smith, F. P. to F. E. Harper 7-22-1876 (7-23-1876) Dy
Smith, Fenton to Livia? Alston 10-5-1874 T
Smith, Francis G. to Elizabeth M. Carrington 12-20-1852 Ma
Smith, Frank to Ann Cotherin 12-2-1869 (12-3-1869) T
Smith, Frank to Judy Ann Whitson 1-17-1877 Dy
Smith, Franklin to Sarah J. P. Mullinix 9-19-1844 Be
Smith, Fred. R. to Martha P. Payne 10-2-1852 (no return) L
Smith, Frederick W. to Cynthia A. Allen 4-11-1849 Sh
Smith, Frederick to Bridget Fallen 5-28-1857 Sh
Smith, G. A. to Clem Staggs 4-20-1876 Dy
Smith, G. F. to A. J. Smith 1-17-1843 Hr
Smith, G. L. to Mary J. Scrobrough 8-4-1866 (8-5-1866) Cr
Smith, G. T. to M. B. Yarbro 11-19-1872 (11-20-1872) T
Smith, G. T. to Samantha Garrett 12-12-1859 Hy
Smith, G. W. A. to Eliza Jane Luny 4-4-1863 Mn
Smith, G. W. to B. I.? Davis 1-10-1869 G
Smith, G. W. to L. F. Beasley 11-14-1853 (no return) F
Smith, G. W. to Lucy Stanley 5-22-1861 O
Smith, G. W. to Mary A. C. Dunn 4-18-1839 Sh
Smith, G. W. to Maryann McCall 1-15-1848 (1-17-1848) F
Smith, G. W. to Sallie E. Hall 1-5-1866 (1-10-1866) F

Smith, G. Washington to Esther Lee 7-10-1841 (7-11-1841) Hr
Smith, Geo. H. to Maria L. Krafft 4-16-1861 Sh
Smith, Geo. W. to M. W. Acock 10-10-1863 (10-12-1863) Sh
Smith, Geor. A. to Elizabeth Grider 12-27-1844 (1-7-1845) F
Smith, George A. to Catherine D. Wormelay 4-19-1849 Sh
Smith, George A. to Martha K. Gleeson 12-8-1847 (12-9-1847) Ma
Smith, George L. to Fanny H. Webb 11-8-1853 Ma
Smith, George M. to Malinda A. Plant 1-11-1843 (1-12-1843) F
Smith, George W. to Elizabeth Phillips 2-11-1852 Hn
Smith, George W. to Louisa Reeves 7-19-1855 Be
Smith, George W. to Parale Linder 2-14-1872 T
Smith, George W. to Virginia E. Smith 10-30-1867 T
Smith, George Y. to Emily Peyton 12-10-1846 Sh
Smith, George to Delia Ann Smith 7-1-1868 (7-19-1868) T
Smith, George to Ella Henderson 3-29-1871 Hy
Smith, George to Emily Glenn 3-26-1868 G B
Smith, George to Joanna Bains 10-12-1878 (no return) L B
Smith, George to Lucy Bernard 1-4-1868 T
Smith, George to Lue Someral 10-12-1873 Hy
Smith, George to Mariah Taylor 9-11-1868 (9-26-1868) F B
Smith, George to Mollie Smith 8-8-1878 Dy
Smith, George to Prissa Coley 12-2-1843 (12-4-1843) G
Smith, George to Selia Boyett 12-11-1839 (12-12-1839) O
Smith, Gideon to Sarah A. Cook 1-4-1869 Ma
Smith, Giles to Everline Pullim 10-27-1866 (10-28-1866) T
Smith, Giles to Margaret Chambers 4-25-1873 (4-26-1873) T
Smith, Gordon to Sarah Beliew 1-8-1861 G
Smith, Green Berry to Cynthia J. Crocker 12-20-1868 G
Smith, Green to Ann Eliza Pewitt 2-15-1865 T
Smith, Green to Emeline Flowers 12-19-1869 G B
Smith, Green to Jane Stevenson 11-13-1852 Cr
Smith, Green to Malissa J. Moore 1-28-1858 Cr
Smith, Green to Rachael A. Davie 2-17-1866 Hy
Smith, Green to Susan Bradshaw 3-10-1880 (3-11-1880) Dy
Smith, H. B. to Elmira Elizabeth Gates 2-26-1879 L
Smith, H. B. to Sarah E. Winburn 10-13-1866 Hy
Smith, H. F. to Maggie A. Bell 11-12-1867 Ma
Smith, H. R. to F. J. Crowder 9-5-1871 Hy
Smith, H. to E. (Mrs.) Stewart 4-24-1860 Sh
Smith, Hamilton to Mary Bone 8-21-1866 (8-23-1866) F
Smith, Hampton to Polly Grisman 12-6-1877 Dy
Smith, Hampton to Tabitha Patterson 3-11-1861 (3-15-1861) G
Smith, Hansford to Elizabeth Barnes 9-13-1839 (9-19-1839) Ma
Smith, Hardin to Matilda Smith 7-18-1883 (7-26-1883) L
Smith, Harrison to Florence Gilland 9-5-1872 T
Smith, Harrison to Louisa Bunch 7-26-1842 Sh
Smith, Harvey P. to Margaret E. Walker 10-6-1842 Hr
Smith, Hasting J. to Emelina Birmingham 2-19-1840 Ma
Smith, Haywood to Jane Wilson 6-24-1861 (6-25-1861) Hr
Smith, Hemphill to Margaret Jane Thompson 11-13-1867 T
Smith, Henry C. to Catharine Hunley 1-1-1857 G
Smith, Henry D. (of Ala.) to Lizzie V. Fenner 4-28-1869 (4-29-1869) Ma
Smith, Henry D. to Drucilla C. Greer 12-8-1853 Hn
Smith, Henry D. to Mary A. Davis 3-8-1866 (3-10-1866) O
Smith, Henry H. to Mary G. Peay 11-17-1853 Hn
Smith, Henry P. to Mary J. Leslie 11-9-1872 (11-10-1872) Cr
Smith, Henry W. to Mary S. Jackson 7-4-1841 Sh
Smith, Henry to Ann Douglass 12-30-1865 T
Smith, Henry to Ellen Burrough 12-4-1869 (no return) F B
Smith, Henry to Emiline Stone 6-25-1867 Hy
Smith, Henry to Fannie Williamson 1-12-1871 Hy
Smith, Henry to Jane Robertson 4-8-1861 (no return) Dy
Smith, Henry to Liza Slack 2-24-1872 O
Smith, Henry to Lureta G. Lowry 1-1-1846 Hn
Smith, Henry to Margaret Miller 1-12-1846 (1-15-1846) T
Smith, Henry to Mary Brodie 6-24-1871 (no return) L
Smith, Henry to Mary Jane McRee 9-14-1854 O
Smith, Henry to Maud Hunter Jacob 4-18-1871 T
Smith, Henry to Nancy Sewell 9-11-1865 Mn
Smith, Henry to Sarah Bradshaw 9-15-1873 (9-16-1873) Dy
Smith, Henry to Sarah Whitfield 4-6-1878 Hy
Smith, Hilliard to Bettie Prichard 12-22-1874 (12-23-1874) Dy
Smith, Hiram to M. C. Carroll 7-20-1872 (no return) Cr
Smith, Hugh H. (Lt US Army) to Mary A. Kelly 5-20-1864 Sh
Smith, Hughes to Louisa T. Hamette 8-26-1848 Cr
Smith, I. H. to Sarah I. Neely 1-9-1867 (1-10-1867) O
Smith, I. K. to S. J. Neely 1-9-1867 O
Smith, Isaac B. to Cornelia A. Bartlett 10-13-1856 Sh
Smith, Isaac to Delia Harris 11-26-1869 (no return) F B
Smith, Isaac to Ellen Norris 12-5-1835 Hr
Smith, Isaac to Martha Clark 3-1-1870 (3-2-1870) T
Smith, Isham N. to America A. Thompson 10-29-1838 Hr
Smith, Isham N. to Clemant A. Mallory 11-23-1846 (11-26-1846) Hr
Smith, J. A. to L. A. Taylor 8-29-1862 (8-30-1862) O
Smith, J. A. to M. A. Scobey 12-11-1878 (12-19-1878) Dy
Smith, J. B. to Bettie Lumley 7-27-1872 (8-1-1872) Dy
Smith, J. B. to Mary F. Lucas 4-8-1885 L
Smith, J. B. to Susan C. Medlin 12-19-1851 Cr
Smith, J. D. to N. W. Turnage 1-7-1861 (1-10-1861) T
Smith, J. E. to Amanda F. Fleming 10-24-1874 (10-25-1874) T
Smith, J. E. to Annie R. Glenn 7-4-1872 Hy
Smith, J. F. to M. J. Atkins 11-20-1872 T
Smith, J. F. to Rebecca Smith 1-3-1867 Dy
Smith, J. G. to Louisa C. Butler 12-4-1868 Be
Smith, J. Green to Lula Nixon 12-26-1884 L
Smith, J. H. to Alice Laurison 2-23-1886 (3-12-1886) L
Smith, J. H. to M. J. King 1-23-1860 Hy
Smith, J. H. to Polly Trout 10-4-1871 (no return) Dy
Smith, J. L. to Athenia Hysmith 7-24-1862 Mn
Smith, J. L. to Mary E. Cherry 1-2-1856 (1-3-1856) Sh
Smith, J. M. to Ann E. Linson 9-1-1860 Hy
Smith, J. M. to M. S. Johnson 12-22-1885 L
Smith, J. M. to Mary G. Davenport 11-19-1856 (no return) L
Smith, J. M. to S. J. Russom 3-10-1880 (3-11-1880) L
Smith, J. N. to Sallie Campbell 9-1-1860 (9-2-1860) F
Smith, J. P. to Mollie B. Alexander 3-25-1865 (3-29-1865) F
Smith, J. P. to W. M. McDearmon 12-19-1878 Dy
Smith, J. R. to Mary (Mrs.) Roberts 3-29-1879 (3-30-1879) Dy
Smith, J. R. to Mary F. Burks 8-20-1865 Mn
Smith, J. S. to Mary Urbey(Irby) 4-20-1865 Be
Smith, J. S. to Nancy A. Guinn 6-7-1863 Hn
Smith, J. Sid to Mary F. Roberts 3-17-1874 (3-19-1874) L
Smith, J. T. to C. C. Hawkins 11-7-1863 (11-8-1863) O
Smith, J. V. to Mary (Mrs.) Patterson 12-18-1852 (no return) F
Smith, J. W. C. to Martha L. Taylor 1-19-1861 Hr
Smith, J. W. to Drucilla A. Baird 11-24-1860 G
Smith, J. W. to E. F. Harris 5-29-1866 (6-3-1866) Cr
Smith, J. W. to Emily C. Combs 1-7-1866 W
Smith, J. W. to J. N. Walters 12-2-1869 Cr
Smith, J. W. to Mary J. Darnall 12-7-1865 O
Smith, J. W. to Nancy G. Love 11-19-1857 We
Smith, J. c. to Mary Jane Currin 10-31-1885 (11-2-1885) L
Smith, Jack to Eliza T. Smith 1-4-1869 T
Smith, Jackson to Ann Foust 12-14-1872 (12-26-1872) Dy
Smith, Jackson to Sarah Jane Mayo 2-23-1858 Ma
Smith, Jackson to Susan Jones 10-17-1874 (10-20-1874) T
Smith, Jacob F. to Samuella McIntosh 10-24-1867 T
Smith, Jacob to Elanor Wiseman 8-17-1841 T
Smith, James A. to Jessie E. Curry 12-31-1870 (1-2-1871) T
Smith, James A. to Mary A. Williams 2-19-1849 Cr
Smith, James A. to Sarah L. Williams 12-17-1868 (no return) L
Smith, James B. to Edny Jane Gore 8-25-1855 (8-28-1855) Hy
Smith, James C. to Julia A. J. E. Williams 2-14-1856 (2-18-1856) G
Smith, James E. to Rebecca Pankey 11-6-1848 (11-8-1848) Hr
Smith, James E. to Tennessee Brown 11-3-1865 L
Smith, James F. to Mary Ann Hunt 12-4-1839 Hn
Smith, James F. to Mary M. Bell 3-19-1845 (3-20-1845) G
Smith, James F. to Nancy Ann Bell 6-4-1860 (6-6-1860) Hr
Smith, James F. to Nancy C. Brooks 9-4-1851 Hn
Smith, James G. to Sarah Eliza Allen 1-2-1854 T
Smith, James H. to Lucinda C. Mathis 3-15-1859 (3-16-1859) G
Smith, James H. to Lucy Ann Gaines 11-25-1841 Cr
Smith, James H. to Lydia Wilson 6-26-1845 Sh *
Smith, James H. to Mollie J. Drane 12-1-1857 Sh
Smith, James H. to Nancy A. Carver 12-17-1854 Cr
Smith, James H. to R. M. McKelvy 9-12-1867 G
Smith, James J. to Jennie A. White 11-6-1876 (no return) Dy
Smith, James K. Polk to Maria Doyle 1-30-1867 Dy
Smith, James M. to Eliza Ann Permelia Mullinix 9-23-1847 Be
Smith, James M. to Harriet C. Jones 3-6-1855 Sh
Smith, James M. to Mary Anne Rankin 10-2-1856 Sh
Smith, James N. P. to Ann P. Summers 1-23-1868 Be
Smith, James N. to Julia Catharine Turnage 4-17-1850 T
Smith, James R. to Celia Atts(Alts) 8-18-1830 (8-19-1830) Hr
Smith, James S. to Jane W. Tennant 8-5-1858 T
Smith, James S. to Lyde Wethers 1-19-1870 (1-20-1870) Ma
Smith, James Spencer to Susan McClelland 2-9-1853 (2-15-1853) T
Smith, James T. to Callia M. McMurry 2-3-1864 O
Smith, James T. to Jane C. Grady 3-12-1846 G
Smith, James T. to Josephine Page 2-6-1868 G
Smith, James V. to Syrena Ann Chism 8-6-1862 (8-7-1862) L
Smith, James V. to Syrina Ann Chism 8-6-1862 (no return)
Smith, James W. to Anna Coyne 8-7-1863 Sh
Smith, James W. to Fredonia Young 10-27-1835 Sh
Smith, James W. to Julia Ann Wright 11-30-1844 (no return) F
Smith, James W. to R. O. Durham 12-27-1843 (12-28-1843) F
Smith, James to Adaline Mayfield 4-7-1870 G
Smith, James to Amanda Gossett 12-24-1860 Ma
Smith, James to Astalyssa Shettie 1-10-1841 Sh
Smith, James to Callie Williams 1-8-1874 Dy
Smith, James to Caroline Osburn 11-15-1877 Dy
Smith, James to Charity Manley 12-26-1870 (12-28-1870) Dy
Smith, James to Charlotte Henson 9-21-1858 Sh
Smith, James to Elizabeth Reed (Reece) 1-26-1830 G

Smith, James to Louvisa Long 6-26-1883 (6-29-1883) L
Smith, James to Maggie Ross 12-21-1876 (12-24-1876) Dy
Smith, James to Martha A. Gordon 11-27-1856 Cr
Smith, James to Mary A. Liggett 5-10-1855 Hn
Smith, James to Mary E. Hopkins 3-13-1860 Hy
Smith, James to Nancy Marsh 9-9-1851 Hr
Smith, James to Sarah Barns 11-15-1830 O
Smith, James to Sarah Jane Smith 4-8-1852 Hn
Smith, James to Sopha Rogers 11-24-1841 Sh
Smith, Janier? L. to Patricia Denton 7-31?-1859 (maybe 7-21) Cr
Smith, Jas. B. to Eliza J. Lokey 8-18-1859 Hr
Smith, Jas. H. to Ann H. Patterson 7-5-1858 G
Smith, Jas. M. to Linda Callicott 1-13-1867 O
Smith, Jas. M> to Harriet E. Yarbroh 2-7-1864 T
Smith, Jas. P. to Sarah F Willis 3-12-1868 (no return) F B
Smith, Jasper N. to Mary E. Miller 6-30-1855 (7-1-1855) Hr
Smith, Jefferson to Mary Jane (Miss) James 7-26-1849 Sh
Smith, Jeremiah to Margarett Cook 10-4-1853 G
Smith, Jerry to Cath Taylor 1-1-1868 Hy
Smith, Jerry to Celia Flowers 12-22-1884 (12-23-1885?) L
Smith, Jerry to Hettie Roberson 12-5-1872 Hy
Smith, Jesse J. to Martha C. Batts 10-12-1846 F
Smith, Jessee J. to Katharine J. Massey 9-7-1846 (9-6?-1846) G
Smith, Jessee to Sallie Taliaferro 2-8-1871 Hy
Smith, Jessie to Rhoena Jane Davis 7-14-1877 (7-16-1877) L
Smith, Jno. B. to Frances H. McLary 7-27-1858 Ma
Smith, Jno. W. to Emily C. Marshall 5-5-1864 O
Smith, Jo. Fletcher to Rebecca A. Mahan 7-25-1867 (no return) Dy
Smith, Joel R. to Dorothy Bledsoe 1-12-1841 Cr
Smith, Joel W. to Sue A. Lancaster 11-20-1877 (11-22-1877) O
Smith, John A. to Elizabeth J. Berry 2-27-1871 Hn
Smith, John A. to Jerusah D. Walker 10-25-1859 (10-28-1859) T
Smith, John A. to Mary M. Mathis 7-18-1849 Cr
Smith, John A. to Susan Mathis 12-9-1874 Hy
Smith, John C. to Mary E. Mitchel 3-9-1857 G
Smith, John D. to Isabella M. Dickson 12-19-1840 Ma
Smith, John D. to Nancy C. Reagan 12-1-1854 (12-3-1854) Hr
Smith, John D. to T. A. Archibald 2-25-1865 (2-28-1865) Dy
Smith, John D. to Vetury White 12-8-1850 Be
Smith, John Douglas to Sadie (Sallie?) Cage 7-21-1874 T
Smith, John E. to Hannah Fowler 1-23-1851 (1-28-1851) G
Smith, John E. to Malinda Harris 4-10-1848 (4-15-1848) T
Smith, John F. to Ava Holly 3-18-1844 (3-19-1844) Hr
Smith, John H. to M. J. Thompson 11-1-1865 Hy
Smith, John H. to Parthenia C. Henry 9-13-1853 (9-14-1853) G
Smith, John H. to Susan Smith 12-22-1858 (12-23-1858) T
Smith, John Henry to Elizabeth Sneed 1-22-1866 Hn
Smith, John J. to Emily E. Hogue 8-12-1850 (8-13-1850) Hr
Smith, John J. to Peggy Ann Jenkins 1-2-1849 Hn
Smith, John L. to Margaret Conner 4-15-1869 Ma
Smith, John M. to M. A. Uptegrove 7-24-1865 Be
Smith, John M. to Permenda A. Roberts 1-6-1849 Cr
Smith, John M. to Rutha Ann Vann 10-15-1858 Ma
Smith, John N. to Fannie M. Shaw 9-20-1854 (9-19?-1854) Ma
Smith, John P. to Martha Jane Hodge 10-31-1848 Hr
Smith, John P. to Mary C. Reid 9-11-1845 Sh
Smith, John P. to Sarah Cleaves 3-10-1843 (no return) F
Smith, John T. to Ann E. Lafloore 12-11-1868 (12-13-1868) Cr
Smith, John T. to Christain A. Wooley 7-19-1858 (7-21-1858) Ma
Smith, John W. to Elizabeth E. Searcey 12-4-1866 (12-5-1866) T
Smith, John W. to Emily Murphy 9-27-1849 Sh
Smith, John W. to Jelpha Ann Ayeres 11-7-1856 (11-8-___) O
Smith, John W. to Luce Threlkill 10-10-1862 Mn
Smith, John W. to Lydia A. McDaniel 2-1-1848 Hn
Smith, John W. to M. M. Bishop 10-31-1849 Hn
Smith, John W. to M. Teresa McDonald 1-8-1862 (1-16-1862) Sh
Smith, John W. to Martha Herron 1-30-1850 Cr
Smith, John W. to Mary F. Saint 5-31-1860 Sh
Smith, John W. to Sarah Clarkson 3-23-1861 (3-26-1861) Sh
Smith, John to Ann Pool 9-26-1870 T
Smith, John to Awlla D. Hill 1-22-1840 (1-23-1840) G
Smith, John to Bettie Fumbanks 3-11-1880 Dy
Smith, John to Cela Hurt (Hust) 10-12-1872 Hy
Smith, John to Delila Nowel 2-16-1839 Be
Smith, John to Elizabeth G. Pullen 1-31-1826 G
Smith, John to Elizabeth Longley 4-?-1844 (4-20-1844) O
Smith, John to Elizabeth Stoker 3-5-1851 Cr
Smith, John to Emily Johnson 2-5-1878 Dy
Smith, John to Fanny Earp 12-22-1844 Be
Smith, John to Frances Moore 9-25-1861 Mn
Smith, John to Harriet Vaulx 6-10-1868 Hy
Smith, John to Lottsy Parker 2-21-1873 Hy
Smith, John to Lou Cobb 10-13-1875 Dy
Smith, John to Mandy Bolen 1-28-1866 T
Smith, John to Margaret Bringle 1-1-1873 (1-2-1873) T
Smith, John to Margaret Williams 10-23-1869 (10-24-1869) F
Smith, John to Mary A. Martin 12-1-1836 (12-8-1836) G
Smith, John to Mary Bowers 12-13-1877 Hy
Smith, John to Mary Nancy Lemons 1-3-1869 G
Smith, John to Matilda Jane Wilson 1-20-1844 F
Smith, John to Mildred Smith 12-29-1868 (12-31-1868) T
Smith, John to Minerva Smith 3-23-1862 G
Smith, John to Missouri C. Jerrell 10-31-1844 Be
Smith, John to Nancy Malin 4-9-1854 Be
Smith, John to Nancy Mitchell 5-20-1866 G
Smith, John to Nora Woods 8-30-1877 (no return) Dy
Smith, John to Perlenza Howe 1-1-1857 Be
Smith, John to R. I. Taylor 1-28-1877 Hy
Smith, John to Rosanna Oliver 2-2-1869 Hy
Smith, John to Sarah Ann Clark 1-26-1843 (1-?-1843) T
Smith, John to Sarah Bartlett 3-20-1839 G
Smith, John to Sarah Doak 1-20-1871 (1-22-1871) Dy B
Smith, John to Sarah M. Tyrus 12-14-1836 Sh *
Smith, John to Sina Wagner 1-15-1874 T
Smith, John to Susan Winningham 5-30-1861 Mn
Smith, Jonas? M. to Mary McCauley 11-1-1848 F
Smith, Jonathan B. to Martha C. Muston 5-26-1858 (5-29-1858) Sh
Smith, Joseph C. to Mary E. Miranda 2-18-1862 Sh
Smith, Joseph D. to Mary F. McKelvey 5-30-1857 (5-31-1857) G
Smith, Joseph E. to Mary E. Barnett 8-24-1840 (8-25-1840) Ma
Smith, Joseph H. to Nancy C. Green 9-2-1858 Cr
Smith, Joseph H. to Virginia A. Hall 1-2-1869 (1-6-1869) F
Smith, Joseph L. to Drew J. Doty 6-27-1848 Sh
Smith, Joseph M. to Nancy Manasco 12-30-1845 Sh
Smith, Joseph to Abigal McLeod 8-9-1845 Cr
Smith, Joseph to Amanda Compton 11-14-1868 (no return) L
Smith, Joseph to Fannie Barbee 1-12-1875 Hy
Smith, Joseph to Harriet Lea 10-23-1839 (10-24-1839) Hr
Smith, Joseph to Indianna Marshall 7-18-1874 (7-21-1874) L B
Smith, Joseph to Lidia Eaton 10-14-1852 (1-10-1854) Hr
Smith, Joseph to Mariah J. Lunsford 10-29-1870 (10-30-1870) L
Smith, Joseph to Phoebe Heathscott 1-4-1881 (1-5-1881) L
Smith, Joseph to Rebecca Lax 8-24-1840 (no return) Hn
Smith, Joseph to Sarah W. Wormack 2-25-1834 Sh
Smith, Joseph to Sinora Fields 5-24-1871 T
Smith, Joshua V. to Elizabeth A. Plant 6-14-1841 (6-15-1841) F
Smith, Josiah to Cynthia Ann Williams 8-29-1850 Hn
Smith, Julus F. to Martha S. McCoy 5-29-1862 Mn
Smith, Killis McDonald to Eliza Jane Walker 6-13-1853 (6-14-1853) Hr
Smith, L. B. to Catharine R. Bowers 1-23-1861 (1-24-1861) T
Smith, L. B. to Mary J. Devaughn 11-5-1862 G
Smith, L. B. to Nancy Dickey 5-11-1874 (5-13-1874) T
Smith, L. C. to Maggie Drumonds 8-16-1864 G
Smith, L. D. to Rebecca C. Foust 3-14-1840 (3-16-1840) O
Smith, L. J. to Katherine Darden 12-18-1868 (12-20-1868) F
Smith, L. J. to Martha McCalley 9-19-1855 (no return) F
Smith, L. S. to Frances Cunningham 2-7-1859 (2-8-1859) O
Smith, L. W. to M. A. Shearon 12-25-1867 O
Smith, Lafayette to Louisanna Pettigrew 3-5-1866 (3-6-1866) Ma
Smith, Landon H. to Maria Schutt 2-21-1851 (2-22-1851) Sh
Smith, Lemuel B. to Sarah E. Roson 1-15-1861 O
Smith, Leonard Brantlin to Caroline Bowers 10-2-1848 (10-4-1848) T
Smith, Leroy to Flora Sherrill 10-6-1870 T
Smith, Levi S. to Eliza B. Carter 12-20-1855 O
Smith, Levi to Sarah Norris 1-22-1839 (1-25-1839) Hr
Smith, Lewis to Alsey Scott 9-3-1854 Cr
Smith, Lewis to Louisa A. Fisher 12-10-1857 Sh
Smith, Lewis to Portia H. Jones 3-3-1842 G
Smith, Limerick to Adaline Bendon? 8-3-1867 (8-4-1867) Dy
Smith, Lucien W. to Mary E. Butterworth 8-14-1877 (8-15-1877) Dy
Smith, Ludwell to Elizabeth Provine 1-1-1858 Hn
Smith, Ludwell to Nancy McConnell 3-16-1842 (no return) Hn
Smith, M. A. to Helen D. VanPelt 10-12-1864 (10-13-1864) Sh
Smith, M. H. to Lucy B. Wilson 3-7-1859 (3-9-1859) Hr
Smith, M. W. to Bettie B. Hewitt 10-24-1869 F
Smith, Madison D. to Elvira C. Ellington 1-26-1841 (2-2-1841) Hr
Smith, Manuel to Milley Archer 8-30-1866 (8-31-1866) T
Smith, Marcus D. to Jennie May 11-8-1864 Sh
Smith, Marion to Annabella Huzza 10-5-1858 O
Smith, Marion to Martha Perkins 12-7-1866 (12-16-1866) F
Smith, Marshall E. to Mollie A. Moore 12-6-1866 Ma
Smith, Martin to Clarrisa Pearson 3-30-1867 (4-14-1867) L B
Smith, Matt to Clarissa Tyus 8-12-1875 Hy
Smith, Michael to Bridget Silver 6-11-1857 Sh
Smith, Middleton to Hannah Hunter 4-18-1878 L
Smith, Middleton to Mary Nelson 4-15-1875 L B
Smith, Milton to Nancy C. Crums(Crews?) 3-27-1845 Hr
Smith, Milton to Susan C. Gray 3-4-1831 Hr
Smith, Monk to Ellen McCorkle 10-27-1875 (10-28-1875) Dy B
Smith, Mose to Lucretia Fumbanks 2-14-1878 Dy
Smith, Moses to Celia Sherrid 8-4-1866 T
Smith, Moses to Elizabeth Ewart 5-22-1858 (6-2-1858) Sh
Smith, Moses to Frances M. Campbell 3-10-1845 (3-17-1845) T
Smith, Moses to Jane Dangerfield 12-1-1877 (12-2-1877) L B

Smith, Mrion to Isabella Huzza 10-5-1853 O
Smith, Nathan C. to Eliza Thompson 5-17-1871 (5-18-1871) Dy B
Smith, Nathan C. to Rebecca Haislip 7-31-1854 (8-1-1854) Ma
Smith, Nathan to Frances Harris 4-19-1870 (no return) Dy
Smith, Nathan to Marilda J. Nunnery 1-8-1858 Be
Smith, Nathan to Mary Carter 7-17-1838 Cr
Smith, Nathaniel M. to Nancy Shipman 10-24-1851 Cr
Smith, Ned to Jane Smith 11-18-1870 Hy
Smith, Needham to Becka Walton 4-14-1874 (4-15-1874) T
Smith, Nehemiah to Elizabeth Jane Warren 11-23-1840 (12-23-1840) O
Smith, Neil to Elizabeth Pingleton 5-20-1861 (5-26-1861) Hr
Smith, Nelson P. to Barbrey B. Wilks 2-11-1846 Cr
Smith, Nelson to Jane Epperson 7-6-1870 G B
Smith, Nicholas P. to Cele Glass 2-8-1842 (2-10-1842) L
Smith, Noah C. to Sarah P. Sandford 5-20-1850 (5-21-1850) G
Smith, O. J. to Martha Ferguson 2-12-1868 (2-13-1868) L
Smith, Oliver to Sarah Billing 12-13-1867 T
Smith, Owen to Louana Sphere 9-7-1833 (10-8-1833) G
Smith, P. E. to C. D. Boling 4-27-1853 (no return) F
Smith, P. N. to M. A. Goodin 7-11-1864 (no return) Hn
Smith, P. W. to Dis Ann Smith 2-28-1865 Be
Smith, Parke to Sarah E. Tippet 12-23-1862 Mn
Smith, Parker to Nancy J. Clark 9-9-1863 (no return) L
Smith, Peas A. to E. S. Jones 8-5-1858 Cr
Smith, Peter Perkins to Elizabeth Moore 6-6-1845 (6-15-1845) T
Smith, Peyton C. to Ellen F. West 12-11-1855 (no return) L
Smith, Peyton J. to Emma C. Sherrod 12-7-1870 (12-11-1870) F
Smith, Peyton J. to Teressa H. Dickins 12-16-1848 (12-17-1848) G
Smith, Peyton to Mary Lewis 1-8-1879 (1-9-1879) L
Smith, Peyton to Melissa Owen 11-8-1851 (11-10-1851) L
Smith, Philip N. to Mary Parker 4-28-1842 Hr
Smith, Philip to Adline Blan? 1-13-1872 (no return) Cr B
Smith, Philip to Jane Pipkins 1-2-1845 We
Smith, Phill to Claricy Trigg 7-2-1872 (9-30-1872) T
Smith, Phillip to Malvina Mansfield 7-4-1867 Dy
Smith, Philoman W. to M. A. Willbanks 2-21-1861 We
Smith, Pleas to Ann Fowlkes 1-2-1871 (1-8-1871) Dy
Smith, Pompey to Emma Fowlkes 2-16-1879 Dy
Smith, Preston L. to Kate Smith 6-5-1867 (6-6-1867) L
Smith, Pryor H. to Sarah A. Allen 10-18-1860 (no return) Hn
Smith, R. C. to Hattie Cocke 6-12-1867 T
Smith, R. C. to Lucy A. Scruggs 11-28-1867 Hn
Smith, R. E. D. to Bettie C. Carson 1-28-1868 Cr
Smith, R. E. D. to Elizabeth H. Bagby 1-11-1848 Hn
Smith, R. E. to S. E. Perkins 4-24-1860 (5-1-1860) F
Smith, R. H. to Elizabeth McGlohn 9-4-1860 Be
Smith, R. J. to L. R. Gammon 2-6-1869 (no return) Dy
Smith, R. P. to Mary Jane Bragg 8-7-1857 T
Smith, R. T. to E. L. C. Babb 12-7-1865 G
Smith, Raleigh to Sarah Ann Ryne 6-16-1847 (6-17-1847) L
Smith, Richard J. to Unity Campbell 7-2-1831 G
Smith, Richard S. to Maggie F. Parks 7-25-1874 L
Smith, Richard to Martha Ann Henderson 12-25-1851 Hn
Smith, Richard to Mollie Spence 3-16-1878 Dy
Smith, Richard to Nella Walker 1-18-1866 G
Smith, Robert B. to Mary M. Sturdivant 3-28-1836 Sh
Smith, Robert E. to Fannie Statler 1-27-1858 Hr
Smith, Robert L. to Elizabeth Carroll 9-4-1841 G
Smith, Robert L. to M. J. (Mrs.) Sidle 9-27-1853 Sh
Smith, Robert L. to Mary Jane Dewoody 7-11-1849 Sh
Smith, Robert M. to Mary K.(H?) Fisher 12-23-1885 L
Smith, Robert W. to Minerva Jane McGuire 1-24-1852 (1-28-1852) T
Smith, Robert to Ann Rlayner 3-8-1867 (3-9-1867) T
Smith, Robert to Charlotte Johnson 9-11-1869 (no return) F B
Smith, Robert to Clarinda Murphy 2-1-1843 Sh
Smith, Robert to Louisa Brooks 1-6-1868 T
Smith, Robert to Lucinda Blount 1-16-1878 Hy
Smith, Robert to Martha Browning 5-18-1855 (5-20-1855) G
Smith, Robert to Martha Jane Dobson 12-11-1867 T
Smith, Robert to Mary E. Adams 3-17-1863 Sh
Smith, Robert to Mary M. Bodican? 6-7-1843 Sh
Smith, Robert to Missouri Angeline Tims 5-2-1857 (5-1?-1857) Ma
Smith, Robert to Nicey Hodge 8-11-1868 (no return) Dy
Smith, Robert to Rhody York 5-9-1855 (12-9-1855) L
Smith, Rogers to Mattie Johnson 11-17-1877 Hy
Smith, Rufus to Adelaide Wilson 9-23-1857 Sh
Smith, Rufus to Minerva McDaniel 1-22-1880 (1-21?-1880) Dy
Smith, Rupert to Angaline Mahon 5-10-1867 (5-11-1867) Dy
Smith, S. E. to Sarah E. Scarbrough 2-4-1865 Cr
Smith, S. H. to Nancy W. Coil 2-28-1861 G
Smith, S. M. to L. J. Harden 7-27-1862 Mn
Smith, S. M. to Minerva Connell 1-22-1852 We
Smith, S. R. to Hariet L. Rice 2-27-1866 (2-28-1866) T
Smith, S. R. to Jane Maley 6-20-1872 T
Smith, S. S. to Permedie Luter 12-2-1867 Hn
Smith, S. W. to Mary Inman 6-27-1863 (6-28-1863) Sh
Smith, Sam H. to Virginia C. Sugget 8-20-1855 (no return) F

Smith, Sam to Harriet Taylor 9-6-1870 (9-21-1870) F B
Smith, Sam to Nancy Jones 12-4-1869 (no return) F B
Smith, Saml. Robert to Nancy Smith 1-13-1844 (1-14-1844) T
Smith, Saml. to Annie? Archer 4-5-1871 T
Smith, Samuel to Clarissa Evans 1-17-1873 (1-18-1873) L B
Smith, Samuel to Elizabeth J. Martin 3-30-1849 Hn
Smith, Samuel to Moriah S. Waddle 10-24-1844 Cr
Smith, Samuel to Narcissa Haley 10-10-1843 We
Smith, Sandy to Eliza Ragland 2-11-1868 Hy
Smith, Sandy to Emiline Williams 7-5-1877 Dy
Smith, Sandy to Sylva Smith 9-6-1869 (9-7-1869) T
Smith, Scott to Rebecca Payne 12-3-1872 (12-4-1872) T
Smith, Sidney to Clicey Garrison 3-16-1878 Hy
Smith, Sidney to E. P. Smith 6-11-1831 Hr
Smith, Simeon T. to Phebe A. Hawks 11-1-1860 We
Smith, Simpson to Ellen Earp 11-16-1856 Be
Smith, Solomon to Louisa E. Jackson 7-16-1856 (7-17-1856) Ma
Smith, Solomon to Martha King 3-12-1848 Sh
Smith, Solomon to Susan Bledsoe 1-28-1870 T
Smith, Spead to Mollie Owen 12-14-1868 (no return) L
Smith, Stephen A. to Adaline Woodall 7-24-1844 Hn
Smith, Stephen R. to Elizabeth Smith 8-4-1856 (8-7-1856) O
Smith, Stephen to Mary Ann Cole 2-3-1844 (2-8-1844) T
Smith, Stephen to Mary Polly Alman 11-1-1830 Ma
Smith, Stephen to Samatha J. Blilder? 8-24-1856 Cr
Smith, T. A. to V. E. Moore 10-27-1877 (10-28-1877) L
Smith, T. C. to Susan Ray 10-17-1868 (10-21-1868) Cr
Smith, T. H. B. to E. M. L. Jones 5-16-1861 Mn
Smith, T. Lewis to Meloria S. Burrow 6-11-1856 (7-3-1856) Hr
Smith, T. R. to A. M. Fowler 6-15-1876 We
Smith, Taylor to Ann Chipman 2-16-1869 L B
Smith, Thomas H. to Susan C. Newsom 9-11-1862 (9-15-1862) Ma
Smith, Thomas J. to R. F. Whitehead 9-6-1853 (no return) F
Smith, Thomas J. to Saluda C. Massengill 1-17-1868 Be
Smith, Thomas J. to Sarah A. Bristoe 10-13-1858 Hn
Smith, Thomas Othello to Mary A. Cheatham 11-24-1857 Sh
Smith, Thomas R. to Catharine Miller 4-28-1853 Hr
Smith, Thomas W. to Sarah A. Borran 5-14-1842 (5-15-1842) G
Smith, Thomas to Elizabeth Key 3-7-1860 Be
Smith, Thomas to Julia Drum 11-12-1856 Sh
Smith, Thomas to Lucinda Wells 3-27-1843 Hn
Smith, Thomas to Margaret Carson 1-7-1870 (no return) L
Smith, Thomas to Mariah Haliburton 9-10-1875 (9-11-1875) L
Smith, Thomas to Mary Ann Ross 3-2-1836 (3-3-1836) G
Smith, Thomas to Mary Pirtle 8-6-1827 (8-7-1827) Hr
Smith, Thomas to Sarah Ann Lowell 1-?-1862 (1-13-1862) Cr
Smith, Thomas to Susan Fisher 8-7-1875 (no return) L
Smith, Thos. G. N. to Mary Upton 12-7-1854 Ma
Smith, Thos. H. to Agnes Arnold 4-27-1841 Cr
Smith, Thos. J. to Sarah F. Hatchell 2-19-1870 (2-20-1870) T
Smith, Thos. L. to Mary J. Campbell 6-20-1844 Cr
Smith, Thos. to Mary Carter 12-3-1856 Cr
Smith, Tonneleuke P? B. to Pernina S. Jones 5-21-1862 (5-24-1864?) Sh
Smith, V. J. to Ann E. Cothran 2-20-1863 (2-24-1863) Dy
Smith, Vincent to Tennessee McGary 12-27-1880 (12-29-1880) Dy
Smith, W. A. to Frances J. Klink 3-11-1859 (3-15-1859) Sh
Smith, W. A. to Mary J. Sharp 12-10-1866 (12-12-1866) Ma
Smith, W. A. to Susan C. Young 8-10-1862 Mn
Smith, W. B. to Mary B. Walker 2-6-1861 (2-7-1861) Dy
Smith, W. D. to Mary Ann Wommack 5-24-1855 We
Smith, W. D. to Tennessee Starkey 7-2-1851 Sh
Smith, W. E. to F. M. Kinney 12-10-1872 (12-11-1872) T
Smith, W. E. to Mary Ann Farrow 7-24-1867 Be
Smith, W. H. to Mollie Lanier 1-21-1875 Hy
Smith, W. J. to A. M. Case 1-6-1864 O
Smith, W. J. to Martha J. Helms 1-11-1864 Be
Smith, W. M. to Julia Meadows 6-1-1867 (no return) Dy
Smith, W. M. to L. E. Butler 11-11-1872 (11-13-1872) Cr
Smith, W. M. to Lizzie Simms 3-3-1873 Dy
Smith, W. M. to M. A. Crider 9-22-1870 G
Smith, W. M. to Mattie Williams 12-16-1865 G
Smith, W. P. to E. H. Bevill 2-4-1867 (2-7-1867) Cr
Smith, W. R. to Ann Eliza Holder 2-27-1855 (no return) We
Smith, W. R. to M. A. E. Brooks 1-17-1870 Hy
Smith, W. S. to A. T. Bevell 8-12-1867 (8-13-1867) Cr
Smith, Wash to Lucinda Cherry 8-28-1868 (8-30-1868) L B
Smith, Washington to Isabella Adams 7-26-1869 (7-27-1869) F B
Smith, Washington to Maggie Bunton 3-15-1871 G
Smith, Washington to Sarah Warren 11-18-1841 (11-22-1841) O
Smith, Watkin? to Fannie Dyson 11-9-1872 (11-15-1872) T
Smith, Wesley to Emily Taylor 9-16-1863 G
Smith, Wesley to Emma Morgan 8-28-1880 (8-29-1880) Dy
Smith, Will to Bettie McNail 1-5-1880 (1-15-1880) Dy
Smith, William A. to Jane A. Smith 8-10-1848 F
Smith, William C. to Amelia Overton 7-17-1851 Hr
Smith, William C. to Sally A. Cotton 6-3-1847 (6-10-1847) F
Smith, William D. to Caroline A. Palmer 7-25-1868 (7-26-1868) T

Smith, William F. to Nancy M. Pinkerten 5-31-1859 We
Smith, William G. to Cynthia J. Warlick 1-18-1848 Ma
Smith, William H. to Henrietta Mebane 7-27-1870 (no return) F B
Smith, William H. to Mahala Simpson 1-12-1850 (1-14-1850) G
Smith, William H. to Saphronia H. Pace 10-8-1859 (10-9-1859) G
Smith, William H. to Sarah Ann Chambers 2-25-1861 (2-27-1861) L
Smith, William H. to Sarah Ann Ray 6-2-1849 (6-6-1849) O
Smith, William K. to Delilah M. Caviness 12-26-1853 Hr
Smith, William L. to Mary G. Alexander 10-19-1859 Hn
Smith, William M. to Martha Ann Thompson 2-21-1866 L
Smith, William M. to Mary E. Phillips 9-29-1869 (12-3-1869) F
Smith, William M. to Sussanah S. Sterritt (Stenett) 1-22-1853 (1-23-1853) O
Smith, William P. to Margaret F. Sinclair 7-25-1854 O
Smith, William P. to Velandeo A. Hines 10-2-1860 (10-3-1860) O
Smith, William R. to Elvira Bryant 10-22-1856 G
Smith, William R. to Eveline Reed 6-19-1857 (6-23-1857) G
Smith, William W. to Elizabeth J. Easley 7-29-1860 Hn
Smith, William W. to Emoline Canady 1-30-1857 (2-3-1857) G
Smith, William to Angelin Winston? 7-9-1869 T
Smith, William to Caroline Griggs 8-19-1874 L
Smith, William to Drucilla Presson 12-20-1855 Be
Smith, William to Elizabeth Barrow 2-8-1830 (2-16-1830) O
Smith, William to Elizabeth Webb 9-24-1846 Hr
Smith, William to Fanny Turner 2-17-1869 (2-20-1869) F B
Smith, William to Harriet Jane Bledsoe 4-25-1832 G
Smith, William to Huldy Williams 12-4-1830 Ma
Smith, William to Juliann Loving 4-14-1844 Hn
Smith, William to Kesiah Kannaday 1-12-1844 (2-17-1844) G
Smith, William to Leah E. Johnston 12-19-1852 Hn
Smith, William to Louisa Marsh 1-29-1856 (1-31-1856) Hr
Smith, William to Louiza Tennessee Lewellen 3-15-1870 (no return) L
Smith, William to Lucinda Douglas 9-23-1835 Sh
Smith, William to Martha A. Palmer 8-7-1855 Hn
Smith, William to Mary Moffitt 10-29-1838 (10-30-1838) Hr
Smith, William to Marya M. Terry 1-23-1851 O
Smith, William to Prissilla Gilliam 8-12-1841 (no return) F
Smith, William to Sarah B. Smith 9-10-1868 G
Smith, William to Sarah Fitzpatrick 7-6-1868 (7-10-1868) L B
Smith, William to Susan Fussell 6-12-1860 Ma
Smith, William to Susan M. Walker 1-5-1852 (no return) F
Smith, William to Susan Smith 1-15-1868 T
Smith, Willis to Dollie Tucker 10-19-1870 (10-10?-1870) Dy B
Smith, Willis to Emma Lawrence 8-2-1884 L
Smith, Wilson to Mila Bradford 3-16-1878 Hy
Smith, Wm. H. to Morgan E. Forbess 12-29-1857 Cr
Smith, Wm. A. J. to Manerva James? 12-28-1846 (12-31-1846) Hr
Smith, Wm. C. to Pamela Ellisono 8-12-1847 Sh
Smith, Wm. F. to M. E. Huntington 7-27-1859 (7-28-1859) Sh
Smith, Wm. H. to Annie Develin 6-1-1863 Sh
Smith, Wm. Henry to Jane Mildred Black 11-13-1852 (11-16-1852) T
Smith, Wm. J. to Tennessee McClohn 5-30-1858 Be
Smith, Wm. M. to E. Julia Taylor 9-22-1853 (no return) F
Smith, Wm. N. to Martha Jane Whitley 10-26-1869 G
Smith, Wm. P. to Virginia E. Hughes 11-24-1850 Sh
Smith, Wm. S. to Ann Hall 9-23-1857 Cr
Smith, Wm. W. to Mary L. Burns 1-16-1857 (1-23-1857) Sh
Smith, Wm. to Chany Merriweather 1-9-1878 Hy
Smith, Wm. to Dollie Daniel 12-1-1877 (12-2-1877) Dy
Smith, Wm. to Elizabeth Coats 3-30-1872 (4-14-1872) T
Smith, Wm. to Elizabeth Gilliland 5-8-1838 (5-12-1838) G
Smith, Wm. to Fanny N. Short 4-2-1858 (no return) We
Smith, Wm. to July Ann Wiley 10-1-1849 (10-2-1849) F
Smith, Wm. to Margaret Anderson 3-23-1875 (3-25-1875) Dy
Smith, Wm. to Mary Williams 4-1-1844 Hr
Smith, Wm. to Millie Silsby 6-14-1876 (6-15-1876) Dy
Smith, Wm. to Sarah A. Porter 3-6-1853 Cr
Smith, Wm. to Sarah McMahan 1-21-1842 Sh
Smith, Wm. to Susan Shaw 11-24-1853 Cr
Smith, Woodson L. to Lydia Ann Beloat 1-23-1849 Sh
Smith, Wyat to Elizabeth Saunders 3-22-1846 (no return) L
Smith, Wyatt to Alice Ledsinger 4-13-1871 (4-14-1871) Dy
Smith, Zachariah to Mary Ann White 9-5-1831 (9-11-1831) G
Smith, Zack to H. E. Bryant 2-7-1867 G
Smith, Zelman to Susan Reach 6-2-1846 Cr
Smitheal, Green W. to Florence S. Menefee 10-27-1870 T
Smitheel, Henry to Emily Link 12-20-1877 Hy
Smither, Jos. H. to Verginia L. Richardson 10-10-1870 (10-11-1870) Dy
Smithern, William H. to Elizabeth R. Neil 2-4-1843 Ma
Smithern, William H. to Evoline Neill 1-9-1830 Ma
Smithers, James L. to Caroline M. Markham 1-6-1852 (1-7-1852) Sh
Smithey, John to Elizabeth Sharp 1-9-1825 H
Smithey, William T. to Susan Causey 1-20-1856 Hn
Smithin, Wilkins to Ann Taylor 12-22-1868 T
Smithson, J. W. to Bertha Ann Hansberry 10-4-1855 Hn
Smithson, John M. to Anne Hassler 11-7-1872 T
Smithson, John S. to Eliza J. Sanford 2-24-1853 Ma
Smithson, S. P. to Elizabeth Earls 12-14-1854 (no return) We

Smithwich, William G. to Rebecca Hoppers 1-5-1850 (1-9-1850) Ma
Smithwick, G. W. L. to Mary J. Bowlin 12-16-1856 (no return) We
Smithwick, J. G. to Roanna Williams 5-24-1850 (5-26-1850) F
Smithwick, James T. to Lucy V. Strange 11-25-1847 Sh
Smithwick, John J. to Sarah J. Thompson 12-20-1855 We
Smithwick, John to Isabel J. Thomas 5-9-1860 Hy
Smithwick, Samuel S. S. to Mary Jane Hopper 1-27-1862 (1-29-1862) Ma
Smoot, Hesekiah to Mariah Booker 6-13-1869 G B
Smoot, I. T. to Nancy J. Henderson 2-20-1861 Hn
Smoot, J. M. to Sue O. Baynes 10-3-1877 Hy
Smoot, John to Jane G. Polk 5-3-1842 Sh
Smoot, John to Mary Casteel 11-1-1857 Hn
Smoot, Lewis to Mary Hines 9-4-1857 Sh
Smotherman, Azariah to Mary R. Cooper 5-3-1849 Hn
Smotherman, Elisha D. to Nancy M. Mathis 3-15-1860 Hn
Smotherman, James G. to Elizabeth J. Mathis 12-13-1854 Hn
Smotherman, Lewis S. to Martha Ann Stewart 12-24-1857 Hn
Smotherman, P. N. to Elizabeth Lamn? 7-9-1851 (no return) Hn
Smothers, A. L. to Mary E. E. Henry ?-?-1850 Cr
Smothers, E. G. to Martha C. Ayers 1-15-1859 Cr
Smothers, Edward to Susan Jenkins 11-25-1842 Cr
Smothers, F. J. to Martha Hatley 8-29-1867 Be
Smothers, Green to Martha Pinkston 10-22-1845 Cr
Smothers, Jacob to Deliah Pinkston 10-14-1848 Cr
Smothers, James to Sarah E. Barns 4-29-1857 Be
Smothers, Jesse to Harriet Pinkston 4-5-1846 Cr
Smothers, John C. to Mary E. Farrow 1-19-1869 G
Smothers, Sebrom to Sarah E. Laycock 6-11-1870 (6-12-1870) Cr
Smothers, Sebron to Frances McCoy 12-18-1868 (12-22-1868) Cr
Smothers, T. J. to Adline Harrell 12-26-1867 Hy
Smothers, Wiley to Catharine Dillion? 6-30-1869 Cr
Smothers, Wiley to Isabella Sanders 3-24-1859 Cr
Smothers, Wilie to A. Rumley 7-20-1843 Cr
Smothers, Z. T. to S. E. Crockett 4-25-1872 (no return) Cr
Smyth, A. D. to Malenda Smyth 1-7-1858 We
Smyth, J. P. to Lucinda Powers 12-9-1858 We
Smyth, John M. to G. A. Alexander 10-27-1854 We
Smyth, John O. to P. E. Risin 7-22-1863 We
Smyth, Larkin T. to Jane Wire(Wise)? 11-2-1825 Hr
Smyth, P. H. to M. W. _____ 12-1-1858 We
Snead, A. R. to Z. H. Herron 1-20-1849 Sh
Snead, Garland to Anny Elizabeth Kelly 12-17-1850 We
Snead, Israel to Mary Jordan 11-17-1874 (11-18-1874) Dy
Snead, John to Cornelia A. Jones 9-21-1854 Cr
Sneathan, Joshua to Sarah Clack 8-24-1839 (8-25-1839) O
Sneathen, Joshua to Levina Gwinn 1-25-1842 (1-26-1842) O
Sneed, A. J. to Elizabeth Sneed 1-11-1871 (1-12-1871) Cr
Sneed, Archibald J. to Ella B. Mays 1-19-1869 (1-20-1869) Ma
Sneed, Garland to Lydia Keting 6-21-1869 (6-22-1869) Cr
Sneed, Isreal to Mary Kee 11-5-1851 Cr
Sneed, J. G. to Victoria Winston 11-26-1862 (11-27-1862) F
Sneed, J. G. to Victoria Winston 11-26-1862 (not endorsed) F
Sneed, J. to M. Sneed 12-25-1865 (no return) Hn
Sneed, James to Sarah Jane Williams 2-28-1866 Hn
Sneed, Jno. L. T. to Mary A. Shephard 8-26-1848 (8-27-1848) Hr
Sneed, John to Elizabeth Hodges 6-8-1843 (7-?-1843) Hr
Sneed, M. R. to Sophia A. Herron 2-2-1848 Sh
Sneed, Nathaniel M. to Virginia E. Law 6-9-1856 (6-10-1856) Sh
Sneed, Richard A. to Ann R. Bullock 12-15-1869 Ma
Sneed, Richard to Rosa Tinley 5-19-1846 Sh
Sneed, Samuel B. to Elizabeth Cashen 8-1-1859 We
Sneed, Thomas F. to Mattie A. Mulvaney 9-25-1861 Sh
Sneed, Wm. B. G. to E. G. Anderson no dates (with Sep 1844) F
Sneed, Wm. H. to Eliza Bayers (Bayliss)? 4-28-1838 Sh
Sneed, Wm. R. to Mary Jane Brigance 2-25-1847 Cr
Sneede, J. A. to Martha Belvin 10-7-1855 We
Sneedon, Abraham to Ellen Eden 10-30-1850 Hn
Snell, David M. to Eliza Jane Byram 2-1-1851 (2-4-1851) Sh
Snell, James to Emma Harrison 7-20-1867 G
Snell, James to Francis Rodgers 5-4-1853 Sh
Snell, John C. to Susan J. Foster 11-26-1868 G
Snellgroves, Saml. to Jane Stone 2-16-1856 (2-17-1856) Hr
Snelling, Charles to Ellen Connell 10-23-1861 (10-27-1861) Sh
Snelling, Henry to Judy J. Holloway 12-17-1849 (12-20-1849) F
Snelling, Rubin to Rachal Green 12-10-1870 T
Snider, Carroll to Susan Ann Myrick 2-2-1867 (no return) Hn
Snider, George W. to Nancy M. Matheny 12-20-1860 Hn
Snider, Hugh B. to Vicy Ramsay 8-15-1840 Hn
Snider, James to N. E. Diggs 2-3-1863 Hn
Snider, Jonas B. to Martha F. Rogers 11-7-1858 Hn
Snider, Jonathan to Missouri A. Marsh 1-15-1849 (12-24-1848?) T
Snider, Marion Alexander to Martha Jane Acre 5-18-1866 (no return) Hn
Snider, Peter to Catherine Upchurch 5-6-1847 Hn
Snider, Peter to Mary Emery 10-21-1847 Hn
Snider, Robert to Martha A. Rhodes 5-18-1867 (no return) Hn
Snider, Thomas to Maranda Reed 6-13-1854 Hn
Snider, Uriah to Susan Snider 12-1-1838 O

Snider, W. D. to Elizabeth Farmer 8-7-1868 Be
Snider, William R. to Nancy E. Meadows 12-16-1840 Hn
Snider, William to Nancy E. Hagood 2-27-1862 (no return) Hn
Snipes, Doctor to Lina Gill 3-11-1869 Hy
Snipes, Farrington B. to Elizabeth Bond 5-3-1854 Ma
Snipes, Farrington B. to Tempie Johnston 11-30-1868 (12-3-1868) Ma
Snipes, James A. to Elizabeth Murphy 12-19-1853 (12-20-1853) L
Snipes, Robert to Elisabeth Allen 7-13-1877 Hy
Snoddy, James P. to S. J. Bobbitt 10-16-1867 G
Snoden, Wm. H. to Sarah Taylor 6-17-1844 (6-26-1844) F
Snodgrass, H. J. to M. A. Jenkins 1-21-1856 (no return) Hn
Snodgrass, Morgan to Mary A. Freeman 4-13-1873 Hy
Snodgrass, Thomas T. to Eliza P. Jenkins 3-27-1856 We
Snody, James K. to A. L. Grier 6-24-1863 G
Snoor, Anthony to Amelia Haase 8-23-1862 Sh
Snotgrass, Allen to Caroline Freeman 11-3-1877 Hy
Snow, Edmond to Leah Simms 2-10-1831 Sh
Snow, Edmund to Mary A. Young 3-10-1844 Sh
Snow, Elijah to Martha Helen Jones 5-10-1862 (5-18-1862) Dy
Snow, Green P. to Matilda D. Halley 1-30-1843 Sh
Snow, Henry to Amelia Morris 4-14-1860 (4-22-1860) F
Snow, Henry to Mary Shinalt 12-11-1844 (12-12-1844) F
Snow, J. F. to Dicey E. Grills 10-31-1873 (11-4-1873) Dy
Snow, J. W. to Nancy E. Thomas 9-28-1859 (9-29-1859) Hr
Snow, James to Sarah Williams 1-18-1861 (1-20-1861) O
Snow, Jno. M. to Kittie C. Buckner 4-8-1861 Sh
Snow, John F. to Nancy Ann Garner 4-21-1869 G
Snow, John to Frances C. Ramsey 11-17-1840 Sh
Snow, Rufus S. to Lucretia Justice 5-17-1855 Hr
Snow, Stephen H. to Margaret Radford 8-19-1850 (8-22-1850) F
Snow, T. P. to F. E. Seawright 2-17-1864 (no return) Hn
Snow, W. F. to Ellen Sloan 6-28-1860 G
Snow, William to Isabella Gause 12-25-1867 (12-26-1867) L B
Snow, Wm. to Anna Spencer 10-22-1849 (10-24-1849) F
Snowde, H. P. to T. P. Foster 3-31-1866 Cr
Snowden, David L. to Lucinda Bryant 10-7-1850 Cr
Snowden, Enoch F. to Martha Wood 11-26-1847 Sh
Snowden, Francis to Lucy Ann Berry 12-11-1852 (12-23-1852) Sh
Snowden, J. L. to Vina A. Petty 11-14-1867 Cr
Snowden, J. N. to M. A. Williams 8-23-1860 Sh
Snowden, James to Mahala Renfro 4-16-1855 (no return) F
Snowden, Nathan to Mary Gregory 3-18-1841 Sh
Snowden, Samuel to Mary Jane Marks 10-23-1856 (11-20-1856) Sh
Snowden, Stephen to Nancy Fletcher 1-25-1836 (1-?-1836) G
Snowden, Thos. P. to Mary Worl 12-24-1838 Ma
Snowden, W. T. to Mary J. McDowell 2-23-1860 Sh
Snowden, Wm. to Mary J. Davis 12-16-1841 Cr
Snyder, Elihu to Dicy Griffin 9-27-1840 Hn
Snyder, George to Mary Ann Smith 11-18-1857 Sh
Snyder, James to Susan Baker 5-19-1861 We
Snyder, Thomas A. to Polly Myrick 7-20-1845 Hn
Soap, James S. to Jane Raiford 1-25-1840 (no return) F
Sodden?, Phill to Lucy Bradshaw 12-24-1869 T
Soemrs, John B. to Henrietta Weints 2-1-1854 Sh
Soemrs, Joseph to Sarah P. C. Morgan 9-21-1854 Sh
Soger, Peter to Annie Crime 7-15-1863 Sh
Solan, Michael to Bridget Gaffaney 10-3-1860 Sh
Solan, Micheal to Sarah Pendegraft 4-14-1855 (4-23-1855) Sh
Solea, Edward to Peggie Elcan 6-23-1871 Hy
Sollis, Adam to Sina Sollis 2-3-1843 (2-4-1843) G
Sollis, B. L. to Jane Boone 12-14-1867 (12-15-1867) Dy
Sollis, Buckner S. to Martha Boon 11-21-1851 G
Sollis, Geo. D. to M. Amanda Lowe 2-1-1879 Dy
Sollis, W. H. to L. W. (Mrs.) Ferrill 3-5-1867 G
Solmon, R. H. to Sarah J. Thomas 2-10-1867 Hn
Solmon, Robert H. to Nancy A. Bridges 10-18-1860 Hn
Soloman, Jordon to Harriett C. Bagg 10-22-1850 Cr
Soloman, Patrick H. to Mariah J. Butler 1-30-1844 Cr
Solomon, Isaac to Avira R. Bryant 2-10-1852 (2-12-1852) G
Solomon, J. H. to Melissa Alexander 12-26-1860 G
Solomon, J. to Mary A. Alexander 10-8-1866 G
Solomon, Louis to Rachel Goldzinsky 8-17-1871 Ma
Someraner (Somorer), Henry to Caroline Best 11-3-1864 Sh
Somerow, James H. to Sarah Wright 11-26-1849 (11-28-1849) L
Somers, Geo. Tho. to Sarah J. E. Lunsford 8-5-1875 Hy
Somers, John to Martha Jane Hogue 11-10-1853 (11-?-1853) O
Somers, John to Sarah J. Brown 2-4-1851 (2-5-1851) O
Somers, W. D. to Maria H. Ewell 12-25-1864 F
Somervell, Willis L. to Mary Ann Martin 1-11-1834 (1-16-1834) Hr
Somervill, A. C. to M. B. Somervill 10-10-1859 (10-11-1859) T
Somervill, Charles to Tinah Sumervill 12-27-1867 T
Somervill, Richard B. to Virginia Triplett Taylor 3-13-1847 (3-16-1847) T
Somerville, A. C. to E. C. Saunders 10-27-1875 (10-28-1875) L
Somerville, Charles to Susan Gill 11-11-1869 Hy
Somerville, John M. to Ellin G. Somerville 8-3-1868 (8-4-1868) T
Somerville, John to Catherin Luster 3-22-1869 (3-24-1869) T
Somerville, John to Nerva Locket 2-16-1874 (2-25-1874) T
Somerville, Peyton to Margaret Hopper 12-26-1865 (no return) F B
Sommehalder, F. to Elizabeth Zimmermann 3-4-1858 (3-8-1858) Sh
Sommer, John to Mary A. Harrison 5-30-1859 Sh
Sommers, William G. to Sarah A. Batt 11-19-1862 We
Sommerville, Ben to Ellen Simmons 10-18-1870 T
Sommerville, R. B. to Elizabeth T. Hunt 1-9-1853 (1-12-1853) T
Sommerville, Thomas to Mary A. Siler 4-26-1838 Hr
Sommerville, W. F. to Mary Sommervill 12-28-1865 (12-30-1865) T
Sonnemann, Frederick to Augusta (Mrs.) Dollman 11-25-1863 Sh
Sonthers, Jessee A. to Christina M. Jones 5-9-1849 G
Sooter, Rutherfer D. to Susan Price 10-4-1838 Cr
Soper, Jones L. to Jane Martin 1-2-1841 (no return) F
Sorbet, Bernard to Margaret Peters 7-8-1856 Sh
Sorel, Thomas to Christiana Kerbrugh 4-7-1877 (4-8-1877) L
Sorrel, Arris to Malinda Hall 12-7-1848 F
Sorrell, A. C. to Leonie Yow 9-12-1870 (9-13-1870) Dy
Sorrell, A. S. to Malissy Ferrell 5-3-1855 (no return) F
Sorrell, Albert B. to Mary L. Neely 4-21-1866 Dy
Sorrell, J. H. to M. R. Yowe 12-22-1870 Dy
Sorrell, Jeptha O. to Rachael Eeson 3-28-1865 Dy
Sorrell, N. J. to Mary Jane Rochell 10-9-1861 Hy
Sorrell, N. W. to Mattie Page 1-3-1872 Dy
Sorrell, S. C. to E. F. Lovelace 7-29-1868 (no return) Dy
Sorrell, Thomas to Keziah Battle 9-7-1861 (9-8-1861) Ma
Sorrell, W. W. to Viola Turnley 10-23-1877 (10-24-1877) Dy
Sorrels, John to F. C. Shettlesworth 9-23-1847 Sh
Sorrels, John to Martha Peak 2-21-1856 Sh
Sorrels, William B. to Mary Boon 5-14-1846 Sh
Sorter, T. G. to Nancy Ball 7-2-1867 G
Sory, M. L. to P. J. Winford 5-11-1857 (5-12-1857) Sh
Sossaman, Edward to Lydia A. McIlvain 8-26-1858 Sh
Souls?, Clem Y. to Martha Murphy 8-5-1841 Hn
Soung, John A. to Jane Rorrell 5-8-1847 (5-28-1847) F
Southall, A. L. to Julia A. Buffaloe 4-3-1857 (4-5-1857) Hr
Southall, Austin to Martha Shaw 1-2-1873 Hy
Southall, George D. to Belle Chamblin 9-5-1855 Sh
Southall, James T. to Mary A. Rose 10-15-1859 Hy
Southall, Payton to Mary E. Harp 9-24-1845 Cr
Southall, Wash to Minnie Nixon 8-11-1878 Hy
Southard, B. F. to Rebecca Burford 11-9-1873 Hy
Souther, J. H. to Joe Williams 4-5-1875 (4-6-1875) L
Sutherland, J. E. to Elizabeth Hicks 1-8-1857 Cr
Southerland, James B. to Jane Spain 10-29-1860 (no return) Dy
Southern, B. F. to Cynthia Averett 5-14-1859 (5-15-1859) F
Southern, James H. to Lorenda Doxey 12-24-1832 Hr
Southern, Louis to Isabella Pierce 12-?-1865 (12-30-1865) Dy
Southern, Millard to Julia Talley 4-6-1878 (4-7-1878) Dy
Southwell, Thomas to Bridget Devney 1-11-1860 Sh
Soward, Bird to Mollie Miller 2-7-1878 Dy
Soward, Handy to Low Currin 8-30-1871 (8-31-1871) L
Soward, J. E. to Iola Pottow(Pillow?) 5-1-1880 (5-4-1880) L
Soward, Jesse M. to Indiana Wright 1-23-1850 L
Soward, John to Anna Branch 12-23-1880 (12-24-1880) L B
Soward, John to Caroline Davis 10-27-1856 (12?-4-1856) L
Soward, John to Edwina? Parr 2-24-1876 (no return) Dy
Soward, John to Jane Davis 7-14-1856 L
Soward, Samuel to Lucinda Mize 10-23-1837 Sh
Soward, W. F. to M. A. Moore 2-22-1882 (2-23-1882) L
Soward, William P. to Susannah R. Eison 6-28-1856 (7-2-1856) L
Sowell, Cader to Elizabeth I. Odle 2-27-1840 Ma
Sowell, E. A. to Lovina Massey 1-18-1858 Cr
Sowell, E. B.(D?) W. to Betty A. Johns 10-18-1865 G
Sowell, Henry F. to Frances E. White 12-30-1869 Ma
Sowell, Major to Pink Wilson 12-24-1866 G
Sowers, J. P. to M. E. Williams 8-1-1871 Dy
Spain, A. H. to Frances L. Morris 11-26-1869 (11-28-1869) Cr
Spain, D. C. to Angelian Killough 9-21-1852 Cr
Spain, David T. to Mary E. Hickman 2-4-1869 Cr
Spain, Edmund to Sarah Shadwick 12-18-1845 Hn
Spain, Edward H. to Milly Taylor 7-24-1844 Be
Spain, J. H. to M. R. House 10-14-1871 (10-15-1871) Cr
Spain, J. H. to M. T. Porter 2-19-1873 Cr
Spain, James H. to Anne E. Rudd 4-9-1860 Hy
Spain, James T. to Sophronia A. Brown 8-9-1870 G
Spain, Joe H. to Sarah B. Vincent 12-29-1845 Cr
Spain, Littleberry to Debby Rossin? 9-30-1850 Cr
Spain, Littleberry to Mary McBride 7-28-1858 Hr
Spain, Sterling G. to Martha White 11-24-1847 Cr
Spain, T. C. to M. J. Adams 2-25-1873 (2-27-1873) Cr
Spain, T. C. to Mary C. Edwards 12-30-1840 Cr
Spain, W. W. to M. E. Miller 5-23-1860 Dy
Spain, William D. to Jennie Nichols 7-12-1875 (7-13-1875) Dy
Spain, William to Mary J. Dyson 12-1-1854 (12-2-1854) Hr
Spain, Wm. W. to E. F. Swinney 9-13-1855 Cr
Spainham, Emanuel to Nancy Russell 6-27-1847 O
Spake, Samuel D. to Susan Mays 7-7-1846 (7-9-1846) G
Spalding, Arthur to Culine? Barns 7-22-1860 Cr

Spalding, Don Alonzo to Mary A. McCarty 8-3-1853 Sh
Spangle, Rodolphus to Mary Ann Smaller 8-17-1861 (8-20-1861) Sh
Spann, Samuel F. to Martha M. Killebrew 11-16-1848 Hn
Spann, T. W. to Elizabeth Watson 9-12-1861 G
Spann, Willis W. to Analiza? Lampkins 2-23-1854 Hn
Sparkman, Henderson to Elizabeth Roberts 12-25-1854 (12-27-1854) G
Sparkman, Ivey (Irey?) W. to Elizabeth J. Carlisle 6-29-1853 Sh
Sparkman, Levi to Nancy H. L. Carlisle 12-19-1855 (12-20-1855) Sh
Sparkman, William R. to Ann M. Selph 8-30-1847 (9-1-1847) G
Sparks, Benjamin to Betsy Carson 7-3-1869 (7-4-1869) Cr
Sparks, Burel J. to Mary J. Chandler 12-9-1857 Hn
Sparks, Daniel to Polly Tuel 9-17-1827 Ma
Sparks, David to Cumfort Moffitt 9-17-1827 Ma
Sparks, George to Asena Snider 12-10-1845 Hn
Sparks, J. E. to L. J. D. Matthews 9-28-1859 Hn
Sparks, James L. to Laura Mays 11-3-1870 F
Sparks, James to Clara Baucum 3-8-1870 Cr
Sparks, James to Dorah Carson 12-31-1872 (1-2-1873) Cr B
Sparks, Jefferson to Penelope Futrel 9-4-1833 (9-5-1833) Hr
Sparks, Minas to Sarah Shinn 1-27-1851 Hr
Sparks, Mitchel to Nannie Swayne 12-23-1872 (12-24-1872) Cr B
Sparks, Neal B. to Nancy A. Winford 3-23-1846 Sh
Sparks, Ross to Margaret Lankford 1-18-1869 (1-21-1869) Cr
Sparks, S. G. to M. C. McClellan 5-16-1866 F
Sparks, Solomon C. to Martha C. Smith 3-23-1841 Hr
Sparks, W. R. to Susan G. Harper 3-8-1873 (3-28-1873) Cr
Sparks, William F. to Rebecca A. L. Thornton 10-19-1853 Hn
Sparks, William to Lucy Davis 4-16-1855 (4-10?-1855) Ma
Sparks, William to Matilda White 10-7-1874 Hy
Sparks, Wm. H. to Sarah Swarringer? 10-?-1859 Cr
Sparrow, George to Lucinda Demril? 4-17-1869 (no return) F B
Spate, Saml. D. to Rebecca Richardson 9-26-1839 G
Spates, John to Susan Beeman 12-18-1846 Hn
Spaugh, P. S. to Rena McIntyre 12-30-1879 (12-31-1879) L
Spaulding, Richard to Phoeba Baird 10-8-1870 F B
Speake, Saml. D. to Lucy D. Richardson 10-27-1841 G
Speaks, Jessee to Elvira Jane Odom 1-3-1854 Sh
Spear, George to Margaret Mason 11-8-1829 Sh
Spear, J. P. to W. A. (Mrs.) Henly 6-21-1870 G
Spear, John to Elizabeth Munn? 2-4-1845 Sh
Spear, Joseph N. to Nancy M. Ezell 5-6-1866 G
Spear, Joseph to Spicy Spear 7-2-1851 Sh
Spear, W. E. to Susan J. Quin 10-30-1856 (no return) We
Spear, William to Mariah Darnall 8-16-1849 Hn
Spear, Willis to Sarah McMinn 1-18-1840 (1-30-1840) G
Spearman, Henry to Martha Wyly 2-25-1867 Be
Spears, Abram to Nancy Simmons 9-8-1841 Sh
Spears, E. T. to Margaret E. Baxter 11-8-1849 Cr
Spears, End to Katy Nelson 7-28-1867 Hy
Spears, George to Melinda Loyd 1-9-1838 Sh
Spears, Hudson J. to Sarah Graves 6-3-1850 (6-30-1850) Ma
Spears, James D. to Nancy S. Pearce 9-23-1862 G
Spears, James F. to Sarah J. Covington 12-30-1843 (1-4-1844) Hr
Spears, James M. to Emma E. Shivers 12-31-1869 (1-2-1870) Ma
Spears, John M. to Mariah Graves 4-28-1846 (4-29-1846) Ma
Spears, Thomas to Elizabeth Everett 3-22-1869 (3-23-1869) Cr
Spears, Thomas to Queen A. Gordon 12-18-1856 (12-22-1856) Ma
Speck, E. B. to Sarah Philips 12-12-1864 Sh
Spedder, Wm. E. M. to Elizabeth Roundtree 9-17-1851 Cr
Speed, C. C. to N. J. Pender 3-24-1862 Hy
Speed, C. C. to V. C. Bowden 1-14-1867 O
Speed, J. S. to Ann E. Branch 3-10-1863 Hy
Speed, Jno. H. to Mary E. Deadrick 4-18-1849 Sh
Speer, Dennis to Lucinda Moncreef 11-7-1838 (11-15-1838) F
Speer, J. B. D. to Mary Jane Wright 2-4-1857 (2-5-1857) Sh
Speer, Stephen to Mary Counts 2-25-1834 Sh
Speers, Noah S. to Maggie A. Ellis 12-25-1865 Hy
Speight, F. M. to R. C. Hatler 12-28-1865 Hn
Speight, J. H. to Fannie Hilliard 11-10-1873 (no return) Dy
Speight, J. M. to M. Coley 12-10-1865 Hn
Speight, John M. to Eliza Ann A. Baylis 10-13-1858 (no return) Hn
Speight, John M. to Martha Barton 5-2-1856 Hn
Speight, S. W. to V. A. Carter 1-11-1866 Hn
Speller, Nelson to Macia Jackson 12-22-1873 Hy
Spelling, John to E. T. O. Hamilton 9-19-1867 (no return) Cr
Spellings, Benjamin F. to Louisa Genest 2-20-1838 G
Spellings, G. C. to Melvina Aden 6-8-1858 Be
Spellings, J. M. to Adaline Butler 1-20-1851 Cr
Spellings, Robert to Lucy Browning 8-17-1847 (8-18-1847) G
Spellings, William J. C. to Harriott Wilkerson 12-20-1843 G
Spellings, William to A. P. Jordon 3-22-1871 (3-23-1871) Cr
Spellings, Wm. H. to Susan Jane McCracken 10-28-1869 G
Spellman, Lewis B. to Cinnie Carey? 8-3-1863 Sh
Spellman, Patrick to Hannah Brown 10-3-1863 Sh
Spence, Brittan to Bettie Cox 2-24-1868 (2-26-1868) Ma
Spence, Charles to Tennessee Anderson 8-23-1866 (8-24-1866) Dy
Spence, G. E. to Lucinda Thompson 10-1-1867 (no return) Dy
Spence, George William to Samanthia Octavia Cates 2-24-1879 (2-25-1879) L
Spence, Henry to Lizzie Bell 6-30-1876 Dy
Spence, J. E. to Catharine Jackson 11-12-1860 (11-13-1860) Sh
Spence, J. L. to Nancy H. Wingo 3-28-1871 O
Spence, James to Marcella Johnson 3-9-1858 Be
Spence, John N. P. to Martha J. Boyd 10-27-1846 (10-28-1846) L
Spence, Joseph S. to Lucinda C. Buck 7-10-1865 Hy
Spence, K. R. to S. P. (Mrs.) Harvey 12-16-1867 F
Spence, Samuel to Sarah Wood 12-22-1845 (no return) We
Spence, W. H. to Nad Corbett 1-7-1862 Be
Spence, William G. to Jane Bibb 6-24-1852 L
Spence, Wm. J. to Ann E. Johnson 6-19-1866 Hy
Spence, Wm. W. to Mary E. Butterworth 12-6-1847 (12-8-1847) F
Spence, Wm. to Frances Smith 2-22-1878 (2-23-1878) Dy
Spence, Wm. to Susan Fields 1-15-1868 Dy
Spencer, Benj. Marion to Sarah (Mrs.) Woollard 7-6-1869 Ma
Spencer, Charles to Mary Lefever 4-2-1838 Hn
Spencer, Dabna to Sallie Bowers 11-9-1874 T
Spencer, Duncan M. to Harriet A. Connor 12-29-1859 (1-1-1860) Ma
Spencer, Eli B. to Parthenia Stephens 7-22-1830 Sh
Spencer, Elijah H. to Amanda Johnson 7-26-1851 (7-31-1851) Ma
Spencer, Elijah to Hannah Jackson 2-27-1836 (2-28-1836) G
Spencer, Isaac to May F. Lyons 5-11-1874 Dy
Spencer, Isaac to Susan (Mrs.) Flowers 9-21-1841 (9-26-1841) G
Spencer, J. A. to H. A. Rutlidge 8-19-1866 G
Spencer, J. C. to Joan Dodson 12-9-1866 G
Spencer, J. P. to Elizabeth Jackson 9-19-1878 (9-20-1878) Dy
Spencer, J.E. to Celestia A. Nutall 9-21-1859 Hr
Spencer, Jacob to Rebecca Reynolds 1-18-1870 (1-16?-1870) Dy
Spencer, James M. to Tennessee Davis 8-26-1858 (8-29-1858) Hr
Spencer, James to Mary Odle 2-6-1828 (2-7-1828) Ma
Spencer, Jesse H. to Jermima Blackburn 12-28-1858 G
Spencer, Jesse to Madaline Weathers 3-27-1844 Hn
Spencer, Jno. C. to Lizzie Gordon 2-28-1871 (3-2-1871) Ma
Spencer, John A. to Catherine M. Farrow 3-30-1844 (no return) Hn
Spencer, John to Martha Taylor 1-22-1831 (1-23-1831) Ma
Spencer, John to Tabitha Hopper 10-8-1853 (10-9-1853) G
Spencer, Jonathan to Nancy A. Moore 9-3-1860 (9-5-1860) T
Spencer, Jonathan to Nancy A. Moore 9-5-1860 T
Spencer, Mark to Nancy McCollum 3-9-1829 Ma
Spencer, Thomas to Harrett A. Miller 4-8-1852 G
Spencer, W. G. to Nancy R. McClain 5-26-1850 Hn
Spencer, William J. to Elizabeth Spencer 6-27-1826 G
Spenser, Albert to Sarah Foster 7-24-1869 Hy
Sperbeck, Geo. C. to Fanny Rodner 5-17-1864 (5-19-1864) Sh
Sperlin, Elias to Susan R. Binkley 1-25-1858 Hr
Sperling, Benj. to Milly Hamilton 9-25-1833 Hr
Sperling, John to Sarah Mayfield 1-31-1833 (2-5-1833) Hr
Sperry, R. A. to Amanda Goodner 10-1-1850 (10-2-1850) F
Spesard, Charles M. to Elizabeth Archer 12-29-1866 (12-30-1866) T
Spicer, Isaac to Dinah Davis 12-23-1871 Hy
Spicer, James M. to Pacena Spicer 1-31-1846 Be
Spicer, K. S. to F. S. Frazier 2-8-1863 O
Spicer, Saml. S. to Fannie L. Horton 11-28-1860 Sh
Spicer, Spencer A. to Martha Jane Smith 12-16-1852 Be
Spicer, W. D. to Matilda Williams 6-7-1855 Be
Spicer, Wm. P. to Susan E. Hogg 4-18-1853 Be
Spicers, John W. to Nancy Robertson 1-14-1856 (no return) We
Spickenagle, John M. to Mary Jane Davis 2-18-1832 Sh
Spickenagle, Wm. to Isabella Haralson 12-28-1842 Sh
Spickernagle, Horace to Lean Smith 12-31-1853 (1-1-1854) Sh
Spiegel, Christian to Martha E. Cockerill 3-26-1856 (3-27-1856) Sh *
Spier, Samuel to Ann Mccoy 3-5-1861 G
Spight, Ira to Mary R. Dickson 1-24-1832 (1-31-1832) G
Spight, James W.(M?) to Mary E. D. Rucker 12-31-1840 Hr
Spight, Thomas to Catharine Evans 6-5-1834 (6-6-1834) G
Spights, Jansy J. to Mary Gauntlet 5-23-1866 O
Spiker, Wm. H. to Mary E. Head 12-5-1864 O
Spiller, D. C. to Mary M. Hollingshead 9-3-1879 (9-4-1879) L
Spiller, Geo. F. A. to Sarah (Mrs.) Hood 11-11-1862 (11-12-1862) F
Spilman, Michael to Catherine Daugherty 6-3-1848 Sh
Spine, Alexander to Catherine Whitlock 4-29-1830 Hr
Spinks, C. A. to Elmira Shoemaker 10-6-1875 (10-11-1875) L
Spinks, John C. to Sarah Jane Lake 1-26-1848 Hr
Spinks, Windsor J. to Cynthia C. Laks 10-31-1860 Hr
Spinson, Benjamin to Louisa Crisenberry 3-16-1854 Hn
Spires, Joseph to D. T. P. Megee 1-8-1861 Be
Spires, Robert to Caroline Greer 5-14-1846 Be
Spitznagel, J. to Elizabeth Timmons 12-30-1858 Sh
Spivey, Calvin to Elizabeth Preson 1-6-1842 Ma
Spivey, Calvin to Mary E. A. Mizell 1-28-1847 Ma
Spivey, Jacob to Calodonia Smith 1-30-1851 Sh
Spivey, Joe to Venus Pugh 1-2-1874 Hy
Spivey, Turner to Prisie Davie 12-28-1871 Hy
Spivy, John H. to Martha Howard 10-31-1845 (11-2-1845) Hr
Spivy, W. D. to Jane Simmons 10-22-1857 (10-26-1857) Hr
Spoon, Eliza to Sarah Butler 6-8-1845 Cr

Spoon, W. R. to E. T. Cochrane 12-1-1876 (12-3-1876) Dy
Spoon, William R. to L. E. Jones 7-20-1878 (7-21-1878) Dy
Spoon, Wm. B. to Elizabeth Towsend 1-2-1866 (1-5-1866) Cr
Spotswood, Edwin A. to Jannitte Armour 5-21-1862 Sh
Spradlin, Thomas J. to Martha Bransford 12-10-1852 O
Spradlin, William to Amanda I. Johnson 4-3-1876 (4-12-1876) Dy
Spraggins, H. T. to Annie Williams 1-25-1879 (1-26-1879) Dy
Spraggins, James W. to Lucinda Jane Brewer 11-24-1869 (11-25-1869) Ma
Spraggins, W. F. to Mary Edwards 5-5-1877 Dy
Spragins, Noel to Eliza Jones 1-30-1844 (2-1-1844) Ma
Sprague, Geo. (Capt.) to Ellen Pierce 6-13-1863 (6-14-1863) Sh
Spring, Berry L. to Mary J. Wilie 12-18-1860 (12-19-1860) Ma
Springer, Aaron to Cornelia Belew 10-8-1853 (10-10-1853) G
Springer, H. T. to Nancy E. Sellars 12-7-1871 (no return) Cr
Springer, Hosea to Nancy C. Settles 11-8-1865 (11-8-1865) Cr
Springer, J. M. to M. E. Laws 11-13-1867 Cr
Springer, Jason to Matilda Scott 11-12-1853 Cr
Springer, Joseph to Mary Smith 10-24-1866 G
Springer, R. B. to Clementine Sellers 12-9-1865 (12-19-1865) Cr
Springer, Thos. to Lucy C. Brandon 12-5-1872 (12-6-1872) Cr
Springer, Thos. to Zelphia Gulledge 2-15-1846 Cr
Springer, Urias to Elizabeth Gullage 12-13-1870 Cr
Springer, W. D. to Sarah J. Beasley 12-21-1867 (12-22-1867) L
Springer, Wm. M. to Susan Jane Scott 9-18-1847 Cr
Springer, Wm. P. to Zetha A. Phillips no date (1838-1859) Cr
Springfield, Baker C. to Callie E. Totten 11-23-1869 (11-24-1869) Ma
Springfield, Blunt to Elizabeth Degraftenreid 12-4-1843 (no return) F
Springfield, Chas. to Millie Horton 12-2-1871 Hy
Springfield, Edward to Matilda Green 12-25-1866 (12-26-1866) F B
Springfield, Gentry to Alice Turner 8-1-1883 (8-2-1883) L
Springfield, John to Mary Ann Gray 7-7-1856 (7-8-1856) Hr
Sprouce, William to Lucinda H. Broadwaters 12-9-1839 (12-10-1839) F
Sprout, John w. to Chaney Palmer 10-18-1838 Hn
Sprowl, S. B. to Rebecca Smiley 11-13-1867 Hn
Sprowls, Alexander to Margaret Brundage 6-10-1858 Hn
Spruce, Joseph to Winopard Leary 6-8-1830 Ma
Spruwell, Andrew J. to Martha Millone 5-17-1845 (5-23-1845) G
Spry, A. A. to Ellen Hargate 1-21-1859 (1-23-1859) L
Spures, D. to M. Davis 11-30-1841 Be
Spurlin, A. C. to Elizabeth Hamlin? 11-30-1849 (11-31?-1849) Hr
Spurlin, Absolom C. to Rebecca H. Spurlin 12-19-1847 Sh
Spurlin, Berry to Milly Marler 7-21-1837 Hr
Spurling (Sparling?), Harry to Jane H. Posey 5-1-1854 Sh
Spurling, Geo. W. to Minervia J. Crews 3-1-1858 Hr
Spurling, Levi to Lavina(Lavivian) Cooper 6-22-1827 (6-23-1827) Hr
Spurlock, Timothy P. to Ann Huntsman 12-21-1840 (12-22-1840) Ma
Spurm, Lot to E. P. McPherson 2-5-1868 G
Spurrell, Oliver to Amanda Ferrell 2-18-1877 Hy
St. Clair, Francis to Catherine (Miss) Talty 4-21-1864 Sh
St. John, Benjamin T. to S. L. Nailling 5-12-1863 We
St. John, Daniel to Permelia J. Youchman 8-15-1838 (8-16-1838) O
St. John, J. Y. to Martha Glenn 12-4-1865 O
St. John, Michael to Mary O'Brien 9-20-1856 (9-21-1856) Sh
St. John, William to Sarah F. Martin 1-25-1875 (1-26-1875) L
Stacey, J. M. to Nellie Boydston 9-27-1883 L
Stacey, John B. to Elizabeth Smith 3-17-1852 O
Stacey, John to Arminta Linsey 11-6-1844 (11-?-1844) O
Stack, Ed to Maggie Fogarty 11-26-1861 Sh
Stack, William to Hannonah Donley 2-1-1860 Sh
Stacy, Abner to Mary F. Boyd 2-23-1854 L
Stacy, B. F. to C. M. Hamner 9-25-1852 (no return) F
Stacy, Edward M. to Darthula E. Byrn 2-4-1871 (2-5-1871) L
Stacy, Jacob to Nancy Bennett 1-14-1840 Cr
Stacy, James D. to Matilda Hulon 10-13-1821 Hn
Stacy, James H. to Sopha Ann Cruse 9-4-1852 (no return) F
Stacy, R. F. to Z. A. Farrar 7-21-1866 (7-22-1866) F
Stacy, Thomas W. to Nancy C. Leigh 8-23-1871 (8-24-1871) Cr
Stacy, Thos. to Rebecca Whitehorn 7-31-1845 Cr
Stacy, Will A. to Mary Ann Knight 10-3-1827 Hr
Stadtmiller, John A. to Elizabeth Haley 8-9-1851 (8-11-1851) Sh
Stafford, B. R. to D. C. Atkins 4-26-1854 (no return) F
Stafford, B. R. to Julia A. Snelling 12-19-1856 (no return) F
Stafford, Daniel J. to Hesterann Harrison 8-2-1841 (8-12-1841) F
Stafford, Diocles S. to Rebbecca White 1-10-1853 Cr
Stafford, George to Melinda Craddac 4-12-1856 (4-13-1856) G
Stafford, Isaac to Nancy A. Pipkins 7-19-1855 Hy
Stafford, J. B. to H. A. Stafford 6-22-1867 (6-23-1867) F
Stafford, J. P. to Mary F. Stafford 10-6-1862 (10-7-1862) F
Stafford, J. S. to M. A. Erwin 8-27-1872 (8-28-1872) O
Stafford, James W. to Catharine Ray 8-26-1840 (no return) We
Stafford, Jessee to Catharine Taylor 10-17-1851 (no return) F
Stafford, John L. to Judah Malone 4-19-1837 (4-20-1837) Hr
Stafford, John L. to Rebecca Ann Ralls 7-27-1848 O
Stafford, John to Caroline Brown 7-10-1861 We
Stafford, John to Martha Cox 6-19-1850 Cr
Stafford, John to Sally Hatley? 2-6-1837 Hr
Stafford, Joseph A. to Cynthia Montgomery 12-24-1834 (12-25-1834) Hr
Stafford, L. M. to Elizabeth Quinn 8-3-1840 Cr
Stafford, Noah to Martha Montgomery 6-23-1868 (7-2-1868) F
Stafford, Pinkney to Lucinda Robertson 2-14-1867 (2-15-1867) F
Stafford, Reuben to Jane Wilson 10-5-1867 Hy
Stafford, Reuben to Violett Davis 1-6-1876 Hy
Stafford, Thos. J. to Mary E. Bomer 2-24-1840 (2-27-1840) F
Stafford, Uriah to Elizabeth Hanks 11-76-1825 (11-8-1825) Hr
Stafford, Vincent R. to Anna A. Burton 12-19-1838 (12-20-1838) F
Stafford, W. B. to Martha C. Bowers 9-14-1847 (no return) F
Stafford, W. J. to Sallie J. Talls (Falls?) 1-25-1868 (no return) F
Stafford, Willis to America Walton 8-16-1866 (no return) F B
Stafford, Willis to Elizabeth Robertson 12-22-1868 F
Stafford, Wm. H. to Maryann D. Hood 2-17-1845 (2-18-1845) F
Staggs, Etheridge to Sarah M. Hood 1-11-1877 Dy
Staggs, Henry to Martha Ann Redding 12-23-1863 (no return) Dy
Staggs, Henry to Martha Davidson 12-24-1864 (1-2-1865) Dy
Staggs, R. to Darcus (Mrs.) Swann 4-3-1871 (4-9-1871) Dy
Stagner, George to Margaret Roberts 2-8-1848 Hn
Stagner, Henry to Louisa Merrick 3-27-1851 Be
Stagner, J. N. to Judith Elizabeth Miller 1-11-1863 Hn
Stagner, J. W. to Eugene Mitchner 3-2-1878 (3-23-1878) Dy
Stagner, Joseph to Manerva Claton 9-28-1856 Be
Stagner, Josiah to Mary E. West 6-15-1856 Hy
Stagner, Nathan to Christian Mannon 12-31-1861 Be
Stagner, William to Eliza Thornton 8-24-1853 Be
Stagner, Wm. A. to Lucinda Wyatt 12-22-1853 Be
Stags, Henry to Mary Thompson 10-22-1866 O
Staid, Charles to Ann O'Brien 10-7-1861 Sh
Stailey, Samuel to Matilda Wright 8-16-1850 Sh
Stainback, F. E. to Elizabeth Picot 2-15-1854 Sh
Stainback, Henry to Jennie Trent 7-13-1866 (not executed) F B
Stainback, Littleberry to Rebecca B. Cross 3-6-1844 (3-7-1844) Hr
Stainback, W. E. to Priscilla A. Williamson 4-25-1865 (4-26-1865) F
Stalcup, B. S. M. to H. I. Hall 1-19-1871 Dy
Stalcup, John R. to Susan Allen 1-3-1850 Cr
Stalens, A. G. to Mary C. Ragan 12-5-1859 G
Staley, George to Paulina Loure 9-4-1851 Sh
Stalkup, J. F. to M. A. Lawhorn 1-27-1870 (1-28-1870) Dy
Stallcupp, W. J. to Sarah J. Taylor 4-10-1869 Dy
Stallings, Bryant B. to Tabitha Alvis 10-18-1865 G
Stallings, G. W. to Pathena Evans 2-16-1866 G
Stallings, H. D. to Rosaline Pavid 5-21-1854 Sh
Stallings, John to Elizer Cooper 1-24-1867 G
Stallings, Kemp to Harrett Bates 12-19-1845 (12-23-1845) Hr
Stallings, L. M. to Elizabeth Alvis 1-14-1867 (2-14-1867) G
Stallings, N. F. to Mary Carr 4-28-1860 (4-29-1860) G
Stallings, William to Emaline Amouse 1-8-1862 (1-9-1862) F
Stallings, Willis to Jane Law 11-19-1830 (11-24-1830) Ma
Stallings, Wm. S. to E. J. Rideout 12-25-1860 (not executed) F
Stallion, Archy to Nancy Ann Epps 12-13-1869 (12-26-1869) F B
Stallions, Kemp to Keziah Brown 5-23-1829 (5-24-1829) Hr
Stalls, Geo. A. to Margaret C. Burke 1-8-1861 Sh
Stalls, W. M. to Lucinda Ray 12-13-1860 Hn
Stamfield, John A. to Fannie McDaniel 6-3-1867 Hy
Stamp, J. T. to S. A. Bui? 12-6-1865 (12-13-1865) Dy
Stamper, W. H. to M. A. Stamper 7-23-1879 (7-24-1879) L
Stamps, Daniel to Sarah Price 7-10-1860 F
Stamps, E. G. to Nancy A. Robins 7-20-1875 (7-21-1875) L
Stamps, J. D. to Ann (Mrs.) Brown 2-15-1860 Sh
Stamps, J. T. to S. A. Bell 12-6-1865 (12-13-1865) Dy
Stamps, Nathan to Margaret Willis 7-17-1867 (8-10-1867) Dy
Stanback, Henderson to Matilda Powell 1-4-1871 (1-11-1871) F
Stanbrough, Ira to Sarah A. Crane 2-26-1856 (2-27-1856) Sh
Standback, Henry to A. Jane Turner 4-30-1868 G B
Standfield, Harvey D. to Hester Ann Griggs 3-13-1840 (3-15-1840) Hr
Standley, J. F. to E. L. Halford 6-14-1864 G
Standley, Jos. H. to Martha F. Atkins 12-26-1859 Hy
Standley, William to Gatsey Caraway 12-30-1851 (1-1-1852) Hr
Standley, Wm. to Mary Walker 1-28-1849 (2-1-1849) O
Standly, Major to Cassa Johnson 11-10-1835 (11-12-1835) Hr
Stanfield, J. A. to Mary M. Yancy 12-12-1881 (12-15-1881) L
Stanfield, James S. to Garzilla K. McCord 3-6-1853 Hn
Stanfield, Oliver to Mandy Jane Conder 2-28-1871 (3-1-1871) Ma
Stanfield, R. E. to S(arah) A(melia) Ford 1-2-1877 (no return) L
Stanfield, Robert P. to Sarah Hasting 11-27-1856 Hn
Stanfield, T. H. to V. A. Ricks 8-21-1865 Hy
Stanfield, Wm. H. to Roxana O. Davis 11-4-1868 (no return) Dy
Stanford, Marion to Emma McClish 1-30-1869 Hy
Stanford, Thomas L. to Mary L. Massey 10-8-1865 (10-12-1865) Cr
Stanford, Thos. to Candes Lassiter 4-20-1840 Cr
Stanford, William to Isabel Tinnen 5-18-1867 (5-19-1867) T
Stanley, Aaron to Mary Lacey 9-11-1833 (7?-23-1833) G
Stanley, B. F. to Elizabeth Stanley 8-24-1867 O
Stanley, David W. to Nancy Grey 1-30-1860 F
Stanley, Eli to Luriraney Smith 4-6-1828 Ma
Stanley, H. J. to Georgia A. Mewborn 1-10-1871 (1-12-1871) F
Stanley, Harrison L. H. to Malinda Mays 3-7-1861 Ma

Stanley, Hays to Nancy Meacham 6-2-1853 (7-2-1853) Ma
Stanley, Henry to Nancy Rogers 8-24-1878 (8-25-1878) Dy
Stanley, Isaac to Nancy McElvain 7-16-1836 (7-17-1836) O
Stanley, J. A. to P. T. Smith 1-14-1880 (1-15-1880) L
Stanley, J. F. to H. A. Stanley 8-24-1867 O
Stanley, J.(I.?) N. to Mollie McMahon 5-28-1866 Hy
Stanley, James E. to Mary E. Midgett 10-9-1847 Hy
Stanley, James to Ann O'Brien 4-14-1860 (4-22-1860) Sh
Stanley, James to Sarah J. Jackson 12-13-1859 (12-15-1859) O
Stanley, John B. to Harriet D. Edwards 9-28-1847 Hn
Stanley, John B. to Lucinda J. Crawford 8-26-1846 (no return) F
Stanley, John J. to Darcus A. Heathcott 2-21-1867 L
Stanley, John L. to Mary Perkinson 8-2-1827 Sh
Stanley, John W. to Mary T. Harris 2-24-1842 O
Stanley, Joseph B. to Frances S. Terrill 2-26-1852 (3-9-1852) G
Stanley, Joseph to Mary Hatchett 10-1-1864 (not exec) O *
Stanley, O. C. to Mollie L. Stanley 11-26-1872 Hy
Stanley, Omer H. to Jane M. W. Langford 12-22-1852 (12-23-1852) Ma
Stanley, Richard to Mahulda Hatchett 11-6-1862 (11-7-1862) O
Stanley, Richard to Parmelia Lewis Davis 4-2-1858 (4-4-1858) O
Stanley, Richard to Parmelia Louisa Davis 4-2-1838 (4-4-1838) O
Stanley, Samuel H. to Susannah French 6-24-1846 Hn
Stanley, Solomon H. to Nancy A. Gilerland 12-16-1839 (no return) F
Stanley, Thomas W. to Nancy E. Lusk 9-26-1859 L
Stanley, William W. to Eliza Jane Wilks 2-14-1854 G
Stanly, Hillery H. to Mary Z. Sasser 2-2-1847 Hr
Stanly, J. C. to Harriet J. Pratt 4-16-1847 F
Stanly, J. M. to Mary E. Martin 7-23-1878 Hy
Stanly, Newton C. to Martha C. Gullage 9-12-1860 Cr
Stanney, Napoleon to Frances Brown 2-1-1871 (2-4-1871) F B
Stansbury, William to Elenor Applegate 8-16-1843 (8-17-1843) O
Stanton, Edward to Eve Stanton 12-24-1867 Hy
Stanton, John S. to Georgia B. Gwyn 10-19-1863 (10-21-1863) Sh
Stanton, Priest to Amanda Scott 3-20-1873 Hy
Stanup?, Hamilton to Canna? Cage 5-8-1869 (2-19-1871?) T
Stanus, John Wesley to Mary E. Manasco 9-6-1860 (9-13-1860) T
Staples, Nathl. W. to Lydia M. Smith 10-2-1852 (10-21-1852) Sh
Staples, Robert to Elizabeth Clowe 11-1-1842 M
Stapleton, William K. to Margaret Boyd 4-15-1841 Ma
Stapleton, Wm. to Margaret Marcey 5-3-1854 (5-4-1854) Sh
Staret, William to Mary M. Farmer 1-10-1867 T
Staritt, John to Frances D. Rhodes 5-16-1865 T
Stark, Alexander to Elizabeth Robinson 1-21-1861 Sh
Stark, F. P. to E. A. Hamner 11-13-1863 Sh
Stark, H. C. to Lucy W. Fanales 6-12-1848 Hr
Stark, John to Susan Reid 11-24-1858 (11-26-1858) Sh
Stark, Joseph B. to Margaret A. Little 12-22-1868 (no return) F
Stark, Joseph C. to Lamiza Ann Baird 4-22-1847 F
Starke, Stephen G. to Caroline C. McGehe(e) 2-12-1848 Sh
Starkey, Elijah to Valenia Johnson 9-5-1859 (9-6-1859) Hr
Starkey, Jarvis to Nancy C. Butler 10-25-1858 (10-27-1858) Ma
Starkey, William to Matilda Tims 2-11-1829 Ma
Starks, John F. to Martha J. Orr 2-16-1854 Hn
Starks, P. W. to L. E. King 9-7-1855 We
Starks, Peter to Patsy Bond 12-18-1877 Hy
Starks, Pharaoh to Angeline Wynne 12-23-1879 Dy
Starks, R. L. to Mary Mickelbury 1-7-1847 Sh
Starks, Reuben to Martha Ann Innes? 10-19-1854 Hn
Starks, S. R. to Eliza K. Scott 8-26-1847 Sh
Starks, Thomas C. to Winnie Humphries 8-11-1842 Hn
Starks, Thomas to Susanah Page 1-20-1858 We
Starling, Thos. to Sarah Louisa Sturges 4-6-1859 (4-7-1859) Sh
Starling, William Shadrach to Mary Quimmly? 7-20-1846 (7-20-1846) T
Starnes, A. Pinckney to Ann Boothe 3-23-1844 T
Starnes, Ebenezer to Mary F. Robison 9-22-1848 (no return) L
Starnes, H. C. to Mary M. Manasco 3-7-1865 (3-8-1865) T
Starnes, Harvey C. to Delila M. Shultz 6-1-1867 (6-2-1867) T
Starnes, Henry T. to Mary E. Craig 2-24-1872 (no return) L
Starnes, J. R. to Josephine Stokes 7-20-1853 (7-21-1853) T
Starnes, James to D. Ann Davidson 3-13-1866 (3-14-1866) T
Starnes, John W. to Sarah Johnson 12-2-1867 (12-4-1867) T
Starnes, John to Hanah E. Huggens 1-12-1861 (1-13-1861) L
Starnes, Jonathan to Mildred Hannah 7-6-1845 Sh
Starnes, Marsall to Sarah Golding 12-5-1838 L
Starnes, Marshall to Parlee Johnson 5-27-1851 (5-28-1851) L
Starnes, Stroder to Harriet Ray 7-16-1864 L
Starnes, T. F. to Sarah A. Forest 2-29-1861 Be
Starnes, Wm. to Nancy Timms 7-9-1860 (7-12-1860) T
Starns, William to Catherine Hutchens 7-24-1844 Sh
Starr, William to Mary Ann (Mrs.) Dickey 2-27-1861 Sh
Starrett, Robert C. to Amanda J. Hogan 2-15-1851 (2-18-1851) O
Statham, Robert H. to Martha E. Gills 4-15-1858 O
Staton, Charles to Martha A. Syler 3-12-1845 Hn
Staton, Daniel H. to Martha E. Dickson 6-27-1856 (6-28-1856) G
Staton, Everet to Kissiah Berry(Beny) 7-26-1828 (7-28-1828) Hr
Staton, J. J. to T. A. Anderson 5-31-1865 Hn
Staton, Thomas to Lavina Spellings 1-21-1836 (1-22-1836) G

Staton, William to Elizabeth Little 9-10-1846 G
Staton, Wm. F. to Martha S. H. Gray 6-3-1867 (6-6-1867) T
Statum, George to Josephine Livingstone 10-25-1877 Dy
Stayton, E. F. to N. P. Robertson 3-1-1873 (3-3-1873) Cr
Steadman, Jno. A. to Annie E. Haskins 11-8-1869 (11-11-1869) Ma
Steadman, Nathan W. to Nancy Stewart 12-19-1855 Ma
Stearns, John to Martha Massey no date (with 1862) T
Stearns, Lamotte to Lizzie L. Klyce 1-22-1866 (1-23-1866) F
Stearns, Marshall to Maggie Churchwell 9-2-1884 (9-3-1884) L
Steart, T. W. to Hellen T. Brown 10-18-1871 (no return) Dy
Steavans, Alx. to Lucy Rogers 2-8-1878 Hy
Steaverson, Walter P. to Harriet Gansey 4-19-1871 L
Steavins, Clark to Anna Ware 12-26-1877 Hy
Stedham, Anderson to Jane C. Johnson 4-12-1839 F
Stedham, William to Eliza Sowell 12-14-1848 (no return) F
Stedham, Wm. to F. L. Henley 7-2-1860 (7-12-1860) F
Stedman, H. W. to Susan A. Horne 6-3-1863 Sh
Steed, Calier A. to Ellen B. Burus 1-20-1857 Ma
Steed, George to Malisa Snellings 1-2-1869 G B
Steed, James N. to Jane Ewing 1-11-1859 Ma
Steed, Noah G. to Emiline O. Burke 1-31-1850 We
Steel, David M. to P. E. Johnson 8-17-1845 We
Steel, I. to A. D. Klyce 12-22-1868 Hy
Steel, J. E. to Elizabeth Morris 3-8-1870 Hy
Steel, J. W. to Hulda Ann Steeley 6-6-1865 Hn
Steel, James to Sarah Johnson 1-21-1845 Cr
Steel, James W. to Frances Moody 10-14-1857 Hn
Steel, James to Lucy Ann Guill 12-23-1852 Hn
Steel, Jno. B. to P. E. Slow 9-27-1859 (9-28-1859) F
Steel, John A. to Nancy E. Sloan 7-10-1856 (7-21-1856) G
Steel, John J. to Mary Ann Phelps 4-22-1847 Hn
Steel, John to Eliza P. Shankle 11-15-1848 Cr
Steel, John to Nancy Mathis 6-14-1860 Cr
Steel, Minor to Elizabeth L. Allen 3-26-1850 Be
Steel, Ninian F. to Phebe A. Wilson 8-27-1846 (no return) F
Steel, Samuel S. to Clarissa E. Bryson 5-5-1867 Hn
Steel, Sidney to Ann J. Freeland 5-20-1846 Cr
Steele, D. P. to Sallie Williamson 2-1-1875 Hy
Steele, David P. to Mary Currie 12-16-1858 L
Steele, Doctr. G. T. to E. A. Williams 9-4-1851 (no return) F
Steele, Frederick to Precilla Raffo 7-15-1861 Sh
Steele, Geo. to Eliza Pannell 5-16-1860 Hr
Steele, Henry to Mary Ann Stein 10-19-1882 (no return) L
Steele, James M. to Unity A. Parham 11-21-1850 We
Steele, John H. to Annie Stein 11-20-1882 (no return) L
Steele, John S. to G. A. Moore 10-4-1869 (10-6-1869) Cr
Steele, John T. to Mary J. Smith 5-29-1867 (5-30-1867) Cr
Steele, John to Margaret L. Wilson 1-6-1845 (1-9-1845) T
Steele, Ninian to Hannah Harvey 11-2-1826 H
Steele, S. H. to Mary P. Looney 12-25-1866 (12-26-1866) L
Steele, S. W. to Mary A. Neely 8-4-1852 Sh
Steele, Stephen H. to Cornelia E. Stith 4-28-1858 (no return) L
Steele, W. F. to M. E. Ayers 1-10-1876 (1-12-1876) Dy
Steele, W. to M. Allen 3-21-1842 Be
Steele, William to Malissa Thomas 2-19-1869 G B
Steele, Wm. A. to Mary V. Willis 9-2-1866 Be
Steeley, Robert T. to Jane Shipley 12-15-1841 (no return) Hn
Steelman, Alison T. to Elizabeth J. Steelman 10-10-1848 Sh
Steelman, D. to Nancy Harris 8-19-1880 L
Steelman, James to Frances Sim (Linn?) 5-6-1850 Sh
Steelman, W. H. to Z. C. Gurley 8-11-1862 (9-11-1862) O
Steely, J. M. to Martha Bowman 11-27-1867 Hn
Steepleton, Jonathan to Polly Covington 4-2-1844 Ma
Steepleton, William K. to Delilah Lambert 11-8-1850 Ma
Steffey, W. A. to L. Lizzie Grant 6-13-1860 (6-14-1860) Sh
Stegall, W. L. to Mary M. McIlwaine 4-16-1872 T
Steger, Anderson to Cherry Jones 2-14-1870 (2-23-1870) F B
Steger, John J. to Evalina A. Raiford 6-9-1848 (6-11-1848) F
Steim, Andrew to Louisa Marshall 7-3-1856 Sh
Stein, George F. to Amanda R. Croff 9-1-1881 (9-4-1881) L
Stein, Jefferson W. to Sarah A. Dyre 3-13-1843 (no return) F
Steinbrecker, Peter to Mary Senn 10-2-1858 Sh
Steinkuhl, Jacob to Margaret Wenderoth 7-3-1849 Sh
Stell, Charles C. to Mary C. Hague 5-13-1848 (5-17-1848) G
Stell, J. to Mary Jane Brown 12-20-1864 Sh
Stell, John T. to Lucinda Johnson 4-1-1861 (4-2-1861) Cr
Stell, Lewis to Ann Knowles 4-22-1854 (4-23-1854) Sh
Stell, Lewis to Sarah J. Douglass 2-24-1855 Sh
Stelle, Edward to Amanda Broughton 9-3-1883 (no return) L
Steller, John P. to Julian Butler 11-17-1832 (11-18-1832) G
Stem, Alfred W. to Elizabeth Vancleave 11-27-1850 Hn
Stem, James to Edith A. Kendall 10-2-1853 Hn
Stem, Leonard B. to Mary M. Baucum 8-21-1856 Hn
Stem, Wilson to Drucilla Potts 2-5-1845 (no return) Hn
Stennett, William C. to Emily C. Pigg 12-11-1848 (12-18-1848) O
Step, Calvin H. to Gatsy Richardson 1-22-1853 Be
Step, James to Priscilla (Mrs.) Conway 2-10-1845 G

Stephen, Isaac C. to Mary Jane York 10-29-1839 Ma
Stephen, R. H. to M. W. Nowell 5-10-1854 Cr
Stephen, S. M. to Ellen P. Capps 7-6-1851 Cr
Stephen, Thos. to Mary Little 9-17-1848 Cr
Stephen, William to Elizabeth Hubert 4-26-1825 (4-28-1825) O
Stephen, Wm. to Elizabeth Huffman 8-22-1844 Cr
Stephens(on), James L. to Mary Ann Box 8-17-1853 (8-18-1853) O
Stephens, Andrew to Minerva Jane Griffin 8-21-1860 Ma
Stephens, B. S. to Elizabeth (mrs.) Huett 8-8-1867 G
Stephens, C. G. to Ellen S. Clehorn 5-3-1857 We
Stephens, C. H. to Louisa Bailey 11-11-1844 (11-14-1844) Hr
Stephens, D. H. to S. E. Gillis 3-11-1875 Dy
Stephens, D. M. to Lizzie Hobson 1-14-1878 (1-16-1878) Dy
Stephens, Daniel to Ann B. McDonald 2-17-1848 Sh
Stephens, Ehu A. to Elizabeth Betts 7-6-1852 Hn
Stephens, Ervin to Caroline Haris 12-8-1847 O
Stephens, Ervin to Matilda Taylor 11-28-1862 (12-4-1862) O
Stephens, Fielden to E. M. Williford 8-30-1840 Hn
Stephens, Henry P. to Nancy M. Chandler 1-22-1854 Hn
Stephens, Isaac to Julia Ann Miller 1-7-1852 O
Stephens, Isaiah to Mary A. Lovin 4-26-1855 Sh
Stephens, Israel to Parmelia Johnson 6-23-1857 O
Stephens, J. M. to Jane Joyner 11-26-1874 (11-27-1874) T
Stephens, J. R. G. to Sarah A. Ball 2-7-1871 Hy
Stephens, James E. to Sarah A. Little 12-14-1853 (12-15-1853) Hr
Stephens, James to Mary Hodge 3-22-1839 Hr
Stephens, Jeremiah to Margaret F. Elder 5-1-1854 (5-4-1854) O
Stephens, Jeremiah to Martha Ann Taylor 11-27-1856 (11-28-1856) O
Stephens, Jeremiah to Martha C. Sanders 10-2-1855 (10-3-1855) O
Stephens, John M. to Lucinia House 2-3-1839 Hn
Stephens, John M. to Manda M. Master 8-6-1860 (8-7-1860) O
Stephens, John to Maring Jones 5-5-1841 (5-17-1841) Ma
Stephens, John to Mary A. Halbrooks 8-11-1863 Dy
Stephens, John to Polly McCain 2-10-1848 (2-11-1848) Ma
Stephens, Joseph O.(C.) to Mary F. Richardson 6-21-1858 (6-23-1858) Hr
Stephens, Joseph to Rebecca Coker 7-30-1879 L
Stephens, Lawrence to Elizabeth Brock 12-8-1840 (12-13-1840) Hr
Stephens, Lawrence to Margaret Siser? 12-4-1854 (12-15-1854) T
Stephens, Marion J. to Martha P. White 11-19-1855 (11-21-1855) G
Stephens, Mortimer to S. B. Robbins 1-30-1878 (no return) Dy
Stephens, Ransom to Betsy A. Sasser 11-26-1849 (12-3-1849) Hr
Stephens, Ruben K. to Minerva Williams 11-2-1870 (11-3-1870) Ma
Stephens, S. J. to Sarah A. Hall 1-16-1861 G
Stephens, T. P. to Mary P. Thompson 12-20-1866 Hn
Stephens, Thomas to Adaline Young 8-2-1861 We
Stephens, Thos. N. to Elizabeth Alison 10-10-1843 (10-12-1843) Ma
Stephens, Truman W. to Rutha G. Poynter 12-18-1848 (no return) Hn
Stephens, W. D. to Jane Hertle 12-23-1868 (12-25-1868) F
Stephens, W. W. to Jane Norvell 3-19-1874 Hy
Stephens, William C. to Julia Ann Ward 3-9-1853 G
Stephens, William G. to Jane Smith 11-23-1832 (11-24-1832) G
Stephens, William H. to Barbara Miller 12-31-1838 (1-2-1839) Ma
Stephens, William P. to Mary E. Moultrie 11-19-1859 (11-20-1859) O
Stephens, William to Irene H. Campbell 1-14-1885 (1-15-1885) L
Stephens, Wm. A. to Harriet M. Gaskins 11-19-1866 (11-21-1866) Ma
Stephens, Wm. H. to Candas Stafford 11-20-1867 (11-21-1867) F
Stephens, Wm. L. to Sarah A. Hamilton 9-21-1862 G
Stephens, Wm. to Maria McNamara 4-3-1853 (4-6-1853) Sh
Stephenson, C. L. to Mary E. Graham 6-26-1848 O
Stephenson, David to Elizabeth Ammons 9-12-1843 (9-14-1843) Hr
Stephenson, Elijah to Dovey L. M. Ammons 10-25-1842 Hr
Stephenson, F. C. to Emily C. Germany? 12-25-1849 Sh
Stephenson, Geo. to Nancy Burns 12-31-1851 Sh
Stephenson, J. J. to Cate S. James 4-9-1860 (4-10-1860) O
Stephenson, James M. to Martha A. Rooks 3-16-1866 (3-18-1866) Ma
Stephenson, James to Delia M. Hall 11-7-1868 (11-8-1868) Cr
Stephenson, James to Violi (Mrs.) Cobb 5-4-1864 Sh
Stephenson, John to Martha Hisaw 8-8-1844 Cr
Stephenson, M. D. to Rebecca Olive 12-5-1848 (no return) Hn
Stephenson, Oscar S. to Sarah H. Todd 2-12-1845 (no return) Hn
Stephenson, Thomas N. to Alsa Ann Alison 4-25-1843 Ma
Stephenson, Thomas N. to Catherine Kendrick 3-15-1848 Ma
Stephenson, W. C. to Susan Gentry 1-12-1876 Dy
Stephenson, Wm. G. to Louisa B. Stephenson 12-30-1861 Sh
Stephenson, Wm. J. to Elizabeth W. Ward 4-1-1839 Cr
Stephenson, Wm. to Elizabeth Smith 7-5-1840 Cr
Stephison, Daniel to Martha Shane 11-7-1831 G
Sterbler, F. Geo. to M. A. Sommerauer 2-1-1860 Sh
Sterling, Allen to L. B. Billings 9-7-1864 Sh
Sterling, Edward Canfield to Cordilia Seavey 9-7-1860 Sh
Sterling, Jno. to Araminta A. Smith 8-4-1846 Sh
Sterling, John A. to Mary J. Raines 12-23-1866 Hn
Sterling, Robert to Penelope P. Campbell 6-5-1856 Ma
Stern (Storm?), Adriance to Carrie Willis 11-2-1859 (11-3-1859) Sh
Sternberger, Joseph to Lena Schafer 5-31-1876 Hy
Stevans, Eli to Hester Perry 3-26-1878 Hy
Steven, W. A. to Mary Shelton 9-18-1869 (9-19-1869) T

Stevens, A. M. to Julia A. Brackin 12-19-1865 (12-21-1865) Dy
Stevens, A. to Sophronia Adams 10-23-1862 Ma
Stevens, Alfred to Fannie Anderson 9-30-1863 (10-1-1863) L
Stevens, Andrew to Rebecca Ann Gendren 8-20-1845 (8-21-1845) T
Stevens, Atkins to Sarah Ann Carter 12-8-1835 Hr
Stevens, Christopher to Mary Burkett 4-18-1840 Cr
Stevens, Edmond to Amand Winn? 1-27-1873 (1-28-1873) T
Stevens, Edwin to Eliza Cranford 6-26-1832 Hr
Stevens, Elliot to Elizabeth Boyte 2-13-1832 Hr
Stevens, G. H. to Elizabeth Joyner 10-24-1856 T
Stevens, George to Vinetta Morgan 2-18-1877 Hy
Stevens, Haywood to Nancy J. Rose 12-17-1851 (12-18-1851) T
Stevens, Henry to Eliza Sinclair 3-8-1870 (no return) Dy
Stevens, Henry to Sarah Smith 1-30-1866 Hn
Stevens, Henry to Winny Hall 12-28-1870 (12-29-1870) T
Stevens, J. B. G. to Sarah H. Klyce 9-26-1870 Hy
Stevens, J. H. to Mary A. Feezor 1-3-1865 T
Stevens, J. M. to M. E. Stokes 2-26-1872 T
Stevens, James H. to D. Stevens 3-2-1859 Hn
Stevens, James J. to Mary Virginia Case 1-14-1862 Sh
Stevens, James to Marth E. McBride 4-3-1867 T
Stevens, Joel to Martha Ann Stevens 8-18-1852 (8-19-1852) T
Stevens, John B. to Mary Williams 3-22-1850 T
Stevens, John to Anna? Beavers 5-10-1869 (5-13-1869) T
Stevens, John to Cordelia Tatum 12-25-1866 (12-26-1866) F
Stevens, John to Mary Rice 11-6-1866 T
Stevens, John to Winnie Smith 9-17-1866 T
Stevens, Julius to Eliza Pender 3-12-1870 Hy
Stevens, Lewis to Frances Stevens 1-19-1844 (1-24-1844) F
Stevens, Lewis to Mary Jane Menafee 5-5-1871 (5-7-1871) T
Stevens, Lovod to Nancy Eleanor Fortner 1-20-1878 T
Stevens, M. C. H. to Mary A. Jones 1-11-1857 Hn
Stevens, Moore to Catharine McDonald 12-24-1849 T
Stevens, Needham to Laura E. Smith 12-15-1874 (12-16-1874) T
Stevens, Peter H. to Eliza Heckle (Hooker) 1-16-1838 Sh
Stevens, Robert to Ann Maddox 9-23-1860 (not endorsed) F
Stevens, S. to Polly Ann Simpson 9-29-1856 T
Stevens, Samuel L. to Mary Rosan 8-18-1840 (no return) F
Stevens, Thomas D. to Martha A. Blount 11-16-1856 Hn
Stevens, Thomas to Jane Kincaid 1-31-1829 Sh
Stevens, W. A. to Mary Shelton 9-18-1869 T
Stevens, Wiley to Sarah Wiseman 3-18-1865 (3-21-1865) T
Stevens, William C. to Mildrid W. Moore 8-22-1832 Sh
Stevens, William C. to Rosa L. Sanford 12-23-1871 (no return) L
Stevens, William to Fannie Balis 11-25-1871 T
Stevens, Willis to Clarisa Field 1-14-1874 T
Stevens, Wm. H. to Mary M. Stafford 11-1-1862) (not endorsed) F
Stevens, Wylie to Nancy Jane Searcey 6-3-1855 T
Stevenson, A. J. to Adeline Weatherall 12-18-1860 Sh
Stevenson, George W. to Jane Hubbs 12-12-1862 O
Stevenson, J. B. M. to Mary F. Viah? 1-3-1866 (no return) Dy
Stevenson, J. B. to Martha J. Hudgens 8-13-1856 Hn
Stevenson, J. C. to Martha Stewart 8-12-1863 F
Stevenson, James to Jane Smith 1-6-1855 Ma
Stevenson, M. A. to A. E. Stunston 5-6-1863 (no return) We
Stevenson, N. K. to Emma Brown 1-1-1863 Dy
Stevenson, Noah to Julia Pullims 12-16-1865 (12-26-1865) T
Stevenson, Noah to July Pullim 12-16-1865 T
Stevenson, Saml. E. to Rebecca Owen 4-24-1866 (4-29-1866) T
Stevenson, W. G. to M. C. Clutch 6-25-1863 (6-28-1863) F
Stevenson, William M. to Emeline Darnall 10-23-1841 O
Stevenson, Wm. to Ann Quinn 10-1-1859 (10-2-1859) Sh
Steward, A. A. to Mollie E. Pierce 12-23-1875 L
Steward, Asberry to Winniford Pittman 12-5-1878 L
Steward, B. S. to M. I. Meadows 1-9-1873 L
Steward, Edward H. to Mary Hale 12-18-1852 (12-19-1852) Hr
Steward, George to Amanda Wood 1-1-1878 Dy
Steward, J. F. to S. A. Braden 12-7-1875 (12-8-1875) L
Steward, James A. to Emma Dodson 4-22-1862 (4-23-1862) F
Steward, M. to M. Crausby 11-4-1850 (no return) L
Steward, Wm. M. to Sarah J. Stram 12-14-1850 (12-17-1850) F
Stewart, A. R. to Martha A. Dallas 2-16-1858 Sh
Stewart, Able to Ann Mitchell 12-26-1853 Hr
Stewart, Albert G. to Susan H. Rea 1-2-1840 Sh
Stewart, Alexander to Mira Tuberville 5-12-1827 (5-15-1827) Hr
Stewart, Alfred to Join Goff 10-7-1839 L
Stewart, Allen G. to Malinda Peak 4-5-1869 G
Stewart, Allen to Elvira Scott 7-18-1869 Hy
Stewart, Andrew C. to Mary A. Bradberry 2-16-1846 Ma
Stewart, Andrew to Josephine T. Pharr 9-16-1857 Sh
Stewart, Andrew to Triona L. Springer 12-5-1865 (12-6-1865) Cr
Stewart, B. C. to M. L. Hilliard 8-23-1860 Hy
Stewart, B. G. to Mary A. Goodrich 12-19-1839 (12-23-1839) Ma
Stewart, B. L. to Eliza (Mrs.) Scott 8-30-1869 (9-2-1869) L
Stewart, Benager to Lydia B. Dill 4-4-1868 (4-5-1868) Cr
Stewart, C. B. to J. Lou Hamilton 6-13-1871 Ma
Stewart, C. M. to V. A. Walker 2-13-1860 Sh

Stewart, Calvin E. to Catharin Baw 12-28-1851 (no return) F
Stewart, Charles L. to Ann Eliza Brent 1-31-1848 Ma
Stewart, Charles to Nancy A. Maxwell 6-3-1841 Hn
Stewart, Daniel M. to Mary H. McMurray 11-27-1866 Hy
Stewart, David A. to Anna E. Joyner 1-17-1877 Hy
Stewart, David C. to Jane Marshall 8-13-1878 Hy
Stewart, David H. to Sarah Walker 7-3-1845 Sh
Stewart, E. A. to Margaret Neel 12-5-1860 F
Stewart, E. B. to S. C. Turner 10-12-1878 (no return) L
Stewart, E. P. to Mary Batte 9-11-1840 Sh
Stewart, E.B. to Lucy M. Farriss 1-26-1859 (1-27-1859) Hr
Stewart, Edward D. to Winny Ann Baw 12-30-1845 F
Stewart, Edward H. to Charlotte Short 10-25-1849 (11-17-1849) Hr
Stewart, Edward to Lucindy Ross 11-16-1843 Cr
Stewart, Elisha T. to Mary E. Huddleston 7-20-1859 Hr
Stewart, Enock to Adaline O. Hancock 12-3-1851 (12-4-1851) Hr
Stewart, F. H. to Mary A. Tanner 4-7-1852 Sh
Stewart, Finney to Sarah M. Mathis 5-7-1861 Hn
Stewart, Frank to Nannie Barbee 12-9-1866 Hy
Stewart, G. W. to Josephine A. McCoy 11-23-1876 Hy
Stewart, Geo. M. to Angelina Branch 1-7-1846 F
Stewart, Geo. Washington to Sarah Quimby 7-4-1822 Sh
Stewart, George W. to Sarah Lucinda Goode 1-19-1860 Hn
Stewart, George to Frances Fletcher 12-20-1869 F B
Stewart, H. Alexander to Elizabeth C. Cole 3-17-1853 (3-23-1853) Hr
Stewart, Ham to Ann Caldwell 11-27-1865 (no return) F
Stewart, Henry A. to Rachel Grady 12-17-1858 (12-20-1858) Sh
Stewart, Henry B. to Jane Catherine Redditt 12-1-1848 Sh
Stewart, Henry to Ada Austen 2-24-1882 (no return) L
Stewart, Henry to Joanna Joiner 5-11-1867 (no return) F B
Stewart, Henry to Mary Ann Harral 8-27-1845 Sh
Stewart, Henry to _____ 1-23-1869 L
Stewart, Hugh M. to Susan A. Mathews 1-18-1847 Sh
Stewart, J. B. to B. J. Dinwiddie 3-13-1859 Cr
Stewart, J. C. to Elizabeth Anderson 3-2-1853 (3-8-1853) O
Stewart, J. D. to N. M. Taylor 6-8-1861 (6-11-1861) Sh
Stewart, J. P. to Mary E. Rodgers 3-27-1842 Sh
Stewart, J. S. to Mary L. Gillispie 8-15-1849 Sh
Stewart, James A. to Frances Barker 9-22-1841 Cr
Stewart, James A. to Mary C. Keaton 12-12-1849 Cr
Stewart, James C. to Martha Morgan 3-22-1866 G
Stewart, James D. to Annie J. Price 3-9-1869 G
Stewart, James D. to Jarusha Jane (Mrs) Taylor 11-3-1867 Cr
Stewart, James Donald to Mary Ann Epperson 6-1-1848 Sh
Stewart, James E. to Christiana E. Adams 5-9-1854 Hr
Stewart, James E. to Margaret F. Bryant 8-27-1861 Mn
Stewart, James F. to Celina Blow 8-28-1848 Cr
Stewart, James L. to Alice G. Anderson 3-30-1830 Sh
Stewart, James M. to Jane Epperson 8-30-1849 Sh
Stewart, James M. to Nancy Ann Simpson 2-8-1864 (2-11-1864) O
Stewart, James P. to Jane Cross 9-7-1837 (9-8-1837) G
Stewart, James W. to Mary Dye 8-21-1845 Sh
Stewart, James to Eliza Ledsinger 12-28-1870 (12-29-1870) Dy
Stewart, James to Margaret B. Fife 11-4-1863 Sh
Stewart, James to Mary Ann Rose 6-29-1867 (7-1-1867) Ma
Stewart, James to Sarah J. Hendren 11-7-1866 T
Stewart, Jerry to Clarissa Wadd 6-10-1866 Hn B
Stewart, Jerry to Ella Taliaferro 5-7-1874 Hy
Stewart, John A. to F. E. Byrn 12-31-1878 (1-1-1879) L
Stewart, John C. to Elizabeth Bond 12-13-1847 Sh
Stoat, John C. to Hettie E. Hale 2-6-1854 (2-14-1854) Sh
Stewart, John M. to Elizabeth M. Carr 1-16-1845 Hn
Stewart, John M. to Nancy Elizabeth Crews 10-12-1870 (10-13-1870) Dy
Stewart, John T. to L. E. Bradshaw 1-13-1864 (1-14-1864) Sh
Stewart, John W. to Martha J. Haynes 2-18-1847 Hn
Stewart, John Wesley to Elizabeth Williams 7-18-1867 G
Stewart, John to Elizabeth W. Taliaferro 6-16-1835 G
Stewart, John to Mary Burch 4-8-1846 T
Stewart, John to Roseana M. Bates 8-23-1837 (8-24-1837) G
Stewart, John to Sallie Shaw 1-2-1866 Hy
Stewart, Joseph H. to Margaret Brooks 2-23-1860 We
Stewart, Joseph L. to Nancy Jane Collins 10-9-1845 We
Stewart, L. J. to Irene Lucas 11-18-1885 L
Stewart, M. A. to Sarah F. Farriss 12-26-1854 (12-27-1854) Hr
Stewart, M. D. L. to Sallie Coleman 10-18-1854 Sh
Stewart, Marcus H. to Mary Ann Leznik 12-19-1848 (12-21-1848) F
Stewart, Martin to Martha Crausby 11-4-1850 (no return) L
Stewart, N. J. to Sarah McCoy 9-4-1869 Hy
Stewart, N. R. to Elizabeth Webb 12-29-1855 (no return) F
Stewart, P. B. to Sarah E. Matthews 4-26-1847 Sh
Stewart, Patrick to Ann L. Witherington 1-13-1859 G
Stewart, R. A. to Caroline P. Goodgion 10-13-1867 Hn
Stewart, R. J. to Kate Hays 11-19-1864 Sh
Stewart, R. M. to Nancy Gordon 1-10-1869 Hy
Stewart, Richard to Linthia Spencer 9-11-1867 O
Stewart, S. G. to Martha J. Via 6-8-1864 G
Stewart, S.(L?) P. to Mahuldah Carr 2-19-1847 (2-21-1847) Hr

Stewart, Samuel D. to Mourning Ingram 4-5-1852 (4-6-1852) Hr
Stewart, Samuel M. to Nancy W. Sanders 1-1-1851 Sh
Stewart, Samuel to Cheslina? Smith 7-13-1861 (7-18-1861) L
Stewart, Samuel to Fanny Gravitt 1-3-1870 G B
Stewart, Seaborn J. to Dicey King 1-14-1845 (1-19-1845) Ma
Stewart, T. P. to Sarah Parrish 2-5-1868? (1-6-1868) O
Stewart, Thomas to Fanny S. Freeman 9-1-1842 Hn
Stewart, Thomas to Jane Wynn 9-25-1827 Ma
Stewart, Thos. J. to Cathrine Ross 1-22-1842 Cr
Stewart, Thos. to Margaret Linkston 11-4-1863 Sh
Stewart, Thos. to Nancy Smith 12-8?-1846 Cr
Stewart, Tom to Emily Armour 11-18-1865 F B
Stewart, U. T. to Mary Baugh 9-?-1854 (no return) F
Stewart, W. D. to M. J. Turner 12-30-1879 (12-31-1879) L
Stewart, W. F. to A. A. Neighbors 2-9-1856 Hr
Stewart, W. P. to R. M. Gray 2-11-1856 Sh
Stewart, William E. to Elizabeth B. Duffy 3-7-1853 (3-8-1853) Ma
Stewart, William E. to Mary Elizabeth Parrish 9-21-1860 (9-23-1860) Ma
Stewart, William P. to Susan E. Adams 11-9-1842 G
Stewart, William to Cela Ann Bailey 2-12-1849 (2-17-1849) Hr
Stewart, Wilson E. to Margaret C. Bostick 10-17-1859 Ma
Stewart, Wilson E. to Mary A. Alexander 8-5-1878 (8-10-1868?) Ma
Stewart, Wilson to Hannah Tyson 1-12-1871 Hy
Stewart, Wm. N. to Martha E. Blankenship 12-7-1868 G
Stewart, Wm. to Carolina Kirby 7-5-1846 Cr
Stewart?, Andrew to Triona L. Springer 12-5-1865 (12-6-1865) Cr
Stice?, H. M. to Sarah C. Futrell 2-11-1856 (no return) Hn
Stigal, Wm. T. to Martha J. Presson 5-17-1863 Be
Stigall, Elijah to Martha A. Raines 5-25-1858 (5-27-1858) G
Stigall, H. to Martha J. Weakes 11-16-1854 Hn
Stigall, Hartwell to Mary Rains 10-24-1853 Hn
Stigall, Henry F. to Margaret A. Williams 9-10-1865 Be
Stigall, Thomas R. to Delila Lamb 8-11-1858 Hn
Stigall, William A. to Jane Somers 1-29-1852 Hn
Stigler, William J. to Margaret E. Lackey 12-28-1867 (no return) Hn
Stiles, Marshall to America J. Bell 11-10-1855 Sh
Stiles, Marshall to Charlotte E. Bell 3-26-1860 (3-28-1860) Sh
Stiles, Samuel to Anne E. Carter 3-24-1855 (3-25-1855) Sh
Stiles, Thomas to Eliza Reynolds 12-16-1852 Sh
Still, Alexander to Ann Ellis 12-26-1873 (12-29-1873) T
Still, Dick to Rebecca Calhoun 6-20-1872 T
Still, J. H. to Eliza Compton 12-1-1854 (no return) F
Still, Thos. W. to Mary Rankins 7-6-1843 We
Still, Wiert F. to Millisy W. Stone 8-5-1839 (no return) L
Still, William to Mary Church 7-3-1857 (7-5-1857) G
Stillwell, Coleman to Ann Banks 12-28-1868 (12-29-1868) T
Stillwell, W. H. to Mary A. Hockaday 8-8-1845 (8-11-1845) G
Stilwell, William H. to Mary Ann Gillespie 11-26-1850 (11-28-1850) G
Stinnett, John to Martha Vaughan 11-2-1854 Hn
Stinson, C. L. to Mary E. Graham 6-26-1848 (7-2-1848) O
Stinson, David to Mary Parker 12-28-1868 (12-29-1868) Dy
Stinson, J.C. to Mary F. Prewett 9-26-1860 (10-24-1860) Hr
Stires, John to Mary Albright 1-2-1845 Be
Stirman (Sturman), Joel H. to Cinthia Jones 4-9-1829 Sh
Stith, R. S. to A. M. Phillips 2-14-1854 (no return) F
Stitt, Alex to Siller Sherrill 7-20-1872 T
Stitt, James Leander to Elizabeth R. Hall 8-9-1854 T
Stitt, Jas. L. to Addie Sraynie? 9-12-1860 (9-13-1860) T
Stitt, Samuel W. to Mollie J. Calhoun 1-10-1860 (1-11-1860) T
Stitt, Thos. W. to Mary Rankin 7-6-1843 (no return) We
Stoat, Jacob A. to Mary A. Clancy 7-29-1846 Sh
Stobaugh, Albert to Nancy Jane Taylor 2-10-1857 Ma
Stobaugh, Ansolem to Julia R. Rooks 8-31-1870 (9-1-1870) Ma
Stobaugh, James to Rebecca Edwards 5-24-1838 Ma
Stobaugh, Robert to Nancy Buffalo 1-4-1869 (1-6-1869) Ma
Stockard, C. C. to Mary E. Green 3-26-1859 (3-27-1859) G
Stockard, C. H. to Patience E. White 4-4-1867 G
Stockard, Thomas to Nancy Edward 10-10-1850 G
Stockard, W. H. to Sarah F. White 9-18-1860 G
Stockdale, George to Martha Winns 5-20-1866 Hn B
Stockdale, W. R. to Mary E. McDaniel 8-2-1863 Be
Stockley, Charles A. to Lucy Jane Trigg 5-13-1846 Sh
Stocks, Caswell to Almira Stocks 5-30-1842 Sh
Stocks, John to Almira Evetts 3-9-1837 Sh
Stocks, Lemon to Sarah Ann Mackey 11-27-1840 Sh
Stockslager, Geo. K. to Susan Burton 10-15-1857 Sh
Stockton, Daniel E. to Lizie Palmer 12-26-1859 Sh
Stockton, Daniel L. to Nancy Ann Jones 8-26-1833 (9-5-1833) Hr
Stockton, J. S. to M. A. Scobey 12-2-1878 (12-5-1878) Dy
Stockton, J. T. to Jennie Pace 9-15-1874 (9-17-1874) Dy
Stockton, John C. to Rhoda Young 8-3-1826 Hr
Stockton, Wm. to Elizabeth Barkley 1-22-1837 Hr
Stoddard, Henry, jr. to Sarah L. C. Kemper 2-7-1859 (2-9-1859) Sh
Stoder, Lecusgal to Haner L. Collins 10-4-1849 Cr
Stoe, William N. to Elizabeth C. (Mrs.) Rowsey 12-30-1868 (12-31-1868) Ma
Stofle, Thomas to Frances Haggard 4-23-1849 Hn
Stofle, William to Nancy J. Bevill 12-23-1838 Hn

Stokeley, D. W. to Ellen Pender 3-22-1880 (3-18?-1880) L
Stokeley, Johnston to Rosa Watson 12-27-1883 L
Stokeley, William to Amy Green 3-9-1881 (3-2?-1881) L
Stokely, A. R. to Patience Rogers 5-18-1875 Hy
Stokely, Ben to Rose Stokely 12-13-1869 Hy
Stokely, Peter to Jane Rogers 7-7-1867 Hy
Stoker, Francis M. to Harinah J. Wright 10-12-1856 Cr
Stoker, Francis M. to Margaret A. Wyatt 10-31-1857 Cr
Stoker, Haywood C. to Jimmie Ann Cox 4-18-1870 (4-19-1870) Cr
Stoker, Isa. to R. L. Smith 1-25-1845 We
Stoker, Robert to Louisa J. Bennett 12-17-1846 Cr
Stoker, W. W. to M. A. Townsel 2-8-1867 Cr
Stoker, William to M. F. Wetherly 7-23-1865 (7-28-1865) O
Stokes, Benjamin G. to Martha Gaines 10-29-1856 (11-9-1856) L
Stokes, C. H. to M. A. Ballard 5-11-1883 (5-13-1883) L
Stokes, Charles T. to Nancy H. Cowell 8-15-1868 (no return) L
Stokes, Charles Thomas to Dollie Stalcupple 9-15-1879 L
Stokes, D. H. to Martha J. Rooks 8-23-1868 Hy
Stokes, D. M. to Nancy E. Waller 11-22-1853 Hn
Stokes, F. M. to R. E. McCord 8-18-1846 Cr
Stokes, Galin to Martha Kirby 1-31-1844 Cr
Stokes, Henry to Ann Macklin 2-13-1869 G B
Stokes, Henry to Clara A. J. Hilliard 10-23-1856 Cr
Stokes, J. L. to Laura Green Clay 9-1-1885 L
Stokes, J. L. to Mary Warren 4-24-1883 (4-27-1883) L
Stokes, James to Lorenda Lucas 12-6-1838 Cr
Stokes, Jasper T. to Mary A. Tucker 12-20-1853 Cr
Stokes, John A. to Nancy P. Hill 11-28-1861 T
Stokes, John Adams to Sarah Sopornia? Freeman 8-6-1851 (8-7-1851) T
Stokes, John B. to Mary E. Cox 11-28-1841 Cr
Stokes, John H. to Louvinia Rogers 11-29-1871 Hy
Stokes, Loyd to Adline Cole 10-26-1870 (10-27-1870) Cr
Stokes, M. L. to N. C. Rose 1-3-1881 (1-4-1881) L
Stokes, Micajah to Virginia A. Hedges 7-7-1870 L
Stokes, P. H. to A. M. Kerbrugh 9-1-1877 (9-13-1877) L
Stokes, W. B.(Green B.) to Masie McBee 3-30-1827 (3-31-1827) Hr
Stokes, W. H. to Martha Manning 8-5-1865 (8-6-1865) L
Stokes, W. L. to Mary Jane Bettis 1-30-1858 (2-2-1858) Sh
Stokes, William T. to Alvina M. Nobles 9-11-1850 L
Stokley, Alex to Chena Vanbunn 11-6-1871 Hy
Stokley, Henry to Kittie Howell 2-25-1869 Hy
Stone, Aaron R. to Louiza Kercey 1-8-1846 Cr
Stone, Alfred to Zelphia Stone? 12-6-1838 Cr
Stone, Asher to Mary Susan Allen 12-26-1849 Sh
Stone, B. B. to H. A. Andrew 12-12-1867 G
Stone, B. R. to Martha Wheatley 2-22-1858 (2-24-1858) L
Stone, Benjamin to Harriet Cross 5-26-1855 (5-28?-1855) Hr
Stone, Bird B. to Mary Fly 5-21-1834 (5-27-1834) G
Stone, Clark L. to Margarett Yerout 2-15-1842 Ma
Stone, Clark to Sary E. Wood 5-4-1840 Cr
Stone, Coburn to Rachael Etheredge 10-5-1833 (10-6-1833) G
Stone, David to Charlotte Bell 6-18-1841 Cr
Stone, G. D. to Mary Bratton 9-23-1840 (9-24-1840) G
Stone, G. W. to Lusey Ann Staples 10-22-1860 (10-25-1860) L
Stone, George D. to Anney Jones 1-6-1840 (1-8-1840) G
Stone, George to Margarett Hicks 11-28-1865 G
Stone, Gordan W. to Elizabeth C. Thompson 6-19-1839 L
Stone, Grief G. to Elizabeth Eastridge 6-14-1836 (6-16-1836) O
Stone, Hartwell M. to Sarah Eveline Delph 3-31-1856 Ma
Stone, Hendley to C. J. Bass 9-4-1858 (9-5-1858) Hr
Stone, Hendley to Emily F. Rankin 9-7-1843 (9-14-1843) Hr
Stone, Henry C. to N. C. Harvy 8-29-1866 (no return) Cr
Stone, Hiram H. to Mary Sanders 3-3-1827 Ma
Stone, Hugh S. to Mary Ann Nuckles ?-14-1839 G
Stone, J. C. to Charlotte Walker 1-4-1875 Hy
Stone, J. L. to Elizabeth Winford 12-18-1860 (12-20-1860) Sh
Stone, J. R. to Fannie E. Parsons 12-20-1870 (12-21-1870) L
Stone, Jacob to Mary Jane Williams 5-30-1842 F
Stone, James M. to Nancy C. Baldwin 1-15-1861 Sh
Stone, James M. to Nancy Jane Roach 3-7-1866 Ma
Stone, James to A. C. Farrington 1-2-1866 (1-3-1866) T
Stone, Joel M. to Lilphia Butler 8-23-1826 Hr
Stone, John A. to Sarah Hall 3-5-1838 Hn
Stone, John D. to Nancy E. McKnight 2-6-1837 (2-7-1837) G
Stone, John G. to Mary Nolen 3-27-1838 (3-29-1838) Ma
Stone, John H. to Louisa Alford 2-17-1874 (2-15-1874) L
Stone, Lemuel to Margaretti Lacey 1-23-1849 (1-24-1849) Ma
Stone, Lemuel to Narcissa M. Newsom 5-31-1854 Sh
Stone, Levi to Eliza Ann Price 8-16-1845 (8-17-1845) G
Stone, M. E. to Sal___ A. Thompson 4-11-1839 L
Stone, Medlin to Rebecca Kilpatrick 2-17-1869 (2-21-1869) Ma
Stone, Nicholas C. to Martha T. Fly 10-18-1834 (10-26-1834) G
Stone, Nicholas P. to Margaret M. Alexander 8-7-1832 Sh
Stone, R. C. to B. A. Thomas 12-31-1866 (1-3-1867) F
Stone, Reubin to Martha Bailey 4-13-1835 Hr
Stone, Richard W. to Lucinda Boone 6-2-1832 (6-6-1832) O
Stone, Robert to Mary A. Fowler 7-8-1846 (7-13-1846) F
Stone, Samuel M. to Elizabeth Cribbs 11-23-1852 G
Stone, Samuel P. to Helen M. Hadley 8-31-1865 Hn
Stone, Samuel S. to Kizia M. Argo 2-10-1848 Cr
Stone, Samuel to Elizabeth Rogers 8-3-1863 (no return) Cr
Stone, Samuel to Nancy Stone 12-21-1843 Cr
Stone, T. to Fanny Slaton (Staton?) 1-17-1867 G
Stone, Thomas B. to Jane Cochran 4-23-1833 O
Stone, Thomas S. to Matilda J. Fielding 5-17-1834 (5-18-1834) G
Stone, Tilford to Dallia Russell 2-5-1839 Cr
Stone, W. A. to M. C. Manley 10-17-1874 (no return) Dy
Stone, W. E. to Alice Byrne 10-6-1858 (10-7-1858) Sh
Stone, W. T. to Maggie B. Owen 12-31-1867 Hy
Stone, Wesly to Adeline Toone 8-30-1844 Ma
Stone, William K. to Sarah E. Emmerson 11-25-1844 Ma
Stone, Wm. M. to Maria Jane Lea 9-22-1867 Hy
Stone, Wm. M. to Sarah J. Cribbs 10-31-1846 G
Stone, Wm. to Margaret Love 2-14-1834 (2-16-1834) Hr
Stone, Zedekiah to Eliza Carter 9-9-1840 Sh
Stone, Zedekiah to Mary Roach 12-26-1854 (12-27-1854) Sh
Stoodley, S. G. to Mary C. Wheller 9-20-1860 L
Stoops, Geo. N. to J. J. Earnheart 7-2-1869 (7-4-1869) F
Storer, Thomas to Sarah E. Coop 12-23-1863 G
Storey, James L. to Narcissa Johnson 5-15-1841 (5-19-1841) Ma
Storey, Littleton to Margarett Johnson 3-5-1844 Ma
Storks, Sam to Eliza Adams 1-30-1869 Hy
Story, Alexander to Elizabeth Johnson 2-10-1843 Ma
Story, J. W. to Frances McClain 2-1-1866 Hn
Story, John R. to Narcissa Lefever 1-9-1859 Hn
Story, N. E. to Susan Yow 9-28-1864 Hn
Story, Otis L. to Rebecca M. Reeves 3-5-1841 (3-1?-1841) Ma
Story, Samuel J. to Mary L. Nance 7-24-1866 Hn
Story, Wm. D. to Elizabeth L. Hill 5-25-1863 Sh
Stott, Henry to Allice Bridgewater 2-18-1871 (3-1-1871) F B
Stott, J. P. to Ann Avery 10-3-1865 G
Stott, John M. to Mattie S. Stott 5-10-1874 Hy
Stott, Oliver to Adeline House 12-26-1870 Hy
Stott, Washington to Jane Marshall 12-27-1871 Hy
Stoup, Henry to Lydia Boyd 11-16-1864 Sh
Stout, Abraham Madison to Maria Pateet 10-24-1849 Sh
Stout, Charles to Elizabeth Caps 8-26-1843 (no return) We
Stout, Chas. to Irene L. McClure 5-10-1864 Sh
Stout, Elihu to Sarah J. Moore 5-11-1855 (5-13?-1855) Hr
Stout, J. W. (Dr.) to Rhody (Mrs.) Frazier 3-13-1838 Sh
Stout, J. to N. E. Brackett 1-3-1859 (1-5-1859) Sh
Stout, James M. to Mary Gray 7-14-1848 Hr
Stout, John W. to Sarah J. Sanders 7-31-1851 Cr
Stout, Levi to Ann Earles 6-15-1843 We
Stout, Lorenzo D. to Catharine (Mrs.) Green 2-18-1858 (7-15-1858) Ma
Stout, M. D. to Elizabeth M. Parker 10-24-1843 We
Stout, Oliver P. to Manivesy E. Upshaw 1-2-1843 Hn
Stout, Samuel L. to Eliza Stubblefield 8-16-1861 We
Stout, Stokely to Fannie Maddox 3-30-1861 (3-31-1861) Sh
Stout, William to Emeline Hunter 12-26-1868 (12-27-1868) F B
Stovall, Benton L. to Malinda Bright 2-11-1862 (2-10?-1862) O
Stovall, Daniel to Mary Barham 3-28-1867 G
Stovall, George A. to Laura J. Williams 4-7-1859 Sh
Stovall, H. D. to Kate E. Mitchell 1-8-1855 We
Stovall, J. E. to T. A. Spikes 12-17-1873 O
Stovall, L. B. to Susan L. Watt 3-19-1860 Sh
Stovall, Samuel to Maggie Moss 12-27-1870 (12-28-1870) O
Stovall, Thomas to Harriett Morris 5-24-1876 (5-25-1876) O
Stovall, W. G. to S. E. Leftwick 2-8-1859 Sh
Stovall, William C. to Martha Ann Matthews 10-30-1847 (11-4-1847) Ma
Stovall, Wm. B. to Sarah Brantley 6-13-1840 (6-14-1840) Hr
Stoveall, John H. to Martha A. Nance 4-8-1858 Hn
Stover, G. W. to Adaline Mitchel 12-26-1866 O
Stover, George W. to Ann Burk 12-20-1854 Ma
Stover, L. E. to Elmira P. Eaves 3-6-1852 (3-7-1852) O
Stover, Lemuel to Rachel Adkerson 8-3-1854 (8-6-1854) O
Stover, R. B. to Phereby Whyte 9-8-1866 (9-10-1866) F
Stover, Wm. H. to Mary Mitchell 12-23-1862 O
Stow, Isaac C. to Susan R. Turbeville 10-24-1861 We
Stow, Lemuel C. to Nancy B. Eskridge 2-12-1859 We
Stow, Samuel A. to Luraney Morris 5-24-1846 Sh
Stowes, Edmund to Clarisa Sheen 12-26-1867 Hy
Straer, Thomas to Sarah E. Coop 12-23-1863 G
Straessler, Henrich (Henry) to Ann Heidrieger 2-26-1846 Sh
Strain, A.(N?) B. to Mary W. Lovelace 2-19-1866 (2-21-1866) L
Strain, Charles T. to Mary Jane McCorkle 12-26-1860 (1-2-1860?) Ma
Strain, Elbert F. to Margaret S. Gardner 12-20-1842 (12-22-1842) L
Strain, John D. to Winny Holloman 9-8-1830 Ma
Strain, John to Dinah Baxter 8-20-1879 L B
Strain, John to Mattie Nelson 12-20-1882 (12-21-1882) L
Strain, Joseph Hagans to Jane Forsyth 1-26-1854 T
Strain, Peter to Martha Walker 12-25-1866 T
Strain, Robert M. to Mary A. Foster 7-13-1842 (7-14-1842) G
Strain, Robert to Mariah C. Tucker 1-27-1859 L

Strain, William D. to Jennette McQuiston 12-17-1847 T
Strain, Wm. Druffin to Eliz. Agnes Faulkner 4-8-1851 T
Straing, R. P. to Margaret E. McQuiston 11-22-1870 T
Strange, Henry to Lucinda Parham 6-7-1848 Cr
Strange, J. to Delila J. Burns 4-11-1842 (4-12-1842) F
Strange, Jesse A. to Mildred Jane Dickson 3-15-1855 Sh
Strange, Jesse to Martha G. Boyd 10-11-1849 Sh
Strange, Jessee to Susan Giles Smith 11-17-1842 T
Strange, John R. to Lucy J. Doyle 5-17-1873 (5-18-1873) L
Strange, Joseph to Amanda Dowd 11-1-1860 G
Strange, Sam to Mollie Cothran 6-18-1874 T
Strange, Wm. H. to Sallie E. Boyd 10-10-1866 (10-11-1866) T
Strange, Wm.R. to Maria E. Murrill 2-9-1857 Sh
Strans, Parminue to Mary Jeffries 8-1-1840 (8-4-1840) Ma
Straton, Ed to Patsey Willis 12-23-1868 (12-24-1869?) G B
Straton, John to M. F. Kirk 10-27-1863 O
Stratten, D. A. to Ugenia Smith 2-3-1864 L
Stratton, Asa S. to Mary E. Chamberlain 7-10-1849 Sh
Stratton, James to Nancy Pride 2-5-1857 O
Stratton, John T. to Emma P. Furguson 9-18-1851 Sh
Stratton, John to Esther Pride 1-21-1850 (1-22-1850) O
Stratton, Samuel to Julia Ann Crowder 1-4-1868 G B
Stratton, Uriah to L(e)acy Pride 1-2-1849 O
Stratton, Uriah to Leacy Pride 1-2-1849 O
Stratton, Wm. H. to Sally A. Waldran 5-4-1859 (5-5-1859) Sh
Straughn, James M. to Mary L. Abbernathy 7-11-1846 F
Straughn, S. H. to Nancy Scott 4-24-1861 Sh
Strausberg, Henry to July Jackson 12-6-1869 G
Strawn, J. A. to S. J. Minton 3-31-1865 (4-1-1865) Dy
Stray, Wesley to Laura Broils 2-27-1868 G B
Strayhorn, Hudson to Elizabeth McLemore 10-7-1871 (no return) Cr B
Strayhorn, Jesse D. to Martha Ann Shepherd 3-10-1873 T
Strayhorn, John A. to Mollie E. Medlin 2-28-1866 Hy
Strayhorn, John Y. to Francis T. Bryan 12-4-1854 Ma
Strayhorn, L. O. to L. F. Hunt 3-2-1869 G
Strayhorn, Newell T. to Lucy A. Smith 1-3-1844 Ma
Strayhorn, Robert J. to Frances N. Pope 1-26-1859 (1-27-1859) Ma
Strayhorn, S. H. to Sarah M. Biggs 12-8-1868 (12-9-1868) Dy
Strayhorn, Willis to Fannie Blair 1-31-1872 (2-1-1872) Dy
Straylin, P. C. to Sarah B. Anderson 5-26-1853 Cr
Strederick?, Gilford to Laura Dent 3-30-1874 (5-31-1874) O
Street, A. G. to E. C. Kinney 5-7-1870 (5-9-1870) T
Street, George C. to Martha J. Powell 9-2-1852 Hn
Street, H. D. to H. E. Cox 12-26-1844 Hn
Street, J. C. to M. J. Kinney 8-2?-1871 (8-3-1871) T
Street, John H. to Elizabeth K. Jernigan 4-15-1861 (no return) Hn
Street, John W. to Nancy A. C. Harrison 8-31-1848 (9-7-1848) Hr
Street, T. J. to Cynthia A. McCommon 12-15-1860 (1-1-1861) Hr
Strehl, G. J. to Louise Biele 11-15-1858 Sh
Strehl, Jacob to Louisa Reebner 6-18-1851 (6-19-1851) Sh
Strehl, Joseph to Sarah Rest 1-22-1851 (1-23-1851) Sh
Strength, E. C. to Mattie Campbell 3-28-1878 Hy
Strength, W. F. to Mollie E. Thomas 3-12-1878 Hy
Stribbling, John Q. to Susan Little 1-26-1853 (no return) Cr
Stribbling, Thades to Elizabeth N. Browning 1-11-1850 Cr
Stribling, S. R. to Mary Cates 5-6-1863 Mn
Stricklan, Jackson to Hasentine Thurmond 2-18-1871 (2-19-1871) Dy
Strickland, A. M. to Elizabeth Prigg 7-23-1849 Cr
Strickland, C. L. to R. L. Davis 7-3-1876 (7-4-1876) L
Strickland, Charles to Gelina Cooper 9-9-1849 Be
Strickland, Cullen to Eliza Porter 6-6-1849 (6-7-1849) Hr
Strickland, E. P. to Emer Eugenia Long 6-23-1862 (no return) L
Strickland, E. P. to Martha Turner 5-24-1854 (no return) L
Strickland, J. S. to Susan D. Conghley 7-29-1866 G
Strickland, James to Harriet Jones 8-26-1866 Hy
Strickland, John A. to Rody Holland 8-24-1853 Be
Strickland, John S. to Mary Jane Allison 12-20-1841 (12-29-1841) Hr
Strickland, L. W. to Charlott Harbet 9-18-1862 (10-30-1862) L
Strickland, Noah to Elizabeth Davidson 3-3-1861 Hy
Strickland, Robt. to Caledonia Grantham 7-10-1868 (no return) F
Strickland, William to Amanda Watkins 5-8-1875 (5-9-1875) Dy
Stricklen, Janus M. to Amanda J. Strange 3-10-1868 Dy
Stricklin, Elijah P. to Melissa Ann Hooper 3-13-1849 L
Stricklin, G. W. to Sarah E. Anderson 5-21-1861 Mn
Stricklin, George W. to Elizabeth White 9-30-1843 (no return) F
Stricklin, J. S. to Mary E. Jones 12-25-1865 Hy
Stricklin, J. W. to Martha E. Jones 4-23-1861 (4-24-1861) Hr
Stricklin, James to Virginia D. Drummond? 7-5-1869 (no return) Dy
Stricklin, Job to F. J. Simpson 10-2-1861 (10-3-1861) Hr
Stricklin, John R. to Biddie Clark 9-2-1869 Hy
Stricklin, John to Elizabeth Ray 1-27-1857 Hy
Stricklin, John to Jane Clark 12-24-1849 G
Stricklin, Nathaniel to Mary Miller 10-14-1840 (10-15-1840) Hr
Stricklin, W. H. to Martha A. Chamberlaine 1-5-1856 Sh
Stricklin, W. L. to M. E. R. Jones 1-26-1863 Mn
Stricklin, Wm. P. to Mary E. Reece 12-6-1851 (12-11-1851) Hr
Strickling, Richard E. to Louisa Bishop 7-20-1846 Sh
Strickling, Washington to Mary E. Jones 1-21-1863 Mn
Stricklun, Wm. to Joanna Howard 11-10-1866 T
Stringer, Leonard to Emaline Rose 3-26-1849 Hn
Stringer, Roland to Mary Williams 1-23-1849 Hn
Stringer, Thomas L. to Allice J. Dodd 1-12-1875 (1-14-1875) L
Stringfellow, H. M. to Lucy T. Brooks 5-30-1860 (5-31-1860) Sh
Strohwig, F. to Louia Countz 4-20-1858 Sh
Strong, Alfred to Caroline McCain 12-2-1865 (12-7-1865) T
Strong, Andrew to Laura Wood? 10-26-1869 T
Strong, Belfast to Amanda McCain 1-19-1869 (1-21-1869) T
Strong, Benjamin to Charlott Hanness 3-15-1847 (no return) F
Strong, C. F. to Sallie Simonton 9-25-1860 (9-26-1860) T
Strong, Charles to Martha Ann Dickson 1-21-1857 (1-22-1857) T
Strong, Henry to Matilda Reed 12-19-1866 T
Strong, James W. to Susan Temple 1-28-1858 We
Strong, James to Mary L. Hubbard 11-12-1844 Sh
Strong, K.? to Martha Moffit 11-15-1871 T
Strong, Morris to Franky Williams 1-1-1868 (1-2-1868) Dy
Strong, O. B. to Lucy A. Williams 2-10-1864 G
Strong, Osborne to T. S. Talley 12-27-1876 Dy
Strong, R. S. to Isabella Jackson 4-12-1870 (4-13-1870) T
Strong, Saml. to Charletta Yarbro 12-11-1867 T
Strong, Thos. J. to Martha Williams 11-11-1870 (11-16-1870) F
Strong, William James to Lauretta L. Bernard 11-16-1847 T
Strong, William to Mary A. Baxter 1-25-1841 Sh
Strong, Wm. James to Mary Ann McCreight 9-25-1850 (9-26-1850) T
Strongham, Lorenza D. to Frances Ellison 7-23-1832 (7-24-1832) Hr
Strook, Daniel H. to Ellen J. Bailey 1-5-1854 (no return) Hn
Strother, Christopher C. to Susan C. Dawtry 1-27-1851 (1-28-1851) G
Strother, G. W. to Harriett Saine? 11-26-1867 (no return) Hn
Strother, Henry to Ann Ferguson 12-24-1868 Dy
Strother, Henry to Harriet Ann Beard 7-18-1873 (no return) Dy B
Strother, Hesikiah to Eliza Smith 10-4-1880 (10-17-1880) Dy
Strother, Hezekiah to Mollie Maddra 7-18-1873 (10-31-1873) Dy
Strother, Sterling to Mary Daughtry 8-30-1842 (9-1-1842) G
Strothers, Solomon G. to Lidia Kilgore 7-13-1830 Hr
Stroud, A. J. to Penelope McFadden 6-7-1857 Hn
Stroud, B. J. to Rebeca Hutchison 10-6-1866 G
Stroud, E. H. to Margaret Wilson 12-26-1883 (12-27-1883) L
Stroud, F. M. to Mary York 2-25-1864 (2-30-1864) Sh
Stroud, Howel to Matilda Hailey 2-24-1842 Hn
Stroud, J. M. to Susan J. Jones 7-24-1871 (7-26-1871) T
Stroud, James (John) to Jane Almon 10-2-1849 O
Stroud, James H. to Mary Jane Haley 1-13-1848 O
Stroud, James W. to Mary A. Stroud 11-27-1857 Hn
Stroud, Jesse to Francess Childress 12-20-1842 (no return) Hn
Stroud, John D. to Emarilla J. Hallum 9-20-1869 (9-22-1869) Cr
Stroud, R. F. to Martha E. Barnett 1-4-1866 Hn
Stroud, R. W. to Emily E. Pool 10-29-1854 Hn
Stroud, Richard A. to C. M. Shelton 4-15-1851 O
Stroud, Silas to Clarissa Jane McLeroy 7-3-1848 (8-4-1848) O
Stroud, Stokeley to Nancy M. Thomas 2-8-1856 Sh
Stroud, Thomas J. to Anna F. Craig 5-19-1864 Hn
Stroud, Thomas M. to Eliza Jarry (Jenny) 6-1-1850 Sh
Stroud, Thos. M. to Rebecca Gaine 4-11-1854 Sh
Stroud, William to Elizabeth Longly 3-10-1829 O
Stround, T. to Sarah J. Phifer 12-26-1860 Be
Stroup, D. S. to Elizabeth Mooney 9-22-1867 Hn
Strouse, Richard to Sarah E. Austin 12-31-1867 (1-1-1868) L
Strown, James M. to Jane E. Hern 12-25-1843 Cr
Stuart, Alfred to Amanda J. Allen 3-12-1844 G
Stuart, Andrew C. to Nancy J. Nowell 2-15-1855 Cr
Stuart, B. C. to H. S. Thornton 12-22-1869 Hy
Stuart, Jno. L. to Martha E. Nickleson 1-26-1871 Hy
Stuart, John B. to Mahaly Allen 1-2-1837 (1-5-1837) G
Stuart, Johnson to Eliza Anderson 10-30-1871 (11-4-1871) T
Stuart, William C. to Elizabeth Fuqua 2-13-1844 (2-14-1844) G
Stubblefield, Alexander to Nancy J. Stubblefield 11-12-1844 We
Stubblefield, B. M. to N. M. A. D. Lewis 9-13-1867 G
Stubblefield, James W. to Mary A. Manard 9-8-1847 Cr
Stubblefield, R. W. to M. Fanny Coleman 11-16-1866 Hn
Stubblefield, Richard to Louisa E. Lawson 8-20-1858 Hn
Stubblefield, Riley to Sarah Neese? 12-7-1851 Hn
Stubblefield, Thomas to Margaret Ellis 10-28-1862 Hn
Stubblefield, W. F. to Martha A. Echols 11-1-1853 Sh
Stubblefield, W. R. to Narcissa (Mrs.) Crider 12-7-1865 G
Stubblefield, William to Lucinda Reed 5-14-1867 G
Stubbs, Berry to Susan Weaver 3-9-1866 Hn
Stubbs, John to Mary Jones 7-6-1846 (7-14-1846) O
Stubbs, John to Mourning Stubbs 11-4-1856 (11-5-1856) O
Stubbs, Julius to Susan Clements 12-27-1866 T
Stubbs, N. J. to E. K. Anderson 11-26-1870 (12-1-1870) Cr
Stubbs, Thomas J. to Jane C. Anderson 1-3-1870 (1-20-1870) Cr
Stubenfield, Jerry S. to Sarah M. A. Taylor 12-17-1857 Hn
Stubenrauck, John Geo. to Louisa Brockmann 4-22-1854 (4-23-1854) Sh
Stubilfield, J. W. to Margaret Robinson 6-5-1856 We
Stublefield, A. H. to Emeline Bridges 6-2-1859 Hn

Stublefield, William R. to Mary Belch 6-1-1858 (6-3-1858) G
Stuck, H. J. to A. V. Bointon 5-9-1860 Sh
Stuckey, Alexander to Caroline Hutchison 5-15-1861 (no return) L
Stuckey, Alexander to Mary E. M. Black 1-31-1855 (2-7-1855) L
Stuckey, D. M. C. to Fredonia M. Ruth 4-10-1867 (4-11-1867) L
Stuckey, Doctor McC___ to Ruthy Ann Hipp 12-26-1855 (12-27-1855) L
Stuckey, James to Malinda Meadows 9-6-1847 (9-7-1847) L
Stuckey, Jesse S. L. to Sarah Hutchison no date (with Aug 1862) L
Stuckey, Noah to Elizabeth Langley 5-9-1848 (5-11-1848) L
Studdard, Melton to Catherine Woodard 10-8-1840 Cr
Studivant, Ned to Amanda Jeffreys 3-26-1870 Hy
Studvant, Andrew J. to Frances A. Reeves 9-7-1852 (no return) F
Stull, Abram to Paulina Carter 7-4-1855 Sh
Stull, R. D. to Joseph Isabella Staggs 1-30-1877 Dy
Stull, Stephen to Phoebe Cannon 7-21-1866 (7-22-1866) F B
Stults, William to S. A. Wilson 12-1-1857 G
Stump, Harrison to Bridget O'Hara 11-20-1860 (11-24-1860) Sh
Stump, John to Margaret Braden 4-15-1861 Mn
Stunson, Lewis to Louiza A. Alexander 1-9-1845 Hn
Stunston, Rufus to Rosina Carroll 8-12-1866 Hn
Stunten, Levi to Ammana F. Stephens 5-12-1857 We
Sturdevant, Frank to Ellen Lea 12-1-1878 Hy
Sturdevant, John Ingram to Lydia A. Bradford 11-24-1868 (11-25-1868) Ma
Sturdevant, Thomas J. to Mary Ann A. Garrett 9-14-1858 Ma
Sturdevant, William J. to Joanna Dew 1-15-1861 (1-16-1861) Ma
Sturdivant, Anderson to Elizabeth Hart 10-12-1854 Hn
Sturdivant, Benjamin to Elizabeth Templeton 1-4-1848 Ma
Sturdivant, Davidson P. to Elizabeth Hart 12-27-1866 Hn
Sturdivant, Jacob to Harriet Golden 7-17-1869 G B
Sturdivant, Oliver to Tennessee Oliver 2-10-1868 G
Sturdivant, Richard B. to Adaline Wynns 10-14-1846 Hn
Sturdivant, Washington to Mary Ann Ford 7-21-1852 (7-23-1852) Ma
Sturdivant, Wm. J. to Amelia Smith 9-4-1855 (9-5-1855) Hr
Sturges, Franklin to Elizabeth Furguson 3-22-1848 Sh
Sturges, Samuel M. to Emily Grigery 5-9-1835 Sh
Sturges, William to Lucata Exum 12-23-1858 O
Sturgin, J. P. to Fannie Rainey 7-6-1859 Sh
Sturgis, Hiram to Nally (Hally) Furguson 9-17-1847 Sh
Sturgis, Joshua L. to Mary D. Hays 3-14-1861 T
Sturkie, John A. to Emily C. Moxley 4-9-1866 (4-10-1866) Ma
Sturla, Angelo to Elizabeth Stephens 8-11-1849 Sh
Sturt, John C. to Sarah J. Freeman 9-19-1856 We
Sturtivant, Jess to Elizabeth Smith 7-10-1841 (7-14-1841) Ma
Stute, William G. to Cynthia W. Rucker 10-31-1842 (11-4-1842) Ma
Stutham, William to Martha Russell 5-30-1849 (5-31-1845) T
Stutman, Isaac to Martha Huskey 7-3-1842 Sh
Styers, George W. to Mary C. Thompson 12-23-1885 L
Styers, J. E. to Frances E. Addison 2-21-1885 (2-24-1885) L
Styers, J. H. to Jennie (Mrs.) Bates 10-3-1885 (10-4-1885) L
Styers, J. H. to Matilda C. Vardeman 11-28-1869 Hy
Styers, T. H. to M. I. Loving 11-25-1869 Hy
Styles, James to Nancy E. Shepherd 9-10-1839 (no return) Hn
Styles, L. A. to Savannah A. Airy? 2-21-1850 Hn
Subject, Elick to Sarah Robinson 9-22-1877 Hy
Sudberry, J. W. to Rachel James 3-19-1860 Hy
Sudberry, James F. to M. E. Smith 11-25-1873 (no return) Dy
Suddith, John W. to Mary Jane Clark 1-5-1853 Hn
Sudsberry, G. W. to Harriet E. Gibson 12-31-1884 L
Suesberry, Billy to Nancy Perry 11-25-1871 Hy
Sufferin, Henry to Margaret Loghlen 5-21-1864 Sh
Suffield, W. to Mary Rogers 12-21-1841 (12-25-1841) F
Sugg, J. D.? to T. J. King 9-7-1866 (9-9-1866) Cr
Sugg, W. S. to Louisa J. Walker 1-18-1864 (1-20-1864) L
Sugg, Wiley P. to Almedia C. V. Parr 12-18-1855 L
Sugg, Wiley P. to Sue Anderson 2-8-1868 (2-12-1868) L
Suggett, Benjamin B. to Parthena B. Holloway 1-27-1846 (1-28-1845?) F
Suggs, Isaac J. to Margaret Jackson 5-4-1848 Sh
Suggs, Isaac J. to Susan E. Epps 4-7-1851 (4-9-1851) Sh
Suggs, Joseph to Martha J. Bridges 8-2-1846 Cr
Suggs, Sims to Laura Ann Johnson 7-1-1839 Cr
Suggs, Sylvester to Sarah C. Capell 11-15-1884 L
Suggs, William H. to Josephine Maniss 1-18-1872 L
Suggs?, Wm. A. to Mary C. Bridges 8-18-1860 Cr
Suiter, W. J. to L. M. Nelson 11-1-1871 (11-2-1871) Cr
Sulenger, Roger T. to Elizabeth Hill 8-25-1828 (8-27-1828) Hr
Sulfrige, W. to Margaret Johnson 12-31-1872 (1-2-1873) T
Sulivan, G. W. to L. A. Gregory 11-25-1874 Hy
Sulivan, Henry to Elizabeth McCain 12-12-1850 We
Sulivan, Jacob to Abigail Young 9-1-1850 We
Sulivan, Nathan to Mary Jane Ross 10-8-1840 Sh
Suliven, Jacob to Eliza McKane 11-18-1860 We
Sulivine, W. M. to Martha Ann Sanderson 3-22-1852 We
Sullender, Samuel to Elizabeth Goodman 8-5-1834 Hr
Sullens, Columbus to Lavinia Webb 1-31-1864 Be
Sullinger, John E. to Patsey A. Clanton 9-5-1868 T
Sullinger, John E. to Patsey Clanton 9-5-1868 (9-7-1868) T
Sullivan, A. C. to S. Sullivan 11-9-1839 Ma

Sullivan, Albert G. to Mary F. Crisp 5-4-1843 Hr
Sullivan, Andrew to Margaret Wellehan 4-14-1863 Sh
Sullivan, B. H. to Anna Stephens 2-23-1876 Dy
Sullivan, Calvin W. to Julia Ann Horn 6-27-1858 Hn
Sullivan, Charles L. to Margaret L. Anderson 5-14-1860 (5-15-1860) Sh
Sullivan, Daniel to Mary (Mrs.) Kenney 12-21-1863 (1-6-1864) Sh
Sullivan, Eliazer to Martha Glidewell 9-26-1870 (9-28-1870) Ma
Sullivan, Eugene to Mary (Mrs.) Foley 1-25-1864 (1-26-1864) Sh
Sullivan, Geo. to Ellen McKinney 10-1-1854 Sh
Sullivan, H. to Mary Jane Pennel 10-23-1856 (11-3-1856) T
Sullivan, Hyram W. to Frances J. Bowles 8-2-1848 Hn
Sullivan, Isaac T. to Caroline Kirk 11-13-1866 (11-15-1866) O
Sullivan, J. A. to G. A. McLeary 2-18-1869 G
Sullivan, J. B. to M. J. Wetherspoon 2-19-1864 G
Sullivan, J. P. to Mary M. Hays 8-15-1857 Sh
Sullivan, Jacob A. to Mary F. Wooten 9-7-1869 (9-8-1869) T
Sullivan, Jacob to Elizabeth J. Trobough 12-21-1842 (12-23-1842) T
Sullivan, James to Bridget McDonnell 11-1-1855 (11-4-1855) Sh
Sullivan, James to Susan Balew 11-7-1867 G
Sullivan, Jeff to Mariah McNeill 8-10-1870 (8-11-1870) F B
Sullivan, Jeremiah to Mary Daly 3-14-1863 Sh
Sullivan, Jerimiah to Eliza Lambert 1-17-1843 Ma
Sullivan, John E. to Sally Galbreath 9-23-1867 T
Sullivan, John J. to Martha J. Stroud 6-30-1857 (no return) Hn
Sullivan, John to Bridget Ryan 1-6-1862 Sh
Sullivan, John to Elizabeth Wilson 1-9-1855 (1-11-1855) T
Sullivan, John to Polly Harrison 8-11-1855 (8-15-1855) Hr
Sullivan, Mitchell to Lizzie Baison 4-24-1878 Hy
Sullivan, N. A. to N. W. Mears 11-25-1871 (11-30-1871) T
Sullivan, Owen to M. Galoven (Currie) 9-11-1875 Hy
Sullivan, Patrick to Margaret Pickett 7-6-1852 Sh
Sullivan, Patrick to Mary Rigney 2-21-1857 (2-22-1857) Sh
Sullivan, Patrick to Mary Shea 10-2-1851 Sh
Sullivan, Paulding A. to Nancy Elizabeth Hastings 8-4-1867 Hn
Sullivan, Peter to Julia Sullivan 8-7-1858 (8-8-1858) Sh
Sullivan, Preston to Mary Sprows 4-3-1841 (5-5-1841) Ma
Sullivan, Ramsom to Mary Nichelson 3-4-1830 Sh
Sullivan, Robt. P. to Clara Rousan 5-29-1867 (5-30-1867) T
Sullivan, Thomas to Elizabeth Ann Darley 6-11-1855 (no return) F
Sullivan, Thomas to Mary Holcomb 9-20-1866 (9-3?-1866) Cr
Sullivan, W. to Catherine Crimmins 2-10-1862 Sh
Sullivan, William to Sarah Redford 12-23-1860 Hn
Sullivant, Charles W. to Mary E. Davis 7-23-1850 (no return) F
Sullivant, Jeremiah to Martha Gray 1-3-1842 Hr
Sullivant, Jesse H. to Mary An Bell 12-12-1848 (12-14-1848) F
Sullivant, Mitchel to Maria Walker 1-18-1866 Hy
Sullivant, Rhesa? R. to Elizabeth Edwards 1-4-1842 (1-11-1842) F
Sumerow, Charley L. to Hester Ann Carnall 3-29-1867 (3-30-1867) L B
Sumerow, George H. to Elvira Smith 11-21-1854 (11-23-1854) L
Sumerow, Henry T. to Ellen Smith 12-20-1853 (12-21-1853) L
Sumerow, Jasper to Sarah Parr 8-2-1872 (8-3-1872) L B
Sumerow, Jesse M. to Sarah E. Sumerow 10-3-1854 (10-5-1854) L
Sumerow, W. F. to E. R. Somerow 10-28-1874 L
Sumerow, William to Mary Cherry 10-18-1880 (10-20-1880) L
Sumers, J. W. to A. E. Sumers 3-31-1874 (4-3-1874) O
Sumers, John to Martha Harris 2-16-1857 We
Sumner, John W. to Emmaline Trimble 2-21-1843 (no return) Hn
Summerell, G. C. to Elizabeth J. Baugh 9-13-1849 Sh
Summers, Charles L. to Elizabeth Key 9-26-1838 Hn
Summers, Edward to Abegale C. Roberts 5-12-1857 We
Summers, Eli A. to Martha Jane Daw 11-12-1856 G
Summers, F. F. to P. T. Evans 12-10-1868 Hy
Summers, George P. to Martha J. Lane 11-7-1843 (11-8-1843) O
Summers, George W. to Sarah (Miss) Bradford 11-3-1864 (11-5-1864) O
Summers, Ivory to J. E. (Mrs.) Morris 1-11-1876 Hy
Summers, J. A. to Callie E. Burnett 1-25-1869 (1-27-1869) F
Summers, James to Unity M. Terrell 12-12-1844 We
Summers, Jesse L. to Ellen Nowell 9-12-1866 Be
Summers, Jesse L. to Rebecca J. Owens 8-2-1849 Hn
Summers, Jesse L. to Sarah E. Owen 9-6-1857 (no return) L
Summers, John D. to Rebecca Wilson 5-14-1853 (no return) Hn
Summers, John W. to Elizabeth Davidson 1-8-1851 (no return) Hn
Summers, John W. to Margaret E. Turner 10-1-1870 (10-6-1870) F
Summers, Joseph to Sarah C. Utley 8-25-1862 Be
Summers, P. L. to M. E. Kelly 10-9-1862 Hn
Summers, Patrick to Mary O'Brien 6-10-1856 (6-15-1856) Sh
Summers, Thomas to Mary L. Scott 3-19-1865 Be
Summers, William C. to Luvenia Caraway 1-14-1857 We
Summers, William D. to Sarah E. Sexton 8-8-1854 Hn
Summers, William to Sealy Downing 2-25-1829 O
Summers, Wm. to Margaret Hawley 5-26-1863 Sh
Summers, Wm. to Martha A. Nolan 10-11-1857 We
Summers, Zera to Elizabeth Thurston 9-30-1863 Hn
Summons(Summers?), lJohn G. to Eliza Lakey 7-17-1838 Hr
Sumner, David W. to Catharine E. Redd 6-7-1841 (not endorsed) F
Sumner, Henry to Jane Taliaferro 1-1-1870 Hy
Sumner, Isaac to Catharine Wester 5-24-1853 Be

Sumner, James to Susan Sherrod 11-14-1866 Hy
Sumner, Marcus D. L. to Sarrah D. Higganson 4-18-1843 (4-25-1843) F
Sumner, T. J. to Mary A. Watson 11-28-1867 Hy
Sumner, Thomas J. to Mary Ann Fielder 6-29-1869 (no return) L
Sumners, J. R. to Burdie Ellis 10-19-1880 (10-20-1880) L
Sumners, James A. to Ellen A. Vernon 2-23-1852 (2-24-1852) Hr
Sumpter, Andrew J. to Martha A. Want 8-20-1858 (8-23-1858) Sh
Sumption, John to C. Snider 2-13-1861 Sh
Sumroe, Josiah to Eliza Currie 12-25-1866 Hy
Sumrow, R. W. to Nancy Warren 1-7-1867 Dy
Suratt, Joseph to Malissa Baker 8-16-1831 G
Suratt, S. B. to Alice B. Tate 12-21-1857 (12-22-1857) Sh
Surber, R. H. to N. E. Fussell 3-4-1872 (3-7-1870?) Cr
Surratt, J. L. to C. E. Pearson 11-8-1864 Mn
Surratt, Walter to Anna Ridgeway 7-22-1829 (7-23-1829) O
Suser, Wiley to Eliz. J. Chipman 5-13-1853 Ma
Suter, J. J. to Margaret Ridley 12-28-1854 Sh
Suter, J. J. to Mary Fisher 10-28-1856 Sh
Suter, R. D. to Jane Bird 12-24-1850 (no return) Cr
Suthen, Andrew J. to Martha A. Dunavant 3-17-1866 (3-18-1866) L
Sutherland, B. F. to Martha Averitt 1-24-1866 Hy
Sutherland, J. T. to Sarah E. Hopkins 8-17-1873 Hy
Sutherland, Jesse to Martha A. Jones 5-6-1857 We
Sutherland, John B. to Martha M. Edwards 10-5-1868 L
Sutherland, John to Sallie Cherry 1-16-1861 L
Sutherland, Johnson to Matilda Burns 11-24-1881 L B
Sutherland, Jos. T. to Mary C. Moore 12-14-1871 Hy
Sutherland, Nathan to Lou Henning 2-20-1877 (2-23-1877) L B
Sutherlin, M. P. to Ludie J. Dumas 1-22-1867 Hn
Sutherlin, William S. to Sarah P. Routon 11-12-1853 Hn
Suttle, L. D. to Frances A. Young 12-29-1856 (12-30-1856) L
Suttlemore, James to Jennie Colvin 12-29-1875 (1-2-1876) Dy
Sutton, A. S. to L. W. Right 12-11-1871 Hy
Sutton, Albert to Susan Hurt 12-27-1865 Hy
Sutton, Archabald to Sarah E. Petty 7-9-1864 Mn
Sutton, Austin to Tamasia Buck 12-23-1869 Hy
Sutton, B. J. to Martha E. Hampton 9-2-1865 (9-4-1865) F
Sutton, B. L. to L. N. J. Garrett 11-15-1869 L
Sutton, Ben to Marthy Leigh 4-6-1867 Hy
Sutton, Benjamin to Frances Robertson 2-10-1845 (2-13-1845) Hr
Sutton, Buck to Elisabeth Parmer 1-12-1878 Hy
Sutton, Charles to E. F. Marr (Mearr) 4-29-1861 Hy
Sutton, E. P. to Lou A. Mullins 7-2-1866 (7-5-1866) L
Sutton, E. P. to Lou A. Mullins 7-2-1867? (7-5-1866) L
Sutton, Elijah to Vina Mebane 12-12-1867 (12-15-1867) F B
Sutton, F. L. to Mollie Williams 12-29-1868 L
Sutton, Filemore to Jenny Sweet 2-19-1876 Hy
Sutton, George W. to Amanda C. Simpson 10-26-1853 (11-12-1853) Hr
Sutton, J. E. to Mattie Taliaferro 2-7-1885 (2-8-1885) L
Sutton, J. S. to N. H. Sutton 8-15-1868 Hy
Sutton, Jackson to Jane Slanty 1-17-1857 Cr
Sutton, James T. to Mary Ann Pinchback 4-18-1848 (4-19-1848) F
Sutton, James to Mary Dudley 3-4-1877 O
Sutton, James to Susan Brinkly 10-18-1844 (10-19-1844) F
Sutton, John P. to Gafa P. Pinson 2-5-1855 Cr
Sutton, Joseph B. to Matilda J. Marr 2-4-1860 Hy
Sutton, Lewis R. to Sydney Harriss 12-16-1850 (12-17-1850) Hr
Sutton, N. E. to A. E. Wells 8-5-1878 L
Sutton, Norborne E. to Eleanor C. Fisher 10-19-1848 L
Sutton, Norborne E. to Sarah F. Wells 9-9-1867 (9-11-1867) L
Sutton, P. H. to America K. Black 2-16-1867 Hy
Sutton, Patrick Henry to Evilina Fisher 4-30-1850 (no return) L
Sutton, Perry to Cintha McCabe 7-24-1859 Hy
Sutton, Robert to Roxanna Taylor 7-10-1869 Hy
Sutton, Stephen to Eliza Green 2-5-1863 Mn
Sutton, W. C. to Judith A. Sutton 12-4-1878 Hy
Sutton, Wesley to Anna Walker 1-9-1878 Hy
Sutton, Wiley to Letha Mebane 10-24-1868 Cr
Sutton, William T. to Tennessee Campbell 8-3-1865? (9-5-1866?) L
Sutton, William to Tabitha Carter 12-6-1852 O
Swaggard, Jeremiah to Elizabeth Cullum 6-7-1847 O
Swaggart, Littleberry S. to Ruthy Jane Yarbrough 1-17-1842 (no return) F
Swailes, John to Mary Jane Scott 2-18-1851 (2-20-1851) Sh
Swaim, A. J. to E. B. Montgomery 7-21-1855 (7-22-1856) We
Swaim, A. J. to Lora M. Dallohite 3-22-1857 We
Swaim, M. D. to S. P. Ward 8-28-1852 We
Swaim, S. H. to Eliza H. Montgomery 4-20-1858 We
Swain, Chas. to M. A. Mathews 4-25-1851 (4-26-1851) Hr
Swain, Edmond to Amanda Smith 8-28-1868 (8-29-1868) T
Swain, John W. to Catharine Taylor 11-8-1841 Sh
Swain, William A. to Dely C. Russell 12-25-1865 Mn
Swan, W. H. to L. M. Collins 6-22-1864 Sh
Swann, B. M. to M. M. Mobly 10-8-1865 G
Swann, T. B. to L. A. Freeman 5-15-1860 F
Swanner, J. G. to Jennie Jackson 10-26-1871 Dy
Swanson, Henry to Ella Lowery 8-4-1871 Hy
Swanson, J. J. to F. P. Dodson 1-11-1868 Hy

Swanson, J. W. to M. H. Alexander? 12-21-1837 Sh
Swanson, James to Sinda Mann 12-20-1868 Hy
Swaringin, W. T. to M. J. Crawford 12-3-1864 (12-5-1864) Cr
Swayne, Adam to Ann Odum 5-11-1867 (no return) Dy
Swayne, H. N. to P. R. Thopson 10-14-1865 O
Swayne, Hugh W. to Martha J. Covington 10-8-1858 Cr
Swayne, J. N. to Rose E. Collier 10-25-1871 Hy
Swayne, John T. to Mary C. Porter 4-29-1851 Sh
Swayne, John to Jane Huffman 4-27-1872 (no return) Cr B
Swayne, Phillip C. to Leah S. Miller 3-1-1854 Hn
Swearengin, Champ to M. E. Blalock 10-12-1871 Cr
Swearengin, J. W. to Sarah T. Butler 1-10-1855 Cr
Swearengin, Samuel to Mary Thomason 7-29-1846 Cr
Swearingen?, S. T. to Charley M. Wilson 10-16-1849 (no return) Hn
Sweat, Columbus to I. Ann Buryman 10-27-1861 Mn
Sweat, Emery to Emma Pane 3-30-1868 (4-2-1868) F
Sweat, J. A. to C. S. Spencer 3-31-1861 Mn
Sweat, John D. to Louisa M. Simpson 12-23-1845 (no return) Hn
Sweat, Joseph to Nannie Taylor 3-29-1886 (4-22-1886) L
Sweat, L. T. to Thedonia Harris 3-14-1868 (3-16-1868) F
Sweat, T. F. to Amanda Wooten 4-28-1858 Sh
Sweate, Luke Thomas to Georgianna Everette 4-2-1878 (4-3-1878) L
Sweatt, A. W. to Adley Taylor 9-15-1866 Hn
Sweeney, Hugh to Mahala Anderson 8-30-1862 (8-31-1862) Ma
Sweeney, James J. to Elizabeth Barbee 6-18-1844 Hn
Sweeney, John to Johanna Myers 7-27-1857 Sh
Sweeney, Samuel to Nellie S. Shinness 12-24-1862 Sh
Sweeny, J. L. to Margaret Whitsett 5-3-1831 Sh
Sweeny, Jame to Anna (Mrs.) Martin 4-11-1864 Sh
Sweeny, James to Sarah Jane Harrison 1-11-1848 Ma
Sweet, Clinton to Ann Jarrett 12-27-1869 Hy
Sweet, Fonzo to Eliza Meux 12-12-1872 Hy
Sweet, Hubbard R. to Chloe L. Parsons 5-1-1863 Sh
Sweet, Isaac to Emmer Taylor 12-28-1876 Hy
Sweet, Joe to Frances James 9-24-1881 (9-29-1881) L
Sweet, Spencer to Parthena Campbell 5-7-1878 Hy
Sweet, Washington to Mollie Harvey 2-1-1877 Hy
Sweeten, Eli to Sarah C. Mayhew 8-17-1830 Sh
Sweetland, Samuel to Mary Jane Abernathy 5-15-1854 (5-17-1854) Sh
Sweeton, A. E. to Mariah J. Lambert 10-24-1854 (10-25-1854) Hr
Sweeton, Dutton M. to Serena Anderson 7-19-1836 Hr
Sweeton, Dutton to Lucy Davis 10-4-1841 (10-10-1841) Hr
Sweeton, Jarvis to Betsy Yarbroy? 2-2-1836 Hr
Sweeton, W. B. W. to Nancy H. Lambert 1-18-1860 Hr
Swenny, Levy to Eliza A. Summonds? 9-25-1855 (no return) Hn
Swetland (Sweetland), Samuel to Martha A. V. Abernathy 4-20-1847 Sh
Swift, Alex to Mattie Bell 2-28-1885 L
Swift, Allen to Louisa Porter 2-5-1870 G B
Swift, Andrew to Lotta Morris 2-2-1870 (no return) F B
Swift, Carns M. to Mary E. Mayo 7-29-1844 F
Swift, E. J. to Sarah Webb 3-12-1859 Cr
Swift, Frank to Matilda Morgan 3-5-1878 Hy
Swift, George to Elizabeth Watson 10-17-1848 Sh
Swift, Isaac N. to Frances J. Jackson 5-22-1859 Hn
Swift, J. M. to Anna Brown 6-21-1868 G
Swift, James to Eliza Curtis 8-2-1871 (8-19-1871) Dy
Swift, Levi to Amanda Roper 12-5-1869 G B
Swift, R. M. to Latalia B. Cole 10-13-1853 Cr
Swift, Robert to Rhoda Emeline Lynch 6-3-1846 Be
Swift, Thomas B. to Kitta A. R. Edwards 9-6-1853 Hn
Swift, Thos. J. to Sarah L. Mayo 2-1-1850 (2-5-1850) F
Swift, V. H. to Ada Raff 11-2-1863 Sh
Swift, V. H. to Caledonia Harrell 11-12-1859 (11-13-1859) F
Swift, Washington to Rosetta Kelton 1-16-1870 G B
Swift, William to Cresa Reid 4-20-1867 (no return) F B
Swift, Willie to Victoria McGaughey 7-26-1873 (no return) Dy
Swift, Willis to Victoria McGaughen 7-26-1873 (8-27-1873) Dy
Swim, B. M. to M. M. Mobly 10-8-1865 G
Swimm, Ambrose M. to Rose Buchannan 11-29-1858 Sh
Swindell, B. W. to Nancy Moon 10-4-1838 Cr
Swindell, G. Y. to Mary Ann Young 2-6-1866 Hn
Swindell, John M. to Jemima L. Curtis 4-7-1861 (4-8-1861) G
Swindell, Robert H. to Sarah C. Abernathy 3-14-1864 (no return) Cr
Swindell, Robt. H. to Sarah C. Abernathy 3-14-1864 (3-20-1864) Cr
Swindle, A. D. R. to Nancy J. Leggett 9-13-1859 (9-14-1859) G
Swindle, A. R. to Fannie Taylor 2-6-1873 Dy
Swindle, E. H. to I. J. Bruithwick 2-26-1866 Dy
Swindle, G. C. to Elizabeth Anderson 10-25-1840 Be
Swindle, G. P. to Margret M. Summers 8-19-1868 Be
Swindle, Holloway to Rebecca Adamson 7-17-1838 Hr
Swindle, J. H. to Isabela Box 4-23-1863 Be
Swindle, J. H. to Rebecca Cox 1-15-1863 Be
Swindle, J. S. to Nancy White 12-14-1857 Be
Swindle, James M. to Hannah Thomason 1-29-1863 Be
Swindle, James T. to Isabella E. McCalister 11-8-1842 (11-10-1842) G
Swindle, Jas. M. to Susan Mathews 12-17-1857 Hr
Swindle, John H. to Missouri A. Johnson 12-10-1868 G

Grooms

Swindle, John to Permilia Roberts 7-26-1836 Hr
Swindle, Joseph A. to Mary Tune 3-15-1837 (3-16-1837) Hr
Swindle, Joshua to Drucella Holt 2-18-1853 (2-19-1853) G
Swindle, Joshua to Prissilla Hancock 12-9-1845 (12-17-1845) G
Swindle, Moses B. to Clarissa L. Westmoreland 9-11-1868 (9-12-1868) Cr
Swindle, R. D. to Elizabeth Lambert 3-30-1849 (4-1-1849) Hr
Swindle, Thomas to Matilda Ann Bright 12-16-1856 Be
Swindle, W. A. to Mary Lewis 7-20-1864 Be
Swindle, William H. to Sarah E. Nevil 11-24-1858 (11-25-1858) G
Swindle, William to Sarah White 5-22-1856 Be
Swindle, Wm. A. to Angelina Smith 11-10-1850 Be
Swiney, C. to Mary Roberts 1-11-1870 (1-12-1870) F
Swink, Geo. W. to Ann E. Buchanan 5-14-1869 Ma
Swink, Henry H. to Sallie M. Williams 5-23-1871 Ma
Swink, James to Sarah A. Mays 11-2-1852 (12-2-1852) Ma
Swink, Jesse W. to Mary E. Robinson 2-14-1843 Cr
Swink, John to Selah Walls 11-23-1865 G
Swinney, Em. A. to Leweellen Swinney 2-13-1842 Cr
Swinney, F. M. to Martha Wood 1-29-1852 Hn
Swinney, H. W. to Martha Davidson 9-6-1849 Hn
Swinney, J. A. to Sallie Bolton 6-14-1871 (6-15-1871) Cr
Swinney, John to Mary Ann Bradshaw 3-23-1869 (3-24-1869) F
Swinney, Samuel L. to Sarah Harris 4-17-1868 (no return) Cr
Swinny, Calvin to Hannah Cheek 3-2-1863 Hn
Swinny, Lewis to Elizabeth Wright 12-25-1852 (no return) F
Switzer, David to Lively Collins 2-24-1833 Sh
Switzer, John to Mary Collins 3-26-1833 Sh
Swoboda, Frank to Mary E. Olmstead 5-30-1885 (5-31-1885) L
Swoope, Charles C. to Fannie Hutchens 7-13-1858 Sh
Swor, Armstrong to Harriet D. Hendricks 12-10-1839 Hn
Swor, Benjamin F. to Sarah L. A. Ballard 12-30-1866 Hn
Swor, Cave to Parthenia McGehee 2-15-1867 Hn B
Swor, G. W. to M. J. Memmonds 12-21-1865 Hn
Swor, James W. to R. A. Etheridge 11-5-1855 (no return) Hn
Swor, John to Elizabeth Alexander 9-24-1857 Hn
Swor, John to Martha B. Harris 4-1-1846 (no return) Hn
Swor, Joseph to Sarah Ellinor 9-9-1841 Hn
Swor, William R. to Mary Hart 8-27-1846 (no return) Hn
Sykes, Allen R. to Hester Ann Cuff 2-23-1845 Be
Sykes, H. O. to Nancy Cooper 7-3-1861 (7-4-1861) Hr
Sykes, James to F. J. Holland 10-16-1847 Be
Sykes, Jas. to Pheby Melton 11-7-1839 Be
Sykes, Jno. W. to Mary E. Williamson 1-10-1871 (1-11-1871) Ma
Sykes, John W. to Sarah T. Vick 8-28-1866 Ma
Sykes, Miles W. to Jane Fitshugh 11-25-1847 (11-27-1847) F
Sykes, Samuel S. to Carolina A. Williams 4-10-1848 Ma
Sykes, Thomas to Isabella Holland 7-2-1850 Be
Sykes, W. D. to Emma Sheppeson 10-11-1882 L
Sykes, William J. to Arabella L. Kennon 1-31-1848 Ma
Sykes, William to Delia Hall 1-21-1879 (1-27-1879) L
Sykes, William to Manerva B. Holland 9-9-1851 Be
Sykes, Wm. J. to Mary G. Waggoner 11-20-1866 Ma
Symes, Burrel to Elizabeth Edward 10-6-1869 G
Synnott, J. B. to Julia A. Dorsey 6-9-1859 (6-13-1859) Sh
Sypes, John F. N. to Susana Maria Johnson 11-6-1868 (11-8-1868) Ma
Szerinzi, Armin (Dr.) to Kate (Mrs.) Wellingstone 9-14-1863 Sh

T___, James to Martha Ann Frances Smith 12-10-1842 (12-15-1842) T
Taber, John to Safronia Armstrong 8-28-1832 Hr
Taber, William H. to Louisa T. Hullum 11-25-1831 (12-1-1831) Hr
Tabner, Richard to Susan Lawler 5-1-1847 Sh
Tabor, Jno. S. to Mary J. Harris 9-26-1859 (9-28-1859) Hr
Tackett, Geo. to Mary Hunter 7-3-1860 Hr
Tackett, George to Sarah Hodges 7-31-1834 (8-5-1834) Hr
Tackett, Manin to Lethe Shelton 5-17-1858 (5-18-1858) Hr
Tackett, Wm. to Susan Fortner 3-1-1859 (3-2-1859) Hr
Taflor, Fredrick to Catharine Williams 9-6-1859 Sh
Tagart, William R. to Nancy E. Prewitt 7-10-1852 (7-13-1852) Hr
Tagg, Joseph to Hattie Wzant 11-1-1858 (11-17-1858) Sh
Tagg, Joseph to Matilda Miller 2-29-1848 Sh
Taggart, John P. to Elizabeth Prewitt 4-3-1848 (4-4-1848) Hr
Taggart, William to Catherine McBee 2-26-1827 Hr
Tait, Caleb to Nancy Ramey 7-30-1846 O
Tait, William to Mary A. Marks 1-31-1857 (2-1-1857) Sh
Talafairo, John F. to Ann Mariah Leonard 2-24-1851 (2-26-1851) F
Talbert, P. L. to Elizabeth Hays 1-28-1863 We
Talbot, Edward to Missouri P. Wheeler 9-26-1870 (9-27-1870) Ma
Talbot, Geo. W. to Orva Ann Jayne 6-25-1849 (6-27-1849) Ma
Talbot, J. Eugene to Sarah R. Wilson 11-27-1849 Sh
Talbot, Joseph H. to Martha Freeman 8-16-1842 Ma
Talbot, Lawrence E. to Joe May Rice 2-16-1871 Ma
Talbot, William W.(H?) to Rosanna Hipp 12-4-1852 (12-5-1852) L
Taler, W. H. to Sarah H. Edwards 12-6-1859 (12-22-1859) O
Taler, Wm. H. to Chartally Scallions 7-29-1841 F
Taliafero, L. V. to Mattie L. Halliburton 1-10-1885 (1-11-1885) L
Taliaferro, B. D. to Mollie E. Boyd 7-19-1861 Hy
Taliaferro, B. L. to Martha C. Dupree 12-10-1861 Hy
Taliaferro, C. C. to Eliza Prather 8-31-1854 Hn
Taliaferro, C. C. to Ora E. Grigg 1-18-1872 Hy
Taliaferro, C. M. to Laura E. Sherman 2-4-1875 Hy
Taliaferro, Charles to Rebecca Jones 10-30-1862 Mn
Taliaferro, Chas. S. to Mary Ellen Jones 6-15-1875 Hy
Taliaferro, Chas. S. to Mattie S. Turner 3-16-1870 Hy
Taliaferro, D. C. to Massey L. Dupree 7-25-1860 Hy
Taliaferro, David to Chloe Dickson 1-10-1872? Hy
Taliaferro, Ed to Sophrona Anderson 2-9-1871 Hy
Taliaferro, Edwin T. to Jane B. Pope 5-27-1845 G
Taliaferro, Edwin to Elsia Walker 12-23-1869 Hy
Taliaferro, Ernest L. to Mollie F. Lankford 2-9-1886 (2-11-1886) L
Taliaferro, Garland to Jane King 9-4-1878 Hy
Taliaferro, George to Cora Currie 12-27-1876 Hy
Taliaferro, George to Mollie Thomas 1-18-1878 Hy
Taliaferro, James E. to Susan Norman 2-14-1868 G
Taliaferro, Jno. R. S. to A. R. (Mrs.) Hamilton 10-23-1868 G
Taliaferro, John A. to Caroline Harrisson 6-24-1830 G
Taliaferro, L. V. to Mary E. Clements 12-20-1868 Hn
Taliaferro, Simon to Elmirah Claiborne 12-31-1870 Hy
Taliaferro, Thad to Julia Barbee 1-26-1877 L
Taliaferro, Thomas J. to Martha D. Woods 5-2-1866 Hn
Taliaferro, Walker to Sarah A. Yancy 3-28-1843 G
Taliaferro, Wash. to Martha Hodge 12-28-1870 Hy
Taliaferro, Wm. H. to Laura Jones 2-6-1866 Hy
Taliferro, Henry to Jennie Walker 12-27-1874 Hy
Talkington, Samuel G. to Frances Goodman 4-3-1852 G
Tallent, John H. to Rebecca Adkins 5-16-1842 F
Talley, Benjamin to Thurza Ann Stewart 2-28-1841 Ma
Talley, Charles to Tarissa M. Henderson 4-4-1848 O
Talley, Charles to Tarissa M. Henderson 4-4-1848 (4-6-1848) O
Talley, Chas. B. to Mariah Yandell 10-3-1869 G B
Talley, D. F. to E. M. Brooks 2-8-1871 Ma
Talley, Dock to Martha Chamber 2-25-1873 (2-26-1873) T
Talley, Dudley C. to Martha A. (Mrs.) Exum 1-13-1870 Ma
Talley, E. F. to N. E. Williams 2-18-1880 L
Talley, Foster D. to Lucy E. Crewsdon 7-6-1858 (7-7-1858) Sh
Talley, G. W. to Sarah Jones 8-9-1859 (8-10-1859) G
Talley, Henry to Rose Allen 1-19-1871 T
Talley, J. Thomas to M. E. Harrison 12-24-1873 Dy
Talley, James E. to Nancy P. Durley 11-24-1858 G
Talley, James to Adaline Harris 4-29-1876 (4-30-1876) Dy B
Talley, John H. to Panthia Bowers 10-8-1845 We
Talley, John to Emma Waller 11-21-1874 T
Talley, Joseph J.? to Caroline L. Wissen 4-22-1840 (4-23-1840) T
Talley, Martin to Sarah Carter 1-12-1848 (1-13-1848) O
Talley, Robertson P. to Fanny A. Lery 4-8-1854 Sh
Talley, T. S. to Lola Jones 6-20-1878 Dy
Talley, William F. to Ellen D. Young 2-28-1857 (3-18-1857) L
Talley, Wm. F. to Anna R. Crewdson 6-1-1858 (6-2-1858) Sh
Talley, Wm. H. to Julia A. E. Davidson 1-17-1867 G
Talliaferro, B. F. to Miss Smith 2-24-1846 (no return) We
Tallley, Martin to Arcada Organ 4-27-1836 M
Tally, Benj. F. to Elizabeth N. Bowers 12-11-1845 G
Tally, Edward F. to Lucy A. F. Bibb 9-6-1850 (9-12-1850) L
Tally, Fletcher H. to M. C. Leake 2-24-1858 Sh
Tally, Frank to Gibson Mary 6-2-1864 Sh B
Tally, Gib. to Puss Coldwell 12-10-1870 Hy
Tally, Kentiance G. to Clemsa Watts 11-18-1842 G
Tally, Martin to Catharine Hornsby 1-1-1839 O
Tally, Martin W. to Paralee E. Bennett 8-20-1849 Hn
Talty, John to Ann Brown 5-24-1861 Sh
Tamm, Emanuel to Hannah Auker 2-4-1874 Hy
Tamplin, Patrick to Margaret Brodie 6-9-1849 Sh
Tan___?, Joihn F. to Easter Williams 2-26-1839 Hn
Tancel, A. L. to Sarah A. Spence 6-18-1868 Dy
Tanksley, G. W. to Elizabeth Jones 1-19-1863 Sh
Tannehill, B. N. D. to Sallie Lynch 11-4-1857 (11-5-1857) Hr
Tanner, D. B. to Mollie Trimble 12-6-1869 Hy
Tanner, Elyer? to Amanda Calhoun 1-4-1867 (1-14-1867) T
Tanner, F. Thad. to Jane Hardin 2-12-1876 Hy
Tanner, George W. to Mary Ann Meadows 8-14-1838 (8-16-1838) O
Tanner, John A. to M. A. Mosley 11-21-1844 Hy
Tanner, John to Susan A. Orr 6-15-1854 (6-17-1854) O
Tanner, L. to Sarah A. Prewitt 4-9-1856 (4-23-1856) Hr
Tanner, Lafayette to Minerva Robertson 4-7-1854 (4-13-1854) Hr
Tanner, N. H. to Eliza Golding 10-24-1851 (no return) L
Tanner, Perry to Sue Nelson 10-26-1872 Hy
Tanner, R. F. to Elizabeth Hopkins 11-15-1865 Mn
Tanner, Richard to Elenor Cardwell 3-29-1863 Mn
Tanner, Richard to Mary Ellen Cardwell 11-25-1865 Mn
Tanner, Samuel to Mary Jane Byrn 12-18-1873 L B
Tanner, Simon P. to Mary A. Price 4-23-1851 Sh
Tanner, T. A. to Eoma Smith 1-7-1854 G
Tanner, Thad to Angeline Henderson 1-19-1868 Hy
Tanner, Tyra H. to Corina B. White 1-18-1854 (1-19-1854) O
Tanner, Wm. A. to Virginia A. Crowder 9-13-1851 (9-17-1851) Hr

Tanner, Wm. W. to Sarah A. Reeves 7-19-1856 (7-22-1856) O
Tansel, Thomas E. to Mary McBride 10-12-1871 Dy
Tansil, Benjamin A. to Mary D. Glass 12-8-1862 We
Tansil, M. to Mollie Jones 1-13-1874 Dy
Tansil, Sain A. to Dolly Wherry 5-7-1875 Dy
Tansill, J. T. to Mary A. Fonville 11-5-1858 We
Tapley, John P. to Delphia Ann Stokes 2-13-1860 Hy
Tapp, Frank to Fannie Brumley 3-4-1878 Hy
Tappan, Isaac to Emily Williams 1-4-1867 F B
Tappan, Mose to Martha Littlejohn 3-1-1869 (3-5-1869) F B
Tappan, Thos. to Amy Carpenter 12-22-1870 F B
Tapps, P. H. to Hettie Wisdom 10-9-1865 Mn
Tapscott, A. B. to Mary Jones 5-21-1866 G
Tapscott, Taylor to Moriah Read 1-24-1878 Hy
Tarble, Melvin to Elisabeth A. Skur 9-24-1864 (9-25-1864) Sh
Tarbrok, Elias D. to Eliza Clark 2-11-1857 T
Tarbutten, John to Emily Vincent 12-5-1855 (12-13-1855) O
Targart, A. J. to M. C. Durham 12-18-1854 (no return) F
Tarkington, A. W. to E. R. Tipton 1-5-1867 (1-7-1867) Dy
Tarkington, F. M. to Rebecca B. Anderson 10-2-1854 (10-10-1854) Sh
Tarkington, James C. to Mary E. Donaldson 7-28-1863 O
Tarkington, Joseph to Mary A. Alvis 3-21-1848 Sh
Tarkington, Wm. D. to Fannie Sorrell 4-3-1878 (4-4-1878) Dy
Tarkinton, Jos. C. to Martha L. Davis 2-12-1852 Sh
Tarpley, Jas. to Mary E. Belch 5-6-1869 Hy
Tarply, F. P. to Margrarett? J. McMullin 9-24-1860 (9-25-1860) Cr
Tarply, J. M. to Louisa Biggs 6-27-1867 Be
Tarrant, John D. to Anna Alexander 7-24-1879 L
Tarrant, John H. to M. A. S. Graw (McGraw?) 9-24-1866 (9-25-1866) Dy
Tarrant, N. B. to S. V. Smith 1-4-1870 (1-5-1870) Dy
Tarrentine, James F. to Sarah Jane West 10-1-1857 O
Tarrey, Edward to Holland Dots 12-25-1874 (12-27-1874) T
Tarry, Allen to Bell Blackwell 12-31-1872 T
Tarry, James J. to Ann C. Byram 6-20-1863 Sh
Tarry, Jim to Rosa Alexander 12-21-1873 T
Tarry, Wm. Little to Sallie Anderson Hunt 4-4-1850 (4-10-1850) T
Tart, Thadeus C. S. to Nancy C. Poyner 6-7-1859 Hn
Tarver, Julian to Monian Yates 12-17-1867 (12-18-1867) Ma
Tarver, Thomas D. to Wilmouth O. Edmondson? 8-22-1854 (no return) F
Tarvin, Milton T. to Mary L. McClary 7-8-1836 (7-14-1836) G
Tarvoaler, W. M. to Gussie M. Somervill 10-27-1859 (11-17-1859) T
Tarwater, George T. to Lucy Ann E. Lane 12-3-1844 (12-5-1844) F
Tary, Joseph W. to Elizabeth Morgan 8-20-1851 O
Tatam, George W. to Rachael Aronhart 5-25-1865 Dy
Tate, A. M. to Katie Sloss 4-20-1881 (4-25-1881) L
Tate, Andrew to Ann Malone 12-24-1869 (no return) F B
Tate, Caleb to Nancy Roney 7-30-1847 O
Tate, Daniel to Randy Collins 8-25-1848 Cr
Tate, Edmond to Mary Clark 3-4-1869 T
Tate, Edmund to Lila Heaslett 1-22-1869 (no return) F B
Tate, Elisha to Miriah David 5-15-1858 Cr
Tate, George W. to Eliza Cooper 3-11-1835 Hr
Tate, George W. to Sarah Whitford 8-13-1836 Hr
Tate, Henry to Margaret Haselett 7-19-1867 (no return) F B
Tate, James to Eliza N. Hill 2-5-1852 Sh
Tate, Jerome B. to Nancy A. Hardage 12-24-1859 Ma
Tate, Jesse M. to Lucy Ann Greenlaw 3-30-1842 Sh
Tate, Magnis to Elizabeth Roberts 11-12-1848 Hr
Tate, Nathaniel to Martha Hams 1-7-1858 Cr
Tate, Robert A. to Mary Bolam 4-4-1864 Sh
Tate, Robert to Elizabeth Long 7-25-1847 Cr
Tate, Robert to Parthenia Lee 9-29-1877 L
Tate, Saml. to Catharine P. Young 3-10-1852 We
Tate, Samuel to Mary Carnes 4-19-1843 F
Tate, T. F. to M. A. Ramsey 11-23-1872 (11-26-1872) O
Tate, T. S. to Ann Eliza Jones 12-11-1860 (12-12-1860) Hr
Tate, Thomas S. to Francisco C.(K.) Ford 3-19-1835 Sh
Tate, Thomas W. to Mary J. Mooney 12-3-1859 Hr
Tate, Thos. G. to Mary P. Clay 8-10-1869 Hy
Tate, Thos. S. to Mollie C. Alexander 2-9-1865 (no return) Cr
Tate, W. G. to Elizabeth Peoples 9-20-1872 (9-29-1872) Dy
Tate, William P. to Sophia Kelly 2-7-1840 (7-30-1840) G
Tate, William to Jane Crook 12-24-1869 (no return) F B
Tate, Wm. E. to Nanny W. Bond 10-23-1861 Sh
Tate, Wm. M. to E. W. Rodgers 12-18-1856 Cr
Tate, Wm. R. to Mary H. Weatherford 11-18-1867 (12-19-1867) T
Tate, Z. M. to Susan M. Williams 10-31-1839 W
Tatem, Edward W. to Rebecca H. Copeland 2-10-1849 F
Tatom, G. W. to Mary E. Morris 10-8-1867 (10-12-1867) F
Tatum, A. H. to J. E. Henderson 11-20-1867 G
Tatum, A. H. to Lizie Jeter 9-28-1875 Hy
Tatum, A. J. G. to Susan McAdams 12-26-1839 F
Tatum, A. R. to Allice B. Stewart 12-20-1869 (12-23-1869) F
Tatum, Absolum H. to Emly A. M. Avery 3-7-1855 (3-9-1855) G
Tatum, Andy to Harriett Palmer 12-26-1870 (12-29-1870) Dy
Tatum, Ben to Susan Turner 8-29-1873 Hy
Tatum, Ben to Tabby Scales 12-17-1873 Hy
Tatum, David to Tennesee Pillow 12-24-1872 (12-26-1872) L B
Tatum, Dick to Sophia Rivers 1-1-1870 (1-27-1870) F B
Tatum, E. W. to H. A. E. Oats 12-27-1849 (no return) F
Tatum, Edward W. to Elizabeth B. Manning 4-7-1851 (4-8-1851) F
Tatum, Frank to Lucinda Taylor 3-31-1866 (4-1-1866) F B
Tatum, G. W. to Alletha T. Turnbow 9-28-1852 (no return) F
Tatum, G. W. to E. F. Morton 12-23-1868 G
Tatum, G. W. to Elizabeth C. Sims 8-31-1850 (9-3-1850) G
Tatum, Geo. W. to Mattie L. Holt 11-13-1860 G
Tatum, George F. to Elizabeth Hall 5-14-1865 G
Tatum, George M. to Eunice Bloomingdale 11-27-1877 (11-28-1877) Dy
Tatum, George to Martha Ward 2-12-1878 L
Tatum, George to Rhoda E. Ward 8-6-1857 (no return) L
Tatum, H. A. to Elizabeth N. Ingram 9-19-1851 (no return) F
Tatum, J. G. to E. A. Brown 1-11-1866 (1-14-1866) F
Tatum, J. H. to Mary E. Roberson 12-28-1865 Hy
Tatum, Jackson to Martha Jane Holliday 9-11-1847 F
Tatum, James B. to Martha A. P. Avery 12-29-1857 (12-31-1857) G
Tatum, John G. to Mary P. Clifton 1-18-1841 (1-21-1841) F
Tatum, John P. to Sarah Hopper 6-12-1851 G
Tatum, John P. to Sarah Jane Batts 11-12-1869 G
Tatum, L. W. to Martha A. Barcroft 3-18-1860 Hy
Tatum, Nathaniel to Matilda Broyles 11-23-1843 (11-25-1843) F
Tatum, P. B. to Emma A. Wood 4-24-1866 Dy
Tatum, R. E. to Susan H. Oates 11-15-1852 (no return) F
Tatum, Richard to Margaret Eason 11-4-1845 (no return) F
Tatum, Samuel G. to Edith Campbell 8-19-1859 L
Tatum, Samuel G. to Mary Ann Strain 9-14-1854 L
Tatum, Sihon to Julia Jeanes 2-11-1862 Mn
Tatum, Thos. E. to Martha Morton 5-31-1866 Hy
Tatum, W. M. to Jane A. Klyce 7-4-1866 G
Tatum, Waddie to Alice Kellar 10-19-1882 L
Tatum, Waddy S. to Martha Tucker 3-9-1844 (3-13-1844) L
Tayler, T. L. to Mary A. King 6-18-1873 Cr
Tayloe, Thomas H. to Sally Palmer 10-25-1859 Hn
Taylor, A. B. to Maria Fuller 10-25-1864 (10-26-1864) Sh
Taylor, A. C. to C. A. Davis 1-31-1867 G
Taylor, A. D. to Elizabeth Stevens 12-25-1860 (no return) Hn
Taylor, A. H. to Mary E. Turner 11-26-1861 G
Taylor, A. J. to Fannie E. Holland 9-15-1869 G
Taylor, A. T. to Parthenia Ramey 5-10-1868 G
Taylor, A. to M. Swift 8-20-1841 Be
Taylor, Aaron to Julias Taliaferro 7-20-1867 Hy
Taylor, Aaron to Moriah Shaw 12-19-1872 Hy
Taylor, Aaron to Nellie Baily 12-29-1869 Hy
Taylor, Abner to Laura Manley 3-30-1832 (3-31-1832) Hr
Taylor, Albert to Philis Taylor 5-6-1867 T
Taylor, Alex to Catherine Morgan 12-25-1878 Hy
Taylor, Alex to Ede Moody 1-16-1868 Hy
Taylor, Alexander to Patsey Williamson 2-27-1867 T
Taylor, Alexander to Veria Mason 12-23-1874 T
Taylor, Alison to Cinda Jacocks 7-6-1876 Hy
Taylor, Allen to Adelia Taylor 7-4-1866 O
Taylor, Allen to Fanny Jane Clay 2-8-1854 G
Taylor, Allen to Susan B. Johnson 10-20-1847 (10-21-1847) G
Taylor, Alvin E. to Martha A. Taylor 1-2-1860 (1-3-1860) F
Taylor, Alx to Rose Jackson 4-18-1868 Hy
Taylor, Anderson to Matty Mathews 12-26-1868 (12-28-1868) F B
Taylor, Andrew to Clarissa Polk 6-7-1824 (6-11-1824) Hr
Taylor, Andrew to Mary C. Mitchell 3-31-1846 (4-2-1846) F
Taylor, Andrew to Nancy Alexander 6-1-1877 Hy
Taylor, Andrew to Nancy Kimbro 9-6-1869 T
Taylor, Andrew to Reny Perkins 10-31-1871 (no return) Cr B
Taylor, Andrew to Sue Utley 9-14-1870 (9-15-1870) Ma
Taylor, Anthony to Peggy Miller 12-28-1865 (no return) F
Taylor, Archibald Henderson to Lee R. Turnage 6-30-1858 Sh
Taylor, Arden to Sylvia Bledsoe 5-7-1870 (5-8-1870) Cr
Taylor, Arthur K. to Susan P. Rose 1-12-1856 (1-13-1856) Sh
Taylor, Augustus to Marmu? Ferrell 7-18-1855 Hr
Taylor, B. J. to Lucretia Spellings 1-11-1869 G
Taylor, Ben to Rachael Jackson 9-23-1874 Hy
Taylor, Benajah S. to Martha H. Ward 9-21-1854 Sh
Taylor, Benj. F. to Ann M. Stanton 11-4-1847 Hy
Taylor, Benjamin F. to Louisa C. Porch 4-18-1861 (no return) We
Taylor, Benjamin F. to Margaret A. Crockett 12-26-1862 (no return) We
Taylor, Benjamin F. to Margaret E. Frierson 6-8-1842 G
Taylor, Beverly to Alice Allman 4-7-1872 Hy
Taylor, Bevley to Mary Westbrook 3-9-1870 (no return) Hy
Taylor, Billington to Eliza Ann Parks 8-12-1861 We
Taylor, Branch to Polly Frazer 7-30-1867 Hy
Taylor, Brister to Mary Jane Fulton 10-24-1872 O
Taylor, C. A. G. to A. L. Hall 9-19-1867 Dy
Taylor, C. M. to Francis M. Jones 3-14-1865 (3-15-1865) L
Taylor, Caldwell to Laura Maclin 12-28-1868 Hy
Taylor, Caldwell to Sallie Taylor 2-20-1866 T
Taylor, Calvin to Em Moore 1-7-1868 Hy
Taylor, Cambridge to Mary Burrel 12-28-1869 T

Grooms

Taylor, Charles N. to Martha L. Fuller 12-29-1852 Sh
Taylor, Charles to Annie Eliza Parker 12-23-1873 (12-26-1873) T
Taylor, Charles to Beckey Johnson 12-28-1869 T
Taylor, Charles to Mary Davison 12-30-1856 Hn
Taylor, Charley to Nannie Cobb 3-24-1875 (no return) L B
Taylor, Charlie to Fannie Taylor 8-16-1877 Hy
Taylor, Chas. F. to Emma A. Hall 6-20-1864 Sh
Taylor, Chas. to R. Goodman 1-1-1872 T
Taylor, Coleman to Anna Palmer 1-5-1869 Hy
Taylor, Craven L. to Elizabeth Tull 11-7-1854 Ma
Taylor, Crofford to Katharin Duncan 5-16-1865 Dy
Taylor, D. F. to Margaret E. Wilkinson 6-2-1879 Dy
Taylor, D. F. to S. J. Hawkins 1-7-1879 (1-8-1879) Dy
Taylor, D. H. to S. E. Winget 10-12-1865 Hy
Taylor, Daniel to Mary Lane 11-27-1870 T
Taylor, Daniel to Nancy Read 9-10-1857 Ma
Taylor, Deal to Allice Green 11-13-1873 Hy
Taylor, Dewery to Rose Barbie 12-27-1867 Hy
Taylor, Duncan D. to Nancy Ellis 10-14-1868 (10-15-1868) Dy
Taylor, Duncan E. to Selesta Nixon 9-5-1856 L
Taylor, Duncan to Sophia Kelly 1-12-1876 Hy
Taylor, Dunkin to Rebecca Nixon 1-3-1869 Hy
Taylor, E. F. to Jane A. Flowers 2-11-1857 (2-12-1857) G
Taylor, Ed. H. to Neppie L. Harbert 3-14-1876 Hy
Taylor, Edmond to Finie Green 1-5-1875 Hy
Taylor, Edmond to Parasade M. Meriweather 3-23-1843 (3-28-1843) Ma
Taylor, Edmund F. to Nancy A. Hopper 12-17-1852 (12-25-1852) G
Taylor, Edmund to Sarah E. Rawlins 9-26-1878 Hy
Taylor, Edmund to Sarah Taylor 10-3-1878 Hy
Taylor, Egbert to Mandy Wood 12-25-1874 Hy
Taylor, Eliga to Siller Owen 2-21-1878 Hy
Taylor, Ellis to Lucinda Taylor 6-30-1877 Hy
Taylor, F. to Elizabeth Manley 1-31-1848 Cr
Taylor, Fayette to Sarah J. Taylor 12-26-1874 Hy
Taylor, Fayette to Sarah Taylor 12-31-1875 Hy
Taylor, Frank M. to Mollie D. Thompson 11-24-1868 (11-26-1868) F
Taylor, Frank to Sarah Ann Evans 9-22-1869 O
Taylor, Franklin to Flora Thomas 12-21-1868 (12-25-1868) F B
Taylor, G. A. to Catherine Edmunds 12-5-1864 (no return) Hn
Taylor, G. N. to Barbara Leap 6-11-1863 O
Taylor, G. W. to Nannie Roberts 2-11-1869 G
Taylor, Gabriel to Eliza Jackson 6-10-1857 O
Taylor, Gem to Georgeanna Blades 7-21-1866 Hy
Taylor, Geo. Ardmore? to Ann F. Sommervill 11-16-1852 T
Taylor, George M. to Sophonia E. Gowan 1-17-1853 G
Taylor, George W. to Massa Parker 9-10-1828 (9-12-1828) Hr
Taylor, George to Juda Estis 6-30-1883 (7-1-1883) L
Taylor, George to Julia Taylor 11-5-1867 Hy
Taylor, George to Margarett M. Gray 1-21-1864 (no return) Cr
Taylor, George to Rachel Murphy 7-26-1856 (9-18-1856) Sh
Taylor, George to Sally Ann Milener 2-8-1864 (2-11-1864) O
Taylor, George to Sarah Green (Greer?) 6-19-1869 G B
Taylor, George to Tomasia Speller 7-5-1877 Hy
Taylor, Gideon to Nancy Cobb Jones 6-24-1857 Sh
Taylor, Giles to Sarah Crouse 11-17-1842 Hr
Taylor, Granderson to Jane Davis 7-21-1872 Hy
Taylor, Granville to Sarah Tucker 12-25-1877 (12-27-1877) Dy
Taylor, H. A. to Rhody Ann Clark 3-23-1864 Sh
Taylor, H. B. to Ellen Murphy 1-27-1867 G
Taylor, H. C. to Molly Hess 12-25-1874 Hy
Taylor, H. H. to Roann Houston 7-21-1864 F
Taylor, H. M. to L. C. Rainey 2-4-1875 Dy
Taylor, H. P. to Fannie High 12-6-1864 Hn
Taylor, H. S. to Jane Eliza Mayo 9-18-1846 (no return) F
Taylor, Hal to Lucenda Sulivan 7-12-1868 Hy
Taylor, Hark to Sue Smith 7-17-1874 Hy
Taylor, Heck to Harriett Watten 10-5-1871 Hy
Taylor, Henderson to Lindie (Ludie) Taylor 2-19-1870 Hy
Taylor, Henry C. to Dorothy A. Read 2-16-1864 (no return) Cr
Taylor, Henry Ligen to Sarah Gill 11-9-1874 Hy
Taylor, Henry M. to Mary F. Carter 2-15-1869 (2-9?-1869) L
Taylor, Henry S. to Louise E. Hunter 10-16-1838 F
Taylor, Henry to Caroline Alexander 8-3-1870 (8-4-1870) Dy
Taylor, Henry to Layer McClish 8-14-1877 Hy
Taylor, Henry to Lizzie Glevur? 11-30-1872 (12-1-1872) Dy
Taylor, Henry to Mary Crow 11-21-1874 (11-24-1874) Dy B
Taylor, Henry to Millie Adams 2-26-1870 Hy
Taylor, Henry to Nancy E. Ayers 1-28-1874 (1-29-1874) Dy
Taylor, Henry to Venus Alphin 10-12-1867 Hy
Taylor, Hirian A. to Elizabeth A. Moore 2-15-1853 Cr
Taylor, Howell to Fannie Green 12-10-1878 Hy
Taylor, Hutson to Martha Kilbreah 2-19-1868 Be
Taylor, Hyman to Lucy Randle 2-3-1839 Hn
Taylor, Ike to Hettie Elcan 3-10-1873 T
Taylor, Isaac to Eliza M. Tally 5-19-1852 Sh
Taylor, Isaac to Margaret J. Blakemore 7-8-1856 We
Taylor, J. A. to L. C. Briant 2-28-1872 (3-1-1872) Cr

Taylor, J. B. to Lizzie Griffiths 2-17-1870 G
Taylor, J. B. to Susan Anna Jones 12-27-1876 (12-28-1876) Dy
Taylor, J. C. to E. H. (Mrs.) Adams 11-30-1865 G
Taylor, J. C. to Laura Gardner no date (not executed) Hy
Taylor, J. C. to Nancy J. Mohundro 12-30-1865 Hn
Taylor, J. C. to Sarah Cole 3-5-1874 Hy
Taylor, J. C. to Winnie Privett 12-21-1870 Hy
Taylor, J. D. to M. W. Williams 1-6-1862 (1-8-1862) F
Taylor, J. F. to Martha Chambers 12-29-1866 (12-30-1866) F
Taylor, J. H. to L. E. Edwards 9-21-1871 Cr
Taylor, J. H. to Maria M. Valentine 2-1-1867 Hn
Taylor, J. H. to Mary E. Allen 7-8-1871 (7-9-1871) Cr
Taylor, J. J. to Susan Clark 2-24-1846 We
Taylor, J. L. to Mary A. Pollock 4-12-1851 O
Taylor, J. M. to A. C. Allen 6-22-1865 O
Taylor, J. P. to D. E. Curlin 12-23-1885 L
Taylor, J. P. to M. J. Wheeler 11-21-1857 G
Taylor, J. R. to Jane Busby 12-28-1865 Hn
Taylor, J. to Caroline Thompson 12-3-1874 T
Taylor, Jack to Ann Taylor 12-12-1872 Hy
Taylor, Jack to Lydia A. Taylor 2-19-1868 Hy
Taylor, Jacob I. to Annie Tucker 9-12-1873 Hy
Taylor, Jacob to Emily Smith 9-16-1876 Hy
Taylor, James A. to Jane Caroline Meriwether 12-5-1839 Ma
Taylor, James A. to Mary Ann Ray 7-29-1854 O
Taylor, James A. to Mattie Taylor 12-28-1875 Hy
Taylor, James Allan to Frances A. Taylor 2-6-1843 (2-8-1843) T
Taylor, James Allen to Margaret (Mrs.) Tysen 9-14-1869 (9-16-1869) Ma
Taylor, James B. to Mary E. Amonett 12-20-1848 Sh
Taylor, James B. to Merinda Senonah 7-30-1832 Sh
Taylor, James Carroll to Mary Hood McCauley 1-8-1845 (1-9-1845) T
Taylor, James F. to A. C. Cox 9-21-1869 (9-23-1869) Cr
Taylor, James M. to Mary Phillips 2-2-1849 O
Taylor, James N. to Margaret E. C. Taylor 10-16-1866 (10-18-1866) Dy
Taylor, James R. to Susan Briley 9-11-1842 Sh
Taylor, James T. to Meoma S. McBroom 8-7-1867 (no return) L
Taylor, James to Deborah Parker 11-15-1827 (11-18-1827) G
Taylor, James to Dyzer Baily 2-7-1878 Hy
Taylor, James to Elizabeth Sullins 1-18-1850 Be
Taylor, James to Elizabeth Yarbrough 5-23-1848 Be
Taylor, James to Fanny Taylor 2-11-1869 T
Taylor, James to Kittie Turnley 5-18-1867 F B
Taylor, James to Louza Green 9-4-1865 (no return) Cr
Taylor, Jarrett to Nancy French 6-4-1864 Cr
Taylor, Jas. R. to Emily J. Spencer 10-19-1858 G
Taylor, Jemy to Feby A. Rayner 3-21-1868 Hy
Taylor, Jerry T. to Sarah T. Strong 1-2-1878 Hy
Taylor, Jesse to Julia Wilson 2-20-1872 Hy
Taylor, Jesse to M. F. Bradford 12-26-1867 Hy
Taylor, Jesse to Polly Ann Townzen 11-2-1853 Be
Taylor, Jim to Fannie Taylor 4-18-1868 (no return) F B
Taylor, Jim to Julia Mann 8-20-1870 Hy
Taylor, Jim to Linda McNeil 1-6-1866 (no return) F B
Taylor, Jno. P. to Jane E. (Sarah) Manning 9-29-1847 Sh
Taylor, Jno. W. to Lucy M. Nash 3-30-1842 Sh
Taylor, Joe to Adaline Bradford 12-28-1869 Hy
Taylor, Joe to Rebecca Crockett 8-27-1880 L B
Taylor, John H. to Lucy A. Moser 4-30-1859 (5-1-1859) O
Taylor, John C. to Malissa M. Rogers 10-3-1855 (no return) Hn
Taylor, John C. to Susan Sedberry 8-6-1854 Cr
Taylor, John G. to Matilda C. Taylor 3-17-1864 G
Taylor, John G. to Nancy W. Biles 6-27-1844 Hn
Taylor, John H. to Sallie W. Strange 3-20-1855 Sh
Taylor, John Henry to Rachel Northcross 12-27-1851 (1-1-1852) Hr
Taylor, John I. to Martha D. Meacham 2-19-1828 Ma
Taylor, John J. to Dicey Ham 3-19-1850 Ma
Taylor, John J. to Lucy Mills 11-16-1857 Ma
Taylor, John J. to Mary Alexander 7-20-1846 Ma
Taylor, John K. to N. J. Farrow 11-30-1858 (12-1-1858) Sh
Taylor, John L. to C. E. Manley 11-17-1849 Cr
Taylor, John M. to Judis A. Lemons 10-9-1848 (10-11-1848) F
Taylor, John M. to Martha Ann Wadrill 10-11-1858 Cr
Taylor, John M. to Tobitha Speer 8-16-1838 F
Taylor, John P. to Elizabeth E. Garrison 4-1-1856 (4-2-1856) O
Taylor, John P. to Mary L. Smith 6-2-1858 T
Taylor, John S. to Araminta Matheney 10-10-1844 Hn
Taylor, John S. to M. A. K. Enoch 12-23-1865 (12-27-1865) Dy
Taylor, John T. to Maggie Strong 11-25-1874 Hy
Taylor, John T. to Polly Ann Cottingham 3-9-1845 Be
Taylor, John W. to Amanda Smith 9-28-1863 Hn
Taylor, John W. to Malinda J. Drake 10-16-1866 Hn
Taylor, John W. to Sarah Evans 1-25-1860 Sh
Taylor, John to Catharine Mahar 2-3-1857 Sh
Taylor, John to Ellen Davis 8-18-1867 Hy
Taylor, John to Jennie Lane 1-11-1872 Hy
Taylor, John to Kittie E. Taylor 1-29-1874 Hy
Taylor, John to Margaret Johnson 1-5-1870 T

Taylor, John to Martha Morgan 12-7-1872 (12-28-1872) L B
Taylor, John to Martha Stegall 2-2-1864 (2-3-1864) Dy
Taylor, John to Mary Williams 2-17-1876 Hy
Taylor, John to Mrs. Gary 12-1-1863 T
Taylor, Jonathan N. to Rebecca Green 9-5-1831 Ma
Taylor, Jordan to Emeline Hunter 2-27-1866 (12-28-1866) F B
Taylor, Joseph R. to Mary Claiborne 2-27-1843 G
Taylor, Joseph W. to Elizabeth Morgan 8-20-1851 O
Taylor, Joseph to Ann Williams 1-5-1841 L
Taylor, Joseph to Ellen Groves 6-2-1866 (6-17-1866) F B
Taylor, Joseph to Jane Green 7-6-1826 (7-19-1826) Hr
Taylor, Joseph to Mary F. Jackson 3-17-1851 O
Taylor, Joseph to Mary F. Jackson 3-17-1857 O
Taylor, Joseph to Mary Shea 6-29-1857 (6-27?-1857) Sh
Taylor, Joseph to Sally Elison 10-14-1828 Ma
Taylor, Joshua J. to Elmina F. Ragan 3-11-1868 G
Taylor, Josiah to Elizabeth Biddy 10-19-1831 (10-20-1831) Hr
Taylor, Josiah to Tempe Webster 2-27-1832 (3-1-1832) Hr
Taylor, Kelly to Patsy Davis 8-23-1868 Hy
Taylor, Kinchen to Nancy C. Cox 1-27-1850 Be
Taylor, Kinchen to Sarah Capps 12-7-1855 Be
Taylor, Lawson D. to Lacy J. Fry 11-26-1849 (11-29-1849) Ma
Taylor, Lawson to Sarah Reeves 8-13-1870 T
Taylor, Legvi to Mary A. Sedberry 8-17-1854 Cr
Taylor, Lemiel to Teressa Wallace 9-8-1830 Ma
Taylor, Lemuel to Jane Hawkins 9-26-1844 Cr
Taylor, Lewis H. to Elizabeth Strother 1-8-1840 Sh
Taylor, Lewis to Amelia Taylor 12-30-1870 Hy
Taylor, Lewis to Edmonia Rogers 11-14-1878 Hy
Taylor, Lewis to Eliza Morrow 3-27-1869 (4-1-1869) F B
Taylor, Lewis to Florence Wilson 3-7-1869 Hy
Taylor, Lewis to Hannah Melisa Hays 12-4-1872 Hy
Taylor, Lewis to Isabel Johnson 12-21-1867 Hy
Taylor, Lewis to Julia P. Whitelaw 12-16-1875 Hy
Taylor, Lewis to Malinda Evans 4-3-1872 Hy
Taylor, Lewis to Sarah Dickenson 5-29-1863 (5-30-1863) O
Taylor, Lewis to Sophy Williams 10-13-1867 Hy
Taylor, Lihue to Elenida Woldram 7-29-1839 (8-1-1839) F
Taylor, Louis to Polly Montgomery 12-24-1867 T
Taylor, M.W. to America J. Ralph 4-16-1857 T
Taylor, Mansel M. to Nancy F. Duncan 7-20-1858 O
Taylor, Martin Y. to Susan Whitley 2-21-1849 (2-22-1849) G
Taylor, Mat to Adeline Hart 2-5-1869 (2-9-1869) F B
Taylor, Mathew M. to Martha W. Patton 8-6-1856 (8-7-1856) G
Taylor, Milton to Margaret Ann Lefever 8-25-1838 Hn
Taylor, Mortimer to Laura Buck 12-25-1866 Hy
Taylor, Moses to Cynthia Alexander 1-9-1843 (1-12-1843) Ma
Taylor, Moses to Liza Shirly 12-27-1867 Hy
Taylor, N. W. to Ellender Hickman 9-30-1847 Cr
Taylor, Nathan to Ellie Jones 6-1-1877 Hy
Taylor, Nathaniel to Elizabeth Richardson 11-27-1843 (11-30-1843) G
Taylor, Nathaniel to Nancy Taylor 1-2-1866 T
Taylor, Nelson to Ann Sumerow 1-25-1869 (2-17-1869) L
Taylor, Nelson to Crecy Walker 7-28-1866 Hy
Taylor, Nelson to Linn Rutherford 11-20-1869 Hy
Taylor, Nelson to Phebe Taylor 12-25-1866 Hy
Taylor, Newborn to Joanna White 12-22-1866 Hy
Taylor, Nicles to Mahaly Wills 2-4-1868 Hy
Taylor, Nowell to Lutish Taylor 1-9-1869 T
Taylor, Oliver to Elizabeth Lockhart 7-8-1839 Sh
Taylor, Osburn to Susan Ann Davis 5-29-1867 Hy
Taylor, Peter to Anna Watkins 11-8-1875 Hy
Taylor, Peter to Bettie Reddick 3-2-1866 (3-3-1866) F B
Taylor, Polk to Alice Whitmore 12-30-1885 (12-31-1885) L
Taylor, Polk to Critina Hess 12-28-1870 Hy
Taylor, Powell S. to Margaret E. Spain 7-18-1867 Dy
Taylor, Profeit to Sallie Elkin 3-3-1869 T
Taylor, R. C. to Mary E. Browning 7-22-1864 (no return) Cr
Taylor, R. H. to J. Volney Gift 10-6-1859 Sh
Taylor, Rasmus to C. Gammelle 10-13-1871 T
Taylor, Reuben to Amanda Wright 10-10-1868 (10-11-1868) L B
Taylor, Reuben to Malinda J. Nevels 3-22-1861 (3-27-1861) L
Taylor, Reuben to Penney L. Slater 7-26-1864 L
Taylor, Rev. R. V. to Sarah L. Chunn 7-21-1853 Hr
Taylor, Richd. to Emma Taylor 12-12-1872 Hy
Taylor, Riley to Mary Ann Gooch 11-22-1838 Cr
Taylor, Robert H. to Mary A. Jackson 7-20-1847 (7-21-1847) G
Taylor, Robert L. to Rebecca E. Spence 11-18-1879 (11-19-1879) L
Taylor, Robert Z. to America C. Ivie 10-6-1869 G
Taylor, Robert to D. Baptist 12-23-1872 T
Taylor, Robert to Joana Thompson 3-14-1870 (3-17-1870) L
Taylor, Robert to Mary D. Hale 5-12-1842 Ma
Taylor, Robert to Nancy S. Hoover 1-23-1852 G
Taylor, Robert to Sophia Umphries 3-2-1865 (3-8-1865) L
Taylor, Robert to Tempy Clark 5-16-1872 L B
Taylor, Robt. W. to Mary E. Pentecost 6-22-1866 Ma
Taylor, Robt. to Jennie Taylor 8-22-1872 Hy

Taylor, Ruff & Ready to Susan Morris 4-28-1866 Hy
Taylor, Rufus C. to Mollie Shaw 5-7-1869 (no return) F
Taylor, S. A. to Callie Davis 9-18-1873 Hy
Taylor, S. G. to Sarah J. Baldridge 2-13-1859 We
Taylor, S. J. to Mollie E. Crenshaw 10-13-1873 (10-15-1873) Dy
Taylor, S. P. to N. L. White 9-20-1866 G
Taylor, Sam to Levinia Taylor 1-25-1868 T
Taylor, Sam to Norah Taylor 3-19-1874 Hy
Taylor, Samuel J. to Mary S. Bludworth 8-4-1867 Be
Taylor, Samuel L. to Sarah M. Mitchell 10-31-1860 T
Taylor, Samuel M. to Virginia E. Fuqua 9-29-1859 (no return) We
Taylor, Samuel to Fanny M. Watts 1-22-1849 (1-25-1849) G
Taylor, Samuel to Sally Owen 1-16-1877 Hy
Taylor, Sandy to Mollie Smith 7-25-1872 Hy
Taylor, Senson to Amy Coffin 8-21-1869 (8-22-1869) F B
Taylor, Shareons to Susan Cox 1-27-1846 Cr
Taylor, Shelton D. to Parthenia H. M. Martin 10-11-1846 T
Taylor, Sidney to Edie Lewis Taylor 12-15-1875 Hy
Taylor, Sim to Ellen Harland 12-12-1867 G
Taylor, Sinclar to Elizabeth Gleason 11-30-1848 O
Taylor, Stephen S. to Eliza Bradford 12-21-1880 (12-22-1880) L
Taylor, Stephen to Alice Moore 12-24-1872 Hy
Taylor, Stephen to Ann McNeil 1-6-1866 (no return) F B
Taylor, Stephen to Mary Curry 9-14-1867 Hy
Taylor, Steven to Ellen Currie 5-5-1867 Hy
Taylor, Steven to Kate Taliaferro 1-10-1869 Hy
Taylor, Sylvanus to Henretta J. Kirby 10-12-1850 Ma *
Taylor, T. T. to Lucy Coleman 9-10-1860 (9-11-1860) Sh
Taylor, Thomas B. to Bella Cornelius 11-11-1863 Hy
Taylor, Thomas H. to Jane Ingram 5-1-1849 Ma
Taylor, Thomas J. to Hannah M. Walker 1-7-1868 (1-8-1868) L
Taylor, Thomas L. to Mary E. Taylor 8-29-1867 G
Taylor, Thomas T. to Elizabeth Hathaway 12-21-1859 Ma
Taylor, Thomas to C. B. Hanks 4-1-1861 Mn
Taylor, Thomas to Jane L. Littleton 2-23-1867 (no return) Hn B
Taylor, Thomas to Juliana Gilchrist 9-19-1831 (9-21-1831) G
Taylor, Thomas to Martha Davis 11-18-1850 (11-19-1850) Ma
Taylor, Thomas to Mary Ann Ross 10-13-1856 Sh
Taylor, Thos. C. to Celina Phillips 2-25-1841 G
Taylor, Thos. G. to Ann T. Reeves 12-14-1854 G
Taylor, Thos. L. to S. A. Fowler 5-28-1873 (no return) Cr
Taylor, Tom to Fannie Shaw 1-20-1874 Hy
Taylor, V. M. L. to Sarah F. Dodd 10-29-1858 G
Taylor, Vinson M. L. to Margaret Patterson 9-17-1844 (9-19-1844) G
Taylor, W. (Dr.) to Emaline M. McFarlen 2-9-1847 (2-11-1847) G
Taylor, W. A. to Hattie Taylor 10-11-1877 Hy
Taylor, W. A. to J. Butler 8-18-1867 G
Taylor, W. B. to N. A. Ward (Word?) 5-8-1866 G
Taylor, W. C. to Sarah E. Martin 3-5-1867 G
Taylor, W. H. to Bettie Williams 2-22-1882 (2-23-1882) L
Taylor, W. H. to Helen E. Bowen 9-17-1856 Sh
Taylor, W. H. to Rutha E. Christman 2-12-1853 (no return) F
Taylor, W. H. to Sally Cottingham 10-12-1842 Be
Taylor, W. M. to Ann Robertson 1-1-1867 Hn
Taylor, W. M. to R. C. Ruse 10-7-1862 (10-12-1862) Cr
Taylor, W. N. to Miranda G. Nash 11-25-1878 (11-27-1878) Dy
Taylor, W. N. to Rebecca L. Harton 11-14-1870 (11-15-1870) Dy
Taylor, W. T. to Sarah E. Spenser 2-5-1854 Hn
Taylor, W. W. to Elizabeth Punch 4-6-1848 Hr
Taylor, W. W. to M. P. Horton 10-5-1865 G
Taylor, Ward, jr. to Amanda Gibson 2-29-1860 (3-2-1860) Sh
Taylor, Washington S. to Ann E. Park 3-31-1853 Sh
Taylor, Wat to Rachel Moore 11-12-1870 Hy
Taylor, Weddle to Maria Claibourne 3-6-1871 T
Taylor, Wedly to Sallie Macklin 9-6-1866 T
Taylor, Whitfield to Nancy Crockett 6-24-1844 We
Taylor, Whitfield to Nancy Gaines 10-16-1845 We
Taylor, Wiley P. to Fannie Lenow 1-12-1858 (1-13-1858) Sh
Taylor, Wiley to Clara Taylor 5-19-1867 Hy
Taylor, Wiley to Mariah S. Watt 11-15-1849 (11-18-1849) G
Taylor, Wiley to Sarah E. King 1-28-1867 G
Taylor, William A. to Martha W. N. Bland 4-17-1839 (4-24-1839) F
Taylor, William D. to C. A. Garrison 8-7-1878 (8-8-1878) Dy
Taylor, William J. to Catharine Goodrich 12-2-1846 (12-9-1846) G
Taylor, William J. to Mahala L. Stewart 7-18-1870 (7-21-1870) Ma
Taylor, William O. to Mary Jane Brogden 12-21-1868 G
Taylor, William P. to Manerva A. Brooks 1-6-1851 (1-7-1851) F
Taylor, William T. to Mary E. Volentine 4-28-1844 Hn
Taylor, William to Ann (Mrs.) Baber 11-21-1864 Sh
Taylor, William to Clementine P. Hosford 12-15-1850 Hn
Taylor, William to E. V. McCree 12-1-1864 G
Taylor, William to Elizabeth Jane Gibson 1-6?-1847 (1-7-1847) Hr
Taylor, William to Elizabeth McIlroy 7-6-1824 (7-8-1824) Hr
Taylor, William to F. E. Enochs 10-8-1872 (10-9-1872) Dy
Taylor, William to Lizzie Green 1-10-1877 Hy
Taylor, William to Lucinda Gage 12-15-1827 Hr
Taylor, William to Lucinda Gage 12-15-1829 (12-24-1829) Hr

Taylor, William to Lucinda Sanford 7-7-1857 G
Taylor, William to Mary Patterson 3-7-1846 (3-11-1846) G
Taylor, William to Nancy Thornton 9-1-1866 Hy
Taylor, William to R. Clement 3-23-1866 (4-1-1866) T
Taylor, William to Rutha McFarland 3-13-1838 (3-22-1838) Ma
Taylor, Willis R. to Elizabeth Mabury 8-6-1850 Be
Taylor, Willis V. to Sarah K. Vincent 1-14-1840 Hr
Taylor, Willis to Dina Dukes 2-20-1873 Hy
Taylor, Willis to Louisa Hart 4-9-1829 (5-11-1829) Hr
Taylor, Willis to Mary Peebles 12-31-1873 Hy
Taylor, Wilson to Ann Link 2-18-1875 Hy
Taylor, Wily to Eliza Sweet 4-14-1866 Hy
Taylor, Wm. H. to S. J. Adams 12-24-1851 Cr
Taylor, Wm. J. to Martha Jane Roberts 5-12-1850 We
Taylor, Wm. O. to Susan Green no date (with 1868) T
Taylor, Wm. to Florenc Jackson 9-17-1868 (9-18-1868) T
Taylor, Wm. to Frances Collier 6-6-1868 F B
Taylor, Wm. to Frankie Maclin 1-28-1870 T
Taylor, Wm. to L. Jane Cumins 1-10-1870 T
Taylor, Wm. to Mary A. Jones 2-2-1847 Cr
Taylor, Wyatt A. to Tennessee V. Collins 7-29-1858 Ma
Taylor, Wyley to Rose Morgan 12-23-1873 (12-31-1873) L B
Taylor, wiley to Nany Dozer 7-7-1838 (7-8-1838) G
Tayne?, Banyan to Nancy M. Wright 7-22-1841 T
Teadford, John J. to Phoebe N. Rosson 2-14-1850 (2-19-1850) Hr
Teaffe, Philip to Ann Jane Collins 7-28-1858 Hy
Teagner, Henry to Caroline Ross 12-26-1867 F B
Teague, Abner to Mary J. Allison 3-16-1866 Ma
Teague, Anderson to Ellen Strickland 8-25-1866 (8-26-1866) F B
Teague, C. M. to N. A. Baird 10-27-1860 (10-30-1860) F
Teague, Caswell to Paralee McCullough 5-21-1866 (no return) Hn B
Teague, Charles to Elizabeth Tharpe 11-17-1866 Hn B
Teague, Henry M. to Frances Daniel 1-27-1851 Hr
Teague, James Welborn to Julia Ann Torrance 12-18-1860 (12-19-1860) F
Teague, James to Mary A. Duke 10-23-1866 (10-24-1866) F
Teague, Joseph B. to Elizabeth Comer 1-1-1844 Hr
Teague, Joshua M. to Catharine A. Dean 1-16-1856 Hr
Teague, Joshua to Rosie Atkins 5-21-1866 (no return) Hn B
Teague, Josiah to Mary Ann Upton 10-19-1852 (10-20-1852) Hr
Teague, Spencer to Lavinia Crutcher 9-20-1866 (9-21-1866) F B
Teague, Thos. J. to Susan A. Robertson 12-23-1857 Sh
Teague, W. L. to Sarah McCullough 1-31-1861 Hn B?
Teague, W. S. to M. R. Chambers 1-31-1864 (2-2-1864) F
Teague, William G. to Molly Thomas 10-14-1831 Hr
Teague, William H. to Sarah E. Brag 2-24-1863 We
Teague, William to Amanda Williams 8-27-1846 Ma
Teague, William to Temperance Whitehead 12-6-1845 (12-11-1845) F
Teague, Wm. T. to Mattie C. Dean 3-9-1870 (3-10-1870) Ma
Teahen, Wm. M. to Mattie Matthews 12-20-1870 (12-21-1870) Ma
Teal, James C. to Penelope Fairless 3-10-1838 Ma
Teater, B. W. to Margaret M. Hendricks 10-30-1867 (no return) Dy
Teater, Shelby to Sarah M. Bedford 3-15-1840 O
Tedder, E. M. to Malinda ___ 1-3-1861 Be
Tedder, James to Martha J. Lewis 8-19-1866 Be
Tedder, James to Nancy Burns 6-14-1846 Be
Tedder, John to Emily Yates 1-13-1864 Be
Teddleton, Joseph to Elizabeth Ursery 8-9-1867 (8-10-1867) Ma
Tedford, John J. to Ailsy Warren 12-5-1859 (12-15-1859) Hr
Tedrow, John C. to Selina Hogue 12-4-1866 O
Tedwell, James to Nancy Ann Manasco 7-3-1867 (7-4-1867) T
Teel, James E. to Mary Ann Gailor 10-18-1841 F
Teel, Luther to Nancy Mitchell 12-2-1861 Sh
Teel, P. M. to A. Johnson 11-13-1847 (11-18-1847) F
Teel, Westley C. to A. F. Holland 3-23-1843 (3-24-1843) F
Tegethoff, Wm. to Louisa Stoemer 9-1-1860 Sh
Tel, G. W. to Jane E. Forrest 1-20-1863 (1-22-1863) Sh
Telfair, Edward to Mary R. Davie 10-28-1850 Ma
Temple, Charles to Charlett Hunter 11-3-1828 Ma
Temple, J. S. to Mary C. Hunter 12-4-1883 L
Temple, J. W. to Harriet E. Wells 12-17-1862 (12-28-1862) F
Temple, John H. to Catherine E. Maltbie 9-16-1847 Sh
Temple, John S. to Lavinia F. Sherrill 9-15-1856 Ma
Temple, John S. to Mary F. Gains 12-14-1868 (12-16-1868) L
Temple, William S. to Elizabeth Sherl 11-27-1854 (11-30-1854) Ma *
Temple, Wm. S. to Margarett M Ballard 4-18-1843 Ma
Temples, John I. to Elizabeth S. Marsh 3-24-1869 (3-28-1869) Ma
Templeton, Augustus A. to C. E. Brooks 12-3-1872 (12-5-1872) T
Templeton, Charles M. to Malinda C. Adams 1-14-1861 (no return) We
Templeton, David I. H. to Mary M. Knox 2-7-1854 (2-10-1854) G
Templeton, J. S. to Sarah Lunsford 5-18-1861 (5-19-1861) L
Templeton, John J. to Margaret E. Stevenson 3-12-1866 (3-14-1866) T
Templeton, R. F. to S. A. Akin 1-21-1868 (1-22-1868) Dy
Templeton, Richard S. to Eliza K. Cherry 12-18-1860 (12-20-1860) T
Templeton, S. G. to S. E. Williams 8-21-1865 (8-22-1865) Dy
Temus, William D. to Amanda E. Underwood 7-4-1860 We
Tennant, Marsh to Lou Nichols 3-4-1886 (3-6-1886) L
Tennant, William to Elizabeth McGowan 10-25-1850 (10-27-1850) T

Tenney, Oliver G. to Nancy L. Farmer 8-31-1850 O
Tenning, Ransom to Malinda Voss 8-4-1878 Hy
Tennis, Reubin to Nancy Mathews 7-2-1831 (7-3-1831) Ma
Tenny, J. R. to Rosa Futhery? 1-27-1868 (1-29-1868) T
Tensly, Henry B. to Lucy Sherman 3-13-1872 Hy
Tepe, F. A. to Fannie J. Douglass 7-20-1858 Sh
Terell, William H. to Rachael M. Thomas 1-29-1849 G
Terrell, A. A. to Josephine Castaloe 12-28-1876 Hy
Terrell, Banister to Josephine Moore 12-20-1856 Ma
Terrell, Benjamin F. to Mary J. Davis 10-31-1839 G
Terrell, Benjamin H. to G.? A. Clark 12-19-1868 (12-22-1868) T
Terrell, Constantine to Elizabeth Tyson 12-11-1872 Hy
Terrell, G. W. to Ann Fonville 4-11-1867 G
Terrell, George J. to Penelope Gregory 5-9-1861 G
Terrell, Henry C. to Marina Craft 7-2-1855 Sh
Terrell, Isaac to Artemisia Glass 1-25-1856 T
Terrell, J. B. to N. A. Clag 8-23-1860 Sh
Terrell, J. J. to Mary Holloway 9-26-1870 G
Terrell, J. to V. H. Jackson 1-29-1867 G
Terrell, James M. to Mary A. Long 2-17-1863 We
Terrell, James M. to Sarah Dickson 10-8-1856 G
Terrell, John H. to Elizabeth B. Fleming 7-4-1843 We
Terrell, Joseph M. to Jean V. Dodson 6-29-1863 G
Terrell, Joseph M. to Sarah E. Corley 8-3-1863 G
Terrell, William B. to Sarah E. Dodson 1-7-1859 (12-10-1859) G
Terrell, Wm. to Nancy C. Haney 2-24-1878 Hy
Terrett, William to Mary Chambers 8-19-1846 (8-23-1846) O
Terril, Thadeous N. to Lew A. W. Clay 3-15-1853 (3-16-1853) G
Terril, Thomas to Sarah Roth 4-30-1867 Hy
Terril, Wm. R. to Paralee Booth 3-14-1873 Hy
Terrill, Buford to Julia Bouchier 2-15-1854 E
Terrill, Franklin J. to Sarah A. Roberson 5-16-1850 G
Terrill, George W. to Ann Bell 9-5-1839 G
Terrill, Robert to Catharine Jackson 12-25-1852 O
Terrill, S. T. to Jennie E. Pervis 6-16-1866 Hy
Terrill, Thomas J. to Mary M. Starrett 3-23-1842 (3-24-1842) O
Terrill, William to Winnie M. Troxer 3-12-1874 Hy
Terrill, Wm. A. to Maranda Tosh 11-16-1873 Hy
Terry, A. L. to Elizabeth Haynes 9-25-1856 O
Terry, Alexander to Emeline R. Bell 3-6-1843 G
Terry, Andrew to Nancy Johnston 3-4-1847 O
Terry, Champion to Mary Howlett 1-25-1855 Hn
Terry, Henry to Elizabeth Crague 2-7-1867 O
Terry, Hiram to Elizabeth Cooksey 11-3-1843 (11-5-1843) Hr
Terry, Hiram to Mary Ann Jackson 6-9-1850 Hn
Terry, Isaac N. to Elizabeth Bradley 9-9-1855 Hn
Terry, J. M. to Susan Kinney 7-2-1874 T
Terry, James F. to E. T. (Mrs.) Wood 6-1-1861 (6-3-1861) Sh
Terry, James M. to Mary A. R. Stone 11-26-1841 (12-7-1841) G
Terry, James M. to Sarah Elenor Kelley 9-20-1858 (9-21-1858) T
Terry, John C. to Sarah E. Stroud 12-4-1853 Hn
Terry, John H. to Frances A. White 5-29-1837 G
Terry, John S. to Mary V. Hansboro 1-1-1858 Cr
Terry, John to Caroline Sewell 12-13-1865 Mn
Terry, John to Louisa Tansel 12-15-1863 (12-20-1863) O
Terry, John to Maggie Marshall 9-29-1877 (10-4-1877) L
Terry, John to Susannah Rogers 1-15-1838 (1-16-1838) Hr
Terry, Joseph B. to Joanna Parker 11-26-1856 Hr
Terry, Joseph to Elizabeth Lake 5-30-1885 (5-31-1885) L
Terry, M. T. to Clara A. Olive 12-21-1868 (12-22-1868) F
Terry, Monroe E. to Louisa P. Williamson 11-18-1868 G
Terry, Pleasant to Matilda Ferguson 12-14-1864 Dy
Terry, R. S. J. to Murphy M. Williams 11-1-1859 (11-2-1859) Sh
Terry, Ras.? to Hester Ann Taylor 4-7-1866 (4-29-1866) T
Terry, Steven to Rebeca Kelly 1-3-1853 (1-25-1853) T
Terry, Thomas J. to Nancy Ann Baker 3-20-1852 Hn
Terry, William H. to Sarah E. Scott 12-16-1852 Ma
Terry, William to S. A. M. N. C. Flowers 2-8-1866 G
Terry, William to T. S. Rankins 11-30-1852 Hn
Tesh, John to Elizabeth Gist 9-26-1861 Cr
Test (West), George to Nancy McKinney 2-5-1836 O
Tetterton, Matthew to Martha M. Greenwell 1-31-1849 (2-1-1849) Ma
Tettleton, Bryant to Elizabeth Parker 12-30-1846 Ma
Tettleton, Silas to Jane Langston 10-14-1841 Ma
Tevilla, E. P. to T. A. Peery 11-10-1868 Dy
Tevilla, H. C. to Sarah Edwards 11-28-1868 (11-30-1868) Dy
Thacher, Pleasant to Sarah Byars 12-14-1852 We
Thacher, Wm. C. to Rachel Hearn 1-15-1846 We
Thacker, G. W. to Sophia Catherine Armer 9-19-1869 G
Thacker, Levi to Martha Avery 3-23-1867 (3-24-1867) Ma
Thacker, Moses to Rachel Lovelace 12-21-1868 (no return) Dy
Thacker, William L. D. to Susan Wilcox 8-14-1831 Sh
Thadwick, John R. to Martha Taylor 12-23-1849 G
Tharp, Gilliam to Rebecca Jane Nail 12-25-1847 (12-28-1847) F
Tharp, Granville to Dora Wells 12-14-1870 F B
Tharp, Isaac to Sopha Mayfield 2-18-1847 G
Tharp, J. C. to E. A. Neal 7-13-1865 G

Grooms

Tharp, J. Coleman to M. Precilla Shaw 7-30-1856 G
Tharp, Jessee J. to Sarah Ann Moor 1-29-1851 (1-30-1851) F
Tharp, Jessee to Catharine Dalton 4-2-1846 G
Tharp, Lafayette to Susan Walker 6-5-1863 Sh
Tharp, W. H. (Dr.) to Susan P. Whitmore 11-22-1852 (no return) F
Tharp, William A. to Candis A. Evans 2-23-1846 (3-3-1846) F
Tharpe, Anthony to Caroline Miller 5-30-1844 Hn
Tharpe, Edward to Dorcas Tharpe 12-25-1866 Hn B
Tharpe, H. H. to Maranda C. Williams 2-23-1863 Hn
Tharpe, H. W. to Tennessee Palmer 11-24-1852 Hn
Tharpe, Henry to Lucy Frazier 11-28-1839 (no return) Hn
Tharpe, Luco M. to Mary Crockett 10-10-1845 Hn
Tharpe, Mark to Eveline Tharpe 5-21-1866 (no return) Hn B
Tharpe, Thomas R. to M. C. Porter 6-9-1851 Hn
Tharpe, W. A. to Alice A. Crockett 8-1-1854 Hn
Tharpe, W. L. to Mary V. Stewart 11-1-1866 Hn
Tharpe, William to Nancy Hudgens 8-31-1848 Hn
Tharpe, William to Rebecca McCullough 6-8-1867 (no return) Hn B
Tharpe, ____? to Jane Newton 1-13-1840 Hn
Thatcher, Wm. to Elizabeth Hill 8-4-1847 Sh
Thayer, Wm. H. to Nellie Manning 12-5-1863 (12-6-1863) Sh
Thebold, Augustus to Sarah Piles 11-14-1860 (11-15-1860) Hr
Thedford, Constant to Lucretia Sherron 10-2-1843 (10-12-1843) G
Thedford, Denis to Hester H. Gray 8-4-1829 (8-5-1829) G
Thedford, Edward to Louiza Peel 11-4-1850 (11-6-1850) G
Thedford, Jacob to Agnis H. Mathews 8-3-1866 G
Thedford, James W. to Emeline Hill 9-25-1862 G
Thedford, James to Sarah Williams 3-12-1862 G
Thedford, John L. to Margaret Jane Cribbs 1-30-1850 G
Thedford, John R. to Sarah Pounds 3-12-1851 G
Thedford, Josiah L. to Polly Kennedy 9-28-1828 (9-29-1828) G *
Thedford, Josias to Hannah Thedford 12-27-1859 G
Thedford, Sandford to Manerva Gilliland 2-6-1843 (2-9-1843) G
Thedford, Thomas J. to Margarett W. (Mrs.) McKnight 8-15-1844 G
Thedford, Thos. J. N. K. H. to Elvira Thedford 2-10-1846 (2-12-1846) G
Thedford, Walter L. to Nancy N. Cash 1-16-1869 (1-20-1869) Ma
Thedford, Walter M. to Rutha Canaday 7-3-1838 (7-8-1838) G
Thedford, Walter N. to Mary M. Herndon 10-22-1855 (10-24-1855) G
Thedford, Walter to Elizabeth Runalds 11-3-1845 (11-6-1845) G
Thedford, William T. to Sarah Cantrell 9-9-1860 (9-10-1860) G
Thedford, William to Elizabeth Crockett 11-3-1829 G
Thedford, William to Harriet Littleford 10-18-1828 (10-19-1828) G
Thedford, William to Polly Williams 10-13-1837 (10-15-1837) G
Thedford, William to Sophronia Edwards 10-4-1849 (1-8-1849?) Ma
Thedford, Wm. to Nany Fox 11-16-1841 G
Thedford, Walter to Barbary Holt 10-4-1834 (10-9-1834) G
Theure (Theurer), ____ to Susan Williams 7-21-1846 Sh
Thielemann, Capt. Milo to Minnie (Mrs.) Wilson 11-24-1862 Sh
Thitford, J. A. to P. J. Aikin 1-8-1867 (1-9-1867) Dy
Thogmodden, J. D. to Lucra Price 2-19-1867 (3-22-1867) Dy
Thom, Wily to Amelia Welch 11-26-1838 (11-29-1838) Ma
Thomas, A. J. to M. A. (Mrs.) Brown 5-3-1868 G
Thomas, A. L. to Mary Pate 10-3-1849 Sh
Thomas, A. R. to Mary J. Hale 10-18-1856 G
Thomas, Abner D. to Margarett Ann Thomas 2-12-1845 (no return) F
Thomas, Abner D. to Nancy Bean 4-15-1840 (4-16-1840) G
Thomas, Abner D. to Nancy Taner 6-19-1834 G
Thomas, Abner S. to Chana Lovett 7-29-1850 (8-8-1850) G
Thomas, Alex to Mattie Helm 4-13-1882 (no return) L
Thomas, Alfred A. to Manervia S. Murphy 9-29-1841 G
Thomas, Alfred James to Polly S. Childress 12-23-1845 G
Thomas, Alfred to Amanda Morgan 10-11-1849 O
Thomas, Alfred to Eliza Wood 10-2-1873 Hy
Thomas, Alfred to Martha Hall 3-12-1873 (4-5-1873) T
Thomas, B. F. to M. A. Neblett 12-2-1867 Hy
Thomas, B. F. to Zady F. Hammonds 8-27-1856 Hr
Thomas, Bedford to Elizabeth J. Hendricks 1-10-1849 (1-12-1849) Hr
Thomas, Ben to Charlott McCulloch 8-24-1867 G B
Thomas, Benj. to Sally Brodnax 2-2-1867 (no return) F B
Thomas, Benjamin to Millea Reaves 2-1-1877 Hy
Thomas, Burk to Darcy Gardner 11-28-1872 (11-30-1872) O
Thomas, C. C. to Margaret E. Bateman 5-12-1857 (5-13-1857) Sh
Thomas, C. C. to N. E. Cowan 7-15-1867 Hy
Thomas, C. P. to Elizabeth Holm 2-5-1880 Cr
Thomas, C. R. to Mary A. Stanley 12-24-1860 Hy
Thomas, Calvin P. to Susan Hansburrow 1-18-1851 Cr
Thomas, Charles to Jane Carroll 7-9-1846 Hn
Thomas, Charlie to Fannie Taylor 4-5-1871 Hy
Thomas, D. M. to Hariette Mason 10-11-1860 G
Thomas, D. M. to Levinia Mount 10-9-1862 (no return) Cr

Thomas, Daniel to Mary Laws (Lane) 4-22-1849 Sh
Thomas, David J. to Lafronia A. Lowry 11-30-1858 Hn
Thomas, David to Malinda Murphy 2-25-1828 G
Thomas, David to Mary Patterson 3-2-1867 Hy
Thomas, E. A. to M. Ella Shofner 2-17-1873 (2-19-1873) Cr
Thomas, E. S. to Mary McAskille 2-26-1873 (2-27-1873) Cr
Thomas, Ed to Mary Bennett 12-4-1877 Hy
Thomas, Edward to Amanda Owen 12-13-1877 Hy
Thomas, Edward to Ann Craighead 9-10-1872 T
Thomas, Edward to Susan Smith 3-31-1870 T
Thomas, Elam F. to Alice A. Rhodes 9-3-1844 T
Thomas, Ezekeil to Etseta Sparks 1-19-1853 Cr
Thomas, F. G. to M. A. Greer (Green?) 12-23-1869 G
Thomas, Francis M. to Mary A. Hammond 8-20-1852 (8-22-1852) Hr
Thomas, Francis to Nannie McClenahan 1-14-1869 (1-20-1869) T
Thomas, Fred to Bridget Nagle 12-8-1862 Sh
Thomas, Friday to Dinah Henderson 1-5-1867 F B
Thomas, George E. to Lucy Ann Blaydes 2-11-1862 Hy
Thomas, George R. to Mary F. Clark 10-1-1867 Hy
Thomas, George to Charlotte Kney 8-19-1863 (8-20-1863) Sh
Thomas, George to Henrietta Morrow 5-10-1867 (5-20-1867) F B
Thomas, Green to Dilly Currie 10-30-1878 Hy
Thomas, Green to Eugenia Montgomery 12-22-1866 Be
Thomas, Guriah to Sarah Moreland 2-28-1871 (4-3-1871) F B
Thomas, H. B. to S. A. Roach 10-31-1867 (11-5-1867) Cr
Thomas, Henry A. to Sarah Jane Vanpelt 2-7-1850 (2-8-1850) Ma
Thomas, Henry P. to Eliza Roberts 4-10-1841 (4-15-1841) Hr
Thomas, Henry to Elizabeth Burton 2-20-1867 Hy
Thomas, Henry to Emily Adison 2-4-1867 (2-6-1867) L B
Thomas, Henry to Frances Hendren 5-27-1871 Hy
Thomas, Henry to Martha A. Peery 3-23-1858 (no return) We
Thomas, Henry to Nellie Short 12-23-1869 Hy
Thomas, Henry to S. Turnage 12-24-1873 (12-27-1873) T
Thomas, Henry to Susan Haliburton 7-1-1845 (7-2-1845) G
Thomas, Hugh B. to Mary E. Fletcher 10-19-1864 G
Thomas, Isaac to Elizabeth Gilbert 8-14-1838 Cr
Thomas, Isaac to Rachel Walker 12-27-1876 Dy
Thomas, Isaiah to Francis Cason 12-24-1877 L
Thomas, Isham to Elizabeth Holt 7-10-1855 (7-11-1855) G
Thomas, Isham to Martha A. Waldroup 11-15-1861 We
Thomas, J. A. to Nancy Pinson 1-10-1870 T
Thomas, J. A. to Nancy Pinson 1-10-1870 (1-13-1870) T
Thomas, J. B. to C. B. Maury 12-21-1865 F
Thomas, J. B. to Emily W. Seward 3-23-1858 (3-26-1858) Sh
Thomas, J. B. to Katie Bruce (Brown) 2-28-1872 Hy
Thomas, J. H. to Mary E. Alexander 12-17-1860 Hy
Thomas, J. Henry? to Martha Perry 3-25-1858 We
Thomas, J. J. to Nancy E. Hendrick 2-17-1847 Hr
Thomas, J. M. to Amanda Clark 12-6-1851? (12-9-1862) F
Thomas, J. S. to Anna Powell 9-11-1867 L
Thomas, J. S. to Martha L. Ing 1-18-1860 (1-19-1860) G
Thomas, J. W. B. to Serritha J. Kirkman 12-28-1865 Hy
Thomas, J. W. to Fannie Elam 3-11-1863 G
Thomas, J. W. to Margaret Thompson 2-27-1865 F
Thomas, J. W. to Nancy F. Couch 6-22-1861 (6-25-1861) Sh
Thomas, Jackson to Mary L. Holt 5-23-1859 (no return) We
Thomas, James A. to Elizabeth Edmundson 10-28-1852 G
Thomas, James A. to Malinda Porter 11-29-1841 (11-30-1841) G
Thomas, James F. to Caroline Thomas 10-28-1861 Sh
Thomas, James G. to Phoebe R. Smith 11-15-1868 G
Thomas, James H. to Jane Sharp 11-3-1868 (11-4-1868) Ma
Thomas, James N. to Martha L. J. Hallen 4-25-1858 Cr
Thomas, James W. B. to Jane M. Mcclish 3-13-1844 Ma
Thomas, James to Elizabeth Ethridge 11-30-1865 G
Thomas, James to Emma Wood 7-29-1877 Hy
Thomas, James to Mary Neal 7-25-1872 Hy
Thomas, Jas. F. to M. A. Cathey 1-12-1875 (1-14-1875) O
Thomas, Jesse W. to Mary J. Somers 12-3-1845 (12-4-1845) Ma
Thomas, Jesse to Penelope McClellan 5-6-1828 Hr
Thomas, Jim to Lucy A. Adams 10-8-1870 Hy
Thomas, Jno. G. to Louisa McCoy 12-20-1875 Hy
Thomas, Joel A. to Mary E. Emerson 1-27-1869 (1-28-1869) Ma
Thomas, John D. to Mary Parker 1-31-1849 O
Thomas, John F. to Bettie Connell 12-25-1865 G
Thomas, John F. to Mary F. Temple 1-6-1862 We
Thomas, John F. to Phebe A. Furgerson 7-16-1867 (no return) L B
Thomas, John H. to Alice Silsby 12-28-1872 Dy
Thomas, John H. to Mary J. Lusker 10-27-1864 Sh
Thomas, John H. to N. E. Taylor 10-26-1857 (10-27-1857) Ma
Thomas, John H. to Nannie D. Cole 10-29-1859 (11-1-1859) Ma
Thomas, John H. to Virgina A. (Mrs.) Sharp 1-26-1869 Ma
Thomas, John J. to Sarah Jane McIver 12-8-1845 (12-9-1845) Ma
Thomas, John M. to Lucy Q. (Mrs.) Beasly 4-8-1844 (no return) F
Thomas, John T. to H. A. P. Barbee 11-21-1864 Sh
Thomas, John W. to Mary C. Arnold 3-20-1864 G
Thomas, John W. to Susan Busbee 12-24-1866 Hn B

Thomas, John to Amy Fleming 6-19-1873 Hy
Thomas, John to Eliza A. Carey 6-10-1857 (6-28-1857) G
Thomas, John to Elizabeth Braden 9-21-1847 (no return) L
Thomas, John to Elizabeth Brown 8-8-1851 Be
Thomas, John to Etta Bond 2-3-1885 L
Thomas, John to Marina Boon 12-20-1828 (12-23-1828) Ma
Thomas, John to Mary E. Nichols 10-15-1861 O
Thomas, John to Mollie Bivens 7-18-1885 (7-19-1885) L
Thomas, John to Pink Warren 9-7-1867 (no return) F B
Thomas, Joseph to Jane McDowell 2-28-1871 (9-22-1873) F B
Thomas, Joseph to Martha Jones 3-22-1877 Hy
Thomas, Joseph to Racheal Simons 8-10-1867 Hy
Thomas, L. L. to Bettie J. Rives 11-1-1877 Hy
Thomas, Lemuel A. to Julia A. Moody 11-28-1867 Hy
Thomas, Levin to Elizabeth A. Goodrich 3-7-1861 Dy
Thomas, Levy S. to Martha Stringfellow 7-30-1864 Sh
Thomas, Lewis to Malinda Ashburn 11-27-1843 T
Thomas, Lewis to Nancy Carr 9-13-1828 Hr
Thomas, Louis to Allis Hudson 7-13-1871 (7-14-1871) Cr B
Thomas, Lucius J. to Rebecca J. Hays 7-27-1859 Ma
Thomas, Luke to Mary E. Covington 11-19-1870 (11-24-1870) Cr
Thomas, Luke to Rachel Williams 12-16-1870 (12-28-1870) Cr B
Thomas, M. V. B. to Emily Owens 7-17-1855 (7-19-1855) Sh
Thomas, Mack to Amanda Hillman 1-25-1873 (1-26-1873) Cr
Thomas, Marshall to Lavenia Mount 3-3-1863 (no return) Cr
Thomas, Marshall to Sallie Karr 9-4-1868 (9-12-1868) F B
Thomas, Mathew to Rebecca Roberson 9-30-1863 L
Thomas, Milton to Lyda Dolan 3-11-1848 (3-12-1848) G
Thomas, Monroe to Rhoda Saunders 11-16-1866 G
Thomas, Moses to Caroline Deason 12-7-1869 (no return) L
Thomas, Moses to Margaret Whitesides 1-6-1844 (1-7-1844) L
Thomas, N. D. to Mary A. Boucher 8-12-1848 Cr
Thomas, Nathan P. to Elizabeth B. Tipton 3-30-1846 O
Thomas, Nathan to Bettie Turner 8-6-1867 (no return) L B
Thomas, Newton M. to Mary M. Allen 1-30-1855 (1-31-1855) Sh
Thomas, Olivar to Ellen Lewis 1-27-1872 Hy
Thomas, Owen to Jenny Clements 11-23-1866 (11-24-1866) T
Thomas, Pate to Lou Enochs 1-3-1878 Dy
Thomas, Peter to Dina Brown 10-1-1874 (10-3-1874) T
Thomas, Plumer to Keziah Burns 3-28-1872 Hy
Thomas, Polk to Angaline Barker 1-22-1873 (1-23-1873) Cr B
Thomas, R. G. to Parale F. Sinclair 8-29-1855 O
Thomas, R. H. to Mary E. Biggs 3-24-1863 G
Thomas, Redden C. to Martha E. Hobbs 1-12-1846 (1-15-1846) G
Thomas, Robert H. to Elizabeth P. Morris 10-14-1856 G
Thomas, Robert to Morning Ann J.(Mrs.) Garlington 6-22-1863 Sh
Thomas, Robt. H. to Margaret M. Teater 7-27-1878 (7-28-1878) Dy
Thomas, S. A. to Hdy? Arnold 11-12-1865 G
Thomas, Sam to Adaline Tyus 10-5-1871 Hy
Thomas, Saml. H. to Mattie E. Polk 2-8-1871 (no return) F
Thomas, Saml. to Sarah Porter Carter 12-19-1873 (12-20-1873) T
Thomas, Samuel M. to Elizabeth Reavis 11-6-1849 Ma
Thomas, Samuel M. to Martha Ann Hopkins 4-11-1843 Sh
Thomas, T. C. to A. L. Cole 7-19-1864 G
Thomas, Thomas D. to Susan M. Hamilton 5-4-1847 G
Thomas, Thomas J. to Mollie E. Howard 7-29-1866 Hy
Thomas, Tunce to Rebecca Rutherford 12-11-1869 Hy
Thomas, W. A. to Hattie (Mrs.) Martin 12-26-1870 Dy
Thomas, W. F. to Mary Clark 12-17-1866 Hy
Thomas, W. R. to Mary W. Crafton 10-19-1865 G
Thomas, W. T. to E. F. (Mrs.) Todd 10-19-1869 Cr
Thomas, W. T. to Malinda Hedgecock 10-9-1862 (no return) Cr
Thomas, W. W. to Catherine Kohn 1-3-1863 Sh
Thomas, W. W. to Florinda Saunders 2-13-1861 Be
Thomas, Wiley W. to Margarett H. Patterson 7-16-1849 (7-17-1849) Ma
Thomas, William A. to Rebecca L. Brim 6-4-1867 (6-6-1867) L
Thomas, William A. to Sarah A. H. Davis 10-27-1852 (10-28-1852) G
Thomas, William F. to Lucy A. E. Hally 3-3-1841 F
Thomas, William J. to Louisa J. Sharp 12-21-1858 Ma
Thomas, William L. to Sarah L. Thomas 1-15-1868 G
Thomas, William to Bettie Richardson 4-10-1869 (4-11-1869) L
Thomas, William to Lucinda Sample 3-9-1857 (3-12-1857) Sh
Thomas, William to Margrette S. J. Coffman 8-30-1855 (9-9-1855) G
Thomas, William to Mary E. Hall 1-9-1870 G
Thomas, William to Mattie Thomas 10-24-1870 F B
Thomas, William to Virginia Carr 7-16-1849 Be
Thomas, Wm. T. to Mary J. Fraser 9-12-1861 F
Thomas, Wm. to Frances A. Walker 2-17-1842 Sh
Thomas, Wm. to Nancy Pearson 12-20-1831 (12-22-1831) Hr
Thomas, Zachariah to Mary Geno 5-15-1836 Sh
Thomason, A. J. to Sarah Hyatt 5-24-1863 Be
Thomason, Arnold D. to Sarah Blacksheer 10-18-1843 Hn
Thomason, G. J. G. to Ann M. Miller 2-21-1871 Hn
Thomason, G. W. to Mary Groom 2-15-1866 Hn
Thomason, George to Catherine Sanders 9-28-1867 O
Thomason, H. M. to M. A. Seals 8-14-1869 (no return) Dy
Thomason, J. W. to Eliza Jane Turner 9-15-1862 (no return) Hn

Thomason, J. W. to Louisa Parish 12-24-1869 (12-28-1869) Cr
Thomason, James G. to Mary E. Knowles 11-13-1878 Dy
Thomason, James H. to Lucy Vaughn 11-20-1851 Hn
Thomason, James P. to Ader Wyly 12-17-1867 Be
Thomason, James to Sarah Jane Rogers 11-17-1847 G
Thomason, Jasper to Sarah F. McCampbell 11-11-1857 Hn
Thomason, Mark to Katy Dillion 9-15-1861 Be
Thomason, R. C. A. to Nancy C. Taylor 2-13-1861 (2-16-1861) Cr
Thomason, R. D. to Piety J. Phelps 2-8-1859 Hn
Thomason, Richard to Amanda J. Bracken 10-20-1859 (no return) Cr
Thomason, Robert H. to Caroline Blacksheer 9-8-1842 Hn
Thomason, Thomas to Betsy Norvill 8-1-1867 G
Thomason, W. C. to Eliza Ann Sims 5-17-1868 G
Thomason, William C. to E. Jane Box 2-12-1862 Be
Thomason, Willis Clinton to America Foster 9-3-1867 (no return) Hn
Thomason, Wm. R. to Temperance A. Gully 1-30-1851 Be
Thomasson, Osborn to Lucy Ferrill 12-27-1880 (no return) Dy
Thomerson, Alford B. to Winiford Britt 1-3-1841 Cr
Thomerson, G. F. to Allis Wilson 2-12-1866 O
Thomison, William to Eveline Vaulx 5-29-1875 Hy
Thomison, Wm. J. to Elizabeth Spinster 12-10-1840 Cr
Thompkins, Alphine (Alpheus?) to Elizabeth Cloude 12-24-1868 G
Thompkins, Lewis to Lucinda Price 12-7-1872 (12-29-1872) L B
Thompkins, S. to Lee Beasly 2-1-1882 (2-2-1882) L
Thompson, A. H. to E. N. Taylor 12-24-1851 Cr
Thompson, A. J. to Mary C. F. Thompson 12-19-1871 (no return) Cr
Thompson, A. L. to Edney V. Conley (Corley?) 7-24-1862 G
Thompson, A. M. to Martha A. Martin 1-26-1875 Hy
Thompson, A. S to Eliza Jane Wilcox 8-12-1849 Hn
Thompson, A. S. to Alice Turner 1-31-1886 L
Thompson, A. T. to A. W. Baucum 5-1-1856 We
Thompson, A. W. to Mary J. Mullins 10-16-1855 (no return) L
Thompson, Abraham to Rebecca Simpson 8-18-1855 O
Thompson, Albert to Elizabeth F. Gaines 2-25-1847 L
Thompson, Albert to Mary Mayes 1-21-1862 Hn
Thompson, Albert to Nancy Fagan 1-26-1870 T
Thompson, Alexander to Mary Eliza Barnett 12-19-1866 (12-20-1866) Ma
Thompson, Alexander to Patsey Lawrence 3-21-1829 Ma
Thompson, Allen M. to Mary A. H. Pipkin 9-17-1855 (9-18-1855) Hr
Thompson, Allen to Edith Mathews 12-28-1872 T
Thompson, Allen to Emiline Dancy 1-8-1874 Hy
Thompson, Allen to Ida Mercy 11-16-1877 Hy
Thompson, Allen to Sallie Turner 1-3-1872 L
Thompson, Anely to Sarah Holland 11-27-1860 Dy
Thompson, Archells to Unica McGeehe 8-6-1835 G
Thompson, Archibald to Mary Holland 3-9-1840 (3-12-1840) Ma
Thompson, B. F. to S. E. Webb 12-20-1871 (no return) Cr
Thompson, B. H. to Mary Martin 3-6-1851 (5-13-1851) Sh
Thompson, B. H. to Perlina Collins 1-15-1859 (1-16-1859) Sh
Thompson, B. L. to Cornelia Grissom 11-15-1851 (no return) F
Thompson, Ben to Rozetta Debow 12-22-1873 (12-25-1873) O
Thompson, Benj. A. F. to Mary A. Baker 3-10-1846 We
Thompson, Benjamin F. to L. B. Bassham 8-7-1849 O
Thompson, Benjamin L. to Susan Guthrie 3-15-1840 (3-25-1840) Ma
Thompson, Benjamin to Lucretia J. Edmondson 1-17-1857 (1-20-1857) Sh
Thompson, Benjamin to Mary Hallebirton 9-20-1870 (9-22-1870) L
Thompson, Benjamin to Permelia Jane Wiseman 10-31-1844 Be
Thompson, Bonaparte to Harriett Reed 1-22-1870 F B
Thompson, Burrell M. to Mary Heard 6-3-1854 (6-4-1854) G
Thompson, C. H. to Phredonia A. Utly 3-26-1854 Be
Thompson, C. K. to Maryann King 12-16-1865 (12-18-1865) Cr
Thompson, Calvin L. to Angeline E. Johnston 2-8-1870 (2-9-1870) Cr
Thompson, Calvin to Lucy Nance 8-4-1877 (8-26-1877) L
Thompson, Calvin to Mary Bell Thurmond 6-19-1884 L
Thompson, Cary to Fanny King 5-2-1867 (5-5-1867) F B
Thompson, Charles L. to Nancy Mayfield 1-27-1844 (1-30-1844) G
Thompson, Columbus W. to Elizabeth F. Moore 1-17-1871 Dy
Thompson, Cyrus to Adelia Cardozo 9-25-1842 Sh
Thompson, D. C. to M. J. Burnes 8-5-1859 Hr
Thompson, D. W. to C. Andrews 3-3-1847 Hr
Thompson, David to Bettie Gibbs 12-25-1883 (no return) L
Thompson, David to Harriet Wilson 5-4-1866 (5-6-1866) F
Thompson, David to Minerva J. James 8-16-1842 Hr
Thompson, David to Salitha E. Yeates 8-2-1849 Be
Thompson, Dennis to Nancy Edmondson 10-10-1853 (10-13-1853) G
Thompson, E. E. to Mary J. Finly 7-23-1867 Be
Thompson, E. G. to Frances Crain 11-16-1833 (11-?-1833) Hr
Thompson, E. H. to Nannie Clemins 10-14-1856 Cr
Thompson, E. T. to Susan J. Hammons 11-8-1855 (11-9-1855) Hr
Thompson, Edward to Elizabeth Oliver? 11-1-1866 Cr
Thompson, Elijah D. to Amarantha Dillion 3-26-1863 Be
Thompson, Ephram to Elizabeth Brown 12-4-1838 G
Thompson, F. N. to Sarah A. Wheeler 8-14-1860 (no return) Dy
Thompson, F. M. to Panthia M. Henderson 12-19-1860 Hy
Thompson, G. W. to Mary M. Robbins 10-22-1871 Hy
Thompson, Geo. W. to Catharine G. Green 12-10-1845 F
Thompson, Geo. W. to Martha B. Meriwether 12-22-1842 (1-3-1843) O

Thompson, George B. to Tabita Saunders 3-10-1831 (3-11-1831) Hr
Thompson, George G. to Mary E. Ruddle 12-14-1870 Ma
Thompson, George W. to Penelope G. Webster 12-20-1849 Sh
Thompson, George W. to Sarah Ann McCommon 1-1-1851 (1-2-1851) Hr
Thompson, George to Lizzie Turner 10-15-1883 (10-20-1883) L
Thompson, George to Rachel Wood 1-18-1869 (1-20-1869) L
Thompson, George to Sallie Howell 1-31-1866 (no return) L
Thompson, Gilbert to Catherine Wimberly 10-22-1838 Hn
Thompson, Glasgow to Callie Weddington 3-20-1861 G
Thompson, Henry P. to Elizabeth York 12-14-1841 Sh
Thompson, Henry to Polly Whitley 8-31-1866 T
Thompson, Henry to Rachael Tatom 12-6-1870 (12-21-1871) F B
Thompson, Henry to Sarah Lane 3-1-1856 O
Thompson, Henry to Virginia L. Moor 1-26-1853 G
Thompson, Heyborrow? to Betsy Titcomb 5-19-1866 (no return) F B
Thompson, Hezekiah C. to Susan Parker 7-3-1852 (7-8-1852) G
Thompson, Hilyard M. to Mary E. Ashlock 1-10-1861 Hn
Thompson, Hiram to Margrett Calahan 12-29-1846 Hr
Thompson, Hugh A. to Josephine Rone 11-21-1862 (12-3-1862) Ma
Thompson, Hugh H. to Ellen Ferrald 6-12-1860 We
Thompson, Isaac N. to Mary J. Ayers 3-9-1840 (3-12-1840) Hr
Thompson, Isuah? to Rachel Wood 11-18-1871 (no return) L
Thompson, J. B. to Lizzie Spain 2-25-1878 (2-27-1878) Dy
Thompson, J. C. C. to Mary F. Gowen 12-12-1865 (12-14-1865) Cr
Thompson, J. C. to Martha L. Scott 7-13-1857 O
Thompson, J. D. to E. J. Hamilton 10-17-1867 (no return) Cr
Thompson, J. H. to Elizabeth Fergason 1-20-1857 (no return) L
Thompson, J. H., jr. to M. E. Carson 6-3-1880 (6-5-1880) L
Thompson, J. M. to Mariah J. A. Kreighton 3-25-1864 (4-6-1864) Sh
Thompson, J. M. to Mary Ann Cole 2-19-1866 (no return) Hn
Thompson, J. N. to Mary Griffin 4-8-1866 Hy
Thompson, J. Q. A. to Florida C. Pettit 9-19-1860 (9-20-1860) Sh
Thompson, J. R. to Nancy C. Taylor 1-11-1841 (no return) Hn
Thompson, J. S. to M. F. Smith 8-12-1867 (8-13-1867) Dy
Thompson, J. S. to Mary McCutchen 12-30-1868 (no return) Dy
Thompson, J. T. to Margarett J. Crafton 12-23-1858 G
Thompson, J. W. to G. A. Byrn 12-22-1880 L
Thompson, J. W. to Martha Massey 3-25-1869 G
Thompson, J. W. to Mollie Edwards 2-23-1876 Dy
Thompson, J. W. to Rebecca A. Stewart 12-29-1869 (12-30-1869) L
Thompson, Jacob L. to Margarett Brooks 5-14-1841 Sh
Thompson, Jake to Lucinda A. Willson 10-11-1867 (no return) L B
Thompson, James B. to Sarah A. Dickinson 3-5-1859 (3-7-1859) G
Thompson, James B. to Sarah Jane Barnett 5-2-1842 Ma
Thompson, James F. to Harriet M. Wharton 3-24-1841 Hn
Thompson, James H. to Julia N. P. Koonce 12-11-1850 F
Thompson, James J. to Elizabeth A. Rollens 7-13-1863 (no return) Cr
Thompson, James J. to Mary Jane McCauley 12-?-1858 (12-9-1858) Ma
Thompson, James M. to Louisa Harrison 10-5-1843 F
Thompson, James M. to Martha C. Davis 5-9-1854 (5-11-1854) O
Thompson, James M. to Mollie F. Chambers 12-17-1869 (12-19-1869) L
Thompson, James P. to Nancy Brightwell 2-2-1852 (2-5-1852) G
Thompson, James R. to Arabella Thomas 12-30-1868 (12-31-1868) Cr
Thompson, James T. to Mary J. Worrell 2-31-1852 Ma
Thompson, James W. to Elizabeth M. J. Yarbrough 12-28-1850 (1-2-1851) G
Thompson, James W. to Lucy Janie Waller 2-9-1839 (2-12-1839) F
Thompson, James W. to Mollie Ann Morison 4-1-1878 (4-4-1878) L
Thompson, James to Eveline Thompson 2-15-1869 (2-17-1869) O
Thompson, James to Letha Campbell 3-22-1839 G
Thompson, James to Mary F. Mebane 8-?-1859 F
Thompson, James to Mary Philpot 6-1-1833 (6-4-1833) Hr
Thompson, James to Sarah Yates 2-22-1845 (2-23-1845) G
Thompson, Jarret to Martha A. R. Thompson 5-15-1865 Dy
Thompson, Jas. M. to Malvina Hamwick 5-26-1851 (5-29-1851) Sh
Thompson, Jas. P. to Nancy Eckford 11-10-1865 (11-12-1865) T
Thompson, Jas. to Sarah Drue Bonner 12-22-1851 Sh
Thompson, Jerry to Sarah Ball 12-31-1869 G B
Thompson, Jno. to J. A. Stephenson 12-24-1863 (12-25-1863) O
Thompson, Jno. to S. E. Bloodworth 11-3-1839 Be
Thompson, Joe to Sopha Hathorn 10-15-1872 Hy
Thompson, John B. to Martha Ann Reid 12-24-1861 T
Thompson, John B. to Susan Orr 5-25-1870 (5-26-1870) T
Thompson, John C. to Sarah E. McCaleb 3-1-1853 (3-10-1853) G
Thompson, John D. to Annie A. Miller 2-21-1865 (2-22-1865) T
Thompson, John J. to Polly Ann Clifft 3-14-1846 (3-24(14?)-1846 Hr
Thompson, John K. to L. C. Lawler 4-6-1854 We
Thompson, John M. to Clarissa Norris 12-23-1847 (12-26-1847) Hr
Thompson, John M. to Mary Robinson 1-20-1843 Cr
Thompson, John M. to Sarah Barnes 1-19-1836 (1-20-1836) G
Thompson, John P. to F. M. Burks 12-23-1879 L
Thompson, John T. to Jane McGehee 5-3-1838 (no return) F
Thompson, John T. to Martha Ann Bounds 8-10-1846 (8-13-1846) F
Thompson, John W. to Emily S. Jones 12-9-1858 Cr
Thompson, John to Cloe Cadwell 1-28-1824 (2-5-1824) Hr
Thompson, John to Ebediance Jackson 12-6-1849 O
Thompson, John to Eliza Duke 12-22-1870 (12-25-1870) F
Thompson, John to Elizabeth Lewis 11-23-1864 (11-24-1864) Sh
Thompson, John to Laura Gardner 12-22-1875 Hy
Thompson, John to Lavina Farrar 10-10-1866 (10-15-1866) F B
Thompson, John to Mary J. Wilkins 11-10-1843 (no return) F
Thompson, John to Mary Scott 3-6-1872 (3-10-1872) O
Thompson, John to Nancy Ann Wright 10-11-1853 (10-13-1853) G
Thompson, John to Nancy Gee 3-10-1857? (3-10-1858) Hr
Thompson, John to Polly Cross 2-16-1828 (2-17-1828) Hr
Thompson, John to Tabitha Bradberry 12-19-1848 Cr
Thompson, Jonthan to Nancy Clampitt 3-30-1844 Ma
Thompson, Joseph D. to Mary J. Beadles 12-27-1859 We
Thompson, Joseph H. to Mary P. Blankinship 1-15-1863 G
Thompson, Joseph S. to Ann C. Allen 3-9-1847 (3-10-1847) Hr
Thompson, Joseph to Perlina McFadden 3-2-1870 (3-17-1870) F B
Thompson, Joseph to _____ Kellin no date (with Mar 1838) F
Thompson, Joshua to _____ Skillen no dates (with May 1838) F
Thompson, Josiah H. D. to Eliza Ann Rainey 10-8-1855 (10-16-1855) Hr
Thompson, Judison L. to Mary P. Hopper 12-15-1858 Cr
Thompson, Keeble T. to Sarah A. Hammons 9-30-1846 (10-1-1846) Hr
Thompson, L. N. to Mary E. McIver 2-25-1874 L
Thompson, L. to Mary E. Wills 11-25-1852 Hn
Thompson, LaFayette to Hanley Crocker 3-24-1834 (3-30-1834) Hr
Thompson, Lee to Emily M. Derribery 3-21-1853 Hr
Thompson, Lemuel to Angeline Wiseman 2-24-1850 Be
Thompson, Lon O. to Bolinda F. Rush 7-5-1870 (7-13-1870) L
Thompson, Lycurgus to Mary C. Webb 5-28-1856 Sh
Thompson, Lycurgus to Sarah J. Corley 2-9-1860 G
Thompson, M. to L. C. Parks 12-10-1872 (12-11-1872) Dy
Thompson, Major to Elizabeth Ward 2-6-1834 Sh
Thompson, Marion to Eliza Williams 7-15-1856 (7-16-1856) O
Thompson, Miners L. to Sarah A. Tidwell 4-29-1844 (5-1-1844) Ma
Thompson, Monroe to Vic Williamson 12-25-1867 F B
Thompson, Moses G. to Martha Warmick 7-6-1839 (no return) Hn
Thompson, Neil to Sarah Jane Mullins 9-11-1866 (9-13-1866) Ma
Thompson, Nep to Tempy Ann Bumpass 10-30-1871 Hy
Thompson, P. C. to Bettie Ray 11-2-1863 T
Thompson, P. C. to Virginia A. Hodges 12-3-1868 (no return) F
Thompson, P. H. to Nancy C. Mashburn 2-3-1858 (2-4-1858) Hr
Thompson, Paul to Ella King 10-2-1873 Hy
Thompson, Peter to Louisa F. New 1-1-1843 Cr
Thompson, Peter to Penny Williamson 2-13-1867 (2-15-1867) T
Thompson, Phil to Amona Person 1-30-1873 (1-31-1873) L
Thompson, R. C. to Mollie Dickson 12-28-1869 (12-30-1869) T
Thompson, Ransom to S. Willis 8-19-1854 G
Thompson, Richard to Mariah Lyons 1-7-1847 G
Thompson, Robert C. to Mary E. Morris 1-8-1860 Hn
Thompson, Robert L. D. to Mary Ann Bates 2-13-1850 L
Thompson, Robert L. to Elizabeth J. McCarter 9-21-1835 (10-1-1835) Hr
Thompson, Robert M. to Nancy N. Sammons 1-10-1866 O
Thompson, Robert S. to Caroline L. Simmons 11-10-1868 G
Thompson, Robert to E. J. Davis 11-23-1857 (11-24-1857) O
Thompson, Robert to Emily Norris 6-17-1835 (6-26-1835) Hr
Thompson, Robert to Polly(Mary) Rogers 11-24-1834 Hr
Thompson, Ruff to Ema Wardlaw 12-3-1874 L B
Thompson, S. F. to M. L. Baker 11-5-1873 (11-6-1873) Dy
Thompson, S. R. to M. R. Kirk 12-10-1873 T
Thompson, Sam to Polly Ann Baldridge 10-22-1870 G
Thompson, Sam to Sarah Ann Temple 3-26-1868 (no return) F B
Thompson, Saml. Alexr. to Jane Campbell 2-13-1843 (2-16-1843) T
Thompson, Saml. to Julia Ann Anthony 7-25-1841 Hr
Thompson, Saml. to Nancy E. Hughes 1-31-1854 (2-1-1854) O
Thompson, Samuel A. to S. H. Watson 5-14-1846 L
Thompson, Samuel W. to Ellen A. Bunch 9-4-1857 Hn
Thompson, Sheppard B. to Margaret Jane Gibson 3-20-1858 (4-6-1858) O
Thompson, Sidney I. to Martha I. Redden 3-12-1842 Ma
Thompson, Spencer to Viney McAndless 11-7-1837 O
Thompson, Stephen S. to Sarah E. McBride 5-25-1867 (5-27-1867) Dy
Thompson, Steven M. to Percinda Peacock 6-4-1859 Cr
Thompson, T. G. to Sally M. Rose 11-1-1841 (11-6-1841) Hr
Thompson, Talbert to Eliza Wood 3-6-1871 (3-8-1871) T
Thompson, Terrel to Neely A. M. Freeman 9-1-1845 (9-4-1845) Ma
Thompson, Thoas to Emily Ford 1-24-1849 T
Thompson, Thomas A. to Kerah H. Sellers 7-29-1834 (7-31-1834) Hr
Thompson, Thomas B. to Elizabeth Hamlett 10-25-1856 (10-26-1856) Ma
Thompson, Thomas B. to Mary A. Rob nson 2-2-1853 Ma
Thompson, Thomas C. to Margaret A. Simmons 1-1-1861 (1-3-1861) Hr
Thompson, Thomas D. to Fannie A. Williams 1-16-1865 (1-17-1865) L
Thompson, Thomas I. to M. L. Crunk (Crank?) 9-9-1865 G
Thompson, Thomas J. to Sarah J. Naylor 9-9-1854 (9-13-1854) O
Thompson, Thomas T. to Eliza Jane Ellington 5-13-1861 (5-17-1861) Ma
Thompson, Thomas to Amanda R. Moseley 12-24-1873 Dy
Thompson, Thomas to Elizabeth E. Alexander 8-18-1846 (8-19-1846) Ma
Thompson, Tobe to Eveline Glisson 12-10-1867 (12-12-1867) T
Thompson, W. A. to Mariah S. Clopton 8-6-1859 Cr
Thompson, W. A. to Nora Lannom 5-1-1867 G
Thompson, W. D. to Ann Caroline Allison 3-10-1867 Hn
Thompson, W. E. to Susan Adams 5-12-1873 (5-13-1873) Cr
Thompson, W. F. to A. M. Poe 1-10-1864 Be

Thompson, W. G. to Emily Hale 6-11-1854 Cr
Thompson, W. G. to Sabina A. Bennett 1-8-1852 Hn
Thompson, W. H. H. to Ellen Sneed 1-19-1871 (1-20-1871) Cr
Thompson, W. J. to Martha J. Davidson 6-14-1859 Sh
Thompson, W. J. to Martha Jane Cole 12-17-1860 (12-19-1860) T
Thompson, W. N. to S. M. Chester 1-28-1857 We
Thompson, W. P. to J. A. Whitehurst 12-23-1857 (12-24-1857) Sh
Thompson, W. R. to Drusilla Webb 1-18-1881 L
Thompson, W. W. to Clarissa Ammons 12-23-1852 Hr
Thompson, Washington to Mary Forbs 12-5-1839 (12-18-1839) F
Thompson, William A. to Mary Harris 1-24-1838 Hn
Thompson, William B. to Sophia Lowry 5-22-1850 Sh
Thompson, William B. to Susan E. Stevens 11-7-1849 (11-8-1849) Hr
Thompson, William D. to Susan Owens 10-16-1861 (no return) Hn
Thompson, William F. to Mosiah Bregance 2-21-1838 Ma
Thompson, William F. to Susan Clowe 11-15-1843 Sh
Thompson, William H. to Margarett L. Bell 4-4-1855 (no return) F
Thompson, William H. to Sarah J. Corley 12-27-1858 G
Thompson, William H. to Susan M. Gibson 8-1-1863 (8-2-1863) Dy
Thompson, William M. to Emily Fields 12-24-1860 O
Thompson, William P. to Margaret E. Wilson 3-14-1853 (3-15-1853) G
Thompson, William W. to Jerutia Rose 8-12-1837 (8-17-1837) Hr
Thompson, William to Abby Green 4-6-1870 (4-7-1870) Dy
Thompson, William to Dona Osborn 5-3-1871 T
Thompson, William to Elizabeth A. Crenshaw 12-6-1842 (12-8-1842) G
Thompson, William to Emily Hays 10-26-1847 Hr
Thompson, William to Julia A. L. Holmes 9-9-1856 G
Thompson, William to Mary E. Moore 4-5-1864 Mn
Thompson, William to Sarah Williams 11-26-1843 Be
Thompson, William to Susan H. Nelson 1-3-1839 Sh
Thompson, William to T. F.? Cunningham 8-4-1883 (8-5-1883) L
Thompson, Willouby L. to Elizabeth Ann Crawford 10-23-1837 Hr
Thompson, Wm. A. to Martha J. Heely 1-6-1865 (no return) Cr
Thompson, Wm. A. to Mattie A. D. Moore 12-8-1870 Hy
Thompson, Wm. D. to Fannie Senter 12-11-1866 (12-12-1866) Ma
Thompson, Wm. G. to Mary H. Nelson 10-19-1857 (10-20-1857) Sh
Thompson, Wm. H. to Sarah Ann McClerkin 12-1-1873 T
Thompson, Wm. J. to Maggie J. Sims 12-10-1870 (12-11-1870) Ma
Thompson, Wm. J. to Nancy Chamberlin 1-27-1857 Cr
Thompson, Wm. J. to Sarah A. Hale 11-23-1852 Cr
Thompson, Wm. T. to Catherine Ormsberry 9-21-1827 Sh
Thompson, Wm. to Delia Jacocks 5-26-1869 Hy
Thompson, Wm. to Mary Bremer 12-9-1846 Sh
Thompson, Wm. to Nancy E. Higgs 10-24-1859 Hr
Thompson, Woolsey to Juanna Conner 1-31-1863 Sh
Thompson, ____ to Sarah Lane 3-1-1858 (3-6-1858) O
Thomson, Alex to Ann Love 12-26-1866 Hy
Thomson, J. H. to Martha A. Dell 5-5-1861 Mn
Thomson, John B. to Eliza F. Beaver 12-23-1867 (12-24-1867) F
Thomson, Willis to Mary F. tAlly 12-18-1860 (12-20-1860) Sh
Thomson, ____ to Mary C. Suggs 1-30-1844 Sh
Thorgmorten, Abner to Mary Powel 1-10-1846 (no return) We
Thorgmorton, Elisha to Susan Curtis 11-30-1844 We
Thorn, Joseph to Martha Ann Blythe 12-18-1848 (12-21-1848) Ma
Thorn, Martin to Halma A. Brown 11-23-1845 (11-28-1845) Ma
Thorn, Thomas A. to Mary E. McElwee 11-1-1871 Hy
Thorn, Thomas to Judy Hast 1-11-1844 G
Thorn, W. W. to Sophronia J. Crider 1-26-1870 G
Thornton, A. H. to Sallie F. Thornton 5-2-1866 (5-3-1866) F
Thornton, Dennis to Polly Fry 8-18-1867 Be
Thornton, Ed to Emma Newby 3-2-1871 Hy
Thornton, Ed to Louisa Purham 12-29-1880 (12-30-1880) L B
Thornton, George M. to Elizabeth L. Malin 8-14-1855 Be
Thornton, Hamilton to Mary A. Johnson 12-17-1856 (no return) F
Thornton, I. C. to Milly Patterson 11-23-1858 We
Thornton, I. to Hanah Morris 12-28-1839 (12-30-1839) Ma
Thornton, J. V. to M. C. Lay 9-27-1859 (9-28-1859) F
Thornton, James B. to Mary E. Cox 4-21-1870 F
Thornton, James to Lourena (Mrs.) Reeves 5-17-1867 (5-19-1867) Ma
Thornton, John H. to Sarah J. Olds 12-2-1868 Dy
Thornton, John to Jennie Bruce 4-3-1876 Hy
Thornton, John to M. J. Black 12-27-1866 G
Thornton, John to Martha R. Dowland 9-22-1867 G
Thornton, Josiah to Elizabeth Vaught 8-27-1833 (9-3-1833) Hr
Thornton, Lee to Hannah J. Lake 5-15-1869 L
Thornton, Patrick to Lucy Whitmore 7-26-1867 (7-27-1867) F B
Thornton, Peter to Charlotte Shaw 12-26-1876 Hy
Thornton, Presley to Mary Ann Birdwell 1-20-1853 Be
Thornton, Riley to Josephine Sims 9-27-1870 Hy
Thornton, Rolly to Susie Barrett 12-15-1878 Hy
Thornton, S. L. to M. A. King 11-18-1874 (11-19-1874) Dy
Thornton, Samuel M. to Delila Dunt 7-15-1842 (7-21-1842) O
Thornton, Seth L. to Lillian C. King 12-3-1867 (no return) Dy
Thornton, Shover to Mary Washington 5-15-1884 (5-13?-1884) L
Thornton, T. A. to Mollie Hartsfield 10-24-1867 G
Thornton, T. H. to M. R. Griffin 1-16-1878 Dy
Thornton, Theopilus to Delilah Deen 11-17-1827 (12-3-1827) Hr
Thornton, W. B. to Lucinda Mary Cox 1-29-1857 Be
Thornton, W. H. to Nancy Mass 11-28-1848 (11-6?-1848) F
Thornton, William to Dorthula Greer 6-30-1859 G
Thornton, William to Mary Stamps 12-25-1867 (no return) Hn B
Thorp, S. A. to Jennette Hitchcock 5-16-1866 (5-20-1866) Dy
Thorpe, J. H. to Celia A. Rogers 8-6-1860 Hr
Thorton (Horton?), James B. to Susan S. Thornton 5-8-1854 (no return) L
Thorton?, Edward to Easter Berry? no date (with 1874) T
Thrailkill, Morgan to Rhoda C. Barrett 6-5-1861 (6-9-1861) Hr
Thrasher, Franklin to Fatha Lock 12-1-1825 Hr
Thrasher, Jesse A. to Caroline Pankey 8-12-1858 Hr
Threadgill, W. C. to Mary C. Reeves 7-18-1848 (8-1-1848) O
Threadgill, Wm. A. to Harriet A. Mills 11-28-1860 (no return) Cr
Threlkeld, John to Delilah Highfield 3-28-1828 (3-30-1828) Hr
Throgmortin, William to Harriett Parker 1-14-1852 We
Throgmorton, James P. to Mary C. Davidson 1-20-1864 Hn
Throgmorton, James P. to Sarah A. Gallimore 8-3-1847 (no return) Hn
Throgmorton, James W. to Margaret Throgmorton 9-4-1848 (no return) Hn
Throgmorton, John C. to Martha A. Watkins 2-22-1862 Hn
Throgmorton, John H. to Susan E. Perry 9-15-1867 Hn
Throgmorton, Julius S. to Margaret J. Moten 1-5-1842 Hn
Throgmorton, Robert to Lucinda C. Bevil 3-9-1848 Hn
Throgmorton, Robertson to Rilla A. Swor 6-10-1841 Hn
Throgmorton, William N. to Frances N. Tilly 1-12-1859 Hn
Throgmorton, William to Theatus Pierce 12-29-1841 Hn
Thron, David to Mary A. Toone 6-8-1857 Hr
Thrukill, Wm. T. to Sarah A. McColun 10-13-1847 Cr
Thrulkiler, William to Jossiphia Brann 10-9-1859 We
Thues, Henry L. to Caroline Satterfield 2-12-1859 (2-13-1859) Ma
Thum, D. G. to Ula Lloyd 10-26-1885 (10-28-1885) L
Thum, David G. to Mary Ann Wardlaw 12-20-1853 (maybe 12-21) L
Thum, G. W. to Nettie A. Jenkins 11-26-1873 L
Thum, John G. to M. A. Pipkin 1-10-1878 L
Thum, John G. to Sarah Francis Barfield 12-19-1870 (12-21-1870) L
Thuman, Joseph to Ann Turner 12-9-1830 Ma
Thuran, John P to Sallie Ecklin 9-15-1856 (9-16-1856) Sh
Thurgood, John to Mary Sweat 9-20-1869 Hy
Thurman, David T. to Frances Pippin 1-30-1854 Ma
Thurman, David T. to Moniza Lawrence 10-28-1858 Ma
Thurman, G. W. to Mary Fuller 5-26-1863 Sh
Thurman, Harrison to Paralee Davidson 12-25-1862 Mn
Thurman, Henry to Amanda Maxville 12-24-1868 G
Thurman, Meridith M. to Martha J. Lowe 5-17-1851 (5-20-1851) Hr
Thurman, Thomas J. to Ann Lane 11-20-1867 (no return) Hn
Thurman, Thomas to Cortin L. White 3-12-1863 Mn
Thurman, Wash to Bettie Thornton 8-26-1869 (8-28-1869) F B
Thurman, William to Malsina Miller 6-11-1849 (6-12-1849) Ma
Thurman, Wm. M. to M. A. Nash 3-9-1866 (3-11-1866) Dy
Thurmon, Jmaes A. to Martha E. Moore 3-19-1867 (3-21-1867) L
Thurmond, A. P. to Eliza Jane Frost 2-26-1884 (2-27-1884) L
Thurmond, Andrew to Mary Ann Fisher 4-12-1867 (4-13-1867) L B
Thurmond, E. D. to Sarah Frances Frost 7-14-1883 (7-23-1883) L
Thurmond, Erasmus to Eliza E. Walpole 9-13-1879 (no return) L
Thurmond, Erasmus? to Fannie Walpole 1-1-1884 L
Thurmond, F. J. to N. T. Tomlinson 11-27-1876 (11-28-1876) L
Thurmond, Guy to Jane McDearman 1-19-1878 L
Thurmond, J. N. to Emiline Johnson 9-11-1873 Dy
Thurmond, J. P. to C. A. Wood 2-15-1865 Dy
Thurmond, James L. to L. D. E. Reynolds 8-25-1877 (8-29-1877) L
Thurmond, James L. to Sarah L. Moore 7-21-1856 (7-22-1856) L
Thurmond, John H. to Mary L. Tucker 6-21-1847 (no return) L
Thurmond, John L. to Elizabeth Sawyer 2-4-1867 (no return) L
Thurmond, Lewis to Nannie Sowerson 9-28-1876 L B
Thurmond, M. M. to S. A. Low 10-8-1860 (10-9-1860) Hr
Thurmond, O. L. to Sarah Jane Elizabeth Vale 3-2-1868 (3-10-1868) L
Thurmond, Orvill L. to Sarah C(aroline) Chambers 1-11-1848 (1-13-1848) L
Thurmond, Richard to Callie Grace 8-28-1877 (8-29-1877) Dy
Thurmond, Robert to Mary McDearmon 12-28-1871 L
Thurmond, Robert to Sarah Smith 12-22-1885 (12-24-1885) L
Thurmond, W. A. to Mary J. Smith 6-6-1884 (6-15-1884) L
Thurmond, W. A. to W. P. Wilson 8-28-1877 (8-29-1877) L
Thurmond, William A. to Elza New 2-27-1866 (3-1-1866) L
Thurston, James to Jane Spence 4-30-1851 Hn
Thurston, William H. to Emily A. Wade 9-8-1855 Hn
Thurston, Wm. to Mary Johnson 9-30-1845 We
Thweatt, Frederick to Docy D. Manning 3-11-1840 Hn
Thweatt, William K. to Mary Wildur 10-25-1842 (10-27-1842) G
Tibbs, Nacie to Claira Mathews 1-5-1871 Hy
Tibbs, Wesley to Dorcas Clack 10-10-1871 Hy
Tice, John W. to Rebecca A. Madry 11-1-1855 Be
Ticer, James to Mary E. Moore 10-4-1859 (10-6-1859) Sh
Ticer, William H. to Susan Cooper 11-4-1858 (1-28-1859) T
Tidrow, Charles H. to Nancy E. Sellers 6-10-1851 (6-11-1851) G
Tidwell, C. J. to C. E. Smothers 2-1-1870 Hy
Tidwell, Charles W. to Sarah J. Richardson 3-26-1868 Cr
Tidwell, Franklin B. to Prior A. J. Lane 11-23-1842 (11-24-1842) Ma
Tidwell, J. M. to Ann Eliza Bussey 3-22-1850 (3-26?-1850) Sh

Tidwell, John F. to Mary J. Blassingame 1-9-1862 Mn
Tidwell, Joseph D. to Eliza A. Harris 10-31-1866 Ma
Tidwell, R. P. to M. J. Barnes 1-7-1868 O
Tidwell, William M. to Mary Person 6-17-1841 Ma
Tidwell, William to Mary F. Tidwell 12-11-1861 Mn
Tighe, Edward to Ann Butler 2-20-1860 Sh
Tigrett, A. B. to Lutie A. Parks 5-14-1873 (5-15-1873) Dy
Tilghman, A. G. to Catharine M. Boyet 11-24-1855 (no return) F
Tilghman, A. J. to Mahala Tyson 10-21-1845 (10-29-1845) G
Tilghman, E. R. to C. W. Moore 8-5-1864 Sh
Tilghman, Eli to Cintha A. Ward (Word?) 3-3-1862 G
Tilghman, Eli to H. L. Denney 10-3-1860 (10-4-1860) O
Tilghman, Eli to Nancy Crain 7-20-1839 (7-23-1839) G
Tilghman, Eli to Sarah E. Bavard 12-22-1866 O
Tilghman, J. C. to Nancy Ann Needham 7-21-1864 G
Tilghman, M. M. to Susan Minton 11-29-1868 G
Tilghman, Pinkney to Louiza Norton 1-15-1853 (1-18-1853) G
Tilghman, Robert C. to Lydia Tyson 10-31-1851 G
Tilghman, W. B. to M. A. Tyson 3-28-1866 G
Tillar, William to Mildred W. Lundy 7-5-1845 Sh *
Tiller, George W. to Maryann Robinson 10-19-1839 (5-13-1840?) F
Tiller, John W. to Mary E. Rodgers 8-6-1860 (8-16-1860) F
Tiller, Thos. H. to Martha J. Williams 11-7-1868 (11-9-1868) F
Tillery, A. F. to Bettie P. Wright 12-21-1866 (12-23-1866) L
Tilley, James H. to Delila McMicken 12-30-1861 (1-1-1862) Hr
Tilliman, William E. to Martha Sammons 12-23-1852 G
Tillman, Bryan to Mary Ann Murrin 6-17-1865 T
Tillman, Damman to Nancy C. Caudle 4-18-1861 We
Tillman, E. L. to Susan E. Barret 5-29-1865 G
Tillman, Geo. to Margaret Wiseman 2-27-1871 (2-28-1871) T
Tillman, James M. to Nancy C. Davis 7-31-1869 (8-3-1869) F
Tillman, James to Mary Cannon 4-20-1839 (4-25-1839) Hr
Tillman, Jas. Henry to America J. Wood 1-8-1872 (1-11-1872) T
Tillman, M. M. to Eliza F. Clark 1-17-1861 G
Tillman, Thomas J. to Allice McBomer 8-5-1872 (8-7-1872) L
Tillman, Thos. H. to Frances Wiseman 1-1-1862 T
Tillman, W. Thos. to Jane Bealtin? 1-30-1869 (2-4-1869) T
Tillman, Wm. P. to Elizabeth Robinson 12-11-1865 Hy
Tillmon, A. D. to E. A. Moffett 11-9-1859 F
Tilly, William F. to Sarah E. Gibbs 11-26-1860 Hn
Tilman, A. G. to Isilla Waldrope 2-16-1854 G
Tilman, F. to M. O. T. West 6-10-1879 (6-11-1879) Dy
Tilman, J. L. to Laura J. Simms 3-1-1884 (3-2-1884) L
Tilman, Jeremiah A. to Mary A. Rutledge 7-24-1851 G
Tilman, S. L. to V. J. Smith 12-17-1879 (12-18-1879) L
Tilman, Thomas J. to Alice J. Trimble 1-19-1882 L
Tilman, W. A. to N. J. Olds 9-28-1881 (9-29-1881) L
Tilman, William F. to Susan Ann Bryant 6-15-1866 (6-17-1866) T
Tilman, William F. to Mary Ann Voss 8-17-1850 L
Tilmartin, John to Joanna Dillon 8-4-1853 Sh
Tilmon, John to Martha Windham 10-13-1842 (10-17-1842) T
Tilmon, Joseph to Frances Childress 9-29-1838 Hr
Tilson, Henry to Burda Williamson 4-1-1871 (4-2-1871) F B
Tilson?, Elijah to America Williams 6-23-1863 T
Tilton, J. C. to Jane Elizabeth Smally 2-2-1848 (2-3-1848) Hr
Tilton, William to Francis S. Turner 1-22-1861 Sh
Timberlake, John W. to Elizabeth A. Howard 1-6-1840 (1-7-1840) Hr
Timberlick, Saml. R. to Marth J. Delashmet 5-6-1867 (5-14-1867) T
Timbs, James to Elizabeth Wade Davidson 12-21-1853 (12-22-1853) T
Timmon, J. F. to Mrs. E. A. Byrd 12-19-1867 (12-22-1867) T
Timmons, F. T. to Nancy M. Barnes 6-28-1845 (no return) L
Timmons, G. A. to Mattie M. Overall 8-16-1870 G
Timmons, Ira to Susan Ann Lloyd 2-6-1878 L B
Timmons, James to Margaret Nolan 8-29-1853 Sh
Timmons, John to Louisa Goan 1-19-1874 (no return) L B
Timms, Alexander to Margaret J. P. Wade 12-17-1873 (12-23-1873) T
Timms, Benjam. to Sarah Walker 8-31-1869 (9-1-1869) T
Timms, H. M. to A. V. Bird 1-4-1871 (1-12-1871) T
Timms, Jabus to Ellen C. Davidson 12-28-1859 (12-29-1859) T
Timms, John N. to Sarah C. Hannis? 4-9-1867 (4-10-1867) T
Timms, M. C. to Mary T. Timms 12-28-1871 (12-29-1870?) T
Timms, Nathaniel to Sarah Hardin 1-20-1849 (1-21-1849) Ma
Timms, Sidney R. to Marteller Ann Hammond 10-16-1867 (10-19-1867) T
Timms, Vinson to Matilda Timms 7-23-1849 Ma
Tims, Alexander to Sarah Narcissa Bayse 3-1-1854 (3-2-1854) T
Tims, Benj. to Sarah Booth 12-17-1871 (12-19-1871) T
Tims, E. D. L. to Louisa M. King 7-10-1861 Hr
Tims, George W. to Missouri Ann Tims 2-27-1856 (2-28-1856) Ma
Tims, J. C. to Lyda Hammers 3-2-1854 (3-3-1854) Hr
Tims, James T. to Medira Boothe 12-13-1877 Hy
Tims, John C. to Cynthia Ann Savage 9-23-1830 Hr
Tims, John C. to Mary A. Ballard 12-5-1877 L
Tims, John H. to Tamer Richardson 7-31-1861 (8-1-1861) Hr
Tims, John T. to Jane (Mrs.) Glidwell 9-7-1858 (9-9-1858) Ma
Tims, John to Martha C. Helms 12-13-1871 (12-14-1871) T
Tims, Larkin to Rebecca Roberts 6-10-1843 (6-11-1843) Ma
Tims, Nathaniel to Irena E. L. Tims 2-15-1871 T

Tims, Samuel to Nancy C. Moore 2-18-1845 (2-19-1845) T
Tims, Thomas to Martha Ann Scheen 9-11-1858 (9-12-1858) T
Tims, Valentine to Martha Horn 12-23-1846 Ma
Tims, William to Mary Glidewell 8-6-1852 Ma
Tincher, T. S. to Mary S. McKencie 8-3-1864 (8-4-1864) Sh
Tindell, Augustus S. to Nancy M. Timmons 12-27-1848 L
Tiner, Jessee to Mary J. Taylor 3-8-1859 G
Tiner, John W. to Sarah A. Williamson 11-24-1859 Ma
Tiner, W. H. R. to Ellen Green? 10-29-1867 Dy
Tines, Henry to Jane Goode 6-17-1867 (6-22-1867) F B
Tines, J. M. to M. J. Alexander 7-11-1868 (7-11-1870?) G
Tines, Jack to Milly Crews 9-30-1868 G B
Tines, T. H. to Martha A. Denton 3-28-1858 We
Tines, W. C. to Sarah E. Bondurant 12-28-1858 We
Tinin, Welton to Hannah Nixon 10-25-1885 (no return) L
Tinker, John B. to Martha Maxwell 4-23-1848 Be
Tinkle, B. L. to A. R. Light 10-4-1870 G
Tinkle, Daniel to Amanda Katharine Williams 10-11-1828 G
Tinkle, Daniel to Nancy H. Vernon 4-14-1858 (4-15-1858) G
Tinkle, George W. to Elizabeth Ann Hall 3-18-1840 (3-19-1840) G
Tinkle, H. H. to Josephine Ward 1-11-1869 G
Tinkle, Lindsey K. to Rebecka McWhorter 2-23-1831 G
Tinkle, R. F. to L. J. Light 7-21-1864 G
Tinkle, S. A. to J. A. Petty 6-1-1874 (no return) Dy
Tinkle, Thos. W. to Sarah A. Moore 2-2-1861 (2-3-1861) Dy
Tinkle, W. E. to E. J. Strother 12-25-1866 G
Tinkle, W. T. to Elizabeth Davidson 8-26-1866 G
Tinkle, Wm. E. to Willie S. Harvy 10-1-1838 (10-2-1838) G
Tinnen, J. F. to Sarah E. Hurt 8-10-1861 (8-14-1861) T
Tinnen, John to Nancy Jane Davis 2-7-1859 T
Tinnen, W. H. to Susan Billings 2-4-1869 (1?-31-1869) T
Tinnen, William M. to Julia L. Mitchell 12-11-1858 (12-12-1858) T
Tinner, William A. to Cassa L. Carlton 11-12-1856 G
Tinnin, Currie to Dona Parker 4-18-1877 L
Tinslay, W. D. to Lucinda Jane Curtis 2-28-1873 (3-20-1873) L
Tinsley, Charles A. to Amanda L. Simms 3-17-1868 (no return) Dy
Tinsley, Charles to Jane Summers 10-10-1854 G
Tinsley, G. P. to Callie Maxwell 5-7-1873 (5-8-1873) Dy
Tinsley, Geo. B. to Margaret C. White 11-17-1850 (11-20-1850) G
Tinsley, J. W. to Claudia Lovelace 3-21-1877 Dy
Tinsley, James G. to Frances M. Yeates 8-7-1852 (8-12-1852) G
Tinsley, Wm. to Sarah P. Harpole 8-21-1841 (8-30-1841) G
Tinsly, Aubner to Tempe Fields 2-21-1871 T
Tipler, George to Sillah?(Lillah?) Cox 3-24-1841 (3-25-1841) Hr
Tipler, John H. to Mary Conly 1-9-1851 (1-15-1851) Hr
Tipler, John to Lucinda Harrison 11-7-1843 (11-9-1843) Hr
Tipler, Thomas J. to Militha Tedford 1-22-1842 (2-3-1842) Hr
Tipler, W. F. to Matilda L. Burke 3-7-1856 (3-8-1856) Hr
Tipler, William F. to Sarah Bishop 1-6-1838 Hr
Tippett, A. R. to Katharine S. Morris 2-16-1845 Be
Tippett, L. H. to Delaney Bruce 8-25-1844 Be
Tippitt, Sanford to Elizabeth Mathis 12-14-1866 (12-16-1866) Cr
Tipton, Alex to Jane Hutson 2-20-1878 (no return) Dy
Tipton, Alex to Lucy Smith 6-3-1879 Dy
Tipton, Alex to Mary Spence 5-30-1866 (6-2-1866) Dy
Tipton, Alle G. to Margaret Harris 6-30-1840 (7-9-1840) O
Tipton, Dallas to Sallie Jackson 8-13-1868 T
Tipton, Daniel F. to Elizabeth F. Babb 10-15-1860 Hn
Tipton, Dick to Rosina Morgan 11-16-1865 T
Tipton, Fillmore to Caroline Ruff 2-28-1877 Dy
Tipton, F. T. to Mattie E. Tipton 2-20-1866 Dy
Tipton, J. Cas to Mamie J. Want? 6-5-1870 Dy
Tipton, J. D. B. to Ella F. Pate 8-15-1874 (8-16-1874) Dy
Tipton, J. H. to M. J. Smith 4-12-1871 (no return) Dy
Tipton, Jack to Minerva Miller 6-22-1867 (6-23-1867) T
Tipton, James to Rachael Puckett 9-20-1832 G
Tipton, John to Candis Clements 3-12-1870 T
Tipton, John to Matilda Bell 12-26-1873 (12-27-1873) T
Tipton, Lee to Sarah Frazier 10-10-1874 (10-19-1874) Dy
Tipton, Nat to Laura A. Stone 11-21-1850 T
Tipton, P. C. to Ella Sulivan 2-10-1875 Hy
Tipton, P. L. to Sallie A. Light 10-3-1874 (10-4-1874) Dy
Tipton, P. M. to Barbary Walker 11-16-1865 Dy
Tipton, P. M. to Charity Tumbough 8-3-1843 F
Tipton, Pleasant to Mary E. Tarkington 11-3-1868 Dy
Tipton, Preston M. to Mollie P. Leight 2-6-1878 Dy
Tipton, Quincy A. to Mary C. Chrismon 9-1-1841 F
Tipton, Sam to Alice Pickett 12-14-1881 (12-26-1881) L B
Tipton, William A. to Eliza Galihar 10-22-1839 (11-1-1839) O
Tipton, William to Clary Spence 5-8-1879 (5-9-1879) Dy
Tipton, William to Mariah Ruff 10-31-1874 Dy
Tipton, Wm. M. to Nancy Pooch 12-25-1866 Dy
Tipton, Wm. to Harriet Morgan 8-11-1866 T
Tipton, jr., Wiley B. to Rebecca A. McDavid 10-9-1866 Dy
Tisdale, James H. to Betsy P. Smith 1-16-1832 (1-17-1832) Hr
Tisdale, Lewelyn T. to Susannah W. Bell 12-16-1854 (12-17-1854) T
Tisdale, P. E. to Lucetta P. Townsend 10-10-1857 (10-15-1857) T

Tisdale, William H. to Mary Willey 3-21-1825 (3-24-1825) Hr
Tisdel, W. H. to Ann Beck 3-24-1851 Sh
Tison, John to Martha Sparks 12-24-1846 Cr
Tison, Lemuel B. to Desha Briley 8-9-1832 Sh
Tittle, Anthony M. to Rebecca Malin 8-19-1841 Be
Tittle, John M. to Matilda Harrison 11-6-1845 Be
Tittle, Samuel to Delany Pope 11-13-1838 Be
Tittle, T. G. to A. J. Utley 3-20-1842 Be
Titus, Andrew J. to Jane Brown 7-27-1836 Sh
Titus, Criss to Oriann Washingto Calaway 12-27-1877 L B
Titus, David to Mary Halfacre 6-15-1872 (6-16-1872) L B
Titus, Frazor to Sarah Ann Wilson 8-21-1843 Sh
Titus, Joe to Matilda Bedford 10-29-1877 L
Titus, Peter W. to Susan T. Hynes 11-23-1836 Sh
Titus, Robert E. to Indiana Buntyn 5-16-1843 Sh
Toben, Dennis to Ellen Malenay 5-17-1862 Sh
Tod, Francis to Julia Pryor 10-8-1851 Sh
Todd, A. F. to Sallie Armstrong 9-6-1866 Dy
Todd, Adam to Harriett Wakelan 4-6-1867 (no return) Hn B
Todd, Benjamin to Sarah F. Drinkard 10-21-1865 (10-29-1865) Cr
Todd, C. W. to S. A. Carter 10-1-1879 Dy
Todd, David to Amey P. Mayfield 8-19-1836 (8-20-1836) G
Todd, Edward S. to Emma R. Hale 4-14-1846 Sh
Todd, Eli to Sintha Bell 12-29-1857 Hn
Todd, F. H. to Josephine Brewer 12-3-1866 (12-5-1866) Cr
Todd, Fleming C. to Eliza F. Gee 10-21-1861 (10-22-1861) Cr
Todd, George H. to Amanda Ross 4-13-1852 (4-15-1852) Ma
Todd, Harey to Amanda C. Demoss 8-16-1865 (no return) Cr
Todd, Henry to Keziah C. Edwards 4-6-1864 G
Todd, Hugh S. to Nancy Bailey 2-16-1864 (no return) Cr
Todd, J. K. to Harriet J. Barker 1-1-1867 F
Todd, J. L. to L. J. Todd 3-3-1866 (3-4-1866) F
Todd, J. M. to Mary E. Watson 4-5-1864 Hn
Todd, J. M. to S. E. Denning 9-10-1869 (9-12-1869) Cr
Todd, James A. to Prudence Calahan 1-14-1859 Hn
Todd, James A. to Sarah Ann Ward 9-3-1844 (9-4-1846) F
Todd, James A. to Sarah Ann Ware 9-3-1846 (no return) F
Todd, James L. to Roenna M. E. Walden 8-2-1848 Ma
Todd, James to Jane Wallace 1-6-1861 Hn
Todd, John B. to Mary Margaret Hendly 11-8-1867 (11-10-1867) Cr
Todd, John C. to Mary A. R. Stockard 11-6-1861 G
Todd, John T. to Larren T. Martin 12-16-1844 O
Todd, John to Hester Ann Blake 10-22-1850 Hn
Todd, John to Marge A. Bowden 11-16-1844 Hn
Todd, John to Mary Disley 3-3-1848 Sh
Todd, John to Sarah Frensley 8-5-1841 Hn
Todd, M. B. to Harriett N. Hood 10-4-1860 We
Todd, M. L. to Sarah A. C. Boston 3-26-1868 G
Todd, Richard to Theney High 8-27-1838 (no return) Hn
Todd, Rufus to Jane Coley 11-17-1853 Hn
Todd, Samuel W. to Sarah Ann Breedlove 11-11-1856 Hn
Todd, Solomon to Elizabeth Steel 7-23-1862 Hy
Todd, Thomas to Rebecca C. Wallace 9-15-1857 Hn
Todd, Thos. H. to Mary G. (Mrs.) Ayres 2-13-1856 Sh
Todd, W. C. to Fannie E. Boatwright 8-31-1870 G
Todd, W. C. to Nancy A. Jones 12-20-1866 G
Todd, W. H. L. to R. L. Smith 11-19-1866 O
Todd, William to Emily Rawlings 11-27-1832 Hr
Todd, William to Jane C. Pipkin 1-12-1858 (1-14-1858) Ma
Todd, William to Virginia Breedlove 1-14-1852 Hn
Todd, Wm. J. to Sarah Jane Turner 3-14-1846 We
Todd, Wm. W. to Frances C. Suggett 8-26-1865 F
Tolbert, Daniel to Bridget Murphey 7-3-1862 (7-6-1862) Sh
Tolbert, W. S. to Mollie Blackman 2-27-1876 (2-28-1876) Dy
Tolbert, Wm. to Caroline Klyce 10-25-1868 Hy
Tolen, Jessee L. to Adalaid V. Cherry 4-8-1854 G
Toler, Jesse to Francis J. Douglas 11-24-1866 O
Toler, John S. to Mary Ann Dickey 5-5-1849 (5-7-1849) G
Toley, Hugh to Margaret Barry 5-13-1863 Sh
Toliver, E. D. to Agnes Crittendon 1-10-1876 O B
Toliver, Frank to Meter Mayo 12-28-1869 (1-1-1870) T
Toller, Thomas E. to Narcissa Rhodes 9-6-1845 (9-14-1845) Hr
Tolley, Wilson to Martha Johnson 3-28-1840 (3-1?-1840) Ma
Tolley, Wm. to Mary Jarrett 9-27-1843 Cr
Tolliver, James to Sarah Adams 11-22-1871 (11-23-1871) T
Tolliver, Riley to Martha Alford 11-19-1878 (11-20-1878) L
Tolls, Author to Eliza Jones 2-28-1869 Be
Tolls, Oliver to Joly Wyly 2-28-1869 Be
Tolston, Wm. to Mariah Crews 5-8-1844 Cr
Tom, Dock to Jane _____ 1-31-1873 (no return) L
Tomberlin, Prince to Aimy Sp_ill 10-20-1869 G B
Tombs, J. H. to Mary Armstrong 12-30-1864 Mn
Tombs, Owen to Lucenda Glasscock 2-28-1835 G
Tomery, J. M. to Fanny Webb 5-17-1861 (5-23-1861) Sh
Tomiss, E. M. to Lucinda Williamson 10-12-1850 We
Tomlin, George M. to Sarah M. Carpenter 11-27-1850 (11-28-1851?) Ma
Tomlin, James W. to Martha A. McClellen 2-17-1852 Ma

Tomlin, James W. to Penelope Estes 12-14-1861 (12-15-1861) Ma
Tomlin, John L. H. to Amanda C. Elder 5-19-1846 G
Tomlinson, Elias to Flora M. Alexander 11-14-1848 (no return) Hn
Tomlinson, Elias to Virginia Winston 3-4-1856 (3-5-1856) O
Tomlinson, H. C. to D. T. Turner 6-14-1865 (6-15-1865) F
Tomlinson, H. M. to Caroline Caldwell 8-5-1850 Sh
Tomlinson, James M. to Rachel Askew 3-9-1848 Ma
Tomlinson, James T. to Elizabeth Jeans 11-1-1855 (11-6-1855) O
Tomlinson, James to Lucy E. Dunaway 6-25-1884 (6-26-1884) L
Tomlinson, John A. to Frances C. Jackson 4-25-1848 Ma
Tomlinson, John to Lucy H. Moore 9-3-1850 (9-12-1850) F
Tomlinson, Junius to G. A. Yates 2-5-1868 F
Tomlinson, N. C. to Tempey Everett 7-17-1872 (no return) Cr
Tomlinson, Quince to Eliza Jane Porter 1-1-1872 (1-3-1872) L B
Tomlinson, Sidney H. to Martha T. Phillips 4-8-1848 (4-15-1848) G
Tomlinson, T. G. to Mary F. Bohannon 2-21-1850 Hn
Tomlinson, Thomas D. to Martha E. Person 8-27-1866 (8-28-1866) Ma
Tomlinson, W. A. to Mary E. Cardwell 2-5-1863 We
Tomlinson, Wilie J. to Susan C. Williams 6-1-1858 Hn
Tomlinson, William E. to Emma G. Harris 11-19-1866 (11-21-1866) Ma
Tomlinson, William to Frances Huckabee 7-26-1860 L
Tomlinson, William to Louisa Jackson 10-1-1839 (10-2-1839) Ma
Tompkins, Socrates to Mary Gilliland 1-10-1872 L
Toms, E. H. to Mary W. Ragan 11-8-1870 G
Tomson, George W. to Mary Ann Brown 12-16-1848 (12-23-1848) Hr
Tomson, Thos. G. N. to Martha E. F. Brewer 9-29-1848 (with 1858) Hr
Tonage, David E. to Mary J. Askew 11-25-1851 (no return) F
Toney, Joseph to Mary Ann Sikes 6-2-1848 Sh
Tood?, M. L. to Susan C. Alexander 1-?-1866 (1-17-1866) Cr
Tooky, Daniel to Mary Ann Galligan 7-5-1856 (7-6-1856) Sh
Tool, Jas. to Susan Hamilton 7-26-1874 (7-29-1874) T
Toole, William to Ann McGhee 2-12-1861 Sh
Toombes, H. B. to F. G. Puckett 2-21-1857 (3-1-1857) Hr
Toombs, Charlie to Emma Gunter 6-16-1879 (6-29-1879) L
Toombs, H. C. to E. A. Flowers 9-20-1869 Cr
Toombs, J. G. to Margaret Smith 1-3-1866 (SB 1867) G
Toombs, O. P. T. to Martha Mann 10-6-1870 (10-7-1870) O
Toombs, O. P. T. to Martha Mann? 10-6-1870 O
Toombs, William A. G. to Sarah M. Ward 12-19-1855 G
Tooms, J. E. to Fannie Hooper 12-27-1878 Hy
Toomy, John to Bridget Nugent 2-20-1860 Sh
Toon, Jesse A. to Caroline H. Dickson 12-11-1844 Sh
Toone, Coleman to Elizabeth Marsh 7-26-1852 Ma
Toone, James jr. to Ruth Harriss 1-16-1861 (1-17-1861) Hr
Toony, John to Mary Dillard 2-13-1858 Sh
Topp, Ben to Phillip Johnson 2-21-1868 (2-22-1868) Dy
Topp, John WEsley to Phillis Campbell 1-31-1868 G B
Topp, Thos. C. to Mary E. Ware 1-15-1855 Sh
Topp, Wash to Amanda Edwards 12-28-1870 (12-29-1870) Dy
Torbiss?, Arthur to Eliza Hutcherson 12-10-1842 (12-15-1842) T
Torian, Robt. S. to Nannie C. Buck 4-24-1872 Hy
Tornton, Henry to Nancy Walk 8-18-1870 (8-19-1870) T
Torpey, John to Hannevah Donnevan 5-30-1864 (5-31-1864) Sh
Torrence, H. H. to Martha Wood 9-12-1869 Cr
Torrence, James M. to Emma M. Brown 4-26-1870 Dy
Torrey, J. A. to N. M. Patterson 2-2-1858 Sh
Tosh, H. H. to M. E. Eskew 11-30-1871 (12-15-1871) Cr
Tosh, Harrison B. to Nancy Neely 12-13-1831 Cr
Tosh, J. G. to Frances Scott 3-1-1866 Cr
Tosh, James M. to Elizabeth C. Dodd 1-9-1871 (1-10-1871) Cr
Tosh, James M. to Saletha Neely 11-13-1845 Cr
Tosh, L. M. to L. J. Louis 3-11-1868 Cr
Tosh, Lafayette to Margaret A. Grant 11-8-1858 Cr
Tosh, R. H. to Evaline Scott 12-11-1870 (12-13-1870) Cr
Tosh, Thos. J. to Sarah I. Phillips 12-26-1854 Cr
Tosh, W. H. to Elizabeth Wilson 1-22-1852 Cr
Tosper, Elijah B. to Martha E. Needham 12-30-1858 G
Toten, Archibald W. O. to Harriett C. Hurt 3-29-1843 Ma
Totten, Benjamin to Elizabeth C. Lancaster 3-3-1847 (3-14-1847) O
Totten, James L. to Sarah Eliza Dyer 6-19-1833 (6-20-1833) G
Totty, Arthur to Mary C. Lunsford 3-20-1855 L
Totty, Bolen A. to Virginia R. Atchison 9-1-1867 Be
Totty, J. E. to Lucinda Williams 2-9-1861 Be
Totty, James E. to Josie (Mrs.) Hope 4-14-1873 (4-24-1873) Cr
Totty, James E. to Louisa Hawley 9-10-1857 Be
Touchton, K. B. to M. E. Bandy 9-18-1878 Hy
Tourtello, William to Anna (Mrs.) kirkby 7-1-1856 Sh
Towell, W. R. to Lidia Waddle 12-23-1839 (1-7-1840) Ma
Tower, George A. to E. M. Hull 7-6-1870 Dy
Towhey, John to Catharine Burke 5-13-1860 Sh
Towler?(Lowler?), W. M. to Frances Bowers 9-13-1850 (9-18-1850) Hr
Towles, Anthony to Sally Boals 12-28-1868 (12-30-1868) F B
Towlkes, T. J. to Julia A. Burton 7-16-1857 F
Town, D. R. to Sallie A. Cocke 2-4-1864 Sh
Townes, Beverly to Eveline Shoffner 8-1-1868 (8-3-1868) Cr
Townes, Henry C. to Alice C. Crockett 12-17-1868 Cr
Townes, James M. to Mary Jane Fortune 4-26-1870 (4-27-1870) Ma

Grooms

Townes, Richard r. to Mary Jane Waddle 10-18-1838 Sh
Townes, Stephen P. to Mollie E. Patton 5-4-1864 G
Townes?, George E. to Jane Oswald 4-22-1850 Sh
Townley, G. C. to Mary E. Chilton 9-13-1866 Hn
Townly, John to Harriet E. Simpson 9-16-1865 (no return) Hn
Towns, Archy to Adaline Knox 12-4-1868 (12-7-1868) F B
Towns, Bevily to Nancy Davis 11-1-1871 (11-15-1871) Cr
Towns, Geo. to Caroline Montgomery 12-24-1870 Hy
Towns, Henry to Chatherine Taylor 3-6-1871 T
Towns, Henry to Clara Caldwell 9-26-1885 L
Towns, James M. to Anna T. Persons 4-5-1865 (no return) Cr
Towns, Jesse to Mary Robinson 11-19-1840 Sh
Towns, Robert W. to Margaret W. Temple 11-27-1854 (11-30-1854) Ma
Towns, Samuel to Belle Wilson 1-27-1875 Hy
Townsend, Albert to Abigail (Mrs) Butler 6-25-1862 (no return) Cr
Townsend, David H. to Elizabeth A. McManus 12-5-1844 Sh
Townsend, Edward C. to Elizabeth Rickets 9-1-1855 (9-2-1855) Sh
Townsend, George Goodram to Priscilla Sanford 11-10-1842 T
Townsend, George W. W. to Nancy E. Townsend 8-2-1865 T
Townsend, George to Mary A. Hallmark 7-29-1871 Cr
Townsend, Gideon to Fanny McDaniel 7-16-1846 Be
Townsend, Henry to Octavy Peacock 11-3-1880 (11-4-1880) Dy
Townsend, J. C. G. to Nancy E. Adams 9-13-1860 Hy
Townsend, James to Henrietta L. Sellers 6-3-1871 (6-11-1871) Cr
Townsend, James to Isabell Richard 2-9-1867 T
Townsend, John P. to Sarah Elizabeth Hill 3-16-1852 (3-17-1852) T
Townsend, John R. to Dicy M. Byars 12-17-1872 (12-18-1872) T
Townsend, John to Judith Moore 5-2-1868 T
Townsend, John to Lizzie Enochs 12-29-1873 (12-30-1873) Dy
Townsend, Nathaniel to Lanna Butler 9-18-1871 Cr
Townsend, Nathn. to Carolina Marchbanks 1-15-1846 Be
Townsend, O. L. to Sallie E. Bass 12-16-1868 (12-17-1868) F
Townsend, Peter to Maria Ketuna Townsend 2-6-1850 (2-7-1850) T
Townsend, Prince to Elvira Williams 12-30-1885 L
Townsend, R. M. to Sarah A. Anderson 11-23-1869 T
Townsend, Robert to Ann Smith 5-11-1867 Be
Townsend, Stephen to Lou Beaumont 8-16-1877 Dy
Townsend, Sy to N. P. Berchun 3-12-1873 (3-16-1873) Cr
Townsend, William J. to Ortha A. Butler 8-27-1868 (8-28-1868) Cr
Townsend, Wm. Hunley to Permelia Foster 2-10-1855 (2-14-1855) T
Townsley, John S. to Henrietta (Mrs.) Alexander 6-11-1863 Sh
Townsley, M. T. to Dilly Gause 3-4-1882 (3-15-1882) L
Townson, Franklin to Mary Westmoreland 1-6-1872 (1-7-1872) O B
Towsen, Henry to Ella Byas 1-28-1882 (1-29-1882) L
Towsend, George W. to Amanda Townsend 4-8-1864 (4-9-1864) Cr
Towson, John W. to M. Walker 2-2-1865 (2-6-1865) Cr
Toy, Elijah to Jane Cheatham 12-13-1846 Be
Tozier, Samuel to Ophelia Ann Scott 7-18-1861 Hr
Tr___?, Henry to Mattie Wade 11-22-1873 (11-23-1873) O
Trabue, R. D. to Martha H. Witherspoonn 1-12-1860 Sh
Trace, William to Mary F. Pamplin 7-11-1846 Sh
Tracey, Daniel to Julia Clara 7-28-1856 Sh
Trader, Doddridge to Mary C. May 8-2-1859 (8-3-1859) Ma
Trafford, George to Martha H. Clay 6-19-1868 Ma
Trafford, J. V. to Frances Richardson 6-11-1870 (6-12-1870) Dy
Trafton, Benjamin to Elizabeth Flowers 12-28-1842 (12-29-1842) G
Trail, Valentine to Martha E. Dickey 4-23-1864 (4-26-1864) Dy
Trailer, Joseph to Martha E. Tatum 9-25-1861 Hy
Trailor, William to Emeline (Mrs.) Hooker 1-1-1868 G
Trainam, William to Virginia Denton 2-9-1859 (2-10-1859) L
Trainer, Barnett M. to Elizabeth Brumley 6-27-1839 (7-4-1839) F
Trainer, J. C. to E. C. Towns 3-7-1871 (3-8-1871) Cr
Trainer, John H. to Adaline R. Wiles 1-23-1867 (1-24-1867) F
Trainer, Thomas to Elizabeth Ward 1-3-1833 (1-4-1833) G
Trainham, John to Mary Burks 12-21-1866 (12-24-1866) L
Transau, Edward T. to Mary T. Pearson 12-7-1855 (12-13-1854?) Ma
Transee, Benjamin F. to Sarah Ann Wilson 10-4-1847 Ma
Transon, Wm. to Dealy Bond 1-11-1878 Hy
Trantham, A. D. to Mary L. Grissom 7-12-1855 We
Trantham, Hyram to Nancy Key 8-15-1839 Hn
Trantham, Jesse to Charlotte Victory? 7-22-1849 Hn
Trantham, R. F. to Rebeca Deeson 5-10-1855 We
Trantham, William to Margaret Goforth 1-11-1845 (1-13-1845) T
Trap, Samuel to Sally A. Burchit 1-16-1864 (1-18-1864) Cr
Trase, Joseph to Sarah Finch 8-20-1843 We
Trask, William l. to Lucy Delapp 6-19-1858 (6-21-1858) Ma
Trass?, Allen to Louisa Nelson 1-26-1867 (2-18-1867) T
Trat, Samuel to Sally Ann Burchit 1-16-1864 (no return) Cr
Travathan, William A. to Sarah A. Kendall 11-22-1854 Hn
Travis, Albert to M. A. V. Wood 12-24-1851 Sh
Travis, Benjamin W. to Mary J. Dismukes 12-29-1840 Hn
Travis, Diggo to Frances Hagler 5-20-1866 Hn B
Travis, Edward to Elizabeth R. Shell 10-23-1847 (no return) Hn
Travis, Fielding to M. Kicks 10-29-1845 (no return) We
Travis, Franklin to Rebecca H. Hogan 3-7-1855 Cr
Travis, Geo. to Bettie Copeland 1-28-1874 (1-29-1874) Dy
Travis, Henry C. to Emly Turner 2-4-1860 We

Travis, Henry to Mary Ann Parker 9-14-1848 (9-?-1848) T
Travis, J. W. to Ellen S. White 11-27-1866 Hn
Travis, James L. to Lizzie A. Calhoun 10-15-1860 Sh
Travis, James to Catharin Fowler 11-23-1846 We
Travis, James to Martha Flowers 3-28-1863 Hy
Travis, James to Sophia L. Covington 1-12-1852 Hn
Travis, John B. to Mary Turner 8-4-1842 Cr
Travis, John B. to Rhoda Turner 9-27-1840 Cr
Travis, John to Amanda Swanner 12-12-1877 Dy
Travis, John to Mary A. Foley 7-5-1862 (7-6-1862) Sh
Travis, Joseph N. to S. E. Wynn 10-28-1863 Hn
Travis, Joseph to Eliza J. Crump 11-24-1842 Hn
Travis, L. M. to Sophia A. Crump 8-6-1851 Hn
Travis, L. W. to Narcissa J. Roberts 7-17-1855 (no return) We
Travis, M. H. to Mary Seymore 12-16-1866 G
Travis, M. L. to Eliza Barnett 1-18-1844 Be
Travis, Miles H. to Frances Gilliland 8-28-1863 G
Travis, Miles H. to Martha Jane Woodson 4-28-1849 (4-29-1849) G
Travis, Miles H. to Sarah R. Woodson 4-2-1853 (4-3-1853) G
Travis, N. M. to Ann Witherington 1-4-1854 G
Travis, Owen to Rosetta Porter 11-24-1867 Hn B
Travis, Peter to Bell Hagler 5-20-1866 Hn B
Travis, R. B. to Mary J. Gillespie 12-10-1857 Be
Travis, R. B. to Sarah Jane Cowell 2-10-1861 Be
Travis, T. M. to Susan Jonett 12-30-1872 (1-1-1873) Cr
Travis, Tazwell to Martha Atkins 5-20-1866 H
Travis, Thomas O. to E. C. Renfro 10-12-1861 (no return) Hn
Travis, W. E. to N. G. Hagler 9-10-1846 Hn
Travis, William O. to Emily McCullough 5-8-1866 Hn B
Travis, William to E. F. Cody 3-16-1840 (no return) Hn
Travis, William to M. J. Bobo 1-3-1868 (1-6-1868) Cr
Travis, Wm. to Sarah A. Gregory 4-14-1845 Cr
Trawick, Andrew M. M. to Martha B. R. McSwayne 6-30-1867 Hn
Traylor, John to Nancy P. Tugwell 6-25-1864 Hy
Traylor, Pascall G. to Catherine B. C. Gaylor? 11-16-1836 Hr
Traylor, T. L. to Mary E. Shumate 9-10-1875 Hy
Traylor, Thomas to Ramola N. Angus 1-5-1841 Ma
Traylor, W. G. to Harrett M. Roney 8-2-1853 Cr
Traynor, Jerry to Harriet Forran 4-23-1836 (4-29-1836) G
Traywick, Elvis R. to Nannie B. Coleman 12-26-1872 Cr
Traywick, H. A. to Martha J. Moore 1-1-1867 Cr
Traywick, Rufus L. to T. J. Heuey 6-2-1858 Cr
Traywick, W. H. to E. Thomas 10-20-1852 Cr
Traywick, Wm. H. to Mary A. Enochs 10-2-1844 Cr
Treadway, Richmond to Anna Snow 12-27-1877 (no return) L B
Treadway, Richmond to Anna Snow 4-2-1879 L B
Treadwell, Albert to Septimus Dunnegan 1-31-1874 (2-8-1874) Dy
Treadwell, Danl. C. to Drucilla Sandeford 12-2-1830 Sh
Treadwell, Robt. A. to Susie Long 2-9-1869 Ma
Treadwell, Stephen C. to Louisa Crenshaw 10-10-1835 Sh
Treadwell, Timmon S. to Elizabeth E. Haynie 10-1-1850 Hr
Treadwell, W. L. to Lew A. Farabee 12-21-1858 (12-22-1858) Sh
Treanthan, N. to P. Mitchell 7-30-1852 We
Tredway, Richard to L. J. Scott 9-21-1869 (1-1-1870) T
Treece, James G. to Susan A. Box 8-10-1858 (8-12-1858) Hr
Treese, Boyd to Jane Goad 3-7-1852 (3-18-1852) Hr
Treesse, George W. to Sarah Mahaffy 8-13-1845 Sh
Trellien, M. L. to Lanorea L. Ward (Word?) 9-6-1865 G
Trent, Adam to Judith Alford 9-2-1866 F
Trent, R. T. to Martha Gillam 1-25-1845 (no return) We
Trent, W. C. to A. E. Freeman 12-7-1865 Hn
Trent, William H. to Martha G. Jackson 3-14-1846 (3-17-1846) F
Trevathan, Henry H. to Susan L. Frazier 1-19-1858 Hn
Trevathan, James L. to Sarah E. Howell 3-22-1848 Hn
Trevathan, John W. to Martha V. Caldwell 6-29-1858 Hn
Trevathan, John W. to Mary E. Venable 4-2-1858 Hn
Trevathan, V. C. to Eliza J. Kendall 3-5-1854 Hn
Trew, Robert to Ada Jones 8-26-1870 (8-29-1870) Dy
Trezevant, Edward B. to Hattie M. Walton 7-6-1858 Sh
Trezevant, Jno. Pollard to Louisa R. Rembert 12-2-1841 Sh
Trezevant, John T. to Eleanor L. Beatty 1-31-1838 Sh
Trezevant, Nathl. M. to Amanda A. Avery 11-30-1848 Sh
Trible, James O. to Elizabeth Field 1-2-1858 Hn
Trice, Francis to Jane E. Wenstram? 10-22-1855 (10-23-1855) T
Trice, John to Augusta B. Hill 1-11-1854 (1-12-1854) Sh
Trice, John to Effie J. Bourden 7-15-1848 Hn
Trice, John to Elizabeth M. Nelson 1-1-1842 Sh
Trice, John to Fanney Adams 3-19-1874 Hy
Trice, N. S. to Mary F. Frayser 3-28-1860 (3-29-1860) Sh
Trice, Stephen E. to Susan E. Crossno 3-25-1852 Be
Trice, W. C. to Sarah A. Butler 8-21-1854 Sh
Trice, William to Sarah Edwards 12-19-1868 Ma
Trigalez, E. to Rose Goilliot 4-23-1864 Sh
Trigallez, Emmanuel to Louisa Noeimi Esther Louvet 4-2-1859 Sh
Trigg, A. to Sarah McMillan 7-14-1841 Sh
Trigg, Anthony to Martha Proctor 1-16-1869 G B
Trigg, Isaac to Maria _____ 7-2-1872 T

Trigg, James to Rebecca Thompson 11-17-1840 Sh
Trigg, Jas. W. to Katy Williams 2-20-1869 (3-1-1869) T
Trigg, John A. to E. R. Gift 3-13-1854 (3-14-1854) Sh
Trigg, John to Julia S. (Mrs.) Chester 12-10-1855 Sh
Trigg, John to Martha Haskell 1-14-1858 Sh
Trigg, Moses to Elsie Manna Sims 12-31-1873 T
Trigg, William to Eliza Rawlings 10-27-1827 Ma
Triller?, John to Virginia Whitney 4-22-1853 (no return) F
Trim, Samuel H. to Martha E. McKnatt 9-10-1872 T
Trimble, E. C. to C. E. Porter 10-28-1850 Hn
Trimble, Frank to Lilly Shelton 1-6-1870 F
Trimble, G. E. to Rosa E. Patton 12-19-1866 Hy
Trimble, J. L. to T. C. Scott 2-26-1873 (2-27-1873) Dy
Trimble, R. E. to Delia Rainey 2-28-1885 (3-5-1885) L
Trimble, Robert B. to Lucinda J. Nance 10-27-1851 G
Trimble, Thomas B. to Margaret P. Carpenter 6-19-1882 L B
Triplet, William G. to Elizabeth Avery 10-30-1863 Mn
Tripp, G. W. to Mary Cusick 10-30-1880 (11-5-1880) L
Tripp, George to Malinda Gaskins 6-4-1879 (6-22-1879) Dy
Tripp, H. A. to Minnie L. White 7-10-1864 Sh
Tripp, J. M. to Selina Fisher 1-4-1855 Sh
Tripp, Jno. W. to Louiza Brace 5-4-1868 (5-10-1868) F B
Tripp, Thomas A. to Adelia (Dibzorah?) Galloway 3-10-1866 (3-11-1866) F
Tripp, Thos. A. to Sallie Hicks 5-26-1869 (5-27-1869) F
Trobaugh, Henry G. to Martha D. Bond 8-21-1854 Sh
Trobaugh, William A. to Mary R. Boyd 5-18-1849 Sh
Trobough, Daniel Adams to Mary Ann Burton 6-24-1846 (6-25-1846) T
Trobough, J. W. to Jane D. Bambridge 6-4-1872 (6-5-1872) T
Trobough, Jas. W. to Mary Louisa Tyree? 10-24-1856 (10-25-1855?) T
Trobough, L. W. to M. E. Pool 5-21-1862? T
Trobough, Littleton W. to Patsey W. McCraw 5-29-1844 T
Trobough, R. H. to Jane Boyd 12-14-1865 T
Trobough, Tho. B. to Eliza Jane Jackson 3-16-1850 (3-19-1850) T
Trobough, ___ to Mary? A. Williams 4-18-1863 (4-21-1863) T
Trosper, James to Rachael Glasscock 7-12-1834 G
Trosper, Robert to Elizabeth Short 8-19-1841 (8-22-1841) G
Trosper, T. J. to M. F. Long 5-2-1864 G
Trotman, Charlie to Matilda Mann 5-12-1867 Hy
Trotman, Clinton to Martha C. Newborn 6-17-1866 Hy
Trott, Asa L. to Margaret Whitesides 10-30-1828 Sh
Trotter, Adam to Mary Ann Greaves 1-10-1878 Hy
Trotter, B. Y. to Obediance E. Hall 10-10-1848 F
Trotter, G. W. to Lucy A. Abernathy 7-21-1851 (7-22-1851) F
Trotter, George W. to Elizabeth Ball 1-10-1844 F
Trotter, George W. to Sarah Elizabeth Meriwether 4-28-1857 Ma
Trotter, Harvey to Louisa Atkins 4-3-1844 Sh
Trotter, Henry J. to Melvina Conner 1-26-1848 F
Trotter, Joseph H. to Ruth W. Harrison 7-6-1846 (7-9-1846) F
Trotter, Joseph H. to Sarah Jane Cloyed 9-22-1852 (no return) F
Trotter, Richard B. to Marina W. Simmons 10-5-1837 Sh
Trotter, Richard to Mary Carolin Hutchinson 9-3-1867 T
Trotter, T. H. to Lucy L. Drumwright 1-5-1881 L
Trotter, W. B. to Frances Jordan 1-13-1844 (1-6-1844) F
Trotter, William A. to Annie Todd 4-29-1861 (5-2-1861) Dy
Trotter, William to Angeline McNeill 9-4-1871 (9-7-1871) Cr B
Trought, Henry to Sabeany Benton 12-26-1848 Cr
Trousdale, A. C. to S. D. Crank 12-2-1866 F
Trousdale, Allen to Ann Burgner(Burger) 9-7-1827 Hr
Trousdale, B. F. to M. W. B. Hunt 6-28-1853 Hn
Trousdale, J. M. to Nancy J. Perry 12-2-1867 (no return) Hn
Trousdale, John to Elizabeth Mooney 12-26-1842 (12-27-1842) Ma
Trousdale, Leonidas to Virginia F. Joy 12-21-1853 Hr
Trout, Adam to Frances Gilliland 11-23-1834 G
Trout, Alfred to Sarah a. Carter 4-6-1852 Cr
Trout, Charles M. to Mary A. Mosier 12-23-1865 (12-24-1865) O
Trout, Daniel H. to Mary Cox 10-15-1870 (10-16-1870) Dy
Trout, Granvill M. to Sarah C. Pinkston 11-18-1864 Be
Trout, Granville to Lydia Pinkston 2-12-1857 Cr
Trout, H. C. to Mary E. Brackins 4-22-1875 Be
Trout, Hiram C. to Frances C. Clements 7-15-1845 G
Trout, Hiram C. to Sally N. Shelton 3-13-1854 (3-14-1854) G
Trout, J. B. to E. C. Tucker 3-25-1867 (2?-28-1867) Dy
Trout, J. U. to Mary Green 1-7-1869 G
Trout, J. W. to M. E. Turrentine 12-20-1866 (12-23-1866) Dy
Trout, J. W. to N. L. Hendricks 12-24-1876 (12-26-1876) Dy
Trout, John to Sarah J. Gibson 7-15-1850 (7-16-1850) G
Trout, Leland to Marietta Swift 12-10-1866 (no return) F
Trout, W. E. to Maggie Simons 12-31-1878 (1-1-1879) Dy
Trout, W. S. to Susan A. Wood 11-20-1866 (no return) Dy
Trout, Wm. to Catherine N. Henkle 4-26-1859 Hy
Trout, Wm. to Delia Smith no date (c. Sep 1866) T
Troutman, Geo. W. to Alice Williamson 9-20-1860 Sh
Troutt, E. H. to Lonesome Howard 1-28-1870 (1-29-1870) Dy
Trowell, Francis to Sarah Cook 8-12-1846 F
Troy, Edgar to Margaret Burnham 2-10-1869 (no return) Dy
Troy, Elmer to Ethel Maybell Gross 12-4-1854 Be CC
Troy, F. A. to M. A. Crow 12-11-1872 Dy

Troy, J. P. to M. J. Smith 9-14-1863 (9-15-1863) Dy
Troy, James F. to E. A. King 8-25-1866 (8-26-1866) Dy
Troy, William E. to Harriet Garrison 5-27-1862 (no return) Dy
Troy, Zach T. to S. A. Crow 12-28-1867 (12-29-1867) Dy
Truce, P. G. to Mary L. Bolton 11-1-1859 Sh
Trudeau, F. H. to Louisa Baner 5-6-1861 Sh
Truehart, George W. to Mary (Mrs.) Scruggs 12-5-1850 Sh
Truehart, Thomas J. to Mary Ellen Dupuy 12-2-1852 (12-22-1852) Sh
Truelove, Harry to Mattie Archibald 2-9-1876 Hy
Truesdale, Jack to Josephine Ragland 12-4-1866 (no return) F B
Trulove, Jas. H. to Mary A. Honey 6-17-1846 (6-18-1846) F
Trulove, John to Mary A. Atkinson 8-5-1843 Sh
Trumen, Jas. to Mary Williams 12-31-1851 (1-1-1852) Sh
Trump, H. to Mitta Beasley 11-2-1867 (11-4-1867) F
Trusdale, Andrew to Abby E. Braden 11-22-1869 (no return) F B
Trusty, Benj. F. to Ellender McCarey 1-1-1845 (1-2-1845) G
Trusty, Henderson to Julian Mitchell 1-16-1830 G
Trusty, R. B. to Eliza F. A. Lipard 11-21-1859 (11-23-1859) O
Trusty, Thomas T. to Mary F. Cooper 8-21-1872 Dy
Trusty, W. T. to Rebecca Wright 2-7-1872 (no return) Dy
Truthman, Olloise to Johanna Veragut 5-21-1862 Sh
Tschudi, Henry to Elizabeth Runck 11-25-1859 (11-27-1859) Sh
Tubberville, James C. to Matilda A. Myirack 1-27-1862 (no return) We
Tubbs, Francis M. to Olive V. (Mrs.) Shelby 11-19-1870 (11-20-1870) Ma
Tubbs, J. to Susan Parks 1-3-1860 Be
Tuck, Ferdinand N. to Elizabeth L. Hill 9-16-1858 We
Tuck, Isham to Catherine Brown 11-8-1844 We
Tucker, A. C. to M. B. G. Palmer 12-7-1864 (12-8-1864) Cr
Tucker, A. E. to Sarah Colly 3-13-1856 We
Tucker, A. J. to Lottie Hughes 3-3-1875 Hy
Tucker, A. R. to M. A. Laws 2-13-1851 Cr
Tucker, A. to Mariah Blackwell 10-17-1840 (no return) L
Tucker, Alexander R. to Susan Fields 4-3-1858 (4-6-1858) L
Tucker, Allen J. to Martha Jane Smally 11-7-1859 Sh
Tucker, Allen to Sarah A. Carter 6-20-1850 Sh
Tucker, Augustus to Mary Anderson 11-23-1867 Hy
Tucker, B. P. to Susan E. (Mrs.) Vining 10-31-1859 Sh
Tucker, Benj. F. to K. C. Pope 10-13-1857 (9?-18-1857) Hr
Tucker, Calvin to Martha Ramsey 2-17-1845 (2-20-1845) T
Tucker, Coleman H. to Julianne C. Finger 7-14-1845 (7-15-1845) Ma
Tucker, Daniel S. to M. L. (Mrs.) Walker 2-19-1872 (2-20-1872) Dy
Tucker, E. K. to M. E. Huie 8-13-1866 G
Tucker, Ebenezer D. to Caroline T. Dickey 9-4-1855 (9-5-1855) G
Tucker, Edmond to Merry Spivey 5-30-1871 Hy
Tucker, Edmond to Sophronia A. White 4-10-1874 L B
Tucker, Edmund V. to Elizabeth A. Horskins 8-20-1838 L
Tucker, Edward A. to Angey E. Shoemake 1-11-1863 We
Tucker, Ellic to Rosa Nixon 6-12-1867 Hy
Tucker, Frank to Fannie Burns 5-6-1878 Hy
Tucker, G. W. to Rebecca Jane King 1-22-1868 Be
Tucker, George to Harriett Shelton 1-8-1869 (1-9-1869) F B
Tucker, George to Minnie Scott 7-1-1867 (7-6-1867) T
Tucker, George to Nina Easley 4-9-1876 Hy
Tucker, Gideon to Ann Bradberry 6-11-1834 G
Tucker, Gideon to Cely Johnson 7-28-1832 G
Tucker, Gratten to Fannie Halliburton 2-19-1873 L
Tucker, H. J. to Anne E. Norris 3-26-1851 Sh
Tucker, Hartwell P. to Katie Ida Parrish 2-17-1857 Sh
Tucker, Haywood to City Ross 1-15-1852 Hn
Tucker, Ike to Amanda Wilkerson 12-26-1866 Hy
Tucker, J. B. to Eudora Parker 4-1-1879 (4-2-1879) Dy
Tucker, J. N. to E. H. Calhoun 10-23-1868 G
Tucker, J. R. to N. C. Stall 9-25-1856 Sh
Tucker, J. T. to Jane E. Claxton 9-19-1860 G
Tucker, J. W. to Sallie A. Mayfield 9-26-1866 (9-27-1866) F
Tucker, James A. to Sarah A. Bowls 7-13-1855 We
Tucker, James H. to Elizabeth Goldsby 12-15-1849 Hn
Tucker, James P. to Mollie J. Tucker 9-4-1862 Hy
Tucker, James W. to Sarah S. McCallester 11-1-1841 G
Tucker, James to Emaly V. Patton 1-23-1848 (1-27-1848) G
Tucker, James to Laura A. Correthers 12-5-1857 (12-8-1857) T
Tucker, James to Martha F. Morgan 6-4-1851 G
Tucker, Jesse C. to Mary Jane Murrell 3-14-1850 Hr
Tucker, Jesse D. to Marinda C. Haltom 12-2-1869 (12-5-1869) Ma
Tucker, Jessee to Kate M. Smith 10-24-1857 (10-25-1857) G
Tucker, Jessie to Sallie Ann Tucker 4-10-1869 (4-11-1869) F B
Tucker, Jno. B. to Mozella Perry 10-1-1866 (10-10-1866) Dy
Tucker, Joel A. to Martha P. Elender 3-17-1861 We
Tucker, John P. to Martha Boytt 7-19-1842 (7-20-1842) G
Tucker, John W. to Amanda C. Guffe 1-2-1869 Hy
Tucker, John W. to Virginia McMahan 5-23-1855 We
Tucker, John to Louisa Gregory 8-9-1874 Hy
Tucker, John to Rose Mathews 2-22-1868 Hy
Tucker, John to Sarah A. Mayfield 8-14-1844 Sh
Tucker, Joseph C. C. to Mary A. Jackson 7-3-1843 (7-6-1843) F
Tucker, Joseph H. to Caroline Black 2-22-1866 (2-25-1866) Cr

Grooms

Tucker, Joseph S. to Frances E. Tucker 8-23-1869 (8-24-1869) T
Tucker, Julias M. to Clarissa Ann Ammons 12-8-1851 G
Tucker, Lewis to Nancy Jones 11-9-1868 (11-13-1868) F B
Tucker, Mareau? J. to Mary Jane Rogers (Royers?) 1-3-1866 (no return) L
Tucker, Monroe to Hannah Hare 12-28-1865 (1-1-1866) F B
Tucker, Morris to Ann Bailey 2-5-1878 Hy
Tucker, N. S. to Alice Lunsford 3-24-1886 L
Tucker, P. G. to Mary F. Harrison 5-6-1863 (5-7-1863) O
Tucker, P. G. to Nancy Jane Ross 11-9-1846 We
Tucker, Paschal G. to Nancy Jane Ross 11-9-1846 (11-19-1846) We
Tucker, Phillip to Elizabeth Dunlap 3-1-1867 Hn
Tucker, R. A. to Elizabeth Carnes ?-?-1849 Cr
Tucker, Richard to Betty Crider 4-2-1872 (4-3-1872) Cr B
Tucker, Robert A. to Nancy C. Cox 3-22-1875 L
Tucker, Robert to Mary Gillett 12-31-1840 Cr
Tucker, Robert to Mary Williams 12-25-1868 (12-26-1868) F B
Tucker, Robt. G. to Sallie E. Lanier 10-5-1868 (10-6-1868) F
Tucker, S. T. to N. M. Mathis 7-20-1865 G
Tucker, Samuel R. to Marilda M. Dale 6-7-1848 G
Tucker, Sandy to Edmony Rogers 1-7-1875 Hy
Tucker, Stephen to D. N. Wilson 3-13-1867 (3-14-1868?) G
Tucker, Stephen to M. A. T. Bean 10-25-1870 (no return) Dy
Tucker, Steven to Martha Clark 10-2-1846 G
Tucker, Steven to Martha Williams 1-18-1875 Hy
Tucker, T. B. to Martha Jane Bonds 8-13-1854 Hn
Tucker, T. O. to F. M. Roberts 1-11-1860 We
Tucker, Thomas to Molly Smith 4-18-1876 Hy
Tucker, Thos. A. to Ester C. Etchison 12-19-1853 (12-22-1853) G
Tucker, Tom to Mary E. Read 4-12-1872 Hy
Tucker, W. H. to Fanny Johnson 11-1-1859 Hy
Tucker, W. J. to Mary A. Hering 7-8-1865 (7-9-1865) O
Tucker, W. J. to Sarah C. Stoker 12-21-1854 We
Tucker, William A. to Hulen H. Tucker 12-20-1867 (12-23-1867) T
Tucker, William to Annie Watkins 2-26-1873 L
Tucker, Willis T. to Mary Emar Jordan 1-22-1868 Hy
Tucker, Wm. J. to Mary A. Anderton 1-9-1861 Sh
Tucker, Wm. M. to Evalene Hancock 1-22-1876 (1-28-1876) L
Tucker, Wm. to Mary Lemons 5-23-1844 Cr
Tudor, Jesse G. to Eliza Cutberth 6-20-1833 (7-19-1833) Hr
Tudor, Kenny L. to Emily Davis 7-7-1833 (8-8-1833) Hr
Tue, Joab to Julian Reddick 9-20-1840 Be
Tue, Joab to Polly Coley 6-18-1843 Be
Tuft, James to Amanda M. McKinney 5-10-1860 (5-13-1860) Sh
Tufts, Peter E. to Lovina Mulford 1-25-1855 (1-27-1855) Sh
Tuggle, Phillip to Elizabeth S. A. Green 5-2-1842 (no return) L
Tuggle, Tho. R. to Elizabeth Burford 10-1-1846 (no return) F
Tuggle, Thos. I. to Ann Elvill 11-6-1841 (11-12-1841) Ma
Tuggle, William H. to Martha P. Alvis 10-4-1854 G
Tugwell, John L. to Jacky Ann Jones 6-20-1861 Sh
Tugwell, R. R. to B. A. Finch 8-18-1867 Hy
Tuikler, John to May J. McCamack 12-17-1856 T
Tuley, James A. to Susan R. Denney 8-22-1859 (8-23-1859) O
Tull, C. W. to L. E. Glimp 1-3-1883 (1-10-1884) L
Tull, D. G. to Tennessee Hamilton 2-5-1868 G
Tull, E. C. to Lucy Ann Ballard 6-1-1881 L
Tull, E. C. to S. F. Maxfield 5-5-1875 L
Tull, John H. to Tabitha J. McCarver 8-22-1859 Hr
Tull, John to Jane A. Burgh 1-27-1842 Ma
Tull, T. J> to Marinda Drennon 1-5-1857 (1-9-1857) Hr
Tull, Thomas J. to Miranda McCarver 3-14-1854 Hr
Tulley, Britain to Martha Grant 2-20-1841 Cr
Tully, A. to Sarah W. Aldridge 4-15-1843 Ma
Tully, Britton to Exery Ponder 1-28-1846 Cr
Tully, Edward to Catherine Montgomery 7-1-1849 Sh
Tully, John L. to Martha Rose 9-12-1839 Cr
Tully, Patrick to Mary Parker 5-17-1861 Sh
Tully, T. P. to Susan Cole 1-19-1865 Mn
Tumer, Sipio to Susan A. Taylor 12-20-1872 (12-26-1872) T
Tunadge, John D. to Susan Montague 1-22-1844 (1-24-1844) F
Tune, Alfred T. to Elizabeth A. Edwards 9-17-1849 (9-19-1849) O
Tune, Louis H. to Virginia M. Hudson 7-22-1867 G
Tunely?, H. L. W. to N. (Mrs.) Conwell 8-3-1868 (8-4-1868) Dy
Tupell, James T. to Louis A. Stone 10-3-1844 Ma
Turbeville, B. to Sarah Wright 5-19-1852 Hn
Turbeville, C. F. to Lucinda Turbeville 2-12-1851 Hn
Turbeville, James E. to Elizabeth Wright 2-10-1859 Hn
Turbeville, John D. to Henrietta S. Turbeville 12-25-1867 Hn
Turfim, Wm. to Nancy Ann Wright 2-17-1863 (2-18-1863) Dy
Turk, G. W. to Mary J. Wilson 2-13-1856 (2-14-1856) Sh
Turley, A. J. to Catharine Marrick 3-7-1856 Sh
Turley, Thos. to Flora C. Battle 4-26-1843 Sh
Turlington, J. K. to N. A. Reader 2-16-1858 We
Turnage, E. J. to A. F. Beaver 7-10-1872 (7-11-1872) T
Turnage, Emanuel to Ann E. Baker 5-22-1848 We
Turnage, Green to Alice Stevens 8-23-1872 (8-25-1872) Dy
Turnage, Henry M. to Eliz. Murphy Tucker 10-14-1850 (10-16-1850) T
Turnage, Henry Martin to Rebecka Frances Manly 12-30-1857 (12-31-1857) T

Turnage, Ily D. to Susan M. Phelps 10-26-1847 (11-10-1847) T
Turnage, J. B. to M. A. Hatton 1-12-1874 (1-14-1874) T
Turnage, James B. to Charlotte Ammonet 10-20-1852 Sh
Turnage, James B. to Eliza F. Robinson 12-3-1866 (12-4-1866) T
Turnage, James W. to Mary Manasco 12-16-1868 (12-17-1868) T
Turnage, John L. to Mariah W. Delashmeit 7-1-1865 T
Turnage, Owen to V. Carolin Cocke 10-30-1867 (10-31-1867) T
Turnage, T. G. to M. A. E. Moore 7-9-1862 Sh
Turnage, Walker to Martha A. Simpson 3-27-1844 (3-28-1844) T
Turnage, William B. to Elizabeth Caroline Hughes 6-5-1843 (6-6-1843) T
Turnage, Wm. A. jr. to Mildred Beaver 2-14-1865 T
Turnbow, R. L. to Permelia W. Cochran 1-4-1855 Hy
Turnbow, Thomas J. to Mary J. Cochran 7-25-1861 Hn
Turnbull, Chas. J. to Francis G. Torrey 2-23-1856 (2-24-1856) Sh
Turnbull, William to Judy Jenkins 4-13-1866 (4-15-1866) F B
Turner, Able C. to Elizabeth Philips 1-21-1851 (1-26-1851) O
Turner, Albert to _____ 3-19-1886 (no return) L
Turner, Alexander to Colann Gordon 1-10-1827 Ma
Turner, Alexander to Martha Scipper 12-9-1842 (12-10-1842) G
Turner, Alfred H. to J. T. Berry 8-20-1840 Cr
Turner, Andrew to Levina Chisham 1-1-1827 Hr
Turner, Antny to Lucy Walker 1-28-1870 (1-30-1870) F B
Turner, Arch to Mary Brown 10-18-1873 Hy
Turner, Arthur to Nancy Ferril 12-25-1848 G
Turner, Ben F. to Alice C. Loving 11-5-1874 Hy
Turner, Benjamin to Eliza Golding 5-28-1853 (5-29-1853) L
Turner, Benjamin to Nancy Jamison 2-26-1854 Hn
Turner, Benjamin to Sarah Johnson 11-21-1831 Hr
Turner, Bob to Lila Armstrong 5-2-1868 (no return) F B
Turner, C. F. to Martha Irwin 8-6-1853 Sh
Turner, C. L. to India D. Graves 10-28-1867 (10-31-1867) F
Turner, Charles B. to Susan A. Keeton 1-7-1867 (1-8-1867) F
Turner, Charles W. to Frances Myrick 7-14-1851 (no return) Hn
Turner, Charles W. to Margaret C. Peeples 1-24-1860 Hn
Turner, Charles to Alice Ryan 9-15-1855 (9-16-1855) Sh
Turner, Chas. to Frances Williamson 4-17-1866 T
Turner, Cyrus to Nancy Harper 3-18-1868 G
Turner, D. C. to Mary A. Roberts 12-21-1854 We
Turner, D. W. to Catherine O'Connel 2-22-1864 Sh
Turner, David W. to Emma J. Mathis 3-2-1870 (3-8-1870) Ma
Turner, David W. to Melcenia V. Barnett 2-16-1857 (2-19-1857) Ma
Turner, David to Catherine O'Connell 2-9-1861 Sh
Turner, Dority to Susan M. Lewis 10-23-1846 (10-27-1846) G
Turner, E. B. to Roena R. Ruffin 9-21-1867 (9-25-1867) F
Turner, E. W. to Catherine O'Conner 2-22-1864 Sh
Turner, Edward to Caroline Cochran 6-28-1847 (no return) L
Turner, Elijah to Nancy Jane Morgan 4-8-1867 (4-9-1867) Ma
Turner, F. W. to S. A. Wren 6-27-1870 (6-29-1870) Cr
Turner, F. W. to Susan A. Berry 11-27-1840 Cr
Turner, Francis M. to Lucy A. Landrum 12-12-1859 (12-13-1860) We
Turner, Frank to Margaret Arnold 12-21-1870 Dy
Turner, G. M. to M. A. Dieta 9-16-1846 Hn
Turner, Geo. to Eliza Tyus 7-25-1872 Hy
Turner, George M. to Elizabeth A. Brown 1-3-1843 Hn
Turner, George W. to Caroline C. Hobbs 1-18-1848 (1-19-1848) Ma
Turner, George W. to Susan A. Miller 10-31-1854 (11-2-1854) T
Turner, George to Caroline Bond 7-31-1879 (8-8-1879) L
Turner, George to Caroline Tyus 6-12-1875 Hy
Turner, George to Mary Anderson 6-28-1839 Hr
Turner, H. B. to C. C. Smith 12-16-1867 (12-19-1867) F
Turner, Harden J. to Margaret O. Braden 8-22-1863 (8-23-1863) L
Turner, Henery M. to Sarah Foster 1-29-1846 Cr
Turner, Henry P. to Frances Ann Morgan 4-19-1848 Sh
Turner, Irvin L. to L. M. Brown 1-28-1874 L
Turner, J. A. to Mary Frances Searcy 9-13-1868 G
Turner, J. C. to Margaret Ann Dodson 11-3-1857 (11-4-1857) Sh
Turner, J. D. P. to Mary E. Lynch 2-21-1869 Be
Turner, J. F. to Ivana A. Bland 5-6-1864 Sh
Turner, J. L. to Martha J. Sweat 12-14-1863 (no return) Hn
Turner, J. L. to Mary A. Locke 12-26-1853 (no return) F
Turner, J. M. to Lucinda Lumley 1-31-1877 (2-1-1877) Dy
Turner, J. M. to Sarah E. Bryan? 4-29-1869 G
Turner, J. T. to M. J. Gowan 2-8-1873 (2-18-1873) Cr
Turner, J. W. to Sarah J. Mitchell 12-9-1846 (no return) F
Turner, Jack to Nancy Davis 12-27-1866 G
Turner, Jackson to Dicey Goforth 4-13-1855 (4-14-1855) Hr
Turner, Jackson to Jane Rogers 6-20-1858 We
Turner, Jackson to Sarah Young 9-27-1854 Be
Turner, Jacob to Elvira Lewis 6-2-1865 (no return) Hn
Turner, Jacob to L. S. Mizell 5-21-1873 (5-22-1873) Cr
Turner, James C. to Martha J. Paschall 8-6-1861 We
Turner, James F. to Mary J. Cunningham 3-23-1868 (3-24-1868) Cr
Turner, James H. to Eliza J. Gore 12-6-1860 Hn
Turner, James J. to Susan Mary 1-6-1852 Be
Turner, James N. to E. C. Culbreth 2-19-1868 (no return) F
Turner, James to Anna Jennings 1-25-1879 L
Turner, James to Carrie White 4-20-1876 (4-21-1876) L B

Grooms

Turner, James to Eliza Jane Craig 1-28-1864 (no return) Dy
Turner, James to Jane Goodrich 12-23-1864 Dy
Turner, James to Julia A. West 10-9-1850 G
Turner, James to Lucinda Patterson 7-23-1862 G
Turner, James to Mary Patterson 12-5-1842 (12-8-1842) G
Turner, James to Nancy Nicholson 1-12-1856 (1-13-1856) Ma
Turner, Jesse to Elizabeth Alford 6-15-1835 (6-16-1835) G
Turner, Jessee J. to Malvina Buck 8-29-1855 Sh
Turner, Joe to Nannie Jordan 12-26-1883 (12-27-1884?) L
Turner, John B. to Arminda D. Johnson 4-7-1863 F
Turner, John C. to Caroline Wytt 2-10-1881 G
Turner, John C. to Frances E. Cardwell 12-21-1857 Ma
Turner, John H. to Rebecca Gunter 4-13-1862 We
Turner, John S. to Mary F. Stell 11-14-1861 Sh
Turner, John T. to Eliza Ann Goode 10-28-1858 Hn
Turner, John W. to Margaret B. McLemore 2-10-1855 (2-13-1855) Ma
Turner, John to Bettie Wynne 8-21-1878 (8-28-1878) Dy
Turner, John to Eliza Hale 1-30-1861 Hr
Turner, John to Elizabeth Johnson 12-20-1834 Hr
Turner, John to Elizabeth Savage 12-20-1860 Hr
Turner, John to Harriett Ware 4-14-1877 Hy
Turner, John to Mary C. Etheridge 8-14-1854 We
Turner, John to Mary Richley 5-7-1862 Sh
Turner, John to Nancy P. McWherter 1-26-1858 We
Turner, John to Peggy Reed 7-8-1833 (7-9-1833) Hr
Turner, John to Phebe Read 5-28-1870 Hy
Turner, Joseph B. to Martha A. Galemore 2-17-1852 Hn
Turner, Joseph to Matilda C. Smith 10-11-1841 (10-21-1841) F
Turner, L. C. to B. P. Mobley 8-25-1856 We
Turner, L. G. to B. Sisco 1-6-1863 O
Turner, L. W. to C. A. Ramsey 1-23-1866 G
Turner, L. W. to M. F. Ramsey 8-19-1863 G
Turner, Levi J. to Margarett Patterson 4-9-1855 (4-10-1855) G
Turner, Luther to Georgian Thomas 4-10-1858 (4-11-1858) Ma
Turner, M. C. to Sarah Stanly 10-12-1859 O
Turner, M. J. to Henrietta Y. Garrett 1-17-1854 (1-19-1854) Sh
Turner, M. L. to Marthann Allen 10-13-1847 (10-19-1847) F
Turner, M. T. to Laura J. Johnson 12-30-1859 (1-3-1860) Sh
Turner, Pleasant G. to Sarah F. Fowler 11-29-1854 (12-10-1854) Hr
Turner, Presley to Mary D. Gillmore 1-4-1869 (1-6-1869) F
Turner, R. to Mary H. Bunn 10-19-1870 (10-20-1870) Cr
Turner, Reeves to Sophia Curry 12-17-1862 We
Turner, Richard to Martha M. Flowers 7-25-1859 (7-31-1859) G
Turner, Robert B. to Lucy M. Bragg 9-27-1869 (9-28-1869) T
Turner, Robert S. to Martha Ann Camp 6-21-1856 O
Turner, S. B. to B. L. Goodman 12-21-1869 T
Turner, Samuel G. to Desdamonia Patterson 6-19-1863 G
Turner, Samuel G. to Mary Jane Senter 12-6-1852 (12-7-1852) Ma
Turner, Scott to Rachel M. Lunsford 12-25-1868 (no return) L
Turner, Seth B. to Rebecca A. Lundy (Lindy) 11-15-1850 Sh
Turner, Silas to Martha Stanley 12-17-1866 Hy
Turner, Simon T. to Martha Eddins 5-24-1831 Sh
Turner, Simon to Julia M. Leonard 6-28-1853 (no return) F
Turner, Sion to Sallie Skipper 3-19-1870 G
Turner, T. R. to Martha Howell 6-20-1838 (6-24-1838) G
Turner, T. T. W. to Nancy R. Edleman 8-15-1869 G
Turner, Terrish to Peggy Brightwell 5-4-1853 (5-5-1853) G
Turner, Terry to Almedy Barham 3-11-1867 Hy
Turner, Thomas A. to Mary Massey 10-10-1868 (10-11-1868) Cr
Turner, Thomas H. to Sarah A. Williams 12-23-1863 G
Turner, Thomas J. to Mary P. Pittman 12-5-1860 (12-6-1860) L
Turner, Thomas to Mariah Wilson 6-12-1878 (6-13-1878) Dy
Turner, Thos to Elizabeth A. Shepherd 3-4-1843 Hr
Turner, Thos. A. to Susannah Foster 3-13-1845 G
Turner, Vinis to Martha A. (Mrs.) Smith 7-14-1873 (7-15-1873) L
Turner, W. A. to Ann Eliza Jones 5-14-1850 F
Turner, W. A. to Elizabeth F. Koen 9-18-1849 Sh
Turner, W. A. to Patsy A. Corley 12-22-1858 (1-22-1859) G
Turner, W. G. to Mollie Perkins 1-17-1877 (1-18-1877) L
Turner, W. H. to Alice Carigan 1-24-1882 (1-25-1882) L
Turner, W. S. to Laura J. McIntosh 4-8-1867 Dy
Turner, Wade H. to Martha Lynn 5-21-1828 O
Turner, Walter to Ann Cotten 12-30-1874 T
Turner, William C. to Martha A. Nesbitt 3-13-1852 (3-15-1852) G
Turner, William D. to Mariah Espy 12-31-1828 (1-1-1829) Ma
Turner, William E. (Mrs.) Chambers 12-5-1847 Sh
Turner, William E. to Maggie E. Wade 1-3-1866 T
Turner, William H. to Elizabeth Cole 2-5-1844 (2-13-1844) Ma
Turner, William W. to Tryphena Pearson 11-1-1845 (no return) F
Turner, William to Cassandra Garnett 6-23-1852 (6-29-1852) L
Turner, William to Jane Pinkston 6-1-1861 (no return) Dy
Turner, William to Josephine H. Goodman 3-23-1871 T
Turner, Wm. J. to Mary Ann Nance 1-9-1845 Be
Turner, Wm. to Adaline Huston 7-15-1871 T
Turner, Wm. to Martha Walker 5-12-1869 (no return) Dy
Turner, Wyatt to Rebeca Tyus 12-16-1869 Hy
Turner, Y. B. to Mary E. Tucker 11-19-1866 (11-20-1866) T

Turney, Reuben S. to Mary H. Cunningham 9-17-1850 Hn
Turney, W. R. to E. M. Wright 12-11-1866 O
Turnham, Joseph to Sarah Williams 11-7-1857 (11-8-1857) O
Turnham, P. W. to Nancy M. West 7-15-1851 O
Turnipseed, Louis to Julea Ivey 5-18-1870 G B
Turnipseed, Mance to Caroline Hale 4-6-1867 G B
Turnley, George W. to Anna Miller 7-19-1853 (no return) F
Turnley, S. M. to Olie Alexander 2-8-1877 Hy
Turpin, Alfred to Emma Crook 12-6-1884 (12-11-1884) L
Turpin, Alfred to Frankie Henning 9-13-1883 L
Turpin, Buster to Martha King 9-10-1881 (no return) L B
Turpin, Frank to Winnie Whirl 7-8-1876 Hy
Turpin, Henderson to Margaret Langsford 9-18-1870 Hy
Turpin, I. H. to S. J. McLean 9-16-1868 Hy
Turpin, Joseph to Juntha J. Steward 12-5-1860 (12-26-1860) Dy
Turpin, Richmond to Ann Eliza Harris 9-22-1863 (9-23-1863) Dy
Turpin, Richmond to Louisa T. Hassell 6-13-1864 (no return) Dy
Turrantine, R. J. to Julia Powers 11-4-1857 O
Turrentine, Saml. M. to Isabella Edwards 8-28-1858 (9-2-1858) Sh
Turrentine, Van to Linnie Hazel 3-18-1880 (3-19-1880) L B
Tusley, David to Frances Skinner 6-22-1867 G B
Tuter, John F. to Elizabeth Kinsey 9-13-1842 (9-15-1842) G
Tuttle, Nathan W. to Elizabeth Ann Riddle 2-2-1826 Hr
Tweady, Asa to Alean Nunn 2-8-1869 Hy
Twedle, A. to Mary Jane Riplett 7-10-1863 Sh
Tweedle, Alexander to Mary Leggett 2-20-1844 Sh
Tweedle, James to Amanda Gray 9-15-1857 (9-27-1857) O
Twigg, Jacob M. to Minerva Meritt 3-23-1850 (3-26-1850) G
Twigg, Thomas to Mary A. East 1-30-1855 We
Twisdale, D. M. to Miss Jane Huison? 12-12-1865 (12-13-1865) T
Twitty, Marion to Virginia W. Curley 9-16-1847 Sh
Twitty, Wm. to Nancy M. Burress 8-19-1851 Sh
Twohig, Ptrick to Bridget Sullivan 11-12-1861 Sh
Twyman, J. K. to Naomi Norris 12-19-1881 L
Tyas, June to Mary Gaither 3-6-1886 (12-30-1886) L
Tyas, T. J. to Lucy Scott 4-18-1878 L B
Tybass, William E. to Amelia A. Moody 4-5-1859 We
Tycen, George W. to Msary Barnes no date (with 1862) T
Tycen, Robert E. to Martha Flanakin 10-3-1857 T
Tycer, ____ to Anne? McCraw 5-18-1863 T
Tyer, Wm. S. to Sarah Wright 3-11-1877 Hy
Tyler, Alfred to Ann Janes 12-24-1865 Hn
Tyler, David C. to Celia A. Askew 3-1-1869 F
Tyler, E. W. to Nancy J. Kail 8-26-1870 Hy
Tyler, Gabriel S. to Steve Johnston 3-18-1833 (3-19-1833) G
Tyler, Gary to Margaret Dickson 6-27-1865 G
Tyler, Geo. to Anna Clay 10-13-1864 Sh
Tyler, George to Betsey Willson 1-2-1869 F B
Tyler, H. A. to Amanda Kirkland 12-19-1866 Hn
Tyler, H. A. to Bettie Fowlkes 4-1-1868 (4-2-1868) Dy
Tyler, Hugh to Elizabeth A. Stephens 8-20-1846 Hn
Tyler, J. B. to Mary E. Stephens 6-29-1864 (6-30-1864) O
Tyler, James to Mollie Campbell 3-18-1879 (3-19-1879) L B
Tyler, John to Sarah Lane 1-16-1855 (1-17-1855) Sh
Tyler, Mark to Mary Jane Watson 5-12-1879 Dy
Tyler, Miles F. to Laurey F. Olive 1-5-1864 Hn
Tyler, Miles F. to Susan B. Chance 12-14-1852 Hn
Tyler, Nerv to Harriet Fisher 12-27-1867 Hy
Tyler, Peter to Lanie Campbell 10-25-1874 Hy
Tyler, Richard C. to Martha Bell 10-28-1858 G
Tyler, Richard L. to Mary W. Donaldson 1-22-1850 (2-5-1850) O
Tyler, Wm. M. to Martha E. Bridger 10-27-1859 Hy
Tylor, John H. to Maryt Bloys 4-24-1849 (5-14-1849) O
Tylor, John W. to Mary Bloys 4-24-1849 O
Tylor, Richard L. to Mary W. Dollerson 1-22-1850 (2-5-1850) O
Tyner, J. W. to Lucinda Barnes 12-8-1847 Be
Tyner, James M. D. to Elizabeth Cora Dillian 3-23-1858 Be
Tyner, Jessee to Frances Watson 12-22-1841 (12-23-1841) G
Tyner, Thomas to Lucinda Douglass 7-14-1847 Be
Tynsen, Alexander to Catharine Skelly 4-26-1858 (4-27-1858) Sh
Tyre, David W. to Mary J. Joyner 1-29-1860 Cr
Tyre, William S. to Lavenia King 11-12-1846 Sh
Tyre, Zachariah to Mary Elizabeth McCraw 2-9-1842 T
Tyree (Tyne?), C. H. to Mollie E. Dance 12-19-1866 G
Tyree, George to Jennie Smith 2-24-1868 G B
Tyrell, Michael to Mary Ryan 6-11-1853 (6-12-1853) Sh
Tysen, Enoch to Mary Stewart 12-23-1870 Hy
Tyson, B. B. to B. P. Pryor 12-23-1867 O
Tyson, Benj. P. to Mary V. Bledsoe 10-27-1859 (10-26?-1859) G
Tyson, Eddie A. to Bettie Owen 2-7-1877 Hy
Tyson, Gaither to Fannie Meriwether 12-11-1866 (12-12-1866) Ma
Tyson, James E. to Mary Elizabeth Miles 10-27-1855 (11-1-1855) O
Tyson, James R. to Elizabeth M. Beard 12-18-1848 Hn
Tyson, Joel S. to Martha E. Lowin? 11-4-1844 Hn
Tyson, John A. to Ann Jane Cartmell 2-1-1843 (2-2-1843) Ma
Tyson, Johnson B. to Mary M. Alston 6-27-1849 (6-28-1849) Ma
Tyson, Reuben to Exaline Boyt 7-30-1831 (8-4-1831) G

Tyson, Samuel to Sarah Sparks 1-8-1845 Cr
Tyson, W. F. to Elmira J. Thomason 4-2-1867 Hn
Tyson, William A. to Mary A. Beard 9-22-1852 Hn
Tyson, William R. to Ann E. Rutledge 11-13-1845 (11-16-1845) G
Tyson, William to Elizabeth Parish 4-10-1857 Hn
Tytus, Henry to Catherine Jennings 6-13-1868 L B
Tytus, Henry to Fannie Parr 3-7-1883 (3-15-1883) L
Tytus, T. J. to Sabre Fuller 9-30-1877 (not executed) L
Tyus, B. S. to F. V. Jarrett 2-2-1872? Hy
Tyus, Clarance to Febby Byars 3-5-1875 Hy
Tyus, David to Angeline Marr 4-30-1870 Hy
Tyus, Doc to Mary Jane Beard 2-24-1880 (2-25-1880) L
Tyus, Ed to _____ 10-26-1875 Hy
Tyus, Esquer to Winnie Pettie 2-21-1872 Hy
Tyus, Green to Martha Capell 12-24-1867 Hy
Tyus, Haskin to Louisa Pilly? 1-26-1875 L
Tyus, Henry to Virginia Tyus 12-6-1873 Hy
Tyus, Isaac to Liza Graves 9-16-1869 Hy
Tyus, Jack to Rose Bond 2-1-1872 Hy
Tyus, James to Ida Bradford 12-29-1869 Hy
Tyus, John E. to Fanny M. Jarratt 11-29-1865 Hy
Tyus, John to Daphne Glenn 12-18-1878 L B
Tyus, Lawrence to Ellen Jarrett 12-24-1871 Hy
Tyus, Lawrence to Mary Winn 4-16-1883 (no return) L
Tyus, Louis to Frances Ridley 9-1-1876 (no return) L
Tyus, Nelson to Adeline Mann 10-11-1867 Hy
Tyus, Peter to Elizabeth Thompson 10-12-1869 Hy
Tyus, Taylor to Chaney Marley 12-13-1872 (12-19-1872) L
Tyus, Wm. B. to Zula Belle Johnson 3-29-1876 Hy
Tyus, Wm. to Virginia Stanton 3-18-1877 Hy

Udaley, Andrew to Jane Rogers 12-23-1841 G
Umback, John to Annette Peker 3-28-1861 (4-7-1861) Sh
Umphery, David to Narsissa Kelly 1-24-1852 Cr
Umphlett, John to Rachell W. Croom 6-4-1853 (no return) F
Umphrey, Henry to Martha Blythe 2-29-1844 Sh
Umphries, Silvester to Mary Ann Daily (Danby?) 6-17-1854 (7-12-1854) Sh
Umpstead, Edgmere? to Catharine Adams 1-24-1868 (no return) Cr
Umstard, William D. to Martha W. Shelton 1-4-1847 G
Umstead, Daniel to Louise Hill 4-12-1856 Cr
Umstead, Paul to Catherine Jones 1-30-1850 Cr
Umstead, Wilie to Mary P. Campbell 10-3-1833 G
Umsted, John to Nancy A. Shane 12-6-1858 (12-7-1858) G
Umsted, M. B. to S. V. Graves 11-21-1866 G
Underhill, John to Elizabeth Tate 1-15-1862 Sh
Underhill, W. D. to Sarah Bartlett 10-18-1854 We
Underwood, A. S. to Sarah J. Nuckles 12-13-1843 (12-14-1843) G
Underwood, Abel V. to Malissa Moore 12-2-1857 Hn
Underwood, Benjamin F. to Julia Sammons 4-5-1854 O
Underwood, C. to Mary F. Durnay 6-27-1863 (6-28-1863) O
Underwood, Charles to Susan Jane Gailor 2-27-1878 Hy
Underwood, David N. to Julia Ann Underwood 5-2-1863 Hn
Underwood, David to Amanda C. Alexander 1-17-1850 Hn
Underwood, David to Susan Bushart 1-27-1864 Hn
Underwood, Edmund G. to Lucy J. Boswell 1-17-1853 Ma
Underwood, Edward to Malinda C. Reynolds 12-23-1868 L
Underwood, F. H. to Sarah J. Wade 10-1-1867 Hn
Underwood, G. J. to Anna Keltner 11-19-1884 (11-20-1884) L
Underwood, G. V. to M. A. Winters 3-16-1871 (3-17-1871) O
Underwood, Granville to Mary A. Brockwell 10-21-1867 O
Underwood, H. F. to Caroline Crawford 1-2-1861 We
Underwood, Henry to Mary Lowry 8-30-1880 L B
Underwood, Hickman F. to Caroline Crawford 1-1-1861 (no return) We
Underwood, J. A. to Caroline Scarborough 12-25-1838 (12-27-1838) O
Underwood, J. R. to C. D. Crihfield 3-31-1880 L
Underwood, J. N. to E. J. Isbell 6-30-1863 (7-2-1863) O
Underwood, James A. to I.(J?S?) E. Elder 3-2-1885 (3-4-1885) L
Underwood, James H. to Sarah A. Emerson 12-17-1860 (no return) Hn
Underwood, James to Mary S. Hughes 10-7-1856 We
Underwood, Jeremiah E. to Morning E. Rudd 10-10-1852 We
Underwood, John to Elvery Nasbitt 3-28-1867 G
Underwood, John to Nancy Bevill 12-26-1850 Hn
Underwood, M.K. to F. A. Luton 10-4-1884 (10-5-1884) L
Underwood, Matthew to Julia Welch 12-4-1862 Hn
Underwood, R. C. to Emeline Myers 11-4-1842 Hn
Underwood, Robt. H. to A. E. Alexander 12-8-1875 (12-16-1875) O
Underwood, Thomas F. to Cincinnatti T. Harpool 2-27-1869 (3-4-1869) O
Underwood, Thomas to Mary (Mrs.) Edmondson 9-26-1849 Sh
Underwood, Thos. G. to Marinda Thomas 8-16-1848 Sh
Underwood, W. A. to Cornelia Holmes 10-20-1870 G
Underwood, W. L. to Margarett Myres 11-5-1838 (11-6-1838) F
Underwood, W. S. to Mary J. Linden 3-15-1855 We
Underwood, Wm. to Sarah Waters 12-14-1877 (12-20-1877) Dy
Unthank, James H. to Mary Bell Neely 7-24-1855 Hr
Upchurch, Bayliss H. to Surania A. Simmons 10-6-1859 Hn
Upchurch, C. H. to Annie Bardell 2-2-1860 (2-3-1860) Sh
Upchurch, Calvin to Adaline Jackson 2-24-1873 (2-26-1873) T

Upchurch, David to Martha Glover 11-7-1851 Hn
Upchurch, David to Tabitha Jenkins 6-1-1849 (no return) Hn
Upchurch, F. M. to Ann Eliza F. Greene 12-14-1858 Hn
Upchurch, F. M. to M. E. Jones 1-21-1864 (no return) Hn
Upchurch, James W. to Sallie J. Yarbroh 2-18-1861 T
Upchurch, James to Caron H. Rumley 4-3-1842 Hn
Upchurch, Jameson to Matilda Williams 10-9-1862 Be
Upchurch, John F. to Martha Ann Wynns 2-14-1855 Hn
Upchurch, John to Ellen Taylor 1-20-1866 (1-21-1866) T
Upchurch, John to Jane Hill 7-20-1867 (7-21-1867) T
Upchurch, John to Margaret Jackson 1-2-1869 O
Upchurch, Overton to Sarah Smith 1-13-1850 Hn
Upchurch, Ovid to Mary J. Blakemore 12-22-1867 Hn B
Upchurch, P. Green to Ann Elmore 10-16-1873 T
Upchurch, Reuben to Clementine Jackson 7-17-1852 O
Upchurch, Rubinn to Julia L. Jenkins 1-22-1860 Hn
Upchurch, Seth to Frances Evans 3-24-1867 Be
Upchurch, Thomas A. to Catherine Arnold 10-8-1865 Hn
Upchurch, W. G. to Julia Clark ?-21-1861 (1-20-1861) T
Upchurch, Wesby to Lucy Bradford 12-26-1867 Hn B
Upchurch, William to Lucy A. Jackson 2-26-1845 Hn
Updegraff, Joseph H. to Sarah T. Akin 9-18-1848 Sh
Upshaw, James R. to Bettie W. Eppes 5-5-1856 (5-6-1856) Sh
Upshaw, John to Sarah Cotner 5-5-1845 Hn
Upshaw, John to Temperance Randle 8-23-1842 Hn
Upshaw, Lindsey to Amanda Hardin 6-6-1868 G B
Uptegrove, Nathanel F. to Martha Faulden 12-2-1847 Cr
Uptegrove, Wm. C. to Elizabeth Chambers 4-16-1845 Cr
Uptigrove, Elisha to Adaline Smith 6-24-1860 Be
Upton, A. I. to S. C. Blankenship 8-31-1867 O
Upton, A. J. to S. C. Blankenship 8-31-1867 O
Upton, D. M. to Mary S. Gilbert 11-15-1865 Hn
Upton, Edward to Susan Malugin 1-17-1872 T
Upton, George W. to Martha J. Parlow 7-1-1867 (7-17-1867) Ma
Upton, George W. to Mary F. Clymor 5-26-1860 (5-27-1860) O
Upton, James to Sarah Welborne 12-1-1864 O
Upton, John D. to Elizabeth Gilbert 5-18-1852 Hn
Urbey, William H. to Caroline J. Kellison 12-20-1861 We
Urguhart, A. to Mary A. McDonaugh 11-5-1859 Hn
Urguhart, Edmond to Henrietta Thompson Blood 10-7-1864 (10-12-1864) Sh
Ursery (Ussery?), John to Susan Tedington 9-25-8170 G
Ursery, Calvin to Elizabeth Hutchins 12-20-1844 (12-19?-1844) F
Ursery, Dempsey to Emily Johnson 3-22-1852 (3-23-1852) Ma
Ursery, Jno. M. to Mahala A. Jordan 1-13-1869 Ma
Ursery, John Harvey to Sarah Hogan 8-22-1866 Ma
Ursery, William H. to Fannie Dixon 9-13-1867 (9-15-1867) Ma
Ursery, William to Abigail F. Mason 8-3-1837 (8-3-1847?) Ma
Usery, John W. to Mary E. Usery 9-24-1870 (9-27-1870) Ma
Usher, William to N. C. Hankins 1-17-1835 (1-22-1835) Hr
Using, George to Lucy Eastwood 10-16-1839 Ma
Usrey, Nathan to Lucinda Seay 4-9-1846 Sh
Ussery, Noah R. to Martha Jane Beavers 12-20-1852 (1-4-1853) Hr
Ussery, Persan to Alsa Pullam 2-7-1840 Hr
Ussy(Ussery?), John D. to Elizabeth Bailey 2-8-1848 (2-17-1848) Hr
Utley, Albert to Rebecca A. Thornton 10-2-1853 Be
Utley, Andrew J. to Judd D. Thomas 9-10-1850 Be
Utley, B. L. to Frances Camp 3-23-1851 Be
Utley, Burrell W. to Mary C. Hellard 12-11-1855 (12-12-1855) Ma
Utley, Charles to Tilla Martin 7-23-1870 G B
Utley, Columbus to Sarah Estus 12-23-1873 L
Utley, F. M. to M. P. Cusick 2-17-1881 (2-28-1881) L
Utley, F. M. to T. A. Utley 2-5-1867 Hy
Utley, G. W. to Elizabeth V. Camp 8-29-1860 Be
Utley, George to Bettie Clay 8-29-1872 Cr
Utley, J. A. R. to M. J. Lee 11-24-1870 Cr
Utley, J. B. to M. P. Scruggs 5-30-1873 (no return) Cr
Utley, J. H. to Martha J. Flatt 10-28-1862 Mn
Utley, James A. to Martha E. Fox 1-1-1853 Cr
Utley, Jonathan to Lucinda D. Oliver 5-23-1846 Ma
Utley, Joseph S. to Perline Duncan 5-14-1849 (5-17-1849) Ma
Utley, L. J. to Uphemia Pickins 4-27-1870 Hy
Utley, M. V. to Sarah P. Gossett 9-26-1867 Be
Utley, Ned to Amy Lucas 1-4-1869 (1-8-1869) Cr
Utley, Panes T. to Susan C. Alexander 2-8-1841 Ma
Utley, Samuel J. to Elizabeth E. Flatt 12-10-1865 Mn
Utley, Saunders to Nancy Robertson 1-14-1834 G
Utley, T. J. to Martha J. Glover 8-19-1861 Mn
Utley, Thos. B. to Ellen Woolfolk 11-3-1868 (11-4-1868) Ma
Utley, William H. to Emaline Farror 9-21-1852 Be
Utley, Wm. to Julet A. Portis 11-17-1848 Cr
Utterback, A. P. to Jane Smith 10-15-1857 Hn
Utterback, John L. to M. A. Curd 9-17-1851 Hn
Uzzell, Elisha T. to Susan Towns 1-31-1834 Sh

Vaccaro, Frank to Natina Maelatesta 4-8-1859 (4-12-1859) Sh
Vaccaro, John B. to Mary questa 4-2-1861 (4-7-1861) Sh
Vaccaro, Lewis to Alice Wildberger 8-29-1855 Sh

Vaden, D. D. to Martha Parr 7-29-1856 G
Vaden, D. D. to Polly Davis 3-11-1854 G
Vaden, Henry C. to Eliza E. Woodrum 11-6-1862 G
Vaden, Henry C. to Louiza J. Hailey 1-11-1860 G
Vaden, Joseph L. to Mary P. McLeary 1-16-1867 G
Vaden, R. W. to Eugenia E. Gaines 12-1-1868 L
Vaden, Richard S. to Cyntha I. Boon 12-16-1845 G
Vaden, T. J. to H. J. Reaves 5-21-1881 (no return) L
Vaden, William to Sarah A. Thomas 5-16-1855 We
Vail, George to Mary Lions 6-22-1852 (6-24-1852) G
Vail, I.J. N. to D. E. Bettis 8-5-1871 (no return) Dy
Vail, R. M. to M. E. Moore 10-25-1871 (10-26-1871) L
Vail, Robert to Teresa Griffin 6-13-1845 Sh
Vail, Rowan H. to Martha Hooper 6-18-1850 (no return) L
Vail, Travis P. to Nancy Jane Damson-Damron-Dawson 12-11-1848 (12-26-1848) Hr
Vail, W. M. to D. A. Timmes? 12-19-1878 Dy
Vails, Samuel jr. to Eliza Jane Roberts 3-28-1844 Hr
Vails, William to Sarah Blunt 1-18-1842 (1-23-1842) Hr
Valentine, B. G. to Sarah Jane Welch 9-7-1856 Hn
Valentine, Henry to Rebecca C. Thomas 10-2-1846 We
Valentine, Henry to Sarah E. Dibrell 3-4-1850 (3-6-1850) G
Valentine, Hiram to Eliza S. Jones 4-16-1851 Hn
Valentine, James B. to Malissa J. Weathers 3-8-1842 Hn
Valentine, Janes to Mary Jane Webb 9-8-1853 (9-11-1853) Ma
Valentine, Thomas J. to Mariah Tyson 7-3-1857 (no return) Hn
Valentine, Thomas S. to Missouri E. Taylor 12-23-1860 Hn
Valentine, W. T. to Nancy Jane Gross 7-21-1865 T
Valentine, William T. to Lucy Ann Holiman 7-1-1846 O
Vales (Voles?), Live (Levi?) to Harriet Carter 5-15-1854 Sh
Vales, W. S. to M. M. Meter 1-10-1876 (1-20-1876) L
Vallen, Andrew J. to Aly A. Kemp 2-8-1859 We
Vamer, Adgion M. to Mary Ann Warren 11-26-1864 (11-27-1864) Sh
Van Buren, Martin to Isabella Roberts 12-27-1870 (12-29-1870) F B
Van Buren, Martin to Marie White 8-12?-1868 T
Van Campber, Cornelius to Eleanor Waley 6-28-1848 Sh
Van Davelt?, M. to Caroline Field 1-18-1871 (1-19-1871) T
Van Eaton, R. N. to E. Holmes 12-30-1869 G
Van Gilder, John W. to Louisa A. Massey 9-11-1849 Sh
Van Pelt, John W. to Sarah Ann Bounds 9-7-1840 (9-24-1840) F
Van Pelt, William to Daruishia Belmont Jones 7-22-1868 (7-17?-1868) Ma
Van Rinkel, Jojada S. to Eva Huligens 5-14-1864 Sh
Van, Charley to Harriet Haselett 5-15-1868 (no return) F B
VanLien, Henry Clay to Hannah Jane Foster 6-15-1848 (6-24-1848) T
VanWagener, J. W. to Annie T. Wolfe 10-29-1855 Sh
Vanallstine, R. B. to Mollie Clark 3-5-1878 (3-6-1878) L
Vance, Andrew to Nancy M. Haynis 12-9-1850 Sh
Vance, F. M. to T. R. Orsborn 9-26-1867 O
Vance, Hezekiah to Mary Newsom 10-23-1869 (10-29-1869) F B
Vance, Martin to Mary Jane Calhoun 12-31-1844 O
Vance, jr., William to Frances C. W. Winchester 10-4-1846 Sh
Vancleave, James A. to Angeline Vice 12-23-1866 Hn
Vancleave, James E. to Amanda P. Carver 7-24-1868 (7-26-1868) Cr
Vancleave, John B. to Narissa C. Rice 5-23-1858 Hn
Vancleave, R. W. to Susan Jackson 10-4-1855 Hn
Vancleave, Wm. H. to Mary J. Carver 4-1-1869 Cr
Vandal, Washington G. to Sarah S. Young 11-25-1846 Sh
Vanderbilt, Mark to Amanda Jane Smith 10-23-1845 T
Vanderbilt, Mark to Amanda Jordan 11-14-1854 (11-15-1854) L
Vandergrift, Wm. H. to Rebecca Wright 3-14-1861 Sh
Vanderpool, Samson to Arilia D. Rogers 5-26-1842 (5-29-1842) F
Vanderville, T. J. to M. A. Porter 10-18-1858 (10-19-1858) Sh
Vandike, Calvin A. to Ellenor B. Wingate 8-4-1859 Hy
Vandike, Robert A. to Mahala A. J. Hays 4-29-1868 Hy
Vandyck, Adam to Mary McCampbell 9-11-1866 Hn B
Vandyke, William to Sarah J. Martin 10-14-1852 (no return) Hn
Vaneaton, B. S. to Sarnisa Huie 3-13-1860 (3-14-1860) G
Vanhog, Hugh to Elvy Fletcher 12-31-1840 G
Vanhog, John to Ann N. Brightwell 12-6-1852 (12-7-1852) G
Vanhog, J. S. to Cornelia D. Malone 2-12-1862 Hn
Vanhook, Jacob E. to Nancy S. Whitlow 11-19-1844 Ma
Vanhook, John T. to Frances Tuttle 7-22-1849 Hn
Vanhook, Jon S. to Elizabeth E. Smith 4-26-1851 Hn
Vanhook, Solomon W. to E. K. Williams 1-25-1871 Ma
Vann, J. C. to Sue M. Fuller 10-28-1868 (11-29-1868) Dy
Vann, James S. to Eliza Gregory 8-30-1846 (no return) F
Vann, Valentine to Susan A. Robinson 1-3-1855 (1-4-1855) Ma
Vannoy, R. B. to Nancy A. Hampton 12-7-1864 O
Vanpelt, Israel to Susan Crawford 11-29-1870 (12-20-1870) F B
Vanpelt, William to Nancy Emily Jones 7-28-1866 (7-29-1866) Ma
Vanpelt, Wm. T. to Eliza Roffner? 9-27-1844 F
Vantrease, Valentine to Rebecca B. Baskwell 1-13-1851 Hr
Vantreece, Benj. F. to S. C. (Mrs.) Adams 1-15-1867 (1-17-1867) Ma
Vantrees, William to Martha A. Nanny 4-16-1850 (4-17-1850) Ma
Vantreese, Benjamin F. to Elizabeth Weaks 9-29-1852 G
Vantreese, John to Nancy Hicks 10-2-1847 (10-6-1847) Ma
Vantreese, Thomas to Jane Williams 1-31-1855 (2-1-1855) Ma

Vantreese, William C. to Sabetha W. Lovelace 6-8-1840 (6-10-1840) Ma
Vantreese, Wm. A. to Mary Ann Williams 12-8-1866 (12-20-1866) Ma
Vantress, William to Mary A. Stone 4-22-1848 (4-26-1848) Ma
Vantresse, John to Tebitha D. Pool 12-25-1840 Hr
Vantrice, William to Martha I. Hayley 1-10-1845 (SB 1843?) Ma
Vanwinkle, William to Margaret Mitchel 2-27-1843 Sh
Varden, Lafayett to Rebecca Elender Gill 5-23-1854 G
Varner, J. F. to Lucy Purvis 11-8-1870 Hy
Varner, John W. to Deborah J. Battle 3-11-1852 G
Varner, William A. to Frances Martin 4-19-1849 G
Vasser, William V. to Mary A. M. Anderson 8-10-1846 Sh
Vasser?, George H. to Frances E. P. Williams 1-13-1851 Sh
Vastbinder, Samuel to Laura Farce 11-9-1874 Hy
Vaugh, G. B. to Susan Fields 10-1-1858 Cr
Vaugh, Wm. G. to Mary E. Wright 3-28-1855 Cr
Vaughan, Craddock to Mary Margaret McCoy 1-20-1846 (1-21-1846) T
Vaughan, Edward to Elizabeth C. Morgan 10-26-1854 We
Vaughan, George to Delila Norman 1-15-1842 (1-16-1842) Hr
Vaughan, Gilbert to Renetta Somervill 3-24-1869 T
Vaughan, Henry to Mary Houseman 4-1-1866 (no return) Cr
Vaughan, J. A. to Elizabeth A. Motley 11-13-1848 Sh
Vaughan, J. A. to Sarrah J. White 6-28-1866 G
Vaughan, J. H. to Anne Colvin 9-7-1878 (9-8-1878) Dy
Vaughan, J. L. to M. H. Steward 12-15-1856 (12-17-1856) Hr
Vaughan, James D. to Martha Carter 12-4-1869 (12-5-1869) T
Vaughan, James L. to Parmelia Frances Young 9-6-1854 (9-7-1854) Sh
Vaughan, James T. to Isabella C. Hagler 6-2-1863 We
Vaughan, James to Caroline Winkle 9-10-1843 Sh
Vaughan, James to Martha Haily 3-11-1846 (no return) Hn
Vaughan, James to Melissa P. Wlkinson 11-9-1860 (11-11-1860) Hr
Vaughan, James to Selia Raynor 8-1-1868 (8-2-1868) L
Vaughan, Jas. L. to Martha C. Robinson 8-16-1851 Sh
Vaughan, John D. to Mary R. Loving 9-5-1866 Hy
Vaughan, John W. to Hattie Welch 12-11-1860 Sh
Vaughan, John to Jane Cooksey 3-2-1844 Hr
Vaughan, John to Maranda Haley 3-2-1845 Hn
Vaughan, L. M. to Hettie C. Arwood 9-24-1879 L
Vaughan, Louis to Ann Bond 10-31-1879 (11-11-1879) L B
Vaughan, Moses to Martha S. Smith 11-20-1865 (11-22-1865) T
Vaughan, Nat to Malinda Brown 12-10-1868 (no return) F B
Vaughan, Noah to Judy Taylor 12-26-1867 G B
Vaughan, Patrick to Julia Carter 2-22-1852 (2-23-1852) Sh
Vaughan, R. M. to Susan E. Williams 1-7-1856 Sh
Vaughan, Richard to Martha Allen 4-23-1870 Hy
Vaughan, Richard to Matilda P. Trotter 1-8-1840 (1-10-1840) F
Vaughan, Richd. to Sarah L. Downing 8-4-1868 T
Vaughan, S. H. C. to Mary E. Moody 11-24-1867 G
Vaughan, Sterling to Mary Cannon 8-14-1851 Hn
Vaughan, T. S. to Nancy M. Montgomery 9-7-1870 T
Vaughan, T. W. to Sarah Sanders 4-15-1865 (5-24-1865) T
Vaughan, Tobe to Carolinie Elder 8-7-1867 G
Vaughan, W. A. to Nancy E. Baucum 4-29-1861 G
Vaughan, William to Didama Cook 1-22-1828 (1-24-1828) Hr
Vaughan, William to Narissa Williams 8-13-1834 Sh
Vaughan, Wm. H. to M. E. Olive 9-10-1872 (9-11-1872) Dy
Vaughn, A. J. to F. A. Alexander 8-5-1855 We
Vaughn, Alexander H. to Fanny Bradford 4-7-1830 G
Vaughn, Benjamin to Giney Hamilton 4-16-1831 H
Vaughn, Ebenezer to Martha A. Pearce 3-29-1856 (no return) Hn
Vaughn, Henry to Mariah Jackson 12-26-1867 T
Vaughn, James M. to C. V. Strickland 1-2-1878 (1-4-1878) L
Vaughn, James to Sarah Burnett 4-26-1855 Hr
Vaughn, Joel B. to Susan Jane Spencer 2-11-1858 G
Vaughn, John W. to Frances A. Parr 12-21-1843 Sh
Vaughn, John W.. to Elizabeth T. Ward 1-10-1861 Hn
Vaughn, John to Lethia Jamison 11-12-1870 T
Vaughn, John to Rebecca Jane Lester 7-22-1837 (7-23-1837) Hr
Vaughn, Josephus to Nancy M. Sumers 12-23-1856 We
Vaughn, Josephus to Sophia Alexander 11-6-1858 We
Vaughn, Melvill to Fannie Hall 3-9-1869 (3-11-1869) T
Vaughn, Nathaniel to Sisly Burk 3-18-1856 Hn
Vaughn, Peter A. to Mary E. Whitmore 12-18-1848 (1-2-1849) F
Vaughn, Peter to Elizabel? H. Hill 4-4-1867 T
Vaughn, Purcell C. to Sarah Nobles 1-10-1835 (1-13-1835) G
Vaughn, Richard to Mary L. Brooks 10-9-1838 Hn
Vaughn, Richmond to Leutitia Jiles 10-4-1873 T
Vaughn, Slarter to H. A. Costen 5-25-1856 We
Vaughn, Stephen to Matilda Stroud 7-11-1857 Hn *
Vaughn, T. M. to Martha Salmon 12-20-1865 Hn
Vaughn, Thomas to Sarah P. Gunter 7-4-1853 Sh
Vaughn, W. B. to Martha Dennie 12-24-1877 (12-25-1877) L
Vaughn, Walton H. to Frances Richardson 9-10-1832 (9-15-1832) Hr
Vaughn, William F. to Mary E. Pierce 4-2-1867 Hn
Vaughn, William to Arbelia Reden 1-2-1849 Hn
Vaughn, William to Elizabeth Davis 8-19-1858 G
Vaughn, William to Margaret Smith 2-10-1859 Hn
Vaughn, Wm. E. to Martha Mitchell 2-7-1853 (2-17-1853) Sh

Vaughn, Wm. F. to Mary A. E. Douglass 2-21-1866 Hy
Vaught, A. M. to Nancy Daughty 11-10-1856 G
Vaught, Bayless D. to Bennie Harper 4-2-1866 O
Vaught, L. C. to Rachel Wicker 12-1-1858 (12-2-1858) O
Vaught, Samuel F. to Mary Hood 7-6-1857 (7-22-1857) O
Vaught, T. K. to Sally Berry 2-21-1866 G
Vaughter, John L. to Ann Bishop 1-4-1859 Cr
Vaughter, Richard B. to Martha Ann Gregory 12-4-1854 (12-7-1854) Ma
Vaughter, Wat to Fannie Wilkes 5-7-1874 Hy
Vault, Stephen to Martha Gates 5-4-1846 (5-6-1846) Hr
Vaulx, Claiborne to Amanda Morris 7-2-1870 Hy
Vaulx, Hesekiah to Menervia Jeter 4-6-1872 Hy
Vaulx, Horace to Annie Miller 12-19-1878 Hy
Vaulx, Jackson to Mealey Colwell 12-13-1874 Hy
Vaulx, Jacob H. to America Litle 3-21-1878 Hy
Vaulx, John W. to Eliza J. Caldwell 5-31-1869 Ma *
Vaulx, John to Dovy Hart 5-13-1876 Hy
Vaulx, Stephen to Sila (Lila) Elder 8-16-1867 Hy
Vaulx, Thos. to Sarah Hughs 12-23-1867 Hy
Vauters, Thomas D. to Elen Priest 1-18-1865 Cr
Vawter, A. J. to Frances P. Rhodes 1-2-1866 (no return) Cr
Vawter, Robert to Sarah M. Crossett 1-11-1870 (no return) Cr
Vawter, T. D. to Nancy E. Coffman 12-24-1870 (12-25-1870) Cr
Vawter, Wm. H. to M. J. Harrell 1-2-1866 (1-3-1866) Cr
Vawton, R. L. to A. J. Rhodes 11-15-1869 (no return) Cr
Vaysor?, Mack to Cornelius Dobbins 4-16-1868 (no return) F B
Veach, F. B. to Lucy B. Williamson 12-30-1858 Be
Veach, S. J. to C. T. Burns 12-5-1853 (12-11-1853) O
Veach, Thomas to Unity Cole 1-7-1848 Be
Veal, Lafayette to Sarah R. Nabors 3-31-1863 (4-2-1863) Sh
Veasey, Robert L. to Caroline B. Bowden 11-22-1843 Hn
Veasey, Thomas B. to C. L. Patterson 1-29-1848 Hn
Veazey, B. F. to M. E. W. Williams 12-31-1869 G
Veazey, R. L. to Ann E. Pearce 11-29-1862 Hn
Veazey, William B. to Mary Ann Crowder 11-17-1844 (no return) Hn
Vedder, Nicholas J. to Mary Jane Hamilton 4-16-1837 Sh
Velasques, Claudius to Lee Ann Smith 7-30-1850 Sh
Velse, James to Mary Glenn 4-11-1848 Sh
Veltilla, Jeramiath to Mary E. Tully 3-11-1839 Cr
Venable, C. D. to Mary Kendall 2-1-1848 Hn
Venable, Ephraim S. to Sally Ann Holly 11-12-1861 Hn
Venable, J. B. to Sarah J. Ethridge 1-19-1854 Hn
Venable, Joseph B. to Hester Ann Bidwell 8-26-1856 Hn
Venable, Leander B. to Sarah R. Cowan 5-25-1843 Hn
Venable, Luther R. to Margaret Winns 3-14-1838 (no return) Hn
Vencir, Pleasant A. to Mary Hobbs 11-19-1849 (11-20-1849) G
Ventress, Amos to Susan Browder 12-29-1870 (12-31-1870) O B
Venturini, Daniel to F. A. Fransioli 1-5-1855 (1-7-1855) Sh
Venturini, David to Susan Berry (Beary?) 8-20-1853 Sh
Verhin, Isaac to Isabella F. Mathews 12-12-1850 O
Verhine, Augustus to Martha F. Roland 8-28-1866 (8-29-1866) O
Verhine, E. H. to Martha P. Guinn 3-5-1866 (3-8-1866) O
Verhine, Elisha Howard to Mary E. Mitchell 10-21-1845 O
Verhine, Everett H. to Rebecca Carter 4-9-1839 O
Verhine, Isaac to Margaret M. Wilson 12-12-1853 (12-15-1853) O
Verhine, John D. to Emily Green 3-2-1859 (3-3-1859) O
Verhine, John D. to Nancy Cullum 1-5-1846 (1-25-1846) O
Verhines, S. D. to Z. T. Turner 1-28-1873 (1-29-1873) O
Vermillon, F. M. to Eliza A. Dement 12-28-1858 We
Verner, J. H. to M. J. (Mrs.) Latta 2-26-1866 G
Vernon, A. P. to Martha Lethers 6-29-1844 (7-4-1844) Hr
Vernon, E. F. to Elizabeth Givens 6-4-1884 (6-8-1884) L
Vernon, E. F. to L. J. Strange 9-11-1878 (9-16-1878) L
Vernon, E. F. to Tennessee Bell Holden 12-26-1885 (12-29-1885) L
Vernon, E. R. (Dr.) to Sallie Clark 12-25-1867 Dy
Vernon, John E. to Mary E. Wesson 9-22-1871 (9-25-1871) Dy
Vernon, Pryor L. to Sarah Robinson 9-27-1852 Hr
Vernon, Tho. to Easther Kelly 3-19-1837 (3-26?-1837) Hr
Vernon, William to Elizabeth Gossett 3-12-1850 Be
Verser, Calvin C. to Annie M. Conner 11-10-1885 L
Verser, John L. to Mary A. Dickason 11-23-1846 (11-24-1846) F
Verser, Wm. A. to Jane Broom 10-1-1841 F
Vesperman, Henry to Malam Zouk 7-20-1863 Sh
Vesser, Calvin C. to Mary E. Day 9-30-1867 Ma
Vest, LeeRoy to Sarah A. Wassen 2-14-1856 Sh
Vest, William to N. A. Ross 7-29-1870 (8-4-1870) F
Vestal, James W. to Amanda Jane Barr 9-17-1867 (9-18-1867) Ma
Vestal, Thos. N. to Demaris Starrett 1-1-1845 (1-2-1845) F
Vester, David Y. to Pheby Melton 2-1-1849 Be
Vester, J. H. to Elizabeth Ann Benton 7-4-1844 Be
Vetetoe, J. W. to Melissa McDonnel 8-5-1861 Mn
Via, Pleasant to Louisa A. Webb 11-14-1876 Dy
Via, Rufus A. to Mary J. Blankenship 1-16-1856 G
Via, Stephen A. to Nancy J. Jarrett 7-19-1871 (no return) Dy
Via, William A. to Mary M. Key 11-5-1855 (11-7-1855) G
Viar, John N. to Nancy M. E. Younger 10-24-1860 (10-25-1860) Cr
Viar, R. F. to Martha E. Pitts 8-22-1866 (8-23-1866) Dy

Viar, Thomas to Melissa E. Viar 11-16-1865 (no return) Dy
Vican, John A. to Jennie Williams 6-6-1879 (6-15-1879) Dy
Vicary, John to Margaret Williams 1-11-1851 Sh
Vick, A. R. to Sarah J. West 10-21-1859 F
Vick, Allen P. to Elvira G. Sykes 10-27-1869 (10-28-1869) Ma
Vick, Americus to Susanah Pafford 3-23-1848 Be
Vick, Howel to Martha A. Pinington 1-6-1846 G
Vick, John T. to Lucy M. Belote 11-15-1851 (no return) F
Vick, John to Celia Marshall 3-7-1859 Cr
Vick, Joshua S. to Susan Castles 1-22-1845 Ma
Vick, Josiah to Ester E. Waldrope 1-3-1851 (1-9-1851) G
Vick, Nathan to Sarah Prewitt 1-5-1843 Ma
Vick, Wm. S. to Susan A. Brimingham 11-16-1864 Dy
Vicker, John to Martha Brantley 12-16-1842 (12-22-1842) Hr
Vickers, ?. S. to C. Morrell 1-1-1852 Cr
Vickers, A. N. to Mary Y. Vickers 6-25-1857 Cr
Vickers, Benj. C. to Sallie Houston 4-16-1862 Sh
Vickers, David C. to Mary A. Darnall 3-4-1863 Cr
Vickers, David C. to Mary A. Darnall 3-4-1863 (no return) Cr
Vickers, E. M. to K. J. Forest 11-7-1861 Mn
Vickers, G. W. to N. E. Bennett 10-6-1858 Cr
Vickers, Hiram to Alice E. Western 5-29-1872 Hy
Vickers, James E. to Sarah Carroll 6-10-1839 G
Vickers, James to Jane Avant 12-23-1846 (12-24-1846) Hr
Vickers, John S. to L. A. Humphreys 4-9-1873 (4-10-1873) Cr
Vickers, Joseph G. to Laura E. Western 5-29-1872 Hy
Vickers, R. a. to Charlotte Swinney 1-8-1858 Cr
Vickers, Robert to Margarett Churchwell 12-23-1852 Cr
Vickers, Rufus to Martha B. Hicks 8-10-1854 Cr
Vickers, Thomas J. to Mary E. McCaslin 12-7-1867 (12-12-1867) Cr
Vickery, John B. to Mary Ann Peacock 2-27-1861 Hn
Vickery, Robert to Melinda Nichols 5-24-1838 Sh
Vicky, William H. to Delphia E. Hamm 1-10-1864 Mn
Victor, James W. to M. C. Mitchell 10-31-1864 Sh
Viers, William to Mary Disek (Disch) 9-28-1848 Sh
Viers, Wm. to Rebecca Locke 1-6-1853 Sh
Vigus, Albernon S. to Mary L. Pickett 10-13-1859 Sh
Vincen, John to Martha Ann Sergant 4-20-1873 Hy
Vincent, Abner to Abby McCall 12-7-1868 (12-20-1869?) T
Vincent, Amos to Mary Harris 9-21-1835 Sh
Vincent, B. to Eliza E. Jourdan 6-25-1840 Cr
Vincent, Benjamin D. to Elizabeth Felps 1-29-1868 (no return) Cr
Vincent, Charles to Polly Hayes 4-12-1834 Sh
Vincent, Geo. W. to Jane Hughes 7-14-1858 Hr
Vincent, J. M. to Nancy B. Moore 11-14-1868 G
Vincent, Jacob G. to Rebecca Robins 8-24-1843 We
Vincent, James to Gletha Smith 1-27-1842 (1-28-1842) G
Vincent, James to Sarah McAlilly 6-16-1867 G
Vincent, Jesse to Sarah Hicks 4-22-1855 Cr
Vincent, John A. to Mary M. Shelton? 2-14-1843 T
Vincent, John A. to Sarah A. Anderson 1-9-1850 Ma
Vincent, N. P. to Sarah J. Ball 3-10-1866 (no return) Dy
Vincent, Orren B. to Margaret A. Chambers 7-11-1861 We
Vincent, Peter to Nancy Maburn 1-3-1871 (1-14-1871) T
Vincent, Solimon to Lemess? Phillips 12-25-1867 T
Vincent, Thomas S. to Leonilla E. Gamewell 12-1-1869 Ma
Vincent, Uriah M. to Amanda M. Easterwood 1-6-1858 (1-7-1858) O
Vincent, William to Evaline Brown 9-26-1866 (9-27-1866) Ma
Vincent, William to Jane Dockins 7-23-1841 (7-28-1841) O
Vincent, William to Martha Kennedy 1-1-1871 T
Vincent, Willis to Sarah Davis 10-4-1855 Hr
Vincent, jr., Parsons to Henrietta Sellers 3-28-1838 Cr
Vines, Seaborn to Mary English 8-29-1860 (not executed) Sh
Vining, O. K. to Susan Jukes 12-13-1854 Sh
Vinsen, P. A. to Eldenor Campbell 11-30-1852 Cr
Vinsent, J. D. to Ella J. Hord 4-25-1864 Sh
Vinson, A. J. to Mill Lilly Livermore 10-6-1864 Sh
Vinson, Andrew to Margarett Moore 1-17-1872 (1-18-1872) Cr
Vinson, C. D. to Peneler Jackson 3-7-1866 O
Vinson, George to Sarah Hardin 6-24-1852 Ma
Vinson, Hiram C. to Martha Kendall 11-19-1844 F
Vinson, James M. to Matilda Chisolm 2-5-1842 (2-10-1842) Ma
Vinson, James R. to Elizabeth Diggs 1-31-1872 Cr
Vinson, Jas. H. to Addie Spradlin 10-3-1871 O
Vinson, L. to Sarah R. Hatchett 2-18-1844 Cr
Vinson, Monroe to Lucinda Smith 2-15-1871 L
Vinson, Thomas to Elizabeth Johnson 11-13-1848 (11-14-1848) G
Vinson, Thomas to Mary J. Fuller 1-2-1851 Cr
Vinson, Wm. to Elizabeth Lucus 12-2-1840 Cr
Vinston, Eli to Agness Cyle 8-23-1866 (8-26-1866) T
Vinyard, W. F.? to Nancy J. Humphreys 12-24-1868 (no return) Dy
Vioujas (Virugus?), Chas. Edmonds to M. Tourant 12-1-1859 Sh
Vire, M. R. to Ann Gammons 12-21-1866 (12-27-1866) Dy
Vires, William R. to M. J. Beard 10-29-1865 Mn
Viser, Wm. C. to Jane E. Watkins 6-25-1844 (no return) F
Vogts, George to Augusta Samse 9-18-1856 Sh
Volentine, B. G. to Sarah J. Gullage 12-23-1851 Hn

Volentine, Emery H. to Mary W. Gately 6-30-1848 Hn
Volentine, John R. to Elizabeth Cobb 5-24-1869 Ma
Volentine, Jon C. to Mary A. S. Taylor 4-18-1848 Hn
Volentine, Martin W. B. to Sarah C. Samford 12-24-1860 Hn
Volentine, Thomas to Sarah Norman 10-28-1853 Hn
Volkmar, C. F. to Belle Jenney? 12-9-1879 (12-9-1880?) L
Vollentine, Wesley to M. J. Graham 4-24-1869 O B
Von Negler, Henry to Mary F. Muller 12-24-1866 F
Voss, Ezekiel F. to Mary Jane Patterson 12-28-1847 (12-30-1847) L
Voss, J. T. to Ann E. Fisher 8-28-1857 (no return) L
Voss, J. W. W. to M. L. Voss 11-3-1883 (11-4-1883) L
Voss, John T. to Nancy E. Olds 2-6-1866 L
Voss, John to Ailcy Jordan 7-4-1877 (7-17-1877) L
Voss, John to Cally Hues 11-30-1874 (12-2-1874) L
Voss, John to Elizabeth M. McCauley 12-12-1849 T
Voss, John to Mary Ann Frances Haslip 9-12-1885 (9-13-1885) L
Voss, John to Sarah Smith 8-22-1853 L
Voss, John to Sintha Hughs 2-31-1869 Hy
Voss, Joseph to Sarah Jane Chrismus 4-15-1862 (4-17-1862) L
Voss, P. G. to Cornelia Ann Davis 8-12-1879 (8-13-1879) L
Voss, P. G. to Louisa Scallions 10-8-1873 (10-9-1873) L
Voss, R. W. to Julia A. Johnston 12-26-1882 (12-27-1882) L
Voss, S. J. to Margrate Childers 3-11-1876 (3-12-1876) L
Voss, T. E. to Emma E. Scott 12-28-1880 (12-29-1880) L
Voss, T. L. to Ema E. Emerson 5-11-1876 L
Voss, W. G. to Rebecca Salisbury 2-22-1881 (2-23-1881) L
Voss, Wilie to Emily Rainey 7-27-1858 (7-28-1858) L
Voss, Wm. J. to Sarah C. Walpole 3-18-1861 (3-19-1861) L
Voss, Zelmon to Elizabeth Parker 4-29-1857 Ma
Voss, Zilmon to Nancy Pewett 2-8-1855 L
Voss, jr., John to Rosa Wood 5-12-1877 Hy
Vowel, Nicholas to Henrietta E. Branch 2-23-1873 Hy
Vowell, Alfred W. to Matilda P. Hatler 10-17-1862 We
Vowell, Huston L. to Margaret J. Young 10-9-1862 We

Wachter, John George to Anna Shoenman 1-18-1856 (1-19-1856) Sh
Waddall, C. W. to M. C. Smith 8-21-1838 F
Waddel, Sneed to Mat Shirley 12-10-1878 Hy
Waddell, Alex P. to Isabella S. Miller 6-6-1853 (no return) F
Waddell, Buren B. to Fannie L. Tarver 6-9-1857 Ma
Waddell, Joe to Harriet Newburn 12-31-1865 Hy
Waddell, John C. to Elizabeth D. Bugg 8-15-1846 F
Waddell, Marcus to Apalipa (Assalissa?) Sturges 1-22-1853 (1-24-1853) Sh
Waddell, Phillip E. to Sarah E. Moore 11-5-1846 G
Waddell, Wm. to Ella Houston 2-8-1868 (no return) F B
Waddill, John E. to Fannie E. James 10-6-1869 (10-7-1869) Cr
Waddington, James to Fanny Patton 1-28-1875 (1-29-1875) O
Waddle, James W. to Amanda L. Gause 6-1-1861 Hy
Waddle, Samuel A. to Sarah C. Furgerson 12-20-1853 (12-21-1853) Sh
Waddle, Thomas to Sarah Wood 11-30-1847 Sh
Waddle, W. M. to Elizabeth A. Smith 2-8-1868 Cr
Waddle, Wm. E. to Susan H. Brach 2-4-1868 (2-5-1868) Cr
Waddley, Thomas J. to Mary Jones 7-30-1851 Hn
Waddy, Joseph K. to Virginia H. Vaden 9-20-1851 (9-24-1851) Sh
Waddy, Marion to Juddath D. Waddy 12-3-1860 O
Waddy, W. K. to Elizabeth W. Clark 9-5-1860 G
Waddy, William to Annie Turner 12-23-1871 (12-24-1871) Dy
Wade, Alex to Winey Jetton 6-16-1870 G
Wade, B. R. to Frances J. Harlen 2-18-1858 We
Wade, Edmond to Manna E. Ayers 7-30-1829? Hr
Wade, Edward to Rebecca Lacy 7-29-1829 Hr
Wade, Edwin to Manna Ayers 7-30-1832 (8-8-1832) Hr
Wade, G. N. to Marietta Mitchell 11-17-1866 O
Wade, G. R. to Jennie Apperson 11-23-1863 Sh
Wade, George to Basora McClaland 11-15-1854 (11-18-1854) Ma
Wade, George to L. Harper 3-7-1867 G
Wade, George to Mary (Mrs.) Everett 12-23-1867 G
Wade, Henry E. to Mary E. Terrence 10-24-1854 (no return) F
Wade, Hezekiah J. to Margaret J. Harper 2-13-1856 O
Wade, Isham to Lou Freeman 2-4-1869 G
Wade, J. E. to M. R. Crudup 8-20-1878 (8-21-1878) Dy
Wade, J. L. to Mattie McGee 9-14-1865 H
Wade, James T. to Frances A. Wade 12-24-1840 G
Wade, James to Frances C. McKaughan 5-13-1846 Hr
Wade, Jas. T. to Wealthy Clouse (Clove) 12-26-1850 Sh
Wade, John F. to Margarett Farmer 12-22-1870 (12-23-1870) F
Wade, John to Rebecca Lawson 3-22-1875 O
Wade, Joseph M. to Cintha A. Alexander 10-19-1839 Hn
Wade, Josiah L. to Martha A. Underwood 10-6-1853 (10-7-1853) G
Wade, Lemuel to Ellen Davis 11-22-1867 Hy
Wade, Lemuel to Siller Peebles 7-20-1868 Hy
Wade, Madison to Lucinda Payne 6-17-1869 G B
Wade, Michael to Mary Canford 12-13-1851 Sh
Wade, Osias to Bolsoa Vann 7-30-1855 Ma
Wade, R. A. to Martha E. Albritton 3-18-1862 Hn
Wade, R. C. to E. J. Felts 1-22-1855 (1-23-1855) G
Wade, R. D. to Mary A. Arnold 3-5-1868 Be

Wade, R. P. to Charlotte L. Jackson 12-20-1867 (12-28-1867) Dy
Wade, R. P. to Nancy J. Forshee 11-12-1868 Dy
Wade, Richard T. to Sarah J. Terrence 12-19-1853 (no return) F
Wade, Robert to Elizabeth Henderson 8-24-1847 Hn
Wade, Robert to Susan E. Catron 11-3-1857 (11-5-1857) O
Wade, Thomas to Nancy Hutchinson 1-29-1855 (1-30-1855) O
Wade, Thos. P. to Martha W. Freeman 11-4-1853 G
Wade, Tinzel to H. Mitchuer 1-20-1872 (1-21-1872) Dy
Wade, W. J. to Sallie Shaw 12-21-1871 Hy
Wade, W. W. to Nancy L. Vinson 9-27-1865 (9-28-1865) O
Wade, Washington H. to Mary C. Murry 5-9-1841 (5-18-1841) T
Wade, William E. to Elizabeth C. Davis 2-9-1832 G
Wade, William to Eliza E. Cooper 11-29-1866 Be
Wadkin, John S. to T. N. Hamilton 12-13-1839 Ma
Wadkins, Aaron to Mary D. Pierce 8-15-1861 Be
Wadkins, G. H. to M. A. Comton 6-1-1868 (6-4-1868) Cr
Wadkins, Hiram W. to Mary Jane Beasley 7-29-1846 We
Wadkins, Thomas to Sarah Frazier 2-16-1853 Sh
Wadkins, William C. to Angeline Griffin 9-27-1867 Hn
Wadkins, William to Mahaly Francisco 11-17-1853 Be
Wadkins, Willie B. to Ann E. Kincaid 4-14-1829 Ma
Wadley, Robert B. to Mary Ann Clark 9-12-1839 Cr
Wadley, William R. to Mary Jane Brower 10-15-1862 (10-19-1862) Ma
Wadlingford, John W. to Julia Anderson 1-31-1878 (2-3-1878) Dy
Wadlington, Ben C. to M. T. Enochs 9-24-1877 (9-27-1877) Dy
Wadlington, John to Sarah Jane Gravit 8-15-1859 (8-16-1859) Ma
Wafer, Leander to R. Ritter Clementine Lee 2-13-1855 G
Wagener, J. L. to S. B. Stafford 10-23-1866 (10-30-1866) F
Wages, W. W. to Mary A. Morgan 1-16-1866 G
Waggener(Wagner), Solomon to Mary Wilson 4-14-1834 Hr
Waggener, J. M. to Fannie R. Kirkland 10-17-1850 Sh
Waggener, J. N. to Fannie R. Kirkland 12-17-1860 Sh
Waggener, John H. to Sallie A. Cheeke 10-22-1851 Sh
Waggener, William to Caroline Angus 3-24-1866 T
Wagginer, Thomas to E. L. Crittendon 2-2-1852 (2-12-1852) O
Waggoner, Daniel jr. to Kassandre M. Farley 8-21-1842 Be
Waggoner, David to S. E. Cobb 10-22-1879 (10-23-1879) Dy
Waggoner, Fredrick to Martha Ann Rains 1-8-1863 Mn
Waggoner, G. W. to Angeline Chitwood 1-20-1869 (1-21-1869) Dy
Waggoner, George to Margaret C. Whitworth 4-26-1861 Ma
Waggoner, Henry G. to Sarah E. Baker 10-12-1856 We
Waggoner, John W. to Lucy Bradford 3-18-1862 Ma
Waggoner, John to Lean Owens 12-13-1864 Mn
Waggoner, Leonard to Jennie Green 12-13-1878 (12-18-1878) Dy
Waggoner, Peter to Emeline Pettigrew 4-13-1845 We
Waggoner, Richard to Sarah M. Dalning 3-13-1846 (no return) We
Waggoner, Stephen B. to Mary G. Whitworth 12-23-1856 Ma
Waggoner, T. H. to Jane Rainbo 11-14-1855 (no return) We
Waggoner, W. L. to J. C. Watkins 12-24-1873 Hy
Wagner, C. L. to Mollie Davis 12-21-1869 G
Wagner, Henry to Sarah C. Miller 10-26-1851 Hn
Wagner, Martin to Dinah Graves 8-24-1847 Sh
Wagner, Oliver C. to Joy Catherine Olive 6-20-1850 (no return) Hn
Wagoner, B. F. to Emerine Pots 4-20-1854 We
Wagoner, William to Jane Brooks 7-20-1865 Mn
Wagster, Crittenden to Kidy Jones 10-3-1838 O
Wagster, David S. to M. A. Bynum 12-31-1850 We
Wagster, J. H. to M. A. Snider 12-1-1868 We
Wagster, John A. to Parolee Carlton 3-30-1862 We
Wagster, John to S. C. Hunt 1-19-1864 G
Wagster, R. A. to S. E. Corley 2-28-1867 Dy
Wagster, R. W. to M. P. Ward 8-20-1877 (8-21-1877) L
Wagster, Rich D. to Bashly Smith 9-11-1845 We
Wagster, Richard to Amanda J. Cooper 12-31-1857 We
Wagster, S. L. to E. L. Conley (Corley?) 10-17-1869 G
Wagster, William to Elizabeth Crittenden 1-6-1843 Hn
Waher?, David to Mary Ann McCarty 1-21-1849 Hn
Wahl, Lewis to Harriett E. Thomas 3-7-1861 G
Wahls, George to Elizabeth P. Bagby 3-1-1871 (3-2-1871) Cr
Wain, John to Frances Fartherlain 8-12-1838 F
Wainright, Zachariah to Esper Ann Clement 1-3-1852 (7-8-1852) G
Wainscot, John W. to Nancy A. Hill 9-2-1856 We
Wainscott, William to Martha Wimberley 2-27-1843 Hn
Wainwright, A. J. to Martha E. Evans 4-14-1860 Hy
Wainwright, Charles to Cornelia Taylor 4-23-1866 (4-28-1866) F B
Wainwright, Crocket to Pena Steele 12-27-1866 Hy
Wainwright, Geo. F. to Sarah O. Limon? 1-4-1847 (1-13-1847) F
Wainwright, Z. to Amanda Montague 6-26-1870? Hy
Wainwright, Z. to C. M. Cook 11-28-1861 Hy
Wair, Wm. W. to Frances E. Fort 2-15-1841 (2-17-1841) Hr
Wakefield, August to Sallie Sawyers 4-17-1869 (4-18-1869) T
Wakefield, E. S. to Hannah Pate 7-20-1881 (no return) L
Wakefield, E. S. to Mary Nelson 12-11-1865 (12-12-1865) L
Wakefield, Ezekiel to Rebecca Hutchison 9-25-1841 (9-30-1841) L
Wakefield, Ezekiel to Sarah Williams 8-13-1846 L
Wakefield, Thomas A. to Nancy C. Haynes 1-19-1858 (1-20-1858) L
Wakefield, Thomas N. to D. M. Glimp 3-7-1871 (3-8-1870?) L

Wakefield, Thomas to Rebecca L. Williams 7-14-1849 (7-19-1849) L
Wakeland, Milton to Lucy Jane Forest 10-29-1840 Hn
Walbridge, Frederick G. to Amarillas Mitchell 6-29-1853 Sh
Walden, B. A. to Unity Cammond 10-3-1853 (no return) F
Walden, George I. to Louisa A. C. Rutherford 12-29-1830 (1-2-1831) Hr
Walden, Isaac to Laura Holcombe 10-29-1857 Hr
Walden, John E. to Lavina P. Crutchfield 1-30-1845 (no return) We
Walden, John F. to Ana E. Doyle 10-27-1862 (10-28-1862) Sh
Walden, Joseph to Sarah (Mrs.) Hall 1-13-1864 Sh
Walden, W. H. to M. M. V. Churchhill 11-7-1865 (11-9-1865) F
Walding, J. A. to C. J. Hughs 10-13-1868 Hy
Waldow, Charles to Frances Robins 7-5-1856 (7-6-1856) O
Waldran, Francis M. to Mathia (Martha) Kehoe 2-21-1845 Sh
Waldran, James S. to Eliza E. Rodgers 8-29-1850 Sh
Waldran, James S. to Malinda A. Neal 9-1-1853 Sh
Waldran, Jesey to Jane Corbitt 12-14-1852 (12-16-1852) Sh
Waldran, Jesse to Elizabeth H. Jones 12-13-1843 Sh
Waldran, William B. to Sabra Ann Cook 2-13-1840 Sh
Waldren, G. W. to Nancy J. Palmer 2-25-1875 Hy
Waldren, J. H. to Adaline Featherston 2-12-1873 (no return) Dy
Waldron, Henry to Mary G. Jones 1-3-1861 We
Waldron, J. W. to Mollie Wofford 1-1-1877 (1-4-1877) Dy
Waldrop, Alfred to Ann Jones 7-19-1838 Hn
Waldrop, B. to Georgia Hubbard 10-14-1875 O
Waldrop, Enoch D. to Martha A. Waldrop 7-12-1846 G
Waldrop, H. H. to Cathrine Bats 1-7-1863 Mn
Waldrop, J. W. to Louisa (Mrs.) Sanders 3-1-1865 G
Waldrop, John D. to Cordelia Beaver 7-27-1851 Hn
Waldrop, John D. to Susanna Peak 10-18-1842 Hn
Waldrop, John R. to Susan Harris 10-22-1845 (10-23-1845) G
Waldrop, Obadiah to Flavis Crass 10-9-1838 Hn
Waldrop, Presley to Charity Aslin 1-23-1856 G
Waldrop, Wiley A. to Julia Pounds 1-3-1846 (1-8-1846) G
Waldrop, jr., John Wesley to Lucy Jane Pounds 6-9-1867 G
Waldrum, Jno. W. to Martha J. Stratton 2-19-1867 O
Waldrum, John W. to M. A. Roney 3-2-1860 (3-8-1860) O
Waldrup, James R. to Harriet Ann Stegall 12-7-1867 (12-10-1867) Ma
Wales, James to Frances Craddick 10-1-1859 (10-2-1859) Sh
Wales, John Irvin to Susanna Jane Craddock 9-26-1859 (9-27-1859) Sh
Wales, William to Caroline (Mrs.) Cowgill 12-30-1863 (1-7-1864) Sh
Walis, John to Mary E. McCully 1-3-1853 (no return) F
Walk, Augustus W. to Mary L. White 8-?-1866 (8-30-1866) T
Walk, Thos. B. to Mrs. Sarah Upchurch 1-5-1865 T
Walker, A. B. to Harriet (Mrs.) Walker 11-15-1865 Hy
Walker, A. C. to Allice J. Cayce 10-13-1858 (10-15-1858) Sh
Walker, A. C. to M. A. Walker 8-3-1869 (8-4-1869) Dy
Walker, A. C. to Martha J. Allen 11-30-1853 Sh
Walker, A. F. to Nannie Blanton 1-30-1868 G
Walker, A. H. to Frances Clark 9-4-1877 (9-9-1877) O
Walker, A. H. to Mary A. Crook 12-30-1856 We
Walker, Aaron to Frances Cheatham 4-6-1885 (no return) L
Walker, Alenn to Regina M. Richie 10-16-1850 We
Walker, Alford M. to Nancy Duff 1-24-1829 (1-27-1829) Hr
Walker, Allen to Margarette Jones 7-29-1846 We
Walker, Andrew to Mooney Patterson 9-9-1869 (9-11-1869) T
Walker, Andrew to Silvia Wilson 1-4-1873 (1-9-1873) Cr B
Walker, Archer to Letheann Fowlkes 12-25-1877 (no return) Dy
Walker, B. C. to H. A. Walker 2-1-1862 Hy
Walker, B. D. to Mary F. Moorer 5-11-1858 (5-12-1858) L
Walker, B. F. to Eugenia Epps 2-13-1864 Hy
Walker, Bailey to Cheney Fowlkes 6-22-1872 (6-30-1872) Dy
Walker, Bartlett to Bettie Jayro 5-6-1873 (5-7-1873) L B
Walker, Ben T. to Ellen Pinyan 11-3-1877 (11-4-1877) Dy
Walker, Benjamin W. to Mary A. Dickerson 8-16-1861 We
Walker, Benjamin to Mariah Nevils 10-15-1851 (10-17-1851) G
Walker, Bob to Jinney Norman 1-9-1869 (no return) F B
Walker, Bruce to Julia Banks 3-14-1878 Hy
Walker, C. P. to Lula E. Puckett 10-18-1866 Hn
Walker, Cato to Lucinda Perry 1-2-1871 (1-5-1871) F B
Walker, Charles D. to Elizabeth Trotman Hoffler 2-11-1850 T
Walker, Charles D. to Emily R. Walker 3-3-1847 (3-4-1847) T
Walker, Chas. William to Mary Magee 12-27-1852 (12-28-1852) Sh
Walker, Cubit to Pattie Gause 1-22-1868 (1-23-1868) L B
Walker, Cyrus to Susan Shipard 12-31-1872 (1-1-1873) L
Walker, D. A. to Fannie Hurdle 2-2-1884 (2-7-1884) L
Walker, D. C. to Florella White 2-5-1856 Be
Walker, Dan A. to Mary Jane Mabane 2-20-1871 Hy
Walker, Daniel to America Williams 1-16-1869 G B
Walker, David B. to Martha A. McKane 3-17-1868 (no return) Dy
Walker, David G. to Nonnanda A. Young 11-4-1849 Sh
Walker, David to E. Ann Baylor 11-11-1865 Hn
Walker, David to Louisa Rice 8-24-1876 L B
Walker, David to Sally M. Blake 3-7-1831 (3-8-1831) Hr
Walker, E. A. to Elizabeth Edwards 8-18-1857 (8-20-1857) T
Walker, E. F. to Mary C. Doldon? 9-14-1859 T
Walker, E. P. to Emma C. Bratton 10-25-1870 (10-30-1870) T
Walker, E. T. to Nancy Simmons 4-9-1861 G

Walker, E. to Mary A. Gorden 11-21-1862 (3-25-1862?) O
Walker, Ebenezer T. to Lucy Culbreath 1-3-1842 (1-4-1842) T
Walker, Ebenezer to Elizabeth Long 10-27-1861 G
Walker, Eli to Malinda Jane Steely 7-9-1857 Hn
Walker, Elias to Sarah Dilliard 10-1-1830 Ma
Walker, Elson C. to Darcas Laster 2-18-1875 Hy
Walker, Emerine to Sallie Keeling 1-6-1849 Cr
Walker, Enoch R. to Nancy Ann Sewell 11-18-1868 (11-19-1868) Ma
Walker, Enoch to Elizabeth Walker 12-23-1834 G
Walker, Epps to Lucinda Williams 10-30-1869 F B
Walker, Felix to Ellen Cromwell 10-4-1838 (10-4-1838) Ma
Walker, Felix to Mary Brooks 7-1-1866 Hy
Walker, Francis M. to Phebe Gibson 8-20-1849 (8-23-1849) O
Walker, Frank to Eady Harris 12-16-1867 T
Walker, Frank to Eady Harris 8-12-1867 T
Walker, Franklin to Elizabeth Coleman 4-15-1858 We
Walker, G. G. to Nannie Seymore 12-21-1868 (12-22-1868) Cr
Walker, G. H. to Mary B. Jenkins 12-3-1878 (no return) L
Walker, G. L. to H. L. Barcley 9-6-1871 Hy
Walker, G. W. to Julia Colvin 4-13-1876 Dy
Walker, G. W. to Mary A. Mathis 9-8-1870 Hy
Walker, G. W. to S. E. Shelton 3-5-1879 (3-6-1879) Dy
Walker, George A. to Nannie M. Cavenor 12-26-1870 (12-29-1870) T
Walker, George W. to Alice Mitchell 3-12-1870 (3-13-1870) Cr
Walker, George W. to Mary E. Longworth 1-2-1861 (1-3-1861) Cr
Walker, George to Jane Lewis 12-22-1875 Hy
Walker, George to Lucy Sheals 2-22-1872 L B
Walker, George to Syntha Ann Williams 7-10-1865 G
Walker, Graves H. to Nancy L. Burns 2-24-1870 G
Walker, Green to India Merriwether 12-23-1872 Hy
Walker, H. A. to A. E. Holmes 9-13-1866 (9-16-1866) Cr
Walker, H. B. to Malinda Southerland 2-9-1842 (2-10-1842) F
Walker, H. C. to U. D. Willis 5-25-1864 G
Walker, H. H. to Mima Twyman 2-11-1873 T
Walker, H. S. to Elizabeth Gammons 12-14-1870 (12-15-1870) Dy
Walker, H. S. to L. C. Harrison 12-24-1862 (1-8-1863) Dy
Walker, H. W. to Caroline Seymore 2-7-1861 G
Walker, Harrison to Lucinda White 1-11-1868 O
Walker, Hartwell to Rhoda Deninney 7-26-1841 Sh
Walker, Henry C. to Lizzie J. Trigg 3-22-1852 Sh
Walker, Henry D. to Sarah Gray 12-22-1845 (12-23-1845) L
Walker, Henry H. to Louisa F. Overton 11-22-1866 Hy
Walker, Henry Ray to Mary Ann Light 6-5-1866 Dy
Walker, Henry W. to Mary E. Archie? 11-10-1850 Hn
Walker, Henry W. to Nancy Goode 12-28-1842 Hn
Walker, Henry to Hannah Shaw 2-16-1847 (3-14-1847) G
Walker, Henry to Martha E. Linder 8-31-1863 (no return) We
Walker, Henry to Mary A. Straton 1-6-1869 G B
Walker, Henry to Sarah Newton 12-30-1848 O
Walker, Hilman to Kesiah P. Collier 1-1-1846 We
Walker, Hilman to Susan M. Winstead 10-27-1856 We
Walker, Hiram S. to Maryann Biggs 11-29-1847 F
Walker, Isaac W. to Nancy P. Bayles 7-20-1858 Cr
Walker, Isham to Rachell P. Hampton 8-15-1850 Hn
Walker, Iverson to Louisa Bennett 12-18-1878 Hy
Walker, J. A. to M. M. Shelton 10-16-1869 (10-17-1869) Dy
Walker, J. E. to M. E. Graitt? 11-20-1871 L
Walker, J. J. to Margarett A. Steel 10-30-1865 G
Walker, J. K. P. to Rossa A. McDonald 7-17-1865 (7-19-1865) O
Walker, J. K. to Mattie Barclay 4-2-1872 Hy
Walker, J. M. to S. L. McCoy 12-19-1869 G
Walker, J. N. to Hester Ann Balis 5-30-1855 Be
Walker, J. P. to Emma Harris 10-29-1873 Dy
Walker, J. R. to Sarah Ann Young 10-22-1850 F
Walker, Jackson to Mariah J. Anderson 12-11-1871 Hy
Walker, James B. to Lucy Ann Walker 7-13-1852 Be
Walker, James D. to Mary E. Garrison 2-?-1862 (no return) Cr
Walker, James H. to Isabella S. Meridith 4-20-1831 Ma
Walker, James H. to Lucy Page 2-7-1850 Hn
Walker, James M. to Nancy Boyles 12-9-1835 G
Walker, James S. to Martha George 12-10-1868 (12-15-1868) T
Walker, James S. to Sarilda T. Matlock 12-6-1846 Be
Walker, James V. to Nancy Boyls 12-9-1833 (12-12-1833) G
Walker, James to Ann Janes 10-3-1845 O
Walker, James to Ann Jones 10-3-1843 O
Walker, James to Catharine Andrews 3-27-1828 Sh
Walker, James to Clara Suggs 6-2-1881 (no return) L B
Walker, James to Ellen Anthony 3-4-1868 Hy
Walker, James to Jane Walker 10-2-1844 (10-15-1844) G
Walker, James to Mary Long 6-30-1866 (7-1-1866) Cr
Walker, James to Mary W. Bailey 10-19-1836 (10-18?-1836) O
Walker, James to Mattie Howard 9-26-1881 (no return) L
Walker, James to Sarah Street 4-12-1849 Hn
Walker, Jas. P. to Maria L. Wilson 1-13-1842 (no return) L
Walker, Jasper N. to M. F. Moore 12-2-1867 (12-3-1867) Ma
Walker, Jerry to Peggie Alexander 8-23-1875 (8-24-1875) O
Walker, Jesse to Emily Stovall 7-4-1853 (7-7-1853) O

Walker, Jim to Lucy McLemore 1-18-1878 Hy
Walker, Jim to Mary Pulliam 12-24-1867 (12-25-1867) F B
Walker, Jno. to Martha E. Privett 10-14-1868 (10-21-1868) F
Walker, Joe to Ann Pirtle 12-31-1866 (1-1-1867) F B
Walker, Joel to Mary E. Brimingham 10-3-1853 (10-4-1853) Ma
Walker, John B. to Elizabet J. Walker 3-4-1852 T
Walker, John B. to Mrs. Harriett Mcguire 8-14-1858 (8-17-1858) Hr
Walker, John B. to Sarah C. Sellers 4-5-1844 (no return) F
Walker, John B. to Sarah J. P. Nowell 1-24-1867 Be
Walker, John B. to Tabitha A. McFadden 2-11-1856 Hn
Walker, John C. to Mary Wesson 1-15-1846 Sh
Walker, John C. to Mary Wesson 7-11-1838 Sh
Walker, John F. to Amelia Ann Brown 3-20-1855 (3-21-1855) Ma
Walker, John F. to Sarah A. Barten 9-13-1843 (9-14-1843) G
Walker, John H. to Tennie M. Moore 12-25-1848 Cr
Walker, John J. to Jane Dickerson 3-31-1849 O
Walker, John K. to Rachael Ross 10-20-1849 (10-21-1849) O
Walker, John N. to Martha Ann Hudson 10-26-1867 (11-7-1867) Ma
Walker, John N. to Mary B. Lewis 5-14-1870 (5-19-1870) Ma
Walker, John R. to Sarah Linton 11-17-1848 G
Walker, John Rhodes to Fanny Evans 6-22-1876 Hy
Walker, John W. to Luetta Jane Stovall 4-6-1857 (4-8-1857) O
Walker, John W. to Lydia Frances Marshall 12-13-1847 (12-?-1847) T
Walker, John to Eliza Hall 11-25-1852 (no return) F
Walker, John to Elizabeth Dildy 1-30-1867 (no return) Cr
Walker, John to Hattie Peterson 11-14-1878 Hy
Walker, John to Lucinda Broom 1-4-1868 (no return) F B
Walker, John to Sally Rice 3-30-1843 Hn
Walker, John to Sarah A. Gibbons 2-19-1855 Cr
Walker, John to Tempy Jane Hicks 3-22-1848 Cr
Walker, John to Tissie Lea 12-28-1871 Hy
Walker, Jordan to Adaline Harte? 3-15-1872 T
Walker, Joseph H. to Mary Tenant 1-12-1850 T
Walker, Joseph Newton to Zillah Syrena Roberts 7-6-1866 (7-8-1866) Ma
Walker, Joseph to Eliza Marchbanks 10-14-1847 Be
Walker, Joseph to Mary Baker 12-26-1871 (12-27-1871) L
Walker, L. R. to Hannah E. Carter 1-15-1849 (1-18-1849) O
Walker, Lacy B. to Sarah M. Carter 4-5-1858 (4-8-1858) O
Walker, Lee to Amanda Perry 4-3-1873 Hy
Walker, Leonard A. to Margaret Bever 11-7-1858 Cr
Walker, Levi to Addie M. Wells 2-14-1876 Hy
Walker, Lewis to Thomis? Poor 4-3-1830 Ma
Walker, Liberty to Martha A. Pierce 9-18-1852? (9-18-1851) Sh
Walker, M. B. to M. J. Benson 3-17-1848 (3-29-1848) F
Walker, Madison to Harriett Smith 12-28-1871 Hy
Walker, Manuel to Annie Fossett 1-6-1883 (1-8-1883) L
Walker, Matthew to Nancy Davis 1-28-1868 (2-1-1868) F B
Walker, Maxy H. to Sylvia Williams 12-23-1875 Hy
Walker, Milton to Allice Hughs 12-23-1872 (12-26-1872) Cr B
Walker, Milton to Lucy Hill 9-12-1873 T
Walker, Minn to Pheby Sherrod 3-6-1872 L
Walker, Mose? to Mary Jane Jones 7-23-1873 Dy
Walker, Moses to Frances Perry 10-19-1870 Hy
Walker, Moses to Josephine Johnson 9-12-1866 (9-27-1866) Dy
Walker, Moses to Mary Bridgewater 5-1-1867 (5-4-1867) F B
Walker, Ned to Hannah Holt 12-24-1877 (12-26-1877) L
Walker, Needham to Lucy Hutchins 2-10-1836 Sh
Walker, Oswill C. to Elizabeth Parks 12-18-1849 Be
Walker, Ovid to Mattie Pender 2-9-1874 Hy
Walker, P. A. to E. C. Milam 10-16-1866 (no return) Dy
Walker, Parris to Adeline Smith 1-11-1871 (no return) L
Walker, Peter to Mary Crowder 3-28-1871 Hy
Walker, Peter to Rachel Payne 8-12-1874 Hy
Walker, Pleasant D. to Adeline E. Emberson 11-30-1841 Hn
Walker, Pli to Sarah B. Hamblet 12-31-1849 (1-2-1850) F
Walker, R. L. to Sallie A. Pulliam 12-4-1866 (12-29-1866) F
Walker, R. S. to J. P. Sampson 11-7-1861 Cr
Walker, Reubin to Sarah Sevier 2-21-1872 Hy
Walker, Robert A. to Mary A. Daniel 5-8-1873 (5-3?-18730 T
Walker, Robert L. to Martha McNair 4-24-1865 T
Walker, Robert T. to Ellen Archer 11-27-1859 Hn
Walker, Robert to Ruth Harrison 5-11-1859 (5-15-1859) O
Walker, Rubin to Tiller Hunter 2-8-1877 Hy
Walker, S. H. to N. J. Taylor 12-24-1865 Hn
Walker, Samuel to Mary Parker 9-28-1842 Sh
Walker, Silas to Louisa Fields 6-8-1854 O
Walker, Simon H. to Edna B. Frazier 7-3-1849 (7-4-1849) F
Walker, Spencer to Roberta Brown 2-4-1880 (2-5-1880) L B
Walker, Stephen to Cumiah Nash 12-26-1865 Hy
Walker, Stephen to Hannah Thomason 7-22-1850 Be
Walker, Stephen to Jane Rogers 9-26-1852 Be
Walker, Stephen to Rachel Easley 7-11-1874 Hy
Walker, T. A. to Bettie Maclin 11-1-1865 Hy
Walker, T. J. (Dr.) to Bettie Sweet 3-4-1868 Hy
Walker, T. J. to L. E. Price 1-14-1867 (1-20-1867) Dy
Walker, Temple C. to Mary C. Buly? 5-6-1848 (5-7-1848) F

Walker, Thomas W. to Florida E. Wood 8-23-1858 (8-25-1858) Ma
Walker, Thomas W. to Rebecca Reynolds 3-29-1858 Hr
Walker, Thomas to Agnes Rogers 5-9-1850 We
Walker, Thomas to Elizabeth Anthony 1-21-1869 Hy
Walker, Thomas to Fanny Green 2-13-1844 G
Walker, Thomas to Martha Willoughby 3-1-1841 Hr
Walker, Thomas to Mary L. McFall(McFarlin) 11-14-1833 (11-27-1833) Hr
Walker, Thos. J. to Elizabeth A. Little 2-19-1859 Cr
Walker, Thos. M. to Susan Henderson 6-1-1846 We
Walker, Thos. M. to Susan Hendson 7-11-1846 (no return) We
Walker, Thos. P. to Cairly W. Moore 10-7-1856 Cr
Walker, Thos. to Catherine Plummer 6-18-1853 Sh
Walker, Tillmon P. to Elizabeth Jackson 12-25-1848 O
Walker, Tom to Easter Winfield 1-12-1871 Hy
Walker, Uriah to Huldah Porter 12-12-1876 (12-13-1876) Dy
Walker, Valentine to Elizabeth White 3-14-1853 (3-15-1853) Hr
Walker, Valintine to Otey Walker 1-18-1850 (1-20-1850) Ma
Walker, Vincent B. to Louisa J. Kenfall 12-12-1854 Hn
Walker, Volentine to Liuisa? Walker 11-1-1870 (11-2-1870) Ma
Walker, W. A. J. to Mary A. Smith 9-7-1870 (no return) Dy
Walker, W. A. to M. V. Sutton 5-16-1859 We
Walker, W. A. to Mary Ann Wood 2-1-1855 Be
Walker, W. C. to M. C. Willis 12-18-1866 G
Walker, W. H. to V. A. Baird 7-20-1869 G
Walker, W. P. to A. E. Allen 1-15-1867 O
Walker, W. S. to Martha J. King 8-12-1869 (8-13-1869) Dy
Walker, W. S. to Molly Hight 12-24-1865 Hn
Walker, W. T. to Bettie E. Jones 7-25-1877 Dy
Walker, W. W. to Myra McGaughy 7-31-1867 Dy
Walker, Ward to Mary Ann Willis 7-2-1868 G
Walker, Washington to Sarah Word 12-23-1871 (12-26-1871) Dy
Walker, William B. to Sarah Ann Page 6-2-1838 F
Walker, William D. to Susan E. Barton 12-2-1853 Hn
Walker, William F. to Dorcas J. Cline 8-5-1860 Hn
Walker, William J. to Adaline Moore 11-4-1846 F
Walker, William J. to Jane A. R. Jackson 10-3-1846 (10-6-1846) G
Walker, William P. to Martha A. Bailey 9-23-1852 (9-24-1852) Ma
Walker, William P. to Temperance Y. Anderson 4-21-1858 Hn
Walker, William Thomas to Gilly Oakly 11-21-1867 Hn B
Walker, William W. to Nancy H. Taylor 6-22-1848 (no return) F
Walker, William to Amanda Freeman 11-6-1872 Hy
Walker, William to Lucy A. Whitfield 6-15-1848 Hn
Walker, William to Martha Belew 2-28-1842 G
Walker, William to Martha J. Smith 5-30-1840 (no return) Hn
Walker, William to Mary Ann Fowler 8-3-1833 (8-?-1833) Hr
Walker, William to Neely Ellender Walker 8-8-1846 (8-9-1846) Ma
Walker, William to Nellie Baker 12-31-1868 F
Walker, William to Susan Franklin 12-20-1866 (12-23-1866) O
Walker, William to Susan Grizzard 2-8-1867 (2-10-1867) L B
Walker, William to Tempy Norris 4-20-1836 Sh
Walker, Willis to Mary Thomas 1-20-1876 Hy
Walker, Wilson R. to Nancy Weeks 1-5-1850 (no return) Hn
Walker, Wm. N. to Jessie L. (Mrs.) Wright 6-20-1863 (6-28-1863) Sh
Walker, Wm. to Adie Cates 2-2-1872 Hy
Walker, Wyatt to Malvina Stanley 12-23-1854 (12-24-1854) O
Walker, Wyly to Narcessa J. Melton 3-24-1839 Be
Walker, Z. R. to Julia A. S. Fisher 4-21-1866 (no return) Cr
Walker, Zach to Susan Conner 12-13-1868 Hy
Walker?, James A. to Nancy C. Radford 2-20-1859 Be
Walkers, Elisha to Ann Williams 1-1-1866 (1-2-1866) O
Walkup, James to Mollie Cogbill 8-17-1867 (8-18-1867) F
Wall (Mall), Wm. to Eliza Keoppen 6-24-1862 Sh
Wall, A. J. to Martha Ann Hill 1-11-1863 Hn
Wall, Abner M. to Ruth M. Wright 1-23-1840 (1-25-1840) O
Wall, Burel P. to Emaretta Marberry 5-10-1861 Hn
Wall, Burrell to Frances E. Reynolds 5-27-1862 (no return) Hn
Wall, Ezekiel to Maria H. Hatly 1-6-1834 (1-4?-1834) Hr
Wall, F. F. to Ann Ashford 4-23-1857 T
Wall, Gabriel to Mary Williams 11-20-1869 G B
Wall, Henry C. to Delpha A. Flake 10-20-1871 (10-22-1871) Cr
Wall, J. B. to E. M. Love 1-23-1866 (1-24-1866) F
Wall, J. D. to Irene O. Wright 12-20-1866 O
Wall, J. J. to Fannie Champion 1-10-1867 F
Wall, J. N. to M. J. Seymour 4-27-1853 F
Wall, J. P. to Axie McDaniel 12-22-1873 T
Wall, J. W. to M. A. Lovett 9-28-1868 (no return) Dy
Wall, Jesse E. to Frances A. Marberry 12-7-1858 Hn
Wall, John O. to Martha J. Grogan 1-6-1870 (1-7-1870) Cr
Wall, Milton to Ada Fitzpatrick 1-2_-1882 (1-23-1882) L B
Wall, Nelson to Susan Tharp 8-3-1847 (8-11-1847) F
Wall, Oney C. to Fanny Caraway 2-14-1867 F
Wall, Phil to T. Hayslett 2-12-1869 (no return) F B
Wall, Spencer to Susan Avery 11-18-1850 Hn
Wall, W. B. to Susan Herron 1-24-1866 (1-25-1866) F
Wall, W. T. to N. B. OKelly 11-22-1864 (11-24-1864) F
Wall, W. W. to S. E. Russell 5-1-1868 G
Wall, Wilsons to Elizabeth A. Huffman 6-25-1848 Cr

Wall, Wm. H. to Miss Fannie Steele 11-28-1864 (11-29-1864) T
Wallace, Alex to Araminta Madison 8-1-1856 We
Wallace, Alexander S. to Adaline Laurance 4-26-1851 G
Wallace, Alexander to Maria Solon 3-18-1857 Sh
Wallace, Alfred to Mary Horn 2-16-1842 Cr
Wallace, Alvan to Isabella Hair 2-27-1863 Mn
Wallace, Asa to Mary Denie (Dennis) 7-7-1847 Sh
Wallace, B. F. to Isabell V. McGehee 12-17-1857 Hn
Wallace, B. P. to Fannie Lacey 1-15-1868 Hy
Wallace, Benjamin to Caty Williams 1-2-1862 Mn
Wallace, David C. to Malissa Lawrence 12-18-1856 Hn
Wallace, Dew H. C. to Anna Eaker 3-30-1858 Hn
Wallace, E. C. to Sarah E. White 5-8-1877 (5-9-1877) L
Wallace, Edward to Esshia C. Revel 1-16-1834 O
Wallace, Eli to ____ Crowel 1-21-1840 Hn
Wallace, Everett to Mary Jane Williams 7-28-1857 (7-30-1857) Ma
Wallace, Francis M. to Pernina A. Taylor 1-21-1858 Hn
Wallace, George to Mary Adams 6-12-1874 T
Wallace, Gideon to Martha Dickson 4-22-1830 Sh
Wallace, Henderson C. to Mary C. Gahagan 5-25-1841 Hr
Wallace, J. A. to Susana Wallace 3-25-1873 (3-27-1873) Dy
Wallace, J. B. to A. H. Martin 2-3-1874 Hy
Wallace, J. B. to Celia Richardson 12-8-1855 Hr
Wallace, J. N. to Jane Betts 9-28-1856 Hn
Wallace, J. N. to Mary Ann Crowley 10-11-1838 (no return) Hn
Wallace, Jacob to Nancy Caroline Morrison 1-19-1854 T
Wallace, James A. to Mary C. Jack 11-11-1862 (11-13-1862) Dy
Wallace, James W. to Margaret Lewis 12-10-1865 Mn
Wallace, James to Anne Flaherty 10-4-1864 Sh
Wallace, James to Catherine Hood 5-26-1853 Cr
Wallace, Jas. R. to Laura F. Marshall 10-13-1868 (10-17-1868) F
Wallace, Jno. G. to Eliza M. Barnes 10-4-1850 Sh
Wallace, John C. to Martha Vinson 4-15-1855 Hn
Wallace, John H. to Phebe A. Featherston 11-10-1853 G
Wallace, L. D. to M. E. Trimble 2-28-1869 Hy
Wallace, R. C. to M. T. Crawford 3-5-1850 (no return) F
Wallace, Rhea to Sally Hicks 3-1-1848 Sh
Wallace, Richard to Eliz. Rogers 3-3-1829 Ma
Wallace, Richard to Lucy T. Nelson 10-15-1840 Sh
Wallace, Richard to Winnifred H. Landrum 11-14-1842 Sh
Wallace, Riley E. to Julia A. Naigle 3-17-1856 Sh
Wallace, Robert to Phereby (Mrs.) Davis 8-17-1867 G B
Wallace, S. F. to E. C. Haywood 2-20-1855 Cr
Wallace, Stephen to Lucretia Foren 1-27-1853 (1-28-1853) G
Wallace, Thomas W.(M?) to Malissa Price 2-24-1840 (2-25-1840) Hr
Wallace, Thos. to Sarah White 8-3-1847 Cr
Wallace, W. A. to M. Reed 3-9-1863 (3-25-1863) Dy
Wallace, W. J. to Lucy J. Whitehead 3-30-1875 Hy
Wallace, W. M. to M. A. Jones 12-20-1877 Hy
Wallace, Wilee to Sarah F. Bird 3-25-1854 (3-26-1854) G
Wallace, Will W. to Elizabeth L. Mathews 1-4-1848 (1-6-1848) Hr
Wallace, William B. to Mary E. Williams 3-28-1848 Ma
Wallace, William R. to Ethreal Leggett 12-6-1849 Sh
Wallace, William to Mary Fullerton 1-26-1847 Be
Wallace, William to Mollie Thomas 1-19-1874 Hy
Wallace, William to Nancy Miller 5-24-1864 Hn
Wallace, Wm. H. to S. E. Herbert 10-29-1860 Hy
Wallace, Wm. to Mary Montague 10-29-1867 (11-6-1867) F
Wallace, Wm. to Nancy Cirk 1-20-1855 Cr
Wallace, ____ to Mary Gillum 5-25-1867 T
Waller, A. C. to Mariah C. Hatley 8-4-1845 (8-5-1845) F
Waller, A. to M. E. Blain 12-20-1852 (no return) F
Waller, Albert to Tina King 12-14-1853 (12-15-1853) Hr
Waller, C. M. to A. E. Pulliam 2-7-1859 (2-8-1859) F
Waller, David W. to Sarah Ingram 9-23-1844 (9-26-1844) O
Waller, E. M. to Lucy Reed 1-21-1851 (no return) F
Waller, Edward G. to Martha F. Waller 2-7-1845 (2-18-1845) F
Waller, H. B. to R. E. Wiggins 12-14-1869 (no return) F
Waller, J. S. to M. E. White 8-1-1870 (8-5-1870) T
Waller, Jesse to Jennie Culp 1-29-1870 (3-6-1870) F B
Waller, John to Mary Scott 10-11-1849 Hr
Waller, John to Susan Jonagan 9-2-1854 (9-3-1854) Hr
Waller, Jonas M. to Mary Gardner 2-26-1862 (2-27-1862) Ma
Waller, Joseph S. to Agnes W. Douglas 7-27-1835 Sh
Waller, Joseph S. to Mary Frances Culbreth 11-14-1857 (3-20-1858) T
Waller, L. G. to Susan A. Waller 4-27-1846 (5-3-1846) F
Waller, M. M. to Margarett N. Leonard 9-30-1847 (no return) F
Waller, Samuel to Emaline Spivey 8-11-1848 Sh
Waller, Thomas J. to Clarissa Reed 1-1-1847 (1-7-1847) F
Waller, Thomas to Altamyra Roberts 8-9-1842 (8-11-1842) Hr
Waller, Thos. to Eliza Johnston 11-15-1843 G
Waller, William D. to Ann L. Rogers 2-27-1862 Ma
Waller, Wm. C. to Elizabeth Walker 12-29-1858 Sh
Wallice, Daniel M. to Bitha Lavina Northcutt 6-14-1834 G
Wallice, John to Rebecca Reed 1-7-1862 G
Wallice, Jonathan to S. A. Wallice 1-13-1857 G
Wallice, M. S. to Sarah E. Conley 1-16-1856 G

Wallice, Stephen to Eliza Wallice 9-20-1862 G
Wallick, P. M. to Virginia C. Towns 10-14-1867 (10-16-1867) Cr
Wallingford, Isaac B. to Mary S. McMinn 9-12-1850 (9-13-1850) G
Wallingford, John B. to Nancy Fowler 9-16-1833 G
Wallingford, Thomas W. to Unity Jane Brigget Bell 12-17-1855 Ma
Wallingford, Washington to Mildred E. Scott 10-9-1859 Hn
Wallingsford, George W. to Elizabeth H. Stone 1-23-1841 (1-24-1841) G
Wallingsford, Moses B. to Martha Fowler 1-15-1835 (1-20-1835) G
Wallis(Wilson), Jesse W. to Elizabeth W. Hubard 12-13-1845 (12-18-1845) Hr
Wallis, C. D. C. to H. E. Hopkins 2-6-1861 G
Wallis, C. J. to Louisa E. Bell 5-15-1862 O
Wallis, C. T. to M. E. Cummings 11-9-1865 O
Wallis, Evander to Jane Tilor 8-8-1845 We
Wallis, Hiran to S. Wallice 3-12-1852 Cr
Wallis, James C. to Susan Rodgers 8-16-1858 Cr
Wallis, John M. to Juley Bell 12-11-1864 (no return) Hn
Wallis, Levi to Elizabeth Ferrell 11-20-1867 O
Wallis, Lunsford M. R. to Ann E. Boon 3-17-1846 G
Wallis, Robt. Mathews to Mahala Jane Kelley 3-11-1856 T
Wallis, Stephen to Mary Jack 12-30-1856 Cr
Wallis, Wesley to Harriett Harper 4-7-1866 O
Wallis, Wm. R. to Penny E. Wollard 1-17-1840 G
Wallis, Wm. to Mary Harper 7-20-1866 O
Wallon, E. S. W. to Lucy Head 3-22-1860 O
Wallpool, R. C. to Mary A. Lee 8-7-1870 G
Walls, Edmond to Susan Hunt 2-16-1867 G
Walls, George to Julia Blessing 12-3-1863 G
Walls, J. B. to A. C. Richey 1-30-1869 F
Walls, J. H. to Mary F. Coker 4-24-1876 Hy
Walls, J. J. to W. F. Jones 2-23-1870? (2-23-1871) L
Walls, J. M. to Julia A. Dover 9-8-1870 F
Walls, James B. to Harriet A. Harvey 12-13-1836 (12-21-1836) Hr
Walls, James M. to Polly McCrackin 9-11-1861 (no return) Dy
Walls, James to Matilda Sevier? 10-24-1866 Dy
Walls, John M. to Keziah E. Bland 12-17-1857 Hn
Walls, Rayland R. to Gabrella Waldrop 3-13-1851 G
Walls, Richard to Susan Hicks 8-31-1854 G
Walls, Riland to Patience White 2-26-1845 We
Walls, Solomon to Eliza J. Barns 8-5-1841 (8-6-1841) G
Walls, William A. to Rachel Hicks 1-5-1854 (1-8-1854) G
Walls, William H. to Alpha Guin 7-16-1873 Hy
Walpole, Cilas to Millie Moore 5-24-1876 L
Walpole, E. W. to M. O. Duncan 8-13-1879 (8-14-1879) L
Walpole, J. B. to Hanah M. Moor 1-11-1861 (1-13-1861) L
Walpole, J. R. to Agnes C. Taylor 3-29-1865 (no return) L
Walpole, James to Margaret Taylor 12-22-1865 (12-24-1865) L
Walpole, John B. to Elizabeth Roberson 7-31-1839 (no return) L
Walpole, John R. to Agnus C. Taylor 3-29-1865 (3-30-1865) L
Walpole, Peyton to Sarah Moore 2-19-1880 (no return) L
Walpole, S. W. to M. A. Ballenger 8-23-1884 (8-26-1884) L
Walpole, Thomas G. to Martha E. Taylor 1-12-1871 Hy
Walpole, Thomas L. to Frances E. Johnson 2-14-1861 L
Walpole, Thomas to Martha Hurley 9-15-1859 L
Walsh (Welsh), Thomas to Martha McClaskey 1-20-1848 Sh
Walsh, James R. to Susan V. Parker 12-19-1876 (12-20-1876) L
Walsh, James to Margarett McGrath 11-12-1862 Sh
Walsh, John L. to Martha C. Garland 11-18-1856 (11-30-1856) Ma
Walsh, John L. to Martha J. Murchison 2-16-1849 Ma
Walsh, John to Berdelia Moran 8-9-1861 Sh
Walsh, John to Elizabeth Dunn 3-7-1852 Sh
Walsh, John to Mary Daly 10-11-1854 Sh
Walsh, Michael to Hannah Barnes 4-14-1858 Hn
Walsh, Richard to Lucy A. Crouch 2-3-1838 Sh
Walsh, Thomas to Ellen Burk (Buck?) 1-3-1853 (1-29-1853) Sh
Walsh, Thomas to Margaret Scanerlin 5-10-1862 (5-11-1862) Sh
Walsh, Wm. F. (Dr.) to Margaret B. Pharr 11-5-1851 Sh
Walston, William to Mary E. Pennington 2-12-1845 G
Walt, James L. to Mary R. Bateman 12-5-1859 (12-8-1859) T
Walt, Mathew to Martha McCarrol 1-12-1869 (1-28-1869) T
Walter, Frederick to Louisa Brei 1-27-1862 Sh
Walter, G. W. to R. E. Deloach 4-1-1869 (4-6-1869) L
Walter, Hermann to Mary Weisler 3-10-1863 Sh
Walter, Joseph to Katharine Staap (Stoop?) 11-4-1862 Sh
Walter, Lewis to Mary W. Harvey 5-15-1855 Sh
Walter, Louis to Rosina Cutz 7-28-1856 Sh
Walters, A. J. to I. N. Moore 2-19-1873 (2-20-1873) Cr
Walters, A. J. to S. E. Gragsdon 1-30-1866 Hn
Walters, Frank M. to Lucy Ann Tooms 12-7-1857 (12-10-1867?) Ma
Walters, Henry B. to Emily Allen 7-18-1850 Hn
Walters, J. W. to Anna Cole 2-22-1872 Cr
Walters, Jno. W. to Mary F. King 1-1-1869 (1-3-1869) Ma
Walters, Joell W. to Martha J. Hinson 2-1-1868 (2-5-1868) Cr
Walters, John B. to Josephine Baker 12-19-1861 (12-21-1861) Sh
Walters, John to Ann Boman? 5-8-1842 Hn
Walters, Moses P. to Mahaly F. Wamble 1-28-1863 Mn
Walters, Samuel to Julia Ann Muzzall 8-31-1843 (no return) Hn
Walters, Samuel to Lucy Muzzle? 9-17-1860 Hn

Walters, Spencer to Tabitha E. Randle 2-1-1842 Hn
Walters, Thomas B. to Martha J. Southerland 3-27-1855 We
Walters, Thomas to Martha Hagler 5-13-1845 Hn
Walters, William W. to Mary Miller 10-20-1859 We
Walters, ____ to Theodotia Noel 3-26-1839 (no return) Hn
Walthall, Edward C. to Sophia A. Bridgers 8-16-1855 Sh
Walthall, John A. to Sarah ann Elder 6-13-1848 (6-18-1848) F
Walthall, Samuel G. to Mary Faulkner 1-2-1866 Hy
Walton (Walter?), James A. to Sarah Robinson 12-29-1846 (12-30-1846) L
Walton, Alfred J. to Ann E. Currin 3-20-1843 (no return) F
Walton, Anthony to Martha Green 4-17-1872 T
Walton, C. J. to Jane Nichols 5-3-1879 Dy
Walton, Charles C. to Mary K. Phillips 7-30-1879 (7-31-1879) Dy
Walton, Daniel to Emiline Webster 1-20-1872 (2-1-1872) Dy
Walton, David to Mahala Brown 12-28-1870 (12-29-1870) F B
Walton, E. T. to Analiza Cherry 2-25-1864 Hn
Walton, Frank to Malinda Reams 12-24-1868 F B
Walton, Geo. Washington to Minerva Jane Myers 3-21-1849 T
Walton, George W. to Elizabeth A. Brown 12-25-1867 (12-29-1867) T
Walton, George W. to Frances e. Breedlove 1-11-1848 Hn
Walton, George W. to Mary Yarbro 6-8-1870 (6-9-1870) T
Walton, George to Ann Haskins 7-14-1877 (7-15-1877) Dy
Walton, George to Emaly Acock 8-19-1872 (8-20-1872) T
Walton, Isaac D. to Lucy Ann Fenner 3-1-1859 (3-2-1859) Ma
Walton, J. H. to Sallie C. Bell 12-7-1868 (no return) Dy
Walton, J. M. to Almeda G. Sutton 11-3-1850 Hn
Walton, Jackson to Isau? Taylor 12-15-1874 T
Walton, Jackson to Mary Hearn 12-30-1841 Cr
Walton, James M. to Catharine Teague 11-24-1847 (11-25-1847) Hr
Walton, Jas. M. to Georgiana Wair 7-15-1858 Hn
Walton, Jerimiah to Rebecca Eskew 5-3-1840 Cr
Walton, John J. to Elizabeth Teague 12-27-1838 Hr
Walton, John to Nancy Rivers 12-26-1870 (1-2-1871) F B
Walton, Joseph G. to Elizabeth Jane Flynn 10-2-1851 Hr
Walton, L. M. to Mattie L. Swinney 1-1-1866 (1-4-1866) Cr
Walton, Nelson to Charity Evans 10-26-1885 (10-28-1885) L
Walton, Nelson to Metisla Shofner 4-28-1846 Cr
Walton, P. T. to Martha Pate 5-23-1865 (no return) Cr
Walton, Peter to Rosena Dickinson 12-25-1866 (12-27-1866) F B
Walton, Robert H. to Sarah Kearney 1-8-1842 (1-9-1842) Hr
Walton, Solomon R. B. to Issaballa T. Cobb 4-25-1839 F
Walton, Stephen to Mollie Davis 3-5-1873 (3-6-1873) Dy
Walton, T. H. to Elizabeth F. Payne 6-23-1862 (no return) Dy
Walton, Thomas J. to M. A. E. Mitchell 7-2-1836 G
Walton, Thomas to Lucy Walton 1-9-1867 (1-17-1867) F B
Walton, William D. to Sarah Frances Cox 2-12-1844 (2-13-1844) T
Walton, William H. to Mariah J. McIntosh 11-25-1869 T
Walton, William to Emily McIver 11-23-1836 Hr
Walton, William to Mariah A. Freeland 8-15-1864 (no return) Hn
Walton, Willis to Malinda Waller 12-11-1860 F
Walton, Wm. D. to Martha A. A. Rice 4-16-1856 T
Wamble, John to Elizabeth Sasser 1-5-1852 (1-8-1852) Hr
Wandle?, John R. to Ruth Kendle? 7-11-1866 Hn
Wands, John D. to Mary A. (Mrs.?) Bishop 10-13-1863 Sh
Wanniger, Fred to Hannah Gibbs 4-9-1857 Sh
Warbriton, N. G. to Frances A. Gee 12-12-1864 Cr
Warbritten, B. F. to Mary Harris 12-21-1864 (12-22-1864) Cr
Warbritton, David to Conne Gibson 8-10-1856 Cr
Warbritton, Harrison to Margaret Harris 11-18-1851 Cr
Warbritton, J. N. to S. F. Traywick 2-5-1870 (2-6-1870) Cr
Warbritton, Wm. J. to Mary F. Hamilton 8-18-1854 Cr
Warburton, Thomas to Mary Eubanks 6-25-1848 Sh
Ward (Word), J. C. to Paulina Henderson 2-12-1856 Sh
Ward, A. M. to Martha A. McClaron 2-16-1859 (2-17-1859) F
Ward, Benj. to Elizabeth Johnson 11-27-1854 W
Ward, Burrel F. to Partheny Ward 12-26-1866 Be
Ward, Calvin H. to Maday W. Cates 2-19-1852 We
Ward, Charles H. to Nancey J. Rainey 12-18-1866 L
Ward, Charles to Harriet Rice 2-21-1872 (2-23-1872) Dy
Ward, Chas. to Julia A. F. Canada 12-16-1867 (12-20-1867) F
Ward, Danel to Delia Cats 12-26-1854 (12-28-1855) We
Ward, Doctor M. to Matilda O. Wilson 10-9-1863 G
Ward, E. T. to M. E. Edmondson 9-29-1868 G
Ward, Edward to Sarah Ward 10-18-1839 Sh
Ward, Elijah to Nancy Michael 1-1-1838 Hn
Ward, Enoch to Francis Bramblett 6-28-1845 (6-29-1845) O
Ward, Frank to Louisa Freeman 11-20-1866 Hy
Ward, Geo. to Minerva Hass 11-25-1850 (11-26-1850) F
Ward, George to Laura Ferris 2-23-1867 G
Ward, H. S. to Jane Morrell 2-20-1862 (2-21-1862) Sh
Ward, Harvell M. to Mary C. Thomas 3-14-1850 O
Ward, Henry I. to America C. Williams 10-12-1852 (10-14-1852) G
Ward, Henry to Jane Pratt 1-6-1867 G
Ward, Henry to Louvinia Yong 9-22-1869 (9-23-1869) L B
Ward, Henry to Mary Silsby 12-20-1865 (12-24-1865) Dy
Ward, I.(J?) R. to S. A. Hood 12-31-1875 Hy
Ward, J. B. to M. J. Hampden 9-7-1872 (no return) Dy

Ward, J. H. to Annie Miller 10-1-1877 (no return) Dy
Ward, J. P. to Susan Heath 8-30-1865 G
Ward, J. S. to Mary E. Thompson 1-27-1868 Dy
Ward, J. W. to Rebecca A. Ward 11-29-1860 Be
Ward, J. W. to Sarah P. Lett 1-14-1869 G
Ward, James J. to Almeda Hatcher 10-14-1845 (no return) We
Ward, James M. to Martha Ann Kelly 12-8-1841 T
Ward, James N. to Elizabeth R. Harget 10-5-1857 (10-13-1857) O
Ward, James T. to Benvilla Nichols 9-4-1839 Ma
Ward, James T. to Elvy Jane Edwards 8-16-1854 (8-18-1854) Ma
Ward, James T. to Lucinda C. Chamber 8-31-1869 (9-1-1869) L
Ward, James to Martha A. Cooper 6-15-1844 (6-18-1844) G
Ward, James to Mary Blair 2-13-1836 Hr
Ward, James to Mary F. Dement 5-12-1853 G
Ward, James to Nancy Nabers 6-12-1830 (6-13-1830) Hr
Ward, Jeremiah to Nancy Lane 1-6-1840 (1-7-1840) O
Ward, Jerry to Mollie Cambell 11-11-1870 G
Ward, Jesse B. to Jane C. Haynes 11-24-1866 Ma
Ward, Jesse N. (W.?) to Susan Ward 4-3-1867 G
Ward, John A. to Jane H. Morton 1-2-1871 (1-5-1871) F
Ward, John A. to Sarah McCollum 7-5-1853 Cr
Ward, John C. to Elizabeth R. Smith 4-3-1859 Hn
Ward, John C. to Lexey Redden 2-24-1841 Hn
Ward, John E. to Mary Emeline Wren 9-1-1869 G
Ward, John F. to Elizabeth C. Pounds 1-26-1860 (no return) We
Ward, John J. to Susan E. Caldwell 1-22-1858 (2-2-1858) O
Ward, John M. to Zylpha Dinkins 9-27-1838 G
Ward, John N. to Mary P. Alexander 11-11-1858 We
Ward, John to Martha Cearley 8-12-1867 Dy
Ward, John to Nancy C. (Mrs.) Porter 1-12-1864 (1-13-1864) Sh
Ward, John to Sallie Mayes 9-9-1870 G
Ward, John to Sarah Mills 10-30-1848 (no return) F
Ward, Joseph H. to Frances A. McAdams 11-19-1856 We
Ward, Joseph Pheland to Mary H. Swanson 9-17-1840 Sh
Ward, Joseph R. to Elizabeth P. McGill 11-13-1856 Be
Ward, Josiah to Louisa Henley 6-8-1843 T
Ward, Josiah to Margaret A. Harly 3-26-1863 We
Ward, K. K. to Mary F. Duncan 3-31-1865 Hn
Ward, K. L. to R. A. Pearce 2-3-1841 Be
Ward, King W. to Martha Jane White 4-15-1851 (5-1-1851) Hr
Ward, L. L. to E. C. Morgan 5-1-1861 Sh
Ward, Lee to Margaret Bert 3-21-1874 T
Ward, Levie J. to Martha J. Sanders 7-30-1862 We
Ward, Littleton to Elizabeth Mitchell 9-7-1831 (9-13-1831) G
Ward, M. F. to J. E. Harrison 1-3-1868 G
Ward, Matthew to Luisa G. Turner 6-19-1842 Hn
Ward, Minus M. to Susan Green 11-8-1856 (11-11-1856) Ma
Ward, Nathen to Nancy D. Little 11-12-1846 Cr
Ward, O. D. to Jane McCoy 3-5-1849 (3-14-1849) Ma
Ward, R. D. to Alabama Boyett 1-3-1865 O
Ward, R. M. to A. Oneal 10-21-1867 (10-24-1867) Dy
Ward, Robert to Celia Green 7-11-1871 (7-13-1871) L
Ward, Robert to Sabina Brown 1-5-1859 Cr
Ward, Simeon to Elizabeth E. McAdoo 11-20-1844 Hn
Ward, T. H. to E. J. Whitly 11-22-1864 (11-23-1864) Sh
Ward, Theophilus J. to Dicy Ward 12-20-1853 Be
Ward, Thomas H. to Alabama S. Sims 11-30-1859 We
Ward, Thomas H. to Mary A. Gurganus 11-12-1853 G
Ward, Thomas M. to Mary Catharine Cannon (Cameron) 9-15-1845 Sh
Ward, Thomas to Mary F. Young 11-8-1865 Hn
Ward, Thos. A. to Martha J. Ward 2-2-1860 Be
Ward, Timothy W. to Mary E. Cooper 1-10-1849 F
Ward, Van to E. E. C. (Mrs.) Rowland 10-1-1848 Sh
Ward, W. A.(H?) to A. V. Wingo 12-23-1868 G
Ward, W. C. to E. F. Fowlkes 3-19-1864 G
Ward, W. D. to Nancy I. Simpson 12-22-1853 Hr
Ward, W. G. to Susan A. Provow 12-20-1866 Hn
Ward, W. H. to E. H. Thomas 4-8-1861 (4-9-1861) O
Ward, W. L. to Margarett R. Whitchard 3-15-1866 G
Ward, W. T. to N. C. Walker 11-26-1873 T
Ward, William G. to Jane W. Brown 12-5-1849 (12-6-1849) G
Ward, William H. to Eliza P. Rushing 10-14-1860 Hn
Ward, William L. to Sarah Jane Cook 6-14-1847 F
Ward, William to Eveline Ward 7-15-1852 Be
Ward, William to Jane Arbrough 3-11-1851 (3-13-1851) G
Ward, William to Ophelia Theadford 9-28-1860 (10-20-1860) O
Ward, William to Perlina McClain 8-5-1841 Hn
Ward, William to Rebeca Deck 8-12-1845 We
Ward, Willis C. to Lucy A. Gillespie 1-1-1851 G
Ward, Willis to Ann Powell 12-2-1869 (no return) Dy
Ward, Wm. G. to Timitha E. Burrow 6-13-1854 G
Ward, Wm. H. to Maranda H. Bush 4-14-1853 Be
Ward, enj. to C. J. McNamee 3-20-1860 (3-21-1860) F
Ward, jr., Matthias to Elizabeth L. Sanders 5-25-1836 Sh
Wardeau (Wardlaw), W. I. to F. A. Campbell 9-6-1876 L
Warden, Horace to Lula Lockhart 10-5-1882 (no return) L
Warden, Thos. F. to Eliza Owens 1-30-1860 (2-7-1860) G

Wardlaw, Abe to Alice Dark 12-18-1878 (12-20-1878) L B
Wardlaw, Campbell to Bettie Meadows 9-22-1868 (9-26-1868) L
Wardlaw, James to Alesta? Norris 9-18-1849 (9-22-1849) L
Wardlaw, Jeff to Rachel Scott 12-27-1879 (12-28-1879) L B
Wardlaw, Jim Brown to Callie Burks 1-5-1876 (2-6-1876) L
Wardlaw, Joseph H. to Julia D. Smith 7-10-1850 L
Wardlaw, Joseph H. to Lou P. Sampson 9-5-1866 L
Wardlaw, Joseph H. to Martha F. Palmer 1-23-1860 (no return) L
Wardlaw, Nat to Sarah J. Tening 9-17-1885 L
Wardlaw, Ned to Delia Oldham 5-30-1877 L
Wardlaw, Thomas to Martha Halliburton 8-23-1853 (8-25-1853) L
Wardlaw, William to Charity Henning 10-10-1871 (10-12-1871) L
Wardlowe, William C. to Louisa Jones 9-1-1864 Mn
Ware, A. V. to A. G. Isbell 2-6-1860 (2-8-1860) F
Ware, Adam to Solona Ware 12-21-1870 Hy
Ware, Alfred to Elizabeth Crane 3-9-1848 Sh
Ware, Allen to Minnie Rogers 10-30-1873 Hy
Ware, Berry to Frances Broadnax 11-27-1878 Hy
Ware, C. W. to Dora Ripley 12-7-1864 Sh
Ware, Charles to Fannie N. Maclin 12-27-1875 Hy
Ware, Edward S. to Mary A. Marshall 1-11-1868 Hy
Ware, Griffin G. to Emily J. Ferguson 3-26-1854 Hn
Ware, H. B. to Mary E. Maclin 12-27-1874 Hy
Ware, Hamilton to Ada Bowers 4-14-1873 Hy
Ware, Henry to Elizabeth Wainwright 9-7-1867 Hy
Ware, Hickman to Nannie Maclin 1-24-1876 Hy
Ware, James D. to Ann Fife 11-2-1868 Hy
Ware, James to Kizar Robinson 6-13-1844 Cr
Ware, James to Laura Pullman 5-17-1877 Hy
Ware, Jim to Lizzie Johnson 1-3-1871 Hy
Ware, John C. to Elizabeth B. Green 1-28-1857 Cr
Ware, Joseph J. to Permelia Dodd 11-5-1853 Cr
Ware, L. H. to Elizabeth H. Vinson 1-20-1846 Ma
Ware, Lewis to Edmny? Thompson 11-3-1868 (10?-5-1868) L
Ware, Lewis to Manda Anderson 8-27-1870 Hy
Ware, Mitchell to Lucindy Brodenax 1-6-1875 Hy
Ware, Monroe to Anna Johnson 11-21-1875 (5-3-1876) L B
Ware, Nick to Sally Shapard 7-5-1873 Hy
Ware, Robert P. to Eliza Jane Waldran 5-13-1850 Sh
Ware, Samel D. to Sarah E. Blaydes 2-22-1851 (2-27-1851) F
Ware, William to Dinah Nunn 11-27-1873 Hy
Ware, William to Nancy C. Crockett 8-5-1848 (8-6-1848) O
Ware, William to Nancy Crockett 8-5-1848 O
Ware, Wm. P. to Nancy E. Gibson 4-17-1858 Hr
Ware, Wm. W. to Margaret S. Young 10-3-1854 (10-4-1854) Sh
Warell, Henry to Sarah Rust 11-8-1856 Cr
Waren, James W. to Eliza J. Glasgow 8-3-1856 We
Warf, Burrell to Athey Wooten 1-3-1850 T
Warfield, John to Susan Tyree 7-8-18__ (probably 1870) G B
Warford, Jas. H. to Eliza J. Galloway 11-27-1856 Hr
Warford, R. S. to S. C. Goins 10-17-1870 O
Warington, John to Emily Ann Stacy 9-20-1847 (9-23-1847) F
Warlick, P. D. to M. E. Mitchiner 7-15-1867 (no return) Cr
Warlick, Walton to Filbis Moore 1-5-1871 Cr B
Warmack, Benjamin to Frances C. Arnold 9-4-1846 (9-6-1846) G
Warmack, Burwell to Avy Cook 5-9-1840 (5-12-1840) G
Warmack, James to Mary Shelton 11-28-1873 (12-11-1873) Dy
Warmack, James to Pernelia Humphreys 11-25-1841 Hn
Warmack, Jno. D. to Addie L. Calhoun 12-15-1873 (12-16-1873) T
Warmack, John H. to Nancy King 1-28-1853 Be
Warmack, T. J. to Margaret N. McGlohn 11-16-1854 Be
Warmack, Thomas J. to Elizabeth Baker 9-18-1867 Be
Warmack, William to Eliza McNeal 12-12-1854 Be
Warmack, William to Lavina Grayum 4-17-1870 (8-29-1870) Dy
Warmath, Henry H. to Frances A. Clement 6-12-1855 Ma
Warmath, Henry to Mary Jarratt 11-3-1842 (11-5-1842) Ma
Warmath, J. C. to L. J. Mann 11-15-1876 L
Warmath, Micajah W. to Martha Eudaley 8-23-1850 (8-27-1850) G
Warmath, Thos. D. to Harrett M. Green 9-20-1854 G
Warmath, William to Caroline Quimblay 10-7-1828 Ma
Warmic, William to Winnie Austin 2-10-1878 Hy
Warmoth, Chesterfield to Mary Jane Roseman 1-10-1859 (1-11-1859) Ma
Warmoth, R. H. to A. S. Clement 3-26-1867 G
Warmouth, Robert W. to Catharine Yarbrok 2-3-1858 (2-4-1858) T
Warner, B. W. M. to Jo Ann E. Parrish 10-28-1844 (no return) F
Warner, Fred L. to Matilda Young 8-6-1859 (8-7-1859) Sh
Warner, George to Mary A. Weatherforf 9-15-1867 Hn
Warner, Gregory to Emma Jones 3-29-1874 Hy
Warner, James W. to Martha J. Slone 10-29-1839 (11-7-1839) F
Warner, John G. to Anne M. McIver 9-11-1845 Sh
Warner, Joseph to Martha Alexander 9-24-1857 Ma
Warner, Joseph to Mary G. Whitworth 9-4-1856 (noncomeatibus) Ma
Warner, Thos. L. to Sarah A. Prescott 1-4-1851 (1-7-1851) L
Warner, William to E. W. Moore 9-14-1847 Sh
Warner, William to Melenda Luker 6-1-1855 We
Warner, Wm. E. to C. P. Terry 5-8-1863 (5-10-1863) Cr
Warner, Wm. E. to C. R. Terry 5-8-1863 (no return) Cr

Warpole, James to Ellen E. Allen 2-11-1870 G B
Warpool, B. F. to Emily Keaton 12-4-1865 (12-17-1865) Cr
Warr, L. L. to Sallie Wiseman 9-9-1868 T
Warr, Miles to Martha Williamson 5-5-1871 (5-6-1871) F B
Warr, Rufus to Betty Blain 12-25-1868 (12-27-1868) F B
Warr, Scott to Mattie Isbell 3-1-1869 (3-3-1869) F
Warr, Thomas J. to Annie E. Wiggins 11-21-1865 (no return) F
Warran, A. J. to M? A. Thompson 1-22-1884 L
Warran, William J. to Mary J. Moplin 8-2-1870 (not executed) L
Warran, William to Elizabeth C. Keathley 5-11-1839 (5-15-1839) G
Warrel, Cardy to Frances J. Strain 7-3-1852 Ma
Warren, A. J. to Susan Jane Witt 9-26-1874 Hy
Warren, Abner to Marcilla? Glenn 8-17-1846 (8-20-1846) Hr
Warren, Alexander to Elizabeth T. Puett 6-7-1858 (6-8-1858) O
Warren, Alvin to Ruthey Wellman 12-24-1834 (12-28-1834) Hr
Warren, Alvis to Susan Hamm 9-15-1862 Mn
Warren, Anderson to Salak? McCully 4-20-1866 (no return) F B
Warren, Archibald to Matilda J. Walker 6-8-1858 Sh
Warren, Asbury to Eliza Anne Williams 7-23-1847 (8-4?-1847) Hr
Warren, B. E. to Tabitha Carter 1-4-1853 (1-5-1853) O
Warren, Charles H. to Mattie E. Linsey 12-22-1874 T
Warren, Daniel E. to Sarah A. Williams 4-6-1853 Hr
Warren, E. I. to L. Chisenhall 9-22-1867 O
Warren, Ebenezer to Sarah Moody 6-6-1833 Sh
Warren, Ed to Mary Wirt 12-26-1866 F B
Warren, Edwin to Mary Blankenship 5-9-1840 (5-14-1840) G
Warren, Elijah F. to Louisa J. Riggs 8-12-1854 (8-17-1854) Hr
Warren, Elijah F. to Sarah Dawson 6-20-1845 (6-22-1845) Hr
Warren, George to Mary Jane Harriss 10-15-1859 (10-16-1859) Hr
Warren, George to Mary Mankins 5-2-1857 Hn
Warren, H. A. to J. F. Knight 1-23-1867 Mn
Warren, H. F. to Matilda Bobbitt 12-22-1877 Hy
Warren, Henry to Elizabeth E. Burton 11-1-1838 Sh
Warren, Henry to Martha Stott 1-29-1873 Hy
Warren, Henry to Mary Ann Hainey 8-10-1877 Hy
Warren, Henry to Susan Temple 12-24-1869 (2-26-1870) F B
Warren, J. R. to M. C. C. Ellis 9-13-1867 O
Warren, James A. to Elizabeth Holladay 10-10-1840 Hn
Warren, James M. to Rutha L. Roseman 12-9-1862 Ma
Warren, James W. to Arella Futrell 10-6-1847 (10-6-1847) Ma
Warren, James to Martha J. Stucken 11-22-1860 Dy
Warren, James to Mary F. Willson 3-15-1859 (no return) We
Warren, Jefferson to Elizabeth Owen 12-21-1831 (1-5-1832) Hr
Warren, Joe to Alice Thompson 3-25-1885 (3-26-1885) L
Warren, John B. to Mary A. Smith 2-9-1858 Cr
Warren, John C. to Sarah Murphy 9-10-1828 (9-11-1828) Hr
Warren, John G. to Eliza Avery 3-25-1831 G
Warren, John M. to Mildred F. Brandon 10-15-1856 O
Warren, John M. to Sophronia Clarke 11-15-1834 Hn
Warren, John to Cora Johnson 1-11-1834 (1-16-1834) Hr
Warren, John to E. E. Lock 10-8-1863 Mn
Warren, John to Emily S. PSankey 1-29-1855 (1-30-1855) Hr
Warren, John to Mary Sanders 2-3-1844 Hn
Warren, John to Sarah G. Duncan 6-21-1842 (6-22-1842) O
Warren, Jonathan to Mary A. Halliburton 10-24-1869 G
Warren, Joseph to Bettie McFadden 2-2-1868 G
Warren, Joseph to Caroline Bell 4-14-1868 (no return) Dy
Warren, Joseph to Henny Myly 12-3-1865 Hn
Warren, Joseph to Lucinda Clift 11-7-1840 (11-26-1840) Hr
Warren, Lane to Liller Williams 8-4-1870 (8-7-1870) L
Warren, London to Jane Jones 3-22-1870 (4-9-1870) F B
Warren, M. M. to Laura Young 5-19-1883 (5-24-1883) L
Warren, Nathaniel W. to Harriet R. Vail 4-2-1864 (4-4-1864) Dy
Warren, Nathaniel to Martha J. Smith 10-27-1851 (10-29-1851) Sh
Warren, Newton W. to Susan G. Mitchell 7-19-1853 (7-21-1853) G
Warren, P. A. to T. L. Drake 10-9-1856 Cr
Warren, Perry to Caroline Warren 12-3-1866 (12-8-1866) F B
Warren, Pomfrett H. to Fanny A. Levy 11-22-1870 F
Warren, R. B. to L. E. Altome? 2-2-1865 Hn
Warren, R. F. to Mary E. Baugh 2-17-1868 (2-20-1868) F
Warren, R. H. to Laura L. Glenn 12-26-1866 (12-27-1866) L
Warren, R. W. to Lourana L. Glenn 12-26-1866 (12-27-1866) L
Warren, Robert W. to Ann R. Grammer 10-21-1854 (10-25-1854) L
Warren, Robert to Amanda Ann Mace 12-17-1840 (12-22-1840) Hr
Warren, Robert to Mary E. Duffer 12-8-1864 G
Warren, Samuel H. to Emily Ann Kimbrough 11-7-1839 Sh
Warren, Thomas C. to Clara Corden 7-16-1857 Cr
Warren, Thomas R. to Elizabeth E. T. Kerr 9-19-1860 (9-20-1860) Hr
Warren, Thomas R. to Rebecca Ann Gattis 12-15-1848 (12-20-1848) Ma
Warren, Thomas to Elizabeth Snider 11-25-1841 (11-28-1841) O
Warren, Thomas to Mollie Scot 2-4-1885 (2-5-1885) L
Warren, Thomas to Narcissa Sewell 7-27-1862 Mn
Warren, Thomas to Roxanna Neel 2-27-1869 (3-28-1869) F B
Warren, W. M. to Mary L. Evans 10-10-1860 (not executed) Cr
Warren, W. S. to Mariah O. Striclin 2-19-1869 (no return) Dy
Warren, Wesley to Sarah Millington Travis 8-6-1839 (no return) Hn
Warren, William Thomas to Emiline G. Crowder 11-19-1840 (12-2-1850) Hr

Warren, William to Balm Hughes 6-20-1868 G
Warren, Wm. D. to Angeline Edwards 12-13-1852 Sh
Warren, Wm. J. to Mary Eliza Caraway 8-19-1854 (8-24-1854) O
Warren, Y. H. to Emily F. Thompson 3-3-1858 Cr
Warren, Z. T. to E. C. Canaday 1-11-1868 O
Warren, Zachariah P. to Sarah E. Brown 11-3-1862 Hy
Warren, Zedrick to Lizzie Baxler 12-23-1867 (12-24-1867) F B
Warrick, Hyram to Charity Melton 10-28-1847 Be
Warrick, W. R. to Mary A. Pafford 5-21-1868 Be
Warrick, William to Mary Ann Presson 3-27-1851 Be
Warrin, Edwin to Elizabeth Hendrick 5-8-1831 G
Warrin, Robert to Sina Keathley 9-11-1839 (9-12-1839) G
Warrin, William C. to Nancy L. Driskell 12-25-1843 G
Warrington, L. E. to Emma Glass 1-1-1856 Sh
Warson (Watson), Absalom to Sarah Tucker 5-10-1849 Sh
Warters, William W. to Sally Reynolds 2-13-1844 Be
Wasborn, Andrew J. (I?) to Mary A. Hendrix 4-12-1860 We
Wash, William to Harrett L. Guarrant 3-30-1840 F
Washam, Richard to Mahaily White 5-20-1866 Hn B
Washam, William to Sarah E. Hale 10-11-1859 O
Washbern, Belfred C. to Nancy Baker 1-27-1847 (1-18?-1847) O
Washburn, Elmer to E. J. Knight 1-19-1860 Sh
Washburn, John A. to W. (Mrs.) Rockwell 5-3-1838 Sh
Washburn, John W. to Nancy J. Jackson 8-4-1867 Hn
Washington, Andrew to Tennessee Jones 7-22-1874 Hy
Washington, Boswell to Bettie Nelson 1-13-1876 Hy
Washington, Caesar to Mary Burrell 1-15-1870 G B
Washington, Dock to Sally Yancy 8-22-1868 Hy
Washington, Frank to Etta Parker 1-2-1873 Hy
Washington, Geo. W. to Charlotte Exum 12-21-1868 (no return) F B
Washington, Geo. to Matilda Keener 9-3-1866 (9-8-1866) F
Washington, George to Clary Warr 9-11-1869 (9-26-1869) F B
Washington, George to Harriet Jones 9-22-1870 F B
Washington, George to Jack Ann Rhodes 8-6-1870 (8-7-1870) T
Washington, George to Martha Fitzpatrick 7-25-1876 (7-27-1876) L
Washington, George to Millie Taylor 2-26-1870 Hy
Washington, George to Moriah Taylor 2-23-1871 Hy
Washington, George to Sallie Dison 8-21-1873 T
Washington, George to Sally A. Staten? 1-13-1843 Hr
Washington, George to Sarah Lewis 3-10-1868 (no return) F B
Washington, Henry to Jane Walls 12-28-1868 (1-18-1869) F B
Washington, Henry to Susan Henderson 3-21-1868 (3-22-1868) O
Washington, James to Annie Morgan 12-28-1867 F B
Washington, Lewis to Fannie White 5-17-1877 Dy
Washington, Samuel to Elizabeth Poole 3-22-1830 Hr
Washington, Tillman to Mollie Moore 9-8-1867 G B
Washington, W. B. to Louisa M. Dickason 5-1-1850 F
Washington, Wm. B. to Virginia Dickason 8-7-1860 (8-8-1860) F
Wass?, James to Elisabeth Jones 8-22-1868 (8-23-1868) T
Wasson, J. B. to Julia C. Farnsworth 1-28-1864 Sh
Wasson, William to Elizabeth Pitts 7-28-1844 Sh
Waterfield, A. P. to Isabella Feser 4-21-1857 We
Waterfield, N. B. to F. A. Dent 4-13-1855 We
Wateridge, D. H. to Mary Ivey 10-11-1866 Hy
Wateridge, D. W. to E. J. Marcom 11-28-1877 Hy
Wateridge, W. H. to Z. E. Castalaw 12-24-1868 Hy
Waterman, L. A. to M. F. Goode 9-21-1857 Sh
Waters, E. A. to Margaret McCord 12-2-1863 Hn
Waters, F. M. to Frances Simpson 1-1-1870 (1-3-1870) Dy
Waters, J. B. to Sarah L. Bond 7-21-1853 Be
Waters, J. N. to Eliza A. Murray 6-13-1868 Dy
Waters, John to Ann Adam 1-9-1830 Ma
Waters, John to Jane Pareson? 12-6-1857 Be
Waters, Joseph to Nancy Hutcherson 1-12-1863 Mn
Waters, L. H. to Hattie Nash 4-10-1880 (4-18-1880) Dy
Waters, Obadiah to Jemima Rushing 1-1-1845 Be
Waters, Robert S. to Nancy V. Bush 11-2-1865 (no return) Hn
Waters, Robert to Polly Ann Jones 3-8-1854 Be
Waters, Thos. to Mary Moore 1-30-1845 (no return) We
Waters, Wm. H. to Sarah G. Palma 6-18-1855 (6-21-1855) Sh
Watford, Henry to Harriet A. Bond 1-9-1872 Hy
Watfort, King to Anner Neal 2-3-1877 Hy
Watfort, Nelson to Eliza Bell 2-3-1877 Hy
Watkins, B. F. to Sarah Emarson 2-18-1860 G
Watkins, Benj. to Emiline Morris 7-29-1866 Hy
Watkins, Benj. to Sarah A. Winfrey 1-23-1851 (no return) F
Watkins, Benjamin F. to Sarah P. Harding 1-19-1857 Ma
Watkins, Bob to Lina Read 3-31-1872 Hy
Watkins, Elbert to Aggie Baldwin 12-31-1871 Hy
Watkins, Frank to Matha King 1-30-1873 Hy
Watkins, G. D. to M. Owen 1-4-1872 Hy
Watkins, George to Isabella Holmes 12-31-1843 Hn
Watkins, George to Rachel Freeman 6-20-1878 Hy
Watkins, Henry C. to Malvina H. Day 11-5-1845 Ma
Watkins, Hezekiah to Eliza Jackson 12-23-1854 Sh
Watkins, Hiram to Martha Ann Bussel 12-25-1850 Be
Watkins, Isaac to Esther Ann Hudspeth 12-3-1860 (no return) Hn

Watkins, Isaac to Margaret J. Grainger 1-29-1867 Hn
Watkins, Isaac to Margaret J. Grainger 2-6-1866 (no return) Hn
Watkins, Isaiah to Olivia C. Crews 12-24-1849 Hr
Watkins, Israel to Elizabeth McKinnen 6-6-1836 Hr
Watkins, J. O. C. to Permelia A. Wright 9-22-1856 (no return) L
Watkins, J. S. to Lucy A. Dodson 9-13-1865 G
Watkins, J. W.? to Martha J. Mathis 11-28-1867 Hn
Watkins, James T. to Mary Jones 7-28-1858 (8-4-1858) O
Watkins, James to Lucinda Barrett 11-14-1850 Hn
Watkins, James to Lucinda Cargill 12-28-1866 (no return) F B
Watkins, James to Mollie Morris 6-25-1875 Hy
Watkins, Jas. B. to L. M. Lankford 12-6-1871 Hy
Watkins, John S. to Eliza S. Brown 4-7-1868 Ma
Watkins, John S. to Jane S. Todd 11-8-1843 (11-9-1843) Ma
Watkins, John W. to Martha Jane Oliver 3-13-1850 Hn
Watkins, John W. to Nancy Jane Mathis 5-16-1864 (no return) Hn
Watkins, John to Clarissa Turner 11-24-1840 Hn
Watkins, Jonas to Jennett Jones 11-16-1882 (11-18-1882) L
Watkins, Joseph H. to Parilee J. Crews 12-5-1870 (12-6-1870) Cr
Watkins, L. B. to Mattie Foster 12-2-1878 (12-4-1878) L
Watkins, Major to Dolly Phillips 10-17-1868 (10-31-1868) F B
Watkins, Nathan to Harriett Williams 11-6-1877 Hy
Watkins, Nelson to Parilee Douglass 8-12-1866 Hy
Watkins, Newton P. to Martha J. Watson 2-6-1869 (no return) Dy
Watkins, R. H. to C. A. Peoples 6-18-1850 We
Watkins, R. to L. M. E. Sneed 7-20-1838 T
Watkins, Robert W. to Mary E. Fisher 11-24-1856 (no return) L
Watkins, Samuel S. to Louisa C. Harris 12-20-1847 (12-21-1847) Ma
Watkins, Simeon to Mary McNutt 9-1-1840 Hn
Watkins, Stephen K. to Grace Humphreys 12-12-1866 F
Watkins, Thomas J. to Rutha J. Kelley 10-28-1847 F
Watkins, Thomas P. to Martha A. Booth 9-18-1838 F
Watkins, Thomas to Martha Stagner 7-14-1851 Hn
Watkins, W. G. to Sarah J. Harden (Haiden) 5-19-1847 Sh
Watkins, W. L. to Mary K. Weakley 2-14-1866 Dy
Watkins, Wade to Ella Foster 8-21-1873 Hy
Watkins, Walton to Susie Trezevant 10-17-1871 (10-18-1871) Ma
Watkins, Wesley to Martha Nickleson 1-21-1870 Hy
Watkins, Will M. to Eliza A. Phillips 9-27-1860 Dy
Watkins, William F. to Mary E. Richardson 4-30-1878 Hy
Watkins, William to Annie Read 12-12-1876 Hy
Watkins, William to Frances Cash 11-12-1857 Hn
Watkins, Wyatt B. to Mary E. Wall 8-23-1853 (no return) F
Watkins, Zach to Fannie Stevens 10-11-1876 (10-12-1876) Dy
Watlington, Francis W. to Mollie J. Anderson 4-26-1867 (4-27-1867) Ma
Watlington, Sterling M. to Catharine Croom 5-14-1866 Ma
Watlington, William T. to Elizabeth Ozier 8-5-1847 Ma
Watson, A. E. to W. Bowden 3-21-1854 Cr
Watson, A. S. to S. J. Mead 1-31-1849 (2-1-1849) O
Watson, A. T. to Harriet S. Baugh 10-4-1859 Sh
Watson, A. W. to L. C. Jordan 1-15-1863 Be
Watson, Albert to Mary J. Simpson 11-20-1868 (11-22-1868) Dy
Watson, Alfred to Sarah Ann Halbrooks 2-27-1850 Be
Watson, Anail to Mary Elizabeth White 7-1-1854 (7-2-1854) Ma
Watson, Andrew J. to Sarah F. Devenport 11-11-1867 (11-13-1867) L
Watson, B. B. to Luizer Ashley 12-6-1865 G
Watson, B. H. to M. E. Parker 9-26-1863 (9-27-1863) O
Watson, Beverly B. to Nancy E. Page 3-4-1850 G
Watson, Bob to Callie Bates 12-29-1883 (12-30-1883) L
Watson, Dav? to Mary Presson 9-29-1840 Be
Watson, David to Catharine Stiller 7-5-1834 G
Watson, David to Patience A. Smith 1-13-1868 Be
Watson, David to Rebecca C. Ballard 7-22-1851 Be
Watson, David to Rhoda Jordan 2-2-1865 Be
Watson, E. A. to M. A. Booth 12-18-1873 Hy
Watson, E. D. to S. Y. Jorden 10-17-1876 Hy
Watson, E. J. to Sarah? Bumpass 3-1-1842 F
Watson, Edward F. to Nancy Akmaugh 11-14-1855 Cr
Watson, F. M. to S. A. Jackson 2-6-1878 (no return) L
Watson, Frank E. to Alice Grogan 12-29-1885 (12-30-1885) L
Watson, G. R. to Eliza Cathen 3-14-1878 Hy
Watson, Geo. M. to Frances C. Duke 4-26-1849 We
Watson, George W. to Cassa Ann Hendricks 2-8-1854 Ma
Watson, Henry to Drusilla Parks 9-26-1884 L
Watson, Henry to Louisa Estes 5-28-1876 Hy
Watson, Henry to Martha J. Scarborough 12-4-1860 We
Watson, Henry to Rowena Lake 8-21-1879 L
Watson, Isaac to Lucinda Greer 6-10-1846 Be
Watson, Izeral Crain to Martha Elizabeth Pollard 9-20-1870 L
Watson, J. A. to A. E. Brooks 3-23-1852 (3-24-1852) Sh
Watson, J. A. to Susan A. Ellison 10-27-1874 (10-28-1874) T
Watson, J. H. to Martha M. Colly 3-4-1861 We
Watson, J. H. to Rebecca Surber 12-20-1867 (12-22-1867) Cr
Watson, J. W. to Ellen Harris 10-18-1860 G
Watson, J. W. to Virginia C. Jones 5-14-1866 Hn
Watson, Jack to Tilla Bowden 2-28-1866 Hn
Watson, Jacob D. to M. A. Johnston? 11-21-1847 Hn

Watson, James G. to Mencus J. Goodlow 3-12-1855 (no return) F
Watson, James M. to L. L. Wade 11-24-1868 (11-26-1868) T
Watson, James N. to Mary Capps 9-18-1864 Be
Watson, James T. to Nancy L. Edwards 1-27-1869 (1-28-1869) Ma
Watson, James to Elizabeth Floyd 12-6-1836 Hr
Watson, James to Talisha C Presson 12-12-1851 Be
Watson, Joe to Eddie Jackson 1-22-1876 Hy
Watson, Joe to Lucy Halliburton 3-16-1871 Hy
Watson, John E. to Sarah J. Chambers 12-25-1860 (12-26-1860) L
Watson, John R. to Phebe Fielder 1-6-1869 (no return) L
Watson, John S. to Margaret Sammons 3-18-1863 O
Watson, John W. to C. Helen Reville 6-21-1861 Sh
Watson, John W. to Juliet V. Castleman 7-25-1854 Sh
Watson, John W. to Rebecca J. Parker 12-18-1860 Cr
Watson, John to Louisa Dunnahoe 12-21-1846 (12-23-1846) L
Watson, John to Martha Burton 2-15-1870 Hn
Watson, John to Martha Hazelwood 1-16-1843 G
Watson, John to Nancy Smith 1-29-1868 Be
Watson, John to Sarah Holt 11-3-1852 (11-4-1852) Sh
Watson, Joseph A. to Minerva E. Hilliard 11-5-1856 Cr
Watson, Joseph to Sarah Davenport 12-23-1835 Hr
Watson, K. J. to N. A. Weaver 9-12-1849 (9-13-1849) F
Watson, L. L. to A. L. Johnston 9-24-1857 G
Watson, L. M. to Eliza Sea 10-9-1864 Mn
Watson, Landy to Unissa J. Dial 9-7-1846 (9-10-1846) L
Watson, Lemuel to Elizabeth Faulkes 3-1-1856 (3-25-1856) O
Watson, Lemuel to Mary E. Underwood 9-26-1863 (10-?-1863) O
Watson, Lucian N. to Mary Jane McFall 8-26-1850 (8-29-1850) O
Watson, Lusian N. to Mary Jane McFall 8-26-1850 (8-29-1850) O
Watson, Mack to Manervy Jane Rushing 12-15-1867 Be
Watson, Nathan to Minerva Murray 5-15-1868 (10-25-1868) F B
Watson, Nelson to Mary A. Shofner 1-6-1842 Cr
Watson, P. D. to M. M. Russell 1-13-1869 G
Watson, Richard R. to Sarah J. Cunningham 1-4-1859 G
Watson, Robert D. to Mary E. Darnall 7-29-1853 (8-2-1853) O
Watson, Robert D. to Susan A. Marr 2-12-1849 O
Watson, Robert Z. to Francis Ann Burras 9-8-1853 (9-7?-1853) Ma
Watson, Sam'l. to Sarah Ann Nash 12-4-1856 (12-6-1856) O
Watson, Sammie S. to Emaline Wildon 7-14-1853 Cr
Watson, Samuel G. H. to Sarah Barker 6-21-1841 (6-24-1841) O
Watson, Samuel Z. to Jane A. Burton 2-12-1857 Hn
Watson, Sidney Y. to Priscilla S. (Mrs.) Adams 10-1-1860 (10-2-1860) Sh
Watson, T. A. to Nancy A. E. Darough 9-26-1867 Hy
Watson, T. W. to Caldonia Pitts 12-13-1871 (12-14-1871) L
Watson, T. to Jane McGill 6-16-1841 Be
Watson, Thomas A. to Elizabeth Craigue(Craig) 6-27-1863 Be
Watson, Thomas M. to Kisiah Sellars 6-29-1835 (7-2-1835) G
Watson, Thomas to Narcissa Anderson 9-20-1859 Ma
Watson, Thos. J. to Louiza Clark 9-18-1850 Hn
Watson, W. F. to Francis E. Hipp 12-28-1877 (12-29-1877) L
Watson, W. F. to S. A. Hawkins 5-23-1874 (5-24-1874) O
Watson, W. H. to Jennie Jordon 8-2-1869 Hy
Watson, W. H. to Martha E. Combs 12-24-1860 Be
Watson, W. H. to Mary Jones 11-27-1871 (11-28-1871) Dy
Watson, W. S. to Mattie Johnston 7-8-1878 Hy
Watson, W. T. to Cora E. Harris 1-14-1861 (1-15-1861) F
Watson, William H. to Sarah R. Tyner 2-4-1843 (2-10-1843) Ma
Watson, William H. to Virginia J. Abernathy 10-29-1845 Sh
Watson, William to Frances Coleman 9-12-1857 (9-18-1857) G
Watson, William to Martha J. Campbell 2-8-1853 Ma
Watson, Wm. to Mary Armer 10-26-1839 Be
Watt, Bowlen to Pamelia Trimble 4-12-1854 We
Watt, Daniel to Margarett Thurston 4-14-1867 G B
Watt, J. F. to Annie C. Foster 11-9-1869 G
Watt, J. M. to Marsilla Keel 9-17-1860 (9-26-1860) Sh
Watt, James N. to Elizabeth Lyon 4-3-1841 (4-4-1841) G
Watt, James S. to Susan L. Robinett 4-19-1853 (4-21-1853) Sh
Watt, Jas. N. to Mary P. Austin 12-6-1858 (12-12-1858) G
Watt, John M. to Catharine Ann McClure 9-8-1848 G
Watt, John M. to Trifena Jester 9-1-1851 (9-2-1851) G
Watt, Saml. M. to Arminta Peel 12-28-1859 (12-29-1859) Sh
Watt, Samuel to Eliza Stern (Starnes) 8-19-1847 Sh
Watt, Samuel to Martha C. Quinly 12-18-1841 (12-19-1841) Ma
Watt, Samuel to Thursday Sires? 9-28-1861 G
Watt, Thomas J. to Nancy E. Lyon 9-4-1867 (9-5-1867) Ma
Watt, Thomas J. to Sarah A. Lyon 1-4-1854 (1-12-1854) Ma
Watt, Thomas to M. J. Dowdy 10-6-1867 G
Watt, Thomas to Mary Fowler 12-21-1842 G
Watt, Thos. to Avolina G. Bledsoe 9-29-1857 (9-28-1857) G
Watt, William to M. C. Taylor 12-29-1865 G
Watt, Wm. M. to Cordelia Browne 6-2-1845 (no return) F
Watt, jr., James N. to Sarah Jane Lyon 3-16-1850 Ma
Watters, Joel to Mary Wood 3-4-1841 Hn
Wattes, Benj. to Meboly Wattes 5-6-1852 Cr
Watts, Alison M. to Mary Jane Lynn 10-24-1854 (10-26-1854) Sh
Watts, Benjamin to Mary J. Younger 10-16-1860 (10-6?-1860) Cr
Watts, Benjamine F. to Elizabeth Miller 10-8-1859 We
Watts, Bowlin to Pamelia Tinbee 4-12-1854 We
Watts, C. H. to Mahulda Boyett 1-23-1866 O
Watts, Edmond to Susan Hunt 2-16-1867 G
Watts, J. H. to Virginia A. P. Watts 1-22-1862 G
Watts, John F. to Matilda Simmons 12-5-1861 (no return) We
Watts, Milichi to Matilda Totten 11-13-1830 G
Watts, Richard to Eliza J(ackson) McElyea 12-20-1850 Sh
Watts, Solomon to Elizabeth Ann Nedrey 9-2-1839 (9-11-1839) O
Watts, Vinson to Nancy Watts 9-28-1841 O
Watts, W. J. to Ana H. Jackson 10-7-1871 (10-8-1871) O
Watts, W. J. to Evelly Eckley 1-21-1873 (1-22-1873) O
Watts, William to Nancy A. Howard 1-8-1862 We
Wattson, William to Nancy A. Howard 1-8-1862 We
Wayatt, Pinkney A. to Ann Oakley 8-13-1863 (no return) We
Wayman, J. P. to Eliza A. Snowden 12-13-1854 (12-14-1854) Sh
Wayman, John to Frances McKinney 8-18-1841 T
Wayman, Wm. McG. to Kate Wood 11-22-1860 Sh
Waymon, Kirtley to Eliza Dorsey 2-8-1847 Sh
Wayne, B. F. to Emma Pots 6-20-1854 We
Waynick, A. R. to Mollie J. Lanier 10-13-1856 (10-30-1856) Ma
Wayson, Alex to Nancy Stricklin 1-15-1878 Dy
Weakes, John R. to Mary Ann Hopper 12-21-1869 (12-23-1869) Ma
Weakes, Tilley to Barbara McMackins 2-8-1844 Cr
Weakley, D. R. to Sallie E. Curtis 3-8-1872 Dy
Weakley, Henry to Agnes Hale 8-1-1877 Dy
Weakley, M. H. P. to Mary Morris 12-24-1870 (3-15-1871) Dy
Weakly, James to Mary Hall 5-22-1867 Dy
Weaks, Andrew R. to Nancy Baucum 8-7-1842 Hn
Weaks, Andrew to Lusetta Cole 7-8-1867 Hn
Weaks, Benjamin to Frances Fitch 9-24-1857 Hn
Weaks, Benjamin to Frances W. Foster 8-21-1843 (no return) Hn
Weaks, David to Mary Webb 10-27-1837 Sh
Weaks, Hewitt to Nancy C. Upchurch 5-5-1853 Hn
Weaks, James H. to Ann E. Tyler 4-11-1851 G
Weaks, James R. to Susan Walker 1-15-1867 Hn
Weams, J. W. to Mathe Houston 1-20-1868 (1-21-1868) Cr
Wear, Ben H. to Lyde Read 5-2-1869 Hy
Wear, Geo. W. to M. F. Nash 12-19-1872 (12-20-1872) O
Weare, Franklin H. to Belviretta Cain 11-16-1857 (11-19-1857) Ma
Weas, Samuel C. to Leanna Jackson 2-4-1861 O
Weatherall, James to Sarah Adison 1-16-1869 Hy
Weathered, James to Elvira Nealy 8-30-1837 Sh
Weatherford, Charles to Mollie Hogan 11-29-1866 (11-2?-1866) Cr
Weatherford, E. A. to Sarah E. Tate 12-11-1866 T
Weatherford, James W. to Eliza Ann Cox 6-16-1836 Sh
Weatherford, James to Sarah Moss 7-21-1865 (7-26-1865) T
Weatherford, W. R. to Minerva J. Griffen 9-17-1863 G
Weatherford, William to Lucinda E. Mickleberry 12-3-1835 Sh
Weatherington, Joshua to Mary Billings 1-8-1857 T
Weatherington, Robert to Martha Collier 9-11-1869 (9-12-1869) T
Weatherley, Joseph J. to Margaret M. Hughes 11-10-1858 (no return) Hn
Weatherley, Wm. Henry Clay to Mary Jane Clark 6-18-1866 (no return) Hn
Weatherly, Andrew D. to Asenith M. Marshall 12-7-1858 (12-8-1858) Ma
Weatherly, George to Jane Stephens 9-22-1866 (9-30-1866) T
Weatherly, James H. (W.?) to M. J. Crawford 2-7-1871 F
Weatherly, James to Mary J. Volentine 11-7-1860 Ma
Weatherly, Joseph J. to Virginia Woodson 1-31-1839 Hn
Weatherly, Lucius L. to Virginia L. (Mrs.) Stratton 5-4-1869 (5-6-1869) Ma
Weatherly, R. T. to Eliza Ann Best 12-15-1875 Hy
Weatherly, Robert to Melissa Ann Wood 11-13-1866 Ma
Weatherly, Rufus A. to Rutha Jane Dickinson 12-12-1859 Ma
Weatherly, Saml. H. to Martha Ann Valentine 11-13-1866 Ma
Weatherly, William M. to Mary Ann Reevely 12-15-1856 Ma
Weatherly, William W. to Sarah F. Winston 12-15-1858 (12-5?-1858) Ma
Weatherred, William D. to Lavina Adams 12-20-1870 (12-22-1870) T
Weathers, Charles H. to Mary Holloman 12-11-1867 (12-12-1867) Ma
Weathers, J. E. to Arabella Eason 10-16-1855 Cr
Weathers, James E. to Mary J. Crisp 2-28-1844 G
Weathers, Jordan to Lucinda Wright 2-23-1874 T
Weathers, Moses to Sina Ann Trusdale 12-30-1873 (12-3?-1873) T
Weatherspoon, Jas. to Rosa Whitelaw 1-19-1878 Hy
Weatherspoon, Joseph to Emaly Rentfro 12-16-1843 (12-21-1843) G
Weaver, Alfred N. to Hawkins Mangrum 11-12-1860 (11-13-1860) Ma
Weaver, B. W. to Sarah A. Knox 12-7-1860 (12-11-1860) Sh
Weaver, Charles A. to Mary Coward 12-28-1869 T
Weaver, Charles to Martha Turner 11-26-1860 Dy
Weaver, Claiborne to Hannah Taylor 11-1-1875 Hy
Weaver, Claibourne to Sarah A. E. Harton 7-19-1843 (7-20-1843) Ma
Weaver, Emmor to Mary E. Womble 9-6-1867 Hy
Weaver, G. C. to Margaret Blakeley 4-3-1880 (4-4-1880) L
Weaver, George to Edmony Johnson 1-2-1868 Hy
Weaver, Governor to Amanda Wilson 10-14-1874 T
Weaver, J. D. to J. A. Caigle 11-22-1882 (11-23-1882) L
Weaver, J. J. to M. C. Elmore 11-7-1867 (11-8-1867) T
Weaver, James to Ann Mcguire 5-26-1838 F
Weaver, James to H. W. Tate 6-24-1841 Sh
Weaver, John A. to Martha J. Lancer 10-15-1844 (no return) F
Weaver, John B. to Susan M. Mathis 4-7-1855 (4-8-1855) G

Weaver, John C. to Jane E. Wheatley 9-19-1860 (9-20-1860) Sh
Weaver, John G. to Elizabeth A. Minton 12-31-1865 Mn
Weaver, John W. to Mary Cass Peters 9-30-1835 Sh
Weaver, John to Rebecca Marvan 3-22-1856 (3-23-1856) G
Weaver, Jonathan W. to Julia (Mrs.) Bland 3-22-1856 (4-2-1856) Sh
Weaver, Joseph H. to Mary Jane Freeland 12-30-1851 Hn
Weaver, Joshua to Nancy Sanford 8-28-1830 Ma
Weaver, Lafayette to Elizabeth I. Parker 9-11-1852 Hr
Weaver, M. W. to Jane Markham 11-13-1847 (11-14-1847) F
Weaver, Phillip to Nancy G. Taylor 11-15-1841 Ma
Weaver, Simpson to Louisa Dement 10-2-1857 (10-4-1857) O
Weaver, Tip to Patra Brown 10-14-1874 T
Weaver, U.(N?) A. to A. M. Holland 8-31-1865 G
Weaver, W. G. to Nancy A. D. Porter 12-26-1869 G
Weaver, W. J. to Cerilla J. Parteet 2-18-1869 (no return) Dy
Weaver, Wm. L. to Lucy L. Weever 11-14-1863 Sh
Weaver, Yancy to Lucinda Poff 1-15-1874 Hy
Webb, A. H. to Mary J. Wadkins 12-19-1853 (12-22-1853) L
Webb, A. H. to Susan J. Williams 9-18-1850 L
Webb, A. to Mary D. Knox 2-1-1850 (no return) F
Webb, Albert J. to Virginia F. Sanderford 10-2-1847 (10-3-1847) G
Webb, Andrew C. to Winefred C. Corburn 5-25-1847 Hr
Webb, Andrew J. to Elizabeth Richey 2-18-1838 F
Webb, Asberry M. to Eliza Jane Freeman 10-5-1833 (10-10-1833) G
Webb, Asberry M. to Nancy C. Ward 7-9-1853 G
Webb, Asberry to Louiza A. Robbins 9-12-1860 Dy
Webb, B. F. to M. A. Dean 10-31-1866 (11-5-1865?) F
Webb, C. W. to Mary C. Phillips 10-30-1858 Cr
Webb, Chas. Wm. to Rosanna Kulbreath 12-19-1850 T
Webb, Claiborne to Susan J. McCrory 2-4-1856 Ma
Webb, Crockett D. to Elizabeth Braden 11-21-1849 L
Webb, David Taylor to Sarah E. Fullen 1-19-1871 L
Webb, E. J. to S. M. Williams 8-13-1879 (8-14-1879) L
Webb, E. O. to F. J. Stiers 7-19-1865 Be
Webb, E. W. to E. F. Baker 10-18-1879 (10-19-1879) Dy
Webb, Elisha A. to Amanda Craig 7-7-1858 (7-27?-1858) L
Webb, G. W. to Ann B. Tatum 8-12-1868 (8-20-1868) Dy
Webb, G. W. to Fannie L. Bylor 1-24-1877 L
Webb, Gardner to Clarissa Judkins 4-25-1870 G
Webb, Geo. C. to Malinda Craig 6-17-1864 (6-19-1864) L
Webb, George C. to Elizabeth F. Pitts 11-12-1857 (no return) L
Webb, George D. to P. E. Foster 12-22-1885 G
Webb, George H. to Mary Jane Winberry 10-21-1855 Be
Webb, George H. to Mary Jane Winberry 10-21-1855 Be CC
Webb, George W. to Henrietta Owen 6-11-1845 Sh
Webb, George to Leoma Capps 12-24-1857 We
Webb, George to Malissa Heath 1-8-1861 We
Webb, Henry to Elizabeth Liddle 1-1-1846 (no return) We
Webb, Henry to Fanny Smothers 10-23-1853 Be
Webb, Henry to Fanny Smothers 10-23-1853 Be CC
Webb, Henry to Martha Foster 10-17-1867 Cr
Webb, Henry to Sarah A. Childress 11-18-1852 Hn
Webb, Hugh to Racal (Mrs.) Copeland 3-19-1846 G
Webb, I. H. D. to Mary Cooper 11-15-1848 L
Webb, Isah to Mary Moore 6-21-1837 (6-22-1837) G
Webb, J. A. to Ann E. Singleton 11-15-1854 L
Webb, J. A. to Ida Colvin 9-11-1877 (9-12-1878?) L
Webb, J. A. to Lula F. Harrison 12-24-1877 (12-26-1877) L
Webb, J. A. to M. T. Wakefield 12-16-1885 L
Webb, J. M. to Docia E. Ferrell 10-24-1853 (10-28-1853) Hr
Webb, J. M. to Ellen H. Taylor 11-17-1865 (11-20-1865) F
Webb, J. M. to M. E. Love 12-20-1865 F
Webb, J. R. to Mary E. Chitwood 9-30-1865 (no return) Dy
Webb, Jacob M. to Elizabeth J. Rogers 11-23-1843 Hr
Webb, Jacob to Elizabeth J. Bell 7-12-1846 Sh
Webb, James A. to Nancy J. Barr 11-14-1860 We
Webb, James F. to Malissa C. Gowan 7-31-1878 (8-1-1878) Dy
Webb, James G. to Mary J. Johnson 11-29-1857 We
Webb, James J. to Louisa K. Taylor 8-23-1867 (8-25-1867) Cr
Webb, James K. to Celia A. Duncan 11-19-1847 (11-20-1848?) Ma
Webb, James M. to Patina C. Perry 1-14-1848 (1-18-1848) F
Webb, James R. to Elizabeth Adams 7-27-1846 (7-30-1846) F
Webb, James W. to America Cunningham 6-5-1854 G
Webb, James W. to Mary Elizabeth Easterwood 8-27-1867 G
Webb, James to Eady Brown 3-23-1874 Hy
Webb, James to Elizabeth Foster 8-4-1865 (8-6-1865) Cr
Webb, Jas. A. to M. L. Winborn 1-20-1868 (1-21-1868) F
Webb, Jeremiah to Peggy Stafford 10-31-1838 (11-3-1838) G
Webb, Jesse to Mahaley Swift 8-10-1848 (no return) Hn
Webb, Jno. C. to Isadore Ketchum 12-2-1858 F
Webb, John L. to Louisa J. Ellison 2-19-1850 (2-23-1850) F
Webb, John L. to Nancy Adams 8-29-1846 (8-31-1846) F
Webb, John P. to Harriett Pemberton 11-12-1862 G
Webb, John R. to Adeline Lee 1-30-1866 Hn
Webb, John S. to Amanda Jane Henderson 12-2-1864 (12-6-1854) O
Webb, John W. to J. A. David 6-17-1871 (6-19-1871) T
Webb, John W. to Martha W. Ragan 12-21-1836 G

Webb, John to Caroline Box 12-4-1854 (12-6-1854) Hr
Webb, John to Ella (Mrs.) Tucker 12-24-1866 (12-25-1866) Dy
Webb, John to Hetta Rodgers 4-26-1870 G
Webb, John to Rachel Baty 12-28-1867 (12-29-1867) T
Webb, Joseph B. to Jennie M. Bunch 12-5-1872 T
Webb, Joseph to Gincy Willborn 12-25-1867 G
Webb, Joseph to Joycy Peeler 9-20-1854 Hr
Webb, Leroy D. to Euvilinah M. Carroll 6-13-1846 (7-14-1846) G
Webb, Levi to Elizabeth Dement 12-9-1844 (12-10-1844) G
Webb, Lewis E. to Susan A. Halstead 9-16-1852 Hn
Webb, M. C. to Mary J. Hogan 11-21-1856 (11-23-1856) Hr
Webb, M. D. to Manurva C. Meadows 7-3-1865 (7-6-1865) L
Webb, M. J. to Sallie L. Black 10-4-1860 (10-5-1860) F
Webb, Madison M. to Eliza Ann Haislip 12-11-1871 L
Webb, Mansil to Frances Rogers 1-25-1853 (1-27-1853) Hr
Webb, McDaniel to Mary E. McKinnie 12-3-1849 (12-5-1849) Hr
Webb, Micajah to Drucilla Farmer 1-11-1828 Ma
Webb, Miles D. to Mary E. Whitamore 4-24-1854 (4-25-1854) L
Webb, Miles D. to Susan A. Rhea 6-4-1844 (no return) L
Webb, N. to M. Morgan 11-29-1882 (no return) L
Webb, Norman to Wethly Webb 12-7-1843 Ma
Webb, Prior to Mary Mashburn 10-10-1849 (10-11-1849) Hr
Webb, R. A. to M. E. White 12-8-1865 Hy
Webb, R. C. to Elizabeth E. Dortch 4-30-1851 (5-1-1851) F
Webb, R. F. to N. M. Foster 8-15-1871 (no return) Cr
Webb, R. M. to M. J. Hicks 12-29-1879 (12-30-1879) L
Webb, R. W. to Mattie J. Ballard 12-28-1867 Hy
Webb, Richard to Sarah A. Patton 9-1-1864 G
Webb, Robert M. to Martha Cooper 11-7-1848 (11-9-1848) G
Webb, Robert T. to Harriet M. White 10-31-1860 (11-1-1860) Ma
Webb, Robert to Eliza Ann Taylor 8-26-1854 (8-26-1854) Hr
Webb, Rufus W. to Sarah R. Webb 2-13-1856 G
Webb, Russell to Nillie Winbush 12-13-1875 (12-19-1875) L B
Webb, S. H. to Mattie E. Finley 1-28-1869 Be
Webb, Samuel J. to Margarette C. Ennis 12-20-1860 G
Webb, Samuel to Emily Bennett 3-19-1857 Be
Webb, Samuel to Emily Burnett 3-19-1857 Be CC
Webb, Samuel to Polly Smith 8-25-1828 G
Webb, Samuel to Polly Smith 8-28-1827 (8-30-1827) G
Webb, Shadrack to Frances Owen 1-16-1850 Sh
Webb, Soloman P. F. to Caroline M. Jenkins 12-16-1857 L
Webb, T. J. to Mary E. Williams 9-9-1873 Hy
Webb, T. S. to Milly Moore 10-16-1858 (10-17-1858) G
Webb, Thomas to Mary Caldwell 11-24-1866 G
Webb, Thos. H. to Emma H. Hamer 5-27-1858 Hr
Webb, Thos. H. to M. S. Macomb 9-4-1867 (no return) Dy
Webb, Travis to Margaret Brown 9-17-1839 Cr
Webb, W. A. to Mollie Grace 8-22-1877 Dy
Webb, W. G. to Susan Webb 12-12-1860 (12-13-1860) Cr
Webb, W. M. to Nannie L. Childress 1-21-1880 L
Webb, W. R. to Henrietta Green 9-7-1880 (9-9-1880) L B
Webb, Washington to Fanny Sturdivant 11-28-1868 G B
Webb, Watson to Franky Jane Field 1-19-1847 (1-21-1847) Hr
Webb, Wilban to Nancy Crockett 6-11-1835 G
Webb, William A. to Mary Ann Sanders 4-9-1841 (4-13-1841) Ma
Webb, William C. to Hester Crockett 1-7-1836 G
Webb, William H. to Martha C. Moore 12-21-1873 L
Webb, William H. to Martha Jane Crockett 9-6-1847 G
Webb, William J. to Fannie P. Love 2-20-1861 Sh
Webb, William R. to Cynthia Ann Elliot 12-22-1866 (12-26-1866) Ma
Webb, William to Eliza Perrett 9-27-1860 L
Webb, Wm. A. to Elizabeth Botton 12-29-1868 (12-31-1868) Ma
Webber, A. J. to Mary J. West 6-8-1862 G
Webber, A. W. to Arretta Bryant 1-11-1853 (no return) F
Webber, Albert to M. F. Ivy 10-24-1866 (11-11-1866) F
Webber, Andrew J. to Susan M. Patterson 1-1-1851 G
Webber, E. B. to Sarah Ann Edmindston 10-2-1855 (10-14-1855) Sh
Webber, James A. to Martha A. Simons 5-3-1875 (5-4-1875) Dy
Webber, James to Ace Catherine Jackson 2-28-1869 G
Webber, John W. to Melinda N. McAlexander 11-19-1862 Sh
Webber, John to Nancy Loving 2-4-1837 Sh
Webber, Philip R. to Joella S. Duvall 10-28-1861 (10-31-1861) Sh
Webber, Phillip to Martha A. Moncreif 12-18-1849 (no return) F
Webber, W. R. to Ally C. Swift 11-16-1867 (no return) F
Weber, J. to Levina Brady 1-6-1840 Sh
Weber, N. to Catherine Haas 8-8-1850 Sh
Webster, Daniel to Louisa Turner 12-25-1869 (12-31-1869) F B
Webster, Henry to Hannah Shinault 12-6-1827 Hr
Webster, Henry to Virginia J. Blackwell 1-18-1869 (1-19-1869) L
Webster, J. M. to M. A. Gentry 1-10-1872 Dy
Webster, James to Isabella Bankhead 3-11-1841 F
Webster, James to Jane Dillingham 9-8-1827 Hr
Webster, Jas. M. to Adaline Ayers 8-8-1832 (9-11-1832) Hr
Webster, Jesse to Sarah Casey 12-12-1835 (12-17-1835) Hr
Webster, John H. to Matilda F. Ussery 7-15-1861 (7-18-1861) Hr
Webster, John to Caroline Mosier 3-28-1865 Mn
Webster, John to Chincy Norment 7-3-1867 Dy

Webster, John to Harriet Paine 11-5-1869 F B
Webster, Joseph H. to Narcissus Woods 1-17-1851 (1-19-1851) T
Webster, L. L. to Mattie J. T. Linn 7-13-1874 (7-15-1874) T
Webster, R. M. to N. M. A. Capps 2-4-1857 We
Webster, Samuel to Martha Ragan 2-6-1827 Hr
Webster, Shadrick to Elizabeth J. Cunningham 4-19-1857 Hn
Webster, William to Mary Ann Moore 12-21-1867 (12-22-1867) L
Webster, Wm. M. to A. E. Lowry 11-10-1878 Hy
Weddington, James to Nancy M. Cloud 11-29-1859 We
Weddington, W. B. to J. M. Spadder 8-15-1857 Cr
Weddington, W. B. to Josaphine McMackin 2-15-1871 Dy
Weddington, W. B. to S. M. Gallian 8-11-1859 (8-14-1859) G
Weddle, J. G. to Martha Gentry 2-24-1863 G
Weddle, James B. to Harriet Melear 9-18-1861 Hn
Weddle, Jeremiah G. to Jane Ann Gardner 2-15-1847 G
Weddle, Sam to Fanny Harbert 3-14-1876 Hy
Weddle, Sam to Kisza Cotter 12-23-1877 Hy
Wedgestaff, Wm. to Charlett Anderson 10-17-1872 Hy
Wedgewood, P. D. to Mary A. B. Major 8-30-1856 (8-31-1856) Sh
Wedington, R. G. to Jane T. Whitaker 1-4-1858 (1-5-1858) G
Weed, James P. to Mary L. Moffatt 8-21-1847 (8-23-1847) O
Weed, John L. to Maria A. James 4-19-1854 Sh
Weeks, John H. to Mary S. Alexander 1-27-1852 Hn
Weeks, W. R. to Keran H. Uprchurch 9-15-1859 Hn
Weeks, W. S. to Sarah Branch 9-6-1868 Be
Weems, Perry to Ann Hess 12-18-1873 Hy
Weener (Werner?), Phillip to Eva Sultsman 2-4-1861 Sh
Weever, E. J. to M. E. C. Hobs 12-17-1874 T
Weever, Wm. L. to Lucy L. Weaver 11-14-1863 (11-15-1863) Sh
Weglesworth, A. J. to E. A. Hollowell 12-27-1856 Sh
Wegmann, Nickolas to Mary Statzle 4-26-1856 Sh
Wehrum (Warham?), John to Harriet Vanhorn 2-19-1861 Sh
Wehrum, Philip to Elizabeth Stephen 2-10-1858 Sh
Weick, James T. to Eliza R. Terry 11-3-1853 (no return) Hn
Weidgwoood, P. D. to Sarah Haynes 5-8-1847 Sh
Weigand, Wm. F. to Nancy Maceer 8-12-1862 Sh
Weigel, Louis to Elizabeth Hassel 3-21-1857 Sh
Weight, Francis to Barborah Fullbright 12-15-1828 Ma
Weiler (Weiblen), Philipp to Madaline Lienhardt 2-7-1850 Sh
Weiner, W. to Hellen Geiberger 9-18-1860 Sh
Weinr (White), George to Louise Kney 12-15-1855 Sh
Weir, David D. to Margaret Weir 8-10-1830 Ma
Weir, Donald D. to Ann B. Weir 2-14-1842 (2-15-1842) Ma
Weir, John P. to Elizabeth W. Rogers 5-5-1842 Ma
Weirich, Peter to Salomea Woerne 9-6-1864 Sh
Weiser, John to Ellen Welsh 12-7-1857 Sh
Weisheiver, John C. to Nanny Freeman 8-15-1870 (8-16-1870) T
Weiss, Emanuel to Margaret Schroeder 10-23-1849 Sh
Welb, James R. to Sarah Ballard 8-26-1857 (8-31-1857) T
Welborne, Isaac Y. to Sarah Blankenship 10-22-1856 (10-25-1856) O
Welbourn, C. C. to Annie Show 1-5-1860 F
Welch, Charles H. to Cordelia T. Lyle 12-22-1868 (12-24-1868) T
Welch, Esquire to Rachel Jones 6-19-1877 Dy
Welch, F. M. to Emily S. Gee 10-4-1858 (10-7-1858) Hr
Welch, F. M. to Hannah J. Mayfield 5-3-1850 (5-9-1850) Hr
Welch, Francis E. to Ann B. Carlten 8-12-1858 We
Welch, George to Polly Ward 1-6-1844 (1-7-1844) Hr
Welch, Harrod P. to Martha Pruitt 12-22-1829 G
Welch, Henry to Caroline Smith 2-15-1836 (2-18-1836) G
Welch, J. A. to Sarah S. E. Rogers 7-30-1850 (not endorsed) We
Welch, J. M. to Nancy Hutchens 7-9-1857 We
Welch, Jacob W. to Francis J. (Mrs.) Taylor 4-15-1862 (4-27-1862) Ma
Welch, James to Frances Fields 9-29-1835 (9-30-1835) G
Welch, James to Mary Smith 6-26-1845 Sh
Welch, James to Mary Whaling 6-30-1845 Sh
Welch, John H. to Anna Dallas 10-24-1849 O
Welch, John L. to Mary Snowden 1-1-1859 (1-4-1859) Sh
Welch, John S. to Judeth Roberts 7-29-1846 We
Welch, John to Nancy I. Vaugan 12-27-1852 (12-28-1852) Hr
Welch, M. D. to Sallie E. Harris 10-5-1858 Sh
Welch, Michael to Margarett Hartigan 4-9-1864 (4-10-1864) Sh
Welch, Miles to Lucretia Forsythe 9-24-1859 (9-25-1859) G
Welch, Patrick J. to Louiza Cunningham 5-28-1873 Cr
Welch, Patrick to Catharine Mullins 5-9-1853 (5-10-1853) Sh
Welch, Richard to July Wade 6-17-1843 (6-18-1843) G
Welch, S. J. to M. L. E. Johnson 8-18-1871 Dy
Welch, Thomas to Eviline Butler 10-29-1866 G
Welch, Thos. to Ann Williams 4-?-1866 (4-19-1866) O
Welch, W. G. to M. F. Rainey 10-29-1870 (10-30-1870) Dy
Welch, William to Florence Claiss 7-29-1874 Dy
Welch, Willie J. to Mary A. Brown 9-27-1866 Ma
Welch, Wm. H. to Roseann Hale 4-16-1863 Sh
Weld, Jno. B. to Mary C. Christian 7-20-1846 Sh
Weldon, Andrew J. to Sarah C. McSwain 12-22-1852 Hn
Weldon, James W. to Harriet A. Gould 5-27-1850 Hn
Weldon, William W. to Nancy E. P. Chilcutt 2-3-1846 Hn
Wellborn, Henry E. to Jane Talbott 12-5-1853 (no return) F

Weller(Miller?), Cyrus W. to Elizabeth E. McLeary 9-1-1840 (9-2-1840) T
Weller, W. H. to Henrietta Wenderoth 10-30-1861 Sh
Wellingham, Anderson to Nancy Stitt 3-19-1869 (4-11-1869) T
Wellington, W. F. to Angeline Lackey 12-19-1869 Hy
Wellions, Henry C. to Lenora M. F. Guy 12-11-1851 Hr
Wellions, Henry to Susan Ann Rainer 3-13-1843 (3-13?-1843) Hr
Wellons, Charles M. to Cela M. Crawford 11-28-1850 Hr
Wellons, Henry C. to Martha C. Boston 4-12-1859 (4-14-1859) Hr
Wellons, Larkin M. to Nancy T. Hannis 9-25-1841 (9-30-1841) Hr
Wells, A. D. to Mary F. Smith 1-16-1867 L
Wells, A. Dolphis to Mary J. Garrison 1-11-1847 (no return) F
Wells, Alexander to Julia C. McWhirter 12-18-1868 Ma
Wells, Alexander to Rachel Reid 9-30-1841 Sh
Wells, B. B. to D. M. H. Browning 11-13-1874 Hy
Wells, Benjamin L. to Jane Bunn 11-18-1866 Be
Wells, Charles W. to Elizabeth Bullock 6-12-1843 (no return) We
Wells, Daniel I. to Mary E. Suggett? 11-24-1836 Hr
Wells, Danl. to Frances Currie 10-12-1872 Hy
Wells, G. W. to Sallie G. Hubbard 7-24-1869 Hy
Wells, Geo. G. to Callie Hooks 11-19-1867 Hy
Wells, George W. to Louisa M. Moore 12-19-1854 (12-20-1854) O
Wells, George to Emma Currie 6-14-1876 Hy
Wells, Henry W. to Mary S. Bassinger 8-1-1859 G
Wells, Horatio S. to Mary High 10-26-1842 F
Wells, J. C. to M. A. Ferguson 3-28-1859 (3-29-1859) Hr
Wells, J. G. to E. C. Vincent 2-9-1842 (2-10-1842) F
Wells, J. W. to Nannie L. B. Strong 10-21-1872 L
Wells, James Grayer to Mary Ida Currey 12-23-1868 G
Wells, James S. to M. C. Barton 8-6-1852 Hn
Wells, James to Fannie Votter 2-23-1878 Hy
Wells, James to Martha Barber 1-15-1873 Hy
Wells, James to Nancy Jones 6-5-1870 G B
Wells, Jas. B. to Louisa Powell 3-24-1842 Sh
Wells, Jas. T. to Mary E. Lancaster 6-12-1860 O
Wells, Jim to Harriet Moffit 9-5-1868 (9-6-1868) F B
Wells, John L. to Polly M. McBride 1-13-1831 Hr
Wells, John M. to Sarah Patterson 9-27-1845 (9-28-1845) G
Wells, John S. to Julia F. Ford 7-15-1862 (7-16-1862) L
Wells, John to Josey White 4-19-1873 (4-20-1873) T
Wells, John to Mary Burk 8-13-1857 Sh
Wells, John to Mary Jane Peyton 6-6-1857 (6-7-1857) Ma
Wells, Joseph M. to Sally Burns 1-2-1830 (1-9-1830) Hr
Wells, Lee to Dinkie Light 10-26-1871 Dy
Wells, Lewis to Margaret H. Guthrie 10-29-1850 Hr
Wells, M. D. to Annie Summers 12-9-1884 L
Wells, M. M. to Nannie J. Black 11-28-1870 Hy
Wells, Martin R. to Lizzie Schully 2-20-1861 Sh
Wells, Moses to Eudora Nunn 5-13-1877 Hy
Wells, Nelson to Ann Whitthorn 12-27-1869 F B
Wells, Nelson to Judy Mason 12-31-1868 (no return) F
Wells, Peter to B. A. Clements 1-5-1869 Hy
Wells, Pleasant B. to Emily Little 1-14-1832 Hr
Wells, R. M. to Elizabeth Jennings 7-13-1880 L
Wells, R. W. to Ella V. Skelton 11-3-1860 Hy
Wells, Robert to Paralee Pierce 10-7-1868 L
Wells, S. Wesley to Sarah Long 3-26-1849 O
Wells, Saml. A. to Mary L. Thorp 9-16-1857 (9-20-1857) Sh
Wells, T. Lee to Ella Pell 2-26-1879 Dy
Wells, Thomas H. to Julian Farran 2-12-1838 Hn
Wells, Thomas S. to Sarah Rogers 8-18-1830 Hr
Wells, Thomas to Mary Smith 2-17-1866 (2-18-1866) Dy
Wells, Trenton to V. M. Anderson 11-24-1866 (11-28-1866) F
Wells, W. T. to Lizzie Venable 2-10-1875 Hy
Wells, W. T. to Martha Davis 7-11-1859 (7-14-1859) Hr
Wells, William H. to Martha G. Evans 12-10-1838 (12-11-1838) F
Wells, William H. to Mary Ann Latham 12-23-1850 (12-24-1850) Ma
Wells, William H. to Mary J. Burnett 5-29-1858 (5-30-1858) L
Wells, William H. to Nancy Rogers 6-18-1827 Hr
Wells, William T. to Melissa Dougan 9-25-1843 (no return) F
Wells, William to Delilah A. Crockett 6-2-1858 (6-14-1858) L
Wells, Wm. T. to Zelia A. Hullum 9-24-1859 (9-25-1859) Hr
Wells, Z. M. to Elizabeth Moon 5-27-1851 O
Wellsman, J. C. to Eliza Buff 10-10-1868 T
Welsh, Caswell to Elizabeth Finley 3-19-1844 Sh
Welsh, Henry A. to Mary Jane Harding 9-11-1854 (9-13-1854) Ma
Welsh, James to Catharine Calahan 3-28-1864 Sh
Welsh, James to Ellen Dalsy (Daley) 11-18-1849 Sh
Welsh, John J. to Frances Kerr 10-27-1874 Hy
Welsh, John to Kate Agnes Mahan 1-5-1864 Sh
Welsh, W. to Margaret Egan 8-13-1864 (8-14-1864) Sh
Welty, Elbert to Amanda E. Riley 7-3-1861 (7-4-1861) Hr
Wenbury, Alfred to Mary Ross 9-1-1842 Cr
Wence, James Owen to Mary Jane Pipkin 9-20-1847 Sh
Wend?, Jourdan? P. to Sarah A. Luth 12-9-1846 Hn
Wenner, Philip to Rosina Heidel 6-28-1860 Sh
Werkmeister, John to Mary Wegman 9-30-1854 Sh
Werne, Joseph to Annie M. Chivvis 11-28-1860 Sh

Werner, W. T. to Mollie E. Turner 6-22-1871 Hy
Werrick, John to Mary Pafford 11-28-1844 Be
Wesbrook, R. A. to Marry J. Phillips 12-4-1854 (no return) F
Wesche, F. to Margaret (Mrs.) Reis 10-26-1864 Sh
Wesimen, Robert to Frances Oliver 9-23-1846 Cr
Wesley, J. W. to Mattie Williams 12-25-1874 (no return) Dy
Wesling, Harman H. to Catherine Imbush (Imlish) 8-13-1846 Sh
Wesser, H. H. to Nancy Cox 8-12-1841 Be
Wesson, Alfred to Susan H. Thompson 3-27-1847 Sh
Wesson, Benjamin to Cary Ann Wesson 1-5-1841 Sh
Wesson, Benjamin to Frances Holman 12-3-1850 Hn
Wesson, Bolivar C. to Ann Rebecca Ford 11-22-1848 (11-23-1848) T
Wesson, E. A. F. to Martha A. Grace 2-3-1857 Hr
Wesson, George W. to Mary Ann Wesson 2-11-1851 (2-14-1851) F
Wesson, H. H. to Barbary Burns 10-14-1847 Be
Wesson, H. H. to Nancy East 8-12-1841 Be CC
Wesson, Isaac to Mary Ann Wood 1-24-1856 Sh
Wesson, J. D. to P. A. Dickey 2-3-1875 (2-4-1875) Dy
Wesson, J. W. to M. M. Dodd 5-24-1869 (5-27-1869) Dy
Wesson, John A. to Barbery Warden 7-19-1849 F
Wesson, Joseph N. to Emma Eliza Anderson 12-23-1858 Sh
Wesson, Nat to Mary F. Williams 12-24-1867 (no return) Dy
Wesson, Sterling L. to Martha G. Rideout 9-22-1855 Sh
Wesson, Wilkins to Sarah Farley 7-10-1839 F
Wesson?, James D. to Rebecca McFarlane 1-14-1844 (1-16-1844) T
West, A. G. to Susan M. Hargett 2-20-1865? (2-22-1863) O
West, Abram M. to Mary T. Wilson 7-19-1856 (7-22-1856) O
West, B. F. to Jane R. Davis 10-12-1857 Sh
West, B. F. to Margaret J. Dearmond 11-8-1855 Sh
West, Benjamin to Elizabeth Cozart 4-18-1831 Ma
West, Benjamin to Mary Mims 7-4-1838 Sh
West, Charles to Theresa Hendricks 1-12-1863 Sh
West, Columbus to Elizabeth Cosby 4-30-1854 Hn
West, Daniel to Martha A. Lea 5-28-1844 (6-15-1844) G
West, Geo. H. to Martha A Gardner 10-22-1859 (10-27-1859) G
West, George to Johnella Th___ton 11-13-1874 (11-27-1874) L
West, George to Seigniora P. Elcan 10-21-1845 Sh
West, Gilbert A. to Martha E. Sexton 9-2-1848 (9-10-1848) G
West, H. C. to S. L. Harrison 1-29-1879 L
West, Henry to Mary J. Lanier 12-30-1873 Hy
West, J. A. to S. A. Duncan 9-28-1881 (9-29-1881) L
West, J. L. to Josephin T. Coats 1-13-1872 (1-16-1872) L
West, J. P. to Mary A. West 2-13-1878 L
West, J. R. to Lucinda George 10-3-1866 G
West, J. Y. to Mary A. Shenon 1-8-1874 Hy
West, James A. to Mary J. Nipp 9-25-1861 O
West, James F. to Sarah J. Owen 11-4-1838 Sh
West, James M. to Martha J. Watts 12-22-1862 (1-14-1863) O
West, James M. to Mary L. Huggans 12-24-1857 We
West, James R. to Jerome W. Harris 9-4-1841 Ma
West, James R. to Lucy Gill 5-23-1859 (5-24-1859) G
West, James R. to Mary E. Robinson 5-31-1862 G
West, James to Ann Florence 10-25-1858 (11-7-1858) Ma
West, James to Susan Stone 11-3-1851 (11-12-1851) Sh
West, John Allen to Martha Jane Ballard 2-24-1874 L
West, John D. to Elizabeth Lett 2-10-1871 (2-11-1871) Ma
West, John F. to Minerva (Mrs.) Watson 3-31-1870 (4-3-1870) L
West, John W. to Mary Woodward 8-14-1867 G
West, John W. to Nancy Kelly 12-17-1855 (12-20-1855) G
West, John to Lizzie Lee 9-15-1880 L B
West, John to Mary Beaton 10-10-1844 Be CC
West, John to Mary Beaton 10-12-1844 Be
West, John to Sarah Ann Dickinson 1-13-1853 Ma
West, L. M. to Sally Bazemore 8-15-1853 (8-17-1853) Sh
West, M. G. to Sabrina Todd 9-1-1874 (no return) L
West, Moses to Nancy Jane Crose 7-6-1849 Be
West, Noel E. to Mary Jane Harington 2-18-1839 (2-20-1839) F
West, Olen to Martha Ann Johnson 11-1-1841 Ma
West, Owen to Jane McClur 10-12-1841 G
West, Peter to Elizabeth McKnight 3-2-1827 (3-4-1827) Hr
West, Philip H. to Nancy E. Autry 12-17-1858 (not executed) Ma
West, Phillip to Deby D. Butler 1-3-1849 F
West, Phillip to Mary Basemore 9-6-1852 (9-28-1852) Sh
West, R. C. to Elizabeth (Mrs.) Furgason 1-4-1872 Hy
West, R. L. to M. R. Waddy 2-26-1863 G
West, Reuben to Elizabeth Jane D___wns? 5-1-1853 Hn
West, Reubin to Lucinda Womble 11-24-1872 Hy
West, Richard L. to Mary E. Blair 12-21-1849 (12-23-1849) G
West, Robert C. to Elizabeth Bowers 4-29-1861 (5-2-1861) L
West, Robert C. to Martha Borum 10-18-1854 (10-19-1854) L
West, Robert to Mary Conner 10-8-1861 G
West, Samuel M. to Rebecca E. Ward 1-23-1862 Sh
West, T. H. to Martha Moore 2-15-1859 (no return) We
West, Thomas to Eliza J. Lea 3-16-1846 (3-19-1846) G
West, W. B. to Mary E. Reeves 12-14-1871 (12-16-1871) O
West, W. D. to Martha J. Sherron 8-14-1872 Hy
West, W. M. to Lucy Bowers 5-14-1872 L
West, Wiley W. to Elizabeth McMinn 8-9-1847 G
West, William H. to Sarah Jane Foutch 4-23-1851 (5-1-1851) G
West, William M. to Mariah J. Barfield 2-3-1874 L
West, William to Eliza Caroline Hammond 12-29-1862 Sh
West, William to Joanna Mangrum 7-17-1850 (7-18-1850) Hr
West, William to Susan McCarver 5-2-1837 (5-7-1837) Hr
West, Wm. F. to Phebe Gateley 8-6-1850 (8-7-1850) Ma
Westbrook, Ethelred E. to Jane R. Meriweather 5-23-1855 (6-24-1855) O
Westbrook, Ira O. to Katie M. Lawrence 11-15-1884 (11-16-1884) L
Westbrook, James M. to Mary S. Willson 8-30-1860 We
Westbrook, James R. to Frances Watson 8-31-1853 Hr
Westbrook, James to Winifred Jordan 8-27-1831 (9-1-1831) Ma
Westbrook, John R. to Martha A. Williams 9-3-1850 Hr
Westbrook, M. F. to Manervia Huddleston 7-19-1858 Hr
Westbrooks, Fagan to Mary Shelton 3-6-1867 T
Westbrooks, Iszrell to Mahalia Holloway 10-17-1877 Hy
Wester, James M. to Martha L. Bostick 11-18-1858 We
Weston, A. M. to Nanny Jane Moone? 12-6-1855 Hn
Weston, Benjamin to Amanda Price 10-8-1846 Hn
Weston, Edward to Nancy Johnson 10-7-1867 G B
Weston, John M. to Mary Anne Worsham 10-2-1862 Hn
Weston, William to Kate Seymour 2-3-1863 Sh
Wetherford, I. A. to Mary I. Dismuke 1-1-1861 Hn
Wetherford, Stephen F. to Harrett Lottis 11-22-1852 G
Wetherington, Henry T. to Sophonia E. Keathley 10-21-1851 (10-29-1851) G
Wethington, Allen to Mary Elkins 6-21-1853 (6-23-1853) T
Wever (Weaver), Benjamin to Harriet R. Knox 12-19-1863 (12-23-1863) Sh
Wever, Benjm. F. to Ann R. Chambers 1-9-1854 (1-10-1854) Sh
Whalen, Michael to Bridget Cusick 4-2-1864 (4-3-1864) Sh
Whaley, Jesse H. to Eliza Swand (Sword) 12-31-1842 Sh
Whaley, John N. to Susan Jane Taylor 1-17-1842 (1-20-1842) Hr
Whaling (Whiting?), John to Emma Wright 4-6-1869 (4-9-1869) L
Whaling, Richard to Betsy Ryan 11-26-1846 Sh
Whalon, Edward to Mary Madden 5-23-1857 (5-26-1857) Sh
Wharton, Austin to Elvira Batchelor 11-15-1877 Hy
Wharton, C. F. to A. E. Hodges 12-9-1862 Mn
Wharton, G. B. to Mary Sheppard 12-16-1847 Hn
Wharton, George W. to Elizabeth Aycock 7-29-1851 Hn
Wharton, James C. to Amanda Jane Lunsford 6-7-1842 (6-9-1842) T
Wharton, James R. to Sarah E. McAfee 11-26-1862 Mn
Wharton, James to Elizabeth Marberry 2-28-1849 Hn
Wharton, Sam to Nancy Pender 2-26-1871 Hy
Wharton, W. H. to Sarah J. Faulkner 4-22-1877 Hy
Whaton, James C. to Mary Jane Murchison 9-2-1841 (9-?-1841) Ma
Whealan, Ed to Mary Mullarney 2-12-1861 Sh
Whealor, Charles M. to Susan A. Roberts 12-7-1852 We
Wheatley (Wheartly), Alexander to Fanny A. Harmon (Hannon) 5-22-1856 We
Wheatley, A. J. to Rebecca E. Smith 11-25-1871 (10?-29-1871) L
Wheatley, Allen J. to Elizabeth Carter 4-19-1857 Be
Wheatley, Allen J. to Elizabeth Carter 4-19-1857 Be CC
Wheatley, B. W. to Lucy W. Brooks 12-10-1856 Be CC
Wheatley, H. N. to Mary Ann Lunsford 8-3-1876 L
Wheatley, Hansel L. to Lamyra Melton 12-9-1866 Be
Wheatley, Isaac to Annie Chipman 11-11-1876 (11-12-1876) L
Wheatley, James A. to Emma E. Kirk 11-17-1868 (11-18-1868) L
Wheatley, John to Susan Simons 9-24-1866 (9-27-18??) O
Wheatley, T.R. to Mattie G. Smith 10-16-1869 (10-17-1869) L
Wheatley, Thomas J. to Margaret E. Hendon 9-6-1856 Be CC
Wheatley, Thomas R. to Louisa Smith 12-23-1871 (12-24-1871) L
Wheatley, W(illiam) W. to Marian Carter 4-25-1850 Sh
Wheatley, W. W. to Martha Hall 12-1-1864 Be
Wheatley, W. W. to Martha Hall 12-10-1864 Be CC
Wheatley, Wm. A. to Susan R. Brigham 11-30-1848 Be
Wheatly, B. W. to Lucy W. Brooks 12-10-1856 Be
Wheatly, Caesar to Ellen Currie 6-9-1866 Hy
Wheatly, Thomas J. to Margaret E. Herndon 9-6-1856 Be
Wheeler, A. J. to Jennie S. Chadwick 12-22-1859 Sh
Wheeler, B. P. to Martha E. Pegram 5-1-1855 We
Wheeler, Benjm. H. to Margaret E. Rodgers 11-18-1853 (11-19-1853) Sh
Wheeler, C. M. to Lucy J. Jones 10-9-1857 G
Wheeler, Charles to Manda White 2-2-1839 Be
Wheeler, Charles to Manda White 2-2-1839 Be CC
Wheeler, George T. to Sarah L. Bennett 1-16-1867 F
Wheeler, George W. to Caroline Baker 9-10-1867 Be
Wheeler, J. A. J. to Susan Glover 3-2-1859 (3-3-1859) Sh
Wheeler, J. E. to M. J. Hart 2-17-1872 (2-18-1872) Dy
Wheeler, J. T. to F. M. Hart 1-14-1879 (1-15-1879) Dy
Wheeler, Jack to Sarah Jones 3-29-1875 Hy
Wheeler, James H. to Mary A. Ramsey 10-24-1842 (10-27-1842) F
Wheeler, James M. to Nancy A. Williams 10-19-1863 G
Wheeler, James to Mary Hill 12-5-1859 (12-11-1859) F
Wheeler, Jno. P. to Sarah R. Webster 7-29-1849 Hr
Wheeler, John A. to E. A. Horton 9-26-1869 G
Wheeler, John to Lucinda Crockett 12-5-1854 (12-9-1854) O
Wheeler, John to Mary Watson 7-25-1843 Sh
Wheeler, King to Amanda Jefferson 5-2-1868 (no return) F B
Wheeler, Meredith to Amanda Cannon 8-4-1862 G

Wheeler, Saml. H. to Sarah A. Taylor 10-13-1854 (10-14-1854) G
Wheeler, Samuel R. to Mary Laws 10-9-1843 We
Wheeler, Solomon P. to Nancy Choate 10-6-1828 Hr
Wheeler, William H. to Almedia Ann McCrean 9-26-1846 (10-4-1846) F
Wheeler, William W. to Emma Richardson 2-1-1871 L
Wheeless, Wm. to Margrit Ketton 12-10-1846 We
Wheelock, John Ambrose to Ellen Rose Newman 9-19-1850 T
Wheelons, William to Sallie West 11-21-1872 L
Wheelus, Thos. to Huldah Davis 10-8-1846 We
Whelan, Michael to Sarah Donlan 7-26-1864 Sh
Whelan, Thomas to Loretta O'Neil 2-8-1853 Sh
Whelen, John to Alice Ryan 1-17-1860 Sh
Whelen, Patrick to Mary Folay 7-30-1859 We
Wheless, Joseph C. to Matilda E. Ayres 4-5-1853 Sh
Wherry, John to Margaret Geary 10-24-1832 Sh
Wherry, Silas to Sarah Jane Faulkner 10-11-1843 Sh
Wherry, Silas to Sarah Land 7-22-1833 Sh
Wherry, Thomas J. to Mary Herring 4-24-1840 Sh
Wherten, H. C. to Martha Corely 2-1-1844 Cr
Whetty, Felise G. to Carline M. Goff 2-6-1841 (2-10-1841) G
Whevelin, Patrick to Martha Baker 8-26-1861 (no return) We
Whichard, J. W. to Susan Ann Woods 3-25-1879 (3-28-1879) Dy
Whichard, James to Harriet Canada 3-19-1867 G
Whichard, Reuben to Lucrecca Nobles 12-13-1835 G
Whicker, Thomas A. to Martha A. Williams 3-28-1863 G
Whillis, Benj. to Mary Bennett 2-11-1841 Cr
Whipple, David H. to Jane S. Caldwell 3-15-1836 O
Whistler, Wm. H. to Eliza McDonough 3-15-1851 (3-17-1851) Sh
Whitaker, Eli to Emiline Davenport 4-9-1835 Hr
Whitaker, Henry to Amanda Board 5-22-1875 (5-30-1875) O
Whitaker, J. C. to M. A. Hughes 8-2-1860 Sh
Whitaker, Jno. W. to Lucy J. Strickland 12-15-1868 (12-16-1868) F
Whitaker, John C. to Nancy Riddle 1-14-1833 (1-15-1833) Hr
Whitaker, Lusnford to Sarah Teague 7-8-1835 Hr
Whitaker, W. W. to Kate M. Critchlow 1-6-1862 Hy
Whitaker, Wesley to Sarah A. E. Chambers 12-24-1865 Mn
Whitaker, William D. to Dolly A. Nichols 9-7-1866 Hn
Whitbey, Richardson to Camilla Wright 12-15-1827 Sh
Whitbey, Richardson to Permintia Barnhart 9-1-1831 Sh
Whitby, Andrew J. to Mary E. Stafford 12-21-1868 (12-24-1868) F
Whitby, Melvin to Fannie Wiley 10-12-1864 Sh
White, A. B. to M. F. Lynn 9-19-1860 We
White, A. B. to R. J.(I?) Kellar 11-30-1882 L
White, A. J. to Eliza C. Rawlinigs 4-4-1864 (4-5-1864) Sh
White, A. J. to Martha M. Jacobs 9-18-1854 (9-20-1854) G
White, A. S. to Julia A. Archer 9-6-1875 (9-8-1875) Dy
White, A. to Dora Walker 3-18-1861 Cr
White, Aaron to Susan Ward 11-30-1878 (12-1-1878) Dy
White, Abe to Ellen W. Denton 11-10-1869 (11-11-1869) Cr
White, Abraham to Elizabeth Brown no date (with Dec 1856) F
White, Absolum A. to Nancy Harley 12-1-1836 G
White, Albert C. to R. F. Hilliard 12-22-1869 Ma
White, Alexander to Mary Eliza Simmons 2-22-1847 (2-23-1847) Hr
White, Alfred A. to Martha J. Cook 12-18-1862 We
White, Allen B. to Isabella Lamb 10-11-1853 Hn
White, Allen B. to Nancy B. Roachell 3-12-1838 Cr
White, Allen to Mary Clark 1-10-1862 Hy
White, Allen to Nancy Cribbs 12-19-1827 G
White, Alonza to Jane Thomas 6-22-1848 Ma
White, Andrew J. to Sarah M. Thetford 11-9-1852 (11-11-1852) G
White, Archibald I. T. to Ann E. Ward 1-25-1859 (1-26-1859) O
White, B. A. to Nancy E. White 2-6-1860 Hy
White, Benj. F. to Emeline Bushard 12-19-1866 (12-20-1866) Ma
White, Berry to Margaret White 9-3-1859 Cr
White, Boyd to Eliza A. Nixon 4-5-1860 Hn
White, Bryant to Margaret Walker 3-24-1870 (no return) Dy
White, C. B. R. to Amanda Yow 10-20-1874 (10-21-1874) Dy
White, C. D. to Sopronia J. Jackson 8-14-1856 We
White, Calvin to Sarah E. Hensley 7-21-1856 Sh
White, Charles to Josephine Dudley 3-4-1863 We
White, Charles to Julia Borden 7-2-1859 (5?-2-1859) Sh
White, Clinton I. to Matilda C. Fuller 2-18-1841 Sh
White, Daniel T. to Martha A. James 4-30-1860 (5-1-1860) Sh
White, Daniel to Margarett Dowin 8-20-1838 Ma
White, David C. to Mary V. Webster 1-8-1848 (1-13-1848) F
White, David Ewing to Welthy Ann Hopper 5-26-1855 (5-27-1855) T
White, David to Jane Harden 7-12-1858 Sh
White, Drewberry to Levina Higdon 9-5-1855 Be
White, Drewberry to Levina Higdon 9-5-1855 Be CC
White, E. to E. J. (Mrs.) Wyse 1-26-1870 Hy
White, E. to Rebecca Shaw 2-22-1861 (no return) Cr
White, Ed to Amand Porter 2-21-1873 (2-23-1873) Cr
White, Edward H. to Jane R. M. Kenely 3-31-1845 (no return) L
White, Edward to Armenta Cannon 11-29-1849 Cr
White, Edward to Elizabeth Culp 8-11-1869 (8-12-1869) Cr
White, Edward to Susan Picket 4-12-1871 (4-13-1871) L
White, Elbert A. to S. Almeda Waldran 2-6-1849 Sh

White, Elgin C. to Mary C. Page 4-21-1838 (4-22-1838) G
White, Elisha M. to Mary J. Fain 12-21-1857 Hn
White, Ellis to Mary Barlow 4-20-1872 L
White, Eton J. to Mary Neeley 5-23-1844 (no return) We
White, Fell to Harriet Hagler 8-15-1867 Hn B
White, Franklin to Julia Ann Outlaw 10-1-1836 O
White, Franklin to Mary Franklin 12-18-1854 Cr
White, G. W. D. to Amanda E. Hamil 10-24-1865 Hy
White, G. W. D. to Eliza J. Dodd 7-13-1868 (7-15-1868) L
White, G. W. to Susan Simore 4-7-1852 Cr
White, George Allen to Lucy Jordan 2-25-1875 L B
White, George S. to Margaret V. Frazor 9-3-1857 O
White, George T. to Tennessee Wilbourn 10-19-1853 O
White, George W. to Louisa Shelby 7-11-1836 Hr
White, George W. to Sarah Hood 1-16-1844 (1-18-1844) T
White, George to Elizabeth Henderson 10-4-1846 (10-5-1846) O
White, George to Lucy Ivory 4-17-1882 (4-18-1882) L
White, George to Mary J. Gardner no date (with Feb 1863) Cr
White, Glouster to Nicey White 3-31-1867 Hy
White, Green L. to Theodocia Davis 9-9-1845 (9-11-1845) O
White, H. B. to Francetta V. Bell 1-16-1863 Sh
White, Harrison to Elizabeth Lamb 8-2-1848 Hn
White, Harrison to Elizabeth Ray 11-27-1839 Hn
White, Henry W. to Sarah E. Edwards 12-2-1861 Dy
White, Henry to Martha (Mrs.) Scott 10-30-1850 Sh
White, Hugh L. to Josephine O. Walker 6-30-1867 Be
White, Isaiah to Mary M. Heath? 5-10-1860 Hn
White, J. A. to Sarah E. McAfee 7-5-1869 (7-7-1869) Dy
White, J. B. to E. C. Betts 7-5-1876 Hy
White, J. B. to Malvina Harris 7-10-1884 (7-15-1884) L
White, J. C. to Ann Kelly 7-20-1872 (no return) Cr
White, J. C. to Mary Reddick 6-18-1855 We
White, J. E. to E. F. Ray 12-19-1864 G
White, J. E. to J. L. Jackson 3-15-1877 Dy
White, J. E. to J. L. Jackson ?-?-1877 (no return) Dy
White, J. F. to S. A. Herring 10-11-1875 Hy
White, J. M. to Carroline Bryant 11-6-1837 G
White, J. M. to F. L. Dodd 9-10-1865 (9-11-1865) Dy
White, J. M. to N. J. Wilcox 11-9-1870 (11-10-1870) Cr
White, J. W. to Jennie Plummer 7-25-1871 (7-13?-1871) Cr
White, Jackson to Margaret Strader (Shader) 12-25-1842 Sh
White, Jacob D. to Eliza J. Evans 9-22-1843 Cr
White, James D. to Mary Jane Hubbard 8-8-1837 Hr
White, James Henry to Margrett E. Jones 2-8-1870 (2-9-1870) Dy
White, James Henry to Nancy Johnson 5-23-1866 Ma
White, James L. to Martha S. Riddle 9-19-1866 O
White, James M. to Ann C. Johnston 10-2-1838 Ma
White, James M. to Elizabeth McCartney 9-17-1859 (9-22-1859) G
White, James M. to Martha A. Wolton 11-4-1852 Sh
White, James N. to Sarah Jane Edwards 9-7-1868 Ma
White, James R. to Sarah R. Rider 12-22-1840 (12-24-1840) Ma
White, James T. to Martha A. Allen 7-8-1846 Sh
White, James W. to Mary Jones 6-12-1882 L B
White, James to Emily H. Davie 9-19-1855 Ma
White, James to Joanna Bradshaw 11-6-1855 Sh
White, James to Lanty Price 8-6-1863 We
White, James to Laura A. White 7-19-1876 Hy
White, James to Marilyn Freeman 7-5-1851 (7-?-1851) T
White, James to Matilda Brewer 8-5-1863 Be
White, James to Matilda Brewr 8-5-1863 Be CC
White, James to Patience E. Flippin 10-3-1853 (10-13-1853) G
White, Jas. L. to H. A. J. Cobb 7-2-1872 Hy
White, Jas. P. to Lucy Jackson 12-31-1870 Hy
White, Jas. W. to Martha C. Blackwell 11-3-1850 Sh
White, Jeremiah F. to Ferriby (Lenity) Naile 9-5-1835 Sh
White, Jerry to C. A. E. Brand 1-22-1863 (1-25-1863) O
White, Jessie to Janie Jones 9-4-1871 Cr
White, Jno. T. to Lucy A. Carlton 12-18-1850 We
White, Joel M. to Rosanah J. Gorden 2-23-1854 Be
White, John B. to Sarah J. Chandler 3-10-1868 Ma
White, John H. to Harriet E. Boyd 6-17-1873 (6-18-1873) L
White, John H. to Sarah Straden (Staden) 3-11-1844 Sh
White, John M. to Jane M. Simpson 8-4-1846 Ma
White, John M. to Nancy Handcock 5-26-1836 (5-27-1836) G
White, John S. to Jane Marshall 2-11-1847 (2-21-1847) O
White, John S. to Syntha Logan 5-31-1851 (6-1-1851) O
White, John T. to Nancy Parker 11-6-1844 We
White, John W. to Elizabeth James 9-20-1848 O
White, John W. to Elizabeth James 9-20-1848 (9-21-1848) O
White, John W. to Josephine Wilhelm 9-8-1866 (9-9-1866) Ma
White, John W. to Mary N. Finch 1-8-1857 O
White, John to Charity Johnson 1-15-1874 Hy
White, John to Charlotte Sadler 5-6-1871 (5-7-1871) F B
White, John to Clarisa Fuller 1-17-1848 Sh
White, John to Hannah Wright 7-27-1877 (no return) L B
White, John to Julia Browning 2-1-1851 Cr
White, John to Sarah Brandon 3-4-1856 Sh

White, John to Sarah Wright 6-9-1833 Sh
White, Jordan to Nancy Cove 1-29-1867 (2-5-1867) F B
White, Joseph B. to Elvina Taylor 8-3-1868 Ma
White, Joseph E. to Mary C. Curtis 1-31-1883 (2-1-1883) L
White, Joseph H. to Fedelia Jones 10-4-1857 We
White, Joseph M. to Margaret Blakemore 3-6-1860 We
White, Joseph R. to Dorthy Minton 10-6-1862 Mn
White, Joseph to Amelia Anderson 1-21-1871 Hy
White, Joseph to M. F. Holifield 2-16-1869 O
White, Joseph to Matilda J. Turner 11-11-1851 Sh
White, Joseph to Tabitha Baker 8-4-1852 Ma
White, Josiah S. to Rebecca W. Minter 4-20-1849 (4-24-1849) Hr
White, Lemuel to Elizabeth Gaines 8-11-1847 (8-12-1847) L *
White, Lemuel to M. A. Davenport 5-5-1883 (5-7-1883) L
White, Lewis to Martha Pearce 2-5-1852 Be CC
White, Littleberry to Susan Branch 7-7-1830 Ma
White, Luder(Leeder?) to Martha Pearce 2-5-1852 Be
White, M. J. M. to Elizabeth Brown 10-3-1862 (not solemn.) O
White, M. M. to Mary E. Booth 11-10-1868 Hy
White, M. T. to Mary Hamil 12-1-1869 Hy
White, M. V. to E. P. C. Curtis 5-22-1867 (5-23-1867) Dy
White, Major J. M. to Caroline Bassham 8-24-1838 (8-25-1838) O
White, Micheal to Nancy Wisner 8-20-1842 Sh
White, Moses to Lucy Rucker 3-4-1877 Hy
White, Nolen S. to Maria E. Mason 9-19-1871 (9-20-1871) Ma
White, P. E. to O. E. Claibourne 12-26-1878 Hy
White, Patrick Y. to Sarah J. Hibbitts 2-6-1866 (2-7-1866) Dy
White, Patrick to Penelope Garrett 12-29-1856 Sh
White, Peter to Eliza Daniel 8-26-1872 Hy
White, Phillip W. to Eliza R. Hornbeak 6-17-1846 We
White, Phillip W. to Eliza R. Hornbeak 6-18-1846 We
White, Pompy to Violet Castellow 3-16-1871 Hy
White, R. B. to Caroline Jones 1-28-1863 Be CC
White, R. B. to Caroline Jones 2-28-1863 Be
White, R. B. to S. M. Nowell 2-24-1869 Hy
White, R. H. to S. C. Wyatt 11-28-1870 (11-30-1870) Cr
White, Reddick T. to Mary W. Parker 11-7-1867 Hy
White, Redding to Mary L. A. Eason 5-3-1830 Ma
White, Richard to Mattie Taylor 3-27-1875 Hy
White, Richardson P. to Malinda Gilliland 1-13-1845 (1-16-1845) G
White, Ro L. to Mary C. Bright 3-21-1855 (3-22-1855) Hr
White, Robert H. to Willie Helen Dalle? 3-23-1871 T
White, Robert K. to Martha J. Terrill 1-4-1874 Hy
White, Robt. P. to Lavinia A. (Louisa?) Firth 10-20-1866 (10-23-1866) F
White, Samuel N. to Nancy E. Hale 1-1-1855 (1-4-1855) G
White, Samuel to Rebecca H. Scott 6-28-1842 (6-29-1842) Hr
White, Sanford to Mary Watson 7-16-1857 O
White, T. A. to Emma J. Dozier 6-12-1871 Cr
White, T. H. to A. L. Law 8-12-1856 Sh
White, Terrell to Malinda Covington 4-14-1868 (4-16-1868) L
White, Thomas S. to Sally Gullet 10-2-1832 (10-8-1832) Hr
White, Thomas to Elizabeth Anderson 3-6-1834 Sh
White, Thomas to Julia Bevins 9-5-1872 T
White, Thomas to Martha Squiers 9-5-1872 T
White, Thomas to Martha Squires 9-5-1872 (9-13-1872) T
White, Thompson to Nancy Patrick 5-20-1863 G
White, Thos. D. to Martha Johnson 8-16-1849 Be
White, Thos. E. to Sophia B. Fitzhugh 4-2-1834 (4-3-1834) Hr
White, Thos. to Sindy Freeman 1-5-1873 Hy
White, Tom to Amanda McCain 8-1-1874 T
White, W. A. to C. T. Tilghman 2-11-1867 G
White, W. C. to Louisa Lemons 2-13-1860 Cr
White, W. C. to Nancy B. Bibbs 1-19-1871 Cr
White, W. F. to Commency A. Glover 10-25-1856 (10-26-1856) Sh
White, W. G. to M. E. C. Morris 10-15-1857 We
White, W. H. to M. J. H. Hill 10-15-1863 T
White, W. H. to Mahaly J. Wilker 7-28-1857 Sh
White, W. H. to Martha W. Simmons 3-5-1866 (3-28-1866) O
White, W. L. to M. C. Cox 2-15-1886 (2-16-1886) L
White, W. T. to Mary A. Baird 12-14-1866 G
White, West to Belle Nixon 8-4-1878 L
White, William C. to Frances Attwood 6-22-1838 (6-24-1838) Hr
White, William H. to Lizzie Conner 12-19-1882 (12-23-1882) L
White, William H. to Mary Jane Griffin 6-25-1866 (6-26-1866) L
White, William L. to Mary E. Partlow 9-9-1839 (no return) F
White, William R. to Julia A. Armstrong 3-11-1846 (3-12-1846) G
White, William R. to Winneford Simmons 10-29-1863 G
White, William T. to Eliza E. Parchman 2-20-1841 (2-23-1841) F
White, William to Amanda Hyett 1-5-1850 (1-4?-1850) G
White, William to Ellen Benson 3-18-1867 L
White, William to Hannah E. Caldwell 3-9-1842 (3-10-1842) O
White, William to Manirva Hammil 2-18-1871 (2-19-1871) L
White, William to Maria J. McMacken 9-21-1869 (9-23-1869) Cr
White, William to Mary E. Shankle 3-3-1869 O
White, Wilson to Ellen Palmer 7-2-1869 (7-4-1869) Cr
White, Wm. C. to Octavia Harris 11-20-1859 (11-21-1859) Hr
White, Wm. H. to Jane Williams 4-9-1870 Hy

White, Wm. L. to Mary Price 3-1-1848 (3-2-1848) O
White, Wm. R. to Charlotty Little 10-12-1843 Cr
White, Wm. T. to Henrietta Harmes (Hannes?) 9-10-1851 (9-13-1851) Sh
White, Wm. to Agnes Wright 7-21-1877 Hy
White, Wm. to Dilsy Allen 7-9-1866 (6?-10-1866) Dy
White, Wm. to Sophena Horton 6-26-1856 Cr
White, Z. R. to A. A. Stone 11-7-1866 (no return) Cr
Whitefield, Johnson J. to Agnis Gregory 11-19-1839 (no return) F
Whitehead (White), Dennis C. to Pauline Imes 7-18-1841 Sh
Whitehead, Alex to Anna Wallace 11-13-1879 (12-27-1879) L B
Whitehead, Alex to Maria Colter 9-14-1874 Hy
Whitehead, Ephraim to Betsy Alexander 1-31-1867 Hn B
Whitehead, Fletcher to Adaline Boyd 7-20-1867 (8-10-1867) F B
Whitehead, G. P. to S. C. Dryhall 11-21-1867 O
Whitehead, J. Hugh to Elizabeth Zane 7-12-1868 G
Whitehead, James W. to Martha M. Hart 10-20-1846 Hn
Whitehead, R. H. to M. A. Conkey 12-19-1859 (12-20-1859) F
Whitehead, Reding to Sarah E. Blanchard 2-4-1852 (no return) F
Whitehead, Richd. H. to Virginia Mills 1-15-1868 Hy
Whitehead, S. D. to Isadora Hollis 3-20-1851 F
Whitehead, T. to Kisiah Petty 2-20-1840 Be
Whitehead, T. to Kisiah Petty 2-20-1840 Be CC
Whitehead, W. J. to Alice B. Medlin 10-11-1871 Hy
Whitehead, W. J. to M. E. Richards 11-8-1876 Hy
Whitehead, W. W. to M. W. Arnold 8-15-1854 (no return) F
Whitehead, William J. to Charity A. Seigler 1-13-1848 Sh
Whitehead, William to Hannah Allison 7-1-1849 Be
Whiteherst, Ashville B. to Elizabeth Breckhouse 2-11-1854 (2-14-1854) G
Whiteherst, H. D. to F. A. Winningham 3-4-1868 Hy
Whitehorn, Elvis B. to A. P. Williams 8-10-1867 (8-11-1867) Cr
Whitehorn, James S. to Sarah F. Parsons 11-27-1869 (11-28-1869) Cr
Whitehorn, Joseph N. to Sarah J. Vaughn 1-30-1856 Cr
Whitehorn, Nicholas H. to Elizabeth I. Glass 11-26-1849 (11-29-1849) Hr
Whitehorn, Thomas to Elizabeth Farr 7-9-1844 (7-10-1844) Hr
Whitehorn, W. W. to Lizzie Reasons 7-9-1872 (7-15-1872) Dy
Whitehorne, John R. P. to Sarah Ann Cherry 9-9-1857 O
Whitehurst, Allen to Caroline Moore 2-29-1872 Hy
Whitehurst, Delaney to Martha Powell 2-28-1868 Hy
Whitehurst, Henry to Margaret Fawcett 5-10-1881 (5-11-1881) L B
Whitehurst, Isham to Sarah Capell 4-4-1866 Hy
Whitehurst, Moses F. to Elizabeth J. Crockett 12-7-1844 (12-8-1844) G
Whiteker, James to Mariah Parsons 2-27-1864 Hn
Whitelaw, David A. to Amanda Buntyn 1-27-1841 Sh
Whitelaw, David to Hannah Whitelaw 10-30-1878 Hy
Whitelaw, Dick to Hannah Read 1-17-1872 Hy
Whitelaw, Fed to Annie Marrs 12-25-1871 Hy
Whitelaw, J. H. to Charity Smith 1-4-1876 Hy
Whitelaw, James P. to Bittie Whitelaw 2-17-1869 Hy
Whitelaw, Jas. A. to Becky Read 2-14-1878 Hy
Whitelaw, John F. to Maria L. Cole 11-5-1849 (11-8-1849) Ma
Whitelaw, John to Margaret Taylor 1-13-1866 Hy
Whitelaw, Jordan to Rosa Jarrett 1-1-1883 (no return) L
Whitelaw, M. F. to Amelia Henderson 12-1-1885 (12-3-1885) L
Whitelaw, Moses to Caldona Young 12-13-1876 (12-14-1876) L
Whitelaw, Thomas to Emily Rennolds 3-28-1853 (3-29-1853) Sh
Whitelaw, Thomas to Mary S. Hatch 2-4-1841 (2-11-1841) F
Whitelaw, Tom to Frances Love 1-16-1870 Hy
Whitelaw, W. L. to C. H. Whitelaw 2-17-1869 Hy
Whitelaw, W. L. to Cornelia Houck 6-10-1878 Hy
Whitelaw, W. L. to Frolens Frazier no date (not executed) Hy
Whitelaw, Wm. to Lizzie Roberson 1-6-1867 Hy
Whitelaw, Wm. to Moria Whitelaw 11-15-1876 Hy
Whitelow, Jordon to Martha Buck 4-16-1868 Hy
Whitelow, Spencer to Harriet Scarbrough 10-27-1866 Hy
Whitelsy, C. J. to Albina Morris 2-18-1840 F
Whiteman, John to Deffilue? Jones 12-23-1870 T
Whitemore, Joshua to Martha D. Botts 9-2-1857 Sh
Whiten, F. to Mary Walker 12-13-1855 Hn
Whitenton, Othneil to Christenia R. Cock 1-13-1858 Ma
Whiteside(s), John N. to Eliza L. Harper 11-21-1839 O
Whiteside, James H. to Margarett A. Harper 9-20-1848 (9-21-1848) O
Whiteside, John to Susan Brown 10-1-1850 Cr
Whiteside, Jonathan to Margarett Long 10-22-1846 O
Whiteside, Joseph E. to Margaret A. Alexander 11-21-1855 (11-22-1855) Ma
Whiteside, Robert to Nancy Ann Alexander 3-24-1855 Ma
Whiteside, William H. to Martha M. Harper 6-23-1840 (6-25-1840) O
Whiteside, William H. to Mary D. Harper 1-9-1843 (1-12-1843) O
Whitesides, Holly to Annie Forbush 12-19-1883 (12-20-1883) L
Whitesides, John N. to Mahala H. Calhoun 2-6-1845 O
Whitesides, Thomas to Diannah Cox 9-20-1866 Ma
Whiteworth, Able to Nancy Hargress 1-10-1869 Hy
Whitfield, F. C. to Margaret Williams 2-3-1867 Hn
Whitfield, Geo. W. to Mrs. Elizabeth Wilson 9-7-1850 (9-10-1850) Hr
Whitfield, H. C. to Amanda Boswell 1-22-1862 T
Whitfield, John to Elizabeth Graves 11-4-1838 Hn
Whitfield, John to Sally Nealy 3-16-1841 (3-18-1841) F
Whitfield, Lemuel H. to Lucy E. Ruffin 4-14-1854 (4-15-1854) Sh

Whitfield, Needham to Araminta Gray 6-18-1848 Hn
Whitfield, Richard M. to Mary F. Love 1-1-1855 Ma
Whitfield, William H. to Elizabeth Hill 8-18-1854 (8-20-1854) O
Whitfield, William to Elizabeth Wimberly 11-7-1850 Hn
Whitford, David to Sarah Brooks 9-26-1837 Hr
Whitford, Jessee to Elizabeth Brooks 5-5-1838 (5-6-1838) Hr
Whitford, John W. to Fanny Smith 12-8-1872 Hy
Whithorne, Frank C. to Florence A. Orr 10-9-1866 Hn
Whiting, Silas to Sarah Hester 6-21-1848 (6-23-1848) F
Whitington, James to Cottury Betts 2-5-1844 Ma
Whitington, Joseph A. to Susan V. West 12-23-1869 (no return) L
Whitis, Benjamine to Amanda Lanier 2-5-1861 (2-20-1861) Dy
Whitis, Lafayett to Mollie Stitt 12-22-1869 (12-23-1869) T
Whitlaw, Henry to Elizabeth Smith 4-28-1849 (4-29-1849) Ma
Whitley (Wheatley), Asberry to Isabella Melton 1-17-1867 Be
Whitley, A. D. to Elizabeth Glover 7-31-1867 O
Whitley, Alexander D. to Sarah Frances Edwards 2-26-1856 (2-28-1856) O
Whitley, Alfred A. to Elizabeth Herring 12-17-1846 Sh
Whitley, Andrew J. to Henrietta Roane 8-25-1851 T
Whitley, B. F. to Susan A. Munn 4-30-1861 (5-1-1861) Sh
Whitley, Claiburn to Jenny Maclin 7-18-1868 T
Whitley, Daniel R. to Sarah Jett 1-5-1852 (1-6-1852) L
Whitley, David to Rhode Macklin 6-16-1866 (6-17-1866) T
Whitley, Doctor F. to Nancy Rooks (Brook) 8-27-1846 Sh
Whitley, E. to S. A. Flowers 1-27-1870 G
Whitley, E.B. to Sarah E. Peeler 12-31-1866 (1-1-1867) T
Whitley, Frank J. to Mary T. Somerville 4-5-1874 (4-13-1874) T
Whitley, Isaac W. to Sarah Ann Boon 5-3-1851 Be
Whitley, Isaac W. to Sarah Ann Boon 5-3-1851 Be CC
Whitley, James D. to Mary A. C. Hubbs 11-3-1852 (11-4-1852) O
Whitley, John to Frances Baptist 2-12-1872 T
Whitley, John to Lizzy Powel 1-4-1868 Hy
Whitley, Jos. D. to Annie M. Field 5-11-1866 (5-15-1866) F
Whitley, Joseph D. to Eliza Rufina Sherrod 12-16-1854 T
Whitley, Needham to Matilda C. Biggs 2-22-1854 G
Whitley, R. D. to M. R. Harmon 12-5-1867 Hy
Whitley, Robert E. to Amanda Rose 1-6-1869 T
Whitley, William to Mary McCall 5-26-1844 Mn
Whitley, Wm. S. to Emily Ann Banks 12-21-1854 T
Whitlock, David to Fannie Manning 10-8-1869 Hy
Whitlock, George W. to Rosa V. Maten 6-29-1869 (7-1-1869) T
Whitlock, Thos. to Elizabeth A. _____ 7-28-1832 Hr
Whitlock, William to C. F. Jones 3-6-1874 (3-7-1874) Dy
Whitlock, Wm. Ray to Evaline Smith 2-5-1849 (2-8-1849) T
Whitlock, Wm. to Nancy Watson 1-19-1867 (1-21-1867) Dy
Whitlocke, John D. to Martha A. Roberts 7-31-1864 G
Whitlow, Francis M. to Ann Fenner 2-2-1857 (2-5-1857) Ma
Whitlow, Nathan H. to Mary Elizabeth Webb 11-1-1854 Ma
Whitly (Whitby), Jesse to Susanna Whitly 6-15-1841 Sh
Whitly, F. G. to M. C. Anderson 3-14-1849 (no return) F
Whitly, John to Susan James 1-9-1869 G B
Whitly, Joseph to Caroline Ballowe 10-26-1849 Be
Whitman, F. S. to Lucinda Beard 11-2-1864 Sh
Whitman, J. D. to Elisabeth Findley 2-14-1862 (2-16-1862) Sh
Whitman, John F. to Louisa Neal 11-29-1862 Dy
Whitman, L. Milton to Sarah E. Henry 7-12-1848 Sh
Whitmore, Aleck to Harriet Daniel 8-6-1868 Hy
Whitmore, Alfred to Dora Rogers 10-27-1873 Hy
Whitmore, Alfred to Sallie Hendren 7-11-1878 Hy
Whitmore, Edwin to Betty B. McLeod 12-18-1864 Hy
Whitmore, Geo. L. to Rebecca A. Usher 11-10-1845 (11-12-1845) Hr
Whitmore, Geo. S. to Nancy D. Cagle 9-6-1850 Sh
Whitmore, Henry to Tennessee Williams 12-11-1884 L
Whitmore, James A. to Jane Snider 7-24-1876 T
Whitmore, R. A. to Cornelia A. Brown 6-30-1851 Hr
Whitmore, Wm. A. to Mollie J. Norton 12-5-1860 Sh
Whitmore, jr., Edwin to Ida B. Oliver ?-21-1864 Hy
Whitnell, David T. to Phitney M. Looney 9-25-1843 Hn
Whitney, Abraham to Hanah Shell 10-11-1862 Sh
Whitney, Elijah to Mary Anderson 2-17-1842 (2-22-1842) F
Whitney, James M. to Amanda E. Hardin 11-19-1867 (11-20-1867) F
Whitney, James to Sharlott Adams 8-29-1848 (no return) F
Whitsett, Wm. I. to Frances E. Stockard 10-25-1843 Cr
Whitsitt, B. A. to Lucy R. Hardaway 12-18-1845 Sh
Whitsitt, H. L. to Elizabeth Adkins 4-1-1843 Sh
Whitson, Aden to Susie Seviere 1-5-1874 (1-8-1874) L
Whitson, Andrew J. to Elvira A. Lindsey 12-18-1866 L
Whitson, Charles B. to Nancy ann Whitfield 2-13-1855 (no return) F
Whitson, Christopher to Mary J. Anderson 8-29-1849 (8-30-1849) L
Whitson, G. N. to Margarett Neely 12-7-1864 G
Whitson, G. W. to Mary E. Cooper 5-6-1871 Dy
Whitson, George W. to Malvina? Ray 9-8-1853 L
Whitson, J. T. to M. E. Gaines 12-7-1878 (12-8-1878) L
Whitson, James C. to Sallie A. Robinson 9-14-1868 (9-15-1868) L
Whitson, Jno. G. to Jemimah Ann Young 7-9-1846 (no return) F
Whitson, John D. to Elizabeth G. Fields 5-14-1834 (5-15-1834) G
Whitson, John G. to Sallie M. Gregg 3-30-1872 T

Whitson, John T. to Emaline Wynne 4-4-1861 Dy
Whitson, John T. to Mary L. McKnight 7-24-1879 Dy
Whitson, John W. to Mary J. Johnson 10-10-1850 (no return) L
Whitson, John to Nancy Williams 12-10-1867 (12-11-1867) L
Whitson, S. B. to Huldah A. Soap 10-31-1845 (no return) F
Whitson, T. J. to E. J. Lamb 9-17-1861 (9-18-1861) T
Whitson, Thomas E. to Nancy W. Glimp 2-27-1851 L
Whitson, W. W. to Elizabeth Cowrie? 4-13-1881 L
Whitson, William to Minerva Newman no date (before 1851) Sh
Whitt, P. H. to Sarah E. Archer 10-23-1865 Mn
Whittaker, A. W. to C. M. Donalson 2-11-1856 (2-13-1856) Sh
Whittaker, B. H. to Lucretia J. Strickland 1-18-1871 F
Whittaker, James Ables to Nancy Upchurch 6-24-1856 Hn
Whittaker, John to Sarah Ann J. P. Ralls 5-10-1866 Hn
Whittaker, Orange to Mollie Patterson 1-17-1876 (no return) Dy
Whittaker, Wm. D. to Sally Ann Abbington 5-18-1846 (5-22-1846) F
Whitten, A. to Nancyann Malone 4-25-1842 F
Whitten, J. F. to Ema Griffin 3-15-1869 G
Whitten, J. M. to Mary A. J. Hopkins 3-9-1857 Hr
Whitten, James W. to Jennie Wright 6-16-1874 (no return) Dy
Whitten, Kent H. to Estell Curry 9-25-1871 T
Whitten, M. H. to Dora Wiseman 5-30-1874 (no return) Dy
Whitten, Masslon to Mary Ann E. M. Miller 11-11-1841 G
Whitten, S. D. to Maggie E. Jarrett 9-24-1865 L
Whitten, William E. to Susan Lovell 2-23-1850 (2-24-1850) Hr
Whittenton, George A. to Elizabeth Bledsoe 2-5-1846 Ma
Whittenton, J. R. to M. Troy 8-26-1869 (8-27-1869) Dy
Whittenton, James M. to Mattie A. Moore 1-6-1870 Ma
Whittenton, Quintillian T. to Delilah Owen 10-11-1862 Ma
Whittick, D. T. to M. F. Dickerson 7-17-1864 G
Whittier, Jessie to Catharine Allen 9-1-1833 Sh
Whittington, Amos to Lucinda Ann Magee 10-4-1851 (10-29-1851) O
Whittington, C. to Louisa Christie 5-3-1849 Sh
Whittington, Gibson to Elizabeth Williams 8-20-1840 Ma
Whittington, John to Viny M. King 10-30-1865 (10-31-1865) Dy
Whittington, Nathan W. to Malvina Irvin 9-6-1842 Ma
Whittle, George J. to Fannie Poindexter 5-1-1867 (5-11-1867) F B
Whittle, M. (Rev.) to Mary Foard 1-3-1863 (no return) Dy
Whitton, David to Susan A. Boone 2-19-1856 (2-21-1856) Sh
Whitton, Henry to Mary Crawford 11-27-1869 F B
Whitton, Jack to Sarah Stokley 3-28-1878 Hy
Whittsett, Willie W. to Elizabeth Whitsett 11-28-1832 Sh
Whitworth, Creed to Martha Hutchins 3-5-1836 Sh
Whitworth, Ezekiel T. to Catherine Collins 3-5-1856 Ma
Whitworth, Filmore J. to Sarah B. Furguson 2-18-1852 (2-19-1852) Sh
Whitworth, Francis M. to Amanda M. Waggoner 3-16-1854 Ma
Whitworth, George W. to Margaret J. Shankle 10-17-1858 Hn
Whitworth, George to Angelina Hutchison 5-8-1851 L
Whitworth, George to Elizabeth Nevels 5-15-1861 L
Whitworth, J. M. to Amanda F Allen 7-2-1863 Hn
Whitworth, John H. to Elizabeth J. Reay 2-18-1852 (2-19-1852) Sh
Whitworth, John H. to Malinda Grainger 2-18-1846 Hn
Whitworth, P. M. to Nancy M. Brasfield 11-23-1857 We
Whitworth, P. to Lucinda Roark 9-5-1850 Sh
Whitworth, Robert W. to Rosa Dougherty 8-19-1851 Sh
Whitworth, Robert to Isabella Hobbs 10-15-1857 (10-16-1857) Ma
Whoohon?, George to Hudah Lain 12-2-1851 Be
Whooten, George to Hulda Lain 12-2-1851 Be CC
Whooten, George to Matilda Carolina George 6-9-1852 Be CC
Whooton, George to Matilda Caroline George 6-9-1852 Be
Whorton, John to Emily Cox 12-4-1872 Hy
Whorton, Samuel to Artelia E. Walker 9-14-1852 (no return) F
Whyte, James C. to Martha C. Wray 10-24-1840 (10-25?-1840) F
Whyte, James E. to Barthinia S. Webb 7-22-1847 Ma
Wichard, Rubin to Eliza J. Brent 11-12-1847 (11-14-1847) G
Wicker, Coleman to Nancy Wright 1-2-1841 Hn
Wicker, Jno. W. to Virginia Sampson 8-15-1864 (8-16-1864) O
Wicker, John W. to Louisa Pryor 4-13-1852 O
Wicker, Matthew to Mary A. Kelly 5-15-1849 Hn
Wicker, Neal to M. A. (Mrs.) Hoffman 11-2-1867 O
Wicker, William G. to Nancy M. Smith 3-17-1866 (3-18-1866) O
Wicker, William R. to Martha D. Wright 5-22-1861 O
Wickham, W. G. to Lucy Braswell 4-27-1847 Sh
Wicks, G. A. to Mary Gibson 1-4-1875 (1-5-1875) Dy
Wicks, Tobe to Cynthia A. Ledsinger 12-27-1875 Dy
Widdis, William to Charlotte Grant 4-12-1869 (4-13-1869) Cr
Widener, James K. to Mary A. Bursbe 5-31-1870 L
Widener, M. H. to M. E. Nowell 9-30-1874 Hy
Widick, E. M. to M. O. Jones 12-9-1868 Hy
Wiegand, George to Mary Essig 11-15-1854 G
Wieners, B. to Anna Duerkap 11-17-1856 Sh
Wier, John Wesley to F. R. Burford 8-27-1863 Sh
Wigam, Wm. F. to N. H. Maceer 8-12-1862 Sh
Wigfall, R. F. to Margaret McCutchen 7-23-1875 (7-24-1875) Dy
Wiggans, John to Nancy Roads 4-10-1854 We
Wiggens, W. T. to Nancy Willingham 9-14-1861 Sh
Wiggin, J. R. to Sarah Jane Arnold 4-12-1871 (4-13-1871) Dy

Wiggin, John W. to Mary E. Rainey 8-15-1843 (no return) Hn
Wiggin, Norris J. to Annie E. Sevier 1-19-1864 Sh
Wiggins, Archer to Nancy Taliaferro 4-6-1866 Hy
Wiggins, Archibald to Judy Pulliam 2-7-1871 (2-15-1871) F B
Wiggins, Finny to Nancy Harris 10-10-1866 (10-13-1866) F B
Wiggins, Harris to Betsy Mitchell 12-31-1827 Hr
Wiggins, Harris to Ellen Chisum 7-1-1851 Ma
Wiggins, James R. to Elizabeth S. Jones 6-27-1859 (6-30-1859) Hr
Wiggins, James T. to Jane Kurby 6-15-1832 Hr
Wiggins, Jas. W. to Sallie P. Smith 1-14-1871 (1-15-1871) F
Wiggins, Ned to Fanny Jones 11-22-1870 (no return) F
Wiggins, Ned to Liza Shackelford 5-18-1866 (no return) F B
Wiggins, West W. to Mary Ann Smith 6-1-1839 (6-5-1839) Hr
Wiggins, Wiley W. to Mary Ann Johnson 3-10-1843 Sh
Wiggins, Wm. W. to Sophia H. Miller 11-16-1859 Hr
Wiggins, Zang to Celena Granberry 12-23-1869 (no return) F B
Wiggs, Jonathan S. to Zelphia J. Lea 8-21-1856 G
Wiggs, Loi R. to Caroline Wiggs 10-1-1840 Ma
Wiggs, Matthew to Rebecca Lee 4-9-1857 G
Wiggs, W. W. to Martha P. Fonville 10-27-1869 G
Wiggs, Wm. B. to Laura R. Taylor 6-3-1861 Sh
Wikmiller, Jacob to Mary Jerk 11-29-1864 Sh
Wikoff, B. D. (Rev.) to Melissa Johnson 5-30-1860 Sh
Wilbanks, J. S. to Mary A. Wilbanks 5-11-1860 (5-20-1860) Hr
Wilber (Milber?), A. to Milla (Mrs.) Wright 1-1-1863 Sh
Wilber, Needham to Mary Balentine 11-7-1864 Sh
Wilbon, John R. to Mattie Hall 12-22-1869 Ma
Wilborn, E. B. to Malissa Jane Rowland 8-14-1868 (8-16-1868) Cr
Wilborn, John to Harriett Allison 10-4-1851 (10-28-1851) O
Wilborne, George to Sallie A. Finch 1-5-1876 Dy
Wilbourn, Elijah to Nancy Stuard 11-29-1843 (11-30-1843) G
Wilbourn, Isaac Y. to Sarah Blankenship 10-22-1856 (10-23-1856) O
Wilbourn, J. G. to Mary S. Shaw 12-18-1867 F
Wilbourn, William J. N. to Rebecca J. McLamore 11-17-1846 G
Wilbourn, William to Narcissus E. O'Neal 12-161852 O
Wilburn, George M. to Elizabeth Fite 3-3-1853 (3-?-1853) G
Wilburn, John K. to Mary D. Mayfield 5-7-1866 (5-10-1866) F
Wilburn, Joshua to Jane Bryant 2-19-1829 Hr
Wilburn, Joshua to Jane Bryant 2-19-1829 (2-20-1829) G
Wilcox, Charles B. to Mary M. Carter 3-14-1859 Cr
Wilcox, John S. to Martha A. Taylor 9-18-1859 Hn
Wilcox, S. B. to Mary (Mrs.) Beckner 11-2-1857 Sh
Wilcox, Thomas to Jane C. Caruth 8-16-1842 (8-24-1842) L
Wilcox, Thomas to Melinda Caruth 12-22-1851 L
Wilcox, W. L. to S. J. Hendrix 10-22-1867 (no return) Dy
Wilcox, W. W. to Mary E. Goling 6-18-1874 Hy
Wildbenga, Jno. to Caroline I.(J) Cheek 5-17-1849 Sh
Wildberger, John to Eliza Gaccer 3-27-1855 Sh
Wilder, C. to F. J. Sayles 1-11-1867 Cr
Wilder, J. C. to Fannie Jones 6-25-1872 (no return) Cr
Wilder, James W. to Corar Guthrie 9-24-1867 (no return) Cr
Wilder, Jas. A. to Emma Taylor 10-8-1867 Hy
Wilder, W. L. to S. A. Jackson 12-6-1859 (12-8-1859) F
Wilder, W. O. to Louisa McKnight 12-10-1869 (12-15-1869) F
Wilds, Columbus J.? to Ellen C. Colvet 10-15-1872 (10-6?-1872) Cr
Wilds, M. D. L. to L. C. Belote 11-15-1858 Sh
Wiles (Wiley?), M. D. Lafayette to Arabella V. Haynes 3-17-1856 Sh
Wiles, Gillum to Leah Rutledge 4-4-1840 Sh
Wiles, H. J. to E. J. Wilson 3-24-1866 F
Wiles, Hiram to Martha A. Thompson 6-28-1849 Sh
Wiles, Hiram to Martha J. Simmons 7-2-1853 (7-4-1853) Sh
Wiles, LaFayette to Martha A. Wallis 12-12-1855 (12-13-1855) Sh
Wiles, Robert to Fanny G. Mills 11-24-1851 O
Wiles, Samuel to Delina Davis 9-23-1833 (9-26-1833) O
Wiles, Stephen to Dora Taylor 1-6-1871 Hy
Wiles, William A. to Mary V. Dunlap 3-6-1855 G
Wiles?, W. Z.? to Susan Webb? no date (with 12-1860) Cr
Wiley, A. S. to Martha E. Meek 9-9-1859 Hr
Wiley, Adison to Hrrett Taylor 11-20-1849 Cr
Wiley, Brown to Fannie Bond 12-11-1873 Hy
Wiley, Charles P. to Caroline H. Harper (Hanssen?) 6-8-1854 Sh
Wiley, Giles to Caledonia Sneed 11-22-1867 (11-24-1867) F B
Wiley, Harris to Poka Bruce 4-3-1865 Hn
Wiley, James to Elizabeth Taylor 2-8-1836 Hr
Wiley, Jerry to Ellen Whitelaw 4-27-1871 Hy
Wiley, Jesse to Martha James 1-6-1841 Sh
Wiley, John H. to Lula A. Haven 12-2-1856 Cr
Wiley, John W. to Jennie Jones 9-30-1871 (10-1-1871) T
Wiley, John to Anna Erwin 11-16-1867 (11-20-1867) T
Wiley, John to Catherine Yancey 8-17-1864 (no return) F B
Wiley, John to Delly Ann Jones 9-14-1846 Sh
Wiley, Nelson to Sarah L. Conner 2-4-1842 (2-6-1842) Hr
Wiley, R. C. to _____ 3-14-1849 (3-15-1849) F
Wiley, Richard to Louisa Frierson 12-29-1865 (12-30-1865) F B
Wiley, Rufus to Lidda Crop (Cross) 1-2-1872 Hy
Wiley, Samuel H. to Martha C. Patterson 1-12-1860 Hn
Wiley, Seaborn? J. to Pamela Powers 6-16-1853 (6-17-1853) Sh
Wiley, Smith to Catherine Hardin 6-12-1875 L
Wiley, T. H. to Jenny A. Cockram 1-23-1862 Mn
Wiley, T. P. to Mary Anderson 8-24-1848 Sh
Wiley, Thomas? James to Sarah Jane Davis 8-10-1854 T
Wiley, William to Adaline James 5-17-1848 Sh
Wiley, William to Claricy Bostic 2-3-1867 Hy
Wiley, William to Martha Yarbrough 10-1-1853 (10-3-1853) Sh
Wilhauks, John to Delila Gaskins 5-9-1860 (no return) We
Wilhelm, Frederick to Martha F. (Mrs.) Coble 1-26-1864 Sh
Wilhelm, John D. to Annie C. White 8-28-1866 (8-30-1866) Ma
Wilhight, Julius to Polly Friar 3-2-1837 Hr
Wilhite, Matthew to Nancy Moss 9-5-1833 Hr
Wiliamson, Louis to Bettie Adkisson 12-26-1871 (12-28-1871) Cr B
Wilie, James M. to Jane Delapp 4-11-1853 (4-12-1853) Ma
Wilie, John McW. to Nancy Lovel 12-28-1843 Sh
Wilie, John W. to Nancy E. Miller 7-31-1855 (8-2-1855) T
Wilie, Nelson to Caroline Brown 1-7-1872 (1-9-1872) T
Wilk, G. W. to Margaret A. Lacy 1-4-1866 (1-14-1866) Cr
Wilkerson, Benjamin to Cavell F. Birdsong 8-17-1839 (8-21-1839) Hr
Wilkerson, Charles to Ann Wilkerson 11-18-1866 Hy
Wilkerson, Edward to S. J. Trent 12-31-1849 Sh
Wilkerson, Elgie to Sarah J. Tyler 7-8-1877 Hy
Wilkerson, F. A. to Martha J. Bransford 7-24-1866 O
Wilkerson, George W. to Sarah B. Wood 10-20-1843 Hr
Wilkerson, George to Margaret A. Giles 1-17-1850 Sh
Wilkerson, Isaac A. to Sarah Swor 12-5-1848 Hn
Wilkerson, J. W. to S. A. (Mrs.) Want 11-3-1863 Sh
Wilkerson, Jackson to Mary Suttles 3-28-1859 Hr
Wilkerson, James R. to Sylvester Elinder 12-21-1848 Hn
Wilkerson, John J. to Julia Ann Coursey 9-14-1860 Hn
Wilkerson, John to Charlotty Sullivan 1-19-1853 Cr
Wilkerson, John to Eliza Jerman 1-27-1843 (1-30-1843) Ma
Wilkerson, Joseph E. to Berthenia Frailkill 9-17-1864 Sh
Wilkerson, Lamb to Easter Williamson 3-12-1870 T
Wilkerson, Littleberry G. to Elizabeth G. Oliver 1-24-1844 (no return) F
Wilkerson, R. P. to L. V. Moore 9-11-1865 Mn
Wilkerson, Tom to Nancy Armstrong 7-5-1867 (no return) F B
Wilkerson, W. A. to L. M. Moody 11-10-1868 Hy
Wilkerson, W. A. to Mary E. Martin 8-5-1867? Hy
Wilkerson, W. D. to Mary J. Harris 10-9-1854 (no return) F
Wilkerson, Wiley to Matilda Kemp 3-20-1866 (no return) F B
Wilkerson, Wm. D. to Mary E. (Mrs.) Freding 8-8-1870 (8-9-1870) Ma
Wilkerson, Wm. to Sarah Rivers 12-22-1869 F B
Wilkerson, jr., William D. to Mattie M. Mays 4-3-1866 (4-4-1866) L
Wilkes, Andrew to Mollie Lindsey 2-8-1871 (2-9-1871) F B
Wilkes, Benjamin B. to Anna Summers 3-17-1877 Hy
Wilkes, Benjamin to Mary McMahon 2-27-1834 Hr
Wilkes, Frank to Nancy Douglas 11-26-1874 Hy
Wilkes, J. B. to Mary D. Porter 1-21-1868 G
Wilkes, James B. to Annie E. Halliburton 2-23-1885 (12-24-1885) L
Wilkes, James to Laura F. Doyle 8-21-1854 (8-23-1854) Hr
Wilkes, John M. to Mary Thomas 4-21-1858 G
Wilkes, John W. to E. J. Mitchell 3-13-1858 (3-17-1859?) Hr
Wilkes, John to Mary Coritt 10-31-1855 Cr
Wilkes, Joseph to Naoma M. Barnett 3-12-1829 Hr
Wilkes, Perry C. to A. E. J. Wilkes 11-12-1856 (11-13-1856) Hr
Wilkes, Samuel to Delly Miller 12-26-1872 Hy
Wilkes, W. H. to M. J. Thomas 4-20-1868 G
Wilkes, W. S. to E. T. Barfield 2-13-1883 (2-14-1883) L
Wilkes, W. S. to Ella Blackwell 12-23-1880 L
Wilkes, William H. to Amandy J. C. P. Howell 2-4-1860 G
Wilkes, William S. to Mary N. Barfield 11-28-1871 L
Wilkins, A. S. to C. V. Taylor 3-24-1863 G
Wilkins, Alfred to Mary Brown 6-15-1869 F B
Wilkins, Allen to Letta Sane? 7-14-1870 G
Wilkins, Anderson to Etta Boyd 10-15-1868 Hy
Wilkins, Charles Thos. to Molly Catherine Townzel 5-20-1870 (5-22-1870) Ma
Wilkins, Feereby to Catherine Sturdivant 12-9-1850 (12-11-1850) Ma
Wilkins, Geo. W. to Telissa Ann Kirk 11-9-1854 (11-8?-1854) Hr
Wilkins, George to Nancy Shaw 4-28-1857 (4-29-1857) L
Wilkins, Henry S. to Elizabeth Owens 10-18-1859 We
Wilkins, Henry to Harriet Ann Deak 4-14-1880 (4-15-1880) Dy
Wilkins, J. C. to Mary J. Stephenson 2-22-1871 (2-25-1871) T
Wilkins, James A. to Martha Estes 9-1-1845 (9-4-1845) Ma
Wilkins, James J. to Sarah Ann Stocks 2-28-1863 Sh
Wilkins, James Y. to Sarah Ann Stocks 2-28-1863 (3-1-1863) Sh
Wilkins, James to Ann H. Owen 7-19-1855 T
Wilkins, James to Josephine Timms 4-21-1868 (4-23-1869?) T
Wilkins, John to Ellen McCree 12-12-1866 G
Wilkins, L. J. to Addie Jones 6-30-1863 Sh
Wilkins, Michaels H. to Susan A. Malin 9-22-1859 Hn
Wilkins, Newton Benjamin to Lucinda Elizabeth A. Campbell 12-20-1873 (12-21-1873) Dy
Wilkins, Samuel J. to Miranda Webb 8-3-1843 G
Wilkins, W. P. to L. S. Burns 10-8-1860 (10-9-1860) Cr
Wilkins, W. P. to M. E. Patton 10-12-1869 (10-13-1869) Cr
Wilkins, W. to America F. McGuin 5-4-1859 T

Wilkins, West to Melissa Trantham 5-19-1840 T
Wilkins, William to Catharine H. Smith 7-14-1852 (7-15-1852) T
Wilkins, Wm. E. to Mary R. Adair 11-27-1854 (11-29-1854) Hr
Wilkinson, Eli to Sarah Curry 1-12-1862 Mn
Wilkinson, F. M. to A. E. Arnold 9-14-1865 G
Wilkinson, F. M. to M. A. R. Halliburton 1-10-1867 (no return) L
Wilkinson, J. M. to Ella Harris 9-19-1870 (9-24-1870) F
Wilkinson, James F. to Mary E. Spain 3-19-1878 (3-25-1878) Dy
Wilkinson, James to Eliza (Mrs.) Smith 11-13-1864 Sh
Wilkinson, John R. to Sallie E. Reddick 3-7-1871 Ma
Wilkinson, John to Seletha Gage 5-8-1830 Hr
Wilkinson, R. B. to Louisa Drane 5-16-1878 (5-17-1878) Dy
Wilkinson, Stephen G. to Louisa Broyls 12-11-1850 (12-13-1850) L
Wilkinson, T. W. to E. T. Gossitt 5-28-1856 Sh
Wilkinson, Threlbut to Narsalyce? Lane 3-14-1850 Sh
Wilkinson, Wm. B. to Maggie L. Locke 1-27-1859 (2-2-1859) F
Wilkirson, William Asberry to Lula Henry? 10-28-1873 L
Wilkison, James G. to Lucinda Hannis 7-4-1827 (7-5-1827) Hr
Wilkison, James to L. P. Halliburton 1-10-1861 Be
Wilks, Armstead to Harriet Barnum 1-26-1884 (2-17-1884) L
Wilks, Burwell to Nancy P. Elston 3-2-1829 Ma
Wilks, E. B. to Julia A. Mitchell 3-25-1869 Cr
Wilks, Joseph to Rebecca J. Kirkpatrick 12-6-1847 (12-7-1847) Ma
Wilks, Modnaca to Mary Flowers 4-7-1845 (4-10-1845) G
Wilks, Roger to Sarah Mathews 3-17-1869 Hy
Wilks, T. J. to L. J. Thomas 11-19-1870 Hy
Wilks, William R. to Nancy Bishop 1-4-1874 Hy
Wilks, Yancy E. to Mary E. Rhodes 12-16-1869 Cr
Willard, Clarence B. to Lear Elizabeth Grimes 5-25-1863 Sh
Willard, J. H. to A. R. Hatchett 12-17-1863 G
Willard, R. W. to Lucy E. Bowen 10-17-1859 Sh
Willbanks, Henry to Mary Jane Rogers 12-25-1862 Hn
Willbanks, Jesse to Elizabeth Suiter 11-29-1862 (no return) Hn
Willbanks, William to Rhody Cross 8-12-1866 Hy
Willcher, C. A. to Sarah Ann (Mrs.) Pierce 12-3-1864 (12-4-1864) Sh
Willcox (Nilcex), Robert F. to Virginia Wallace 7-21-1863 (7-22-1863) Sh
Willeford, J. L. to S. E. Abbott 5-6-1863 Sh
Willeford, Thomas Y. to America Upchurch 12-30-1846 Hn
Willeford, Willis W. to Rebecca Row 9-26-1839 Hn
Willenberg, Charles to Enna Beckert 5-13-1861 Sh
Willes, J. S. to Miranda Huss (Hemp) 4-9-1854 We
Willet, Wm. D. to Martha J. Brewer 11-14-1867 Hy
Willett, D. S. to J. A. Buckhannon 11-18-1852 Hn
Willett, E. Miles to Mary A. Magevney 9-28-1861 (10-1-1861) Sh
Willett, James T. to Mary E. Day 11-15-1862 (11-19-1862) Ma
Willett, John to Martha Mitchell 4-4-1842 (4-7-1842) Ma
Willett, Joseph to Lucretia Choate 9-27-1831 L
Willett, Warren P. to Alabama T. Buchanan 2-16-1853 (no return) Hn
Willey, Joseph to Margaret Fergason 3-13-1845 Sh
Willheit, Louis to Ursulina Sesselman 11-3-1859 Sh
Willi, G. W. to Priscilla Hodge 9-6-1852 Hr
Willi, George W. to Serena Atkinson 1-5-1847 (1-6-1847) Hr
Willialms, Theophilus to Elizabeth Huzza 5/31/1847 (6-1-1847) O
William, Calvin to Milly Narvin 1-23-1830 Ma
William, John G. to Lydia L. Holt 1-22-1856 (1-24-1856) G
William, Napolian to Lucy Thomas 8-1-1867 (8-2-1867) T
William, Riley to Belgona Palston 1-11-1846 Hn
William, Zibia H. to Mary Potts 1-7-1839 (no return) Hn
Williams, A. B. to Sally Ann Harrison 1-4-1866 Dy
Williams, A. H. to Nancy Carr 12-13-1847 Sh
Williams, A. J. to F. A. Williams 10-12-1863 (10-13-1863) O
Williams, A. J. to Mary Jane Seat 9-29-1840 (10-1-1840) G
Williams, A. L. to Susan Kirk 11-18-1874 (no return) Dy
Williams, A. M. to Zylphia J. Williams 6-24-1873 Dy
Williams, A. R. to Martha B. Johnson 5-13-1858 G
Williams, A. W. to Sarah Ann Adams 3-23-1845 Be
Williams, A. W. to Sarah Ann Adams 3-23-1845 Be CC
Williams, A. to N. A. Freeman 10-17-1854 We
Williams, A. to Parolee Anderson 6-5-1849 Hn
Williams, Albert C. to Mary Williams 8-17-1866 Hy
Williams, Albert J. to Rebecca Lowery 2-21-1850 Hn
Williams, Albert to Marget Dinwoody 9-19-1859 T
Williams, Alex to Caroline Aikins 11-26-1872 Hy
Williams, Alex to Mary E. Norton 9-3-1867 Dy
Williams, Alex to Priscilla Hammons 8-4-1856 (8-10-1856) G
Williams, Alex to Sylvia Mays 2-15-1877 Dy
Williams, Alexander to Emmer Badaw 12-27-1870 (12-28-1870) T
Williams, Alexander to Galaney Rigsby 10-18-1847 (10-19-1847) T
Williams, Alfred to Ammarilla Harris 8-6-1839 F
Williams, Alfred to Edney Fainer 4-11-1872 Hy
Williams, Alfred to Matilda Jones 12-29-1869 (12-30-1869) F B
Williams, Allen C. to Harriet M. Alexander 8-4-1852 (8-5-1852) G
Williams, Allen to Emily C. Mitchell 11-20-1843 Be
Williams, Allen to Emily C. Mitchell 11-20-1843 Be CC
Williams, Allen to Lucy Bledsoe 7-21-1842 L
Williams, Allen to Nancy Brooks 2-3-1847 Cr
Williams, Allen to Sarah Scot 3-13-1858 (3-14-1858) T

Williams, Alvin R. to Mary M. Dickerson 12-14-1859 (12-15-1859) Ma
Williams, Alvin to Sarah Ann Crawford 9-3-1837 Hr
Williams, Anderson to Harriet Cullin 1-1-1844 (1-4-1844) L
Williams, Anderson to Molly Hancock 2-2-1870 G B
Williams, Anderson to Phillis Harper 12-28-1868 (12-30-1868) T
Williams, Andrew J. to Caroline C. Stewart 12-17-1846 F
Williams, Andrew J. to Louisa F. Barnes 7-8-1857 L
Williams, Andrew J. to Sarah Jane Thomas 9-26-1860 (10-2-1860) Ma
Williams, Andrew to Emiline Boo 3-1-1858 Hr
Williams, Anthony T. to Margarett L. Eddins 3-27-1850 Ma
Williams, Aron W. to Uphrasia America Fr. Browder 12-17-1855 (12-20-1855) Ma
Williams, Arthur A. to Margaret Conell 8-8-1846 G
Williams, Arthur to Gilly Hundley 11-4-1857 Ma
Williams, Arthur to Mary McBride 12-21-1829 (12-24-1829) G
Williams, Arthur to Nancy Holloman 2-16-1869 (2-17-1869) Ma
Williams, Arthur to Susan J. Orr 2-19-1849 (2-20-1849) F
Williams, Augustus to Nancy Jones 10-9-1860 Sh
Williams, B. E. to J. A. Hays 1-7-1878 L
Williams, B. M. to Didema Abernathy 10-13-1862 (no return) Cr
Williams, B. W. to Mary Ann Spain 3-9-1848 Hn
Williams, Barney to Victoria Mason 9-9-1867 (9-12-1867) F B
Williams, Baxter J. to Mary C. Taylor 9-23-1841 (9-30-1841) Ma
Williams, Ben to Cynthia Stedman 11-16-1870 (11-18-1870) Dy
Williams, Ben to Hanah Rake 1-27-1866 Hy
Williams, Benj. F. to Dortha A(labama) Smith 12-12-1865 (12-13-1865) Dy
Williams, Benj. J. to Frances C. Moore 1-7-1845 Be
Williams, Benj. to Carolina Enochs 7-5-1840 Cr
Williams, Benj. to Sarah C. Jenkins 3-23-1859 Cr
Williams, Benjamin A. to Jobie A. Wright 6-26-1861 (6-27-1861) Cr
Williams, Benjamin F. to Mary A. Minter 3-22-1842 H
Williams, Benjamin J. to Martha J. (Mrs.) Sanders 3-17-1847 G
Williams, Benjamin J. to Martha V. Chandler 6-20-1853 Hr
Williams, Benjamin M. to Martha Elizabeth Williams 3-21-1843 Hr
Williams, Benjamin to Caroline Wood 1-13-1847 (1-14-1847) Hr
Williams, Benjamin to Frances C. Moore 1-7-1845 Be CC
Williams, Benjamin to Louisa Bird 6-4-1852 (6-6-1852) O
Williams, Benjamin to Martha A. R. Harly 10-26-1853 (3-13-1854) Hr
Williams, Benjamin to Mildred Thomason 12-5-1839 We
Williams, Benjamin to Peggy Medly 9-4-1839 (9-1?-1839) Ma
Williams, Bennett B. to Sarah J. Bynum 1-5-1863 We
Williams, Benton to Eliza J. Moore 11-3-1863 O
Williams, Berry H. to Frances Ellington 12-22-1868 (12-23-1868) Ma
Williams, Berry H. to Mary Ritty Freno 2-4-1857 (2-5-1857) Ma
Williams, Bill to Jane Tanner 11-3-1867 Hy
Williams, Bill to Sarah Thomas 12-24-1877 (12-25-1877) L B
Williams, Billie to Manda Hathway 12-31-1874 O
Williams, Billy to Elizabeth Kelly 10-27-1869 (no return) F B
Williams, Boyed to Rebeca Willis 2-13-1839 (2-14-1839) F
Williams, Buck to Patsy Mathis 2-2-1867 G
Williams, Buck to Percilla West 6-8-1867 (6-11-1867) T
Williams, Buck to Vinie Austin 2-11-1875 Hy
Williams, Burrie T. to Cornelia Sedberry 2-28-1856 Cr
Williams, Butler to Chainey Smith 9-12-1871 (9-16-1871) T
Williams, C. C. to Eliza A. Johnson 7-26-1853 Be
Williams, C. C. to Eliza A. Johnson 7-26-1853 Be CC
Williams, C. E. to Mary O. Little 1-7-1840 Sh
Williams, C. H. to Mary A. Birdsong 10-29-1851 (10-31-1851) Hr
Williams, C. H. to Mary James 9-19-1860 G
Williams, C. L. to Mannie House 10-7-1851 Cr
Williams, C. M. to Eliza Jane Calbert 2-8-1858 Sh
Williams, C. T. to Mattie A. Jeter 1-6-1875 Hy
Williams, C. W. to Frances R. Mastin (Martin?) 12-17-1861 Sh
Williams, Calvin to Eliza H. Rankin 2-13-1835 Hr
Williams, Calvin to Sarah Ann McFarland 4-8-1853 (4-10-1853) O
Williams, Cato to Candis Goodlett 2-11-1868 (2-16-1868) F B
Williams, Chapman to Eliza Detherage 11-28-1838 Ma
Williams, Charles H. to Mary F. Parson 2-16-1860 Hn
Williams, Charles W. to Clarissa Young 12-16-1835 (12-17-1835) G
Williams, Charles W. to Clarissa Young 12-16-1836 G
Williams, Charles to Bettie E. Williams 8-9-1880 (8-15-1880) L
Williams, Charles to Clarinda Crenshaw 1-21-1874 T
Williams, Charles to Louisa Fink 5-7-1873 T
Williams, Charley to Lottie Bond 11-21-1878 Hy
Williams, Charlie to Cina Tyus 12-10-1878 Hy
Williams, Claude to Emily Williams 1-23-1866 (no return) F B
Williams, Cloyd to Amanda Badaw 12-29-1869 (no return) F B
Williams, Cokely P. to Lety Tally 2-17-1831 Hr
Williams, Coleman to Louisa Mooreland 8-14-1868 (no return) F
Williams, Collin to Catherine Massey 1-10-1854 (1-11-1854) Ma
Williams, Colliver to Sarah House 3-1-1853 Cr
Williams, D. H. to M. J. Pritchard 1-28-1868 (1-30-1868) Cr
Williams, Dan to Pricilla Carlin 2-17-1827 (2-18-1827) Hr
Williams, Daniel L. to Lucinda C. English 2-29-1848 (2-30?-1848) G
Williams, Daniel to Martha Harris 2-25-1846 (2-26-1846) T
Williams, Dave to Ada Halliburton 12-31-1885 (1-1-1886) L
Williams, Dave to Nellie Alison 12-2-1871 Hy

Williams, David A. to Mary E. Wright 12-16-1845 (12-17-1845) L
Williams, David C. to Frances A. Williams 1-12-1848 Hn
Williams, David to Cary Porter 5-14-1850 Sh
Williams, David to Elizabeth V. Seaton 9-26-1834 Hr
Williams, David to Elve (Elsie?) A. Walker 2-7-1842 (no return) L
Williams, David to Emaline Stockley 11-10-1870 (12-14-1870) T
Williams, David to Margarett L. Morrison 2-10-1849 Ma
Williams, David to Mary A. Bearden 8-13-1849 Sh
Williams, David to Mary McKangham 9-27-1828 Hr
Williams, Drew to Mary Powers 7-13-1843 We
Williams, Drury B. to Martha Taylor 8-31-1852 (9-5-1852) Ma
Williams, Drury B. to Rebecca Jane Davis 10-20-1857 (10-22-1857) Ma
Williams, E. J. to Almira P. Smith 11-24-1858 (11-28-1858) Sh
Williams, E. L. to M. A. Hamilton 9-23-1864 (9-27-1864) O
Williams, E. N. to Caroline Swinney 1-18-1859 Cr
Williams, E. P. to Mariah Archer 3-29-1838 Sh
Williams, E. S. to R. B. Inman 6-30-1872 (7-1-1872) O
Williams, Ed to Siloa Bone 6-9-1870 (6-25-1870) F B
Williams, Edward D. to L. I. Alison 1-12-1870 Hy
Williams, Edward E. to Mary A. Fields 9-3-1842 (9-6-1842) O
Williams, Edward to Amanda Crowder 12-23-1873 Hy
Williams, Edward to Lyd A. Gillaland 1-30-1861 (no return) Dy
Williams, Edwin to Mary E. Caudle 9-25-1865 Cr
Williams, Eleanor to Mary Thornton 12-21-1845 We
Williams, Elias to Dina Carter 6-12-1879 (6-18-1879) L
Williams, Elias to Elizabeth Moody 1-19-1830 Sh
Williams, Elijah F. to Emma E. Martin 2-2-1871 L
Williams, Elijah H. to Amanda J. Davis 12-23-1867 (12-27-1867) Ma
Williams, Elijah to Louisa H. Harris 5-29-1852 (5-30-1852) Sh
Williams, Elisha C. to Hannah E. Carter 11-22-1854 O
Williams, Elisha to Mary Rogers 2-15-1844 (no return) F
Williams, Elkanor to Cynthia A. Hilliard 6-18-1855 O
Williams, Emery E. to Dorcas Jones 11-25-1834 Hr
Williams, Ephram W. to Windsor J. Edwards 7-29-1850 Cr
Williams, Ephran to Adaline Peter 11-27-1856 Cr
Williams, Essex to Ruth Wilson 10-20-1871 T
Williams, Evans to Celia High 4-18-1870 (5-1-1870) F B
Williams, Everett to Wincy Jane Williams 10-13-1866 G
Williams, Ezekial to Smith Ann Green? 12-18-1872 (12-25-1872) L B
Williams, Ezekiel Smith to Mary A. H. Wright 1-29-1855 (1-31-1855) T
Williams, Ezekiel to Virginia Pinson (Pierson?) 4-24-1869 (4-29-1869) L B
Williams, F. A. to M. E. Winn 8-10-1867 (8-11-1867) Cr
Williams, F. G. to Anna E. Priest 10-19-1871 (no return) Cr
Williams, F. M. to Eliza Hartwell 6-6-1857 (6-7-1857) Sh
Williams, F. to Jane Cole 5-15-1867 O
Williams, Fayett to Eliza Lenier 3-6-1867 Hy
Williams, Francis to Ellinor Jones 9-24-1836 (9-29-1836) O
Williams, Francis to Livina Harris 7-30-1870 T
Williams, Frank H. to Mary B. Tucker 5-24-1856 Sh
Williams, Frank to Catharine J. Trigg 7-31-1854 Sh
Williams, Franklin to Tibitha Connell 1-27-1858 G
Williams, Frederick to Margaret Hays 11-30-1868 Hy
Williams, G. D. to Martha J. Waterage 12-15-1868 Hy
Williams, G. H. to Nancy C. Huffman 7-14-1866 (7-15-1866) Cr
Williams, G. P. to M. L. Benton 1-11-1873 (1-12-1873) Cr
Williams, G. R. to Adeline McPherson 8-17-1874 (8-19-1874) L
Williams, G. W. to M. J. Ledsinger 10-7-1871 (10-8-1871) Cr
Williams, G. W. to Martha A. Smith 2-27-1868 G
Williams, Geo. to Moriah Carter 5-24-1868 Hy
Williams, George L. to Elender Bivins 2-6-1850 Be
Williams, George M. to E. C. Glraham 12-5-1853 (12-7-1853) Hr
Williams, George R. to Louisa Hutcherson 8-13-1849 (8-14-1849) L
Williams, George W. to Jane Fergerson 2-13-1845 Sh
Williams, George to Amanda Wadkins 8-24-1862 (no return) Hn
Williams, George to Caroline E. G. Johnston 9-7-1846 (no return) Hn
Williams, George to Dathie McAdoo 11-5-1866 G
Williams, George to Harriet Jackson 10-15-1870 (10-18-1870) L
Williams, George to Helen Young 6-23-1866 Hy
Williams, George to Jemima Neeey 3-27-1847 (3-28-1847) O
Williams, George to Jemima Neely 3-27-1847 (3-28-1847) O
Williams, George to Lidda Lewis 2-18-1839 (2-25-1839) F
Williams, George to Lizzie Bond 3-16-1872 Hy
Williams, George to Louisa Chambers 11-16-1867 Hy
Williams, George to Mosella Green 9-15-1880 L B
Williams, George to P. A. Jones 6-3-1877 Hy
Williams, George to Rebecca A. Chumney 10-24-1866 O
Williams, Green to Nancy A. Philips 1-1-1839 (1-3-1839) G
Williams, Greenbury to Louisa M. Tate 8-26-1849 Be
Williams, H. B. to Martha Hardican 10-19-1863 Dy
Williams, H. H. to Elizabeth Perry 12-30-1867 (12-31-1867) F
Williams, H. J. to V. C. Williams 6-7-1879 (6-8-1879) L
Williams, Hamblin L. to Lucina Moore 1-12-1832 (1-17-1832) Hr
Williams, Hansel to Nancy Pridgeon 11-?-1844 Hn
Williams, Harbird to Manerva? C. Dodd 8-11-1859 O
Williams, Hardy to Mary Newhouse 12-30-1867 G B
Williams, Harrison to Rebecca Rushing 5-30-1866 Be
Williams, Hartwell T. to Margaret Wesson 7-19-1852 Sh

Williams, Henders. to Crecy Adams 9-6-1866 Hy
Williams, Henry L. to Elizabeth Barnes 7-13-1848 Hn
Williams, Henry L. to Margaret Reeth? 3-12-1859 (3-24-1859) O
Williams, Henry W. to Jane Dukes 2-21-1878 Hy
Williams, Henry to Belle Townes 9-18-1878 (9-25-1878) L B
Williams, Henry to Catherine Taylor 3-5-1870 Hy
Williams, Henry to Clarisa Pierson 9-16-1873 (9-17-1873) L B
Williams, Henry to Ella B. Moore 9-2-1874 L
Williams, Henry to Eller Williams 8-31-1875 (9-3-1875) L B
Williams, Henry to Harriet Richardson 12-28-1868 (12-30-1868) T
Williams, Henry to Mary Black 12-3-1838 Sh
Williams, Hillman to Matilda A. Kennen 9-22-1863 Sh
Williams, Hiram to Polly Grant 12-27-1824 (1-13-1825) Hr
Williams, Howlbert? to Tempe Reddick 9-1-1866 (no return) F
Williams, Hudson to Caroline Parker 11-2-1830 Ma
Williams, I. S. to T. C. Jones 9-9-1867 O
Williams, Isaac A. to Mollie R. J. Wells 12-25-1866 (12-28-1866) F
Williams, Isaac B. to Adaline Fitzgerald 4-27-1841 Hn
Williams, Isaac E. to Meriah E. Ellis 12-27-1844 Cr
Williams, Isaac Volentine to Artie Caroline Smith 11-20-1855 Ma
Williams, Isaac to Catherine Palmer 11-27-1843 Hn
Williams, Isaac to Martha Harrison 3-1-1870 (3-3-1870) F B
Williams, Isaac to Nancy J. Taylor 1-16-1867 G
Williams, Isham to Rose Walker 8-29-1874 Hy
Williams, J. A. to E. J> Howard 1-1-1882? (1-2-1883) L
Williams, J. D. to Mary Whitehead 1-16-1860 (1-17-1860) O
Williams, J. F. to Emily Robertson 1-2-1869 L
Williams, J. F. to Mary A. Baucum 1-13-1867 Hy
Williams, J. F. to Susan Christopher 3-10-1867 Be
Williams, J. G. to A. W. Clark 12-9-1850 (12-11-1850) Hr
Williams, J. G. to M. C. Chaney 9-8-1865 Hy
Williams, J. H. to A. M. Nelson 12-14-1877 (12-16-1877) Dy
Williams, J. J. to A. M. Sneed 9-14-1851 (no return) F
Williams, J. J. to Ann R. Watkins 10-30-1865 (10-31-1865) F
Williams, J. J. to Sarah E. Lemmon 12-20-1852 (no return) F
Williams, J. L. to Artie Woolfolk 12-6-1870 (12-7-1870) Ma
Williams, J. L. to Elizabeth McCarroll 10-13-1842 Be
Williams, J. M. to Martha Watkins 7-8-1848 Cr
Williams, J. N. to L. E. Quinley 4-7-1876 Hy
Williams, J. N. to M. A. Harrell 10-29-1860 (11-1-1860) F
Williams, J. N.(W?) to Nancy E. Baker 11-17-1870 G
Williams, J. R. to Callie Odle 8-22-1870 (8-28-1870) Dy
Williams, J. R. to Margaret E. Tidwell 2-14-1857 We
Williams, J. S. to Elizabeth Glover 10-22-1864 (10-23-1864) O
Williams, J. T. to B. J. Boen 6-12-1870 G
Williams, J. T. to H. E. Moore (Monroe-Munn) 1-16-1878 L
Williams, J. T. to M. J. Moore 10-1-1866 (no return) F
Williams, J. W. to Almina T. Outlaw 12-27-1848 O
Williams, J. W. to Cleary Shelton 4-25-1850 (4-27-1850) O
Williams, J. W. to Elvira M. Burrow 12-4-1865 (12-6-1865) Cr
Williams, J. W. to Joan Harrison Duncan 4-28-1860 (4-29-1860) Hr
Williams, J. W. to Sallie Shubell 2-17-1869 Hy
Williams, J. W. to Soprona E. Whitt 5-8-1869 (no return) Dy
Williams, J. Y. to Mary M. Gray 1-30-1873 O
Williams, J.L. to Elizabeth McCarroll 10-13-1842 Be CC
Williams, Jack to Tennessee Rose 1-4-1878 Hy
Williams, Jackson to Dena A. Henderson 11-11-1871 Hy
Williams, Jackson to Letha Clifton 6-16-1866 (no return) F B
Williams, Jacob E. to Sarah E. Bailey 11-8-1855 Sh
Williams, Jacob N. (M?) to M. A. (Mrs.) Allen 7-10-1864 (7-11-1864) Sh
Williams, Jacob to Delilah Allison 1-12-1854 Ma
Williams, James A. to Ellen L. Weatherford 9-20-1859 T
Williams, James A. to Jane Olivar 8-27-1873 (8-28-1873) L
Williams, James A. to Susan M. Lowery 10-24-1854 Cr
Williams, James A.(O?) to Louiza McNair 4-28-1863 G
Williams, James B. to Frances Davis 5-3-1857 Cr
Williams, James B. to Mary (Mrs.) Elder 10-9-1862 (10-12-1862) O
Williams, James B. to Mary J. Allen 9-24-1840 (no return) F
Williams, James C. to Lorindo Roach 9-26-1832 (10-14-1832) G
Williams, James C. to Sarah Hale 9-30-1851 (10-20-1851) Sh
Williams, James C. to Sarah Hale 9-5-1851 Sh
Williams, James E. to Emma Wood 11-12-1878 (11-13-1878) L
Williams, James F. to Susanna Johnson 2-8-1858 (2-11-1858) Hr
Williams, James G. to Celia A. White 7-29-1855 Hn
Williams, James H. to Mary Ann Bradford 10-31-1843 Hn
Williams, James J. to Martha J. Maxwell 3-15-1854 Hn
Williams, James J. to Missouri A. B. Williams 6-22-1857 T
Williams, James K. to Sacisa Bradberry 1-10-1861 (no return) We
Williams, James L. to Ellen A. Neagle 7-5-1859 Sh
Williams, James M. to M. B. P. Peler 11-10-1870 Cr
Williams, James M. to Mary M. Moody 10-3-1859 (10-5-1859) O
Williams, James M. to Marze M. H. Fallwell 12-12-1858 Hn
Williams, James P. to Catharine Bevins 12-25-1841 F
Williams, James R. to Caroline Perkins 10-10-1849 Be
Williams, James T. to Eliza Jane Grove 9-28-1841 (9-29-1841) Hr
Williams, James T. to Harriet R. Harris 1-29-1850 (1-31-1850) Hr
Williams, James T. to Parthema McDogal 10-4-1857 We

Williams, James T. to Sarah M. Caldwell 12-8-1859 Hn
Williams, James T. to Sarah T. Gray 1-29-1870 (2-3-1870) Cr
Williams, James W. to Nancy Box 12-22-1857 O
Williams, James Wesley to Margaret Hart 9-28-1868 Ma
Williams, James to Ann S. Lane 12-26-1860 (12-27-1860) Hr
Williams, James to Eliza Hall 3-27-1859 Hn
Williams, James to Elizabeth Flowers 3-24-1859 (3-27-1859) G
Williams, James to Elizabeth Johnson 12-24-1849 Sh
Williams, James to Jane Brown 11-18-1835 Sh
Williams, James to Jenny Blair 1-15-1868 G B
Williams, James to Lula Sullivan 1-7-1880 (1-8-1880) L
Williams, James to Maattie Jones 1-1-1873 (1-2-1873) T
Williams, James to Mariah Mitchell 9-10-1853 (9-23-1853) L
Williams, James to Mary A. Davidson 12-4-1856 Be
Williams, James to Mary Ann Davidson 12-6-1856 Be CC
Williams, James to Matilda Roads 10-1-1845 (no return) We
Williams, James to Sarah E. Hunt 7-8-1870 G
Williams, James to Susan Menley 11-23-1833 Hr
Williams, James to Uminie Partlow 9-11-1873 T
Williams, James to Vina Henderson 1-20-1874 Hy
Williams, James to Virginia Blancet 3-24-1861 G
Williams, Jerry to Sallie Short 12-24-1868 Hy
Williams, Jesse A. to C. Belle Kelly 9-22-1866 (9-25-1866) F
Williams, Jesse J. to Lucindy F. Mabry 1-4-1848 Cr
Williams, Jesse K. to Nelly E. Cornell 6-29-1854 We
Williams, Jessee K. to Nancy Sanderlin 9-15-1842 Sh
Williams, Jett to Mariah Thompson 3-16-1875 Hy
Williams, Jim to Anias Davie 3-16-1867 Hy
Williams, Jim to Susan Cavenaugh 8-24-1869 Hy
Williams, Jno. A. (Dr.) to Harriet J. Wynne 3-27-1877 (no return) Dy
Williams, Jno. G. to Sarah A. Knight 5-6-1858 (5-7-1858) Hr
Williams, Jno. Wesley to Amanda Neville 7-18-1867 G
Williams, Jno. to Milla Newby 7-11-1868 (7-12-1868) F B
Williams, Jo. to Martha Olds 2-10-1872 (2-19-1872) Dy
Williams, Joe to Clara Campbell 12-29-1866 G
Williams, Joe to Hannah Schums 12-26-1878 Hy
Williams, Joe to Julia Taliaferro 5-1-1872 Hy
Williams, Joe to Sanna? Williams 9-21-1867 (9-22-1867) F B
Williams, John A. to Fannie T. Henley 11-17-1869 (11-18-1869) L
Williams, John A. to Jennie Downs 1-22-1876 (1-28-1876) L
Williams, John A. to Martha J. Corley 3-3-1845 (3-6-1845) L
Williams, John A. to Sally T. Thompson 11-21-1853 Sh
Williams, John A. to Sarah A. Webb 12-22-1858 Hn
Williams, John B. to Elizabeth Hanlin? (Harlen?) 12-22-1862 Sh
Williams, John B. to Martha C. Bobbett 1-29-1851 (1-31-1851) G
Williams, John C. to M. A. (Mrs.) Love 9-1-1864 Sh
Williams, John C. to Nancy A. Terry 10-5-1849 Hr
Williams, John C. to Sarah O. Williams 11-5-1868 T
Williams, John Ed. Jefferson to Eliza Perkins 1-21-1886 L
Williams, John F. to Indiana Hill 9-19-1865 (9-20-1865) T
Williams, John F. to Indianna Hill 9-19-1865 T
Williams, John F. to Susan Marshall 6-13-1842 (6-16-1842) Ma
Williams, John G. to Adeline Hamilton 1-14-1864 G
Williams, John H. to Elizabeth Lee 4-10-1845 Hn
Williams, John J. to Canely? M. Norvell 3-27-1864 (3-27-1864) Cr
Williams, John J. to S. J. C. McDonald 7-5-1864 G
Williams, John K. to Milberby Collier 6-10-1855 Be
Williams, John K. to Milbery Callus 6-10-1855 Be CC
Williams, John L. to Martha Zachry 2-9-1858 G
Williams, John M. to Barbary A. Cooper 11-18-1860 Hn
Williams, John M. to Karen M. F. McGehee 8-27-1855 Hn
Williams, John P. to Eliza Cruse 10-27-1831 Sh
Williams, John R. to Elizabeth A. Anesworth 12-14-1847 (12-15-1847) F
Williams, John S. to Frances S. Lawrence 4-14-1846 Hn
Williams, John S. to Mary C. Adams 2-9-1870 (no return) Dy
Williams, John T. to Sarah E. Spicer 6-18-1848 Be
Williams, John Thomas to Martha Whitson 6-?-1854 (6-14-1854) L
Williams, John W. to Almira Williams 1-15-1852 O
Williams, John W. to Bettie Baker 5-4-1878 (5-5-1878) L
Williams, John W. to Bettie Whitley 3-29-1861 (3-31-1861) Sh
Williams, John W. to Francis Clug (Clay?) 5-28-1850 (5-31-1850) L
Williams, John W. to Laurine Choate 5-15-1831 Sh
Williams, John W. to Lavina E. Clemant 6-6-1854 (6-7-1854) T
Williams, John W. to Margarett Worley 1-6-1851 F
Williams, John W. to Mary O. Elum 12-21-1850 (12-24-1850) G
Williams, John W. to Sarah I. J. Carter 9-24-1858 Cr
Williams, John to America Lawson 6-15-1882 (6-17-1882) L
Williams, John to Catharine Flynn 5-23-1861 Sh
Williams, John to Catharine Morrison 7-7-1853 Sh
Williams, John to Dinarza M. Jones 9-2-1862 Cr
Williams, John to Frances Buford 11-2-1866 (11-3-1866) F B
Williams, John to Jane Kelly 8-4-1867 Hn
Williams, John to Malvina Scott 7-7-1866 (no return) F B
Williams, John to Martha Arnold 1-9-1855 Cr
Williams, John to Martha Walker 9-6-1879 (9-7-1879) L B
Williams, John to Mary Conway 8-2-1854 Sh
Williams, John to Mary L. Humphrey 12-2-1858 Hr

Williams, John to Mary Rayner 9-8-1827 (9-13-1827) Hr
Williams, John to Mollie Reeder 12-29-1874 (12-30-1874) L
Williams, John to Nannie Purkins 12-26-1868 Hy
Williams, John to Parmela Armstrong 11-10-1841 (11-11-1841) G
Williams, John to Rebeccah Roberts 8-21-1866 Cr
Williams, John to Sarah Ann Pankey 5-26-1857 (5-27-1857) O
Williams, John to Sarah Currie 12-31-1865 Hy
Williams, John to Sarah Hampton 4-29-1839 (3-1-1839?) O
Williams, John to Sarah Scales 12-24-1868 (12-25-1868) Cr
Williams, Johnathan (Norman?) to Sarah A. F. Gilleland 10-7-1873 (10-9-1873) T
Williams, Johnson to Elizabeth D. Robb 8-27-1833 G
Williams, Jon F. to Rebeca C. Bennett 2-28-1867 Cr
Williams, Jones J. to Amanda L. Powell? 12-21-1841 (12-27-1842?) T
Williams, Jones to Susan Anderson 1-25-1853 Ma
Williams, Joseph A. to Elizabeth Palmer 2-3-1863 (2-4-1863) Cr
Williams, Joseph C. to Mary Lake 9-19-1840 Hr
Williams, Joseph F. to Elizabeth T. Collins 11-21-1843 Sh
Williams, Joseph to Ann Jordan 3-22-1833 G
Williams, Joseph to Elizabeth Haskins 6-11-1879 (6-12-1879) Dy
Williams, Joseph to Josie Mack 1-2-1873 Hy
Williams, Joseph to Mary Chairs 2-17-1855 Sh
Williams, Joshua P. to Mela Cooke 11-21-1844 Hn
Williams, Joshua S. to Martha Jane Griffin 12-30-1848 O
Williams, Josiah to Jane Singleton 9-2-1880 L
Williams, Kenion to Roena Babb 10-21-1870 G
Williams, L. D. to Louisa Roberts 1-8-1865 Cr
Williams, L. F. to C. J. McCall 11-16-1866 (11-21-1866) Cr
Williams, L. L. to Virginia C. Carter 4-27-1854 G
Williams, L. T. to Elizabeth Walls 8-13-1872 (8-15-1872) Cr
Williams, L. W. to Allice Adams 11-6-1881 L
Williams, Lawrence P. to Caroline Chasum 9-9-1847 (9-10-1847) Ma
Williams, Lazarus to Mary J. Cooper 7-19-1858 Hn
Williams, Lemuel to Rachel Jackson 10-9-1852 (10-12-1852) T
Williams, Lemuel to Sarah C. Kelly 8-31-1867 (9-3-1867) T
Williams, Levi D. to Martha J. Ruff 8-4-1852 Cr
Williams, Lewis A. to E. P. Algea 1-21-1843 Cr
Williams, Lewis L. to Ruth E. Huzza 12-13-1844 (12-19-1844) O
Williams, Lewis M. to Virginia D. Harrison 10-19-1857 Hr
Williams, Lewis to Elizabeth Stephenson 12-15-1842 Sh
Williams, Lewis to Matilda Estes 9-23-1866 Hy
Williams, Lewis to Mattie Rice 4-9-1875 (4-21-1875) L
Williams, Lewis to Susan Holmes 9-30-1871 T
Williams, Licurgas W. to Amanda C. Walker 4-19-1855 (4-22-1855) G
Williams, Livra? to Martitia Ray 2-28-1868 (3-1-1868) Cr
Williams, Lorenzo D. to Dialtha Emeline Bomar 6-5-1857 (6-7-1857) Ma
Williams, Louis to Katie Jones 9-4-1869 (10-7-1869) L B
Williams, Luke L. to Rebecca C. Blair 7-20-1846 (no return) F
Williams, Luke to Martha Johnson 11-23-1870 (11-24-1870) Dy
Williams, M. H. to Isabella R. Bray 8-17-1854 We
Williams, M. H. to R. C. Richardson 12-25-1866 Hy
Williams, M. J. to Martha J. Cunningham 10-12-1869 Dy
Williams, M. L. to Eugenia A. Little 11-10-1852 Sh
Williams, M. S. to Elizabeth Steele 9-25-1860 Hn
Williams, M.? J. to Jane Fisher 9-3-1867 (no return) Dy
Williams, Mabry D. to Anvalina Belote 6-30-1856 (7-3-1856) Hr
Williams, Maddison to Susan Norman 5-16-1868 (no return) F B
Williams, Madison to Eliza Adams 2-18-1872 Hy
Williams, Madison to Sene? Cain 12-13-1867 Hy
Williams, Markens to Almeda Moss 12-21-1842 Ma
Williams, Mathew to Harriett Medlin 5-16-1840 (5-17-1840) Ma
Williams, Meekins to Penina Bogant 3-29-1866 (4-1-1866) Ma
Williams, Miles to E. M. McKinney 9-15-1863 Mn
Williams, Mose to Fancy Isbell 1-18-1868 (no return) F B
Williams, Moses H. to Priscilla Ward 5-27-1838 (5-30-1838) Hr
Williams, Moses M. to Fanny Nicholas 7-29-1861 Sh
Williams, Moses P. to Maggie Jester 8-27-1873 (8-28-1873) L
Williams, N. R. to Magdalaine Fisher 10-21-1858 (11-3-1858) Sh
Williams, N. W. to Tomantana Johnson 7-8-1845 (7-9-1846?) F
Williams, N. to Elizabeth A. Reece 1-9-1871 (1-11-1871) Dy
Williams, Nathan to Eliza H. Martin 9-20-1841 Cr
Williams, Nathan to Jennie Gause 10-1-1873 Hy
Williams, Nathan to Mary A. Butler 1-1-1853 Cr
Williams, Nathan to Nancy Pierce 3-25-1857 Be
Williams, Nathan to Nancy Pierce 3-25-1857 Be CC
Williams, Nathanial to Hannah Robertson 2-8-1842 (2-10-1842) G
Williams, Nathaniel to Sarah J. Wallice 4-5-1856 (4-6-1856) G
Williams, Nathiel W. to Paradise Huntsman 5-30-1855 Ma
Williams, Newton to Sophronia Ellington 12-15-1850 (12-17-1850) Ma
Williams, Normon to Jane Hurley 12-17-1847 (12-22-1847) F
Williams, Orville to Rebecca Elam 9-23-1856 Sh
Williams, Oswald to Clementine Thomas 3-20-1860 (3-22-1860) Sh
Williams, Otho to Mary E. Winter 11-4-1857 Sh
Williams, P. M. to Cynthia Houston 2-12-1842 F
Williams, P. M. to M. C. Britt 8-25-1858 (9-1-1858) Sh
Williams, P. T. to T. C. Johnson 11-14-1865 O
Williams, Peter to Elvira Bradford 2-3-1881 L B

Williams, Peter to Sylvia Jonakin 5-19-1866 (8-11-1866) F B
Williams, Peter to Viola Jackson 12-14-1849 (12-19-1849) Ma
Williams, Pink to Dona Broddie 1-7-1874 (1-8-1874) L B
Williams, Pleasant B. to Mary Flinn 2-5-1847 T
Williams, Po A. to Deborah Gilmon(Gilmore?) 3-16-1847 (3-23-1847) Hr
Williams, Providence to Miss Walker 2-5-1838 (no return) F
Williams, R. A. to Margarett A. Kile 6-22-1856 Cr
Williams, R. A. to S. V. Walton 11-13-1867 Hn
Williams, R. F. to S. J. Roane 1-1-1872 (1-4-1872) T
Williams, R. M. to Mary C. Caloway 4-26-1866 Hn
Williams, R. T. to Bethe Taylor 12-25-1861 (no return) Cr
Williams, R. W. to Jane H. Williams 7-20-1856 Hn
Williams, R. W. to N. V. Tart 11-2-1864 (no return) Hn
Williams, Ralph to Mary Jane Emerson 12-15-1868 (12-17-1868) Ma
Williams, Ralph to Sarah C. White 5-28-1844 Hn
Williams, Reuben W. to Susan E. Davidson 10-19-1859 (10-20-1859) L
Williams, Richard N. to Eliza H. Sauls 12-24-1844 F
Williams, Richard to Lucinda Taylor 11-8-1877 Hy
Williams, Richard to Millie MacKey 11-18-1864 Sh
Williams, Richard to _____ 7-10-1868 (7-11-1868) L
Williams, Richmond to Silva Fields 12-24-1868 (12-25-1868) F B
Williams, Riley to Annis Walker 4-13-1873 Hy
Williams, Riley to Malinda Anderson 3-29-1870 Hy
Williams, Robert A. to Emily E. Pitts 10-25-1876 (no return) L
Williams, Robert B. to Martha E. Manley 7-19-1853 Ma
Williams, Robert C. to Malinda Merritt 9-23-1843 Cr
Williams, Robert J. to Martha J. Johnson 12-22-1852 Ma
Williams, Robert Sevier to Tebitha Emaline Smith 2-13-1854 (2-15-1854) T
Williams, Robert W. to Sarah Wimberley 2-9-1858 Hn
Williams, Robert to Betsy Perkins 11-8-1867 Hy
Williams, Robert to Louisa House 1-28-1871 (2-22-1871) L
Williams, Robert to Mary O. Williams 10-4-1858 (10-6-1858) Sh
Williams, Robert to Sarah Jane Keith 9-15-1852 (9-16-1852) O
Williams, Robt. Alex to Mary Catharine Wilkins 2-18-1861 (2-19-1861) T
Williams, Robt. to Martha Morris 4-3-1868 (no return) F B
Williams, Rounsville to Ann Elizabeth Whitworth 12-28-1859 (12-29-1859) Ma
Williams, Runion to Martha I. Barker 9-10-1866 G
Williams, S. B. to Sallie Ophelia Polk Rust 7-30-1868 G
Williams, S. B. to Sarah Godby 2-10-1848 (no return) F
Williams, S. R. to A. R. Stalkup 10-17-1878 (10-18-1878) Dy
Williams, S. to N. J. Lewis 6-18-1858 G
Williams, S. to Sarah Ann Beaver 7-23-1845 (8-7-1845) F
Williams, Sam A. to Linnie Fields 11-23-1876 Dy
Williams, Sam to Elizabeth James 4-6-1859 (4-7-1859) Sh B
Williams, Sam to Lucinda Hale 5-27-1866 Hy
Williams, Saml. M. to Manerva A. E. Davis 2-11-1857 (2-12-1857) T
Williams, Samuel C. to Margaret J. Braden 11-19-1853 (11-20-1853) Sh
Williams, Samuel G. to Martha M. Tailor 9-17-1846 We
Williams, Samuel H. to Eddy Carter Haskins 12-23-1874 (12-24-1874) Dy
Williams, Samuel H. to Margaret Deauran 4-17-1867 G
Williams, Samuel to Mary Jane Hill 12-13-1842 (12-15-1842) Ma
Williams, Samuel to Sarah Low 5-29-1861 (5-30-1861) Hr
Williams, Samuel to Susan A. Pucker 8-19-1867 (8-20-1867) Cr
Williams, Sanders to Geraldine Garrison 11-21-1870 (11-23-1870) Ma
Williams, Sandy to Emmer Moore 2-11-1869 Hy
Williams, Seth to Mary Dunwoody 2-15-1834 (2-20-1834) G
Williams, Shadrach to Elizabeth Glenn 1-26-1871 (2-9-1871) L
Williams, Shadrack to Annie Jones 10-18-1873 (10-19-1873) L
Williams, Sidney J. to Mary Jane Parker 12-6-1852 (12-7-1852) Sh
Williams, Soloman to Milia Kirby 7-21-1842 Cr
Williams, Spencer to Paralee Heaslett 2-2-1867 (no return) F B
Williams, Stephen E. to Nancy E. Bishop 5-2-1859 Sh
Williams, Sterling E. to Elizabeth D. Flint 2-14-1834 (2-18-1834) Hr
Williams, Sumpter to Dillah Murrell 3-22-1869 (no return) F B
Williams, T. B. to Rebecca Murphy 1-2-1850 Sh
Williams, T. F. to Frances M. Hall 11-26-1849 (no return) F
Williams, T. J. to Bethany J. Naylor 6-29-1865 Mn
Williams, T. T. to M. E. Mebane 10-26-1870 Cr
Williams, Thomas A. to Margaret Brogdon 9-25-1860 Hn
Williams, Thomas B. to Matilda Haynes 5-21-1861 Ma
Williams, Thomas E. to Katherine Bakere 12-1-1853 Hn
Williams, Thomas J. to Martha R. Cole 11-8-1852 (11-11-1852) G
Williams, Thomas K. to Virginia W. Wilbourn 11-1-1855 (11-3-1855) O
Williams, Thomas M. to Jane M. Smith 5-25-1861 T
Williams, Thomas M. to Mary A. Clements 10-9-1848 (10-11-1848) T
Williams, Thomas P. to Narcissa Roberts 9-25-1861 (no return) Cr
Williams, Thomas R. to Mary Ann Elizabeth Putnam 12-11-1857 (12-12-1857) O
Williams, Thomas to E. J. Terrill 11-23-1869 G
Williams, Thomas to Lovey Radford 8-19-1849 Hn
Williams, Thomas to Martha Simpson 3-29-1855 Hn
Williams, Thomas to Martha Woodson (Hutcherson) 7-19-1868 G B
Williams, Thomas to Mary Ann Craft 1-30-1860 (2-1-1860) Hr
Williams, Thomas to Mollie Ozier 1-7-1870 (1-10-1870) F B
Williams, Thomas to Nancy Busseck 8-3-1840 Cr
Williams, Thomas to Nancy J. Simpson 12-23-1845 (no return) Hn
Williams, Thomas to Nancy Warren 1-21-1870 (2-19-1870) F B
Williams, Thomas to Sabry Davidsson 10-18-1828 G
Williams, Thomas to Tabitha Moore 12-2-1846 Hn
Williams, Thos. J. to Lydia Cooper 8-9-1864 (8-14-1864) O
Williams, Thos. M. to Malinda J. Morris 10-13-1857 We
Williams, Thos. M. to Mary White 2-16-1845 Cr
Williams, Thos. P. to Susan A. Hicks 8-4-1846 Cr
Williams, Thos. W. to Hester R. McBride 12-16-1842 (12-21-1842) G
Williams, Thos. W. to Sarah Barrett 10-7-1858 G
Williams, Thos. to Lucinda W. Duke 2-24-1848 F
Williams, Thos. to Lucindia Reed 10-12-1830 Hr
Williams, Thos. to Marthaann Yarborough 12-24-1839 (no return) F
Williams, Tias to Cary Ann Berry 7-16-1869 (7-17-1869) T
Williams, Tom to Susan Camden 1-13-1870 G B
Williams, W. A. to E. P. Thetford 10-11-1877 (no return) Dy
Williams, W. A. to L. P. Huffman 1-24-1873 (1-30-1873) Cr
Williams, W. A. to Mary Ida Fly 10-2-1867 G
Williams, W. B. to Margaret C. Bostick 7-28-1856 Ma
Williams, W. B. to Mary A. Wade 3-30-1858 G
Williams, W. B. to Tennessee Tatum 7-14-1849 (no return) F
Williams, W. C. to L. D. Brown 5-16-1857 (5-22-1857) Sh
Williams, W. C. to Malisa Naron 5-4-1865 Hn
Williams, W. D. to Siddy Ann M. Medlin 12-16-1859 (12-18-1859) Ma
Williams, W. F. to V. P. Churchwell 10-24-1871 Cr
Williams, W. H. to Mary A. Kelley 7-4-1868 O
Williams, W. H. to Mary Frances Dickens 2-2-1868 G
Williams, W. L. C. to Julianna E. Craft 12-9-1850 (12-12-1850) Hr
Williams, W. M. to Sarah E. Pickler 1-14-1858 Cr
Williams, W. N. to Elizabeth A. Canada 10-17-1859 Sh
Williams, W. N. to Lucy A. Forester 3-19-1855 (no return) We
Williams, W. P. to Almedia L. Jackson 10-19-1870 (10-20-1870) Ma
Williams, W. P. to Julia Ann Eliza Edwards 11-22-1860 (11-25-1860) Ma
Williams, W. R. to Mary A. Fowler 6-19-1850 We
Williams, W. to Cleary Shelton 4-2-1850 (4-7-1850) O
Williams, Wash to Mary Rice 4-4-1876 Hy
Williams, Wash. to Alice Short 10-13-1874 Hy
Williams, Wesley to Elizabeth Johnson 11-19-1869 (11-21-1869) Dy
Williams, Westly to Darthula Cravens 11-21-1865 Cr
Williams, William A. P. to Mary Ann Billington 5-2-1854 (5-4-1854) Ma
Williams, William A. to Emeritta Tosh 12-11-1865 (12-12-1865) Cr
Williams, William C. to Jane A. Dugger 10-8-1857 Hn
Williams, William F. to Malessa Eudaly 7-22-1856 (7-29-1856) G
Williams, William H. to Aly Hall 9-12-1840 (9-25-1840) Ma
Williams, William N. to Margaret E. Gray 6-25-1858 (6-27-1858) O
Williams, William R. to Amza N. Sneed 2-5-1860 Hn
Williams, William R. to M. E. Rees 7-27-1863 (7-28-1863) Cr
Williams, William R. to Martha E. Rees 7-27-1863 Cr
Williams, William S. to Malissa Waldrip 1-18-1836 (1-19-1836) G
Williams, William S. to Nancy (Mary) Bustin 1-22-1846 Sh
Williams, William W. to Margarett Lee 10-11-1850 O
Williams, William W. to Sarah C. Andrews 7-10-1864 Mn
Williams, William to Bethsheba Marberry 4-7-1842 Hn
Williams, William to Caroline Dawson 11-28-1854 G
Williams, William to Clementine Taylor 12-30-1845 (12-31-1845) G
Williams, William to Delilia Houston 11-13-1872 (11-27-1872) T
Williams, William to Eliza Collier 3-30-1854 Sh
Williams, William to Elizabeth Thompson 7-19-1841 (7-20-1841) L
Williams, William to Emma M. Newberry 7-9-1859 Sh
Williams, William to Henrietta Edgar 4-17-1860 Hn
Williams, William to Jane Crenshaw 2-7-1833 Sh
Williams, William to Lucinda Webb 12-12-1868 G B
Williams, William to Martha Brinkley 5-1-1863 (5-13-1863) Sh
Williams, William to Martha Mathis 9-24-1856 (no return) L
Williams, William to Mary Morgan Adams 12-18-1848 (12-19-1848) Ma
Williams, William to Mary Patrick 4-2-1873 (4-3-1873) Dy
Williams, William to Nancy Joiner 5-5-1841 (5-6-1841) G
Williams, William to Polly Wynn 3-7-1855 (3-8-1855) O
Williams, William to Rebecca Polly 2-13-1858 (2-14-1858) O
Williams, William to Sarah Ann Sanderford 9-4-1849 (9-5-1849) G
Williams, William to Sarah Arnold 7-2-1853 (7-3-1853) G
Williams, William to Sarah Odum 7-12-1862 Hn
Williams, William to Susan Thedford 4-28-1846 (5-29-1846) G
Williams, Williford to Mary Ann Richards 1-8-1862 (1-9-1862) Ma
Williams, Willis G. to Easter C. Pettyjohn 9-5-1850 Hn
Williams, Willis L. to Lucy Moody 10-4-1840 Hn
Williams, Willis W. to Mary E. (Mrs.) Morrill 2-25-1867 (2-27-1867) Ma
Williams, Wilson to Elizabeth V. Baker 10-1-1859 (10-2-1859) Ma
Williams, Winfield to Jane Robinson 12-11-1847 (12-22-1847) Ma
Williams, Wm. A. to Elizabeth Elliott 1-29-1845 (no return) We
Williams, Wm. A. to Marsher A. Lygote 11-20-1850 Cr
Williams, Wm. H. H. to Nancy C. Oates 1-24-1871 (1-26-1871) F
Williams, Wm. H. to Esther Gordon 11-20-1844 (no return) F
Williams, Wm. J. to Susan A. George 12-14-1854 Cr
Williams, Wm. to Eleanor Ammons 5-6-1847 (5-9-1847) F
Williams, Z. N. to M. J. Williams 2-1-1866 G
Williams, Z. to Annis Greer 7-6-1869 T
Williams, Zack to Charlotte Yarbro 4-18-1873 (4-13?-1873) T
Williams, daniel to Jane Sanders 1-19-1870 (no return) F B

Williams, sr., Tho. to Nancy White 8-5-1844 We
Williamson, A. G. to Nanie (Mrs.) Gordon 5-10-1864 Sh
Williamson, Alfred to Catie McFarland 2-5-1869 (1?-14-1869) F B
Williamson, Archabald to Lutisha R. Hill 4-15-1852 (no return) F
Williamson, B. M. to Nancy Yancy 12-13-1860 Hy
Williamson, Bill to Lucy Willingham 3-2-1871 Hy
Williamson, Bill to Priscilla Deener? 4-22-1871 (no return) F B
Williamson, C. A. to Harriett Williams 1-15-1861 G
Williamson, Cater to Matilda Williamson 3-19-1866 F B
Williamson, Clark to Fanny Irvens 5-2-1871 (5-13-1871) F B
Williamson, Ed to Elvora Smith 11-27-1868 Cr
Williamson, F. M. to Alice A. Nash 9-16-1868 G
Williamson, Francis M. to Nercissa L. Cherry 8-1-1871 L
Williamson, Frank to Dolly Holloway 5-23-1868 (5-25-1868) F B
Williamson, G. W. to Elizabeth J. Williamson 9-7-1864 (no return) Cr
Williamson, George S. to Emanda E. Whitlow 2-11-1871 Ma
Williamson, George to Amanda Ross 1-7-1869 F B
Williamson, George to Eliza Walker 3-30-1867 (4-7-1867) F B
Williamson, George to George R. Haskins 4-15-1844 Ma
Williamson, George to L. Thornton 7-21-1866 (7-22-1866) F
Williamson, George to Mam Clark 12-24-1871 Hy
Williamson, George to Mary Ray 9-23-1865 (9-24-1865) Dy
Williamson, George to Mary Wright 2-20-1869 (no return) F B
Williamson, George to Tabitha Ann Lane 5-30-1828 Ma
Williamson, Hardy to Emiline McClusky 12-4-1867 (12-5-1867) Dy
Williamson, Haywood to Elizabeth Maroney 1-3-1856 Ma
Williamson, Henry to Clarissa C. Butler 12-13-1856 (12-14-1856) G
Williamson, Henry to Eliza Robison 5-3-1870 (no return) Cr
Williamson, Henry to Louisa Moor 12-23-1841 Cr
Williamson, Horace to Amanda Trip 2-10-1866 (2-17-1866) F B
Williamson, I. A. to Sophia Goff 12-27-1865 (12-28-1865) O
Williamson, I. N. to S. E. Smith 10-6-1868 G
Williamson, J. F. to Susan E. Coleman 8-31-1860 Dy
Williamson, J. L. to Emma J. Cornwell 6-22-1858 Sh
Williamson, J. M. to Callie Boo 10-21-1879 (10-23-1879) Dy
Williamson, J. M. to Mary J. McCollum 4-26-1866 Cr
Williamson, J. W. to Mary Ann Walls 4-21-1868 Be
Williamson, J. W. to Mary L. Taylor 3-5-1860 (3-7-1860) F
Williamson, J. W. to S. L. Cheatham 7-8-1868 O
Williamson, Jack to Barthenia Coe 12-23-1865 (12-26-1865) F B
Williamson, James A. to Mary Jane Cleaver 8-11-1852 G
Williamson, Jas. A. to Cyntha C. Stone 4-21-1863 (no return) Cr
Williamson, Jas. M. to Rachal Bulleton 1-29-1845 (1-30-1845) G
Williamson, Jeff to Harriet Maggard 1-20-1872 (1-21-1872) Dy
Williamson, Jerry to Harriet Gaither 12-31-1866 (no return) F B
Williamson, Jesse to Ann Smith 12-11-1869 (12-12-1869) Cr
Williamson, John A. to Rebecca C. Fly 6-30-1857 (7-1-1857) Ma
Williamson, John H. to Molly T. Brooks 8-10-1857 Sh
Williamson, John J. to Elizabeth J. Reynolds 4-4-1857 (no return) Hn
Williamson, John M. to Billie Anders 3-27-1872 (3-28-1872) Cr
Williamson, John N. to Mary E. H. McClure 1-6-1868 (1-7-1868) Cr
Williamson, John to Jane Blanton 9-12-1867 (no return) Hn B
Williamson, John to Leaner Malone 2-23-1867 (2-28-1867) T
Williamson, John to Mary Morris 7-20-1840 (7-23-1840) L
Williamson, Joseph T. to Julia A. Cozart 4-8-1856 (4-9-1856) Ma
Williamson, Lawson to Sissee Hunt 1-31-1870 T
Williamson, Leroy H. to Angeline Johnson 1-5-1856 Cr
Williamson, Lewin? to F. E. Carter 7-21-1873 (7-22-1873) Cr
Williamson, Lewis to Lutia Tarry 3-21-1866 T
Williamson, Mathew to Mary Jane Halton 1-22-1868 (1-26-1868) Ma
Williamson, Monroe to Moriah Collier 12-28-1867 Hy
Williamson, Ned to Martha Orgain 1-12-1867 F B
Williamson, P. G. to Elizabeth Aden 12-31-1865 Be
Williamson, Primus to Maggie Harwell 3-25-1870 F B
Williamson, R. D. to C. A. Stanfield 11-19-1865 Hy
Williamson, Robert to Caroline McKinney 11-3-1858 Cr
Williamson, Robin to Rachel Fisher 4-18-1866 F B
Williamson, S. E. to Cordelia Hammer 4-1-1871 (4-4-1871) Cr
Williamson, S. W. to M. J. Huddle 9-15-1869 (no return) Cr
Williamson, Samuel B. to Mary E. Abernathy 10-26-1869 (10-31-1869) Cr
Williamson, Samuel B. to Mary E. Eanes 5-1-1845 Sh
Williamson, Samuel L. to Virginia G. Carter 11-24-1858 Cr
Williamson, Samuel M. to Mary Jane Sneed 9-29-1841 (10-4-1841) F
Williamson, Samuel to Martha E. Patterson 12-15-1859 O
Williamson, Spencer to Delilah Carpenter 5-2-1878 Dy
Williamson, T. M. to Cynthia Houston 2-12-1842 (no return) F
Williamson, Thomas to Eliza Jane Prewitt 11-16-1850 (11-28-1850) Hr
Williamson, Thos. H. to Catherine Wood 4-25-1844 Sh
Williamson, Thos. P. to Lucy J. Rowland 9-21-1866 Hy
Williamson, Tilghman D. to Jane   4-19-1863 G
Williamson, W. B. to Mollie Ann Shelly (Shelby?) 3-26-1860 (3-27-1860) Sh
Williamson, W. C. to F. E. Lawhorn 1-20-1863 (1-21-1863) Dy
Williamson, William to Prudence Richardson 9-8-1856 (9-10-1856) Hr
Williamson, William to Wils Eliza Williamson 5-25-1867 F B
Williamson, Wm. K.? to Mary J. Vincent 7-9-1861 (7-10-1861) Cr
Williamson, Wm. L. to Sallie P. Taylor 3-5-1860 (3-7-1860) F
Williamson, Wm. to Annis Lea 11-10-1866 Hy

Williamson, buck to Frances Williamson 1-13-1866 (1-14-1866) F B
Willias, Wm. Walker to Margret L. Pearl 5-14-1871 Hy
Willie, Harrison to Columbia Wilson 1-29-1836 Sh
Willie, Joseph to Leaner Jackson 2-1-1847 (2-2?-1847) Hr
Williford, Charles to Charlotte Wade 12-27-1868 G B
Williford, David J. to Granada Tyler 1-5-1870 (1-6-1870) Ma
Williford, John F. to Reubicca Foster 12-27-1868 G
Williford, John to Ella Green 12-27-1880 (12-28-1880) L
Williford, Nathan W. to Frances Milegan 2-16-1838 F
Williford, R. A. to S. V. Westbrook 4-25-1864 (4-26-1864) Sh
Williford, Richard Y. to Evalina Potts 1-1-1854 Hn
Williford, W. T. to Sarah J. Dial 6-15-1869 G
Willingham, H. T. to Nancy Wallace 11-8-1847 (11-9-1847) F
Willingham, John C. to Elizabeth J. Shelton 10-28-1844 (no return) We
Willingham, W. H. to Nancy McGee 9-22-1841 (9-27-1841) F
Willis (Willy?), Morris to Rachel Jones 1-19-1861 Sh
Willis, Albert to Ann Baker 2-7-1850 Ma
Willis, Alfred to Janie Collins 12-6-1852 (no return) L
Willis, Anderson to Phoebe Cockram 10-5-1838 Hn
Willis, David G. to Malissa Jane Quarles 7-18-1860 (7-19-1860) O
Willis, David G. to Zebu H. Williams 10-5-1846 Hn
Willis, David to Catherine Earhart 11-24-1840 Cr
Willis, E. E. to M. J. Lee 10-8-1860 O
Willis, Edmond to Molly Kid 2-11-1869 G B
Willis, Edward to Margaret M. Hommel 12-31-1860 (1-1-1861) Dy
Willis, G. M. to Mary June Bradford 7-22-1842 Hn
Willis, G. W. to Laura Walker 2-13-1884 (no return) L
Willis, George W. to Efarilla Swanner 12-23-1863 (no return) Dy
Willis, George to Malissa Parks 12-23-1847 Sh
Willis, H. M. to E. F. Holder 12-23-1866 G
Willis, Henderson to Elizabeth Forest 12-27-1855 Be
Willis, Henderson to Elizabeth Forest 12-27-1855 Be CC
Willis, Hinton to Ann Holder 11-15-1832 G
Willis, James T. to Julia Hutchins 4-9-1845 F
Willis, James W. to Mary A. Caldwell 2-3-1853 Hn
Willis, James to Julia Harrison 1-1-1868 G
Willis, John J. to Misa (Miza?) Simpson 7-7-1839 (7-8-1839) L
Willis, M. H. to Angeline   1-27-1848 Hn
Willis, N. W. to Elender A. (Mrs.) Hollis 12-16-1854 (no return) F
Willis, Newton A. to Nancy A. Crawford 10-4-1849 Hn
Willis, Nick to Anne Freeman 5-16-1870 G B
Willis, Nick to Julia Davis 5-18-1868 G
Willis, P. H. to Emila T. Jackson 7-6-1847 (7-7-1847) F
Willis, Ruffin to Jane Hutchins 1-10-1844 F
Willis, Thomas to Malinda Enochs 2-23-1872 (2-24-1872) Dy
Willis, W. L. to Emeline A. King 11-5-1860 G
Willis, W. S. to Sarah E. English 9-12-1852 Hn
Willis, W. to E. T. Williamson 12-11-1860 Sh
Willis, William N. to Elizabeth O'Brian 7-31-1866 Hn
Willis, William to Catherine Parkes 12-19-1849 Sh
Willis, William to Elizabeth Neely 6-9-1866 (6-10-1866) Ma
Willis, Willis H. to Margaret L. Newport 5-9-1857 Hn
Williva, Washington to Nancy T. Etheridge 8-12-1862 Dy
Willougby, John to Mollie Sulivan 7-23-1874 Hy
Willoughby, Andrew to Elizabeth Huddleston 3-28-1843 (no return) Hn
Willoughby, Ashly G. to Mary Jane Taylor 7-3-1841 (7-5-1841) Hr
Willoughby, Edward to Elizabeth J. Yarbrough 6-15-1854 (6-22-1854) Hr
Willoughby, Eugene R. to Susan A. Deloach 12-3-1866 (12-6-1866) Ma
Willoughby, Ewing to Emily Taylor 1-13-1836 Hr
Willoughby, Hiram B. to Catharine M. Cooper 2-3-1830 Hr
Willoughby, Isaac to Matilda Netherland 8-26-1842 (no return) Hn
Willoughby, James to Fanny Marsh 8-25-1857 Hr
Willoughby, James to Harriet Marsh 12-17-1851 (12-16?-1851) Hr
Willoughby, John V. to E. G. Roberts 8-23-1855 (no return) Hn
Willoughby, John W. to Nannie J. Watkins 6-27-1867 Ma
Willoughby, John to Emily Findley 11-12-1845 Hr
Willoughby, John to Nancy Lenorah Hunter 1-12-1848 (1-13-1848) Hr
Willoughby, Thos. B. to Eliza Ann Thompson 6-15-1854 (6-29-1854) Hr
Willoughby, W. H. to Mary Weaver 2-24-1860 (2-26-1860) Sh
Willoughby, William A. to Mary Finley 9-11-1859 Hr
Willoughby, William to Mary J. Ford 11-25-1861 (no return) Hn
Willowby, A. J. to Mary E. Puckett 10-28-1866 Hn
Willowford, William S. to Almira J. Vaughn 12-17-1859 (no return) Hn
Wills (Wells), M. S. to Lizie Aikin 1-3-1876 Hy
Wills, Anthony to Sue Yancey 12-24-1867 Hy
Wills, E. L. to Ann E. Wills 1-12-1848 Be
Wills, H.S. to Frances M. High 5-4-1845 Hr
Wills, Jessie J. to Sarah M. Grayer 1-1-1846 G
Wills, John B. to Harriet C. Alexander 6-29-1838 F
Wills, Mack to Elizabeth Johnson 1-10-1869 Hy
Wills, W. T. to Lizzie C. Mann 6-22-1869 Hy
Willsford, Michael to Elizabeth Morris 9-19-1857 O
Willson, Berry to Nancy Murphey 12-20-1850 (no return) Hn
Willson, Cirk (Kirk) to Elizabeth Kidd 6-23-1864 Hn
Willson, George W. to Siryna E. Story 10-26-1863 Hn
Willson, Henry to Elizabeth Smith 10-3-1863 Sh
Willson, James T. to Mary S. Butler 2-22-1871 Cr

Willson, John to Martha M. Lenimon 9-20-1870 L
Willson, R. A. to Carey Willis 12-13-1864 (no return) Hn
Willson, S. D. to Amanda Bill (Bell?) 10-2-1875 (10-3-1875) L
Willson, T. C. to Margaret D. Allen 8-21-1866 (8-23-1866) Cr
Willson, Thomas to Catherine Keller 10-12-1874 (10-13-1874) L
Willson, Thomas to Jerusha Vaughn 4-25-1843 (4-27-1843) F
Willson, William R. to Harriet _____ 2-10-1849 (no return) Hn
Wilman, James to Catharine Brown 10-22-1855 Sh
Wilmans, Frederick A. to Adelia T. Deburgan 10-15-1864 Sh
Wils?, Wash to Maria Bowers 9-12-1873 (9-15-1873) T
Wilson, A. B. to Margaret Adams 3-23-1840 (3-29-1840) F
Wilson, A. C. to Ann E. Gilliland 9-16-1859 Sh
Wilson, A. J. to E. L. Hunt 9-9-1885 L
Wilson, A. J. to Eliza H. McCain 12-15-1857 T
Wilson, A. J. to Frances Davis 1-15-1867 L
Wilson, A. M. to Sue E. Adams 12-8-1871 Hy
Wilson, A. R. to C. A. Mannitt 10-22-1857 Cr
Wilson, A. R. to Mary P. James 7-1-1863 G
Wilson, A. R. to Susan C. Coleman 11-29-1859 G
Wilson, A. to Mary Ann Greene 1-20-1864 Hn
Wilson, A. to Mary Ann Willis 12-28-1865 Hn
Wilson, A. to Susan Jane King 8-28-1861 (8-29-1861) Sh
Wilson, Adolphus B. to Sarah A. Trainer 2-22-1869 (2-24-1869) F
Wilson, Adolphus to Adelia Oldham 5-18-1878 Hy
Wilson, Aldred to C.L. Dobyn 12-23-1845 Sh
Wilson, Alfred to Sarah Jane Wilson 4-4-1861 Be
Wilson, Alfred to Sarah Jane Wilson 4-4-1861 Be CC
Wilson, Allen I. to Ellener Chandler 12-7-1843 Ma
Wilson, Allen J. to Mary M. Chandler 9-10-1855 Ma
Wilson, Allen King to Amie Hicks 11-10-1829 (11-9?-1829) Hr
Wilson, Anders to Gaberila A. McCan 10-21-1845 (10-30-1845) Hr
Wilson, Anderson to Margaret Watterson? 2-1-1870 (no return) F B
Wilson, Anthony to Martha Bolls 12-24-1868 Hy
Wilson, Ashley R. to Elizabeth A. Coleman 6-7-1853 G
Wilson, B. F. to Mary W. Williams 3-10-1848 Sh
Wilson, Ben to Mary Mann 9-19-1865 Hy
Wilson, Benjamin to Elizabeth Jane Styles 1-25-1862 O
Wilson, Bennit to Harriet Cogbill 2-15-1869 (2-16-1869) F B
Wilson, Berry F. to Elizabeth Fisher 11-30-1854 Hn
Wilson, Billy to Betty Mann 7-20-1881 L B
Wilson, Bob to Amey Edwards 11-14-1874 T
Wilson, Bob to Margret Read 2-21-1870 Hy
Wilson, C. H. to Emaline Moore 11-3-1866 O
Wilson, C. T. to Martha N. Campbell 10-28-1848 (no return) Hn
Wilson, Calvell to Emeline Reeves 1-12-1838 (12-13-1838) Ma
Wilson, Charles M. to Tizzina Mathews 8-26-1853 Cr
Wilson, Charles W. to Margaret Waldrop 10-8-1839 Hn
Wilson, Charles to Georgia Ann Walsh 8-26-1874 O B
Wilson, Charles to Julia Morris 12-24-1866 (12-27-1866) F B
Wilson, Charles to Mittie Bradford 4-4-1876 Hy
Wilson, Charley to Ella Haywood 1-23-1873 Hy
Wilson, Claiburn to Martha Hunnell 3-28-1842 (3-29-1842) Hr
Wilson, Cornelius to Fanny Sweet 3-16-1876 Hy
Wilson, Cyrus to Louisa Hamilton 1-21-1840 Ma
Wilson, Dan T. to Lizzie Chadwick 6-6-1869 (no return) Dy
Wilson, Dave to Roberta Cook 7-2-1878 (12-13-1878) L
Wilson, David N. to Mary F. Cooper 12-25-1869 (12-26-1869) Cr
Wilson, David R. to Mary Conway 12-27-1849 F
Wilson, David to A. E. Crider 8-18-1841 Cr
Wilson, David to Elizabeth Boothe 7-21-1851 (7-22-1851) T
Wilson, David to Frances Wilson 2-4-1857 Cr
Wilson, David to Sarah A. Briggers 12-23-1844 Cr
Wilson, David to Sarah Luny 8-31-1848 Sh
Wilson, Dennis to Martha Clure 12-25-1870 (no return) F B
Wilson, Dolphin to Jane Young 10-30-1875 Hy
Wilson, E. H. to Lydia Heckle 12-20-1852 (12-23-1852) Sh
Wilson, E. S. to Jane Addfield 3-29-1861 Sh
Wilson, E. T. to Bettie Calhoun 8-21-1860 (8-22-1860) T
Wilson, Earl to Martha Jane Deloach 2-10-1856 Be CC
Wilson, Edward M. to N. E. Dyer 2-21-1866 O
Wilson, Fed to Kitty Brinkley 9-3-1870 (9-4-1870) F B
Wilson, Ferdenand to Mary Ann Mulvin 9-14-1863 Sh
Wilson, Fin to E. N. L. Roach 1-5-1857 Cr
Wilson, Francis A. to Hadnah? Boyd 1-29-1850 F
Wilson, Francis M. to F. M. McClaney 5-6-1863 Sh
Wilson, Fred Wm. to Famia Haywood 11-9-1871 T
Wilson, G. B. to E. G. Williamson 10-17-1867 O
Wilson, G. H. to Amanda Owens 2-15-1865 (2-20-1865) Cr
Wilson, G. W. to M. A. (Mrs.) Stokes 7-23-1885 L
Wilson, G. W. to Milley Jane Harris 6-23-1863 (6-24-1863) L
Wilson, Geo. W. to Susan Ann Potts 11-9-1857 (11-12-1857) Sh
Wilson, Geo. to Emma Hughlett 1-18-1868 (1-19-1868) T
Wilson, Geo. to Mary C. Smith 2-2-1846 (2-5-1846) Hr
Wilson, Geor. W. to Martha Ruffin 12-15-1842 Ma
Wilson, George N. to Amanda Todd 8-5-1868 Cr
Wilson, George W. to Angeline Howard 9-25-1866 Hn
Wilson, George to Charlotte Murrell 1-22-1870 (1-29-1870) F B
Wilson, George to Clara Eliza Wilkinson 12-11-1830 (12-12-1830) O
Wilson, George to Darcus Hathcot 3-7-1861 G
Wilson, George to Louisa Thorton 2-14-1875 Hy
Wilson, George to Mariah Mitchell 5-11-1864 (5-15-1864) O
Wilson, George to Sallie Amos 2-1-1883 (no return) L
Wilson, Gobe to Amanda Yarbro 8-11-1874 (8-12-1874) T
Wilson, H. B. to Martha A. Henry 11-11-1862 G
Wilson, H. H. to Bettie (Mrs.) Ivie 7-2-1867 L
Wilson, H. M. to B. A. Jackson 1-1-1866 O
Wilson, H. P. R. to M. F. Greenway 10-15-1854 (no return) F
Wilson, H. S. to Cyntha A. Law? 11-28-1844 Hn
Wilson, H. W. (W. H.) to Nancy L. Porter 1-4-1865 G
Wilson, H. to Tennessee A. Swor 10-12-1865 Hn
Wilson, Harman M. to Martha J. Gooch 9-29-1862 O
Wilson, Henry to Margaret O'Donner 9-10-1863 (9-11-1863) Sh
Wilson, Henry to Mitty Smith 12-22-1875 Hy
Wilson, Henry to Nancy Ann Ragsdale 10-27-1830 Ma
Wilson, Horace to Elmira J. Thomas 9-29-1857 (10-1-1857) G
Wilson, Horace to Lucy Eliza Dinkins 2-6-1850 Sh
Wilson, Hugh to Aggy Snidy?(Sniedy?) 6-5-1828 Hr
Wilson, Hugh to Jane Webb 10-8-1844 (10-10-1844) O
Wilson, Ingram to Louisa Hullum(Hull?) 9-2-1840 (9-6-1840) Hr
Wilson, Isaac to Frances Bowles 2-18-1846 (could be 1847) Sh
Wilson, Isaac to Jane M. Burden 9-28-1855 (9-30-1855) Hr
Wilson, Isaac to _____ 12-20-1869 T
Wilson, Isaiah to Mary Wilson 12-12-1855 Hn
Wilson, J. A. to M.F. Reeves 10-19-1870 (10-20-1870) F
Wilson, J. B. to Alliner Morris 3-24-1849 Cr
Wilson, J. B. to Mary Jones 9-25-1865 G
Wilson, J. C. to M. D. Etheridge 10-8-1874 Hy
Wilson, J. D. to J. H. Kelso 10-31-1865 Hn
Wilson, J. D. to Mary E. Houston 11-28-1857 Sh
Wilson, J. E. to S. P. Williamson 9-14-1874 (9-17-1874) T
Wilson, J. G. to Jane Miller 10-15-1876 Hy
Wilson, J. H. to E. M. Robey 1-11-1872 O
Wilson, J. H. to Mary D. Mitchell 9-29-1872 T
Wilson, J. M. to S. E. Long 8-6-1863 G
Wilson, J. P to Matilda Cochran 12-8-1855 Hn
Wilson, J. T. to Elizabeth L. Berger 12-18-1866 (no return) Cr
Wilson, J. W. to Eliza M. Luen 2-17-1858 We
Wilson, J. W. to Martha Patterson 5-10-1879 (5-11-1879) L
Wilson, J. W. to Mary E. Hood 7-10-1884 L
Wilson, J. W. to Mary Y. Harrell 9-26-1856 Cr
Wilson, J. W. to Rebecca Winser 5-13-1858 Hn
Wilson, Jacob to Emelia Cotten 1-13-1866 (8-27-1866) T
Wilson, James A. to Elizabeth Dyer 8-31-1865 O
Wilson, James B. to Emeline Whitington 8-22-1843 (8-23-1843) Ma
Wilson, James G. to Elizaeth C. French 2-24-1870 Cr
Wilson, James J. to Ann Matlock 11-12-1852 Hn
Wilson, James P. to Celestia Hawkins 9-17-1855 (no return) We
Wilson, James R. to Malinda Moody 11-21-1856 Sh
Wilson, James R. to Melvina Jordan 8-15-1863 Mn
Wilson, James W. to Rebecca E. Cole 6-19-1856 Hn
Wilson, James W. to Sally H. Lutin 8-23-1852 (no return) L
Wilson, James to A. E. Hall 3-23-1852 (no return) F
Wilson, James to Amelia Vincent 5-21-1832 Hr
Wilson, James to Ann E. Griffin 10-23-1860 (10-25-1860) Sh
Wilson, James to Ceralda Keeth 12-13-1872 G
Wilson, James to Elizabeth Sevier 10-13-1841 Ma
Wilson, James to Harriet Murrell 2-21-1868 (2-26-1868) F B
Wilson, James to Letitia Braden 12-22-1836 Sh
Wilson, James to Margarett Wyles 8-21-1833 (8-22-1833) O
Wilson, James to Matilda Tyson 2-6-1851 (2-9-1851) G
Wilson, James to Nancy Vinson 4-23-1872 (4-24-1872) Dy
Wilson, James to Sarah Barker 9-27-1858 O
Wilson, Jason H. to Elizabeth Hutchings 5-10-1828 Ma
Wilson, Jason to Emily Hicks 2-28-1848 (3-2-1848) Hr
Wilson, Jason to Lucinda Hamilton 2-2-1833 (2-5-1833) Hr
Wilson, Jefferson to Mary Mayfield 12-22-1832 O
Wilson, Jerry to Frances Parker 11-28-1867 G B
Wilson, Jesse to Temperance Fish 9-23-1851 (9-25-1851) Hr
Wilson, Jim to Hettie Burnet 11-7-1874 (11-9-1874) L
Wilson, Jno. R. to Sarah F. Mills (Wills) 8-9-1862 Hy
Wilson, Jo. to Sarah Parker 5-10-1883 (no return) L
Wilson, John A. to Elizabeth Caruthers 11-5-1838 (11-6-1838) Ma
Wilson, John A. to Jane Ward 10-13-1842 L
Wilson, John A. to Juliah Benett 1-30-1845 Cr
Wilson, John A. to Louisa E. Gable 4-19-1863 (4-22-1863) Sh
Wilson, John A. to M. M. Lane 12-13-1856 (12-18-1856) G
Wilson, John A. to Nancy Jane Trail 1-8-1861 Hy
Wilson, John A. to Nancy Rodgers 1-3-1853 (no return) F
Wilson, John A. to Susey H. Wray 8-3-1869 Hy
Wilson, John B. to Demarias Taylor 10-9-1868 (no return) L
Wilson, John C. to Hester Welsh 6-14-1864 Sh
Wilson, John C. to Louisa Sheets 7-3-1828 O
Wilson, John G. to Mary Davis 12-7-1843 Hr
Wilson, John J. to Sarah Holloway 1-16-1839 (no return) F

Wilson, John T. to Elizabeth Epps 1-24-1844 Sh
Wilson, John T. to Julia A. Sparkman 7-13-1867 (7-14-1867) Dy
Wilson, John T. to Sarah W. Williams 10-6-1852 Cr
Wilson, John W. P. to Zilpha Sellers 10-4-1838 Cr
Wilson, John W. to Lou Harris 10-21-1867 (no return) Dy
Wilson, John W. to Mattie A. James 10-22-1861 (no return) Hn
Wilson, John to Alice Burk 7-12-1856 (7-14-1856) Sh
Wilson, John to Annie Woodruff 1-22-1881 L
Wilson, John to Catharine Smith 12-28-1868 (12-31-1868) T
Wilson, John to Delila C. Reams 6-18-1864 Sh
Wilson, John to Dianna Clarke 3-30-1837 Sh
Wilson, John to Edmonia Link 3-28-1878 Hy
Wilson, John to Elizabeth Kelly 12-8-1840 Hn
Wilson, John to F. R. Rebecca Mitchel 4-15-1841 Sh
Wilson, John to Frances Coldwell 9-27-1882 L
Wilson, John to Frances Martin 3-16-1857 (no return) Hn
Wilson, John to Jane Darmon 9-22-1842 (9-?-1842) Ma
Wilson, John to Jane Lotty 2-22-1854 (3-7-1854) Sh
Wilson, John to Jane McClure 12-20-1831 Sh
Wilson, John to Lena E. Graddy 9-29-1856 (10-2-1856) G
Wilson, John to Mary Murrell 12-28-1870 (12-31-1870) F B
Wilson, John to Sarah Taylor 7-24-1869 (7-25-1869) F B
Wilson, John to Susana Wells 9-20-1873 (9-21-1873) L
Wilson, Joseph F. to Elizabeth Swor 3-30-1843 Hn
Wilson, Joseph to Amanda L.? Carter 12-17-1867 (12-18-1867) Cr
Wilson, Joseph to Elmira Poindexter 12-20-1869 (12-30-1869) F B
Wilson, King (Cain) to Mary Bradford 10-18-1868 Hy
Wilson, L. J. to E. C. Skipwith 2-27-1860 (2-28-1860) Sh
Wilson, Lafayett to L. B. Byrn 11-16-1867 O
Wilson, Lewis to Catherine Lott 1-1-1873 Hy
Wilson, Lewis to Eliza Oldham 12-22-1877 Hy
Wilson, Lewis to Maggie Johnson 12-24-1875 (12-24-1874?) T
Wilson, Lindsay to Rebecca F. Lofland 4-26-1850 O
Wilson, Linzey to Rebecca F. Loffland 4-26-1850 O
Wilson, Louis to Eliza Oldham 8-9-1878 Hy
Wilson, Loyd to Nancy Coker 10-22-1839 (11-9-1839) F
Wilson, M. F. to Mary Eliza Gafford 9-16-1861 Sh
Wilson, M. W. to Mary J. Tosh 8-14-1844 (no return) Cr
Wilson, Mack to Mary Eliza Gafford 7-10-1861 Sh
Wilson, Matthew to Mary Jane Halliburton 7-11-1869 G
Wilson, Maxfield to Rachael S. Glass 1-25-1856 (1-30-1856) Hr
Wilson, Mercer D. to Louisa Gorden 9-1-1844 We
Wilson, Merida to Mary E. Swor 11-27-1855 Hn
Wilson, Miles to Liddy McCord 3-23-1839 Hr
Wilson, Miles to Margrett Anderson 2-25-1847 Hr
Wilson, Mines P. to Charlotte M. Campbell 3-19-1845 Hn
Wilson, Montravile G. to Catharine McManus 10-28-1854 Sh
Wilson, Moses to Malinda Jordan 6-29-1867 (7-3-1867) F B
Wilson, Munford to Martha T. Pegran 6-8-1835 M
Wilson, Nathan to Mary Josephine Simmons 1-9-1867 Be
Wilson, P. B. to Elizabeth Wilson 6-14-1852 Hn
Wilson, P. H. to N. E. Wiley 12-17-1872 T
Wilson, P. W. to Celestia Kinsey 12-24-1874 O
Wilson, Perry to Lucretia Moore 9-5-1846 (9-6-1846) O
Wilson, Peter M. to Viney Dacus 1-12-1869 T
Wilson, Peter P. to Frances L. Davis 9-24-1856 We
Wilson, Peter to Martha C. Fletcher 3-15-1853 (3-19-1853) G
Wilson, R. C. to Susie A. Cox 5-31-1879 (6-1-1879) L
Wilson, R. D. to Lydia R. Harwood 2-17-1869 G
Wilson, R. L. to Mattie Ellis 12-9-1869 (12-14-1870?) G
Wilson, R. N. J. to Emma Deloach 9-11-1861 (9-12-1861) Sh
Wilson, R. T. to Margaret A. Simeton? 2-24-1866 T
Wilson, R. W. to Eveline Keathley 1-2-1864 (12-30-1864?) G
Wilson, R. to M. Sane 12-14-1856 We
Wilson, Richard B. to Martha Burriss 10-14-1847 F
Wilson, Richard to Frances Sneed 3-4-1870 Cr
Wilson, Robert D. to Nancy J. Calhoun 2-26-1866 O
Wilson, Robert L. to Nancy A. Reed 1-17-1841 (1-18-1841) Ma
Wilson, Robert to Elizabeth Furlong 10-21-1857 We
Wilson, Robert to Susan Paschall 5-17-1846 Hn
Wilson, Robert to Susan Word 6-21-1883 (6-29-1883) L
Wilson, Robt. to Minnie Rogers 9-30-1873 Hy
Wilson, Rufus to Ann Love 12-31-1872 Hy
Wilson, S. A. to C. L. Redson (Reason?) 1-4-1861 G
Wilson, S. C. to Sarah C. Barton 10-5-1865 Hn
Wilson, S. H. to Sarah Oliver 1-5-1857 (no return) Hn
Wilson, S. O. to M. J. Lovel 11-28-1872 O
Wilson, S. P. to R. E. Rivers 12-13-1864 O
Wilson, Sam'l H. to Mary P. Calhoun 1-31-1856 O
Wilson, Samuel D. to Matilda M. Henderson 12-27-1839 (SB 1838) F
Wilson, Samuel D. to Ruth C. Martain 1-29-1824 O
Wilson, Samuel D. to Susan Motherel 3-13-1860 O
Wilson, Samuel H. to Alice L. Hunter 1-23-1869 (1-27-1869) F
Wilson, Samuel J. to Susan S. Turner 12-26-1864 (12-29-1864) Sh
Wilson, Samuel McK. to Mary E. Vaughan 6-11-1855 (6-12-1855) Sh
Wilson, Samuel W. to Crissa Paschal 3-12-1863 Hn
Wilson, Samuel to Adeline Bledsoe 10-13-1865 (10-24-1865) Cr

Wilson, Samuel to M. E. Brewer 3-15-1843 Be
Wilson, Samuel to M. E. Brewer 3-15-1843 Be CC
Wilson, Samuel to Malinda Key 3-14-1854 Hn
Wilson, Samuel to Susan McDougal 3-15-1861 Sh
Wilson, Scott to Rose Cooper 10-12-1864 Sh
Wilson, Shadrack to Margaret A. McWherter 6-8-1852 G
Wilson, Simon to Nancy Farmington 6-20-1840 (could be July) Sh
Wilson, Solomon to Eliza Wilks 2-23-1878 Hy
Wilson, Spencer to Mary Wallis 10-1-1866 (10-5-1866) T
Wilson, Squire to Elizabeth McCan 3-16-1840 Hr
Wilson, Stephen to Martha Whitess 9-11-1837 Hr
Wilson, Syrus to E. Laycook 12-29-1851 Cr
Wilson, T. I. to S. A. Christie 1-12-1878 Hy
Wilson, T. to M. E. Griffini 5-8-1884 (5-9-1884) L
Wilson, Taylor to Anna S. Addyman 1-12-1860 Sh
Wilson, Thaddeus to Sina Matthews 11-26-1860 (11-27-1860) F
Wilson, Thadios to Marinett Cartwright 9-8-1849 (10-3-1849) F
Wilson, Thomas A. to Catherine A. Taylor 1-1-1873 Hy
Wilson, Thomas C. to Margaret Bond 10-2-1827 Sh
Wilson, Thomas E. to Harriett Murphy 5-22-1858 (no return) Hn
Wilson, Thomas H. to Rhodia Roberts 10-14-1856 Hn
Wilson, Thomas M. to Martha A. Fisher 1-1-1850 Hn
Wilson, Thomas M. to Zilphy Gullage 9-1-1842 (no return) Hn
Wilson, Thomas to Ann Wyatt 3-4-1869 Be
Wilson, Thomas to Catharine Hutchens 8-28-1845 Sh
Wilson, Thomas to Eveline Brayden 9-9-1830 Sh
Wilson, Thomas to Frances Shoemaker 2-20-1869 (2-25-1869) L
Wilson, Thos. H. to Martha Solomon 2-13-1861 (2-14-1861) T
Wilson, Tolbert to Burtie Oldham 12-1-1869 Hy
Wilson, Truston to P. J. Mendenall 1-21-1847 Sh
Wilson, W. A. to Lucretia Maxedon 12-21-1865 Mn
Wilson, W. A. to Sarah A. Glass 10-20-1866 (10-21-1866) L
Wilson, W. J. W. to Alvira H. Eckles 9-25-1856 (9-27-1856) G
Wilson, W. J. to Mary Agnes Lawhorn 3-17-1858 Sh
Wilson, W. L. to Amanda Ryon 4-17-1874 L
Wilson, W. M. to Georganna Brookens 7-11-1876 Hy
Wilson, W. N. to Elizabeth A. Harrison 8-25-1853 Be
Wilson, W. N. to Elizabeth A. Harrison 8-25-1853 Be CC
Wilson, W. N. to Margaret Saunders 4-25-1878 (4-28-1878) L
Wilson, W. N. to Nancy S. Fisher 10-31-1866 Hn
Wilson, W. N. to R. Mathews 3-24-1865 O
Wilson, W. P. to Mary Ashley 2-11-1866 G
Wilson, W. P. to Sarah J. Taylor 3-10-1855 (no return) F
Wilson, W. W. to Melinda W. Duncan 11-24-1852 Hn
Wilson, WM. A. to M. J. Paisley 1-31-1854 (2-2-1854) Ma
Wilson, Walker B. to Jane Owen 6-8-1838 (6-11-1838) Hr
Wilson, Walter A. to Della Williams 5-28-1881 L
Wilson, Wash to Burtie Taylor 12-24-1874 Hy
Wilson, Wesley to Martha Street 12-29-1866 Hy
Wilson, West to Nancy Johnson 1-16-1873 Hy
Wilson, Whitson H. to Martha F. Johnson 10-4-1858 (10-6-1858) Ma
Wilson, William A. to Rebecca Hall 12-18-1846 Hn
Wilson, William B. to Artamissa J. Smith 9-18-1865 Cr
Wilson, William C. to May Y. Coats 12-21-1855 (no return) Hn
Wilson, William D. to Eliza Williamson 9-3-1842 (9-4-1842) Ma
Wilson, William H. to Elvira Hughes 9-12-1844 Hn
Wilson, William H. to Margaret C. Stricklin 1-13-1846 (no return) L
Wilson, William H. to Mary J. Mosby 5-18-1861 (5-19-1861) Sh
Wilson, William Henry to Margaret L.? Harris 4-16-1840 T
Wilson, William M. to Nancy Ann Carithers 5-24-1853 O
Wilson, William P. to Emily Crabtree 12-28-1858 Hn
Wilson, William P. to Nancy Clemons 1-26-1835 (2-9-1835) G
Wilson, William P. to Sarah Jane Taylor 12-27-1854 Ma
Wilson, William P. to Sarah Jane Taylor 3-12-1855 Sh
Wilson, William R. to Elizabeth Murphy 3-19-1855 (no return) Hn
Wilson, William R. to Harriet _____ 2-10-1849 (no return) Hn
Wilson, William Robert to Lucinda Leake 1-18-1856 Ma
Wilson, William W. to Martha Strain 3-28-1829 Ma
Wilson, William W. to Sarah E. Kirby 1-26-1858 Hn
Wilson, William jr. to Sarah Ann King 12-15-1848 (12-17-1848) Hr
Wilson, William to Betsy Williams 6-6-1831 Sh
Wilson, William to Cynthia Still? 11-17-1829 (11-25-1829) Hr
Wilson, William to Elizabeth Johnson 3-7-1828 Sh
Wilson, William to Ellen Byrn? 10-3-1'70 (not executed) L
Wilson, William to Louisa Webb 12-2-_830 Sh
Wilson, William to Lydia Beard 4-30-1873 T
Wilson, William to Mary Jane Goodman 12-8-1852 (12-9-1852) Sh
Wilson, William to Nancy Howard 6-30-1830 (7-1-1830) G
Wilson, William to Sallie Fields 8-4-1873 (8-9-1873) T
Wilson, William to Sarah Ann Parker 8-18-1845 Sh
Wilson, William to Sarah McCulough 12-31-1857 T
Wilson, Willis A. to Martha C. Kelly 3-21-1868 T
Wilson, Willis to Viney Burks 9-30-1879 (10-1-1879) L B
Wilson, Wm. L. to Nancy McCarroll 9-8-1854 (9-14-1854) T
Wilson, Wm. M. to Nancy A. Shelby 12-14-1845 Sh
Wilson, Wm. P. to M. A. Hall 12-14-1874 (12-17-1874) O
Wilson, Wm. to Julia Maxey 2-7-1871 Hy

Wilson, Wm. to Lea Wear 3-30-1866 O
Wilson, Wm. to Susannah Hughes 12-13-1843 Sh
Wilson, Younger to Betsy Anderson 9-11-1876 (9-15-1876) L B
Wilson, Z. N. to Saphronia J. Morris 4-19-1863 G
Wilson, Zacheus to Mary Jane Patton 8-30-1848 Hn
Wilson, Zebadr to Martha A. James 1-11-1858 We
Wilson, jr., P. to M. E. Carter 7-25-1863 (7-29-1863) F
Wilsons, William to Rhoda Walker 12-21-1853 (12-22-1853) Sh
Wily, C. P. to Ellen Wade 1-23-1867 O
Wily, W. L. to Sallie Shinault 2-1-1860 F
Wimberley, A. J. to Sarah A. Pfleuger 1-31-1867 Hn
Wimberley, B. F. to Nancy E. Stewart 4-27-1868 Dy
Wimberley, Benjamin F. to Hannah A. Walker 3-26-1858 Hn
Wimberley, F. M. to Mary Smith 12-2-1866 F
Wimberley, George W. to Nancy Clayton 1-20-1850 Hn
Wimberley, Henry P. to Hannah M. Roberts 7-24-1860 Hn
Wimberley, Henry to Lucina P. Stroud 11-16-1847 Hn
Wimberley, Isaac to Sarah Shankle 11-8-1838 Hn
Wimberley, James H. to Martha T. Hardin 11-26-1867 Hn
Wimberley, James S. to Eliza Irby 12-24-1861 Hr
Wimberley, John to Jane Frazier 5-13-1849 Hn
Wimberley, Lewis to Mary C. Roberts 4-20-1851 Hn
Wimberley, Noah to Martha Lee 5-13-1853 Hn
Wimberley, W. D. to R. S. Lee Milberry 9-5-1852 Hn
Wimberley, William P. to Elizabeth Whitfield 3-12-1850 Hn
Wimberly, Richard C. to Mary Pursell 9-28-1842 Sh
Winberry, Alfred to Mima Edwards 11-3-1869 Dy
Winberry, G. W. to Elizabeth Pinkston 6-17-1861 Be
Winberry, George to Carolina Johnson 6-21-1857 Be CC
Winberry, George to Caroline Johnson 6-21-1857 Be CC
Winberry, James to Judy Dennis 1-26-1852 Be CC
Winberry, John H. to Susan A. Hill 7-3-1855 Sh
Winberry, R. M. to Mary L. James 1-3-1871 (1-5-1871) Dy
Winberry, Willis C. to Sarah E. Reddit 12-22-1858 Sh
Winburn, Burton to Letta A. Jones 7-7-1874 Hy
Winburn, Henry C. to Nancy E. Bess 11-19-1866 Hy
Winburn, Henry to Mary Claybrook 11-23-1857 (11-26-1857) Sh
Winburn, J. F. to S. L. Alford 4-22-1882 (4-24-1882) L
Winburn, J. J. to Annie Baxter 12-12-1878 Hy
Winburn, Jas. T. to Nancy Maxwell 9-22-1855 T
Winbury, James to Judy Dennis 1-26-1852 Be
Winbury, James to Rachel Ross 3-22-1849 Be
Winbury, John H. to Loucretia Jane Slate 10-30-1850 Sh
Winbush, John to Mary Tildon (Gildon?) 1-5-1884 (1-6-1884) L
Winbush, Nathan to Sisan? Turner 1-5-1884 (1-6-1884) L
Winbush, W. M. to Helen Greer 3-6-1866 Hn
Winchell, James A. to Callie C. Jameson 9-3-1856 (9-4-1856) Sh
Wincheste, Gilbert to Cherry Sumerow 12-29-1871 L
Winchester, Henry to Eliza Johnson 3-7-1874 (3-11-1874) Dy
Winchester, Henry to Martha Ann King 12-24-1867 (12-25-1867) Dy
Winchester, J. G. to Patsy Melton 8-26-1842 Be
Winchester, J. P. to Patsy Melton 8-26-1842 Be CC
Winchester, Madison to Sarah L. Lee 2-17-1858 Hn
Winchester, William to N. E. Morgan 10-23-1862 Hn
Winchester, Wm. D. to Mary Ann Currie 2-6-1858 Ma
Wind, John to Eliza Weckesser 10-21-1856 Sh
Winders, Henry H. to Therina Temple 1-16-1840 Sh
Windgo, German U. to Lemmende E. Alexander 1-20-1865 Hn
Windiss, Henry to Nancy Jane Ralph 4-21-1847 (4-22-1847) T
Windrow, Henry to Fanny A. Beard 11-6-1885 (11-7-1885) L
Windrow, Thomas to Ida Moorer 10-29-1880 (10-30-1880) L B
Windsor, ____ to Josephine Lafever 11-4-1857 Hn
Winegardner, Samuel to Mollie Foley 2-17-1863 Sh
Winfield, Casso to Mary Jarrett 12-24-1872 Hy
Winfield, Curtis to Eleander Brown 12-16-1848 F
Winfield, G. H. to Eliza A. Reed 5-17-1866 Hy
Winfield, Henry to Nan Cox 6-26-1869 (6-25?-1869) F B
Winfield, Isaac to Mary E. Smith 10-9-1872 F
Winfield, J. L. to Mary H. Guinn (Gause-Green?) 2-9-1860 (2-15-1860) L
Winfield, Miles to Mollie Loving 10-30-1868 Hy
Winfield, W. W. to Mary E. Harwell 6-1-1859 (6-26-1859) F
Winfield, William E. to Lucinda M. Malone 11-10-1845 (11-12-1845) F
Winford, Andrew to S. V. Winford 7-25-1865? (7-26-1866) T
Winford, Benjamin to Lucinda Sulivan 10-5-1843 Sh
Winford, Harvey to Mary Jane Hopper 11-1-1849 Sh
Winford, Isaac T. to Margaret A. Brimley 6-9-1870 (6-12-1870) T
Winford, J. S.? to Viola S. Crenshaw 4-13-1857 T
Winford, John S. to Viola S. Crenshaw 4-13-1857 (4-16-1857) T
Winford, Jonathon to Mary J. Taylor 11-20-1843 T
Winford, Mat to Sarah Claiburn 10-17-1869 (1-3-1869?) T
Winford, Samuel H. to Narcissa Shetter 8-4-1842 T
Winford, Thomas B. to America Jane Gardner 10-13-1841 T
Winford, Timothy to Nancy Galloway 6-16-1838 T
Winford, William L. to Eliza Jane Anderson 12-1-1846 Sh
Winford, William W. to Mary Read 12-30-1868 T
Winfree, Frank B. to Nannie E. Williams 2-28-1871 Ma
Winfree, Saml. to Mary E. Culbreath 2-26-1868 T

Winfrey, Dick to Mary Levy 7-13-1867 G
Winfrey, Jessey to Patsy Cocke 2-24-1869 F B
Winfrey, William to Ann Dortch 5-3-1869 (no return) F B
Winfrow?, Mat. to Sarah Claiburn 10-17-1868 T
Wing, W. H. to Eliza Hood 12-17-1866 (12-20-1866) F
Wingard, J. W. to B. Carr 2-21-1861 Sh
Wingo, J. W. to M. E. Giles 9-4-1865 G
Wingo, John J. to Mary A. Cooper 5-8-1864 Cr
Wingo, John W. to Elizabeth A. Campbell 2-7-1859 G
Wingo, T.? R. to Mary J. C. Jones 2-18-1867 (no return) Cr
Wingo, Thomas to Delia A. Bradford 9-20-1868 G
Wingo, Thos. G. to Elizabeth Simmons 11-17-1847 Cr
Wingo, William to Nancy H. Ferrell 1-5-1859 O
Wingrove, Edwin L. to Virginia Howlett 1-8-1862 (1-9-1862) Ma
Winkelman, Henry to Mary Schlatter 8-31-1857 (9-1-1857) Sh
Winkler, Richmond to Eleanor Goss 1-13-1841 (1-14-1841) T
Winkley, C. P. to S. M. Bond 2-15-1854 (2-16-1854) Sh
Winn, A. M. to Roxanna Griffith 12-9-1875 Hy
Winn, C. R. to Susan J. Nicks 10-21-1847 (no return) Hn
Winn, Charles to Maria Smith 2-23-1866 (2-24-1866) T
Winn, Daniel to Susan Landrum 6-26-1845 O
Winn, James to Mary A. Hickman 11-18-1864 Sh
Winn, Joel to Rebecca A. Stanley 12-14-1854 Cr
Winn, John to Adeline Jackson 2-2-1871 T
Winn, Joseph M. to Nancy C. Jackson 12-9-1855 Hn
Winn, Minor M. to Nancy Yarbory 3-15-1846 G
Winn, O. D. to S. A. Griffith 4-11-1872 (4-14-1872) L
Winn, Peter to Kessandria Pitts 3-7-1840 (3-27-1840) O
Winn, Philip S. to Martha Jane Punch? 1-11-1843 T
Winn, Robt to Fannie Hall 11-1-1873 (11-2-1873) T
Winn, Sam to Louisa Dyson 3-26-1874 Hy
Winn, Samuel C. to Catherine Carlton 12-10-1846 Cr
Winn, T. W. to Susan A. Malone 10-23-1856 T
Winn, W. F. to Emma Griffith 11-13-1871 (11-14-1872) L
Winn, W. M. to Sscotin Flippin 6-14-1870 G
Winn, William A. to Sarah A. Bailey 12-19-1866 (12-25-1866) Ma
Winn, William H. to Mary Pitt 3-1-1865 (3-3-1865) T
Winn, William to Emma Hunt 4-13-1874 T
Winn, William to Polly Burton? 4-25-1846 Hn
Winn, Wm. Alexr. to Elizabeth Jane Norvell 12-15-1857 (12-17-1857) Ma
Winn, Wm. R. to Casandra Shinault 11-24-1841 F
Winn, Wm. to Emma Hunt 4-13-1874 T
Winn, Wm. to Jennie Taylor 1-17-1866 (1-20-1866) T
Winn?, G. W. to Rebecca J. Howard 6-10-1873 T
Winne, Peter C. to Lizzie M. Eaton 12-23-1869 Ma
Winningham, Peter R. to Sarah K. Kent 10-8-1842 (no return) L
Winns, D. O. to Araminta Causey 7-20-1840 (no return) Hn
Winrow, Abe to Judy Townes 9-5-1878 (9-6-1878) L B
Winrow, H. to Judith M. H. Henning 8-12-1850 (no return) L
Winrow, Philip to Ellen Turner 2-7-1874 (no return) L B
Winrow, Phill to Lou Pain 12-27-1877 L B
Winscot?, W. C. to Sarah Hamlin 5-8-1845 Hn
Winsett, Berry R. to Sarah Hasting 3-1-1838 Hn
Winsett, Daniel to Martha Joiner 7-5-1852 Hn
Winsett, Henry D. to Susan E. Tombs 7-8-1860 Hn
Winsett, James A. to Isabella J. Roach 11-18-1845 (11-19-1845) F
Winsett, James E. to Eliza A. Bell 5-16-1867 F
Winsett, James M. to Isabella C. Craig 1-24-1860 Hn
Winsett, John H. to Lydia A. Aden 12-27-1841 Hn
Winsett, Joseph to Nancy Myrick 1-15-1852 Hn
Winsett, R. D. to Anna M. Finney 1-22-1868 (12-23-1868) F
Winsett, William B. to Adaline Trevathan 5-5-1859 Hn
Winsett, William F. to Nancy J. Pearse 11-11-1866 Hn
Winsett, William M. to Sarah Ann Broach 1-2-1861 Hn
Winslow, Alson G. to Lenora Andrews 1-28-1853 (1-3-1853?) Ma
Winslow, Thomas H. to Melvina Harris 10-5-1866 (10-7-1866) Ma
Winsore, J. A. to Elizabeth Berry 4-7-1852 Cr
Winstad, John S. to Victora Rucker 11-18-1860 We
Winstad, William F. to Martha Rose 12-20-1860 We
Winstead, Charles C. to Sarah J. Wheeler 1-11-1855 We
Winstead, Saml. to Ann Eliza Sanson 12-12-1850 We
Winstead, Samuel A. to Lavenia V. Yates 12-20-1861 (not endorsed) We
Winstead, Samuel to Julia Byars 8-13-1856 We
Winstead, W. T. M. to Mary Gates 1-5-1858 We
Winsten, James M. to Thirza Thornton 8-28-1861 We
Winston, Allison S. to Sarah F. Hunter 2-21-1853 O
Winston, Arnold to Nancy (Mrs.) Denton 11-9-1857 (11-10-1857) Ma
Winston, David to Eliza Ferris 10-9-1866 G
Winston, Ed to Annie Estes 12-29-1870 Hy
Winston, Edmond to Sallie A. Fry 5-21-1852 (no return) F
Winston, F. B. to Julia Taylor 11-24-1868 Hy
Winston, George to Nancy Johnson 1-15-1846 We
Winston, George to Polly Willoughby 2-25-1858 We
Winston, Hiram to Martha Watkins 4-18-1873 Hy
Winston, Isaac J. to Nancy E. Sumerow 9-18-1873 L
Winston, Isaac to Olivia B. Michee 10-11-1852 (no return) F
Winston, James H. to Martha M. Jones 1-11-1843 (1-12-1843) Ma

Winston, John A. to Polly Walker Logwood 10-18-1843 F
Winston, John W. to Julia F. McCaig 5-28-1870 (5-31-1870) Ma
Winston, Joseph E. to Margaret Nicholson 2-26-1848 (3-1-1848) Ma
Winston, M. to Cathrine Jenkins 2-8-1852 We
Winston, N. B. to Margaret C. Garland 9-13-1856 (9-17-1856) Ma
Winston, Reuben to Arley Williams 5-19-1883 (no return) L
Winston, Robert J. to Eliza W. Bondurant 11-19-1850 We
Winston, S. A. to E. R. Glenn 2-4-1857 We
Winston, Thomas B. to Maria L. Nelson 10-31-1853 Sh
Winston, William J. to Martha F. Huddleseton 6-4-1855 (6-7-1855) O
Winston, William N. to Winney Ann Conger 9-28-1848 Ma
Winston, Wm. to Marcia S. McLean 7-24-1836 Sh
Winters, Aaron to Alice Purvise 4-10-1827 O
Winters, C. T. to S. E. Hinson 11-18-1863 Hn
Winters, Dock to Elin Moses 12-19-1877 Hy
Winters, James Carroll to Jane Ballard 7-28-1855 (7-29-1855) T
Winters, James to Amanda Edwards 1-2-1877 Hy
Winters, Jo to Harriat Suggs 12-30-1875 (12-31-1875) L B
Winters, John to Catherine Pilcher 4-22-1839 Sh
Winters, Joseph to Mary Ann Knight 9-9-1850 (9-10-1850) F
Winters, Lewis C. to Ellen Shaw no date (Spring 1852) L
Winters, Marshal to Mary Eliza Powell 2-29-1872 Hy
Winters, Owen to Nancy Daly 9-8-1858 Sh
Winters, Patrick to Mary Black 5-8-1858 Hn
Winters, Thomas to Catherine Douherty 9-12-1862 Sh
Wintz, L. P. to Julian Nance 11-29-1864 Hn
Wipper, Henry to Jane Wright 3-21-1849 Sh
Wirt, Finis E. to Eliza W. Royal 1-27-1833 Sh
Wirt, Green to Mary Warren 1-2-1866 (no return) F B
Wirt, Harry to Henrietta Patterson 12-27-1867 (12-31-1867) F B
Wirt, Martin to Eliza Cheatham 4-25-1857 O
Wirt, S. P. to S. E. Crabtree 5-4-1868 (5-5-1868) F
Wirwa, C. W. to Henrietta Richardt 9-21-1868 (9-22-1868) F
Wisdom, Scott to Mattie Pate Smith 6-17-1870 (6-18-1870) Ma
Wise, Andrew to Nancy Devalt 4-24-1874 Hy
Wise, Burrell to Martha Yancey 12-27-1831 (12-25?-1831) Hr
Wise, D. S. to Frances Jefferson 6-30-1868 Hy
Wise, Ernst to Annie Couster 4-15-1851 Sh
Wise, J. A. to Elisabeth J. Mitchell 6-5-1854 Sh
Wise, James C. to Martha Ann Mullins 7-4-1846 Hr
Wise, Jessee to Tilda Anthony 1-12-1877 Hy
Wise, Joseph to Rebecca Butler 4-1-1877 Hy
Wise, Marshall M. to Martha (Mrs.) Root 4-17-1837 Sh
Wise, S. B. to Rebecca Armstrong 8-3-1865 Mn
Wise, Wm. P. to Elizabeth L. Hill 4-20-1861 (4-21-1861) Hr
Wisehart, Benjamin F. to Mary A. Chilcutt 1-17-1867 Hn
Wisehart, George W. to Lucy C. Bucy 12-8-1859 Hn
Wiseman, A. C. to Jane C. Combs 5-8-1856 Be
Wiseman, A. C. to Jane E. Combs 5-8-1856 Be CC
Wiseman, A. L. to Charlotte Jane Presson 10-23-1847 Be
Wiseman, A. N. to Liza Ann French 10-18-1866 Hn
Wiseman, Aaron to Matilda Hinton 3-3-1882 (no return) L
Wiseman, Franklin to Bettie Coats 2-18-1871 (2-19-1871) T
Wiseman, Franklin to Mary E. Wiseman 11-4-1852 Be
Wiseman, Franklin to May E. Wiseman 11-4-1852 Be CC
Wiseman, H. H. to Miss M. E. Winn 12-27-1860 T
Wiseman, Isaac to Emeline Spencer 9-25-1866 T
Wiseman, J. H. to Nancy J. Hudson 8-13-1868 Be
Wiseman, J. to J. A. Wiseman 4-5-1841 Be
Wiseman, J. to J. S. Wiseman 4-5-1841 Be CC
Wiseman, James M. to Mary Ann Capps 2-18-1845 Be
Wiseman, James M. to Mary Ann Capps 2-18-1845 Be CC
Wiseman, John Bowen? to Elizabeth Lamb 12-12-1846 (12-24-1846) T
Wiseman, John P. to Mariah Blain 12-17-1860 (12-20-1860) F
Wiseman, John to Polly Ann Presson 1-26-1854 Be
Wiseman, John to Polly Ann Presson 1-26-1854 Be CC
Wiseman, Joseph F. to Martha F. Feezor 11-16-1865 T
Wiseman, L. W. to Martha Coats 12-1-1874 (12-2-1874) T
Wiseman, Milton to Elender Wiseman 3-3-1850 Be
Wiseman, O. O. to J. E. Kinny 12-22-1873 (1-7-1874) T
Wiseman, R. J. to Louisa McCarroll 4-9-1853 Be
Wiseman, R. J. to Louisa McCarroll 4-9-1853 Be CC
Wiseman, Saml. to Marietta McCarroll 7-2-1848 Be
Wiseman, William to Nancy J. Harrison 12-17-1860 T
Wiseman, Wm. O. to Mary A. Ralph 8-14-1852 T
Wiseman, Zachariah to Emeline Morriss 5-4-1842 (no return) F
Wiseman, ___ to Jane Martin 1-26-1874 (1-28-1874) T
Wisener?, HGenry to Mary Elizabeth Goodnoe 2-13-1844 (2-16-1844) T
Wisenor, James H. to Priscilla Morris 12-19-1853 Sh
Wissmer, Frank to Eliza Wilder 6-6-1860 (6-9-1860) Sh
Wiswell, A. M. to Caroline E. Mann 5-21-1857 Sh
Witham, A. J. to Nancy E. Craig 8-3-1869 L
Witherington, A. to S. C.(H.?) Bond 6-23-1870 G
Witherington, Absolum to Harrett Glisson 11-26-1851 G
Witherington, Alexander to Ann Eliza Keathley 1-14-1859 (1-16-1859) Sh
Witherington, Benton to Sarrah Ann Brit 10-13-1865 G
Witherington, D. M. to Sarah E. Gillespie 12-20-1853 Sh
Witherington, Daniel to Julia F. Holland 3-1-1863 G
Witherington, J. M. to Harriet J. Smith 1-27-1866 (1-28-1866) T
Witherington, Maj. W. to Mary Phelps 5-26-1853 (6-26-1853) G
Witherington, Stephen to Elizabeth Wilson 5-16-1861 G
Witherington, William S. to Mary A. Hunt 12-16-1862 We
Witherington, Willis to Rachael E. Ridgeway 2-26-1856 (2-27-1856) G
Withers, Elihu to Maria Trantham 3-15-1838 Hn
Witherspoon, H. H. to Bettie Bond 10-24-1871 (10-25-1871) Ma
Witherspoon, James R. to America Barnes no date (with Aug 1838) G
Witherspoon, Jas. M. to L. A. Hanmon 1-5-1861 G
Witherspoon, Joseph to Susan Y. Bledsoe 3-22-1850 G
Witherspoon, N.J. to S. A. Driskell 2-1-1865 G
Witherspoon, Thos. M. to Roenna McCalvy 1-23-1838 G
Witherspoon, W. C. to Sarah A. Nichols 12-22-1862 (12-30-1862) O
Witherspoon, jr., William to Hallie Rice 3-29-1868 (4-2-1868) Ma
Withington, John Clark to Francis Elizabeth Roy 4-10-1870 (4-13-1870) L
Witt, Alford M. to Louisa Hammonds 11-21-1855 (11-22-1855) G
Witt, Bud to Emma Landers 8-18-1864 Sh
Witt, C. J. to M. C. Hale 8-26-1868 G
Witt, Coleman H. to Susan F. Hoskins 11-21-1853 (11-23-1853) G
Witt, D. to Hannah Loving 10-9-1883 L
Witt, E. J. to Mollie P. Umsted 9-18-1869 G
Witt, E. A. to Elvira A. Shane 11-24-1860 G
Witt, E. M. to Mary H. Williams 12-20-1865 G
Witt, Geo. R. to Isabella R. Yancey 9-1-1846 F
Witt, George R. to Mary A. Yancy 2-10-1841 (2-11-1841) F
Witt, Isaac to Nancy Hamilton 12-23-1846 (no return) We
Witt, J. W. to Lula Cheatham 4-9-1863 Sh
Witt, James S. to Juda Dickens 12-2-1845 G
Witt, John to Queen Jones 12-30-1869 (1-1-1870) F B
Witt, Joseph to Juby Ann Atkins 9-8-1842 (no return) Hn
Witt, P. C. to Susan J. Young 3-18-1872 Hy
Witt, P. J. to Georga A. Murphy 12-4-1876 (12-6-1876) L
Witt, S. B. to Mary E. Goodman 10-9-1873 Hy
Witt, Silas D. to Nancy G. Palmore 2-23-1861 (2-24-1861) Cr
Witt, Simeon P. to Caroline H. Ward 2-23-1853 (2-24-1853) Sh
Witt, W. H. to Minerva Nowell 5-3-1865 G
Witt, William H. to Mary N. Arnold 7-2-1845 G
Woerne, Frederick to Madelia Enhel 9-10-1857 Sh
Wofford, Benton to Dolly Cox 3-28=1848 Hn
Wofford, James M. to Traney Burton 1-16-1839 (no return) Hn
Wofford, James to Viann W. Phelps 9-11-1856 Hn
Woford, William R. to Louisa J. Hullum 3-12-1849 (3-21-1849) Hr
Wohrum, Lewis to Hellena Dutlinger 5-13-1856 Sh
Wolard, John to Peney Pope 10-30-1839 (10-31-1839) G
Woldridge, D. H. to Martha J. Senter 1-24-1860 (1-25-1860) G
Wolf, Chas. E. to Rosena Lunge 8-19-1864 (9-1-1864) Sh
Wolfe, Benjm. F. to Louisa Black (Block) 9-7-1848 Sh
Wolfe, G. A. to Louisa Thomas 3-16-1859 (3-21-1859) Sh
Wolfe, Henry to Nancy Powell 1-2-1862 Mn
Wolfe, J. T. to Nancy Miller 4-4-1864 Sh
Wolfe, Jesse to Temperance Sloan 6-29-1850 (6-30-1850) Hr
Wolfe, Joe to Mahala Tillman 3-20-1871 Hy
Wolff, Emil to Christiana Schlosser 12-26-1853 Sh
Wolff, J. F. to Fanny Miller 4-4-1864 (4-5-1864) Sh
Wolfkill, H. B. to Susan A. Hightower 4-24-1857 (4-26-1857) Sh
Wollard, James M. to Julia R. (Mrs.) Mylor 5-21-1868 Ma
Wolsey, Robt. to Mariah Orgain 12-15-1868 (12-19-1868) F B
Wolverton, Bird to Ann Jane Tucker 10-27-1835 Hr
Wolverton, J. M. to Mary Holeman 8-27-1861 Mn
Wolverton, William A. to Martha A. Justice 1-17-1851 (1-23-1851) Hr
Womack, A. P. to Eliza Jones 1-3-1842 (1-6-1842) F
Womack, Daniel to Soniza C. Fawbess 8-20-1849 (8-27-1849) G
Womack, E. P. to Rebecca Wagnon 12-2-1842 Sh
Womack, Henry to Mary Bookers(Brookran) 9-22-1835 Hr
Womack, Hezekiah to Caroline N. Hutchens 11-18-1849 (11-13?-1849) G
Womack, James G. to Elizabeth Lager Theus 12-24-1844 Ma
Womack, John C. to Martha A. Noles 7-3-1859 O
Womack, John F. to Lockey Ann Wagnon 3-7-1843 Sh
Womble, B. F. to Matilda Ezzell 7-23-1857 We
Womble, D. W. to P. A. Montgomery 10-20-1861 We
Womble, J. W. to Mary Jane Stephens 1-4-1841 (1-7-1841) F
Womble, James to Bettie Davis 1-29-1873 Hy
Womble, Jefferson H. to Martha A. Kemp 2-24-1862 We
Womble, P. G. to Nancy McDade 10-22-1844 (10-31-1844) F
Womble, W. W. to Mary E. Foust 12-22-1856 We
Womble, William W. to Narcissa C. Sherman 3-9-1848 Ma
Womick, Oscar H. to Laura D. Bywater 12-22-1864 Sh
Wommack, John C. to Martha A. Noles 7-3-1859 O
Wommack, Wm. to Alabama Jones 3-27-1878 Hy
Wood, Albert M. to Mary E. Mosly (Mosby) 10-2-1844 Sh
Wood, Alexander Carroll to Camdis D. Taylor 4-10-1854 (4-12-1854) T
Wood, Alexander to Catharine Bringle 6-4-1846 T
Wood, Allen L. to Polly Adair 8-8-1839 G
Wood, Augustin to Sarah Gouger 8-11-1855 (8-12-1855) G
Wood, B. F. to Julia A. Thom 3-17-1863 G
Wood, C. T. to Susan R. Satterfield 6-27-1856 (6-28-1856) Sh

Wood, Charles L. to Ama L. Read 4-5-1856 (4-6-1856) Ma
Wood, Charles to E. B. Whaley 6-21-1858 (6-22-1858) Sh
Wood, Cole to Jenny Gause 6-6-1885 (no return) L
Wood, Currie to Ella Barfield 1-24-1883 L
Wood, D. F. to M. C. Williams 2-4-1880 L
Wood, David H. to Mary E. Deakins 12-17-1850 (12-19-1850) T
Wood, David to Martha A. Gracy 4-19-1855 T
Wood, Dock to Rebecca Richardson 12-18-1866 (1-20-1867) Dy
Wood, Ferd. to Laura Shaw 5-8-1871 (5-9-1871) Ma
Wood, Francis J. to Frances R. Gregory 2-7-1871 Hy
Wood, Franklin to Mary Ann McKee 10-10-1838 (10-15-1838) G
Wood, G. W. to Louizer R. Stockard 12-20-1860 G
Wood, G. W. to N. C. Palmer 2-20-1869 (2-21-1869) Cr
Wood, G. W. to N. J. Anderson 10-6-1875 O
Wood, G. to Nicey Lake 1-6-1883 (1-25-1883) L
Wood, George W. to Lucy Ann W. Comer 5-24-1867 (no return) Hn
Wood, George W. to Mary S. Jackson 11-4-1852 Hn
Wood, George W. to Mattie P. Pipkins 9-10-1879 L
Wood, George W. to Nancy F. Lewis 7-25-1855 (no return) Hn
Wood, George to Ann Macon 1-2-1866 Hy
Wood, George to Eliza Haskins 2-13-1835 Hr
Wood, George to Mary J. (Mrs.) Williamson 6-8-1853 (no return) F
Wood, George to Matilda Butler 10-7-1869 T
Wood, Green to Martha Ann Lowry 11-18-1844 (7-24-1845) F
Wood, H. W.(M?) to S. C. Duggel 12-6-1865 G
Wood, H. to A. G. Algee 10-1-1869 (10-3-1869) Cr
Wood, Handy to Mary Ann Alston 12-11-1860 (12-12-1860) L
Wood, Henry to Juda Williamson 1-20-1874 T
Wood, Henry to Sarah McGary 5-6-1876 (5-7-1876) Dy
Wood, Isaac to Easter Jones 9-27-1866 G
Wood, J. J. to Isabella J. Wessen 9-13-1864 (10-18-1864) Sh
Wood, J. J. to Martha D. Wesson 1-22-1857 Sh
Wood, J. L. to N. E. Hall 12-12-1865 (12-15-1865) Cr
Wood, J. M. to M. M. Lett 11-10-1869 G
Wood, J. S. to Susana F. Alston 12-8-1866 (12-12-1866) L
Wood, J. T. to Susanah Warren 6-6-1851 (6-7-1851) Hr
Wood, J. W. to B. A. Roberson 5-5-1873 (5-7-1873) L
Wood, J. W. to N. E. Roberson 6-2-1877 (6-3-1877) L
Wood, James B. to Jane Willis 5-13-1828 Ma
Wood, James E. to Mary D. Moody 8-21-1852 (8-22-1852) G
Wood, James E. to Milly Grant 11-15-1858 (11-16-1858) Ma
Wood, James H. to Mary C. Porter 10-23-1876 (10-24-1876) Dy
Wood, James S. to Elizabeth W. Yancy 2-12-1849 (2-13-1849) G
Wood, James S. to Rhoda A. Robertson 9-1-1852 G
Wood, James T. to Elizabeth J. Cartwright 11-12-1844 (11-14-1844) G
Wood, James T. to S. L. Hart 12-13-1876 L
Wood, Jas. S. to M. F. Hazlewood 1-20-1857 G
Wood, Jas.R. to Sarah Buffalo 12-11-1856 Hy
Wood, Jason L. to Nannie C. Pentecost 1-4-1870 Ma
Wood, Jeromiah P. to Martha Woods 5-27-1868 (5-28-1868) Ma
Wood, Jesse to Adaline Williamson 10-19-1867 (10-20-1867) F B
Wood, Jno. L. to Elizabeth Warren 1-3-1848 (1-4-1848) Hr
Wood, John A. to Mary Hendricks 6-9-1860 L
Wood, John E. to S. E. Walker 8-3-1874 (8-6-1874) T
Wood, John H. to Frances M. McCoy 6-18-1856 (6-19-1856) T
Wood, John H. to Margaret Timmonds 6-5-1862 (6-8-1862) Sh
Wood, John M. to Huldah M. Cochran 3-26-1850 Sh
Wood, John R. to Angeline Baughman 11-22-1860 (5-21-1861) O
Wood, John R. to Pauline E. Guy 9-21-1859 Hr
Wood, John S. to Martha A. Hastings 8-11-1853 Hn
Wood, John S. to Sidy Burr 10-30-1849 L
Wood, John T. to Catharine T. Taylor 2-5-1869 Cr
Wood, John T. to Mary Lewis 10-26-1857 Hn
Wood, John T. to T. B. McDowell 2-7-1852 (2-8-1852) Hr
Wood, John to Ana Bradley 9-21-1832 (9-23-1832) G
Wood, John to Elizabeth B. Butts 6-27-1859 Sh
Wood, John to Indiania Shelton 7-27-1868 T
Wood, John to Nancy Lockard 9-16-1841 L
Wood, Jordan C. to Mary F. Wood 12-16-1868 T
Wood, Joseph H. to Francis H. Keller 9-21-1875 L
Wood, Joseph to Sophilia Spence 8-7-1845 We
Wood, Kircus to Dolly Taylor 1-5-1868 Hy
Wood, Lander L. to Nancy D. Lee 12-2-1856 (12-3-1856) G
Wood, Lewis to Kitty Klyce 12-25-1865 Hy
Wood, Lewis to Lillie Shelton 10-31-1873 Hy
Wood, M. L. to Walker McCord 2-6-1883 L
Wood, Marion to Sarah A. Penick 12-18-1866 (12-19-1866) Cr
Wood, Miles to Eliza J. Baker 4-2-1840 Hn
Wood, Miles to Francis Atkins 10-20-1845 We
Wood, Minor to Lucy Smith 1-20-1869 Dy
Wood, Nathaniel G. to Tennessee McEwen 9-10-1861 (9-16-1861) G
Wood, O. H. P. to Rebecca J. H. Durham 5-7-1840 T
Wood, P. M. to Sarah Worly 1-28-1867 (1-30-1867) O
Wood, Patrick to Judah Wood 5-24-1866 Hy
Wood, Peter P. to Eliza Ralph 4-12-1849 T
Wood, Peter P. to Sarah Elizabeth Hartsfield 7-7-1869 (7-8-1869) T
Wood, R. L. to Sarah Adaline Burks 11-28-1881 (11-29-1881) L

Wood, R. W. to Margaret Mason 3-14-1870 (3-15-1870) Ma
Wood, Rezin S. to Sarah J. Currie 1-2-1850 L
Wood, Richard to Candis Furnandez 9-19-1867 (9-21-1867) T
Wood, Robert F. to Eliza Jane Whitson 12-23-1869 (no return) Dy
Wood, Robert H. to Mary Carolin Bills 1-12-1847 Hr
Wood, Robert L. to Sarah B. Norman 3-2-1835 Hr
Wood, Robert W. to S. F. Williams 3-1-1871 L
Wood, Robert to Margaret Campbell 4-27-1867 (4-28-1867) L B
Wood, Robt. to Maseriah Ragland 3-4-1871 Hy
Wood, S. A. to Dona Chitwood 5-11-1875 Dy
Wood, S. A. to Mary E. Coker 10-16-1879 Dy
Wood, S. R. to Mary E. Cole 10-10-1876 Hy
Wood, Sabert to Eliza Jane Alston 10-28-1856 (10-29-1856) L
Wood, Silas to L. A. (Mrs.) Seawell 10-13-1845 Sh
Wood, Spiner to Mary M. Alen 3-20-1848 (no return) F
Wood, Stephen to Alice Barnett 12-30-1874 (12-31-1874) Dy
Wood, T. J. to M. J. Williford 9-13-1865 G
Wood, T. P. to Sallie A. Alston 12-24-1873 L
Wood, Tamberlin to Margaret Lucinda Baxter 11-11-1829 (2-5-1830) O
Wood, Thomas A. to Sarah F. Smith 1-3-1874 (1-4-1874) T
Wood, Thomas D. to Louisa Jane Witherington 7-1-1842 T
Wood, Thos. J. to Lamanios Joslin 3-12-1857 G
Wood, Thos. to Sarah M. Roe 12-11-1865 (12-13-1865) T
Wood, W. C. to M. G. Blaylock 9-7-1856 We
Wood, W. H. to Martha H. Wood 4-21-1853 G
Wood, W. L. to Nancy Burks 2-14-1872 L
Wood, Washington to Lucy Allison 1-17-1869 Hy
Wood, Wesley W. to Elizabeth C. Dement 9-24-1858 We
Wood, William A. to Pamelia A. Thompson 9-14-1843 L
Wood, William H. to Martha E. Hogan 11-22-1842 Hn
Wood, William to Amanda A. Warren 11-1-1842 Hn
Wood, William to Margaret Wilson 12-23-1870 T
Wood, William to Mariah Greer 4-2-1874 (4-24-1874) L B
Wood, William to Pheaby Collier 1-5-1855 Be CC
Wood, William to Pheraby Collier 1-5-1855 Be
Wood, Willie to Margaret Pierce 4-4-1858 Hn
Wood, Willis to Elizabeth Smith 6-23-1846 Ma
Wood?, James to Mary E. Davis 8-15-1867 (8-16-1867) Dy
Woodall, B. F. to Martha S. Harrell 9-16-1861 (no return) Cr
Woodall, Turner to Rebecca Mathis 7-13-1842 G
Woodard, Aaron W. to Zelpha Woodard 3-12-1838 (5-20-1838) Ma
Woodard, Amos to Maryline Mills 4-30-1861 Dy
Woodard, Benjamine to Mary Justine 12-7-1830 (12-9-1830) Ma
Woodard, David to Judith Taylor 8-8-1864 (8-10-1864) T
Woodard, F. M. to Lyra Sanford 9-18-1866 O
Woodard, Frank to Hannah Mitchell 6-10-1877 O B
Woodard, Frank to Martha (Mrs.) Bishop 11-10-1864 Sh
Woodard, George W. to Mary Hysinger 7-25-1878 Hy
Woodard, H. L. to Jane Angus 1-13-1857 (1-14-1857) T
Woodard, H. P. to Elizabeth Finley 5-9-1845 Cr
Woodard, J. H. to M. M. Wimpy 7-11-1868 Hy
Woodard, J. H. to Susannah Mosgraves 3-12-1878 L
Woodard, J. P. to Septempa Carson 9-3-1845 Cr
Woodard, Jackson to M. J. A. Hooks 10-27-1848 (no return) F
Woodard, James E. to Susan A. Shuford 3-17-1868 (3-18-1868) Cr
Woodard, James M. to Lucy Jane Smith 8-3-1869 (no return) Cr
Woodard, James M. to Sarah McFarland 12-19-1840 (12-14?-1840) Ma
Woodard, James to Martha Fletcher 9-18-1862 G
Woodard, Jerramiah P. to Elizabeth Thompson 9-29-1836 (10-2-1836) G
Woodard, Jessee to Cynthia Chipman 1-1-1878 L
Woodard, John R. to Mary E. (Mrs.) Chitman 2-25-1867 (2-26-1867) Ma
Woodard, Jonathan to Elizabeth James 10-30-1828 G
Woodard, Joseph to Martha Jane Spivey 2-12-1863 L
Woodard, Joseph to Mary E. (Mrs.) Cowel 2-11-1867 L
Woodard, L. C. to Amanda S. E. Long 2-18-1868 L
Woodard, L. C. to Jennie Ferrell 12-16-1874 Hy
Woodard, L. C. to Mollie J. Hawkens (Nankens?) 1-9-1870? (1-11-1871) L
Woodard, Lewis H. to Mary A. Thomas 9-4-1855 (no return) L
Woodard, R. A. to Catharine Gardner 3-19-1878 (3-20-1878) L
Woodard, Richard R. to Matilda R. B. Cowel 4-26-1878 (no return) L
Woodard, Robert A. to M. A. Ferrill 12-21-1881 (no return) L
Woodard, W. F. to Jane Fletcher 7-24-1862 G
Woodard, W. J. to Sarah Ann Fulkerson 10-8-1867 (10-10-1867) L
Woodard, W. P. to Cintha J. Graham 1-8-1868 (1-9-1868) Cr
Woodard, Wm. J. to Rachel B. Fulkerson 10-8-1857 L
Woodard, Wm. P. to Tennessee Roberson 12-24-1866 (12-25-1866) Ma
Woodburry, Henry to Charlotte L. Bradley 1-31-1861 (1-30?-1861) Dy
Wooddell, William J. to Harriet B. Caruthers 2-21-1853 (2-22-1853) Ma
Woodell, Isaac to Elizabeth E. Roach 4-9-1859 Hr
Woodell, John to Eady Bruce 9-27-1847 (9-29-1847) Ma
Woodelle, David C. to Louisa J. Harston 9-5-1849 Ma
Woodfin, C. to Mary J. Crawford 4-27-1843 Hr
Woodfin, John to Frances Edgarton 4-23-1841 Hr
Woodfin, John to Minta Thompson 4-4-1868 F B
Woodfin, W. N. to Ellen Porter 2-12-1856 Hn
Woodfolk, John R. to Almera Niel 2-23-1842 (2-24-1842) Ma
Woodford, William to Nelly Lindsey 2-21-1866 Hn

Woodfork, Ed to Peep Shelton 1-5-1870 (no return) F B
Woodide, Francis E. to Martha E. Day 12-6-1853 G
Woodrough, William H. to Sarah C. Willson 12-15-1860 (no return) We
Woodruff, B. F. to Christiana Gidcomb 9-23-1880 L
Woodruff, D. W. to E. C. Hill 4-15-1854 (4-20-1854) G
Woodruff, S. F. to Miss ____ Harrison 9-20-1855 (no return) F
Woodruff, W. C. to Lillie Bayley 2-19-1861 (2-21-1861) Sh
Woods, Allen L. to Polly Adair 8-8-1838 G
Woods, Andrew D. to Mary A. Woods 2-14-1870 (2-15-1870) Ma
Woods, Andrew to Ann Harlan 12-15-1867 G B
Woods, Andrew to Mary J. Harden 12-1-1877 (12-2-1877) L
Woods, B. F. to Sarah Page 4-14-1867 G
Woods, Benjamin F. to Elizabeth N. Fletcher 10-6-1852 (10-12-1852) G
Woods, Bill to Ella? Smith 10-4-1873 T
Woods, Caleb to Ann E. Murchison 8-5-1846 (8-13-1846) Ma
Woods, Callus to Cinda Clay 2-16-1876 Hy
Woods, Daniel to Emma Fowlkes 1-6-1872 (no return) Dy
Woods, David H. to Ann Eliza Deakins 12-8-1847 (12-?-1847) T
Woods, David to Delia Walker 12-6-1879 (12-8-1879) Dy
Woods, David to Mary Ann Brown 4-4-1832 (4-5-1832) O
Woods, Edmond to Rebecka Crockett 11-22-1826 G
Woods, Frank to Lucinda Green 4-2-1881 (4-5-1881) L B
Woods, George B. to Mary Robinus 4-24-1849 Cr
Woods, George H. to Leona Vincent 5-1-1843 Cr
Woods, George W. to Mary S. Williams 10-28-1882 (10-29-1882) L
Woods, Granderson to Jane Willis 3-8-1842 Hn
Woods, Henry to M. A. E. Bryant 3-19-1868 Be
Woods, J. M. to S. A. Bullock 11-7-1856 We
Woods, J. M. to T. B. Butler 2-1-1868 (2-5-1868) Cr
Woods, James D. to Susan J. S. Porter 12-16-1857 Hn
Woods, James H. to Martha A. Dunn 12-21-1843 Cr
Woods, James M. to Sarah S. White 6-18-1836 (6-19-1836) G
Woods, James T. to Eudora M. Booth 7-19-1845 (7-29-1845) G
Woods, James to Margaret Mack 6-4-1864 (6-6-1864) Sh
Woods, Jeremia to A. L. J. Snyder 10-8-1857 Sh
Woods, John D. to Emily Daverson 4-30-1839 Cr
Woods, John H. to Martha J. Blous? 7-25-1860 T
Woods, John J. to Elizabeth P. Wesson 2-24-1853 Sh
Woods, John to Frances Jones 3-25-1874 (3-26-1874) T
Woods, John to Lutitia M. Locke 1-3-1842 (12?-23-1842) F
Woods, John to Mary Nailon 5-9-1857 (5-10-1857) Sh
Woods, Joseph to Elizabeth Dancer 8-21-1829 Sh
Woods, Levi S. to Mary Jarman 12-31-1853 (1-5-1854) G
Woods, Lucas to Mary Johnson 10-20-1855 (no return) Hn
Woods, Monan to Sarah J. Fifer 7-15-1859 (no return) Hn
Woods, Patrick to Joanah (Mrs.) Keaf 10-27-1864 (10-30-1864) Sh
Woods, Peter H. to V. F. Harris 12-18-1850 Cr
Woods, R. J. to J. B. Standfield 7-27-1871 Cr
Woods, R. N. to O. Ozier 2-27-1840 Cr
Woods, Robert P. to Louiza J. Willson 12-31-1861 (1-5-1862) Cr
Woods, Robert to Nancy Chitwood 12-16-1879 (no return) Dy
Woods, S. P. to Harriett Moore 12-31-1868 (1-1-1869) Cr
Woods, Saml. D. to Mary C. Keas 1-2-1850 G
Woods, Sampson to Nancy Almond 1-16-1848 Hn
Woods, Smith to Patsy Fakes 2-29-1868 G B
Woods, Sylvester to Cynthia Skinner 1-13-1848 Hn
Woods, Taylor to Zoa Ann Deener 12-26-1867 (no return) F B
Woods, Thomas to Paralee Price 2-21-1867 Be
Woods, Thomas to Sarah T. Harmon 1-11-1862 (1-12-1862) Dy
Woods, Thos. to Silvian Harbor 12-26-1854 (12-28-1854) G
Woods, W. H. to H. E. Cawthan 1-27-1868 (1-29-1868) Cr
Woods, W. H. to J. P. Green 10-2-1869 (10-6-1869) Dy
Woods, W. to Susan Herald 3-6-1878 (3-7-1878) Dy
Woods, Will to Rachel Harris 4-5-1879 (4-7-1879) Dy
Woods, William H. to Benigna Polk 7-12-1834 W
Woods, William H. to Jane Barnett 10-22-1847 (10-26-1847) Ma
Woods, William T. to Susan Goodloe 11-28-1862 (12-?-1862) Dy
Woods, William to Fanny Dowdy 1-31-1870 (2-10-1870) F B
Woods, William to Martha Hastings 7-9-1848 Hn
Woods?, Saml. M. to Narcissa Robinson 1-13-1844 (1-18-1844) T
Woods?, Thomas to Margret C. Downey 2-3-1843 (2-5-1843) O
Woodside, Amaziah to Frances Montgomery 10-3-1860 (no return) Dy
Woodside, D. P.(T) to Harriett Blackwell 9-27-1846 Sh
Woodsides, J. M. to Alice Jackson 8-23-1875 (8-25-1875) Dy
Woodson, Charles to Matilda Yancy 4-20-1870 G
Woodson, Creed T. to N. E. P. (Mrs.) Chrisp 2-19-1868 G
Woodson, Creed to Emeline T. Shaw 12-20-1847 F
Woodson, Dave to Myrah Jordan 10-17-1868 G B
Woodson, Doctor to Betty Cunningham 6-28-1871 (6-29-1871) Cr B
Woodson, George A. to Mary L. Smith 3-4-1851 F
Woodson, Henry L. to Elizabeth C. Johnson 7-16-1854 (7-15?-1854) Hr
Woodson, Henry to Charton Bell 1-3-1868 G B
Woodson, J. P. to Mary L. McMullen 10-13-1856 (10-15-1856) G
Woodson, John R. to Amanda E. Pitman 10-7-1848 F
Woodson, John to Martha Rebecca Ann Lewis 8-26-1867 (8-28-1867) Ma
Woodson, Josh R. to Mary N. McCrory 2-2-1856 Hr
Woodson, Matthew to Marrilla I. Rash 4-18-1839 Sh

Woodson, Mitchell to Melissa Donner (Danner?) 7-29-1869 G
Woodson, Ned to Alice Cunningham 1-22-1869 (1-23-1869) Cr
Woodson, Richard to Fannie Smith 2-12-1874 Dy
Woodson, Thomas to Jane Edwards 10-31-1846 (11-1-1846) G
Woodson, Thos. L. to Luzun M. Fields 12-14-1849 G
Woodson, W. A. to Mary Jane George 9-17-1856 (9-18-1856) T
Woodson, W. D. to Mary E. Smith 12-18-1850 Be
Woodson, W. G. to Josephine Howard 6-6-1869 G
Woodson, Warren to Mildred Dowel 6-19-1842 Sh
Woodson, William H. to Julia Bullington 4-9-1842 G
Woodson, William to Emily Crouch 8-26-1841 Sh
Woodson, Williie to Luizer Donner 2-23-1867 G
Woodward, Archieleus to Julia Hawley 9-20-1855 Sh
Woodward, Asa to Mary Penn 12-10-1831 (12-11-1831) Ma
Woodward, Asa to Sarah Bennett 3-22-1846 (3-24-1846) F
Woodward, Bennet to Nancy Powel 10-25-1862 (10-26-1862) Ma
Woodward, David to Adelene Cordoza 2-14-1844 Sh
Woodward, David to Ann Eliza Scruggs 10-20-1840 Sh
Woodward, J. Marshall to Mary K. Williams 2-23-1857 Sh
Woodward, John to Melinda McCarey 5-16-1825 O
Woodward, Oliver C. to Sallie A. Clark 12-6-1852 (12-7-1852) Sh
Woodward, Wiley A. to Lucinda Holland 7-11-1854 Cr
Woodworth, Jeremiah to Harriet E. Bailey 12-26-1853 Sh
Woolard, Cornelas to Sarah Bradley 11-19-1840 (11-22-1840) G
Woolard, Cornelias to Mary Foren 7-21-1857 G
Woolard, Henry to Mahaly A. Crocker 2-18-1864 G
Woolard, Thomas C. to Sarah J. Mathis 2-6-1862 G
Wooldridge, Robert to Mary P. Crouch 9-3-1839 Sh
Woolen, A. T. M. to M. C.? Rogers 4-2-1860 (4-10-1860) Cr
Wooley, D. W. to Maryline E. Moody 11-28-1874 (12-1-1874) Dy
Wooley, John W. to Sarah E. Shaw 12-6-1858 Ma
Woolfirk, Wesley to Catherine Rose 4-4-1873 (4-8-1873) T
Woolfolk, John G. to Sue Pearson 11-3-1868 (11-5-1868) Ma
Woolfolk, John R. to Julia Preston 2-18-1861 (6-18-1861) Ma
Woollen, W. H. to Betty Capers 2-223-1880 (2-24-1880) L
Woolner, Charles to Mary (Mrs.) Foley 2-10-1863 Sh
Woolverton, D. W. M. to Sarah Jane Farris 1-12-1861 (1-15-1861) Hr
Woolverton, R. T. to A. C. Jernagin 5-11-1861 (5-22-1861) Hr
Wooston, B. to Mary Jane Savington 12-20-1879 (no return) L B
Wooten, Arthur F. to Ann Eliza Joice 5-14-1842 (5-15-1842) T
Wooten, Bailey L. to Sarah E. Smith 11-8-1855 Sh
Wooten, Ben to Aanda Miller 1-20-1869 T
Wooten, H. F. to Sarah A. Gregory 11-14-1857 We
Wooten, James L. to Laura F. Whitley 12-17-1855 Sh
Wooten, James L. to Serenia E. Griffin 12-9-1850 Sh
Wooten, James to Mary E. Haynes 5-19-1846 Hn
Wooten, John to Phillis Clements 1-13-1866 (1-14-1866) T
Wooten, Memory to Elizabeth Henderson 12-31-1868 Ma
Wooten, W. H. to Mahala Pickard 9-24-1861 T
Wooten, William Henry to Caroline Winiford Howerton 12-14-1841 T
Wooten, William L. to Mary N. Baugh 12-31-1851 (no return) F
Wooten, Wm. E. to Sally Ash 11-13-1867 Hy
Wooten, Wm. S. to Margaret A. Outland 12-15-1870 Ma
Wooton, Cannon Smith to Helen Tucker 9-28-1843 T
Wooton, Weems to Lucy S. Ashe 1-9-1871 Hy
Wootten, Benjamin to America D. Blanton 9-10-1855 Sh
Worashum, Senior to Jane Swiney 12-28-1854 Cr
Word (Ward), E. H. to Martha E. Morgan 12-13-1848 Sh
Word, Aaron to Precilla H. Freeman 4-15-1836 (4-21-1836) G
Word, Alfred to Maco Bishop 5-25-1872 Hy
Word, Benj. A. (of AR) to Ida Hutcherson 2-22-1870 Ma
Word, Bryant to Banna E. Wilson 2-3-1843 (2-5-1843) G
Word, Cornelius to Martha Word 1-13-1870 G B
Word, Daniel W. to Louisa Simpson 8-22-1844 G
Word, Daniel W. to Lucinda Hawkins 5-16-1837 (5-?-1837) G
Word, H. H. to Anne M. Rains 9-23-1841 G
Word, Henry to Della Fields 12-25-1879 Dy
Word, Isack to Rachael Freeman 12-5-1836 (12-8-1836) G
Word, J. C. to M. D. Wilbourn 2-4-1864 (2-10-1864) F
Word, Jack to Eliza Boyd 3-27-1869 (no return) F B
Word, John to Drucilla M. Conel 11-16-1842 G
Word, Thomas to Rosanna Crider 9-25-1834 (9-25-1834) G
Word, Timothy H. to Mary E. Abbott 12-21-1843 G
Worden, D. D. to Roberta Smither 11-21-1864 Sh
Worden, James B. to Jamima Nobles 1-4-1841 (1-7-1841) G
Wordlow, Albert to Callie Johnson 10-14-1875 Hy
Wordlow, Jordan to Marsha Thompson 12-28-1871 Hy
Wordsworth, Jim to Melisa McFarland 12-26-1871 Hy
Wordum, Branch H. to Amanda Little 1-22-1855 Cr
Worel, Franklin to Nancy I. Searcy 3-4-1867 O
Worel, W. H. to L. J. Morrow 10-17-1865 O
Worel?, John M. to Martha A. Cawthan 1-9-1863 (no return) Cr
Work, E. E. to Adline Rucker 12-25-1867 Hy
Work, Z. C. to F. B. Flippin 2-21-1873 (2-26-1873) L
Workman, James H. to Margarett Gurgaras 10-19-1858 We
Workman, Jefferson J. to Delany C. Adams 5-6-1858 Be CC
Workman, Jefferson P. to Delaney C. Adams 5-6-1858 Be

Workman, Jefferson P. to Narcissa J. Hamonds 3-27-1864 G
Workman, John C. to Elenor E. Gargus 6-26-1844 We
Workman, John E. to Eliza D. Hugganes 2-27-1857 We
Workman, John M. to Matilda S. Bolden 1-11-1859 Hn
Workman, Wm. to Margaret Gargus 10-10-1844 We
Works, Alex to Provie Clark 9-8-1877 Dy
Works, Frank to Jane Oldham 2-10-1872 (2-15-1872) Dy
Worlds, Turner to Millie Rhodes 1-20-1872 Hy
Worley, Leonard to Aney Harley 3-2-1824 (3-3-1824) G
Worley, W. C. to N. J. Hightower 12-12-1874 (12-27-1874) T
Wormack, M. A. to Sarah McGuin 6-21-1869 Hy
Wormack, Richard to Mary L. Billingsley 1-9-1847 (1-12-1847) G
Wormack, William to Adaline E. Billingsley 7-18-1850 (7-23-1850) G
Wormath, John R. to Mary Elizabeth Prewitt 10-23-1874 (10-24-1874) T
Wormell, W. E. to Cordelia L. Molitor 7-23-1859 (7-26-1859) Sh
Wormley, Nathaniel Green to Mary Hardy Alston 6-22-1850 (6-23-1850) T
Worrel, Caswell to Nancy Williams 1-2-1866 (no return) Dy
Worrel, Jesse to Lenora Foshee 1-1-1870 (1-2-1870) Cr
Worrel, L. J. to Martha J. Jackson 10-17-1871 (10-19-1871) O
Worrell, Alfred to Harriet H. D. Crain 10-16-1837 (10-22-1837) O
Worrell, Amus to Mary Barron 1-13-1840 Hr
Worrell, Davis to Julia H. Fife 2-9-1863 Hy
Worrell, Henry H. to Nancy Ann Adams 10-3-1842 O
Worrell, Henry to Mary A. L. Butts 11-26-1849 Ma
Worrell, J. R. to A. J. Roberson 1-1-1866 Hy
Worrell, J. R. to A. J. Roberson 1-2-1866 Hy
Worrell, John to Martha Adams 10-31-1878 Hy
Worrell, Peter to Nancy Bell 6-2-1856 Ma
Worrell, Ransom T. to Martha Sanders 5-14-1862 Hy
Worrell, Saml. to Malinda Norman 10-18-1867 (10-19-1867) F B
Worrell, T. B. to A. M. (Mrs.) Simpson 3-1-1853 (no return) F
Worrell, William B. to Mary A. Hudson 9-14-1849 (9-20-1849) Hr
Worrell, William to Mary C. Guthrie 10-4-1855 O
Worrell, Wm. B. to Martha Hamilton 12-21-1857 (12-23-1857) Hr
Worsham, G. H. to Margaret V. Marshall 5-21-1856 Sh
Worsham, Gloster to Mary Jane Travis 5-20-1866 Hn
Worsham, James W. to Elizabeth Morris 6-12-1856 Hn
Worsham, Leigh to Mary Ann Henley 12-24-1872 (1-5-1873) L
Worshum, J. T. to Mississippi E. Weldon 11-16-1846 (no return) We
Worsly, William H. to Lena Holland 1-21-1884 (1-22-1884) L
Wortham, Augustine W. to Mary Jane Ealey 2-20-1862 Sh
Wortham, Benj. H. to Mary J. Burrow 9-8-1846 (no return) F
Wortham, Charles L. to Luticia C. Betts 1-9-1861 Sh
Wortham, Edward H. to Martha Redditt 5-17-1849 Sh
Wortham, Green to M. P. E. Mason 11-26-1860 (11-27-1860) Ma
Wortham, James M. to Rebecca Edwards 9-28-1853 (10-?-1853) Sh
Wortham, Johnson W. to Clarissa McBee 8-30-1837 Hr
Wortham, Lee to Emma Larrison 2-4-1881 (not executed) L
Wortham, Moses to Mary Bess 10-19-1866 G
Wortham, Nathaniel to Henrietta Smith 4-29-1852 T
Wortham, Pinkney to Julia Ann Hise 3-26-1868 T
Wortham, Pleasant to Susanna J. Stokes 10-5-1845 Sh
Wortham, Richard to Allavana Edwards 6-21-1848 Sh
Worthy, Greenbury to Diana Gunter 9-19-1853 We
Woton, Levi to Elizabeth Oliver (Olum) 3-18-1841 Sh
Wrather, James A. to Elizaeth Haneline 12-3-1846 Hn
Wray, Aleck to Fanny Barby 7-9-1870 F B
Wray, J. A. to Sallie A. Neal 9-6-1862 (9-8-1862) F
Wray, J. H. to C. F. Clancy 10-17-1866 Hy
Wray, James M. to Sallie Permenter 12-15-1868 Hy
Wray, Jas. Rich to Harriett Reinhardt 1-5-1846 Hn
Wray, John to Mary Atkins 10-27-1859 (11-3-1859) F
Wray, Joseph to Caroline Harmon 1-20-1846 (no return) We
Wray, Thomas J. to Sarah Ann Harper 12-9-1849 Hn
Wray, William J. to Martha A. Johnson 8-23-1862 We
Wray, Wm. to W. M. (Mrs.) Thurston 6-2-1850 Sh
Wrays, Doctor P. to Elizabeth Gilbert 8-6-1856 We
Wreen, W. H. to Cemantha L. Tinkle 2-28-1860 (3-1-1860) G
Wren, Elijah to T. E. Greer 10-6-1856 (10-16-1856) G
Wren, J. B. to M. A. Cooper 10-22-1868 Cr
Wren, N. J. to Julie Edwards 11-18-1867 (11-20-1867) Cr
Wren, R. D. to Sarah A. Deliny? 12-22-1858 Cr
Wren, Richmond L. to Sarah A. Delaney 2-23-1858 Cr
Wren, Robert to Mary A. Smith 8-1-1865 (no return) Cr
Wrenn, David J. to Lucinda Evans 7-5-1841 (7-6-1841) Ma
Wrenn, N. W. to Sarah A. Williams 11-23-1859 (11-24-1859) G
Wrenn, Thomsa J. to Martha M. Temple 5-10-1847 (5-13-1847) G
Wrey, Joseph to Satey Bray 7-31-1848 Hr
Wright, A. C. to Ariel Upchurch 8-30-1863 Hn
Wright, A. J. to Emaline Smart 12-1-1855 (no return) We
Wright, A. M. to Rebecca Williams 1-2-1866 G
Wright, A. N. to Sallie Sandlin 10-20-1874 (10-22-1874) Dy
Wright, A. W. to Georgiana Craig 2-22-1870 F
Wright, Abraham G. to Parmelia Duncan 11-19-1853 (11-21-1853) Sh
Wright, Adogria? to Mary Nance 11-28-1864 Be
Wright, Anderson to Mary Nance 11-28-1864 Be CC
Wright, Andrew J. to Eliza A. McQuiston 1-29-1868 (1-30-1868) T

Wright, Arrim (Orrin?) to Sarah Mathews 7-23-1868 G B
Wright, Astley C. to Mollie E. Loving 10-29-1860 Hn
Wright, Austem to Eliza Hill 2-27-1871 (2-28-1871) T
Wright, Bascom to Alice Locke 7-28-1875 (no return) Dy
Wright, Ben to Fosey Eggleston 12-26-1868 (1-1-1869) L B
Wright, Benjamin to Melinda Frazer 2-9-1844 Sh
Wright, Bill to A. Waid 4-9-1870 G
Wright, Bob to Amelia Hardin 12-27-1877 (12-28-1877) L
Wright, C. H. to Mary Jane Turner 8-30-1860 (9-4-1860) Cr
Wright, C. P. H. to Emily Dickson 9-17-1843 Cr
Wright, Carter to Mattie F. Fisher 11-30-1878 (no return) L B
Wright, Charles W. to Mary T. Hudgins 2-24-1869 (2-25-1869) Ma
Wright, Charles to Elmeranda M. Caruthers 7-27-1858 (11-21-1858) O
Wright, Cirus to Nancy Siler 3-1-1867 (3-2-1867) T
Wright, Columbus to Nancy Moore 2-24-1869 Cr
Wright, D. W. to Christiana A. Duke 5-30-1853 (no return) F
Wright, D. W. to Miss ____ Duke 5-23-1853 (no return) F
Wright, Daniel W. to Catharine A. Thompson 6-28-1860 Sh
Wright, David L. to L. Beckworth 9-12-1842 (9-15-1842) O
Wright, David to Lucinda Truel 4-7-1870 Hy
Wright, Dennis to Elizabeth Thomas 1-18-1879 (1-22-1879) L
Wright, Doctor Henry to Elizabeth W. Cody 9-1-1827 (9-6-1827) Hr
Wright, E. D. to Margaret A. Hagans 1-31-1853 Sh
Wright, E. G. to Ann Hersch? 10-16-1856 Be
Wright, E. G. to Ann Hussah 10-16-1856 Be CC
Wright, E. to Elizabeth Gwin 1-1-1845 Cr
Wright, Edmund to Emma Finley 6-3-1873 (6-4-1873) O
Wright, Edward to Sarah Wright 2-20-1875 (2-21-1875) L
Wright, F. D. H. to Sarah Ann Carper 12-4-1850 (12-11-1850) Hr
Wright, F. M. to Julia M. Nored 11-29-1860 Hn
Wright, F. M. to Mary E. Cotton 10-26-1844 (10-29-1844) F
Wright, Francis M. to Catharine Gallop 8-14-1852 (8-16-1852) O
Wright, Francis to Elizabeth Latham 8-21-1853 (8-23-1853) Ma
Wright, Franklin to Matilda Phillips 3-7-1857 (3-12-1857) O
Wright, G. P. to C. E. Campbell 11-19-1866 O
Wright, G. W. to Nancy L. Ruce? 1-31-1870 (2-10-1870) Cr
Wright, General M. to Martha H. Frazier 1-8-1858 O
Wright, George H. to Margarett H. Doak 11-26-1839 Ma
Wright, George S. to Rebecca D. Pettey 2-26-1861 F
Wright, George W. to Mary E. Turbeville 8-28-1854 (no return) Hn
Wright, George to Julia Alexander 8-27-1883 (8-28-1883) L
Wright, George to Mary J. Norman 3-6-1855 Sh
Wright, Griffin to Vilett C. Jetton 5-7-1846 G
Wright, H. B. to M. A. Brewer 1-21-1857 Be CC
Wright, H. B. to M. A. Brewer 1-21-1858 Be
Wright, H. W. to Lucinda McCane 11-16-1865 Cr
Wright, H. W. to Margarett L. Hall (Nall?) 1-30-1866 G
Wright, H. W. to Mary Terrell 5-9-1831 (5-10-1831) G
Wright, Harrison to Malinda Lake 4-3-1877 (4-4-1877) L B
Wright, Henry to Henrietta Alsobrooks 7-8-1881 (7-10-1881) L B
Wright, Henry to Milly Pierson 12-25-1873 L B
Wright, Herris to Lucy Watson 12-23-1873 (12-24-1873) L B
Wright, Isaiah R. to Cecilia A. Hollomon 8-29-1842 (9-1-1842) O
Wright, Isham A. to Mary Bernard 1-3-1848 (1-6-1848) T
Wright, J. A. to Mary J. Barville 11-2-1874 (11-6-1874) T
Wright, J. A. to S. E. Rodgers 12-24-1850 Cr
Wright, J. A. to Winna R. Rogers 8-22-1864 (8-25-1864) Cr
Wright, J. B. to M. E. Dancy 2-24-1870 G
Wright, J. C. to E. Richardson 1-10-1867 G
Wright, J. D. to Lucinda Oldham 6-21-1874 Hy
Wright, J. M. C. Q. to C. J. Nelson 8-15-1856 (8-21-1856) G
Wright, J. M. to C. B. Neville 8-23-1864 Hn
Wright, J. N. to Mary Flowers 11-27-1856 G
Wright, J. P. to Nancy Tilmon 3-5-1867 (3-10-1867) Cr
Wright, J. R. to Martha Storeer 6-15-1861 (6-16-1861) O
Wright, J. S. to Margaret N. Shaw 1-29-1869 (1-30-1869) T
Wright, J. W. to Elizabeth Martin 12-25-1863 (12-27-1863) Sh
Wright, J. W. to S. I. Bidix 2-25-1869 G
Wright, Jacob A. to Mary A. Cook 11-5-1846 We
Wright, James A. to Angeline C. Wright 12-5-1850 Hn
Wright, James A. to Cornelia B. Adams 9-29-1860 Hr
Wright, James C. to A. M. (Mrs.) Siler 12-15-1858 Sh
Wright, James L. to Mary McCrare? 9-1-1853 T
Wright, James M. to Elizabeth McQuisten 3-20-1841 (3-23-1841) T
Wright, James M. to Mary R. Orr 12-5-1865 Hn
Wright, James W. to Elizabeth Talley 5-14-1861 Dy
Wright, James to Jane Boyd 10-22-1862 O
Wright, James to Mary McGregor 1-?-1871 (1-19-1871) T
Wright, James to Mary Smith 5-4-1861 Sh
Wright, James to Urshula Crocker 11-8-1847 (11-10-1847) Hr
Wright, Jeremiah to Frances Jeffers 10-2-1835 G
Wright, Jerry to Laura Davis 1-10-1874 (1-12-1874) L B
Wright, Jesse to Willie Ross 11-21-1872 (11-22-1872) T
Wright, Jessee to Virgina C. Hurt 10-11-1873 (10-13-1873) T
Wright, Jo? to Eva Ann Cole 3-11-1871 (3-12-1871) Dy
Wright, John B. to Sarah M. Landrum 3-28-1877 (3-29-1877) Dy
Wright, John C. to Elizabeth A. Fleming 8-20-1868 G

York, Eugene to Susan F. Adcock 7-24-1875 (no return) Dy
York, George W. to Fannie Watkins 4-18-1870 (no return) Dy
York, John B. to V. C. McGill 10-18-1870 (10-20-1870) Dy
York, John S. to Milla Hight 11-20-1838 Hy
York, Robert F. to C. Catharine Ware 12-23-1854 (12-24-1854) Sh
York, W. B. (Dr.) to Mollie Parker 1-14-1867 (1-15-1867) Dy
York, William C. to Rosa T. Graham 12-18-1867 Ma
York, William P. to Elizabeth C. Sloan 9-22-1850 Sh
Young, A. to Catharine Cobb 11-27-1867 (11-28-1867) Cr
Young, Al to Dinah Pitts 1-13-1880 (1-14-1880) L
Young, Alexander to H. E. J. Mullins 10-29-1867 G
Young, Alfred to Jane Pinner? 12-7-1852 T
Young, Amos to Elizabeth McLain 11-9-1868 (no return) F B
Young, Archie A. to Amelia R. Anthony 12-18-1878 L
Young, Augustus to Eliza Nayce 12-26-1866 Hy
Young, B. F. to Laura A. Hopper 3-20-1878 (3-21-1878) Dy
Young, B. N. to Sarah Ann Morris 12-19-1850 We
Young, Benj. F. to Harriet Young 9-13-1849 (9-12?-1849) G
Young, Beverly to Sallie Robins 5-27-1861 Hy
Young, C. C. to Nancy Elizabeth Fox 6-21-186_ (probably 1869) G
Young, C. M. to Margaret Brandon 8-30-1870 (9-1-1870) Dy
Young, Charles to Ada Pitts 3-13-1884 L
Young, Charlie to Lucy White 10-21-1870 (1-22-1871) Dy
Young, Cornelius to Ellen Hargett 2-23-1880 (no return) L
Young, Crockett to Susan A. Price 1-15-1859 We
Young, Dan C. to Charlotte J.(C) Harris 10-21-1840 Sh
Young, Daniel A. to Angy Dollar 4-8-1868 Ma
Young, Daniel A. to E. P. Johnson 2-18-1849 Hn
Young, Daniel A. to Kedie H. (Mrs.) Duffery 1-4-1870 (1-6-1870) Ma
Young, Daniel J. to Mary Ann Calhoun 1-14-1863 We
Young, David A. to Emiline Mullens 1-1-1861 G
Young, David E. to Mary Nichols 10-22-1866 Be
Young, Dennis to Nancy Thompson 1-19-1870 Hy
Young, Doremus N. to Martha Mebane 9-26-1865 Cr
Young, E. G. to Susan Jane Morton 12-21-1869 Hy
Young, Edmund to Turah Warren 1-17-1839 Hn
Young, Elbert Allen to Matilda Jane Reed 2-1-1868 G
Young, Elijah to Ann C. Steeley 12-20-1841 (no return) Hn
Young, Elijah to Henrietta Piercy 6-13-1884 (no return) L
Young, Fountain P. to Susan A. Van Pelt 12-9-1862 (12-11-1862) Ma
Young, Frederick to Fereby Bates 12-26-1866 Hy
Young, Fredrick to Leathie Clark 2-9-1871 Hy
Young, G. A. to M. E. Cox 7-15-1880 L
Young, Geo. W. to Elizabeth Bonds 12-28-1859 Hr
Young, George M. to Margaret Kerr 3-13-1850 Sh
Young, George to Adda Thompson 2-13-1871 (no return) L
Young, George to Ella Coltart 12-2-1880 L B
Young, George to Flora Trice 12-17-1870 Hy
Young, Green B. to Elizabeth Leach 11-14-1849 T
Young, Greene to Lucy Cooper 1-3-1856 Cr
Young, H. S. to Lillie E. Flowers 10-23-1883 (10-24-1883) L
Young, Isaac to Eliza Clements 4-12-1870 G B
Young, J. B. to S. A. Watson 11-22-1860 G
Young, J. E. to M. J. Prescott 7-21-1885 L
Young, J. F. to Emily Rodgers 12-28-1866 (1-2-1867) F
Young, J. G. to Annie Hall 1-15-1873 T
Young, J. M. to Mary R. E. Walker 9-4-1876 (9-6-1876) Dy
Young, J. M. to Susan M. Buck 6-5-1867 Hy
Young, J. R. to Martha J. Ross 10-9-1860 Be CC
Young, J. R. to Marthy J. Ross 10-9-1860 Be
Young, J. R. to Nancy E. Askew 11-4-1867 Be
Young, Jackson to Frances Currie 9-13-1882 L
Young, James A. to Girldine Plunk 2-15-1864 Mn
Young, James B. to Josephine Calloway 10-11-1863 Hn
Young, James B. to Sarah J. Reagan 11-4-1858 Hr
Young, James Franklin to Erena Lamb 9-2-1844 (9-4-1844) T
Young, James H. to Alevia W. Williams 6-16-1857 (6-21-1857) Ma
Young, James L. to Clementine Claughlin Laughlin 7-14-1835 Hr
Young, James M. to Martha Enochs 3-23-1844 G
Young, James S. to Mary A. Carter 8-24-1854 Hn
Young, James f. to Tabitha E. Johns 1-8-1863 G
Young, James to Claricy J. Vaughan 1-13-1857 T
Young, James to Ellen Balknight 8-21-1873 (8-23-1874?) L B
Young, James to Jane McDaniel 5-28-1840 Hn
Young, James to Martha A. A. Cearley 11-23-1854 Hr
Young, James to Mary J. Woods 1-4-1869 (no return) L B
Young, James to Nelly Nelson 11-20-1879 (no return) L
Young, Jeff to Louisa Brim 2-3-1881 L B
Young, Jno. W. to Martha Roe 8-4-1874 (8-12-1874) T
Young, John A. to Elizabeth Parsons 4-10-1866 Cr
Young, John B. to Sallie E. Spain 11-6-1866 (11-8-1866) F
Young, John W. to Emeline Dunigan 10-11-1848 G
Young, John to Jane Chandler 10-29-1846 Ma
Young, John to Lony Clark 2-20-1868 G
Young, John to Luousia Taylor 2-26-1872 L B
Young, John to Margaret Burk 4-7-1864 Sh
Young, John to Margaret Burke 7-5-1864 Sh
Young, John to Margrett C. Belote 12-15-1846 (12-17-1846) Hr
Young, John to Martha Ann Little 3-17-1854 G
Young, John to Nancy Flippins 8-23-1863 G
Young, John to Polly Wallace 2-8-1845 (2-9-1845) G
Young, Jonas to Margaret Beard 8-5-1847 Ma
Young, Jonathan J. to Nancy Sanders 8-17-1843 Hr
Young, Jordan to Catherine Helm 11-28-1883 (11-19-1884) L
Young, Joseph to Elizabeth Rebecca Mills 3-2-1854 O
Young, Joseph to Tibitha Sanders 9-7-1847 Sh
Young, Joseph to W. A. T. McKinza 3-21-1846 (3-22-1846) Hr
Young, Joshua D. to Sarah Cunningham 10-16-1851 G
Young, Josiah to Maletta Ferrell 6-28-1838 Ma
Young, Lafayette to Eurilda Yarbrough 11-22-1860 Hn
Young, Levi to Sarah Bledsoe 11-1-1867 (no return) L B
Young, Levy to Malinda Patterson 2-18-1832 (2-21-1832) Ma
Young, Lilburn to D. R. (Mrs.) Mill 1-18-1861 (1-20-1861) O
Young, Louis to Julia Ann Martin 5-26-1862 (5-27-1862) O
Young, Louis to Louisa Prato 9-17-1868 (no return) Dy
Young, M. C. to Pheriby Stevens 9-28-1853 (9-29-1853) Hr
Young, M. C. to Rachael Trezevant 5-8-1861 (5-9-1861) Hr
Young, Martin to Elizabeth Erwin 7-27-1841 (7-29-1841) Hr
Young, Matthew to Lorenza Pate 2-13-1830 (2-14-1830) O
Young, Milton C. to Holly S. Thompson 1-2-1854 (2-1-1854) Hr
Young, Milton R. to Tach Mathenor 1-5-1869 (1-10-1869) O
Young, Moody to Sarah Reasons 7-22-1852 (7-23-1852) G
Young, Moses to Sarah Coltart 11-4-1865 Hy
Young, Nathan to Emily Coltart 4-25-1874 Hy
Young, Nathaniel M. to Tempy M. Darnell 3-1-1850 (3-3-1850) Hr
Young, Nelson to Margaret Pitts 1-11-1883 L
Young, Newton to Magdaline Carr 1-30-1840 Hn
Young, Nicholas to Hellen Gills 1-29-1867 Hy
Young, Norflet T. to Mary Davis 1-11-1869 (1-14-1869) F
Young, O. D. to Mary E. Ingraham 1-5-1865 Mn
Young, Peter to Jane Bently 6-30-1866 (no return) F B
Young, Peter to Nancy Carley 10-30-1854 Hr
Young, Phillip to Sally Anna Tucker 12-24-1866 (no return) F B
Young, R. C. to Lucinda Dillahunty 3-19-1874 T
Young, R. P. to Dora Adams 12-24-1877 (12-30-1877) L
Young, R. W. to Alice Mann 10-2-1878 Hy
Young, Richard to Mary Hurley 11-17-1862 Sh
Young, Robert to Mary Ferguson 3-12-1856 (3-13-1856) T
Young, S. H. to Misouri Buck 7-16-1867 Hy
Young, Samuel A. to Sarah Ann Person 10-12-1852 Sh
Young, Samuel to Ida Buck 12-15-1882 (12-19-1882) L
Young, Samuel to Lutitia Jones 4-28-1855 (4-30-1855) Hr
Young, Samuel to Martha Wright 1-18-1877 L B
Young, Simeon to Abagail Fields 11-12-1860 Hn
Young, Sye to Mariah Jones 10-31-1868 (11-1-1868) F B
Young, T. T. to Mariah E. Taylor 8-2-1856 (8-4-1856) L
Young, Thomas E. to S. C. Richie 12-22-1877 (12-23-1877) Dy
Young, Thomas to Elizabeth Smith 9-10-1849 Hr
Young, Thomas to Mareny Eleonor Goodman 1-11-1836 Hr
Young, Thomas to Martha Greer 12-19-1856 (12-21-1856) O
Young, Thos. to Norvella Nelson 3-24-1867 Hy
Young, W. A. to Elizabeth Coleman 1-22-1867 Hy
Young, W. F. to Maria Cook 4-22-1850 Sh
Young, W. H. to Betty Rutherford 10-5-1876 Hy
Young, W. L. to Elizabeth Farmer 10-7-1855 We
Young, Will to Harrit Evans 2-15-1869 Hy
Young, William C. to Salina E. Follis 10-2-1857 (10-5-1857) Ma
Young, William F. to Agnes Medlin 7-31-1848 (8-1-1848) Ma
Young, William H. to Sarah Ann Wilson 12-6-1836 Sh
Young, William to Leir Smith 11-11-1826 G
Young, William to S. E. Lowry 1-2-1856 (no return) Hn
Young, jr., George W. to Mariah E. Anthony 6-28-1871 L
Youngblood, Cadda W. to Lucy Reed 1-30-1844 Hn
Youngblood, Jonathan to Margaret Kendrick 2-1-1836 Hr
Younge, Jas. M. to Pining B. O'Neill 11-7-1865 (11-9-1865) Cr
Younger, David to Delilah Moore 8-15-1863 Mn
Younger, George to Nancy Haley 8-23-1857 Hn
Younger, J. G. to F. V. Hart 11-22-1870 Hy
Younger, J. T. to M. F. Brasfield 7-21-1864 (7-25-1864) Cr
Younger, James to S. C. Frizzell 1-12-1853 Hn
Younger, John to Lucinda P. Emery 9-28-1859 Hn
Younger, T. W. to H. M. Haynes 2-10-1865 (2-12-1865) Cr
Younger, Thomas A. to Tamer J. North 10-1-1860 (no return) Cr
Younger, W. T. to Callie T. Hansbro 1-16-1869 (no return) Cr
Younger, William to Selva A. Pepper 9-18-1855 We
Younger, Wm. M. to Mary Ann Younger 2-20-1839 Cr
Youngs, John W. to Martha G. Burford 12-21-1840 (12-23-1840) F
Yount, Henry to Ann Batewright 7-24-1868 T
Yount, Hiram Malachi to Mary Catharine Starnes 3-12-1851 (3-13-1851) T
Youre, John to Mary Crutchfield 4-13-1871 O
Youree, Cornelius to Harriet D. Davis 8-7-1874 (8-9-1874) O
Youree, Francis M. to Nancy R. Dickey 8-26-1858 O
Youree, J. W. to G. T. McFerson 9-29-1870 G
Youree, Stephen to S. J. Clark 11-16-1874 O B

Youree, William B. to Margaret E. Calhoun 1-1-1861 O
Youree, William P. to America W. Moss 4-2-1838 F
Yousman, George to Mary W. Crow 11-15-1843 O
Yow, John W. to Susannah Hooker 11-6-1859 Hn
Yow, Wyatt c. to Siphronia Jones 12-23-1841 Hn

Zanone, John B. to Mary Signaigo 9-12-1857 (9-13-1857) Sh
Zant, John to Mary A. Jones 11-1-1853 Sh
Zarber, J. T. to E. T. Smalley 4-10-1842 Be CC
Zaricor, S. S. to Emma Boone 2-23-1874 (2-24-1874) O
Zearicor, William M. to Mary N. Baldridge 11-18-1850 G
Zedwitz, Otto Haensel to Julia Koch 6-29-1852 Sh
Zeller, F. W. to Martha A. Farmer 12-24-1856 Sh
Zellers, Thomas to Lucy Stone 4-29-1826 O
Zellner, J. A. to E. J. Robinson 2-26-1872 (2-27-1872) Cr
Zellner, J. W. to Willie E. Patton 11-3-1866 (11-6-1866) F
Zender, Alexander to Laura? Edition 8-26-1881 (8-27-1881) L
Zericor, Samuel to Nancy S. Blakemore 1-4-1827 (1-7-1827) G
Zimmerman, John to Alice A. Keneley 2-14-1870 (no return) L
Zornes (Zanes?), W. H. to Martha E. Wooden 9-9-1863 G
Zunkermann, G. A to Rosinna Batz 3-21-1856 Sh
Zweifel, D. to Ernstine Schuhmann 1-25-1858 (1-26-1858) Sh

BIBLIOGRAPHY

BOOKS

Carroll County Historical Society, Carroll County, Tennessee Marriages 1838-1859, McKenzie, TN (no date)

Davis, Bettie B., Lauderdale County, Tennessee Marriages 1838-1867, Memphis, TN, 1983

____, Shelby County, Tennessee Marriage Bonds & Licenses 1850-1865, Memphis, TN, 1983

Fischer, Marjorie Hood, Haywood County, Tennessee Marriage Records, 1859-1878, Vista, CA, 1987

Gary, Grace Dietzel and Carolyn West Stricklin, Obion County, Tennessee Marriage Records 1824-1877, Union City, TN, 1978

Gossum, Mary Louise and Emily B. Walker, Gibson County, Tennessee Marriage Records Volume A, June, 1860 - November, 1870, South Fulton, TN, 1984

Inman, W. O., Henry County, Tennessee Marriages 1838-1852, Paris, TN, 1974

____, Henry County, Tennessee Marriages 1853-1867, Paris, TN, 1974

Lydia Russell Bean Chapter, NSDAR, Benton County, Tennessee Marriages 1832-1857, Knoxville, TN 1962

Sistler, Byron and Barbara, Carroll County, TN Marriages 1860-1873, Nashville, TN, 1988

____, Dyer County, TN Marriages 1860-1879, Nashville, TN, 1989

____, Fayette County, TN Marriages 1838-1871, Nashville, TN, 1989

____, Hardeman County, TN Marriages 1823-1861, Nashville, TN, 1986

____, Madison County, TN Marriages 1838-1871, Nashville, TN, 1983

____, Tipton County, TN Marriages 1840-1874, Nashville, TN, 1987

Smith, Jonathan K. T., Genealogical Gleanings in Benton County, Tennessee, Memphis, TN, 1974

Tennessee Genealogical Society, Shelby County, Tennessee Marriage Records 1819-1850, Memphis, TN, 1957

Weakley County Genealogical Society, Weakley County, Tennessee Marriage Records 1843-1863, Martin, TN, 1980

Whitley, Edythe Rucker, Marriages of Gibson County, Tennessee 1824-1860, Baltimore, MD, 1982

PERIODICALS

Brown, Albert, "McNairy County, Tennessee Marriages 1861-1865", Ansearchin' News, Vol. 34, p. 147 and Vol. 35, p. 33, published Memphis, TN

Mitchell, Mary Ann and Charlotte Thornton, "Madison County, Tennessee, Loose Marriage Bonds 1823-1832", Family Findings, Vol. 1, pp. 9, 39, published Jackson, TN.